A

TOPOGRAPHICAL DICTIONARY

OF

ENGLAND,

IN FOUR VOLUMES.

A TOPOGRAPHICAL DICTIONARY OF ENGLAND

By Samuel Lewis

VOLUME IV

CLEARFIELD

Originally published, London, 1831
Reprinted, four volumes in two, 1996, by
Genealogical Publishing Co., Inc.
Baltimore, Maryland

Reprinted in the original four-volume format, 2018, by
Genealogical Publishing Company for
Clearfield Company
Baltimore, Maryland

ISBN Volume IV: 9780806358703
Set ISBN: 9780806315089

A

TOPOGRAPHICAL DICTIONARY

OF

ENGLAND,

COMPRISING THE

SEVERAL COUNTIES, CITIES, BOROUGHS, CORPORATE AND MARKET TOWNS,
PARISHES, CHAPELRIES, AND TOWNSHIPS,
AND THE ISLANDS OF GUERNSEY, JERSEY, AND MAN,

WITH

HISTORICAL AND STATISTICAL DESCRIPTIONS;

ILLUSTRATED BY

MAPS OF THE DIFFERENT COUNTIES AND ISLANDS;

AND EMBELLISHED WITH

ENGRAVINGS OF THE ARMS OF THE CITIES, BISHOPRICKS, UNIVERSITIES, COLLEGES, CORPORATE TOWNS,
AND BOROUGHS; AND OF THE SEALS OF THE SEVERAL MUNICIPAL CORPORATIONS.

BY SAMUEL LEWIS.

IN FOUR VOLUMES.

VOL. IV.

LONDON:
PUBLISHED BY S. LEWIS AND CO., 87, ALDERSGATE-STREET.
M. DCCC. XXXI.

A

TOPOGRAPHICAL DICTIONARY

OF

ENGLAND.

SABRIDGEWORTH, county of HERTFORD.——See SAWBRIDGEWORTH.

SACOMB, a parish in the hundred of BROAD-WATER, county of HERTFORD, 4 miles (N. by W.) from Ware, containing 341 inhabitants. The living is a rectory, in the archdeaconry of Huntingdon, and diocese of Lincoln, rated in the king's books at £10. 3. 4. Samuel Smyth, Esq. was patron in 1807. The church, dedicated to St, Mary, is situated upon an eminence on the north side of the Ware and Wotton road; it has a tower on the south side of the nave, formerly embattled; and, in the chancel, two stone stalls, and a piscina under trefoil arches, with memorials of the Rolt family. There is a bequest of £5 per annum by the Rev. John Meriton, late rector, for apprenticing one poor child.

SADBERGE, a chapelry in that part of the parish of HAUGHTON le SKERNE which is in the south-western division of STOCKTON ward, county palatine of DURHAM, 4¼ miles (E. N. E.) from Darlington, containing 315 inhabitants. The chapel is dedicated to St. Andrew: around the base of the hill upon which it stands are traces of an ancient intrenchment. This was formerly a place of great importance, and the capital of a district, or county, of the same name, having had its gaol, sheriff, coroner, and other civil officers. A school is supported by small annual subscriptions. The Stockton and Darlington railway passes in the vicinity.

SADDINGTON, a parish in the hundred of GARTREE, county of LEICESTER, 6 miles (N. W. by W.) from Market-Harborough, containing 232 inhabitants. The living is a rectory, in the archdeaconry of Leicester, and diocese of Lincoln, rated in the king's books at £19. 2. 6., and in the patronage of the Crown. The church is dedicated to St. Helen. The Union canal passes through a tunnel partly in this parish and partly in that of Kibworth-Harcourt.

SADDLEWOOD, a tything in the parish of HAWKESBURY, upper division of the hundred of GRUMBALDS-ASH, county of GLOUCESTER, 5 miles (W. S. W.) from Tetbury. The population is returned with Hillesley.

SADDLEWORTH, a chapelry in that part of the parish of ROCHDALE which is in the upper division of

the wapentake of AGBRIGG, West riding of the county of YORK, 12 miles (S. W. by W.) from Huddersfield, containing, with Quick, 13,902 inhabitants. The living is a perpetual curacy, in the archdeaconry and diocese of Chester, endowed with £200 private benefaction, £200 royal bounty, and £1200 parliamentary grant, and in the patronage of the Vicar of Rochdale. The chapel is dedicated to St. Chad. There are five places of worship for dissenters. A free school was founded in 1729, by Ralph Hawkyard, who endowed it with £280, and, in augmentation of the master's salary, John Walker, in 1755, bequeathed £200; the income arising from these sums is applied to teaching poor children of the parish, and supplying them with books. The Huddersfield canal passes through the parish, and the manufacture of woollen and cotton goods is carried on to a very great extent; the number of looms employed in the former exceeding three thousand five hundred, and in the latter four hundred; there are more than one hundred mills on the river Tame and its tributary streams. A few coal mines are worked, and excellent freestone abounds within the chapelry. It is in contemplation to establish a market, and to revive a fair formerly held at the village. There are some interesting natural curiosities at Greenfield, consisting of huge caverns, rocks, and a stupendous rocking-stone, with many Druidical remains. Castle Shaw is said to have been a fortress of the Britons, round beads, similar to those contained in the barrows on Salisbury plain, and a brazen celt, having been discovered near it.

SAFFRON - WALDEN, county of ESSEX. — See WALDEN (SAFFRON).

SAHAM-TONEY, a parish in the hundred of WAYLAND, county of NORFOLK, 1¾ mile (N.W.) from Watton, containing 925 inhabitants. The living is a rectory, in the archdeaconry and diocese of Norwich, rated in the king's books at £21. 19. 4½., and in the patronage of the Warden and Fellows of New College, Oxford. The church is dedicated to St. George: the tower, erected about 1480, has upon it a representation of St. George and the Dragon, carved in stone. There is a place of worship for Wesleyan Methodists. Edward Goffe, in 1611, bequeathed a house and land for a free school, to which another benefactor subsequently left other houses and land.

SAIGHTON, a township in that part of the parish of St. Oswald, Chester, which is in the lower division of the hundred of Broxton, county palatine of Chester, 4½ miles (S.E.) from Chester, containing 291 inhabitants.

SAINTBURY, a parish in the upper division of the hundred of Kiftsgate, county of Gloucester, 2¼ miles (W.) from Chipping-Campden, containing 156 inhabitants. The living is a rectory, in the archdeaconry and diocese of Gloucester, rated in the king's books at £19. 9. 4½., and in the patronage of James Roberts West, Esq. The church, dedicated to St. Nicholas, has undergone various alterations, but there is still a Norman door remaining. Castle Bank, an ancient camp in this parish, is ascribed to the Danes, and supposed to have been dependent upon a larger one upon the summit of the same hill in the adjoining parish.

SALCOMBE, a chapelry in the parish of Malborough, hundred of Stanborough, county of Devon, 5½ miles (S.) from Kingsbridge. The population is returned with the parish. A chapel existed here so early as 1401; it was rebuilt in 1801, chiefly through the exertions of Mr. Yates, and is served by a curate appointed by the vicar of West Allington. There is a place of worship for Wesleyan Methodists. Salcombe, which is situated on the western side of the entrance to Kingsbridge harbour, is the principal station for that port, and contains several shipwrights yards. A pleasure fair is held here at Whitsuntide.

SALCOMBE (REGIS), a parish in the eastern division of the hundred of Budleigh, county of Devon, 2 miles (E.N.E.) from Sidmouth, containing 436 inhabitants. The living is a discharged vicarage, in the peculiar jurisdiction and patronage of the Dean and Chapter of Exeter, rated in the king's books at £14. 12. 8., endowed with £1000 royal bounty. The church is dedicated to St. Peter and St. Mary. There was formerly a chapel, dedicated to St. Clement and St. Mary Magdalene. The parish is bounded on the south by the English channel, and was anciently held in royal demesne. Courts leet and baron are occasionally held. Gypsum and chalk for lime are obtained here.

SALCOTT, a parish in the hundred of Winstree, county of Essex, 8½ miles (S.S.W.) from Colchester, containing 138 inhabitants. The living is a discharged vicarage, with Great Wigborough, in the archdeaconry of Colchester, and diocese of London, endowed with £400 private benefaction, and £1200 royal bounty, and in the patronage of the Bishop of London. The church is dedicated to St. Mary.

SALDEN, a hamlet in the parish of Mursley, hundred of Cottesloe, county of Buckingham, 4½ miles (E.N.E.) from Winslow. The population is returned with the parish.

SALE, a township in the parish of Ashton upon Mersey, though locally in that of Great Budworth, hundred of Bucklow, county palatine of Chester, 2 miles from Ashton upon Mersey, containing 1049 inhabitants. The Duke of Bridgewater's canal passes through the township.

SALEBY, a parish in the Wold division of the hundred of Calceworth, parts of Lindsey, county of Lincoln, 1½ mile (N. by E.) from Alford, containing with Thoresthorpe, 235 inhabitants. The living is a vicarage, in the archdeaconry and diocese of Lincoln, rated in the king's books at £4, and in the patronage of the Trustees of Alford school. The church is dedicated to St. Margaret.

SALEHURST, a parish in the hundred of Henhurst, rape of Hastings, county of Sussex, ¾ of a mile (N.E.) from Robertsbridge, containing, with Robertsbridge, 2121 inhabitants. The living is a vicarage, in the archdeaconry of Lewes, and diocese of Chichester, rated in the king's books at £14, and in the patronage of S. B. P. Micklethwaite, Esq. The church, dedicated to St. Mary, exhibits portions in the early and later styles of English architecture. The river Rother runs through the parish, and is here crossed by a bridge. John Cooper, in 1699, devised land for the establishment of a free school, which, by the returns made to parliament in 1786, was of the annual value of £45, but the donor's directions have never been complied with.

SALESBURY, a chapelry in the parish and lower division of the hundred of Blackburn, county palatine of Lancaster, 4½ miles (N.) from Blackburn, containing 427 inhabitants. The living is a perpetual curacy, in the archdeaconry and diocese of Chester, endowed with £400 private benefaction, £600 royal bounty, and £600 parliamentary grant, and in the patronage of R. B. W. Bulkeley, Esq.

SALFORD, a parish in the hundred of Manshead, county of Bedford, 4½ miles (N. by W.) from Woburn, containing 312 inhabitants. The living is a discharged vicarage, united, in 1750, to the rectory of Holcutt, in the archdeaconry of Bedford, and diocese of Lincoln, rated in the king's books at £7. 16. 3. The church is dedicated to St. Mary. There is a place of worship for Wesleyan Methodists.

SALFORD, county palatine of Lancaster. — See MANCHESTER.

SALFORD, a parish in the hundred of Chadlington, county of Oxford, 2 miles (W.N.W.) from Chipping-Norton, containing 293 inhabitants. The living is a rectory, in the archdeaconry and diocese of Oxford, rated in the king's books at £9. 11. 3., and in the patronage of the Rev. R. J. Skillicorne. The church is dedicated to St. Mary.

SALFORD, a parish in the Stratford division of the hundred of Barlichway, county of Warwick, 5¾ miles (S. by W.) from Alcester, containing 813 inhabitants. The living is a vicarage, in the archdeaconry and diocese of Worcester, rated in the king's books at £9, endowed with £800 parliamentary grant, and in the patronage of Lady Skipwith. The church is dedicated to St. Matthew. The river Avon and its tributary stream, the Arrow, run through the parish. William Perkins, in 1656, gave £232 for the support of a free grammar school; the annual income, now upwards of £40, is applied to instructing, in English, the children of parishioners; the classics were formerly taught, but they have of late years been discontinued. An ancient mansion, the property of Mr. Berkeley, is now occupied as a nunnery, the society consisting of an abbess, sixteen professed nuns, and a school for young ladies, noviciates.

SALHOUSE, a parish in the hundred of Taverham, county of Norfolk, 4¼ miles (S.E. by S.) from

Coltishall, containing 475 inhabitants. The living is a discharged vicarage, with that of Wroxham, in the archdeaconry and diocese of Norwich. The Rev. D. Collyer was patron in 1801. The church is dedicated to All Saints. There is a place of worship for Baptists.

SALING (BARDFIELD), county of Essex. — See BARDFIELD-SALING.

SALING (GREAT), a parish in the hundred of HINCKFORD, county of ESSEX, 5 miles (N. W. by W.) from Braintree, containing 326 inhabitants. The living is a discharged vicarage, in the jurisdiction of the Commissary of Essex and Herts, concurrently with the Consistorial Court of the Bishop of London, rated in the king's books at £7, endowed with £200 royal bounty. B. Goodrich, Esq. was patron in 1816. The church is dedicated to St. James.

Arms.

SALISBURY, a city having separate civil jurisdiction, locally in the hundred of Underditch, county of WILTS, 82 miles (S. W. by W.) from London, containing 8763 inhabitants. This city owes its origin to the ruin of Old Sarum, where the bishops of the diocese of Wiltshire had fixed their seat; which place being very inconvenient, from its exposed situation on an eminence, want of water, and from its military tenants, who not only levied contributions on their property, but insulted the priests in the exercise of their devotions, they solicited permission to transfer the see to a more appropriate situation. Bishop Poore having obtained license from Pope Honorius, selected the site of the present city, which lies in a pleasant vale, about two miles from the remains of Old Sarum, and laid the foundation of the present magnificent cathedral in the year 1220. The completion of that edifice was soon followed by the removal not only of the members of the establishment, but also of the inhabitants, who gradually deserting the old town, and building houses near the new cathedral church, Salisbury soon increased in extent, and grew into importance. Its progress was much accelerated by a charter of Henry III., constituting the new establishment a free city, and conferring on the inhabitants the same privileges and immunities as were enjoyed by the inhabitants of Winchester. This monarch also empowered the bishop to surround the city and the cathedral close with walls and ditches, to repair the roads and bridges, and to levy tallage for the completion of the walls. Disputes, however, arising between the bishop and the citizens respecting these aids, in the reign of Edward I., both parties appealed to the king in council, and that monarch, deciding in favour of the bishop, deprived the citizens of their charter, which was subsequently restored to them upon an amicable arrangement of the dispute by the parties themselves. About this period, Bishop Bridport built a bridge at Harnham, and thus changing the direction of the great western road, which formerly passed through Old Sarum, that place was completely deserted, and Salisbury became one of the most flourishing cities in the kingdom.

Edward I. assembled a parliament there, to deliberate upon measures for recovering the province of Gascoigne, which had been seized upon by Philip of France; at which parliament none of the clergy assisted, the king having suspended them from the exercise of their secular functions for having refused him aid. In the reign of Edward III., a second parliament, for enquiring into the state of the kingdom, was held at Salisbury, at which Mortimer, Earl of March, and his partisans, were attended by their followers in arms : the Earls of Kent, Norfolk, and Lancaster, who, on being summoned to attend this parliament, were prohibited by Mortimer from appearing with an armed force, finding, on their arrival, that his own partisans were armed, retreated for the purpose of assembling their retainers, and, returning with an army, were about to take vengeance on Mortimer, when the quarrel was compromised through the intervention of the clergy. From the time of Edward I., the bishops and the citizens appear to have lived in a state of mutual harmony, till the reign of Richard II., when the prelate requiring the corporation to concur with him in his efforts to suppress the meetings of the Lollards, who assembled here in great numbers, the latter refused, and the bishop, appealing to the king, obtained an order in council compelling them to assist him in that object. In the reign of Richard III., the Duke of Buckingham, who had headed an unsuccessful insurrection against him, was taken prisoner in his retreat, and, being brought hither, was immediately executed, in 1483, without any trial. No event of historical importance appears, in connection with this city, till after the close of the parliamentary war, when, during the interregnum, Col. Wyndham, with other gentlemen of this county, marched into Salisbury with two hundred armed men, and proclaimed Charles II. king; but they were not supported by the inhabitants of the surrounding country.

The city is pleasantly situated in a spacious valley, near the confluence of the rivers Nadder and Willey with the Avon, and consists of several principal streets regularly formed, and intersected at right angles by smaller ones, dividing the town into a number of squares, called Chequers, which derive their form from the original grant of the bishops of a certain number of perches in front and in depth allotted for building; the areas, round which the houses have been erected, are laid out in gardens. Most of the houses are built of brick, and of modern erection, many of them being of handsome appearance, but there are some of a more ancient date, constructed of timber and brick-work plastered over, of irregular form and size. The waters of the rivers run through most of the streets of the city, in canals lined with brick, and contribute greatly to their cleanliness, and to the health of the inhabitants. The city is connected, by two stone bridges of six arches each, with the suburb of Fisherton, including which it occupies an area nearly three quarters of a mile square, and, with the suburb of East Harnham, by an ancient bridge of ten arches : this bridge is divided into two parts by a small islet, on which was formerly a chapel, dedicated to St. John, where three chaplains were appointed to say mass, and to receive the contributions of passengers towards the keeping of it in repair. Some improvement has lately taken place in paving and lighting the town, which is amply supplied with water. The Salisbury and Wiltshire library and news-room was established in 1819 : the library amounts to more than two thousand volumes, in the various departments of literature, and annexed to it is a small museum, containing a collection of various fossils peculiar to this neighbourhood : this institution is supported by a proprietary and by annual subscriptions. A small neat theatre is opened for some months in the winter, and assemblies and concerts are held during the same season, in rooms well adapted to the purpose, though, as public buildings, not entitled to architectural notice. Races take place annually in August, and are in general well attended. The environs are pleasant, containing, in addition to several villas with which they are ornamented, the seat of Wadham Wyndham, Esq., on the north-east ; and, on the bank of the Avon, Longford castle, the seat of the Earl of Radnor, originally built in the reign of James I., and subsequently enlarged and considerably improved. Salisbury was formerly celebrated for its manufactures of flannels, druggets, and the cloths called Salisbury Whites ; but these branches of trade are now almost extinct, and what remains is confined to a very inconsiderable number of persons : the town is still noted for its manufacture of the more select articles of cutlery of superior quality, but the sale is very limited. The Salisbury canal, joining with the Andover canal near Romsey, was originally intended to be continued westward to Bath and Bristol, connecting the Bristol and English channels, but the design has been abandoned, barges at present proceeding no further in this direction than Romsey, though it has a communication with Southampton and the English channel. The market days are Tuesday and Saturday ; the former for corn, of which there is an abundant supply, and the latter for cheese and all kinds of provisions ; there is also a large cattle market every alternate Tuesday. The fairs, which are falling into disuse, are on the Tuesday after January 6th for cattle, Tuesday after the 25th of March for cloth, Whit-Monday and Tuesday for horses and pedlary, and October 20th for butter and cheese. The poultry cross, which appears to have been built in the reign of Edw. III., and of which only the lower part is remaining, where butter, eggs, and poultry are sold, is situated without the south-west corner of the marketplace : this is an extensive quadrilateral area, well arranged for the general uses of the market.

The government of the city, by charter of incorporation granted in the reign of Henry III., and confirmed by successive sovereigns till that of Anne, is vested in a mayor, recorder, deputy recorder, twenty-four aldermen, and thirty common council - men, assisted by a town clerk and two chamberlains, with three serjeants at mace, and other subordinate officers. The mayor is elected annually by the corporation at large, and sworn into office by the bishop, at his court, or, in his absence, by the late mayor, recorder, and aldermen. The high steward and the recorder are usually noblemen possessing influence in the county, and hold their offices for

Corporate Seal.

life. The mayor, recorder, late mayor, and ten of the aldermen, are justices of the peace within the city, and hold quarterly courts of session for all offences : the corporation, by their charter, have the power to try for capital offences, but generally transfer prisoners charged with such crimes to the judge travelling the western circuit. On the part of the bishop are a bailiff and deputy bailiff, who are empowered to hold a court of record, for the recovery of debts to any amount, on the first Saturday in every month, the jurisdiction of which extends over the city and the cathedral close : they also hold a court leet for the bishop, as lord of the manor. The bailiff and deputy bailiff are both appointed by the bishop, and, by charter, are chosen for the same offices on behalf of the corporation : their powers resemble those of the sheriff of the county, and it is their duty to summon the juries for the sessions held in the city. The Close of Sarum is a corporation, consisting of the bishop, the recorder, and the canons residentiary, who are justices ; they may hold sessions of the peace for the liberty of the Close, either in the guildhall of the city, or the Close itself, at the pleasure of the bishop. The bishop is not entitled to a place in the chapter when it consists of the dean and the residentiary canons only, that is, a common chapter ; in an extraordinary, or what is commonly called a general, chapter, which is composed of all the members, the bishop is entitled to a seat, as prebendary of Pottern. The assizes and the Lent quarter sessions for the county are regularly held here. The council-house, erected in 1795 (the former building having been destroyed by fire) under the provisions of an act of parliament, at the expense of the late Earl of Radnor, on the site of the ancient guildhall, is a substantial and handsome building of white brick, ornamented with rustic quoins and cornices of stone, and consisting of two wings, connected by a central vestibule, to which is an entrance through a receding portico of four Doric columns, supporting an entablature enriched with triglyphs, and surmounted by an open balustrade, with a tablet in the centre, inscribed with the name of the founder, and the date of its erection. The right wing is occupied entirely by the council-chamber and other offices, in which the business of the corporation is transacted, and the public entertainments are held : the council-chamber is seventy-five feet in length, twenty-four in breadth, and twenty-four feet in height, and is ornamented with a whole-length picture of Queen Anne, by Dahl ; and half-length portraits of the Earl of Radnor, and William Hussey, Esq., one of the members for the city, by Hopner. The left wing comprises the courtrooms, in which are held the sessions for the city, the assizes and sessions for the county, and the bishop's court ; above is a grand jury room, and other offices : the grand jury room is decorated with portraits of James I.; John, Duke of Somerset; Seth Ward, Bishop of the diocese ; Sir Robert Hyde, Chief Justice of England; Sir Samuel Eyre, also Chief Justice ; and several other distinguished characters. The building at first erected, being found too small for holding the assizes, has been enlarged by public subscription. The county gaol and bridewell, a substantial and spacious edifice, erected in 1818, at the western extremity of Fisherton-Anger, at an expense of about £30,000, comprises ten wards, ten day-rooms, and ten airing-yards, for the classification of prisoners, who are employed in cultivating the land within the boundary wall of the gaol, and receive a certain sum of money on their discharge : the buildings contain apartments for the governor, a chapel, and two infirmaries, and the regulations are judicious and humane. The city exercised the elective franchise in the 23rd of Edward I., since which time it has regularly returned two members to parliament : the right of election is vested in the mayor and corporation : the mayor is the returning officer.

The seat of the diocese was originally established at Wilton, in this county, about the beginning of the tenth century, where it remained under the superintendence of eleven successive bishops, of whom Hermannus, the last, having been appointed to the see of Sherborne, annexed that bishoprick to Wilton, and founded, for the united sees,

Arms of the See of Sarum.

a cathedral church at Old Sarum, which was afterwards completed by Osmund, who, having accompanied William the Conqueror into England, was, by that monarch, appointed bishop. The see remained at Old Sarum till the year 1217, when Richard le Poore transferred the episcopal chair to Salisbury in 1220, where it has ever since remained. The establishment consists of a bishop, dean, precentor, chancellor, treasurer, six canons residentiary, who are also prebendaries, three archdeacons (for Berks, Sarum, and Wilts), subdean, succentor, thirty-eight prebendaries, four priest vicars, six singing men, eight choristers, organist, and other officers. The cathedral, dedicated to the Blessed Virgin Mary, begun by Richard le Poore in 1220, and completed in 1258, is one of the most magnificent and interesting ecclesiastical edifices in the kingdom. It is in the form of a double cross, with a highly enriched tower and lofty spire rising from the intersection of the nave and larger transepts, to the height of four hundred feet from the pavement, being the highest in England : the whole building, with the exception only of the upper part of the tower, and the spire, which are of a later date, are in the purest style of early English architecture. The west front is divided into five compartments by buttresses ornamented with canopied niches filled with statues: between the two central buttresses is the principal entrance through a richly-moulded arch of spacious dimensions, with a smaller on each side: above the entrance is a large and beautiful window, and at the angles of the front are square embattled towers beautifully enriched, and crowned with angular pinnacles surmounted by spires. The north front is of considerable beauty, and the end fronts of the transepts, projecting boldly from the sides of the main building, and displaying, in successive series of arches, a pleasing variety of composition, corresponding with the general style, are a fine relief to the exterior. The interior, of which the perspective is impressively striking, is exquisitely beautiful, from the loftiness of its elevation and the delicacy and lightness of its construction : the nave is separated from the aisles by a handsome range of ten clustered columns and finely-pointed arches ; the roof, which is plainly groined, is

eighty-four feet high, and the space above the columns is occupied by a triforium of elegant design, and a range of clerestory windows of three lights, of which the central is higher than the rest, and which is continued round the whole extent of the building ; the larger transepts, of the same character with the nave, consist of three arches of similar arrangement, and the smaller of two arches. The choir, separated from the nave by a screen of modern workmanship supporting the organ, which was the gift of his Majesty George III., consists of seven arches, and, by the removal of the altar-screen, has been connected with the Lady chapel, of which the roof, being lower than that of the choir, in a great degree destroys the effect : the bishop's throne, the pulpit, and the prebendal stalls, are of finely-executed tabernacle-work, and harmonise with the prevailing character of the building : the floor is of black and white marble ; the east window is embellished with a painting of the Resurrection, by Eginton, from a design by Sir Joshua Reynolds ; the choir is also ornamented with a painting of the Elevation of the Brazen Serpent in the Wilderness, from a design by Mortimer, executed by Pearson, the gift of the late Earl of Radnor ; and many of the other windows are painted in Mosaic. The cathedral was repaired, under the superintendence of Mr. Wyatt, at an expense of £26,000. The chapels in the transepts have been removed, and their principal ornaments have been distributed in various parts of the building. In the nave, choir, and transepts are numerous monuments to the bishops of the see, among which are those of Bishops Joceline and Roger, the latter being perhaps the earliest specimen of monumental sculpture extant; also of a chorister bishop, one of the children of the choir, who died while personating the character of a bishop, according to custom, during the festival of St. Nicholas ; exclusively of several to the Earls of Salisbury, and the neighbouring nobility and gentry. The length of the cathedral, from east to west, is four hundred and fifty feet within the walls ; and the breadth, along the greater transept, two hundred and five feet. The cloisters are the largest and most magnificent of any in the kingdom, and the cathedral close has some entrance gateways of ancient character and of beautiful design. The chapter-house, of an octagonal form, of which the roof is supported by one central clustered column, is a beautiful building lighted by lofty windows; the frieze is ornamented with subjects from the sacred writings in bas relief, which is in tolerable preservation. The episcopal palace is the work of different times, and combines various styles of architecture ; a considerable portion was added by the late Dr. Shute Barrington : it contains portraits of nearly all the modern prelates of the see.

The city comprises the parishes of St. Edmund, St. Martin, and St. Thomas, in the jurisdiction of the Subdean, and diocese, of Salisbury : the Cathedral Close is extra-parochial, and under the jurisdiction of the Dean. The living of St. Edmund's is a rectory not in charge, endowed with £1600 parliamentary grant, and in the patronage of the Bishop : the church, formerly collegiate, is a handsome structure, in the later style of English architecture, with a tower, which, having fallen down in 1653, was rebuilt in a style of appropriate character : the interior is neatly arranged, but the chancel has been modernised : at the east end is a beautiful painted window of the Ascension, by Eginton, the gift of the late Samuel Whitchurch, Esq.: the churchyard, which contains many monuments, is finely planted with lime-trees, which, interweaving their branches, form avenues of great beauty. The living of St. Martin's is a discharged rectory, rated in the king's books at £11.3.1½., endowed with £1000 parliamentary grant, and in the patronage of Mr. Wyndham: the church is a spacious structure, combining different styles of architecture, with a tower surmounted by a spire; the chancel is in the early English, and other parts in the decorated and later styles of English architecture. The living of St. Thomas' is a perpetual curacy, endowed with £1200 parliamentary grant, and in the patronage of the Dean and Chapter: the church is a spacious and handsome structure, in the later style of English architecture, with a tower on the south side of the south aisle; the nave is lighted with a handsome range of clerestory windows; the chancel and other parts are specimens of considerable merit: among the monuments is one supposed to be that of the Duke of Buckingham, who was executed here, in the reign of Richard III. There are two places of worship for Independents, and one each for Baptists, Wesleyan Methodists, Unitarians, and Roman Catholics. The grammar school, in the Close, for the education of the choristers, is under the superintendence of the Dean and Chapter: among the scholars educated in it was Addison, the poet and essayist, who was a native of Milston, near Amesbury, in this county, of which parish his father was rector. The city grammar school was founded by Queen Elizabeth, for the education of the sons of citizens, and is under the control of the mayor and commonalty. A school, in which eight orphan females are maintained and educated, was founded by a member of the Godolphin family: a school is also supported by the bishop, in which twenty boys and twenty girls are clothed and educated; and National and Sunday schools are supported by subscription.

The infirmary, a spacious and commodious brick building, near Fisherton bridge, is more adapted to its use than calculated for ornament: it owes its origin to Lord Feversham, who bequeathed £500 to the first institution of the kind which should be established in the county; it is further liberally supported by contributions. The College of Matrons was founded for the maintenance of the widows of ten poor clergymen, by Seth Ward, Bishop of the diocese, who endowed it with property producing £200 per annum; the income has been much augmented by the increased value of the original property and subsequent donations: the buildings are within the Close, and the establishment is under the direction of the Bishop and the Dean and Chapter, who elect the matrons, to each of whom a handsome pension is allowed. Bishop Richard le Poore founded, near Harnham bridge, an hospital for a master, eight aged men, and four women, which was completed by his successor, Bishop Bingham: it is occupied by a master, six aged men, and six women, among whom the income arising from the endowment is divided. Trinity hospital, founded in the reign of Richard II., still maintains twelve aged brethren; the mayor and commonalty exercise the office of master. Among other similar establishments are Bricket's hospital, in Exeter-street, founded in 1519, for six aged widows, who receive each three shillings and sixpence per week; Eyre's hospital, founded in 1617, for six men

and their wives, who also receive each three shillings and sixpence per week; Blechynden's hospital, founded in 1683, for six aged women, who receive two shillings and sixpence each per week; Taylor's hospital, founded in 1698, for six aged men nominated by the corporation, and who have a weekly allowance of three shillings and sixpence each; and Frowd's hospital, in Bedwin-street, founded in 1750, for six aged men and six women, who have each four shillings and sixpence per week. There are also several unendowed almshouses for the residence of poor people, of which the principal are three in St. Ann's-street, the bequest of Mrs. Sutton; six in Culver-street, supposed to be the donation of Bishop Poore; twenty in Bedwin-street, the gift of Mrs. Marks; and thirteen in Castle-street, presented to the corporation by William Hussey, Esq., M.P., for the use of the poor: these last were subsequently endowed by the will of the donor, and are occupied by men and their wives, who receive three shillings and sixpence per week. There are various charitable bequests for apprenticing poor children, and for distribution among the poor: the principal is the charity of Joan Popple, who gave to the mayor and commonalty, for the use of the poor, considerable property in Basinghall-street London, producing, at present, a rental of nearly £400: she was interred in St. Thomas's church, in this city, in 1572, and the mayor and commonalty have lately erected a monument to her memory. John, Duke of Somerset, who died in 1671, gave to the mayor and commonalty a considerable sum for the purchase of an estate, the rental of which is applied to the apprenticing of poor children of the city. A college was founded here by Egidius de Bridport, in 1260, in which many of the students who had retired from Oxford, in consequence of their quarrel with Otho, the pope's legate, in 1238, afterwards continued their studies: and there were formerly remains of a monastery of Grey friars, founded by the Bishop of Salisbury, in the reign of Henry III., on a site of ground given by that monarch; a convent of Black friars, to which Edward I., if not the founder, was at least a considerable benefactor; and of the hospital of St. Michael, and the college of St. Erith. The neighbourhood abounds with flints found in the alluvial soil, and in strata of chalk; these flints, both the nodular from the chalk, and the fractured found in the gravel, yield a variety of organic remains of the *spongia* and *alcyonia genera*; several valuable collections have been formed in the neighbourhood, and it has been reckoned that there are not less than twelve distinct species of that submarine substance. Among the eminent natives of this city were, Walter Winterton, Cardinal of St. Sabric; William Herman, author of several works in prose and verse; John Thornborough, Bishop of Worcester; George Coryate, author of "The Crudities;" Michael Muschant, an able civilian and poet; Sir Toby Matthews, a celebrated Jesuit and politician; Dr. Thomas Bennet, a noted divine and writer; Thomas Chubb and John Eden, distinguished controversial writers; John Greenhill, a celebrated portrait-painter; William and Henry Lawes, musicians and composers; Dr. Harris, an eminent historian and biographer; James Harris, author of "Hermes;" and John Tobin, author of "The Honeymoon," and other dramatic works. Salisbury gives the title of marquis to the family of Cecil.

SALKELD (GREAT), a parish in LEATH ward, county of CUMBERLAND, 3 miles (S. by W.) from Kirk-Oswald, containing 403 inhabitants. The living is a rectory, held with the archdeaconry of Carlisle, in the diocese of Carlisle, rated in the king's books at £22.10.10., and endowed with £200 private benefaction, and £600 royal bounty. The church is dedicated to St. Cuthbert: the tower, which appears to have contained four rooms above each other, was formerly resorted to as a place of security; under it is a dungeon. There are places of worship for Presbyterians and Primitive Methodists. The parish is intersected by the river Eden, which is crossed by a bridge of singular construction, having elliptical, semicircular, and pointed arches; it was partly built with the materials of an old bridge taken down about fifty years ago: the remains of a pier belonging to a still more ancient structure, demolished by a great flood in 1360, are still visible in the stream of the Eden. A school-house, erected by subscription in 1686, is endowed with about £3 per annum. In the neighbourhood are vestiges of an ancient encampment, the ramparts of which are twelve feet high; and on the common is a chalybeate spring. Among the several eminent natives of this parish were, Dr. George Benson, a nonconformist divine and biblical critic, born in 1699; the late Lord Ellenborough, Lord Chief Justice of the King's Bench; and Rowland Wetheral, the celebrated mathematician and astronomer, born in the middle of the last century.

SALKELD (LITTLE), a township in the parish of ADDINGHAM, LEATH ward, county of CUMBERLAND, 3½ miles (S.) from Kirk-Oswald, containing 111 inhabitants. Here was anciently a chapel.

SALL, a parish in the hundred of EYNSFORD, county of NORFOLK, 1¾ mile (N. N. E.) from Reepham, containing 245 inhabitants. The living is a rectory, in the archdeaconry of Norfolk, and diocese of Norwich, rated in the king's books at £12. 19. 7., and in the patronage of the Master and Fellows of Pembroke Hall, Cambridge. The church, dedicated to St. Peter and St. Paul, is a stately cruciform structure, principally in the later style of English architecture, with a western tower of elegant proportions.

SALMONBY, a parish in the hundred of HILL, parts of LINDSEY, county of LINCOLN, 5¼ miles (E. N. E.) from Horncastle, containing 89 inhabitants. The living is a discharged rectory, in the archdeaconry and diocese of Lincoln, rated in the king's books at £5. 10. 2½. The Rev. John Hall was patron in 1812. The church is dedicated to St. Margaret. Edward Richardson, in 1714, bequeathed land for teaching poor children of the parishes of Salmonby and Thetford.

SALPERTON, a parish in the hundred of BRADLEY, county of GLOUCESTER, 5 miles (N. W. by N.) from North Leach, containing 173 inhabitants. The living is a perpetual curacy, in the archdeaconry and diocese of Gloucester, endowed with £600 private benefaction, £600 royal bounty, and £600 parliamentary grant, and in the patronage of John Browne, Esq.

SALT, a joint township with Enson, in that part of the parish of ST. MARY, LICHFIELD, which is in the southern division of the hundred of PIREHILL, county of STAFFORD, 4 miles (N. E. by N.) from Stafford, containing 439 inhabitants. There is a place of worship for Wesleyan Methodists.

SALTASH, a borough, market town, and chapelry, in the parish of ST. STEPHEN, having separate jurisdiction, though locally in the southern division of the hundred of East, county of CORNWALL, 21 miles (S.S.E.) from Launceston, and 220 (W. S. W.) from London, containing 1548 inhabitants. This is a place of considerable antiquity, the county

Seal and Arms.

assizes having been held here so early as 1393. In the civil commotions between Charles I. and the parliament, its local importance was evinced in the repeated contests for possession by both the conflicting parties, which terminated in its final abandonment by the royalists in 1646; during this collision the town was fortified. It is pleasantly situated on a steep rocky elevation rising from the western bank of the river Tamar, and consists principally of three narrow streets irregularly formed; the houses in general are of ancient appearance. The market is on Saturday; and fairs are held on Candlemas-day, and July 25th, for cattle; there are likewise four quarterly shows for cattle. The inhabitants are, for the greater part, fishermen, or persons connected with the docks of Devonport. The first charter of incorporation was granted in the reign of Henry III., which was confirmed by Richard II., and renewed, with additional privileges, by Charles II., in 1682, under the provisions of which the municipal body consists of a mayor and six aldermen, styled "the council of the borough," with an indefinite number of free burgesses, assisted by a recorder and other officers. The mayor is chosen annually from among the aldermen, by the aldermen and free burgesses; the aldermen out of the free burgesses, and the town clerk by the aldermen. The property of the oyster-fishery, to the mouth of the Tamar, except between Candlemas and Easter, with river dues for anchorage, buoyage, and salvage, and a right of ferry, are vested in the corporation, and their coroner sits upon all bodies found drowned in the river. Holding the manor under the duchy of Cornwall, they are empowered, by the charter, to hold a court of admiralty for the borough, and liberty of the river Tamar. A court of record, established by charter of the 35th of George III., for the recovery of debts to any amount, is held every week, at which the mayor and aldermen, or any two of them, preside. Sessions for the division are held quarterly in the guildhall: the assizes have not been held here for many years. Saltash first returned members to parliament in the reign of Edward VI.: the elective franchise is in the freeholders of the borough possessing burgage tenements, about seventy in number: the mayor is the returning officer. The living is a perpetual curacy, in the archdeaconry of Cornwall, and diocese of Exeter, and in the patronage of the Mayor and Corporation. The chapel, dedicated to St. Nicholas, is an ancient structure, with a fine massive tower: in the interior is a magnificent monument to the memory of three brothers who were drowned. There is a place of worship for Baptists. Here are endowments of uncertain date; one by John Francis Buller, to the amount of £15 per annum, for the instruction of poor children at the National school, and the other by the Crown, of £6. 17. 2. per annum, in aid of the grammar school.

SALTBY, a parish in the hundred of FRAMLAND, county of LEICESTER, 8¼ miles (N. E.) from Melton-Mowbray, containing 234 inhabitants. The living is a discharged vicarage, consolidated with that of Sproxton, in the archdeaconry of Leicester, and diocese of Lincoln, rated in the king's books at £7. The church is dedicated to St. Peter. The small river Eye has its source in this parish.

SALTER, an extra-parochial district, in ALLERDALE ward above Darwent, county of CUMBERLAND, 8 miles (E. by S.) from Whitehaven, containing, with Eskat, 37 inhabitants.

SALTERFORTH, a township in the parish of BARNOLDWICK, eastern division of the wapentake of STAINCLIFFE and EWCROSS, West riding of the county of YORK, 8¼ miles (S. W. by W) from Skipton, containing 686 inhabitants.

SALTERSFORD, a chapelry in the parish of PRESTBURY, hundred of MACCLESFIELD, county palatine of CHESTER, 6 miles (E. N. E.) from Macclesfield. The population is returned with the parish. The living is a perpetual curacy, in the archdeaconry and diocese of Chester, endowed with £200 private benefaction, and £800 royal bounty, and in the patronage of the Vicar of Prestbury. Saltersford gives the inferior title of baron to the family of Stanhope, Earls of Courtown.

SALTFLEET-HAVEN, a hamlet (formerly a market town) in the parish of SKIDBROOK, Marsh division of the hundred of LOUTH-ESKE, parts of LINDSEY, county of LINCOLN, 38 miles (N. E. by E.) from Lincoln. The population is returned with the parish. This was a town of some importance about half a century ago, but it is now decayed : the old town is said to have been destroyed by an inundation of the sea. There is a place of worship for Wesleyan Methodists. A fair is held on October 3rd, and is celebrated for the show of good foals. Here is a very fine bed of oysters.

SALTFLEETBY (ALL SAINTS), a parish in the Marsh division of the hundred of LOUTH-ESKE, parts of LINDSEY, county of LINCOLN, 10¼ miles (E. by N.) from Louth, containing 218 inhabitants. The living is a rectory, in the archdeaconry and diocese of Lincoln, rated in the king's books at £12. 19. 4½., and in the patronage of the President and Fellows of Magdalene College, Oxford. The church is dedicated to All Saints.

SALTFLEETBY (ST. CLEMENT'S), a parish in the Marsh division of the hundred of LOUTH-ESKE, parts of LINDSEY, county of LINCOLN, 10½ miles (E. N. E.) from Louth, containing 126 inhabitants. The living is a discharged rectory, in the archdeaconry and diocese of Lincoln, rated in the king's books at £7. 0. 1., and in the patronage of Earl Brownlow. The church is dedicated to St. Clement.

SALTFLEETBY (ST. PETER'S), a parish in the Marsh division of the hundred of LOUTH-ESKE, parts of LINDSEY, county of LINCOLN, 8½ miles (E. by N.) from Louth, containing 185 inhabitants. The living is a rectory, in the archdeaconry and diocese of Lincoln, rated in the king's books at £5, and in the patronage of the Provost and Fellows of Oriel College, Oxford. The church is dedicated to St. Peter.

SALTFORD, a parish in the hundred of KEYNSHAM, county of SOMERSET, 5¼ miles (W. N. W.) from Bath, containing 327 inhabitants. The living is a discharged rectory, in the archdeaconry of Bath, and diocese of Bath and Wells, rated in the king's books at £10. 5. 10., and in the patronage of the Duke of Buckingham. The church is dedicated to St. Mary. The parish is bounded on the east and on the north by the river Avon, on the banks of which there are extensive brass works.

SALT-HILL, a village partly in the parish of FARNHAM-ROYAL, hundred of BURNHAM, and partly in the parish of UPTON, hundred of STOKE, county of BUCKINGHAM, 2 miles (N.) from Eton. The population is returned with the parishes, This village, which is situated on the road to Bath, is distinguished by two exceedingly large and splendid inns, and is further noted as being connected with the triennial ceremony of the Eton scholars, termed the Montem, the procession repairing hither to a tumulus on the south side of the road, which probably acquired the name Salt-hill from the money collected by the boys being called "Salt Money."

SALTHOUSE, a parish in the hundred of HOLT, county of NORFOLK, 2¼ miles (E.) from Clay, containing 281 inhabitants. The living is a discharged rectory, annexed to that of Kelling, in the archdeaconry and diocese of Norwich, rated in the king's books at £20. The church is dedicated to St. Nicholas.

SALTMARSH, a township in the parish of HOWDEN, wapentake of HOWDENSHIRE, East riding of the county of YORK, 4½ miles (S. E.) from Howden, containing 179 inhabitants. Three poor children are educated for £1 a year, the gift of Richard Jewitt, in 1735.

SALTON, a parish in the liberty of St. PETER of YORK, East riding, though locally in the wapentake of Ryedale, North riding, of the county of YORK, comprising the townships of Brawby and Salton, and containing 336 inhabitants, of which number, 148 are in the township of Salton, 6¾ miles (W. S. W.) from Pickering. The living is a discharged vicarage, in the peculiar jurisdiction of the Impropriator, rated in the king's books at £4. 10. 10., and in the patronage of G. W. Dowker, Esq. The church is dedicated to St. John of Beverley.

SALTWICK, a township in the northern division of the parish of STANNINGTON, western division of CASTLE ward, county of NORTHUMBERLAND, 5 miles (S. S. W.) from Morpeth. The population is returned with the parish.

SALTWOOD, a parish in the hundred of HAYNE, lathe of SHEPWAY, county of KENT, ¾ of a mile (N. by W.) from Hythe, containing 570 inhabitants. The living is a rectory, with the perpetual curacy of Hythe, in the peculiar jurisdiction and patronage of the Archbishop of Canterbury, rated in the king's books at £34. The church, dedicated to St. Peter and St. Paul, is principally in the decorated style of English architecture. Saltwood was distinguished at an early period for its castle, which is said to have been first built by the son of Hengist, the Saxon, in 448, and, in the reign of John, to have become one of the palaces of the Archbishops of Canterbury. The remains, which are so considerable as to create some idea of its former magnificence, are situated on Saltwood Green, commanding a fine view of the sea, which it is supposed formerly came up to this place, an anchor having been dug up near the spot. The Rev. George Barnesley, in 1723, bequeathed a rent-charge of £5. 5. for teaching poor children.

SALWARPE, a parish in the upper division of the hundred of HALFSHIRE, county of WORCESTER, 2½ miles (W. S. W.) from Droitwich, containing 462 inhabitants. The living is a rectory, in the archdeaconry and diocese of Worcester, rated in the king's books at £14. 14. 7. The Rev.J.V.Vashon was patron in 1808. The church, dedicated to St. Michael, exhibits portions in the Norman, and in the decorated and later styles of English architecture. The Droitwich canal passes through the parish. Thomas Trimmell bequeathed £24 per annum for teaching poor children, and repairing the church; but the charity commissioners report it as lost. A small Benedictine priory, a cell to the abbey of Fontevrault, was founded here in the reign of Richard II., the site of which is occupied by an old mansion erected in the time of Henry VIII. Richard Beauchamp, the celebrated Earl of Warwick, was born here, in 1351.

SAMBOURN, a hamlet in the parish of COUGHTON, Alcester division of the hundred of BARLICHWAY, county of WARWICK, 3¾ miles (N. W. by N.) from Alcester, containing 653 inhabitants.

SAMLESBURY, a chapelry in the parish and lower division of the hundred of BLACKBURN, county palatine of LANCASTER, 4 miles (E. by N.) from Preston, containing 1979 inhabitants. The living is a perpetual curacy, in the archdeaconry and diocese of Chester, endowed with £600 private benefaction, £400 royal bounty, and £700 parliamentary grant, and in the patronage of the Vicar of Blackburn. The chapel is dedicated to St. Leonard. Six poor children are educated for £8 a year by a master, who occupies the school-house rent-free.

SAMPFORD (GREAT), a parish in the hundred of FRESHWELL, county of ESSEX, 3¾ miles (N.E. byN.) from Thaxted, containing 756 inhabitants. The living is a vicarage, with the perpetual curacy of Hempstead, in the jurisdiction of the Commissary of Essex and Herts, concurrently with the Consistorial Court of the Bishop of London, rated in the king's books at £18. E. Hervey, Esq. was patron in 1801. The church is dedicated to St. Michael. There is a place of worship for Baptists.

SAMPFORD (LITTLE), a parish in the hundred of FRESHWELL, county of ESSEX, 3¾ miles (N. E. by E.) from Thaxted, containing 365 inhabitants. The living is a rectory, in the jurisdiction of the Commissary of Essex and Herts, concurrently with the Consistorial Court of the Bishop of London, rated in the king's books at £11, and in the patronage of the Warden and Fellows of New College, Oxford. The church is dedicated to St. Mary.

SAMPFORD-ARUNDEL, a parish in the hundred of MILVERTON, county of SOMERSET, 2¾ miles (S. W.) from Wellington, containing 376 inhabitants. The living is a discharged vicarage, in the archdeaconry of Taunton, and diocese of Bath and Wells, rated in the king's books at £6. 3. 1½., endowed with £800 royal bounty, and in the patronage of W. Bellet, Esq. The church is dedicated to the Holy Cross.

SAMPFORD-BRETT, a parish in the hundred of WILLITON and FREEMANNERS, county of SOMERSET, 7¼ miles (E.S.E.) from Dunster, containing 194 inhabitants. The living is a rectory, in the archdeaconry of Taunton,

and diocese of Bath and Wells, rated in the king's books at £7. 19. 7., and in the patronage of — Tanner, Esq. The church is dedicated to St. George.

SAMPFORD-COURTENAY, a parish in the hundred of BLACK TORRINGTON, county of DEVON, 5¼ miles (N. E. by N.) from Oakhampton, containing 1017 inhabitants. The living is a rectory, in the archdeaconry of Totness, and diocese of Exeter, rated in the king's books at £47. 12. 1., and in the patronage of the Provost and Fellows of King's College, Cambridge. The church is dedicated to St. Andrew. At Sticklepath, which in the time of Henry V. was a separate parish, is a chapel, wherein service is occasionally performed. Near it a mine of copper was opened a few years ago, but with so little success that it is now closed. It was here that a serious commotion, owing to the alteration in the church service, broke out in 1549. At Brightley, in this parish, a monastery of Cistercians was founded, in 1136, by Richard Fitz-Baldwin de Brioniis, Baron of Oakhampton, which was afterwards removed to Ford; but the ruins of a chapel, supposed to have belonged to it, are still remaining.

SAMPFORD-PEVERELL, a parish in the hundred of HALBERTON, county of DEVON, 5 miles (E. by N.) from Tiverton, containing 739 inhabitants. The living is a rectory, in the archdeaconry and diocese of Exeter, rated in the king's books at £23. 8. 11½., and in the patronage of J. Sillifant and T. Hugo, Esqrs. The church, dedicated to St. John the Baptist, has some elegant screen-work; one of the aisles is said to have been built by Margaret, Countess of Richmond, mother of Henry VII. The manor-house, in which she resided, afterwards belonged to Sir Amias Paulett, who had custody of Mary, Queen of Scots, at the time of her execution. It was a castellated building, erected about 1337, and taken down in 1775. Sampford-Peverell was anciently a borough, and had a considerable woollen manufactory. The Grand Western canal passes through the parish. There are a place of worship for Wesleyan Methodists, and an endowed school.

SAMPFORD-SPINEY, a parish in the hundred of ROBOROUGH, county of DEVON, 4½ miles (E. by S.) from Tavistock, containing 333 inhabitants. The living is a perpetual curacy, with that of Shaugh, in the archdeaconry of Totness, and diocese of Exeter, endowed with £400 royal bounty, and in the patronage of the Dean and Canons of Windsor. The church has lately received an addition of thirty-two free sittings, the Incorporated Society for the enlargement of churches and chapels having granted £15 towards defraying the expense. The parish is situated on the verge of Dartmoor, and is intersected by the Plymouth railway. In the vicinity is a mine where cobalt and silver have been found.

SAMPSON'S (ST.), a parish in the eastern division of the hundred of POWDER, county of CORNWALL, 4 miles (S. S. E.) from Lostwithiel, containing 248 inhabitants. The living is a perpetual curacy, annexed to the vicarage of Tywardreth, in the archdeaconry of Cornwall, and diocese of Exeter, endowed with £200 private benefaction, and £600 royal bounty. W. Rashleigh, Esq. was patron in 1815. The river Fowey is navigable on the east of this parish. Here was anciently a castle of the Earls of Salisbury, the site of which is called Castle-Dore.

C

SANCREED, a parish in the hundred of PENWITH county of CORNWALL, 4 miles (W. by S.) from Penzance, containing 1001 inhabitants. The living is a vicarage, in the archdeaconry of Cornwall, and diocese of Exeter, rated in the king's books at £8, and in the patronage of the Dean and Chapter of Exeter. Besides the church, here were three ancient chapels, of which there are still some remains. There is a place of worship for Wesleyan Methodists.

SANCTON, a parish in the Hunsley-Beacon division of the wapentake of HARTHILL, East riding of the county of YORK, comprising the townships of North Cliff, and Sancton with Houghton, and containing 423 inhabitants, of which number, 334 are in the township of Sancton with Houghton, 2½ miles (S. E.) from Market-Weighton. The living is a discharged vicarage, in the archdeaconry of the East riding, and diocese of York, rated in the king's books at £6. 1. 10½., endowed with £600 royal bounty, and in the patronage of J. Broadley, Esq. The church is dedicated to All Saints. There is a place of worship for Wesleyan Methodists. A free school is endowed with a rent-charge of £20, which is paid for teaching about thirty boys.

SANDALL (GREAT), a parish in the lower division of the wapentake of AGBRIGG, West riding of the county of YORK, comprising the townships of Crigglestone, Great Sandall, Walton, and part of that of West Bretton, and containing 2692 inhabitants, of which number, 888 are in the township of Great Sandall, 2 miles (S. by E.) from Wakefield. The living is a discharged vicarage, in the archdeaconry and diocese of York, rated in the king's books at £13. 7. 8., endowed with £200 private benefaction, and £200 royal bounty, and in the patronage of the Crown. The church is dedicated to St. Helen. Richard Taylor, in 1686, bequeathed certain houses in Wakefield, producing an annual income of £18, of which sum, £10 is paid for teaching eight poor children, and £6 to two widows in almshouses founded by the same individual. There are two other almshouses for poor women, founded by George Grice, and rebuilt in 1823. A castle was built here, about 1320, by John Plantagenet, the last Earl of Warren, for his favourite mistress, Maude, the wife of Thomas, Earl of Lancaster. It was occupied by Edward Baliol in the reign of Edward III., during the preparations for placing him on the Scottish throne. It subsequently became the residence of Richard Plantagenet, Duke of York, and lastly of the Duke of Gloucester, afterwards Richard III. During the great civil war it was held for Charles I., till surrendered in 1645, and in 1646 it was completely demolished, insomuch that there are now only a few very inconsiderable fragments.

SANDALL (KIRK), a parish in the southern division of the wapentake of STRAFFORTH and TICKHILL, West riding of the county of YORK, 4¼ miles (N. E. by N.) from Doncaster, containing 192 inhabitants. The living is a discharged vicarage, in the archdeaconry and diocese of York, rated in the king's books at £9. 0. 2½., and in the patronage of the Crown. The church, dedicated to St. Oswald, is a cruciform structure, with a tower rising from the intersection : it contains a curious monument to the memory of John Rokeby, a native of this place, and Archbishop of Dublin, who directed his body to be buried here, and his heart

and bowels at Halifax. A free school was founded, in 1626, by Robert Wood, and endowed with a messuage and land, of the annual value of £60, which is enjoyed by the master, who at his own cost has lately rebuilt the school-house : he receives annually £15 from another source, and educates about forty children.

SANDALL (LONG), a joint township with Wheatley, in that part of the parish of DONCASTER which is in the soke of DONCASTER, West riding of the county of YORK, 3½ miles (N. E. by N.) from Doncaster, containing, with Wheatley, 160 inhabitants.

SANDBACH, a parish comprising the market town of Sandbach, the chapelries of Church-Hulme, and Goostrey with Barnshaw, and the townships of Arclid, Blackden, Bradwell, Cotton, Cranage, Leese, Twemlow, Wheelock, and a small portion of Rudheath, in the hundred of NORTHWICH, and the townships of Bechton and Hassall, in that of NANTWICH, county palatine of CHESTER, and containing 6369 inhabitants, of which number, 2905 are in the town of Sandbach, 26 miles (E. by S.) from Chester, and 162 (N.W.) from London. This town occupies a pleasant eminence near the small river Wheelock, which falls into the Dane, in the midst of a fertile tract, and commands, from certain points, extensive views of a rich landscape, embracing the Vale Royal, the hills of Staffordshire and Derbyshire, and the distant mountains of Wales. The worsted trade, and the manufacture of shoes, formerly prevailed; but they have been succeeded by the throwing of silk, and the manufacture of this article, in its various branches, by which the town has considerably advanced in importance and prosperity within the last twenty years : the malt trade, which was formerly carried on, has also declined : here are some brine springs. The Grand Trunk canal passes through the parish. A charter for a market was obtained in the seventeenth century; it is held on Thursday; and fairs are on Easter Tuesday and Wednesday, the first Thursday after the 11th of September, and a statute and pleasure fair on December 27th, for cattle and wearing apparel : in the market-place are some ancient crosses, which were repaired in 1816. A court is held occasionally by the lord of the manor, and two constables are appointed at the petty sessions of the county magistrates.

The living is a vicarage, in the archdeaconry and diocese of Chester, rated in the king's books at £15. 10. 2½., and in the patronage of the Rev. Mr. Armitstead. The church, dedicated to St. Mary, is principally in the later English style. There are places of worship for Independents, and Primitive and Wesleyan Methodists. Some small benefactions have been made at different periods for the instruction of poor children, the principal of which are, a school-house, erected in 1694, at the expense of Francis Wells; and a bequest of £200, for teaching three boys in it, and preparing them for the University; also £420 as an endowment for the school, which is under the superintendence of trustees, for the instruction of twenty children of this parish in the rudiments of an English education. A National school is supported by voluntary contributions.

SANDERINGHAM, a parish in the Lynn division of the hundred of FREEBRIDGE, county of NORFOLK, 3¼ miles (N. E.) from Castle-Rising, containing 72 inhabitants. The living is a discharged rectory, with that of Babingley annexed, in the archdeaconry and diocese of Norwich, rated in the king's books at £5. 6. 8., and in the patronage of H. H. Henley, Esq. The church is dedicated to St. Mary.

SANDERSTEAD, a parish in the first division of the hundred of WALLINGTON, county of SURREY, 3 miles (S. S. E.) from Croydon, containing 189 inhabitants. The living is a rectory, in the archdeaconry of Surrey, and diocese of Winchester, rated in the king s books at £7, and in the patronage of the Rev. A. W. Wigsell. The church is dedicated to All Saints. Purley, in this parish, is memorable as having been the residence of the late John Horne Tooke, and the place where he wrote his work on English grammar, fancifully entitled "The Diversions of Purley."

SANDFORD, a chapelry in that part of the parish of St. HELEN's, ABINGDON, which is in the hundred of HORMER, county of BERKS, 3 miles (N.W. by N.) from Abingdon, containing 92 inhabitants.

SANDFORD, a joint township with Woodley, in that part of the parish of SONNING which is in the hundred of SONNING, county of BERKS, 5½ miles (E.) from Reading, containing, with Woodley, 759 inhabitants.

SANDFORD, a parish in the hundred of CREDITON, county of DEVON, 2 miles (N. by W.) from Crediton, containing 1906 inhabitants. The living is a perpetual curacy, in the peculiar jurisdiction of the Bishop of Exeter, and in the patronage of the Governors of the Crediton Charity. The church, dedicated to St. Swithin, was formerly a chapel of ease to that of Crediton. Sir John Davie, Bart., in 1677, bequeathed a rent-charge of £16 for teaching and clothing twenty children; the Rev. Robert Ham, in 1730, gave £3 a year for the instruction of ten, and Mary Lock, in 1773, a similar sum for teaching six, poor children, all which charities are applied according to the directions of the donors.

SANDFORD, a parish in the hundred of BULLINGTON, county of OXFORD, 3¼ miles (S. S. E.) from Oxford, containing 193 inhabitants. The living is a donative, in the patronage of the Duke of Marlborough. The church is dedicated to St. Andrew. The parish is bounded on the west by the river Isis, on which there is an extensive paper-mill. Here was formerly a preceptory of Knights Templars, founded by Queen Maud, Consort of Stephen, the preceptor and brethren of which had the management of most of the estates belonging to that order in the neighbouring counties.

SANDFORD, a parish in the hundred of WOOTTON, county of OXFORD, 3¾ miles (E. N. E.) from Neat-Enstone, containing, with the hamlets of Grove-Ash and Ledwell, 489 inhabitants. The living is a discharged vicarage, in the archdeaconry and diocese of Oxford, rated in the king's books at £7. 0. 5., endowed with £200 private benefaction, and £200 royal bounty, and in the patronage of William Taylor, Esq. for two turns, and the Duke of Marlborough for one. The church is dedicated to St. Martin. Fifteen children are educated for six guineas a year, the bequest of Henry Meads, in 1750.

SANDFORD, a township in the parish of PREES, Whitchurch division of the hundred of BRADFORD (North), county of SALOP, 5½ miles (N. E.) from Wem, containing, with the hamlets of Darleston, Fauls, and Mickley, 561 inhabitants.

SANDFORD, a hamlet in the parish of WARCOP, EAST ward, county of WESTMORLAND, 4¼ miles (W.

N. W.) from Brough, containing 163 inhabitants. There are several ancient intrenchments and tumuli in the vicinity: the largest of the latter was opened in 1766, and found to contain calcined human bones and some military weapons; near them was formerly a circle of stones about fifty yards in diameter.

SANDFORD-ORCAS, a parish in the hundred of HORETHORNE, county of SOMERSET, 6 miles (N. E.) from Yeovil, containing 332 inhabitants. The living is a rectory, in the archdeaconry of Wells, and diocese of Bath and Wells, rated in the king's books at £11. 9. 9½. John Hutchins, Esq. was patron in 1816. The church is dedicated to St. Nicholas. There is a place of worship for Wesleyan Methodists.

SANDGATE, a chapelry partly within the liberty of the town of FOLKESTONE, and partly in the parish of CHERITON, hundred of FOLKESTONE, lathe of SHEPWAY, county of KENT, 1¼ mile (W. by S.) from Folkestone. The name of this village is a contraction of Sandygate, and is derived from its situation in one of those openings from the sea between the hills, formerly called gates, and the sandy nature of the soil on which it stands: it emerged from obscurity and insignificance about fifty years ago, when two yards were established here for shipbuilding, and six twenty-eight gun frigates, of about eight hundred tons' each, were built. A castle, similar to those at Deal and Walmer, was erected by HenryVIII., in 1539, on the site, as it is supposed, of a more ancient one which stood here in the reign of Richard II., and was formerly an object of much curiosity, but has undergone considerable alterations of late years, the large circular tower forming the centre having been converted into a martello tower: it is within the jurisdiction of the lord-warden of the cinque-ports. During the late war with France there was a summer camp on Shorn-cliff, a hill at the north side of the village; where also, about thirty years since, some extensive barracks were erected. At the bottom of the hill commences the New Military canal, cut about twenty years ago, which extends in a straight line along the coast, passes Hythe, where it crosses the Romney road, and, following the course of the hills for twenty-three miles, terminates at Cliff End in Sussex; it is about thirty yards wide, and six in depth. The situation of the village is in the highest degree salubrious and pleasant: it lies along the shore, with hills rising immediately behind it, consists of good modern buildings, which are rapidly increasing, possesses bathing-machines, and every requisite for hot and cold bathing, with a circulating library and reading-rooms, and is rising into estimation as a watering-place. A fair is held on the 23rd of July.

The living is a perpetual curacy, in the archdeaconry of Canterbury, endowed with £300 royal bounty, and in the patronage of the Earl of Darnley, who erected a neat chapel in 1822: it contains six hundred sittings, of which two hundred are free, the Incorporated Society for building and enlarging churches and chapels having contributed £150 towards defraying the expense. There is a place of worship for Wesleyan Methodists. A National school for one hundred boys and fifty girls is supported by voluntary contributions. On the summit of a hill in this neighbourhood is an ancient camp, of elliptic form, comprising nearly two acres: the north and west sides are defended by a triple ditch, the south

C 2

by a single one very steep, and the east by a double one; its formation is attributed to King Ethelbert.

SANDHOE, a township in the parish of St. John Lee, southern division of Tindale ward, county of Northumberland, 2½ miles (E. N. E.) from Hexham, containing 180 inhabitants. This township contains some fine mansions, commanding prospects of a richly diversified country; and near the gardens of Beaufront is a Roman Catholic chapel, now in disuse.

SANDHOLME, a joint township with Stockhill, in that part of the parish of St. John which is within the liberties of the borough of Beverley, East riding of the county of York. The population is returned with Stockhill. There is a place of worship for Wesleyan Methodists.

SANDHURST, a parish in the hundred of Sonning, county of Berks, 5¼ miles (S. by E.) from Wokingham, containing 771 inhabitants. The living is a perpetual curacy, in the peculiar jurisdiction and patronage of the Dean of Salisbury, endowed with £600 royal bounty, and £1600 parliamentary grant. The church is dedicated to St. Michael. John Moseley, in 1773, bequeathed a trifling annuity for teaching six children. In this parish is the Royal Military College, for the scientific instruction of cadets intended for the army, and of officers already possessing military commissions. The two branches of this national institution were first temporarily placed at High Wycombe, in 1799, and removed to Great Marlow, in 1802, by their founder, His Royal Highness the late Duke of York, on a plan furnished by Major-General J. G. Le Marchant, who fell gallantly fighting at the battle of Salamanca. In 1812, the establishment at Marlow was removed to the present magnificent structure, which had been erected at the national expense, and where, since the year 1820, both branches of the institution have been concentrated. The senior department, as it is called, is a school for the staff, where officers of all ranks already in the service are admitted to study: the junior department is appropriated to the professional education of young gentlemen intended for the cavalry and infantry. Since its foundation the college has afforded instruction to above three thousand young gentlemen for the service, besides qualifying above four hundred and fifty other officers for the staff. Its affairs are under the control of a board of commissioners, under the presidency of the Commander in Chief, consisting of the Secretary at War, the Master General of the Ordnance, and the principal general officers on the home staff of the army. The institution, however, is immediately governed by a general, having under him a colonel, as lieutenant-governor, with other officers. The instruction, both of the senior students and the gentlemen cadets, is conducted under the superintendence of the military authorities of the college, by professors and masters in the various branches of study; of which the chief are mathematics, practical astronomy, the theory of fortification and actual construction of field works, military drawing and surveying, the principal modern languages, the Latin classics, and general history: the young gentlemen are also regularly instructed in military exercises and riding.

The college stands in the midst of extensive and picturesque grounds, with a fine sheet of water in front of it, and surrounded by many thriving and beautiful plantations. The edifice, which has a fine Doric portico of eight columns, is of a simple and majestic character: it is calculated for the reception of four hundred gentlemen cadets, and thirty students of the senior department; the length of the main building being four hundred and thirty-four feet, and that of the whole principal façade no less than nine hundred. The house of the governor stands detached in its own grounds; that of the lieutenant-governor closes the western extremity of the front range; and the quarters of the officers of the establishment form, with the main building, a square in its rear; while the masters' houses, at the distance of about a quarter of a mile in front, are built on a terrace overlooking the high western road. A well-situated observatory, and a spacious riding-house, one hundred and ten feet by fifty, are among the detached buildings; and the principal edifice, besides the halls of study, the dining-halls, and dormitories of the gentlemen cadets, and servants' offices, contains a handsome octagonal room, in which the public examinations are held, and a very neat and chastely decorated chapel.

SANDHURST, a parish in the upper division of the hundred of Dudstone and King's Barton, county of Gloucester, 3 miles (N.) from Gloucester, containing 473 inhabitants. The living is a discharged vicarage, in the archdeaconry and diocese of Gloucester, endowed with £400 private benefaction, and £400 royal bounty, and in the patronage of the Bishop of Bristol. The church is dedicated to St. Lawrence. The navigable river Severn bounds the parish on the east and north.

SANDHURST, a parish in the hundred of Selbrittenden, lathe of Scray, county of Kent, 7 miles (S. W. by W.) from Tenterden, containing 1182 inhabitants. The living is a rectory, in the archdeaconry and diocese of Canterbury, rated in the king's books at £20, and in the patronage of the Archbishop of Canterbury. The church, dedicated to St. Nicholas, is principally in the later style of English architecture. There are places of worship for Baptists and Wesleyan Methodists. A National school has been recently established. A fair for cattle and pedlary is held on May 25th. The river Kennet separates this extensive parish from the county of Sussex.

SANDIACRE, a parish in the hundred of Morleston and Litchurch, county of Derby, 9½ miles (E.) from Derby, containing 587 inhabitants. The living is a perpetual curacy, in the peculiar jurisdiction and patronage of the Prebendary of Sandiacre in the Cathedral Church of Lichfield, endowed with £400 royal bounty, and £1000 parliamentary grant. The church, dedicated to St. Giles, exhibits an admixture of the various styles of English architecture, from the Norman downwards, though the decorated predominates, with some slight remains of stained glass in the windows, and in the chancel three elegant stone stalls. There is a place of worship for Wesleyan Methodists. The Erewash and Derby canals form a junction near the village, at which a market and a fair were formerly held.

SANDON, a parish in the hundred of Chelmsford, county of Essex, 2 miles (W. by S.) from Danbury, containing 488 inhabitants. The living is a rectory, in the archdeaconry of Essex, and diocese of London, rated in the king's books at £13. 6. 8., and in the patronage of the President and Fellows of Queen's

College, Cambridge. The church is dedicated to St. Andrew. The Chelmer and Blackwater navigation passes along part of the boundary of this parish.

SANDON, a parish in the hundred of ODSEY, county of HERTFORD, 4¾ miles (N. W. by N.) from Buntingford, containing 646 inhabitants. The living is a vicarage, in the archdeaconry of Huntingdon, and diocese of Lincoln, rated in the king's books at £9, and in the patronage of the Dean of St. Paul's, London. The church is dedicated to All Saints.

SANDON, a parish in the southern division of the hundred of PIREHILL, county of STAFFORD, 4½ miles (N. N. E.) from Stafford, containing 513 inhabitants. The living is a discharged rectory, in the archdeaconry of Stafford, and diocese of Lichfield and Coventry, rated in the king's books at £7. 10., and in the patronage of the Earl of Harrowby. The church, dedicated to All Saints, contains an elegant monument to the memory of the well-known genealogist and antiquary, Sampson, the last of the Eardwicks, formerly proprietors of the manor, who was born here, and died in 1603; the site of their ancient mansion, encompassed by a moat, is still distinguishable. In the grounds of the hall, a noble stone structure belonging to the Earl of Harrowby, is an obelisk, erected to the memory of the late Rt. Hon. William Pitt, which bears date 1806, and is encircled with iron palisades. The stone with which this mansion and pillar are built was obtained in a quarry on the spot. The Grand Trunk canal passes through the parish, in a line parallel with the Trent. Sandon is in the honour of Tutbury, duchy of Lancaster, and within the jurisdiction of a court of pleas held at Tutbury every third Tuesday, for the recovery of debts under 40s. Sandon confers the inferior title of viscount on the family of Ryder, Earls of Harrowby.

SANDON-FEE, a tything in the parish of HUNGERFORD, hundred of KINTBURY-EAGLE, county of BERKS, 1¾ mile (S. W. by S.) from Hungerford, containing 474 inhabitants.

SANDRIDGE, a parish in the hundred of CASHIO, or liberty of ST. ALBANS, county of HERTFORD, 2¾ miles (N. E.) from St. Albans, containing 823 inhabitants. The living is a discharged vicarage, in the archdeaconry of St. Albans, and diocese of London, rated in the king's books at £8, endowed with £200 private benefaction, and £200 royal bounty, and in the patronage of Earl Spencer. The church is dedicated to St. Leonard. A National school was erected by subscription in 1824, on ground given by Earl Spencer, and is supported by voluntary contributions.

SANDWICH, a cinque-port, borough, and market town, having separate jurisdiction, locally in the hundred of Eastry, lathe of St. Augustine, county of KENT, 39 miles (E.) from Maidstone, and 68 (E. by S.) from London, containing 2912 inhabitants. This place, which appears to have risen into reputation upon the decline of the *Portus Rutupensis*, derived its Saxon name *Sondwic*, signifying a town on the sands, from its situation on a point of

Arms.

land which had been gained from the sea, on its retiring from that ancient port. It is by most antiquaries supposed to have been also the *Lunden-wic*, noticed in the Saxon chronicle as the principal place of resort for merchants trading with the port of London, and to have been at a very early period a place of considerable importance. In 851, Athelstan defeated a large party of the Danes, who had landed on this part of the coast, and destroyed nine of their ships; soon after which an army of those invaders landed from three hundred and fifty ships, and plundered this town and Canterbury; and in 993, Anlaf, another Danish chieftain, arrived with a fleet of ninety sail, and laid waste the town. In 1011, a Danish fleet having landed at Sandwich, ravaged the coasts of Kent and Sussex, besieged Canterbury, massacred the inhabitants, and set fire to that city. In 1014, Canute, on leaving England, touched at this port, and set on shore his English hostages, whom he had barbarously mutilated; and subsequently, after being established on the throne of England, granted the port of Sandwich, and all its revenues, to Christ Church, Canterbury, for the support of the monks, and partly rebuilt the town, which from this time began to flourish, and had attained such eminence as to be made one of the principal cinque-ports of the kingdom, by Edward the Confessor, who resided for some time in it, and, in 1052, fitted out a fleet to oppose Earl Godwin and his sons, who in the same year entered this harbour, whence they sailed for London. In the Norman survey Sandwich is described as a borough, held by the Archbishop of Canterbury, and as a fort rendering to the king the same services as Dovor, yielding then a rent of £50, and forty thousand herrings for the monks' food. In the reign of Henry III., the French having effected a landing, burnt the town, which, from the opulence of the inhabitants, was soon rebuilt in a more substantial manner, and obtained from that monarch the grant of a weekly market and other privileges. Edward I. fixed the staple of wool here for a short time; and in the same reign, the monks of Canterbury, in exchange for other lands in Kent, surrendered to the king all their rights and customs in the town, with the exception only of their houses and quays, a free passage across the ferry, and the privilege of buying and selling in the market free of toll, which reservations were afterwards abandoned in exchange for lands in Essex, in the reign of Edward III. At this time Sandwich contributed to the armament destined for the invasion of France, twenty-two ships and five hundred and four mariners, and was the general place of rendezvous for the fleets of Edward, who usually embarked here on his several expeditions against that country. Richard II., in the seventh year of his reign, issued an order for enclosing and fortifying the town, which, from its naval importance, had become a principal object of attack with the French, who, preparing to invade England, had constructed a wall of wood, three thousand paces in length, and twenty feet in height, with towers at short intervals, to protect their troops from the English archers, which it was their intention to fix up on the coast after they had effected a landing; parts of this wall being found on board of two large ships which were taken in the following year, were used in strengthening the fortifications of the town. In 1416, Henry V., while waiting

to embark for Calais, took up his residence in the monastery of the Carmelite friars. In the 16th and 35th of Henry VI., the French plundered the greater part of the town; which, however, in the reign of Edward IV., was in a very prosperous state, its trade having greatly increased. In 1456, the French made another attempt on the town; and in the following year, Marshal De Bréze landed a force of five thousand men, and, after a sanguinary battle, succeeded in obtaining possession of the town, which they plundered, and after setting it on fire, returned to their ships and escaped: it was soon afterwards pillaged by the Earl of Warwick, in his insurrection against the king. To guard against similar assaults, Edward IV. fortified the town with a wall strengthened with bastions, and surrounded it with a fosse, appropriating £100 per annum of the custom-house dues towards its restoration, which, together with the advantages of its haven, soon enabled it to regain its former prosperity; and its trade so much increased, that the net amount of the customs was £16,000 per annum, and there were ninety-five vessels belonging to the port, furnishing employment to one thousand five hundred seamen. The harbour soon after this began to decay, from the quantity of light sand which was washed into it by the sea; and this detriment was further increased by the sinking of a large vessel at its mouth. In 1493, a mole was constructed, and many attempts were made, during the reigns of Henry VIII. and Elizabeth, to remove the obstructions and improve the harbour, but they were not attended with success; and so much had the trade declined in consequence, that in the eighth year of the reign of Elizabeth, there were only sixty-two seamen belonging to the port. The persecutions on account of religious tenets in the Netherlands drove away many artisans, who, with their families, sought an asylum in England; and Elizabeth encouraged the refugees, of whom not less than four hundred were settled here by letters patent, dated at Greenwich in 1561, to whom she granted two weekly markets for the sale of their manufactures. They introduced the weaving of silk, and the manufacture of baizes and flannels, bringing them in a short time to a great degree of perfection; and, by their industry and good conduct, they soon became a flourishing and opulent community. Among them were some gardeners, who, finding the ground favourable for the production of esculent plants, employed themselves in their cultivation, to the great benefit of the landholders; they also introduced the cultivation of flax, teasel, and canary seed, which are at present grown here in greater abundance than in any other part of Kent; and, shortly after their introduction, were propagated with success in every part of the island. The settlement of the Flemings tended greatly to compensate for the decay of the harbour, and sustained the prosperity and importance of the town. Elizabeth paid it a visit in 1573, and was hospitably entertained by the corporation for three days. In the reign of James I., the trade of the port had revived in some degree, and the amount of the customs was £3000 per annum: the descendants of the Flemish refugees had laid aside their original employment, and were intermingled with the rest of the inhabitants in the general occupations of the town.

The town is situated on the navigable river Stour, about two miles from its influx with the sea, near the commencement of the Roman Watling-street, and is surrounded on all sides by a considerable extent of low ground; the houses, many of which are of very ancient appearance, are irregularly built; the streets are narrow, though some improvements have been effected under the provisions of an act passed in 1787, by which the town is paved, and lighted with oil: the inhabitants are amply supplied with water from the river Stour, and from a small stream which rises near the village of Eastry, the water of which is conveyed to the town by a canal, nearly three miles in length, called the Delf, which was constructed under letters patent granted in the 13th of Edward I. Considerable portions of the walls are still remaining, and till the year 1784 five of the ancient gates were entire, the only one now standing being Fisher's Gate, a plain ancient structure, facing the quay. A bridge of two arches, in the centre of which is a swing-bridge, to admit vessels to pass without lowering their masts, connects the town with Stonar and the Isle of Thanet. The port extends from the North Foreland, in a north-easterly direction, to eleven fathoms of water, six miles distant from the shore, and in a southerly direction to the head of the Goodwin sands, along which it continues for five miles to Sandown castle; in a south-westerly direction up the haven, and thence in a southerly direction to the quay at the mouth of the Gestling; including within its jurisdiction as a cinque-port, the ports of Fordwich, Sarre, Ramsgate, Deal, Walmer, and Stonar. The harbour is at present so much choked up with sand that only vessels of small burden can enter it with safety. The foreign trade is principally with Norway, Sweden, and the Baltic, for timber and iron; and the home trade with Wales and Scotland, in which corn, flour, seeds, hops, malt, fruit, &c., are shipped. The custom-house is a branch of that of Ramsgate, though the trade of this port is more considerable than that of the latter. Ship-building and rope-making are carried on to a limited extent, but there are no vestiges of the ancient manufactories. The market days are Wednesday and Saturday, the former for corn, with which it is abundantly supplied: a large cattle market is held every alternate Monday, and an annual fair on the 4th of December, which generally continues a week.

Corporate Seal.

Obverse.   Reverse.

By a succession of charters, of which the last was granted by Charles II., in the thirty-sixth year of his reign, the government is vested in a mayor, high steward, recorder, twelve jurats, and twenty-four common council-men, assisted by a town clerk and other officers. The mayor is annually chosen by the resident freemen; the recorder, who holds his office for life, is appointed by the mayor and jurats; and the common council consists of such of the freemen as have served the office of treasurer. The mayor and the jurats are justices of the peace within the town and liberties, and additional cinque-port magistrates are appointed, by act of parliament, for the several members of the port. Since 1437, the town has consisted of twelve wards, each of which is under the jurisdiction of a jurat, who appoints a constable and deputy constable. The freedom of the borough is inherited by birth, or obtained by marriage with the daughter of a freeman, by servitude, gift, or by the purchase of a frank tenement of the yearly value of £5. Among the numerous privileges enjoyed by Sandwich, as a cinque-port, is that of sending three barons to assist in supporting the canopy over the king at coronations; and when a queen consort is crowned, six are sent, who enjoy the favour of dining at the coronation feast, at a table placed on the right of their Majesties. The corporation hold courts of session, three times a year, for all offences within the borough, and have the power of inflicting capital punishment, which formerly was by drowning, a document being extant, of the date of 1315, in which a complaint is preferred against the prior of Christchurch, "for that he had diverted the course of a certain stream, called the Gestling, so that the felons could not be executed for want of water." The corporation also hold a court of record, for the recovery of debts to any amount; and a court of requests, for the recovery of debts not exceeding £5, is held by commissioners appointed under an act passed in the 47th of George III. The guildhall, usually called the court-hall, was erected in 1579, and contains, on the basement story, the several rooms for holding the courts, and on the first story, the council-chamber, and offices in which the public business of the corporation is transacted; in the upper story are kept the ancient cucking-stool and wooden mortar, for the punishment of scolds, and arms for the train bands. All municipal elections, decrees, and ordinances, are made by the whole corporate body in a general assembly, held twice in the year at the guildhall, and convened, according to ancient usage, by the sound of a brass horn. The borough gaol and house of correction, a small and inconvenient building, having been found inadequate for the classification of prisoners, a larger and more handsome edifice is now being erected, which will afford the necessary convenience for this arrangement, and will contain a house for the gaoler, &c. This borough first exercised the elective franchise in the 42nd of Edward III., since which time it has regularly returned two members to parliament, who are styled barons: the right of election is vested in the mayor, jurats, and freemen, resident and non-resident, not receiving alms, of whom the number is about nine hundred: the mayor is the returning officer.

The town comprises the parishes of St. Clement, St. Mary the Virgin, and St. Peter the Apostle, all in the archdeaconry and diocese of Canterbury, and the extra-parochial liberty of the hospital of St. Bartholomew. The living of St. Clement's is a vicarage, rated in the king's books at £13. 16. 10½., and in the patronage of the Archdeacon of Canterbury: the church is an ancient and spacious structure, combining various styles of architecture, with a massive central tower of Norman character, enriched with several

series of arches of very fine composition; the interior has portions in the early and later styles of English architecture, and contains several monuments, and an octagonal font. The living of St. Mary's is a discharged vicarage, rated in the king's books at £8. 1., endowed with £200 private benefaction, and £200 royal bounty, and in the patronage of the Archdeacon of Canterbury: the church, an ancient building, consists of a nave, north aisle, and chancel, in which are some interesting remains of the early style; the south aisle has been destroyed. The living of St. Peter's is a discharged rectory, rated in the king's books at £8, endowed with £800 private benefaction, £200 royal bounty, and £1500 parliamentary grant, and in the alternate patronage of the Crown, and of the Mayor and Corporation: the church appears to have been originally in the Norman style of architecture, but, from frequent alterations, its original character is nearly lost among the additions which have been made of Kentish ragstone and flint: the south aisle was destroyed by the fall of the steeple, in 1661, but the latter was rebuilt with the materials of the former as high as the nave, and finished with bricks made from the mud in the harbour. There was formerly a chapel, dedicated to St. James, the cemetery of which is still used as a burial-place. There are places of worship for Independents and Wesleyan Methodists.

The free grammar school was founded by subscription among the inhabitants, in the reign of Elizabeth, and in 1563, endowed with lands for its support by Sir Roger Manwood, then recorder of the borough, and subsequently Chief Baron of the Exchequer, who appointed the mayor and corporation governors: the revenue is about £37. 19. per annum, which is paid to the master, who resides in the school-house. Mrs. Joan Trapps, of London, in 1568, founded four scholarships in Lincoln College, Oxford, of which two are in the appointment of the Governors of this school, and two in that of the Rector and Fellows of the college, without any distinction of place: these scholarships were afterwards augmented with £3 per annum, by Mrs. Joyce Frankland. Sir Roger Manwood, in 1581, founded four scholarships in Caius College, Cambridge, in the alternate nomination of the Governors of the school, and the Master and Fellows of the college. A charity school, established by subscription, in 1711, and principally supported by the same means, is under the direction of the mayor and three trustees chosen from each parish: the rents for its support amount to £25 per annum, besides some bequests made in 1811 and 1817: eighty boys and sixty girls are instructed in this establishment on the National system. St. Thomas' hospital was founded, about the year 1392, by Mr. Thomas Ellis, a wealthy draper of this town, who endowed it for eight aged men and four women, each of whom, from the improved state of the funds, receives an allowance of £25 per annum. St. Bartholomew's was founded prior to the year 1244, when Sir Henry de Sandwich made a considerable addition to its original endowment; sixteen aged men and women, appointed by the mayor and jurats, receive a considerable annual pension, which, during the last lease, amounted to £52 per annum each, but is at present rather less. The buildings occupy a spacious triangular area, and afford healthy and pleasant dwellings for the inmates. The site is extra-parochial; and there is a small neat chapel attached to the charity, the mayor and jurats appointing the chaplain. St. John's hospital, supposed to have been founded about the year 1287, has been taken down, and six small houses have been erected on its site, for the reception of six aged men and women, who are appointed by the mayor, and receive each an annual sum of £20. Sir John Manwood, Chief Baron of the Exchequer, and author of the "Forest Laws;" and Mr. Richard Knolles, master of the grammar school, and author of the "History of the Turkish Empire," were natives of this place. Sandwich gives the title of earl to the family of Montague.

SANDWITH, a township in the parish of St. Bees, Allerdale ward above Darwent, county of Cumberland, 2¼ miles (S. by W.) from Whitehaven, containing 358 inhabitants. It extends to St. Bees' Head, where there is a lighthouse; and upon the cliffs adjacent grows an abundance of samphire.

SANDY, a parish partly in the hundred of Wixamtree, but chiefly in that of Biggleswade, county of Bedford, 3¾ miles (N. by W.) from Biggleswade, containing, with the hamlets of Beeston and Gritford, 1392 inhabitants. The living is a rectory, in the archdeaconry of Bedford, and diocese of Lincoln, rated in the king's books at £32. 2. 11., and in the patronage of F. Pym, Esq. The church is dedicated to St. Swithin. The river Ivel runs through the parish, and is crossed by a bridge at Gritford. Galley hill is the site of the ancient Roman station Salinæ, which commanded another at Chesterfield, a piece of ground, still so called, near the village, through which passed the great road from Baldock in Herts, across this county, into Cambridgeshire. The ramparts, which enclose an area of thirty acres, are surrounded by a deep fosse, and in the centre is a mount, probably thrown up for the prætorium. At some distance, on the other side of the valley, are the remains of Cæsar's camp. Several Roman urns, coins, and fragments of a beautiful red pottery, have been discovered at Chesterfield; the latter, which was ornamented with figures, has been deemed the ancient Samian ware. Owing to the sandy nature of the soil, cucumbers are cultivated in the open air in such abundance, that Covent-Garden market, London, is almost wholly supplied with that vegetable from this place.

SANKEY (GREAT), a chapelry in the parish of Prescot, hundred of West Derby, county palatine of Lancaster, 2¾ miles (W.) from Warrington, containing 551 inhabitants. The living is a perpetual curacy, in the archdeaconry and diocese of Chester, endowed with £1000 private benefaction, £600 royal bounty, and £600 parliamentary grant. R. Gwillim, Esq. was patron in 1814. The first canal navigation in modern times originated here, in 1755.

SANTON, a joint township with Melthwaite, in the parish of Irton, Allerdale ward above Darwent, county of Cumberland, 4½ miles (N. N. E.) from Ravenglass, containing, with Melthwaite, 297 inhabitants.

SANTON, a parish in the hundred of Grimshoe, county of Norfolk, 4 miles (N. W. by N.) from Thetford, containing 21 inhabitants. The living is a discharged rectory, in the archdeaconry of Norfolk, and diocese of Norwich, and in the patronage of the Mayor and Corporation of Thetford. The church is dedicated to St. Helen.

SAPCOTE, a parish in the hundred of Sparkenhoe, county of Leicester, 4¼ miles (E. by S.) from Hinckley, containing 797 inhabitants. The living is a rectory, in the archdeaconry of Leicester, and diocese of Lincoln, rated in the king's books at £10. 11. 10½., and in the patronage of John Frewen Turner, Esq. The church is dedicated to All Saints. There is a place of worship for Wesleyan Methodists. The river Saor runs through the parish, in which upwards of two hundred frames are employed in the manufacture of hosiery. A house of industry, also a common mill for grinding corn, were built by subscription in 1806, the expense of each amounting to £1300; and in the same year handsome bathing rooms were erected, at an expense of £600, defrayed by J. F. Turner, Esq., over a spring called Golden Well, the water of which is serviceable in nervous, consumptive, scorbutic, and scrophulous disorders. A school for the instruction of poor children was endowed by the Rev. Mr. Burroughs, formerly rector of this parish, and is further supported by J. F. Turner, Esq. There are vestiges of a mount and moat of an ancient castle, which once occupied the site of the family mansion of the Bassetts. In a field called Black Piece, a curious tesselated pavement was discovered in 1770.

SAPEY (UPPER), a parish in the hundred of Broxash, county of Hereford, 6½ miles (N. N. E.) from Bromyard, containing 323 inhabitants. The living is a rectory, in the archdeaconry and diocese of Hereford, rated in the king's books at £9. 5. 7½., and in the patronage of Sir T. Winnington, Bart. The church is dedicated to St. Michael. A charity school, founded by Mr. Addingbroke, is endowed with about £10 per annum. In the neighbourhood are the remains of a single-intrenched Roman camp.

SAPEY-PRITCHARD, a parish in the upper division of the hundred of Doddingtree, county of Worcester, 5¾ miles (N. E. by N.) from Bromyard, containing 200 inhabitants. The living is a discharged rectory, in the archdeaconry of Salop, and diocese of Hereford, rated in the king's books at £4. 4. 2., and in the patronage of P. Rufford, Esq. The church is dedicated to St. Bartholomew. A court leet is annually held here.

SAPISTON, a parish in the hundred of Blackbourn, county of Suffolk, 3¼ miles (N. by W.) from Ixworth, containing 242 inhabitants. The living is a perpetual curacy, in the archdeaconry of Suffolk, and diocese of Norwich, endowed with £1200 royal bounty, and in the patronage of the Duke of Grafton. The church is dedicated to St. Andrew.

SAPLEY, an extra-parochial district, in the hundred of Hurstingstone, county of Huntingdon, 2 miles (E.) from Huntingdon.

SAPPERTON, a township in the parish of Church-Broughton, hundred of Appletree, county of Derby, 12 miles (W.) from Derby. The population is returned with the parish.

SAPPERTON, a parish in the hundred of Bisley, county of Gloucester, comprising the tythings of Frampton-Marshall and Sapperton, and containing 476 inhabitants, of which number, 295 are in the tything of Sapperton, 5¼ miles (W. N. W.) from Cirencester. The living is a rectory, in the archdeaconry and diocese of Gloucester, rated in the king's books at £17, and in the patronage of Earl Bathurst. The church is dedicated to St. Kenelm. The Thames and Severn canal, in its course through this parish, is conducted, by a tunnel four thousand one hundred and eighty feet long, underneath Hagley wood. At Frampton, two urns filled with denarii and copper coins, were discovered, in 1759, by the sinking of a wagon-wheel, near which spot are vestiges of an ancient camp, and south-east of it there was a beacon.

SAPPERTON, a parish in the soke of GRANTHAM, parts of KESTEVEN, county of LINCOLN, 4½ miles (W.) from Falkingham, containing 55 inhabitants. The living is a discharged rectory, in the archdeaconry and diocese of Lincoln, rated in the king's books at £5. 9. 9½., endowed with £600 private benefaction, and £400 royal bounty, and in the patronage of Sir W. E. Welby, Bart. The church is dedicated to St. Nicholas.

SAREDON (GREAT and LITTLE), a township in the parish of SHARESHILL, eastern division of the hundred of CUTTLESTONE, county of STAFFORD, 7 miles (N. N. E.) from Wolverhampton, containing 297 inhabitants.

SARNESFIELD, a parish in the hundred of WOLPHY, county of HEREFORD, 2½ miles (W. by S.) from Weobley, containing 102 inhabitants. The living is a discharged rectory, in the archdeaconry and diocese of Hereford, rated in the king's books at £5. 6. 8., and in the patronage of Thomas Monnington, Esq. The church is dedicated to All Saints. A court leet is occasionally held here.

SARR, a ville in the cinque-port liberty of SANDWICH, though locally in the hundred of Ringslow, or Isle of Thanet, lathe of St. AUGUSTINE, county of KENT, 8¾ miles (N. E.) from Canterbury, containing 191 inhabitants.

SARRATT, a parish in the hundred of CASHIO, or liberty of St. ALBANS, county of HERTFORD, 3½ miles (N. W. by N.) from Rickmansworth, containing 397 inhabitants. The living is a vicarage, in the archdeaconry of St. Albans, and diocese of London, rated in the king's books at £9, and in the patronage of Mrs. Harriet Gordon. The church is dedicated to the Holy Cross : it is a cruciform structure, consisting of a nave, chancel, transepts, and a square tower, being built of a mixture of brick, stone, and flints : it contains a piscina beneath an embattled cornice ornamented with roses, and two stone seats. The village is situated on a ridge of land forming the western boundary of a vale watered by a small river, commonly called the Sarret stream.

SARSDEN, a parish in the hundred of CHADLINGTON, county of OXFORD, 3¾ miles (S. W. by S.) from Chipping-Norton, containing 128 inhabitants. The living is a rectory, in the archdeaconry and diocese of Oxford, rated in the king's books at £8. 18. 1½. J. H. Langston, Esq. was patron in 1817. Ann Walker, in 1705, gave £600, now producing an annual income of £52. 10., for which twenty-four girls are educated.

SARSON, a tything in the parish of AMPORT, hundred of ANDOVER, Andover division of the county of SOUTHAMPTON. The population is returned with the parish.

SARUM (OLD), an ancient borough in the parish of STRATFORD under the CASTLE, hundred of UNDERDITCH,

county of WILTS, 1½ mile (N.) from Salisbury. The population is returned with the parish. This place was originally a British settlement of some importance previous to the time of the Romans, who, on their establishment in the island, fixed here their station *Sorbiodunum*, situated on the *Via Iceniana*, or Iknield-street. By the Saxons, who, under their leader Kenric, son of Cerdic, second king of Wessex, took this town from the Britons in 552, it was called *Searesbyrig*, from the dryness of its situation, and continued to be a residence of the West Saxon kings till the union of the Octarchy under Egbert, after which time it still continued to be a royal castle. Alfred issued an order to the sheriff of Wiltshire to fortify this place with a trench and palisades, which order is given by Ledwiche, in his "*Antiquitates Sarisburienses*," and the remains of the present fortifications are evidently of Saxon character. In 960, Edgar convoked a wittenagemote, or great council of the state here, the especial object of which was to deliberate upon the best mode of defending the northern counties against the incursions of the Danes, by whom this part of the kingdom was particularly infested. In 1003, Sweyn, King of Denmark, having landed on the western coast, to retaliate the massacre of his countrymen in the reign of Ethelred, pillaged the town and burnt the castle. Soon after the Norman Conquest, pursuant to a decree of a synod held in St. Paul's cathedral, in 1076, for removing episcopal sees from obscure villages into fortified cities, the seat of the bishoprick of Wiltshire was, by Bishop Herman, removed from Sherborne (which had fallen into decay) to this place, where he laid the foundation of a cathedral church, which was completed by his successor, Bishop Osmund, in 1092. On the completion of the Norman survey, in 1086, William the Conqueror summoned all the bishops, abbots, barons, and knights of the kingdom, to attend him at Sarum, and do homage for the lands which they held by feudal tenure. In 1095. or 1096, William Rufus assembled a great council here, in which William, Count of Eu, was impeached of high treason against the king, in conspiring to raise Stephen, Earl of Albemarle, to the throne. Henry I. held his court here several months during the year 1100, where he received Archbishop Anselm, on his arrival in England, whom he required to do homage, and swear fealty to him, and to receive from his hands the investiture of his see. This demand gave rise to a dispute between the king and the pope, which was at length compromised, the pope allowing the prelates to do homage to the king, and reserving to himself alone the right of investiture, which was the first attempt to establish papal supremacy in the island. This monarch again fixed his residence here in 1106, and in 1116 assembled the prelates and barons of the realm, to swear allegiance and do homage to his son William, as his successor on the English throne, previously to his embarkation for Normandy, on his return from which place that prince was unfortunately drowned. In the reign of Stephen, Bishop Roger held the castle for the king; and soon after the instalment of his successor, Joceline, in 1142, the partisans of the Empress Matilda took possession of the town, which, in the course of the contest, was alternately occupied by both parties. On the accession of Henry II., in 1154, the castle was found to be in a dismantled state, and a considerable sum was expended **D** in putting it into repair. From the time of Stephen, disputes had arisen between the castellans and the clergy, which became so violent, that in the reign of Richard I., Herbert, then bishop, induced by these annoyances, and other inconveniences attending the situation of his church, among which was the difficulty of obtaining water, which could not be accomplished, except by permission of the governor, obtained license from the king to remove the see, and to erect a new church in the valley, at the distance of nearly two miles from the castle. This design was carried into execution by his successor, who having obtained a special indulgence from the pope, laid the foundation of the present cathedral of New Sarum, or Salisbury, to which place the episcopal chair was transferred. From that period the town of Old Sarum began to decay, and was gradually deserted by its inhabitants, who established themselves in the more immediate vicinity of the new cathedral church. Of the old town there is scarcely a single vestige, except a few fragments of foundation walls of some of the houses, on the declivity of an eminence rising from the western side of a valley, and forming the extremity of a ridge which extends towards the east. The vast ditches and ramparts of the ancient city, and the site of the castle, may be traced, and, while they constitute the only visible remains of this once flourishing city, are among the most interesting objects of antiquarian research : there were houses remaining down to the time of Henry VIII., and service was performed in the old chapel of the cathedral until nearly the same period. Old Sarum is a borough by prescription, and first exercised the elective franchise in the 23d of Edward I., but made no other return till the 34th of Edward III., since which time it has continued to send two members to parliament : the right of election is vested in the burgage freeholders, of whom the number is seven : the bailiff is the returning officer. A temporary house is erected under a large tree for holding the election. John of Salisbury, one of the most eminent scholars of his time, and celebrated as an historian and biographer, was born at Old Sarum, in the early part of the twelfth century.

SATLEY, a chapelry in that part of the parish of LANCHESTER which is in the western division of CHESTER ward, county palatine of DURHAM, 5 miles (N. E. by N.) from Wolsingham, containing 103 inhabitants. The living is a perpetual curacy, in the archdeaconry and diocese of Durham, endowed with £1000 royal bounty, and in the patronage of the Perpetual Curate of Lanchester. There is a school supported by subscription.

SATTERLEIGH, a parish in the hundred of SOUTH MOLTON, county of DEVON, 3¾ miles (S. W. by W.) from South Molton, containing 55 inhabitants. The living is a discharged rectory, in the archdeaconry of Barnstaple, and diocese of Exeter, rated in the king's books at £4. 0. 7½., endowed with £400 private benefaction, and £400 royal bounty, and in the patronage of John Bawden, Esq. The church is dedicated to St. Peter.

SATTERTHWAITE, a chapelry in the parish of HAWKESHEAD, hundred of LONSDALE, north of the sands, county palatine of LANCASTER, 4 miles (S. by W.) from Hawkeshead, containing 307 inhabitants. The living is a perpetual curacy, in the archdeaconry of

Richmond, and diocese of Chester, endowed with £200 private benefaction, and £400 royal bounty, and in the patronage of the Landowners in Hawkeshead parish.

SATTERTHWAITE, a chapelry in the parish of ULVERSTONE, hundred of LONSDALE, north of the sands, county palatine of LANCASTER, 7½ miles (N. by W.) from Ulverstone, containing 154 inhabitants. Here are quarries of slate for roofing houses.

SAUGHALL (GREAT), a township in the parish of SHOTWICK, higher division of the hundred of WIRRALL, county palatine of CHESTER, 4 miles (N. W. by W.) from Chester, containing 343 inhabitants.

SAUGHALL (LITTLE), a township in the parish of SHOTWICK, higher division of the hundred of WIRRALL, county palatine of CHESTER, 3¼ miles (N. W. by W.) from Chester, containing 38 inhabitants.

SAUGHALL-MASSEY, a township in the parish of BIDSTONE, lower division of the hundred of WIRRALL, county palatine of CHESTER, 9 miles (N. N. W.) from Great Neston, containing 165 inhabitants.

SAUL, a parish in the upper division of the hundred of WHITSTONE, county of GLOUCESTER, 9 miles (N. W. by W.) from Stroud, containing 467 inhabitants. The living is a perpetual curacy, in the archdeaconry and diocese of Gloucester, endowed with £200 private benefaction, and £600 royal bounty, and in the patronage of the Vicar of Standish. The church is dedicated to St. James. There is a place of worship for Wesleyan Methodists. The navigable river Severn runs on the northern side of the parish, through which passes the Thames and Severn, and the Gloucester and Berkeley, canals.

SAUNDBY, a parish in the North-clay division of the wapentake of BASSETLAW, county of NOTTINGHAM, 2½ miles (S. W. by W.) from Gainsborough, containing 101 inhabitants. The living is a rectory, in the archdeaconry of Nottingham, and diocese of York, rated in the king's books at £14. 8. 6½., and in the patronage of Lord Viscount Midleton. The church, dedicated to St. Martin, is in the later style of English architecture, with portions of an earlier date.

SAUNDERTON, a parish in the hundred of DESBOROUGH, county of BUCKINGHAM, 1½ mile (S. W.) from Princes-Risborough, containing 210 inhabitants. The living is a rectory, in the archdeaconry of Buckingham, and diocese of Lincoln, rated in the king's books at £13. 9. 7., and in the patronage of the President and Fellows of Magdalene College, Oxford. The church is dedicated to St. Mary. This formerly constituted two parishes, but coming into the possession of one individual, they were united, in 1457, and the church dedicated to St. Nicholas was suffered to go to ruin.

SAUSTHORPE, a parish in the hundred of HILL, parts of LINDSEY, county of LINCOLN, 3 miles (N.N.W.) from Spilsby, containing 167 inhabitants. The living is a discharged rectory, in the archdeaconry and diocese of Lincoln, rated in the king's books at £6. 3. 6¼. George D. Kent, Esq. was patron in 1819. The church is dedicated to St. Andrew.

SAVERNAKE-PARK, or NORTH-SIDE, an extra-parochial district, in the hundred of SELKLEY, county of WILTS, 1½ mile (S.E. by E.) from Marlborough, containing 127 inhabitants.

SAVERNAKE-FOREST, or SOUTH-SIDE, an extra-parochial district, in the hundred of KINWARD-

STONE, county of WILTS, 2 miles (S.) from Marlborough.

SAWBRIDGEWORTH, a parish in the hundred of BRAUGHIN, county of HERTFORD, 11½ miles (E. by N.) from Hertford, containing 2071 inhabitants. The living is a vicarage, in the archdeaconry of Middlesex, and diocese of London, rated in the king's books at £17, and in the patronage of the Bishop of London. The church is dedicated to St. Michael. There are places of worship for Independents and Wesleyan Methodists.

SAWDON, a township in the parish of BROMPTON, PICKERING lythe, North riding of the county of YORK, 9 miles (W. S. W.) from Scarborough, containing 139 inhabitants. There is a place of worship for Wesleyan Methodists.

SAWLEY, a parish in the hundred of MORLESTON and LITCHURCH, county of DERBY, comprising the chapelries of Breason and Wilne, the townships of Long Eaton, Risley, and Sawley, and the liberties of Draycott and Hopwell, and containing 3643 inhabitants, of which number, 958 are in the township of Sawley, 4 miles (N. by W.) from Kegworth. The living is a perpetual curacy, in the peculiar jurisdiction and patronage of the Prebendary of Sawley in the Cathedral Church of Lichfield, endowed with £400 private benefaction, and £2000 parliamentary grant. The church is dedicated to All Saints. There is a place of worship for Wesleyan Methodists. The rivers Trent, Derwent, and Erewash run through the parish, which is also intersected by the Derby and the Erewash canals. Sawley had anciently a market and a fair; the market, having fallen into disuse, was revived about 1760, and was again discontinued before 1770; the market-house still remains. Harrington bridge, across the Trent, was completed in 1790. A National school is partly supported by a trifling sum bequeathed by Francis Hacker, in 1676.

SAWLEY, a chapelry in that part of the parish of RIPON which is in the liberty of RIPON, West riding of the county of YORK, 5½ miles (S. W. by W.) from Ripon, containing 490 inhabitants. The living is a perpetual curacy, in the peculiar jurisdiction of the Archbishop of York, endowed with £400 private benefaction, £400 royal bounty, and £300 parliamentary grant, and in the patronage of the Dean and Chapter of Ripon. The chapel is dedicated to St. Michael. The Wesleyan Methodists have a place of worship here. Six poor children are taught for the interest arising from £100, the gift of Ralph Lowther, in 1770.

SAWLEY, an extra-parochial liberty, in the western division of the wapentake of STAINCLIFFE and EWCROSS West riding of the county of YORK, 4 miles (N. E.) from Clitheroe, containing, with Tosside, 561 inhabitants. A Cistercian abbey, in honour of the Blessed Virgin, was founded here, in 1146, by William de Percy, the revenue of which, at the dissolution, was estimated at £221. 15. 8. The ruined gate-house has been converted into a cottage, and the greater part of the nave and transept, with the foundations of the choir and chapter-house, still remain.

SAWSTON, a parish in the hundred of WHITTLESFORD, county of CAMBRIDGE, 5¼ miles (W. N. W.) from Linton, containing 699 inhabitants. The living is a vicarage, in the archdeaconry and diocese of Ely, rated in the king's books at £13. 10. 2½., endowed with £200 parliamentary grant, and in the patronage of R. Hud-

dleston, Esq. The church is dedicated to St. Mary. There is a place of worship for Independents.

SAWTRY (ALL SAINTS), a parish in the hundred of NORMAN-CROSS, county of HUNTINGDON, 3½ miles (S.) from Stilton, containing 501 inhabitants. The living is a rectory, in the archdeaconry of Huntingdon, and diocese of Lincoln, rated in the king's books at £8. 15. 7½., and in the patronage of the Duke of Devonshire. The church, which is ancient, has three seats, or stalls, on the north side of the chancel. There is a place of worship for Wesleyan Methodists. A monastery, in honour of the Blessed Virgin, was founded in 1146, by Simon, Earl of Northampton who brought hither from the abbey of Wardon, or Sartis, in Bedfordshire, a convent of Cistercian monks, whose revenue at the dissolution was estimated at £199. 11. 8.

SAWTRY (ST. ANDREW), a parish in the hundred of NORMAN-CROSS, county of HUNTINGDON, 3¼ miles (S. by E.) from Stilton, containing 319 inhabitants. The living is a rectory, in the archdeaconry of Huntingdon, and diocese of Lincoln, rated in the king's books at £8. 1. 0½. A. Annesley, Esq. was patron in 1812.

SAWTRY (ST. JUDITH), an extra-parochial liberty (formerly a parish), in the hundred of NORMAN-CROSS, county of HUNTINGDON, 4 miles (S. by E.) from Stilton, containing 207 inhabitants. The church has long been demolished. Here, it is said, was formerly a cell to the abbey of Ramsey.

SAXBY, a parish in the hundred of FRAMLAND, county of LEICESTER, 4½ miles (E. by N.) from Melton-Mowbray, containing 153 inhabitants. The living is a discharged rectory, consolidated with the vicarage of Stapleford, in the archdeaconry of Leicester, and diocese of Lincoln, rated in the king's books at £5, and in the patronage of the Earl of Harborough. The church is dedicated to St. Peter. The Melton-Mowbray and Oakham canal passes through the parish. The neighbourhood presents the appearance of having been the scene of some sanguinary contest; the skeletons of horses and men, earthen urns, which are supposed to have contained the hearts of the slain, bridle bits, fibulæ, &c., and weapons in use before the introduction of fire arms, having been discovered three feet below the soil, and immediately upon the surface of the gravel, in digging for which the workmen invariably found heaps of pebbles laid upon the bodies.

SAXBY, a parish in the eastern division of the wapentake of ASLACOE, parts of LINDSEY, county of LINCOLN, 7¼ miles (W. by S.) from Market-Rasen, containing 105 inhabitants. The living is a discharged rectory, in the archdeaconry and diocese of Lincoln, rated in the king's books at £7. 4. 1., endowed with £200 royal bounty, and £200 parliamentary grant, and in the patronage of the Earl of Scarborough. The church is dedicated to St. Helen.

SAXBY, a parish in the northern division of the wapentake of YARBOROUGH, parts of LINDSEY, county of LINCOLN, 5 miles (S. W.) from Barton upon Humber, containing 233 inhabitants. The living is a rectory, in the archdeaconry and diocese of Lincoln, rated in the king's books at £12. 18. 6½., and in the patronage of J. Harman, Esq. and others. The church is dedicated to All Saints.

SAXELBY, a parish in the eastern division of the hundred of GOSCOTE, county of LEICESTER, 4 miles (W. N. W.) from Melton-Mowbray, containing, with the hamlet of Shoby, 134 inhabitants. The living is a rectory, in the archdeaconry of Leicester, and diocese of Lincoln, rated in the king's books at £9, and in the patronage of the Earl of Aylesford. The church is dedicated to St. Peter. The late Mr. Houghton left £5 per annum for the education of poor children.

SAXELBY, a parish in the wapentake of LAWRESS, parts of LINDSEY, county of LINCOLN, 6½ miles (N. W. by W.) from Lincoln, containing, with the township of Ingleby, 561 inhabitants. The living is a discharged vicarage, in the archdeaconry of Stow, and diocese of Lincoln, rated in the king's books at £10, endowed with £200 royal bounty, and in the patronage of the Bishop of Lincoln. The church is dedicated to St. Botolph. There is a place of worship for Wesleyan Methodists.

SAXHAM (GREAT), a parish in the hundred of THINGOE, county of SUFFOLK, 5 miles (W. by S.) from Bury-St. Edmund's, containing 260 inhabitants. The living is a rectory, in the archdeaconry of Sudbury, and diocese of Norwich, rated in the king's books at £11. 13. 11½., and in the patronage of Robert Muir, Esq. The church is dedicated to St. Andrew.

SAXHAM (LITTLE), a parish in the hundred of THINGOE, county of SUFFOLK, 3¾ miles (W.) from Bury-St. Edmund's, containing 202 inhabitants. The living is a rectory, in the archdeaconry of Sudbury, and diocese of Norwich, rated in the king's books at £8. 11. 5½., and in the patronage of Earl Cornwallis. The church is dedicated to St. Nicholas.

SAXLINGHAM, a parish in the hundred of HOLT, county of NORFOLK, 3¾ miles (W. by N.) from Holt, containing 147 inhabitants. The living is a rectory, with that of Sharrington annexed, in the archdeaconry and diocese of Norwich, rated in the king's books at £12. 17. 3½. R. P. Joddrell, Esq. was patron in 1812. The church, dedicated to St. Margaret, contains a large and costly monument in the form of an Egyptian pyramid, ornamented with numerous hieroglyphics, erected by Sir Christopher Heydon to the memory of his lady, who died in 1593. There is a place of worship for Wesleyan Methodists.

SAXLINGHAM-NETHERGATE, a parish in the hundred of HENSTEAD, county of NORFOLK, 3½ miles (N. E.) from St. Mary Stratton, containing 595 inhabitants. The living is a discharged rectory, with that of Saxlingham-Thorpe united, in the archdeaconry of Norfolk, and diocese of Norwich, rated in the king's books at £13. 11. 8., and in the patronage of J. Steward, Esq. The church is dedicated to St. Mary.

SAXLINGHAM-THORPE, a parish in the hundred of HENSTEAD, county of NORFOLK, 3¼ miles (N. E. by E.) from St. Mary Stratton, containing 133 inhabitants. The living is a discharged rectory, united to that of Saxlingham-Nethergate, in the archdeaconry of Norfolk, and diocese of Norwich, rated in the king's books at £6. 18. 4. The church, which has fallen into ruins, was dedicated to St. Mary.

SAXMUNDHAM, a market town and parish in the hundred of PLOMESGATE, county of SUFFOLK, 20 miles (N. E. by N.) from Ipswich, and 89 (N. E.) from London, containing 989 inhabitants. This town, supposed to be of Saxon origin, is situated in a valley, near a small stream which flows on the eastern side into the Alde, on the high road to London : it consists chiefly of one street running north and south, of modern and newly-fronted houses, and is of neat and respectable appearance : the inhabitants are plentifully supplied with water from springs : there is an assembly-room, in which balls and concerts are occasionally held. The only branch of business is that in malt. The market is on Thursday, and is noted for corn, which is shipped in large quantities from Snape and Iken wharfs for London. Fairs are on Whit-Tuesday, and on the first Thursday in October, for toys, &c. The living is a discharged rectory, in the archdeaconry of Suffolk, and diocese of Norwich, rated in the king's books at £8. 15. 10., and in the patronage of Dudley Long North, Esq. The church, a neat edifice embosomed in trees, and standing a little southward of the town, is dedicated to St. John the Baptist, and has recently undergone a thorough repair, one hundred and eighty sittings having been added, of which ninety are free; towards defraying the expense the Incorporated Society for the building and enlargement of churches and chapels contributed £75 : it contains several monuments. There is a place of worship for Independents. William Corbold gave a rent-charge of £5 for the instruction of four poor children.

SAXONDALE, a township in the parish of SHELFORD, southern division of the wapentake of BINGHAM, county of NOTTINGHAM, 8 miles (E.) from Nottingham, containing 118 inhabitants.

SAXTEAD, a parish in the hundred of HOXNE, county of SUFFOLK, 2¼ miles (N.W.) from Framlingham, containing 453 inhabitants. The living is a perpetual curacy, annexed to the rectory of Framlingham, in the archdeaconry of Suffolk, and diocese of Norwich. The church is dedicated to All Saints.

SAXTHORPE, a parish in the southern division of the hundred of ERPINGHAM, county of NORFOLK, 5¼ miles (N.W. by W.) from Aylsham, containing 342 inhabitants. The living is a discharged vicarage, in the archdeaconry and diocese of Norwich, rated in the king's books at £4. 13. 4., endowed with £200 private benefaction, and £200 royal bounty, and in the patronage of the Master and Fellows of Pembroke Hall, Cambridge. The church is dedicated to St. Andrew.

SAXTON, a parish in the upper division of the wapentake of BARKSTONE-ASH, West riding of the county of YORK, comprising the townships of Saxton with Scarthingwell, and Towton, and containing 472 inhabitants, of which number, 378 are in the township of Saxton with Scarthingwell, 4¼ miles (S. by W.) from Tadcaster. The living is a perpetual curacy, in the archdeaconry and diocese of York, endowed with £200 private benefaction, and £400 royal bounty. R. O. Gascoigne, Esq. was patron in 1805. The church is dedicated to All Saints. Lords Dacre and Westmorland, with a vast number of the slain in the sanguinary battle of Towton, fought on March 29th, 1461, between the houses of York and Lancaster, were interred here.

SCACKLETON, a township in that part of the parish of HOVINGHAM which is in the wapentake of BULMER, North riding of the county of YORK, 10 miles (W. by N.) from New Malton, containing 171 inhabitants.

SCAFTWORTH, a township in the parish of EVER-TON, liberty of SOUTHWELL and SCROOBY, though locally in the wapentake of Bassetlaw, county of NOTTINGHAM, 1¼ mile (S. E. by E.) from Bawtry, containing 100 inhabitants.

SCAGGLETHORPE, a township in the parish of SETTRINGTON, wapentake of BUCKROSE, East riding of the county of YORK, 3 miles (E. by N.) from New Malton, containing 222 inhabitants. There is a place of worship for Primitive Methodists, with a Sunday school.

SCALBY, a township in the parish of BLACKTOFT, wapentake of HOWDENSHIRE, East riding of the county of YORK, 6¼ miles (E. by N.) from Howden, containing 179 inhabitants.

SCALBY, a parish in PICKERING lythe, North riding of the county of YORK, comprising the chapelry of Cloughton, and the townships of Burniston, Newby, Scalby, Stainton-Dale, and Throxenby, and containing 1559 inhabitants, of which number, 446 are in the township of Scalby, 3¼ miles (N. W. by W.) from Scarborough. The living is a discharged vicarage, in the archdeaconry and diocese of York, rated in the king's books at £6. 13. 4., and in the patronage of the Dean and Chapter of Norwich. The church is dedicated to St. Lawrence. At Scalby Mill, in this parish, are tea-gardens, resorted to by the company that visit Scarborough during the season for bathing.

SCALDWELL, a parish in the hundred of ORLING-BURY, county of NORTHAMPTON, 8½ miles (N. by E.) from Northampton, containing 323 inhabitants. The living is a rectory, in the archdeaconry of Northampton, and diocese of Peterborough, rated in the king's books at £14. 0. 10., and in the patronage of the Duke of Buccleuch. The church is dedicated to St. Peter and St. Paul. Thomas Rowe, in 1665, bequeathed a rent-charge of £10 for teaching ten children of Scaldwell, and ten of Brixworth; and in 1735, Edward Palmer gave another of £2, for the instruction of three more.

SCALEBY, a parish in ESKDALE ward, county of CUMBERLAND, comprising the townships of East and West Scaleby, and containing 618 inhabitants, of which number, 255 are in the township of East Scaleby, 6½ miles, and 363 in that of West Scaleby, 5½ miles, (N. E. by N.) from Carlisle. The living is a discharged rectory, in the archdeaconry and diocese of Carlisle, rated in the king's books at £7. 12. 1., endowed with £400 royal bounty, and £400 parliamentary grant, and in the patronage of the Bishop of Carlisle. The church, dedicated to All Saints, was repaired in 1827. There is a trifling sum for the support of a school, left by Joseph Jackson, in 1773. Richard Tilliol, called Richard the Rider, received a grant of this territory from Henry I., and built a castle upon it with materials brought from the Picts' wall. In the early part of the parliamentary war, Scaleby castle was garrisoned for Charles I. ; in 1645 it surrendered to the parliamentarians; in 1648 it again fell into the hands of the royalists, but was soon after re-captured and kept for the parliament; it is still in tolerable preservation. The late Rev. William Gilpin, author of the Lives of the Reformers, Forest Scenery, &c., was born in it, in 1724.

SCALERGATE, a township in the parish of AP-PLEBY, ST. LAWRENCE, EAST ward, county of WEST-MORLAND, containing 108 inhabitants. The remains of Appleby castle are within this township.

SCALES, a joint township with Bromfield and Crookdake, in that part of the parish of BROMFIELD which is in ALLERDALE ward below Darwent, county of CUMBERLAND 5½ miles (S. W. by W.) from Wigton. The population is returned with Bromfield.

SCALES, a joint township with Newton, in the parish of KIRKHAM, hundred of AMOUNDERNESS, county palatine of LANCASTER, 2¾ miles (S. E.) from Kirkham. The population is returned with Newton.

SCALFORD, a parish in the hundred of FRAM-LAND, county of LEICESTER, 4 miles (N. by E.) from Melton-Mowbray, containing 438 inhabitants. The living is a vicarage, in the archdeaconry of Leicester, and diocese of Lincoln, rated in the king's books at £8. 1. 10½., and in the patronage of the Duke of Rutland. The church is dedicated to St. Egelwin the Martyr.

SCAMBLESBY, a parish in the northern division of the wapentake of GARTREE, parts of LINDSEY, county of LINCOLN, 6¾ miles (N. by E.) from Horncastle, containing 347 inhabitants. The living is a perpetual curacy, in the peculiar jurisdiction of the Dean and Chapter of Lincoln, and in the patronage of the Prebendary of Melton-Ross with Scamblesby in the Cathedral Church of Lincoln, endowed with £400 private benefaction, £600 royal bounty, and £600 parliamentary grant.

SCAMMONDEN, a chapelry in the parish of HUD-DERSFIELD, upper division of the wapentake of AG-BRIGG, West riding of the county of YORK, 7½ miles (W.) from Huddersfield, containing, with Dean-Head, 855 inhabitants. The living is a perpetual curacy, in the archdeaconry and diocese of York, endowed with £440 private benefaction, and £400 royal bounty, and in the patronage of the Vicar of Huddersfield.

SCAMPSTON, a chapelry in the parish of RIL-LINGTON, wapentake of BUCKROSE, East riding of the county of YORK, 5¼ miles (N. E. by E.) from New Malton, containing 200 inhabitants. The living is a perpetual curacy, in the archdeaconry of the East riding, and diocese of York, endowed with £800 royal bounty, and £400 parliamentary grant, and in the patronage of the Vicar of Rillington.

SCAMPTON, a parish in the wapentake of LAW-RESS, parts of LINDSEY, county of LINCOLN, 5¾ miles (N. N. W.) from Lincoln, containing 238 inhabitants. The living is a discharged rectory, in the archdeaconry of Stow, and diocese of Lincoln, rated in the king's books at £8. 16. 8., and in the patronage of Sir George Cayley, Bart. The church is dedicated to St. John the Baptist.

SCARBOROUGH, a borough, market town, and parish, having separate jurisdiction, locally in Pickering lythe, North riding of the county of YORK, 39 miles (N. E.) from York, and 216 (N.) from London, containing, with the township of Falsgrave, 8533 inhabitants. The origin of this town has not been satisfactorily ascertained : it

Corporate Seal.

is supposed to have derived its name from the Saxon Scear, a rock, and Burgh, a fortified place. No mention of it occurs in the Norman survey, attributable to its having been one of those towns which, in the sanguinary conflicts between the Saxons and the Danes, were laid desolate, or to its having shared in the devastation that marked the progress of the Conqueror. The earliest authentic record is a charter of Henry II., conferring certain privileges on the inhabitants; and in the reign of Henry III., a charter was granted for making a new pier at *Scardeburgh*, as it was then called. Prior to the construction of the pier, the town began to rise into importance, and was defended by walls and a fosse, of which some vestiges may still be traced. In the reign of Stephen, a castle had been erected by William le Gros, Earl of Albemarle and Holdernesse, which that nobleman was compelled to surrender to Henry II., who made considerable additions to it. In this castle Piers Gaveston took refuge from the attacks of the confederate barons, and for a considerable time maintained it against their assaults, till a scarcity of provisions obliged him to surrender. In this reign the town was burnt by the Scottish forces, who, headed by Robert Bruce, their king, made an irruption into England. Robert Aske, the leader of the insurrection called the Pilgrimage of Grace, made an unsuccessful attempt to gain possession of the castle, in 1536; and during Wyatt's rebellion, in 1553, it was surprised and taken by a party headed by Thomas, second son of Lord Stafford, who, disguising themselves as peasants, obtained possession of it: but it was soon retaken by the Earl of Westmorland, and Stafford and three of his accomplices being made prisoners, were sent to London, and executed for high treason.

During the civil war in the reign of Charles I., the parliamentarian forces, commanded by Sir John Meldrum, besieged the castle, which held out under its brave governor, Sir Hugh Cholmley, for more than twelve months, and after the death of their leader, who fell in the assault, the command devolved upon Sir Matthew Boynton, to whom the fortress was surrendered, in 1645, upon honourable terms, after the exhaustion of its military stores. Col. Boynton, who succeeded Sir Matthew in the command of the castle, having declared for the king, it came again into the possession of the royalists; but the garrison mutinying, he was obliged to capitulate, and it was finally surrendered to the parliament in 1648, and soon afterwards dismantled. George Fox, founder of the Society of Friends, was confined in it in 1665. During the rebellion in 1745, the castle was put into a state of temporary repair; and since that time three batteries have been erected for the protection of the town and harbour, of which two are on the south and one on the north side of the castle-yard, and within the enclosure are barracks for the accommodation of one hundred and twenty men. This once formidable fortress comprised within the boundary walls an area of more than nineteen acres, and occupied the summit of an eminence three hundred feet above the level of the sea, which surrounds it on all sides except on the west, by which it is connected with the town, and on the north, east, and south, is a vast range of perpendicular rocks; the entrance is through an arched gateway, on the summit of a narrow isthmus, flanked by bastions, and defended by a draw-bridge within the gates, and a deep fosse. The principal parts now remaining are the keep, a square tower, the walls

of which are twelve feet thick, and some portions of the semicircular towers which defended the ramparts, now falling rapidly to decay; some slight remains of the chapel are still discernible within the walls: the castle and its precincts are extra-parochial.

The town is beautifully and romantically situated in the recess of a fine open bay, on the coast of the North sea, and consists of several spacious streets of handsome well-built houses, rising in successive tiers from the shore, in the form of an amphitheatre: the beach, of firm and smooth sand, slopes gradually towards the sea, and affords at all times safe and commodious sea-bathing, for which the town is celebrated. On the cliffs are many new and handsome houses for private residence, and numerous lodging-houses have been erected for the accommodation of visitors, who repair hither, either for the convenience of sea-bathing, for which the water of the bay, unimpaired in its quality by the influx of any stream of fresh water, is peculiarly favourable; or for the benefit of the mineral springs, the efficacy of which, in numerous diseases, has been for more than two centuries in the highest repute. These springs, which are saline chalybeates, varying in the proportions of their several ingredients, were for some time lost by the sinking of a large mass of the cliff, in 1737, but were recovered after a diligent search. The principal are the south and the north wells, situated at the base of the cliff, south of the town, near the sea-shore, where a convenient and handsome building has been erected for the accommodation of visitors. The water of the south well contains ninety-eight ounces, and that of the north well one hundred ounces, of carbonic acid gas in a gallon; the former is purgative, and the latter tonic. A fine terrace, one hundred feet above the level of the sands, forms a pleasant marine promenade. A handsome iron bridge of four arches on stone pillars, connecting the dissevered cliffs, in the chasm between which runs the stream called Mill-beck, and affording facility of access to the spas, was erected in 1827: it is four hundred and fourteen feet in length, and seventy-five in height, and constitutes one of the principal ornaments of the town. Adjacent to the bridge is the museum, an elegant circular building with a dome, erected by subscription in 1829, for the investigation and illustration of the natural history of the district, and already displaying many most valuable specimens. There are five separate bathing establishments, where warm sea-water baths may be obtained at any time: three of them are situated on the cliff, and the others near the pier; they are under the super intendence of medical practitioners residing in the town. There is also a general sea-bathing infirmary, supported by subscription, for the use of poor invalids, who, on the plan of the infirmary at Margate, are boarded and lodged upon very moderate terms, and during their residence in it, have the gratuitous use of the waters. The theatre, a commodious and well-arranged building, is open during the season; and assemblies are held occasionally under the superintendence of a master of the ceremonies, in a handsome suite of rooms elegantly fitted up for that purpose. A Scientific Institution is forming, to support which a considerable sum has been subscribed: the situation selected for the museum to be attached is on the cliffs near the bridge. The environs are beautifully diversified with hill and dale, and include much picturesque and romantic scenery; Olivers' mount, about a mile from the town, approached by a gradual ascent, forms a magnificent natural marine terrace, five hundred feet above the level of the sea, commanding an interesting view of the Castle hill, with its venerable ruins, the town, the harbour, and the piers on one side, and an extensive view of the ocean on the other. The rides are pleasant; and the salubrity of the air, and the numerous objects of interest with which the neighbourhood abounds, have rendered Scarborough a favourite place of fashionable resort. The town is supplied with fresh water by means of a reservoir, capable of containing four thousand hogsheads.

The port is a member of the port of Hull, and its limits extend from the most easterly part of Flamborough Head, in a direction northward, to Peaseholme Beck, including all the sea-coast to fourteen fathoms of water, at low water mark. The foreign trade is principally with Portugal, Holland, and the Baltic, from which places it imports wine, brandy, geneva, timber, deals, hemp, flax, and iron : it carries on also a considerable coasting trade in corn, butter, bacon, and salt-fish, with Newcastle, Sunderland, and other places on the coast, and with the port of London for groceries. There are one hundred and seventy-three ships belonging to the port, averaging a burden of one hundred and sixty-four tons. The harbour, though confined at the entrance, is easy of access, and safe and commodious within : it is protected by two piers, of which the one was considerably enlarged by act of parliament obtained in the 5th of Geo. II.; it is one thousand two hundred feet in length, and forty-two feet broad at the extremity, and in the intermediate line varies from thirteen to eighteen feet in breadth. This pier having been found insufficient to prevent the accumulation of sand in the harbour, an act was obtained for the construction of a new pier, of which the breadth at the foundation is sixty feet, and at the curvature, where it is most subject to the action of the waves, sixty-three feet; it is forty feet high, forty-two feet in breadth at the top, and one thousand two hundred feet in length, and was designed by Smeaton, the celebrated engineer. To defray the expense of this undertaking, a duty of one halfpenny per chaldron was granted on all coal brought from Newcastle, with other duties on shipping frequenting the port. The custom-house, a neat building on the sand side, is under the superintendence of the usual officers ; and three steam-packets touch at this port twice every week, on their passage between London and Edinburgh. The fishery was formerly carried on to a considerable extent, and was a source of great profit to the town, but has of late greatly declined. There are some establishments for shipbuilding, and several manufactories for cordage and sail-cloth. An attempt was made, in 1794, to form a canal, but it was never accomplished. The market days are Thursday and Saturday, the former for corn ; the fish market is held on the sands near the harbour : the fairs are on Holy Thursday and November 22nd, chiefly for cattle. The borough received a charter of incorporation from Henry II., under which, ratified and extended by succeeding monarchs, the government is vested in two bailiffs, two coroners, four chamberlains, and thirty-six common council-men, assisted by a town clerk, a recorder, and subordinate officers. The bailiffs are annually chosen by the common council, and are justices of the peace within the borough. The corporation hold quarterly courts of session, for all offences not capital, and a manorial court every month, for the recovery of debts to any amount. The town hall is a spacious and commodious building, in which the several courts are held, and the public business of the corporation is transacted. The borough gaol and the house of correction, distinct buildings, are but ill adapted for the classification of prisoners ; the former, chiefly for debtors, contains four rooms, and the latter only three, without airing-yards. The borough first exercised the elective franchise in the 23rd of Edward I., since which time it has regularly returned two members to parliament : the right of election is vested in the bailiffs and corporation : the bailiffs are the returning officers.

The living is a discharged vicarage, in the archdeaconry of the East riding, and diocese of York, rated in the king's books at £13. 6. 8., endowed with £1800 parliamentary grant, and in the patronage of Lord Hotham. The church, dedicated to St. Mary, was anciently the conventual church of the Cistercian monastery, and was formerly a spacious and magnificent cruciform structure, with three noble towers : it sustained considerable damage during the siege of the castle, in the time of the parliamentary war, and retains but few portions of its ancient character : the present steeple stands at the eastern end. Christ-church, a handsome edifice in the later style of English architecture, with a square embattled tower crowned with pinnacles, and containing one thousand two hundred sittings, of which six hundred are free, was erected in 1828, at an expense of £5000, by grant from the parliamentary commissioners, exclusively of a local subscription of £3000, and the stone, which was the gift of Sir John V. B. Johnstone, Bart. There are places of worship for Baptists, the Society of Friends, Independents, and Wesleyan Methodists, and a Roman Catholic chapel. The grammar school is of very obscure origin ; in 1648 the corporation ordered a part of St. Mary's church to be fitted up and appropriated to its use, the expense of which was defrayed by the sale of the old school-house ; the income, arising from donations of land and money, is about £12 per annum ; gratuitous instruction is afforded to four scholars only. A society, consisting of about two hundred members, was established in 1729, under the patronage of Robert North, Esq., for clothing and educating the poor children of the town, which is, to a considerable extent, accomplished by weekly contributions of its members, and general subscription. The spinning school was established, in 1788, under the patronage of the ladies of Scarborough, for the clothing and education of girls, who are also instructed in useful domestic occupations; a Lancasterian school is supported by subscription, and there are Sunday schools in connexion with the established church, and the dissenting congregations. The Seamen's hospital was erected, in 1752, by the ship-owners of the town, for the maintenance and support of aged seamen, their widows, and children : it is supported by a contribution of sixpence per month from the owner of every vessel belonging to the port, for each person on board during the time the vessel is at sea, or in actual service, and is under the superintendence of a president and trustees, annually elected: the income of this hospital, arising from donations, is about £200 per annum. St. Thomas' hospital was founded by the corporation, for aged and infirm persons, and is under the direction of the bailiffs and common council; the buildings are low and of ancient appearance. There are also several amicable societies, and various charitable bequests for distribution among the poor. To the north of St. Sepulchre's street are the remains of a Franciscan convent, supposed to have been founded about the 29th of Henry III., and now used as a workshop. Among other monastic establishments anciently existing here were, a monastery of Dominicans, founded in the reign of Edward I., by Adam Say, Knt., or by Henry Percy, Earl of Northumberland; and a house of Carmelite friars, founded by Edward II., in 1319. Scarborough gives the title of earl to the family of Lumley.

SCARCLIFF, a parish in the hundred of SCARSDALE, county of DERBY, 6 miles (N. N. W.) from Mansfield, containing 494 inhabitants. The living is a discharged vicarage, in the archdeaconry of Derby, and diocese of Lichfield and Coventry, rated in the king's books at £5, endowed with £1000 royal bounty, and £200 parliamentary grant, and in the patronage of the Duke of Devonshire. The church, dedicated to St. Leonard, contains a monument in the 11th century, representing a lady in robes, with a coronet on her head, and an infant on her left arm: the inscription, in Lombardic capitals, has become illegible from time and mutilation. Ten poor children are instructed for an annuity of £6 bequeathed by Kithe Vaughan, in 1813, and another of 10s. by Elizabeth Saxton, in 1815.

SCARCROFT, a township in the parish of THORNER, lower division of the wapentake of SKYRACK, West riding of the county of YORK, 6¼ miles (S. S. W.) from Wetherby, containing 105 inhabitants.

SCARGILL, a township in the parish of BARNINGHAM, western division of the wapentake of GILLING, North riding of the county of YORK, 3½ miles (S. W. by W.) from Greta-Bridge, containing 136 inhabitants.

SCARISBRICK, a township in the parish of ORMSKIRK, hundred of WEST DERBY, county palatine of LANCASTER, 2 miles (N. W.) from Ormskirk, containing 1584 inhabitants.

SCARLE (NORTH), a parish in the lower division of the wapentake of BOOTHBY-GRAFFO, parts of KESTEVEN, county of LINCOLN, 10 miles (W. S. W.) from Lincoln, containing 434 inhabitants. The living is a discharged rectory, in the archdeaconry and diocese of Lincoln, rated in the king's books at £4. 17. 3½., and in the patronage of Lord Egremont. The church is dedicated to All Saints. There is a place of worship for Wesleyan Methodists. The river Trent forms a boundary of this parish.

SCARLE (SOUTH), a parish in the northern division of the wapentake of NEWARK, county of NOTTINGHAM, 7½ miles (N. E. by N.) from Newark, containing, with the chapelry of Besthorpe, 422 inhabitants. The living is a discharged vicarage, in the archdeaconry of Nottingham, and diocese of York, rated in the king's books at £5. 2. 5., endowed with £200 private benefaction, and £200 royal bounty, and in the patronage of the Prebendary of South Scarle in the Cathedral Church of Lincoln. The church is dedicated to St. Helen.

SCARNING, a parish in the hundred of LAUNDITCH, county of NORFOLK, 2 miles (W. S. W.) from East Dereham, containing 498 inhabitants. The living is a discharged vicarage, in the archdeaconry and diocese of Norwich, rated in the king's books at £9. 19. Sir John Lombe, Bart. was patron in 1808. The church is dedicated to St. Peter and St. Paul. A free school was founded here and liberally endowed by William Secker, in 1604.

SCARRINGTON, a parish in the northern division of the wapentake of BINGHAM, county of NOTTINGHAM, 12½ miles (E. by N.) from Nottingham, containing 171 inhabitants. The living is a perpetual curacy, annexed to the vicarage of Orston, in the archdeaconry of Nottingham, and diocese of York. There is a place of worship for Wesleyan Methodists. Scarrington is in the honour of Tutbury, duchy of Lancaster, and within the jurisdiction of a court of pleas held at Tutbury every third Tuesday, for the recovery of debts under 40s.

SCARTHINGWELL, a joint township with Saxton, in the parish of SAXTON, upper division of the wapentake of BARKSTONE-ASH, West riding of the county of YORK, 4¾ miles (S. by E.) from Tadcaster. The population is returned with Saxton.

SCARTHO, a parish in the wapentake of BRADLEY-HAVERSTOE, parts of LINDSEY, county of LINCOLN, 2¼ miles (S.) from Great Grimsby, containing 148 inhabitants. The living is a discharged rectory, in the archdeaconry and diocese of Lincoln, rated in the king's books at £8. 10. 10., and in the patronage of the Principal and Fellows of Jesus College, Oxford. The church is dedicated to St. Giles.

SCATHWAITERIGG-HAY, a joint township with Hutton i' th' Hay, in that part of the parish of KENDAL which is in KENDAL ward, county of WESTMORLAND, 2 miles (N. E.) from Kendal, containing 348 inhabitants.

SCAWBY, a parish in the eastern division of the wapentake of MANLEY, parts of LINDSEY, county of LINCOLN, 2¼ miles (W. S. W.) from Glandford-Bridge, containing, with the township of Sturton, 838 inhabitants. The living is a discharged vicarage, in the archdeaconry of Stow, and diocese of Lincoln, rated in the king's books at £7, and in the patronage of Sir H. Nelthorpe, Bart. The church is dedicated to St. Hibald. There is a place of worship for Wesleyan Methodists. A free school, founded in 1705, by Richard Nelthorpe, is endowed with land now let for £30 a year, for the instruction of the children of the Nelthorpe tenantry.

SCAWTON, a parish in the wapentake of RYEDALE, North riding of the county of YORK, 5 miles (W.) from Helmsley, containing 154 inhabitants. The living is a discharged rectory, in the archdeaconry of Cleveland, and diocese of York, rated in the king's books at £2. 19. 2., and in the patronage of — Worsley, Esq. The church, dedicated to St. Mary, is in the early style of English architecture.

SCHOLES, a joint township with Morwick, in the parish of BARWICK in ELMETT, lower division of the wapentake of SKYRACK, West riding of the county of YORK, 7 miles (E.N.E.) from Leeds. The population is returned with Morwick. There is a place of worship for Wesleyan Methodists.

SCILLY ISLANDS. These islands, of which there are seventeen, varying in extent from one thousand six hundred and forty acres to ten, besides twenty-two smaller islets, and numerous naked rocks, form a cluster lying off the south-west coast of Cornwall, about 17 leagues due west from the Lizard point, and 10 leagues nearly west by south from the Land's End. By the Greeks they were called *Hesperides* and *Cassiterides*; by the Romans *Sellinæ* and *Siluræ Insulæ*: their present name of Scilly, anciently written Sully, or Sulley, appears to be British, and they are reported to take it from a small island, containing only one acre, which is called Scilly Island. Except what relates to their trading intercourse with the Phœnicians and the Romans, and the circumstance of their having been occasionally appropriated by the latter as a place of banishment for state criminals, the first mention we find of them in history is in the tenth century, when they were subdued by King Athelstan. After this there is no record of any remarkable historical event respecting them until the reign of Charles I., when they became of considerable importance as a military post. In 1645, they afforded a temporary asylum to Prince Charles and his friends, Lords Hopton and Capel. In 1649, Sir John Grenville being governor of the Scilly Islands, fortified and held them for Charles II. The parliament finding their trading vessels much annoyed by his frigates, fitted out an expedition for the reduction of the islands, under the command of Admiral Blake and Sir George Ascue, who first took possession of those of Trescaw and Bryer, and threw up fortifications for the purpose of attacking Sir John Grenville, at St. Mary's. The Dutch admiral, Van Tromp, is said to have made insidious, but ineffectual, proposals to the governor to take the islands under his protection. Resistance being found vain, they were delivered up to the parliament, in the beginning of June of the same year, this having been one of the last rallying points for the royalists: the garrison consisted of eight hundred soldiers, with numerous commissioned officers.

The total surface of the islands is about four thousand seven hundred acres, and the number of inhabitants from two to three thousand. The extent of St. Mary's Island, the largest, including the garrison, which is joined to it by an isthmus, is one thousand six hundred and forty acres, and its population is from 1200 to 1500. The principal town, called Hugh-town, or Heugh-town, was much damaged by inundation during the great storm in 1744. The pier was finished in 1750, having been constructed at the expense of Lord Godolphin; vessels of one hundred and fifty tons' burden may ride here in safety. Near this town are the ruins of an old fortress, with a mount, and the remains of several block-houses and batteries, supposed to have been constructed in the civil war. About two furlongs to the eastward is a bay, called Pomellin, or Porthmellin, where a fine white sand, composed of crystals and talc, much esteemed as a writing sand, and for other purposes, is procured in abundance. About a mile from Hugh-town is the Church-town, consisting of a few houses and the church, in the chancel of which are interred Sir John Narborough, Bart., son of the celebrated admiral of that name; Henry Trelawney, son of a Bishop of Winchester; and Captain Edmund Loades, of the Association man of war, all of whom shared the fate of Rear-Admiral Sir Cloudesley Shovel, who was lost on the Gilston rock, October 22nd, 1707. Two furlongs further, bordering on the sea, is Old-town, formerly the principal town of the island. On a promontory, called the Giant's Castle, are traces of an ancient fortress, supposed to be of remote origin. On the west side of the island are St. Mary's garrison, with the barracks and several batteries, and Star castle: the latter was built by Sir Francis Godolphin, in 1593. The island next in magnitude is Trescaw, anciently called Iniscaw, and St. Nicholas, which contains eight hundred and eighty acres, and about 500 inhabitants. In it are some remains of the conventual church of St. Nicholas, the ruins of Old-castle, and Oliver's Battery. Old-castle, which appears to have been built in or about the reign of Henry VIII., is spoken of by Leland as "a little pile, or fortress:" it appears to have been afterwards enlarged, as its ruins shew it to have been a considerable building. Oliver's castle, as it is called, from its having been built by the parliamentarians, was repaired in 1740; but is described by Borlase, in 1756, as being then already much decayed. St. Martin's island, though next in size to St. Mary's and Trescaw, containing seven hundred and twenty acres, was uninhabited until the reign of Charles II.; it now contains about 250 inhabitants. Mr. Ekins, in 1683, built a tower on this island, as a land-mark, twenty feet high, with a spire upon it of the same height. On St. Agnes' island, which contains 250 inhabitants, is a lighthouse. Bryer, or Brehar, contains three hundred and thirty acres, and about 120 inhabitants.

The principal employment and trade of the islanders consist in fishing and making kelp: about one hundred boats are used for fishing, piloting, &c.: the quantity of kelp annually made varies from one to two hundred tons. Tin is found in several of the islands, and in some, lead and copper; but no mines are now worked. Some of them produce grain, chiefly barley, peas, and oats, with a small portion of wheat; a few acres are sown with the pillis, or naked oat: potatoes are cultivated in great quantities in St. Mary's. Cattle are fed on most of them, and though not very abundant, are sometimes sold to masters of vessels. Samphire, for pickling, is collected in abundance in the isle of Trescaw. The tamarisk and *lavatera arborea* grow plentifully in that of St. Mary.

The property and temporal jurisdiction of these islands were anciently attached to the earldom, as they now are to the duchy, of Cornwall (excepting those of Trescaw), St. Sampson, St. Elid, St. Teon, and Nullo, and some lands in other islands, which were given, in or before the reign of Edward the Confessor, to certain monks, or hermits, who had their abode in the island of St. Nicholas (now Trescaw), and were subsequently granted by King Henry I. to the abbot of Tavistock. The present lessee of the whole is the Duke of Leeds, the representative of the Godolphin family, to whom they appear to have been first leased in the 13th of Elizabeth; the duke holds them at a rent of £40, for thirty-one years, from 1800, so that the lease is now about to expire. The government of them appears to have been vested, at least since the Reformation, uniformly in the proprietors, except in the instances of Sir John Grenville and Joseph Hunkin, Esq., during the interregnum, and Major Bennet, previously to the year 1733. Before the Reformation, it appears that the proprietor kept the peace of the islands, with the assistance of twelve armed men; and that there were frequent feuds between them and the king's coroner, who came hither to hold assizes for the trial of prisoners accused of greater offences. It is most probable that all minor offences were cognizable, as they now are, by a court delegated by the lord proprietor, whose authority for exercising the civil jurisdiction is derived from a patent of the 10th of King William. The lord proprietor appoints a court, or council of twelve, consisting of some of the principal inhabitants, among whom are generally the military commandant, steward, chaplain, and commissary of musters. Vacancies are supplied by election ; but the whole may be dissolved, and a fresh appointment made, at any time, by the lord proprietor. After the death of a lord proprietor, a new council is necessarily appointed. The court generally sits monthly, for the trial of plaints, suits, &c., between the islanders, excepting such causes as affect life and limb, and such as are cognizable by the court of Admiralty. Persons charged with transportable offences are tried here, such as receiving stolen goods, &c.; but the punishment is only fines, or whipping, and sometimes imprisonment. Those accused of murder, burglaries, &c., are conveyed before the nearest Cornish magistrate, and sent to be tried at the assizes for the county of Cornwall.

These islands have always been deemed to be under the spiritual jurisdiction of the Bishop of Cornwall, or Exeter, and to have formed part of the archdeaconry of Cornwall ; but there is no record of any ecclesiastical jurisdiction having been exercised, except in proving wills. In early times the abbot of Tavistock held the tithes of the whole, and certain lands, by the title of finding two monks to reside there, and to provide for the spiritual wants of the inhabitants. Since the Reformation the tithes have been vested in the lord proprietor, who is patron of the donative, and pays the minister an optional salary. The minister receives neither institution nor induction, nor is he licensed by the bishop ; and neither he nor the churchwardens are cited to visitations : the latter are sworn in at the lord's council court, where cognizance is taken of all offences usually brought before spiritual courts. It was formerly customary to punish such offenders by ducking in salt water at the quay head. Until of late years the minister of St. Mary's was the only clergyman in the islands, officiating constantly at St. Mary's, where a register of baptisms and marriages was kept for all the islands ; at Trescaw, only on the Sunday after Easter ; and at St. Martin's, on Trinity Sunday : the chapels of the other islands were served by laymen, or, as they were called, island clerks, usually fishermen. The Society for promoting Christian Knowledge now employs two missionaries, who officiate at what are called the Off-islands. There are chapels at Trescaw, St. Martin's, St. Agnes', Bryer, and St. Sampson's, for the most part built by the Godolphin family, since the Reformation ; that of Bryer, about 1746 : that of St. Agnes' was built at the expense of the Society for promoting Christian Knowledge, which also gave £400 towards erecting a house for the missionary, at Trescaw. The Wesleyan Methodists have four places of worship in these islands. The Earl of Godolphin, in 1747, established a school for instructing twelve boys in reading, writing, and arithmetic. The Rev. Richard Corbet Hartshorne, rector of Broseley in Shropshire, about the year 1753, gave the sum of £250 towards the support either of a minister or schoolmaster at Trescaw, under the direction of the Society for promoting Chris-

tian Knowledge. The only considerable benefaction which the society has received towards the religious instruction of the islanders, since that time, is the sum of £500, given by Charles Etty, Esq. About £300 per annum is expended by the society, on the missions and schools, chiefly out of their general funds. On St. Helen's island, now uninhabited, are the ruins of houses, and of an ancient chapel.

SCOLE, otherwise OSMONDISTON, a parish in the hundred of DISS, county of NORFOLK, 19½ miles (S. S. W.) from Norwich, containing 468 inhabitants. The living is a discharged rectory, in the archdeaconry of Norfolk, and diocese of Norwich, rated in the king's books at £9, and in the patronage of Sir E. Kerrison, Bart. The church is dedicated to St. Andrew. The village is a great thoroughfare on the high road from Ipswich to Norwich and Yarmouth, and contains a very good inn, built in the seventeenth century by a merchant of London, at the expense of £1500.

SCOPWICK, a parish in the second division of the wapentake of LANGOE, parts of KESTEVEN, county of LINCOLN, 8¼ miles (N.) from Sleaford, containing 232 inhabitants. The living is a discharged vicarage, in the archdeaconry and diocese of Lincoln, rated in the king's books at £8, endowed with £400 royal bounty, and in the patronage of the Crown. The church is dedicated to the Holy Cross.

SCORBROUGH, a parish in the Bainton-Beacon division of the wapentake of HARTHILL, East riding of the county of YORK, 4½ miles (N. N. W.) from Beverley, containing 88 inhabitants. The living is a discharged rectory, in the archdeaconry of the East riding, and diocese of York, rated in the king's books at £7, and in the patronage of the Earl of Egremont. The church is dedicated to St. Leonard.

SCOREBY, a joint township with West Stamford-Bridge, in that part of the parish of CATTON which is in the wapentake of OUZE and DERWENT, East riding of the county of YORK, 6½ miles (E. by N.) from York. The population is returned with West Stamford-Bridge.

SCORTON, a township in that part of the parish of CATTERICK which is in the eastern division of the wapentake of GILLING, North riding of the county of YORK, 2½ miles (N. N. E.) from Catterick, containing 496 inhabitants. A free grammar school here is endowed with £200 a year, the bequest of Leonard Robinson, Esq. The school-house, erected in 1760, stands on the north side of a spacious green, around which the village, which is well built, is situated. The buildings on the east side are occupied by a religious community of thirty nuns, of the order of St. Clair, who emigrated to this country from Normandy, in 1795. There are also about twenty boarders, and they have a neat chapel belonging to the establishment. Within the parish is a spring, called St. Cuthbert's well, the water of which is efficacious in cutaneous and rheumatic disorders.

SCOSTHORPE, a township in that part of the parish of KIRKBY in MALHAM-DALE which is in the western division of the wapentake of STAINCLIFFE and EWCROSS, West riding of the county of YORK, 6½ miles (S. E. by E.) from Settle, containing 102 inhabitants.

SCOTBY, a township in that part of the parish of WETHERAL which is in CUMBERLAND ward, county of CUMBERLAND, 3½ miles (E. by S.) from Carlisle, containing 318 inhabitants. There is a meeting-house, with a burial-ground, for the Society of Friends. A rail-road from Carlisle to Newcastle passes through the township. A school is endowed with land, now producing £14 a year, for teaching poor children, who pay each a small quarterage.

SCOTFORTH, a township in that part of the parish of LANCASTER which is in the hundred of LONSDALE, south of the sands, county palatine of LANCASTER, 1½ mile (S.) from Lancaster, containing 579 inhabitants. Eight poor children are instructed for £2. 5. a year, the interest of a legacy by John Taylor, in 1799.

SCOTHERN, a parish in the wapentake of LAWRESS, parts of LINDSEY, county of LINCOLN, 5¾ miles (N. E. by N.) from Lincoln, containing 366 inhabitants. The living is a discharged vicarage, in the archdeaconry of Stow, and diocese of Lincoln, rated in the king's books at £4. 5. 2½., endowed with £800 royal bounty, and in the patronage of the Earl of Scarborough. The church is dedicated to St. German.

SCOTTER, a parish in the wapentake of CORRINGHAM, parts of LINDSEY, county of LINCOLN, 9¼ miles (N. E. by N.) from Gainsborough, containing 938 inhabitants. The living is a rectory, in the archdeaconry of Stow, and diocese of Lincoln, rated in the king's books at £22. 4. 2., and in the patronage of the Bishop of Peterborough. The church is dedicated to St. Peter. There is a place of worship for Wesleyan Methodists. The river Eau runs through the parish, and falls into the Trent, which forms its north-west boundary. A charter for a market on Thursday, and a fair on July 10th, was granted by Richard I., but the former has been discontinued. There is a fair for horses and cattle on July 6th, called Scotter shew.

SCOTTON, a parish in the wapentake of CORRINGHAM, parts of LINDSEY, county of LINCOLN, 8¾ miles (N. E.) from Gainsborough, containing, with the chapelry of East Ferry, 515 inhabitants. The living is a rectory, in the archdeaconry of Stow, and diocese of Lincoln, rated in the king's books at £23, and in the patronage of Sir Richard Frederick, Bart. The church is dedicated to St. Genewys. There is a place of worship for Wesleyan Methodists. The parish is bounded on the west by the river Trent.

SCOTTON, a township in that part of the parish of CATTERICK which is in the eastern division of the wapentake of HANG, North riding of the county of YORK, 3½ miles (S. S. E.) from Richmond, containing 128 inhabitants.

SCOTTON, a township in the parish of FARNHAM, lower division of the wapentake of CLARO, West riding of the county of YORK, 2¼ miles (N. W.) from Knaresborough, containing 297 inhabitants. It is within the peculiar jurisdiction of the court of the honour of Knaresborough.

SCOTTOW, a parish in the southern division of the hundred of ERPINGHAM, county of NORFOLK, 2½ miles (N.) from Coltishall, containing 434 inhabitants. The living is a vicarage, with the rectory of Belaugh, in the archdeaconry and diocese of Norwich, rated in the king's books at £8. 13. 6½., and in the patronage of the Bishop of Norwich. The church is dedicated to All Saints.

SCOULTON, a parish in the hundred of WAYLAND, county of NORFOLK, 4¼ miles (E.) from Watton, containing 339 inhabitants. The living is a discharged rectory, in the archdeaconry and diocese of Norwich, rated in the king's books at £10. 4. 2., and in the patronage of John Weyland, Esq. The church, dedicated to All Saints, has a low steeple, the basement being square, and the upper story octangular. At the end of each aisle there was formerly a chapel.

SCRAFTON (WEST), a township in the parish of COVERHAM, western division of the wapentake of HANG, North riding of the county of YORK, 4½ miles (S. W.) from Middleham, containing 146 inhabitants.

SCRAPTOFT, a parish in the hundred of GARTREE, county of LEICESTER, 4 miles (E. by N.) from Leicester, containing 126 inhabitants. The living is a vicarage, in the archdeaconry of Leicester, and diocese of Lincoln, rated in the king's books at £8. 10., and in the patronage of — Hartopp, Esq. The church is dedicated to All Saints. Here is a curious and ancient stone cross.

SCRATBY, a parish in the eastern division of the hundred of FLEGG, county of NORFOLK, 2½ miles (N. by W.) from Caistor. The population is returned with the parish of Ormsby St. Margaret. The living is a discharged vicarage, united to that of Ormsby St. Margaret, in the archdeaconry and diocese of Norwich. The church is dedicated to All Saints.

SCRAYFIELD, a parish in the hundred of HILL, parts of LINDSEY, county of LINCOLN, 3 miles (E. by S.) from Horncastle, containing 23 inhabitants. The living is a discharged rectory, united to that of Hameringham, in the archdeaconry and diocese of Lincoln, rated in the king's books at £4. 19. 4½.

SCRAYINGHAM, a parish in the wapentake of BUCKROSE, East riding of the county of YORK, comprising the chapelry of Leppington, and the townships of Howsham and Scrayingham, and containing 511 inhabitants, of which number, 157 are in the township of Scrayingham, 9½ miles (N. W. by N.) from Pocklington. The living is a rectory, in the archdeaconry of the East riding, and diocese of York, rated in the king's books at £21. 11. 10½., and in the patronage of the Crown. The church is dedicated to St. Peter.

SCREDINGTON, a parish in the wapentake of ASWARDHURN, parts of KESTEVEN, county of LINCOLN, 4¼ miles (S. E. by S.) from Sleaford, containing 256 inhabitants. The living is a discharged vicarage, in the peculiar jurisdiction and patronage of the Dean and Chapter of Lincoln, rated in the king's books at £6. 15. 4., and endowed with £600 royal bounty. The church is dedicated to St. Andrew.

SCREMBY, a parish in the Wold division of the wapentake of CANDLESHOE, parts of LINDSEY, county of LINCOLN, 3½ miles (E. N. E.) from Spilsby, containing, with Grebby, 200 inhabitants. The living is a discharged rectory, in the archdeaconry and diocese of Lincoln, rated in the king's books at £16. 10. 2½. The Rev. H. Brackenbury was patron in 1813. The church is dedicated to St. Peter and St. Paul.

SCRENWOOD, a township in the parish of ALNHAM, northern division of COQUETDALE ward, county of NORTHUMBERLAND, 8 miles (N. W.) from Rothbury, containing 37 inhabitants.

SCREVETON, a parish in the northern division of the wapentake of BINGHAM, county of NOTTINGHAM, 8½ miles (S. W. by S.) from Newark, containing 292 inhabitants. The living is a discharged rectory, in the archdeaconry of Nottingham, and diocese of York, rated in the king's books at £6. 19. 1., and in the patronage of Col. Hildyard. The church, dedicated to St. Winifred, contains an altar-tomb and effigy to the memory of Gen. Whalley, the supposed executioner of Charles I., who commanded under Cromwell : figures of his three wives and twenty-two children are represented on the same monument : he died in 1683. A small river, called the Car Dyke, runs through the parish, which is in the honour of Tutbury, duchy of Lancaster, and within the jurisdiction of a court of pleas held at Tutbury every third Tuesday, for the recovery of debts under 40s. Dr. Thoroton, the antiquary and topographer, was born in an ancient mansion here belonging to his family.

SCRIVELSBY, a parish in the southern division of the wapentake of GARTREE, parts of LINDSEY, county of LINCOLN, 2½ miles (S.) from Horncastle, containing 153 inhabitants. The living is a rectory, united, in 1731, with that of Dalderby, in the archdeaconry and diocese of Lincoln, rated in the king's books at £12. 17. 6. The church is dedicated to St. Benedict. The Dymokes hold the manor of Scrivelsby, by inheritance from the Marmions, by " the service of grand serjeantry, that, whenever any king of England is to be crowned, the lord of this manor for the time being, or, in case of sickness, some one for him, shall come well armed for battle, on a good horse, into the presence of our lord the king, at his coronation, and make proclamation that, if any one will say that our said lord the king has not a title to his kingdom and crown, he shall be ready and prepared to defend the right of the king and his kingdom, and the dignity of his crown, in his own person, against him and any other whatsoever." The small river Bane runs through the parish.

SCRIVEN, a joint township with Tentergate, in that part of the parish of KNARESBOROUGH which is in the lower division of the wapentake of CLARO, West riding of the county of YORK, 1 mile (N. by W.) from Knaresborough, containing, with Tentergate, 1373 inhabitants. It is within the peculiar jurisdiction of the court of the honour of Knaresborough.

SCROOBY, a parish within the liberty of SOUTHWELL and SCROOBY, though locally in the wapentake of Bassetlaw, county of NOTTINGHAM, 1½ mile (S.) from Bawtry, containing 269 inhabitants. The living is a discharged vicarage, with that of Sutton, in the archdeaconry of Nottingham, and diocese of York. The church is dedicated to St. Wilfred. In this parish are some remains of an ancient palace of the Archbishops of York, converted into a farm-house; in the garden is a mulberry-tree, said to have been planted by Cardinal Wolsey.

SCROPTON, a parish in the hundred of APPLETREE, county of DERBY, 11½ miles (W. S. W.) from Derby, containing, with Foston, 510 inhabitants. The living is a perpetual curacy, in the archdeaconry of Derby, and diocese of Lichfield and Coventry, and in the patronage of J. Broadhurst, Esq. The church is dedicated to St. Paul. The river Dove runs through the parish.

SCRUTON, a parish in the eastern division of the wapentake of HANG, North riding of the county of YORK, 4¼ miles (N. E. by N.) from Bedale, containing 411 inhabitants. The living is a rectory, in the archdeaconry of Richmond, and diocese of Chester, rated in

the king's books at £14. 0. 5., and in the patronage of Henry Gale, Esq. The church is dedicated to St. Radegund.

SCULCOATES, a parish in the Hunsley-Beacon division of the wapentake of HARTHILL, East riding of the county of YORK, 1¼ mile (N.) from Kingston upon Hull, containing 10,449 inhabitants. The living is a discharged vicarage, in the archdeaconry of the East riding, and diocese of York, rated in the king's books at £5. 6. 8., endowed with £600 royal bounty, and in the patronage of the Crown. The parish church, dedicated to St. Mary, was rebuilt in 1760. An act was obtained, in 1814, for the erection of an additional church, called Christ-church, which was consecrated in 1822 : it is a handsome structure of white brick and Roche abbey stone, and cost upwards of £7000, part of which has been defrayed by subscription. By the same act the presentation was vested in subscribers of £100, and their survivors, till the number be reduced to eight, vacancies in which are to be filled up by the pew-holders, and these eight trustees, together with the vicar of Sculcoates, are to possess the patronage. The population of Sculcoates, less than a century ago, did not exceed one hundred, but the southern part of the parish, since the construction of its dock on the western bank of the river Hull, in 1774, has been extensively built upon, and now forms a large and populous part of the environs of Hull. The petty sessions for the division are held in a hall recently erected. This place is noticed in Domesday-book as one of the lordships granted to Ralph de Mortimer, a follower of the Conqueror.

SCULTHORPE, a parish in the hundred of GALLOW, county of NORFOLK, 2 miles (N. W.) from Fakenham, containing 466 inhabitants. The living is a rectory, in the archdeaconry of Norfolk, and diocese of Norwich, rated in the king's books at £16. Mrs. Jones was patroness in 1811. The church, dedicated to All Saints, was erected by Sir Robert Knollys, K. G., who, from a common soldier, rose to rank and eminence as a commander under Edward III., acquired an immense fortune, and, for his good services in subduing Wat Tyler's rebellion, received the freedom of the city of London. He died in the 92nd year of his age, and was buried in the church of the Carmelites, Fleet-street, London.

SCUNTHORPE, a township in the parish of FRODINGHAM, eastern division of the wapentake of MANLEY, parts of LINDSEY, county of LINCOLN, 8½ miles (W. N. W.) from Glandford-Bridge, containing 210 inhabitants. There is a place of worship for Wesleyan Methodists.

SEA-BOROUGH, a parish in the hundred of CREWKERNE, county of SOMERSET, 2½ miles (S. by W.) from Crewkerne, containing 92 inhabitants. The living is a discharged rectory, in the archdeaconry of Taunton, and diocese of Bath and Wells, rated in the king's books at £6. 15. Sir James Mansfield, Bart. was patron in 1806.

SEABRIDGE, a township partly in the parish of SWINNERTON, but chiefly in that of STOKE upon TRENT, northern division of the hundred of PIREHILL, county of STAFFORD, 1½ mile (S. by W.) from Newcastle under Lyne, containing 140 inhabitants.

SEABROOK, a joint hamlet with Horton, in the parish of IVINGHOE, hundred of COTTESLOE, county of BUCKINGHAM, $1\frac{1}{2}$ mile (W. N. W.) from Ivinghoe. The population is returned with Horton.

SEACOMB, a joint township with Poulton, in the parish of WALLAZEY, lower division of the hundred of WIRRALL, county palatine of CHESTER, $11\frac{3}{4}$ miles (N. N. E.) from Great Neston. The population is returned with Poulton. There is a place of worship for Independents.

SEACOURT, a hamlet in the parish of WYTHAM, hundred of HORMER, county of BERKS, containing 29 inhabitants.

SEACROFT, a township in the parish of WHITKIRK, lower division of the wapentake of SKYRACK, West riding of the county of YORK, $4\frac{1}{2}$ miles (E. N. E.) from Leeds, containing 886 inhabitants. There is a place of worship for Wesleyan Methodists.

Corporate Seal of Seaford.

Obverse. Reverse.

SEAFORD, a cinque-port, borough, and parish (formerly a market town), locally in the hundred of Flexborough, rape of Pevensey, county of SUSSEX, 42 miles (E. by S.) from Chichester, and $59\frac{1}{4}$ (S. S. E.) from London, containing 1047 inhabitants. This was formerly a considerable town, and had four churches and chapels, until burnt by the enemy; but it has greatly declined, being only resorted to for sea-bathing: it is defended by a small fort. Prawns of a large size and good flavour are caught here. The river Ouse, the æstuary of which formerly constituted its harbour, now empties itself into the sea at Newhaven, about three miles westward. The market, which was on Saturday, is disused: fairs are held on March 15th and July 25th. Seaford was originally a member of the port of Hastings, but was made a port of itself by charter of Henry VIII., who incorporated the inhabitants, under the style of "the bailiffs, jurats, and commonalty of the town, parish, and borough of Seaford:" the bailiff, and other officers, are chosen annually on the 29th of September; the jurats are twelve in number. The borough first sent barons to parliament in the 26th of Edward I., and continued to the 21st of Richard II., from which time a suspension took place until the reign of Edward IV., when the privilege was restored: the right of election was formerly exercised by the freemen only, in number about five; but, by a decision of the House of Commons in 1792, it is vested in the inhabitant housekeepers paying scot and lot: the bailiff is the returning officer. The living is a discharged vicarage, with that of Sutton annexed, in the archdeaconry of Lewes, and diocese of Chichester, rated in the king's books at £11. 15., and in the alternate patronage of the Prebendaries of Seaford and Sutton in the Cathedral Church of Chichester. The church, dedicated to St. Leonard, is in the decorated style of English architecture. A National school, in which about one hundred boys and fifty girls are instructed, is supported by the representatives of the borough. Seaford gives title of baron to the family of Ellis, conferred on the present lord by patent, dated July 15th, 1826.

SEAGRAVE, a parish in the eastern division of the hundred of GOSCOTE, county of LEICESTER, $3\frac{1}{4}$ miles (N. E. by E) from Mountsorrel, containing 424 inhabitants. The living is a rectory, in the archdeaconry of Leicester, and diocese of Lincoln, rated in the king's books at £19. 8. $11\frac{1}{2}$., and in the patronage of the President and Fellows of Queen's College, Cambridge. The church is dedicated to All Saints.

SEAGRY (LOWER and UPPER), a parish in the hundred of MALMESBURY, county of WILTS, $4\frac{1}{4}$ miles (S. S. E.) from Malmesbury, containing 215 inhabitants. The living is a discharged vicarage, in the archdeaconry of Wilts, and diocese of Salisbury, rated in the king's books at £7. 13. $1\frac{1}{2}$., endowed with £200 private benefaction, and £400 royal bounty, and in the patronage of the Earl of Carnarvon. The church is dedicated to St. Mary.

SEAHAM, a parish in the northern division of EASINGTON ward, county palatine of DURHAM, comprising the townships of Seaham, and Seaton with Slingley, and containing 198 inhabitants, of which number, 103 are in the township of Seaham, $4\frac{3}{4}$ miles (S. by E.) from Sunderland. The living is a vicarage, in the archdeaconry and diocese of Durham, rated in the king's books at £5. 0. 5., and in the patronage of A. J. C. Baker, Esq. The church, dedicated to St. Mary, is a small plain structure, principally in the Norman style.

SEAL, a parish in the hundred of CODSHEATH, lathe of SUTTON at HONE, county of KENT, $2\frac{1}{4}$ miles (N. E.) from Seven-Oaks, containing 1320 inhabitants. The living is a perpetual curacy, annexed to the vicarage of Kemsing, in the archdeaconry and diocese of Rochester. The church is dedicated to St. Peter. A school for eight girls is endowed with certain lands, bequeathed by John Porter, in 1678, and Francis Bickerstaff, in 1731.

SEAL, a parish in the hundred of FARNHAM, county of SURREY, $3\frac{1}{2}$ miles (E. by N.) from Farnham, containing, with the hamlet of Tongham, 364 inhabitants. The living is a perpetual curacy, in the archdeaconry of Surrey, and diocese of Winchester, endowed with £600 royal bounty, and in the patronage of the Archdeacon of Surrey.

SEAL (NETHER and OVER), a parish in the western division of the hundred of GOSCOTE, county of LEICESTER, $5\frac{3}{4}$ miles (S. W. by W.) from Ashby de la Zouch, containing, exclusively of a portion of the hamlet of Donisthorpe which is in this parish, 1160 inhabitants. The living is a rectory, in the archdeaconry of Leicester, and diocese of Lincoln, rated in the king's books at £17. 8. $11\frac{1}{2}$., and in the patronage of the Rev. William Gresley. The church is dedicated to St. Peter. This parish is in the honour of Tutbury, duchy of Lancaster, and within the jurisdiction of a court of pleas held at Tutbury every third Tuesday, for the recovery of debts under 40*s*.

SEAMER, a parish in the western division of the liberty of LANGBAURGH, North riding of the county of

YORK, 2¼ miles (N. W. by W.) from Stokesley, containing 226 inhabitants. The living is a perpetual curacy, in the archdeaconry of Cleveland, and diocese of York, endowed with £600 royal bounty, and £200 parliamentary grant, and in the patronage of R. G. Russell, Esq. The church is dedicated to St. Martin. John Coulson, in 1679, bequeathed a rent-charge of £8 for the education of ten boys at the village of Newby. In the neighbourhood is a remarkable tumulus, and on the acclivity of a hill adjoining are vestiges of an ancient intrenchment, in the valley beneath which many human bones and warlike weapons have been discovered, conjectured to be relics of the great battle of Baden-hill, in which Prince Arthur overthrew the Saxons, in 492.

SEAMER, a parish in PICKERING lythe, North riding of the county of YORK, comprising the chapelry of East Ayton, and the townships of Irton and Seamer, and containing 1034 inhabitants, of which number, 596 are in the township of Seamer, 4½ miles (S. W. by S.) from Scarborough. The living is a vicarage, in the archdeaconry of the East riding, and diocese of York, rated in the king's books at £18. 16. 5½., and in the patronage of W. J. Denison, Esq. The church, dedicated to St. Martin, is a handsome structure, in the cathedral form. There is a place of worship for Wesleyan Methodists. A noted fair is held annually on July 15th, and a market on the first Monday in every month, for cattle and sheep. Schools for children of both sexes, with a dwelling-house for the master, were built and liberally endowed by the lord of the manor, in 1814. An insurrection, headed by the parish clerk and two others, broke out here in the reign of Edward VI., in 1549, which had for its objects the restoration of the Roman Catholic religion, the abolition of monarchy, and the equalization of all ranks. The rebels, to the number of three thousand, after committing great excesses, laid down their arms upon being offered the king's pardon; but the ringleaders were taken and executed at York, in September of the same year.

SEARBY, a joint parish with Owmby, in the southern division of the wapentake of YARBOROUGH, parts of LINDSEY, county of LINCOLN, 4¾ miles (N. W.) from Caistor, containing, with Owmby, 247 inhabitants. The living is a discharged rectory, with the vicarage of Owmby annexed, in the peculiar jurisdiction and patronage of the Dean and Chapter of Lincoln, rated in the king's books at £8. The church is dedicated to St. Nicholas.

SEASALTER (LIBERTY), a parish in the hundred of WHITSTABLE, lathe of ST. AUGUSTINE, county of KENT, 5¼ miles (N. W. by N.) from Canterbury, containing 654 inhabitants. The living is a discharged vicarage, in the archdeaconry and diocese of Canterbury, rated in the king's books at £11, endowed with £200 private benefaction, and £200 royal bounty, and in the patronage of the Archbishop of Canterbury. The church is dedicated to St. Alphage. Mrs. Frances Fagg, in 1794, bequeathed £800 three per cents. for the support of a school, built by subscription, in which seventeen children are educated. On the sea-shore is an extensive oyster bed, called the Pollard, belonging to the Dean and Chapter of Canterbury, who let it to a certain number of dredger-men, parishioners. Four annual fairs were held here, but they have been long discontinued.

SEASONCOTE, a parish in the upper division of the hundred of KIFTSGATE, county of GLOUCESTER, 2 miles (W. by S.) from Moreton in the Marsh, containing 86 inhabitants. The living is a discharged rectory, united with the vicarage of Longborough, in the archdeaconry and diocese of Gloucester, rated in the king's books at £9. 12. 11., and endowed with £400 royal bounty.

SEATHWAITE, a chapelry in the parish of KIRKBY-IRELETH, hundred of LONSDALE, north of the sands, county palatine of LANCASTER, 8 miles (W. by N.) from Hawkeshead, containing 208 inhabitants. The living is a perpetual curacy, in the peculiar jurisdiction of the Dean and Chapter of York, endowed with £400 private benefaction, and £600 royal bounty, and in the patronage of William Penny, Esq.

SEATON, a township in the parish of CAMMERTON, ALLERDALE ward below Darwent, county of CUMBERLAND, 1¾ mile (N. E.) from Workington, containing 620 inhabitants. Here are extensive collieries and ironworks, near which the Derwent is crossed by a stone bridge, opposite to Workington.

SEATON, a parish in the hundred of COLYTON, county of DEVON, 2½ miles (S.) from Colyton, containing, with the chapelry of Beer, 1745 inhabitants. The living is a vicarage, in the archdeaconry and diocese of Exeter, rated in the king's books at £17. 0. 7½., and in the patronage of Lord Rolle. The church is dedicated to St. Gregory. There are places of worship for Wesleyan Methodists and Unitarians. Seaton is situated on the sea coast, and is supposed to have been the Moridunum of Antoninus, and a landing-place of the Danes. Leland speaks of it as having "a notable haven," and of the unsuccessful attempts of the inhabitants "to make a waul within the haven." In 1820, commissioners were appointed, under an act of parliament, to improve the harbour, and the lord of the manor was authorised to take dues. The town has been much improved of late years, and is now a well-frequented bathing-place: a pleasure fair is held on Whit-Tuesday.

SEATON, a joint township with Slingley, in the parish of SEAHAM, northern division of EASINGTON ward, county palatine of DURHAM, 4½ miles (S. by W.) from Sunderland, containing, with Slingley, 95 inhabitants.

SEATON, a parish in the hundred of WRANDIKE, county of RUTLAND, 2½ miles (E. by S.) from Uppingham, containing, with the hamlet of Thorpe by Water, 457 inhabitants. The living is a rectory, in the archdeaconry of Northampton, and diocese of Peterborough, rated in the king's books at £20. 7. 6., and in the patronage of the Hon. J. Monckton. The church is dedicated to All Saints.

SEATON, a township in the parish of SIGGLESTHORNE, northern division of the wapentake of HOLDERNESS, East riding of the county of YORK, 10¼ miles (N. E. by E.) from Beverley, containing 301 inhabitants. A place of worship for Wesleyan Methodists was erected by subscription, in 1810.

SEATON (NORTH), a township in the parish of WOODHORN, eastern division of MORPETH ward, county of NORTHUMBERLAND, 6¾ miles (E.) from Morpeth, containing 159 inhabitants.

SEATON-CAREW, a township in the parish of STRANTON, north-eastern division of STOCKTON ward county palatine of DURHAM, 10½ miles (N. E. by N.) from Stockton upon Tees, containing 312 inhabitants. Here was a chapel, dedicated to St. Thomas à Becket, but it has been long since demolished, there being no traces of it. There is a place of worship for Wesleyan Methodists. The village is considerably resorted to during the bathing-season, and contains respectable public, as well as private, accommodation for the visitors. The beach is smooth, and the sands firm and level to an extent of several miles, so that the convenience for bathing machines is exceedingly good. A priory of Gilbertine canons, subordinate to that of Sempringham, founded here by Alan de Wilton, was valued, at the dissolution, at £11. 2. 8. per annum.

SEATON-DELAVAL, a township in the parish of EARSDON, eastern division of CASTLE ward, county of NORTHUMBERLAND, 6¼ miles (N. by W.) from North Shields, containing 240 inhabitants. Here are the ruins of one of the most magnificent mansions in the north of England; it was erected from a design by Sir John Vanburgh, in 1707, by Admiral Delaval, and was destroyed by fire on January 3rd, 1822. Near it is the site of the ancient castle of Seaton-Delaval, of which little remains, except the chapel, which is a fine specimen of Norman architecture, containing monuments of a Knight Templar and his lady, and ornamented with numerous escutcheons, banners, and pieces of ancient armour: divine service is still performed in it every Sunday. At a short distance from the chapel is a handsome mausoleum, erected by the late Lord Delaval, in memory of his son, the interior of which is fitted up as a chapel, having arched catacombs underneath for the reception of the dead.

SEATON-HOUSE, a joint township with Boulmer, in the parish of LONG HOUGHTON, southern division of BAMBROUGH ward, county of NORTHUMBERLAND, 6 miles (E.) from Alnwick. The population is returned with Boulmer.

SEATON-ROSS, a parish in the Holme-Beacon division of the wapentake of HARTHILL, East riding of the county of YORK, 7¼ miles (W. by S.) from Market-Weighton, containing 477 inhabitants. The living is a perpetual curacy, in the archdeaconry of the East riding, and diocese of York, endowed with £1200 parliamentary grant, and in the patronage of W. C. Maxwell, Esq. The church is dedicated to St. Edmund. There is a place of worship for Wesleyan Methodists.

SEATON-SLUICE, or HARTLEY-PANS, a small sea-port in the township of HARTLEY, parish of EARSDON, eastern division of CASTLE ward, county of NORTHUMBERLAND, 6 miles (N.) from North Shields. The population is returned with Hartley. It is situated at the mouth of a rivulet, called Seaton-burn, where the late Sir Ralph Delaval, with great difficulty and expense, formed a new haven, and to prevent its being choked with sand, constructed an immense sluice upon the brook, with flood-gates to retain the water, from the flow of the tide till the ebb, when a sufficient body is collected every twelve hours, to cleanse the bed of the harbour, and remove from it every impediment to its navigation. Considerable improvements upon the original plan were subsequently made by Lord Delaval, who also formed a second entrance, which is crossed by a draw-bridge nine hundred feet in length. From twelve to fifteen vessels, of three hundred tons' burden each, can now ride in

safety at this port, and sail in or out with any wind. Coal is shipped here for the London and other markets, in very large quantities, from the neighbouring collieries. There are extensive glass-bottle works, malt-kilns, and a brewery, and there were formerly considerable manufactories for salt and copperas. The Presbyterians have a place of worship here. A blockhouse and battery were erected during the late war, for the defence of the port, which is subordinate to that of Newcastle. A whale, upwards of fifty feet long, was taken on this coast, in 1766.

SEAVINGTON (ST. MARY), a parish in the southern division of the hundred of PETHERTON, county of SOMERSET, 3 miles (E.) from Ilminster, containing 319 inhabitants. The living is a perpetual curacy, in the archdeaconry of Taunton, and diocese of Bath and Wells, endowed with £600 royal bounty, and £200 parliamentary grant, and in the patronage of Earl Poulett.

SEAVINGTON (ST. MICHAEL), a parish in the southern division of the hundred of PETHERTON, county of SOMERSET, 3½ miles (E.) from Ilminster, containing, with the chapelry of Dinnington, 420 inhabitants. The living is a rectory, in the archdeaconry of Taunton, and diocese of Bath and Wells, rated in the king's books at £6. 15., and in the patronage of Earl Poulett.

SEBERGHAM, a parish in the ward and county of CUMBERLAND, comprising the townships of Church, or Low Sebergham, and Castle, or High, Sebergham, and containing 903 inhabitants, of which number, 338 are in the township of Church-Sebergham, 8¼ miles, and 565 in that of Castle-Sebergham, 6¼ miles, (S. E. by E.) from Wigton. The living is a perpetual curacy, in the archdeaconry and diocese of Carlisle, endowed with £200 private benefaction, and £400 royal bounty, and in the patronage of the Dean and Chapter of Carlisle. The church, dedicated to the Virgin Mary, occupies the site of an ancient hermitage; it was repaired in 1774, and again in 1785. In this parish a considerable quantity of limestone is quarried and burned; there are also extensive mines of coal, and a powerful mineral spring. Near the church, the river Caldew is crossed by a bridge, erected in 1689, by Alexander Denton, one of the justices of the common pleas; and about a mile below it is Bell bridge, a structure of one arch, built in 1772, near the site of an ancient one demolished by a great flood in 1771.

SECKINGTON, a parish in the Tamworth division of the hundred of HEMLINGFORD, county of WARWICK, 3¾ miles (N. E. by E.) from Tamworth, containing 126 inhabitants. The living is a rectory, in the archdeaconry of Coventry, and diocese of Lichfield and Coventry, rated in the king's books at £5. 16. 0½., and in the patronage of Sir Francis Burdett, Bart. The church is dedicated to All Saints: near it are vestiges of a large ancient encampment. In the neighbourhood is the site of a small priory, founded by William Burdett, in the reign of Henry II.

SEDBERGH, a parish in the western division of the wapentake of STAINCLIFFE and EWCROSS, West riding of the county of YORK, comprising the market town of Sedbergh, and the chapelries of Dent and Garsdale, and containing 4483 inhabitants, of which number, 2022 are in the town of Sedbergh, 77 miles (W. N. W.) from York, and 260 (N. W. by N.) from London. This town is situated in a secluded vale, in a mountainous district, and contains two cotton mills, in which several persons are employed. Coal is obtained from a mine rather more than two miles distant, near which the river Rother passes. The market, now almost disused, is on Wednesday; and fairs are held on March 20th, the Wednesday in Whitsun-week, and October 29th, chiefly for live stock. A constable is annually elected by the ley payers, and a court for the recovery of small debts has been recently instituted. The living is a discharged vicarage, in the archdeaconry of Richmond, and diocese of Chester, rated in the king's books at £12. 8., endowed with £200 private benefaction, and £200 royal bounty, and in the patronage of the Master and Fellows of Trinity College, Cambridge. The church is dedicated to St. Andrew. There are places of worship for the Society of Friends, Independents, and Wesleyan Methodists. The free grammar school was founded and endowed by Roger Lupton, D.D., Provost of Eton College, in the 5th of Edward VI., for all boys duly qualified to enter upon a course of classical instruction, without restriction : by his Majesty's letters patent it was ordained, that there should be one master and one usher, and twelve of the inhabitants of Sedbergh were incorporated governors : his Majesty likewise endowed the school with the rectory and church of Weston, and various messuages and lands, now producing a rental of £500, which sum is paid to the master, who allows the usher £100 per annum : the appointment to the mastership is vested in the Master and Fellows of St. John's College, Cambridge, who are visitors : from thirty to forty boys are educated. Exhibitions to two fellowships and eight scholarships in St. John's College, Cambridge, were founded in favour of this school, by Dr. Lupton ; one fellowship and two scholarships, in the same college, were also founded for boys from this school, by Henry Hebblethwayte, citizen and draper of London ; and a further exhibition for one of the scholars, being a native of Sedbergh, to either of the Universities, is given by the governors, as the appropriation of three bequests at their disposal. A small annual sum, the interest of various bequests, is applied towards the instruction of poor children. At Howgill, in this parish, is a school, erected near the chapel, and endowed with land by John Robinson, the income of which is £26 per annum : about sixty children are instructed.

SEDGEBERROW, a parish in the middle division of the hundred of OSWALDSLÓW, county of WORCESTER, 4 miles (S. S. W.) from Evesham, containing 250 inhabitants. The living is a rectory, in the archdeaconry and diocese of Worcester, rated in the king's books at £13. 15. 7½., and in the patronage of the Dean and Chapter of Worcester. The church has a small octagonal tower, surmounted by a spire, and exhibits portions in the decorated and later English styles of architecture.

SEDGEBROOK, a parish in the wapentake of WINNIBRIGGS and THREO, parts of KESTEVEN, county of LINCOLN, 4 miles (W. N. W.) from Grantham, containing 230 inhabitants. The living is a rectory, in medieties, one rated in the king's books at £7. 18. 9., and the other at £7. 4. 7., and both in the patronage of the Crown. The church is dedicated to St. Lawrence. Lady Margaret Thorold, in 1718, gave land, directing

that £15 of the income arising therefrom should be applied for teaching fifteen poor children, £5 for apprenticing one boy, and £5 to the poor.

SEDGEFIELD, a parish in the north-eastern division of STOCKTON ward, county palatine of DURHAM, comprising the market town of Sedgefield, and the townships of Bradbury, Butterwick, Embleton, Fishburn, Foxton with Shotton, and Mordon, and containing 1955 inhabitants, of which number, 1268 are in the town of Sedgefield, 11 miles (S. E. by S.) from Durham, and 255½ (N. by W.) from London. The town, which rather presents the appearance of a large genteel village, occupying a gentle eminence commanding an extensive prospect to the south and south-east, is remarkable for the peculiar salubrity of its atmosphere, and the longevity of its inhabitants, attributable, in a great degree, to the openness of its situation, and the fine gravel soil on which it stands : the inhabitants are supplied with water from springs. The centre of the town forms a spacious square, where the market is held, on Fridays, which was granted in 1312, by the charter of Bishop Kellaw, and is well supplied with provisions : a large fair, provincially called the Month-day, is held on the first Friday in every month, for the sale of hogs, and there are fairs for cattle on the first Fridays in April and October. A parochial lending library, on the plan of those recommended by the Society for the promotion of Christian Knowledge, has been established, under the patronage of Lord Barrington. This parish is a member of the great episcopal manor at Middleham, and is divided into seven constableries ; that of Sedgefield includes the town itself, Hardwick, and Layton. A halmote court is held here, once in eighteen months, in rotation with those at Cornforth and Middleham, for the recovery of debts under 40s., at which the bishop's steward presides. The living is a rectory, in the archdeaconry and diocese of Durham, rated in the king's books at £73. 18. 1½., and in the patronage of the Bishop of Durham. The church, which is dedicated to St. Edmund, is a handsome cruciform structure, combining the early and later styles of English architecture ; the windows are principally in the decorated style : the nave is separated from the aisles by a row of pillars supporting pointed arches, and from the chancel by an oak screen of rich tabernacle-work ; in the latter are some canopied stalls : the font is an octagonal structure of black marble ; the tower, at the west end, is embattled and pinnacled ; and the interior of the church contains several brasses and mural tablets. There is a place of worship for Wesleyan Methodists. A free grammar school, of unknown foundation and endowment, has an income of about £50 per annum, for which six poor children are instructed ; six are also educated and clothed from a benefaction of £400 three per cent. Bank Annuities by Richard Wright, Esq., in the year 1790: the master is appointed by the rector and the vestry. In 1782, John Lowther, Esq. bequeathed £600 three per cent. Bank Annuities, for the instruction and clothing of six poor girls. An almshouse for five poor men, and five poor women, inhabitants of this town, was founded and endowed with £44 per annum, arising from land, by Thomas Cooper : additional benefactions were made by William Wrightson, Esq. and Thomas Foster, the latter of whom bequeathed the interest of £2000 for the benefit of the inmates. Upwards of ninety-one acres of land, under the superintendence of eight trustees, belong to a charity, founded by Dame Eliz. Frevill, in 1630, for apprenticing poor children, and for purposes of general benevolence; in addition to which there are several minor charitable benefactions. Mrs. Elizabeth Elstob, the celebrated Saxon scholar, who died in 1756, was a native of Elstob, in this parish, of which the pious and erudite Bishop Lowth was rector, prior to his elevation to the see of London.

SEDGEFORD, a parish in the hundred of SMITH-DON, county of NORFOLK, 8½ miles (N. N. E.) from Castle-Rising, containing 534 inhabitants. The living is a vicarage, in the peculiar jurisdiction and patronage of the Dean and Chapter of Norwich, rated in the king's books at £8. The church is dedicated to St. Mary.

SEDGHILL, a parish in the hundred of DUN-WORTH, county of WILTS, 4½ miles (S. W.) from Hindon, containing 213 inhabitants. The living is a perpetual curacy, annexed to the rectory of Berwick St. Leonard, in the archdeaconry and diocese of Salisbury, and in the patronage of the Rev. C. H. Grove. The church is dedicated to St. Catherine.

SEDGLEY, a parish in the northern division of the hundred of SEISDON, county of STAFFORD, 3½ miles (S.) from Wolverhampton, containing 17,195 inhabitants. This populous parish is situated in the midst of a country abounding with coal, iron-stone, and limestone, the working of which furnishes employment to the greater part of the inhabitants, who have increased nearly three thousand in number since 1821. The iron is manufactured in a variety of ways, both into pig-iron in furnaces, and into wrought or malleable in mills, which latter is again converted into bars, rods, hoops, hurdles, nails, coffee-mills, locks, &c. A great extent of the Essington and Wyrley canal intersects the parish in various directions, affording a ready transit for these articles. A court leet is annually held, at which a constable is chosen. The living is a vicarage, in the archdeaconry of Stafford, and diocese of Lichfield and Coventry, rated in the king's books at £5. 12. 8½., and in the patronage of the Earl of Dudley. The church, dedicated to All Saints, is a beautiful edifice in the purest style of English architecture, with side aisles, vaulted nave, and clerestory windows: it was completed in 1829, at the sole expense of the Earl of Dudley, and will contain one thousand three hundred persons. In the hamlet of Lower Gornall, in this parish, is a chapel dedicated to St. James, which was erected about nine years ago, and in which are five hundred free sittings, the Incorporated Society for the building and enlargement of churches having contributed £500 towards defraying the expense: the living is a perpetual curacy, endowed with £400 private benefaction, £600 royal bounty, and £200 parliamentary grant, and in the patronage of the Earl of Dudley. A chapel of ease has also been recently erected at Coseley, calculated to contain nearly two thousand persons, with one thousand one hundred and fifty-six free sittings, at an expense of £10,536, partly arising from subscriptions in the parish, and from a grant by the parliamentary commissioners. There are two places of worship belonging to the Particular Baptists, three to Wesleyan Methodists, one to Primitive Methodists, and one each to Independents and Presbyterians; the Roman Catholics have also two chapels. Here is a small bequest by Samuel Timmins, for teaching poor

children; and an excellent National school, for two hundred boys and two hundred girls, has been recently erected by the Earl of Dudley: there is also one at Gornall, for one hundred boys and one hundred girls, both supported by voluntary contributions. The emerinite, and the singular fossil called the "Dudley locust," are found chiefly in this parish, the latter only in an isolated limestone rock, termed the Wren's Nest Hill.

SEDGWICK, a township in the parish of HE-VERSHAM, KENDAL ward, county of WESTMORLAND, 4½ miles (S.) from Kendal, containing 184 inhabitants. There is a place of worship for Independents. A mill for the manufacture of gunpowder was established here about 1770. The river Kent and the Lancaster canal pass through the township. Here is a free school with a trifling endowment.

SEDLESCOMB, a parish in the hundred of STAPLE, rape of HASTINGS, county of SUSSEX, 3 miles (N. E.) from Battle, containing 667 inhabitants. The living is a rectory, in the archdeaconry of Lewes, and diocese of Chichester, rated in the king's books at £9. 4. 2., and in the patronage of the Crown. The church, dedicated to St. John the Baptist, is principally in the early style of English architecture. There is a place of worship for Wesleyan Methodists. The Rev. George Barnsley, in 1723, bequeathed £150 for the education of children, which sum, added to subsequent gifts, was laid out in the purchase of an estate now let for £20 per annum, for which twenty boys are instructed. Here was formerly a preceptory of Knights Templars.

SEEND, a chapelry in the parish and hundred of MELKSHAM, county of WILTS, 3½ miles (S. E. by E.) from Melksham, containing 1011 inhabitants. The chapel is dedicated to the Holy Cross. There is a place of worship for Wesleyan Methodists. The Kennet and Avon canal passes through the chapelry.

SEER-GREEN, a hamlet in the parish of FARN-HAM-ROYAL, hundred of BURNHAM, county of BUCK-INGHAM, 2¼ miles (N. N. E.) from Beaconsfield, containing 264 inhabitants.

SEETHING, a parish in the hundred of LODDON, county of NORFOLK, 5¾ miles (N. by W.) from Bungay, containing 386 inhabitants. The living is a perpetual curacy, in the archdeaconry of Norfolk, and diocese of Norwich, and in the patronage of the Mayor and Corporation of Norwich. The church is dedicated to St. Margaret.

SEIGHFORD, a parish in the southern division of the hundred of PIREHILL, county of STAFFORD, 2¾ miles (W. N. W.) from Stafford, containing, with the townships of Aston and Doxey, 851 inhabitants. The living is a discharged vicarage, in the archdeaconry of Stafford, and diocese of Lichfield and Coventry, rated in the king's books at £6, and in the patronage of the Crown. The church is dedicated to St. Chad. Six children are instructed for about £3. 3. a year, arising from a bequest by Dame Dorothy Bridgman.

SEISDON, a township in the parish of TRYSULL, southern division of the hundred of SEISDON, county of STAFFORD, 6 miles (W. S. W.) from Wolverhampton. The population is returned with the parish.

SELATTYN, a parish in the hundred of OSWESTRY, county of SALOP, 3¼ miles (N. N. W.) from Oswestry, containing 959 inhabitants. The living is a rectory, in the archdeaconry and diocese of St. Asaph, rated in the king's books at £12. 9. 9½., and in the patronage of William Lloyd, Esq. The church is dedicated to St. Mary. James Wylding, one of the assembly of divines during the Interregnum, and the celebrated Dr. Henry Sacheverell, were rectors here. Offa's Dyke forms part of the western boundary of the parish, wherein formerly stood the ancient "Castle Brogyntyn," of which there are now scarcely any remains. A National school has been recently established.

SELBORNE, a parish in the hundred of SELBORNE, Alton (North) division of the county of SOUTHAMPTON, 4½ miles (S. E. by S.) from Alton, containing 893 inhabitants. The living is a vicarage, in the archdeaconry and diocese of Winchester, rated in the king's books at £8. 2. 1., and in the patronage of the President and Fellows of Magdalene College, Oxford. The church, dedicated to St. Mary, is principally in the early style of English architecture: the altar-piece is ornamented with a fine painting, by Albert Durer, representing the offerings of the Magi, presented by the late Rev. Gilbert White, author of "The History of Selborne," and other works on Natural History, who was born here in 1720, where he chiefly resided. In the time of the Saxons Selborne was held in royal demesne. A fair is held at the village on May 29th. Gilbert White, in 1719, bequeathed £100, now producing an annual income of £8. 10., for teaching the poor children of the parish to read. A priory of Black canons, in honour of the Blessed Virgin Mary, was founded here, in 1233, by Peter de Rupibus, Bishop of Winchester; it was subsequently suppressed, and became part of the endowment of Magdalene College, Oxford. At Temple, in this parish, resided Sir Adam Gurdon, the celebrated freebooter in the time of Henry III.

SELBY, a market town and parish, partly within the liberty of ST. PETER of YORK, East riding, and partly in the lower division of the wapentake of BARKSTONE-ASH, West riding, of the county of YORK, 14 miles (S. by E.) from York, and 177 (N. by W.) from London, containing 4097 inhabitants. The Saxon name of this place was *Salebeia*, whence its present appellation is obviously derived. The first remarkable event in its history is the foundation of a Benedictine abbey by William the Conqueror, in 1070, which was dedicated to St. German, and, in process of time, acquired such extensive possessions and immunities, as to render it equal in rank to the church of St. Peter at York; the superior of this establishment, with that of St. Mary's, in that city, being the only mitred abbots north of the Trent: at the dissolution the revenue was valued at £819. 2. 6.: of this magnificent fabric the church is the only part remaining. In the early period of the great civil war, the town appears to have been held for the parliament, and, although subsequently taken by the royalists, it was eventually recaptured by Sir Thomas Fairfax, when the majority of the king's party were made prisoners, with several horses, pieces of ordnance, and a large quantity of ammunition.

The town is situated on the river Ouse, on the great road from London to Edinburgh: the streets are well paved, and lighted with oil, and the houses in general well built. A new street has been formed, called the Crescent, which consists of excellent and commodious houses, and adds considerably to the improved appearance of the town. The fertility of the surrounding district has been greatly increased by a process of irrigation, whereby the water of the rivers Ouse and Aire is detained upon the land until a sediment has been deposited, which forms excellent manure, and has contributed most materially to the increased value of the soil. A large quantity of weld, for the use of dyers, is produced in the vicinity, and formerly flax was cultivated and prepared to a considerable extent; this branch of trade, however, has greatly declined, owing to the importation of that article from France and the Netherlands, but flax-spinning is still carried on to some extent; there are also some iron-foundries, and manufactories for sail-cloth and leather. The general trade of the town has been much improved by means of a canal connecting the navigable rivers Ouse and Aire, thus opening a more direct communication with Leeds and the West riding of Yorkshire, so that the greater quantity of the goods sent to that district is disembarked here. A bridge of timber across the Ouse was opened in 1795, and is remarkable for the facility with which it can be turned round, though weighing seventy tons, being opened and closed within the space of a minute. A branch custom-house has been recently established, whereby vessels are enabled to clear out without touching at the port of Hull. The chief article exported is stone, which is sent coastwise: ships of one hundred and fifty to two hundred tons' burden navigate to Selby; steam-boats pass daily to and from Hull, and there are daily communications with London, and every port on the coast: here is a ship-yard, in which vessels of considerable burden are built. It is in contemplation to construct a railway from Selby to Leeds, which, if effected, will materially promote the trading interests of the town. The market is on Monday, and fairs are held on Easter-Tuesday, Monday after June 22nd, and on Michaelmas-day, for cattle, horses, cloth, &c.: in the centre of the market-place is a handsome cross, in the ancient style of English architecture. A petty session for the wapentake of Barkstone-Ash is held every alternate Monday; and courts leet and baron twice a year, by the lord of the manor, the Hon. E. R. Petre, who gave the site for the erection of a town hall, which was built in 1825, at an expense of £800, raised by subscription; it is a neat edifice of brick, enclosed with an iron railing.

The living is a perpetual curacy, in the jurisdiction of the peculiar court of Selby, endowed with £800 royal bounty, and £1600 parliamentary grant, and in the patronage of the Hon. E. R. Petre. The church, formerly conventual, and belonging to the abbey, is dedicated to St. Mary and St. German, and was made parochial by letters patent of James I., dated March 20th, 1618. The ancient monastery stood on the west side of the river Ouse, and the principal buildings were on the west and south side of the church; the barn and granary are yet remaining, but the gateway was taken down about thirty years ago: over it was the abbot's court-house, with two rooms on the sides for the jury and the witnesses; on one side was the porter's lodge, and on the other a room in which to serve the poor. The appearance of this venerable pile is strikingly impressive: the magnificence, yet comparative simplicity, of the west front, render it deserving of particular notice, as its proportions and decorations merit remark from their singularity and elegance. The entrance is by a large and richly-ornamented Norman doorway, supported by six columns, with simply ornamented capitals. The triple arches above the doorway are in the English style, and the decorations partake in character with many found on the north and west doorways, and internal parts of the church. The centre arch forms the west window, being considerably larger than those at the sides, and filled with tracery. The walls of the nave and north transept are Norman, though few exterior arches of that character now remain, being mostly replaced by windows, &c., in the English style, at different periods. The most striking feature on this side is the porch, in that mixed style which prevailed soon after the formation of the pointed arch, having circular and pointed arches indiscriminately introduced, composed of the same mouldings. Under it is a Norman doorway less enriched, but more elegantly proportioned than that at the west end. With the simple and massive nave is contrasted the beautiful choir, a perfect and splendid example of the early style of English architecture. The proportions are extremely elegant, and the ornaments richly disposed, forming on the whole, perhaps, one of the most chaste and magnificent designs in the kingdom. The upper part of the centre tower fell down, destroying the south transept and the roof of the western part of the south aisle, on March 30th, 1690. The present tower was probably rebuilt about the year 1700, but in a style by no means corresponding with the original. The chapter-house is a beautiful building attached to the south side of the choir: the room used for that purpose, now the vestry-room, appears, from its style and simplicity, to be of an earlier date: over it is a room now used as a school. The internal architecture of the choir is magnificent, the ornaments being of the most splendid and elaborate kind; but the object which most attracts the attention is the east window; the proportion of all its parts, the beauty of its tracery, and the slender lofty mullions, supported by transoms, are unsurpassed. In the last century this window contained the Genealogy of Christ, but only a few scattered fragments now remain. The priests' stalls, of stone, are on the south side of the choir: there are several wooden stalls now remaining. The four Norman arches at the intersection of the great cross aisles are composed of a few mouldings and ornaments: the nave in this style is particularly grand and well-proportioned, and almost every pier and cluster of columns differ in design and decoration. Among the many striking architectural peculiarities which this magnificent edifice exhibits are two clusters of columns, or piers, supporting arches in the gallery, on the north side of the nave. The front is simple, with a beautiful and lofty cover of carved wood suspending from the second arch, on the north side of the nave. In the year 1826, a fine-toned organ was erected by private subscription, and adds considerably to the beauty of the choir. The only monuments of consequence are those of a knight and a lady, and two slabs, one for Abbot Selby, dated 1504, and the other for Abbot Berwich, 1526: this church has lately received four hundred and twenty-two additional sittings, of which three hundred and twenty-two are free, the Incorporated Society for the building and enlargement of churches and chapels having contributed £300 towards defraying the expense. Its appearance has been much improved by an addition to the church-yard, and the removal of some houses which obstructed the view of the west end, whereby the whole edifice has been thrown open to the market-place: these improvements were effected by the Hon. E. R. Petre, at an expense of not less than £2000 : the whole has been since enclosed with an iron railing, three hundred and fifty yards in length, at the cost of £600, which was defrayed by the voluntary contribution of the parishioners. There are places of worship for the Society of Friends, Independents, Calvinistic and Wesleyan Methodists, Unitarians, and Roman Catholics. A Blue-coat school for boys is principally supported by voluntary contributions, augmented by a legacy of £100 from John Herbert, in 1775, which, with other donations, was vested in land; and £13 per annum is paid to the master by the trustees under the will of Joseph Rayner, who, in 1710, bequeathed £100 to be vested in land for the instruction of poor children: twenty boys are clothed and educated on this foundation, and £22. 10. per ann. is likewise paid for the instruction of thirteen poor boys and ten girls on the foundation of Leonard Chamberlain, in 1716, who also endowed an almshouse for seven poor widows. Henry I., the youngest son of William the Conqueror, was born here, during the visit of that monarch and his queen, the year after the foundation of the abbey. Thomas Johnson, a botanist, who published the first local catalogue of plants in the kingdom, besides an improved edition of Gerard's Herbal, and who fell in a skirmish with the parliamentarians, in 1644, was also a native of this place.

SELBY'S-FOREST, a township in the parish of KIRK-NEWTON, western division of GLENDALE ward, county of NORTHUMBERLAND, containing 63 inhabitants. This extensive district consists chiefly of moors and mountains ; the principal of the latter is the Cheviot, from which the celebrated range of hills so called derives its name ; on its summit is a large lake occasionally frozen in the summer.

SELHAM, a parish in the hundred of EASEBOURNE, rape of CHICHESTER, county of SUSSEX, 3½ miles (W by S.) from Petworth, containing 80 inhabitants. The living is a discharged rectory, in the archdeaconry and diocese of Chichester, rated in the king's books at £4. 15. 11½., endowed with £200 private benefaction, and £200 royal bounty, and in the patronage of the Principal and Fellows of Brasenose College, Oxford. The church, dedicated to St. James, is in the early style of English architecture. The Rother, or Arundel, navigation passes through the parish.

SELLACK, a parish in the upper division of the hundred of WORMELOW, county of HEREFORD, 4¼ miles (N. W.) from Ross, containing 301 inhabitants. The living is a vicarage, with the perpetual curacy of King's Caple, in the peculiar jurisdiction of the Bishop of Hereford, rated in the king's books at £16. 6. 8., and in the patronage of the Dean and Chapter of Hereford. The church is dedicated to St. Tesiliaii.

SELLING, a parish in the hundred of BOUGHTON under BLEAN, lathe of SCRAY, county of KENT, 4 miles (S. S. E.) from Faversham, containing 573 inhabitants. The living is a discharged vicarage, in the archdeaconry and diocese of Canterbury, rated in the king's books at £6. 13. 4., endowed with £200 private benefaction, and £200 royal bounty, and in the patronage of Lord Sondes. The church, dedicated to St. Mary, is partly in the early and partly in the later style of English architecture.

F 2

On Shottendon Hill is an ancient fortification of an irregular form, thought by some to be Roman, and by others Danish; but it seems probable that it was a work of the former, from the extensive Roman intrench-ments still visible in a wood two miles to the south-east of it: there is also a tumulus in the neighbourhood.

SELLINGE, a parish in the hundred of STREET, lathe of SHEPWAY, county of KENT, 5¼ miles (N. W. by W.) from Hythe, containing 469 inhabitants. The living is a discharged vicarage, in the archdeaconry and diocese of Canterbury, rated in the king's books at £7. 4. 5., and in the patronage of the Crown. The church, dedicated to St. Mary, has an admixture of the various styles of English architecture. Five children are educated for £5 a year, bequeathed by Mr. God-frey.

SELMESTON, a parish in the hundred of DANE-HILL-HORSTED, rape of PEVENSEY, county of SUSSEX, 6¼ miles (E. S. E.) from Lewes, containing 208 inhabit-ants. The living is a discharged vicarage, in the arch-deaconry of Lewes, and diocese of Chichester, rated in the king's books at £7. 5. 8., and in the patronage of the Prebendary of Heathfield in the Cathedral Church of Chichester. The church, dedicated to St. Mary, is in the early style of English architecture.

SELSEY, a parish in the hundred of MANHOOD, rape of CHICHESTER, county of SUSSEX, 8 miles (S.) from Chichester, containing 766 inhabitants. The living comprises a discharged vicarage and a sinecure rectory united, in the archdeaconry and diocese of Chiches-ter, the former rated in the king's books at £8, and the latter at £11. 3. 4., and in the patronage of the Bishop of Chichester. The church, dedicated to St. Peter, is a stately pile, principally in the early style of English architecture: in the middle aisle are several coffin-shaped gravestones, with crosses and various other devices; and against the north wall of the chancel is a monument to John and Agatha Lewes, of the time of Henry VIII. This parish is peninsular, having Pagham harbour on the north, the English channel on the east and south, and, at high water, a narrow stream on the west, which is crossed by a ferry a little below Littlesham, and also by a small bridge. Its name, ac-cording to Bede, is derived from the Saxon *Seals-ey*, sig-nifying the island of Seals, for the resort of which animals it was anciently noted. The village, consisting principally of one street of neatly-built houses, occu-pies a dry gravelly site. A court baron is annually held here, and there is a fair for toys, &c., on July 14th. A school-house was erected for children of the parish by the late Rev. William Walker. Near the church is a circular intrenched mound, supposed to be an ancient British work. A monastery, dedicated to the Blessed Virgin, was founded here, about 681, by St. Wilfred, who, having previously converted many of the South Saxons to Christianity, and obtained of King Ædilwach the lands of this peninsula for its endowment, placed therein some religious who had been his companions in exile, of whom Eadbercht, abbot in 711, was consecrated first bishop of the South Saxons, and fixed his episco-pal seat at this place, but Bishop Stigandus, in 1075, procured its translation to Chichester. Vestiges of this ancient little city are mentioned, in ancient re cords, as being plainly visible at ebb-tide, and at such times are said to be still discernible, with remains of its

cathedral. Selsey gives the title of baron to the family of Peachy.

SELSIDE, a chapelry in that part of the parish of KENDAL which is in KENDAL ward, county of WEST-MORLAND, 4 miles (N. N. E.) from Kendal, containing, with the township of Whitwell, 291 inhabitants. The living is a perpetual curacy, in the archdeaconry of Richmond, and diocese of Chester, endowed with £400 private benefaction, and £400 royal bounty, and in the patronage of the Inhabitants. The chapel, dedicated to Christ, was built about 1720, by the inhabitants, on site given by William Thornburgh, Esq., the descendant of a Roman Catholic family, proprietors of Selside Hall, in consideration of his being allowed to devote the original chapel, attached to the hall of his ances-tors, to his own religion; it is now the kitchen of a farm-house. The free school, which was rebuilt by subscription in 1793, is supported from several sources, the principal being an estate left by John Kitching, in 1730, now producing an annual income of £50, for the education of all the poor children of the chapelry.

SELSTON, a parish in the northern division of the wapentake of BROXTOW, county of NOTTINGHAM, 9 miles (S. W.) from Mansfield, containing 1321 inhabit-ants. The living is a discharged vicarage, in the archdea-conry of Nottingham, and diocese of York, rated in the king's books at £5, endowed with £800 royal bounty, and in the patronage of Sir W. Dixie, Bart. The church is dedicated to St. Helen. The Mansfield and Pinxton railway intersects the parish, in the neighbour-hood of which are extensive collieries.

SELWORTHY, a parish in the hundred of CAR-HAMPTON, county of SOMERSET, 4 miles (W.) from Minehead, containing 483 inhabitants. The living is a rectory, in the archdeaconry of Taunton, and diocese of Bath and Wells, rated in the king's books at £12. 15. 5., and in the patronage of Sir T. D. Acland, Bart. The church, dedicated to All Saints, is a neat edifice in the decorated style, with a plain embattled tower; the roofs of the nave, chancel, and south aisle, are each divided into small square compartments, enriched with figures curiously carved in wood, and supported by two rows of pillars and arches of a peculiarly light and graceful construction. There are remains of two chapels, one at Tivington, now used as a school-room, the other at West Lynch, converted into a barn. On a hill to the north-west of the church are vestiges of an ancient encampment, called Bury Castle; it is of an elliptical form, with a rampart of earth and stones, enclosing an area of about an acre and a half.

SEMER, a parish in the hundred of COSFORD, county of SUFFOLK, 2 miles (S. by E.) from Bildeston, containing 262 inhabitants, exclusively of 169 inmates of the house of industry for the hundred of Cosford, which is in this parish. The living is a rectory, in the archdeaconry of Sudbury, and diocese of Norwich, rated in the king's books at £11. 7. 1., and in the pa-tronage of the Rev. C. Cooke. The church is dedicated to All Saints. The river Brett runs through the parish. The house of industry, capable of holding five hundred persons, was erected in 1799, at the expense of the hundred.

SEMINGTON, a chapelry in the parish of STEE-PLE-ASHTON, hundred of WHORWELSDOWN, county of WILTS, 3 miles (N. E. by E.) from Trowbridge, containing 244 inhabitants. The chapel is dedicated to St. George. There is a place of worship for Wesleyan Methodists. Thomas Somner, in 1699, bequeathed land producing a trifling income for the education of two children.

SEMLEY, a parish forming a detached portion of the hundred of CHALK, county of WILTS, 4¾ miles (S. by W.) from Hindon, containing 675 inhabitants. The living is a rectory, in the archdeaconry and diocese of Salisbury, rated in the king's books at £17. 2. 8½., and in the patronage of the Dean and Canons of Christ Church, Oxford. The church is dedicated to St. Leonard. There is a place of worship for Baptists. Dr. William Thorn, a celebrated divine and Hebrew scholar, was born here, towards the close of the sixteenth century.

SEMPERINGHAM, a parish in the wapentake of AVELAND, parts of KESTEVEN, county of LINCOLN, 3¼ miles (E.S.E.) from Falkingham, containing, with the chapelries of Birthorpe and Pointon, 462 inhabitants. The living is a discharged vicarage, in the archdeaconry and diocese of Lincoln, rated in the king's books at £2. 15. 8., endowed with £400 royal bounty, and £200 parliamentary grant, and in the patronage of the Crown. The church, dedicated to St. Andrew, appears to have been originally a larger structure, and is principally in the Norman style, with a plain tower of later date, crowned with eight rich pinnacles. Gilbert de Sempringham, rector of this parish, and founder of the Gilbertine, or Sempringham, order, erected here, about 1139, a priory in honour of the Blessed Virgin Mary, for nuns and canons, whose revenue, at the dissolution, was valued at £359. 19. 7.: it was the superior establishment of the Sempringham order, where their general chapters were held: the buildings stood a little to the northward of the church, where the site only is discernible, being surrounded by a moat.

SEND, a parish in the second division of the hundred of WOKING, county of SURREY, 3 miles (S.W. by W.) from Ripley, containing, with the chapelry of Ripley, 1283 inhabitants. The living is a vicarage, in the archdeaconry of Surrey, and diocese of Winchester, rated in the king's books at £8. 18. 1½., and in the patronage of Earl Onslow. The church, dedicated to St. Mary, is principally in the early style of English architecture. There is a place of worship for Wesleyan Methodists. A church and priory of Black canons, in honour of the Blessed Virgin Mary and St. Thomas à Becket, was founded, in the time of Richard I., at Newark, in this parish, by Ruald de Calva, and Beatrix, his wife, which at the dissolution possessed a revenue of £294. 18. 4. The Wey and Arun canal passes through the parish.

SENNEN, a parish in the hundred of PENWITH, county of CORNWALL, 8¼ miles (W.S.W.) from Penzance, containing 637 inhabitants. The living is a perpetual curacy, in the jurisdiction of the royal peculiar court of St. Burian, and in the patronage of the King, as Prince of Wales. There is a place of worship for Wesleyan Methodists. In this parish are, the Land's End, which, according to Dr. Berger, is three hundred and ninety-one feet above the level of the sea; Cape Cornwall; and Whitsand bay: it was in this bay that King Stephen landed, on his first arrival in England; also King John, on his return from the conquest of Ireland; and Perkin Warbeck, in the reign of

Henry VIII.: near it are the site of an ancient castle, called Castle-Mean, and the remains of a chapel. On one of the rocks, called the Longships, off this part of the coast, is a lighthouse, constructed, in 1797, under the direction of the Master and Wardens of the Trinity House.

SEPHTON, a parish in the hundred of WEST DERBY, county palatine of LANCASTER, comprising the chapelry of Great Crosby, and the townships of Aintree, Little Crosby, Ince-Blundell, Litherland, Lunt, Netherton, Orrell with Ford, Sephton, and Thornton, and containing 3433 inhabitants, of which number, 389 are in the township of Sephton, 7 miles (N.) from Liverpool. The living is a rectory, in the archdeaconry and diocese of Chester, rated in the king's books at £30. 1. 8., and in the patronage of the Rev. R. R. Rothwell. The church, dedicated to St. Helen, was rebuilt in the reign of Henry VIII., by the Rev. Anthony Molyneaux, a distinguished preacher, then rector: it is principally in the later style of English architecture, with a lofty spire; the interior is remarkably elegant, the chancel in particular, which is separated from the nave by a magnificent screen, and contains sixteen richly-sculptured stalls, with numerous monuments of the family of Molyneaux, of whom Sir William fought and performed signal acts of valour under the banner of the Black Prince, at Navaret, as did Sir Richard in the battle of Agincourt, and another Sir William in that of Flodden Field. This place confers the title of earl on their descendants.

SERLBY, a township in the parish of HAUGHTON, Hatfield division of the wapentake of BASSETLAW, county of NOTTINGHAM, 2¾ miles (S.S.W.) from Bawtry. The population is returned with the parish. Here was formerly a chapel of ease to the vicarage of Harworth, which has long been in ruins.

SESSAY, a parish in the wapentake of ALLERTONSHIRE, North riding of the county of YORK, comprising the townships of Hutton-Sessay and Sessay, and containing 493 inhabitants, of which number, 364 are in the township of Sessay, 6¾ miles (N. W. by W.) from Easingwould. The living is a rectory, in the archdeaconry of Cleveland, and diocese of York, rated in the king's books at £17. 0. 2½., and in the patronage of Lord Viscount Downe. The church is dedicated to St. Cuthbert.

SETCHEY, a parish in the Lynn division of the hundred of FREEBRIDGE, county of NORFOLK, 5 miles (S.) from Lynn-Regis, containing 94 inhabitants. The living is a rectory, annexed to that of North Runcton, in the archdeaconry and diocese of Norwich.

SETMURTHEY, a chapelry in the parish of BRIGHAM, ALLERDALE ward above Darwent, county of CUMBERLAND, 4 miles (E. N. E.) from Cockermouth, containing 188 inhabitants. The living is a perpetual curacy, in the archdeaconry of Richmond, and diocese of Chester, endowed with £800 royal bounty, and £400 parliamentary grant, and in the patronage of the Earl of Lonsdale. A school-house was built by subscription among the inhabitants, in 1795, but it is not endowed.

SETTLE, a market town in the parish of GIGGLESWICK, western division of the wapentake of STAINCLIFFE and EWCROSS, West riding of the county of YORK, 59 miles (W. by N.) from York, and 234 (N. W. by N.) from London, containing 1508 inhabitants. The name of this town is derived from the Saxon word *Setl*, a seat : its situation is singular and picturesque, at the base of an almost perpendicular limestone rock, which rises to the height of two hundred feet; it is neat and well built, the houses being chiefly of stone : the streets are partially paved, and the inhabitants are well supplied with water from numerous springs and wells. There is a subscription library and news-room. The surrounding vale consists of rich pastures, and is enclosed on each side by a long range of craggy mountains, including the lofty elevations of Pendle hill on the south, of Pennigant on the north, and Ingleborough on the north-west. Considerable business is done in the cotton trade, and there are several roperies and a paper manufactory. The market is on Tuesday : fairs are held on April 26th, Whit-Tuesday, August 18th and the two following days, and Tuesday after October 27th ; in addition to which there are fairs every alternate Tuesday from Easter to Whitsuntide, for lean cattle, and every second Monday in the year for fat cattle. A constable is appointed annually at a court baron of the lord of the manor, which is always held once, and sometimes twice, a year. There are places of worship for Independents and Wesleyan Methodists. A National school is supported by voluntary contributions.

SETTRINGTON, a parish in the wapentake of BUCKROSE, East riding of the county of YORK, comprising the townships of Scogglethorpe and Settrington, and containing 757 inhabitants, of which number, 535 are in the township of Settrington, 4 miles (E. S. E.) from New Malton. The living is a rectory, in the archdeaconry of the East riding, and diocese of York, rated in the king's books at £42. 12. 6., and in the patronage of the Trustees of the late Earl of Bridgewater. The church is dedicated to All Saints.

SEVENHAMPTON, a parish in the hundred of BRADLEY, county of GLOUCESTER, 4¼ miles (S.) from Winchcombe, containing 386 inhabitants. The living is a perpetual curacy, in the archdeaconry and diocese of Gloucester, endowed with £200 private benefaction, £400 royal bounty, and £200 parliamentary grant, and in the patronage of William Morris and John Hincksman, Esqrs. The church is dedicated to St. Andrew.

SEVENHAMPTON, a chapelry in the parish of HIGHWORTH, hundred of HIGHWORTH, CRICKLADE, and STAPLE, county of WILTS, 1½ mile (S. E. by S.) from Highworth, containing 242 inhabitants. The chapel is dedicated to St. Andrew : the chapelry is within the peculiar jurisdiction of the Prebendary of Highworth in the Cathedral Church of Salisbury.

SEVEN-OAKS, a township in that part of the parish of GREAT BUDWORTH which is in the hundred of BUCKLOW, county palatine of CHESTER, 4 miles (N. W. by N.) from Northwich, containing 141 inhabitants.

SEVEN-OAKS, a market town and parish in the hundred of CODSHEATH, lathe of SUTTON at HONE, county of KENT, containing, with the chapelry of Riverhead, and the liberty of Weald, 3942 inhabitants, of which number, 2114 are in the town, 17½ miles (W.) from Maidstone, and 24 (S. E. by S.) from London. This place, which in the Textus Roffensis is written *Seovan Acca*, is supposed to have derived its name from seven large oaks which stood upon the eminence on which the town is built : the period of its origin is uncertain, and the only historical event connected with it is the defeat and death of Sir Humphry Stafford, by Jack Cade and his followers, when sent to oppose the rebels by Henry VI., in 1450. The manor, formerly an appendage to Otford, and as such belonging to the see of Canterbury, was conveyed, about the time of the dissolution of the monastic establishments, by Archbishop Cranmer to Henry VIII., and it subsequently became the property of the Dukes of Dorset. The town is situated on the ridge of hills which crosses the county, separating the Upland from the Weald, or southern part, near the river Darent, in a fertile and beautiful part of the country : it is well built, being divided into two principal streets, and is most respectably inhabited, being generally esteemed a very desirable place of residence. There are some silk-mills in the neighbourhood. The market is on Saturday, principally for corn ; and there is also a market on the third Tuesday in every month, for cattle, which is very numerously attended : the fairs are on the 10th of July and the 12th of October, the latter being also a statute fair. The town is under the jurisdiction of the county magistrates : a bailiff, high constable, and several inferior officers, are chosen annually at a court leet, but their authority embraces little more than the superintendence of the charities. The petty sessions for the lathe of Sutton at Hone are held here; and a court of requests, for the recovery of debts not exceeding £5, the jurisdiction of which extends throughout the hundreds of Codsheath, Somerden, Westerham, and Wrotham, and the ville and liberty of Brasted. In the reign of Queen Elizabeth the assizes were held in the ancient market-house, near the middle of the High-street, and also two or three times at subsequent periods.

The living comprises a sinecure rectory and a vicarage, in the exempt deanery of Shoreham, which is within the peculiar jurisdiction of the Archbishop of Canterbury ; the rectory is rated in the king's books at £13. 6. 8., and the vicarage at £15. 3. 1½., both being in the patronage of the Rev. Thomas Sackville Curteis. The church, dedicated to St. Nicholas, is a spacious and handsome edifice at the southern end of the town, and on so elevated a situation as to be a conspicuous object many miles around. A new church, or chapel, with a house for the minister, was erected a few years since in the Weald liberty, by Lord Amherst and Multon Lambard, Esq. ; it will contain about two hundred persons, and is endowed with £200 private benefaction, and £2100 parliamentary grant : another, which will accommodate six hundred persons, is being erected by the same persons, in the Riverhead liberty : the right of presentation to both, after the decease of the founders, will be vested in the vicar. The Baptists have two places of worship, and the Supralapsarians and Wesleyan Methodists one each. The free grammar school was founded and endowed by Sir William Seven-oake, usually written Sennocke, in 1432 ; who, having been deserted by his parents, was brought up by some charitable persons, and apprenticed to a grocer in London, from which humble station he rose to be lord mayor of that city, and its representative in parliament, and left a portion of his wealth to found this school and an hospital for decayed elderly tradespeople. Queen Elizabeth granted a charter to the school, which places the management in the hands of the wardens and assistants of the town, who are elected annually, and appoint the master; and it is in consequence called " The Free Grammar School of Queen Elizabeth." It has seven scholarships; four of £15 per annum each, founded by direction of the court of Chancery, in 1735, from the surplus of money received under this endowment in the hands of the trustees, in any college at either of the Universities; two of £12 a year each, founded by Lady Boswell, in Jesus' College, Cambridge; and one of £4 per annum, founded by Robert Holmden, paid by the Leather-sellers' Company, at either University : in default of scholars from this school, that at Tonbridge has the right to appoint to the three last-named scholarships. The income at present derived from Sir William Sennocke's endowment, including some additions to it, particularly that of Anthony Pope, in 1571, is between £700 and £800 per annum, of which sum, exclusively of repairs, &c., of the house, £50 a year is appropriated as a salary to the master, who has also a house and excellent premises : about seven boys are generally on the foundation. Lady Margaret Boswell founded a school, in 1675, for educating poor children of the town, with funds for apprenticing them : the present income is nearly £700 per annum, from which a considerable deduction is made for repairing the sea wall at Burnham Level, which, on an average of six years, amounted to upwards of £200 per annum : a new school-house was erected, in 1827, on the site of the former, at an expense of about £2000, defrayed by savings from the income, and nearly three hundred children are instructed on the National system : a premium of £12 is given, as an apprentice fee, with each boy on leaving the school, the number of whom averages about six yearly. In the almshouse founded by Sir William Sennocke are thirty-two persons, who are maintained ; and sixteen out-pensioners receive an allowance from the endowment.

SEVINGTON, a parish in the hundred of CHART and LONGBRIDGE, lathe of SCRAY, county of KENT, 2¼ miles (S. E. by E.) from Ashford, containing 86 inhabitants. The living is a discharged rectory, in the archdeaconry and diocese of Canterbury, rated in the king's books at £8. 14. 0½., and in the patronage of the Rev. Edward Norwood. The church is dedicated to St. Mary.

SEWARDSTONE, a hamlet in the parish of WALTHAM-ABBEY, or HOLY CROSS, hundred of WALTHAM, county of ESSEX, 1¼ mile (S.) from Waltham-Abbey, containing 808 inhabitants. There is a heap of rubbish in the vicinity, called " the ruins of the old church." The Wesleyan Methodists have a place of worship here.

SEWERBY, a joint township with Marton, in the parish of BRIDLINGTON, wapentake of DICKERING, East riding of the county of YORK, 1¾ miles (E. N. E.) from Bridlington, containing, with Marton, 317 inhabitants.

SEWSTERN, a chapelry in the parish of BUCKMINSTER, hundred of FRAMLAND, county of LEICESTER, 9 miles (E. by N.) from Melton-Mowbray, containing 298 inhabitants. The chapel is dedicated to St. Michael. The Independents and Wesleyan Methodists have each a place of worship.

SEXHOW, a township in the parish of RUDBY in CLEVELAND, western division of the liberty of LANGBAURGH, North riding of the county of YORK, 5 miles

(S. W. by W.) from Stokesley, containing 38 inhabitants.

SHABBINGTON, a parish in the hundred of ASHENDON, county of BUCKINGHAM, 3 miles (W. by N.) from Thame, containing 241 inhabitants. The living is a vicarage, in the archdeaconry of Buckingham, and diocese of Lincoln, rated in the king's books at £10. 9. 7., and in the patronage of the Rev. Philip Wroughton and Mary Anne his wife. The church is dedicated to St. Mary Magdalene.

SHACKERSTONE, a parish in the hundred of SPARKENHOE, county of LEICESTER, 5 miles (N. W.) from Market-Bosworth, containing, with the hamlet of Odestone, and exclusively of a portion of the township of Barton in the Beans, which is in this parish, 486 inhabitants. The living is a discharged vicarage, in the archdeaconry of Leicester, and diocese of Lincoln, rated in the king's books at £5. 2. 3½., and in the patronage of G. Greenaway, Esq. The church is dedicated to St. Peter. The Ashby de la Zouch canal passes through the parish.

SHADFORTH, a township in the parish of PITTINGTON, southern division of EASINGTON ward, county palatine of DURHAM, 4½ miles (E. by S.) from Durham, containing 223 inhabitants. One of the towers of an ancient castellated mansion still remains.

SHADINGFIELD, a parish in the hundred of WANGFORD, county of SUFFOLK, 4¾ miles (S.) from Beccles, containing 189 inhabitants. The living is a discharged rectory, in the archdeaconry of Suffolk, and diocese of Norwich, rated in the king's books at £12, and in the patronage of Lord Braybrooke. The church is dedicated to St. John the Baptist.

SHADOXHURST, a parish in the hundred of BLACKBOURNE, lathe of SCRAY, county of KENT, 5¼ miles (S. W.) from Ashford, containing 244 inhabitants. The living is a discharged rectory, in the archdeaconry and diocese of Canterbury, rated in the king's books at £7. 13., endowed with £200 private benefaction, and £200 royal bounty, and in the patronage of the Crown. The church is dedicated to St. Peter and St. Paul.

SHADWELL, a parish in the Tower division of the hundred of OSSULSTONE, county of MIDDLESEX, 1½ mile (E. by S.) from London, containing 9557 inhabitants. This parish is situated on the northern bank of the river Thames, and comprises several streets, which are lighted with gas, and supplied with water from the East London water-works. It is within the jurisdiction of the New Police, the Thames Police Office, and a court of requests held in Whitechapel. There are some roperies in the parish. The living is a discharged rectory, in the archdeaconry of Middlesex, and diocese of London, and in the patronage of the Bishop of London. The church, dedicated to St. Paul, is a handsome modern edifice, the old structure having, within the last few years, been taken down, and the present building erected upon its site, but within the original foundations. There are places of worship for Independents and Primitive and Wesleyan Methodists. A parochial school, in which forty-five boys, and thirty-five girls are instructed, is supported by subscription. The British Union school, instituted in 1816, in Shakspeare's walk, affords instruction to four hundred and sixty boys, and one hundred and eighty girls; it is conducted on the Lancasterian plan, and is supported by voluntary contributions. The Protestant dissenters' original charity school was founded in 1712, and is situated in Shakspeare's walk: since its institution, one thousand five hundred and ninety-two boys have been received and one thousand five hundred and twenty-two apprenticed: at present there are seventy boys, who are educated and clothed by subscription. A chapel is attached to the institution. Thirty-one almshouses for the widows of poor seamen, founded and endowed in 1713, by Captain James Cooke and Alice his wife, are situated in this parish.

SHADWELL, a township in the parish of THORNER, lower division of the wapentake of SKYRACK, West riding of the county of YORK, 5¾ miles (N. N. E.) from Leeds, containing 197 inhabitants. There is a place of worship for Wesleyan Methodists.

Arms.

SHAFTESBURY, or SHASTON, a borough and market town, having separate jurisdiction, though locally in the hundred of Monckton up Wimborne, Shaston (East) division of the county of DORSET, 28 miles (N. N. E.) from Dorchester, and 101 (W. S. W.) from London, on the great western road from London to Exeter, containing, with the liberty of Alcester, 2903 inhabitants. The origin and derivation of the name of this town have given rise to much conjecture, it being supposed by some to have had existence even prior to the birth of Christ, and to have been called *Caer Palladur* by the Britons: other periods have been assigned for its foundation, but that which appears to be most probable is the reign of King Alfred; in confirmation of which, Camden states, that in the time of William of Malmesbury was to be seen an old stone, brought from the ruins of a wall into the nuns' chapter-house, with an inscription purporting that King Alfred built this city (if so we may render " *fecit* ") in 880, and in the eighth year of his reign. Its Saxon derivation from *Sceaft*, signifying the point of a hill, is supposed to be in allusion to the situation of the town. A Benedictine nunnery, founded here about the same period, has also been ascribed to various persons. Camden, following William of Malmesbury, attributes it to Elgiva, wife of Edmund, great grandson to King Alfred; whilst Leland and many other writers assert this latter monarch to be its founder, and that his daughter was the first abbess. To this abbey the remains of Edward the Martyr were removed after his murder at Corfe-Castle, and it appears to have been much resorted to by pilgrims, amongst whom was King Canute, who died here; and the extent of its endowments may be estimated from their value at its dissolution being £1166 per annum: the remains are very inconsiderable. The importance of the abbey naturally increased that of the town, which is reported at an early period to have contained ten parish churches. In the time of Edward the Confessor three mints were established here; and, according to a survey made shortly before the Norman Conquest, Shaftesbury contained one hundred and four houses, and three mint-masters. The town is situated on a high hill, with a gradual rise

on the east and south-east, but more precipitous on the west and south-west, at the extremity of the county of Dorset, and bordering on that of Wilts: it commands extensive views over both counties. The streets, which are neither paved nor lighted, are narrow and irregular; the houses are principally built of stone, and the inhabitants are badly supplied with water: on the hill is a well of prodigious depth, from which water is drawn up by machinery worked by a horse; but the inhabitants are principally supplied from the adjoining parish of Motcomb. The manufacture of shirt buttons was formerly carried on to a considerable extent, but it has very much declined, and there is now but very little trade. The market is on Saturday, and well supplied with all kinds of commodities; and there are fairs on the Saturday before Palm-Sunday, 24th of June, and 23rd of November.

Corporate Seal.

Obverse.   Reverse.

This is a very ancient borough, being described as such in Domesday-book, but it was not incorporated till the reign of Queen Elizabeth, who, according to Hutchins, granted its first charter, appointing a mayor, recorder, twelve aldermen, a bailiff, and common council; but no charter can be found prior to that granted by James I., in 1604, which, confirmed by one of Charles II., vests the government in a mayor and twelve capital burgesses, assisted by a recorder, who elect annually a town clerk, coroner, and two serjeants at mace. The mayor, the preceding mayor, and the recorder, are justices of the peace, and, with the capital burgesses, have power to hold a court of record every Saturday, for debts under £10, contracted within the borough; three of them form a quorum, the mayor or preceding, mayor, being one. A town hall, which is a handsome building, has been recently erected, at an expense of about £3000, defrayed by Earl Grosvenor. The borough first sent members to parliament in the 23rd of Edward I., and has since continued to do so without interruption: the right of election is vested in the inhabitants paying scot and lot, about four hundred in number: the mayor is the returning officer, and the prevailing influence is exercised by Earl Grosvenor.

The town comprises the three parishes of St. Peter, the Holy Trinity, and St. James, in the archdeaconry of Dorset, and diocese of Bristol. The living of St. Peter's is a discharged rectory, rated in the king's books at £11. 10. 2½., and united to that of the Holy Trinity, which union comprehends the ancient parishes of St. Lawrence and St. Martin: the living of Holy Trinity parish is rated in the king's books at £4. 1. 10½. St. Peter's church is of considerable antiquity, but contains many modern alterations: it possesses a curiously carved font, and a very ancient monument, supposed to have been removed from the abbey. That of the Holy Trinity is also ancient, and is said to have been enlarged by Sir Thomas Arundel, in the early part of the reign of Queen Elizabeth; it has a square embattled tower, ornamented with pinnacles; the churchyard is spacious, and adjoining it may still be seen the remains of the wall of the abbey. The living of St. James' (a portion of which parish, in the liberty of Alcester, is without the borough) is a rectory, rated in the king's books at £1. 11. 0½. : the church is a small and ancient fabric. The ancient parishes into which the town was formerly divided are now comprised in the above three, the livings of all which are in the patronage of the Earl of Shaftesbury. The Society of Friends, Independents, and Wesleyan Methodists, have each places of worship here. The free school, for educating, clothing, and apprenticing twenty poor boys, was founded and endowed by Mr. William Lush, in 1719. Spiller's spittal, for ten poor men, was founded and endowed by Sir Henry Spiller, in 1646; and an almshouse for sixteen poor women was founded by Matthew Chubb, and endowed by him and several other benefactors. On Castle Green, an eminence near the town, is a small mount, surrounded by a shallow ditch, which some have conjectured to be the site of a castle, but of which no mention can be found; by others it is supposed to have been a Roman intrenchment. The old city, which tradition reports to have existed prior to the time of Alfred, is said to have been near this mount. Shaftesbury was the birthplace of the Rev. James Granger, author of the Biographical History of England : it gives the title of earl to the family of Ashley Cooper.

SHAFTO (EAST), a township in that part of the parish of HARTBURN which is in the north-eastern division of TINDALE ward, county of NORTHUMBERLAND, 11¾ miles (W. S. W.) from Morpeth, containing 35 inhabitants. Here was formerly a chapel. Behind the ancient hall rises a lofty verdant hill, termed Shafto Crag, adjacent to which there is a spacious cave formed in the solid rock.

SHAFTO (WEST), a township in that part of the parish of HARTBURN which is in the north-eastern division of TINDALE ward, county of NORTHUMBERLAND, 12½ miles (W. by S.) from Morpeth, containing 54 inhabitants.

SHAFTON, a township in the parish of FELKIRK, wapentake of STAINCROSS, West riding of the county of YORK, 5 miles (N. E.) from Barnesley, containing 235 inhabitants. There is a place of worship for Wesleyan Methodists.

SHALBOURN, a parish partly in the hundred of KINTBURY-EAGLE, county of BERKS, and partly in the hundred of KINWARDSTONE, county of WILTS, 4 miles (S. S. W.) from Hungerford, containing, with the township of West Shalbourn, 941 inhabitants. The living is a vicarage, in the peculiar jurisdiction and patronage of the Dean and Canons of Windsor, rated in the king's books at £14. 17. 6. The church, dedicated to St. Michael, is principally in the Norman style. In that part of the parish which is in the county of Wilts is an ancient chapel, in a dilapidated state, with a house attached to it, called Westcourt, and supposed to have been a retreat for the monks of Sarum, or rather a place of occasional relaxation from the austerities of the

VOL. IV.

monastery. On the edge of the down, a continuance of Salisbury plain, is a tumulus, commanding very extensive prospects over several counties. Fragments of human skeletons and of horses, supposed to be the remains of those slain in the wars during the Octarchy, are often met with in the neighbourhood. Wansdyke, the boundary between the kingdoms of Mercia and the West Saxons, runs along one side of the parish, on the north side of which is a chalybeate spring, formerly in great repute.

SHALBOURN (WEST), a township in that part of the parish of SHALBOURN which is in the hundred of KINWARDSTONE, county of WILTS, 4 miles (S. S. W.) from Hungerford, containing 410 inhabitants.

SHALDEN, a parish in the hundred of ODIHAM, Basingstoke division of the county of SOUTHAMPTON, 2¾ miles (N. W.) from Alton, containing 149 inhabitants. The living is a rectory, in the archdeaconry and diocese of Winchester, rated in the king's books at £9. 15. 10., and in the patronage of the Crown. The church is dedicated to St. Peter and St. Paul.

SHALDON-GREEN, a township in the parish of STOKEINTINHEAD, in a detached portion of the hundred of WONFORD, county of DEVON, 5¼ miles (E.) from Newton Abbots. The population is returned with the parish. A chapel was erected in this township about one hundred and fifty years ago, by the Carews of Haccombe. There are places of worship for Baptists and Independents. Shaldon, which contains many genteel villas, is pleasantly situated on the south bank of the river Teign, across which a bridge has been lately erected opposite to Ringmore, and a ferry-boat is constantly passing between this and Teignmouth, so that a more direct communication is thus established, both for vehicles and foot-passengers, with Teignmouth and Torquay.

SHALFLEET, a parish in the liberty of WEST MEDINA, Isle of Wight division of the county of SOUTHAMPTON, 3¼ miles (E. by S.) from Yarmouth, containing 878 inhabitants. The living is a discharged vicarage, in the archdeaconry and diocese of Winchester, rated in the king's books at £18. 12. 1., and in the patronage of the Crown. The church is partly Norman and partly of later date, with a low tower of considerable magnitude. The navigable river Newton bounds the parish on the north-east.

SHALFORD, a parish in the hundred of HINCKFORD, county of ESSEX, 5 miles (N. N. W.) from Braintree, containing 670 inhabitants. The living is a discharged vicarage, in the jurisdiction of the Commissary of Essex and Herts, concurrently with the Consistorial Court of the Bishop of London, rated in the king's books at £7, and in the patronage of the Prebendary of Shalford in the Cathedral Church of Wells. The church is dedicated to St. Andrew.

SHALFORD, a parish in the first division of the hundred of BLACKHEATH, county of SURREY, 1 mile (S. S. E.) from Guildford, containing 744 inhabitants. The living is a discharged vicarage, in the archdeaconry of Surrey, and diocese of Winchester, rated in the king's books at £8. 4. 7½., and in the patronage of the Crown. The church is dedicated to St. Mary. The Wey and Arun Junction canal passes through the parish; and in the neighbourhood the two rivers meet and form one stream.

G

SHALSTONE, a parish in the hundred and county of BUCKINGHAM, 4 miles (N. W. by W.) from Buckingham, containing 201 inhabitants. The living is a rectory, in the archdeaconry of Buckingham, and diocese of Lincoln, rated in the king's books at £8. 0. 5., and in the patronage of the Rev. Sir S. C. Jervoise, Bart. The church is dedicated to St. Edward.

SHAMBLEHURST, a tything in the parish of SOUTH STONEHAM, hundred of MANSBRIDGE, Fawley division of the county of SOUTHAMPTON, 4¼ miles (W. by S.) from Bishop's Waltham. The population is returned with the parish.

SHANGTON, a parish in the hundred of GARTREE, county of LEICESTER, 6¼ miles (N. by W.) from Market-Harborough, containing 44 inhabitants. The living is a rectory, in the archdeaconry of Leicester, and diocese of Lincoln, rated in the king's books at £10 13. 4., and in the patronage of Sir J. Isham, Bart. The church is dedicated to St. Nicholas : about three quarters of a mile from it is "Gartre Bush," the spot where the hundred court was formerly held.

SHANKLIN, a parish in the liberty of EAST MEDINA, Isle of Wight division of the county of SOUTHAMPTON, 9½ miles (S. E.) from Newport, containing 155 inhabitants. The living is a perpetual curacy, annexed to the rectory of Bonchurch, in the archdeaconry and diocese of Winchester. In the church is an oak chest, curiously carved, with a Latin inscription, dated 1512, and the arms of the see, the gift of Thomas Silksted, Prior of Winchester. At a short distance from the village is a prodigious chasm, called Shanklin Chine, which, extending a considerable way inland from the coast, and being overgrown with shrubs and brushwood, forms a picturesque and extremely romantic scene.

SHAP, a parish in WEST ward, county of WESTMORLAND, 6 miles (N. W.) from Orton, containing, with portions of the chapelry of Mardale, the township of Fawcet-Forest, and of the hamlet of Birbeck-Fells, 969 inhabitants. The living is a discharged vicarage, in the archdeaconry and diocese of Carlisle, rated in the king's books at £8. 15. 7½., endowed with £400 private benefaction, £600 royal bounty, and £1100 parliamentary grant, and in the patronage of the Earl of Lonsdale. The church, dedicated to St. Michael, has lately received an addition of one hundred and ten free sittings, the Incorporated Society for the enlargement of churches and chapels having granted £50 towards defraying the expense. The river Lowther runs through the parish, which is bounded on the west by the lake Hawswater, and contains quarries of limestone and blue slate. In 1687, a charter was obtained for a market on Wednesday, and three fairs on April 23rd, August 1st, and September 17th, each for two days, but they have been long in disuse. At present a small market is held on Monday, and a fair for cattle and pedlary on May 4th. About one mile west from the town, which consists of a long straggling street, on the high road between Penrith and Kendal, are the venerable ruins and tolerably perfect tower of Shap abbey, founded about 1150, by Thomas Fitz-Gospatrick, in honour of God and St. Mary Magdalene, for Premonstratensian canons, whom he caused to be removed hither from an abbey which he had previously established at Preston in Kendal : at the dissolution it contained twenty monks, whose revenue was estimated at £166. 10. 6. Thomas Jackson, in 1703,

gave a messuage and land for the erection and support of a school ; the annual income is £25, for which about twenty children are instructed. In this parish is the site of a remarkable Druidical monument, or temple, upwards of half a mile in length, and from twenty to thirty yards in breadth : it is encompassed by huge masses of granite, many of them three or four yards in diameter, placed at irregular distances, having at the upper end a circus, or hippodrome, supposed to have been the place of sacrifice. Shap Well, the water of which is impregnated with sulphur, and serviceable in scorbutic cases, is within the adjoining parish of Crosby-Ravensworth. At Hardendale, in this parish, Dr. John Mill, the learned editor of the Greek Testament, was born, in 1645; he died in 1701.

SHAPWICK, a parish in the hundred of BADBURY, SHASTON (East) division of the county of DORSET, 4½ miles (S. E.) from Blandford-Forum, containing 409 inhabitants. The living is a vicarage, in the archdeaconry of Dorset, and diocese of Bristol, rated in the king's books at £7. 9. 4½., and in the patronage of Lord Rivers. The church is dedicated to St. Bartholomew. The navigable river Stour bounds the parish on the south. James Alexander, Esq., in 1818, gave a moiety of the dividends arising from £300 three per cents. for the education of poor children. Here was a small Carthusian priory, a cell to that of Sheen in Surrey.

SHAPWICK, a parish in the hundred of WHITLEY, county of SOMERSET, 6¾ miles (W. by S.) from Glastonbury, containing 414 inhabitants. The living is a discharged vicarage, with the perpetual curacy of Ashcott annexed, in the archdeaconry of Wells, and diocese of Bath and Wells, rated in the king's books at £9. 13. 4., and in the patronage of the Rev. G. H. Templar. The church is dedicated to St. Mary.

SHARDLOW, a township in the parish of WILN, hundred of MORLESTON and LITCHURCH, county of DERBY, 7 miles (S. E by E.) from Derby. The population is returned with the parish. The Trent and Mersey canal passes through the township.

SHARESHILL, a parish in the eastern division of the hundred of CUTTLESTONE, county of STAFFORD, 5¾ miles (N. N. E.) from Wolverhampton, containing, with the township of Great and Little Saredon, 583 inhabitants. The living is a perpetual curacy, with that of Penkridge, in the archdeaconry of Stafford, and diocese of Lichfield and Coventry, endowed with £200 private benefaction, and £600 royal bounty, and in the patronage of E. J. Littleton, Esq. The church, dedicated to the Assumption of the Virgin Mary, is a brick building, with an ancient tower of stone. The Staffordshire and Worcestershire canal crosses the north-western angle of the parish.

SHARLSTON, a township in the parish of WARMFIELD, lower division of the wapentake of AGBRIGG, West riding of the county of YORK, 4¼ miles (E. by S.) from Wakefield, containing 330 inhabitants.

SHARNBROOK, a parish in the hundred of WILLEY, county of BEDFORD, 4 miles (N. E.) from Harrold, containing 691 inhabitants. The living is a discharged vicarage, in the archdeaconry of Bedford, and diocese of Lincoln, rated in the king's books at £8, and in the patronage of the Crown. The church, dedicated to St. Peter, is of early English architecture, with a spire. There is a place of worship for Baptists.

SHARNFORD, a parish in the hundred of SPARK-ENHOE, county of LEICESTER, 4¼ miles (E.S.E) from Hinckley, containing 460 inhabitants. The living is a rectory, in the archdeaconry of Leicester, and diocese of Lincoln, rated in the king's books at £9. 18. 9., and in the patronage of the Crown. The church is dedicated to St. Helen. The river Soar runs through the parish.

SHARPENHOE, a hamlet in the parish of STREAT-LEY, hundred of FLITT, county of BEDFORD, 4 miles (S.S.W.) from Silsoe. The population is returned with the parish. This hamlet contains a charity school for the instruction of eight children, founded by Richard Norton, in 1686, and endowed with a rent-charge of £10. Thomas Norton, a dramatic writer, was born here in the early part of the sixteenth century : he died about 1600.

SHARPERTON, a township in the parish of AL-LENTON, western division of COQUETDALE ward, county of NORTHUMBERLAND, 6½ miles (W. by N.) from Roth-bury, containing 107 inhabitants.

SHARPLES, a township in the parish of BOLTON, hundred of SALFORD, county palatine of LANCASTER, 2¾ miles (N.) from Great Bolton, containing 2065 inhabitants. In this township are a large power-loom factory, and a bleaching establishment, affording employment to about one thousand three hundred persons. Coal abounds in the neighbourhood; and there are reservoirs for supplying the town of Bolton with water. Children of this place have the benefit of a free education at Eagley-bridge school, in the township of Turton.

SHARRINGTON, a parish in the hundred of HOLT, county of NORFOLK, 4¼ miles (W.S.W.) from Holt, containing 235 inhabitants. The living is a discharged rectory, annexed to that of Saxlingham, in the archdeaconry and diocese of Norwich, rated in the king's books at £10. The church is dedicated to All Saints.

SHARROW, a township in that part of the parish of RIPON which is in the liberty of RIPON, West riding of the county of YORK, 1½ mile (E. by N.) from Ripon, containing 103 inhabitants. A chapel has been lately erected, containing five hundred and fifty sittings, of which two hundred and eighty are free, the Incorporated Society for building additional churches having granted £400 towards defraying the expense. This township is within the peculiar jurisdiction of the Archbishop of York. The Rev. Thomas Savage, in 1782, bequeathed £5 per annum for teaching eight poor children. The sum of £4. 10. a year is also paid out of the chapel rates, on account of sundry small gifts for the education of six others.

SHATTON, a joint hamlet with Brough, in the parish of HOPE, hundred of HIGH PEAK, county of DERBY, 6 miles (N.E. by N.) from Tideswell. The population is returned with Brough. Shatton is in the honour of Tutbury, duchy of Lancaster, and within the jurisdiction of a court of pleas held at Chapel en le Frith every third Tuesday, for the recovery of debts under 40s.

SHAUGH, a parish in the hundred of PLYMPTON, county of DEVON, 6 miles (N.) from Earl's Plympton, containing 551 inhabitants. The living is a perpetual curacy, annexed to that of Sampford-Spiney, in the archdeaconry of Totness, and diocese of Exeter, endowed with £22. 10. per annum and £100 private be-nefaction, £200 royal bounty, and £1800 parliamentary grant, and in the patronage of the Dean and Canons of Windsor. The scenery in the immediate vicinity is of the most romantic description.

SHAVINGTON, a joint township with Gresty, in the parish of WYBUNBURY, hundred of NANTWICH, county palatine of CHESTER, 4¼ miles (E.) from Nant-wich, containing 274 inhabitants. The old manorial seat of the Wodenothes, of whom was descended John, the celebrated antiquary, born in 1624, was highly curious, from its age, and the abundance of stained glass and other ancient relics it contained.

SHAW, a chapelry in the parish of OLDHAM cum PRESTWICH, hundred of SALFORD, county palatine of LANCASTER, 5 miles (S.E.) from Rochdale. The population is returned with the parish. The living is a perpetual curacy, in the archdeaconry and diocese of Chester, endowed with £400 private benefaction, £400 royal bounty, and £1000 parliamentary grant, and in the patronage of the Vicar of Prestwich. There is a place of worship for Wesleyan Methodists.

SHAW cum DONNINGTON, a parish in the hundred of FAIRCROSS, county of BERKS, 1¼ mile (N.E.) from Speenhamland, containing 531 inhabitants. The living is a rectory, in the archdeaconry of Berks, and diocese of Salisbury, rated in the king's books at £12. 11. 8., and in the patronage of the Rev. Thomas Penrose, D.C.L. The church is dedicated to St. Mary. The river Lambourn runs through the parish. An attempt was made by a soldier of Cromwell's army, in 1644, to assassinate Charles I. at the manor-house, his usual place of rest, when journeying to the West of England : a brass plate fixed on the spot where the ball entered still records the event. In the second battle of Newbury this mansion was garrisoned for the king, and attacked by a large body of the enemy, which was repulsed with great loss. Several cannon balls, since found at intervals about the grounds, are preserved; as are also a cloak, hat, bridle, and spur belonging to the Protector, and a bed on which Queen Anne reposed. Here are almshouses for twelve poor persons, founded about 1618, by Sir Richard Abberbury, Knt.

SHAWBURY, a parish comprising the townships of Besford and Preston-Brockhurst, in the hundred of PIMHILL, the township of Acton-Reynold, in the liberties of SHREWSBURY, and the townships of Edgbolton and Shawbury, in the Whitchurch division of the hundred of BRADFORD (North), county of SALOP, and containing 1133 inhabitants, of which number, 339 are in the township of Shawbury, 7¼ miles (E.) from Shrewsbury. The living is a discharged vicarage, in the archdeaconry of Salop, and diocese of Lichfield and Coventry, rated in the king's books at £7. 1. 5½., and in the patronage of William Marvin, Esq. The church is dedicated to St. Mary.

SHAWDON, a township in the parish of WHIT-TINGHAM, northern division of COQUETDALE ward, county of NORTHUMBERLAND, 7½ miles (W.) from Alnwick, containing 77 inhabitants. Two ancient urns of common earthenware were found in the neighbourhood some years ago.

SHAWELL, a parish in the hundred of GUTHLAX-TON, county of LEICESTER, 3 miles (S.) from Lutter-worth, containing 209 inhabitants. The living is a rectory, in the archdeaconry of Leicester, and diocese of

Lincoln, rated in the king's books at £9, and in the patronage of the Crown. The church is dedicated to All Saints. A free grammar school for children of this parish and that of Newton, founded here by John Eckington, has an endowment of £20 per annum, with a house and garden for the master. The founder also erected an almshouse for six poor men.

SHEARSBY, a chapelry in that part of the parish of KNAPTOFT which is in the hundred of GUTHLAX-TON, county of LEICESTER, 7 miles (N. E.) from Lutterworth, containing 310 inhabitants. The chapel is dedicated to St. Mary Magdalene. Here is a saline spring, the water of which has been found serviceable in scorbutic affections.

SHEBBEAR, a parish in the hundred of SHEBBEAR, county of DEVON, 7¾ miles (W. N. W.) from Hatherleigh, containing 1006 inhabitants. The living is a discharged vicarage, with the perpetual curacy of Sheepwash annexed, in the archdeaconry of Barnstaple, and diocese of Exeter, rated in the king's books at £11. 8. 4., and in the patronage of the Crown. The church is dedicated to St. Lawrence. The parish is bounded on the west by the river Torridge.

SHEEN, a parish in the southern division of the hundred of TOTMONSLOW, county of STAFFORD, 10 miles (E. by N.) from Winster, containing 429 inhabitants. The living is a perpetual curacy, in the archdeaconry of Stafford, and diocese of Lichfield and Coventry, endowed with £800 royal bounty, and in the patronage of Sir H. Bateman. Fourteen poor children are educated for £7. 10. a year, the produce of sundry bequests.

SHEEN (EAST), a hamlet in the parish of MORT-LAKE, western division of the hundred of BRIXTON, county of SURREY, |6½ miles (S. W. by W.) from London. The population is returned with the parish.

SHEEPSHEAD, a parish in the western division of the hundred of GOSCOTE, county of LEICESTER, 4 miles (W.) from Loughborough, containing 3464 inhabitants. The living is a discharged vicarage, in the archdeaconry of Leicester, and diocese of Lincoln, rated in the king's books at £8. 10. 10., endowed with £200 private benefaction, and £200 royal bounty, and in the patronage of C. M. Phillipps, Esq. The church is dedicated to St. Botolph. There are places of worship for Baptists, the Society of Friends, and Wesleyan Methodists. Many of the inhabitants are employed in the weaving of stockings. A National school established here is supported by subscription.

SHEEPSTOR, a parish in the hundred of Ro-BOROUGH, county of DEVON, 7 miles (S. E. by E.) from Tavistock, containing 129 inhabitants. The living is a perpetual curacy, annexed to the vicarage of Bickleigh, in the archdeaconry of Totness, and diocese of Exeter. Sheepstor rock is one of the most remarkable granite heaps upon Dartmoor, and is a conspicuous object from Roborough down : at the foot of it is situated the village, on the little river Mew. At Ailsborough, in this parish, a lofty eminence on Dartmoor, are very extensive tin mines.

SHEEPWASH, a parish in the hundred of SHEB-BEAR, county of DEVON, 4 miles (W. N. W.) from Hatherleigh, containing 436 inhabitants. The living is a perpetual curacy, annexed to the vicarage of Shebbear, in the archdeaconry of Barnstaple, and diocese of Exeter.

There is a place of worship for Baptists. The river Torridge runs through the parish. A market and three annual fairs were formerly held here. In 1743, the village was almost destroyed by fire. In this parish are the remains of a very large mansion, called Upcott Avenel, to which a chapel was formerly annexed ; the few rooms still in being have been converted into a farm-house, and the fine old gateway was removed some years ago, for the purpose of building a handsome residence.

SHEEPWASH, a parish with Bothall, in the eastern division of MORPETH ward, county of NORTHUM-BERLAND, 4¾ miles (E.) from Morpeth, containing, with Ashington, 50 inhabitants. The living is a rectory, united to that of Bothall, in the archdeaconry of Northumberland, and diocese of Durham, rated in the king's books at £3. 17. 1. The church, which has been demolished, was dedicated to the Holy Sepulchre. The river Wansbeck, which is navigable for keels and small boats, is here crossed by a bridge.

SHEEPY (MAGNA), a parish in the hundred of SPARKENHOE, county of LEICESTER, 3 miles (N. E. by N.) from Atherstone, containing, with the chapelry of Ratcliffe-Culey, 638 inhabitants. The living is a mediety of the rectory of Sheepy Magna and Parva, in the archdeaconry of Leicester, and diocese of Lincoln, rated in the king's books at £13. 4. 9½., and in the patronage of the Rev. T. C. Fell. The church is dedicated to All Saints. At the Mythe, which formerly belonged to the monks of Merevale, are some slight remains of an ancient chapel. This parish is in the honour of Tutbury, duchy of Lancaster, and within the jurisdiction of a court of pleas held at Tutbury every third Tuesday, for the recovery of debts under forty shillings.

SHEEPY (PARVA), a parish in the hundred of SPARKENHOE, county of LEICESTER, 3¼ miles (N. E.) from Atherstone, containing 87 inhabitants. The living is a mediety of the rectory of Sheepy Magna and Parva, in the archdeaconry of Leicester, and diocese of Lincoln, rated in the king's books at £13. 4. 9½., and in the patronage of the Rev. T. C. Fell. The church is dedicated to All Saints.

SHEERING, a parish in the hundred of HARLOW, county of ESSEX, 3 miles (N. E.) from Harlow, containing 439 inhabitants. The living is a rectory, in the archdeaconry of Middlesex, and diocese of London, rated in the king's books at £13. 13. 4., and in the patronage of the Dean and Canons of Christ Church, Oxford. The church is dedicated to St. Mary.

SHEERNESS, a sea-port, market town, and chapelry, in the parish of MINSTER, having separate jurisdiction, though locally in the liberty of the Isle of Sheppy, lathe of SCRAY, county of KENT, 21 miles (N. E.) from Maidstone, and 50 (E. by S.) from London, containing 817 inhabitants. This place, which is situated at the north-western point of the Isle of Sheppy, on the river Medway, at its junction with the Thames, was a mere swamp until the reign of Charles II., when the importance of its situation being appreciated, that monarch, early in 1667, directed the construction of a strong fort, and twice personally ascertained its progress. In the same year, before the new fortifications were in a very advanced state, the Dutch fleet entered the Thames, and made their memorable attack on the shipping in the Medway, having in their passage destroyed that portion of the works which was completed, and landed some men, who took possession of the fort. In consequence of this, a regular fortification, with a line of heavy artillery and of smaller forts higher up, on each side of the Medway, was formed, to which other works have since been added. A garrison is kept up, under the command of a governor, lieutenant-governor, fort-major, and inferior officers; and the construction of a royal dock-yard, for repairing ships and building frigates and smaller vessels, has caused Sheerness to become a naval station of the first importance. In 1798, the mutiny of the fleet stationed at the Nore threatened this town with the most alarming consequences, and induced many of the inhabitants to make a precipitate retreat to Chatham and other places; but the fortunate suppression of this formidable insurrection saved the town from the apprehended danger. In 1827, it suffered from a dreadful fire, which destroyed fifty houses, and property of the value of £60,000; but the houses, which were before principally of wood, have been replaced by others built of brick.

Owing to the naval establishment formed here, Sheerness has grown up into a considerable town, consisting of two divisions, Blue Town and Mile Town: it has been recently much enlarged, some new streets and a spacious hotel having been erected, the latter fitted up in a very superior style; but there are not sufficient houses for the population, many of the poorer inhabitants residing in the hulls of old vessels, though, in consequence of recent reductions in the dock-yards and arsenals, the number has considerably decreased. A pier and causeway extend from the town to low water mark, which are kept in good repair; and the town is paved, lighted, and cleansed under the authority of two acts of parliament passed in the 41st and 49th of George III. There was formerly a great scarcity of water, but it is now supplied, and of a very excellent quality, at one half-penny per pail, from four subscription wells, which have been sunk to a depth of three hundred and sixty feet: the principal one, called King's well, is within the fort, and supplies the vessels at the Nore. This place has latterly become the resort of a great deal of company, attracted by the facility of sea-bathing; the beach, on which the machines are stationed, being very clean, and forming a delightful promenade. On the cliffs leading from the beach towards Minster there is, perhaps, one of the most splendid and interesting views in the kingdom: the German Ocean on the east; the rivers Thames and Medway, bearing innumerable vessels of all sizes, with the town and harbour of Sheerness, to the north and west; and the fertile valleys of Kent, with the Medway winding through them, and the towns and villages interspersed, towards the south, combine in presenting a diversity and sublimity of landscape rarely excelled. The harbour has of late years been much enlarged and improved, and is now safe and commodious, often presenting a splendid appearance from the number of vessels in it; passage boats ply with every tide, and a steam-boat daily, to and from Chatham, and there is in summer a regular communication by steam-boats with London.

The dock-yard has been greatly extended and improved within the last fifteen years, at a cost of about three millions, and is now one of the finest in Europe:

it covers an area of sixty acres, and is surrounded by an extremely well built brick wall, which cost £40,000. The docks are sufficiently capacious to receive men of war of the first class, with all their guns, stores, equipments, &c., on board; and two steam-engines, each of fifty horse power, have been erected for the purpose of pumping them dry. There is a basin, with a depth of water of twenty-six feet, which will hold six ships of the first class; and two of a smaller size, for store-ships and boats. The storehouse, which is the largest building in the country, is six stories high, with iron joists, beams, window-frames, and doors, and will contain at least thirty thousand tons of naval stores: there is also a handsome victualling storehouse, smithy, navy pay office, mast-houses, &c. The commissioners and principal officers of the establishment have handsome houses in the yard, and a noble residence has been erected in the garrison for the port-admiral, in which are state rooms for the reception of the royal family, the lords of the admiralty, &c. The principal establishment of the ordnance departments has been removed hence to Chatham, where the stores for the fleet at the Nore, &c., are kept, and the ground formerly occupied by it has been added to the dock-yard. An office connected with this department is still, however, retained here; and it is said that government contemplates the re-establishment of the department at this place on a very enlarged scale, and the extension of the present line of fortifications from the garrison point, outside the town, to the sea wall, called Queenborough wall, for which purpose they have purchased two hundred acres of land surrounding the town. The principal government officers residing here are clerks of the cheque and survey, store-keeper, master shipwright and his assistant, master attendant, master caulker, boatswain, surgeon, and porter. Many convicts are employed in the hulks and in the improvements here.

The chief trade in the town arises from the dock-yard and other establishments connected with government, though considerable quantities of corn and seed, the produce of the isle, as well as oysters (of which the beds extend all along the coast, as far as Milton), are shipped for the London market. There are copperas works of considerable extent, within a few miles of the town: the pyrites, or copperas stones, are collected in heaps upon the beach, from the falling cliffs, and carried away in vessels. The market is on Saturday, but there is no regular market-place. The parish church was formerly at Minster, about four miles distant, but a very elegant church has lately been erected at the east end, and just outside the wall, of the dock-yard, the area of which is appropriated for the officers, &c., of the dock-yard, and the galleries for the public. The chaplain is appointed by the Board of Admiralty. The living is distinct from that of Minster, though it is in contemplation to unite them, and the ecclesiastical government is in the jurisdiction of the Consistorial Court of Canterbury, concurrently with the Archidiaconal court. There are two places of worship each for the Baptists and Independents, and one each for the Primitive and Wesleyan Methodists, the Unitarians, and Roman Catholics, also a Synagogue. Sunday schools are attached to the chapels of the Baptists, Independents, and Wesleyan Methodists, in which more than one thousand children are instructed: there are several reading societies. In sinking the wells here, the workmen, at the depth of two hundred feet, discovered a complete prostrate forest, through which, in the prosecution of their work, they were obliged to burn their way ; which is considered to be a remarkable confirmation of the history of the deluge, and specimens are in the possession of most of the Philosophical Institutions in Europe. Stones well adapted for the composition of Roman cement, in consequence of being impregnated with copperas, are dredged up from the sea in the neighbourhood of the cliffs.

SHEET, a tything in the parish of PETERSFIELD, hundred of FINCH-DEAN, Alton (South) division of the county of SOUTHAMPTON, ¾ of a mile (N.E. by E.) from Petersfield, containing 306 inhabitants. John Lock, in 1674, bequeathed a rent-charge of £2. 10. for the education of children.

SHEFFIELD, a parish comprising the market town of Sheffield, the chapelries of Attercliffe and Ecclesall-Bierlow, the townships of Nether Hallam, and Upper Hallam, and the hamlet of Darnall, in the southern, and the township of Brightside-Bierlow in the northern, division of the wapentake of STRAFFORTH and TICKHILL, West riding of the county of YORK, and containing 65,275 inhabitants, of which number, 42,157 are in the town of Sheffield, 55 miles (S. W. by S.) from York, and 163 (N. N. W.) from London. This place, which is of great antiquity, and was formerly called *Sheaffield*, derived its name from its situation on the river Sheaf, near its confluence with the Don, and forms the chief town of the extensive Saxon manor of Hallam, now called Hallamshire. The parish formed a portion of this large manor, which, although dismembered, and its jurisdiction dissolved, has imparted name to the more extensive tract called Hallamshire, the limits of which are undefined, but of which Sheffield may be considered the chief town. At the time of the Norman survey, the manor of Sheffield was held, under Judith, niece of William the Conqueror, by Roger de Busli, and the widowed countess of the Saxon Earl Waltheof, who had been decapitated for entering into a conspiracy against William, and subsequently, with other manors, by the family of De Lovetot, the first of that family who owned the manor being supposed to have erected the ancient castle, which, with the lordship of Hallamshire, afterwards descended to the Earls of Shrewsbury, from whom the estate finally passed to the Dukes of Norfolk. Edward I. granted the lords of the manor various privileges, who in turn releasing the inhabitants from the feudal tenure by which they held their estates, in consideration of a fixed annual payment, occasioned Sheffield to become a free town. Cardinal Wolsey, after his arrest in 1530, was detained in the manor-house here for eighteen days, in custody of the Earl of Shrewsbury ; and Mary, Queen of Scots, was, with the exception of a few short intervals, held in captivity in the same place, or in the castle, for nearly fourteen years. During the civil war in the reign of Charles I., the inhabitants being in the interest of the parliamentarians, made a feeble effort to maintain the town and castle for the parliament ; but the Earl of Newcastle, with a party of royalists, quickly gained possession for the king, and placed a garrison in the castle, under the command of Sir William Saville, who was appointed governor. The Earl of Manchester sent a force, under Major-General Crawford, to attempt its reduction, and after a protracted siege, it was surrendered on honourable terms, and soon afterwards demolished by order of the parliament.

The town is pleasantly situated on a gentle eminence rising out of a spacious valley, which, with the exception of an opening to the north-east, is sheltered by a chain of lofty hills richly clothed with wood, and nearly surrounded by the rivers Don, Sheaf, and Porter. Over the river Don a stone bridge of three arches was erected in 1485, and called Lady bridge, from a religious house near it, dedicated to the Blessed Virgin, which was taken down, on widening the bridge, in 1768. An iron bridge of three arches has been also constructed over the same river ; and, in 1828, an additional stone bridge of three arches was erected, for the purpose of affording an easier communication between the Rotherham and Barnesley roads, and the new corn and cattle markets : a bridge over the Sheaf, consisting of one arch, was rebuilt in 1769, by Edward, Duke of Norfolk. The town extends for nearly a mile from north to south, and for three-quarters of a mile from east to west, and consists of numerous streets, which, with the exception of one or two of the principal, are narrow and inconvenient : the houses, chiefly of brick, have obtained from the works a sombre appearance, and are intermixed with many of very ancient character. The chief portion is within the angle formed by the rivers, but there are considerable ranges of building on the opposite banks : considerable improvements have taken place, under the provisions of an act obtained in 1818, by which the town is partially paved, lighted with gas by a company whose extensive works are situated at Shude Hill, near the bridge over the river Sheaf, and formerly supplied with water, conveyed from springs in the neighbouring hills, by means of works, situated on Crook's moor, erected by a few private individuals, in 1782 ; but the supply becoming inadequate to the increasing demands of the town, a company was formed in 1829, with a capital of £ 100,000, and incorporated by act of parliament. The environs abound with beautiful scenery and pleasant walks, and are ornamented with elegant villas, inhabited by the more opulent families. The barracks, forming an extensive range of building, and, with the parade ground, occupying a large tract of land to the north-east of the town, were erected in 1794, and are pleasantly situated on the bank of the river Don ; they contain accommodation for two troops of cavalry. The public subscription library, originally in Surrey-street, has been removed into a commodious room fitted up for it in the music hall, and is supported by a proprietary of two hundred members, who pay an annual subscription of £1. 1. each : connected with the establishment is a reading-room, which is well supplied with periodical works. A Literary and Philosophical Society was instituted in 1822, the members of which hold their meetings in an elegant apartment in the music hall, containing their apparatus, a collection of fossils, botanical specimens, and curiosities from the South Sea islands,

Seal of the Town's Trust, or Sheffield Free Tenants.

and ornamented with a full-length portrait of Mr. Montgomery, the poet: the society deliver their public lectures in the saloon of the music hall. The public news-room, a neat stone building, forming part of the East Parade, recently erected, is well attended by a number of annual subscribers of £1. 6. each; and a commercial news-room has been also established in the music hall. The mechanics' library, established in 1824, contains more than two thousand volumes, and is open every evening, under the superintendence of six of the members. Concerts are occasionally held, during the season, in the music hall, under the direction of the choral concert committee. The music hall is a spacious and elegant building, in the Grecian style of architecture, erected in Surrey-street, in 1824; it comprises on the ground-floor a room for the public library, thirty-eight feet long, and thirty-five feet wide, of which the roof is supported on pillars; a reading-room and a saloon; and a spacious room for the Literary and Philosophical Society, thirty-seven feet long, and thirty-six feet wide: the buildings also contain an elegant music-room, ninety-nine feet in length, and thirty-eight feet wide, with a well-arranged orchestra; adjoining are a handsome saloon, thirty-eight feet long, and twenty feet wide, with four recesses, two large refreshment-rooms, and housekeeper's apartments. The theatre and assembly-rooms were erected in 1762, and form an extensive building of brick, handsomely ornamented with stone, and having a central portico supporting a pediment; the theatre is generally open from October to January, and the assembly-rooms, which are elegantly fitted up, are well attended during the season. The Town's Trust has arisen from a grant made by a member of the ancient family of Furnival, about the year 1300, and consists of property in lands and tenements, shares in the river Don navigation, &c., producing about £1400 per annum, which is under the management of twelve trustees, resident in the town, elected by the freeholders, who have been lately incorporated, under the title of the "Town's Trust," or "Sheffield Free Tenants:" the income is applied to the maintenance of Lady's bridge, the keeping in order of Barker pool, the repair of the church and the highways, the payment of the stipendiary clergy, and other charitable and public uses.

This town appears to have been distinguished at a very early period for the manufacture of articles of cutlery, for which the numerous mines of coal and iron in the neighbourhood rendered its situation peculiarly favourable. Chaucer, in his Canterbury Tales, mentions the "Sheffield Thwytel, or Whittel," a kind of knife worn by such as had not the privilege of wearing a sword, for the making of which, as well as the iron heads for arrows, before the general use of fire-arms, Sheffield had, even at so early a period, become celebrated. From that time the principal articles manufactured were, implements of husbandry, including scythes, sickles, shears, and other sharp instruments of steel, till the middle of the last century, when considerable improvements were introduced, and great ingenuity displayed in the finer articles of cutlery. The superintendence of the trade was entrusted to twelve master cutlers, appointed at the court leet of the lord of the manor, with power to enforce the necessary regulations for its protection and improvement. In 1624, the

Seal of the Cutlers' Company.

cutlers were incorporated by an act of parliament entituled "an act for the good order and government of the makers of knives, scissors, shears, sickles, and other cutlery wares, in Hallamshire, in the county of York, and parts near adjoining;" and the government was invested in a master, two wardens, six searchers, and twenty-four assistants, consisting of freemen only, in number about six hundred. The master, who, with the other officers of the company, is chosen annually by the whole corporation, on retiring from office, nominates the senior warden as his successor, whom if rejected by the company, he nominates another member, till one is approved of by the body: the wardens are chosen by the officers of the company from among the searchers for the time being. The master, wardens, and assistants, have power to make by-laws for the regulation of the trade, and to inflict penalties for the neglect of them; and the jurisdiction of the company, which is restricted exclusively to affairs relating to the trade, extends throughout the whole district of Hallamshire, and all places within six miles of it. By an act obtained in 1814, permission is given to all persons, whether sons of freemen or not, and without their having served an apprenticeship, or obtained from the company a mark for their goods, to carry on business any where within the limits of Hallamshire. The privilege thus bestowed has been a great means of advancing the trade to its present state of perfection, by affording encouragement to men of genius from every part of the country to settle in this town; and the competition thus produced, has furnished exquisite specimens of workmanship in the finer branches of the trade, which abound in the show-rooms of the principal manufacturers, particularly in those of Messrs Rodgers and Sons, and excite the admiration of the spectator. The cutlery trade employs from eight to ten thousand persons. The principal articles are table knives and forks; pen and pocket knives of every description; scissors; razors; surgical, mathematical, and optical instruments; engineers' and joiners' tools; scythes, sickles, and files, of which great quantities are manufactured and exported; and an endless variety of steel wares, which may be considered the staple trade of the town, though various other branches of manufacture have been subsequently introduced and carried to a high degree of perfection.

Connected in some degree with the cutlery, but embracing a great variety of other objects, are ivory articles of every description; but the principal branches of manufacture which have more recently been established, and for which the town has obtained an unrivalled superiority, are spoons, tea and coffee pots, candlesticks, and a great variety of articles of Britannia metal, which are made in great quantities, and of every pattern; likewise silverplated goods of every kind, among which are dessert knives and forks plated upon steel, tureens, epernes, and services for the table, candelabras, ice-pails, urns, and a variety of similar articles, of the most elegant patterns, and of the richest workmanship, being generally known by the name of "Sheffield plate with silver edges." The manufacture of silver plate in all its branches, from the most minute to the most massive articles, is also carried on to a considerable extent, and has obtained deserved celebrity. The most ingenious and highly-finished specimens of cutlery displayed in the principal shops in the metropolis, and in those of the principal towns in England, notwithstanding their being stamped with the venders' names, are manufactured here, and so highly are the manufactures of this town esteemed, that they are found in every market in Europe, and exported in great quantities to every part of the globe. The making of buttons and button-moulds, wire-drawing, and the refining of silver, are also carried on; and along the banks of the rivers are numerous iron and steel works, in which the heavier castings are produced, and extensive works for slitting and preparing the iron and steel for the use of the manufacturers: among the manufactured iron goods are boilers for steam-engines, stove-grates (of most elegant design and exquisite workmanship), fenders, fire-irons, and various smaller articles. There are also extensive factories for the weaving of carpets, and of horse-hair seating for chairs. In 1806, a type-foundry was established with considerable success; and another was commenced in 1818, the proprietors having purchased the business of a house in London: both these establishments are now considerable, and supply type not only to printers in the provincial towns, but to several highly respectable houses in the metropolis. The trade of the town is greatly facilitated by its advantageous line of inland navigation. The river Don was, in 1751, made navigable to Tinsley, about three miles from the town; and in 1815, a bill was obtained for enabling the proprietors of the Sheffield canal to connect the Don, at Tinsley, with the town, by means of a navigable cut, which was accomplished in 1819, forming a direct communication with the German sea. Adjoining the basin of this canal, at the eastern extremity of the town, is a commodious wharf, where vessels can load and unload under cover, and spacious warehouses and offices for the transaction of business. The basin is capable of containing more than forty vessels of about fifty tons' burden, which arrive here from Hull, York, Gainsborough, Manchester, Leeds, Liverpool, and Thorn, at which last place, vessels from London generally unload goods intended for Sheffield. The market was granted, in 1296, to Thomas, Lord Furnival; the market days are Tuesday and Saturday: the former, chiefly for corn, is held in the corn exchange, a handsome building, erected under an act of parliament obtained, in 1827, by the Duke of Norfolk, on the site of the Shrewsbury hospital, which has been removed. The market for butchers' meat is held in a convenient situation near Newmarket-street, at the end of which is the market for eggs, poultry, and butter: the vegetable market is on the outside of the enclosure for the butchers' meat, and consists of ranges of shops; the fruit market is held on the south side of Newmarket-street; and the fish market, in King-street, is well supplied with salt-water fish on Monday and Thursday, and with fresh-water fish every day during the season. The fairs are on the Tuesday in Trinity week and November 28th, for cattle and toys; and

a cheese fair, held at the same time with the latter, has been established within the last few years, in which are sold many hundred tons of cheese from the counties of Derby, Stafford, Chester, and Lancaster. The town is within the jurisdiction of the magistrates for the district, who meet in the town hall every Tuesday and Friday, for the determination of petty causes: the October sessions for the West riding are also held here. A court is held every third week, under the steward of the manor of Eccleshall, for the recovery of debts under £5; and a court of requests every Thursday, under commissioners appointed by an act passed in the 48th of George III., for the recovery of debts not exceeding £5, of which the jurisdiction extends for several miles round the parish. The town hall, a spacious and commodious building of plain architecture, with a cupola, was erected in 1808, at the foot of the hay market, on the site of an old building, which was taken down: it contains a large and well-arranged room in which the sessions are held, and apartments for the use of the police magistrates, the commissioners of the court of requests, and for the transaction of public business; on the ground-floor is a prison for felons within the liberty of Hallamshire, with apartments for the keeper. The Cutlers' Hall, in Church-street, in which the business of that company is transacted, and their public meetings held, was erected in 1726: it is a neat and capacious stone building, ornamented with the arms of the company well sculptured, and contains three large rooms in front for the transaction of business, and other offices; on the second floor is a spacious dining-room, elegantly fitted up, and ornamented with several well-executed portraits. In addition to an excise-office and post-office, there is also an assay-office, erected in 1773, in order to relieve the manufacturers from sending their silver goods to London to receive the Hall mark.

The living is a vicarage, in the archdeaconry and diocese of York, rated in the king's books at £12. 15. 2½., and in the alternate patronage of Marmaduke Lawson, Esq., and Philip Gell, Esq., as representatives of Robert and William Swyft, Esqrs., to whom the advowson was granted in the reign of Henry VIII.; the latter of those gentlemen presented in 1805. Three stipendiary clergymen, who are independent of the vicar, are appointed to assist him by twelve burgesses of the town and parish, incorporated by charter of Queen Mary, who hold certain lands and estates in trust, for the payment of the stipendiary assistants, and for the repairs of the church: they are called the "Twelve Capital Burgesses," and hold their meetings in a room over the vestry-room of the church, vacancies in their number being filled up by vote among themselves. The church, erected in the reign of Henry I., and dedicated to St. Peter, is a spacious cruciform structure, with a central tower and spire, most probably in the Norman style of architecture; but it has been so altered by repairs, that, with the exception of part of the tower and spire, and a few small portions of the inte-

Seal of the Twelve Capital Burgesses.

rior, very little of its original character can be distinguished. The chancel contains the first production from the chisel of Chantrey, a mural tablet, with the bust of the Rev. James Wilkinson, late vicar, canopied with drapery, in Carora marble, erected at the public expense, as a tribute of respect to his memory. Many illustrious persons have been interred in this church, among whom were Mary, Countess of Northumberland ; Elizabeth, Countess of Lennox, mother of the unfortunate Lady Arabella Stuart ; Lady Elizabeth Butler ; four of the Earls of Shrewsbury ; and Peter Roflet, French secretary of Mary, Queen of Scots. St. Paul's, a chapel of ease to the vicarage, was erected in 1720, by subscription, towards which Mr. R. Downes, silversmith, contributed £1000 : it is a handsome edifice in the Grecian style of architecture, with a tower surmounted by a well-proportioned dome, and a cupola of cast-iron ; the interior is light, and elegantly ornamented, and contains a bust by Chantrey of the Rev. Alexander Mackenzie, with emblematical sculpture finely executed. St. James', also a chapel of ease to the vicarage, a neat structure in the Grecian style of architecture, with a campanile turret, was erected by subscription in 1788 : the interior is well arranged, and the east window is embellished with a beautiful painting of the Crucifixion, by Peckett. St. George's church, on an eminence at the western extremity of the town, containing two thousand and three sittings, of which one thousand and eleven are free, erected, in 1824, by grant from the parliamentary commissioners, at an expense of £15,129. 9. is a very handsome structure, in the later style of English architecture, with a lofty square embattled tower, crowned with pinnacles : the living is a perpetual curacy, in the patronage of the Vicar. St. Philip's church, near the infirmary, containing two thousand sittings, of which seven hundred and fifty-five are free, was erected, in 1827, by grant from the parliamentary commissioners, at an expense of £13,970. 16.: it is a neat edifice, in the later English style of architecture, with a square embattled tower, crowned with pinnacles: the living is a perpetual curacy, in the patronage of the Vicar. St. Mary's church, of which the first stone was laid by the Countess of Surrey, in 1826, is a handsome structure in the later style of English architecture, with a tower, and a porch of beautiful design : it was erected by grant from the parliamentary commissioners, at an expense of £13,946. 11. 9., and contains one thousand nine hundred and ninety-two sittings, of which seven hundred and forty are free : the site, and the cemetery, were given by His Grace the Duke of Norfolk : the living is a perpetual curacy, in the patronage of the Vicar. There are also other churches in the townships belonging to the parish, which are noticed under their proper heads. There are five places of worship for Independents, four for Wesleyan Methodists, and one each for Baptists, the Society of Friends, Unitarians, and Roman Catholics.

The free grammar school was founded by letters patent in the reign of James I., and endowed by Thomas Smith, of Crowland, in the county of Lincoln, with lands producing, in 1603, £30 per annum, which have been since exchanged for lands at Wadsley, producing, together with subsequent benefactions, a revenue of £175. 10. : the school is under the control of the vicar and twelve inhabitants of the town, who appoint

the master, with a salary of £60 per annum : there are at present about twenty scholars on the foundation, who are gratuitously instructed in the classics. The boys' charity school, at the north-east corner of the churchyard, was established in 1706, and the present school-house, a neat and commodious edifice of stone, has been recently erected on the site of the original building : it has an income arising from a benefaction of £5000 by Mr. Parkins, in 1766, aided by a donation from Mr. T. Hanby, which maintains six boys on the establishment, at an expense of upwards of £60 per annum, the past masters of the Cutlers' Company being his principal trustees : the whole revenue is about £284 per annum, with which, and annual subscriptions, eighty boys are maintained, clothed, educated, and apprenticed. At the opposite corner of the churchyard is a similar school, in which sixty girls are maintained, clothed, and educated, and afterwards placed out in service : a convenient school-house was erected, in 1786, at an expense of £1500. A school for reading, writing, and arithmetic, has also been established here, in pursuance of the will of Mr. William Birley, who, in 1715, bequeathed £900 in trust for the purchase of an estate, of the rental of which, one-third was to be appropriated to the establishment of the school, one-third towards the maintenance of indigent tradesmen, or their widows, and the remainder towards the support of a minister to officiate in the chapel of the hospital. The school of industry was established in 1795, and removed to its present situation in 1815 : the buildings, which are upon an extensive scale, and well adapted to their use, were erected by subscription : there are three hundred and fifty children in this establishment. A Lancasterian school for boys, established in 1809, and a similar institution for girls, established in 1815, are supported by subscription. National schools for children of both sexes are maintained in connexion with the National Society, and there are numerous Sunday schools.

The Earl of Shrewsbury's hospital was projected by Gilbert, Earl of Shrewsbury, in 1616, and completed, in pursuance of his will, by the Earl of Norfolk, Earl Marshal of England, and the buildings erected in 1673 : it is amply endowed for eighteen men and eighteen women, who have each a comfortable dwelling, ten shillings per week for each man, and eight shillings for each woman, and an allowance of coal, coats, and a gown, annually : the original buildings were recently taken down to make room for the market-place, and the erection of the corn exchange, and a neat range of buildings, in the later style of English architecture, has been erected on the southern side of the town, in the centre of which is a chapel. Hollis' hospital was founded, in 1703, by Mr. Thomas Hollis, a native of the town, who, with others of his descendants, endowed it for sixteen aged women, widows of cutlers, or of persons connected with the trade, who receive each seven shillings per week, an annual allowance of coal, and a gown once in two years : a part of the funds is also applied to the support of a school. The general infirmary was first opened for the reception of patients in 1797, and, in a manufacturing town, where so many artisans are continually exposed to accidents, and their health materially injured by the processes of many of the trades in which they are employed, has been deserv-

H

edly regarded as an object entitled to the most liberal patronage and support. The premises, occupying an extensive site about a mile to the north-west of the town, and guarded against the too near approach of other buildings by the purchase of thirty-one acres of surrounding land, were erected by public subscription, at an expense of nearly £20,000, including the purchase of the land: they are handsomely built of stone, and form a conspicuous ornament in the principal approaches to the town. In front of the building is a neat portico, ornamented with statues of Hope and Charity, finely sculptured, and the grounds are enclosed by an iron palisade, with a central gateway, and a porter's lodge on each side. The internal arrangements are extensive and complete, and the institution is supported by an income arising from donations and bequests, and by annual subscription. Among the principal benefactions are, £200 by the Rev. James Wilkinson, late vicar; £200 by Dr. Browne, under whose auspices the establishment was materially promoted; £1000 by Mrs. Fell, of Newhall; a donation of £2000, and a subsequent legacy of £500, by Francis H. Sitwell, Esq.; and £6337. 2. 10. bequeathed by the late Rev. Thomas Gisborne, who also gave like sums to the infirmaries of Nottingham and Derby.

Several extensive charitable benefactions have been made for the benefit of the inhabitants. Mr. Thomas Hanby left £8000, of which the interest of £3000 was for the benefit of the boys' charity school, and that of the remaining £5000 for distribution among the poor and creditable housekeepers, members of the church of England, and not under fifty years of age, two-thirds of the number to be men, and one-third women: the nomination is in the Master and Wardens of the Cutlers' Company, the past masters, the vicar and churchwardens, and the Town's Trust. Mrs. Eliza Parkins bequeathed £10,000, one-half of which is appropriated to the support of the boys' charity school, and the interest of the remainder divided annually among such poor persons as the vicar, the three assistant ministers, and the churchwardens, shall select. Mrs. Mary Parsons bequeathed £1500 to be invested in the funds, and the proceeds annually divided among forty-eight aged and infirm silver-platers; Mr. John Kirby left £400, the interest of which is annually divided between two poor widows; and Mr. Joseph Hudson, of London, gave £200 in trust to the Cutlers' Company, to divide the proceeds annually among sixteen of the most needy file-makers: there are also various other charitable bequests for distribution among the indigent; a humane society for recovering persons apparently drowned; a society for ameliorating the condition of the poor, and various others. The neighbourhood, which is rich in mines of iron and coal, abounds also with quarries of excellent stone, some of which, especially that at Grimsthorpe, contain many admirable specimens of calamites; and the coal shale and iron-stone have beautiful impressions of various vegetable productions. On Spital Hill, near the town, was an hospital, founded in the reign of Henry II., by William de Lovetot, and dedicated to St. Leonard, of which there is no vestige; and of the ancient manor-house, in which Cardinal Wolsey and Mary Queen of Scots were confined, the ruins can but faintly be traced. In 1761, two thin plates of copper were ploughed up on a piece of land, called the Lawns, each

containing an inscription commemorating the manumission of some Roman legionaries, and their enrolment as citizens of Rome. From the prevalence of iron-ore, the waters of Sheffield have a slight chalybeate property. The Rev. Dr. Robert Saunderson, Regius Professor of Divinity in the University of Oxford, and Bishop of Lincoln; the Rev. Mr. Balguay, Prebendary of North Grantham in the Cathedral Church of Salisbury, and an eminent disputant in the Bangorian controversy, were natives of this place: and Chantrey, the celebrated sculptor, was born at Norton, a village about three miles from the town. Sheffield gives the titles of baron and earl to the family of Holroyd.

SHEFFORD, a chapelry (formerly a market town) in the parish of CAMPTON, hundred of CLIFTON, county of BEDFORD, 9½ miles (S. E. by S.) from Bedford, containing 618 inhabitants. The chapel, dedicated to St. Michael, has lately received an addition of two hundred and two free sittings, the Incorporated Society for the enlargement of churches and chapels having granted £250 towards defraying the expense. The market, which was on Friday, has been discontinued. The river Ivel has been rendered navigable to Biggleswade, by the assistance of a canal recently cut. Robert Bloomfield, the poet, died here in 1823.

SHEFFORD (EAST), a parish in the hundred of KINTBURY-EAGLE, county of BERKS, 5¾ miles (N.E.) from Hungerford, containing 59 inhabitants. The living is a rectory, in the archdeaconry of Berks, and diocese of Salisbury, rated in the king's books at £9. 11. 3., and in the patronage of the Rev. C. B. Coxe. This parish is entitled to send children to the school founded by Lady Frances Winchcombe at Thatcham.

SHEFFORD (WEST), a parish in the hundred of KINTBURY-EAGLE, county of BERKS, 5½ miles (N.E. by N.) from Hungerford, containing 490 inhabitants. The living is a rectory, in the archdeaconry of Berks, and diocese of Salisbury, rated in the king's books at £14. 3. 4., and in the patronage of the Principal and Fellows of Brasenose College, Oxford. The church, dedicated to St. Mary, is principally in the Norman style, with a circular tower at the west end. Near the north door is a niche enriched with pinnacles, &c., and the font is richly and curiously carved with foliage. There is a place of worship for Wesleyan Methodists. This parish is entitled to send one boy to the school founded by W. Saunders at Chaddleworth. Charles I. took up his quarters here on the 19th of November, 1644.

SHEINTON, a parish in the hundred of STOTTESDEN, though locally in that of Condover, county of SALOP, 3½ miles (N. by W.) from Much Wenlock, containing 182 inhabitants. The living is a discharged rectory, in the archdeaconry of Salop, and diocese of Lichfield and Coventry, rated in the king's books at £6. 9. 2., endowed with £200 private benefaction, and £200 royal bounty, and in the patronage of W. Hill, Esq. The church is dedicated to St. Peter and St. Paul. The parish is bounded on the north by the river Severn.

SHELDING, a township in that part of the parish of RIPON which is in the lower division of the wapentake of CLARO, West riding of the county of YORK, 6¼ miles (W. by S.) from Ripon, containing 56 inhabitants.

SHELDON, a chapelry in the parish of BAKEWELL, hundred of HIGH PEAK, county of DERBY, 3 miles (W.)

from Bakewell, containing 143 inhabitants. The living is a perpetual curacy, in the peculiar jurisdiction of the Dean and Chapter of Lichfield, endowed with £200 private benefaction, £600 royal bounty, and £200 parliamentary grant, and in the patronage of the Vicar of Bakewell. The chapel is dedicated to All Saints. There are lead mines in the neighbourhood. Mary Frost, in 1756, gave £200 for apprenticing poor boys. Sheldon is in the honour of Tutbury, duchy of Lancaster, and within the jurisdiction of a court of pleas held at Chapel en le Frith, for the recovery of debts under 40s.

SHELDON, a parish in the hundred of HAYRIDGE, county of DEVON, 7 miles (E. by N.) from Cullompton, containing 186 inhabitants. The living is a perpetual curacy, in the archdeaconry and diocese of Exeter, endowed with £600 private benefaction, and £800 royal bounty, and in the patronage of John R. Drewe, Esq, The church is dedicated to St. James.

SHELDON, a parish in the Birmingham division of the hundred of HEMLINGFORD, county of WARWICK, 4¾ miles (S. W.) from Coleshill, containing 423 inhabitants. The living is a rectory, in the archdeaconry of Coventry, and diocese of Lichfield and Coventry, rated in the king's books at £8. 10. 10., and in the patronage of Earl Digby. The church, dedicated to St. Giles, is principally in the decorated style, with a fine tower of later architecture.

SHELDWICK, a parish in the hundred of FAVERSHAM, lathe of SCRAY, county of KENT, 2¼ miles (S. by W.) from Faversham, containing 545 inhabitants. The living is a discharged vicarage, in the archdeaconry and diocese of Canterbury, rated in the king's books at £6. 16. 8., and in the patronage of the Dean and Chapter of Canterbury. The church, dedicated to St. James, is principally in the decorated style of English architecture.

SHELF, a township in the parish of HALIFAX, wapentake of MORLEY, West riding of the county of YORK, 3½ miles (N. E. by N.) from Halifax, containing 1998 inhabitants. There is a place of worship for Primitive Methodists. A Lancasterian school has been established for children of all persuasions.

SHELFANGER, a parish in the hundred of DISS, county of NORFOLK, 2¼ miles (N. by W.) from Diss, containing 440 inhabitants. The living is a rectory, in the archdeaconry of Norfolk, and diocese of Norwich, rated in the king's books at £17, and in the patronage of the Duke of Norfolk. The church is dedicated to All Saints. There is a place of worship for Baptists.

SHELFORD, a parish in the southern division of the wapentake of BINGHAM, county of NOTTINGHAM, 8 miles (E. N. E.) from Nottingham, containing, with the township of Saxondale, and part of that of Newton, 671 inhabitants. The living is a perpetual curacy, in the archdeaconry of Nottingham, and diocese of York, endowed with £200 private benefaction, and £300 parliamentary grant, and in the patronage of the Earl of Chesterfield. The church, dedicated to St. Peter and St. Paul, is the burial-place of the noble family of Stanhope, and contains the remains of Philip, the accomplished Earl of Chesterfield, who died in 1773. This parish forms part of the vale of Trent, which river bounds it on the west and north, and the Fosse-road touches its south-eastern boundary. It is in the honour of Tutbury, duchy of Lancas-

ter, and within the jurisdiction of a court of pleas held at Tutbury every third Tuesday, for the recovery of debts under 40s. A priory, in honour of the blessed Virgin Mary, was founded here, in the time of Henry II., by Ralph Hanselyn, which, at the dissolution, had a revenue of £151. 14. 1. An hospital, called the Bede Houses, was founded and endowed, in 1694, by Sir William Stanhope, for the reception and support of six of his decayed tenants, but the number has been reduced to four. The manor-house was garrisoned by Col. Stanhope and most of his men were slain.

SHELFORD (GREAT), a parish in the hundred of THRIPLOW, county of CAMBRIDGE, 4½ miles (S. by E.) from Cambridge, containing 718 inhabitants. The living is a discharged vicarage, in the peculiar jurisdiction and patronage of the Bishop of Ely, rated in the king's books at £13. 6. 8., endowed with £600 royal bounty, and £1600 parliamentary grant. The church, dedicated to St. Mary, is said to have been built by Bishop Fordham, who died in 1425; the steeple was blown down by the great storm of 1703, and again, in 1798; it has since been rebuilt by subscription.

SHELFORD (LITTLE), a parish in the hundred of THRIPLOW, county of CAMBRIDGE, 5 miles (S. by E.) from Cambridge, containing 438 inhabitants. The living is a rectory, in the archdeaconry and diocese of Ely, rated in the king's books at £15. 9. 7. The Rev. H. Finch was patron in 1806. The church is dedicated to All Saints. There is a place of worship for Independents. Near the bridge over the Cam, which separates Great and Little Shelford, stood anciently a hermitage.

SHELL, a hamlet in the parish of HIMBLETON, middle division of the hundred of OSWALDSLOW, county of WORCESTER, containing 45 inhabitants.

SHELLAND, a parish in the hundred of STOW, county of SUFFOLK, 3½ miles (W. N.W.) from Stow-Market, containing 104 inhabitants. The living is a perpetual curacy, in the archdeaconry of Sudbury, and diocese of Norwich.

SHELLEY, a parish in the hundred of ONGAR, county of ESSEX, 1½ mile (N.) from Chipping-Ongar, containing 179 inhabitants. The living is a rectory, in the archdeaconry of Essex, and diocese of London, rated in the king's books at £9. 15. J. Tomlinson, Esq. was patron in 1812. The church is dedicated to St. Peter.

SHELLEY, a parish in the hundred of SAMFORD, county of SUFFOLK, 2¼ miles (S.) from Hadleigh, containing 130 inhabitants. The living is a perpetual curacy, in the archdeaconry of Suffolk, and diocese of Norwich, endowed with £16 per annum and £200 private benefaction, and £800 royal bounty, and in the patronage of Sir W. B. Rush, Knt. The church is dedicated to All Saints.

SHELLEY, a township in the parish of KIRK-BURTON, upper division of the wapentake of AGBRIGG, West riding of the county of YORK, 6 miles (S. E.) from Huddersfield, containing 1329 inhabitants. There are places of worship for Independents and Wesleyan Methodists.

SHELLOW-BOWELS, a parish in the hundred of DUNMOW, county of ESSEX, 6¼ miles (N. E.) from Chipping-Ongar, containing 114 inhabitants. The living is

H 2

a discharged rectory, consolidated with that of Willingale-Doe, in the jurisdiction of the Commissary of Essex and Herts, concurrently with the Consistorial Court of the Bishop of London, rated in the king's books at £7. 13. 4. The church is dedicated to St. Peter and St. Paul.

SHELSLEY (KING'S), a hamlet in that part of the parish of SHELSLEY-BEAUCHAMP which is in the upper division of the hundred of DODDINGTREE, county of WORCESTER, 9½ miles (S. W. by W.) from Stourport, containing 264 inhabitants.

SHELSLEY-BEAUCHAMP, a parish partly in the lower, and partly in the upper, division of the hundred of DODDINGTREE, county of WORCESTER, 8¼ miles (S. W.) from Stourport, containing 546 inhabitants. The living is a rectory, in the archdeaconry and diocese of Worcester, rated in the king's books at £9. 4. 4½., and in the patronage of Lord Foley. The church is dedicated to All Saints. Caleb Avenant, in 1723, gave certain land in support of a school.

SHELSLEY-WALSH, a parish in the upper division of the hundred of DODDINGTREE, county of WORCESTER, 9 miles (S. W.) from Stourport, containing 57 inhabitants. The living is a discharged rectory, in the archdeaconry and diocese of Worcester, rated in the king's books at £3. 8. 9., and in the patronage of Lord Foley. The church is dedicated to St. Andrew.

SHELSWELL, a parish in the hundred of PLOUGHLEY, county of OXFORD, 6 miles (N. N. E.) from Bicester, containing 51 inhabitants. The living is a rectory, annexed to that of Newton-Purcell, in the archdeaconry and diocese of Oxford, rated in the king's books at £4. The church, which was dedicated to St. Ebbe, has been long desecrated.

SHELTON, a parish in the hundred of STODDEN, county of BEDFORD, 4 miles (W. by N.) from Kimbolton, containing 129 inhabitants. The living is a rectory, in the archdeaconry of Bedford, and diocese of Lincoln, rated in the king's books at £13, and in the patronage of Lord St. John. The church is dedicated to St. Mary. This parish has the privilege of sending five boys to the free school which was founded, in 1702, by Joseph Neale, in the adjoining parish of Nether Dean.

SHELTON, a parish in the hundred of DEPWADE, county of NORFOLK, 2½ miles (S. E. by S.) from St. Mary Stratton, containing 236 inhabitants. The living is a rectory, with that of Hardwick annexed, in the archdeaconry of Norfolk, and diocese of Norwich, rated in the king's books at £8, and in the patronage of the King, by reason of lunacy. The church dedicated to St. Mary, was built by Sir Ralph Shelton, who also erected the manor-house, now in ruins : it was a spacious castellated structure, with a chapel attached, encompassed by an embattled wall and a moat.

SHELTON, a parish in the southern division of the wapentake of NEWARK, county of NOTTINGHAM, 6½ miles (S. by W.) from Newark, containing 105 inhabitants. The living is a rectory, in the archdeaconry of Nottingham, and diocese of York, rated in the king's books at £6. 14. 4½. The Rev. J. J. Maltby was patron in 1814. The church is dedicated to St. Mary.

SHELTON, a chapelry in the parish of STOKE upon TRENT, northern division of the hundred of PIREHILL, county of STAFFORD, 2 miles (E. N. E.) from New-castle under Lyne, containing, with Etruria, and part of Cobridge, 7325 inhabitants. This, like many other places in this part of the county, has risen from the extensive potteries carried on in the vicinity, and consists chiefly of the houses of the proprietors, which are handsome buildings, and of the dwellings of the numerous workmen. The village is amply supplied with water, and is paved with brick, and lighted with gas, under the superintendence of commissioners appointed under an act of parliament obtained in 1815, and amended in 1828, for its regulation and improvement. A mechanics' institution was established in 1826, under the patronage of the Marquis of Stafford, Josiah Wedgwood, Esq., and others ; lectures are delivered in a spacious and commodious room over the British and Foreign school-rooms, in which also concerts, generally for the benefit of some charitable institution, take place occasionally, and the public meetings of the inhabitants are held. Races have been recently established in the neighbourhood, and are generally well attended. The principal articles of manufacture are, porcelain, china, and earthenware, for which there are thirty-four factories, affording employment to more than two thousand five hundred men, women, and children. The works are on the bank of the Trent and Mersey canal, which passes through the village, and affords great facility for the transport of goods, which are sent in great quantities to the London market, and to the principal towns in England : there are also convenient wharfs on its banks, and extensive gas-works have been erected. The regulation of the police, like that of the adjoining township of Hanley, is under the superintendence of the commissioners appointed under the act, and all public meetings of the inhabitants are convened by the chief bailiff of that township, in which the public market for both townships is held. Shelton is in the honour of Tutbury, duchy of Lancaster, and within the jurisdiction of a court of pleas held at Tutbury every third Tuesday, for the recovery of debts under 40s.

This chapelry is, by act of parliament passed in 1827, for the further endowment of the living, about to be erected into a parish and district rectory, and a new church is at present being built by grant from the parliamentary commissioners. There are places of worship for Baptists, Independents, Wesleyan Methodists of the Old and New Connexions, and Unitarians. The British and Foreign school, in which more than six hundred children are instructed, was established in 1821, and is supported by subscription ; and there are also Sunday schools in connexion with the established church, and the various dissenting congregations, in which several thousand children are instructed. In the immediate vicinity is the North Staffordshire Infirmary, a noble institution, of extensive public utility, forming a valuable school of medicine, and a source of incalculable benefit to the population of this large manufacturing district. Elijah Fenton, the poet, was born and resided in a house in the village, which is still existing ; he was buried in the parish church of Stoke upon Trent, where a monument has been erected to his memory. In this township are the Potteries, and the beautiful villa of Etruria, erected by the late Josiah Wedgwood, Esq., the former a considerable hamlet, and the latter remarkable for the beauty of its situation and style of architecture, and for the many splendid Etruscan vases with which it is ornamented : these elegant specimens of art, produced under his own superintendence, are imitations of the original vases found in Italy, to the discovery of which that gentleman was chiefly indebted for the elegance of form, and purity of taste, which he has introduced into the manufacture of porcelain, china, and stone ware, for which this place is so deservedly celebrated, and which, by the use of flint in the composition of these articles, also introduced by Mr. Wedgwood, has been progressively brought to its present state of perfection.

SHELVE, a parish in the hundred of CHIRBURY, county of SALOP, 7¾ miles (N. by E.) from Bishop's Castle, containing 55 inhabitants. The living is a discharged rectory, in the archdeaconry of Salop, and diocese of Hereford, rated in the king's books at £2. 13. 4., endowed with £600 royal bounty, and in the patronage of Robert Bridgeman More, Esq. The church is dedicated to All Saints. Here are numerous veins of lead-ore, which is considered to vie in richness with any in England : one of the mines was worked by the Romans in the time of Adrian, as is evident from an inscription on a pig of lead found in the vicinity. A market on Friday, and a fair on the festival of the Invention of the Cross, were granted by Henry III.

SHELWICK, a township in the parish of HOLMER, hundred of GRIMSWORTH, county of HEREFORD, 2¼ miles (N. E. by N.) from Hereford. The population is returned with the parish.

SHENFIELD, a parish in the hundred of BARSTABLE, county of ESSEX, 1 mile (N. E. by N.) from Brentwood, containing 619 inhabitants. The living is a rectory, in the archdeaconry of Essex, and diocese of London, rated in the king's books at £14. 18. 4., and in the patronage of the Countess de Grey. The church is dedicated to St. Mary.

SHENINGTON, a parish in the upper division of the hundred of TEWKESBURY, county of GLOUCESTER, 6 miles (W. N. W.) from Banbury, containing 381 inhabitants. The living is a rectory, in the archdeaconry and diocese of Gloucester, rated in the king's books at £15. 3. 4. Robert Dent, Esq. and others were patrons in 1801. The church, dedicated to the Holy Trinity, has lately received an addition of one hundred and thirteen sittings, of which ninety are free, the Incorporated Society for the enlargement of churches and chapels having granted £60 towards defraying the expense.

SHENLEY, a parish in the hundred of DACORUM, county of HERTFORD, 6 miles (N. W.) from Chipping-Barnet, containing 1132 inhabitants. The living is a rectory, in the archdeaconry of Huntingdon, and diocese of Lincoln, rated in the king's books at £16. 8. 1½. The Rev. T. Newcome was patron in 1801. The church, dedicated to St. Botolph, is built with flints, and has a wooden tower on the south side. A chapel is supposed to have formerly stood on a moated site in the park belonging to the house called Colney Chapel.

SHENLEY, a parish comprising the hamlet of Brook-End in the hundred of COTTESLOE, and the township of Church-End in that of NEWPORT, county of BUCKINGHAM, 3½ miles (N. W. by W.) from Fenny-Stratford, and containing 449 inhabitants. The living is a rectory, in the archdeaconry of Buckingham, and diocese of Lincoln, rated in the king's books at £22. 9. 7., and in the patronage of the Rev. P. Knapp.

The church is dedicated to St. Mary. An almshouse was founded here by Thomas Stafford, Esq., with an endowment of £35 per annum, for four men and two women, each of whom receives a small weekly stipend, and an annual allowance for clothing.

SHENSTONE, a parish in the southern division of the hundred of OFFLOW, county of STAFFORD, 3½ miles (S. by W.) from Lichfield, containing 1699 inhabitants. The living is a discharged vicarage, in the archdeaconry of Stafford, and diocese of Lichfield and Coventry, rated in the king's books at £6. 5. 8., endowed with £200 private benefaction, and £200 royal bounty, and in the patronage of Sir Robert Peel, Bart. The church, dedicated to St. John the Baptist, exhibits specimens of the various styles of English architecture. There is a chapel of ease at Upper Stonnal. An unknown benefactor gave £27 towards building a school-room, for the support of which there is a trifling endowment. There was once a castle, or fortification, at Upper Stonnal, of which only the remembrance is preserved in the name of Castle field. A fair for cattle is held on the last Monday in February.

SHENTON, a chapelry in the parish of MARKET-BOSWORTH, hundred of SPARKENHOE, county of LEICESTER, 2½ miles (S. W. by S.) from Market-Bosworth, containing 194 inhabitants. The Ashby de la Zouch canal crosses the north-eastern angle of the chapelry.

SHEPHALL, a parish in the hundred of CASHIO, or liberty of ST. ALBANS, county of HERTFORD, 2¼ miles (S. E. by S.) from Stevenage, containing 187 inhabitants. The living is a vicarage, in the archdeaconry of St. Albans, and diocese of London, rated in the king's books at £9. 5. 10., and in the patronage of the Crown. The church is dedicated to St. Mary.

SHEPLEY, a township in the parish of KIRK-BURTON, upper division of the wapentake of AGBRIGG, West riding of the county of YORK, 7 miles (S. E. by S.) from Huddersfield, containing 1000 inhabitants.

SHEPPERTON, a parish in the hundred of SPELTHORNE, county of MIDDLESEX, 2¼ miles (E. by S.) from Chertsey, containing 782 inhabitants. The living is a rectory, in the archdeaconry of Middlesex, and diocese of London, rated in the king's books at £26. S. H. Russell, Esq. was patron in 1817. The church is dedicated to St. Nicholas.

SHEPRETH, a parish in the hundred of WETHERLEY, county of CAMBRIDGE, 5¾ miles (N. by W.) from Royston, containing 320 inhabitants. The living is a discharged vicarage, in the archdeaconry and diocese of Ely, rated in the king's books at £6. 11. 1., and in the patronage of Hale Wortham, Esq. The church is dedicated to All Saints. The river Cam runs through the parish.

SHEPSCOM, a chapelry in the parish of PAINSWICK, hundred of BISLEY, county of GLOUCESTER, 2 miles (E. by N.) from Painswick, containing 725 inhabitants. The living is a perpetual curacy, in the archdeaconry and diocese of Gloucester, endowed with £1800 parliamentary grant, and in the patronage of the Vicar of Painswick. The chapel has lately received an addition of sixty free sittings, the Incorporated Society for the enlargement of churches and chapels having granted £60 towards defraying the expense.

SHEPTON-BEAUCHAMP, a parish in the southern division of the hundred of PETHERTON, county of

SOMERSET, 3¾ miles (N. E. by E.) from Ilminster, containing 567 inhabitants. The living is a rectory, in the archdeaconry of Taunton, and diocese of Bath and Wells, rated in the king's books at £14. 8. 11½., and in the patronage of Robert Dent, Esq. and others. The church is dedicated to St. Michael. The poor children of this parish are instructed for £12. 12. a year, arising from the rent of certain land bequeathed by Thomas Rich, in 1723, and from £200, the gift of Elizabeth Morgan, in 1763.

SHEPTON-MALLET, a market town and parish in the hundred of WHITESTONE, county of SOMERSET, 14 miles (N. E.) from Somerton, and 125 (W. by S.) from London, containing 5021 inhabitants. The origin of this town is not comparatively of very remote antiquity, the charter for its market having been granted by Edward II., in the 11th year of his reign. The manor, at the time of the Norman survey, was subordinate to that of Pilton, which had been granted by King Ina to the abbot of Glaston; and its pastures, from the sheep fed on which it is supposed to derive its name, are noticed in that work; the additional and distinguishing appellation having been received from the Barons Mallet, lords of Shepton in the reigns of Henry I. and II. The consequences of the Duke of Monmouth's rebellion were severely felt in this part; thirteen persons of the town, having been convicted at the "bloody western assizes," suffered here for their participation in it. The town is situated chiefly on the southern bank of a deep valley, and consists of a number of streets and lanes, the principal of which, crossing the valley from north to south, is spacious and well built, paved, and lighted with oil, but the others are mostly narrow and irregular: the recent erection of a bridge, and the opening of a new road, have materially improved the town. It is well supplied with water, and a stream runs through the bottom of the valley, turning several mills in its course. The manufacture of woollen goods, silk, lace, stockings, sail-cloth, and hair-seating, is carried on to a considerable extent, and affords employment to a great number of persons. The parish comprises a portion of the Mendip range of hills, prior to the enclosure of which lead-ore was obtained in it. The market days are Tuesday and Friday, the latter a very large one for all kinds of agricultural produce. The market cross, erected by Walter and Agnes Buckland, in 1500, is a fine old structure: it originally consisted of five arches, but it has lately undergone a thorough renovation (funds having been left to keep it in repair by the founders), and a sixth arch has been added in the centre: elevated above two rows of steps is an hexagonal pillar, supporting a flat roof, surmounted by a pyramidal spire, and ornamented with niches. The fairs are on Easter-Monday, 18th of June, and 8th of August. The management of the local affairs is vested in a high constable and subordinate officers, who are chosen at a court leet held annually in October, by the householders generally; and a court for the recovery of debts under £2 has been held here from time immemorial.

The living is a rectory, in the archdeaconry of Wells, and diocese of Bath and Wells, rated in the king's books at £33. 12. 1., and in the alternate patronage of the King, as Duke of Cornwall, and the Rev. Provis Wickham. The church, dedicated to St. Peter and St. Paul, is a venerable cruciform pile of building, to which are attached two small chapels; the roof of the nave is curiously wrought, and the pulpit and font, which are of stone, are much admired: it contains some ancient monuments. There are places of worship for Baptists, Independents, Wesleyan Methodists, and Roman Catholics. The nuns of the order of the Visitation have a convent here, which is the only one of that order in the kingdom; its inmates are about thirty in number. The free school, founded by Sir George Strode and others, in 1639, is endowed with property at present producing about £75 per annum, principally arising from the rectorial tithes of the parish of Meare, subject to the master's keeping the school-house, and the chancel of the parish church of Meare, in repair, and paying a crown-rent of £10. 18. per annum to the Earl of Radnor, for the rectory of Meare: the present master has had no scholar on the foundation. Four poor boys are educated, and an apprentice fee of £7 given with each, by means of a charity founded by Mr. John Curtis, in 1730, now producing about £20 per annum; and sixteen poor girls are clothed and educated from the produce of a bequest made by Mrs. Mary Gapper, in 1783, now amounting to £27 per annum. Almshouses for four poor men were founded and endowed, in 1699, by Mr. Edward Strode, with property now yielding about £360 per annum, of which amount about £80 per annum is appropriated to the repairs of the almshouses, and allowances to the inmates, and about £200 to the purchase of bread for weekly distribution among the poor of the parish, for whose benefit there are several other smaller benefactions. The county bridewell, or house of correction, is in this town: it has been materially enlarged of late years, and is capable of receiving from two to three hundred prisoners; it comprises fourteen wards, fifteen day-rooms, and thirty-one cells, besides workshops and tread-mills: the building was erected by prison labour, the stone being quarried within the walls. The Roman Fosse-way to Ilchester passes through the parish to the eastward of the town. Shepton-Mallet was the birthplace of Hugh Inge, Chancellor of Ireland, who died in 1528; of Walter Charlton, an eminent physician, author of a work on Stonehenge, and other productions; and of Simon Browne, a celebrated dissenting minister.

SHEPTON-MONTAGUE, a parish in the hundred of NORTON-FERRIS, county of SOMERSET, 2½ miles (S.) from Bruton, containing 367 inhabitants. The living is a perpetual curacy, in the archdeaconry of Wells, and diocese of Bath and Wells, rated in the king's books at £8. 15., endowed with £200 royal bounty, and in the patronage of the Earl of Ilchester. The church is dedicated to St. Peter.

SHERATON, a township in the parish of MONK-HESLETON, southern division of EASINGTON ward, county palatine of DURHAM, 11½ miles (N.) from Stockton upon Tees, containing 116 inhabitants.

SHERBORNE, a market town and parish in the hundred of SHERBORNE, Sherborne division of the county of DORSET, 18 miles (N. by W.) from Dorchester, and 120 (W. S. W.) from London, containing 3622 inhabitants. This place, though of remote antiquity, does not appear to have emerged from comparative insignificance until the Saxon era: the name, anciently written Schiraburn, Schireburn, and Scyreburn, and of which its present appellation is a corruption, is derived from the Saxon words *Scire* clear, and *Burn* a spring, or fountain, and was usually written in old Latin records *Fons clarus*. In 670, a house was founded here for Secular canons, by Cenwalh, King of the West Saxons, and others ; and in the year 704, Sherborne was made the head of an episcopal see, which included the counties of Dorset, Somerset, Wilts, Devon, and Cornwall, by Ina, of which his kinsman, Aldhelm, was the first bishop. About 998, the Secular canons were displaced, and a society of Benedictines, established under license from Ethelred, by Wlffin, bishop of this see, who also rebuilt the monastery, and dedicated it to St. Mary, which institution became richly endowed, and at the dissolution its revenue was valued at £682. 14. 7.: the only remains of the convent are the cloister, the abbey barn, and the ancient refectory, now used as a silk manufactory. It is evident that a castle was built here at a very early period, but the founder, and the time of its erection and demolition, are unknown. Previously to the time of Henry I., however, another had succeeded it, which was built by Roger, the third Bishop of Salisbury, and became an episcopal palace: it was an octagonal structure, situated on a hill eastward of the town, and fortified by a moat and several drawbridges: having been seized by Stephen, it remained in the possession of the crown for some time, but about 1350 was recovered by Bishop Wyvil, and reverted to the bishoprick. During the civil war in the reign of Charles, it was garrisoned in the royal interest, and although gallantly defended and one of the last that yielded, it was eventually taken by the parliamentary forces under the command of Fairfax, and was demolished in 1645. Considerable portions of the ruins are remaining: the present mansion, called Sherborne castle, the seat of the Earl of Digby, was built by Sir Walter Raleigh. About 1103 Sherborne is stated to have been burnt by a detachment of the Danish invaders, and the entire destruction of the town and its ecclesiastical buildings, although doubtful, is a matter of great probability. The see continued for nearly three centuries, when it was removed first to Wilton, afterwards to Old Sarum, and finally to New Sarum, or Salisbury ; this event contributed much to depress the prosperity of Sherborne, and for a long period afterwards it was in comparative obscurity. The town is situated principally on the side of a hill near the border of the White Hart Forest, and the vale of Blackmore, and is divided by a small stream into two parts, of which one is called Castle Town ; it is well paved by a rate on the inhabitants, lighted by subscription, and amply supplied with excellent water. The woollen trade, which formerly flourished, was succeeded by the making of buttons, haberdashery, and lace : in 1740 the first silk-mill was erected, and the various branches of this manufacture, especially the making of silk twist and buttons, afford employment to a great number of the working class. Markets are held on Tuesday, Thursday, and Saturday ; and fairs on May 22nd, July 18th and 26th, and the first Monday after the 10th of October. The town is within the jurisdiction of the county magistrates : and formerly a court for the recovery of debts under 40s. was held by the steward of the hundred, but has been for some years discontinued.

The living is a vicarage, in the peculiar jurisdiction of the Dean of Salisbury, rated in the king's books at £20. 4. 7., and in the patronage of the Crown. The church, anciently the cathedral of the bishops of Sherborne, and originally erected by Bishop Aldhelm, stands south of the town, and is dedicated to St. Mary : it was partially destroyed by fire in the reign of Henry VI., and having been rebuilt by the abbots during the three succeeding reigns, it consequently exhibits specimens of different styles of architecture : the semicircular arches and zigzag mouldings in the porch, transept, west end, and north side of the building, are Norman, while the upper part of the nave, the tower, east end, aisles, and some of the chapels, are in the later style of English architecture : the roof is supported by groins springing from the aisles, and at the intersection of the tracery is a variety of arms and emblematical devices. It is a cruciform structure of freestone, with a tower rising from the intersection, one hundred and fifty-four feet high, and containing six bells, the largest of which, weighing more than three tons, was the gift of Cardinal Wolsey, and is considered the largest bell ever rung in a peal. The Saxon kings, Ethelbald and Ethelbert, and many Saxon nobles, bishops and abbots, have been interred here : the church contains some very ancient monuments : it has been enlarged with one hundred free sittings, towards which the Incorporated Society for the building and enlargement of churches and chapels contributed £50. There are places of worship for the Society of Friends, Independents, and Wesleyan Methodists. The free grammar school was founded by Edward VI., who endowed it with property belonging to the several chantries in the churches of Gillingham, Lychett-Matravers, and Marnhull, in the county of Dorset ; and at Martock, in the county of Somerset ; producing an income of £1200 per annum, and placed it under the government of twenty of the inhabitants, whom he incorporated, and appointed the Bishop of Bristol special visitor : the masters are required to be clergymen and graduates in one of the Universities. There are four exhibitions of £60 per annum each to either of the Universities, tenable for four years by boys on the foundation only, of whom the present number is fifty : the school is in high repute, and, in addition to the scholars on the foundation, there are sixty private boarders, under the care of the masters. One of the principal benefactors to this town was Mr. Benjamin Vowell, who by will gave the dividends of £1000 three per cent. consols., to be annually distributed in clothing, besides two sums of £300, and one of £400, to various benefit societies : he was also a liberal contributor to the funds of the British and Foreign Bible Society, and the Church and London Missionary Societies. The Bluecoat school was founded, in 1640, by Richard Foster, who gave land for the instruction of ten boys and ten girls, directing £5 per annum from the surplus rents to be applied towards maintaining one of the boys at the University, if required. A charity school for boys was founded, in 1717, by John Woodman, who gave £250 to the vicar and churchwardens, for the instruction of poor boys, which sum was vested in land for that purpose. In 1743, William, Lord Digby, gave land for teaching and clothing thirteen poor girls. The churchwardens and overseers have the right of sending three boys to Christchurch Hospital, in London, for whose support Giles Russel gave lands, in 1670. A National school, in which one hundred and twenty boys are taught ; and a Lancasterian school, in which sixty boys and girls receive instruction, are supported by subscription. The almshouse, originally an hospital of the order of St. Augustine, was, by license from Henry VI., refounded and dedicated to St. John the Baptist and St. John the Evangelist, for twenty brethren, twelve poor men, four poor women, and a chaplain ; and was governed by a master and trustees : it now contains sixteen men and eight women, under the superintendence of a master and nineteen brethren, elected from among the inhabitants of the town ; a chaplain officiates daily. There is a very considerable fund for the relief of the poor, arising from land and houses given for that purpose, in 1448, by Robert Neville, Bishop of Sarum, and others; also a small sum for apprenticing poor children, given by Agnes Broughton, in 1633, under the management of the trustees of the almshouse.

SHERBORNE, a parish in the lower division of the hundred of SLAUGHTER, county of GLOUCESTER, 6 miles (N. W. by W.) from Burford, containing 525 inhabitants. The living is a discharged vicarage, with that of Windrush united, in the archdeaconry and diocese of Gloucester, rated in the king's books at £15. 6. 8., and in the patronage of Lord Sherborne. The church is dedicated to St. Mary Magdalene. James Bradley, D.D., Regius Professor of Astronomy, and Astronomer Royal, was born here, in 1692 : he died in 1762, and was buried at Minchinhampton.

SHERBORNE, a parish in the Snitterfield division of the hundred of BARLICHWAY, county of WARWICK, 2¾ miles (S. W. by S.) from Warwick, containing 217 inhabitants. The living is a perpetual curacy, in the archdeaconry and diocese of Worcester, endowed with £16 per annum and £400 private benefaction, and £800 royal bounty, and in the patronage of the Rev. Elias Webb. The church is dedicated to All Saints.

SHERBORNE (ST. JOHN), a parish in the hundred of BASINGSTOKE, Basingstoke division of the county of SOUTHAMPTON, 2¾ miles (N. N. W.) from Basingstoke, containing 596 inhabitants. The living comprises a sinecure rectory and a vicarage, in the archdeaconry and diocese of Winchester, the former rated in the king's books at £9. 8. 1½., endowed with £200 private benefaction, and £200 royal bounty, and in the patronage of William L. W. Chute, Esq., and the latter rated at £7, and in the patronage of the Rector. The church is dedicated to St. Andrew. There is a private chapel at the Vine, containing a tomb in memory of Chaloner Chute, Esq., Speaker of the House of Commons in Richard Cromwell's parliament, and the purchaser of this noble mansion, which was erected in the reign of Henry VIII., by the first Lord Sandys. A school for the instruction of upwards of one hundred children of both sexes is liberally supported by Mrs. Chute and Miss Wiggatt.

SHERBORNE (MONKS'), a parish partly in the hundred of BASINGSTOKE, Basingstoke division, but chiefly in the hundred of CHUTELY, Kingsclere division, of the county of SOUTHAMPTON, 3½ miles (N. W. by N.) from Basingstoke, containing, with the tything of Chineham, 494 inhabitants. The living is a discharged vicarage, in the archdeaconry and diocese of Winchester, rated in the king's books at £8. 0. 7½., and in the patronage of the Provost and Fellows of Queen's

College, Oxford. The church is dedicated to All Saints. Here was a Benedictine priory, dedicated to St. Mary and St. John, a cell to the abbey of Cerasy in Normandy, which, at its suppression, was given by Henry VI. to Eton College, but it was finally granted by Edward IV. to the hospital of St. Julian in Southampton, and is enjoyed by the Provost and Fellows of Queen's College, as masters of that hospital.

SHERBURN, a township in the parish of PITTINGTON, southern division of EASINGTON ward, county palatine of DURHAM, 2¾ miles (E.) from Durham, containing 281 inhabitants.

SHERBURN, a parish in the wapentake of BUCKROSE, East riding of the county of YORK, 11¼ miles (E. N. E.) from New Malton, containing 496 inhabitants. The living is a discharged vicarage, in the archdeaconry of the East riding, and diocese of York, rated in the king's books at £6. 0. 2½., endowed with £400 royal bounty, and £400 parliamentary grant, and in the patronage of Sir W. Strickland, Bart. The church is dedicated to St. Hilda. There is a place of worship for Wesleyan Methodists.

SHERBURN, a parish partly in the liberty of ST. PETER of YORK, East riding, and partly in the upper division of the wapentake of BARKSTONE-ASH, West riding, of the county of YORK, comprising the market town of Sherburn, and the townships of Barkston, Huddleston with Lumby, Lotherton with part of Aberford, Micklefield, South Milford, and Newthorp, and containing 2916 inhabitants, of which number, 1144 are in the town of Sherburn, 15 miles (S. W. by S.) from York, and 184 (N. by W.) from London. The name of this place appears to be of Saxon derivation, being compounded of *Scire*, clear or pure, and *Burn*, a spring or fountain, with reference to a small stream by which it is watered. It was anciently of more importance than it is at present, when King Athelstan had a palace here, which was subsequently given to the Archbishop of York, but of which only the site remains, and the present church, which was constructed out of its ruins. In the great civil war, Sherburn was the scene of a remarkable conflict between Lord Digby, Lieutenant-General of the forces north of the Trent, and Colonel Copley, an officer in the interest of the parliament, when, owing to a misunderstanding as to the relative position of the parties, the army of the former was broken up and discomfited, and his baggage and cabinet papers fell into the enemy's hands. The town is situated on the direct road from Tadcaster to Ferrybridge, the vicinity abounding with fine orchards : a species of plum, called the Winesoms, is abundantly prolific and fine in this soil. Flax is cultivated to some extent, and is sent to the Leeds market ; teasel also forms a prominent article of trade. About a mile and a half from the town is a quarry of fine stone, and upon a stream, called Bishop Dyke, are several corn-mills. The market, now almost disused, is on Friday; and there is a fair on September 25th. The living is a discharged vicarage, in the peculiar jurisdiction and patronage of the Prebendary of Fenton in the Cathedral Church of York, rated in the king's books at £10. 17. 1. The church, which is dedicated to All Saints, is a spacious and handsome structure, the nave presenting a rare and beautiful specimen of ancient architecture. There is a place of worship for Wesleyan Methodists. Sherburn hospital and school-house were erected, in 1619, in pursuance of the will of Robert Hungate, Esq., who gave a rent-charge of £225. 6. 8. for the maintenance, clothing, and education of twenty-four male orphans of the parishes of Sherburn, Saxton, and Sand-Hutton, the city of York, or elsewhere; also for the support of four scholars at St. John's College, Cambridge, from this foundation: the salary of the master is about £40 per annum, and eight boys of the parish are instructed, clothed, and maintained, until they are fifteen years of age: this school is also entitled to send candidates for Lady Hastings' exhibitions at Queen's College, Oxford. A charity school for poor girls was founded and endowed, in 1731, with certain land, and the sum of £1450, by the Rev. Samuel Duffield. A rich and elegant cross was found, some years ago, in the churchyard, in digging amongst the foundations of an old chapel: traces of a Roman road from this place to Aberford are yet visible.

SHERBURN-HOUSE, an extra-parochial liberty, in the southern division of EASINGTON ward, county palatine of DURHAM, 2¼ miles (E. by S.) from Durham, containing 67 inhabitants. An hospital for lepers was founded here, previously to 1181, by Hugh Pudsey, Bishop of Durham: it was dedicated to St. Mary Magdalene, and its revenue, in the reign of Henry VIII., was certified as of the value of £142. 0. 4., the society consisting of a master, several priests, and sixty-five lepers. It is yet in being, having been incorporated in 1585, by Queen Elizabeth, for a master and thirty brethren, and is still subject to the regulations then adopted: the Bishop of Durham appoints the master, who must be in holy orders, and of the degree of M.A. at least; and the master nominates the brethren, who each receive a handsome yearly stipend, besides being comfortably lodged, fed, and clothed. At present this is one of the most richly endowed charitable foundations in the North of England, its income amounting to several thousand pounds per annum. The hospital was enlarged in 1819, by fifteen additional lodging-houses, for the accommodation of as many out-brethren, before which period there were only fifteen inmates. The building, to which is attached a chapel and apartments for the master, is of a quadrangular form, situated in an agreeable vale on the eastern side of Sherburn water.

SHERE, a parish in the second division of the hundred of BLACKHEATH, county of SURREY, 6 miles (E. by S.) from Guildford, containing 1077 inhabitants. The living is a rectory, in the archdeaconry of Surrey, and diocese of Winchester, rated in the king's books at £26. 1. 5½. The Bishop of Winchester, by lapse, presented in 1805. The church, dedicated to St. James, is principally in the early style of English architecture, with a tower and spire rising from the centre. There are two places of worship for Wesleyan Methodists. Courts leet and baron are occasionally held by the lord of the manor, William Bray, Esq., the county historian. Thomas Galton, in 1758, gave £400 for teaching poor children. There is a smaller bequest, for a like purpose the gift of Mr. Duncomb, in 1746.

SHEREFORD, a parish in the hundred of GALLOW, county of NORFOLK, 2¼ miles (W.) from Fakenham, containing 98 inhabitants. The living is a discharged rectory, in the archdeaconry and diocese of Norwich,

rated in the king's books at £9, and in the patronage of Marquis Townshend. The church is dedicated to St. Nicholas.

SHERFIELD upon LODON, a parish in the hundred of ODIHAM, Basingstoke division of the county of SOUTHAMPTON, 3¾ miles (N. E. by N.) from Basingstoke, containing 522 inhabitants. The living is a rectory, in the archdeaconry and diocese of Winchester, rated in the king's books at £11. 3. 6½. The King, by reason of lunacy, presented in 1815. The church is dedicated to St. Leonard. James Sherfield, in 1735, gave £100 to build a school-house, and £25 a year for the education of the children of this parish, including four from Stratfield-Saye.

SHERFIELD-ENGLISH, a parish in the hundred of THORNGATE, Andover division of the county of SOUTHAMPTON, 4¾ miles (W. N. W.) from Romsey, containing 327 inhabitants. The living is a rectory, in the archdeaconry and diocese of Winchester, rated in the king's books at £6. 10. 2½., and in the patronage of R. Bristow, Esq. The church is dedicated to St. Leonard.

SHERFORD, a parish in the hundred of COLERIDGE, county of DEVON, 3¼ miles (E.) from Kingsbridge, containing 429 inhabitants. The living is a perpetual curacy, annexed to the vicarage of Stokenham, in the archdeaconry of Totness, and diocese of Exeter. The church, dedicated to St. Martin, contains some good screen-work. Attached to an old farm-house at Kennedon are some remains of the manorial seat of Justice Hals, who lived in the reign of Henry V.

SHERIFF-HALES, a parish partly in the Newport division of the hundred of BRADFORD (South), county of SALOP, but chiefly in the western division of the hundred of CUTTLESTONE, county of STAFFORD, 3 miles (N. by E.) from Shiffnall, containing, with the hamlet of Woodcote, 1064 inhabitants. The living is a vicarage, in the archdeaconry of Stafford, and diocese of Lichfield and Coventry, rated in the king's books at £11.1.8., and in the patronage of the Marquis of Stafford. The church is dedicated to St. Mary. There is a place of worship for Wesleyan Methodists. A milky vitriolic water is found among the iron mines in the neighbourhood.

SHERMANBURY, a parish in the hundred of WINDHAM and EWHURST, rape of BRAMBER, county of SUSSEX, 7½ miles (N. E. by N.) from Steyning, containing 320 inhabitants. The living is a rectory, in the archdeaconry of Lewes, and diocese of Chichester, rated in the king's books at £4. 19. 4½., and in the patronage of the Rev. J. G. Challen, D.D. The church is dedicated to St. Giles. The river Adur, which divides into two branches in the parish, is navigable hither from Shoreham. The springs here are strongly impregnated with iron, and there are some of a saline quality. Here are the groined gateway and some other remains of a castellated mansion, surrounded by a moat called Ewhurst, and anciently a seat of the Lords De la Warr.

SHERMANS-GROUNDS, an extra-parochial district, in the western division of the hundred of Goscote, county of LEICESTER, containing 19 inhabitants.

SHERNBORNE, a parish in the hundred of SMITHDON, county of NORFOLK, 6¼ miles (N. E. by N.) from Castle-Rising, containing 135 inhabitants. The living is a discharged vicarage, in the archdeaconry of Norfolk, and diocese of Norwich, rated in the king's books at £8, and in the patronage of the Bishop of Ely. The church, dedicated to St. Peter and St. Paul, was built by one Thorpe, lord of Shernborne, when Felix, Bishop of the East Angles, came to convert the inhabitants to Christianity, and is said to be the second founded in that kingdom; it has no tower, and the chancel has been long in ruins.

SHERRINGHAM, a parish in the northern division of the hundred of ERPINGHAM, county of NORFOLK, 5¼ miles (W.) from Cromer, containing 694 inhabitants. The living is a vicarage, in the archdeaconry and diocese of Norwich, endowed with £600 royal bounty, and £1200 parliamentary grant, and in the patronage of the Bishop of Ely. The church is dedicated to All Saints. Here was formerly a monastery of Black canons, a cell to Nutley abbey, Buckinghamshire.

SHERRINGTON, a parish in the hundred of NEWPORT, county of BUCKINGHAM, 1¾ mile (N. N. E.) from Newport-Pagnell, containing 796 inhabitants. The living is a rectory, in the archdeaconry of Buckingham, and diocese of Lincoln, rated in the king's books at £20. 0. 2½., and in the patronage of the Bishop of Lincoln. The church is dedicated to St. Laud.

SHERRINGTON, a parish forming a detached portion of the hundred of BRANCH and DOLE, county of WILTS, 5½ miles (N. E. by N.) from Hindon, containing 165 inhabitants. The living is a rectory, in the archdeaconry and diocese of Salisbury, rated in the king's books at £11, and in the patronage of E. Lambert, Esq. The church is dedicated to St. Michael.

SHERSTON (MAGNA), a parish in a detached portion of the hundred of CHIPPENHAM, county of WILTS, 5¾ miles (W. by S.) from Malmesbury, containing 1146 inhabitants. The living is a discharged vicarage, with the rectory of Sherston Parva united, in the archdeaconry and diocese of Salisbury, rated in the king's books at £10. 2., endowed with £1000 parliamentary grant, and in the patronage of the Dean and Chapter of Gloucester. The church, dedicated to the Holy Cross, exhibits portions of Norman and of the several styles of English architecture: it is a large structure, with a lofty tower rising from the centre. Mrs. Hodges, in 1726, bequeathed a rent-charge of £5 for teaching poor children; besides which there are a trifling sum, the gift of Thomas Byrton, in 1721, and £200 left by Ann Brain, in 1780, for the like purpose. Two small streams, forming the river Avon, unite in this parish. Sherston, from its situation near the Consular way, and from the coins of Antoninus, Faustinus, Gordianus, Flavius, Julianus, and others found here, was evidently occupied by the Romans. In the neighbourhood are the foundations and fragments of three stone crosses; and here was fought, in 1016, an obstinate battle between Edmund Ironside and Canute the Great.

SHERSTON (PARVA), or SHERSTON-PINKNEY, a parish in a detached portion of the hundred of CHIPPENHAM, county of WILTS, 4¾ miles (W.) from Malmesbury, containing 123 inhabitants. The living is a discharged rectory, united to the vicarage of Sherston Magna, in the archdeaconry and diocese of Salisbury, rated in the king's books at £3. 14. 4½. The church has long been demolished, no institution having taken place since 1640, when the patronage was in the Crown.

SHERWILL, a parish in the hundred of SHERWILL, county of DEVON, 4 miles (N. E.) from Barnstaple, containing 645 inhabitants. The living is a rectory, in the archdeaconry of Barnstaple, and diocese of Exeter, rated in the king's books at £30. 3. 11½., and in the patronage of Sir Arthur Chichester, Bart. The church is dedicated to St. Peter.

SHEVINGTON, a township in the parish of STANDISH, hundred of LEYLAND, county palatine of LANCASTER, 3¼ miles (N. W. by W.) from Wigan, containing 836 inhabitants.

SHEVIOCK, a parish in the southern division of the hundred of EAST, county of CORNWALL, 3 miles (S. by E.) from St. Germans, containing 491 inhabitants. The living is a rectory, in the archdeaconry of Cornwall, and diocese of Exeter, rated in the king's books at £26. 14. 7., and in the patronage of the Rt. Hon. R. P. Carew. The church, dedicated to St. Mary, is an ancient structure, containing a sumptuous monument to the memory of Sir Edward and Lady Courtenay, and several curious tombs of the family of Dawnay. The parish is bounded on the north by the Lynher river, and on the south by the English channel. At Wrinkle Cove is an ancient pier, and off the coast a considerable pilchard fishery.

SHIELDS (NORTH), a sea-port and market town, partly in the township of NORTH SHIELDS, partly in that of TYNEMOUTH, partly in that of PRESTON, and partly in that of CHIRTON, parish of TYNEMOUTH, eastern division of CASTLE ward, county of NORTHUMBERLAND, 8 miles (E. N. E.) from Newcastle, and 276 (N. by W.) from London; the township of North Shields contains 8205 inhabitants, and the present population of the town is supposed to be about 20,000. The earliest notice of this place occurs in the reign of Edward I., from which it appears, that in the preceding reign the only buildings on the site of the present town consisted of fishermens' huts, or *Shielings*, of which the name is supposed to be a corruption. At about the same period, the prior and monks of Tynemouth erected houses here, formed a harbour, established a market, and encouraged the settlement of ship-builders and tradesmen, thereby exciting the jealousy of the burgesses of Newcastle, who possessed the exclusive trade of the Tyne, and commenced proceedings against the prior, who, by a judgment of the court of King's Bench, was obliged to destroy the buildings that he had erected, and to give up the commerce which he was creating, and the town consequently returned to its former obscurity, and remained in that state until the middle of the seventeenth century, when Cromwell used exertions to remove the restrictions which prevented it from assuming that station as a commercial town which its situation was entitled to, by causing an act to be passed for the erection of quays, &c., and the establishment of a market twice a week; but his death interfered with these plans, and it was not until the close of the seventeenth century, that any of the restrictions crippling its trade were removed: since that period the facilities afforded by the increase of knowledge to the freedom of trade having caused the abolition of the remaining restrictions, North Shields has advanced rapidly to its present importance, and the immense augmentation in its commerce may be estimated from the circumstance of its population having increased, in the period between the census of 1801 and that of 1821, upwards of nine thousand seven hundred persons, being more than three-fourths of the whole number of inhabitants at the former period.

The town is situated on the northern shore of the river Tyne, at its confluence with the German Ocean, and opposite to South Shields, which is on the southern bank of the river. The older part consists chiefly of narrow lanes and alleys, and its appearance has been compared to that of Wapping in London, but the more recent additions comprise several spacious streets, three handsome squares, and many houses of a very superior description, both in the town and its immediate vicinity. The theatre is a small brick building, fitted up in a neat and appropriate manner, and is open for a few months in the winter season. A subscription library was established in 1807, and the valuable collection of books of which it is composed is kept in a handsome building erected for the purpose. A scientific and mechanics' institution was formed in 1825, which is rapidly advancing in prosperity. The town is lighted with gas; and water, which formerly in dry seasons was difficult to be procured, is now abundantly supplied from the reservoirs at Percy Main, Whitley, and Waterville, and conveyed by pipes into the town, by a company incorporated in 1786. The harbour is capable of containing two thousand sail of vessels, and in spring tides ships of five hundred tons' burden can pass the bar crossing its mouth in safety. The principal article of trade is coal, which is exported in large quantities to London and places on the eastern coasts of England and Scotland, and this trade employs the greater part of the vessels belonging to the port, the number of which, in 1827, was two hundred and seventy-nine, a few being engaged in the American and Baltic trade, and in the Greenland and Davis' Straits fishery. Ships of three hundred tons' burden can load or unload at the quay, which is spacious, and has a crane for facilitating the landing or shipping of goods. The principal manufactures are such as are connected with the shipping, there being six ship-builders' yards, two sail-cloth manufactories, two salt-works, and a chain-cable and anchor manufactory; in addition to which are rope-walks, and manufactories for tobacco, gloves, and hats. Some inconvenience is felt from ships being obliged to clear out at the custom-house at Newcastle; here is an office belonging to that establishment, and at Clifford's Fort is a watch-house, where officers are stationed, with a lighthouse adjoining to it: a life-boat is also kept here, which was presented to the town by the Duke of Northumberland, in 1798, with a donation of £20 towards keeping it in repair. A weekly market is held on Friday, in a spacious and commodious market-place, formed in 1804, by the Duke of Northumberland, as lord of the manor; and there is a statute fair annually on the first Friday in November. A meeting of magistrates is held every Tuesday; and a court leet and baron, for making presentments, and for the recovery of debts under 40s., is held at Easter and Michaelmas, by the steward of the manor of Tynemouth.

North Shields has had no place of worship belonging to the established church (the inhabitants having attended the church at Tynemouth) until recently, when a chapel of ease was erected in the market-place. There are two places of worship belonging to Metho-

dists in the New Connexion, and one each to Particular Baptists, the Society of Friends, Independents, Primitive and Wesleyan Methodists, Presbyterians, United Secession Church, and Roman Catholics, also a synagogue: that belonging to the Wesleyan Methodists is a spacious building, erected in 1807, at an expense of £2500. A free school, with houses for the master and mistress, was erected by subscription in 1810, in commemoration of the royal jubilee; it is supported by subscriptions, and nearly three hundred children of both sexes are instructed on the Lancasterian plan. Another school was founded and liberally endowed by Mr. Thomas Kettlewell, in 1825, for which a handsome and commodious house has been erected, at an expense of £1200, and nearly two hundred boys are gratuitously instructed. The dispensary, which was established in 1802, is supported by donations and annual subscriptions, and has afforded most extensive relief to the poor. In addition to the institutions already noticed, there are several benefit societies, particularly that formed in 1824, for the mutual relief of sailors suffering from sickness, shipwreck, or want, and consisting of upwards of two thousand members. Steamboats pass regularly every day between this town and Newcastle, and a constant intercourse is maintained by boats with South Shields. It has been frequently proposed to connect this latter town with North Shields, to accomplish which a tunnel, to pass under the bed of the river, was at one period proposed; and it was more recently thought that a chain bridge would be the most desirable mode of opening a communication between the two places; but this appears to have been abandoned, from a fear that it might obstruct the progress of the shipping.

SHIELDS (SOUTH), a sea-port, and market town, partly in the chapelry of SOUTH SHIELDS, and partly in that of WESTOE, parish of JARROW, eastern division of CHESTER ward, county palatine of DURHAM, 20 miles (N.N.E.) from Durham, and 278 (N.N.W.) from London; the township of South Shields contains 8885 inhabitants, and the present population of the town is supposed to exceed 17,000. Although this town has only attained its present size and importance in very recent times, its origin appears to lay claim to considerable antiquity; many remains of the Romans, consisting of altars, an hypocaust, coins, and other memorials, discovered on Lawe hill, near the town, indicating that it was one of the stations occupied by that people, though the name by which it was then known has not been ascertained. The military road, called the "Wreken Dyke," terminated here, and an elevated pavement at the western end of the town appears to be a Roman work. It is situated on the southern bank of the Tyne, at its junction with the German Ocean, nearly opposite to North Shields: the old part of the town consists principally of a long, narrow, and inconvenient street, running along the shore of the river, but the higher and more modern part of it comprises many spacious and well-built houses: it is lighted with gas, supplied by works completed in 1824, at an expense of £4000. In the large square near the centre of the town is the town hall, erected, about 1768, by the Dean and Chapter of Durham, in which the petty sessions for this part of the eastern division of Chester ward are held, on the second and fourth Wednesdays in each month; and a court leet and court baron by the Dean and Chapter, as lords of the manor, for making presentments, and for the recovery of small debts: it is also used as an exchange by the merchants, and as a public news-room; the under part is composed of a colonnade, in which the market for butter, eggs, and poultry, is held. A subscription library was established in 1803, and "a Literary, Scientific, and Mechanics' Institution" in 1825; the latter, in addition to its library, possesses apparatus for mechanical and scientific experiments, and has very much contributed to increase a desire for knowledge in its neighbourhood. The theatre, erected in 1791, on the Bank Top, is a neat building. This town owes much of its present importance to the salt trade, which was established about 1499; and during the reigns of Elizabeth, James, and Charles I., it attracted many strangers, who settled here. When in its most flourishing state, in 1696, it employed nearly one hundred and fifty salt-pans, and many hundred individuals; but it has so much declined, that the number of pans does not now exceed five, producing about six tons of salt weekly. It has, however, been succeeded by other branches of business, from which the town derives equal benefit, the principal being the coal trade: in addition to the coal brought down the river in keels and shipped here, two mines are worked in the immediate neighbourhood; connected with them are staiths on the banks of the river, for facilitating the loading of vessels, by means of which a cargo is frequently shipped in one tide. The number of vessels belonging to the port in 1827 was two hundred and fifty-nine, though within the last century the number was only four or five: the majority of them are employed as colliers, and a few in the American, Baltic, and Indian trades. Here are thirteen dry docks, which will contain nineteen large vessels, and extensive yards for ship-building are attached to each dock: during the late war, when the trade of the port was most flourishing, thirty vessels have been launched in a year, but the number is now very far short of this. There are nine glass-houses in the neighbourhood, in which the different kinds of crown and flint glass, and glass bottles, are made, and some mills for grinding it; the duty paid in one year, during the war, on this branch of manufacture amounted to £89,334. There are also three breweries, and seven rope-walks, in some of which patent cordage is made. The market is on Wednesday; and fairs, granted by charter of Bishop Trevor, in 1770, are held on June 24th and September 1st, but they are indifferently attended.

The living is a perpetual curacy, in the archdeaconry and diocese of Durham, and in the patronage of the Dean and Chapter of Durham. The chapel, dedicated to St. Hilda, is of great antiquity, although very little remains of the original edifice, it having been, with the exception of the old tower, modernised and nearly rebuilt in 1810, at an expense of nearly £5000; the altar is placed in a circular recess, ornamented with three transparent paintings of scriptural subjects: a lectureship has been established, with an allowance of about £200 per annum, raised by subscription among the inhabitants, who appoint the lecturer. A chapel of ease was erected in 1818, in that part of the town which is in the township of Westoe, at an expense of about £2400, raised by subscription, towards which, £1000 was given by the Dean and Chapter of Durham,

and £500 by the trustees of Lord Crewe: it contains one thousand two hundred sittings, seven hundred of which are free. The ground-floor of the building is used for a school, which was established at the same time, and in which upwards of three hundred children of both sexes are instructed on the National system. There are two places of worship each belonging to the Particular Baptists, Wesleyan Methodists, and Presbyterians, and one each to Independents, Methodists of the New Connexion, and Primitive Methodists, and the United Secession Church: nearly all of which have Sunday schools attached. A charity school was founded, in 1772, by subscriptions amounting to upwards of £1400, which, by the aid of subsequent liberal donations, affords instruction to about one hundred and twenty children: it is under the superintendence of five trustees, elected annually, one of whom is always the minister for the time being. The dispensary, established in 1821, has been productive of great benefit, having afforded relief to nearly three thousand poor persons: there are several other benevolent and benefit societies established in the town. The invention of the life-boat originated with a few benevolent individuals of the town, who assisted Mr. Greathead to construct one, which was found effectual for its purpose, and to whom parliament voted a reward of £1200. To Mr. Marshall, another native, the seamen of the eastern coast are indebted for the construction of the floating-light off Newarp Sand, on the coast of Norfolk.

SHIFFNALL, a parish in the Shiffnall division of the hundred of BRIMSTREE, county of SALOP, comprising the market town of Shiffnall, the chapelry of Priors-Lee, the townships of Hatton and Woodside, and the hamlet of Oakengates, and containing 4411 inhabitants, of which number, 1463 are in the town of Shiffnall, 17½ miles (E. by S.) from Shrewsbury, and 143 (N. W.) from London. This place, formerly called Idsall, appears to have been of greater note than it is at present, although the origin of its name and history is involved in obscurity. It belonged to Earl Morcar prior to the Conquest and, at a period considerably later, it was the property of the family of Dunstanville, one of whom, Walter de Dunstanville, by the special command of Henry III., resided in the marches of Wales, to protect them against the ravaging incursions of the Welch. It afterwards came into the possession of the Badlesmeres, who obtained from Edward I. a market for two days in the week, and two yearly fairs. Bartholomew de Badlesmere having been executed for his participation in the battle of Boroughbridge, it subsequently became the property of various persons of distinction, among whom were the families of Bohun, Tiptoft, Ap Rees, Mortimer, Talbot, &c. The town is supposed to have been destroyed by fire, and subsequently built on its present site, to the eastward of the church, it being, prior to its destruction, situated to the westward; and a book printed towards the end of the fifteenth century, entitled "the Burnynge of the town of Idsall, alias Shiffnall," is said to be in existence, though very scarce. It is situated on the high road from London to Holyhead, in a country abounding with coal and iron-ore, and is indifferently paved and not lighted, but the inhabitants are supplied with good water from wells: there are two paper-manufactories, and the coal and iron mines in the neighbourhood are worked on an extensive scale by a company at Priors-Lee. A subscription library has been established. The market is on Tuesday; and there are fairs on the first Monday in April, August 5th, and November 23rd, for hops, horses, and cattle of different kinds. A petty session is held monthly by the magistrates, and a court leet annually.

The living is a vicarage, with the perpetual curacy of Priors-Lee annexed, in the archdeaconry of Salop, and diocese of Lichfield and Coventry, rated in the king's books at £15. 6. 8., and in the patronage of George Brooke, Esq. The church, dedicated to St. Andrew, is a large ancient cruciform structure, with a tower in the centre; the prevailing style of architecture is the later Norman, with many modern alterations, and the four pointed arches supporting the tower are good specimens of that style: the chancel, in which are two round-headed windows (now blocked up), with slender-shafted columns and decorated capitals, is evidently of earlier date, and is separated from the tower by a large semicircular arch, which is a fine specimen of the early Norman style: the roof of the nave, composed of oak richly carved, is covered by a plaister ceiling, added in 1810, when the church underwent a thorough repair: there are some ancient monuments, and a tablet to the memory of one William Wakeley, stating that he died in 1714, having lived in the reigns of eight kings and queens. The Baptists and Independents have each places of worship here. A free school, founded in 1595, by John Aaron, had, from other endowments, an income of £13. 17. 4., which was paid to the master until 1816, when an addition was made from a fund raised by subscription, making the income £30 per annum, and the National system was adopted; about one hundred and thirty children of both sexes are instructed. Three exhibitions to Christ Church College, Oxford, founded, in 1689, by Edward Careswell, are attached to this school, but the course of education pursued not qualifying the scholars for the University, the benefit of them is enjoyed by a private classical school, the master of which is nominally classical master of the free school. Six poor girls are clothed and instructed in reading and working, from a small endowment by Beatrice Jobber, and there are some minor bequests for the benefit of the poor. In a field near the town are the remains of a military station, consisting of a circular mound with a ditch. Shiffnall was the birthplace of Dr. Beddoes, a physician eminent as well for his literary attainments as for professional skill.

SHIFFORD, a chapelry in the parish and hundred of BAMPTON, county of OXFORD, 6 miles (S.E.) from Witney, containing 42 inhabitants.

SHILBOTTLE, a parish in the eastern division of COQUETDALE ward, county of NORTHUMBERLAND, comprising the townships of Guyson, Hazon, Newton on the Moor, Shilbottle, Whittle, and Woodhouse, and containing 1153 inhabitants, of which number, 548 are in the township of Shilbottle, 4½ miles (S. by E.) from Alnwick. The living is a discharged vicarage, in the archdeaconry of Northumberland, and diocese of Durham, rated in the king's books at £4. 14. 8., and in the partonage of the Crown. The church, dedicated to St. James, was thoroughly repaired about 1793. Coal of a superior quality is obtained here. Henry Strother, in 1741, founded and endowed a school for teaching

poor children, the income of which was augmented by Francis Strother, in 1765 and 1770.

SHILDON, a township in that part of the parish of St. ANDREW AUCKLAND which is in the north-western division of DARLINGTON ward, county palatine of DURHAM, 3½ miles (S. E. by S.) from Bishop-Auckland, containing 115 inhabitants. Here is an extensive depôt for goods, on the line of the railway from Witton park to Darlington and Stockton. A free school, erected by Mrs. Edward Whalton, is endowed with £25 a year, and a house and land occupied by the master.

SHILLINGFORD, a parish in the hundred of GANFIELD, county of BERKS, 2¼ miles (S. E. by E.) from Great Farringdon, containing 271 inhabitants. The living is a rectory, in the archdeaconry of Berks, and diocese of Salisbury, rated in the king's books at £17. 8. 11½. W. Y. Mills, Esq. was patron in 1810. The church, dedicated to St. Faith, is partly Norman, and partly in the early style of English architecture: it contains some ancient and curious monuments, particularly an altar-tomb to the memory of John de Blewbury, a priest, who died in 1372.

SHILLINGFORD (ST. GEORGE), a parish in the hundred of EXMINSTER, county of DEVON, 3½ miles (S. S. W.) from Exeter, containing 70 inhabitants. The living is a discharged rectory, recently consolidated with that of Dunchideock, in the archdeaconry and diocese of Exeter, rated in the king's books at £9, and in the patronage of Sir L. V. Palk, Bart. The church contains an old monument to one of the Courtenay family.

SHILLINGSTONE, or SHILLING-OKEFORD, a parish in the hundred of CRANBORNE, in a detached portion of the Shaston (West) division of the county of DORSET, 5¾ miles (N. W.) from Blandford-Forum, containing 430 inhabitants. The living is a rectory in medieties, in the archdeaconry of Dorset, and diocese of Bristol, the first mediety rated in the king's books at £7. 9. 9½., and the second at £6. 16. 5½., and in the patronage of J. Thompson, Esq. The church, dedicated to the Holy Rood, has an embattled tower, crowned with pinnacles: it contains a small altar-tomb, erected, it is said, to the memory of the founder. The parish is bounded on the north by the river Stour.

SHILTON, a parish partly in the hundred of FARRINGDON, county of BERKS, and partly in the hundred of BAMPTON, county of OXFORD, 2½ miles (S. S. E.) from Burford, containing 256 inhabitants. The living is a discharged vicarage, in the archdeaconry and diocese of Oxford, rated in the king's books at £5. 5. 5. Miss Georges and others were patrons in 1808. The church is in Oxfordshire, the greater part of the parish in Berkshire, and the vicarage-house upon the boundary of the two counties. A charity school is supported by subscriptions.

SHILTON, a parish in the Kirby division of the hundred of KNIGHTLOW, county of WARWICK, 5¾ miles (N. E.) from Coventry, containing 396 inhabitants. The living is a perpetual curacy, in the archdeaconry of Coventry, and diocese of Lichfield and Coventry, endowed with £800 royal bounty, and in the patronage of the Crown. The church is dedicated to St. Andrew. The Oxford canal crosses the southern portion of the parish.

SHILTON (EARL), county of LEICESTER.—See EARL-SHILTON.

SHILVINGTON, a township in that part of the parish of MORPETH which is in the western division of CASTLE ward, county of NORTHUMBERLAND, 5 miles (S. W. by S.) from Morpeth, containing 110 inhabitants.

SHIMPLING, a parish in the hundred of DISS, county of NORFOLK, 3¾ miles (N. E.) from Diss, containing 179 inhabitants. The living is a discharged rectory, in the archdeaconry of Norfolk, and diocese of Norwich, rated in the king's books at £10. 13. 4. P. J. Harrison, Esq. was patron in 1821. The church, dedicated to St. George, was erected early in the thirteenth century, but the steeple appears to be of more ancient date; a representation of St. George and the Dragon, and the arms of the Shimplings, are carved on the front of it.

SHIMPLING, a parish in the hundred of BABERGH, county of SUFFOLK, 4 miles (W. N. W.) from Lavenham, containing 450 inhabitants. The living is a rectory, in the archdeaconry of Sudbury, and diocese of Norwich, rated in the king's books at £16. 17. 1. The Rev. Thomas Fiske was patron in 1800. The church is dedicated to St. George.

SHINCLIFFE, a chapelry in that part of the parish of ST. OSWALD, DURHAM, which is in the southern division of EASINGTON ward, county palatine of DURHAM, 1¾ mile (S. E.) from Durham, containing 367 inhabitants. The living is a perpetual curacy, in the archdeaconry and diocese of Durham, and in the patronage of the Vicar of St. Oswald. The chapel was built and endowed, in 1826, by the Dean and Chapter of Durham.

SHINETON, county of SALOP. — See SHEINTON.

SHINFIELD, a parish comprising Shinfield East side, in the hundred of CHARLTON, and the liberty of Hartley-Dammer, in that of THEALE, county of BERKS, and Shinfield West side, in the hundred of AMESBURY, county of WILTS, 3 miles (S. by E.) from Reading, and containing 1065 inhabitants. The living is a vicarage, with the perpetual curacy of Swallowfield annexed, in the archdeaconry of Berks, and diocese of Salisbury, rated in the king's books at £20. 3. 1½., and in the patronage of the Dean and Chapter of Hereford. The church is dedicated to St. Mary. There is a place of worship for Independents. A free school was founded here, in 1707, by Richard Piggot, who endowed it with £42 per annum, for teaching and clothing twenty boys. There is another school, endowed by Mary Spicer in 1697, in which fifteen children are taught by a schoolmistress for £9 a year, arising from the rent of a house and land.

SHINGAY, a parish in the hundred of ARMINGFORD, county of CAMBRIDGE, 6½ miles (N. W. by N.) from Royston, containing 86 inhabitants. The living is a perpetual curacy, annexed to the vicarage of Wendy, in the archdeaconry and diocese of Ely. The church is dedicated to St. Mary. A preceptory of the Knights Hospitallers of St. John of Jerusalem was founded here in 1140, the revenue of which, at the suppression, was estimated at £175. 4. 6.

SHINGHAM, a parish in the hundred of CLACKCLOSE, county of NORFOLK, 4¼ miles (S. W. by W.) from Swaffham, containing 58 inhabitants. The living

is a discharged rectory, annexed to that of Beechamwell All Saints, in the archdeaconry of Norfolk, and diocese of Norwich, rated in the king's books at £4. 6. 8., endowed with £200 royal bounty.

SHIPBORNE, a parish in the hundred of WROTHAM, lathe of AYLESFORD, county of KENT, 3¾ miles (N.) from Tonbridge, containing 402 inhabitants. The living is a donative, in the patronage of John Simpson, Esq. The church is dedicated to St. Giles the Abbot, on whose festival (Sep. 1st) a fair is still held. Christopher Smart, a poet and miscellaneous writer of some eminence, was born here in 1722, and died in a state of derangement in 1771.

SHIPBROOK, a township in the parish of DAVENHAM, hundred of NORTHWICH, county palatine of CHESTER, 3 miles (S. E.) from Northwich, containing 92 inhabitants. The Grand Trunk canal passes through the township.

SHIPDEN, formerly a parish in the northern division of the hundred of ERPINGHAM, county of NORFOLK, adjacent to Cromer. The living was a rectory, but the church, which was dedicated to St. Peter, having been destroyed by an inundation of the sea, the parochial rights of Shipden have, for a very long period, been lost.

SHIPDHAM, a parish in the hundred of MITFORD, county of NORFOLK, 4¾ miles (S. W. by S.) from East Dereham, containing 1642 inhabitants. The living is a rectory, in the archdeaconry of Norfolk, and diocese of Norwich, rated in the king's books at £27. 7. 6., and in in the patronage of the Rev. B. Barker. The church, dedicated to All Saints, is a stately pile, with a strong western tower embattled and crowned with a handsome turret. Thomas Bullock, in 1735, bequeathed land, producing upwards of £45, for teaching the poor children of the parish. There was anciently an hermitage within the parish, with a chapel dedicated to St. Thomas à Becket, for the repair of which the Bishop of Ely, in 1487, granted forty days' indulgence to all who might contribute.

SHIPHAM, a parish in the hundred of WINTERSTOKE, county of SOMERSET, 3 miles (N. E. by N.) from Axbridge, containing 635 inhabitants. The living is a discharged rectory, in the archdeaconry of Wells, and diocese of Bath and Wells, rated in the king's books at £10. 3. 11., endowed with £200 royal bounty, and in the patronage of the Dean and Chapter of Wells. The church is dedicated to St. Leonard. There are lead and calamine works in operation in the parish.

SHIPLAKE, a parish in the hundred of BINFIELD, county of OXFORD, 2¾ miles (S.) from Henley upon Thames, containing 528 inhabitants. The living is a discharged vicarage, in the archdeaconry and diocese of Oxford, rated in the king's books at £7. 1., and in the patronage of the Dean and Canons of Windsor. The church is dedicated to St. Peter and St. Paul.

SHIPLEY, a township in the parish of HEANOR, hundred of MORLESTON and LITCHURCH, county of DERBY, 9½ miles (N. E. by E.) from Derby, containing 595 inhabitants. The Nutbrook canal and several railways communicate with the coal mines here.

SHIPLEY, a township in the parish of ELLINGHAM, southern division of BAMBROUGH ward, county of NORTHUMBERLAND, 4½ miles (N. W. by N.) from Alnwick, containing 129 inhabitants.

SHIPLEY, a parish in the hundred of WEST GRINSTEAD, rape of BRAMBER, county of SUSSEX, 6 miles (S. S. W.) from Horsham, containing 1159 inhabitants. The living is a perpetual curacy, in the archdeaconry and diocese of Chichester, endowed with £200 private benefaction, £200 royal bounty, and £600 parliamentary grant, and in the patronage of the Rector of Coombs. The church, dedicated to St. Mary, is principally in the Norman style.

SHIPLEY, a parochial district, in the parish of BRADFORD, wapentake of MORLEY, West riding of the county of YORK 3¼ miles (N.N.W.) from Bradford, containing 1606 inhabitants. A church was founded in 1825, under the authority of His Majesty's Commissioners, and in 1828 it was constituted a district church; the estimate, including incidental expenses, was £7622. 7. There are places of worship for Baptists and Wesleyan Methodists. A branch of the Leeds and Liverpool canal passes through the township, in which the manufacture of worsted, woollen cloth, paper, &c., is carried on to some extent.

SHIPMEADOW, a parish in the hundred of WANGFORD, county of SUFFOLK, 3 miles (W. by S.) from Beccles, containing 133 inhabitants. The living is a discharged rectory, in the archdeaconry of Suffolk, and diocese of Norwich, rated in the king's books at £10. Robert Suckling, Esq. was patron in 1803. The church is dedicated to St. Bartholomew. The navigable river Waveney bounds the parish on the north.

SHIPPON, a chapelry in that part of the parish of ST. HELEN, ABINGDON, which is in the hundred of HORMER, county of BERKS, 1 mile (W.N.W.) from Abingdon, containing 138 inhabitants.

SHIPSTON upon STOUR, a market town and parish forming, with the parishes of Tidmington and Tredington, a detached portion of the upper division of the hundred of OSWALDSLOW, county of WORCESTER, being locally in the Kington division of the hundred of Kington, county of Warwick, 16 miles (S. by W.) from Warwick, and 83 (N.W. by W.) from London, containing 1562 inhabitants. This town is said to derive its name from having been formerly one of the largest markets for sheep in the kingdom; it is situated on the river Stour, in a fertile and rather hilly country, at about two miles distance from the Stratford upon Avon and Moreton railway: there was formerly a large manufacture of shag, which has quite declined, and it has now little trade of any description. The Dean and Chapter of Worcester, who possess the manorial rights, hold a court annually, at which a constable is appointed. The market is on Thursday, and there are fairs on the third Tuesday in April, June 22nd, the last Tuesday in August, and the Tuesday after the 10th of October. The living is a rectory, with the perpetual curacy of Tidmington annexed, in the archdeaconry and diocese of Worcester, rated in the king's books at £5. 7. 8½., and in the patronage of the Dean and Chapter of Worcester, and of the Principal and Fellows of Jesus College, Oxford, the former presenting to every third vacancy. The church is dedicated to St. Edmund. The Baptists, Society of Friends, and Wesleyan Methodists, have each a place of worship. Endowments for the instruction of children were bequeathed by John Pittway, in 1706, and by George Marshall, in 1747, the latter amounting to £39 per annum, and the National

school is well attended; there are also various small bequests for the poor of the town.

SHIPTON, a parish within the liberties of the borough of WENLOCK, county of SALOP, 7 miles (S. W. by S.) from Much-Wenlock, containing 126 inhabitants. The living is a perpetual curacy, in the archdeaconry of Salop, and diocese of Hereford. The church is dedicated to St. James. This was formerly a chapelry in the parish of Wenlock.

SHIPTON, a chapelry in the parish of MARKET-WEIGHTON, partly within the liberty of ST. PETER of YORK, and partly in the Holme-Beacon division of the wapentake of HARTHILL, East riding of the county of YORK, 1½ mile (N. W. by W.) from Market-Weighton, containing 369 inhabitants. It is within the peculiar jurisdiction of the Prebendary of Weighton in the Cathedral Church of York. There is a school for the education of ten boys, endowed with a rent-charge of £5. 14., by John Hutchinson, in 1714, and another of £2 by John and Elizabeth Barker, in 1742.

SHIPTON, a township in that part of the parish of OVERTON which is in the wapentake of BULMER, North riding, and extending into the liberty of ST. PETER of YORK, East riding, of the county of YORK, 5½ miles (N. W. by N.) from York, containing 377 inhabitants. There are places of worship for Calvinistic and Wesleyan Methodists. A free grammar school was founded, in 1655, by Ann Middleton, who endowed it with £40 per annum, which is paid to the master, who also occupies a house rent-free, for teaching about fifty children reading, writing, and accompts.

SHIPTON upon CHERWELL, a parish in the hundred of WOOTTON, county of OXFORD, 2¼ miles (E.) from Woodstock, containing 147 inhabitants. The living is a rectory, in the archdeaconry and diocese of Oxford, rated in the king's books at £11. 9. 4½. Mrs. Payne was patroness in 1813. The church is dedicated to St. Mary.

SHIPTON under WHICHWOOD, a parish in the hundred of CHADLINGTON, county of OXFORD, 4 miles (N.N.E.) from Burford, comprising the chapelries of Langley, Leafield, Lyneham, Milton, and Ramsden, and containing 2275 inhabitants. The living is a vicarage, in the archdeaconry and diocese of Oxford, rated in the king's books at £16, and in the patronage of the Professor of Civil Law in the University of Oxford. The church is dedicated to St. Mary.

SHIPTON-BELLINGER, a parish in the hundred of THORNGATE, Andover division of the county of SOUTHAMPTON, 4¼ miles (S. W. by S.) from Ludgershall, containing 267 inhabitants. The living is a discharged vicarage, in the archdeaconry and diocese of Winchester, rated in the king's books at £8, and endowed with £200 royal bounty. J. Gilbert, Esq. was patron in 1812. The church is dedicated to St. Mary. This parish is within the jurisdiction of the Cheyney Court held at Winchester every Thursday, for the recovery of debts to any amount.

SHIPTON-LEE, a hamlet in the parish of QUAINTON, hundred of ASHENDON, county of BUCKINGHAM, 5½ miles (S. W. by S.) from Winslow, containing 106 inhabitants. Here was formerly a chapel, now demolished.

SHIPTON-MOYNE, a parish in the hundred of LONGTREE, county of GLOUCESTER, 2¼ miles (S. by E.)

from Tetbury, containing 390 inhabitants. The living is a rectory, in the archdeaconry and diocese of Gloucester, rated in the king's books at £18. 1. 10½., and in the patronage of W. Hodges, Esq. The church is dedicated to St. John the Baptist.

SHIPTON-OLIFFE, a parish in the hundred of BRADLEY, county of GLOUCESTER, 6¼ miles (N.W. by W.) from North Leach, containing 177 inhabitants. The living is a discharged rectory, with that of Shipton-Sollars united, in the archdeaconry and diocese of Gloucester, rated in the king's books at £7. 5. 9., and in the alternate patronage of the families of Peachy and Chapeau. The church is dedicated to St. Oswald. Limestone exists in the parish.

SHIPTON-SOLLARS, a parish in the hundred of BRADLEY, county of GLOUCESTER, 6½ miles (W. N.W.) from North Leach, containing 62 inhabitants. The living is a discharged rectory, united with that of Shipton-Oliffe, in the archdeaconry and diocese of Gloucester, rated in the king's books at £7. 3 4. The church is dedicated to St. Mary.

SHIRBURN, a parish in the hundred of PIRTON, county of OXFORD, 4 miles (S. by E.) from Tetsworth, containing 332 inhabitants. The living is a discharged vicarage, in the archdeaconry and diocese of Oxford, rated in the king's books at £10. 16. 0½., endowed with £800 private benefaction, and £200 royal bounty, and in the patronage of the Earl of Macclesfield. The church is dedicated to All Saints. Shirburn castle, the seat of the Earl of Macclesfield, is surrounded by a moat, over which is a drawbridge.

SHIREHAMPTON, a chapelry in the parish of WESTBURY upon TRIM, lower division of the hundred of HENBURY, county of GLOUCESTER, 5 miles (N.W. by W.) from Bristol, containing 635 inhabitants. The chapel, dedicated to St. Michael, has lately received an addition of one hundred and fifty-four sittings, of which ninety-one are free, the Incorporated Society for the enlargement of churches and chapels having granted £100 towards defraying the expense. There is a place of worship for Wesleyan Methodists. King-road and Hung-road, two noted anchorages for ships, are within the precincts of this chapelry.

SHIREHEAD, a chapelry in that part of the parish of COCKERHAM which is in the hundred of AMOUNDERNESS, county palatine of LANCASTER, 4 miles (N. W. by N.) from Garstang. The population is returned with the parish. The living is a perpetual curacy, in the archdeaconry of Richmond, and diocese of Chester, endowed with £200 private benefaction, and £800 royal bounty.

SHIRE-NEWTON, a parish in the upper division of the hundred of CALDICOTT, county of MONMOUTH, containing 689 inhabitants, of which number, 261 are in the village of Shire-Newton, 4½ miles (W.) from Chepstow. The living is a discharged rectory, in the archdeaconry and diocese of Llandaff, rated in the king's books at £9. 8. 1½., and in the patronage of the Crown. The church is dedicated to St. Thomas à Becket.

SHIRLAND, a parish in the hundred of SCARSDALE, county of DERBY, 2 miles (N. by W.) from Alfreton, containing, with the hamlet of Higham, 1205 inhabitants. The living is a rectory, in the archdeaconry of Derby, and diocese of Lichfield and Coventry, rated in the king's books at £7. 15. 5., and in the alternate pa-

tronage of the Earl of Thanet, and W. E. Nightingale, and John Charge, Esqrs. The church, dedicated to St. Leonard, contains several ancient monuments of the De Greys. Higham was formerly a market town, but the market was discontinued about 1785 ; a fair, chiefly for cattle, is still held on the Wednesday after New Year's day. At Hatfield-gate is a charity school, endowed by Edward Revell, Mr. Stocks, and others, with about £25 per annum, and a house for the master, who educates twenty-four children : the premises have been recently rebuilt by subscription.

SHIRLEY, a parish in the hundred of APPLETREE, county of DERBY, 4¼ miles (S.E. by S.) from Ashbourn, comprising the chapelry of Yeaveley, and the township of Stydd, and containing 589 inhabitants. The living is a discharged vicarage, in the archdeaconry of Derby, and diocese of Lichfield and Coventry, rated in the king's books at £6. 13. 4., endowed with £200 private benefaction, and £300 parliamentary grant, and in the patronage of the Rev. W. A. Shirley. The church, dedicated to St. Michael, is a small building with a wooden tower. Part of the old manor-house of the Shirleys, who settled here in the reign of Henry II., still remains attached to a farm-house.

SHITLINGTON, a parish partly in the hundred of CLIFTON, and partly in that of FLITT, county of BEDFORD, 4 miles (E. S. E.) from Silsoe, containing, with the hamlets of Holywell and Lower Stondon, 1149 inhabitants. The living is a discharged vicarage with Gravenhurst, in the archdeaconry of Bedford, and diocese of Lincoln, rated in the king's books at £18, endowed with £200 private benefaction, and £200 royal bounty, and in the patronage of the President and Fellows of Trinity College, Cambridge. The church, dedicated to All Saints, is a large and handsome edifice ; the tower was rebuilt by the parishioners in 1750.

SHITLINGTON, a township in the parish of THORNHILL, lower division of the wapentake of AGBRIGG, West riding of the county of YORK, 5¾ miles (S. W. by W.) from Wakefield, containing 1635 inhabitants.

SHITLINGTON (HIGH), a township in the parish of WARK, north-western division of TINDALE ward, county of NORTHUMBERLAND, 3 miles (W.) from Wark, containing 104 inhabitants.

SHITLINGTON (LOW), a township in the parish of WARK, north-western division of TINDALE ward, county of NORTHUMBERLAND, 2½ miles (W. by N.) from Wark, containing 105 inhabitants.

SHITTERTON, a tything in the parish and hundred of BEER - REGIS, Blandford (South) division of the county of DORSET, containing 127 inhabitants.

SHOBDON, a parish in the hundred of STRETFORD, county of HEREFORD, 5½ miles (E. S. E.) from Presteigne, containing 536 inhabitants. The living is a rectory, in the archdeaconry and diocese of Hereford, rated in the king's books at £5. 7. 11., and in the patronage of William Hanbury, Esq. The church, dedicated to St. John the Evangelist, is the burial-place of the Bateman family ; it was partially rebuilt, in 1757, by John Viscount Bateman. A court leet is annually held here. Two schools, one for boys, the other for girls, are supported by Mr. and Mrs. Hanbury. Near the church is a mount, called Castle Hill, encompassed with a moat supposed to be the remains of a Roman, or Danish, fortification.

SHOBROOKE, a parish in the western division of the hundred of BUDLEIGH, county of DEVON, 2 miles (E.N.E.) from Crediton, containing, exclusively of a portion of the tything of Fulford which is in this parish, 737 inhabitants. The living is a rectory, annexed to the bishoprick of Exeter, in the archdeaconry and diocese of Exeter, rated in the king's books at £36. There is a place of worship for Independents. Various bequests, producing about £6 a year, are applied to the education of poor children.

SHOBY, a chapelry in the parish of SAXELBY, eastern division of the hundred of GOSCOTE, county of LEICESTER, 5 miles (W. by N.) from Melton-Mowbray, containing 31 inhabitants.

SHOCKLACH, a parish in the higher division of the hundred of BROXTON, county palatine of CHESTER, comprising the townships of Caldecott, Church-Shocklach, and Oviatt-Shocklach, and containing 422 inhabitants, of which number, 158 are in the township of Church-Shocklach, 4½ miles (N. W. by W.), and 180 in that of Oviatt-Shocklach, 3¼ miles (W.N.W.), from Malpas. The living is a perpetual curacy, in the archdeaconry and diocese of Chester, endowed with £200 private benefaction, and £200 royal bounty, and in the patronage of Sir R. Puleston, Bart. The church, dedicated to St. Edith, is a small ancient building, with an enriched Norman door. The parish is bounded on the west by the river Dee, which is crossed by a bridge at Castle-Town, where is the moated site of Shocklach castle.

SHOEBURY (NORTH), a parish in the hundred of ROCHFORD, county of ESSEX, 3¼ miles (E.N.E.) from South End, containing 210 inhabitants. The living is a discharged vicarage, in the archdeaconry of Essex, and diocese of London, rated in the king's books at £9, endowed with £200 private benefaction, and £200 royal bounty, and in the patronage of the Crown. The church is dedicated to St. Mary.

SHOEBURY (SOUTH), a parish in the hundred of ROCHFORD, cuonty of ESSEX, 4 miles (E.) from South End, containing 153 inhabitants. The living is a rectory, in the archdeaconry of Essex, and diocese of London, rated in the king's books at £14. 13. 4. R. Bristow, Esq. was patron in 1812. The church is dedicated to St. Andrew. The parish is bounded on the south by the Thames, and lies opposite to the Nore. On Shoebury Ness is a signal station. A school is supported by small annual subscriptions.

SHOPLAND, a parish in the hundred of ROCHFORD, county of ESSEX, 2 miles (N.E. by E.) from Prittlewell, containing 34 inhabitants. The living is a discharged vicarage, in the archdeaconry of Essex, and diocese of London, rated in the king's books at £9, and endowed with £200 royal bounty. Thomas Mutlow, Esq. was patron in 1803. The church is dedicated to St. Mary Magdalene.

SHOREDITCH (ST. LEONARD), a parish in the Tower division of the hundred of OSSULSTONE, county of MIDDLESEX, adjoining the north-eastern portion of the metropolis, and, with Haggerstone and Hoxton, which, by a recent act of parliament, have been constituted distinct parishes, containing 52,966 inhabitants. This parish, in ancient records called Sordig, Soresdich, and Shordych, appears to have derived its name from the great common sewer, or ditch, which passed through

it, and to have given name to the family of Sir John de Sordig, lord of the manor, and one of the ambassadors of Edward III. to Philip of France, more than a century prior to the time of Jane Shore, from whom, according to a legendary tradition, it is supposed to have been originally derived. The Roman military way leading from London wall to the ford at Hackney, passed through part of the churchyard, and there are still some vestiges of the old artillery ground, anciently a Roman Campus Martis, which was subsequently celebrated for archery and other military exercises practised there by the citizens of London, but now covered with houses. The parish, which is very extensive, consists of numerous streets connecting it with the metropolis, and of several ranges of building on the roads to Kingsland, Hackney, and Bethnal Green ; it is well paved, lighted with gas, and amply supplied with water. There are some remains of ancient houses, but by far the greater number are of modern appearance, and many of them of recent erection. Among the more ancient is one near the bath of St. Agnes de Clare, rebuilt after the fire of London, in which the practice of inoculation for the small-pox was first brought to perfection, previously to the erection of the Small-pox hospital in the parish of St. Pancras, to which the original establishment was removed in 1765. The only branches of manufacture carried on in the parish are such as are connected with the silk-factories of the adjoining parish of Spitalfields, and there are several breweries, and some extensive foundries for church bells. The parish is within the jurisdiction of a court of requests for the Tower Hamlets, established under an act passed in the 23rd of George II., and 19th of George III., for the recovery of debts under 40s., and within the limits of the new police act.

The living is a vicarage, in the archdeaconry and diocese of London, rated in the king's books at £17, and in the patronage of the Archdeacon of London. The church, rebuilt in 1740, is a handsome edifice in the Grecian style of architecture, with a tower, from which rises an open turret surrounded with Corinthian pillars, supporting an elliptical dome surmounted by a small, but well-proportioned, spire ; the western entrance is through a stately portico of four columns of the Doric order, supporting an enriched entablature and cornice, and surmounted by a triangular pediment. The interior is well arranged ; the east window is embellished with stained glass, and there are numerous ancient monuments, among which may be noticed an altar-tomb, with recumbent effigies, of Sir John Elrington and his lady ; a monument of Sir Thomas Leigh, in a kneeling posture ; one for four ladies of the Rutland family, whose figures are represented kneeling at an altar, two on each side, in a recess ; some erect statues, and various other memorials. There are places of worship for Baptists, Independents, and Wesleyan and other Methodists. The charity school, for the maintenance, clothing, and education, of boys, was established in 1705, and a school-house erected by subscription, in 1722 : a similar institution for girls was established in 1709, and the school-house was erected in 1723 ; the former has an annual income of £100, and the latter one of £160, arising from rents and personal estates ; they are further supported by subscription, and afford maintenance and instruction to fifty boys and forty girls. There are National and Sunday schools in connexion with the established church and the various dissenting congregations. On the south side of Old Street-road are twelve almshouses, built, in 1591, by Judge Fuller, who endowed them with £50 per annum, for twelve aged widows of the parish : on the opposite side of the road are eight almshouses, founded, in 1658, by Mr. John Walter, who endowed them for aged widows, who have an allowance of money weekly, and an annual supply of coal : adjoining these are almshouses erected by the Company of Weavers, for decayed members, to which Mr. William Watson was a great benefactor in 1670 : there are also some almshouses belonging to the Dutch church in Austin Friars, among which are two tenements, the gift of Egbert Guede, of Overyssel, Gent., for the maintenance and habitation of four poor men belonging to that church. The Refuge for the Destitute, in Kingsland-road, a spacious building, in every respect adapted to its purpose, is also within the parish.

SHOREHAM, a parish in the hundred of CODS-HEATH, lathe of SUTTON at HONE, county of KENT, 4½ miles (N.) from Seven-Oaks, containing 891 inhabitants. The living, a discharged vicarage, is one of the three which constitute the deanery of the Arches, in the peculiar jurisdiction of the Archbishop of Canterbury, rated in the king's books at £14. 6. 8., and in the patronage of the Dean and Chapter of Westminster. The rectory of Shoreham, with the curacy of Otford, is rated in the king's books at £34. 9. 9½., and is an impropriation belonging to the Dean and Chapter of Westminster, a certain stipend being allowed to the curate. The church, dedicated to St. Peter and St. Paul, is an ancient structure, containing several elegant monuments. The river Darenth runs through the parish in its course to Dartford. Castle farm was built with the remains, and upon the site, of Shoreham castle. An old mansion-house, built by Inigo Jones, and formerly belonging to the D'Aranda family, is fast going to decay.

Corporate Seal of New Shoreham.

Obverse.   Reverse.

SHOREHAM (NEW), a borough, market town, sea-port, and parish, in the hundred of FISHERGATE, rape of BRAMBER, county of SUSSEX, 23 miles (E.) from Chichester, and 56 (S. by W.) from London, containing, according to the last census, 1047 inhabitants, which number has since increased to about 1500. This town is indebted for its origin to the decay of Old Shoreham, situated not far distant, which, though anciently a place of importance, is now an inconsiderable village. In ancient history it is chiefly remarkable for having been built on the spot where Ælla, the Saxon, landed with supplies from Germany, in aid of his countrymen, Hengist and Horsa. The town is situated about one mile from the English channel, on the river Adur, across which is a long wooden bridge, on the main road between Brighton and Portsmouth. A suspension bridge, on a design similar to that at Hammersmith, is now in progress over the river, at the western entrance into the town, at the expense of His Grace the Duke of Norfolk; which, when completed, will reduce the distance between Shoreham and Worthing about two miles. Shoreham is noted for its ship-building, and vessels of seven hundred tons have been launched here. From its proximity to Brighton and Worthing, the trade and importance of the port has, of late years, rapidly increased; its revenue, within the last twenty years, has been augmented five-fold, having been, in 1810, about £7000, and now amounting to £35,000. The harbour, which is a tide harbour, is very commodious : in spring tides it has about nineteen feet of water, in common ones about fourteen feet, and not more than three feet at ebb. The river runs by the side of the town, parallel with the sea, with which it communicates about half a mile eastward, and is frequented by ships of considerable burden. The imports consist principally of timber, deals, merchandise from France, wine, spirits, coal, &c.; and considerable quantities of oak timber are exported. Cement manufactories have been established here. The custom-house, lately erected, under the direction of Mr. Smirke, is an elegant building in the Grecian style, situated in the centre of the town. A large market for corn is held every fortnight; and a fair on July 25th. Shoreham is a borough by prescription, and is governed by a high constable appointed by the lord of the manor. It has sent two members to parliament since the 1st of Edward I.; the right of election being in the inhabitants paying scot and lot, and the freeholders of the rape of Bramber : the high constable is the returning officer. At the election in 1791, a majority of the electors having formed themselves into a society, called the Christian Club, the real object of which was to sell their votes to the best bidder, an act of parliament was passed, disfranchising every member of the society, and extending the votes for New Shoreham to the whole rape of Bramber, so that the right of election was imparted to about one thousand six hundred freeholders, instead of two hundred, to which it had been previously confined.

The living is a discharged vicarage, annexed to that of Old Shoreham, in the archdeaconry of Lewes, and diocese of Chichester, rated in the king's books at £6. 1. 8., endowed with £200 private benefaction, £800 royal bounty, and £800 parliamentary grant, and in the patronage of the President and Fellows of Magdalene College, Oxford. The church, dedicated to St. Mary, is an extremely interesting specimen of Norman architecture. At present only the choir is fitted up and appropriated to divine worship, the nave having been entirely destroyed. It was originally cruciform, and one of the largest in the neighbourhood, as well as perhaps the most elegant; the architectural details within being still remarkable for their richness and diversity. The Independents and Wesleyan Methodists have each a place of worship. There are National schools for boys and girls. Here was anciently a priory for Carmelites, or White friars, founded by Sir John Mowbray, Knt.;

also an hospital, dedicated to St. James, but no remains of either are now discernible.

SHOREHAM (OLD), a parish in the hundred of FISHERGATE, rape of BRAMBER, county of SUSSEX, ½ a mile (N. W. by N.) from New Shoreham, containing 235 inhabitants. The living is a discharged vicarage, with that of New Shoreham annexed, in the archdeaconry of Lewes, and diocese of Chichester, rated in the king's books at £7. 18. 6., and in the patronage of the President and Fellows of Magdalene College, Oxford. The church is dedicated to St. Nicholas. Here was an ancient hospital, dedicated to St. James, which was valued, in the reign of Elizabeth, at £1. 6. 8. per annum.

SHORESWOOD, a township in the parish of NORHAM, otherwise Norhamshire, county palatine of DURHAM, though locally to the northward of the county of Northumberland, 6½ miles (S. W. by S.) from Berwick upon Tweed, containing 261 inhabitants, who are chiefly employed in the adjacent coal mines.

SHORNCUTT, a parish in the hundred of HIGHWORTH, CRICKLADE, and STAPLE, county of WILTS, 5¾ miles (W. N. W.) from Cricklade, containing 25 inhabitants. The living is a discharged rectory, in the archdeaconry and diocese of Salisbury, rated in the king's books at £4. 7. 6., and in the patronage of the Crown. The church is dedicated to All Saints.

SHORNE, a joint parish with Merston, in the hundred of SHAMWELL, lathe of AYLESFORD, county of KENT, 3¾ miles (S. E.) from Gravesend, containing, with Merston, 776 inhabitants. The living is a vicarage, in the archdeaconry and diocese of Rochester, rated in the king's books at £13. 1. 8., and in the patronage of the Dean and Chapter of Rochester. The church, dedicated to St. Peter and St. Paul, contains a fine monument to the memory of Sir Henry de Cobham. Courts leet and baron are occasionally held. National and Sunday schools established here are supported partly by subscription, but principally by the dividends arising from £900 three per cent. consols., the bequest of the Rev. R. G. Ayerst, in 1812. A battery, mounting twenty-four pounders, for the protection of this part of the Medway, was constructed in 1796.

SHORTFLATT, a township in that part of the parish of BOLAM which is in the north-eastern division of TINDALE ward, county of NORTHUMBERLAND, 10¾ miles (W. S. W.) from Morpeth, containing 22 inhabitants.

SHORTHAMPTON, a chapelry in that part of the parish of CHARLBURY which is in the hundred of CHADLINGTON, county of OXFORD, 5 miles (S. by E.) from Chipping-Norton. The population is returned with the tything of Chilson. The living is a perpetual curacy, annexed to the vicarage of Charlbury, in the archdeaconry and diocese of Oxford. The chapel is dedicated to All Saints.

SHORWELL, a parish in the liberty of WEST MEDINA, Isle of Wight division of the county of SOUTHAMPTON, 5 miles (S. W. by S.) from Newport, containing 576 inhabitants. The living comprises a sinecure rectory, rated in the king's books at £20. 0. 2½., and a discharged vicarage, to which is united the rectory of Mottiston, rated at £17. 16. 0½., endowed with £200 private benefaction, and £200 royal bounty, in the archdeaconry and diocese of Winchester, and both in the patronage of Lady St. John Mildmay. The church is dedicated to St. Peter.

SHOSTON, a township in the parish and northern division of BAMBROUGH ward, county of NORTHUMBERLAND, 8 miles (E. by S.) from Belford, containing 63 inhabitants.

SHOTFORD, a hamlet (formerly a chapelry) in the parish of MENDHAM, hundred of EARSHAM, county of NORFOLK, 1 mile (S. E.) from Harleston. The population is returned with the parish. The chapel is desecrated, having been converted into a malt-house.

SHOT-HAUGH, a joint township with East and West Thriston, in that part of the parish of FELTON which is in the eastern division of MORPETH ward, county of NORTHUMBERLAND. The population is returned with East and West Thriston.

SHOTLEY, a parish in the eastern division of TINDALE ward, county of NORTHUMBERLAND, comprising the chapelry of High Blanchland, and the townships of Newbiggin and Shotley, and containing 1090 inhabitants, of which number, 609 are in the township of Shotley, 10½ miles (S. E.) from Hexham. The living is a perpetual curacy, in the archdeaconry of Northumberland, and diocese of Durham, endowed with £10 per annum and £200 private benefaction, and £400 royal bounty, and in the patronage of Lord Crewe's trustees. The church, dedicated to St. Andrew, is situated upon an eminence about a mile and a half from the village of Shotley: in the cemetery is an elegant mausoleum in memory of the Hopper family. Here are several extensive and productive lead and coal mines. A school is supported by annual contributions amounting to about £20.

SHOTLEY, a parish in the hundred of SAMFORD, county of SUFFOLK, 8¼ miles (S. E. by S.) from Ipswich, containing 339 inhabitants. The living is a rectory, in the archdeaconry of Suffolk, and diocese of Norwich, rated in the king's books at £20, and in the patronage of the Marquis of Bristol. The church, dedicated to St. Mary, is remarkable for its elegance, which it owes to a former incumbent, the Hon. Hervey Aston, D.D., who completely pewed, paved, and beautified it in 1744. The parish is situated at the confluence of the navigable rivers Orwell and Stour, opposite to the town of Harwich, with which there is a communication by a regular ferry.

SHOTOVER, an extra-parochial liberty, in the hundred of BULLINGTON, county of OXFORD, 4¼ miles (E. by N.) from Oxford, containing 85 inhabitants.

SHOTTESBROOK, a parish in the hundred of BEYNHURST, county of BERKS, 5 miles (S. W.) from Maidenhead, containing 135 inhabitants. The living is a rectory not in charge, united, in 1744, to the vicarage of White Waltham, in the archdeaconry of Berks, and diocese of Salisbury. The church, dedicated to St. John the Baptist, though small, is an elegant cruciform structure, principally in the decorated style, with a tower and spire rising from the intersection: it was erected in 1337, and contains three stone stalls under trefoil arches, with a piscina adjoining, an octangular font, enriched with crocketed pinnacles, and several interesting monuments and inscriptions. In the chancel lie the remains of the learned Henry Dodwell, some time Camden Professor of History at Oxford, and an able chronologist and historian: his celebrated work "De cyclis Veterum" was written here. A chantry, or college, for a warden, five priests, and two clerks, was founded here, in 1337, by Sir William Trussell, Knt., the revenue of which at the dissolution was estimated at £42. 2. 8. Smewins, in this parish, was a hunting-seat of Prince Arthur, eldest son of Henry VII., but it is now a farm-house.

SHOTTESHAM (ALL SAINTS), a parish in the hundred of HENSTEAD, county of NORFOLK, 4¾ miles (N. E. by N.) from St. Mary Stratton, containing 458 inhabitants. The living is a discharged vicarage, in the archdeaconry of Norfolk, and diocese of Norwich, rated in the king's books at £6. 13. 4., and in the patronage of the Earl of Albemarle. Elizabeth Bayspoole, in 1711, bequeathed £4. 12. per annum for a school and other charitable purposes.

SHOTTESHAM (ST. MARTIN), a parish in the hundred of HENSTEAD, county of NORFOLK, 4½ miles (N. E. by N.) from St. Mary Stratton. The population is returned with the parish of Shottesham St. Mary. The living is a discharged rectory, in the archdeaconry of Norfolk, and diocese of Norwich, rated in the king's books at £4, and in the patronage of the Bishop of Norwich. The church has been demolished.

SHOTTESHAM (ST. MARY), a parish in the hundred of HENSTEAD, county of NORFOLK, 4¾ miles (N. N. E.) from St. Mary Stratton, containing, with the parish of Shottesham St. Martin, 383 inhabitants. The living is a discharged vicarage, in the archdeaconry of Norfolk, and diocese of Norwich, rated in the king's books at £5, and in the patronage of the Earl of Albemarle. The church of St. Botolph has been demolished; and the living, a discharged vicarage, was annexed in 1311 to this parish.

SHOTTISHAM, a parish in the hundred of WILFORD, county of SUFFOLK, 5¼ miles (S. E.) from Woodbridge, containing 235 inhabitants. The living is a discharged rectory, in the archdeaconry of Suffolk, and diocese of Norwich, rated in the king's books at £4. 16. 0½., endowed with £200 royal bounty, and in the patronage of Mrs. Elizabeth Darby and Miss Mary Kett. The church is dedicated to St. Margaret. The navigable river Deben runs on the western side of the parish, where there is an inlet, called Shottisham creek. Crag or shell pits, supposed to be diluvial remains, abound here.

SHOTTLE, a joint township with Postern, in the parish of DUFFIELD, hundred of APPLETREE, county of DERBY, 2¼ miles (W. by S.) from Belper, containing, with Postern, 607 inhabitants. The sum of £6 per annum, arising partly from a bequest by Ralph Dowley, in 1740, is paid to a schoolmaster for teaching the poor children of the township, in a school-room erected by subscription among the inhabitants.

SHOTTON, a joint township with Langley-Dale, in the parish of STAINDROP, south-western division of DARLINGTON ward, county palatine of DURHAM, 5½ miles (N. E. by E.) from Barnard-Castle. The population is returned with Langley-Dale.

SHOTTON, a township in the parish of EASINGTON, southern division of EASINGTON ward, county palatine of DURHAM, 9 miles (E. by S.) from Durham, containing 264 inhabitants. A free school, with a house for the master, was founded here, in 1668, in pursuance of the will of Edward Walton; the annual income is £25, of which sum £20 is paid for the instruction of twenty children, and £5 is appropriated for books and repairs, under the superintendence of the Society of Friends.

SHOTTON, a joint township with Foxton, in the parish of SEDGEFIELD, north-eastern division of STOCKTON ward, county palatine of DURHAM, 8½ miles (N. W.) from Stockton upon Tees, containing 63 inhabitants.

SHOTTON, a joint township with Plessey, in the parish of STANNINGTON, western division of CASTLE ward, county of NORTHUMBERLAND, 6¼ miles (S. by E.) from Morpeth. The population is returned with Plessey.

SHOTTSWELL, a parish in the Burton-Dassett division of the hundred of KINGTON, county of WARWICK, 4½ miles (N. N. W.) from Banbury, containing 268 inhabitants. The living is a discharged vicarage, in the archdeaconry of Coventry, and diocese of Lichfield and Coventry, rated in the king's books at £5. 13. 4., and in the patronage of the Earl of Guildford. The church is dedicated to St. Lawrence. There is a place of worship for Wesleyan Methodists.

SHOTWICK, a parish in the higher division of the hundred of WIRRALL, county palatine of CHESTER, comprising the townships of Cappenhurst, Kingswood, Great Saughall, Little Saughall, Shotwick, and Woodbank, otherwise Rough Shotwick, and containing 719 inhabitants, of which number, 94 are in the township of Shotwick, 6 miles (N. W.) from Chester. The living is a perpetual curacy, in the archdeaconry and diocese of Chester, endowed with £18 per annum, and £240 private benefaction, £600 royal bounty, and £400 parliamentary grant, and in the patronage of the Dean and Chapter of Chester. The church, dedicated to St. Michael, has a curious Norman door, and some portions in the later style of English architecture.

SHOTWICK-PARK, an extra-parochial liberty, in the higher division of the hundred of WIRRALL, county palatine of CHESTER, 4¼ miles (N. W.) from Chester, containing 23 inhabitants. This was the site of a castle formerly belonging to the crown. Henry II. is said to have lodged here on his journey to and from Ireland; and Edward I. occupied it in 1278. The castle was standing in Leland's time, and there were some remains in 1622, since which period every vestige has been gradually removed.

SHOULDEN, a parish in the hundred of CORNILO, lathe of ST. AUGUSTINE, county of KENT, 1½ mile (W.) from Deal, containing 285 inhabitants. The living is a perpetual curacy, annexed to the vicarage of Northbourne, in the archdeaconry and diocese of Canterbury. The church is dedicated to St. Nicholas.

SHOULDHAM, a parish in the hundred of CLACKCLOSE, county of NORFOLK, 6½ miles (N. E.) from Downham-Market, containing 679 inhabitants. The living is a perpetual curacy, consolidated with that of St. Margaret, in the archdeaconry of Norfolk, and diocese of Norwich, and in the patronage of Sir Thomas Hare, Bart. The church is dedicated to All Saints; that of St. Margaret was standing in 1512, but after the dissolution was suffered to go to decay. There is a place of worship for Wesleyan Methodists. A Gilbertine priory, in honour of the Holy Cross and the Blessed Virgin, was founded, in the time of Richard I., by Jeffrey Fitz-Piers, Earl of Essex, which, at the dissolution, possessed a revenue of £171. 6. 8.

SHOULDHAM-THORPE, a parish in the hundred of CLACKCLOSE, county of NORFOLK, 5 miles (N. E.)

from Downham-Market, containing 305 inhabitants The living is a perpetual curacy, in the archdeaconry of Norfolk, and diocese of Norwich, and in the patronage of Sir Thomas Hare, Bart. The church is dedicated to St. Mary.

SHOWELL, a chapelry in the parish of SWERFORD, hundred of CHADLINGTON, county of OXFORD, 2½ miles (E. N. E.) from Chipping-Norton.

SHRAWARDINE, a township in that part of the parish of ABBERBURY, which is in the hundred of FORD, county of SALOP, 6½ miles (N. W.) from Shrewsbury, containing, with Benthal, 48 inhabitants.

SHRAWARDINE, a parish in the hundred of PIMHILL, county of SALOP, 6¾ miles (W. N. W.) from Shrewsbury, containing 177 inhabitants. The living is a rectory, in the archdeaconry of Salop, and diocese of Hereford, rated in the king's books at £9. 12. 6., and in the patronage of the Earl of Powis. The church is dedicated to St. Mary. Shrawardine castle was built by Alan, a follower of the Conqueror, and ancestor of the celebrated Fitz-Alans, who held it under the crown for many ages, to check the invasions of the Welch. After having been the scene of many remarkable events, it was, in the reign of Elizabeth, purchased by Lord Chancellor Bromley : the site and remains, together with other estates in the parish, are now the property of the Earl of Powis.

SHRAWLEY, a parish in the lower division of the hundred of DODDINGTREE, county of WORCESTER, 4¼ miles (S. by W.) from Stourport, containing 484 inhabitants. The living is a rectory, in the archdeaconry and diocese of Worcester, rated in the king's books at £9. 17. 1., and in the patronage of Thomas Taylor Vernon, Esq. The church is dedicated to St. Mary. The river Severn passes through the parish, in which there are vestiges of some ancient intrenchments.

SHREWLEY, a chapelry in the parish of HATTON, Snitterfield division of the hundred of BARLICHWAY, county of WARWICK, 4 miles (N. W. by W.) from Warwick, containing 250 inhabitants.

SHREWSBURY, a borough and market town, having separate jurisdiction, locally in the liberties of Shrewsbury, county of SALOP, of which it is the chief town, 154 miles (N. W.) from London, containing, exclusively of the parish of Meole-Brace, which is within the liberties, 18,254 inhabitants, according to the census of 1821, since which period the number has increased to about 2000 more. This ancient borough is said to have risen from the ruins of Uriconium, now Wroxeter, a celebrated Roman station on the line of the Watling-street, which, passing through the present town in a direction from east to west, divides it into two nearly equal parts. From its situation on two hills, richly covered with shrubs and trees, it obtained from the Britons the appellations of Pengwerne and Amwithic, or Y Mwythig, and was by the Saxons called Scrobbes-byrig, from which, written in Domesday-book Sciropesberie, its present name is derived ; from what source it obtained the appellation of

Arms.

Salopesberie, by which it is mentioned in some ancient records, and from which it has, with the county, been denominated " Salop," has not been satisfactorily ascertained. During the octarchy, it was the capital of the district called Powysland, which comprised a portion of the Saxon and British frontier territories ; and the residence of the princes of Powys, whom, in 778, Offa, King of Mercia, expelled from their possessions, adding them to his own kingdom ; and, to secure his conquest, raised that stupendous barrier still called Offa's Dyke. In the reign of Alfred the Great, this town was numbered among the principal cities of Britain : it had a mint, which it retained till the reign of Henry III., there being several of the coins extant, struck in the reigns of Athelstan, Edgar, Athelred, Canute, Edward the Confessor, and Harold II., besides several between the years 1066 and 1272. When Canute was pursuing his conquests through the northern parts of the kingdom, the inhabitants revolted in his favour and surrendered the town, which, in 1016, Edmund Ironside, a short time previously to the partition of the kingdom, recovered from the Danes, inflicting signal vengeance on the townsmen for their treachery. At the time of the Conquest, Shrewsbury, with nearly the whole of the county, was bestowed by William on his kinsman, Roger de Montgomery, whom he created Earl of Shrewsbury, Chichester, and Arundel, that nobleman erecting here a formidable castle for his baronial residence. In 1069, the town was besieged by Edric Sylvaticus, and Owen Gwynedd, Prince of Wales, but was relieved by King William, who advanced from York, and defeated the assailants with great slaughter. In 1102, Robert de Belesme, son of Earl Roger, having espoused the cause of Robert, Duke of Normandy, and commenced measures for raising him to the throne of England, in opposition to his brother Henry I., that monarch marched against the town with an army of sixty thousand men ; and the earl, although he had previously fortified it with a wall on each side of the castle, across the isthmus formed by the river Severn, submitted on the approach of the king, acknowledged his treasonable conduct, and was banished to Normandy ; his estates were thus forfeited, and the castle became a royal fortress. The importance of Shrewsbury as a frontier town has rendered it the scene of many and various transactions of historical interest. In 1116, the nobles of the realm assembled here to do homage, and take the oaths of allegiance, to William, son of the Empress Matilda. Stephen, in 1138, laid siege to the castle, while Fitz-Alan, the governor, was absent in forwarding the claims of the empress, and having taken it by storm, hanged several of the garrison.

The frequent inroads of the Welch induced John to assemble a council here, in order to concert measures for suppressing them ; and, in 1215, Llewellyn, who had married Joan, natural daughter of that monarch, appeared before Shrewsbury with a numerous army, and obtained possession of it and the castle. Henry III. soon dispossessed him of his capture, and drove him back to his own territory ; but in the war with the barons, Richard, Earl of Pembroke, retired into Wales and, being assisted by that prince, laid waste the intermediate district, and plundered and burnt the town, after having put many of the inhabitants to the sword. Simon de Montfort, whilst prosecuting the war against

Henry III., obtained possession of the town, which he held only for a short time. In 1241 and 1267, the same monarch assembled an army here for the invasion of Wales, but was diverted from his purpose by the submission of Llewellyn, with whom he subsequently concluded a treaty of peace. About this time the king recommended the inhabitants to complete the fortifications of the town, of which only one side was defended, but notwithstanding the aid of royal bounty, the work was not accomplished in less than thirty years. The continued incursions of the Welch upon the English frontier induced Edward I., in 1277, to fix his residence in Shrewsbury, to which he removed the courts of King's Bench and Exchequer, and, in 1283, assembled the parliament here; the king and his court were accommodated at Acton-Burnell, the seat of Bishop Burnell, the Lord High Chancellor; the lords held their sittings in the castle, and the commons, who for the first time had any voice in the national councils, assembled in a barn in the town. This monarch having sent a force against the Welch without success, took the field in person, at the head of a numerous army, and an engagement took place at the foot of Snowdon, in which they were completely routed, Llewellyn slain, and his brother David, who had instigated him to this insurrection, taken prisoner, and, after a short confinement in Rhyddlan castle in Flintshire, brought to Shrewsbury, where, having been tried by the parliament, he was condemned and executed as a traitor, with a degree of degradation and severity previously unknown in this country, and which, till a very late period, furnished a precedent for the punishment of treason. Edward II. was received in this town with the greatest pomp in 1322, where, in the same year, he celebrated a grand tournament, which was attended by a numerous assemblage of knights and noblemen. In 1397, Richard II. convened the parliament at Shrewsbury, gave a splendid entertainment to the lords and commons, and created several peers, who at this time first assumed their seats in parliament : this, from the number of noblemen and others who attended, was called the Great Parliament; but the measures enacted, though ratified by the pope's bull, were repealed during the following reign, and the king's conduct while in this town was made the subject of one of those charges which subsequently led to his deposition.

In 1403, a sanguinary battle was fought in the immediate vicinity, between the forces of Henry IV. and those of the Earl of Northumberland, who had rebelled against the king, assisted by a considerable body of Scottish troops under the command of Earl Douglas, amounting to fourteen thousand men. After a severe and protracted conflict, the victory was decided in favour of Henry : two thousand three hundred knights and gentlemen, among whom was Hotspur, son of Earl Percy, after performing prodigious exploits of valour, and six thousand common soldiers, were slain on both sides ; the dead were interred on the spot, which has since been called Battlefield, where a church was afterwards erected by the king, in memory of his victory. Owen Glyndwr, who had raised an army to co-operate with the insurgents, remained inactive with twelve thousand men at Oswestry, and, on their defeat, retired into Wales. During the contest between the houses of York and Lancaster, the inhabitants embraced the cause of the former ; and on the defeat of Richard Plantagenet, Duke of York, at the battle of Wakefield, in which he was slain, his son Edward, Earl of March, afterwards Edward IV., levied in this town and neighbourhood a powerful army, with which he avenged the death of his father at the battle of Mortimer's Cross, where he gained a signal victory. Edward, on his elevation to the throne, selected Shrewsbury as an asylum for his queen during the agitation of the times, and in the convent of the Dominican friars, in which her Majesty resided, the princes Richard and George were born, the latter of whom died in childhood, and the former, with his elder brother, Prince Edward, was inhumanly murdered in the Tower of London by their uncle, the Protector, afterwards Richard III. The Earl of Richmond, on landing at Milford Haven, proceeded to this town, where he was proclaimed king, and, having strengthened his army with considerable reinforcements raised in the neighbourhood, advanced into Leicestershire, where he gained the battle of Bosworth Field, which terminated in the death of Richard III., and his own elevation to the throne, under the title of Henry VII. This monarch on his accession visited the town, with his queen and Prince Arthur ; and after celebrating the festival of St. George in the church of St. Chad, granted the inhabitants several privileges, in acknowledgment of the alacrity with which they had supported his claims to the crown.

On the breaking out of the parliamentary war, Charles I. came to Shrewsbury, where he was received with every demonstration of loyalty by the inhabitants, and was soon afterwards joined by Prince Rupert, Prince Charles, the Duke of York, and several noblemen and gentlemen : the king kept his court in an ancient building, called the Council-house, and having established a mint for the supply of his exigencies, the inhabitants liberally presented their plate to be melted and coined into money for his use, of which considerable sums were expended in extending and strengthening the fortifications of the town. In 1664, Col. Mytton made two attempts to obtain possession of the town and castle for the parliament, but was repulsed in both, with considerable loss ; but having obtained a reinforcement, he made a third effort, in which he carried the place by storm, and was appointed governor. In 1651, Charles II. summoned it to surrender, but, on the refusal of the governor, marched on to Worcester ; after which disastrous battle he took refuge in the Royal Oak at Boscobel, on the confines of this county. During that monarch's retreat on the continent, a plan was formed by a party of royalists to besiege the castle ; but their scheme was frustrated, and several of them were punished. James II. visited the town in 1687, and, attended by the nobility and gentry of the county, kept his court for several days at the council-house. During this reign the castle was dismantled, and all its ammunition and military stores removed. This castle, originally of such great extent and formidable strength that, to make room for its erection, Earl Roger pulled down nearly one-fifth of the town, was a fortress of very great importance till the final subjugation of Wales, after which period it was entrusted to a constable, generally the sheriff, who made it the county prison : its importance as a frontier garrison having ceased, it fell into decay, and was repaired during the parliamentary war, as a garrison for the king : after it came into the possession of the parliament, Cromwell erected an additional fort, called Roushill, which is among the most entire of the remaining portions. The remains are situated at the northern entrance into the town, on the summit of a bold eminence overlooking the Severn, by which it is nearly surrounded, and are composed principally of the keep, a spacious modernised structure of red stone, consisting of two round embattled towers connected by a quadrangular building, one hundred feet in length ; the walls of the inner court ; and the great arch of the interior gateway : these include a grassy area, in which, though now private property, the knights of the shire, according to immemorial usage, are girt with their swords, on their election to parliament. On the south side of the court is a lofty mount rising abruptly from the river : the summit is surrounded with a wall, and in one angle of the enclosure was a barbican, which has been converted into a summer-house, and commands an extensive, varied, and picturesque view of the surrounding country. The ramparts formerly environing the town, together with the towers by which they were defended, have, with the exception of the part erected by Cromwell, and one of the towers on the south side of the town, been demolished. Adjoining the castle precinct, and formerly within its walls, are the remains of the ancient Council-house, where the courts for the Marches of Wales were occasionally held, and which afforded a temporary residence to several of the English monarchs.

The town is pleasantly situated on two eminences rising gently from the river Severn, which, by its windings, forms a peninsula : it consists of several streets irregularly formed, and, with some exceptions, inconveniently narrow. Various improvements have been made under the provisions of an act obtained in 1821, and others are in progress, for removing numerous obstructions arising from the style of building, and widening the approaches to the town. The houses are in general of ancient character, though greatly intermixed with others of handsome appearance and modern erection ; and, under the influence of a situation admirably adapted to commercial purposes, and affording in its environs delightful spots for private residence, a very rapid degree of improvement is progressively taking place. It is well paved, lighted with gas by a company established in 1820, and supplied with excellent water from a remarkably fine spring, called Bradwell, about two miles distant, from which, since 1574, it has been conveyed by pipes, into numerous conduits in several parts of the town, and with water from the river Severn, by a company established in 1827. Over this river are two bridges of stone, one called the English bridge, a handsome structure of Grinshill freestone of seven circular arches, crowned with a balustrade, erected in 1774, at an expense of £16,000, defrayed by public subscription, and connecting the suburb of Abbey Foregate with the town ; the other, called the Welch bridge, a neat plain structure of five spacious arches, erected in 1795, at a cost exceeding £8000, affording a passage over the river into Wales. Near the Abbey Foregate is the military depôt, a handsome brick building, one hundred and thirty-two feet in length, and forty feet in width, erected in 1806, from a design by Wyatt, at an expense of £10,000 : within the enclosure are two magazines for ammunition, and

at each angle a neat house for the store-keeper and armourer : the building is capable of containing twenty-five thousand stand of arms. At the entrance into the town from the London road is a lofty column of the Grecian Doric style, rising from a base, ornamented at the angles with lions couchant, to the height of one hundred and thirty-two feet, and supporting on its summit a well-executed statue of Lieut. Gen. Rowland, Lord Hill, in honour of whose achievements in the late continental war it was erected, by general subscription, in 1814. The public subscription library, near St. John's Hill, containing more than five thousand volumes in various departments of literature, is conducted by a president and a committee, rising from a base, and supported by proprietary members, who pay £2. 2. admission, and an annual subscription of £1. 11. 6. ; attached to it is a news-room well supplied with periodical publications. A mechanics' institution was established in 1825, where lectures are occasionally delivered. The theatre was formerly part of the palace of the Princes of Powysland, of which it still retains some vestiges, though materially altered by its appropriation to dramatic uses : it is at present in a dilapidated condition, and performances take place in the circus. Assemblies are held monthly, during the season, in a suite of rooms well fitted up ; and races annually in September, continuing three days ; the course is on Bicton heath, about two miles west of the town. The river Severn, in addition to the salmon for which it is celebrated, and with which it formerly abounded to a much greater extent, produces trout, pike, perch, carp, eels, shad, flounders, lampreys, &c. On the south-western side of the town is a beautiful walk, called the Quarry, comprising about twenty acres, and extending along the winding margin of the Severn for five hundred yards in length, forming a noble avenue of full-grown lime-trees, from which diverge three other walks leading to the town. In the vicinity also are numerous pleasant walks and rides, through a country abounding in beautiful and picturesque scenery. The richly-cultivated plain of Shrewsbury, extending thirty miles from north to south, and twenty-eight from east to west, is divided into two nearly equal parts by the river Severn, and surrounded by a noble range of lofty mountains and beautiful hills. Among the former are the famed Wrekin, the Lawley, the Caradoc, the Longmynd, the Stiperstones, and the Breyddin chain, on which is an obelisk in honour of Admiral Lord Rodney ; and among the latter, the beautiful wood-crowned eminences of Grinshill, Pymhill, Hawkstone, Haughmond, and others, forming a finely varied range of hills of different elevation and character.

The trade, which was formerly of considerable extent and importance, has been materially diminished by the growth of other places ; but the town has, notwithstanding, always maintained a respectable share of internal commerce. Its ancient traffic in Welch cloths and flannel was formerly the principal source of its opulence, and at present, though not restricted to the Drapers' Company as before, produces no inconsiderable profit : the greater portion of those made in the counties of Montgomery and Merioneth, and part of Denbighshire, is sent to Shrewsbury. Two extensive manufactories for thread, linen yarn, and canvas, situated near the castle, adjoining the suburb of Castle Foregate, afford employment to a considerable number of persons ; and on the banks of the river, in Coleham, are the extensive iron-foundries of Mr. Hazledine, in which the immense chains that support the stupendous bridge over the Menai straits, and the iron work in many similar erections, were cast. This town is also noted for its brawn, and for a particular kind of sweet cakes, called Shrewsbury cakes. The river affords a convenient transit for goods of every description to Worcester, Gloucester, Bristol, and other towns; and considerable quantities of grain, in which the trade is extensive, and of lighter manufactured articles, are forwarded by land-carriage to Edstaston wharf, and thence, by the Ellesmere canal, to Chester and Liverpool. The Shrewsbury canal, which is the great medium of supplying the town with coal of excellent quality, terminates near the Castle Foregate, where convenient wharfs have been constructed by the canal company, for the use of persons connected with the coal-works on the line of the canal, which, when the Birmingham and Liverpool junction canal is completed, will open a new and extensive species of traffic for the town. The market days are Wednesday and Saturday, the latter being for grain : the general market is held in a stone building, erected in 1819, and about to be enlarged by subscription ; and that for corn, in the area under a spacious building of stone, erected in 1595, in the later style of English architecture ; in the centre of the principal front is a spacious portal, above which are the arms of Queen Elizabeth in alto relievo, and on each side of the central arch, pillars, supporting lions with shields on their breasts, well sculptured : the building is one hundred and five feet in length, and twenty-four feet wide, and over the ground-floor is a room of the same dimensions, appropriated formerly to the Drapers' Company, for the sale of flannel, and now used as a warehouse.

This town has received a succession of charters of incorporation, from the time of William the Conqueror to the reign of James II. : the earliest preserved in the archives of the corporation is dated Nov. 11th, 1st of Richard I., under which, as extended and confirmed by succeeding sovereigns, and remodelled by Charles I., the government is vested in a

Corporate Seal.

mayor, recorder, steward, twenty-four aldermen, and forty-eight common council-men, assisted by a town clerk, two chamberlains, two coroners, sword-bearer, serjeants at mace, and subordinate officers. The mayor is elected annually on the Friday after St. Bartholomew's day, the charter directing the mayor, aldermen, and assistants, to choose the senior alderman, who hath not before served for that dignity, which course is usually followed ; they also appoint the other officers of the corporation. The mayor, late mayor, recorder, three senior aldermen, and the Bishop of Lichfield and Coventry, with his commissary, are justices of the peace within the town and liberties. The freedom is acquired by descent, as well as by being born in the town, or obtained by apprenticeship to a member of one of the Incorporated Companies, of which there were sixteen, the Drapers' being the principal, but they are now much reduced in number.

It was formerly the custom for the several companies to celebrate the festival of Corpus Christi in St. Chad's church, after which three days were devoted to festivity and recreation ; the religious part of this ceremony was discontinued at the Reformation, but they still meet on the second Monday after Trinity, and go in procession to Kingsland, where they hold a rural festival, in arbours erected for the purpose, in which they are visited by the mayor and corporation. All persons above the age of twenty-one, born in the town, and all persons having served an apprenticeship in it, may demand their freedom on payment of £6. 19. 1. ; and all sons of burgesses, and those claiming by descent from burgesses, on paying £1. 3. 6. The corporation hold quarterly courts of session, on the Friday after the county quarter sessions, for all offences not capital ; and the mayor, assisted by some of the other magistrates, holds a session every Tuesday and Friday, for the determination of petty causes : they also hold a court of record, the jurisdiction of which extends over the liberties, every Tuesday, at which the mayor and the recorder preside, for the recovery of debts to any amount. A court of requests is also held, every alternate Wednesday, by commissioners appointed under an act passed in the 23rd of George III., for the recovery of debts exceeding 2s. and under 40s. : and courts leet are held annually in May and October, at the latter of which constables and other officers for the town are appointed. The assizes and general quarter sessions for the county are held here. The town and shire hall is a spacious, handsome, and commodious building of stone, erected in 1785, containing, on the ground-floor, a vestibule and two courts for the assizes, under one of which, appropriated to the Crown bar, is a cell for prisoners awaiting their trial : a handsome geometrical staircase leads to the upper story, where are a large room, occasionally used for county meetings, and for those of the corporation, and the incorporated and trading companies, and for other purposes ; a grand jury room, ornamented with portraits of George I., II., and III., Queen Charlotte, Admiral Benbow, Lord Hill, and Admiral Owen ; offices for the court of record, and for transacting the public business of the corporation. The town and county gaol, and house of correction for the county and the several boroughs therein, an extensive building of brick, pleasantly situated on the bank of the Severn, was erected in 1793, at an expense of £30,000 : the entrance is through a freestone gateway, over which is a bust of the celebrated Howard, and on each side a lodge for the inspection of prisoners previously to their admission : it contains a house for the governor, a chapel, an infirmary, twenty-three wards, nine work-rooms, twenty-three day-rooms and airing-yards, and is admirably adapted to the classification, employment, and reformation of prisoners, of whom it is capable of receiving five hundred. The borough has exercised the elective franchise from the 23rd of Edward I., and has regularly returned two members to parliament : the right of election is vested in the resident burgesses paying scot and lot, and not receiving alms, of whom the number is about nine hundred : the mayor is the returning officer.

Shrewsbury comprises the parishes of St. Alkmond, St. Chad, Holy Cross, St. Julian, and St. Mary, all, with the exception of St. Mary's, which is a royal peculiar, in the archdeaconry of Salop, and diocese of Lichfield and Coventry. The living of St. Alkmond's is a vicarage, rated in the king's books at £6, and in the patronage of the Crown. The church was made collegiate by King Edgar, who endowed it for the support of ten canons, one of whom acted as dean; but the society was dissolved on the establishment of Lilleshull abbey, to which its revenue was appropriated. The old edifice, a cruciform structure of great antiquity, was, with the exception of the tower and spire, which are one hundred and eighty-four feet in height, taken down, from an apprehension of insecurity, and rebuilt in 1795: the east window is embellished with a painting by Eginton, in stained glass, emblematical of faith. The living of St. Chad's is a perpetual curacy, in the patronage of the Crown: the church, erected in 1792, at an expense of nearly £20,000, in lieu of an older edifice, which, while undergoing repair, fell down in 1788, is a handsome circular building, in the Grecian style of architecture, with a square rustic tower supporting an octagonal belfry surmounted by a dome resting on eight Corinthian pillars: the body of the church forms a rotunda one hundred feet in diameter, surrounded by a range of duplicated Ionic pillars between the lofty arched windows, rising from the basement, and supporting a handsome cornice surmounted by a balustrade: the entrance is through a stately portico of four Doric columns, supporting a triangular pediment; the interior has a rich and pleasing effect; the galleries are supported by a duplicated range of Ionic pillars, from which rise Corinthian pillars supporting the roof; the chancel is adorned with a painting of the Resurrection, in stained glass, by Eginton, from a design by West, removed from Lichfield cathedral. The remains of the ancient church, formerly collegiate, and once a royal free chapel, consist only of the south aisle of the chancel, containing portions in the Norman, early English, and decorated styles of architecture: it was fitted up for the performance of the funeral service, and is at present appropriated to the use of the charity school. The living of the parish of the Holy Cross is a vicarage, with the chapel of St. Giles', rated in the king's books at £8, and in the patronage of Lord Berwick. The church, occupying a low site in the eastern suburb, to which it gives name, and surrounded on the south and west by the river Rea, commonly called Meole brook, is part of the conventual church of a splendid abbey, founded for Benedictine monks, by Roger de Montgomery, in 1083, (on the site of a religious institution established prior to the Conquest, with the revenue of which it was partly endowed,) and dedicated to St. Peter and St. Paul: it was a mitred abbey, and the abbots exercised episcopal authority in their house, being in some respects exempt from the jurisdiction of the diocesan: at the dissolution, in 1513, its revenue was estimated at £615. 4. 3. The king intended to make Shrewsbury the seat of a diocese, and to raise the abbey church into a cathedral, Dr. Bourchier, the last abbot of Leicester, having been actually nominated bishop; but pecuniary exigencies compelled him to abandon the design. The abbey was further distinguished by the resort of many pilgrims to the shrine of St. Winifred, whose remains had been removed hither from Gwytherin, in Denbighshire. The walls of this establishment included ten acres, and the buildings, principally in the Norman style of

architecture, were extensive and magnificent: the principal remains are the western tower, the north porch, nave, and aisles of the abbey, now the parish church, besides some small portions of the conventual buildings: the former retains several features of its ancient grandeur, though many alterations have been made, particularly the introduction of a large window of seven lights, of elegant tracery, and emblazoned with armorial bearings in stained glass, in the later English style, over the west doorway, which was originally a handsome circular arch, within which, at a much later period, a painted one has been placed; on each side of which are niches, one of them containing a statue of St. Peter, and the other a statue of St. Paul. The interior has a solemn grandeur of effect; the roof is finely vaulted, and supported on circular arches and massive piers, and in other parts the slender clustered column and the pointed arch prevail: the east window is enriched with armorial bearings, including those of Lord Berwick, by whom it was presented, and, in the central compartment, with paintings of St. Peter and St. Paul, in stained glass, by Mr. D. Evans, of Shrewsbury: there are various altar-tombs and ancient monuments, and within an arch, which formerly led to the south aisle of the transept, is an ancient figure in armour, supposed to be that of its founder, Earl Roger, who, having assumed the cowl toward the close of his life, died and was buried here. Among the ruins of the conventual buildings is a fragment, supposed to be part of the refectory, on which is an exquisitely beautiful octagonal structure of stone, resting partly on a corbel, projecting from the wall, and supposed to have been an oratory, or pulpit, from which one of the monks, according to their custom, read to his brethren while at dinner: it is an unrivalled specimen of the decorated style of English architecture, ornamented with lofty and finely-pointed windows, divided only by enriched mullions rising from the corbel, and crowned with trefoiled arches, deeply moulded; the spaces between the three northern arches are filled up to the height of four feet with stone panels, in which are enshrined figures, and the exterior is crowned with an obtuse dome almost concealed by the ivy which has overspread the building: the interior is six feet in diameter, and the roof is elaborately groined, and ornamented in the centre, where the ribs unite, with an alto relievo of the Crucifixion. The chapel of St. Giles, which was originally attached to the hospital belonging to the abbey church, stands at the eastern extremity of the Abbey Foregate, and divine service is performed in it only twice a year, being principally appropriated to the performance of the funeral service: it is a small ancient building, having recently undergone considerable repair, with a diminutive turret, and an elegant eastern window of stained glass. The living of St. Julian's is a perpetual curacy, endowed with £200 private benefaction, and £200 royal bounty, and in the patronage of the Earl of Tankerville: the church, with the exception of the tower, which is in the Norman style of architecture, was rebuilt of brick in 1750; the interior, which is neatly arranged, is decorated with some relics of the ancient structure; in the east wall of the chancel is a small female figure, enshrined in rich tabernacle-work, probably representing St. Juliana the patroness, and in the ceiling is preserved a considerable portion of the ancient fret-work; the east window is embellished with a painting of St. James, in stained glass, brought from Rouen during the French revolution, above which are some armorial bearings; among the monuments is a slab of coarse alabaster, inscribed with Longobardic characters. The living of St. Mary's is a perpetual curacy, in the patronage of the Corporation and Head Master of the free grammar school: the church is an ancient cruciform structure, partly in the Norman, and partly in the early English, style of architecture, with a western tower surmounted by a lofty spire of beautiful proportion; the lower part of the tower and the south porch are of the Norman style: the interior is well arranged, and, from its frequent enlargement and alteration, comprises specimens of various styles; the nave, of which the oak roof is finely panelled and carved, and supported on circular arches and massive piers, is lighted by a double range of clerestory windows, and separated from the chancel by a highly enriched pointed arch; the windows at the ends of the transepts, and on the north side of the chancel, are early English, and the east window of the latter is embellished with stained glass, formerly in the old church of St. Chad, representing the genealogy of Christ from the root of Jesse, and containing in each of the numerous oval compartments a king, or patriarch, of the ancestry of Joseph, the husband of the Virgin Mary: among the monuments is one to the memory of Robert Cadman, who, attempting a second time to perform his descent from the summit of the spire, by means of a rope, the other end of which was secured in a field on the opposite side of the river, was killed by the accidental breaking of the rope. A chapel of ease to St. Mary's, dedicated to St. Michael, has recently been built near the Castle Foregate, by public subscription, aided by a grant of £500 from the Incorporated Society for building and enlarging churches and chapels: it contains eight hundred and ten sittings, of which six hundred and thirty are free. A chapel of ease to the parish of St. Chad is also in progress of erection, in Frankwell. There are places of worship for Baptists, the Society of Friends, Independents, Wesleyan and Welch Methodists, Sandemanians, Unitarians, and Roman Catholics.

The royal free grammar school was founded by Edward VI.; its endowment, augmented by Queen Elizabeth, produces an annual income of about £3000: it is under the superintendence of the Bishop of Lichfield and Coventry, as visitor, and thirteen trustees, the mayor of Shrewsbury, who presides at the several meetings, being one: it is conducted by a head and second master, with salaries of £300 and £150 respectively, appointed by the Master and Fellows of St. John's College, Cambridge, and is open for gratuitous instruction to all sons of burgesses, and has maintained, for many years, a distinguished rank among the public schools of the country. Belonging to it are four exhibitions of £70 per annum each, and four of £15 per annum each, to St. John's College, Cambridge; four, of £60 per annum, each, to Christ Church College, Oxford; and two of £25 per annum each, and one of £23 per annum, to either of the Universities; four scholarships of £63 per annum each, and two of £40 each, in Magdalene College, Cambridge; a by-fellowship in the same college, of £126 per annum, and three contingent exhibitions.

Exclusively of boys on the foundation, there are more than two hundred boarders in this establishment, for whose accommodation the ample houses of the masters, contiguous to the school, afford every advantage. The premises, in the later style of English architecture, occupy two sides of a quadrangle, with a square turret crowned with pinnacles in the angle, and comprise spacious school-rooms, and a chapel, over which is a fine library, rebuilt in 1815, at an expense of £1860, and containing an extensive and valuable collection of books and manuscripts, to which is annexed a museum of antiquities from Wroxeter, and fossils peculiar to this part of the country. Among the eminent persons who have received the rudiments of their education in this school are, Sir Philip Sydney; Sir Fulke Greville (Lord Brooke); Dr. John Thomas, Bishop of Salisbury; the Rev. Dr. John Taylor, a learned critic and philologist; Dr. Waring, Lucasian Professor of Mathematics in the University of Cambridge; W. Wycherly and Ambrose Phillips, the poets; William Clark, a learned divine and antiquary; and various others. A school was founded in 1800, and a handsome freestone building erected, at an expense of £2000, containing spacious school-rooms, and a convenient house for the master and mistress, by Mr. John Allat, formerly chamberlain of the borough, who endowed it for the clothing, instruction, and apprenticing of poor children: there are twenty boys and twenty girls in the establishment, and, from the same funds, coats and gowns are annually distributed among a considerable number of aged men and women. A school for instructing, clothing, and apprenticing poor children of the parish of St. Julian, was founded, and a neat brick building erected for it, in 1724, by Mr. Thomas Bowdler, alderman and draper. The public subscription charity school, near the abbey church, was established in 1778, at which time houses for the master and mistress were built; there are one hundred and seventy boys and one hundred and forty girls in this school, who are instructed on Dr. Bell's system, and annually clothed. The royal Lancasterian school was established, and a commodious building, comprising two school-rooms, with apartments for the master and the mistress, was erected by subscription in 1812: there are one hundred and seventy boys, and one hundred and thirty girls in this institution. Sunday schools have also been instituted in connexion with the established church and with the several dissenting places of worship. St. Chad's almshouses were founded, in 1409, by Mr. Bennet Tupton, with a small endowment; there were originally thirteen, but for want of funds two have fallen into decay: the inmates receive sixteen shillings per annum each. St. Mary's almshouses, sixteen in number, were founded, in 1460, by Mr. Degory Watur, draper; the inmates, who must be inhabitants of St. Mary's parish, receive from his endowment £2. 6. 10½. per annum each, and an upper garment every other year from the Drapers' Company: the old almshouses were taken down in 1827, and a new building has been erected opposite St. Mary's church. St. Giles' almshouses, four in number, are inhabited by aged persons nominated by the Earl of Tankerville, who allows them one shilling and sixpence each per week, with a quantity of coal and an upper garment annually.

The house of industry, beautifully situated on an eminence adjoining Kingsland, on the south bank of the Severn, was erected in 1765, at an expense of £12,000, by the governors of the Foundling Hospital in London, as a branch establishment; on the relinquishment of that design it was closed, and afterwards opened as a woollen manufactory for the employment of the children of the poor : it was subsequently rented by Government for the confinement of prisoners during the American war, and on the incorporation of the parishes for the maintenance of their poor, in 1784, it was purchased by the guardians and appropriated to its present use : the buildings, in addition to the inhabited apartments, comprise a chapel, school-rooms, work-rooms, an infirmary, &c., with about twenty acres of land adjoining it. The general infirmary, established in 1745, was the second formed in the kingdom, that of Winchester being the first ; it is liberally supported by subscription, and is under the superintendence of a president and a committee, and, in addition to the gratuitous attendance of the physicians and surgeons in the neighbourhood, has a resident surgeon, a matron to superintend the domestic arrangements, a secretary, and other officers : the premises, originally of brick, being found too small for the increased population of the town and neighbourhood, were taken down in 1827, and have been handsomely rebuilt of stone, upon a much more extensive scale, at an expense of £18,735. 17. 10., of which, £13,044. 1. 3. was raised by subscription, forming one of the most commodious and splendid establishments of the kind in England. In the suburb of Frankwell is an hospital, founded, in 1734, by Mr. James Millington, draper, who bequeathed nearly the whole of his property for its erection and endowment : it is a neat brick building, with a turret rising from the centre, in which is a chapel (used also as a school-room), with houses for the master and mistress, and on each side are six small houses, for twelve single men or women chosen from the poor housekeepers of Frankwell, or that part of the parish of St. Chad which is nearest to it; they receive £6 per annum each, an allowance of coal, and a gown or coat ; a gown or coat, with £2, is also given annually to each of ten poor housekeepers resident in Frankwell, who, on vacancies occurring in the hospital, have the preference of appointment: twenty poor boys and twenty girls, natives of Frankwell, are completely clothed, educated, and apprenticed on leaving the school; the master has a salary of £40 per annum, with £10 additional for keeping the accounts; the mistress a salary of £40 per annum, and the chaplain a stipend of £25 per annum. On the expiration of the first year of his apprenticeship, each boy, producing a certificate of good conduct, receives a present of £5, and each girl has £5 on being apprenticed. Two exhibitions of £40 per annum each, to Magdalene College, Cambridge, were given by the same founder, to which boys educated in the hospital have the first claim, and which, in default of such, revert to boys born in Frankwell, and educated in the free grammar school. Among the monastic institutions anciently existing here were, a convent of Grey friars, founded in the reign of Henry III., by Hawise, wife of John de Charleton, Lord of Powis, of which there are some remains ; a convent of Dominican friars, founded by Lady Genevile, of which there is not a vestige, the foundations having been lately dug up; and a convent of Augustine friars, founded by one of the family of Stafford, of which some small portions are remaining. Of the numerous chapels, the only one of which there are any remains is that of St. Nicholas, near the old Councilhouse, now converted into a stable. Among the eminent natives of this town were, Richard and George Plantagenet, sons of Edward IV.; Ralph of Shrewsbury, Bishop of Bath and Wells ; Robert, Bishop of Bangor; Thomas Bower, and John Thomas, Bishops of Salisbury ; Edward Wooley, Bishop of Clonfert ; Sneyd Davies ; Lord Chief Justice Jones ; Richard Onslow, Speaker of the House of Commons ; the Rev. Job Orton ; George Costard, a distinguished mathematician ; Thomas Churchyard, the poet ; Vice-Admiral Benbow ; Dr. John Taylor, a learned critic, and editor of Demosthenes ; Hugh Farmer, an eminent divine ; and Dr. Charles Burney, a celebrated musician. Ordericus Vitalis, one of the best of early English historians, born at Atcham, in 1074, was educated in the abbey. Shrewsbury gives the title of earl to the family of Talbot.

SHREWTON, a parish in the hundred of BRANCH and DOLE, county of WILTS, 5¾ miles (W. N. W.) from Amesbury, containing 461 inhabitants. The living is a discharged vicarage, in the archdeaconry and diocese of Salisbury, rated in the king's books at £8, and in the patronage of the Bishop of Salisbury. The church is dedicated to St. Mary. There are two places of worship for Baptists.

SHRIPPLE, a tything in the parish of IDMISTON, hundred of ALDERBURY, county of WILTS, 7 miles (E. by N.) from Salisbury, containing 51 inhabitants.

SHRIVENHAM, a parish (formerly a market town) in the hundred of SHRIVENHAM, county of BERKS, 5 miles (S. W. by S.) from Great Farringdon, containing, with the chapelries of Longcot and Watchfield, the hamlet of Fernham, and the tythings of Beckett and Bourton, 1879 inhabitants. The living is a vicarage, in the archdeaconry of Berks, and diocese of Salisbury, rated in the king's books at £20, and in the patronage of the Crown. The church, dedicated to St. Andrew, is a large structure, principally in the Norman style, with a tower rising from the centre. A chantry was founded here, in 1336, by John de Burghton and Agnes his wife. William de Valence obtained a charter, in 1257, for a weekly market on Thursday, and an annual fair on the festival of St. Mary Magdalene, which were confirmed by another charter in 1383, but both have been long disused. The Wilts and Berks canal passes through the parish. Thomas Stratton, in 1703, gave a rent-charge of £4, for which sum ten boys are educated in a school-house purchased by the parish, with aid from private subscriptions. In 1788, the materials of an old chapel at Watchfield were sold, and the produce vested in the purchase of £260. 4. 1. three per cents., the dividends arising from which are applied for teaching six poor children, and six others are instructed by a schoolmistress, for the annual proceeds of £100, left by Richard Smith, in 1818. Here are eight almshouses, founded in 1642, by Sir Henry Martin, with an endowment of about £40 per annum.

SHROPHAM, a parish in the hundred of SHROPHAM, county of NORFOLK, 4 miles (N. by W.) from East Harling, containing 457 inhabitants. The living is a discharged vicarage, in the archdeaconry of Norfolk, and diocese of Norwich, rated in the king's books at £8. 13. 9., and in the patronage of the Mayor and Corporation of Norwich. The church is dedicated to St. Peter. Shropham, which gave name to the hundred, was anciently a town of some importance, though it is now only a small village.

SHROPSHIRE, an inland county, bounded on the north by Cheshire, and a detached portion of the Welch county of Flint; on the east by Staffordshire; on the south-east by Worcestershire; on the south by Herefordshire; and on the south-west, west, and north-west, respectively, by the counties of Radnor, Montgomery, and Denbigh, in Wales. It extends from 52° 20′ to 53° 4′ (N. Lat.), and from 2° 17′ to 3° 14′ (W. Lon.), and comprises an area of upwards of one thousand three hundred and forty-one square miles, or about eight hundred and fifty-eight thousand two hundred and forty statute acres. The population, in 1821, was 206,153. The name has been corrupted from the Saxon *Scrob-scire*, a contraction of *Scrobbes-byrig-scyre*, meaning the shire of *Scrobbes-byrig*, the Saxon name for Shrewsbury. The aboriginal inhabitants of this district were of the tribes called the Cornavii and the Ordovices, the former occupying the country on the north-eastern side of the Severn; the latter, the opposite shores of that river, and the south-western tracts. Little is known of the Cornavii, but the Ordovices joined with the Silures, under Caractacus, in defending their territory against the Roman invaders; and it is thought by some that the battle in which the Britons under that leader were finally defeated, by Ostorius Scapula, was fought within the limits of this county. Gough supposes it to have been at the hill called Caer Caradoc, or the Gaer, near the junction of the small rivers Clun and Temd, on the point of which are the remains of a very large and strongly fortified camp. Under the Roman dominion, Shropshire was included in the division called *Flavia Cæsariensis*. After that people had abandoned Britain, this county was the theatre of numerous sanguinary contests between the Britons and the Saxons, by the former of whom it was held as part of the kingdom of Powysland, of which Shrewsbury, called by them *Pengwerne*, was the capital. In the year 642, at Oswestry, then called Maserfeld, Oswald, King of Northumbria, was defeated and slain, by Penda, the Pagan king of Mercia. Though the British princes long disputed the possession of this territory, they were ultimately obliged to retreat; and in 777, their seat of royalty was transferred to Mathrafael, among the mountains of Powys, and Shropshire became part of the kingdom of Mercia. They still, however, made frequent inroads; and the warlike Saxon monarch, Offa, partly to avert the evils attendant upon these hostilities, caused a deep dyke and rampart to be made, which extended one hundred miles along the mountainous border of Wales, from the Clwyddian hills to the mouth of the Wye, crossing the westernmost parts of Shropshire; but the Welch continued their incursions far within this boundary, and in their hasty retreats often carried off immense booty. In the ninth century, when the Danes invaded the island, this part of Mercia, although it suffered less than some others, experienced much calamity, and its chief city, *Uriconium*, was destroyed. Shrewsbury then sprang up, and flourished in consequence; and Alfred, having subdued these ravagers, ranked it among his principal cities, and gave its name to the shire of which it

was the capital. In 1016, Shrewsbury was taken by Edmund Ironside, who severely punished the inhabitants for having taken part with Canute, in opposition to his father Ethelred. The Welch continued their incursions both before and after this event with great fierceness, particularly in the time of Edward the Confessor, under their reigning prince Griffydd. Harold, afterwards king of England, undertook an expedition against this prince, both by land and sea, and harassed the Welch so much, that they sent him the head of their chief in token of subjection: he afterwards endeavoured to secure the advantages thus gained by a decree, forbidding any Welchman to appear on the eastern side of Offa's Dyke, on pain of losing his right hand.

At the period of the Norman Conquest, nearly the whole of Shropshire, together with extensive possessions in other parts of England, was bestowed on Roger de Montgomery, a relation of William's, and one of his chief captains, in reward for his services. But the hostilities of the Welch disturbed this warrior in the enjoyment of his good fortune; and, in 1067, Owen Gwynnedd, their prince, in alliance with Edric Sylvaticus, or Edric the Forester, the Saxon Earl of Shrewsbury, laid siege to that town, with a force so formidable as to require the presence of the Conqueror, who repulsed the assailants with great slaughter, and bestowed the title of Earl of Shrewsbury upon Roger de Montgomery. This county, in like manner, was frequently the scene of contest, or of preparation for military enterprise, so long as the ancient British inhabitants of Wales maintained their independence. William the Conqueror, and his more immediate successors, for the purpose of subduing the resolute Britons, issued grants to certain of his nobles of all the lands they should be able to wrest from them; and hence originated the seigniories and jurisdictions of the lords marchers. The precise extent of the territory designated as the Marches it is difficult to determine, the word meaning, in a general sense, the borders between the Welch and the English: but the western border of Shropshire certainly formed a principal portion. The tenure by which these lords marchers held under the king was, in case of war, to serve with a certain number of vassals, to furnish their castles with strong garrisons, and with sufficient military implements and stores for defence, to keep the king's enemies in subjection: to enable them to perform this, they were allowed to exercise, in their respective territories, absolute power. For their better security they fortified old castles and built new ones, garrisoning them with their own retainers; and thus it was that the greater part of the numerous castles on the Welch border were erected. They had particular laws in their baronies, termed *Angletheria* and *Waltheria*, where all suits between them and their tenants were commenced and determined; but if a question arose concerning the barony and its title, it was referred to the king's courts. There was also, so early as the reign of John, a lord warden of the marches, whose jurisdiction resembled that of a lord-lieutenant.

In the year 1102, Bridgenorth and Shrewsbury, both which had been garrisoned for Robert, Duke of Normandy, by Robert de Belesme, Earl of Shrewsbury, were taken by Henry I., and that earl having incurred forfeiture of his estates, the county was bestowed by

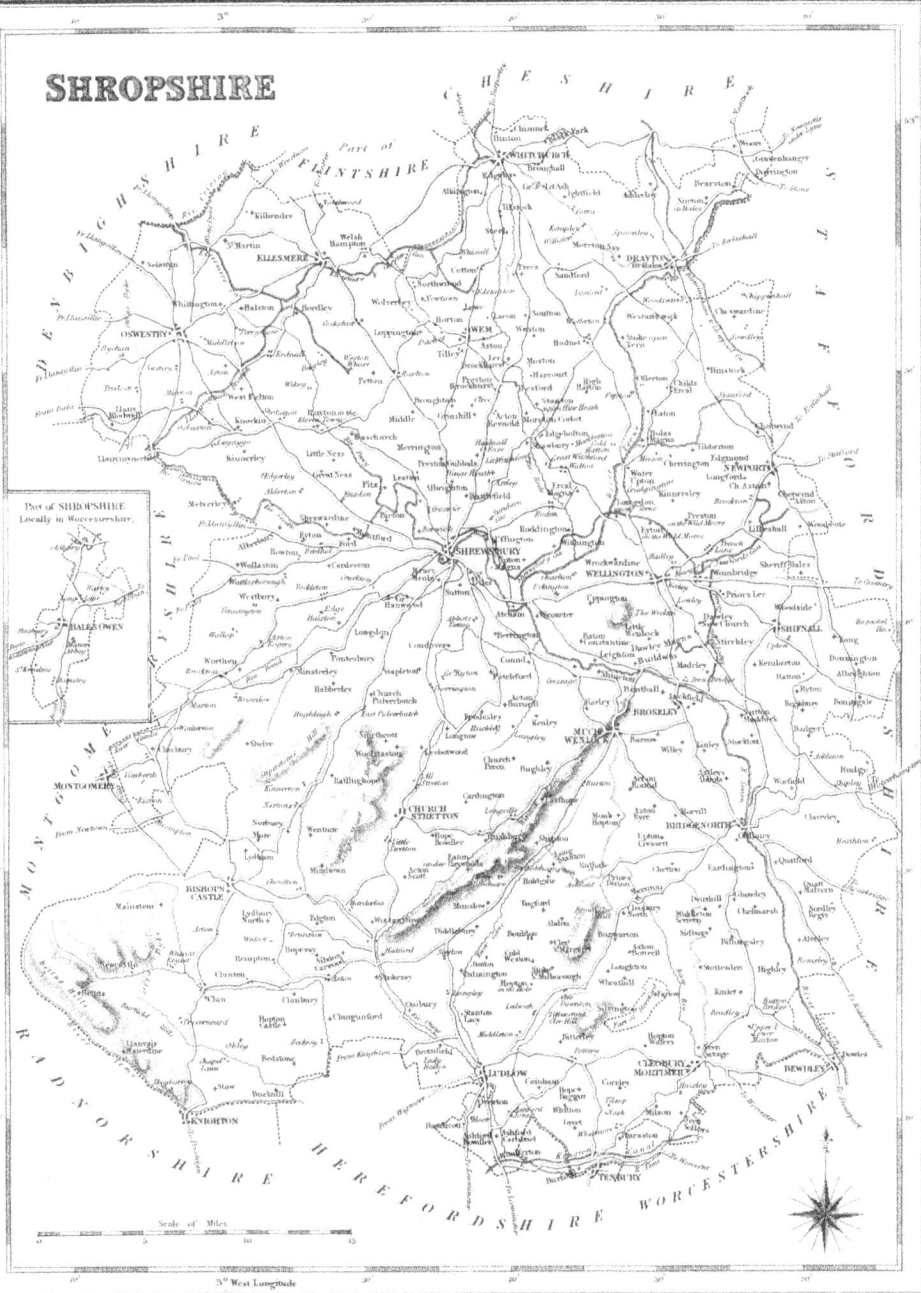

SHROPSHIRE

Scale of Miles

3° West Longitude

the king upon his queen Adeliza. In 1138, Ludlow, which had been seized by Henry I. from Robert de Belesme, being held by Gervaise Paganel, its governor, for the empress Matilda, was besieged by King Stephen; and, in 1139, Shrewsbury, which had been seized by William Fitz-Alan, Lord of Oswestry, for the empress, was taken by the same monarch, after a vigorous defence. In 1156, Bridgenorth, then held by Hugh de Mortimer against the authority of its royal owner, Henry II., was besieged and reduced by that monarch, who, in 1164, assembled an army in Shropshire, and attempted the subjugation of the Welch; near the Ceiriog, in the north-western part of the county, a strong body of his troops, which had been sent from Oswestry, where the king was then lying, to attempt the passage of that river, was attacked by the Welch, in a wood of birches at the farther end of Selattyn Hill, opposite to Chirk castle, and very few of the men who composed it escaped. In 1212, Oswestry was taken and burned by King John, who afterwards entered Wales, where he made great devastation. In the year 1215, Shrewsbury surrendered without resistance to Llewellyn, Prince of Wales, whose forces had previously gained many advantages on the marches; and, in 1233, Oswestry was taken and burned by the same chieftain, in alliance with the Earl of Pembroke, who afterwards again obtained possession of Shrewsbury. At that town, in 1241, Henry III. assembled his army to attack David ap Llewellyn, Prince of Wales; but on submission made by him, Henry, after remaining there fifteen days, returned to London. In 1253, the gentry of the county incurred the king's displeasure, by refusing to obey the new constitutions then enjoined for the keeping of arms and musters, and being answerable for robberies on the highway; the penalties exacted in punishment of which disobedience were so severe, that for some years after the people were destitute of necessaries, and without means of tilling the ground. In the war between that monarch and the insurgent barons, the latter took Shrewsbury, in 1260, but it was shortly afterwards retaken by the forces of Henry. In 1263, Bridgenorth was captured by Simon de Montfort, Earl of Leicester. Henry III., in 1267, again came to Shrewsbury with an army, designing to attack the Welch; but the expedition was abandoned on the submission of their prince, Llewellyn. The frequent hostilities of the Welch still rendered it necessary that vigorous measures should be taken against them; and in 1277, in the reign of Edward I., that monarch being personally engaged in the final reduction of Wales, the court of Exchequer, and the court of King's Bench, were removed to Shrewsbury for a few months. In 1283, during the same reign, a parliament was assembled at Shrewsbury, the king and his court being lodged at Acton-Burnell.

During the interval which had elapsed between the reign of the Conqueror and that of Edward I., as the English arms had continued to prevail, so the dominion of the marches had penetrated at length into the very heart of Wales; but on the death of Llewellyn, in the eleventh year of the latter monarch's reign, when the Welch submitted to his power, the necessity for such grants as those before mentioned existed no longer, and after this period no more lords marchers were created: the power of these once absolute baronial chieftains was also diminished by the erection of the court of the mar-

ches, which was held at Ludlow. In the year 1397, Richard II., in the twentieth year of his reign, held a parliament at Shrewsbury, called by Speed, from the numbers that attended it, "the Great Parliament;" on its dissolution the king went to Oswestry, where the Duke of Hereford, afterwards Henry IV., and the Duke of Norfolk, appeared before him, and it was there determined that they should decide the quarrel which had arisen between them by single combat, at Coventry. In 1403, on July 22nd, the partisans of the Earl of Northumberland, who were to have been joined by an army under Owen Glyndwr, were defeated near Shrewsbury by Henry IV.; their commander, Henry Percy, surnamed Hotspur, was slain, and the Earl of Worcester taken prisoner, as also was the Scotch Earl Douglas, in his flight after the action, on Haughmond hill: the total number of slain on both sides was about two thousand three hundred knights and gentlemen, and six thousand common soldiers. In gratitude for this victory, Henry built and endowed a collegiate church upon the spot where most of the slain were buried, which has ever since been called Battle-field. Glyndwr's forces, amounting to twelve thousand men, which had remained inactive at Oswestry, after the defeat of their allies, retired into Wales. During the war between the rival houses of York and Lancaster, in the year 1455, Richard, Duke of York, published at Ludlow a declaration of allegiance to the reigning monarch, Henry VI., saying also that the army which he had raised was only for the redress of grievances and the public weal: in 1459, however, Henry having advanced against this nobleman with superior forces, was joined at Ludford, a village near Ludlow, on October 13th, by Sir Andrew Trollope, with a large body of troops, which had deserted from the Duke of York at Ludlow; and on this, the duke, with his sons, the Earls of March and Rutland, and his friends, the Earls of Salisbury and Warwick, fled from the country: the king's forces then entered Ludlow, which they sacked. After the death of the Duke of York at the battle of Wakefield, his son Edward, afterwards Edward IV., went to Shrewsbury, in 1460, and obtained from the surrounding country a powerful levy, with which he obtained the victory at the great battle of Mortimer's Cross in Herefordshire. The Earl of Richmond, afterwards Henry VII., in his march from Milford Haven towards Leicestershire, in which county he soon after fought the great battle of Bosworth Field, passed with his increasing army through Shropshire: he was admitted into Shrewsbury without resistance, and thence marched by Newport, where he was joined by Sir Gilbert Talbot, with two thousand of the tenantry and retainers of the Earl of Shrewsbury, then a minor, to whom Sir Gilbert was uncle and guardian.

In the great civil war of the seventeenth century, this county was the scene of much violence and bloodshed. On September 20th, 1642, at Wellington, Charles I., at the head of his army, with which he had marched from Nottingham, issued a proclamation, promising to preserve the Protestant religion, the laws and liberty of his subjects, and the privileges of parliament; and thence marched to Shrewsbury, where he was joined by his two sons, Prince Charles, and James Duke of York, by Prince Rupert, and a great number of noblemen and gentlemen: the king remained here until the 12th of October, when he marched to Bridgenorth, and thence advanced towards Edge-hill in Warwickshire, where occurred the first great conflict of that memorable struggle. In 1644, Longford house, on April 3rd, and Tong castle, on April 6th, were captured from the parliamentarians by Prince Rupert; but on the other hand, in June of the same year, Oswestry was taken from the royalists by the Earl of Denbigh. In July, the latter place was besieged by a party of royalist forces under Col. Marrowe, but was relieved by Sir Thomas Middleton, who took about two hundred prisoners. In February, 1645, Apsley house was taken by the parliamentarians under Sir John Price; and on the 9th of the same month, Shrewsbury was taken by suprise by Col. Mytton, the parliamentarian governor of Wem; its governor, Sir Michael Earnley, was slain, sixty gentlemen and two hundred soldiers made prisoners, and fifteen pieces of ordnance fell into the hands of the victors. By the loss of this important station the royal communication with North Wales was cut off, and a check given to the plan which had been formed by the united counties of Salop, Worcester, Chester, and Flint, of augmenting the king's forces at Stokesay, near Ludlow. In the summer of this year, a royalist force of nearly two thousand horse and foot, drawn from the garrisons at Ludlow, Hereford, Worcester, and Monmouth, was defeated by an inferior number of parliamentarians; and to a party of the latter, under Sir William Brereton, the castle of Ludlow was delivered up on the 9th of June in the year following. In 1646, Bridgenorth castle also, after an obstinate resistance of a month, surrendered to the parliamentarians. In 1651, when Charles II. was fleeing, after the disastrous issue of the battle of Worcester, he arrived, at three o'clock in the morning of September 4th, at White Ladies' priory, on the eastern side of this county; from that place, after having concealed himself in the neighbourhood during the two following days, he was conducted to Boscobel house, and the day after his arrival there was concealed, in company with Col. Careless, in the Royal Oak, in an adjoining wood: having passed two nights at this place, he removed to another and more secure hiding-place in Staffordshire. The last hostile movement made in Shropshire was an ineffectual attempt, in 1654, by Sir Thomas Harris and others, to surprise the castle of Shrewsbury for the king. The jurisdiction of the president and council of the marches, which had been re-established at Ludlow by Edward IV., in honour of the Earl of March, from whom he was descended, and whose title he had borne, was abolished by act of parliament, in the first year of the reign of William and Mary, at the humble suit of the gentlemen and other inhabitants of the principality of Wales.

Shropshire includes parts of the several dioceses of Hereford, Lichfield and Coventry, and St. Asaph: a detached portion, containing the parishes of Claverley, Hales-Owen, and Worfield, is in that of Worcester: the whole is contained in the province of Canterbury. That part of the diocese of Hereford which is in Shropshire, forming about one-half of the county, is almost wholly included in the archdeaconry of Salop, together with parts of Montgomeryshire, Radnorshire, Herefordshire, and Worcestershire: only one parish in this county is in the archdeaconry of Hereford. The

archdeaconry of Salop, which comprises most of that part of the diocese of Lichfield and Coventry contained in Shropshire, which is very considerable, is for the most part within the limits of this county; five parishes only, in the same diocese, being in the arch deaconry of Stafford. The archdeaconry of St. Asaph is co-extensive with the diocese. Shropshire contains the deaneries of Burford, Clun, Ludlow, Marchia, Newport, Pontesbury, Salop, Stottesden, and Wenlock. The boundaries of the ecclesiastical divisions are extremely irregular: some parishes are contained partly in this and partly in other counties. The number is two hundred and fourteen, of which one hundred and five are rectories, fifty-eight vicarages, and the remainder perpetual curacies. For purposes of civil government the county is divided into fifteen hundreds, or districts answering thereto, viz. the hundreds of Bradford (North), comprising the Drayton and Whitchurch divisions; Bradford (South), comprising the Newport and Wellington divisions; and Brimstree, comprising the Hales-Owen and Shiffnall divisions; and the hundreds of Chirbury, Condover, Ford, Munslow, Oswestry, Overs, Pimhill, Purslow (with which that of Clun has been incorporated), and Stottesden; the liberty of Shrewsbury; and the franchise of Wenlock. It contains the borough and market towns of Shrewsbury, Bishop's Castle, Bridgenorth, Clun, Ludlow, and Wenlock; and the market towns of Broseley, Cleobury-Mortimer, Drayton in Hales, Ellesmere, Hales-Owen, Newport, Oswestry, Shifnall, Church-Stretton, Wellington, Wem, and Whitchurch. Two knights are returned to parliament for the shire, and two representatives for each of the boroughs. The county members are elected at Shrewsbury. Shropshire is included in the Oxford circuit: the assizes and general quarter sessions are held at Shrewsbury, where is the county gaol. It is the seat of judicature for all suits of the inhabitants of North Wales, commenced by Quo Minus in the Exchequer at Westminster, which are tried at the assizes here, as they are for those of South Wales at Hereford. There are one hundred and nine acting magistrates. The rates raised in the county for the year ending March 25th, 1827, amounted to £96,921. 3., the expenditure to £96,461. 10., of which £ 80,753. 18. was applied to the relief of the poor.

The form of the county is an irregular parallelogram. It possesses almost every variety of fine scenery; bold and lofty mountains; woody and secluded vallies; fertile and widely-cultivated plains; a majestic river, which divides it into two nearly equal portions; and sequestered lakes. Though no part of the surface is absolutely flat, yet the north-eastern districts are comparatively so, as contrasted with the hills on the southern and western borders, approaching the Welch mountains, and form an important part of the immense plain, or vale, which also includes the whole of the county of Cheshire, and the southern part of Lancashire, and is bounded on the east by the hills of Staffordshire, Derbyshire, and the western borders of Yorkshire; and on the west by the mountains of North Wales, and by the sea. The extent of the plain of Salop is about thirty miles long from north to south, or from Whitchurch to Church-Stretton; and twenty-eight miles broad, from Oswestry to Colebrook-dale: it is divided into two unequal portions by the Severn, and is bounded, with other parts of Shropshire, on the west by a line of limestone hills, extending from Ruabon to Llanymynech, and the Breydden hills ; on the east by the hills on the Staffordshire border, the Wrekin, the hills of Acton-Burnell, Frodgesley, the Lawley, and Caer-Caradoc ; and on the south by the Longmynd, or Longmont, and the Stiperstones. The famed Wrekin mountain, celebrated for the magnificent and extensive prospects which it commands, rises singly out of the plain, to the height of nearly one thousand two hundred feet above the level of the Severn, near which it is situated : north of it are excrescences of rock and partial swells. To the south-west the hills are more frequent ; and on the western and south-western borders of the county is a striking succession of mountainous elevations, divided by beautiful vallies : some of the highest ground in the county is considered to be the summits of the hills in the vicinity of Oswestry. Lying to the east of the Wrekin, and on the eastern borders of the county, the coal district of Colebrookdale, which extends from north-east to south-west, about eight miles in length, and two in breadth, is considerably above the level of the plain of Shropshire, more especially its southern parts ; so that at Horsehay it is five hundred feet above the level of the Severn, which there approaches it : the scenery of this vale is particularly beautiful. South-west of the Severn, the limestone ridge of hills, which commences at Lincoln hill in Colebrook-dale, proceeds in a south-westerly direction towards Church-Stretton, near which place it turns southward from the hills, around Hope-Bowdler, and descends nearly in a direct line to Ludlow, on the southern border of the county. Westward is a vale about two miles broad, and nearly fifteen in length, from Colebrookdale to the Stretton valley. Its western side is bounded by the line of low hills ranging, without any intermediate valley, along the base of a much more elevated ridge, of which the Wrekin forms the northern extremity : this chain is continued on the south-western side of the Severn, in a line with the Wrekin, and constitutes the Acton-Burnell hills, the Frodgesley hills, the Lawley, Caer Caradoc, and the Hope-Bowdler hills ; all which have craggy summits, ascend abruptly from the plain, at an angle of about sixty degrees, and command remarkably fine prospects. The vale in which Church-Stretton is situated separates from these the singular mass of hills called the Longmynd, which ascends gradually from the plain to a height much superior to that of the Wrekin, and then stretches, with a level and unvaried summit, for several miles towards Bishop's Castle. The peculiar characteristic of these hills is their squareness, both in plan and outline, and from the vale just mentioned three or four lines of them are seen rising above each other, the form of each being nearly a cube, or, from the wasting of the summit and accumulations at the base, a truncated pyramid : almost every hill is separated from the others by a deep narrow valley, or glen, occasionally overhung with wood, and watered by a stream, which here and there forms small cascades : some of these streams flow northward into the plain of Shrewsbury ; and others take a southerly course, watering the country between Bishop's Castle and Ludlow. Following the mountainous line that forms the boundary of the plain of Salop, a high and rocky district occurs between the high road from Shrewsbury to Bishop's Castle and the vale of Montgomery. The most elevated peak of this assemblage of lofty hills is called the Stiperstones, its summit being extremely craggy, and overspread with enormous loose blocks of quartz, which, at a distance, look like the ruins of some great fortress. This hill is somewhat higher than the Wrekin, and forms the abrupt termination of a line of mountains that hence extends south-westward into Radnorshire. From the Stiperstones a range of low hills stretches, in a north-easterly direction, as far as Shrewsbury, under the names of Lyth hill, Baystone hill, and the Sharpstones. In the southern parts of the county, the Clee hills, like the Wrekin, have their bases projecting towards the low lands, which accompany the course of the Severn : the Brown Clee hill, and the Titterston Clee hill, are amongst the highest in Shropshire, and have flat tops, but very irregular sides, and, like many others similarly situated, have vestiges of ancient fortifications upon their summits. Of the Berwyn mountains only a small portion, the slate mountain of Selattyn, is within the boundary of Salop. The views obtained from many of the heights are remarkably grand and beautiful. The lakes, though neither numerous nor of great extent, form a variety in the landscape rarely met with in the midland counties ; that adjoining Ellesmere covers one hundred and sixteen acres, and there are several others in the neighbourhood, but of smaller extent. Near Whitchurch are two other meres ; besides which, on the northern side of the Severn, are those of Fennymere, Llynclyspool, and Ancot. On the western side of the county is Marton pool, occupying about forty acres ; and at Shrawardine is a fine piece of water of nearly the same size : there is another Marton pool, on the northern side of the Severn, of nearly the same size as the former. South of the Severn, at the distance of a few miles from Shrewsbury, is Beaumere, a small but beautiful sheet of water, and almost adjoining it is Shomere.

These irregularities of surface and of soil produce great diversity in the climate. The corn harvest on the eastern side of the county, where the land is warm and flat, frequently commences a fortnight sooner than in the more central districts, where, although the vales are extensive, the soils are heavier, and frequently rest upon clay ; hay and grain are both, however, gathered earlier in the central than in the western parts of the county, where the ground is not in general so stiff, but where the vales are narrow, and the high lands frequent and extensive. The air is generally very salubrious, and the inhabitants are remarkable for their longevity.

The variations of soil are as great as those of surface ; and the different kinds are so intermingled as to render it difficult to define the limits of each. There is nearly an equal quantity of wheat and turnip land, though the proportions of the former somewhat preponderate. That part of the county which lies north-eastward of the Severn consists chiefly of a turnip soil under tillage, intermingled with large portions of meadow and pasture. The flat lands on the banks of that river, which are frequently overflowed, form rich meadows. On its south-western side, from Alderbury, in a district about eight miles wide, down to Cressage, the soils are chiefly of a good quality, but very variable ;

comprising pasture, wheat, and turnip land, each in small quantities. From Cressage, in a tract about six miles in width, to Bridgenorth, and thence to Cleobury and Ludlow, is chiefly a mixed soil upon clay, in some places very thin. The remaining south-western portion of the county has soils of almost every species, except chalk and flint : they are generally thin, some resting upon clay, others upon hard rock of different kinds, and compose extensive tracts of hilly wastes. In the hundred of Oswestry, on the northern side of the Severn, and occupying the north-western extremity of the county, is a considerable quantity of deep loam and gravelly soil, with some marl, in the parish of that name ; while in that of West Felton, in the vicinity of the same town, is a large tract of black peaty bog. Towards the south-east the soil becomes sandy ; and Pimhill hundred, which adjoins it on the east, contains a mixture of boggy land and of sand lying over a red sandstone, with a still greater proportion of sound wheat land. North Bradford, forming the north-eastern part of the county, has some low land of a peaty nature, good meadow land, a considerable quantity of sand lying upon a red sand-stone, and some gravelly soils. South of this, and on the eastern border, the hundreds of South Bradford and Brimstree consist for the most part of sandy loam. The franchise of Wenlock, immediately to the west of the latter, is chiefly occupied by pale-coloured clays, locally called dye-earth, which at a considerable depth are blue, but near the surface become a pale yellow : there is also some light sand, and a considerable quantity of soil formed chiefly of the decomposed matter upon which it rests. In the hundreds of Stottesden, Overs, and Munslow, which adjoin the south-eastern and southern borders of the county, there is also much clay, and a varying stony soil upon a substratum of limestone : they have also a shallow rocky loam lying upon freestone, and sometimes slate marl ; sands covering red sand-stone, particularly in the vicinity of Bridgenorth, and some clays of a reddish colour, especially near Ludlow. In Condover hundred, nearly in the centre of the county, and on the southern side of the Severn, is a good deal of gravelly loam, sand, and clay, frequently blending in very small beds. In the liberties of Shrewsbury, around that town, and in the hundred of Ford, which lies on the south side of the Severn, between it and the western border of the county, there is also much pebbly loam : north of Shrewsbury is some reddish clay upon red rock, and on the northern border of Ford hundred are some lighter-coloured clays upon limestone : the southern part of this division consists for the most part of a deep clayey soil, and, proceeding still southward and westward, becomes gravelly, rocky, and uneven. The small hundred of Chirbury, southward of this, is still more rugged, but has plains of a deep light-coloured loam, or clay. In the hundred of Purslow, forming the south-western extremity of the county, although the surface is very uneven, yet several of the hills are smooth, and there are some pale-coloured clays, and a considerable quantity of lighter soils.

The red soils are in general very productive. On the arable lands the courses of husbandry vary ; but there is not much difference between the culture of the sandy and gravelly soils of this county, and that practised on similar soils in Norfolk, or any other

light soils where turnips are grown. The crops most common are, wheat, barley, oats, peas, and turnips. The average produce of wheat per acre is from fifteen to twenty bushels, that of barley from eighteen to thirty-five, and that of peas from ten to twenty-four. Rye was formerly much cultivated on the arenaceous soils, but to a great extent it has been superseded by wheat. A small quantity of vetches is grown, as green food for horses ; and a little buck-wheat is sown on the light soils : scarcely any beans are cultivated : in the eastern part of the county turnips are almost universally grown ; as also to a great extent on the rocky lands of the western side of it. The principal artificial grasses are the broad-leafed clover, Dutch clover (both red and white), trefoil, and ray-grass. Hops are cultivated in a small district on the Herefordshire side of the county ; hemp and flax only in small quantities ; potatoes are extensively grown. Grass land for hay is seldom manured : on the banks of the Severn, and in other flat tracts, intersected by smaller streams that occasionally overflow their banks, are natural meadows regularly mown ; but the crops are often much damaged by floods : the hay harvest is generally in July. In the vales of the south-western parts of the county, the grass lands are very good : the pasture lands are not, however, on the whole, of the richest kind. The meadows, in different parts, are irrigated by means of levels preserved from the natural streams, and continued along their banks. Shropshire is not famous for its dairies : in the south-eastern portion of that part of it lying to the north-east of the Severn they are small, and, as much butter is made, the cheese is of an inferior quality : on the north-western side of the same district, and bordering upon Cheshire, the dairies are much larger, and are chiefly for cheese : on the other side of the Severn, small dairies are kept, both for butter and cheese. Lime and marl are very extensively employed as manures : with the former, which is most generally used, every part of the county is tolerably well supplied : soot and malt-dust are sometimes scattered over the meadows, or pastures, in the vicinity of the towns.

The neat cattle are considered to be for the most part of the same kind as those which prevail in Warwickshire and Staffordshire : the Old Shropshire ox was remarkable for a large dewlap. Many are also reared of the improved breeds of Lancashire, Cheshire, Leicestershire, and Staffordshire ; and upon the southern confines, the Herefordshire breed prevails. In the vicinity of Bishop's Castle the cattle are good and uniform in shape and colour, the latter being a dark red. The neat cattle on the north-eastern side of the Severn are an inferior sort of the Lancashire long-horned breed, in general for the dairy. Most farmers rear a few calves yearly for the regular supply of their dairies : a still greater number is reared on the south-western side of the Severn, where they are worked young, and then sold, when about six years old, at the great fairs in the county, to the Northamptonshire and Leicestershire graziers. The old Shropshire sheep are horned and have black or mottled faces and legs : their size is about that of the South-Down sheep, but their necks are rather longer, and the carcass not quite so compact ; they are extremely hardy, and so seldom drink, that if one of them be seen to do so, it is immediately regarded as diseased. On the Longmynd is a horned breed of sheep with black faces, apparently indigenous to the tract they inhabit; they are nimble and hardy; when fat, they weigh near ten pounds per quarter, and carry a fleece of about two pounds and a half, of which half a pound is coarse wool, and is sold separately from the rest. Upon the hills nearer Wales the flocks are without horns and with white faces; have rather shorter legs and heavier and coarser fleeces than the Longmynd sheep, and are of about the same weight. Perhaps in no county of equal size are reared or fattened so many hogs as in this: the original hog of Shropshire was a high-backed, large-eared animal, but this is now rarely to be met with unmixed with other breeds: pork and bacon are much consumed by the poorer classes of inhabitants.

There are some considerable rabbit-warrens upon the Longmynd and the Brown Clee hill. Geese are reared on the commons, and sold to the farmers, who fatten them: some farmers also, particularly in the honour of Clun, rear great numbers of turkeys, which are purchased by persons who drive them to Birmingham and other large towns. Many farmers have small orchards, from which they make cider for their own consumption; and on the confines of Herefordshire and Worcestershire, the orchards are larger, and the cider is made for sale. This county has been cleared at different times of much of its timber, great supplies having been sent to Bristol, for ship-building; but it still retains more fine woods of oak than most other counties, there being sufficient for the home consumption, and a considerable surplus for exportation. The coppice-woods are extensive, and consist chiefly of oak. Large quantities of oak poles are used in the coal-pits, and as they are required to be of considerable strength, the trees of which they are formed are seldom felled under twenty-four years' growth. On the side of Shropshire, towards Bewdley in Worcestershire, is a large tract of coppices, which are cut at from eighteen to twenty-one years' growth, to be converted into charcoal for manufacturing bar iron. There is much timber in the hedge-rows, consisting principally of oak and ash, with a few elms, and still fewer beech, lime, and sycamore trees: poplars are common by the sides of brooks and the smaller rivers: birches, both as trees and fences, are frequent in the south-western district. There are many modern plantations, generally of various kinds of fir and pine, intermingled with different deciduous trees: indeed, there are few trees which do not flourish in the soil. Exclusively of the heathy mountainous tracts before described, which are chiefly sheep-walks, there are some flat open heaths in the north-eastern part of the county, and in the parishes of Worfield and North Cleobury, in the vicinity of Bridgenorth. Clun Forest, an extensive sheep-walk, contains above twelve thousand acres, and is a fine extent of smooth turf, with every variation of swelling banks and retired dingles: a part of the Longmynd has been enclosed. There are several large mosses and a great number of smaller ones: the largest district of swampy moor-land surrounds the village of Kinnersley.

The whole of the county is plentifully supplied with coal; but in the south-western district, the common articles of fuel are peat and wood. The mineral productions are various and considerable; the principal are, coal, iron, lead, and stone of different kinds. The coal district of Colebrook-dale is about six miles long

from north-east to south-west, and two miles broad: it commences on the south-western side of the Severn, in the parishes of Barrow and Much-Wenlock, and runs across that river through those of Broseley, Madeley, Little Wenlock, Wellington, Dawley, Malins-Lea, Shiffnall, Lilleshall, and some others. Red sandstone is found immediately to the eastward of this tract, and the coal strata dip rapidly towards it. The whole of this "independent coal formation" is composed of the usual members, viz. quartzose sandstone, indurated clay, clay porphyry, slate clay, and coal, alternating with each other without much regularity, except that each bed of coal is always immediately covered by indurated, or slaty, clay. Trop, or greenstone, appears in some places between the coal formation and the limestone upon which it rests, and which rises to the west of it. The strata are found most complete in Madeley colliery, where a pit has been sunk to the depth of seven hundred and twenty-nine feet, through all the beds, eighty-six in number, that constitute the formation. The sand-stones, which make part of the first thirty strata, are fine-grained, and often contain thin plates, or minute fragments, of coal: and the thirty-first and thirty-third strata are coarse-grained sand-stone, entirely penetrated by petroleum. Below these, at different depths, are three thick beds of sand-stone, varying in quality: vegetable impressions are found in most of them, excepting those nearest the surface. The clay porphyry occurs but once, at the depth of seventy-three feet from the surface. The indurated clay is, in some beds, compact, dull, and smooth, when it is termed clod; in others it is glossy, unctuous, and tending to a slaty texture, and is then called clunch: it encloses beds of clay iron-stone, in the form of compressed balls, or broad flat masses, and some vegetable impressions, and a few shells: the beds of iron-ore are five or six in number, and in the iron-stone nodules, vulgarly called ball-stone, impressions of various ferns are common. The slaty clay, called by the miners basses, is of a blueish black colour, usually containing pyrites, and is always either mixed with coal, or combined with petroleum. The first bed of coal occurs at the depth of one hundred and two feet from the surface; it is not more than four inches thick, and is very sulphureous: nine other beds of a similar nature, but somewhat thicker, lie between this and the depth of nearly four hundred feet; they are used only in burning lime. The first bed capable of being worked is five feet thick, and occurs at the depth of nearly five hundred feet: below it are thirteen other beds of different quality and thickness; some possess the quality of caking: they are usually a mixture of slate-coal and pitch-coal, but rarely of cannel coal. Of these numerous beds, some are wanting in the neighbouring collieries, and the thickness of others varies considerably. The whole formation rests either upon die-earth, which is of a greyish colour, and contains petrifactions, chiefly of the Dudley fossil kind, and is so named because the beds of coal die, or cease, beneath it; or upon limestone, except in one place, where the greenstone trop interposes between the coal and the limestone. The principal faults, or breaks, in the strata run nearly north-east and south-west: two of these have thrown the strata on both sides of the district, from one to two hundred feet lower than they are in the middle of it, but have not at all affected the surface; and it is in this middle tract, on account of the greater facility of working the mines, that by far the greatest quantity of coal and iron-ore is raised. The limestone formation consists of beds of lime-stone and sand-stone, forming two mountain ranges westward of this, in the direction of north-east and south-west: at the northern extremity of one range, where it comes in contact with the coal formation, the limestone contains cavities, some of which are lined with, and some full of, petroleum. The combination of coal, iron-ore, &c., together with the advantages of water-carriage which it possesses, renders Colebrook-dale the centre of some of the most extensive iron-works in the kingdom, which consume by far the greater part of the coal raised there. In the Clee hills, from twenty to thirty miles southward of Colebrook-dale, are other coal-works, where the strata consist also of both coal and iron-stone, and dip towards the centre of the hills: this coal and iron-stone is in some places covered by a thick bed of basalt, which forms irregular ridges, higher than any other parts of the hills: the strata of coal in Brown Clee hill are much thinner than in the Tillerston, where the principal stratum is six feet thick: cannel coal is also found in this hill, and the strata are, as elsewhere, disarranged by faults. There are coal fields at Billingsley, two or three miles north-eastward of these, where a stratum of spatous iron-ore has been found; and valuable coal-works lie southward of the Clee hills, some of which produce cannel coal: coal is also found in most other parts of the hundred of Stottesden. Some miles westward of the first-mentioned coal district, pits have been sunk with success; and, indeed, out of the fifteen civil divisions of this county, ten are known to produce this valuable mineral: it is chiefly the south-western districts that are deficient of it. Nearly parallel with the Welch border is a bank of coal strata, extending from the Dee to the Severn, and a portion of these is worked in the western and north-western parts of Shropshire, the coal having the caking quality of the Newcastle coal, and yielding a powerful heat; the principal works are near Chirk bridge: a stratum of coal seven feet thick has here been met with: spatous iron-ore, and common argillaceous iron-stone, are also found. The strata dip towards the east, and rest upon an irregular band of limestone, which in some places rises to a great height above the plain, but in others scarcely appears above the surface. In many parts, especially near Oswestry, this limestone changes into a kind of marble, and small quantities of both lead and copper are found through its whole extent.

There are mines of lead-ore of a good quality adjoining the Stiperstones, and in their vicinity; in the western parts of the county, the veins are in argillaceous schistus, and produce sulphuret of lead, both galena and steel-ore (which latter contains silver), carbonate of lead chrystal-lized, red lead-ore, and blende, or black-jack: the Bog mine has been worked to the depth of one hundred and fifty yards, and a ton of the ore raised here yields fifteen hundred-weight of pure lead: the ore of the White grit mine does not yield so much. At Snailbach, a vein, which is in some parts four yards in width, has been worked to the depth of one hundred and eighty yards: calamine is also here met with. Ancient tools, judged to be Roman,

have been found in these mines. The lead-ore is reduced at Minsterley and other places near the mines, whence it is sent by land-carriage to Shrewsbury, and there shipped, together with the raw calamine, in barges, for Bristol. There are appearances both of lead and cop-per in different other parts of the county. The various beds of stone are too numerous and diversified for mi-nute description: besides those of limestone, a long range extends from Colebrook-dale, by Wenlock, to Ludlow, on the southern border of the county; the lime-works at Lilleshall are very considerable: limestone is also found in the Clee hills, and to a limited extent in the south-western districts, and in many places south of Shrewsbury, as well as in the parishes of Cardeston and Alberbury to the west of that town. At the eastern extremity of the Wrekin, and at some other lime-works, is produced a red lime, which sets very hard in water; in some parts of Shropshire limestone is found under very thick argillaceous strata. At Grinshill, seven miles north of Shrewsbury, is a noted quarry of white sand-stone, the bed of which is sixty feet thick: great use has been made of this stone in the more mo-dern edifices of Shrewsbury and the vicinity. There are large extents of red sand-stone in the same neigh-bourhood, and westward and south-westward, as well as in the eastern parts of the county; and near Bridge-north, beds of red sand-stone are found under white sand-stone, and vice versa. Further south, sand-stone prevails; and at Orton bank is a stratum similar to the Bath and Portland stone, enclosed in strata of lime-stone. In the western district is a siliceous grit, difficult to work; but the more common stone is ar-gillaceous. A kind of stony slate is found in the parish of Bettws, on the south-western verge of the county, and is used for covering roofs; and good flag-stones are obtained in Corndon-hill, west of Bishop's Castle. In the Swinney mountain, near Oswestry, is a superior white sandstone; and the same is found at Bowden quarry, in the hundred of Munslow. At Soudley, in the parish of Eaton and franchise of Wenlock, is a very good flag-stone for floors. At Pitchford, about seven miles south-east of Shrewsbury, is a red sand-stone, approaching the surface in many places, from which exudes a mineral pitch: from this rock is ex-tracted an oil, called "Betton's British oil," used medi-cinally. Clay slate occurs as the supporting rock of the trop formation of this county, which extends from the Wrekin to Church-Stretton. Lawley hill is in part formed of a kind of granite; but a still greater part consists of toadstone: Caer Caradoc hill is composed of a shivery kind of schistus: the Wrekin chiefly com-prises reddish chert-stone, with granulated quartz im-bedded in it: the hills near Oswestry are of coarse-grained sand-stone: this county affords throughout a rich field of enquiry for the mineralogist.

The rich stores of iron and lead ores, coal, and stone; the increasing manufactures, and the agricultural im-provements of the district, have raised Shropshire to a high position in the scale of national importance; while its inland navigation has rendered it the emporium of the trade between England and Wales, and a grand centre of communication with the inland counties. The chief manufacture is that of iron: the number of blast furnaces for this metal between Ketley and Willey, in the great eastern coal district, in a space of about seven miles, exceeds that in any other tract of equal extent in the kingdom. Some of these produce iron of the best quality : the number of persons employed in them is about six thousand. The quantity of coal annually raised is nearly three hundred thousand tons : the number of steam-engines employed on both sides of the Severn is remarkably great. In Colebrook-dale, coked coal was first employed, on an extensive scale, as a substitute for charcoal, in the manufacture of iron. Various branches of the flannel manufacture are carried on near Shrewsbury ; and there are mills at different places for dyeing woollen cloth. A consider-able manufacture of gloves is carried on at Ludlow, chiefly for the London market, at which place paper is also made. Near Coalport, on the Severn, coloured china of all sorts, and of exquisite taste and beauty, is made : and at the same newly-formed town is a manu-facture of earthenware in imitation of that made at Etruria, commonly called Wedgewood ware. Glass is made at Donington; earthenware, pipes, bricks and tiles, and nails, at Broseley; and at Coalport, in the neigh-bourhood of the last-mentioned place, is a china ma-nufacture of great excellence : at Coalport are also ma-nufactures of ropes and chains for the mines. There is a manufacture of carpets at Bridgenorth ; paper and horse-hair seating are made at Drayton ; and at nearly all the towns in the county the malting business is carried on to a very considerable extent. The staple trade of Shrewsbury is in fine flannels and Welch webs, but it has very much declined. The ultimate markets for the strong, or high country cloth, which is woven in Denbighshire, are Holland, Germany, and America: the small cloth, which is about one-eighth of a yard narrower than the other, and is sometimes brought for sale to Oswestry market, is generally dyed before it is exported : it is sent to South America, and to the West Indies, as clothing for the slaves.

The Severn, which, among British rivers, is next in magnitude and importance to the Thames, runs nearly through the centre of the county, in an irregular bend-ing course of between sixty and seventy miles, and in a general direction of from north-west to south-east. Entering on the western border below Welch-Pool in Montgomeryshire, it proceeds eastward across the great plain to Shrewsbury, which it nearly encircles, its course being in that vicinity more circuitous than in any other part within the limits of this county: hence it continues in a south-easterly direction until it has passed Colebrook-dale, shortly below which it turns southward to Bridgenorth, and the rest of its course through Shropshire is thenceforward nearly in the same direction; it finally quits the county, after having formed, for the distance of a few miles, the eastern boundary of a projecting portion of Stottesdon hundred, which it separates first from Staffordshire, and afterwards from Worcestershire, which latter county it then enters near Bewdley. During the whole of its course through Shropshire, this river is navigable for barges of from twenty to eighty tons' burden, which are towed up it; and for vessels called trows, which are larger, and navigate the ports lower down the river : by far the greater part of the barges are employed in exporting downwards the produce of the mines near Colebrook-dale ; wines, groceries, &c., are brought up the Severn, for the consumption of this county, that of Montgomery,

and others : and besides the exports of coal and iron by means of it, are those of lime, lead, flannel, grain, and cheese, with some others of minor importance. The inconveniences and interruptions attendant on the na-vigation of this river are very great, and are chiefly occasioned by the frequent fords and shoals that occur in its channel, which has a rapid fall ; by a deficiency of water in times of drought; and by the superabundance of it in rainy seasons, when it rushes down with irre-sistible force. The fish found in it, within the limits of Shropshire, are salmon, flounders, a few pike, trout, graylings, perch, eels, shad, bleak, gudgeons, chub, roach, and dace (in great abundance), carp, a few lampreys, and ruff. The fishermen very com-monly use a kind of canoe, being a very short wide boat, made of osiers covered with hides, and worked with a paddle, answering exactly to the description of the boats of the Britons in the time of Cæsar, and called a coracle : this bark is so light that the fisher-man, on quitting the river, carries it upon his back, one end being pulled over his head, in the manner of a large basket. By the statute of the 30th of Charles II., cap. 9th, the conservancy of the Severn, within the county, is vested in the county magistrates, with power to appoint one or more under-conservators. The smaller streams and brooks are extremely numerous, and the waters of almost all of them finally reach the Severn ; its most important tributaries are, the Camlet, the Vyrnyw, the Tern, the Clun, the Ony, and the Teme. The Camlet, rising on Corndon Marsh, within a few miles of its source, runs parallel with the Ony for some distance, but upon a different level, and then turns towards the west, and afterwards to the north-west, falling into the Severn a little beyond the western confines of the county. The river Vyrnyw, on the entrance of the Severn into the county, joins it from the north, having for some miles before its confluence formed the boundary be-tween the counties of Salop and Montgomery. The Tern rises in Staffordshire, but shortly entering this county, pursues a southerly course of nearly thirty miles to the Severn, between four and five miles east-ward of Shrewsbury. South of the Severn, and ris-ing not far from the course of the Camlet, the Clun runs southward to the Teme near Leintwardine. The Ony, from near the source of the Camlet, joins the Teme near Oakley park. The Teme, rising on the bor-ders of Radnorshire, runs along the southern side of this county, sometimes forming its boundary, and at others deviating on either side of it : at Ludlow this river is augmented by the Corve, which flows towards it through a long valley to which it gives name : the Teme is joined by different other minor streams, and finally quits this county, near Tenbury in Worcester-shire : it is celebrated for grayling, and contains, be-sides, abundance of trout.

The want of a navigable canal for conveying the produce of the more remote coal and iron mines of the eastern districts to the river Severn was long ex-perienced, owing to the peculiar unevenness of the surface of the country over which it must pass, and the impossibility of obtaining a sufficient quantity of water for lockage ; until, at last, the remedy for these obstacles was supplied by a canal from the neighbour-hood of the Oaken Gates to the iron-works at Ketley, a distance of about a mile and a half, with a fall of seventy-three feet, in which, instead of lockage, an inclined plane was formed. An act of parliament was then obtained for the Shropshire canal, which was finished in 1792, and which, commencing on the north side of the London road from Shrewsbury, at a place called Donnington-Wood, and taking a course nearly southward, proceeds about one hundred yards on a level, and then ascends one hundred and twenty feet, by means of an inclined plane three hundred and twenty yards in length : from the top of this inclined plane, which is the highest level of the canal, it proceeds by the Wrockwardine and Snedshill coal and iron works, and near the Oaken Gates, where it is joined by the small Ketley canal : from this junction it is continued past other iron-works to Southall-bank, where a branch, striking off to the right, terminates at Brierly hill : the main line of the canal, turning to the left at Southall-bank, goes on to the Windmill Farm, where it descends one hundred and twenty-six feet, by means of an inclined plane six hundred yards long, from the bottom of which it passes by the east of Madeley to the banks of the Severn, where it descends two hundred and seven feet, by an inclined plane three hundred and fifty yards in length, and then proceeds parallel with that river, but on a level above the reach of floods, to Coalport, where it terminates : its total extent, including the branch, which is two miles and three-quarters long, is upwards of ten miles and a half : the boats navigating it are only of five tons' burden, and are drawn up the inclined planes by means of machinery worked by steam. Immediately after the completion of this, the Shrewsbury canal was projected, for supplying that town with coal, which was conveyed thither, before its completion, only by an expensive land-carriage of about fourteen miles. From the bottom of the first inclined plane of the Shropshire canal, a short cut had been made to diverge along the side of the hill towards Ketley; and of this, the Shrewsbury Canal Company purchased about a mile in extent, at the northern extremity. At the end of this is an inclined plane of seventy-five feet fall, and two hundred and twenty-three yards in length, from the bottom of which the canal passes by Eyton mill to Long-lane, a distance of four miles and a half, in which is a fall in lockage of thirty-nine feet; hence it proceeds to Long, where it crosses the river Tern and its valley, at the height of sixteen feet above the level of the latter, by means of an aqueduct of cast-iron, sixty-two yards in length, and an embankment : near this place it also crosses the road from Wellington to Shrewsbury, &c., and thence proceeds to Roddington, where it crosses the small river Roden, by an embankment and aqueduct, at the height of twenty-one feet above the surface of the stream : it then passes through Withington to near Atcham, where it crosses another turnpike-road, and half a mile further north enters a tunnel nine hundred and seventy yards in length, from the northern end of which the canal is continued to Pimley, where it crosses another valley, by means of a small aqueduct and embankment, and then proceeds along the banks of the Severn to its termination in a large basin and coal-yard at that entrance to Shrewsbury which is called the Castle-Foregate. As only small boats navigate this canal, the locks are so formed, as to admit of two,

three, or four of them passing through at a time. The Ellesmere canal, or rather system of canals, which unites the Severn, the Dee, and the Mersey, crosses the river Ceiriog into the north-western parts of Shropshire, by an aqueduct two hundred yards in length, and sixty-five in height, and then passes about a mile, in an easterly direction, along the southern bank of that river, after which it turns towards the south-east, and passes by St. Martin's moor, where it descends thirteen feet, by means of two locks, to Frankton common, where it falls thirty feet, by four locks, to Hordley : from this latter place it passes to Weston-Llullingfields, where it terminates. At Frankton common, a branch strikes off eastward, which, after having passed close by the town of Ellesmere, proceeds by Welch-Hampton to Fens-moss, where it divides, one branch proceeding to the town of Whitchurch, the other terminating at Prees heath, near the village of Prees : this Whitchurch and Prees branch is altogether twenty-one miles in length, and entirely upon one level : from Whitchurch, however, it descends northward, by one hundred and twenty-eight feet of lockage, towards the Chester canal, near Nantwich. At Hordley is a branch from the Ellesmere canal, in a south-westerly direction, which, proceeding on a level to Aston moor, in the parish of Oswestry, there descends nineteen feet, by means of three locks, and afterwards passes by Crick heath, and through Llanymynech, to about half a mile beyond that village, where it joins the Montgomeryshire canal : this branch is upwards of eleven miles in length : it was intended to carry this canal near Leaton heath, to pass by Newton, Baschurch, &c., and to enter the Severn near Fitz, but it is doubtful whether or not this will ever be carried into effect. A canal, formed by the Marquis of Stafford, commences at Donnington-Wood, and proceeds on a level to Pave-lane, near Newport, a distance of seven miles : there is a branch from this to his lordship's lime-works at Lilleshall. Iron railways, for the conveyance of heavy articles, have been adopted to a considerable extent in this county : the whole of the extensive iron and coal tract in the vicinity of Colebrook-dale is intersected by numerous tram-roads leading from the coal-works to the different foundries, and the wharfs on the banks of the canal and the river Severn.

The great road from London to Holyhead, through Buckingham and Shrewsbury, enters this county from Shatterford in Staffordshire, and passes through Bridge-north, Much Wenlock, Shrewsbury, and Oswestry, to Llangollen in Denbighshire. The road from London to Holyhead, through Birmingham, enters from Wolver-hampton in Staffordshire, and passes through Wellington, Shrewsbury, and Ellesmere, to Overton in Flint-shire. The road from London to Holyhead, through Worcester, enters the county from Tenbury in Worcestershire, passes through Burford, and (after crossing a corner of Herefordshire) through Ludlow and Bishop's Castle, to Montgomery in Wales. The road from London to Holyhead, through Chester, enters from Weston under Lizard in Staffordshire, and passes through Newport and Whitchurch, to Chester. That from London to Chester, through Birmingham, enters from Muckleston in Staffordshire, and passes through Dormoton and Woore, to Nantwich in Cheshire.

The relics of antiquity contained in the county are

numerous and diversified. Remains of encampments, supposed by antiquaries to have been of early British formation, are to be seen in Brocard's Castle, near Church-Stretton; Bury ditches, on Tongley-hill, near the village of Basford; on the Clee hills; on the hills called Caer Caradoc, two miles and a half from Church-Stretton, and the Caer Caradoc, or Gear, near Clun; at Old Port, near Oswestry, and on the Wrekin. The principal Roman stations were *Uriconium*, or *Viroconium*, now Wroxeter, which was a chief city of the Cornavii, fortified by the Romans; and *Rutunium*, at Rowton; but of the exact site of the last there is a difference of opinion : there were also *Bravinium*, at Rushbury; *Sariconium*, at Bury hill; and *Usacona*, at Sheriff-Hales. The Roman station *Mediolanum*, is by some fixed near Drayton, but with more probability at Meifod. Vestiges of Roman encampments and fortifications are found in the Bury Walls, near Hawkstone; the Walls, near Chesterton; and the remains of the ancient city of *Uriconium*, near Wroxeter. A great Roman road enters Shropshire on the east between Crackley bank and Weston, and passes through it in a bending line, in the vicinity of Church-Stretton, which town derives its name from it, to Leintwardine in Herefordshire, on the southern borders of this county : there are besides numerous minor vestiges of that people. Part of Offa's Dyke may be traced in the south-western part of Shropshire, which it enters from Knighton, in Radnorshire, and quits for Montgomeryshire, between Bishop's Castle and Newton ; it is again visible in this county, near Llanymynech, on the western border, whence it proceeds across the race-course, near Oswestry, and then descends to the river Ceiriog, the northwestern boundary of the county, near Chirk, where it again enters Wales. There are the remains of a Danish camp near Cleobury-Mortimer. A very singular cave, in which were human bones, was discovered in 1809, in digging the bottom of a rock, at Burncote, near Worfield : Kynaston's Cave, in the almost perpendicular side of Nesscliffe rock, and the traditions connected with it, are worthy of notice.

The number of religious houses, including collegiate establishments and hospitals, was about forty-seven. The remains of some of them are interesting, either for beauty or antiquity : the principal are those of the abbeys of Buildwas, Hales-Owen, Haughmond, Lilleshall, Much Wenlock, Shrewsbury, and White abbey, near Alberbury; and of the priories of Bromfield, Chirbury, and White Ladies. Several of the churches, too, are interesting for their beauty and antiquity. Among the most worthy of notice are those of Burford, Cleobury-Mortimer, Ellesmere, Hales-Owen, Hodnet (which has a circular tower), Kinlet, Ludlow, Morvill, Newport, Shiffnall, Tong, and St. Mary's and St. Alkmond's, Shrewsbury. Of the ancient castles contained within the limits of the county, the great number of which has before been accounted for, some of the most remarkable that still remain, wholly, or in part, are those of Acton-Burnell; Alberbury; Bridgenorth, which was founded so far back as the year 912, by Ethelfleda, daughter of Alfred the Great; Caus; Clun; Hopton; Ludlow, so long the seat of the Lords President of the Marches; Middle; Moreton-Corbet; Oswestry; Red Castle, Shrewsbury; Sibdon; Stoke; Wattlesborough, and Whittington. Among the most

remarkable ancient mansions are those of Boscobel, where Charles II. was concealed after the battle of Worcester; White-hall, and Bellstone-house : Shrewsbury Council-house is also remarkable for its antiquity. Of the more modern residences of nobility and gentry, this county includes considerably more than a hundred. Shropshire contains numerous medicinal springs of various properties. At Kingley Wick, about two miles to the west of Lilleshall hill, is a strong spring of impure brine, from which salt was formerly made. There are medicinal springs of different qualities at Smeithmore and Moreton-Say, in the hundred of North Bradford; at Broseley, and at Admaston near Wellington, besides others near Ludlow ; between Welbatch and Pulley common, in the vicinity of Wenlock, and on Prolley moor : that best known is Sutton Spa, about two miles to the south of Shrewsbury, and close to the village of Sutton, the waters of which are saline and chalybeate, and somewhat resemble those of Cheltenham : near Colebrook-dale is a bituminous spring of fossil tar. Numerous fossils are found among the strata of this county, particularly in the Colebrook-dale coal district. The *reseda luteola*, or dyers' weed, which affords a beautiful yellow dye, grows wild in many parts of the county; and the *berberis vulgaris*, or common barberry, is also occasionally found in a similar uncultivated state.

SHROTON, county of DORSET.—See IWERNE-COURTNAY.

SHUCKBURGH (LOWER), a parish in the Burton-Dassett division of the hundred of KINGTON, county of WARWICK, 5 miles (E.) from Southam, containing 166 inhabitants. The living is a perpetual curacy, annexed to the vicarage of Priors' Hardwick, in the archdeaconry of Coventry, and diocese of Lichfield and Coventry. The church is dedicated to St. John the Baptist. The Oxford canal passes through the parish.

SHUCKBURGH (UPPER), a parish in the Southam division of the hundred of KNIGHTLOW, county of WARWICK, 5½ miles (E.) from Southam, containing 47 inhabitants. The living is a perpetual curacy, in the archdeaconry of Coventry, and diocese of Lichfield and Coventry, and in the patronage of Sir F. Shuckburgh, Bart. The church is dedicated to St. John the Baptist.

SHUDY-CAMPS, a parish in the hundred of CHILFORD, county of CAMBRIDGE, 4¼ miles (E. S. E.) from Linton, containing 333 inhabitants. The living is a discharged vicarage, in the archdeaconry and diocese of Ely, rated in the king's books at £9, and in the patronage of the Master and Fellows of Trinity College, Cambridge. The church is dedicated to St. Mary.

SHURDINGTON (GREAT), a parish in the upper division of the hundred of DUDSTONE and KING's BARTON, county of GLOUCESTER, 2¾ miles (S. W.) from Cheltenham, containing 102 inhabitants. The living is a perpetual curacy, annexed to the vicarage of Badgeworth, in the archdeaconry and diocese of Gloucester, and in the patronage of W. L. Lawrence, Esq. The church is dedicated to St. Paul. On opening a large tumulus here a stone coffin was found, at the depth of sixteen feet, which contained the body of a man, with a helmet almost consumed by rust.

SHURLACH, a township in the parish of DAVENHAM, hundred of NORTHWICH, county palatine of

CHESTER, 1¾ mile (E. S. E.) from Northwich, containing 64 inhabitants. The Grand Trunk canal passes through the parish.

SHUSTOCK, a parish in the Atherstone division of the hundred of HEMLINGFORD, county of WARWICK, 2¾ miles (E. N. E.) from Coleshill, containing, with the hamlets of Bentley and Blythe, 577 inhabitants. The living is a discharged vicarage, in the archdeaconry of Coventry, and diocese of Lichfield and Coventry, rated in the king's books at £5. 7., endowed with £200 royal bounty, and in the patronage of the Crown. The church is dedicated to St. Cuthbert. Thomas and Charles Huntback, in 1714, gave certain houses and land to endow a school for poor children, and an almshouse for six widows.

SHUTE, a parish in the hundred of COLYTON, county of DEVON, 2 miles (N.) from Colyton, containing 593 inhabitants. The living is a perpetual curacy, annexed to the vicarage of Colyton, in the peculiar jurisdiction of the Dean and Chapter of Exeter. The church, dedicated to St. Michael, contains a memorial of Charles Bickford Templar, Esq., who was lost in the wreck of the Halsewell East Indiaman, in 1786.

SHUTFORD (EAST), a chapelry in that part of the parish of SWALCLIFFE which is in the hundred of BANBURY, county of OXFORD, 5 miles (W. by N.) from Banbury, containing 33 inhabitants. The chapel is dedicated to St. Martin.

SHUTFORD (WEST), a township in that part of the parish of SWALCLIFFE which is in the hundred of BANBURY, county of OXFORD, 5½ miles (W.) from Banbury, containing 344 inhabitants.

SHUTTINGTON, a parish in the Tamworth division of the hundred of HEMLINGFORD, county of WARWICK, 3¾ miles (E. by N.) from Tamworth, containing 169 inhabitants. The living is a perpetual curacy, in the archdeaconry of Coventry, and diocese of Lichfield and Coventry, endowed with £400 private benefaction, and £600 royal bounty, and in the patronage of Sir Francis Burdett, Bart. The Coventry canal crosses the south-western angle of the parish.

SHUTTLEHANGER, a chapelry in the parish of STOKE-BRUERNE, hundred of CLELEY, county of NORTHAMPTON, 2¾ miles (E. N. E.) from Towcester, containing 308 inhabitants.

SIBBERTOFT, a parish in the hundred of ROTHWELL, county of NORTHAMPTON, 5 miles (S. W.) from Market-Harborough, containing 406 inhabitants. The living is a vicarage, annexed to that of Welford, in the archdeaconry of Northampton, and diocese of Peterborough, rated in the king's books at £6. 4. 9½. The church is dedicated to St. Helen. There is a place of worship for Wesleyan Methodists. A spot here, called Castle-yard, is supposed to be the site of an ancient castle.

SIBBERTSWOLD, a parish in the hundred of BEWSBOROUGH, lathe of ST. AUGUSTINE, county of KENT, 6¼ miles (N. W.) from Dovor, containing 299 inhabitants. The living is a vicarage, with that of Coldred annexed, in the archdeaconry and diocese of Canterbury, rated in the king's books at £6, and in the patronage of the Archbishop of Canterbury. The church, dedicated to St. Andrew, is principally in the early style of English architecture.

SIBDON-CARWOOD, a parish in the hundred of PURSLOW, county of SALOP, 7 miles (S. E. by E.) from Bishop's Castle, containing 61 inhabitants. The living is a perpetual curacy, in the archdeaconry of Salop, and diocese of Hereford, and in the patronage of the Vicar of Clun.

SIBFORD-FERRIS, a hamlet in that part of the parish of SWALCLIFFE which is in the hundred of BLOXHAM, county of OXFORD, 7¼ miles (W.S. W.) from Banbury, containing 216 inhabitants. It is within the peculiar jurisdiction of the manorial court of Sibford.

SIBFORD-GOWER, a hamlet in that part of the parish of SWALCLIFFE which is in the hundred of BLOXHAM, county of OXFORD, 7¾ miles (W. by S.) from Banbury, containing 494 inhabitants. One-third of the rents of the poor's estate is paid to a schoolmaster for teaching about sixty children. It is within the peculiar jurisdiction of the manorial court of Sibford.

SIBSEY, a parish in the western division of the soke of BOLINGBROKE, parts of LINDSEY, county of LINCOLN, 5¼ miles (N. N. E.) from Boston, containing 1354 inhabitants. The living is a discharged vicarage, in the archdeaconry and diocese of Lincoln, rated in the king's books at £11. 11.3., and in the patronage of the Crown. The church is dedicated to St. Margaret. There is a place of worship for Wesleyan Methodists.

SIBSON, a hamlet in the parish of STIBBINGTON, hundred of NORMAN-CROSS, county of HUNTINGDON, 1½ mile (S. E.) from Wansford. The population is returned with the parish.

SIBSON, a parish in the hundred of SPARKENHOE, county of LEICESTER, 4 miles (W. S. W.) from Market-Bosworth, containing, with the township of Upton, 378 inhabitants. The living is a rectory, in the archdeaconry of Leicester, and diocese of Lincoln, rated in the king's books at £15. 18. 11½., and in the patronage of the Master and Fellows of Pembroke College, Oxford. The church is dedicated to St. Botolph.

SIBTHORPE, a parish in the southern division of the wapentake of NEWARK, county of NOTTINGHAM, 6¾ miles (S.S.W.) from Newark, containing 142 inhabitants. The living is a donative, in the patronage of Duke of Portland. The church, dedicated to St. Peter, was originally much larger than it is at present: the north and south aisles have been taken down, so that the pillars and lofty arches of the nave are now worked into the outer wall of the building. In the reign of Edward II., Thomas de Sibthorpe founded a chantry in the church, and subsequently erected it into a college for a warden, nine chaplains, three clerks, and four choristers; he also added four chapels, in honour of St. Anne, St. Katharine, St. Margaret, and St. Mary; the revenue, at the dissolution, was estimated at £31. 1. 2. Thomas Secker, D. D., Archbishop of Canterbury, was born here in 1693 : he died in 1768.

SIBTON, a parish in the hundred of BLYTHING, county of SUFFOLK, 2 miles (N. W. by W.) from Yoxford, containing 569 inhabitants. The living is a discharged vicarage, with the perpetual curacy of Peasenhall annexed, in the archdeaconry of Suffolk, and diocese of Norwich, rated in the king's books at £8. 8. 4., endowed with £200 private benefaction, and £200 royal bounty. M. B. Kingsbury, Esq. and others were patrons in 1821. The church is dedicated to St. Peter. John and Dorothy Scrivener, in 1719, gave a rent-charge of

£ 12. 15. 6. for teaching ten or twelve children. Here are extensive remains of a Cistercian abbey, founded, in 1149, by William de Cayneto; it was dedicated to the Blessed Virgin Mary, and at the dissolution possessed a revenue of £250. 15. 7. There was an hospital at the gate of the abbey.

SICKLINGHALL, a township in the parish of KIRKBY-OVERBLOWS, upper division of the wapentake of CLARO, West riding of the county of YORK, 3 miles (W.) from Wetherby, containing 257 inhabitants. There is a place of worship for Wesleyan Methodists.

SIDBURY, a parish in the eastern division of the hundred of BUDLEIGH, county of DEVON, 2½ miles (N. N. E.) from Sidmouth, containing 1612 inhabitants. The living is a vicarage, in the peculiar jurisdiction and patronage of the Dean and Chapter of Exeter, rated in the king's books at £28. The church is dedicated to St. Giles. There is a place of worship for Independents. Sidbury is a decayed market town, but there are still two annual fairs for cattle, on the Tuesday before Ascension-day, and at Michaelmas. On the Barton, or manor, of Sand is an old mansion, with the inscription *Hortus Johannis Capelli* over the garden door. A school is supported by small annual subscriptions.

SIDBURY, a parish in the hundred of STOTTESDEN, county of SALOP, 5¼ miles (S. S. W.) from Bridgenorth, containing 93 inhabitants. The living is a discharged rectory, in the archdeaconry and diocese of Hereford, rated in the king's books at £4. 17. 8½., and in the patronage of Thomas Wood, Esq., and Miss Hayley. The church is dedicated to the Holy Trinity.

SIDDINGTON, a chapelry in the parish of PRESTBURY, hundred of MACCLESFIELD, county palatine of CHESTER, 5 miles (N. by W.) from Congleton, containing 481 inhabitants. The living is a perpetual curacy, in the archdeaconry and diocese of Chester, endowed with £403 private benefaction, and £400 royal bounty, and in the patronage of D. Davenport, Esq. The chapel is built partly of wood and plaster, and partly of brick. Courts leet and baron are held annually at Martinmas. John Fowden, in 1712, founded a school, and endowed it with £8 per annum.

SIDDINGTON, a village in the hundred of CROWTHORNE and MINETY, county of GLOUCESTER, 1¼ mile (S. S. E.) from Cirencester, containing 349 inhabitants, and comprising the united parishes of St. Mary and St. Peter, in the archdeaconry and diocese of Gloucester; the former is a rectory, rated in the king's books at £8. 12. 1.; and the latter, a discharged vicarage, rated at £5. 12. 3½.; both being in the patronage of the Crown. The church, dedicated to St. Peter, exhibits portions in the several styles of English architecture, and some Norman remains; the south door and the arch leading into the chancel, in particular, are fine specimens of the former style. The river Churn, and the Thames and Severn canal, run through the parish.

SIDE, a parish in the hundred of RAPSGATE, county of GLOUCESTER, 7 miles (E.) from Painswick, containing 40 inhabitants. The living is a rectory, in the archdeaconry and diocese of Gloucester, rated in the king's books at £3. 18. 4., endowed with £200 royal bounty. Joseph Pitt, Esq. was patron in 1813. The church i- ‥ dicated to St. Mary.

SIDESTRANDS, a parish in the northern division of the hundred of ERPINGHAM, county of NORFOLK, 3 miles (S. E. by E.) from Cromer, containing 146 inhabitants. The living is a discharged rectory, in the archdeaconry of Norfolk, and diocese of Norwich, rated in the king's books at £5. 10., endowed with £200 royal bounty, and in the patronage of the King, as Duke of Lancaster. The church is dedicated to St. Michael.

SIDLESHAM, a parish in the hundred of MANHOOD, rape of CHICHESTER, county of SUSSEX, 4 miles (S.) from Chichester, containing, 1029 inhabitants. The living is a discharged vicarage, in the archdeaconry and diocese of Chichester, rated in the king's books at £7. 10., and in the patronage of the Prebendary of Sidlesham in the Cathedral Church of Chichester. The church, dedicated to St. Mary, is in the early style of English architecture. The parish is bounded on the south by Selsey harbour. It has a convenient quay, near which is a superior tide-mill, which for justness of principle is equal to any in the kingdom : it was erected, at a considerable expense, by the late Mr. Woodroffe, under the direction of Benjamin Basle, the inventor and constructor of the machinery, which will grind a load of corn in an hour.

SIDMONTON, a chapelry in that part of the parish of KINGSCLERE which is in the hundred of KINGSCLERE, Kingsclere division of the county of SOUTHAMPTON, 7 miles (N. by E.) from Whitchurch, containing 156 inhabitants.

SIDMOUTH, a sea-port, market town, and parish, in the eastern division of the hundred of BUDLEIGH, county of DEVON, 13½ miles (E. S. E.) from Exeter, and 158 (W. S. W.) from London, containing 2747 inhabitants. The earliest account of this place is in the time of William the Conqueror, who bestowed the manor on the monastery of St. Michael in Normandy, from which, during the subsequent wars with France, it was alienated to the abbey of Sion, and has since belonged to various persons. In the reign of Edward III., the town appears to have been governed by a portreeve, and to have furnished that monarch, in his attack on Calais, with two vessels and twenty-five seamen. It is said to have been formerly famous for its fishery, and to have traded with Newfoundland; but the harbour, which then existed, is supposed, from the discovery of an old anchor and fragments of vessels, to have been in the Ham meadow, near the town; it has been choked up with sand and pebbles, and boats and fishing-smacks can now only approach the shore. To its great attractions as a watering-place its present prosperity owing, the extent of which may be estimated by the circumstance of the population having increased more than one thousand since 1821. The town is situated at the entrance of a narrow valley, on a small stream called the Sid, from which it derives its name: the surrounding country is remarkably picturesque and beautiful, and the hills bounding it on the east and west sides are of very great altitude, and extremely precipitous, terminating abruptly on the shore, and, in addition to their scenic beauty, affording great shelter to the town, which, though irregularly built, is very neat, and is skirted with numerous detached residences, altogether occupying a site of considerable extent. The inns and boarding-houses are of the best description, and every accommodation is provided for persons requiring sea-bathing. On the beach is a public walk more than half a mile in length, fronting which are the warm baths, public rooms, library, &c.

Assemblies and concerts take place during the season. The markets, on Tuesday and Saturday, are well supplied; and there are fairs annually on Easter Monday and Tuesday, and the third Monday in September. Petty sessions are held on the first Monday in every month, by two resident magistrates, who include Salcombe, Branscombe, Sidbury, and Sidford, within their jurisdiction; and at a court leet and baron held annually by the lord of the manor, two constables and tythingmen are appointed.

The living is a vicarage, in the archdeaconry and diocese of Exeter, rated in the king's books at £18. 15. 5., and in the patronage of the Rev. William Jenkins. The church, dedicated to St. Nicholas, is an ancient structure, with a well-built tower: it has recently received an addition of two hundred and sixty sittings, one hundred and sixty of which are free; and in aid of the expense, £200 was granted by the Incorporated Society for the enlargement of churches and chapels. Amongst the monuments is one to the memory of Dr. Currie, the distinguished biographer of Robert Burns. There are places of worship for Baptists, Independents, and Unitarians. A charity school, on the National system, is supported partly by a small endowment, and partly by subscriptions; and the poor of the parish are relieved by bequests from Anthony Isaack, in 1639, and John Minshull, in 1663, and others of small amount: some charitable institutions are supported by donations and subscriptions from the inhabitants and visitors of the town. A fraternity of Augustine monks is said to have once existed near Sidmouth, and there are still the remains of a building, which tradition affirms to have been a chapel of ease at a period when Sidmouth belonged to the parish of Otterton, on the road to which place there is an ancient stone cross. A fort, mounting four pieces of ordnance, formerly stood near the town. At Wolbrook cottage, in the vicinity, His Royal Highness the late Duke of Kent died. Sidmouth gives the title of viscount to the family of Addington.

SIGGLESTHORNE, a parish in the northern division of the wapentake of HOLDERNESS, East riding of the county of YORK, comprising the townships of Catfoss, Little Hatfield, Seaton, and Sigglesthorne, and containing 538 inhabitants, of which number, 163 are in the township of Sigglesthorne, 10 miles (E. N. E.) from Beverley. The living is a rectory, in the archdeaconry of the East riding, and diocese of York, rated in the king's books at £31. 1. 3., and in the patronage of the Crown. The church is dedicated to St. Lawrence. Marmaduke Constable, in 1810, gave £200 to be applied for the education of poor children: the annual income is £16. 15., and fifteen are instructed.

SIGHILL, a township in the parish of EARSDON, eastern division of CASTLE ward, county of NORTHUMBERLAND, 6¾ miles (N. W.) from North Shields, containing 138 inhabitants.

SIGNET, a joint hamlet with Upton, in the parish of BURFORD, hundred of BAMPTON, county of OXFORD, 1¼ mile (S. by W.) from Burford. The population is returned with Upton.

SIGSTON (KIRBY), a parish in the wapentake of ALLERTONSHIRE, North riding of the county of YORK, comprising the townships of Kirby-Sigston, Sowerby under Cotliffe, and Winton, and containing 322 inhabitants, of which number, 131 are in the township of Kirby-Sigston, 3½ miles (E. by N.) from North Allerton. The living is a rectory, in the peculiar jurisdiction of the Dean and Chapter of Durham for Allerton and Allertonshire, rated in the king's books at £12. 13. 4., and in the patronage of Sir T. Slingsby, Bart. The church is dedicated to St. Lawrence.

SILCHESTER, a parish in the hundred of HOLDSHOTT, Basingstoke division of the county of SOUTHAMPTON, 7½ miles (N.) from Basingstoke, containing 407 inhabitants. The living is a rectory, in the archdeaconry and diocese of Winchester, rated in the king's books at £9. 6. 0½., and in the patronage of the Bishop of Winchester. The church, dedicated to St. Mary, is partly in the early, and partly in the later, style of English architecture. There is an endowed school for five children. This place, situated near the borders of Berkshire, was the Caer Seiont, or Segont, of the Britons, and the Vindonum of the Romans, having been one of the principal stations of the latter in the south of England. The usurper Constantine was invested with the purple in this city, in the year 407. About 493, it was destroyed by the Saxon chief, Ælla, on his march to Bath, from the coast of Sussex, where he had made his landing. The enclosed area is in the form of an irregular octagon, nearly a mile and a half in circumference. The walls are most perfect on the south side, being in some places nearly twenty feet high. About one hundred and fifty yards from the north-east angle of the walls is a Roman amphitheatre, now covered with trees; and about a mile and a half to the north-west, near a village called the Soak, are some remains of a camp. Silchester confers the title of baron upon the family of Pakenham, Earls of Longford.

SILEBY, a parish in the eastern division of the hundred of GOSCOTE, county of LEICESTER, 1½ mile (E.) from Mountsorrel, containing 1328 inhabitants. The living is a discharged vicarage, in the archdeaconry of Leicester, and diocese of Lincoln, rated in the king's books at £8. 15. 5., endowed with £200 private benefaction, and £200 royal bounty, and in the patronage of George Pochin, Esq. The church, dedicated to St. Mary, has a highly enriched tower. There are places of worship for Baptists and Wesleyan Methodists. The manufacture of hosiery is carried on to a considerable extent. The Rev. William Staveley, in 1702, founded a small free school, with an endowment of £5 per annum, to which George Pochin, in 1706, bequeathed £50. The parish, which is bounded on the west by the river Soar, is in the honour of Tutbury, duchy of Lancaster, and within the jurisdiction of a court of pleas held at Tutbury every third Tuesday, for the recovery of debts under 40s.

SILFIELD, a township in the parish of WYMONDHAM, hundred of FOREHOE, county of NORFOLK, 1½ mile (S.E.) from Wymondham, containing 444 inhabitants.

SILKSTONE, a parish in the wapentake of STAINCROSS, West riding of the county of YORK, comprising the chapelries of Barnesley and Stainbrough, and part of those of West Bretton and Cumberworth, and the townships of Dodworth, Hoyland-Swaine, Silkstone, and Thurgoland, and containing 13,728 inhabitants, of which number, 807 are in the township of Silkstone, 4¼ miles (W. by S.) from Barnesley. The living is a vicarage, in the archdeaconry and diocese of York, rated in the king's books at £17. 13. 4., and in the patronage of the Archbishop of York. The church, dedicated to All Saints, is partly Norman, and partly of later date, with some elegant screen-work. There is a place of worship for Wesleyan Methodists. In this parish the various kinds of linen are manufactured; wire-drawing is also carried on, and there are extensive iron-foundries and collieries in the neighbourhood. The Rev. John Clarkson, in 1734, assigned his interest in the profits arising from certain messuages and lands, under lease for five hundred years, for the education of poor children of the township of Silkstone; the income is £28. 15., and there are at present fifteen free scholars.

SILKSWORTH, a township in the parish of Bishop-Wearmouth, northern division of Easington ward, county palatine of Durham, 3 miles (S. W. by S.) from Sunderland, containing 210 inhabitants.

SILPHO, a joint township with Harwood-Dale, in the parish of Hackness, liberty of Whitby-Strand, North riding of the county of York, 6¼ miles (N.W. by W.) from Scarborough, containing, exclusively of Harwood-Dale, 96 inhabitants.

SILSDEN, a chapelry in the parish of Kildwick, eastern division of the wapentake of Staincliffe and Ewcross, West riding of the county of York, 4 miles (N. by W.) from Keighley, containing 1904 inhabitants. The living is a perpetual curacy, in the peculiar jurisdiction of the manorial court of Silsden, endowed with £400 private benefaction, £400 royal bounty, and £400 parliamentary grant, and in the patronage of the Earl of Thanet. The chapel is dedicated to St. James. There is a place of worship for Wesleyan Methodists. The manufacture of woollen cloth, calico, and nails, is carried on. Five poor children are taught for £3. 6. 8. a year, the bequest of William Laycock, in 1612.

SILSOE, a chapelry (formerly a market town) in the parish of Flitton, hundred of Flitt, county of Bedford, 10 miles (S. by E.) from Bedford, containing 568 inhabitants. The chapel, dedicated to St. James, has a tower in the decorated style, with a wooden spire, and over the altar a representation of the Adoration of the Shepherds, painted and presented by Mrs. Mary Lloyd. A market, now disused, was granted in 1319; also a fair, which is held on the festival of St. Peter and St. James, besides which there is another on September 21st.

SILTON, a parish in the hundred of Redlane, Sturminster division of the county of Dorset, 3 miles (S.S.W.) from Mere, containing 409 inhabitants. The living is a rectory, in the archdeaconry of Dorset, and diocese of Bristol, rated in the king's books at £7. 9. 7. H. C. Sturt, Esq. was patron in 1815. The church is dedicated to St. Nicholas.

SILTON (NETHER), a chapelry in that part of the parish of Leak which is in the wapentake of Birdforth, North riding of the county of York, 8 miles (N. by E.) from Thirsk, containing 202 inhabitants. The living is a perpetual curacy, annexed to the vicarage of Leak, in the peculiar jurisdiction of the Bishop of Durham. There is a place of worship for Wesleyan Methodists.

SILTON (OVER), a parish in the wapentake of Birdforth, North riding of the county of York, comprising the townships of Kepwick and Over Silton, and containing 264 inhabitants, of which number, 94

VOL. IV.

are in the township of Over Silton, 8½ miles (N. by E.) from Thirsk. The living is a perpetual curacy, in the archdeaconry of Cleveland, and diocese of York, endowed with £600 royal bounty, and £200 parliamentary grant. The church is dedicated to All Saints.

SILVERDALE, a chapelry in the parish of Warton, hundred of Lonsdale, south of the sands, county palatine of Lancaster, 4¾ miles (W. by S.) from Burton in Kendal, containing 243 inhabitants. The living is a perpetual curacy, in the archdeaconry of Richmond, and diocese of Chester, endowed with £200 private benefaction, and £600 royal bounty, and in the patronage of the Vicar of Warton. The chapel has lately received an addition of two hundred and seven free sittings, the Incorporated Society for the enlargement of churches and chapels having granted £80 towards defraying the expense. The parish is situated on Morecambe bay.

SILVERLEY, a parish in the hundred of Cheveley, county of Cambridge, 3¾ miles (E.) from Newmarket. The population is returned with the parish of Ashley. The living is a vicarage, united to the rectory of Ashley, in the archdeaconry of Sudbury, and diocese of Norwich, rated in the king's books at £7. 17. 3½. The church is dedicated to All Saints.

SILVERSTONE, a parish in the hundred of Greens-Norton, county of Northampton, 3 miles (S. by W.) from Towcester, containing 837 inhabitants. The living is a perpetual curacy, with that of Whittlebury, annexed to the rectory of Greens-Norton, in the archdeaconry of Northampton, and diocese of Peterborough. The church is dedicated to St. Michael. There is a place of worship for Wesleyan Methodists.

SILVERTON, a parish in the hundred of Hayridge, county of Devon, 5¼ miles (S.W. by W.) from Cullompton, containing 1308 inhabitants. The living is a rectory, in the archdeaconry and diocese of Exeter, rated in the king's books at £51. 8. 4., and in the patronage of the Earl of Ilchester and the Hon. P. C. Wyndham. The church, dedicated to St. Mary, is a handsome specimen of the later style of English architecture: adjoining it are some slight remains of an ancient chapel, dedicated to the Virgin Mary. There is a place of worship for Wesleyan Methodists. The river Exe marks the northern boundary of the parish. A market was formerly held here weekly : there are cattle fairs on the first Thursday in March and July, and a pleasure fair on September 4th. The free school was founded, in 1724, by John Richards, who gave £1200 for its erection and support; the present annual income is £90, and the number of boys taught about seventy. Sixty girls are also instructed in a school supported by voluntary contributions and an annuity of £2. 10., the gift of the Rev. Richard Troyle, in 1730.

SILVINGTON, a parish in the hundred of Overs, county of Salop, 6 miles (N. W.) from Cleobury-Mortimer, containing 38 inhabitants. The living is a discharged rectory, in the archdeaconry of Salop, and diocese of Hereford, rated in the king's books at £3. 6. 8., endowed with £400 private benefaction, and £400 royal bounty, and in the patronage of the Rev. Thomas Hill. The church is dedicated to St. Michael.

SIMONBURN, a parish in the north-western division of Tindale ward, county of Northumberland, comprising the chapelry of Humshaugh, and the townships

N

of Haughton and Simonburn, and containing 1030 inhabitants, of which number, 569 are in the township of Simonburn, 9 miles (N. W. by N.) from Hexham. The living is a rectory, in the archdeaconry of Northumberland, and diocese of Durham, rated in the king's books at £34. 6. 3., and in the patronage of the Governors of Greenwich Hospital. The church, dedicated to St. Simon, was repaired and beautified in 1821 : it contains monuments to the family of Allgood. This parish was formerly the largest in the county, having, in 1814, been divided, pursuant to an act obtained in 1811, into six parishes and rectories, the livings of all which are in the gift of the Governors of the Hospital, to which institution the manor of the ancient parish belongs, and from its funds the churches were erected. None but chaplains in the navy who have served ten years, or lost a limb in the service, can be inducted to these benefices; they are not allowed to hold any other preferment, but by an act passed in 1820, may receive their half-pay. The ancient parish was about thirty-three miles in length, and fourteen in breadth, diversified with mountains and vallies of picturesque character : the Roman wall passed on the northern side of it, and within its limits coal is abundant, and iron-ore was formerly obtained. A very small portion of its surface is in tillage, the land being chiefly applied to depasturing sheep and Scotch and Irish cattle. Giles Heron, a liberal benefactor to the poor, founded and endowed, in 1679, a school for teaching poor children, and for apprenticing them. The ancient castle was entirely destroyed in expectation of finding some hidden treasure, but part of the west end was rebuilt in 1766. In 1735, a stone inscribed VLPI. SABI., to Ulpias and Sabinus, Roman lieutenants in Britain, was found in taking down part of the rectory-house.

SIMONDSLEY, a township in the parish of GLOSSOP, hundred of HIGH PEAK, county of DERBY, 8 miles (N. by W.) from Chapel en le Frith, containing 340 inhabitants.

SIMONSTONE, a township in that part of the parish of WHALLEY which is in the higher division of the hundred of BLACKBURN, county palatine of LANCASTER, 4¾ miles (W. by N.) from Burnley, containing 396 inhabitants.

SIMONSWOOD, a township in the parish of WALTON on the HILL, hundred of WEST DERBY, county palatine of LANCASTER, 5 miles (S. by E.) from Ormskirk, containing 390 inhabitants.

SIMPSON, a parish in the hundred of NEWPORT, county of BUCKINGHAM, 1½ mile (N. by E.) from Fenny-Stratford, containing, exclusively of the chapelry of Fenny-Stratford, part of which is in this parish, 395 inhabitants. The living is a rectory, in the archdeaconry of Buckingham, and diocese of Lincoln, rated in the king's books at £17. 6. 8., and in the patronage of Sir J. Hanmer, Bart. The church is dedicated to St. Nicholas.

SINDERBY, a township in that part of the parish of PICKHILL which is in the wapentake of HALLIKELD, North riding of the county of YORK, 6¼ miles (W. by S.) from Thirsk, containing 86 inhabitants.

SINGLEBOROUGH, a hamlet in the parish of GREAT HORWOOD, hundred of COTTESLOE, county of BUCKINGHAM, 3 miles (N.) from Winslow, containing 104 inhabitants.

SINGLETON, a chapelry in the parish of KIRKHAM, hundred of AMOUNDERNESS, county palatine of LANCASTER, 3 miles (E. by S.) from Poulton, containing 501 inhabitants. The living is a perpetual curacy, in the archdeaconry of Richmond, and diocese of Chester, endowed with £1000 private benefaction, and £1200 royal bounty, and in the patronage of — Shaw, Esq. The chapel, consecrated in 1754, is dedicated to St. Anne. There is a great fair for sheep and cattle on September 21st.

SINGLETON, a parish in the hundred of WESTBOURN and SINGLETON, rape of CHICHESTER, county of SUSSEX, 5½ miles (S. by W.) from Midhurst, containing, with the tything of Charlton, 484 inhabitants. The living is a discharged rectory, annexed to the vicarage of West Dean, in the archdeaconry and diocese of Chichester, rated in the king's books at £6. 13. 4., and in the patronage of the Dean and Chapter of Chichester for two turns, and of the Duke of Richmond for one. The church is in the later style of English architecture.

SINNINGTON, a parish comprising the townships of Marton and Sinnington in PICKERING lythe, and the township of Little Edstone, in the wapentake of RYEDALE, North riding of the county of YORK, and containing 614 inhabitants, of which number, 343 are in the township of Sinnington, 4¾ miles (W. N. W.) from Pickering. The living is a perpetual curacy, in the archdeaconry of Cleveland, and diocese of York, endowed with £200 royal bounty, and in the patronage of the Master of Hemsworth school. There is a place of worship for Wesleyan Methodists. An annuity of £5 is paid from the estate of Lady Lumley, for the free instruction of the poor.

SINWELL, a tything in the parish of WOTTON under EDGE, upper division of the hundred of BERKELEY, county of GLOUCESTER. The population is returned with the parish.

SISLAND, a parish in the hundred of LODDON, county of NORFOLK, 6¼ miles (N. by E.) from Bungay, containing 101 inhabitants. The living is a discharged rectory, in the archdeaconry of Norfolk, and diocese of Norwich, rated in the king's books at £4. 3. 9. The Rev. William Hobson was patron in 1819. The church is dedicated to St. Mary.

SISTON, a parish in the hundred of PUCKLE-CHURCH, county of GLOUCESTER, 6½ miles (E. by N.) from Bristol, containing 902 inhabitants. The living is a rectory, in the archdeaconry and diocese of Gloucester, rated in the king's books at £5. 14. 4½. F. Trotman, Esq. was patron in 1815. The church is dedicated to St. Anne.

SITHNEY, a parish in the hundred of KERRIER, county of CORNWALL, 2 miles (N.W.) from Helston, containing 2238 inhabitants. The living is a discharged vicarage, in the archdeaconry of Cornwall, and diocese of Exeter, rated in the king's books at £19. 11. 5¼., and in the patronage of the Bishop of Exeter. The church is dedicated to St. Sithney. There is a place of worship for Wesleyan Methodists. The parish is bounded on the south by the English channel. Here was an ancient hospital, dedicated to St. John.

SITTINGBOURNE, a parish (formerly a corporate and market town) in the hundred of MILTON, lathe of SCRAY, county of KENT, 10 miles (E. N. E.) from Maidstone, containing 1537 inhabitants. The only incident worthy of notice in the ancient history of this town is the fact that Henry V. was entertained at the Red Lion here, by one John Northwood, a gentleman then resident in the vicinity, at the small expense of nine shillings and ninepence; and several other English monarchs have occasionally conferred a like distinction on the place. The town is situated on the main road from Canterbury to London, and consists of one long wide street. By means of Milton creek, which bounds the parish on the north, and is navigable at Crown quay, hoys sail hence to London. In the neighbourhood is a manufactory for bruising seed. A weekly market and two annual fairs were granted by charter of Elizabeth; the former was soon discontinued; the latter are held on Whit-Monday and October 10th, for linen and woollen goods, hardware, &c.; and a great monthly market is held on Tuesdays. By the same charter the inhabitants were incorporated, under the style of " Guardian and Free Tenants," which was subsequently changed by another charter into that of " Mayor and Jurats;" they likewise had the privilege of sending two members to parliament, but all these were merely nominal, as it seems they were never exercised.

The living is a vicarage, in the archdeaconry and diocese of Canterbury, rated in the king's books at £10, and in the patronage of the Archbishop of Canterbury. The church, dedicated to St. Michael, was, with the exception of the walls, destroyed by fire in 1762; the present edifice exhibits specimens in the decorated and later styles of English architecture, and contains a fine enriched octagonal font, and some curious and ancient monuments: it has received an addition of two hundred and sixty-eight sittings, of which one hundred and seventy-five are free, the Incorporated Society for the building and enlargement of churches and chapels having contributed £45 towards defraying the expense. There is a place of worship for Wesleyan Methodists. A National school is supported by voluntary contributions. In the vicinity are some remains of ancient fortifications.

SIX-HILLS, a parish in the eastern division of the wapentake of WRAGGOE, parts of LINDSEY, county of LINCOLN, 5 miles (E. S. E.) from Market-Rasen, containing 141 inhabitants. The living is a discharged vicarage, in the archdeaconry and diocese of Lincoln, rated in the king's books at £6, and in the patronage of George Robert Heneage, Esq. The church is dedicated to All Saints. A Gilbertine priory of nuns and canons, in honour of the Blessed Virgin, was founded here by one Grella, or Greslei, which at the dissolution had a revenue of £170. 8. 9.

SIZEWELL, a hamlet in the parish of LEISTON, hundred of BLYTHING, county of SUFFOLK, 4¼ miles (N. by E.) from Aldborough. The population is returned with the parish. Here was formerly a chapel, dedicated to St. Nicholas, but it has been demolished.

SKECKLING, a parish in the southern division of the wapentake of HOLDERNESS, East riding of the county of YORK, 10½ miles (E.) from Kingston upon Hull, containing 436 inhabitants. The living is a discharged vicarage, with the perpetual curacy of Burstwick annexed, in the archdeaconry of the East riding, and diocese of York, rated in the king's books at £7, and in the patronage of Sir T. A. Clifford Constable, Bart. The

church is dedicated to All Saints; in the chancel is a fine painting of the Lord's Supper.

SKEEBY, a township in that part of the parish of EASBY which is in the western division of the wapentake of GILLING, North riding of the county of YORK, 2¼ miles (E. N. E.) from Richmond, containing 163 inhabitants.

SKEFFINGTON, a parish in the eastern division of the hundred of GOSCOTE, county of LEICESTER, 9½ miles (W. by N.) from Uppingham, containing 169 inhabitants. The living is a rectory, in the archdeaconry of Leicester, and diocese of Lincoln, rated in the king's books at £12. 13. 9., and in the patronage of the Rev. George Crum. The church is dedicated to St. Thomas à Becket.

SKEFFLING, a parish in the southern division of the wapentake of HOLDERNESS, East riding of the county of YORK, 4½ miles (S. E. by E.) from Patrington, containing 201 inhabitants. The living is a discharged vicarage, in the archdeaconry of the East riding, and diocese of York, rated in the king's books at £5, endowed with £600 royal bounty, and in the patronage of the Rector of Rise. The church, dedicated to St. Helen, is principally in the later style of English architecture. There is a place of worship for Wesleyan Methodists.

SKEGBY, a parish in the northern division of wapentake of BROXTOW, county of NOTTINGHAM, 3 miles (W.) from Mansfield, containing 584 inhabitants. The living is a perpetual curacy, annexed to that of Mansfield-Woodhouse, in the archdeaconry of Nottingham, and diocese of York, endowed with £600 royal bounty, and £1400 parliamentary grant. The church is a small stone edifice, in a very dilapidated state, situated on an eminence some distance from the village. The manufacture of earthenware is carried on here, and on Skegby moor are extensive collieries.

SKEGNESS, a parish in the Marsh division of the wapentake of CANDLESHOE, parts of LINDSEY, county of LINCOLN, 3¾ miles (E. by S.) from Burgh, containing 150 inhabitants. The living is a discharged rectory, in the archdeaconry and diocese of Lincoln, rated in the king's books at £15. 6. 8., and in the patronage of the Earl of Scarborough. The church is dedicated to St. Clement. According to Leland, here was once a considerable town, having a haven and a castle, and surrounded by walls, which was swallowed up by the sea.

SKELBROOKE, a chapelry in the parish of SOUTH KIRBY, upper division of the wapentake of OSGOLD-CROSS, West riding of the county of YORK, 7¼ miles (N. W. by N.) from Doncaster, containing 115 inhabitants. The living is a perpetual curacy, in the archdeaconry and diocese of York, endowed with £200 private benefaction, and £600 royal bounty. Sir R. Perryn, Knt. was patron in 1800. The chapel is dedicated to St. Michael. The ancient Forest of Barnsdale, part of which is comprised in this parish, is said to have been one of the haunts of the famous Robin Hood, whose name is given to a well not far distant. It is further remarkable for the meeting which took place, in 1541, between Henry VIII. and the clergy of York, headed by the archbishop, who on their knees presented the king with £600.

SKELLINGTHORPE, a parish in the lower division of the wapentake of BOOTHBY-GRAFFO, parts of KESTEVEN, county of LINCOLN, 5½ miles (W.) from Lincoln, containing 370 inhabitants. The living is a discharged vicarage, in the archdeaconry and diocese of Lincoln, rated in the king's books at £6. 18. 9., endowed with £200 royal bounty, and £400 parliamentary grant, and in the patronage of the Misses F. and S. Dowbiggin. The church is dedicated to St. Lawrence. There is a place of worship for Wesleyan Methodists.

SKELLOW, a township in the parish of Owston, upper division of the wapentake of Osgoldcross, West riding of the county of York, 5½ miles (N.N.W.) from Doncaster, containing 146 inhabitants.

SKELMANTHORPE, a township partly in the parish of Emley, lower division, partly in the chapelry of Cumberworth, parish of Kirk-Burton, upper division, of the wapentake of Agbrigg, and partly in the parish of High Hoyland, wapentake of Staincross, West riding of the county of York, 7¾ miles (S. E. by E.) from Huddersfield. The population is returned with Cumberworth. There is a place of worship for Wesleyan Methodists.

SKELMERSDALE, a chapelry in the parish of Ormskirk, hundred of West Derby, county palatine of Lancaster, 4 miles (E. S. E.) from Ormskirk, containing 622 inhabitants. The living is a perpetual curacy, in the archdeaconry and diocese of Chester, endowed with £200 private benefaction, £600 royal bounty, and £1500 parliamentary grant, and in the patronage of the Vicar of Ormskirk. The chapel has lately received an addition of one hundred and forty sittings, of which seventy are free, the Incorporated Society for the enlargement of churches and chapels having granted £90 towards defraying the expense. There is a small endowment, bequeathed by Evan Swift, in 1720, for a school. Skelmersdale gives the title of baron to the family of Bootle-Wilbraham.

SKELSMERGH, a township in that part of the parish of Kendal which is in Kendal ward, county of Westmorland, 2½ miles (N. by E.) from Kendal, containing 258 inhabitants. The township is bounded on every side, except on the east, by the small rivers Kent, Mint, and Sprint, upon which there are corn, worsted, bobbin, and dye-wood mills. Here are remains of a chapel, dedicated to St. John the Baptist; and at Doddington Green there is one for Roman Catholics. A school is supported by small annual subscriptions.

SKELTON, a parish in Leath ward, county of Cumberland, comprising the townships of Lamonby, Skelton, and Unthank, and containing 858 inhabitants, of which number, 332 are in the township of Skelton, 6¾ miles (N.W. by W.) from Penrith. The living is a rectory, in the archdeaconry and diocese of Carlisle, rated in the king's books at £43. 3. 6½., and in the patronage of the President and Fellows of Corpus Christi College, Oxford. The church, dedicated to St. Mary, is an ancient structure: it was thoroughly repaired in 1794, and formerly contained a richly-endowed chantry. Freestone and limestone are obtained in the parish. A free school, erected in 1750, by Isaac Milner, was endowed in 1817, by the Rev. Joseph Nelson, with £1000, now producing upwards of £32 a year, for which twenty-eight children are instructed.

SKELTON, a township in the parish of Howden, wapentake of Howdenshire, East riding of the county of York, 2 miles (S. E. by S.) from Howden, containing 221 inhabitants.

SKELTON, a parish partly in the liberty of St. Peter of York, East riding, but chiefly in the wapentake of Bulmer, North riding, of the county of York, 3¾ miles (N. W. by N.) from York, containing 273 inhabitants. The living is a perpetual curacy, in the jurisdiction of the peculiar court of Alne and Tollerton, and in the patronage of — Hepworth, Esq. The church is dedicated to All Saints.

SKELTON, a parish in the eastern division of the liberty of Langbaurgh, North riding of the county of York, comprising the townships of Great Moorsham, Skelton, and Stranghow, and containing 1235 inhabitants, of which number, 791 are in the township of Skelton, 4 miles (N. E. by N.) from Guilsbrough. The living is a perpetual curacy, in the archdeaconry of Cleveland, and diocese of York, endowed with £200 private benefaction, and £200 royal bounty, and in the patronage of the Archbishop of York. The church is dedicated to All Saints. There is a place of worship for Wesleyan Methodists. A market, formerly held on Sunday, but afterwards changed to Saturday, and a fair at Whitsuntide, have been discontinued. Skelton castle was built by Robert de Brus, a Norman baron, who came over with the Conqueror, and from whom descended some of the kings of Scotland and the present family of Bruce, Marquises of Ailesbury. There are now but few remains of the ancient building, the whole having been entirely modernised, or renovated, in 1794.

SKELTON, a chapelry in that part of the parish of Ripon which is in the liberty of Ripon, West riding of the county of York, 4 miles (S. E. by E.) from Ripon, containing 314 inhabitants. The living is a perpetual curacy, in the jurisdiction of the peculiar court of Ripon, belonging to the Archbishop of York, endowed with £200 private benefaction, and £800 royal bounty, and £800 parliamentary grant, and in the patronage of the Dean and Chapter of Ripon. The chapel is small, but handsomely built in the early style of English architecture.

SKELWITH, a joint township with Monk-Coniston, in the parish of Hawkeshead, hundred of Lonsdale, north of the sands, county palatine of Lancaster, 2½ miles (S. W. by W.) from Ambleside. The population is returned with Monk-Coniston.

SKENDLEBY, a parish in the Wold division of the wapentake of Candleshoe, parts of Lindsey, county of Lincoln, 4 miles (N. E. by N.) from Spilsby, containing 210 inhabitants. The living is a discharged vicarage, in the archdeaconry and diocese of Lincoln, rated in the king's books at £4. 0. 5., endowed with £400 royal bounty, and in the patronage of Lord Gwydir and Baroness de Eresby. The church is dedicated to St. Peter. There is a place of worship for Wesleyan Methodists.

SKENFRETH, a parish in the upper division of the hundred of Skenfreth, county of Monmouth, 6¾ miles (N. N. W.) from Monmouth, containing 488 inhabitants. The living is a discharged vicarage, in the archdeaconry and diocese of Llandaff, rated in the king's books at £5. 16. 10½., and in the patronage of W. Cecil, Esq. The church, dedicated to St. Bridget, is a large handsome structure, the windows of which are enriched with fine stained glass. The parish is intersected by the river Mon, over which a bridge was erected in 1825, at an expense to the county of £1000, the road from London to Milford Haven being thus shortened by seven miles. Courts leet and baron are annually held here. Of the ancient castle, which stood on an eminence rising gently from the bank of the Mon, nothing remains but the outer wall: it was defended by six towers and a moat supplied from the river.

SKERNE, a parish in the Bainton-Beacon division of the wapentake of HARTHILL, East riding of the county of YORK, 2¾ miles (S. E. by S.) from Great Driffield, containing 251 inhabitants. The living is a discharged perpetual curacy, in the archdeaconry of the East riding, and diocese of York, endowed with £200 private benefaction, and £400 royal bounty. R. Arkwright, Esq. was patron in 1808.

SKERTON, a township in that part of the parish of LANCASTER which is in the hundred of LONSDALE, south of the sands, county palatine of LANCASTER, ¾ of a mile (N.) from Lancaster, containing 1283 inhabitants. Skerton is a considerable village, separated from the town of Lancaster by the river Lune, in which there is a considerable salmon fishery. A free school was erected by Jane Jephson, and endowed with £12 a year by Henry Williamson, in 1767, for twenty children.

SKETCHLEY, a hamlet in the parish of ASTON-FLAMVILLE, hundred of SPARKENHOE, county of LEICESTER, 1¼ mile (S. by W.) from Hinckley. The population is returned with the chapelry of Burbage. Here was formerly a chapel, now in ruins.

SKEWSBY, a township in the parish of DALBY, wapentake of BULMER, North riding of the county of YORK, 8¾ miles (E. by N.) from Easingwould. The population is returned with the parish.

SKEYTON, a parish in the southern division of the hundred of ERPINGHAM, county of NORFOLK, 3¾ miles (E. by S.) from Aylsham, containing 324 inhabitants. The living is a discharged rectory, with that of Oxnead and the vicarage of Buxton annexed, in the archdeaconry and diocese of Norwich, rated in the king's books at £9. 10., endowed with £200 royal bounty, and in the patronage of George Anson, Esq. The church is dedicated to All Saints.

SKIDBROOK, a parish in the Marsh division of the hundred of LOUTH-ESKE, parts of LINDSEY, county of LINCOLN, 10½ miles (N. E. by E.) from Louth, containing, with the hamlet of Saltfleet-Haven, 365 inhabitants. The living is a discharged vicarage, in the archdeaconry and diocese of Lincoln, rated in the king's books at £11. 3. 6., and in the patronage of the Rev. J. M. Phillips. The church is dedicated to St. Botolph.

SKIDBY, a parish in the Hunsley-Beacon division of the wapentake of HARTHILL, East riding of the county of YORK, 4 miles (S. by W.) from Beverley, containing 313 inhabitants. The living is a perpetual curacy, annexed to the vicarage of Cottingham, in the archdeaconry of the East riding, and diocese of York. The church is dedicated to St. Michael. Eight children are educated for the proceeds of £150, the gift of John Marshall in 1803.

SKILGATE, a parish in the hundred of WILLITON and FREEMANNERS, county of SOMERSET, 6½ miles (W. by S.) from Wiveliscombe, containing 226 inhabitants. The living is a rectory, in the archdeaconry of Taunton, and diocese of Bath and Wells, rated in the king's books at £9. 9. 4½. The Rev. R. Bere was patron in 1817. The church is dedicated to St. John the Baptist.

SKILLINGTON, a parish in the wapentake of BELTISLOE, parts of KESTEVEN, county of LINCOLN, 3 miles (N. W. by W.) from Colsterworth, containing 364 inhabitants. The living is a discharged vicarage, in the peculiar jurisdiction of the Dean and Chapter of Lincoln, rated in the king's books at £4. 19. 4½., endowed with £200 royal bounty, and in the patronage of — Whitelock, Esq. The church is dedicated to St. James. There is a place of worship for Wesleyan Methodists.

SKINBURNESS, a village in the parish of HOLME-CULTRAM, ALLERDALE ward below Darwent, county of CUMBERLAND, 11½ miles (N. W. by W.) from Wigton. The population is returned with Low Holme. This place had anciently a market and a fair, granted to the abbot of Holme-Cultram; it was of considerable importance as a depôt from which the army employed against the Scots was supplied with stores. About 1303, the town was washed away by an irruption of the sea, and the abbot, in consequence having obtained license to erect a church, or chapel, at Arlosh, a new town was also built, and called Newton-Arlosh. Skinburness is now a pleasant village and respectable sea-bathing place, affording public and private accommodation to its numerous visitors, and commanding a most extensive view over the Solway Frith, and of the Scottish mountains beyond. A very productive herring fishery is carried on here.

SKINNAND, a parish in the higher division of the wapentake of BOOTHBY-GRAFFO, parts of KESTEVEN, county of LINCOLN, 11½ miles (N. W.) from Sleaford, containing 14 inhabitants. The living is a discharged rectory, in the archdeaconry and diocese of Lincoln, rated in the king's books at £5. 13. 11½., and in the patronage of Lord Viscount Falkland. The church is in ruins.

SKINNINGROVE, a township in the parish of BROTTON, eastern division of the liberty of LANGBAURGH, North riding of the county of YORK, 8 miles (N. E.) from Guisbrough, containing 60 inhabitants. It has a small fishing village, situated on a creek, almost secluded from view by the lofty heights which closely environ it on every side.

SKIPLAM, a township in that part of the parish of KIRKDALE which is in the wapentake of RYEDALE, North riding of the county of YORK, 5½ miles (N. E. by E.) from Helmsley, containing 170 inhabitants.

SKIPSEA, a parish in the northern division of the wapentake of HOLDERNESS, East riding of the county of YORK, comprising the chapelry of Ulrome, and the townships of Bonwick, Dringhoe with Upton and Brough, and Skipsea, and containing 693 inhabitants, of which number, 329 are in the township of Skipsea, 11¼ miles (E. by S.) from Great Driffield. The living is a discharged vicarage, in the archdeaconry of the East riding, and diocese of York, rated in the king's books at £9. 16., endowed with £200 private benefaction, £400 royal bounty, and £1000 parliamentary grant, and in the patronage of the Archbishop of York. The church, dedicated to All Saints, is principally in the later style of English architecture. There are places of worship for Independents and Wesleyan Methodists. The parish is bounded on the east by the North sea. A lofty mount, termed Skipsea Brough, was anciently the site of the baronial castle of the lords of Holderness.

SKIPTON, a township in that part of the parish of TOPCLIFFE which is in the wapentake of BIRDFORTH, North riding of the county of YORK, 5 miles (S. W. by W.) from Thirsk, containing 110 inhabitants. There is a place of worship for Wesleyan Methodists. The Rev. Mr. Day, in 1764, bequeathed a small sum towards the support of a school.

SKIPTON, a parish comprising the market town of Skipton, the chapelry of Bolton-Abbey, and the townships of Barden, Draughton, Embsay with Eastby, East Halton with Bolton, and Stirton with Thorlby, in the eastern division of the wapentake of STAINCLIFFE and EWCROSS, and the township of Hazlewood with Storiths, and part of that of Beamsley, in the upper division of the wapentake of CLARO, West riding of the county of YORK, and containing 5479 inhabitants, of which number, 3411 are in the town of Skipton, 44 miles (W.) from York, and 211 (N.N.W.) from London. The name, which is variously spelt in Domesday-book, as *Sciptone, Sceptone,* or *Sceptetone,* was probably acquired from the vast number of sheep anciently fed in the vicinity. About the close of the reign of William the Conqueror, a castle was built here by Robert de Romille, which, in the great civil war, was garrisoned for the royal cause; but having been invested by the opposing party, it was surrendered, after a siege of three years, December 20th, 1645, having held out longer than any other fortress in the northern part of the country: in the following year an order was issued from the parliament for its demolition, which, in 1649, was partially carried into effect, but it was soon after restored by the Countess of Pembroke, who occasionally resided in it; in more modern times it has undergone a thorough repair, and is still a magnificent and commodious residence. The town is situated in a valley of great fertility and beauty, near the river Aire, and is skirted on the south-west by the Leeds and Liverpool canal, which partly passes through it, affording great facility for the conveyance of goods. It consists chiefly of two long and wide streets, one crossing the other at its termination, nearly at right angles, which are partly paved, and well supplied with water, conveyed through pipes from a spring that rises upon Rumbles moor: the houses are neatly built of stone, obtained in the immediate vicinity. The adjacent vale is celebrated for its productiveness, and is a fine grazing district: from the surrounding hills are some beautiful and picturesque views. There is a small subscription library. The situation of the town is highly advantageous to the purposes of trade, of which the spinning and weaving of cotton form the principal branch: there are several cotton-mills upon the neighbouring streams, and an extensive brewery for porter and ale. The market is on Saturday, when a small quantity of grain is brought for sale; and there is a large market every second Monday for fat cattle and sheep: fairs are held on March 25th, Saturdays before Palm and Easter Sundays, the first and third Tuesdays after Easter, on Whitsun-eve, August 5th, and November 23rd, chiefly for sheep, horned cattle, pedlary, &c.; and September 23rd for horses. The local affairs are under the superintendence of a constable, who is appointed annually at the manorial court leet: the general quarter sessions for the West riding are held here at Midsummer, in the town hall, which is a neat stone building, situated on the east side of Sheep-street Hill.

The living comprises a rectory and a discharged vicarage, in the archdeaconry and diocese of York, the former rated in the king's books at £4. 0. 10., and the latter, which is endowed with £200 private benefaction, and £200 royal bounty, rated at £10. 12. 6., and both in the patronage of the Dean and Canons of Christ Church, Oxford. The church is dedicated to the Holy Trinity: it immediately adjoins the castle, and is the work of different periods, but principally in the later style of English architecture; four stone seats, with pointed arches and cylindrical columns, in the south wall of the nave, are supposed to be the only remaining parts of the original edifice: the tower, which stands at the west end, was repaired by Lady Clifford, Countess Dowager of Pembroke, in the year 1655: there are several monuments to different members of the family of Clifford, Earls of Cumberland; and beneath the altar is a family vault, which was their place of interment from the dissolution of Bolton priory to the death of the last Earl of Cumberland. There are places of worship for the Society of Friends, Independents, and Wesleyan Methodists. The free grammar school was founded in 1548, and endowed with lands in Addingham, Eastby, and Skipton, by the Rev. William Ermystead, the annual proceeds of which amount to upwards of £600: the master is appointed by the vicar and churchwardens, and has an agreeable residence, with pleasure grounds and gardens attached: boys are admissible from all parts, and there are about sixty in the school. They are eligible to the exhibitions of Lady Elizabeth Hastings, in Queen's College, Oxford; and the school has two exhibitions in Christ's College, Cambridge, founded by William Petyt, Esq., who gave £200 to the college for that purpose. The Clerk's school was originally endowed, by the Rev. William Ermystead, with lands of great value at Wike, near Harewood, in Yorkshire, which, by mismanagement of the trustees, have been lost, and a prescriptive payment, amounting to £12 per annum, is made to the master of the boys' National school, who is also clerk of the parish: this school and a National school for girls are further supported by voluntary contributions, the school-house having been also erected from a similar fund: the number of children in both is one hundred and sixty. Sylvester Petyt, Esq., Principal of Bernard's Inn, and a native of this parish, bequeathed a library for the use of the parishioners, which is preserved in the church; and the sum of £24,048 South Sea Annuities, for various charitable purposes, especially for the payment of £20 per annum to Christ's College, Cambridge, for an augmentation of exhibitions for the free grammar school, for apprenticing twelve poor children of parishioners annually, the interest of £100 for the librarian, and of £50 to buy books for poor boys at the grammar school. The principal remains of the old castle are the western doorway, and several round towers. George Holmes, an eminent antiquary, who republished the first seventeen volumes of Rymer's Fœdera, was a native of this town.

SKIPWITH, a parish in the wapentake of OUZE and DERWENT, East riding of the county of YORK, comprising the townships of North Duffield and Skipwith, and containing 748 inhabitants, of which number, 315 are in the township of Skipwith, 5½ miles (N.N.E.)

from Selby. The living is a discharged vicarage, in the jurisdiction of the Peculiar Court of Howdenshire, rated in the king's books at £ 10. 11. 3., and in the patronage of the Crown. The church is dedicated to St. Helen. The Rev. Joseph Nelson, in 1813, bequeathed £400 for the education of the poorest children of the parish; the annual income is upwards of £13. 10., for which about fourteen children are instructed in a school founded by Dorothy Wilson, in 1717.

SKIRBECK, a parish partly in the wapentake of Kirton, but chiefly in that of Skirbeck, parts of Holland, county of Lincoln, 1 mile (S. E. by S.) from Boston, containing, with the hamlet of Skirbeck-Quarter, 1307 inhabitants. The living is a rectory, in the archdeaconry and diocese of Lincoln, rated in the king's books at £34. 17. 8½., and in the patronage of the Rev. William Volans. The church is dedicated to St. Nicholas. An ancient hospital, for ten poor persons, founded in honour of St. Leonard, was given, in 1230, by Sir Thomas Multon, Knt., to the knights hospitallers of St. John of Jerusalem, who settled here, and dedicated it anew to St. John the Baptist. In the time of Edward II., its revenue was sufficient for the maintenance of four priests, also twenty poor people in the infirmitory, and for the daily relief of forty more at the gate.

SKIRBECK-QUARTER, a hamlet in that part of the parish of Skirbeck which is in the wapentake of Kirton, parts of Holland, county of Lincoln, containing 325 inhabitants.

SKIRCOAT, a township in the parish of Halifax, wapentake of Morley, West riding of the county of York, 1¾ mile (S. S. W.) from Halifax, containing 3323 inhabitants. The manufacture of cotton and woollen goods is carried on here to a considerable extent.

SKIRLAUGH (NORTH), a chapelry in that part of the parish of Swine which is in the northern division of the wapentake of Holderness, East riding of the county of York, 9 miles (N. N. E.) from Kingston upon Hull, containing, with the township of Rowton, and part of that of Arnold, 260 inhabitants. The chapel, dedicated to St. Augustine, was built by Walter Skirlaw, Bishop of Durham; it is an elegant specimen of the later English style. There is a place of worship for Wesleyan Methodists.

SKIRLAUGH (SOUTH), a chapelry in that part of the parish of Swine which is in the middle division of the wapentake of Holderness, East riding of the county of York, 8¾ miles (N. N. E.) from Kingston upon Hull, containing 211 inhabitants. Marmaduke Langdale, about 1609, bequeathed £200, directing the interest to be applied for teaching and apprenticing children, and other charitable purposes.

SKIRLINGTON, a township in the parish of Atwick, northern division of the wapentake of Holderness, East riding of the county of York, 13½ miles (E. S. E.) from Great Driffield. The population is returned with the parish.

SKIRPENBECK, a parish partly in the wapentake of Buckrose, and partly in the liberty of St. Peter of York, East riding of the county of York, 7¾ miles (N. W. by N.) from Pocklington, containing 263 inhabitants. The living is a rectory, in the archdeaconry of the East riding, and diocese of York, rated in the king's books at £14. 7. 8½., and in the patronage of the Crown.

SKIRWITH, a township in the parish of Kirkland, Leath ward, county of Cumberland, 7½ miles (E. N. E.) from Penrith, containing 238 inhabitants. There is a place of worship for Wesleyan Methodists. A school was erected by subscription in 1828, towards which Lady le Fleming and W. Parker, Esq. each contributed £20. The mansion of the latter is supposed to occupy the site of a preceptory of Knights Templars.

SKUTTERSKELFE, a township in the parish of Rudby in Cleveland, western division of the liberty of Langbaurgh, North riding of the county of York, 2 miles (W. by S.) from Stokesley, containing 32 inhabitants. Near the village is an excellent land-mark called Folly Hill, which is sometimes discernible twenty leagues at sea.

SLAIDBURN, a parish in the western division of the wapentake of Staincliffe and Ewcross, West riding of the county of York, comprising the townships of High Bowland-Forest, Low Bowland-Forest, Easington, Newton, and Slaidburn, and containing 2583 inhabitants, of which number, 904 are in the township of Slaidburn, 8 miles (N. by W.) from Clitheroe. The living is a rectory, in the archdeaconry of the East riding, and diocese of York, rated in the king's books at £32, and in the patronage of J. Wigglesworth, Esq. The church is dedicated to St. Andrew. There is a chapel of ease, dedicated to St. Peter; also a place of worship for Wesleyan Methodists. A free grammar school was founded here, in 1717, by John Brannord, who bequeathed an estate in trust, to apply £200 for the erection of the school-house, with £50 a year to a master, and £30 to an usher, for teaching the classics, or English grammar, to all the children of the parish. Another school was endowed, in 1732, by Mr. William Clayton, with £250, and by Mr. Johnson with £100, the interest of which sums, amounting to about £14. 14. per annum, is applied to the gratuitous instruction of from twenty to thirty poor children. A chantry was founded, in 1332, by Stephen de Hamerton, in the chapel of St. Mary, then existing on his manor of Hamerton, for a Secular chaplain, to celebrate mass for the repose of the souls of himself, his father, and his mother.

SLAITHWAITE, a chapelry in the parish of Huddersfield, upper division of the wapentake of Agbrigg, West riding of the county of York, 5 miles (W. S. W.) from Huddersfield, containing 2871 inhabitants. The living is a perpetual curacy, in the archdeaconry and diocese of York, endowed with £200 private benefaction, and £600 royal bounty, and in the patronage of the Vicar of Huddersfield. The chapel, rebuilt in 1784, will accommodate upwards of one thousand five hundred persons. The canal, and the new line of road from Huddersfield to Manchester, pass through this place. The manufacture of woollen and cotton goods is carried on to a great extent, and the prosperity of the village is likely to be promoted by the recent discovery of an excellent spa, thought to be equal in its chalybeate properties to the springs at Harrogate. A free school was founded and endowed here, in 1721, by the Rev. Robert Meek; the income, with subsequent benefactions, amounts to £42 per annum, for which twenty boys are instructed.

SLALEY, a parish in the eastern division of Tindale ward, county of Northumberland, 5½ miles (S. E. by S.) from Hexham, containing 582 inhabitants.

The living is a perpetual curacy, in the archdeaconry of Northumberland, and diocese of Durham, endowed with £200 private benefaction, £200 royal bounty, and £1200 parliamentary grant, and in the patronage of T. W. Beaumont, Esq. At Dukesfield, in this parish, is a large mill for smelting and refining lead-ore, which is brought from Wardle, in the county of Durham. Ochre is obtained and manufactured on Slaley fell. A small school is supported by the bequests of Matthew Carr, in 1729, and Ralph Carr, in 1769.

SLAPTON, a parish in the hundred of COTTESLOE, county of BUCKINGHAM, 3¼ miles (N. by W.) from Ivinghoe, containing 312 inhabitants. The living is a rectory, in the archdeaconry of Buckingham, and diocese of Lincoln, rated in the king's books at £14. 9. 7., and in the patronage of the Dean and Canons of Christ Church, Oxford. The church is dedicated to the Holy Cross. There is a place of worship for Wesleyan Methodists. The Grand Junction canal passes through the parish. A charity school is supported by voluntary subscriptions.

SLAPTON, a parish in the hundred of COLERIDGE, county of DEVON, 6 miles (S. W.) from Dartmouth, containing 689 inhabitants. The living is a discharged perpetual curacy, in the archdeaconry of Totness, and diocese of Exeter, endowed with £600 private benefaction, £400 royal bounty, and £1200 parliamentary grant, and in the patronage of the Parishioners. The church is dedicated to St. Mary. John and Charles Kelland, about 1690, bequeathed £150, which, with accumulations, now produces about £20 per annum, applied to the instruction and apprenticing of poor children.

SLAPTON, a parish in the hundred of GREENSNORTON, county of NORTHAMPTON, 3¾ miles (W. S. W.) from Towcester, containing 201 inhabitants. The living is a rectory, in the archdeaconry of Northampton, and diocese of Peterborough, rated in the king's books at £9. 9. 9½., and in the patronage of the Rev. Thomas C. Welch. The church is dedicated to St. Botolph. There is a place of worship for Wesleyan Methodists. Three poor children are educated by means of a trifling bequest from Thomas Knight, in 1723.

SLAUGHAM, a parish in the hundred of BUTTINGHILL, rape of LEWES, county of SUSSEX, 4¼ miles (N. W. by W.) from Cuckfield, containing 933 inhabitants. The living is a rectory, in the archdeaconry of Lewes, and diocese of Chichester, rated in the king's books at £10. 19. 2. Mrs. Sergison was patroness in 1800. The church, dedicated to St. Mary, is in the decorated style of English architecture, and has lately received an addition of two hundred free sittings, the Incorporated Society for the enlargement of churches and chapels having granted £100 towards defraying the expense.

SLAUGHTER (LOWER), a parish in the lower division of the hundred of SLAUGHTER, county of GLOUCESTER, 3 miles (S. W.) from Stow on the Wold, containing 242 inhabitants. The living is a perpetual curacy, annexed to the rectory of Bourton on the Water, in the archdeaconry and diocese of Gloucester. The parish is crossed on the south-east by the Fosseroad, near which a figure of Pallas, sculptured in stone, was discovered about 1770.

SLAUGHTER (UPPER), a parish in the lower division of the hundred of SLAUGHTER, county of

GLOUCESTER, 3¼ miles (S. W. by W.) from Stow on the Wold, containing 245 inhabitants. The living is a rectory, in the archdeaconry and diocese of Gloucester, rated in the king's books at £14. 14. 2., and in the patronage of Walter Lawrence Lawrence, Esq. The church is dedicated to St. Peter. Two brooks run through the parish, and afterwards fall into another, all which uniting form the river Windrush. There is a small endowment by the late rector, the Rev. F. T. Travell, for the support of a Sunday school.

SLAUGHTERFORD, a parish in the hundred of CHIPPENHAM, county of WILTS, 5½ miles (W. by N.) from Chippenham, containing 121 inhabitants. The living is a perpetual curacy, annexed to the rectory of Biddestone, in the archdeaconry of Wilts, and diocese of Salisbury. The church, dedicated to St. Nicholas, has lately received an addition of one hundred and thirty sittings, of which one hundred are free, the Incorporated Society for the enlargement of churches and chapels having granted £100 towards defraying the expense.

SLAWSTON, a parish in the hundred of GARTREE, county of LEICESTER, 5¾ miles (N. E. by N.) from Market-Harborough, containing 228 inhabitants. The living is a discharged vicarage, in the archdeaconry of Leicester, and diocese of Lincoln, rated in the king's books at £6. 5. 7½., endowed with £200 private benefaction, and £200 royal bounty, and in the patronage of the Crown. The church is dedicated to All Saints.

SLEAFORD (NEW), a market town and parish in the wapentake of FLAXWELL, parts of KESTEVEN, county of LINCOLN, 18 miles (S. S.E.) from Lincoln, and 116 (N. by W.) from London, containing, with the hamlet of Holdingham, 2220 inhabitants. The name in ancient records is written La Ford and Eslaforde, which has been corrupted into Sleaford, and the epithet New given to distinguish it from Old Sleaford, an adjoining parish. A castle appears to have been erected here at an early period, but of its history there are few records, and of the building only some trifling remains. The town is situated on the main road from London to Lincoln; it is of respectable appearance, and is gradually improving in buildings and importance; it is well paved and lighted, and the inhabitants are supplied with water from an adjacent spring, called Bully, or Boiling, wells. A small theatre was erected in 1824. A canal connects this town with Boston, Lincoln, and the Trent navigation, and thus promotes the prosperity of its general trade. The market is on Monday; and fairs are on Plough-Monday, Easter-Monday, Whit-Monday, August 11th, and October 20th, for horses, cattle, sheep, and provisions. The quarter sessions for the parts of Kesteven are held here by adjournment from Bourne. The old town hall, being greatly dilapidated, has been pulled down, and a handsome edifice, in the later style of English architecture, erected.

The living is a discharged vicarage, in the peculiar jurisdiction and patronage of the Prebendary of Lafford, or New Sleaford, in the Cathedral Church of Lincoln, rated in the king's books at £8. The church, dedicated to St. Denis, exhibits some fine specimens of almost every style of English architecture, and consists of a nave, aisles, a large chapel on the north side, and a chancel: at the west end is a tower, erected about

1150, which is by far the most ancient part of the building; it is in the early style of English architecture, and is surmounted by a spire of later date, one hundred and forty-four feet high; an enriched spiral staircase leads to it on the south side. In the chancel are three fine stalls, in the later style; at its entrance are the screen and canopy of the ancient rood-loft. The entire structure is replete with interest: there are several ancient monuments, chiefly belonging to the family of Carr, formerly lords of the manor. There are places of worship for those in the Connexion of the late Countess of Huntingdon, Independents, and Wesleyan Methodists. The free grammar school was founded, in 1604, by Robert Carr, Esq., who endowed it with £20 per annum: the master, who must be a graduate of one of the Universities, is appointed by the Marquis of Bristol, as owner of the "late fair castle of Sleaford," for which he pays to the crown £40 per annum: the children of the town and neighbourhood are instructed gratuitously. A school was endowed with lands by William Alvey, in 1729, for the instruction of poor children: twenty boys and twenty girls are educated. An hospital, for a chaplain and twelve poor men, was founded and endowed by Sir Robert Carr, Bart., in 1636; the almsmen have weekly allowances of ten shillings and sixpence each, and a certain quantity of coal, with comfortable apartments, and the chaplain a salary of £20 per annum, to officiate in a chapel attached. The Bishop of Lincoln had anciently a magnificent palace here, in which King John sojourned a few days, but no part remains except the foundations: it is supposed to have been destroyed by Cromwell. A branch of the Ermin-street passes through this parish, and that of Old Sleaford.

SLEAFORD (OLD), a parish in the wapentake of ASWARDHURN, parts of KESTEVEN, county of LINCOLN, 1 mile (S. E.) from New Sleaford, containing 215 inhabitants. The living is a vicarage, in the archdeaconry and diocese of Lincoln, rated in the king's books at £4. 10., and in the patronage of the Marquis of Bristol. The church, which was dedicated to St. Giles, has been demolished upwards of two hundred years, for which period there has been no presentation, the vicarage being now supposed to have merged into the impropriation: the inhabitants attend divine service at Quarrington, or New Sleaford. The Roman street passes through the parish.

SLEAGILL, a township in the parish of MORLAND, WEST ward, county of WESTMORLAND, 8¼ miles (N. by W.) from Orton, containing 157 inhabitants. Coal is obtained here.

SLECKBURN (EAST), a township in the parish of BEDLINGTON, a detached portion of the eastern division of CHESTER ward, county palatine of DURHAM, locally on the east side of the county of Northumberland, 6¼ miles (E. S.E.) from Morpeth. The population is returned with the parish.

SLECKBURN (WEST), a township in the parish of BEDLINGTON, a detached portion of the eastern division of CHESTER ward, county palatine of DURHAM, locally on the east side of the county of Northumberland, 5¾ miles (E. by S.) from Morpeth. The population is returned with the parish.

SLEDDALE (LONG), a chapelry in that part of the parish of KENDAL which is in KENDAL ward,

county of WESTMORLAND, 8 miles (N. by W.) from Kendal, containing 185 inhabitants. The living is a perpetual curacy, in the archdeaconry of Richmond, and diocese of Chester, endowed with £600 royal bounty, and in the patronage of the Land-owners. The chapel was rebuilt in 1712. A school, termed the Chapel school, is supported by the Hon. F. G. Howard, lord of the manor, who allows £15 a year to the master. Here are quarries of a fine blue slate, situated amid mountain scenery of the most romantic and picturesque character.

SLEDMERE, a parish in the wapentake of BUCKROSE, East riding of the county of YORK, 7½ miles (N.W. by W.) from Great Driffield, containing, with the hamlet of Croom, 425 inhabitants. The living is a perpetual curacy, in the archdeaconry of the East riding, and diocese of York, endowed with £400 royal bounty, and £200 parliamentary grant, and in the patronage of Sir Tatton Sykes, Bart. The church is dedicated to St. Mary.

SLEEP, a hamlet in that part of the parish of ST. PETER, ST. ALBANS, which is in the hundred of CASHIO, or liberty of ST. ALBANS, county of HERTFORD, containing 639 inhabitants.

SLIMBRIDGE, a parish in the upper division of the hundred of BERKELEY, county of GLOUCESTER, 4 miles (N. by W.) from Dursley, containing 807 inhabitants. The living is a rectory, in the archdeaconry and diocese of Gloucester, rated in the king's books at £28. 2. 11., and in the patronage of the President and Fellows of Magdalene College, Oxford. The church, dedicated to St. John the Evangelist, is a handsome structure with a fine spire. There is a place of worship for Independents. The Gloucester and Berkeley canal passes through the parish, and the Severn is navigable along the north-west boundary. Dr. Jenner, who discovered and introduced the practice of vaccination, was a native of this parish.

SLINDON, a township in the parish of ECCLESHALL, northern division of the hundred of PIREHILL, county of STAFFORD, containing 130 inhabitants. It is within the peculiar jurisdiction of the Prebendary of Eccleshall in the Cathedral Church of Lincoln.

SLINDON, a parish in the hundred of ALDWICK, rape of CHICHESTER, county of SUSSEX, 4¼ miles (W. by N.) from Arundel, containing 471 inhabitants. The living is a rectory, in the peculiar jurisdiction of the Archbishop of Canterbury, rated in the king's books at £14. 13. 1½. The Rev. M. Smelt was patron in 1815. The church, dedicated to St. Mary, is in the early style of English architecture.

SLINFOLD, a parish partly in the hundred of EAST EASWRITH, rape of BRAMBER, but chiefly in the hundred of WEST EASWRITH, rape of ARUNDEL, county of SUSSEX, 4 miles (W. by N.) from Horsham, containing 644 inhabitants. The living comprises a sinecure rectory and a vicarage united, in the archdeaconry and diocese of Chichester, rated jointly in the king's books at £12. 14. 2., and in the patronage of the Bishop of Chichester. The church is dedicated to St. Peter. Two branches of the river Arun form a junction here, and a Roman road passes through the parish.

SLINGLEY, a joint township with Seaton, in the parish of SEAHAM, northern division of EASINGTON ward, county palatine of DURHAM, 5¾ miles (S. by W.)

from Sunderland. The population is returned with Seaton.

SLINGSBY, a parish in the wapentake of RYEDALE, North riding of the county of YORK, 6 miles (W. N. W.) from New Malton, containing 548 inhabitants. The living is a rectory, in the archdeaconry of Cleveland, and diocese of York, rated in the king's books at £12. 1. 10½., and in the patronage of the Earl of Carlisle. The church, dedicated to All Saints, is partly in the early and partly in the later style of English architecture. The Rev. Robert Wood, in 1712, in exercise of a power reserved to him, gave a rent-charge of £5 for teaching ten poor children, to which the Earl of Carlisle adds £10 per annum. Here is a fine bed of limestone, abounding with organic fossil remains. A Roman road from Malton to the westward passes through the parish, and here was a castle belonging to the family of Lacy before the Conquest, and afterwards to that of Mowbray, which Richard III. subsequently held, and died possessed of: it was partly rebuilt, in the later style of English architecture, by Sir C. Cavendish, in 1603, but the walls only are remaining.

SLIPTON, a parish in the hundred of HUXLOE, county of NORTHAMPTON, 3¾ miles (W. by N.) from Thrapstone, containing 135 inhabitants. The living is a discharged vicarage, in the archdeaconry of Northampton, and diocese of Peterborough, rated in the king's books at £5. 12. 3½., and in the patronage of the Heirs of the Duke of Dorset. The church is dedicated to St. John the Baptist.

SLOLEY, a parish in the hundred of TUNSTEAD, county of NORFOLK, 3½ miles (N. N. E.) from Coltishall, containing 308 inhabitants. The living is a discharged rectory, in the archdeaconry of Norfolk, and diocese of Norwich, rated in the king's books at £5. 6. 8., and in the patronage of the Earl of Orford. The church is dedicated to St. Bartholomew.

SLOUGH, a village, partly in the parish of STOKE-POGES, and partly in that of UPTON, hundred of STOKE, county of BUCKINGHAM, 41 miles (S. E. by S.) from Buckingham, and 21 (W.) from London. The population is returned with the parishes. A cattle market is held on Tuesday. Herschel, the celebrated astronomer, resided at this place, and here he constructed his powerful telescope; the frame of it is visible from the Bath road.

SLYNE, a joint township with Hest, in the parish of BOLTON le SANDS, hundred of LONSDALE, south of the sands, county palatine of LANCASTER, 2½ miles (N.) from Lancaster, containing 317 inhabitants. At Hest bank, in this township, a breakwater was constructed in 1820, along the side of which vessels from Liverpool and Glasgow load and unload their cargoes; and, by means of a canal extending to within a short distance of the shore, a considerable trade is carried on with Kendal and other inland places. The road across the sands to Ulverstone commences at Hest; and the great road to Kendal, Carlisle, and Glasgow, passes through the village of Slyne. Courts leet and baron are held here. There are traces of salt-works which formerly existed in the neighbourhood.

SMALESMOUTH, a township in the parish of GAYSTEAD, north-western division of TINDALE ward, county of NORTHUMBERLAND, 8 miles (W. by N.) from Bellingham, containing 163 inhabitants.

SMALLBURGH, a parish in the hundred of TUNSTEAD, county of NORFOLK, 5¼ miles (N. E. by E.) from Coltishall, containing 722 inhabitants. The living is a discharged rectory, in the archdeaconry of Norfolk, and diocese of Norwich, rated in the king's books at £10. 4., and in the patronage of the Bishop of Norwich. The church is dedicated to St. Peter; the steeple fell down in 1677, and occasioned great injury to the edifice.

SMALLEY, a chapelry in the parish of MORLEY, hundred of MORLESTON and LITCHURCH, county of DERBY, 7 miles (N. E.) from Derby, containing 727 inhabitants. The chapel is dedicated to St. John the Baptist. John and Samuel Richardson, in 1712, conveyed certain property to trustees, for the erection and support of a school for twelve poor boys, each to receive eightpence per week; the present annual income is £88, and twenty-eight boys are educated, viz., fourteen from this chapelry, eight from Heanor, and six from Horsely-Woodhouse. There are extensive collieries in the neighbourhood.

SMALLFORD, a ward partly in the parish of ST. STEVEN, and partly in that part of the parish of ST. PETER, ST. ALBANS, which is in the hundred of CASHIO, or liberty of ST. ALBANS, county of HERTFORD. The population is returned with the parish. Here are almshouses for three widows.

SMALL-HYTHE, a chapelry in the parish and hundred of TENTERDEN, lathe of SCRAY, county of KENT, 2 miles (S. by E.) from Tenterden. The chapel is dedicated to St. John the Baptist.

SMALLWOOD, a township in that part of the parish of ASTBURY which is in the hundred of NORTHWICH, county palatine of CHESTER, 3 miles (E. by S.) from Sandbach, containing 584 inhabitants. There is a place of worship for Wesleyan Methodists.

SMARDALE, a township in the parish of KIRKBY-STEPHEN, EAST ward, county of WESTMORLAND, 2¾ miles (W. S. W.) from Kirkby-Stephen, containing 55 inhabitants. A chapel was anciently situated at a place now called Chapel Well.

SMARDEN, a parish (formerly a market town) in the hundred of CALEHILL, lathe of SCRAY, county of KENT, 8 miles (N. E. by E.) from Cranbrooke, and 46 (S. E. by E.) from London, containing 1038 inhabitants. The living is a rectory, in the archdeaconry and diocese of Canterbury, rated in the king's books at £24. 2. 6., and in the patronage of the Archbishop of Canterbury. The church is dedicated to St. Michael. There are places of worship for Baptists and Wesleyan Methodists: the former has a school attached. A free school was founded, in 1716, by Stephen Dadson, who endowed it with property now producing upwards of £45 a year, for which from forty to fifty children are instructed: six of the parish of Bethersden have the privilege of admittance here. The market has fallen into disuse, but the market-house is still standing: a fair is held on October 10th, for toys and pedlary.

SMEATON (GREAT), a parish partly in the wapentake of ALLERTONSHIRE, and partly in the eastern division of GILLING, North riding of the county of YORK, 6½ miles (N. by W.) from North Allerton, containing, with the township of Hornby, 488 inhabitants. The living is a rectory, in the archdeaconry of Richmond (with the perpetual curacy of Appleton upon

Wisk in that of Cleveland), and diocese of Chester, rated in the king's books at £13. 13. 4., and in the patronage of Henry Hewgill, Esq. The river Wisk runs through the parish, and the Tees flows along the northern side of it.

SMEATON (KIRK), a parish in the upper division of the wapentake of Osgoldcross, West riding of the county of York, 6½ miles (S. E.) from Pontefract, containing 321 inhabitants. The living is a rectory, in the archdeaconry and diocese of York, rated in the king's books at £10. 1. 0½., and in the patronage of Earl Fitzwilliam. The church is dedicated to St. Mary.

SMEATON (LITTLE), a township in the parish of Birkby, wapentake of Allertonshire, North riding of the county of York, 5½ miles (N. by W.) from North Allerton, containing 64 inhabitants.

SMEATON (LITTLE), a township in the parish of Womersley, lower division of the wapentake of Os-goldcross, West riding of the county of York, 6½ miles (S. E. by E.) from Pontefract, containing 176 inhabitants. Ann Jackson, in 1675, bequeathed £30 in support of a school for teaching poor children.

SMEETH, a parish in the franchise and barony of Bircholt, lathe of Shepway, county of Kent, 4¾ miles (E. S. E.) from Ashford, containing 393 inhabitants. The living is a perpetual curacy, annexed to the rectory of Aldington, in the peculiar jurisdiction and patronage of the Archbishop of Canterbury. The church, dedicated to St. Mary, is principally in the Norman style of architecture. Smeeth was formerly a market town; fairs are still held on May 12th and Michaelmas-day, for toys and pedlary. Timothy Bedingfield, in 1691, bequeathed an estate producing a considerable income for teaching poor children, and maintaining two aged women.

SMEETON-WESTERBY, a township in the parish of Kibworth-Beauchamp, hundred of Gartree, county of Leicester, 5¼ miles (N. W.) from Market-Harborough, containing 388 inhabitants.

SMERRILL, a joint chapelry with Middleton, in that part of the parish of Youlgrave which is in the hundred of Wirksworth, county of Derby, 5 miles (S. S.W.) from Bakewell. The population is returned with Middleton. It is in the honour of Tutbury, duchy of Lancaster, and within the jurisdiction of a court of pleas held at Tutbury every third Tuesday, for the recovery of debts under 40s.

SMETHCOTT, a parish in the hundred of Condover, county of Salop, 9½ miles (S. by W.) from Shrewsbury, containing 347 inhabitants. The living is a discharged rectory, in the archdeaconry of Salop, and diocese of Lichfield and Coventry, rated in the king's books at £4. 9., and in the patronage of Mrs. Lacey. The church is dedicated to St. Michael.

SMETHWICK, a township in the parish of Brereton, hundred of Northwich, county palatine of Chester, 4 miles (N. E. by E.) from Sandbach. The population is returned with the parish.

SMETHWICK, a chapelry in the parish of Harbone, southern division of the hundred of Offlow, county of Stafford, 4 miles (W. by N.) from Birmingham, containing 1950 inhabitants. The living is a perpetual curacy, annexed to the vicarage of Harbone, in the peculiar jurisdiction of the Dean and Chapter of

Lichfield. There are places of worship for Independents and Calvinistic Methodists. The Birmingham canal passes through the chapelry. About fifteen children are instructed by a schoolmistress for £9. 9. a year, the bequest of Dorothy Parkes, who erected the school premises in 1723.

SMISBY, a parish in the hundred of Repton and Gresley, county of Derby, 2½ miles (N. N. W.) from Ashby de la Zouch, containing 322 inhabitants. The living is a perpetual curacy, in the archdeaconry of Derby, and diocese of Lichfield and Coventry, endowed with £400 royal bounty, and in the patronage of the Marquis of Hastings.

SNAILWELL, a parish in the hundred of Staploe, county of Cambridge, 2¾ miles (N.) from Newmarket, containing 222 inhabitants. The living is a rectory, in the archdeaconry of Sudbury, and diocese of Norwich, rated in the king's books at £27. 11. 0½., and in the patronage of the Trustees of the late J. Tharp, Esq. The church is dedicated to St. Peter.

SNAINTON, a chapelry partly in the parish of Ebberston, but chiefly in that of Brompton, Pickering lythe, North riding of the county of York, 9¼ miles (S. W. by W.) from Scarborough, containing 603 inhabitants. The chapel is subordinate to the vicarage of Brompton. There is a place of worship for Wesleyan Methodists.

SNAITH, a parish comprising the market town of Snaith, the chapelries of Armin, Hooke, and Rawcliff, and the townships of Balne, Cowick, Goole, Gowdall, Hick, Hensall, and Pollington, in the lower division of the wapentake of Osgoldcross, and the chapelry of Carleton, in the lower division of the wapentake of Barkstone-Ash, West riding of the county of York, and containing 6909 inhabitants, of which number, 834 are in the town of Snaith, 23 miles (S. by E.) from York, and 175 (N. by W.) from London. The town is situated on a gentle declivity on the south bank of the river Aire: it is small and irregularly built; the streets are lighted with oil; the houses are chiefly of brick, and rather of mean appearance, but a few handsome and substantial dwellings have been lately erected; the inhabitants are well supplied with water from wells. Flax is cultivated in the neighbourhood to a considerable extent, and conveyed to the market at Leeds by the river Aire: the canal from Knottingley to Goole passes southward of the town. The market is on Thursday, and fairs are held on the last Thursday in April, and August 10th, for cattle, &c. Courts are occasionally held for the manor. The living is a perpetual curacy, in the jurisdiction of the peculiar court of Snaith, and in the patronage of Nicholas Edmund Yarburgh, Esq. The church, dedicated to St. Mary, is an ancient and spacious structure, in the later style of English architecture, with a low square tower surmounted with pinnacles and a belfry of wood. There is a place of worship for Wesleyan Methodists. The free grammar school is of unknown foundation: in 1741, Nicholas Waller gave a rent-charge of £30 for its endowment: twenty boys are educated, but classical instruction has been long discontinued, There are almshouses for six poor persons, founded by the Yarburgh family; and others for six poor widows, which were rebuilt, in 1802, by Lord Viscount Downe.

SNAPE, a parish in the hundred of Plomesgate, county of Suffolk, 2¾ miles (S. by E.) from Saxmundham, containing 518 inhabitants. The living is a discharged vicarage, consolidated with that of Friston, in the archdeaconry of Suffolk, and diocese of Norwich, rated in the king's books at £5. 5. 7½., endowed with £400 royal bounty, and in the patronage of R. W. H. H. Vyse, Esq. The church is dedicated to St. John the Baptist; the front is hexagonal and much enriched in the later English style. The parish is bounded on the south by the river Alde, or Orr, which is crossed by a bridge, where there is a quay for shipping corn, &c. A society of Benedictine monks from the abbey of St. John at Colchester settled here in 1155, and in 1400 was exempted from all subjection to that house, and raised into a distinct priory; it was dedicated to the Blessed Virgin Mary, and at its suppression, in 1524, was granted to Wolsey towards the endowment of his intended colleges, when its revenue was valued at £99. 1. 11.

SNAPE, a township in the parish of WELL, eastern division of the wapentake of HANG, North riding of the county of YORK, 3¼ miles (S.) from Bedale, containing 689 inhabitants, who are principally employed in wool-combing for the worsted-spinners in this part of the county. There is a place of worship for Wesleyan Methodists. An almshouse for eight aged persons, and free schools for children of each sex, have been founded and liberally endowed by the Nevilles.

SNAREHILL-HOUSE, an extra-parochial district, in the hundred of GUILT-CROSS, county of NORFOLK, 1¾ mile (S.) from Thetford. This place and Thetford Lodge are all that remain of two villages, called Great and Little Snareshill.

SNARESTON, a parish in the hundred of SPARKEN-HOE, county of LEICESTER, 7 miles (N. W.) from Market-Bosworth, containing 356 inhabitants. The living is a perpetual curacy, annexed to the rectory of Sweepstone, in the archdeaconry of Leicester, and diocese of Lincoln. The church is dedicated to St. Bartholomew. The Ashby de la Zouch canal passes through the parish. Snarestone is in the honour of Tutbury, duchy of Lancaster, and within the jurisdiction of a court of pleas held at Tutbury every third Tuesday, for the recovery of debts under 40s.

SNARFORD, a parish in the wapentake of LAW-RESS, parts of LINDSEY, county of LINCOLN, 7 miles (S. W.) from Market-Rasen, containing 64 inhabitants. The living is a discharged rectory, in the archdeaconry of Stow, and diocese of Lincoln, rated in the king's books at £4, endowed with £200 royal bounty, and in the patronage of the Subdean of Lincoln. The church is dedicated to St. Lawrence.

SNARGATE, a parish in the liberty of ROMNEY-MARSH, though locally in the hundred of Aloesbridge, lathe of SHEPWAY, county of KENT, 5½ miles (N. W. by W.) from New Romney, containing 93 inhabitants. The living is a rectory, in the archdeaconry and diocese of Canterbury, rated in the king's books at £17. 6. 8., and in the patronage of the Archbishop of Canterbury. The church is dedicated to St. Dunstan.

SNAVE, a parish in the liberty of ROMNEY-MARSH, though locally in the hundred of Aloesbridge, lathe of SHEPWAY, county of KENT, 4½ miles (N. W. by N.) from New Romney, containing 108 inhabitants. The living is a rectory, in the archdeaconry and diocese of Canterbury, rated in the king's books at £19. 7. 11.,

and in the patronage of the Archbishop of Canterbury. The church is dedicated to St. Augustine.

SNEAD, a hamlet in the parish of ROCK, lower division of the hundred of DODDINGTREE, county of WORCESTER, 5½ miles (S. W.) from Bewdley. The population is returned with the parish.

SNEATON, a parish in the liberty of WHITBY-STRAND, North riding of the county of YORK, 2¼ miles (S. by W.) from Whitby, containing 251 inhabitants. The living is a rectory, in the archdeaconry of Cleveland, and diocese of York, rated in the king's books at £13. 2. 6., and in the patronage of James Wilson, Esq., at whose expense the present church, which is in the decorated style, was lately erected, the former edifice having fallen to decay. He also established a free school for all the children of parishioners. Courts leet and baron are held here.

SNELLAND, a parish in the western division of the wapentake of WRAGGOE, parts of LINDSEY, county of LINCOLN, 5 miles (W. N. W.) from Wragby, containing 133 inhabitants. The living is a rectory, in the archdeaconry and diocese of Lincoln, rated in the king's books at £3. 17. 6., and in the patronage of Earl Brownlow. The church is dedicated to All Saints.

SNELSMORE, a tything in the parish of CHIEVE-LEY, hundred of FAIRCROSS, county of BERKS, 3¾ miles (N.) from Newbury. The population is returned with the parish.

SNELSON, a township in that part of the parish of ROSTHERN which is in the hundred of MACCLESFIELD, county palatine of CHESTER, 5¼ miles (S. E.) from Nether Knutsford, containing 137 inhabitants.

SNELSTON, a parish in the hundred of APPLETREE, county of DERBY, 2½ miles (S. W.) from Ashbourn, containing 462 inhabitants. The living is a perpetual curacy, annexed to the rectory of Norbury, in the archdeaconry of Derby, and diocese of Lichfield and Coventry. The church is dedicated to St. Peter. There is a place of worship for Wesleyan Methodists. Snelston is in the honour of Tutbury, duchy of Lancaster, and within the jurisdiction of a court of pleas held at Tutbury every third Tuesday, for the recovery of debts under 40s. Children of this parish are entitled to the benefit of a school at Norbury, founded by Thomas Williams.

SNENTON, a parish in the southern division of the wapentake of THURGARTON, county of NOTTINGHAM, ¾ of a mile (E.) from Nottingham, containing 1212 inhabitants. The living is a perpetual curacy, in the archdeaconry of Nottingham, and diocese of York, endowed with £600 royal bounty, and £200 parliamentary grant, and in the patronage of Earl Manvers. The church is dedicated to St. Stephen. The village, which a few years ago consisted of a few scattered houses, and contained not more than two hundred and fifty inhabitants, now presents a most respectable appearance, new streets and many elegant houses having been recently erected. The county asylum for lunatics is in this parish: it is a large brick building, capable of accommodating one hundred and thirty patients: the establishment is well conducted, and is supported by voluntary contributions. In the neighbourhood are some curious excavations in the stone rock, used as dwellings.

SNETTERTON, a parish in the hundred of SHROP-HAM, county of NORFOLK, 3 miles (N.) from East Harling, containing 225 inhabitants. The living comprises the consolidated rectories of All Saints and St. Andrew the Apostle, with the rectory of Quiddenham, in the archdeaconry of Norfolk, and diocese of Norwich, rated in the king's books at £12. 17. 1. The church is dedicated to St. Andrew.

SNETTISHAM, a parish in the hundred of SMITH-DON, county of NORFOLK, 6¾ miles (N. by E.) from Castle-Rising, containing 959 inhabitants. The living is a discharged vicarage, in the archdeaconry of Norfolk, and diocese of Norwich, rated in the king's books at £5. 6. 8., endowed with £400 private benefaction, £200 royal bounty, and £300 parliamentary grant. Henry Styleman, Esq. was patron in 1815. The church is dedicated to St. Mary. There is a place of worship for Wesleyan Methodists. A market on Friday was formerly held here : the town was then called Snetham. Ancient brass instruments, in the shape of axe heads, with handles to them, usually termed celts, have been discovered in the neighbourhood.

SNEYD, a township in the parish of BURSLEM, northern division of the hundred of PIREHILL, county of STAFFORD, ½ a mile (N.) from Hanley. The population is returned with the parish. There is a place of worship for Wesleyan Methodists. The manufacture of earthenware is carried on here, and there are extensive coal-works in the vicinity.

SNIBSTON, a chapelry in that part of the parish of PACKINGTON which is in the western division of the hundred of GOSCOTE, county of LEICESTER, 4½ miles (S. E.) from Ashby de la Zouch. The population is returned with the parish

SNITTER, a township in the parish of ROTHBURY, western division of COQUETDALE ward, county of NORTH-UMBERLAND, 2¾ miles (N. W. by W.) from Rothbury, containing 160 inhabitants.

SNITTERBY, a parish in the eastern division of the wapentake of ASLACOE, parts of LINDSEY, county of LINCOLN, 11¼ miles (N. W. by W.) from Market-Rasen, containing 153 inhabitants. The living is a perpetual curacy, annexed to the rectory of Wading-ham, in the archdeaconry of Stow, and diocese of Lincoln. The church is dedicated St. Nicholas.

SNITTERFIELD, a parish in the Snitterfield division of the hundred of BARLICHWAY, county of WAR-WICK, 4 miles (N. by E.) from Stratford upon Avon, containing 642 inhabitants. The living is a vicarage, in the archdeaconry and diocese of Worcester, rated in the king's books at £8, and in the patronage of the Bishop of Worcester. The church, dedicated to St. James, exhibits portions in the early, decorated, and later styles of English architecture.

SNITTERTON, a joint hamlet with Winsley, in that part of the parish of DARLEY which is in the hundred of WIRKSWORTH, county of DERBY, 1½ mile (W. by N.) from Matlock. The population is returned with Winsley. It is in the honour of Tutbury, duchy of Lancaster, and within the jurisdiction of a court of pleas held at Tutbury every third Tuesday, for the recovery of debts under 40s.

SNITTLEGARTH, a joint township with Bewald-eth, in the parish of TORPENHOW, ALLERDALE ward below Darwent, county of CUMBERLAND, 1¼ mile (W. S. W.) from Ireby. The population is returned with Bewaldeth.

SNODLAND, a joint parish with Paddlesworth, in the hundred of LARKFIELD, lathe of AYLESFORD, county of KENT, 3¾ miles (N. E. by N.) from West Malling, containing, with Paddlesworth, 438 inhabitants. The living is a rectory, with that of Paddlesworth, in the archdeaconry and diocese of Rochester, rated in the king's books at £20, and in the patronage of the Bishop of Rochester. The church is dedicated to All Saints. On a stream tributary to the Medway there is a paper-mill. John May, Esq., in 1800, founded a school for the instruction of forty children, and vested the government of it in the magistrates for the lathe.

SNOREHAM, a parish in the hundred of DENGIE, county of ESSEX, 5 miles (S. S. E.) from Maldon. The living is a rectory, in the archdeaconry of Essex, and diocese of London, rated in the king's books at £3, and in the patronage of Col. Strutt. The church, which was dedicated to St. Peter, is in ruins. Snoreham is rated with the parish of Latchingdon.

SNORING (GREAT), a parish in the northern division of the hundred of GREENHOE, county of NOR-FOLK, 1¾ mile (S. S. E.) from Little Walsingham, containing 360 inhabitants. The living is a rectory, with that of Thursford annexed, in the archdeaconry and diocese of Norwich, rated in the king's books at £24, and in the patronage of the Master and Fellows of St. John's College, Cambridge. The church is dedicated to St. Mary.

SNORING (LITTLE), a parish in the hundred of GALLOW, county of NORFOLK, 3¼ miles (N. E. by E.) from Fakenham, containing 271 inhabitants. The living is a rectory, annexed to the vicarage of East Bars-ham, in the archdeaconry and diocese of Norwich, rated in the king's books at £12, and in the patronage of Sir J. D. Astley, Bart.

SNOWSHILL, a parish in the lower division of the hundred of KIFTSGATE, county of GLOUCESTER, 6 miles (N. E.) from Winchcombe, containing 301 inhabitants. The living is a perpetual curacy, annexed to the rectory of Stanton, in the archdeaconry and diocese of Gloucester.

SNYDALE, a parish in the hundred of NORMAN-TON, lower division of the wapentake of AGBRIGG, West riding of the county of YORK, 4 miles (W. by S.) from Pontefract, containing 119 inhabitants.

SOBERTON, a parish in the hundred of MEON-STOKE, Portsdown division of the county of SOUTH-AMPTON, 3¾ miles (E. by S.) from Bishop's Waltham, containing 882 inhabitants. The living is a perpetual curacy, annexed to the rectory of Meon-Stoke, in the peculiar jurisdiction of the Incumbent of that parish. The church is principally in the early style of English architecture. Soberton is within the jurisdiction of the Cheyney Court held at Winchester every Thursday, for the recovery of debts to any amount.

SOCKBRIDGE, a township in the parish of BAR-TON, WEST ward, county of WESTMORLAND, 3 miles (S. S. W.) from Penrith, containing 190 inhabitants. It is situated on the south bank of the river Eamont, and abounds with limestone. The ancient hall, a quadrangular building, with a tower, has been converted into a farm house.

SOCKBURN, a parish partly in the south-western division of STOCKTON ward, county palatine of DUR-HAM, but chiefly in the wapentake of ALLERTONSHIRE,

North riding of the county of YORK, 7 miles (S. E.) from Darlington, containing, with the townships of Over-Dinsdale and Girsby, 194 inhabitants. The living is a discharged vicarage, in the archdeaconry and diocese of Durham, rated in the king's books at £3. 18. 1½., endowed with £400 royal bounty, and £400 parliamentary grant, and in the patronage of the Master and Brethren of Sherburn Hospital. The church, dedicated to All Saints, is principally in the early English style, and contains some ancient monuments, one of which is that of the valorous Sir John Conyers, representing him with his feet resting upon a lion, that appears to be contending with a winged dragon. In an adjoining field is the Grey Stone, where, according to legendary story, the dauntless knight slew the "monstrous venemous and poysonous wyveron, ask, or worm, which overthrew and devoured many people in fight." In reference to this is the curious tenure of the manor of Sockburn, for an account of which, see NEASHAM. The river Tees runs through the parish.

SODBURY (CHIPPING), a market town and parish in the lower division of the hundred of GRUMBALD'S ASH, county of GLOUCESTER, 28 miles (S. S. W.) from Gloucester, and 113 (W. by S.) from London, containing 1059 inhabitants. This town, which existed in the twelfth century, and was endowed by King Stephen with the same privileges as Bristol, is a great thoroughfare on the road from Bristol to Cirencester, at the foot of a hill near the source of the Little Avon. It is said to be one of the greatest marts for the sale of cheese in England, and many of the inhabitants are engaged in the malt trade, and the carriage of lime and coal. The market is on Thursday; and fairs are held May 23rd and June 24th for cattle, cheese, and pedlary, on the Friday before Lady-day and Michaelmas-day, both statute fairs. The town was governed by a bailiff until 1681, when the inhabitants were incorporated by charter of Charles II., which ordained that the municipal body should consist of a mayor, six aldermen, and twelve burgesses; but this grant was annulled by proclamation of James II., in 1688, at the request of the inhabitants : constables are now elected annually at the court leet of the lord of the manor. The living is a perpetual curacy, annexed to the vicarage of Old Sodbury, in the archdeaconry and diocese of Gloucester, endowed with £1000 royal bounty. The church, a large edifice, is dedicated to St. John the Baptist. There are places of worship for Baptists and the Society of Friends. A free grammar school is endowed with £20 per annum from the funds of the town and church lands, for which the master, who has also a good residence rent-free, instructs twenty boys.

SODBURY (LITTLE), a parish in the lower division of the hundred of GRUMBALD'S ASH, county of GLOUCESTER, 2¾ miles (E. N. E.) from Chipping-Sodbury, containing 107 inhabitants. The living is a rectory, in the archdeaconry and diocese of Gloucester, rated in the king's books at £6. 10. 10. The Rev. W. H. H. Hartley was patron in 1822. The church is dedicated to St. Adeline. On the brow of a hill, in this parish, are traces of an ancient camp, probably of Roman origin. A slight skirmish took place in its vicinity previously to the fatal battle of Tewkesbury, between the forces of Queen Margaret and the advanced guard of Edward IV., when several of the latter were taken prisoners.

SODBURY (OLD), a parish in the lower division of the hundred of GRUMBALD'S ASH, county of GLOUCESTER, 1¾ mile (E.) from Chipping-Sodbury, containing 803 inhabitants. The living is a vicarage, with the perpetual curacy of Chipping-Sodbury annexed, in the archdeaconry and diocese of Gloucester, rated in the king's books at £14. 8. 1½., and in the patronage of the Dean and Chapter of Worcester. The church is dedicated to St. John the Baptist.

SOFTLEY, a joint township with Lynesack, in that part of the parish of ST. ANDREW AUCKLAND which is in the north-western division of DARLINGTON ward, county palatine of DURHAM, 8 miles (S. S. E.) from Walsingham. The population is returned with Lynesack. This township, which is commonly called South Side, is bounded on the south by the river Gaunless, and contains several coal-works.

SOHAM, a market town and parish in the hundred of STAPLOE, county of CAMBRIDGE, 5¾ miles (S. E.) from Ely, and 69 (N. N. E.) from London, containing 2856 inhabitants. This was a place of some note at a very early period. About 630, St. Felix, first Bishop of the East Angles, is said to have founded a monastery here, which he made the seat of his diocese, prior to the removal of the see to Dunwich, and where his remains were interred, they were afterwards taken up and conveyed to Romney abbey, when the cathedral church was erected by Luttingus, a Saxon nobleman. This building, as well as the bishop's palace, was destroyed by fire, and the monks, who at that time were a flourishing society, were killed by the Danish army under the command of Inguar and Ubba, in 870. Before the draining of the fens, here was a large lake, or mere, over which was anciently a dangerous passage by water to Ely, but it was subsequently rendered more safe by the construction of a causeway through the marshes, at the expense of Hervey, Bishop of Ely. The town is situated on the east bank of the river Cam, on the verge of the county; the streets are irregularly built, and the houses of mean appearance. Horticulture is carried on to a considerable extent, especially in the article of asparagus; the dairies are abundant, and cheese of a most excellent quality, and very similar to that of Stilton, is made here. A market, formerly held on Thursday, has been disused for more than a century : the present market is on Saturday : fairs are held on May 9th, for horses, cattle, and pedlary; and on the Monday before Midsummer, which is a pleasure fair; another, formerly held three days before Michaelmas, has been discontinued.

The living is a vicarage, with the chapel of Barraway, in the archdeaconry of Sudbury, and diocese of Norwich, rated in the king's books at £32. 16. 5½., and in the patronage of the Master and Fellows of Pembroke Hall, Cambridge. The church, which is dedicated to St. Andrew, is a venerable cruciform structure, with a lofty square embattled tower, visible at a great distance; in the interior are several monuments. There are places of worship for Baptists, Independents, Wesleyan Methodists, and Unitarians. The free school is endowed with the profits of an estate of moor land allotted for that purpose on the division of the commons, in 1685 : the master's salary is about £50 per annum; poor children are apprenticed from the same fund. Three almshouses were founded for poor widows, in 1502, by Richard Bond; and nine others, in 1581, by Thomas Peachey, but neither has any endowment, excepting an allowance for fuel. Some few vestiges of the ancient palace and cathedral church are yet visible, and several human bones were dug up at the east end of the street, near the church, a few years ago.

SOHAM (EARL), a parish in the hundred of LOES, county of SUFFOLK, 3½ miles (W.) from Framlingham, containing 641 inhabitants. The living is a rectory, in the archdeaconry of Suffolk, and diocese of Norwich, rated in the king's books at £10, and in the patronage of the Rev. J. H. Groome. The church is dedicated to St. Mary. There is a place of worship for Baptists. A fair is held on August 4th, for lambs.

SOHAM (MONK), a parish in the hundred of HOXNE, county of SUFFOLK, 6 miles (W. by N.) from Framlingham, containing 388 inhabitants. The living is a rectory, in the archdeaconry of Suffolk, and diocese of Norwich, rated in the king's books at £19. 5. 2½., and in the patronage of the Rev. J. H. Groome. The church is dedicated to St. Peter.

SOHO, a hamlet in the parish of HANDSWORTH, southern division of the hundred of OFFLOW, county of STAFFORD, 2¼ miles (N.W.) from Birmingham, which see.

SOKEHOLME, a township in the parish of WARSOP, Hatfield division of the wapentake of BASSETLAW, county of NOTTINGHAM, 4 miles (N. by E.) from Mansfield, containing 69 inhabitants.

SOLIHULL, a market town and parish in the Solihull division of the hundred of HEMLINGFORD, county of WARWICK, 13 miles (N. W.) from Warwick, and 105 (N.W.) from London, containing 2817 inhabitants. This town is situated on the road from Warwick to Birmingham, and consists principally of one street, with another branching off from the high road to the market-place: the houses in general are modern and well built, and many of them large and handsome; the inhabitants are well supplied with water from the river Blythe, which flows through the eastern extremity of the town, and from springs: the air is salubrious, and the surrounding scenery of a pleasing character. The Warwick and Birmingham, and the Stratford on Avon, canals pass through the parish. The market is on Wednesday; and fairs are held on April 29th, for cattle and horses; Sep. 11th for horses and the hiring of servants; and Oct. 12th, for cattle. A court leet, at which a constable is appointed, is held occasionally in the town hall, a neat modern brick building, beneath which is the marketplace, and in the upper part assemblies sometimes take place. Petty sessions are also held every alternate Wednesday. The living is a rectory, in the archdeaconry of Coventry, and diocese of Lichfield and Coventry, rated in the king's books at £24. 18. 4., and in the patronage of E. B. Clive, Esq. The church, which is dedicated to St. Alphege, is a large cruciform structure, partly in the later and partly in the decorated style of English architecture, with an embattled tower and octagonal spire rising from the intersection: the tracery, mouldings, and corbels, in the interior are extremely elegant, and there are some fine specimens of tabernacle and screen-work; near the west entrance is an ancient stone font of octagonal form, and having round Norman pillars at the angles: in the chancel and tran-

septs are several piscinæ in trefoil niches, with triangular canopies: the vestry-room was formerly a chapel dedicated to St. Thomas à Becket. In 1757, the spire fell on the north transept, and broke the roof and some monuments; it was afterwards rebuilt. There are places of worship for Independents and Roman Catholics. Sundry donations prior to 1697 were directed by the court of Chancery to be applied, under the management of fifteen trustees, among other purposes, to the instruction of poor children of this parish; the annual income is upwards of £317, of which sum, the headmaster, who must be a graduate of one of the Universities, receives £100 for teaching the classics, and an under-master £65, for conducting the English department: the number of scholars is from fifty to sixty, all of whom must be sons of parishioners. Shenstone, the poet, was educated here. Fifteen poor girls are instructed by a schoolmistress for £8 per annum, arising from the united bequest of Mrs. Martha Palmer and Mrs. Fisher, in 1746. A Benedictine nunnery, in honour of St. Margaret, was founded at Hean-wood, in this parish, in the time of Henry II., by Ketelburn de Langdon, the revenue of which was valued at the dissolution at £21. 2.

SOLPORT, a township in the parish of STAPLETON, ESKDALE ward, county of CUMBERLAND, containing 360 inhabitants.

SOMBOURN (KING'S), a parish in the hundred of KING'S SOMBOURN, Andover division of the county of SOUTHAMPTON, 3 miles (S.) from Stockbridge, containing 991 inhabitants. The living is a vicarage, with the perpetual curacies of Little Sombourn and Stockbridge annexed, in the archdeaconry and diocese of Winchester, rated in the king's books at £21. 1. 10½., and in the patronage of Sir Charles Mill, Bart. The church, dedicated to St. Peter and St. Paul, is an ancient structure, containing, in a recess enriched with the trefoil ornament, the effigy of an ecclesiastic in robes. There was formerly a chapel of ease at Compton, but it has long since gone to decay. The Andover canal passes through the parish, and is crossed by Horse bridge, at a place so called, on the line of the old Roman road from Winchester to Old Sarum. Courts leet and baron are annually held here, the former on the Thursday in Easter week, at which two constables, tythingmen, and other officers for the hundred are appointed. Considerable quantities of chalk are sent hence to Redbridge, for the improvement of the strong clay soil in the New Forest. The spinning of silk for the Winchester manufacturers affords employment to about fifty women and children of the village. A Sunday school is attended by about two hundred boys and girls. This place, before the Conquest, was held in royal demesne, and now forms part of the duchy of Lancaster. John of Gaunt had a palace here, of which there are still some slight remains, and what is supposed were the stables, &c., have been converted into a farm-house. The ancient gardens and pleasure grounds may still be traced, as well as the park, the fish-ponds, and an extensive bowling-green, encompassed by an earthwork about three feet high. On a commanding eminence, three miles to the northward of the church, are the remains of a Roman, or Danish, fortification, called the Ring, with a deep intrenchment enclosing an area of about twenty-one acres; and on the adjoining down are some of smaller dimensions, apparently subordinate to the former, but within the parish of Stockbridge.

SOMBOURN (LITTLE), a parish in the hundred of KING's SOMBOURN, Andover division of the county of SOUTHAMPTON, 2 miles (S. E.) from Stockbridge, containing 59 inhabitants. The living is a perpetual curacy, annexed to the vicarage of King's Sombourn, in the archdeaconry and diocese of Winchester. The church is dedicated to All Saints.

SOMERBY, a parish forming, with the parishes of Cold Overton and Withcote, a detached portion of the hundred of FRAMLAND, county of LEICESTER, 6 miles (S. by E.) from Melton-Mowbray, containing 384 inhabitants. The living is a discharged vicarage, in the archdeaconry of Leicester, and diocese of Lincoln, rated in the king's books at £6. 16. 8. W. Hanbury, Esq. was patron in 1814. The church, dedicated to All Saints, is an ancient structure, with a tower and spire rising from the centre. There is a place of worship for Wesleyan Methodists.

SOMERBY, a chapelry in the parish and wapentake of CORRINGHAM, parts of LINDSEY, county of LINCOLN, 2¾ miles (E.) from Gainsborough. The population is returned with the parish.

SOMERBY, a parish in the wapentake of WINNIBRIGGS and THREO, parts of KESTEVEN, county of LINCOLN, 4 miles (S. E. by E.) from Grantham, containing, with the hamlet of Great Humby, 246 inhabitants. The living is a rectory, in the archdeaconry and diocese of Lincoln, rated in the king's books at £11. 12. 3½., and in the patronage of Lord Gwydir. The church is dedicated to St. Mary Magdalene.

SOMERBY, a parish in the southern division of the wapentake of YARBOROUGH, parts of LINDSEY, county of LINCOLN, 4½ miles (E.) from Glandford-Bridge, containing 79 inhabitants. The living is a discharged rectory, in the archdeaconry and diocese of Lincoln, rated in the king's books at £7. 7. 6. Robert Burton, Esq. was patron in 1816. The church is dedicated to St. Margaret.

SOMERCOATES (NORTH), a parish in the Marsh division of the hundred of LOUTH-ESKE, parts of LINDSEY, county of LINCOLN, 8¼ miles (N. E.) from Louth, containing 684 inhabitants. The living is a vicarage, in the archdeaconry and diocese of Lincoln, rated in the king's books at £9. 18. 4., and in the patronage of the King, as Duke of Lancaster. The church is dedicated to St. Peter. There is a place of worship for Wesleyan Methodists.

SOMERCOATES (SOUTH), a parish in the Marsh division of the hundred of LOUTH-ESKE, parts of LINDSEY, county of LINCOLN, 7¼ miles (N. E. by E.) from Louth, containing 301 inhabitants. The living is a rectory, in the archdeaconry and diocese of Lincoln, rated in the king's books at £22. 6. 3., and in the patronage of the King, as Duke of Lancaster. The church is dedicated to St. Mary.

SOMERFORD (GREAT), a parish in the hundred of MALMESBURY, county of WILTS, 4 miles (S. E. by S.) from Malmesbury, containing 481 inhabitants. The living is a rectory, in the archdeaconry of Wilts, and diocese of Salisbury, rated in the king's books at £12. 14. 7., and in the patronage of the Rector and Fellows of Exeter College, Oxford. The church is dedicated to St. Peter and St. Paul.

SOMERFORD (LITTLE), a parish in the hundred of MALMESBURY, county of WILTS, 3½ miles (S. E.) from Malmesbury, containing 330 inhabitants. The living is a rectory, in the archdeaconry of Wilts, and diocese of Salisbury, rated in the king's books at £8. 7. 1., and in the patronage of the Earl of Ilchester. The church is dedicated to St. John the Baptist.

SOMERFORD-BOOTHS, a township in that part of the parish of ASTBURY which is in the hundred of MACCLESFIELD, county palatine of CHESTER, 2¾ miles (N. W. by N.) from Congleton, containing 285 inhabitants.

SOMERFORD-KEYNES, a parish in the hundred of HIGHWORTH, CRICKLADE, and STAPLE, county of WILTS, 6½ miles (W.) from Cricklade, containing 324 inhabitants. The living is a vicarage, in the archdeaconry of Wilts, and diocese of Salisbury, rated in the king's books at £8. G. J. Foyle, Esq. was patron in 1803. The church is dedicated to All Saints.

SOMERLEYTON, a parish in the hundred of MUTFORD and LOTHINGLAND, county of SUFFOLK, 4½ miles (N. W. by W.) from Lowestoft, containing 349 inhabitants. The living is a rectory, in the archdeaconry of Suffolk, and diocese of Norwich, rated in the king's books at £12. The Rev. G. Anguish was patron in 1817. The church is dedicated to St. Mary.

SOMERSALL-HERBERT, a parish in the hundred of APPLETREE, county of DERBY, 3½ miles (E. by N.) from Uttoxeter, containing 104 inhabitants. The living is a discharged rectory, in the archdeaconry of Derby, and diocese of Lichfield and Coventry, rated in the king's books at £4. 18. 10., and in the patronage of the Earl of Chesterfield. The church is dedicated to St. Peter.

SOMERSBY, a parish in the hundred of HILL, parts of LINDSEY, county of LINCOLN, 7 miles (N. W.) from Spilsby, containing 95 inhabitants. The living is a discharged rectory, in the archdeaconry and diocese of Lincoln, rated in the king's books at £4. 16. 5½., and in the patronage of Lady Willoughby D' Eresby, The church is dedicated to St. Margaret.

SOMERSETSHIRE, a maritime county, bounded on the north-west by the Bristol channel, on the south-west by Devonshire, on the south-east by Dorsetshire, on the east by Wiltshire, and on the north-east by Gloucestershire. It extends from 50° 48' to 51° 27' (N. Lat.), and from 2° 35' to 4° 5' (W. Lon.); and comprises an area of one thousand six hundred and forty-two square English miles, or one million fifty thousand eight hundred and eighty statute acres. The population, in 1821, was 355,314. At the period of the Roman Conquest, the district now forming the county of Somerset was part of the territory of the Belgæ, a people of Celtic origin, who had migrated hither out of Gaul, about three centuries before the commencement of the Christian era. Between the native Britons and this tribe continued hostilities existed, in consequence of the efforts of the former to regain possession of the territory which had been taken from them. About two hundred and fifty years after the first settlement of the Belgæ, Divitiacus, King of the Suessones, brought over to them from the continent a considerable army of their fellow-countrymen, and a treaty was concluded between the contending nations, in which a line of demarcation between the territories of each was agreed

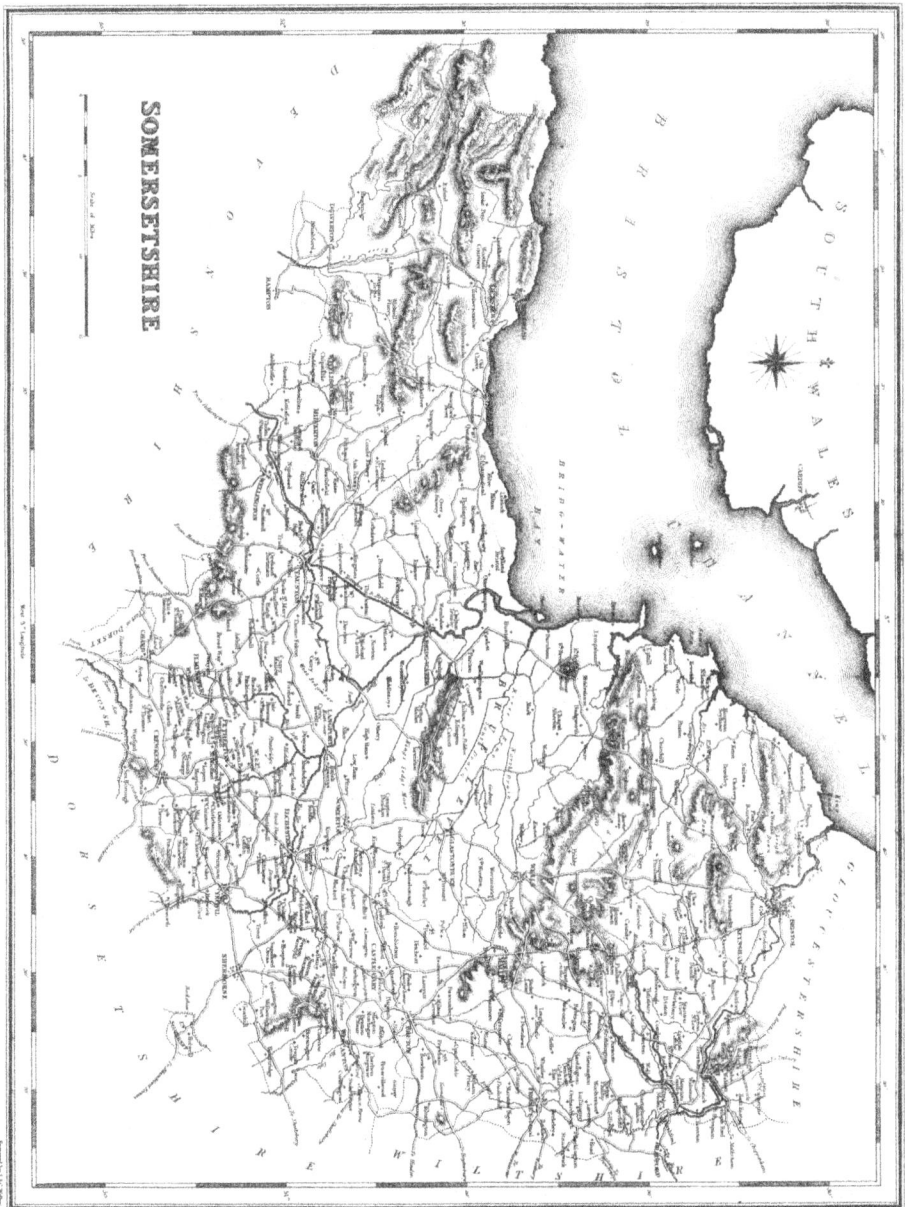

SOMERSETSHIRE

upon : this line consisted of a large and deep fosse defended by a rampart, called Wansdike, parts of which may still be traced : commencing at Andover, in Hampshire, it traverses the county of Wilts, and, on approaching Somersetshire, crosses the Avon near Binacre, and again at Bathampton, whence it continues over Claverton down to Prior Park, Inglish-Combe, Stanton-Prior, Publow, Norton, and Long Ashton, and terminates on the shores of the Bristol Channel at Portishead, being eighty miles in length. Thus nearly the whole of Somersetshire was included in the territory of the Belgæ; and of the three chief cities of that people, two, Bath and Ilchester, were situated within its limits. In the Roman division of the kingdom it was included in Britannia Prima. On the abandonment of Britain by that people, Somersetshire soon became the scene of sanguinary contention between the Saxons and the Britons, who were compelled gradually to retire into the fastnesses of Wales. In the year 493, a large body of Saxons, under the command of Ælla and his three sons, encamped on Lansdown, and laid siege to Bath; but that city was relieved by the renowned King Arthur, who attacked and, after a sanguinary conflict, defeated the Saxon leader. About 520, Arthur again delivered Bath from the assaults of these invaders, led by three lieutenants of the Saxon chief, Cerdic, and repulsed them with great slaughter. In 577, however, the Saxon leaders Ceawlin and Cuthwin, the former of whom was monarch of the newly-founded kingdom of Wessex, led their forces towards the north-eastern part of the county, and advanced to Deorham, a village about eight miles from Bath, in the county of Gloucester, where they defeated three British kings, and added to their conquests the three royal cities of Bath, Gloucester, and Cirencester. In 658, a battle was fought at Pen between a party of Danes and some Saxon forces. In the year 775, Offa, King of Mercia, wrested the city of Bath from the sovereignty of Wessex, and restored much of its ancient splendour. In 845, a great battle was fought at Stoke-Courcy between the Saxons under the conduct of Elstan, Bishop of Sherborne, and an army of Danish marauders, in which the latter were totally defeated. In the early part of the reign of Alfred the Great, the Danes, who had previously desolated almost every other part of England, extended their ravages to this county. In 873 they destroyed Glastonbury, and in 877 Somerton shared the same fate. The king himself, having recourse to flight and concealment, took refuge for some time in the cottage of a neatherd, situated on a spot of ground, a few acres in extent, surrounded by water, and almost impassable marshes, at the confluence of the rivers Parret and Tone, in this county. Here, when the pursuit and search of his enemies had abated, he collected a few faithful adherents, built a habitation, and constructed a long bridge, one end of which was fortified, so as to prevent all hostile approach. From this strong hold, called in Saxon *Etheling-ege*, or the *Isle of the Nobles*, and now written *Athelney*, he made frequent and sudden excursions, harassing the Danes, and maintaining himself and his followers by the booty that he acquired. His successes continuing, the number of his followers increased; and the news of his preservation, and his being in arms, having been spread among the Saxons, a day was appointed for a general rising against the Danes. The place of rendez-

vous was at a spot called Egbert's Stone, on the eastern side of the Forest of Selwood, in the vicinity of Frome, where the Saxons accordingly assembled in great numbers, and whence their monarch led them to the great victory of Ethandune, in Wiltshire. After the total subjection of these Pagan warriors, Alfred brought their leader, Guthrum, to his court at Aller, on the banks of the Parret, in this county, where he received the rite of baptism. In gratitude for his complete successes, Alfred founded a monastery in the isle of Athelney, to the honour of our Saviour and St. Peter the Apostle. In 918, Somersetshire was again visited by the Danes, a band of whom landed at Porlock; but being attacked with bravery by the inhabitants, the greater part of them were killed, and the remainder compelled to embark : another body landed at Watchet, and there met with a similar reception. This latter town, however, was plundered by them in 987; and again in 997, when they burned it and slaughtered the inhabitants. In 1001, a battle was fought between the Danes and the Saxons at Pen, where also, in 1016, occurred a similar conflict, the Saxons being commanded by Edmund Ironside. In 1052, in the time of Edward the Confessor, Harold, afterwards king of England, landed at Porlock from Ireland, on his return from banishment, with a large body of troops which he had there collected; and having formed an intrenched camp in the vicinity of that town, which he garrisoned, he marched into the interior with the remainder of his troops, spreading desolation on every side : at last, returning to his ships loaded with booty, he set sail, after having fired the town of Porlock and the adjacent woods. In the reign of William Rufus, during the insurrection headed by Odo, Bishop of Baieux, and other Norman barons, in favour of Robert, Duke of Normandy, the city of Bath was plundered and burned by the insurgents, who, however, received a check before the walls of Taunton. No event peculiarly affecting this county occurs on record from this period until the year 1607, when some of the low marshy tracts, for an extent of twenty miles in length, and about four in breadth, were overflowed by an irruption of the sea, and eighty persons drowned.

In the great struggle between Charles I. and the parliament, Somersetshire, owing to the strength of the royal party in the south-west of England, was a scene of active warfare. The first hostile encounter was a skirmish which occurred at Martial's Elm, in 1642. In 1643, on July 5th, was fought the obstinately contested battle of Lansdown, between a portion of the parliamentarian army under the command of Sir William Waller, and the king's forces under the Marquis of Hertford and Prince Maurice, after which the former retired into Bath. In 1644, Lieut. F. Doddington and Sir W. Courtney, with some royalist troops, engaged with Lieutenant-General Middleton and his forces, a few miles from Bridg-water, where the latter were defeated, with the loss of eighty men killed, and one hundred and forty taken prisoners. In October, the loyal inhabitants of this county petitioned the king for liberty to arm themselves in his cause, which was granted; and in the same year occurred an action at Aller, a few miles to the north-west of Langport, between some royal and some parliamentarian forces, commonly called the battle of Aller-Moor. At Wiveliscombe, on February 9th, 1645,

P

Col. Lutterell, the parliamentarian sheriff of Devonshire, with twenty men, was shot dead by the royalists ; and on the same day, Major Stephens, having advanced from Taunton to drive Sir Francis Mackworth from his quarters at Langport, was received so warmly by the latter, that very few of his party escaped : the Major and all the chief officers were made prisoners and sent to Bristol. On March 20th of the same year, a party of the parliamentarian forces from Taunton having fixed their quarters at Wiveliscombe, were defeated in a skirmish, which took place in a field near Nettlecombe, by Col. Windham, the royalist commander of Dunster castle, with a small body of horse. At Langport, on July 12th, a party of the king's forces, under Lord Goring, were defeated by the parliamentarians : Nunney castle was afterwards burned by the latter. In 1646, the siege of Dunster castle, which had been some time commenced by the parliamentarians, was suddenly raised by the royalists, Lord Wentworth, Sir Richard Grenville, and Col. Webbe, who routed the besiegers, many of whom were slain, and one thousand taken prisoners.

Somersetshire was the principal theatre of the rebellion in favour of the Duke of Monmouth, in 1685. That ill-advised nobleman having landed at Lyme-Regis in Dorsetshire, with scarcely a hundred followers, and published his audacious manifesto, he was immediately joined by great numbers, chiefly of the lower orders, insomuch that, in four days, he found himself at the head of two thousand horse and foot. Advancing by Axminster towards Taunton, in this county, he received considerable reinforcements, and on his arrival was welcomed by the people of the latter town with every demonstration of joy. There he assumed the title of king, and asserted the legitimacy of his birth : his forces were now augmented to six thousand, and many others who flocked to join him were dismissed for want of arms. From Taunton he proceeded to Bridg-water, Wells, and Frome, and was proclaimed king at all. He then returned to Bridg-water, where being cordially received, he resolved to fortify himself, and maintain his position until he should receive further news from London. The rapid approach of the king's forces, however, caused him to alter his plan : on Saturday, July 4th, intelligence was brought that the king's troops were encamped at Sedgemoor, within a mile and a half of his own army. On the following day he reconnoitred them, in company with Lord Grey and other officers, and considering their position extremely injudicious, he called a council of war, in which it was determined to surprise the enemy in the middle of the following night. The ill conduct and consequent failure of this attack, and the unsparing slaughter of the duke's misguided followers in the rout that followed it, are well known. In the punishment subsequently inflicted upon the favourers of this enterprise, the people of Somersetshire were marked as principal victims, the military executions of Kirk, although not so numerous, exceeding in violence and barbarity the judicial cruelties of Judge Jeffreys. In 1688, the Prince of Orange, shortly after his landing at Torbay, attacked a party of the royal guards at Wincanton, and put many of them to the sword : this event is remarkable as being the first and almost only instance in which blood was spilt during the progress of that glorious revolution.

This county is co-extensive with the diocese of Bath and Wells, in the province of Canterbury, and is divided into the archdeaconries of Bath, Wells, and Taunton, the first having no archidiaconal court, and in the two latter the bishop exercising jurisdiction concurrently with the archdeacons; the first of which contains the two deaneries of Bath, and Redcliffe with Bedminster; the second those of Axbridge, Cary, Frome, Ilchester, Marston, and Pawlett, and the jurisdiction of Glastonbury; and the last those of Bridg-water, Crewkerne, Dunster, and Taunton : the total number of parishes is four hundred and sixty-nine, of which two hundred and forty-one are rectories, one hundred and thirty-eight vicarages, and the remainder perpetual curacies. For purposes of civil government it is divided into the hundreds of Abdick and Bulstone, Andersfield, Bath-Forum, Bempstone, Brent with Wrington, Bruton, Cannington, Carhampton, Catsash, Chew, Chewton, Crewkerne, North Curry, Frome, Glaston-Twelve-Hides, Hampton and Claverton, Hartcliffe with Bedminster, Horethorne, Houndsborough, Berwick and Coker, Huntspill and Puriton, Keynsham, Kilmersdon, Kingsbury (East and West), Martock, Mells and Leigh, Milverton, Norton-Ferris, Petherton (North and South), Pitney, Portbury, Somerton, Stone, Taunton and Taunton-Dean, Tintinhull, Wellow, Wells-Forum, Whitestone, Whitley, Williton and Freemanners, and Winterstoke. It contains the cities of Bath and Wells ; the borough, market, and sea-port towns of Bridg-water and Minehead ; the borough and market town of Taunton ; the borough towns of Ilchester and Milborne Port ; the market and sea-port town of Watchet ; the small sea-port town of Porlock ; and the market towns of Axbridge, Bruton, Chard, Crewkerne, Dulverton, Dunster, Frome-Selwood, Glastonbury, Ilminster, Langport-Eastover, Milverton, Shepton-Mallet, Somerton, Wellington, Wincanton, Wiveliscombe, and Yeovil. Two knights are returned for the shire ; two representatives for each of the cities ; and two for each of the boroughs : the county members are elected at Ilchester. Somersetshire is included in the western circuit : the Lent assizes are held at Taunton ; the summer assizes at Bridg-water and Wells, alternately. The quarter sessions are held on January 11th and April 19th at Wells, on July 12th at Bridg-water, and on October 18th at Taunton. There are one hundred and thirty acting magistrates. The rates raised in the county for the year ending March 25th, 1827, amounted to £189,692. 5.; the expenditure to £186,809. 13.; of which £163,225. 4. was applied to the relief of the poor.

To describe the variety of surface with some degree of perspicuity, it is necessary to consider it as divided into three districts : the first comprehends the north-eastern portion of the county, included between the harbours of Uphill and King-road, on the west, and the towns of Bath and Frome on the east : the next and central division, which is much the largest, comprising the entire middle part of the county, from the borders of Wiltshire and Dorsetshire to the Bristol channel, is bounded on the north-east by the Mendip hills, and on the south-west by the Quantock hills and the forest of Neroche : the third forms the remaining western part of the county. The general surface of the north-eastern district is finely varied by lofty hills, which command magnificent views over the fertile plains that lie beneath them.

The western part of it, however, including the hundreds of Winterstoke and Portbury, consists of low moor-lands, as they are called, which are subject to frequent inundation, sometimes for several successive months; but the herbage produced on them, when cleared from stagnant water, is remarkably luxuriant. In the parishes of Congresbury, Yatton, Banwell, Winscombe, Churchill, and Puxton, there are not less than three thousand acres, which, for the most part, discharge their waters into the small river Yeo, and are under the inspection of commissioners of sewers : at spring-tides the waters of the river rise five feet above the level of the adjacent lands. To the northward of these parishes lie nearly four thousand acres, in the parishes of Kenn, Kingston-Seymour, Clevedon, Nailsea, and Chelvey, alike subject to inundation, being secured from the sea by a wall of stone, elevated about ten feet above the level of the lands within : this wall is sometimes over-flowed by high tides, and when strong westerly winds prevail at the equinoxes, it is frequently broken down by the impetuosity of the waves, so that many hundred acres are laid under water. This tract discharges its waters by two rivers, called the Little Yeos, at the mouths of which are sluices : it is also subject to frequent land-floods. South-westward of these parishes lie six others, liable to the same circumstance, and discharging their waters by a sluice at Uphill. Northward of these is Leigh down, a tract of elevated land of nearly three thousand acres, extending from Clevedon to the Hot Wells, near Bristol ; south-eastward of which is a vale of rich grass land, extending from Bedminster, on the north-east, in a south-westerly direction, to the low districts just mentioned. The extensive mountainous range, called the Mendip hills, stretches from Cottle's Oak, near the town of Frome, on the eastern side of the county, in a direction nearly west-north-west, immediately northward of Wells and Axbridge, to a place called Black Rock, on the Bristol channel, near Uphill, a distance of more than thirty miles. In the middle division, on the borders of Wilts and Dorset, the lands are high, and chiefly occupied either as sheep-walks, or in the production of corn. The country around Shepton, Bruton, Castle-Cary, Ilchester, Somerton, Langport, Petherton, and Ilminster, is exceedingly productive, both in corn and pasture, and abounds with good orchards and fine luxuriant meadows : westward of this extensive tract rise the Polden and Ham hills, with a bold aspect. A distinguishing feature in this division is its marshes, or fen lands, which are divided into two districts, called Brent marsh, and the Bridg-water, or South marsh. By far the greater part of Brent marsh, about twenty thousand acres, has been drained and converted into fine grazing and dairy lands : there yet remain considerable tracts of turf bog, upon which much improvement remains to be effected. The river Brue drains the greater portion of this marsh, and has a barrier against the tide, with sluices at Highbridge. The two principal bogs of this district, comprising several thousand acres, situated one on each side of this river, a little to the westward of Glastonbury, are five or six feet higher than the adjacent lands, and consist of a mass of porous earth, saturated with, and floating in, water : some parts of the drained lands are occasionally subject to land-floods. The Ax has no barrier against

the tide ; and the waters, both of this river and of the Brue, are much obstructed in their progress towards the sea by accumulations of mud. The divisions of property are here marked by ditches eight feet wide at the top, three feet and a half at the bottom, and five feet deep, which discharge their waters into the rivers : sluices are occasionally formed on them in time of drought, to keep back the water for the use of the cattle. The South marsh is bounded on the north-east by the Polden hill, which extends chiefly between Bridg-water and Glastonbury ; on the south-east by Ham hill and others ; on the south-west by the river Parret ; and on the north-west by Bridg-water bay. That part of it lying nearest the sea has a surface more elevated than the interior, owing to the great deposit of mud by the tides, in the course of successive ages : the same observation is also applicable to Brent marsh. The river Parret is the principal drain of this marsh ; but it has no barrier against the tides, the consequence being that in rainy seasons many thousand acres are laid under water for a considerable time, rendering the herbage unwholesome, and the air unhealthy. These tracts having, in former times, been constantly subject to occasional inundations from the sea, it was found necessary to establish a Commission of Sewers, the members of which should examine and inspect the sea-banks, ditches, gutters, and sewers, and order the requisite cleansings and repairs : the first commission of this kind upon record was in 1304 ; and the like offices are continued to the present day. Part of this marsh, which has been more recently drained (about the end of the last century), is called King's Sedgmoor, and contains nearly fourteen thousand acres. There are other tracts similar to this, on the borders of the rivers Tone and Parret, nearly all of which were, in like manner, and about the same period, drained and improved ; viz., Normoor, near North Petherton; Stanmoor, Currymoor, West Sedgmoor, &c., near North Curry; West-moor, near Kingsbury ; and Wet-moor, near Muchelney; amounting in the whole to about ten thousand acres, independently of many other low enclosed tracts, which are liable to occasional inundation.

The south-western division of the county has nearly an equal proportion of lofty hills and fertile slopes and vales. In the vale of Taunton-Dean, which comprises thirty parishes, and the market towns of Taunton, Wellington, and Milverton, the prospect is agreeably relieved by a mixture of arable and pasture ground ; but to the north-west are wild and mountainous tracts. The Quantock hills, extending nearly the whole of the distance between the town of Taunton and the sea ; the Brandon hills, to the westward of these ; and others in this part of the county, are noted for their wild and picturesque scenery. The highest point of the Quantock hills is one thousand two hundred and seventy feet above the level of the sea ; and these heights command views, not only of the fertile country immediately around them, but also of the Welch coast : the elevation called Dundry-beacon, situated near the sea, is the highest point of land, being, according to the Ordnance survey, one thousand six hundred and sixty-eight feet above the level of the sea. Thus we find the surface of Somerset-shire varied by lofty hills and fertile plains : it is also adorned by numerous noble woods. Some of the most remarkable heights, besides those before-mentioned, commanding very rich and extensive views, are, Broad-field down, between Bristol and Wrington; Dundry hill, near Bristol; Lansdown, near Bath; White-down, to the eastward of Chard; Black-down, to the south-westward of the same town; and on the confines of Devon, the hills of Hamden, Montacute, St. Michael's, and Brent-Knoll; the Tor, near Glastonbury; Bratton, near Minehead; Snowden, near Chard; Ash-Beacon; Brad-ley-Knoll; Dundon hill; Halston Round hill; Moor-linch; and North hill: fine views are also obtained from Enmore castle, which commands the Mendip hills; Hinton St. George; and the vicinity of Taunton. The mountainous parts of the county have a smooth, undu-lating, and rounded outline, seldom presenting cliffs, or precipitous faces, except on the sea-shore. The exten-sive line of sea-coast is very irregular; in some places projecting in lofty and rocky promontories, and in others receding into fine bays, with low and level shores. From Stert-point, at the mouth of the Parret, northward, the shore is for a considerable distance entirely flat, and composed of vast sand-banks, repel-ling the waters of the ocean, which anciently spread over these shoals, and covered the extensive district now called Brent Marsh. The general direction of the Somersetshire coast, from the western extremity until near the mouth of the Parret, is from west to east; here, however, commence the shores of the marshes of the middle district, which, extending in a direction nearly from north to south, form, with the last-mentioned, the bay of Bridg-water, so called from the sea-port of that name, situated some miles up the river Parret. This bay is terminated on the north by the promontory formed by Breane down; beyond this are two smaller bays and promontories, between which and the mouth of the Avon the coast runs nearly in a north-easterly direction.

In such an extent and diversity of surface the cli-mate varies considerably. Near the sea-coast the win-ters are never severe; and from Minehead and Dul-verton, on the west, to Milborne-Port and Wincanton, on the east, the climate is mild and temperate, the Quantock, Branden, and Dundry hills alone excepted. Proceeding northward and ascending Poulden hill, it changes, and becomes colder and more stormy; and still further northward, on the Mendip hills, the cold increases, and the air in winter is moist, and the wea-ther boisterous, the whole country being sometimes en-veloped in dense fogs: in summer, however, the air on these hills is clear, salubrious, and invigorating; and it also frequently happens that spring crops in the vales are destroyed by frosts in April or May, while those on the hills remain uninjured. In the beautiful and exten-sive vale of Taunton-Dean, in the western part of the county, the climate is peculiarly mild and serene; but the north-western and mountainous parts of this division are subject to great mutability in the state and temper-ature of the atmosphere. In consequence of the con-tiguity of the Bristol channel, which fills the air with watery vapours, unfavourable to the ripening of corn, considerable tracts of hilly country, which would other-wise be employed in the production of grain, are kept under grass: still, even in the more elevated tracts, there is a very large portion of arable land. The seed-time and harvest in the mountainous districts are

nearly a month later than in the vales; excepting only as regards the seeds that are commonly sown in the Autumn, which, in the first-mentioned tracts, on account of the greater degree of cold, are put in the ground a fortnight earlier than is generally done elsewhere.

For its general fertility Somersetshire is particularly eminent; and the variety of soil is so great, that almost every species may be found within its limits. That of the moor-lands of the north-eastern division is, for the most part, a deep and rich mixture of clay and sand, a marine deposit. Leigh down has a thin gravelly soil, lying im-mediately upon limestone, and frequently not more than three inches from the surface, being therefore unfavour-able for tillage: that of Broadfield down, a few miles further south, is of the same nature. The soil of the Mendip hills is for the most part deep and loamy; but tracts of an inferior quality, light, spongy, and black, occasionally intervene; and the loam is sometimes in-termingled with pieces of stone, and with gravel, clay, or other substances that alter its quality in different degrees. The soil of the Polden and Ham hills is of an inferior quality and a very thin staple. That of the marshes, or moors, of the middle district is generally very fertile, and consists of four kinds, viz., strong, dry, and fertile clay, of considerable depth, which is es-teemed the most valuable; red earth, varying in depth from one foot to six feet, and covering the black moory earth; black moory earth, having a substratum of clay at various depths; and what is called turf-bog, which is of a light spongy texture, and so full of the fibrous roots of plants that it is with difficulty cut with a spade: under it is found a stratum of black earth, from one to two feet thick; and next occurs the peat, which is from three to fifteen feet in depth, full of flaggy leaves and the hollow stalks of rushes, together with bituminous matter: it is employed as the common fuel of the district. Southward of this extensive level is an elevated tract of great fertility, composed chiefly of sea-sand and shells, well adapted for tillage. The soil of the fruitful vale of Taunton-Dean is a rich loam, interspersed in some places with clay, and in others with sand, and that of some other parts of the western division is little inferior; but the hills and forests are for the most part left in a state of nature: the Quan-tock hills have various thin soils, covering a thin shaly rock, and sometimes limestone. The soil of White-down is very various; that of Black-down consists of a thin surface of black earth on a bed of sand and gra-vel. On the sea-coast, for some distance westward of the mouth of the river Parret, the remains of a forest are discoverable at low water, which is described in the Geological Transactions, Vol. III., p. 380.

In the north-eastern district the proportion of ara-ble land is very small; in the middle division it is greater, but almost wholly on the south-eastern side, in the vicinities of Shepton-Mallet, Bruton, Castle-Cary, Wincanton, Millborne-Port, Yeovil, Ilchester, South Petherton, Crewkerne, Chard, and Ilminster; there is, however, some on the hills near the great marshes also: in the vale of Taunton, in the western part of the coun-ty, is much arable land, and on the northern side, ap-proaching Watchet: the whole amounts to nearly three hundred thousand acres. The rotations of crops are various: those commonly cultivated are wheat, barley, oats, beans, and peas, the produce of which varies greatly. The wheat produced on the rising lands to the south of Bridg-water marsh is of very superior quality; and the best barley in the county is supposed to grow in the parishes of Chedzoy, Weston-Zoyland, Middlezoy, and Othery, in the same district: on the Mendip hills the favourite crop is oats, which are there produced in abundance and of good quality. In the north-eastern district turnips are seldom seen; but in the arable parts of the middle division they are cultivated to a great extent: vetches are sometimes grown. The most common artificial grass is the broad clover: sanfoin is much cultivated in the north-eastern districts, as also are ray-grass, marl-grass, and White Dutch clover: the marl-grass grows spontaneously on the marl ground, and bears a striking resemblance to red, or broad clover. Potatoes are very extensively cultivated in different districts, more especially on the fertile soils in the vicinity of Castle-Cary, where one hundred and sixty sacks per acre is a common produce. In the parishes of Wrington, Blagdon, Ubley, Compton-Martin, and Harptree, in the north-eastern district, teasel is extensively grown, chiefly on a strong rich clay; the produce is very uncertain. The head of this plant, which is composed of well-turned vegetable hooks, is used in dressing cloth; and the manufactures of Somersetshire and Wiltshire are for the most part supplied from these parishes: large quantities are also exported from Bristol to Yorkshire. Woad is also cultivated in this district, chiefly in the vicinity of Keynsham, the quality of which is much esteemed: three or four crops are commonly gathered in the season; and the average produce per acre is about a ton and a half. In the rich tract extending from Wincanton, by Yeovil, to Crewkerne, a great deal of flax and hemp is grown. Turkey rhubarb is occasionally cultivated in small quantities. In some of the western parts of the county the common mode of getting in the corn is by carrying it on the backs of horses, a large wooden crook on each side of the saddle being laden with the sheaves: this is in consequence of the unevenness of the country, and the steepness of the hills: even manure is carried upon the land in a similar manner. The arable lands are not near sufficient to supply the consumption of grain, many thousand quarters being annually brought from the counties of Wilts and Dorset. The grass lands are of very great extent, occupying about six hundred thousand acres; and the plains are remarkable for their luxuriant herbage, furnishing a supply of produce much more than sufficient for consumption; London, Bristol, Salisbury, and other markets, receiving great quantities of fat oxen, sheep, and hogs, besides cider, cheese, butter, and different other articles from this county. Many of these tracts, when not chilled by an excess of moisture, bear an almost perpetual verdure. In the northern district, on the rich marsh land near the Bristol channel, the grazing system prevails; in the vicinity of Bristol and Bath, the meadows are almost universally mown, while in the parts more remote from those towns, dairying is almost the only object: to whatever purpose applied, these lands are respectively good and profitable. Nearly the whole of the rich marshes and low lands of the middle division are under grass, and applied partly to grazing and partly to dairying. In the western part of the county, in the parishes of Crowcombe, Stogumber, Monksilver, Nettlecombe, Dun-

ter, Dulverton, &c., are some irrigated meadows of excellent quality, the greater part lying on steep declivities. Lime is the principal manure: marl is applied in those parts where it is found of good quality, and some of the marsh farmers on the river Brue cut openings in the banks of that river, in the winter, and thus irrigate their land with the muddy water descending from the hills. In parts of the county where stone is easily procured the fences frequently consist of stone walls, though they are commonly of white thorn: the beech hedges about Dulverton, Dunster, &c., are not only beautiful to the eye, but are an annual source of profit, yielding much fuel. The cattle of Somersetshire form an object of great importance in its agricultural economy. In the north-western district, the cows, which are all for the dairy, are almost entirely of the short-horned breed: both butter and cheese are made here; many dairy farmers in the vicinity of Bath and Bristol make butter and cheese of half-skimmed milk.

From Crewkerne, extending southward into Dorsetshire, is one of those deep large vales for which this county is remarkable, containing the villages of Clapton, Seaborough, Wayford, Woolmington, &c., and in which commences a district about twenty miles square (one half in Dorsetshire, and the other in Somersetshire), noted for supplying the summer markets at Exeter with calves, which are there bought by the Devonshire farmers, and, after being pastured three or four years in that county, are sold to the Somersetshire graziers, who fatten them for the London market: these are of the kind called Devonshire cattle. The neat cattle of Taunton-Dean are of the North Devon breed, and are held in high esteem by the graziers; and, indeed, the oxen of the whole western district are remarkably well shaped; they are almost universally red, yoked at three years old, and worked until they are five or six; they perform the greater part of the agricultural labour: in the other parts of the county also, oxen are often similarly employed. The summer-fattened oxen are for the most part of the Devonshire kind, and bred either in the northern part of that county, or the lower parts of Somerset: the winter-fattened cattle are of an inferior kind, partly home-bred and partly from Wales: heifers are sometimes grazed in preference to oxen. Lean cattle of the red Devonshire and Somersetshire breed are bought at the fairs of this county by the graziers of Leicestershire, Oxfordshire, Warwickshire, &c.; and besides the numerous fairs for the sale of cattle, both in the counties of Somerset and Devon, a large market is held every three weeks, during the summer months, at Somerton, on the southern side of the great central marshes, to which many lean cattle are brought, together with an immense number of lean sheep, the latter chiefly of the Dorsetshire breed: this is a market for fat cattle also. In the vicinity of Bath is a valuable breed of large sheep, some of which, when fattened, weigh from thirty to forty pounds per quarter. The Mendip hills have a native and very hardy breed, with fine wool, which thrive on very scanty pasturage; their flesh is also much esteemed. In the south-eastern part of the middle division the sheep are an improved sort of the Dorsetshire breed; the number kept, chiefly in breeding flocks, is exceedingly great. Many sheep of this kind are fed in the marshes, besides others of the Mendip breed, and great numbers from Dorsetshire. In Taunton-Dean they are of the Dorsetshire breed; and in this western portion of the county are two other kinds of sheep; one, a native breed, without horns, well made, somewhat resembling the Leicester sheep, and having a thick fleece, which generally weighs about seven or eight pounds, is found in the neighbourhood of Dulverton, Bampton, Wiveliscombe, &c., and is highly esteemed by the graziers in the marshes : many of them are taken to the Bristol market; the fat wethers, at two years old, weigh about twenty-five pounds per quarter. The other is a small horned sort, which is bought when young at South Molton in Devonshire, and is kept on the Forest of Exmoor, or the adjoining hills, for two or three years, merely for the sake of their wool, the weight of the fleece seldom exceeding four pounds; when fat, these sheep weigh from fourteen to eighteen pounds per quarter. A few Leicester sheep have been introduced into the county. The extraordinary number of hogs fattened in the north-eastern district are, for the most part, procured from the Bristol market, to which they are brought by men from Wales, or by drovers; they are fed chiefly upon whey, and their flesh is of a fine colour and delicate flavour. The few bred are of different sorts, viz., the native white breed, which has large ears and a long body; the Berkshire black and white kind; the Chinese breed; and a mixed sort. But few horses are bred in the county; the northern district is supplied by dealers, who bring them from the great fairs in the North of England. The great demand for poultry in the cities of Bristol and Bath causes great attention to be paid in the adjoining districts to the rearing and fattening of all kinds of fowls. In the same tracts are also many large pieces of garden-ground for supplying those cities with vegetables; and in the vicinity of the town of Somerton are numerous gardens, which supply the surrounding markets, even as far as Wells and Shepton-Mallet, with early peas, beans, potatoes, &c., and, in the month of August, with great quantities of cucumbers. The northern district contains innumerable orchards; those which have a northern aspect, and are sheltered from the westerly winds, are considered the most regular in bearing; the fruit produced at the northern base of the Mendip hills, as at Langford, Burrington, Rickford, Blagdon, Ubley, Compton-Martin, and Harptree, affords a strong and palatable cider : the favourite apple is here the Court of Wick pippin, which takes its name from the place where it was first cultivated. In the middle division are also many orchards, from which a considerable quantity of cider is made. In the vale of Taunton-Dean cider of the very finest quality is made with particular care.

The woods and plantations occupy about twenty thousand acres; the north-eastern district is but partially covered, and, according to the demand at the collieries, the wood it contains is cut at very irregular intervals. Kingswood, the timber of which is chiefly oak, covers about two hundred and thirty acres. On the northern declivity of the Mendip hills are some good coppices, the principal of which are those of Blagdon, Hasel, and Ubley : the scenery of these woods is very picturesque, and being sheltered from the strong south-westerly winds, their growth is rapid. On the opposite declivity are other coppices, of which Stoke-wood is the principal; these, from their exposed situation, are less productive. In the eastern part of this district are other woods, large and productive, such as those of Mells, Leigh, Edford, Harwich, Compton, Cameley, &c., being, from their vicinity to the coal-works, very valuable : in the same part are also many beautiful plantations. The vallies of the north-eastern district are richly adorned with elms. In the eastern part of the middle division is an extensive chain of woodland, several miles in length, from the parish of East Cranmore, through Downhead, Cloford, Whatley, Elm, &c., besides other woods of considerable size. On the borders of Wiltshire was the large forest of Selwood, extending from Penscellwood to within three miles of Frome, which was disafforested in the reign of Charles I : it appears to have extended over a vale of about twenty thousand acres, eighteen thousand of which have been cleared and converted into arable and pasture land, with a small portion of meadow : the remainder continues in coppice woods, the chief sorts of timber being oak and ash, while the underwood is principally hazel, ash, alder, willow, and birch : the chief natural defects of these woods are the coldness of the soil upon which they are situated, and their exposure, for the most part, to violent south-west winds : the coal-pits near Mendip are a constant market for the poles cut from the underwood. Numerous modern plantations have been made in this tract, in which the Scotch fir thrives best. The marsh lands have few trees of any kind. On the declivities of the Quantock and other hills, in the western part of the county, are many coppice-woods, chiefly of oak. This district does not otherwise abound with oak, but elms grow in the hedge-rows, sometimes to a considerable size.

This county has different uncultivated wastes : in the north-western district are several unenclosed commons, the principal of which are Broadfield down and Lansdown, the former containing about two thousand five hundred acres, the latter nearly one thousand : the surface of Lansdown is perfectly smooth, and it is remarkable for its excellence in feeding sheep. The large open tract called Leigh down, to the west of Bristol, is also subject to a right of commonage, and is chiefly depastured with sheep. More than one half of the ancient royal forest of Mendip, on the hills of that name, is now enclosed : the remainder is covered to the extent of several miles with heath and fern, and furnishes pasturage for large flocks of sheep. On the highest parts of this tract is a considerable flat, containing several swamps, which often prove dangerous to travellers. In the middle division, the largest unenclosed upland common is the forest of Neroche, near Ilminster, containing eight or nine hundred acres, and upon which different parishes have a right of commonage without stint : the next in size is White-down, near Chard : the low marshy wastes comprise several thousand acres. At the western extremity of the county, and partly in Devonshire, is the great forest of Exmoor, extending from east to west for a distance of ten or twelve miles, and from north to south about eight, and containing nearly twenty-thousand acres. Near the centre of this large tract is an enclosed estate, called Simonsbath, of about two hundred acres, with a dwelling-house, licensed and frequented as an inn. On the summits of the hills, more especially on the western and northern sides, are swamps many acres in extent, in which turf is cut. The small river Barl, which rises in the waste, runs on the border of the Simonsbath estate, but loses its name about two miles further eastward, on joining the Ex, which rises in a low swampy spot of ground, about two miles to the north-east of the above-mentioned estate, and gives name to the forest : the Ex, at the confluence of the Barl, becomes a considerable stream, and soon after, in its course southward, quits the county for Devonshire : numerous small rivulets discharge themselves into the above-mentioned streams, from every quarter. Excepting a few willows and thorns by the sides of these rivulets, not a tree or bush, out of the limits of the Simonsbath estate, is any where to be seen. The roads are in general, as might be expected in so large a tract devoid of inhabitants, extremely bad, and in some places scarcely passable. Upon this forest, about twenty-two thousand sheep are depastured every summer, and about four hundred small horses are kept the whole year round ; but the value of the latter is so trifling, that very little profit is derived from them. When the snow covers the ground to the depth of many feet, these hardy animals are seen in droves, traversing the narrow vallies and sheltered parts, gathering their scanty fare from the banks of the rivulets and warm springs ; but the sheep are all driven off as the severer part of the winter season approaches. At Simonsbath, the forester has an annual sale for the small horses that are bred on the surrounding hills ; and here also, in the month of May, he meets the farmers from all the country round, who enter in his books the number of sheep to be depastured on the forest. There are also several hundred acres of uncultivated land on the Quantock and Brandon hills, and in some other parts. The wastes of that part of Black-down which lies within this county are supposed to exceed a thousand acres : the occupiers of estates contiguous to these hills stock them with young cattle in the summer months. In the northern district the fuel is chiefly coal ; in the middle division much turf is burned ; while the western part of the county is supplied with coal from Wales, which, however, is of an inferior quality.

The chief mineral productions are coal, lead, calamine, limestone, freestone, and various other kinds of stone : fullers' earth, marl, and ochre, are also occasionally found. The coal beds are the nearest to London of any yet discovered, and constitute the most southern deposit of that mineral in England. This deposit is comparatively small, and lies northward of the eastern parts of the Mendip hills : it may be divided into the northern and the southern ; the former including the parishes of High Littleton, Timsbury, Paulton, Radstock, and the northern part of Midsummer-Norton ; the latter, the southern part of Midsummer-Norton, Stratton on the Foss, Kilmersdon, Babington, and Mells. This southern division comprises what have long been known as the Mendip collieries, and it is probable that they were once within the verge of the extensive forest of Mendip, but they are now in the midst of old enclosures, and their ancient name has become obsolete. In the northern collieries the strata of coal dip about nine inches in the yard, their thickness varying from ten inches to upwards of three feet ; they are seldom worked if less than fifteen inches. The coal is of excellent quality : it is firm, of a strong grain, and commonly raised in large pieces, which ensure its conveyance to almost any distance without injury : in burning, it makes a clear and durable fire. Bath is the principal market for its consumption, to which may be added the western parts of Wiltshire; and the adjacent parts of Somersetshire : about fifteen hundred men and boys are employed at the various collieries. The southern division is worked on a more limited scale : the strata here dip from eighteen to thirty inches in the yard, while in some places they descend perpendicularly : their number is twenty-five, varying in thickness from six inches to seven feet, but they are seldom worked when less than eighteen inches. The quality of the coal raised in this district varies, some of it being nearly equal to that of the northern collieries, but the greater part is softer, of shorter grain, and less adapted for distant carriage. The south-western parts of Wiltshire, the northern parts of Dorsetshire, and the eastern and southern parts of Somersetshire, are the chief markets. At Clapton, a village lying to the north-west of Leigh down, and west of Bristol, is a coal-work, possessing the advantage of a land-level of forty-four fathoms : at this pit are landed about two hundred and forty bushels daily : the small coal is shipped at Portishead point for Wales, where it is used in burning lime. Under the rich and extensive vale lying to the south-east of Leigh down are beds of coal thought to be inexhaustible : some thousands of bushels are now daily raised at the pits in this district. The principal stratum is five feet thick, sometimes rather more : this and the other strata generally dip towards the south, about nine inches in the yard, seldom more than a foot in the same extent : the rocks above the coal being full of fissures, considerable inconvenience is experienced from the influx of water. The Mendip hills, which consist chiefly of limestone of that kind called, in mineralogical language, mountain-limestone, are famous for their mines, chiefly of lead and lapis calaminaris. Those of the former metal are nearly exhausted, or, at least, the deep working is so encumbered with water, that little can be done in them. In former times, however, many thousand pounds have been annually paid to the see of Wells for the lord's share (one-tenth) of the lead dug in the forest, in the parish of Wells only : on Broadfield down also there are veins of lead. In the parishes of Rowberrow, Shipham, and Winscombe, are valuable mines of lapis calaminaris : this mineral is sometimes found within a yard of the surface, and is seldom worked deeper than thirty fathoms : between four and five hundred miners are here constantly employed in raising it. In the parishes of Compton-Martin and East Harptree are mines of the same kind. From these parishes, eastward, through the whole tract of Mendip, to Mells, at its eastern extremity, are also found marks and indications of calamine ; and at Merchant's hill, in the parish of Binegar, several tons of it have been raised. The Mendip mines are governed by a set of laws and orders, commonly called Lord Choke's Laws, which were enacted in the time of Edward IV., when, on some disputes arising, that monarch sent Lord Choke, the Lord Chief Justice of England, down to his royal forest of Mendip, and the said laws and orders were agreed upon by the lords royal of Mendip, viz., the Bishop of Bath, Lord

Glaston, Lord Benfield, the Earl of Chewton, and my Lord of Richmond, at a great meeting then held at a place called the Forge. According to these, the miners are allowed to turn upon the forest as many cattle in summer as they are able to keep in winter : but before becoming such they must crave license of the lord of the soil, where they purpose to work, or, in his absence, of his officers, after which they proceed to break the ground : a tenth part of the ore must be paid to the lord, and a tenth part of the lead also, if it be smelted on his territory : every lord of the soil ought to hold a miner court twice a year, and to swear twelve men of the same occupation, for the redress of misdemeanors : the lord, or lords, may issue arrests for strife between man and man, on account of their works, and for obtaining the payment of their own duties : and if any miner should by misfortune meet his death by the earth falling in upon him, or by any other accident, the other miners are bound to fetch him out of the earth, and bring him to Christian burial, at their own costs and charges ; nor shall any coroner, or officer at large, have to do with him in any respect. The mountain limestone formation near Bristol, forming a feature in English geology, constitutes the hills rising from beneath the red marl to the west of Bristol, and forms a range of considerable elevation, through which the Avon passes, in its course to the Severn. These hills consist of a prodigious number of strata, of very different natures, but chiefly of limestone of several varieties, the dip of which is about forty-five degrees. Some of the limestone strata contain different organic remains ; and an assemblage of numerous strata, called the Black Rock, from the colour of the limestone, which is here quarried for paving-stones, contains numerous fossils and round concretions, penetrated by petroleum, which sometimes exudes from the rock. Very few of these numerous beds of limestone are quarried, and many of them will not burn into good lime. Calamine, accompanied by heavy spar and galena, is found in veins of calcareous spar, crossing the limestone. Manganese is found in a vein of iron-stone, crossing the limestone. The strata alternating with the limestone are beds of clay of various kinds, which sometimes contain nodules of coral and geodes of iron-ore : thin beds of iron-stone and quartzose sand are also found ; besides a bed of coal about two inches thick. The mountain limestone ranges round Bristol, in almost every direction, forming a kind of irregular basin, and reposes on the red sand-stone, which visibly passes beneath it. On the top of the limestone strata forming the cliffs, on the side of the Avon, lies a yellowish sand-stone, which has sometimes the appearance of a breccia, occurring also in some other parts of the same district. The red clay in the neighbourhood of Bristol contains gypsum, and abounds with sulphate of strontian, in veins and large beds. Red sand-stone is found under the limestone of the Mendip hills. The mountainous part of the western district of this county is formed of a series of rocks, differing much in mineralogical character, but a great proportion of them having the structure of sand-stones : some of the finest of these sand-stones graduate into a fine-grained slate, divisible into laminæ as thin as paper, and having a smooth, silky, and shining surface : their prevailing colours are reddish brown and greenish grey, with many intermediate mixtures ; but some of the slaty varieties

are of a purplish hue, occasionally spotted with green. In many places large beds of limestone, full of madrepores, are contained in the slate, which, towards the external parts of the beds, is interstratified with limestone. Copper, in the state of sulphuret and of malachite, and veins of hematite, are frequently met with ; and nests of copper-ore, of considerable magnitude, have been found in the subordinate beds of limestone. The Quantock hills, Grabbist hill, Croydon hill, Brendon hill, and some others to the west of them, consist chiefly of the kind of stone called grey wacké, in some places interstratified with limestone : the quarries of limestone in the eastern side of the Quantock hills are very numerous. North hill, extending along the sea-shore from Minehead to Porlock, and forming a very bold and precipitous coast, is of grey wacké ; and the whole of the precipitous coast of the county presents a great variety of mineralogical strata. Granite, of small grain, occurs near the foot of a hill a few miles to the north-east of Taunton, where it is quarried to a small extent ; the inhabitants of the neighbourhood call it pottle-stone. The kind of limestone called by mineralogists *lias*, and which extends in a direction nearly north-east and south-west almost to the banks of the Humber, commencing in Dorsetshire a little to the west of Ilchester, passes by Bath, and occupies a large tract of this county ; it is also found on the coast of Somerset, whence it extends for some distance inland ; proceeding eastward, it first occurs a little distance to the west of Watchet, and forms some very high cliffs to the eastward of that place ; the Polden hills consist chiefly of lias : this stone burns into a very strong quick lime, valuable, when made into mortar, for its increasing hardness under water. Coombe down is the place where the greatest quantity of freestone is raised, in doing which the ground has been undermined for several miles. The parishes of Midsummer-Norton, Sutton on the Foss, Kilmersdon, Radstock, Timsbury, High Littleton, Farmborough, Paulton, Stone-Easton, Binegar, and Chilcompton, comprehend a tract of land rendered remarkably fertile by the application of marl, which is found at various depths from the surface, of a black colour, and in inexhaustible quantities.

The principal manufactures are those of woollen and worsted goods at Frome, Taunton, Wellington, and Wiveliscombe ; of gloves, at Yeovil, Stoke, and Martock ; of lace, at Chard and Taunton ; of silk, at Taunton, Bruton, and Shepton-Mallet ; of crape, at Taunton ; and of knit worsted stockings, at Shepton-Mallet. Upon the Avon are several mills for preparing iron and copper, and others for the spinning of worsted, and the spinning and weaving of cotton. Many of the lower classes derive cheap and wholesome food from the salmon and herring fisheries of Porlock, Minehead, and Watchet, which are carried on to a considerable extent : the other fish found off this coast, and which are occasionally taken at different places upon it, are tublin, flounders, sand-dabs, hakes, pipers, soles, plaice, skate, conger-eels, shrimps, prawns, crabs, muscles, and star-fish.

The chief rivers are the Lower Avon, the Parret, the Tone, the Brue, and the Ax. The Lower Avon, rising in the hilly district of North Wiltshire, after forming, for some distance, the boundary between Somerset and Wilts, enters this county crossing the north-eastern extremity of it. After partly encircling the city of Bath, a few miles lower, it becomes the north-eastern boundary of the county, and separates it from Gloucestershire during the rest of its very irregular course, which it pursues for the most part in a north-westerly direction, by the town of Keynsham, and the city of Bristol, to its junction at Kingroad with the æstuary of the Severn, which there assumes the name of the Bristol Channel. This river, besides constituting the harbour of Bristol, is navigable for small craft as high as Bath, a distance of sixteen miles above that port. The Parret rises at South Parret in Dorsetshire, and soon entering this county, flows nearly northward by Crewkerne to Langport, where it is joined on the east by the small river Yeo, and assumes a north-easterly direction to Bridg-water, having nearly midway between these towns received the waters of the Tone from the west : forming the harbour of Bridg-water, it thenceforward pursues a very devious course, for the most part in a northerly direction, and finally falls into Bridg-water bay, at Stert point. The navigable part of its course commences at Langport, whence to Stert point is a distance of about twenty miles. The Tone rises in the Quantock hills, near the town of Wiveliscombe, and, flowing for some miles southward to the borders of Devon, afterwards takes an easterly course by the town of Taunton, where it becomes navigable to the Parret at Boroughbridge, about eight miles from Taunton, and near the centre of the county. The Brue rises on the western borders of Wiltshire, not far from the town of Bruton, past which it flows nearly in a south-westerly direction : some miles lower, however, it assumes a north-westerly course, and passes at a short distance south-westward of Glastonbury, to the Bristol Channel, near the mouth of the Parret : from the vicinity of Glastonbury, the course of this river is entirely through the marshes : it is navigable up to Highbridge, a distance of two miles from its mouth. The Ax originates in two small streams from the south-western side of the Mendip hills, one of which has its source in the natural cavern called Wokey Hole; its course is north-westward, and for a considerable distance through the marshes; passing to the south-west of Axbridge, it falls into the Bristol Channel near Black Rock. The Ex rises on Exmoor Forest, at the western extremity of this county, which it soon quits for that of Devon. The smaller streams are very numerous; they all flow through fertile tracts, and the banks of many of them are adorned with extensive ornamented grounds belonging to the various seats of the nobility and gentry, with which this county abounds : some of the principal are the Yeo, the Cale, the Chew, the Frome, the Ivel, and the Barl. Of fish, the rivers contain salmon, trout, pike, perch, roach, dace, eels, carp, tench, and gudgeons. The Kennet and Avon canal enters the county from Bradford in Wiltshire, and joins the Lower Avon at Bath. Previously to the year 1798, acts had been obtained for the following canals, the construction of which was then in progress, viz : the Somersetshire coal canal, which has two branches, the one commencing at Paulton, the other at Radstock, and both communicating with the Kennet and Avon canal near Bath; the Dorset and Somerset canal, which was never carried into execution, was intended to commence near Nettlebridge, in the district of the

southern collieries, to pass through the town of Frome, and then to divide into two branches, one of them joining the Kennet and Avon canal near Bradford, and the other to pass through Wincanton, to the borders of Dorsetshire ; and the Ilchester and Langport canal. The turnpike roads of this county are good. The road from London to Wells, Bridg-water, and Minehead, enters the county from Warminster in Wilts, and passes through Frome, Shepton-Mallet, Wells, Glastonbury, Bridg-water, Watchet, and Dunster, to Minehead. That from London to Wells, through Marlborough, falls into the former at Frome. The road from London to Exeter and Dartmouth, by Taunton, enters from Stourhead in Wilts, and passes through Castle-Cary, Somerton, Langport, Taunton, and Wellington, to Cullompton in Devonshire : this is also the road from London to Barnstaple and Ilfracombe. The road from London to Bath, Bristol, and Milford Haven, enters the county from Chippenham in Wilts, and passes through Bath-Ford, Bath-Easton, Bath, Keynsham, and Bristol, to New Passage in Gloucestershire. That from London to Bath, through Devizes, enters from Melksham in Wilts, and falls into the last-mentioned road at Bath-Ford.

The remains of antiquity that have been found are very various. The parish of Stanton-Drew, in the north-eastern district, is remarkable as containing the remains of four clusters of huge massive stones, forming two circles, an oblong, and an ellipsis, which are supposed to have anciently constituted a Druidical temple. The ancient boundary called Wansdyke may be traced in several places; in the vicinity of its course, near Great Bedwin, celts and ancient instruments of war have been discovered. Besides the Roman cities of Bath and Ilchester, there are numerous places which, although their names have been changed, or altered, since that remote period, still bear evident marks of Roman origin in the foundations of some of their walls, and in various remains that have from time to time been dug from them ; such are Camalet, Hamden, Wellow, Coker, Chilcompton, Conquest, Wiveliscombe, Bath-Ford, Warley, Street, Long Ashton, Postlebury, South Petherton, Watergore, Wigborough, Yeovil, Putsham, Kilton, Stogumber, Edington, Inglish-Combe, &c. Among the many miscellaneous remains of this people which have been discovered, more especially at Bath, are included temples, sudatories, tesselated pavements, altars, hypocausts, and coins of different ages. Traces of ancient encampments are still visible at Blacker's hills, Bow-ditch, Brompton, Bury Castle, and Burwalls ; in the parish of South Cadbury, near Chesterton, in the parish of Chew Magna, Cowes Castle, Doleberry, Douxborough Castle, Godshill, Hawkridge Castle, on Hampton down, Masbury, Mearknoll, Modbury, on the forest of Neroche, Newborough, Norton-Hautville, Stantonbury, Stokeleigh, Tedbury, Trendle Castle, Turk's Castle, Wiveliscombe Castle, and Worleberry. The principal Roman road was the Fosse-way, which extended across this county from Bath, in a south-westerly direction to Perry Street, on the confines of Devonshire. In a direction nearly parallel with this ran another road from the forest of Exmoor, through Taunton, Bridg-water, and Axbridge, to Portishead, whence there was a *trajectus*, or ferry, across the Bristol Channel to the city of *Isca Silurum*, now Caerleon. On Salisbury hill are traces of the earthworks thrown up at the time of the siege of Bath by the Saxons. An encampment called Jack's Castle, near Wilmington, is supposed to have been of Danish formation. The intrenchments formed by the forces of Harold, near Porlock, in 1052, are still to be seen.

According to Tanner, the number of religious houses in the county of all denominations, before the Reformation, including two Alien priories, was about forty-four. There are remains of the abbey in the Isle of Athelney, founded by King Alfred; of that of Banwell, founded in the same reign; of those of Bath, Bruton, Cliff, Glastonbury, Hinton, Keynsham, Muchelney, and Wells; of the priories of Barlinch, Barrow, Bath, Berkeley, Buckland, Sordrum, Cannington, Chewton, Dunster, Frome, Hinton-Charterhouse, Ilchester, Kewstoke, Montacute, Portbury, Stavordale, Stogursey, Taunton, Woodspring, and Yeanston; and of the nunneries of Nunney, Walton, and Whiteball. Of ancient church architecture, the most interesting specimens are in the churches of Allen, Ashill, Axbridge, Barton St. David, St. James at Bath, Bath-Easton, North Cadbury, Camerton, Chew Magna, Crewkerne, Dunster, Goathurst, Ilminster, Keynsham, Lansdown, Martock, Nunney, St. Magdalene and St. James Taunton, Walton, Wincanton, and Yeovil. The greater number of the churches of Somersetshire exhibit fine specimens of the decorated and later styles of English architecture; from which it has been thought probable that they were rebuilt by that prince, in reward for the zeal in his cause displayed by its inhabitants. There are several ancient chapels; and the fonts of Beckington, East Camel, Corfe, and Pendomer, are remarkable for their antiquity. Remains still exist of the ancient castles of Bridg-water, Dunster, Montacute, Stoke under Hamdon, Stowey, Taunton, and Walton. Combe-Sydenham, near Stogumber, is a very ancient mansion, the seat of the family of the Sydenhams. The more modern seats of nobility and gentry are particularly numerous. Besides the celebrated waters of Bath, there are mineral springs of different properties at Alford, Ashill, Castle-Cary, East Chinnock, Glastonbury, Queen-Camel, Wellington, and Wells: at Nether Stowey is a petrifying spring. In the Mendip hills, and surrounded by wild and magnificent scenery, is Wokey Hole (so called from the neighbouring village of Wokey), an extensive natural cavern, the most celebrated in the West of England, in which the waters of the Ax take their rise, issuing from it in a clear and rapid stream : in the parish of Cheddar, in the same district, is an immense chasm in the hills, called Cheddar Cliffs, the scenery of which is particularly rugged and striking. Mr. Collinson, in his history of this county, mentions the following birds as the most remarkable that are found in it, or upon its coasts, viz., the heath-hen, the wild duck, the curlew, the rail, the gull, and the wheat-ear; and adds, that on Exmoor Forest, and some other lower and uncultivated tracts, red deer are found. Somersetshire abounds with rare and curious plants : on the hilly wastes occur the dwarf juniper, the cranberry, and the wortleberry, the last being here provincially called *hurts*. The rocks on the coast have great quantities of the *lichen marinus*, or sea-bread : in the low moors grows the *gale*, or candleberry myrtle. The county of Somerset gives the title of duke to the family of Seymour.

SOMERSHAM, a parish (formerly a market town) in the hundred of HURSTINGSTONE, county of HUNTINGDON, 8½ miles (E. N. E.) from Huntingdon, and 64¼ (N.) from London, containing 1166 inhabitants. This town, formerly called *Summersum*, is supposed to have derived its name from an adjacent hill, which was the site of a summer camp of the Romans : it is situated in a fertile country, abounding with springs of remarkable purity, some of which were considered to possess medicinal qualities, but are now disused. Several of the inhabitants are employed in preparing wicks for rushlights, which are extensively transmitted hence to various parts of the kingdom. The market, long since discontinued, was on Friday : fairs are held on June 23rd and November 12th, but they are very inconsiderable. The living is a rectory, with the perpetual curacies of Colne and Pidley annexed, in the archdeaconry of Huntingdon, and diocese of Lincoln, rated in the king's books at £40. 4. 7., and annexed to the Regius Professorship of Divinity in the University of Cambridge. The church, standing in the centre of the town, is dedicated to St. John the Baptist. There is a place of worship for Baptists. A free school is endowed with the proceeds of £200, the bequest of Thomas Hammond, in 1730, and with some land assigned by the commissioners in 1765. The Bishops of Ely had formerly a palace here.

SOMERSHAM, a parish in the hundred of BOSMERE and CLAYDON, county of SUFFOLK, 6 miles (N. W. by W.) from Ipswich, containing 377 inhabitants. The living is a rectory, in the archdeaconry of Suffolk, and diocese of Norwich, rated in the king's books at £8. Mrs. Stubbin was patroness in 1807. The church is dedicated to St. Mary. There is a place of worship for Independents.

SOMERS-TOWN, a chapelry in the parish of ST. PANCRAS, Holborn division of the hundred of OSSULSTONE, county of MIDDLESEX, 2 miles (N. W.) from St. Paul's Cathedral, London. This place has, within the last thirty years, become a very populous neighbourhood, a particular description of which is given in the article on ST. PANCRAS.

SOMERTON, a parish in the hundred of PLOUGHLEY, county of OXFORD, 3½ miles (S. E.) from Deddington, containing 400 inhabitants. The living is a rectory, in the archdeaconry and diocese of Oxford, rated in the king's books at £15. 1. 10½., and in the patronage of the Rev. H. Wintle. The church is dedicated to St. James. On the north side of the tower is represented, in stone, our Saviour between two thieves, and over the communion table is a painting (after the manner of L. Da Vinci) of Christ and the Eleven Apostles at the Last Supper. In the churchyard is a handsome stone cross, having on its south side a fine crucifix in basso relievo. The river Cherwell and the Oxford and Birmingham canal pass through the parish. Here was a castle, probably built in the reign of Stephen, as appears from the will of Thomas Fernor, Esq., dated 1580, by which he bequeathed "the castle yard and chapel therein" to his executors, who erected on its site a free school, with a house for the master, and endowed it with £10 per annum, for which about fifteen boys are instructed. There is also a girls' school, endowed by the Countess of Jersey with £20 a year. Some remains of the old mansion of the Fermors still exist, particularly the large western window, which gave light to the grand hall; and very recently an apartment could be traced, termed the Prince's chamber, from its having been once occupied by James II., who, on coming to the crown, granted a charter for a fair at Somerton, which was held in a place now called Broad Pound. There is a powerful petrifying spring in the parish, forming a small cascade.

SOMERTON, a market town and parish, in the hundred of SOMERTON, county of SOMERSET, 5 miles (N. N. W.) from Ilchester, and 123 (W.S.W.) from London, containing 1643 inhabitants. This was anciently the chief town in the county. During the Saxon era, a castle was erected here which became a royal residence; it was subsequently converted into a state prison, and was the place of custody of many distinguished persons, among whom was John, King of France, who was removed hither from Hertford castle by Edward III.: its site is now occupied by the gaol, in the erection of which the materials of the ancient edifice were used. The town is situated near the river Cary, over which is a stone bridge, and consists of several narrow streets. The market is on Tuesday: fairs are on the Tuesday in Passion week, and the third, sixth, ninth, and twelfth Tuesdays following, for cattle; and September 30th and November 8th, for cattle, sheep, hogs, and pedlary. The town is governed by a bailiff and constables, annually chosen by the inhabitants; and the county magistrates hold petty sessions in the town hall, which stands in the centre of the market-place. The living is a vicarage, in the archdeaconry of Wells, and diocese of Bath and Wells, rated in the king's books at £16. 0. 7½., and in the patronage of the Earl of Ilchester. The church, which is dedicated to St. Michael, is an ancient structure, with an octagonal embattled tower on the south side. There is a place of worship for Independents. The free school was founded, in the 27th of Charles II., by Thomas Glover, who endowed it with an estate producing £10. 10. per annum, in addition to which is a rent-charge of £5, given by Alice Yates, for the education of twelve poor boys of Hurcot and Easter, in this parish. On the eastern side of the hill above the village of Hurcot are considerable quantities of fine white alabaster.

SOMERTON, a parish in the hundred of BABERGH, county of SUFFOLK, 7 miles (N. E. by N.) from Clare, containing 156 inhabitants. The living is a rectory, in the archdeaconry of Sudbury, and diocese of Norwich, rated in the king's books at £6. 16. 8., and in the patronage of the Marquis of Downshire. The church is dedicated to St. Margaret.

SOMERTON (EAST), a parish in the western division of the hundred of FLEGG, county of NORFOLK, 6¼ miles (N. N. W.) from Caistor, containing 76 inhabitants. The living is a perpetual curacy, annexed to the rectory of Winterton, in the archdeaconry and diocese of Norwich. The church, which was dedicated to St. Mary, has been long since demolished.

SOMERTON (WEST), a parish in the western division of the hundred of FLEGG, county of NORFOLK, 6¼ miles (N. W. by N.) from Caistor, containing 197 inhabitants. The living is a perpetual curacy, in the archdeaconry and diocese of Norwich, endowed with £400 private benefaction, £1000 royal bounty, and £600 parliamentary grant, and in the patronage of Thomas Groves, Esq. The church, dedicated to St.

Mary, is thatched, and has a tower round at the base, and octangular above.

SOMPTING, a parish in the hundred of BRIGHTFORD, rape of BRAMBER, county of SUSSEX, 2 miles (E. N. E.) from Worthing, containing 472 inhabitants. The living is a discharged vicarage, in the archdeaconry and diocese of Chichester, rated in the king's books at £8. 7. E. Barker, Esq. was patron in 1815. The church is a cruciform structure, principally in the early English style, with a curious tower at the west end, apparently of more ancient date: it has lately received an addition of one hundred and fourteen sittings, of which eighty-eight are free, the Incorporated Society for the enlargement of churches and chapels having granted £70 towards defraying the expense.

SONNING, a parish comprising the liberty of Eye with Dunsden, in the hundred of BINFIELD, county of OXFORD, the liberty of Early, in the hundred of CHARLTON, and the township of Sandford with Woodley, in that of SONNING, county of BERKS, 3½ miles (E.N.E.) from Reading, and containing 2493 inhabitants. The living is a vicarage, in the peculiar jurisdiction and patronage of the Dean of Salisbury, rated in the king's books at £20. 7. 1. The church is dedicated to St. Andrew. There is a place of worship for Independents. The river Thames runs through the village. During the separation of Berkshire and Wiltshire from the ancient diocese of Sherborne, this is said to have been a bishop's see, though the fact has not been clearly established: it is certain, however, that the bishops of Salisbury had a palace here, in which Isabel Queen of Richard II. resided, from the period of the king's imprisonment at Pomfret, till his lamentable death. Sir Thomas Rich, in 1766, founded a free school, and endowed it with an estate now producing about £52. 10. a year, for educating and clothing twenty poor boys, and apprenticing three of them annually in London. There are also a rent-charge of £5, the bequest of Mr. Payne, in 1709, for placing out an additional apprentice, and the interest of £500 South Sea annuities, bequeathed by Dame Harriet Read, towards educating, clothing, and apprenticing children, at the discretion of the vicar, but the latter fund has hitherto been expended in clothing only.

SOOTHILL, a township in that part of the parish of DEWSBURY which is in the lower division of the wapentake of AGBRIGG, West riding of the county of YORK, 6 miles (N. W. by W.) from Wakefield, containing 3099 inhabitants. An ancient building, now used as a malt-house, is supposed to have been originally a church, or chapel.

SOPLEY, a parish in the hundred of CHRISTCHURCH, New Forest (West) division of the county of SOUTHAMPTON, 2¾ miles (N.) from Christ-church, containing 978 inhabitants. The living is a vicarage, in the archdeaconry and diocese of Winchester, rated in the king's books at £12. 16. 10½., and in the patronage of — Willis, Esq. The church, dedicated to St. Michael, and the village, are situated on the left bank of the river Avon. There is a place of worship for Baptists.

SOPWORTH, a parish in a detached portion of the hundred of CHIPPENHAM, county of WILTS, 7½ miles (W. by S.) from Malmesbury, containing 222 inhabitants. The living is a rectory, in the archdeaconry of

Wilts, and diocese of Salisbury, rated in the king's books at £8. 10. 5., and in the patronage of the Duke of Beaufort. The church is dedicated to St. Mary.

SOTBY, a parish in the eastern division of the wapentake of WRAGGOE, parts of LINDSEY, county of LINCOLN, 5 miles (E. by N.) from Wragby, containing 128 inhabitants. The living is a discharged rectory, in the archdeaconry and diocese of Lincoln, rated in the king's books at £9. 0. 10., and in the patronage of the Crown. The church is dedicated to St. Peter.

SOTHERTON, a parish in the hundred of BLYTH-ING, county of SUFFOLK, 4¼ miles (E. N. E.) from Halesworth, containing 178 inhabitants. The living is a discharged rectory, annexed to that of Uggeshall, in the archdeaconry of Suffolk, and diocese of Norwich, rated in the king's books at £5. 6. 8. The church is dedicated to St. Andrew.

SOTTERLEY, a parish in the hundred of WANG-FORD, county of SUFFOLK, 4½ miles (S.E. by S.) from Beccles, containing 287 inhabitants. The living is a discharged rectory, in the archdeaconry of Suffolk, and diocese of Norwich, rated in the king's books at £10. M. Barne, Esq. was patron in 1805. The church is dedicated to St. Margaret.

SOTWELL, a parish in the hundred of MORETON, county of BERKS, 1¾ mile (N. W. by W.) from Walling-ford, containing 145 inhabitants. The living is a perpetual curacy, annexed to the rectory of St. Leonard, Wallingford, in the archdeaconry of Berks, and diocese of Salisbury. The church is dedicated to St. James.

SOUGHTON, a township in that part of the parish of LLANSILLIN which is in the hundred of OSWESTRY, county of SALOP, 3¾ miles (S. W. by W.) from Oswes-try, containing 249 inhabitants.

SOULBURY, a parish in the hundred of COTTES-LOE, county of BUCKINGHAM, 3 miles (W. N. W.) from Leighton-Buzzard, containing 547 inhabitants. The living is a perpetual curacy, in the archdeaconry of Buckingham, and diocese of Lincoln. Sir John Lovett, Bart. was patron in 1808. The church is dedicated to All Saints. There is a place of worship for Wesleyan Methodists. Robert Levet, in 1710, and the Rev. John Sambee, in 1728, liberally endowed with land a school for twenty-four boys and girls, one of the former to be apprenticed annually.

SOULBY, a township in the parish of DACRE, LEATH ward, county of CUMBERLAND, 5 miles (S. W.) from Penrith. The population is returned with the parish. The village is situated on the margin of the beautiful lake Ullswater.

SOULBY, a chapelry in the parish of KIRKBY-STEPHEN, EAST ward, county of WESTMORLAND, 2½ miles (N. W.) from Kirkby-Stephen, containing 251 inhabit-ants. The living is a perpetual curacy, in the archdea-conry and diocese of Carlisle, endowed with £200 pri-vate benefaction, and £200 royal bounty, and in the patronage of the Rev. Sir C. J. Musgrave, Bart. The chapel was erected in 1663, at the expense of Sir Philip Musgrave, Bart. Soulby is a considerable village, situ-ated on the river Eden, which is here crossed by a bridge of three arches, erected in 1819. Two fairs for cattle and sheep are held on the Tuesday before Easter, and August 30th; they are of recent establishment, and well attended. Three poor boys are educated for a tri-

fling annuity, the gift of several individuals since 1768.

SOULDERN, a parish in the hundred of PLOUGH-LEY, county of OXFORD, 4 miles (E. by S.) from Ded-dington, containing 491 inhabitants. The living is a rectory, in the archdeaconry and diocese of Oxford, rated in the king's books at £8. 14. 2., and in the patronage of the Master and Fellows of St. John's College, Cambridge. The church is dedicated to St. Mary. There is a place of worship for Wesleyan Me-thodists. The Oxford and Birmingham canal passes through the parish, and the river Cherwell forms the western boundary. A National school is supported partly by contributions, and partly by a sum of money left by Miss Westcarr for that purpose.

SOULDROP, a parish in the hundred of WILLEY, county of BEDFORD, 5½ miles (N. E. by N.) from Har-rold, containing 223 inhabitants. The living is a discharged rectory, united to that of Knotting, in the archdeaconry of Bedford, and diocese of Lincoln, rated in the king's books at £10. The church, dedicated to All Saints, has been rebuilt, but the ancient steeple remains.

SOULTON, a township in that part of the parish of WEM which is in the Whitchurch division of the hundred of BRADFORD (North), county of SALOP, con-taining 30 inhabitants.

SOUND, a township in the parish of WYBUNBURY, hundred of NANTWICH, county palatine of CHESTER, 3 miles (S. W. by S.) from Nantwich, containing 247 inha-bitants.

SOURTON, a parish in the hundred of LIFTON, county of DEVON, 4½ miles (S. W.) from Oakhampton, containing 546 inhabitants. The living is a perpetual curacy, annexed to the rectory of Bridestowe, in the archdeaconry of Totness, and diocese of Exeter. The church is dedicated to St. Thomas à Becket.

SOUTH-ACRE, a parish in the southern division of the hundred of GREENHOE, county of NORFOLK, 3½ miles (N. by W.) from Swaffham, containing 100 inha-bitants. The living is a rectory, in the archdeaconry of Norfolk, and diocese of Norwich, rated in the king's books at £10. 18. 1½. B. Fountain, Esq. was patron in 1802. The church is dedicated to St. George. At Rache-ness, in this parish, there was, in the time of Henry II., an hospital for lepers, subordinate to the priory of Castle-Acre.

SOUTHAM, a hamlet in the parish of BISHOP'S CLEEVE, hundred of CLEEVE, or BISHOP'S CLEEVE, county of GLOUCESTER, 2½ miles (N. E.) from Chel-tenham. The population is returned with Brock-hampton.

SOUTHAM, a market town and parish in the Southam division of the hundred of KNIGHTLOW, county of WARWICK, 10 miles (E. S. E.) from Warwick, and 84 (N.W.) from London, containing 1161 inhabit-ants. This town, anciently called Suthau, is a place of great antiquity, and had formerly a mint. In an old mansion near the centre of the town, which appears to have been built prior to the reign of Elizabeth, King Charles and his two sons are said to have slept, on the night before the battle of Edge Hill, in which a son of the Earl of Pembroke, whose monument is in the church, was slain. The parochial register for the year 1641 contains an entry of money paid to the king's footman for opening the church doors, which had been locked up and sealed by the king's order, as a punishment to the inhabitants for not ringing the bells on his entering the town. The monks of Coventry had a religious establishment here, and in Bury orchard, near the churchyard, foundations have been discovered, and many skeletons dug up : in 1741, a considerable part of the town was destroyed by fire. At Haliwell, in this parish, was a cell of Black canons, subordinate to the abbey of Rowcester in Staffordshire, whither it was removed in the 19th of Edward II. The town is pleasantly situated on an eminence rising from the eastern bank of the river Sowe, and consists of two streets: the houses in general are modern and well built, the inhabitants are well supplied with water from springs, and the surrounding scenery is pleasingly diversified. The river Stowe is crossed by a neat stone bridge of two arches, at the lower extremity of the town, and on the rising ground on the opposite side an antique mansion forms a striking contrast with the other buildings. The market, formerly on Wednesday, is now held on Monday, and is well supplied with corn : fairs are held on Easter-Monday, the Monday after Holy Thursday, and July 10th, for cattle and horses ; the last of these is a show fair, at which, in imitation of that at Coventry, the procession of Lady Godiva is celebrated. A constable and headborough are appointed annually at the court leet of the lord of the manor.

The living is a rectory, in the archdeaconry of Coventry, and diocese of Lichfield and Coventry, rated in the king's books at £22. 17.. 6., and in the patronage of the Crown. The church, which is dedicated to St. James, is a stately structure, principally in the decorated style of English architecture, with a fine tower, surmounted by a lofty spire ; in the roof of the nave, which is lighted by eight clerestory windows, adorned with tracery, is some tabernacle-work, well carved in oak. There is a place of worship for Baptists. A free school was founded in 1762, and endowed with lands, previously given for the relief of the poor, the proceeds of which amount to about £30 per annum, and the funds have been further augmented with £30 per annum from the rents of the town lands. There is also an endowment of £200 per annum for the relief of the poor and the repairs of the bridge. A self-supporting dispensary, for the relief of the sick poor, was established here, on a peculiar plan, by Mr. Smith, a resident surgeon, who has been the means of founding similar institutions in different parts of the country. An infirmary for curing diseases of the eye and ear, established by the same indefatigable gentleman, in 1818, under the patronage of the nobility and gentry of the neighbourhood, is supported by annual subscriptions and donations : it is under the management of a president, vice-president, treasurer, and a committee, and is attended by the professional gentlemen in the town and neighbourhood : the building is in the later English style, and is highly ornamental to the town. Here is a mineral spring, of similar properties to the waters at Leamington, and another called Holywell, of considerable antiquity, remarkable for the intense coldness of the water. The Rev. Mr. Holyoake, author of the first collection of English words ever published in the form of a dictionary, was at one time rector of this parish.

SOUTHAMPTON, a seaport, borough, and market town, and a county of itself, under the designation of " The Town and County of the Town of Southampton," locally in the county of Hants, 75 miles (S. W. by W.) from London, containing, according to the last census, 12,913 inhabitants, which number has since much increased. This place

Arms.

probably derives its name from the ancient British *Ant*, the original name of one of the rivers which empty themselves into its fine æstuary. To the north-east of the present town, on the opposite bank of the Itchen, the Romans had a military station, called *Clausentum*, which was succeeded by the Saxon town of *Hantune*, on the site of the present Southampton. In 838, the Danes, with a fleet of thirty-three ships, effected a landing on the coast, but were repulsed with considerable loss by Wulphere, governor of the southern part of the county, under Ethelwolf ; and in 860 they again penetrated into the county, and burned the city of Winchester. In the reign of Athelstan, two mints were established here. In 981, a party of Danish pirates having made a descent from seven large vessels, plundered the town, and laid waste the neighbouring coast. In the reign of Ethelred II., Sweyn, King of Denmark, and Olave, King of Norway, landed here with a considerable force, plundered and burned the town, massacred the inhabitants, and committed the most dreadful depredations in the surrounding country, till Ethelred purchased peace by the payment of £16,000, on the receipt of which, the invaders retired to Hantune, where they embarked for their own kingdom. Canute, after his establishment on the throne, made this town his occasional residence ; and it was whilst seated on the beach here, at the influx of the tide, that he took occasion to make that memorable reproof of his courtiers, for their gross flattery, which has been recorded by historians. At the time of the Conquest, the town was so much reduced by the repeated incursions of the Danes, that, at the Norman survey, the king had only seventy-nine demesne tenants. Henry II. and his queen landed at this port, on their return from France, in 1174. In the reign of John, Adam de Port was governor of the castle ; and in that of Edward III., the town was completely destroyed by the French and their allies, the Spaniards and Genoese, but they were repulsed, with the loss of the Prince of Sicily and other commanders. Richard II. enlarged the castle, and strengthened the fortifications that had been erected for the defence of the town and harbour. Henry V., previously to the battle of Agincourt, marshalled his army here for his expedition against France, and, during his stay in the town, detected a conspiracy formed against him by the Lords Cambridge and Scroop, and Sir Thomas Grey, who were here executed for treason, and buried in the chapel of an ancient hospital, still remaining, called God's House. In the reign of Edward IV., Southampton was the scene of a sanguinary contest between the partisans of the houses of York and Lancaster, in which the former having gained the victory, many of the Lancastrian chiefs were, by the king's order, executed with extreme barbarity. The town had increased materially in extent and importance, and its trade had become so flourishing that, in the reign of Edward V., the Lord Mayor of London was appointed collector of the king's duties at this port. In 1512, Grey, Marquis of Dorset, embarked here with a force for the assistance of Ferdinand, King of Spain; and ten years after, the Emperor Charles V. sailed from it, on his return to his own dominions, after having visited Henry VIII. Edward VI., in his tour through the western and southern parts of the kingdom, for the benefit of his health, visited the town, and was sumptuously entertained by the mayor and corporation. Philip, King of Spain, on his arrival in England to espouse Queen Mary, landed at this port, and was entertained at the sheriff's house by the mayor and his brethren, who sent him a present of wine, which he received on board his ship, the *Grace de Dieu*, then lying in the harbour.

The town is beautifully situated on a peninsular tract of ground, rising with a gradual ascent from the north-eastern shore of Southampton water, and bounded on the east by the river Itchen, over which is a bridge leading to Gosport; and on the south and west by the fine open bay formed by the confluence of the Itchen with the river Test. The shores of the bay, or æstuary, are richly clothed with wood, and afford a succession of beautifully diversified scenery, the vicinity being studded with villages, mansions, and villas. Southampton water, about two miles broad at its entrance near Calshot castle, stretches north-westward nearly seven miles : on the eastern shore are the ruins of Netley abbey, forming an object romantically picturesque. The town, rising gradually from the margin of the water, is distinguished for the beauty of its situation; and the approach from the London road, through an avenue of stately elms and a well-built suburb, is striking. The principal entrance is through Bar gate, one of the ancient gates, on the north front of which are two gigantic figures representing Sir Bevois of Southampton and the giant Ascupart, whom, according to legendary tale, Bevois is said to have slain in combat. From this gate, which is embattled and machicolated, a spacious street, more than half a mile in length, and equal to many of the finer streets of the metropolis, leads directly to the quay, for the improvement of which the old Water gate was taken down about twenty-five years since. The ancient part of the town was formerly enclosed with walls nearly a mile and a quarter in circuit, of which, with their ruined circular towers, considerable portions are still entire, the principal being that reaching from the south-east of West gate, along the shore northward. Of the ancient gates, the principal now remaining are West gate and South gate, in addition to Bar gate, in relation to which last the more modern part of the town is distinguished, by the appellation of Above Bar, from the other part, which is called Below Bar. In that part Above Bar are many fine ranges of building. A new street of handsome houses has been recently erected, leading from the street Above Bar to the western shore, with a terrace, commanding a fine view of the surrounding scenery. The town is well paved, lighted with gas, and supplied with excellent water, chiefly from springs collected on an adjoining

common, and conveyed from a reservoir into public conduits, as well as into many of the houses. The handsome iron pillars for the gas-lights were presented by William Chamberlayne, Esq., late member for the borough, in commemoration of whose munificence, the inhabitants have erected on the quay a lofty cast-iron column, supporting a splendid gas-light. A Literary and Philosophical Society, recently established by a proprietary of thirty members, is further supported by an unlimited number of annual subscribers of £1. 1. : lectures are given periodically, and the business of the institution is conducted by a president and committee. In the lecture-room of this institution, during the six months of the year in which it is unoccupied by the society, there is an exhibition of paintings for sale, which is well attended, and considerably resorted to by the numerous visitors frequenting this place. The library and reading-rooms in the High-street, at which a book of arrivals is regularly kept, are amply supplied with volumes in every department of literature, and with periodical works, and the establishment is liberally supported by subscription : there are also two circulating libraries and several reading-rooms in other parts of the town, together with billiard-rooms elegantly fitted up. Near the platform is a subscription bowling-green. There are two sets of assembly-rooms, one called the Long Rooms, erected on the west side of the town, in 1761 ; and the other, recently erected, called the Archery Rooms : these rooms command an extensive view of the bay and the scenery of the opposite shore. The theatre, in French-street, is well arranged and tastefully decorated : performances take place three evenings in the week during the season, which commences in August. Races are held annually in the autumn, and continue two days : the course, which is well adapted to the purpose, is pleasantly situated on Southampton common, and was given to the town by the corporation. The Botanic gardens, on the west bank of the Southampton water, form an agreeable promenade, and contain a very extensive collection of indigenous and exotic plants, constantly keeping pace with the improved state of botanical science and discovery. There are three lodges of Freemasons. An annual regatta takes place during the summer, in which prizes, given by subscription, are contested for by yachts and small vessels belonging to the fishermen of Itchen, on the Southampton river; than which none can be more favourably adapted to aquatic excursions, from the bay being so beautiful and finely sheltered.

The salubrity of the air, and the beauty of its situation, have made Southampton a resort for sea-bathing; and hot, cold, medicated, and vapour baths have been constructed. In addition to those previously established, a handsome and commodious building has been erected, in the Grecian style of architecture, at an expense of £7000, near the platform on the beach, and provided with baths of every kind, with an elegant and spacious promenade-room attached, commanding a good view of the water, which, during the summer season, is covered with pleasure boats, and with fine yachts. Numerous respectable lodging-houses are let for the accommodation of visitors. On the beach is a causeway planted with trees, extending above half a mile. On the platform, which has been much enlarged, is an ancient piece of ordnance, presented by Henry VIII., and recently mounted on a handsome cast-iron carriage, the gift of John Fleming, Esq., member for the county. The barracks, erected here during the late war, and occupying about two acres of land, were, in 1816, considerably enlarged, and converted into a military asylum, as a branch of the institution at Chelsea, under the patronage of the late Duke of York, for the orphan children of soldiers, and of those whose mothers are dead, and their fathers absent on service : the buildings are of brick, handsome and commodious, and are appropriated to the reception of female children only. At Itchen Ferry, and on the western side of the town, are bathing-machines, with experienced guides. The environs are equally remarkable for the varied beauty of their scenery, and for the number of elegant mansions and villas. In addition to the numerous attractions which the town itself possesses, and the facilities afforded for aquatic excursions, there are, in various directions, extensive rides through a country abounding with objects of extreme interest, and enriched with a great variety of scenery.

The port, of which the jurisdiction extends from Langstone harbour, on the east, to Hurst castle on the west, and midway from Calshot castle to the Isle of Wight, carries on a considerable foreign trade: the imports are wine and fruit from Portugal; hemp, iron, and tallow, from Russia; pitch and tar from Sweden ; and timber from other ports of the Baltic: it has also a considerable trade with Jersey and Guernsey. By act of parliament of Edward III., making Southampton one of the staple ports for the exportation of wool, all cargoes of that material, not originally shipped to those islands from this port, must either be re-landed here, or pay a duty at the custom-house. A coasting trade is also carried on with Wales, from which it imports iron and slates ; with Newcastle, from which it imports coal, lead, and glass ; and with various other places. The quay, on which stands a convenient custom-house, is accessible to vessels of two hundred and fifty tons' burden, and is commodiously adapted to the dispatch of business. Belonging to the port are one hundred and seventy-five vessels, averaging a burden of forty-five tons. The harbour is spacious, and affords good anchorage for ships, which may ride at all times in security, being sheltered from all winds. Steam vessels proceed regularly, all the summer and autumn, from this port to Havre, and to Jersey and Guernsey ; and there are sailing-packets on the same destination at all other seasons daily : steam-packets afford a constant communication with the Isle of Wight and Portsmouth in summer and autumn, and sailing vessels at other times. The trade of the town principally arises from the wants of the inhabitants and visitors. The trade is facilitated by the Itchen canal navigation to Winchester, the river itself being navigable as far as Northam ; and a seventy-four gun ship and several frigates were built in the docks here during the late war. A canal to Salisbury, with a view to open a communication between this town and Bristol, was projected about thirty-five years since ; but the design, after having been partly carried into effect, was abandoned, the capital having been expended before half of the work was completed. The market days are Tuesday, Thursday, Friday, and Saturday ; the market on Friday is for corn : the markets are well supplied with fish, eggs, poultry, and provisions of every kind. The fairs are on May 6th and 7th, for cows and pigs, and on Trinity Monday and Tuesday : the latter, a very ancient fair, is proclaimed by the mayor with particular ceremony on the preceding Saturday, and continues till the Wednesday noon following ; during which time the senior bailiff presides and entertains the corporation in a booth erected on the occasion : this fair, which is principally for horses, cattle, and pigs, is held on the eastern side of the town, near the site of an ancient hermitage, formerly occupied by William Geoffrey, to whom its revenue, arising from standings, &c., was originally granted ; a court of pie-powder is attached to it, and during its continuance all persons are free from arrest for debt within the precincts of the borough.

Corporate Seal.

Obverse. Reverse.

The inhabitants were first incorporated in the reign of Henry I., whose charter was confirmed by Richard I., and by John, who assigned the customs of the port, together with those of Portsmouth, to the burgesses, for an annual payment of £200 : their privileges were extended and confirmed by Henry VI., who erected the town, with a surrounding district, into a county of itself, and were modified by Charles I., by whose charter the government is vested in a mayor, sheriff, two bailiffs, an indefinite number of aldermen, and twenty-four common council-men, assisted by a recorder, town clerk, two coroners, four serjeants at mace, and subordinate officers. The mayor, who is also admiral of the port, the late mayor, the recorder, five senior aldermen, and two senior common council-men, together with the Bishop of Winchester, are justices of the peace within the borough and liberties. The freedom is obtained only by election of the corporation, who have the right of nominating an indefinite number of burgesses ; among many illustrious personages to whom the freedom of the borough has been given were, Frederick, Prince of Wales, the then Dukes of York and Cumberland, George III., the late Duke of Cumberland, and his late Majesty George IV. The corporation hold quarterly courts of session for all offences not capital ; and they have the privilege of holding assizes, when the judges are travelling the western circuit, to try for capital crimes committed within the limits of the town and county of the town. The mayor and bailiffs hold a court of record every Tuesday, for the recovery of debts to any amount. The inhabitants paying scot and lot have right of common on the Town Lands, adjoining the town, the most extensive of which is Southampton common, containing about three hundred and fifty acres. The audit-house is a handsome building, erected about fifty years since, comprising in the upper story a spacious hall, in which the business of the corporation is transacted, and the records and regalía are deposited; among the latter, which are splendid, is a silver oar borne before the mayor on public occasions, as the ensign of his admiralty jurisdiction. The guildhall is a spacious room above the arches of the ancient Bar gate, which is a beautiful and venerable structure in the Norman style of architecture : the principal archway is deeply moulded and enriched, and is flanked by circular embattled turrets, and the approach is ornamented with two lions sejant, cast in lead, presented to the corporation in 1744, in lieu of two which were decayed, by William Lee, Esq., on his being elected a burgess ; the south side of the gateway is neatly faced with stone, with a niche in the centre, in which is a statue of George III., presented to the corporation by the late Marquis of Lansdowne, to replace a decayed figure of Queen Anne : the hall, in which the borough sessions and other courts are held, is fifty-two feet in length, and twenty-one feet wide, and is lighted with four handsome windows ; adjoining it are a room for the grand jury, and other apartments. The common gaol for the borough comprises four rooms for twelve prisoners, but does not admit of classification. The bridewell, to which female prisoners alone are committed, contains three rooms, capable of receiving ten prisoners, and a small chapel, in which divine service is performed once in the week. The sheriff's prison for debtors contains two wards, and is adapted to the reception of ten prisoners. The borough exercised the elective franchise in the 23rd of Edward I., since which time it has regularly returned two members to parliament : the right of election is vested in the burgesses, resident and non-resident, and in the inhabitants generally paying scot and lot, of whom the number exceeds nine hundred : the mayor and bailiffs are the returning officers.

Southampton comprises the parishes of All Saints, Holy Rood, St. John and St. Lawrence united, St. Mary, and St. Michael, all, with the exception of St. Mary's, in the archdeaconry and diocese of Winchester. The living of All Saints' is a discharged rectory, rated in the king's books at £8. 1. 10½., endowed with £300 private benefaction, and £200 royal bounty, and in the patronage of the Crown : the church, rebuilt on the enlarged site of an ancient structure, is in the Grecian style of architecture, with a turret at the east end rising from a square pedestal, and surrounded by six Corinthian columns, supporting a circular entablature surmounted by a dome. The west entrance is ornamented with four three-quarter columns of the Ionic order, supporting a triangular pediment; an entablature, resting upon Ionic pilasters, surrounds the building, which is of brick stuccoed ; the interior, of which the roof is arched and handsomely panelled, is neatly arranged ; the altar is within a deep recess, formed by the arch supporting the tower, and is lighted by a handsome window on each side : the area underneath the church is divided into arched catacombs, in one of which are deposited the remains of Captain Carteret, the clebrated circumnavigator, and of Bryan Edwards, author of the "History of the West Indies ;" and on the north side of the altar is a mural tablet to the memory of the Rev. Dr. Mant, many years rector of the parish. The living of Holy Rood parish is a discharged vicarage, rated in the king's books at £12. 1. 10½., and in the patronage of the Provost and Fellows of Queen's College, Oxford :

the church is an ancient structure in the High-street; with a tower and spire at the south-west angle, and has a portico in front, within which the hustings are erected at elections of members for the borough : among the monuments is one by Rysbrach to Miss E. Stanley, sister of the Rt. Hon. Hans Stanley, with an epitaph written by the poet Thomson, who has immortalized her memory in his poem of the Seasons. The living of St. John's is a discharged rectory, rated in the king's books at £6. 13. 4., and united to that of St. Lawrence : the church is demolished. The living of the parish of St. Lawrence is a discharged rectory, with that of St. John's annexed, rated in the king's books at £7. 10., endowed with £800 royal bounty, and £800 parliamentary grant, and in the patronage of the Crown: the church is a small ancient building. The living of St. Mary's is a rectory, in the precinct of the town, rated in the king's books at £37. 5. 5., in the peculiar jurisdiction of the Rector, and in the patronage of the Bishop of Winchester: the church is modern, with a very extensive churchyard, which is the principal cemetery of the town. The living of St. Michael's is a discharged vicarage, rated in the king's books at £12. 11. 10½., endowed with £400 private benefaction, £400 royal bounty, and £400 parliamentary grant, and in the patronage of the Crown : the church is an ancient and spacious structure, principally in the Norman style of architecture, with a tower between the nave and the chancel, surmounted by a lofty and well-proportioned octagonal spire: the interior has been recently repaired, and has undergone considerable alterations, with the addition of nine hundred seats, seven hundred of them free, by grant of £350 from the Incorporated Society for the enlargement of churches and chapels : the massive circular columns that supported the roof have been replaced with lighter octangular pillars, and sharply pointed arches ; the windows are of a later style, and the tracery of the large west window has been carefully restored, and the upper compartments embellished with stained glass ; a new window of elegant design has been placed by the corporation in the chapel of this church, in which, from time immemorial, the mayors have been sworn into office: the ancient font, of Norman character and highly enriched, has been removed from an obscure situation at the east end of the church, and placed in the central area underneath the tower : there are some ancient monuments, and in the chapel is an old cenotaph of Lord Chancellor Wriothesley, who in the reign of Henry VIII. passed sentence of death on Queen Anne Boleyn. St. Paul's, a proprietary chapel in the parish of All Saints, a handsome edifice in the later style of English architecture, has been recently erected, under the superintendence of a committee. There is a handsome and commodious place of worship for Independents ; a neat one for Baptists ; others for the Society of Friends and Wesleyan Methodists ; one in which the liturgy of the Church of England is read, but the service is conducted by a dissenting minister ; and a neat Roman Catholic chapel of recent erection.

The free grammar school was founded in the reign of Edward VI.: the master is appointed by the corporation, who have recently erected a convenient schoolhouse, capable of accommodating forty boarders, on the site of an ancient edifice, called Westhall : the endowment produces not more than about £30 per annum :

among other eminent men who have been educated in this school was the celebrated Dr. Watts, a native of Southampton, whose father kept a boarding-school in the town. A charity school was founded, in 1760, for qualifying twenty boys for the sea service, by Alderman Taunton, of this town, who left considerable funds for charitable uses: the original number of scholars has, by a decree of the court of Chancery, been reduced to ten, who are permitted to choose any mechanical trade, if they prefer it, and receive an apprentice fee of £5, and, on the expiration of their indentures, a present of £5.5., on producing a certificate of good conduct: pensions of £10 per annum were also paid from these funds to six decayed persons of the town, of whom the number has been increased to sixteen by a bequest of the late Charles D'Aussy, Esq.; and £40 per annum is appropriated from the same funds, as a reward for female servants, and a portion on their marriage. A National school, in which are one hundred and fifty boys, and the same number of girls, and a Lancasterian school, in which nearly the same number of both sexes are educated, are supported by subscription. There are also several infant schools, and various Sunday schools in connexion with the established church and the dissenting congregations. The ancient hospital of Domus Dei, or God's House, was originally founded in the reign of Henry III., partly as a convent for nuns, and as a chapel to a neighbouring friary, which was burned by the French in the reign of Edward III., by whom it was given to Queen's College, Oxford; after various changes it was established as an hospital for a warden, four brothers, and four sisters, who, in addition to their residence, have an allowance of two shillings a week from the college, and an annual supply of coal from other bequests: the buildings are ancient, and retain much of their original character; the ancient chapel was long used as a place of worship by the French Protestants. The hospital of St. John, on the site of which the present theatre has been built, consisted of a master and six boys; the latter are now taught the woollen manufacture in the workhouse, a spacious building well adapted to that and other purposes. Thorner's almshouses, a neat and commodious range of building, receiving their name from the funds for erecting them having arisen from a bequest by Robert Thorner, Esq., in 1690, for gradual accumulation, were originally built in 1789, and have lately been enlarged: they now accommodate twenty-six widows, who are allowed four shillings a week each. The same benefactor also bequeathed funds for apprenticing a certain number of poor children, with a premium of £5 each, and a present of £5 on expiration of the term of apprenticeship. Almshouses in St. Mary's parish were founded, in 1565, by Richard Butler, mayor, and built on ground given by Thomas Lynton, mayor, in 1545. Six small unendowed tenements, near the workhouse, of which the origin is unknown, are appropriated by the corporation as residences for the poor. The penitentiary, or refuge for destitute females, supported by donations and subscription, is a spacious and commodious building, with a handsome chapel attached to it, recently erected in front of Kingsland-place, and conducted on a plan well calculated to reclaim and restore to society unfortunate females, who are here accustomed to regular and industrious habits, and qualified for employment as servants. The public dispensary was established in

1823, for the relief of poor invalids not receiving parochial aid, and is gratuitously attended by the physicians and surgeons of the town, who visit patients at their own houses: it is under the direction of a president and committee, and is liberally supported by subscription. The ladies' lying-in charity was established in 1812, and, under the direction of a committee of ladies, administers extensive relief and assistance to the poor at their own houses. Miss Elizabeth Bird bequeathed £1400 three per cents. to the mayor and corporation, in trust, for the annual payment of £5 each to six unmarried women, members of the church of England, and upwards of sixty years of age, who must appear every Sunday at church, wearing a silver medal with the device of the testator, and dine together, at a table prepared for them by the rector of All Saints' parish, to whom she bequeathed a sum for that purpose. There are a Royal Humane Society, and several benefit and friendly societies. A repository for the sale of works, drawings, and other productions of the necessitous, was established in 1828, under the patronage of Her present Majesty, when Duchess of Clarence: by this institution, fifty children are taught and employed in netting, till of an age to go to service; they pursue their employment in the cottages of their parents, and generally earn about five shillings a week. There are various charitable bequests for distribution among the poor. The ancient castle, which was repaired and strengthened by Richard II., was situated on the west side of the town: the walls included a semicircular area, the town wall towards the sea forming the chord; the keep was situated in the south part of the area. Of this fortress there are no vestiges: the ruins and the site became the property of the late Marquis of Lansdowne, who erected a handsome castellated mansion on the spot, at an expense of £70,000, which, after his death, was sold as building materials, and taken down, and a chapel and several tenements were erected on its site. At Bittern, about a mile and a quarter from the town, supposed to have been the old station *Clausentum*, numerous Roman antiquities have been discovered, among which were considerable vestiges of a fortification, and a portion of a Roman wall, coins from the reign of Claudius to those of Valentinian and Valens, tesselated pavements, bricks, fragments of pottery, urns, vases, and sculptured stones, on several of which were Roman inscriptions. Southampton gives the title of baron to the family of Fitzroy.

SOUTHAMPTON (COUNTY of), a maritime county on the southern coast, bounded on the east by the counties of Surrey and Sussex, on the north by that of Berks, on the west by Wiltshire and Dorsetshire, and on the south by the English Channel. Including the Isle of Wight, it extends from 50° 36' to 51° 23'(N. Lat.), and from 45' to 1° 53' (W. Lon.); and comprises an area of upwards of one thousand six hundred and twenty-eight square miles, or one million forty-one thousand nine hundred and twenty statute acres. The population, in 1821, was 283,298.

At the period of the invasion of Britain by Cæsar, the southern parts of this district formed a portion of the territory of the Regni; and the more northern tracts, part of that of the Belgæ, who had come over from Gaul, and violently dispossessed the former inhabitants. Under the Romans, it was included in the division called *Britannia Prima*. The Isle of Wight, called by the Ro-

R

mans *Vectis*, is mentioned by Suetonius as having been conquered by Vespasian, about the year 43: no other traces of Roman occupation have, however, been at any time discovered in it than a few coins. At a subsequent period, the inhabitants of this part of the country bravely defended themselves against the fierce invasions of the Saxons. In the year 501, about fifty years after the first arrival of Hengist in Kent, Cerdic made a descent upon these shores at Charford, and a band of his allies, under Porta, effected a landing, with the crews of two ships, at Portsmouth. On the establishment of the kingdom of Wessex, by Cerdic, a great part of the county was included within the limits of that kingdom, at the same time that a part of its southern shores, together with the Isle of Wight, was comprised in the Saxon kingdom of Kent. The only British king whom the Saxons mention in the battles that preceded the establishment of this West Saxon kingdom, was Natanleod, who appears only in one great battle, fought in the tract now constituting the New Forest, in 508, in which he fell, with five thousand of his men; and such was the extent of his disaster, that all the territory near the scene of conflict was afterwards called by his name. In 519, Cerdic and his son Cynric obtained a victory over the Britons at Cerdices-ford, and from this time the Saxon Chronicle dates the reign of the West Saxon kings. In 528, another conflict is mentioned at Cerdices-leah, but its issue is not stated; and, in 530, Cerdic and his son conquered the Isle of Wight with great slaughter. This chieftain, who died in 534, appears only to have maintained himself in the district where he landed, and Mr. Whitaker thinks that all his operations were confined to this county; but his posterity enlarged his settlement into a kingdom so powerful as finally to absorb every other similar establishment in the island: its capital city was Winchester. In the year 661, the Isle of Wight was subdued by Wulfere, King of Mercia, who bestowed it upon the king of the South Saxons; but Ceadwalla, King of Wessex, a descendent of Cerdic's, retook it about fifteen years afterwards.

The next remarkable occurrence upon record is, that a large fleet of the northern *vikingr*, or sea-kings, suddenly appeared off the coast of this county, in 860, and ravaged the country as far as Winchester, which city they plundered; but, being pursued on returning to their ships, they were overtaken, and defeated by the Earls of Hampshire and Berkshire. In 787, the Isle of Wight was seized by the Danes, who apparently designed to make it a place of retreat, whither they might retire with their plunder from the neighbouring coasts. How long they maintained themselves here is uncertain; but, in the reign of Alfred, they again landed on the island, and plundered the inhabitants. At Basing, in 870, the kings of Wessex, Ethelred and Alfred, were defeated by the North men. In 1001, in the reign of Ethelred, the Danes once more seized the Isle of Wight, and kept possession of it for many years after; and at Winchester, on November 13th, 1002, began the general massacre of that people, by Ethelred order. In the reign of Edward the Confessor, the Isle of Wight was twice plundered by Earl Godwin, and again, in the reign of Harold, by Earl Tosti. The ancient British name of this district was *Gwent*, or *Y Went*, a term descriptive of its open downs; and hence the appellation *Caer Gwent*, or the city of the

Gwentians, now Winchester. When the Saxon dominions in Britain were divided into shires, this district received the name of *Hamtunscyre*, from the ancient name of the present town of Southampton: this was afterwards corrupted into *Hamptescyre*, and hence its modern appellations of Hampshire and Hants. The name of the Isle of Wight is considered, by Mr. Whitaker and other antiquaries, to have been derived from the British word *Guith*, or *Guict*, signifying, the divorced or separated, and apparently indicating a supposition of its having once been connected with the main land: hence also arose its Roman name of *Vectis*, or the separated region: by the Saxons it was called *Weet*. It was off this island, in 1080, that William the Conqueror surprised his brother, the Bishop of Baieux, when setting out on his expedition to Italy; and in it he assembled the Norman chiefs, in whose presence he sentenced the bishop to imprisonment for quitting the realm without his permission.

Between the period of the battle of Hastings, in 1066, and the Norman survey in 1086, William laid waste a large tract of country, in the south-western part of Hampshire, for the purpose of making a royal chase, destroying a great number of villages, together with no fewer than thirty-six parochial churches. The accidents that occurred to the family of the Conqueror in the New Forest (as this extensive waste has ever since been called) were regarded, by the oppressed Saxons, with a sort of patriotic superstition, as judgments for the cruelty of which that monarch had been guilty in forming it. In 1081, Richard, son of William, died, in consequence of having been dashed against a tree by his horse, in this forest; in 1100, Richard, son of Duke Robert, and nephew to William Rufus, was killed there by an arrow discharged inadvertently; and William II. himself perished in this forest by a similar accident, in July of the same year. Winchester, from the earliest period of the Saxon kingdom of Wessex, had been the residence of the West Saxon monarchs; and, after the subjection of the other kingdoms of the Octarchy to the dominion of the sovereigns of Wessex, it continued to be one of the principal seats of the Saxon kings of England, as it was also of those of the Norman race, after the Conquest. The proximity of the New Forest to this city occasioned it to be the most frequented of the royal chases. Immediately on the death of William Rufus, his younger brother, Henry, hastened to Winchester, possessed himself of the royal treasure, and thence returned to London, where he was crowned. In 1101, however, Robert, Duke of Normandy, the Conqueror's eldest son, landed from the continent, with an army, at Portsmouth, to dispossess his brother of the crown which he had usurped, when an accommodation was effected through the mediation of the barons. At Portsmouth also, in 1140, the Empress Maud and her brother Robert, Earl of Gloucester, landed, with only one hundred and forty attendants, designing to wrest the crown from the usurper Stephen; and, in the internal commotions that ensued, this county was the scene of much bloodshed. At Winchester, the king's forces and those of the empress carried on active military operations against each other for the space of seven weeks, the latter being ultimately compelled to retreat into the castle, which was thereupon vigorously

SOUTHAMPTON

besieged: the empress escaped by stratagem, and fled to Gloucester ; but her troops, marching out, were pursued by the royal army, and the Earl of Gloucester was taken prisoner at Stockbridge. On an exchange of prisoners (the earl being given up by one party, and King Stephen by the other), the earl again came to Winchester, but was compelled to abandon it by an army collected from the surrounding country.

King John, having been compelled to sign Magna Charta, at Runymede, retired to the Isle of Wight, where he remained pending his correspondence with the pope for absolution from the oaths that he had then taken, and whilst raising, on the continent, the mercenary troops which he afterwards employed to revenge himself on the barons. In 1016, in the sequel of the same contest, Odiham castle was defended for John, by only three officers and ten men, against Louis the Dauphin and his army, for the space of fifteen days. In the year 1338, the town of Southampton was plundered and burned by a force consisting of French, Spaniards, and Genoese ; but the son of the king of Sicily, one of three hundred of the invaders, was slain. In the year 1346, on July 6th, Edward III., and his son, Edward, the Black Prince, sailed from Southampton with the army with which they afterwards gained the victory of Crecy. In the reigns of Edward III. and Richard II., the Isle of Wight was several times assaulted by the French, and partially plundered. Carisbrooke castle, then the only fortress in it, was besieged by these invaders in the year 1377, but without success, and with great loss to the assailants. In this expedition, the French burned the village of Rye, and the towns of Yarmouth and Newtown, and levied a contribution of one thousand marks upon the inhabitants, whose non-resistance on oath they exacted in the event of their revisiting it within a year. In 1415, at Southampton, where Henry V. was preparing to embark with the army that afterwards distinguished itself on the plain of Agincourt, the conspiracy against the life of that monarch was discovered, for which the Earl of Cambridge and Sir Thomas Grey suffered death. The lordship of the Isle of Wight, in the 17th of Henry VI., came into the possession of Humphrey, Duke of Gloucester, to whom it had been granted in reversion, who seems to have enjoyed it until his death; although, two years previously to that event, Henry Beauchamp, Duke of Warwick, was made king of the Isle of Wight, by patent from Henry VI., the king himself assisting at the ceremony of his coronation : this nobleman died soon after, without male issue. At Beaulieu abbey, in 1471, Margaret of Anjou, and her son, Prince Edward, took sanctuary, on hearing of the defeat and death of the Earl of Warwick, until, being joined by the Duke of Somerset and other partisans, the queen was persuaded once more to enter the field. Sir Edward Widville, in the first of Henry VII., was made captain of the Isle of Wight ; and, about three years afterwards, to ingratiate himself with the king, he persuaded the inhabitants to undertake an expedition to France, in aid of the Duke of Brittany, who was then in arms against the French monarch. From the numbers that flocked to his standard he selected about forty gentlemen and four hundred of the commonalty, and embarked with them for Brittany, in four vessels. In a battle fought at St. Aubin's, Sir Edward and all the English were slain, excepting one boy, who brought

home the melancholy tidings. To encourage the population of the island, so much reduced by this slaughter, an act was soon afterwards passed, prohibiting any of the inhabitants from holding lands, farms, or tithes, above the annual rent of ten marks. Perkin Warbeck, after his repulse before Exeter, in 1498, took sanctuary at Beaulieu, whence he surrendered himself to Henry VII., on promise of his life being spared. In 1573, the Emperor Charles V., who had been entertained at Winchester by Henry VIII., embarked at Southampton to return to Spain. In the thirty-sixth of the same reign, the French landed two thousand men in the Isle of Wight, from the fleet commanded by D'Annebaut, who began to plunder and burn the villages, but were suddenly attacked by the captain of the island, Sir R. Worsley, and compelled to retreat to their ships, with the loss of their general and a considerable number of men : several forts were soon after constructed on different parts of the coast of this island. At Southampton, July 21st, 1554, Philip, Prince of Spain, afterwards Philip II., landed, and was united in marriage, on July 25th, at Winchester, to Mary, Queen of England. At Portsmouth, in 1628, George Villiers, Duke of Buckingham, whilst preparing to embark, as commander of an expedition to relieve the Protestants of Rochelle, was assassinated by Felton.

Early in the civil war of the seventeenth century, the parliament obtained possession of the Isle of Wight, by the removal of Jerome, Earl of Portland, who was attached to the royal cause ; and, shortly after, Carisbrook castle was taken from the Countess of Portland and Col. Brett, to whom the king had entrusted it, by the Newport militia, aided by four hundred auxiliaries from vessels lying in the Medina river. The other forts in the island were also, in like manner, seized for the parliament, who appointed Philip, Earl of Pembroke, its governor ; and it thenceforward happily escaped being a scene of that warfare which soon after desolated almost every other part of the kingdom : indeed, the security here enjoyed induced many families from the main land to take refuge in the island, until the period of the Restoration. In December 1643, in an engagement at Alton, in this county, the royalist Col. Bowles was killed, and his regiment taken prisoners, by the parliamentarian forces under Sir William Waller; and, in October 1645, Basing House, which had been heroically defended by the Marquis of Winchester, from August 1643, was at length stormed and taken by Cromwell in person. In 1647, Charles I., after his escape from Hampton Court, remained in concealment at Titchfield House, in this county, until he there surrendered himself to Col. Hammond, then Governor of the Isle of Wight, by whom he was conveyed to Carisbrook castle. After having been detained there, first as guest, and afterwards as prisoner, for the space of thirteen months, he was removed in close custody to Hurst castle, by a detachment of the parliamentarian army, on November 29th, 1648, whence he was shortly after conducted to London. At Portsmouth, on May 14th, 1662, landed Catherine, Infanta of Portugal, who was the next day given in marriage to Charles II. Bishop's Waltham and its neighbourhood, in the early part of the last century, were infested by a daring gang of depredators, who, from their custom of blacking their faces to prevent discovery, were termed

"Waltham Blacks," and to repress whose excesses the famous Black Act was passed, in the 9th of George II., 1723. Shortly after the termination of the decisive campaign of 1815, His Majesty's ship Bellerophon appeared off Portsmouth, having on board Napoleon Buonaparte, who had submitted himself to the mercy of the British government.

William the Conqueror, on his accession to the throne of England, granted the lordship of the Isle of Wight, with a palatine jurisdiction, to his kinsman, William Fitz-Osbert. It afterwards several times escheated to, and otherwise became vested in, the crown, and was as often granted to different noble families. Whether the Sir Edward Widville in the time of Henry VII., before mentioned, had received a grant of the lordship of it, is uncertain; but since the period of his death it has remained in the possession of the Crown, although some lands annexed to the castle at Carisbrook continue to be holden by the governor *jure officii*. From the time that Edward I. purchased this lordship of Isabella de Fortibus, the defence of the island was generally entrusted to some person nominated by the crown, who was at first distinguished by the appellation of warden, afterwards by that of captain and, in later times, by that of governor.

This county is included in the diocese of Winchester, and province of Canterbury: the archdeaconry of Winchester is co-extensive with the county, and comprises the deaneries of Alresford, Alton, Andover, Basingstoke, Droxford, Fordingbridge, Sombourn, Southampton, Isle of Wight, and Winchester: the total number of parishes is three hundred and five, of which one hundred and fifty-four are rectories, seventy-two vicarages, and the remainder perpetual curacies. For purposes of civil government it is parcelled into the divisions of Alton (North), comprising the liberty of Alresford, and the hundreds of Alton, Bishop's Sutton, and Selborne; Alton (South), comprising the hundreds of East-Meon and Finch-Dean; Andover, comprising the hundreds of Andover, Barton-Stacey, King's-Sombourn, Thorngate, and Wherwell; Basingstoke, comprising the hundreds of Basingstoke, Bermondspit, Crondall, Holdshott, Mitcheldever, and Odiham; Fawley, comprising the hundreds of Bountisborough, Buddlesgate, Fawley, Mainsborough, and Mansbridge; Kingsclere, comprising the hundreds of Chutely, Evingar, Kingsclere, Overton, and Pastrow; New Forest (East), comprising the liberties of Beaulieu, Dibden, and Lymington, and the hundreds of New Forest (East), New Forest (North), and Redbridge, and parts of Ringwood and Bishop's-Waltham; New Forest (West), comprising the liberties of Breamore and Westover, and the hundreds of Christchurch, Fordingbridge, and part of Ringwood; Portsdown, comprising the liberties of Alverstoke with Gosport, and Havant, and the hundreds of Bosmere, Fareham, Hambledon, Meon-Stoke, Portsdown, Titchfield, and part of Bishop's-Waltham; and Isle of Wight, comprising the liberties of East and West Medina. It contains the city of Winchester; the borough, market, and sea-port towns of Christchurch, Lymington, Newport, Portsmouth, Southampton, and Yarmouth; the borough and market towns of Andover, Petersfield, Stockbridge, and Whitchurch; the borough and sea-port town of Newtown; the small sea-port towns of Emsworth (a dependency

on the harbour of Portsmouth) and Brading; and the market towns of New Alresford, Alton, Basingstoke, Fareham, Fordingbridge, Gosport, Havant, Kingsclere, Odiham, Ringwood, Romsey, and Bishop's-Waltham. Two knights are returned to parliament for the shire, two representatives for the city of Winchester, and two for each of the boroughs: the county members are elected at Winchester. Hampshire is included in the western circuit: the assizes and quarter sessions are held at Winchester. There are one hundred and ten acting magistrates. The rates raised in the county for the year ending March 25th, 1827, amounted to £213,406. 4. 0., the expenditure to £210,526. 13., of which, £184,928. 18., was applied to the relief of the poor.

The form of the county, exclusively of the Isle of Wight, approaches nearly to a square, having a triangular projection at its south-western corner. The Isle of Wight is separated from the main land by a strait of unequal breadth, formerly called the Solent Sea, now the Sound, or, more usually, the West Channel, the distance across which, at its western extremity, is only about a mile, while, towards its eastern end, it is as much as seven miles. The form of the island is somewhat rhomboidal, the greatest diagonal breadth being twenty-three miles from east to west, and the transverse diameter, from north to south, about thirteen miles. The surface of the whole county is beautifully varied by gently rising hills and fruitful valleys, and, in some parts, with extensive tracts of woodland. In the southern districts, approaching the coast, the population is much more dense than elsewhere; the mildness of the seasons, the beauty of the landscapes, and the proximity to the ports, operating as strong inducements to the continued residence of many families, besides those engaged in commercial pursuits. The agricultural report drawn up by Charles Vancouver, Esq., for the consideration of the Hon. the Board of Agriculture, divides the main land into five districts. The first, called the woodland district, occupies the northern portion of the county, comprising an area of one hundred and three thousand nine hundred and forty-four acres, and may be separated from the other parts by a line passing from the borders of Surrey, near Farnham in that county, immediately to the south of Odiham, to the north of Basingstoke, and to the south of Kingsclere and Highclere, to the confines of Berkshire, near East Woodhay: this includes the woodlands and wastes of Bagshot, &c. Its soil and substrata are various: in the eastern part of it are some darkish-coloured sands and a gravelly mould of good depth resting upon a dry subsoil, but intermingled with a stronger and wetter brown loam. The borders of the streams have narrow tracts of meadow and pasture land, the soil of which is, for the most part, a dark-coloured sandy, or gravelly, loam, lying on a variety of substrata of clay, loam, peat, and gravel, and abounding in springs, which render it of a wet and spongy nature, and cause it to produce herbage of inferior quality. The great mass of this district, however, has a strong brown and grey loam, resting upon a tough blue and yellow clay, having generally an excess of moisture, with numerous unsound and boggy places. Ascending from the woodland valley northward, the soil becomes of a rather lighter quality; but, still proceeding northward, this improvement is lost on a thin sandy and gravelly mould, lying upon deep beds of white, red, and yellow sand and gravel, and a wet hungry loam, upon a moist, loose, white and yellow clay, which constitute the soil of part of Bagshot heath and Frimley common, in the county of Surrey. Along the southern side of this district, is a tract composed of a temperate mixed soil, situated between the heavy clays, just mentioned, and the chalk district, which will hereafter be described; upon this is found a large proportion of valuable grass land. Peat is got on the wastes, and in some of the enclosed grounds: a large quantity is annually dug on the commons of Cove, Farnborough, and Aldershot. The second district comprises the whole body of the county, from the borders of Wiltshire to those of Sussex and Surrey, being bounded, on the north, by the last-mentioned tract, and, on the south, by a line drawn from the vicinity of Sherfield-English, on the western confines of the county, near Lockerley, Mottisfont, Mitchelmarsh, and Hursley, to the south of Bishop's-Waltham, and to the north of Hambledon and Catherington, towards the eastern boundary: it is computed to contain two hundred and fifty-four thousand two hundred and ninety-five acres; and the higher parts of this large central district have much the appearance of an elevated plain, divided into many unequal portions, and intersected by deep hollows, through which the brooks and rivulets rising in these elevated tracts descend, for the most part in a southerly course, towards the sea. In these vallies are considerable tracts of meadow and pasture land, and by far the greater number of the habitations in this district is situated in them. The higher tracts are almost wholly in open and extensive sheep downs: the substratum is throughout a firm unbroken bed of chalk. The soil covering some of them is provincially called *hazel-mould*, being light, dry, friable, and arenaceous, resting upon a chalk rubble containing flint, and naturally producing a short, but excellent, pasturage for sheep: another kind of the down land consists of a black vegetable mould, resting on a nearly similar substratum: a third is a thin grey loam, lying immediately on a firm bed of chalk, and constituting a very great proportion of the downs: a fourth sort consists of a deep, strong, red, flinty loam, lying at the various depths of from one to eight or ten feet, upon the firm chalk rock; this is usually found on the flat summits of the lesser eminences, of which the brows and acclivities are occupied by a fifth description, which is of a thin staple, and chiefly consists of decomposed chalk, being favourable to the production of turnips and sainfoin. Below these hills a deep, strong, grey loam frequently occurs, the tillage of which, together with that of the red loam, is very difficult: the crops of wheat produced upon it are great. In other parts of this district, soils of a darker colour, equally strong, are met with; and in the numerous hollows intersecting the whole, exclusively of the valleys traversed by running streams, the surface is formed of an assemblage of small flat flints, combined together by a proportionably small quantity of extremely tough loam. This is provincially termed *shrave*; and there is another sort of it, consisting of a coarse red pebbly gravel, mixed with a small proportion of tough red loam, or, more commonly, with a dry sand, or small gravel. The soil of the deeper valleys is a black vegetable mould, resting on a strong

calcareous loam, in which occur large chasms occupied by masses of peat, which is occasionally dug for fuel, or to be burned for manuring the ground with its ashes; numerous trunks of trees are found in this earth. The third district is small, containing only forty-nine thousand five hundred and twenty-five acres, and including the forests of Woolmer and Alice-Holt, the hills of Binfield, Great and Little Worldham, Selborne, and Empshot, together with all the lower sides of the chalk hills surrounding and forming the vale of Petersfield, the soil of which is, for the most part, a grey sandy loam of good staple, lying on a kind of soft sand rock, being provincially termed *malmy* land. In the vale of Petersfield, formed by the chalk downs and the heaths of Woolmer Forest and its appendages, and traversed by a small branch of the river Loddon, the soil consists of a tough, brown, flinty clay, found at a certain distance from the chalk, interspersed with tracts of light sandy loam. Ascending from this valley, in a north-easterly direction from the town, from which it takes its name, is an extensive tract of sandy and gravelly heath, part of which has been applied to the culture of Scotch fir, and which extends along the borders of Sussex, within and upon the confines of Woolmer Forest. Still further, in the same direction, is found a considerable tract of convertible sandy loam, which forms good turnip land: small quantities of stronger soil are also found, while the vallies have a thin moory soil upon a clay of different colours: peat is obtained here also, chiefly upon the wastes, and in Woolmer and Alice-Holt Forests. The fourth district includes the whole southern part of the county situated on the main land (excepting a tract of twenty-six thousand eight hundred and ninety-five acres, at its south-eastern extremity), and comprises an area of three hundred and thirty-three thousand four hundred and eighty-nine acres. This large division, besides many extensive wastes and commons, comprehends the Forest of Bere, the New Forest, and Waltham Chase: its soils are various, but consist chiefly of light sandy and gravelly loams, intermixed with clay and brick-earth, and resting on substrata of argillaceous and calcareous marl. The heaths and commons chiefly comprise the higher lands between Gosport and Titchfield, between Titchfield, Bursledon, and Botley, and between the two latter places and the river Itchen: the cultivated district lying north of Southampton, Millbrook, and Redbridge, is also much contracted in extent by the extensive commons of Shirley and Southampton. Descending southward from the heaths, the surrounding country preserves a smooth and uniform appearance, until broken on the south-west by Hill-common and Tatchbury Mount, beyond which occurs a considerable extent of flat low ground, including Netley marsh, and thence extending towards Eling, and, for some distance westward, into the New Forest. Along the confines of the New Forest, and bordering upon the western side of Southampton water, the surface is much broken by hills. On the western side of the Avon the country rises suddenly, and spreads into extensive heaths and commons, upon which many plantations of forest trees have been made: a portion of Poole heath, so called from the vicinity of the town of Poole, in Dorsetshire, is included within the limits of Hampshire. Much peat and turf moor is found on the heaths, low grounds, and wastes. Hayling

Island, forming the south-western extremity of the county, and Portsea Island, containing the town of Portsmouth, together with the tracts on the main land immediately opposite to them, constitute the fifth district, comprising an area of twenty-six thousand eight hundred and ninety-five acres. In the islands and low grounds of the main land, a strong flinty and a tender hazel-coloured loam prevail. The soil and substrata of Portsdown hill, in the different degrees of its elevation, are similar to those of the chalk district. A large extent of Portsea Island is occupied as garden ground, and is very productive: on the coasts of this island, particularly on its eastern side, as well as on those of Hayling Island, is much loamy marsh land, subject to occasional inundation by spring tides, and chiefly appropriated as salterns. Its southern side is generally sandy, and the bed of shingles, on its south-eastern coast, affords large supplies of ballast to the coasting vessels, as well as an inexhaustible store of materials, of a good quality, for making and repairing the roads between Fareham and Chichester.

Some of the finest views in the main land are from Farley hill; Portsdown hill, on which a large fair is held on July 26th; Weyhill, on which is held another on October 11th; Danebury hill, Sidon hill, and Eagle-hurst cliff. Through the centre of the Isle of Wight, from east to west, extends a range of lofty hills, affording only pasturage for sheep, and commanding views over every part of the island, with the ocean on the south, and the beautiful shores of Hampshire on the north. Its surface is otherwise much diversified: on the coast the land is, in some parts, very high, particularly on the south, where the cliffs are very steep, and vast fragments of rock, which the waves have at some time undermined, lie scattered below: on the northern side, the ground slopes to the water in easy declivities, excepting towards the Needles, or western extremity, where the rocks are bare, broken, and precipitous. The height of the cliffs, of which the Needles form the extreme point, is, in some places, six hundred feet above the level of the sea; in some parts they are perpendicular, and in others overhanging; they contain many deep caverns. The Needles derive their name from a lofty pointed rock rising to the height of about one hundred and twenty feet above low water mark, and severed, with others, from the main land, by the force of the waves: part of this rocky projection, about sixty years ago, having been undermined by the sea, fell, and totally disappeared. St. Catherine's hill, the highest point in the island, rises seven hundred and fifty feet above the level of high water mark, and commands magnificent prospects; as also do the Culver cliffs, at the eastern end of the island; Carisbrook castle, and Bem-bridge down. The soil and substrata of the Isle of Wight are extremely various. It may be said, generally, however, that the soil of the enclosed and depastured marshes and low grounds bordering on the Yarmouth river, on the inlets of Shalfleet and Newtown, on the Medina river between Newport and Cowes, on the Wooton and Ryde rivers, and of the embanked marshes above Brading haven, is composed of a tender hazel-coloured loam, lying, in some places, upon a blue, or rather black, sea-clay, but from which it is most frequently separated by a bed of coarse sand, or fine gravel. The surface mould of the low grounds and meadows, bordering the higher parts of the courses of these streams, is variable, in

proportion to the quantity and quality of the adventitious matter washed down from the surrounding hills. On the whole northern side of the island, and for a considerable distance along its southern shores, the prevailing character of the soil is a rough strong clay, of different colours, in which are a blueish argillaceous marl, and a pure white shell marl. In the other parts are chiefly found tender red sand, and a gravelly mould, with argillaceous and calcareous marl, chalk, and its usual accompaniments, red loam and flints; and though the superior fruitfulness of most of these soils generally corresponds with the high estimation in which they are held by the inhabitants, yet some heaths and commons occur, and there are several small tracts of morass, the chief of which is on the western branch of the Medina river. The chalk downs of Brading and Arreton form an unbroken range from Culver cliff, on the eastern coast, to the valley that separates them from Staple's heath: those of Gatcombe and Shorwell are isolated from the western range by a highly-cultivated valley, extending from Shorwell to Newport, and terminating northward in the waste called Parkhurst Forest. From the vale of Shorwell to the western extremity of the island the high chalk downs are broken only by three gaps, or carriage-roads, one of which is the passage between the head of the Yarmouth river and the innermost cove of Freshwater bay. The tract of downs situated towards the southern extremity of the island terminates abruptly towards the sea, in a precipice of limestone rock, having the appearance, particularly when seen from a distance, of an immense stone wall, and overhanging the romantic tract called the Undercliff, which extends along the sea-shore for a distance of nearly six miles.

In the northern, or woodland, district of the county, and in that comprising the forests of Woolmer and Alice-Holt, &c., the climate is generally mild, but a considerable degree of cold damp is exhaled. The most prevalent winds in the former are from the south-west, and are frequently accompanied by fogs that last for several days. In the elevated and extensive chalk district the air is dry, thin, and healthy, and the westerly winds, which are by far the most frequent, are often experienced with great violence. In the lower tracts, approaching the coast, the climate is very mild, and the westerly winds are by much the most common and violent. Along the borders of the Southampton water agues are still experienced, though by no means to the extent that they formerly were. In the islands of Hayling and Portsea, and upon the surrounding shores, the same malady very commonly appears towards the close of summer; but the higher parts of this south-western district have a dry, and generally a keen, air. In the Isle of Wight is experienced all the variety of climate felt in other parts of the county: the air is, however, favourable to human health; and its mildness and salubrity are particularly remarkable on the southern borders, where much advantage is annually derived by invalids resorting thither for a short period, particularly by such as are afflicted with pulmonary diseases. The southern shores are much exposed to the fury of westerly gales, while the northern side, although in a great measure exempt from the like violent visitations, is, nevertheless, later in its seasons than the southern, by the space of ten days or a fortnight.

On the arable lands of the county, the rotations of crops are various : the grain generally cultivated consists of wheat, barley, oats, rye, peas, and beans. The early wheat is almost universally eaten off by sheep, in the month of March, and sometimes even a little later. The produce of this grain varies greatly: that of barley, sown after turnips, averages thirty-five bushels, and of the same corn sown after wheat, from four and a half to five bushels less per acre. Oats are generally cultivated as food for horses only : the common produce is little above thirty bushels per acre, and .frequently less: the straw, as well as that of barley, is found of much value as winter food for cattle. Rye is chiefly grown as a corn crop in the valley of the Avon, and in the parish of Christchurch ; the produce is about eighteen bushels per acre : in most other parts of the county it is cultivated for the purpose of being eaten green by cattle. Peas of different sorts are in common cultivation ; but beans are not so frequently met with : the produce of both is uncertain : the bean crop is generally cut with a reaping-hook. Turnips and tares are commonly cultivated : coleseed, or rape, by which latter name this plant is here most generally designated, is cultivated as food for sheep only. Cabbages are seldom grown for the purpose of feeding cattle with them ; but, as a vegetable, for supplying the large towns and the immense quantity of shipping resorting to the southern coast, they are extensively raised in all convenient situations : potatoes are largely cultivated for the like purpose. The most common artificial grasses are the common broad clover, ray-grass, trefoil, sainfoin, and lucern : burnet is a plant that forms a large portion of the herbage of the downs : a much larger and stronger species is found on many of the low grounds, and upon the cold clay loams, where, as upon the downs, it has every appearance of being indigenous. In the parish of Alton and its vicinity, upon the borders of Surrey, hops are grown to a great extent : the produce varies greatly, but may be estimated, on an average, at about five hundred weight per acre : their culture has been much encouraged by the reputation of the Farnham hops, that town, in Surrey, being situated only at the distance of a few miles. Hemp and flax are sometimes cultivated. Several of the manures employed are remarkable : the principal are, marl, which is found, of different colours and properties, in many of the parishes within, and upon the confines of, the New Forest, towards Lymington, and in some of the more cultivated parts, particularly on the northern side of the Isle of Wight, as well as on the wastes between Southampton water and the Beaulieu river; *malme*, a kind of marl, or chalky clay, found at Timsbury, above Romsey, and many other places along the valley of the Test, as high as the parish of Romsey, both of a black and of a white kind, as also in one or two other places ; and chalk, which is extensively used, more especially on the strong lands, within a convenient distance of the Southampton water, to which it is brought from Fareham, from Portsdown hill, and even from the coasts of Kent and Essex. Much chalk is also employed in the islands of Portsea and Hayling, and in the northern, or woodland district ; as are also turf, peat, and coal-ashes, in situations where they can be procured; on the sea-coast, *rack,* or sea-weed, is some-

times used. The most extensive and valuable tracts of meadow land are upon the borders of the various rivers : those of the best quality produce about thirty-six hundred weight of hay per acre. This county is particularly noted for its irrigated meadows, some of the principal of which are situated on the respective courses of the Test, the Anton, the Itchen, and the stream which passes through Titchfield to the sea, at Hilt Head. The green sward of the southern side of the Isle of Wight is, in numerous places, of a very rich quality : pastures of the same description are situated on the Medina river, above Newport, and upon some of the principal branches of the Brading river. The embanked marshes of Brading and Yaverland, in this island, form a valuable tract of rich feeding land : almost all the other embanked lands on the coasts of the islands, as well as of the main land of the county, have been appropriated as salterns for the manufacture of sea and medicinal salts : many of these salt-works are now abandoned, but the brine and bitumen with which the ground is saturated, prevent their being brought into tillage.

Hampshire possesses no particular breed of cattle : those of Sussex, Suffolk, Hereford, Glamorgan, and North and South Devon, are indiscriminately met with, and are generally preferred for draught: many cattle of the Leicester breed are also seen. In dairy establishments the same indiscriminate intermixture is observed. Many cows are kept, in different parts of the county, for the purpose of suckling calves to supply the markets of London, Portsmouth, Chichester, Winchester, Newbury, Reading, Salisbury, &c., with veal. The number of sheep kept is remarkably great. In the woodland district the heath sheep, or the Old Hampshire, or Wiltshire breed, were formerly the most common, but have now, in many places, given way to breeds crossed between the New Leicester and others. The South Down breed occupies a great extent of the county, particularly of the open downs of the chalk district : upon the chalk downs of the Isle of Wight it is equally prevalent, although in that island are found many of the Dorsetshire breed, sometimes intermingled with the New Leicester. Numerous hogs are fed for a few weeks, at the close of the autumn, upon the mast produced in the forest and other woodlands ; and a superior mode of curing being practised, the Hampshire bacon has become famous for its excellence. The native hog is a coarse, raw-boned, flat-sided animal, now seldom met with, the common stock being either of the Berkshire breed, or of a mixed kind between that and different other breeds. The horses have generally a coarse and heavy appearance. Upon the heaths and forests vast numbers of light small horses are bred, generally about twelve hands high, and provincially termed *heath-crop pers*, which propagate indiscriminately upon these wastes, where they succeed in maintaining an existence throughout the year. The cliffs, at the western extremity of the Isle of Wight, are frequented by an immense number of marine birds, such as puffins, razor-bills, willcocks, gulls, cormorants, and Cornish choughs, as well as by daws, starlings, and wild pigeons, some of which come only for a certain season, while others remain the whole year. Vipers, in this island, are very numerous, and many of them are caught for medicinal purposes ; great quantities of poultry are bred for the supply of the out-ward-bound shipping. Gardening is carried on to a gerat extent in the vicinity of all the large towns, and Portsea island is considered to produce the finest brocoli in the kingdom. In the northern and middle parts of the county the orchards are few and small; but upon the marly and clayey substrata of the southern and south-western districts they are more numerous, and some cider is made. In the Isle of Wight most farmers make annually several hogsheads of cider, which is of excellent quality, and chiefly for home consumption. This county has long been celebrated for its honey, called heath honey and down honey, from the different districts in which the bees collect it; the latter being the more valuable. The woods are numerous and extensive: the coppices in different parts are cut at various ages: their produce is formed into hop poles, wattled hurdles, hoops, rafter poles, and bavins and fagots. From those of the southern district, a number of straight hoops are also exported to the West Indies: woods of this kind, in the northern woodland district, consist chiefly of birch, willow, alder, hazel, wild cherry, ash, and sometimes oak; in the chalk district, of hazel, willow, oak, ash, maple, white thorn, and a little beech and wild cherry; and, in the southern part of the county, of hazel, willow, alder, birch, holly, and some ash, beech, and wild cherry. The coppice wood of the north-eastern part of the Isle of Wight is overshadowed by a heavy growth of timber. In the northern district a very fine growth of oak is generally observed; but the annual produce of this timber, in the southern parts, has been greatly diminished. In almost every part of the chalk district beech woods and groves flourish with peculiar vigour; and the forests and other woodlands are found to contain large proportions of this timber. Ash is found in different parts; but elm is generally of scarce growth, although it is occasionally seen, more especially in the southern districts; the largest elms are much in demand at the Royal Dock-yard for keel-pieces. The abele and aspen poplar, the lime or linden tree, and the Turin, or Lombardy poplar, are frequently met with. Fir-trees of different kinds are seen to flourish in mixed plantations. In the Isle of Wight, the woods of Swainston are of considerable extent, and those of Wooton and Quarr occupy an area of a thousand acres.

The New Forest comprises a very extensive tract in the south-western part of the county. Its ancient boundaries, according to the oldest perambulation extant, which is dated 8th of Edward I., were, the Southampton river, on the east; the Sound and the British Channel, on the south; and the river Avon, on the west: northward, it extended as far as North Charford, on the west; and to Wade and Ower bridge, on the east. Different other perambulations are on record; but, according to that made in the 22nd of Charles II., the forest extends from Godshill, on the northwest, south-eastward to the sea, a distance of about twenty-three miles; and from Hardley, on the east, to Ringwood on the west, about fifteen miles; and contains ninety-two thousand three hundred and sixty-five statute acres. The extent of the woods and waste lands of this tract were, however, at that time, reduced to sixty-three thousand eight hundred and forty-five acres, by several manors and other freeholds within the perambulation, amounting to twenty-

four thousand seven hundred and ninety-seven acres; by six hundred and twenty-five acres of copyhold, or customary lands, belonging to the king's manor of Lyndhurst; by one thousand and four acres of leasehold, granted for certain terms of years; by nine hundred and one acres of purprestures, or encroachments on the forest; and by one thousand one hundred and ninety-three acres of enclosed lands held by the master-keepers and groom-keepers, with their respective lodges. The remainder belonged to the crown, as it does at present, and in each kind of the property above mentioned, as being included within the limits of the forest, the king has also various rights and interests: in the freeholds he has certain rights relative to the deer and game; the copyholds are subject to quit-rents and fines, and the timber trees upon such property belong to the crown. The encroachments consist chiefly of cottages built by poor persons, with small parcels of enclosed land adjoining: such, however, as had been made by the proprietors of neighbouring estates, and had been held without any acknowledgment, the crown is authorised, by a modern act of parliament, to grant on lease, for valuable considerations, and provision is made against future encroachment. The forest lands, containing, as before stated, sixty-three thousand eight hundred and forty-five acres, are subject to certain rights of commonage, pasturage, pannage, and fuel, possessed by the proprietors of estates within, or adjacent to, the forest; which rights, and those of the crown, are defined by an act of the 9th and 10th of William III., for the increase and preservation of timber in the forest. By this act, the crown was empowered to enclose six thousand acres, as a nursery for timber, until the trees should be past danger of being injured by the deer or cattle, when the same should be thrown open, and an equal quantity might, in like manner, be enclosed, afterwards to be thrown open, in any other part of the forest. The crown has also the right of keeping deer in the unenclosed part of the forest, at all times and without limitation. In consequence of this act, the woodlands, which, according to surveys made at different periods, had been long remaining in a neglected state, received, for a while, some portion of attention; but that, ere long, was withdrawn from them, when the superintendence of the surveyor-general of the crown lands ceased, and the whole fell, by degrees, under the sole direction of a surveyor-general of the woods. For local purposes the New Forest is divided into nine bailiwicks, which are subdivided into fifteen walks. It is under the government of a lord-warden, who is appointed by letters patent under the great seal, during his Majesty's pleasure; and by his patent are granted to him the manor of Lyndhurst, and hundred of Redbridge, with various other privileges and emoluments; he appoints a steward for the king's house at Lyndhurst. A riding forester is appointed in the same manner as the lord-warden, whose office it is to ride before the king when he enters the forest. A bow-bearer, and two rangers, are appointed by the lord-warden, during pleasure. A woodward is appointed by letters patent from his Majesty, during pleasure, and acts by deputy. Four verderers, the judges of the swanimote and attachment courts, are chosen by the freeholders of the county, in pursuance of the king's writ. A high-steward, and an under-steward, are appointed by the lord-warden, during pleasure : the duty of the latter is to attend at and enrol the proceedings of the courts of attachment and swanimote, and hold the court leet for the hundred of Redbridge, and the courts baron for the manor of Lyndhurst. Twelve regarders are chosen by the freeholders of the county. There are, besides, nine foresters, or master-keepers, and an indefinite number of under-foresters, or groom-keepers, though commonly one to each walk. A purveyor of the navy acts also for the forest, whose office is a naval appointment, and whose duty is to assign timber for the navy, and to prevent any fit for that use from being cut for other purposes. The limits of the forest were finally ascertained, and disputed boundaries settled, by an act of parliament passed in the year 1800. Of the perquisites of the under-keepers, which, at the period of the investigation made in 1789, arose chiefly from deer, browse-wood, rabbits, and swine, only the first and last are now allowed them, and the rabbits are nearly destroyed. The forest courts are regularly held by the verderers, who preside in them at Lyndhurst. The scenery is remarkable for its sylvan beauty, presenting magnificent woods, extended lawns, and vast sweeps of wild heath, unlimited by artificial boundaries, together with numerous river views and the prospect of distant shores. In some parts also are extensive bogs, the most considerable of which is at a place called Longsdale, on the road between Brockenhurst and Ringwood, which extends for about three miles. The oaks seldom rise into lofty stems, and their branches, which are more adapted to what the ship-builders call knees and elbows, are commonly twisted into the most picturesque forms : this is supposed to be owing to the nature of the soil through which their roots have to penetrate, it being generally an argillaceous loam, tempered in different degrees with sand, or gravel. The advantage of water-carriage to the various royal or private dockyards in which its produce is employed, is superior to that of any other forest in the kingdom.

The forest of Bere, situated in the south-eastern part of the county, and extending northward from the Portsdown hills, which, according to the perambulation made in 1688, is now considered the boundary, comprises about sixteen thousand acres, upwards of one-third being enclosed. It is divided into two walks, named East and West, to each of which are annexed several smaller divisions, called purlieus, all of them being subject to the forest laws. Its officers are a warden, four verderers, two master-keepers, two under-keepers, a ranger, a steward of the swanimote court, twelve regarders, and two agistors. North-westward of it is the Chase of Bishop's-Waltham, containing about two thousand acres, which belongs to the see of Winchester. The forest of Alice-Holt and Woolmer, on the eastern border of the county, approaching the confines of Surrey and Sussex, and to the north-east of Petersfield, is divided into two parts by intervening private property : its limits comprehend fifteen thousand four hundred and ninety-three acres, of which, eight thousand six hundred and ninety-four belong to the crown: the division called Alice-Holt contains about two thousand seven hundred and forty acres of crown land. Parkhurst, or Carisbrooke forest, lying at a short distance to the north-west of Newport, in the Isle of Wight, occurs in Domesday-book under

the appellation of the King's park, and was afterwards called the King's forest : it includes about three thousand acres, nearly destitute of valuable trees. The total quantity of waste land in Hampshire, exclusively of the forests, falls little short of one hundred thousand acres.

A sandy and gravelly character of soil prevails on the greater part of the heaths and commons, which produce ling, or heather, fern, coarse aquatic plants and grasses, furze, and dwarf alder : a superior kind of land occasionally found produces also a particularly sweet herbage for deer and cattle. Upon the inlets and southern coasts of the main land, as also of the Isle of Wight, are large tracts of sea mud, generally less elevated than the highest level of the spring tides, which consequently overflow them. A long range of this kind of marsh extends on the western side of Southampton river, through the parish of Fawley, and a like tract occurs between Calshot castle and the Salterns of Fawley : the extent of these, together with others situated higher up the Southampton river, is estimated at about two thousand acres. The rivers of Beaulieu and Lymington, and the harbour of Christchurch, present similar tracts ; and about four thousand acres of this kind of mud are found along the shore, between Hurst castle and the mouth of the Beaulieu river. The inlet, or harbour, of Portsmouth comprises about three thousand acres, and about five thousand five hundred are included in the harbour of Langport, and the portion of that of Emsworth which is within the limits of this county. In the Isle of Wight, similar tracts of marsh are found bordering on the Yarmouth river, on the inlets of Shalfleet and Newtown, and in Brading haven, the area of which is stated at seven hundred and fifty acres. In this latter marsh, different small tracts have been at various periods embanked against the flow of the tide ; and an attempt was made by Sir Bevis Thelwall, and Sir Hugh Middelton, the constructor of the New River, to exclude the sea entirely by an embankment thrown across its narrow outlet, which was completed ; but in a wet season, when the inner part of the haven was full of water, and there was a high spring tide, the waters met under the bank, and made a breach, which was never repaired, and these marshes still remain in their ancient state, notwithstanding that the outlet is, at low water, only about twenty yards in width, and its surface appears for the most part to be more elevated than the embanked marshes lying westward of it, in the parishes of Brading and Yaverland. Throughout all the woodland parts of Hampshire the peasantry are tolerably well supplied with fuel ; they obtained it formerly by a claim of snap-wood, meaning the fallen branches and such withered pieces as they could snap off by hand, or with a hook fastened at the end of a long pole, but having improperly exercised this privilege they have been deprived of it. Turf is pared on the heaths and commons, and peat is sometimes used. A vast quantity of furze is also cut on the waste lands, as fuel; and the parishes contiguous to the forests have generally a right of turbary in them : coal can only be procured, and that at a high price, at the ports, or along the canals.

The mineral productions are not numerous. On its southern shores, particularly near the mouth of the

Beaulieu river, iron-stone is washed up by the sea, and was formerly gathered, and conveyed to the iron-works at Sowley, but these have been discontinued. It is also occasionally found in small quantities in different other parts of the county, particularly in the cliffs near Hordwell, which are upwards of one hundred feet high, and abound with nodules of iron-ore, together with pebbles, or flints, many of them containing fossil shells, or their impressions, of various and scarce species, found in a blueish kind of clay, or marl. A thin stratum of coal discovers itself at the foot of Bembridge cliff, in the Isle of Wight, and extends through the southern part of the island, appearing again at Warden Ledge, in Freshwater parish: near it is a stratum of fullers' earth. The range of chalk hills crossing the county from east to west, and occupying the central part of it, forms a portion of the vast formation that constitutes so considerable a feature in the geology of England. The strata constituting the southern part of the main land, and the northern part of the Isle of Wight, lie upon a depressed portion of the chalk beds, which, in geological language, is termed the Chalk Basin of the Isle of Wight. The chalk raised in this county is of two kinds, white and grey, both of them burned into lime of a good quality, that from the latter being also particularly serviceable as a cement under water, for which it is extensively employed. Between Milton and Christchurch is found a hard reddish stone, of which several ancient structures in that part of the county are built. The numerous strata of various kinds and formations, and exhibiting great diversity of position, of which the Isle of Wight consists, form a remarkably rich field of study for the geologist. At Alum-bay, at the north-western extremity of the island, is found a vein of white sand, in great demand for the glass-works of Bristol and Liverpool, as also for others situated on the western coasts of England and Scotland, and in Ireland. Eastward of this, along the northern foot of the downs, grist or quarry stone, of a yellowish grey colour, and very porous texture, is found in detached masses, and used for building. A strong liver-coloured building-stone, rising in cubical masses, encrusted with a brownish kind of ochre, and enclosing specimens of rich iron-stone, occurs on the southern side of the island : a rough calcareous freestone is frequently found in the marl pits, in loose detached pieces. Eastward of Staple's heath, and northward of Arreton downs, a close grey lime-stone is raised, the beds of which are separated from each other by small layers of marine shells, cemented together by alum, that substance being well known to pervade the western parts of the island. Freestone is sometimes found under marl in the northern districts of it : a plum-pudding stone exists in large quantities near Sandown fort, and is much used for paving and flooring. Potters' clay occurs in great variety, in different parts of the county ; and ochres of divers colours in the Isle of Wight.

The manufactures are various, but not extensive ; ship-building, however, in addition to the works of the royal dock-yard at Portsmouth, is extensively carried on in most of the numerous creeks and harbours. The other productions are chiefly woollen goods, bed-ticking, light silk articles, sacking, leather, and a coarse kind of earthenware. At Overton are very extensive silk-mills, and the young female peasantry in the vicinity are much employed in the platting of straw for bonnets, the straw-hat manufacture being carried on at many towns in the county. There are paper-mills in different parts of the county, those in the vicinity of Overton being of considerable importance. At Lymington is a manufacture of salt. The advantages for maritime commerce may be estimated from the following list of harbours and roadsteads viz.: Hayling and Portsmouth harbours, with their dependencies ; the inlet of Southampton, with the mouths of the Itchen and Test rivers, their ship-yards, and the smaller havens of Redbridge, Eling, Hythe, Cadland, and Fawley, and of Botley, Bursledon, and Hamble, on the river Hamble ; the Beaulieu river, with its dependencies, slips, and private dock-yards ; Lymington, or Boldre water, with a number of small creeks through the salterns, including Keyhaven ; and the harbour of Christchurch, with its branches, forming the mouth of the Avon and Stour rivers. In the Isle of Wight are the harbours of Hithe, Cowes, South Yarmouth, and Brading. The roadsteads separating that island from the rest of the county are those of St. Helen's, Motherbank, Spithead, Cowes, Southampton bay, and Yarmouth roads, the latter of which is terminated westward by the Needles, the passage, or channel, of which is contracted to the space of only about a mile, by a broad bank of shingles thrown up by the sea, which beats upon it with great violence : this bank, from the main land in the parish of Milton, projects south-eastward, and upon its furthest extremity stands Hurst castle, built in the reign of Henry VIII., and commanding the passage. The shores of this county, particularly of the Isle of Wight, are much resorted to during the summer for the purpose of sea-bathing, &c. : the most frequented places are, on the main land, Christchurch, Muddiford, Lymington, and Southampton ; and in the Isle of Wight, Yarmouth, Cowes, Hythe, Brading, and Shanklin. Whatever may be yielded to the public by the exertions of the fishermen, a small portion only of the fish they take is consumed within the limits of the county, and that generally of an inferior quality, being such as would not pay for its carriage to the metropolis, for which purpose light vans are kept in constant use. In all the rivers and creeks that discharge their waters directly into the sea, salmon are caught : the fisheries of the Southampton water are particularly extensive, and the boats engaged in them often make long coasting voyages to procure other fish, which are taken thence to the markets of London, Oxford, Bath, &c. Several persons are employed on the flat and rocky shores of the Isle of Wight, in catching shrimps and prawns, and, on its bolder shores, in taking crabs and lobsters. Across the vallies and low places of the heaths of Farnborough, Cove, and Aldershot, the soil of which is very retentive of water, dams have been constructed for stopping the descending waters, and thus forming ponds of various extent, which are usually stocked with carp and tench, and are very profitable to their owners, who send nearly the whole of these fish to the London market.

The principal rivers are the Test, the Anton, the Itchen, the Avon, the Boldre water, and the Exe. The Test, rising in the vicinity of Whitchurch, and being, at the distance of about a mile below Wherwell, joined by the Anton, which rises in the north-western part of the county, and flows through Andover, takes a southerly course to Stockbridge, and thence through Romsey to Redbridge, below which it expands and forms the head of the Southampton water, an arm of the sea extending from the "Above Town" of Southampton to the Sound, at Calshot castle, and rendered exceedingly picturesque by its woody and irregular shores : the general direction of the Southampton water is from north-west to south-east. The Itchen, also called the Arbre, has its source at Chilton-Candover, near Alresford, and, being soon increased by the small river Alne, flows westward to King's Worthy, where it suddenly assumes a southerly course, which it pursues by Winchester, Twyford, and Bishop's Stoke, to the Southampton water, at the distance of about half a mile eastward of the town of Southampton : this river was brought into a regular channel, and made navigable up to Winchester, by Godfrey de Lacy, Bishop of Winchester, in 1215 : towards its mouth it expands considerably. The Avon, traversing the projecting south-western portion of the county, in a direction from north to south, enters it from Wiltshire, a few miles above Fordingbridge, and meandering, frequently in separate channels, near the western border of the New Forest, is much increased by numerous rivulets rising in that district : from Fordingbridge it passes by Ringwood to Christchurch, near which town it receives the waters of the Stour, and soon falls into Christchurch bay : by an act passed in 1665, it was made navigable up to Salisbury, but the works having been swept away by a flood, the navigation was destroyed. The Boldre water is formed by several small streams rising in the New Forest, most of which unite above Brockenhurst, thence proceeding southward, by Boldre and Lymington, to the sea. The Exe, frequently called the Beaulieu river, from similar sources in the same district, flows south-eastwardly, and, beginning to expand near Beaulieu, opens into a broad æstuary to the sea, below Exbury. The principal river of the Isle of Wight is the Medina, anciently [called the Mede, which rises near the bottom of St. Catherine's down, in the southern part of the island, and flowing directly northward, divides it into two equal parts, each constituting a liberty, which derives its name from its position on the eastern or western side of this stream : passing on the eastern side of the town of Newport, the Medina mingles its waters with those of the sea in Cowes harbour. The other principal streams of this island are the Yar, the Wooten and the Ear ; its shores are also indented by various creeks and bays. A navigable canal has been made, along the valleys of the Test and Anton, from Andover to the head of the Southampton water : from Barlowes-Mill, near Andover, its course is by Stockbridge and Romsey to its termination at Redbridge, in the parish of Millbrook : from Redbridge a branch proceeds directly to Southampton, and a collateral branch extends from it in a westerly direction, up the valley between East Dean, Lockerley, and East Tytherley, to Alderbury common, within two miles of Salisbury, but neither of them is navigable. The Andover canal is of considerable advantage to the inland districts through which it passes. From Basingstoke a canal has been made, under the authority

of an act of parliament obtained in 1778, to the river Wey in Surrey, by which the navigation is maintained to the Thames : the total length of this canal, which from Basingstoke is carried directly eastward, in the vicinity of Odiham, and across the eastern borders of the county, is thirty-seven miles and a quarter : the cost of cutting it amounted to about £100,000, a large portion of which was expended in forming a tunnel through Grewill hill, near Odiham, which is arched with brick, and is nearly three quarters of a mile in length : the articles of traffic conveyed upon it are chiefly corn, flour, coal, and timber. The Winchester and Southampton canal is one of the oldest in the kingdom : the act for its construction was obtained in the reign of Charles I., but from the want of a suitable trade upon it, however advantageous to the city of Winchester and the surrounding country, it does not appear to have realized the expectations of the projectors.

At the north-eastern angle of the county, the London road branches off in two directions, each line crossing the county somewhat diagonally : the upper, or great western road, passing through Basingstoke, Whitchurch, and Andover, quits the county at Lobcomb Corner, seven miles east-north-east of Salisbury ; from this a minor branch diverges at Basingstoke, which dividing at Popham Lane, a little beyond that town, one line proceeds through Winchester to Southampton, and the other passes through Stockbridge, and joins the great western road at Lobcomb Corner. The lower road passes through Farnham, Alton, New Alresford, and Winchester, to Southampton, whence the line is continued across the New Forest to Ringwood, a little beyond which town it quits the county. The road from London to Portsmouth enters this county at Seven Thorn, on its eastern side, and passes through Petersfield to the latter port. Various other turnpike-roads, in connexion with these, intersect the county in different directions, all of which are remarkably good. Within the limits of the county were the stations of *Venta Belgarum*, supposed to have been at Winchester ; *Vindonum*, at Silchester ; *Clausentum*, at Bittern ; *Brigæ*, at Broughton ; and *Andaoreon*, at Andover. The principal remains of Roman occupation discoverable are at Silchester, approaching the confines of Berkshire, where gold coins and rings, Roman bricks, and pottery, &c., have been dug up. About three-quarters of a mile north of Lymington is Buckland Rings, the remains of a Roman camp. Traces of other encampments of different periods are visible in various parts ; some of the most extensive and remarkable are those of the camp on Danebury hill, to the west and north-west of which are several barrows, many more of these monuments being found in different parts of the county. Three Roman roads branch from Silchester, one of them proceeding to the northern gate of Winchester ; another, by Andover, to Old Sarum ; and the third, northward, across Mortimer heath : from Winchester also was a road leading to Old Sarum. The number of ancient religious establishments was about fifty-three. There are still interesting remains of the abbeys of Hide, Netley, Beaulieu, and Quarr ; as also of the hospital of St. Cross, near Winchester. The cathedral of Winchester is one of the most interesting edifices in England : in that city the college, the cross, the west gate, and the episcopal palace of Wolvesey, are also remarkable for their antiquity. Among the finest ancient churches are those of Christchurch, Romsey, and St. Michael, Southampton. The most remarkable ancient fonts are those of Winchester cathedral; of the church of St. Michael, Southampton; and of that of East Meon. Some of the gates and other parts of the fortifications of the town of Southampton are still standing; as are also the castles of Hurst, Porchester, and Carisbrooke, in the Isle of Wight: there are remains also of the castles of Christchurch, Odiham, and Warblington. The modern seats of the nobility and gentry are extremely numerous, more especially the villas. The cottages of the peasantry are in general remarkable for their comfortable appearance. In many parts of the chalk district, and in that part of the county bordering on Dorsetshire, mud, or *cob* walls, as they are provincially termed, are very commonly used to form enclosures. Several chalybeate springs are found in different parts of the Isle of Wight: at Pitland is a spring impregnated with sulphur; and at Shanklin another, the water of which is slightly tinctured with alum. The waters of the streams in the northern woodland part of the county are of a strong chalybeate quality: that which issues from the bogs and swampy ground is charged with a solution of iron. In the strong loam, woodland clay, and chalk, districts, the want of a regular supply of water during seasons of drought is severely felt. Fossil remains of different kinds are found in some of the strata of this county; among the natural curiosities of which may also be mentioned the immense chasms near the sea-shore in the Isle of Wight, called Blackgang Chine, Luccombe Chine, and Shanklin Chine; and there is a large natural cavern at Freshwater Gate, a small creek in the centre of Freshwater bay. Samphire grows in great plenty on some of the high cliffs of the Isle of Wight, and is gathered by the inhabitants.

SOUTHBOROUGH, a chapelry in the parish and lowey of TONBRIDGE, lathe of AYLESFORD, county of KENT, 2¾ miles (S. by W.) from Tonbridge, with which the population is returned. It is situated about midway between Tonbridge and the Wells, and consists of a number of scattered houses. A new district church, in the early style of English architecture, has been recently erected, and endowed at an expense of £8436, defrayed by subscriptions. It contains four hundred and eighty-six sittings, two hundred and eighty-six of which are free. The property is vested in five trustees, who have also the appointment of the minister. In 1785, premises for a school were erected by the Executors of the Rev. Edward Holmes, and endowed with £1050 four per cents., for the education of fifty children: it is managed by trustees.

SOUTH-BURN, a township in the parish of KIRK-BURN, Bainton-Beacon division of the wapentake of HARTHILL, East riding of the county of YORK, 3¾ miles (S. W.) from Great Driffield, containing 103 inhabitants.

SOUTHCHURCH, a parish in the hundred of ROCHFORD, county of ESSEX, 1 mile (N. N. E.) from South-End, containing 353 inhabitants. The living is a rectory, in the peculiar jurisdiction and patronage of the Archbishop of Canterbury, rated in the king's books at £27. 0. 10. The parish is bounded on the south by the Thames; where are considerable oyster beds.

SOUTHCOATES, a township in the parish of DRYPOOL, middle division of the wapentake of HOLDERNESS, East riding of the county of YORK, 1½ mile (N. E. by E.) from Kingston upon Hull, containing 798 inhabitants.

SOUTHCOT, a tything in that part of the parish of ST. MARY, READING, which is in the hundred of READING, county of BERKS, 1½ mile (W. S. W.) from Reading, containing 121 inhabitants.

SOUTHEASE, a parish in the hundred of HOLMSTROW, rape of LEWES, county of SUSSEX, 3¾ miles (S. by E.) from Lewes, containing 112 inhabitants. The living is a rectory, in the archdeaconry of Lewes, and diocese of Chichester, rated in the king's books at £16. 0. 10., and in the patronage of the Rev. — Todd. The church is principally in the early style of English architecture, with a circular tower.

SOUTHEND, a hamlet in the parish of PRITTLEWELL, hundred of ROCHFORD, county of ESSEX, 1¼ mile (S. S. E.) from Prittlewell, and 42 miles (E.) from London. This village, which has of late years risen into repute as a bathing-place, and considerably increased in size, is pleasantly situated on the declivity and at the base of a well-wooded hill, at the mouth of the Thames, directly opposite to the river Medway: it is divided into the Upper and the Lower town, the latter having been anciently a small fishing village, and consists of an irregular line of houses fronting the sea; of late years some handsome dwellings have been added, between which and the beach a small parade has been partly enclosed. Here are several neat rows of houses, and at the eastern extremity is a small but neat theatre, erected in 1804, and open during the season. The Upper town, which has received the appellation of New Southend, occupies an eminence fronting the sea: it is considered the more fashionable part of the town, being, both in situation and style of building, far preferable. A handsome range of houses, called the Terrace, has been finished, in a neat and uniform style. Adjoining is the Royal Hotel, which contains many good suites of apartments, an assembly-room sixty feet by twenty-four in dimensions, a music-gallery, and other apartments. On the brow of the hill is the library, an elegant building, partaking of the later English style, with a circular front, and adjoining it is a billiard-room. In front of the terrace is a fine broad gravel promenade, and between this and the sea is a shrubbery extending its whole length, and containing a neat cottage, in which are all the requisite accommodations for warm baths. A pier of frame-work has recently been constructed by an incorporated company of proprietors. The surrounding scenery is of a rich and picturesque character, and the views extend across the channel from the Isle of Thanet along the rich hills of the opposite county of Kent, and, up the river Thames nearly to Gravesend, including also the Medway, and the government works and dock-yards at Sheerness. There is a place of worship for Independents.

SOUTHERNBY-BOUND, a township in the parish of CASTLE-SOWERBY, LEATH ward, county of CUMBERLAND, 11½ miles (N. W. by W.) from Penrith, containing 160 inhabitants.

SOUTHERY, a parish in the hundred of CLACK-CLOSE, county of NORFOLK, 6½ miles (S.) from Downham-Market, containing 663 inhabitants. The living is a rectory, in the archdeaconry of Norfolk, and diocese of Norwich, rated in the king's books at £7. 10., and in the patronage of Robert Martin, Esq. The church, dedicated to St. Mary, is a very ancient structure, with a wooden screen separating the nave and chancel: it has lately received an addition of one hundred and twenty free sittings, the Incorporated Society for the enlargement of churches and chapels having granted £150 towards defraying the expense.

SOUTH-FIELDS, a liberty in the hundred of GUTHLAXTON, county of LEICESTER, containing 762 inhabitants.

SOUTHFLEET, a parish in the hundred of AXTON, DARTFORD, and WILMINGTON, lathe of SUTTON at HONE, county of KENT, 3½ miles (S. W.) from Gravesend, containing 577 inhabitants. The living is a rectory, in the archdeaconry and diocese of Rochester, rated in the king's books at £31. 15., and in the patronage of the Bishop of Rochester. The church, dedicated to St. Nicholas, is principally in the decorated style of English architecture, and exhibits many marks of antiquity, including six stone stalls under pointed arches, a piscina, a window of stained glass, and a font much admired for its curious workmanship. This was a place of importance during the Octarchy, when it was called *Sudfleta :* from its proximity to the old Watling-street, its distance from the station *Durobrivis* (Rochester), and the numerous Roman relics found on the spot, it is supposed to occupy the site of the *Vagniacæ* of Antoninus. Among other antiquities a Roman milliary and a stone tomb, containing two leaden coffins, have been discovered in the parish. A school-house has been erected, and is endowed with a rent-charge of £20, bequeathed by the family of Sedley.

SOUTHGATE, a chapelry in the parish and hundred of EDMONTON, county of MIDDLESEX, 8 miles (N. by W.) from London. The population is returned with the parish. The name of this place is derived from its situation at the south gate, or entrance, of Enfield Chase, and it is still called South-street division. The village contains many handsome houses : the New River runs at its extremity. The neighbourhood is well wooded; the Duke of Buckingham and Chandos having a residence here, in the grounds of which is a very fine old oak tree, that covers with its shade nearly an acre of ground. The chapelry is within the jurisdiction of a court of requests held at Enfield, for the recovery of debts under 40s. The living is a perpetual curacy, in the patronage of the Vicar of Edmonton. The chapel, built in 1615, at the sole expense of Sir John Weld, has been recently pulled down and rebuilt: it is endowed with an estate in Essex, called Orsett. There is a place of worship for Independents. A Lancasterian school was built by John Walker, Esq., and is supported solely by his widow. Mrs. Cowley left a sum of money to clothe nine boys and nine girls in this school. In an adjacent field, called 'Camp Field,' have been found several pieces of cannon, and a gorget belonging to Oliver Cromwell, having his initials handsomely inlaid with jewels, now in the British Museum; and in 1829, several ancient coins were dug up in the neighbourhood.

SOUTH-HAMLET, a hamlet in the parish of HEMPSTEAD, middle division of the hundred of DUD-STONE and KING'S BARTON, county of GLOUCESTER, containing 391 inhabitants.

SOUTH-HILL, a parish in the middle division of the hundred of EAST, county of CORNWALL, 3¼ miles (N. W.) from Callington, containing 534 inhabitants. The living is a rectory, with the perpetual curacy of Callington annexed, in the archdeaconry of Cornwall, and diocese of Exeter, rated in the king's books at £38, and in the patronage of Lord Clinton. The church is dedicated to St. Sampson. John Knill, in 1747, gave £5 per annum for teaching children and relieving the poor.

SOUTHILL, a parish in the hundred of WIXAM-TREE, county of BEDFORD, comprising the hamlets of Broom and Stanford, and the township of Southill, and containing 1165 inhabitants, of which number, 682 are in the township of Southill, 4 miles (S. W. by W.) from Biggleswade. The living is a discharged vicarage, with that of Old Warden annexed, in the archdeaconry of Bedford, and diocese of Lincoln, rated in the king's books at £11. 15., and in the patronage of W. H. Whitbread, Esq. The church, dedicated to All Saints, contains monuments of several of the Byng family, among which are those of the celebrated naval officer, Sir George Byng, the first Viscount Torrington, and of his son, Vice-Admiral the Hon. John Byng, who was executed for an alleged professional crime, though the inscription upon his coffin, engraved in brass, represents him to have fallen a martyr to political persecution. The Baptists have a place of worship here.

SOUTH-MEAD, an extra-parochial liberty, in the middle division of the hundred of DUDSTONE and KING'S BARTON, county of GLOUCESTER, adjacent to the south side of the city of Gloucester.

SOUTHOE, a parish in the hundred of TOSELAND, county of HUNTINGDON, 3¼ miles (N. by W.) from St. Neot's, containing 268 inhabitants. The living is a vicarage, with the perpetual curacy of Hale Weston annexed, in the archdeaconry of Huntingdon, and diocese of Lincoln, rated in the king's books at £14. 2. 3½., and in the patronage of the Rev. R. Pointer. The church is dedicated to St. Leonard.

SOUTHOLT, a parish in the hundred of HOXNE, county of SUFFOLK, 5 miles (S. E. by S.) from Eye, containing 203 inhabitants. The living is a perpetual curacy, annexed to the rectory of Worlingworth, in the archdeaconry of Suffolk, and diocese of Norwich. The church is dedicated to St. Margaret.

SOUTHORPE, an extra-parochial liberty, in the wapentake of CORRINGHAM, parts of LINDSEY, county of LINCOLN, 7 miles (N. E.) from Gainsborough, containing 34 inhabitants.

SOUTHORPE, a hamlet in the parish of BARNACK, liberty of PETERBOROUGH, county of NORTHAMPTON, 3¼ miles (N. by E.) from Wansford, containing 117 inhabitants.

SOUTHOVER, county of SUSSEX.—See LEWES.

SOUTHPORT, a chapelry in the parish of NORTH MEOLS, hundred of WEST DERBY, county palatine of LANCASTER, 9 miles (N. W.) from Ormskirk, and 22 (N.) from Liverpool. The population is returned with the parish. This place, situated at the mouth of the Ribble, on the shore of the Irish sea, has of late years been much resorted to for sea-bathing, and possesses most of the usual accommodations for visitors: it consists of one principal street, formed by handsome houses of brick, with gardens in front, and is surrounded by meols, or sand hills, resembling small tumuli. A theatre, news-rooms, and libraries, with other places of public resort, supply the means of amusement and relaxation. An episcopal chapel, called Christ church, was built in 1820, the right of presentation to which belongs to — Hesketh, Esq. There are places of worship for Independents and Wesleyan Methodists. The Strangers' charity furnishes to the sick poor the means of obtaining the benefits of sea air and bathing ; and a dispensary, erected in 1823, supplies the requisite medical aid.

SOUTHPORT, county of SOUTHAMPTON. — See PORTSEA.

SOUTHROP, a parish in the hundred of BRIGHTWELL'S BARROW, county of GLOUCESTER, 3 miles (N.) from Lechlade, containing 313 inhabitants. The living is a discharged vicarage, in the archdeaconry and diocese of Gloucester, rated in the king's books at £5. 16. 8., and in the patronage of the Warden and Fellows of Wadham College, Oxford. The church is dedicated to St. Peter.

SOUTHROP, a tything in the parish of HERRIARD, hundred of BERMONDSPIT, though locally in that of Odiham, Basingstoke division of the county of SOUTHAMPTON, 5 miles (N. W.) from Alton. The population is returned with the parish.

SOUTHROPE, a township in the parish of HOOK-NORTON, hundred of CHADLINGTON, county of OXFORD, containing 279 inhabitants.

SOUTHSEA, county of SOUTHAMPTON.——See PORTSEA.

SOUTH-TOWN, a parish in the hundred of MUTFORD and LOTHINGLAND, county of SUFFOLK, 1 mile (S. by W.) from Great Yarmouth, containing 1039 inhabitants. The living is a discharged rectory, consolidated, in 1520, with the vicarage of Gorleston, in the archdeaconry of Suffolk, and diocese of Norwich. The church, now demolished, was dedicated to St. Nicholas. South-town, or Little Yarmouth, which forms a populous suburb to Great Yarmouth, extends from Yarmouth bridge about half a mile to the southward, along the western bank of the river, one side of the road being occupied by elegant private houses, and the opposite, by timber wharfs, docks, and yards for ship-building, which afford employment to a great number of shipwrights and others.

SOUTHWARK, county of SURREY.—See LONDON.

SOUTHWELL, a market town and parish, in the liberty of SOUTHWELL and SCROOBY, county of NOTTINGHAM, 14 miles (N. E.) from Nottingham, and 132 (N. N. W.) from London, containing 3051 inhabitants. This place, which is of great antiquity, derived its name from one of many large springs, or wells, that formerly existed in the neighbourhood, few of which are now remaining. It was distinguished, at a very early period, by the foundation of one of the first Christian churches in this part of the country, by Paulinus, who, at the request of Ethelburga, wife of Edwin, King of Northumberland, had been sent over to England by Pope Gregory VII., to preach the doctrine of Christianity, which she had herself embraced, and who, having converted Edwin to the Christian faith, was made Archbishop of York, in 627. The history of the town relates chiefly to the progress of its religious establish-

ment, which flourished, under a succession of prelates, till the Conquest, at which time the church had become collegiate, had ample revenues, and contained ten prebends, the number of which was subsequently increased to sixteen. From the time of the Conquest till the period of the Reformation, the revenue of the church continued to increase, and the establishment to prosper, during the reigns of Henry I., Henry II., Henry III., Edward I., and other sovereigns, who contributed largely to its endowment. Popes Alexander III. and Urban III. were also beneficent patrons ; every succeeding archbishop was anxious to promote its independence, and the zeal and liberality of its own members were constantly devoted to its improvement. Soon after the dissolution of the monasteries by Henry VIII., the archbishop, and the prebendaries of Southwell, surrendered the church into the possession of that monarch, by whom, at the request of Cranmer, Archbishop of Canterbury, the chapter was refounded, in 1541, and Southwell subsequently erected into a see, of which, in 1543, Dr. Cox, afterwards translated to Ely, was appointed bishop. Edward VI., soon after his accession to the throne, dissolved the chapter, and granted the prebendal estates to John, Earl of Warwick, upon whose attainder, in 1553, they reverted to the crown, and were restored by Queen Mary, who re-established the chapter upon its ancient foundation, and the prebendal establishment was finally confirmed by Queen Elizabeth, in 1585, and a new code of laws instituted. During the parliamentary war, Charles I. was frequently at this town, and held his court generally at the archiepiscopal palace, and occasionally at the King's Arms Inn, now the Saracen's Head, at which latter place, on the 6th of May, 1646, he privately surrendered himself to the Scottish commissioners. The parliamentary troops, during their stay in the town, converted the church into a stable, broke the monuments, defaced the ornaments, and demolished the episcopal palace, in which Cardinal Wolsey resided during the summer previous to his death ; the lands belonging to the see were sold for £4061. They destroyed all the ancient records, except the Registrum Album, or white book, which is still in the possession of the chapter, and contains most of the grants to the church, from the year 1109 to 1525.

The town is pleasantly situated on a gentle eminence richly clothed with wood, and surrounded by an amphitheatre of hills of various elevation, near the small river Greet, which is celebrated for the red trout abounding in it, and comprises the districts of the Burgage, the High Town, East Thorpe, and West Thorpe, together forming a considerable, though scattered, town : it is well paved and abundantly supplied with water : the houses are in general well built, and the town has a neat and prepossessing appearance. Assemblies are held in a commodious suite of rooms erected in 1806 ; a harmonic society, established in 1786, is well supported, and a small neat theatre was opened in 1816. A pleasant promenade has been formed on the north side of the churchyard, and planted with trees, called the Parade : the roads in the vicinity have been recently improved. The air is salubrious, and the environs afford some agreeable walks. There is not much trade carried on, and the only branch of manufacture is that of silk, for which a mill has been recently erected on the river Greet by a firm at Nottingham. The market is on Saturday : the airs are on Whit-Monday, which is a pleasure fair, and October 21st, a statute fair. The town is under two separate jurisdictions, called the Burgage and the Prebendage: the former, denominated the Soke of Southwell *cum* Scrooby, includes twenty townships, for which quarterly courts of session are held by a *Custos Rotulorum*, and justices of the peace, nominated by the Archbishop of York and the Chapter of Southwell, and appointed by a commission under the great seal, for the trial of all but capital offenders. The prebendage includes twenty-eight parishes, over which the chapter, their vicar-general, exercise ecclesiastical jurisdiction, and all episcopal functions, except confirmation and ordination: the subdivisions of the town are under the superintendence of the constable, or bailiff, assisted by two thirdboroughs for each district. The house of correction for the county, a spacious and commodious building, which, after having been several times enlarged, was completed in 1829, comprises eleven wards, thirty-four work and day rooms, eleven airing-yards, and a tread-mill with four wheels, being well adapted to the classification of prisoners, who are employed in framework knitting, spinning yarn, shoe-making, &c., and receive a portion of their earnings on their discharge: the buildings consist of the governor's house, chapel, infirmary, baths, and the requisite offices.

The living is a discharged vicarage, in the peculiar jurisdiction of the Chapter, and in the patronage of the Prebendary of Normanton in the Collegiate Church, rated in the king's books at £7. 13. 4., endowed with £200 private benefaction, £600 royal bounty, and £400 parliamentary grant. The church, dedicated to St. Mary, (both parochial and collegiate), is a spacious and magnificent cruciform structure, chiefly of Norman architecture, with some portions in the early, decorated, and later styles of English architecture, having a low central tower, and two others of the same height at the west end, of seven stages, richly ornamented, between which is the principal entrance, through a fine circular arch, with a large window above it, of the later style, highly enriched with elegant tracery. The nave and transepts are of Norman character; the former has a flat roof of panelled oak finely carved, and supported upon a range of low massive circular columns and arches, and is lighted by a range of clerestory windows of small dimensions, above a triforium of large and undivided arches. The roof of the aisles is finely groined in stone; the arches and piers supporting the central tower are strikingly beautiful, from the simplicity of their style, and the stateliness of their elevation: the choir and the eastern transepts are beautiful specimens of the early English style, perhaps unrivalled for their purity of design, and fidelity of minute detail; the former is lighted by two tiers of lancet-shaped windows, and is fitted up as a parochial church, with galleries; the stalls and the screen are in the later period of the decorated style. There are few monuments deserving notice, except that of Archbishop Sandys, in the south transept, the principal having been destroyed during the occupation of the church by the parliamentarian troops. On the eastern side of the north transept was formerly a chantry, or singing school, which has been converted into a library for the college, containing a valuable and extensive collection of works, chiefly on divinity. On the north side of the

church is the chapter-house, in the decorated style of English architecture: the entrance doorway, which is double, is elegantly enriched with foliage of a character not very prevalent in England; the tracery in the windows, and in the stalls under them, is very beautiful. The prebendal houses, and especially that for the residentiary prebendary, are handsome buildings. In the church-yard are some remains of the ancient collegiate buildings the establishment of which is still retained, consisting of sixteen prebendaries, six vicars choral, an organist, six singing men, six choristers, and six boys as probationers, with a registrar, treasurer, auditor, and other officers : two annual synods are held, at which all the Nottinghamshire clergy attend, over whom a certain number of the prebendaries are appointed by the archbishop to preside. There are places of worship for Baptists and Wesleyan Methodists.

The free grammar school, which occupies the site of the college of the chantry priests, is under the superintendence of the chapter of the collegiate church, by which body the master is appointed, subject to the approval of the Archbishop of York; it has two scholarships founded in St. John's College, Cambridge, by the Rev. Dr. John Keyton, Canon of Salisbury in the reign of Henry VIII., for boys who have been choristers in the collegiate church: the school, which has a small endowment, is open to all boys of the town for gratuitous instruction in the classics. In 1744, Mr. Thomas Bailsford bequeathed lands for teaching ten poor children; Mr. Richard Stenton, in 1771, left £150 for building a school-room; and, in 1775, Mr. John Leverock gave land for clothing and instructing children. There are Sunday schools in connexion with the established church and the dissenting congregations. Of the ancient episcopal palace there are considerable remains, consisting chiefly of the chapel and great hall, which are almost entire, and have been fitted up as a modern residence: in this portion of the building is a room lighted by the great west window of the hall, which is appropriated to the holding of the sessions: the quadrangle, once surrounded with offices, has been converted into a garden. Vestiges of a Roman fosse are perceptible on the Burgage hill. Of the springs which formerly distinguished this vicinity, and from one of which the town derived its name, St. Catherine's well, at West Thorpe, celebrated for the cure of rheumatism, and South well, about half a mile to the south-east of the town, are still open. The ruins of the palace, which are overspread with ivy, form an interesting and romantic ornament to the town: the northern portion of the building is nearly entire, and has been fitted up as a modern residence, and the extensive quadrangle converted into a garden. Near them were found, in 1780, a large ring of pure gold, on the inside of which was inscribed *Mieu mouri que change ma foi*, and, in 1828, a large brass seal, with the device of a female kneeling, and holding in her right hand a tilting spear bearing a breast-plate, out of which rises a unicorn's head, and in her left hand a shield, with the arms of Cavendish and Kemp quartered, and on a scroll encircling the device the legend *Gorge Rygmayden*, in Saxon characters: this seal is preserved in the museum at York.

SOUTHWELL-PARK, in the parish of HARGRAVE, hundred of THINGOE, county of SUFFOLK, 7 miles (W.

s. w.) from Bury-St. Edmund's. The population is returned with the parish.

SOUTHWICK, a township in the parish of MONK-WEARMOUTH, eastern division of CHESTER ward, county palatine of DURHAM, 1¾ mile (N. W. by W.) from Sunderland, containing 1004 inhabitants. There is a place of worship for Wesleyan Methodists. On the banks of the Wear, in this township, are several lime-kilns, ship-yards, and earthernware and glass manufactories. Human bones, and sometimes entire skeletons, have been found on removing the soil above the limestone quarries on Southwick hills.

SOUTHWICK, a parish in the hundred of WILLY-BROOK, county of NORTHAMPTON, 2¾ miles (N. N. W.) from Oundle, containing 109 inhabitants. The living is a discharged vicarage, in the archdeaconry of Northampton, and diocese of Peterborough, rated in the king's books at £8. 7. 6., and in the patronage of George F. Lynn, Esq. The church is dedicated to St. Mary.

SOUTHWICK, a parish in the hundred of PORTS-DOWN, Portsdown division of the county of SOUTHAMPTON, 3¼ miles (N. E. by E.) from Fareham, containing 711 inhabitants. The living is a donative, in the patronage of T. Thistlethwayte, Esq. The church is dedicated to St. James. A priory of Black canons, founded by Henry I., and originally established at Porchester, in 1133, was soon after removed hither, and flourished till the dissolution, when its revenue was valued at £314. 17. 10. per annum : it acquired some historical celebrity from its having been the scene of the marriage of Henry VI., with Margaret of Anjou ; and there are still some small remains of the monastic buildings in Southwick Park. The manor-house is a large building of some antiquity, having two wings terminating in gables, and embattled. King Charles I. was on a visit to the owner of this mansion at the time when the Duke of Buckingham, whom he had accompanied thus far from London, was assassinated by Felton, at Portsmouth : George I. was also entertained here. The publicans at Southwick enjoy the peculiar privilege, under a charter of Queen Elizabeth, of having no soldiers billeted upon them, nor quartered in their houses. A fair for horses is held on April 5th ; and here was formerly a market, granted to the priory, in 1235, but it has long been disused.

SOUTHWICK, a parish in the hundred of FISHER-GATE, rape of BRAMBER, county of SUSSEX, 1½ mile (E.) from New Shoreham, containing 374 inhabitants. The living is a discharged rectory, in the archdeaconry of Lewes, and diocese of Chichester, rated in the king's books at £9. 13. 9½., and in the patronage of the Crown. The church, dedicated to St. Michael, is principally in the Norman style, though the upper story of the tower and some smaller portions are of later date. John Gray, in 1751, left a small sum towards the support of a school.

SOUTHWICK, a chapelry in the parish of NORTH BRADLEY, hundred of WHORWELSDOWN, county of WILTS, 2½ miles (S. W. by S.) from Trowbridge, containing 1562 inhabitants. The living is a perpetual curacy, annexed to the vicarage of North Bradley, in the archdeaconry and diocese of Salisbury, endowed with £1200 private benefaction, and £3400 parliamentary grant. There are places of worship for Baptists and Wesleyan Methodists.

SOUTHWOLD, a sea-port, borough, market town, and parish, having separate jurisdiction, though locally in the hundred of Blything, county of SUFFOLK, 36 miles (N. E.) from Ipswich, and 104 (N. E.) from London, containing 1676 inhabitants. The ancient names of this place were *Suwald, Suwalda, Sudholda, and Southwood*, probably de-

Arms.

rived from an adjacent wood, the western confines still retaining the appellation of Wood's-end Marshes, and Wood's-end Creek. In the year 1659, a dreadful conflagration took place, which in a few hours consumed the town hall, market-house, prison, several other buildings, and two hundred and thirty-eight dwelling-houses, at an estimated loss ·of more than £40,000 ; the court baron rolls were all destroyed, and in consequence the copyholders under the corporation became freeholders. Another remarkable event was the memorable sea-fight between the English, under the command of His Royal Highness the Duke of York, and the Dutch under Admiral Ruyter, which took place in Sole bay, to the east of the town, on the 26th of May, 1672, in which, though the former proved victorious, many brave and distinguished officers were slain, among whom was the Earl of Sandwich, second in command. In 1747, the haven, which had become choked up with sand, was cleared out by act of parliament. In 1749, a pier was erected on the north side ; and in 1751, another on the south side, by the same authority. The town is pleasantly situated on a hill overlooking the German Ocean, and is rendered peninsular by the sea and a creek, called the Buss creek, which runs into the river Blyth, over which there is a bridge, formerly a drawbridge, leading into the town : it consists principally of one paved street ; the houses are mostly well built and of modern appearance, and the inhabitants are well supplied with water from numerous excellent springs. On St. Edmund's, commonly called Gun, Hill, are six eighteen-pounders, presented by His Royal Highness the Duke of Cumberland, who landed here October 17th, 1745. There was formerly an ancient fort, probably in the possession of the Danes on their invasion of the country in 1010, of which the foss is still discernible. From the nature of its situation and the convenience of the beach, Southwold is admirably adapted for sea-bathing, and has for several years been much resorted to for that purpose : there is a good promenade ; also a reading-room, called the *Casino*, on the Gun Hill, with an assembly-room : races are held annually. In consequence of the encroachments of the sea, a breakwater has been made under Gun Hill cliff, extending upwards of three hundred yards. The trade of the town consists in the home fishery, which employs several small boats ; in the preparation and exportation of salt, for which there is a manufactory ; and of red herrings, red sprats, and malt : the imports are coal and cinders : the coasting trade is chiefly in timber, lime, wool, and corn. The entrance into the haven is on the south side of the town : they superintendence of it is vested in commissioners, its revenue being about £1400 per annum, which is expended in repairing the piers and haven. The river Blyth is navigable to Halesworth, and, besides the bridge crossing it on the north, there is a ferry to Walberswick. The market is on Thursday, and fairs are held on Trinity-Monday and St. Bartholomew's day, for toys, &c.

The first charter of incorporation was granted by Henry VII., and confirmed, with extended privileges, by Henry VIII. and subsequent sovereigns: that under which it is now governed was granted by William and Mary. The government is vested in two bailiffs, a high steward, town clerk, coroner, and other officers. The

Corporate Seal.

bailiffs and the inferior officers are elected annually on the 6th of December : the bailiffs and high steward are justices of the peace, with exclusive jurisdiction, and hold regular sessions for the trial of felons and other offenders. A court of record, for the recovery of debts to any amount, is held every Monday, at which the bailiffs and the high steward preside. Here is also a court of admiralty, of which the bailiffs are the judges, its jurisdiction extending not further than the limits of the town, although those of the port reach from Cove-hithe to Thorpe-ness. The guildhall was erected by the corporation, at an expense of £800; and the old gaol having been taken down, a new one was built, in the year 1819. The living is a perpetual curacy, annexed to the vicarage of Reydon, in the archdeaconry of Suffolk, and diocese of Norwich, endowed with £400 private benefaction, £600 royal bounty, and £1000 parliamentary grant. The church, dedicated to St. Edmund, and completed about 1460, is a very elegant structure, in the later style of English architecture, with a large and lofty tower, surmounted with a spire, and constructed with freestone intermixed with flint of various colours. At each angle of the east end of the chancel is a low hexagonal embattled tower, decorated with crosses : the south porch is very elegant, and above the clerestory roof is a light open lantern : the ceiling is handsomely painted : the interior was, in former times, very richly ornamented, as appears by the carved work of the rood-loft, screen, and the seats of the magistrates. On the south side of the churchyard are three gravestones, in memory of Thomas Gardner, the historian of Dunwich and Southwold, and his two wives and daughter, on which are some singular inscriptions. The church has lately received an addition of one hundred free sittings, towards defraying the expense of which the Incorporated Society for building and enlarging churches and chapels contributed £50. There are places of worship for Baptists, Independents, and Wesleyan Methodists. On a hill, called Eye cliff, at a small distance from the town, are vestiges of ancient encampments, and, in many parts, of circular tents, now called Fairy hills, most probably of Danish origin. Fossil remains of the elephant and mammoth are frequently found in the cliffs.

SOUTHWOOD, a parish in the hundred of BLO-FIELD, county of NORFOLK, 3¾ miles (S. by W.) from Acle, containing 40 inhabitants. The living is a dis-

VOL. IV.

charged rectory, annexed to the vicarage of Limpenhoe, in the archdeaconry and diocese of Norwich. The church is dedicated to St. Edmund.

SOUTHWORTH, a joint township with Croft, in the parish of WINWICK, hundred of WEST DERBY, county palatine of LANCASTER, 3¼ miles (S. E. by E.) from Newton in Mackerfield, containing 1257 inhabitants. The hall once belonged to the Roman Catholic college of Stonyhurst, and part of it is still used as a chapel by persons of that persuasion.

SOW, a parish partly in the Kirby division of the hundred of KNIGHTLOW, but chiefly in the county of the city of COVENTRY, county of WARWICK, 3 miles (E. N. E.) from Coventry, containing 1212 inhabitants. The living is a vicarage, in the archdeaconry of Coventry, and diocese of Lichfield and Coventry, and in the patronage of the Crown. The church, dedicated to St. Mary, has lately received an addition of one hundred and eighty-one sittings, of which one hundred and sixty-six are free, the Incorporated Society for the enlargement of churches and chapels having granted £100 towards defraying the expense. Considerable coal-works are in operation in this parish, and many of the inhabitants are engaged in the riband manufacture, in connexion with the trade of Coventry.

SOWERBY, a joint township with Inskip, in the parish of ST. MICHAEL, hundred of AMOUNDERNESS, county palatine of LANCASTER, 4¼ miles (S. S. W.) from Garstang. The population is returned with Inskip.

SOWERBY, a chapelry in the parish of THIRSK, wapentake of BIRDFORTH, North riding of the county of YORK, 1 mile (S.) from Thirsk, containing 748 inhabitants. The living is a perpetual curacy, in the archdeaconry of Cleveland, and diocese of York, endowed with £200 private benefaction and £400 royal bounty, and in the patronage of the Archbishop of York.

SOWERBY, a chapelry in the parish of HALIFAX, wapentake of MORLEY, West riding of the county of YORK, 4 miles (S. S. W.) from Halifax, containing, with Ramble, 6890 inhabitants. The living is a perpetual curacy, in the archdeaconry and diocese of York, endowed with £200 private benefaction, £200 royal bounty, and £800 parliamentary grant, and in the patronage of the Vicar of Halifax. The chapel, dedicated to St. Peter, contains a fine statue, erected about half a century ago, to the memory of John Tillotson, D.D., Archbishop of Canterbury, who was born at Haugh-End, his father having been a manufacturer, in 1630 ; he died in 1694. There are places of worship for Independents and Wesleyan Methodists. The manufacture of woollen and cotton goods is extensively carried on here. Paul Bairslow, in 1711, bequeathed £16 per annum for the support of a school. In 1678, a considerable number of Roman coins was ploughed up in the neighbourhood.

SOWERBY (CASTLE), a parish in LEATH ward, county of CUMBERLAND, 3¼ miles (S. E. by E.) from Hesket-Newmarket, containing, with the townships of Bustabeck, How-bound, Row-bound, Southernby-bound, and Stocklewath-bound, 1012 inhabitants. The living is a discharged vicarage, in the archdeaconry and diocese of Carlisle, rated in the king's books at £17. 10. 5., and in the patronage of the Dean and Chapter of Carlisle. The church is dedicated to St. Kentigern. At Birks-ceugh are the remains of a chapel, formerly called Lady

T

chapel; and in the township of How-bound is Castle Hill, the site of an ancient castle, from which the parish derives its distinguishing prefix. Four poor children are instructed for a rent-charge of £5, the bequest of John Sowerby, in 1783.

SOWERBY under COTLIFFE, a township in the parish of KIRBY-SIGSTON, wapentake of ALLERTON-SHIRE, North riding of the county of YORK, 3 miles (E. by S.) from North Allerton, containing 53 inhabitants.

SOWERBY (TEMPLE), a chapelry in the parish of KIRKBY-THORE, EAST ward, county of WESTMORLAND, 7 miles (N. W.) from Appleby, containing 371 inhabitants. The living is a perpetual curacy, in the archdeaconry and diocese of Carlisle, endowed with £500 private benefaction, and £400 royal bounty, and in the patronage of the Earl of Thanet. The chapel, dedicated to St. James, is a handsome structure of red freestone, with a square tower and portico, rebuilt and enlarged, in 1770, at the expense of the late Sir William Dalston. There is a place of worship for Independents. The village, situated on the river Eden, which is crossed by a bridge rebuilt in 1748, is considered to be the neatest in the county: it consists of two spacious streets of well-built houses, with several commodious inns, and near it are many handsome villas inhabited by genteel families. Fairs for sheep and cattle are held here on the last Thursdays in February, March, and October, and on the second Thursday in May. The Knights Templars had a preceptory here, which, when suppressed in 1312, was given to the Knights Hospitallers.

SOWERBY-BRIDGE, a chapelry in the parish of HALIFAX, wapentake of MORLEY, West riding of the county of YORK, 2¾ miles (S. W. by W.) from Halifax, with which the population is returned. The living is a perpetual curacy, in the archdeaconry and diocese of York, endowed with £200 private benefaction, and £400 royal bounty, and in the patronage of the Vicar of Halifax. The old chapel being insufficient to accommodate the increased population of the place, a more commodious structure has been built, containing nearly one thousand sittings, of which three hundred and seven are free, the Incorporated Society for the enlargement of churches and chapels having granted £800 towards defraying the expense. There is a place of worship for Wesleyan Methodists. Woollen and cotton goods are manufactured here to a considerable extent. There are also three large iron-foundries, and a great number of corn-mills on the Calder, which river and the Rochdale canal pass through this district. Great quantities of stone are obtained here.

SOWTON, a parish partly in the eastern division of the hundred of BUDLEIGH, but chiefly in that of WONFORD, county of DEVON, 4 miles (E.) from Exeter, containing 339 inhabitants. The living is a rectory, in the archdeaconry and diocese of Exeter, rated in the king's books at £11. 16. 3., and in the patronage of the Bishop of Exeter. The church is dedicated to St. Michael. Five poor children are instructed for a small annuity left by Thomas Weare, in 1691.

SOYLAND, a township in the parish of HALIFAX, wapentake of MORLEY, West riding of the county of YORK, 5½ miles (S. W. by W.) from Halifax, containing 3242 inhabitants, many of whom are employed in the manufacture of cotton and woollen goods.

SPALDING, a market town and parish in the wapentake of ELLOE, parts of HOLLAND, county of LINCOLN, 44 miles (S. E. by S.) from Lincoln, and 100 (N.) from London, containing, according to the last census, 5207 inhabitants, now supposed to amount to upwards of 6000. This place is said to have derived its name from a Spa, or spring of chalybeate water, in the market-place: it is of considerable antiquity, being mentioned at an early period of the Saxon annals as one of the points on the boundary line of the estate belonging to Crowland abbey, to which a subordinate cell for a prior and five monks was founded here, in 1051, by Thorold de Buckenhale ; but at the Conquest, on the presentation of this manor to Ivo Talbois, Earl of Angiers, and nephew of the Conqueror, who built a castle here, the society was so harassed by their new neighbour as to be compelled to abandon their cell, which, falling into his hands, was given, in 1074, with the church of St. Mary and the manor, to the abbey of St. Nicholas at Angiers, whereupon some Benedictine monks were sent over, and it became an Alien priory to that monastery, being dedicated to St. Mary and St. Nicholas : it did not share the fate of other Alien houses, but was raised to the dignity of an abbey, and so continued until the general suppression, when its revenue was valued at £878. 18. 3. The town is situated on the river Welland, in a fenny district, but remarkably well drained : the streets are clean and well paved, the houses of neat appearance, and the inhabitants are well supplied with water. An Antiquarian Society was established here, many years ago, by Mr. Maurice Johnson, a native of the town, of which Sir Isaac Newton, Sir Hans Sloane, Dr. Stukeley, and several other distinguished persons, were members; many of the valuable books are still preserved, some in the vestry-room of the church, and others in the grammar school, as are also some manuscripts, relics of antiquity, and natural curiosities : the room is now used for a permanent subscription library. A literary club has also been recently established. The theatre, a small and neat edifice, is open about three weeks in the year : assemblies are occasionally held in commodious rooms in the town hall. The land in the vicinity is extensively appropriated to grazing, and the fenny tracts have been drained by means of steam-engines. Wool forms a principal article of trade, and some of the manufacturing towns of Yorkshire are supplied from this neighbourhood. Since the river Welland was made navigable to Crowland and Stamford, Spalding has acquired a considerable traffic in corn and coal; sloops of from fifty to seventy tons' burden come up to the centre of the town, and by these a regular coasting trade is maintained with London, Hull, Lynn, and other places : there is a quay for landing goods, with spacious storehouses for their reception. The port is a member of the port of Boston. The market, on Tuesday, is the largest in the county for cattle. Fairs are held April 27th, June 30th, August 28th, September 25th, and December 6th, chiefly for live stock. Spalding has been the principal seat of jurisdiction for the parts of Holland for many centuries. In the Saxon times the courts of law were held here by the earls, and subsequently to the Conquest the priors were invested with the judicial authority, and possessed the power of life and death. At present the quarter sessions for these parts are held here, and petty sessions for the wapentake every week. Courts of sewers, and of requests for the recovery of debts not exceeding £5, for the hundred of Elloe; and also courts leet and baron, at which the steward presides, are held. The town hall, situated at the north-west end of the market-place, was erected at the expense of Mr. John Hobson: the lower part is let for shops, and the rental given to the poor, according to the will of the donor. A new house of correction for the parts of Holland was built in 1824 : it is an airy and commodious edifice, under very good regulations.

The living is a perpetual curacy, in the archdeaconry and diocese of Lincoln, and in the patronage of certain Trustees, who are seized of the rectory, which is of considerable annual value, in trust for the incumbent. The church, which is dedicated to St. Mary and St. Nicholas, is principally in the later style of English architecture, with a fine tower and crocketed spire : it was erected in 1284, instead of the conventual church, then pulled down, and considerable additions were made in 1466, amongst which was a very beautiful north porch. There are places of worship for Baptists, the Society of Friends, Independents, and Wesleyan Methodists. A free grammar school was erected in the reign of Elizabeth, and endowed, by the will of John Blanche, with eighty-nine acres of land, for the support of a master to instruct the children of householders born in the parish : the original endowment has been considerably augmented by Mr. Atkinson: the trustees are incorporated, and have a common seal. Another, called the Petit school, was founded, in 1682, by Thomas Willesley, and endowed with nearly sixty acres of land. The Blue-coat school, founded by one of the Gamlyn family, is supported by a small endowment of land, aided by voluntary contributions. An almshouse, for the reception of twenty-two poor persons, was founded and endowed, in 1590, by Sir Matthew Gamlyn; and another for eight poor widows, in 1709, by Mrs. Elizabeth Sparke. There are also considerable estates vested in trustees, called "Town Husbands," for the benefit of the poor. A portion of the abbey buildings yet remains, which has been partly converted into tenements, and is partly in ruins. Many relics of antiquity have at different periods been discovered in the neighbourhood, and others taken out of the river Welland.

SPALDINGTON, a township in the parish of BUBWITH, Holme-Beacon division of the wapentake of HARTHILL, East riding of the county of YORK, 4½ miles (N. by E.) from Howden, containing 361 inhabitants. There is a place of worship for Wesleyan Methodists. Spaldington hall, formerly the seat of the ancient family of Vavasour, is a fine specimen of the Elizabethan style of architecture.

SPALDWICK, a parish in the hundred of LEIGH-TONSTONE, county of HUNTINGDON, 3¾ miles (N. E. by N.) from Kimbolton, containing 332 inhabitants. The living is a discharged vicarage, in the peculiar jurisdiction and patronage of the Prebendary of Long-stowe in the Cathedral Church of Lincoln, rated in the king's books at £12. 0. 10., and endowed with £200 royal bounty. The church is dedicated to St. James. There are places of worship for Baptists and Independents. Fairs for cattle are held on Whit-Monday and November 28th.

SPALFORD, a hamlet in the parish of NORTH CLIFTON, northern division of the wapentake of NEWARK, county of NOTTINGHAM, 7 miles (E. by S.) from Tuxford, containing 86 inhabitants.

SPANBY, a parish in the wapentake of AVELAND, parts of KESTEVEN, county of LINCOLN, 4¼ miles (N. N. E.) from Falkingham, containing 73 inhabitants. The living is a vicarage, in the archdeaconry and diocese of Lincoln, and in the patronage of Jerome Knapp, Esq. The church is dedicated to St. Nicholas.

SPARHAM, a parish in the hundred of EYNSFORD, county of NORFOLK, 3 miles (S. W.) from Reepham, containing 330 inhabitants. The living is a rectory, in the archdeaconry of Norfolk, and diocese of Norwich, rated in the king's books at £9. 17. 11., and in the patronage of Edward Lombe, Esq. The church is dedicated to St. Mary.

SPARKFORD, a parish in the hundred of CATS-ASH, county of SOMERSET, 4¼ miles (S. W. by S.) from Castle-Cary, containing 273 inhabitants. The living is a rectory, in the archdeaconry of Wells, and diocese of Bath and Wells, rated in the king's books at £12. 16. 3., and in the patronage of James Bennett, Esq. The church, dedicated to St. Mary Magdalene, has lately received an addition of sixty-seven sittings, of which sixty-two are free, the Incorporated Society for the enlargement of churches and chapels having granted £40 towards defraying the expense.

SPARSHOLT, a parish partly in the hundred of SHRIVENHAM, but chiefly in that of WANTAGE, county of BERKS, 3¼ miles (W.) from Wantage, containing, with the joint chapelry of Kingston-Lisle with Farlow, 817 inhabitants. The living is a discharged vicarage, in the archdeaconry of Berks, and diocese of Salisbury, rated in the king's books at £20. 2. 3½., and in the patronage of the Provost and Fellows of Queen's College, Oxford. The church, dedicated to the Holy Cross, is principally in the Norman style : it contains three stone stalls, and a piscina, highly enriched with trefoil ornaments and crocketed pinnacles. The Wilts and Berks canal passes through the parish, and the Iknield road through the vale of White Horse, to the southward of the village. Abraham Atkins, in 1788, gave a school-house, and endowed with a moiety of the rents arising from a certain estate : the annual income is about £63, for which the master instructs all the children of the parish who apply. Eight others are taught for £2. 10. a year, the gift of Richard Edmondson, in 1713.

SPARSHOLT, a parish in the hundred of BUDDLES-GATE, Fawley division of the county of SOUTHAMPTON, 3¾ miles (W. N. W.) from Winchester, containing, with Lainson, 370 inhabitants. The living is a vicarage, in the archdeaconry and diocese of Winchester, rated in the king's books at £16. 10. 2½., and in the patronage of the Crown. The church is dedicated to St. Stephen. Sparsholt is within the jurisdiction of the Cheyney Court held at Winchester every Thursday, for the recovery of debts to any amount.

SPAUNTON, a township in the parish of LAST-INGHAM, wapentake of RYEDALE, North riding of the county of YORK, 7½ miles (N. W.) from Pickering, containing 109 inhabitants.

SPAXTON, a parish in the hundred of CANNING-TON, county of SOMERSET, 5 miles (W.) from Bridgwater, containing 816 inhabitants. The living is a rectory, in the archdeaconry of Taunton, and diocese of Bath and Wells, rated in the king's books at £24. 8. 9., and in the patronage of the Rev. William Gordon. The church is dedicated to St. Margaret. The Rev. Joseph Cook, in 1708, bequeathed lands producing a liberal income for the maintenance of six poor persons in an hospital, for teaching poor children, and other charitable purposes.

SPECTON, a chapelry in the parish of BRIDLINGTON, wapentake of DICKERING, East riding of the county of YORK, 5½ miles (N. N. W.) from Bridlington, containing 116 inhabitants. The living is a perpetual curacy, in the archdeaconry of the East riding, and diocese of York, endowed with £800 royal bounty, and in the patronage of W. J. Denison, Esq.

SPEEN, a parish comprising the tythings of Benham and Church-Speen, in the hundred of KINTBURY-EAGLE, and the township of Wood-Speen with Bagnor, and the tything of Speenhamland, in that of FAIRCROSS, county of BERKS, and containing 2392 inhabitants, of which number, 600 are in the tything of Church-Speen, ¾ of a mile (W.) from Speenhamland. The living is a vicarage, in the archdeaconry of Berks, and diocese of Salisbury, rated in the king's books at £14. 0. 10., and in the patronage of the Bishop of Salisbury. The church, dedicated to St. Mary, contains some curious monumental figures. The parish is bounded on the south by the river Kennet and the Kennet and Avon canal, and on the north by the river Lambourn. This was the *Spinæ* of the Romans, a station on the road from Gloucester to Silchester. To the north of the church traces of an agger, or fortification, are distinctly visible; and on Speen moor a large urn was found under a tumulus of earth eight feet high; a Roman altar, consecrated to Jupiter, was also discovered, in 1730, at Fulsham, in this neighbourhood. This was the principal scene of the second battle of Newbury, fought October 27th, 1644, between what is now the castle and the village. Here was formerly a market on Monday, but it has been long disused.

SPEEN (WOOD), a joint township with Bagnor, in that part of the parish of SPEEN which is in the hundred of FAIRCROSS, county of BERKS, 2 miles (N. W. by N.) from Speenhamland, containing, with Bagnor, 594 inhabitants.

SPEENHAMLAND, a hamlet in that part of the parish of SPEEN which is in the hundred of FAIRCROSS, county of BERKS, adjoining the town of Newbury, containing 818 inhabitants. An almshouse was founded here, in 1664, by Mrs. Anne Watts, for two poor widows, with an allowance of two shillings each per week.

SPEKE, a township in the parish of CHILDWALL, hundred of WEST DERBY, county palatine of LANCASTER, 7 miles (S. S. W.) from Prescot, containing 462 inhabitants.

SPELDHURST, a parish partly in the hundred of SOMERDEN, lathe of SUTTON at HONE, but chiefly in the hundred of WASHLINGSTONE, lathe of AYLESFORD, county of KENT, 3 miles (N. W.) from Tonbridge-Wells, containing 2297 inhabitants. The living is a rectory, in the archdeaconry and diocese of Rochester, rated in the king's books at £15. 5., and in the patronage of R. Burgess, Esq. The church, dedicated to St. Mary, was struck by lightning and burned down in 1791; it was rebuilt in the following year, and has lately received an addition of one hundred and fifty free sittings, the In-

corporated Society for the enlargement of churches and chapels having granted £150 towards defraying the expense. A branch of the river Medway runs through the parish, upon which there are several mills, and a large iron-foundry, called Barden Furnace. Iron-ore abounds here, and, in consequence, the springs are more or less chalybeate. Tonbridge-Wells, situated partly in this parish, is the place most resorted to for drinking these waters; for a detailed account of it, see the article on that place.

SPELSBURY, a parish in the hundred of CHADLINGTON, county of OXFORD, 5 miles (S. E. by S.) from Chipping-Norton, containing, with the hamlets of Dean, Ditchley, Fullwell, and Taston, 610 inhabitants. The living is a vicarage, in the archdeaconry and diocese of Oxford, rated in the king's books at £9. 8. 9., endowed with £200 private benefaction, and £200 royal bounty, and in the patronage of the Dean and Canons of Christ Church, Oxford. The church, dedicated to All Saints, contains the remains of John, the celebrated Earl of Rochester. On an eminence near the village is an extensive triangular intrenchment, called Castle Ditches, enclosing a space of about twenty-four acres.

SPENNITHORN, a parish in the western division of the wapentake of HANG, North riding of the county of YORK, comprising the townships of Bellerby, Harmby, and Spennithorn, and containing 850 inhabitants, of which number, 249 are in the township of Spennithorn, 1 mile (N. E. by N.) from Middleham. The living is a rectory, in the archdeaconry of Richmond, and diocese of Chester, rated in the king's books at £20. 10. 5., and in the patronage of Marmaduke Wyvill, Esq. The church is dedicated to St. Michael. John Hutchinson, a philosophical writer, was born here, in 1667.

SPERNALL, a parish in the Alcester division of the hundred of BARLICHWAY, county of WARWICK, 4 miles (N.) from Alcester, containing 113 inhabitants. The living is a discharged rectory, in the archdeaconry and diocese of Worcester, rated in the king's books at £3. 18. 1½., and in the patronage of the Rev. F. Chambers. The church is dedicated to St. Leonard.

SPETCHLEY, a parish in the lower division of the hundred of OSWALDSLOW, county of WORCESTER, 3¾ miles (E. by S.) from Worcester, containing 121 inhabitants. The living is a discharged rectory, in the archdeaconry and diocese of Worcester, rated in the king's books at £6. 11. 3. The Rev. George Dineley was patron in 1811. The church, dedicated to All Saints, contains several monuments worthy of notice, particularly two very handsome ones to the Berkeley family.

SPETISBURY, a parish in the hundred of LOOSEBARROW, Shaston (East) division of the county of DORSET, 3 miles (S. E. by S.) from Blandford-Forum, containing 546 inhabitants. The living is a rectory, with the perpetual curacy of Charlton-Marshall annexed, in the archdeaconry of Dorset, and diocese of Bristol, rated in the king's books at £28. 18. 1½., and in the patronage of Thomas Rackett, Esq. The church is dedicated to St. John the Baptist. The navigable river Stour runs close past the village. Dr. Sloper, in 1728, founded and endowed with £20 per annum a school for teaching poor children. There is also a bequest by Bishop Hall, for supplying the poor with bibles. Here was a priory, a cell to the abbey of Preaux in Normandy, founded in the time of Henry I., but afterwards considered part of the cell of Monk Toftes in Norfolk, belonging to the same house. In the neighbourhood are the remains of a fortification, in which many coins and other relics of the Saxons have been found.

SPEXHALL, a parish in the hundred of BLYTHING, county of SUFFOLK, 2 miles (N. by W.) from Halesworth, containing 172 inhabitants. The living is a discharged rectory, in the archdeaconry of Suffolk, and diocese of Norwich, rated in the king's books at £14, and in the patronage of the Crown. The church is dedicated to St. Peter.

SPILSBY, a market town and parish in the eastern division of the soke of BOLINGBROKE, parts of LINDSEY, county of LINCOLN, 31 miles (E.) from Lincoln, and 133 (N.) from London, containing 1234 inhabitants. The town is situated upon an elevated spot of ground which commands an extensive south-easterly view of a tract of marsh and fen land bounded by Boston deeps and the North sea: it consists of four principal streets diverging from a spacious square, forming the market-place, which is ornamented on its east side by a cross, consisting of a plain octagonal shaft rising from a quadrangular base, and resting on five steps. A subscription library and news-room is connected with the principal inn. The market is on Monday; and fairs are held on the Monday before, and the two next after, Whit-Monday (when Whitsuntide falls in May, otherwise there is no fair on the latter day), and on the third Monday in July, for cattle and wearing apparel. The general quarter sessions for the south division of the parts of Lindsey are held here twice a year, in January and July. A court-house and house of correction, begun in June 1824, were completed within two years, at an expense of £25,000: the latter contains sixty-three cells, eighteen day-rooms, and nine apartments for the turnkeys, with an infirmary and yards for the prisoners, so arranged that the governor's house commands a complete view of the whole: the site occupies about two acres of ground, and is surrounded by a lofty brick wall, in which, in front of the building, is a handsome Doric portico.

The living is a perpetual curacy, in the archdeaconry and diocese of Lincoln, endowed with £600 royal bounty, and £1200 parliamentary grant, and in the patronage of the Rector of Partney. The church, dedicated to St. James, is an ancient irregular stone edifice, with a handsome embattled tower at the west end, supposed to have been erected about the time of Henry VII., at a much later date than the body of the building. Amongst several ancient monuments is one in memory of the celebrated Lord Willoughby de Eresby, who, in the reign of Elizabeth, commanded four thousand English troops despatched to France, in aid of Henry IV., King of Navarre: he died in 1601, and was interred here. There are places of worship for Independents and Wesleyan Methodists, with Sunday schools attached. The grammar school, rebuilt in 1826, is endowed for the gratuitous education of thirty scholars. In 1735, the Duke of Ancaster and others endowed a school for the education and clothing of twenty poor boys. At Eresby, near this town, are extensive remains of the foundations of a chapel, made collegiate in 1349, for a master and twelve priests, by Sir John Willoughby, and dedicated to the Holy Trinity. At the same place was formerly an elegant mansion belonging to the late Duke of Ancaster, which, in 1769, was destroyed by fire, one pillar alone remaining.

SPINDLESTONE, a township in the parish of BAMBROUGH, northern division of BAMBROUGH ward, county of NORTHUMBERLAND, 3¼ miles (E. by S.) from Belford, containing 97 inhabitants. Here was anciently a military station of considerable extent, vestiges of mounds and intrenchments being conspicuous.

SPITTAL on the STREET, a chapelry in the parish of GLENTWORTH, western division of the wapentake of ASLACOE, parts of LINDSEY, county of LINCOLN, 10 miles (E.) from Gainsborough. The chapel is dedicated to St. Nicholas. An hospital for poor women, with a chapel dedicated to St. Edmund, existed here in the reign of Edward II., was augmented in that of Richard II., and is now under the superintendence of the Dean and Chapter of Lincoln.

SPITTLE, a joint township with Poulton, in the parish of BEBBINGTON, lower division of the hundred of WIRRALL, county palatine of CHESTER, 5½ miles (N.E. by N.) from Great Neston. The population is returned with Poulton.

SPITTLE, or SPITTAL, a considerable fishing and sea-bathing village in the parish of TWEEDMOUTH, in ISLANDSHIRE, forming a part of the detached portion of the county palatine of DURHAM, locally northward of the county of Northumberland, 1 mile (S. E.) from Berwick upon Tweed. The population is returned with the parish. There is a place of worship for Presbyterians. This place, which is situated on the coast of the North sea, at the mouth of the river Tweed, consists of two principal streets. It was formerly inhabited by smugglers and others of disreputable character, but, since the enclosure of the adjacent common, these have gradually given place to honest and industrious fishermen. Here are six herring houses for curing red and white herrings, and good accommodation for persons who resort hither for sea-bathing and for drinking the water of a powerful chalybeate spring in the neighbourhood. On Sunnyside hill, half a mile from the village, is an extensive colliery, the property of the corporation of Berwick.

SPITTLE, a township in the parish of OVINGHAM, eastern division of TINDALE ward, county of NORTHUMBERLAND, 11 miles (W. by N.) from Newcastle upon Tyne, containing 3 inhabitants.

SPITTLE, a township in the parish of FANGFOSS, Wilton-Beacon division of the wapentake of HARTHILL, East riding of the county of YORK, 3½ miles (N. W.) from Pocklington. The population is returned with the parish.

SPITTLE-HILL, a township in that part of the parish of MITFORD which is in the western division of MORPETH ward, county of NORTHUMBERLAND, 1¾ mile (W. by N.) from Morpeth, containing 9 inhabitants. An hospital, dedicated to St. Leonard, was founded here, and endowed with lands by Sir William Bertram; the site is occupied by a modern mansion.

SPITTLEGATE, a township in that part of the parish of GRANTHAM which is in the wapentake of WINNIBRIGGS and THREO, parts of KESTEVEN, county of LINCOLN, 1 mile (S. by E.) from Grantham, containing 709 inhabitants.

SPIXWORTH, a parish in the hundred of TAVERHAM, county of NORFOLK, 4¾ miles (N. by E.) from

Norwich, containing 74 inhabitants. The living is a discharged rectory, in the archdeaconry and diocese of Norwich, rated in the king's books at £6. E. Longe, Esq. was patron in 1808. The church, dedicated to St. Peter, contains many monuments and inscriptions.

SPOFFORTH, a parish in the upper division of the wapentake of CLARO, West riding of the county of YORK, comprising the chapelry of Wetherby, and the townships of Follifoot, Linton, Plompton, Little Ribston, Spofforth, and Stockeld, and containing 3044 inhabitants, of which number, 895 are in the township of Spofforth, 3¼ miles (N.W. by W.) from Wetherby. The living is a rectory, in the archdeaconry and diocese of York, rated in the king's books at £73. 6. 8., and in the patronage of the Earl of Egremont. The church is dedicated to All Saints. There is a place of worship for Wesleyan Methodists. This was for several ages, prior to Alnwick, or Warkworth, the seat of the Percy family, who had a princely castle here, which was demolished by the Yorkists after the battle of Towton, in which the Earl of Northumberland and Sir Charles Percy, his brother, were slain. The grand hall of this once magnificent mansion, though in ruins, still remains ; it is nearly seventy-six feet in length, and about thirty-seven in breadth, and is lighted by one of those large cathedral windows introduced subsequently to the reign of Edward I. A school for fifteen poor children is supported by an annuity of £5, the gift of the Earl of Egremont, in 1786, and another of £2. 10., by the Rev. Dr. Trip.

SPONDON, a parish in the hundred of APPLETREE, county of DERBY, 3¼ miles (E. by S.) from Derby, containing, with the chapelry of Stanley, 1543 inhabitants. The living is a discharged vicarage, in the archdeaconry of Derby, and diocese of Lichfield and Coventry, rated in the king's books at £6. 14. 7., and in the patronage of the Executors of the late H. D. Lowe, Esq. The church, dedicated to St. Mary, is in the decorated style of English architecture, and has in the chancel three stone stalls : it has lately undergone a thorough repair, at an expense of £1200, and received an addition of one hundred and eighty sittings, of which one hundred and two are free, the Incorporated Society for the enlargement of churches and chapels having granted £65 towards defraying the expense : in the churchyard is an antique stone, apparently Saxon. The Derby canal passes through the parish, which was formerly more extensive, the chapelries of Chaddesden, Lockhay, and Stanley, having been recently separated from it, and erected into distinct parishes. The village of Spondon, on a commanding eminence, overlooking the beautiful vale of Derwent, is of considerable size, and the residence of several highly respectable families. The inhabitants are principally employed at the extensive cotton-mills, established here, and in the manufacture of stockings, lace, and net, for the Nottingham market. There is a place of worship for Wesleyan Methodists. A parochial library has been established. A free school for ten boys was endowed with a rent-charge of £3, by Thomas Gilbert, Esq., in 1657, and an annuity of £5, the gift of the Rev. George Stanhope, in 1727 : the school-room was built in 1699. A National school is supported by subscription.

SPOONBED, a tything in the parish of PAINSWICK, hundred of BISLEY, county of GLOUCESTER, containing 880 inhabitants.

SPORLE, a parish in the southern division of the hundred of GREENHOE, county of NORFOLK, 2½ miles (N. E. by E.) from Swaffham, containing, with the hamlet of Palgrave, 706 inhabitants. The living is a vicarage, in the archdeaconry of Norfolk, and diocese of Norwich, rated in the king's books at £10. 3. 6½., and in the patronage of the Provost and Fellows of Eton College. The church, dedicated to St. Mary, is an ancient and spacious building of flint, with a western tower, quoined and embattled with freestone, annexed to which is a large porch, also embattled, with a dilapidated room over it, supposed to have been once inhabited by a recluse. In the chancel are many old gravestones, stripped of their brasses, and on the north side a small chapel, separated from the aisle by screen-work. A priory of Black monks, a cell to the abbey of Saumers in Anjou, was founded here, as it is thought, by Henry II., in honour of the Blessed Virgin Mary, and at the suppression was granted, by Henry VI., towards the endowment of Eton College. Eight children are instructed for a small sum arising from the rent of certain land bequeathed by Sir Matthew Colworthy.

SPOTLAND, a chapelry, consisting of the townships of Spotland Further Side and Spotland Nearer Side, in that part of the parish of ROCHDALE which is in the hundred of SALFORD, county palatine of LANCASTER, 1¼ mile (N. W.) from Rochdale, containing 13,453 inhabitants. The living is a perpetual curacy, in the archdeaconry and diocese of Chester, and in the patronage of Vicar of Rochdale. This chapelry forms an extensive suburb to the town of Rochdale, and largely participates in the cotton and every other branch of trade and manufacture carried on there. It is in contemplation to erect a new chapel, his Majesty's commissioners for building churches having proposed a grant for that purpose. Samuel Taylor and Robert Jacques, in 1740, conveyed to trustees a school-house and sundry other property, for the free education of children ; the annual income is about £31, which is paid to a school-mistress, for teaching twenty girls. The premises were rebuilt in 1819, at an expense of £400, the amount of accumulations.

SPRATTON, a parish in the hundred of SPELHOE, county of NORTHAMPTON, 6¾ miles (N. N. W.) from Northampton, containing, with the hamlet of Little Creaton, 945 inhabitants. The living is a vicarage, in the archdeaconry of Northampton, and diocese of Peterborough, rated in the king's books at £15, and in the patronage of John Bartlett, Esq. The church, dedicated to St. Luke, has a Norman tower, and the body presents a mixture of that and the early and decorated styles of English architecture.

SPREYTON, a parish in the hundred of WONFORD, county of DEVON, 8 miles (E. by N.) from Oakhampton, containing 398 inhabitants. The living is a discharged vicarage, in the archdeaconry and diocese of Exeter, rated in the king's books at £10. 5. 8., and in the patronage of the Rev. Richard Holland. The church is dedicated to St. Michael. A lead mine has been opened here, but it has hitherto proved unsuccessful.

SPRIDLINGTON, a parish in the eastern division of the wapentake of ASLACOE, parts of LINDSEY, county of LINCOLN, 9 miles (W. S. W.) from Market-Rasen, containing 199 inhabitants. The living is a rectory, in the archdeaconry of Stow, and diocese of Lincoln, rated in the king's books at £11. 10., and in the patronage of the Rev. Frederick Gildart. The church is dedicated to St. Hilary.

SPRINGFIELD, a parish in the hundred of CHELMSFORD, county of ESSEX, 1 mile (N. E.) from Chelmsford, containing 1450 inhabitants. The living is a rectory in two portions, called Bosworth's and Richard's, but consolidated by Bishop Sherlock, in the archdeaconry of Essex, and diocese of London, the former rated in the king's books at £11. 6. 8., and the latter at £11. 4. 9½., and in the patronage of the Earl of Arran. The church is dedicated to All Saints. The river Chelmer runs through the parish, which derives its name from an extraordinary number of springs within its limits. Dr. Goldsmith composed his "Deserted Village" whilst residing at a farm-house nearly opposite the church here. Joseph Strutt, the engraver and antiquary, was born here in 1749; he died in 1802.

SPRINGTHORPE, a parish in the wapentake of CORRINGHAM, parts of LINDSEY, county of LINCOLN, 4½ miles (E. by S.) from Gainsborough, containing 200 inhabitants. The living is a rectory, in the archdeaconry of Stow, and diocese of Lincoln, rated in the king's books at £14. 3. 4., and in the patronage of the Crown. The church is dedicated to St. George and St. Lawrence.

SPROATLEY, a parish in the Middle division of the wapentake of HOLDERNESS, East riding of the county of YORK, 7 miles (N. E. by E.) from Kingston upon Hull, containing 357 inhabitants. The living is a rectory, in the archdeaconry of the East riding, and diocese of York, rated in the king's books at £7. 0. 10., and in the patronage of the Earl of Cardigan. The church, dedicated to All Saints, was built in 1819, upon the site of the old edifice, which was dedicated to St. Swithin: it is of white brick, principally in the later style of English architecture, and has lately received an addition of one hundred free sittings, the Incorporated Society for the enlargement of churches and chapels having granted £150 towards defraying the expense. In laying the foundation of the church some antique tombstones were found, one of them bearing a Saxon inscription. There is a place of worship for Wesleyan Methodists. Bridget Biggs, in 1733, gave an estate for the erection and support of a school for twenty children, and for apprenticing them: the income is about £90 per annum, for which sixteen boys and fifteen girls are educated and apprenticed.

SPROSTON, a township in that part of the parish of MIDDLEWICH which is in the hundred of NORTHWICH, county palatine of CHESTER, 2¼ miles (E.) from Middlewich, containing 148 inhabitants.

SPROTBROUGH, a parish in the northern division of the wapentake of STRAFFORTH and TICKHILL, West riding of the county of YORK, comprising the chapelry of Cateby and the township of Sprotbrough, and containing 487 inhabitants, of which number, 318 are in the township of Sprotbrough, 2¾ miles (W. S. W.) from Doncaster. The living is a rectory, in the archdeaconry and diocese of York, rated in the king's books at £44. 18. 9., and in the patronage of Sir J. Copley, Bart. The church, dedicated to St. Mary, contains monuments of the Fitzwilliams and Copleys: one of the former family founded an hospital here, before 1363, in honour of St. Edmund, the revenue of which at the dissolution was valued at £9. 13. 11.

SPROUGHTON, a parish in the hundred of SAMFORD, county of SUFFOLK, 3 miles (W. by N.) from Ipswich, containing 506 inhabitants. The living is a rectory, in the archdeaconry of Suffolk, and diocese of Norwich, rated in the king's books at £20. 18. 9., and in the patronage of the Marquis of Bristol. The church is dedicated to All Saints. The Stow-Market and Ipswich navigation passes through the parish.

SPROWSTON, a parish in the hundred of TAVERHAM, county of NORFOLK, 3 miles (N. E. by N.) from Norwich, containing 832 inhabitants. The living is a perpetual curacy, in the peculiar jurisdiction and patronage of the Dean and Chapter of Norwich, endowed with £400 royal bounty, and £1000 parliamentary grant. The church, dedicated to St. Mary and St. Margaret, contains a mural monument of marble to the memory of Sir Miles Corbet, and Catharine his lady, a descendant of whom, Thomas Corbet, Esq., was one of the judges that signed the death warrant of Charles I., and, after the Restoration, was arrested and executed as a traitor, in 1661.

SPROXTON, a parish in the hundred of FRAMLAND, county of LEICESTER, 8 miles (N. E. by E.) from Melton-Mowbray, containing 372 inhabitants. The living is a discharged vicarage, consolidated with that of Saltby, in the archdeaconry of Leicester, and diocese of Lincoln, rated in the king's books at £7. 4. 4., endowed with £200 royal bounty, and in the patronage of the Duke of Rutland. The church is dedicated to St. Bartholomew. There is a place of worship for Wesleyan Methodists. The small river Eye runs through the parish.

SPROXTON, a township in the parish of HELMSLEY, wapentake of RYEDALE, North riding of the county of YORK, 1½ mile (S.) from Helmsley, containing 167 inhabitants.

SPURSTOW, a township in that part of the parish of BUNBURY which is in the first division of the hundred of EDDISBURY, county palatine of CHESTER, 4¼ miles (S. by E.) from Tarporley, containing 553 inhabitants. A mineral spring here, called Spurstow Spa, was formerly much frequented, and baths were erected by Sir Thomas Mostyn, for the accommodation of visitors; but the waters are not at present in much repute.

STADHAMPTON, a parish in the hundred of DORCHESTER, county of OXFORD, 8 miles (S. E. by E.) from Oxford, containing 254 inhabitants. The living is a perpetual curacy, in the jurisdiction of the peculiar court of Dorchester, endowed with £16 per annum private benefaction, £600 royal bounty, and £400 parliamentary grant, and in the patronage of C. Peers, Esq. The church is dedicated to St. John the Baptist. Sundry benefactions, producing £10 a year, are applied for the education of nine poor children. The parish is bounded on the west by the river Thame. The Rev. John Owen, D.D., the celebrated and learned nonconformist, Dean of Christ Church, and Vice Chancellor of the University of Oxford, in the time of the Commonwealth, was born here.

STADMERSLOW, a township in the parish of WOLSANTON, northern division of the hundred of PIREHILL, county of STAFFORD, containing 264 inhabitants.

STAFFIELD, or STAFFOL, a township in the parish of KIRK-OSWALD, LEATH ward, county of CUMBERLAND, 1½ mile (N. N. W.) from Kirk-Oswald, containing 309 inhabitants.

Arms.

STAFFORD, a borough, market town, and parish, having separate jurisdiction, locally in the southern division of the hundred of Pirehill, county of STAFFORD, of which it is the capital, 136 miles (N.W. by N.) from London, on the road to Chester, containing, with the township of Worston, 5759 inhabitants. This place, which is of great antiquity, was originally called *Stadeford*, or *Stadford*, from the Saxon *Stade*, signifying a place on a river, and the *trajectus*, or ford, across the river Sow, on which it is situated. It is said to have been, in 705, the devotional retirement of St. Bertelin, the son of a Mercian king, upon whose expulsion from his hermitage, at a spot called Berteliney, and Betheney, meaning the island of Bertelin, several houses were built, which formed the origin of the present town. In 913, Ethelfleda, Countess of Mercia, erected a castle on the north side of the river, and surrounded the town with walls and a fosse, of which the only vestige is a small portion of the East gate. Edward the Elder, brother of Ethelfleda, about a year after the erection of the castle, built a tower, the site of which Mr. Pennant supposes to have been the mount called, by Speed, Castle hill. From this period till the Conquest, the town appears to have increased considerably in extent and importance, and though it had not received any charter of incorporation, it is, in Domesday-book, called a city, in which the king had eighteen burgesses in demesne, and the Earls of Mercia twenty mansions. William, out of all the manors in the county, reserved this only for himself, and built a castle to keep the barons in subjection, appointing, as governor, Robert de Toeni, the progenitor of the house of Stafford, on whom he bestowed all the other manors, with the title of Baron de Stafford. The castle, after having been rebuilt by Ralph de Stafford, a celebrated warrior, in the reign of Edward III., remained till the parliamentary war, when it was garrisoned by the royal forces under the Earl of Northampton, but was at length taken by the parliamentary troops under the command of Sir William Brereton, and subsequently demolished by order of the parliament. The remains consisted chiefly of the keep, and were situated on the summit of a lofty eminence, about a mile and a half to the south-west of the town; the walls were eight feet thick, and at each angle was an octagonal turret, with a tower similarly shaped on the south-west side. About fifty years since, the only visible remains were part of a wall, which the late Sir William Jerningham underbuilt, to prevent it from falling; in doing which it was discovered, that the basement story lay buried under the ruins of the upper parts. Sir George Jerningham afterwards began to rebuild the castle on the old foundation, but has completed only one front, flanked with two round towers, in which are deposited some ancient armour and other curiosities. The town is pleasantly situated on the river Sow, about six miles distant from its confluence with the Trent: the entrance from the London road is by a neat bridge over the river, near which was one of the ancient gates:

the houses are in general well built of brick, and roofed with slate, and many of them are handsome and of modern erection; the streets are well paved, at the expense of the corporation, and the inhabitants are amply supplied with water. The environs are pleasant, abounding with noble mansions and elegant villas. Assemblies are held in a suite of rooms in the town hall; and races take place annually in May. The principal branch of manufacture is that of shoes, for supplying the London market, and for exportation; and the tanning of leather is carried on to a considerable extent. Stafford, in common with the neighbourhood, is also noted for the quality of its ale. The river Penk joins the Sow near Rudford bridge, an elegant structure of three arches, nearly a mile distant, and the Staffordshire and Worcestershire canal passes near the town. The market is on Saturday: the fairs are April 5th, May 14th, June 25th, October 3rd, and December 5th, principally for horses and cattle.

Corporate Seal.

The inhabitants first received a regular charter of incorporation in the reign of John, confirming all privileges previously enjoyed; it was dated one year prior to that of London, and seven years before the signing of Magna Charta. After various confirmations and additions, in the subsequent reigns, it became forfeited in 1826, by the common council neglecting to fill up vacancies in the body corporate; and, on petition, a new charter was granted by George IV., in 1827, restoring and confirming all previous rights and privileges, with the exception only of exemption from serving on juries for the county. By this charter, the government is vested in a mayor, ten aldermen, and ten principal burgesses, assisted by a recorder, town clerk, serjeants at mace, and subordinate officers. The mayor is annually elected by the aldermen and capital burgesses, who fill up vacancies in their respective bodies as they occur: the mayor and the two senior aldermen are justices of the peace within the borough. The freedom is inherited by birth, or obtained by servitude to a resident freeman. The corporation have power to hold quarterly courts of session within the borough, for all offences not capital; but they transfer to the judges travelling the circuit all causes requiring the decision of a jury: they have power also to hold a court of record, for the recovery of debts to any amount, but no process has issued from it for the last twenty years. The custom of Borough English prevails within the town and liberties. The assizes and sessions for the county, which had previously been held here, were restored by Queen Elizabeth, the inhabitants having represented to her, on visiting the town, that to their removal its decay, at that time, was, among other causes, to be attributed. The borough first exercised the elective franchise in the 23rd of Edward I., since which time it has regularly returned two members to parliament: the right of election is vested in all resident burgesses: non-residents, who are eligible to become burgesses, may vote on being sworn in, but if they continue to reside out of the borough, they lose their franchise, unless they again become inhabitants for six months before the election. The number of electors is upwards of eight hundred : the mayor is the returning officer. The county hall is a spacious and handsome modern building of stone, in the centre of the High-street, and occupying nearly the whole of one side of a spacious square, appropriated as a market-place, over part of which is a room for one thousand stand of arms, for the Staffordshire militia; towards its erection the corporation contributed £1050 : it is one hundred and twenty feet in length, ornamented in the front with finely-sculptured figures of Justice and Peace, and contains several handsome apartments, with an assembly-room in the centre, elegantly fitted up, and occupying nearly the whole length of the front; on each side of it are the court-rooms for the assizes and sessions, approached by a central staircase, on the landing of which are the grand jury room and other apartments. The county gaol and house of correction is a spacious and substantial modern edifice, comprising the governor's house, an infirmary, a chapel (in which service is performed regularly every Sunday, and twice during the week), a school-room, nineteen wards, nineteen day-rooms, seventeen work-rooms and shops, and nineteen airing yards, with two tread-mills, of which one is used for the grinding of corn, and the other for raising water for the supply of the prison, which is well adapted to the classification of prisoners, who are employed at their trades, and receive a portion of their earnings on discharge: the building occupies an airy and healthy situation, and is under excellent regulations, being calculated for the reception of two hundred prisoners in separate cells.

Stafford comprises the united parishes of St. Mary and St. Chad, in the archdeaconry of Stafford, and diocese of Lichfield and Coventry. The living of St. Mary's is a rectory not in charge, in the patronage of the Crown: the church, formerly collegiate for a dean and thirteen prebendaries, is an ancient and spacious cruciform structure in the early style of English architecture, with a lofty octagonal tower rising from the intersection, the upper part of which is of later date : the north entrance is richly ornamented with delicate shafts, and bold hollows embellished with flowers and foliage: the interior is beautifully arranged; the piers and arches are of the early English, passing into the decorated, style, and, to the east of the transepts, diminish gradually in height; the windows are generally in the decorated style, though intermixed with others of the later English, of which the east window is an elegant specimen; the chancel is spacious, and the roof is supported on finely-pointed arches, and piers of clustered columns; in the north transept is an ancient font of great beauty, and highly ornamented with sculptured figures and animals; there are many ancient monuments, among which the most conspicuous are those of the family of Aston of Tixall. The living of St. Chad's is a perpetual curacy, in the patronage of the Prebendary of Pipa Minor in the Cathedral Church of Lichfield : the church is a small edifice, originally in the Norman style of architecture, with a tower of the later English style between the chancel and the nave; the former is still in good preservation, and, with the exception of a modern east window, retains its original character; but the nave is of more recent date. There are places of worship for the Society of Friends,

Independents, Wesleyan Methodists of the Old and New Connexion, and a Roman Catholic chapel ; which last, in that part of the environs called Forebridge, is a small but handsome edifice, erected by the late Edward Jerningham, Esq., and contains several of the ancient stone stalls removed from Lichfield cathedral.

The free grammar school, which, according to Leland, was originally established by " Sir Thomas, Countre Parson of Ingestre by Heywodde, and Syr Randol, a chauntre preste of Stafford," and further endowed with subsequent benefactions, was, on petition of the inhabitants, refounded by Edward VI., who augmented the endowment, in 1550 : the income exceeds £370 per annum, of which two-thirds are paid to the headmaster, and the remainder to the usher, both of whom are appointed by the corporation, subject to the approval of the bishop of the diocese: the school is open to all boys of the town, of whom there are at present thirteen on the foundation. A Lancasterian school is supported by subscription; and there are Sunday schools in connexion with the established church and the dissenting congregations. The institution for the relief of the widows and orphans of poor clergymen of the " Archdeaconry, the several Peculiars, and County, of Stafford," is supported by liberal donations and annual subscription, and has also an income arising from property vested in old South Sea stock, amounting to £2400 : such clergymen as are disabled by age, sickness, or infirmity, and have not an income sufficient for the necessary support of themselves and their families, participate also in the benefits of this institution. The county infirmary was instituted in 1766, and the present building erected in 1772 : the premises, situated in the Foregate, were considerably enlarged a few years since, and are well adapted to the reception of eighty patients, who receive professional assistance from two physicians, three surgeons, and a chaplain attached to the institution, which is under the superintendence of a president and committee : the average number of patients admitted in the course of a year is six hundred, and about eight hundred out-patients receive the benefit of medical assistance at their own dwellings : attached to it is a house of recovery from fever, recently erected, designed for the reception of twenty-four patients : this institution has funded property, amounting to £2347, and is further supported by donations and annual subscriptions : within the last few months it has received the name of hospital, and confers, on pupils who have attended it, the same advantages and privileges as the hospitals of London. The county general lunatic asylum was established in 1818, for patients from all parts of the kingdom, upon moderate terms, regulated according to the circumstances of the patients; those from the county are received upon lower terms than others, and in all cases the deficiency is made up from the funds of the institution, which is liberally supported by subscription, and has funded property to the amount of £2351. 15. in the three per cent. consols. It is admirably conducted, and ranks among the principal establishments of this kind in the kingdom. The buildings are spacious, and well adapted to the health and comfort of the patients ; the gardens and pleasure grounds comprise thirty acres, in which they may take exercise, and every kind of rational amusement is afforded them ; a small stream runs through the enclosure, and warm air is introduced into the buildings, which are well ventilated, arranged according to the rank and condition of the patients, and provided with warm and cold baths; one hundred and seventy patients may be received into the institution. Almshouses for twelve aged and infirm persons were erected, in 1640, by Sir Martin Noel, at an expense of £1000; twenty poor families at present reside in them, and receive among them fifteen shillings and sixpence weekly, paid by the corporation from the rental of land in the Coton fields; which sum will be increased with £12 per annum, arising from the Marston tithes, and the interest of £50 left by Dr. Binns: these houses are in a very dilapidated state; two of them have been repaired by Lord Talbot, who appoints two inmates, the rest being nominated by the corporation. A priory of Black canons was founded by Richard Peche, Bishop of Coventry and Lichfield, in 1181, and dedicated to St. Thomas à Becket, the revenue of which at the dissolution was £198. 0. 9.: a small portion of the buildings now converted into a farm-house remains, about two miles east of the town. A house of Friars Eremites, of the order of St. Augustine, was founded in the suburb of Forebridge, by Ralph, Lord Stafford, to which, on the suppression of the priory of Stone, the monuments of the Stafford family were removed; it continued till the dissolution, at which time these splendid monuments were destroyed. A priory of Franciscan friars was founded at the north end of the town walls by Sir James Stafford of Sandon, in the reign of Edward I., the revenue of which at the dissolution was £35. 13. 10. In addition to these were a free chapel, in the castle, dedicated to St. Nicholas; a free chapel, or hospital, of St. John, near the river, in Forebridge, for a master and poor brethren, the revenue of which at the dissolution was £10; and a free chapel, or hospital, dedicated to St. Leonard, of which the revenue was £4. 12. 4. Several silver coins, of a later date than the reign of Edward VI., a silver cross, the lower portion of an ancient font or piscina, a cannon ball, and two small millstones, were found, on repairing the walls of the castle, some few years since. Among eminent natives were, John de Stafford, a Franciscan monk; Edmund Stafford, Bishop of Exeter, and Chancellor of England, in the reigns of Richard II. and Henry IV.; Thomas Ashebourn, a strenuous opponent of Wickliffe; Thomas Fitz-herbert, a learned Roman Catholic divine of the sixteenth and seventeenth centuries, and principal of the English college at Rome; and Izaak Walton, the well-known author of the treatise on the art of angling. Stafford gives the title of baron to the family of Jerningham, and that of marquis to the family of Gower.

STAFFORD, a hamlet in the parish of BARWICK, hundred of HOUNDSBOROUGH, BERWICK, and COKER, county of SOMERSET, 2 miles (S. by E.) from Yeovil. The population is returned with the parish.

STAFFORD (WEST), a parish in the hundred of CULLIFORD-TREE, Dorchester division of the county of DORSET, 2½ miles (S.E. by E.) from Dorchester, containing 184 inhabitants. The living is a rectory, with that of Frome-Billet united, in the archdeaconry of Dorset, and diocese of Bristol, rated in the king's books at £10. 8. 1½. Mrs. Elizabeth Floyer was patroness in 1820. The church, by the date 1640 over the porch, seems to have been rebuilt in that year. At Bingham

Court are the remains of a free chapel, which has been long desecrated. Frome-Billet was formerly a parish, but the church having been destroyed, and the parish becoming almost depopulated, the living was united, about the middle of the fifteenth century, to that of West Stafford.

STAFFORDSHIRE, an inland county, bounded on the north and north-west by Cheshire, on the west by Shropshire, on the south by Worcestershire and a detached portion of Shropshire, on the south-east by Warwickshire, and on the east and north-east by a small projecting portion of the county of Leicester, and by Derbyshire. It extends from 52° 23′ to 53° 14′ (N. Lat.), and from 1° 33′ to 2° 22′ (W. Lon.); and includes an area of one thousand one hundred and forty-eight square miles, or seven hundred and thirty-four thousand seven hundred and twenty statute acres. The population, in 1821, was 341,040. Its ancient British inhabitants were the Cornavii, whose territory, on its subjection by the Romans, was included in the division called *Flavia Cæsariensis*. On the completion of the Anglo-Saxon Octarchy, it was included in the powerful kingdom of Mercia, several of the principal towns of which were situated within its limits. In the year 705, a battle was fought between Cenred, King of Mercia, and Osred, King of Northumbria, near Maer, in this county. Staffordshire shared largely in the calamitous results of the Danish invasions. The Danes, however, were defeated with great slaughter by the Saxons in a battle fought in the reign of Edward the Elder, early in the tenth century, either near Tettenhall, or at Wednesfield, in the south-western part of the county. In the reign of Henry I., Robert de Belesme, Earl of Shrewsbury, in open revolt, in support of the claim of Robert Duke of Normandy to the English crown, committed great ravages in Staffordshire. In the year 1322, Thomas, Earl of Lancaster, in rebellion against Edward II., was defeated at Burton upon Trent, whence he was pursued to Pontefract. During the sanguinary struggle between the houses of York and Lancaster, the Earl of Salisbury, proceeding, with a body of about five thousand men, to join the Duke of York, who then lay at Ludlow, was intercepted at Blore heath by the royal army, amounting to ten thousand men, under the command of Lord Audley: an engagement ensued, in which, by a skilful manœuvre, the earl succeeded in gaining the victory, and Lord Audley himself was slain, together with two thousand four hundred of his men, almost all from Cheshire: Margaret of Anjou, consort of Henry VI., who beheld the contest, fled to Eccleshall castle. In the great civil war of the seventeenth century, both parties had numerous active supporters in this county. In 1643, a smart action occurred on Hopton heath, near Stafford, between a small party of royalists, under the Earl of Northampton, and some parliamentarian forces, under Sir John Gell and Sir William Brereton: the royalists gained some advantage, but the earl, being too eager in the pursuit, was surrounded and slain. Stafford soon after surrendered to the parliament, as also did the town of Wolverhampton and the castle of Eccleshall, the latter only after a severe siege, during which Sir William Brereton signally defeated a party of royalists under Col. Hastings, who attempted its relief: in the early part of this contest also, Sir William Brereton had reduced the castle of Tutbury,

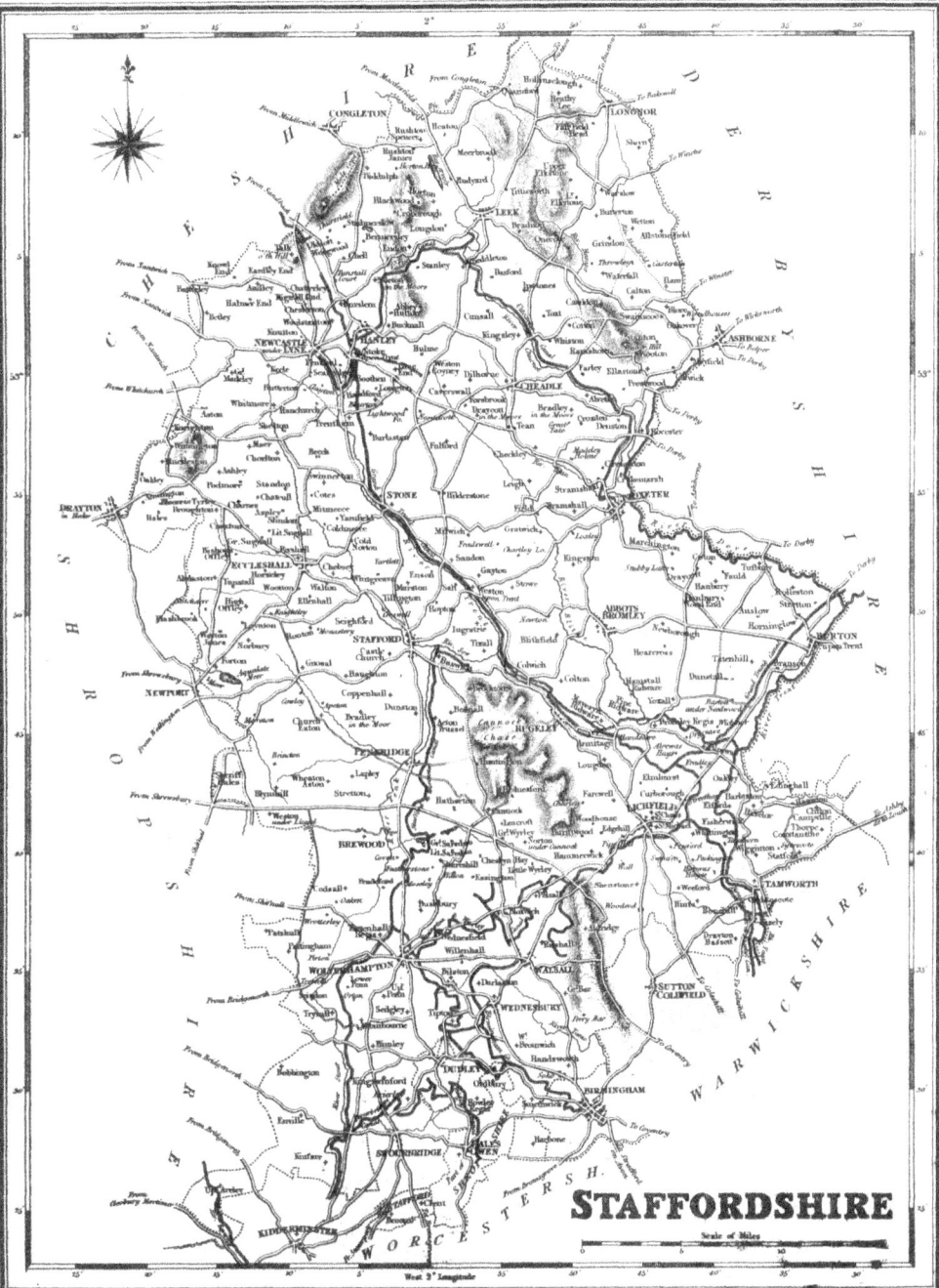

STAFFORDSHIRE

Scale of Miles

West 2° Longitude

DRAWN AND ENGRAVED FOR LEWIS' TOPOGRAPHICAL DICTIONARY.

after a vigorous siege. In 1643, Burton upon Trent was plundered by the parliamentarian army, who left a garrison in it. Lichfield Close, the fortified part of that city, which was held by the royalists, was first be sieged in March 1643, by Lord Brook, who, being slain in the course of the operations, was succeeded in the command by Sir J. Gell, to whom the place shortly after surrendered; but the parliamentarian garrison left by this commander, after a brave resistance, was, on the 21st of the following month, compelled to deliver it up to Prince Rupert, who advanced hither from the reduction of Birmingham: this place remained in the hands of the royalists until about twelve months after the decisive battle of Naseby. From Lichfield Prince Rupert proceeded to Burton, and gained possession of it, leaving a garrison, which was soon compelled to surrender the town to Lord Grey. In 1644, Dudley castle, locally situated just within the southern confines of the county, after being besieged for the space of three weeks by the parliamentarians, was relieved, on July 11th, by a party of the king's forces from Worcester. Stourton castle surrendered to the king this year; and the parliamentarians were also defeated by Col. Bagot, in an attack upon Lord Paget's manor-house, near Burton upon Trent. In the course of the year 1646, the fortresses held by the royalists were surrendered to the opposite party. In 1745, the Scotch rebels halted at Leek, while the army under the Duke of Cumberland was drawn up on Stone field, near the town of Stone, to oppose them; the rebels, however, resumed their retreat, closely followed by the duke's forces.

Staffordshire is in the diocese of Lichfield and Coventry (excepting the two parishes of Brome and Clent), and in the province of Canterbury: it forms an archdeaconry, containing the deaneries of Tamworth, Tutbury, Lapley, Treizull, Alveton, Leek, Newcastle under Line, and Stone, and comprises one hundred and forty-six parishes, of which forty-five are rectories, forty-four vicarages, and the remainder perpetual curacies. For purposes of civil government it is divided into the hundreds of Cuttlestone (East and West), Offlow (North and South), Pirehill (North and South), Seisdon (North and South), and Totmonslow (North and South). It contains the city of Lichfield; the borough and market towns of Newcastle under Line, Stafford, and Tamworth; and the market towns of Burslem, Burton upon Trent, Cheadle, Eccleshall, Hanley, Lane-End, Leek, Longnor, Penkridge, Rugeley, Stone, Uttoxeter, Walsall, Wednesbury, and Wolverhampton. Two knights are returned to parliament for the shire, two representatives for the city of Lichfield, and two for each of the boroughs. This county is included in the Oxford circuit: the assizes and quarter sessions are held at Stafford. There are sixty-two acting magistrates. The rates raised in the county for the year ending March 25th, 1827, amounted to £165,518. 12., and the expenditure to £158,808. 13., of which £124,958. 19. were applied to the relief of the poor.

Its surface is various. The northern part rises into hills, called the Moorlands, constituting the southern extremity of the long mountainous range which extends hence through the north of Derbyshire, and along the western confines of Yorkshire, towards the mountainous borders of Scotland. These moorlands are situated to the north of a supposed line drawn from Uttoxeter to Newcastle under Line, and comprise large tracts of waste and uncultivated land, appropriated almost entirely to the pasturage of sheep. A large portion of them has been enclosed with stone walls, almost the only fence to be seen in this part of the county; but these enclosures have not been subdivided, and large breadths have never undergone the least improvement. The pleasant vale, in which is situated the town of Cheadle, in this part of the county, is bounded, in the vicinity of that town, by high barren hills, composed of huge heaps of gravel: the wastes upon these hills, and others equally dreary and barren, extending both northward and westward of Cheadle, are extensive; almost their only produce being heath, broom, whortleberries, and mountain cinquefoil. Eastward of this town also, approaching the borders of Derbyshire, are similar desolate wastes, one of which, near the banks of the Dove, is called Oak-moor, from its being nearly covered with dwarf oaks. A little to the north of this commences an extensive tract of limestone country, included between the rivers Dove and Churnet, extending westward as far as Ipstones, and northward as far as Longnor, and comprising an area of fifty or sixty square miles: this is the most valuable part of the moorlands, the soil naturally producing a fine herbage: many of the hills, which are composed of immense masses of limestone, rise to a very considerable height, and in various places present huge perpendicular cliffs: the Weaver hills, in the southern part of it, of very considerable extent, rise, in common with some other of the highest peaks of the moorlands, to the height of a thousand feet and upwards above the level of the tide in the Thames at Brentford, and command remarkably extensive views, in which are included the Peak hills of Derbyshire; these are almost covered with irregular excrescences, clothed with moss or lichens. Large tracts of the other parts of the moorlands, notwithstanding their great superiority of elevation, are entirely wet peat moors, or mosses; such are Morrage, Axedge, the Cloud heath, High Forest, Leek Frith, and Mole Cop. The summits of some of the hills terminate in huge cliffs, particularly those called Leek Rocks, or Roches, composed of a coarse gritstone; and Ipstones' Sharp Cliffs, large rugged rocks piled in remarkably striking forms, and overhanging a precipice, at the base of which are scattered prodigious masses, which have fallen from the rocks above. Indeed, one of the greatest obstacles to the improvement of much of the moorlands consists in the immense quantities of stones lying on, or of rocks rising above, the surface soil: some of the most striking of these masses, besides those just mentioned, are Wetley rocks, those to the west of Flash, and others on High Forest, the Cloud heath, and Mole Cop common, with the waste to the north of it. The scenery of Dove Dale is celebrated for its romantic beauty; and in the limestone part of the moorlands are various narrow, deep, and picturesque vallies, bounded on each side by precipices of rock, among the principal of which are Mill Dale, near Allstonefield, and the vale of the small river Manifold.

The middle and southern parts of the county are level, or diversified only by gently rising eminences. The following tracts, however, are exceptions to this observation, viz., the limestone hills of Dudley and Sedgley; the parish of Rowley-Regis, principally composed of an isolated mountain, terminating in various peaks, the loftiest of them, called Turner's Hill, being the highest spot of ground in the south of Staffordshire, rising to the height of nine hundred feet above the level of high water in the Thames at Brentford; the hills of Clent, in the detached portion of the county lying to the south of Stourbridge in Worcestershire, and nearly equal in height to those of Rowley; Bar-beacon, rising to the height of six hundred and fifty-three feet, and many others of less elevation; all of which command striking and extensive prospects over this and some of the neighbouring counties. The soil of the Rowley hills is a strong marly loam, through which the rocky substratum frequently rises in innumerable fragments; that of the Clent hills is of the kind commonly called stone-brash, the lower parts being of stronger staple than the summits: much of these latter hills consists of sheepwalks of good herbage. Magnificent views may also be obtained from Beaudesert park, Sherholt park, Tamworth castle, and Tutbury castle. The lowest points of land are supposed to be the banks of the Severn at Upper Arely, which are only sixty feet above the level of high water at Brentford; and the banks of the Trent, at its junction with the Dove below Burton, about one hundred feet above the same level: those of the Tame at Tamworth are fifty feet higher than the last-mentioned. The lakes are neither numerous nor very extensive: the principal is Aqualate meer, on the borders of Shropshire, near Newport in that county, which is one thousand eight hundred and forty-eight yards long, and six hundred and seventy-two broad; the extent of Ladford Pool is about sixty acres. The climate, in its general character, is cold and wet; in the moorlands the very great quantity of rain that falls is attributed to the attractive force of the mountains acting upon the passing vapours; and in this district the snow, which is here always of greater depth than elsewhere in the county, continues upon the ground for a very long time; and its fences, being almost entirely uncemented stone walls, do not at all mitigate the piercing coldness of the atmosphere. The average annual quantity of rain which falls in Staffordshire is estimated at thirty-six inches.

The arable soils have been distinguished, by Mr. Pitt, in his general view of the agriculture of the county, into four species, viz.: first, strong, or clayey soils, which are of two kinds, the harsh, stiff, and untractable, and the more mild and friable, both of them commonly resting on a substratum of marl, with a hard stone rock underneath. Lands of this nature occupy a very extensive tract, stretching across the middle of the county, from the border of Derbyshire to that of Shropshire, but excluding the extensive waste of Cannock heath, and the country to the east of Stafford, between that town and the Trent. That part of the county lying eastward of the river Tame has the same kind of soil, as also have several parishes in the southwestern extremity approaching the banks of the Severn. Secondly, loose, light, sandy land, adapted to the culture of turnips, and occupying a tract bounded on the north by the Trent, on the east by the Tame, on the south by the confines of the county, and on the west by an imaginary line drawn from the village of Armitage, near the Trent, southward by Longdon, Hammerwich, Aldridge, and a short distance eastward of Walsall, to the verge of the county, near Birmingham: of the

same kind also are, a considerable tract lying to the south-west of Dudley and Wolverhampton, extending from the border of Worcestershire to that of Shropshire; and another, of much smaller size, extending westward from Brewood, and including the village of Sheriff-Hales. Thirdly, the calcareous soils, or those resting on a substratum of limestone; such are the soils of the great northern limestone district before described, as also of one of very small extent to the north and north-west of Dudley, and of another to the north-east of Walsall. Fourthly and lastly, mixed soils and loams, formed of the above in different proportions, frequently with the addition of gravel and various adventitious matter, and occupying the remaining extensive portions of the county: the substrata are various, including sand, gravel, clay, marl, and stone of different kinds. In some of the uncultivated tracts, and in one or two other places, are found small pieces of ground of a thin light black earth of a peaty nature, generally lying upon gravel. The meadow soils are in many places similar to those of the adjoining arable lands, with the addition, when within reach of natural inundation, of the accumulating sediment so deposited; and in others composed of peat-earth, varying in thickness, sometimes to the depth of several feet, and containing trunks of trees. This kind of land, which must be drained on converting it to meadow, or pasture land, for which it is very valuable, sinks several inches during that process.

The quantity of land devoted to agricultural purposes is estimated at six hundred thousand acres, of which five hundred thousand are arable, the rest meadow, or pasture. Of the arable lands, two hundred thousand acres are of the clayey, or of the more friable of the mixed loams; an equal quantity is of gravelly or sandy loam, or of the calcareous soils, while the remaining hundred thousand acres are, for the most part, of light sandy or gravelly loams, suitable for turnips. The courses of crops are various: it may be observed, however, that the famous Norfolk system, including the rotation of turnips, barley, clover, and wheat, is in common practice on the light soils. The crops of grain and pulse commonly cultivated are wheat, barley, oats, beans, and peas: the average of what are considered good crops of wheat is twenty-five bushels per acre; of barley, thirty; and of oats, from thirty to forty: that of peas and beans varies greatly. Rye is little grown, though some is sown as early spring food for sheep. On the moorlands oats are almost the only grain ever cultivated, and are commonly sown for three succeeding years, after which the ground is laid down for grass: a considerable quantity of oaten bread is eaten in the moorlands. Buck-wheat, here called French wheat, is sometimes cultivated, both as a crop and for ploughing under as manure. Hemp and flax are also grown, though upon a small scale; and many leases are subject to restrictions to prevent the cultivation of these plants to any great extent. Cabbages are a common agricultural crop in many parts of the county. The common and the Swedish turnip are both extensively grown, as also are vetches and rape. The common artificial grasses are red clover, white clover, trefoil, and ray-grass: burnet and rib-grass are sown in considerable quantities, as are also mixed hay-seeds. The low lands adjoining the rivers and brooks consist of meadows and pastures, as also do considerable tracts of flat land, which, by the backing on of water in former times, have acquired a stratum of peaty earth upon their surface. Considerable tracts of meadow land, lying near the larger streams, are rendered very productive by the occasional overflow of their waters, which, however, sometimes sweep away, or greatly damage, the produce. The meadows on the banks of the Dove, in the higher part of its course, before it is joined by the Churnet, are rendered proverbially fertile by the calcareous particles deposited by the overflowing of that river, the plain within reach of which is in some places nearly a mile broad. There is a considerable extent of grass land in the vicinity of all the principal towns: the vale of the Trent is regarded as the richest tract in the county for its extent: there are several irrigated pieces of meadow land in different parts of the county. Lime is extensively applied as manure upon all kinds of land: an extraordinary quantity of marl also is used for the same purpose, being found under the loamy soils, and in gravelly land; numerous marl-pits, the formation of which is of unknown date, occur in most parts where that substance is to be found.

The feeding of cattle is not practised extensively, although there are more bred than are consumed: the surplus is sold to dealers for the London market. The cattle are for the most part of the long-horned breed: the dairies, to which they are almost all appropriated, vary in size, containing from ten to forty, and, in some instances, even to seventy cows each: the few oxen that are bred are scarcely ever worked. Staffordshire contains the following distinct native breeds of sheep. First, the grey-faced, without horns, which is the native breed of Cannock heath, and the neighbouring commons. Secondly, the black-faced horned sheep, with fine wool, which are peculiar to the commons on the western side of the county, towards Drayton in Shropshire. Thirdly, the white-faced polled breed, with long combing wool, peculiar to the eastern parts of the moorlands. Fourthly, the mixed waste-land breed, which is found upon the wastes and uncultivated enclosures of the western parts of the moorlands, and is much inferior to the last-mentioned. The sheep on the commons of the southernmost part of the county are also of mixed breeds; their wool is tolerably fine, and of a clothing quality. Lastly, the pasture flocks, of various sorts and crosses, but chiefly of the Old and New Leicester breeds: those of the Cotswold, Wiltshire, and Dorsetshire, are also occasionally met with. Hogs are fattened upon most farms, both for pork and bacon: the breed most esteemed is a cross between the large slouch-eared kind and a dwarf breed, which is finer boned, broad, and plump: part of the consumption of bacon, which is very great in this county, is supplied from Shropshire and North Wales. Rabbits are very abundant upon the sandy parts of the waste lands. The gardens and orchards are not remarkable either for their extent or the nature of their productions, except that in the parish of Tettenhall, near Wolverhampton, great quantities of a peculiar kind of pear, called from the name of the place where it is produced, are grown: a great quantity of fruit is brought to the markets of this county from Worcestershire. The woods, wastes, and impracticable lands, are supposed to occupy an extent of upwards of one hundred thousand acres. The county is well stocked with

almost every species of thriving English timber, growing on the numerous estates of the nobility and gentry. Plantations to a great extent have been made on various parts of the steep moorland hills, particularly those of Dilhorne, Kingsley, and Oakmoor: from the underwood of these, many rods and staves, to make crates for the use of the potteries, are cut. Needwood Forest, in the eastern part of the county, situated between the rivers Trent and Dove, before the passing of an act of enclosure about the commencement of the present century, was an entirely wild tract of nearly ten thousand acres, presenting much romantic and beautiful scenery, and affording pasturage to numerous herds of deer: it was also subject to a common-right for cattle and horses. Of the wastes at present remaining, Cannock heath is far the most extensive: it contains upwards of twenty-five thousand acres, and is situated near the centre of the county, lying chiefly to the north and east of the small town of Cannock, whence it extends to the southern banks of the Trent. The northern and western parts of this common have for the most part a light soil, but the eastern and southern are of a cold, wet, gravelly nature; the best sheep-land is a tract on the western side, towards Tiddesley, and another in the northern part of it, near Rugeley and Beaudesert Park, to which may also be added the vicinity of Hedgford: the southern and eastern parts are in a great measure barren, producing little besides heath, whortleberries, lichens, and mosses. Although now a bleak and dreary tract, entirely devoid of trees, this waste in former times is asserted to have been covered with a profusion of majestic oaks, and to have been a favourite chase of the Saxon monarchs of Mercia. In addition to Walsall wood, Whittington heath, and the Weeford Flats, the other principal waste lands are those of Swindon and Wombourne, and that near Stewponey, on the south; those of Morrage, Wetley moor, Stanton moor, Hollington heath, and Caverswall common, in the north; and, in the middle districts, those of Essington wood, Snead common, Wyrley and Pelsal commons, Tirley, Ashley, Maer, Swinnerton, Tittensor, and Shelton heaths, Houlton, Milwich, Hardwick, and Fradswell commons, and others of smaller extent, chiefly used as sheep-walks. Most of them bear evident marks of ancient cultivation. Fuel is very plentiful, the principal article being coal from the numerous mines of the county; on the moorlands a good deal of peat is dug, particularly on Morrage and Axedge commons.

The mineral productions are numerous and valuable, consisting chiefly of coal, iron, lead, copper, marble, alabaster, and stone of various kinds. The coal strata have been found to exist to a superficial extent of fifty thousand acres. The coal district of the southern part of the county extends in length from Cannock heath, a part of which it includes, to near Stourbridge in Worcestershire; and in breadth from Wolverhampton to Walsall. In the north of the county this mineral is raised in abundance, in the neighbourhood of Newcastle and the Potteries, near Lane-End and Holly-bush, and again in the vicinity of Cheadle and Dilhorne: the thickness of the strata in the southern district is frequently as much as eight, ten, and even twelve yards: these and all the other beds of this formation dip westward towards the red sandstone, which occupies a tract twelve miles in breadth between this and the Shropshire coal formation. In the colliery of Birch hill, near Walsall, occurs a bed of trap, or green-stone, as it is here called, lying upon indurated sand-stone, and covered by a bed of slaty clay : the effect it has upon the coal is that of depriving it of its bitumen, and thus reducing it to what is called blind coal : the whole of the strata of this mine are inter-rupted faults, as the miners call them, of this green-stone. A singular species of coal, called peacock-coal, from the prismatic colours it exhibits, is raised at Han-ley. In the district called the Potteries, the strata in-tervening between the beds of coal consist chiefly of clays of different kinds, some of which make excellent fire-bricks for building the kilns, and making the sag-gars, or cases in which the ware is burned. Iron-ore abounds in all the coal-mines : the strata of it that are found in the neighbourhood of Wednesbury, Tipton, Bil-ston, in part of the parish of Sedgley, and to the west of Newcastle, are very extensive, lying generally under a vein of coal : the iron-ore found on Cannock heath is of a peculiar kind, called Cannockstone, of very little value. In the numerous mines of coal and iron, and in the foundries, blast-furnaces, slitting-mills, and other iron manufactories, an immense number of work-men are employed : the works on the banks of the Birmingham canal are particularly numerous and ex-tensive. The other metallic ores obtained are those of copper and lead, of both which considerable quantities are raised at Ecton, near Warslow, approaching the north-eastern border of the county : a copper-mine is also worked at Mixon, within a few miles of Leek ; and a lead mine near Stanton moor, in the same part of the county. Limestone forms the substratum of a very great extent of country, already described : an immense quantity of it is raised for burning into lime ; the lime-works on Caldon Low, and in the neigh-bourhood of the Weaver hills, are particularly extensive. Under several of the limestone hills, in the southern part of the county, that are perforated by tunnels, large caverns have been hollowed out, without dis-turbing the surface soil, some of them penetrating to a distance of three hundred yards from the canal. The limestone of this county, in different places, has some of the qualities of marble, and is susceptible of a high polish ; in others it is composed, in a great measure, of petrified marine substances. The kind of marble called rance-marble, which is white, with red veins formed of shining gritty particles, and takes so good a polish, as to be frequently used for chimney-pieces and monuments, is found in great abundance in Yelpersley Tor and the adjoining hills : there is a con-siderable quantity of grey marble at Stansop, and at Powke hill is obtained a very hard black marble. In the great limestone district, particularly on the banks of the river Dove, are some veins of alabaster, which is also dug between Needwood Forest and Tutbury : many of the moulds used in the potteries are composed of this material, after it has been ground. Extensive quarries of excellent freestone are numerous : at Bilston is obtained a particularly fine kind : Gornall, near Sedgley, has different quarries of a coarser sort ; and among the numerous other places where freestone is obtained may be specified, more particularly, Tixall, Wrottesley, Brewood park, and Pendeford. The hills of Rowley have for their basis a peculiar kind of

quartzose stone, devoid of any gritty quality, called Rowley rag-stone, a great quantity of which is carried to Birmingham and elsewhere, for paving, &c. : this stone lies in no regular strata, but in rude heaps and masses, which sometimes project above the surface. Clays of almost every description are found in this county : potters' clay, of several sorts, abounds chiefly in the vicinity of Newcastle under Line, where the pot-tery wares were formerly manufactured from it. At Amblecot, in the southern part of the county, is a clay of a dark blueish colour, of which glass-house pots of a remarkably superior quality are made, great quan-tities of them being sent to different parts of the kingdom, and many consumed in the neighbouring glass-works. Yellow and red ochre are also found in Staffordshire ; and a blue clay, obtained at Darlaston near Wednesbury, is used by glovers. A kind of black chalk exists, in beds of grey marble, in Langley-close ; and a fine reddish earth, little inferior to the red chalk of France, is obtained near Himley hall.

The manufactures are various and extensive : that of hardware, in the southern district, is very im-portant, and affords employment to many thousand per-sons. At Wolverhampton, and in its vicinity, are made locks of every kind, edge-tools, files, augers, japanned goods, and a great variety of other articles of the same material. The town and neighbourhood of Wal-sall are famous for the manufacture of saddlers' iron-mongery, such as bridle-bits, stirrup-irons, spurs, &c., sent thence to every part of the kingdom. The ma-nufacture of nails employs many thousand persons in some of the most populous parishes in this part of the county, particularly in those of Sedgley, Rowley, West Bromwich, Smethwick, Tipton, Wombourne, and Pelsall, and in the Foreign of Walsall : many women and children are employed in making the lighter and finer sorts. The other kinds of hardware produced are chiefly plated, lackered, japanned, and some ena-melled goods, toys, tobacco and snuff boxes, of iron and steel ; and machinery for steam-engines. Some places also partake of the manufacture of guns ; and there are several works for making brass, and for pre-paring tin plates, chiefly in the northern part of the county. In those parts of Staffordshire situated in the vicinity of Stourbridge and Dudley, in Worcestershire, are a number of large glass-houses, where the manufac-ture is carried on to a great extent. The manufacture of china and earthenware, in the north-western part of the county, is the most extensive and important in the kingdom : the district called the Potteries consists of numerous scattered villages occupying an extent of about ten square miles, and containing about twenty thousand inhabitants ; it is crossed by the Trent and Mersey, or Grand Trunk, canal. This manufacture, though of very ancient establishment in this part of the country, was of inferior importance until the latter part of the eighteenth century, when, chiefly by the exer-tions of the late Josiah Wedgwood, Esq., it was raised to such a pitch of excellence, as confers honour upon that gentleman's ingenuity and taste ; and in conse-quence, several of the villages of this district, particu-larly Burslem and Hanley, have grown rapidly into po-pulous market towns. The several species of ware invented by Mr. Wedgwood, varied by the industry and ingenuity of the manufacturers into an infinity of forms, and variously painted and embellished, constitute nearly the whole of the fine earthenwares at present manufactured in England, which are the object of a very extensive traffic. They are chiefly the following, *viz.*, the Queen's ware, which is composed of the whitest clays from Derbyshire and Dorsetshire, and different other parts of England, mixed with a due proportion of ground flint; terra cotta, resembling porphyry, granite, and other stones of the silicious, or crystalline, order; basaltes, or black ware; porcelain biscuit, of nearly the same properties as the natural stone of that name; a white porcelain biscuit, of a smooth wax-like surface, of the same properties as the preceding; jasper, a white porcelain biscuit of exquisite beauty and delicacy, possessing the general properties of the basaltes, together with the singular one of receiving, through its whole substance, from the mixture of metallic calces with other materials of the same colours which those calces communicate to glass, or enamels, in fusion, a property that no other porcelain, or earthenware, of either ancient or modern composition has been found to possess; bamboo, or cane-coloured porcelain biscuit, possessing the same qualities as the white porcelain biscuit; and a porcelain biscuit, remarkable for great hardness, little inferior to that of agate: the glazes are of vitreous composition. A very great number of persons is constantly employed in raising and preparing the raw materials for this manufacture in different parts of the kingdom, more especially upon the southern coasts, from Norfolk round to North Devon, and on the shores of Wales and Ireland. Vessels, which in the proper season have been employed in the Newfoundland fishery, convey these materials coastwise to the most convenient ports, whence they are forwarded by the inland small craft to the Potteries. Notwithstanding that almost every part of the kingdom receives supplies of pottery from this manufacture, yet by far the greater portion of its produce is exported to foreign countries. The exports of earthenware and china to the United States alone amount to sixty thousand packages annually. The quantity of wool manufactured is small; nearly the whole of the produce of the county being sold to the clothing and hosiery districts. The cotton manufacture is considerable; the works at Rochester and other places near the Dove are on a large scale, as are also those at Fazeley, and Tutbury. The town of Leek and its neighbourhood has a considerable manufacture of silk, and mohair, the articles being chiefly sewing-silk twist, buttons, ribands, ferrets, shawls, and handkerchiefs. Tape is manufactured at Cheadle and Tean, affording employment to many of their inhabitants. Stafford has manufactures of shoes and boots, for exportation and home consumption; tanning and hat-making are carried on to a great extent in several of the towns. This county is also celebrated for its ale, particularly that made at Burton upon Trent.

The principal rivers are the Trent, the Dove, the Tame, the Blythe, the Penk, and the Sow: the Severn also, though not considered a Staffordshire river, takes its navigable course by the parish of Upper Arely, at the south-western extremity of the county. The Trent, which ranks as the third largest river in England, rising from New Pool, near Biddulph, on the borders of Cheshire, flows southward through the district of the Potteries to Trentham, and thence south-

eastward by the town of Stone: having received the waters of the Penk and the Sow, near the centre of the county, its winding course gradually assumes an easterly direction, and, as it approaches Derbyshire, it forms several islands: having been joined by the Tame from the south, the Trent almost immediately becomes the boundary between this county and that of Derby, which it continues to be, pursuing a north-north-easterly direction, and passing by the town of Burton, where it becomes navigable, and a little below which, being joined by the Dove, it wholly enters Derbyshire, after a course, through this county and bordering upon it, of upwards of fifty miles. During its progress through Staffordshire the Trent is a bold, clear, and rapid stream, bordered by luxuriant meadows, the banks of which are in several places adorned with fine seats and ornamented grounds. The Dove, which, throughout its course, forms the boundary between this county and that of Derby, rises in the moorland hills, near the point to the north-west of Longnor, at which the three counties of Stafford, Derby, and Chester, meet: not far from its source it enters the beautiful and sequestered Dove Dale, flowing through it, in a southerly direction, to the vicinity of Ashbourn in Derbyshire, whence it proceeds southwestward towards Uttoxeter, near which town it assumes a south-easterly direction, by Tutbury, to its junction with the Trent to the north-east of Burton: from the great inclination of the bed of this river its waters flow with great rapidity, in some places dashing over rugged masses of rock, in others forming gentle cascades. Near the village of Ilam, in this county, the Dove is greatly augmented by the waters of the rivers Manifold and Hamps: the former, rising near the source of the Dove, takes a very circuitous route through a romantic vale situated in the north-eastern part of the county, and, sinking into the earth to the south of Ecton hill, between the villages of Butterton and Wetton, it emerges again at Ilam, shortly before its junction with the Dove, and at the distance of about four miles from the spot where it sinks into the ground: this stream is joined during its subterraneous transit by the Hamps, which in like manner passes under ground for a considerable distance. A little below Rochester, and a few miles above Uttoxeter, the Dove is joined from the north-west by the powerful stream of the Churnet, formed by the junction of two moorland rivulets near Leek. The Tame rises from several sources in the vicinity of Walsall, whence it takes a south-easterly direction, and enters Warwickshire near Aston *iuxta* Birmingham: after making a sweep through the northern part of that county it re-enters Staffordshire at Tamworth, after having formed the boundary of the county for a short distance above that town, whence its course, though irregular, is generally in a northerly direction towards the Trent, with which river it forms a junction immediately before it reaches Derbyshire. The Blythe rises near Watley moor, in the northern and mountainous part of the county, and takes a course nearly parallel with the Trent to its junction with that river near King's Bromley. The Penk, rising near the western border of the county, and flowing northward, a little to the east of Brewood, by the town of Penkridge, forms a junction with the Sow, which descends by Eccleshall and Stafford, at a short distance to the eastward of the latter town, whence their united waters proceed directly to the Trent. The small river Dane, rising near the source of the Dove, but assuming an irregular westerly course, forms the boundary between this county and Cheshire for upwards of ten miles. Several streams from the south-western part of the county take their course to the Severn: the principal of these is the Stour.

The extent of artificial navigation for the ready transport of the produce of the mines, manufactures, &c., is remarkably great. The Grand Trunk canal, which was planned, and in a great measure executed, by the celebrated engineer Brindley, enters this county from Cheshire, near Lawton, and almost immediately passes through the Harecastle tunnel, which is two thousand eight hundred and eighty yards long: hence it proceeds in the vicinity of Newcastle under Line, and soon gaining the valley of the Trent, it closely follows the course of that river by Stone and Rugeley, crossing it several times: a few miles below the latter town, however, it makes an extensive sweep, leaving the Trent some miles to the north, but afterwards again crosses it, along the northern bank of which it proceeds, at a little distance to the north of Burton, until it quits the county for Derbyshire. The highest level of this canal is at Harecastle, near which it enters Stafford-shire, and from which, on the south-eastern side, there is a fall of three hundred and sixteen feet, the greater part of which occurs in this county: the ordinary breadth of it is twenty-nine feet at the top, and sixteen at the bottom, and its usual depth four feet and a half, but in the part of its course below Burton it is several feet broader, and five feet and a half deep. The Staffordshire and Worcestershire canal branches from this, at Haywood, near the confluence of the rivers Sow and Trent, up the valley of the former of which it proceeds for some miles in a westerly direction, and then assumes a course nearly southerly, which it pursues by Penkridge and near Wolverhampton, quitting the county, in its course to the Severn, a short distance to the south of Kinver: this canal, with the Grand Trunk, completes the communication between the ports of Bristol, Liverpool, and Hull. The Coventry and Oxford canal branches from the Grand Trunk at Fradley heath, whence it takes a circuitous route, in a south-south-easterly direction, by the village of Whittington, to that of Fazely, near which it enters Warwickshire: from Fazely, a branch proceeds to Birmingham, and is called the Birmingham and Fazely canal. The Wyrley and Essington canal, commencing at a place called Wyrley Bank, passes through Oldfield, over Essington wood and Snead commons, and across the road from Wednesfield to Bloxwich, soon after which it turns west-ward to Wednesfield, and a little beyond that village, near Wolverhampton, forms a junction with the Bir-mingham canal: its branches are, one from the vicinity of Wolverhampton to Stow heath, another from Pool-Hayes to Ashmore Park, and a third from Lapley-Hayes to Ashmore Park. At Huddlesford commences a branch from the Coventry canal, called the Wyrley and Essington Extension, which, proceeding to the south of Lichfield, and over part of Cannock heath, forms a junction with the Wyrley and Essington canal, near Bloxwich: on the western side of this part of Cannock heath, a branch is carried southward, by Walsall wood, to the lime-works at Hayhead; its whole extent, includ-ing the branches, is thirty-four miles and a half; and from Cannock heath to the Coventry canal it has a fall of two hundred and sixty-four feet. The Birmingham canal, from that town in Warwickshire, takes a north-westerly course, and soon enters this county, proceed-ing to the north-east of the town of Dudley in Worces-tershire, and by Tipton and Bilston to Wolverhampton, and thence to the Staffordshire and Worcestershire canal, a little to the north of the latter town, after a course of twenty-two miles. Of the very numerous branches of this canal, one proceeds northward, over Ryder's Green, to the collieries of Wednesbury, and the vicinity of Walsall; while another, commencing about a mile from Dudley, passes south-westward by Brierly-Hill, and to the left of Brockmore Green joins a canal which, commencing in a large reservoir at Pensett's Chase, and passing nearly in a straight line by Words-ley, crosses the river Stour, and joins the Staffordshire and Worcestershire canal, a few miles to the west of Stourbridge in Worcestershire, to which town there is a small branch. The cut which connects the Dudley canal with that of Birmingham, called the Dudley Ex-tension canal, has part of its course in this county. Sir Nigel Gresley's canal extends from the Grand Trunk, near Newcastle under Line, past that town, to the coal-mines in Ape-dale.

Several large single stones at Cannock are supposed to be Druidical, as also are the eight upright stones, called "the Bridestones," near Biddulph, on the north-western border of the county; and on Drood, or Druid, heath, where there are several singular earth-works, Mr. Shaw, the historian of this county, considers the chief seat of the Arch-Druid of Britain to have been situated. Thyrsis, or Thor's house, a cavern, situated in the side of a lofty precipice in the vale of the Manifold, near the village of Wetton, is also supposed to have been the scene of Druidical rites. Some very ancient artificial caves have been discovered at Biddulph. The encamp-ment of Billington, about three miles to the west of Stafford, and that on Castle hill, near Beaudesert park, in the vicinity of Rugeley, are of ancient British for-mation. Under the Roman dominion, the tract now constituting Staffordshire contained the stations of *Etocetum*, at Wall, near Lichfield; and *Pennocrucium*, now Penkridge. Sheriff-Hales, near the confines of Shropshire, is supposed by some antiquaries to have been the site of the station *Uxacona*, or *Usacona*. Two of the great prætorian ways also crossed Staffordshire: the Watling-street, entering it from Warwickshire, near Tamworth, proceeded westward across the southern part, and quitted it for Shropshire, to the west of the town of Brewood: the Iknield-street, which entered from Warwickshire, at the village of Handsworth, near Birmingham, proceeded thence, in a north-north-east-erly direction, to a little beyond Shenstone, where it crossed the Watling-street, and afterwards pursued a north-easterly course, entering Derbyshire at Monks' Bridge, on the Dove. Roman domestic remains, and traces of their roads, are discoverable in different places; and Roman earth-works are visible at Arely wood, Ashton heath, Ashwood heath, near Kinver at Oldbury, near Shareshill, and in Tiddesley park. Near Maer are intrenchments supposed to have been thrown up by Cenred, in the progress of his hostilities against Osred, King of Northumbria; and on Sutton-Coldfield there is a camp, considered to be of Danish formation. The number of religious houses in this county, including free chapels, hospitals, and colleges, was about forty. Remains of the abbeys of Burton and Croxden, and of the priories of Rowton, Stafford, and Stone, are still visible. The present religious edifices most worthy of notice for beauty or antiquity are, the cathedral of Lichfield, St. Chad's church in that city, and the churches of Armitage, Audley, Barton, Burslem, Bushbury, Caverswall, Checkley, Colwich, Clifton-Campville (remarkable for its magnificent spire), Draycott Elford, Gayton, Gnosall, Kinver, Madeley, Mavesyn-Ridware, Muckleston, Pipe-Ridware, Rushall, Sandon, St. Mary's and St. Chad's at Stafford, Stoke, Tettenhall, Trysull, Wednesbury, and Wolstanton. The most remarkable fonts are those of Armitage, Ashley, St. Chad's in Lichfield, Pipe-Ridware, Norton under Cannock, St. Mary's at Stafford, Tettenhall, and Wolverhampton. The remains of ancient castles are chiefly those of Alveton, Caverswall, Chartley, Dudley, Healy, or Heyley, castle, Tamworth, and Tutbury. Among the most remarkable ancient mansions are Bentley hall and Moseley hall, in both which Charles II. remained concealed for some time after the battle of Worcester. Staffordshire contains numerous modern seats of the nobility and gentry, many of which are elegant, and several magnificent: among the most distinguished are Trentham, the property and residence of the Marquis of Stafford; and Beaudesert, that of the Marquis of Anglesey. Most modern houses of the ordinary class are built of brick, and roofed with tile or slate, the latter brought along the canals, chiefly from Wales and Westmorland: near Newcastle, and in one or two other places, large quantities of a peculiar kind of blue tiles are made, which, owing to their superior durability, are in great demand. Salt springs exist in different places; the principal are in the parish of Weston; and there are other mineral springs of various qualities, the most remarkable being that near Codsall, formerly famous for the cure of leprosies; St. Erasmus' well, between Ingestre and Stafford; and that at Willoughby. Numerous fossil remains occur in different parts of the strata of this county, more particularly in some of the limestone beds. At Bradley, a hamlet immediately adjoining the village of Bilston, to the east of Wolverhampton, a stratum of coal, about four feet thick, and eight or ten yards below the surface, having been set on fire, burned for about fifty years, and has reduced a considerable extent of land to a complete calx, used for the mending of roads: sulphur and alum are found in its vicinity. Some of the most remarkable plants and shrubs occasionally found growing wild are, the wild teasel, on moist ground; the *reseda luteola*, or dyers' weed; the periwinkle; the daffodil; geraniums of various sorts; the black currant; the *ribes alpinum*, or mountain currant, on the moorlands; the cranberry, on the moist parts of Cannock heath; and the barberry. The original calendar of the Norwegians and Danes was, till lately, used by many of the inhabitants of this county, where it has the appellation of the Staffordshire Clog: this is a quadrangular piece of wood, on each of the four sides of which are contained three months of the year, the days being expressed by notches, to which are added the symbols of the several saints, to denote the day of their festival, &c.

STAGBATCH, a hamlet in the parish of Leominster, hundred of Wolphy, county of Hereford, 2 miles (W.S.W.) from Leominster. The population is returned with the chapelry of Ivington.

STAGSDEN, a parish in the hundred of Willey, county of Bedford, 5½ miles (W. by S.) from Bedford, containing 542 inhabitants. The living is a discharged vicarage, in the archdeaconry of Bedford, and diocese of Lincoln, rated in the king's books at £8, endowed with £200 royal bounty. Lord Hampden was patron in 1811. The church is dedicated to St. Leonard.

STAINBROUGH, a chapelry in the parish of Silkstone, wapentake of Staincross, West riding of the county of York, 3¼ miles (S.W.) from Barnesley, containing 194 inhabitants. Here is a school, founded by the family of Cutler, with a house for the master, and an endowment of £8 per annum, which, with an annuity of £2 from F. T. V. Wentworth, Esq., is applied for teaching fifteen children.

STAINBURN, a township in the parish of Workington, Allerdale ward above Darwent, county of Cumberland, 1 mile (E.) from Workington, containing 138 inhabitants. Here was formerly an oratory, subordinate to the priory of St. Bees.

STAINBURN, a chapelry in the parish of Kirkby-Overblows, upper division of the wapentake of Claro, West riding of the county of York, 4¼ miles (N.E. by E.) from Otley, containing 364 inhabitants. The living is a perpetual curacy, in the peculiar jurisdiction of the court of the honour of Knaresborough, endowed with £12 per annum private benefaction, and £400 royal bounty, and in the patronage of the Vicar of Kirkby-Overblows.

STAINBY, a parish in the wapentake of Beltisloe, parts of Kesteven, county of Lincoln, 2½ miles (W.S.W.) from Colsterworth, containing 158 inhabitants. The living is a rectory, with that of Gunby annexed, in the archdeaconry and diocese of Lincoln, rated in the king's books at £6. 6. 8., and in the patronage of the Earl of Harborough. The church is dedicated to St. Peter.

STAINDROP, a parish in the south-western division of Darlington ward, county palatine of Durham, comprising the market town of Staindrop, and the townships of Hilton, Langley-Dale with Shotton, Raby with Keverstone, Wackerfield, and Woodland, and containing 2047 inhabitants, of which number, 1273 are in the town of Staindrop, 5½ miles (N.E. by E.) from Barnard-Castle, and 244 (N.N.W.) from London. This place, formerly called also Stainthorp, or the stony town, is of great antiquity, having been granted by King Canute, who had a mansion at Raby, in this parish, to the monastery at Durham. The town is pleasantly situated in a valley, and consists chiefly of one long well-built street. Here is a subscription library and news-room. In Langley-dale are very extensive works for smelting lead-ore. A weekly market on Saturday, and fairs annually on the Vigil of St. Thomas the Martyr and the two following days, were granted in 1378, by Bishop Hatfield, which, after a time, fell into disuse, but the market has been revived, and is well supplied with provisions. The magistrates hold petty sessions every alternate Saturday; and a court leet and court baron for the lordship of Raby are held at Michaelmas by the lord of the manor, at which constables are sworn in at the former, and debts under 40s. are recoverable at the latter : the jurisdiction extends over the other townships in the parish. The living is a perpetual curacy, annexed to the rectory of Cockfield, in the archdeaconry and diocese of Durham, endowed with £400 royal bounty, and £400 parliamentary grant, and in the patronage of the Marquis of Cleveland. The church, dedicated to St. Mary, was formerly collegiate: it is a handsome structure, exhibiting portions in the early, decorated, and later styles of English architecture, with a square embattled tower rising from the centre, and contains some ancient and handsome monuments. The Society of Friends, Independents, Wesleyan Methodists, and Presbyterians, have each a place of worship here. A charity school, for the education of thirty poor children, is endowed with £15 per annum, arising from land left by Mr. Granger. A collegiate establishment was founded here, in the reign of Henry IV., by Ralph Nevill, Earl of Westmorland, in honour of the Virgin Mary, for a master, six priests, six clerks, six decayed gentlemen, six poor officers, and other poor men : its revenue at the dissolution was estimated at £170. 4. 6.

STAINES, a market town and parish, in the hundred of SPELTHORNE, county of MIDDLESEX, 10 miles (W. S. W.) from Brentford, and 17 (W. S. W.) from London, containing 1957 inhabitants. This place has by some been conjectured to derive its name from a Roman milliarium, which is stated to have been placed here, and the traces of a Roman road pointing towards Staines' bridge, mentioned by Dr. Stukeley, who also states the town to have been surrounded by a ditch, may in some degree strengthen this conjecture; but the more general opinion is, that its name is owing to a stone which, standing on the banks of the river near it, marks the extent of the jurisdiction of the Lord Mayor of London, as conservator of the Thames ; the inscription on it bears date 1284. An army of Danes on their way from Oxford (which they had burned) to their ships, crossed the river here, in 1009, on hearing that an army was marching from London to oppose them. The town, which has been much improved of late years, consists principally of one wide street, containing some good houses, terminating at the river Thames, across which is an iron bridge of one arch. In lieu of this, which has been considered unsafe, a handsome stone bridge has been erected, and a new street formed in a line with it, which will avoid the sharp turn over the former, where many accidents have occurred. The market is on Friday : the market-house, standing near the bridge, is a small building surmounted by a spire. There are fairs on May 11th and September 19th. The living is a vicarage, with the perpetual curacies of Ashford and Laleham annexed, in the archdeaconry of Middlesex, and diocese of London, rated in the king's books at £12. 3. 4., and in the patronage of the Crown. The church, dedicated to St. Mary, erected in 1631, by Inigo Jones, has been recently rebuilt ; it is a neat structure, with a square embattled tower ; the interior, which is well arranged and handsomely fitted up, contains three hundred and forty-four free sittings, towards defraying the expense of which, the Incorporated Society for the building and enlargement of churches and chapels granted the sum of £250. There are places of worship for Baptists, the Society of Friends, and In-

dependents. Here are a National and a Lancasterian school for boys, and a National school and a school of Industry for girls. Duncroft House, in which King John is said to have slept, the night after he signed Magna Charta at Runnymede, is in this parish. A forest anciently extended from Staines to Hounslow, but part of it, consisting of about three hundred acres, has been enclosed.

STAINFIELD, a chapelry in the parish of HACCONBY, wapentake of AVELAND, parts of KESTEVEN, county of LINCOLN, 3½ miles (N. N. W.) from Bourne, containing 58 inhabitants.

STAINFIELD, a parish in the western division of the wapentake of WRAGGOE, parts of LINDSEY, county of LINCOLN, 4 miles (S. W. by S.) from Wragby, containing 103 inhabitants. The living is a perpetual curacy, annexed to that of Apley, in the archdeaconry and diocese of Lincoln, endowed with £600 royal bounty, and £200 parliamentary grant. A priory of Benedictine nuns was founded here, in the reign of Henry II., by Henry Percy, which at the dissolution possessed a revenue of £112. 5.

STAINFORTH, a township in the parish of GIGGLESWICK, western division of the wapentake of STAINCLIFFE and EWCROSS, West riding of the county of YORK, 2 miles (N.) from Settle, containing 235 inhabitants.

STAINFORTH, a township in the parish of HATFIELD, southern division of the wapentake of STRAFFORTH and TICKHILL, West riding of the county of YORK, 3¼ miles (W. S. W.) from Thorne, containing, with South Bramwith, 694 inhabitants. There are places of worship for Wesleyan Methodists and Unitarians. Henry Travers, in 1706, bequeathed certain land, directing the rental to be applied for teaching poor children.

STAININGHALL, a parish in the hundred of TAVERHAM, county of NORFOLK, 2 miles (S. W. by S.) from Coltishall. The population is returned with the parish of Horstead. The living is a discharged rectory, annexed to that of Frettenham, in the archdeaconry and diocese of Norwich, rated in the king's books at £1. 13. 6½. The church is desecrated.

STAININGTON, a chapelry in the parish of ECCLESFIELD, northern division of the wapentake of STRAFFORTH and TICKHILL, West riding of the county of YORK, 4 miles (W. by N.) from Sheffield. The chapel, erected under the late act for promoting the building of additional churches, &c., was finished in November 1829, at an expense of £2607. 19. 3., defrayed by the parliamentary commissioners : it is in the later style of English architecture, with a cupola, and contains seven hundred and twenty-two sittings, of which three hundred and sixty-six are free.

STAINLAND, a township in the parish of HALIFAX, wapentake of MORLEY, West riding of the county of YORK, 4½ miles (S. by W.) from Halifax, containing 2814 inhabitants, who are extensively employed in the manufacture of worsted, woollen cloth, cotton, and paper. There is a place of worship for Independents. Various Roman coins have been found in the neighbourhood.

STAINLEY (NORTH), a joint township with Sleningford, in that part of the parish of RIPON which is in the liberty of RIPON, West riding of the county of YORK, 4½ miles (N. W. by N.) from Ripon, containing, with Sleningford, 385 inhabitants. It is within the peculiar jurisdiction of the Archbishop of York.

STAINLEY (SOUTH), a parish in the lower division of the wapentake of CLARO, West riding of the county of YORK, 2¾ miles (N.E. by N.) from Ripley, containing, with the township of Clayton, 232 inhabitants. The living is a perpetual curacy, in the peculiar jurisdiction of the court of the honour of Knaresborough, endowed with £200 private benefaction, £800 royal bounty, and £300 parliamentary grant, and in the patronage of Horner Reynard, Esq., and the heirs of the late Mrs. Gibson.

STAINMORE, a chapelry in the parish of BROUGH, EAST ward, county of WESTMORLAND, 4 miles (E.S.E.) from Brough, containing 616 inhabitants. The living is a perpetual curacy, in the archdeaconry and diocese of Carlisle, endowed with £400 private benefaction, and £400 royal bounty, and in the patronage of the Earl of Thanet. The chapel was erected as a school-house in 1594, consecrated for divine service in 1608, and repaired, in 1699, by Thomas, Earl of Thanet, who built the school-house adjoining, in which about thirty children are instructed, but the only permanent income attached to it is an annuity of £8, devised by Sir Cuthbert Buckle, Knt., in 1594. At a place called Maiden Castle is a Roman fort, and there is another at Rere Cross, which, according to tradition, was erected, in the first or second century, by Marius, a petty king of the Britons, in memory of a victory which he obtained there over the Picts.

STAINSBY, a township in the parish of AULT-HUCKNALL, hundred of SCARSDALE, county of DERBY, 5¾ miles (S.E.) from Chesterfield. The population is returned with the parish.

STAINSIKER, or STAINSACRE, a joint township with Hawsker, in the parish of WHITBY, liberty of WHITBY-STRAND, North riding of the county of YORK, 1¾ mile (S.E.) from Whitby. The population is returned with Hawsker.

STAINTON, a township in that part of the parish of STANWIX which is in CUMBERLAND ward, county of CUMBERLAND, 1½ mile (N.W.) from Carlisle, containing 71 inhabitants.

STAINTON, a township in the parish of DACRE, LEATH ward, county of CUMBERLAND, 2¾ miles (S.W. by W.) from Penrith. The population is returned with the parish. Eight children of this township are instructed for the dividends arising from £100 three per cents., the gift of Mark Scott, in 1758.

STAINTON, a township in the parish of URSWICK, hundred of LONSDALE, north of the sands, county palatine of LANCASTER, 1½ mile (S.E.) from Dalton. The population is returned with the parish.

STAINTON, a chapelry in the parish of HEVERSHAM, KENDAL ward, county of WESTMORLAND, 4 miles (S. by E.) from Kendal, containing 397 inhabitants. The living is a perpetual curacy, in the archdeaconry of Richmond, and diocese of Chester, endowed with £400 private benefaction, and £800 royal bounty, and in the patronage of the Vicar of Heversham. The chapel, called Cross-Crake chapel, was founded, in the reign of Richard II., by Anselm de Furness, son of the first Michael le Fleming; it was rebuilt in 1773, and had a burial-ground attached in 1823. There is a place of worship for Independents. The Lancaster canal passes

through the parish, and on a rivulet, tributary to the Belo, are two flax-mills and a woollen-mill : the manufacture of bobbin is also carried on. Cross-Crake school, adjoining the chapel, has been lately rebuilt by subscription ; it has an endowment by Mr. Threlfall of £5 per annum, which, with small quarterages, is paid to the schoolmaster for teaching about seventy children.

STAINTON, a township in the parish of DOWN-HOLME, western division of the wapentake of HANG, North riding of the county of YORK, 5½ miles (S.W. by W.) from Richmond, containing 54 inhabitants.

STAINTON, a parish in the western division of the liberty of LANGBAURGH, North riding of the county of YORK, comprising the townships of Hemlington, Ingleby-Barwick, Maltby, Stainton, and Thornaby, and containing 968 inhabitants, of which number, 356 are in the township of Stainton, 5 miles (N. W by N.) from Stokesley. The living is a vicarage, with the perpetual curacy of Thornaby annexed, in the archdeaconry of Cleveland, and diocese of York, rated in the king's books at £5. 14. 2., and in the patronage of the Archbishop of York. The church, dedicated to St. Peter, is an ancient structure, partially repaired and modernised about 1820. Six poor children are taught for a rent-charge of five guineas, the gift of Mary Burdon, in 1817.

STAINTON, a parish in the southern division of the wapentake of STRAFFORTH and TICKHILL, West riding of the county of YORK, 7 miles (S. by W.) from Doncaster, containing, with the township of Hellaby, 218 inhabitants. The living is a discharged vicarage, in the archdeaconry and diocese of York, rated in the king's books at £5. 15., endowed with £200 private benefaction, and £200 royal bounty, and in the patronage of the Earl of Scarborough. The church is dedicated to St. Winifred.

STAINTON (GREAT), a parish in the north-eastern division of STOCKTON ward, county palatine of DURHAM, comprising the townships of Elstols and Great Stainton, and containing 154 inhabitants, of which number, 126 are in the township of Great Stainton, 7 miles (N. E. by N.) from Darlington. The living is a rectory, in the archdeaconry and diocese of Durham, rated in the king's books at £12. 13. 4., and in the patronage of the Crown. The church is dedicated to All Saints. A school was founded and endowed, in 1749, by the Rev. Thomas Nicholson, and has since received considerable donations, chiefly from Lord Crewe's charity. Mr. Hubbock of Stainton-Grange gave £60 for the instruction of three or four children from Little Stainton.

STAINTON by LANGWORTH, a parish in the western division of the wapentake of WRAGGOE, parts of LINDSEY, county of LINCOLN, 5 miles (W.) from Wragby, containing, with the hamlets of Newball and Reasby, 182 inhabitants. The living is a discharged vicarage, in the archdeaconry and diocese of Lincoln, rated in the king's books at £4. 18. 4., and in the patronage of the Earl of Scarborough. The church is dedicated to St. John the Baptist.

STAINTON (LITTLE), a township in the parish of BISHOPTON, south-western division of STOCKTON ward, county palatine of DURHAM, 5½ miles (N.E.) from Darlington, containing 62 inhabitants.

STAINTON (MARKET), a parish in the northern division of the wapentake of GARTREE, parts of LIND-

SEY, county of LINCOLN, 7 miles (E. by N.) from Wragby, containing 131 inhabitants. The living is a perpetual curacy, in the archdeaconry and diocese of Lincoln, endowed with £800 royal bounty, and £200 parliamentary grant. — Dickenson, Esq. was patron in 1818. The church is dedicated to St. Michael. Here was formerly a market on Monday, and an annual fair on October 29th; the latter was removed to Horncastle in 1768, the sum of £200 having been paid in compensation to the lord of this manor.

STAINTON le VALE, a parish in the southern division of the wapentake of WALSHCROFT, parts of LINDSEY, county of LINCOLN, 6 miles (N. E.) from Market-Rasen, containing 121 inhabitants. The living is a discharged rectory, in the archdeaconry and diocese of Lincoln, rated in the king's books at £4. 17. 6., endowed with £200 royal bounty. J. Angerstein, Esq. was patron in 1819. The church is dedicated to St. Andrew.

STAINTON - DALE, a township in the parish of SCALBY, PICKERING lythe, North riding of the county of YORK, 8½ miles (N. W. by N.) from Scarborough, containing 294 inhabitants.

STALBRIDGE, a market town and parish in the hundred of BROWNSHALL, Sturminster division of the county of DORSET, 7½ miles (E. by N.) from Sherborne, and 111 (W. S.W.) from London, containing, with the tythings of Gomershay, Thornhill, and Weston, 1571 inhabitants. The name of this place, in Domesday-book, is written Staplebridge, and at the time of the Conquest belonged to the abbey of Sherborne. The town and the greater part of the parish are situated upon a rock, which supplies building materials for the neighbourhood; the streets are not regularly paved, but are partially lighted by subscription, and the inhabitants are well supplied with water. From the south end of the main street another diverges, and at the intersection is an ancient stone cross, thirty feet in height, including the pedestal (ornamented on the sides with sculptured emblematical figures), from which rises the frustum of a pyramid, twelve feet high, with fluted angles, and decorated on one of the faces with a figure of our Saviour with a lamb at his feet, and at the bottom with shields of arms, and surmounted with canopied shrines, in one of which is a representation of the Crucifixion; above these are enriched canopies, terminating in a crocketed pinnacle, formerly surmounted by a cross, the whole being supported on three octagonal flights of steps, which diminish in the ascent. In the park formerly belonging to the manor-house the Anglesea cricket club is held: a building has been erected for the accommodation of the members, who meet weekly during the season, but the rest is converted to agricultural purposes, and is surrounded by a wall five miles in circumference. Stalbridge was formerly noted for the manufacture of stockings: several of the inhabitants are now employed in winding silk. A branch of the river Stour, and the Dorsetshire and Somersetshire canal, pass through the parish. In the reign of Edward I., a grant of a market and fair was made to the abbot of Sherborne; the present market is on Tuesday, and on every alternate Tuesday is a great market for cattle: fairs are held May 6th and September 4th. The living is a rectory, in the archdeaconry of Dorset, and diocese of Bristol, rated in the king's books at £27. 4. 7., and in the patronage of the Senior Bachelor of Christ's College, Cambridge. The

church, which is dedicated to St. Mary, is a spacious and ancient structure, with a lofty embattled tower; on the capitals of the pillars supporting the chancel are figures of angels holding scrolls inscribed with texts of Scripture: it contains some ancient monuments. There is a place of worship for Independents. A National school for children of both sexes is supported by subscription.

STALHAM, a parish in the hundred of HAPPING, county of NORFOLK, 7¼ miles (S.E. by E.) from North Walsham, containing 492 inhabitants. The living is a discharged vicarage, in the archdeaconry of Norfolk, and diocese of Norwich, rated in the king's books at £5, endowed with £200 royal bounty, and in the patronage of the Marquis of Cholmondeley. The church is dedicated to St. Mary. There is a place of worship for Wesleyan Methodists.

STALISFIELD, a parish in the hundred of FAVERSHAM, lathe of SCRAY, county of KENT, 2¼ miles (N. N.E.) from Charing, containing 340 inhabitants. The living is a vicarage, in the archdeaconry and diocese of Canterbury, rated in the king's books at £5. 6. 8., and in the patronage of the Archbishop of Canterbury. The church, dedicated to St. Mary, is a large, handsome, and ancient cruciform structure.

STALLINGBOROUGH, a parish in the eastern division of the wapentake of YARBOROUGH, parts of LINDSEY, county of LINCOLN, 7¼ miles (W. N. W.) from Great Grimsby, containing 343 inhabitants. The living is a discharged vicarage, in the archdeaconry and diocese of Lincoln, rated in the king's books at £11. 10. 10., endowed with £400 royal bounty, and in the patronage of the Bishop of Lincoln. The church, dedicated to St. Peter and St. Paul, with its tower, fell down in 1746; the chancel, and the burial-place of the Ayscough family, were afterwards rebuilt. There is a place of worship for Wesleyan Methodists. Four poor children are instructed for a trifling annuity, the bequest of John Appleby.

STALLING-BUSK, a chapelry in the parish of AYSGARTH, western division of the wapentake of HANG, North riding of the county of YORK, 17 miles (W. by S.) from Middleham. The population is returned with the parish. The living is a perpetual curacy, in the archdeaconry of Richmond, and diocese of Chester, endowed with £200 private benefaction, and £800 royal bounty, and in the patronage of the Vicar of Aysgarth. The river Ure here forms a fine cataract.

STALMINE, a chapelry in that part of the parish of LANCASTER which is in the hundred of AMOUNDERNESS, county palatine of LANCASTER, 5 miles (N. N. E.) from Poulton, containing, with the township of Stanall, 507 inhabitants. The living is a perpetual curacy, in the archdeaconry of Richmond, and diocese of Chester, endowed with £200 private benefaction, and £200 royal bounty, and in the patronage of the Vicar of Lancaster. The chapel is dedicated to St. James.

STALYBRIDGE, a market town and chapelry, partly in the township of HARTSHEAD, parish of ASHTON under LINE, hundred of SALFORD, county palatine of LANCASTER, partly in that of DUCKINFIELD, parish of STOCKPORT, and partly in that of STALYBRIDGE, parish of MOTTRAM in LONGDEN DALE, hundred of MACCLESFIELD, county palatine of CHESTER, 8 miles (N. E. by N.) from Stockport, containing upwards of 12,000 inhabitants; which population is included in the returns for the several townships in which it is situated. It is on the banks of the Tame, and derives its name, which was originally Staveleigh, from the family of the Staveleighs, who formerly had their residence here, which is still in existence, and the addition from the bridge, which has been recently rebuilt, at an expense of £4000, and, crossing the river here, connects the two palatine counties of Lancaster and Chester : it is partially paved and lighted with gas, and considerable improvements are in progress, under an act of parliament for that purpose obtained in 1828 ; it is well supplied with water. The principal market day is Saturday, and there is a fair for pedlary on the 5th of March. The court of requests, held at Ashton under Line, for the recovery of debts under £5, comprises this place within its jurisdiction. The advance of the trade and population of the town has been singularly rapid; the first cotton-mill was erected in 1776, into which a steam-engine was introduced in 1795, and in 1828 there were twenty-four factories, worked by thirty-three steam-engines and by six water-wheels, of the aggregate power of eight hundred and ninety-eight horses, which turned three hundred and ninety-eight thousand one hundred and sixteen spindles, and worked two thousand nine hundred power-looms, giving employment to about six thousand four hundred persons; besides which, other mills are in progress of erection, which will add, when completed, nearly one hundred thousand spindles. Upwards of eight hundred houses have been erected within the last three years : large quantities of excellent fire-bricks are manufactured. The new road from Manchester to Sheffield runs on the north side of the town, and the Huddersfield canal, passing in the vicinity, affords great facility to commerce.

The living is a perpetual curacy, in the archdeaconry and diocese of Chester, endowed with £800 royal bounty, and £1600 parliamentary grant, subject to the rector of Ashton under Line, and in the patronage of the Earl of Stamford. The chapel, dedicated to St. George, is a handsome octagonal structure, occupying an elevated site. There are places of worship for General and Particular Baptists, Wesleyan Methodists, and Methodists of the New Connexion, to which Sunday schools are attached, affording instruction to upwards of two thousand children. A Society for Mutual Instruction has been established here, with a library and apparatus for lecturing, and there are also a news-room, and several benefit societies. A temporary place of confinement, termed a "Lock-up," has been recently erected. The neighbourhood, formerly much covered with wood, presents some bold scenery ; and from the "Wild Bank," which rises one thousand three hundred feet above the level of the sea, the prospect is extensive.

STAMBORNE, a parish in the hundred of HINCKFORD, county of ESSEX, 5¼ miles (N. W. by W.) from Castle-Hedingham, containing 432 inhabitants. The living is a rectory, in the jurisdiction of the Commissary of Essex and Herts, concurrently with the Consistorial Court of the Bishop of London, rated in the king's books at £15, and in the patronage of the King, as Duke of Lancaster. The church is dedicated to St. Peter. There is a place of worship for Independents. A school is supported by annual subscription.

STAMBRIDGE (GREAT), a parish in the hundred of ROCHFORD, county of ESSEX, 1¾ mile (E.) from Rochford, containing 401 inhabitants. The living is a rectory, in the archdeaconry of Essex, and diocese of London, rated in the king's books at £20, and in the patronage of the Governors of the Charter-house, London. The church is dedicated to St. Mary and All Saints.

STAMBRIDGE (LITTLE), a parish in the hundred of ROCHFORD, county of ESSEX, 1½ mile (N. E. by N.) from Rochford, containing 100 inhabitants. The living is a discharged rectory, in the archdeaconry of Essex, and diocese of London, rated in the king's books at £12, and in the patronage of the Crown.

STAMFORD, a borough and market town, having separate jurisdiction, though locally in the wapentake of Ness, parts of KESTEVEN, county of LINCOLN, 46 miles (S. by E.) from Lincoln, and 89 (N. by W.) from London, containing 5050 inhabitants. Its original name, which was *Steanforde*, is derived from the Saxon *stean*, a stone, and *forde*, from the passage across

Seal and Arms.

the river Welland being paved with stones ; it was afterwards called Stanford, which was subsequently changed to its present name. The town is of very remote antiquity, its origin being ascribed by tradition to a period long before the Christian era; but the earliest authentic account respecting it is by Henry of Huntingdon, who records it as the place where the Picts and Scots, after having ravaged the country to Stamford, were defeated, in a battle fought betwixt them and the Britons, assisted by the Saxons under the command of Hengist, who had been called to the assistance of the Britons by their king Vortigern. It was one of the five cities into which the Danes were distributed by Alfred the Great, when, after defeating them, he allowed that people, with Guthrum their prince, to settle in the kingdom, and who were thence called *Fif-burgenses*, or Five-burghers (the other places being Derby, Nottingham, Leicester, and Lincoln), and subsequently *Seafen-burgenses*, on the addition of two more cities, namely, Chester and York. A castle was erected by Edward the Elder, early in the tenth century, on the bank of the river, opposite the town, to check the incursions of the Danes, and of the Five-Burghers and other internal enemies, but every vestige of it has long since disappeared. Another castle, on the north-west of the town, the foundations of which are still visible, was fortified by Stephen, during the war with the Empress Matilda, but was captured by Henry of Anjou, her son, afterwards Henry II., and the town appears to have been at this period surrounded by a wall, of which no traces are discernible. The barons met at Stamford in the 17th year of the reign of John, to concert those measures which led to the signing of Magna Charta by that monarch. In the reign of Henry III., the Carmelites and members of other religious establishments here commenced giving lectures on divinity and the liberal arts, which being attended by a great number of youths of good family, led to the erection of colleges, and Stamford became celebrated as a place for education; insomuch that, from dissensions occurring in the reign of Edward III., in the University of Oxford, amongst the students from the southern and those from the northern parts of England, a considerable number of the latter, with several professors, removed hither; but they soon returned to Oxford, in consequence of a royal proclamation, and statutes were passed by both Universities, by which any person taking a degree at either of them bound himself by oath not to attend any lectures at Stamford: a part of the gate of Brasenose College, standing in St. Paul's street, is all that now remains of its university. The town suffered much during the war between the houses of York and Lancaster, a great portion of it having been burnt and otherwise destroyed about the year 1461, and it never afterwards regained its former importance.

The town is pleasantly situated on the side of a hill, rising gradually from the northern bank of the Welland, across which a stone bridge of five arches connects it with Stamford-Baron, or St. Martin's, in Northamptonshire: the houses are chiefly built of freestone, obtained from the neighbouring quarries of Ketton and Barnoak, and covered with slate: the streets are partially paved, and lighted with gas, the works for which were erected in 1824, at an expense of upwards of £9000: it is well supplied with water, which is brought by pipes from Wothorpe, about a mile distant, and the approach from the south is pleasing and picturesque. The theatre, erected in 1768, is a neat and commodious edifice, lighted with gas, and there are assembly-rooms in St. George's square. Races are held in March and July, on a good course, a mile in circumference, on Wittering heath, near the town. On the banks of a stream are excellent cold and hot water baths. The trade is principally in coal, rafts, malt, and beer, and is much promoted by the Welland being navigable hither for boats and small barges. There was formerly a school for spinning and winding raw silk, which has been discontinued. The market days are Monday and Friday, the latter being noted for corn: the butchers' and fish markets were erected, in 1807, by the corporation. The fairs are on Tuesday before February 13th, Monday before Mid-Lent, Mid-Lent Monday, Monday before May 12th, Monday after the festival of Corpus Christi, and November 8th. At the time of the Conquest, Stamford was governed by *lagemen*, or aldermen, but was not incorporated by charter until the 1st of Edward IV. In 1663, a charter was granted by Charles II., in which the chief magistrate is first styled mayor; it was confirmed in 1685 by James II., being that under which the town is now governed. The corporation consists of a mayor, twelve aldermen, and twenty-four capital burgesses, who appoint a recorder, coroner, town clerk, and subordinate officers. The mayor and aldermen are elected annually by the members of the corporation, and the office of coroner is held in succession to that of mayor. The mayor and aldermen are justices of the peace, and hold quarter sessions, and a court of record for the recovery of debts to the amount of £40, contracted within the limits of the borough, every Thursday; they have also the privilege of trying for capital offences, but this they do not exercise. The freedom is acquired by birth, apprenticeship, purchase, or gift of the corporation. The custom of Borough English prevails here, by which,

when the father dies intestate, the youngest son inherits the lands and tenements, to the exclusion of the elder branches of the family. The town hall, wherein the business of the corporation is transacted, was rebuilt in 1776; it is a large and handsome detached building, standing in the main street, near the end of the bridge, and containing a sessions-room, house of correction, gaol, guard-room, and other apartments. This borough first sent members to parliament in the reign of Edward I., and continued to do so, with occasional intermissions, until that of Edward IV., since which period it has exercised this privilege without interruption: the right of voting is vested in the resident inhabitants paying scot and lot, and not receiving alms: the number of voters is about eight hundred, and the mayor is the returning officer: the prevailing influence is exercised by the Marquis of Exeter.

Stamford formerly contained fourteen parish churches, but several of those in the liberties were destroyed by the northern soldiers, in 1461; and the number was again reduced, in 1538, at the dissolution of the monastic institutions: by an act of parliament, passed in 1547, five were allowed to remain, which still continue, the livings being in the archdeaconry and diocese of Lincoln. The living of All Saints' is a vicarage, with the rectory of St. Peter consolidated, rated in the king's books at £12. 7. 8., and in the patronage of the Crown for one turn, and the Marquis of Exeter for two: the church is a large and handsome structure, combining some fine specimens of the early and later styles of English architecture, with a lofty embattled tower surmounted by an elegant octangular crocketed spire, in the later English style; it was built, about 1465, at the expense of Mr. John Brown, a merchant at Calais, who was buried in it. The living of St. George's is a discharged rectory, with that of St. Paul's consolidated, rated in the king's books at £5. 3. 11½., endowed with £200 private benefaction, and £200 royal bounty, and in the patronage of the Marquis of Exeter: the church, a spacious plain edifice with a square embattled tower, was rebuilt in 1450, by William Bruges, Esq., the first Garter King at Arms. The living of St. John's the Baptist is a rectory, with that of St. Clement's consolidated, rated in the king's books at £8. 8. 6½., and in the patronage of the Mayor and Corporation for one turn, and the Marquis of Exeter for two: the church, rebuilt about the year 1452, is principally in the later English style; it has a neat embattled tower, adorned with pinnacles, and a handsome porch at the south end; the screen separating the chancel from the nave and aisles, and the roof, are both very handsome. The living of St. Mary's is a discharged rectory, rated in the king's books at £4. 18. 9., endowed with £400 private benefaction, and £600 royal bounty, and in the patronage of the Marquis of Exeter: this handsome church, supposed to have been built about the end of the thirteenth century, is considered the mother church; it is principally in the later English style, with some portions, particularly a very fine tower and spire, of early English architecture. The living of St. Michael's is a discharged rectory, with the vicarage of St. Andrew's and the rectory of St. Stephen's consolidated, rated in the king's books at £8. 14. 2., endowed with £200 private benefaction, and £200 royal bounty, and in the patronage of the King, as Duke of Lancaster, for one turn, of the Mayor for one, and of the Marquis of Exeter for two: the church, situated near the centre of the town, is probably the oldest, having been built early in the thirteenth century; it has been much altered and modernised, the embattled tower at the west end having been erected in 1761. There are places of worship for Independents, Wesleyan Methodists, and Roman Catholics.

The free grammar school was founded by Alderman William Radcliffe, about the year 1500, and endowed by him with estates now producing £470 per annum: the election of the master is, by an act of parliament passed in 1548, vested in the aldermen of Stamford, with the advice and consent of the Master of St. John's College, Cambridge; a house is provided for him, and he receives the whole income, from which he pays the salary of the under-master, and keeps in repair the schoolhouse, which is situated in St. Paul's street, and has been recently rebuilt by subscription. The school is open to all boys of the town and its vicinity, but at present there are only a few on the foundation: it is entitled to one of the twenty-four scholarships at St. John's College, Cambridge, augmented by the first Lord Burghley, who was educated here, and Thomas, Lord Exeter, who, in 1613, also founded three fellowships and eight scholarships at Clare Hall, Cambridge, directing by his will that the Master and Fellows should, when vacancies occurred, prefer candidates educated at Stamford school, provided they are equally qualified in other respects with their competitors. Mr. Thomas Truesdale, in 1700, vested £50 in trust of the corporation for scholars going to the university, and £12 per annum was bequeathed by Mr. Marshall, for an exhibition for a scholar from the grammar school of Southwark, or Stamford. The Blue-coat school was established, in 1704, by subscription among the inhabitants, with which an estate at Hogsthorpe was purchased, the proceeds, aided by other contributions, affording instruction and clothing to about forty boys. Wells', or the petty school, was endowed in 1604. A National school for girls was established, in 1815, from the surplus fund of a lying-in charity, assisted by voluntary contributions.

The charitable institutions are numerous and liberally endowed. The principal is the hospital, or bead-house, founded and largely endowed by William Browne, in 1493, for a warden, confrater, twelve poor aged men, and a nurse, who are incorporated, and have a common seal: the edifice, situated in the cattle market, is now appropriated for decayed tradesmen of the town and neighbourhood, each of whom receives a weekly allowance, and some clothing once a year. Truesdale's hospital, in Scot-gate, was founded in 1700, and eight poor men, with their wives, are lodged in it, receiving a weekly allowance of five shillings, and some coal and clothing annually; and as, on the decease of any male inmate, his widow must quit the hospital, the sum of five shillings a week was bequeathed by H. Fryer, Esq. to each widow so leaving it, for the remainder of her life. Snowden's hospital, endowed in 1604, affords an asylum to eight poor women, with a small weekly allowance of two shillings. Williamson's callis, or almshouse, has apartments for ten poor women, with a weekly allowance of five shillings, arising from various legacies. All Saints' callis, for men and women, is supported by incidental legacies, and by subscriptions from the corporation; and Peter's Hill callis, for an unlimited number of poor women, is endowed by the corporation with the interest of £200, arising from the Black Sluice drainage. The principal bequests for charitable purposes are, one of £1800, by John Warrington, Esq., for the benefit, in equal proportions, of the poor widows of All Saints' callis and Snowden's hospital; £3000, left by Mr. Fryer, for the poor of Snowden's hospital and Peter's Hill callis; the rent of four houses, left by Mrs. Williamson, to be paid, in sums of three shillings and sixpence a week, to six poor women; and an estate producing £50 per annum, left by Mr. W. Wells for the education of children under ten years of age belonging to the parish of All Saints. A handsome infirmary, for Stamford and the county of Rutland has recently been erected near the town, by subscription, which receives thirty-two patients, and towards the support of which, upwards of £7000 stock was bequeathed by Mr. Henry Fryer, and £2000 collected by the ladies at a bazaar; it is further supported by voluntary contributions. A Benedictine priory, dedicated to St. Leonard, and valued at the dissolution at £36. 17. per annum, is supposed to have been founded here in the seventh century, and refounded in the time of William the Conqueror, when it was made a cell to the monastery of Durham; the site is a small distance from the town, though formerly included within it; a portion of the conventual church still remains. Of the Carmelite friary, founded in 1291, the west gate exists, and is a handsome specimen of the architecture of that period; the infirmary occupies a portion of the site. Part of an outer wall, and a postern, are the only remains of the convent of Grey friars, founded by Henry III. A Dominican priory was founded prior to the year 1240; a Gilbertine priory in 1291; an Augustine priory before 1346; and an hospital, or house of lepers, in 1493. A custom, called bull-running, is practised here on St. Brice's day (the 13th of November), and is said to have originated in William, Earl of Warren, having, in the reign of King John, granted a meadow for the common use of the butchers of the town, on condition that they should find a bull to be hunted and baited annually on that day, for the diversion of the inhabitants. Stamford gives the title of earl to the family of Grey of Groby.

STAMFORD, a township in the parish of EMBLETON, southern division of BAMBROUGH ward, county of NORTHUMBERLAND, 5 miles (N. E. by N.) from Alnwick, containing 120 inhabitants.

STAMFORD-BARON, county of NORTHAMPTON.—See MARTIN'S (ST.) STAMFORD-BARON.

STAMFORD-BRIDGE (EAST), a township partly in the liberty of ST. PETER of YORK, but chiefly in that part of the parish of CATTON which is in the Wilton-Beacon division of the wapentake of HARTHILL, East riding of the county of YORK, 8 miles (E. N. E.) from York, containing 298 inhabitants.

STAMFORD-BRIDGE (WEST), a joint township with Scoreby, in that part of the parish of CATTON which is in the wapentake of OUZE and DERWENT, East riding of the county of YORK, 7½ miles (E.N.E.) from York, containing, with Scoreby, 151 inhabitants. There is a place of worship for Wesleyan Methodists. The river Derwent separates this township from that of East Stamford. Christopher Wharton, in 1787, gave £600 in support of a school, for twelve boys and six girls; the annual income is about £30, and the expense of the school-house, erected in 1795, was defrayed out of previous accumulations. The celebrated battle between Harold and Tosti, in 1066, was fought near this place.

STAMFORD-HILL, county of MIDDLESEX.—See HACKNEY.

STAMFORDHAM, a parish (formerly a market town) in the north-eastern division of TINDALE ward, county of NORTHUMBERLAND, 12½ miles (W. N. W.) from Newcastle upon Tyne, comprising the chapelry of Ryall, and the townships of Bitchfield, Blackheddon, Cheeseburn-Grange, Fenwick, Hawkwell, Heugh, Ingoe, Kearsley, East Matfen, West Matfen, Nesbit, Ouston, and Walridge, and containing 1827 inhabitants. The living is a vicarage, in the archdeaconry of Northumberland, and diocese of Durham, rated in the king's books at £14. 18. 1½., and in the patronage of the Crown. The church is dedicated to St. Mary. There is a place of worship for Presbyterians. Lime and coal abounds within the parish. The market has fallen into disuse, but the market cross, erected by Sir John Swinburne, Bart., in 1735, is still standing. Fairs, for the sale of cattle, pigs, &c., are held on the second Thursday in April, and on the 14th of August, if on Thursday, if not, on the Thursday following; there are also statute fairs for hiring servants, on the Thursdays before Old May-day and November 14th, and on the last Thursday in February. A free school was founded, in 1663, by Sir Thomas Widdrington, Knt., who endowed it with property now producing about £220 per annum.

STANALL, a township in that part of the parish of LANCASTER which is in the hundred of AMOUNDERNESS, county palatine of LANCASTER, 4¼ miles (N. by E.) from Poulton. The population is returned with the chapelry of Stalmine.

STANCILL, a joint township with Wellingley and Wilsick, in the parish of TICKHILL, southern division of the wapentake of STRAFFORTH and TICKHILL, West riding of the county of YORK, 3 miles (N. N. E.) from Tickhill, containing, with Wellingley and Wilsick, 54 inhabitants.

STANDBRIDGE, a chapelry in the parish of LEIGHTON-BUZZARD, hundred of MANSHEAD, county of BEDFORD, 3¼ miles (E. by S.) from Leighton-Buzzard, containing 407 inhabitants. The living is a perpetual curacy, in the peculiar jurisdiction of the Prebendary of Leighton-Buzzard in the Cathedral Church of Lincoln, endowed with £800 royal bounty, and in the patronage of the Vicar of Leighton-Buzzard. The chapel is dedicated to St. John the Baptist.

STANDBRIDGE, county of DORSET.—See HINTON (PARVA).

STANDERWICK, a parish in the hundred of FROME, county of SOMERSET, 4 miles (E. N. E.) from Frome, containing 86 inhabitants. The living is a rectory, annexed to that of Beckington, in the archdeaconry of Wells, and diocese of Bath and Wells, rated in the king's books at £2. 9. 7.

STANDFORD, a parish in the hundred of STOUTING, lathe of SHEPWAY, county of KENT, 3½ miles (N. W.) from Hythe, containing 229 inhabitants. The living is a perpetual curacy, annexed to the rectory of Lyminge, in the archdeaconry and diocese of Canterbury. The

church is dedicated to All Saints. The ancient Stane-street passes through the village. A trifling bequest from the Rev. Dr. Lynch, in 1789, is applied for the education of two poor children.

STANDGROUND, a parish in the hundred of NORMAN-CROSS, county of HUNTINGDON, 1 mile (S. E. by S.) from Peterborough, containing, with the chapelry of Farcett, 1024 inhabitants. The living is a vicarage, in the archdeaconry of Huntingdon, and diocese of Lincoln, rated in the king's books at £6. 6. 10½., and in the patronage of the Master and Fellows of Emanuel College, Cambridge. The church is dedicated to St. John the Baptist.

STANDHILL, a hamlet in the parish and hundred of PIRTON, county of OXFORD, 3 miles (W. S. W.) from Tetsworth. The population is returned with the parish.

STANDISH, a parish in the upper division of the hundred of WHITSTONE, county of GLOUCESTER, 6 miles (N. W.) from Stroud, containing 525 inhabitants. The living is a vicarage, in the archdeaconry and diocese of Gloucester, rated in the king's books at £44. 2. 8½., and in the patronage of the Bishop of Gloucester. The church, dedicated to St. Nicholas, is principally in the decorated style of English architecture.

STANDISH, a parish in the hundred of LEYLAND, county palatine of LANCASTER, comprising the chapelry of Coppull, and the townships of Adlington, Anderton, Charnock-Heath, Charnock-Richard, Duxbury, Shevington, Standish with Langtree, Welsh-Whittle, and Worthington, and containing 7616 inhabitants, of which number, 2065 are in the township of Standish with Langtree, 3¼ miles (N. W. by N.) from Wigan. The living is a rectory, in the archdeaconry and diocese of Chester, rated in the king's books at £45. 16. 8., and in the patronage of Sir R. Perryn, Knt. The church, dedicated to St. Wilfrid, was built in 1584, by the Rev. Richard Moodie, the first Protestant rector; it is an elegant structure of the Tuscan order. The free grammar school, founded in 1603, by Mary Langton, is endowed with lands, &c., producing an annual income exceeding £100, for the support of a master and an usher. Mary Smalley, in 1794, bequeathed £1000 for the endowment of a school, in which twenty poor girls are taught and clothed: the income amounts to £50 per annum. Fairs for horses, cattle, toys, &c., are held on June 29th and November 22nd. Two of the twelve ancient castles of Lancashire, viz., Standish and Penwortham, stood here, but their sites only can now be distinguished.

STANDLAKE, a parish in the hundred of BAMPTON, county of OXFORD, 5½ miles (S. S. E.) from Witney, containing, with part of the hamlet of Brighthampton, 643 inhabitants. The living is a rectory, in the archdeaconry and diocese of Oxford, rated in the king's books at £16. 10. 10., and in the patronage of the President and Fellows of Magdalene College, Oxford. The church is dedicated to St. Giles. Twelve poor children are instructed for about £8. 10. per annum, arising from the united gifts of William Plaisterer, in 1711, and John Chambers, in 1732.

STANDLINCH, a parish in the hundred of DOWNTON, county of WILTS, 4¾ miles (S. E. by S.) from Salisbury, containing 42 inhabitants. It is bounded on the west and south-west by the river Avon. A chantry was founded here by Queen Elfrida, in expiation of the murder of Edward the Martyr, on the site of which a small chapel was erected in 1147, and rebuilt in 1677; but, though still in existence, no living is attached to it, nor is it used for divine service, except occasionally by the family of the lord of the manor, Farl Nelson, of Trafalgar House.

STANDON, a parish (formerly a market town) in the hundred of BRAUGHIN, county of HERTFORD, 8 miles (N. E.) from Hertford, containing 2135 inhabitants. The living is a discharged vicarage, in the archdeaconry of Middlesex, and diocese of London, rated in the king's books at £14. 13. 4., and in the patronage of the Rev. Henry Law. The church, dedicated to St. Mary, is a large ancient building, with a tower on the north side. There are places of worship for Baptists and Wesleyan Methodists. About five miles from Ware, on the Cambridge road, in this parish, is St. Edmund's College, established for the education of the sons of the English nobility, clergy, and gentry, of the Roman Catholic religion. The building was erected in 1795, under the direction of Mr. James Taylor, architect, and consists of a range of buildings four stories high, and, with its two wings, three hundred feet long; more than eighty students can be conveniently accommodated. The course of education is commercial, classical, and theological: the institution is under the management of a president and vice-president, and there are eight professors and masters. The usual period for continuing at college is twelve years; the first seven are devoted to history, the mathematics, the ancient and modern languages, &c., and the remaining five are appropriated to logic, metaphysics, theology, and divinity. The occasion of founding this institution was the expulsion of the English Roman Catholics from their college at Douay, at the commencement of the French Revolution. A free school for the instruction of poor children was endowed with £33 per annum, by Thomas Fisher, in 1612, and other benefactions. The market, which was on Friday, was granted by Charles II., together with two fairs; a pleasure fair is held on the 25th of April. The ancient Ermin-street runs through this parish.

STANDON, a parish in the northern division of the hundred of PIREHILL, county of STAFFORD, 4 miles (N. N. W.) from Eccleshall, containing 415 inhabitants. The living is a rectory, in the archdeaconry of Stafford, and diocese of Lichfield and Coventry, rated in the king's books at £6. 18. 4., and in the patronage of the Rev. Thomas Walker. The church is dedicated to All Saints. The river Sow bounds the parish on the south. Ten poor children are taught to read for £6 a year, the interest of bequests by Ann Tagg and Margaret Plant.

STANE, a parish in the Marsh division of the hundred of CALCEWORTH, parts of LINDSEY, county of LINCOLN, 6½ miles (N.) from Alford. The population is returned with Witherne. The living is a rectory, united to that of Mablethorpe, St. Mary, in the archdeaconry and diocese of Lincoln, rated in the king's books at £5. 6. 8. The church is dedicated to All Saints.

STANFIELD, a parish in the hundred of LAUNDITCH, county of NORFOLK, 6 miles (N. W. by N.) from East Dereham, containing 209 inhabitants. The living is a discharged rectory, in the archdeaconry and diocese of Norwich, rated in the king's books at £6. 14. 2.,

and in the patronage of the Rev. W. Newcome. The church is dedicated to St. Margaret.

STANFORD, a hamlet in the parish of SOUTHILL, hundred of WIXAMTREE, county of BEDFORD, 3¼ miles (S. W. by S.) from Biggleswade, containing 257 inhabitants.

STANFORD, a parish in the hundred of GRIMSHOE, county of NORFOLK, 6 miles (S. W.) from Watton, containing 150 inhabitants. The living is a discharged vicarage, in the archdeaconry of Norfolk, and diocese of Norwich, rated in the king's books at £5. 13. 1½., endowed with £400 royal bounty, and in the patronage of the Bishop of Ely. The church, dedicated to All Saints, is built of brick, now much decayed; it has a tower of flint at the west end, is circular at the base, and octangular above.

STANFORD, a parish in the hundred of GUILSBOROUGH, county of NORTHAMPTON, 5 miles (S.E.) from Lutterworth, containing 20 inhabitants. The living is a discharged vicarage, in the archdeaconry of Northampton, and diocese of Peterborough, rated in the king's books at £9. 10. 5., endowed with £200 private benefaction, and £600 royal bounty. Lady Cave was patroness in 1818. The church is dedicated to St. Nicholas. The river Avon, and the Grand Union canal, pass through the parish.

STANFORD, a parish in the upper division of the hundred of DODDINGTREE, county of WORCESTER, 8 miles (N. E. by N.) from Bromyard, containing 194 inhabitants. The living is a rectory, in the archdeaconry of Salop, and diocese of Hereford, rated in the king's books at £7. 4. 2., and in the patronage of Sir T. E. Winnington, Bart. The church, dedicated to St. Mary, was erected in 1768, in the later style of English architecture. The river Teme runs through the parish, which produces hops and abounds with limestone.

STANFORD (BISHOP'S), a parish in the hundred of BROXASH, county of HEREFORD, 3½ miles (S. E. by S.) from Bromyard, containing, with the township of King's Stanford, 317 inhabitants. The living is a perpetual curacy, in the archdeaconry and diocese of Hereford, endowed with £800 royal bounty, and £200 parliamentary grant, and in the patronage of the three Portionists of Bromyard. The church is dedicated to St. James.

STANFORD le HOPE, a parish in the hundred of BARSTABLE, county of ESSEX, 1½ mile (S. E. by E.) from Horndon on the Hill, containing 301 inhabitants. The living is a rectory, in the archdeaconry of Essex, and diocese of London, rated in the king's books at £12. 19. 9½., and in the patronage of Sir H. Fetherstonhaugh, Bart. The church is dedicated to St. Margaret. The parish is bounded on the south by a portion of the Thames, called the Hope.

STANFORD (KING'S), a township in the parish of BISHOP'S STANFORD, hundred of BROXASH, county of HEREFORD, 3½ miles (S. S. E.) from Bromyard, containing 80 inhabitants. Here is a petrifying spring.

STANFORD upon SOAR, a parish in the southern division of the wapentake of RUSHCLIFFE, county of NOTTINGHAM, 2½ miles (N. by E.) from Loughborough, containing 160 inhabitants. The living is a rectory, in the archdeaconry of Nottingham, and diocese of York, rated in the king's books at £9. 7. 6., and in the patronage of the Rev. S. F. Dashwood. The church is dedicated to St. John the Baptist. The river Trent enters the county here, and runs through the parish. Roman coins have been discovered.

STANFORD in the VALE, a parish partly in the hundred of OCK, but chiefly in that of GANFIELD, county of BERKS, 4 miles (E. S. E.) from Great Farringdon, containing, with the joint chapelry of Goosey with Circourt, 931 inhabitants. The living is a discharged vicarage, in the archdeaconry of Berks, and diocese of Salisbury, rated in the king's books at £21. 1. 10½., and in the patronage of the Dean and Chapter of Westminster. The church is dedicated to St. Denis. About twenty-five children are instructed for £7 per annum, arising from the united bequests of John Hulton, in 1750, and William Shilton, in 1753. Here was formerly a market on Thursday, with a fair on the festival of St. Dionysius, by corruption St. Denis, granted in 1230 to Ferrars, Earl of Derby, by Henry III.

STANFORD-DINGLEY, a parish in the hundred of FAIRCROSS, county of BERKS, 8½ miles (E. N. E.) from Speenhamland, containing 135 inhabitants. The living is a rectory, in the archdeaconry of Berks, and diocese of Salisbury, rated in the king's books at £8. 1. 8., and in the patronage of the Rev. John E. W. Valpy. The church, dedicated to St. Denis, is principally in the Norman style of architecture. The small river Fawley runs through the parish.

STANFORD-RIVERS, a parish in the hundred of ONGAR, county of ESSEX, 2 miles (S. W. by W.) from Chipping-Ongar, containing 792 inhabitants. The living is a rectory, in the archdeaconry of Essex, and diocese of London, rated in the king's books at £26. 13. 4., and in the patronage of the King, as Duke of Lancaster. The church is dedicated to St. Margaret. There is a place of worship for Independents. A workhouse for eleven contiguous parishes is now being erected.

STANHOE, a parish in the hundred of SMITHDON, county of NORFOLK, 4 miles (S. W. by S.) from Burnham-Westgate, containing, with Barwick, 445 inhabitants. The living is a rectory, in the archdeaconry of Norfolk, and diocese of Norwich, rated in the king's books at £16, and in the patronage of Mr. and Mrs. Hoste. The church is dedicated to All Saints.

STANHOPE, a parish in the north-western division of DARLINGTON ward, county palatine of DURHAM, comprising the townships of Forest-Quarter, Newland-Side, Park-Quarter, and Stanhope-Quarter, and containing 7341 inhabitants, of which number, 1584 are in the township of Stanhope-Quarter, 5¾ miles (W. N. W.) from Walsingham. The village is situated on the north bank of the river Wear, and many of the inhabitants are employed in the adjacent lead mines, which are very extensive. The magistrates hold here petty sessions every alternate Friday; and at Frosterley, in this parish, a court baron is held occasionally. In 1421, a charter was obtained from Bishop Langley for a market and two annual fairs: fairs only are now held on the Wednesday before Easter, the second Friday in September, and December 21st, the last for the sale of cattle. A savings' bank has been established. Adjacent to the western extremity of the village is Stanhope hall, formerly the mansion of the Fetherstonhaugh family, an ancient edifice, regularly protected by a curtain. The living is a rectory, with the perpetual curacy of Weardale St. John's annexed, in the archeaconry and diocese of

Durham, rated in the king's books at £67. 6. 8., and in the patronage of the Bishop of Durham. The church, which stands on elevated ground to the north of the town, is dedicated to St. Thomas the Apostle. There is a place of worship for Wesleyan Methodists, with a Sunday school attached. Stanhope school was endowed, in 1681, by Richard Bainbridge, which was increased in 1724, by the Rev. William Hastwell, for the education of ten poor children: the income is about £25 per annum, and one hundred boys and girls are educated: the latter likewise bequeathed a small estate to supply funds for apprenticing two poor boys. A National school, with which a subscription library is connected, was erected at the expense of Bishop Barrington, and endowed with a portion of the interest of £2000 given by that prelate for the support of six schools in this parish: it is further supported by annual subscriptions and a small quarterage from the children. On the incursion of the Scots, in the reign of Edw. III., that sovereign encamped his forces in this neighbourhood, but the enemy retired without coming to an engagement: the remains of an ancient fortress are visible to the west of the village, on a lofty eminence one hundred and eighty-eight feet above the river. Several altars and Roman antiquities have been dug up here. A little northward are some natural excavations, called Hetherburn Caves, and, except on the banks of the Wear, the neighbourhood is rugged and mountainous; on this river, a little above the town, are the extensive lead-works of the London Company. A tenth of the produce of the mines belongs to the rector, which renders the living exceedingly valuable. This parish also abounds with limestone.

STANION, a parish in the hundred of CORBY, county of NORTHAMPTON, 4¾ miles (S. E.) from Rockingham, containing 297 inhabitants. The living is a perpetual curacy, annexed to the vicarage of Brigstock, in the archdeaconry of Northampton, and diocese of Peterborough. The church is dedicated to St. Peter. There is a place of worship for Wesleyan Methodists.

STANLEY, a chapelry in the parish of SPONDON, hundred of APPLETREE, though locally in that of Morleston and Litchurch, county of DERBY, 6 miles (N. E. by E.) from Derby, containing 357 inhabitants. The chapel is dedicated to St. Andrew. This parish is entitled to one-fifth of the benefits of West Hallam school, founded by John Scargill.

STANLEY, a township in that part of the parish of LEEK which is in the northern division of the hundred of TOTMONSLOW, county of STAFFORD, 5 miles (S. W.) from Leek, containing 113 inhabitants. The Rev. Richard Shaw bequeathed £10 a year for teaching poor children.

STANLEY, a chapelry in the parish of WAKEFIELD, lower division of the wapentake of AGBRIGG, West riding of the county of YORK, 1¾ mile (N. N. E.) from Wakefield, containing, with the township of Wrenthorp, 4620 inhabitants. A lunatic asylum for paupers has been established in this township. This was the site of a Roman station, where a vast quantity of Roman crucibles, moulds, and silver and copper coins, has been found ; of the latter forty pounds weight was dug up in 1812. Many of these relics are deposited in the British museum and other similar establishments. The scene of the battle fought by Robin Hood, Scarlet, and Little John, against the Pindar of Wakefield, is laid here, according to the ancient ballad.

STANLEY (KING'S), a parish in the lower division of the hundred of WHITSTONE, county of GLOUCESTER, 3¼ miles (W. by S.) from Stroud, containing 2269 inhabitants. The living is a rectory, in the archdeaconry and diocese of Gloucester, rated in the king's books at £18. 15. 2½., and in the patronage of the Master and Fellows of Jesus College, Cambridge. The church is dedicated to St. George. There are places of worship for Baptists and Wesleyan Methodists. Three small schools, conducted by females, in different parts of the parish, are partly supported with £18 a year, arising from several bequests. Here are vestiges of an ancient encampment, at some distance from which eight Roman altars, a large brass of Alexander Severus, and other relics, were discovered some years since.

STANLEY (ST. LEONARD), a parish (formerly a market town) in the lower division of the hundred of WHITSTONE, county of GLOUCESTER, 4¼ miles (W.S.W.) from Stroud, containing 757 inhabitants. The living is a perpetual curacy, in the archdeaconry and diocese of Gloucester, endowed with £700 private benefaction, and £400 royal bounty, and in the patronage of Mrs. Cumberland. The church, dedicated to St. Swithin, is an ancient cruciform structure, partly in the early, and partly in the later, style of English architecture, with a low tower in the centre, singularly constructed with double walls, and a passage and recesses between them: it formerly belonged to a priory of Benedictine monks, founded here in 1146, and dedicated to St. Leonard, as a cell to the abbey of St. Peter, Gloucester, which at the dissolution possessed a revenue of £126. 0. 8. There are considerable remains of the conventual buildings, of which, the kitchen has been converted into a dairy. Stanley, before 1686, when a great fire destroyed most of its buildings, was a considerable town, with two fairs, on St. Swithin's day and November 6th, which are still held, but the market, which was on Saturday, under a grant of Edward II., renewed in 1620, has been discontinued. There is an extensive manufacture of woollen cloth in the village; the houses in which are now scattered and irregular. Thomas Vobes, in 1708, bequeathed certain lands, which, with sundry smaller bequests, now produce an annual income of about £41, for the education of forty children. There is also a Sunday school, erected and supported by voluntary contributions.

STANLEY-PONTLARGE, a parish in the lower division of the hundred of KIFTSGATE, county of GLOUCESTER, 2¾ miles (N. W.) from Winchcombe, containing 48 inhabitants. The living is a perpetual curacy, annexed to the vicarage of Toddington, in the archdeaconry and diocese of Gloucester.

STANLOW-HOUSE, an extra-parochial liberty, in the higher division of the hundred of WIRRALL, county palatine of CHESTER, 8 miles (N. by E.) from Chester, containing 16 inhabitants. An abbey of Cistercian monks was founded here, in 1178, by John Lacy, constable of Chester, which, on account of the inundations of the Mersey in 1296, was removed to Whalley in Lancashire, a cell being left at this place: some small remains of the conventual buildings are visible in a farm-house.

STANMER, a parish in the hundred of RINGMER, rape of PEVENSEY, though locally in that of Lewes, county of SUSSEX, 4 miles (N. N. E.) from Brighton, containing 123 inhabitants. The living is a rectory, united to the vicarage of Falmer, in the peculiar jurisdiction of the Archbishop of Canterbury, rated in the king's books at £16. The church is an ancient structure in the early English style.

STANMORE (GREAT), a parish in the hundred of GORE, county of MIDDLESEX, 10 miles (N. W.) from London, containing 990 inhabitants. The living is a rectory, in the jurisdiction of the Commissary of London, concurrently with the Consistorial Court of the Bishop of London, rated in the king's books at £10, and in the patronage of George Drummond, Esq. The church is dedicated to St. John the Evangelist. There is a place of worship for Independents. The first meeting, after the conclusion of the late war, of the Prince Regent and his illustrious guests, the Emperor of Russia and the King of Prussia, with Louis XVIII., took place here. The celebrated Dr. Parr kept a school on the site of a house now belonging to Mr. Barren. Here is a monument in memory of Cassibelaunus, also a mound called Belmont, thrown up at the expense of the late Duke of Chandos.

STANMORE (LITTLE), a parish in the hundred of GORE, county of MIDDLESEX, ½ a mile (N. W.) from Edgware, containing, with part of the village of Edgware, 712 inhabitants. The living is a perpetual curacy, in the jurisdiction of the Commissary of London, concurrently with the Consistorial Court of the Bishop of London, and in the patronage of G. Drummond, Esq. The church, dedicated to St. Lawrence, stands about half a mile from the village, and was rebuilt, with the exception of the tower, about 1715, by the Duke of Chandos, whose splendid mansion of Canons was in this parish, but the internal decorations were not completed until 1720: the ceiling and walls were painted by Laguerre; on each side of the altar is a painting of the Nativity, and a dead Christ, by Belluchi; and behind it is a recess for the organ, supported by columns of the Corinthian order; in the back ground are paintings of Moses receiving the Law, and Christ preaching. Handel, who resided at Canons as chapel-master, is said to have composed his sacred drama of Esther for its consecration; the anthems used in it were composed by him, and the morning and evening services by Pepusch. On the 25th of September, 1790, a grand miscellaneous concert of sacred music, selected from Handel's works, was performed to his honour in this church. A vault was constructed on the north side of the chancel by the Duke of Chandos, for the interment of his family, and in a large chamber over it is a monument of his ancestor, James, first Duke of Chandos. The free grammar school was founded and endowed by Sir Lancelot Lake, in 1656; the income is derived from a field producing £50 per annum, of which £30 is paid to the master, and the remainder applied to charitable purposes. Almshouses were founded, in 1640, by Dame Mary Lake, for seven poor persons, having an endowment of about £45 per annum; and this parish is entitled to send three poor persons to the almshouses in Edgeware, founded in 1828, by Charles Day, Esq.

STANNEY (GREAT), a township in the parish of STOKE, higher division of the hundred of WIRRALL.

county palatine of CHESTER, 6¾ miles (N.) from Chester, containing 18 inhabitants. The Chester canal passes through this township. A court leet is occasionally held. Excellent marl, composed of alluvial matter, abounds here, and large trees have been dug up in the meadows.

STANNEY (LITTLE), a township in the parish of STOKE, higher division of the hundred of WIRRALL, county palatine of CHESTER, 5½ miles (N.) from Chester, containing 228 inhabitants.

STANNINGFIELD, a parish in the hundred of THEDWESTRY, county of SUFFOLK, 5¼ miles (S. by E.) from Bury-St. Edmunds, containing 290 inhabitants. The living is a rectory, in the archdeaconry of Sudbury, and diocese of Norwich, rated in the king's books at £8. 0. 2½. T. A. Cook, Esq. and others were patrons in 1809. The church is dedicated to St. Nicholas. Mrs. Inchbald, an ingenious novelist and dramatic writer, was a native of this place : she died at Kensington in 1821.

STANNINGTON, a parish in the western division of CASTLE ward, county of NORTHUMBERLAND, 5 miles (S. by E.) from Morpeth, containing, with the townships of Blagdon, and Plessey with Shotton, 963 inhabitants. The living is a vicarage, in the archdeaconry of Northumberland, and diocese of Durham, rated in the king's books at £5. 13. 4., and in the patronage of the Bishop of Durham. The church, dedicated to St. Mary, is an ancient structure ; it had formerly a chantry, and the windows exhibit some fine old specimens of stained glass. There are places of worship for Wesleyan Methodists and Unitarians. The river Blythe runs through the parish, which abounds with coal. Here is an extensive manufacture of oil-cloth. Mrs. Grey, in 1720, gave a rent-charge of £2, and John Moor, in 1813, bequeathed the interest of £200, which, together amounting to £11 per annum, is applied for teaching eleven poor children.

STANNINGTON, a chapelry in the parish of ECCLESFIELD, northern division of the wapentake of STRAFFORTH and TICKHILL, West riding of the county of YORK, 4 miles (W.) from Sheffield. The population is returned with the parish. The chapel has been recently completed, at the expense of £2607. 19. 3., defrayed by the parliamentary commissioners, and contains seven hundred and twenty-two sittings, of which, three hundred and sixty-six are free ; it is in the patronage of the Vicar of Ecclesfield. The manufacture of cutlery is here extensive.

STANSFIELD, a parish in the hundred of RISBRIDGE, county of SUFFOLK, 5¼ miles (N. by E.) from Clare, containing 451 inhabitants. The living is a rectory, in the archdeaconry of Sudbury, and diocese of Norwich, rated in the king's books at £11. 9. 4½., and in the patronage of the Crown. The church is dedicated to All Saints.

STANSFIELD, a township in the parish of HALIFAX, wapentake of MORLEY, West riding of the county of YORK, 4¼ miles (S. W.) from Halifax, containing 7275 inhabitants. It is bounded on the south by the river Calder. Here is the site of a manor-house, formerly belonging to the Warrens ; and the rocky height above was once crowned with a castle.

STANSTEAD, a parish in the hundred of WROTHAM, lathe of AYLESFORD, county of KENT, 2 miles (N.) from Wrotham, containing 292 inhabitants. The living is a perpetual curacy, annexed to the vicarage of Wrotham, in the peculiar jurisdiction of the Archbishop of Canterbury. The church is dedicated to St. Mary.

STANSTEAD, a parish in the hundred of BABERGH, county of SUFFOLK, 5¼ miles (N. E. by E.) from Clare, containing 341 inhabitants. The living is a rectory, in the archdeaconry of Sudbury, and diocese of Norwich, rated in the king's books at £10, and in the patronage of the Rev. S. Sheen. The church is dedicated to St. James.

STANSTEAD (ABBOTS'), a parish in the hundred of BRAUGHIN, county of HERTFORD, 2¾ miles (N.E. by E.) from Hoddesdon, containing 950 inhabitants. The living is a discharged vicarage, in the archdeaconry of Middlesex, and diocese of London, rated in the king's books at £10, and in the patronage of the Rev. T. Feilde. The church, dedicated to St. James, situated on an eminence one mile south-east from the village, was built, in 1578, by Ralph Baesh, Esq. The parish is bounded on the west by the navigable river Lea, on the north by the Ashe, and on the east and south-east by the navigable river Stort, being nearly insulated. The Rye House, noted for the plot laid there, in 1683, against the lives of Charles II. and James, Duke of York, was built, in the reign of Henry VI., by Andrew Ogard. It was formerly surrounded by a moat, but the only remains of the structure now existing is an embattled gate-house of brick, with a handsome stone doorway, long since converted into a workhouse for the parish. Almshouses for six poor widows were founded, in 1636, by Sir Edward Baesh, who endowed them with certain lands and a rent-charge of £25, for the payment of two shillings per week to each ; the residue to be applied for apprenticing poor children. He also founded a free grammar school, with an endowment of £20 per annum, and gave a small cottage for the use of the parish clerk.

STANSTED-MOUNTFITCHET, a parish partly in the hundred of CLAVERING, but chiefly in that of UTTLESFORD, county of ESSEX, 18 miles (N. W.) from Chelmsford, containing, with the hamlet of Bentfield, 1518 inhabitants. The living is a discharged vicarage, in the jurisdiction of the Commissary of Essex and Herts, concurrently with the Consistorial Court of the Bishop of London, rated in the king's books at £13. 6. 8., and in the patronage of E. F. Maitland, Esq. The church, dedicated to St. Mary, has lately received an addition of two hundred free sittings, the Incorporated Society for the enlargement of churches and chapels having granted £200 towards defraying the expense. There is a place of worship for Independents. A Sunday school, attended by about one hundred children, is supported by voluntary contributions. Here are slight remains of a castle erected by William Gernon, surnamed Montfichet ; and about two miles from the church was the priory of Thremhall, founded by Richard de Montfichet, and dedicated to St. James.

STANTHORNE, a township in the parish of DAVENHAM, hundred of NORTHWICH, county palatine of CHESTER, 1¼ mile (W. N. W.) from Middlewich, containing 148 inhabitants.

STANTON, a chapelry in that part of the parish of YOULGRAVE which is in the hundred of HIGH PEAK, county of DERBY, 3½ miles (N.) from Winster, containing 710 inhabitants. It is in the honour of Tutbury, duchy of Lancaster, and within the jurisdiction of a court of pleas held at Chapel en le Frith every third Tuesday, for the recovery of debts under 40s.

STANTON, a joint township with Newhall, in the parish of STAPENHILL, hundred of REPTON and GRESLEY, county of DERBY, 3 miles (S. S. E.) from Burton upon Trent, containing, with Newhall, 1099 inhabitants. It is in the honour of Tutbury, duchy of Lancaster, and within the jurisdiction of a court of pleas held at Tutbury every third Tuesday, for the recovery of debts under 40s.

STANTON, a parish in the lower division of the hundred of KIFTSGATE, county of GLOUCESTER, 4¾ miles (N. E. by N.) from Winchcombe, containing 269 inhabitants. The living is a discharged rectory, with the perpetual curacy of Snowshill annexed, in the archdeaconry and diocese of Gloucester, rated in the king's books at £17. 11. 5½., and in the patronage of the Rev. R. Wynniatt. The church is dedicated to St. Bartholomew. The navigable river Wye bounds the parish on the north, and the Monmouth railway passes on the south.

STANTON, a township in the parish of LONGHORSLEY, western division of MORPETH ward, county of NORTHUMBERLAND, 6 miles (N. W. by W.) from Morpeth, containing 168 inhabitants. Here are a colliery, several quarries of limestone, and kilns for burning lime. The ancient manor-house has been converted into a poor-house : a chapel which stood a little to the northward of it has quite disappeared. From the foundations in the neighbourhood, Stanton seems to have been once a considerable place.

STANTON, a township in the parish of ELLASTONE, southern division of the hundred of TOTMONSLOW, county of STAFFORD, 3½ miles (W.) from Ashbourn, containing 373 inhabitants. It is in the honour of Tutbury, duchy of Lancaster, and within the jurisdiction of a court of pleas held at Tutbury every third Tuesday, for the recovery of debts under 40s.

STANTON, a parish in the hundred of BLACKBOURN, county of SUFFOLK, 3¼ miles (N. E.) from Ixworth, containing, with Stanton St. John, 939 inhabitants. The living comprises the united discharged rectories of All Saints and St. John, in the archdeaconry of Sudbury, and diocese of Norwich, rated jointly in the king's books at £18. 10. 10. Capel Lofft, Esq. was patron in 1811.

STANTON upon ARROW, a parish partly in the hundred of STRETFORD, but chiefly in that of WIGMORE, county of HEREFORD, 5½ miles (E. N. E.) from Kington, containing 385 inhabitants. The living is a discharged vicarage, in the archdeaconry and diocese of Hereford, rated in the king's books at £5. 17. 10., and in the patronage of the Crown. The church is dedicated to St. Peter.

STANTON under BARDON, a chapelry in the parish of THORNTON, hundred of SPARKENHOE, county of LEICESTER, 9 miles (W. N. W.) from Leicester, containing, with the township of Horsepool, 302 inhabitants. There is a place of worship for Wesleyan Methodists. It is within the jurisdiction of the peculiar court of the lord of the manor of Groby.

STANTON (ST. BERNARD), a parish in the hundred of SWANBOROUGH, county of WILTS, 5¾ miles (E. by N.) from Devizes, containing 332 inhabitants.

The living is a discharged vicarage, in the archdeaconry of Wilts, and diocese of Salisbury, rated in the king's books at £7, and in the patronage of the Earl of Pembroke. The church is dedicated to All Saints.

STANTON by BRIDGE, a parish in the hundred of REPTON and GRESLEY, county of DERBY, 6¾ miles (S. by E.) from Derby, containing 190 inhabitants. The living is a rectory, in the archdeaconry of Derby, and diocese of Lichfield and Coventry, rated in the king's books at £6. 12. 8½., and in the patronage of Sir George Crewe, Bart. The church, dedicated to St. Michael, is partly in the Norman and partly in the decorated style of architecture. The distinguishing appellation arises from the ancient bridge over the Trent, termed Swarkston bridge, which connects these two parishes.

STANTON by DALE, a parish in the hundred of MORLESTON and LITCHURCH, county of DERBY, 9 miles (E. by N.) from Derby, containing, with the township of Weston-Underwood, 686 inhabitants. The living is a perpetual curacy, in the archdeaconry of Derby, and diocese of Lichfield and Coventry, endowed with £200 private benefaction, and £200 royal bounty, and in the patronage of the Earl of Stanhope. The church is dedicated to St. Michael. The Erewash and the Nutbrook canals pass through the parish. Almshouses for six poor persons were founded, in 1711, by a bequest from Joseph Middlemore, with an endowment of more than £100 per annum. The inhabitants are entitled to the benefit of the free school at Risley. Stanton is in the honour of Tutbury, duchy of Lancaster, and within the jurisdiction of a court of pleas held at Tutbury every third Tuesday, for the recovery of debts under 40s.

STANTON (FEN), county of HUNTINGDON. — See FEN-STANTON.

STANTON (ST. GABRIEL), a chapelry in the parish and hundred of WHITCHURCH-CANONICORUM, Bridport division of the county of DORSET, 4 miles (W. by S.) from Bridport, containing 112 inhabitants. The living is a perpetual curacy, annexed to the vicarage of Whitchurch-Canonicorum, in the archdeaconry of Dorset, and diocese of Bristol. There is a signal station on the coast of the English channel, which forms the southern boundary.

STANTON upon HINE-HEATH, a parish in the Whitchurch division of the hundred of BRADFORD (North), county of SALOP, comprising the townships of Booley, Harcourt, High Hatton, Moston, and Stanton, and containing 700 inhabitants, of which number, 273 are in the township of Stanton, 5½ miles (S. E. by E.) from Wem. The living is a discharged vicarage, in the archdeaconry of Salop, and diocese of Lichfield and Coventry, rated in the king's books at £5. 10. 10., endowed with £200 private benefaction, and £200 royal bounty. The Rev. R. Hill was patron in 1819. The church is dedicated to St. Andrew.

STANTON (ST. JOHN'S), a parish in the hundred of BULLINGTON, county of OXFORD, 4½ miles (N. E. by E.) from Oxford, containing 468 inhabitants. The living is a rectory, in the archdeaconry and diocese of Oxford, rated in the king's books at £16. 9. 4½., and in the patronage of the Warden and Fellows of New College, Oxford. The church is dedicated to St. John the Baptist. Lady Elizabeth Holford, in 1717, gave £500 in support of a charity school for the children of this parish and that of Forest Hill : this bequest, having accumulated to £1550 Old South Sea annuities, produces an annual dividend of about £46. 10., which is applied for teaching fifty children, in a school-house erected in 1767.

STANTON (LACY), a parish in the hundred of MUNSLOW, county of SALOP, 3 miles (N. N. W.) from Ludlow, containing 1267 inhabitants. The living is a vicarage, in the archdeaconry of Salop, and diocese of Hereford, rated in the king's books at £16, and in the patronage of the Earl of Craven. The church is dedicated to St. Peter.

STANTON (LONG), a parish in the hundred of MUNSLOW, county of SALOP, 7¾ miles (S. W. by S.) from Much-Wenlock, containing 261 inhabitants. The living is a discharged vicarage, in the archdeaconry of Salop, and diocese of Hereford, rated in the king's books at £7, endowed with £200 private benefaction, and £200 royal bounty, and in the patronage of the Dean and Chapter of Hereford. The church is dedicated to St. Michael.

STANTON (LONG) ALL SAINTS, a parish in the hundred of NORTHSTOW, county of CAMBRIDGE, 6¼ miles (N. W. by N.) from Cambridge, containing 370 inhabitants. The living is a discharged vicarage, in the archdeaconry and diocese of Ely, rated in the king's books at £13. 13. 4½., and in the patronage of the Bishop of Ely, whose predecessors had a palace here, at which Queen Elizabeth was entertained on the day after her visit to the University of Cambridge, in August 1564. There is a place of worship for Wesleyan Methodists.

STANTON (LONG) ST. MICHAEL, a parish in the hundred of NORTHSTOW, county of CAMBRIDGE, 5½ miles (N. W. by N.) from Cambridge, containing 134 inhabitants. The living is a discharged vicarage, in the archdeaconry and diocese of Ely, rated in the king's books at £6. 12. 8½., and in the patronage of the Master and Fellows of Magdalene College, Cambridge. The church is a small thatched building.

STANTON (ST. QUINTIN), a parish in the hundred of MALMESBURY, county of WILTS, 4¼ miles (N. by W.) from Chippenham, containing 285 inhabitants. The living is a rectory, in the archdeaconry of Wilts, and diocese of Salisbury, rated in the king's books at £10. 5. 7½., and in the patronage of the Earl of Radnor. The church, dedicated to St. Giles, has lately received an addition of eighty free sittings, the Incorporated Society for the enlargement of churches and chapels having granted £40 towards defraying the expense. Good slate, limestone, and a very hard blue stone for building, abound within the parish. Here were formerly the ruins of an ancient castle, but they have entirely been removed within the last few years.

STANTON on the WOLDS, a parish in the northern division of the wapentake of RUSHCLIFFE, county of NOTTINGHAM, 7½ miles (S. E. by S.) from Nottingham, containing 119 inhabitants. The living is a discharged rectory, in the archdeaconry of Nottingham, and diocese of York, rated in the king's books at £2. 13. 4. The Rev. John Hallward was patron in 1819. The church is dedicated to All Saints. The parish is bounded on the east by the old Fosse road.

STANTON-BURY, a parish in the hundred of NEWPORT, county of BUCKINGHAM, 3 miles (W. by S.) from Newport-Pagnell, containing 40 inhabitants. The living is a discharged vicarage, in the archdeaconry of Buckingham, and diocese of Lincoln, rated in the king's books at £7. 6. 8., endowed with £200 royal bounty, and £400 parliamentary grant, and in the patronage of Earl Spencer. The church, dedicated to St. Peter, exhibits many Norman remains, particularly a fine and richly decorated arch between the nave and the chancel.

STANTON-DREW, a parish in the hundred of KEYNSHAM, county of SOMERSET, 1½ mile (W. by S.) from Pensford, containing 622 inhabitants. The living is a discharged vicarage, with the perpetual curacy of Pensford annexed, in the archdeaconry of Bath, and diocese of Bath and Wells, rated in the king's books at £7. 2. 8½., and in the patronage of the Archdeacon of Bath. The church is dedicated to St. Mary. The river Chew runs through the parish, and is crossed by a stone bridge. Richard Jones, in 1688, bequeathed two-fifths of the proceeds of an estate for educating and apprenticing poor children : the income is £60 a year, and about thirty boys have the benefit of it. Six poor girls are instructed for £5 per annum, the gift of Elizabeth Lyde, in 1772. The neighbourhood abounds with various objects of interest to the antiquary, the most prominent of which are, *Maes Knoll Tump*, a stupendous barrow, and an extensive Druidical temple of three circles of stones, whose diameters are respectively one hundred and twenty, forty-three, and thirty-two yards, spreading itself over ten acres of ground : the stones, which are of amazing proportions, were apparently brought from the neighbouring quarries; many of them, however, now lie prostrate on the ground. The name of Belton, or Belluton, a hamlet at nearly an equal distance from each of these British monuments, is thought to be a corruption of Belgeton, a town of the Belgæ, being situated on the line of Wansdyke, the ancient boundary of their territory.

STANTON-FITZWARREN, a parish in the hundred of HIGHWORTH, CRICKLADE, and STAPLE, county of WILTS, 2¼ miles (S. W. by W.) from Highworth, containing 262 inhabitants. The living is a rectory, in the archdeaconry of Wilts, and diocese of Salisbury, rated in the king's books at £10. 2. 6., and in the patronage of the Rev. Dr. Trenchard. The church is dedicated to St. Leonard.

STANTON-HARCOURT, a parish in the hundred of WOOTTON, county of OXFORD, 4½ miles (S. E.) from Witney, containing 606 inhabitants. This place was granted by Queen Adeliza, second wife of Henry I., to her kinswoman Milicent, wife of Richard de Camville, whose daughter Isabel married Robert de Harcourt. It is situated near the confluence of the small river Windrush with the Thames. The living is a discharged vicarage, in the archdeaconry and diocese of Oxford, rated in the king's books at £16. 13. 4., endowed with £200 private benefaction, and £200 royal bounty, and in the patronage of the Bishop of Oxford. The church is dedicated to St. Michael ; in the ancient tower are three chambers above each other, in good repair, the uppermost of which retains the name of Pope's study, being the room in which the poet translated his fifth volume of Homer: in the church are two epitaphs written by Pope, one by Congreve, and one by Dr. Friend ; in the Harcourt aisle are some good monuments. Here is a kitchen, which bears marks of remote antiquity; the date of its erection is uncertain, but it was repaired about the reign of Henry IV., and has a great resemblance to the abbot's kitchen at Glastonbury. A school for the education of poor children is supported by the proceeds of various benefactions; the income is £18 per annum, and from thirty to forty children are instructed at small charges. Some ancient remains, called the Devil's Quoits, were probably placed here to commemorate a victory of the Saxon Princes Cynegil and Chwichelm over the Britons, on which occasion about two thousand of the latter were slain.

STANTON-PRIOR, a parish in the hundred of KEYNSHAM, county of SOMERSET, 5 miles (W. S. W.) from Bath, containing 158 inhabitants. The living is a discharged rectory, in the archdeaconry of Bath, and diocese of Bath and Wells, rated in the king's books at £10. 1. 10½., and in the patronage of W. G. Langton, Esq. The church is dedicated to St. Lawrence. On a long isolated eminence, called Stanton Bury, are the remains of an ancient intrenchment, enclosing more than thirty acres: it has been thought a work of the Romans, some of their coins having been found near it; but being situated on the Wansdyke, it had probably a more remote origin, and might have been subsequently occupied by them. Gilbert Sheldon, Archbishop of Canterbury, was born here, in 1598; he died in 1677.

STANTON-STONEY, a parish in the hundred of SPARKENHOE, county of LEICESTER, 4¼ miles (E. by N.) from Hinckley, containing 533 inhabitants. The living is a rectory, in the archdeaconry of Leicester, and diocese of Lincoln, rated in the king's books at £14. 13. 1½., and in the patronage of the Marquis of Hastings. The church is dedicated to St. Michael.

STANWAY, a parish in the Colchester division of the hundred of LEXDEN, county of ESSEX, 4 miles (W. by S.) from Colchester, containing 479 inhabitants. The living is a rectory, in the archdeaconry of Colchester, and diocese of London, rated in the king's books at £10. 17. 6., and in the patronage of the President and Fellows of Magdalene College, Oxford. The church, dedicated to All Saints, has lately received an addition of eighty sittings, of which fifty are free, the Incorporated Society for the enlargement of churches and chapels having granted £50 towards defraying the expense. A number of large bones and other remains, probably of elephants brought over by Claudius in 43, was found here, in 1764, lying in a stratum of sea-sand and shells.

STANWAY, a parish in the upper division of the hundred of TEWKESBURY, county of GLOUCESTER, 3½ miles (N. E.) from Winchcombe, containing 415 inhabitants. The living is a discharged vicarage, in the archdeaconry and diocese of Gloucester, rated in the king's books, at £9, endowed with £200 private benefaction, and £200 royal bounty, and in the patronage of the Earl of Wemyss and March. The church is dedicated to St. Peter. Limestone is obtained in the parish. The Earl of Wemyss supports two schools for the education of poor children.

STANWELL, a parish in the hundred of SPELTHORNE, county of MIDDLESEX, 2¾ miles (N. E. by N.) from Staines, containing, with a portion of the town of Colnbrook, which is in this parish, 1225 inhabitants. The living is a discharged vicarage, in the archdeaconry of Middlesex, and diocese of London, rated in the king's

books at £9, and in the patronage of the Crown. The church, dedicated to St. Mary, is principally in the later style of English architecture. There is a place of worship for Independents.

STANWICK, a parish in the hundred of HIGHAM-FERRERS, county of NORTHAMPTON, 2¼ miles.(N. N. E.) from Higham-Ferrers, containing 424 inhabitants. The living is a rectory, in the archdeaconry of Northampton, and diocese of Peterborough, rated in the king's books at £12. 9. 4½., and in the patronage of the Crown. The church, dedicated to St. Lawrence, exhibits portions in the early, decorated, and later, styles of English architecture; it has an octangular tower of the former character, surmounted by an enriched spire, in the decorated style. There is a place of worship for Wesleyan Methodists. Mrs. Pacey, in 1784, bequeathed a rent-charge of £10 for teaching poor children, and £5 yearly for clothing five of them. Richard Cumberland, the dramatist, was born here, in 1732.

STANWICK (ST. JOHN), a parish in the western division of the wapentake of GILLING, North riding of the county of YORK, comprising the townships of Aldbrough, Caldwell, East Layton, and Stanwick St. John, and containing, exclusively of a portion of the township of Stapleton, which is in this parish, 928 inhabitants, of which number, 59 are in the township of Stanwick St. John, 7½ miles (N. by E.) from Richmond. The living is a vicarage, in the archdeaconry of Richmond, and diocese of Chester, rated in the king's books at £6. 13. 4., and in the patronage of John Wharton, Esq. The church, dedicated to St. John the Baptist, is a very ancient stone structure, and contains two fine marble statues to the memory of Sir Hugh and Lady Smithson. In this parish is a most extensive intrenchment, enclosing an area of nearly one thousand acres: it has been ascribed to the Romans, and also to the Scots; but Whitaker, the learned antiquary, considers it the site of an ancient camp, or city, of the Britons.

STANWIX, a parish comprising the townships of Cargo, or Craghow, and Stainton, in CUMBERLAND ward, and the townships of Etterby, Houghton, Linstock, Rickerby, Stanwix, and Tarraby, in ESKDALE ward, county of CUMBERLAND, and containing 1592 inhabitants, of which number, 400 are in the township of Stanwix, ½ a mile (N.) from Carlisle. The living is a vicarage, in the archdeaconry and diocese of Carlisle, rated in the king's books at £9, and in the patronage of the Bishop of Carlisle. The church, dedicated to St. Michael, is an ancient edifice, built upon the site and out of the ruins of the Congavata of the Romans, of which station Severus' Wall formed the northern rampart, and near which many altars and inscriptions have been found. The parish is bounded on the south by the river Eden, which is crossed by a handsome stone bridge, connecting it with the city of Carlisle: the village is beautifully situated on the northern bank of that river. A soft freestone abounds in the neighbourhood.

STAPELEY, a township in the parish of WYBUNBURY, hundred of NANTWICH, county palatine of CHESTER, 1¾ mile (S. E.) from Nantwich, containing 329 inhabitants.

STAPELEY, a joint tything with Rye, in the parish and hundred of ODIHAM, Basingstoke division of the county of SOUTHAMPTON, 2½ miles (S. S. W.) from

Hartford-Bridge. The population is returned with the parish.

STAPENHILL, a parish in the hundred of REPTON and GRESLEY, county of DERBY, 1 mile (S.E.) from Burton upon Trent, containing, with the chapelry of Cauldwell, and the township of Stanton with Newhall, 1791 inhabitants. The living is a discharged vicarage, in the archdeaconry of Derby, and diocese of Lichfield and Coventry, rated in the king's books at £5. 6. 0½., and in the patronage of the Marquis of Anglesey. The church is dedicated to St. Peter. There is a place of worship for Baptists. The river Trent runs through the parish, in which there are very extensive collieries. Stapenhill is in the honour of Tutbury, duchy of Lancaster, and within the jurisdiction of a court of pleas held at Tutbury every third Tuesday, for the recovery of debts under 40s. John Hieron, an eminent nonconformist divine and critic, was born here, in 1608.

STAPLE, a tything in the parish of TISBURY, hundred of DUNWORTH, county of WILTS. The population is returned with the parish.

STAPLE next WINGHAM, a parish in the hundred of DOWNHAMFORD, lathe of St. AUGUSTINE, county of KENT, 1¾ mile (E. by S.) from Wingham, containing 467 inhabitants. The living is a perpetual curacy, annexed to the rectory of Adisham, in the archdeaconry and diocese of Canterbury. The church is dedicated to St. James.

STAPLE-FITZPAINE, a parish in the hundred of ABDICK and BULSTONE, county of SOMERSET, 5 miles (S.E. by S.) from Taunton, containing 385 inhabitants. The living is a rectory, with the perpetual curacy of Bickenhall annexed, in the archdeaconry of Taunton, and diocese of Bath and Wells, rated in the king's books at £17. 14. 2., and in the patronage of E. B. Portman, Esq. The church is dedicated to St. Peter.

STAPLEFORD, a parish in the hundred of THRIPLOW, county of CAMBRIDGE, 5½ miles (S.S.E.) from Cambridge, containing 408 inhabitants. The living is a vicarage, in the archdeaconry and diocese of Ely, rated in the king's books at £7. 18. 9., and in the patronage of the Dean and Chapter of Ely. The church is dedicated to St. Andrew.

STAPLEFORD, a parish in the hundred and county of HERTFORD, 3¾ miles (N. by W.) from Hertford, containing 212 inhabitants. The living is a rectory, in the archdeaconry of Huntingdon, and diocese of Lincoln, rated in the king's books at £8. 8. 6½., and in the patronage of Samuel Smith, Esq. The church is dedicated to St. Mary. The river Bean runs through the parish, and there is a large watercourse, called the New Cut, made at the expense of S. Smith, Esq., to diminish the violence of the floods.

STAPLEFORD, a parish in the hundred of FRAMLAND, county of LEICESTER, 4 miles (E. by S.) from Melton-Mowbray, containing 218 inhabitants. The living is a discharged vicarage, in the archdeaconry of Leicester, and diocese of Lincoln, rated in the king's books at £13, and in the patronage of the Earl of Harborough. The church, dedicated to St. Mary Magdalene, was erected in 1783, and contains some fine monuments of the Sherard family, among which is one by Rysbrach, in memory of the first Earl of Harborough. The river Wreake and the Melton-Mowbray and Oakham canal run through the parish. Here is an endowed hospital.

STAPLEFORD, a parish in the lower division of the wapentake of BOOTHBY-GRAFFO, parts of KESTEVEN, county of LINCOLN, 6½ miles (N.E. by E.) from Newark, containing 213 inhabitants. The living is a discharged vicarage, annexed to that of Carlton le Moorland, in the archdeaconry and diocese of Lincoln, rated in the king's books at £5. 3. 4., endowed with £600 royal bounty. The church is dedicated to All Saints.

STAPLEFORD, a parish in the southern division of the wapentake of BROXTOW, county of NOTTINGHAM, 5¾ miles (W.S.W.) from Nottingham, containing 1104 inhabitants. The living is a perpetual curacy, in the archdeaconry of Nottingham, and diocese of York, and in the patronage of the Crown. The church, dedicated to St. Helen, underwent a thorough repair in 1785. There is a place of worship for Wesleyan Methodists. The river Erewash bounds the parish on the west and north-west: the stocking manufacture is here carried on to a considerable extent. There is a school for a limited number of girls, endowed by Lady Warren; also a National school, supported by subscription. An obelisk, apparently of Saxon construction, and a Druidical monument, called the Hemlock Stone, are the only remains of antiquity here. Stapleford Hall was the residence of that distinguished admiral, Sir John Borlase Warren.

STAPLEFORD, a parish in the hundred of BRANCH and DOLE, county of WILTS, 4½ miles (N.N.W.) from Wilton, containing 305 inhabitants. The living is a discharged vicarage, in the archdeaconry and diocese of Salisbury, rated in the king's books at £10, endowed with £15 per annum and £200 private benefaction, and £600 royal bounty, and in the patronage of the Dean and Canons of Windsor. The church is dedicated to St. Mary.

STAPLEFORD (ABBOT'S), a parish in the hundred of ONGAR, county of ESSEX, 5¾ miles (S.E. by S.) from Epping, containing 458 inhabitants. The living is a rectory, in the archdeaconry of Essex, and diocese of London, rated in the king's books at £16. 15., and in the patronage of the Crown. The church is dedicated to St. Mary. There is a school-house, endowed with three old cottages and £25 a year, in which forty boys are instructed.

STAPLEFORD (BRUEN), a township in that part of the parish of TARVIN which is in the second division of the hundred of EDDISBURY, county palatine of CHESTER, 4½ miles (W.N.W.) from Tarporley, containing 268 inhabitants. At Hargrave Stubbs, in this township, is a grammar school, founded by Sir Thomas Moulson, Bart., who endowed it with a rent-charge of £20 on certain lands then given by him for charitable uses, and now let for £155 per annum.

STAPLEFORD (FOULK), a township in that part of the parish of TARVIN which is in the lower division of the hundred of BROXTON, county palatine of CHESTER, 5½ miles (W.) from Tarporley, containing 263 inhabitants.

STAPLEFORD (TAWNEY), a parish in the hundred of ONGAR, county of ESSEX, 3¾ miles (S.E. by E.) from Epping, containing 283 inhabitants. The living is a rectory, with that of Mount-Thoydon united, in the archdeaconry of Essex, and diocese of London, rated in the king's books at £15. 8. 9., and in the patronage of

Sir Thomas Smyth, Bart. The church is dedicated to St. Mary.

STAPLEGATE, an extra-parochial district, forming the northern suburb of the city of Canterbury, in the hundred of WESTGATE, lathe of St. AUGUSTINE, county of KENT, containing 257 inhabitants.

STAPLEGROVE, a parish in the hundred of TAUNTON and TAUNTON-DEAN, county of SOMERSET, 1¾ mile (N. W.) from Taunton, containing 403 inhabitants. The living is a rectory, in the archdeaconry of Taunton, and diocese of Bath and Wells, and in the patronage of Vincent Stuckey, Esq. It was separated from Taunton, and made a distinct parish, in 1554. The church has lately received an addition of one hundred sittings, of which sixty are free, the Incorporated Society for the enlargement of churches and chapels having granted £30 towards defraying the expense. A gift of land, producing a trifling sum, is applied for teaching poor children.

STAPLEHURST, a parish partly in the hundred of CRANBROOKE, and partly in that of MARDEN, lathe of SCRAY, county of KENT, 4 miles (N. by E.) from Cranbrook, containing 1513 inhabitants. The living is a rectory, in the archdeaconry and diocese of Canterbury, rated in the king's books at £26. 5. 10., and in the patronage of the Master and Fellows of St. John's College, Cambridge. The church is dedicated to All Saints. There is a place of worship for Independents. Three schools are supported here for about £60 per annum, arising from the united bequests of Lancelot Bathurst, in 1539, and John Gibbon, Esq., in 1707. A fair for cattle, corn, and hops, is held on October 11th.

STAPLETON, a parish in ESKDALE ward, county of CUMBERLAND, comprising the townships of Belbank, Solport, Stapleton, and Trough, and containing 1127 inhabitants, of which number, 487 are in the township of Stapleton, 10 miles (E. N. E.) from Longtown. The living is a discharged rectory, in the archdeaconry and diocese of Carlisle, rated in the king's books at £1.8.11½., endowed with £200 royal bounty, and £600 parliamentary grant, and in the patronage of the Earl of Carlisle for one turn, and Sir J. R. G. Graham, Bart., for two. The church is dedicated to St. Mary. The river Line, which is here crossed by a bridge, runs through the parish, and on its northern bank are the ruins of Shank castle. Limestone abounds here, and a colliery has been lately opened in the vicinity. A small school is endowed with £2 per annum.

STAPLETON, a parish in the hundred of BARTON-REGIS, county of GLOUCESTER, 2½ miles (N. E. by N.) from Bristol, containing 2137 inhabitants. The living is a perpetual curacy, in the peculiar jurisdiction of the Bishop of Bristol, endowed with £200 private benefaction, and £200 royal bounty, and in the patronage of Sir John Smith, Bart. The church, dedicated to the Holy Trinity, has lately received an addition of seven hundred sittings, of which five hundred and seventy-four are free, the Incorporated Society for the enlargement of churches and chapels having granted £500 towards defraying the expense. Mary Webb, in 1729, bequeathed £450, which, with other subsequent donations, produces an annual income of £42. 10., for teaching thirty children, and for the maintenance of three poor women in an almshouse adjoining the school, both of them founded by the above testatrix.

STAPLETON, a joint township with Frog-Street, in that part of the parish of PRESTEIGNE which is in the hundred of WIGMORE, county of HEREFORD, containing, with Frog-Street, 150 inhabitants.

STAPLETON, a chapelry in the parish of BARWELL, hundred of SPARKENHOE, county of LEICESTER, 3 miles (N. by E.) from Hinckley, containing 260 inhabitants. The chapel is dedicated to St. Martin.

STAPLETON, a parish in the hundred of CONDOVER, county of SALOP, 6 miles (S. by W.) from Shrewsbury, containing 240 inhabitants. The living is a rectory, in the archdeaconry of Salop, and diocese of Lichfield and Coventry, rated in the king's books at £6. 7. 6., and in the patronage of Mrs. Downs. The church is dedicated to St. John.

STAPLETON, a township partly in the parish of ST. JOHN STANWICK, western division, but chiefly in the parish of CROFT, eastern division, of the wapentake of GILLING, North riding of the county of YORK, 2¼ miles (S.W.) from Darlington, containing 113 inhabitants.

STAPLETON, a township in the parish of DARRINGTON, upper division of the wapentake of OSGOLDCROSS, West riding of the county of YORK, 4¼ miles (S. E. by E.) from Pontefract, containing 109 inhabitants.

STARBOTTON, a township in the parish of KETTLEWELL, eastern division of the wapentake of STAINCLIFFE and EWCROSS, West riding of the county of YORK, 17 miles (N. E. by N.) from Settle. The population is returned with the parish.

STARCROSS, a small sea-port in the parish of KENTON, hundred of EXMINSTER, county of DEVON, 1½ mile (W. by N.) from Exmouth. The population is returned with the parish. The chapel, recently erected, contains five hundred sittings, of which three hundred and fifty are free, the Incorporated Society for promoting the building of additional churches, &c., having contributed £400 towards the expense. There is a place of worship for Wesleyan Methodists. Starcross is a pleasant watering-place, situated on the western side of the mouth of the river Exe, south of Powderham castle, and opposite to Exmouth. The trade consists principally in the importation of coal and timber, for landing which there is a convenient quay. A fair is held on the Wednesday in Whitsun-week. On an eminence in the neighbourhood is a conspicuous landmark, called Belvidere, consisting of a lofty triangular tower, with a hexagonal turret rising from each corner: it was erected, in 1773, by Lord Courtenay, and commands interesting views of the rich and diversified scenery of the vicinity, including Powderham castle, erected by Isabella, the last of the great family of Rivers, in the reign of Edward I., the park, grounds, and plantations of which are nearly ten miles in circumference.

STARSTON, a parish in the hundred of EARSHAM, county of NORFOLK, 1¼ mile (N. N. W.) from Harleston, containing 437 inhabitants. The living is a rectory, in the archdeaconry of Norfolk, and diocese of Norwich, rated in the king's books at £15, and in the patronage of the Duke of Norfolk, who appoints a Fellow of St. John's College, Cambridge.

STARTFORTH, a parish in the western division of the wapentake of GILLING, North riding of the county of YORK, ¾ of a mile (W. S. W.) from Barnard-Castle, containing 460 inhabitants. The living is a discharged

Z

vicarage, in the archdeaconry of Richmond, and diocese of Chester, rated in the king's books at £4. 0. 10., endowed with £200 private benefaction, and £200 royal bounty, and in the patronage of the Earl of Lonsdale. The church, dedicated to the Holy Trinity, is of great antiquity.

STATFOLD, a parish in the southern division of the hundred of Offlow, county of Stafford, 3¾ miles (N.E.) from Tamworth, containing 29 inhabitants. The living is a perpetual curacy, annexed to the vicarage of St. Mary, Lichfield, in the archdeaconry of Stafford, and diocese of Lichfield and Coventry. The church, now used only as a chapel for interment, is in decent repair. Statfold, under its ancient name Stotfold, is one of the prebends in the Cathedral Church of Lichfield, the revenues of which have been formed by act of parliament into a "Fabric Fund," for repairs, &c., no prebendary being appointed.

STATH DIVISION, a tything in the parish of Stoke St. Gregory, hundred of North Curry, county of Somerset, containing 267 inhabitants.

STATHERN, a parish in the hundred of Framland, county of Leicester, 8¾ miles (N. by E.) from Melton-Mowbray, containing 456 inhabitants. The living is a rectory, in the archdeaconry of Leicester, and diocese of Lincoln, rated in the king's books at £16. 3. 1½., and in the patronage of the Master and Fellows of Peter House, Cambridge. The church is dedicated to St. Guthlake. The Grantham canal passes through the parish. There is a trifling endowment for a school, the gift of Joseph Westley, in 1735.

STAUGHTON (GREAT), a parish comprising the divisions of North Side and South Side, in the hundred of Toseland, county of Huntingdon, 3¼ miles (S.E. by S.) from Kimbolton, and containing 1173 inhabitants. The living is a vicarage, in the archdeaconry of Huntingdon, and diocese of Lincoln, rated in the king's books at £20, and in the patronage of the President and Fellows of St. John's College, Oxford. The church is dedicated to St. Andrew. There are two small bequests in support of a school, by Elizabeth Conyers, in 1709, and John Poachby, in 1727.

STAUGHTON (LITTLE), a parish in the hundred of Stodden, county of Bedford, 4 miles (S. by E.) from Kimbolton, containing 406 inhabitants. The living is a rectory, in the archdeaconry of Bedford, and diocese of Lincoln, rated in the king's books at £13. 8. 4., and in the patronage of the President and Fellows of Corpus Christi College, Oxford. The church is dedicated to All Saints. There is a place of worship for Baptists.

STAUNTON, a joint township with Streatlam, in that part of the parish of Gainford which is in the south-western division of Darlington ward, county palatine of Durham, 1¾ mile (N.E. by N.) from Barnard-Castle, containing, with Streatlam, 251 inhabitants.

STAUNTON, a parish in the hundred of St. Briavells, county of Gloucester, 3½ miles (E. by N.) from Monmouth, containing 200 inhabitants. The living is a discharged rectory, in the archdeaconry and diocese of Gloucester, rated in the king's books at £7, and in the patronage of Lord Viscount Gage. The church is dedicated to All Saints.

STAUNTON, a parish in the southern division of the wapentake of Newark, county of Nottingham, 6¾ miles (S.) from Newark, containing, with portions of the chapelry of Flawborough, and the hamlet of Alverton, 227 inhabitants. The living is a rectory, in the archdeaconry of Nottingham, and diocese of York, rated in the king's books at £16. 13. 11½., and in the patronage of the Rev. Dr. Staunton. The church is dedicated to St. Mary.

STAUNTON, a parish forming, with the parishes of Chaseley and Eldersfield, a distinct portion of the lower division of the hundred of Pershore, county of Worcester, 6 miles (N.E. by E.) from Newent, containing 308 inhabitants. The living is a rectory, in the archdeaconry and diocese of Worcester, rated in the king's books at £11. 5., and in the patronage of Joseph Hill, Esq. The church, dedicated to St. James, is partly in the decorated, and partly in the later, style of English architecture, with a tower and spire.

STAUNTON upon WYE, a parish in the hundred of Grimsworth, county of Hereford, 8¼ miles (W. N.W.) from Hereford, containing 514 inhabitants. The living is a rectory, in the archdeaconry and diocese of Hereford, rated in the king's books at £13. 13. 4., and in the patronage of the Dean and Canons of Christ Church, Oxford. The church is dedicated to St. Mary.

STAUNTON-HARROLD, a chapelry in the parish of Breedon, western division of the hundred of Goscote, county of Leicester, 3½ miles (N.N.E.) from Ashby de la Zouch, containing 329 inhabitants. The chapel, dedicated to the Holy Trinity, is a domestic chapel belonging to Earl Ferrars. Staunton is in the honour of Tutbury, duchy of Lancaster, and within the jurisdiction of a court of pleas held at Tutbury every third Tuesday, for the recovery of debts under 40s.

STAVELEY, a parish in the hundred of Scarsdale, county of Derby, 4¾ miles (N.E. by E.) from Chesterfield, containing, with the chapelry of Barlow, 2759 inhabitants. The living is a rectory, in the archdeaconry of Derby, and diocese of Lichfield and Coventry, rated in the king's books at £12. 7. 6., and in the patronage of the Duke of Devonshire. The church, dedicated to St. John the Baptist, contains several monuments of the Frecheville family, and the east window exhibits some stained glass presented by Lord Frecheville in 1676. The river Rother runs through the parish; and the Chesterfield canal, and several rail-roads, pass between it and the neighbouring collieries. A considerable quantity of iron-stone, obtained here, is smelted near the village, where are two blast furnaces. A free grammar school was founded at Netherthorp, in 1537, by Judge Rodes, in support of which and of two scholarships in St. John's College, Cambridge, he bequeathed £20 per annum. A new house was erected by subscription, in 1804, for the master, whose annual income, including the bequests of Margaret Frecheville, in 1599, Lord James Cavendish, in 1742, and the Rev. Francis Gisborne, in 1796, is about £30 a year. There are also some smaller donations for the education of girls. An hospital for four aged persons of each sex was erected at Woodthorpe, in 1632, by Sir Peter Frecheville, who endowed it with £4 per annum to each of the inmates; but Richard Robinson, in 1777, having augmented the original endowment with a donation of £18 per annum, the allowances have been since doubled. Staveley was for many generations the chief seat of the Frechevilles.

In the reign of Charles I., Sir John Frecheville, an active royalist, strongly fortified his house here with twelve pieces of cannon, but capitulated in August 1644.

STAVELEY, a chapelry in the parish of CARTMEL, hundred of LONSDALE, north of the sands, county palatine of LANCASTER, 9 miles (N. E.) from Ulverstone, containing 350 inhabitants. The living is a perpetual curacy, in the archdeaconry of Richmond, and diocese of Chester, endowed with £800 royal bounty, and in the patronage of Lord G. Cavendish.

STAVELEY, a parish in the lower division of the wapentake of CLARO, West riding of the county of YORK, 3 miles (S. W. by S.) from Boroughbridge, containing 331 inhabitants. The living is a rectory, in the peculiar jurisdiction of the Honour court of Knaresborough, rated in the king's books at £8. 17. 11., and in the patronage of the Rev. G. Astley. The church is dedicated to All Saints.

STAVELEY (NETHER), a township in that part of the parish of KENDAL which is in KENDAL ward, county of WESTMORLAND, 4¾ miles (N. W. by N.) from Kendal, containing 189 inhabitants.

STAVELEY (OVER), a chapelry in that part of the parish of KENDAL which is in KENDAL ward, county of WESTMORLAND, 5 miles (N. W. by N.) from Kendal, containing 312 inhabitants. The living is a perpetual curacy, in the archdeaconry of Richmond, and diocese of Chester, endowed with £200 private benefaction, and £600 royal bounty, and in the patronage of the Inhabitants. The manufacture of woollens and bobbin is carried on to some extent. Edward III. granted a charter for a market on Friday, and an annual fair on the festival of St. Luke, but both have been long disused. George Jopson, in 1696, gave two tenements, now let for £40 per annum, to the minister, provided he should instruct all the children of the chapelry ; at present about forty partake of the benefit of this charity.

STAVERTON, a parish in the hundred of HAYTOR, county of DEVON, 3¼ miles (N. by W.) from Totness, containing 1042 inhabitants. The living is a vicarage, in the peculiar jurisdiction and patronage of the Dean and Chapter of Exeter, rated in the king's books at £32. 14. 9½. The church, dedicated to St. George, contains some good screen-work. This parish is bounded on the south and south-west by the river Dart, and is famous for its cider : there are about forty presses, and the average quantity produced annually is seven thousand hogsheads. In the neighbourhood are quarries of blue and grey marble, and excellent limestone. The Rev. Thomas Baker, in 1802, gave £200 for charitable uses, of the proceeds of which £8 is applied to the instruction of young children ; and Thomas Bradridge, in 1805, gave a trifling annuity for the education of four.

STAVERTON, a parish in the lower division of the hundred of DEERHURST, county of GLOUCESTER, 4¾ miles (W. by N.) from Cheltenham, containing 262 inhabitants. The living is a vicarage, in the peculiar jurisdiction of the Bishop of Salisbury, rated in the king's books at £12, and in the patronage of the Crown by reason of lunacy. The church is dedicated to St. John the Baptist. The Gloucester and Cheltenham rail-road passes through the parish.

STAVERTON, a parish in the hundred of FAWSLEY, county of NORTHAMPTON, 2 miles (W. S. W.) from Daventry, containing 474 inhabitants. The living is a discharged vicarage, in the archdeaconry of Northampton, and diocese of Peterborough, and in the patronage of the Dean and Canons of Christ Church, Oxford. The church is dedicated to St. Mary. The Rev. Francis Baker, in 1767, gave certain land, now producing an annual income of £44, which is applied to the instruction of twenty-five children in a house occupied by the master, and purchased with a bequest of £100 by Catharine Burbidge, in 1767. There is also a Sunday school, supported by the annual proceeds of a legacy of £200, bequeathed by the late Rev. Sir John Knightley.

STAVERTON, a chapelry in the parish of TROWBRIDGE, hundred of MELKSHAM, county of WILTS, 2½ miles (N.) from Trowbridge, with which the population is returned. The chapel has lately received an addition of one hundred and twenty sittings, of which one hundred are free, the Incorporated Society for the enlargement of churches and chapels having granted £125 towards defraying the expense. Here is a large cloth manufactory.

STAWELL, a chapelry in the parish of MOORLINCH, hundred of WHITLEY, county of SOMERSET, 5 miles (E. by N.) from Bridg-water, containing 200 inhabitants.

STAWLEY, a parish in the hundred of MILVERTON, county of SOMERSET, 3 miles (S. W. by S.) from Wiveliscombe, containing 195 inhabitants. The living is a discharged rectory, in the archdeaconry of Taunton, and diocese of Bath and Wells, rated in the king's books at £8. 8. 6½. G. Hyde, Esq. was patron in 1819. The church is dedicated to St. Michael.

STAXTON, a township in the parish of WILLERBY, wapentake of DICKERING, East riding of the county of YORK, 6½ miles (S. by W.) from Scarborough, containing 213 inhabitants. There is a place of worship for Wesleyan Methodists.

STAYLEY, a township in the parish of MOTTRAM, in LONGDEN-DALE, hundred of MACCLESFIELD, county palatine of CHESTER, 1 mile (N. E.) from Ashton under Line, containing, with a part of the town of Stalybridge, (which is described under its own head), 1609 inhabitants. The Huddersfield canal passes through the township.

STAYTHORPE, a township in the northern division of the wapentake of THURGARTON, county of NOTTINGHAM, containing 69 inhabitants.

STEAN, a parish in the hundred of KING'S SUTTON, county of NORTHAMPTON, 2¼ miles (N.W.) from Brackley, containing 33 inhabitants. The living is a discharged rectory, with that of Hinton in the Hedges, in the archdeaconry of Northampton, and diocese of Peterborough, rated in the king's books at £5. 9. 7., and endowed with £200 private benefaction, and £400 royal bounty. The church is dedicated to St. Peter.

STEARSBY, a hamlet in the parish of BRANSBY, wapentake of BULMER, North riding of the county of YORK, 7½ miles (E. N. E.) from Easingwould. The population is returned with the parish.

STEBBING, a parish in the hundred of HINCKFORD, county of ESSEX, 3¼ miles (N. E. by E.) from Great Dunmow, containing 1311 inhabitants. The living is a vicarage, in the jurisdiction of the Commissary of Essex and Herts, concurrently with the Consistorial Court of the Bishop of London, rated in the king's books at £ 12. Thomas Batt, Esq. was patron in 1802. The church, dedicated to St. Mary, has lately received an addition of one hundred and forty free sittings, the Incorporated Society for the enlargement of churches and chapels having granted £30 towards defraying the expense. There is a place of worship for Independents.

STEDHAM, a parish in the hundred of EASE-BOURNE, rape of CHICHESTER, county of SUSSEX, 2¼ miles (W. N.W.) from Midhurst, containing 453 inhabitants. The living is a rectory, with that of Heyshot united, in the archdeaconry and diocese of Chichester, rated in the king's books at £17. 18. 6½., and in the patronage of Lord Selsey. The church is dedicated to St. James.

STEEP, a parish in the hundred of EAST MEON, Alton (South) division of the county of SOUTHAMPTON, 1¾ mile (N.) from Petersfield, containing, with the tythings of North Ambersham and South Ambersham, 808 inhabitants. The living is a perpetual curacy, annexed to the vicarage of East Meon, in the archdeaconry and diocese of Winchester. Steep is within the jurisdiction of the Cheyney Court held at Winchester every Thursday, for the recovery of debts to any amount.

STEEP-HOLMES ISLAND, in the parish of UP-HILL, hundred of WINTERSTOKE, county of SOMERSET, 2 leagues (W. by N.) from Uphill. It is a vast rock, about a mile and a half in circumference, rising perpendicularly out of the Bristol channel to the height of four hundred feet above the level of the sea, and inaccessible at all points except two. A few rabbits burrow here, and great numbers of sea-fowl build their nests within the recesses of its overhanging rocks. A house was erected, in 1776, for the accommodation of fishermen, who occasionally make this island their resort. A priory is supposed to have been founded here, about the reign of Edward II., by Maurice, Lord Berkeley.

STEEPING (GREAT), a parish in the Wold division of the wapentake of CANDLESHOE, parts of LINDSEY, county of LINCOLN, 3 miles (E. S. E.) from Spilsby, containing 278 inhabitants. The living is a discharged vicarage, united to the rectory of Firsby, in the archdeaconry and diocese of Lincoln, rated in the king's books at £7. 18. 4. The church is dedicated to All Saints. There is a place of worship for Wesleyan Methodists. The parish is bounded on the south by the river Steeping. The remains of an old mansion, surrounded by a moat, are now occupied as a farm-house, and a moated enclosure in the neighbourhood is said to have been the site of a monastery.

STEEPING (LITTLE), a parish in the eastern division of the soke of BOLINGBROKE, parts of LINDSEY, county of LINCOLN, 3¼ miles (S.E. by E.) from Spilsby, containing 278 inhabitants. The living is a discharged rectory, in the archdeaconry and diocese of Lincoln, rated in the king's books at £9. 19. 4., and in the patronage of Lord Gwydir. The church is dedicated to St. Andrew.

STEEPLE, a parish in the hundred of HASILOR, Blandford (South) division of the county of DORSET, 4¼ miles (W. by S.) from Corfe-Castle, containing 233 inhabitants. The living is a rectory, united by act of parliament in the 8th of George I. to that of Tyneham, in the archdeaconry of Dorset, and diocese of Bristol,

rated in the king's books at £9. 15. 5., and in the patronage of W. Richards, Esq. The church, dedicated to St. Michael, has a plain but lofty tower. The hamlet of West Creech, in this parish, formerly belonged to the abbey of Bindon, and had the privileges of a market and fair, granted by Henry III.

STEEPLE, a parish in the hundred of DENGIE, county of ESSEX, 5½ miles (W. S. W.) from Bradwell near the Sea, containing 533 inhabitants. The living is a discharged vicarage with Stanesgate, in the archdeaconry of Essex, and diocese of London, rated in the king's books at £15. 18., and in the patronage of J. K. and T. Hunt, Esqrs., and Miss Hunt. The church is dedicated to St. Lawrence and All Saints. Blackwater river is navigable on the north side of the parish. At Stanesgate, a priory of Cluniac monks, subordinate to that of Lewes, existed before 1176; it was dedicated to St. Mary Magdalene, and at the dissolution had a revenue of £38. 18. 3.

STEEPLE-MORDEN, county of CAMBRIDGE.— (See MORDEN STEEPLE.)

STEEPLETON-PRESTON, formerly a parish, now considered extra-parochial, in the hundred of PIM-PERNE, Blandford (North) division of the county of DORSET, 4¼ miles (N. N. W.) from Blandford-Forum, containing 23 inhabitants. The living is a discharged rectory, in the archdeaconry of Dorset, and diocese of Bristol, rated in the king's books at £6. 18. 4., and endowed with £200 royal bounty. P. Beckford, Esq. was patron in 1810. The church is dedicated to St. Mary.

STEETON, a township in the parish of BOLTON-PERCY, ainsty of the city, and East riding of the county, of YORK, 3½ miles (E. by N.) from Tadcaster, containing 83 inhabitants.

STEETON, a joint township with Eastburn, in the parish of KILDWICK, eastern division of the wapentake of STAINCLIFFE and EWCROSS, West riding of the county of YORK, 2¾ miles (N. W.) from Keighley, containing, with Eastburn, 753 inhabitants. There is a place of worship for Wesleyan Methodists. William Laycock, in 1612, gave a rent-charge of £3. 6. 8. in support of a school.

STELLA, a township in the parish of RYTON, western division of CHESTER ward, county palatine of DURHAM, 7½ miles (W. by N.) from Gateshead, containing 421 inhabitants. There is a Roman Catholic chapel at Stella hall. The navigable river Tyne runs past the village, where is a wharf belonging to the London Lead Company, and a coal-staith. A considerable English army was defeated here, August 28th, 1640, by the Scots, who passed the Tyne under cover of several pieces of cannon, which they had planted in Newburn church.

STELLING, a parish partly in the hundred of Lo-NINGBOROUGH, but chiefly in that of STOUTING, lathe of SHEPWAY, county of KENT, 6 miles (S. by W.) from Canterbury, containing 295 inhabitants. The living is a perpetual curacy, annexed to the rectory of Upper Hardres, in the archdeaconry and diocese of Canterbury. The church is dedicated to St. Mary. The parish is bounded on the west by the ancient Stane-street.

STELLING, a township in the parish of BYWELL St. PETER, eastern division of TINDALE ward, county of NORTHUMBERLAND, 8½ miles (E. by N.) from Hexham, containing 12 inhabitants.

STENIGOT, a parish in the northern division of the wapentake of GARTREE, parts of LINDSEY, county of LINCOLN, 5¾ miles (S. W. by W.) from Louth, containing 107 inhabitants. The living is a discharged rectory, in the archdeaconry and diocese of Lincoln, rated in the king's books at £7. 12. 3½., and in the patronage of Mrs. Arlington. The church is dedicated to St. Nicholas.

STENSON, a township in that part of the parish of BARROW which is in the hundred of APPLETREE, county of DERBY, 4¼ miles (S. S. W.) from Derby. The population is returned with the chapelry of Twyford. The inhabitants are entitled to the benefit of Alsop's school at Findern.

STEPHENS (ST.), a parish in the northern division of the hundred of EAST, county of CORNWALL, ¾ of a mile (N. N. W.) from Launceston, containing, with the borough of Newport, 977 inhabitants. The living is a perpetual curacy, in the archdeaconry of Cornwall, and diocese of Exeter, endowed with £200 private benefaction, £600 royal bounty, and £800 parliamentary grant. John Horwell, in 1717, bequeathed funded property amounting to £1705. 15. 2., to be applied for teaching poor children.

STEPHENS (ST.), a parish in the hundred of CASHIO, or liberty of ST. ALBANS, county of HERTFORD, 1 mile (S. W.) from St. Albans, containing, with Park, Smallford, and Windridge wards, 1580 inhabitants. The living is a discharged vicarage, in the archdeaconry of St. Albans, and diocese of London, rated in the king's books at £15, endowed with £200 private benefaction, and £200 royal bounty, and in the patronage of — Cator, Esq. The church, situated on the Roman Watling-street, occupies the site of that built, in the reign of King Eldred, by Ulsinus, sixth abbot of St. Albans. A fine brass eagle with expanded wings, on an ornamented pedestal of the same metal, was dug up some years ago in the churchyard, and is now used as a stand in the chancel for Fox's Martyrology. The rivers Ver and Colne run through the parish, in which many Roman coins have been found.

STEPHENS (ST.), county of KENT.—See HACKINGTON.

STEPHENS (ST.) in BRANNEL, a parish in the eastern division of the hundred of POWDER, county of CORNWALL, 4½ miles (W. by N.) from St. Austell, containing 2479 inhabitants. The living is a perpetual curacy, annexed, with that of St. Denis, to the rectory of St. Michael Carhaise, in the archdeaconry of Cornwall, and diocese of Exeter, and in the patronage of Lord Grenville. The church is an ancient building, principally in the Norman style, with a detached square tower. There is a place of worship for Independents. A school is endowed with a small annual income. Several tin and copper mines have been opened in the neighbourhood, but have been found unproductive, except one, called Strawberry mine, which is worked on a small scale. The parish abounds with moor-stone, which is much used in building, and with a species of fine white clay. In the clay-works are found a black kind of spar, and some beautiful transparent regular polygonal chrystals, called Cornish diamonds. Here are vestiges of a circular intrenchment, surrounded by a foss, comprising about an acre.

STEPHENS (ST.) by SALTASH, a parish in the southern division of the hundred of EAST, county of CORNWALL, 1 mile (W. by S.) from Saltash, containing, with the borough of Saltash, 2873 inhabitants. The living is a vicarage, in the archdeaconry of Cornwall, and diocese of Exeter, rated in the king's books at £26, endowed with £15 per annum private benefaction, £200 royal bounty, and £700 parliamentary grant. Thomas Edwards, Esq. was patron in 1815. In this parish are considerable remains of the ancient castle of Trematon, in a beautiful situation on the banks of the Lyner : the area covered more than an acre of ground, and was enclosed by embattled walls; the keep is situated on the summit of a conical elevation, and is approached by a circular arched doorway ; the principal gateway consists of three arches, supporting a square embattled tower, containing a museum for natural curiosities : this castle was erected prior to the Conquest.

STEPNEY, a parish in the Tower division of the hundred of OSSULSTONE, county of MIDDLESEX, 2½ miles (E.) from London, comprising the hamlets of Mile-End New Town, Mile-End Old Town, and Ratcliff, and containing, according to the last census, 36,940 inhabitants, which number has since been progressively increasing, and at present may be estimated at nearly 80,000. This parish, called in various ancient records Stebunhithe and Stebenhythe, occurs in Domesday-book under the name Stibenhede, from which its present appellation is obviously deduced. It anciently included a widely extended district, comprising, in addition to its present parochial limits, the hamlets of Stratford le Bow, Limehouse, Poplar and Blackwall, Shadwell, St. George's in the East, Wapping, Spitalfields, White-chapel, and Bethnal-Green, which, owing to their increased extent and importance, have been successively separated from it, and erected into distinct parishes, at present constituting some of the most populous districts in the vicinity of the metropolis. The present parish of St. Paul, Shadwell, was separated from Stepney in 1666 ; St. Mary's, Whitechapel, in 1673 ; St. John's, Wapping, in 1694 ; St. Mary's, Stratford le Bow, in 1717 ; the parishes of Christchurch (Spitalfields) and St. George in the East, in 1729 ; St. Anne's, Limehouse, in 1730 ; St. Matthew's, Bethnal-Green, in 1743 ; and the parish of All Saints', Poplar, including Blackwall, in 1817. According to Stowe, Edward I. held a parliament at Stepney, in the mansion of Henry Walleis, mayor of London, in which he conferred several valuable privileges on the citizens. The manor was, in 1380, annexed to the see of London, and the bishops had a palace, called Bishop hall, now included in the parish of Bethnal-Green, in which they continued to reside till 1550, when it was alienated from the see by Bishop Ridley, who gave it to Edward VI. In the rebellion under Jack Cade, in the reign of Henry VI., the insurgents who attacked the metropolis, encamped for some time at the hamlet of Mile-End; and, in 1642, at the commencement of the parliamentary war, fortifications were constructed in this parish for the defence of the city.

From the then pleasantness of its situation, and the beauty of its scenery, which are noticed in a letter from Sir Thomas More to Dean Colet, Stepney was formerly the favourite residence of many persons of distinction. Isabel, Countess of Rutland, had a seat here in the latter part of the sixteenth century, at which time Sir Thomas Lake, secretary of state in the reign of James I., was also a resident; but there are no vestiges of the houses which they occupied. Henry, the first Marquis of Worcester, had a mansion near the parsonage-house, of which the gateway, handsomely built of brick, with a turret at one of the angles, is still remaining, and forms part of a house wherein Dr. Richard Mead was born, and where he resided for many years: the site of the ancient mansion is now occupied by an academy for the education of young men intended for ministers of the Baptist denomination. Sir Henry Colet, father of Dean Colet, the founder of St. Paul's school, lived in a spacious residence to the west of the church, called the Great Place, the site being now partly occupied by a place of public entertainment, called Spring Gardens; on two sides of the pleasure grounds, traces are still discernible of the moat that surrounded the ancient mansion. During part of the seventeenth century, Stepney suffered severely from the ravages of the plague, of which two thousand nine hundred and seventy-eight persons died in the year 1625; and in the year 1665, not less than six thousand five hundred and eighty-three. In the course of the latter year, one hundred and sixteen sextons and grave-diggers, belonging to this parish, died of the plague, and so greatly was the parish, then principally inhabited by sea-faring men, depopulated, that it is recorded, in the Life of Lord Clarendon, that "there seemed an impossibility to procure seamen to fit out the fleet." In 1794, a most calamitous and destructive fire, occasioned by the boiling over of a pitch kettle in a barge-builder's yard, broke out, and consumed more than half of the hamlet of Ratcliff, communicated to the shipping in the river, and destroyed several ranges of warehouses, among which was one belonging to the East India Company, containing more than two hundred tons of saltpetre. Of one thousand two hundred houses then in that hamlet, only five hundred and seventy escaped the conflagration, and thirty-six warehouses, chiefly stored with articles of combustion, were totally consumed. By this dreadful calamity several hundred families were reduced to the utmost distress, deprived of shelter, and made dependent for subsistence on the public benevolence. One hundred and fifty tents, furnished by government from the Tower, were pitched for their reception in an enclosed piece of ground near the churchyard, and provisions were daily supplied to them from the vestry-room of the church. A public subscription was opened at Lloyd's coffee-house, by which, together with the contributions of thousands who came to visit the extensive ruins caused by this desolating conflagration, more than £16,000 was collected for the relief of the sufferers.

The parish is situated on the northern bank of the Thames, and is chiefly inhabited by persons connected with the shipping: it extends for a considerable distance from the river to the principal road leading into Essex, and comprises many handsome ranges of building, among which are Tredegar-square on the north, and Beaumont-square on the south, side of the Mile-End road, together with numerous handsome houses in detached situations. The commercial-road, leading from Whitechapel to the East and West India docks, passes through the parish: this road, which is

seventy feet wide, with a pavement on each side eight feet in width, was begun in 1802, and towards the fund for making it and keeping it in repair, all houses within the distance of one hundred feet on each side pay a contribution of two shillings and ninepence in the pound. On the south side of this road, a tram-road has been laid down within the last year, at a very great expense. The basin, or dock, at the junction of the Regent's canal with the Thames, capable of containing one hundred ships, occupies a portion of the east side of the hamlet of Ratcliff. The ancient house in which Dean Colet resided, after his resignation of the vicarage of Stepney, and which he gave to the head-master of St. Paul's school, as a place of retirement, has been converted into two handsome houses, now called "Collet Place," the front of which is ornamented with a bust of the dean: the greater portion of the buildings in this part of the parish are of modern date, having been erected subsequently to the fire in 1794. The parish is paved, and lighted with gas, under the superintendence of commissioners appointed by act of parliament, and supplied with water by the East London Company, from their works at Old Ford, about two miles distant, the reservoir of which, excavated in 1827, and covering ten acres of ground, is situated to the north of the high road. On the banks of the Regent's canal, which crosses the Mile-End road under a stone bridge, are several coal and timber wharfs; in the hamlets of Mile-End Old Town and Mile-End New Town are some extensive breweries, a large distillery, an extensive floor-cloth manufactory, a manufactory for tobacco-pipes, and a very spacious nursery-ground; in the hamlet of Ratcliff there are extensive manufactories for sail-cloth, sails, chain-cables, and mooring-chains, steam-engines, and machinery connected with the docks and shipping, and large establishments belonging to coopers for the West India trade, timber and hoop merchants, ship-chandlers, sugar-bakers, rope-makers, and various other trades, for which its situation renders it peculiarly favourable. The market, granted by Charles II., in 1664, is now held at Whitechapel; and the fair, granted at the same time, and originally held on Mile-End green, was afterwards removed to Stratford le Bow, and subsequently suppressed.

Stepney is within the jurisdiction of the county magistrates, who sit at the police-office in Lambeth-street, Whitechapel, for the despatch of business relating to the hamlets of Mile-End Old and New Towns; and at the Thames police office, Wapping, for the hamlet of Ratcliff: its local affairs are under the superintendence of twelve trustees, who, pursuant to the provisions of an act passed in 1810, are annually elected by the inhabitants, at the town hall in White Horse-street, on Easter-Monday; where also, at the same time, the churchwardens, two overseers, a constable, and fourteen headboroughs, are chosen. It is within the limits of the new police establishment, and under the jurisdiction of the court of requests for the "Tower Hamlets," held in Osborne-street, Whitechapel, for the recovery of debts under 40s. A notion has for many years been very generally entertained, that all persons born at sea are, from that circumstance alone, parishioners of Stepney; to counteract the influence of this error, which has subjected the parish to serious expense, the overseers, in 1813, applied for a criminal information against a magistrate of the county of Chester, for having removed a vagrant, who stated that he was born at sea, from the parish of Stockport to Stepney. On this occasion Lord Ellenborough observed, that "this was a great blunder on the part of the magistrate;" and in the hope that the promulgation of his lordship's decision, that "certainly it must be understood, that all these sea-born persons are not to be marched off, at the pleasure of the magistrate, to the parish of Stepney," would produce the desired effect, the overseers forbore to press further proceedings.

The church of Stepney, together with the manor, was appropriated to the see of London, in 1380, and the bishops of that diocese appointed to the rectory, which was a sinecure, the rectors being patrons of the vicarage: in 1544, the great tithes were impropriated, and the impropriator presented both to the rectory and to the vicarage; in 1708, they were purchased by the Principal and Fellows of Brasenose College, Oxford, which purchase was afterwards confirmed by act of parliament, and they were annexed to the vicarage, subject to an annual payment of £40 to the college, and divided into moieties, of which the incumbents were styled portionist of Church-Stepney and Spitalfields-Stepney. After the separation of the several parishes, and the consequent diminution of the value of the benefice, the arrangement was altered, and the living became vested in one person. It is a rectory, in the peculiar jurisdiction of the Commissary of London, concurrently with the Consistorial Court of the Bishop, rated in the king's books at £73. 6. 8., and in the patronage of the Principal and Fellows of Brasenose College, Oxford. The church, dedicated to St. Dunstan and All Saints, is a spacious structure of flint and stone, principally in the later style of English architecture, with a low broad tower, strengthened with buttresses, and surmounted by a turret crowned with a small dome. Near the western entrance is a bas-relief, indifferently executed and much decayed, representing the Virgin and Child, with a female figure in the attitude of supplication; and over the south door is a rudely-sculptured representation of the Crucifixion, in tolerable preservation. The nave is separated from the aisles by clustered columns and pointed arches; and on the south side of the chancel are two arched recesses. There are many ancient monuments in the church; on the north side of the chancel is the altar-tomb of Sir Henry Colet, Knt., under an arched canopy, finely groined, and near it a monument to Benjamin Kenton, Esq., on which is a finely sculptured representation of the Good Samaritan, by Westmacott: this benevolent individual, who died in 1800, at the advanced age of eighty-three, bequeathed to different charitable institutions the sum of £63,550. On the east wall is a monument to Lady Dethic, and on the south, a tablet to Sir Thomas Spert, Knt., founder and first master of the corporation of the Trinity: the church was thoroughly repaired and beautified in 1828. The churchyard is spacious, and the various walks are shaded with double rows of elm-trees; there are numerous monuments to distinguished persons who have been buried here, among whom were, the Rev. Matthew Mead, who was ejected from the living of Shadwell for nonconformity; Admiral Sir John Leake, Knt., a distinguished officer in the reign of Queen Anne; and various others. A church in the later style of English architecture, containing one thousand three hundred and thirty-eight sittings, of which nine hundred and thirty are free, was erected in 1822, towards the expense of which, the parliamentary commissioners granted the sum of £3500. There are places of worship for Baptists, the Society of Friends, those in the connexion of the late Countess of Huntingdon, Calvinistic Methodists, and three for Independents; of one of which, near the church, founded by the lecturer, the Rev. Wm. Greenhill, and built in 1674, the Rev. Matthew Mead became the first minister.

The charity schools at Ratcliff were established in 1710, and the school-house was erected in 1719; the endowment of this institution, originally for the clothing and instruction of thirty boys and twenty girls, consists of an estate at Edmonton, given to the school by Mr. Wakeling; a legacy of £500, by Edward Turner, Esq., and other benefactions, amounting in the whole to £2000: the school was enlarged in 1814, and adapted to the instruction, on the National system, of two hundred additional boys and one hundred and twenty girls, of whom forty boys and twenty-five girls are annually clothed in green, and apprenticed. The charity school at Mile-End Old Town was established by subscription in 1714, and has been subsequently endowed with various benefactions, producing £143. 16. per annum: one hundred and sixty boys, and one hundred and five girls, are instructed on the National plan; a school-room for the girls, and other apartments, were erected at Stepney Green, in 1786, behind which is a school for the boys. The Stepney Meeting charity school, in which one hundred and thirty boys and sixty girls are instructed, partly on the National and partly on the Lancasterian plan, was founded in 1783, and the present building erected in 1828: it has an endowment of £188 per annum, arising from various benefactions, and is further supported by subscription. The charity school for Mile-End New Town was established by subscription, in 1785, for the instruction of thirty boys and thirty girls; the permanent income arises from £715, vested in the four per cents., the deficiency being supplied by subscription. There are also Sunday schools in connexion with the established church and the dissenting congregations. In School-house-lane, Ratcliff, are the almshouses of the Coopers' Company, founded in 1538, by Toby Wood, Esq., and Mr. Cloker, members of that company, for fourteen aged persons of both sexes, who were to receive £1. 6. 8. each per annum. Adjoining them is a free grammar school, largely endowed by Nicholas Gibson, Esq., master of the company, and sheriff of London, in the reign of Henry VIII., for the instruction of thirty boys; in this school Bishop Andrews, and several other distinguished persons, received the rudiments of their education. These premises were destroyed by the fire of 1794, but were rebuilt in 1796, and the almshouses more liberally endowed by the company; they now afford an asylum to sixteen men and six women, who receive each £15, and a chaldron and a half of coal yearly: in the school there are at present fifty boys, who are instructed in reading, writing, and arithmetic, by a master whose salary is £73. 10. per annum, with a house and an allowance of coal, and the privilege of receiving private pupils: the buildings occupy three sides of a quadrangle, with a chapel in the central range.

The almshouses belonging to the Vintners' Company, originally founded in Thames-street, in 1357, were destroyed in the great fire of London, in 1666, and were afterwards rebuilt at Mile-End; they were taken down and rebuilt in 1802, upon a larger scale, in appropriation of a bequest of £2250 by Mr. Benjamin Kenton of Stepney; they consist of twelve separate tenements and a chapel, and are endowed for twelve widows of freemen of the Vintners' Company, who receive £36 per annum each; a chaplain performs divine service weekly, and has a stipend of £52. 10. per annum. Almshouses, erected by the Brethren of the Trinity House, comprise twelve sets of apartments, with a handsome chapel in the centre, in the front windows of which are some armorial bearings in stained glass. Francis Bancroft, in 1727, bequeathed in trust to the Drapers' Company, property then worth £28,000, for the erection and endowment of twenty-four almshouses for aged men, members of that company, and a school for one hundred boys : the present income, arising from £40,800 three per cent. consols., £33,400 three per cent. reduced annuities, and from landed property, exceeds £4000 per annum; the almsmen receive each £20 per annum, and a chaldron and a half of coal, with a gown every third year. The head-master of the school receives a salary of £120 per annum, and the second master one of £90, with houses free of rent, taxes, and repairs, and four chaldrons of coal annually; the boys are instructed in reading, writing, and arithmetic, and on leaving school receive an apprentice fee, or a sum of £2. 10. to fit them out for service. The buildings, in the Mile-End-road, consist of two ranges of houses occupying two sides of a quadrangular area, of which the school-room, chapel, and other apartments form the third side. A chaplain, who is appointed by the Master and Wardens of the Drapers' Company, has an annual stipend of £31. 10., and performs divine service in the chapel every Sunday morning, and on Christmas-day and Good Friday. Mr. John Fuller, in 1592, founded twelve almshouses, which he endowed with £50 per annum, for twelve aged and unmarried men. Near the churchyard are the Mercers' almshouses, founded in 1691, by Dame Jane Mico, relict of Sir Samuel Mico, which she endowed for ten aged widows, who receive each £30 per annum. Mrs. Bowry, in 1715, bequeathed a leasehold estate and a sum of money in the South Sea annuities, amounting to £2636. 13., for the erection and endowment of eight almshouses between Mile-End and Stratford le Bow, for decayed seamen and their widows, of this parish. Cap. James Cook, and his widow, Dame Alice Row, founded four almshouses in the Grove-road, Mile-End, for widows of seamen of Stepney, to which the hamlet of Mile-End exclusively presents, on condition of keeping them in repair. Eight almshouses were erected in Mile-End Old Town, in 1698, by Mr. John Pennell, who endowed them for aged widows, of whom four are to be widows of seamen belonging to the Hon. East India Company's service; each of the inmates receives an allowance of six shillings and eightpence per month, seven sacks of coal yearly, and a gown every alternate year. The East London Institution for lying-in women, established by

subscription, is well supported and judiciously regulated. At Mile-End Old Town is the Jews' hospital for aged poor, and for the education and employment of children, founded in 1806, and enlarged in 1818 : the building, which is on the south side of the road, is spacious, and ornamented in front with a central pediment and Ionic pilasters. Nearly opposite is the hospital for Spanish and Portuguese Jews, established in 1747, for the reception of sick poor and lying-in women, and intended also as an asylum for the aged and infirm. On the north side of the high road are two spacious cemeteries belonging to the Portuguese Jews, and a third for German or Dutch Jews, in which several of the Rabbins, and other eminent individuals of that class are interred.

STEPPINGLEY, a parish in the hundred of REDBORNESTOKE, county of BEDFORD, 2½ miles (S. W. by S.) from Ampthill, containing 323 inhabitants. The living is a discharged rectory, in the archdeaconry of Bedford, and diocese of Lincoln, rated in the king's books at £6. 16. 3., and in the patronage of the Duke of Bedford. The church is dedicated to St. Lawrence.

STERNDALE (EARL), a chapelry in the parish of HARTINGTON, hundred of WIRKSWORTH, county of DERBY, 5½ miles (S. E. by S.) from Buxton, containing, with Middle Quarter, 417 inhabitants. The living is a perpetual curacy, in the peculiar jurisdiction of the Dean's court for the manor of Hartington, endowed with £400 private benefaction, £600 royal bounty, and £1300 parliamentary grant, and in the patronage of the Vicar of Hartington. The chapel was erected in 1829, at the expense of £1000. The Peak Forest and Cromford rail-road passes through the chapelry. Four poor children are instructed for £2 a year, the gift of James Hill, in 1712.

STERNFIELD, a parish in the hundred of PLOMESGATE, county of SUFFOLK, 1½ mile (S. S. E.) from Saxmundham, containing 180 inhabitants. The living is a rectory, in the archdeaconry of Suffolk, and diocese of Norwich, rated in the king's books at £8. 14. 4½., and in the patronage of C. Long, Esq. The church is dedicated to St. Mary Magdalene.

STERT, a parish in the hundred of SWANBOROUGH, county of WILTS, 2 miles (S. E.) from Devizes, containing 193 inhabitants. The living is a perpetual curacy, annexed to the vicarage of Urchfont, in the peculiar jurisdiction of the Bishop of Salisbury. The church is dedicated to St. James.

STETCHWORTH, a parish in the hundred of RADFIELD, county of CAMBRIDGE, 2¾ miles (S. by W.) from Newmarket, containing 462 inhabitants. The living is a discharged vicarage, in the archdeaconry and diocese of Ely, rated in the king's books at £10. 12. 1. R. Eaton, Esq. was patron in 1809. The church is dedicated to St. Peter. An almshouse for two poor persons of each sex was founded here, in 1700, by Lord and Lady Gorges, who endowed it with £30 per annum.

STEVENAGE, a market town and parish in the hundred of BROADWATER, county of HERTFORD, 12 miles (N. W. by N.) from Hertford, and 31 (N. N. W.) from London, containing 1664 inhabitants. The ancient name of this town was *Stigenhaght*, signifying the hills by the highway, evidently derived from six barrows, or hills, near the road side, half a mile south of the town : about the period of the Octarchy it was called *Stigenhace*, and in Domesday-book *Stevenach*, or *Stevenadge*. It formed a part of the demesne of the Saxon kings, and was given, by Edward the Confessor, to the abbey of Westminster, on the suppression of which it was granted, by Edward VI., to the see of London, to which the manor still belongs. The town is pleasantly situated on the great North road from London to Edinburgh, and consists principally of one long and spacious street, with two or three smaller ones, comprising some well-built brick residences, and a few good shops, and is well supplied with water. The trade is principally that of carcass butchers, who dispose of the slaughtered cattle principally at Hertford, and in the London market. The platting of straw furnishes employment to many of the females in the town and its vicinity. In the reign of James I., Monteine, Bishop of London, procured the grant of a weekly market, and three fairs annually, which was confirmed, with liberty to alter the market-day, by a charter of William and Mary ; but, from the contiguity of other towns, in which large markets are held, that of Stevenage has fallen into disuse ; and the fairs, except one on the 22nd of September, have also been nearly discontinued. Petty sessions for the division are held here, and a manorial court annually by the Bishop of London.

The living is a rectory, in the archdeaconry of Huntingdon, and diocese of Lincoln, rated in the king's books at £33. 6. 8., and in the patronage of William Baker, Esq. The church, dedicated to St. Nicholas, is situated on a chalky eminence about half a mile from the town, approached by a fine avenue of trees ; it is a neat well-built edifice, with a square tower at the west end, surmounted by a spire covered with lead ; attached to the chancel are two small chapels. There are places of worship for Independents and Wesleyan Methodists. The free school was founded, in the reign of Queen Mary, by the Rev. Thomas Allen, who devised all his estates to the Society of Trinity College, Cambridge, for certain charitable uses, amongst which was an endowment of £13. 6. 8. per annum to this school, which has been increased by subsequent benefactions. The master is appointed by the Master and Fellows of that college, and the trustees are chosen from among the gentlemen in the neighbourhood : the poor children of the parish pay two shillings and sixpence a quarter, and those out of it five shillings. The school-room is at the northern extremity of the town, and upon it is an inscription in old English characters directing, by authority of the king's commissioners in 1632 and 1640, that the master, having the income of the school, shall teach the poor children of the parish, or those resorting to it. Near it stands a commodious house, with garden and orchard attached, for the master, who formerly received a considerable number of boarders. The almshouse for three poor persons, called "All Christians' Souls' House," was founded by Stephen Hellard, in 1501, who directed that the inmates should daily repeat a certain prayer for his soul, and for all Christian souls. There are various other bequests to the poor. Henry Trigg, an eccentric inhabitant of this town, by his will, dated in 1724, directed his body after death to be deposited on a floor, to be erected in one of the outbuildings of his house, leaving his property to his brother on condition that he complied with this direction, which was accord-

ingly done, the corpse still remaining where it was deposited. The six barrows supposed to give name to the town have been conjectured to be sepulchral monuments, although in those that have been opened no human remains were discovered. It is generally supposed that they were erected by the Danes, several battles having been fought between them and the Saxons in this county, some fields, at the distance of about three-quarters of a mile, still retaining the name of Danes' Blood. In a wood about half a mile eastward of the barrows, called Humbley wood, are the apparent remains of an intrenched camp, or fortification, of unknown construction, consisting of a large and perfectly square area, surrounded with a deep moat containing water, with only one entrance on the north side. Richard de Stevenage, abbot of St. Albans at the dissolution, was a native of this place.

STEVENTON, a parish in the hundred of Ock, county of Berks, 5 miles (S. W. by S.) from Abingdon, containing 652 inhabitants. The living is a vicarage, in the archdeaconry of Berks, and diocese of Salisbury, rated in the king's books at £9. 5. 2½., and in the patronage of the Dean and Chapter of Westminster. The church is dedicated to St. Michael. There is a place of worship for Baptists. The Berks and Wilts canal passes through the parish. In the village is an ancient cross, consisting of a tall shaft rising from a base of several steps. A castle was formerly erected here by Baldwin Wake, in 1281, of which there are no vestiges. A priory of Black monks, a cell to the abbey of Bec in Normandy, was founded in the time of Henry I., which, at the suppression of Alien houses, was bestowed upon the abbot and convent of Westminster. Twelve children are instructed daily, and a Sunday school is partly supported, for about £11 per annum, arising from the sum of £210, bequeathed by John Anns, in 1811.

STEVENTON, a parish in the hundred of Basingstoke, Basingstoke division of the county of Southampton, 6¼ miles (E.) from Whitchurch, containing 151 inhabitants. The living is a rectory, in the archdeaconry and diocese of Winchester, rated in the king's books at £11. 4. 7., and in the patronage of Edward Knight, Esq. The church is dedicated to St. Nicholas. The manor-house has a very antiquated appearance, and bears evident marks of former grandeur.

STEVINGTON, a parish in the hundred of Willey, county of Bedford, 5¼ miles (N. W. by W.) from Bedford, containing 485 inhabitants. The living is a discharged vicarage, in the archdeaconry of Bedford, and diocese of Lincoln, rated in the king's books at £12. 13. 4., endowed with £200 private benefaction, and £200 royal bounty, and in the patronage of the Duke of Bedford. The church is dedicated to St. Mary.

STEWKLEY, a parish in the hundred of Cottesloe, county of Buckingham, 6 miles (E. by S.) from Winslow, containing 933 inhabitants. The living is a vicarage, in the archdeaconry of Buckingham, and diocese of Lincoln, rated in the king's books at £9. 9. 7., and in the patronage of the Bishop of Oxford. The church, dedicated to St. Mary, is one of the most enriched and complete specimens of the Norman style of architecture now remaining. There is a place of worship for Wesleyan Methodists.

STEWTON, a parish in the Wold division of the hundred of Louth-Eske, parts of Lindsey, county of

LINCOLN, 2¾ miles (E.) from Louth, containing 63 inhabitants. The living is a discharged rectory, in the archdeaconry and diocese of Lincoln, rated in the king's books at £7. Dudley North, Esq. was patron in 1817. The church is dedicated to St. Andrew.

STEYNING, a borough, market town, and parish, in the hundred of STEYNING, rape of BRAMBER, county of SUSSEX, 24 miles (E. by N.) from Chichester, and 49½ (S. by W.) from London, containing 1324 inhabitants. The name is supposed to be derived from the Steyne-street, an ancient road which passed through this part of the county from Arundel to Dorking. Camden considers it to have been mentioned in Alfred's will by the name of *Steyningham.* It appears in the Saxon age to have been a place of considerable note; a church, or monastery, having been here built, wherein St. Cadman was buried; and in the Catalogue of Religious Houses, ascribed to Gervase of Canterbury, in the time of Richard I., mention is made of a Dean and Secular canons. It is more certain that King Edward the Confessor gave lands to the monastery of Feschamp in Normandy, which included this place; these being taken away by Earl Godwin, and restored by William the Conqueror, some Benedictine monks were sent from that house, who erected an Alien priory here, which was given to the monastery of Sion by Edward IV., and continued part of its possessions till the dissolution. Speed says, the conventual church was dedicated to St. Mary Magdalene, and contained the sacred relics of St. Cuthman (Cadman), and Ethelwulph, father of Alfred the Great: here anciently was also a parochial church of St. Cuthman. Camden speaks of its market as well frequented in his time: the town afterwards became reduced, and is, in the Magna Britannia, a century later, mentioned as "a mean, contemptible place, with hardly a building fit to put a horse in," being said then to have contained not more than one hundred and fifty families; but since that period it has been considerably enlarged. It stands at the foot of a lofty hill near the river Adur, over which is a bridge, and consists of four streets, crossing each other. It is supplied with water by a celebrated spring, issuing from a mountain half a mile distant, its stream turning two mills belonging to the town. Great improvement in the buildings and general appearance of the town has been lately made, through the liberality of the Duke of Norfolk. Here were extensive barracks for infantry, which have been pulled down; and within one mile of the town, on the downs, is a racecourse, but races have not been held for the last fifty years. The land in the vicinity of the town is fertile, and the adjoining downs afford good pasturage for sheep. The chief traffic is in cattle, for which there is a monthly market: great numbers are also sold at the fairs. The market is on Wednesday: the fairs are June 9th, September 20th, and October 10th; at the Michaelmas fair more than three thousand head of Welch oxen alone have been disposed of, exclusively of other kinds, together with sheep, horses, hogs, wheat, seeds, &c. Steyning is a borough by prescription, under the authority of a constable, appointed at the court leet of the lord of the manor. It sends two members to parliament: the right of election, which has been frequently contested, is in the inhabitant householders paying scot and lot, about eighty in number: the constable is the returning officer. The members were formerly elected in conjunction with Bramber, but at present each town is entitled to return two representatives, although one part of Bramber is in the centre of Steyning.

The living is a vicarage, in the archdeaconry and diocese of Chichester, rated in the king's books at £15, and in the patronage of Sir J. C. Honywood, Bart. The church, which is dedicated to St. Andrew, consists of the nave only of a larger cruciform structure, presenting beautiful specimens of the Norman style of architecture. The interior is magnificently enriched: four diagonally ornamented circular arches, surmounted, or terminated, each with a small round-headed window, form the south side of the nave, have, for their beauty and variety, been copied in the repairs of Arundel Castle; the side aisles are much and disproportionably lower. At the east end, where the transept is intersected, are clusters of columns, and arches for supporting a central tower: a lofty Norman arch leads into the chancel. The present tower on the west, of more modern date, is of flint and rubble stone, laid checquer-wise, with angular buttresses. The free school was founded and endowed, in 1614, by William Holland, a native and alderman of Chichester, who bequeathed for that purpose to trustees a garden and messuage, called "Brotherhood Hall," then used as a school-house, together with his manor of Festoes, &c., to pay from the proceeds of the latter £20 yearly for the instruction of children of persons dwelling within Steyning and its liberty; the master not to board more than six pay-scholars: the income is £81 10. per annum, and ten boys receive a classical education. Brotherhood Hall is still standing, and most likely received its name from having been the hall of some guild, or fraternity, prior to the dissolution. It consists of a centre, with a large arched entrance and two wings, the roofs split into five divisions and pointed, with large square windows of the time of Henry VIII. No children have been elected to this foundation for some years. A National school is supported by voluntary contributions. John Pell, the mathematician, was educated here.

STIBBARD, a parish in the hundred of GALLOW, county of NORFOLK, 4¼ miles (E. by S.) from Fakenham, containing 426 inhabitants. The living is a discharged rectory, annexed to that of Colkerk, in the archdeaconry of Norfolk, and diocese of Norwich, rated in the king's books at £11. 13. 4. The church is dedicated to All Saints.

STIBBINGTON, a parish in the hundred of NORMAN-CROSS, county of HUNTINGDON, 1 mile (E. by S.) from Wansford, containing, with the hamlet of Sibson, 374 inhabitants. The living is a rectory, in the archdeaconry of Huntingdon, and diocese of Lincoln, rated in the king's books at £7. 13. 6½., and in the patronage of the Duke of Bedford. The church is dedicated to St. John the Baptist.

STICKFORD, a parish in the western division of the soke of BOLINGBROKE, parts of LINDSEY, county of LINCOLN, 5½ miles (S. W.) from Spilsby, containing 343 inhabitants. The living is a discharged vicarage, in the archdeaconry and diocese of Lincoln, rated in the king's books at £6. 3. 6., endowed with £800 royal bounty, and in the patronage of the Bishop of Lincoln. The church is dedicated to St. Helen. There is a place of worship for Wesleyan Methodists.

STICKNEY, a parish in the western division of the soke of BOLINGBROKE, parts of LINDSEY, county of LINCOLN, 2½ miles (E. by N.) from Bolingbroke, containing 763 inhabitants. The living is a rectory, in the archdeaconry and diocese of Lincoln, rated in the king's books at £13. 11. 3., and in the patronage of the Rev. R. Loxham. The church is dedicated to St. Luke. There is a place of worship for Wesleyan Methodists. A grammar school was founded, in 1678, by William Lovell, who endowed it with land producing a liberal income to the master.

STIDD, or STEDE, an extra-parochial liberty, in the lower division of the hundred of BLACKBURN, county palatine of LANCASTER, 7 miles (N. N. W.) from Blackburn. The population is returned with Ribchester. Here are the ruins of an ancient chapel, in the early style of English architecture, endowed with £25 a year, to preserve which stipend, service has occasionally been performed within its walls since the Reformation, by the vicar of Ribchester.

STIFFKEY, a parish in the northern division of the hundred of GREENHOE, county of NORFOLK, 3¾ miles (E.) from Wells, containing 350 inhabitants. The living comprises the united rectories of St. John and St. Mary, with the rectory of Morston annexed, in the archdeaconry and diocese of Norwich, rated in the king's books at £25, and in the patronage of Marquis Townshend. The old hall, having been in a state of dilapidation for some years, is now used as a farm-house. It was built, in 1604, by Sir Nicholas Bacon, Knt., Lord Keeper of the Great Seal, and the west front, flanked by two embrasured towers, still remains. To the westward of the village is Warborough hill, on the summit of which is a circular camp.

STIFFORD, a parish in the hundred of CHAFFORD, county of ESSEX, 1¾ mile (N. by W.) from Gray's Thurrock, containing 206 inhabitants. The living is a rectory, in the archdeaconry of Essex, and diocese of London, rated in the king's books at £15, and in the patronage of the Master and Fellows of Pembroke College, Oxford. The church is dedicated to St. Mary.

STILLINGFLEET, a parish partly in the ainsty of the city of YORK, partly in the liberty of ST. PETER of YORK, but chiefly in the wapentake of OUZE and DERWENT, East riding of the county of YORK, comprising the townships of Acaster-Selby, Kelfield, and Stillingfleet with Moreby, and containing 878 inhabitants, of which number, 404 are in the township of Stillingfleet with Moreby, 7½ miles (S. by W.) from York. The living is a discharged vicarage, in the archdeaconry of Cleveland, and diocese of York, rated in the king's books at £9. 7. 6., endowed with £200 private benefaction, and £200 royal bounty, and in the patronage of the Dean and Chapter of York. The church, dedicated to St. Helen, is an ancient structure, exhibiting some portions in the Norman style; attached to it is a chapel, in which is a cross-legged figure in armour, one of the ancient family of Moreby. There is a place of worship for Wesleyan Methodists. Four poor children are instructed for an annuity of £1. 10., the bequest of the Rev. Mr. Turey.

STILLINGTON, a chapelry in the parish of RED-MARSHALL, south-western division of STOCKTON ward, county palatine of DURHAM, 8 miles (N. W. by W.) from Stockton upon Tees, containing 49 inhabitants.

STILLINGTON, a parish in the liberty of ST. PETER of YORK, East riding, though locally in the wapentake of Bulmer, North riding of the county of YORK, 4½ miles (E. S. E.) from Easingwould, containing 698 inhabitants. The living is a discharged vicarage, in the peculiar jurisdiction and patronage of the Prebendary of Stillington in the Cathedral Church of York, rated in the king's books at £4. 15. 5., and endowed with £200 royal bounty. The church is dedicated to St. Nicholas. There is a place of worship for Wesleyan Methodists. A National school has been established in the village. The celebrated Laurence Sterne held this living, and resided at Sutton in the neighbourhood.

STILTON, a parish (formerly a market town) in the hundred of NORMAN-CROSS, county of HUNTINGDON, 12½ miles (N. N. W.) from Huntingdon, containing 710 inhabitants. The living is a rectory, in the archdeaconry of Huntingdon, and diocese of Lincoln, rated in the king's books at £11. 5. 10., and in the patronage of the Bishop of Lincoln. The church is dedicated to St. Mary. There is a place of worship for Wesleyan Methodists. Stilton gives name to the famous cheese so called, great quantities of which are sold here, though it is made in Leicestershire, twenty miles off. There is a small charitable endowment for poor widows. The place takes its name from *Stivecle*, signifying stiff clay, according to Stukeley, and is situated upon the Roman road, Ermin-street ; though formerly a market town, it has dwindled into comparative insignificance. There is a fine spring about a quarter of a mile from the town, at one period celebrated for the cure of ulcerated legs, which properties are said to have ceased ; and to the south-east are the remains of an ancient circular encampment.

STINCHCOMBE, a parish in the upper division of the hundred of BERKELEY, county of GLOUCESTER, 2 miles (W. by N.) from Dursley, containing 432 inhabitants. The living is a perpetual curacy, in the archdeaconry and diocese of Gloucester, endowed with £200 private benefaction, and £200 royal bounty, and in the patronage of the Bishop of Gloucester. The church is dedicated to St. Cyr.

STINSFORD, a parish in the hundred of GEORGE, Dorchester division of the county of DORSET, 1¼ mile (E. N. E.) from Dorchester, containing 337 inhabitants. The living is a vicarage, in the archdeaconry of Dorset, and diocese of Bristol, rated in the king's books at £12. 17. 1., and in the patronage of the Earl of Ilchester. The church is dedicated to St. Michael.

STIRCHLEY, a parish in the Wellington division of the hundred of BRADFORD (South), county of SALOP, 3 miles (W. by S.) from Shiffnall, containing 172 inhabitants. The living is a discharged rectory, in the archdeaconry of Salop, and diocese of Lichfield and Coventry, rated in the king's books at £6. 5. 10., and in the patronage of John Oakeley, Esq. The church is dedicated to St. James. The Shropshire canal passes through the parish.

STIRTON, a joint township with Thorlby, in the parish of KILDWICK, eastern division of the wapentake of STAINCLIFFE and EWCROSS, West riding of the county of YORK, 1¼ mile (N. W.) from Skipton, containing, with Thorlby, 168 inhabitants.

STISTED, a parish in the hundred of HINCKFORD, county of ESSEX, 3½ miles (E. N. E.) from Braintree, containing 790 inhabitants. The living is a rectory, in

2 A 2

the peculiar jurisdiction and patronage of the Archbishop of Canterbury, rated in the king's books at £22. The church is dedicated to All Saints.

STITHIANS, a parish in the hundred of KERRIER, county of CORNWALL, 4¾ miles (N. W. by W.) from Penryn, containing 1688 inhabitants. The living is a vicarage, with the perpetual curacy of Perran-Arworthal annexed, in the archdeaconry of Cornwall, and diocese of Exeter, rated in the king's books at £14. 0. 10., and in the patronage of the Earl of Falmouth. There is a place of worship for Wesleyan Methodists.

STITTENHAM, a township in the parish of SHERIFF-HUTTON, wapentake of BULMER, North riding of the county of YORK, 8¼ miles (W. S. W.) from New Malton, containing 81 inhabitants.

STIVICHALL, a parish in the county of the city of COVENTRY, 1¾ mile (S. by W.) from Coventry, containing 96 inhabitants. The living is a perpetual curacy, in the archdeaconry of Coventry, and diocese of Lichfield and Coventry, endowed with £400 private benefaction, £800 royal bounty, and £300 parliamentary grant, and in the patronage of Francis Gregory, Esq. The church is dedicated to St. James.

STIXWOULD, a parish in the southern division of the wapentake of GARTREE, parts of LINDSEY, county of LINCOLN, 6¾ miles (W. S. W.) from Horncastle, containing 214 inhabitants. The living is a discharged vicarage, in the archdeaconry and diocese of Lincoln, rated in the king's books at £7. 10., endowed with £400 royal bounty, and £200 parliamentary grant, and in the patronage of Edmund Turnor, Esq. The church is dedicated to St. Peter. A convent of Cistercian nuns, in honour of the Blessed Virgin, was founded here, in the reign of Stephen, by the Countess Lucy, relict of Ranulph, first Earl of Chester, which at the dissolution possessed a revenue of £163. 1. 2.

STOBOROUGH, a liberty in the parish of the HOLY TRINITY, borough of WAREHAM, Blandford (South) division of the county of DORSET, ¾ of a mile (S.) from Wareham, containing 280 inhabitants. It was formerly governed by a mayor, chosen annually at Michaelmas; but the inhabitants declining to qualify themselves, when the Schism act came into operation, in 1714, the office no longer exists, but a bailiff is appointed in the same manner as the mayor was, viz:, by a jury at the court held by the lord of the manor.

STOCK, a parish in the hundred of CHELMSFORD, county of ESSEX, 3 miles (N. N. E.) from Billericay, containing 610 inhabitants. The living is a rectory, with that of Ramsdon-Bellhouse annexed, in the archdeaconry of Essex, and diocese of London, rated in the king's books at £10, and in the patronage of John Unwin, Esq. The church is dedicated to All Saints.

STOCK, a hamlet in the parish of FLADBURY, middle division of the hundred of OSWALDSLOW, county of WORCESTER, 6¾ miles (E. S. E.) from Droitwich. The population is returned with the chapelry of Bradley.

STOCK-DENNIS, a tything in the parish and hundred of TINTINHULL, county of SOMERSET, containing 10 inhabitants. This was formerly a parish, the living of which was a rectory, valued in 1294 at £20, but the church having been destroyed, and the parish almost depopulated, it has long since lost its parochial rights.

STOCK-GAYLAND, a parish in the hundred of BROWNSHALL, Sturminster division of the county of

DORSET, 7 miles (E. S. E.) from Sherborne, containing 63 inhabitants. The living is a discharged rectory, in the archdeaconry of Dorset, and diocese of Bristol, rated in the king's books at £5. 7. 1. The Rev. H. F. Yeatman was patron in 1819.

STOCKBRIDGE, a borough, market town, and parish, having separate jurisdiction, though locally in the hundred of King's Sombourn, Andover division of the county of SOUTHAMPTON, 18 miles (N. by W.) from Southampton, and 66 (W. S. W.) from London, containing 715 inhabitants. This small town is situated on the great western road from London to Exeter, and

Seal and Arms.

consists of one long street, which is intersected at the west end by the river Test, and at the east by the Andover canal, over each of which is a bridge; that over the former was rebuilt in 1799, and is a handsome structure: five smaller streams cross the street in the intermediate space, with bridges over them: it is lighted at the expense of Earl Grosvenor, and watched by subscription, and the inhabitants are supplied with excellent water. On Houghton down, about two miles west of the town, was formerly a race-course; but a new one has been formed, immediately adjoining it, in the parishes of Wallop and Longstock, under Danebury hill, from the area and intrenchments of which the whole of it may be seen: a stand is being erected, which is also intended for the members of the Bibury Racing club, which is to be removed to Danebury down from Gloucestershire: races are held in June, and, for some years past, a plate has been given by Earl Grosvenor. The streams are particularly favourable for trout-fishing, the principal nobility and gentry of this and the adjoining counties meeting here three or four times a year, and spending several weeks in this favourite recreation during the season. The preparation of parchment and glue affords employment to a few persons. Some thousand bushels of peat ashes are annually disposed of to the neighbouring farmers for manure, that article being much used for fuel by the inhabitants, though they are also well supplied with coal by means of the canal. The market, on Thursday, is well attended, and a large and handsome market-room, adjoining the Grosvenor Arms, has been built, at the expense of Earl Grosvenor: there were formerly three fairs, of which one only is now held, on the 10th of July, which is one of the largest in the county for lambs, several thousands being annually sold.

Stockbridge is a borough by prescription, under a bailiff and a constable, who are elected annually by the jury, at the court leet of the manor, held by the steward on Easter-Wednesday, the constable for the year preceding being generally made bailiff for the following year: the jury are summoned by a serjeant at mace. Petty sessions are held monthly. The town hall, a neat edifice, is situated near the centre of the town, and was rebuilt in 1810, on the site of the previous structure, at an expense of £1500; defrayed by the inhabitants. It first sent representatives to parliament in the 1st of Elizabeth: the right of election is vested in the inhabitant householders paying scot and lot: the number of resident voters is about one hundred : the bailiff is the returning officer, and the influence of Earl Grosvenor is predominant. The living is a perpetual curacy, annexed to the vicarage of King's Sombourn, in the archdeaconry and diocese of Winchester. The church is dedicated to St. Peter. There is a place of worship for Independents. About two miles and a half from the town is Danebury hill, a circular intrenchment, in good preservation, enclosing an extensive area, with very high ramparts. On the north and west are several barrows, one of which is named Canute's barrow. On the east, at the distance of about one mile and a half, is another circular intrenchment, with a high rampart, enclosing an area of about twenty acres, called Woolberry, on the east side of which is the representation of a white horse, cut, many years since, at the expense of W. P. Powlett, Esq., of Sombourn House. Robert, Earl of Gloucester, natural brother of the Empress Matilda, was taken prisoner in this town on his flight from Winchester : according to tradition, he took refuge in the church, after having effected the escape of the empress, who was conveyed thence in funeral procession through the besieging army, under the pretence of her being dead, but, having arrived at a certain distance, she mounted a horse, and reached Gloucester in safety.

STOCKBURY, a parish in the hundred of EYHORNE, lathe of AYLESFORD, county of KENT, 4½ miles (W. by S.) from Milton, containing 594 inhabitants. The living is a vicarage, in the archdeaconry and diocese of Canterbury, rated in the king's books at £9. 11. 0½., and in the patronage of the Dean and Chapter of Rochester. The church, dedicated to St. Mary Magdalene, is a spacious cruciform structure, in the early English style, the columns and arches of which, on the north side, are of Bethersdon marble, and peculiarly elegant. There are several streets of straggling houses in the parish, namely, Stockbury-street, Yelsted-street, South-street, North-dean, and Hill Green, an eminence commanding extensive views of the surrounding country, with the sea in the distance. A fair for toys, &c., is held on August 2nd. Mrs. Jane Bentley, in 1752, bequeathed an annuity of £2. 10. a year, for teaching three children of each sex, and £2 every fourth year to purchase bibles and prayer-books for their use. A dreadful tempest, attended with the most destructive effects, happened here in 1746.

STOCKELD, a township in the parish of SPOFFORTH, upper division of the wapentake of CLARO, West riding of the county of YORK, 2 miles (W.) from Wetherby, containing 69 inhabitants. On the margin of a lake, within this township, is a rock of a peculiar form, sixty-five feet in girth, and in height thirty, which probably gave name to the place, Stockheldt being the Dutch term for a misshapen figure of stone.

STOCKERSTON, a parish in the hundred of GARTREE, county of LEICESTER, 2¾ miles (W. S. W.) from Uppingham, containing 50 inhabitants. The living is a rectory, in the archdeaconry of Leicester, and diocese of Lincoln, rated in the king's books at £13, and in the patronage of the Master and Fellows of St. John's College, Cambridge. The church is dedicated to St. Peter. Near it, John Boyvile, Esq., in 1465, obtained leave of Edward IV. to erect, in honour of the Blessed

Virgin, an almshouse for a chaplain and three poor persons, and to settle lands upon them in mortmain, of the annual value of £10.

STOCKHAM, a township in the parish of RUNCORN, hundred of BUCKLOW, county palatine of CHESTER, 3½ miles (N. E.) from Frodsham, containing 52 inhabitants.

STOCKHILL, a joint township with Sandholme, in that part of the parish of ST. JOHN which is within the liberties of the borough of BEVERLEY, East riding of the county of YORK, 1¾ mile (N. E.) from Beverley, containing, with Sandholme, 48 inhabitants.

STOCKHILL, a joint township with Middleton, in that part of the parish of ILKLEY which is in the upper division of the wapentake of CLARO, West riding of the county of YORK, 6½ miles (N. W.) from Otley. The population is returned with Middleton.

STOCKINGFORD, a hamlet in the parish of NUNEATON, Atherstone division of the hundred of HEMLINGFORD, county of WARWICK, 1½ mile (W.) from Nuneaton. The population is returned with the parish.

STOCKLAND, a parish forming a detached portion of the hundred of WHITCHURCH-CANONICORUM, Bridport division of the county of DORSET, though locally in the county of Devon, 6¼ miles (N. E. by E.) from Honiton, containing 1147 inhabitants. The living is a vicarage, in the archdeaconry of Dorset, and diocese of Bristol, rated in the king's books at £15. 13. 11½., and in the patronage of the Freeholders and Inhabitants. The church, dedicated to St. Michael, is a large ancient structure. The parochial school is well supported by annual donations.

STOCKLAND-BRISTOL, a parish in the hundred of CANNINGTON, county of SOMERSET, 7 miles (N. W. by N.) from Bridg-water, containing 199 inhabitants. The living is a discharged vicarage, in the archdeaconry of Taunton, and diocese of Bath and Wells, rated in the king's books at £6. 9. 4., and in the patronage of the Mayor and Corporation of Bristol. The church has lately received an addition of one hundred and twenty sittings, of which eighty are free, the Incorporated Society for the enlargement of churches and chapels having granted £50 towards defraying the expense.

STOCKLEWATH-BOUND, a township in the parish of CASTLE-SOWERBY, LEATH ward, county of CUMBERLAND, 8 miles (S. by W.) from Carlisle, containing 213 inhabitants. Castle-Steads, a Roman camp, one hundred and eighty-eight yards long, and one hundred and sixty broad, is within this township : it has an inner and an outer rampart, and is placed in a triangular position with, and at an equal distance from, two other fortifications, called Whitestones and Stoneraise, the latter of which, it is supposed, was originally a burial-ground of the Druids, afterwards occupied by the Romans. About a mile from these are vestiges of a Druidical temple, where three stone coffins, containing human bones and other relics, have been found ; and a little to the southward are fragments of a large rocking-stone, to which an avenue of stones seems to have once led.

STOCKLEY, a township in the parish of BRANCEPETH, north-western division of DARLINGTON ward, county palatine of DURHAM, 4¾ miles (S. W. by W.) from Durham. containing 103 inhabitants.

STOCKLEY-ENGLISH, a parish in the western division of the hundred of BUDLEIGH, county of DEVON, 5¼ miles (N. by E.) from Crediton, containing

127 inhabitants. The living is a rectory, in the archdeaconry and diocese of Exeter, rated in the king's books at £7, and in the patronage of the Crown. The church is dedicated to St. Mary.

STOCKLEY-POMEROY, a parish in the western division of the hundred of BUDLEIGH, county of DEVON, 4¼ miles (N. E. by E.) from Crediton, containing 226 inhabitants. The living is a rectory, in the archdeaconry and diocese of Exeter, rated in the king's books at £15. 6. 8., and in the patronage of the Bishop of Exeter. The church, dedicated to St. Mary, is partly of Norman architecture, having an enriched doorway in that style.

STOCKLINCH (MAGDALENE), a parish in the hundred of ABDICK and BULSTONE, county of SOMERSET, 2¾ miles (N.E.) from Ilminster, containing 79 inhabitants. The living is a discharged rectory, in the archdeaconry of Taunton, and diocese of Bath and Wells, rated in the king's books at £4. 4. 7., endowed with £200 private benefaction, £200 royal bounty, and £300 parliamentary grant. Robert Dent, Esq. and others were patrons in 1803. The church is dedicated to St. Mary Magdalene.

STOCKLINCH (OTTERSAY), a parish in the hundred of ABDICK and BULSTONE, county of SOMERSET, 2½ miles (N. E.) from Ilminster, containing 140 inhabitants. The living is a discharged rectory, in the archdeaconry of Taunton, and diocese of Bath and Wells, rated in the king's books at £6. 9. 2., and in the patronage of Jefferys Allen, Esq. The church is dedicated to St. Mary.

Arms.

STOCKPORT, a parish in the hundred of MACCLESFIELD, county palatine of CHESTER, comprising the market town of Stockport, the chapelries of Disley, Marple, and Norbury, and the townships of Bramhall, Bredbury, Brinnington, Duckinfield, Hyde, Offerton, Romilly, Torkington, Wernith, and part of that of Etchells, and containing, according to the last census, 44,957 inhabitants (since greatly increased), of which number, 21,726 are in the town of Stockport, 39 miles (N. E. by E.) from Chester, and 179 (N. W. by N.) from London. This place, from its situation near a common centre from which several Roman roads diverged, is supposed to have been a Roman military station, and the fort to have occupied the summit of Castle hill, on the site of which the Saxons subsequently erected a baronial castle; from which, expressive of its situation in the woods, the town derived its name, Stokeport, or Stockport. Though not mentioned in Domesday-book, it is of considerable antiquity, and, till the Conquest, was a military station of some importance, most probably one of those laid waste by the Normans on their conquest of the island. In confirmation of this opinion may be adduced the name of an adjacent vill, called Portwood, also omitted in the survey, the first notice of it occurring in the records of the lands of the Baron of Dunham, under the name of Brinnington, or the burnt town. In 1173, the castle of Stokeport was held by Geoffrey de Costen-

tyn, against Henry II., but whether in his own right, or not, is uncertain. The first baron appears, from the best authority, to have been Ranulph le Dapifer, the progenitor of the family of the De Spencers, from whom it passed to Robert de Stokeport, who, in the reign of Henry III., made the town a free borough. In 1260, it obtained the grant of an annual fair for seven days, commencing on the festival of St. Wilfrid, and a weekly market on Friday. It is not distinguished by many events of historical importance : during the parliamentary war, it was garrisoned for the parliament; but Prince Rupert advancing against it with a party of the royal troops, expelled the garrison, and took possession of it for the king; it was subsequently retaken by the parliamentarians, who retained it till the termination of the war. In 1745, Stockport was twice visited by the troops under the Pretender, on their approach to Derby, and in their retreat : on the latter occasion, the bridge over the Mersey was destroyed, and the rebels, with Prince Charles, were compelled to wade through the river, in order to effect their escape. Of the ancient castle not a vestige can be traced ; a circular brick building was erected on the site, by the late Sir George Warren, as a hall for the sale of muslin, for which article of manufacture it was his wish to make this town a mart ; but since the failure of that project, the building has been converted into an inn.

Stockport is romantically situated on elevated ground of irregular and precipitous ascent, on the south bank of the river Mersey, which here sweeps round its eastern and northern boundary, and is joined by the Tame: from the banks of the former the houses rise in successive tiers round the sides of the hill, from the base to the summit, and the numerous extensive factories elevated above each other, and spreading over the extent of the town, present, when lighted during the winter months, an appearance strikingly impressive. The most ancient part surrounds the church and market-place, on the high ground overlooking the Mersey, from the bank of which several steep streets, ascending the acclivity, lead into the market-place, whence various other streets diverge in different directions : many of the houses at the base of the hill have apartments excavated in the rock, which is of soft red sand-stone. The principal street, here called the Underbank, follows the direction of the old Roman road, leading southward to Buxton, and contains an ancient timber and brick mansion, formerly occupied by the family of Arderne of Harden and Alvanley, now a banking house. On the summit of the hill is a range of houses surrounding the market-place, and to the north of the church is the site of the ancient castle, and of the Roman military works. The town extends, on the south-east, a very great distance along the road to Chester ; and on the north-east, by a bridge over the Mersey, to Portwood ; on the west towards Cheadle, and towards Manchester by another bridge across the Mersey on the north, on which side of the river is the township of Heaton-Norris, forming part of this town, though in the county of Lancaster. To prevent the inconvenience and delay of travelling through the narrow and hilly part of the town, the trustees of the Manchester and Buxton turnpike-roads applied, in 1824, for an act of parliament to empower them to construct a new line of road from Heaton-Norris chapel, on the north side of the Mersey, to Bramhall-lane, at the southern extremity of the town, through an open and airy situation, affording eligible sites for the erection of houses, and an admirable opportunity for improving and extending the town. This important work was commenced in the same year, and completed under the superintendence of Mr. Thomas Broadhurst, general surveyor and architect for the trustees. Its especial object was, to cross the river without the necessity of descending from the high grounds on each side to the level of the vale of the Mersey, which has been accomplished by the construction of a noble bridge, of eleven arches, across the valley and the river, of which nine are on the Cheshire, and two on the Lancashire, side of the Mersey. The arch over the river has a span of more than ninety feet, and an elevation of forty feet above the water, and is built of hard white stone from the Saddleworth and Runcorn quarries; the two arches on the Lancashire side are of brick, each nine yards in span: those on the Cheshire side are carried over several of the streets, the thoroughfare being continued underneath, and others are closed up, forming commodious warehouses. From the last of them the road is carried for a considerable distance over an artificial embankment, formed of earth cut from the hill through which it passes, to its junction with the Warrington road, near which it again joins the old road at Heaviley, at the distance of three miles from its commencement. The whole expense of this work, which was completed in less than two years, was £40,000: the road throughout is twenty-four yards in width, and it was opened to the public in 1826, with a splendid procession, on the anniversary of the battle of Waterloo, in reference to which event it has been called the Wellington road. Between this and the Lancashire bridge, a foot bridge, termed Vernon bridge, over the Mersey, forming an intermediate and more direct communication between the town and the township of Heaton-Norris, has been built by subscription, the first stone having been laid in 1828.

The town is well paved, and lighted with gas, and the inhabitants are amply supplied with water. An act of parliament for incorporating a gas company, and another for the construction of water-works, were obtained in 1825, and in the following year an act for the general improvement of the town was passed, under which commissioners are appointed for that purpose. A handsome library and news-room was erected, in 1830, by Mr. W. Turner; this institution, which combines the four subscription libraries formerly established, is liberally supported by numerous proprietary subscribers: there is also a neat theatre, which is open for four months during the winter. The surrounding scenery is richly diversified with hill and dale, wood and water. The winding and throwing of silk, for which mills were first established here upon the Italian plan, have been nearly superseded by the introduction of the cotton manufacture, which has for some years been the staple trade of the town: of the former there are still some respectable factories; but the latter, since its introduction, has been rapidly increasing, and has attained, both for its extent and the perfection to which it has been brought, a very high degree of celebrity. There are within the town, including Heaton-Norris and Portwood, not less than fifty cotton factories, worked by sixty-five steam-engines, of the aggregate power of one thousand nine hundred

and eighty horses, and by water-wheels; and in the manufacture of the different cottons and calicos, six thousand three hundred and fifty power-looms are constantly employed: the printing of calico is carried on to a very great extent, and there are many large establishments and dye-houses in the vicinity. Of these the most extensive, belonging to Messrs. Marsland and Son, which is also connected with the blue dye-works, has paid to Government duties in one year amounting to more than £100,000. The weaving of calico has spread over all the neighbouring villages, which in some instances have become virtually a part of the town. The manufacture of hats has been long established, and is carried on to a very considerable extent for the supply of the London, and many of the principal country, markets. The manufacture of a very superior kind of woollen cloth, equal in the smoothness of its texture and the silkiness of its surface to the best cloths of France, was established by the late Peter Marsland, Esq. with great success, and is deservedly encouraged: there are also several extensive thread manufactories. Connected with the various branches of manufacture, the construction of machinery affords employment to a great number of persons, and of several additional steam-engines, others again being used in grinding corn and for other purposes. The importance of Stockport, as a manufacturing town, has been materially promoted by the facility and the abundance of its supply of coal from Poynton, Worth, and Norbury, and the neighbouring districts on the line of the Manchester and Ashton canal, which joins the Peak Forest canal, a branch of the latter extending to this town, and affords also a direct communication with the principal towns in the kingdom. The market, on Friday, is more abundantly supplied with corn, meal, and cheese, than any other market in the county: in the higher part of the town (the Hillgate), extensive and convenient shambles, covering an area of two thousand square yards, have been built for the inhabitants of the vicinity. The fairs are March 4th and 25th, May 1st, and October 23rd, for cattle. Stockport was anciently incorporated: it still retains the office of mayor, which, however, is merely nominal, and it is now within the jurisdiction of the county magistrates, who sit daily at the court-house, and hold a petty session every alternate week. The police is regulated by commissioners appointed by act of parliament in 1826, for this and the general improvement of the town. Courts leet and baron are held twice in the year; at the Michaelmas court the mayor is chosen, by the jury, from four burgesses, nominated by the lord of the manor, who appoints two constables and other officers, to the number of fifty, who are sworn into office at an adjourned court. The churchwardens are appointed by the four lords of the manors of Bramhall, Bredbury, Brinnington, and Norbury, who from time immemorial have represented the parish in ecclesiastical matters. The ancient court baron, for the recovery of debts under 40s., has fallen into disuse; and a court for the recovery of debts not exceeding £5 has been established, by an act passed in the 46th of George III., the jurisdiction of which extends over the townships of Stockport and Brinnington, and the hamlets of Edgeley and Brinksway.

The living is a rectory, in the archdeaconry and diocese of Chester, rated in the king's books at £70. 6. 8., endowed with £200 private benefaction, and £200 royal bounty, and in the patronage of the Hon. Frances Maria Warren. The ancient church, dedicated to St. Mary, and supposed to have been erected in the fourteenth century, having been built of the soft red sand-stone in the neighbourhood, and fallen to decay, was, with the exception of the chancel, rebuilt, at an expense of £30,000, by act of parliament passed in the 50th of George III., and an extensive cemetery added to it. The present structure, situated on the eastern side of the market-place, is a handsome building in the later style of English architecture, with a lofty square tower, crowned with a pierced parapet and pinnacles; the pillars of the nave are carried up to the roof, producing an unusual, but impressive, effect from the loftiness of their elevation (an arrangement affording ample accommodation for galleries, which the increasing population of the parish rendered highly necessary). The chancel, which was in the decorated style of English architecture, has undergone considerable alteration, but still retains some of the ancient stone stalls, which are of elegant design, and the original window has been removed only within the last few years. Several of the ancient monuments have been preserved, and are distributed in various parts of the church. St. Peter's chapel, a neat edifice of brick, was erected in 1768, at the sole expense of William Wright, Esq., of Mottram, St. Andrew, to whom a handsome mural monument has been erected in the centre of the north aisle. The living is a perpetual curacy, endowed with £120 per annum, arising from lands in Mobberley, £200 private benefaction, and £200 royal bounty, and in the patronage of Lawrence Wright, Esq. The church dedicated to St. Thomas, containing one thousand nine hundred and ninety-two sittings, of which nine hundred and seventy-two are free, was erected in 1825, by grant from the parliamentary commissioners, at an expense of £14,555. 13.: it is a handsome structure, in the Grecian style of architecture, with a tower surmounted by a cupola; the principal entrance is at the east end, through a noble portico of six lofty Ionic pillars: the interior is handsomely decorated; from the panelled pedestals that support the galleries rises a beautiful range of fluted Corinthian columns, sustaining the roof; corresponding with which is a series of pilasters of the same order, supporting a handsome entablature and cornice; the ceilings are panelled in large compartments; and above the altar, which occupies the whole central breadth, is a pediment, resting on Ionic pillars, and surmounted on the apex by a gilt cross. The living is a perpetual curacy, in the patronage of the Hon. Frances Maria Warren. There are three places of worship for Independents, three for Wesleyan Methodists, and one each for the Society of Friends, Primitive Methodists, Methodists of the New Connexion, Unitarians, and Roman Catholics.

The free grammar school was founded, in 1482, by Sir Edmund Shaa, or Shaw, citizen and goldsmith of London, who endowed it with £10 per annum, to which several subsequent benefactions have been added. The Goldsmiths' Company, who are patrons, have erected, on the Wellington road, a handsome and extensive school-room, with a house for the master, in the later style of English architecture, at an expense of £4000, on a site of land comprising seven hundred and fifty square yards,

presented for that purpose by the Hon. Frances Maria Warren, Lady Vernon. The National school was established in 1826, and is supported by subscription; the school-rooms are a handsome and spacious edifice of brick, fronted with stone, and well adapted to the purpose; there are two thousand five hundred children of both sexes instructed in this establishment. A school upon a very extensive and comprehensive plan, admitting children of all denominations, was established in 1805, and a very extensive building of brick, four stories high, was erected for its use, at an expense of £10,000, raised by subscription; there are four thousand children belonging to this institution, who are instructed by three hundred gratuitous teachers: attached to it are four branch schools, in the vicinity of the town, erected at an expense of £6000, in which one thousand five hundred children are taught, who cannot conveniently attend the parent establishment. These and some others, all supported by subscription, afford instruction to more than ten thousand children. Sunday schools are also supported in connexion with the established church and the several dissenting congregations. On the eastern side of the old churchyard are six almshouses, founded by an ancestor of the late Sir George Warren, in 1685, for six aged men. The allowance was augmented to £1. 5. by Humphrey Warren, Esq., who died in the middle of the last century, and the late Lady Bulkeley bequeathed £1200, vesting it in trustees, for the same purpose, and £1000 for the poor of Stockport. A dispensary was established, and a commodious building erected, by subscription, in 1797, to which nine fever wards were added in 1799: it is liberally supported, and affords relief to two thousand patients annually. There is a bequest by Mr. Wright, for apprenticing four children, besides some other bequests for distribution among the poor.

STOCKSFIELD-HALL, a township in the parish of Bywell St. Andrew, eastern division of Tindale ward, county of Northumberland, 9 miles (E. by S.) from Hexham, containing 23 inhabitants. It is bounded on the north by the Tyne.

STOCKTON, a township in the parish of Malpas, higher division of the hundred of Broxton, county palatine of Chester, 1¾ mile (S. S. W.) from Malpas, containing 32 inhabitants.

STOCKTON, a parish in the hundred of Clavering, county of Norfolk, 3 miles (N. W. by N.) from Beccles, containing 92 inhabitants. The living is a discharged rectory, in the archdeaconry of Norfolk, and diocese of Norwich, rated in the king's books at £8. Philip Rundell, Esq. was patron in 1816. The church is dedicated to St. Michael.

STOCKTON, a parish in the Shiffnall division of the hundred of Brimstree, county of Salop, 4¾ miles (N. by E.) from Bridgenorth, containing 500 inhabitants. The living is a rectory, with the perpetual curacy of Boningale, in the archdeaconry of Salop, and diocese of Lichfield and Coventry, rated in the king's books at £13. 11. 3. T. Whitmore, Esq. was patron in 1811. The church is dedicated to St. Chad.

STOCKTON, a parish in the Southam division of the hundred of Knightlow, county of Warwick, 2¼ miles (N. E. by E.) from Southam, containing 344 inhabitants. The living is a rectory, in the archdeaconry of Coventry, and diocese of Lichfield and Coventry, rated in the king's books at £10. 7. 1., and in the patronage of the Warden and Fellows of New College, Oxford. The church is dedicated to St. Michael. The Warwick and Napton canal passes in the vicinity. The Rev. Charles Crane, in 1807, gave a house towards the support of a school, in which fifty children are instructed for £12 a year, arising from the church lands.

STOCKTON, a parish forming a detached portion of the hundred of ELSTUB and EVERLEY, county of WILTS, 6¼ miles (N.E.) from Hindon, containing 267 inhabitants. The living is a rectory, in the archdeaconry and diocese of Salisbury, rated in the king's books at £18. 2. 1., and in the patronage of the Bishop of Winchester. The church is dedicated to St. John the Baptist.

STOCKTON, a parish in the lower division of the hundred of DODDINGTREE, county of WORCESTER, 7¼ miles (S. W.) from Bewdley, containing 168 inhabitants. The living is a discharged rectory, in the archdeaconry of Salop, and diocese of Hereford, rated in the king's books at £5. 13. 11½., and in the patronage of the Rev. T. Houlbrooke. The church is dedicated to St. Andrew. The river Teme runs through the parish.

STOCKTON on the FOREST, a parish partly within the liberty of ST. PETER of YORK, East riding, and partly in the wapentake of BULMER, North riding, of the county of YORK, 5¼ miles (N. E.) from York, containing 357 inhabitants. The living is a perpetual curacy, in the peculiar jurisdiction and patronage of the Prebendary of Bugthorpe in the Cathedral Church of York, endowed with £600 royal bounty, and £200 parliamentary grant. There is a place of worship for Wesleyan Methodists.

STOCKTON upon TEES, a parish in the south-western division of STOCKTON ward, county palatine of DURHAM, comprising the incorporated market town and port of Stockton upon Tees, and the townships of Hartburn and Preston upon Tees, and containing 5184 inhabitants, of which number, 5006 are in the town

Corporate Seal.

of Stockton upon Tees, 20 miles (S. S. E.) from Durham, and 244 (N. by W.) from London. This place is of considerable antiquity, and the discovery of a Roman coin, near the site of the castle, has led to the conjecture that it was a Roman station, but nothing farther to confirm this opinion is recorded : it formed a part of the possessions of the see of Durham at an early period, and the castle was occupied by Hugh de Pudsey, Bishop of that diocese in the reign of Richard I. His successor Philip de Poictou entertained King John here in 1214, and the charter granted by that monarch to the burgesses of Newcastle bears date at Stockton. It continued to be the occasional residence of the Bishops of Durham, and seems to have escaped in a great measure the commotions and border feuds which then agitated this part of England, with the exception of an inroad of the Scots in 1322, who plundered and burnt the town. At the period of the parliamentary war the castle was taken

possession of by the royalists, some importance being attached to its commanding the old passage of the Tees; it was afterwards surrendered to the parliamentary forces, and in 1645 was garrisoned by the Scots but delivered by them to the English ; in 1647 it was ordered by the parliament to be dismantled, and about five years afterwards its complete destruction was accomplished, no part of the structure now remaining, although the fosse may still be traced. The town is said to have felt the shock of an earthquake in 1780, and to have suffered severely from the overflowing of the river in 1771, 1783, and 1822. It is situated on an eminence on the northern bank of the Tees, and has advanced rapidly in prosperity since the middle of the seventeenth century, at which period it consisted principally of mean hovels, the better houses being constructed with "post and pile," and not one built of brick. It is now one of the cleanest and handsomest towns in the northern part of the kingdom : the main street, which is about half a mile in length, is broad, and contains some good houses, chiefly of brick, the few of stone having been erected with the materials of the dilapidated castle : from this street smaller ones branch off towards the river, and on the western side of the town a great number of new houses has been recently built : the streets are well paved, and lighted with gas, under the authority of an act of parliament passed in 1822. A handsome stone bridge crosses the river, which was commenced in 1764, and completed in 1769, at an expense of £8000, raised by subscription on shares ; it has five elliptical arches, the span of the central arch being seventy-two feet, and its height from low water mark twenty-three : an annuity of £90 per annum, with £3 for every acre of land occupied by the road leading to the bridge, was directed, by the act of parliament under which it was constructed, to be paid to the Bishop of Durham, as a compensation for the tolls of the ferry which existed previously ; land was purchased for the bishop in lieu of this annuity, and the debt having been paid off, the tolls ceased in 1820. The theatre, in Green Dragon yard, Finkle-street, is a neat building. A Mechanics' institute and library was established in 1824 ; it contains upwards of three hundred volumes, with apparatus for lecturing, and the members are increasing annually in number : there is also a subscription library and news-room. Races are held annually in August, a week after those of York, on the Carrs, on the opposite side of the river ; and assemblies occasionally in a room in the town hall.

The situation of Stockton, on a river navigable ten miles above it, and within the same distance of the sea, affords it many commercial advantages, and the increased shipping, and amount of duties, evince the progressive extension of its mercantile interests. The port is a member of that of Newcastle upon Tyne ; the dues are the property of the bishop, and are held on lease by the corporation, vessels from the cinque-ports being exempted from the payment of them. Ships of large size were formerly obliged to receive and unload their cargoes at Portrack, a mile down the river, or at Cargo-Fleet, or Cleveland Port, a mile lower on the Yorkshire side ; but, in 1808, a company was incorporated by act of parliament, called the "Tees Navigation Company," and a canal was cut from Portrack to the town, capable of admitting vessels of three hundred tons'

burden, which has greatly benefited the trade of the town, and amply repaid the shareholders : another act was recently obtained for the extension of this canal to Newport, a distance of nearly two miles. In 1815, this port was made a bonding-port for certain goods : its principal trade coastwise is with London, Hull, Leith, Sunderland, &c., and comprises the exportation of most articles of agricultural produce, linen and worsted yarn, and more particularly lead, of which many hundred tons, brought chiefly from Yorkshire and the borders of Durham and Northumberland, are annually shipped ; it also forms the chief article of exportation in its foreign trade, which is with the Baltic, Holland, Hamburgh, and the British and American colonies, whence it receives in return materials for ship-building, timber for other purposes, tallow, &c. Two shipping companies in the London, and two in the foreign, trade have been established. The principal branches of manufacture are those connected with the shipping, there being two ship-builders' yards, five manufactories for sail-cloth, two rope-walks, two iron-foundries, and a block and pump manufactory; there are also three breweries, some corn-mills, a mill for spinning yarn, and one for worsted. The fishery of the Tees was formerly a great source of prosperity to the town, but it has considerably declined; eastward of the bridge it belongs to the bishop, but is open to poor fishermen under certain regulations. A rail-road from Witton Park and other collieries, by Darlington, to this place, was constructed in 1825, and is productive of great advantage : by a recent act of parliament the line has been extended to Middlesbro', about four miles lower down the river, where commodious staiths have been erected. On the decline of Hartlepool, in 1680, Stockton was selected as the port for the establishment of the principal officers of the customs, and three legal, or free, quays were appointed. The custom-house, a plain commodious building, was erected, in 1730, by the corporation, on the site of the old building ; the out-stations are Hartlepool and Seaton. The market, granted by Bishop Anthony Beck, in 1310, is on Wednesday and Saturday, and is well attended ; and the shambles, erected in 1825, in front of the town hall, form a neat range of enclosed brick buildings : a handsome stone column, of the Doric order, thirty-three feet high, stands in the centre of the market-place. Fairs are held on the last Wednesday before the 13th of May, and the 23rd of November, which are general and statute fairs, and there are cattle fairs on the last Wednesday in every month.

The period at which Stockton was incorporated is uncertain, but is supposed to be about the commencement of the thirteenth century ; the last charter was granted by Bishop Cosin, in 1666. The corporation consists of a mayor and an indefinite number of aldermen and burgesses, assisted by a recorder, steward of the borough court, town serjeant, and inferior officers. The mayor, who must be an admitted burgess, is chosen annually, at a court leet held on the first Tuesday after the 29th of September, by a majority of burgesses ; there is no specific nomination of aldermen, but the burgesses who have served the office of mayor are so denominated. The mayor is a justice of the peace ; his jurisdiction on the river, under the bishop, empowers him to levy a duty on all vessels entering the harbour ;

it extends from the bar to the Wathstead, betwixt Aislaby and Middleton St. George. The town comprises two constablewicks, one called the Borough, including that part which is wholly freehold, and the other called the Town, consisting of that portion which is held by copy of court roll under the Bishop of Durham ; they form, however, but one township, uniting in the maintenance of the poor. The bishop is lord of the borough, and holds courts leet and baron by his steward, who is generally the recorder ; suits of trespass and debts under 40s. are cognizable by these courts, the jurisdiction of which is limited to the borough. A halmote court is also held twice a year, in which similar causes are tried as in the court baron. Petty sessions for Stockton ward are holden here. The municipal business is transacted in the town hall, built in 1735, and enlarged in 1744 : it stands nearly in the centre of the main street, and is a handsome quadrangular brick building, surmounted by a light clock-tower and a spire, with a piazza stretching along the lower story on its north side ; the upper part of the building contains a court-room, an assembly-room, and other apartments, and the lower part is disposed in shops, &c.

Stockton was formerly a chapelry in the parish of Norton, from which it was separated by an act of parliament obtained in 1713, and constituted a distinct parish. The living is a vicarage not in charge, in the archdeaconry and diocese of Durham, and in the patronage of the Bishop of Durham. The ancient chapel, supposed to have been built about the year 1237, was taken down, and the building of the present church was completed in 1712, at an expense of about £1600 : it is dedicated to St. Thomas, and is a neat and commodious edifice of brick, with a tower, eighty feet high, at the western end ; in the vestry-room is a small library, chiefly of theological works. There are places of worship for Particular Baptists, the Society of Friends, Independents, Primitive and Wesleyan Methodists, Unitarians, and Roman Catholics, several of which have Sunday schools attached. A charity school was founded, in 1721, by subscription ; and since that period has been supported by various benefactions, which have been chiefly laid out in the purchase of land, aided by voluntary contributions. The building, comprising separate school-rooms for the boys and the girls, and a dwelling-house for the master and the mistress, was erected in 1786, George Browne, Esq. having given £1000 for that purpose ; twenty boys and twenty girls are clothed, and upwards of two hundred boys and sixty girls instructed, in this establishment. A school of industry for girls, instituted in 1803, is supported by voluntary subscription ; it affords instruction to about forty children. In 1785, a room for a grammar school was erected by subscription ; it possesses no endowment, but the corporation give a small annual stipend towards its support. Stockton, in conjunction with Norton, is entitled to a scholarship at Brasenose College, Oxford, with an endowment of £8 per annum, founded by Dr. Claymond, formerly vicar of Norton. The almshouses were originally erected about the year 1682, and were rebuilt in 1816, from a bequest of £3000 by George Browne, Esq.; they contain eighteen apartments, in which thirty-six poor persons are lodged, who are appointed by the overseers, and a committee for managing the affairs of the poor, and have a small endowment; there are some other tri-fling bequests for the benefit of the poor. The dispensary, founded in 1792, and revived in 1815, occupies a part of the workhouse. The savings' bank, established in 1815, is held in a room in the almshouses. There are several benefit societies in the town. Stockton is the birthplace of Joseph Ritson, a refined critic, and author of "Ancient Songs and Metrical Romances;" of Brass Crosby, Lord Mayor of London at the period of the commotions occasioned by the prosecution of Wilkes, who was committed to the Tower for refusing to allow a warrant, issued by the Speaker of the House of Commons, to be executed in the city; and of Joseph Reed, a dramatic poet.

STOCKWELL, a chapelry in the parish of LAMBETH, eastern division of the hundred of BRIXTON, county of SURREY, 3 miles (S. S. W.) from London. The population is returned with the parish. The streets are lighted with gas, and the inhabitants are supplied with water from the South London water-works. Here is an extensive ale brewery. The chapel, erected by certain proprietors, is dependent on the mother church at Lambeth, and has been repaired within the last few years. There are places of worship for Baptists and Independents. A National school, for one hundred and eighty boys and one hundred and twenty girls, is supported by voluntary contribution; the school-house was erected in 1818. This chapelry is within the jurisdiction of the court of requests held in the borough of Southwark, and within the limits of the new police act.

STOCKWITH (EAST), a hamlet in the parish of GAINSBOROUGH, wapentake of CORRINGHAM, parts of LINDSEY, county of LINCOLN, 3¾ miles (N. N. W.) from Gainsborough, containing 224 inhabitants. There is a place of worship for Wesleyan Methodists.

STOCKWITH (WEST), a chapelry in the parish of MISTERTON, North-clay division of the wapentake of BASSETLAW, county of NOTTINGHAM, 4 miles (N. N. W.) from Gainsborough, containing 618 inhabitants. There is a place of worship for Wesleyan Methodists. Ten poor children are instructed for £10 a year, paid by the trustee of the late William Huntington. It is within the peculiar jurisdiction of the manorial court of Gringley on the Hill.

STOCKWOOD, a parish in the liberty of SUTTON-POINTZ, Dorchester division, though locally in the Sherborne division, of the county of DORSET, 8 miles (S. S. W.) from Sherborne, containing 33 inhabitants. The living is a discharged rectory, in the peculiar jurisdiction of the Dean of Salisbury, rated in the king's books at £5. 13. 4., and in the patronage of Thomas Bellamy, Esq. The church is dedicated to St. Edwold.

STODDAY, a joint township with Ashton, that part of the parish of LANCASTER which is in the hundred of LONSDALE, south of the sands, county palatine of LANCASTER, 2 miles (S. S. W.) from Lancaster. The population is returned with Ashton.

STODMARSH, a parish in the hundred of DOWN-HAMFORD, lathe of ST. AUGUSTINE, county of KENT, 4½ miles (E. N. E.) from Canterbury, containing 122 inhabitants. The living is a perpetual curacy, in the archdeaconry and diocese of Canterbury, endowed with £200 private benefaction, and £200 royal bounty, and in the patronage of the Archdeacon of Canterbury. The

church, dedicated to St. Mary, is in the early style of English architecture.

STODY, a parish in the hundred of HOLT, county of NORFOLK, 3 miles (S. W. by S.) from Holt, containing 125 inhabitants. The living is a discharged rectory, with that of Hunworth united, in the archdeaconry and diocese of Norwich, rated in the king's books at £6. 3. 4., and in the patronage of Lord Suffield. The church is dedicated to St. Mary. Three pounds per annum, the gift of a Mr. Symonds, is applied for teaching poor children.

STOGUMBER, a parish in the hundred of WILLITON and FREEMANNERS, county of SOMERSET, 7 miles (N. by E.) from Wiveliscombe, containing 1281 inhabitants. The living is a discharged vicarage, in the archdeaconry of Taunton, and diocese of Bath and Wells, rated in the king's books at £11. 18. 7½., and in the patronage of the Dean and Chapter of Wells. The church is dedicated to St. Mary. There is a place of worship for Baptists. A market was formerly held on Saturday, and fairs are still held on May 6th and Aug. 1st. Roman coins have been discovered here.

STOGURSEY, or STOKE-COURCY, a parish in the hundred of CANNINGTON, county of SOMERSET, 8½ miles (N. W. by W.) from Bridg-water, containing, with the hamlet of Fairfield, 1362 inhabitants. The living is a vicarage, with the perpetual curacy of Lilstock annexed, in the archdeaconry of Taunton, and diocese of Bath and Wells, rated in the king's books at £16. 7. 6., and in the patronage of the Provost and Fellows of Eton College. The church is dedicated to St. Andrew. The parish is bounded on the north by the Bristol channel. Ten children are instructed for a rent-charge of £2, bequeathed by Mr. Daniel, in 1764. A Benedictine priory, a cell to the abbey of L'Onley in Normandy, was founded here in the reign of Henry II., which at the suppression was valued at £58 per annum, and granted by Henry VI. to Eton College.

STOKE, a township in the parish of ACTON, hundred of NANTWICH, county palatine of CHESTER, 3½ miles (N. W.) from Nantwich, containing 137 inhabitants. The Chester canal passes through the township.

STOKE, a parish in the higher division of the hundred of WIRRALL, county palatine of CHESTER, comprising the townships of Great Stanney, Little Stanney, and Stoke, and part of that of Whitby, and containing 461 inhabitants, of which number, 129 are in the township of Stoke, 4¾ miles (N. by E.) from Chester. The living is a perpetual curacy, in the archdeaconry and diocese of Chester, endowed with £200 private benefaction, and £200 royal bounty, and in the patronage of Sir H. E. Bunbury, Bart. The church, which is the burial-place of the Bunbury family, has a Norman doorway, some ancient wooden screen-work, and a small chapel attached to the south side of the chancel: it was partially rebuilt in 1827, and has received an addition of fifty-five free sittings, the Incorporated Society for the enlargement of churches and chapels having granted £50 towards defraying the expense. A school, founded here about 1670, by Sir Thomas Bunbury, Bart., is endowed with the interest of £200.

STOKE, a parish in the county of the city of Coventry, 1½ mile (E.) from Coventry, containing 572 inhabitants. The living is a vicarage not in charge, with that of Sow, or Walsgrave, annexed, in the archdeaconry of Coventry, and diocese of Lichfield and Coventry, and in the patronage of the Crown. The church, dedicated to St. Michael, has lately received an addition of forty-four free sittings, the Incorporated Society for the enlargement of churches and chapels having granted £20 towards defraying the expense. The Coventry canal passes through the parish.

STOKE, a township in the parish of HOPE, hundred of HIGH PEAK, county of DERBY, 1½ mile (N. E.) from Stoney-Middleton, containing 74 inhabitants. It is in the honour of Tutbury, duchy of Lancaster, and within the jurisdiction of a court of pleas held at Chapel en le Frith every third Tuesday, for the recovery of debts under 40s.

STOKE, a parish in the hundred of Hoo, lathe of AYLESFORD, county of KENT, 8 miles (N. E.) from Rochester, containing 350 inhabitants. The living is a discharged vicarage, in the archdeaconry and diocese of Rochester, rated in the king's books at £8. 11. 8., endowed with £200 private benefaction, and £200 royal bounty. B. Duppa, Esq. was patron in 1811. The church is dedicated to St. Peter.

STOKE (BISHOP'S), a tything in the parish of WESTBURY upon TRIM, lower division of the hundred of HENBURY, county of GLOUCESTER, 2¼ miles (N. W. by N.) from Bristol, containing 1883 inhabitants.

STOKE (BISHOP'S), a parish in the hundred of FAWLEY, Fawley division of the county of SOUTHAMPTON, 6½ miles (W. by N.) from Bishop's Waltham, containing 1007 inhabitants. The living is a rectory, in the archdeaconry and diocese of Winchester, rated in the king's books at £14. 17. 6., and in the patronage of the Bishop of Winchester. The church is dedicated to St. Mary.

STOKE by CLARE, a parish in the hundred of RISBRIDGE, county of SUFFOLK, 2¼ miles (S. W. by W.) from Clare, containing 746 inhabitants. The living is a perpetual curacy, in the archdeaconry of Sudbury, and diocese of Norwich, endowed with £1200 parliamentary grant, and in the patronage of Sir W. B. Rush, Bart. The church is dedicated to St. Augustine. The navigable river Stour passes on the south of the parish. Sir Gervaise Elwes, Bart., in 1678, bequeathed a rent-charge of £10 for teaching poor children.

STOKE (DRY), a parish partly in the hundred of GARTREE, county of LEICESTER, but chiefly in the hundred of WRANDIKE, county of RUTLAND, 3½ miles (S. S. W.) from Uppingham, containing, with the liberty of Holy-Oakes, 59 inhabitants. The living is a rectory, in the archdeaconry of Northampton, and diocese of Peterborough, rated in the king's books at £11. 2. 1., and in the patronage of the Marquis of Exeter. The church is dedicated to St. Andrew.

STOKE (EARL), county of WILTS.—See EARL-STOKE.

STOKE (EAST), a parish in the hundred of WINFRITH, Blandford (South) division of the county of DORSET, 4 miles (W. by S.) from Wareham, containing, with the tything of Worgret, 519 inhabitants. The living is a rectory, in the archdeaconry of Dorset, and diocese of Bristol, rated in the king's books at £14. 12. 11., and in the patronage of Sir W. Oglander, Bart. The church is dedicated to St. Mary.

STOKE (EAST), near NEWARK, a parish in the northern division of the wapentake of THURGARTON,

county of NOTTINGHAM, 3¾ miles (S. W.) from Newark, containing 424 inhabitants. The living is a discharged vicarage, with the perpetual curacies of Coddington and Syerston annexed, in the archdeaconry of Nottingham, and diocese of York, rated in the king's books at £8. 13., and in the patronage of the Chancellor of the Cathedral Church of Lincoln. The church is dedicated to St. Oswald. The river Trent and the old Fosse road pass through the parish. An hospital, dedicated to St. Leonard, was founded here before the time of Henry I. for a master and brethren, chaplains, and several sick persons, whose revenue at the dissolution was valued at £9. On Stoke field was fought, in 1487, the decisive battle between the armies of Henry VII. and John de la Pole, Earl of Lincoln, who had espoused the cause of the impostor Lambert Simnel, in which the earl and four thousand of his followers were slain : this is said to be the first action wherein cannon was used with success : human bones, fragments of armour, coins, &c., have been frequently ploughed up on the spot.

STOKE (ST. GREGORY), a parish in the hundred of NORTH CURRY, county of SOMERSET, 5 miles (W. by N.) from Langport, containing, with the tythings of Higher, Middle, Morland, and Stath divisions, 1369 inhabitants. The living is a perpetual curacy, annexed to the vicarage of North Curry, in the peculiar jurisdiction of the Dean and Chapter of Wells. The parish is bounded on the north-east by the navigable river Parret, and on the north-west by the Tone, which latter is crossed by three bridges, one of them forming a connexion with the Isle of Athelney, famous as the retreat of the renowned Alfred.

STOKE next GUILDFORD, a parish in the first division of the hundred of WOKING, county of SURREY, ¾ of a mile (N.) from Guildford, containing 1120 inhabitants. The living is a rectory, in the archdeaconry of Surrey, and diocese of Winchester, rated in the king's books at £18. 0. 5., and in the patronage of F. Paynter, Esq. The church, dedicated to St. John the Evangelist, is in the later style of English architecture. The Wey and Arun canal passes through the parish.

STOKE under HAMDON, a parish in the hundred of TINTINHULL, county of SOMERSET, 5¾ miles (W. by N.) from Yeovil, containing 1072 inhabitants. The living is a rectory, in the archdeaconry of Wells, and diocese of Bath and Wells, rated in the king's books at £5. 10. 2½., and in the patronage of Andrew Bain, Esq. The church is dedicated to St. Denis. A free chapel, or chantry, for a provost and four priests, in honour of St. Nicholas, was founded in 1304, by Sir John Beauchamp, Knt., in the ancient castle of which, in the time of Leland, there were extensive remains near the village, as also in the chapel many old sepulchral monuments, statues, &c., without inscriptions, and a flat marble stone, with the effigy of Maheu de Gurney, dated 1406. Here is a considerable manufacture of gloves.

STOKE (HOLY CROSS), a parish in the hundred of HENSTEAD, county of NORFOLK, 5½ miles (N. E. by N.) from St. Mary Stratton, containing 303 inhabitants. The living is a vicarage, in the archdeaconry of Norfolk, and diocese of Norwich, and in the patronage of the Dean and Chapter of Norwich. The church is dedicated to the Holy Cross.

STOKE (LIMPLEY), a joint chapelry with Winsley, in the parish of GREAT BRADFORD, hundred of BRADFORD, county of WILTS, 3 miles (W. by S.) from Bradford. The population is returned with Winsley. The chapel is dedicated to St. Mary.

STOKE (ST. MARY), a parish in the hundred of TAUNTON and TAUNTON-DEAN, county of SOMERSET, 3¼ miles (S. E. by E.) from Taunton, containing 248 inhabitants. The living is a rectory, annexed to the perpetual curacy of Thurlbear, in the archdeaconry of Taunton, and diocese of Bath and Wells. There is a place of worship for Independents.

STOKE (ST. MILBOROUGH), a parish partly in the hundred of MUNSLOW, but chiefly in the liberty of the borough of WENLOCK, county of SALOP, 7 miles (N. E. by N.) from Ludlow, containing, with the chapelry of Heath, 595 inhabitants. The living is a vicarage, in the archdeaconry of Salop, and diocese of Hereford, rated in the king's books at £6. 13. 4. The Rev. George Morgan was patron in 1819. The church is dedicated to St. Milburgh.

STOKE near NAYLAND, a parish in the hundred of BABERGH, county of SUFFOLK, 2 miles (N. E. by N.) from Nayland, containing 1393 inhabitants. The living is a vicarage, in the archdeaconry of Sudbury, and diocese of Norwich, rated in the king's books at £19. 0. 10., and in the patronage of Sir William Rowley, Bart. The church, dedicated to St. Mary, is a spacious structure, in the later style of English architecture, with a finely-proportioned tower. A monastery existed here in the middle of the tenth century, to which Earl Alfgar and his daughters Æthelfled and Ægelfled made considerable donations, it being the burial-place of that noble family.

STOKE (NORTH), a township in that part of the parish of SOUTH STOKE which is in the wapentake of WINNIBRIGGS and THREO, parts of KESTEVEN, county of LINCOLN, 2¾ miles (N. by W.) from Colsterworth, containing 128 inhabitants.

STOKE (NORTH), a parish in the hundred of LANGTREE, county of OXFORD, 2½ miles (S.) from Wallingford, containing 203 inhabitants. The living is a vicarage, with the perpetual curacy of Newnham-Murren annexed, in the archdeaconry and diocese of Oxford, rated in the king's books at £14. 10., and in the patronage of the Master and Fellows of St. John's College, Cambridge. The church is dedicated to St. Mary.

STOKE (NORTH), a parish in the hundred of BATH-FORUM, county of SOMERSET, 4¼ miles (N. W.) from Bath, containing 129 inhabitants. The living is a discharged rectory, in the archdeaconry of Bath, and diocese of Bath and Wells, rated in the king's books at £5. 7. 6., and in the patronage of the Crown. The church is dedicated to St. Martin. The parish is bounded on the west by the river Avon, the ground gradually rising from that river to the heights of Lansdown, which gives the title of marquis to the family of Petty.

STOKE (NORTH), a parish in the hundred of POLING, rape of ARUNDEL, county of SUSSEX, 3 miles (N. by E.) from Arundel, containing 63 inhabitants. The living is a vicarage, in the archdeaconry and diocese of Chichester, rated in the king's books at £5. 14. 4½., endowed with £600 royal bounty, and £400

parliamentary grant, and in the patronage of the Earl of Egremont. The river Avon separates this parish from that of South Stoke.

STOKE (RODNEY), a parish in the hundred of WINTERSTOKE, county of SOMERSET, 5 miles (N. W. by W.) from Wells, containing 272 inhabitants. The living is a discharged rectory, in the archdeaconry of Wells, and diocese of Bath and Wells, rated in the king's books at £8. 12. 8½., endowed with £200 royal bounty, and in the patronage of the Bishop of Bath and Wells. The church, dedicated to St. Leonard, is principally in the Norman style of architecture, and has a curious ancient font. Here is a small endowed almshouse. This was long the seat of the knightly family of Rodney, whose descendant, the distinguished admiral, was elevated to the peerage, as Baron Rodney of Rodney-Stoke, in 1782, for the memorable victory he had achieved over the French fleet commanded by the Compte de Grasse.

STOKE (SEVERN), a parish in the lower division of the hundred of PERSHORE, county of WORCESTER, 3 miles (N. by E.) from Upton upon Severn, containing 666 inhabitants. The living is a rectory, in the archdeaconry and diocese of Worcester, rated in the king's books at £21. 17. 4., and in the patronage of the Earl of Coventry. The church is dedicated to St. Denis. A market and a fair were granted to be held here by Edward II., but both of them have been long since disused.

STOKE (SOUTH), a parish partly in the wapentake of WINNIBRIGGS and THREO, but chiefly in the soke of GRANTHAM, parts of KESTEVEN, county of LINCOLN, 2 miles (N. by W.) from Colsterworth, containing, with the township of North Stoke, and the hamlet of Easton, 428 inhabitants. The living is a rectory, formerly in medieties, which were united in 1776, in the archdeaconry and diocese of Lincoln, rated jointly in the king's books at £18. 15., and in the patronage of the Prebendary of South Grantham in the Cathedral Church of Salisbury. The church is dedicated to St. Andrew and St. Mary. The river Witham runs through the parish, in which are the remains of a Roman villa and baths. Here is an endowed almshouse.

STOKE (SOUTH), a parish in the hundred of DORCHESTER, county of OXFORD, 4¼ miles (S. by W.) from Wallingford, containing, with the chapelry of Woodcote, 739 inhabitants. The living is a discharged vicarage, in the archdeaconry and diocese of Oxford, rated in the king's books at £12. 16. 0½., endowed with £600 private benefaction, £200 royal bounty, and £600 parliamentary grant, and in the patronage of the Dean and Canons of Christ Church, Oxford. The church is dedicated to St. Andrew. There is a place of worship for Independents. Ten poor children are taught for £14.7.8. a year, arising from a bequest by the Rev. Griffith Higgs, D.D., in 1659.

STOKE (SOUTH), a parish in the hundred of BATH-FORUM, county of SOMERSET, 2½ miles (S.) from Bath, containing 258 inhabitants. The living is a discharged vicarage, with the perpetual curacy of Moncton-Combe annexed, in the archdeaconry of Bath, and diocese of Bath and Wells, rated in the king's books at £7. 18. 9., endowed with £200 private benefaction, and £200 royal bounty, and in the patronage of the

Rev. John Wood. The church is dedicated to St. James. The river Avon and the Radford canal run through the parish; the former is crossed by a bridge near its junction with the Kennet.

STOKE (SOUTH), a parish in the hundred of AVISFORD, rape of ARUNDEL, county of SUSSEX, 2½ miles (N.N.E.) from Arundel, containing, with the tything of Offham, 115 inhabitants. The living is a rectory, in the archdeaconry and diocese of Chichester, rated in the king's books at £11. 15. 10., and in the patronage of the Duke of Norfolk. The river Arun forms part of the boundary line of this parish.

STOKE upon TERN, a parish in the Drayton division of the hundred of BRADFORD (North), county of SALOP, comprising the townships of Eaton, Ollerton, Stoke, and Westanswick, and containing 985 inhabitants, of which number, 541 are in the township of Stoke, 6 miles (S. W. by S.) from Drayton in Hales. The living is a rectory, in the archdeaconry of Salop, and diocese of Lichfield and Coventry, rated in the king's books at £20, and in the patronage of — Corbet, Esq. The church, dedicated to St. Peter, contains a handsome monument of alabaster to the memory of Sir Reginald Corbet, a judge of the Common Pleas in the reign of Elizabeth. The ancient mansion-house of the Corbets has been demolished, and a farm-house erected upon its site.

STOKE upon TRENT, a parish in the northern division of the hundred of PIREHILL, county of STAFFORD, 1¾ mile (E.) from Newcastle under Line, comprising the chapelries of Hanley, Lane-End, and Shelton, with part of Cobridge and Etruria, the townships of Bagnall, Botteslaw, Bucknall, Eaves, Fenton-Calvert, Fenton-Vivian, Longton, Penkhul with Boothen, and part of that of Seabridge, and the liberty of Clayton, and containing 29,233 inhabitants. This extensive parish, in common with others in this part of the county, owes its increase to the establishment of numerous potteries, for which its situation on the Trent renders it favourable, and for which it has been for many years particularly distinguished. The streets are paved with brick, and the town is lighted with gas from works established at Shelton, and amply supplied with water. The principal articles of manufacture are china and earthenware in all their various branches, of which there are many extensive factories, employing more than one thousand eight hundred men; of these, the principal is that of Messrs. Spode. On the banks of the Trent and Mersey canal, which passes through the parish, and is carried over the river Trent by an aqueduct near the village, are numerous wharfs and warehouses, from which great quantities of the manufactures are sent by boats daily to all parts of the kingdom. Connected with the works are several mills for the preparation of flint, of which a considerable quantity is used in the manufacture of the finer articles of china, material improvement having been effected by its introduction. The market is on Saturday, and is well supplied with provisions of every kind. The parish is within the jurisdiction of the county magistrates, and the police is under the superintendence of commissioners appointed by act of parliament in 1825, and amended in 1828, under the provisions of which also a chief bailiff is elected, who convenes and presides at all public meetings of the inhabitants.

This parish, at present including a district of more than seventeen square miles, was originally much more extensive, having at different times been subdivided and parts of it formed into independent parishes. In 1807, an act of parliament was obtained for separating from it the chapelries of Newcastle under Line, Burslem, Whitmore, Bucknall with Bagnall, and Norton on the Moors, and erecting them into distinct parishes. In 1818, the perpetual advowson of the remaining parish, of Stoke upon Trent, comprising Botteslaw, Clayton, part of Cobridge, Etruria, Fenton-Calvert, Fenton-Vivian, Hanley, Longton with Lane-End, Penkhul with Boothen, Seabridge, and Shelton, was purchased from the trustees under the will of the late Rev. William Robinson, by the present patron, John Tomlinson, of Cliff Ville, Esq., who in 1827 obtained an act of parliament authorising the sale, to the respective landowners, of all the tithes and rectorial dues belonging to the present rectory, and for endowing two new churches, which the parliamentary commissioners had agreed to build, one at Longton, and the other at Shelton, the livings to be distinct rectories; the same act contains also a provision for converting the chapelries of Lane-End and Hanley into distinct rectories.

The living is a rectory, in the archdeaconry of Stafford, and diocese of Lichfield and Coventry, rated in the king's books, for the original parish, at £41. 0. 10., and in the patronage of J. Tomlinson, Esq. The old church, dedicated to St. Peter, a very ancient structure, having probably been built at the time of the Conquest, is mentioned in the taxation of Pope Nicholas, in 1291, at which time it was, with its several dependent chapels, valued at sixty marks. Being not only too small but also in a state of decay, a new church was erected in 1826, near the site of the former, which is intended to be pulled down, partly by subscription among the inhabitants (towards which £3000 was given by the Rev. John C. Woodhouse, Dean of Lichfield, and rector of the parish, and £500 by Josiah Spode, Esq.), by a parochial rate, and by contributions (spontaneously bestowed) arising from the extra labours of the workmen employed in the potteries: it is a handsome edifice in the later style of English architecture, containing one thousand six hundred sittings. In the chancel of the old church is a mural tablet and bust of the late Josiah Wedgwood, of Etruria, Esq. There are places of worship for Baptists, Independents, Wesleyan Methodists, and Methodists of the New Connexion. A National school, in which seven hundred children of both sexes are instructed, is supported by subscription, and there are also similar schools in the various hamlets. Dr. John Lightfoot, an eminent Hebrew scholar, and one of the principal persons employed in finally arranging the liturgy of the church of England, was born at Stoke, in 1602.

STOKE (WEST), a parish in the hundred of BOSHAM, rape of CHICHESTER, county of SUSSEX, 3½ miles (N. W.) from Chichester, containing 92 inhabitants. The living is a discharged rectory, in the archdeaconry and diocese of Chichester, rated in the king's books at £9. 11., and in the patronage of the Crown.

STOKE-ABBAS, a parish in the hundred of BEAMINSTER-FORUM and REDHONE, Bridport division of the county of DORSET, 2 miles (W. by S.) from Beaminster, containing 615 inhabitants. The living is a rectory, in the archdeaconry of Dorset, and diocese of Bristol, rated in the king's books at £9. 15., and in the patronage of the Warden and Fellows of New College, Oxford. The church is dedicated to St. Mary.

STOKE-ALBANY, a parish in the hundred of CORBY, county of NORTHAMPTON, 5 miles (S. W. by W.) from Rockingham, containing 363 inhabitants. The living is a rectory, in the archdeaconry of Northampton, and diocese of Peterborough, rated in the king's books at £13. 6. 8., and in the patronage of Lord Sondes. The church is dedicated to St. Botolph.

STOKE-ASH, a parish in the hundred of HARTISMERE, county of SUFFOLK, 3½ miles (S. W.) from Eye, containing 330 inhabitants. The living is a rectory, in the archdeaconry of Sudbury, and diocese of Norwich, rated in the king's books at £11. 1. 3., and in the patronage of the Rev. John Ward. The church is dedicated to All Saints. There is a place of worship for Baptists. A branch of the river Waveney flows through the parish.

STOKE-BARDOLPH, a township in the parish of GEDLING, southern division of the wapentake of THURGARTON, county of NOTTINGHAM, 5 miles (E. N. E.) from Nottingham, containing 173 inhabitants.

STOKE-BLISS, a parish partly in the upper division of the hundred of DODDINGTREE, county of WORCESTER, but chiefly in the hundred of BROXASH, county of HEREFORD, 6¼ miles (N.) from Bromyard, containing, with the chapelry of Little Kyre, 303 inhabitants. The living is a rectory, in the archdeaconry and diocese of Hereford, rated in the king's books at £6. 16. 8., and in the patronage of the Crown.

STOKE-BRUERNE, a parish in the hundred of CLELEY, county of NORTHAMPTON, 3½ miles (E. N. E.) from Towcester, containing, with the chapelry of Shuttlehanger, 732 inhabitants. The living is a rectory, in the archdeaconry of Northampton, and diocese of Peterborough, rated in the king's books at £30, and in the patronage of the Principal and Fellows of Brasenose College, Oxford. The church is dedicated to St. Mary. The Grand Junction canal passes through a tunnel two miles long, partly in this parish, and partly in that of Blisworth. Ten pounds a year, the bequest of Elizabeth Prowse, is applied in support of a day and a Sunday school chiefly maintained by the Dowager Lady Mordaunt.

STOKE-CANNON, a parish in the hundred of WONFORD, county of DEVON, 3½ miles (N. N. E.) from Exeter, containing 337 inhabitants. The living is a perpetual curacy, in the peculiar jurisdiction and patronage of the Dean and Chapter of Exeter. The church, dedicated to St. Mary Magdalene, has a curious ancient font. It was given, with the manor, by King Athelstan to the Cathedral of Exeter. The rivers Exe and Culm flow through the parish.

STOKE-CHARITY, a parish in the hundred of BUDDLESGATE, Fawley division of the county of SOUTHAMPTON, 6½ miles (S. by E.) from Whitchurch, containing 144 inhabitants. The living is a rectory, in the archdeaconry and diocese of Winchester, rated in the king's books at £15. 13. 6¼., and in the patronage of the President and Fellows of Corpus Christi College, Oxford. The church is dedicated to St. Michael. This parish is within the jurisdiction of the Cheyney Court

held at Winchester every Thursday, for the recovery of debts to any amount.

STOKE-CLIMSLAND, a parish in the northern division of the hundred of EAST, county of CORNWALL, 3½ miles (N.) from Callington, containing 1524 inhabitants. The living is a rectory, in the archdeaconry of Cornwall, and diocese of Exeter, rated in the king's books at £40, and in the patronage of the Crown. The church is a very spacious structure, with a fine tower. There is a place of worship for Wesleyan Methodists. The parish is bounded on the north by the river Inney, which runs into the Tamar on the east, and near the romantic and picturesque rocks of Carthartmartha. A fair for cattle is held on May 29th. There are two small sums, bequeathed by Ralph Tope in 1718, and Joan Clarke, in 1783, in support of a school.

STOKE-D'ABERNON, a parish in the second division of the hundred of ELMBRIDGE, county of SURREY, 1½ mile (S. E. by E.) from Cobham, containing, with the hamlet of Oakshot, 317 inhabitants. The living is a rectory, in the archdeaconry of Surrey, and diocese of Winchester, rated in the king's books at £13. 11. 3. — Smith, Esq. was patron in 1801. The church is dedicated to St. Mary.

STOKE-DAMERALL, a parish in the hundred of ROBOROUGH, county of DEVON, adjoining the borough of Plymouth, containing 33,578 inhabitants. This parish, which includes Devonport and Morice Town, is one of the most extensive in the county: the village occupies an elevated site, and comprises several rows of excellent houses, a crescent, and some private mansions of more than ordinary beauty. Among the important public structures are, the immense reservoir of the Devonport Water Company, which supplies the government establishments and the neighbourhood in general; the military hospital, a spacious edifice of grey marble, erected in 1797, on the west side of Stonehouse creek, comprising four large square buildings, of similar size and form, connected by a piazza of forty-one arches; and the Blockhouse, occupying an eminence north of the village, surrounded by a fosse and drawbridge, commanding a most magnificent prospect: in addition to the military use of this fortress, it forms an admirable land-mark for ships entering the Sound. The living is a rectory, in the archdeaconry of Totness, and diocese of Exeter, rated in the king's books at £18. 18. 9., and in the patronage of Sir John St. Aubyn, Bart. The church is a spacious edifice, with a low square tower. A new church is in progress of erection by His Majesty's commissioners. There are places of worship for Independents, and Calvinistic and Wesleyan Methodists. On the eastern bank of the Hamoaze, in this parish, is Morice Town, so named from the former lord of the manor, now commonly called the New Passage, where a ferry was established in 1800, to communicate with Cornwall, at Torpoint, on the opposite shore; it consists of four principal streets. The sides of the harbour are lined with various wharfs, and in the town is a large establishment, called the Tamar Brewery. At a short distance is the powder magazine, which, although it covers an area of five acres, was insufficient in time of war, when line-of-battle ships were fitted up as floating magazines. A fair is held here on Whit-Monday. In the vicinity, at Cross hill, is a very extensive quarry of slate of a durable quality.

STOKE-DOYLE, a parish in the hundred of NAVIS-FORD, county of NORTHAMPTON, 1½ mile (S. W. by S.) from Oundle, containing 141 inhabitants. The living is a rectory, in the archdeaconry of Northampton, and diocese of Peterborough, rated in the king's books at £20. 2. 11., and in the patronage of Sir J. Langham, Bart. The church is dedicated to St. Rumbald.

STOKE-EDITH, a parish in the hundred of RAD-LOW, county of HEREFORD, 7¼ miles (E.) from Hereford, containing, with the chapelry of Westhide, 495 inhabitants. The living is a rectory, with the perpetual curacy of Westhide annexed, in the archdeaconry and diocese of Hereford, rated in the king's books at £15, and in the patronage of Edward Foley, Esq. The church is dedicated to St. Mary. A school is supported by small annual donations. An ancient sword, some curious beads, several human skeletons with their faces downwards, and other relics, were found at Radlow Bush some years ago.

STOKE-FERRY, a market town and parish in the hundred of CLACKCLOSE, county of NORFOLK, 38 miles (W. by S.) from Norwich, and 88½ (N. N. E.) from London, containing 703 inhabitants. The living is a perpetual curacy, in the archdeaconry of Norfolk, and diocese of Norwich, endowed with £400 royal bounty, and in the patronage of G. Nightingale, Esq. The church, dedicated to All Saints, had formerly a square tower. This town is situated on the banks of the river Wissey, on the turnpike-road from London to Newmarket. In the reign of Henry III. it obtained a grant for holding a weekly market and an annual fair, which was confirmed by Henry VI.: the market was for a long period disused, but has been recently revived, and is now held on Friday, principally for corn; and the fair on December 6th, for cattle. The population has considerably increased since the last census, and now exceeds nine hundred persons, many of whom are employed in the very extensive malting establishments of Messrs. Whitbread and Co., whose superintendent has successfully adopted a superior plan for drying the malt, and has obtained a patent for his improvements. Twenty-five boys of Stoke-Ferry and Wretton are gratuitously educated in a school founded by the late James Bradfield, Esq.

STOKE-FLEMING, a parish in the hundred of COLERIDGE, county of DEVON, 2 miles (S. S. W.) from Dartmouth, containing 686 inhabitants. The living is a rectory, in the archdeaconry of Totness, and diocese of Exeter, rated in the king's books at £31. 6. 0½., and in the patronage of Charles Farwell, Esq. The church, dedicated to St. Peter, contains some interesting monuments.

STOKE-GABRIEL, a parish in the hundred of HAYTOR, county of DEVON, 4 miles (S. E. by E.) from Totness, containing 638 inhabitants. The living is a discharged vicarage, in the peculiar jurisdiction of the Bishop of Exeter, rated in the king's books at £16. 11. 10½., and in the patronage of Sir Stafford Northcote, Bart., the Rev. John Templar, and the Rev. F. Belfield, alternately. The church contains an ancient wooden screen, and at Watton there was formerly a chantry chapel. There is a place of worship for Baptists. The navigable river Dart bounds the parish on the south. Capt. John Davies, the discoverer of Davies' Straits, was born here.

STOKE-GIFFORD, a parish in the upper division of the hundred of HENBURY, county of GLOUCESTER, 5 miles (N. N. E.) from Bristol, containing 376 inhabitants. The living is a discharged vicarage, in the peculiar jurisdiction of the Bishop of Bristol, rated in the king's books at £6, endowed with £275 private benefaction, and £600 royal bounty, and in the patronage of the Duke of Beaufort. The church is dedicated to St. Michael. John Silcocks, in 1741, bequeathed £200, directing the interest to be applied for teaching poor children of this parish and those of Almondsbury, Filton, and Winterborne; and a school is supported, partly by this charity, and partly by the Dowager Duchess of Beaufort, in which twelve boys and twenty-four girls are educated.

STOKE-GOLDING, a chapelry in the parish of HINCKLEY, hundred of SPARKENHOE, county of LEICESTER, 2¾ miles (N. W.) from Hinckley, containing 594 inhabitants. The chapel is dedicated to St. Margaret. The Ashby de la Zouch canal passes through the chapelry.

STOKE-GOLDINGTON, a parish in the hundred of NEWPORT, county of BUCKINGHAM, 4 miles (W. S. W.) from Olney, containing 818 inhabitants. The living is a rectory, united in 1736 to that of Gayhurst, in the archdeaconry of Buckingham, and diocese of Lincoln, rated in the king's books at £14. 6. 3. The church is dedicated to St. Peter. The river Ouse runs through the parish, in which lime and other stone abound. There was formerly a chapel at Eakley, which is said to have been once a distinct parish.

STOKE-HAMMOND, a parish in the hundred of NEWPORT, county of BUCKINGHAM, 2¼ miles (S.) from Fenny-Stratford, containing 320 inhabitants. The living is a rectory, in the archdeaconry of Buckingham, and diocese of Lincoln, rated in the king's books at £19. 9. 4½., and in the patronage of the Bishop of Lincoln. The church is dedicated to St. Mary. There is a place of worship for Wesleyan Methodists. John Hillersdon, in 1707, founded a free school, and endowed it with land producing upwards of £11 per annum.

STOKE-LACY, a parish in the hundred of BROX-ASH, county of HEREFORD, 4¼ miles (S. W. by S.) from Bromyard, containing 358 inhabitants. The living is a rectory, in the archdeaconry and diocese of Hereford, rated in the king's books at £8, and in the patronage of the Rev. T. Apperley. The church is dedicated to St. Peter and St. Paul. A court leet is held once in seven years. Limestone abounds in the neighbourhood. The late Archdeacon of Hereford bequeathed property for the erection and endowment of a free school for children of both sexes, which gift has recently been augmented by Mr. Brown, of Evington, with £20 per annum, and £50 towards the building of the school-house.

STOKE-LANE, or STOKE (ST. MICHAEL), a parish in the hundred of WHITESTONE, county of Somerset, 4 miles (N. E.) from Shepton-Mallet, containing 1000 inhabitants. The living is a perpetual curacy, annexed to the vicarage of Doulting, in the archdeaconry of Wells, and diocese of Bath and Wells. The church is dedicated to St. Michael. There is a place of worship for Wesleyan Methodists.

STOKE-LYNE, a parish in the hundred of PLOUGH-LEY, county of OXFORD, 4¼ miles (N. by W.) from Bicester, containing, with the hamlets of Bainton and Fewcot, 509 inhabitants. The living is a discharged vicarage, in the archdeaconry and diocese of Oxford. John Coker, Esq. was patron in 1812. The church is dedicated to St. Peter.

STOKE-MANDEVILLE, a parish in the hundred of AYLESBURY, county of BUCKINGHAM, 2¾ miles (N. W. by W.) from Wendover, containing 402 inhabitants. The living is a perpetual curacy, annexed to the vicarage of Bierton, in the peculiar jurisdiction of the Dean and Chapter of Lincoln. The church is dedicated to St. Mary.

STOKE-ORCHARD, a chapelry in the parish of BISHOP's CLEEVE, hundred of CLEEVE, or BISHOP's CLEEVE, county of GLOUCESTER, 4¼ miles (S. E.) from Tewkesbury, containing 239 inhabitants. It is within the peculiar jurisdiction of the Rector of Bishop's Cleeve.

STOKE-PERO, a parish in the hundred of CARHAMPTON, county of SOMERSET, 6¾ miles (W. S. W.) from Minehead, containing 81 inhabitants. The living is a discharged rectory, in the archdeaconry of Taunton, and diocese of Bath and Wells, rated in the king's books at £4. 10. 10., endowed with £400 private benefaction, and £600 royal bounty, and in the patronage of John Quick, Esq. The rusty appearance of the water among the hills indicates the probability of iron-ore lying beneath. Dunkry Beacon, a large and lofty mountain, is partly in the parishes of Cutcombe, Luccombe, Wotton-Courtney, Stoke-Pero, and Exford : its base is about twelve miles in circuit, and its height above the sea at high water is one thousand seven hundred and seventy feet, being the highest eminence in the western part of England : it serves as a distant landmark, but the summit is often obscured by clouds. On the top are many loose stones of large dimensions, and among them the ruins of three large fire-hearths, the remains of beacons. Collinson says, when the air is serene and clear, the line which bounds the horizon cannot be less than five hundred miles in circumference.

STOKE-POGES, a parish in the hundred of STOKE, county of BUCKINGHAM, 2 miles (N.) from Slough, containing, with a part of the town of Slough, 1073 inhabitants. The living is a discharged vicarage, in the archdeaconry of Buckingham, and diocese of Lincoln, rated in the king's books at £7. 17., and in the patronage of Lord F. G. Osborne. The church is dedicated to St. Giles. There is a place of worship for Wesleyan Methodists. A fair is held here on Whit-Tuesday. A school, now conducted on the National system, was erected, at the expense of the parishioners, in 1798, and is supported by sundry bequests, including one by Lady Elizabeth Hatton, in 1645, the whole producing an annual income of about £30. "The hospital of Stoke-Poges," now containing a master, four poor men, and two women, was founded, in 1557, by Lord Hastings of Sloughborough, who endowed it with a rent-charge of about £53, for the support of a chantry priest and four bedesmen. It was originally built in Stoke park, and its noble founder, becoming one of its inmates, ended his days within its walls, and was buried in the chapel attached. The ancient building having been pulled down, in 1765, in pursuance of an act obtained by Mr. Penn, who also augmented the endowment, the hospital was refounded on its present site. The vicar is eligible

to the mastership, and the visitors are the Dean of Windsor and the Provost of Eton. The churchyard of this parish is the scene of "Gray's Elegy," and contains the remains of the poet himself ; and in the field adjoining a large sarcophagus was erected, in 1799, by Mr. Penn of Stoke Park, to the memory of Mr. Gray, who died at Cambridge in 1771, when his body was removed hither, and deposited, with those of his mother and aunt, in a vault constructed at his own expense.

STOKE-PRIOR, a parish in the hundred of WOLPHY, county of HEREFORD, comprising the townships of Stoke-Prior and Wickton with Risbury, and containing 477 inhabitants, of which number, 337 are in the township of Stoke-Prior, 3 miles (S. E.) from Leominster. The living is a perpetual curacy, annexed, with that of Docklow, to the vicarage of Leominster, in the archdeaconry and diocese of Hereford, endowed with £200 private benefaction, and £600 royal bounty.

STOKE-PRIOR, a parish in the middle division of the hundred of OSWALDSLOW, county of WORCESTER, 1¾ mile (S.) from Bromsgrove, containing 900 inhabitants. The living is a discharged vicarage, in the archdeaconry and diocese of Worcester, rated in the king's books at £12, and in the patronage of the Dean and Chapter of Worcester. The church is dedicated to St. Michael. The Birmingham and Worcester canal passes through the parish. In the great civil war, the court-house was almost destroyed by the royalists.

STOKE-RIVERS, a parish in the hundred of SHERWILL, county of DEVON, 5 miles (E. by N.) from Barnstaple, containing 291 inhabitants. The living is a rectory, in the archdeaconry of Barnstaple, and diocese of Exeter, rated in the king's books at £14. 14. 7., and in the patronage of the Rev. Charles Hierns. The church is dedicated to St. Bartholomew.

STOKE-TALMAGE, a parish in the hundred of PIRTON, county of OXFORD, 2 miles (S. S. W.) from Tetsworth, containing 140 inhabitants. The living is a rectory, in the archdeaconry and diocese of Oxford, rated in the king's books at £12. 17. 1., and in the patronage of the Earl of Macclesfield. The church is dedicated to St. Mary Magdalene.

STOKE-TRISTER, a parish in the hundred of NORTON-FERRIS, county of SOMERSET, 2 miles (E.) from Wincanton, containing, with the hamlet of Bayford, 377 inhabitants. The living is a discharged rectory, united to that of Cucklington, in the archdeaconry of Wells, and diocese of Bath and Wells, rated in the king's books at £7. 15. 2½.

STOKE-WAKE, a parish in the hundred of WHITEWAY, Cerne subdivision of the county of DORSET, 10 miles (W.) from Blandford-Forum, containing 139 inhabitants. The living is a rectory, in the archdeaconry of Dorset, and diocese of Bristol, rated in the king's books at £8. 8. 9. H. Seymour, Esq. was patron in 1817. The church is dedicated to All Saints.

STOKEHAM, a parish in the South-clay division of the wapentake of BASSETLAW, county of NOTTINGHAM, 5 miles (N. E. by N.) from Tuxford, containing 45 inhabitants. The living is a perpetual curacy, annexed to the vicarage of East Drayton, in the peculiar jurisdiction of the Dean and Chapter of York.

STOKEINTINHEAD, a parish forming, with Combintinhead, Haccombe, and Shaldon Green, a detached portion of the hundred of WONFORD, county of DEVON,

4 miles (E. by S.) from Newton-Bushell, containing, with the township of Shaldon Green, 610 inhabitants. The living is a rectory, in the archdeaconry and diocese of Exeter, rated in the king's books at £36. 15. 10., and is the patronage of the Bishop of Exeter. The church, dedicated to St. Andrew, contains some ancient screen-work : it was formerly collegiate, for a warden and several chaplains, established in honour of the Virgin Mary and St. Andrew, by John de Stanford, in the reign of Edward III.

STOKENCHURCH, a parish in the hundred of LEWKNOR, county of OXFORD, 6 miles (S. E. by E.) from Tetsworth, containing 1102 inhabitants. The living is a perpetual curacy, annexed to the vicarage of Aston-Rowant, in the archdeaconry and diocese of Oxford. There is a place of worship for Wesleyan Methodists. Twelve poor children are educated, clothed, and apprenticed for a rent-charge of £41, the bequest of Bartholomew Tipping, in 1675.

STOKESAY, a parish in the hundred of MUNSLOW, county of SALOP, 7 miles (N.W.) from Ludlow, containing 564 inhabitants. The living is a discharged vicarage, in the archdeaconry of Salop, and diocese of Hereford, rated in the king's books at £4. 13. 4., and in the patronage of William Smith, Esq. The church is dedicated to St. John the Baptist. A small endowment in land, the gift of Roger Powell, in 1716, is applied in support of the poor, and for teaching children : there is also a bequest of £5 per annum, by Mary Pierce, in 1761, for purchasing books.

STOKESBY, a parish in the eastern division of the hundred of FLEGG, county of NORFOLK, 2¼ miles (E.) from Acle, containing, with the parish of Herringby, 294 inhabitants. The living is a rectory, with that of Herringby united, in the archdeaconry and diocese of Norwich, rated in the king's books at £13. 6. 8., and in the patronage of William Downes, Esq. The church is dedicated to St. Andrew. There is a place of worship for Wesleyan Methodists.

STOKESLEY, a parish in the western division of the liberty of LANGBAURGH, North riding of the county of YORK, comprising the market town of Stokesley, and the townships of Great and Little Busby, Easby, and New-by, and containing 2290 inhabitants, of which number, 1897 are in the town of Stokesley, 41 miles (N. by W.) from York, and 242 (N. by W.) from London. The living is a rectory, in the archdeaconry of Cleveland, and diocese of York, rated in the king's books at £30. 6. 10½., and in the patronage of the Archbishop of York. The church is dedicated to St. Peter. There are places of worship for Independents and Primitive and Wesleyan Methodists. This place is situated on the northern bank of the river Leven, in the centre of the fruitful tract called Allertonshire, which, at the distance of about five miles from the town, is bounded by the Cleveland hills, forming a vast and majestic amphitheatre. The houses are neatly built in a modern style, and are ranged chiefly in one spacious street, from east to west : the market, which is held on Saturday, is abundantly supplied with provisions. There are fairs for horses, cattle, &c ; on the Saturdays before Trinity and Palm Sundays, and before Old Lammas-day. The trade is principally in linen ; one of the mills for its manufacture is worked by a powerful steam-engine. A court leet is held annually, and the magistrates hold petty sessions every week. Two National schools, one for each sex, have been established, in connexion with the diocesan schools, and are partly supported by subscription, and partly by the dividends arising from £2780. 1. 5. five per cents., bequeathed, in 1805, by John Preston. The Society for the Promotion of Christian Knowledge, in 1818, established a depository of books in the vestry-room of the church, from which many thousand volumes have been since distributed.

STOKINGHAM, a parish in the hundred of COLE-RIDGE, county of DEVON, 5¼ miles (E. by S.) from Kings-bridge, containing 1487 inhabitants. The living is a vicarage, with the perpetual curacies of Chivelstone and Sherford annexed, in the archdeaconry and diocese of Exeter, rated in the king's books at £48. 7. 8½., and in the patronage of the Crown. The church, dedicated to St. Barnabas, has an ancient wooden screen. There is a place of worship for Independents.

STONALL (OVER), a chapelry in the parish of SHENSTONE, southern division of the hundred of OFF-LOW, county of STAFFORD, 6 miles (S. W.) from Lichfield. The population is returned with the parish. The living is a perpetual curacy, in the archdeaconry of Stafford, and diocese of Lichfield and Coventry, endowed with £2000 parliamentary grant, and in the patronage of the Vicar of Shenstone.

STONAR, a parish in the hundred of RINGSLOW, or Isle of THANET, lathe of St. AUGUSTINE, county of KENT, ¼ of a mile (N. by E.) from Sandwich, containing 44 inhabitants. The living is a rectory, in the archdeaconry and diocese of Canterbury, rated in the king's books at £3. 6. 8., and in the patronage of the Crown, by lapse. The church has been destroyed. It is supposed that the site of this place, in the time of the Romans, was entirely covered with water. On the sea retiring from Ebbs-fleet, it became a common landing-place, at an early period, and, in consequence, a town and port of considerable importance, having, in 1090, so increased, that the seigniory of Stonar was claimed by the citizens of London, as subject to that port. After sustaining repeated injuries from the Danes and other marauders, as well as from inundations of the sea, it began, about the reign of Richard II., to decay. Leland, who wrote in the time of Henry VIII., describes it as " sometime a pretty town," but then " having only the ruin of the church, which some people call Old Sandwich." Abundant remains of former dwellings may be traced, though at present there are not more than four or five inhabited houses. Salt-works are carried on near the site of the church, the produce of which serves all the purposes of bay salt.

STONDON (LOWER), a hamlet in that part of the parish of SHITLINGTON which is in the hundred of CLIFTON, county of BEDFORD, 3 miles (S. by E.) from Shefford, containing 135 inhabitants.

STONDON (UPPER), a parish in the hundred of CLIFTON, county of BEDFORD, 2¾ miles (S.) from Shefford, containing 33 inhabitants. The living is a rectory, in the archdeaconry of Bedford, and diocese of Lincoln, rated in the king's books at £6. 6. 10½., and in the patronage of the Rev. Mr. Hull. The church is dedicated to All Saints.

STONDON-MASSEY, a parish in the hundred of ONGAR, county of ESSEX, 2 miles (E. S. E.) from Chipping-Ongar, containing 230 inhabitants. The living is a rectory, in the archdeaconry of Essex, and diocese of London, rated in the king's books at £13. 6. 8., and in the patronage of the Rev. J. Oldham. The church is dedicated to St. Peter and St. Paul.

STONE, a parish in the hundred of AYLESBURY, county of BUCKINGHAM, 3 miles (W. S. W.) from Aylesbury, containing 716 inhabitants. The living is a discharged vicarage, in the archdeaconry of Buckingham, and diocese of Lincoln, rated in the king's books at £9, and in the patronage of the Rev. Sir G. Lee, Bart. The church, dedicated to St. John the Baptist, is partly in the Norman, and partly in the early English, style of architecture. There are two places of worship for Methodists. The parish is separated from Waddesdon by the river Thame. The manufacture of lace, which was formerly more considerable, is still carried on. A National school has been erected and is supported by the parishioners.

STONE, a chapelry in the parish and upper division of the hundred of BERKELEY, county of GLOUCESTER, 2¾ miles (S. by W.) from Berkeley. The population is returned with the tything of Ham. The living is a perpetual curacy, in the archdeaconry and diocese of Gloucester, endowed with £10 per annum private benefaction, £200 royal bounty, and £400 parliamentary grant, and in the patronage of the Bishop of Gloucester, by lapse. The church, dedicated to All Saints, is partly in the early, and partly in the later, style of English architecture.

STONE, a parish in the hundred of OXNEY, lathe of SHEPWAY, county of KENT, 6½ miles (S. E.) from Tenterden, containing 425 inhabitants. The living is a vicarage, in the archdeaconry and diocese of Canterbury, rated in the king's books at £8. 14. 4½., and in the patronage of the Dean and Chapter of Canterbury. The church, dedicated to St. Mary, is a spacious and handsome structure. The Grand Military canal passes through the parish. A fair is held here on Holy-Thursday. A free school is supported by voluntary contributions.

STONE, a parish in the southern division of the hundred of PIREHILL, county of STAFFORD, comprising the market town of Stone, and the liberties of Beech, Hilderstone, Kibblestone, and Normicott, and containing 7251 inhabitants, of which number, 2855 are in the town of Stone, 7 miles (N. by W.) from Stafford, and 141 (N. W. by N.) from London. The name is traditionally reported to be derived from a monumental heap of stones, which, according to the custom of the Saxons, had been placed over the bodies of the Princes Wulford and Rufinus, who were here slain by their father Wulfhere, King of Mercia, on account of their conversion to Christianity. The king himself becoming subsequently a convert, founded, in 670, a college of Secular canons, dedicating it to his children, in expiation of his crime, and to this establishment the town is supposed to owe its origin. The canons having been expelled, during the war with the Danes, the college fell into the possession of some nuns, who established themselves here. No mention is made of it in Domesday-book, but it appears to have been granted by Henry I. to Robert de Stafford, who displaced the nuns, and made it a cell to the monastery of Kenilworth, which it continued to be until 1260, when it became independent, with the exception of paying a small sum

annually to that monastery, and an acknowledgment of its patronage ; its revenue was valued, at the dissolution, at about £119. The town is situated on the high road from London to Liverpool, on the eastern bank of the river Trent, over which there is a bridge to Walton, and is paved, and well supplied with water : it consists chiefly of one long street, with several others branching off. The Trent and Mersey canal (commonly called the Grand Trunk) passes through the town, running parallel for several miles with the river ; and the principal office of the Company of Proprietors of this prosperous and important navigation is here. Races are occasionally held in the neighbourhood, and assemblies sometimes in the town. The prevailing branch of manufacture is that of shoes, and there are two considerable breweries : on a stream which falls into the Trent are also several flour and flint mills. The market is on Tuesday : about fifty years since, a great deal of business in corn was transacted at it, but it has very much declined, owing probably to the rapidly increasing population, and additional markets, in the neighbouring potteries. The fairs are on the Tuesday after Mid-Lent, Shrove-Tuesday, Whit-Tuesday, August 5th, and the Tuesday next before the Feast of St. Michael, the two last only being much frequented. Petty sessions are held by the county magistrates every fortnight, and two constables are annually chosen at the court leet of the lord of the manor. The house of industry, erected about forty years since, is governed by the directors and guardians of the parish, under the authority of an act of parliament : the paupers manufacture their own clothing and a few other articles.

The living is a perpetual curacy, in the archdeaconry of Stafford, and diocese of Lichfield and Coventry, endowed with £13 per annum private benefaction, and £200 royal bounty, and in the patronage of the Crown. The church, dedicated to St. Michael, is a modern structure in the later English style, with a square tower : the altar-piece is a fine painting, by Sir William Beechey, of St. Michael binding Satan. The old church fell down about the middle of the last century, occasioned, it is said, by the undermining of one of the pillars in digging a vault ; in consequence of which, no interment is allowed to take place within the walls of the present edifice. There are places of worship for Independents and Wesleyan Methodists, and a Roman Catholic chapel at Aston Hall, in this parish. The free school was founded and endowed with a small annual income by the Rev. Thomas Alleyn, in 1558. The master and Fellows of Trinity College, Cambridge, are the trustees, and appoint the master : the school-house adjoins the churchyard, but there are no boys on the foundation. A bequest of £100 per annum to ten poor widows, charged on the Stone Park estate, is paid by Viscount Granville, though void by the mortmain act ; there are other small charitable endowments. The remains of the abbey adjoin the churchyard, and consist of one perfect arch and rather extensive cloisters. On clearing away some of the rubbish, in 1828, a stone coffin was discovered under the foundation of one of the walls, with the remains enclosed, in a tolerably perfect state. In a field, now allotted to the poor, at a short distance from the town, the army under the Duke of Cumberland was encamped, in 1745, expecting the Pretender to pass that way, but he avoided them by taking the route by Leek. The late celebrated naval commander, Earl St. Vincent, was born at Meaford, in this parish, and is buried in the churchyard here.

STONE, a parish in the lower division of the hundred of HALFSHIRE, county of WORCESTER, 2¼ miles (S.E. by E.) from Kidderminster, containing 464 inhabitants. The living is a vicarage, in the archdeaconry and diocese of Worcester, rated in the king's books at £15, and in the patronage of the Crown. The church, dedicated to St. Mary, contains, over the northern door, some small remains of Norman architecture: this was formerly a chapelry in the parish of Chaddesley-Corbet. There are two spinning-mills in the parish. The free school, founded pursuant to the will of the Rev. Mr. Hill, B. D., is endowed with upwards of twenty acres of land, and a house for the master. This parish possesses a valuable charity of unknown origin, consisting of some land, near Stourbridge, containing clay for making fire-bricks, and producing, on an average, nearly £700 per annum, which, with the dividends of about £5000 three per cent. stock, is applied to repairing the church, and for charitable purposes.

STONE near DARTFORD, a parish in the hundred of AXTON, DARTFORD, and WILMINGTON, lathe of SUTTON at HONE, county of KENT, 2 miles (E. by N.) from Dartford, containing 514 inhabitants. The living is a rectory, in the archdeaconry and diocese of Rochester, rated in the king's books at £26. 10., and in the patronage of the Bishop of Rochester. The church, dedicated to St. Mary, is much admired as being a peculiarly fine specimen of the later style of English architecture: it contains several ancient stalls, remarkable for the elegance of their workmanship and the delicacy of their pillars, which are of crown marble. The river Thames bounds the parish on the north. Stone Castle stands to the south of the high Dovor road, and is said to be one of the one hundred and fifteen castles which were not dismantled in accordance with an express stipulation to that effect between Stephen and Henry II. From the rents of the lands attached to it twenty-six sermons are annually preached, one on each Wednesday during summer, alternately at Gravesend and Dartford, agreeably to the will of Dr. Plume, founder of the Plumian Professorship at Cambridge.

STONE next FAVERSHAM, a parish in the hundred of FAVERSHAM, lathe of SCRAY, county of KENT, 2½ miles (W. by N.) from Faversham, containing 75 inhabitants. The living is a perpetual curacy, in the archdeaconry and diocese of Canterbury.

STONE-DELPH, a joint township with Almington, in that part of the parish of TAMWORTH which is in the Tamworth division of the hundred of HEMLINGFORD, county of WARWICK, 3 miles (S.E.) from Tamworth. The population is returned with Almington.

STONE-EASTON, a parish in the hundred of CHEWTON, county of SOMERSET, 6½ miles (N.) from Shepton-Mallet, containing 419 inhabitants. The living is a perpetual curacy, annexed to the vicarage of Chewton-Mendip, in the archdeaconry of Wells, and diocese of Bath and Wells.

STONEBECK (DOWN), a township in the parish of KIRKBY-MALZEARD, lower division of the wapentake of CLARO, West riding of the county of YORK, 14 miles (W. by S.) from Ripon, containing 568 inhabitants.

STONEBECK (UPPER), a township in the parish of KIRKBY-MALZEARD, lower division of the wapentake of CLARO, West riding of the county of YORK, 16 miles (W. by N.) from Ripon, containing 361 inhabitants.

STONEFERRY, a township in the parish of SUTTON, middle division of the wapentake of HOLDERNESS, East riding of the county of YORK, 1½ mile (N. by E.) from Kingston upon Hull. The population is returned with the parish. There is a place of worship for Wesleyan Methodists. Ann Waters, in 1720, bequeathed property for the erection and endowment of almshouses for seven widows, or poor old maids, who each receive £13 per annum: she also left an annuity of £5 to be paid to one of the almswomen for teaching ten poor girls.

STONEGRAVE, a parish in the wapentake of RYEDALE, North riding of the county of YORK, comprising the townships of East Ness, West Ness, East Newton with Laysthorpe, and Stonegrave, and containing 373 inhabitants, of which number, 177 are in the township of Stonegrave, 4¾ miles (S. E. by S.) from Helmsley. The living is a rectory, in the archdeaconry of Cleveland, and diocese of York, rated in the king's books at £33. 6. 8., and in the patronage of the Crown. The church is partly in the decorated, and partly in the later, style of English architecture.

STONEHAM (NORTH), a parish in the hundred of MANSBRIDGE, Fawley division of the county of SOUTHAMPTON, 4¾ miles (N. N. E.) from Southampton, containing 750 inhabitants. The living is a rectory, in the archdeaconry and diocese of Winchester, rated in the king's books at £21. 9. 7., and in the patronage of John Fleming, Esq. The church, dedicated to St. Nicholas, contains the remains of the celebrated admiral, Lord Hawke, to whose memory there is a superb monument, composed of white and variegated marble, bearing the family arms and other appropriate emblems, with a sculptured representation of his victory over the French admiral, Conflans, in Quiberon bay. Two miles south of the village is an old mansion, formerly the residence of his lordship. The Itchen navigation passes through the parish, which is within the jurisdiction of the Cheyney court held at Winchester every Thursday, for the recovery of debts to any amount. Edmund Dummer, in 1720, gave £300 for erecting a school-house, and an annuity of £5, for which five boys are instructed.

STONEHAM (SOUTH), a parish partly in the county of the town of SOUTHAMPTON, but chiefly in the hundred of MANSBRIDGE, Fawley division of the county of SOUTHAMPTON, 3 miles (N. N. E.) from Southampton, containing, with the tythings of Allington, Barton, Bittern, Eastley, Pollick, Portswood, and Shamblehurst, and the extra-parochial liberty of Swathling, 2702 inhabitants. The living is a vicarage, in the peculiar jurisdiction of the Incumbent, rated in the king's books at £12, and in the patronage of the Rector of St. Mary's, Southampton. The church is dedicated to St. Mary. The river Itchen, which is navigable from Winchester to Northam, where it falls into Southampton water, passes through the parish, which is well situated for trade. At Wood Mills blocks and pumps were formerly manufactured for the supply of nearly the whole of the Royal Navy, but the factory was destroyed by fire a few years since, and there is now a flour-mill upon its site. At Bittern, in this parish, is a National school, supported by voluntary contributions, and attended by about sixty children. At Swathling is a mineral spring, said to be very efficacious for curing diseases of the eye. Stoneham is within the jurisdiction of the Cheyney court held at Winchester every Thursday, for the recovery of debts to any amount.

STONEHOUSE, a parish in the lower division of the hundred of WHITSTONE, county of GLOUCESTER, 4 miles (W.) from Stroud, containing 2126 inhabitants. The living is a vicarage, in the archdeaconry and diocese of Gloucester, rated in the king's books at £22, and in the patronage of the Crown. The church, dedicated to St. Cyr, though much modernised, retains some portions in the Norman style, particularly the north door. There are places of worship for Independents and Wesleyan Methodists. The river Froome, and the Stroudwater canal, pass through the parish. Fairs are held on May 1st and October 11th. The clothing manufacture is carried on to a considerable extent. Limestone is obtained in the parish. Here is a mineral spring, near which a house was erected, some years since, for the accommodation of visitors, but it is not much resorted to. John Elliott and others, in 1774, subscribed £612. 10. for establishing a free school here, and another in the hamlet of Ebley : the income is £47 a year ; the number of scholars at Stonehouse is twenty-eight, and at Ebley sixteen.

STONEHOUSE (EAST), a parish in the suburbs of the borough of PLYMOUTH, county of DEVON, containing 6043 inhabitants. This place, originally called Hipperston, was, in the reign of Henry III., the property of Joel de Stonehouse, from whom it derives its present name : it was then situated more southerly, but, after subsequent improvements and extension to the northward, the ancient buildings were allowed to fall into decay. It now consists of several streets, which are mostly paved, and lighted with gas ; the houses are handsome and commodious ; and the inhabitants are well supplied with water by means of pipes leading from the reservoir of the Devonport Water Company, situated in the parish of Stoke-Damerall, and from a fine stream brought into the town under an act passed in the 35th of Elizabeth. A communication was made with Devonport by means of a stone bridge across Stonehouse creek, erected at the joint expense of the Earl of Mount-Edgecumbe and Sir John St. Aubyn : the tolls are let annually, at a public survey, and the income derived from them is very considerable. Higher up the creek, to the north, is a mill dam, affording a passage to Stoke. On the Devil's Point is the picturesque ruin of a blockhouse, erected in the time of Elizabeth ; and over this old edifice is a modern battery, occupied by the Royal Marine Artillery. At a short distance is Eastern King's battery, commanding the mouth of the Hamoaze : there is also a fort for the protection of the creek. The three towns of Stonehouse, Plymouth, and Devonport, are brilliantly lighted from the gas-works in this parish : the gasometer presents a conspicuous object from the road from Plymouth to Devonport. The road to the ferry at New Passage passes through this place. At the quays in Stonehouse pool vessels unload their cargoes of wood and coal. In addition to the general business arising

from the maritime relations of this town, and its naval and military establishments, are some large manufactories for varnish for the dock-yards, soap, and tallow. A customary market is held on Wednesday, in a neat and convenient building, in Edgecumbe-street ; and there are fairs on the first Wednesday in May, and the second Wednesday in September. The town is within the jurisdiction of the county magistrates, who hold their sessions in the town hall at Devonport. A manorial court leet and baron is held annually. Among the most important public establishments is the Royal Naval Hospital, for the reception of wounded seamen and marines, opened in 1762 : it is situated on an eminence near the creek, and comprises ten buildings, each containing six wards, each ward affording accommodation for about twenty patients, with a chapel, store-room, operating-room, small-pox ward, and dispensary ; they form an extensive quadrangle, ornamented on three sides with a piazza, and the entire edifice, with its spacious lawn, is said to occupy an area of twenty-four acres. In 1795, the government of this institution was vested in a post-captain ; the other officers are, the first and second lieutenants, physician, surgeon, dispenser, chaplain, agent, and steward : the chapel is open to the public. The Royal Marine barracks, on the west shore of Mill bay, comprise a handsome range of buildings forming an oblong square, and are adapted for the accommodation of about one thousand men : the Long Room barracks, built chiefly of wood, will contain nine hundred. A new victualling establishment, now in progress of erection at Devil's Point, is designed upon a scale of great magnitude : among the more remarkable features of the work are, the removal of three hundred thousand cubic yards of limestone rock, and the erection of a granite sea-wall, one thousand five hundred feet in length, the foundation of which was laid by means of a diving bell. The water for the brewery is supplied, at the rate of three hundred and fifty tons per day, from the Plymouth Leat : it first runs into a reservoir capable of receiving two thousand tons, and is thence conveyed through iron pipes into a second basin, of six thousand tons. The Royal Military Hospital is situated on the opposite side of the creek, in the parish of Stoke-Damerall ; its government is similar to that of the Naval Hospital. Stonehouse was formerly a chapelry in the parish of St. Andrew, Plymouth. The living is a perpetual curacy, in the archdeaconry of Totness, and diocese of Exeter, endowed with £200 royal bounty, and in the patronage of the Vicar of St. Andrew's, Plymouth. The church, dedicated to St. George, was built in 1787, when the old chapel was taken down. A grant for a new church was made by the parliamentary commissioners, in 1828. There are places of worship for Baptists, Independents, Wesleyan Methodists, and Roman Catholics. A National school is supported by voluntary contributions.

STONELEIGH, a parish in the Kenilworth division of the hundred of KNIGHTLOW, county of WARWICK, 3¼ miles (E. by N.) from Kenilworth, containing 1391 inhabitants. The living is a vicarage, in the archdeaconry of Coventry, and diocese of Lichfield and Coventry, rated in the king's books at £6. 15. 5., and in the patronage of the Crown. The church, dedicated to St. Mary, is a large and venerable structure, with a square tower supported by strong buttresses, and surmounted by another of smaller size, crowned with pinnacles at the angles: between the chancel and the nave is a large Norman arch, richly ornamented, and supported by columns, whose shafts and capitals are greatly embellished; around the east end is a series of small Norman arches, which for many years were filled up with plaster, but have been restored. On the south side of the chancel is the mausoleum of the Leigh family, lately erected, the ceiling of which is beautifully worked in groined and ribbed arches; in the chancel is a splendid monument to the memory of Lady Alice Leigh, Duchess of Dudley; also a recumbent stone figure, found in an upright position in a wall, in digging the foundation of the mausoleum; it is supposed to be in memory of Geoffrey de Muschamp, Bishop of Coventry and Lichfield in the reign of John. The south aisle is separated from the nave by three pointed arches supported on octagonal pillars; on the south side is a fine Norman porch and doorway, the arch and pillars ornamented with flat and round mouldings: the ancient stone font is cylindrical, and is surrounded by figures of the twelve Apostles, in Norman arches. The free school was founded, in 1708, by Thomas, Lord Leigh, who bequeathed an annuity of £20 for its support; in 1731, the Hon. Ann Leigh gave £1000, as an augmentation of its funds: the annual income is £102; seventy boys and about fifty girls are educated in a large house, containing separate school-rooms, with apartments for the master and the mistress. Almshouses for five aged persons of each sex were founded and endowed, in 1575, by Dame Alice Leigh, whose descendants have for many years past doubled the endowment. The village is situated on the Sow, near its junction with the Avon, and consists of a few red cottages, interspersed with some modern detached houses. About one mile from it is Stoneleigh abbey, the seat of Chandos Leigh, Esq., originally founded by Henry II., in 1154, for Cistercian monks, and dedicated to the Virgin: at the dissolution, its revenue was valued at £178. 2. 5. In 1245, the abbey suffered greatly from fire, and was repaired by Robert de Hockele, the sixteenth abbot, about 1300, who built the gateway-tower, which is entire, and in the early decorated style, leading through a lofty arch-way to the lawn before the house: its situation on an extensive plain, rising gently from the Avon, is peculiarly beautiful. Many privileges were granted to the monks by Henry II., and amongst them power to hold a market and a fair. Of the ancient building, the remains are formed into cellars and domestic offices belonging to the modern elegant mansion, erected by the family of Leigh: among the specimens of ancient architecture are, groined arches, resting on massive pillars; and Norman arches and pillars, in the latest and most finished character of that style, which prevails generally throughout the lower part of the abbey. The rivers Avon and Sow run through the parish; the former nearly surrounds the abbey, and is crossed by a handsome stone bridge, and the latter passes through the village, where it is crossed by an ancient bridge of eight arches, about half a mile before its confluence with the Avon. On the south side of the river, opposite the church, is Motstow hill, where the tenantry used to assemble to render suit and service to the lord of the manor.

STONERAISE, a joint township with Brocklebank, in the parish of WESTWARD, ALLERDALE ward below Darwent, county of CUMBERLAND, 2¼ miles (S. S. E.) from Wigton. The population is returned with Brocklebank. In this township are the ruins of Old Carlisle, where was a considerable Roman city, supposed by Horsley to have been the *Olenacum* of the Notitia. The site is an oblong square, including an area of one hundred and seventy, by one hundred and twenty, yards, and was defended by a double vallum, with an entrance on each side. Both within and without the vallum foundations of numerous dwellings are discernible, and a very great number of altars, statues, coins, and inscriptions, has been found. The Roman road from Carlisle (*Lugovallum*) to Ellenborough (*Volantium* or *Virosidum*) passed by this station, and there are traces of various intrenchments in the vicinity.

STONESBY, a parish in the hundred of FRAMLAND, county of LEICESTER, 6 miles (N. E.) from Melton-Mowbray, containing 246 inhabitants. The living is a discharged vicarage, in the archdeaconry of Leicester, and diocese of Lincoln, rated in the king's books at £5. 0. 7½., and endowed with £600 royal bounty. R. Norman, Esq. was patron in 1820. The church is dedicated to St. Peter.

STONESFIELD, a parish in the hundred of WOOTTON, county of OXFORD, 4¼ miles (W.) from Woodstock, containing 498 inhabitants. The living is a discharged rectory, in the archdeaconry and diocese of Oxford, rated in the king's books at £4. 19. 9½., and in the patronage of the Duke of Marlborough. The church is dedicated to St. James.

STONHAM (ASPEL), a parish in the hundred of BOSMERE and CLAYDON, county of SUFFOLK, 5 miles (N. E.) from Needham-Market, containing 633 inhabitants. The living is a rectory, in the archdeaconry of Suffolk, and diocese of Norwich, rated in the king's books at £19. 10. 2½., and in the patronage of Sir W. Middleton, Bart. The church is dedicated to St. Lambert. In the churchyard is a fine, though mutilated, monument of alabaster to the memory of Anthony Wingfield, Esq., whose statue is represented in a recumbent posture, grasping a serpent. Here is a free school, founded about 1574, by the Rev. John Metcalf.

STONHAM (EARL), a parish in the hundred of BOSMERE and CLAYDON, county of SUFFOLK, 3 miles (N. N. E.) from Needham-Market, containing 677 inhabitants. The living is a rectory, in the archdeaconry of Suffolk, and diocese of Norwich, rated in the king's books at £17. 2. 6., and in the patronage of the Master and Fellows of Pembroke College, Cambridge. The church is dedicated to St. Mary. There is a place of worship for Baptists. John Punchard, about 1475, gave a house for the use of a school, which George Reeve, in 1599, endowed with land, now producing more than £20 a year, for the education of poor children.

STONHAM (PARVA), a parish in the hundred of BOSMERE and CLAYDON, county of SUFFOLK, 4 miles (N. N. E.) from Needham-Market, containing 311 inhabitants. The living is a discharged rectory, in the archdeaconry of Suffolk, and diocese of Norwich, rated in the king's books at £9. 18. 11½. Miss Bevan was patroness in 1816. The church is dedicated to St. Mary.

STONTON-WYVILLE, a parish in the hundred of GARTREE, county of LEICESTER, 5½ miles (N. by E.) from Market-Harborough, containing 122 inhabitants. The living is a rectory, in the archdeaconry of Leicester, and diocese of Lincoln, rated in the king's books at £9. 18. 11½., and in the patronage of the Earl of Cardigan. The church is dedicated to St. Denis.

STOODLEY, a parish in the hundred of WITHERIDGE, county of DEVON, 4 miles (S. W.) from Bampton, containing, with Highley St. Mary, 466 inhabitants. The living is a rectory, in the archdeaconry of Barnstaple, and diocese of Exeter, rated in the king's books at £20. 0. 2½., and in the patronage of N. Fazakerley, Esq. The church is dedicated to St. Margaret. On Warbrightsleigh hill, in this parish, are the remains of an ancient beacon, said to have been erected by Edward II.

STOPHAM, a parish in the hundred of ROTHERBRIDGE, rape of ARUNDEL, county of SUSSEX, 4¼ miles (S. E. by E.) from Petworth, containing 139 inhabitants. The living is a discharged rectory, in the archdeaconry and diocese of Chichester, rated in the king's books at £5. 12. 8½., and in the patronage of Walter Smith, Esq. The church, dedicated to St. Mary, is partly in the early, and partly in the decorated, style of English architecture. The river Rother flows through the parish, which is bounded on the east by the Avon.

STOPSLEY, a hamlet in the parish of LUTON, hundred of FLITT, county of BEDFORD, 2 miles (N. N. E.) from Luton, containing 477 inhabitants.

STORETON, a township in the parish of BEBBINGTON, lower division of the hundred of WIRRALL, county palatine of CHESTER, 4¾ miles (N. by E.) from Great Neston, containing 220 inhabitants.

STORITHS, a joint township with Hazlewood, in that part of the parish of SKIPTON which is in the upper division of the wapentake of CLARO, West riding of the county of YORK, 7½ miles (E.) from Skipton. The population is returned with Hazlewood.

STORMORE, an extra-parochial liberty, in the hundred of GUTHLAXTON, county of LEICESTER. The population is returned with Westrill.

STORRINGTON, a parish in the hundred of WEST EASWRITH, rape of ARUNDEL, county of SUSSEX, 8½ miles (N. E.) from Arundel, containing 901 inhabitants. The living is a rectory, in the archdeaconry and diocese of Chichester, rated in the king's books at £18, and in the patronage of the Duke of Norfolk. The church is dedicated to St. Mary. A market was formerly held here on Wednesday, and there are still fairs on May 12th and November 11th. Jane Downer, in 1763, bequeathed a sum of money, now producing £15 a year, for the education of twenty children; and John Hooper, in 1806, left certain premises, now let for £28 per annum, for teaching ten; which bequests, aided by parochial subscriptions, are applied to the instruction of sixty boys and girls on the National system.

STORTFORD (BISHOP), a market town and parish (formerly a borough) in the hundred of BRAUGHIN, county of HERTFORD, 14 miles (E. N. E.) from Hertford, and 30 (N. N. E.) from London, containing, according to the last census, 3358 inhabitants, now about 4500. This place derives its name from its situation on each side of a ford on the river Stort, now crossed by two bridges, and its prefix from having been bestowed by

William, soon after the Conquest, upon Maurice, Bishop of London, and his successors. In the reign of Stephen, the Empress Matilda negotiated to obtain, by exchange, from the Bishop of London, the castle erected here by William the Conqueror, and not succeeding, threatened its demolition; it, however, remained till the eighth year of King John's reign, who, exasperated at the bishop's promulgation of the pope's menace of laying the kingdom under an edict, razed it to the ground, seized the town into his own hands, incorporated the inhabitants, and granted them the elective franchise, which they continued to exercise only from the fourth of Edward II. till the reign of Edward III., when their privileges ceased. In the reign of Mary, this town became the scene of religious persecution, and Bishop Bonner made use of a prison formerly attached to the castle, for the confinement of convicted Protestants, of whom one was burnt on Goose Green adjoining. The town is situated on two gentle acclivities, that on the east being called Hockerhill, in a fertile valley on the banks of the river Stort, and consists principally of four streets, in the form of a cross, of which Windhill is the western, and Hockerill the eastern, extremity. The inhabitants are well supplied with water from springs. There are a public library, instituted in 1827, and several book societies. The trade consists chiefly in malt and other grain, of which considerable quantities are sent by the river, which is navigable, and a canal, on the banks of which are commodious wharfs and quays: a silk-mill affords employment to many of the inhabitants. The market, for which a very handsome and spacious market-house, or corn-exchange, was erected in 1828, is on Thursday: this building is of the Ionic order, and the area of a semicircular form, with a colonnade supported by iron pillars: the other parts contain an assembly and coffee rooms, and magistrates' chamber, on the first floor, and underneath a spacious hall where the corn-exchange is kept: at the southern extremity are the fish, flesh, poultry, and vegetable markets. It was constructed by means of £100 shares, which promise amply to repay the subscribers. Fairs are held annually on Holy Thursday, the Thursday after Trinity-Sunday, and on the 11th of October, for horses and cattle. Bishop-Stortford is within the jurisdiction of the county magistrates, who hold a petty session every fortnight, in a room at the corn-exchange, where the public business of the town is transacted.

The living is a vicarage, in the jurisdiction of the Commissary of Essex and Herts, concurrently with the Consistorial Court of the Bishop of London, rated in the king's books at £12, and in the patronage of the Precentor of St. Paul's Cathedral, London. The church, dedicated to St. Michael, is an elegant and spacious structure, standing at the south-west angle of the town, with a fine tower surmounted by a lofty spire; it was built in the reign of Henry VI., and partly rebuilt in 1820, and contains many ancient and curious monuments, among which is that of Chas. Denny, grandson to Sir Anthony Denny, Knt., Privy Counsellor to Henry VIII. There are places of worship for Baptists, the Society of Friends, Independents, and Methodists, with which are connected Sunday schools, affording instruction to several hundred children. The free grammar school, in High-street, facing the church, was founded and endowed, in 1579, by Mrs. Margaret Dean, of London; an excellent library was presented to it by Thomas Leigh, Esq., and increased by the Rev. Thomas Leigh, vicar, and other benefactors, of which some part still remains preserved in the tower of the church: this school, in which Sir Henry Chauncey, a native of this town, and author of the History and Antiquities of Hertfordshire, was educated, has declined, nothing remaining of its former celebrity but the libraries of Leigh, the founder, and Tooke, the reviver of it on its former failure, together with the books presented by the boys on their leaving school. The National school, established in 1818, in which two hundred boys and one hundred girls are instructed, is supported by voluntary subscription. There are five newly-erected almshouses for poor people, which have been established with the proceeds of the sale of two almshouses in Potter-street, endowed by Mr. R. Pilston, in 1572; and several estates, producing about £200 per annum, are intended for the apprenticing of poor children, the relief of the poor, and the repair of the church; to which latter purpose about £60 per annum, arising from the revenue of a dissolved chantry, and some ancient guilds, formerly established here, is applied. There are some small remains of the castle, in the garden of which Roman coins have been found, and among them one of Marcus Aurelius Antoninus; and near the castle an ancient well, dedicated to St. Osyth, the water of which is esteemed beneficial in diseases of the eye. Bishop-Stortford was the birthplace of Hoole, the translator of Tasso.

STORWOOD, a township in that part of the parish of THORNTON which is in the Holme-Beacon division of the wapentake of HARTHILL, East riding of the county of YORK, 8¼ miles (S. W. by W.) from Pocklington, containing 116 inhabitants.

STOTFOLD, a parish in the hundred of CLIFTON, county of BEDFORD, 2½ miles (N. W.) from Baldock, containing 693 inhabitants. The living is a discharged vicarage, in the archdeaconry of Bedford, and diocese of Lincoln, rated in the king's books at £5. 17. 1., endowed with £1200 private benefaction, £400 royal bounty, and £900 parliamentary grant, and in the patronage of the Master and Fellows of Trinity College, Cambridge. The church is dedicated to St. Mary. There is a place of worship for Wesleyan Methodists.

STOTFORD, a township in that part of the parish of HOOTON-PAGNELL which is in the southern division of the wapentake of STRAFFORTH and TICKHILL, West riding of the county of YORK, 7 miles (N. W.) from Doncaster, containing 9 inhabitants.

STOTTESDEN, a parish partly in the hundred of WOLPHY, county of HEREFORD, but chiefly in the hundred of STOTTESDEN, county of SALOP, 5¼ miles (N.) from Cleobury-Mortimer, containing, with the chapelry of Farlow, 1608 inhabitants. The living is a vicarage, in the archdeaconry of Salop, and diocese of Hereford, rated in the king's books at £15. 10. 10. Sir W. Pulteney, Bart. was patron in 1822. The church, dedicated to St. Mary, was built by Robert de Belesme, Earl of Shrewsbury, who gave it to the abbey of that place.

STOUGHTON, a chapelry in the parish of THURNBY, hundred of GARTREE, county of LEICESTER, 4 miles (E. S. E.) from Leicester, containing 167 inhabitants. The chapel is dedicated to St. Mary.

STOUGHTON, a parish in the hundred of WEST-BOURN and SINGLETON, rape of CHICHESTER, county

of SUSSEX, 6 miles (N. W.) from Chichester, containing 519 inhabitants. The living is a discharged vicarage, in the archdeaconry and diocese of Chichester, rated in the king's books at £8. 10., and in the patronage of the Bishop of Chichester. The church, dedicated to St. Mary, is in the early style of English architecture.

STOULTON, a parish in the lower division of the hundred of OSWALDSLOW, county of WORCESTER, 3¾ miles (N. W.) from Pershore, containing 380 inhabitants. The living is a perpetual curacy, in the archdeaconry and diocese of Worcester, endowed with £600 private benefaction, £200 royal bounty, and £900 parliamentary grant, and in the patronage of Earl Somers. The church is dedicated to St. Edmund.

STOURBRIDGE, a chapelry in the parish of ST. ANDREW the LESS, or BARNWELL, hundred of FLENDISH, county of CAMBRIDGE, 1½ mile (N. E. by N.) from Cambridge. This place is remarkable for its celebrated fair, one of the largest in the kingdom: it is held in a field to the eastward of Barnwell, and commences September 18th, on which day it is proclaimed by the vice-chancellor, doctors, and proctors of the University of Cambridge, and by the mayor and aldermen of that borough, and continues more than three weeks: the staple commodities exposed for sale are, leather, timber, cheese, hops, wool, cattle, and, on the 25th, horses. The hospital of St. Mary Magdalene, for lepers, was anciently at the disposal of the burgesses of Cambridge; but, about 1245, Hugh, Bishop of Ely, possessed the patronage of it, which was also enjoyed by his successors, till the suppression in 1497: its chapel, called St. Mary's chapel, has been converted into a barn.

STOURBRIDGE, a market town in that part of the parish of OLD SWINFORD which is in the lower division of the hundred of HALFSHIRE, county of WORCESTER, 21 miles (N. by E.) from Worcester, and 124 (N. W.) from London, containing 5090 inhabitants. This place, originally called Bedcote (the manor still retaining that name), derives its present appellation from the erection of a bridge, about the time of Henry VI., across the small river Stour, which here separates the counties of Worcester and Stafford. The surrounding country abounds with coal and iron stone, the mines of which appear, by a manuscript in the possession of the Lyttelton family, to have been worked so early as the reign of Edward III.; and the manufacture of glass was established here in 1557, about the period it was introduced into this country from Lorraine. The town consists chiefly of one long street, called the High-street, which is well flagged and Macadamized, and the lower part spacious, and containing some good houses; the upper is somewhat narrow. A subscription library was established in 1790: it contains about three thousand volumes, and is under the management of a president and a committee of twelve members: Parkes, the self-taught and celebrated chemist, was the first president. There are races on two days in the last week in August, during which the theatre, a small and mean looking building, is open; assemblies are held monthly during the season. The principal branches of trade and manufacture are those of glass, iron, and fire-bricks: the first is now carried on to a very great extent, there being twelve houses in the immediate neighbourhood in which the different varieties of flint, crown, bottle, and window glass, are manufactured, besides several cutting-mills. The flourishing state of this branch of manufacture is chiefly owing to the plentiful supply of fuel, and to the existence, near the town, of that superior species of clay used in making glass-house pots, crucibles, and fire-bricks, which is found here in large quantities, and furnishes a considerable article of export, by the name of "Stour-bridge fire clay:" the best lies at about one hundred and fifty feet below the surface of the earth, in strata of three or four feet thick, in the compass of about two hundred acres, near the town: large quantities of these fire-bricks are made, and sent to London and other places. The manufacture of iron forms also a most important branch of the trade of this town and neighbourhood, and the manufactories are generally on a most extensive scale, particularly that of Bradley and Co., which covers nearly four acres, and gives employment usually to about one thousand men: nearly every article in wrought or cast iron is here manufactured, comprehending in the foundry, steam-engines, boilers, gasometers, and every description of heavy machinery; the bearers, roofs, and fire-proof guards belonging to the custom-house, the new post office, and the recently erected portion of the British Museum, were cast here: in the wrought-iron manufactory are made merchant, wire, and sheet, iron; hoops; nail-rods; small rounds and squares, &c. In the other manufactories are made the various articles of hammered iron, besides scythes, spades, anvils and vices, plantation tools, chains, called gearing, &c.; but that branch of the trade which is carried on to the largest extent is the making of nails, which, in the town and neighbourhood, affords employment to some thousand men, women, and children. The trading interests are greatly benefited by a canal, which, running from the town to the Staffordshire and Worcestershire canal, connects it with that extensive line of inland navigation which spreads in various branches over the mining and manufacturing districts of the country, and also with the Severn, affording an opening for the transit of goods to all parts of the kingdom. The market, granted in 1486, by Henry VII., is on Friday, and is well attended: the market-house, recently erected, at an expense of about £15,000, is a handsome brick building; the principal front, looking towards the High-street, is stuccoed, in the Doric order of architecture: it consists of a spacious triangle, the sides being formed by an arcade, under which those who attend the market expose their goods for sale; the area in the centre is left open, and that portion of the front not occupied by the entrance is disposed in shops. The fairs are on the 29th of March and 8th of September; the former, which continues seven days, is a celebrated horse fair; the latter is for horses, horned cattle, sheep, and pedlary. A court of requests, for the recovery of debts under 40s., the jurisdiction of which extends over the parish of Old Swinford, is held here.

An episcopal chapel, dedicated to St. Thomas, was erected, by subscription among the inhabitants, under an act of parliament obtained about a century since; it is a neat brick edifice, with a square tower, and is not within the jurisdiction of the bishop; the inhabitants possess the power of appointing the minister. There are places of worship for Baptists, the Society of Friends, Independents, Wesleyan Methodists, Presbyterians, and

Roman Catholics. The free grammar school was founded and endowed by letters patent, granted in 1553, by Edward VI.: it has a very considerable endowment, from which £150 is paid to the head-master, and £90 to the second master; the remainder, according to a special clause in the deed of endowment, after deducting for repairs of the school, &c., is divided between them; each master has also a good rent-free residence. The government is vested in eight of the principal inhabitants, who are a body corporate, and elect the masters. For several years there were no pupils on the foundation, but at present there are a few: attached to the school is a library of ancient books. Dr. Johnson received the rudiments of his education in this school until he was fifteen years of age; but the report of his having been a candidate for the head-mastership is void of truth. A National school was erected in 1815, and is supported by voluntary contributions; nearly three hundred children are instructed in it, and it is also used as a Sunday school. This town has the privilege of sending four boys to a noble institution called the Blue-coat hospital, founded by Thomas Foley, Esq.; and it also participates in the advantages of the endowments of John Wheeler and Henry Glover; but as these institutions are for the benefit of the parish generally, an account of them will be given under the article OLD SWINFORD. There are twenty-two friendly societies, composed of about one thousand five hundred members, who assemble on Whit-Monday, and proceed to church, with banners and music. In a sandy tract of ground to the westward of the town, numerous detached portions of jasper, porphyry, rock-salt, granite, chalcedony, agate, cornelian, and several varieties of marble, supposed to be diluvial remains, have been discovered.

STOURMOUTH, a parish in the hundred of BLEAN-GATE, lathe of ST. AUGUSTINE, county of KENT, 8 miles (E.N.E.) from Canterbury, containing 257 inhabitants. The living is a rectory, in the archdeaconry and diocese of Canterbury, rated in the king's books at £19, and in the patronage of the Bishop of Rochester. The church is dedicated to All Saints. The navigable river Stour passes through the parish.

STOURPAIN, a parish in the hundred of PIMPERNE, Blandford (North) division of the county of DORSET, 3 miles (N.W. by N.) from Blandford-Forum, containing 499 inhabitants. The living is a discharged vicarage, in the peculiar jurisdiction and patronage of the Dean and Chapter of Salisbury, rated in the king's books at £7.18.6½., and endowed with £200 parliamentary grant. The church is dedicated to the Holy Trinity. The river Stour is navigable on the west and south of this parish. Lacerton, formerly a distinct parish, was united, in 1431, to Stourpain, to which it is now only a hamlet. In a field, called Chapel Close, adjoining a farm-house, the foundations of its ancient church, which was dedicated to St. Andrew in 1331, may be still traced. On an eminence, called Hod-hill, are the remains of a Danish camp, in the form of the letter D, with a double rampart and fosse, which, on the north and south sides, are almost inaccessible: there are five entrances, and, within the area, which comprises several acres, are many circular trenches, four and five yards in diameter, and some round pits, contiguous to each other, supposed to have been so deep and numerous, at one period, as to be capable of concealing a large army.

STOURPORT, a market town in the chapelry of MITTON, parish of KIDDERMINSTER, lower division of the hundred of HALFSHIRE, county of WORCESTER, 4 miles (S. S. W.) from Kidderminster, and 130 (W. N. W.) from London. The population is returned with Mitton. This place, which is of modern date, owes its origin and present importance to the junction of the Staffordshire and Worcestershire canal with the river Severn, on the south side of the town, near the confluence of the Stour with that river. Its name is derived from its situation on the Stour, and from its being the port, or depôt, to which the manufactured articles and produce of the adjoining counties are brought for transmission to different commercial towns; a communication being opened between the Severn and the Trent by the Grand Trunk canal, and a connexion thus formed with most parts of the kingdom. Prior to the completion of the Staffordshire and Worcestershire canal, in 1770, the only part of the town in existence was a few cottages, forming a part of Lower Mitton. The trade principally arises from its being the depôt for goods intended for transmission by canal navigation, extensive basins having been formed, and warehouses erected, for their reception; and the conveyance of them is a source of lucrative employment to many of the inhabitants, as well as the building of boats and barges, for which docks have been constructed. A canal was projected from this town to Kington in Herefordshire, but it has only been executed as far as Mamble. Stourport is a neat well-built town, principally of brick; the chief streets are paved, and it is partially lighted with gas. A subscription library was established in 1821, and there are two reading societies. The Severn is here crossed by a handsome iron bridge to Arely-King's, consisting of one arch, one hundred and fifty feet in breadth, and fifty in height from the surface of the water, with several land-arches, to afford a more free course for the water, in case of a high flood. The former bridge, built in 1775, had three arches over the river, the centre arch being forty-eight feet wide, and the one on each side of it forty-two feet: this bridge having been swept away by a great quantity of ice brought down by the flood after a sudden thaw, the present handsome structure was erected. The market is held on Wednesday, in a market-house erected on a piece of ground purchased by the proprietors, who receive the tolls, and is beginning to assume considerable importance as a corn market. A great quantity of hops was at one time sold, but this branch of trade has very much declined. There are three fairs annually, on the 31st of March, 15th of September, and 18th of December. The inhabitants attend divine service at Mitton chapel. The Wesleyan Methodists have a place of worship, with a Sunday school attached, in which eighty boys and sixty girls are instructed. The Sunday school-rooms are spacious and airy, in which one hundred and twenty boys and girls receive education by means of voluntary contributions.

STOURTON, a parish partly in the hundred of NORTON-FERRIS, county of SOMERSET, but chiefly in the hundred of MERE, county of WILTS, 2½ miles (W. N. W.) from Mere, containing, with the hamlet of Brook, otherwise Gasper, 658 inhabitants. The living is a rectory, in the archdeaconry and diocese of Salisbury, rated in the king's books at £17, and in the patronage of Sir R. C. Hoare, Bart. The church, dedicated to St. Peter, is in the decorated and later styles of English architecture, and contains some monuments of the ancient family of Stourton. Henry Hoare, Esq., in 1724, gave £2000, to be applied for the erection of charity schools and workhouses within the parish. On the site of a large castle, built by John de Stourton, an elegant mansion, of Italian architecture, has been built by the Hoare family, the present proprietors of the estate; and on the highest point in this demesne is a lofty tower, erected, in 1772, by the late Henry Hoare, Esq., in honour of Alfred, the illustrious king of the West Saxons, who, on issuing from his retreat in the Isle of Athelney, is said to have fixed his standard on this ground, bearing the name of Kingsettle Hill: it lies directly on the line of his march to *Petra Ecbricta*, now Brixton-Deverill, and Edington, where he fought the Danes, and gained a signal victory over them. Under a statue is the following inscription: "Alfred the Great, A. D. 879, on this summit erected his standard against the Danish invaders. To him we owe the origin of juries, and the creation of a naval force. Alfred, the light of a benighted age, was a philosopher and a Christian, the father of his people, and the founder of the English monarchy and liberties." In 656, Cenwallus, King of Wessex, defeated the Britons here, and drove them to Petherton, on the river Parret. In 1001, another obstinate battle was fought near the same spot, in which the Danes overthrew the Saxons under Cola and Edsigus. And again, in 1016, King Edmund here defeated the Danes under King Canute. At the south-western extremity of the parish, and partly in Somersetshire, is a wide boggy tract of country, part of which exhibits a great number of curious excavations, known by the name of Pen Pits: of these there are several thousand, of various forms and dimensions, scattered over a surface of nearly seven hundred acres. Stourton gives the title of baron to the family of Stourton, so created in 1448.

STOUTING, a parish in the hundred of STOUTING, lathe of SHEPWAY, county of KENT, 8 miles (E. by S.) from Ashford, containing 236 inhabitants. The living is a rectory, in the archdeaconry and diocese of Canterbury, rated in the king's books at £7. 17. 11., and in the patronage of the Rev. Jacob Geo. Wrench, D.C.L. The church, dedicated to St. Mary, is principally in the early style of English architecture. The parish is bounded on the east by the Roman Stane-street, and a branch of the river Stour rises here. In the neighbourhood is a mound overgrown with wood, around which was a double moat, but the origin of it is now buried in obscurity. Some urns and Roman coins have been discovered in this parish.

STOVEN, a parish in the hundred of BLYTHING, county of SUFFOLK, 5¼ miles (N. E. by E.) from Halesworth, containing 116 inhabitants. The living is a perpetual curacy, in the archdeaconry of Suffolk, and diocese of Norwich, endowed with £600 royal bounty, and in the patronage of the Rev. N. T. O. Leman. The church, dedicated to St. Margaret, contains a Norman arch of great beauty.

STOW, a hamlet in the parish of THRECKINGHAM, wapentake of AVELAND, parts of KESTEVEN, county of LINCOLN, 2¼ miles (N. E. by E.) from Falkingham. The population is returned with the parish.

STOW, a parish in the wapentake of WELL, parts of LINDSEY, county of LINCOLN, 7½ miles (S. E.) from

Gainsborough, containing, with the townships of Normanby, and Sturton with Bransby, 698 inhabitants. The living is a perpetual curacy, in the peculiar jurisdiction of the Prebendary of Stow in Lindsey in the Cathedral Church of Lincoln, endowed with £1200 parliamentary grant, and in the alternate patronage of the Prebendaries of Corringham and Stow in the Cathedral Church of Lincoln. The church, dedicated to St. Mary, is a large structure, principally in the Norman style, with the upper part of the tower, the west window, and a few other portions, of later date. It was founded for Secular priests by Eadnoth, Bishop of Dorchester, its revenue having been greatly augmented by Earl Leofric and his Lady Godiva. After the Conquest these religious became Benedictine monks, under the government of an abbot, and Bishop Remigius obtained for them, from William Rufus, the then desolate abbey of Eynsham in Oxfordshire, where they soon afterwards settled. There is a place of worship for Wesleyan Methodists. Courts leet and baron are annually held here, and a fair for horses and cattle on October 10th. A school for the education of poor children is endowed with about £12 per annum. Watling-street passes near this place, which is supposed to be the ancient *Lidnacester* of the Romans.

STOW, a parish in the hundred of PURSLOW, county of SALOP, 1½ mile (N. E.) from Knighton, containing 157 inhabitants. The living is a discharged vicarage, in the archdeaconry of Salop, and diocese of Hereford, rated in the king's books at £4. 7. 4., endowed with £200 royal bounty, and in the patronage of the Crown. The church is dedicated to St. Michael. The river Team runs through the parish.

STOW (LONG), a parish in the hundred of LONG-STOW, county of CAMBRIDGE, 2¾ miles (S. S. E.) from Caxton, containing 191 inhabitants. The living is a rectory, in the archdeaconry and diocese of Ely, rated in the king's books at £4. 8. 4. The Rev. W. Wright was patron in 1820. An hospital for poor sisters was founded here, and dedicated to the Blessed Virgin, in the reign of Henry III., by Walter, the then vicar.

STOW (LONG), a parish in the hundred of LEIGHTONSTONE, county of HUNTINGDON, 2½ miles (N. by E.) from Kimbolton, containing, with Little Catwick, 194 inhabitants. The living is a perpetual curacy, in the archdeaconry and diocese of Lincoln, endowed with £4 per annum, and £120 private benefaction, and £400 royal bounty, and in the patronage of the Prebendary of Long-Stow in the Cathedral Church of Lincoln. The church is dedicated to St. Botolph.

STOW *cum* QUY, a parish in the hundred of STAINE, county of CAMBRIDGE, 5 miles (N. E.) from Cambridge, containing 378 inhabitants. The living is a perpetual curacy, in the archdeaconry and diocese of Ely, and in the patronage of the Bishop of Ely. The church is dedicated to St. Mary. There is a small endowed school. Jeremy Collier, the celebrated nonjuring divine, was born here in 1650; he died in 1730.

STOW (WEST), a parish in the hundred of BLACKBOURN, county of SUFFOLK, 5¼ miles (N. N. W.) from Bury-St. Edmund's, containing 179 inhabitants. The living is a discharged rectory, in the archdeaconry of Sudbury, and diocese of Norwich, rated in the king's books at £9. 17. 3½., and in the patronage of R. B. de Beauvoir, Esq. The church is dedicated to St. Mary.

STOW on the WOLD, a market town and parish in the upper division of the hundred of SLAUGHTER, county of GLOUCESTER, 25 miles (E. by N.) from Gloucester, and 82 (W. N. W.) from London, containing, with the hamlets of Donnington and Mangersbury, 1731 inhabitants. This place was the scene of a battle between the royalists and the parliamentary forces in the great civil war, on which occasion the former were put to flight. In old records the town is called Stow St. Edward: it is situated on the summit of a steep elevation; the houses in general are of stone, but low, irregularly built, and of ancient appearance; and it is so indifferently supplied with fuel and water, and having no common field attached, that it is vulgarly remarked, it has only one of the four elements, namely air. There is little trade, except a small woollen business: it was formerly noted for the making of shoes. A charter for a market was procured, in the reign of Edward III., by the abbot of Evesham, then lord of the manor: it is held on Thursday; and fairs are held May 12th and October 24th, for the sale of hops, cheese, and sheep, of which last twenty thousand are said to have been sold at one fair. The inhabitants were incorporated by Henry VI., but at present the town is governed by two bailiffs, who are appointed annually at the manorial court leet. The living is a rectory, in the archdeaconry and diocese of Gloucester, rated in the king's books at £18, and in the patronage of the Rev. H. Hippesley. The church, dedicated to St. Edward, is a spacious edifice, in the ancient English style, erected at different periods in the fourteenth and fifteenth centuries. The tower is conspicuous at a great distance. There is a place of worship for Baptists. A National school for children of both sexes is supported by voluntary contributions. An almshouse for nine poor persons, on the south side of the churchyard, was founded, in the 16th of Edward IV., under the will of William Chestre, and subsequent endowments have been given for the maintenance of its inmates. A park, house, and garden, named St. Margaret's chapel, at a place called Merke in this parish, constituted part of the estates of Charles I. and his queen. The Foss-way intersects the town and the northern part of the parish.

STOW-BARDOLPH, a parish in the hundred of CLACKCLOSE, county of NORFOLK, 2 miles (N. N. E.) from Downham-Market, containing 702 inhabitants. The living is a discharged vicarage, annexed to the rectory of Wimbotsham, in the archdeaconry of Norfolk, and diocese of Norwich, rated in the king's books at £6. 6. 8. The church, dedicated to the Holy Trinity, has a large square tower with brick buttresses, and on the north side of the chancel is a chapel, the burial-place of the Hare family. South of the church are the remains of an ancient hermitage, of flint and brick, now converted into a farm-house. Near a bridge, which crosses the Ouse, about two miles from the village, a fair is held for horses and cows, on the eve of the festival of the Holy Trinity.

STOW-BEDON, a parish in the hundred of WAYLAND, county of NORFOLK, 4¾ miles (S. E. by S.) from Watton, containing 290 inhabitants. The living is a discharged vicarage, in the archdeaconry and diocese of Norwich, rated in the king's books at £4. 19. 4½., endowed with £200 private benefaction, and £200 royal bounty, and in the patronage of the Rev. John Eade. The church, dedicated to St. Botolph, was anciently appropriated to Marham abbey, and had a guild founded in honour of the Virgin Mary.

STOW-LANGTOFT, a parish in the hundred of BLACKBOURN, county of SUFFOLK, 2½ miles (S. E.) from Ixworth, containing 172 inhabitants. The living is a rectory, in the archdeaconry of Sudbury, and diocese of Norwich, rated in the king's books at £8. 7. 8½., and in the patronage of — Wilson, Esq. The church is dedicated to St. George.

STOW-MARIES, a parish in the hundred of DENGIE, county of ESSEX, 5½ miles (S. by W.) from Maldon, containing 242 inhabitants. The living is a rectory, in the archdeaconry of Essex, and diocese of London, rated in the king's books at £18. 6. 8., and in the patronage of the Rev. G. H. Storie. The church is dedicated to St. Mary and St. Margaret. The parish is bounded on the south by Crouch river.

STOW-MARKET, a market town and parish in the hundred of STOW, county of SUFFOLK, 12 miles (N. N. W.) from Ipswich, and, by way of that town, through which the mail travels, 81 (N.E.) from London, but only 75 through Sudbury; containing 2252 inhabitants. The adjunct was given to the name to distinguish the town from Stow-Upland, in the adjoining parish. It is the most central town in the county, is situated at the confluence of three rivulets, which form the river Gippen, on the high road from Ipswich to Bury and Cambridge, and consists of several streets, which are, for the most part, regularly built and paved; many of the houses are handsome, especially those near the market-place; and the inhabitants are well supplied with water from land-springs and wells. The commercial interests of the town are essentially promoted by its locality, and have been much improved by making the Gippen navigable to Ipswich, which was effected under an act obtained in 1790. Over one of the tributary streams called the Orwell, which name the united streams assume from Ipswich to the sea at Harwich, is a bridge southward of the town. From the basin of this navigable river extends a pleasant walk, about a mile in length, chiefly through the hop plantations, with which the neighbourhood abounds. The trade consists chiefly in the making of malt, for which there are more than twenty houses, the manufacture being rapidly increasing; and the exportation of corn, to a considerable extent, to London, Hull, Liverpool, and other places: there are also small manufactories for rope, twine, and sacking, and an iron-foundry. At Combs, about two miles distant, is a considerable tannery. By means of the navigation to Ipswich, grain and malt are conveyed thither, the returns consisting of timber, deals, coal, and slate, for the supply of the central parts of the county. The market is on Thursday, for corn, cattle, and provisions: fairs are held on August 12th, for cattle; July 10th, a pleasure fair; and in the month of September, for hops, cheese, butter, and cattle. The meetings for the nomination of the county members, from its central situation, are generally held in this town; as is also a petty session of magistrates, every alternate Monday; and a manorial court baron is held annually.

The living is a discharged vicarage, with that of Stow-Upland annexed, in the archdeaconry of Sudbury, and diocese of Norwich, rated in the king's books at £16. 15., and in the patronage of Miss Bevan. The

church, which is dedicated to St. Peter and St. Mary, is a spacious and handsome edifice, in the centre of the town, partly in the decorated, and partly in the later, style of English architecture, with a square tower surmounted by a slender wooden spire of tasteful appearance, one hundred and twenty feet in height; the latter was erected from the proceeds of a legacy left for that purpose in the reign of Anne. There are places of worship for Baptists and Independents. Some small benefactions are applied in teaching poor children. A large National school, for an unlimited number of children of both sexes, and two Sunday schools, are supported by voluntary contributions. There are also several benevolent institutions for the relief of the poor, the funds arising from the same source. Abbots' hall, the seat of J. Rust, Esq., was formerly a cell, subordinate to the abbey of St. Osyth, in the county of Essex. In a stone pit near the entrance to the town, the tusks and bones of a species of elephant have been found. Here is a spring slightly impregnated with iron. Dr. Young, tutor to the poet Milton, was vicar of this parish from 1630 to 1655, and was interred here.

STOW-UPLAND, a parish in the hundred of STOW, county of SUFFOLK, adjoining Stow-Market, and containing 836 inhabitants. The living is a discharged vicarage, annexed to that of Stow-Market, in the archdeaconry of Sudbury, and diocese of Norwich.

STOW-WOOD, a parish in the hundred of BULLINGTON, county of OXFORD, 4 miles (N. E.) from Oxford, containing 26 inhabitants. There being no church here, the inhabitants resort to the adjoining parish church of Beckley.

STOWE, a parish in the hundred and county of BUCKINGHAM, 2½ miles (N. N. W.) from Buckingham, containing, with the extra-parochial liberty of Luffield-Abbey, 478 inhabitants. The living is a vicarage, in the archdeaconry of Buckingham, and diocese of Lincoln, rated in the king's books at £11. 14. 7., and in the patronage of the Duke of Buckingham. The church is dedicated to St. Mary. There is a place of worship for Wesleyan Methodists. Stowe is celebrated for the princely mansion of the Duke of Buckingham. Hammond, the elegiac poet, died whilst on a visit here, in 1742.

STOWE, a parish in the wapentake of NESS, parts of KESTEVEN, county of LINCOLN, 2¼ miles (W. N. W.) from Market-Deeping, containing 21 inhabitants. The living is a discharged vicarage, with which that of Barholme was united, in 1772, in the archdeaconry and diocese of Lincoln, rated in the king's books at £4. 3. 9., endowed with £200 royal bounty, and in the patronage of the Governors of Oakham and Uppingham schools. The church is dedicated to St. John the Baptist.

STOWE, a parish in the southern division of the hundred of PIREHILL, county of STAFFORD, 7 miles (N. E. by E.) from Stafford, containing 1185 inhabitants. The living is a perpetual curacy, in the archdeaconry of Stafford, and diocese of Lichfield and Coventry, endowed with £200 private benefaction, £400 royal bounty, and £1200 parliamentary grant, and in the patronage of Earl Ferrers. The church is dedicated to St. John the Baptist. Fourteen children are educated for about £15 a year, arising from land given by an individual whose name is unknown.

STOWE-NINE-CHURCHES, a parish in the hundred of FAWSLEY, county of NORTHAMPTON, 5½ miles

(S. E. by E.) from Daventry, containing 395 inhabitants. The living is a rectory, in the archdeaconry of Northampton, and diocese of Peterborough, rated in the king's books at £18, and in the patronage of the Rev. J. L. Crawley. The church, dedicated to St. Michael, contains a magnificent monument, erected by Nicholas Stone, in 1617, to the memory of Elizabeth, fourth daughter of John, Lord Latimer. The Grand Junction canal passes through the parish, and the ancient Watling-street forms its eastern boundary. The Rev. Edward Williams bequeathed the interest of £120 for teaching poor children, and providing them with books.

STOWELL, a parish in the hundred of BRADLEY, county of GLOUCESTER, 2 miles (W. S. W.) from North Leach, containing 33 inhabitants. The living is a discharged rectory, annexed, in 1660, to that of Hampnett, in the archdeaconry and diocese of Gloucester, rated in the king's books at £5. 17. 1. The church is dedicated to St. Leonard. Sir William Scott, Judge of the court of Admiralty, was created Baron Stowell, of Stowell Park, in 1821.

STOWELL, a parish in the hundred of HORETHORNE, county of SOMERSET, 5 miles (S. S. W.) from Wincanton, containing 102 inhabitants. The living is a discharged rectory, in the archdeaconry of Wells, and diocese of Bath and Wells, rated in the king's books at £6. 15., and in the patronage of W. M. Dodington, Esq. The church is dedicated to St. Mary Magdalene.

STOWELL, a tything in that part of the parish of OVERTON which is in the hundred of ELSTUB and EVERLEY, county of WILTS, 6½ miles (S. W. by S.) from Marlborough. The population is returned with the chapelry of Alton-Priors.

STOWER (EAST), a parish in the hundred of REDLANE, Sturminster division of the county of DORSET, 4¼ miles (W.) from Shaftesbury, containing 476 inhabitants. The living is a perpetual curacy, annexed to the vicarage of Gillingham, in the archdeaconry of Dorset, and diocese of Bristol. The church is dedicated to St. Mary. Henry Fielding, Esq., the celebrated novelist, resided for some time on his estate in this parish.

STOWER (WEST), a parish in the hundred of REDLANE, Sturminster division of the county of DORSET, 5¼ miles (W.) from Shaftesbury, containing 205 inhabitants. The living is a perpetual curacy, annexed to the vicarage of Gillingham, in the archdeaconry of Dorset, and diocese of Bristol. The church is dedicated to St. Mary. William Watson, M. D., author of some theological productions, was a native of this place, where, though he regularly graduated as a physician, and was distinguished for knowledge of his profession, he practised as a quack.

STOWER-PROVOST, a parish and liberty in the Sturminster division of the county of DORSET, 4½ miles (W. by S.) from Shaftesbury, containing 800 inhabitants. The living is a rectory, to which that of Todbere was annexed in 1746, in the archdeaconry of Dorset, and diocese of Bristol, rated in the king's books at £16. 4. 9½., and in the patronage of the Provost and Fellows of King's College, Cambridge. The church is dedicated to St. Michael. In the reign of William the Conqueror, a cell to the nunnery of St. Leger de Pratellis, or Preaux, in Normandy, was founded here, which

at the suppression was granted to Eton College, and then to King's College, Cambridge. Rebecca Stonstreet, in 1785, bequeathed a small annuity for teaching poor children.

STOWERTON, a hamlet in the parish of WHICHFORD, Brails division of the hundred of KINGTON, county of WARWICK, 4 miles (S. E.) from Shipston upon Stour, containing 203 inhabitants.

STOWEY, a parish in the hundred of CHEW, county of SOMERSET, 3½ miles (S. S. W.) from Pensford, containing 208 inhabitants. The living is a discharged vicarage, in the archdeaconry of Bath and Wells, rated in the king's books at £6. 12., and in the patronage of the Bishop of Bath and Wells. The church is dedicated to St. Mary. Richard Jones, in 1688, bequeathed £3000 for teaching and apprenticing poor children of Stowey and Chew.

STOWEY (NETHER), a market town and parish in the hundred of WILLITON and FREEMANNERS, county of SOMERSET, 8 miles (W. N. W.) from Bridgwater, and 147 (W. by S.) from London, containing 773 inhabitants. The living is a vicarage, in the peculiar jurisdiction of the Consistorial Decanal Court of Wells, rated in the king's books at £5. 2. 8½., and in the patronage of the Dean and Canons of Windsor. The church, dedicated to St. Mary, stands at the entrance of the town from Bridg-water. There is a place of worship for Independents. This is a small clean town, situated on a tributary stream to the river Parret: it consists of three streets, nearly in the form of the letter Y, neither paved nor lighted, at the intersection of which stands a rudely built market-house, where a market is held on Saturday, but, from its proximity to Bridg-water, very little business is transacted: there is a fair for cattle on September 18th. A small manufacture of silk affords employment to some of the juvenile part of the population. A Sunday school, in which are one hundred and thirty children, is supported by means of sundry small bequests and subscriptions. On a hill, at the western extremity of the town, a castle is said formerly to have stood; but there is no other vestige of it than a small circular earthwork, which commands fine views of the channel and the Mendip hills. Courts leet and baron are held annually at Michaelmas, when constables and other officers are appointed.

STOWEY (OVER), a parish in the hundred of CANNINGTON, county of SOMERSET, 8 miles (W. by N.) from Bridg-water, containing 587 inhabitants. The living is a discharged vicarage, in the archdeaconry of Taunton, and diocese of Bath and Wells, rated in the king's books at £7. 1. 5½., and in the patronage of a Bishop of Bath and Wells. The church is dedicated to St. Mary Magdalene. The manufacture of silk is here carried on to a small extent.

STOWFORD, a parish in the hundred of LIFTON, county of DEVON, 8¼ miles (E. by N.) from Launceston, containing 394 inhabitants. The living is a rectory, in the archdeaconry of Totness, and diocese of Exeter, rated in the king's books at £11. 12. 6. J. D. Harris, Esq. was patron in 1807. In the church is a marble statue of C. Harris, Esq., in the ancient Roman costume. Margaret Doyle, in 1777, bequeathed the interest of £200 to be applied for teaching poor children. Dr. John Prideaux, a learned divine, was born here in 1578; he died in 1650.

STOWICK, a tything in that part of the parish of HENBURY which is in the lower division of the hundred of HENBURY, county of GLOUCESTER, containing 467 inhabitants.

STRADBROOK, a parish in the hundred of HOXNE, county of SUFFOLK, 5¾ miles (E.) from Eye, containing 1400 inhabitants. The living is a discharged vicarage, in the archdeaconry of Suffolk, and diocese of Norwich, rated in the king's books at £9. 18. 6½., and in the patronage of the Bishop of Ely. The church is dedicated to All Saints. There is a place of worship for Baptists. William Greenling in 1599, bequeathed land to be applied, among other purposes, in support of a school; and Michael Wentworth, in 1687, gave the town house for the use of the poor, with a chamber for a school. Mary Warner also, in 1746, left an annuity of £10 for teaching twelve children.

STRADISHALL, a parish in the hundred of RIS-BRIDGE, county of SUFFOLK, 5 miles (N. by W.) from Clare, containing 433 inhabitants. The living is a rectory, in the archdeaconry of Sudbury, and diocese of Norwich, rated in the king's books at £9. 11. 0½., and in the patronage of John Vernon, Esq. The church is dedicated to St. Margaret.

STRADSETT, a parish in the hundred of CLACK-CLOSE, county of NORFOLK, 3¾ miles (E. N. E.) from Downham-Market, containing 176 inhabitants. The living is a discharged vicarage, in the archdeaconry of Norfolk, and diocese of Norwich, rated in the king's books at £3. 6. 8., and endowed with £200 royal bounty. T. P. Bagge, Esq. was patron in 1817. The church is dedicated to St. Mary: the east window exhibits the arms of the see of Ely, those of the East Angles, and of Bury and Dereham abbeys, in stained glass; the north window also is decorated with various emblems.

STRAGGLESTHORPE, a parish in the wapentake of LOVEDEN, parts of KESTEVEN, county of LINCOLN, 8 miles (E. by S.) from Newark, containing 100 inhabitants. The living is a perpetual curacy, annexed to the rectory of Beckingham, in the archdeaconry and diocese of Lincoln. The church is dedicated to St. Michael.

STRAMSHALL, a township in the parish of UT-TOXETER, southern division of the hundred of TOT-MONSLOW, county of STAFFORD,1¾ mile (N.N.W.) from Uttoxeter. The population is returned with the parish. St. Modwenna, on her arrival from Ireland, early in the ninth century, founded a nunnery here, and presided as abbess in it. Stramshall is in the honour of Tutbury, duchy of Lancaster, and within the jurisdiction of a court of pleas held at Tutbury every third Tuesday, for the recovery of debts under 40s.

STRANGHOW, a township in the parish of SKEL-TON, eastern division of the liberty of LANGBAURGH, North riding of the county of YORK, 4½ miles (E.) from Guilsbrough, containing 91 inhabitants.

STRANTON, a parish in the north-eastern division of STOCKTON ward, county palatine of DURHAM, comprising the townships of Brierton, Seaton-Carew, and Stranton, and containing 704 inhabitants, of which number, 371 are in the township of Stranton, 5 miles (S.W. by W.) from Hartlepool. The living is a discharged vicarage, in the archdeaconry and diocese of Durham, rated in the king's books at £17. 16. 0½., and in the patronage of Sir M.W. Ridley, Bart. The church,

dedicated to All Saints, exhibits specimens of various styles of architecture. There is a place of worship for Wesleyan Methodists. A great quantity of limestone is here quarried and burnt into lime. The village is situated on the south side of Hartlepool harbour : a school was erected by subscription in 1777, before which period the north porch of the church was used as a school-room. An immense quantity of human bones was discovered in draining a morass bordering on the Slake, supposed to have been those of the Scots who fell at the siege of Hartlepool, in 1644.

STRATFIELD-MORTIMER, a parish partly in the hundred of HOLDSHOTT, Basingstoke division of the county of SOUTHAMPTON, but chiefly in the hundred of THEALE, county of BERKS, 7 miles (S.W. by S.) from Reading, containing, with the tythings of West Mortimer and Wokefield, 1092 inhabitants. The living is a discharged vicarage, in the archdeaconry of Berks, and diocese of Salisbury, rated in the king's books at £8. 19. 4½., endowed with £200 private benefaction, and £200 royal bounty, and in the patronage of the Provost and Fellows of Eton College. The church is dedicated to St. Mary, and in the east window is a portrait of William of Wykeham, in stained glass. There is a place of worship for Independents. Fairs are held on April 27th and November 6th.

STRATFIELD-SAYE, a parish partly in the hundred of READING, county of BERKS, but chiefly in the hundred of HOLDSHOTT, Basingstoke division of the county of SOUTHAMPTON, 7¾ miles (N.E. by N.) from Basingstoke, containing, with the tything of Beech-Hill, 769 inhabitants. The living is a rectory, in the archdeaconry and diocese of Winchester, rated in the king's books at £24. 13., and in the patronage of the Duke of Wellington. The church is dedicated to St. Mary. Lora Pitt, and others, in 1739, erected a school-house, and endowed it with £400, now producing an annual income of about £18. 18., for which thirty-six children are instructed. There is also an annuity of £5, the bequest of James Christmas, for the education and relief of the poor. A Benedictine priory, in honour of St. Leonard, was founded here, in 1170, by Nicholas de Stotevile, as a cell to the abbey of Vallemont in Normandy, and at the suppression was granted to Eton College : it stood in that part of the parish which is in Berkshire.

STRATFIELD-TURGIS, a parish in the hundred of HOLDSHOTT, Basingstoke division of the county of SOUTHAMPTON, 6½ miles (N.E. by N.) from Basingstoke, containing 238 inhabitants. The living is a rectory, in the archdeaconry and diocese of Winchester, rated in the king's books at £6. 10. 2½., and in the patronage of the Duke of Wellington. The church is dedicated to All Saints.

STRATFORD (ST.ANDREW), a parish in the hundred of PLOMESGATE, county of SUFFOLK, 3 miles (S. W.) from Saxmundham, containing 213 inhabitants. The living is a discharged rectory, in the archdeaconry of Suffolk, and diocese of Norwich, rated in the king's books at £5, endowed with £200 royal bounty, and in the patronage of the King, as Duke of Lancaster.

STRATFORD (ST. ANTHONY), a parish in the hundred of CAWDEN and CADWORTH, county of WILTS, 4 miles (S. W. by W.) from Salisbury, containing 148 inhabitants. The living is a rectory, in the archdeaconry and diocese of Salisbury, rated in the king's books at £12, and in the patronage of the President and Fellows of Corpus Christi College, Oxford. The church is dedicated to St. Mary.

STRATFORD upon AVON, a borough and market town in the parish of OLD STRATFORD, having separate jurisdiction, though locally in the Stratford division of the hundred of Barlichway, county of WARWICK, 8 miles (S. W.) from Warwick, and 94 (N. W.) from London, on the road through Oxford to Shrewsbury, containing 3069 inhabitants. This place, originally called *Streat-ford* and *Stretford*, derived its name from its situation in the great north road, and from a Saxon ford on the river Avon, at the entrance to the town. It was a place of considerable importance prior to the Conquest, and was distinguished for its monastery, founded, in the reign of Ethelred, on or near the site of the present church. In 1197, Richard I. granted the inhabitants a weekly market; and, during the succeeding reigns, various other privileges were conferred upon the town. In the 36th and 37th of Elizabeth it suffered materially from accidental fires, which destroyed the greater part of it; and again, in 1614, it experienced a similar calamity. In 1588, both ends of the bridge over the Avon were carried away by a flood that inundated the lower part of the town. During the parliamentary war, a party of royalists stationed here was driven out by a superior force of parliamentarians, under the command of Lord Brooke, in 1642; but the inhabitants still maintained their adherence to the royal cause, and, in the following year, Henrietta Maria, queen of Charles I., at the head of three thousand infantry, one thousand five hundred cavalry, and with a train of artillery, and one hundred and fifty wagons, advanced to the town, where she was met by Prince Rupert; and, after remaining for some days at New Place, the residence of Shakspeare, where she was hospitably entertained by the family, proceeded to Kington, to meet the king, whom she accompanied to Oxford. The parliamentarians, having subsequently obtained possession of the town, demolished one of the arches of the bridge, over the deepest part of the river, to prevent the approach of the royalists.

The town is beautifully situated on the south-west border of the county, on an eminence rising gently from the west bank of the Avon, which, here expanding, winds round its base. The entrance from the London road is over a handsome stone bridge of fourteen pointed arches, originally, with the causeway, three hundred and seventy-six yards in length, defended on each side by a stone parapet, and having on the north side a foot-path, with an iron palisade, supported by brackets of iron, resting on the piers. This bridge was built by Sir Hugh Clopton, in the reign of Henry VII., and widened by act of parliament in 1814. Nearly parallel with it is another of nine cycloidal arches, built of brick, and exclusively used as a rail-road to the wharfs at this extremity of the

town. At the southern termination of the town, over a branch of the river, which has been diverted to form a mill dam, is a foot bridge of wood, resting upon strong piers of stone; from the hill beyond which is a fine view of the town, the church, the surrounding scenery, and the distant woods. The town consists of several spacious streets, intersecting each other, some at right angles, and others crossing obliquely: the houses in that part which is called the Old Town, though rather of ancient appearance, are commodious and well built, occasionally interspersed with modern buildings of large dimensions and handsome appearance, and in some of the streets are smaller houses of frame-work timber and plaster; among these, part of the ancient house in which Shakspeare was born is still preserved in its antique state, and is an object of much interest. The house in which he lived in retirement, for a few years previously to his decease, was originally the mansion of the Clopton family, and was purchased by the bard, who, after repairing and improving it, called it "New Place:" it has been taken down by a late proprietor, who also cut down the mulberry tree planted by Shakspeare in the gardens. The town is partially paved, and lighted with oil by lamps adapted to the future introduction of gas, and the inhabitants are amply supplied with water from pumps attached to their houses. The public library and reading-rooms are supported by subscription; the Shaksperian library, also supported by private subscription, was established in 1810, and is a permanent and useful institution. The theatre is a neat building of brick, within the precincts of Shakspeare's garden, and is internally well arranged and elegantly fitted up; the exterior is decorated with a portico, and when completed according to the original plan, will be an ornament to the town; it is generally open for three months in the season, and assemblies are held occasionally, during the winter, at the town hall. To the south of the town is a racecourse, where races formerly took place, and were in general well attended; but since 1786 they have been discontinued. A jubilee, in honour of Shakspeare, was instituted by Garrick, in the year 1769, when the town hall, which had been recently rebuilt, was dedicated to the poet; and his statue, finely sculptured, and presented to the town by Garrick, at the close of the ceremony, was placed in a niche at the north end of the building; this festival has been recently revived, and is celebrated every third year. The environs, abounding with diversified scenery and objects of considerable interest, afford many beautiful walks; and the salubrity of the air, and its central situation in a neighbourhood enlivened with the elegant villas of respectable families, and the noble mansions of the wealthy, make it eligible as a place of residence. There is not much trade carried on, the inhabitants being principally employed in agriculture; the only manufacture is that of patent Florentine silk buttons, a branch of a larger factory at Bromsgrove, employing from fifty to sixty persons. The Stratford canal, passing close to the north of the town, and joining the Birmingham, Warwick, and Oxford canals, connects them with the Avon, which is navigable, for barges of forty tons, to Tewkesbury, where it joins the Severn, thus affording a line of inland navigation to the principal towns in the kingdom : near the bridge are some extensive wharfs for lime, timber, coal, and other articles of merchandise. The market, which was formerly on Thursday, is now, by charter granted in the 59th of George III., held on Friday, and is very considerable for corn and other grain, and for cattle. The fairs, to which are attached courts of pie-powder, are on May 14th and the three following days, for cattle, horses, and toys; and September 25th, for cattle and cheese; besides these there are great cattle markets on the third Monday in February, the Friday after the 25th of March, the last Monday in July, the second Friday after the 25th of September, and on the second Monday in December; there is also a statute fair on the morrow after Old Michaelmas. The corn market is held in the area near the town hall; the poultry market in a neat stuccoed building erected at the east end of Wood-street, near the spot where the ancient cross formerly stood, and surmounted by a cupola and vane, representing a falcon grasping a tilting spear, Shakspeare's family crest; and the cattle market in a spacious area formed by the intersection of the streets leading to the London, Birmingham, Evesham, and Alcester roads.

The town received its first regular charter of incorporation from Edward VI., which, reciting and confirming former grants of privileges to the "Bailiff and Burgesses of Stratford on Avon," was extended by James I., and subsequently by Charles II., in the sixteenth and twenty-sixth years of his reign. Under this last charter the government is vested in a mayor, a high steward, recorder, two chamberlains, twelve aldermen, and twelve burgesses, assisted by a steward of the borough court, clerk of the peace, two serjeants at mace, and subordinate officers. The mayor, who is also coroner and clerk of the market, is chosen annually, on the first Wednesday in September, by the aldermen and burgesses in council; the high steward, recorder, and steward of the borough court are elected by the corporation, and hold their offices for life; the aldermen and the chamberlains are chosen from the common council, by the corporation. The mayor, the late mayor, the high steward, the recorder, and the two senior aldermen, are justices of the peace within the borough; and, by the second charter of Charles II., the mayor, recorder, and the senior aldermen, are also justices of the peace for part of the parish of Old Stratford not otherwise within the jurisdiction of the borough, which includes Old Town, and the church and churchyard. The corporation are, by their charter, empowered to hold quarterly courts of session for all offences not capital, and a court of record for the recovery of debts not exceeding £40; but they have nearly fallen into disuse. The guildhall, in which the courts were held, and the business of the corporation is now transacted, is an ancient building, possessing few claims to architectural notice: it occupies the west side of a small quadrangular area, of which the chapel of the ancient guild of the Holy Cross forms the north side, the vicar's and schoolmaster's houses the east, and the entrance to the school the south side; above the hall are rooms appropriated to the use of the free grammar school. The town hall was rebuilt, in 1768, by the corporation, assisted by the nobility and gentry of the neighbourhood, on the site of the former, of which the upper room, having been used during the civil war as a magazine, by an accidental explosion was destroyed, and

the building greatly damaged. The present building is a plain and substantial structure, of the Tuscan order, on piazzas: at the north angle are two small cells for the temporary confinement of prisoners, and the rest of the area is appropriated to the use of the market: on the west front are the arms of the corporation, and in a niche at the north end of the building is the statue of Shakspeare, presented by Garrick. The upper story comprises a handsome banqueting-room, sixty feet long, and thirty feet wide, decorated with paintings, among which are a full-length portrait of Shakspeare, sitting in an antique chair, by Wilson, and, at the opposite end, one of Garrick, reclining against a bust of the poet, by Gainsborough; besides several smaller apartments, which are also ornamented with paintings: the larger meetings of the corporation, the mayor's feast, and the town meetings, are held here; and the celebration of the jubilee, concerts, and assemblies, take place in this suite of rooms.

The living is a vicarage, in the jurisdiction of the peculiar court of the Rector of Stratford upon Avon, rated in the king's books at £20, and in the patronage of the Earl of Plymouth. The church, dedicated to the Holy Trinity, and formerly collegiate, is a spacious and venerable cruciform structure, in the early style of English architecture, with a square embattled tower rising from the centre, and surmounted by a lofty octagonal spire; the west entrance is through a richly-moulded and deeply-recessed archway, above which is a large window in the later style, its lower central compartment being filled up with three richly-canopied shrines: an avenue of lime trees, with their branches entwined, forms a pleasing approach to the north porch, over which is an apartment originally lighted by a window, now covered by a tablet. The effect of the interior is destroyed by the closing up of the east end of the nave by the organ, excluding the transepts and the chancel: the nave, of which the fine oak roof is richly carved, and supported on clustered pillars and pointed arches, is very lofty, and is lighted by a range of twelve large clerestory windows enriched with tracery of the later style. In the south aisle, which is in the decorated style, is a chapel, dedicated to St. Thomas à Becket; and in the north aisle is a sepulchral chapel, separated by a richly-carved stone screen, containing several altar-tombs, with recumbent figures of the Clopton family, finely sculptured in marble, and painted to represent the natural complexion of the persons. In the transept are several ancient and some handsome modern monuments, and at the extremity of each is a large enriched window: massive piers of clustered columns, and lofty arches, support the tower, but lose their effect by the exclusion of the nave on one side, and of the chancel on the other. The chancel, parted off by an oak screen, which has been glazed, is much disfigured by a flat ceiling of plaster, in the room of the original oak roof: it is lighted by a handsome range of five windows on each side, in the later style, and a large east window of rich tracery, in which are placed several portions of stained glass that have been preserved: on the south side, near the altar, is a piscina, and near it are stone stalls of elegant design; but the beauty of these, and of the ornamental carvings in the church, is greatly defaced by the thick coat of whitewash which conceals the minuter details. On a slab at the entrance to the altar, covering the ashes of the bard, is an inscription written by Shakspeare, and on the north wall is his monument, in which is his bust, representing him in the act of composing, with a pen in the right hand, and the left arm resting upon a scroll on a cushion : this bust, which is a well-attested likeness, and was originally painted with strict resemblance to the complexion, and colour of the eyes and hair, of the poet, has, by the direction of his commentator Malone, been painted to resemble stone, and forms a lamentable contrast to the complexioned monuments of the Clopton family, and others in the church. The ancient stone font in which Shakspeare was baptized having been removed, to make room for a modern one of marble, was carefully preserved by the late Captain Saunders, of Stratford, who placed it on the pedestal of the ancient market cross, and, upon the erection of the new market-house, removed it into his garden. The chapel of ease, also dedicated to the Holy Trinity, is a handsome edifice in the later style of English architecture : it formerly belonged to the ancient guild of the Holy Cross, and was rebuilt, by Sir Hugh Clopton, in the reign of Henry VII. It has a square embattled tower, and a beautiful north porch, of which the entrance is a deeply-recessed and highly-enriched arch, surmounted by a canopy embellished with scrolls and flowers ; the nave is lofty, and is lighted on each side by a range of four windows ; the chancel appears, from frequent alteration and repair, which have been made at different times without due regard to the prevailing style of the structure, to have lost its original character : in repairing the chapel, the walls were found to have been originally decorated with various legendary paintings of great antiquity. The master of the grammar school is usually appointed chaplain, to whom the corporation pay a stipend of £ 50 per annum. There are places of worship for Baptists, Independents, and Wesleyan Methodists.

The free grammar school was founded, in 1482, by Thomas Jolyffe, a native of the town, and one of the brethren of the ancient guild of the Holy Cross : at the dissolution the estate was seized by Henry VIII., but was afterwards restored by Edward VI., for pious and charitable uses, to the corporation, who refounded the school, which is open to all inhabitants of the town for gratuitous instruction in the classics, writing, and arithmetic : the number of scholars on the foundation is about fifteen. The income arising from the endowment is about £ 130 per annum, of which £ 115 is paid by the corporation to the master, who is appointed by the Earl of Plymouth, as lord of the manor ; in addition to which he has £ 30 per annum for a house, the original building being too small for residence, and the chaplainship of the chapel of the Holy Trinity. In this school Shakspeare received his education, but he was removed at an early age. The National school, in which ninety boys and eighty girls are instructed, is supported by subscription ; a Lancasterian school is supported by the Independents ; and an infant school was founded by Miss Mason, at whose expense a neat building, capable of receiving two hundred children, was erected. The almshouses nearly adjoining the guildhall, and in a similar style of building, were refounded and endowed under the charter of Edward VI., for twelve men and twelve women, of whom the most aged and infirm are placed out in case of illness, where they can receive more at-

tention : they have an allowance of five shillings each per week, to which, from the charities of the families of Clopton and Lord, clothing is added every alternate year : there are numerous other charitable bequests for distribution among the poor. About a mile to the west of the town, in the hamlet of Bishopton, is a mineral spring, which, having been analysed by Dr. Perry, in 1744, was found to be of a saline quality, strongly impregnated with sulphur, in its properties like the water of Leamington. At Welcombe, about one mile to the north of the town, are the remains of a military intrenchment, formed of deep ravines meeting obliquely in a common point : in the neighbourhood are several tumuli, in which human bones, spear-heads, and other military weapons, have been found : in opening one of these, in 1795, the proprietor discovered a human skull, transfixed with a spear, which appeared to be the gilded head of a standard pike. On the surface of Borden Hill, about a mile to the west, astroites, or star stones, are found in profusion, in small columns apparently formed of successive layers, which are easily separated : the soil is calcareous, and in the region of limestone, to the north-west, large specimens of testaceous fossils are found : the star stone is found also at Shuckburgh near Southam, and the arms of the family of that name are three of these stones of five points, parted by a chevron. Of the ancient monastery, or of the college that succeeded it, the site of which was near the parish church, not the slightest vestige is discernible. So intimately is the name of Shakspeare associated with every recollection and description of this borough, that every circumstance connected, however remotely with his memory, is deemed worthy of being recorded. It is singular that, though a letter addressed to him has been discovered, which was in the possession of the late Captain Saunders, no traces of his hand-writing, nor any thing that was ever known to have belonged to him, have ever been fully authenticated. In 1810, a large gold seal ring, which had evidently lain there many years, was found near the churchyard, bearing the initials W.S., tied together with a string and tassels, according to the fashion of his time : this, which with great probability is supposed to have been his signet, is in the possession of Mr. Wheler, author of the history of Stratford. Stratford is eminently distinguished as the place where Shakspeare was born, on the 23rd of April, 1564, and in which, after having lived a few years in retirement, he ended his days, on the anniversary of his birth, in 1616, in the 52nd year of his age. Among other eminent natives were John de Stratford, Lord Treasurer in the reign of Edward II., and Lord Chancellor in that of Edward III., who promoted him to the see of Canterbury ; Robert de Stratford, his brother, Archdeacon of Canterbury, and afterwards Lord Chancellor, on the translation of his brother to the primacy, and who, together with him and the Bishop of Lichfield and Coventry, was committed to the Tower, on a charge of having detained the supplies for the war with France, but was subsequently liberated and promoted to the see of Chichester ; Ralph de Stratford, Bishop of London, who, during the great pestilence, in the year 1348, purchased a piece of ground near Smithfield, for the interment of those who died of the contagion ; John Huckell, educated in the free grammar school, author of a poem on the Avon, who assisted Garrick in the composition of the Ode, and other poetical addresses, delivered at the celebration of the jubilee, in 1769; and Francis Ainge, a memorable instance of longevity, who was baptized on the 23rd of August, 1629, left England in his youth and died in North America, on the 13th of April, 1767, having attained the extraordinary age of one hundred and thirty-seven years.

STRATFORD le BOW, county of MIDDLESEX.— See BOW.

STRATFORD under the CASTLE, a parish in the hundred of UNDERDITCH, county of WILTS, 1¾ mile (N. W. by N.) from Salisbury, containing, with the borough of Old Sarum, 385 inhabitants. The living is a perpetual curacy, in the archdeaconry and diocese of Salisbury, and in the patronage of the Dean and Chapter of Salisbury. The church is dedicated to St. Lawrence.

STRATFORD (FENNY), a market town and chapelry, partly in the parish of BLETCHLEY, and partly in that of SIMPSON, hundred of NEWPORT, county of BUCKINGHAM, 13½ miles (E.) from Buckingham, and 45 (N. W.) from London, containing 521 inhabitants. The distinguishing prefix is derived from the nature of the surrounding land; the town itself stands on an eminence. In 1665, it was much depopulated by the plague, on account of the ravages of which the inns were shut up, and the road turned in another direction: it contains two streets. The Grand Junction canal crosses the high road at the bottom of the town. Lace-making employs a considerable number of poor females. The market, which has never flourished since the time of the plague, is on Monday; and fairs for cattle are held on April 19th, July 18th, October 10th, and November 28th. The living is a perpetual curacy, in the archdeaconry of Buckingham, and diocese of Lincoln, endowed with £400 private benefaction, and £600 royal bounty, and in the patronage of John Willis, Esq. The chapel, situated in Bletchley, having been dilapidated since the reign of Elizabeth, was rebuilt by subscription, through the exertions of Mr. Browne Willis, the antiquary, who resided here, and who may be considered its founder. The first stone was laid by him, on St. Martin's day, in 1724, and the building was dedicated to St. Martin, because his grandfather died on St. Martin's day, in St. Martin's lane. On its consecration, in May 1730, he delivered a speech to the diocesan, in which he represented the decline of morality among the inhabitants, from the want of a place of worship: it has received an addition of two hundred and forty free sittings, to which the Incorporated Society for the building and enlargement of churches and chapels contributed £195. The living is a perpetual curacy, in the archdeaconry of Bucks, and diocese of Lincoln, and in the gift of the patron of Bletchley. The remains of Mr. Willis are interred within the rails of the communion-table: he bequeathed a benefaction for a sermon to be preached on St. Martin's day, and requested that the rector of Bletchley may never have the cure of Fenny-Stratford, but directed that, if he would contribute £6 per annum towards the salary of the curate, he should have the appointment; this has never been done. Baptists and Wesleyan Methodists have each a place of worship. A National school, supported by voluntary contributions, was erected in 1817. A guild, dedicated to St. Margaret and St. Catherine, was founded, in 1494, by Roger and John Hobbes.

STRATFORD (ST. MARY), a parish in the hundred of SAMFORD, county of SUFFOLK, 5¼ miles (W. N. W.) from Manningtree, containing 614 inhabitants. The living is a discharged vicarage, in the archdeaconry of Suffolk, and diocese of Norwich, rated in the king's books at £13, and in the patronage of the King, as Duke of Lancaster. The river Stour is navigable on the west of this parish, also on the south, where it is crossed by a bridge. Lettice Dikes, in 1589, gave a rent-charge of £1, and Robert Clarke, in 1731, another of £5, for teaching poor children. This parish is entitled also to the benefit of Littlebury's school, founded at Dedham, in 1575.

STRATFORD (OLD), a hamlet partly in the parishes of COSGROVE, FURTHO, PASSENHAM, and POTTERS-PURY, hundred of CLELEY, county of NORTHAMPTON, ¼ of a mile (N. W.) from Stony-Stratford. The population is returned with the parishes. At a place called Chapel Close there formerly stood a hermitage and a free chapel.

STRATFORD (OLD), a parish in the Stratford division of the hundred of BARLICHWAY, county of WARWICK, adjacent to the town of Stratford upon Avon, containing, with the hamlet of Luddington, and the town of Stratford upon Avon, 4229 inhabitants. The living is a discharged vicarage, in the peculiar jurisdiction of the Rector of Stratford upon Avon, rated in the king's books at £20, endowed with £400 royal bounty, and in the patronage of the Earl of Plymouth. The church is dedicated to the Holy Trinity.

STRATFORD (STONY), a market town comprising the united parishes of West Side and East Side, in the hundred of NEWPORT, county of BUCKINGHAM, 8 miles (N. E.) from Buckingham, and 52 (N.W.) from London, containing 1499 inhabitants. At or near this spot appears to have been the *Lactodorum* of the Itinerary. Camden is of opinion that it was at the town, because the derivation of *Lactodorum*, in the ancient British language, agrees with the present name, both signifying "a river forded by means of stones." Dr. Stukeley supposes it was at Old Stratford, on the Northamptonshire side of the river; and Dr. Salmon, at Claverston, an eminence close to the old road which led to the ford at Passenham, where the army of Edward the Elder was stationed, whilst he fortified Towcester. Through Stratford passes the Roman road, Watling-street, in its course in a direct line through the county from Brickhill. One of the crosses in memory of Eleanor, queen of Edward I., was erected here, but it was demolished in the great civil war. At an inn in this town, Richard III., when Duke of Gloucester, accompanied by the Duke of Buckingham, seized the unfortunate young prince, Edward V., and, in his presence, arrested Lord Richard Grey and Sir Thomas Vaughan. In 1736, an accidental fire destroyed fifty-three houses; and, in 1742, a similar catastrophe consumed one hundred and thirteen, and the church of St. Mary Magdalene, which has never been rebuilt: the tower, however, escaped the flames, and is yet standing. The damage was estimated at £10,000, of which £7000 was raised for the sufferers by a brief and subscriptions. The town consists of one long street, composed of houses built of freestone, of which some are very good: it is partially paved with pebbles, and well supplied with water, but not lighted, though an act for lighting and paving was obtained in 1800. This place consisted originally of only a few inns, but its traffic (which is now very great) increasing, its enlargement followed, and a stone bridge, with five arches, was constructed over the Ouse. The manufacture of bone-lace gives employment to many families. A market was granted to the Veres in 1460 : in 1663, Simon Bennet, lord of the manor of Calverton, procured a charter for a market on Friday (the present market-day), and four fairs, but only three are now held, *viz.* August 2nd, Friday next after October the 10th, and November 12th; the first and last are for cattle. The government is in the county magistrates, who sit every alternate Friday.

The livings of the two parishes, having been united, form a perpetual curacy in the archdeaconry of Buckingham, and diocese of Lincoln, endowed with £8 per annum and £200 private benefaction, and £600 royal bounty, and in the patronage of the Bishop of Lincoln. The church, dedicated to St. Giles, formerly a chantry, was erected in 1451, and endowed in 1482, but rebuilt, except the tower, in 1776, by Mr. Irons of Warwick. Till of late years it was included in the parish of Calverton, on the west side of the street, whilst that of St. Mary Magdalene belonged to that of Wolverton, on the east side ; there are not at present, in either district, twenty acres of land not covered with buildings. There are places of worship for Baptists, Independents, and Wesleyan Methodists. Two Sunday schools, in which upwards of three hundred children are instructed, were opened in 1786 ; and in 1819, a National school, for an unlimited number of boys, supported by voluntary contributions, was also opened, to which an endowment for ten boys, bequeathed by Mr. M. Hipwell, of this place, has since been appropriated. Here is also a fund of £70 per annum, for apprenticing poor children.

STRATFORD (WATER), a parish in the hundred and county of BUCKINGHAM, 3 miles (W. by N.) from Buckingham, containing 167 inhabitants. The living is a rectory, in the archdeaconry of Buckingham, and diocese of Lincoln, rated in the king's books at £7. 0. 5., and in the patronage of the Duke of Buckingham. The church, dedicated to St. Giles, is partly Norman, having an enriched doorway in that style.

STRATFORD-LANGTHORNE, a ward in the parish of WEST HAM, hundred of BEACONTREE, county of ESSEX, 4 miles (N. E. by E.) from London. The population is returned with the parish. The village, which is situated on the high road to Harwich, is well lighted with gas by the trustees of the road, and supplied with water from the East London water-works. It is in contemplation to erect a new church in this part of the parish, his Majesty's commissioners having proposed a grant for that purpose. There are places of worship for Independents, Wesleyan Methodists, and Roman Catholics. The printing and dyeing of calico and silk are extensively carried on. There are also two chemical establishments, and a porter brewery, on the river Lea, which is navigable to the Thames. A charity school was founded in 1802, and is supported by voluntary contributions and the work of the children, for clothing and educating thirty girls. John Hiett, in 1719, bequeathed £5 a year for apprenticing one poor boy. About 1135, a Cistercian abbey, dedicated to the Virgin Mary and All Saints, was founded here by William of Montfichet, the society of which, being in danger from the floods, the abbey occupying a low situation in the marshes, removed to a cell at Burghstead, near Billericay ; but the damages sustained from the waters being repaired, they returned, and continued here till the dissolution, at which period the revenue was valued at £573. 15. 6.

STRATTON, a market town and parish in the hundred of STRATTON, county of CORNWALL, 17½ miles (N. N. W.) from Launceston, and 223 (W. by S.) from London, containing 1580 inhabitants. This place has acquired considerable note, as having been the scene of the great victory obtained, in the early part of the civil war, by the royalist forces over their opponents : in consideration of the eminent services rendered by Sir Ralph Hopton, on this occasion, he was created Lord Hopton of Stratton, in 1643 ; and after his death in 1654, Charles II., then in exile, in 1658, created Sir John Berkley, to whose prowess and courage the victory at Stratton was mainly owing, Baron Berkley of Stratton. The town is situated in a flat country, and the streets are but indifferently paved ; the inhabitants are tolerably supplied with water : it is in contemplation to build a market-house and two bridges. The Bude canal passes within a mile of the town, and extends to Draxton bridge, about three miles north of Launceston : upon it are six inclined planes, worked by very powerful machinery, particularly that near Bude. The market is on Tuesday, and fairs are on May 19th, November 8th, and December 11th. A court leet is held annually by the lord of the manor, and a court baron by the lord of the manor of Efford ; petty sessions for the hundred are also held on the first Tuesday in every month. The living is a discharged vicarage, in the archdeaconry of Cornwall, and diocese of Exeter, rated in the king's books at £10. 11. 8., and in the patronage of the King, as Duke of Cornwall. The church is dedicated to St. Andrew. There is a place of worship for Wesleyan Methodists. Here is a small charitable donation for the education of fifteen boys and ten girls. Some lands, now let for about £115 per annum, are vested in feoffees for the benefit of the poor of this parish.

STRATTON, a parish in the hundred of GEORGE, Dorchester division of the county of DORSET, 3½ miles (N. W.) from Dorchester, containing, with the tything of Grimstone, 262 inhabitants. The living is a perpetual curacy, annexed to that of Charminster, in the peculiar jurisdiction of the Dean of Salisbury, endowed with £200 private benefaction, £200 royal bounty, and £200 parliamentary grant, and in the patronage of J. Trenchard, Esq. The church, dedicated to St. Mary, has a lofty tower, but no chancel, the latter having been pulled down in 1547. A Roman road from Dorchester to Ilchester passes through the parish.

STRATTON, a parish in the hundred of CROWTHORNE and MINETY, county of GLOUCESTER, 1¾ mile (N. W.) from Cirencester, containing 271 inhabitants. The living is a rectory, in the archdeaconry and diocese of Gloucester, rated in the king's books at £12. 7. 6., and in the patronage of Mrs. Masters. The church, dedicated to St. Peter, is a small ancient structure with a steeple rising from between the nave and the chancel. The ancient Ermin-street passes through the parish, and by a bush, called Crowthorne, which gives name to the hundred.

STRATTON, an extra-parochial liberty, in the hundred of COLNEIS, county of SUFFOLK, adjoining the parish of Levington, and containing but one house, the ancient hall. In Chapel-field, between Levington and Trimley, are the ruins of a church or chapel, almost concealed by trees and bushes.

STRATTON (EAST), a parish in the hundred of MITCHELDEVER, Basingstoke division of the county of SOUTHAMPTON, 6 miles (N. N. W.) from New Alresford, containing 386 inhabitants. The living is a perpetual curacy, annexed to the vicarage of Mitcheldever, in the archdeaconry and diocese of Winchester. The church is dedicated to All Saints.

STRATTON on the FOSS, a parish in the hundred of KILMERSDON, county of SOMERSET, 6 miles (N. N. E.) from Shepton-Mallet, containing 317 inhabitants. The living is a discharged rectory, in the archdeaconry of Wells, and diocese of Bath and Wells, rated in the king's books at £9. 11. 5½., and in the patronage of the King, as Duke of Cornwall. The church is dedicated to St. Vigor. The village is situated on the ancient Fosse way, which now forms part of the turnpike-road leading from Bath to Shepton-Mallet. On the eastern side of the road is Downside College, an elegant and stately edifice, established for the education of Roman Catholic children, and those designed for the service of that church. Coal, iron-stone, and marl, are found in abundance, the former affording considerable employment to the poor. The Bath market is principally supplied with butter from the dairy farms in this neighbourhood.

STRATTON (LONG) ST. MARY, a parish in the hundred of DEPWADE, county of NORFOLK, 10½ miles (S. by W.) from Norwich, containing 636 inhabitants. The living is a rectory, annexed to that of St. Clement's, Norwich, in the archdeaconry of Norfolk, and diocese of Norwich, rated in the king's books at £10, and in the patronage of the Master and Fellows of Caius College, Cambridge. The church, in old records, is called Stratton *cum* turri, whence it appears that the other two Strattons had churches without steeples : it contains a handsome monument to Judge Reve and his lady. There is a place of worship for Independents. The Roman road leading to *Ad Tuam*, or Tasburgh, passes through the parish. A fair was granted by King John to Roger de Stratton, in 1207, but it is now disused. Here was anciently a hermitage, with an oratory attached. Several Roman urns, one of them curiously ornamented, were found, in 1773, on opening a gravel pit, near which a sepulchral hearth has since been discovered, with a mixture of ashes and burnt earth upon it.

STRATTON (ST. MARGARET), a parish in the hundred of HIGHWORTH, CRICKLADE, and STAPLE, county of WILTS, 2¾ miles (N. E. by N.) from Swindon, containing, with the tything of Upper Stratton, 745 inhabitants. The living is a discharged vicarage, in the archdeaconry of Wilts, and diocese of Salisbury, rated in the king's books at £8. 12. 3½., endowed with £200 royal bounty, and in the patronage of the Warden and Fellows of Merton College, Oxford, on the nomination of the Bishop of Salisbury. John Hurring, in 1720, bequeathed lands producing a small income for teaching poor children. An Alien priory was founded here soon after the Conquest, which, at the dissolution, was given by Henry VI. to King's College, Cambridge.

STRATTON (ST. MICHAEL), a parish in the hundred of DEPWADE, county of NORFOLK, 1 mile (N. by E.) from St. Mary Stratton, containing 229 inhabitants. The living is a rectory, with that of St. Peter consolidated, in the archdeaconry of Norfolk, and diocese of Norwich, rated in the king's books at £6. 12. 8½., and in the patronage of the Warden and Fellows of New College, Oxford. The church of St. Peter has been long since demolished.

STRATTON (UPPER), a tything in the parish of STRATTON ST. MARGARET, hundred of HIGHWORTH, CRICKLADE, and STAPLE, county of WILTS, 4¼ miles (S. W.) from Highworth. The population is returned with the parish.

STRATTON (WEST), a tything in the parish and hundred of MITCHELDEVER, Basingstoke division of the county of SOUTHAMPTON, 6¾ miles (N. W. by N.) from New Alresford. The population is returned with the parish.

STRATTON-AUDLEY, a parish partly in the hundred and county of BUCKINGHAM, but chiefly in the hundred of PLOUGHLEY, county of OXFORD, 3 miles (N. E. by N.) from Bicester, containing 342 inhabitants. The living is a perpetual curacy, in the archdeaconry and diocese of Oxford, endowed with £200 private benefaction, and £200 royal bounty, and in the patronage of the Dean and Canons of Christ Church, Oxford. The church is dedicated to St. Mary.

STRATTON-STRAWLESS, a parish in the southern division of the hundred of ERPINGHAM, county of NORFOLK, 4¼ miles (S. S. E.) from Aylsham, containing 187 inhabitants. The living is a discharged rectory, in the archdeaconry and diocese of Norwich, rated in the king's books at £8. 8., endowed with £200 royal bounty, and in the patronage of R. Marsham, Esq. The church, dedicated to St. Margaret, contains numerous monuments and inscriptions, and the windows some curious specimens of ancient stained glass.

STREATHAM, a parish in the eastern division of the hundred of BRIXTON, county of SURREY, 6 miles (S. by W.) from London, comprising the hamlets of Upper Tooting and Balham Hill, and containing 3616 inhabitants. This parish, which derives its name from its situation near the great Roman road from Arundel to London, is almost connected with the metropolis by continuous ranges of building, and extends along the principal road to Brighton for nearly three miles. The houses, which are mostly modern, are well built, and interspersed with several detached villas and stately mansions, particularly in the neighbourhood of the common. Streatham park was formerly the residence of Mrs. Thrale, afterwards Madame Piozzi, where Dr. Johnson spent much of his time. The neighbourhood is richly wooded, and is diversified with hills and vallies, and the surrounding scenery is finely varied : the air, which is considered particularly salubrious and invigorating, combining with other local advantages, has rendered this village a favourite residence of many opulent families. Among the attractions is a mineral spring, which was discovered in 1660, and is still held in esteem, being highly efficacious in scorbutic eruptions, and in many other cases. The only branch of manufacture is that of silk, recently introduced. The parish is within the jurisdiction of the court of requests for the eastern division of the hundred of Brixton, held in the borough of Southwark, for the recovery of debts under £5, and within the limits of the new police establishment. The living is a rectory, in the archdeaconry of Surrey, and diocese of Winchester, rated in the king's books at £18. 13. 9., and in the patronage of the Duke of Bedford. The ancient church, dedicated to St. Leonard, with the exception of the tower, which is of flint, and surmounted by a spire of shingles, forming a picturesque object in the distant landscape, was taken down in 1830, and is now being rebuilt upon an enlarged scale. A chapel has been erected at Upper Tooting, within the last few years, of which the living is a perpetual curacy, in the patronage of the Rector. There are places of worship for Independents and Wesleyan Methodists. A National school is supported by subscription. Mrs. Elizabeth Howland, in 1716, bequeathed £20 per annum for clothing and educating ten girls; and Mrs. Dorothy Appleby, in 1681, left £5 per annum for apprenticing a poor child annually. The St. Anne's Society for the maintenance, clothing, and education of poor children of both sexes was originally established in 1709, and for nearly a century had only a day school in London for clothing and instructing thirty children of each sex from all parts of the kingdom. The first asylum which this society established in the country was at Lavenham, in Suffolk, in 1794, where twenty boys were admitted on the foundation; this establishment was subsequently removed to Peckham in Surrey, where the number of boys increased to sixty-eight, but the efforts of the committee to extend the benefit of the institution, rendered it necessary to provide more ample accommodation, and the present handsome building, adapted to the reception of one hundred and fifty children, was, in 1830, erected at Brixton Hill, in this parish, at an expense of £8000. It is a handsome edifice of brick, having a basement of stone, channelled in horizontal lines, with a central piazza, from which rises a portico of four Ionic columns, supporting a triangular pediment with frieze and cornice continued round the building, which is also decorated at the angles with antæ of corresponding character: it occupies, with the grounds attached, more than two acres of freehold land. The internal arrangements are well adapted to the purposes of the institution, and the management is under the superintendence of a committee of governors, chosen from the subscribers, by whom the institution is supported. The funds have been materially assisted by a liberal contribution of £3000 by Mrs. Partis, of Bath, towards the erection of the new asylum; in acknowledgment of which benefit, Mrs. Partis has the right, in perpetuity, of placing two boys and two girls in the institution, which, after her decease, will devolve to the trustees of Partis' College, near Bath, noticed in our account of that city. There are at present seventy-eight boys and twenty-eight girls, who are educated, clothed, and wholly maintained, the boys till they are fourteen, and the girls till they are fifteen, years of age, when they are apprenticed and placed out at the expense of the society. Thirty boys and thirty girls are still clothed and instructed in the school in London, of whom ten boys, and five girls, are annually admitted on the foundation at Brixton, according to seniority and merit; the remainder are elected by the governors at large, without reference to any particular district, the asylum being open to necessitous children from every part of the

kingdom; any person may place a child in the institution by paying the sum of £105. The celebrated Dr. B. Hoadley, Bishop of Bangor, was for several years rector of this parish, previously to his promotion to the see of Salisbury.

STREATLAM, a joint township with Staunton, in that part of the parish of GAINFORD which is in the south-western division of DARLINGTON ward, county palatine of DURHAM, 2¾ miles (N. E. by E.) from Barnard-Castle. The population is returned with Staunton. Here was anciently a chapel, but no traces of it are discernible. In the neighbourhood are extensive quarries, from which stone has been raised for the erection of the principal buildings in this part of the county; among which is Streatlam castle, a stately structure, built in the seventeenth century, on the site of the old castle, by Sir William Bowes, whose ancestors resided here for many generations.

STREATLEY, a parish in the hundred of FLITT, county of BEDFORD, 5 miles (N. by W.) from Luton, containing, with the hamlet of Sharpenhoe, 309 inhabitants. The living is a discharged vicarage, in the archdeaconry of Bedford, and diocese of Lincoln, rated in the king's books at £6. 15. 2., endowed with £600 royal bounty, and in the patronage of — Cuthbert, Esq. The church is dedicated to St. Margaret. Richard Norton, in 1686, gave a rent-charge of £10 in support of a school, wherein eight boys are educated.

STREATLEY, a parish in the hundred of MORETON, county of BERKS, 5½ miles (S. by W.) from Wallingford, containing 590 inhabitants. The living is a vicarage, in the archdeaconry of Berks, and diocese of Salisbury, rated in the king's books at £10. 7. 6., and in the patronage of the Bishop of Salisbury. The church is dedicated to St. Mary. Streatley is supposed to have taken its name from its situation on the ancient Iknield-street, or Ickleton Long, as it is here called, which crosses the Thames from this place to Goring in Oxfordshire. Eight boys and girls are taught to read and write for an annuity of £2. 5., the bequest of Mr. Richard Tull. Here was formerly a convent of the Dominican order, part of which was remaining a few years since.

STREET, a parish in the hundred of WHITLEY, county of SOMERSET, 1¾ mile (S. S. W.) from Glastonbury, containing 791 inhabitants. The living is a rectory, with the perpetual curacy of Walton annexed, in the archdeaconry of Wells, and diocese of Bath and Wells, rated in the king's books at £24. 12. 3½., and in the patronage of the Marquis of Bath. The church, dedicated to the Holy Trinity, has lately received an addition of two hundred and fifty-six sittings, of which two hundred and forty are free, the Incorporated Society for the enlargement of churches and chapels having granted £120 towards defraying the expense. There are places of worship for Baptists and the Society of Friends. A large fair for all kinds of cattle is held at Christmas. Blue lias and limestone, abounding with marine impressions, are found here.

STREET, a parish in the hundred of STREET, rape of LEWES, county of SUSSEX, 6¼ miles (N. W.) from Lewes, containing 152 inhabitants. The living is a discharged rectory, in the archdeaconry of Lewes, and diocese of Chichester, rated in the king's books at £6. 19. 7., endowed with £200 private benefaction, and £200 royal bounty. Mrs. Lane was patroness in 1822. The church is a small ancient structure of flint, partly in the early English, and partly in the decorated, style of architecture, containing several monuments to the Dobell family and others.

STREETHALL, a parish in the hundred of UTTLESFORD, county of ESSEX, 4 miles (W.N.W.) from Saffron-Walden, containing 54 inhabitants. The living is a discharged rectory, in the archdeaconry of Colchester, and diocese of London, rated in the king's books at £13, endowed with £200 private benefaction, and £200 royal bounty, and in the patronage of Lieut. General Raymond.

STREETHAY, a hamlet in that part of the parish of ST. MICHAEL, LICHFIELD, which is in the northern division of the hundred of OFFLOW, county of STAFFORD, 2¼ miles (N.E. by E.) from Lichfield, containing 90 inhabitants.

STRELLY, a parish in the southern division of the wapentake of BROXTOW, county of NOTTINGHAM, 4½ miles (W.N.W.) from Nottingham, containing 350 inhabitants. The living is a discharged rectory, in the archdeaconry of Nottingham, and diocese of York, rated in the king's books at £6. 4. 8., endowed with £400 royal bounty, and in the patronage of T. Webb Edge, Esq. The church, dedicated to All Saints, is a large handsome cruciform structure, with a lofty tower; the nave is separated from the chancel by a richly-carved oaken screen: it contains several tombs of the Strelley family, and the windows exhibit some ancient stained glass in good preservation. Though the hall has been much modernised, there still remain slight traces of the style of Edward III. In the park is an extensive area, surrounded by a moat, and in the neighbourhood are considerable coal mines. Richard Smedley, in 1744, gave land for the endowment of a school, in which twenty poor children are educated.

STRENSALL, a parish within the liberty of ST. PETER of YORK, East riding, though locally in the wapentake of Bulmer, North riding, of the county of YORK, 6 miles (N.N.E.) from York, containing 378 inhabitants. The living is a discharged vicarage, in the peculiar jurisdiction and patronage of the Prebendary of Strensall in the Cathedral Church of York, rated in the king's books at £4. 13. 4. The church is dedicated to St. Mary. Robert Wilkinson, in 1718, gave by deed £14. 6. per annum in support of a school; the present annual income, arising from this and other sources, is £34, for which the master instructs all the poor children of the parish.

STRENSHAM, a parish in the upper division of the hundred of PERSHORE, county of WORCESTER, 4½ miles (S. W. by S.) from Pershore, containing 312 inhabitants. The living is a rectory, in the archdeaconry and diocese of Worcester, rated in the king's books at £12, and in the patronage of John Taylor, Esq. The church, dedicated to St. John the Baptist, is a noble structure: it contains many memorials of the Russel family, among which are some fine specimens of Italian sculpture, in Parian and other marbles. Strensham, which is pleasantly situated on the river Avon, between the hills of Malvern and Bredon, is renowned in history for the siege it sustained against the parliamentary forces, and for the signal bravery displayed by the then lord of the manor, Sir William Russel, here, as well as

in the memorable battle of Worcester: it is further distinguished as the birthplace, in 1612, of Samuel Butler, author of Hudibras. Blue stone abounds in every part of the parish, and, in some places, fossils and minerals are met with. Lady Ann Russel bequeathed a rent-charge of £10 for teaching poor children; and there are nine almshouses, endowed by some members of the same family.

STRETFORD, a parish in the hundred of STRETFORD, county of HEREFORD, 4¾ miles (S. W. by W.) from Leominster, containing 48 inhabitants. The living is a discharged rectory, in the archdeaconry and diocese of Hereford, rated in the king's books at £6. 19. 8., endowed with £200 royal bounty, and in the patronage of the Representatives of the late John Morris, Esq. The church is dedicated to St. Peter.

STRETFORD, a hamlet in the parish of LEOMINSTER, hundred of WOLPHY, county of HEREFORD, 2½ miles (E. by S.) from Leominster. The population is returned with the township of Broadward.

STRETFORD, a chapelry in the parish of MANCHESTER, hundred of SALFORD, county palatine of LANCASTER, 4 miles (S. W.) from Manchester, containing 2173 inhabitants. The living is a perpetual curacy, in the archdeaconry and diocese of Chester, endowed with £230 private benefaction, £600 royal bounty, and £800 parliamentary grant, and in the patronage of the Wardens and Fellows of the Collegiate Church of Manchester. The chapel has lately received an addition of one hundred and seventy-six sittings, of which ninety-five are free, the Incorporated Society for the enlargement of churches and chapels having granted £95 towards defraying the expense.

STRETHAM, a parish [in the southern division of the hundred of WITCHFORD, Isle of ELY, county of CAMBRIDGE, 4¼ miles (S. W. by S.) from Ely, containing, with the chapelry of Thetford, 1104 inhabitants. The living is a rectory, in the peculiar jurisdiction and patronage of the Bishop of Ely, rated in the king's books at £22. The church is dedicated to St. James. There are places of worship for Baptists and Wesleyan Methodists.

STRETTON, a township in the parish of TILSTON, higher division of the hundred of BROXTON,' county palatine of CHESTER, 4½ miles (N. W. by N.) from Malpas, containing 106 inhabitants.

STRETTON, a chapelry in that part of the parish of GREAT BUDWORTH which is in the hundred of BUCKLOW, county palatine of CHESTER, 4½ miles (S. by E.) from Warrington, containing 277 inhabitants. In 1827 a new chapel, with a tower, in the early English style, was erected, towards defraying the expense of which the Incorporated Society for promoting the building of additional churches granted £1800: it contains five hundred sittings, half of them free.

STRETTON, a township in the parish of NORTH WINGFIELD, hundred of SCARSDALE, county of DERBY, 4½ miles (N. by W.) from Alfreton, containing 489 inhabitants.

STRETTON, a parish in the hundred of ALSTOE, county of RUTLAND, 8¼ miles (N. E. by E.) from Oakham, containing 195 inhabitants. The living is a rectory, in the archdeaconry of Northampton, and diocese of Peterborough, rated in the king's books at £7. 17. 1., and in the patronage of Sir G. Heathcote, Bart. The church is dedicated to St. Nicholas. The Rev. John Turner, in 1786, bequeathed £ 20 in support of a school.

STRETTON, a chapelry in that part of the parish of PENKRIDGE which is in the western division of the hundred of CUTTLESTONE, county of STAFFORD, 3 miles (S. W. by W.) from Penkridge. The population is returned with the parish. The living is a perpetual curacy, in the jurisdiction of the royal peculiar court of Penkridge, endowed with £710 private benefaction, and £800 royal bounty, and in the patronage of E. J. Littleton, Esq. The chapel is dedicated to St. John. The Grand Trunk canal passes in the vicinity. This is now an obscure place, supposed to occupy the site of the Roman *Pennicrocium*, agreeing in distance with the account given by Antoninus, in his Itinerary, and there having been several Roman coins, with other relics, found upon the spot.

STRETTON, a township in that part of the parish of BURTON upon TRENT which is in the northern division of the hundred of OFFLOW, county of STAFFORD, 2¼ miles (N.) from Burton upon Trent, containing 374 inhabitants. It is within the peculiar jurisdiction of the manorial court of Burton upon Trent.

STRETTON (CHURCH), a market town and parish in the hundred of MUNSLOW, county of SALOP, 13 miles (S. by W.) from Shrewsbury, and 153 (N.W.) from London, containing, with the townships of All Stretton, Little Stretton, and Minton, 1226 inhabitants. This place, which, by its adjunct, is distinguished from its townships as the seat of the parish church, derived its name Stretton, or Street-town, from its situation within a quarter of a mile of the ancient Watling-street, which passes in a direction parallel with the road from Shrewsbury to Ludlow. The town is romantically situated in a rich and fertile vale, enclosed on one side by a bold range of mountains, among which are the Caer Caradoc, the lofty and precipitous retreat of Caractacus; the Lawley; and the Raglish; and on the other by the extensive chain of hills called the Longmynd, flat on the summit, but deeply indented, on the south-eastern acclivity, with numerous vallies, from which many mountain streams descend with impetuosity. It consists of one street only, in the wider part of which is the market-house, erected in 1617, an antique building of timber and plaster, consisting of two upper rooms now used for storing wool, and supported on pillars of wood, resting on stone plinths, affording a sheltered area for the use of the market. The houses are in general built of brick, and of neat and modern appearance, occasionally interspersed with handsome dwellings and many small cottages : the inhabitants are amply supplied with water by pumps attached to the more respectable houses, and from a stream which, descending from the Longmynd, flows at one extremity of the town. The secluded and romantic situation of the place, its proximity to scenes of deep interest, the mildness and salubrity of the air, and various other attractions, render it a place of resort for parties from the neighbouring towns. But little trade is carried on: a manufactory for flannel was established in 1816, which is now flourishing; but the principal part of the inhabitants are employed in agriculture : large flocks of sheep are depastured on the neighbouring hills, and a fair for wool was established in 1819. The market is on Thursday,

chiefly for provisions : the fairs are March 10th, for cattle, horses, and sheep; May 14th, a statute fair; July 3rd, a great wool fair; September 25th, a very large sheep fair; and the last Thursday in November, for cattle, sheep, and horses. The county magistrates hold a court of petty sessions at the Talbot hotel, on the third Thursday in every month; and two constables for each township are annually appointed at the court leet held in the old manor-house, now an inn, at which also, under the steward, who must be a lawyer, a court of requests for the recovery of debts under 40s. was formerly held by letters patent of Charles II., granted to the Marquis of Bath, then lord of the manor.

The living is a rectory, in the archdeaconry of Salop, and diocese of Hereford, rated in the king's books at £15. 10., and in the patronage of the Rev. Robert Norgrave Pemberton. The church, dedicated to St.Lawrence, is an ancient and venerable cruciform structure, principally in the early style of English architecture, with a square embattled tower rising from the centre, strengthened by buttresses, and crowned with pinnacles : in the buttress at the south angle is a figure of St. Lawrence, and in other parts of the tower are groups of figures, well sculptured. The south porch and the entrance on the north are of Norman character, and the interior contains several portions in the Norman style, with insertions in the decorated style of English architecture. The nave, chancel, and transepts, are separated by four lofty clustered columns and pointed arches, which support the tower; the chancel is beautifully ornamented with richly carved oak in antique devices, collected from ancient manorial and ecclesiastical edifices, and put up by the present rector, who has bestowed much care and expense on the embellishment of the church; and in the central compartment of the altar is an elegant and well-carved representation of a dead Christ in the lap of the Virgin. The windows, principally in the decorated style, with rich and flowing tracery, are embellished with stained glass; and in the south transept, the ancient oak roof, finely carved, is carefully preserved. A large stone coffin with a lid, now broken, and an alabaster slab, with an illegible inscription, were taken from under a low arch in the south transept. The triennial visitation is held in this church by the bishop of the diocese, in August, and in the intermediate years by the archdeacon, in May.

The free school was endowed by successive benefactors, of whom the principal were, Edward Lloyd, Esq., who in 1790 bequeathed £100; John Bridgman, Esq., who in 1803 gave £100; and the Rev. John Mainwaring, who in 1807 left £200 for the same purpose. In addition to these legacies, of which a portion is appropriated to apprenticing the children, it has an endowment of forty acres of land, under the late enclosure act. The building, which is neat and well adapted to its use, comprises two school-rooms, with apartments for the master and the mistress; the school is free for all children of the parish, and combines the objects of a National school, (in which one hundred children, of whom the more respectable pay a quarterage to the trustees, are instructed in reading, writing, and arithmetic,) with the advantages of a Sunday school : the income is about £70, out of which the master is allowed £40, per annum. The almshouses, which have been recently erected, are appropriated as residences for four poor people, who pay a rent of one shilling per quarter : the rental of four acres of land in the parish, and several charitable bequests, are distributed among the poor, on Easter-day, by the rector and churchwardens. On Caer Caradoc are the remains of a large encampment, defended on the steepest acclivities with one, and on the more accessible ascents with two, and in some places with three, intrenchments hewn out of the solid rock ; this was probably an exploratory station of Caractacus, from whom the hill received its name. In the neighbourhood of Clun is another, in which the British hero, after his escape from the Roman conquerors, took refuge, and from which he was betrayed into their power, and led captive to Rome. On the summit of Longmynd a pole has been erected, denoting the highest point in that extensive range of hills, commanding a panoramic view of a wide extent of country in every direction : the prospect includes, on the west, the Stiperstones, the Welch mountains, the Sugar loaf in Abergavenny, the Table mountain, the Cader Idris, and the intervening range from that mountain to Snowdon; on the south-east, the Edgewood, between Wenlock and Ludlow, the Wrekin, and the Clee and Malvern hills; and the Radnorshire hills on the south-west. On the Longmynd are many low tumuli and cairns of stones ; and on one of the eminences, called Bodbury, is a large intrenchment of earth: this mountain was the scene of many battles between the Romans and the Britons, and afterwards between the Welch and the English. In 1825, one of the tumuli was opened, under the superintendence of the Rev. Mr. Pemberton, rector of the parish : on the level of the base was found a circular enclosure of loose stones, appearing to have endured the action of fire, and several pieces of bone were discovered in a calcined state, supposed to have been parts of the bodies burnt there according to the rites of Roman sepulture : this tumulus was surrounded by the trench, from the excavation of which it had been raised. On an eminence at Minton is a very lofty tumulus, supposed to be one of those mounts upon which, in the earlier times of the Britons, justice was administered to the people. One mile to the south-west of Church-Stretton was Brockard's Castle, of which the site, the intrenchments, the moat, and foundations, with the approaches from the Watling-street, may be traced. Among the eminent natives of this town were William Thynne, Receiver of the Marches, in 1546 ; Sir John Thynne, Knt., who founded Longleat House, in the county of Wilts; and Dr. Roger Mainwaring, vicar of St. Giles' in the Fields, London, and chaplain to Charles I., who, for preaching two sermons, called " Religion " and " Allegiance," was censured by parliament, and imprisoned and suspended for three years ; being afterwards by the king made Bishop of St. David's, he retained that dignity till the abolition of episcopacy, when he again underwent various persecutions till his death, in 1653.

STRETTON upon DUNSMOOR, a parish in the Rugby division of the hundred of KNIGHTLOW, county of WARWICK, 5½ miles (W. by N.) from Dunchurch, containing, with the hamlet of Princethorpe, 760 inhabitants. The living is a vicarage, in the archdeaconry of Coventry, and diocese of Lichfield and Coventry. The Rev. H. T. Powell was patron in 1817. The church is dedicated to All Saints. William Herbert, in 1694, bequeathed land, directing the rental to be applied to

charitable purposes, among which £10. 10. is paid to a schoolmaster for teaching poor children.

STRETTON en le FIELDS, a parish in the hundred of REPTON and GRESLEY, county of DERBY, though locally in the western division of the hundred of Goscote, county of Leicester, 5 miles (S. W.) from Ashby de la Zouch, containing 116 inhabitants. The living is a rectory, in the archdeaconry of Derby, and diocese of Lichfield and Coventry, rated in the king's books at £9. 10. 5., and in the patronage of Sir William Browne Cave, Bart. The church, dedicated to St. Michael, contains some ancient tombs of ecclesiastics.

STRETTON on the FOSS, a parish forming a detached portion of the Brails division of the hundred of KINGTON, county of WARWICK, 3 miles (W. S. W.) from Shipston upon Stour, containing 410 inhabitants. The living is a rectory, with that of Ditchford annexed, in the archdeaconry of Gloucester, and diocese of Worcester, rated in the king's books at £11, and in the alternate patronage of the two Coheiresses of the Rev. W. Hawes. The church is dedicated to St. Peter. The old Roman Fosse-way passes through the parish, also an unfinished rail-road. There is a spring in the neighbourhood, the water of which is slightly impregnated with salt. Ditchford friary is divided into three farms, but there are no remains of its ancient chapel.

STRETTON under FOSS, a hamlet in the parish of MONK'S KIRBY, Kirby division of the hundred of KNIGHTLOW, county of WARWICK, 6¼ miles (N. W. by N.) from Rugby, containing, with Newbold-Revel, 261 inhabitants. There is a place of worship for Independents. The Oxford canal is crossed by the old Fosse-road to the westward of this place.

STRETTON (MAGNA), a chapelry in the parish of GLEN MAGNA, hundred of GARTREE, county of LEICESTER, 5½ miles (S. E. by E.) from Leicester, containing 17 inhabitants. The chapel is dedicated to St. John the Baptist. The Roman *Via Devana* passes through the chapelry.

STRETTON (PARVA), a chapelry in the parish of KING'S NORTON, hundred of GARTREE, county of LEICESTER, 6 miles (E. S. E.) from Leicester, containing 128 inhabitants.

STRETTON-BASKERVILLE, a parish in the Kirby division of the hundred of KNIGHTLOW, county of WARWICK, 3 miles (E. by S.) from Nuneaton, containing 85 inhabitants. The living is a sinecure rectory, in the archdeaconry of Coventry, and diocese of Lichfield and Coventry, rated in the king's books at £6. Miss Pinchin and Mrs. Wilcox were patronesses in 1822. The church, which was dedicated to All Saints, is in ruins.

STRETTON-GRANDSOME, a parish in the hundred of RADLOW, county of HEREFORD, 7¾ miles (N. W.) from Ledbury, containing 150 inhabitants. The living is a vicarage, with the perpetual curacy of Ashperton annexed, in the archdeaconry and diocese of Hereford, rated in the king's books at £9. 4. 2., and in the patronage of the Rev. W. Hopton. The church is dedicated to St. Lawrence.

STRETTON-SUGWAS, a parish in the hundred of GRIMSWORTH, county of HEREFORD, 3¼ miles (N. W. by W.) from Hereford, containing 151 inhabitants. The living is a discharged rectory, in the archdeaconry and diocese of Hereford, rated in the king's books at £9. 7. 1., and in the patronage of the Governors of Guy's Hospital, London. The church is dedicated to St. Mary Magdalene.

STRICKLAND (GREAT), a township in the parish of MORLAND, WEST ward, county of WESTMORLAND, 6 miles (S. E. by S.) from Penrith, containing 246 inhabitants. There is a meeting-house belonging to the Society of Friends, with a burial-ground attached. A school, for which the building was erected in 1790, is endowed with land purchased with £10 left, in 1757, by Wm. Fletcher, and £20 by Wm. Stephenson, in 1797.

STRICKLAND (LITTLE), a township in the parish of MORLAND, WEST ward, county of WESTMORLAND, 8¾ miles (N. N. W.) from Orton, containing 115 inhabitants.

STRICKLAND-KETTLE, a township in that part of the parish of KENDAL which is in KENDAL ward, county of WESTMORLAND, 2 miles (N. by W.) from Kendal, containing 390 inhabitants. It is bounded on the east by the Kent river. The chapel and part of the village of Burneside is within this township.

STRICKLAND-ROGER, a township in that part of the parish of KENDAL which is in KENDAL ward, county of WESTMORLAND, 4 miles (N.) from Kendal, containing 341 inhabitants. It is bounded on the west by the river Kent, and on the east by the Sprint, and contains part of the village of Burneside. Near Garnet bridge is a mill for the manufacture of bobbin, and at Cowen Head there is a paper-mill. At a place called Hundhow was anciently a chapel, called Chapel en le Wood.

STRINGSTON, a parish in the hundred of CANNINGTON, county of SOMERSET, 10¼ miles (W. N. W.) from Bridg-water, containing 131 inhabitants. The living is a vicarage, with the rectory of Kilve united, in the archdeaconry of Taunton, and diocese of Bath and Wells. There is a place of worship for Independents. In the neighbourhood is an ancient fortification, called Danes-burrow, or Douseborough, Castle, with a double embankment and wide ditch; it is about three quarters of a mile in circumference, and is wholly covered with oak coppice wood, among which a prætorium may be distinctly traced. There is a trifling bequest by George Paddon, in 1734, for the education of children.

STRIXTON, a parish in the hundred of HIGHAM-FERRERS, county of NORTHAMPTON, 4¼ miles (S. by E.) from Wellingborough, containing 56 inhabitants. The living is a discharged rectory, consolidated with the vicarage of Bozeat, in the archdeaconry of Northampton, and diocese of Peterborough, rated in the king's books at £7, and in the patronage of Earl Spencer. The church, dedicated to St. John the Baptist, is small, but affords a good specimen of the early style of English architecture.

STROUD, a tything in the parish of CUMNER, hundred of HORMER, county of BERKS, containing 76 inhabitants.

STROUD, or STROUDWATER, a market town and parish in the hundred of BISLEY, county of GLOUCESTER, 10 miles (S. by E.) from Gloucester, and 102 (W. by N.) from London, containing 7097 inhabitants. This place, which formerly belonged to the parish of Bisley, derives its name from its situation on the Slade, or Stroud water, near its confluence with the Frome. It stands on a considerable declivity, in the midst of a most beautiful country, and consists principally of a long street extending up the side of the hill, which is crossed by another at its base: the streets are paved, and contain many handsome houses, and the inhabitants are well supplied with water conveyed by pipes from two springs in the neighbourhood. Stroud has long been famous as the centre of the woollen manufacture in Gloucestershire, and is supposed to owe much of its prosperity to the peculiar properties of the stream called the Stroud water, which is admirably adapted for dyeing scarlet, and which, consequently, was the means of attracting, at an early period, many clothiers and dyers to its banks. It possesses great advantages in water-carriage, the Thames and Severn canal passing close to the south of the town. The inhabitants of the neighbourhood and surrounding villages are employed in different processes of this manufacture, several thousand pieces of broad and narrow cloth being annually made, and conveyed by the canal to different parts of the empire. The town has been greatly improved recently, in consequence of an act of parliament obtained, within a few years, for paving, lighting, and widening the streets; and many new roads have been formed extending in various directions, to connect it more closely with the contiguous towns. The market, which is on Friday, is well supplied; and there are fairs on the 10th of May and the 21st of August, for cattle, sheep, and pigs. The petty sessions for the hundred are held here, on the first and third Fridays in every month. Stroud is also within the jurisdiction of the court of requests, for the recovery of debts under 40s., held at Cirencester, on Thursday every three weeks; and in that of a court baron held annually by the lord of the manor of Bisley. The living is a perpetual curacy, in the archdeaconry and diocese of Gloucester, endowed with £400 private benefaction, £400 royal bounty, and £800 parliamentary grant, and in the patronage of the Bishop of Gloucester : there is an endowed lectureship, in the gift of the parishioners. The church, dedicated to St. Lawrence, is a large building, erected and enlarged at several different periods, with a tower at its western end, surmounted by a lofty octangular steeple. There are places of worship for Particular Baptists, Independents, and Wesleyan Methodists. Thomas Webb, in 1642, gave an endowment, now amounting to about £54 per annum, by means of which four poor boys are boarded, clothed, and educated; and, in 1734, Henry Windowe bequeathed £21 for the maintenance and clothing of two more : there are other small endowments for educating and apprenticing poor boys, and several hundred children are instructed in the Sunday schools. The parochial school, instituted, in 1700, by the Rev. William Johns, is supported by annual subscriptions. Many endowments also provide relief for the poor, and several friendly societies for the benefit of such as are sick have been established. Stroud is the birthplace of John Canton, F.R.S., a celebrated natural philosopher, who died in 1772; and Joseph White, D.D., Professor of Arabic at Oxford, who died in 1814; both these distinguished men were the sons of weavers.

STROUD, a parish partly within the jurisdiction of the borough of ROCHESTER, and partly in the hundred of SHAMWELL, lathe of AYLESFORD, county of KENT, ¼ a mile (N. W.) from Rochester, containing 2704 inhabitants. The village consists of one principal street, on the high road from London to Rochester, to which latter place it is joined by a bridge over the Medway, at its eastern extremity: the houses are irregularly built, and equally destitute of uniformity and respectability of appearance; but since the last act of parliament for paving, watching, and lighting the village, it has been considerably improved: the adjoining heights command interesting and extensive prospects. The inhabitants are principally engaged in maritime pursuits, in the fisheries on the Medway, and in dredging for oysters, of which large quantities, as well as shrimps, are sent to the London and other markets: the trade principally arises from the resort of sea-faring men, from its situation as a thoroughfare, and, more particularly, from its proximity to Rochester. The fair is on August 17th, and the three following days, by grant of King John, and has become very considerable. That part of the parish, called Stroud Extra, which is not within the borough of Rochester is under the jurisdiction of the county magistrates, and within that of the court of requests held at Rochester, for the recovery of debts not exceeding £5. The living is a perpetual curacy, in the archdeaconry and diocese of Rochester, endowed with £200 private benefaction, and £400 royal bounty, and in the patronage of the Dean and Chapter of Rochester. The church, dedicated to St. Nicholas, is a neat building of stone, situated at the western extremity of the village, and consists of a nave and aisles; in the south aisle is a chapel, the floor of which contains some handsome specimens of Mosaic work. There is a place of worship for Independents. Francis Barrell, Esq., in 1718, bequeathed £1100 for the endowment of three charity schools, one to be in Stroud, for instructing thirty children, of which number twenty were to be of this parish; and, in 1721, Mr. William Turner gave a rent-charge of £2 for the same purpose. Of Stroud Temple, originally a preceptory founded for Knights Templars, and valued at the dissolution at £52. 6. 10., there are some interesting remains on the Temple farm; and of Stroud hospital, founded by Bishop Gilbert de Glanville, in the reign of Richard I., for infirm and indigent travellers, the almonry, which has been converted into a stable, and some other portions, are remaining. About two miles from Stroud, on the London road, is Gadshill, celebrated by Shakspeare as the scene of Falstaff's valorous exploits.

STROUD-END, a tything in the parish of PAINS-WICK, hundred of BISLEY, county of GLOUCESTER, containing 812 inhabitants.

STROXTON, a parish in the wapentake of WIN-NIBRIGGS and THREO, parts of KESTEVEN, county of LINCOLN, 3¾ miles (S. S. W.) from Grantham, containing 140 inhabitants. The living is a discharged rectory, in the archdeaconry and diocese of Lincoln, rated in the king's books at £3. 8. 6½., and in the patronage of Sir W. E. Welby, Bart. The church is dedicated to All Saints.

STRUBBY, a parish in the Wold division of the hundred of CALCEWORTH, parts of LINDSEY, county of LINCOLN, 4 miles (N.) from Alford, containing, with Woodthorp, 255 inhabitants. The living is a discharged rectory, in the peculiar jurisdiction and patronage of the Dean and Chapter of Lincoln, rated in the king's books at £4. 13. 4., and endowed with £200 royal bounty. The church is dedicated to St. Oswald.

STRUMPSHAW, a parish in the hundred of BLO-FIELD, county of NORFOLK, 3½ miles (S. W. by W.) from Acle, containing 318 inhabitants. The living is a discharged rectory, united to that of Bradeston, in the archdeaconry and diocese of Norwich, rated in the king's books at £8. The church is dedicated to St. Peter. Here is a windmill, standing on the highest ground in the county, and forming a conspicuous landmark.

STUBBS, a joint township with Hamphall, in the parish of ADWICK le STREET, northern division of the wapentake of STRAFFORTH and TICKHILL, West riding of the county of YORK, 7 miles (N. W.) from Doncaster. The population is returned with Hamphall.

STUBBY-LANE, a hamlet in the parish of HAN-BURY, northern division of the hundred of OFFLOW, county of STAFFORD, 4½ miles (S. E.) from Uttoxeter, containing 177 inhabitants. It is in the honour of Tutbury, duchy of Lancaster, and within the jurisdiction of a court of pleas held at Tutbury every third Tuesday, for the recovery of debts under 40s.

STUBLACH, a township in that part of the parish of MIDDLEWICH which is in the hundred of NORTH-WICH, county palatine of CHESTER, 3 miles (N. by E.) from Middlewich, containing 64 inhabitants.

STUBTON, a parish in the wapentake of LOVEDEN, parts of KESTEVEN, county of LINCOLN, 6¾ miles (S. E. by E.) from Newark, containing 174 inhabitants. The living is a rectory, in the archdeaconry and diocese of Lincoln, rated in the king's books at £12. 3. 9., and in the patronage of Sir Robert Heron, Bart. The church is dedicated to St. Martin.

STUDHAM, a parish partly in the hundred of DACORUM, county of HERTFORD, but chiefly in the hundred of MANSHEAD, county of BEDFORD, comprising the hamlets of Humbershoe, Studham, and part of that of Market-Street, and containing 774 inhabitants, of which number, 173 are in the hamlet of Studham, 3¼ miles (W. by S.) from Market-Street. The living is a discharged vicarage, in the archdeaconry of Bedford, and diocese of Lincoln, rated in the king's books at £9, endowed with £400 royal bounty, and in the patronage of the Crown. The church is dedicated to St. Mary.

STUDLAND, a parish in the hundred of ROWBAR-ROW, Blandford (South) division of the county of DOR-SET, 5½ miles (E. by N.) from Corfe-Castle, containing 382 inhabitants. The living is a discharged rectory, in the archdeaconry of Dorset, and diocese of Bristol, rated in the king's books at £7. 10. 5., endowed with £200 private benefaction, and £200 royal bounty, and in the patronage of Edmond Morton Pleydell, Esq. The church, dedicated to St. Nicholas, is supposed to have been built about the time of the Conquest. The parish, which includes Brownsea and several smaller islands, is bounded on the north by Poole harbour, on the east by Studland bay, and by Swanage bay on the south-east, where there is a signal station, on a hill called Ballard down. The bay, though an open roadstead, affords excellent anchorage for ships drawing fourteen or fifteen feet of water. Brownsea island is of an oval form, about three miles in circumference, and contained anciently a hermitage and chapel, dedicated to St. Andrew, of which there are now no remains. The castle, at its eastern extremity, was built in the reign of Elizabeth, by the inhabitants of Poole, for the defence of that port: adjoining it is a platform, upon which, in time of war, a few pieces of ordnance are mounted. There is also a quay, where vessels of considerable burden can lie conveniently for taking in, or discharging, their cargoes. On Studland common there are many ancient barrows, which 'must be either British or Danish, the principal of them is ninety feet in perpendicular height, and is called Agglestone, or Stone Barrow, from its being surmounted by an enormous circular red sand-stone, eighteen feet high, and computed to weigh four hundred tons.

STUDLEY, a chapelry in the parish of BECKLEY, partly in the hundred of ASHENDON, county of BUCKINGHAM, and partly in that of BULLINGTON, county of OXFORD, 6½ miles (N. E. by E.) from Oxford, containing, with the hamlet of Horton, 429 inhabitants. A priory of Benedictine nuns, in honour of the Blessed Virgin Mary, was founded here, in the reign of Henry II., by Bernard de S. Walerico, which at the dissolution had a revenue of £102. 6. 7.

STUDLEY, a parish in the Alcester division of the hundred of BARLICHWAY, county of WARWICK, 4¾ miles (N. by W.) from Alcester, containing 1338 inhabitants. The living is a perpetual curacy, in the archdeaconry and diocese of Worcester, rated in the king's books at £8, endowed with £200 private benefaction, £600 royal bounty, and £1000 parliamentary grant, and in the patronage of R. Knight, Esq. The church is dedicated to St. Mary. There is a place of worship for Wesleyan Methodists. Studley is situated on the river Arrow, and has a large manufacture of needles and fish-hooks, which affords employment to many of the inhabitants. Eight children are taught free, and two are annually clothed, from a small income arising from bequests by William Mortiboys, in 1733, and William Ayres, in 1739: the school-house was built by subscription in 1810. There are considerable remains of a priory, founded, in honour of St. Mary, early in the reign of Henry II., by Peter de Studley, who translated hither a Society of Augustine canons, which he had previously established at Wicton in Worcestershire: this house, at the dissolution, had a revenue of £181. 3. 6., and at its gate William de Cantilupe erected an hospital for the relief of poor impotent people.

STUDLEY-ROGER, a township in that part of the parish of RIPON which is in the lower division of the wapentake of CLARO, West riding of the county of YORK, 1¾ mile (W. S. W.) from Ripon, containing 144 inhabitants. It is within the peculiar jurisdiction of the Archbishop of York.

STUDLEY-ROYAL, a hamlet in that part of the parish of RIPON which is in the lower division of the wapentake of CLARO, West riding of the county of YORK, 2½ miles (W. S. W.) from Ripon, containing 19 inhabitants. It is within the peculiar jurisdiction of the Archbishop of York.

STUKELEY (GREAT), a parish in the hundred of HURSTINGSTONE, county of HUNTINGDON, 2½ miles (N. W.) from Huntingdon, containing 341 inhabitants. The living is a discharged vicarage, in the archdeaconry of Huntingdon, and diocese of Lincoln, rated in the king's books at £6. 14. 2., and in the patronage of the Master and Fellows of Trinity Hall, Cambridge. The church, dedicated to St. Bartholomew, is principally in the Norman style of architecture.

STUKELEY (LITTLE), a parish in the hundred of HURSTINGSTONE, county of HUNTINGDON, 3¼ miles (N. W. by N.) from Huntingdon, containing 385 inhabitants. The living is a rectory, in the archdeaconry of Huntingdon, and diocese of Lincoln, rated in the king's books at £13. 13. 1½., and in the patronage of Lady Olivia Sparrow. The church is dedicated to St. Martin.

STUNTNEY, a chapelry in the parish of the HOLY TRINITY, ELY, hundred and Isle of ELY, county of CAMBRIDGE, 1½ mile (S. E.) from Ely. The population is returned with the parish. The living is a perpetual curacy, in the archdeaconry and diocese of Ely, endowed with £200 private benefaction, and £400 royal bounty, and in the patronage of the Vicar of Holy Trinity parish, Ely. The chapel is in the Norman style of architecture.

STURBRIDGE, county of CAMBRIDGE. — See STOURBRIDGE.

STURMER, a parish in the hundred of HINCKFORD, county of ESSEX, 6 miles (W. by S.) from Clare, containing 311 inhabitants. The living is a rectory, in the jurisdiction of the Commissary of Essex and Herts, concurrently with the Consistorial Court of the Bishop of London, rated in the king's books at £8. 10., and in the patronage of the Duke of Rutland. Sturmer, though now an obscure place, was formerly of considerable importance: it extended into the counties of Suffolk and Cambridge, and also included Haverhill and Kedington, then hamlets, but now distinct parishes, each exceeding it both in extent and population.

STURMINSTER-MARSHALL, a parish in the hundred of COGDEAN, Shaston (East) division of the county of DORSET, 5 miles (W.) from Wimborne-Minster, containing, with the tything of Coombe-Almer, 715 inhabitants. The living is a vicarage, with the perpetual curacy of Lytchett-Minster annexed, in the jurisdiction of the peculiar court of Sturminster-Marshall, rated in the king's books at £31. 5., and in the patronage of the Provost and Fellows of Eton College. The church, dedicated to St. Mary, is a spacious structure, with an embattled tower, a remarkably large chancel, and, at the west end of the north aisle, an apartment partitioned off with wainscoting, for holding the peculiar court. The navigable river Stour bounds the parish on the north-east, and is there crossed by Whitmill bridge, of eight arches. In the centre of the village is an open space, still called the market-place, though no market has been held within the memory of man. Early in the reign of Henry I., a fair was granted to William, Earl of Pembroke, then Earl Marshal, from whom the place probably obtained its distinguishing appellation, the name itself being derived from the church, or minster, on the river Stour. A charity school is well supported by annual subscriptions. Cogdean-Elmes, an eminence in this parish, near which are several barrows and some large elms, gives name to the hundred, the courts of which were anciently held upon it.

STURMINSTER-NEWTON-CASTLE, a market town and parish in the hundred of STURMINSTER-NEWTON-CASTLE, Sturminster division of the county of DORSET, 8 miles (S. W.) from Shaftesbury, and 108 (W. S. W.) from London, containing 1612 inhabitants. This place, which derives its name from the river on the northern bank of which it stands, and the minster, or church, is supposed to be the *Anicetis* of Ravennas, and was early known to the Saxons ; some lands here having been given by Alfred to his son Ethelwald. In 968, Edgar gave the manor of Sturre, or Stour, to the abbey of Glastonbury, and the grant was confirmed by Edmund Ironside ; and in the Norman survey it was included in Newenton, or Newton. At the dissolution it was given by Henry VIII. to Catherine Parr, and, after her death, by Edward VI. to his sister Elizabeth, who devised it to Sir Christopher Hatton, from whom it passed to the family of Lord Rivers. In 1645, some hundred clubmen of Dorsetshire and Wiltshire forced the quarters of the parliamentary troops here, and, after some slaughter on both sides, were victorious, taking sixteen dragoons, with several horses and arms. In 1681, and 1729, the town suffered by conflagrations, having sustained damage at the latter period to the amount of £13,000. Sturminster-Newton is formed by the two townships of Sturminster and Newton, occupying different sides of the river Stour, and connected by a causeway and bridge of six arches ; the latter has been lately widened and improved, and the formed raised, so as to prevent the inundation to which it was previously subject. The streets are in general narrow, and the houses low and indifferently built, except in the market-place, where there is a large oblong market-house, with ware-rooms above and shambles below. A turnpike road, lately completed, runs through this town to Sherborne, and the Dorset and Somerset canal passes eastward of it. Some trade is carried on with Newfoundland, and the little manufacture in the town consists of baizes, though woollen goods were formerly made. The market is held on Thursday, and on every alternate Thursday is a large market for cattle : fairs are May 12th and October 24th. A court leet is held annually, at which the constable for the hundred, and tythingmen, are appointed. The living is a vicarage, in the archdeaconry of Dorset, and diocese of Bristol, rated in the king's books at £16. 16. 8., and in the patronage of Lord Rivers. The church, a handsome edifice dedicated to St. Mary, is situated on the south side of the town, and was originally built by John Selwood, abbot of Glastonbury, but has been lately rebuilt by the Rev. Thomas Lane Fox ; it consists of a chancel, nave, and two aisles, with an embattled tower. A chapel of ease, which stood at Bagbere in this parish, has fallen into decay. There is a place of worship for Wesleyan Methodists. A National school, for children of both sexes, has been also recently erected by the Rev. T. L. Fox, by whom it is principally supported. The principal object of interest is an ancient fortification, or camp, called the Castle, situated on an eminence in Newton, near the south bank of the river, supposed to have been constructed by the Romans, or not later than the Saxon era : it consists of a vallum and deep foss, in the shape of the Roman letter D, and on the top, near the centre, is a small artificial mount, or keep, near which are the ruins of an ancient house, where the courts were formerly held.

STURRY, a parish in the hundred of BLEANGATE, lathe of ST. AUGUSTINE, county of KENT, 2½ miles (N. E.) from Canterbury, containing 878 inhabitants. The living is a vicarage, in the archdeaconry and diocese of Canterbury, rated in the king's books at £13. 1. 8., and in the patronage of the Archbishop of Canterbury. The church, dedicated to St. Nicholas, is in the early style of English architecture, with a tower surmounted by a spire. The river Stour runs through the parish, and is crossed by a bridge at the village, which is large and well built, on the road between Canterbury and the Isle of Thanet. A fair is held here on Whit-Monday.

STURSTON, a hamlet in that part of the parish of ASHBOURN which is in the hundred of APPLETREE, county of DERBY, 1 mile (E.) from Ashbourn, containing 561 inhabitants.

STURSTON, a parish in the hundred of GRIMSHOE, county of NORFOLK, 5¼ miles (S. W. by S.) from Watton, containing 42 inhabitants. The living is a perpetual curacy, in the archdeaconry and diocese of Norwich, endowed with £200 royal bounty, and in the patronage of Lord Walsingham. The church is dedicated to the Holy Cross.

STURTON, a township in the parish of SCAWBY, eastern division of the wapentake of MANLEY, parts of LINDSEY, county of LINCOLN, 2¾ miles (S. W.) from Glandford-Bridge. The population is returned with the parish.

STURTON, a joint township with Bransby, in the parish of STOW, wapentake of WELL, parts of LINDSEY, county of LINCOLN, 8¼ miles (S. E.) from Gainsborough, containing 268 inhabitants. It is within the peculiar jurisdiction of the Prebendary of Stow in Lindsey in the Cathedral Church of Lincoln. There is a place of worship for Wesleyan Methodists. The Countess Dowager of Warwick, in 1626, gave an annuity of £5 for teaching poor children ; and Edward Burgh subsequently bequeathed property, producing about £7 per annum, for a like purpose.

STURTON, a parish in the North-clay division of the wapentake of BASSETLAW, county of NOTTINGHAM, 6 miles (E. N. E.) from East Retford, containing 605 inhabitants. The living is a vicarage, in the archdeaconry of Nottingham, and diocese of York, rated in the king's books at £5. 7. 3½., endowed with £600 parliamentary grant, and in the patronage of the Dean and Chapter of York. The church is dedicated to St. Peter. The Roman road from Lincoln to Doncaster passes through the parish, and the river Trent forms its southern boundary. A National school, erected in 1830, is partly supported by a rental of £6. 14., the gift of George Green, in 1710, for teaching eight poor children. Several coins were lately discovered here, and among them one of Louis XIII., and a leaden seal of Pope Innocent III.

STURTON (GREAT), a parish in the northern division of the wapentake of GARTREE, parts of LINDSEY, county of LINCOLN, 5½ miles (N. W. by N.) from Horncastle, containing 145 inhabitants. The living is a discharged vicarage, in the archdeaconry and diocese of Lincoln, rated in the king's books at £8, endowed with £200 royal bounty, and in the patronage of the Crown. The church is dedicated to All Saints.

STURTON-GRANGE, a township in that part of the parish of WARKWORTH which is in the eastern division of COQUETDALE ward, county of NORTHUMBERLAND, 2½ miles (W. N. W.) from Warkworth, containing 72 inhabitants.

STURTON-GRANGE, a township in the parish of ABERFORD, lower division of the wapentake of SKYRACK, West riding of the county of YORK, 7 miles (E.) from Leeds, containing 92 inhabitants.

STUSTON, a parish in the hundred of HARTIS-MERE, county of SUFFOLK, 3 miles (N. by W.) from Eye, containing 208 inhabitants. The living is a discharged rectory, in the archdeaconry of Sudbury, and diocese of Norwich, rated in the king's books at £6. 16. 8., and in the patronage of Sir Edward Kerrison, Bart. The church is dedicated to All Saints.

STUTCHBURY, a parish in the hundred of KING'S SUTTON, county of NORTHAMPTON, 5 miles (N. by W.) from Brackley, containing 32 inhabitants. The living is a rectory, in the archdeaconry of Northampton, and diocese of Peterborough, rated in the king's books at £3. 6. 8., and in the patronage of the University of Oxford. The church, which was dedicated to St. John the Baptist, is destroyed.

STUTTON, a parish in the hundred of SAMFORD, county of SUFFOLK, 6¼ miles (S. by W.) from Ipswich, containing 475 inhabitants. The living is a rectory, in the archdeaconry of Suffolk, and diocese of Norwich, rated in the king's books at £12. 17. 6., and in the patronage of the Rev. Thomas Mills. The church is dedicated to St. Peter. The river Stour separates this parish from Essex, and, at high tides, is here from two to three miles broad. The gateway and other remains of Stutton hall are good specimens of the domestic style of architecture prevalent in the reign of Elizabeth : it was formerly the residence of the ancient family of Jermys, and is now occupied by a tenant.

STUTTON, a joint township with Hazlewood, in that part of the parish of TADCASTER which is in the upper division of the wapentake of BARKSTONE-ASH, West riding of the county of YORK, 1¾ mile (S. by W.) from Tadcaster, containing 256 inhabitants. In the neighbourhood are quarries of excellent limestone, and several limekilns.

STYDD, a township in the parish of SHIRLEY, hundred of APPLETREE, county of DERBY, 4¾ miles (S. by W.) from Ashbourn, containing 30 inhabitants.

STYFORD, a township in the parish of BYWELL ST. ANDREW, eastern division of TINDALE ward, county of NORTHUMBERLAND, 7 miles (E. by S.) from Hexham, containing 69 inhabitants. It is bounded on the south by the river Tyne.

STYRRUP, a township in the parishes of BLYTH, HARWORTH, and HOUGHTON, Hatfield division of the wapentake of BASSETLAW, county of NOTTINGHAM, 3½ miles (W. S. W.) from Bawtry, containing 444 inhabitants.

SUCKLEY, a parish in the upper division of the hundred of DODDINGTREE, county of WORCESTER, 5½ miles (E. S. E.) from Bromyard, containing, with the chapelries of Alfrick and Lulsley, 1187 inhabitants. The living is a rectory, in the archdeaconry and diocese of Worcester, rated in the king's books at £26. 19. 4½., and in the patronage of the Crown. The church is dedicated to St. John the Baptist. There is a place of worship for Wesleyan Methodists. Courts leet and baron are annually held here. A school for the education of the poor is endowed with about £8 per annum.

SUDBORNE, a parish in the hundred of PLOMES-GATE, county of SUFFOLK, 1½ mile (N. by E.) from Orford, containing 561 inhabitants. The living is a rectory, with the perpetual curacy of Orford annexed, in the archdeaconry of Suffolk, and diocese of Norwich, rated in the king's books at £33. 6. 8., and in the pa-

tronage of the Crown. The church is dedicated to All Saints. The parish is bounded on the east by the North sea : on the shore is a lighthouse, called, with another in the adjoining parish of Orford, " The Orfordness Lights."

SUDBOROUGH, a parish in the hundred of HUX-LOE, county of NORTHAMPTON, 4¼ miles (N.W.) from Thrapstone, containing 294 inhabitants. The living is a rectory, in the archdeaconry of Northampton, and diocese of Peterborough, rated in the king's books at £10. 5. 10., and in the patronage of the Bishop of London. The church, dedicated to All Saints, is in the early, decorated, and later English, styles of architecture.

SUDBROOK, a parish in the upper division of the hundred of CALDICOTT, county of MONMOUTH, 5¼ miles (S. W. by S.) from Chepstow. The living is a discharged rectory, in the archdeaconry and diocese of Llandaff, rated in the king's books at £4. 14. 7., endowed with £200 royal bounty, and in the patronage of R. C. Vaughan, Esq. The church, dedicated to the Holy Trinity, is in ruins : the parish has greatly declined in importance.

SUDBROOKE, a parish in the wapentake of LAW-RESS, parts of LINDSEY, county of LINCOLN, 4½ miles (N. E.) from Lincoln, containing 103 inhabitants. The living is a discharged rectory, in the archdeaconry of Stow, and diocese of Lincoln, rated in the king's books at £7. 10., and in the patronage of the Bishop of Lincoln. The church is dedicated to St. Edward.

SUDBURY, a parish in the hundred of APPLETREE, county of DERBY, 5 miles (E. by S.) from Uttoxeter, containing 628 inhabitants. The living is a rectory, in the archdeaconry of Derby, and diocese of Lichfield and Coventry, rated in the king's books at £14. 13. 1½., and in the patronage of Lord Vernon. The church, dedicated to All Saints, contains some very ancient monuments. Here are almshouses for seven poor persons.

SUDBURY, a borough and market town, having separate jurisdiction, locally in the hundred of Babergh, county of SUFFOLK, 22 miles (W. by S.) from Ipswich, and 56 (N.E. by N.) from London, containing, according to the last census, 3950 inhabitants, which number has since increased to nearly 5000. This place, which was originally called *South Burgh*,

Arms.

is of great antiquity, and at the period of the compilation of Domesday-book was of considerable importance, having a market and a mint. A colony of the Flemings, who were introduced into this country by Edward III., for the purpose of establishing the manufacture of woollen cloth, settled here, and that branch of trade continued to flourish for some time, but at length fell to decay. The town is situated on the river Stour, which is crossed by a bridge leading into Essex. For some years after its loss of the woollen trade, it possessed few attractions, the houses belonging principally to decayed manufacturers, and the streets being very dirty : it has, however, within the last few years, been greatly improved, having been paved and lighted

in 1825, under an act obtained for the purpose, and some good houses built. The town hall, recently erected by the corporation, in the Grecian style of architecture, is a great ornament to the town, in which is also a neat theatre. The trade principally consists in the manufacture of silk, crape, and buntings used for ships' flags: that of silk was introduced by the manufacturers from Spitalfields, in consequence of disputes with their workmen, and now affords employment to a great number of persons, about one thousand five hundred being engaged in the silk, and four hundred in the crape and bunting, business. The river Stour, navigable hence to Manningtree, affords a facility for the transmission of coal, chalk, lime, and agricultural produce. The statute market is on Saturday, and the corn market on Thursday: fairs are held on the 12th of March and 10th of July, principally for earthenware, glass, and toys.

The first charter of incorporation was granted by Queen Mary, in 1554, and confirmed by Elizabeth, in 1559 : another was given by Oliver Cromwell, but that under which the corporation derives its power was bestowed by Charles II. The government is in a mayor, six aldermen, and twenty-four capital burgesses, with a recorder, town clerk, bailiff, chief constable, and subordinate officers. The mayor

Corporate Seal.

is elected from among the aldermen by the capital burgesses, with the assent of twenty-four freeholders, and the capital burgesses are elected by the court. The mayor and his immediate predecessor are justices of the peace, the former holding courts of quarter session, and a court of record, every Monday, for the recovery of debts to the amount or damage of £20, the jurisdiction of which is co-extensive with the borough. The freedom is obtained by birth, apprenticeship, purchase, or gift of the corporation. The borough first sent members to parliament in the commencement of the reign of Elizabeth, when the elective franchise was vested in the body corporate; but it has since been decided to be in the freemen, who are about eight hundred in number : the mayor is the returning officer.

Sudbury comprises the parishes of All Saints, St. Gregory, and St. Peter, in the archdeaconry of Sudbury, and diocese of Norwich. The living of All Saints' is a discharged vicarage, rated in the king's books at £4.11.5½., endowed with £400 royal bounty, and £1200 parliamentary grant. Henry Sperling, Esq. was patron in 1811. The living of St. Gregory's is a perpetual curacy, with that of St. Peter annexed, endowed with £400 private benefaction, and £1400 parliamentary grant, and in the patronage of Sir Lachlan Maclean. The churches are all of considerable antiquity, and are spacious and handsome structures, mostly in the later English style of architecture, of which they present some fine specimens, though generally much defaced. St. Gregory's, which is the most ancient, was formerly collegiate, until Henry VIII. granted its site and other possessions, for a sum of £1280, to Sir T. Paston, Knt.: it contains a very magnificent font, and in a niche in the wall of the vestry-room, enclosed with an iron grating, is a human

head, supposed to be that of Symon de Theobald, alias de Sudbury, Archbishop of Canterbury in the time of Richard II., a native of this town, who was beheaded by the mob in Wat Tyler's rebellion. One hundred and thirty free seats have been added to the church of St. Peter, towards defraying the expense of which the Incorporated Society for the enlargement of churches and chapels gave £30. The free grammar school was founded, in 1491, by William Wood, who endowed it with a farm, called the School farm, in the parish of Little Maplestead, in the county of Essex, worth about £100 per annum ; a good house is provided for the master, with a large school-room, and about one acre of land, for which he pays a moderate rent : there are six boys on the foundation, whose parents must be inhabitants of Sudbury. There is also a National school, with a small endowment, in which about one hundred and thirty children are instructed. The hospital of St. Leonard, for lepers, was founded by John Colneys, and endowed, by Simon Theobald de Sudbury, with about five acres of land, a chapel, and a dwelling-house : it is now in the possession of the corporation of the poor, and is applied towards their maintenance. From a bequest by Thomas Carter, fifty poor men receive coats and fifty poor women gowns annually on St. Thomas' day, and there are several other smaller charities for the benefit of the poor. The college of St. Gregory, for Secular priests, founded by Simon de Theobald, was richly endowed, and valued, at the period of the dissolution, at £122 per annum : its only remains are the gateway, and portions of a wall now forming a part of the workhouse. A gateway, part of a monastery of Augustine friars, standing in Friars'-street, also exists. About half a mile from the town is a spring of exceedingly pure water, which, from its supposed efficacy in curing many painful diseases, is called by the inhabitants "Holy water." Sudbury is the birthplace of Gainsborough, the celebrated painter. It gives the inferior title of baron to the Duke of Grafton.

SUDELEY-MANOR, a parish in the lower division of the hundred of KIFTSGATE, county of GLOUCESTER, 1 mile (S. S. E.) from Winchcombe, containing 90 inhabitants. The living is a rectory, in the archdeaconry and diocese of Gloucester, rated in the king's books at £6. 11. 5½., and in the patronage of Lord Rivers. The church, which has remained in a dilapidated state ever since the injury it sustained in the great civil war, was the burial-place of Queen Catharine Parr, and of several of the family of Bridges. The ancient castle is said to have been built, ex spoliis Gallorum, by Boteler, Lord Sudeley, a celebrated warrior in the reigns of Henry V. and VI., who sold it to Edward IV., for fear of confiscation. It was granted by Edward VI. to his uncle, Lord Seymour, who espoused Queen Catharine Parr. Mary bestowed it upon Sir John Bridges, created by her Baron Chandos of Sudeley, whose grandson, the third Lord Chandos, here entertained Queen Elizabeth, in 1592. George, the sixth lord, having embraced the cause of Charles I., the castle was twice besieged by the parliamentary forces, who reduced it to its present state of ruin : the remains are considerable and interesting.

SUDELEY-TENEMENTS, a hamlet in the parish of WINCHCOMBE, lower division of the hundred of KIFTSGATE, county of GLOUCESTER. The population is returned with the parish.

SUFFIELD, a parish in the northern division of the hundred of ERPINGHAM, county of NORFOLK, 3¼ miles (W. by N.) from North Walsham, containing 238 inhabitants. The living is a discharged rectory, in the archdeaconry of Norfolk, and diocese of Norwich, rated in the king's books at £14, and in the patronage of Lord Suffield. The church is dedicated to St. Margaret. Suffield gives the title of baron to the family of Harbord.

SUFFIELD, a joint township with Everley, in the parish of HACKNESS, liberty of WHITBY-STRAND, North riding of the county of YORK, 5 miles (W. N. W.) from Scarborough, containing, with Everley, 97 inhabitants.

SUFFOLK, a maritime county, bounded on the east by the North Sea, or German Ocean, on the north by the county of Norfolk, on the west by that of Cambridge, and on the south by that of Essex. It extends from 51° 56' to 52° 36' (N. Lat.), and from 23' to 1° 44' (E. Lon.), comprising an area of about one thousand five hundred and twelve square miles, or nine hundred and sixty-seven thousand six hundred and eighty statute acres. The population, in 1821, was 270,542. At the period of the Roman invasion this county formed part of the territory inhabited by the Iceni, or Cenomanni, who, according to Whitaker, were descended from the Cenomanni of Gaul. Under the Roman dominion it was included in the division called *Flavia Cæsariensis*. After the withdrawal of the Roman legions, Cerdic, one of the earliest Saxon invaders, and founder of the kingdom of Wessex, landed, in 495, at a place afterwards called Cerdic Sand, in the hundred of Mutford and Lothingland, forming the north-eastern extremity of the county, and, after gaining some advantages over the opposing Britons, set sail for the western parts of the island. During the succeeding invasions of the Saxons, the territory now comprised in the counties of Suffolk, Cambridge, and Norfolk, was erected by Uffa, about the year 575, into the kingdom of East Anglia, in which the relative position of this district obtained for its inhabitants the name of *Suthfolc*, or southern people (in contradistinction to those of Norfolk, who were called the *North-folc*, or northern people), whence, by contraction, its modern name. The Christian religion was permanently established in this kingdom by King Sigebert, who brought over with him a Burgundian ecclesiastic, named Felix, whom he made bishop of East Anglia, and who fixed his seat at Dunwich, in this county, where he died, in 647. Bisa, or Bosa, on succeeding to this see, in 669, divided it into two bishopricks, the seat of one of which was fixed at North Elmham, in Norfolk, the other remaining at Dunwich; but these were re-united about the year 870, when North Elmham became the sole seat of the diocese. In 655, during the struggles for independence maintained by East Anglia against the powerful kingdom of Mercia, then under the sway of Penda, a battle was fought at Bulcamp, near Dunwich, in which Anna, monarch of the East Angles, and his son Ferminus, were slain. East Anglia was again the scene of desolation, at the period of its subjugation by Offa, King of Mercia, who had basely assassinated its king, Ethelbert. It remained tributary to Mercia until, in the reign of Egbert, the kingdom of Wessex obtained a preponderating influence in the Octarchy: under that

monarch it continued to have its own sovereigns, until the reign of the East Anglian king, Edmund, who, after being barbarously murdered by the Danes under Inguar and Ubba, was surnamed the Martyr. These marauders directing their early attacks chiefly upon this part of the island, possessed themselves of the whole of East Anglia before the death of Egbert, making lamentable ravages in their progress. After the total defeat of the Danes by Alfred, in the West of England, East Anglia was one of the principal portions of territory allotted to them, for their limited residence, by that monarch. Suffolk suffered severely on the invasion by Sweyn, King of Denmark, who landed at Ipswich in 1010, and at Rushmere, or, according to some, at a place called Seven Hills, in the parish of Nacton, signally defeated the Saxons under Earl Ulfketel.

Some time after the Norman Conquest had changed the political system of the whole kingdom, in the year 1153, Ipswich was besieged and taken by King Stephen; his son Eustace also made some ravages in the vicinity of Bury, at which town he died, on St. Lawrence's day in the same year. During the reign of Henry II., in 1173, the Earl of Leicester, in support of the demands of Prince Henry, the king's eldest son, landed at Wadgate haven, in this county, with an army of Flemings, and was immediately joined by Hugh Bigod, Earl of Norfolk: their united forces overran the whole county, which, in a great measure, they laid waste; but, being met at Fornham St. Genevève, near Bury, by Richard de Lucy, Chief Justice of England, and Humphrey de Bohun, the constable, they were defeated with great slaughter, and Leicester and his countess made prisoners. In 1215, during the baronial war, Saher de Quincy, Earl of Winchester, withdrew, with his army of foreign mercenaries, from the siege of Colchester to Bury St. Edmund's; and Louis the Dauphin, in the two following years, in conjunction with the barons opposed to the king, reduced the whole of this county to subjection, committing great devastation in it. In 1267, Henry III. mustered a large body of his forces at Bury, the insurgent barons being at that time strongly posted in the Isle of Ely. In 1326, Isabella, queen of Edward II., landed with an army on the coast of Suffolk, and thence marched to Bury, where she remained a considerable time, recruiting her forces, and collecting her adherents. In the reign of Richard II., at the period of Wat Tyler's rebellion, many of the men of Suffolk joined the Norfolk insurgents in their formidable revolt, which was at last suppressed by the military exertions of Spencer, Bishop of Norwich. In 1486, Henry VII. made a progress through Suffolk, under the apprehension of its being invaded by the supporters of Lambert Simnel, the pretended Edward Plantagenet. In the fifteenth year of this reign, Ralph Wilford, the son of a shoemaker, was instructed, by an Augustine friar of this county, to personate the Earl of Warwick, and the story soon gained credit, the friar asserting its authenticity from the pulpit: both master and pupil were, however, soon arrested; the latter was hanged, and the former condemned to perpetual imprisonment. In 1526, the Dukes of Norfolk and Suffolk met at Bury, and succeeded in quelling an alarming insurrection which had broken out in the southern parts of Suffolk, at Lavenham, Hadleigh, Sudbury, &c. In 1549, it being reported that the leader of the Norfolk rebels, named Kett, had formed a camp on Mousehold heath, near Norwich, the lower orders of the people assembled in great numbers, and, having made themselves masters of Lothingland, seized six pieces of cannon at Lowestoft, with which they proceeded to batter Yarmouth, but their design was frustrated by the inhabitants of that port, and many of them were made prisoners. On the death of Edward VI., the inhabitants of Suffolk showed great zeal in supporting the claims of the Princess Mary, in opposition to the adherents of Lady Jane Grey; and Mary, at this period, removed from Norfolk to Framlingham castle, in this county. In 1561, Queen Elizabeth made a progress through Suffolk; as also in 1578, when she was received on its confines by a magnificent cavalcade, headed by the high sheriff, which again attended her Majesty on her departure.

In the civil war of the seventeenth century, this was one of the eastern counties that were associated in the cause of the parliament, and placed under the command of the Earl of Manchester. Sir Edward Barker, Sir John Petty, and other loyal gentlemen, endeavoured to raise a force to secure it for the king, but were surprised and reduced to obedience to the parliament by Cromwell. During the war with the Dutch, in the reign of Charles II., on June 3rd, 1665, the memorable engagement between the English and Dutch fleets, in which the latter was defeated, with the loss of eighteen ships taken, and fourteen sunk or burned, and about six thousand men, of whom two thousand were made prisoners, occurred off Lowestoft. In 1667, the Dutch landed three thousand men under Felixstow cliff, near the southern extremity of the coast, who, marching to the adjacent fort, after an hour's incessant firing with small arms, were put to flight by the discharge of two or three small guns on board a galliot lying among the shingles. Southwold bay, commonly called Sole bay, is celebrated as the scene of the sanguinary and obstinate conflict, on the 28th of May, 1672, between the united fleets of England and France on the one side, and the Dutch fleet on the other, in which the French squadron, sheering off soon after the commencement of the action, left the engagement to the English and the Dutch: the Dutch vessels that were not either sunk or burned, being dreadfully shattered, were at last obliged to retreat; while the English, having suffered in an equal degree, were unable to pursue. In the year 1782, Lowestoft, and various other points on this coast, were strongly fortified, on account of a threatened foreign invasion.

Suffolk is comprised in the diocese of Norwich, and province of Canterbury. Its western part, with such parishes in Cambridgeshire as belong to the same diocese, constitute the archdeaconry of Sudbury, which is divided into eight deaneries, seven of which are in the county, viz., those of Blackbourn, Clare, Hartismere, Stow, Sudbury, Thedwestry, and Thingoe; its eastern part forms the archdeaconry of Suffolk, which contains the fourteen deaneries of Bosmere, Carlford, Claydon, Colneis, Dunwich, Hoxne, Ipswich, Loes, Lothingland, Orford, Samford, South Elmham, Wangford, and Wilford: the total number of parishes is five hundred, of which three hundred and twenty-two are rectories, ninety-seven vicarages, and the remainder perpetual curacies. For purposes of civil government

it is divided into the twenty-one hundreds of Babergh, Blackbourn, Blything, Bosmere and Claydon, Carlford, Colneis, Cosford, Hartismere, Hoxne, Lackford, Loes, Mutford and Lothingland, Plomesgate, Risbridge, Samford, Stow, Thedwestry, Thingoe, Thredling, Wangford, and Wilford. It contains the borough, market town, and sea-port of Ipswich; the boroughs and sea-ports of Aldborough, and Dunwich; the borough and market towns of Bury St. Edmund's, Eye, and Sudbury; the borough of Orford; the market towns and sea-ports of Lowestoft, Southwold, and Woodbridge; and the market towns of Beccles, Bungay, Clare, Debenham, Framlingham, Hadleigh, Saxmundham, and Stow-Market. Two knights are returned to parliament for the shire; and two representatives for each of the boroughs: the county members are elected at Ipswich, where stands the county gaol. Suffolk is included in the Norfolk circuit: the assizes are held at Bury. There are one hundred and ten acting magistrates. The rates raised in the county for the year ending March 25th, 1827, amounted to £253,475. 19., and the expenditure to £252,283. 14., of which £223,037. 2. was applied to the relief of the poor.

The two grand civil divisions are, the franchise, or liberty, of Bury St. Edmund's, and the remaining part, or body of the county, as it is termed, each at the county assizes, furnishing a distinct grand jury. In its civil government Suffolk is also divided into the Geldable portion, in which the issues and forfeitures are paid to the king; and the franchises, in which they are paid to the lords of the liberties. The former comprises the hundreds of Blything, Bosmere and Claydon, Hartismere, Hoxne, Mutford and Lothingland, Samford, Stow, and Wangford: the sessions for Blything, Mutford and Lothingland, and Wangford, are held at Beccles; and for the rest of the Geldable hundreds at Ipswich. The franchises are three in number; first, the franchise, or liberty, of St. Ethelred, which formerly belonged to the prior and convent, now to the Dean and Chapter, of Ely, containing the hundreds of Carlford, Colneis, Loes, Plomesgate, Thredling, and Wilford, the sessions for which are held at Woodbridge. Secondly, the franchise, or liberty, of St. Edmund, given to the abbot of Bury by Edward the Confessor, and comprising the hundreds of Babergh, Blackbourn, Cosford, Lackford, Risbridge, Thedwestry, and Thingoe, the sessions for which are held at Bury. And thirdly, the liberty of the duchy of Norfolk, granted by letters patent from Edward IV., dated December 7th, 1468, in which the duke has the returning of all writs, and the right of appointing a special coroner, and of receiving all fines and amerciaments: it comprises, within the limits of this county, his manors of Bungay, Kelsale, Carlton, Peasenhall, the three Stonhams, Dennington, Brundish, the four Ilketshalls, and Cratfield. The counties of Suffolk and Norfolk formed only one shrievalty until the year 1576, when a sheriff for each was first appointed. With regard to the government and management of the poor, the most remarkable circumstance is the incorporation of several hundreds for the erection and support of houses of industry, on a very large scale, and in situations chosen for their pleasantness and salubrity. Thus, Colneis and Carlford hundreds were incorporated in the 29th of George II., and have their house of industry in the parish of Nacton; the hundred of Blything was

SUFFOLK

CAMBRIDGESHIRE

NORFOLK

ESSEX

GERMAN OCEAN

incorporated in 1764, and has its house of industry in the hamlet of Bulcamp, near Blythburgh; that of Mutford and Lothingland in the same year, having its house of industry in the parish of Oulton, near Lowestoft; and that of Wangford also in 1764, which has its house of industry at Shipmeadow, between Bungay and Beccles. The following hundreds were incorporated in 1765: viz., those of Loes and Wilford (since dis-incorporated), which had their house of industry in the parish of Melton; that of Samford, in the parish of Tattingstone; and that of Bosmere and Claydon, in the parish of Barham. The hundred of Cosford, and the parish of Polstead, which have theirs in the parish of Semer, were incorporated in the 19th of George III. The hundred of Stow was incorporated in the 20th of George III., and has its house of industry in the parish of One-House.

The climate, which is very salubrious, is also remarkably dry: its other chief peculiarities are, that frosts are here experienced with great severity; and that, in the spring months, the north-easterly winds, which are very prevalent, are sharp, and injurious to vegetation. The soils are various, but the limits of each may be clearly traced. Strong clayey loams, on a substratum of clay marl, occupy the largest tract, which extends from the confines of Cambridgeshire and Essex, on the south-west, across the central parts of the county, to those of Norfolk, on the north-east: on the north-west this district is bounded by an irregular imaginary line, passing from the western border of the county, near Dalham, by Barrow, Little Saxham, the vicinity of Bury St. Edmund's, Rougham, Pakenham, Ixworth, and Honington, to the northern boundary at Knettishall; and on the south-east by another, drawn from the banks of the Waveney, near North Cove, a few miles to the east of Beccles, southward by Wrentham and Wangford, and then south-westward by Blythford, Holton, Bramfield, Yoxford, Saxmundham, Campsea-Ash, Woodbridge, Culpho, Bramford, Hadleigh, and along the high lands bordering on the western side of the river Bret, to the confluence of that stream with the Stour: it must be observed, that the bottoms of the vales traversed by running streams, which are numerous, and the slopes descending to them, are of a soil superior in quality to the rest of this district, generally consisting of a rich friable loam. Rich loams, of various qualities, occupy that portion of the county included between the south-eastern part of the strong loams and the æstuaries of the rivers Stour and Orwell, lying to the south of a line drawn from Ipswich to Hadleigh: some of these are of a sandy quality, others much stronger: from Debtford and Higham, on the borders of the Stour, eastward, across the Orwell, to the banks of the river Stour, near its mouth, extends a tract of friable and putrid vegetable mould of extraordinary fertility; more especially at Walton, Trimley, and Felixstow. In the projecting north-eastern district, lying between the river Waveney and the ocean, is much land of the same rich quality; but as it is interspersed with many sandy tracts, and on the sea-coast is of a sandy character throughout, it may be considered to form part of the great sandy maritime district extending from the river Orwell, between the clayey loams and the sea, to the north-eastern extremity of the county: the lands in this district are generally of excellent staple, and are

among the best-cultivated in England; although, in the country lying between the towns of Woodbridge, Orford, and Saxmundham, and north-eastward, as far as Leiston, there is a large extent of poor, and in some places even blowing, sands, which have caused this south-eastern part of the county to receive the name of "Sandlings," or "Sandlands:" the substratum of the eastern district, though sometimes marl, is generally sand, chalk, or crag; which last is a singular mass, consisting of cockle and other shells, found in numerous places, from Dunwich, southward, to the Orwell, and even beyond that river. Another district of sand occupies the whole extent between the clayey soils and the fenny tract, which latter forms the north-western angle of the county, and may be separated from the sand by an irregular line drawn from near where the river Larke begins to form the western boundary of Suffolk, to the Little Ouse, a short distance below Brandon: these western sands, unlike much of the last-mentioned, are seldom of a rich loamy quality, but comprise numerous warrens and poor sheep-walks; much of that now under tillage is apt to blow, that is, to be driven by the wind, and consequently ranks among the worst soils: the chief exceptions to the general inferiority of this district lie to the south-east of a line drawn from Barrow to Honington, and at Mildenhall: the substratum is throughout a perfect chalk, at various depths. Of the Fens, it is only necessary to observe, that the surface, to the depth of from one foot to six, consists of the ordinary peat of bogs, some of which is very solid and black; but in other places it is more loose, porous, and of a reddish colour: the substratum is generally a white clay, or marl.

By far the greater part of the county is under tillage: the modes of culture on the clayey loams are various; but, on the rich loam and lighter soils, the Norfolk system has been generally introduced: on the sand, turnips are everywhere employed as a preparative crop before corn or grass: paring and burning is practised only in the Fens, where the course of crops, after this operation, is generally cole-seed; then oats twice in succession, with the last crop of which are sown ray-grass and clover, under which the land remains for six or seven years, and afterwards is again pared and burned. The crops commonly cultivated are wheat, barley, oats, beans, peas, buck-wheat, turnips, cabbages, carrots, potatoes, tares, cole-seed, red and white clover, trefoil, sainfoin, hemp, and hops. The produce of the corn crops varies greatly on the different soils: that of wheat is estimated to average twenty-two bushels per acre; that of barley thirty-two bushels, and that of oats thirty-six bushels. Rye, though formerly much sown, is now only seen on the poorest sands, where the produce is about sixteen bushels per acre. Peas are more frequently cultivated than beans, as they flourish on a greater diversity of soils. Buck-wheat is often grown on the poor sands, and is chiefly employed in fattening hogs and poultry. The culture of carrots in the Sandlings is of very ancient practice, great quantities having been formerly sent from that district by sea to the London market; but the chief object for which they are now grown is as food for horses: the produce on good land is generally from four hundred to five hundred bushels per acre: they are left in the field during winter, and taken up only as wanted. Potatoes are grown in every part of the county : the tares are employed chiefly as green food for horses. Much cole-seed is sown, and in the fen district it constitutes one of the principal crops : it is chiefly applied as food for sheep; but when left for seed, it is reaped and left on the ground until fit to thresh, which operation is performed in the field on cloths, and the straw burned : the average produce of seed is about twenty bushels per acre. Of the artificial grasses above-mentioned, great quantities of clover are seeded; as also is trefoil occasionally : the cultivation of sainfoin is particularly extensive, and in the chalky districts it is everywhere found; this also is not unfrequently seeded. Hemp is chiefly grown in a tract of about ten miles broad, extending in length from Eye to Beccles : the average produce per acre is forty-one stones. The culture of hops is confined to an extent of about one hundred and fifty acres, in the vicinity of Stow-Market. The most remarkable agricultural implement is the well-known light Suffolk swing-plough : drilling is much practised.

The grass lands are not remarkable for excellence, and the extent occupied by dairy farms is not so great as formerly, though large quantities of butter are still sent to the London market. Large tracts of grass land are also mown for the supply of the towns with hay : the produce varies from one to two tons per acre; the herbage, which springs up after the gathering of the hay crop, is here called *rawings*. Clay and marl are extensively employed as manures; as also is chalk, which the inhabitants of the hundreds of Colneis and Samford obtain from Kent and Essex, by means of the corn-hoys: besides these substances, the shell-marl, or crag, as it is provincially termed, that is found in the Sandlings, is much used for this purpose, and considerable quantities of manure are brought from London. The Suffolk cows have long been famous for the great quantity of their milk, which, however, is not remarkable for richness: they are universally polled, and of a small size, few, when fattened, weighing more than fifty stone: their general character is that of having a snake-like head, a small dewlap, short and slender legs, a large body with flat loins, and a large udder; the colour is various. In some parts of the county black cattle are fattened, part of them being brought from Ireland and Wales, but by far the greater number from Scotland. The number of sheep kept is very great, the South Down breed being most prevalent. The only remarkable breed of hogs is a particularly good one, which is found in the dairy district : they are well made, small-boned, and have thick, short noses. There are many rabbit warrens, particularly in the western district. Poultry is exceedingly plentiful, especially turkies, for which this county is nearly as famous as Norfolk. The Suffolk breed of horses is as celebrated as that of the cows; it is found in the greatest perfection in the tract included between the coast and the towns of Woodbridge, Debenham, and Eye, extending as far north as Lowestoft.

The woods are of very small extent, and are not generally of luxuriant growth : the strong loams formerly bore considerable quantities of fine oak, a great proportion of which has been cleared off, and various plantations made, but only with a view to ornament. The amount of waste lands at the time of the publication of Mr. Young's Agricultural Survey, in 1804, was nearly one hundred thousand acres, the most important tracts

being the immense wastes that occupy nearly all the country from Newmarket, on the borders of Cambridgeshire, to the confines of Norfolk, near the towns of Thetford and Brandon; and those lying between Woodbridge, Orford, and Saxmundham, in the eastern part of the county; besides which, numerous heaths of smaller extent are scattered in every quarter of it : the chief use of these wastes is as sheep-walks. Wood and coal are both much used as fuel, the former chiefly in the habitations of the poorer classes; in the vicinity of the heaths, fens, and commons, turf is also burned.

The manufactures and commerce are very inconsiderable, in comparison with those of many other counties. The chief manufacture is the combing and spinning of wool, in a great measure for the Norwich manufacturers, which is carried on, though not to any great extent, in most parts of the county, excepting the hemp district before mentioned, where the latter material is spun and woven into linen. At Sudbury are manufactories for silk, and woollen goods : there is also a silk manufactory at Mildenhall, a branch of an extensive concern at Norwich. The imports are merely the ordinary supplies of foreign articles for the inhabitants : the chief exports are corn and malt. The principal fishery on the coast is that of herrings, which is the chief support of the town of Lowestoft, where about forty boats, of forty tons' burden each, are engaged in it : the season commences about the middle of September, and lasts until towards the latter end of November. This town also partakes in the mackarel fishery, in which the same boats are employed, the season commencing about the end of May, and continuing until the end of June. In the Orford river there is a considerable oyster fishery.

This is a well-watered county : the principal rivers are the Stour, the Gippen, or Orwell, the Deben, the Ore, the Waveney, the Little Ouse, or Brandon river, and the Lark; besides which the smaller streams are almost innumerable. The Stour, rising on the Cambridgeshire border of the county, runs southward, across its south-western extremity, to the vicinity of Haverhill, eastward of which town it begins to form the southern boundary of Suffolk, and continues so throughout the rest of its course, passing by the towns of Clare, Sudbury, and Nayland : a few miles to the eastward of the latter place it is augmented by the powerful stream of the Bret, descending from the north-west : at Manningtree in Essex it first meets the tide, and begins to expand into a broad æstuary, which at high water has a beautiful appearance; but at low water the river shrinks into a narrow channel, bordered by extensive mud banks. Proceeding eastward, it is joined near Harwich by the Orwell, and their united waters, having formed the port of Harwich, discharge themselves into the North sea, between that town in Essex, and Landguard fort at the south-eastern extremity of this county : this river is navigable up to Sudbury. The Gippen is formed by the confluence of three rivulets at Stow-Market, from which place it was made navigable in 1793 : it takes a south-easterly course by Needham-Market to Ipswich, below which town it assumes the name of Orwell, expands into an æstuary, and continues its course to its junction with the Stour opposite Harwich : the Orwell is navigable for ships of considerable burden up to

Ipswich, and the scenery on its banks is beautiful. The Deben rises near Debenham, and, passing that town, runs south-eastward to the vicinity of the village of Rendlesham, whence it takes a south-westerly course to Woodbridge, at which place it expands into an æstuary, and thence proceeds in a southerly direction to the North sea: towards its mouth it takes the name of Woodbridge haven, which joins the sea about ten miles below that town, to which it is navigable for vessels of considerable burden. The Ald rises north of Framlingham, and, running south-eastward, expands into an æstuary as it approaches Aldborough, where, having arrived within a very short distance of the sea, it suddenly takes a southerly direction, and discharges its waters into the North sea below Orford: it is navigable to a short distance above Aldborough. The Waveney, rising in a swampy meadow near the village of Lopham in Norfolk, immediately becomes the boundary of the county, which it henceforward continues to be, proceeding first eastward and then north-eastward to Bungay, where it makes an extensive horseshoe bend, and then reassumes its easterly course by Beccles, at a short distance beyond which town, having approached within a very few miles of the sea, it is compelled by rising grounds abruptly to assume a northerly course to the river Yare, which it joins at the head of Bredon-water, an expansion formed by these united rivers, which, contracting again near Yarmouth, pursues a nearly southerly course to the sea, below that town: this river, the meadows on the banks of which are among the richest in England, is navigable for barges as high as Bungay bridge. The Little Ouse, or Brandon river, though rising within a very short distance of the course of the Waveney, assumes a directly contrary course, and, forming the northern boundary of the county, proceeds westward to the neighbourhood of the village of Barnham, where it assumes a northerly course, by the town of Thetford in Norfolk, below which it again takes a westerly course, passing by the town of Brandon, in this county, and quitting Suffolk at its north-western extremity: this river is navigable up to Thetford. The Larke, rising in the south-western part of the county, flows northward to Bury, and thence north-westward to Mildenhall, below which place it soon becomes the western boundary of the county, which it finally quits near its north-western extremity, shortly to join the Little Ouse: this river is navigable to within a mile of Bury St. Edmund's. The Blythe, rising near Laxfield, in the hundred of Hoxne, thence runs east-north-eastward to Halesworth, where it becomes navigable, and whence it flows eastward by Blythburgh to Southwold, where it falls into the North sea. The only artificial navigation is that in the channel of the Gippen, from Stow-Market to Ipswich: it is sixteen miles and forty rods long, and has fifteen locks, each sixty feet in length and fourteen in width: this canal was opened in the year 1793: the total expense of its formation was about £26,380. The roads, in every part of Suffolk, are excellent. That from London to Norwich, through Newmarket, enters this county from the latter town in Cambridgeshire, and passes through Mildenhall to Thetford; and that to Norwich, through Ipswich, enters from Colchester, and passes through Stratford, Ipswich, and Thwaite. The road from London to Lynn, through Newmarket, branches from the first Norwich road at Mildenhall, and passes through Brandon. The road from London to Yarmouth, through Ipswich, branches from the second Norwich road at Ipswich, and passes through Woodbridge, Saxmundham, and Lowestoft.

Within the limits of the county were comprised the Roman stations *Ad Ansam*, at Stratford, on the border of Essex; *Cambretonium*, at Brettenham, or Icklingham; *Garianonum*, at Burgh Castle (though some fix it at Caistor, near Yarmouth); and *Sitomagus*, probably at Woolpit. Remains of Roman military works exist at Burgh Castle, Brettenham, Icklingham, Stow - Langtoft, and Stratford, on the banks of the Stour. Numerous domestic and sepulchral relics of that people have also been dug up in different places, such as pavements, coins, medals, urns, rings, &c. That stupendous work of human labour, called the Devil's Ditch, on Newmarket heath, is supposed to have served as the line of demarcation between the kingdoms of Mercia and East Anglia. On a hill called Eye Cliff, and several others situated in its vicinity, are some earthworks, supposed to have constituted a Danish camp; and near Barnham, on the borders of the Little Ouse, is a range of eleven tumuli, on a spot supposed to have been the scene of one of the conflicts between the Danes, under Inguar, and the forces of Edmund, King of East Anglia: others occur in different places, the most remarkable group of them being that called the Seven Hills, at Fornham St. Geneveve, near Bury. The number of religious houses, of all denominations, was about fifty-nine, including four Alien priories. There are remains, more or less extensive, of the abbeys of Bury St. Edmund's and Leiston; of the priories of Blythburgh, Butley, Clare, Herringfleet, Ipswich, Mendham, and Sudbury; and of the nunneries of Bungay and Redingfield. Some of the most remarkable churches are those of Alderton, Ashfield, and Barnham, all which are now in ruins; of Beccles, which is remarkable for its noble steeple; Blythburgh; St. Mary, and St. James, at Bury; Buxlow, in ruins; Creeting All Saints, Corton, Dunwich, Flixton, and Fordley, all in ruins; Framlingham; Haslewood, in ruins; St. Lawrence, St. Mary at Quay, and St. Mildred at Ipswich, part of the latter of which has been converted into a town hall; Lavenham, the most beautiful in the county; Lowestoft; Sibton; Stow-Langtoft; and Thurlston, now used as a barn: in addition to these, may be enumerated the churches of Eye, Hoxne, Laxfield, Long Melford, Southwold, Bungay St. Mary (partly in ruins), Covehithe, Walberswick (in ruins), Kessingland, Walton, &c. The fonts in the following churches are worthy of notice for their antiquity, or other peculiarities, *viz.*, those of Blythburgh, Clare, Framlingham, Hawstead, Hengrave, St. Peter's (Ipswich), Letheringham, Lowestoft, Melton, One-House, Orford, Snape, Ufford, and Worlingworth. The remains of ancient fortresses are chiefly those of the castles of Bungay, Clare, Framlingham, Haughley, Lidgate, Mettingham, Orford, and Wingfield. Ancient mansions are seen in different parts of the county; the most remarkable is Hengrave Hall. There are many elegant seats, among the most distinguished of which is Euston Park, the property and residence of the Duke of Grafton; and Heveningham Hall, the seat of Lord Huntingfield. Suffolk gives the title of earl to the family of Howard.

2 G 2

SUGLEY, a township in that part of the parish of NEWBURN which is in the western division of CASTLE ward, county of NORTHUMBERLAND, 3¾ miles (W.) from Newcastle, containing 266 inhabitants. The extensive manufactory termed the Tyne Iron Works is within this township.

SUGNALL (MAGNA), a township in the parish of ECCLESHALL, northern division of the hundred of PIREHILL, county of STAFFORD, 2½ miles (N. W. by W.) from Eccleshall, containing 109 inhabitants. It is within the peculiar jurisdiction of the Prebendary of Eccleshall in the Cathedral Church of Lichfield.

SUGNALL (PARVA), a township in the parish of ECCLESHALL, northern division of the hundred of PIREHILL, county of STAFFORD, 3 miles (N. W.) from Eccleshall, containing 79 inhabitants. It is within the peculiar jurisdiction of the Prebendary of Eccleshall in the Cathedral Church of Lichfield.

SULBY, an extra-parochial district, in the hundred of ROTHWELL, county of NORTHAMPTON, 6¼ miles (S. W.) from Market-Harborough, containing 59 inhabitants. An abbey of the Premonstratensian order, in honour of the Blessed Virgin Mary, was founded here, about 1155, by Robert de Querceto, Bishop of Lincoln, and its possessions were so much increased by Sir Robert de Paveley, Knt., that, at the dissolution, its revenue was estimated at £305. 8. 5.

SULGRAVE, a parish in the hundred of CHIPPING-WARDEN, county of NORTHAMPTON, 8½ miles (N. by W.) from Brackley, containing 578 inhabitants. The living is a discharged vicarage, in the archdeaconry of Northampton, and diocese of Peterborough, rated in the king's books at £9. 17., and in the patronage of W. Harding, Esq. The church is dedicated to St. James. Near it, to the westward, is Castle hill; and about a mile to the northward is an artificial mount, called Burrough hill, crowned with an ancient fortification, forty feet square, and commanding a most extensive prospect, nine counties being visible from its summit. There are several bequests for the education and relief of the poor, the principal of which are, a rent-charge of £8 by John Hodges, in 1724, another of £12. 16. by Robert Gardiner, in 1763, who also gave the interest of £500 to put out apprentices.

SULHAM, a parish in the hundred of THEALE, county of BERKS, 5 miles (W. by N.) from Reading, containing 152 inhabitants. The living is a rectory, in the archdeaconry of Berks, and diocese of Salisbury, rated in the king's books at £6. 4. 2. J. Wilder, Esq. was patron in 1814. The church is dedicated to St. Nicholas.

SULHAMPSTEAD-ABBOTTS, a parish in the hundred of READING, county of BERKS, 7 miles (S. W. by W.) from Reading, containing, with the tything of Graisley, 364 inhabitants. The living is a rectory, to which, in 1782, that of Sulhampstead-Bannister was annexed, in the archdeaconry of Berks, and diocese of Salisbury, rated in the king's books at £10. 6. 0½., and in the patronage of the Provost and Fellows of Queen's College, Oxford. The church is dedicated to St. Bartholomew. The river Kennet runs through the parish. There is a Sunday school for the children of both parishes, superintended by a benevolent lady, who has endowed it with £573. 5. 3. three per cent. consols., also a school-room and house for the master and mistress.

SULHAMPSTEAD-BANNISTER, a parish in the hundred of THEALE, county of BERKS, 6¾ miles (S. W. by W.) from Reading, containing 315 inhabitants. The living is a rectory, annexed to that of Sulhampstead-Abbotts, in the archdeaconry of Berks, and diocese of Salisbury, rated in the king's books at £6. 5. The church is dedicated to St. Michael. The river Kennet runs through the parish.

SULLINGTON, a parish in the hundred of EAST EASWRITH, rape of BRAMBER, county of SUSSEX, 5½ miles (W.) from Steyning, containing 287 inhabitants. The living is a rectory, in the archdeaconry and diocese of Chichester, rated in the king's books at £12. 17. 6., and in the patronage of the Rev. G. Palmer. The church, dedicated to St. Mary, is principally in the early style of English architecture.

SUMMERFORD, a township in that part of the parish of ASTBURY which is in the hundred of NORTHWICH, county palatine of CHESTER, 1¾ mile (N. W.) from Congleton, containing 107 inhabitants.

SUMMERHOUSE, a township in that part of the parish of GAINFORD which is in the south-western division of DARLINGTON ward, county palatine of DURHAM, 6¾ miles (N. W. by W.) from Darlington, containing 189 inhabitants. There is a place of worship for Wesleyan Methodists. A school was built by subscription in 1821.

SUNBURY, a parish in the hundred of SPELTHORNE, county of MIDDLESEX, 15 miles (S. W. by W.) from London, containing 1777 inhabitants. The living is a vicarage, in the archdeaconry of Middlesex, and diocese of London, rated in the king's books at £13. 6. 8., and in the patronage of the Dean and Chapter of St. Paul's, London. The church is dedicated to St. Mary.

SUNDERLAND, a township in the parish of ISALL, ALLERDALE ward below Darwent, county of CUMBERLAND, 6 miles (N. E.) from Cockermouth, containing 48 inhabitants.

SUNDERLAND, a sea-port, market town, and parish, in the northern division of EASINGTON ward, county palatine of DURHAM, on the southern bank of the river Wear, 13 miles (N. E.) from Durham, and 269 (N. by W.) from London, containing, exclusively of Bishop-Wearmouth and Monk-Wearmouth, 14,725 inhabitants. The early history of this place is interwoven with that of Bishop-Wearmouth, until the end of the twelfth century, when, in a charter of privileges and free customs, granted to those then enjoyed at Newcastle, granted to it, under the name of South Wearmouth, by Bishop Pudsey, we meet with the first authentic record of its distinct maritime and commercial character as a port. The etymology and date of its present name are somewhat obscure; the more probable conjecture is that it was intended to designate its original peninsular situation, occasioned by the influx of the river Wear into the sea, and a deep ravine at Hendon Dean, which separated it from the main land. Its prosperity having been essentially promoted by the provisions of the above-mentioned charter, it gradually increased in population and importance, and, in the reign of Henry VIII., was becoming a place of considerable note. At the commencement of the seventeenth century, some Scottish families and foreign merchants came to reside here, and the charter of Bishop Morton raised it to the dignity of a corporate town. Soon after the Conquest, Malcolm, King of Scotland, when traversing the eastern coast in one of his destructive incursions, met with Edgar Atheling, heir to the English crown, his sister Margaret, the future queen of Scotland, and a train of distressed Saxons, whilst waiting in the harbour of Sunderland for a wind and tide favourable to their escape from the victorious Normans into Scotland. During the great civil war the inhabitants were entirely devoted to the interests of the parliament, and, in 1642, the town was garrisoned in its behalf, in consequence of the seizure of Newcastle by the royalists, and the exportation of coal from that port to London being prohibited; a parliamentary commissioner also was sent to reside here until the surrender of that town. In 1644 and 1645, repeated skirmishes occurred in Sunderland and the neighbourhood, between the contending parties, during which period the resident Scots suffered greatly from want of provisions, owing to the wreck of some vessels laden with supplies from Scotland, and the capture of others by the royalists, in the river Tyne, whither adverse winds had most inopportunely driven them.

The town comprises several streets, of which the principal is broad and handsome, nearly a mile long, and communicates with the High-street of Bishop-Wearmouth. In general the houses are well built, except in the lower part of the town: by virtue of an act of parliament, passed in 1809, considerable improvements were made, in the removal of nuisances; and, in 1823, a company was formed for lighting the streets with gas, supplied from two gasometers, which are calculated to contain twenty-five thousand cubic feet, the works having been built at an expense of £8000. The inhabitants are supplied with water from a large well, by means of a steam-engine, which raises it into two reservoirs, at the rate of one hundred and fifty gallons per minute, whence it is conveyed to the houses through pipes: the expense of these works is estimated at £5000, which was defrayed by shares of £25 each. The facilities and accommodations afforded to bathers, during the season, have rendered this town a place of fashionable resort: in 1800, hot and cold baths were established at Hendon; and, in 1821, a suite of hot, cold, vapour, and medicinal baths was erected on the town moor: on the sands, which are peculiarly favourable to bathing, are several machines for the purpose. A mechanics' institute for Sunderland and its vicinity, established in 1825, is in a very flourishing condition, and comprises a library of four hundred volumes, with the requisite apparatus for lectures. Among various other literary institutions is a subscription library, originally established in 1795: the present handsome edifice was completed in 1802, and contains upwards of four thousand five hundred volumes. There are a commodious theatre in Drury-lane, and an assembly-room. Races were formerly held on the town moor, but they have for some time been discontinued. Barracks were erected on the Sands in 1794; they afford accommodation for one thousand eight hundred men, stabling for ten horses, and an hospital adapted to the reception of eighty patients. Monk-Wearmouth and the opposite batteries have been constructed for the protection of the port. Of all the improvements which the town has received during the last fifty years, the cast-iron bridge across the Wear, which

connects it with Monk-Wearmouth, may be considered the chief. Previously to 1792 the river had been crossed by means of two ferries: the first project entertained was that of erecting a stone bridge, which was abandoned for the present structure, of which the first stone was laid September 24th, 1793, and the work completed in 1796, at a total expense of £33,400, of which sum, £30,000 was advanced by Rowland Burdon, Esq., M. P. for the county; the tolls are let annually for £3000. The bridge was built under the direction of Mr. Thomas Wilson, of Bishop-Wearmouth, and consists of one magnificent arch, two hundred and thirty-six feet in the span, and one hundred feet in height from low water mark, admitting vessels of from two to three hundred tons' burden to pass underneath: the abutments are nearly solid masonry, twenty-four feet thick, forty-two broad at the bottom, and thirty-seven at the top; the breadth of the carriage-way is thirty-two feet, with flagged foot-paths on each side, defended by an iron balustrade: the whole weight of iron is two hundred and sixty tons, forty-six of which are malleable, and the remainder cast.

Sunderland is mainly indebted to its advantageous situation on the coast, and near the influx of a navigable river, which flows through a district abounding with coal and limestone, for its present importance. The export of coal, which is the staple article of commerce, appears to have commenced so early as the reign of Elizabeth, or the beginning of that of James; the quantity shipped at present is about five hundred and sixty thousand chaldrons (Winchester Measure) annually. The town dues on exports are sixpence each chaldron, three halfpence of which are paid by the fitters. The metropolis and the western part of England are the principal marts; a large quantity is also sent to the Baltic. The next in importance is the trade in lime, of which upwards of thirty thousand chaldrons are annually shipped for the ports of Yorkshire and those on the eastern coast of Scotland; from twenty-five to thirty vessels, of from forty to one hundred tons' burden, are employed. The remainder of the export trade is supplied by the numerous manufactories in the town and its vicinity, which consist of those for flint and crown glass, copperas-works, extensive potteries, roperies, chain cable and sail-cloth manufactories, and a brass foundry: there are also three sawing-mills, wrought by steam, and grindstone quarries, in one of which is a fine vein of black marble, from which various chimney and other ornaments are constructed. Of these, the patent ropery at Deptford is worked by a steam-engine of sixteen-horse power, and is capable of producing five hundred tons of cordage in the year: within the usual hours of labour, in 1804, eight hundred tons were manufactured, but the average annual sale is from three to four hundred, being nearly half of the whole quantity made in the neighbourhood. The principal imports are flour, wine, spirituous liquors, timber, tallow, iron, and flax. Ship-building is here carried on more extensively, perhaps, than at any other port in the empire, about twenty eight builders being resident: on the shores of the river, from eighty to one hundred vessels may be placed on the stocks at a time; there are thirty yards for building ships, five for boats, four dry-docks, and four floating-docks. The largest vessel ever constructed here was the Lord Duncan, launched from Southwick quay, in

1798; its extreme length was one hundred and forty-four feet, the breadth thirty-nine feet, and the burden nine hundred and twenty-five tons: the number of vessels built, from 1824 to 1826 inclusive, was two hundred and fifty-two. The salmon fishery was formerly very extensive, and, so late as the year 1788, seventy-two were taken at one draught; but this pursuit has been wholly abandoned, and the supplies now consist of cod, ling, turbot, haddock, skate, herrings, crabs, and lobsters, all of them being caught in great abundance. By the parliamentary returns printed by the House of Commons in 1828, it appears that Sunderland, as it respects the gross amount of the tonnage, and the average size and number of its ships, is the fourth port in the united kingdom; the tonnage being the one twenty-first part of the aggregate tonnage of the united kingdom, one-seventeenth part of the tonnage of England, one-third of the whole tonnage of Scotland, and exceeding, by five thousand and eighty-seven tons, the gross amount of the tonnage of all Ireland. In the year 1829, the number of ships belonging to the port was six hundred and twenty-five, the tonnage one hundred and seven thousand eight hundred and eighty; and the magnitude of its maritime trade is evinced by the circumstance of nine thousand one hundred and eighty ships having been, during that year, cleared to foreign parts and coastwise at the custom-house. The general importance of this sea-port has increased, within the last fifty years, to a height and with a rapidity almost incredible; the population and shipping having within that period, become doubled in number; and as the exports and imports are annually greater, and as the formation of capacious wet docks, to afford additional accommodation for ships, is now in contemplation, it may be expected to rise still higher in commercial character and maritime consequence.

The harbour is formed by two piers: the depth of water at the highest spring tide is from fifteen to twenty feet, and at the lowest neap tides from ten to eleven; vessels of four hundred tons' burden can enter it. In 1669, letters patent were obtained from Charles II., by Edward Andrew, Esq., empowering certain commissioners to levy contributions for the purpose of cleansing the harbour, and erecting a pier and lighthouse. Under this authority the southern pier had been partially constructed, at an expense of £50,000, and, in 1765, its completion was expected to require as much more: its present length is about six hundred and twenty-six yards, and a tide light is placed at its extremity. The northern pier was begun in 1787, and is now one thousand eight hundred and fifty feet in length. Near its extremity is an elegant octagonal lighthouse of freestone, sixty-eight feet high from the pier to the under side of the cap, lighted with gas by means of nine argand lamps and reflectors, each of the latter being eighteen inches in diameter. A gasometer, and two neat cottages, for the residence of the men who attend to the lights, have been erected on the pier: the disasters incident to this rocky and somewhat dangerous coast are additionally provided against by having in constant readiness two life-boats of peculiar construction. All the improvements connected with the harbour were placed under the superintendence of commissioners appointed, for twenty-one years, by an act passed in the 3rd of George I., of which the

provisions have been subsequently enlarged and confirmed: their jurisdiction extends up the river as far as to Biddick Ford, and from Sooter point to Ryhope Dean on the coast. The exchange, a neat structure in High-street, erected in 1814, at an expense of £8000, advanced on shares of £50 each, comprises an auction mart, a commercial-room, a news-room, merchants' walk, and justice-room. The custom-house is situated on the moor, and the excise-office in East Cross-street. The market, formerly held on Friday, is now on Saturday; and fairs are, May 13th and 14th, and October 12th and 13th, for toys, &c.

The first charter of privileges was granted to the inhabitants, in the twelfth century, by Bishop Pudsey, which conferred upon them similar privileges to those enjoyed by the burgesses of Newcastle, likewise the right to determine all pleas arising within the borough, excepting those of the crown; other privileges and appointments having been made by subsequent Bishops of Durham. Previously to 1634, the town was governed by a bailiff appointed by letters patent from the bishop; but in that year the inhabitants were incorporated by charter of Bishop Morton, under the style of mayor, twelve aldermen, and commonalty of the borough of Sunderland, which also stated that it had been a borough from time immemorial, known as the new borough of Wearmouth: the mayor was clerk of the market. Although the practical operation of this charter ceased almost immediately after it was granted (the original nominees having been the only individuals who acted under it), a body of the influential tradesmen and neighbouring gentlemen have, for some years past, formed a private corporation, under the title of "Freemen and Stallingers," and in that capacity have claimed, and are in possession of, the town moor as their corporate property: they do not interfere in the regulation, or government, of the town, and their right to hold the moor is disputed by the inhabitants. There are twelve freemen, and eighteen stallingers: the sole right of election is vested in the freemen. The various interests in the town are let on two leases by the Bishop of Durham; one includes the borough courts, fairs, market, tolls, anchorage, and beaconage, and the office of water-bailiff; the other comprises the ferry-boats, and metage and tolls of fruits, herbs, and roots. The bishop holds his baronial court annually, with the court leet for the recovery of debts under 40s. A petty session of the county magistrates is held every Friday at the exchange.

Anterior to 1719, Sunderland formed a portion of the parish of Bishop-Wearmouth, but in that year, an act was obtained to make it a distinct parish. The living is a rectory, in the archdeaconry and diocese of Durham, and in the patronage of the Bishop of Durham. The endowment is only £80 per annum, which is assessed, under the act, upon all estates real and personal, stock in trade, &c.; and this sum, with the surplice fees, constitutes the only income of the incumbent. The church, dedicated to the Holy Trinity, was erected in 1720, and repaired in 1803: it stands in the upper part of the town, and is a commodious handsome brick edifice, with a square tower: the altar is placed in a recess, covered with a dome opening into the nave, under fluted pilasters, with Corinthian capitals. The parochial business is transacted by twenty-four vestrymen, who are elected, on possessing the requisite qualification of a freehold estate of at least £10 per annum, by the parishioners, and continue in office three years. St. John's chapel was built in 1769, chiefly at the expense of John Thornhill, of Thornhill, Esq.; the site, at the head of Barrack-street, having been given by Marshall Robinson, of Herrington: it has received five hundred additional sittings, towards defraying the expense of which, the Incorporated Society for the enlargement of churches and chapels contributed £200: it has also been endowed with £2800 private benefaction, royal bounty, and parliamentary grant: the living is a perpetual curacy, in the patronage of the Bishop, generally held by the rector of Sunderland. Another church was erected, in John-street, in 1827, at the expense of the parliamentary commissioners. There are places of worship for Baptists; Scotch Burghers; the Society of Friends; Independents; Calvinistic, Primitive, and Wesleyan, Methodists, and Methodists of the New Connexion; Presbyterians; Unitarians; Roman Catholics, and Jews; forming in all nineteen dissenting places of worship. A school for instructing and clothing poor girls was endowed, in 1778, under the will of Elizabeth Donnison, widow, with £1500; the management is vested in eight trustees, of whom the rector of Sunderland is one: the interest arising from the property, which is vested in the three per cents., is £78. 8. 6.; thirty-six poor girls are educated and clothed. A school for children of members of the Society of Friends was established, pursuant to the will of Edward Walton, in 1768; the master's income is £26 per annum, and twenty boys receive instruction. A school of industry, in which girls belonging to the poorhouse are taught the platting of straw, is supported by the overseers. A National school, established in 1808, and containing about three hundred and twenty boys and sixty girls, is supported by voluntary contributions: the building consists of two stories, and cost the sum of £500, which was collected by parochial subscription, aided by donations from the executors of Dr. Paley, the trustees of Lord Crewe, Dr. Bell, and several other benevolent individuals. In addition to these are numerous Sunday schools. The almshouses in Assembly Garth, for the residence of thirty-eight superannuated seamen and their widows, belonging to the "Muster Roll," were purchased, in 1750, by the trustees of the "Seamen's Fund," appointed by virtue of an act passed in the 20th of George II., which obliges the masters of all vessels to levy sixpence per month from each sailor towards this provident institution, to be under the management of fifteen trustees, who are elected annually; upwards of seven hundred individuals derive benefit from it. The Sunderland and Bishop-Wearmouth Marine almshouse, for ten widows, or unmarried daughters, of master-mariners, was founded and endowed, in 1820, by Mrs. Eliz. Woodcock; each candidate must have passed her fifty-sixth year: each inmate receives an annuity of £10 for life. Almshouses in Churchlane, Bishop-Wearmouth, for the maintenance of twelve poor women, were built and endowed by a legacy of £1400, the bequest of Mrs. Jane Gibson, in 1725; the appointment of the inmates is vested in the family of Mowbray. On Wearmouth Green are almshouses for twelve poor persons, erected about 1712, under the will of John Bowes, rector of Bishop-Wearmouth, and endowed, in 1725, by Thomas Ogle, with a bequest of

£100; the Dean and Chapter of Durham are trustees. The infirmary, comprising a dispensary, house of recovery, and humane society, each instituted at different periods, but now combined in one establishment, was erected in 1822, at an expense of £3000: it is in the patronage of the Bishop of Durham, and under the management of eight presidents, twelve vice-presidents, four physicians, four surgeons, a matron, apothecary, and other subordinate officers: the building is situated in Durham-lane. Amongst the several friendly societies are four lodges of freemasons, having a masonic hall in Queen-street, erected in 1785. Here are also numerous benevolent societies for the benefit of the sick and poor of the town and its vicinity. Sunderland confers the inferior title of earl upon the family of Churchill, Dukes of Marlborough.

SUNDERLAND (NORTH), a township in the parish and northern division of BAMBROUGH ward, county of NORTHUMBERLAND, 8½ miles (E. by S.) from Belford, containing 566 inhabitants. There is a place of worship for Presbyterians. Seven children are educated for £5 a year, with a house and garden for the master, allowed by the trustees of Lord Crewe's estate. This township has the North sea on the east, and possesses a small port, subject to Berwick, from which corn, fish and lime are exported; of the latter article considerable quantities are burned at the kilns in the neighbourhood.

SUNDERLAND-BRIDGE, a township in that part of the parish of AUCKLAND ST. ANDREW, which is in the south-eastern division of DARLINGTON ward, county palatine of DURHAM, 3½ miles (S. S. W.) from Durham, containing 204 inhabitants. It is situated between the river Wear and Croxdale water, the former being crossed by a bridge on the great north road. On the manor of Butterby are saline and sulphureous springs.

SUNDERLAND-WICK, a township in the parish of HUTTON-CRANSWICK, Bainton-Beacon division of the wapentake of HARTHILL, East riding of the county of YORK, 2½ miles (S. S. W.) from Great Driffield, containing 60 inhabitants.

SUNDON, a parish in the hundred of FLITT, county of BEDFORD, 4¾ miles (N. W. by N.) from Luton, containing 387 inhabitants. The living is a discharged vicarage, in the archdeaconry of Bedford, and diocese of Lincoln, rated in the king's books at £8. 6. 8., endowed with £200 royal bounty, and in the patronage of J. R. Cuthbert, Esq. The church, dedicated to St. Mary, is partly in the decorated style of architecture. A market and fair, formerly held by royal grant in 1316, have been long disused.

SUNDRIDGE, a parish in the hundred of CODSHEATH, lathe of SUTTON at HONE, county of KENT, 4 miles (W. by N.) from Seven-Oaks, containing 1129 inhabitants. The living is a rectory, in the peculiar jurisdiction and patronage of the Archbishop of Canterbury, rated in the king's books at £22. 13. 4. The church has some fine windows in the later English style. The river Darent flows through the parish, part of which lies below the great ridge of sand hills in the Weald. The manufacture of paper is carried on here. A National school is attended by about two hundred children, each paying threepence a week, and by ten others who are taught for a rent-charge of £6 left by Humphrey Heide, Esq. Sundridge gives the English title of baron to the Duke of Argyll.

SUNK-ISLAND, an extra-parochial district, in the southern division of the wapentake of HOLDERNESS, East riding of the county of YORK, 20 miles (S. E. by E.) from Kingston upon Hull, containing 216 inhabitants. Here is a small chapel, in the patronage of the Archbishop of York, also a place of worship for Wesleyan Methodists. This island has been gradually recovered from the Humber; a century ago it comprised only eight hundred acres, but it now contains five thousand, in a high state of cultivation, and more is expected to be embanked within a very short period. It was originally two miles from the opposite shore, and vessels formerly passed through the channel, which is now so narrow as to be crossed by a bridge to the main land.

SUNNINGHILL, a parish in the hundred of COOKHAM, county of BERKS, 6 miles (S. S. W.) from New Windsor, containing 1125 inhabitants. The living is a vicarage, in the peculiar jurisdiction of the Dean of Salisbury, endowed with £200 private benefaction, and £200 royal bounty, and in the patronage of the Master and Fellows of St. John's College, Cambridge. The church, dedicated to St. Michael, is principally in the Norman style of architecture. There is a place of worship for Baptists. Two chalybeate springs, in the garden of an inn called Sunning Wells, were formerly in great repute, and adjoining them is a room where public breakfasts have been given. At a place called Bromehall, in this parish, there was formerly a small convent of Benedictine nuns, founded before the reign of John; it was deserted by these sisters in 1522, when it escheated to the crown, and was granted to St. John's College, Cambridge.

SUNNINGWELL, a parish in the hundred of HORMER, county of BERKS, 2½ miles (N.) from Abingdon, containing, with part of the chapelry of Kennington, 277 inhabitants. The living is a rectory, in the archdeaconry of Berks, and diocese of Salisbury, rated in the king's books at £12. 14. 7., and in the patronage of Sir G. Bowyer, Bart. The church, dedicated to St. Leonard, is an ancient structure of a singular form, and contains a monument to the memory of Bishop Jewell. The village is pleasantly situated on the banks of the Thames, across which there is a wooden bridge.

SURFLEET, a parish in the wapentake of KIRTON, parts of HOLLAND, county of LINCOLN, 4 miles (N.) from Spalding, containing 812 inhabitants. The living is a vicarage, in the archdeaconry and diocese of Lincoln, rated in the king's books at £11, endowed with £1400 parliamentary grant, and in the patronage of — Pickworth, Esq. The church, dedicated to St. Lawrence, is partly in the later style of English architecture, and partly of earlier date, with a tower and spire. There is a canal, called the Glen, by which the waters of Pinchbeck are conveyed to the Welland river; and another, termed the Grand Sluice, that conveys the waters of the fen to Boston. This parish contains one of the largest heronries in England. Here are two endowed schools, one free for twenty children, the other for children inhabiting Fen Ends.

SURLINGHAM, a parish in the hundred of HENSTEAD, county of NORFOLK, 5½ miles (E. S. E.) from Norwich, containing 403 inhabitants. The living is a rectory, with the perpetual curacy of St. Saviour's annexed, in the archdeaconry of Norfolk, and diocese of Norwich, rated in the king's books at £ 6. 13. 4., and in the patronage of the Rev. W. Collett. The church is dedicated to St. Mary. Here is a ferry across the Yare, which is much frequented.

SURRENDRAL, a tything in that part of the parish of HULLAVINGTON which is in the hundred of CHIPPENHAM, county of WILTS, 5¾ miles (S. W.) from Malmesbury, containing 34 inhabitants.

SURREY, an inland county, bounded on the north by the river Thames, which separates it from Middlesex and the south-eastern extremity of Buckinghamshire; on the north-west by Berkshire; on the west by Hampshire; on the south by Sussex; and on the east by Kent: it extends from 51° 5′ to 51° 31′ (N. Lat.), and from 3′ (E. Lon.) to 51′ (W. Lon.); comprising an area of seven hundred and fifty-eight square miles, or about four hundred and eighty-five thousand one hundred and twenty statute acres. The population, in 1821, was 398,658. The most ancient British inhabitants of this district, of whom we have authentic information, were the Segontiaci, or, as they are called by Ptolemy, the Regni, a people who had been expelled from Hampshire by the invading Belgæ. Cæsar, in his exploratory invasion of Britain, crossed the north-eastern part of Surrey, from the county of Kent to the Thames, which he is supposed to have passed at a place now called Cowey Stakes, at Walton on Thames, into the territory of Cassivellaunus, though the Britons endeavoured to prevent his passage by driving stakes into the bed of the river. Under the Roman dominion Surrey was included in the division called Britannia Prima. On the complete establishment of the Saxon kingdom of Wessex, it appears to have included the greater part of this county. In 568, Ethelbert, in defence of his own kingdom, having invaded the territories of Ceawlin, King of Wessex, a great battle was fought between them at Wimbledon, in which the former was signally defeated: this was the first battle fought between the Saxon kings. This county suffered severely from the ravages of the Danes, who entered it in 852, after sacking London, but were defeated with great slaughter at Ockley, near its southern border, by Ethelwulph and his son Ethelbald. In 893, Wada, or Huda, the only Saxon recorded to have borne the title of Earl of Surrey, was slain in battle against the Danes, in the Isle of Thanet, whither he had marched with the men of Surrey to the assistance of the Earl of Kent; and in the same year the invaders made great devastations in this county, particularly in the vicinity of Gödalming. When Canute besieged London, in 1016, finding that the citizens had taken possession of London bridge, so as to prevent the passage of his vessels under it, he proceeded to construct a canal through the marshes on the south side of the Thames, with which river it communicated at Rotherhithe and at Chelsea-reach, thus enabling the Danish monarch to attack the city from that part of the river which is above the bridge. William the Conqueror after London after the battle of Hastings, in 1066, in order to terrify the inhabitants into submission, reduced Southwark to ashes. The first who enjoyed the dignity of Earl of Surrey, after the Conquest, was William de Warren, Earl of Warren in Normandy, who had distinguished himself in the battle of Hastings, and was united in marriage to a daughter of the Conqueror. In 1215, at

SURREY

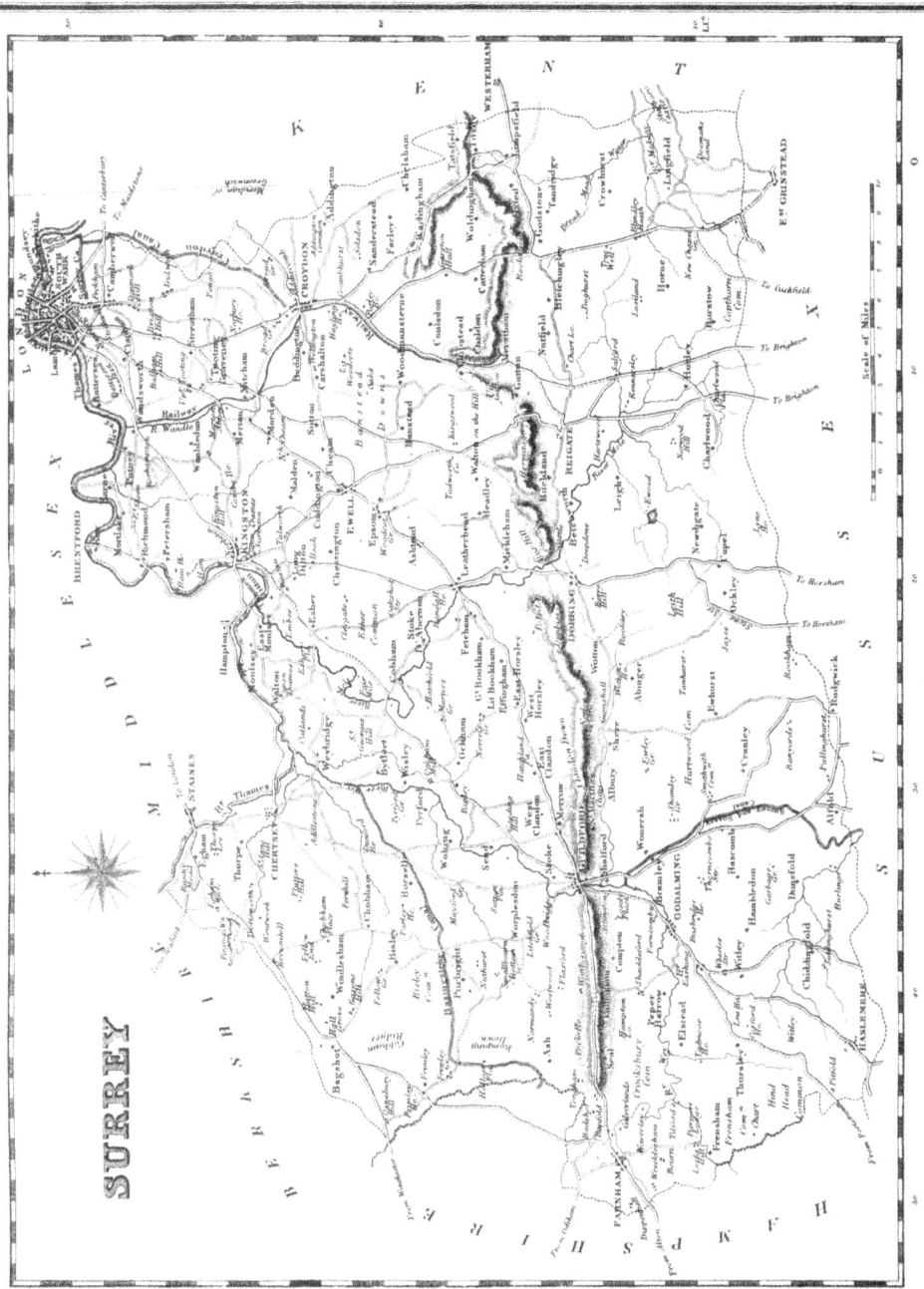

DRAWN AND ENGRAVED FOR LEWIS' TOPOGRAPHICAL DICTIONARY.

Scale of Miles

Runymede, near Egham, the armed barons compelled King John to grant the famous Magna Charta: this monarch having afterwards broken faith with his people, and desolated England with bands of armed mercenaries, Louis the Dauphin, who had been invited by the barons to assume the crown, possessed himself, in 1216, of the castles of Guildford and Farnham, which, however, were shortly retaken, on the death of John, by the forces of his son and successor, Henry III. In the sixteenth year of the reign of this monarch, Hubert de Burgh, Chief Justice of England, having incurred the displeasure of his sovereign, took refuge in the convent of Merton, whither Henry ordered the citizens of London to proceed and seize him; they marched towards that place, to the number of twenty thousand, but the king's anger having in the meantime been appeased, their march was countermanded. In 1264, immediately after the battle of Lewes, in which Henry III. was defeated and taken prisoner by the disaffected barons, a party of the king's forces then lying in garrison at Tonbridge castle, marched into this county, destroyed Blechingley castle, and advanced upon Croydon, where they surprised the men of London, who had espoused the cause of the barons, and had been driven out of the field at Lewes, slew many of them, and gained a considerable booty. During Wat Tyler's rebellion, in 1381, the men of Essex attacked the archiepiscopal palace at Lambeth, and destroyed all the furniture, books, registers, and public papers. In 1472, the bastard Falconbridge, with an army of seventeen thousand men, came to Kingston, intending to cross the Thames; but finding the bridge broken down, he marched to St. George's Fields near London, and, in an attack upon that city, was repulsed by its inhabitants. Sir Thomas Wyatt, in his military operations to prevent the marriage of Queen Mary with Philip of Spain, marched with a force of about two thousand men to Southwark, where he arrived on February 3d, 1554: after staying there three days, his entrance into London being vigorously opposed, he marched to Kingston, with the design of crossing the Thames into Middlesex: there he found the bridge broken, and the opposite bank of the river defended by two hundred men, who, however, soon retired, on two pieces of ordnance being pointed against them, and Sir Thomas, having repaired the bridge, passed over.

During the contest between Charles I. and the parliament, a great majority of the inhabitants strenuously supported the proceedings of the latter; and, in the early part of the dispute, a petition was presented to the House of Commons, signed by two thousand of them, and another to the Lords, congratulating them on the measures which they had adopted, and complaining of there being evil counsellors about the king, and popish lords in the House. In January 1642, Col. Lunsford assembled at Kingston a body of four or five hundred cavalry, for which he was proclaimed a traitor by the parliament, and apprehended. In August of the same year, by order of the parliament, Captain Royden, with two hundred foot and a troop of horse, seized and took away the arms in Lambeth House. In October, the Earl of Essex was at Kingston, with an army of three thousand men; and at the beginning of November, Sir Richard

Onslow, one of the knights of the shire, and a parliamentarian, went with the trained bands of Southwark to the defence of that town, but being ill-received by the inhabitants, he abandoned it. On the 8th of the same month, a party of soldiers took possession of Lambeth House, by order of the parliament, after the battle of Brentford; on November 12th, the king marched to Kingston. In December, Farnham castle, which had been well garrisoned for the king by Sir John Denham, high sheriff of the county, was besieged by the parliamentarian forces, and, after an obstinate resistance, surrendered to Sir William Waller. Although armed bands were occasionally moving in different parts of the county, yet no other important event seems to have taken place within its limits until the year 1647, when the inhabitants of Southwark, not approving of the conduct of the citizens of London towards them, privately sent word to General Fairfax, that they were willing to surrender the borough to him: the General immediately sent a brigade, under the command of Col. Rainsborough, who took possession of it. Fairfax then visited Croydon, whence, on August 10th, he removed his head-quarters to Kingston. On the 27th of the same month Cromwell removed his head-quarters from Kingston, and fixed them at Putney, whence the parliamentarian army took its departure, on November 13th, two days after Charles I. had made his escape from Hampton Court, and on the 18th held a grand rendezvous on Ham common. The Earl of Holland, the Duke of Buckingham, and Lord Francis Villiers, making a last attempt on behalf of the royal cause, assembled at Kingston a body of six hundred horse, their avowed object being to release the king, then confined in the Isle of Wight, and bring him to parliament, to establish peace in the kingdom, and preserve the laws: the parliament immediately sent some troops of horse from Windsor, under the command of Col. Pritty, who found the royalists but ill prepared for defence: a skirmish took place near Surbiton common, in which the Earl of Holland and his party were soon defeated, and Lord Francis Villiers was slain. On the Restoration, the Lord Mayor and Aldermen of London met Charles II., in his approach towards the capital, on May 29th, in St. George's Fields, where a magnificent tent was erected, in which the king partook of a sumptuous collation. In 1768, during the riots of the populace of London and its environs, occasioned by the imprisonment of John Wilkes, Esq., in the King's Bench, the rioters were opposed by the military in St. George's Fields, and some lives were lost: and in 1780, Lord George Gordon assembled on the same spot upwards of fifty thousand persons, who afterwards were engaged in the memorable disturbances of that year. Lambeth Palace was threatened with the popular vengeance, but was preserved by the timely interference of the military.

Surrey is included in the diocese of Winchester, and province of Canterbury; excepting the exempt deanery of Croydon, which contains nine parishes, and is in the peculiar jurisdiction of the Archbishop of Canterbury: it forms an archdeaconry, in which are the deaneries of Ewell, Southwark, and Stoke: the total number of parishes is one hundred and forty-one, of which seventy-nine are rectories, thirty-four vicarages, and the remainder perpetual curacies. For purposes of civil government it is divided into the hundreds of Blackheath, Brixton, Copthorne, Effingham, Elm-bridge, Farnham, Godalming, Godley, Kingston, Reigate, Tandridge, Wallington, Woking, and Wotton, all of them having first and second divisions, except Brix-ton, which is divided into east and west, and Farnham, which has no division. It contains the borough and market town of Southwark, with the populous subur-ban parishes of Rotherhithe, Bermondsey, Newington, Camberwell, Lambeth, Clapham, and Battersea; the borough and market towns of Guildford, Haslemere, and Reigate; the boroughs of Blechingley and Gatton; the market towns of Chertsey, Croydon, Dorking, Farn-ham, Godalming, and Kingston; and the large and elegant village of Richmond. Two knights are returned to parliament for the shire, and two representatives for each of the boroughs: the county members are elected at Guildford. Surrey is included in the Home circuit: the lent and winter assizes are held at Kingston, and the summer assizes at Guildford and Croydon, alternately: the county gaol is in Horsemonger-lane, in the parish of Newington. The quarter sessions are held at the New Sessions House, Newington, on January 12th; at Rei-gate, on April 20th; at Guildford, on July 13th; and at Kingston, on October 19th. There are one hundred and sixty-five acting magistrates. The rates raised in the county, for the year ending March 25th, 1827, amounted to £288,108. 15., and the expenditure to £291,830. 9., of which £241,582. 4. was applied to the relief of the poor. According to the earliest authentic accounts, the county of Surrey had always a sheriff of its own until the beginning of the reign of John, when it was placed under the same shrievalty with Sussex; and though, during the reigns of succeeding monarchs, it was occasionally under a distinct sheriff, yet the regular appointment of a separate sheriff for it did not com-mence until 1615.

Its form is nearly oblong, except that the northern border is rendered extremely irregular by the devious course of the Thames. The scenery, celebrated for its beauty, possesses also great variety; presenting in some parts wild and naked heaths, which form a powerful contrast with the adjoining highly cultivated and orna-mented districts. The surface, for the most part, is gent-ly undulating, excepting the Weald, a district of about thirty miles in length, and varying from three to five in breadth, which extends along the whole southern bor-der, and forms, with the Wealds of Kent and Sussex, one immense plain, the flat surface of which is of very inferior elevation: some of the hills, however, rise to a very considerable height, and command rich and extensive views. The middle of the county is crossed from east to west by the Downs, which rise with a gentle acclivity from the north, but on the south are broken into precipitous cliffs of great height and romantic irregularity: the prospects from the most ele-vated of them are remarkably beautiful and diversified. Southward of the Downs rise the hills that overhang the Weald, in the vicinities of Oxted, Godstone, Rei-gate, and Dorking. Approaching the western side of the county, this range becomes of greater extent, and near Wonersh, Godalming, and Pepper - Harrow, is covered with rich woods, and intersected by pleasing vallies, watered by streams tributary to the Wey; the whole forming one of the most picturesque por-tions of the county. The largest tracts of the very ex-

tensive heaths lie in the western part: from Egham, on the banks of the Thames, south-south-westward as far as the village of Ash, the district consists, with little exception, of heath and moor; as also does that extend-ing in a transverse direction from Bagshot, on the north-western confines, by Chobham and Byfleet, to Cobham, Ripley, and Oatlands: the whole south-west-ern angle is of the same barren character, from Hasle-mere to Farnham, in one direction, and from Elstead to Frensham in the other.

The climate in general is remarkable for its dryness, but it varies considerably in different situations. The greatest quantity of rain falls in that portion of the county which is included in the vale of London; and the atmosphere of this district is moist, as also is that of the southern border, from the flatness of the surface, the immense number of trees obstructing the free circulation of air, and the wet nature of the soil. On the other hand, the air on the Downs is dry, keen, and bracing; and a similar climate prevails on the heaths about Bagshot, Aldershot, Hindhead, &c. The spring is generally early, vegetation being here little checked by the easterly winds, which often so much retard it in other counties. On the whole, the climate is esteemed particularly salubrious; and the atmosphere, being kept clear of the smoke of the metropolis, by the prevalence of westerly and southerly winds, is remarkable for its superior purity.

The soils, which are extremely various, are by no means so clearly discriminated as in many other coun-ties, the different species lying in small patches much intermixed: they may, however, be reduced under the four general heads of clay, loam, chalk, and heath. The most extensive tract bearing a uniform character is that denominated the Weald of Surrey, where the surface consists of a pale, cold, retentive clay, upon a subsoil of the same nature, in which iron is found: still deeper occurs a white clay of a slaty texture, the laminæ of which are extremely thin. In some places, particularly on the northern border of the Weald, where the soil is more of a loamy character, rag-stone is the prevailing substratum: the difficulties experienced in the cultiva-tion of this soil are extremely great. Northward of it lies a district of sandy loam, stretching across the whole county, and forming the range of hills overlooking the Weald: this soil is every where of great depth, though variable in colour and fertility, and rests on a sand-stone, veined with oxyde of iron; the richest portion of it lies around Godalming. Although this district, in the eastern part of the county, is in few places more than half a mile broad, yet, proceeding westward, in the neighbourhood of Godalming, it expands to a breadth of five or six miles. The chalky soil of the Downs ad-joins this to the north, the most fertile portions of it being a pure hazel loam of various depths, while the substratum of the whole is chalk rock. A less fri-able soil, mixed with flints, intervenes between Croy-don and Godstone, and is found on all the declivities of the chalk hills. Along the elevated summit of the Downs, particularly about Walton and Headley, is a large extent of heathy land, consisting of ferruginous and barren sand. A peculiar kind of clay, of a blueish-black colour, here called "black land," extends in a long narrow tract along the southern side of the chalk hills, from the vicinity of Reigate, into the county of Kent.

Proceeding northward from the eastern extremity of the Downs, a variety of soils occurs, chiefly strong clays, interspersed with tracts of sandy loam, and these again with patches of gravel, which continue nearly to Dulwich, whence, to the north-eastern extremity of the county, a strong pure clay occupies the whole tract. Northward from the chalk, at Banstead Downs, is also a long tract of clay, continuing by Sutton, Mordon, and the eastern side of Merton, to the sandy loams of Wimbledon, Putney heath, and Mortlake. A similar soil is found on descending northwards from any part of the Downs, between Banstead and Clandon, near Guildford; but the breadth of clay separating the sandy loam from the chalk continues decreasing as it proceeds westward. The rich sandy soil lying between the clay and the Thames is intermingled, especially on the banks of the Mole and the Wey, with loams of various qualities, and even with clay: the subsoil of nearly the whole of these northern sands is a yellow silicious gravel. North-westward from Guildford, sandy loams first occur in the vicinity of Stoke, and afterwards strong retentive clays, which extend beyond Warplesdon, where they unite with the heaths. The soil on the banks of the Thames consists partly of a sandy loam, and partly of a rich strong loam.

The proportion of arable land greatly exceeds that of meadow and pasture: the drill husbandry is general in the western part of the county, about Bagshot, Esher, Send, Cobham, Ripley, &c. The corn and pulse crops are, wheat, barley, oats, beans, and peas: wheat is cultivated to a great extent; the barley, being of a superior quality, is generally appropriated to the making of malt. The field varieties of peas and beans are extensively cultivated, as an agricultural crop, in most parts of the county, especially on the chalk hills; while the finer sorts are grown in the vicinity of the metropolis, and on the sandy loams in the vale of the Thames, chiefly for the supply of the London market. The cultivation of turnips and cabbages is now carried on to a great extent, partly for the supply of the metropolitan markets, and partly for the consumption of cattle. Great quantities of carrots are grown in the northern part of the county, to the west of the river Mole, and parsnips on the rich deep lands in the district lying between Wandsworth and Kingston, for the London markets, being seldom given to cattle. Tares, and sometimes rye, are grown as green food for sheep and horses. Red clover has long been in general cultivation: the greater part of this crop is made into hay, but though within a short distance of London, much is cut green for horses and cows. Trefoil, white clover, and ray-grass, are occasionally sown, and large tracts of chalky soil are occupied by sainfoin, most of which is made into hay: lucerne is also grown, but on a small scale. The Farnham hops are cultivated to a considerable extent on the borders of Hampshire, and have long been celebrated for their excellent quality, always bringing a higher price than any other hops in the kingdom. Woad flourishes on the chalk hills about Banstead Downs, where it is generally sown with barley. By far the most extensive and valuable tracts of meadow are situated along the banks of the Thames, in the north-western part of the county, and on the banks of the Wey, near Godalming: there is also a small extent of meadow in its north-eastern angle, near the metropolis.

Of dairy pastures there are scarcely any: the greatest extent lying together is on the estate of the Duke of Norfolk, in the parishes of Newdigate and Charlwood, on the southern border. Large quantities of manure, of different kinds, are carried from the metropolis into the northern parts of Surrey; in the more remote districts lime and chalk are procured from the quarries and works on both sides of the range of chalk downs.

A great variety of cattle is kept in this county; but few oxen are worked. The large Wiltshire, the South Down, and the Dorsetshire, are the principal breeds of sheep, the latter being kept chiefly for the rearing of early house lambs, for which Surrey was formerly much celebrated, though the number sent to the London market has greatly decreased: many grass lambs are prepared for the butcher in April and May. Great numbers of hogs are fed at the distilleries and starch-manufactories, whither they are brought chiefly from Berkshire, Shropshire, and the East riding of Yorkshire; those from the first-named district are preferred. Most of the farmers keep hogs of the Berkshire and Chinese breeds: Budgwick, on the border of Sussex, is remarkable for a breed of swine that fatten to an enormous size. Numerous flocks of geese are kept on the commons, especially in the Weald: the Dorking breed of fowls is much celebrated. The quantity of garden ground employed in raising vegetables for the London market is very considerable: the parishes of Mortlake and Battersea are particularly distinguished for the cultivation of asparagus of excellent quality; in the latter much ground is also occupied in the cultivation of vegetables for seed. Orchards are numerous, but of very limited extent. It is considered that a greater extent of land is employed in the cultivation of medicinal plants in this county than in any other in England: those grown in the largest quantity are peppermint, lavender, wormwood, camomile, aniseed, liquorice, and poppies, which, with a few others for the druggists and perfumers, occupy a large portion of land in the parishes of Mitcham and Tooting.

The part most remarkable for its woods is the Weald, on the southern side of the county, which, there is every reason to believe, was formerly wholly covered with wood, much of which has been cleared off at no very remote period. The coppices consist chiefly of oak, birch, ash, chesnut, sallow, hazel, and alder; and their produce is formed into hoops, poles for the hop plantations, hurdles, and fagots; great quantities are also made into charcoal, for gunpowder and other purposes. The woodlands in the other parts of the county, particularly on the chalk hills, have a greater proportion of coppice, and fewer timber trees, than those in the Weald. The most common kinds of timber are oak, beech, walnut, ash, elm, box, yew, birch, Scotch fir, larch, and maple; besides which, lime and chesnut trees are found in the numerous plantations about gentlemens' seats. The oaks of the finest and largest growth are those in the Weald; the beeches thrive best on the chalk hills, where they are every where seen; walnut trees, of a large size, are found scattered in many parts, but no where in great numbers; the ash and elm are seldom seen any where but in the hedge-rows, and the latter chiefly to the north of the chalk hills, about Croydon, Cheam, &c., and in the more immediate vicinity of the metropolis. The box in this county, and chiefly on Box hill, near Dorking, attains a considerable size; its wood is bought principally by the mathematical instrument makers, and by the turners, in London and Tonbridge. Surrey is noted for the great number of yew-trees that are scattered in a wild state over its chalk hills, and for the size to which some of those that have been artificially planted have attained. Besides forming a considerable portion of the underwoods, the birch flourishes on the heaths: great quantities of brooms are made of its small branches, and sold chiefly at Southwark. Extensive plantations of fir and larch have been made on the heathy lands in the western part of the county. In the western and northern parts the osier and willow are much cultivated, particularly about Byfleet, Chertsey, &c.; the common furze is also cultivated in different places for fuel.

Under the early Norman sovereigns a large portion of Surrey was reserved as part of the royal demesne. By Henry II. the limits of Windsor Forest were gradually extended until he had afforested nearly the whole of this county; but Richard, his son and successor, in the first year of his reign, consented to disafforest all the county lying eastward of the river Wey, and southward of Guildford Down, his charter to that effect having been confirmed by King John. That part still enclosed in the forest, according to the provisions of this charter, was called the Bailiwick of Surrey, being exempt from the jurisdiction of the sheriff, and subject only to that of its own bailiff: it contained the parishes and townships of Ash, Bisley, Byfleet, Chobham, Horsell, Purbright, Pyrford, Stoke, Tongham, Wanborough, Worplesdon, Windlesham, and Woking: within the same district also lay Chertsey, Egham, and Thorpe, but these being estates of the abbey of Chertsey, were not subject to the bailiff's jurisdiction. Notwithstanding the charter of forests granted by King John, this part of the county remained in forest until after the granting of another charter by Henry III., in the ninth year of his reign, which disafforested the whole, excepting only the park of Guildford. Edward I. and Edward II. attempted to set aside this grant, but without effect; and Edward III., in the first year of his reign, fully confirmed it. The royal pretensions were revived in the seventh of Charles I., but without success; and from that period the district known, since the time of Richard I., as the Bailiwick of Surrey, has been regarded as only a purlieu of the forest of Windsor; and the king has still a right and property over the deer escaping into it, which may be destroyed by none, except the owners of woods, or lands, in which they may be found, which are especially exempted from the operation of the forest laws: it is, however, so far free and open to all owners of land within its limits, that, under certain restrictions, they may chase and kill any of the deer actually found therein. For the better preservation of the deer escaping out of the forest into this purlieu, the king has a ranger, appointed by letters patent, whose office it is to chase them back again, and to whom, in his official capacity, belongs Fangrove Lodge, near Chertsey.

It appears surprising, that a county so near the metropolis should contain so large a quantity of waste land. About the commencement of the present century it was computed, that one-sixth lay in a wild and un-

cultivated state; and though this extent has been greatly lessened by numerous enclosures, there yet remain in heaths about forty-eight thousand acres, and in commons about seventeen thousand. The principal heaths are, that of Bagshot, on the western border of the county, which, with Romping Downs, and the wastes of Purbright, Windlesham, &c., contains upwards of thirty thousand acres, almost entirely covered with short heath; Frensham, Thursley, and Witley heaths, comprising together five thousand eight hundred acres; Hindhead heath, which, with the last-mentioned tracts, is situated on the south-western confines of Surrey, and occupies an extent of upwards of three thousand acres; the heaths of Farnham and Crooksbury, containing about three thousand seven hundred acres; Blackheath, about four miles south of Guildford, comprising about one thousand acres; and Headley heath, containing about nine hundred acres. From their vicinity to the metropolis, Addington heath and Shirley common, containing about three hundred acres, and situated to the south-east of Croydon, are worthy of notice. The surface of the heaths is in general flat, and their value is very trifling, being only used for grazing a very few lean cattle. In the low swampy parts, about Bagshot, Windlesham, Frimley, and Chobham, peat is cut, though the places which supply it are few; some of the heath is cut for making into brooms; they also produce whortleberries, which are sometimes gathered for sale. In the western heaths, as well as in several other parts, fish-ponds have been made, by means of dams in the narrow vallies, in which fish, chiefly carp, are fed for the London market. Two of the most extensive of these are, Spire pond, between Chobham and Byfleet, and another near Frensham, each containing about one hundred and fifty acres. The most extensive commons still remaining unenclosed are, those of Leith hill and Hurtwood, containing upwards of three thousand acres; those of Walton, Kingswood, and Banstead, occupying about one thousand five hundred acres; and those of Epsom, Leatherhead, and Ashtead, extending over one thousand two hundred acres. Those in the more immediate vicinity of the metropolis are Wimbledon and Putney, containing about one thousand acres; Barnes common, about two hundred; Wandsworth common, about three hundred and fifty; Battersea and Clapham commons, together about fifty; Streatham common, about two hundred and fifty; and Kennington common, about twenty. Coal from the port of London is carried into every part of the county, and in the vicinity of the metropolis is the only fuel that is used; but in the more remote districts, furze, turf, and peat, are commonly burned in all the cottages.

A sand-stone, commonly called rag-stone, containing oxyde of iron, abounds along the line of junction of the Weald with the sand hills, which skirt that tract on the north: the oxyde of iron sometimes prevails so greatly, as to have been formerly worked and smelted as iron-ore; but in consequence of the high price of fuel, these works have long been totally abandoned. Stone of a similar kind to the above is found in smaller quantities about Send and Chobham; and iron-ore appears in the sand in the vicinities of Puttenham and Godstone. At Purbright, and in many parts of the surrounding country, are found loose blocks of stone bearing a strong resemblance, both in quality and appearance, to those termed the Grey Wethers, on the downs of Berkshire and Wiltshire. In the neighbourhoods of Godstone, Gatton, Merstham, Reigate, and Blechingley, are extensive quarries of a peculiar kind of stone, which, when first dry, is soft and unable to bear the action of a damp atmosphere; but after being kept under cover for a few months, its texture becomes so firm and compact, that it can resist the heat of an ordinary fire, and is, in consequence, in great demand for fire-places. On the White hills near Blechingley this stone is softer than elsewhere, and is now chiefly dug for the glass-manufacturers, who, by means of it, have been enabled to produce plate-glass of much larger dimensions than they formerly could: great quantities are taken by water to Liverpool and the north of England. Limestone, of a blueish-grey colour, containing a very small proportion of flint, is extensively quarried near Dorking, and affords lime of great purity and strength, particularly serviceable in works under water, having been employed in the construction of the West India and Wapping docks: limestone is also dug and burned at Guildford, Sutton, and Carshalton. Some of the most extensive chalk-pits are those at Croydon, Sutton, Epsom, Leatherhead, Bookham, Effingham, Horsley, Clandon, Stoke, Guildford, and Puttenham, on the northern side of the Downs; and those at Godstone, Catterham, Reigate, Merstham, Buckland, and Betchworth, on the southern side. The sand about Tandridge, Reigate, and Dorking, is in great request for hour-glasses, writing, and a variety of other purposes; that about Reigate, more especially, is considered unequalled in the kingdom for purity and colour; great quantities are sent to London. Fullers' earth is found in very extensive beds about Nutfield, Reigate, and Blechingley, to the south of the Downs; and some, though of an inferior quality, near Sutton and Croydon, to the north of them: it is of two kinds, blue and yellow, the latter, which is the most valuable, being chiefly employed in fulling the finer cloths of Wiltshire and Gloucestershire, while the former is sent into Yorkshire, for the coarser manufactures: this earth is sent in wagons to the railway commencing at Merstham, along which it is conveyed to the Thames, where it is shipped. Brick-earth is found in most parts of the county, though not of the finest quality: at Nonsuch, in the parish of Cheam, however, there is a particularly valuable bed, from which a kind of brick, capable of resisting intense heat, is made.

Though Surrey cannot be regarded as a manufacturing county, yet its vicinity to the metropolis, and the convenience of its streams for the working of mills, have caused several manufactures of importance to be established in it. On the Wandle is situated a great number of flour, paper, snuff, and oil mills, besides mills for preparing leather and parchment, and for grinding logwood: upon its banks also, chiefly in the parishes of Croydon and Mitcham, are large calico, bleaching, and printing works. This river, which is usually not more than three feet deep, and eight broad, is remarkable for turning ninety mills in a course of only ten miles. On the Mole are several flour-mills, some iron-mills at Cobham, and several flatting-mills at Ember. There are extensive powder-mills near Malden, to the north of

Ewell; and several paper-mills on the different tributary branches of the Wey. At Godalming are considerable factories for the weaving of all kinds of stockings and the making of patent fleecy hosiery; at the same place are also establishments for the combing of wool, and the manufacture of worsteds, blankets, tilts, and collar-cloths. At Stoke, near Guildford, is a sawing-mill for staves, ship-pins, &c.; and at Mortlake a manufacture of delft and stone ware. In the neighbourhood of London, particularly at Battersea and Lambeth, are several distilleries on a very extensive scale; and at the latter place, manufactories for patent shot and artificial stone: the manufactures carried on in Southwark, and its immediate vicinity, are of different kinds, being chiefly such as are connected with the varied trade of the port of London. This north-eastern extremity of the county has a very large share in the vast commerce of the port of London; and, besides its numerous wharfs and quays on the banks of the Thames, it possesses various large commercial docks, among which may be noticed, more particularly, the Grand Surrey docks (Outer and Inner), by which the Grand Surrey canal connects with the river.

The principal rivers are the Thames, the Wey, and the Mole. The Thames, forming the entire northern boundary of the county, first touches it at its north-western extremity, above Egham, whence it takes a south-easterly course, by the town of Chertsey, to the confluence of the Wey, where it assumes an irregular north-easterly direction to the village of Kew, passing by the town of Kingston (to which and the village of Thames-Ditton it makes an extensive sweep on the south-east), the village of Petersham, and the bold heights of Richmond: at Kew it takes a winding easterly course, which it pursues by Mortlake, Barnes, Putney, Wandsworth, and Battersea: then forming Chelsea Reach, it pours its majestic stream through the spacious arches of the six magnificent bridges which connect the cities of London and Westminster with the borough of Southwark and the southern suburbs of the metropolis; and, immediately eastward of the last of them forms the pool, or harbour of London; between Rotherhithe and Deptford it quits Surrey, as it approaches the superb pile of Greenwich hospital: above London bridge it is navigable for barges of large burden during the whole of its course past this county; the tide flows to Richmond bridge. The Wey, rising on the eastern border of Hampshire, to the south-west of Haslemere, makes a small circuit through that county, and then enters Surrey, on its south-western border, near Frensham, proceeding eastward to Godalming, where it becomes navigable, and whence its course to the Thames is generally in a north-north-easterly direction: at the village of Shalford, a little to the south of Guildford, it is joined by a stream which rises near Leith hill, to the south of Wotton, and passing through Guildford, by the villages of Stoke and Send, and close to the south-east of that of Woking, it proceeds to Weybridge, to which place it gives name, and near which it falls into the Thames at Harn Haw. The Mole rises from several springs on the southern borders of the county, and in the forest of Tilgate in Sussex, the waters of which unite in the parish of Horley, to the south of Reigate, whence this river takes a south-westerly course, at first through a flat and uninteresting county : approaching the downs near Dorking, the scenery changes, and passing beneath the venerable groves around Betchworth castle, the river enters a narrow defile, and pursues its course through a romantic valley beneath the almost perpendicular height of Box hill : its course from the vicinity of Dorking is nearly northward to Leatherhead, where it emerges from among the hills, flowing northwestward by the village of Stoke to that of Cobham, a little distance beyond which it takes a north-easterly direction by Esher to West and East Moulsey, at which latter place it joins the Thames opposite to Hampton Court. This river is famed for, and is supposed to derive its name from, the circumstance of a part of its waters pursuing a subterraneous passage : this is occasioned by the porous and cavernous nature of the soil over which the river runs during several miles of its course below Dorking : when its waters are at their ordinary height, no particular irregularity in its stream is here observable ; but in seasons of drought its current is wholly carried through the swallows, as the subterranean passages are called, and its ordinary channel, similar to that of any other river of the same size, is left dry, except here and there a stagnant pool : by the bridge at Thorncroft it rises again, and thenceforward the current is uninterrupted. The small river Wandle, rising from some very strong springs near Croydon, flows eastward by Beddington and Wollington, and having been greatly increased by the waters of some other powerful springs situated near Carshalton, flows northward by Mitcham, Mordon, Merton, and Tooting, to Wandsworth, where it falls into the Thames, after a course of about ten miles : its waters are remarkable for their purity. A powerful stream rises in the town of Ewell, whence it pursues its course to the Thames, at Kingston. One of the streams which, by their junction in Kent, form the river Medway, rises in the parishes of Godstone and Horne, and flowing through that of Lingfield, passes eastward into that county. The small river Loddon forms the western boundary of Surrey for the distance of nine or ten miles near its source.

Under the head of canals it may be proper to observe, that the navigation of the Wey is artificial, and has locks upon it, which are supposed to have been the first constructed in the kingdom ; the navigable channel also is, in some places, wholly separate from the natural course of the river : the bill for the formation of this navigation up to Guildford was passed in 1651, but the work was not carried into execution until towards the close of the century : it was extended to Godalming in 1760, and by its means timber, flour, and paper, are now exported to London. The Basingstoke canal enters Surrey from Hampshire near Dradbrook, crossing the river Loddon, from which it derives its chief supply of water ; immediately turning northward, it proceeds in that direction to the neighbourhood of Frimley, where it pursues an easterly course, a little inclining northward, by Purbright, to the river Wey, a short distance below Byfleet ; from Dradbrook to its junction with the navigable channel of the Wey, a distance of about fifteen miles, it has a fall of one hundred and ninety-five feet ; from Hook common there is a branch to Turgis Green, six miles long, and on

the same level : the act for the formation of this navigation was passed in 1778, and it was completed in 1796 : the chief articles of traffic upon it are timber, corn, and coal. The Grand Surrey canal, the act for constructing which was obtained in 1801, commencing a little to the west of the road from London to Camberwell, is carried eastward across the Kent road, and then northward to the Grand Surrey docks, through which it communicates with the Thames. The Croydon canal, the act for making which was obtained in 1801, commencing on the northern side of that town, is carried north-by-east by the hamlet of Sydenham to the Grand Surrey canal, in the parish of Deptford; part of its course lies just within the north-eastern confines of Kent : it is navigable for boats of twenty-five tons' burden. The Surrey and Sussex canal forms a junction between the navigable channel of the Arun in Sussex, and that of the Wey, a little above Guildford. The Surrey railway, which was projected and commenced in the year 1802, proceeds from Wandsworth, in a double line, up the valley of the Wandle to Croydon, whence it is continued southward to Merstham : the part from Wandsworth to Croydon, about ten miles in length, was soon completed ; and the success of the undertaking shortly induced the proprietors to form the further line, which is about seven miles long, but has not near the same extent of traffic as the lower part, from which short branches are carried to many of the manufactories on the banks of the Wandle ; at Wandsworth the railway terminates at a basin, capable of holding more than thirty barges, which communicates with the Thames : the breadth of the two lines, with a foot-path, is twenty-four feet. In forming the railway between Croydon and Merstham, it was found necessary, for the purpose of preserving the level, to raise embankments across several vallies, of from ten to thirty feet deep, with arched carriage roads through them.

Owing to the inferiority of the materials for making and repairing the ordinary roads, they are not generally in a good condition. The road from London to the Land's End enters from Staines, and passes through Egham and Bagshot to Basingstoke : this is also the road from London to Truro, through Launceston ; that from London to Wells, Bridg-water, and Minehead ; that to Exeter and Dartmouth, through Taunton ; that to Barnstaple and Ilfracomb ; and that to Stratton. The road from London to Winchester, Poole, and Weymouth, branches off near Bagshot, and passes through Farnham to Alton in Hampshire : this is also the road from London to Southampton, to Gosport, and to Portsmouth. The road from London to Portsmouth, through Guildford, passes through Wandsworth, Kingston, Esher, Guildford, and Godalming, to Petersfield. The road from London to Chichester branches from the last near Godalming, through Haslemere, to Midhurst. The road from London to Brighton, by Lewes, passes through Streatham and Croydon, to East Grinstead in Sussex. That from London to Brighton, through Reigate, passes by Clapham common, Tooting, Mitcham, Sutton, and Reigate, to Crawley in Sussex : that by Horsham, branches from the last at Lower Tooting, and passes through Ewell, Epsom, Leatherhead, and Dorking. The road from London to Dovor quits Surrey at New Cross turnpike.

This county contained the Roman station of *No-*

viomagus, situated at Woodcote, near Croydon; besides two others, supposed to have been respectively at Kingston on Thames and Walton on the Hill. It was traversed by the roads leading from the southern and eastern coasts to the capital, which met in St. George's Fields, near Southwark, the principal of them being the Ermin-street, which ran nearly parallel to, and at a very short distance to the eastward of, the present turnpike-road through Clapham, Tooting, Merton, Ewell, and Epsom, to Ashtead, thence proceeding, nearly in a southerly direction, to Dorking, where it took a westerly course, about a mile southward of Guildford, to Farnham, beyond which town it soon entered Hampshire; the Stane-street, which, branching from the Ermin-street at Dorking, proceeded southward, through the parish of Ockley, into Sussex; and another Stane-street, which from the metropolis passed through Streatham, Croydon, Coulsdon, Catterham, and Godstone, also into Sussex; and the Watling-street, from Dovor, which crossed its north-eastern extremity to London. Remains of ancient encampments, supposed to be Roman, may be seen at Bottle hill, in the parish of Warlingham; on Castle hill, in that of Hascomb; near Chelsham; on Holmbury hill, in the parish of Ockley; at Ladlands and Oatlands; and on St. George's hill, near Walton on Thames. Foundations of Roman edifices have been discovered at Walton on the Hill, and on Blackheath, in the parish of Albury, both surrounded by intrenchments. Other remains of buildings, supposed to be of the like origin, have been traced in the vicinities of Wollington, Carshalton, and Beddinton; and near Kingston on Thames, Roman sepulchral urns, coins, earthenware, and foundations of buildings, have been found. Many Roman coins and pavements have also been found in St. George's Fields, Southwark. Different ancient encampments, the date of the formation of which is uncertain, exist in various places, besides those above mentioned; that at the south-western angle of Wimbledon common is supposed by Camden to mark the site of the battle fought in 568; while those of Hanstie Bury, on a projection of Leith hill, and War Coppice hill, in the parish of Catterham, are attributed to the Danes.

The number of religious houses in Surrey, of all denominations, prior to the general dissolution, was about twenty-eight. Remains yet exist of the abbeys of Chertsey and Waverley, and of the priories of Merton, Newark, or Newstead, and Southwark. Of ecclesiastical architecture and antiquities, the most remarkable specimens are in the churches of Addington, Barnes, Beddington, Camberwell, Carshalton, Chaldon, Chipstead, Compton, Croydon, Dunsfold, St. Mary and St. Nicholas (at Guildford), Kingston, Lambeth, Leatherhead, Leigh, Merstham, Merton, Merrow, Mickleham, Shere, St. Mary Overy, commonly called St. Saviour's, in Southwark (one of the largest and finest parochial churches in the kingdom), and in the chapel of St. Martha on the Hill. The most remarkable fonts are those of the churches of Beddington, Chelsham, Dunsfold, Elstead, Ewhurst, Frensham, Hambledon, Haslemere, Horne, Merstham, Mitcham, Mordon, Mortlake, Shere, Thames-Ditton, and Walton on the Hill. There are extensive remains of the castles of Farnham and Guildford. The most remarkable ancient residence is Lambeth palace: there are also remains of the ancient palace of the Archbishops

of Canterbury, at Croydon. Few counties in England can vie with Surrey in the number and elegance of its seats of nobility and gentry, and certainly none not exceeding it in size: this circumstance is owing chiefly to its vicinity to the metropolis, and the superior pleasantness of its scenery. Of its parks, the royal one of Richmond, to the south-east of that elegant resort, is the most extensive, being nearly eight miles in circumference, and containing upwards of two thousand two hundred and fifty acres. Many of the farm-houses in the Weald have a mean and dilapidated appearance; but in the other parts of the county they are neat and commodious: the oldest are built entirely of brick, and generally roofed with large heavy flag-stones; while many are constructed on a wooden frame, with lath and plaster; others again are rough-cast. The mineral springs are numerous, and were formerly in high repute and much frequented, more particularly those of Epsom. On the northern side of the chalk hills, and in the vallies by which they are traversed, in the eastern part of the county, copious streams of water, in the shape of remarkably powerful springs, provincially called bourns, are periodically discharged. In sinking wells on the chalk it is often found necessary to bore to the depth of three hundred feet; and the thick beds of clay lying in the north-eastern part of the county must, for the same purpose, be bored entirely through, frequently to an equal depth. There are several remarkable excavations, of unknown date, in the chalk hill upon which Guildford castle stands. Surrey gives the title of earl to the family of Howard, Dukes of Norfolk.

SUSSEX, a maritime county, bounded on the west by Hampshire, on the north by Surrey, on the north-east and east by Kent, and on the south by the English Channel. It extends from 50° 44′ to 51° 9′ (N. Lat.), and from 50′ (E. Lon.) to 57′ (W. Lon.); comprising an area of upwards of one thousand four hundred and sixty-three square miles, or about nine hundred and thirty-six thousand three hundred and twenty statute acres. The population, in 1821, was 233,019. At the period of the invasion of Britain by the Romans, Sussex formed part of the territory of the Regni. The reduction of this part of the island was effected by Flavius Vespasian, who was commissioned by the Emperor Claudius, about the year 47, to establish the Roman dominion in the maritime provinces, which he accomplished without much difficulty, and fixed his head-quarters near the site of the present city of Chichester. This territory was included in the division called *Britannia Prima*. No particular mention of it occurs in history until after the departure of the Romans from Britain, when, in 477, a Saxon chieftain, named Ælla, landed, with his three sons and a considerable number of followers, at West Wittering, a village about eight miles south-west of Chichester: they soon made themselves masters of the adjacent coasts, but were too weak to penetrate into the country, which was vigorously defended by its inhabitants. Hostilities appear to have been carried on for several years between Ælla and the Britons, the former occasionally receiving reinforcements; and, in 485, a sanguinary but indecisive battle was fought near *Mercreadesbourne*, in the vicinity of Pevensey. Ælla's forces having, however, been recruited by fresh arrivals of his countrymen, he undertook, in 490, the siege of *Anderida*, the capital of the Regni (the precise situation of which has not been ascertained), and at last succeeded in taking it by assault; as a punishment for the obstinacy of its defenders, he ordered them all to be put to the sword. From this period may be dated the foundation of the kingdom of the South Saxons, called in Saxon *Suth Seaxe*, of which Sussex is a contraction. Ælla, on the death of Hengist, founder of the Saxon kingdom of Kent, became the most influential of the Saxon chieftains in Britain, which he continued to be until his death in 504, or 505. Cissa, the only surviving son of Ælla, succeeded his father in the government of the South Saxons, and employed much of his time and treasure in rebuilding and improving the capital of his kingdom, to which he gave the name of *Cissa-ceaster*, now Chichester. About the year 650, Adelwalch succeeded to the throne of Sussex, and was attacked, vanquished, and made prisoner, by Wulfhere, monarch of the more powerful kingdom of Mercia. Having at the court of the latter embraced the Christian religion, Adelwalch, was reinstated in his dominions, and made every exertion to propagate the same faith among his subjects, receiving into his dominions Bishop Wilfrid, who had been expelled from Northumbria, at the same time assigning the peninsula of Selsea as his abode, and granting to him and his companions that and other lands for their maintenance. Ceadwalla, a prince of the blood royal of Wessex, having failed in an attempt to usurp the supreme authority in that kingdom, fled to the great forest of *Anderida*, which occupied the Weald of Sussex, Surrey, and Kent, where he succeeded in maintaining himself for some time at the head of a band of freebooters : Adelwalch attacked and expelled him from his territories ; but Ceadwalla, having undertaken an expedition against Kent, which proved unsuccessful in his retreat from that kingdom, again encountered Adelwalch, whom he defeated and slew. On the death of the king, Berthun and Anthun, two South Saxon nobles, rallied their countrymen around them, and compelled the invader, Ceadwalla, to retire. The latter, however, on the death of the reigning monarch of Wessex, soon after succeeded peaceably to the throne of that kingdom, and renewing his contests with the South Saxons, entered their country with a powerful army, defeated them, and made great devastations throughout their whole territory : the final subjugation of Sussex was, however, left for Ceadwalla's successor, who, in 728, united it to his other dominions. Bishop Wilfrid returned to Northumbria about the year 658, and after his departure it appears that the ecclesiastical affairs of Sussex were under the government of the bishops of Winchester, until the year 711, when Eadbert, abbot of Selsea, was appointed bishop of the South Saxons, and for more than three succeeding centuries Selsea was the episcopal see, until it was removed to Chichester, in the reign of the Conqueror, about the year 1082. In the year 876, the Danes, returning from the siege of Exeter, landed on the coast of Sussex, but were attacked and routed by the men of Chichester, who slew many of them and captured some of their vessels. In 893, they visited the eastern part of the county, and proceeding up the river Rother, seized the town of Appledore in Kent. The famous Danish pirate, Hesting, or Hastings,

also landed near the site of the present town of Hastings, where he raised some kind of fortifications. In 902, a battle was fought at Holmwood, in this county, between the Danes and the men of Kent ; and in 904, Sweyn, King of Denmark, and Olave, King of Norway, retreating from the siege of London, ravaged both Surrey and Sussex. It was at this period also that a sanguinary battle was fought, near Lewes, between the North-men and the Saxons, in which the former were defeated, and Olave taken prisoner. In 1009, the Danish chiefs, Heming and Anlaf, laid waste Sussex, which experienced a similar devastation in 1013. In 1051, its coasts were ravaged by Godwin, Earl of Kent. William, Duke of Normandy, in his invasion of England, made his descent upon this coast, landing his army in Pevensey bay, where he arrived with a fleet of nine hundred sail, on September 29th, 1066. On the 14th of October the Saxon and the Norman armies came to an engagement at a place then called *Epiton*, but which, in commemoration of this victory, has ever since been called Battle. Thence William marched along the coast, north-eastward, to Dovor. In 1087, or 1088, William II. invested Pevensey castle, where the rebellious Bishop of Baieux had taken refuge, the garrison in which, after a siege of six weeks, was compelled by famine to surrender. On May 14th, 1264, the decisive battle between the forces of Henry III. and those of his barons, under Simon de Montfort, was fought near Lewes, in which the king and his son, Prince Edward, were made prisoners. In 1266, Prince Edward attacked Winchelsea, and took it by storm. In 1287, Old Winchelsea and Rye harbours suffered greatly by a tremendous tempest, which choked up the mouth of the Rother, and changed its course. Sussex, at various periods, has suffered severely from partial invasions, to which its locality seems to have peculiarly exposed it. In 1340, the French burned several ships at Hastings, and made an attempt upon Winchelsea, which failed : in this year also they landed at Rottingdean, and advanced across the Downs towards Lewes, but were met by the gentlemen and other inhabitants of the neighbouring county, whom they defeated, but withdrew immediately to their ships, and carried off their prisoners. In 1380, the French and Spaniards landed at Winchelsea, which town they burned. In 1447, Rye suffered the like infliction from the French only. In 1513, the French made a descent on the coast, at Brighton, and having pillaged that town, set fire to it. In 1545, after they had retired from the Isle of Wight, they made another descent at the same place, but were driven back to their ships : they shortly after made an attempt to land at Newhaven, when all who approached the shore were either killed or drowned : from Newhaven they sailed to Seaford, and there attempted to land, but with the same unfavourable result ; after which they retired to their ships and proceeded to France, with diminished forces. In 1551, the Princess, afterwards Queen Elizabeth, visited Halnaker, Petworth, Cowdray, and Chichester ; and in 1573, after her accession, she made a tour along the coast : she also visited different parts of Sussex in 1591.

In 1642, while Charles I. lay at Reading, he was waited upon by a deputation from this county, requesting his authority to raise the southern counties in arms in his behalf. Having obtained the necessary commis-

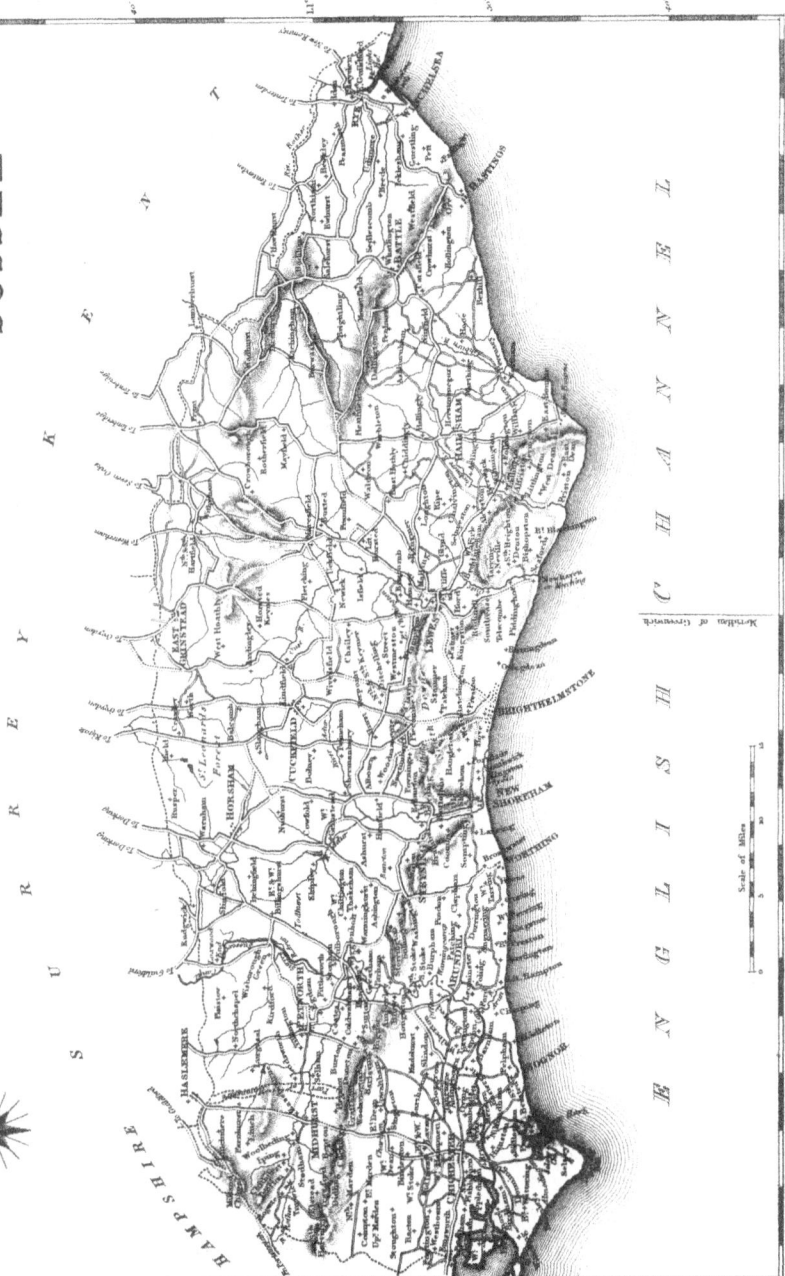

SUSSEX

S U R R E Y

K E N T

HAMPSHIRE

ENGLISH CHANNEL

Scale of Miles

Meridian of Greenwich

DRAWN AND ENGRAVED FOR LEWIS' TOPOGRAPHICAL DICTIONARY.

Drawn by R. Creighton

Engraved by J & C Walker

sions, Chichester was chosen, as being a walled town, for the place of rendezvous ; but the mass of the people were little inclined to defend the royal cause, and, in 1643, Sir William Waller was sent by the parliament, with a considerable force, to attack the royalists, and dislodge them from that city, which he invested, and which, after a brisk siege of ten or twelve days, was surrendered to him, on December 29th. Near the close of the year 1644, Lord Hopton suddenly appeared with his forces before Arundel castle, which was given up to him on the first summons ; but in less than two months after, it was as suddenly retaken by Sir William Waller. After the battle of Worcester, Charles II. was conducted, by Lord Wilmot and Col. Gunter, to the house of a Mr. Maunsell of Ovingdean, in this county, where he lay concealed for a few days, whilst his friends were devising the means of his escape to the continent, in effecting which he proceeded to Brighton, on October 14th, and the next morning embarked at Shoreham on board a coal vessel, which conveyed him to Fescamp in Normandy. In the year 1690, on June 30th, the combined fleets of the English and Dutch were defeated, off Beachy Head, by that of the French. Different places on the coast suffered severely, from violent gales and unusually high tides, in January 1775, and in the same month of the year 1792.

Sussex is co-extensive with the diocese of Chichester, in the province of Canterbury, and is divided into the two archdeaconries of Chichester and Lewes, the former containing the deaneries of Arundel, Boxgrove, Chichester, Midhurst, and Storrington, and, locally that of Pagham ; the latter those of Dallington, Hastings, Lewes, and Pevensey, and, locally that of South Malling ; all the parishes comprised in the exempt deaneries of Pagham and South Malling, with those of All Saints at Chichester, and St. Thomas in the Cliffe at Lewes, are in the peculiar jurisdiction of the Archbishop of Canterbury. The total number of parishes is three hundred, of which one hundred and fifty-seven are rectories, one hundred and twenty-seven vicarages, and the remainder, with the exception of three, which have both a rectory and a vicarage, perpetual curacies. The great civil divisions are called *rapes*, a term peculiar to this county : they are six in number, *viz.*, Arundel, comprising the hundreds of Arundel, Avisford, Bury, Poling, Rotherbridge, and West Easwrith ; Bramber, comprising those of Brightford, Burbeach, East Easwrith, Fishergate, Patching, Singlecross, Steyning, Tarring, Tipnoak, West Grinstead, and Windham and Ewhurst ; Chichester, those of Aldwick, Bosham, Box and Stockbridge, Dumpford, Easebourne, Manhood, and Westbourn and Singleton ; Hastings, those of Baldslow, Battle, Bexhill, Foxearle, Goldspur, Gostrow, Guestling, Hawkesborough, Henhurst, Netherfield, Ninfield, Shoyswell, and Staple ; Lewes, those of Barcomb, Buttinghill, Dean, Fishergate, Holmstrow, Lewes, Poynings, Preston, Street, Swanborough, Whalesbone, and Younsmere ; and Pevensey, those of Alciston, Bishopstone, Burley-Arches, or Burarches, Danehill-Horsted, Dill, Eastbourne, East Grinstead, Flexborough, Hartfield, Longbridge, Loxfield-Dorset, Loxfield-Pelham, Ringmer, Rotherfield, Rushmonden, Shiplake, Totnore, and Willingdon, and the lowey of Pevensey. It contains the city and port of Chichester ; the following members of the cinque-ports, *viz.*, Hastings, Rye, Seaford, and

Winchelsea, all which have markets except Seaford ; the borough, market town, and sea-port of Horsham ; the borough and market towns of Arundel, East Grinstead, Lewes, Midhurst, Shoreham, and Steyning ; the borough of Bramber ; the market towns and sea-ports of Brighton and Hastings ; and the market towns of Cuckfield, Hailsham, Little Hampton, Petworth, and Worthing. Two knights are returned to parliament for the shire, two citizens for the city of Chichester, two barons for each of the members of the cinque-ports, and two burgesses for each of the boroughs : the county members are elected at Chichester. This is one of the counties forming the Home Circuit : the Lent assizes are held at Horsham, and the summer and winter assizes at Lewes : the county gaols are at Lewes and Horsham, a portion of the former being used as the county house of correction. The quarter sessions are held at Petworth, Horsham, Lewes, and Chichester : there are one hundred and thirty-four acting magistrates. The rates raised in the county for the year ending March 25th, 1827, amounted to £274,185. 2., and the expenditure to £273,664. 1., of which £239,778. 12. was applied to the relief of the poor.

The most remarkable feature in the surface and scenery of Sussex is the bold and open range of chalk hills, called the South Downs, extending into it from Hampshire, and stretching, in nearly an easterly direction, for the greater part of its length, gradually approaching the sea : their northern declivity is precipitous, but on the south their descent is gradual, except in the vicinity of Brighton, where they form a shore broken into stupendous cliffs, terminated on the east by the bold promontory of Beachy Head, which rises perpendicularly above the strand to the height of five hundred and sixty-four feet, and is the most elevated point on the southern coast of England. The rest of the coast is flat, excepting the vicinity of Selsea Bill, where a few rocks present themselves, and the rocks of Hastings. The district generally understood to constitute the South Downs consists only of the chalk hills lying to the east of Shoreham : many parts of the Downs westward of the river Arun are overgrown with much beech wood, chiefly of a dwarf size, furze, &c., so that the herbage is much inferior to that covering them further eastward. Southward of the chalk hills, extending from their base to the sea, lies a fertile and richly-cultivated vale, which towards its eastern extremity, between Brighton and Shoreham, is, for the most part, less than a mile in breadth : proceeding westward, between the rivers Adur and Arun, this is increased to three miles ; and from the Arun to the borders of Hampshire its breadth varies from three to seven miles : its length is about thirty-six. Extensive tracts of marsh land lie adjacent to the coast, between the eastern extremity of the South Downs at Beachy Head and the confines of Kent, in the vicinity of Rye ; others also are situated on the lower part of the course of the rivers Ouse, Adur, and Arun. "The Weald" comprises a tract of country, the exact limits of which are not defined : in a legal sense it means the large woodland district contained in the three counties of Sussex, Surrey, and Kent, in which the woods pay no tithe. The large portion of it within the limits of this county, called the Weald of Sussex, comprises nearly the whole of the level tract lying to the north of the Downs, together with the range of hills running the whole length of the county, at a short distance from its northern and north-eastern boundaries, a great part of which is completely barren. Such is the quantity of timber and other trees in the low plains of the Weald, that, when viewed from the chalk hills, they present to the eye the appearance of one mass of wood ; this is, in part, owing to the common practice, at the period that this tract was first reclaimed from its condition of a wild forest, of leaving a shaw of wood, several yards in width, around each enclosure, as a nursery for timber. On the whole, the scenery of Sussex is pleasing and picturesque, much resembling that of the adjoining county of Surrey, except that its maritime districts, including the noble Downs, command a wide expanse of sea studded with numerous vessels, and terminated on the west by the Isle of Wight. The climate in the western maritime tracts is particularly mild, and favourable for vegetation ; as is also that of the South Downs, though not to so great a degree. These hills are bleak, and completely exposed to the violent westerly and south-westerly winds, which sometimes do considerable damage, by shaking the corn out of the ear : the gales also carry with them saline particles, from the spray of the sea, (which beats with extreme violence upon the coast,) that destroy the vegetation of all the hedges and trees over which it more immediately sweeps : the same matter penetrates even through the walls of houses, particularly those in exposed situations.

The different soils of chalk, clay, sand, loam, and gravel, are found in this county. The first is the soil of the South Downs, consisting, in its natural state, of a rich light hazel mould, lying upon a substratum of loose chalk, or chalk rubble, which covers the more compact rock of the same nature : when brought under cultivation it becomes intermixed with a great portion of chalk by the action of the plough. In some places along the summit of the Downs, nearly the whole surface consists of flints covered by a natural turf : descending from these hills the soil becomes of a deeper staple, and near their base is every where of a good and sufficient depth for the plough. Westward of the river Arun this soil is very gravelly, and contains large flints, and between the Adur and the Ouse has a thin substratum of reddish sand. Along the northern base of the chalk hills, throughout nearly their whole length, and lying between them and the clay of the Weald, is a narrow tract of rich and strong arable land, consisting of an excessively stiff, deep, calcareous loam, on a substratum of pure clay, which, from the admixture of chalk, has generally a whitish appearance. The soil of the fertile vale lying to the south of the Downs consists of a rich loam, in some places rather stiff, more particularly in the projecting south-western angle of the county, and in the peninsula of Selsea Bill, though more commonly light and sandy, and resting upon a substratum of brick-earth, or gravel ; the latter, in the western part of it, being by far the most prevalent. Between this and the chalk hills extends a narrow tract, inferior to the former in richness, but consisting of excellent land for turnips ; its breadth is greatest on the confines of Hampshire, the flints lying upon its surface in such abundance as entirely to hide the mould : vegetation, however, flourishes through

these beds of stone with singular luxuriance. The prevailing soil of the Weald, namely, that of its low plains, is a very stiff clayey loam, on a substratum of brick-clay, and that again upon one of sand-stone. Upon the hills before mentioned, as traversing it in a direction nearly from east to west, the soil is in some places a sandy loam, resting upon a sandy gritstone ; and in others, a poor, black, sandy, vegetable mould on a soft clay. A long line of these poor sandy tracts, in an unimproved state, crosses the northern part of this county from Kent, and extends into Hampshire : these wastes are, however, wholly separated from each other by extensive districts of clay and others under cultivation. The soil of the marsh lands is composed of decayed vegetable substances, intermixed with sand and other matter, deposited by inundations : in the rape of Lewes this vegetable mould is about twelve inches thick ; while in that of Pevensey it is many feet deep, and rests upon a heavy black silt, or sea-sand, containing various kinds of shells : stumps of trees, and timber of large size, have been dug from both these tracts.

The rich arable lands lying to the south of the Downs, and those at the foot of their northern declivity, amount to about one hundred thousand acres : of Down land there is about sixty-eight thousand acres, of which a great proportion is under its native green sward : the arable and grass lands of the Weald, which are of nearly equal extent, amount together to about four hundred and twenty-five thousand acres. The whole county is enclosed with good hedge-rows, excepting the greater part of the Downs, and the wastes towards its northern confines. The rotations of crops are regulated chiefly by the nature and properties of the soil, and are therefore various : the common system in the Weald is a fallow, two crops of corn, and one of clover. The corn and pulse commonly grown are wheat, barley, oats, and peas. A valuable species of wheat, called the *Chidham white*, or hedge wheat, takes the former name from the village of Chidham, in this county, where it was first cultivated, the plant which produced the original seed having been found growing wild in a hedge in that neighbourhood. The soil of the extensive tract of the Weald being generally too heavy for the culture of barley, the quantity produced is consequently inferior. Oats are grown on the largest scale in the Weald. Peas are very extensively cultivated, especially on the South Downs, and in the maritime districts : beans are very little grown. Tares are frequently cultivated as green food for cattle and horses. Coleseed, barley, and rye are sown, and are in great esteem among the flock-masters of the Downs, as green food for their sheep. Turnips are also much cultivated, more particularly as food for the flocks during the winter and the spring. Potatoes are extensively and very successfully grown, particularly in the vicinities of Battle, East Bourne, and Chichester : they are chiefly applied to the fattening of cattle.

The principal artificial grasses are, red and white clover, trefoil, and ray-grass : lucerne is commonly cultivated in the neighbourhood of Brighton and East Bourne, and is seen in a few other places, particularly about Chichester : sainfoin is also occasionally sown. In the eastern and north-eastern parts, hops are very extensively cultivated. The meadow lands are mown every year, and afterwards grazed. It is only in the western part of the county that there are any extensive tracts of irrigated meadows; these are chiefly on the course of the small river Lavant. The marshes may be classed among the finest and most profitable of their kind, having undergone great improvement : the brooks, or levels, as they are called, by which they are traversed, are sometimes, especially in winter, so much swollen by violent rains, as to overflow their banks : when one of these inundations occurs during summer, as is sometimes the case, the whole produce of the flooded land is, for that year, entirely spoiled by the stagnant muddy water, and no kind of cattle will eat the herbage ; the tides also sometimes overwhelm parts of them, as the banks are not every where strong enough to resist their force. These marshes occupy about thirty thousand acres, and are wholly employed in the feeding of cattle and sheep ; the level of Pevensey is preferred for the cattle, while the marshes about Winchelsea and Rye, adjoining the western side of Romney-Marsh in Kent, not possessing fresh water, are better calculated for sheep. An act of parliament was obtained, about the commencement of the present century, for widening the channel of the Ouse, near Lewes, and making a shorter cut to the sea, the execution of which design has been of essential benefit to the Lewes and Laughton levels. The great extent of Down land having its native green sward is applied to the feeding of numerous flocks of sheep : the herbage is short, sweet, and aromatic, and of an excellent kind, peculiar to these hills, which is supposed to give to the flesh of the sheep fed upon them that firmness and exquisite flavour for which it is so remarkable. Several of the manures are peculiar : chalk is used in immense quantities, as also is lime burned from it ; and as the chalk hills extend no further eastward than East Bourne, it is shipped in sloops from Holywell pits at Beachy Head, and conveyed to the kilns at Bexhill, Hastings, and Rye : lime is also burned from a kind of limestone dug in the Weald. The lands in the maritime district are extensively manured with marl, which is found almost every where on the south side of the Downs, at the depth of only a few feet from the surface : great quantities are also dug from pits on the sea-shore, which are generally covered at high water. Sea mud, provincially called *sleech*, is frequently used as manure near the coast ; wood ashes are employed in the Weald.

The chief object of the cattle system is the breeding and rearing of stock, for the purposes of working, and fattening for the butcher, the dairy being only a secondary object. The native cattle are ranked among the best in the kingdom : their colour is universally red, and they have a great disposition to fatten ; they yield but very little milk, but the quality of it is peculiarly rich : many oxen are employed in the labours of the farm. When fat, the ordinary weight of the oxen is about one hundred and forty stone : the other sorts are principally Welch. Besides its valuable native breed of cattle, Sussex has a breed of sheep, the South Down, one of the most celebrated and numerous in the kingdom : this breed has of late years been introduced in great numbers into various parts of England, more particularly the southern and midland counties; and its excellence is every where acknowledged. The wool is of a very fine carding kind, and its lightness is in proportion to its fineness. The other kinds are the celebrated Romney-Marsh breed, and Hampshire, Dorsetshire, Wiltshire, and Somersetshire sheep. The hogs bear much affinity to those of Berkshire; some of them are of a mixed breed, between this and a smaller species. Great numbers of rabbits occupy the extensive sandy wastes, many of them being sent to the London market. Northchapel, Kindford, and their vicinities, are famous for fowls. Most of what are called Dorking fowls are bred in the Weald of Sussex, the chief market for them being at Horsham.

In the western parts of the county are some considerable orchards, from which cider is made : it is only to the south of the Downs that orchards for cider are much attended to, though the vicinity of Petworth is considered to produce the best in the county : nearly all that is made is for home consumption. Sussex has, from the remotest period of antiquity, been celebrated for its fine growth of timber, chiefly oak : the extent of its woodlands cannot be estimated at less than one hundred and seventy thousand acres, nearly all included within the Weald, the timber produced in which is preferred by the navy contractors to that of any other district. In the Saxon times here appears to have been one continued forest, stretching from Hampshire into Kent, which, at the time of the Norman Conquest, was valued, not according to the quantity of timber it produced, but the number of hogs that could be fed on the acorns. The quantity of timber in the remaining portions of this ancient woodland has, of late years, been much lessened by extensive falls. The coppices contain oak, ash, beech, Spanish chesnut, willow, maple, and red and white birch ; the natural produce of the sands consists chiefly of birch, hazel, and beech underwood. The produce of these coppices is converted principally into poles for the hop-plantations, and for fuel : new plantations have been formed in several places. The waste lands are chiefly situated on the northern side of the county, occupying an extent of about one hundred thousand acres : their soil has a discouraging aspect, generally consisting of a poor blackish sand, frequently very wet ; and their chief value is as rabbit warrens. Among the most extensive are, St. Leonard's Forest, containing about ten thousand acres ; Ashdown Forest, occupying nearly twenty thousand ; and the forests of Waterdown and Tilgate. The principal articles of fuel are coal and wood; in a few places turf is used.

The chief mineral productions are the various descriptions of limestone obtained in the Weald : one of these is the Sussex marble, which, when cut and polished, is equal in beauty to most marbles : it is frequently used for chimney-pieces, and for building, paving and burning into lime: much of it was employed in building the cathedral at Canterbury, where it is called Petworth marble, being found in the neighbourhood of that town in the highest degree of perfection. The limestone and the iron-stone in contact with it often rise to within a very few feet of the surface. Alternate strata of sand-stone and iron-stone occur every where in the Weald ; and under these, at a considerable depth, are numerous strata of limestone, which, when burned, makes the finest cement in the kingdom. The sand-stone, though often extremely friable, is in some places solid enough for the purposes of masonry : the iron-stone is of various kinds, each having a provincial name. Anciently the iron-stone of this district was very extensively worked as ore, until the successful establishment of the great iron and coal works in the midland and northern districts of the kingdom occasioned the works in the Weald, the fuel of which was supplied by the extensive surrounding woodlands, to be wholly abandoned. Fullers' earth is found at Tillington, and used in the neighbouring fulling-mills ; red ochre is obtained at Graffham, Chidham, and several other places on the coast, some of it being sent to London. The manufacture of charcoal, chiefly for gunpowder, has been of considerable importance in this county, from which large quantities have been annually sent to London over land. At Chichester a small woollen manufacture is carried on: sacks, blankets, linen and worsted yarn, cotton and stuff goods, and other articles, are made in the workhouses. There are paper-mills at Iping and a few other places. Potash is made at Bricksill hill, near Petworth, for the soap-makers of that town. Brick-making is common in many parts of the county : near Petworth are kilns for the burning of bricks and tiles to be exported to the West Indies. Ship and boat building is carried on in some of the small harbours of Sussex ; yet, notwithstanding the great extent of sea-coast, its maritime commerce is of nearly as little importance as its manufactures. Corn is exported in different directions, much of it being sent to Portsmouth. A considerable quantity of timber is exported ; as are charcoal, cord-wood, and oak-bark ; horned cattle and sheep, hides, and wool, are among its agricultural exports. There are several fisheries upon the coast, chiefly for herrings, mackerel, and flat-fish, much of the produce being sent to London. In the Weald are very numerous ponds for feeding fresh water fish for the London markets : these are chiefly carp ; though tench, perch, eels, and pike, are also kept : many of the ponds were originally formed for the purpose of working the machinery of the iron-manufactories long since abandoned. The most fashionable places of resort for sea-bathing are Brighton, Worthing, and Hastings.

All the principal rivers rise in the Weald, within the limits of the county, and take a tolerably direct course to the English channel, so that their length is not great. They are, the Arun, with its tributary, the Rother ; the Ouse ; and the Adur. The Arun has its source in St. Leonard's Forest, whence it flows, for a few miles, by Horsham, and then turns due south : having received the waters of the Rother, which rises in the north-western part of the county, and joins it near the village of Stopham, its course becomes very serpentine, as it flows through a rich tract of marshes, and by the town of Arundel, to the sea at Little Hampton : this river, with the aid of several artificial cuts, has been made navigable up to New-bridge, near Guillenhurst ; and the Rother, with the like assistance, as high as the town of Midhurst. A small canal also branches from the Rother to the village of Haslingbourne, within half a mile of Petworth. The largest barges navigating these rivers are of thirty tons' burden : the tide flows up the Arun, a distance of seventeen miles, to the vicinity of the village of Amberley : this river is celebrated for its mullets, which, in the summer season, proceed up it, in large shoals, as far as Arundel, as also for its trout and eels. The Ouse is formed by the junction of two

streams, one of which rises in the forest of Worth, the other in that of St. Leonard, uniting near Cuckfield, whence the Ouse, proceeding first eastward, and then southward, passes the town of Lewes, to the sea at Newhaven : this river has been made navigable beyond Lewes to within five miles of Cuckfield. The Adur, sometimes called the Beeding, also rises in St. Leonard's Forest, and pursues a course southward, by Steyning and Bramber, to Shoreham, where it suddenly takes an easterly direction, nearly parallel with the coast, and only at a short distance from it, falling into the sea a little westward of Brighton : it is navigable for ships of considerable burden to Shoreham, and for barges to the vicinity of the village of Ashurst. The Rother has its source at Rotherfield, near Ashdown Forest, whence it proceeds eastward, and soon becomes the boundary between this county and that of Kent : after passing the Isle of Oxney, in the latter county, it suddenly turns southward across the eastern extremity of Sussex, expanding into an æstuary, and falling into the sea below the town of Rye, the harbour of which it forms ; it is navigable as far as Newenden. The Lavant, a much smaller stream than any of the above, rises in the chalk hills near East Dean, and flows southward by Chichester, some distance below which it becomes navigable for ships, and expands into an æstuary, which opens into the sea between the village of Wittering and the south-eastern point of Hayling island in Hampshire : remarkably fine lobsters are bred in this river, near its mouth. The shores of the south-western part of the county are rendered very irregular by several other arms of the sea, one of which separates Thorney island from the rest of the county. One of the four streams which, by their junction immediately within the south-western confines of Kent, form the river Medway, rises in the north-eastern part of this county. The Portsmouth and Arundel canal, the act for the formation of which was obtained in 1815, commencing from the river Arun, a little below the latter town, proceeds westward, in nearly a direct line, to the broad æstuary of the Lavant, below Chichester, to which city there is a short branch northward : from the Lavant the navigation is continued through the channels which separate Thorney and Hayling islands from the main land to the eastern side of Portsea island, where the artificial navigation recommences, and proceeds westward across that island to Portsmouth.

The roads are generally good. That from London to Chichester enters the county from Haslemere in Surrey, and passes through Midhurst, where it is joined by another road from London to the same place, entering from Godalming, near Cripple-Crouch, whence there is a branch to Petworth. The road from London to Brighton, through Lewes, entering from Surrey, passes through East Grinstead and Lewes, or through Maresfield and Lewes, to Brighton ; that from London to Brighton through Reigate passes through Crawley and Cuckfield, in this county ; and that from London to Brighton by Horsham, through West Grinstead and Steyning : the road to Newhaven and Seaford branches from the first of these at Lewes ; and those to Arundel, Tarring, and New Shoreham, from the last at Steyning. The road from London to Rye and Winchelsea runs for upwards of twenty miles along the confines of the counties of Sussex and Kent : the road to Hastings branches from it at Flimwell, and thence proceeds through Robertsbridge and Battle to Hastings.

This county is supposed to have contained the Roman stations of *Anderida Civitas*, at East Bourne; *Anderida Portus*, at Pevensey; *Cilindunum*, at Slindon; *Mida*, at Midhurst; *Mantantonis*, or *Mutuantonis*, at Lewes; *Portus Adurni*, at Aldrington; and *Regnum*, at Chichester. The present roads from Portsmouth, from Midhurst, and from Arundel, to Chichester are considered to have been originally of Roman formation; and from this city the Roman road, commonly called the Stane-street, proceeded, in a north-easterly direction, towards Dorking in Surrey, where it fell into the Ermin-street, being traceable in many parts of its course. Various Roman domestic remains have been dug up in different places, particularly at Chichester, Bognor, and East Bourne, including tesselated pavements and baths: coins of the Lower Empire have been found in various other places. The number of ancient encampments upon the Downs and in other parts of the county, near the sea, evince that they have been frequently the scene of military operations: some of these ancient fortifications are supposed to have been made by the Romans, others by the Saxon and the Danish invaders, while one on Mount Caburn, about a mile and a half from Lewes, on the northern edge of the Downs, is thought to be British. Near the western confines of the county, to the west of Chichester, are, the encampment of the Broile, of an oblong form, about half a mile in length and a quarter in breadth; and another, called Gonshill, of the same form. On the northern brow of the Downs, overlooking the Weald, and proceeding from west to east, occur the following camps; Chenkbury, about two miles west of Steyning, which is circular, and the circumference about two furlongs; eight miles further, above Poynings, a large camp of an oval form, not less than a mile round, and accessible only at one narrow neck of land, which is defended by a deep broad ditch and high bank; Wolstenbury, about three miles further, on a hill projecting from the rest like a bastion, nearly circular, and about a furlong in diameter; Ditchling, three miles from the last, nearly square, about sixty rods long, and fifty broad; and lastly, that on Mount Caburn, already mentioned, which is round, and scarcely three furlongs in circumference; and a quarter of a mile westward of it is another fortification, much larger, but not so perfect. Those on the southern side of the Downs, proceeding in the same direction, are, that on St. Roche's, or St. Rook's, hill, which is circular, and about two furlongs in diameter; that on High down, four miles eastward of Arundel, a small square; and Cissbury, four miles south-west of Steyning. The only one on the central heights of the chalk hills is Hollingbury, two miles north of Brighton, which is square, and the area about five acres. About a mile eastward of the same town, on the top of a hill near the sea, is a camp with a triple ditch and bank, also square, except that the angles are rounded off: its outer circumference is about three quarters of a mile. In the parish of Telscombe, about five miles from the last, are two other squares; and at Newhaven, on the point of a hill overlooking the mouth of the Ouse, is a strong fortification of an oval form, and containing an area of about six acres. About a mile eastward of Seaford is another

work of the same kind, also situated close to the sea, but of a semicircular form, and containing about twelve acres; and lastly, about three miles east of Cuckmere haven, near Burling Gap, are other earthworks, enclosing a hill, of a semi-elliptical form, and about three quarters of a mile in circumference: traces of several more earthworks of less extent and importance are discoverable in other places.

The number of religious houses in this county, before the general dissolution, including hospitals and colleges, was about fifty-eight. There are yet extensive remains of the magnificent abbey of Battle, founded, in 1067, by William the Conqueror, in commemoration of his victory over Harold; and of that of Bayham, on the confines of Kent; and considerable relics of the priories of Boxgrove, Hardham, Lewes, Michelham, and Shelbred, about four miles north of Midhurst. The churches most remarkable for antiquity, or other peculiarities, are, those of Aldrington (in ruins), Arundel, Barnham, Battle, Bramber, Broadwater, Cuckfield, East Marden, St. Clement and All Saints at Hastings, Horsham, St. John sub Castro and St. Anne at Lewes, New Shoreham, Old Shoreham, Rye, Selsea, Steyning, South Stoke, Up-Waltham, St. Thomas at Winchelsea, and West Hampnett. There are also interesting remains of ancient chapels at several places. Some of the fonts most worthy of notice are those of Aldingbourn, a curious specimen of the very ancient fonts of black marble, standing on five pillars of unequal size, which are common in this county; Bosham, Brighton, St. Clement's at Hastings, North Mundham, Stedham, Tortington, West Wittering, Woolbeding, and Yapton. The most considerable remains of ancient castles are those of Amberley, Arundel, Bodiham, Bramber, Eridge, in the parish of Frant, Hastings, Hurstmonceaux, Ipres at Rye, Lewes, Pevensey, Scotney, and Winchelsea. The most remarkable ancient mansion is that of Cowdray House, now in ruins. Several of the modern seats of the nobility and gentry are magnificent; and the Pavilion at Brighton is distinguished as one of the residences of the monarch. Some of the seats most worthy of notice are, Petworth Park, the residence of the Earl of Egremont, the lord-lieutenant of the county; Arundel Castle, that of the Duke of Norfolk; the episcopal palace of Chichester; Eridge Castle, the residence of the Earl of Abergavenny; Goodwood, that of the Duke of Richmond; Parham Park, that of Lord de la Zouche; Penshurst Place, that of Sir John Shelley Sidney, Bart; Sheffield Park, that of the Earl of Sheffield; Slindon House, that of the Earl of Newburgh; and Stanmer Park, that of the Earl of Chichester. The ordinary houses, as well as the gentlemen's seats, when situated near the quarries, are generally built of the kinds of stone that are found in the northern and eastern parts of the county. On the Downs, and in their vicinity, flints are almost the only material for the former. The houses in different parts, particularly those in exposed situations, are frequently faced with tile. There is a chalybeate spring at Brighton, and another at East Bourne: near Hastings there is a singular dropping well, and, in the same vicinity, a fine waterfall of forty feet perpendicular. The following parishes are incorporated for the common support of their poor; *viz.*, Repton, Cocking, Chithurst, East Bourne, Farnhurst, Iping, Linchmere, Lodsworth, Lurgasall, Selham, Stedham, Tillington, Trayford, Trotton, Woolbeding, and Wollavington, which have their common house of industry at East Bourne ; and Bersted, Bignor, Burton, Bury, Clapham, Coates, Duncton, Egdean, Patching, Slindon, and Sutton, which have their house of industry at the last-mentioned place. The title of the Duke of Sussex is borne by His Royal Highness Prince Augustus Frederick, sixth son of George III., upon whom it was conferred in the year 1801.

SUSTEAD, a parish in the northern division of the hundred of ERPINGHAM, county of NORFOLK, 4¼ miles (S. W.) from Cromer, containing 134 inhabitants. The living is a perpetual curacy, in the archdeaconry of Norfolk, and diocese of Norwich, endowed with £600 royal bounty, and in the patronage of the Rev. John Boldero. The church is dedicated to St. Peter and St. Paul.

SUTCOMBE, a parish in the hundred of BLACK TORRINGTON, county of DEVON, 5½ miles (N. by E.) from Holsworthy, containing 405 inhabitants. The living is a rectory, in the archdeaconry of Totness, and diocese of Exeter, rated in the king's books at £17. 10. 7½., and in the patronage of the Rev. W. H. Coham. The church, dedicated to St. Andrew, has a Norman doorway, but is mostly of later date. There is an almshouse for six poor persons, founded and endowed by Sir William Morice, Secretary of State to Charles II.

SUTTERBY, a parish in the Wold division of the wapentake of CANDLESHOE, parts of LINDSEY, county of LINCOLN, 4¾ miles (W. S. W.) from Alford, containing 33 inhabitants. The living is a rectory, in the archdeaconry and diocese of Lincoln, rated in the king's books at £5. 10. 2½., endowed with £200 royal bounty, and in the patronage of the Crown. The church is dedicated to St. John the Baptist.

SUTTERTON, a parish in the wapentake of KIRTON, parts of HOLLAND, county of LINCOLN, 8¼ miles (N. W. by N.) from Holbeach, containing 1014 inhabitants. The living is a vicarage, in the archdeaconry and diocese of Lincoln, rated in the king's books at £23. 3. 4., and in the patronage of the Crown. The church, dedicated to St. Mary, is principally in the later style of English architecture, with a tower, surmounted by an elegant crocketed spire.

SUTTON, a parish in the hundred of BIGGLESWADE, county of BEDFORD, 1¾ mile (S.) from Potton, containing 369 inhabitants. The living is a rectory, in the archdeaconry of Bedford, and diocese of Lincoln, rated in the king's books at £20, and in the patronage of the President and Fellows of St. John's College, Oxford. The church is dedicated to All Saints. Here were the seat and royalty of the celebrated Sutton John of Gaunt, Duke of Lancaster, who conferred Sutton and Potton upon Sir Roger Burgoyne and his heirs, by a curious laconic deed in doggerell verse, which is preserved among the ancient records in the Arches, Doctors' Commons. The manor-house was burned down in 1826. There is a fine chalybeate spring near the parsonage-house. The learned Bishop Stillingfleet was rector of Sutton, about the middle of the seventeenth century, where he wrote his *Origines Sacræ*.

SUTTON, a parish in the southern division of the hundred of WITCHFORD, Isle of Ely, county of CAMBRIDGE, 6¼ miles (W. by S.) from Ely, containing 1157 inhabitants. The living is a vicarage, with the rectory of Mepal united, in the peculiar jurisdiction of the Bishop of Ely, rated in the king's books at £10, and in the patronage of the Dean and Chapter of Ely. The church, dedicated to St. Andrew, was built by Barnet, Bishop of Ely, who died in 1373 : it is a beautiful specimen of the decorated style of English architecture. There are places of worship for Baptists and Wesleyan Methodists. This place had anciently a market and a fair, granted to the first abbot of Ely. A charity school is supported by the Dean and Chapter, the master of which receives a salary of £20 per annum. In 1634, some labourers discovered, near this place, several ancient coins and gold rings, and three silver plates, one of which had a curious inscription engraven upon it.

SUTTON, a township in the parish of RUNCORN, hundred of BUCKLOW, county palatine of CHESTER, 2 miles (N. E. by E.) from Frodsham, containing 266 inhabitants.

SUTTON, a township in the parish of PRESTBURY, hundred of MACCLESFIELD, county palatine of CHESTER, 2¼ miles (S. E. by S.) from Macclesfield, containing 2991 inhabitants, who are principally employed in the silk manufacture. Here are two small bequests, by Catherine Nixon, in 1689, and John Upton, applied to the instruction of poor children. This was the seat of the family of Holinshed, the historian, and is supposed to have been his birthplace.

SUTTON, a township in that part of the parish of MIDDLEWICH which is in the hundred of NORTHWICH county palatine of CHESTER, 1¼ mile (S.) from Middlewich, containing 32 inhabitants.

SUTTON, a parish in the hundred of SCARSDALE, county of DERBY, 4 miles (E. S. E.) from Chesterfield, containing, with Duckmanton, 685 inhabitants. The living is a discharged rectory, with the vicarage of Duckmanton annexed, in the archdeaconry of Derby, and diocese of Lichfield and Coventry, rated in the king's books at £12. 16. 0½., and in the patronage of Richard Arkwright, Esq. The church is dedicated to St. Mary ; the windows exhibit some remains of ancient stained glass. Twenty poor children are instructed for about £20 per annum, arising from the rent of sixteen acres of land allotted by the lord and freeholders of the manor. Nicholas Deincourt, Earl of Scarsdale, in 1643, fortified the hall, which he had previously erected here, for Charles I. ; it was taken by assault, and the works demolished by Sir John Gell, and, some time afterwards, was plundered by the parliamentarian garrison of Bolsover : this mansion is situated in an extensive and beautiful park.

SUTTON, a parish in the hundred of ROCHFORD, county of ESSEX, 1½ mile (S. E. by S.) from Rochford, containing 89 inhabitants. The living is a rectory, in the archdeaconry of Essex, and diocese of London, rated in the king's books at £11, and in the patronage of W. Cockerton, Esq. and others.

SUTTON, a township in the parish of PRESCOT, hundred of WEST DERBY, county palatine of LANCASTER, 1½ mile (S. E. by E.) from St. Helen's, containing 2329 inhabitants, who are extensively employed in the manufacture of crown and flint glass, earthenware, and watch movements.

SUTTON, a township in the parish of WYMONDHAM, hundred of FOREHOE, county of NORFOLK, 1½ mile (S. W. by S.) from Wymondham, containing 645 inhabitants.

SUTTON, a parish in the hundred of HAPPING, county of NORFOLK, 8¼ miles (E. N. E.) from Coltishall, containing 317 inhabitants. The living is a discharged rectory, in the archdeaconry of Norfolk, and diocese of Norwich, rated in the king's books at £6. 16. 8., and in the patronage of the Earl of Abergavenny. The church is dedicated to St. Michael.

SUTTON, a chapelry in the parish of CASTOR, liberty of PETERBOROUGH, county of NORTHAMPTON, 1¼ mile (E. by S.) from Wansford, containing 113 inhabitants. The chapel is dedicated to St. Michael. The river Nene runs through the chapelry, in which there is a fine stone quarry, producing stone resembling that at Ketton.

SUTTON, a hamlet in the parish of GRANBY, northern division of the wapentake of BINGHAM, county of NOTTINGHAM, 14 miles (E. by S.) from Nottingham. The population is returned with the parish.

SUTTON, a parish in the liberty of SOUTHWELL and SCROOBY, though locally in the wapentake of Bassetlaw, county of NOTTINGHAM, 3¼ miles (N. N. W.) from East Retford, containing, with the township of Lound, 717 inhabitants. The living is a discharged vicarage, with that of Scrooby annexed, in the archdeaconry of Nottingham, and diocese of York, rated in the king's books at £10, endowed with £200 private benefaction, and £200 royal bounty, and in the patronage of the Duke of Portland. The church is dedicated to St. Bartholomew. The river Idle runs through the parish, in which there is a very ancient mansion of singular appearance, said to have been formerly much larger than at present, and the country residence of some of the ancestors of Earl Fitzwilliam. A school, erected by subscription in 1783, is endowed with the proceeds of £70, the gift of Richard Taylor, in 1737, and with two allotments of the waste lands, enclosed in 1773 : the annual income is about £28, for which, and the payment of threepence each per week, thirty children are educated. Sutton is in the honour of Tutbury, duchy of Lancaster, and within the jurisdiction of a court of pleas held at Tutbury every third Tuesday, for the recovery of debts under 40s.

SUTTON, a township in the parish of DIDDLEBURY, hundred of MUNSLOW, county of SALOP, 6 miles (N.) from Ludlow, containing 180 inhabitants.

SUTTON, a parish in the liberties of the borough of SHREWSBURY, county of SALOP, 2¼ miles (S. S. E.) from Shrewsbury, containing 71 inhabitants. The living is a discharged rectory, in the archdeaconry of Salop, and diocese of Hereford, rated in the king's books at £3, endowed with £200 royal bounty, and in the patronage of Lord Berwick. The church is dedicated to St. John. Sutton Spa, a fine mineral spring issuing from a stratum of ash-coloured clay, close to the village, is nearly similar in its properties to sea water, and has been found efficacious in cases of scrofula.

SUTTON, a parish in the hundred of WILFORD, county of SUFFOLK, 3½ miles (S. E. by E.) from Woodbridge, containing 577 inhabitants. The living is a discharged vicarage, in the archdeaconry of Suffolk, and diocese of Norwich, rated in the king's books at £8. 2. 1., and in the patronage of the Rev. Robert Field. The church is dedicated to All Saints. There is a place of worship for Baptists. The navigable river Deben bounds the parish on the west, where there is a ferry to Wood-

ford. Sutton Hall is a fine specimen of ancient domestic architecture.

SUTTON, a parish in the second division of the hundred of WALLINGTON, county of SURREY, 2¾ miles (E. N. E.) from Ewell, containing 911 inhabitants. The living is a rectory, in the archdeaconry of Surrey, and diocese of Winchester, rated in the king's books at £16. 18. 4., and in the patronage of the Rev. Thomas Hatch. The church, dedicated to St. Nicholas, is partly in the decorated style of English architecture; it had formerly a wooden tower, which has been replaced by one of brick, and contains, among other handsome monuments, chiefly of the Talbots, one to the memory of Lady Dorothy Brownlow. In Domesday-book two churches are mentioned to have existed in this place. There is a place of worship for Independents. The Wey and Arun canal passes through the parish. Nine poor children are educated for £6 per annum, the gift of William Beck, in 1789; and the interest of a bequest of £100 by Susannah Bentley, in 1823, is paid in aid of the National school, which is further supported by voluntary contributions. There are also two Sunday schools, endowed by Mrs. Lucy Manners, with £700 three per cent. consols. Mary Gibson left £500 three per cent. annuities, directing the interest to be distributed annually in the following manner; £5 to the rector, £5 to the poor, £2 each to the two churchwardens, and £1 to the parish clerk, provided that, on the 12th of August, the mausoleum of her family be opened and inspected by them, and that they then repair to the church, to hear a sermon preached by the rector. There is a large chalk pit in the parish, in which a variety of curious fossils has been found.

SUTTON, a parish in the hundred of ROTHERBRIDGE, rape of ARUNDEL, county of SUSSEX, 5 miles (S.) from Petworth, containing 353 inhabitants. The living is a rectory, in the archdeaconry and diocese of Chichester, rated in the king's books at £15. 0. 10., and in the patronage of the Earl of Egremont. The church, dedicated to St. John, is partly in the early, and partly in the decorated, style of English architecture.

SUTTON, a hamlet in the parish of TENBURY, upper division of the hundred of DODDINGTREE, county of WORCESTER, 2½ miles (S. by E.) from Tenbury, containing 205 inhabitants.

SUTTON, a township in the parish of NORTON, wapentake of BUCKROSE, East riding of the county of YORK, 1 mile (S. by E.) from New Malton, containing 87 inhabitants.

SUTTON, a parish in the middle division of the wapentake of HOLDERNESS, East riding of the county of YORK, 3½ miles (N. N. E.) from Kingston upon Hull, containing, with the township of Stoneferry, 3658 inhabitants. The living is a perpetual curacy, in the archdeaconry of the East riding, and diocese of York, endowed with £600 royal bounty, and £1000 parliamentary grant, and in the patronage of H. Broadley, Esq. The church, dedicated to St. James, had formerly a chantry of six priests, endowed by John of Sutton, and valued, at the dissolution, at £13. 18. 8. per annum. Many of the most opulent merchants of Hull have residences in this neighbourhood. In the village are two hospitals; one of them founded by Leonard Chamberlain, and rebuilt in 1800, for the maintenance of two poor aged widowers and eight widows, each having a separate house and three shillings a week; the other erected in 1819, by the trustees of the late Mrs. Watson, for the reception of the widows and daughters of poor clergymen deceased. A house of White friars existed here in the time of Edward I.

SUTTON, a joint township with Howgrave, in the parish of KIRKLINGTON, wapentake of HALLIKELD, North riding of the county of YORK, 5¼ miles (N.) from Ripon, containing 122 inhabitants. There is a place of worship for Wesleyan Methodists.

SUTTON, a joint township with Healey, in the parish of MASHAM, eastern division of the wapentake of HANG, North riding of the county of YORK, 6½ miles (S. W.) from Bedale. The population is returned with Healey.

SUTTON, a township in the parish of BROTHERTON, partly within the liberty of ST. PETER of YORK, East riding, and partly in the lower division of the wapentake of BARKSTONE-ASH, West riding, of the county of YORK, 1 mile (N. E. by E.) from Ferry-Bridge, containing 74 inhabitants.

SUTTON, a township in the parish of CAMPSALL, upper division of the wapentake of OSGOLDCROSS, West riding of the county of YORK, 6¼ miles (N. by W.) from Doncaster, containing 145 inhabitants.

SUTTON, a township in the parish of KILDWICK, eastern division of the wapentake of STAINCLIFFE and EWCROSS, West riding of the county of YORK, 5 miles (W. N. W.) from Keighley, containing 1092 inhabitants, several of whom are employed in the manufacture of cotton goods and worsted. There is a place of worship for Baptists.

SUTTON in ASHFIELD, a parish in the northern division of the wapentake of BROXTOW, county of NOTTINGHAM, 3½ miles (W. S. W.) from Mansfield, containing, with the hamlet of Hucknall under Huthwaite, 4655 inhabitants. The village is situated on an eminence, and comprises several streets, covering a considerable extent of ground. The inhabitants are chiefly engaged in the manufacture of cotton hose and lace: in the former about one thousand seven hundred frames are in operation, affording employment to more than two thousand five hundred persons; and there are twenty machines for making the latter: a large factory for spinning cotton, and making checks and nankeens, has long been conducted here. A few also find employment in making a coarse kind of red pottery ware. The Mansfield and Pinxton railway passes through this parish. Limestone of excellent quality abounds in the vicinity. A book society has been established for several years. A small customary market, for provisions, is held on Saturday. The living is a perpetual curacy, in the peculiar jurisdiction of the manorial court of Mansfield, endowed with £400 private benefaction, £400 royal bounty, and £1800 parliamentary grant, and in the patronage of the Duke of Devonshire. The church, situated north-west of the town, is dedicated to St. Mary. There are places of worship for General and Particular Baptists, Independents, and Primitive and Wesleyan Methodists. A National school for boys is principally supported by voluntary contributions, excepting about £10 per annum, which is now appropriated for that purpose, arising from two small benefactions in land, given, some years ago, for the general purposes of education, by James Mason and Elizabeth Root. A Sunday school, in which twenty-one boys and

one hundred and twenty girls are instructed, is connected with this institution; and the Sunday schools attached to the dissenting religious communities contain not less than five hundred children of both sexes. Joseph Whitehead, a frame-work knitter, eminent for his attainments in astronomy and mechanics, who constructed an orrery upon Ferguson's principle, and other complicated pieces of machinery, and was also an excellent musician, was a native of this place; he died in 1811, at the early age of twenty-seven years.

SUTTON (BISHOP'S), a parish in the hundred of BISHOP'S SUTTON, Alton (North) division of the county of SOUTHAMPTON, 1¾ mile (E. S. E.) from New Alresford, containing 474 inhabitants. The living is a vicarage, with the perpetual curacy of Ropley annexed, in the archdeaconry and diocese of Winchester, rated in the king's books at £19. 10. 2½., and in the joint patronage of Sir Thomas Baring, Bart., and John Deacon, Esq. The church is dedicated to St. Nicholas. There is a place of worship for Independents. Fairs are held on the Thursday after the festival of the Holy Trinity, and on November 6th. The Bishops of Winchester had anciently a palace here, the remains of which have been converted into a malt-house.

SUTTON under BRAILS, a parish in the upper division of the hundred of WESTMINSTER, county of GLOUCESTER, though locally in the hundred of Kington, county of Warwick, 4¾ miles (S. E.) from Shipston upon Stour, containing 236 inhabitants. The living is a rectory, in the archdeaconry and diocese of Gloucester, rated in the king's books at £13. 13. 4., and in the patronage of the Bishop of London. The church is dedicated to St. Thomas à Becket.

SUTTON upon DERWENT, a parish in the Wilton-Beacon division of the wapentake of HARTHILL, East riding of the county of YORK, 6½ miles (W. by S.) from Pocklington, containing 400 inhabitants. The living is a rectory, in the archdeaconry of the East riding, and diocese of York, rated in the king's books at £14. 14. 7., and in the patronage of Sir T. Clarges, Bart. The church is dedicated to St. Michael. There is a place of worship for Wesleyan Methodists. The village is pleasantly situated on the banks of the Derwent, which is here crossed by a substantial stone bridge, and near it is a spring strongly impregnated with iron.

SUTTON by DOVOR, a parish in the hundred of CORNILO, lathe of ST. AUGUSTINE, county of KENT, 4 miles (S. W. by W.) from Deal, containing 154 inhabitants. The living is a perpetual curacy, annexed to the vicarage of Northbourne, in the archdeaconry and diocese of Canterbury, endowed with £200 private benefaction, and £200 royal bounty. The church, dedicated to St. Peter and St. Paul, is a small ancient structure, in the early English style, with a circular east end, but no tower.

SUTTON (EAST), a parish in the hundred of EYHORNE, lathe of AYLESFORD, county of KENT, 6 miles (S. E.) from Maidstone, containing 312 inhabitants. The living is a perpetual curacy, annexed to the vicarage of Sutton-Valence, in the archdeaconry and diocese of Rochester. The church is dedicated to St. Peter and St. Paul. The parish is crossed by the ridge of hills bounding the Weald, of which its southern side forms a part.

SUTTON (ST. EDMUND'S), a chapelry in the parish of LONG SUTTON, wapentake of ELLOE, parts of HOLLAND, county of LINCOLN, 10 miles (E. by N.) from Crowland, containing 549 inhabitants. The living is a perpetual curacy, in the archdeaconry and diocese of Lincoln, endowed with £600 royal bounty, and in the patronage of the Vicar of Long Sutton.

SUTTON in the ELMS, a township in the parish of BROUGHTON-ASTLEY, hundred of GUTHLAXTON, county of LEICESTER, 6½ miles (E.) from Hinckley, containing 150 inhabitants. There is a place of worship for Baptists.

SUTTON on the FOREST, a parish in the wapentake of BULMER, North riding of the county of YORK, comprising the townships of Huby and Sutton on the Forest, and containing 940 inhabitants, of which number, 443 are in the township of Sutton on the Forest, 8¼ miles (N. by N.) from York. The living is a vicarage, in the archdeaconry of Cleveland, and diocese of York, rated in the king's books at £17. 3. 4., and in the patronage of the Archbishop of York. The church, dedicated to All Saints, is a very handsome structure. The celebrated Lawrence Sterne was vicar of this parish. There is a place of worship for Independents.

SUTTON (FULL), a parish in the Wilton-Beacon division of the wapentake of HARTHILL, East riding of the county of YORK, 5¼ miles (N. W. by N.) from Pocklington, containing 125 inhabitants. The living is a discharged rectory, in the archdeaconry of the East riding, and diocese of York, rated in the king's books at £10. 12. 8½., and in the patronage of Lord Feversham.

SUTTON (GREAT), a township in the parish of EASTHAM, higher division of the hundred of WIRRALL, county palatine of CHESTER, 7 miles (N.N.W.) from Chester, containing 182 inhabitants.

SUTTON (GUILDEN), a parish in the lower division of the hundred of BROXTON, county palatine of CHESTER, 3¼ miles (E.N.E.) from Chester, containing 131 inhabitants. The living is a perpetual curacy, in the archdeaconry and diocese of Chester, endowed with £600 royal bounty, and in the patronage of Sir J. T. Stanley, Bart.

SUTTON on the HILL, a parish in the hundred of APPLETREE, county of DERBY, 8 miles (W. by S.) from Derby, containing, with the township of Osleston and Thurvaston, and the hamlet of Ash, 638 inhabitants. The living is a vicarage, in the archdeaconry of Derby, and diocese of Lichfield and Coventry, rated in the king's books at £4. 16. 8., and in the patronage of the Rev. W. Ward. The church is dedicated to St. Michael. Twelve poor children are educated and apprenticed for an annuity of £20, bequeathed in 1722, by Anne Jackson. The school-house was erected by subscription in 1736. All the lands in the township, except one farm, were given, some years ago, by Humphrey Chetham, Esq., to the Blue-coat hospital at Manchester.

SUTTON at HONE, a parish in the hundred of AXTON, DARTFORD, and WILMINGTON, lathe of SUTTON at HONE, county of KENT, 2½ miles (S. by E.) from Dartford, containing 863 inhabitants. The living is a vicarage, in the archdeaconry and diocese of Rochester, rated in the king's books at £10, and in the patronage of the Dean and Chapter of Rochester. The church, dedicated to St. John the Baptist, is a spacious structure,

principally in the decorated style. This extensive parish anciently gave name to the lathe ; it is intersected by the river Darent, on the banks of which is the village, in a pleasing situation. Sutton Place, or St. John's, is an ancient brick structure, formerly belonging to the knights of St. John of Jerusalem, who had a commandery here. Dr. Pitcairn, the eminent physician, resided at Hextable, in this parish.

SUTTON (ST. JAMES), a chapelry in the parish of LONG SUTTON, wapentake of ELLOE, parts of HOLLAND, county of LINCOLN, 5½ miles (S.E. by S.) from Holbeach, containing 343 inhabitants. The living is a perpetual curacy, in the archdeaconry and diocese of Lincoln, endowed with £800 royal bounty, and in the patronage of the Vicar of Long Sutton. The chapel was built of a large sort of brick ; but the chancel, and, at the distance of about twenty-one yards to the westward, the steeple, composed of brick and stone, are the only remains. Near it is a remarkable stone, called Ivy Cross. Six children are educated for a small annuity, bequeathed by William Preston, in 1777.

SUTTON (KING'S), a parish in the hundred of KING'S SUTTON, county of NORTHAMPTON, 6 miles (W. by S.) from Brackley, containing, with the hamlets of Astrop, Purson, and Walton, 1323 inhabitants. The living is a discharged vicarage, in the jurisdiction of the peculiar court of Banbury, rated in the king's books at £5. 6. 8., and in the joint patronage of Sir J. Willes, and R. C. Elwes, Esq. The church, dedicated to St. Peter, is a beautiful specimen of the later English style of architecture, and the tower is surmounted by a lofty crocketed spire. There are places of worship for Independents and Wesleyan Methodists. At Astrope there is a mineral spring, called St. Rumbald's well, which formerly attracted many visitors.

SUTTON (LITTLE), a township in the parish of EASTHAM, higher division of the hundred of WIRRALL, county palatine of CHESTER, 7¾ miles (N.N.W) from Chester, containing 329 inhabitants.

SUTTON (LONG, or ST. MARY'S), a parish in the wapentake of ELLOE, parts of HOLLAND, county of LINCOLN, 4¼ miles (E. by S.) from Holbeach, containing, with the chapelries of Sutton St. Edmund and Sutton St. James, and the hamlet of Sutton-Bourne, or Sutton St. Nicholas, 3955 inhabitants. The living is a vicarage, in the archdeaconry and diocese of Lincoln, rated in the king's books at £40, and endowed with £400 royal bounty. The Rev. T. L. Bennett was patron in 1816. The church, dedicated to St. Mary, is a fine structure, with an ancient stone steeple, and a lofty spire covered with lead. There is a place of worship for Independents.

SUTTON (LONG), a parish in the hundred of So-MERTON, county of SOMERSET, 2¾ miles (S. S.W.) from Somerton, containing 856 inhabitants. The living is a discharged vicarage, in the peculiar jurisdiction and patronage of the Dean and Chapter of Wells, rated in the king's books at £8. 18. The church is dedicated to the Holy Trinity. The river Yeo, or Ivel, is navigable along the southern boundary of the parish. Roman coins, pateræ, and other antiquities, have been found in the neighbourhood.

SUTTON (LONG), a parish in the hundred of CRONDALL, Basingstoke division of the county of SOUTHAMPTON, 2¼ miles (S.) from Odiham, containing

328 inhabitants. The living is a perpetual curacy, in the archdeaconry and diocese of Winchester, endowed with £400 royal bounty. R. Potenger, Esq. was patron in 1806. The church, dedicated to All Saints, has lately received an addition of one hundred and ninety sittings, of which one hundred and sixty-four are free, the Incorporated Society for the enlargement of churches and chapels having granted £190 towards defraying the expense. Eight poor children are educated for a rent-charge of £4, the gift of Stephen Terry, in 1737.

SUTTON in the MARSH, a parish in the Marsh division of the hundred of CALCEWORTH, parts of LINDSEY, county of LINCOLN, 6½ miles (N.E. by E.) from Alford, containing 135 inhabitants. The living is a discharged vicarage, in the archdeaconry and diocese of Lincoln, rated in the king's books at £6. 13. 4., and in the patronage of the Prebendary of Sutton in Marisco in the Cathedral Church of Lincoln. The church is dedicated to St. Clement.

SUTTON (ST. MICHAEL), a parish in the hundred of BROXASH, county of HEREFORD, 4¼ miles (N. N. E.) from Hereford, containing 51 inhabitants. The living is a perpetual curacy, in the archdeaconry and diocese of Hereford, endowed with £1000 royal bounty, and in the patronage of the Unitt family.

SUTTON (ST. NICHOLAS), a parish in the hundred of BROXASH, county of HEREFORD, 4¼ miles (N. B. by N.) from Hereford, containing 202 inhabitants. The living is a rectory, in the archdeaconry and diocese of Hereford, rated in the king's books at £8. 1. 8., and in the patronage of the Unitt family.

SUTTON near SEAFORD, a parish in the hundred of FLEXBOROUGH, rape of PEVENSEY, county of SUSSEX, ¾ of a mile (N. E. by E.) from Seaford, with which the population is returned. The living is a discharged vicarage, annexed to that of Seaford, in the archdeaconry of Lewes, and diocese of Chichester. The church is desecrated.

SUTTON upon TRENT, a parish in the northern division of the wapentake of THURGARTON, county of NOTTINGHAM, 5½ miles (S. E.) from Tuxford, containing 884 inhabitants. The living is a discharged vicarage, in the archdeaconry of Nottingham, and diocese of York, rated in the king's books at £5. 6. 8., endowed with £200 royal bounty, and in the patronage of Sir Charles Hulse, Bart. The church, dedicated to All Saints, exhibits a mixture of various styles of architecture. There are places of worship for Baptists and Wesleyan Methodists. Six poor children are instructed in the parochial school-house for £6 per annum, the bequest of Mary Sprigg, in 1816.

SUTTON under WHITESTONE-CLIFFE, a township in that part of the parish of FELIX-KIRK which is in the wapentake of BIRDFORTH, North riding of tne county of YORK, 3½ miles (E. by N.) from Thirsk, containing 325 inhabitants. There is a place of worship for Calvinistic Methodists.

SUTTON-BASSETT, a parish in the hundred of CORBY, county of NORTHAMPTON, 3¼ miles (N. E.) from Market-Harborough, containing 142 inhabitants. The living is a vicarage, united with that of Weston by Welland, in the archdeaconry of Northampton, and diocese of Peterborough. The church is dedicated to St. Mary.

SUTTON-BENGER, a parish in the hundred of MALMESBURY, county of WILTS, 5 miles (N. N. E.) from Chippenham, containing 458 inhabitants. The living is a discharged vicarage, in the archdeaconry of Wilts, and diocese of Salisbury, rated in the king's books at £6. 3. 4., endowed with £200 private benefaction, and £200 royal bounty, and in the patronage of the Dean and Chapter of Salisbury. The church is dedicated to All Saints. There is a place of worship for Independents.

SUTTON-BINGHAM, a parish in the hundred of HOUNDSBOROUGH, BERWICK, and COKER, county of SOMERSET, 3½ miles (S. by W.) from Yeovil, containing 78 inhabitants. The living is a rectory, in the archdeaconry of Wells, and diocese of Bath and Wells, rated in the king's books at £4. 15. 10. W. Helyar, Esq. was patron in 1820. The church is principally in the early style of English architecture.

SUTTON-BONNINGTON, a parish in the southern division of the wapentake of RUSHCLIFFE, county of NOTTINGHAM, 2 miles (S. E. by E.) from Kegworth, containing 983 inhabitants. The living consists of the united rectories of St. Anne and St. Michael, in the archdeaconry of Nottingham, and diocese of York, the former rated in the king's books at £4. 17. 6., and in the patronage of the Crown, and the latter rated at £15. 2. 1., and in the patronage of the Dean and Chapter of Bristol. There is a place of worship for Wesleyan Methodists.

SUTTON-BOURNE, a hamlet in the parish of LONG SUTTON, wapentake of ELLOE, parts of HOLLAND, county of LINCOLN, 5 miles (E. by N.) from Holbeach, containing 673 inhabitants.

SUTTON-CHENEY, a chapelry in the parish of MARKET-BOSWORTH, hundred of SPARKENHOE, county of LEICESTER, 2 miles (S. S. E.) from Market-Bosworth, containing 354 inhabitants. The chapel, dedicated to St. James, has lately received an addition of one hundred and fifty sittings, of which one hundred and twenty are free, the Incorporated Society for the enlargement of churches and chapels having granted £60 towards defraying the expense. There is a place of worship for Wesleyan Methodists. The Ashby de la Zouch canal passes through the parish.

SUTTON-COLDFIELD, a market town and parish, having separate jurisdiction, though locally in the Birmingham division of the hundred of Hemlingford, county of WARWICK, 26 miles (N. W. by N.) from Warwick, and 110 (N. W. by N.) from London, containing 3466 inhabitants. This town, formerly called *Sutton-Colville*, and *King's Sutton*, is of considerable antiquity, having been of some note in the Saxon times. During the reign of Edward the Confessor, the manor was in the possession of Edwin, Earl of Mercia, but subsequently William the Conqueror held it in his own hands, and Henry I. exchanged it with the Earl of Warwick for other manors. In later times, the town having nearly fallen into decay, it was indebted to the attachment of Vesey, Bishop of Exeter, and chaplain to

Seal and Arms.

Henry VIII., who was a native of this place, for that munificence which led to its revival, and laid the foundation of its future prosperity. It occupies a bleak and exposed situation on rising ground of steep acclivity, and consists principally of one long street; the houses are mostly modern, well built, and of handsome appearance, and the inhabitants are well supplied with water from springs. Adjacent to it is a very extensive and finely-wooded park, in which the inhabitants have the privilege of pasturage, for a small payment to the corporation: it is crossed by the Iknield-street, which is distinctly traceable for two miles, entering the park near a small artificial mount, called King's Standing on the Coldfield, from the circumstance of Charles having harangued his troops from Shropshire on this spot, and taking thence a direction into the Lichfield road. Here is a medicinal spring, called Rounton Well; another, possessing sulphureous qualities, is now disused. The principal occupation is the manufacture of spades, saws, axes, and other implements: mills for grinding gun-barrels are worked by streams of water issuing from pools in the park, of which one covers from thirty to thirty-five acres. The Birmingham and Fazely canal passes through the parish. The market is held on Monday; and fairs are on Trinity-Monday and November 8th, for cattle, sheep, and pedlary. The town is governed by a corporation, which obtained its charter from Henry VIII., at the instance of Bishop Vesey, consisting of a warden, two capital burgesses, and twenty-two other corporate members. The warden, who is chosen annually, and the capital burgesses, for life, by the corporation, from their own body, are justices of the peace by virtue of their office: the warden acts as coroner for the town, manor, and lordship of Sutton. The corporation are lords of the manor, and elect a lord high steward and park-keepers: the former appoints his deputy, who must be a lawyer, and presides at the courts leet and baron. The other members are also chosen by the corporation; the inhabitants are free and eligible by residence. Under the charter they were empowered to hold courts of Oyer and Terminer, and of gaol delivery, which, from disuse, have been transferred to the county town, the corporation paying a quota towards the county rate: they hold a petty session at the town hall, on the Friday in the week of general quarter sessions. A court of record was formerly held, but it has been discontinued since 1727. In the town hall, a neat brick building, are the arms of Bishop Vesey, emblazoned on a shield surmounted with a mitre.

The living is a rectory, in the archdeaconry of Coventry, and diocese of Lichfield and Coventry, rated in the king's books at £33. 9. 2., and in the patronage of William Bedford, Esq. The church, dedicated to the Holy Trinity, is a fine ancient structure, built probably in the thirteenth century, though combining different styles of English architecture: the aisles were added by Bishop Vesey, whose effigy, in a recumbent posture, with a mitre on his head and crosier in his right hand, is in the chancel: part of the nave fell down about seventy years ago, and was rebuilt by the corporation, at the expense of £1500. The free grammar school was founded, in the reign of Henry VIII., and endowed with land in the parish, by Bishop Vesey: the salary of the master is from £300 to £400 per annum, and a handsome house was erected for him, chiefly at the expense of the corporation, on the condition of his teaching twenty-four poor boys additionally in reading, writing, and arithmetic. National schools, in which about two hundred and forty children of both sexes are educated and clothed, are supported from funds belonging to the corporation. Almshouses for five aged men and five aged women, with gardens attached, were built and are supported by the corporation. Among various charitable benefactions, four marriage portions, of £24 each, are allowed annually to four poor maidens, natives or long resident. Near Driffold house, so called from the custom of driving and folding the cattle of the parishioners, a farm-house occupies the site of the old manor-house, formerly an episcopal palace of great strength, of which a few remains are still visible. At the north-west extremity of Sutton, near the Chester road, is a pool called the Bowen, at the extremity of which are the remains of a fortification, called Loaches Banks, enclosing a quadrangular area of nearly two acres, surrounded by three large mounds and three narrow trenches, supposed to be an ancient British camp, from the neighbouring heath being named Drude heath (i. e. Druids' heath): it is defended on three sides by a morass, and accessible only on the side from the Coldfield, where it is protected by a larger mound.

SUTTON-COURTNEY, a parish in the hundred of Ock, county of Berks, 3 miles (S. by E.) from Abingdon, containing, with the chapelry of Appleford, and township of Sutton-Wick, 1147 inhabitants. The living is a vicarage, in the archdeaconry of Berks, and diocese of Salisbury, rated in the king's books at £18. 13. 4., endowed with £400 parliamentary grant, and in the patronage of the Dean and Canons of Windsor. The church, dedicated to All Saints, is very ancient: it has a wooden rood-loft, also a Norman font surrounded with pillars and enriched with sculptured foliage, &c. There is a place of worship for Independents. The Wilts and Berks canal passes through that portion of the parish which borders upon Steventon common. A paper-mill here employs about twenty-five persons. Edmund Bradstock, in 1607, bequeathed a house and lands, of the present annual value of £55, for the education of children: the premises are now in the occupation of a school-master, who teaches fifteen boys. An almshouse was erected, in 1820, pursuant to the will of Francis Elderfield, Esq., who endowed it with £60 per annum for ever.

SUTTON-GRANGE, a township in that part of the parish of Ripon which is in the liberty of Ripon, West riding of the county of York, 3 miles (N. W. by N.) from Ripon, containing 86 inhabitants.

SUTTON-MADDOCK, a parish in the Shiffnall division of the hundred of Brimstree, county of Salop, 6 miles (N.) from Bridgenorth, containing 417 inhabitants. The living is a discharged vicarage, annexed to the rectory of Kemberton, in the archdeaconry of Salop, and diocese of Lichfield and Coventry, rated in the king's books at £5. The church is dedicated to St. Mary. The Severn bounds the parish on the west, and the Shropshire canal forms a junction with that river, near the china manufactory established on its banks.

SUTTON-MALLET, a chapelry in the parish of Moorlinch, hundred of Whitley, county of Somerset, 5¼ miles (E.) from Bridg-water, containing 164 inhabitants. The chapel has lately received an addition of eighty free sittings, the Incorporated Society for the enlargement of churches and chapels having granted £50 towards defraying the expense.

SUTTON-MANDEVILLE, a parish in the hundred of CAWDEN and CADWORTH, county of WILTS, 7 miles (W. S. W.) from Wilton, containing 250 inhabitants. The living is a rectory, in the archdeaconry and diocese of Salisbury, rated in the king's books at £13. 6. 8., and in the patronage of — Hibberd, Esq. The church is dedicated to All Saints.

SUTTON-MONTIS, or MONTAGUE, a parish in the hundred of CATSASH, county of SOMERSET, 5¼ miles (S.) from Castle-Cary, containing 165 inhabitants. The living is a rectory, in the archdeaconry of Wells, and diocese of Bath and Wells, rated in the king's books at £6. 12. 1. R. Leach, Esq. was patron in 1825. The church is dedicated to the Holy Trinity.

SUTTON-POINTZ, a tything in the parish of PRESTON, liberty of SUTTON-POINTZ, Dorchester division of the county of DORSET, 4 miles (N. N. E.) from Melcombe-Regis, containing 337 inhabitants. It is within the peculiar jurisdiction of the Prebendary of Preston in the Cathedral Church of Salisbury. Here was formerly a chapel, dedicated to St. Giles, some remains of which are still visible.

SUTTON-SCOTNEY, a chapelry in the parish of WONSTON, hundred of BUDDLESGATE, Fawley division of the county of SOUTHAMPTON, 5¾ miles (S.) from Whitchurch. The population is returned with the parish.

SUTTON-VALENCE, a parish in the hundred of EYHORNE, lathe of AYLESFORD, county of KENT, 4½ miles (S. E. by S.) from Maidstone, containing 1058 inhabitants. The living is a vicarage, with the perpetual curacy of East Sutton annexed, in the archdeaconry and diocese of Canterbury, rated in the king's books at £7. 9. 7., and in the patronage of the Dean and Chapter of Rochester. The church, dedicated to St. Mary, is a handsome structure in the later English style, with the remains of a lofty spire, injured by lightning : it has lately received an addition of three hundred sittings, of which two hundred and eighty are free, the Incorporated Society for the enlargement of churches and chapels having granted £100 towards defraying the expense. There is a place of worship for Independents. The village, called Town Sutton, is situated below the ridge of hills bounding the Weald, and was anciently distinguished for a strong castle, of which part of the keep still remains : it is a highly picturesque ruin, being overgrown with ivy, and having branches of trees sprouting from its walls. A free grammar school, founded here pursuant to letters patent of the 18th of Elizabeth, by which the master and four wardens of the Clothworkers' Company were constituted governors, is endowed with a rent-charge of £30, by William Lambe and John Franklin, in support of a master and an usher ; another of £5, bequeathed in 1713, by George Maplisden, for the usher ; and with £200, the gift of Francis Robins, in 1721, to found two exhibitions, of £10 a year each, in St. John's College, Cambridge ; Mr. Lambe also left £4 per annum for a visitation, and the master occupies a house rent-free. Thirty boys receive an English education, and instruction in the classics when required.

SUTTON-VENEY, a parish in the hundred of WARMINSTER, county of WILTS, 2 miles (W. S. W.) from Heytesbury, containing 689 inhabitants. The living is a rectory, in the archdeaconry and diocese of Salisbury, rated in the king's books at £21, and in the patronage of — Thring, Esq. The church, dedicated to St. Leonard, has lately received an addition of one hundred and fifteen sittings, of which seventy-five are free, the Incorporated Society for the enlargement of churches and chapels having granted £75 towards defraying the expense.

SUTTON-WALDRON, a parish in the hundred of REDLANE, Sturminster division of the county of DORSET, 5½ miles (S.) from Shaftesbury, containing 206 inhabitants. The living is a rectory, in the archdeaconry of Dorset, and diocese of Bristol, rated in the king's books at £9. 9. 4½., and in the patronage of H. C. Sturt, Esq. The church is dedicated to St. Bartholomew.

SUTTON-WICK, a township in the parish of SUTTON-COURTNEY, hundred of OCK, county of BERKS, 1¾ mile (S. by W.) from Abingdon, containing 217 inhabitants.

SWABY, a parish in the Marsh division of the hundred of CALCEWORTH, parts of LINDSEY, county of LINCOLN, 5½ miles (W. by N.) from Alford, containing 302 inhabitants. The living is a discharged rectory, in the archdeaconry and diocese of Lincoln, rated in the king's books at £12. 1. 10., and in the patronage of the President and Fellows of Magdalene College, Oxford. The church is dedicated to St. Nicholas. There is a place of worship for Wesleyan Methodists.

SWADLINCOTE, a chapelry in the parish of CHURCH-GRESLEY, hundred of REPTON and GRESLEY, county of DERBY, 4¾ miles (S. E. by E.) from Burton upon Trent, containing 459 inhabitants. There is a place of worship for Wesleyan Methodists. This township is in the honour of Tutbury, duchy of Lancaster, and within the jurisdiction of a court of pleas held at Tutbury every third Tuesday, for the recovery of debts under 40s. Here are extensive potteries for the manufacture of yellow earthenware : coal is obtained in the neighbourhood.

SWAFFHAM, a market town and parish in the southern division of the hundred of GREENHOE, county of NORFOLK, 28 miles (W. by N.) from Norwich, and 95 (N. N. E.) from London, containing 2836 inhabitants. This ancient town is situated on an eminence commanding an extensive view of the surrounding country, and is remarkable for the salubrity of its air, and the longevity of its inhabitants : it consists of four principal, and several inferior, streets ; the houses in general are well built, and the inhabitants are well supplied with water from springs. A book club is supported by subscriptions among the clergy and gentry in the town and neighbourhood ; a neat theatre has been recently erected, and an elegant assembly-room, on the market hill, was lately repaired and modernised, at a considerable expense ; subscription assemblies are held monthly. On the north-west side of the town is a fine heath of some thousand acres, admirably adapted for the diversions of racing and coursing : greyhounds are annually entered here for the latter amusement, in the month of November, being subject to the same restrictions as race-horses. A charter for a market and two annual fairs was granted by King John to one of the Earls of Richmond, who were anciently lords of the manor. The market is on Saturday; and fairs are held on May 12th for sheep, July 21st, and November 3rd, for sheep and cattle. The market-place, a fine area surrounded by handsome buildings, contains a beautiful cross, erected in 1783, by Lord Orford, consisting of a circular dome covered with lead, supported on eight pillars, and crowned with a figure of Ceres, the whole being enclosed with palisades. The county magistrates hold a weekly petty session: the general quarter sessions are held here at Midsummer only, by adjournment from Norwich; manorial courts leet and baron are held annually in April or May. This town having formerly been held in royal demesne, the inhabitants are exempt from toll, and from being empannelled on juries, or any recognizances, except in the court of the manor. Anciently the Earl of Richmond had a prison in the town, and a house of correction, or bridewell, was erected in the 41st of Elizabeth, for the convenience of several adjoining hundreds. The New Bridewell was built about 1787, and will hold upwards of one hundred prisoners: attached to it is a chapel, the chaplain, who has a stipend of £200 per annum, being elected by the justices: a tread-mill was erected in 1822, and, in 1825, a handsome residence for the governor.

The living is a vicarage, with the rectory of Thrixton annexed, in the archdeaconry of Norfolk, and diocese of Norwich, rated in the king's books at £14. 5. 10., and in the patronage of the Bishop of Norwich. The church, which is dedicated to St. Peter and St. Paul, is a splendid and spacious cruciform structure, with a stately and well-proportioned embattled tower and turreted spire, in the later style of English architecture; in the transept are three chapels: the vaulted roof of the nave, richly adorned with figures of angels carved in Irish oak, and that of the side aisles, rest on fourteen arches, supported on fine slender clustered pillars, and are surmounted by twenty-six clerestory windows; in the interior are several handsome monuments, and some brasses, bearing a variety of inscriptions; and in a library attached to the church is a curious missal. The north aisle is commonly reported to have been built by John Chapman, a tinker of this town; concerning which circumstance, there is a curious monkish legend, and there are various devices of a pedlar, and others representing a person keeping a shop, in different parts of the church, which are, in all likelihood, only rebuses on the name of Chapman, a conceit very prevalent in former times; the founder having probably been a person of that name, who was churchwarden in 1462. This church has lately received an addition of one hundred and seventy sittings, of which one hundred and four are free, the Incorporated Society for the enlargement of churches and chapels having contributed £50 towards defraying the expense. Here was anciently a free chapel, dedicated to St. Mary; and about half a mile distant, in a hamlet formerly called Guthlac's Stow, now Goodluck's Close, stood another, dedicated to St. Guthlac. There are places of worship for Baptists and Wesleyan Methodists. The grammar school was founded by Nicholas Hammond, Esq., who by will bequeathed £500 for erecting a school-house, and £500 for the instruction of twenty boys in reading, writing, and arithmetic. A National and Evening school is

supported by subscription. Several houses have been given, at different periods, as rent-free residences for the poor, for whom there is also a workhouse, which was the residence of the rector before the impropriation took place. John de Swaffham, a man of great learning, and a strenuous opponent of Wickliffe, who was raised to the see of Bangor by Pope Gregory II., was a native of this town.

SWAFFHAM-BULBECK, a parish in the hundred of STAINE, county of CAMBRIDGE, 6 miles (W. by S.) from Newmarket, containing 684 inhabitants. The living is a discharged vicarage, in the archdeaconry and diocese of Ely, rated in the king's books at £16. 10., and in the patronage of the Bishop of Ely. The church is dedicated to St. Mary. The parish is partly bounded by the Cam, of which river there is a branch, called Swaffham Lode, navigable to the village. A charity school was founded here, in 1721, by Mrs. Frances Towers, and endowed with £50 per annum. Here are the remains of a Benedictine nunnery, founded before the reign of John, by one of the Bolebecs, and dedicated to St. Mary. At the dissolution its revenue was estimated at £46. 18. 10., and the house is now occupied by paupers.

SWAFFHAM-PRIOR, a parish in the hundred of STAINE, county of CAMBRIDGE, 5½ miles (W. by N.) from Newmarket, containing 979 inhabitants. The living consists of the consolidated vicarages of St. Cyriac and St. Mary, in the archdeaconry and diocese of Ely, the former rated in the king's books at £16. 18. 11½., and the latter at £14. 12. 11., and in the alternate patronage of the Bishop, and the Dean and Chapter, of Ely. Here were formerly two churches in the same cemetery; that of St. Mary has fallen to ruin, except the tower, which, from the peculiarity of its situation, still forms an interesting object. The church dedicated to St. Cyriac has been lately rebuilt. The parish, which includes part of Newmarket heath, is bounded on the north by the Cam, and several navigable drains, or lodes, communicating with that river, pass through it. A market and fair, anciently granted to the prior of Ely, have been long disused. There are two endowed schools, one of which is conducted upon the National plan.

SWAFIELD, a parish in the hundred of TUNSTEAD, county of NORFOLK, 1½ mile (N. by E.) from North Walsham, containing 131 inhabitants. The living is a discharged rectory, in the archdeaconry of Norfolk, and diocese of Norwich, rated in the king's books at £6, and in the patronage of the King, as Duke of Lancaster. The church is dedicated to St. Nicholas.

SWAINBY, a joint township with Allarthorp, in that part of the parish of PICKHILL which is in the wapentake of HALLIKELD, North riding of the county of YORK, 6 miles (E. S. E.) from Bedale, containing, with Allarthorp, 33 inhabitants. There are places of worship for Primitive and Wesleyan Methodists. Butchers' knives, and some other articles of cutlery, are manufactured. A Premonstratensian abbey, founded here by Hellewise, daughter of Ranulph de Glanville, in the time of Henry II., was afterwards translated to Coverham.

SWAINSCOE, a joint township with Blore, in the parish of BLORE, northern division of the hundred of TOTMONSLOW, county of STAFFORD, 4 miles (W. N. W.) from Ashbourn. The population is returned with Blore.

SWAINSTHORPE, a parish in the hundred of HUMBLEYARD, county of NORFOLK, 4¼ miles (N.N.E.) from St. Mary Stratton, containing 185 inhabitants. The living consists of the united rectories of St. Mary and St. Peter, in the archdeaconry and diocese of Norwich, rated in the king's books at £12. 13. 4., and in the patronage of the Rev. R. C. Long. The church, dedicated to St. Peter, is a small ancient structure, with a steeple, round at the basement, and sexangular above; that of St. Mary was pulled down at the Reformation.

SWAINSWICK, a parish in the hundred of BATH-FORUM, county of SOMERSET, 3 miles (N. by E.) from Bath, containing 381 inhabitants. The living is a discharged rectory, in the archdeaconry of Bath, and diocese of Bath and Wells, rated in the king's books at £9. 17. 8., endowed with £200 private benefaction, and £200 royal bounty, and in the patronage of the Provost and Fellows of Oriel College, Oxford. The church, dedicated to St. Mary, contains the remains of the celebrated William Prynne, barrister at law, an active statesman and public writer during the disturbed reign of Charles I. He was born at this place in 1600, and died in 1669.

SWALCLIFFE, a parish comprising the chapelries of Epwell and East Shutford, and the township of West Shutford, in the hundred of BANBURY, and the hamlets of Sibford-Ferris and Sibford-Gower, in that of BLOXHAM, county of OXFORD, 6 miles (W. S. W.) from Banbury, and containing 1798 inhabitants. The living is a vicarage, in the archdeaconry and diocese of Oxford, rated in the king's books at £7. 9. 4½., and in the patronage of the Warden and Fellows of New College, Oxford. The church is dedicated to St. Peter and St. Paul. One-third of the sum of £72. 15. per annum, arising from the rent of certain land, bequeathed by an unknown individual, is paid in support of a school, and the residue for other charitable purposes.

SWALECLIFFE, a parish in the hundred of BLEANGATE, lathe of ST. AUGUSTINE, county of KENT, 6½ miles (N.) from Canterbury, containing 143 inhabitants. The living is a rectory, in the archdeaconry and diocese of Canterbury, rated in the king's books at £11. 9. 4½., and in the patronage of Earl Cowper. The church is dedicated to St. John the Baptist.

SWALLOW, a parish in the wapentake of BRADLEY-HAVERSTOE, parts of LINDSEY, county of LINCOLN, 3¾ miles (E. N. E.) from Caistor, containing 122 inhabitants. The living is a rectory, in the archdeaconry and diocese of Lincoln, rated in the king's books at £7. 10. 10., and in the patronage of Lord Yarborough. The church is dedicated to the Holy Trinity.

SWALLOWCLIFFE, a parish in the hundred of DUNWORTH, county of WILTS, 6½ miles (S. E.) from Hindon, containing 252 inhabitants. The living is a perpetual curacy, and constitutes also the endowment of a prebend in the church of Heytesbury, in the peculiar jurisdiction and patronage of the Dean of Salisbury, as Dean of Heytesbury, rated in the king's books at £8. 13. 4.

SWALLOWFIELD, a parish partly in the hundred of CHARLTON, county of BERKS, but chiefly in the hundred of AMESBURY, county of WILTS, 6 miles (S. by E.) from Reading, containing 983 inhabitants. The living is a perpetual curacy, annexed to the vicarage of Shinfield, in the archdeaconry of Berks, and diocese of Salisbury. The church is dedicated to All Saints. There

is a place of worship for Wesleyan Methodists. A fair is held here on June 9th. The celebrated Lord Chancellor Clarendon, after his retirement from public life, resided at the manor-house, then the property of his son, where he wrote "The History of the Rebellion."

SWALWELL, a township in the parish of WHICKHAM, western division of CHESTER ward, county palatine of DURHAM, 4¾ miles (W. by S.) from Gateshead, containing 1320 inhabitants, the greater number of whom are employed at the extensive iron-works of Messrs. Crawley, Millington, and Co., where anchors of the largest size, chain cables, pumps, and cylinders for steam-engines, with every other description of cast and wrought iron articles, are produced. This factory was founded, about 1690, by Sir Ambrose Crawley, who was originally a blacksmith: he also benevolently established schools for instructing the children of his workmen, provided asylums for their widows and orphans, and adopted the most laudable regulations for orderly conduct among them. There are places of worship for Presbyterians and Wesleyan Methodists. An annual festival is held, on May 22d, in the village, which is of considerable size: a freemasons' lodge is occasionally held at the Queen's Head Inn. William Shield, the celebrated musical composer, was a native of this place.

SWANAGE, a market town and parish in the hundred of ROWBARROW, Blandford (South) division of the county of DORSET, 7 miles (E. S. E.) from Corfe-Castle, and 122 from London, containing 1607 inhabitants. In the Saxon Chronicle this place is called Swanawic; Asser Menevensis names it Swanavine and Gnavewic, and in Domesday-book it is written Swanwic and Sonwic. The earliest and principal historical circumstance which we find on record connected with it is the destruction, by a violent storm in 877, of a Danish fleet, on its way from Wareham to the relief of Exeter, in the bay on which the town stands; and a similar disaster is said to have befallen another of their fleets, after its defeat by Alfred, in the same place and year. The town, which is situated on the small bay of the same name, consists principally of one street about a mile long, containing many neat houses, built and roofed with stone; and the bay having of late years become a place of resort for sea-bathing, has led to the erection of some new houses in the town, and considerable improvements in the neighbourhood, land having been levelled and drives formed for the visitors. The manufacture of straw-plat employs many of the females, but the chief occupation of the inhabitants is derived from working the many quarries in the parish, which produce great quantities of the freestone called Purbeck stone, which is conveyed in carts to boats, and by them to the larger vessels in the bay, by which it is conducted to various parts of the kingdom, a small quantity being sent abroad. The bay affords a tolerable harbour for vessels of three hundred tons' burden. In addition to other public works, Ramsgate pier was constructed of this stone, fifty thousand tons having been conveyed thither for the purpose. The quarry men are governed by local laws or regulations, by which none but their sons, who must serve an apprenticeship of seven years, are allowed to work. The market is on Tuesday and Friday.

The living is a rectory, in the archdeaconry of Dorset, and diocese of Bristol, rated in the king's books at

£27. 9. 9½., and in the patronage of John Calcraft, Esq. The church, dedicated to St. Mary the Virgin, is an extremely ancient structure, with a very large chancel and a lofty tower : it was formerly a chapel to the vicarage of Worth-Matravers, but was made parochial in 1500. There are places of worship for Independents and Wesleyan Methodists. Fossils of different fish, particularly bream, are frequently found in the quarries, and there are also some mineral springs in the parish, recommended for their medicinal qualities.

SWANBOURNE, a parish in the hundred of COTTESLOE, county of BUCKINGHAM, 2¼ miles (E.) from Winslow, containing 616 inhabitants. The living is a vicarage, in the archdeaconry of Buckingham, and diocese of Lincoln, rated in the king's books at £9. 9. 7., and in the patronage of the Crown. The church is dedicated to St. Swithin. There is a place of worship for Baptists. Nicholas Godwin, in 1712, bequeathed £15 per annum for teaching poor children.

SWANLAND, a township in the parish of NORTH FERRIBY, county of the town of KINGSTON upon HULL, 6¾ miles (W. by S.) from Kingston upon Hull, containing 418 inhabitants. There is a place of worship for Independents.

SWANNINGTON, a chapelry in the parish of WHITWICK, western division of the hundred of Goscote, county of LEICESTER, 4½ miles (E. by S.) from Ashby de la Zouch, containing 541 inhabitants. There is a place of worship for Wesleyan Methodists.

SWANNINGTON, a parish in the hundred of EYNSFORD, county of NORFOLK, 3½ miles (S. E.) from Reepham, containing 365 inhabitants. The living is a discharged rectory, with the vicarage of Wood-Dalling annexed, in the archdeaconry of Norfolk, and diocese of Norwich, rated in the king's books at £6. 11. 5., and in the patronage of the Master and Fellows of Trinity Hall, Cambridge. The church is dedicated to St. Margaret.

SWANSCOMBE, a parish in the hundred of AXTON, DARTFORD, and WILMINGTON, lathe of SUTTON at HONE, county of KENT, 4 miles (E.) from Dartford, containing 908 inhabitants. The living is a rectory, in the archdeaconry and diocese of Rochester, rated in the king's books at £25. 13. 4., and in the patronage of the Master and Fellows of Sidney Sussex College, Cambridge. The church, dedicated to St. Peter and St. Paul, is principally in the early style of English architecture. The parish is bounded on the north by the river Thames, from which the village, agreeably surrounded by woods, has a highly picturesque appearance. Swanscombe, anciently Swanes-Camp, is celebrated for the landing and encampment of Sweyn, King of Denmark; also as the place where the men of Kent enclosed William the Conqueror with boughs in their hands, when, casting them down, they prepared for battle, demanding the enjoyment of their former rights, which they obtained. From Greenhithe, a hamlet in this parish, immense quantities of chalk and lime are sent to the neighbouring ports.

SWANTHORPE, a joint tything with Crondall, in the parish and hundred of CRONDALL, Basingstoke division of the county of SOUTHAMPTON, 3 miles (S. E.) from Odiham. The population is returned with Crondall.

SWANTON-ABBOTT, a parish in the southern division of the hundred of ERPINGHAM, county of NOR-

FOLK, 3 miles (S. S. W.) from North Walsham, containing 424 inhabitants. The living is a discharged rectory, in the archdeaconry and diocese of Norwich, rated in the king's books at £6. 10., and in the patronage of Lord Viscount Anson. The church is dedicated to St. Michael.

SWANTON-MORLEY, a parish in the hundred of LAUNDITCH, county of NORFOLK, 3¾ miles (N. E.) from East Dereham, containing 723 inhabitants. The living is a rectory, with that of Worthing annexed, in the archdeaconry and diocese of Norwich, rated in the king's books at £15. 10. 2½., and in the patronage of Edward Lombe, Esq. The church, dedicated to All Saints, was erected in 1379, on an eminence in the centre of the village. Near it stood the ancient manor-house, surrounded by a moat. William Small, in 1651, bequeathed a rent-charge of £8 for teaching and apprenticing children.

SWANTON-NOVERS, a parish in the hundred of HOLT, county of NORFOLK, 6¼ miles (S. W.) from Holt, containing 302 inhabitants. The living is a discharged rectory, annexed to that of Wood-Norton, in the archdeaconry and diocese of Norwich, rated in the king's books at £4. 15. 2½. The church is dedicated to St. Edmund.

SWANWICK, a hamlet in the parish of ALFRETON hundred of SCARSDALE, county of DERBY, 1½ mile (S. by W.) from Alfreton, with which the population is returned. There are places of worship for Baptists and Wesleyan Methodists. A free school, erected in 1740, was endowed by Mrs. Elizabeth Turner with £500, which was laid out in the purchase of a house and lands of the annual value of £60, now in the occupation of the schoolmaster, who educates forty children. In the neighbourhood are extensive collieries.

SWARBY, a parish in the wapentake of ASWARDHURN, parts of KESTEVEN, county of LINCOLN, 5½ miles (N. W. by N.) from Falkingham, containing 143 inhabitants. The living is a discharged vicarage, in the archdeaconry and diocese of Lincoln, rated in the king's books at £6, endowed with £200 royal bounty, and in the patronage of Sir T. Whichcote, Bart. The church, dedicated to St. Mary and All Saints, is a handsome structure, principally in the later English style.

SWARDESTON, a parish in the hundred of HUMBLEYARD, county of NORFOLK, 4½ miles (S. S. W.) from Norwich, containing 291 inhabitants. The living is a discharged vicarage, in the archdeaconry of Norfolk, and diocese of Norwich, rated in the king's books at £6, endowed with £400 private benefaction, £200 royal bounty, and £600 parliamentary grant, and in the patronage of J. Steward, Esq. The church is dedicated to St. Andrew.

SWARKESTONE, a parish in the hundred of REPTON and GRESLEY, county of DERBY, 5¼ miles (S. by E.) from Derby, containing 243 inhabitants. The living is a rectory, in the archdeaconry of Derby, and diocese of Lichfield and Coventry, rated in the king's books at £5, and in the patronage of Sir George Crewe, Bart. The church, dedicated to St. James, is principally in the Norman style, though much disfigured by the insertion of modern windows : it has lately received an addition of one hundred sittings, of which seventy are free, the Incorporated Society for the enlargement of churches and chapels having granted £35 towards defraying the expense. Swarkestone is in the honour of

Tutbury, duchy of Lancaster, and within the jurisdiction of a court of pleas held at Tutbury every third Tuesday, for the recovery of debts under 40s. The Trent and Mersey canal passes through the parish, and is here joined by the Derby canal. The bridge over the Trent is constructed so as to secure a passage over the low grounds, which are usually flooded in the winter : the span over the river is only one hundred and thirty-eight yards, but the whole length of the bridge is one thousand three hundred and four yards : it was originally not more than eleven or twelve feet broad, but has been widened in many places, so that carriages can now pass each other at very small intervals. About the beginning of the year 1643, Col. Hastings fortified Sir John Harpur's house at Swarkestone, and threw up some works at the bridge, to secure the passage of the Trent. Sir John Gell marched thither with Sir George Gresley's troops, when the garrison at the bridge offered a determined resistance, on the part of the royalists, but the men were at length driven from their works with considerable loss.

SWARLAND, a township in that part of the parish of FELTON which is in the eastern division of COQUET-DALE ward, county of NORTHUMBERLAND, 8¼ miles (S. by W.) from Alnwick, containing 211 inhabitants. An obelisk of white freestone, erected by the late Alexander Davison, Esq. to the memory of Admiral Lord Nelson, stands near Swarland Hall, and close to the great road between Morpeth and Alnwick.

SWARRATON, a parish in the hundred of BOUN-TISBOROUGH, Fawley division of the county of SOUTH-AMPTON, 3 miles (N. N. W.) from New Alresford, containing 109 inhabitants. The living is a discharged rectory, in the archdeaconry and diocese of Winchester, rated in the king's books at £4. 5. 2½., and in the patronage of Alexander Baring, Esq.

SWATON, a parish in the wapentake of AVELAND, parts of KESTEVEN, county of LINCOLN, 5¼ miles (N. E.) from Falkingham, containing 298 inhabitants. The living is a vicarage, with the rectory of Spanby annexed, in the archdeaconry and diocese of Lincoln, rated in the king's books at £12. 7. 1., and in the patronage of J. W. Knapp, Esq. The church is dedicated to St. Michael.

SWAVESEY, a parish in the hundred of PAPWORTH, county of CAMBRIDGE, 5¼ miles (E. S. E.) from St. Ives, containing 1029 inhabitants. The living is a vicarage, in the archdeaconry and diocese of Ely, rated in the king's books at £7. 6. 8., and in the patronage of the Master and Fellows of Jesus College, Cambridge. The church, dedicated to St. Andrew, anciently belonged to an Alien priory of Black monks, founded here, soon after the Conquest, as a cell to the abbey of St.Sergius and St. Bachus, and that of St. Briocus, at Angiers ; at the suppression it was given by Richard II. to the priory of St. Anne, Coventry, and some slight remains of the monastic buildings are still visible. There is a place of worship for Baptists. A market and fair were granted, in 1243, to the family of Zouch, the site of whose ancient castle is about half a mile south-west from the church.

SWAY, a hamlet in that part of the parish of BOLDRE which is in the hundred of CHRISTCHURCH, New Forest (West) division of the county of SOUTH-AMPTON, 3½ miles (N. W.) from Lymington. The population is returned with the parish. There is a place of worship for Baptists.

SWAYFIELD, a parish in the wapentake of BEL-TISLOE, parts of KESTEVEN, county of LINCOLN, 2 miles (S. by W.) from Corby, containing 206 inhabitants. The living is a rectory, in the archdeaconry and diocese of Lincoln, rated in the king's books at £11. 2. 11., and in the patronage of the Crown. The church is dedicated to St. Nicholas.

SWEEPSTONE, a parish in the western division of the hundred of GOSCOTE, county of LEICESTER, 4¾ miles (S. by E.) from Ashby de la Zouch, containing, with Newton, 625 inhabitants. The living is a rectory, with the perpetual curacy of Snareston annexed, in the archdeaconry of Leicester, and diocese of Lincoln, rated in the king's books at £21. 18. 4., and in the patronage of the Representatives of the Charnel family. The church is dedicated to St. Peter. The river Mease, and the Ashby de la Zouch canal, run through the parish. At Snarestone there is a free school for forty boys, endowed by the Charnels. Sweepstone is in the honour of Tutbury, duchy of Lancaster, and within the jurisdiction of a court of pleas held at Tutbury every third Tuesday, for the recovery of debts under 40s.

SWEETHOPE, a township in the parish of THOCK-RINGTON, north-eastern division of TINDALE ward, county of NORTHUMBERLAND, 9¾ miles (E. by S.) from Bellingham, containing 25 inhabitants. The river Wansbeck has its source in the neighbourhood.

SWEFLING, a parish in the hundred of PLOMES-GATE, county of SUFFOLK, 2¾ miles (W. N. W.) from Saxmundham, containing 367 inhabitants. The living is a rectory, in the archdeaconry of Suffolk, and diocese of Norwich, rated in the king's books at £9. 2. 8½. The Rev. R. Turner was patron in 1813. The church is dedicated to St. Mary.

SWELL, a parish in the hundred of ABDICK and BULSTONE, county of SOMERSET, 4 miles (W. S. W.) from Langport, containing 133 inhabitants. The living is a discharged vicarage, in the archdeaconry of Taunton, and diocese of Bath and Wells, rated in the king's books at £5. 10. 5., and in the patronage of the Dean and Chapter of Bristol. The church is dedicated to St. Catherine.

SWELL (LOWER), a parish in the upper division of the hundred of SLAUGHTER, county of GLOUCESTER, 1 mile (W.) from Stow on the Wold, containing 263 inhabitants. The living is a discharged vicarage, in the archdeaconry and diocese of Gloucester, rated in the king's books at £6. 12. 3½., and in the patronage of the Dean and Canons of Christ Church, Oxford. The church is dedicated to St. Mary.

SWELL (UPPER), a parish in the upper division of the hundred of KIFTSGATE, county of GLOUCESTER, 1¼ mile (N. W.) from Stow on the Wold, containing 82 inhabitants. The living is a discharged rectory, in the archdeaconry and diocese of Gloucester, rated in the king's books at £6. 14. 6., and in the patronage of Charles Pole, Esq. The church has lately received an addition of fifty-one free sittings, the Incorporated Society for the enlargement of churches and chapels having granted £10 towards defraying the expense. The Roman Foss-way bounds the parish on the east.

SWERFORD, a parish in the hundred of CHADLING-TON, county of OXFORD, 4¼ miles (N. E. by E.) from Chipping-Norton, containing 395 inhabitants. The living is a rectory, in the archdeaconry and diocese of

Oxford, rated in the king's books at £15. 7. 1., and in the patronage of the Master and Fellows of Magdalene College, Oxford.

SWETTENHAM, a parish in the hundred of NORTHWICH, county palatine of CHESTER, comprising the townships of Kermincham and Swettenham, and containing 435 inhabitants, of which number, 259 are in the township of Swettenham, 5 miles (N.W.) from Congleton. The living is a rectory, in the archdeaconry and diocese of Chester, rated in the king's books at £5. 1. 3., and in the patronage of the Rev. J. D'Arcey. The church is a brick structure, with a tower, forming a conspicuous object in the romantic scenery on the banks of the Dane.

SWILLAND, a parish in the hundred of BOSMERE and CLAYDON, county of SUFFOLK, 6 miles (N. by E.) from Ipswich, containing 195 inhabitants. The living is a discharged vicarage, in the archdeaconry of Suffolk, and diocese of Norwich, rated in the king's books at £7. 8. 4½., and in the patronage of the Crown. The church is dedicated to St. Mary.

SWILLINGTON, a parish in the lower division of the wapentake of SKYRACK, West riding of the county of YORK, 6½ miles (E. S. E.) from Leeds, containing 510 inhabitants. The living is a rectory, in the archdeaconry and diocese of York, rated in the king's books at £16. 1. 8., and in the patronage of Sir John Lowther, Bart. The church, dedicated to St. Mary, is partly in the decorated, and partly in the later, style of English architecture. Sir William Lowther, Bart., and others, gave £92 for the erection of a school, which the former endowed with land producing a small annuity for teaching six poor children.

SWIMBRIDGE, a parish in the hundred of SOUTH MOLTON, county of DEVON, 4¼ miles (S. E. by E.) from Barnstaple, containing 1374 inhabitants. The living is a perpetual curacy, with that of Landkey annexed, in the jurisdiction of the Consistorial Court of the Bishop of Exeter, endowed with £400 private benefaction, £400 royal bounty, and £800 parliamentary grant, and in the patronage of the Dean of Exeter. The church, dedicated to St. James, is a fine specimen of the later style of English architecture, with a spire : it contains a stone pulpit, enriched with figures of saints, and the nave and chancel are separated by a handsome wooden screen. There is a place of worship for Wesleyan Methodists. Sixteen children are instructed for £6 per annum, arising from the parish estate. The village is situated in a hollow surrounded by verdant hills of singular formation. Limestone is found here, enclosed in a strata of hard blueish building stone.

SWINBROOK, a parish in the hundred of CHADLINGTON, county of OXFORD, 2½ miles (E.) from Burford, containing 208 inhabitants. The living is a perpetual curacy, in the archdeaconry and diocese of Oxford, endowed with £16 per annum and £290 private benefaction, £200 royal bounty, and £300 parliamentary grant, and in the patronage of the Chancellor of the Cathedral Church of Salisbury. The church, dedicated to St. Mary, is partly Norman, and partly of later date, with a remarkable tower open with an arch to the west ; it has some remains of a rood-loft and wooden screen-work. The river Windrush runs through the parish, which possesses a very considerable right in the forest of Whichwood. Mrs. Anne Pytts, in 1715, endowed a school with £30 per annum, for teaching boys of Swinbrook and the parish of Widford.

SWINBURN, a joint township with Colwell, in the parish of CHOLLERTON, north-eastern division of TINDALE ward, county of NORTHUMBERLAND, 7 miles (N.) from Hexham. The population is returned with Colwell. It is bounded on the west by a rivulet of the same name, tributary to the North Tyne. There is a domestic Roman Catholic chapel at Swinburn castle, a handsome stone structure belonging to Ralph Riddell, Esq.

SWINBURN (LITTLE), a joint township with Whiteside-Law, in the parish of CHOLLERTON, north-eastern division of TINDALE ward, county of NORTHUMBERLAND, 9½ miles (N. by E.) from Hexham. The population is returned with the township of Chollerton.

SWINCOMB, a parish in the hundred of EWELME, county of OXFORD, 5¼ miles (E. by N.) from Wallingford, containing 345 inhabitants. The living is a rectory, in the archdeaconry and diocese of Oxford, rated in the king's books at £7. 9. 4½., and in the patronage of the Crown. The church is dedicated to St. Botolph.

SWINDALE, a chapelry in the parish of SHAP, WEST ward, county of WESTMORLAND, 12 miles (W. N.W.) from Orton. The population is returned with the parish. The living is a perpetual curacy, in the archdeaconry and diocese of Carlisle, endowed with £1200 royal bounty, and in the patronage of the Vicar of Shap. The chapel was built at the expense of the inhabitants, in 1749. Near it is a school, founded in 1703, by Mr. Baxter, and endowed with a rent-charge of £25.

SWINDEN, a township in the parish of GISBURN, western division of the wapentake of STAINCLIFFE and EWCROSS, West riding of the county of YORK, 7½ miles (S.E.) from Settle, containing 37 inhabitants.

SWINDERBY, a parish in the lower division of the wapentake of BOOTHBY-GRAFFO, parts of KESTEVEN, county of LINCOLN, 8½ miles (S.W. by W.) from Lincoln, containing 365 inhabitants. The living is a vicarage, in the archdeaconry and diocese of Lincoln, rated in the king's books at £3. 19. 9½., and in the patronage of Charles Moor, Esq. The church is dedicated to All Saints. There is a place of worship for Wesleyan Methodists. Daniel Disney, in 1732, bequeathed a rent-charge of £3 for teaching eight children, and Elizabeth Upsall, in 1770, another of £4, for the education of six.

SWINDON, a parish in the hundred of CHELTENHAM, county of GLOUCESTER, 2¼ miles (N. N.W.) from Cheltenham, containing 201 inhabitants. The living is a discharged rectory, in the archdeaconry and diocese of Gloucester, rated in the king's books at £13. 1. 0½. The Rev. W. Romney was patron in 1807. The church is dedicated to St. Lawrence.

SWINDON, a market town and parish in the hundred of KINGSBRIDGE, county of WILTS, 41 miles (N.) from Salisbury, and 81 (W.) from London, containing 1580 inhabitants. This place is mentioned in Domesday-book, but nothing further connected with its ancient history is on record. The town is pleasantly situated on the summit of a considerable eminence, commanding extensive and beautiful views of parts of Berkshire and Gloucestershire : the principal street is wide, and contains some good houses; and many of the inhabitants being persons in easy circumstances, the general aspect of the town is prepossessing: there is a good supply of water, which is of excellent quality. No branch of manufacture is carried on. The market is on Monday, for corn, &c., and on every second Monday for cattle; the latter is termed the great market. Fairs are held on the Monday before April 5th, the second Monday after May 12th, the second Monday in September, and the second Monday after September 11th, for cattle of all kinds, pedlary, &c. The petty sessions for the Swindon division of the hundred are held here. The living is a vicarage, in the archdeaconry of Wilts, and diocese of Salisbury, rated in the king's books at £17, and in the patronage of the Crown. The church, dedicated to the Holy Rood, and situated at the south-eastern extremity of the town, is a small unadorned edifice, with a low tower; the interior is neatly fitted up. There are places of worship for Independents and Wesleyan Methodists. The free school, which was established in 1764, was founded by the gentry of the town and neighbourhood, and is supported partly by an endowment of about £40 per annum, arising from several bequests, and partly by voluntary contributions; there is a house for the master, and about forty boys are instructed in reading, writing, and arithmetic. Some very extensive quarries are worked in the immediate vicinity, the stones raised from which are usually very large, and of an excellent quality. The Wilts and Berks canal passes about half a mile from the town, and a reservoir, covering about seventy acres, for its supply in dry seasons, has been constructed about a mile and a half from it, and is partly in this parish, adding much to the beauty of the scenery.

SWINDON, a township partly in the parish of PANNALL, lower division, and partly in that of KIRKBY-OVERBLOWS, upper division, of the wapentake of CLARO, West riding of the county of YORK, 6 miles (W. by S.) from Wetherby, containing 52 inhabitants. It is within the peculiar jurisdiction of the Honour Court of Knaresborough.

SWINE, a parish comprising the chapelries of Bilton and South Skirlaugh, and the townships of Benningholme with Grange, Coniston, Ellerby, Ganstead, Marton, Swine, Thirtleby, and Wyton, in the middle, and the joint township of North Skirlaugh with Rowton, in the northern, division of the wapentake of HOLDER-NESS, East riding of the county of YORK, and containing 1604 inhabitants, of which number, 229 are in the township of Swine, 6½ miles (N. N. E.) from Kingston upon Hull. The living is a discharged vicarage, in the archdeaconry of the East riding, and diocese of York, rated in the king's books at £8, endowed with £200 private benefaction, £200 royal bounty, and £1200 parliamentary grant, and in the patronage of W. Wilberforce, Esq. The church, dedicated to St. Mary, is partly in the early, and partly in the later, style of English architecture. Six poor children are educated for £6 a year, the bequest of Mrs. Lamb. A nunnery of the Cistercian order, dedicated to the Blessed Virgin Mary, was founded here, in the reign of Stephen, by Robert de Verli, which at the dissolution possessed a revenue of £134. 6. 9.

SWINEFLEET, a chapelry in the parish of WHIT-GIFT, lower division of the wapentake of OSGOLDCROSS,

West riding of the county of YORK, 4¾ miles (S. S. E.) from Howden, containing 956 inhabitants. The living is a perpetual curacy, annexed to that of Whitgift, in the archdeaconry and diocese of York, endowed with £1000 royal bounty, and £1000 parliamentary grant. There is a place of worship for Wesleyan Methodists.

SWINESHEAD, a parish in the hundred of LEIGH-TONSTONE, county of HUNTINGDON, though locally in the hundred of Stodden, county of Bedford, 3½ miles (S. W. by W.) from Kimbolton, containing 245 inhabitants. The living is a rectory, in the archdeaconry of Huntingdon, and diocese of Lincoln, rated in the king's books at £12. 13. 6½., and in the patronage of the Duke of Manchester. The church is dedicated to St. Nicholas.

SWINESHEAD, a parish (formerly a market town) in the wapentake of KIRTON, parts of HOLLAND, county of LINCOLN, 7 miles (W. by S.) from Boston, containing 1696 inhabitants. An abbey for Cistercian monks was founded here by Robert de Greslie, in 1134, the revenue of which at the dissolution was valued at £175. 19. 10.; many valuable coins and several skeletons have, at various periods, been dug up near the spot, and, in 1825, on sinking a well, one of the latter was discovered, which measured six feet four inches. King John, in passing the Cross Keys wash, near this place, lost his carriages and baggage, and escaped to the monastery only with his life, where he died. The ruins of the monastery have entirely disappeared, but its site is still visible, and a mansion, recently modernised, was erected with a portion of its materials, about two hundred and twenty years since. The sea formerly flowed up to the town, and near the market-place was a harbour. About thirty years ago, a bridge was taken down, which crossed a river then navigable for small craft, but now choked up. The market, nearly disused, is on Thursday, and a fair is held on October 2nd. The living is a discharged vicarage, in the archdeaconry and diocese of Lincoln, rated in the king's books at £14. 9., endowed with £30 per annum private benefaction, £200 royal bounty, and £900 parliamentary grant, and in the patronage of the Master and Fellows of Trinity College, Cambridge. The church, dedicated to St. Mary, is a handsome edifice with a lofty spire. A free school was founded, in 1720, by Thomas Cowley, Esq., who endowed it with certain lands producing £35 per annum, for which thirty-five children receive instruction, with a small surplus for clothing the poor, who also receive from the interest of various charitable bequests the benefit of a distribution amounting to £200 per annum. About a quarter of a mile north-westward of the town is a circular Danish encampment, called the Man-war-rings, about sixty yards in diameter, and surrounded by a double fosse.

SWINETHORP, an extra-parochial liberty, in the higher division of the wapentake of BOOTHBY-GRAFFO, parts of KESTEVEN, county of LINCOLN, 7 miles (W. by S.) from Lincoln, containing 55 inhabitants. Coal may be obtained here, though the mines have not yet been worked.

SWINFEN, a hamlet in the parish of WEEFORD, southern division of the hundred of OFFLOW, county of STAFFORD, 2¼ miles (S. E. by S.) from Lichfield, containing 109 inhabitants. It is within the peculiar jurisdiction of the Prebendary of Alrewas and Weeford in the Cathedral Church of Lichfield.

SWINFORD, a tything in the parish of CUMNER, hundred of HORMER, county of BERKS, containing 54 inhabitants.

SWINFORD, a parish in the hundred of GUTH-LAXTON, county of LEICESTER, 3½ miles (S. E. by S.) from Lutterworth, containing 450 inhabitants. The living is a discharged vicarage, in the archdeaconry of Leicester, and diocese of Lincoln, rated in the king's books at £5. 7. 11., and in the patronage of Lady Cave. The church, dedicated to All Saints, has lately received an addition of one hundred free sittings, the Incorporated Society for the enlargement of churches and chapels having granted £50 towards defraying the expense. Here was a preceptory of the Knights Templars.

SWINFORD (KING'S), a parish in the northern division of the hundred of SEISDON, county of STAFFORD, 3 miles (N. by W.) from Stourbridge, containing, with the chapelry of Brierly-Hill, and the hamlets of Brockmoor and Wordsley, 11,022 inhabitants. The situation of this parish, in a country abounding with coal and iron mines, has been the means of the establishment of its manufactures, the principal of which are iron and glass, both carried on to a considerable extent, and for the conveyance of which great facilities are afforded by the Stourbridge and the Staffordshire and Worcestershire canals passing through the parish; a rail-road from some of the principal mines to the latter canal has recently been constructed, at a great expense, by Earl Dudley. A court leet and a court baron are held annually, and the inhabitants claim an exemption from tolls, under a charter granted by Queen Elizabeth, and confirmed by Charles I. A copyhold court is also held occasionally. The living is a rectory, with the perpetual curacy of Brierley-Hill annexed, in the archdeaconry of Stafford, and diocese of Lichfield and Coventry, rated in the king's books at £17. 13. 4., and in the patronage of Earl Dudley. The church is dedicated to St. Mary. His Majesty's commissioners are about to erect a new church at Wordsley, in this parish, which, by a recent act of parliament, will become the mother church. Holbeach House, in which Catesby and the other Popish conspirators engaged in the gunpowder plot were taken, is in this parish. There are the remains of a Roman encampment on Ashwood heath, and the spa, at Lady well, is partly in this parish, and partly in that of Dudley. There is a school-house at Brierley-Hill, for the endowment of which the Rev. Mr. Ashenhurst bequeathed £80, but the bequest does not appear to have been ever carried into effect.

SWINFORD (OLD), a parish partly in the southern division of the hundred of SEISDON, county of STAFFORD, but chiefly in the lower division of the hundred of HALFSHIRE, county of WORCESTER, 1 mile (S. S. E.) from Stourbridge, containing, with the town of Stourbridge, and the hamlet of Amblecoat, 11,227 inhabitants. The living is a rectory, in the archdeaconry and diocese of Worcester, rated in the king's books at £26. 6. 8. and in the patronage of Lord Foley. The church is dedicated to St. Mary. The Blue-coat hospital, in this parish, was founded by Thomas Foley, Esq., ancestor of the noble family of that name, and endowed by him with estates now producing upwards of £2000 per annum: it is a commodious brick building, somewhat in

the style of a college, pleasantly situated on the road to Bromsgrove. In this noble institution seventy poor boys are boarded, clothed and educated: the original number was sixty, but the increase of income has enabled the feoffees to add ten more. They are chosen from the following parishes and towns, viz., Old Swinford, three; town of Stourbridge, four; Kidderminster, six (three from the borough and three from the foreign); Bewdley, four; Dudley, four; Great Whitley, King's Swinford, Kinver, Harbourn, Hales-Owen, West Bromwich, Bromsgrove, Rowley - Regis, Wednesbury, and Sedgeley, two each; Hagley, Little Whitley, Alvechurch, Pedmore, and Wombourn, one each; and the remaining twenty-four are appointed by the representative of the founder: each boy must, on admission, be between seven and eleven years of age, free from disease, and the son of parents who have never received parochial relief; he is annually provided with a suit of clothes (similar to that worn at Christ's Hospital), a cap, and four pair of shoes and stockings, and, at fourteen years of age, is apprenticed with a premium of £4, and on producing a certificate of good conduct during his apprenticeship, receives at its expiration a gratuity of £15. The establishment is under the direction of nineteen feoffees, who are noblemen, dignitaries of the church, or gentlemen of large landed property, in this or the adjoining counties, and who elect the master, steward, &c. The school at Red-hill is supported with endowments by John Wheeler, Esq., and Henry Glover, Esq., the former of whom granted property for the instruction of twenty poor boys, and for furnishing them with books and stationery, and the latter bequeathed £400, since laid out in lands, for the instruction of six poor boys in reading, writing, and arithmetic, for six years each, providing them with books and stationery, and apprenticing one of them annually, with a premium of £5 : two boys have since been added by the trustees, who are the governors of the Stourbridge free grammar school, and the boys on the foundation of both these charities are instructed by the same master. The remainder of Henry Glover's endowment, after all necessary charges for the school are deducted, is distributed amongst the poor of that part of the parish which is in the county of Worcester who do not receive parochial relief, in sums of not more than one shilling per week to each person. Exclusively of the trade connected with the town of Stourbridge, a detailed account of which is given in the article on that place, many of the inhabitants are engaged in the making of nails.

SWINGFIELD, a parish in the hundred of FOLKSTONE, lathe of SHEPWAY, county of KENT, 5 miles (N.) from Folkestone, containing 304 inhabitants. The living is a perpetual curacy, in the archdeaconry and diocese of Canterbury, endowed with £200 private benefaction, and £800 royal bounty, and in the patronage of Sir J. G. Bridges, Bart. The church is dedicated to St. Peter. A preceptory of Knights Templars was founded here before 1190, to which Sir Waresius de Valoniis and others were considerable benefactors : it subsequently became part of the possessions of the Knights of St. John of Jerusalem, and, at the dissolution, had a revenue of £87. 3. 3. On Swingfield common, during the agitations of 1745, the neighbouring nobility, gentry, and yeomen, to the amount of several thousands, accoutred with arms and ammunition, assembled, to oppose an expected invasion on the coast of Kent.

SWINHOE, a township in the parish and northern division of BAMBROUGH ward, county of NORTHUMBERLAND, 9½ miles (S. E. by E.) from Belford, containing 111 inhabitants.

SWINHOPE, a parish in the wapentake of BRADLEY-HAVERSTOE, parts of LINDSEY, county of LINCOLN, 7¾ miles (S. E. by E.) from Caistor, containing 94 inhabitants. The living is a discharged rectory, in the archdeaconry and diocese of Lincoln, rated in the king's books at £4. 17. 8½., endowed with £400 private benefaction, and £400 royal bounty, and in the patronage of Mrs. Allington. The church is dedicated to St. Helen.

SWINNERTON, a parish in the northern division of the hundred of PIREHILL, county of STAFFORD, 3½ miles (W. N. W.) from Stone, containing 832 inhabitants. The living is a rectory, in the archdeaconry of Stafford, and diocese of Lichfield and Coventry, rated in the king's books at £10. 2. 6., and in the patronage of the Rev. Christopher Dodsley. The church is dedicated to St. Mary. The river Sow forms the boundary between this parish and Eccleshall.

SWINSTEAD, a parish in the wapentake of BELTISLOE, parts of KESTEVEN, county of LINCOLN, 2 miles (S. E.) from Corby, containing 319 inhabitants. The living is a discharged vicarage, in the archdeaconry and diocese of Lincoln, rated in the king's books at £6. 19. 7., and in the joint patronage of Baroness Willoughby De Eresby and Lord Gwydyr. The church is dedicated to St. Mary. There is a place of worship for Wesleyan Methodists.

SWINTON, a joint township with Warthermask, in the parish of MASHAM, partly in the liberty of ST. PETER of YORK, East riding, and partly in the eastern division of the wapentake of HANG, North riding of the county of YORK, 1 mile (S. W.) from Masham, containing, with Warthermask, 177 inhabitants. Many relics of antiquity have been discovered in this neighbourhood, among which were the handle of a shield, of gold, and a Roman battle-axe of brass.

SWINTON, a chapelry in the parish of APPLETON le STREET, wapentake of RYEDALE, North riding of the county of YORK, 2¼ miles (N. W. by W.) from New Malton, containing 334 inhabitants. There is a place of worship for Wesleyan Methodists.

SWINTON, a chapelry in the parish of WATH upon DEARN, northern division of the wapentake of STRAFFORTH and TICKHILL, West riding of the county of YORK, 4¾ miles (N. N. E.) from Rotherham, containing 1050 inhabitants. The living is a perpetual curacy, in the archdeaconry and diocese of York, endowed with £800 private benefaction, £400 royal bounty, and £600 parliamentary grant, and in the patronage of the Vicar of Wath upon Dearn. The chapel, dedicated to St. Mary, has a fine Norman door. There is a place of worship for Wesleyan Methodists. A considerable manufacture of earthenware is carried on in this chapelry.

SWITHLAND, a parish in the western division of the hundred of GOSCOTE, county of LEICESTER, 2¼ miles (S. W. by W.) from Mountsorrel, containing 336 inhabitants. The living is a rectory, in the peculiar jurisdiction of Grooby, under the Commission of the Earl of Stamford and Warrington, rated in the king's books at £10. 4. 7., and in the patronage of the Crown. The church is dedicated to St. Leonard. There are quarries of slate in the parish. Swithland has an interest in the endowed school at Mountsorrel.

SWYRE, a parish in the hundred of UGGSCOMBE, Dorchester division of the county of DORSET, 5½ miles (S. E.) from Bridport, containing 210 inhabitants. The living is a discharged rectory, in the archdeaconry of Dorset, and diocese of Bristol, rated in the king's books at £7. 0. 5., and in the patronage of the Duke of Bedford. The church was dedicated to the Holy Trinity in 1503: it has a lofty tower, and north and south porches. The parish is bounded on the south by the English channel, and the village is situated about one mile from the coast. A wake is annually kept on Trinity Monday.

SYDE, county of GLOUCESTER.—See SIDE.

SYDENHAM, a chapelry in the parish of LEWISHAM, hundred of BLACKHEATH, lathe of SUTTON at HONE, county of KENT, 8¼ miles (S.S.E.) from London. The population is returned with the parish. This place, which formerly consisted only of a few scattered dwellings, was first brought into notice by the discovery, in 1640, of a saline chalybeate spring, the waters of which, similar in their properties to those of Epsom, attracted the notice, and made it the occasional resort, of invalids: and, notwithstanding that the wells have fallen almost into disuse, the salubrity of the air, the pleasantness of its situation, and its proximity to the metropolis, have made it the permanent residence of numerous families of respectability, who have erected in the vicinity many handsome seats and elegant villas. The village is well built, and contains many genteel houses, with detached cottages of pleasing appearance. The upper part of the common commands extensive and richly-varied prospects, and the surrounding scenery possesses much rural beauty: the neighbourhood affords many pleasant walks, and the adjoining woods are much frequented by parties from the metropolis on excursions of pleasure. The Croydon canal passes through the village, which is within the jurisdiction of the court of requests held at Bromley and at Greenwich, for the recovery of debts not exceeding £5. An annual fair, chiefly for pleasure, is held on Trinity-Monday, and is in general well attended. The proprietary episcopal chapel, of which the Rev. P. A. French appoints the minister, was originally a meeting-house, Dr. John Williams, author of a Greek Concordance, having been minister for many years: it is a convenient edifice, but not in any respect entitled to architectural notice. A new church, to contain nine hundred and thirty-six sittings, of which five hundred and forty-six are to be free, is in progress of erection, by grant from the parliamentary commissioners, at an expense of £10,279. 19. 1.: it is a handsome structure of white Suffolk brick, ornamented with stone, in the later style of English architecture, with a square embattled tower, ninety-three feet high, crowned with pinnacles: the interior consists of a lofty nave, lighted by a handsome range of seven clerestory windows, and separated from the aisles by lofty piers and arches of graceful elevation. The living will be a perpetual curacy, in the patronage of the Vicar of Lewisham. There are places of worship for Independents and Wesleyan Methodists. The National school, in which forty-six boys and thirty-four girls are instructed, is supported by subscription.

SYDENHAM, a parish in the hundred of LEWK-NOR, county of OXFORD, 2¾ miles (E.) from Tetsworth, containing 367 inhabitants. The living is a perpetual curacy, annexed to the vicarage of Thame, in the jurisdiction of the Peculiar Court of Thame, subject to the Dean and Chapter of Lincoln. The church is dedicated to St. Mary.

SYDENHAM-DAMAREL, a parish forming, with the parish of Lamerton, a distinct portion of the hundred of LIFTON, county of DEVON, 5¾ miles (W. by N.) from Tavistock, containing 288 inhabitants. The living is a rectory, in the archdeaconry of Totness, and diocese of Exeter, rated in the king's books at £10. 6. 8., and in the patronage of John Carpenter, Esq. The church is dedicated to St. Mary. The river Tamar separates the parish from Cornwall. A copper mine formerly in operation is now neglected.

SYDERSTONE, a parish in the hundred of GAL-LOW, county of NORFOLK, 6¼ miles (S.) from Burnham-Westgate, containing 317 inhabitants. The living is a rectory, in the archdeaconry of Norfolk, and diocese of Norwich, rated in the king's books at £13. 13. 4., endowed with £200 royal bounty, and in the patronage of the Marquis of Cholmondeley. The church is dedicated to St. Mary.

SYDLING (ST. NICHOLAS), a parish and liberty in the Cerne subdivision of the county of DORSET, 8 miles (N. W. by N.) from Dorchester, containing 563 inhabitants. The living is a discharged vicarage, in the archdeaconry of Dorset, and diocese of Bristol, rated in the king's books at £13. 1. 0½., endowed with £200 private benefaction, and £200 royal bounty, and in the patronage of the Warden and Fellows of Winchester College. The church is a neat structure, with a high embattled tower; the chancel has been elegantly rebuilt by the late Sir William Smith, who also constructed a large family vault within it, where his remains were deposited in 1752. There is a place of worship for Independents. Near the ancient mansion-house of the Hardys, at Up-Sydling, there was, before the Reformation, a chapel of ease, but there are no vestiges of it.

SYERSCOTE, otherwise STERSCOTE, a liberty in that part of the parish of TAMWORTH which is in the northern division of the hundred of OFFLOW, county of STAFFORD, 3 miles (N. N. E.) from Tamworth, containing 41 inhabitants.

SYERSTON, a parish in the southern division of the wapentake of NEWARK, county of NOTTINGHAM, 5¾ miles (S. W.) from Newark, containing 129 inhabitants. The living is a perpetual curacy, annexed to the vicarage of East Stoke, in the archdeaconry of Nottingham, and diocese of York. The old Fosse road passes through the parish, which is partly bounded by the river Trent.

SYKEHOUSE, a chapelry in the parish of FISH-LAKE, southern division of the wapentake of STRAF-FORTH and TICKHILL, West riding of the county of YORK, 5½ miles (N. W. by W.) from Thorne, containing 551 inhabitants. The chapel is dedicated to St. Peter.

SYLEHAM, a parish in the hundred of HOXNE, county of SUFFOLK, 3½ miles (S. W.) from Harleston, containing 360 inhabitants. The living is a vicarage, in the archdeaconry of Suffolk, and diocese of Norwich. Miss Isabella Barry was patroness in 1814. The church is dedicated to St. Mary.

SYMONDSBURY, a parish in the hundred of WHITCHURCH-CANONICORUM, Bridport division of the county of DORSET, 1½ mile (W. N. W.) from Bridport, containing 1076 inhabitants. The living is a rectory, in the archdeaconry of Dorset, and diocese of Bristol, rated in the king's books at £36. 3. 4., and in the patronage of the Rev. G. Raymond. The church, dedicated to St. John the Baptist, is a large cruciform structure, partly in the early, and partly in the later style of English architecture, with a tower rising from the intersection. The small river Simene has its source in this parish, and falls into the Birt at Bridport. There are several springs in the neighbourhood, slightly impregnated with iron.

SYMONDS-HALL, a tything in the parish of WOTTON under EDGE, upper division of the hundred of BERKELEY, county of GLOUCESTER, 3 miles (N. E. by E.) from Wotton under Edge, with which the population is returned.

SYNFIN, a joint liberty with Arleston, in that part of the parish of BARROW which is in the hundred of APPLETREE, county of DERBY, 2½ miles (S. by W.) from Derby, containing, with Arleston, 74 inhabitants.

SYRESHAM, a parish in the hundred of KING's SUTTON, county of NORTHAMPTON, 4¾ miles (N. E.) from Brackley, containing 725 inhabitants. The living is a rectory, in the archdeaconry of Northampton, and diocese of Peterborough, rated in the king's books at £13, and in the patronage of Sir S. C. Dormer, Knt. The church is dedicated to St. James. There is a place of worship for Wesleyan Methodists. The Rev. George Hammond, in 1755, bequeathed the interest of £300 for teaching ten poor children, and, in augmentation of the master's salary, Conquest Jones, in 1773, left the interest of £100.

SYSONBY, a parish in the hundred of FRAMLAND, county of LEICESTER, 1 mile (W.) from Melton-Mowbray, containing 67 inhabitants. The living is a perpetual curacy, annexed to the vicarage of Melton-Mowbray, in the archdeaconry of Leicester, and diocese of Lincoln.

SYSTON, a parish in the eastern division of the hundred of GOSCOTE, county of LEICESTER, 5¼ miles (N. N. E.) from Leicester, containing 1264 inhabitants. The living is a discharged vicarage, in the archdeaconry of Leicester, and diocese of Lincoln, rated in the king's books at £7. 2. 7., endowed with £1000 parliamentary grant, and in the patronage of the Vice-Chancellor and Fellows of the University of Oxford. The church is dedicated to St. Peter. Dame Margaret Thorold, in 1718, gave a rent-charge of £5 for teaching poor children. About a mile south-west of the village is a tumulus, on the eastern side of a Roman road passing through the vicinity.

SYSTON, a parish in the wapentake of WINNI-BRIGGS and THREO, parts of KESTEVEN, county of LINCOLN, 4 miles (N. N. E.) from Grantham, containing 188 inhabitants. The living is a vicarage, in the archdeaconry and diocese of Lincoln, endowed with £400 private benefaction, and £200 royal bounty, and in the patronage of Sir John H. Thorold, Bart. The church is dedicated to St. Mary.

SYWELL, a parish in the hundred of HAMFORD-SHOE, county of NORTHAMPTON, 5 miles (W.) from Wellingborough, containing 265 inhabitants. The living is a rectory, in the archdeaconry of Northampton, and diocese of Peterborough, rated in the king's books at £11. 1. 5½., and in the patronage of Earl Brownlow. The church is dedicated to St. Peter and St. Paul.

T.

TABLEY (INFERIOR), a township in that part of the parish of GREAT BUDWORTH which is in the hundred of BUCKLOW, county palatine of CHESTER, 3 miles (S. W. by W.) from Nether Knutsford, containing 110 inhabitants. Here was formerly a chapel, the site of which is still called Chapel field. Tabley confers the title of baron on the family of Leicester, created July 16th, 1826, at which period Sir John Fleming Leicester, Bart., a gentleman distinguished for his munificent patronage of the fine arts, and encouragement of native artists, was raised to the peerage by that title; he died in June 1827.

TABLEY (SUPERIOR), a township in that part of the parish of ROSTHERN which is in the hundred of BUCKLOW, county palatine of CHESTER, 2 miles (W. N. W.) from Nether Knutsford, containing 450 inhabitants. Here are the ruins of an ancient chapel, formerly called, from its situation, "The chapel in the street."

TACHBROOK (BISHOP'S), a parish partly in the Kenilworth division of the hundred of KNIGHTLOW, but chiefly in the Warwick division of the hundred of KINGTON, county of WARWICK, 3¾ miles (S. E.) from Warwick, containing, with the hamlet of Tachbrook-Mallory, 654 inhabitants. The living is a vicarage, in the peculiar jurisdiction of the Prebendary of Tachbrook in the Cathedral Church of Lichfield, rated in the king's books at £5. 13. 4., and in the patronage of the Bishop of Lichfield and Coventry. The church is dedicated to St. Chad. A school was erected and endowed, in 1771, by subscription of Sir William Bagot, the Earl of Warwick, and others, in which about one hundred children are instructed on the National system: the income is £39 per annum, with a good house and garden for the master.

TACHBROOK-MALLORY, a hamlet in that part of the parish of BISHOP'S TACHBROOK which is in the Kenilworth division of the hundred of KNIGHTLOW, county of WARWICK, 3½ miles (S.E. by E.) from Warwick, containing 55 inhabitants.

TACKLEY, a parish in the hundred of WOOTTON, county of OXFORD, 3¼ miles (N.E.) from Woodstock, containing 478 inhabitants. The living is a rectory, in the archdeaconry and diocese of Oxford, rated in the king's books at £19. 9. 4½., and in the patronage of the President and Fellows of St. John's College, Oxford. The church, dedicated to St. Nicholas, is an ancient cruciform structure, but the north aisle appears to have been destroyed by fire. There is a place of worship for Wesleyan Methodists. Earth of a peculiar quality, used for flooring barns, cottages, &c., abounds here. The Roman Akeman-street passes through the parish, and separates the two manors of the Duke of Marlborough and Sir Henry Dashwood, Bart.: on that

of the latter the two gateways of the ancient mansion built by the Harborne family still remain.

TACOLNESTON, a parish in the hundred of DEP-WADE, county of NORFOLK, 4½ miles (N. W. by W.) from St. Mary Stratton, containing 416 inhabitants. The living is a rectory, in the archdeaconry of Norfolk, and diocese of Norwich, rated in the king's books at £12, and in the patronage of Mrs. Warren. The church is dedicated to All Saints. John Tasephans, who was prior of the Carmelite friary at Norwich, was born here in 1404: he was a learned and pious divine, and a powerful orator, but his intolerant zeal brought much persecution upon the Lollards. The hall, a fine brick mansion, is a good specimen of the domestic style of architecture prevalent in the seventeenth century; it is said to have been built, in 1670, by the Browne family, who then held the estate.

TADCASTER, a parish comprising the market town of Tadcaster, and the township of Stutton with Hazlewood (the latter being extra-parochial), in the upper division of the wapentake of BARKSTONE-ASH, West riding, and the townships of Catterton and Oxton, in the ainsty of the city of YORK, East riding, of the county of YORK, and containing 2811 inhabitants, of which number, 2426 are in the town of Tadcaster, 10 miles (S. W.) from York, and 189½ (N.N.W.) from London. This place was the Roman station Calcaria, so named from the nature of the soil, which abounds in calx, or limestone, and one of the outports, or gates, on the Consular way, to their chief military station, Eboracum, the city of York. Under the name Calca-cester, Bede relates that Heina, the first female who assumed the habit of a nun in this country, retired to it, where she built a residence. In all the great civil wars of England, it was regarded as a post of considerable importance, and the possession of it has been repeatedly contested. During the commotions, on the appointment of the Earl of Newcastle to the command of the royal army, in 1642, he advanced from York towards this town, with four thousand men and seven pieces of cannon, and commenced his attack on the enemy's works, which lasted without intermission from eleven in the morning to five in the afternoon: his ammunition being exhausted, the lord general desisted from the assault, in expectation of a fresh supply from York before the following morning; but during the night, Sir Thomas Fairfax, who was posted here with seven hundred men, drew them off to Cawood and Selby, and left the royalists in possession. The town, which is a great thoroughfare, is situated on the river Wharf, over which is a very handsome stone bridge, considered the finest in the county, erected in the beginning of the last century; its centre marks the divisions of the jurisdictions of the West riding and the ainsty of the city of York. On the banks of the river, which is navigable up to the town, are several flour-mills. The streets are arranged on each side, and the houses are neat and modern. The walks on the banks of the river are highly interesting, and have of late been greatly improved. In the immediate neighbourhood are stone quarries, one of which, called Jack-daw-Cragg, (singularly interesting and romantic, and in the possession of the ancient family of Vavasour,) supplied stone for the erection of the magnificent cathedral at York, and is now furnishing materials for its repair, in consequence of the partial conflagration in 1829. The market is on Wednesday; and fairs are held on the last Wednesdays in the months of May and October, for cattle and sheep; and in November, for hiring servants.

The living is a discharged vicarage, in the archdeaconry and diocese of York, rated in the king's books at £8. 4. 9½., endowed with £200 private benefaction, and £200 royal bounty, and in the patronage of the Earl of Egremont. The church, which is dedicated to St. Mary, is a handsome structure in the later style of English architecture, with a fine tower. There are places of worship for Independents, Inghamites, and Primitive and Wesleyan Methodists, the last having a school-room attached, capable of containing three hundred children. The grammar school, and an hospital for four poor men, were founded and endowed with lands and the sum of £600, by Dr. Oglethorpe, Bishop of Carlisle, and confirmed by license in the 5th of Philip and Mary; the number of scholars is twenty, and the annual income is £145. Forty boys and girls are also instructed by four poor women, almshouse pensioners, on the foundation of Mrs. Henrietta Dawson, who, about thirty years ago, bequeathed £15 per annum to ten widows, and £10 per annum to ten spinsters, with an additional £5 per annum to each of the four women for teaching the children. A Sunday school, in connexion with the established church, was built by subscription in 1788, on a plot of ground given by the late William Hill, Esq., whose daughter, the present Miss Hill, has ever since contributed materially towards its support, and has assigned to it a permanent endowment of £20 per annum. Several Roman coins have been found here at different times, and there are some vestiges of a trench, surrounding part of the town, which is supposed to have been thrown up at the time of the civil war in the reign of Charles I.

TADDINGTON, a chapelry in the parish of BAKEWELL, hundred of HIGH PEAK, county of DERBY, 3½ miles (S. S. W.) from Tideswell, containing, with the township of Priestcliffe, 463 inhabitants. The living is a perpetual curacy, in the peculiar jurisdiction of the Dean and Chapter of Lichfield, endowed with £800 royal bounty, and £800 parliamentary grant, and in the patronage of the Vicar of Bakewell. The chapel, dedicated to St. Michael, is fast going to decay: near it is the mutilated shaft of an ancient cross. There is a place of worship for Baptists. The Rev. Roger Wilkson, in 1714, bequeathed lands, now producing £84 per annum, for the education of all children of the Wilkson family, and ten others, by a schoolmaster bearing his name. Twelve poor children are also taught in another school, erected by subscription in 1805, and supported with a rent-charge of £15, the bequest of Michael White in 1798. Taddington is in the honour of Tutbury, duchy of Lancaster, and within the jurisdiction of a court of pleas held at Chapel en le Frith, for the recovery of debts under 40s.

TADLEY, a parish in the hundred of OVERTON, Kingsclere division of the county of SOUTHAMPTON, 6 miles (N. N. W.) from Basingstoke, containing 597 inhabitants. The living is a perpetual curacy, annexed to the vicarage of Overton, in the peculiar jurisdiction of the Incumbent. The church is dedicated to St. Peter. There is a place of worship for Independents. Tadley

is within the jurisdiction of the Cheyney Court held at Winchester every Thursday, for the recovery of debts to any amount.

TADLOW, a parish in the hundred of ARMINGFORD, county of CAMBRIDGE, 4½ miles (E. S. E.) from Potton, containing 147 inhabitants. The living is a discharged vicarage, in the archdeaconry and diocese of Ely, rated in the king's books at £6. 17., and in the patronage of the Master and Fellows of Downing College, Cambridge. The church is dedicated to St. Giles.

TADMARTON, a parish in the hundred of BLOXHAM, county of OXFORD, 4¾ miles (W. S. W.) from Banbury, containing 401 inhabitants. The living is a rectory, in the archdeaconry and diocese of Oxford, rated in the king's books at £13. 11. 0½., and in the patronage of the Provost and Fellows of Worcester College, Oxford. The church, dedicated to St. Nicholas, has lately received an addition of one hundred sittings, of which seventy are free, the Incorporated Society for the enlargement of churches and chapels having granted £40 towards defraying the expense.

TAKELEY, a parish in the hundred of UTTLESFORD, county of ESSEX, 2¾ miles (S. E. by E.) from Stansted - Mountfitchet, containing 1134 inhabitants. The living is a vicarage, in the jurisdiction of the Commissary of Essex and Herts, concurrently with the Consistorial Court of the Bishop of London, rated in the king's books at £11, and in the patronage of the Bishop of London. The church is dedicated to the Holy Trinity. There is a place of worship for Independents. A small priory was founded here, in the reign of Henry I., as a cell to the abbey of St. Valery in Picardy.

TALK o' th' HILL, a chapelry in the parish of AUDLEY, northern division of the hundred of PIREHILL, county of STAFFORD, 5 miles (N. N. W.) from Newcastle under Line, containing 1008 inhabitants. The living is a perpetual curacy, in the archdeaconry of Stafford, and diocese of Lichfield and Coventry, endowed with £200 private benefaction, £600 royal bounty, and £200 parliamentary grant, and in the patronage of the Vicar of Audley. The chapel is a small brick building, surmounted by a cupola. The great north road formerly passed through the village, which is situated upon an eminence commanding a view into nine counties, with the mountains of North Wales in the distance. In the centre is a stone cross, where a market was formerly held. A free school was erected by subscription in 1760, in which fourteen children are instructed for £15 a year. Adjacent to the village is a spring, the water of which is of a blue milky colour, strongly impregnated with sulphur, and much in request for cutaneous diseases.

TALKIN, a township in the parish of HAYTON, ESKDALE ward, county of CUMBERLAND, 3 miles (S. E. by S.) from Brampton, containing 280 inhabitants. It is bounded on the west by the river Gelt, and contains quarries of freestone and limestone, and collieries. A school is supported by small annual subscriptions. Three valuable gold clasps were discovered, in 1790, on Netherton farm, where a battle was formerly fought.

TALLAND, a parish in the hundred of WEST, county of CORNWALL, 2 miles (S. W. by W.) from West Looe, containing, with the borough of West Looe, 1378 inhabitants. The living is a discharged vicarage, in the archdeaconry of Cornwall, and diocese of Exeter, rated in the king's books at £10. The Rev. N. Kendall was patron in 1806. The church is dedicated to St. Tallan. The parish is bounded on the south by the English channel, and includes the decayed market town of West Looe, and part of the small fishing town of Polperro. Mary Kendall, in 1710, left £4 per annum for teaching poor girls; and Charles Kendall, in 1746, gave £6 a year for the instruction of boys.

TALLATON, a parish in the hundred of HAYRIDGE, county of DEVON, 4½ miles (N.W. by N.) from St. Mary Ottery, containing 393 inhabitants. The living is a rectory, in the archdeaconry and diocese of Exeter, rated in the king's books at £32. 3. 1½., and in the patronage of the Rev. R. P. Welland. The church, dedicated to St. James, has an elegant wooden screen, in good preservation. Four poor children are taught by a schoolmistress, for a trifling annuity left by Elizabeth Prideaux, in 1710. At Escot House, which was destroyed by fire in 1808, George III. and three of the princesses were entertained by Sir G. Young, Bart., August 14th, 1789. Dr. Thomas Sprat, Bishop of Rochester, an historian and poet, was born here, in 1636; he died in 1713. Southcote, in this parish, was the occasional residence of Sir William Pole, the antiquary.

TALLENTIRE, a township in the parish of BRIDEKIRK, ALLERDALE ward below Darwent, county of CUMBERLAND, 3¾ miles (N. by W.) from Cockermouth, containing 244 inhabitants. Limestone is quarried and burned in the vicinity. Here is a free school, with a trifling endowment.

TALLINGTON, a parish in the wapentake of NESS, parts of KESTEVEN, county of LINCOLN, 3½ miles (W. by S.) from Market-Deeping, containing 240 inhabitants. The living is a discharged vicarage, in the archdeaconry and diocese of Lincoln, rated in the king's books at £8. 9. 8., endowed with £400 royal bounty, and in the patronage of Lord Gwydyr. The church is dedicated to St. Lawrence.

TALWORTH, a hamlet in the parish of LONG DITTON, second division of the hundred of KINGSTON, county of SURREY, 2¼ miles (S. S. E.) from Kingston upon Thames, containing 234 inhabitants.

TAMERTON (NORTH), a parish in the hundred of STRATTON, county of CORNWALL, 5 miles (S. S. W.) from Holsworthy, containing 479 inhabitants. The living is a perpetual curacy, in the archdeaconry of Cornwall, and diocese of Exeter, and in the alternate patronage of P. Coffin, Esq., and Miss I'Ans. The church is dedicated to St. Denis. The river Tamar and the Bude canal run through the parish, in a parallel direction, from north to south. There is a dilapidated chapel at Hornacot, in this parish.

TAMERTON-FOLIATT, a parish in the hundred of ROBOROUGH, county of DEVON, 4½ miles (N. by W.) from Plymouth, containing 1101 inhabitants. The living is a vicarage, in the archdeaconry of Cornwall, and diocese of Exeter, rated in the king's books at £12. 7. 8½., and in the patronage of the Crown. The church, dedicated to St. Mary, has a remarkably fine tower, and contains, among several handsome memorials of the Coplestone, Bampfylde, and Radcliffe families, an ancient altar-tomb, with the figures of an armed knight and his lady. There is a place of worship for Wes-

leyan Methodists. Tamerton, supposed by Camden to be the ancient Tamara, is delightfully situated on a creek of the Tamar, and is inhabited by many genteel families. A free school for twenty boys was founded, and liberally endowed with land and money, by Mary Deane, in 1734; the income is about £120 a year, for which they are clothed and educated. An almshouse for four widows was erected, in 1669, by Sir C. Bampfylde. In this parish is Maristow, the beautiful, but neglected, domain of Sir M. M. Lopes, Bart., where, in August 1789, he entertained George III. and three of the princesses. A chapel is attached to the mansion, in which divine service is regularly performed.

TAMHORN, a hamlet in the parish of WHITTINGTON, northern division of the hundred of OFFLOW, county of STAFFORD, 3 miles (N. W. by N.) from Tamworth, containing 16 inhabitants. The Birmingham and Fazely canal passes in the vicinity.

TAMWORTH, a parish partly in the northern and partly in the southern division of the hundred of OFFLOW, county of STAFFORD, and partly in the Tamworth division of the hundred of HEMLINGFORD, county of WARWICK, comprising the borough and market town of Tamworth, the chapelry of Wiggington, the townships

Corporate Seal.

of Almington with Stone-Delph, Biddescote, Bolehall with Glascote, Bonehill, and Fazely, the hamlet of Wilnecote with part of Dosthill, the liberties of Syerscote, otherwise Sterscote, and Tamworth Castle, and the extra-parochial liberty of Hopwas-Hayes, and containing 7185 inhabitants, of which number, 1636 are in the borough of Tamworth, 22 miles (S. E. by E.) from Stafford, 27 (N. by W.) from Warwick, and 112 (N. W. by N.) from London. This town is of great antiquity, being considered the most ancient in the county: its name is derived from Tame, the river on which it is situated, and Waert, or Worthidge, a water farm. At a very early period it was the site of a Mercian fortification and royal residence, and was the seat of government under Offa, Cenwulf, Beornwulf, and others, at which period it had also a mint. The town, having been nearly destroyed by the Danes, was rebuilt early in the tenth century, by Ethelfleda, daughter of Alfred the Great, who also erected a castle for its defence, which, having undergone recent repairs, is now a private residence. It stands south-west of the town, and the ancient fosse which surrounded it, called the King's Dyke, is still visible at a short distance. Tamworth, which is about equally divided between the counties of Stafford and Warwick, though commonly considered a Staffordshire town, stands near the confluence of the rivers Tame and Anker, both crossed by bridges about a mile distant from the Coventry canal: it consists of some good streets. The manufacture of lace, cotton, tapes, and patten-ties, affords employment to several persons. Many veins of coal have been found, and are worked, in the vicinity; and bricks and tiles of great durability are made from a clay which abounds here. There is a permanent library, under the direction of a respectable committee. The market is on Saturday : fairs are held by charter on May 4th, July 26th, and October 24th, for cattle and merchandise, and there are five new fairs for the sale of cattle only. The town is governed under a charter granted by Charles II., upon the surrender of a former one, which had been conferred by Elizabeth, authorising the appointment of a high steward, two bailiffs, recorder, twenty-four capital burgesses, a town clerk, and other officers : the members of the body corporate are chosen by the two bailiffs and the capital burgesses ; the high steward, recorder, and town clerk, hold their offices for life ; and the two bailiffs are chosen annually by the capital burgesses, from their own body. The corporation hold courts leet and baron twice a year, and are empowered also to hold a court of record, for the recovery of debts, but this right has not been exercised for many years. Quarter sessions are held regularly, but the trial of criminals has been discontinued, they being now sent to the county gaol for trial by the judges of assize. The borough returns two members to parliament : the elective franchise is in the inhabitants paying scot and lot, and not receiving alms, the number of whom is about six hundred ; the bailiffs are the returning officers, and the influence of the noble family of Townshend and Sir Robert Peel, Bart., is predominant.

The living is a perpetual curacy, in the archdeaconry of Stafford, and diocese of Lichfield and Coventry, endowed with £400 private benefaction, £400 royal bounty, and £800 parliamentary grant, and in the patronage of C. E. Repington, Esq. The church, dedicated to St. Edith, and situated in that part of the parish which is in the county of Stafford, is a spacious and handsome edifice, with a fine tower, in which are two remarkable spiral staircases, communicating with separate floors, their respective entrances being within and without the church : beneath the edifice is a small crypt : the building combines the decorated and later styles of English architecture. It was formerly collegiate, and occupies the site of an ancient monastery : the foundation of the college, which consisted of a dean and six prebendaries, is uncertain, but is attributed, with the greatest probability, to the Marmions, who were successively owners of the castle. Some fine tesselated pavement, now placed in front of the communion-table, was discovered a few years ago, when the church was undergoing repair. There are places of worship for Baptists, the Society of Friends, Independents, Wesleyan Methodists, and Unitarians. The free grammar school was refounded in the reign of Edward VI., and the stipend of £10. 13. 2¼. was confirmed to the master, and made payable from the revenues of the Crown. In the reign of Elizabeth the bailiffs were incorporated governors, and in 1677 the school-room was rebuilt : the revenue has been subsequently increased by various benefactors, and now amounts to £33. 11. 3. : from four to twelve children are instructed. Boys from this school are eligible to a scholarship at Catherine Hall, Cambridge, founded by Mr. Frankland ; and a native of this town to a fellowship in St. John's College, Cambridge, on the foundation of Mr. Bailey. A free school for twelve boys and ten girls has an income of £20 per annum, partially arising from a charitable bequest ; and the Sunday schools are endowed with the interest of £50, the gift of Mrs. Mary Done. In 1686, the Rev. John Rawlett bequeathed lands and houses for teaching and apprenticing poor children. An almshouse for fourteen poor men and women was endowed, in 1678, by Thomas Guy, Esq., of London, founder of Guy's Hospital in the borough of Southwark, who represented this borough in seven parliaments, and, in 1701, rebuilt the town hall. A new bridge has lately been erected at Fazely, over the Thame, along which passes the ancient Watling-street. Edward, Lord Thurlow, was also a representative of this borough until his elevation to the peerage, and recorder until his death. Tamworth confers the inferior title of viscount on Earl Ferrers.

TAMWORTH - CASTLE, a liberty adjoining the borough, and in that part of the parish, of TAMWORTH which is in the Tamworth division of the hundred of HEMLINGFORD, county of WARWICK, containing 19 inhabitants.

TANDRIDGE, a parish in the first division of the hundred of TANDRIDGE, county of SURREY, 1½ mile (E. by S.) from Godstone, containing 421 inhabitants. The living is a perpetual curacy, in the archdeaconry of Surrey, and diocese of Winchester, endowed with £600 royal bounty, and £200 parliamentary grant, and in the patronage of Sir W. Clayton, Bart. The church is dedicated to St. Peter. A National school, established here for the children of Tandridge, Godstone, and Oxted, is partly supported by a small bequest of David Maynard, in 1709. A priory of Augustine canons, in honour of St. James, to which Odo de Dammartin was a great benefactor, was founded in the time of Richard I., and at the dissolution had possessions valued at £86. 7. 6. per annum.

TANFIELD, a chapelry in that part of the parish of CHESTER le STREET which is in the middle division of CHESTER ward, county palatine of DURHAM, 6¾ miles (S. W.) from Gateshead. The population is returned with the townships of Beamish and Lintz-Green. The living is a perpetual curacy, in the archdeaconry and diocese of Durham, endowed with £200 private benefaction, and £200 royal bounty, and in the patronage of Lord Ravensworth. The chapel, dedicated to St. Margaret, was rebuilt by subscription in 1749, with the exception of a portion of the chancel, in the southern wall of which there is a piscina. There are two papermills and extensive collieries in the neighbourhood. Tanfield Arch, a magnificent stone structure, one hundred and thirty feet in the span, springing from abutments, nine feet high, to the height of sixty feet, was erected, upon the site of a wooden arch that had recently fallen, by certain coal owners, at the expense of £12,000, to expedite the passage of their wagons. Elizabeth Davison, in 1762, bequeathed £500 towards the support of a free school and for other charitable uses.

TANFIELD (EAST), a township in the parish of KIRKLINGTON, wapentake of HALLIKELD, North riding of the county of YORK, 6½ miles (N. N. W.) from Ripon, containing 32 inhabitants.

TANFIELD (WEST), a parish in the wapentake of HALLIKELD, North riding of the county of YORK, 6½ miles (N. W. by N.) from Ripon, containing 709 inhabitants. The living is a rectory, in the archdeaconry of Richmond, and diocese of Chester, rated in the king's books at £13. 0. 5., and in the patronage of the Marquis of Ailesbury. The church, dedicated to St. Nicholas, is an ancient structure, containing many curious old monuments: attached to it is the chantry of Maud Marmion, founded, in the time of Henry III., for a master, warden, and two brothers, to pray for the souls of Lord and Lady Marmion. There is a place of worship for Wesleyan Methodists. Eleven poor children are educated for £8 per annum, left by Diana, Countess of Oxford, and a smaller annuity bequeathed by Catherine Allen, in 1769. On the banks of the Ure, which is here of considerable width and crossed by a bridge, are the remains of Tanfield castle, the origin and history of which are involved in obscurity.

TANGLEY, a parish in the hundred of PASTROW, Kingsclere division of the county of SOUTHAMPTON, 5½ miles (N.N.W.) from Andover, containing 256 inhabitants. The living is a perpetual curacy, annexed to the rectory of Faccombe, in the archdeaconry and diocese of Winchester. The church is dedicated to St. John the Baptist. There is a place of worship for Wesleyan Methodists. A fair for sheep is held on April 15th.

TANGMERE, a parish in the hundred of ALDWICK, rape of CHICHESTER, county of SUSSEX, 3 miles (E. by N.) from Chichester, containing 174 inhabitants. The living is a rectory, in the peculiar jurisdiction of the Archbishop of Canterbury, rated in the king's books at £13. 5., and in the patronage of the Duke of Richmond. The church, dedicated to St. Andrew, is in the early style of English architecture. This parish is entitled to send two children to Boxgrove school, which was founded, in 1751, by the Countess Dowager of Derby.

TANKERSLEY, a parish in the wapentake of STAINCROSS, West riding of the county of YORK, comprising the chapelry of Wortley, and the township of Tankersley, and containing 1529 inhabitants, of which number, 625 are in the township of Tankersley, 5¼ miles (S.) from Barnesley. The living is a rectory, in the archdeaconry and diocese of York, rated in the king's books at £26. 0. 2½., and in the patronage of Earl Fitzwilliam. The church, dedicated to St. Peter, is principally in the later style of English architecture.

TANNINGTON, a parish in the hundred of HOXNE, county of SUFFOLK, 4¾ miles (N. W.) from Framlingham, containing 209 inhabitants. The living is a discharged vicarage, in the archdeaconry of Suffolk, and diocese of Norwich, rated in the king's books at £12. 10. 2½., endowed with £200 private benefaction, and £200 royal bounty, and in the patronage of the Bishop of Rochester. The church is dedicated to St. Ethelbert.

TANSHELF, a township in the parish of PONTEFRACT, upper division of the wapentake of OSGOLDCROSS, West riding of the county of YORK, ¼ of a mile (W. by S.) from Pontefract, containing 356 inhabitants. There is a small sum, the bequest of Richard Banister, in 1762, for teaching one child.

TANSLEY, a hamlet in that part of the parish of CRICH which is in the hundred of WIRKSWORTH, county of DERBY, 1½ mile (E.) from Matlock, containing 449 inhabitants. There is a place of worship for Wesleyan Methodists. Two children are educated for a trifling sum, bequeathed by Sir John Statham, in the reign of Anne. Tansley is in the honour of Tutbury, duchy of Lancaster, and within the jurisdiction of a court of pleas held at Tutbury every third Tuesday, for the recovery of debts under 40s.

TANSOR, a parish in the hundred of WILLYBROOK, county of NORTHAMPTON, 2¼ miles (N. N. E.) from Oundle, containing 234 inhabitants. The living is a rectory, in the archdeaconry of Northampton, and diocese of Peterborough, rated in the king's books at £13. 12. 11., and in the patronage of the Dean and Chapter of Lincoln. The church, dedicated to St. Mary, is a small structure, partly in the Norman, and partly in the early English style, with some screen-work and ancient monuments. The parish is partly bounded by the river Nen: at Cotterstock, on its opposite bank, a fine Roman tesselated pavement has been discovered. Clement Bellamy, in 1658, bequeathed £5 per annum for the education of children.

TANWORTH, a parish in the Warwick division of the hundred of KINGTON, county of WARWICK, 4¼ miles (N. W. by N.) from Henley in Arden, comprising the liberty of Monks-Riding, and containing 1993 inhabitants. The living is a discharged vicarage, in the archdeaconry and diocese of Worcester, rated in the king's books at £6. 13. 4., endowed with £200 private benefaction, and £200 royal bounty, and in the patronage of the Earl of Plymouth. The church is dedicated to St. Mary Magdalene. The Stratford on Avon canal passes through the parish. Two charity schools, attended by eighty children, are supported out of the proceeds of several charitable bequests, amounting to £80 per annum.

TAPLOW, a parish in the hundred of BURNHAM, county of BUCKINGHAM, 1 mile (E. N. E.) from Maidenhead, containing 586 inhabitants. The living is a rectory, in the archdeaconry of Buckingham, and diocese of Lincoln, rated in the king's books at £11. 18. 9., and in the patronage of the Crown. The church is dedicated to St. Nicholas: in the chancel lie the remains of Sarah Milton, the mother of the immortal poet, who resided here for some years. Ann Taplow, in 1784, left £1. 10. per annum toward the instruction of the poor. On the river Thames, which separates this parish from Berkshire, is a large paper-mill, employing a considerable number of persons. Cleifden, in this parish, was the residence of the Prince and Princess of Wales, during the infancy of their son, George III. It formerly belonged to a member of the Hamilton family, who fought under the celebrated Duke of Marlborough, and who, on his return from the continent, indulged the curious fancy of figuring the battle of Blenheim, by plantations of trees, now in full vigour.

TAPTON, a township in the parish of CHESTERFIELD, hundred of SCARSDALE, county of DERBY, 1½ mile (N. E. by E.) from Chesterfield, containing 149 inhabitants.

TARBOCK, a township in the parish of HUYTON, hundred of WEST DERBY, county palatine of LANCASTER, 3½ miles (S. by W.) from Prescot, containing 699 inhabitants, of whom a considerable number are employed at the collieries here.

TARDEBIGG, a parish partly in the Alcester division of the hundred of BARLICHWAY, county of WARWICK, but chiefly in the upper division of the hundred of HALFSHIRE, county of WORCESTER, 3 miles (E. S. E.) from Bromsgrove, containing, with the hamlets of Bentley, Redditch, Tutnal with Cobley, and Wibheath-Yields, 3458 inhabitants. The living is a vicarage, in the archdeaconry and diocese of Worcester, rated in the king's books at £8, and in the patronage of the Earl of

Plymouth. The church is dedicated to St. Bartholomew. At Redditch, in this parish, is a manufacture of needles and fish-hooks. The Birmingham and Worcester canal passes through a short tunnel in the parish.

TARLETON, a parish in the hundred of LEYLAND, county palatine of LANCASTER, 8½ miles (N. by E.) from Ormskirk, containing 1616 inhabitants. The living is a rectory, in the archdeaconry and diocese of Chester, endowed with £660 private benefaction, and £600 royal bounty, and in the patronage of the Rev. Streynsham Master. The church, consecrated in 1719, is dedicated to St. Mary. This was formerly a chapelry in the parish of Croston. A free school, the building for which was erected in 1650, is endowed with £30 per annum, for which twenty children are gratuitously instructed.

TARNICAR, a joint township with Upper Rawcliffe, in the parish of ST. MICHAEL, hundred of AMOUNDERNESS, county palatine of LANCASTER, 4¼ miles (S. W.) from Garstang. The population is returned with Upper Rawcliffe.

TARPORLEY, a parish in the first division of the hundred of EDDISBURY, county palatine of CHESTER, comprising the market town of Tarporley, and the townships of Eaton, Rushton, and Utkinton, and containing 2123 inhabitants, of which number, 800 are in the town of Tarporley, 10½ miles (E. S. E.) from Chester, and 172 (N. W.) from London. This town, which is situated on the great road from Chester to London, has a neat appearance, and consists of one long street, which is well paved, and terminated at the southern extremity by the ancient manor-house. At the close of the thirteenth century, a grant of a market and fair was obtained by Hugh de Thorpley, then proprietor of the manor. The market is on Thursday; and fairs are held May 1st, the first Monday after August 24th, and December 11th. The town was governed by a mayor from 1297 to 1348, but now only two constables are appointed. The living is a rectory, in the archdeaconry and diocese of Chester, rated in the king's books at £20. 3. 4., and in the joint patronage of the Dean and Chapter of Chester, Lord Alvanley, and the Rev. Sir P. G. Egerton, Bart. The church, dedicated to St. Helen, is an ancient structure of red stone, and contains some good monuments. There is a place of worship for Wesleyan Methodists. A school, situated in the churchyard, was endowed with £20 per annum by Lady Jane Done, who left also a small bequest for apprenticing poor children, but there are no free scholars. Almshouses have been founded for four poor widows, each of whom receives thirty shillings per annum.

TARRABY, a township in that part of the parish of STANWIX which is in ESKDALE ward, county of CUMBERLAND, 1¾ mile (N. N. E.) from Carlisle, containing 153 inhabitants.

TARRANT-CRAWFORD, county of DORSET.—See CRAWFORD-TARRANT.

TARRANT-GUNVILLE, a parish in that part of the hundred of CRANBORNE which is in the Shaston (West) division of the county of DORSET, 6 miles (N. N. E.) from Blandford-Forum, containing 487 inhabitants. The living is a rectory, in the archdeaconry of Dorset, and diocese of Bristol, rated in the king's books at £19. 7. 11., and in the patronage of the Master and Fellows of University College, Oxford. The church

was dedicated to St. Mary in 1503; the body is raised above the aisles, and the tower is embattled and crowned with pinnacles. The small river Tarrant runs through the parish.

TARRANT - HINTON, county of DORSET. — See HINTON (TARRANT).

TARRANT-KEYNSTON, a parish in the hundred of PIMPERNE, Blandford (North) division of the county of DORSET, 3½ miles (S. E. by E.) from Blandford-Forum, containing 220 inhabitants. The living is a rectory, in the archdeaconry of Dorset, and diocese of Bristol, rated in the king's books at £7. 17. 8½. Charles Hiley, Esq. was patron in 1806. The church, dedicated to All Saints, stands on the western bank of the small river Tarrant, which falls into the Stour on the southern side of the parish.

TARRANT-LAUNCESTON, a parish in the hundred of PIMPERNE, Blandford (North) division of the county of DORSET, 5¼ miles (N. E. by E.) from Blandford-Forum, containing 88 inhabitants. The living is a perpetual curacy, annexed to the vicarage of Tarrant-Monckton, in the archdeaconry of Dorset, and diocese of Bristol.

TARRANT-MONCKTON, county of DORSET.—See MONCKTON (TARRANT).

TARRANT-RAWSTON, a parish in the hundred of PIMPERNE, Blandford (North) division of the county of DORSET, 4½ miles (E. by N.) from Blandford-Forum, containing 58 inhabitants. The living is a discharged rectory, in the archdeaconry of Dorset, and diocese of Bristol, rated in the king's books at £8. 9. 2., and in the patronage of Sir J. W. Smith, Bart. The church is dedicated to St. Mary. The small river Tarrent runs through this parish, and that of Tarrant-Rushton.

TARRANT-RUSHTON, a parish in that part of the hundred of CRANBORNE which is in the Shaston (East) division of the county of DORSET, 3¾ miles (E.) from Blandford-Forum, containing 206 inhabitants. The living is a rectory, in the archdeaconry of Dorset, and diocese of Bristol, rated in the king's books at £4. 19. 2., and in the patronage of the Rev. George E. Saunders. The church was dedicated to St. Mary in 1342. Here was formerly an hospital, or chantry, dedicated to St. Leonard, which was granted to the prior of Christchurch-Twynham in the 7th of Edward III.

TARRETBURN, a township in the parish of BELLINGHAM, north-western division of TINDALE ward, county of NORTHUMBERLAND, 3 miles (N. W.) from Bellingham, containing 264 inhabitants.

TARRING (WEST), a parish in the hundred of TARRING, rape of BRAMBER, county of SUSSEX, 1½ mile (N. W.) from Worthing, containing 650 inhabitants. The living consists of a sinecure rectory, rated in the king's books at £22. 13. 4., and a vicarage consolidated with the rectory of Patching, rated at £8. 13. 4., in the peculiar jurisdiction and patronage of the Archbishop of Canterbury. The church, dedicated to St. Andrew, is principally in the early style of English architecture.

TARRING-NEVILLE, a parish in the hundred of DANEHILL-HORSTED, rape of PEVENSEY, county of SUSSEX, 2½ miles (N.) from Newhaven, containing 81 inhabitants. The living is a rectory with that of Heighton, united in 1660, in the archdeaconry of Lewes, and diocese of Chichester, rated in the king's books at £7, and in the patronage of D. Geere, Esq. The church, dedicated to St. Mary, is a neat structure in the early English style, with a remarkably large chancel.

TARRINGTON, a parish in the hundred of RAD-LOW, county of HEREFORD, 7 miles (W. N. W.) from Ledbury, containing 500 inhabitants. The living is a vicarage, in the archdeaconry and diocese of Hereford, rated in the king's books at £5. 0. 2½., and in the patronage of E. T. Foley, Esq. The church is dedicated to St. James.

TARSET (WEST), a township in the parish of THORNEYBURN, north-western division of TINDALE ward, county of NORTHUMBERLAND, 4 miles (W. N. W.) from Bellingham, containing 169 inhabitants.

TARVIN, a parish partly in the lower division of the hundred of BROXTON, but chiefly in the second division of the hundred of EDDISBURY, county palatine of CHESTER, comprising the townships of Ashton, Bruen-Stapleford, Burton, Clotton-Hoofield, Dudden, Foulk-Stapleford, Hockenhull, Horton with Peele, Kelsall, Mouldsworth, and Tarvin, and containing 3485 inhabitants, of which number, 1022 are in the township of Tarvin, 6 miles (E. by N.) from Chester. The living is a vicarage, in the archdeaconry and diocese of Chester, rated in the king's books at £19. 11. 0½., and in the patronage of the Bishop of Lichfield and Coventry. The church, dedicated to St. Andrew, is in the later style of English architecture, with a fine tower considerably enriched with sculpture, though now much mutilated. Courts leet and baron are held here. A grammar school was founded in 1600, with a house for the master, by John Pickering, who endowed it with £200, which was laid out in lands now producing an annual income of £18, for which twenty children are instructed. The celebrated calligrapher, John Thomason, was master of this school; he died in 1740. About the middle of the sixteenth century, Sir John Savage, lord of the manor, procured a charter for a market and a fair to be held here, which have been long disused. During the great civil war, Tarvin was a considerable military post, often taken and retaken by each party till September 1644, when it fell into the power of the parliament, and so remained to the end or the war.

TASBURGH, a parish in the hundred of DEPWADE, county of NORFOLK, 2 miles (N.) from St. Mary Stratton, containing 469 inhabitants. The living is a rectory, with Rainthorpe, in the archdeaconry of Norfolk, and diocese of Norwich, rated in the king's books at £8, and in the patronage of Sir Thomas Beevor, Bart. The church, dedicated to St. Mary, stands on a lofty eminence, within the area of a square intrenchment containing twenty-four acres, which Gale considers the Roman station Ad Tuam; it was an advantageous position for the defence of the river Tesse, running hence to Caistor, and here forming a convenient harbour. Coins, fibulæ, and other relics of antiquity, have been found.

TASLEY, a parish in the hundred of STOTTESDEN, county of SALOP, 1¾ mile (N. W. by W.) from Bridgenorth, containing 95 inhabitants. The living is a discharged rectory, in the archdeaconry of Salop, and diocese of Hereford, rated in the king's books at £5. 6. 8., and in the patronage of J. White, Esq.

TATENHILL, a parish in the northern division of the hundred of OFFLOW, county of STAFFORD, 3¾ miles (W. S. W.) from Burton upon Trent, containing, with the chapelries of Barton under Needwood and Wichnor, and the township of Dunstall, 2059 inhabitants. The living is a rectory, annexed to the deanery of Lichfield, in the archdeaconry of Stafford, and diocese of Lichfield and Coventry, rated in the king's books at £26. 1. 8. The church is dedicated to St. Michael. The Grand Trunk canal passes through the parish, which is in the honour of Tutbury, duchy of Lancaster, and within the jurisdiction of a court of pleas held at Tutbury every third Tuesday, for the recovery of debts under 40s.

TATHAM, a parish in the hundred of LONSDALE, south of the sands, county palatine of LANCASTER, comprising the townships of Ireby and Tatham, and containing 880 inhabitants, of which number, 765 are in the township of Tatham, 11 miles (N. E. by E.) from Lancaster. The living is a rectory, in the archdeaconry of Richmond, and diocese of Chester, rated in the king's books at £12. 5., and in the patronage of John Marsden, Esq. The church, dedicated to St. James, is a handsome modern structure. An old Roman road passes through the parish, in which there is an extensive colliery. A fair for cattle is held annually on March 12th, in the village of Lowgill. A school is endowed with an estate producing about £28 a year, which is applied for the instruction of all the poor children of the lower division of the parish.

TATHAM-FELL, a chapelry in the parish of TATHAM, hundred of LONSDALE, south of the sands, county palatine of LANCASTER, 12½ miles (E. N. E.) from Lancaster. The population is returned with the parish. The living is a perpetual curacy, in the archdeaconry of Richmond, and diocese of Chester, endowed with £800 royal bounty, and in the patronage of the Rector of Tatham.

TATHWELL, a parish in the Wold division of the hundred of LOUTH-ESKE, parts of LINDSEY, county of LINCOLN, 3¼ miles (S. by W.) from Louth, containing 272 inhabitants. The living is a discharged vicarage, in the archdeaconry and diocese of Lincoln, rated in the king's books at £10, and in the patronage of the Bishop of Lincoln. The church is dedicated to St. Vedast. On a high hill in this parish are six barrows, in a line running from east to west.

TATSFIELD, a parish in the second division of the hundred of TANDRIDGE, county of SURREY, 5½ miles (N. E. by E.) from Godstone, containing 174 inhabitants. The living is a discharged rectory, in the archdeaconry of Surrey, and diocese of Winchester, rated in the king's books at £5. 0. 5., and in the patronage of William L. Gower, Esq. The church is principally in the early style of English architecture.

TATTENHALL, a parish in the lower division of the hundred of BROXTON, county palatine of CHESTER, comprising the townships of Golborn-Bellow, Newton by Tattenhall, and Tattenhall, and containing 1016 inhabitants, of which number, 855 are in the township of Tattenhall, 5¾ miles (S. W. by W.) from Tarporley. The living is a rectory, in the archdeaconry and diocese of Chester, rated in the king's books at £13. 17. 6., and in the patronage of the Bishop of Chester. The church, dedicated to St. Alban, has lately received an addition of one hundred free sittings, the Incorporated Society for the enlargement of churches and chapels having granted £30 towards defraying the expense. There are places of worship for Independents and Wesleyan Methodists. Dr. Paploe, rector of this parish, who died in 1781, gave money, vested in the purchase of £334 three per cents., for the education of twelve children.

TATTENHOE, a parish in the hundred of COTTESLOE, county of BUCKINGHAM, 3¾ miles (W.) from Fenny-Stratford, containing 16 inhabitants. The living is a perpetual curacy, holden by institution as a rectory, in the archdeaconry of Buckingham, and diocese of Lincoln, endowed with £800 royal bounty, and £200 parliamentary grant. W. S. Lowndes, Esq. was patron in 1813. The church was rebuilt in 1540, but the parish containing only a few inhabitants, it fell into disuse and desecration, until the rector of Shealey claimed the tithes of the parish, in 1636, when it was consecrated anew, and the living was presented to as a rectory.

TATTERFORD, a parish in the hundred of GALLOW, county of NORFOLK, 4 miles (W. by S.) from Fakenham, containing 67 inhabitants. The living is a discharged rectory, consolidated with that of Tatterset, in the archdeaconry of Norfolk, and diocese of Norwich, rated in the king's books at £6. 6. 8. The church is dedicated to St. Margaret.

TATTERSET, a parish in the hundred of GALLOW, county of NORFOLK, 5 miles (W.) from Fakenham, containing 150 inhabitants. The living is a discharged rectory, with which that of Tatterford is consolidated, in the archdeaconry of Norfolk, and diocese of Norwich, rated in the king's books at £11. 1. 8., and in the patronage of Sir Charles Chad, Bart. The church is dedicated to St. Andrew.

TATTERSHALL, a market town and parish in the southern division of the wapentake of GARTREE, parts of LINDSEY, county of LINCOLN, 30 miles (S. E. by E.) from Lincoln, and 125 (N.) from London, containing 627 inhabitants. This place, anciently a Roman military station, as two encampments at Tattershall park in its immediate neighbourhood indicate, was granted at the Conquest to Eudo, one of William's followers, whose descendants erected a castle here about 1440, of which some remains are yet visible south-westward from the town: it stood on a moor, and was surrounded by two fosses, which received the waters of the Bane, but the principal part was demolished during the parliamentary war: the north-west tower, a rectangular brick structure one hundred feet high, flanked by four embattled octangular turrets, was built by Sir Ralph Cromwell, treasurer of the Exchequer in the reign of Henry VI., and still remains; he likewise erected a lofty tower, with a spiral staircase leading to its summit, about four miles northward, as an appendage to the larger structure, but this is now in a very dilapidated state. The town, situated on the river Bane, near its junction with the Witham, is much decayed, and the trade inconsiderable: a canal from the Witham to Horncastle passes through it. The market, originally granted by King John to Robert Fitz-Eudo, was formerly on Friday, but is now on Thursday: fairs are on May 15th and September 25th. The living is a perpetual curacy, in the peculiar jurisdiction of the manorial court of Kirstead, and in the patronage of E. Fortescue, Esq. The church, which is dedicated to the Holy Trinity, is situated on the eastern side and in the outer moat of the castle, and

was made collegiate, in the time of Henry VI., for seven chaplains (one of whom was master), six clerks, and six choristers: at the dissolution its revenue was estimated at £348. 5. 11. The collegiate buildings have been taken down, and the church alone remains, which is a beautiful and venerable cruciform structure, consisting of a nave, transept, and choir, of which the last was once much admired for its magnificent painted windows, but since their removal to the chapel of Burleigh, the seat of the Marquis of Exeter, this part of the edifice has been allowed to fall into decay. There is a place of worship for Wesleyan Methodists. A National school, wherein about one hundred and thirty children are instructed, is held in the south side of the transept of the church; and an almshouse for thirteen poor persons, originally established by the license which raised the church into a college, still remains, with a small endowment for its support.

TATTINGSTONE, a parish in the hundred of SAMFORD, county of SUFFOLK, 5½ miles (S. W. by S.) from Ipswich, containing 346 inhabitants, exclusively of 319 in the house of industry for the hundred of Samford, which is in this parish. The living is a rectory, in the archdeaconry of Suffolk, and diocese of Norwich, rated in the king's books at £6. 13. 4. The Rev. J. Bull was patron in 1816. The church is dedicated to St. Mary. There is a place of worship for Wesleyan Methodists.

TATTON, a township in that part of the parish of ROSTHERN which is in the hundred of BUCKLOW, county palatine of CHESTER, 2 miles (N.) from Nether Knutsford, containing 87 inhabitants.

TATWORTH, a joint tything with Forton, in the parish of CHARD, eastern division of the hundred of KINGSBURY, county of SOMERSET, 1¾ mile (S.) from Chard, containing 437 inhabitants.

TAUNTON, a borough and market town in the hundred of TAUNTON and TAUNTON-DEAN, county of SOMERSET, 11 miles (S. by W.) from Bridg-water, and 144 (W. by S.) from London, containing, according to the last census, 8534 inhabitants, which number has since increased to upwards of 10,000. This place, which was called by the Saxons *Tantun*, and subsequently *Tawnton* and *Thoneton*, from its situation on the river Thone, or Tone, is of great antiquity, and the discovery of several urns, containing Roman coins, in the neighbourhood has led to the conjecture that it existed in the time of that people; but the earliest authentic accounts refer to the period of the Octarchy, a castle having been built here for a royal residence by Ina, King of the West Saxons, about the year 700, in which he held his first great council. This castle was afterwards demolished by his queen, Ethelburga, after expelling Eadbricht, King of the South Saxons, who had seized it. The town and manor are supposed to have been granted to the church of Winchester in the following reign; and another castle is said to have been built, on the site of the first, by the Bishops of Winchester, in the reign of William the Conqueror, in which they principally resided for some years. At this period Taunton had a mint, some of the coins bearing the Conqueror's effigy being still in existence. In the reign of Henry VII., in 1497, Perkin Warbeck seized the town and castle, which he quickly abandoned, on the approach of the king's troops. In 1645, it again participated in civil war, being celebrated for the long siege it sustained, and the defence it made, under Colonel (afterwards the renowned Admiral) Blake, who held it for the parliament against ten thousand troops under Lord Goring, until relieved by Fairfax. On this memorable occasion a public thanksgiving was appointed by the Commons, who voted £500 to the Colonel, and £1000 to the men under his command; but the inhabitants incurred the displeasure of the king, who, on his restoration, suspended its charter, and ordered the walls to be razed to the ground, which was so effectually done, that even their site is not now known. Taunton was again implicated in rebellious proceedings by its connexion with James, Duke of Monmouth, who was proclaimed king on the Cornhill of this town, June 21st, 1685; many of whose followers, after his defeat at Sedgmoor, were inhumanly put to death, on the same spot, by the brutal Kirke, without form of trial, besides those who were condemned by the merciless Judge Jeffreys, at the bloody assize which he held here in the following September.

The town is situated in a central part of the singularly beautiful and luxuriant vale of Taunton-Dean, and is upwards of a mile in length : the principal streets, which terminate in the market-place, are spacious, well paved, and lighted with gas by a company established in 1821 : the houses, mostly built of brick, are generally commodious and handsome, and well supplied with excellent water. The respectability of the town, combined with the beauty of the surrounding country, has rendered it very attractive as a place of residence, and many recent improvements have been effected, amongst which the erection of a neat crescent and terrace may be particularly noticed, and the removal of some old houses at East Gate, which has rendered the entrance from London more spacious. The parade, in the centre of the town, is a fine open triangular space, enclosed with iron posts and chains, and on the east side of it is a wide street, erected by the late Sir Benjamin Hammet, which forms a handsome approach to St. Mary's beautiful church. A substantial stone bridge of two arches crosses the Tone, and connects the town with the village of North-town, or Norton. Several detached villas, commanding beautiful views, have also been erected in the suburbs of Wilton, Staplegrove, West Monckton, and adjoining parishes. The Taunton and Somerset Institution, established in 1823, possesses a small but valuable library, particularly works of reference; also various specimens in mineralogy, ornithology, zoology, &c. : it has likewise a noble and spacious public reading and news-room. The theatre, in Silver-street, is usually open two months in the year, and balls and concerts occasionally take place.

Taunton was formerly noted for its woollen manufacture, being one of the first places into which that branch of trade was introduced, but it has long since given place to the silk trade, which was begun here, in 1778, and is now carried on to a considerable extent : the chief articles manufactured are, crapes, persians, sarsnets, and mixed goods; and, as nearly every cottage has a silk-loom, the trade furnishes employment to a great number of persons, principally females. Two patent lace-manufactories have been lately established. The river Tone is navigable, but its course to Bridg-water being circuitous, and the navigation frequently interrupted, a canal, called the Taunton and Bridg-water

canal, has been constructed, and has given increased activity to trade, considerable quantities of Welch coal being brought to the town, and, in return, the produce of the vale of Taunton being exported to Bristol and other parts of England. The markets are on Wednesday and Saturday, the latter being the principal; they are well supplied with fish from both channels, with every other kind of provisions, and with fruit in abundance. The old market-house, standing on the south side of the Parade, is a lofty brick building, supported on each side by an arcade, one of which is used as a corn market, and the other by various tradesmen : it contains the guildhall, and a handsome assembly-room, in which is a full-length portrait of George III. in his robes, presented by the late Sir Benjamin Hammet. The Parade is appropriated to the butchers, who form on it their market of moveable standings, placed in rows ; on the west side is a handsome building of freestone, erected in 1821, in the lower part and rear of which is the market for fish, pork, poultry, and dairy produce; the upper being used as the library and reading-room, with a museum attached : it is of the Ionic order, the entablature supported by four handsome columns, and forms a great ornament to this part of the town. The last Saturday in every month is called the great market, including the sale of live stock. This is one of the towns which, by act of parliament, are obliged to make weekly returns of corn sold; the tolls of the markets are let for about £1400 per annum. There is an annual fair on the 17th of June, for horses and cattle.

The town was for several centuries under the jurisdiction of portreeves and bailiffs, chosen at the courts of the Bishops of Winchester, as lords of the manor, which was formerly very extensive and valuable, the rental, at the time of the Conquest, appearing, from a document found amongst the court rolls, to amount to nearly £700 per annum : it was, however, divided by the Conqueror, and portions of it distributed among his favourites. By the custom of the manor the wife is considered her husband's heir, and succeeds before the children, the youngest son before the eldest, and so on in other relations, the younger succeeding first. It continued in the possession of the Bishops of Winchester until the year 1822, when it was sold by Bishop Tomline to Thomas Southwood, Esq., at whose annual courts, held in the castle, two portreeves, who collect the lord's rents, two bailiffs, two constables, and six tythingmen, are chosen. A charter was granted, in 1627, by Charles I., vesting the civil power in a mayor, justice, aldermen, and burgesses; this was suspended by Charles II., but subsequently confirmed by him, and existed until the year 1792, when, in consequence of the corporation having suffered a majority of the members to die without filling up vacancies, and a majority being required to swear in the officers, none could be legally elected ; whereby the charter became forfeited, and a fruitless application having been made to the Privy Council for its renewal, the town is now under the jurisdiction of the county magistrates, who hold a petty session on Wednesdays and Saturdays at the guildhall. The bailiffs convene, and usually preside at, public meetings, and the constables have the distribution of most of the public charities. The Lent assizes for the county are held in the castle, as are also the Michaelmas general quarter sessions. A court for the recovery of small debts under 40s. is holden, in the same place, for the borough and hundred alternately, every week. The castle is supposed to be part of a stately edifice erected by William Giffard, Bishop of Winchester, in the reign of Henry I.; it was thoroughly repaired by Bishop Langton, towards the end of the fifteenth century, and, in addition to other improvements, the present assize hall was built, by Bishop Horne, in 1577, since which period, various sums have been expended for keeping it in repair. The building consists of a south front, with a gateway in the centre, over which are two escutcheons, one bearing the arms of Henry VII., with the motto *Vive le roi Henri*; the other the inscription *Laus tibi Xte.*, and *T. Langto Winto*, 1495, both in Saxon characters: at its east end is a circular tower. The inner court-yard is an irregular quadrangle, the east side being the shorter, and on the north side are the county courts, grand jury room, &c.: the access to it is through an open court, called Castle Green, formerly enclosed with two gates, but one only remains, over which is what was the porter's lodge, now occupied as a dwelling-house; besides these is another apartment, called the Exchequer chamber, where the rolls of the manor are preserved; the walls are of great strength, and the grooves for the portcullis quite perfect. The moat was filled up in 1785, and the drawbridge removed. The only prison, besides a small place of temporary confinement, called the Nook, is the county bridewell, at Wilton, to confine malefactors until they can be taken before a magistrate. It was erected in 1754, and enlarged in 1815, being now capable of receiving eighty prisoners. Debtors, as well as criminals, are sent to the county gaol at Ilchester, and the latter also to Wilton and Shepton-Mallet prisons. This is a borough by prescription, and first sent members to parliament in the reign of Edward I., in 1295: the right of election is in the potwallers, or persons who boil their own pot, and have resided six months within the limits of the borough (which is not co-extensive with the town, comprising only a part of the parish of St. Mary Magdalene) and do not receive alms: the number of electors is about six hundred, and the bailiffs are the returning officers.

Taunton comprises the parishes of St. James and St. Mary Magdalene, in the archdeaconry of Taunton, and diocese of Bath and Wells, but many of the houses extend into the adjoining parishes. The living of St. James' is a perpetual curacy, endowed with £1000 private benefaction, £800 royal bounty, and £1700 parliamentary grant, and in the patronage of Sir T. B. Lethbridge, Bart.: the church, which is an ancient unadorned structure, with a quadrangular tower, was formerly the conventual church of the priory. The living of St. Mary Magdalene's is a vicarage, endowed with £600 private benefaction, and £600 royal bounty, and in the patronage of E. B. Portman, Esq.: the church, standing near the centre of the town, was originally a chapel to the conventual church of St. James, but was made parochial in 1308, under Walter Huselshaw, then Bishop of Bath and Wells: it is a spacious and magnificent edifice, in the decorated and later styles of English architecture, consisting of a chancel, nave, and five aisles, two of the latter having been probably added at a later date, separated by four rows of clus-

tered columns supporting pointed arches: the quadrangular tower at the west end is an elegant structure in four compartments, containing thirteen windows, which, by the variety of their ornaments, add much to its lightness and beauty; it is one hundred and twenty-one feet in height, exclusively of its pinnacles of thirty-two feet, which are richly adorned with carved work, and the top crowned with most exquisitely delicate battlements; the whole forming a beautiful and conspicuous object for many miles round. There is a place of worship each for Baptists, the Society of Friends, Independents, and Unitarians, and two for Wesleyan Methodists, one of them erected under the immediate direction of their founder, the Rev. John Wesley. The Roman Catholics have lately built a handsome chapel, with a portico supported by two Ionic pillars, and a façade ornamented with windows and pilasters of the same order; they have also a convent of Franciscan nuns, who emigrated from Brussels during the French Revolution in the last century, and first settled at Winchester, until they became possessed of their present residence, which is a noble building standing at the east end of the town, near the entrance from London, originally intended for a public hospital.

The free grammar school was founded, in 1522, by Richard Fox, Bishop of Winchester, and endowed, in 1554, by William Walbee, clerk, with property now producing about £36 per annum: the school-house is on the south side of the Castle green, and adjoining it is a house for the master, whose appointment is vested in the Warden of New College, Oxford; there are no boys on the foundation. The school in Middle-street, in which eighty boys and fifty girls are clothed and instructed, is supported by voluntary subscription; and there are also a school of industry and two infant schools. The almshouses at East Gate were founded, in 1635, by Robert Gray, Esq., a native of this town, and endowed by him with £2000; ten poor women and seven men are lodged in them, who, by direction of the founder, were to receive two shillings a week each, but additional benefactions have enabled the trustees to increase this allowance to three shillings a week. Huish's almshouses, on the north side of Hammet-street, founded and endowed by Richard Huish, Esq., for "thirteen poor, needy, maimed, impotent, or aged men," one of whom is appointed president, and reads prayers daily in the chapel attached to the building; he receives seven shillings, and the rest five shillings, a week each, besides clothing and coal occasionally. Henley's and Pope's almshouses, and seventeen other tenements, are also appropriated to the rent-free residence of the poor, but are not endowed. Of the other charities, the principal is that arising from the Town Lands, consisting of property to which no claimant appeared after a plague had raged in Taunton, which, together with some land and houses purchased under bequests of John Meredith and Margery Acland, is vested in feoffees; the annual produce is about £360, and, after some deductions for expenses, the income from the Town Lands is distributed in money among the poor of the parish of St. Mary Magdalene; that from John Meredith's bequest, in clothing to poor men and women; and that from Margery Acland's, in small sums to poor women: there are also many small sums, as well as bread and clothing, arising from various bequests, annually distributed. The Taunton and Somerset hospital was founded, in 1809, in commemoration of George III. entering upon the fiftieth year of his reign : it was opened on the 25th of March, 1812, and contains four wards, two for men and two for women, being capable of accommodating twenty-six patients. An eye infirmary, established in 1816, is supported by voluntary contributions ; and there is a society for the relief of lying-in women. Taunton is the birthplace of Samuel Daniel, the poet, born in 1562 ; and of the Rev. Henry Grove, in 1683, an eminent dissenting minister, who, in addition to other works, contributed some excellent papers to the Spectator. Amongst the bishops of Winchester who made it their occasional residence are the celebrated names of Cardinals Beaufort and Wolsey.

TAVERHAM, a parish in the hundred of TAVERHAM, county of NORFOLK, 5¾ miles (N. W.) from Norwich, containing 192 inhabitants. The living is a rectory, formerly in medieties, now united, in the archdeaconry and diocese of Norwich, each rated in the king's books at £4. 2. 8½., and in the alternate patronage of the Bishop of Norwich and Mrs. Branthwayte. The church is dedicated to St. Edmund.

Arms

TAVISTOCK, a borough, market town, and parish, in the hundred of TAVISTOCK, county of DEVON, 33 miles (W. by S.) from Exeter, and 204 (W. S. W.) from London, containing 5483 inhabitants. The origin of this town, which derives its name from the river Tavy, on which it is pleasantly situated, appears to have been coeval with the erection of an abbey of Black monks, commenced by Ordgar, Earl of Devonshire, in 961, and completed by his son Ordulf, in 981, the noble founder, according to tradition, having been admonished in a vision to erect a monastery : it was richly endowed, and dedicated to St. Mary the Virgin and St. Rumon in 997 : it was destroyed by the Danes, but afterwards arose from its ruins with considerable enlargement : from Henry I. it received the jurisdiction of the entire hundred of Tavistock, and the grant of a market and a fair. The abbey church was dedicated, in 1318, by Bishop Stapleton ; and in 1513, Richard Barham, the abbot, procured from Henry VIII. the right of a seat among the peers, and from Pope Leo. X. an exemption for the abbey from all episcopal and metropolitan jurisdiction ; in 1539, it was surrendered to the king by John Peryn, the last abbot, and its revenue was valued at £902. 5. 7. The monastery is remarkable as having contained a school for Saxon literature, at an early period (the study of which was discontinued about the period of the Reformation), and an ancient printing-press, soon after the introduction of printing into England. In Exeter College, Oxford, is a copy of the Stannary laws, printed here ; also a perfect copy of Boëthius, translated by Walton, and printed, in 1525, by Dan Thomas Rychard, one of the monks of the abbey ; the possessions of which, with the borough and town, was granted at the dissolution to John, Lord Russell, ancestor of the present noble proprietor, the Duke of Bedford. Of the venerable fabric there are yet sufficient remains, indicating its beauty and extent, although considerably mutilated and appropriated to various uses : among these are the gate-house and several complete buildings near it ; the refectory, now used as an assembly-room ; traces of the boundary walls, and an entire gateway, near the canal bridge. Within the parish there are also some remains of Old Morwell house, once the hunting seat of the monks of Tavistock.. In 1591, while the plague raged at Exeter, the summer assizes were held in this town, and thirteen criminals were executed on the Abbey green. After the defeat of the parliamentary forces on Bradock Down, in 1643, the royalists were quartered here, and Charles I. visited this town on his advance towards Cornwall, after his unsuccessful attempt on Plymouth.

The town occupies a portion of the level and acclivity of a valley, through which the river passes with tumultuous impetuosity over an uneven and rocky bed, and which presents some of the most beautiful and picturesque scenery in this justly admired county : it is irregularly built, but the approach from the Plymouth road is remarkably good. On the right, and opposite the church, are the various embattled and turreted buildings of the old abbey, part of which has been converted into the Bedford hotel, with an extensive façade in the English style of architecture, and several other portions and fragments covered with ivy. It also possesses a good library, with a Doric portico, in which the members of a literary and scientific institution assemble, and lectures are delivered occasionally. Races are held on Whitchurch down. The river is crossed by three bridges, two ancient ones immediately leading from the body of the town, and the third on the Plymouth road, about a quarter of a mile distant : near this is another over the Tavistock canal, which extends hence to the town, parallel with the river ; it was opened in June 1817, to form a junction with the Tamar at Morwell Ham quay, five miles distant : a branch canal extends to the slate quarries at Mill hill. The head of this canal is connected with the above-mentioned quay by an inclined plane, two hundred and forty feet high ; and, in its course, it flows through a tunnel under Morwell Down, one mile and three quarters in length. The boats employed are of iron, and the principal articles conveyed by them are ore, coal, and lime. The serge and coarse woollen manufactures, with the mining business, form the chief employment of the inhabitants, but the former is on the decline. There are a tin-smelting establishment and an extensive iron-foundry in the town. The neighbourhood abounds with mineral productions : a section of the mining field between the Tamar and Tavy rivers exhibits a considerable quantity of the porphyritic rock, in alternate beds, called elvan. From the mines of Morwell, grey and ruby copper is procured ; from Wheal Friendship, native rich, yellow, red, and chrystallized copper, and, in general, arsenic and yellow pyrites may be found. Lead abounds in the district ; and silver is also found, as well as tin, iron, manganese, and the loadstone. The market, noted for its supply of corn, is held on Friday : fairs are on the second Wednesday in January, May, July, September, October, November, and December.

The town, which is one of the four stannary towns in the county, is governed by a portreeve, who is elected annually at the manorial court leet. A court of pie-powder was anciently held, and there is still a court for the recovery of debts not exceeding £20. This borough sent representatives to parliament in the reign of Edward I.: the

Corporate Seal.

elective franchise is vested in the resident freeholders, the number of whom is about thirty; the portreeve is the returning officer, and the influence of the Duke of Bedford is predominant. Amongst the most distinguished members returned for this borough were John Pym, the great opposer of Charles I., and William, the unfortunate Lord Russell, in the reign of Charles II.

The living is a discharged vicarage, in the archdeaconry of Totness, and diocese of Exeter, rated in the king's books at £10. 17. 6., endowed with £600 royal bounty, and £1000 parliamentary grant, and in the patronage of the Duke of Bedford. The church, which is dedicated to St. Eustachius, is a neat and very spacious edifice, with a lofty tower elevated over an arched thoroughfare: it contains some good monuments, especially those in memory of Sir John Fitz and Sir John Glanville, the latter of whom was a judge of the Common Pleas, and died in 1600. There are places of worship for the Society of Friends, Independents, Wesleyan Methodists, and Unitarians. The grammar school is of ancient and uncertain foundation, but has now merely a nominal existence: it was endowed in 1649, by Sir J. Glanville, with certain estates, for the maintenance and education of one boy, and with a small exhibition to either of the Universities, on the completion of his preparatory studies: the master receives £4. 4. per annum from the proceeds of the estates, under an act passed in the 3rd of George III., which are now vested in the Duke of Bedford, who also grants him the use of a house rent-free, and an annual contribution of £20, for which eight boys are instructed. In 1674, Nicholas Watts bequeathed some rent-charges, part of them applicable to assist a youth preparing for the University. A subscription free school for children of both sexes, was erected at the expense, and is chiefly supported by the beneficence, of the Duke of Bedford: it is adapted to the reception of one hundred and forty boys and one hundred and twenty girls, and is conducted on the system of Dr. Bell. An almshouse for four poor widows was founded by one of the Courtenay family, each of the inmates receiving £2 per annum. Couches' almshouses are for the reception of fifteen pensioners, nominated by the Duke of Bedford, each of whom receives £3 per annum. The sum of £15, arising from lands, is applied annually in apprenticing poor children. The workhouse, a large and convenient building, occupies the site of an ancient lazar-house. There are also several benefit societies, and other charities of a public nature. At Brook is a chalybeate spring of reputed medicinal properties. From the summit of a lofty and precipitous cliff at Morwell woods there is a fine view of the river Tamar, winding through a valley of great

beauty. Among the eminent natives were, Sir Francis Drake; Judge Glanville; his son, Sir John Glanville; and William Browne, author of "The Shepherd's Pipe." Tavistock confers the inferior title of marquis on the Duke of Bedford.

TAVY (ST. MARY), a parish in the hundred of LIFTON, county of DEVON, 4 miles (N. E. by N.) from Tavistock, containing 933 inhabitants. The living is a rectory, in the archdeaconry of Totness, and diocese of Exeter, rated in the king's books at £14. 5. 7½., and in the patronage of John Buller, Esq. In this parish is an extensive copper mine, called Weal Friendship.

TAVY (ST. PETER), a parish partly in the hundred of LIFTON, but chiefly in that of ROBOROUGH, county of DEVON, 3½ miles (N. E.) from Tavistock, containing, with the hamlet of Willsworthy, 444 inhabitants. The living is a rectory, in the archdeaconry of Totness, and diocese of Exeter, rated in the king's books at £17.1.8., and in the patronage of the Bishop of Exeter. At Willsworthy there was formerly a chantry chapel, which has been converted into a cow-house.

TAWSTOCK, a parish in the hundred of FREMINGTON, county of DEVON, 2 miles (S.) from Barnstaple, containing 1237 inhabitants. The living is a rectory, in the archdeaconry of Barnstaple, and diocese of Exeter, rated in the king's books at £69. 12. 1., and in the patronage of Sir B. Wrey, Bart. The church is dedicated to St. Peter. There is a place of worship for Independents. Mary Pine, in 1758, left a small sum in support of a school. The manor-house, which was garrisoned by Sir T. Fairfax, in February 1646, was almost consumed by fire in 1787: it has been rebuilt by Sir B. Wrey, except the ancient gateway, which still remains, bearing date 1574.

TAWSTOCK, county of SUFFOLK.—See TOSTOCK.

TAWTON (BISHOP'S), a parish in the hundred of SOUTH MOLTON, county of DEVON, 2 miles (S. by E.) from Barnstaple, containing 1200 inhabitants. The living is a vicarage, in the peculiar jurisdiction of the Bishop of Exeter, rated in the king's books at £21, and in the patronage of the Dean of Exeter. The church, dedicated to St.John the Baptist, is a neat ancient structure, with a handsome stone spire. On the division of the see of Sherborne, about 905, Tawton was made the seat of the Devonshire diocese, by Eadulphus, or Werstan, its first bishop; but under the second (Putta) it was translated to Crediton, and, in 1550, Bishop Vesey conveyed the manor to the Russell family. Some remains of the episcopal palace are still discernible, and in the churchyard are the ruins of the deanery. This parish contains the populous village of Newport, which see.

TAWTON (NORTH), a parish in the hundred of NORTH TAWTON with WINKLEY, county of DEVON, 7 miles (N. E.) from Oakhampton, containing 1563 inhabitants. The living is a rectory, in the archdeaconry of Barnstaple, and diocese of Exeter, rated in the king's books at £32. 4. 7., and in the patronage of the Rev. George Hole. The church is dedicated to St. Peter. There is a place of worship for Independents. This place was anciently called Cheping Tawton, i. e., "a market town on the Taw," which river runs through the parish. Its market charter was confirmed in 1270, at which period it was a borough town, being still governed by a portreeve, elected annually at the manorial court. The market was discontinued about 1720, but cattle fairs are held on the third Tuesday in April, October 3rd, and December 18th. Here was once an extensive woollen manufacture, and there is still a spinning-mill. Ten children are educated for about £14. 14. a year, part of the produce of a messuage and lands, the gift of the Rev. Richard Hole, in 1783. There were formerly chapels at Crook-Burnell, Nichols-Nymet, and Bath-Barton, in this parish; the last is the birthplace of Henry de Bathe, a learned justiciary of the thirteenth century; he died in 1262. Henry Tozer, expelled from Exeter College for his loyalty, in 1648, was a native of this place; he was the author of "Directions for a Devotional Life," which passed through ten editions. In the neighbourhood, a small brook sometimes issues out of a large pit ten feet deep, and continues running for several days together, like that called Woobourne in Hertfordshire.

TAWTON (SOUTH), a parish in the hundred of WONFORD, county of DEVON, 3¼ miles (E. by S.) from Oakhampton, containing 1878 inhabitants. The living is a vicarage, in the archdeaconry and diocese of Exeter, rated in the king's books at £10, endowed with £15 per annum and £200 private benefaction, and £1400 parliamentary grant, and in the patronage of the Dean and Canons of Windsor. The church is dedicated to St. Andrew.

TAXALL, a parish in the hundred of MACCLESFIELD, county palatine of CHESTER, comprising the townships of Taxall, and Whaley with Yeardsley, and containing 662 inhabitants, of which number, 241 are in the township of Taxall, 8¼ miles (N. E. by E.) from Macclesfield. The living is a discharged rectory, in the archdeaconry and diocese of Chester, rated in the king's books at £9. 2. 6., and in the patronage of the Rev. J. Swain. The church, dedicated to St. James, has lately received an addition of two hundred and twenty-four sittings, of which two hundred and two are free, the Incorporated Society for the enlargement of churches and chapels having granted £200 towards defraying the expense. The village occupies a pleasing situation on the banks of the river Goyt, which separates it from Derbyshire.

TAYNTON, a parish in the hundred of BOTLOE, county of GLOUCESTER, 3½ miles (S. S. E.) from Newent, containing 516 inhabitants. The living is a rectory, in the archdeaconry of Hereford, and diocese of Gloucester, rated in the king's books at £9. 6. 8., and in the patronage of the Dean and Chapter of Gloucester. The church, dedicated to St. Lawrence, has lately received an addition of one hundred and sixty-one sittings, of which one hundred and thirty-seven are free, the Incorporated Society for the enlargement of churches and chapels having granted £100 towards defraying the expense. Robert Aldridge, in 1737, bequeathed a rent-charge of £2. 10. for teaching four children to read the Bible.

TAYNTON, a parish in the hundred of CHADLINGTON, county of OXFORD, 1¾ mile (N. W.) from Burford, containing 324 inhabitants. The living is a discharged vicarage, in the archdeaconry and diocese of Oxford, rated in the king's books at £7. 9. 4½., endowed with £600 royal bounty, and in the patronage of Lord Dynevor. The church is dedicated to St. John. The river Windrush runs through the parish, in which are considerable quarries of excellent freestone. Five boys

are educated by a schoolmistress, for the interest of £100, bequeathed by John Collier in 1725.

TEALBY, a parish in the southern division of the wapentake of WALSHCROFT, parts of LINDSEY, county of LINCOLN, 4½ miles (E. N. E.) from Market-Rasen, containing 755 inhabitants. The living is a discharged vicarage, in the archdeaconry and diocese of Lincoln, rated in the king's books at £6. 16. 8. G. Tennyson, Esq. was patron in 1816. The church is dedicated to All Saints. There is a place of worship for Wesleyan Methodists.

TEAN, a hamlet in the parish of CHECKLEY, southern division of the hundred of TOTMONSLOW, county of STAFFORD, 7¼ miles (N. W. by W.) from Uttoxeter. The population is returned with the parish. There is a place of worship for Calvinistic and Wesleyan Methodists. The manufacture of tape, supposed to be the most extensive in Europe, was established at Upper Tean, in 1748, at which, and in the adjoining bleaching grounds, several hundred persons find employment. The proprietors support schools for the children of their workpeople. In the neighbourhood are several fine mansions and elegant villas.

TEATH (ST.), a parish in the hundred of TRIGG, county of CORNWALL, 3 miles (S. W. by W.) from Camelford, containing 990 inhabitants. The living is a vicarage, in the archdeaconry of Cornwall, and diocese of Exeter, rated in the king's books at £12, endowed with £200 private benefaction, and £200 parliamentary grant, and in the patronage of the Bishop of Exeter. The church was formerly collegiate for two prebendaries, or portionists. There is a place of worship for Wesleyan Methodists. The parish is bounded on the west by the Bristol channel, and contains the great slate quarry of Delabole.

TEDBURN (ST. MARY), a parish in the hundred of WONFORD, county of DEVON, 4½ miles (S. W. by S.) from Crediton, containing 709 inhabitants. The living is a rectory, in the archdeaconry and diocese of Exeter, rated in the king's books at £18. 6. 3., and in the patronage of the Rev. Charles Burn. A cattle fair is held on the Monday before Michaelmas-day. At Hackworthy, in this parish, there was formerly a chapel of ease.

TEDDINGTON, a parish in the hundred of SPELTHORNE, county of MIDDLESEX, 11 miles (S. W. by W.) from London, containing 863 inhabitants. The living is a perpetual curacy, in the jurisdiction of the Commissary of London, concurrently with the Consistorial Court of the Bishop of London, and in the patronage of the Earl of Bradford. The church, dedicated to St. Mary, is principally in the later style of English architecture: it contains the remains of Sir Orlando Bridgeman, who died in 1674, and of Dr. Stephen Hall, Clerk of the Closet to the Princess of Wales, mother of George III., and fifty-one years minister of this parish, to which he was a most liberal benefactor: he died in 1761. The village stands on the western bank of the Thames, on the road from London, through Isleworth, to Hampton Court. Here are the wax bleaching grounds and candle manufactory of Messrs. Barclay, the largest and most complete establishment of the kind in the kingdom. During the summer months, nearly four acres of ground are covered with wax, of which about two hundred thousand pounds are annually bleached, and in winter formed into candles by hand. Connected with this manufactory is a very extensive one of spermaceti, chiefly carried on in Leicester-square by the same firm. Twelve girls are instructed for £20 a year, the rent of certain cottages and land purchased with £40 left by Dame Dorothy Bridgeman, and a smaller sum from the parish funds. Bushy Park, the usual country residence of William IV. and his queen Adelaide, before their accession to the throne, is partly in this parish.

TEDDINGTON, a chapelry in the parish of Overbury, middle division of the hundred of Oswaldslow, county of Worcester, 5 miles (E. by N.) from Tewkesbury, containing 146 inhabitants. The chapel is dedicated to St. Nicholas.

TEDSTONE-DELAMERE, a parish in the hundred of Broxash, county of Hereford, 4½ miles (N. E. by E.) from Bromyard, containing 246 inhabitants. The living is a discharged rectory, in the archdeaconry and diocese of Hereford, rated in the king's books at £6. 13. 4., and in the patronage of the Master and Fellows of Brasenose College, Oxford. The church is dedicated to St. James. There is a petrifying spring in the parish.

TEDSTONE-WAFER, a parish in the hundred of Broxash, county of Hereford, 3¾ miles (N. E. by N.) from Bromyard, containing 98 inhabitants. The living is a rectory, united to that of Edvin-Loach, in the archdeaconry and diocese of Hereford, rated in the king's books at £1. 10. A court leet is occasionally held here: limestone abounds in the neighbourhood.

TEETON, a hamlet in that part of the parish of Raventhorpe which is in the hundred of Nobottle-Grove, county of Northampton, 7¾ miles (N. W. by N.) from Northampton, containing 90 inhabitants.

TEFFONT-EVIAS, a parish in the hundred of Dunworth, county of Wilts, 6½ miles (W.) from Wilton, containing 147 inhabitants. The living is a rectory, in the archdeaconry and diocese of Salisbury, rated in the king's books at £8, and in the patronage of the Rev. John Thomas Mayne. The church has been lately rebuilt, on which occasion it received an addition of one hundred free sittings, the Incorporated Society for the enlargement of churches and chapels having granted £100 towards defraying the expense. The river Nadder, and a beautifully clear stream, which rises near the adjoining village of Teffont-Magna, run through the parish; the latter forms a lake, covering two acres, well stocked with trout. There is a fine freestone quarry, now being worked, besides very extensive excavations, from which the stone used in building Salisbury cathedral was taken. The manor-house, a handsome structure in the later style of English architecture, was the birthplace of Henry, Earl of Marlborough, Lord High Treasurer and Chancellor of England in the time of James II.

TEFFONT-MAGNA, a parish, forming a distinct portion of the hundred of Warminster, being locally in that of Dunworth, county of Wilts, 5¼ miles (E.) from Hindon, containing 220 inhabitants. The living is a perpetual curacy, annexed to the rectory of Dinton, in the archdeaconry and diocese of Salisbury.

TEIGH, a parish in the hundred of Alstoe, county of Rutland, 5 miles (N.) from Oakham, containing 178 inhabitants. The living is a rectory, in the archdeaconry of Northampton, and diocese of Peterborough, rated in the king's books at £14. 2. 11., and in the patronage of the Earl of Harborough. The church is dedicated to the Holy Trinity.

TEIGNMOUTH, a sea-port and market town, comprising two parishes, called East and West Teignmouth, in the hundred of Exminster, county of Devon, 15 miles (S. by E.) from Exeter, and 187¾ (W. S. W.) from London, containing 3980 inhabitants, of which number, 2514 are in West Teignmouth. This place was originally an insignificant village, and is stated to have been the first landing-place of the Danes, in 787, on being sent to reconnoitre the British coast; who, having slain the governor, were encouraged by this omen of success to pursue their warlike purpose throughout the island. The town has been twice destroyed by fire, first by a French pirate, in 1340, and subsequently, in the reign of Anne, when the French, having effected a landing, proceeded to ransack the churches, and burnt one hundred and sixteen houses, with a number of ships and small craft lying within the harbour: in commemoration of this calamitous event, one of the streets still retains the appellation of French-street. Alarmed at the threat of a similar attack, in 1744, the inhabitants obtained permission to erect a small fort on the beach of East Teignmouth, and petitioned theAdmiralty for the requisite supply of ordnance. In Camden's time the eastern town was called Teignmouth-Regis, and the other Teignmouth-Episcopi, the manor of the latter having belonged to the see of Exeter, until alienated by Bishop Vesey. The town, as its name implies, is situated on the navigable river Teign, at its influx into the ocean: it occupies a gentle declivity at the foot of a chain of hills, by which it is sheltered on the north and west, the two parts being separated by a small rivulet, called the Tame. East Teignmouth, which is the more modern, is almost entirely appropriated as a watering-place, in which respect it is considered equal, if not superior, in magnitude and fashionable repute, to any on the Devonshire coast: its situation is beautiful, and in the vicinity are prospects, particularly from Little Haldon, of great and deserved celebrity: the cliffs are of a reddish colour, and of considerable height, and at the southern side of the river's mouth is a singular elevation, called the Ness. On the strand fronting the sea are spacious carriage drives, promenades, and an extensive lawn. The public rooms, which form the centre of a crescent, comprise spacious assembly-rooms, with apartments for refreshments, cards, and billiards; the façade of the building is decorated with an Ionic portico over a Doric colonnade; this handsome edifice was lately erected by subscription. There are also a public library, bathing establishments, and a small theatre. A regatta takes place annually about the month of August. West Teignmouth is the port and principal seat of business: in this respect it had risen to some importance at an early period, having sent members to the great council for maritime affairs, and contributed seven ships, with one hundred and twenty men, towards the expedition against Calais, in 1347. The town is roughly paved, and irregularly built, and, with its quay and dock-yard, is situated on the curve formed by the sudden expansion of the river. A post-road, passing through it from Exeter to Torquay, crosses a bridge over the Teign, said to be the longest in England: it is composed of wood and iron, with a drawbridge at each end, for the passage of vessels, and was recently erected by subscription. The quay was constructed, in 1820, by G. Templar, Esq. ; and in the small dock-yard, sloops of war, and vessels of two hundred tons' burden, have been built. The harbour is safe and commodious, though somewhat difficult to enter, on account of a moveable bar, or sand bank, which shifts with the wind. In the middle of the last century, twenty ships, of from fifty to two hundred tons' burden each, were employed in the trade with Newfoundland, and some business of this description is still carried on, but it is on the decline : coal and culm are imported, and the home fishery at present occupies a considerable number of the inhabitants. By means of a rail-road and canal, which latter joins the Teign at Newton-Abbot's, and is navigable thence to the sea at Teignmouth, a communication has been effected between the granite quarries at Haytor and the clay-pits of Bovey, which greatly facilitates the exports of granite, and pipe and potters clay. A grant of a market and a fair was obtained, in the reign of Henry III., by the Dean and Chapter of Exeter, for East Teignmouth, where there is a commodious market-house, which belongs to the lord of the manor. The market is on Saturday, principally for provisions : fairs are held on the third Tuesday in January, the last Tuesday in February, and the last Tuesday in September. The government of both parishes is vested in a portreeve, who is annually elected from a jury of twelve, sworn in at the court leet and baron held by the lord of the manor ; in East Teignmouth two constables are elected by the court, and two by the parish.

The living of East Teignmouth is a perpetual curacy, in the peculiar jurisdiction of the Dean and Chapter of Exeter, endowed with £ 800 royal bounty, and in the patronage of the Vicar of Dawlish. The church, which is dedicated to St. Michael, was almost entirely rebuilt a few years since, the only part of the ancient edifice now remaining being a well-executed doorway, after the enriched Saxon model. The living of West Teignmouth is also a perpetual curacy, in the peculiar jurisdiction of the Bishop of Exeter, and in the patronage of the Vicar of Bishop's Teignton : the church, which is dedicated to St. James, is a spacious modern octagonal structure, with a tower on one of its sides, and surmounted in the centre by a lantern. There are places of worship for Baptists at East Teignmouth, and Independents and Calvinistic Methodists at West Teignmouth. In East Teignmouth, thirteen poor children are instructed from the proceeds of a joint benefaction, made in 1731, by Capts. John and Thomas Coleman. In West Teignmouth is a large school, founded by means of a benefaction from the family of Elwill, and additionally supported by subscription, in which from two hundred to three hundred children are educated on the National system. There is a poor-house in each parish. Teignmouth confers the title of baron on the family of Shore.

TEIGNTON (BISHOP'S), a parish in the hundred of EXMINSTER, county of DEVON, 1¾ mile (W. by N.) from West Teignmouth, containing 946 inhabitants. The living is a discharged vicarage, in the peculiar jurisdiction of the Bishop of Exeter, rated in the king's books at £25. 8. 10., and in the patronage of the Rev. John

Comyns. The church, dedicated to St. John the Baptist, is principally in the Norman style of architecture, with an enriched western doorway, and a low massive tower between the nave and the chancel. The river Teign forms a boundary of the parish, in which are extensive quarries of limestone, affording also compact blocks of various-coloured marble. There is a charity school, with a house for the master, founded in 1729, and endowed by Christopher Coleman and others, the money having been vested in the purchase of an estate in Bovey-Tracey, yielding £40 per annum, for teaching and clothing twenty poor children. Near the church are the remains of a palace and chapel of Bishop Grandison, and an hospital founded by that prelate for poor decayed clerks, the ruins of which are highly picturesque. There was formerly a chapel at Venn, in this parish.

TEINGRACE, a parish in the hundred of TEINGBRIDGE, county of DEVON, 2¼ miles (N. by W.) from Newton-Bushell, containing 131 inhabitants. The living is a rectory, in the archdeaconry of Totness, and diocese of Exeter, rated in the king's books at £5. 9. 4½., and in the patronage of G. Templer, Esq. The church, dedicated to St. Mary, is a handsome edifice, rebuilt in 1787, by James Templer, Esq., George Templer, Esq., and the Rev. John Templer, brothers. Among other monuments of that family, it contains one to the memory of Charles Templer, who perished in the wreck of the Halsewell East Indiaman, on the Dorsetshire coast, in 1786. The Stover canal and railway, constructed by the Templer family, facilitate the exportation of potters' clay found in the neighbourhood, and of granite from the extensive quarries near High Tor. There is a large National school, supported by subscription.

TEINGTON-DREWS, a parish in the hundred of WONFORD, county of DEVON, 4½ miles (N. N. W.) from Moreton-Hampstead, containing 1188 inhabitants. The living is a rectory, in the archdeaconry and diocese of Exeter, rated in the king's books at £40. 13. 4., and in the patronage of the Ponsford family. The church, dedicated to the Holy Trinity, is an interesting old structure, with a beautiful window of stained glass at the east end : it has lately received an addition of seventy free sittings, the Incorporated Society for the enlargement of churches and chapels having granted £40 towards defraying the expense. An almshouse was founded by Richard Eggecomb, in 1542. The name of this place is supposed to signify " the Druids' Town on the Teign," which river here pursues its rapid course through scenery of the wildest description, and is crossed by Fingal's bridge, in a romantic valley ; but the greatest curiosity is a cromleck on the Shilston estate, consisting of three supporting stones, each about six feet and a half high, with a covering stone, twelve feet long, and nine feet across the widest part. On the bank of the Teign is one of the celebrated logan, or rocking, stones, which are thought by some to be a work of design, by others of nature.

TEINGTON (KING'S), a parish in the hundred of TEINGBRIDGE, county of DEVON, 2 miles (N. E. by N.) from Newton-Bushell, containing 1131 inhabitants. The living is a vicarage, with the perpetual curacy of Highweek annexed, in the archdeaconry of Totness, and diocese of Exeter, rated in the king's books at £28. 13. 9., and in the patronage of the Prebendary of King's Teington in the Cathedral Church of Salisbury. The church is dedicated to St. Michael. There is a place of worship for Independents. The river Teign is navigable here, in the neighbourhood of which are large beds of potters' clay of an excellent quality, and a chalybeate spring. Theophilus Gale, a learned nonconformist divine, was born here, in 1628; he died in 1687.

TELLISFORD, a parish in the hundred of WEL-LOW, county of SOMERSET, 6 miles (N. N. E.) from Frome, containing 167 inhabitants. The living is a discharged rectory, in the archdeaconry of Wells, and diocese of Bath and Wells, rated in the king's books at £9. 1. 0½., and in the patronage of the Rev. C. W. Baker. The church is dedicated to All Saints. The parish is separated from Wiltshire by the river Frome, which is here crossed by a bridge. A school is endowed with the interest of £143 three per cents., by Edward Crabb, a native of this place. About a third part of the village was destroyed by fire in 1785.

TELSCOMBE, a parish in the hundred of HOLM-STROW, rape of LEWES, county of SUSSEX, 3½ miles (N. W. by W.) from Newhaven, containing 113 inhabitants. The living is a discharged rectory, in the archdeaconry of Lewes, and diocese of Chichester, rated in the king's books at £13. 13. 4., and in the patronage of John Philpot, Esq. The church, dedicated to St. Lawrence, is a small structure, principally in the Norman style. The Rev. Josiah Povey, in 1727, bequeathed land, &c., yielding about six guineas a year, for teaching poor children. Henry Smith, Esq. bequeathed an estate in this parish, called Court Farm, directing the rents to be applied for the relief of the poor of seven parishes in the north of England.

TEMPLE, a parish in the hundred of TRIGG, county of CORNWALL, 6¼ miles (N. E. by E.) from Bodmin, containing 27 inhabitants. The living is a perpetual curacy, in the peculiar jurisdiction and patronage of Sir B. Wrey, Bart., endowed with £200 royal bounty. The church is quite dilapidated. The extensive moors, which lie between Bodmin and Launceston, take their name from this parish, in which they are partly situated.

TEMPLE-BREWER, an extra-parochial liberty, in the wapentake of FLAXWELL, parts of KESTEVEN, county of LINCOLN, 6¾ miles (N. W. by N.) from Sleaford, containing 52 inhabitants. A preceptory of the Knights' Templars was founded here before 1185, which afterwards belonged to the hospitallers, and had possessions, at the dissolution, valued at £184. 6. 8., per ann.

TEMPLE-HALL, an extra-parochial liberty, in the hundred of SPARKENHOE, county of LEICESTER, 2½ miles (W. by S.) from Market-Bosworth, containing, with Willsborough, 105 inhabitants.

TEMPLE-NEWSOM, a township in the parish of WHITKIRK, lower division of the wapentake of SKY-RACK, West riding of the county of YORK, 4 miles (E. by S.) from Leeds, containing 1166 inhabitants. It is within the peculiar jurisdiction of the manorial court of Temple-Newsom. The Knights Templars had a preceptory here, which, at the suppression of their order, was granted to Sir John D'Arcy.

TEMPLE-SOWERBY, county of WESTMORLAND.— See SOWERBY (TEMPLE).

TEMPLETON, a parish in the hundred of WI-THERIDGE, county of DEVON, 5 miles (W. by N.) from Tiverton, containing 198 inhabitants. The living is a rectory, in the archdeaconry and diocese of Exeter,

rated in the king's books at £8. 15., and in the patronage of Sir W. T. Pole, Bart. The church is dedicated to St. Margaret. Mary Carwithen, in 1741, left a small sum for the education of poor children.

TEMPSFORD, a parish in the hundred of BIG-GLESWADE, county of BEDFORD, 6½ miles (N. N. W.) from Biggleswade, containing 577 inhabitants. The living is a rectory, in the archdeaconry of Bedford, and diocese of Lincoln, rated in the king's books at £24, and in the patronage of the Crown. The church is dedicated to St. Peter. There is a place of worship for Wesleyan Methodists. The village is situated on the river Ivel, which is navigable through the parish, and falls into the Ouse as it passes along the western boundary. This is a place of great antiquity; it was occupied by the Danes before 921, when they were expelled by the Saxons, but they returned in 1010, and reduced it to ashes.

TENBURY, a parish in the upper division of the hundred of DODDINGTREE, county of WORCESTER, comprising the market town of Tenbury, and the hamlets of Berrington, Sutton, and Tenbury-Foreign, and containing 1668 inhabitants, of which number, 1008 are in the town of Tenbury, 22 miles (N. W. by W.) from Worcester, and 134 (N. W. by W.) from London. The town is situated on the southern bank of the river Teme, from which it derives its name, having been originally called Temebury. It consists chiefly of three streets, leading respectively to Worcester, Bromsgrove, and Cleobury-Mortimer, partially paved, and the houses in general but indifferently built. The surrounding country is rich, and very productive of hops and apples, and great quantities of cider and perry are made, forming a principal source of trade: there is also a considerable malting trade, and a tannery. A canal, commenced in 1794, originally intended to extend from Leominster to Stourport, but not completed the whole distance, passes within half a mile of the town. The river Teme, which here separates Worcestershire from Shropshire, is crossed, at the northern entrance into the town, by a bridge of six arches. The market, granted by Henry III. in 1249, is on Tuesday; the building for the corn market is an ancient structure, but the butter-cross is more recent. Fairs are on April 22nd, May 1st, July 18th, and September 26th. Petty sessions are held once in two months, and a court leet and court baron by the lord of the manor. The living is a vicarage, with the perpetual curacy of Rochford annexed, in the archdeaconry of Salop, and diocese of Hereford, rated in the king's books at £21, and in the patronage of the Rev. George Hall. The church, dedicated to the Virgin Mary, was rebuilt in 1777, the old building having been swept away by a flood, in November 1770: it is a spacious and neat edifice, having formerly had a chantry attached to it, which was valued, at the period of the suppression, at £5. 0. 6. per annum. There is a place of worship for Particular Baptists. The National school was founded in 1816, and is supported by voluntary contributions. The principal charity arises from some houses and lands given by Mr. Philip Baylis, which having been let by the feoffees in 1767, on lease for ninety-nine years, at a rental of £7. 10. per annum, little benefit is derived from them. Races are held annually in July, on a good course about a mile south of the town.

TENBURY-FOREIGN, a hamlet in the parish of TENBURY, upper division of the hundred of DODDINGTREE, county of WORCESTER, containing 260 inhabitants.

TENDRING, a parish in the hundred of TENDRING, county of ESSEX, 6½ miles (S.S.E.) from Manningtree, containing 700 inhabitants. The living is a rectory, in the archdeaconry of Colchester, and diocese of London, rated in the king's books at £16, and in the patronage of the Master and Fellows of Balliol College, Oxford. The church is dedicated to St. Edmund. A school is supported by subscription.

Corporate Seal of Tenterden.

Obverse.   Reverse.

TENTERDEN, a market town and parish within the cinque-port liberties, having separate jurisdiction, though locally in the hundred of Tenterden, lathe of Scray, county of KENT, 18 miles (S.E. by S.) from Maidstone, and 53 (S.E. by E.) from London, containing 3259 inhabitants. This place, of which the present name appears to be a corruption of *Theinwarden*, or the ward of Thanes, that is, the guard in the valley, was one of the first places in which the woollen manufacture was established, in the reign of Edward III. It became a scene of opposition to the Church of Rome at an early period, prior to the Reformation, when, in the time of Archbishop Warham, forty-eight inhabitants of the town and its vicinity were publicly accused of heresy, and five of them condemned to be burned. The town stands upon a pleasant eminence, surrounded by some fine plantations of hops: the houses are well built and of respectable appearance. The town-hall was built in 1792, the former having been destroyed by fire, and contains a commodious room occasionally used for public assemblies. The Royal Military canal passes within six miles of the town. The market, principally for corn, is held on Friday; and there is a fair for horses, cattle, and pedlary, on the first Monday in May. The inhabitants were incorporated, by the style of "The Bayliffe and Commonaltie of the Town and Hundred of Tenterden," and the town annexed as a member to the town and port of Rye, by Henry VI.; a new charter was granted in the 42nd of Elizabeth, changing the style to "Mayor, Jurats, and Commons," according to the provisions of which the town is governed by a mayor, twelve jurats, and admitted freemen (not limited as to number), who are the commons: the mayor, who is also coroner, annually elected on the 29th of August, and the jurats, are chosen by the commons, and the latter by the mayor and jurats: a town clerk, chamberlain, and two serjeants at mace, are appointed by the corporation: the mayor and jurats hold a court of quarter sessions, with power to try for all offences, except treason, and choose a high constable and six borsholders for the town and hundred. The mayor, and two or more jurats, also hold a court of record, every fifteen days, for the recovery of debts to any amount, and for trying all pleas, its jurisdiction extending over the hundred, which includes only this parish and part of Ebony.

The living is a vicarage, in the archdeaconry and diocese of Canterbury, rated in the king's books at £33. 12. 11., and in the patronage of the Dean and Chapter of Canterbury. The church, which is dedicated to St. Mildred, is spacious and handsome, with a lofty tower at the west end, to which a beacon was formerly attached. There are places of worship for Baptists, Wesleyan Methodists, and Unitarians. At Smallhythe, in this parish, is a chapel, erected about 1509, dedicated to St. John the Baptist, and licensed by faculty from Archbishop Warham: it is repaired and maintained out of lands in this parish and that of Wittersham, vested in feoffees, and the chaplain is appointed by the inhabitants. It appears that, at the time of the erection of this chapel, the sea came up to Smallhythe, as power was then given to inter in the chapelyard the bodies of shipwrecked persons cast on shore. The free grammar school founded, at an early period, by an ancestor of the late Sir Peter Hayman, was endowed, in 1521, by William Marshall, with a rent-charge of £10, and, in 1702, by John Mantel, with the sum of £200, which was laid out in land: the present income is £58. 15. per annum, which sum is appropriated to the support of the National school, six scholars being always kept distinct, and taught the Latin tongue, on the original foundation: one hundred boys and eighty girls are instructed; and the vicar and the members of the corporation are governors; the remainder of the expense is defrayed by voluntary contributions. In 1660, Dame Jane Maynard bequeathed land for apprenticing children and the maintenance of poor widows. Hoole, the translator of Tasso, resided at this place. Tenterden confers the title of baron on the family of Abbot; Sir Charles Abbot, Lord Chief Justice of the Court of King's Bench, having been raised to the peerage by that title, on the 30th of April, 1827.

TENTERGATE, a joint township with Scriven, in that part of the parish of KNARESBOROUGH which is in the lower division of the wapentake of CLARO, West riding of the county of YORK. The population is returned with Scriven.

TERLING, a parish in the hundred of WITHAM, county of ESSEX, 3¾ miles (W.) from Witham, containing 781 inhabitants. The living is a discharged vicarage, in the archdeaconry of Colchester, and diocese of London, rated in the king's books at £10, and in the patronage of J. Strutt, Esq. The church is dedicated to All Saints. There is a place of worship for Wesleyan Methodists. Benjamin Jocelyne, in 1775, bequeathed an annuity of £10 for teaching ten poor boys. In 1269, the Bishop of Norwich had a palace and park here, which was subsequently the residence of Henry VIII. Its chapel possessed the privilege of sanctuary, and as such afforded shelter to the celebrated Hubert de Burgh, when he had fallen under the indignation of Henry III. On making a new road through the grounds, in 1824, about three hundred gold and silver coins were turned up, and, upon further search, a jar was discovered, containing two large rings, and thirty small pieces of gold, with some silver coins of twelve Roman emperors, as bright as if just taken from the mint, and in regular succession, beginning with Constantius, and ending with Honorius. Terling is at no great distance from the ancient Roman stations at Colchester, Maldon, and Pleshy.

TERRINGTON, a parish partly within the liberty of St. Peter of York, East riding, but chiefly in the wapentake of Bulmer, North riding, of the county of York, comprising the townships of Ganthorpe, and Terrington with Wigginthorpe, and containing 723 inhabitants, of which number, 617 are in the township of Terrington with Wigginthorpe, 8 miles (W. by S.) from New Malton. The living is a rectory, in the archdeaconry of Cleveland, and diocese of York, rated in the king's books at £23. 18. 6½., and in the patronage of the Rev. Dr. Waddilove. The church is dedicated to All Saints. There is a place of worship for Wesleyan Methodists.

TERRINGTON (ST. CLEMENT'S), a parish in the Marshland division of the hundred of Freebridge, county of Norfolk, 5½ miles (W. by N.) from Lynn-Regis, containing 1408 inhabitants. The living is a vicarage, with that of Terrington St. John's, in the archdeaconry and diocese of Norwich, rated jointly in the king's books at £23. 6. 8., and in the patronage of the Crown : the rectory is annexed to the Margaret Professorship in the University of Cambridge. The church is a handsome cruciform structure, in the later style of English architecture, having on the battlements of the south aisle many shields with different armorial bearings. Here was also a chapel, dedicated to St. James. There is a place of worship for Wesleyan Methodists. Though not noticed in Domesday-book, Terrington was an extensive place, and had considerable salt-works in the time of the Saxons, as appears from a grant by Godric, brother to Ednoth, abbot of Ramsey, about 970.

TERRINGTON (ST. JOHN'S), a parish in the Marshland division of the hundred of Freebridge, county of Norfolk, 6 miles (W. S. W.) from Lynn-Regis, containing 583 inhabitants. The living is a vicarage, united to that of Terrington St. Clement's, in the archdeaconry and diocese of Norwich : the rectory is, with that of St. Clement's, annexed to the Margaret Professorship in the University of Cambridge. The church is a regular pile of building, having, at its south-west angle, a square tower crowned with pinnacles.

TESTERTON, a parish in the hundred of Gallow, county of Norfolk, 2¾ miles (S. E. by S.) from Fakenham, containing 31 inhabitants. The living is a discharged rectory, in the archdeaconry and diocese of Norwich, rated in the king's books at £5, and in the patronage of P. M. Case, Esq. The church, which was dedicated to St. Remigius, has been destroyed.

TESTON, a parish in the hundred of Twyford, lathe of Aylesford, county of Kent, 4 miles (W. by S.) from Maidstone, containing 259 inhabitants. The living is a discharged vicarage, in the archdeaconry and diocese of Rochester, rated in the king's books at £6. 10. Mrs. Bouverie was patroness in 1820. The church, dedicated to St. Peter and St. Paul, is a remarkably small

structure. It stands on the banks of the Medway, over which there is a fine bridge of seven arches. A court leet is occasionally held here.

TETBURY, a market town and parish in the hundred of Longtree, county of Gloucester, 20 miles (S. by E.) from Gloucester, and 99 (W. by N.) from London, containing 2734 inhabitants. The town is pleasantly situated on an eminence at the southern verge of the county, bordering on Wiltshire, and near the source of the river Avon, over which is a long bridge or causeway, leading into the main road to Malmesbury : it consists principally of a long street, crossed at right angles by two shorter ones, with a spacious market-house near one of the intersections. An act was obtained, in 1817, for paving and lighting the town, the expense of which was defrayed out of the funds in the hands of trustees appointed in 1814, under the act "for enclosing certain common fields and waste grounds within the parish :" £1000 was also appropriated from the same fund for the repair of the market house. The poor are chiefly employed by wool staplers, and the market was formerly noted for the sale of woollen yarn, but the introduction of machinery has put an end to the trade. The market is on Wednesday ; and fairs are held on Ash-Wednesday, the Wednesday before and after the 5th of April, and July 22nd for corn, cheese, horses, and cattle. A bailiff and a constable are elected annually at the court leet of the feoffees of the manor. Petty sessions for the town and hundred are held here and at Horsley and Rodborough alternately.

The living is a vicarage, in the archdeaconry and diocese of Gloucester, rated in the king's books at £36. 13. 4., and in the patronage of the Trustees of Tetbury charity. The church, which is dedicated to St. Mary, was rebuilt in 1781, in the early style of English architecture, at an expense of £6000, exclusively of the old tower, which is surmounted by a fine modern spire, the ancient church having been undermined by a flood, in 1770 : the nave is separated from the aisles by ornamented clustered pillars, which literally support nothing, the principle on which the roof of the theatre at Oxford was constructed has been applied to this building. There are places of worship for Baptists and Independents. A grammar school was endowed by Sir William Romney, a native of this town, and alderman and sheriff of London, in the reign of James I., who bequeathed to certain trustees a lease for years of the weights of wool and yarn, tolls, and other profits within the town, with the proceeds of which lands have since been purchased, and out of the rents £40 per annum was paid to the master; but since the year 1800 no payments have been made, and the affairs of the institution are under investigation : there is a small bequest for books, which is withheld until the school shall be re-established. Fifteen boys are educated for a rent-charge of £30, devised for that purpose by Elizabeth Hodges, in 1723. The Sunday school, open to all the poor children of the parish, is supported by bequests of £100 each from Ann Wright, in 1788, Sarah Paul, in 1795, and Ann Gastrell, in 1797. An almshouse for eight poor persons was founded and endowed by the above-mentioned Sir W. Romney. In Maudlin meadow, which belongs to Magdalene College, Oxford, and is situated north of the town, is a petrifying spring, impregnated with calcareous earth. Races were formerly held annually on a common, about a mile eastward from the town, but they have been discontinued, and the lands enclosed. A castle is said to have been built here, long before the invasion of Britain by the Romans; and ancient British coins and fragments of weapons have been found within the area of a camp in the vicinity, of which all traces are now obliterated. Roman coins of the Lower Empire have also been discovered.

TETCHWORTH, a hamlet in the parish of LUD-GERSHALL, hundred of ASHENDON, county of BUCK-INGHAM, 10 miles (W. N. W.) from Aylesbury. The population is returned with the parish.

TETCOTT, a parish in the hundred of BLACK TOR-RINGTON, county of DEVON, 5 miles (S. by W.) from Holsworthy, containing 256 inhabitants. The living is a discharged rectory, in the archdeaconry of Totness, and diocese of Exeter, rated in the king's books at £13. 16. 8., and in the patronage of Sir W. Molesworth, Bart. The church is dedicated to the Holy Cross.

TETFORD, a parish in the hundred of HILL, parts of LINDSEY, county of LINCOLN, 6 miles (N. E. by E.) from Horncastle, containing 531 inhabitants. The living is a discharged rectory, in the archdeaconry and diocese of Lincoln, rated in the king's books at £5. 0. 10. Miss Harrison was patroness in 1820. The church, dedicated to St. Mary, has lately received an addition of one hundred and ten sittings, of which sixty are free, the Incorporated Society for the enlargement of churches and chapels having granted £40 towards defraying the expense. There is a place of worship for Wesleyan Methodists.

TETNEY, a parish in the wapentake of BRADLEY-HAVERSTOE, parts of LINDSEY, county of LINCOLN, 10½ miles (N.) from Louth, containing 622 inhabitants. The living is a discharged vicarage, in the archdeaconry and diocese of Lincoln, rated in the king's books at £7. 18. 4., endowed with £200 royal bounty, and in the patronage of the Bishop of Lincoln. The church is dedicated to St. Peter and St. Paul. There is a place of worship for Wesleyan Methodists.

TETSWORTH, a parish in the hundred of THAME, county of OXFORD, 11½ miles (E. S. E.) from Oxford, containing 495 inhabitants. The living is a perpetual curacy, annexed to the vicarage of Thame, in the peculiar jurisdiction of the Dean and Chapter of Lincoln. The church is dedicated to St. Giles. There is a place of worship for Wesleyan Methodists.

TETTENHALL-REGIS, a parish comprising the hamlets of Oaken, Pirton with Trescott, and Tettenhall-Clericorum, in the northern, and the township of Pendeford, and the hamlet of Wrottesley, in the southern, division of the hundred of SEISDON, county of STAF-FORD, 1¾ mile (N. W.) from Wolverhampton, and containing 2478 inhabitants. The living is a perpetual curacy, in the jurisdiction of the royal peculiar court of Tettenhall, endowed with £210 private benefaction, and £200 royal bounty, and in the patronage of Sir J. Wrottesley, Bart. The church, dedicated to St. Michael, is partly in the early, decorated, and later styles of English architecture. It was made collegiate before the Conquest for a dean and four prebendaries, and has lately received an addition of three hundred and seventy-two sittings, of which two hundred are free, the Incorporated Society for the enlargement of churches and chapels having granted £300. towards defraying the

expense. There is a place of worship for Wesleyan Methodists. The Worcestershire and Staffordshire canal passes through the parish, in which there is a considerable manufacture of locks.

TETTON, a township in the parish of WARMING-TON, hundred of NORTHWICH, county palatine of CHES-TER, 3 miles (W. N. W.) from Sandbach, containing 170 inhabitants. The Grand Trunk canal passes the parish.

TETWORTH, a joint parish with Everton, in the hundred of TOSELAND, county of HUNTINGDON, 3 miles (N. by W.) from Potton, containing, exclusively of Everton, 180 inhabitants. See EVERTON.

TEVERSALL, a parish in the northern division of the hundred of BROXTOW, county of NOTTINGHAM, 5¼ miles (W. by N.) from Mansfield, containing 414 inhabitants. The living is a rectory, in the archdeaconry of Nottingham, and diocese of York, rated in the king's books at £9. 19. 2., and in the patronage of Miss Henrietta Howard Molyneux. The church, dedicated to St. Catherine, is principally in the Norman style, and contains several old monuments of the Grenhalghe, Molyneux, and Babington families. South of it are the extensive ruins of the ancient mansion-house built by Gilbert Grenhalghe, in the reign of Henry VII., and the remains of a hanging garden, on a very magnificent scale. Coal and limestone abound in the parish, but neither are now worked.

TEVERSHAM, a parish in the hundred of FLEN-DISH, county of CAMBRIDGE, 3½ miles (E.) from Cambridge, containing 155 inhabitants. The living is a rectory, in the peculiar jurisdiction and patronage of the Bishop of Ely, rated in the king's books at £19. 16. 0½. The church is dedicated to All Saints.

TEW (GREAT), a parish in the hundred of WOOT-TON, county of OXFORD, 3¾ miles (N. N. E.) from Neat-Enstone, containing, with the chapelry of Little Tew, 760 inhabitants. The living is a vicarage, in the archdeaconry and diocese of Oxford, rated in the king's books at £6. 13. 4., endowed with £200 private benefaction, and £400 royal bounty, and in the patronage of G. F. Stratton, Esq. The church, dedicated to St. Michael, has lately received an addition of three hundred and nine sittings, of which two hundred and fifty-seven are free, the Incorporated Society for the enlargement of churches and chapels having granted £200 towards defraying the expense. Thomas Edwards Freeman, in 1781, gave an annuity of £12 for the education of ten children of each sex.

TEW (LITTLE), a chapelry in the parish of GREAT TEW, hundred of WOOTTON, county of OXFORD, 2½ miles (N. by E.) from Neat-Enstone, containing 229 inhabitants.

TEWIN, a parish in the hundred and county of HERTFORD, 3 miles (E. S. E.) from Welwyn, containing 477 inhabitants. The living is a rectory, in the archdeaconry of Huntingdon, and diocese of Lincoln, rated in the king's books at £14, and in the patronage of the Master and Fellows of Jesus' College, Cambridge. The church, dedicated to St. Peter, has a square embattled tower, with a low spire. The Rev. Henry Yarborough, in 1783, bequeathed the rents and profits of four tenements, to be applied for teaching ten children, and increasing the parish clerk's income; and Lady Cathcart, in the same year, gave an annuity of £5 in further support of the school. There are sundry other bequests for the relief of the poor, and apprenticing children.

Seal and Arms.

TEWKESBURY, a borough, market town, and parish, having separate jurisdiction, locally in the lower division of the hundred of Tewkesbury, county of GLOUCESTER, 10 miles (N. N. E.) from Gloucester, and 103 (W. N. W.) from London, containing, according to the last census, 4962 inhabitants, which number has since considerably increased. This place, which is of great antiquity, is supposed to have derived its name from *Theot*, a Saxon recluse, who, during the latter period of the Octarchy, founded a hermitage here, where he lived in solitude and devotion, and from whom it was called *Theotisberg*, from which its present appellation is deduced. In 715, a monastery was founded here by the two brothers Odo and Dodo, Dukes of Mercia, and dedicated to the Blessed Virgin Mary, which, after having experienced great injury during the Danish wars, became a cell to the abbey of Cranborne in Dorsetshire. After the Conquest, Robert Fitz-Haimon, who attended William in his expedition to Britain, enlarged the buildings of this monastery, and so amply augmented its possessions, that the monks of Cranborne removed, in 1101, to Tewkesbury, which they made the principal seat of their establishment: it subsequently was raised into an abbey of Benedictine monks, and continued to flourish till the dissolution, at which time its revenue was estimated at £1598. 1. 3. The last decisive battle between the Yorkists and the Lancastrians took place within half a mile of this town, in 1471; on this memorable occasion, many of the principal nobility were slain on both sides, and not less than three thousand of the Lancastrian troops. Queen Margaret, who headed her own forces, was intrenched on the summit of an eminence, called the Home Ground, at the distance of a mile from the town, on the east side of the road to Gloucester; and the troops of Edward IV., who advanced against his opponents by way of Tredington, occupied the sloping ground to the south, called the Red Piece: the victory was decisive in favour of the Yorkists, the defeat of the Lancastrians having been ascribed to the treacherous inactivity of Lord Wenlock, or of their generals, whom the chief commander, the Duke of Somerset, struck dead on the field with his battle axe. After their defeat, the Duke of Somerset, with about twenty other distinguished persons, took shelter in the church, from which they were dragged with violence, and immediately beheaded. At the commencement of the great civil war in the reign of Charles I., Tewkesbury was occupied by the parliamentarians, who were afterwards driven out, and the town was taken by the royalists, by whom it was again lost and retaken, till, in 1644, it was surprised and captured by Col. Massie, governor of Gloucester, for the parliamentarians, in whose possession it remained till the conclusion of the war.

The town is pleasantly situated in the northern part of the luxuriant vale of Gloucester, and on the eastern bank of the river Avon, near its confluence with the Severn: it is nearly surrounded by the small rivers Carron, over which is a new stone bridge, and Swilgate, which is crossed by two, both these streams falling into the Avon. It is handsome and well built, consisting of three principal streets, well paved, and is amply supplied with water: the houses are in general of brick, but occasionally interspersed with specimens of the ancient timber and brick buildings. Considerable improvements have taken place, under the provisions of an act obtained in 1786, among which may be noticed the ranges of building, erected in 1810, to the east of the High-street, on a tract of land called Oldbury, and the recent formation of a new street. An elegant cast-iron bridge has been lately constructed over the river Severn, near the hamlet of Mythe, within half a mile of the town, at an expense of £36,000, subscribed on shares of £100 each, opening a direct communication between London and Hereford: it consists of one noble arch, one hundred and seventy-two feet in span, with a light iron balustrade, and was opened to the public in 1826. Near the division of the Worcester and Pershore roads is an ancient bridge of several arches over the Avon, from which a level causeway has been raised, extending to the iron bridge. A subscription library, with a news-room, was established in 1828, and is well supported: it contains at present more than one thousand volumes. A small theatre has been recently fitted up, which is occasionally opened by the Cheltenham company. The races, established in 1825, take place annually on the Ham, a large meadow near the town; and assemblies are held at the town hall.

About the beginning of the fifteenth century this place seems to have carried on a considerable trade upon the Severn; and a petition was forwarded to the House of Peers, in the 8th of Henry VI., stating that the inhabitants had been accustomed "to ship all manner of merchandise down the Severn to Bristol," and complaining of the disorderly conduct of the people of the forest of Dean, who are reported "to have come with great riot and strength, in manner of war, as enemies of a strange country, to stop and plunder their ships as they passed by the coasts near the forest; and that the marauders sometimes not only despoiled them of their merchandise, but destroyed their vessels, and even cast overboard their crews, and drowned them." For the redress of these grievances an act was passed in the same year, and, in 1580, Queen Elizabeth made Tewkesbury an independent port, for the loading and discharging of ships with merchandise to and from the parts beyond the seas, which grant was afterwards revoked, on a petition from the inhabitants of Bristol. Tewkesbury formerly enjoyed a considerable trade in woollen cloth, and was celebrated for the manufacture of mustard of superior quality: the principal branch of trade at present is the stocking frame-work knitting, which was introduced about the commencement of the eighteenth century, and in which from seven to eight hundred frames are at work, employing about one thousand five hundred persons. The manufacture of cotton-thread lace, was established at Oldbury in 1825, and is in a flourishing state; a considerable trade is carried on in malt, and some in leather, and there is a large manufactory for nails: an extensive distillery and a rectifying establishment were opened in 1770; the former has been abandoned, but the latter is still conducted on an advantageous scale. A very considerable carrying trade centres here, in connexion with the Avon and the Severn, goods being conveyed by land and water to all parts of the kingdom : on the bank of the Avon are extensive corn-mills, formerly belonging to the abbey. The market days are Wednesday and Saturday; the former for corn, sheep, and pigs; the latter for poultry and provisions. The fairs are on the second Monday in March, the second Wednesday in April, May 14th, the first Wednesday after September 4th, and October 10th, for cattle, leather, and pedlary; fairs were also held in June and December, but they have been recently discontinued : statute fairs are held on the Wednesday before, and the Wednesday after, Old Michaelmas-day, and there are great cattle markets on the second Wednesday in June, August, and December. The market-house, erected by a company, to whom the corporation have mortgaged the tolls for ninety-nine years, is a handsome building, with Doric columns and pilasters, supporting a pediment in front.

Tewkesbury, though a borough by prescription, was first incorporated by Elizabeth, in 1574; whose charter was confirmed by James I., in the 3rd year of his reign, and when that monarch sold the manor to the corporation, in 1609, he granted a new charter, with extended privileges; which being lost, or destroyed, during the parliamentary war, an exemplification of it was obtained under the great seal in the reign of Charles II.: this was surrendered, in 1685, to James II., who, in the following year, incorporated the inhabitants, under the title of "Mayor, Aldermen, and Common Council-men;" but the functions of the municipal body having ceased in 1692, the town remained without a corporation till 1698, when William III. granted the present charter. The government, under this last charter, is vested in two bailiffs, a high steward, recorder, twenty-four principal burgesses, or common council-men, and twenty-four assistants, with a town clerk, who is also clerk of the peace, a coroner, chamberlain, serjeants at mace, and subordinate officers. The bailiffs, who are elected annually, and the high steward and recorder, who hold their offices for life, are appointed from among the principal burgesses, the latter, as vacancies occur, being chosen from the assistants. The bailiffs, with four principal burgesses, appointed annually on the second Thursday in October, are justices of the peace within the borough. There were formerly several trading companies incorporated under the charter, but the only one now in existence is that of Cordwainers. The freedom of the borough is acquired by birth, servitude to a resident freeman, and by gift of the corporation. The eldest son of a freeman, born after his father's admission, is entitled to the freedom on his father's decease, but if the son die first, the right does not devolve upon any other. The bailiffs and justices hold quarterly courts of session, for all offences within the borough not capital; the bailiffs and recorder hold a court of record, every Friday, for the recovery of debts not exceeding £50; and the corporation, as lords of the manor, hold a court leet, the jurisdiction of which extends over all the parishes in the hundred of Tewkesbury. The town hall, in which the courts are held, and the public business of the corporation is transacted, is a handsome building, erected in 1788, by Sir William Codrington, Bart., at an expense of £1200; the lower part is appropriated to

the use of the courts, and the upper part contains a hall for the meetings of the corporation, and an assembly-room. The common gaol, house of correction, and penitentiary for the borough, was built in 1816, at the northern extremity of the High-street, at an expense of £3419. 11. 7½., raised by a rate on the inhabitants, and was subsequently considerably enlarged and improved : it contains four wards for the classification of prisoners, and is under the superintendence of the bailiffs and justices of the peace for the borough, and of two visiting magistrates. The county magistrates hold here a petty session for the division every alternate Wednesday. The borough first received the elective franchise in the 7th of James I., since which time it has continued to return two members to parliament: the right of election is vested in the freemen generally, and in all proprietors of freehold houses within the ancient limits of the borough, of whom the number is about six hundred : the bailiffs are the returning officers.

The living is a vicarage, in the archdeaconry and diocese of Gloucester, endowed with £400 private benefaction, and £600 royal bounty, and in the patronage of the Crown. The church, dedicated to St. Mary, situated at the south-western part of the town, and formerly the collegiate church of the ancient monastery, is a spacious and venerable cruciform structure, principally in the Norman style of architecture, with a noble and richly-ornamented tower rising from the centre, and supported on four massive lofty piers with circular arches. The nave and choir, which latter was repaired in 1796, at an expense of £2000, are separated from the aisles by a noble range of cylindrical columns and circular arches, highly enriched with mouldings and other ornaments peculiar to the Norman style; the former is lighted by a range of clerestory windows in the later style, inserted in the Norman arches of the triforium, and the latter by an elegant range of windows in the decorated style, with rich tracery, and embellished with considerable portions of ancient stained glass; the windows of the aisles and transepts are of the decorated and the later styles, and the large west window of the later style is inserted in a very lofty Norman arch of great depth, with shafts and mouldings richly ornamented; the roof is finely groined, and embellished, at the intersections of the ribs, with figures of angels playing on musical instruments : the east end of the choir is hexagonal, and contains several beautiful chantry chapels, in the decorated style of English architecture: the Lady chapel and the cloisters have been destroyed, but the arches which led to them may be traced on the outside of the building, and on the north side are the remains of the chapter-house, now used for a school. The church contains a fine series of monuments, from the earliest period of the decorated, to the latest period of the later, style of English architecture, among which are several to the early patrons of the abbey, and to those who fell in the battle of Tewkesbury. In a light and elegant chapel on the north side of the choir, erected by Abbot Parker, in 1397, is the tomb of Robert Fitz-Haimon, the founder, who was killed at Falaise in Normandy, in 1107, and whose remains, after having been interred in the chapter-house, were removed into the church, in 1241 : an altar-tomb, enclosed with arches surmounted by an embattled cornice, on which are the figures of a knight and his lady, is supposed to have been erected for Hugh le Despenser and his wife Elizabeth, daughter of William Montacute, Earl of Salisbury. Near this is a beautiful sepulchral chapel, built by Isabel, Countess of Warwick, for her first husband, Richard Beauchamp, Earl of Worcester, who was killed at the siege of Meaux, in 1421 : it is profusely ornamented, and the roof, which is richly embellished with tracery, was supported on six pillars of blue marble, of which only two are remaining. Among the modern monuments is one, by Flaxman, to Anne, wife of Sir S. Clarke, Bart., of finely executed sculpture. Five hundred additional sittings, of which three hundred are free, have lately been made to the church, at an expense of £200, by grant of the Incorporated Society for the enlargement of churches and chapels. There are places of worship for Baptists, the Society of Friends, Independents, and Wesleyan Methodists, all which have Sunday schools annexed.

The free grammar school was founded in 1576, and endowed with £20 per annum, by Mr. Ferrers, payable out of the manor of Skillingthorpe, in the county of Lincoln, also with lands purchased with money left by Sir Dudley Digges, and with some chief rents ; it is under the superintendence of the bailiffs, justices, chamberlain, and town clerk of the corporation, by whom the master is appointed : the room appropriated to it is supposed to have been the chapter-house of the abbey. The Blue-coat school is endowed with one-twelfth part of the rents of a farm in Kent, devised for charitable uses by Lady Capel, in 1721, and with £2. 10. per annum given by Mr. Thomas Merret, in 1724, being further supported by subscription : forty boys are clothed and instructed in it. The National school, under the superintendence of the same master, was established in 1813, and a building for its use, and also for that of the Blue-coat school, was erected adjoining the churchyard, in 1817, the two establishments having been incorporated, at an expense of £1345. 8. 3¼. A Lancasterian school was established in 1813, for which a building had been previously erected, at the cost of more than £600, raised by contribution ; the ground was given by N. Hartland, a member of the Society of Friends : these schools are supported by subscription. In the churchyard are some unendowed almshouses for ten poor widows. A dispensary, established in 1815 ; a lying-in charity, in 1805 ; and a society for the distribution of blankets among the poor, in 1817, are supported by subscription; and there are various charitable bequests for distribution among the poor. Near the entrance into the town from Gloucester is the house of industry, a large brick building well adapted for the purpose. Of the monastic buildings, with the exception of the church, there are few remains : the principal is the gateway of the ancient monastery, which appears to have been erected in the fifteenth century ; it is surmounted with an embattled parapet rising above the cornice, from which are projecting figures, and below it is a canopied niche between two square-headed windows. Roman coins have been frequently dug up in the vicinity, and, in 1828, several were found near the abbey church. At Walton, near the town, is a mineral spring, the water of which resembles that at Cheltenham. The hamlet of Mythe, remarkable for the beauty of its situation,

is on the north-west side of the town, near the confluence of the Severn and the Avon. On the south-west side is a tumulus, from which the descent to the Severn is precipitous and abrupt. George III. visited this spot in 1788, since which time it has obtained the name of Royal Hill : in the immediate vicinity are some handsome seats. Southwick, another hamlet, situated, as its name implies, to the south of the town, is mentioned in the Norman survey, under the name Sudwick, as containing three hides of land. Alan of Tewkesbury, a monk of the abbey, the friend and biographer of Thomas à Becket ; and Estcourt, the celebrated dramatist, who was contemporary with Steele and Addison, were natives of this town. Tewkesbury gave the title of baron to George I., previously to his accession to the throne, which at present is extinct.

TEY (GREAT), a parish in the Witham division of the hundred of LEXDEN, county of ESSEX, 4 miles (N.E. by E.) from Great Coggeshall, containing 625 inhabitants. The living is a discharged vicarage, in the archdeaconry of Colchester, and diocese of London, rated in the king's books at £7, endowed with £200 private benefaction, and £200 royal bounty, and in the patronage of the Rector. The rectory is a sinecure, rated at £18, and in the patronage of G. B. Tyndale, Esq. The church, dedicated to St. Barnabas, exhibits in the interior some columns of the Tuscan order, and has a large square tower rising from the centre.

TEY (LITTLE), a parish in the Witham division of the hundred of LEXDEN, county of ESSEX, 2¾ miles (E. by N.) from Great Coggeshall, containing 49 inhabitants. The living is a discharged rectory, in the archdeaconry of Colchester, and diocese of London, rated in the king's books at £4, and in the patronage of the Bishop of London. The church is dedicated to St. James.

TEY (MARKS), a parish in the Witham division of the hundred of LEXDEN, county of ESSEX, 4 miles (E. by N.) from Great Coggeshall, containing 351 inhabitants. The living is a vicarage not in charge, in the archdeaconry of Colchester, and diocese of London, and in the patronage of the Master and Fellows of Balliol College, Oxford. The church is dedicated to All Saints.

TEYNHAM, a parish in the hundred of TEYNHAM, lathe of SCRAY, county of KENT, 4¼ miles (E.) from Sittingbourne, containing 600 inhabitants. The living is a vicarage, in the archdeaconry and diocese of Canterbury, rated in the king's books at £10, and in the patronage of the Archdeacon of Canterbury. The church, dedicated to St. Mary, is a handsome cruciform structure, principally in the early style of English architecture ; it contains many brasses and other ancient memorials, and the windows exhibit fragments of old stained glass. An accession has lately been made to the parish by the embankment of the island of Fowley. Conyer creek, an inlet of the sea, is terminated by a quay, to which vessels of two hundred and fifty tons burden come up and discharge their cargoes of coal, for the supply of the inhabitants, taking in the produce of the neighbourhood, for the London and other markets. The parish abounds with cherry orchards, and there are a few plantations of hops. Here are vestiges of a Roman encampment, and the ruins of a palace formerly belonging to the Archbishops of Canterbury.

Teynham confers the title of baron on the family of Curzon.

THAKEHAM, a parish in the hundred of EAST EASWRITH, rape of BRAMBER, county of SUSSEX, 6½ miles (N. W.) from Steyning, containing, with the house of industry for six other parishes, 603 inhabitants. The living is a rectory, in the archdeaconry and diocese of Chichester, rated in the king's books at £14. 9. 9½., and in the patronage of the Duke of Norfolk. The church, dedicated to St. Mary, is partly in the early, and partly in the later, style of English architecture.

THAME, a market town and parish in the hundred of THAME, county of OXFORD, 13 miles (E.) from Oxford, and 44½ (N. W. by W.) from London, comprising the townships of Old Thame, New Thame, and Priest-end (which constitute the town), and North Weston, Moreton, and Thame Park, containing 2479 inhabitants. This town is evidently of Roman origin, and is first mentioned, as a place of some importance, at the commencement of the tenth century, when Wulfhere, King of Mercia, granted a charter, dated " in the vill called Thames :" in the year 970, Osketyl, Archbishop of York, died here. It suffered much from the Danish invasions, particularly in 1010, during which period a fortification was erected. At the Conquest it belonged to the Bishop of Lincoln, and formed part of the extensive possessions of the succeeding prelates, in this county, till the reign of Edward VI.: among the many benefits conferred on the town by them was the diverting through it the road which passed on its side. In 1138, a monastery for Cistercian monks was founded at Thame Park, in honour of the Virgin Mary, the revenue of which at the dissolution was valued at £256. 13. 7.: the site is occupied by a modern mansion. About the reign of Edward IV., an hospital for destitute persons was founded and endowed with lands by Richard Quartermaine, a member of an ancient family of high repute. In the civil war of the sixteenth century, Thame was the centre of military operations, and experienced much consequent distress: during the late contest with France, it became one of the depôts for prisoners of war. The town is situated on a gentle declivity on the bank of the river Tame, whence its name is derived, and which empties itself into the Thames at Dorchester, in this county: it consists principally of one long and spacious street, with a commodious market-place in the centre, over which is the town hall, an indifferent building. A little lace is made, but the poor are chiefly employed in husbandry. The market, which is of great antiquity, is on Tuesday, and is well supplied with corn and cattle. Fairs are held on Easter-Tuesday, the Tuesday before Whit-Sunday, the first Tuesday in August, and a statute fair on the 11th of October.

The living, anciently a prebend in the Cathedral Church of Lincoln, valued in the king's books at £82. 12. 3½., but impropriated and dissolved in 1547, is now a discharged vicarage, with the perpetual curacies of Sydenham, Tetsworth, and Towersey annexed, in the peculiar jurisdiction of the Dean and Chapter of Lincoln, rated in the king's books at £18, and in the patronage of Walter Long, Esq. The church, which is dedicated to St. Mary, is a large and handsome cruciform structure, in the early English style of architecture, with an embattled tower rising from the intersec-tion, and supported on four massive pillars: the interior is divided by columns and pointed arches, and is entered by a stone porch with an elegant canopied niche, in which was formerly a statue of the tutelar saint: in the chancel is a tomb of white marble, with an effigy, to the memory of Lord Williams, who, in 1558, bequeathed estates for the foundation of a free grammar school, erected by his executors, in 1574, near the church, and the maintenance of a master and an usher: the Warden and Fellows of New College, Oxford, are trustees, and are empowered to nominate the master, who must be a clergyman and a graduate of one of the Universities, subject to the approbation of the Earl of Abingdon, as heir of the founder: the school is open to all boys of the parish. Dr. Fell; Justice Sir George Crook; Pocock, the learned orientalist; King, Bishop of Chichester; and Anthony à Wood, the antiquary, were educated in this school. A free school was established by bequests from the second Earl of Abingdon and others, the income amounting to £35 annually, in which twenty-five boys are instructed. There are several small annuities for apprenticing poor boys, and other benefactions, amounting to £100 per annum for the poor. An almshouse for five poor men and one woman was also founded and endowed by Lord Williams, upon the dissolved foundation of Richard Quartermaine. A little to the north of the church are the remains of the prebendal house, consisting of nearly three sides of a quadrangle: the refectory is still visible, among other rooms, and the chapel is also preserved; but, though evidently of considerable grandeur formerly, the whole now only serves as farm-buildings. George Hetheridge, an eminent Hebraist and Grecian in the reign of Elizabeth, and Regius Professor of Greek at Corpus Christi College, Oxford; and Lord Chief Justice Holt; were natives of this town.

THANINGTON, a parish in the hundred of WESTGATE, lathe of St. AUGUSTINE, county of KENT, 1¼ mile (S. W. by W.) from Canterbury, containing, with the hamlet of Milton, 374 inhabitants. The living is a perpetual curacy, in the archdeaconry and diocese of Canterbury, endowed with £200 private benefaction, and £200 royal bounty, and in the patronage of the Archbishop of Canterbury. The church is dedicated to St. Nicholas. The ancient road, called Stane-street, passes through the parish.

THARSTON, a parish in the hundred of DEPWADE, county of NORFOLK, 1½ mile (N. W.) from St. Mary Stratton, containing 369 inhabitants. The living is a discharged vicarage, in the archdeaconry of Norfolk, and diocese of Norwich, rated in the king's books at £5. 1. 8., and in the patronage of the Bishop of Ely. The church is dedicated to St. Mary.

THATCHAM, a parish partly in the hundred of FAIRCROSS, but chiefly in that of READING, county of BERKS, 3 miles (E.) from Newbury, containing, with the chapelries of Greenham and Midgham, 3677 inhabitants. This place, according to the Norman survey, appears to have been once a town of some importance; tradition has assigned to it the rank of a borough, but there is no proof that it ever sent representatives to parliament. A market, on Sunday, was confirmed, by charter of Henry II., to the abbot, or monks, of Reading, then possessors of Thatcham, which was subsequently changed to Thursday, in 1218, by Henry III.; but it has long been discontinued : the remains of the butter-cross still exist. The town is pleasantly situated near the navigable river Kennet, on the Bath road : the inhabitants are well supplied with water. The Kennet and Avon canal passes a little to the southward. The chief source of employment is a manufactory for galloons and black ribands ; and there is a paper-mill at Colthropt. A statute fair is held on the first Tuesday after October 12th.

The living is a vicarage, in the archdeaconry of Berks, and diocese of Salisbury, rated in the king's books at £20, and in the patronage of William Hanbury, Esq. The church, which is dedicated to St. Luke, has some portions in the early, and some in the later, style of English architecture : at the south entrance is a fine Norman arch, and in the interior are, an altar-tomb to the memory of William Danvers, Chief Justice of the Court of Common Pleas ; and a mural monument to Nicholas Fuller, Esq., barrister of Gray's Inn. There is a place of worship for Independents. A free school was founded, in 1707, by Lady Frances Winchcomb, who gave, by deed to trustees, a rent-charge of £53 per annum, for the education of thirty poor boys of the parishes of Thatcham, Bucklebury, and Little Shefford, and apprenticing some of them. It was opened about the year 1713, but continued only for a few years, in consequence of the attainder of Lord Bolingbroke, who was the owner of the estate charged, and also the only surviving trustee of the school, &c., the affairs of the charity subsequently came under the direction of the court of Chancery. In 1741, arrears were recovered sufficient to purchase £1406. 9. 7., old South Sea annuities, since which period the funds have continued to increase, the amount of stock being now upwards of £5000, exclusively of the rent-charge of £53, which is regularly received. The school was re-opened in June 1794, under the regulations of the decree of the court of Chancery, and forty boys are educated, upon the Madras system, and clothed, five or six of them being annually apprenticed, with a premium of £10 : those who are not apprenticed receive a small gratuity, on leaving the school, to fit them for service. The school-house was originally a decayed chapel, purchased by Lady Winchcomb for the purpose. A National school, erected in 1826, in which fifty boys and ninety girls are instructed, and an infant school, are supported by subscription. There is an almshouse for nine widows, founded by means of bequests from the Rev. Mr. Herdsman and John Hunt, besides various minor charitable benefactions.

THAXTED, a parish in the hundred of DUNMOW, county of ESSEX, 19 miles (N. N. W.) from Chelmsford, containing 2045 inhabitants. This village, which is of considerable antiquity, is situated on the river Chelmar, on the main road from Chelmsford to Cambridge. Fairs are held on the Monday before Whit-Monday, and August 10th. The living is a vicarage, in the jurisdiction of the Commissary of Essex and Herts, concurrently with the Consistorial Court of the Bishop of London, rated in the king's books at £24, and in the patronage of Lord Viscount Maynard, whose ancestor gave £2000 in augmentation of the vicarage. The church, which is dedicated to St. Mary, is a spacious embattled structure, supported by buttresses terminating in canopied niches, in the later style of English architecture, and with a tower and crocketed spire one hundred and eighty-three feet high, the exact length of the church ; the south porch is much enriched. There are places of worship for Baptists, the Society of Friends, and Independents. A free grammar school for the instruction of thirty boys was founded by Thomas Yardley. Some Roman coins, and a beautiful amphora, were discovered in this parish some years ago.

THEAKSTONE, a township in the parish of BURNESTON, wapentake of HALLIKELD, North riding of the county of YORK, 3¼ miles (S. E. by E.) from Bedale, containing 87 inhabitants.

THEALE, a chapelry in the parish of TILEHURST, hundred of READING, county of BERKS, 4¼ miles (W. by S.) from Reading. The population is returned with the parish. The chapel is a beautiful structure, in the later style of English architecture, recently erected, at the expense of Mrs. Sophia Sheppard. The Rev. Thomas Sheppard, D.D., gave £20 a year for establishing a school on the Madras system.

THEARNE, a township in that part of the parish of ST. JOHN, BEVERLEY, which is within the liberties of the borough of BEVERLEY, East riding of the county of YORK, 3¾ miles (S. E. by E.) from Beverley, containing 90 inhabitants.

THEBERTON, a parish in the hundred of BLYTHING, county of SUFFOLK, 4 miles (N. E. by E.) from Saxmundham, containing 557 inhabitants. The living is a discharged rectory, in the archdeaconry of Suffolk, and diocese of Norwich, rated in the king's books at £26. 13. 4., and in the patronage of the Crown. The church is dedicated to St. Peter. The parish is bounded on the east by the North Sea. There are the ruins of an ancient castle upon the coast.

THEDDINGWORTH, a parish partly in the hundred of ROTHWELL, county of NORTHAMPTON, but chiefly in the hundred of GARTREE, county of LEICESTER, 4½ miles (W. by S.) from Market-Harborough, containing, with the hamlet of Hothorpe, 264 inhabitants. The living is a discharged vicarage, in the archdeaconry of Leicester, and diocese of Lincoln, rated in the king's books at £8. 15. 7. John Cook, Esq. and others were patrons in 1810. The church is dedicated to All Saints. The Grand Union canal passes through the parish.

THEDDLETHORPE (ALL SAINTS'), a parish in the Marsh division of the hundred of CALCEWORTH, parts of LINDSEY, county of LINCOLN, 10½ miles (N. N. E.) from Alford, containing 211 inhabitants. The living is a vicarage, in the archdeaconry and diocese of Lincoln, rated in the king's books at £7. 5. 2½., endowed with £400 private benefaction, £800 royal bounty, and £600 parliamentary grant, and in the patronage of Joseph Alcock, Esq.

THEDDLETHORPE (ST. HELEN'S), a parish in the Marsh division of the hundred of CALCEWORTH, parts of LINDSEY, county of LINCOLN, 9¾ miles (N. by E.) from Alford, containing 239 inhabitants. The living is a rectory, with that of Mablethorpe St. Peter united, in the archdeaconry and diocese of Lincoln, rated in the king's books at £18. 10. 2½., and in the patronage of Lord Gwydyr. There is a place of worship for Wesleyan Methodists.

THELBRIDGE, a parish in the hundred of WITHERIDGE, county of DEVON, 7¼ miles (E. by S.)

from Chulmleigh, containing 168 inhabitants. The living is a rectory, in the archdeaconry of Barnstaple, and diocese of Exeter, rated in the king's books at £10. 6. 5½., and in the patronage of Mr. and Mrs. Daubney. The church is dedicated to St. David. Four children are educated for the interest of £40, bequeathed by Penelope Sydenham.

THELNETHAM, a parish in the hundred of BLACKBOURN, county of SUFFOLK, 3½ miles (N. W.) from Botesdale, containing 512 inhabitants. The living is a discharged rectory, in the archdeaconry of Sudbury, and diocese of Norwich, rated in the king's books at £16. 18. 4. Dover Colby, Esq. was patron in 1816. The church is dedicated to St. Nicholas.

THELVETON, a parish in the hundred of DISS, county of NORFOLK, 1¾ mile (N.) from Scole, containing 162 inhabitants. The living is a discharged rectory, in the archdeaconry of Norfolk, and diocese of Norwich, rated in the king's books at £9, and in the patronage of the Crown. The church is dedicated to St. Andrew.

THELWALL, a chapelry in the parish of RUNCORN, hundred of BUCKLOW, county palatine of CHESTER, 3½ miles (E. S. E.) from Warrington, containing 327 inhabitants. The living is a perpetual curacy, in the archdeaconry and diocese of Chester, endowed with £400 private benefaction, £1000 royal bounty, and £300 parliamentary grant, and in the patronage of T. A. Pickering, Esq. The chapel has lately received an addition of two hundred and forty sittings, of which one hundred and twenty are free, the Incorporated Society for the enlargement of churches and chapels having granted £120 towards defraying the expense. The Duke of Bridgewater's canal passes through the parish, and the river Mersey forms its northern boundary, on the south bank of which river are some gunpowder mills. Thelwall was formerly a considerable town, though now but an obscure village.

THEMELTHORPE, a parish in the hundred of EYNSFORD, county of NORFOLK, 1¾ mile (E. by S.) from Foulsham, containing 109 inhabitants. The living is a discharged rectory, annexed to that of Bintree, in the archdeaconry of Norfolk, and diocese of Norwich, rated in the king's books at £4. 2. 8½. The church is dedicated to St. Andrew.

THENFORD, a parish in the hundred of KING'S SUTTON, county of NORTHAMPTON, 5½ miles (N. W. by W.) from Brackley, containing 234 inhabitants. The living is a discharged rectory, in the archdeaconry of Northampton, and diocese of Peterborough, rated in the king's books at £10, and in the patronage of the Crown. The church is dedicated to St. Mary. A court baron is occasionally held here. There is a mineral spring in the parish.

THERFIELD, a parish in the hundred of ODSEY, county of HERTFORD, 2½ miles (S. W. by S.) from Royston, containing 872 inhabitants. The living is a rectory, in the archdeaconry of Huntingdon, and diocese of Lincoln, rated in the king's books at £50, and in the patronage of the Dean and Chapter of St. Paul's, London. The church is dedicated to St. Mary.

THETFORD, a chapelry in the parish of STRETHAM, southern division of the hundred of WITCHFORD, Isle of ELY, county of CAMBRIDGE, 2¼ miles (S. by W.) from Ely, containing 229 inhabitants. The chapel is dedicated to St. George.

THETFORD, a borough and market town, possessing exclusive jurisdiction, though locally in the hundred of Shropham, county of NORFOLK, but partly in the hundred of LACKFORD, county of SUFFOLK, 30 miles (S. W.) from Norwich, and 80 (N. N. E.) from London, containing, according to the last census, 2922 inhabitants, which number has since increased to 3500.

Arms.

This ancient place, called *Theodford* by the Saxons, evidently derives its name from the river Thet, which, having united its stream with the Lesser Ouse at this spot, the latter passes through the town, separates the two counties, and is navigable hence to Lynn. The majority of antiquaries consider it to be the site of the celebrated *Sitomagus* of the Romans, who possessed it in 435, and it is known to have been the metropolis of East Anglia; on which account, and from its proximity to the North Sea, it was frequently, during the Octarchy, desolated by the Danes, who, having retained possession of the town for fifty years, totally destroyed it by fire in the ninth century. In 1004, it sustained a similar calamity from their king, Sweyn, who had invaded East Anglia; and in 1010, it became for the third time the scene of plunder and conflagration by these marauders, into whose hands it again fell, after a signal victory which they had obtained over the Saxons. In the reign of Canute, Thetford began to recover from the effects of these repeated calamities, and, in that of Edward the Confessor, had nearly regained its former prosperity, containing not less than nine hundred and forty-seven burgesses, who enjoyed divers privileges. In the time of the Conqueror, the episcopal see of North Elmham was transferred hither, and hence to Norwich, by Herbert de Losinga, in the following reign; but Henry VIII. made it the seat of a bishop suffragan to Norwich, which it continued during his reign. From the time of Athelstan to that of John here was a mint, in which coins of Edmund and Canute were struck. The ancient extent and importance of this town may be gathered from the fact that, in the reign of Edward III., it comprised twenty-four principal streets, five market-places, twenty churches, six hospitals, eight monasteries, and other religious and charitable foundations, of all which there are comparatively but few remains. Thetford has been honoured with the presence and temporary residence of several British sovereigns, particularly Henry I., Henry II., and Elizabeth, who rebuilt the ancient mansion of the Earls of Warren, on its lapse to the crown, and occasionally resided in it, as did also James I., for the purpose of hunting; and it is still called the King's House.

The town, which has of late been much improved, comprises five principal streets, which are partly paved, and is connected with the few remaining houses on the Suffolk side by a handsome iron bridge over the Ouse, erected in 1829: the modern buildings are plain and neat, and the inhabitants are well supplied with water from wells and springs. Assemblies are occasionally held, a small theatre is open during the Lent assizes, and there is a subscription library. In addition to a very extensive paper-mill, there are, a large iron-foundry, an agricultural machine manufactory, three good breweries; and several malting establishments. The navigation of the river, in its course to Lynn, having been lately improved between this place and Brandon, a brisk business is carried on in corn, wool, coal, and other articles. The market is on Saturday; the market-house is a neat and commodious building, covered with cast-iron, with a portico and palisades in front. Fairs are held May 14th, August 2nd, and August 16th, for sheep; September 25th, for cattle; and there is a wool fair in July.

The charter of incorporation, granted by Elizabeth, in 1573, was surrendered to the crown in the 34th of Charles II., and a very imperfect one obtained in its stead, which, in 1692, was annulled, and the original charter restored, by a decree in Chancery: the municipal body consists of a mayor, recorder, ten aldermen, and twenty common councilmen, assisted by a town clerk, sword-bearer, serjeant at mace, and inferior officers. The mayor is clerk of the market, and, in the year after his mayoralty, acts as coroner; the mayor, coroner, and recorder, are justices of the peace, with exclusive jurisdiction, within the borough, and hold quarter sessions: there is also a court of requests for the recovery of debts to the amount of £50. The county assizes for the Norfolk circuit have been held here, in Lent, ever since the year 1234. The guildhall is a fine old building, erected at the expense of Sir Joseph Williamson, Knt., Secretary of State to Charles II., in which the assizes are held. The gaol is a plain edifice of flint and white brick, commodiously arranged, and capable of holding one hundred prisoners: on these buildings many thousand pounds have been expended by the inhabitants. This borough sends two members to parliament: the right of election is vested exclusively in the corporation; the mayor is the returning officer.

Thetford comprises the parishes of St. Cuthbert, St. Peter, and St. Mary the Less, all in the archdeaconry and diocese of Norwich, and in the patronage of the Duke of Norfolk. The living of St. Cuthbert's is a discharged rectory, with that of the Holy Trinity united, endowed with £200 royal bounty, and £1400 parliamentary grant: the church has a square embattled tower. The living of St. Peter's is a discharged rectory, with that of St. Nicholas' united, rated in the king's books at £5. 1. 5½., and endowed with £200 private benefaction, and £200 royal bounty: the church is commonly called the black church, being constructed chiefly of flint; the tower and part of the body of the church were rebuilt in 1789. The living of the parish of St. Mary the Less is a perpetual curacy, rated in the king's books at £1. 13. 6½., endowed with £200 private benefaction, and £200 royal bounty: the church, which stands in the county of Suffolk, has a square tower. There were formerly many more parishes in this town, the churches of which have all been demolished. There

Corporate Seal

are places of worship for the Society of Friends, Independents, Wesleyan Methodists, and Roman Catholics. A free grammar school, and an hospital for two poor men and two poor women, were founded, in the reign of James I., under the will of Sir Richard Fulmerston, who died in 1566, having bequeathed property for the erection of a free school, and other buildings, with adequate salaries for the master and usher, and remuneration to a clergyman for the performance of certain prescribed duties; it was therefore decreed, by act of parliament, that this should be a free grammar school and hospital for ever, and that the master, usher, and the four poor people, should be incorporated, under the title of "The Master and Fellows of the School and Hospital at Thetford." A National school, in which about one hundred and fifty children are educated, is supported by subscription. Almshouses for six poor men were erected, in 1680, at the expense of William Harbord, Esq., and endowed with £30 per annum for a limited term, which expired about twenty years since, after having been renewed; the inmates participate in the proceeds of a bequest of £30 per annum, left in 1679, by his father, Sir Charles Harbord, Knt., Surveyor-General to Charles I. A certain number of boys and girls, children of the inhabitants, are apprenticed from a fund of £2000, bequeathed by Sir J. Williamson: of this charity, the mayor and corporation appoint the trustees. In 1818, Mr. P. Sterne, of this place, bequeathed £1000 for the benefit of the poor: there are several minor charitable benefactions.

The relics of antiquity consist chiefly of fragments of the nunnery, founded in the reign of Canute, by Urius, the first abbot of Bury St. Edmund's; some of the walls, buttresses, and windows, with a fine arch and cell, are still visible, the conventual church having been converted into a barn, and a farm-house built with the other ruinous portions. Of the priory, or abbey, founded on the brink of the river, in 1104, by Roger Bigod, for Cluniac monks, which, at the dissolution, was valued at £418. 16. 3., the gateway, constructed with freestone and black flint, and parts of the church, alone remain. Of the monastery of St. Sepulchre, founded in 1109, by the Earl of Warren, and additionally endowed by Henry II., the church has been converted into a barn; and the site of St. Augustine's friary, founded in 1387, by John of Gaunt, for mendicants of that order, still bears the name of Friars' Close: of the rest, no certain traces can be distinguished. At the eastern extremity of the town are remains of an ancient Danish fortification, which consisted of a large keep and double rampart, erected on an artificial mount, called Castle Hill, of which the height is one hundred feet, and the circumference of the summit eighty-one feet, and of the base nine hundred and eighty-four; the remains of the ramparts are twenty feet high, and the surrounding fosse seventy feet wide: it is somewhat singular, that no trace of any steps, or path, by which military stores could be conveyed up the very steep ascent to the fortress, is visible. Among the various fossils found in the vicinity is a perfect nautilus, which has been deposited in the British Museum. A mineral spring, the properties of which are similar to those of Tonbridge, was discovered here, about eighty years ago, by Matthew Manning, Esq. M.D., and about that time much resorted to: it was afterwards shut up for many years, but in 1819 was re-opened, and

the waters having been again analysed by the celebrated operative chemist, F. Accum, were found very effectual in strengthening the stomach and alimentary canal. A handsome pump-room was then erected, to which hot and cold baths are attached, the first stone having been laid by the Duke of Grafton: it is situated near the river side, and is approached by pleasant sheltered walks. Thomas Martin, F.A.S., and author of the "History of Thetford," was born here, in 1696, and educated at the free school, of which his father was master, and also rector of the parish of St. Mary. The notorious Thomas Paine, author of the "Age of Reason," "Rights of Man," &c., was also born at a house in White Hart-street, and educated at the school.

THICKLEY (EAST), a township in that part of the parish of St. ANDREW AUCKLAND which is in the north-western division of DARLINGTON ward, county palatine of DURHAM, 4¼ miles (S. E.) from Bishop-Auckland, containing 11 inhabitants. The Stockton and Darlington railway passes in the vicinity.

THIMBLEBY, a parish in the soke of HORNCASTLE, parts of LINDSEY, county of LINCOLN, 1¼ mile (W. by N.) from Horncastle, containing 384 inhabitants. The living is a discharged rectory, in the archdeaconry and diocese of Lincoln, rated in the king's books at £13.10.10., and in the patronage of John Hotchkin, Esq. The church is dedicated to St. Margaret.

THIMBLEBY, a township in the parish of OSMOTHERLEY, wapentake of ALLERTONSHIRE, North riding of the county of YORK, 5½ miles (E. N. E.) from North Allerton, containing 200 inhabitants, of whom many are employed in the manufacture of worsted. Four children are instructed for about £2 per annum, arising from the rent of certain land bequeathed by Elizabeth Bolton, in 1725.

THINGWELL, a township in the parish of WOODCHURCH, lower division of the hundred of WIRRALL, county palatine of CHESTER, 5½ miles (N. by W.) from Great Neston, containing 78 inhabitants.

THIRKLEBY, a township in the parish of KIRBY-GRINDALYTH, wapentake of BUCKROSE, East riding of the county of YORK, 10 miles (E. by S.) from New Malton, containing 44 inhabitants.

THIRKLEBY, a parish in the wapentake of BIRDFORTH, North riding of the county of YORK, 4 miles (S. E. by E.) from Thirsk, containing 293 inhabitants. The living is a discharged vicarage, in the archdeaconry of Cleveland, and diocese of York, rated in the king's books at £6, and in the patronage of the Archbishop of York. The church, dedicated to All Saints, was rebuilt, in 1722, by Sir Thomas Frankland, Bart.

THIRLBY, a township in that part of the parish of FELIX-KIRK which is in the wapentake of BIRDFORTH, North riding of the county of YORK, 5 miles (E. N. E.) from Thirsk, containing 167 inhabitants.

THIRLWALL, a township in the parish of HALTWHISTLE, western division of TINDALE ward, county of NORTHUMBERLAND, 4 miles (W. N. W.) from Haltwhistle, containing 293 inhabitants. The ancient mansion of Wardrew, situated on the eastern side of the river Irthing, has been handsomely fitted up, to accommodate visitors who resort to the adjacent spa of Gilsland. On the western bank of the Tippal bourn, which is here crossed by the great Roman wall, are the ruins of the once strong castle of Thirlwall, occupying the summit of a rocky precipice. The walls of this fortress were nine feet thick, vaulted within, and defended by an outer wall of great strength.

THIRN, a township in the parish of THORNTON-WATLASS, eastern division of the wapentake of HANG, North riding of the county of YORK, 4 miles (S. W. by W.) from Bedale, containing 126 inhabitants.

THIRNE, a parish in the western division of the hundred of FLEGG, county of NORFOLK, 4½ miles (N. by E.) from Acle, containing 133 inhabitants. The living is a rectory, annexed to that of Ashby and Oby, in the archdeaconry and diocese of Norwich, rated in the king's books at £5.

THIRNTOFT, a township in the parish of AINDERBY-STEEPLE, eastern division of the wapentake of GILLING, North riding of the county of YORK, 3¼ miles (W. by S.) from North Allerton, containing 165 inhabitants.

THIRSK, a parish partly within the liberty of ST. PETER of YORK, East riding, but chiefly in the wapentake of BIRDFORTH, North riding, of the county of YORK, comprising the borough and market town of Thirsk, and the chapelries of Carlton-Islebeck, or Miniot, Sand-Hutton, and Sowerby, and containing 3502 inhabitants, of which number, 2533 are in the borough of Thirsk, 23 miles (N. W. by N.) from York, and 223 (N. N. W.) from London. The conjectural derivation of the name of this place is from *Tre Isk*, two ancient British words, signifying a town and river, or brook. A strong and extensive castle was erected here, about 979, by the ancient family of Mowbray, on which Roger de Mowbray, in the time of Henry II., having become a confederate of the King of Scotland, erected his standard against his lawful sovereign: on the suppression of that revolt, this fortress, with many others, was entirely demolished, by order of the king. In the reign of Henry VII., during a popular commotion, Henry Percy, Earl of Northumberland, and lieutenant of this county, is said to have been put to death here, beneath a very ancient elm-tree, which formerly grew on Elm Green. The town is situated on the road from York to Edinburgh, nearly in the centre of the vale of Mowbray, a tract of country remarkable for the fertility of its soil, and the picturesque beauty and richness of its scenery: it consists of the Old and the New towns, which are separated by a small stream, called Cod-beck, over which are two substantial stone bridges. A neat gravel walk across the fields leads to the adjacent village of Sowerby; it commands a fine prospect of the surrounding country, terminated by the Hambleton hills, and is the favourite promenade of the inhabitants. At the south-western extremity of the town, the moat and rampart, together with some subterranean vaults, and the site of the court-yard of the castle, still exist. Within the precincts of this ancient fortress New Thirsk is situated, with its spacious and commodious market-place in the centre. The Old Town, which alone is included within the limits of the borough, is on the north-east side of the stream, and consists of a long range of cottages on each side of the turnpike road leading from York to Yarm and Stockton, and two squares surrounded by similar buildings, one called St. James' Green, where the cattle fairs are held, the other formerly comprising an ancient church, dedicated to St. James, of which there are no vestiges.

This place is called Elm Green, from the ancient elm that formerly grew there, beneath which the members of parliament for the borough were usually elected. A small quantity of coarse linen and sacking is manufactured. Coal, which is partly brought from the county of Durham, in small carts containing from eighteen to twenty-two bushels each, is sold at a very high price, although the supply has been somewhat increased by the extension of the Darlington railway to Croft Bridge, twenty-one miles distant. The market is on Monday, and is a large one for provisions, of which great quantities purchased here are carried for sale to Leeds and other places. Fairs are held on Shrove-Monday and April 4th and 5th, for cattle, sheep, leather, &c.; Easter-Monday and Whit-Monday, for woollen cloth, toys, &c.; and August 4th and 5th, October 28th and 29th, and the first Tuesday after December 11th, for cattle, sheep, and leather. The municipal regulations of the town are vested in a bailiff, chosen by the burgage-holders, and sworn in before the steward of the lord of the manor, who holds a court leet annually at Michaelmas, for that and other purposes. Old Thirsk is a borough by prescription, and first sent members to parliament in the 23rd of Edward I., but made no other return till the last parliament of Edward VI.: the elective franchise is vested in the burgage-holders, in number about fifty: the bailiff is the returning officer, and the influence of Sir Robert Frankland, Bart., is predominant.

The living is a perpetual curacy, in the archdeaconry of Cleveland, and diocese of York, endowed with £1600 parliamentary grant, and in the patronage of the Archbishop of York. The church, which is dedicated to St. Mary, and situated at the northern extremity of the New Town, is a spacious and handsome structure, in the later style of English architecture, with a lofty embattled tower at the west end, and is supposed to have been constructed from the ruins of the castle. There are places of worship for the Society of Friends, Independents, and Wesleyan Methodists. In 1769, Jane Day bequeathed £100 for the instruction of poor children. There is a school-house under the chancel of the church for instruction in English grammar, writing, and arithmetic. In the town is also a school of industry, for clothing and educating poor girls. A dispensary, supported by voluntary contributions, has recently been established.

THIRTLEBY, a township in that part of the parish of SWINE which is in the middle division of the wapentake of HOLDERNESS, East riding of the county of YORK, 6 miles (N. E.) from Kingston upon Hull, containing 61 inhabitants.

THISTLETON, a joint township with Greenhalgh, in the parish of KIRKHAM, hundred of AMOUNDERNESS, county palatine of LANCASTER, 4¼ miles (N. N. W.) from Kirkham. The population is returned with Greenhalgh.

THISTLETON, a parish in the hundred of ALSTOE, county of RUTLAND, 8 miles (N. N. E.) from Oakham, containing 181 inhabitants. The living is a rectory, in the archdeaconry of Northampton, and diocese of Peterborough, rated in the king's books at £3. 11. 0½., and in the patronage of G. Fludyer, Esq. The church is dedicated to St. Nicholas. The Rev. Henry Foster, in 1692, bequeathed land, producing upwards of £10 per annum, in support of a school.

THIXENDALE, a township in the parish of WHARRAM-PERCY, wapentake of BUCKROSE, East riding of the county of YORK, 8¾ miles (S. S. E.) from New Malton, containing 184 inhabitants.

THOCKRINGTON, a parish in the north-eastern division of TINDALE ward, county of NORTHUMBERLAND, comprising the townships of Little Bavington, Cary-Coats, Sweethope, and Thockrington, and containing 201 inhabitants, of which number, 48 are in the township of Thockrington, 11¼ miles (N. by E.) from Hexham. The living is a perpetual curacy, in the peculiar jurisdiction and patronage of the Prebendary of Thockrington in the Cathedral Church of York, endowed with £200 private benefaction, and £400 royal bounty.

THOLTHORP, a township in the parish of ALNE, partly within the liberty of ST. PETER of York, East riding, and partly in the wapentake of BULMER, North riding, of the county of YORK, 4½ miles (S. W.) from Easingwould, containing 238 inhabitants.

THOMAS (ST.) the APOSTLE, a parish adjoining the borough of Launceston, in the northern division of the hundred of EAST, county of CORNWALL, containing, with the extra-parochial liberty of St. Thomas Street, 608 inhabitants. The living is a perpetual curacy, in the archdeaconry of Cornwall, and diocese of Exeter.

THOMAS (ST.) the APOSTLE, a parish in the hundred of WONFORD, county of DEVON, ½ a mile (S. by W.) from Exeter, containing, with the chapelry of Oldridge, 3245 inhabitants. The living is a vicarage, in the archdeaconry and diocese of Exeter, rated in the king's books at £11. 2. 8½., and in the patronage of James Buller, Esq. The parish is bounded on the east by the river Exe, from which the Exeter canal passes to the southward. Twenty-four children are educated for an annuity of £10, bequeathed by William Gould, and four for £1. 10. a year, the gift of Robert Pate. A small priory of Black canons, a cell to that of Plympton, founded in the time of Henry III., in honour of the Blessed Virgin, stood partly in this parish, and partly in that of Alphington.

THOMAS (ST.) STREET, an extra-parochial liberty, locally in the parish of ST. THOMAS the APOSTLE, northern division of the hundred of EAST, county of CORNWALL, containing 301 inhabitants.

THOMAS-CLOSE, a township in the parish of HUTTON in the FOREST, LEATH ward, county of CUMBERLAND, 8¾ miles (N. W. by N.) from Penrith, containing 95 inhabitants.

THOMPSON, a parish in the hundred of WAYLAND, county of NORFOLK, 3 miles (S. S. E.) from Watton, containing 427 inhabitants. The living is a perpetual curacy, in the archdeaconry and diocese of Norwich, endowed with £800 royal bounty. Mrs. M. S. Hethersett was patroness in 1816. The church is dedicated to St. Martin. Sir Thomas de Shardelow, Knt., and his brother, about 1349, founded in it, in honour of the Blessed Virgin and All Saints, a chantry, or college, for a master and five chaplains, whose revenue, at the dissolution, was valued at £52. 15. 7.

THOMPSON'S-WALL, a joint township with Couldsnouth, in the parish of KIRKNEWTON, western division of GLENDALE ward, county of NORTHUMBERLAND, 8½ miles (W. by N.) from Wooler, containing 44 inhabitants.

THOMSON, a parish in the hundred of Coombs-Ditch, Blandford (North) division of the county of Dorset, 7 miles (S. by E.) from Blandford-Forum, containing 43 inhabitants. The living is a discharged rectory, annexed to that of Anderston, in the peculiar jurisdiction of the Dean of Salisbury, rated in the king's books at £4. 8. 9. The church, dedicated to St. Andrew, is a small brick building without a tower, circular at the east end: it was wholly rebuilt and pewed by Archbishop Wake.

THONG (NETHER), a township in the parish of Almondbury, upper division of the wapentake of Ag-brigg, West riding of the county of York, 5¼ miles (S. by W.) from Huddersfield, containing 927 inhabitants, of whom many are employed in the manufacture of woollen cloth.

THONG (UPPER), a township in the parish of Almondbury, upper division of the wapentake of Ag-brigg, West riding of the county of York, 6¼ miles (S. S. W.) from Huddersfield, containing 1437 inhabitants. There is a place of worship for Wesleyan Methodists. The manufacture of woollen goods is here carried on to a considerable extent.

THORALBY, a township in the parish of Aysgarth, western division of the wapentake of Hang, North riding of the county of York, 8½ miles (W. by S.) from Middleham, containing 342 inhabitants. Four children are instructed for about £8 a year, arising from the rent of certain lands bequeathed by Elizabeth Whithay, in 1748.

THORESBY (NORTH), a parish in the wapentake of Bradley-Haverstoe, parts of Lindsey, county of Lincoln, 8½ miles (N. by W.) from Louth, containing 484 inhabitants. The living is a rectory, in the arch-deaconry and diocese of Lincoln, rated in the king's books at £24. 10. 10., and in the patronage of Richard Bassett, Esq. The church is dedicated to St. Helen. There is a place of worship for Wesleyan Methodists. Dr. Robert Mapletoft, in 1676, bequeathed land, pro-ducing upwards of £20 per annum, for teaching poor children.

THORESBY (SOUTH), a parish in the Marsh division of the hundred of Calceworth, parts of Lindsey, county of Lincoln, 4 miles (W. by N.) from Alford, containing 149 inhabitants. The living is a discharged rectory, in the archdeaconry and diocese of Lincoln, rated in the king's books at £6. 3. 6½., and in the patronage of the King, as Duke of Lancaster. The church is dedicated to St. Andrew.

THORESTHORPE, a hamlet in the parish of Saleby, Wold division of the hundred of Calceworth, parts of Lindsey, county of Lincoln, ¾ of a mile (N. N. E.) from Alford. The population is returned with the parish.

THORESWAY, a parish in the southern division of the wapentake of Walshcroft, parts of Lindsey, county of Lincoln, 5 miles (S. E.) from Caistor, con-taining 116 inhabitants. The living is a discharged rec-tory, in the archdeaconry and diocese of Lincoln, rated in the king's books at £8. 10. 10., and in the patron-age of the Crown. The church is dedicated to St. Mary.

THORGANBY, a parish in the southern division of the wapentake of Walshcroft, parts of Lindsey, county of Lincoln, 6¼ miles (E. S. E.) from Caistor,

containing 102 inhabitants. The living is a discharged rectory, held by sequestration, in the archdeaconry and diocese of Lincoln, rated in the king's books at £6. 0. 10., and endowed with £800 royal bounty. The church is dedicated to All Saints.

THORGANBY, a parish in the wapentake of Ouze and Derwent, East riding of the county of York, 8½ miles (N. E. by N.) from Selby, containing, with the township of West Cottingwith, 381 inhabitants. The living is a perpetual curacy, in the archdeaconry of Cleveland, and diocese of York, endowed with £200 royal bounty, and £200 parliamentary grant, and in the patronage of Mrs. Baldwin. The church is dedi-cated to St. Elen. There is a place of worship for Wesleyan Methodists. Thomas Dunnington, in 1733, gave a school-house, with a residence for the master, and an annuity of £2 towards his support; which, with the annual sums of £2 by Robert Blythe, £2 by Thomas Bradford, and £10. 10. by Robert Jefferson, is paid for teaching twenty children.

THORINGTON, a parish in the hundred of Blyth-ing, county of Suffolk, 4 miles (S. E.) from Hales-worth, containing 158 inhabitants. The living is a dis-charged rectory, in the archdeaconry of Suffolk, and diocese of Norwich, rated in the king's books at £7, endowed with £200 royal bounty, and in the patronage of H. B. Bence, Esq. The church is dedicated to St. Peter.

THORLEY, a parish in the hundred of Braughin, county of Hertford, 2½ miles (S. S. W.) from Bishop's Stortford, containing 386 inhabitants. The living is a rectory, in the archdeaconry of Middlesex, and diocese of London, rated in the king's books at £16. 13. 4., and in the patronage of the Bishop of London. The church, dedicated to St. James, has an embattled tower, surmounted by a lofty spire at the west end, and a Nor-man doorway on the south.

THORLEY, a parish in the liberty of West Medina, Isle of Wight division of the county of Southampton, 1 mile (E. S. E.) from Yarmouth, containing 132 inha-bitants. The living is a discharged vicarage, in the archdeaconry and diocese of Winchester, rated in the king's books at £6. 18. 9. The Rev. Dr. Walker and Edward Roberts, Esq. were patrons in 1802. The church, dedicated to St. Mary, has a belfry over the porch, but no tower.

THORMANBY, a parish in the wapentake of Bul-mer, North riding of the county of York, 4¼ miles (N. W. by N.) from Easingwould, containing 118 inhabit-ants. The living is a discharged rectory, in the arch-deaconry of Cleveland, and diocese of York, rated in the king's books at £8. 2. 11., endowed with £200 private benefaction, and £200 royal bounty, and in the patronage of Lord Viscount Downe. The church is dedicated to St. Mary.

THORN (ST. MARGARET), a parish in the hun-dred of Milverton, county of Somerset, 3 miles (W.) from Wellington, containing 145 inhabitants. The living is a perpetual curacy, in the archdeaconry of Taunton, and diocese of Bath and Wells, endowed with £400 private benefaction, and £600 royal bounty, and in the patronage of the Archdeacon of Taunton.

THORN-COFFIN, a parish in the hundred of Tin-tinhull, county of Somerset, 2½ miles (N. W. by W.) from Yeovil, containing 97 inhabitants. The living is a discharged rectory, in the archdeaconry of Wells, and diocese of Bath and Wells, rated in the king's books at £5. 5. 2½., endowed with £600 private benefaction, £200 royal bounty, and £600 parliamentary grant, and in the patronage of J. Jolly, Esq. The church is dedicated to St. Andrew.

THORN-GUMBALD, a chapelry in the parish of PAUL, southern division of the wapentake of HOLDERNESS, East riding of the county of YORK, 2 miles (S.E.) from Hedon, containing 259 inhabitants. There is a place of worship for Independents.

THORNABY, a chapelry in the parish of STAINTON, western division of the liberty of LANGBAURGH, North riding of the county of YORK, 1¾ mile (S. S. E.) from Stockton upon Tees, containing 197 inhabitants. The living is a perpetual curacy, united to the vicarage of Stainton, in the archdeaconry of Cleveland, and diocese of York.

THORNAGE, a parish in the hundred of HOLT, county of NORFOLK, 2¾ miles (S.W. by W.) from Holt, containing 264 inhabitants. The living is a rectory, with that of Brinton annexed, in the archdeaconry and diocese of Norwich, rated in the king's books at £6. 18. 4., and in the patronage of Sir J. D. Astley, Bart.

THORNBOROUGH, a parish in the hundred and county of BUCKINGHAM, 3½ miles (E.) from Buckingham, containing 572 inhabitants. The living is a discharged vicarage, in the archdeaconry of Buckingham, and diocese of Lincoln, rated in the king's books at £8. 17., endowed with £200 royal bounty, and in the patronage of Sir H. Verney, Bart. The church is dedicated to St. Mary.

THORNBOROUGH, a township in the parish of CORBRIDGE, eastern division of TINDALE ward, county of NORTHUMBERLAND, 5¾ miles (E.) from Hexham, containing 74 inhabitants. Considerable quantities of limestone are quarried and burned in this township. A lead mine anciently wrought here was re-opened in 1801, but the speculation proving unsuccessful, it was soon after abandoned.

THORNBROUGH, a township in the parish of SOUTH KILVINGTON, wapentake of BIRDFORTH, North riding of the county of YORK, 2¾ miles (E.N.E.) from Thirsk, containing 27 inhabitants.

THORNBURY, a parish in the hundred of BLACK TORRINGTON, county of DEVON, 4½ miles (N.E. by E.) from Holsworthy, containing 517 inhabitants. The living is a rectory, in the archdeaconry of Totness, and diocese of Exeter, rated in the king's books at £11. 3. 11½., and in the patronage of William Morris Fry, Esq. The church, dedicated to St. Peter, has a Norman door, and contains a monument of an armed knight and his lady, with several monumental effigies of the Edgecumbe family.

THORNBURY, a market town and parish in the lower division of the hundred of THORNBURY, county of GLOUCESTER, 24 miles (S.W.) from Gloucester, and 124 (W. by N.) from London, containing, with the chapelries of Falfield, Oldbury upon Severn, and Rangeworthy, and the tythings of Kington, and Moorton, 3760 inhabitants. This town, which is of considerable antiquity, is situated on the banks of a small rivulet, two miles westward of the Severn, in the vale of Berkeley, and consists of three principal streets. The chief object worthy of notice is the remains of an old castle at the end of the town, begun by Edward, Duke of Buckingham, in the year 1511, but left in an unfinished state; th outer wall is still in good preservation, and over the arched gateway, which formed the principal entrance, and is greatly admired, is an inscription in raised letters, recording the date of its erection: these ruins command a fine view of the river Severn, which flows on the western side of the parish, and the remote landscape of South Wales. Henry VIII. and Anne Boleyn were sumptuously entertained here, for ten days, in 1539. The clothing business formerly flourished, but has been long discontinued, and there is now no particular branch of trade. The market is on Saturday. Fairs are held on Easter-Monday, August 15th, and the Monday before December 21st, for cattle and pigs. The corporation, now merely nominal, consists of a mayor and twelve aldermen, with a serjeant at mace and two constables. A manorial court leet is held annually, and occasionally a court baron; also a manor court for the surrender of admission to copyholds. A court for the recovery of debts under 40s., for the hundred, is held once in three weeks, on Thursday; and a court of record, for pleas to any amount, for the honour of Gloucester, is also held every three weeks, on Tuesday.

The living is a vicarage, in the archdeaconry and diocese of Gloucester, rated in the king's books at £25. 15. 10., and in the patronage of the Dean and Canons of Christ Church, Oxford. The church, which is dedicated to St. Mary, is a spacious and handsome cruciform structure, in the later style of English architecture, with a lofty tower with open-worked battlements and eight pinnacles: the north and south doors are of much earlier date. There are places of worship for Baptists, the Society of Friends, Independents, and Wesleyan Methodists. A free grammar school was founded and endowed, in 1648, by William Edwards, its funds having been augmented by subsequent benefactors; the present income is £57. 3. 6., and twelve boys are instructed on the foundation. Another free school was founded, in 1729, by means of a bequest of £500 from John Atwells, and endowed with lands in 1789; the income is £70 per annum, and twenty-four boys and twelve girls are educated. Here are six almshouses for fifteen poor people, founded by Sir John Stafford, in the reign of James I.

THORNBURY, a parish in the hundred of BROXASH, county of HEREFORD, 4¼ miles (N.N.W.) from Bromyard, containing, with the township of Westwood, 183 inhabitants. The living is a rectory, in the archdeaconry and diocese of Hereford, rated in the king's books at £5. 6. 8., and in the patronage of Mrs. Pytts. Wall Hill camp, in this parish, has a triple intrenchment, almost perfect, and is supposed to be a work of the ancient Britons. At Netherwood, in this parish, Robert Devereux, Earl of Essex, who was beheaded in 1601, was born, in 1567.

THORNBY, a parish in the hundred of GUILSBOROUGH, county of NORTHAMPTON, 10½ miles (N.N.W.) from Northampton, containing 176 inhabitants. The living is a rectory, in the archdeaconry of Northampton, and diocese of Peterborough, rated in the king's books at £13. The Rev. N. Cotton was patron in 1814. The church is dedicated to St. Helen.

2 P 2

THORNCOMBE, a parish (formerly a market town) forming a detached portion of the hundred of AXMINSTER, county of DEVON, 6½ miles (S. W. by W.) from Axminster, containing 1322 inhabitants. The living is a vicarage, in the archdeaconry and diocese of Exeter, rated in the king's books at £15. 18. 9., and in the patronage of John Bragge, Esq. The church is dedicated to St. Mary. Here is a free school, founded by the Rev. Thomas Cooke, in 1734, with a small endowment for the instruction of eleven poor children. A fair is held on Easter-Tuesday. At Ford, in this parish, an abbey for Cistercian monks was founded, by Adelign, daughter of Baldwin de Brioniis, in 1140, the revenue of which was valued at £381. 10. 8½.: the remains are considerable, consisting partly of the entrance tower, the old abbey walls, with various other parts being now used as a private mansion. The chapel has a groined roof in the early English style, and some arches of late Norman character: the hall and cloisters are in the later English. The possessor of this abbey holds a court at Holditch.

THORNCOTE, a hamlet in the parish of NORTHILL, hundred of WIXAMTREE, county of BEDFORD, 3¼ miles (N. W.) from Biggleswade, containing, with Brookend, Budnor, Hatch, and a part of Beeston, 241 inhabitants.

THORNDON (ALL SAINTS), a parish in the hundred of HARTISMERE, county of SUFFOLK, 3¼ miles (S. by W.) from Eye, containing 638 inhabitants. The living is a rectory, in the archdeaconry of Sudbury, and diocese of Norwich, rated in the king's books at £24. 11. 10½., and in the patronage of the Rev. Thomas Howes.

THORNE, a market town and parish in the southern division of the wapentake of STRAFFORTH and TICKHILL, West riding of the county of YORK, 29 miles (S. by E.) from York, and 165 (N. by W.) from London, containing 3463 inhabitants. This place, in Leland's time only a small village with a castle near it, the foundations of which are still visible, has become a neat and flourishing town: it is situated on the verge of the moors, near Marshland, a fenny district supposed to have been once a forest, from the numerous fossil trees, &c., which have been discovered here; the streets are paved, and many of the houses well built. On the moor large quantities of peat are obtained, and conveyed, by means of a canal, to the town and other places, to be used as a substitute for coal. The inhabitants carry on a considerable trade in grain and other commodities with London; rope is made to some extent. At Hangman's hill, about a mile distant, is the quay, where all merchandise is shipped and landed. Vessels for the coasting trade are built here, and, being launched at spring tides, are conveyed down the river Don to Hull, to be rigged and otherwise completed. A canal from this river to the Trent passes westward of the town, by which its trade is greatly promoted. The market, originally granted by Richard Cromwell, and renewed by Charles II., is on Wednesday; and fairs, chiefly for horses, cattle, and pedlary, are held on the Monday and Tuesday next after June 11th and October 11th.

The living is a perpetual curacy, in the archdeaconry and diocese of York, endowed with £1200 parliamentary grant, and in the patronage of Lord Deerhurst. The church, which is dedicated to St. Nicholas, is principally in the later style of English architecture, with a square tower surmounted by pinnacles. There are places of worship for the Society of Friends, Independents, Primitive and Wesleyan Methodists, Unitarians, and the followers of Joanna Southcote. The free school was endowed with land by William Brook, in 1705, for the perpetual maintenance of a schoolmaster, and the instruction of ten of the poorest boys within the town: the annual income is £148. 19. 9. Another free school was founded and endowed with land, in 1706, by Henry Travis, the income of which is about £35. The Rev. Abraham de la Pryme, F.R.S., a celebrated antiquary and historian, was some time minister of Thorne, and died in 1704, at the early age of thirty-four. At Crowtrees, near this town, resided Sir Cornelius Vermuyden, who, having expended £400,000 in draining Hatfield Chase, and an additional sum in litigation, died in indigent circumstances.

THORNE-FALCON, a parish in the hundred of NORTH CURRY, county of SOMERSET, 3½ miles (E. by S.) from Taunton, containing 221 inhabitants. The living is a rectory, in the archdeaconry of Taunton, and diocese of Bath and Wells, rated in the king's books at £14. 10., and in the patronage of Richard Batters, Esq. The church is dedicated to the Holy Cross.

THORNER, a parish in the lower division of the wapentake of SKYRACK, West riding of the county of YORK, comprising the townships of Scarcroft, Shadwell, and Thorner, and containing 1010 inhabitants, of which number, 708 are in the township of Thorner, 6½ miles (S. by W.) from Wetherby. The living is a discharged vicarage, in the archdeaconry and diocese of York, rated in the king's books at £8. 3. 4., endowed with £400 private benefaction, and £400 royal bounty, and in the patronage of the Crown. The church is dedicated to St. Peter. There is a place of worship for Wesleyan Methodists. A school was erected by subscription in 1787, and endowed with twelve acres of land from the waste, the annual income arising from which, being £15. 10., is applied to the instruction of six children. There is a fine spring of water, called St. Sykes' Well, in the neighbourhood.

THORNES, a township in the parish of WAKEFIELD, lower division of the wapentake of AGBRIGG, West riding of the county of YORK, 1 mile (S. by W.) from Wakefield. The population is returned with the chapelry of Alverthorpe. A grant has recently been made towards erecting a chapel, by the commissioners appointed under the late act for promoting the building of additional churches, &c., of which the Vicar of Wakefield is to be the patron.

THORNEY, a market town and parish in the hundred of WISBEACH, Isle of ELY, county of CAMBRIDGE, 35 miles (N. W.) from Cambridge, and 86 (N.) from London, containing 1970 inhabitants. This place derived its original name of Ankeridge from a monastery for hermits, or anchorites, founded here, in 662, by Saxulphus, abbot of Peterborough, who became its first prior; the edifice having been destroyed by the Danes, the site lay waste until 972, when Ethelwold, Bishop of Winchester, founded upon it a Benedictine abbey, in honour of the Virgin, which became so opulent that, at the dissolution, its revenue was valued at £508. 12. 5.: of this abbey, which was a mitred one, the only remains are portions of the parish church, a gateway, and some fragments of the old walls. A Literary Society was established, in 1823, which possesses a good library. The market, granted in 1638, is on Thursday; and fairs are held on July 1st and September 21st, for horses and cattle, and on Whit-Monday is a pleasure fair. Upwards of three thousand sheep are sent annually from this district to the London market. The petty sessions are held here. The living is a perpetual curacy, in the peculiar jurisdiction and patronage of the Duke of Bedford. The church, which is dedicated to St. Botolph, and originally formed the nave of the conventual church, built about 1128, is partly in the Norman style of architecture, with portions in the later English: in the churchyard are several tombs of the French refugees, of whom a colony settled here about the middle of the sixth century, having been employed, by the Earl of Bedford, in draining the fens. A school-house was erected by a member of the illustrious house of Russell, and the present Duke of Bedford allows the master a salary of £20 per annum for the instruction of poor children: ten or twelve poor families also are supported in some alms-houses by the munificence of his Grace.

THORNEY, a parish in the northern division of the wapentake of NEWARK, county of NOTTINGHAM, 8¾ miles (E. by N.) from Tuxford, containing, with the hamlets of Broadholme and Wiggesley, 264 inhabitants. The living is a discharged vicarage, in the archdeaconry of Nottingham, and diocese of York, rated in the king's books at £4. 7. 6., endowed with £400 royal bounty, and in the patronage of Nevile George Nevile, Esq. The church is dedicated to St. Helen. The Fosse-Dyke canal borders on the parish.

THORNEY (WEST), a parish in the hundred of BOSHAM, rape of CHICHESTER, county of SUSSEX, 7½ miles (W. by S.) from Chichester, containing 111 inhabitants. The living is a rectory, in the archdeaconry and diocese of Chichester, rated in the king's books at £10. 8. 4., and in the patronage of the Earl of Berkeley.

THORNEYBURN, a parish in the north-western division of TINDALE ward, county of NORTHUMBERLAND, comprising the townships of West Tarset and Thorneyburn, and containing 358 inhabitants, of which number, 189 are in the township of Thorneyburn, 5 miles (N. W. by W.) from Bellingham. The living is a rectory, in the archdeaconry of Northumberland, and diocese of Durham, rated in the king's books at £4. 5., and in the patronage of the Governors of Greenwich Hospital, who, in 1818, at the expense of £4000, erected the church, which is a neat structure, situated in a field formerly called Draper Croft. This is one of the five new parishes anciently forming part of the extensive parish of Simonburn: it is a wild and mountainous district, extending from the North Tyne river to Reedsdale, and is bounded on the east by the Tarset bourn. Coal is obtained within the parish.

THORNFORD, a parish in the hundred of SHERBORNE, Sherborne division of the county of DORSET, 3½ miles (S. W.) from Sherborne, containing 329 inhabitants. The living is a discharged rectory, in the peculiar jurisdiction of the Dean of Salisbury, rated in the king's books at £6. 17. 3., and in the patronage of Mrs. Sampson. The church, dedicated to St. Mary Magdalene, was anciently a chapel dependent on Sherborne abbey.

THORNGRAFTON, a township in the parish of HALTWHISTLE, western division of TINDALE ward, county of NORTHUMBERLAND, 5½ miles (E. by N.) from Haltwhistle, containing 247 inhabitants. House Steads, in this township, was the site of the Roman station Borcovicus, adjacent to which passed the Roman wall. It stands on the brow of a rocky eminence, on the western declivity of which are several terraces, one above another. The area of this fort, on the north side, is level, but on the south it exhibits vast and confused heaps of ruins. In the neighbourhood are foundations of houses and traces of streets, squares, baths, &c., extending over several acres, and to the distance of two miles and a half; and on Chapel hill, a little to the south, are the remains of a temple of the Doric order, among which have been found altars, sepulchral inscriptions, and curiously carved figures in relief.

THORNHAM, a parish in the hundred of EYHORNE, lathe of AYLESFORD, county of KENT, 4 miles (N. E. by E.) from Maidstone, containing 523 inhabitants. The living is a vicarage, in the archdeaconry and diocese of Canterbury, rated in the king's books at £8. 0. 10., and in the patronage of the Rev. John Hudson. The church, dedicated to St. Mary, is principally in the decorated style of English architecture. There is a place of worship for Wesleyan Methodists. Edward Godfrey gave a rent-charge of thirty shillings for the education of poor children. The ruins of Thurnham, or Godard's, castle, still exist on the brow of a hill, forming part of the great range of chalk hills; the walls, which are more than thirteen feet high, and three feet thick, enclose an area of a quarter of an acre, including the keep mount. Urns and other vestiges of a Roman station have been found here. A vein of white sand, known by the name of Maidstone sand, though discovered in this parish, is said to have caused the first improvement in the manufacture of glass in this country: it was first worked by experienced Italians, and soon became of infinite importance in the trade: the pits are remarkable for their vast subterranean caverns, which are curiously arched.

THORNHAM, a township in the parish of MIDDLETON, hundred of SALFORD, county palatine of LANCASTER, 3½ miles (S.) from Rochdale, containing 1374 inhabitants.

THORNHAM, a parish in the hundred of SMITHDON, county of NORFOLK, 6¼ miles (W. by N.) from Burnham-Westgate, containing 627 inhabitants. The living is a discharged vicarage, with that of Holme near the Sea annexed, in the archdeaconry of Norfolk, and diocese of Norwich, rated in the king's books at £10. The church is dedicated to All Saints.

THORNHAM (MAGNA), a parish in the hundred of HARTISMERE, county of SUFFOLK, 3¼ miles (W. S. W.) from Eye, containing 342 inhabitants. The living is a discharged rectory, with which that of Thornham Parva was consolidated in 1744; it is in the archdeaconry of Sudbury, and diocese of Norwich, rated in the king's books at £7. 11. 3., and in the patronage of Lord Henniker. The church is dedicated to St. Mary.

THORNHAM (PARVA), a parish in the hundred of HARTISMERE, county of SUFFOLK, 2¾ miles (W. by S.) from Eye, containing 139 inhabitants. The living is a discharged rectory, with that of Thornham Magna, in the archdeaconry of Sudbury, and diocese of Norwich, rated in the king's books at £4. 14. 4½.

THORNHAUGH, a parish in the liberty of PETER-BOROUGH, county of NORTHAMPTON, 1¼ mile (N.) from Wansford, containing 266 inhabitants. The living is a rectory, with the perpetual curacy of Wansford annexed, in the archdeaconry of Northampton, and diocese of Peterborough, rated in the king's books at £17. 1. 3., and in the patronage of the Duke of Bedford. The church, dedicated to St. Andrew, exhibits portions in the various styles of English architecture.

THORNHILL, a hamlet in the parish of HOPE, hundred of HIGH PEAK, county of DERBY, 6¾ miles (N. E. by N.) from Tideswell, containing 139 inhabitants.

THORNHILL, a tything in the parish of STALBRIDGE, hundred of BROWNSHALL, Sturminster division of the county of DORSET, 2 miles (S.) from Stalbridge, containing 272 inhabitants.

THORNHILL, a parish in the lower division of the wapentake of AGBRIGG, West riding of the county of YORK, comprising the chapelry of Flockton, and the townships of Shitlington, Thornhill, and Lower Whitley, and containing 5458 inhabitants, of which number, 1932 are in the township of Thornhill, 6 miles (W. by S.) from Wakefield. The living is a rectory, in the archdeaconry and diocese of York, rated in the king's books at £40. 0. 7½., and in the patronage of the Hon. and Rev. J. Lumley Saville. The church, dedicated to St. Michael, is principally in the early style of English architecture. There are places of worship for Baptists and Wesleyan Methodists. The river Calder runs through the parish, amid scenery the most beautiful and picturesque. In the extensive park sloping to the banks of the river, and ornamented with aged woods, stood the castellated mansion of the Thornhills, which was surrounded by a moat, and garrisoned by Sir George Saville, a descendant of that family, for Charles I., but was taken and destroyed by the parliamentarians. Thornhill, though now only a manufacturing village, was formerly a place of considerable importance, indications of which are still discernible. It had a market and a fair, granted by charter of Edward II., in 1320, now discontinued. The manufacture of woollen cloth, plaids, shawls, and thread, is carried on; there are also brass and iron works, at the latter of which bar and sheet iron, anchor-palms, piston-rods, boiler-plates, and various other articles, are made. The Rev. Charles Greenwood, in 1642, bequeathed £500 for erecting and endowing a free grammar school; the income is £20 a year, for which all children of the parish who apply receive an English education. There is also a free school, founded and endowed, about 1712, by Richard Walker, with a residence for the master, and an annual income of £47, which is applied to the instruction of eighty children of both sexes; and the Sunday school is aided by an annuity of £4. 10., the bequest of the same benefactor.

THORNHOLM, a township in the parish of BURTON-AGNES, wapentake of DICKERING, East riding of the county of YORK, 4¾ miles (S. W. by W.) from Bridlington, containing 94 inhabitants.

THORNLEY, a township in the parish of KELLOE, southern division of EASINGTON ward, county palatine of DURHAM, 6¼ miles (S. E. by E.) from Durham, containing 60 inhabitants. Thornley Hall, now a farmhouse, is supposed to occupy the site of a castle, which was strongly fortified in 1140, when Bishop Barbara and his adherents fled hither from William Comyn, who had usurped the see of Durham. Limestone is obtained in the neighbourhood.

THORNLEY, a joint township with Wheatley, in the parish of CHIPPING, lower division of the hundred of BLACKBURN, county palatine of LANCASTER, 7¾ miles (W.) from Clitheroe, containing, with Wheatley, 506 inhabitants.

THORNSETT, a hamlet in the parish of GLOSSOP, hundred of HIGH PEAK, county of DERBY, 5¾ miles (N. W. by N.) from Chapel en le Frith, containing 758 inhabitants.

THORNTHWAITE, a chapelry in that part of the parish of CROSTHWAITE which is in ALLERDALE ward above Darwent, county of CUMBERLAND, 4 miles (W. N. W.) from Keswick, containing 164 inhabitants. The living is a perpetual curacy, in the archdeaconry and diocese of Carlisle, endowed with £800 royal bounty, and £200 parliamentary grant, and in the patronage of the Vicar of Crosthwaite. The village, in which the manufacture of woollen cloth is carried on, commands most romantic views of Bassenthwaite lake and Skiddaw. There is a smelting-mill, though it has not been in operation since the neighbouring lead-mine was discontinued.

THORNTHWAITE, a chapelry in the parish of HAMPSTHWAITE, lower division of the wapentake of CLARO, West riding of the county of YORK, 7½ miles (W. by S.) from Ripley, containing, with the township of Padside, 309 inhabitants. The living is a perpetual curacy, in the peculiar jurisdiction of the Honour court of Knaresborough, endowed with £200 private benefaction, £800 royal bounty, and £600 parliamentary grant, and in the patronage of the Vicar of Hampsthwaite. Flax-spinning and the manufacture of linen are carried on here. Francis Day, in 1748 and 1757, gave land producing an annual income of £20, for teaching poor children of Thornthwaite, Padside, Menwith Hill, and Darley.

THORNTON, a parish in the hundred and county of BUCKINGHAM, 4½ miles (E. N. E.) from Buckingham, containing 78 inhabitants. The living is a rectory, in the archdeaconry of Buckingham, and diocese of Lincoln, rated in the king's books at £11. 16. 3., and in the patronage of Sir T. C. Sheppard, Bart. The church is dedicated to St. Michael. William Bredon, who died rector of this parish in 1638, was celebrated for his skill in calculating nativities, and had a share in composing Sir Christopher Haydon's Judicial Astrology.

THORNTON, a parish in the second division of the hundred of EDDISBURY, county palatine of CHESTER, comprising the townships of Dunham, Elton, Hapsford, Thornton in the Moors, and Wimbolds-Trafford, and containing 853 inhabitants, of which number, 162 are in the township of Thornton in the Moors, 6¼ miles (N. N. E.) from Chester. The living is a rectory, in the archdeaconry and diocese of Chester, rated in the king's books at £24. 7. 8½., and in the patronage of Lord Berwick. The church, dedicated to St. Mary, is partly in the later style of English architecture, with a handsome tower. The Gowey, a tributary stream to the Mersey, runs through the parish. A school is endowed with about £7. 10. per annum; the schoolhouse was rebuilt about 1790.

THORNTON, a tything in the parish of MARN-HULL, hundred of REDLANE, Sherborne division of the county of DORSET, 3½ miles (N.N.E.) from Sturminster-Newton-Castle. It is now almost depopulated, though formerly a distinct parish, and was united to Marnhull at the Reformation, when the church, dedicated in 1464 to St. Martin, was desecrated, and is still used as a stable.

THORNTON, a township in the parish of NORHAM, otherwise Norhamshire, county palatine of DURHAM, though locally to the northward of the county of Northumberland, 5¼ miles (S. W.) from Berwick upon Tweed, containing 232 inhabitants.

THORNTON, a township in the parish of POULTON, hundred of AMOUNDERNESS, county palatine of LANCASTER, 1¾ mile (N. by E.) from Poulton, containing 875 inhabitants. There is a place of worship for Wesleyan Methodists. James Baines, in 1717, bequeathed land, now producing an annual income of £31. 10., for teaching poor children of both sexes. The school-room has been lately rebuilt by subscription, and there is a house for the master, who instructs from one hundred to one hundred and fifty children on the National system.

THORNTON, a township in the parish of SEPHTON, hundred of WEST DERBY, county palatine of LANCASTER, 6½ miles (N.) from Liverpool, containing 300 inhabitants.

THORNTON, a parish in the hundred of SPARKENHOE, county of LEICESTER, 6 miles (N.E.) from Market-Bosworth, containing, with the chapelries of Bagworth and Stanton under Bardon, the township of Horsepool, and the extra-parochial liberty of Bagworth Park, 1096 inhabitants. The living is a discharged vicarage, in the archdeaconry of Leicester, and diocese of Lincoln, rated in the king's books at £6. 10. 2., and in the patronage of Lord Viscount Maynard. The church is dedicated to St. Peter.

THORNTON, a parish in the southern division of the wapentake of GARTREE, parts of LINDSEY, county of LINCOLN, 1¾ mile (S.W.) from Horncastle, containing 153 inhabitants. The living is a discharged vicarage, in the archdeaconry and diocese of Lincoln, rated in the king's books at £5. 12. 1., and in the patronage of the Dean and Chapter of Lichfield. The church is dedicated to St. Wilfrid.

THORNTON, a parish partly in the Wilton-Beacon, but chiefly in the Holme-Beacon, division of the wapentake of HARTHILL, East riding of the county of YORK, 4¼ miles (S. W.) from Pocklington, containing, with the townships of Melbourn and Storwood, 751 inhabitants. The living is a discharged vicarage, annexed to the perpetual curacy of Allerthorpe, in the peculiar jurisdiction and patronage of the Dean of York, rated in the king's books at £7. 5. 10.

THORNTON, a joint township with Baxly, in the parish of COXWOLD, wapentake of BIRDFORTH, North riding of the county of YORK, 3 miles (N. by E.) from Easingwould, containing, with Baxly, 70 inhabitants.

THORNTON, a chapelry in the parish of BRADFORD, wapentake of MORLEY, West riding of the county of YORK, 4½ miles (W.) from Bradford, containing 4100 inhabitants. The living is a perpetual curacy, in the archdeaconry and diocese of York, endowed with £400 private benefaction, £600 royal bounty, and £400 parliamentary grant, and in the patronage of the Vicar of Bradford. The chapel, dedicated to St. James, is principally in the later style of English architecture. There are quarries of freestone in the neighbourhood, and the manufacture of worsted is carried on to a considerable extent. A school, erected by subscription, is endowed with £50 per annum, arising from the produce of divers benefactions, the principal of which are those of George Ellis and Samuel Sunderland: about eighty children are instructed, some of them in the classics.

THORNTON, a parish in the eastern division of the wapentake of STAINCLIFFE and EWCROSS, West riding of the county of YORK, 5¾ miles (W.S.W.) from Skipton, containing 1829 inhabitants. The living is a rectory, in the archdeaconry of Richmond, and diocese of Chester, rated in the king's books at £19. 5. 2½., and in the patronage of Sir J. L. Kaye, Bart. The church is dedicated to St. Mary. Here was formerly a market on Thursday, granted to Walter de Muncey, in the 28th of Edward I., with a fair for five days, commencing on the eve of the festival of St. Thomas the Martyr. At a short distance from the village is a huge rocky cliff, called Thornton Scar, partly clothed with wood, and rising to the height of three hundred feet. Thornton Force is a beautiful cataract rushing from an aperture in a precipitous rock, and having a fall of ninety feet in one sheet of water sixteen feet wide.

THORNTON le BEANS, a township in that part of the parish of NORTH OTTERINGTON which is in the wapentake of ALLERTONSHIRE, North riding of the county of YORK, 3½ miles (S.E.) from North Allerton, containing 247 inhabitants. There is a place of worship for Wesleyan Methodists.

THORNTON (BISHOP), a chapelry in that part of the parish of RIPON which is in the liberty of RIPON, West riding of the county of YORK, 3½ miles (N.N.W.) from Ripley, containing 647 inhabitants. The living is a perpetual curacy, in the jurisdiction of the peculiar court of Ripon, belonging to the Archbishop of York, endowed with £400 private benefaction, £600 royal bounty, and £900 parliamentary grant, and in the patronage of the Dean and Chapter of Ripon.

THORNTON upon CLAY, a township in the parish of FOSTON, wapentake of BULMER, North riding of the county of YORK, 11 miles (N.N.E.) from York, containing 173 inhabitants.

THORNTON (EAST), a township in that part of the parish of HARTBURN which is in the western division of MORPETH ward, county of NORTHUMBERLAND, 6 miles (W.) from Morpeth, containing, with East Thornton Moor and Meldon Park Corner, 61 inhabitants.

THORNTON le FEN, a township in the soke of HORNCASTLE, parts of LINDSEY, county of LINCOLN, 8½ miles (N.W.) from Boston, containing 141 inhabitants.

THORNTON in LONSDALE, a parish in the western division of the wapentake of STAINCLIFFE and EWCROSS, west riding of the county of YORK, comprising the chapelry of Black-Burton, and the township of Thornton, and containing 1281 inhabitants, of which number, 535 are in the township of Thornton, 11½ miles (N.W.) from Settle. The living is a rectory, in the archdeaconry of Richmond, and diocese of Chester, rated in the king's books at £28. 13. 1½., and in the patronage of the Dean and Chapter of Worcester. The church is dedicated to St. Oswald. The manufacture of cotton is carried on to a limited extent. One of the sources of the river Greta, which bounds the parish to the south and south-east, is in the valley of Kingsdale, the stream flowing through most romantic scenery, and forming several beautiful cascades in its descent. The celebrated Yorda's cave is at the northern extremity of the vale. Ralph Redmayne, Esq., in 1702, founded a free school, and endowed it with £200, which, having been vested in land, produces annually £50, for teaching all the poor children of the parish, in a school-room built by subscription.

THORNTON le MOOR, a parish in the northern division of the wapentake of WALSHCROFT, parts of LINDSEY, county of LINCOLN, 5½ miles (S.W. by W.) from Caistor, containing 115 inhabitants. The living is a discharged rectory, in the archdeaconry and diocese of Lincoln, rated in the king's books at £9. 10. 10., and in the patronage of the Bishop of Ely. The church is dedicated to All Saints.

THORNTON le MOOR, a township in that part of the parish of NORTH OTTERINGTON which is in the wapentake of BIRDFORTH, North riding of the county of YORK, 5 miles (N.W. by N.) from Thirsk, containing 294 inhabitants. Here was formerly a chapel of ease, the remains of which have been converted into a school-room : there is no endowment.

THORNTON le STREET, a parish in the wapentake of ALLERTONSHIRE, North riding of the county of YORK, comprising the townships of North Kilvington and Thornton le Street, and containing 199 inhabitants, of which number, 131 are in the township of Thornton le Street, 3 miles (N.N.W.) from Thirsk. The living is a discharged vicarage, in the peculiar jurisdiction of the court of the Bishop of Durham, for Allerton and Allertonshire, rated in the king's books at £4, endowed with £200 private benefaction, £200 royal bounty, and £500 parliamentary grant, and in the patronage of the Dean and Canons of Christ Church, Oxford. The church is dedicated to St. Leonard.

THORNTON (WEST), a township in that part of the parish of HARTBURN which is in the western division of MORPETH ward, county of NORTHUMBERLAND, 7¼ miles (W. by N.) from Morpeth, containing 43 inhabitants. This is the supposed site of a Roman camp, and it is recorded that, at the commencement of the eighteenth century, vestiges of a town, intersected by a military way, were discernible.

THORNTON-BRIDGE, a township in that part of the parish of BRAFFERTON which is in the wapentake of HALLIKELD, North riding of the county of YORK, 4½ miles (N.E. by N.) from Boroughbridge, containing 43 inhabitants.

THORNTON-CHILDER, a township in the parish of EASTHAM, higher division of the hundred of WIRRALL, county palatine of CHESTER, 5 miles (E.) from Great Neston, containing 177 inhabitants.

THORNTON-CURTIS, a parish in the northern division of the wapentake of YARBOROUGH, parts of LINDSEY, county of LINCOLN, 5 miles (S. E. by E.) from Barton upon Humber, containing 328 inhabitants. The living is a discharged vicarage, in the archdeaconry and diocese of Lincoln, rated in the king's books at £5. 18. 4., endowed with £400 royal bounty, and in the patronage of C. Winn, Esq. The church is dedicated to St. Law-

rence. A priory of Black canons, in honour of the Blessed Virgin, was founded here in 1139, by William le Gros, Earl of Albemarle, and Lord of Holderness, which at the dissolution had a revenue of £730. 17. 2. Henry VIII. applied the greater part of its possessions to the erection of a sumptuous college, in honour of the Holy and Undivided Trinity, for a dean and nineteen prebendaries, which was dissolved in the 1st of Edw.VI., when its site was granted to the Bishop of Lincoln. It occupied an extensive square area, encompassed by a deep fosse and strong ramparts, within which an avenue of large ash trees led to the church, the ruins of which, particularly the chapter-house, are very fine. There are some remains of the gatehouse, approached by a bridge flanked with embattled walls, and arches with loopholes, supporting two round towers. Various other portions of these once magnificent buildings are still standing, and exhibit good specimens of the decorated and later styles of English architecture. Opposite the entrance are four small mounds, called Butts, supposed to be tumuli.

THORNTON-DALE, a parish in PICKERING lythe, North riding of the county of YORK, comprising the townships of Farmanby and Thornton-Dale, and containing 1282 inhabitants, of which number, 879 are in the township of Thornton-Dale, 2½ miles (E. by S.) from Pickering. The living is a rectory, in the archdeaconry of Cleveland, and diocese of York, rated in the king's books at £20, and in the patronage of R. Hill, Esq. The church is dedicated to All Saints. There is a place of worship for Wesleyan Methodists. A free grammar school was endowed, in 1657, by Viscountess Lumley, who also erected twelve almshouses for as many poor people.

THORNTON-MAYOW, a township in the parish of NESTON, higher division of the hundred of WIRRALL, county palatine of CHESTER, 2⅔ miles (N. N. E.) from Great Neston, containing 204 inhabitants.

THORNTON-RUST, a township in the parish of AYSGARTH, western division of the wapentake of HANG, North riding of the county of YORK, 10 miles (W.) from Middleham, containing 135 inhabitants.

THORNTON-STEWARD, a parish in the western division of the wapentake of HANG, North riding of the county of YORK, 3½ miles (E. by S.) from Middleham, containing 265 inhabitants. The living is a discharged vicarage, in the archdeaconry of Richmond, and diocese of Chester, rated in the king's books at £6. 13. 11½., endowed with £200 private benefaction, and £200 royal bounty, and in the patronage of the Bishop of Chester. The church, dedicated to St. Oswald, is principally in the Norman style. The river Ure bounds the parish on the south. A neat school was erected in 1815, at the expense of George Horn, Esq. ; it has an endowment of £10 per annum for the education of the poor children of the parish.

THORNTON-WATLASS, a parish in the eastern division of the wapentake of HANG, North riding of the county of YORK, comprising the townships of Clifton upon Ure, Rookwith, Thirn, and Thornton Watlass, and containing 432 inhabitants, of which number, 180 are in the township of Thornton-Watlass, 2¾ miles (S. W.) from Bedale. The living is a rectory, in the archdeaconry of Richmond, and diocese of Chester, rated in the king's books at £6. 10. 10., and in the patronage of M. Milbank, Esq. The church is dedicated to St. Mary. Eight poor children are instructed for £4 per annum, the gift of an ancestor of the Rev. Frederic Dodsworth, D.D., in 1756.

THORNVILLE, a township in that part of the parish of WHIXLEY which is in the lower division of the wapentake of CLARO, West riding of the county of YORK, 5¼ miles (S. by E.) from Boroughbridge, containing 13 inhabitants.

THOROTON, a parish in the northern division of the wapentake of BINGHAM, county of NOTTINGHAM, 8 miles (S. S. W.) from Newark, containing 145 inhabitants. The living is a perpetual curacy, in the archdeaconry of Nottingham, and diocese of York. The church is a small edifice, dedicated to St. Elena.

THORP, a township in the parish of ROTHWELL, lower division of the wapentake of AGBRIGG, West riding of the county of YORK, 4½ miles (N. by W.) from Wakefield, containing 80 inhabitants.

THORP-ACRE, a parish in the western division of the hundred of GOSCOTE, county of LEICESTER, 1¼ mile (W. N. W.) from Loughborough, containing, with the chapelry of Dishley, 351 inhabitants. The living is a perpetual curacy, in the archdeaconry of Leicester, and diocese of Lincoln, and in the patronage of Sir William Gordon, Bart.

THORP-ARCH, a parish in the ainsty of the city, and East riding of the county, of YORK, 2¾ miles (S. E. by E.) from Wetherby, containing 343 inhabitants. The living is a discharged vicarage, in the archdeaconry and diocese of York, rated in the king's books at £3. 15. 5., endowed with £400 private benefaction, and £400 royal bounty, and in the patronage of the Earl of Huntingdon. The church, dedicated to All Saints, is a handsome structure. There is a place of worship for Wesleyan Methodists. A free school was founded here, in 1738, by Lady Elizabeth Hastings, who endowed it with £15 a year; but from other sources the annual income has been increased to £40, for which twenty children are instructed. A mineral spring, sulphureous and chalybeate, and in high repute, was discovered here by a labourer, in 1744, the water of which, in some disorders, has a decided superiority over that at Harrogate. The rapid river Wharf separates the village from that of Boston, and forms a picturesque cascade, as viewed through the arches of the bridge by which it is crossed. Here are three good inns, and a number of private lodging-houses, recently erected for the accommodation of visitors, of whom, many have not only derived considerable benefit from the spa, but also from the great salubrity of the air of this pleasing district.

THORP-AUDLING, a township in the parish of BADSWORTH, upper division of the wapentake of OS-GOLDCROSS, West riding of the county of YORK, 4½ miles (S. S. E.) from Pontefract, containing 344 inhabitants.

THORP-BASSETT, a parish in the wapentake of BUCKROSE, East riding of the county of YORK, 5 miles (E. by N.) from New Malton, containing 156 inhabitants. The living is a rectory, in the archdeaconry of the East riding, and diocese of York, rated in the king's books at £12, and in the joint patronage of Earl Fitzwilliam and — Watson, Esq. The church is dedicated to All Saints. Ten boys are instructed for the dividends arising from £200, the gift of the Rev. James Graves, in 1804.

THORP-MORIEUX, a parish in the hundred of COSFORD, county of SUFFOLK, 4¼ miles (N. W.) from

Bildeston, containing 369 inhabitants. The living is a rectory, in the archdeaconry of Sudbury, and diocese of Norwich, rated in the king's books at £18. 14. 4½., and in the patronage of J. H. Harrison, Esq. The church is dedicated to St. Mary.

THORP-STAPLETON, a township in the parish of WHITKIRK, lower division of the wapentake of SKY-RACK, West riding of the county of YORK, 3¾ miles (S. E.) from Leeds, containing 25 inhabitants.

THORP-SUB-MONTEM, a joint township with Burnsall, in the parish of BURNSALL, eastern division of the wapentake of STAINCLIFFE and EWCROSS, West riding of the county of YORK, 8½ miles (N. by E.) from Skipton, containing 329 inhabitants.

THORP-UNDERWOODS, a township in that part of the parish of LITTLE OUSEBURN which is in the lower division of the wapentake of CLARO, West riding of the county of YORK, 6½ miles (S. E.) from Aldborough, containing 179 inhabitants.

THORPE, a parish in the hundred of WIRKSWORTH, county of DERBY, 3¼ miles (N. W. by N.) from Ashbourn, containing 203 inhabitants. The living is a discharged rectory, in the archdeaconry of Derby, and diocese of Lichfield and Coventry, rated in the king's books at £6. 1. 6., and in the patronage of the Dean of Lincoln. The church, dedicated to St. Leonard, is partly in the Norman style of architecture. To the northward of the village is a remarkable conical hill of limestone, called Thorpe Cloud; its altitude is three hundred feet above the bed of the river Dove, which flows at its base.

THORPE, a parish in the eastern division of the soke of BOLINGBROKE, parts of LINDSEY, county of LIN-COLN, 1½ mile (N. W.) from Wainfleet, containing 381 inhabitants. The living is a discharged vicarage, in the archdeaconry and diocese of Lincoln, rated in the king's books at £20. 19. 4., and in the patronage of the Bishop of Lincoln, by lapse. The church is dedicated to St. Peter.

THORPE, a hamlet in the parish of TATTERSHALL, southern division of the wapentake of GARTREE, parts of LINDSEY, county of LINCOLN, containing 269 inhabitants.

THORPE, a parish in the southern division of the wapentake of NEWARK, county of NOTTINGHAM, 3¼ miles (S. W.) from Newark, containing 96 inhabitants. The living is a rectory, in the archdeaconry of Nottingham, and diocese of York, rated in the king's books at £8, and in the patronage of the Crown. The church, dedicated to St. Lawrence, exhibits portions in the several styles of English architecture. The Trent bounds the parish on the north-west, and the old Fosse road passes between that river and the village. A fine tesselated pavement, coins, and many other Roman relics, have been discovered in the neighbourhood.

THORPE, a parish in the southern division of the wapentake of RUSHCLIFFE, county of NOTTINGHAM, 6¾ miles (N. E.) from Loughborough, containing 33 inhabitants. The living is a discharged rectory, in the archdeaconry of Nottingham, and diocese of York, rated in the king's books at £12. 9. 4½., and in the patronage of Lord Rancliffe. The church has been destroyed.

THORPE, a hamlet in the parish of ALDRINGHAM, hundred of BLYTHING, county of SUFFOLK, 3¼ miles (N. by E.) from Aldborough. The population is returned with the parish. Here was formerly a chapel, dedicated to St. Mary, now in ruins.

THORPE, a chapelry in the parish of ASHFIELD, hundred of THREDLING, county of SUFFOLK, 2 miles (E. S. E.) from Debenham. The population is returned with the parish. The living is a perpetual curacy, annexed to that of Ashfield, in the archdeaconry of Suffolk, and diocese of Norwich.

THORPE, a parish in the second division of the hundred of GODLEY, county of SURREY, 2 miles (N. W. by N.) from Chertsey, containing 509 inhabitants. The living is a vicarage, in the archdeaconry of Surrey, and diocese of Winchester, rated in the king's books at £5. 13. 4., endowed with £200 private benefaction, and £200 royal bounty, and in the patronage of the Crown. The church is dedicated to St. Mary. This parish is entitled to the benefit of Sir William Perkins' school at Chertsey.

THORPE, a township in the parish of HOWDEN, wapentake of HOWDENSHIRE, East riding of the county of YORK, 1¼ mile (N. by E.) from Howden, containing 53 inhabitants.

THORPE, a township in the parish of WYCLIFFE, western division of the wapentake of GILLING, North riding of the county of YORK, 1½ mile (N. E. by E.) from Greta-Bridge. The population is returned with the parish. This township is situated on the banks of the Tees: there is a private Roman Catholic chapel.

THORPE, a joint township with Whitcliff, in that part of the parish of RIPON which is within the liberty of RIPON, West riding of the county of YORK, 1½ mile (S. by E.) from Ripon. The population is returned with Whitcliff.

THORPE (ST. ANDREW), a parish partly in the city of NORWICH, but chiefly in the hundred of BLO-FIELD, county of NORFOLK, 2¾ miles (E. by S.) from Norwich, containing 1091 inhabitants. The living is a rectory, in the peculiar jurisdiction of the Bishop of Norwich, rated in the king's books at £8. J. P. Maxwell, Esq. was patron in 1813. The county lunatic asylum is in this parish. The village is delightfully situated on the southern declivity of a hill, at the base of which flows the navigable river Wensum: the vicinity is ornamented with rich plantations, finely interspersed with the handsome villas of many of the opulent citizens of Norwich.

THORPE in BALNE, a township in the parish of BARNBY upon DON, southern division of the wapentake of STRAFFORTH and TICKHILL, West riding of the county of YORK, 6½ miles (N. N. E.) from Doncaster, containing 122 inhabitants. A rent-charge of £5, the gift of James Fretwell, in 1751, and sundry smaller bequests, are applied to the instruction of poor children.

THORPE (EAST), a hamlet in the parish of LONDESBOROUGH, Holme-Beacon division of the wapentake of HARTHILL, East riding of the county of YORK, 2¾ miles (N.) from Market-Weighton. The population is returned with the parish.

THORPE next HADDISCOE, a parish in the hundred of CLAVERING, county of NORFOLK, 5¾ miles (N. by E.) from Beccles, containing 96 inhabitants. The living is a discharged rectory, in the archdeaconry of Norfolk, and diocese of Norwich, rated in the king's books at £3. 6. 8., and in the patronage of the Crown. The church is dedicated to St. Matthias.

THORPE on the HILL, a parish in the lower division of the wapentake of BOOTHBY-GRAFFO, parts of KESTEVEN, county of LINCOLN, 6 miles (S. W.) from Lincoln, containing 235 inhabitants. The living is a rectory, in the archdeaconry and diocese of Lincoln, rated in the king's books at £9. 10., and in the patronage of the Dean and Chapter of Lincoln. The church is dedicated to All Saints. There is a place of worship for Wesleyan Methodists.

THORPE by IXWORTH, a parish in the hundred of BLACKBOURN, county of SUFFOLK, ½ a mile (N. W. by N.) from Ixworth, containing 148 inhabitants. The living is a perpetual curacy, in the archdeaconry of Suffolk, and diocese of Norwich, and in the patronage of Sir C. M. Lamb, Bart. The church is dedicated to All Saints. A priory, in honour of the Virgin Mary, was founded for Black canons, by Gilbert le Blund, a follower of the Conqueror, the revenue of which, at the dissolution, was estimated at £280. 9. 5.: the site is encompassed by a moat.

THORPE (LITTLE), a parish in the hundred of DISS, county of NORFOLK, ½ a mile (E.) from Scole. The population is returned with the parish of Scole. The living is a rectory, annexed to that of Billingford, in the archdeaconry of Norfolk, and diocese of Norwich, rated in the king's books at £4. The church, now in ruins, was dedicated to St. Mary.

THORPE (MARKET), a parish in the northern division of the hundred of ERPINGHAM, county of NORFOLK, 4¾ miles (N. W. by N.) from North Walsham, containing 192 inhabitants. The living is a discharged vicarage, with the donative mediety of Bradfield annexed, in the archdeaconry of Norfolk, and diocese of Norwich, rated in the king's books at £5. 11. 3., endowed with £200 royal bounty, and in the patronage of Lord Suffield. The church, dedicated to St. Margaret, was rebuilt, a few years ago, at the expense of Lord Suffield: it is an elegant structure of flint and free-stone, having at each angle a turret, and each side being terminated by a gable, with a stone cross: the windows are adorned with modern stained glass; the chancel is separated from the nave by a light oaken screen, and at the west end is another of similar workmanship.

THORPE le SOKEN, a parish in the hundred of TENDRING, county of ESSEX, 9½ miles (S. E. by S.) from Manningtree, containing 1148 inhabitants. The living is a discharged vicarage, consolidated with those of Kirby le Soken and Walton le Soken, in the jurisdiction of the peculiar court of the Sokens, the wills and records being deposited at the residence of the lord of the manor at Harwich; it is rated in the king's books at £16, and is in the patronage of the Rev. W. Burgess. The church, dedicated to St. Michael, has lately received an addition of two hundred and forty sittings, of which one hundred and fifty are free, the Incorporated Society for the enlargement of churches and chapels having granted £100 towards defraying the expense. There is a place of worship for Baptists. A small customary market is held on Wednesday evenings, and there are fairs on the Monday before Whitsuntide and September 29th. The petty sessions for the division are held here, on Monday, once in five weeks, alternately with Mistley, Manningtree, and Great Bromley. A creek, or arm of the sea, runs up to Landermere, a small hamlet in the parish, where there is a convenient wharf, at which vessels are laden with corn for the London market. There is a house, called the abbey, with land attached, but no traces of its having ever been a religious house. A number of French refugees formerly settled and had a chapel here, of which there are now no remains. The three parishes form what is termed " the liberty of the Soken," having within its limits two or three reputed manors of smaller extent. It was given to the church of St. Paul, London, by King Athelstan, before 941, and belonged to the canons of St. Paul's at the time of the Norman survey. The Dean and Chapter held the manor, with the three advowsons, as their peculiars, until deprived of them by Henry VIII., and Mary placed them under the jurisdiction of the Bishop of London, to whose visitation they are still subject. Edward VI. granted the manors and advowsons, with all their peculiar privileges, to Sir Thomas D'Arcy, from whose descendants, the Lords D'Arcy, they passed to the Earls of Rochford, and have since had various owners, the advowsons being now separate from the manors. The lord of the manor, who styles himself " lord of the liberty, franchise, dominion, and peculiar jurisdiction of the Soken, in the county of Essex," appoints a commissary, by the title of " Official Principal, and Vicar-general in spiritual causes," who holds a court in Thorpe church annually, and proves wills, grants marriage licenses, &c. The lord holds his court, annually on St. Anne's day, at Kirby : he also appoints a coroner, and other officers for the liberty, which has the privilege, though not exercised, that no bailiff, except its own, can arrest within its limits.

THORPE in the STREET, a township in that part of the parish of NUN-BURNHOLME which is in the Holme-Beacon division of the wapentake of HART-HILL, East riding of the county of YORK, 2½ miles (N. W. by W.) from Market-Weighton, containing 37 inhabitants.

THORPE by WATER, a hamlet in the parish of SEATON, hundred of WRANDIKE, county of RUTLAND, 5 miles (S. E. by S.) from Uppingham, containing 80 inhabitants.

THORPE (WEST), a parish in the wapentake of LAWRESS, parts of LINDSEY, county of LINCOLN, 7½ miles (N. W. by N.) from Lincoln, containing 69 inhabitants. The living is a discharged vicarage, annexed to the rectory of Aisthorpe, in the archdeaconry of Stow, and diocese of Lincoln, rated in the king's books at £ 5. 7. 6.

THORPE-ABBOTS, a parish in the hundred of EARSHAM, county of NORFOLK, 2¼ miles (E.) from Scole, containing 246 inhabitants. The living is a discharged rectory, in the archdeaconry of Norfolk, and diocese of Norwich, rated in the king's books at £ 6. W. Carver, Esq. was patron in 1812. The church is dedicated to All Saints.

THORPE-ACHURCH, a parish in the hundred of NAVISFORD, county of NORTHAMPTON, 4¼ miles (N. N. E.) from Thrapstone, containing 239 inhabitants. The living is a rectory, with the vicarage of Lilford annexed, in the archdeaconry of Northampton, and diocese of Peterborough, rated in the king's books at £14. 16. 3., and in the patronage of Lord Lilford. The church is dedicated to St. John the Baptist.

THORPE-ARNOLD, a parish in the hundred of FRAMLAND, county of LEICESTER, 1½ mile (E. N. E.) from Melton-Mowbray, containing 109 inhabitants.

The living is a vicarage, with the curacy of Brentingby annexed, in the archdeaconry of Leicester, and diocese of Lincoln, rated in the king's books at £ 6. 17. 8½., and in the patronage of the Duke of Rutland. The church is dedicated to St. Mary. The Melton-Mowbray and Oakham canal passes through the parish.

THORPE-BRANTINGHAM, a township in that part of the parish of BRANTINGHAM which is in the Hunsley-Beacon division of the wapentake of HART-HILL, East riding of the county of YORK, 3 miles (S. S. W.) from North Cave, containing 174 inhabitants.

THORPE-BULMER, a township in the parish of MONK-HESLETON, southern division of EASINGTON ward, county palatine of DURHAM, 12½ miles (N. by E.) from Stockton upon Tees, containing 24 inhabitants.

THORPE-CONSTANTINE, a parish in the northern division of the hundred of OFFLOW, county of STAFFORD, 5 miles (N. E.) from Tamworth, containing 40 inhabitants. The living is a rectory, in the archdeaconry of Stafford, and diocese of Lichfield and Coventry, rated in the king's books at £5. 5. 5., and in the patronage of William Phillips Inge, Esq. The church is dedicated to St. Constantine. This parish is in the honour of Tutbury, duchy of Lancaster, and within the jurisdiction of a court of pleas held at Tutbury every third Tuesday, for the recovery of debts under 40s.

THORPE-LUBENHAM, a township partly in the parish of LUBENHAM, hundred of GARTREE, county of LEICESTER, but chiefly in the parish of MARSTON-TRUSSEL, hundred of ROTHWELL, county of NORTHAMPTON, 2 miles (W. by S.) from Market-Harborough, containing 2 inhabitants.

THORPE-MALSOR, a parish in the hundred of ROTHWELL, county of NORTHAMPTON, 2 miles (W.N.W.) from Kettering, containing 299 inhabitants. The living is a rectory, in the archdeaconry of Northampton, and diocese of Peterborough, rated in the king's books at £11. 14. 2., and in the patronage of T. C. Mansell, Esq. The church is dedicated to All Saints. Robert Talbot, an early English antiquary, was born here, about the latter end of the fifteenth century.

THORPE-MANDEVILLE, a parish in the hundred of KING'S SUTTON, county of NORTHAMPTON, 6 miles (N. E. by E.) from Banbury, containing 187 inhabitants. The living is a rectory, in the archdeaconry of Northampton, and diocese of Peterborough, rated in the king's books at £10. 2. 11., and in the patronage of R. P. Humfrey, Esq. The church is dedicated to St. John the Baptist.

THORPE-SALVIN, a parish in the southern division of the wapentake of STRAFFORTH and TICKHILL, West riding of the county of YORK, 5¾ miles (W. by N.) from Worksop, containing 199 inhabitants. The living is a perpetual curacy, in the peculiar jurisdiction of the Chancellor of the Cathedral Church of York, endowed with £600 royal bounty, and in the patronage of the Duke of Leeds. The church, dedicated to St. Peter, has a remarkably fine Norman arch. There is a place of worship for Wesleyan Methodists.

THORPE-SATCHVILLE, a chapelry in the parish of TWYFORD, eastern division of the hundred of Gos-COTE, county of LEICESTER, 5½ miles (S. by W.) from Melton-Mowbray, containing 182 inhabitants. The chapel is dedicated to St. Michael.

THORPE-TINLEY, a township in the parish of TIMBERLAND, first division of the wapentake of LANGOE, parts of KESTEVEN, county of LINCOLN, 10½ miles (N. N. E.) from Sleaford, containing 96 inhabitants.

THORPE-UNDERWOOD, a hamlet in the parish and hundred of ROTHWELL, county of NORTHAMPTON, 1¼ mile (W.) from Rothwell, containing 12 inhabitants.

THORPE-WILLOUGHBY, a township in the parish of BRAYTON, lower division of the wapentake of BARKSTONE-ASH, West riding of the county of YORK, 2½ miles (W. S. W.) from Selby, containing 144 inhabitants.

THORPLAND, a hamlet in the parish of WALLINGTON, hundred of CLACKCLOSE, county of NORFOLK, 3¾ miles (N.) from Downham-Market. The population is returned with the parish. Here was formerly a chapel, dedicated to St. Thomas.

THORPLAND, a hamlet in the parish of FAKENHAM-LANCASTER, hundred of GALLOW, county of NORFOLK, 2 miles (N.) from Fakenham. The population is returned with the parish. Here was formerly a chapel, long since destroyed.

THORRINGTON, a parish in the hundred of TENDRING, county of ESSEX, 8¼ miles (S. E. by E.) from Colchester, containing 353 inhabitants. The living is a rectory, with that of Frating annexed, in the archdeaconry of Colchester, and diocese of London, rated in the king's books at £16, and in the patronage of the Master and Fellows of St. John's College, Cambridge. The church is dedicated to St. Mary Magdalene. There is a place of worship for Wesleyan Methodists.

THORVETON, a parish in the hundred of HAYRIDGE, county of DEVON, 5¾ miles (E. by N.) from Crediton, containing 1317 inhabitants. The living is a vicarage, in the archdeaconry and diocese of Exeter, rated in the king's books at £18. 12. 8½., and in the patronage of the Dean and Chapter of Exeter. The church is dedicated to St. Thomas à Becket. There is a place of worship for Presbyterians. The parish is bounded on the west by the river Exe. A school for thirty boys and as many girls is supported partly by the produce of various donations invested in land, and partly by voluntary subscriptions. At East Raddon there was formerly a chapel, dedicated to St. John the Baptist, the remains of which have been converted into a dwelling-house, called "No Man's Chapel."

THOYDON (MOUNT), a parish in the hundred of ONGAR, county of ESSEX, 4 miles (S. E.) from Epping, containing 245 inhabitants. The living is a rectory, annexed to that of Tawney-Stapleford, in the archdeaconry of Essex, and diocese of London, rated in the king's books at £13. 6. 8. The church, dedicated to St. Michael, contains several fine monuments of the family of Smith, among which is one to the memory of Sir Thomas Smith, Chancellor of the Garter and Principal Secretary of State, in the reigns of Edward VI. and Elizabeth ; opposite this is one to Sir William Smith and his lady, with their three sons and four daughters.

THOYDON-BOIS, a parish in the hundred of ONGAR, county of ESSEX, 3½ miles (S.) from Epping, containing 446 inhabitants. The living is a perpetual curacy, in the archdeaconry of Essex, and diocese of London, endowed with £200 private benefaction, and £200 royal bounty, and in the patronage of R. W. H. Dare, Esq. The church is dedicated to St. Mary.

THOYDON-GARNON, or COOPERSHALL, a parish in the hundred of ONGAR, county of ESSEX, 2½ miles (S. S. E.) from Epping, containing 709 inhabitants. The living is a rectory, in the archdeaconry of Essex, and diocese of London, rated in the king's books at £17. J. R. Abdy, Esq. was patron in 1812. The church is dedicated to All Saints. Lady Ann Sydney Fitzwilliam, in 1602, bequeathed a small rent-charge towards the foundation of an almshouse for four poor widows.

THRANDESTON, a parish in the hundred of HARTISMERE, county of SUFFOLK, 3 miles (N. W.) from Eye, containing 330 inhabitants. The living is a rectory, in the archdeaconry of Sudbury, and diocese of Norwich, rated in the king's books at £13. 6. 8., and in the patronage of Earl Cornwallis. The church is dedicated to St. Margaret.

THRAPSTON, or THRAPSTONE, a market town and parish in the hundred of NAVISFORD, county of NORTHAMPTON, 21 miles (N. E. by E.) from Northampton, and 74 (N. N. W.) from London, containing 854 inhabitants. This small town is delightfully situated in a rich and luxuriant valley, on the eastern bank of the river Nen, over which is a handsome wooden bridge of several arches, built in 1795, in lieu of an old stone bridge, which was swept away by the inundation of that year : the houses are neat and regularly built, and the inhabitants are well supplied with excellent water : the vicinity is adorned with numerous residences of the nobility and gentry. The town appears to have been more extensive than it is at present, as several traces of buildings destroyed by fire are visible. The principal articles of manufacture are whips and bobbin-lace : on the river are corn-mills and a paper-mill ; and in the vicinity are some stone and other quarries, which yield a beautiful white sand, much used for domestic purposes. Some trade is carried on in conveying grain, by means of the Nen, which was made navigable in 1737, to Northampton, Peterborough, Lynn, and other places ; and bringing back timber, coal, and other commodities. The market is on Tuesday, for corn and seed, and is the largest hog market in the county. Fairs are held on the first Tuesday in May, for cattle and sheep ; August 5th, for the hiring of servants, and for shoes and pedlary ; and the first Tuesday after Michaelmas, a very large fair for cattle. There is a resident magistrate in the town, and subordinate officers are appointed at the manorial court, the court of the honour of Gloucester, and that for Navisford hundred, all which are held here.

The living is a rectory, in the archdeaconry of Northampton, and diocese of Peterborough, rated in the king's books at £14. 5. 5., and in the patronage of the Crown. The church, dedicated to St. James, is a cruciform structure, with a western tower and spire, combining the early, decorated, and later styles of English architecture ; it was extensively repaired in 1810 : in the chancel are three stone stalls, with rich mouldings and crocketed canopies, and in the church-yard is an ancient and very curious monument. There is a place of worship for Baptists. In 1794, Mrs. Mary Ekins bequeathed £200 for the education of ten poor boys : the interest is paid to a master, under the direction of the trustees of the Baptist chapel. An " Institution for bettering the condition, and increasing the comfort, of the poor," established in 1826, is supported by voluntary contributions, and a weekly subscription of one penny, by the different members of the poorer families, forming a fund which is expended in bedding, clothing, &c., annually distributed on St. Thomas' day : it has been productive of much benefit, and similar institutions have been formed in the surrounding parishes. There are twenty - four villages within five miles of this town, and, from an adjacent eminence, thirty-two churches may be seen.

THREAPLAND, a township in the parish of TORPENHOW, ALLERDALE ward below Darwent, county of CUMBERLAND, 6¾ miles (N. N. E.) from Cockermouth. The population is returned with the township of Bothel.

THRECKINGHAM, a parish in the wapentake of AVELAND, parts of KESTEVEN, county of LINCOLN, 2 miles (N. E. by N.) from Falkingham, containing, with the hamlet of Stow, 202 inhabitants. The living is a discharged vicarage, in the archdeaconry and diocese of Lincoln, rated in the king's books at £6. 8. 9., and in the patronage of Sir G. Heathcote, Bart. The church, dedicated to St. Peter, has a lofty tower and spire, and exhibits a curious admixture of the Norman, early English, and decorated styles of architecture. In the chancel is an elegant stall ; the font is circular, with early English panelling, and there are some old monuments and good screen-work.

THREE-FARMS, a township in the parish of ECCLESHALL, northern division of the hundred of PIREHILL, county of STAFFORD, containing 55 inhabitants.

THRELKELD, a chapelry in the parish of GREYSTOCK, LEATH ward, county of CUMBERLAND, 4 miles (E. N. E.) from Keswick, containing 303 inhabitants. The living is a perpetual curacy, in the archdeaconry and diocese of Carlisle, endowed with £600 royal bounty, and £400 parliamentary grant, and in the patronage of the Rector of Greystock. The chapel, dedicated to St. Mary, was rebuilt by subscription, upwards of fifty years ago.

THRESHFIELD, a township in the parish of LINTON, eastern division of the wapentake of STAINCLIFFE and EWCROSS, West riding of the county of YORK, 9 miles (N.) from Skipton, containing 237 inhabitants. Here is an endowed school.

THREXTON, a parish in the hundred of WAYLAND, county of NORFOLK, 2¼ miles (W. by S.) from Watton, containing 34 inhabitants. The living is a discharged rectory, annexed to the vicarage of Swaffham, in the archdeaconry of Norfolk, and diocese of Norwich, rated in the king's books at £7. 9. 4½. The church has a low round steeple, and in the south window are various armorial bearings in stained glass.

THRIBERGH, a parish in the southern division of the wapentake of STRAFFORTH and TICKHILL, West riding of the county of YORK, 3 miles (N. E.) from Rotherham, containing 315 inhabitants. The living is a rectory, in the archdeaconry and diocese of York, rated in the king's books at £12. 11. 5½., and in the patronage of John Fullerton, Esq. The church, dedicated to St. Leonard, is principally in the later style of English architecture. Elizabeth Finch, in 1760, bequeathed money producing about ten guineas a year, for teaching poor

children. A new school-room has been erected by Mr. Fullerton, and the former converted into a residence for the master.

THRIGBY, a parish in the eastern division of the hundred of FLEGG, county of NORFOLK, 4½ miles (W.) from Caistor, containing 46 inhabitants. The living is a discharged vicarage, in the archdeaconry and diocese of Norwich, rated in the king's books at £6. Thomas Brown, Esq. was patron in 1817. The church is dedicated to St. Mary.

THRIMBY, a chapelry in the parish of MORLAND, WEST ward, county of WESTMORLAND, 9 miles (N. N. W.) from Orton, containing 62 inhabitants. The living is a perpetual curacy, in the archdeaconry and diocese of Carlisle, endowed with £800 royal bounty, and in the patronage of the Vicar of Morland. The chapel, dedicated to St. Mary, was consecrated in 1814, having been rebuilt, together with a school-house, by the Earl of Lonsdale. The school was founded, in 1684, by Thomas Fletcher, Esq., who endowed it with a rent-charge of £10, for teaching eight children.

THRINGSTONE, a joint chapelry with Swannington, in the parish of WHITWICK, western division of the hundred of GOSCOTE, county of LEICESTER, 4¼ miles (E.) from Ashby de la Zouch, containing 1171 inhabitants. The living is a perpetual curacy, annexed to the vicarage of Whitwick, in the archdeaconry of Leicester, and diocese of Lincoln. The chapel has lately received an addition of four hundred and fifty sittings, of which three hundred and eighty are free, the Incorporated Society for the enlargement of churches and chapels having granted £450 towards defraying the expense. There is a place of worship for Wesleyan Methodists.

THRIPLOW, a parish in the hundred of THRIPLOW, county of CAMBRIDGE, 5½ miles (N. N. E.) from Royston, containing 371 inhabitants. The living is a discharged vicarage, in the peculiar jurisdiction and patronage of the Bishop of Ely, rated in the king's books at £4.9.2., and endowed with £200 private benefaction, and £200 royal bounty. The church is dedicated to All Saints. A grand rendezvous of the parliamentarian army, commanded by Fairfax and Cromwell, took place on Thriplow heath, in July 1647.

THRISLINGTON, a township in the parish of BISHOP'S - MIDDLEHAM, north - eastern division of STOCKTON ward, county palatine of DURHAM, 7½ miles (S. S. E.) from Durham, containing 14 inhabitants.

THRISTON (EAST and WEST), a joint township with Shot-haugh, in that part of the parish of FELTON which is in the eastern division of MORPETH ward, county of NORTHUMBERLAND, 9¾ miles (S. by E.) from Alnwick, containing, with Shot-haugh, 325 inhabitants.

THROAPHAM, a township in the parish of LAUGHTON en le MORTHEN, southern division of the wapentake of STRAFFORTH and TICKHILL, West riding of the county of YORK, 6½ miles (S. S. W.) from Tickhill, containing 50 inhabitants.

THROCKING, a parish in the hundred of EDWINSTREE, county of HERTFORD, 2 miles (W. N. W.) from Buntingford, containing, exclusively of the extra-parochial liberty of Wakely, 69 inhabitants. The living is a rectory, in the archdeaconry of Huntingdon, and diocese of Lincoln, rated in the king's books at £8, and in the patronage of Mrs. Elwes. The church is dedicated to the Holy Trinity.

THROCKLEY, a township in that part of the parish of NEWBURN which is in the western division of CASTLE ward, county of NORTHUMBERLAND, 6¼ miles (W. by N.) from Newcastle upon Tyne, containing 159 inhabitants.

THROCKMORTON, a chapelry in the parish of FLADBURY, middle division of the hundred of OSWALDSLOW, county of WORCESTER, 3¼ miles (N. E.) from Pershore, containing 153 inhabitants.

THROPPLE, a township in that part of the parish of MITFORD which is in the western division of MORPETH ward, county of NORTHUMBERLAND, 4 miles (W.) from Morpeth, containing 75 inhabitants. At Whittle Hill are slight remains of a Roman camp; the intrenchments have been almost obliterated by the plough, and the stones removed for repairing the roads. Coins have been found near it, in an ancient barrow, called Money Hill.

THROPTON, a township in the parish of ROTHBURY, western division of COQUETDALE ward, county of NORTHUMBERLAND, 2 miles (W. by N.) from Rothbury, containing 158 inhabitants. There are places of worship for Presbyterians and Roman Catholics. The village is pleasantly situated near the confluence of the river Coquet and the Snitter-burn, over the latter of which a substantial bridge was erected by subscription in 1810, the old bridge having fallen down several years before. There is a cross road at both ends of the village, and a stone cross is situated at each intersection.

THROSTON, a township in the parish of HART, north-eastern division of STOCKTON ward, county palatine of DURHAM, 3¾ miles (W.) from Hartlepool, containing 71 inhabitants.

THROWLEY, a parish in the hundred of WONFORD, county of DEVON, 6¾ miles (E. S. E.) from Oakhampton, containing 386 inhabitants. The living is a rectory, in the archdeaconry and diocese of Exeter, rated in the king's books at £19. 6. 10½., and in the patronage of the Crown. The church is a small plain building. There are some remains of a chapel at Walland Hill. The river Teign forms one of the boundaries of the parish.

THROWLEY, a parish in the hundred of FAVERSHAM, lathe of SCRAY, county of KENT, 4½ miles (S. S. W.) from Faversham, containing 607 inhabitants. The living is a vicarage, in the archdeaconry and diocese of Canterbury, rated in the king's books at £7. 11. 8., and in the patronage of the Prebendary of Rugmere in the Cathedral Church of St. Paul's, London. The church is dedicated to St. Mary. Sir Thomas Sondes, in 1592, endowed a free school for educating fourteen boys. There are also three almshouses, founded by the same family. The vicarage-house occupies the site of a priory, founded as a cell to the abbey of St. Bertin, at St. Omers in Artois, and granted, in the 22nd of Henry VI., to the abbey of Sion.

THROWLEY, a hamlet in the parish of ILAM, northern division of the hundred of TOTMONSLOW, county of STAFFORD, 7¾ miles (N. W. by W.) from Ashbourn. The population is returned with the parish. It is in the honour of Tutbury, duchy of Lancaster, and within the jurisdiction of a court of pleas held at Tutbury every third Tuesday, for the recovery of debts under 40s.

THROXENBY, a township in the parish of SCALBY, PICKERING lythe, North riding of the county of YORK,

2½ miles (W.) from Scarborough, containing 66 inhabitants.

THRUMPTON, a parish in the northern division of the wapentake of RUSHCLIFFE, county of NOTTINGHAM, 4 miles (N.N.E.) from Kegworth, containing 109 inhabitants. The living is a perpetual curacy, in the archdeaconry of Nottingham, and diocese of York. J. Emmerton, Esq. was patron in 1811. The church is dedicated to All Saints. On the banks of the Trent is a fine old mansion in the style of architecture prevalent in the reign of Elizabeth.

THRUP, a hamlet in the parish of KIDLINGTON, hundred of WOOTTON, county of OXFORD, 1½ mile (E. S. E.) from Woodstock, containing 55 inhabitants.

THRUPP, a joint tything with Wadley, otherwise Littleworth, in that part of the parish of GREAT FARRINGDON which is in the hundred of SHRIVENHAM, county of BERKS, 2 miles (N.) from Great Farringdon. The population is returned with Wadley.

THRUPPWICK, a liberty in the parish of RADLEY, hundred of HORMER, county of BERKS, 1½ mile (E.) from Abingdon, containing 30 inhabitants.

THRUSSINGTON, a parish in the eastern division of the hundred of GOSCOTE, county of LEICESTER, 8¼ miles (N. N. E.) from Leicester, containing 466 inhabitants. The living is a discharged vicarage, in the archdeaconry of Leicester, and diocese of Lincoln, rated in the king's books at £6, endowed with £200 private benefaction, and £200 royal bounty, and in the patronage of — Heycock, Esq. The church is dedicated to the Holy Trinity. Thomas Hayne, in 1640, bequeathed an annuity of about £7 for teaching poor children.

THRUXTON, a parish in the hundred of WEBTREE, county of HEREFORD, 6¼ miles (S. W. by W.) from Hereford, containing 54 inhabitants. The living is a discharged rectory, united to the vicarage of Kingstone, in the peculiar jurisdiction of the Dean of Hereford, rated in the king's books at £4. 8. 4. The church is dedicated to St. Bartholomew.

THRUXTON, a parish in the hundred of ANDOVER, Andover division of the county of SOUTHAMPTON, 5 miles (W.) from Andover, containing 240 inhabitants. The living is a rectory, in the archdeaconry and diocese of Winchester, rated in the king's books at £15. 12. 11., and in the patronage of Mrs. Sheppard. The church is dedicated to the Holy Rood. There is a place of worship for Wesleyan Methodists. Here is a beautiful Roman pavement, nearly perfect.

THUNDERLEY, a hamlet (formerly a distinct parish) in the parish of WIMBISH, hundred of UTTLESFORD, county of ESSEX, 2 miles (S. E. by S.) from Saffron-Walden. The population is returned with the parish. The vicarage has been consolidated with that of Wimbish, in the archdeaconry of Middlesex, and diocese of London. The church is in ruins.

THUNDERSLEY, a parish partly in the hundred of ROCHFORD, consisting of the hamlet of Thundersley, but chiefly in the hundred of BARSTABLE, county of ESSEX, 2¼ miles (S. W. by W.) from Rayleigh, containing 546 inhabitants. The living is a discharged rectory, in the archdeaconry of Essex, and diocese of London, rated in the king's books at £14. 13. 4., and in the patronage of the Rev. G. Hemming. The church, dedicated to St. Peter, is an admixture of the Norman and early English styles of architecture.

THUNDRIDGE, a parish in the hundred of BRAUGHIN, county of HERTFORD, 2½ miles (N. N. E.) from Ware, containing 529 inhabitants. The living is a vicarage, annexed to that of Ware, in the archdeaconry of Middlesex, and diocese of London, rated in the king's books at £6. The church, dedicated to St. Mary and All Saints, has an embattled tower with a lofty spire: it had formerly a Norman arch between the nave and the chancel, which having been enlarged, in recently repairing the edifice, its original character has been destroyed.

THURCASTON, a parish in the western division of the hundred of GOSCOTE, county of LEICESTER, 3¼ miles (S. S. W.) from Mountsorrel, comprising the chapelry of Anstey, and the township of Cropston, and containing 1159 inhabitants. The living is a rectory, in the archdeaconry of Leicester, and diocese of Lincoln, rated in the king's books at £23. 7. 8½., and in the patronage of the Master and Fellows of Emanuel College, Cambridge. The church is dedicated to All Saints. The Rev. Richard Hill, in 1730, bequeathed land, directing the produce to be applied for teaching twenty-two children. The zealous and venerable reformer, Dr. Hugh Latimer, Bishop of Worcester, was born here, about 1480. Doctor Hurd, also Bishop of Worcester, was for some time rector of this parish.

THURCROSS, a township in the parish of FEWSTON, lower division of the wapentake of CLARO, West riding of the county of YORK, 9 miles (W. by S.) from Ripley, containing 600 inhabitants.

THURGARTON, a parish in the northern division of the hundred of ERPINGHAM, county of NORFOLK, 4¾ miles (S.W. by S.) from Cromer, containing 248 inhabitants. The living is a discharged rectory, in the archdeaconry of Norfolk, and diocese of Norwich, rated in the king's books at £9. 6. 8., and in the patronage of the Bishop of Norwich. The church, dedicated to All Saints, is a small thatched building without a tower. Here are slight remains of an ancient hall.

THURGARTON, a parish in the southern division of the wapentake of THURGARTON, county of NOTTINGHAM, 3¼ miles (S. by W.) from Southwell, containing 330 inhabitants. The living is a perpetual curacy, in the archdeaconry of Nottingham, and diocese of York, endowed with £600 royal bounty, and £200 parliamentary grant, and in the patronage of the Master and Fellows of Trinity College, Cambridge. The church is dedicated to St. Peter. An Augustine priory, in honour of St. Peter, was founded here, in 1130, by Ralph de Ayncourt, which, at the dissolution, had a revenue of £359. 15. 10.

THURGOLAND, a township in the parish of SILKSTONE, wapentake of STAINCROSS, West riding of the county of YORK, 3¾ miles (E. S. E.) from Penistone, containing 819 inhabitants, many of whom are employed in the manufacture of woollen cloth and wire. There is a place of worship for Wesleyan Methodists.

THURLASTON, a parish in the hundred of SPARKENHOE, county of LEICESTER, 6 miles (N.E. by E.) from Hinckley, comprising the hamlet of Normanton-Turville, and the liberty of Newparks, and containing 549 inhabitants. The living is a rectory, in the archdeaconry of Leicester, and diocese of Lincoln, rated in the king's books at £13. 19. 7., and in the patronage of R. Arkwright, Esq. The church is dedicated to All Saints.

THURLASTON, a hamlet in the parish of DUNCHURCH, Rugby division of the hundred of KNIGHTLOW, county of WARWICK, 1 mile (W.) from Dunchurch, containing 304 inhabitants.

THURLBEAR, a parish in the hundred of NORTH CURRY, county of SOMERSET, 3¼ miles (S. E.) from Taunton, containing 215 inhabitants. The living is a rectory, in the archdeaconry of Taunton, and diocese of Bath and Wells, and in the patronage of the Rt. Hon. W. Arbuthnot. The church is dedicated to St. Thomas. It was anciently a chapel to the vicarage of St. Mary Magdalene, in Taunton, but the tithes were restored by Sir Thomas Petman, Bart.

THURLBY, a parish in the lower division of the wapentake of BOOTHBY-GRAFFO, parts of KESTEVEN, county of LINCOLN, 9½ miles (S. W.) from Lincoln, containing 102 inhabitants. The living is a perpetual curacy, in the peculiar jurisdiction of the Dean and Chapter of Lincoln, and in the patronage of the Prebendary of Carlton *cum* Thurlby in the Cathedral Church of Lincoln. The church, dedicated to St. German, is principally in the later style of English architecture. The parish lies between the rivers Trent and Witham, the latter of which is celebrated for its eels and pike.

THURLBY, a hamlet in the parish of BILSBY, Wold division of the hundred of CALCEWORTH, parts of LINDSEY, county of LINCOLN, 2¼ miles (E.) from Alford. The population is returned with the parish.

THURLBY, a parish in the wapentake of NESS, parts of KESTEVEN, county of LINCOLN, 5¼ miles (N. N. W.) from Market-Deeping, containing, with the hamlets of Northorpe and Obthorpe, 622 inhabitants. The living is a discharged vicarage, in the archdeaconry and diocese of Lincoln, rated in the king's books at £10. 9. 4½., endowed with £600 royal bounty, and in the patronage of the Provost and Fellows of Eton College. The church, dedicated to St. Firmin, is an ancient but handsome structure. The parish is bounded on one side by the river Glen; and the ancient Roman canal, Carr Dyke, passes close by the church, being plainly discernible.

THURLEIGH, a parish in the hundred of WILLEY, county of BEDFORD, 6½ miles (N.) from Bedford, containing 477 inhabitants. The living is a discharged vicarage, in the archdeaconry of Bedford, and diocese of Lincoln, rated in the king's books at £9. — Crawley, Esq. and others were patrons in 1801. The church is dedicated to St. Peter. Eight children are instructed for about £6. 10. per annum, the bequest of George Franklyn, in 1618. Here is the moated site of the ancient mansion of Blackbull Hall, and on Bury hill are vestiges of a circular camp.

THURLESTONE, a parish in the hundred of STANBOROUGH, county of DEVON, 4½ miles (W. by S.) from Kingsbridge, containing 426 inhabitants. The living is a rectory, in the archdeaconry of Totness, and diocese of Exeter, rated in the king's books at £25. 10. B. G. Buller, Esq. was patron in 1806. The parish is bounded on the north-west by the river Avon, and on the south-west by the English channel.

THURLESTONE, a township in the parish of PENISTONE, wapentake of STAINCROSS, West riding of the county of YORK, 8½ miles (W. by S.) from Barnesley, containing 1524 inhabitants. There is a place of worship for Wesleyan Methodists. The manufacture of woollen cloth and hair cloth is extensively carried on, and there are fulling and scribbling mills in the neighbourhood.

THURLOW (GREAT), a parish in the hundred of RISBRIDGE, county of SUFFOLK, 5 miles (N. by E.) from Haverhill, containing 462 inhabitants. The living is a vicarage, in the archdeaconry of Sudbury, and diocese of Norwich, rated in the king's books at £10. 11. 5½., and in the patronage of the Crown. The church is dedicated to All Saints. An hospital, or free chapel, dedicated to St. James, and subordinate to that of Hautpays, or *De Alto Passu*, was founded here in the time of Richard II., which, at the suppression of Alien houses, was valued at £3 per annum, and granted by Edward IV. to God's House College, Cambridge.

THURLOW (LITTLE), a parish in the hundred of RISBRIDGE, county of SUFFOLK, 5½ miles (N. by E.) from Haverhill, containing 436 inhabitants. The living is a rectory, in the archdeaconry of Sudbury, and diocese of Norwich, rated in the king's books at £7. 10. 5., and in the patronage of the Rev. R. C. Barnard. The church is dedicated to St. Peter. Sir Stephen Soame, in 1618, bequeathed an annuity of £30 in support of a free school for the instruction of twelve boys: he also left a like sum for the endowment of almshouses for eight poor persons who had resided in the parish twenty-four years, and, in default thereof, to those of Great Thurlow, or Wratting.

THURLOXTON, a parish in the northern division of the hundred of PETHERTON, county of SOMERSET, 5 miles (S. S. W.) from Bridg-water, containing 178 inhabitants. The living is a rectory, in the archdeaconry of Taunton, and diocese of Bath and Wells, rated in the king's books at £6. 15. 10., and in the patronage of E. B. Portman, Esq. The church is dedicated to St. Giles.

THURLSTON, a parish within the liberty of the borough of IPSWICH, county of SUFFOLK, 2½ miles (N. N. W.) from Ipswich. The population is returned with the parish of Whitton. The living is a rectory, annexed to that of Whitton, in the archdeaconry of Suffolk, and diocese of Norwich. The church is dedicated to St. Botolph.

THURLTON, a parish in the hundred of CLAVERING, county of NORFOLK, 5½ miles (N.) from Beccles, containing 414 inhabitants. The living is a discharged rectory, in the archdeaconry of Norfolk, and diocese of Norwich, rated in the king's books at £6. 13. 4., and in the patronage of the Mayor and Corporation of Norwich. The church is dedicated to All Saints.

THURMASTON (NORTH), a chapelry partly in the parish of BARKBY, and partly in that of BELGRAVE, eastern division of the hundred of GOSCOTE, county of LEICESTER, 3¼ miles (N. N. E.) from Leicester, containing 192 inhabitants. The living is a perpetual curacy, in the archdeaconry of Leicester, and diocese of Lincoln, endowed with £200 private benefaction, £400 royal bounty, and £1200 parliamentary grant, and in the patronage of George Pochin, Esq. The chapel is dedicated to St. Matthew. There was anciently another, dedicated to St. John the Evangelist. There is a place of worship for Wesleyan Methodists. The petty sessions for the eastern division of the hundred of Goscote are held here. The Leicester and Melton-Mowbray navigation, and the old Fosse road, pass in the vicinity.

The most ancient Roman milliarium known in Britain was found here; it is three feet and a half high, and five feet seven inches in circumference, and has been placed on a pillar in the town of Leicester.

THURNBY, a parish in the hundred of GARTREE, county of LEICESTER, 4 miles (E. by S.) from Leicester, comprising the chapelry of Stoughton, and the hamlet of Bushby, and containing 400 inhabitants. The living is a vicarage, in the archdeaconry of Leicester, and diocese of Lincoln, rated in the king's books at £11, and in the patronage of G. A. Legh-Keck, Esq. The church is dedicated to St. Luke.

THURNHAM, a township in that part of the parish of LANCASTER which is in the hundred of LONSDALE, south of the sands, county palatine of LANCASTER, 4¾ miles (S. S. W.) from Lancaster, containing 448 inhabitants. Glasson dock, the modern harbour of Lancaster, is within this township, and the venerable ruins of Cockersand abbey are in the neighbourhood.

THURNING, a parish partly in the hundred of POLEBROOKE, county of NORTHAMPTON, but chiefly in that of LEIGHTONSTONE, county of HUNTINGDON, 4½ miles (S. E.) from Oundle, containing 156 inhabitants. The living is a rectory, in the archdeaconry of Huntingdon, and diocese of Lincoln, rated in the king's books at £11. 4. 2., and in the patronage of the Master and Fellows of Emanuel College Cambridge. The church is dedicated to St. James.

THURNING, a parish in the hundred of EYNSFORD, county of NORFOLK, 4¾ miles (N. by W.) from Reepham, containing 112 inhabitants. The living is a discharged rectory, in the archdeaconry of Norfolk, and diocese o Norwich, rated in the king's books at £7, and in the patronage of the Master and Fellows of Corpus Christi College, Cambridge. The church is dedicated to St. Andrew.

THURNSCOE, a parish in the northern division of the wapentake of STRAFFORTH and TICKHILL, West riding of the county of YORK, 8 miles (E.) from Barnesley, containing 205 inhabitants. The living is a rectory, in the archdeaconry and diocese of York, rated in the king's books at £11. 7. 8½., and in the patronage of Earl Fitzwilliam. The church is dedicated to St. Helen.

THURROCK (GRAYS), a market town and parish in the hundred of CHAFFORD, county of ESSEX, 22 miles (S. S. W.) from Chelmsford, and 20½ (E. by S.) from London, containing 742 inhabitants. The town, consisting of a single street irregularly built, is situated on the verge of the river Thames, from which branches a creek navigable for small craft: this river has a wharf on its northern bank, communicating with some limeworks by means of a railway. Bricks are here manufactured to some extent for the London builders, and are conveyed hence in barges. The market is on Thursday; and fairs for cattle and hardware are held on May 23rd and October 20th. The living is a discharged vicarage, in the archdeaconry of Essex, and diocese of London, rated in the king's books at £5. 0. 10., and in the patronage of the Master and Fellows of Pembroke College, Oxford. The church is dedicated to St. Peter and St. Paul. A free school, situated in the churchyard, was founded and endowed by William Palmer, in 1706, in which ten children are instructed, and four are clothed.

THURROCK (LITTLE), a parish in the hundred of BARSTABLE, county of ESSEX, 1 mile (E.) from Grays-Thurrock, containing 192 inhabitants. The living is a rectory, in the archdeaconry of Essex, and diocese of London, rated in the king's books at £13. 15., and in the patronage of the Rev. Thomas Schreiber. The church is dedicated to St. Mary. The parish is bounded on the south-west by the Thames.

THURROCK (WEST), a parish in the hundred of CHAFFORD, county of ESSEX, 1 mile (W.) from Grays-Thurrock, containing, with the township of Purfleet, 829 inhabitants. The living is a discharged vicarage, in the jurisdiction of the Commissary of Essex and Herts, concurrently with the Consistorial Court of the Bishop of London, rated in the king's books at £15. 13. 4., and in the patronage of S. Whitbread, Esq. The church is dedicated to St. Clement. The parish is bounded on the south by the Thames, where there is a landing-place, opposite to Greenhithe.

THURSBY, a parish in the ward and county of CUMBERLAND, comprising the townships of Crofton-Quarter, Parton, and High Thursby, and containing 515 inhabitants, of which number, 355 are in the township of High Thursby, 6½ miles (S. W.) from Carlisle. The living is a discharged vicarage, in the archdeaconry and diocese of Carlisle, rated in the king's books at £11. 10. 5., endowed with £200 private benefaction, and £300 parliamentary grant, and in the patronage of the Dean and Chapter of Carlisle. The church is dedicated to St. Andrew. A school, founded in 1740 by subscription, was endowed, in 1798, by Thomas Tomlinson, Esq., with £354, producing to the master a salary of £17. 14., for which ten children are educated. Thursby, it is thought, derived its name from Thor, the Saxon deity, to whose honour a temple is said to have been erected at Woodrigs, in this neighbourhood.

THURSFIELD, a chapelry in the parish of WOL-STANTON, northern division of the hundred of PIRE-HILL, county of STAFFORD, 6½ miles (N. by E.) from Newcastle under Lyne, containing 265 inhabitants. Dr. Robert Hulme, in 1708, bequeathed certain lands, now producing an annual income of £63. 4., for which eighteen boys are taught; and two others are instructed for an annuity of thirty shillings, left by Joseph Brown. James Brindley, of Turnhurst, the celebrated engineer, was interred here in 1772; a plain altar-tomb has been erected in his memory.

THURSFORD, a parish in the northern division of the hundred of GREENHOE, county of NORFOLK, 3½ miles (S. E. by E.) from Little Walsingham, containing 356 inhabitants. The living is a discharged rectory, annexed to that of Great Snoring, in the archdeaconry and diocese of Norwich, rated in the king's books at £8. The church is dedicated to St. Andrew.

THURSHELTON, a parish in the hundred of LIFTON, county of DEVON, 11 miles (N. W. by W.) from Oakhampton, containing 397 inhabitants. The living is a perpetual curacy, annexed to the vicarage of Mary-Stow, in the archdeaconry of Totness, and diocese of Exeter. The church is dedicated to St. George.

THURSLEY, a parish in the second division of the hundred of GODALMING, county of SURREY, 5½ miles (S. W. by W.) from Godalming, containing 608 inhabitants. The living is a perpetual curacy, an-

nexed to the vicarage of Witley, in the archdeaconry of Surrey, and diocese of Winchester. The church is dedicated to St. Michael.

THURSTASTON, a parish in the lower division of the hundred of WIRRALL, county palatine of CHESTER, 5 miles (N. W. by N.) from Great Neston, containing 127 inhabitants. The living is a discharged rectory, in the archdeaconry and diocese of Chester, rated in the king's books at £6. 13. 6., endowed with £200 private benefaction, and £300 parliamentary grant, and in the patronage of the Dean and Chapter of Chester. The church, dedicated to St. Bartholomew, is a curious small structure, partly in the Norman style of architecture. The river Dee passes by this place to Chester.

THURSTON, a parish in the hundred of THEDWES-TRY, county of SUFFOLK, 5½ miles (E. by N.) from Bury St. Edmund's, containing 377 inhabitants. The living is a discharged vicarage, in the archdeaconry of Sudbury, and diocese of Norwich, rated in the king's books at £6. 13. 4., and in the patronage of Charles Tyrrell, Esq. The church, dedicated to St. Peter, is a remarkably fine structure, and the pillars of the nave are peculiarly light and airy. Thomas de Multon, of Egremont, in the 18th of Edward I., obtained the grant of a market on Tuesday, and a fair on the eve, day, and morrow of St. Mary Magdalene, at his manor of Thurstanston, in the county of Suffolk, which is supposed to be the same with Thurston.

THURSTONLAND, a township in the parish of KIRK-BURTON, upper division of the wapentake of AGBRIGG, West riding of the county of YORK, 5½ miles (S. by E.) from Huddersfield, containing 989 inhabitants. There is a place of worship for Wesleyan Methodists.

THURTON, a parish in the hundred of LODDON, county of NORFOLK, 8 miles (S. E.) from Norwich, containing 170 inhabitants. The living is a perpetual curacy, in the archdeaconry of Norfolk, and diocese of Norwich, endowed with £1000 royal bounty, and in the patronage of Sir W. B. Proctor, Bart. The church is dedicated to St. Ethelbert.

THURVASTON, a joint township with Osleston, in the parish of SUTTON on the HILL, hundred of AP-PLETREE, county of DERBY, 7¾ miles (W. by N.) from Derby. The population is returned with Osleston. There is a place of worship for Wesleyan Methodists.

THUXTON, a parish in the hundred of MITFORD, county of NORFOLK, 4 miles (N. by E.) from Hingham, containing 78 inhabitants. The living is a discharged rectory, in the archdeaconry of Norfolk, and diocese of Norwich, rated in the king's books at £4. 6. 3., and in the patronage of the Bishop of Norwich. The church is dedicated to St. Paul.

THWAITE, a parish in the southern division of the hundred of ERPINGHAM, county of NORFOLK, 4¾ miles (N.) from Aylsham, containing 116 inhabitants. The living is a discharged rectory, in the archdeaconry and diocese of Norwich, rated in the king's books at £7, and in the patronage of the Bishop of Norwich. The church, dedicated to All Saints, has a fine Norman entrance on the south.

THWAITE, a parish in the hundred of LODDON, county of NORFOLK, 3½ miles (N.) from Bungay, containing 94 inhabitants. The living is a discharged rectory, in the archdeaconry of Norfolk, and diocese of Norwich, rated in the king's books at £4, and in the patronage of the Duke of Norfolk. The church is dedicated to St. Mary.

THWAITE, a parish in the hundred of HARTISMERE, county of SUFFOLK, 4¾ miles (S. W. by S.) from Eye, containing 112 inhabitants. The living is a discharged rectory, in the archdeaconry of Sudbury, and diocese of Norwich, rated in the king's books at £6. 3. 5½., and in the patronage of John Wilson Sheppard, Esq. The church is dedicated to St. George.

THWAITS, a chapelry in the parish of MILLOM, ALLERDALE ward above Darwent, county of CUMBERLAND, 10 miles (S.E) from Ravenglass, containing 315 inhabitants. The living is a perpetual curacy, in the archdeaconry of Richmond, and diocese of Chester, endowed with £200 private benefaction, and £800 royal bounty, and in the patronage of certain Trustees. The chapel was rebuilt in 1715, and dedicated to St. Anne in 1724.

THWING, a parish in the wapentake of DICKERING, East riding of the county of YORK, 8¾ miles (W. N.W.) from Bridlington, containing, with the townships of Octon, Octon-Grange, and Wold-Cottage, 314 inhabitants. The living is a rectory in medieties, in the archdeaconry of the East riding, and diocese of York, each rated in the king's books at £8. 12. 1., and in the patronage of the Crown. The church is dedicated to All Saints.

TIBBENHAM, a parish in the hundred of DEPWADE, county of NORFOLK, 5 miles (W.S.W.) from St. Mary Stratton, containing 553 inhabitants. The living is a discharged vicarage, in the archdeaconry of Norfolk, and diocese of Norwich, rated in the king's books at £7. 6. 8., endowed with £1000 parliamentary grant, and in the patronage of the Bishop of Ely. The church is dedicated to All Saints. About a mile southeast of it is Chanons Hall, occupying the site of the ancient manor-house of Chanons, which was a very extensive building, surrounded by a moat.

TIBBERTON, a parish in the hundred of LANCASTER, county of GLOUCESTER, 4¼ miles (S.E.) from Newent, containing 282 inhabitants. The living is a discharged rectory, in the archdeaconry of Hereford, and diocese of Gloucester, rated in the king's books at £7. 16. 0½., and in the patronage of James Scott, Esq. The church is dedicated to the Holy Trinity. The Herefordshire and Gloucestershire canal passes on the eastern side of the parish.

TIBBERTON, a chapelry in the parish of EDGMOND, Newport division of the hundred of BRADFORD (South), county of SALOP, 4¼ miles (W. by N.) from Newport, containing 303 inhabitants. The chapel is dedicated to All Saints.

TIBBERTON, a parish in the middle division of the hundred of OSWALDSLOW, county of WORCESTER, 4 miles (E. N. E.) from Worcester, containing 288 inhabitants. The living is a discharged vicarage, in the peculiar jurisdiction and patronage of the Dean and Chapter of Worcester, rated in the king's books at £3. 15. 10. The church is dedicated to St. Nicholas. The Birmingham and Worcester canal passes through the parish.

TIBERTON, a parish in the hundred of WEBTREE, county of HEREFORD, 9 miles (W.) from Hereford, con-

taining 146 inhabitants. The living is a perpetual curacy, annexed to the vicarage of Madley, in the peculiar jurisdiction of the Dean of Hereford. The church is dedicated to St. Mary.

TIBSHELF, a parish in the hundred of SCARSDALE, county of DERBY, 4 miles (N. E. by N.) from Alfreton, containing 711 inhabitants. The living is a discharged vicarage, in the archdeaconry of Derby, and diocese of Lichfield and Coventry, rated in the king's books at £4. 5. 3., and in the patronage of Miss Lord. The church, dedicated to St. John the Baptist, was rebuilt in 1729. The manufacture of stockings is carried on, and there are extensive collieries in the parish.

TIBTHORP, a township in the parish of KIRKBURN, Bainton-Beacon division of the wapentake of HARTHILL, East riding of the county of YORK, 5¼ miles (W. S. W.) from Great Driffield, containing 221 inhabitants. There is a place of worship for Wesleyan Methodists.

TICEHURST, a parish in the hundred of SHOYSWELL, rape of HASTINGS, county of SUSSEX, 4 miles (E. S. E.) from Wadhurst, containing 1966 inhabitants. The living is a vicarage, in the archdeaconry of Lewes, and diocese of Chichester, rated in the king's books at £18. 7. 6., and in the patronage of the Dean and Chapter of Canterbury. The church, dedicated to St. Mary, is principally in the later style of English architecture.

TICHFIELD, county of SOUTHAMPTON. — See TITCHFIELD.

TICKENCOTE, a parish in the hundred of EAST, county of RUTLAND, 3 miles (N. W. by W.) from Stamford, containing 126 inhabitants. The living is a discharged rectory, in the archdeaconry of Northampton, and diocese of Peterborough, rated in the king's books at £6. 5. 6., endowed with £200 private benefaction, and £200 royal bounty, and in the patronage of John Wingfield, Esq. The church, dedicated to St. Peter, was in the earliest style of Norman architecture, but it has been partially rebuilt. Stukeley says, " it is the most venerable church extant, and was the entire oratory of Prince Peada, founder of Peterborough abbey."

TICKENHAM, a parish in the hundred of PORTBURY, county of SOMERSET, 9¼ miles (W. by S.) from Bristol, containing 405 inhabitants. The living is a discharged vicarage, united to that of Portbury, in the archdeaconry of Bath, and diocese of Bath and Wells, rated in the king's books at £8. 15. 5., endowed with £200 private benefaction, and £200 royal bounty, and in the patronage of Adam Gordon, Esq. The church is dedicated to St. Quiricus and Julietta. About a mile north of it are the remains of a double-intrenched Roman camp; the ramparts, constructed of limestone, enclose an area of about an acre.

TICKHILL, a parish in the southern division of the wapentake of STRAFFORTH and TICKHILL, West riding of the county of YORK, comprising the town of Tickhill, the township of Stancill with Wellingley and Wilsick, and containing 1884 inhabitants, of which number, 1830 are in the town of Tickhill, 45 miles (S.) from York, and 157 (N. by W.) from London. This manor having been given by William the Conqueror to Roger de Busli, he erected or rebuilt a castle, which, with the honour of Tickhill, being subsequently forfeited, was given by King Stephen to the Count of Eu, in Normandy; but it afterwards reverted to the crown, and was granted, by Richard I., to his brother, Prince John. In the reign of Henry III., it was restored to the Count of Eu, but, after several changes, became again vested in the crown, in the reign of Henry IV. At the commencement of the great civil war, the castle, then considered a very strong fortress, was garrisoned for the king; and, after a siege of two days, was surrendered to the assailants, and soon after dismantled by order of parliament. The town is situated in a fertile valley, on the border of the county of Nottingham: the streets, which are arranged in the form of a cross, are neat and spacious; the houses are in general of respectable appearance, but built in a straggling manner, and the inhabitants are well supplied with water. The trade in malt was formerly extensive, but at present there are not more than three kilns: a small paper manufactory affords employment to a few persons. The market, formerly held on Friday, is entirely disused. A fair is held on August 21st, for cattle and various articles of merchandise. The market cross is a circular building of stone, erected in 1776, and situated in the centre of the town. Manorial courts leet and baron are held annually. The living is a discharged vicarage, in the archdeaconry and diocese of York, rated in the king's books at £7. 2. 6., endowed with £200 royal bounty, and in the patronage of G. S. Foljambe, Esq. The church, which is dedicated to St. Mary, is a handsome structure in the later style of English architecture, having a fine tower with pinnacles; it was greatly injured by lightning in 1825, but has recently undergone an entire repair, at an expense of £1950. In the chancel is an altar-tomb, ornamented at the sides with large quatrefoils, to the memory of William Estfield, seneschal of the lordship of Holderness, and of the honour of Tickhill, who died in 1386: at the east end of the south aisle is an alabaster monument, with the effigies of a knight and his lady. There are places of worship for Independents and Wesleyan Methodists. A National school for children of both sexes is supported by voluntary contributions, aided by an annuity of £4. 8. 8. from the duchy of Lancaster; sixty boys and forty girls are educated. Near the church is a *Maison de Dieu*, comprising fourteen almshouses for poor widows, of uncertain foundation. The remains of the castle, on the south-east side of the town, consist of the mound, on which the foundations of the keep are visible; the ditch, with part of the external walls, and a dilapidated Norman gateway. The northern part, by considerable repairs and additions, has been changed into a modern residence, and the ground within the walls is formed into gardens and shrubberies. The ruins of an ancient Augustine priory, founded in the reign of Henry III., and situated in an adjacent vale, have been converted into a farmhouse. John of Gaunt, Duke of Lancaster, resided at Tickhill castle.

TICKNALL, a parish in the hundred of REPTON and GRESLEY, county of DERBY, 5¾ miles (N. by W.) from Ashby de la Zouch, containing 1274 inhabitants. The living is a perpetual curacy, in the archdeaconry of Derby, and diocese of Lichfield and Coventry, endowed with £200 royal bounty, and £1200 parliamentary grant, and in the patronage of Sir George Crewe, Bart. The church, dedicated to St. Thomas à Becket, is partly in the early and partly in the later style of English archi-

tecture, and has lately been repaired and embellished. There is a place of worship for Wesleyan Methodists. Many of the inhabitants are employed at the extensive limeworks within the parish. A school-house was erected by Dame Catherine Harpur, who, in 1744, conveyed for its support land now producing an annual income of £25, for which forty boys are instructed: the premises were rebuilt, in 1825, at the expense of Sir George Crewe. An hospital for seven decayed housekeepers of Ticknall and Calke was founded, in 1771, by Charles Harpur, Esq., who gave £500 for building it, and endowed it with £2000: seven aged women at present enjoy the benefits of this charity. Ticknall is in the honour of Tutbury, duchy of Lancaster, and within the jurisdiction of a court of pleas held at Tutbury every third Tuesday, for the recovery of debts under 40s.

TICKTON, a joint township with Hull-Bridge, in that part of the parish of ST. JOHN which is within the liberties of the borough of BEVERLEY, East riding of the county of YORK, 2¼ miles (N. E.) from Beverley, containing, with Hull-Bridge, 110 inhabitants.

TIDCOMBE, a parish in the hundred of KINWARDSTONE, county of WILTS, 6¼ miles (N. N. E.) from Ludgershall, containing 237 inhabitants. The living is a vicarage, in the archdeaconry of Wilts, and diocese of Salisbury, rated in the king's books at £6. 13. 4., endowed with £200 private benefaction, and £200 royal bounty, and in the patronage of the Dean and Canons of Windsor. The church is dedicated to St. Michael.

TIDDESLEY-HAY, an extra-parochial liberty, containing about three thousand five hundred acres, in the eastern division of the hundred of CUTTLESTONE, county of STAFFORD, 2¼ miles (N. E.) from Penkridge, containing 43 inhabitants. This was a royal chace, adjoining that of Cannock, till the reign of Elizabeth, who granted it jointly to the Earls of Warwick and Leicester, by whom it was sold to Sir Edward Littleton, of Pillaton Hall: there were at that time no other enclosures upon it than two ancient parks, and in that state it continued till recently, when it was wholly enclosed by E. J. Littleton, Esq. M.P., its present proprietor.

TIDDINGTON, a hamlet in the parish of ALBURY, hundred of BULLINGTON, county of OXFORD, 3¼ miles (N. N. W.) from Tetsworth, containing 176 inhabitants.

TIDENHAM, a parish forming, with the parish of Wollastone, a detached portion of the hundred of WESTBURY, county of GLOUCESTER, 2 miles (N. E. by N.) from Chepstow, containing, with the chapelry of Lancaut, 1102 inhabitants. The living is a discharged vicarage, in the archdeaconry and diocese of Gloucester, rated in the king's books at £7. 14., and in the patronage of — Davis, Esq. The church is dedicated to St. Mary. The parish occupies a considerable tongue of land, formed by the rivers Severn and Wye, which unite at its southern extremity.

TIDESWELL, a parish in the hundred of HIGH PEAK, county of DERBY, comprising the market town of Tideswell, the chapelry of Wormhill, and the hamlets of Litton and Wheston, and containing 2666 inhabitants, of which number, 1543 are in the town of Tideswell, 33 miles (N. N. W.) from Derby, and 160 (N. W. by N.) from London. The first account of this place is in Domesday-book, in which, under the name *Tiddeswall*, it is described as a royal demesne, having a chapel, which, in 1215, was given by King John to the canons of Lichfield. The town is situated in a valley, surrounded by some of the most barren lands in the county, on the road from Chesterfield to Manchester. The houses in general are of very mean appearance, but the inhabitants are supplied with good water, by means of a small stream which flows through the town. The chief branches of trade are calico-weaving and mining. A market and two fairs were granted by Henry III., and confirmed by subsequent sovereigns : the market is on Wednesday ; and fairs are held March 24th, May 15th, the last Wednesday in July, the second Wednesday in September, and October 29th, for cattle and sheep. This parish is in the honour of Tutbury, duchy of Lancaster, and within the jurisdiction of a court of pleas held at Chapel en le Frith, every third Tuesday, for the recovery of debts under £5. A court leet and court baron are held twice a year.

The living is a discharged vicarage, in the peculiar jurisdiction and patronage of the Dean and Chapter of Lichfield, rated in the king's books at £7. 0. 7½., endowed with £200 private benefaction, £200 royal bounty, and £1200 parliamentary grant. The church, which is dedicated to St. John the Baptist, is a remarkably fine cruciform structure of the thirteenth century, principally in the decorated style of English architecture, having an embattled tower at the west end, with crocketed pinnacles : each of the pillars in the north and south transepts supports three arches, and is strikingly beautiful : the chancel is separated from the nave by a light screen of carved oak, and from the vestryroom by an embattled stone screen, enriched with tracery. In the south transept is a tombstone to the memory of John Foljambe, who contributed largely to the erection of the church, in 1358 : in the chancel is an altar-tomb, ornamented with brasses, to the memory of Sampson Meverell, who served under the Duke of Bedford in France, and was knighted upon the field at St. Luce : another altar-tomb records the death of Robert Pursglove, a native of this town, Prior of Gisburn abbey, Prebendary of Rotherham, and Bishop of Hull, who died May 2nd, 1579. The church has received an addition of three hundred and fifty-eight free sittings, towards defraying the expense of which the Incorporated Society for the enlargement of churches and chapels contributed £180. There are places of worship for Wesleyan Methodists and Roman Catholics. The free grammar school was founded, in 1560, under letters patent from Queen Elizabeth, by the above-mentioned Robert Pursglove, and endowed with lands at Priestcliff and Taddington in this county, and at Colmworth in Bedfordshire ; also with £2 per annum, chargeable on the estate of the Earl of Manvers; to be called " The school of Jesus," and to be open to all boys living in this parish ; from eighty to one hundred are instructed. The master is appointed by the Dean and Chapter of Lichfield ; he and the vicar and churchwardens constitute a body corporate. The income arising from the lands is £227 per annum, one-fourth of which has generally been distributed among the poor of Tideswell on New Year's eve.

TIDMARSH, a parish in the hundred of THEALE, county of BERKS, 6 miles (W. N. W.) from Reading, containing 139 inhabitants. The living is a rectory, in the archdeaconry of Berks, and diocese of Salisbury,

rated in the king's books at £5. 2. 6., and in the patronage of Robert Hopkins, Esq. The church, dedicated to St. Lawrence, is partly Norman and partly in the early style of English architecture, the doorway being a particularly fine specimen of the former ; the ceiling of the chancel is of panelled oak, and adjoining it are two slabs of blue marble, with ancient brasses.

TIDMINGTON, a parish forming, with Shipston upon Stour and Tredington, a detached portion of the upper division of the hundred of OSWALDSLOW, county of WORCESTER, being locally in the Kington division of the hundred of Kington, county of Warwick, 1½ mile (S. by E.) from Shipston upon Stour, containing 70 inhabitants. The living is a rectory with Shipston upon Stour, in the archdeaconry and diocese of Worcester. The church is partly in the early style of English architecture, and partly of later date. Tidmington and Shipston upon Stour were formerly townships in the parish of Tredington, from which they were separated by act of parliament, in the 6th of George I., and made a distinct parish; on this occasion the rectory of Tredington was divided into three parts.

TIDWORTH (NORTH), a parish in the hundred of AMESBURY, county of WILTS, 2½ miles (S. W.) from Ludgershall, containing 327 inhabitants. The living is a rectory, in the archdeaconry and diocese of Salisbury, rated in the king's books at £11. 17. 1., and in the patronage of the Crown. The church is dedicated to the Holy Trinity. Robert Maton, a celebrated divine, was born here about 1607. North-west of the village, on the summit of an isolated hill, is the large earthwork called Chidbury Camp, in form resembling a heart, and enclosing an area of seventeen acres.

TIDWORTH (SOUTH), a parish in the hundred of ANDOVER, Andover division of the county of SOUTHAMPTON, 2¾ miles (S. W. by S.) from Ludgershall, containing 198 inhabitants. The living is a rectory, in the archdeaconry and diocese of Winchester, rated in the king's books at £14. 15. 2½., and in the patronage of T. A. Smith, Esq. The church is dedicated to St. Mary.

TIFFIELD, a parish in the hundred of TOWCESTER, county of NORTHAMPTON, 2¾ miles (N. by E.) from Towcester, containing 127 inhabitants. The living is a rectory, in the archdeaconry of Northampton, and diocese of Peterborough, rated in the king's books at £9. 9. 7., and in the patronage of Thomas Flesher, Esq. and others. The church is dedicated to St. John. The old Roman Watling-street passes through the parish.

TILBROOK, a parish in the hundred of STODDEN, county of BEDFORD, 1½ mile (N. W. by W.) from Kimbolton, containing 297 inhabitants. The living is a rectory, in the archdeaconry of Bedford, and diocese of Lincoln, rated in the king's books at £13. 10., and in the patronage of Lord St. John. The church is dedicated to All Saints. Charles Higgins bequeathed £300 in support of a Sunday school, which sum, together with subscriptions, produces £20 a year.

TILBURY juxta CLARE, a parish in the hundred of HINCKFORD, county of ESSEX, 4 miles (N. N. W.) from Castle-Hedingham, containing 213 inhabitants. The living is a rectory, consolidated with that of Ovington, in the archdeaconry of Middlesex, and diocese of London, rated in the king's books at £8.

TILBURY (EAST), a parish in the hundred of BAR-STABLE, county of ESSEX, 5¼ miles (E. by S.) from Grays-Thurrock, containing, with the liberty of East Lee, 264 inhabitants. The living is a discharged vicarage, in the archdeaconry of Essex, and diocese of London, rated in the king's books at £13. 6. 8., and in the patronage of the Crown. The church is dedicated to St. Margaret. The parish is bounded on the south-east by part of the Thames, called the Hope, where, on Hope point, is a battery for the defence of the river below Tilbury Fort. The lofty tower of the manor-house of Gossalyne was battered down by the Dutch fleet, which ascended the Thames in the reign of Charles II. In this parish was an ancient ferry : it is said to be the place where Claudius passed the Thames in pursuit of the Britons.

TILBURY (WEST), a parish in the hundred of BARSTABLE, county of ESSEX, 3¾ miles (E.) from Grays-Thurrock, containing 249 inhabitants. The living is a rectory, in the archdeaconry of Essex, and diocese of London, rated in the king's books at £20, and in the patronage of the Crown. The church is dedicated to St. James. The parish is bounded on the south by the Thames, and lies directly opposite to Gravesend, with which town and the interior of Kent there is a constant traffic, by means of the ferry-boats stationed here for the conveyance of foot passengers, cattle, carriages, and merchandise. In a chalk hill near the village are several caverns, termed Danes' Holes, curiously constructed of stone, being narrow at the entrance, and very spacious at the depth of thirty feet. A medicinal spring was discovered in 1737, which is beneficial in hæmorrhages, scurvy, diabetes, and some other complaints. Tilbury Fort, partly in this parish, and partly in that of Chadwell adjoining, was originally a blockhouse, built in the reign of Henry VIII.; but after the memorable attack of the Dutch fleet, in 1667, upon the English shipping in the Medway, it was converted into a regular fortification, to which considerable additions have since been made. It is encompassed by a deep wide fosse, and its ramparts present several formidable batteries of heavy ordnance, particularly towards the river. It contains comfortable barracks, and other accommodations for the garrison, which at present consists of a fort-major and a detachment of invalids. Some traces of the camp formed in the neighbourhood, to oppose the invasion of the Spanish Armada, during the reign of Elizabeth, are still visible. According to Bede, Tilbury, or Tillaburgh, was the seat of Bishop Cedda, when, about 630, he was engaged in baptizing the East Saxons.

TILEHURST, a parish in the hundred of READING, county of BERKS, 2¾ miles (W.) from Reading, containing 1760 inhabitants. The living is composed of a rectory and vicarage, united in 1586, in the archdeaconry of Berks, and diocese of Salisbury, rated in the king's books at £21. 15. 2½., and in the patronage of Mrs. Sophia Sheppard. The church, dedicated to St. Michael, is a plain brick structure, containing some ancient brasses, and a sumptuous monument to the memory of Sir Peter Vanlore, Knt., who died in 1627. A chapel of ease has been lately erected at Theale, in this parish. There is a place of worship for Wesleyan Methodists. This extensive parish is bounded on the north by the Thames, and on the south by the river Kennet. There are National schools for children of both sexes, erected and supported by Mrs. Sophia Sheppard. Richard Lloyd, the learned Bishop of Worcester, was born here, in 1627; he died in 1717.

TILFORD, a joint tything with Culverlands, in the parish and hundred of FARNHAM, county of SURREY, 3 miles (S.E.) from Farnham. The population is returned with Culverlands.

TILLEY, a township in that part of the parish of WEM which is in the Whitchurch division of the hundred of BRADFORD (North), county of SALOP, 1 mile (S.) from Wem, containing 348 inhabitants.

TILLINGHAM, a parish in the hundred of DENGIE, county of ESSEX, 2¼ miles (S. by W.) from Bradwell near the Sea, containing 946 inhabitants. The living is a vicarage, in the peculiar jurisdiction and patronage of the Dean and Chapter of St. Paul's, London, rated in the king's books at £25. 3. 9. The church, dedicated to St. Nicholas, was rebuilt, at the expense of the inhabitants, in 1708. The parish is situated on the shore of the North sea.

TILLINGTON, a township in the parish of BURGHILL, hundred of GRIMSWORTH, county of HEREFORD, 5 miles (N.W. by N.) from Hereford, containing 392 inhabitants.

TILLINGTON, a township in that part of the parish of ST. MARY LICHFIELD which is in the southern division of the hundred of PIREHILL, county of STAFFORD, 1½ mile (N.N.W.) from Stafford, containing 39 inhabitants.

TILLINGTON, a parish in the hundred of ROTHERBRIDGE, rape of ARUNDEL, county of SUSSEX, 1¼ mile (W. by N.) from Petworth, containing 681 inhabitants. The living is a rectory, in the archdeaconry and diocese of Chichester, rated in the king's books at £13. 10., and in the patronage of the Earl of Egremont. The church is principally in the decorated style of English architecture.

TILMANSTONE, a parish in the hundred of EASTRY, lathe of ST. AUGUSTINE, county of KENT, 6 miles (W. by S.) from Deal, containing 303 inhabitants. The living is a discharged vicarage, in the archdeaconry and diocese of Canterbury, rated in the king's books at £7. 12. 6., and in the patronage of the Archbishop of Canterbury. The church is dedicated to St. Andrew.

TILNEY, a joint parish with Islington, in the Marshland division of the hundred of FREEBRIDGE, county of NORFOLK, 4¼ miles (S.W.) from Lynn-Regis. The population is returned with Islington, which see.

TILNEY (ALL SAINTS), a parish in the Marshland division of the hundred of FREEBRIDGE, county of NORFOLK, 4½ miles (W. S. W.) from Lynn-Regis, containing 404 inhabitants. The living is a vicarage, with Tilney St. Lawrence annexed, in the archdeaconry and diocese of Norwich, rated in the king's books at £30, and in the patronage of the Master and Fellows of Pembroke Hall, Cambridge. The church is principally in the later style of English architecture. Tilney Smeath, a common in this parish, is said to have been so remarkably fertile, as to constantly feed thirty thousand sheep, and all the horned cattle belonging to seven villages, though no more than three miles long and one broad.

TILNEY (ST. LAWRENCE), a chapelry in the parish of TILNEY ALL SAINTS, Marshland division of the hundred of FREEBRIDGE, county of NORFOLK, 6 miles (S. W. by W.) from Lynn-Regis, containing 552 inhabitants.

TILSHEAD, a parish in the hundred of BRANCH and DOLE, county of WILTS, 4 miles (S. S. E.) from East Lavington, containing 425 inhabitants. The living is a discharged vicarage, in the archdeaconry and diocese of Salisbury, rated in the king's books at £7. 16., endowed with £200 private benefaction, and £200 royal bounty, and in the patronage of the Crown. The church is dedicated to St. Thomas a Becket.

TILSOP, a joint township with Nash and Weston, in the parish of BURFORD, hundred of OVERS, county of SALOP, 4½ miles (W. S. W.) from Cleobury-Mortimer. The population is returned with Nash.

TILSTOCK, a chapelry in that part of the parish of WHITCHURCH which is in the Whitchurch division of the hundred of BRADFORD (North), county of SALOP, 2½ miles (S.) from Whitchurch. The population is returned with the parish. The living is a perpetual curacy, in the archdeaconry of Salop, and diocese of Lichfield and Coventry, endowed with £400 private benefaction, and £400 royal bounty, and in the patronage of the Trustees of the late Earl of Bridgewater. The chapel is dedicated to St. Giles.

TILSTON, a parish in the higher division of the hundred of BROXTON, county palatine of CHESTER, comprising the townships of Carden, Grafton, Horton, Stretton, and Tilston, and containing 833 inhabitants, of which number, 370 are in the township of Tilston, 3 miles (N. W. by N.) from Malpas. The living is a rectory, in the archdeaconry and diocese of Chester, rated in the king's books at £12. 2. 11., and in the patronage of the Marquis of Cholmondely. The church is dedicated to St. Mary. The Chester canal passes through the parish, and close to the village.

TILSTON-FERNALL, a township in that part of the parish of BUNBURY which is in the first division of the hundred of EDDISBURY, county palatine of CHESTER, 2¾ miles (S. S. E.) from Tarporley, containing 166 inhabitants.

TILSWORTH, a parish in the hundred of MANS-HEAD, county of BEDFORD, 3½ miles (N. W. by W.) from Dunstable, containing 246 inhabitants. The living is a discharged vicarage, in the archdeaconry of Bedford, and diocese of Lincoln, rated in the king's books at £8, endowed with £600 royal bounty, and in the patronage of Sir G. O. Page Turner, Bart. The church, dedicated to All Saints, contains several old monuments of the Fowler family, one to the memory of Sir Henry Chester, K.B., and an ancient altar-tomb, with an inscription in French, and the effigy of Adam de Tullesworth, in sacerdotal robes.

TILTON, a parish partly in the hundred of GAR-TREE, but chiefly in the eastern division of the hundred of GOSCOTE, county of LEICESTER, 8¼ miles (W. S. W.) from Oakham, containing, with the townships of Halstead and Marefield, 399 inhabitants. The living is a vicarage, in the archdeaconry of Leicester, and diocese of Lincoln, rated in the king's books at £12. 16. 8., and in the patronage of the Rev. George Greaves. The church, dedicated to St. Peter, is partly in the later style of English architecture. Here was an ancient hospital, which Sir William Burdet annexed to Burton-Lazars, in the time of Henry II.

TILTS, a joint township with Langthwaite, in that part of the parish of DONCASTER which is in the northern division of the wapentake of STRAFFORTH and TICKHILL, West riding of the county of YORK, 4 miles (N.) from Doncaster. The population is returned with Langthwaite.

TILTY, a parish in the hundred of DUNMOW, county of ESSEX, 3 miles (S. by W.) from Thaxted, containing 78 inhabitants. The living is a donative, in the patronage of Lord Viscount Maynard. The church, dedicated to St. Mary, constitutes the remains of an abbey church, a fine specimen of the decorated style of English architecture; the east and north windows are ornamented with remarkably elegant tracery, and there are some rich stalls in the chancel. The abbey was founded, about 1152, by Robert Ferrers, Earl of Derby, and Maurice Fitz-Jeffery, for White monks, whose revenue, at the dissolution, was valued at £177. 9. 4.

TIMBERLAND, a parish in the first division of the wapentake of LANGOE, parts of KESTEVEN, county of LINCOLN, 10 miles (N. N. E.) from Sleaford, containing, with the township of Thorpe-Tinley, and the hamlet of Martin, 1183 inhabitants. The living is a discharged vicarage, in the archdeaconry and diocese of Lincoln, rated in the king's books at £12. 2. 11., endowed with £200 royal bounty, and in the patronage of Sir T. Whichcote, Bart. The church is dedicated to St. Andrew. There is a place of worship for Wesleyan Methodists.

TIMBERSCOMBE, a parish in the hundred of CAR-HAMPTON, county of SOMERSET, 2½ miles (W. S. W.) from Dunster, containing 409 inhabitants. The living is a discharged vicarage, in the peculiar jurisdiction and patronage of the Prebendary of Timberscombe, in the Cathedral Church of Wells, rated in the king's books at £6. 10. The church, dedicated to St. Michael, has an embattled tower, surmounted by a low spire. Richard Ellsworth, in 1714, bequeathed £200 towards building a school-house, and an annuity of £20 for clothing and educating poor children. It was not erected till 1824, and the original endowment having accumulated to £50 a year, from fifty to sixty children are instructed on the Madras system. He also left £40 per annum to Balliol College, Oxford, for the endowment of two scholarships, to be enjoyed for seven years by boys of Timberscombe, Cutcombe, Selworthy, Wooton-Courtney, Winchead, or Dunster, in default of which, by two from any other part of the county, to be chosen by the Master and Fellows of that college.

TIMBLE (GREAT), a township in the parish of FEWSTON, lower division of the wapentake of CLARO, West riding of the county of YORK, 5¼ miles (N. by W.) from Otley, containing 233 inhabitants. It is within the peculiar jurisdiction of the Honour court of Knaresborough.

TIMBLE (LITTLE), a township in that part of the parish of OTLEY which is in the upper division of the wapentake of CLARO, West riding of the county of YORK, 5½ miles (N.) from Otley, containing 62 inhabitants.

TIMPERLEY, a township in the parish of BOWDON, hundred of BUCKLOW, county palatine of CHESTER, 1¾ mile (N. E. by E.) from Altrincham, containing 683 inhabitants.

TIMSBURY, a parish in the hundred of CHEW, county of SOMERSET, 5 miles (S. E.) from Pensford, containing 1090 inhabitants. The living is a rectory, in the archdeaconry of Bath, and diocese of Bath and Wells, rated in the king's books at £11. 19. 9½., and in the patronage of the Master and Fellows of Balliol College, Oxford. The church, dedicated to St. Mary, has lately received an addition of three hundred and forty-one sittings, of which two hundred and eighty-five are free, the Incorporated Society for the enlargement of churches and chapels having granted £250 towards defraying the expense. There is a place of worship for Wesleyan Methodists. The Radford canal passes through the parish, in which there are coal mines that supply the city of Bath. Fifteen poor children are taught for about £16 a year, arising from the rental of certain houses and land left by Thomas Deeke, in 1759.

TIMSBURY, a parish in the hundred of KING'S SOMBOURN, Andover division of the county of SOUTHAMPTON, 2¼ miles (N. by W.) from Romsey, containing 188 inhabitants. The living is a perpetual curacy, in the archdeaconry and diocese of Winchester, endowed with £600 royal bounty, and £200 parliamentary grant. William Chamberlayne, Esq. was patron in 1820. The church is dedicated to St. Andrew. There is a place of worship for Wesleyan Methodists. The Andover canal passes through the parish.

TIMWORTH, a parish in the hundred of THEDWESTRY, county of SUFFOLK, 4¼ miles (N. by E.) from Bury St. Edmund's, containing 210 inhabitants. The living is a rectory, consolidated with those of Ingham and Culford, in the archdeaconry of Sudbury, and diocese of Norwich, rated in the king's books at £9. 17. 11. The church is dedicated to St. Andrew.

TINCLETON, a parish in the hundred of PIDDLETOWN, Dorchester division of the county of DORSET, 5¼ miles (E.) from Dorchester, containing 142 inhabitants. The living is a discharged rectory, in the archdeaconry of Dorset, and diocese of Bristol, rated in the king's books at £5. 11. 8. Mrs. Sturt was patroness in 1802. The church is a small structure, the burial-place of the Baynards of Cliff, of which family it contains several sepulchral memorials. The parish is bounded on the south by the river Frome.

TINGEWICK, a parish in the hundred and county of BUCKINGHAM, 2¼ miles (W. by S.) from Buckingham, containing 832 inhabitants. The living is a rectory, in the archdeaconry of Buckingham, and diocese of Lincoln, rated in the king's books at £12. 16. 3., and in the patronage of the Warden and Fellows of New College, Oxford. The church, dedicated to St. Mary Magdalene, exhibits some remains of Norman architecture, and contains a curious brass to the memory of Erasmus Williams, who died rector of this parish in 1608. Here was formerly a market on Tuesday, granted in 1246, to the abbey De Monte Rothomago in Normandy, to which the manor had previously been given by the family of Finmore. The Rev. Francis Edmonds, about the middle of the last century, endowed a charity school with £15 per annum, for teaching and clothing six boys and six girls; it is now conducted on the National system.

TINGRITH, a parish in the hundred of MANSHEAD, county of BEDFORD, 4¼ miles (E. by S.) from Woburn, containing 155 inhabitants. The living is a discharged rectory, in the archdeaconry of Bedford, and diocese of Lincoln, rated in the king's books at £9, and in the patronage of R. Trevor, Esq. The church is dedicated to St. Nicholas.

TINHEAD, a tything in the parish of EDINGTON, hundred of WHORWELSDOWN, county of WILTS, 1 mile (N. by E.) from Edington, containing 472 inhabitants.

TINSLEY, a chapelry in that part of the parish of ROTHERHAM which is in the southern division of the wapentake of STRAFFORTH and TICKHILL, West riding of the county of YORK, 2¾ miles (S. W. by W.) from Rotherham, containing 327 inhabitants. The living is a perpetual curacy, in the archdeaconry and diocese of York, endowed with £400 private benefaction, £200 royal bounty, and £300 parliamentary grant, and in the patronage of Earl Fitzwilliam.

TINTAGELL, a parish in the hundred of LESNEWTH, county of CORNWALL, 1 mile (W. by S.) from Bossiney, containing, with the borough of Bossiney, 877 inhabitants. The living is a vicarage, in the archdeaconry of Cornwall, and diocese of Exeter, rated in the king's books at £8. 11. 3., and in the patronage of the Dean and Canons of Windsor. The church, dedicated to St. Simphorian, contains a curious Norman font. There is a place of worship for Wesleyan Methodists. A fair for cattle is held at Trevenna on the Monday after October 19th. The parish is bounded by the Bristol channel on the north, where, partly on a stupendous crag, almost surrounded by the sea, and partly on the lofty and precipitous cliff of the main land, are the venerable remains of King Arthur's castle, separated into two divisions by a frightful chasm, three hundred feet deep, across which there was formerly a drawbridge. The keep stood on the peninsula, and, in Leland's time, contained "a prety chapel with a tumbe on the left syde." The ruins now existing consist of huge scattered masses, and of walls pierced with small square holes, for the discharge of arrows. This fortress has been occasionally occupied by several of our princes, of whom Richard, Earl of Cornwall, here entertained his nephew, David, Prince of Wales, during the rebellion of the latter against Henry III., in 1245. In subsequent reigns, till within a few years of that of Elizabeth, it had a governor, and was used as a state prison for the duchy of Cornwall. There were formerly two other chapels within the parish, one dedicated to St. Piran, the other to St. Denis.

TINTERN (LITTLE), a parish in the upper division of the hundred of RAGLAND, county of MONMOUTH, 4¾ miles (N.) from Chepstow, containing 285 inhabitants. The living is a discharged rectory, in the archdeaconry and diocese of Llandaff, rated in the king's books at £2. 1. 5½., endowed with £400 private benefaction, and £400 royal bounty, and in the patronage of — Gale, Esq. The church is dedicated to St. Michael.

TINTINHULL, a parish in the hundred of TINTINHULL, county of SOMERSET, 2¼ miles (S. W.) from Ilchester, containing, with the tything of Stock-Dennis, 398 inhabitants. The living is a discharged vicarage, in the archdeaconry of Wells, and diocese of Bath and Wells, endowed with £600 private benefaction, £400 royal bounty, and £300 parliamentary grant, and in the patronage of the Right Hon. W. Arbuthnot. The church is dedicated to St. Margaret. The old Roman Fosse-way passes through the parish, which is bounded on the north by the navigable river Ivel. Stock-Dennis was anciently a very populous place, but at present it contains only two families.

TINTWISLE, a township in the parish of MOTTRAM in LONGDEN-DALE, hundred of MACCLESFIELD, county palatine of CHESTER, 9½ miles (N. E. by E.) from Stockport, containing 1580 inhabitants, who are mostly employed in the manufacture of cotton and woollen goods, and at the quarries of stone in the neighbourhood. There is a place of worship for Calvinistic Methodists, attached to which is a school attended by about four hundred children. Fairs for cattle are held, on May 2nd and November 1st, at the village, which is situated on an acclivity rising from the western bank of the river Etheron. This was anciently a borough, and had a court leet of its own; it is now only a member of the lordship of Mottram in Longden-Dale, and is within the jurisdiction of a court of requests held there, for the recovery of debts under 40s.

TINWELL, a parish in the hundred of EAST, county of RUTLAND, 1½ mile (S. W. by W.) from Stamford, containing, with the hamlet of Ingthorp, 245 inhabitants. The living is a rectory, in the archdeaconry of Northampton, and diocese of Peterborough, rated in the king's books at £12. 10. 5., and in the patronage of the Marquis of Exeter. The church is dedicated to All Saints. There is a small endowment for the instruction of children.

TIPTON, a parish in the southern division of the hundred of OFFLOW, county of STAFFORD, 1½ mile (N.E.) from Dudley, containing, according to the last census, 11,546 inhabitants, which number has since greatly increased. This place, which is situated nearly in the centre of an extensive and rich mining district, has progressively risen from an inconsiderable village to its present extent and importance, from the abundant and apparently exhaustless mines of coal and iron-stone which are found under almost every acre of its surface. The former is of superior quality, and is found in strata of thirty feet in thickness, and the latter is wrought to a very considerable extent, affording together employment to an immense population, of whose dwellings, with the exception of some belonging to the superintendents of the works, the village principally consists. There are not less than nine forges, with blast furnaces and other apparatus, for the manufacture of pig-iron, of which, on an average, more than seventy tons per week are made, and in which the weekly consumption of coal is not less than six hundred tons. Nails and hinges of every kind, fenders, fire-irons, and boilers for steam-engines, are manufactured to a great extent; and there are also large manufactories for tinned plates, soap, muriatic potash, and red lead. The trade is much facilitated by the Birmingham canal and several of its collateral branches, which intersect the parish, whereby a communication is established with almost every line of inland navigation, and the produce of its mines and manufactures is conveyed to many of the principal towns in the kingdom. The river Trent has its source within a few hundred yards of the western boundary of the parish. Tipton is within the jurisdiction of the county magistrates, and also within that of a court of requests for the parishes of Hales-Owen, Rowley-Regis, West Bromwich, Harborne, and the manor of Bradley, in the parish of Wolverhampton, in the counties of Worcester, Salop, and Stafford, respectively, established by an act passed in

the 47th of George III., for the recovery of debts not exceeding £5. Officers for the internal regulation of the parish are annually appointed at the court leet of the lord of the manor. The living is a perpetual curacy, in the peculiar jurisdiction of the Prebendary of Prees, or Pipa Minor, in the Cathedral Church of Lichfield, endowed with £200 private benefaction, and £400 royal bounty, and in the patronage of the Dean and Chapter of Lichfield. The ancient church, dedicated to St. Martin, having become greatly dilapidated many years since, is now a ruin, and a neat and commodious new church of brick has been erected. There is a place of worship for Wesleyan Methodists. In 1796, Mr. Solomon Woodall gave £650 for the foundation and endowment of a school, and several subsequent donations and benefactions have been made, which, aided by subscriptions, are appropriated to the support of several National schools, in which more than one thousand children receive instruction: there are also Sunday schools in connexion with the established church and the dissenting congregation, supported by subscription.

TIRLEY, a parish in the lower division of the hundred of DEERHURST, county of GLOUCESTER, 5¼ miles (S.W. by W.) from Tewkesbury, containing, with the hamlet of Haw, 443 inhabitants. The living is a discharged vicarage, in the jurisdiction of the peculiar court of Deerhurst, rated in the king's books at £9. 6. 8., and in the patronage of the Crown. The church, dedicated to St. Matthew, is partly in the decorated and partly in the later style of English architecture. There is a place of worship for Wesleyan Methodists. The navigable river Severn flows through the parish, and is crossed at Haw by a handsome stone bridge, completed in 1824, on the new line of road leading from Cheltenham into Hertfordshire, Monmouthshire, and South Wales. A National school has been established since 1817, and is supported by a small endowment, aided by annual subscriptions, and the proceeds of a sermon preached on the Sunday before Old Michaelmas-day.

TISBURY, a parish in the hundred of DUNWORTH, county of WILTS, 3½ miles (S. E.) from Hindon, containing, with the tything of Chicksgrove with Staple, 2122 inhabitants. The living is a vicarage, in the archdeaconry and diocese of Salisbury, rated in the king's books at £18. 10. 10., and in the patronage of Mrs. R. Prevost. The church, dedicated to St. John the Baptist, is a large structure, in the best style of Norman architecture, and contains numerous monuments of the Arundels of Wardour. There is a place of worship for Independents. Alice Combes, in 1740, bequeathed £400, directing the interest to be applied in teaching poor children. Wardour castle, the seat of the noble family of Arundel, is a magnificent mansion, erected between the years 1776 and 1784, from a design by Mr. Paine: it is built of freestone, and consists of a centre and two wings, projecting on the north side in a curvilinear form. About a mile from it are the ruins of the ancient castle, the origin of which is very remote: from the time of Edward III., downwards, it was successively the seat of the families of St. Martin, Lovel, Touchet, Audley, Willoughby de Broke, and, lastly, of Sir John Arundel, whose son Thomas was created Lord Arundel of Wardour, by James I. In the history of this baronial castle no event of importance occurs until the time of Charles I., when it was besieged by a detachment of the parliamentarian army, under Sir Edward Hungerford. Lord Arundel being then at Oxford, attending the king, the castle was left in the custody of his wife, the Lady Blanch Arundel, who, with a garrison of only twenty-five men, held out against a bombardment for five days, at the end of which, on May 8th, 1643, she surrendered upon honourable terms, which, however, were not punctually kept by the captors. The castle was then garrisoned for the parliament, and placed under the command of the celebrated Edmund Ludlow. The latter, being in turn besieged in it, in the course of the same summer, by the royalists, under Lord Arundel and Sir Francis Doddington, made an obstinate resistance for several weeks, but was at last compelled to deliver up the fortress to the besiegers, who, according to Ludlow's account, in his own memoirs, observed the terms of capitulation no better than the parliamentarians had done. Owing to the injury which the castle sustained in these two sieges, especially the latter, it thenceforward ceased to be used, either as a fortress, or as a residence. The ruins are situated beneath a grand amphitheatrical hill clothed with wood: the principal are those of a sexagonal court, which formed the centre of the ancient structure, and in which is a very deep well, sunk by Ludlow, to supply the garrison with water during the siege. Almost contiguous are the remains of the mansion, which was occupied by the family, after the destruction of the castle, until their removal to their present residence. In the ancient castle, Sir Nicholas Hyde, Chief Justice of the King's Bench and Lord Treasurer, in the reign of James I., was born, about 1570; and about the same period, Sir John Davies, eminent as a lawyer, a poet, and a political writer, was born at the hamlet of Chisgrove, in this parish.

TISSINGTON, a parish in the hundred of WIRKSWORTH, county of DERBY, 3¾ miles (N.) from Ashbourn, containing 496 inhabitants. The living is a perpetual curacy, in the archdeaconry of Derby, and diocese of Lichfield and Coventry, endowed with £200 royal bounty, and in the patronage of Sir H. Fitzherbert, Bart. The church, dedicated to St. Mary, is partly Norman and partly of later date: it stands on an eminence overlooking the village, where are five springs of the purest water, in connexion with which a curious ancient custom, termed the "Floralia," prevails among the villagers, annually on Holy Thursday; viz., that of decorating these fountains with the choicest flowers, as offerings to the Naïads; this they execute with admirable ingenuity, and then repair to the church, where the ritual of the day is performed, and a sermon preached; the springs are then visited by the minister, choristers, and people; the Psalms, Epistle, and Gospel are read, and a hymn sung, and the remainder of the day is spent in rural festivity. Catherine Port, in 1722, bequeathed £5 a year, and Frances Fitzherbert, in 1735, gave an annuity of £4, for teaching poor children.

TISTED (EAST), a parish in the hundred of SELBORNE, Alton (North) division of the county of SOUTHAMPTON, 4½ miles (S. by W.) from Alton, containing, with the tything of Rotherfield, 278 inhabitants. The living is a rectory, in the archdeaconry and diocese of Winchester, rated in the king's books at £16, and in the patronage of James Scott, Esq. The church is dedicated to St. James. The Rev. Philip Valois, in 1760,

VOL. IV.

bequeathed £300 in support of a school; and the Rev. John Williams, in 1822, gave £400 three per cents. for a like purpose; the united income is about £24, for which fourteen children are instructed.

TISTED (WEST), a parish in the hundred of BISHOP'S SUTTON, Alton (North) division of the county of SOUTHAMPTON, 4¾ miles (S. E. by E.) from New Alresford, containing 206 inhabitants. The living is a perpetual curacy, in the archdeaconry and diocese of Winchester, endowed with £200 private benefaction, and £200 royal bounty, and in the patronage of the President and Fellows of Magdalene College, Oxford.

TITCHBOURN, a parish in the hundred of FAWLEY, Fawley division of the county of SOUTHAMPTON, 2½ miles (S. W. by S.) from New Alresford, containing 257 inhabitants. The living is a perpetual curacy, annexed to the rectory, and in the peculiar jurisdiction of the Incumbent, of Cheriton. The church is dedicated to St. Andrew.

TITCHFIELD, a parish in the hundred of TITCHFIELD, Portsdown division of the county of SOUTHAMPTON, 2¼ miles (W.) from Fareham, containing 3528 inhabitants. This is a small well-built town, pleasantly situated at the mouth of Southampton water, near the Titchfield river, by means of which small vessels can approach the town. A customary corn market is held on Friday; and fairs are on the Saturday fortnight before Lady-day; May 14th; Sept. 25th for hiring servants; and on the Saturday fortnight before Dec. 21. A court baron is held twice a year, and a court leet annually, the latter having jurisdiction in all pleas of debt under 40s. The living is a vicarage, in the archdeaconry and diocese of Winchester, rated in the king's books at £6. 17. 3½., and in the patronage of H. P. Delmé, Esq. The church is dedicated to St. Peter. There is a place of worship for Independents. Twelve poor boys and twelve poor girls are educated, and the former annually clothed, from funds arising out of the rental of land and premises demised, in 1620, by Henry, Earl of Southampton, for charitable uses. In 1703, Richard Godwin bequeathed a rent-charge of £4 for teaching twelve poor children. At a short distance north of the town are the remains of Titchfield House, erected by the first Earl of Southampton, on the site and with the materials of an abbey for Premonstratensian canons, founded by Peter de Rupibus, in 1231, the revenue of which, at the suppression, was valued at £280. 19. 10. In this mansion Charles I. was concealed after his escape from Hampton Court, in 1647, and again previously to resigning himself to Col. Hammond, who conducted him to Carisbrooke castle, in the Isle of Wight. The building is now in a state of ruin, the entrance gateway being the principal part standing: the old stables yet remain, and are worthy of notice. Titchfield confers the title of marquis on the family of Bentinck.

TITCHMARSH, a parish in the hundred of NAVISFORD, county of NORTHAMPTON, 2 miles (E. N. E.) from Thrapston, containing 748 inhabitants. The living is a rectory, in the archdeaconry of Northampton, and diocese of Peterborough, rated in the king's books at £45, and in the patronage of the Earl of Romney and Sir G. Robinson, Bart. The church is dedicated to St. Mary.

TITCHWELL, a parish in the hundred of SMITHDON, county of NORFOLK, 5 miles (W. by N.) from

Burnham-Westgate, containing 136 inhabitants. The living is a rectory, in the archdeaconry of Norfolk, and diocese of Norwich, rated in the king's books at £12, and in the patronage of the Provost and Fellows of Eton College. The church is dedicated to St. Mary. There is a place of worship for Wesleyan Methodists. Four boys of this parish are entitled to the benefit of the free school at Brancaster.

TITLEY, a parish in the hundred of WIGMORE, county of HEREFORD, 3 miles (N. E. by E.) from Kington, containing 304 inhabitants. The living is a perpetual curacy, in the archdeaconry and diocese of Hereford, endowed with £600 private benefaction, and £600 royal bounty, and in the patronage of the Warden and Fellows of Winchester College. The church, dedicated to St. Peter, was erected about sixty years ago, on the site of that which belonged to a priory of Benedictine monks, founded as a cell to the abbey of Tyrone in France, of which there are no vestiges, except the moat that encompassed it, and a remarkably fine spring of water, still called the Priory well. A National school was established here before 1826, when Lady Coffin Greenly erected a new school-house, with the aid of £80 granted by the National School Society. Courts leet and baron are occasionally held here.

TITLINGTON, a township in the parish of EGLINGHAM, northern division of COQUETDALE ward, county of NORTHUMBERLAND, 7¼ miles (W. by N.) from Alnwick, containing 74 inhabitants.

TITSEY, a parish in the second division of the hundred of TANDRIDGE, county of SURREY, 5 miles (N. E. by E.) from Godstone, containing 167 inhabitants. The living is a rectory, in the archdeaconry of Surrey, and diocese of Winchester, rated in the king's books at £7. 17. 3½., and in the patronage of W. L. Gower, Esq. The river Medway has one of its sources in this parish. Lime of a superior quality is burnt from the chalk-pits at the foot of Botley hill.

TITTENHANGER, a hamlet in that part of the parish of ST. PETER, borough of ST. ALBANS, which is in the hundred of CASHIO, or liberty of ST. ALBANS, county of HERTFORD, 2½ miles (S. E. by E.) from St. Albans, containing 622 inhabitants.

TITTENLEY, a township in the parish of AUDLEM, hundred of NANTWICH, county palatine of CHESTER, containing 36 inhabitants.

TITTISWORTH, a township in that part of the parish of LEEK which is in the northern division of the hundred of TOTMONSLOW, county of STAFFORD, 2 miles (N.E. by N.) from Leek, containing 288 inhabitants.

TITTLESHALL, a parish in the hundred of LAUNDITCH, county of NORFOLK, 6¼ miles (S. S. W.) from Fakenham, containing, with the parish of Godwick, 446 inhabitants. The living is a rectory, with those of Godwick and Wellingham annexed, in the archdeaconry and diocese of Norwich, rated in the king's books at £9. 12. 8½., and in the patronage of T. W. Coke, Esq. The church, dedicated to St. Mary, contains, among several other monuments, an altar-tomb and effigy in white marble of the learned and celebrated Sir Edward Coke, in his judicial costume, with an elaborate inscription.

TIVERTON, a township in that part of the parish of BUNBURY which is in the first division of the hun-

dred of EDDISBURY, county palatine of CHESTER, 1¾ mile (S.) from Tarporley, containing 591 inhabitants. There is a place of worship for Wesleyan Methodists. At Four-lane Ends, in this township, is an old established corn market, held every Monday. The Chester canal passes in the vicinity.

TIVERTON, a borough, market town, and parish, possessing exclusive jurisdiction, though locally in the hundred of Tiverton, county of DEVON, 14 miles (N. by E.) from Exeter, and 163 (W. by S.) from London, and containing, according to the last census, 8651 inhabitants. This place derives its name, which was formerly written *Twy-ford-ton* and *Two-ford-ton*, from the fords on the two rivers (the Exe and the Lowman) between which it is situated; and it was known as the village of Twyford so early as 872. A castle was erected here, in 1106, by Rivers, Earl of Devon, which continued for many ages the head of the barony. In 1200, the town had a market and three annual fairs; and, in 1250, it was supplied with water by means of a leat, at the expense of Isabel, Countess of Westmoreland. In 1353, the wool trade was introduced, and in 1500 the inhabitants were largely engaged in the manufacture of baizes, plain cloths, and kerseys, for which, in the time of Elizabeth, the town enjoyed considerable repute; but, in 1591, the plague greatly checked its prosperity, destroying nearly six hundred of the inhabitants. Notwithstanding this event, however, and a destructive fire in 1598, Tiverton was regarded, in 1612, as the chief manufacturing town in the West of England; but about this time a second fire destroyed six hundred houses, and occasioned very great distress among the inhabitants. During the contest between Charles and the parliament, the townsmen were much divided; in 1643, they were for a time subject to the king, but in 1645 the parliamentary forces effected the entire subjugation of the place, and the castle, church, and outworks were taken, together with the governor and two hundred others. In 1731, a third fire destroyed three hundred houses; and, ten years after, one-twelfth of the population was cut off by a severe epidemic fever. In 1745, the introduction of Norwich stuffs, and the subsequent establishment of a manufactory at Wellington, occasioned the decay of the woollen trade, which, in 1815, was entirely superseded by the patent net manufacture, now the staple trade of the place.

The parish is divided into the four following portions; Clare, Pitt, Priors, and Tidcombe. The town is pleasantly situated on elevated ground, the rivers Exe and Lowman uniting their streams a little southward from it, and consists of several streets of respectable appearance, which are paved throughout, under an act obtained, in 1794, for the improvement of the town. Some of the private mansions are spacious and handsome, and the inhabitants are well supplied with water, small streams, from a branch of the Lowman, running through many of the streets. At its eastern extremity is a wharf, whence a canal extends to Burlescombe,

Corporate Seal.

passing in its course near the rocks of Canonsleigh, which yield excellent limestone: the lofty manufactories on the west side of the river have an imposing effect. The Exe is crossed by two bridges, from one of which (a handsome stone structure, originally erected, in 1590, by the munificence of Mr. Walter Tyrrel, a linen-draper of this town, and lately rebuilt) is a fine view of the castle and church. A subscription reading-room, theatre, and assembly-room, are the chief sources of amusement. About two thousand persons are employed in the lace manufacture. The markets are on Tuesday and Saturday, the former being the principal; and on the second Tuesday in every month is a great market for cattle. Fairs are held on the second Tuesday after Whit-Sunday and on Michaelmas-day. The first charter of incorporation was granted by James I., in 1615; but, in 1723, the mayor absconding on the day of election, it became forfeited, and a second was granted by George I., under which the town is now governed, the municipal body consisting of a mayor, twelve capital burgesses, and twelve assistants, with a recorder and town clerk : the mayor, recorder, and town clerk, are elected by the corporation, the mayor annually on the Tuesday following St. Bartholomew's day : the mayor, recorder, and late mayor, are justices of the peace, with exclusive jurisdiction; they hold a court of session quarterly, and a court of record for all pleas not exceeding £100. The bridewell, a commodious edifice, was rebuilt about thirty-five years ago : the other principal public buildings are the corn market and town hall, and a spacious new market-house, erected in 1830, for the sale of butcher's meat, &c. This borough returns two representatives to parliament : the elective franchise is vested exclusively in the twenty-five members of the corporation; the mayor is the returning officer.

At the close of the thirteenth century, the living, which is in the archdeaconry and diocese of Exeter, was divided, by Hugh Courtenay, Baron of Oakhampton and Earl of Devon, into the portions of Clare, Pitt, Tidcombe, and Priors : the last was given to the monastery of St. James, at Exeter, and, having been subsequently assigned, with the monastery, to the Provost and Fellows of King's College, Cambridge, that society, as owners of the impropriate rectory, appoint the curate : the Clare portion is rated in the king's books at £27; the Pitt portion, with Cove chapelry annexed, is rated at £36; and the Tidcombe portion is rated at £27 : these three last, which are rectorial, are in the patronage of Sir W. Carew, Bart., the Representatives of the late Rev. J. Newte, and of Sir J. Vyvyan, Bart., and the Rev. W. Spurway. The church, which is dedicated to St. Peter, is a very ancient and handsome structure, in the later style of English architecture, with portions in the early style, and an enriched Norman doorway : the altar-piece, of which the subject is "The Deliverance of St. Peter from Prison," was painted and presented by the celebrated Mr. Cosway, a native of this town : the chancel is said to have been the original parish church : the churchyard occupies a commanding elevation, and forms an agreeable promenade. A handsome edifice, in the modern style of architecture, has been erected, as a chapel of ease : it is dedicated to St. George, and each of the four portionists officiates in turn. There are places of worship for Baptists, Independents, and Wesleyan Methodists.

The free grammar school was founded and amply endowed, in 1604, pursuant to the will of Peter Blundell, a clothier of Tiverton, who gave £2400 for the purchase of ground and the erection of the building; and, for its maintenance, devised all his lands in Devonshire to twenty-seven trustees, directing his executors to apply £2000 of the proceeds in the establishment and perpetual maintenance of six students at either of the Universities : additional scholarships were founded by John Ham, in 1678; by R. Downe, in 1806; and one to Balliol College, Oxford, by John Newte, in 1715; there are likewise two exhibitions, of £30 per annum each, endowed with the dividends on certain stock bequeathed by Benjamin Gilbert, in 1783. The upper and under master have each a house rent-free: the number of boys educated, the majority of whom are boarders, has varied considerably at different times : the whole income is upwards of £900 per annum. The building is a venerable edifice of stone, having its north front cased with Purbeck marble; the façade exhibits two porches, and is of considerable extent, with a spacious quadrangular court opposite. The free English school, in Peter-street, was founded in 1611, by Robert Comyn, alias Chilcot, who gave £400 for its erection, and an annuity of £20 for the master's salary; one hundred boys are instructed, all of whom pay a small quarterage. The charity school, which is situated in the churchyard, was originally founded by subscription, in 1713, and has been since extensively endowed with various benefactions : about one hundred children of both sexes are instructed. Almshouses for nine poor men, situated in Gold-street, were founded by John Greenway, in 1529; a chapel is attached, which contains some good carved work. The Western almshouse, which has also a small chapel, for eight poor men, was founded in 1579, by John Waldren; and another, in Peter-street, for six aged women, in 1613, by George Slee. A charitable fund was established, pursuant to the will of Mary Rice, in 1697, under the management of trustees, from which sixty-seven poor persons receive life annuities. The other charitable benefactions belonging to Tiverton, too numerous to particularise, are expended in apprenticing poor children, and contributing, in various ways, to the comfort of the poor, and the general improvement and welfare of the town. Mrs. Cowley, the dramatic authoress, was a native of this town; and Bamfylde Moore Carew, the noted King of the Beggars, was born at Bickleigh, about two miles hence, and received his education in the free grammar school. Some few remains of the boundary wall of the old castle, with its flanking and angular towers, are still perceptible; particularly part of the grand east entrance, and fragments on the south-west : the site, which occupies about an acre of ground, is on a level with the churchyard, and overhangs the river.

TIVETSHALL (ST. MARGARET), a parish in the hundred of Diss, county of Norfolk, 5¾ miles (N. E. by N.) from Diss, containing 347 inhabitants. The living is a rectory, annexed to that of Tivetshall St. Mary, in the archdeaconry of Norfolk, and diocese of Norwich.

TIVETSHALL (ST. MARY), a parish in the hundred of Diss, county of Norfolk, 5¼ miles (N. E.) from Diss, containing 332 inhabitants. The living is a rectory, with that of Tivetshall St. Margaret annexed, in the archdeaconry of Norfolk, and diocese of Norwich, rated in the king's books at £20, and in the patronage of the Earl of Orford. The church is a venerable structure, erected before the Conquest.

TIXALL, a parish in the southern division of the hundred of PIREHILL, county of STAFFORD, 3¾ miles (E. by S.) from Stafford, containing 198 inhabitants. The living is a discharged rectory, in the archdeaconry of Stafford, and diocese of Lichfield and Coventry, rated in the king's books at £8. 0. 8., and in the patronage of Sir Clifford Constable, Bart. The church is dedicated to St. John the Baptist. There is a Roman Catholic chapel in the parish. Immense quantities of freestone are quarried in the neighbourhood of Tixall Hall, which fine old mansion was built of that found upon the spot. Much of it has been used also in the construction of the bridges and locks of the Staffordshire and Worcestershire canal, which passes through the parish, and of the Trent and Mersey canal in the vicinity, the stone being peculiarly adapted for resisting the action of water.

TIXOVER, a parish in the hundred of WRANDIKE, county of RUTLAND, 7½ miles (E. by N.) from Uppingham, containing 108 inhabitants. The living is a perpetual curacy, annexed to the vicarage of· Ketton, in the peculiar jurisdiction of the Prebendary of Ketton in the Cathedral Church of Lincoln. The church is dedicated to St. Mary Magdalene.

TOCKENHAM, a parish in the hundred of KINGSBRIDGE, county of WILTS, 2¾ miles (S. W.) from Wooton-Bassett, containing 153 inhabitants. The living is a rectory, in the archdeaconry of Wilts, and diocese of Salisbury, rated in the king's books at £6. 13. 4., and in the patronage of the Crown. The church is dedicated to St. John.

TOCKETTS, a township in the parish of GUILSBROUGH, eastern division of the liberty of LANGBAURGH, North riding of the county of YORK, 1¾ mile (N. by E.) from Guilsbrough, containing 46 inhabitants.

TOCKHOLES, a chapelry in the parish and lower division of the hundred of BLACKBURN, county palatine of LANCASTER, 3 miles (S. S. W.) from Blackburn, containing 1269 inhabitants. The living is a perpetual curacy, in the archdeaconry and diocese of Chester, endowed with £200 private benefaction, and £800 royal bounty, and in the patronage of the Vicar of Blackburn. The chapel is dedicated to St. Michael. There is a place of worship for Independents.

TOCKINGTON (LOWER), a tything in that part of the parish of ALMONDSBURY which is in the lower division of the hundred of LANGLEY and SWINEHEAD, county of GLOUCESTER, 3¾ miles (S. by E.) from Thornbury, containing 298 inhabitants.

TOCKINGTON (UPPER), a tything in the parish of OLVESTON, lower division of the hundred of LANGLEY and SWINEHEAD, county of GLOUCESTER, 3 miles (S. by W.) from Thornbury, containing 670 inhabitants.

TOCKWITH, a township in the parish of BILTON, ainsty of the city, and East riding of the county, of YORK, 5¾ miles (N. E.) from Wetherby, containing 436 inhabitants. There is a place of worship for Wesleyan Methodists.

TODBERE, a parish in the hundred of REDLANE, Sturminster division of the county of DORSET, 4½ miles (S. W. by W.) from Shaftesbury, containing 127

inhabitants. The living is a discharged rectory; united, in 1746, to that of Stower-Provost, in the archdeaconry of Dorset, and diocese of Bristol, rated in the king's books at £5. 19. 4. The church was considered a chapel to Gillingham till 1434, when it was made parochial : the inhabitants, by ancient custom, bury at Stour.

TODBURN, a township in the parish of LONGHORSLEY, western division of MORPETH ward, county of NORTHUMBERLAND, 8 miles (N. W. by N.) from Morpeth, containing 25 inhabitants.

TODDENHAM, a parish in the upper division of the hundred of WESTMINSTER, county of GLOUCESTER, 3¾ miles (N. E.) from Moreton in the Marsh, containing 440 inhabitants. The living is a rectory, in the archdeaconry and diocese of Gloucester, rated in the king's books at £18. 19. 9½., and in the patronage of the Bishop of London. The church, dedicated to St. Thomas à Becket, is a handsome structure, with a tower and spire, and in the chancel are some canopied stone stalls. The old Fosse-way bounds the parish on the west.

TODDINGTON, a market town and parish in the hundred of MANSHEAD, county of BEDFORD, 15 miles (S.) from Bedford, and 39 (N. W. by N.) from London, containing 1665 inhabitants. This small town occupies an elevated site, and is irregularly built; the houses are of ancient appearance. The manufacture of straw-plat employs a great number of the poor inhabitants. The market, granted by charter of Henry III., in 1218, is held on Saturday, but has considerably declined : fairs are held on St. George's day, the first Monday in June, September 4th, November 2nd, and December 16th. The living is a rectory, in the archdeaconry of Bedford, and diocese of Lincoln, rated in the king's books at £29. 2. 11., and in the patronage of the Heirs of the late Lady Louisa Conolly. The church, which is dedicated to St. George, has portions in the later style of English architecture, and contains some ancient monuments ; the exterior is ornamented with a variety of grotesque figures of animals. There is a place of worship for Wesleyan Methodists. Some remains of an old manor-house, erected on the summit of Cinger mount, are still visible, having been converted into a farm-house. An hospital for a chaplain and three poor men was founded here, in 1443, by Sir John Broughton.

TODDINGTON, a parish in the lower division of the hundred of KIFTSGATE, county of GLOUCESTER, 3 miles (N. by E.) from Winchcombe, containing 355 inhabitants. The living is a discharged vicarage, with the perpetual curacy of Stanley-Pontlarge annexed, in the archdeaconry and diocese of Gloucester, rated in the king's books at £7. 15. 4., and in the patronage of C. H. Tracey, Esq. The church is dedicated to St. Leonard. The small river Isbourn runs through the parish.

TODMORDEN, a market town and chapelry in that part of the parish of ROCHDALE which is in the hundred of SALFORD, county palatine of LANCASTER, 20 miles (N. E.) from Manchester, and 207 (N. W. by N.) from London, containing, with the township of Walsden, 4985 inhabitants, according to the return of 1821, which number has increased to upwards of 6000. This town, anciently called Todmaredene, is situated in a picturesque and fertile district, denominated the vale of

Todmorden, or "the valley of the fox mere, or lake," through which flows the river Calder, here separating the counties of Lancaster and York : a considerable portion of it is included within the township of Langfield, parish of Halifax, county of York, the town being situated at the junction of the township of Todmorden and Walsden, in the county of Lancaster, with those of Langfield and Stansfield in the county of York, the aggregate population of which, in 1821, amounted to upwards of 14,000, and is now considerably increased. The manufactories, for calico, fustian, dimities, satteen, and velveteen, are numerous and extensive, worked by water-mills on the river, and by steam-engines, combining, in the aggregate, a power equal to that of two hundred and twenty horses, and that in the three townships amounting to nearly five hundred. Great facility of conveyance is afforded by the Rochdale canal, which skirts the town on the south, and other navigations, which connect this place with the eastern and western ocean. The intended railway from Manchester to Leeds, for the construction of which an act of parliament is expected to be obtained in this present session (1831), will pass through Todmorden ; and it is thought that a branch from Burnley will subsequently be formed, joining the former at this town. The great prosperity of the local manufactures has essentially contributed to the extension and improvement of the town. The market is on Thursday, the first Thursday in every month being noted for the sale of cattle. Fairs are held on the Thursday before Easter and September 27th, the latter continuing three days. The living is a perpetual curacy, in the archdeaconry and diocese of Chester, endowed with £600 private benefaction, £800 royal bounty, and £2000 parliamentary grant, and in the patronage of the Vicar of Rochdale. The chapel, rebuilt about 1770, on the site of a more ancient one, is dedicated to St. Mary, and is situated on an eminence near the centre of the town. A new chapel is being erected, at an estimated expense of between £4000 and £5000, towards defraying which His Majesty's commissioners for building new churches have granted about £3600, the remainder to be raised by subscription among the inhabitants : it is to contain one thousand two hundred and fifty-five sittings, four hundred and fifty-five of them free, and, on its completion, will supersede the old chapel, which will be abandoned. There are places of worship for Baptists, the Society of Friends, Independents, Wesleyan Methodists, and those of the New Connexion, and Unitarians, to all of which Sunday schools are attached, except that of the Society of Friends, who support day schools for the poor of their own communion. A school, adjoining the chapelyard, was endowed, in 1713, with the sum of £100, contributed by the Rev. Richard Clegg, and £50 voluntary subscriptions : the majority of the freeholders appoint the master, who has the gratuitous use of the school-house : four children, two of them elected by the holders of two particular farms, and two by the inhabitants, are taught free.

TODRIDGE, a township in that part of the parish of Hartburn which is in the western division of Morpeth ward, county of Northumberland, containing 8 inhabitants.

TODWICK, a parish in the southern division of the wapentake of Strafforth and Tickhill, West riding of the county of York, 8½ miles (S. E. by S.) from Rotherham, containing 210 inhabitants. The living is a rectory, in the archdeaconry and diocese of York, rated in the king's books at £6. 14. 7., and in the patronage of the Duke of Leeds. The church is dedicated to St. Peter and St. Paul.

TOFT, a parish in the hundred of Longstow, county of Cambridge, 5 miles (E. by S.) from Caxton, containing 259 inhabitants. The living is a rectory, with the vicarage of Caldecote annexed, in the archdeaconry and diocese of Ely, rated in the king's books at £6. 16. 10½., and in the patronage of the Master and Fellows of Christ College, Cambridge. The church is dedicated to St. Andrew.

TOFT, a township in the parish of Knutsford, hundred of Bucklow, county palatine of Chester, 1¼ mile (S.) from Nether Knutsford, containing 236 inhabitants.

TOFT, a joint hamlet with Lound, in the parish of Witham on the Hill, wapentake of Beltisloe, parts of Kesteven, county of Lincoln, 3 miles (S. W.) from Bourne, containing, with Lound, 210 inhabitants.

TOFT, a hamlet in the parish of Dunchurch, Rugby division of the hundred of Knightlow, county of Warwick, ½ mile (S. W.) from Dunchurch. The population is returned with the parish.

TOFT (MONKS'), a parish in the hundred of Clavering, county of Norfolk, 3½ miles (N.) from Beccles, containing 282 inhabitants. The living is a discharged rectory, with that of Haddiscoe annexed, in the archdeaconry of Norfolk, and diocese of Norwich, rated in the king's books at £8, and in the patronage of the Provost and Fellows of King's College, Cambridge. The church is dedicated to St. Margaret. An Alien priory, a cell to the abbey of St. Peter and St. Paul, at Preaux in Normandy, was founded here in the time of Henry I., the revenue of which, at the suppression, was annexed by Henry V. to the Carthusian monastery at Witham, by Henry VI. to Eton College, and by Edward IV. to King's College, Cambridge.

TOFT next NEWTON, a parish in the northern division of the wapentake of Walshcroft, parts of Lindsey, county of Lincoln, 4 miles (W.) from Market-Rasen, containing 65 inhabitants. The living is a rectory, in the archdeaconry and diocese of Lincoln, rated in the king's books at £9. 10. 10., and in the patronage of the Crown. The church is dedicated to St. Peter and St. Paul. John Holdsworth, in 1748, bequeathed £200 in support of a school.

TOFT (TREES), a parish in the hundred of Gallow, county of Norfolk, 2¼ miles (S. W.) from Fakenham, containing 87 inhabitants. The living is a discharged vicarage, in the archdeaconry and diocese of Norwich, rated in the king's books at £7. 18. 6., endowed with £600 royal bounty, and in the patronage of Marquis Townshend. The church is dedicated to All Saints.

TOFT (WEST), a parish in the hundred of Grimshoe, county of Norfolk, 5¼ miles (N. E.) from Brandon-Ferry, containing 128 inhabitants. The living is a discharged rectory, in the archdeaconry of Norfolk, and diocese of Norwich, rated in the king's books at £8. 6. John Moseley, Esq. was patron in 1815. The church, dedicated to St. Mary, is an ancient building of flint and stone, with a large square tower, erected early in the reign of Edward IV., and coped and embattled with freestone; the nave and chancel are separated by a screen, and in the latter is a piscina. In 1720, an oaken coffin was discovered here, containing, among other relics, human bones, the representation of a face cut in jet, a blue cypher, and several beads.

TOGSTON, a township in that part of the parish of WARKWORTH which is in the eastern division of MORPETH ward, county of NORTHUMBERLAND, 10 miles (S. E. by S.) from Alnwick, containing 102 inhabitants. Coal is obtained here.

TOLLAND, a parish in the hundred of TAUNTON and TAUNTON-DEAN, county of SOMERSET, 3¼ miles (N. N. E.) from Wiveliscombe, containing 113 inhabitants. The living is a rectory, in the archdeaconry of Taunton, and diocese of Bath and Wells, rated in the king's books at £7, and in the patronage of the Crown. The church is dedicated to St. John the Baptist.

TOLLARD-ROYAL, a parish partly in that part of the hundred of CRANBORNE which is in the Shaston (West) division of the county of DORSET, but chiefly in the hundred of CHALK, county of WILTS, 6¾ miles (S. E. by E.) from Shaftesbury, containing 288 inhabitants. The living is a rectory, in the archdeaconry and diocese of Salisbury, rated in the king's books at £16, and in the patronage of — Austin, Esq. The church is dedicated to St. Peter. In this parish is an old farmhouse, called King John's hunting seat, thought to be the remains of an ancient royal residence for hunting in Cranborne Chase.

TOLLER-FRATRUM, a parish in the hundred of TOLLERFORD, Dorchester division of the county of DORSET, 9 miles (N. W. by W.) from Dorchester, containing 37 inhabitants. The living is a discharged vicarage, with the perpetual curacy of Winford-Eagle annexed, in the archdeaconry of Dorset, and diocese of Bristol, rated in the king's books at £10. 6., and in the patronage of F. J. Browne, Esq. The church is dedicated to St. Basil. Near the road leading to Maiden-Newton are slight traces of an ancient intrenchment, upon an eminence called White Sheet; and on Farn down a barrow was opened, many years since, which contained seventeen urns, full of firm bones and black ashes. George Brown, in 1772, left a rent-charge of £21, to be applied in support of a school for the children of this parish and that of Toller-Porcorum. This parish formerly belonged to the brethren of the order of St. John of Jerusalem, whence it derived its distinguishing appellation.

TOLLER-PORCORUM, a parish partly in the hundred of BEAMINSTER-FORUM and REDHONE, Bridport division, but chiefly in the hundred of TOLLERFORD, Dorchester division of the county of DORSET, 10 miles (W. N. W.) from Dorchester, containing, with the tything of Over and Nether Kingcombe, 499 inhabitants. The living is a vicarage, in the archdeaconry of Dorset, and diocese of Bristol, rated in the king's books at £5, and in the patronage of F. J. Browne, Esq. The church is dedicated to St. Peter. Toller-Porcorum, or Swine's Toller, derived its distinguishing name from the great number of swine formerly bred here. It partakes, with Toller-Fratrum, in the benefit of a school, founded in 1772, by George Brown.

TOLLERTON, a parish in the southern division of the wapentake of BINGHAM, county of NOTTINGHAM, 4¾ miles (S. E. by S.) from Nottingham, containing 153 inhabitants. The living is a rectory, in the archdeaconry of Nottingham, and diocese of York, rated in the king's books at £15. 9. 4½., and in the patronage of Pendock Barry, Esq. The church, dedicated to St. Peter, is a small structure, with a tower surmounted by eight pinnacles with vanes: the interior is peculiarly neat, though not pewed.

TOLLERTON, a township in the parish of ALNE, partly within the liberty of ST. PETER of YORK, East riding, but chiefly in the wapentake of BULMER, North riding, of the county of YORK, 4½ miles (S. by W.) from Easingwould, containing 481 inhabitants. It is within the jurisdiction of the peculiar court of Alne and Tollerton.

TOLLESBURY, a parish in the hundred of THURSTABLE, county of ESSEX, 8 miles (E. N. E.) from Maldon, containing 958 inhabitants. The living is a vicarage, in the archdeaconry of Colchester, and diocese of London, rated in the king's books at £16. 6. 3., and in the patronage of Sir W. B. Rush, Knt. The church is dedicated to St. Mary. There is a place of worship for Independents. The parish is bounded on the south by Blackwater river, and South-Fleet creek is navigable to this place from the North sea.

TOLLESHUNT (D'ARCY), a parish in the hundred of THURSTABLE, county of ESSEX, 6¼ miles (N. E. by E.) from Maldon, containing 665 inhabitants. The living is a discharged vicarage, in the archdeaconry of Colchester, and diocese of London, rated in the king's books at £18. 10. General and Mrs. Rebow were patrons in 1819. The church is dedicated to St. Nicholas. The parish is bounded on the south-east by Blackwater river and North-Fleet creek. Near the churchyard is an ancient mansion-house surrounded by a moat. New House, or White House farm, in this parish, was purchased, in 1635, by the trustees of the charity of Henry Smith, Esq., who, besides his great munificence to almost every town and village in Surrey, left money to buy lands, directing the rents to be distributed among the poor of fourteen parishes, of which this is one.

TOLLESHUNT (KNIGHTS'), a parish in the hundred of THURSTABLE, county of ESSEX, 7½ miles (N. E.) from Maldon, containing 376 inhabitants. The living is a rectory, in the archdeaconry of Colchester, and diocese of London, rated in the king's books at £16. 13. 4., and in the patronage of the Crown. The church is dedicated to All Saints. Near the manor-house of Barnewalden, in this parish, some Roman pavements were discovered a few years ago.

TOLLESHUNT (MAJOR), a parish in the hundred of THURSTABLE, county of ESSEX, 5½ miles (N. E. by E.) from Maldon, containing 422 inhabitants. The living is a discharged vicarage, in the archdeaconry of Colchester, and diocese of London, rated in the king's books at £8. Mrs. Jegon was patroness in 1810. The church is dedicated to St. Nicholas. The parish extends south to Blackwater river. Here is a venerable remnant of the old manor-house, consisting of a spacious brick gateway, with four embattled turrets.

TOLPUDDLE, a parish in the hundred of PIDDLE-TOWN, Dorchester division of the county of DORSET, 7 miles (E. N. E.) from Dorchester, containing 351 inhabitants. The living is a vicarage, in the archdeaconry of Dorset, and diocese of Bristol, rated in the king's books at £15. 7. 3½., and in the patronage of the Dean and Canons of Christ Church, Oxford. The church is a small ancient fabric, built of rubble. There is a place of worship for Wesleyan Methodists. The parish is bounded on the south by the small river Piddle.

TONBRIDGE, or TUNBRIDGE, a market town and parish in the lowey of TONBRIDGE, lathe of AYLES-FORD, county of KENT, 14 miles (W. S. W.) from Maidstone, and 30 (S. E.) from London, containing, with part of the chapelry of Tonbridge-Wells, 7406 inhabitants. This place is supposed to have been originally called "Town of Bridges," from the stone bridges crossing the five streams into which the river Medway here branches, of which the present name is a contraction. A castle (by some supposed to have been built before the Conquest, but generally believed to have been erected shortly after, early in the eleventh century, by Richard, Earl of Clare, a relation of the Conqueror), which was on a very large scale, and a frequent scene of warfare, stood near the town, to which it probably gave origin: it was besieged by William Rufus, soon after his accession to the throne, the proprietor having declared in favour of Robert, Duke of Normandy: it was afterwards taken by King John, in his war with the barons; and subsequently was besieged by Prince Edward, son of Henry III., on which occasion the town was burned by the garrison, to prevent its giving shelter to the assailants. Having ascended the throne, Edward was sumptuously entertained here by Gilbert, Earl of Clare; and during his absence in Flanders, his son, afterwards Edward II., when administering the government of the kingdom, resided in this castle, and, having been crowned king, took possession of it, in consequence of the rebellion of its owner, after which it became, with three others, the depository of the records of the kingdom. The lordship, some time after, was the property of the family of Stafford; and, on the attainder of the Duke of Buckingham (the last powerful member of that family), in the reign of Henry VIII., it was seized by the crown, with his other possessions, and the castle suffered to fall into decay.

The town consists principally of one long and spacious street, containing some good houses, and its situation, on the declivity of a hill, contributes greatly to its cleanliness: it is partially lighted and paved: the only public buildings are the town hall and market-house. A stone causeway, at its entrance from London, was constructed, in 1528, by John Wilford; and the principal bridge was erected, in 1775, at an expense of £1100. The chief articles manufactured are Tonbridge ware and gunpowder, but both to a less extent than formerly. The river Medway was made navigable to this town about the middle of the last century, and a considerable quantity of coal and timber is brought by it from Maidstone. The weekly market is on Friday, and there is a cattle market on the first Tuesday in every month, which is very numerously attended: a fair is held on the 12th of October. The county magistrates meet on the second and fourth Wednesdays in each month; and a high constable and borsholder are appointed, every third year, at the court leet of the lord of the manor. A court of requests, for the recovery of debts under £5, is held on the third Monday in the month, comprehending within its jurisdiction the hundreds of Brenchley and Horsemonden, Codsheath, Somerden, Washlingstone, Westerham, and Wrotham,

the lowey of Tonbridge, and the ville and liberty of Brasted. Two representatives were sent to parliament from this town in the 23rd of Edward I., but it has not since exercised the elective franchise.

The living is a vicarage, in the archdeaconry and diocese of Rochester, rated in the king's books at £20. 3. 4., and in the patronage of — Deacon, Esq. The church, dedicated to St. Peter and St. Paul, is a spacious and handsome structure, and has been recently repaired and enlarged, with the addition of four hundred and twenty-seven sittings, of which three hundred and eight are free, the Incorporated Society for building and repairing churches and chapels having contributed £550 towards defraying the expense. There are places of worship for Calvinistic and Wesleyan Methodists.

The free grammar school was founded by Sir Andrew Judd, alderman of London, in the 7th of Edward VI.; and, by letters patent of that monarch, it was ordained that, after the death of the founder, the management of the school should be vested in the "Master, Wardens, and Commonalty of the Mystery of Skinners, of London," who should appoint the master, and, with the advice of the Warden and Fellows of All Souls' College, Oxford, should make statutes and ordinances for the due government of the school. The rental of the estates, with some small additional bequests, amounting, in 1819, to upwards of £4500 per annum, a suit was instituted in Chancery, respecting its application, when it was referred to a master to approve of a scheme for the future regulation of the school, whose report being sanctioned by the Lord Chancellor, in 1825, his lordship decreed, that the Skinners' Company might, with the advice of the Society of All Souls' College, Oxford, make such alterations as they should think fit, provided they did not interfere with the plan of such scheme, under authority of which a salary of £500 per annum is paid to the head-master, and £200 per annum to the under-master, both of them having also rent-free residences. Sixteen exhibitions, of £100 a year each, to continue for four years, were also founded from the income, for boys going to either of the Universities. The school is open to boys residing in the town, or within ten miles of it, free of charge, and to boys from any part of the United Kingdom, on payment of £7. 10. per annum to the master, and £3 per annum to the under-master; and the exhibitions are open to all the boys in the school, with preference to those on the foundation, provided they are equally qualified. An examiner, of seven years' standing, and a resident, at one of the Universities, who must have taken the degree of master of arts, or bachelor of civil law, is appointed by the Warden and Fellows of All Souls' College, Oxford; he publicly examines, at an annual visitation, all the boys in the school, to ascertain their progress; and subsequently examines, in the school-room, the candidates for the exhibitions; reporting to the governors and master the names of such as are qualified. The masters are allowed to take boarders, and any housekeeper of the town, having a license from the Skinners' Company, which is granted on testimonials as to their character from the master, may receive scholars, as boarders, the number not to exceed thirty. In addition to the exhibitions founded from the endowments, the pupils are also eligible to a fellowship at St. John's College,

Oxford, founded by Sir Thomas Whyte; to six exhibitions, of £10 per annum each, tenable at any college in either University, founded by Sir Thomas Smith; to a scholarship of £17. 9. 6. per annum, at Brasenose College, Oxford, founded by Mr. Henry Fisher; to an exhibition of £2. 13. 4. per annum, at either of the Universities, founded by Mr. Thomas Lampard; to two exhibitions, of £6 per annum each, at St. John's College, Cambridge, founded by Mr. Worrall; to an exhibition, originally £4, now £8, per annum, at either University (in default of scholars from Seven-Oaks school), founded by Mr. Robert Holmedon; and to two exhibitions, of £75 per annum each, at Jesus' College, Cambridge (also in default of scholars from Seven-Oaks school), founded by Lady Mary Boswell. The National school, for one hundred and fifty boys and one hundred and fifty girls, is supported by voluntary contributions; and the boys who were educated from the funds of the town charity school, which amounted to about £36, are now instructed in this school. The remains of the once celebrated castle consist only of the entrance gateway, which is flanked by two round towers, and an artificial mount, on which the keep stood; but these serve to show the surpassing strength which it once possessed. Near it are the ruins of a priory of Black canons, founded by Richard de Clare, about the end of the reign of Henry I. : at its dissolution, in 1525, the revenue, amounting to £169. 10. 3., was intended to form a part of the endowment of Wolsey's colleges at Ipswich and Oxford; but the cardinal's disgrace occurring before the grant was confirmed, it became vested in the crown: the foundation is still visible, but little remains besides the refectory, or hall, which has been converted into a barn.

TONBRIDGE, or TUNBRIDGE, WELLS, a chapelry partly in the parish and lowey of TONBRIDGE; and partly in that part of the parish of SPELDHURST which is in the hundred of WASHLINGSTONE, lathe of AYLESFORD, county of KENT; and partly in that part of the parish of FRANT which is in the hundred of ROTHERFIELD, rape of PEVENSEY, county of SUSSEX; 20 miles (S. W.) from Maidstone, and 36 (S. E. by S.) from London; containing about 10,000 inhabitants. This attractive and fashionable watering-place owes its importance to its medicinal springs, which were first discovered, in 1606, by Dudley, Lord North, then sojourning at Eridge House, for the benefit of his health; and he being cured by the use of them, Lord Abergavenny, who resided at Eridge, was induced to fit up the wells, and make such improvements as might lead to their becoming a place of public resort. The springs soon acquired celebrity, as Henrietta Maria, queen of Charles I., retired hither to enjoy the benefit of the waters, after the birth of her eldest son, Prince Charles; and there being no suitable residence, she and her suite were lodged in tents upon Bishop's down. Their increasing reputation continuing to attract many visitors, various retail dealers constructed standings, on which they exhibited their wares, under a row of trees in the road by which the company usually passed to the Wells, and finally lodging-houses were erected. Soon after the Restoration, in 1664, the place was visited by Catherine, queen of Charles II., who, residing here for some time, with the gay court of that monarch, gave it additional attraction. It was also a very favourite residence of Queen Anne, prior to her

accession to the throne, and has continued, ever since, to attract a great concourse of company during the season, which is from May to November. The waters, which are chalybeate, are of nearly equal strength with those of the German Spa, and are considered very efficacious in cases of weak digestion, or where tonics are necessary. The town is irregularly but beautifully built, consisting of clusters of houses in different situations. The Well is situated in a sort of dingle, on a sandy bottom, surrounded by hills; and the water, which rises into a stone basin, is served by a woman who lives at an adjoining cottage, and who receives a certain sum for the season from each person drinking it. About forty years since, a marble basin was substituted for that of stone, and, in consequence of the dirt which had accumulated in the latter, a fixed cover was added, and the water drawn off by a spout; but some of the visitors, not experiencing the usual benefit in the succeeding season, fancifully imagined that the marble cover had neutralized the effects of the water, and it was consequently removed, and a stone basin replaced. Near the Well, which is three hundred feet above the level of the sea, are the principal shops and places of amusement. A spacious handsome building, called the Bath House, has been erected, and contains both hot and cold mineral baths. The Parade, which is broad and handsome, is bounded on one side by the assembly-rooms, libraries, and by shops in which Tonbridge ware and fancy articles of every kind are sold, and in front of which is a piazza extending nearly the whole length; and on the opposite side is a row of trees, with an orchestra in the midst, where a band usually plays during a portion of each day in the season: with the Parade is connected what are called the Upper and Lower walk, divided by palisades of iron. The other parts of the town are situated on detached eminences, at short distances from the Wells, called Mount Ephraim, Mount Sion, Mount Pleasant, and Bishop's Down; which, being interspersed with shrubberies and pleasure grounds, and connected with the Wells by beautiful walks regularly disposed, present a combination of interesting scenery. The inns and boarding and lodging houses are generally of a superior description. Some rocks of considerable height, surrounded with wood, about a mile and a half south-west from the town, are much visited and admired. There is a small neat theatre near the Wells; and races are held, annually in August, on the common. The manufacture of wooden toys and articles for domestic use, commonly denominated "Tonbridge ware," is carried on to a considerable extent. The government is vested in the county magistrates, who meet once a week; and constables are appointed at the court leet for the "hundred of Southborough and manor of Rusthall."

The living is a perpetual curacy, in the archdeaconry and diocese of Rochester, and in the patronage of certain Trustees. The chapel, dedicated to King Charles the Martyr, was built about one hundred and fifty years since, by subscription amongst the visitors, on ground given by the lady of the manor, and is supported by an annual collection after a sermon and by subscriptions: it is a plain Grecian building, fitted up and wainscoted with fine old oak, which, with its ornamented ceiling, is much admired. A new church has also been recently erected by subscription, aided by a grant of £6000 from His Majesty's Commissioners for building new churches, in that part of the town which is in the parish of Tonbridge; it is a handsome structure in the later style of English architecture. There are places of worship for those in the Connexion of the late Countess of Huntingdon, Independents, and Wesleyan Methodists. A charity school adjoins the chapel, in which about eighty boys are instructed; and one has been established for about one hundred girls: both are on the National system, and supported by voluntary contributions. The late Richard Cumberland, Esq.,the celebrated dramatist, was for many years a resident on Mount Sion, frequently attracting hither some of the most eminent literary characters of the day.

TONG, a parish in the hundred of MILTON, lathe of SCRAY, county of KENT, 2 miles (E. by N.) from Sittingbourne, containing 216 inhabitants. The living is a vicarage, in the archdeaconry and diocese of Canterbury, rated in the king's books at £8. 6. 8. W: Baldwin, Esq. was patron in 1803. The church, dedicated to St. Giles, has a tower steeple on the south side. The parish is bounded on the north by the East Swale. The ditch and keep mount of Tong castle still remain in a wood at a short distance south from the church. In this ancient fortress Hengist surprised Vortigern and his nobles ; he massacred the latter, and kept the king a prisoner till he surrendered his kingdom. William Housson, in 1779, bequeathed £200, directing the interest to be applied in teaching poor boys of Tong, Bapchild, and Murston. At Puckeshall, in this parish, there was anciently an hospital, dedicated to St. James.

TONG, a parish in the Shiffnall division of the hundred of BRIMSTREE, county of SALOP, 3¼ miles (E. by S.) from Shiffnall, containing 536 inhabitants. The living is a perpetual curacy, in the archdeaconry of Salop, and diocese of Lichfield and Coventry. George Duront, Esq. was patron in 1807. The church, dedicated to St.Bartholomew, is in the decorated style, with a handsome spire rising from the centre : it originally belonged to the abbey of Shrewsbury, and was purchased, in 1410, by Isabel, relict of Sir Fulk Pembridge, Knt., and others, who rebuilt and made it collegiate for a warden, four chaplains, priests, and two clerks, with an hospital for thirteen poor persons, whose revenue, at the dissolution, was valued at £45. 9. 10. Near the church, and within the demesne of the castle, are considerable remains of the old hospital ; new almshouses have been founded in its stead at the village. Tong castle, a magnificent and extensive mansion, was erected, in the last century, upon the site of the ancient structure, which was then demolished : it is crowned with numerous turrets, pinnacles, and two lofty domes, producing a grand and striking effect. There are benefactions by Lady Harris, Lord and Lady Pierrepoint, and the Rev. Lewis Petier, producing £45 a year, for educating and clothing poor boys and girls in the Sunday school.

TONG, a chapelry in the parish of BIRSTALL, wapentake of MORLEY, West riding of the county of YORK, 4¾ miles (E. S. E.) from Bradford, containing 1893 inhabitants. The living is a perpetual curacy, in the archdeaconry and diocese of York, endowed with £450 private benefaction, and £400 royal bounty, and in the patronage of John Plumbe, Esq. The manufac-

ture of woollen cloth, worsted, rope, and twine, is here carried on. Eight poor children are instructed for £6 a year, bequeathed, in 1739, by Sir George Tempest, who erected the school-house.

TONGE, a joint township with Haulgh, in the parish of BOLTON, hundred of SALFORD, county palatine of LANCASTER, 1¼ mile (E. N. E.) from Great Bolton, containing 1678 inhabitants, who are chiefly employed in the manufacture of cotton and counterpanes, and in the extensive bleaching grounds, spinning-mills, and paper-mills, established here. The ingenious Crompton resided at the ancient seat of the Starkie family, Hull-i'-th'-Wood, where he completed his invention of the spinning-mill, which he sold for not more than £100. He, however, received a grant from parliament of £5000, and a subscription was opened, by the cotton spinners and others of Bolton and Manchester, for the purchase of an annuity, which he enjoyed during the remainder of his life. The commissioners of enclosure have awarded land, now let for £5 a year, towards the foundation of a school. · A limited number of boys of this place are annually appointed to the High Style school, founded by Henry Mather, at Kearsley.

TONGE, a township in the parish of OLDHAM *cum* PRESTWICH, hundred of SALFORD, county palatine of LANCASTER, 1¼ mile (E. by S.) from Middleton, containing 1390 inhabitants. This township adjoins Middleton, and forms a populous part of the environs of that town. In 1829, a grant was proposed for building a chapel, by the Incorporated Society for promoting the erection of additional churches and chapels.

TOOTING (LOWER), or TOOTING-GRAVENEY, a parish in the western division of the hundred of BRIXTON, county of SURREY, 7 miles (S. S. W.) from London, containing 1863 inhabitants. This village, consisting of two streets, is situated on the road from London to Worthing; it is lighted with oil, and supplied with water from wells produced by boring. The atmosphere is considered very salubrious, and the environs are studded with elegant cottages and villas. Assemblies are occasionally held during the winter months. The parish is within the jurisdiction of a court of requests held at Wandsworth, for the recovery of debts under £5, and is also within the superintendence of the new police. The living is a rectory, in the archdeaconry of Surrey, and diocese of Winchester, rated in the king's books at £8. 8. 6½., and in the patronage of the Rev. Richard Greaves. The church, which is dedicated to St. Nicholas, is an ancient structure, with a circular tower and wooden spire, now much dilapidated : it is in contemplation to erect a new church, the expense to be defrayed by subscription, by a sale of part of Tooting common, and by a grant from the Incorporated Society for the building and enlargement of churches and chapels. There are places of worship for Independents and Wesleyan Methodists. The parochial school is endowed with the interest of a bequest of £400 in the five per cent. consols., made by Mr. John Avarn, in 1809 ; and by another bequest, from William Powell, Esq., in 1823, of £210, and a share of the residue of his estate, amounting to £1113, which were together laid out in the purchase of £1441 18. 11. three per cent. consols. : it is further supported by voluntary contribu tions : fifty-seven boys and forty-seven girls are educated, and thirty of the latter are clothed. The school-rooms, and separate apartments for the master and mistress, were erected on the site of some former ones, in 1828, at an expense of £1800. In 1718, Sir James Bateman, Knt., bequeathed £100, directing the interest to be applied in apprenticing children.

TOOTING (UPPER), a hamlet in the parish of STREATHAM, eastern division of the hundred of BRIXTON, county of SURREY, 7 miles (S. S. W.) from London. The population is returned with the parish. This village, which is also designated Tooting-Beck, is situated between two hills. On the road between Tooting and Balham Hill is a chapel of ease to the parish church, erected by the inhabitants of Upper and Lower Tooting, at the expense of nearly £7000 : it has been licensed by the Bishop of Winchester, and will accommodate about a thousand persons : over the altar is a painted window : the minister, who must be at least master of arts, is returned by the committee to the ordinary, who, out of three candidates so qualified, elects one. Two school-houses, with houses for the master and mistress, have been erected by subscription, in which eighty boys and sixty girls receive a gratuitous education : they are supported by voluntary contributions.

TOPCLIFFE, a parish comprising the townships of Catton, Dalton, Elmer with Crakehall, Skipton, and Topcliffe, in the wapentake of BIRDFORTH, and the chapelry of Dishforth, and the townships of Asenby, Baldersby, Marton le Moor, and Rainton with Newby, in the wapentake of HALLIKELD, North riding of the county of YORK, and containing 2540 inhabitants, of which number, 659 are in the township of Topcliffe, which extends within the liberty of St. Peter of York, East riding, 5½ miles (S. S. W.) from Thirsk. The living is a vicarage, in the archdeaconry of Cleveland, and diocese of York, rated in the king's books at £19. 19. 2., and in the patronage of the Dean and Chapter of York. The church, dedicated to St. Columb, is of high antiquity. There is a place of worship for Wesleyan Methodists. John Hartforth, in 1588, gave land and money in support of a free grammar school, which, with the subsequent smaller bequests of William Robinson and Henry Roper, produce £70 a year, for the instruction of thirty boys. Here are slight vestiges of the ancient baronial mansion of the Percy family, called Maiden Bower, in which Henry, the fourth Earl of Northumberland, was murdered by the populace, in 1520, for enforcing a tax imposed in the reign of Henry VII.; and in which Thomas, the fifth earl, who was beheaded at York, in 1572, had previously formed a conspiracy against Queen Elizabeth. Charles I. was confined in it, and the sum of £200,000, for giving him up to the parliament, was here paid to the Scottish commissioners.

TOPCROFT, a parish in the hundred of LODDON, county of NORFOLK, 4¾ miles (E. by S.) from Stratton St. Mary, containing 420 inhabitants. The living is a rectory, in the archdeaconry of Norfolk, and diocese of Norwich, rated in the king's books at £10. 13. 4., and in the patronage of the Bishop of Norwich. The church is dedicated to St. Margaret. Near Topcroft Hall there was formerly a free chapel, dedicated to St. Giles.

TOPPESFIELD, a parish in the hundred of HINCKFORD, county of ESSEX, 4 miles (W. N. W.) from Castle-Hedingham, containing 928 inhabitants. The living is a rectory, in the jurisdiction of the Commissary of

Essex and Herts, concurrently with the Consistorial Court of the Bishop of London, rated in the king's books at £26, and in the patronage of the Crown. The church, dedicated to St. Margaret, contains some curious ancient monuments. Robert Edwards, in 1730, left £10 per annum for teaching children.

TOPSHAM, a market town and parish in the hundred of WONFORD, county of DEVON, 3½ miles (S. E.) from Exeter, and 170 (W. S. W.) from London, containing 3156 inhabitants. In the civil war between Charles and the parliament, the Earl of Warwick brought some ships up the river Exe, and captured a small fort here ; but the vessels being left upon the sands, on the ebbing of the tide, two were captured and one burnt by the army under Fairfax, who remained here some time. This neat little town is situated near the influx of the river Exe into the sea, and is within the limits of the port of Exeter; the river expands here to a considerable width, forming, at high tides, a noble sheet of water. About a mile to the south, on the opposite side of it, are the sea locks, opening into the canal leading to Exeter : the prosperity of the commercial interests of Topsham is dependent on the foreign and coasting trade and the manufactures of that city. The chief local occupations consist of ship-building, and the manufacture of paper, sacking, ropes, and twine ; the coal and timber trades employ several persons, and are somewhat extensive ; anchors and chain cables are also wrought here. A quay, built about 1313, by Hugh Courtenay, was purchased by the Chamber of Exeter, in 1778, and is capable of receiving vessels of two hundred tons' burden : it is large and commodious. On the strand are some neat residences, fronted with gardens extending to the water's edge, the view being justly admired for its variety and extent. In 1257, an annual fair for three days was granted to the inhabitants, and, together with a market on Saturdays, confirmed to them by Edward I. The market is still held on Saturday; and there is a small fair on the first Wednesday in August. The living is a perpetual curacy, in the peculiar jurisdiction and patronage of the Dean and Chapter of Exeter, endowed with £15 per annum and £200 private benefaction, £200 royal bounty, and £500 parliamentary grant. The church, which is dedicated to St. Margaret, has been enlarged with one hundred and eighty free sittings, towards defraying the expense of which the Incorporated Society for the building and enlargement of churches and chapels contributed £150 : it contains some good monuments by Chantry, and the view from the churchyard is considered very fine. There are places of worship for Independents and Wesleyan Methodists. Sundry benefactions for the instruction of poor children, producing an income of about £30 per annum, are paid to the National school for the education of ten boys : this school contains about sixty boys and fifty girls, and is further supported by voluntary contributions.

TORBRYAN, a parish in the hundred of HAYTOR, county of DEVON, 4 miles (S. W. by S.) from Newton-Bushell, containing 277 inhabitants. The living is a rectory, in the archdeaconry of Totness, and diocese of Exeter, rated in the king's books at £20. 14. 7., and in the patronage of J. Wolston, Esq. The church, dedicated to the Holy Trinity, has an elegant wooden screen, and an enriched pulpit, also of wood.

TORKINGTON, a township in the parish of Stockport, hundred of Macclesfield, county palatine of Chester, 4½ miles (S. E.) from Stockport, containing 293 inhabitants.

TORKSEY, a parish in the wapentake of Lawress, though locally in the wapentake of Well, parts of Lindsey, county of Lincoln, 8 miles (S. by E.) from Gainsborough, containing, with the chapelry of Brampton, and the hamlet of Harwick, 365 inhabitants. The living is a perpetual curacy, held by sequestration, in the archdeaconry of Stow, and diocese of Lincoln, endowed with £800 royal bounty. The church is dedicated to St. Peter. A priory of Black canons, in honour of St. Leonard, was founded here by King John, which, at the dissolution, was valued at £27. 2. 8. per annum. Torksey is situated at the junction of the Fosse-Dyke with the river Trent, and formerly enjoyed many privileges, on condition that the king's ambassadors, when travelling this way, should be conveyed by the inhabitants, in their own barges, down the Trent to York.

TORLETON, a hamlet (formerly a chapelry) partly in the parish of Coates, hundred of Crowthorne and Minety, and partly in that of Rodmarton, hundred of Longtree, county of Gloucester, 5 miles (W. by S.) from Cirencester. The population is returned with the respective parishes. The chapel is desecrated.

TORMARTON, a parish in the lower division of the hundred of Grumbald's-Ash, county of Gloucester, 4 miles (E. S. E.) from Chipping-Sodbury, containing 320 inhabitants. The living is a rectory, in the archdeaconry and diocese of Gloucester, rated in the king's books at £27, and in the patronage of N. Castleton, Esq. The church is dedicated to St. Mary.

TOR-MOHUN, or TOR-MOHAM, a parish in the hundred of Haytor, county of Devon, ¾ of a mile (N.W.) from Torquay, containing, with the chapelry of Torquay, 1925 inhabitants. The living is a perpetual curacy, annexed to that of Cockington, in the archdeaconry of Totness, and diocese of Exeter. The church has an elegant wooden screen, formerly painted and gilt, also an ancient stone font. Of thirty-two Premonstratensian monasteries in England, that of Torre, founded and endowed by William de Brewer, in 1196, was by far the richest: it was dedicated to our Holy Saviour, the Virgin Mary, and the Holy Trinity, and, at the dissolution, had a revenue of £396. 0. 11. The situation of the abbey is most beautiful; and the remains of the church (which is said to have been richly furnished with cloth of gold), the chapter-house, &c., evince the former magnificence of the buildings: the old refectory has been converted into a Roman Catholic chapel, and of the three gateways mentioned by Leland, the only one now remaining is much admired for the beauty of its architectural proportions. The modern mansion of Torre Abbey is the seat of H. G. Carey, Esq., in whose family it has continued since 1662. On a hill, about half a mile from the church, are the remains of a chapel, which was dedicated to St. Michael.

TORPENHOW, a parish in Allerdale ward below Darwent, county of Cumberland, comprising the townships of Bewaldeth with Snittlegarth, Blennerhasset with Kirkland, Bothel with Threapland, and Torpenhow with Whitrigg, and containing 961 inhabitants, of which number, 256 are in the township of Torpenhow with Whitrigg, 2½ miles (W. by N.) from Ireby.

The living is a vicarage, in the archdeaconry and diocese of Carlisle, rated in the king's books at £33. 6. 8., and in the patronage of the Bishop of Carlisle. The church, dedicated to St. Michael, is principally in the Norman style; the ceiling is of wood, painted and very curious. The parish is bounded on the north by the river Ellen: it abounds with freestone and limestone, and, it is supposed, with coal also. The ancient free school at Bothel was founded and endowed by subscription, and was rebuilt about thirty years ago; the annual income is about £50, for which eighty children are instructed.

TORPOINT, a chapelry in the parish of St. Anthony, southern division of the hundred of East, county of Cornwall, 3 miles (W.) from Devonport. The population is returned with the parish. The living is a perpetual curacy, in the archdeaconry of Cornwall, and diocese of Exeter, endowed with £200 private benefaction, and £1700 parliamentary grant, and in the patronage of the Vicar of St. Anthony. There are places of worship for Independents and Wesleyan Methodists. The village occupies a peninsula, formed by the river Tamer, the Lynher, and St. John's lake, from which the inhabitants derive an abundance of fish. Though small, it is highly respectable; and in the vicinity are many genteel seats, of which, Trematon Castle is the most distinguished. Sir Coventry Carew founded a free school, for teaching and clothing ten children: there is also a National school, supported by subscription.

TORQUAY, a chapelry in the parish of Tor-Mohun, hundred of Haytor, county of Devon, 7 miles (S. E. by S.) from Newton-Bushell. The population is returned with the parish. This place, about forty years since, was an insignificant fishing hamlet, but is now a fashionable and attractive watering-place: it is situated in the most northerly cove of Torbay, and occupies a somewhat irregular, but singularly beautiful, site. The first great improvement was the erection of a pier and quay, for which an act of parliament was obtained by Sir Lawrence Palk, to whom the town is greatly indebted: it was commenced in 1804, and completed in 1807; and another pier has since been constructed, forming a secure basin, five hundred feet long, and three hundred broad. A considerable portion of the town is built on the strand, and consists of neat and comfortable residences, principally lodging-houses; and there are also two very good hotels, warm and cold baths, and a library and news-room. On the north, east, and west sides it is completely sheltered by hills of very considerable elevation, on the declivities of which are detached houses and terraces, some of them very handsome buildings; and the heights on which they are situated being richly clothed with wood, their appearance from the pier-head is strikingly beautiful. An annual regatta takes place in August, which is well attended; and the assembly-room, erected in 1826, is much frequented during the season, which is from September to May. The salubrity and mildness of the air, arising from its contiguity to the sea and its sheltered situation, renders this a most desirable winter residence for persons of a consumptive habit, or those for whom a mild climate is necessary; and it is usually, at this period of the year, very full of company: it is well supplied with water. Torquay has a trifling share in

2 T 2

the Newfoundland trade; and, in addition to several coasting vessels, employed for the importation of coal, &c., it has a weekly communication by water with London. There is a very convenient market-place, well supplied with provisions at the customary markets, which are on Tuesday and Friday: a fair is held annually at Easter. The living is a perpetual curacy, in the archdeaconry of Totness, and diocese of Exeter, endowed with £1600 parliamentary grant, and in the patronage of the Perpetual Curate of Tor-Mohun and Cockington. The chapel is a handsome modern structure. There are places of worship for Calvinistic and Wesleyan Methodists. In the cliffs in this neighbourhood are several remarkable fissures, or openings, particularly that called Kent's Hole, which is of extraordinary magnitude, comprising numerous caves of various elevations, to which are several openings, one of them ninety-three feet deep, one hundred wide, and thirty in height, containing many interesting specimens, both stalactital and organic, and fossil remains of the elephant and several other animals. Druidical knives have also been discovered. A National school has been established by means of voluntary subscriptions.

TORRINGTON (BLACK), a parish in the hundred of BLACK TORRINGTON, county of DEVON, 5¼ miles (W. by N.) from Hatherleigh, containing 880 inhabitants. The living is a rectory, in the archdeaconry of Totness, and diocese of Exeter, rated in the king's books at £22. 8. 9., and in the patronage of Sir George Bampfylde, Bart. The church is dedicated to St. Mary. There is a place of worship for Baptists. The river Torridge runs through the parish.

TORRINGTON (EAST), a parish in the western division of the wapentake of WRAGGOE, parts of LINDSEY, county of LINCOLN, 4 miles (N. N. E.) from Wragby, containing 89 inhabitants. The living is a discharged rectory, united, in 1735, to the vicarage of Wragby, in the archdeaconry and diocese of Lincoln, rated in the king's books at £7. 10. 10. The church is dedicated to St. Michael.

TORRINGTON (GREAT), a market town and parish, having separate jurisdiction, though locally in the hundred of Fremington, county of DEVON, 34 miles (N. W.) from Exeter, and 198 (W. by S.) from London, containing 2538 inhabitants. The name of this place, in old records, is written *Cheping-Toriton*, the Saxon prefix demonstrating its antiquity as a market town. At a very early period, Torrington conferred the title of baron on its possessors, who had the power of life and death over their dependents: in 1340, Richard de Merton erected a castle here, the chapel of which existed till the latter part of the eighteenth century. In 1484, Bishop Courtenay was tried at the sessions, on a charge of treason against Richard III.; and, in 1590, the county sessions having been held here, in consequence of the appearance of the plague at Exeter, that fatal malady was extended to this town. During the civil commotions in the reign of Charles I., the parliamentary forces supplied

Arms.

from Barnstaple, Bideford, and other places, were put to flight here, in 1643, by Col. Digby. Here also, about three years afterwards, the royalists were defeated by Fairfax in a severe contest, and, after the victory, a thanksgiving sermon was preached in the market-place by Hugh Peters, whose eloquence was considered to have been very effective in promoting the parliamentary interests. The general's intention of prolonging his stay, however, was frustrated by a most appalling event, the explosion of eighty barrels of gunpowder in the church, during its occupation by two hundred prisoners, all of whom, with the soldiers on guard, perished, and the edifice itself was destroyed. The situation of the town is singularly bold and picturesque: it occupies the summit and declivities of a lofty cliff, facing the south, and washed at its base by the river Torridge, over which is a bridge, connecting this parish with that of Little Torrington: the banks of the river are enriched with fine landscape scenery, and, in its course above the town, the stream winds beneath some of the richest hanging woods in the kingdom. The bowling-green, which occupies the highest portion of the cliff, is the site of the ancient castle, and commands a prospect extremely beautiful. The town consists of a market-place, surrounded by good houses, and two long streets, variously disposed on the ridge and declivity, with gardens descending towards the river. The inhabitants have a right of pasturage on an extensive and rich common. The woollen trade, formerly considerable, is now confined to the manufacture of a few serges, blankets, and some coarse cloth: the principal articles of trade are kid, chamois, beaver, and other gloves, of which great quantities are sent to London. Here are two tanyards, and on the river is a large corn-mill. Lime, coal, and timber are supplied by a canal extending hence to the sea docks near Bideford, and running nearly parallel with the river, which there becomes navigable for sloops: about two miles northwest from the town the canal crosses the river, by means of a noble aqueduct, and nearer the sea lock it is interrupted by an inclined plane. The aqueduct, of which the first stone was laid August 11th, 1824, and the canal, were undertaken at the sole expense of Lord Rolle, through his own lands, which is said to have exceeded £40,000. Some veins of lead-ore are found in the neighbourhood. The market is held on Saturday; on the third Saturday in March is a very large cattle market, and a smaller one in November: fairs are on May 4th, July 5th, and October 10th.

The charter of incorporation, granted by Mary, was confirmed in the 15th of James I.: the municipal body consists of a mayor, recorder, seven aldermen, and sixteen burgesses, with a town clerk, and two serjeants at mace: the mayor is nominated in August, and sworn in in October, and, with his immediate predecessor, who is termed a justice, exercises magisterial authority. The corporation hold quarter sessions, and a court of record every three weeks: the county magistrates meet weekly on Saturday.

Corporate Seal.

The town hall is a neat modern edifice of brick and stone, with an arched basement: there is a small prison. This town sent members to parliament in the reign of Edward III., but the inhabitants were relieved from the exercise of the franchise, on petition, in that of Henry VI. The living is a vicarage, with the impropriation of Stow St. Giles annexed, in the archdeaconry of Barnstaple, and diocese of Exeter, rated in the king's books at £20, endowed with £600 private benefaction, and £900 parliamentary grant, and in the patronage of the Dean and Canons of Christ Church, Oxford. The church, which is dedicated to St. Michael, is an ancient structure, rebuilt about five years after its destruction by gunpowder, in 1645: it has a north transept, and on the south side is a low tower. There are places of worship for Baptists, Independents, and Wesleyan Methodists. In addition to the grammar school, the Blue school, in Well-street, was established in 1709, by Denys Rolle, Esq., who gave a messuage and lands, with the sum of £200, for the gratuitous education of forty boys: the annual income is £63. 10.: twenty-two boys are educated and clothed, and two apprenticed annually, with a premium of £1 each. A National school, in New-street, is supported by voluntary contributions. An almshouse for eight poor persons was founded and endowed, in 1604, by John Huddle; there is also an unendowed almshouse. On the restoration of Charles II., General Monk was made Earl of Torrington. The town at present confers the title of viscount on the family of Byng.

TORRINGTON (LITTLE), a parish in the hundred of SHEBBEAR, county of DEVON, 2 miles (S.) from Great Torrington, containing 505 inhabitants. The living is a rectory, in the archdeaconry of Barnstaple, and diocese of Exeter, rated in the king's books at £14. 18. 11½., and in the patronage of Lord Rolle and others. At Toddiport, in this parish, separated from that of Great Torrington by a bridge over the Torridge, is an hospital, with a chapel attached, appropriated to the poor of both parishes.

TORRINGTON (WEST), a parish in the western division of the wapentake of WRAGGOE, parts of LINDSEY, county of LINCOLN, 2¾ miles (N. by E.) from Wragby, containing 133 inhabitants. The living is a discharged vicarage, in the archdeaconry and diocese of Lincoln, rated in the king's books at £4, endowed with £200 royal bounty, and £200 parliamentary grant, and in the patronage of the Bishop of Lincoln. The church is dedicated to St. Mary.

TORRISHOLME, a township in that part of the parish of LANCASTER which is in the hundred of LONSDALE, south of the sands, county palatine of LANCASTER, 2 miles (N. W.) from Lancaster, containing 161 inhabitants.

TORTINGTON, a parish in the hundred of AVISFORD, rape of ARUNDEL, county of SUSSEX, 2½ miles (S. W.) from Arundel, containing 88 inhabitants. The living is a vicarage not in charge, in the archdeaconry and diocese of Chichester. Francis Lovell, Esq. was patron in 1817. The church is principally in the early style of English architecture. The parish is bounded on the east by the river Arun. A priory of Augustine canons, in honour of St. Mary Magdalene, was founded by the Lady Hadwisa Corbet, before the reign of John,

which, at the dissolution, possessed a revenue of £101. 4. 1.

TORTWORTH, a parish in the upper division of the hundred of GRUMBALD's ASH, county of GLOUCESTER, 4 miles (W.) from Wotton under Edge, containing 277 inhabitants. The living is a rectory, in the archdeaconry and diocese of Gloucester, rated in the king's books at £16. 3. 9., and in the patronage of the Provost and Fellows of Oriel College, Oxford. The church is dedicated to St. Leonard.

TORVER, a chapelry in the parish of ULVERSTONE, hundred of LONSDALE, north of the sands, county palatine of LANCASTER, 6 miles (W. S. W.) from Hawkeshead, containing 263 inhabitants. The living is a perpetual curacy, in the archdeaconry of Richmond, and diocese of Chester, endowed with £200 private benefaction, and £600 royal bounty, and in the patronage of the Inhabitants. Three children are educated for the interest of £200, the gift of John Fleming, in 1777, in support of a free grammar school.

TORWORTH, a township in that part of the parish of BLYTH which is in the Hatfield division of the wapentake of BASSETLAW, county of NOTTINGHAM, 4¾ miles (N. W. by N.) from East Retford, containing 219 inhabitants.

TOSELAND, a parish in the hundred of TOSELAND, county of HUNTINGDON, 4¾ miles (E. N. E.) from St. Neots, containing 144 inhabitants. The living is a perpetual curacy, annexed to the vicarage of Great Paxton, in the archdeaconry of Huntingdon, and diocese of Lincoln. The church is dedicated to St. Mary.

TOSSEN (GREAT), a township in the parish of ROTHBURY, western division of COQUETDALE ward, county of NORTHUMBERLAND, 2 miles (W. S. W.) from Rothbury, containing 110 inhabitants, who are chiefly employed in the manufacture of woollen cloth, and at the limestone quarries in the neighbourhood. The village, situated on the river Coquet, was formerly a considerable place, and there are still the remains of an ancient tower.

TOSSEN (LITTLE), a township in the parish of ROTHBURY, western division of COQUETDALE ward, county of NORTHUMBERLAND, 2½ miles (W. S. W.) from Rothbury, containing 36 inhabitants. It is bounded on the north by the river Coquet.

TOSSIDE, or TOSSET, a chapelry in the parish of GISBURN, western division of the wapentake of STAINCLIFFE and EWCROSS, West riding of the county of YORK, 7½ miles (S. W. by S.) from Settle. The population is returned with the parish. The living is a perpetual curacy, in the archdeaconry and diocese of York, endowed with £800 royal bounty, and in the patronage of the Vicar of Gisburn. The chapel is dedicated to St. Bartholomew.

TOSTOCK, a parish in the hundred of THEDWESTRY, county of SUFFOLK, 7½ miles (E.) from Bury-St. Edmund's, containing 281 inhabitants. The living is a discharged rectory, in the archdeaconry of Sudbury, and diocese of Norwich, rated in the king's books at £6. 8. 6½., and in the patronage of J. Moseley, Esq. The church is dedicated to St. Andrew.

TOTHAM (GREAT), a parish in the hundred of THURSTABLE, county of ESSEX, 3 miles (N. N. E.) from Maldon, containing 580 inhabitants. The living is a discharged vicarage, in the archdeaconry of Colchester, and diocese of London, rated in the king's books at £10, endowed with £200 private benefaction, and £200 royal bounty, and in the patronage of W. P. Honeywood, Esq. The church is dedicated to St. Peter.

TOTHAM (LITTLE), a parish in the hundred of THURSTABLE, county of ESSEX, 3½ miles (N. E.) from Maldon, containing 267 inhabitants. The living is a perpetual curacy, annexed to the rectory of Goldhanger, in the archdeaconry of Colchester, and diocese of London. The church is dedicated to All Saints. The parish is bounded on the south by Blackwater river, in a creek of which there are salt-works.

TOTHILL, a parish in the Marsh division of the hundred of CALCEWORTH, parts of LINDSEY, county of LINCOLN, 5¼ miles (N. W. by N.) from Alford, containing 72 inhabitants. The living is a discharged rectory, in the archdeaconry and diocese of Lincoln, rated in the king's books at £6.17., and in the patronage of Lord Willoughby de Broke. The church is dedicated to St. Mary.

TOTLEY, a hamlet in the parish of DRONFIELD, hundred of SCARSDALE, county of DERBY, 3½ miles (W. N. W.) from Dronfield, containing 305 inhabitants. Six children are instructed for an annuity of £6, the gift of the Rev. Robert Turie, in a school-room built by subscription, in 1821.

Corporate Seal.

TOTNESS, a borough, market town, and parish, having separate jurisdiction, though locally in the hundred of Coleridge, county of DEVON, 24 miles (S. S. W.) from Exeter, and 196 (W. S. W.) from London, containing, according to the last census, 3128 inhabitants, since increased to near 4000. It is variously denominated in ancient records: in Domesday-book it is called *Totneis*. Camden speaks of its having been once named *Totonese*; and Risdon alludes to it under the name of *Toutaness*, by contraction *Totnes*, or *Totness*. The latter author accedes to the opinion of Leland, who imagines the name to be a modernization of *Dodonesse*, signifying a rocky town, its situation rendering this supposition probable. The antiquity of the place is attested by Venerable Bede, who describes it as the station where the British troops assembled under Ambrosius and Pendragon, prior to their successful attack upon the tyrant Vortigern. The manor of Great Totness, having been a royal demesne in the time of the Confessor, was bestowed by William I. upon Judhel, one of his nobles, who took the title of "de Totneis," and erected the castle at the north-western extremity of the town. It is probable that Totness was fortified at a very early period, having (according to Risdon) undergone alteration under the Romans, Saxons, Danes, and Normans. Of the present town, which is divided into the Higher, Middle, and Lower quarters, the Middle quarter was included within the ancient boundary wall, in which were three gateways, *viz.*, the East, West, and North. At the time of the Norman survey, Totness was rated when Exeter was rated, and, if there was any expedition by land or water, Totness, Barnstaple, and Lidford, paid as much as Exeter: in that record it is described as containing ninety-five burgesses within the borough, and fifteen without. During the civil war of the seventeenth century, this town became the temporary station of General Goring: Fairfax subsequently halted here, on his way to and from the town of Dartmouth.

Totness is a very respectable town: it is neat and clean, contains many good shops and substantial private residences, and occupies a situation of much beauty and salubrity, on the western bank of the river Dart, over which is a handsome bridge of three arches, completed in 1828, at an expense of about £12,000. It consists chiefly of one long street, rising gradually in a westerly direction from the foot of the bridge, till it reaches a considerable elevation near the site of the castle: this street is crossed midway by the East gateway belonging to the old fortifications; and many of the fronts of the houses beyond are supported by pillars, affording a spacious covered way for foot passengers: the inhabitants are well supplied with water. The general aspect of the town, from the bridge, is picturesque, the church tower appearing on the right of the ascent, and the ivied ruins of the castle crowning the summit, of the hill. The surrounding country, particularly as seen from the castle and the hills, is extremely fine; and the course of the Dart between Totness and its influx into the channel is through variegated and interesting scenery. Owing to the improvement of the roads, the town is fast increasing, many new houses being now in progress of erection on the Plymouth and other roads. There are several libraries, a small theatre, and an assembly-room; and races are held annually in July, or August, on a good course. This town has been noted for its serge manufacture, and there is still some weaving carried on, but the trade is on the decline. The Dart is navigable to the bridge, above which, at a short distance, is a salmon weir, that fish being caught in great quantities; the town is also plentifully supplied with other kinds of fish. During spring tides, vessels of one hundred tons' burden can come up to the quay, a convenience which much facilitates the commercial intercourse with London and Plymouth. Cider is the chief article of exportation: coal, grain, and culm (the last chiefly used for the burning of lime, which abounds in the neighbourhood) are the principal imports. Several boats proceed daily to Dartmouth. Below the weir are corn and fulling mills, the latter being employed by the manufacturers of the town, &c. A customary market is held on Saturday, and there is a great cattle market on the first Tuesday in every month. Fairs for cattle are held on the 12th of May and the 28th of October.

The burgesses obtained a charter of privileges from King John, which was confirmed by Edward I., in whose reign, it is understood, Totness first sent members to parliament: the burgesses obtained the right of electing their mayor in the reign of John. Queen Elizabeth, in the 27th of her reign, granted a charter, whereby the government of the town is entrusted to three magistrates, *viz.*, the mayor, recorder, and a justice: there are fourteen masters and counsellors, or aldermen (of which body the mayor is one), and twenty burgesses, elected from those resident in the borough, and called the "Twenty men," whose duty it is to superintend the letting of lands, &c. A majority of the twenty burgesses must be present at all corporate meetings on their own business; but this is not required at the election of the mayor, or a master and counsellor, on which occasion a majority of the masters and counsellors must be present. There are also a town clerk, portreeve, two serjeants at mace, and eight constables (the serjeants being two), and the remaining constables chosen, not under the charter, but at the annual court leet, held by the corporation, for the manor of Great Totness. The mayor is chosen on the 21st of September, when two out of fourteen masters are nominated, and the election decided by the resident burgesses. The burgesses are elected by a majority of aldermen: the heirs of Sir Richard Edgecumbe, to which family the manor belonged prior to its being purchased by the corporation, are entitled to the right of one burgess-ship for ever, by a reservatory clause in the deed of conveyance; but this is not claimed. The magistrates of the corporation hold quarter sessions for all but capital offences arising within the borough: a court of requests was formerly held, but it is now in disuse. There are a guildhall and chamber, and a town prison. The corporation claim many privileges, such as freedom from quayage and wharfage throughout the kingdom, except the port of London, and exemption from serving on juries, except in the borough, for all inhabitants of the borough and parish, whether members of the corporation or not. This borough sends two representatives to parliament, who are elected by the masters and burgesses at large, the mayor being the returning officer.

The living is a discharged vicarage, in the archdeaconry of Totness, and diocese of Exeter, rated in the king's books at £12. 8. 9., endowed with £1400 parliamentary grant, and in the patronage of the Crown. The church, dedicated to St. Mary, is a curious old edifice, in the later style of English architecture, erected in the fifteenth century. The tower is handsome, and surmounted by octagonal pinnacles of lighter-coloured material than the remainder of the building, which is composed of a red stone strongly resembling brick. In the church are, an elegant stone screen; a curious stone pulpit, enriched with tracery; a handsome altar-piece; and a library, in which are many old and valuable books. Three hundred and fifty free sittings have recently been added, towards which the Incorporated Society for the building and enlargement of churches and chapels contributed £250. There are places of worship for Independents, Wesleyan Methodists, and Unitarians. The grammar school was founded in 1554, and endowed, in 1658, with lands now worth £70 a year, by Sir John Maynard, trustee of Elizeeus Hele, Esq., who left considerable property for charitable purposes. The schoolmaster is appointed by the corporation, who have the right of presenting two boys for gratuitous education; and an unlimited number of day scholars are admitted, at the annual charge of £8. 8. The old schoolroom is used for a charity school on Dr. Bell's plan, the schoolmaster renting a house, in which he is allowed to accommodate twelve boarders. The charity school is endowed with lands, of which the proceeds amount to about £40 per annum, but is chiefly supported by voluntary contributions. Between sixty and seventy children are educated, of whom about thirty are annually clothed. Here is also a National school. Among the numerous charitable donations, some are for re-establish-

ing decayed tradesmen in business, and others for apprenticing children. There is an old almshouse, occupied by about twenty people, supposed to be an enlargement of a foundation by Mr. Norris, who bequeathed £250 for its erection, in 1635: his donation was intended for two persons, and the corporation make a weekly allowance to two poor widows, but they do not reside in the almshouse. Here was formerly a lazar-house, the lands appertaining to which now yield an income of about £15, which is applied to the repairs of the church, &c.; there are still some remains of the building. Of Totness castle little remains, except the embattled walls of a circular keep, occupying the summit of a lofty mound at the western extremity of the town, and commanding a delightful prospect, in which the windings of the Dart are prominently conspicuous: near them is the ruin of a gateway, through which the ancient town was entered on the north. Several religious foundations are mentioned as formerly existing at or near Totness, the principal of which was endowed, in the time of the Conqueror, by Judhel de Totneis: it was of the Benedictine order, dedicated to St. Mary, and formed an appendage to an abbey at Angiers: the site is occupied by a dwelling-house, called "the Priory." Here are some remains of an ancient chapel. Leland mentions a Roman Fosse-way, commencing in this vicinity. Dr. Philip Furneaux, a learned nonconformist divine; Benjamin Kennicott, a learned biblical critic; and Edward Lye, a celebrated lexicographer, were natives of Totness.

TOTON, a hamlet in the parish of ATTENBOROUGH, southern division of the wapentake of BROXTOW, county of NOTTINGHAM, 5¼ miles (S. W. by W.) from Nottingham, containing 208 inhabitants.

TOTTENHAM, a parish in the hundred of EDMONTON, county of MIDDLESEX, 5 miles (N. by E.) from London, comprising High-Cross, Lower, Middle, and Wood-Green wards, and containing 5812 inhabitants. This place, written in Domesday-book Toteham, and now frequently called Tottenham High Cross, is a genteel village, consisting chiefly of one long street, formed by houses irregularly arranged, on the line of road from London to Cambridge: it is lighted with gas, and well supplied with water from several fountains produced by boring; and the immediate vicinity is adorned with numerous handsome villas. Near Tottenham Green, a cross has stood for many years: the present structure, superseding the original one of wood, is an octangular brick column, erected, in 1600, by Dean Wood: it was repaired, covered with cement, and decorated with various architectural embellishments, in 1809, for which purpose a subscription, amounting to nearly £300, was raised by the inhabitants. At the entrance of Page Green, on the east side of the high road, is a remarkable circular clump of elm trees, called "the Seven Sisters;" in the centre was formerly a walnut tree, which, according to tradition, never increased in size, though it continued annually to bear leaves: these trees appear to have been at their full growth in 1631, but no authentic account of their being planted is extant. Within a short distance from the high road was Bruce Castle, a mansion rebuilt, in the seventeenth century, on the site of an ancient castellated edifice, erected in the reign of Henry VIII., and honoured, in the year 1516, with the presence of that monarch, who came hither to meet his sister, Margaret, Queen of Scots; in 1578, Elizabeth also honoured it with her presence. The original castle was the residence and property of Robert de Bruce, father of Robert, King of Scotland; the present building has been converted into a school for young gentlemen: a detached brick tower, which covers a deep well, is the only vestige of the ancient edifice. In the parish is a well, of which the water is similar in its properties to that at Cheltenham; also a spring, called Lady's Well, of reputed efficacy for disorders in the eyes; it is said that this water never freezes. Here are extensive flour and oil mills: the former have been established time immemorially; also a pottery for coarse brown ware, and a brewery: a large silk manufactory is unoccupied. The navigable river Lea passes through the parish. Tottenham is within the jurisdiction of a court of requests held at Enfield, for the recovery of debts under 40s. The regulation of the parish is vested in two churchwardens, four overseers, and a constable, who is also the sexton, assisted by two surveyors and an engineer.

The living is a vicarage, in the jurisdiction of the Commissary of London, concurrently with the Consistorial Court of the Bishop of London, rated in the king's books at £14, and in the patronage of the Dean and Chapter of St. Paul's, London. The church, which is dedicated to All Saints, stands about a quarter of a mile west of the high road, and is in the later style of English architecture, with a square embattled and ivy-mantled tower: on the summit was formerly a lofty wooden cross (whence, according to some, the adjunct to the name of the village), which was destroyed during the civil war: on the south side of the church is a large brick porch, erected prior to 1500; and over it a room, called "a church house," for the transaction of parochial business, afterwards appropriated as a residence for a poor pensioner, and now used for a Sunday school. At the east end of the north aisle is a vestry of circular form, surmounted by a dome, erected, in 1696, by Lord Henry Coleraine, and repaired in 1790; underneath this is the family vault: the eastern window, divided into eight compartments, and containing representations of the Evangelists and some of the Prophets, in fine old painted glass, was given to the parish, in 1807, by the late John Eardley Wilmot, Esq.: the font is curious and of great antiquity: many ancient monuments adorn the interior, of which one in white marble, to the memory of the family of Sir Robert Barkham, is worthy of especial notice. This church was repaired, in 1816, at an expense of £3000. A new church has been recently erected on Tottenham Green, in the later style of English architecture, with turrets at each angle, and pinnacles over the aisles: it contains eight hundred and one sittings, of which three hundred and eighty-six are free; his Majesty's Commissioners for building new churches granted £4893. 11. 6., the remainder of the expense having been defrayed by subscription. There are places of worship for Baptists, Independents, Wesleyan Methodists, and Roman Catholics. The grammar school, founded by means of a bequest from Nicholas Reynardson, alderman of London, in 1685, endowed in the following year, by Sarah, Duchess Dowager of Somerset, with £250 for enlarging the buildings, and £1100 for the purpose of extending the benefits of the institution to all children of such

inhabitants of the parish as were not possessed of real property to the amount of £20 per annum; several small bequests have been made since that period: the master is paid according to the number of children, has a good residence, and is allowed to take twelve private scholars: there are now eighty boys on the foundation. The Blue school, instituted in 1735, in which are thirty-six poor girls; and the Green school, established in 1792, in which are forty, are supported by voluntary contributions; all the children are clothed and educated. Lancasterian schools for children of both sexes are similarly supported. Almshouses for four poor men and four poor women were founded and endowed with a small rent-charge by Balthasar Sanches, a Spaniard, about 1600, first pastry-cook to Philip of Spain, with whom he came over to this country, and was the first who exercised that trade in London. An almshouse for six poor men and six poor women, with a small chapel in the centre, was founded and endowed with £2000 by Nicholas Reynardson, Esq., in 1685; some valuable augmentations have been made to the funds, and, in 1828, the buildings were repaired at an expense of £450, defrayed by voluntary contributions. Some almshouses, near the church, are occupied by poor women, placed there by the parishioners.

TOTTENHILL, a parish in the hundred of CLACKCLOSE, county of NORFOLK, 6½ miles (N. N. E.) from Downham-Market, containing 348 inhabitants. The living is a perpetual curacy, in the archdeaconry of Norfolk, and diocese of Norwich, endowed with £800 royal bounty, and £200 parliamentary grant, and in the patronage of the Bishop of Ely. The church is dedicated to St. Botolph.

TOTTERIDGE, a parish in, and forming a detached portion of, the hundred of BROADWATER, though locally in that of Cashio, or liberty of St. Albans, county of HERTFORD, 2 miles (S. by W.) from Chipping-Barnet, containing 490 inhabitants. The living is a perpetual curacy, annexed to the rectory of Bishop's Hatfield, in the archdeaconry of Huntingdon, and diocese of Lincoln. The church, dedicated to St. Andrew, was rebuilt in 1798; it has a latticed square tower, with a spire. There is a place of worship for Independents. A school is partly supported by subscriptions, amounting to about £15 per annum.

TOTTERNHOE, a parish in the hundred of MANSHEAD, county of BEDFORD, 2 miles (W. S. W.) from Dunstable, containing 450 inhabitants. The living is a discharged vicarage, in the archdeaconry of Bedford, and diocese of Lincoln, rated in the king's books at £10, endowed with £400 private benefaction, £200 royal bounty, and £300 parliamentary grant, and in the patronage of the Trustees of the late Earl of Bridgewater. The church is dedicated to St. Giles. On the north side of it passes the Roman Iknield-street, skirting the downs, upon which are the remains of Totternhoe castle, overhanging the village of Stanbridge: the keep mount is lofty and encompassed by a circular fosse within another that is square, the latter enclosing the entire breadth of the ridge. Near this fortification is an ancient camp of a parallelogramic form, and to the eastward are extensive quarries of freestone and limestone, below which, at a great depth, is a bed of clay.

TOTTINGTON, a parish in the hundred of WAYLAND, county of NORFOLK, 3¾ miles (S. S. W.) from

Watton, containing 284 inhabitants. The living is a discharged vicarage, in the archdeaconry and diocese of Norwich, rated in the king's books at £6. 14. 9½., endowed with £800 royal bounty, and in the patronage of the Governors of Chigwell free school. The church, dedicated to St. Andrew, is a large ancient structure : the churchyard wall is coped with coffin stones having crosses on them, supposed to have enclosed the remains of the ancient vicars and other religious buried here.

TOTTINGTON (HIGHER), a township in that part of the parish of Bury which is in the hundred of Salford, county palatine of Lancaster, 3 miles (N. W.) front Bury, containing 1728 inhabitants. Joshua Elton, in 1761, gave certain lands and buildings in support of a free school at the village of Edenfield, in this township, but the income is only £1. 2. 6. a year, for which one child is educated. Samuel Ashton, in 1826, gave land for the enlargement of this charity, for which purpose also a subscription has been entered into.

TOTTINGTON (LOWER), a chapelry in that part of the parish of Bury which is in the hundred of Salford, county palatine of Lancaster, 3 miles (N. W. by W.) from Bury, containing 7333 inhabitants. The living is a perpetual curacy, in the archdeaconry and diocese of Chester, endowed with £800 royal bounty, and £1600 parliamentary grant, and in the patronage of the Rector of Bury. The chapel is dedicated to St. Anne. Here are very extensive establishments for the printing and bleaching of cotton, in which more than two thousand five hundred persons are employed. Courts leet and baron are held twice a year ; and there is a fair on October 12th. A school was erected, in 1715, by Thomas Nuttall, who endowed it with a rent-charge of £3 ; in 1773, the building was enlarged by subscription among the inhabitants, and, with the subsequent bequests of Peter and Ann Baron, the income has been augmented to £24 a year, for which fifteen children are gratuitously instructed. Dr. Wood, the celebrated mathematician, was born at this place.

TOUCHEN, a division in the parish and hundred of Bray, county of Berks, containing 778 inhabitants.

TOULSTON, a township in the parish of Newton-Kyme, upper division of the wapentake of Barkstone-Ash, West riding of the county of York, 2¾ miles (W. by N.) from Tadcaster. The population is returned with the parish.

TOWCESTER, a market town and parish in the hundred of Towcester, county of Northampton, 8½ miles (S. W. by S.) from Northampton, and 60 (N.W.) from London, containing, with the hamlets of Caldicott, Handley, and Wood-Burcot, 2554 inhabitants. The name of this place is written, in Domesday-book, Tovecestre, "a city, or fortified place, on the river Tove." It is considered to have been a Roman station, from the discovery of numerous coins, especially on an artificial mount north-eastward of the town, called Berrymont hill; and on the north-west side are vestiges of a fosse, and the ruins of a tower, supposed to be Saxon : some antiquaries have thought that the station of Lactodorum should be placed here, in preference to Stony-Stratford. During the Saxon era, the town appears to have been so well defended as to have offered a protracted and effectual resistance to the attacks of the Danes : about the year 921, a mandate was issued, by Edward, for rebuilding and fortifying it, and it was surrounded by a

VOL. IV.

stone wall, of which some vestiges are yet discernible. In the reign of Henry VI., a college and chantry were founded here by William Sponne, Archdeacon of Norfolk, the revenue of which, at the dissolution, was valued at £19. 6. 8. per annum. The town, which is situated on the river Tove, consists principally of one long street, composed of well-built houses, and paved under the direction of the trustees of the charities of Archdeacon Sponne, who devised the Tabart Inn, and certain lands, producing about £150 per annum, for that purpose ; the inhabitants are well supplied with water. The manufactures consist of bobbin lace, boots, and shoes ; and great advantages are derived from the situation of the town on the great road from London to Holyhead. The market is on Tuesday ; and fairs are held on Shrove-Tuesday, May 12th, and October 29th, for cattle ; on October 10th is a statute fair for hiring servants. A manorial court is held at Michaelmas, at which the constables for the parish are chosen.

The living is a discharged vicarage, in the archdeaconry of Northampton, and diocese of Peterborough, endowed with £200 private benefaction, and £200 royal bounty, and in the patronage of the Bishop of Lichfield and Coventry. The church, which is dedicated to St. Lawrence, is a neat building of the eleventh century, in the early style of English architecture, and contains the monument of Archdeacon Sponne, who held the living in the time of Henry VI. Among the various incumbents was Pope Boniface VIII., at the time of his promotion to the pontificate, in 1294. Abthorpe, which was formerly a chapelry in this parish, was separated from it by act of parliament, about 1756. There are places of worship for Baptists, Independents, and Wesleyan Methodists. The grammar school was founded, in 1552, by the trustees of Sponne's charity, who, on the dissolution of the college and chantry, purchased and converted them to this use, with a house and garden for the master : the income, arising from bequests and donations, is £56. 2. 8.; the master's salary is about £30 per annum, and twenty-two boys are instructed on the foundation. The Sunday school, in which two hundred and forty children are taught, is aided by the dividends of a bequest from Sir John Knightley, amounting to £5. 14. per annum. Three almshouses were founded and endowed, in 1695, by Thomas Bickerstaff, of this place, and there are a few other bequests for the poor. In the vicinity is a petrifying spring. The Roman Watling-street passed along the site of the town. Sir Richard Empson, once proprietor of the manor, and a celebrated lawyer, who was promoted to the chancellorship of the duchy of Lancaster, in the time of Henry VII., and beheaded on Tower-hill, in the succeeding reign, in the year 1509, was the son of a sieve-maker in this town. About a mile and a half from Towcester, at Easton-Neston, is the seat of Earl Pomfret, formerly celebrated for its splendid collection of paintings and statues, presented, in 1756, to the University of Oxford, by the then Countess of Pomfret.

TOWEDNACK, a parish in the hundred of Penwith, county of Cornwall, 3 miles (S. W. by W.) from St. Ives, containing 582 inhabitants. The living is a perpetual curacy, annexed to the vicarage of Lelant-Uny, in the archdeaconry of Cornwall, and diocese of Exeter. The church is dedicated to St. Twinnock.

2 U

There is a place of worship for Wesleyan Methodists. The mine called Wheal Durla is in this parish.

TOWERSEY, a parish in the hundred of ASHEN-DON, county of BUCKINGHAM, 2¼ miles (E. S. E.) from Thame, containing 367 inhabitants. The living is a vicarage not in charge, annexed to the vicarage of Thame, in the peculiar jurisdiction of the Dean and Chapter of Lincoln. John Blackall, Esq. was patron in 1795. The church is dedicated to St. Catherine. Mrs. Catherine Pye, in 1713, bequeathed property producing more than £40 a year for teaching twenty children.

TOWNGREEN, a township in the parish of WY-MONDHAM, hundred of FOREHOE, county of NORFOLK, containing 889 inhabitants.

TOWNSTALL, county of DEVON.—See DART-MOUTH.

TOWTHORPE, a township in the parish of WHAR-RAM-PERCY, wapentake of BUCKROSE, East riding of the county of YORK, 9 miles (W. N. W.) from Great Driffield, containing 61 inhabitants.

TOWTHORPE, a township partly in the parish of STRENSALL, within the liberty of ST. PETER of YORK, East riding, and partly in that of HUNTINGDON, wapentake of BULMER, North riding, of the county of YORK, 5 miles (N. by E.) from York, containing, in the latter portion, 58 inhabitants, the former part being returned with Strensall.

TOWTON, a township in the parish of SAXTON, upper division of the wapentake of BARKSTONE-ASH, West riding of the county of YORK, 3 miles (S.) from Tadcaster, containing 94 inhabitants. Between this place and Saxton is the celebrated Towton field, where was fought, on Palm-Sunday, 1461, the most important battle between the houses of York and Lancaster, which lasted from nine in the morning till seven in the evening, and ended in the defeat of the latter: in this bloody conflict, it is recorded, one hundred and ten thousand Englishmen were engaged, of whom thirty-six thousand seven hundred and seventy-six were slain.

TOXTETH-PARK, an extra-parochial district, in the hundred of WEST DERBY, county palatine of LANCAS-TER, 3 miles (S. E.) from Liverpool, containing 12,829 inhabitants. This place, which is delightfully situated on the banks of the Mersey, was anciently a park belonging to the Dukes of Lancaster, and afterwards passed to the Molyneaux family. In consequence of its proximity to Liverpool, it has become the residence of numerous merchants, manufacturers, retired tradesmen, &c., and several new streets have been formed within the last few years. It is supposed to have formerly been included in the parish of Walton on the Hill, to which it still pays tithes, though commonly deemed extra-parochial. It possesses two chapels, dedicated to St. James and St. Michael, the latter consecrated in 1818: they are in the patronage of the Rector of Walton. There is a place of worship for Unitarians.

TOYNTON (ALL SAINTS), a parish in the eastern division of the soke of BOLINGBROKE, parts of LIND-SEY, county of LINCOLN, 1½ mile (S.) from Spilsby, containing 342 inhabitants. The living is a discharged vicarage, in the archdeaconry and diocese of Lincoln, rated in the king's books at £5. 11. 3., endowed with £600 royal bounty, and in the patronage of Lord Gwydyr and Lady Willoughby de Eresby.

TOYNTON (HIGH), a parish in the soke of HORN-CASTLE, parts of LINDSEY, county of LINCOLN, 1½ mile (E.) from Horncastle, containing 159 inhabitants. The living is a perpetual curacy, in the archdeaconry and diocese of Lincoln, endowed with £600 royal bounty, and in the patronage of the Bishop of Carlisle. The church is dedicated to St. John the Baptist. There is a place of worship for Wesleyan Methodists.

TOYNTON (LOW), a parish in the soke of HORN-CASTLE, parts of LINDSEY, county of LINCOLN, 1¼ mile (N. E.) from Horncastle, containing 95 inhabitants. The living is a discharged rectory, in the archdeaconry and diocese of Lincoln, rated in the king's books at £11. 1. 8., and in the patronage of Lord Gwydyr and Lady Willoughby de Eresby. The church is dedicated to St. Peter. There is a place of worship for Wesleyan Methodists.

TOYNTON (ST. PETER'S), a parish in the eastern division of the soke of BOLINGBROKE, parts of LIND-SEY, county of LINCOLN, 2¼ miles (S. by E.) from Spilsby, containing 394 inhabitants. The living is a discharged rectory, in the archdeaconry and diocese of Lincoln, rated in the king's books at £12. 0. 2., and in the patronage of Lord Gwydyr and Lady Willoughby de Eresby.

TRAFFORD (BRIDGE), a township in that part of the parish of PLEMONSTALL which is in the second division of the hundred of EDDISBURY, county palatine of CHESTER, 4½ miles (N. E. by N.) from Chester, containing 61 inhabitants.

TRAFFORD (MICKLE), a township in that part of the parish of PLEMONSTALL which is in the lower division of the hundred of BROXTON, county palatine of CHESTER, 3½ miles (N. E.) from Chester, containing 319 inhabitants. Here is a small school, partly supported by subscription.

TRAFFORD (WIMBOLDS), a township in the parish of THORNTON, second division of the hundred of EDDISBURY, county palatine of CHESTER, 6 miles (N. E. by N.) from Chester, containing 117 inhabitants.

TRANMORE, a township in the parish of BEB-BINGTON, lower division of the hundred of WIRRALL, county palatine of CHESTER, 7¼ miles (N. N. E.) from Great Neston, containing 825 inhabitants. The river Mersey is here crossed by a ferry.

TRANWELL, a joint township with High Church, in that part of the parish of MORPETH which is in the western division of CASTLE ward, county of NORTHUM-BERLAND, 2 miles (S. S. W.) from Morpeth, containing, with High Church, 78 inhabitants.

TRAWDEN-FOREST, a township in that part of the parish of WHALLEY which is in the higher division of the hundred of BLACKBURN, county palatine of LANCASTER, 1¾ mile (S. E.) from Colne, containing 2307 inhabitants. There are places of worship for the Society of Friends and Wesleyan Methodists. This district, like other forests in the kingdom, was rejected, as of little value, at the time of the original distribution of land: it comprises ten square miles, and manufactures, similar to those carried on in the neighbouring towns and villages, have been established, and are progressively increasing.

TRAYFORD, a parish in the hundred of DUMP-FORD, rape of CHICHESTER, county of SUSSEX, 5½ miles (S. W. by W.) from Midhurst, containing 137 inhabitants. The living is a rectory, with that of Didling annexed, in the archdeaconry and diocese of Chichester, rated in the king's books at £7. 12. 1., and in the patronage of Lord Selsea.

TREALES, a joint township with Roseacre and Wharles, in the parish of KIRKHAM, hundred of AMOUNDERNESS, county palatine of LANCASTER, 1¼ mile (N. E.) from Kirkham, containing, with Roseacre and Wharles, 760 inhabitants. A school was established, in 1814, from the funds of an estate of William Grumbaldson, bequeathed, in 1725, for charitable purposes : £40 a year is paid for the education of seventy children.

TREBOROUGH, a parish in the hundred of CARHAMPTON, county of SOMERSET, 6¼ miles (S. by E.) from Dunster, containing 113 inhabitants. The living is a discharged rectory, in the archdeaconry of Taunton, and diocese of Bath and Wells, rated in the king's books at £7. 10. 5., and in the patronage of Sir J. Trevelyan, Bart. The church is dedicated to St. Peter.

TREDEGAR, a considerable mining district in the parish of BEDWELTY, lower division of the hundred of WENTLLOOG, county of MONMOUTH, 6 miles (N.) from the parish church. The population, which, in 1821, was returned with the parish, is now calculated at about 6000, mostly employed in the extensive collieries and flourishing iron-works belonging to Messrs. Homfray and Co., at this place, and in those of Messrs. Summers, Harford, and Co., at Sirhowy, in the immediate neighbourhood. These gentlemen have constructed rail-roads in various directions, to facilitate the communication between the respective establishments, one of which extends a distance of twenty-four miles to Newport and Pill-gwenlly, for the conveyance of iron, coal, &c., to be there exported. It is also in contemplation to erect a church, the village of Tredegar having risen, in consequence of their works, to the importance of a market town, with a spacious area in the centre, and a market-house, where a large market is held on Saturday. There are two places of worship for Baptists and three for Wesleyan Methodists, also several commodious inns, and a number of respectable shops, in the village, which now forms a striking contrast to its desolate appearance about thirty years ago, when only one poor family resided near the spot.

TREDINGTON, a parish in the lower division of the hundred of TEWKESBURY, county of GLOUCESTER, 3 miles (S. E. by S.) from Tewkesbury, containing 138 inhabitants. The living is a perpetual curacy, in the archdeaconry and diocese of Gloucester, endowed with £600 royal bounty, and in the patronage of the Bishop of Gloucester. The church is very small, but the churchyard is remarkable for containing a lofty pillar of one single stone, resting upon a basis of four steps.

TREDINGTON, a parish forming, with the parishes of Shipston upon Stour, and Tidmington, a distinct portion of the upper division of the hundred of OSWALDSLOW, county of WORCESTER, being locally in the Kington division of the hundred of KINGTON, county of WARWICK, 2¼ miles (N.) from Shipston upon Stour, containing, with the hamlets of Armscott, Blackwell, Darlingscott, and Newbold, 1032 inhabitants. The living is a rectory, in two portions, in the peculiar jurisdiction of the Rector, jointly rated in the king's books at £99. 17. 6., and in the patronage of the Principal and

Fellows of Jesus' College, Oxford. The church is dedicated to St. Gregory. This parish was divided, under an act passed in the 6th of George I., when the townships of Shipston and Tidmington were separated from it, and constituted a distinct parish. The river Stour runs through the parish. Here was formerly a monastery, the remaining part of which is now the rectory-house. There is a small endowed school in the parish.

TREDUNNOCK, a parish in the upper division of the hundred of USK, county of MONMOUTH, 4½ miles (S.) from Usk, containing 178 inhabitants. The living is a rectory, in the archdeaconry and diocese of Llandaff, rated in the king's books at £10. 0. 5. Capel Hanbury Leigh, Esq. was patron in 1812. The church, dedicated to St. Andrew, contains the monument of a Roman soldier of the second legion; this stone, a kind of blue slate, was discovered fastened by four pins to the foundation of the church, and is now fixed in a similar manner to the wall, near the font.

TREETON, a parish in the southern division of the wapentake of STRAFFORTH and TICKHILL, West riding of the county of YORK, comprising the townships of Brampton en le Morthen, Treeton, and the greater portion of Ulley, and containing, with the whole of the township of Ulley, which is partly in the parish of Aston, 703 inhabitants, of which number, 364 are in the township of Treeton, 4 miles (S. by E.) from Rotherham. The living is a rectory, in the archdeaconry and diocese of York, rated in the king's books at £12, and in the patronage of the Duke of Norfolk. The church is dedicated to St. Helen. A cottage near the churchyard has long been occupied, rent-free, by a schoolmistress, for teaching eight poor children.

TREGARE, a parish in the lower division of the hundred of RAGLAND, county of MONMOUTH, 5½ miles (W. S. W.) from Monmouth, containing 335 inhabitants. The living is a perpetual curacy, annexed to the vicarage of Dingestow, in the archdeaconry and diocese of Llandaff. The church is dedicated to St. Mary.

TREGAVETHAN, a manor in the parish of KEA, western division of the hundred of POWDER, county of CORNWALL, containing 66 inhabitants.

TREGONEY, a borough and market town in the parish of CUBY, western division of the hundred of POWDER, county of CORNWALL, 41½ miles (S.W.) from Launceston, and 248 (S. W. by W.) from London, containing 1035 inhabitants. The old town, which stood at the bottom of the hill on which the present is situated, was of considerable antiquity and importance: it had a castle, supposed to have been built in the reign of Richard I.; and a priory, subordinate to the convent at Merton, in Surrey. The present town consists chiefly of one street, and has greatly declined since the increase of Truro. The Fal, which is here crossed by a bridge, is said to have been once navigable to this place for small barges. The market is on Saturday, for meat and other provisions; and fairs are held on Shrove-Tuesday, May 3rd, July 25th, September 1st, and November 6th. The charter of incorporation was granted by James I., in 1620 : the municipal body consists of a mayor, recorder, and eight capital burgesses, or aldermen : the mayor is elected, annually in September, from among the aldermen, and, with the senior member of that body, exercises magisterial authority. The borough first sent representatives to parliament in the reign of

2 U 2

Edward I., and, after long disuse, recovered the exercise of that privilege in 1559: the elective franchise is vested in potwallers; the number of voters is above three hundred: the mayor is the returning officer, and the influence of J. A. Gordon, Esq. is predominant. The petty sessions for the south division of the hundred of Powder are occasionally held here, and courts are held by the lord of the manor. The living is a vicarage, with that of St. Keby annexed, in the archdeaconry of Cornwall, and diocese of Exeter, rated in the king's books at £10. 4. 2., and in the patronage of J. A. Gordon, Esq. The church, dedicated to St. James, stands without the limits of the borough. There are places of worship for Independents and Wesleyan Methodists. An hospital for decayed housekeepers was founded here, in 1696, by Hugh Boscawen, Esq., and endowed with lands, now let for £30 per annum, but capable of producing three times that amount, on the expiration of the present lease.

TRELLECK, a parish in the upper division of the hundred of RAGLAND, county of MONMOUTH, containing, with the town of Trelleck and the chapelry of Trelleck-Grange, 986 inhabitants, of which number, 138 are in the town of Trelleck, 5 miles (S.) from Monmouth. The living is a vicarage, with the perpetual curacy of Penalth annexed, in the archdeaconry and diocese of Llandaff, rated in the king's books at £8, and in the patronage of the King, as Duke of Cornwall. The church, dedicated to St. Nicholas, has lately received an addition of forty free sittings, the Incorporated Society for the enlargement of churches and chapels having granted £40 towards defraying the expense.

TRELLECK-GRANGE, a chapelry in the parish of TRELLECK, upper division of the hundred of RAGLAND, county of MONMOUTH, 6 miles (N. W. by N.) from Chepstow, containing 92 inhabitants. The living is a perpetual curacy, in the archdeaconry and diocese of Llandaff, endowed with £1000 royal bounty, and £200 parliamentary grant, and in the patronage of the Duke of Beaufort.

TREMAYNE, a parish in the northern division of the hundred of EAST, county of CORNWALL, 6¾ miles (W. N. W.) from Launceston, containing 125 inhabitants. The living is a perpetual curacy, annexed to that of Egloskerry, in the archdeaconry of Cornwall, and diocese of Exeter, endowed with £200 royal bounty.

TRENDLE, a tything in the parish of PITMINSTER, hundred of TAUNTON and TAUNTON-DEAN, county of SOMERSET. The population is returned with the parish.

TRENEGLOS, a parish in the hundred of LESNEWTH, county of CORNWALL, 7½ miles (N. E. by E.) from Camelford, containing 238 inhabitants. The living is a vicarage, with the perpetual curacy of Warbstow annexed, in the archdeaconry of Cornwall, and diocese of Exeter, rated in the king's books at £9. 9. 7., and in the patronage of the King, as Duke of Cornwall. The church is dedicated to St. Werburgh.

TRENT, a parish in the hundred of HORETHORNE, county of SOMERSET, 3 miles (N. E. by E.) from Yeovil, containing 479 inhabitants. The living is a rectory, in the archdeaconry of Wells, and diocese of Bath and Wells, rated in the king's books at £23. 5. 5., and in the patronage of the President and Fellows of Corpus Christi College, Oxford. The church, dedicated to St. Andrew, has a tower at the south-east corner, surmounted by an hexagonal spire. John Young, in 1678, bequeathed £1000 for the erection and endowment of a free school; the annual income is about £95, for which fifteen poor boys are instructed.

TRENTHAM, a parish in the northern division of the hundred of PIREHILL, county of STAFFORD, comprising the chapelry of Blurton with Lightwood-Forest, and the townships of Butterton, Clayton-Griffith, Hanchurch, Handford, and Trentham, and containing 2203 inhabitants, of which number, 589 are in the township of Trentham, 3¼ miles (S. S. E.) from Newcastle under Lyne. The living is a perpetual curacy, in the archdeaconry of Stafford, and diocese of Lichfield and Coventry, endowed with £200 royal bounty, and £1200 parliamentary grant, and in the patronage of the Marquis of Stafford. The church, dedicated to St. Mary, is an ancient structure without a tower, which was taken down about a century ago. A new chapel, erected at Handford, was opened in July 1828. The Trent and Mersey canal passes through the parish, in the neighbourhood of which there is a considerable manufacture of remarkably good bricks and tiles, of a dark blue colour, much in request at Northampton and the intervening places. A court leet is held once a year. Lady Catherine Leveson, in 1670, bequeathed an annuity of £20 for teaching poor children, and a like sum for apprenticing them. Here was anciently a nunnery, of which St. Werburgh, in the seventh century, was appointed abbess, by her brother, King Ethelred. In the reign of Henry I., Randal II., Earl of Chester, converted it into a priory of Augustine canons, in honour of the Blessed Virgin Mary and All Saints, which, at the dissolution, had a revenue of £121. 3. 2., and was granted to Charles, Duke of Suffolk. Trentham gives the title of viscount to the Marquis of Stafford, whose noble mansion is in this parish.

TRENTISHOE, a parish in the hundred of BRAUNTON, county of DEVON, 10½ miles (E. by N.) from Ilfracombe, containing 130 inhabitants. The living is a discharged rectory, in the archdeaconry of Barnstaple, and diocese of Exeter, rated in the king's books at £8. 8. 4., endowed with £200 private benefaction, and £200 royal bounty, and in the patronage of Mrs. A. W. Griffiths. The church is dedicated to St. Peter.

TREPRENAL, a township in the parish of LLANYMYNECH, hundred of OSWESTRY, county of SALOP, 5 miles (S.) from Oswestry. The population is returned with the parish.

TRESCOTT, a joint hamlet with Pirton, in that part of the parish of TETTENHALL which is in the northern division of the hundred of SEISDON, county of STAFFORD, 4 miles (W. by S.) from Wolverhampton. The population is returned with Pirton. It is within the jurisdiction of the royal peculiar court of Tettenhall.

TRESHAM, a chapelry in the parish of HAWKESBURY, upper division of the hundred of GRUMBALD'S-ASH, county of GLOUCESTER, 3½ miles (S. E. by E.) from Wotton under Edge. The population is returned with the tything of Hillesley.

TRESMEER, a parish in the northern division of the hundred of EAST, county of CORNWALL, 6½ miles (W. by N.) from Launceston, containing 173 inhabitants. The living is a perpetual curacy, in the archdeaconry of Cornwall, and diocese of Exeter, endowed with £1000 royal bounty, and in the patronage of the Vicar of North Petherwin. The church is dedicated to St. Nicholas.

TRESWELL, a parish in the South-clay division of the wapentake of BASSETLAW, county of NOTTINGHAM, 5¼ miles (E. by S.) from East Retford, containing 216 inhabitants. The living is a rectory, formerly in two portions, which were united in 1764, in the archdeaconry of Nottingham, and diocese of York; the eastern portion is rated in the king's books at £8. 1. 4., and the western at £9. 15. 8., and in the alternate patronage of the Dean and Chapter of York, and the Rev. Mr. Stephenson. The church is dedicated to St. John the Baptist. There is a place of worship for Wesleyan Methodists.

TRETIRE, a parish in the lower division of the hundred of WORMELOW, county of HEREFORD, 5¾ miles (W.) from Ross, containing, with the chapelry of Michael-Church, 126 inhabitants. The living is a rectory, in the archdeaconry and diocese of Hereford, rated in the king's books at £6. 1. 8., and in the patronage of the Governors of Guy's Hospital, London. The church is dedicated to St. Mary.

TREVALGA, a parish in the hundred of LESNEWTH, county of CORNWALL, 1½ mile (N. E.) from Bossiney, containing 133 inhabitants. The living is a discharged rectory, in the archdeaconry of Cornwall, and diocese of Exeter, rated in the king's books at £7. 6. 0½., and in the patronage of the Dean and Chapter of Exeter. There are quarries of slate in the parish.

TREVENA, county of CORNWALL.—See BOSSINEY and TINTAGELL.

TREVETHAN, a parish in the upper division of the hundred of ABERGAVENNY, county of MONMOUTH, 2 miles (N.) from Pont-y-pool, containing, in 1821, with the market town of Pont-y-Pool, 3931 inhabitants. The living is a perpetual curacy, annexed to the vicarage of Llanover, in the archdeaconry and diocese of Llandaff, endowed with £2000 parliamentary grant. The church, dedicated to St. Cadocus, is a very ancient building, now undergoing a thorough repair. The Monmouthshire and Brecon canals, and numerous rail-roads, pass through the parish. The present number of inhabitants is supposed to be eight thousand, being an increase of more than four thousand in the short space of seven years: nearly the whole are employed in extensive mines of iron and coal, with which the neighbourhood abounds, in the burning of lime, and in the large iron-works established at Pont-y-Pool and in its vicinity. The British Mining Company have established furnaces at the Varteage, three miles from Pont-y-Pool, and new buildings, for the residence of the overseers and workmen, are in progress of erection in almost every direction.

TREVILLE, an extra-parochial liberty, in the upper division of the hundred of WORMELOW, county of HEREFORD, 6½ miles (N. W, by N.) from Ross, containing 74 inhabitants.

TREWEN, a parish in the northern division of the hundred of EAST, county of CORNWALL, 5¼ miles (W. by S.) from Launceston, containing 206 inhabitants. The living is a perpetual curacy, annexed to the vicarage of South Petherwin, in the peculiar jurisdiction of the Bishop of Exeter. The church is dedicated to St. Michael. There is a place of worship for Wesleyan Methodists. Fairs for colts, sheep, and lambs, are held on May 1st and October 10th.

TREWHITT (HIGH and LOW), a township in the parish of ROTHBURY, western division of COQUETDALE ward, county of NORTHUMBERLAND, containing 117 inhabitants. High Trewhitt is 4¼ miles (N. W.), and Low Trewhitt 4½ miles (N. W. by W.), from Rothbury.

TREWICK, a township in that part of the parish of BOLAM which is in the western division of CASTLE ward, county of NORTHUMBERLAND, 7½ miles (S. W.) from Morpeth, containing 50 inhabitants. It is bounded on the south by the river Blyth.

TRIMDON, a parish in the southern division of EASINGTON ward, county palatine of DURHAM, 9 miles (S. E.) from Durham, containing 302 inhabitants. The living is a perpetual curacy, in the archdeaconry and diocese of Durham, endowed with £200 private benefaction, and £200 royal bounty, and in the patronage of William Beckwith, Esq. The church is dedicated to St. Mary Magdalene. A lectureship was endowed here before 1730, with £21. 5. a year, by John Smith, Esq. Henry Airey, in 1680, among other bequests, gave a rent-charge of £5 for the maintenance of a free school: ten poor children are educated for this bequest in a school-house built by subscription, in 1823. The produce of an estate, purchased with the amount of various bequests, is applied partly in apprenticing children, and partly to the relief of the poor. Some large specimens of lead-ore have been dug up in the neighbourhood, but no mine has yet been opened.

TRIMINGHAM, a parish in the northern division of the hundred of ERPINGHAM, county of NORFOLK, 5 miles (S. E. by E.) from Cromer, containing 147 inhabitants. The living is a discharged rectory, in the archdeaconry of Norfolk, and diocese of Norwich, rated in the king's books at £6, endowed with £200 royal bounty, and in the patronage of the King, as Duke of Lancaster. The church is dedicated to St. John the Baptist, whose head, it was pretended, in popish times was deposited here, to which numerous pilgrimages and rich offerings were made.

TRIMLEY (ST. MARTIN), a parish in the hundred of COLNEIS, county of SUFFOLK, 8½ miles (S. E. by E.) from Ipswich, containing 436 inhabitants. The living is a discharged rectory, in the archdeaconry of Suffolk, and diocese of Norwich, rated in the king's books at £12. 0. 5., and in the patronage of the Earl of Rochford. The navigable river Orwell bounds the parish on the south. Thomas Cavendish, celebrated as the first English circumnavigator, was born here.

TRIMLEY (ST. MARY), a parish in the hundred of COLNEIS, county of SUFFOLK, 8¾ miles (S. E. by E.) from Ipswich, containing 379 inhabitants. The living is a discharged rectory, in the archdeaconry of Suffolk, and diocese of Norwich, rated in the king's books at £16. 13. 4., and in the patronage of the Crown. The navigable river Orwell bounds the parish on the south.

TRING, a market town and parish in the hundred of DACORUM, county of HERTFORD, 30 miles (W. by N.) from Hertford, and 31 (N. W. by W.) from London, containing, with the hamlets of Long Marstone and Wilstone, according to the last census, 3286 inhabitants, now about 4000. The origin of this town is of remote antiquity: at the time of the division of the county by

Alfred, it was considered of sufficient importance to give name to the hundred in which it was situated, being then called *Treung*. Antiquaries have attributed the derivation of its name to the supposed original form of the town, being triangular. The opinion that it is of Roman origin receives confirmation from the fact, that the Iknield way from Dorchester to Colchester passed in its vicinity; part of it constitutes a portion of the Chiltern hundreds. The town consists of two principal streets, the larger being crossed at the top by the other, both containing good houses, generally of modern style. Contiguous to it is the elegant mansion of Tring Park (built by Charles II., for his favourite mistress, Eleanor Gwynn, and since modernised), with the hills rising in the back ground, clothed with fine beech trees. The general appearance is exceedingly neat, the atmosphere very salubrious, and the inhabitants are amply supplied with water. A silk-mill, worked partly by water and partly by steam, gives employment to upwards of three hundred persons, and is in progress of great improvement: the manufacture of canvas and straw-plat is also carried on. The Grand Junction canal passes about a mile of the town; and within the parish are four large reservoirs, to supply any loss of water to that navigation. At Wilstone, also within the parish, is one of the sources of the river Thames. The market, granted by charter of Charles II. to Henry Guy, Esq., in 1681 (to whom that monarch had, the year before, granted the manor), is on Friday, for straw-plat, corn, meat, and pedlary; and cattle fairs are held on Easter-Monday and Old Michaelmas-day. The market-house, the property of the lord of the manor, is situated on the north side of the principal street. The living is a perpetual curacy, in the archdeaconry of Huntingdon, and diocese of Lincoln, endowed with £1200 private benefaction, £400 royal bounty, and £2000 parliamentary grant, and in the patronage of the Dean and Canons of Christ Church, Oxford. The church, which is dedicated to St. Peter and St. Paul, situated near the market-house, is a handsome embattled structure in the ancient English style, with a large tower at the west end, surmounted with a low spire: in the interior is an enriched font in the later style of English architecture. There are places of worship for Baptists and Independents. A free school was established, in 1829, by Mr. John Hull; it is conducted on the Lancasterian system, and supported by voluntary contributions: nearly one hundred boys are instructed. A Roman helmet was found in digging the Grand Junction canal, near Northcote hill, between this town and Berkhampstead, of which a drawing was published by the Society of Antiquaries of London, in 1819. Robert Hill, a remarkable self-taught linguist, was born here, in 1699; he died in 1777.

TRITLINGTON, a township in the parish of HEBBURN, western division of MORPETH ward, county of NORTHUMBERLAND, 4¾ miles (N.) from Morpeth, containing 99 inhabitants. A school is partly supported by annual subscriptions.

TROSTON, a parish in the hundred of BLACKBOURN, county of SUFFOLK, 7 miles (N. N. E.) from Bury St. Edmund's, containing 371 inhabitants. The living is a discharged rectory, in the archdeaconry of Sudbury, and diocese of Norwich, rated in the king's books at £10. 4. 7., and in the patronage of the Crown.

The church is dedicated to St. Mary. There is a place of worship for Wesleyan Methodists.

TROSTREY, a parish in the upper division of the hundred of USK, county of MONMOUTH, 2½ miles (N. by W.) from Usk, containing 205 inhabitants. The living is a discharged perpetual curacy, in the archdeaconry and diocese of Llandaff, rated in the king's books at £3. 8. 11½., and endowed with £1000 royal bounty, and in the patronage of — Morris, Esq. The church is dedicated to St. David.

TROTTERSCLIFFE, or TROSLEY, a parish in the hundred of LARKFIELD, lathe of AYLESFORD, county of KENT, 2 miles (N.E. by E.) from Wrotham, containing 243 inhabitants. The living is a rectory, in the archdeaconry and diocese of Rochester, rated in the king's books at £10. 2. 11., and in the patronage of the Bishop of Rochester. The church is dedicated to St. Peter and St. Paul. The Rev. Paul Bariston, in 1711, bequeathed land, producing upwards of £9 a year, for teaching poor children.

TROTTON, a parish partly in the hundred of EASEBOURNE, but chiefly in that of DUMPFORD, rape of CHICHESTER, county of SUSSEX, 3½ miles (W. by N.) from Midhurst, containing, with the chapelry of Milland, 390 inhabitants. The living is a rectory, in the archdeaconry and diocese of Chichester, rated in the king's books at £9. S. Twyford, Esq. was patron in 1813. The church, dedicated to St. George, is principally in the decorated style of architecture. Thomas Otway, the poet, was born here, in 1651; he died in 1685.

TROUGH, a township in the parish of STAPLETON, ESKDALE ward, county of CUMBERLAND, 9½ miles (N.E. by E.) from Longtown, containing 143 inhabitants.

TROUGHEND-WARD, a township in the parish of ELSDON, southern division of COQUETDALE ward, county of NORTHUMBERLAND, 7¼ miles (N. N. E.) from Bellingham, containing 397 inhabitants.

TROUTBECK, a chapelry in the parish of WINDERMERE, KENDAL ward, county of WESTMORLAND, 5½ miles (S.E. by E.) from Ambleside, containing 335 inhabitants. The living is a perpetual curacy, annexed to the rectory of Windermere, in the archdeaconry of Richmond, and diocese of Chester, endowed with £200 private benefaction, and £800 royal bounty. The chapel, called Jesus' chapel, was consecrated in 1562: adjoining is a school-house, built in 1639, with a small endowment. The chapelry is intersected by a rivulet, from which it derives its name. In the neighbourhood are extensive quarries of fine blue slate. There were formerly two cairns, supposed to be British, on the removal of one of which, a rude stone chest was discovered, enclosing a quantity of human bones.

TROUTSDALE, a township in the parish of BROMPTON, PICKERING lythe, North riding of the county of YORK, 8 miles (W.) from Scarborough, containing 45 inhabitants.

TROWAY, a township in the parish of ECKINGTON, hundred of SCARSDALE, county of DERBY, 6½ miles (N. by E.) from Chesterfield, containing 1216 inhabitants.

TROWBRIDGE, a market town and parish in the hundred of MELKSHAM, county of WILTS, 30 miles (N. W.) from Salisbury, and 99 (W. by S.) from London, containing 9545 inhabitants. The origin of this place, and the etymology of its name, are involved in much obscurity: Camden says, it was called by the Saxons *Truthabrig*, a strong and faithful town. It is not mentioned in Domesday-book; but a place called Little Trowle, now a hamlet in the parish, is therein recorded, and hence the present name is, by many, supposed to be a corruption of *Trowlebridge*, by which it is described by Geoffrey of Monmouth; Leland writes it *Through-bridge*, or *Thorough-bridge*. Trowbridge was formerly a royal manor, forming part of the duchy of Lancaster, having been granted by the crown to John of Gaunt: it afterwards reverted to the crown, and was given by Henry VIII., in the 28th year of his reign, to Edward Seymour, Knt., Viscount Beauchamp. Having again lapsed to the crown, Queen Elizabeth, in the 24th of her reign, assigned it, with the profits of the fairs and markets, &c., to Edward, Earl of Hertford: it afterwards became the property of the Duke of Rutland, who alienated it to Thomas Timbrell, Esq., father of the present proprietor. The earliest historical circumstance relating to the town is its defence against King Stephen, by Humphrey de Bohun, who held it for the Empress Matilda, at which period its castle is supposed to have existed, though some writers ascribe its erection to John of Gaunt, Duke of Lancaster: it was demolished previously to the time of Henry VIII., as, when Leland wrote, it was in ruins, only two of its seven towers remaining; not a vestige of it now exists, its site being occupied by other buildings.

The town is situated upon a rocky hill, near the river Were, across which is a stone bridge, and is very irregularly built, the houses being mostly of stone: the principal street is spacious and contains some excellent houses, but the others are generally narrow, and the houses old, and of rather a mean appearance: it is paved, lighted with gas, and tolerably well supplied with water. The manufacture of woollen cloth was introduced here at an early period, and must have very soon become a thriving branch of trade, as Camden mentions that Trowbridge was then famous for the clothing trade: the articles made are chiefly kerseymeres, with some superfine broad cloth. The Kennet and Avon canal passes about a mile north of the town, by which a communication is opened with London and Bristol. The markets are on Tuesday, Thursday, and Saturday, the last being the principal market day, and are well supplied with provisions: there is a fair on the 5th of August, which lasts two days, for cattle, cheese, woollen goods, &c. The town is under the government of the county magistrates, and a petty session is held, by those resident in it, on the first Tuesday in the month, for the transaction of business connected with the parish. A court of requests, for the recovery of debts not exceeding £5, is holden here every Tuesday three weeks, before certain commissioners, under the authority of a local act of parliament, comprehending within its jurisdiction the hundreds of Melksham, Bradford, and Whorwelsdown. A court leet and a court baron are also held by the lord of the manor at Easter, at the former of which, constables, tythingmen, a crier, and cornets of the market, are appointed and sworn.

The living is a rectory, in the peculiar jurisdiction of the Bishop of Salisbury, rated in the king's books at £20. 12. 8½., and in the patronage of the Duke of Rutland. The present incumbent is the Rev. George Crabbe, the poet. The church, dedicated to St. James, is called the new church, in consequence of a more ancient one having existed about seventy yards southeast of the former; it is a large building, with a tower at the west end, surmounted by a lofty spire: the nave and aisles are crowned with battlements and crocketed pinnacles, the former having a flat ceiled roof, ornamented with flowers, &c., and is separated from the aisles by five pointed arches on each side, springing from clustered columns, with rich capitals; there are fragments of painted glass in some of the windows; the font is lofty, and is covered with a profusion of tracery and panelling. Attached to the eastern extremities of the two aisles are two chapels, that on the south belonging to the lord of the manor, and that on the north to the family of Bythesea. At Staverton, in this parish, there is a chapel of ease. There are four places of worship for Particular Baptists, one for General Baptists, one for Independents, two for Wesleyan Methodists, and one for Presbyterians. A free school, for which fifty boys are instructed, is supported by property left for charitable purposes: it stands in the churchyard, and the master is provided with a house, and receives a salary of £70 per annum. There are also seven Sunday schools, in which about one thousand five hundred children are taught to read. In an almshouse, in Hilperton-lane, founded by a person named Yerbury, six poor widows are lodged, and receive a weekly allowance. There was also an almshouse formerly in the churchyard, endowed with considerable funds by John Terumbere, an opulent clothier in the town, the proceeds of which were paid to the inmates, until about the commencement of the present century. The same benefactor devised extensive property in the adjoining parishes for charitable purposes, which was confiscated by Henry VIII., at the time of the Reformation: the poor enjoy the benefit of the moiety of a small estate at Hoddesdon, in Hertfordshire, the rental of which, with the produce of other funds, is distributed in bread, annually at Christmas, among such as do not receive parochial relief. George Keate, a poetical and miscellaneous writer of some celebrity in the last century, was born here, in 1730. Trowbridge formerly gave the title of baron to the family of Seymour, Dukes of Somerset, one of whom is buried here, which title is extinct.

TROWELL, a parish in the southern division of the wapentake of Broxtow, county of Nottingham, 5¼ miles (W.) from Nottingham, containing 464 inhabitants. The living is a rectory in two portions, each rated in the king's books at £4. 14. 4½, in the archdeaconry of Nottingham, and diocese of York; the first portion is endowed with £200 private benefaction, and £200 royal bounty, and both are in the patronage of Lord Middleton. The church is dedicated to St. Helen. The Nottingham canal passes through the parish, which is separated from Derbyshire by the river Erewash. There are coal mines in the neighbourhood.

TROWSE, a parish in the hundred of Henstead, county of Norfolk, 1¾ mile (S.E. by S.) from Norwich, containing, with the hamlet of Newton, 549 inhabitants. The living is a vicarage, with that of Lakenham annexed, in the peculiar jurisdiction and patronage of the Dean and Chapter of Norwich, rated in the king's books at £5. The church is dedicated to St. Andrew.

Trowse-Newton Hall, an ancient building with a chapel, erected by the priors of Norwich, has been converted into a farm-house.

TRUDOX-HILL, a hamlet in the parish of Nunney, hundred of Frome, county of Somerset, 4 miles (S. W.) from Frome, containing 292 inhabitants. Here was formerly a chapel, long since desecrated.

TRULL, a parish in the hundred of Taunton and Taunton-Dean, county of Somerset, 2 miles (S. S. W.) from Taunton, containing 528 inhabitants. The living is a perpetual curacy, in the archdeaconry of Taunton, and diocese of Bath and Wells, endowed with £600 private benefaction, £800 royal bounty, and £500 parliamentary grant, and in the patronage of G. Earle, Esq. The church is dedicated to All Saints. John Wyatt, in 1756, gave the proceeds of £210 in support of a school; the annual income is £24, which is applied for teaching eighteen poor children.

TRUMPINGTON, a parish in the hundred of Thriplow, county of Cambridge, 2½ miles (S.) from Cambridge, containing 540 inhabitants. The living is a vicarage, in the archdeaconry and diocese of Ely, rated in the king's books at £5. 6. 8., and in the patronage of the Master and Fellows of Trinity College, Cambridge. The church is dedicated to St. Mary and St. Michael. William Austin, in 1679, gave ten acres of land, now producing £14 per annum, for teaching four poor children. There are still some remains of the mill, celebrated by Chaucer, in his Reeve's Tale. At Dam Hill, near the river Cam, which runs through the parish, several beautiful vases and pateræ, urns, human bones, and other relics of antiquity, have been discovered. Anstey, author of the poetical "Bath Guide," was born here, in 1724.

TRUNCH, a parish in the northern division of the hundred of Erpingham, county of Norfolk, 3 miles (N. by E.) from North Walsham, containing 441 inhabitants. The living is a rectory, annexed to that of Gimingham, in the archdeaconry of Norfolk, and diocese of Norwich, rated in the king's books at £10. 13. 4. The church is dedicated to St. Botolph. There is a place of worship for Wesleyan Methodists.

TRURO, a borough and market town, in the western division of the hundred of Powder, county of Cornwall, 43 miles (S. W. by W.) from Launceston, and 260 (W. S. W.) from London: the borough contains 2712 inhabitants, which number only forms about a third part of the population of the town, which extends into the parishes of St. Clement and Kenwyn. This place is called, in old records, by the different names of *Trieueru, Trewroe, Truru*, and *Truruburgh*, each signifying three streets, of which the town is supposed to have originally consisted. The manor belonged, in 1161, to Richard de Lucy, Chief Justice of England, who granted certain privileges to the burgesses, which were confirmed by Reginald Fitz-Henry, Earl of Cornwall, as lord paramount, in the reign of Henry I. In 1410, a petition from Truro was presented to the par

Seal and Arms.

liament, praying that the rent payable to the crown, which had been lowered from £12. 1. 10 to £2. 10., for a term of years, by the late king, Richard II., in consequence of their sufferings from pestilence and war, might be so reduced in perpetuity; and stating that, instead of rebuilding their houses, the inhabitants were about to leave the town, which might be considered as the defence of that part of the country from the enemy. During the great civil war, Truro became the headquarters of Sir Ralph Hopton, soon after his arrival in Cornwall with the king's forces, in 1642; and again in 1646, immediately before his surrender to Sir Thomas Fairfax. Prince Charles, afterwards King Charles II., was here for some time in the winter of 1645, and for a few weeks in the early part of 1647.

The town is pleasantly situated in a valley, almost in the centre of the mining district, at the confluence of two small rivers, latterly called the Kenwyn and the St. Allen, which, with a creek of the river Fal, form a body of water sufficient, in spring tides, to enable vessels of one hundred tons' burden to sail up to the town. A considerable increase of buildings has taken place of late years, and it is now handsome and well built : the streets are partially paved, and lighted with gas, the expense being defrayed by an assessment on each house, and the inhabitants are well supplied with water, a stream running through the principal streets. A county library was established in 1792, and a Literary Society, called the Cornwall Institution, with a valuable museum, more recently; there is also a neat assembly-room at the High Cross, which is convertible into a theatre. Truro is a place of considerable trade; its principal manufactures are carpets and paper, and there is an iron-foundry. The chief exports consist of tin and copper-ore; and the imports are, iron, coal, and timber, for the mines. Block tin is converted into ingots and bars; the former are mostly sent to the East Indies, and the latter to the Baltic and Mediterranean : the best description of crucibles are also made from the china stone. There is a large tin smelting-house on the Falmouth road; another near the Redruth road, containing four furnaces, with a chimney upwards of one hundred and eighty feet high, with which the flues of the furnaces communicate; and one on the southern side of the town. The markets are on Wednesday and Saturday; the former is a corn market, and both are well supplied with all kinds of provisions; a cattle market has also been recently established, on the first Wednesday in every month : there are cattle fairs on the Wednesday after Mid-Lent Sunday, Wednesday after Whit-Sunday, November 19th, and December 8th; the November fair belongs to the lord of the manor, and is held in a square area near the church; the others are held on Castle-hill, near the town.

The charter, under which the corporation derives its authority, was granted by Queen Elizabeth, in 1589 : the body corporate consists of a mayor, four aldermen, and, including the mayor, twenty capital burgesses, the vacancies amongst whom are filled up, by the corporation, from among the inhabitants. Although the borough only comprises that part of the town which forms the parish of St. Mary, the jurisdiction of the corporation, by an act passed in the early part of the last century, extends to a distance of half a mile from the limits of the borough, over the environs. It was formerly usual, at the election of a mayor, for the town mace to be delivered to the lord of the manor, who retained it until sixpence was paid for every house in the borough; this custom has ceased, but the sixpence is still exacted from such as occupy certain ancient houses, under the name of Smoke money. The charter states the mayor to be also mayor of Falmouth, and, as such, the corporation formerly exercised jurisdiction over, and received the port dues of, Falmouth harbour; but, early in the last century, this claim was in part successfully resisted by the inhabitants of Falmouth, and the corporation have now authority only over a small portion of the harbour, the extent of which jurisdiction is preserved by the practice of nominally arresting, at this point, in the presence of the members of the corporation, a person for a debt of £999, who is immediately liberated on bail. The Easter quarter sessions for the county are held here; and petty sessions for the west division of the hundred take place on the first Thursday in every month. Truro is one of the coinage towns, and the coinages have, of late years, with few exceptions, been confined to it and Penzance: the hall, in which the process is carried on, is an ancient edifice, situated at the eastern end of Boscawen-street: the vice-warden's court is held on the first Tuesday of every month. The last stannary parliament, which was continued by adjournments to the following autumn, was held here in 1752. The borough first sent members to parliament in the reign of Edward I.: the right of election is vested in the corporation, and the mayor is the returning officer: the preponderating influence is possessed by the Earl of Falmouth.

The living is a discharged rectory, in the archdeaconry of Cornwall, and diocese of Exeter, rated in the king's books at £16, endowed with £200 parliamentary grant, and in the patronage of the Earl of Mount-Edgecumbe. The church, dedicated to St. Mary, is a handsome structure of moor-stone, built about the reign of Henry VIII., in the later style of English architecture, with a lofty spire of modern date, unsuited to the prevailing character of the edifice. A chapel of ease to Kenwyn church has been recently erected in Lemon-street. There are places of worship for Baptists, Bryanites, the Society of Friends, Independents, Wesleyan Methodists, Shouters, and Unitarians. The grammar school is supposed, though not with certainty, to have been founded by a gentleman named Borlase, who resided near the town: the master and usher receive a salary of £25 per annum each. There are two exhibitions, of £30 per annum each, at Exeter College, Oxford, founded for its benefit by the trustees of the charitable bequests of the Rev. St. John Elliot, who died in 1760. Sir Humphrey Davy, the celebrated experimental chemist and natural philosopher, received his education at this school. A charity school, with an endowment of £5 per annum from the same funds, was established here; and there is also a National school for children of both sexes, besides several Sunday schools. An hospital for ten poor housekeepers was founded by Mr. Henry Williams, who died in 1631, and who endowed it with lands now producing about £120 per annum: the corporation have the management, and appoint widows only, to each of whom they allow four shillings a week, and some clothing. The county infirmary, which stands on an elevated and healthy spot, near the town, was opened in 1799, under the patronage of His late Majesty George IV., then Prince of Wales, and is supported by donations and voluntary subscriptions. A convent of Black friars was established, in the latter part of the reign of Henry III., by an ancestor of Rauf Reskiner, who was a benefactor to it in the reign of Edward IV.; it was dissolved, with the other monastic establishments, in the reign of Henry VIII. Samuel Foote, of dramatic celebrity, was born here, in a house now the Red Lion Inn, in 1721.

TRUSHAM, a parish in the hundred of EXMINSTER, county of DEVON, 2¼ miles (N. N. W.) from Chudleigh, containing 192 inhabitants. The living is a rectory, in the archdeaconry and diocese of Exeter, rated in the king's books at £9. 4. 9½., and in the patronage of Sir W. T. Pole, Bart. In the church is a very rich wooden skreen. Ten poor children are instructed for a rent-charge of £5, purchased with the sum of £100, raised by subscription for that purpose.

TRUSLEY, a parish in the hundred of APPLETREE, county of DERBY, 7 miles (W.) from Derby, containing 114 inhabitants. The living is a discharged rectory, in the archdeaconry of Derby, and diocese of Lichfield and Coventry, rated in the king's books at £5. 6. 8., and in the patronage of T. W. Coke, Esq. The church is dedicated to All Saints.

TRUSTHORPE, a parish in the Marsh division of the hundred of CALCEWORTH, parts of LINDSEY, county of LINCOLN, 7 miles (N.E.) from Alford, containing 262 inhabitants. The living is a discharged rectory, in the archdeaconry and diocese of Lincoln, rated in the king's books at £19. 10. 2¼., and in the patronage of the Rev. Owen Marden. The church is dedicated to St. Peter. There is a place of worship for Wesleyan Methodists.

TUBNEY, a parish in the hundred of OCK, county of BERKS, 4¼ miles (W. by N.) from Abingdon, containing 138 inhabitants. The living is a sinecure rectory, in the archdeaconry of Berks, and diocese of Salisbury, rated in the king's books at £3. 1. 10½., and in the patronage of the President and Fellows of Magdalene College, Oxford. The church has been entirely demolished: on the induction of a rector, the ceremony takes place in the open air. The parishioners repair to Fyfield church for the performance of ecclesiastical rites.

TUCKTON, a tything in that part of the parish of CHRISTCHURCH which is in the liberty of WESTOVER, New Forest (West) division of the county of SOUTHAMPTON, 1½ mile (W. S. W.) from Christchurch. The population is returned with the parish.

TUDDENHAM, a parish in the hundred of CARLFORD, county of SUFFOLK, 3¼ miles (N. E. by N.) from Ipswich, containing 308 inhabitants. The living is a discharged vicarage, in the archdeaconry of Suffolk, and diocese of Norwich, rated in the king's books at £10. 13. 4., endowed with £200 royal bounty, and £200 parliamentary grant, and in the patronage of the Rev. C. W. Fonnereau. The church is dedicated to St. Martin.

TUDDENHAM, a parish in the hundred of LACKFORD, county of SUFFOLK, 3 miles (S. E. by S.) from Mildenhall, containing 316 inhabitants. The living is a rectory, in the archdeaconry of Sudbury, and diocese of Norwich, rated in the king's books at £10. 17. 6., and in the patronage of the Marquis of Bristol. The church is dedicated to St. Mary. John Cockerton, in 1723, founded and endowed a free school for twenty children.

TUDDENHAM (EAST), a parish in the hundred of MITFORD, county of NORFOLK, 6¾ miles (E. S. E.) from East Dereham, containing 524 inhabitants. The living is a discharged vicarage, annexed to that of Honingham, in the archdeaconry of Norfolk, and diocese of Norwich, rated in the king's books at £7. 6. 0½., and endowed with £200 private benefaction, and £200 royal bounty. The church is dedicated to All Saints. There are two trifling endowments for the instruction of children.

TUDDENHAM (NORTH), a parish in the hundred of MITFORD, county of NORFOLK, 4¼ miles (E. by S.) from East Dereham, containing 368 inhabitants. The living is a rectory, in the archdeaconry of Norfolk, and diocese of Norwich, rated in the king's books at £10. 5. 5. Mrs. Shelford was patroness in 1814. The church is dedicated to St. Mary. The parish is bounded on the north by the river Lark.

TUDELEY, a parish partly in the hundred of TWY-FORD, but chiefly in that of WASHLINGSTONE, lathe of AYLESFORD, county of KENT, 2½ miles (E. S. E.) from Tonbridge, containing 546 inhabitants. The living is a vicarage, in the archdeaconry and diocese of Rochester, rated in the king's books at £4. 16. 0½., and in the patronage of Lord le Despencer. The church, dedicated to All Saints, is a small modern building of brick, with a square tower and spire.

TUDHOE, a township in the parochial chapelry of WHITWORTH, south-eastern division of DARLINGTON ward, county palatine of DURHAM, 5 miles (S. by W.) from Durham, containing 298 inhabitants.

TUDY (ST.), a parish in the hundred of TRIGG, county of CORNWALL, 6¼ miles (N.) from Bodmin, containing 606 inhabitants. The living is a rectory, in the archdeaconry of Cornwall, and diocese of Exeter, rated in the king's books at £31, and in the patronage of the Dean and Canons of Christ Church, Oxford. There is a place of worship for Wesleyan Methodists. Fairs for sheep and cattle are held on May 20th and September 14th. At Tinten and Kelly Green, in this parish, are the remains of two ancient chapels.

TUFFLEY, a hamlet in that part of the parish of ST. MARY de LODE, city of GLOUCESTER, which is in the middle division of the hundred of DUDSTONE and KING'S BARTON, county of GLOUCESTER, 2¼ miles (S. by W.) from Gloucester, containing 122 inhabitants.

TUFTON, or TUCKINGTON, a parish in the hundred of WHERWELL, Andover division of the county of SOUTHAMPTON, ½ a mile (S. W.) from Whitchurch, containing 156 inhabitants. The living is a perpetual curacy, annexed to the vicarage of Wherwell, in the archdeaconry and diocese of Winchester. The church is dedicated to St. Mary. The river Test passes through the parish.

TUGBY, a parish partly in the hundred of GARTREE, but chiefly in the eastern division of the hundred of GOSCOTE, county of LEICESTER, 7½ miles (W. by N.) from Uppingham, containing, with the liberty of Key-thorpe, 265 inhabitants. The living is a vicarage, in the archdeaconry of Leicester, and diocese of Lincoln, rated in the king's books at £11. 8. 4., and in the patronage of the Crown. The church is dedicated to St.

Thomas à Becket. Robert Wilson, in 1726, bequeathed land, directing the produce to be applied for teaching children and the relief of the poor.

TUGFORD, a parish in the hundred of MUNSLOW, county of SALOP, 10 miles (N. N. E.) from Ludlow, containing 186 inhabitants. The living is a discharged rectory, in the archdeaconry of Salop, and diocese of Hereford, rated in the king's books at £4. 13. 4., and in the patronage of the Bishop of Hereford. The church is dedicated to St. Catherine.

TUGGAL, a township in the parish, and northern division of the ward, of BAMBROUGH, county of NORTHUMBERLAND, 9½ miles (N. by E.) from Alnwick, containing 85 inhabitants.

TUMBY, a township in the parish of KIRKBY upon BAIN, southern division of the wapentake of GARTREE, parts of LINDSEY, county of LINCOLN, 2½ miles (N. E. by N.) from Tattershall, containing 335 inhabitants. There is a place of worship for Wesleyan Methodists.

TUNBRIDGE, county of KENT. — See TON-BRIDGE.

TUNSTALL, a township in the parish of BISHOP-WEARMOUTH, northern division of EASINGTON ward, county palatine of DURHAM, 2¾ miles (S. by W.) from Sunderland, containing 64 inhabitants. Limestone abounds here, imbedded in which have been found fossils, and a considerable quantity of iron-ore. On the Tunstall hills are some vestiges of a Druidical circle; and a rude sepulchre, constructed with fragments of limestone, was discovered in 1814, which contained broken urns, with some small human bones and teeth.

TUNSTALL, a parish in the hundred of MILTON, lathe of SCRAY, county of KENT, 1½ mile (S. W. by W.) from Sittingbourne, containing 160 inhabitants. The living is a rectory, in the archdeaconry and diocese of Canterbury, rated in the king's books at £14. 8. 4., and in the patronage of the Archbishop of Canterbury. The church, dedicated to St. John the Baptist, is principally in the later style of English architecture.

TUNSTALL, a parish in the hundred of LONSDALE, south of the sands, county palatine of LANCASTER, comprising the chapelry of Leck, and the townships of Burrow with Burrow, Cantsfield, and Tunstall, and containing 757 inhabitants, of which number, 155 are in the township of Tunstall, 3¾ miles (S.) from Kirkby-Lonsdale. The living is a discharged vicarage, in the archdeaconry of Richmond, and diocese of Chester, rated in the king's books at £6. 3. 11½., endowed with £400 private benefaction, and £400 royal bounty, and in the patronage of M. Wilson, Esq. The church, dedicated to St. John the Baptist, is very ancient, and occupies a retired situation. Twenty-four children receive a gratuitous education for about £26 a year, arising from sundry bequests, in a school-room built by subscription in 1751.

TUNSTALL, a parish in the hundred of WALSHAM, county of NORFOLK, 2¾ miles (S. S. E.) from Acle, containing 79 inhabitants. The living is a perpetual curacy, in the archdeaconry and diocese of Norwich, endowed with £800 royal bounty. The Rev. George Anguish was patron in 1813. The church is dedicated to St. Peter and St. Paul.

TUNSTALL, a chapelry in the parish of ABDASTON, northern division of the hundred of PIREHILL, county of STAFFORD, containing 102 inhabitants.

TUNSTALL, a parish in the hundred of PLOMES-GATE, county of SUFFOLK, 4½ miles (E. by S.) from Wickham-Market, containing 653 inhabitants. The living is a discharged vicarage, with the rectory of Dunningworth annexed, in the archdeaconry of Suffolk, and diocese of Norwich, rated in the king's books at £21. 0. 5., and endowed with £200 private benefaction, and £200 royal bounty. The Rev. C. Jefferson was patron in 1814. The church is dedicated to St. Michael. There is a place of worship for Baptists.

TUNSTALL, a parish partly within the liberty of ST. PETER of YORK, but chiefly in the middle division of the wapentake of HOLDERNESS, East riding of the county of YORK, 14½ miles (E. by N.) from Kingston upon Hull, containing 163 inhabitants. The living is a discharged vicarage, in the peculiar jurisdiction and patronage of the Succentor of the Cathedral Church of York, endowed with £600 royal bounty. The church, dedicated to All Saints, is principally in the later style of English architecture.

TUNSTALL, a township in that part of the parish of CATTERICK which is in the eastern division of the wapentake of HANG, North riding of the county of YORK, 2 miles (S. W.) from Catterick, containing 253 inhabitants.

TUNSTALL-COURT, a market town and liberty in the parish of WOLSTANTON, northern division of the hundred of PIREHILL, county of STAFFORD, 4 miles (N. by E.) from Newcastle under Lyne, containing 2622 inhabitants. The name is of Saxon derivation, being compounded of ton, or tun, and stall, signifying a town on, or near, a rising ground, appropriately describing the site of the town, which stands on elevated ground in the extensive district of the potteries. Considerable manufactures of porcelain, earthenware, blue bricks and tiles, and some chemical works, afford employment to about one thousand two hundred persons; and there are veins of coal, fine clay, limestone, iron-ore, and other mineral strata, in which the vicinity abounds. The Grand Trunk canal passes near the town, where it has its summit level; the great double tunnel, running two miles under Hare Castle hill, is in the vicinity. A market on Saturday was established in 1818; and the principal inhabitants, under the sanction of the lord of the manor, built, by means of shares, a neat court and market-house. The town is governed by a constable, chosen at the manorial court leet: it is in the honour of Tutbury, duchy of Lancaster, and within the jurisdiction of a court of pleas held at Tutbury every third Tuesday, for the recovery of debts under 40s. His Majesty's Commissioners for building new churches have proposed to make a grant for the erection of a chapel, the right of presentation to belong to the Perpetual Curate of Wolstanton. There are three places of worship for Wesleyan Methodists and Seceders from that community. James Brindley, the celebrated engineer, died at Turnhurst, in this neighbourhood, where his descendants possess considerable property.

TUNSTEAD, a parish in the hundred of TUNSTEAD, county of NORFOLK, 3¼ miles (N.E. by E.) from Coltishall, containing 501 inhabitants. The living is a discharged vicarage, with the perpetual curacy of South Ruston annexed, in the archdeaconry of Norfolk, and diocese of Norwich, rated in the king's books at

£18. 9. 7., and in the patronage of J. C. Clarke, Esq. The church is dedicated to St. Mary.

TUNWORTH, a parish in the hundred of BASING-STOKE, Basingstoke division of the county of SOUTH-AMPTON, 3¾ miles (S.E.) from Basingstoke, containing 119 inhabitants. The living is a rectory, in the archdeaconry and diocese of Winchester, rated in the king's books at £8. 18. 9., and in the patronage of G. P. Jervoise, Esq. The church is dedicated to All Saints.

TUPHOLME, an extra-parochial liberty, in the western division of the wapentake of WRAGGOE, parts of LINDSEY, county of LINCOLN, 9 miles (W. by S.) from Horncastle, containing 71 inhabitants. It appears formerly to have possessed parochial rights : the living was a discharged vicarage, in the archdeaconry and diocese of Lincoln, rated in the king's books at £2. 10. 10., endowed with £600 royal bounty, and in the patronage of the Bishop of Lincoln. An abbey of Premonstratensian canons, in honour of the Blessed Virgin Mary, was founded here, in the time of Henry II., by Allan and Gilbert de Nevill, which, at the dissolution, possessed a revenue of £119. 2. 8.

TUPSLEY, a township in the parish of BISHOP-HAMPTON, hundred of GRIMSWORTH, county of HERE-FORD, 2 miles (E. S. E.) from Hereford, containing 340 inhabitants.

TUPTON, a township in the parish of NORTH WING-FIELD, hundred of SCARSDALE, county of DERBY, 4 miles (S.) from Chesterfield, containing 202 inhabitants.

TURKDEAN, a parish in the hundred of BRAD-LEY, county of GLOUCESTER, 2¼ miles (N. by W.) from North Leach, containing 228 inhabitants. The living is a discharged vicarage, in the archdeaconry and diocese of Gloucester, rated in the king's books at £10, endowed with £210 private benefaction, and £200 royal bounty, and in the patronage of the Dean and Canons of Christ Church, Oxford. The church is dedicated to All Saints. There are quarries of good freestone, from which large quantities were taken and used in the building of Blenheim House.

TURNASTONE, a parish in the hundred of WEB-TREE, county of HEREFORD, 10 miles (E. S. E.) from Hay, containing 60 inhabitants. The living is a discharged rectory, in the archdeaconry and diocese of Hereford, rated in the king's books at £2. 14. 2., endowed with £600 royal bounty, and in the patronage of Mrs. Eliza Boughton. The church is dedicated to St. Mary.

TURNDITCH, a chapelry in the parish of DUF-FIELD, hundred of APPLETREE, county of DERBY, 3¼ miles (W. by S.) from Belper, containing 384 inhabitants. The living is a perpetual curacy, in the archdeaconry of Derby, and diocese of Lichfield and Coventry, endowed with £800 royal bounty, and £200 parliamentary grant, and in the patronage of the Vicar of Duffield. The church is dedicated to All Saints. There is a place of worship for Baptists.

TURNERS-PUDDLE, a parish in the hundred of HUNDREDSBARROW, Blandford (South) division of the county of DORSET, 7½ miles (N.W.) from Wareham, containing 98 inhabitants. The living is a discharged rectory, in the peculiar jurisdiction of the Dean of Salisbury, rated in the king's books at £7. 13. 4., endowed with £200 private benefaction, and £200 royal bounty, and in the patronage of J. Frampton, Esq. The church, dedicated to the Holy Trinity, was partly blown down in 1758, and rebuilt in 1759. The river Piddle runs through the parish.

TURNHAM-GREEN, a hamlet in the parish of CHISWICK, Kensington division of the hundred of Os-SULSTONE, county of MIDDLESEX, 5 miles (W. by S.) from London. The population is returned with the parish. The great western road passes through this village, which contains many handsome houses, is lighted with gas, and supplied with water from the West London water-works. On the south side is the Horticultural Society's garden (see Chiswick), but the principal entrance is here. It is within the jurisdiction of a court of requests held in Kingsgate-street, Holborn, for the recovery of debts under 40s., and is under the superintendence of the new police. There is a place of worship for Wesleyan Methodists. A National school for the parish of Chiswick is situated here: one hundred and twenty-three boys are instructed, and twenty are clothed.

TURNWORTH, a parish forming, with the parishes of Bellchalwell and Shillingstone, a detached portion of that part of the hundred of CRANBORNE which is in the Shaston (West) division, being locally in the hundred of Pimperne, Blandford (North) division, of the county of DORSET, 5 miles (W. by N.) from Blandford-Forum, containing 72 inhabitants. The living is a discharged vicarage, in the archdeaconry of Dorset, and diocese of Bristol, rated in the king's books at £10. 12. 3., and in the patronage of the Bishop of Salisbury. The church is dedicated to St. Mary.

TURTON, a chapelry in the parish of BOLTON, hundred of SALFORD, county palatine of LANCASTER, 4¼ miles (N.) from Great Bolton, containing 2090 inhabitants. The living is a perpetual curacy, in the archdeaconry and diocese of Chester, endowed with £288. 9. 9. private benefaction, £200 royal bounty, and £200 parliamentary grant, and in the patronage of the Lords of the Manor. The chapel is dedicated to St. Bartholomew. There is a place of worship for Unitarians. The chapelry is bounded by two rivulets tributary to the Irwell; these supply the power for various cotton-spinning, bleaching, dyeing, and printing works, of which the most extensive are the Egerton spinning and dye mills, worked by a powerful water-wheel: at these establishments about one thousand persons are employed. The weaving of cotton, by hand-looms, is extensively carried on by the cottagers. A manorial court is held twice a year; and there are fairs for cattle, horses, &c., on the 4th and 5th of September, at the village of Chapel Town. Humphrey Cheetham, Esq., in 1746, endowed a small school for clothing and teaching ten boys: a school-room, with a house for the master, had previously been erected, the former of which was rebuilt and enlarged by subscription about thirty years ago. He also made provision for ten poor boys of this township at Manchester College. Another school was founded by Abigail Cheetham, who endowed it with property now let for £28 a year, for which six boys are clothed and educated in a school-room built by subscription, the master of which has a dwelling-house rent-free. A small sum is also appropriated, from Mrs. Smalley's charity, to the education of poor children at Eagley Bridge school, which was established by subscription, in 1794. A Roman road passed through this chapelry, in which,

among other relics, the remains of a Druidical temple, and the copper head of an old British standard, have been discovered. Turton Tower, an embattled structure four stories high, has been the residence of the Orrells, the Cheethams, and the Greames, but is now occupied as a farm-house.

TURVEY, a parish in the hundred of WILLEY, county of BEDFORD, 8 miles (W. N. W.) from Bedford, containing 882 inhabitants. The living is a rectory, in the archdeaconry of Bedford, and diocese of Lincoln, rated in the king's books at £16, and in the patronage of D. C. Higgins, Esq. The church, dedicated to All Saints, contains several fine monuments of the ancient and noble family of Mordaunt. There is a place of worship for Independents. The parish lies near the border of Buckinghamshire.

TURVILLE, a parish in the hundred of DESBO-ROUGH, county of BUCKINGHAM, 6 miles (N. W. by W.) from Great Marlow, containing 362 inhabitants. The living is a discharged vicarage, in the archdeaconry of Buckingham, and diocese of Lincoln, rated in the king's books at £9. 9. 9½., endowed with £200 royal bounty, and in the patronage of the Bishop of Lincoln. The church is dedicated to St. Mary. The manufacture of lace is carried on here. The celebrated French general, Dumourier, resided at this place during the last two or three years of his life, where he died, and was buried at Henley.

TURWESTON, a parish in the hundred and county of BUCKINGHAM, ¾ of a mile (E.) from Brackley, containing 314 inhabitants. The living is a rectory, in the archdeaconry of Buckingham, and diocese of Lincoln, rated in the king's books at £12. 16. 3., and in the patronage of the Dean and Chapter of Westminster. The church is dedicated to St. Mary. There is a trifling bequest by the Rev. William Fairfax, in 1762, for teaching poor children.

TURWICK, a parish in the hundred of DUMPFORD, rape of CHICHESTER, county of SUSSEX, 5 miles (W. N. W.) from Midhurst, containing 112 inhabitants. The living is a discharged rectory, in the archdeaconry and diocese of Chichester, rated in the king's books at £5. 0. 5., and in the patronage of — Sclater, Esq.

TUSHINGHAM, a joint township with Grindley, in the parish of MALPAS, higher division of the hundred of BROXTON, county palatine of CHESTER, 3¼ miles (E. S. E.) from Malpas, containing 283 inhabitants.

TUSMORE, a parish in the hundred of PLOUGHLEY, county of OXFORD, 6 miles (N. by W.) from Bicester. The population is returned with the parish of Hardwicke. The living is a discharged rectory, in the archdeaconry and diocese of Oxford, rated in the king's books at £3. 5., and in the patronage of Sir G. Dashwood, Bart. The church has been destroyed.

TUTBURY, a parish (formerly a market town) in the northern division of the hundred of OFFLOW, county of STAFFORD, 5¼ miles (N. W. by N.) from Burton upon Trent, containing, according to the last census, 1444 inhabitants, since which the population has considerably increased. The living is a discharged vicarage, in the archdeaconry of Stafford, and diocese of Lichfield and Coventry, rated in the king's books at £7, endowed with £400 private benefaction, £200 royal bounty, and £300 parliamentary grant, and in the patronage of the Vicar of Bakewell. The church, dedicated to St. Mary, is the nave of a more extensive structure, and a fine specimen of the Norman style of architecture : it has lately been enlarged, new pewed, and greatly improved, at an expense of nearly £2000, about one half of which was contributed by his Majesty, by the Society for enlarging churches and chapels, and by the nobility and gentry of the neighbourhood : three hundred and seventy of the sittings are free. There are places of worship for Independents, and Calvinistic, Primitive, and Wesleyan Methodists. Tutbury, situated on the west bank of the river Dove, which is crossed by a stone bridge of five arches, of recent erection, was, at a very early period, erected into a free borough, and possessed many valuable privileges, though it never had the right of sending members to parliament. It had a good market, which gradually declined, as that of Burton increased, till at length it was discontinued altogether; but there are still fairs for horses and cattle, on February 14th, August 15th, and December 1st. On the river are extensive corn and cotton-spinning mills, formerly belonging to an establishment styled the "Tutbury Mill Company," now to John Webb, Esq. ; there is also a considerable cut-glass manufactory. A free school was founded by Richard Wakefield, who, about 1730, endowed it with lands producing about £50 per annum, for the education of poor children : the school-house was rebuilt in 1789. Richard Wakefield also, by his will in 1773, devised land and tithes, now producing about £450, to trustees, for charitable uses. The king, as Duke of Lancaster, is lord of the manor, or honour, of Tutbury, the jurisdiction of which extends over a great portion of Staffordshire, and into several of the neighbouring counties, viz., those of Derby, Leicester, Nottingham, and Warwick ; and, in his Majesty's name, courts leet and baron are here held once a year ; also a court of pleas, every third Tuesday, for the recovery of all debts under 40s., contracted within the honour.

On the division of lands after the Conquest, Tutbury was included in the domain allotted to Henry de Ferrars, a Norman nobleman, who either built the castle, or received it in gift from the Conqueror. His descendant, Robert, joining Leicester in the rebellion against Henry III., was fined £50,000, and, being unable to pay so large a sum, forfeited his castle to the king, who granted it to his son Edmund of Lancaster. After the attainder of Thomas of Lancaster, who, with the Earl of Hereford, had attempted the dethronement of Edward II., the fortress was suffered to fall to ruin, and so remained till 1350, when John of Gaunt becoming its possessor, he rebuilt the greater part of it, with the gatehouse, and surrounded it on three sides by a wall ; the precipitous declivity on the fourth rendering further security unnecessary. Mary, Queen of Scots, was for some time imprisoned in this castle ; and, at the commencement of the parliamentary war, it was garrisoned for the king ; but, by order of the parliament, it was nearly demolished in 1646 : the ruins, however, are still sufficient to indicate its former extent and magnificence, and exhibit good specimens of the early and later styles of English architecture. On the declivity of the commanding eminence upon which the castle stood, a Benedictine priory, in honour of the Blessed Virgin, was founded, in 1080, by Henry de Ferrars, which, though a cell to the ab-

bey of St. Peter super Divam, in Normandy, survived till the general dissolution, when its revenue was valued at £244. 16. 8. Among other curious customs that formerly prevailed here was a minstrel fête, given by the Duke of Lancaster on Assumption-day, to which all the itinerant musicians of the neighbourhood were invited; but the quarrels which almost invariably took place on the occasion rendered it necessary to make certain regulations to preserve order ; a king of the minstrels was, in consequence, elected, and, on the morrow of the festival, a court was held to determine all disputes, and cases of assault and battery, that might have arisen during the fête. There was also a sport termed " Bull running, " which consisted in chasing a bull with a soaped tail, and, if caught in the county, he was conducted to the market-place and there baited, otherwise he remained the property of the Duke of Devonshire, who held the priory on condition of furnishing a bull annually for the purpose : his Grace has, however, compounded with the minstrel king and his subjects, and the bailiff, having purchased his right to the animal, sends him to the manor at Hardwick, for a Christmas feast to the poor. The country between Tutbury and Needwood Forest abounds with alabaster. Ann Moore, who professed the ability to live without food, resided here during the period of her imposture.

TUTNAL, a joint hamlet with Cobley, in that part of the parish of TARDEBIGG which is in the Alcester division of the hundred of BARLICHWAY, county of WARWICK, 2 miles (E. S. E.) from Bromsgrove, containing, with Cobley, 460 inhabitants.

TUTTINGTON, a parish in the southern division of the hundred of ERPINGHAM, county of NORFOLK, 2¾ miles (E.) from Aylsham, containing 228 inhabitants. The living is a discharged vicarage, in the archdeaconry and diocese of Norwich, rated in the king's books at £5. 0. 7½., endowed with £600 royal bounty, and in the patronage of the Bishop of Ely. The church is dedicated to St. Peter and St. Paul.

TUXFORD, a market town and parish in the South-clay division of the wapentake of BASSETLAW, county of NOTTINGHAM, 30 miles (N. E. by N.) from Nottingham, and 139 (N. by W.) from London, on the great north road, containing 979 inhabitants. This place, often denominated Tuxford in the Clay, to designate its situation, is a small town of modern appearance, having been rebuilt since 1702, when the old town was destroyed by fire ; the inhabitants are well supplied with water. The only branch of trade, which is somewhat extensive, is in hops, of which large quantities are grown in the neighbourhood. The market is on Monday : fairs are on May 12th, for cattle, sheep, swine, and poultry ; and on September 28th, for hops. The living is a discharged vicarage, in the archdeaconry of Nottingham, and diocese of York, rated in the king's books at £4. 14. 7., endowed with £200 private benefaction, and £200 royal bounty, and in the patronage of the Master and Fellows of Trinity College, Cambridge. The church, which is dedicated to St. Nicholas, contains portions in various styles of architecture. There is a place of worship for Wesleyan Methodists. The free grammar school was founded, in 1670, by Charles Read, Esq., who bequeathed £200 for the erection of the buildings, endowed it with lands, and directed a salary of £20 per annum to be paid to the master, and £5 per annum towards the maintenance of four boys, " being the sons of poor widows of ministers, and of decayed gentlemen and their widows," from the age of seven to sixteen years : it is under the management of six trustees, freeholders of Tuxford, and subject to the visitation of the mayor and aldermen of Newark, with the minister, and two justices of the peace living in or near the town. There are sundry benefactions for teaching poor children.

TWAMBROOK, a township in that part of the parish of GREAT BUDWORTH which is in the hundred of NORTHWICH, county palatine of CHESTER, ¼ of a mile (E.) from Northwich. The population is returned with the chapelry of Witton.

TWEEDMOUTH, a parish in ISLANDSHIRE, county palatine of DURHAM, though locally northward of the county of Northumberland, adjoining Berwick upon Tweed, and containing 4673 inhabitants. The living is a perpetual curacy, in the archdeaconry of Northumberland, and diocese of Durham, endowed with £200 private benefaction, £400 royal bounty, and £400 parliamentary grant, and in the patronage of the Dean and Chapter of Durham. The chapel, dedicated to St. Bartholomew, which was formerly a chapel of ease to Holy Island, was rebuilt in 1780. There is a place of worship for Scotch Presbyterians. Tweedmouth, situated on the southern bank of the Tweed, forms a handsome suburb to the town of Berwick upon Tweed, to which it is joined by an elegant stone bridge. The inhabitants are principally employed in manufactures, ship-building, and in a very productive salmon-fishery. Petty sessions are held at this place every Saturday. An ancient hospital formerly existed here. In 1203, King John made an attempt to fortify Tweedmouth to repel the Scots, who twice interrupted the design, and the works were entirely demolished by William, surnamed the Lion, who then occupied Berwick. Near the village of East Ord, on the bank of the river, are vestiges of an ancient British intrenchment, where many fragments of military weapons have been found. In this parish is Spittle, a sea-bathing place, which see.

TWEMLOW, a township in that part of the parish of SANDBACH which is in the hundred of NORTHWICH, county palatine of CHESTER, 5¼ miles (E. N. E.) from Middlewich, containing 130 inhabitants.

TWICKENHAM, a parish in the hundred of ISLEWORTH, county of MIDDLESEX, 9 miles (W. S. W.) from London, containing 4206 inhabitants. The name of this place, formerly written *Twicknam*, is said to refer to its situation between two streams, or brooks, that flow into the Thames at each end of the village, which occupies a most delightful position on its western bank, on the road from London, through Isleworth, to Hampton Court. At the southern extremity of the village, fronted by a lawn sloping to the verge of the river, is a modern residence, which occupies the site of Pope's villa, the only remaining vestige of which is the favourite grotto, erected by the poet for his own use. In the centre of the river, nearly opposite to the church, is an island, called Twickenham Ait, comprising about eight acres, the chief part of which is laid out in pleasure ground. The Eel Pie house has been noted for the last two hundred years, as a favourite resort for refreshment and recreation to water parties,

and persons repairing hither for the amusement of fishing ; the old house was taken down in 1830, and a very handsome and commodious edifice, comprising a good assembly-room, measuring fifty feet by fifteen, has been erected on the site by the present proprietor. There are powder and oil mills in the parish. Fairs are held on Holy Thursday and August 9th and 10th. The inhabitants are within the jurisdiction of a court of requests, for the recovery of debts under 40s., held at Brentford during the summer half-year, and at Uxbridge during the winter. The living is a vicarage, in the archdeaconry of Middlesex, and diocese of London, rated in the king's books at £11, and in the patronage of the Dean and Canons of Windsor. The church, which stands near the river, is dedicated to St. Mary, and is a neat structure of brick, ornamented with stone, of the Doric order, with an ancient embattled tower of the eleventh century ; it was rebuilt in 1714 : in the interior is a monument to the memory of Pope, erected by Bishop Warburton ; and another to Mrs. Clive, the actress. Midway between Twickenham and Richmond is a chapel of ease, erected about 1721. There are places of worship for Independents and Wesleyan Methodists. A National school was formed, in 1809, by the union of three schools, and the appropriation of some small endowments belonging to them, amounting to about £135 per annum : one hundred and ten boys and seventy girls are educated, of whom about thirty boys and twenty-four girls are clothed annually : the salary of the master and mistress is £100 per annum. Six boys and one girl of this parish are eligible for instruction and apprenticeship, or to be put to service, on the foundation of John and Frances West, who conveyed estates in trust to the Governors of Christ's Hospital for that purpose ; £20 being paid with each boy, and £5 with each girl. One man or woman of the parish receives £5 per annum also from a benefaction by Frances West of £2600, to be laid out in land for the use of the Clothworkers' Company, to pay to each of ten blind men and ten blind women that sum annually.

TWIGMOOR, a hamlet in that part of the parish of MANTON which is in the eastern division of the wapentake of MANLEY, parts of LINDSEY, county of LINCOLN, 5½ miles (W.) from Glandford-Bridge, containing 33 inhabitants.

TWIGWORTH, a hamlet in that part of the parish of ST. MARY de LODE, GLOUCESTER, which is in the upper division of the hundred of DUDSTONE and KING'S BARTON, county of GLOUCESTER, 2 miles (N. N. E.) from Gloucester, containing 90 inhabitants.

TWINEHAM, a parish in the hundred of BUTTINGHILL, rape of LEWES, county of SUSSEX, 5 miles (S. W.) from Cuckfield, containing 275 inhabitants. The living is a rectory, in the archdeaconry of Lewes, and diocese of Chichester, rated in the king's books at £10. 15. 5., and in the patronage of Sir H. Goring, Bart. The church is dedicated to St. Peter.

TWINING, a parish in the lower division of the hundred of KIFTSGATE, though locally in the lower division of that of Tewkesbury, county of GLOUCESTER, 2¾ miles (N. by E.) from Tewkesbury, containing, with Mythe and Mythe-hook, 849 inhabitants. The living is a discharged vicarage, in the archdeaconry and diocese of Gloucester, rated in the king's books at £7. 9. 7., endowed with £400 private benefaction, £200 royal bounty, and £900 parliamentary grant, and in the patronage of the Dean and Canons of Christ Church, Oxford. The church, dedicated to St. Mary Magdalene, exhibits portions in the Norman style of architecture, and has lately received an addition of one hundred free sittings, the Incorporated Society for the enlargement of churches and chapels having granted £30 towards defraying the expense. The navigable river Avon, which is here crossed by a ferry, separates this parish from Worcestershire.

TWINSTEAD, a parish in the hundred of HINCK-FORD, county of ESSEX, 5½ miles (N. E. by N.) from Halstead, containing 202 inhabitants. The living is a discharged rectory, in the archdeaconry of Middlesex, and diocese of London, rated in the king's books at £6, and in the patronage of the Crown.

TWISTON, a township in that part of the parish of WHALLEY which is in the higher division of the hundred of BLACKBURN, county palatine of LANCASTER, 5 miles (B. N. E.) from Clitheroe, containing 236 inhabitants.

TWITCHEN, a parish in the hundred of SOUTH MOLTON, county of DEVON, 6½ miles (N. E. by E.) from South Molton, containing 162 inhabitants. The living is a perpetual curacy, annexed to the vicarage of North Molton, in the archdeaconry of Barnstaple, and diocese of Exeter. The church is dedicated to St. Peter.

TWIVERTON, a parish in the hundred of WELLOW, county of SOMERSET, 1¾ mile (W. S. W.) from Bath, containing 1500 inhabitants. The living is a discharged vicarage, in the archdeaconry of Bath, and diocese of Bath and Wells, rated in the king's books at £5. 18. 1½., and in the patronage of the Provost and Fellows of Oriel College, Oxford. The church, dedicated to St. Michael, has lately received an addition of one hundred free sittings, the Incorporated Society for the enlargement of churches and chapels having granted £170 towards defraying the expense. There is a place of worship for Wesleyan Methodists. The river Avon runs through the parish, from east to west, and turns numerous mills.

TWIZELL, a township in the parish of NORHAM, otherwise Norhamshire, county palatine of DURHAM, though locally to the northward of the county of Northumberland, 10 miles (S. W.) from Berwick, containing 308 inhabitants. It is situated on the river Till, which is here crossed by a stone bridge of one arch, ninety feet and three-quarters in the span. Twizell castle, a fine, though unfinished, castellated mansion of the Blakes, is seated on a rocky precipice, surrounded by scenery extremely picturesque. Near it is Tillmouth House, the present residence of the family, of whom was the celebrated Admiral Blake, who died in 1657. It has a small chapel attached, and in the neighbourhood are the remains of an ancient chapel, or cell, dedicated to St. Cuthbert.

TWIZELL, a township in that part of the parish of MORPETH which is in the western division of CASTLE ward, county of NORTHUMBERLAND, 6½ miles (S. W. by S.) from Morpeth, containing 38 inhabitants.

TWYCROSS, a parish in the hundred of SPARKEN-HOE, county of LEICESTER, 4¾ miles (W. N. W.) from Market-Bosworth, containing 373 inhabitants. The living is a perpetual curacy, annexed to the vicarage

of Orton on the Hill, in the archdeaconry of Leicester, and diocese of Lincoln. The church is dedicated to St. James. Twycross is in the honour of Tutbury, duchy of Lancaster, and within the jurisdiction of a court of pleas held at Tutbury every third Tuesday, for the recovery of debts under 40s. Charles Jennings, in 1773, bequeathed £333. 6. 8., directing the interest to be applied in support of a school for poor children.

TWYFORD, a chapelry in the parish of HURST, partly in the hundreds of CHARLTON and SONNING, county of BERKS, and partly in that of AMESBURY, county of WILTS, 5 miles (E. N. E.) from Reading. The population is returned with the parish. It is within the peculiar jurisdiction of the Dean of Salisbury. The chapel, dedicated to St. Swithin, was erected at the expense of Mr. Edward Polehampton, who died in 1721. There is a place of worship for Independents. Silk-throwing is extensively carried on. Fairs for horses, toys, &c., are held on July 24th and October 11th. Edward Polehampton, in 1721, bequeathed a rent-charge of £40, with a dwelling-house for the master, to teach ten boys, and another of £10 for clothing them. An hospital was founded here, in 1640, by Lady Frances Winchcombe, for the maintenance of six poor people. A battle was fought near this place in 1688, between the partizans of James II. and those of the Prince of Orange, afterwards William III.

TWYFORD, a parish in the hundred and county of BUCKINGHAM, 5¼ miles (S. W. by S.) from Buckingham, containing, with the hamlets of Charndon and Pounden, 623 inhabitants. The living is a rectory not in charge, annexed to the Rectorship of Lincoln College, Oxford, in the archdeaconry of Buckingham, and diocese of Lincoln. The church is dedicated to St. Mary.

TWYFORD, a chapelry in that part of the parish of BARROW which is in the hundred of APPLETREE, county of DERBY, 5½ miles (S. S. W.) from Derby, containing, with the township of Stenson, 235 inhabitants. The chapel is dedicated to St. Andrew. The Trent and Mersey canal passes through the parish. John Harpur and others, in 1696, bequeathed a rent-charge of £15, to be applied for teaching and apprenticing poor children, or towards their support at the University.

TWYFORD, a parish in the eastern division of the hundred of GOSCOTE, county of LEICESTER, 6¼ miles (S. by W.) from Melton-Mowbray, containing, with the chapelry of Thorpe-Satchville, 495 inhabitants. The living is a discharged vicarage with that of Hungerton, united in 1732, in the archdeaconry of Leicester, and diocese of Lincoln, rated in the king's books at £8. 8. 6., and in the patronage of Sir T. H. Apreece, Bart. The church is dedicated to St. Andrew.

TWYFORD, a township in that part of the parish of COLSTERWORTH which is in the hundred of BEL-TISLOE, parts of KESTEVEN, county of LINCOLN, ¾ of a mile (S.) from Colsterworth, containing 73 inhabitants.

TWYFORD, an extra-parochial liberty, in the Kensington division of the hundred of OSSULSTONE, county of MIDDLESEX, 6 miles (W. N. W.) from London, containing 33 inhabitants. There is a private chapel at Twyford Abbey.

TWYFORD, a parish in the hundred of EYNSFORD, county of NORFOLK, ¾ of a mile (W.) from Foulsham, containing 82 inhabitants. The living is a discharged rectory, in the archdeaconry and diocese of Norwich, rated in the king's books at £4. 19. 9½., endowed with £200 royal bounty, and in the patronage of the Rev. S. H. Savory. The church is dedicated to St. Nicholas. The parish is bounded on the west by the river Wensum.

TWYFORD, a parish in the hundred of FAWLEY, Fawley division of the county of SOUTHAMPTON, 3 miles (S.) from Winchester, containing 1048 inhabitants. The living is a vicarage, with the perpetual curacy of Owslebury annexed, in the peculiar jurisdiction of the Incumbent, rated in the king's books at £12. 12. 8½., and in the patronage of Lady Mildmay, on the nomination of the Master and Fellows of Emanuel College, Cambridge. The church is dedicated to St. Mary. The Itchen navigation passes through the parish. A court baron is held annually. Twyford is within the jurisdiction of the Cheyney Court held at Winchester every Thursday, for the recovery of debts to any amount. Twenty-four poor children are educated for the proceeds of £500, bequeathed by Richard Wooll, in 1780. Here was formerly a Roman Catholic seminary, in which the celebrated poet, Alexander Pope, received part of his education

TWYWELL, a parish in the hundred of HUXLOE, county of NORTHAMPTON, 3½ miles (W. by S.) from Thrapstone, containing 200 inhabitants. The living is a rectory, in the archdeaconry of Northampton, and diocese of Peterborough, rated in the king's books at £9, and in the patronage of J. Williamson, Esq. The church is dedicated to St. Nicholas.

TYDD (ST. GILES'), a parish in the hundred of WISBEACH, Isle of ELY, county of CAMBRIDGE, 5½ miles (N. W. by N.) from Wisbeach, containing 781 inhabitants. The living is a rectory, in the peculiar jurisdiction and patronage of the Bishop of Ely, rated in the king's books at £21. 13. 1½. A school is supported by annual subscriptions, amounting to about £16.

TYDD (ST. MARY'S), a parish in the wapentake of ELLOE, parts of HOLLAND, county of LINCOLN, 6 miles (N. by W.) from Wisbeach, containing 776 inhabitants. The living is a rectory, in the archdeaconry and diocese of Lincoln, rated in the king's books at £17. 6. 5½., and in the patronage of the Crown. The parish is bounded on the east by the river Nene. Martha Trafford, in 1740, gave certain land, the produce of which is applied in teaching poor children, in a school-house lately built by subscription. Nicholas Breakspear, who was raised to the papal dignity, as Adrian IV., was rector of this parish.

TYLDERSLEY, or TILDESLEY, a parochial district in the hundred of WEST DERBY, county palatine of LANCASTER, 2½ miles (E. N. E.) from Leigh, containing 4325 inhabitants. In 1827, the township of Tyldesley was erected into a district parish, as regards ecclesiastical affairs. The living is a perpetual curacy, in the archdeaconry and diocese of Chester, endowed with £600 private benefaction, and £1600 royal bounty, and in the patronage of Lord Lilford. The church, dedicated to St. George, was erected by the commissioners for promoting the building of additional churches, at an expense of more than £12,000, and will accommodate two thousand persons : it is a chaste and handsome structure, designed by Smirke, in the later style of English architecture, with a spire rising to the height of one

hundred and fifty feet, and was consecrated in September 1825. The site was presented by the late Thomas Johnson, Esq. ; and the munificence of George Ormerod, Esq. has supplied the enclosure of the cemetery, a peal of six fine-toned bells, three beautiful painted windows, an organ, an elegant communion cloth, &c. ; the communion plate was the gift of Mrs. Ormerod. There are places of worship for those in the connexion of the late Countess of Huntingdon, and Wesleyan Methodists. The freehold of the village belonged originally to the family of Tildesley ; the present proprietor is George Ormerod, Esq. : about half a century ago, its population consisted of only three families ; it is now estimated at about three thousand individuals, and is still increasing. The Leeds and Liverpool canal, which extends also to Manchester, passes within two miles of the place. Cotton-spinning is extensively carried on, and affords employment to about one thousand persons ; the remainder of the labouring classes are employed in weaving, in agriculture, and in the neighbouring collieries, which are very considerable : there are several cotton-mills, and one for the making of machinery. A National school, erected in 1827, at an expense of £650, on a site given by George Ormerod, Esq., adjacent to the church, is a neat and substantial stone building of two stories, calculated to contain two hundred and fifty boys and as many girls : it is supported by subscription, and by small weekly payments from the scholars. A subscription library was established in 1828. Of the several antique mansions in the neighbourhood, there are considerable remains of Dam House, a very old brick building, with bay windows and gables ; and, near it, the ruins of another, still more ancient : the site of Shackerley Hall is surrounded by a moat.

TYNEHAM, a parish in the hundred of HASILOR, Blandford (South) division of the county of DORSET, 6½ miles (W. by S.) from Corfe-Castle, containing 240 inhabitants. The living is a rectory, united, by an act passed in the 8th of George I., to that of Steeple, in the archdeaconry of Dorset, and diocese of Bristol, rated in the king's books at £11. 0. 10., and in the patronage of W. Richards, Esq. The church, dedicated to St. Mary, was repaired in 1744 ; it is without a tower. There was formerly a chapel at Povington, and another, dedicated to St. Margaret, at North Egleston. The parish is bounded on the south by the English channel, on the coast of which is a circular battery, for the defence of Worbarrow bay. Here was an Alien priory, subordinate to the abbey of Bec in Normandy, which, at the suppression, was given by Henry VI. to St. Anthony's hospital, London ; by Edward IV. to Eton college, and afterwards to the Dean and Prebendaries of Westminster.

TYNEMOUTH, a parish in the eastern division of CASTLE ward, county of NORTHUMBERLAND, comprising the chapelries of North Shields and Whitley, and the townships of Chirton, Cullercoats, Monkseaton, Murton, or Moortown, Preston, and Tynemouth, and containing 24,820 inhabitants, of which number, 9454 are in the township of Tynemouth, 8½ miles (E. N. E.) from Newcastle upon Tyne. This parish is of great extent, occupying the south-eastern section of the county ; the river Tyne bounds it on the south, in its course to the ocean, which forms the eastern limit ; on the north and west are the parishes of Earsdon, Long Benton, and

Wallsend. It abounds with coal; there is also some iron-stone, and the only limestone strata in the county. In the time of the ancient Britons the village was denominated *Penbal Crag,* or "the head of the rampart on the rock:" from remains discovered in 1783, it is conjectured that the Romans had a strong fortress here. A chapel, composed of wood, was built by Edwin, King of Northumberland, in 625; it was afterwards rebuilt with stone by Oswald, in the eighth century, and dedicated to St. Mary, and, having been repeatedly plundered by the Danes, was refounded by Tostig, Earl of Northumberland : in 1074 it was annexed to the monastery of Jarrow, and both institutions were made cells to the abbey of Durham. In 1090, it was elevated into a priory for Black canons by Earl Mowbray, who converted it into a fortress during the period of his conspiracy against William Rufus, when it was again nearly demolished, but rebuilt in 1110. After other ravages, it became the occasional residence of the queens of Edward I. and II., was afterwards plundered by the Scots, and eventually surrendered in 1539, when its revenue was valued at £511. 4. 1. After the dissolution, the church continued parochial until the year 1657, when, having become ruinous, a new parish church was built at North Shields, and dedicated to Christ. Of the ancient priory there are still some interesting and venerable remains, principally in the early style of English architecture, with some portions of earlier date in the north aisle : they consist chiefly of a gateway, exploratory turret, the eastern part of the church, and other parts now converted into a magazine for military stores ; the tower having been appropriated as a barrack, capable of accommodating about four hundred soldiers : they stand within the walls of the castle, near the east end of the village, on a peninsula of stupendous rocks, at the mouth of the Tyne, against which the sea sometimes breaks with great fury. The approach from the west is by means of a drawbridge, and by a gateway of square form, the whole being defended by a double wall, extending to the shore, and a deep outer ditch. During the civil commotions in the reign of Charles, this fortress was defended by the Earl of Newcastle, in 1642, but eventually captured in 1645 : a governor and deputy-governor are still appointed to it. In 1672, Clifford's fort was constructed at the mouth of the river, commanding the entrance to the harbour ; and, in 1758, barracks were erected near the village, for the accommodation of one thousand men ; but, at the general peace, they were sold, and have since been converted into dwelling-houses, which now constitute Percy-square. This place consists principally of one long street, and is much resorted to in the bathing season, having some commodious and elegant baths, erected in 1807. At Collercoats Sands is a mineral spring, which is in considerable repute. The living is a discharged vicarage, in the archdeaconry of Northumberland, and diocese of Durham, rated in the king's books at £24. 19. 4., and in the alternate patronage of the Duke of Northumberland and Sir J. D. Astley, Bart. The church, dedicated to St. Oswin, and formerly belonging to the priory, is in ruins : the parish church is in North Shields. His Majesty's commissioners for building churches have proposed a grant for a new church at Tynemouth. In 1825, Mr. Kettlewell bequeathed the sum of £7000, to build and endow a school in this parish.

TYRLEY, county of STAFFORD. — See BLOORE in TYRLEY.

TYRRINGHAM, a joint parish with Filgrove, in the hundred of NEWPORT, county of BUCKINGHAM, 2¼ miles (N. N. W.) from Newport-Pagnell, containing, with Filgrove, 204 inhabitants. The living is a rectory, with that of Filgrove united, in the archdeaconry of Buckingham, and diocese of Lincoln, rated in the king's books at £13. 6. 10½., and in the patronage of William Praed, Esq. The church is dedicated to St. Peter.

TYSOE, a parish in the Kington division of the hundred of KINGTON, county of WARWICK, 5 miles (S. by E.) from Kington, containing, with the township of Westcote, 1070 inhabitants. The living is a discharged vicarage, united to the rectory of Compton-Wyniates, in the archdeaconry and diocese of Worcester, rated in the king's books at £10, endowed with £200 private benefaction, and £200 royal bounty, and in the patronage of the Earl of Northampton. The church is dedicated to St. Mary. There is a place of worship for Wesleyan Methodists. Twenty boys are educated for £21 per annum, arising from certain property bequeathed to the parish, in 1541, by John Middleton and Edward Richards : the school-room and master's residence were rebuilt a few years ago. Opposite to the church, on the side of a hill, is cut the figure of a horse, which, from the colour of the soil, is called the Red Horse, and gives to the adjacent low lands the name of the Vale of Red Horse. This figure is supposed to have been designed to commemorate the well-known act of Richard Neville, Earl of Warwick, in killing his horse on the day of the battle of Towton, fought on Palm-Sunday, 1461 ; on which day annually it has been customary for the country people to assemble, for the purpose of clearing the figure of the horse from whatever has grown upon it in the course of the year, which is locally termed "scouring the horse."

TYTHBY, a parish in the southern division of the wapentake of BINGHAM, county of NOTTINGHAM, 9 miles (E. S. E.) from Nottingham, containing, with the chapelry of Cropwell-Butler, 635 inhabitants. The living is a perpetual curacy, in the archdeaconry of Nottingham, and diocese of York, endowed with £400 royal bounty, and in the patronage of John Chaworth, Esq. The church is dedicated to the Holy Trinity.

TYTHERINGTON, a township in the parish of PRESTBURY, hundred of MACCLESFIELD, county palatine of CHESTER, 1½ mile (N.) from Macclesfield, containing 382 inhabitants.

TYTHERINGTON, a parish partly in the upper division of the hundred of HENBURY, but chiefly in the lower division of that of THORNBURY, county of GLOUCESTER, 3 miles (S. E.) from Thornbury, containing, with the tything of Itchington, 474 inhabitants. The living is a discharged vicarage, in the archdeaconry and diocese of Gloucester, rated in the king's books at £9. 11. 7. Thomas Hardwick, Esq. was patron in 1817. The church is dedicated to St. James.

TYTHERINGTON, a parish in the hundred of HEYTESBURY, county of WILTS, 4¼ miles (S. E. by E.) from Warminster, containing 147 inhabitants. The living is a perpetual curacy, in the peculiar jurisdiction and patronage of the Dean of Salisbury, as Dean of Heytesbury The church is dedicated to St. James.

TYTHERLEY, otherwise TUDERLEY (EAST), a parish in the hundred of THORNGATE, Andover division of the county of SOUTHAMPTON, 7 miles (S. W.) from Stockbridge, containing 259 inhabitants. The living is a perpetual curacy, in the archdeaconry and diocese of Winchester, and in the patronage of — Bailey, Esq. The church is dedicated to St. Peter. Sarah Rolle, in 1736, conveyed lands, &c., in support of a schoolmaster and schoolmistress; the income is about £ 208 a year, for which all the poor children of this parish and Lockerley, who apply, are gratuitously instructed; forty at present attend, twelve of whom are partly boarded.

TYTHERLEY, otherwise TUDERLEY (WEST), a parish in the hundred of THORNGATE, Andover division of the county of SOUTHAMPTON, 7¾ miles (S. W. by W.) from Stockbridge, containing 494 inhabitants. The living is a rectory, in the archdeaconry and diocese of Winchester, rated in the king's books at £ 8. 5. 10., and in the patronage of C. B. Wall, Esq. This parish is within the jurisdiction of the Cheyney Court held at Winchester every Thursday, for the recovery of debts to any amount.

TYTHERTON-KELLAWAYS, a tything in the parish of BREMHILL, hundred of CHIPPENHAM, county of WILTS, 3¾ miles (E. N. E.) from Chippenham. The population is returned with the parish. This place merits notice from the peculiar circumstances attending its origin and progressive improvement. An individual named Connicker, a native of Reading, having embraced the original doctrines of Whitfield and Wesley, at the period of their first promulgation, became so zealous a devotee, that he expended his patrimonial estates in building meeting-houses in different parts of the country, one of which he erected at Tytherton, and attached to it a burying-ground, &c. Here he fixed his own residence, and propagated his opinions with great success during several years; but, on the schism between Wesley and Whitfield, he joined the Moravians, and induced most of his followers at Tytherton to do the same. Accordingly, two cottages, adjoining each other, were purchased, and converted into a house for the reception of the young unmarried women of the sect. A house for young men, on the same plan, was also attempted to be established, but without success. In this situation, with slow advances towards the end proposed, Tytherton settlement continued till about thirty years ago, when the society, having grown both more numerous and more wealthy, built a new chapel and sister-house, and added to the former a neat residence for their pastor. Since that period, they have erected a large school-house, into which female children of every persuasion are received indiscriminately as boarders, for the purpose of instruction in morality and the elements of knowledge.

TYTHERTON-LUCAS, a chapelry in the parish and hundred of CHIPPENHAM, county of WILTS, 3¼ miles (N. E. by E.) from Chippenham. The population is returned with the parish. The chapel is dedicated to St. Nicholas.

TYTHERTON-STANLEY, a joint tything with Nethermore, in the parish and hundred of CHIPPENHAM, county of WILTS, 2 miles (E. by S.) from Chippenham, containing, with Nethermore, 195 inhabitants.

TYWARDRETH, a parish in the eastern division of the hundred of POWDER, county of CORNWALL, 3¾ miles (W. N. W.) from Fowey, containing 1238 inhabit-

ants. The living is a vicarage, in the archdeaconry of Cornwall, and diocese of Exeter, rated in the king's books at £ 9. 6. 8., endowed with £ 600 private benefaction, £ 600 royal bounty, and £ 2100 parliamentary grant, and in the patronage of W. Rashleigh, Esq. The church, dedicated to St. Andrew, has a richly-ornamented screen. A chapel has been erected by William Rashleigh, Esq., about half a mile from his seat, Menabilly House. There is a place of worship for Wesleyan Methodists. The parish is bounded on the south by the English channel, where, on Greber Head, is a signal station. The petty sessions for the eastern division of the hundred of Powder are held at this place, on the third Monday in every month. Here was a Benedictine priory, a cell to the monastery of St. Sergius and St. Bacchus in Normandy, supposed to have been founded before 1169, by Ricardus Dapifer, steward of the household to the Earl of Cornwall. This house, which was dedicated to St. Andrew, survived the suppression of Alien priories, and continued till the general dissolution, when its revenue was estimated at £ 151. 16. 1: the site is now occupied by a farm-house. There is an almshouse for four poor widows, founded by one of the Rashleigh family.

U.

UBBESTON, a parish in the hundred of BLYTHING, county of SUFFOLK, 5¾ miles (S. W. by W.) from Halesworth, containing 181 inhabitants. The living is a discharged vicarage, in the archdeaconry of Suffolk, and diocese of Norwich, rated in the king's books at £ 6. 13. 4., and in the patronage of Lord Huntingfield. The church is dedicated to St. Peter. The river Blyth rises in the vicinity, and runs through the parish.

UBLEY, or OBLEIGH, a parish in the hundred of CHEWTON, county of SOMERSET, 9 miles (N. by W.) from Wells, containing 393 inhabitants. The living is a discharged rectory, in the archdeaconry of Bath, and diocese of Bath and Wells, rated in the king's books at £ 11. 11. 5½., and in the patronage of the Crown. The church, dedicated to St. Bartholomew, has a tower surmounted by a spire. There is a place of worship for Wesleyan Methodists.

UCKERBY, a township in that part of the parish of CATTERICK which is in the eastern division of the wapentake of GILLING, North riding of the county of YORK, 3½ miles (N. by E.) from Catterick, containing 52 inhabitants.

UCKFIELD, a parish in the hundred of LOXFIELD-DORSET, rape of PEVENSEY, county of SUSSEX, 8 miles (N. E. by N.) from Lewes, containing 1099 inhabitants. The living is a perpetual curacy, annexed to the rectory of Buxted, in the peculiar jurisdiction of the Archbishop of Canterbury. The church, dedicated to the Holy Cross, is principally in the later style of English architecture. There is a place of worship for Baptists. The parish is bounded on the west by the river Ouze: in the neighbourhood are two powerful chalybeate springs. About a mile from the village, which is a well-built, respectable place, is a manufactory for raw and refuse silk. Fairs are held on May 14th and August 29th. Dorothy Ellis, in 1706, bequeathed £ 4. 10. a year, for the instruction of ten young children; and, in the same year, Dr. Anthony Saunders left a messuage, school-house, and land, in trust, for the establishment of a free grammar school for six boys of this parish, and six of Buxted; he also gave his library for the use of the school: the master receives £10 per annum, and the residue, amounting to £20 a year, is applied in apprenticing poor boys of Buxted. This school is now incorporated with a National school, supported by subscription, which affords instruction to about sixty children. In a house once occupied by Bishop Christopherson, confessor to Queen Mary, are massive rings and other vestiges of popery. Dr. Edward Clarke, the celebrated traveller, and librarian to the University of Cambridge, passed much of the early part of his life at Uckfield.

UCKINGTON, a chapelry in that part of the parish of ELMSTONE-HARDWICKE which is in the lower division of the hundred of DEERHURST, county of GLOUCESTER, 2¾ miles (N. W.) from Cheltenham, containing 179 inha-bitants.

UDIMORE, a parish in the hundred of GOSTROW, rape of HASTINGS, county of SUSSEX, 3½ miles (W. N. W.) from Winchelsea, containing 428 inhabitants. The living is a discharged vicarage, in the archdeaconry of Lewes, and diocese of Chichester, rated in the king's books at £8. 5. 2., endowed with £400 private bene-faction, £800 royal bounty, and £200 parliamentary grant, and in the patronage of Lord George Cavendish. The church, dedicated to St. Mary, is principally in the early style of English architecture. The parish is bounded on the south by Brede channel.

UFFCULME, a parish in the hundred of BAMPTON, county of DEVON, 4¾ miles (N. E.) from Cullompton, containing 1979 inhabitants. The living is a vicarage, in the peculiar jurisdiction and patronage of the Pre-bendary of Uffculme in the Cathedral Church of Salis-bury, rated in the king's books at £18. 0. 2½. The church, dedicated to St. Mary, has a rich wooden screen. There are places of worship for Baptists and Independ-ents. Uffculme is a decayed market town : fairs are still held on the Wednesday in Passion week, June 29th, and the middle Wednesday in September. During the last century, a great quantity of serges were made here, and there are still some flannels manufactured. The free grammar school was founded, in 1701, by Nicholas Ayshford, who gave £1200 for its erection and endow-ment, of which sum £400 was expended in building the school-house and master's residence. Two boys of Uffculme, and two of Burlescombe, or Holcombe-Ro-gus, are entitled to gratuitous education for the divi-dends arising from the residue, which amount to about £46 per annum. Bradfield Hall, in this parish, is a perfect ancient mansion, containing several curious apartments, and to which a chapel was formerly attached. On a common in the neighbourhood is a place called Pixy Garden, an ancient earthwork.

UFFINGTON, a parish in the hundred of SHRIVEN-HAM, county of BERKS, 4¼ miles (S. S. E.) from Great Farringdon, containing, with the chapelries of Baulking and Wolstone, 925 inhabitants. The living is a dis-charged vicarage, in the archdeaconry of Berks, and diocese of Salisbury, rated in the king's books at £21. J. A. Houblon, Esq. was patron in 1816. The church, dedicated to St. Mary, is a handsome cruciform struc-ture, in the early style of English architecture : the spire was destroyed by lightning, about 1750. The Wilts

and Berks canal passes through the parish. Thomas Saunders, in 1636, founded and endowed a free school for twelve boys of this parish, and six from Wolstone : the rents applied for its support amount to £41. 15. On White Horse hill, just above the village, is Uffington Castle, a large encampment, surrounded by a double vallum, the inner one very high : it is seven hun-dred feet from east to west, five hundred from north to south, and is supposed to be a work of the Britons, afterwards occupied by the Romans This hill has its name from the rude figure of a horse, three hundred and seventy-four feet in length, cut in the turf, near the summit, said to be commemorative of the victory which Alfred obtained over the Danes in this neighbour-hood, though some consider it a British work. Lands were formerly held here by cleaning, or rather cutting, away the turf, to render the figure more visible ; for which purpose a custom still prevails among the inhabit-ants of assembling to scour, as it is termed, the horse, on which occasion they are entertained by the lord of the manor, and spend the day in festivity. To the west-ward of Uffington Castle is a large tumulus, called Way-land-Smith, and there are various other tumuli scattered on these downs, particularly between Uffington and Lambourn, the most considerable of which are those called the Seven Barrows.

UFFINGTON, a parish in the wapentake of NESS, parts of KESTEVEN, county of LINCOLN, 2¼ miles (E. by N.) from Stamford, containing 466 inhabitants. The living is a rectory, in the archdeaconry and diocese of Lincoln, rated in the king's books at £21. 5. 2½., and in the patronage of the Earl of Lindsey. The church, dedicated to St. Michael, is a handsome structure, partly in the early and partly in the later style of En-glish architecture, with a fine tower and spire, and some fragments of ancient stained glass. An hospital, or priory, of Augustine canons, in honour of the Virgin Mary, was founded in the reign of Henry III., or his predecessor, by William de Albini, which at the dis-solution had a revenue of £42. 1. 3.

UFFINGTON, a parish in the Wellington division of the hundred of BRADFORD (South), county of SALOP, 3¼ miles (E. N. E.) from Shrewsbury, containing 139 inhabitants. The living is a perpetual curacy, in the archdeaconry of Salop, and diocese of Lichfield and Coventry, endowed with £20 per annum private bene-faction, and £600 royal bounty, and in the patronage of John Corbett, Esq. The church is dedicated to the Holy Trinity. The Shrewsbury canal passes through the parish.

UFFORD, a parish in the liberty of PETERBOROUGH, county of NORTHAMPTON, 4¼ miles (N. N. E.) from Wansford, containing, with the hamlet of Ashton, 279 inhabitants. The living is a rectory, in the archdea-conry of Northampton, and diocese of Peterborough, rated in the king's books at £26. 13. 4., and in the patronage of the Master and Fellows of St. John's College, Cambridge. The church is dedicated to St. Andrew. The river Welland runs through the parish, and the Roman road from the station at Castor, leading towards Lincoln, bounds it on the east.

UFFORD, a parish in the hundred of WILFORD, county of SUFFOLK, 2¼ miles (N. E.) from Woodbridge, containing 629 inhabitants. The living is a discharged rectory, in the archdeaconry of Suffolk, and diocese

2 Y 2

of Norwich, rated in the king's books at £8. 5., and in the patronage of the Rev. Charles Brooke. The church, dedicated to St. Mary, contains a curious font, which has been repaired at the expense of the Society of Antiquaries. Here was anciently a chapel, of which there are now no remains. The river Deben runs through the parish. An hospital for four poor men was founded by Thomas Wood, D.D., Bishop of Lichfield and Coventry, who endowed it with £30 per annum.

UFORD, a tything in the parish and hundred of CREDITON, county of DEVON, 3½ miles (W. by S.) from Crediton. The population is returned with the parish.

UFTON, a parish in the hundred of THEALE, county of BERKS, 7¼ miles (S. W. by W.) from Reading, containing 350 inhabitants. The living is a rectory, in the archdeaconry of Berks, and diocese of Salisbury, rated in the king's books at £11. 3. 1½., and in the patronage of the Provost and Fellows of Oriel College, Oxford. The church is dedicated to St. Peter. There are slight remains of a church, which formerly belonged to Upton-Greys, once a distinct parish, but consolidated with this in 1442.

UFTON, a parish in the Kenilworth division of the hundred of KNIGHTLOW, county of WARWICK, 2½ miles (W. by N.) from Southam, containing 154 inhabitants. The living is a perpetual curacy, in the peculiar jurisdiction and patronage of the Prebendary of Ufton in the Cathedral Church of Lichfield, endowed with £200 royal bounty, and £400 parliamentary grant. The church is dedicated to St. Michael.

UGBOROUGH, a parish in the hundred of ERMINGTON, county of DEVON, 3 miles (N. N. E.) from Modbury, containing 1429 inhabitants. The living is a discharged vicarage, in the archdeaconry of Totness, and diocese of Exeter, rated in the king's books at £20, endowed with £400 private benefaction, and £400 royal bounty, and in the patronage of the Master and Wardens of the Grocers' Company. The church contains a Norman font, and some remains of ancient screen-work. There was formerly a chapel at Earlscomb. A fair for cattle is held on the third Tuesday in every month. Sir John Kempthorn, a distinguished admiral, was born at Widescomb, in this parish, in 1620.

UGGESHALL, a parish in the hundred of BLYTHING, county of SUFFOLK, 4¾ miles (N.W.) from Southwold, containing 308 inhabitants. The living is a rectory, with that of Sotherton annexed, in the archdeaconry of Suffolk, and diocese of Norwich, rated in the king's books at £13. 6. 8., and in the patronage of J. Bedingfield, Esq. The church is dedicated to St. Mary.

UGGLEBARNBY, a chapelry in the parish of WHITBY, liberty of WHITBY-STRAND, North riding of the county of YORK, 4 miles (S. S. W.) from Whitby, containing 428 inhabitants. The living is a perpetual curacy, in the archdeaconry of Cleveland, and diocese of York, endowed with £1000 royal bounty, and in the patronage of the Archbishop of York. The chapel was built in 1137, by Nicholas, abbot of Whitby.

UGLEY, a parish in the hundred of CLAVERING, county of ESSEX, 3¼ miles (N.) from Stansted-Mountfitchet, containing 329 inhabitants. The living is a

discharged vicarage, in the jurisdiction of the Commissary of Essex and Herts, concurrently with the Consistorial Court of the Bishop of London, rated in the king's books at £14. 13. 4., endowed with £200 private benefaction, and £400 royal bounty, and in the patronage of the Governors of Christ's Hospital, London. The church is dedicated to St. Peter.

UGTHORPE, a township in the parish of LYTHE, eastern division of the liberty of LANGBAURGH, North riding of the county of YORK, 7½ miles (W.) from Whitby, containing 275 inhabitants. A Roman Catholic chapel was erected here about 1812.

ULCEBY, a parish in the Wold division of the hundred of CALCEWORTH, parts of LINDSEY, county of LINCOLN, 3½ miles (S.W.) from Alford, containing, with the hamlet of Forthington, 214 inhabitants. The living is a discharged rectory, in the archdeaconry and diocese of Lincoln, rated in the king's books at £9. 16. 8. John Robinson, Esq. was patron in 1803. The church is dedicated to All Saints. There is a place of worship for Wesleyan Methodists. The Bull's Head, a lofty hill in this parish, is a noted land-mark.

ULCEBY, a parish in the northern division of the wapentake of YARBOROUGH, parts of LINDSEY, county of LINCOLN, 7¼ miles (S. E.) from Barton upon Humber, containing 455 inhabitants. The living is a discharged vicarage, in the archdeaconry and diocese of Lincoln, rated in the king's books at £11. 18. 4., endowed with £400 royal bounty, and in the patronage of the Crown. The church is dedicated to St. Nicholas.

ULCOMBE, a parish in the hundred of EYHORNE, lathe of AYLESFORD, county of KENT, 7¼ miles (S. E. by E.) from Maidstone, containing 668 inhabitants. The living is a rectory, in the archdeaconry and diocese of Canterbury, rated in the king's books at £16. 5. 10., and in the patronage of the Hon. C. B. Clarke. The church, dedicated to All Saints, is principally in the later style of English architecture; it was formerly collegiate, for an archpresbyter, two canons, a deacon, and one clerk. The parish lies partly in the Weald, and is intersected by several small streams, which empty themselves into the Medway.

ULDALE, a parish in ALLERDALE ward below Darwent, county of CUMBERLAND, 2½ miles (S. S. E.) from Ireby, containing 343 inhabitants. The living is a rectory, in the archdeaconry and diocese of Carlisle, rated in the king's books at £17. 18. 1¾., and in the patronage of the Rev. Joseph Cape. The church was rebuilt by the parishioners in 1730. The river Ellen has its source here, in two small lakes, well stocked with various kinds of fish; about a mile and a half south-east from which, a brook, tumbling from a lofty mountain down several rocky precipices, forms a beautiful cascade, termed White Water Dash. Coal, freestone, limestone, and peat, abound here. A large fair for sheep, established in 1791, is held annually on August 29th. The free school was founded, in 1726, by Matthew Jaldbeck, who endowed it with £100, and the like sum having been raised by subscription, both were expended in the purchase of freehold property; which, with £350 bequeathed by Thomas Tomlinson, produces an annual income of about £47, applied to the education of from fifty to sixty children.

ULEY, a parish in the upper division of the hundred of BERKELEY, county of GLOUCESTER, 2½ miles

(E. by N.) from Dursley, containing 2655 inhabitants. The living is a rectory, in the archdeaconry and diocese of Gloucester, rated in the king's books at £12. 3. 4., and in the patronage of the Crown. The church is dedicated to St. Giles. There are places of worship for Baptists, Independents, and Wesleyan Methodists. The manufacture of woollen cloth is extensively carried on here. On an eminence, north-west of the village, is an ancient encampment, called Uley Bury, where various Roman coins have been found.

ULGHAM, a parochial chapelry in the eastern division of MORPETH ward, county of NORTHUMBERLAND, 5 miles (N. E. by N.) from Morpeth, containing 348 inhabitants. The living is a perpetual curacy, annexed to the rectory of Morpeth, in the archdeaconry of Northumberland, and diocese of Durham. The chapel is dedicated to St. John. Coal is found here, on the banks of the river Line. A market was formerly held, and the ancient market-cross still remains in the village.

ULLENHALL, a chapelry in the parish of WOOTTON-WAVEN, Henley division of the hundred of BARLICHWAY, county of WARWICK, 2¼ miles (N. W. by W.) from Henley in Arden, containing 352 inhabitants. The chapel is dedicated to St. Mary. William Mortiboys, in 1733, bequeathed a rent-charge of £2, for teaching six poor children.

ULLESKELF, a township in that part of the parish of KIRKBY-WHARFE which is within the liberty of St. PETER of YORK, East riding, though locally in the upper division of the wapentake of Barkstone-Ash, West riding, of the county of YORK, 4½ miles (S. E.) from Tadcaster, containing 426 inhabitants.

ULLESTHORPE, a hamlet in the parish of CLAYBROOKE, hundred of GUTHLAXTON, county of LEICESTER, 3¼ miles (N. W.) from Lutterworth, containing 598 inhabitants. There are places of worship for Baptists and Independents.

ULLEY, a township partly in the parish of ASTON, but chiefly in that of TREETON, southern division of the wapentake of STRAFFORTH and TICKHILL, West riding of the county of YORK, 4½ miles (S. E. by S.) from Rotherham, containing 203 inhabitants.

ULLINGSWICK, a parish in the hundred of BROXASH, county of HEREFORD, 5 miles (S. W.) from Bromyard, containing 254 inhabitants. The living is a rectory, with the perpetual curacy of Little Cowarne annexed, in the archdeaconry and diocese of Hereford, rated in the king's books at £9, and in the patronage of the Bishop of Hereford.

ULLOCK, a joint township with Pardsey and Dean-Scales, in the parish of DEAN, ALLERDALE ward above Darwent, county of CUMBERLAND, 5½ miles (S. W. by S.) from Cockermouth, containing, with Pardsey and Dean-Scales, 309 inhabitants.

ULNES-WALTON, a township in the parish of CROSTON, hundred of LEYLAND, county palatine of LANCASTER, 5¼ miles (W. by N.) from Chorley, containing 537 inhabitants.

ULPHA, a chapelry in the parish of MILLOM, ALLERDALE ward above Darwent, county of CUMBERLAND, 9 miles (E. by S.) from Ravenglass, containing 368 inhabitants. The living is a perpetual curacy, in the archdeaconry of Richmond, and diocese of Chester, endowed with £600 royal bounty, and £200

parliamentary grant, and in the patronage of the Vicar of Millom. The chapel is dedicated to St. John. There is a place of worship for Anabaptists. The chapelry extends along the western bank of the river Duddon to the mountains Hard Knot and Wrynose, where is a stone called three-shire stone, marking the boundaries of Cumberland, Lancaster, and Westmorland. A Roman road crosses both these mountains; and about half-way up the former are the remains of Hard Knot Castle, a fortress anciently of great importance, though the period of its erection is involved in obscurity. There are quarries of excellent blue slate, of which about one thousand four hundred tons are annually raised. Copper mines were formerly worked, and zinc is known to exist here. The coppices, with which this district abounds, produce a large supply of wood for making hoops and bobbins, the former being disposed of at Liverpool, and the latter to the manufacturers of cotton, woollen, linen, and silk in other towns. A fair for sheep is held on the first Monday in September, and there were formerly fairs for cloth and yarn, on the Monday before Easter and July 9th, but these are now only resorted to for pleasure. The hall, which bears marks of high antiquity, has been converted into a farm-house: adjoining it is a well, termed "Lady's Dub," where it is said a lady was surprised and killed by one of the wolves that anciently infested the neighbourhood.

ULPHA, a joint township with Methop, in the parish of BEETHAM, KENDAL ward, county of WESTMORLAND, 11 miles (S. S. W.) from Kendal. The population is returned with Methop. It is bounded on the south by the æstuary of the Kent.

ULROME, a chapelry partly in the parish of BARMSTON, but chiefly in that of SKIPSEA, northern division of the wapentake of HOLDERNESS, East riding of the county of YORK, 6¼ miles (N. N. W.) from Hornsea, containing 170 inhabitants. The living is a perpetual curacy, annexed to the rectory of Barmston, in the archdeaconry of the East riding, and diocese of York, rated in the king's books at £3. 19. 2., and endowed with £200 royal bounty. The chapel is very ancient.

ULTING, a parish in the hundred of WITHAM, county of ESSEX, 4½ miles (S. S. W.) from Witham, containing 175 inhabitants. The living is a discharged vicarage, in the archdeaconry of Colchester, and diocese of London, rated in the king's books at £7. 4. 2., endowed with £600 private benefaction, and £600 royal bounty, and in the patronage of R. Nicholson, Esq. The church is dedicated to All Saints. The parish is bounded on the south by the Chelmer and Blackwater navigation.

ULVERCROFT, an extra-parochial liberty, in the western division of the hundred of GOSCOTE, county of LEICESTER, 6 miles (W. by S.) from Mountsorrel, containing 87 inhabitants. At this place, in a deep sequestered valley of Charnwood forest, are the ruins of a church, anciently belonging to an Augustine priory, dedicated to the Blessed Virgin, which was founded by Robert Blanchmains, Earl of Leicester, in the reign of Henry II., and had, at the dissolution, a revenue of £101. 3. 10.

ULVERSTONE, a parish in the hundred of LONSDALE, north of the sands, county palatine of LANCASTER, comprising the market town of Ulverstone, the chapelries of Blawith, Church-Coniston, Egton *cum*

Torver, Lowick, and Satterthwaite, the townships of Newland and Osmotherley, and the extra-parochial district of Mansriggs, and containing 7102 inhabitants, of which number, 4315 are in the town of Ulverstone, 22 miles (N. W.) from Lancaster, and 271 (N.W. by N.) from London. This place derives its name (written in old records *Olvestonam*) from *Ulpha*, a Saxon lord; and was conferred, in 1127, on the abbey of Furness, by Stephen, afterwards King of England: it was afterwards granted to Gilbert, who had succeeded to the barony of Kendal, and who released the inhabitants from their state of feudalism, granting them a charter, which was augmented and confirmed by his successors. Subsequently it reverted to the crown; and being, in 1609, divided into moieties, it was eventually purchased, in 1736, by the Duke of Montague, for £490, and is at present vested in the Duke of Buccleuch. A charter was granted, by Edward I., for a market and an annual fair; but it continued to be merely nominal until the dissolution of the abbey of Furness, near Dalton, the capital of that district, from which event the prosperity of Ulverstone may be dated. The town is situated near the æstuary of the rivers Crake and Leven, and consists principally of four spacious streets; the houses are chiefly of stone. The inhabitants enjoy the advantages of a news-room and two subscription libraries; one of which is general, founded, in 1797, under the auspices of Thomas Sunderland, Esq., and contains three thousand volumes; the other clerical, instituted by the associates of Dr. Bray, and greatly augmented by the donations and exertions of the Rev. Dr. Stonard, the learned commentator on the Prophecies, and by the contributions of other members. The theatre and public rooms, erected by subscription in 1796, were considerably improved in 1828, and, during the hunt week in November, are genteelly attended. The peninsular situation of the town led to the appointment of mounted guides to direct travellers across the sands, who are paid by government, and directed to be there from sunrise to sunset, when the channel is fordable; but this arrangement has been partially superseded by the construction of a new road from Carnforth to Ulverstone, under an act of parliament.

The prevailing branches of manufacture are those of cotton, linen, check, canvas for sails, sacking, candlewicks, hats, axes, adzes, spades, hoes, and sickles. The chief articles of export, in addition to some of the above, are, iron-ore, of which twenty thousand tons were shipped in 1828; copper-ore; pig and bar iron, of the finest quality; the best blue and green slates, about ten thousand tons annually; and limestone, wool, grain, malt, butter, gunpowder, pyrolignous acid, leather, hoops, basket-rods, brush-sticks, baskets called swills, brooms, crate and wheel spoke wood, laths, and oak and larch poles: these are principally sent coastwise, the intercourse with foreign countries being limited. There is a yard for ship-building, and the aggregate registry of ships belonging to the place is nearly three thousand tons: two or three vessels are employed in the American timber trade; and from other ports a few belonging to this town are engaged in the West India trade. Ulverstone is a creek within the limits of the port of Lancaster, and, owing to this circumstance, it has, with the liberty of Furness, lately been released from the heavy duty on coal carried coastwise.

In 1793, an act of parliament was obtained for making a canal, by means of which, ships of four hundred tons' burden are safely moored in a capacious basin with extensive wharfs, and discharge their cargoes close to the town. The tonnage of vessels that entered inwards, for the year ending January 1829, was twenty thousand three hundred and eighty-six; and the tonnage of those cleared outwards, thirty-seven thousand four hundred and thirty-one. The market, granted to Roger de Lancaster, in the 8th of Edward I., is on Thursday: fairs are held on the Tuesday before Easter-Sunday, April 29th, Holy Thursday, October 7th, and the first Thursday after the 23rd of October. Manorial courts leet and baron are held on the Monday next after the 24th of October. The court baron for the liberty of Furness, for the recovery of debts under 40s., is held here every Saturday three weeks; and the baronial court for the manor of Bolton with Adgarley, annually: the petty sessions for the hundred of Lonsdale, north of the sands, are also held here.

Ulverstone anciently formed part of the parish of Dalton. The living is a perpetual curacy, in the archdeaconry of Richmond, and diocese of Chester, endowed with £200 private benefaction, and £200 royal bounty, and in the patronage of T. R. G. Braddyll, Esq. The church, on the south side of a hill, about a quarter of a mile from the town, is dedicated to St. Mary, and is of very ancient and obscure foundation; it was rebuilt in the time of Henry VIII., and again, with the exception of the tower and a Norman doorway, at the commencement of the present century. In the east window is some fine stained glass, the designs from Rubens; the altar-piece, representing the Descent from the Cross, with the three Cardinal graces, was designed by T. R. G. Braddyll, Esq., after the manner of Sir Joshua Reynolds: in the interior are several elegant and sumptuous monuments. The erection of a new church has been approved of by his Majesty's commissioners, to be dedicated to the Holy Trinity, and intended to contain six hundred free sittings. There are places of worship for Independents, Wesleyan Methodists, and Roman Catholics; and about a mile to the south-west is another for the Society of Friends (the first possessed by that community in England), built under the superintendence of George Fox, founder of the sect, who resided at Swartmoor Hall, in this neighbourhood. Townbank school was erected by subscription, and, having been endowed with various bequests, has an income of £35 per annum, for which eighty boys and twenty girls, who pay a small quarterage, are educated. A rent-charge of £1. 10., paid out of Swarthmoor Hall estate, was given by Thomas Fell, for which six boys are instructed. The school-rooms, of which the upper is appropriated to the classics, and the lower to instruction in English, writing, and arithmetic, were rebuilt about 1781. A Sunday school, containing about three hundred children, is supported by voluntary contributions. Conishead priory, in this parish, was founded by Gamel de Pennington, for Black canons, and at the dissolution its revenue was valued at £124. 2. 1.: the buildings were then dismantled, and the materials were sold for £333. 6. 3½., but some remains of the cemetery, pillars of the transept, and foundation walls of the church, with several skeletons, were discovered in 1823: the site is occupied by a modern edifice in the English style of architecture.

UNDERBARROW, a chapelry in that part of the parish of KENDAL which is in KENDAL ward, county of WESTMORLAND, 3¾ miles (W.) from Kendal, containing, with the hamlet of Bradley-field, 504 inhabitants. The living is a perpetual curacy, in the archdeaconry of Richmond, and diocese of Chester, endowed with £400 private benefaction, and £400 royal bounty, and in the patronage of the Landowners, by whom the chapel was rebuilt, in 1708.

UNDERMILBECK, a township in the parish of WINDERMERE, KENDAL ward, county of WESTMORLAND, 8 miles (W. by N.) from Kendal, containing, with the chapelry of Winster, 689 inhabitants. A school is supported by considerable annual subscriptions.

UNDER-SKIDDAW, a township in that part of the parish of CROSTHWAITE which is in ALLERDALE ward below Darwent, county of CUMBERLAND, 6 miles (N. N. W.) from Keswick, containing 487 inhabitants. There is a school at this place, free to the parishioners of Crosthwaite, supported by sundry donations amounting to more than £100 a year.

UNDERWOOD, a joint liberty with Offcoat, in that part of the parish of ASHBOURN which is in the hundred of WIRKSWORTH, county of DERBY. The population is returned with Offcoat.

UNDY, a parish in the lower division of the hundred of CALDICOTT, county of MONMOUTH, 7 miles (E. by S.) from Newport, containing 280 inhabitants. The living is a discharged vicarage, in the archdeaconry and diocese of Llandaff, rated in the king's books at £4. 10. 7½., endowed with £600 royal bounty, and £200 parliamentary grant, and in the patronage of the Chapter of Llandaff.

UNERIGG, a joint township with Ellenborough, in the parish of DEARHAM, ALLERDALE ward below Darwent, county of CUMBERLAND, 1½ mile (S.E.) from Maryport. The population is returned with Ellenborough. A school was founded and endowed, in 1718, by Ewan Christian and others, with about £30 per annum.

UNSTONE, a township in the parish of DRONFIELD, hundred of SCARSDALE, county of DERBY, 4 miles (N. by W.) from Chesterfield, containing 574 inhabitants.

UNSWORTH, a chapelry in the parish of OLDHAM cum PRESTWICH, hundred of SALFORD, county palatine of LANCASTER, 3 miles (S.S.E.) from Bury. The population is returned with the parish. The living is a perpetual curacy, in the archdeaconry and diocese of Chester, endowed with £200 private benefaction, £600 royal bounty, and £1000 parliamentary grant, and in the patronage of the Rector of Prestwich. The chapel, dedicated to St. George, was consecrated in 1730. James Lancaster, in 1737, bequeathed certain property, now producing £12. 12. per annum, for teaching ten poor children.

UNTHANK, a township in the parish of SKELTON, LEATH ward, county of CUMBERLAND, 5½ miles (N.W.) from Penrith, containing 252 inhabitants.

UNTHANK, a township in the parish of ALNHAM, northern division of COQUETDALE ward, county of NORTHUMBERLAND, 8¼ miles (N. N. E.) from Rothbury, containing 21 inhabitants.

UPCHURCH, a parish in the hundred of MILTON, lathe of SCRAY, county of KENT, 5½ miles (E. by S.) from Chatham, containing 414 inhabitants. The living is a vicarage, in the archdeaconry and diocese of Canterbury, rated in the king's books at £11, and in the patronage of the Warden and Fellows of All Souls' College, Oxford. The church, dedicated to St. Mary, is a handsome structure, partly in the decorated, and partly in the later style, of English architecture; with a lofty spire, noted as a land-mark, and some remains of stained glass. The parish is bounded on the north by the Medway, where is Otterham creek and quay, at which corn produced in the neighbourhood is shipped for exportation. By the survey made in the reign of Elizabeth, it appears that twelve vessels belonged to this place.

UP-EXE, a tything in that part of the parish of REWE which is in the hundred of HAYRIDGE, county of DEVON, 6 miles (S.W. by W.) from Cullompton, containing 92 inhabitants.

UPHAM, a parish in that part of the hundred of BISHOP'S WALTHAM which is in the Portsdown division of the county of SOUTHAMPTON, 2¾ miles (N. W. by N.) from Bishop's Waltham, containing 493 inhabitants. The living is a rectory, in the peculiar jurisdiction of the Incumbent, rated in the king's books at £11. 2. 1., and in the patronage of the Bishop of Winchester. Upham is within the jurisdiction of the Cheyney Court held at Winchester, for the recovery of debts to any amount. Dr. Edward Young, author of the "Night Thoughts," whose father was rector of this parish, was born here in 1681; he died in 1707.

UPHAVEN, a parish in the hundred of SWANBOROUGH, county of WILTS, 4 miles (S. W. by S.) from Pewsey, containing 464 inhabitants. The living is a discharged vicarage, in the archdeaconry and diocese of Salisbury, rated in the king's books at £7. 16. 8., and in the patronage of the Crown. The church is dedicated to St. Mary. There is a place of worship for Particular Baptists. A market was granted by Henry III. to Peter de Mauley; and, in the reign of Edward I., Hugh de Spencer procured a charter of free warren and two annual fairs, one of which, as well as the market, is discontinued. A Benedictine priory, a cell to the abbey of Fontanelle in Normandy, was founded here about the commencement of the reign of Henry I., and, at its suppression, was granted by Henry VI. to the monastery of Ivy-Church, in exchange for lands, &c., in Clarendon park.

UPHILL, a parish in the hundred of WINTERSTOKE, county of SOMERSET, 8 miles (N. W. by W.) from Axbridge, containing 270 inhabitants. The living is a discharged rectory, in the archdeaconry of Wells, and diocese of Bath and Wells, rated in the king's books at £11. 7., and in the patronage of John Fisher, Esq. The church, dedicated to St. Nicholas, has a central tower, and occupies the summit of a lofty eminence south of the village. There is a place of worship for Baptists. The river Ax bounds the parish on the south, and falls into the Bristol channel at the village, the proximity of which to Weston-Super-Mare (of late become a fashionable bathing place) has induced capitalists to purchase a considerable portion of land in the neighbourhood, with a view to erect houses upon it Fuel is very abundant and cheap here. A cave was discovered a few years ago, similar to those in the same ridge of hills at Burrington and Banwell.

UP-HOLLAND, county palatine of LANCASTER.—See HOLLAND (UP).

UPLEADON, a parish in the hundred of BOTLOE, county of GLOUCESTER, 3¼ miles (E. by N.) from Newent, containing 182 inhabitants. The living is a perpetual curacy, in the archdeaconry of Hereford, and diocese of Gloucester, endowed with £300 private benefaction, and £200 royal bounty, and in the patronage of the Bishop of Gloucester. The church, dedicated to St. Mary, has a Norman entrance on the north side. The river Leadon runs through the parish.

UPLEATHAM, a parish in the eastern division of the liberty of LANGBAURGH, North riding of the county of YORK, 3¼ miles (N. E. by N.) from Guilsbrough, containing 239 inhabitants. The living is a perpetual curacy, annexed to that of Guilsbrough, in the archdeaconry of Cleveland, and diocese of York, endowed with £200 private benefaction, and £800 royal bounty. The chapel is small and ancient. There is a place of worship for Wesleyan Methodists. From the village, which is pleasantly situated on a declivity, there is a fine prospect of Skelton castle and the rich vale below.

UPLOWMAN, a parish partly in the hundred of HALBERTON, but chiefly in that of TIVERTON, county of DEVON, 4¾ miles (E. N. E.) from Tiverton, containing 425 inhabitants. The living is a rectory, in the archdeaconry and diocese of Exeter, rated in the king's books at £21. 0. 10. John Sillifant and T. Hugo, Esqrs. were patrons in 1822. The church is dedicated to St. Peter. The river Lowman runs through the parish.

UPLYME, a parish in the hundred of AXMINSTER, county of DEVON, 1¼ mile (N. W.) from Lyme-Regis, containing 848 inhabitants. The living is a rectory, in the archdeaconry and diocese of Exeter, rated in the king's books at £20. 8. 11½., and in the patronage of the Rev. H. T. Tucker. The church, dedicated to St. Peter and St. Paul, has lately received an addition of one hundred free sittings, the Incorporated Society for the enlargement of churches and chapels having granted £45 towards defraying the expense. In this parish are extensive beds of blue and white lias, replete with organic marine remains, and applicable to building, paving, or burning into lime.

UPMINSTER, a parish in the hundred of CHAFFORD, county of ESSEX, 4 miles (E. S. E.) from Romford, containing 952 inhabitants. The living is a rectory, in the archdeaconry of Essex, and diocese of London, rated in the king's books at £26. 13. 4, and in the patronage of W. Holden, Esq. The church is dedicated to St. Lawrence. There is a place of worship for Independents. In the neighbourhood are many genteel residences : here is also a mineral spring. Dr. Derham, author of "Physico-Theology," &c., was rector of the parish from 1689 to 1735.

UP-OTTERY, a parish in the hundred of AXMINSTER, county of DEVON, 5¼ miles (N.E. by N.) from Honiton, containing 886 inhabitants. The living is a vicarage, in the archdeaconry and diocese of Exeter, rated in the king's books at £15. 5. 7½., and in the patronage of the Dean and Chapter of Exeter. The church, dedicated to St. Mary, has lately received an addition of one hundred and fifty sittings, of which one hundred are free, the Incorporated Society for the enlargement of churches and chapels having granted £100 towards defraying the expense. There are places of worship for Baptists and Calvinistic Methodists. Fairs for cattle are held here on March 17th and October 24th. There

was a chapel at Roridge, in this parish, at an early period.

UPPERBY, a township in that part of the parish of ST. CUTHBERT, CARLISLE, which is in CUMBERLAND ward, county of CUMBERLAND, 1¾ mile (S. E. by S.) from Carlisle, containing 340 inhabitants, who are chiefly employed in the manufacture of linen.

UPPINGHAM, a market town and parish in the hundred of MARTINSLEY, county of RUTLAND, 6 miles (S.) from Oakham, and 89 (N. N. W.) from London, containing 1630 inhabitants. This town, the name of which is descriptive of its elevated situation, consists chiefly of one street, with a square area in the centre, tolerably well paved, and the houses commodious and well-built. The market, granted by Edward I., in 1280, to Peter de Montfort, is held on Wednesday; and fairs are on March 7th and July 7th, chiefly for horses, horned cattle, sheep, and coarse linen cloth. By statute of the 11th of Henry VII., the standard of weights and measures for the county is kept here. The living is a rectory, in the archdeaconry of Northampton, and diocese of Peterborough, rated in the king's books at £20. 0. 10., and in the patronage of the Bishop of London. The church, dedicated to St. Peter and St. Paul, stands on the southern side of the square; it is a spacious edifice, in the ancient style of English architecture, with a lofty spire, and contains several monuments. There are places of worship for Independents and Wesleyan Methodists. A free grammar school, and an hospital for poor men, adjoining the churchyard, were founded, in 1584, by the Rev. Robert Johnson, Archdeacon of Leicester: these institutions are precisely similar to those at Oakham (which see), the number of scholars varying occasionally at each place. At this school Dr. Charles Manners Sutton, late Archbishop of Canterbury; Lord Manners, late Chancellor of Ireland; Henry Ferne, D.D., Bishop of Chester; and various other eminent persons, were educated. A National school is supported by voluntary contributions.

UPPINGTON, a parish in the Wellington division of the hundred of BRADFORD (South), county of SALOP, 3½ miles (W. S. W.) from Wellington, containing 111 inhabitants. The living is a perpetual curacy, in the archdeaconry of Salop, and diocese of Lichfield and Coventry, and in the patronage of — Kynaston, Esq. The church is dedicated to the Holy Trinity.

UPSALL, a township in the parish of SOUTH KILVINGTON, wapentake of BIRDFORTH, North riding of the county of YORK, 3¼ miles (N.N.E.) from Thirsk, containing 118 inhabitants. There are some remains of a castle of the Mowbrays, which subsequently became the residence of the Scroops.

UPSALL, a township in that part of the parish of ORMSBY which is in the eastern division of the liberty of LANGBAURGH, North riding of the county of YORK, 3 miles (W.) from Guilsbrough, containing 16 inhabitants.

UPSHIRE, a hamlet in the parish of WALTHAM-ABBEY, or HOLY-CROSS, hundred of WALTHAM, county of ESSEX, containing 739 inhabitants. There is a place of worship for Wesleyan Methodists.

UPSLAND, a joint township with Kirklington, in the parish of KIRKLINGTON, wapentake of HALLIKELD, North riding of the county of YORK. The population is returned with Kirklington.

UPTON, a chapelry in that part of the parish of BLEWBERRY which is in the hundred of MORETON, county of BERKS, 4¾ miles (N. N. E.) from East Ilsley, containing, with the liberty of Nottingham-Fee, 215 inhabitants. It is within the peculiar jurisdiction of the Dean of Salisbury.

UPTON, a parish in the hundred of STOKE, county of BUCKINGHAM, ½ a mile (S. E.) from Slough, containing, with the hamlet of Chalvey, and a portion of the town of Slough, which is in this parish, 1268 inhabitants. The living is a discharged vicarage, in the archdeaconry of Buckingham, and diocese of Lincoln, rated in the king's books at £6. 17., endowed with £8 per annum private benefaction, and £200 royal bounty, and in the patronage of the Crown. The church, dedicated to St. Lawrence, has a fine Norman doorway, and is principally in that style of architecture.

UPTON, a township in that part of the parish of ST. MARY, CHESTER, which is in the lower division of the hundred of BROXTON, county palatine of CHESTER, 2¼ miles (N.) from Chester, containing 206 inhabitants.

UPTON, a township in the parish of PRESTBURY, hundred of MACCLESFIELD, county palatine of CHESTER, 1½ mile (N. W.) from Macclesfield, containing 52 inhabitants.

UPTON, or OVER-CHURCH, a parish in the lower division of the hundred of WIRRALL, county palatine of CHESTER, 7¾ miles (N. by W.) from Great Neston, containing 183 inhabitants. The living is a perpetual curacy, in the archdeaconry and diocese of Chester, endowed with £600 royal bounty, and £200 parliamentary grant, and in the patronage of J. Feilden, Esq. At Upton (from which the parish church, called Over-Church, is distant half a mile) a market was held so late as 1662: there are still two fairs for cattle. A court leet is held annually by the lord of the manor. A free school here is conducted on the Madras system.

UPTON, a tything in the parish of HAWKESBURY, upper division of the hundred of GRUMBALD'S ASH, county of GLOUCESTER, containing 548 inhabitants. There is a place of worship for Wesleyan Methodists.

UPTON, a parish in the hundred of LEIGHTONSTONE, county of HUNTINGDON, 6½ miles (N. W.) from Huntingdon, containing 151 inhabitants. The living is a rectory, consolidated with that of Coppingford, in the archdeaconry of Huntingdon, and diocese of Lincoln. The church, dedicated to St. Margaret, is partly in the early style of English architecture, with a curious ancient font.

UPTON, a township in the parish of SIBSON, hundred of SPARKENHOE, county of LEICESTER, 3¾ miles (S. W.) from Market-Bosworth, containing 141 inhabitants. Here was formerly a chapel, now in ruins.

UPTON, a parish in the hundred of WELL, parts of LINDSEY, county of LINCOLN, 5 miles (S. E. by E.) from Gainsborough, containing, with the township of Kexby, 392 inhabitants. The living is a discharged vicarage, in the archdeaconry of Stow, and diocese of Lincoln, rated in the king's books at £7. 4. 2., and in the patronage of Sir. W. A. Ingilby, Bart. The church is dedicated to All Saints. There is a place of worship for Wesleyan Methodists.

UPTON, a parish in the hundred of WALSHAM, county of NORFOLK, 1¾ mile (N.) from Acle, containing, with the parish of Fishley, 465 inhabitants. The living is a discharged vicarage, annexed to that of Ranworth, in the archdeaconry and diocese of Norwich, rated in the king's books at £5. The church is dedicated to St. Margaret.

UPTON, a parish in the hundred of NOBOTTLE-GROVE, county of NORTHAMPTON, 2 miles (W.) from Northampton, containing 45 inhabitants. The living is a perpetual curacy, annexed to the rectory of St. Peter's, Northampton, in the archdeaconry of Northampton, and diocese of Peterborough. The church is dedicated to St. Michael. The parish is bounded on the west by the river Nen. Here are still the remains of a castle founded by Simon de St. Liz. James Harrington, an eminent political writer in the time of the Commonwealth, was born at Upton Hall, in 1611.

UPTON, a chapelry in the parish of CASTOR, liberty of PETERBOROUGH, county of NORTHAMPTON, 2¼ miles (E. N. E.) from Wansford, containing 103 inhabitants. The chapel is dedicated to St. John the Baptist. In the neighbourhood is a quarry of very fine stone, resembling that at Ketton.

UPTON, a parish in that part of the liberty of SOUTHWELL and SCROOBY which separates the northern from the southern division of the wapentake of THURGARTON, county of NOTTINGHAM, 2¾ miles (E.) from Southwell, containing 432 inhabitants. The living is a discharged vicarage, in the peculiar jurisdiction and patronage of the Chapter of the Collegiate Church of Southwell, rated in the king's books at £4. 11. 5½. The church, dedicated to St. Peter, is endowed with lands, of the annual value of £20, for keeping it in repair, the surplus to be given to poor soldiers travelling through the place. Here is a considerable manufactory for starch.

UPTON, a joint hamlet with Signet, in the parish of BURFORD, hundred of BAMPTON, county of OXFORD, 1¼ mile (W.) from Burford, containing, with Signet, 277 inhabitants.

UPTON, a parish in the hundred of WILLITON and FREEMANNERS, county of SOMERSET, 4¼ miles (E. by N.) from Dulverton, containing 297 inhabitants. The living is a perpetual curacy, in the archdeaconry of Taunton, and diocese of Bath and Wells, endowed with £200 private benefaction, and £1000 royal bounty, and in the patronage of T. Hellings, Esq. The church is dedicated to St. James.

UPTON, a township in the parish of RATLEY, Burton-Dassett division of the hundred of KINGTON, county of WARWICK, 4 miles (S. E. by S.) from Kington. The population is returned with the parish.

UPTON, a township in the parish of BADSWORTH, upper division of the wapentake of OSGOLDCROSS, West riding of the county of YORK, 6¼ miles (S. by E.) from Pontefract, containing 184 inhabitants. There are limeworks in the neighbourhood.

UPTON (BISHOP'S), a parish in the hundred of GREYTREE, county of HEREFORD, 4 miles (N. E. by E.) from Ross, containing 613 inhabitants. The living is a vicarage, in the archdeaconry and diocese of Hereford, rated in the king's books at £8. 17. 6., endowed with £300 private benefaction, and in the patronage of the Dean and Chapter of Hereford. The church is dedicated to St John the Baptist. Here is a charity school.

UPTON (ST. LEONARD'S), a parish in the middle division of the hundred of DUDSTONE and KING'S BARTON, county of GLOUCESTER, 3¼ miles (S. E. by S.) from Gloucester, containing 895 inhabitants. The living is a perpetual curacy, in the archdeaconry and diocese of Gloucester, endowed with £400 royal bounty, and £1400 parliamentary grant, and in the patronage of the Bishop of Gloucester. The church is principally Norman, but the tower and some minor parts are in the later style of English architecture.

UPTON (MAGNA), a parish in the Wellington division of the hundred of BRADFORD (South), county of SALOP, 5¼ miles (E.) from Shrewsbury, containing, with the extra-parochial liberty of Haughmond Demesne, 667 inhabitants. The living is a rectory, in the archdeaconry of Salop, and diocese of Lichfield and Coventry, rated in the king's books at £12. The Rev. Corbet Browne was patron in 1808. The church is dedicated to St. Lucia. The Shrewsbury canal passes through the parish.

UPTON upon SEVERN, a market town and parish in the lower division of the hundred of PERSHORE, county of WORCESTER, 10 miles (S.) from Worcester, and 109 (N.W. by W.) from London, containing 2319 inhabitants. According to Dr. Stukeley, this was the *Upoessa* of Ravennas; and the opinion that it was once a Roman station has received confirmation from the discovery of some ancient armour in the neighbourhood. A bridge, consisting of six arches, was erected, pursuant to act of parliament, in the reign of James I., which was broken down, and a battery placed in the churchyard, to prevent the approach of Cromwell and his forces; but the plan was ineffectual, and the parliamentary forces entered the town. Upton is situated on the right bank of the river Severn, which is here navigable for vessels of one hundred tons' burden, and is crossed by a bridge erected in 1606: it is neatly built, and the streets are well paved. There is a subscription library. The surrounding country is in a state of high cultivation, and the prospects are varied and picturesque. A considerable quantity of cider, brought from Hereford and other places, is shipped here for conveyance to different parts of England: there is a harbour for barges, and a wharf on the river, for the convenience of loading and discharging. The market is on Thursday : a plan for the erection of a handsome market-house, to include an assembly-room and apartments for the meetings of the magistrates, has been agreed upon, and the subscription for defraying the expense of its erection nearly completed; an act will be applied for this present session of parliament (1831), soon after which the building will be commenced. Fairs are held April 2nd, June 2nd, July 10th, and the Thursday before the 2nd of October. A manorial court is held occasionally, and petty sessions once a fortnight.

The living is a rectory, in the archdeaconry and diocese of Worcester, rated in the king's books at £27, and in the patronage of the Bishop of Worcester. The church, which is dedicated to St. Peter and St. Paul, is a handsome structure, completed in 1758 : the ancient tower was once surmounted by a spire, which, from an apprehension of insecurity, was taken down, and a wooden cupola substituted. There is a place of worship for Baptists. A charity school for instructing fifteen girls was endowed, in 1718, by Richard and Anne Smith,

with property of the present value of £28 per annum, which was augmented by a bequest of £5 per annum, in 1824, from Miss Sarah Husband : a boys' school was added to it, in 1797, by means of a bequest from George King, of property secured in the purchase of £100 three per cents., and £100 four per cent. consols.; and these are now incorporated into two National schools, which are further supported by voluntary contributions : about one hundred and sixty children are educated. Dr. John Dee, a celebrated astrologer in the reign of Elizabeth, was a native of this town : the Rev. J. Davison, B. D., author of some highly-esteemed theological works, is the present incumbent.

UPTON-CRESSETT, a parish in the hundred of STOTTESDEN, county of SALOP, 5 miles (W. by S.) from Bridgenorth, containing 69 inhabitants. The living is a discharged rectory, in the archdeaconry of Salop, and diocese of Hereford, rated in the king's books at £4. 15. 2½., and in the patronage of Miss Cressett. The church is dedicated to St. Michael.

UPTON-GRAY, a parish in the hundred of BERMONDSPIT, Basingstoke division of the county of SOUTHAMPTON, 4 miles (W. S. W.) from Odiham, containing, with the tything of Hoddington, 388 inhabitants. The living is a perpetual curacy, in the archdeaconry and diocese of Winchester, and in the patronage of the Provost and Fellows of Queen's College, Oxford.

UPTON-HILLIONS, a parish in the western division of the hundred of BUDLEIGH, county of DEVON, 2½ miles (N. N. E.) from Crediton, containing 168 inhabitants. The living is a rectory, in the archdeaconry and diocese of Exeter, rated in the king's books at £10. 6. 8., and in the patronage of the Wellington family. The church is dedicated to St. Mary.

UPTON-LOVELL, a parish in the hundred of HEYTESBURY, county of WILTS, 2 miles (S. E. by E.) from Heytesbury, containing 230 inhabitants. The living is a rectory, in the archdeaconry and diocese of Salisbury, rated in the king's books at £17. 18. 11½., and in the patronage of the Crown. On Upton-Lovell down, about two miles north of Heytesbury, is a single intrenchment, called Knook Castle, including about two acres. On the summit of a hill, to the north-west of Elder-Valley, is a large tumulus, called Bowls Barrow, measuring one hundred and fifty feet in length, ninety-four in breadth, and ten and a half in height, which has been found to contain fourteen human skeletons. There is also, in the neighbourhood of Knook Castle, and near the north bank of the Wily, another large barrow, which, from the number of gold ornaments discovered in it, has been called Golden Barrow.

UPTON-NOBLE, a parish in the hundred of BRUTON, county of SOMERSET, 4 miles (N. N. E.) from Bruton, containing 285 inhabitants. The living is a perpetual curacy, annexed to the rectory of Batcombe, in the archdeaconry of Wells, and diocese of Bath and Wells. There is a place of worship for Wesleyan Methodists.

UPTON-PYNE, a parish in the hundred of WONFORD, county of DEVON, 3½ miles (N. by W.) from Exeter, containing 431 inhabitants. The living is a rectory, in the archdeaconry and diocese of Exeter, rated in the king's books at £23. 6. 8., and in the patronage of Sir S. H. Northcote, Bart. The church contains a good painting of the Last Supper. The river Exe bounds the parish on the south. About £10 per annum, the gift of Thomas Weare, is applied to the education of poor children.

UPTON-SCUDAMORE, a parish in the hundred of WARMINSTER, county of WILTS, 2 miles (N.) from Warminster, containing 343 inhabitants. The living is a rectory, in the archdeaconry and diocese of Salisbury, rated in the king's books at £16. 7. 1., and in the patronage of the Provost and Fellows of Queen's College, Oxford. The church is dedicated to St. Mary.

UPTON-SNODSBURY, a parish in the upper division of the hundred of PERSHORE, county of WORCESTER, 6½ miles (E. by S.) from Worcester, containing 291 inhabitants. The living is a discharged vicarage, in the archdeaconry and diocese of Worcester, rated in the king's books at £8, and in the patronage of the Rev. Henry Green. The church is dedicated to St. Kenelme.

UPTON-WARREN, a parish in the upper division of the hundred of HALFSHIRE, county of WORCESTER, 3½ miles (N.E. by N.) from Droitwich, containing 463 inhabitants. The living is a rectory, in the archdeaconry and diocese of Worcester, rated in the king's books at £11. 2. 3½., and in the patronage of the Earl of Shrewsbury. The church, dedicated to St. Michael, has been partly rebuilt, and the interior is neatly fitted up. A school here is endowed with the rent of certain land in the parish of Bromsgrove, left many years since for that purpose: a house for the master and a school-room are given by the Earl of Shrewsbury, at a nominal rent. There is also an annuity of £10, bequeathed by a person named Saunders, to be paid by the Grocers' Company, for apprenticing, in London, a boy born of poor parents of this parish.

UPTON-WATERS, a parish in the Wellington division of the hundred of BRADFORD (South), county of SALOP, 5½ miles (N. by W.) from Wellington, containing 165 inhabitants. The living is a discharged rectory, in the archdeaconry of Salop, and diocese of Lichfield and Coventry, rated in the king's books at £3. 17. 3½., and in the patronage of the Crown. The church is dedicated to St. Michael.

UP-WALTHAM, county of SUSSEX. — See WALTHAM (UP).

UPWAY, a parish in the liberty of WAYHOUSE, Dorchester division of the county of DORSET, 4½ miles (S. W. by S.) from Dorchester, containing 485 inhabitants. The living is a rectory, in the archdeaconry of Dorset, and diocese of Bristol, rated in the king's books at £18. 3. 1½., and in the patronage of the Bishop of Salisbury. The church, dedicated to St. Lawrence, has an embattled tower crowned with pinnacles. Near it, from the foot of a steep hill, rises the small river Way, which runs through the parish, and falls into the sea at Weymouth. On Ridgway down are numerous barrows, extending from that part of the ridge opposite Sutton-Pointz to beyond Longbridy, a distance of nearly six miles, in a direction parallel to the *Via Iceniana*. In the neighbourhood are extensive quarries of flag-stone and tile-stone.

UPWELL, a parish partly in the hundred of WISBEACH, Isle of ELY, county of CAMBRIDGE, and partly in the hundred of CLACKCLOSE, county of NORFOLK, 5¾ miles (S. E. by S.) from Wisbeach, containing, with the chapelry of Welney, 3782 inhabitants. The living is a rectory, in the archdeaconry of Norfolk, and diocese of Norwich, rated in the king's books at £16. R. G. Townley, Esq. was patron in 1812. The church, dedicated to St. Peter, with the greater part of the parish, is in Norfolk. There is a place of worship for Wesleyan Methodists. The village is intersected by the river Nene, by which the productions of the large garden-grounds here are conveyed to the markets of the various towns situated upon its banks. In that part of the parish which is in Cambridgeshire are the sites of two ancient religious houses, one of which, at Mirmound, was a small priory of Gilbertines, dedicated to the Blessed Virgin Mary, a cell to the priory of Sempringham in Lincolnshire, and valued at the dissolution at £13. 6. 1. per annum.

UPWOOD, a parish in the hundred of HURSTINGSTONE, county of HUNTINGDON, 2¾ miles (S.W. by W.) from Ramsey, containing 388 inhabitants. The living is a perpetual curacy, annexed to that of Great Raveley, in the archdeaconry of Huntingdon, and diocese of Lincoln, endowed with £1400 parliamentary grant. The church is dedicated to St. Peter.

URCHFONT, a parish in the hundred of SWANBOROUGH, county of WILTS, 2¾ miles (N. E.) from East Lavington, containing, with the tythings of Eastcott and Wedhampton, 1294 inhabitants. The living is a discharged vicarage, with the perpetual curacy of Stert annexed, in the archdeaconry and diocese of Salisbury, rated in the king's books at £15. 15. 10., and in the patronage of the Dean and Canons of Windsor. The church is dedicated to St. Michael.

URMSTON, a township in the parish of FLIXTON, hundred of SALFORD, county palatine of LANCASTER, 5½ miles (S. W. by W.) from Manchester, containing 645 inhabitants. John Collier, commonly called Tim Bobbin, the author of the "Lancashire Dialect," was born here. Ten poor children are taught to read for £5 a year, left by Richard Newton, in 1800.

URPETH, a township in that part of the parish of CHESTER le STREET which is in the middle division of CHESTER ward, county palatine of DURHAM, 9 miles (N. by W.) from Durham, containing 650 inhabitants, who are mostly employed in the extensive coal mines adjacent.

URSWICK, a parish in the hundred of LONSDALE, north of the sands, county palatine of LANCASTER, 3 miles (S. W.) from Ulverstone, containing, with the townships of Adgarley, Bardsea, Bolton, and Stainon, 787 inhabitants. The living is a discharged vicarage, in the archdeaconry of Richmond, and diocese of Chester, rated in the king's books at £7. 17. 6., endowed with £200 royal bounty, and £1200 parliamentary grant, and in the patronage of the Parishioners. The church, dedicated to St. Michael, which was re-pewed in 1826, is situated near a deep circular lake, half a mile in diameter. At Bolton are the remains of an ancient chapel, near which, Roman coins and a brass vessel upon three feet have been found. The grammar school was founded, in 1580, by William Marshall, who endowed it with a rent-charge of £15, for which forty boys are instructed.

USHLAWREOED, a hamlet in the parish of BEDWELTY, lower division of the hundred of WENTLLOOG, county of MONMOUTH, containing 3640 inhabitants.

USK, a market town and parish, partly in the lower, but chiefly in the upper, division of the hundred of Usk, county of Monmouth, 13 miles (S. W.) from Monmouth, and 144 (W. by N.) from London, containing, with the hamlets of Glascoed and Gwehellog, 1539 inhabitants. This place, which is of remote antiquity, is generally admitted by antiquaries to have been the *Burrium* of the Romans : it derives its name from the Gaelic *Ysc*, signifying water. The ancient castle, erected on an eminence overlooking the town, experienced repeated assaults during the wars between the Welch chieftains and the Anglo-Norman lords, especially in the time of the celebrated Owen Glyndwr; and, in the civil commotions in the reign of Charles I., it was, with the town, partly demolished by the parliamentary forces. The town is agreeably situated on the river Usk, which is crossed by a stone bridge, and consists of several streets, composed of detached houses, with intervening gardens and orchards. Some of the inhabitants are engaged in husbandry, and others in the salmon-fishery; and there is a small manufactory for Pont-y-pool ware. The market is on Friday, and a cattle market is held on the first Monday in each month. Fairs are, April 20th, a large one for wool; June 20th; October 29th ; and on the Monday before Christmas-day. The town is governed by a corporation, consisting of a portreeve, recorder, and burgesses, assisted by four constables: the portreeve is elected from among the burgesses, who are chosen by the recorder; and the constables are appointed at a borough-leet, held annually : on retiring, the portreeve becomes an alderman. The portreeve possesses magisterial authority, the county magistrates having concurrent jurisdiction. The quarter sessions for the county, and the petty sessions for the division, are held here ; also a court leet once a fortnight, at which the portreeve and recorder preside. The town hall is a handsome edifice over the market-place, built at the expense of the Duke of Beaufort. The prison has been enlarged, and a tread-mill erected, by the county, at an expense of about £600. This borough returns one member to parliament, who is elected by the burgesses of Usk, conjointly with those of Monmouth and Newport; the number of voters is unlimited.

The living is a discharged vicarage, in the archdeaconry and diocese of Llandaff, rated in the king's books at £10. 10., endowed with £200 royal bounty, and in the patronage of William Addams Williams, Esq. The church, which is dedicated to St. Mary, and was formerly conventual, appears to be of Anglo-Norman origin, and was originally cruciform, but has undergone numerous alterations: it contains several ancient monuments, and a modern one, erected, in 1822, to commemorate the extended benevolence of Mr. Roger Edwards, the founder of the grammar school. There are places of worship for Independents, Wesleyan Methodists, and Roman Catholics. The free grammar school was founded and endowed, in 1624, by Mr. Roger Edwards, for an unlimited number of boys : the master has a salary of £70 per annum, with a good residence. The founder also bequeathed £5 per annum, for sending one poor scholar to the University of Oxford. A writing school has been added to this foundation by a decree in Chancery. A National school, for an unlimited number of children of both sexes, is supported by voluntary contributions. Almshouses for twenty-four poor

persons, with a weekly allowance of two shillings and sixpence each, have been erected near the Priory. The remains of the castle, standing on an abrupt eminence to the east of the river, consist of the exterior walls and a tower gateway, forming the entrance, with several apartments, amongst which is the baronial hall : the area is of considerable extent, and is flanked by square and round towers. To the south-east of the church are a few remains of a priory founded here by one of the Earls of Clare.

USSELBY, a parish in the northern division of the wapentake of Walshcroft, parts of Lindsey, county of Lincoln, 3¾ miles (N. by W.) from Market-Rasen, containing 75 inhabitants. The living is a perpetual curacy, in the archdeaconry and diocese of Lincoln, endowed with £1000 royal bounty, and £200 parliamentary grant. J. B. Elliott, Esq. was patron in 1820. The church is dedicated to St. Margaret.

USWORTH (GREAT and LITTLE), a township in the parish of Washington, eastern division of Chester ward, county palatine of Durham, 4¼ miles (S. E.) from Gateshead, containing, with North Biddick, 1365 inhabitants. There is a place of worship for Wesleyan Methodists. The late Mrs. Penrith, in 1814, built a commodious school-house, and endowed it with £30 per annum, for the education of the poor children of the township.

UTKINTON, a township in the parish of Tarporley, first division of the hundred of Eddisbury, county palatine of Chester, 1½ mile (N. by W.) from Tarporley, containing 531 inhabitants.

UTON, a tything in the parish and hundred of Crediton, county of Devon, 2 miles (W. S. W.) from Crediton, with which the population is returned.

UTTERBY, a parish in the wapentake of Ludborough, parts of Lindsey, county of Lincoln, 4¾ miles (N. by W.) from Louth, containing 165 inhabitants. The living is a discharged vicarage, in the archdeaconry and diocese of Lincoln, rated in the king's books at £5. 6. 8., and endowed with £200 royal bounty. The Rev. L. E. Towne was patron in 1807. The church is dedicated to St. Andrew.

UTTOXETER, a market town and parish in the southern division of the hundred of Totmonslow, county of Stafford, 13 miles (N. E. by E.) from Stafford, and 135 (N. W. by N.) from London, containing, with the townships of Crakemarsh, Creighton, Stramshall, and Woodlands, and the liberty of Loxley, 4658 inhabitants. Uttoxeter, anciently called *Uttokeshather*, is a place of great antiquity, and is supposed to have derived its name from the Saxon words *Uttoc*, a mattock, and *Hather*, heath ; it was afterwards called *Utoc Cestre*, and *Utcester*. The town has been properly designated an ancient forest ville, from its situation on the borders of Needwood Forest ; it constituted part of the possessions of the duchy of Lancaster, and formerly belonged to the Peverills of the Peak, Lords of Nottingham. Having come, by marriage, into the possession of William de Ferrars, Earl of Derby, it was forfeited to the crown, together with the other large possessions of that family, by Earl Robert, in the reign of Henry III., and given to Edmund, Earl of Lancaster, the king's second son. In 1308, Thomas, Earl of Lancaster, son of Edmund, obtained for it the grant of a market, and a fair on the eve, day, and morrow of St. Mary Magdalene.

The manor reverted to the crown, as parcel of the duchy of Lancaster, in the person of King Henry IV., son of John of Gaunt, Duke of Lancaster, who obtained it by marriage with Blanche, daughter and co-heiress of Henry, Earl of Lancaster, nephew of Earl Thomas. Charles I., in the first year of his reign, sold it and the demesnes to William, Lord Craven, Sir George Whitmore, Sir William Whitmore, and Mr. Gibson, reserving a fee-farm rent, and it is now vested, in twelve shares, in Earl Talbot and other proprietors : the market and fairs were sold at the same time, and are now the property of Earl Talbot. During the civil war of the seventeenth century, from its proximity to Tutbury castle, it was alternately the head-quarters of the royalist and the parliamentary forces. In May, 1645, the king and Prince Rupert passed through the town, the charges to which, in that year, as appears from the constables' accounts, amounted to £975. 7., and in the following year to nearly £800. The town stands upon a pleasant eminence, rising from the western bank of the river Dove, across which is an ancient stone bridge of six arches, connecting the counties of Stafford and Derby : it consists of several spacious streets, and a good central market-place ; the houses in general are well built, several of them being very genteel. There is no particular branch of manufacture : the local trade in cheese, corn, and other articles, is benefitted by the communication with the Potteries, by means of the Caldon branch of the Trent and Mersey canal, which comes up to a wharf at the northern end of the High-street. The land near the town, and in the vicinity of the Dove, is very fertile in pasturage, and the neighbouring rivers and brooks afford trout, grayling, and other kinds of fish. Near the town is found a pure red brick clay, from one to five yards below the surface, in irregular masses. The market, which is well attended, is held on Wednesday, every alternate Wednesday being a large market for cattle, merchandise, &c. : fairs for cattle are held on the Tuesday before Old Candlemas, May 6th, July 31st, September 1st and 19th, and November 11th and 27th ; those on May 6th and September 19th are the principal. The first charter was granted, in the 36th of Henry III., by William de Ferrars, Earl of Derby, which conferred on the burgesses all the privileges of a free borough. Uttoxeter, though a manor, with power to hold a court baron, was subject to the jurisdiction of the officers of the courts held for the honour of Tutbury ; but, in 1636, an order of the court of the duchy chamber was made, discharging the inhabitants from further attendance at the courts for the honour. Petty sessions for the southern division of the hundred of Totmonslow are held here, every Wednesday, by the county magistrates, who appoint surveyors of the highways, and also constables, head-boroughs, &c., in cases where the lords of the different court leets in the neighbourhood neglect to hold their courts, and make the appointments.

The living is a discharged vicarage, in the archdeaconry of Stafford, and diocese of Lichfield and Coventry, rated in the king's books at £27. 1. 8., endowed with £210 private benefaction, £200 royal bounty, and £800 parliamentary grant, and in the patronage of the Dean and Canons of Windsor, who hold courts for the rectorial manor. The church, dedicated to St. Mary, has been rebuilt, with the exception of the an-cient tower and beautiful and lofty spire, and has received an addition of seven hundred sittings, of which five hundred are free, the Incorporated Society for the building and enlargement of churches and chapels having contributed £500 towards defraying the expense : the spire was damaged by lightning in 1814. There are places of worship for Baptists, Independents, the Society of Friends, and Wesleyan Methodists. A free grammar school, situated in Bridge-street, was founded by the Rev. Thomas Allen, a celebrated mathematician, in the sixteenth century : the management is vested in the Master, Fellows, and Scholars of Trinity College, Cambridge ; fifteen scholars are instructed, and the master's salary is £13. 6. 8. per annum. A National school for an unlimited number of children of both sexes is supported by subscription. There are alms-houses for twelve poor persons, with small endowments ; and a fund, amounting to about £60 per annum, for apprenticing poor children. Thomas Allen, the mathematician ; Sir Simon Degge, the antiquary ; and the distinguished Admiral Gardner, were natives of this place.

UXBRIDGE, a market town and chapelry in the parish of HILLINGDON, hundred of ELTHORNE, county of MIDDLESEX, 15 miles (W. by N.) from London, containing 2750 inhabitants. The most ancient name of this place was Oxebreuge, or Woxbrigge, probably of Saxon origin, which has passed through the several variations of Waxbridge, Woxbridge, and Oxbridge, whence its present name. The town, which was probably founded about the time of Alfred, was surrounded by a ditch, and the whole site comprised about eighty-five acres : in feudal times, it was an important station as a frontier town, and appears to have been fortified at an early period. It afterwards had a regular garrison ; and, during the civil commotions in the reign of Charles, it was the scene of the memorable, but unsuccessful, negociation between the king and his parliament : sixteen commissioners on each side held a conference here, which commenced on the 30th of January, 1645, and continued about three weeks, in an ancient brick mansion, situated at the west end of the town, still designated as the Treaty House ; it has undergone various alterations, and is now the Crown Inn : two of the principal rooms used on this occasion still present specimens of the ancient and curious wainscot, in a fine state of preservation. This edifice was occupied by the Earl of Northumberland, and a mansion in its vicinity was the temporary residence of the Earl of Pembroke : the royal commissioners selected the Crown Inn, which formerly stood opposite the present White Horse ; and the parliamentary commissioners, the George, which, although materially diminished in size, yet remains. In 1647, the head-quarters of the parliamentary army were fixed here ; and there was a garrison so late as 1689.

The town is situated on the high road from London to Oxford, called the Uxbridge road, occupying a gentle declivity on the banks of the river Colne : it is paved, lighted, and supplied with water from numerous wells, and consists of one principal street, about a mile in length, called London, or High-street, which runs south-east and north-west, with another diverging from it, in the direction towards Windsor. The common, which is surrounded by rich and beautiful scenery, has been reduced, by enclosures, to a space of fifteen acres, called the Recreation Ground. Vine-street, branching to the south-east, defines the limits of what was formerly denominated the borough, in that direction; and although the town extends considerably beyond it, eastward, this part, which is called Hillingdon End, is within the parish of Hillingdon, and is neither paved nor lighted. The Grand Junction canal passes through the town. A library and reading-room, called the Uxbridge Book Society, and containing about one thousand three hundred volumes is supported by subscription. An assembly-room, recently fitted up, is attached to one of the inns. The facilities afforded by the river Colne for the erection of water-mills, and by the canal to Paddington, and the Thames, of water-carriage, have rendered Uxbridge remarkable for an extensive flour trade. At the western extremity there are three large flour-mills, and within three or four miles up and down the river, ten more, which are supposed, in the aggregate, to supply upwards of three thousand sacks of flour per week, a great part of it being sent to the metropolis : there are also two small breweries. South-east of the town is a fine soil of brick earth, which extends several miles, and has been sold at £500 or £600 per acre; the burning of bricks on these fields employs several hundred persons. The general trade of the town is very considerable; and manufactories for implements of husbandry, and Windsor and garden chairs, are carried on to a considerable extent. The Colne is crossed by two bridges; over its principal branch is High bridge, which is of brick, and was built about fifty years since, at the joint expense of the counties of Buckingham and Middlesex, instead of an ancient one which had existed from the time of Henry VIII.; over the smaller branch is a short bridge at Mercer's mill. There is likewise a bridge across the Grand Junction canal, and on its bank are warehouses and wharfs for the convenience of trade. The market, granted in the reign of Henry II., is on Thursday, and is one of the largest markets in the kingdom for corn, which is pitched in considerable quantities: there is another market on Saturday, for meat, poultry, eggs, butter, &c. Fairs are held annually on March 25th, July 31st, September 29th, and October 11th; the two latter are now used as statute fairs. The old market-house, erected in 1561, was removed, by act of parliament, in 1785, and the present erected at an expense of nearly £3000: it is a commodious building, one hundred and forty feet in length, by forty-nine in width, constructed with brick, and supported on fifty-one wooden columns, with spacious apartments used for various purposes.

Uxbridge was part of the manor of Colham till 1669, when it became a separate property, and, in 1729, was vested, by purchase and survivorship, in Edmund Baker and Edmund Blount, who conveyed it to trustees and their successors, who must be inhabitants and housekeepers in the town, for charitable uses, certain rights being reserved to the lord of the manor of Colham. The town was anciently a borough: it was governed by bailiffs until the close of the seventeenth century, two of whom were annually chosen at the court baron held for the manor; their office was to superintend the market, gather tolls, proclaim fairs, and collect duties for erecting stalls, called pickage and stallage. It is now under the superintendence of two

constables, four headboroughs, and two ale-conners, who are elected annually, with a beadle and town crier. In the 13th of Edward I. it was ordained that the high constable for the Uxbridge division should be chosen by the justices in quarter session; he generally resides in the town. A petty session for the town and eleven adjoining parishes is held by the magistrates, on the first and third Mondays in every month; and there is a county court of requests, for debts under 40s., on the first Tuesday in every month.

The living is a perpetual curacy, in the archdeaconry of Middlesex, and diocese of London, and in the patronage of the Trustees of G. Townsend, Esq., who are to present a fellow of Pembroke College, Oxford. The chapel, dedicated to St. Margaret, was built about 1447, on the site, and partly from the materials, of an old chapel, which stood here in the thirteenth century, with various subsequent alterations : it stands behind the market-house, and is in the later English style ; it is composed of brick and flint, and consists of a chancel, nave, and two aisles, separated by octagonal pillars and pointed arches, and is surmounted at the north-west end by a low square tower : in the interior are, an ancient octagonal stone font, decorated with quatrefoils and roses, and several fine monuments. The chapel has received an addition of three hundred free sittings, towards defraying the expense of which the Incorporated Society for the building and enlargement of churches and chapels contributed £200. There are places of worship for Baptists, the Society of Friends, and Independents. The free school, for the education of boys in reading, writing, and arithmetic, was founded, in 1809, principally through the benevolent exertions of Thomas Truesdale Clarke, Esq.: it is held in a spacious apartment over the market-place, and is supported by donations and annual subscriptions, together with the interest of £600 given by Mr. J. Hall, to be divided between this school and the school of industry : the lords of the manor and borough lately subscribed £50 per annum. The school of industry for Uxbridge and its vicinity, established in 1809, by uniting two small schools on the improved system of education, is for girls only, and is held in a building in George-yard, erected, in 1816, by subscription among the inhabitants. The Unitarian school at Hillingdon-End was founded, in 1812, by — Brooksbank, Esq., at whose sole expense several girls are clothed and educated. The profits arising from the manor and borough are, by the trustees, according to the deed, appropriated to the payment of £20 per annum amongst six poor men or women, inhabitants of the town, to be nominated by the overseers ; and £10 a year, by weekly payments, the donation of John Clarke; the remainder to be appropriated, at the discretion of a majority of the trustees, "for the benefit and advantage of the town of Uxbridge only." In consequence of an accident, which occasioned the death of a boy, as Lord Osselton's carriage was passing through the town, his lordship gave £100 for the purchase of land, directing the rental to be applied in apprenticing poor boys. In addition to these are several benefactions to the poor by different persons. About four miles from the town, at Breakspear, the seat of J. A. Partridge, Esq., some remains of Roman sepulchres have been recently discovered. Uxbridge gives the inferior title of earl to the Marquis of Anglesey.

V.

VANGE, a parish in the hundred of BARSTABLE, county of ESSEX, 5 miles (N. E. by E.) from Horndon on the Hill, containing 124 inhabitants. The living is a discharged rectory, in the archdeaconry of Essex, and diocese of London, rated in the king's books at £14. C. Smith, Esq. was patron in 1809. The church is dedicated to All Saints.

VAULTERSHOME, a tything in that part of the parish of MAKER which is in the hundred of ROBOROUGH, county of DEVON, 1½ mile (S. by W.) from Devonport, containing 1222 inhabitants.

VEEP (ST.), a parish in the hundred of WEST, county of CORNWALL, 3 miles (N. N. E.) from Fowey, containing 585 inhabitants. The living is a vicarage, in the archdeaconry of Cornwall, and diocese of Exeter, rated in the king's books at £5. 0. 7½., and in the patronage of — Howell, Esq. The church is dedicated to St. Cyricius. The navigable river Fowey bounds the parish on the west, and the Leryn and Penpoll creeks on the south. A fair for cattle and sheep is held on the first Wednesday after June 16th. In this parish are some remains of the chapel of the small priory of St. Cyric and St. Juliett, founded by one of the Earls of Cornwall, as a cell to that of Montacute in Somersetshire. The royalist cavalry were quartered here a short time prior to the capitulation of the Earl of Essex, with his army, in 1644.

VENN-OTTERY, a parish in the eastern division of the hundred of BUDLEIGH, county of DEVON, 3¼ miles (S. W. by S.) from Ottery St. Mary, containing 120 inhabitants. The living is a vicarage, annexed to that of Harpford, in the archdeaconry and diocese of Exeter. The church is dedicated to St. Gregory. The parish is bounded on the east by the river Otter.

VERNHAM-DEAN, a parish in the hundred of PASTROW, Kingsclere division of the county of SOUTHAMPTON, 8 miles (N. by W.) from Andover, containing 628 inhabitants. The living is a perpetual curacy, annexed to the vicarage of Hurstbourn-Tarrant, in the archdeaconry and diocese of Winchester. The church occupies a lonely and romantic situation, in the middle of a wood. There is a place of worship for Wesleyan Methodists. The parish is within the jurisdiction of the Cheyney Court held at Winchester every Thursday, for the recovery of debts to any amount.

VERYAN, a parish in the western division of the hundred of POWDER, county of CORNWALL, 4 miles (S. by W.) from Tregoney, containing 1421 inhabitants. The living is a vicarage, in the archdeaconry of Cornwall, and diocese of Exeter, rated in the king's books at £19, and in the patronage of the Dean and Chapter of Exeter. The church is dedicated to St. Symphoriana. The parish is bounded by the English channel on the south, and includes the fishing cove of Portloe. A school is supported by subscription, aided by a benefaction of about £10 per annum from the Society for Promoting Christian Knowledge.

VIRGINSTOW, a parish in the hundred of LIFTON, county of DEVON, 6¼ miles (N. E. by N.) from Launceston, containing 116 inhabitants. The living is a discharged rectory, in the archdeaconry of Totness, and diocese of Exeter, rated in the king's books at £5. 6. 8., and in the patronage of the Crown. The church is dedicated to St. Bridget.

VIRLEY, a parish in the hundred of WINSTREE, county of ESSEX, 8¼ miles (S. S. W.) from Colchester, containing 58 inhabitants. The living is a discharged rectory, in the archdeaconry of Essex, and diocese of London, rated in the king's books at £7. 13. 4., and in the patronage of the Bishop of London. The church is dedicated to St. Mary. Verley creek is navigable on the east to the North sea.

VOWCHURCH, a parish in the hundred of WEBTREE, county of HEREFORD, 11½ miles (W. by S.) from Hereford, containing, with the townships of Monington and Straddle, 367 inhabitants. The living is a discharged vicarage, in the archdeaconry and diocese of Hereford, rated in the king's books at £5. 9., and in the patronage of the Prebendary of Putson Major in the Cathedral Church of Hereford. The church is dedicated to St. Bartholomew. In the neighbourhood is an ancient square encampment.

VOWMINE, a township partly in the parish of CLIFFORD, hundred of HUNTINGTON, and partly in the parish of DORSTONE, hundred of WEBTREE, county of HEREFORD, 4 miles (E. by S.) from Hay. The population is returned with the parishes.

W.

WABERTHWAITE, a parish in ALLERDALE ward above Darwent, county of CUMBERLAND, 1½ mile (E. S. E.) from Ravenglass, containing 138 inhabitants. The living is a discharged rectory, in the archdeaconry of Richmond, and diocese of Chester, rated in the king's books at £3. 11. 8., endowed with £400 royal bounty, and in the patronage of Lord Muncaster. The church is dedicated to St. John. The parish forms an inclined plane from the mountains to the river Esk, which bounds it on the north-west.

WACKERFIELD, a township in the parish of STAINDROP, south-western division of DARLINGTON ward, county palatine of DURHAM, 7 miles (S. W. by S.) from Bishop-Auckland, containing 105 inhabitants.

WACTON, a parish in the hundred of BROXASH, county of HEREFORD, 4½ miles (N. W. by W.) from Bromyard, containing 113 inhabitants. The living is a perpetual curacy, in the archdeaconry and diocese of Hereford, endowed with £600 royal bounty, and £200 parliamentary grant, and in the patronage of the Portionists of Bromyard.

WACTON (MAGNA), a parish in the hundred of DEPWADE, county of NORFOLK, 1¼ mile (W. by S.) from St. Mary Stratton, containing 233 inhabitants. The living is a discharged rectory, with the sinecure rectory of Wacton Parva annexed, in the archdeaconry of Norfolk, and diocese of Norwich, rated in the king's books at £5, and in the patronage of the Rev. J. Hepworth. The church is dedicated to All Saints.

WACTON (PARVA), a parish in the hundred of DEPWADE, county of NORFOLK, 1½ mile (S. W.) from St. Mary Stratton. The living is a discharged sinecure rectory, annexed to that of Wacton Magna, in the archdeaconry of Norfolk, and diocese of Norwich, rated in the king's books at £2. 13. 4. The church, which was dedicated to St. Mary, is in ruins.

WADBOROUGH, a hamlet in the parish of the HOLY CROSS, PERSHORE, upper division of the hundred of PERSHORE, county of WORCESTER, 3½ miles (W. N. W.) from Pershore, containing 132 inhabitants.

WADDESDON, a parish in the hundred of ASHENDON, county of BUCKINGHAM, 5½ miles (W. N. W.) from Aylesbury, containing, with the hamlets of Westcott and Woodham, 1616 inhabitants. The living is a rectory, in three portions, in the archdeaconry of Buckingham, and diocese of Lincoln, each rated in the king's books at £15, and all in the patronage of the Duke of Marlborough. The church is dedicated to St. Michael: the three portionists officiate alternately. There are places of worship for Baptists and Wesleyan Methodists. Lewis Fetto, in 1724, bequeathed property of the annual value of about £10, for teaching and apprenticing poor children. Almshouses for six poor people were founded, in 1642, by Arthur Goodwin, with an endowment of £30 per annum.

WADDINGTON, a parish within the liberty of the city of LINCOLN, parts of LINDSEY, county of LINCOLN, 4½ miles (S.) from Lincoln, containing, with Meer Hospital, 701 inhabitants. The living is a rectory, in the archdeaconry and diocese of Lincoln, rated in the king's books at £20. 16. 8., and in the patronage of the Rector and Fellows of Lincoln College, Oxford. The church, dedicated to St. Michael, is principally in the Norman style. There is a place of worship for Wesleyan Methodists. This parish participates, with others within the limits of the city and county of the city of Lincoln, in the benefits of the Blue-coat school and hospital founded, in 1602, by Richard Smith, M.D.; and the Jersey school, established, in 1693, pursuant to the will of Henry Stone, Esq.

WADDINGTON, a chapelry in that part of the parish of MITTON which is in the western division of the wapentake of STAINCLIFFE and EWCROSS, West riding of the county of YORK, 1¼ mile (N. W. by N.) from Clitheroe, containing 687 inhabitants. The living is a perpetual curacy, in the archdeaconry and diocese of York, endowed with £200 private benefaction, and £200 royal bounty, and in the patronage of T. L. Parker, Esq. The chapel, dedicated to St. Helen, is principally in the later style of English architecture. There is a place of worship for Wesleyan Methodists. The spinning and manufacture of cotton are carried on here. On the river Ribble is an hospital for ten poor widows, founded by Robert Parker, with a chapel attached.

WADDINGWORTH, a parish in the southern division of the wapentake of GARTREE, parts of LINDSEY, county of LINCOLN, 6 miles (W. by N.) from Horncastle, containing 59 inhabitants. The living is a discharged rectory, in the archdeaconry and diocese of Lincoln, rated in the king's books at £7. 0. 10., and in the patronage of the Crown. The church is dedicated to St. Margaret.

WADEBRIDGE, a market town partly in the parish of ST. BREOCK, hundred of PYDER, and partly in that of EGLOSHAYLE, hundred of TRIGG, county of CORNWALL, 5 miles (E. S. E.) from Padstow. The population is returned with the respective parishes. There are places of worship for Independents and Wesleyan Methodists. This place is chiefly remarkable for its

noble bridge of seventeen arches, nearly three hundred and twenty feet long, over the navigable river Camel: it was built by public contribution, about 1485, and, in the reign of James I., was made a county bridge: there are certain estates vested in trustees, with the rents of which, aided by tolls (from which the inhabitants of the two parishes are exempt), it is kept in repair. The trade of the town principally consists in the exportation of corn, in vessels not exceeding one hundred and fifty tons' burden. The market, which is of ancient establishment, though inconsiderable, is still held on Friday; and there are fairs on May 12th, June 22nd, and October 10th.

WADENHOE, a parish in the hundred of NAVISFORD, county of NORTHAMPTON, 4¼ miles (S. W.) from Oundle, containing 243 inhabitants. The living is a rectory, in the archdeaconry of Northampton, and diocese of Peterborough, rated in the king's books at £11, and in the patronage of the Rev. Dr. Roberts. The church is dedicated to St. Michael.

WADHURST, a parish in the hundred of LOXFIELD-PELHAM, rape of PEVENSEY, county of SUSSEX, 5 miles (S. E.) from Tonbridge-Wells, containing 2136 inhabitants. The living is a vicarage, in the peculiar jurisdiction of the Archbishop of Canterbury, rated in the king's books at £15. 1. 0½., and in the patronage of the Warden and Fellows of Wadham College, Oxford. The church, dedicated to St. Peter and St. Paul, is partly in the early, and partly in the later, style of English architecture. There is a place of worship for Baptists. Mr. Barham, in 1730, left a rent-charge of £5 for the education of twelve poor children; the master's salary is augmented by a further annuity of £5 from the inhabitants.

WADINGHAM, a parish in the eastern division of the wapentake of MANLEY, parts of LINDSEY, county of LINCOLN, 8½ miles (S. by W.) from Glandford-Bridge, containing 447 inhabitants. The living consists of the united rectories of St. Mary and St. Peter, with a chapelry of Snitterby annexed, in the archdeaconry of Stow, and diocese of Lincoln, rated in the king's books at £29. 6. 8., and in the patronage of the Crown. There is a place of worship for Wesleyan Methodists. A new cut, or canal, called the river Ancholme, passes through the parish. A free school is endowed with thirty acres of land.

WADSWORTH, a township in the parish of HALIFAX, wapentake of MORLEY, West riding of the county of YORK, 7½ miles (W. N. W.) from Halifax, containing 4509 inhabitants, who are extensively employed in the manufacture of cotton and worsted goods. Abraham Wall, in 1638, bequeathed a rent-charge of £8, to be applied for teaching poor children; for which purpose also, in 1642, the Rev. Charles Greenwood left houses and lands, now producing a considerable rental.

WADWORTH, a parish in the southern division of the wapentake of STRAFFORTH and TICKHILL, West riding of the county of YORK, 5¼ miles (S.) from Doncaster, containing 614 inhabitants. The living is a discharged vicarage, in the peculiar jurisdiction of the Dean and Chapter of York, rated in the king's books at £4. 2. 6., endowed with £200 royal bounty, and in the patronage of the Impropriator of Wadworth. The church is dedicated to St. Mary. There is a place of worship for Wesleyan Methodists.

WAGHEN, or WAWN, a parish partly within the liberty of St. Peter of York, but chiefly in the middle division of the wapentake of Holderness, East riding of the county of York, comprising the townships of Meux and Waghen, and containing 325 inhabitants, of which number, 251 are in the township of Waghen, 5 miles (S. E. by E.) from Beverley. The living is a discharged vicarage, in the peculiar jurisdiction and patronage of the Chancellor of the Cathedral Church of York, rated in the king's books at £7. 0. 10., and endowed with £200 royal bounty. The church, dedicated to St. Peter, is partly in the decorated style, with a tower of later date: there are three stalls in the chancel.

WAINFLEET, a market town in the Marsh division of the wapentake of Candleshoe, parts of Lindsey, county of Lincoln, 39½ miles (E. S. E.) from Lincoln, and 128 (N. by E.) from London, containing 1422 inhabitants. In the time of the Romans, the whole province is said to have been supplied from this place with salt, made from the sea-water; and a road across the fens, still called the Salters' road, is supposed to have been the Roman road between *Bannovallium* and *Lindum*. Wainfleet returned one burgess to the grand council summoned in the 11th of Edward III.; and, in 1359, it supplied two ships of war for the armament prepared for the invasion of Brittany. The town is situated on a small creek in a marshy district; and, in consequence of the enclosure of the east fen, the waters of the haven have been carried off by a wide drain to Boston Scalf, which has so reduced them as to preclude the entrance of any but small craft. Previously to this event, it is believed that the town was situated higher up the creek, chiefly because the old church of All Saints stood at High Wainfleet, about a mile and a half from the town: it was taken down in 1820. The market is on Saturday; and fairs are held on the third Saturday in May for cattle, and October 24th for sheep, the latter being also a pleasure fair.

The town comprises the following parishes, all in the archdeaconry and diocese of Lincoln: All Saints', a rectory, rated in the king's books at £16. 3. 6½., and in the patronage of the Crown: the church, which has been rebuilt at an expense of £3000, contains six hundred and ten sittings, four hundred of them free; towards defraying the expense of which the Incorporated Society for the building and enlargement of churches and chapels contributed £400. St. Mary's, a perpetual curacy, rated in the king's books at £8. 13. 4., and in the patronage of the Governors of Bethlehem Hospital, London. The church has gone to decay. St. Thomas', a perpetual curacy, in the patronage of — Barnes, Esq. There are places of worship for the Society of Friends and Wesleyan Methodists. The free grammar school was founded, in 1424, by William Patten, generally known as William of Waynflete, Bishop of Winchester, Lord High Chancellor of England in the reign of Henry VI., and founder of Magdalene College, Oxford, from the President and Fellows of which the master receives a small annual stipend, and has, in addition, nineteen acres of land and a rent-free residence.

WAITBY, a township in the parish of Kirkby-Stephen, East ward, county of Westmorland, 1¾ mile (W.) from Kirkby-Stephen, containing 46 inhabitants. A free school was erected, in 1680, by James Highmore, citizen of London, who endowed it with £400,

now producing £40 a year, for which about forty children are instructed.

WAITH, a parish in the wapentake of Bradley-Haverstoe, parts of Lindsey, county of Lincoln, 6¾ miles (S. by E.) from Great Grimsby, containing 30 inhabitants. The living is a discharged vicarage, in the archdeaconry and diocese of Lincoln, rated in the king's books at £2. 14. 2., endowed with £800 royal bounty. Miss Borrell was patroness in 1820. The church is dedicated to St. Martin.

WAKEFIELD, a parish in the lower division of the wapentake of Agbrigg, West riding of the county of York, comprising the market town of Wakefield, the chapelries of Horbury and Stanley, and the townships of Alverthorpe with Thornes, and Wrenthorpe, and containing 22,307 inhabitants, of which number, 10,764 are in the town of

Arms.

Wakefield, 32 miles (S. W. by W.) from York, and 178 (N. N. W.) from London. The discovery of many coins and other relics of the Romans, in the neighbourhood, indicates its existence in the time of that people. In the reign of Edward the Confessor, it formed part of the royal demesne, and was subsequently transferred to the Conqueror: in Domesday-book it is denominated *Wachefeld*. This was the scene of the celebrated battle, at the close of the year 1459, between Richard, Duke of York, and Margaret of Anjou, queen of Henry VI., in which the former lost his life; and the spot of ground where he was buried, a short distance from the town, is still parted off from the adjoining field; his gold ring was found here some years ago. Wakefield again suffered from the calamities of the civil war between Charles I. and the parliament, falling, at different periods, into the hands of each party, according to the various chances of war. The manor, or lordship, which is one of the largest in the kingdom, extending, from east to west, a distance of more than thirty miles, and now comprising a population of upwards of one hundred and twenty thousand, was granted by Henry I., about the year 1107, to William, Earl of Warren, in whose family it continued until the reign of Edward III., when, by default of heirs, it lapsed to the crown, and so remained until granted, by Charles I., to Henry, Earl of Holland; and, after passing through several other families, it was, in 1700, purchased by the Duke of Leeds, to whose descendant, the present duke, it still belongs.

The town is principally situated on the side of an eminence sloping to the river Calder, in the midst of a fertile and picturesque country, and consists of spacious and regular streets, with many well-built and handsome brick houses; it is paved and flagged, lighted with gas, and well supplied with water: very great improvements have been made, of late years more especially, on its northern side, where some handsome rows of houses have been erected, which, with a few detached mansions, standing amidst shrubberies and pleasure grounds, form a great ornament to this part of the town, which is called St. John's. A handsome building,

3 A

situated in Wood-street, near the Court-house, has been erected by subscription, and contains a library and news-room, the upper part being used for concerts, assemblies, and other public amusements. A Literary and Philoso-phical Society, established in 1827, meets every fortnight at the Court-house; and there is also a Phrenological Society. A masonic lodge is held here, of which the Earl of Mexborough is Provincial Grand Master. The theatre, in Westgate, was erected by the late celebrated Tate Wilkinson, Esq., and is usually opened, in August, by the York company. The river, which was made navigable in 1698, is crossed by a handsome stone bridge of nine arches, built in the reign of Edward III., on the eastern side of which is a chapel, supposed to have been founded by that monarch, dedicated to the Virgin Mary, and endowed with £10 per annum, for two chaplains to perform divine service. The present structure was, however, rebuilt by Edward IV., in memory of his fa-ther, the Duke of York, and his followers who fell with him at the battle of Wakefield; it is about ten yards in length and six in width, and is in the later style of English architecture: the eastern window, overhang-ing the river, is ornamented with rich and delicate tra-cery, and the western front has much architectural decoration; it is divided by buttresses into compart-ments, with lofty pedestals, and pointed arches in relief, the spandrils being covered with sculptured ornaments; over these is an entablature, with five shorter compart-ments, in relief, representing scriptural subjects, the whole surmounted by battlements: the revenue ceased at the dissolution of monastic establishments, and the chapel has been long desecrated, being now used as a counting-house by a corn-factor.

The manufacture of woollen cloth and worsted yarn was formerly carried on to a great extent, insomuch that Leland, in speaking of the town, says, "it standeth now al by clothying;" but these branches of trade have greatly declined, and corn and wool are now the staple commo-dities. The Tammy Hall, a building about seventy yards long, and ten broad, consisting of two stories, which was erected by subscription many years since, for the sale of the lighter woollen stuffs, has been converted into a manufactory for stuff pieces by the use of power-looms, the shares of the original proprietors having been bought up. Coal is also procured in great abundance in the sur-rounding country, and is brought to the town by rail-ways from the collieries, and conveyed in barges down the Calder and up the Ouse to York, or by the Hum-ber to Hull. The trade in corn has greatly increased of late years, and warehouses for storing it have been built on a most extensive scale: a corn exchange was erected in 1823. At the foot of the bridge is the soke mill, where persons living in the soke of Wakefield, which comprehends Stanley, Sandal, Alverthorpe, Ossett, Horbury, and Crigglestone, are obliged to have their corn ground. Much barley is also grown in the neighbour-hood, and a considerable quantity is here converted into malt: great quantities of wool are sold, being brought from distant parts of the country, to be disposed of to the neighbouring manufacturers. The Aire and Calder Navigation Company have their principal establishment and wharf near the bridge, whence fly-boats leave for Huddersfield every day; and, by means of their navigation, and the Barnesley and other canals con-nected with it, a direct line of communication is opened

with Hull, Lincolnshire, and Lancashire, which affords great facilities to the trade of the town. The market, on Friday, is well supplied with provisions: the market cross, built by subscription more than one hundred and twenty years since, is a handsome structure of the Doric order, consisting of an open colonnade supporting a dome; a spiral staircase leads to a spacious room, lighted by a lantern at the top, in which business relating to the town is generally transacted: in con-sequence of the confined space of the market-place, the corn market has been removed to the broad street called Westgate. There is also a market for cattle and sheep every alternate Wednesday, which is attended by graziers and butchers from a very considerable distance. Fairs, chiefly for horses, horned cattle, and pedlary, are held on July 4th and 5th, and November 11th and 12th. The town is under the superintendence of a chief constable, who is appointed by the inhabitants, and sworn by the steward of the lord of the manor, at a court leet held at the moot-hall, in Kirkgate. The quarter sessions for the West riding are holden in the second week in January, at the Court-house, a handsome and appropriate edifice, erected in 1806; and a petty session for the district is held weekly, by the county magistrates, on Friday. The manor court, for petty causes and the recovery of debts under £5, is held by the steward, once in three weeks, at the moot-hall. The register-office, established in 1704, and the office of clerk of the peace for the West riding, are both in this town. The house of correction for the West riding is an extensive pile of building, near the bottom of Westgate, constructed on the improved plan of county prisons, comprising a tread-mill for grinding corn, se-parate yards, a chapel, a school for juvenile offenders, day-rooms, and three hundred and seven separate sleeping cells: the prisoners are employed in weaving coarse cloth, calico, and linsey.

The living is a vicarage, in the archdeaconry and dio-cese of York, rated in the king's books at £29. 19. 2., and in the patronage of the Crown. The church, dedi-cated to All Saints, is a spacious and handsome edifice, of English architecture, erected in the reign of Henry III., but, from the many repairs and improvements it has undergone, little of the original style remains. It consists of a nave, separated from the aisles by two rows of clustered columns supporting pointed arches, and from the chancel by a lofty screen: the pulpit and reading-desk are of carved oak; and the font, which bears the date 1611, and the initials of Charles II., was replaced in its present situation, at the west end of the nave (from which it had been removed), in 1821, with the addition of a beautifully wrought canopy. The square tower is adorned with battlements and pinnacles, and surmounted by an octagonal spire, the height of both being about two hundred and thirty-seven feet, exceeding that of any other in the county · in 1715, the vane and about one-third of the spire were blown down, and only partially rebuilt. In 1802, its dilapidated condition exciting alarm as to its safety, it was secured by iron bands; and, in 1823, a portion of it was taken down and rebuilt, so that it is now perfectly secure. There are two lectureships; that in the afternoon, founded in 1652, under the will of Lady Camden, with an income of £100 per annum, is in the gift of the Master and Wardens of the Mercers Company; and that in the evening, established in 1801, is supported by voluntary subscriptions, and in the patronage of seven trustees, of whom the vicar is one. The church dedicated to St. John, standing in that part of the town called St. John's, was commenced in 1792, and completed in 1795, at an expense of about £10,000: the site, and £1000 for the support of the officiating minister, were bequeathed by Mrs. Newstead. It was made parochial, jointly with the church of All Saints, by an act obtained in 1815: the right of presentation belongs to the vicar of All Saints', who has also the patronage of the chapelries of Alverthorpe, Horbury, and Stanley. There are two places of worship each for Independents and Wesleyan Methodists; and the Society of Friends, Primitive Methodists, Unitarians, and Roman Catholics, have each one.

The free grammar school was founded, in 1592, by Queen Elizabeth, and is endowed with property producing rather more than £300 per annum; the number of scholars, who receive a classical education, is about forty. It is under the government of fourteen trustees, who are a corporate body, and appoint the two masters; the first with a salary of £160, and the other with one of £80, per annum, who teach the classics. There is also a writing school, where boys are instructed in writing and arithmetic, on paying a certain sum quarterly to the master. The children of all residents, both in the town and parish, are admissible, and are eligible to the several exhibitions from this school to the Universities; two of which, founded by Thomas Cave, are to Clare Hall, Cambridge; one, founded by Lady Elizabeth Hastings, to Queen's College, Oxford; and three, founded by John Storie, to either of the Universities, each of the value of about £50 per annum. Of the candidates, preference is given, first, to the natives of the town; next, to those born in the parish; and, in failure of these, to residents: but each candidate must have been at the school for three years: the school-room is a commodious building, with a good library attached to it. Several eminent persons have been educated here, amongst whom are Richard Bentley, D.D., who was born in the neighbourhood; Dr. John Potter, Archbishop of Canterbury, a distinguished author, born here in 1674; Dr. John Radcliffe, the munificent benefactor to the University of Oxford, and founder of the Radcliffe library, who was also a native of the town. The Green-coat charity school was founded, about 1707, by the trustees of the poor, from the charity estates; and the present income, amounting to upwards of £600 per annum, arises from the ground on which the fortnight cattle market is held, together with various donations, the principal of which is a grant by John Storie, in 1674, of certain lands, now producing more than £500 per annum: in this school about seventy-five boys and fifty girls are clothed and instructed.

The almshouses, in Almshouse-lane, founded by Cotton Horne, in 1646, and endowed with lands producing nearly £300 per annum, are appropriated to ten poor women, who each receive five shillings a week, and some clothing, coal, and provisions. Adjoining are almshouses endowed by William Horne, in which ten poor men are lodged, and have a weekly allowance, with some clothing and provisions: there are also almshouses at Brooksbank, founded by Leonard Bate, for five poor widows of this parish, who have a weekly allowance. The management of all these establishments is vested in the governors of the grammar school, who have also the distribution of a bequest made, in 1722, by John Bromley, of property now producing upwards of £700 per annum, which is applied to the clothing and apprenticing of poor boys, and the relief of poor housekeepers; and of various other benefactions and bequests for the relief of the poor, producing upwards of £800 per annum. There are also a Lancasterian and two National schools for children of both sexes, and a school of industry, all supported by voluntary contributions, and numerously attended. The West riding pauper lunatic asylum, about a mile north-east of the town, was erected about 1817, and is calculated to contain two hundred and fifty patients: it is a handsome and commodious edifice, and is conducted in a manner admirably adapted both for the bodily comfort and mental relief of its inmates: the establishment is supported by a county rate, but the patients are maintained by the townships from which they are sent. A dispensary and fever ward were established a few years ago, and are supported by voluntary contributions. A mineral spring at Stanley, and another at Horbury, each within about two miles of the town, possess medicinal qualities somewhat similar to those of the waters at Harrogate, or Cheltenham. In addition to those natives of the town who are mentioned as having been educated at the grammar school, the following were also born here: Dr. Thomas Zouch, a learned divine; Joseph Bingham, M.A., author of "Origines Ecclesiasticæ;" and Dr. John Burton, author of the "Monasticon Eboracense."

WAKELY, an extra-parochial liberty, formerly a distinct parish, in the hundred of EDWINSTREE, county of HERTFORD, 2 miles (S. W.) from Buntingford, containing 9 inhabitants.

WAKERING (GREAT), a parish in the hundred of ROCHFORD, county of ESSEX, 4½ miles (E. N. E.) from Southend, containing 776 inhabitants. The living is a vicarage, in the archdeaconry of Essex, and diocese of London, rated in the king's books at £20. 13. 4., and in the patronage of the Bishop of London. The church is dedicated to St. Nicholas. There is a place of worship for Independents. The parish lies at the mouth of the Thames, and has a small haven.

WAKERING (LITTLE), a parish in the hundred of ROCHFORD, county of ESSEX, 4½ miles (N. E. by E.) from Southend, containing 262 inhabitants. The living is a vicarage, in the archdeaconry of Essex, and diocese of London, rated in the king's books at £12, and in the patronage of the Governors of St. Bartholomew's Hospital, London. The church is dedicated to St. Mary. Potten island, in this parish, is formed by Broomhill river and Wakering haven.

WAKERLEY, a parish in the hundred of CORBY, county of NORTHAMPTON, 6¾ miles (E.) from Uppingham, containing 209 inhabitants. The living is a rectory, in the archdeaconry of Northampton, and diocese of Peterborough, rated in the king's books at £11. 12. 6., and in the patronage of the Marquis of Exeter. The church is dedicated to St. Mary.

WALBERSWICK, a parish in the hundred of BLYTHING, county of SUFFOLK, 1¾ mile (S. W. by S.) from Southwold, containing 263 inhabitants. The living is a perpetual curacy, in the archdeaconry of Suffolk, and diocese of Norwich, endowed with £800 royal bounty, and £200 parliamentary grant, and in the patronage of Sir C. Blois, Bart. The church, dedicated to St. Andrew, is partly in ruins. The river Blyth is navigable through the parish, and falls into the North sea on the eastern side of it.

WALBERTON, a parish in the hundred of Avisford, rape of Arundel, county of Sussex, 3½ miles (W. S. W.) from Arundel, containing 687 inhabitants. The living is a discharged vicarage, with that of Yapton united, in the archdeaconry and diocese of Chichester, rated in the king's books at £10. 19. 2., and in the patronage of the Bishop of Chichester. The church, dedicated to St. Mary, is principally in the early style of English architecture. John Nash, in 1732, bequeathed a house and land, with a rent-charge of £12, for teaching eighteen poor children.

WALBURN, a township in the parish of Downholme, western division of the wapentake of Hang, North riding of the county of York, 5 miles (S. W.) from Richmond, containing 37 inhabitants.

WALBY, a township in the parish of Crosby upon Eden, Eskdale ward, county of Cumberland, 4 miles (N. E. by N.) from Carlisle, containing 46 inhabitants.

WALCOT, a parish in the wapentake of Aveland, parts of Kesteven, county of Lincoln, 1½ mile (N. W.) from Falkingham, containing 152 inhabitants. The living is a perpetual curacy, in the archdeaconry and diocese of Lincoln, and in the patronage of Sir G. Heathcote, Bart. The church, dedicated to St. Nicholas, is principally in the decorated style of English architecture, with a tower surmounted by a fine crocketed spire: the clerestory is in the later style. On the edge of the fens is a powerful mineral spring of some repute. The monks of Sempringham abbey had formerly a prison here.

WALCOTE, a hamlet (formerly a chapelry) in the parish of Misterton, hundred of Guthlaxton, county of Leicester, 1¾ mile (E. by S.) from Lutterworth. The population is returned with the parish. The chapel, which was dedicated to St. Martin, has been destroyed.

WALCOTT, a chapelry in the parish of Billinghay, first division of the wapentake of Langoe, parts of Kesteven, county of Lincoln, 8¾ miles (N.E. by N.) from Sleaford, containing 472 inhabitants. The living is a perpetual curacy, annexed to the vicarage of Billinghay, in the archdeaconry and diocese of Lincoln, endowed with £200 private benefaction, and £800 royal bounty. The church is dedicated to St. Oswald. There is a place of worship for Wesleyan Methodists.

WALCOTT, a parish in the hundred of Happing, county of Norfolk, 5¼ miles (E. by N.) from North Walsham, containing 132 inhabitants. The living is a perpetual curacy, in the archdeaconry of Norfolk, and diocese of Norwich, rated in the king's books at £30, endowed with £400 royal bounty, and £200 parliamentary grant, and in the patronage of the Bishop of Norwich. The church is dedicated to All Saints.

WALCOTT, a parish partly within the city of Bath, and partly in the hundred of Bath-Forum, county of Somerset, containing 24,046 inhabitants. This parish includes all those parts of the city of Bath lying on the north, north-east, and north-west, sides of

the parish of St. Michael; also some handsome ranges of buildings on the declivities of Lansdown and Beacon hills. For a more detailed account of this parish, see the article on Bath.

WALCOTT, a joint hamlet with Membris, in the parish of Holy Cross, Pershore, upper division of the hundred of Pershore, county of Worcester, 2 miles (N. by W.) from Pershore, containing, with Membris, 332 inhabitants.

WALDEN, a joint township with Burton, in the parish of Aysgarth, western division of the wapentake of Hang, North riding of the county of York, 10 miles (W. S. W.) from Middleham. The population is returned with Burton.

WALDEN (KING'S), a parish in the hundred of Hitchin and Pirton, county of Hertford, 4½ miles (S. S. W.) from Hitchin, containing 926 inhabitants. The living is a donative, in the patronage of W. Hale, Esq. The church is dedicated to St. Mary. On the north side of the chancel is a chapel, the burial-place of the family of Hale, erected by William Hale, Esq., who died in 1648.

WALDEN (ST. PAUL'S), a parish in the hundred of Cashio, or liberty of St. Albans, county of Hertford, 5¼ miles (N. N. W.) from Welwyn, containing 906 inhabitants. The living is a vicarage, in the archdeaconry of St. Albans, and diocese of London, rated in the king's books at £10, endowed with £800 private benefaction, £800 royal bounty, and £600 parliamentary grant, and in the patronage of the Dean and Chapter of St. Paul's, London. The church is dedicated to All Saints. There are places of worship for Baptists and Independents.

WALDEN (SAFFRON), an incorporated market town and parish, possessing separate jurisdiction, locally in the hundred of Uttlesford, county of Essex, 27 miles (N. N. W.) from Chelmsford, and 42 (N. N. E.) from London. The population, in 1821, was 4154, but now amounts to nearly 4500. The name of Walden is said to be derived from the Saxon words *Weald* and *Den*, signifying a woody hill. At a later period the place was called *Waldenburgh*; and, in the reign of Stephen, when Geoffrey de Mandeville, Earl of Essex, procured from the Empress Matilda the grant of a market, previously held at Newport, the town took the appellation of *Cheping-Walden*. The present designation owes its origin to the culture of saffron in the neighbourhood, which is supposed to have been introduced by Sir Thomas Smith, early in the sixteenth century, but has long since been discontinued: the device of the seal of the corporation is a rebus on the name, being *three saffron flowers walled in*. The Earl of Essex, above-mentioned, was the grandson of Geoffrey de Mandeville, a Norman chief, and one of the most distinguished followers of William I.: he founded a Benedictine priory, near the south-western extremity of the parish, which was richly endowed, and, in 1190, converted into an abbey; its revenue, at the time of the suppression, amounted, according to

Corporate Seal.

Speed, to £406. 5. 11. In 1537, William More, the last abbot, surrendered the abbey, with all its possessions, to the king, who granted them to Sir Thomas Audley, afterwards Lord Chancellor, K.G., and created Baron Audley of Walden. Upon the site of the monastic buildings, and partly out of the ruins, Thomas, first Earl of Suffolk, in 1603, erected a stately fabric, which he called Audley End, in honour of his maternal grandfather, the chancellor; but of this magnificent house, which occupied thirteen years in completing, and was considered the largest mansion within the realm, one court only remains, and even this comparatively small portion of the original building forms a splendid residence. Upon the death of Henry, tenth Earl of Suffolk, in 1745, without issue, the Audley End estates were divided between George William, Earl of Bristol, and Elizabeth, Countess of Portsmouth, as representatives of the daughters and co-heirs of James, third Earl of Suffolk. Lady Portsmouth gave her share of the property, together with the house, in 1762, to her nephew, Sir John Griffin Griffin, K.B., who, in 1784, established his claim, in the female line, to the ancient barony of Howard de Walden; and, dying in 1797, bequeathed his estates to Richard, Lord Braybrooke, the father of the present possessor of Audley End.

Walden contains several good streets, and a spacious market-place, in which there is a neat town hall: the houses are principally built of lath and plaster, and some of them are very ancient. The situation of the town is thus emphatically described by Dr. Stukeley: "A narrow tongue of land shoots itself out like a promontory, encompassed with a valley, in the form of a horse-shoe, enclosed by distant and delightful hills. On the bottom of the tongue, towards the east, stand the ruins of the castle, and on the top, or extremity, the church, the greater part of which is seen above the surrounding houses." The trade in malt and barley is very considerable. The market is on Saturday; and fairs are held annually on Mid-Lent Saturday and November 1st. By the first charter of incorporation, in 1549, the government of the town was vested in twenty persons, a treasurer and two chamberlains being chosen annually from this number; but the present corporation, as re-modelled by the charter of William and Mary, consists of a mayor, recorder, twelve aldermen, deputy recorder, coroner, town clerk, and other officers. The mayor, and his immediate predecessor, and the two senior aldermen, are magistrates, ex officio; the county justices possessing (if they think proper to exercise their right) a concurrent jurisdiction. The sessions are held quarterly, and the court appears, from old records, to possess the power of inflicting capital punishment, which was acted upon more than once in the seventeenth century. A court is also held, every three weeks, for the recovery of debts under £10, at which the mayor, or his deputy, presides, assisted by one of the aldermen. The courts leet and baron for the manors of Brook and Cheping-Walden, belonging to the owner of Audley End, take place at stated times, and at one of these constables are nominated. The magistrates for the division also hold their sessions in the town, once a fortnight.

The living is a vicarage, in the archdeaconry of Colchester, and diocese of London, rated in the king's books at £33. 6. 8., and in the patronage of Lord Braybrooke.

The church, which is a spacious and elegant structure, was erected in the reigns of Henry VI. and VII. : it has an embattled tower and clerestory windows, and two octagonal crocketed turrets, at the east end of the nave. The spire, which was of wood, and much decayed, has been recently removed, and will be replaced by one of stone, more in character, in every respect, with the rest of the building. The east and south ends of the chancel were erected by Chancellor Audley, and the north side by the inhabitants, aided by John Leche, who was vicar from 1489 to 1521, and whose tomb may still be seen near the north chancel door: the chancellor's monument, of black marble, is placed under the east window of the south chancel. The General Baptists, Society of Friends, Independents, Wesleyan Methodists, and Unitarians, have their respective places of worship within the town. The school, in which the classics were formerly taught, owes its foundation to John Leche, before mentioned, and his sister, Johane Bradbury. The learned Sir Thomas Smith, Secretary to Edward VI., a native of Walden, is said to have received his early education here, and through his interest the school was advanced to be a royal foundation: its present income is £74, and the master has a residence. All children born at Walden, Newport, Little Chesterford, or Widdington, are taught gratuitously, subject only to an entrance fee of fourpence. The school-room has lately been repaired, and one hundred and forty boys are now instructed on the National system. There is also a school for one hundred girls, similarly conducted. A range of almshouses is nearly completed, at the south-west end of the town, to replace those founded by Edward VI., for the reception of sixteen decayed housekeepers of each sex, which had been long considered too much dilapidated to admit of reparation. The elevation of the new buildings is handsome and appropriate, and will add much to the general appearance of the town, as well as to the comforts of the inmates : the charity is under the management of the corporation. There are also many other benefactions belonging to the parish, which are all properly administered. Between the town and Audley End Park are the remains of an old embankment, called "The Pell Ditches," respecting which there is no clear or satisfactory tradition. Dr. Stukeley found the south bank to be seven hundred and thirty feet long, twenty feet high, fifty broad at the base, and eight at the top: the length of the western bank is five hundred and eighty-eight feet: both banks and ditches are well preserved and extremely bold. The ruins of the castle, erected soon after the Conquest, by Geoffrey de Mandeville, are only remarkable for the thickness of the walls and the rude character of the building. The hamlet of Little Walden, containing a few straggling houses, stands a mile and a half from the town, on the Linton road. The parish contains seven thousand two hundred and ninety-six acres. Lord Thomas Howard, afterwards Earl of Suffolk, in 1597, took his title of baron from this town, which has descended to the present Lord Howard de Walden, in right of his mother, who was granddaughter to Frederic, fourth Earl of Bristol; the barony, being a female honour, has, at different periods, been disunited from each of the above earldoms.

WALDEN-STUBBS, a township in the parish of WOMERSLEY, lower division of the wapentake of Osgoldcross, West riding of the county of York, 7½ miles (S. E. by E.) from Pontefract, containing 158 inhabitants.

WALDERSHARE, a parish in the hundred of EASTRY, lathe of ST. AUGUSTINE, county of KENT, 4½ miles (N. by W.) from Dovor, containing 69 inhabitants. The living is a discharged vicarage, in the archdeaconry and diocese of Canterbury, rated in the king's books at £5. 8., endowed with £200 private benefaction, and £200 royal bounty, and in the patronage of the Archbishop of Canterbury. The church, dedicated to All Saints, contains some handsome monuments. A fair for toys and pedlary is held on Whit-Tuesday.

WALDINGFIELD (GREAT), a parish in the hundred of BABERGH, county of SUFFOLK, 3¼ miles (N. E. by E.) from Sudbury, containing 711 inhabitants. The living is a rectory, in the archdeaconry of Sudbury, and diocese of Norwich, rated in the king's books at £21. 6. 8., endowed with upwards of £400 private benefaction, and £400 royal bounty, and in the patronage of the Master and Fellows of Clare Hall, Cambridge. The church, dedicated to St. Lawrence, has lately received an addition of one hundred and twenty sittings, of which seventy are free, the Incorporated Society for the enlargement of churches and chapels having granted £30 towards defraying the expense.

WALDINGFIELD (LITTLE), a parish in the hundred of BABERGH, county of SUFFOLK, 4½ miles (N. E. by E.) from Sudbury, containing 386 inhabitants. The living is a discharged vicarage, in the archdeaconry of Sudbury, and diocese of Norwich, rated in the king's books at £4. 18. 11½., and in the patronage of the Rev. R. B. Syer. The church is dedicated to St. Lawrence. There is a place of worship for Wesleyan Methodists.

WALDRIDGE, a township in that part of the parish of CHESTER le STREET which is in the middle division of CHESTER ward, county palatine of DURHAM, 5½ miles (N. by W.) from Durham, containing 125 inhabitants.

WALDRINGFIELD, a parish in the hundred of CARLFORD, county of SUFFOLK, 3½ miles (S. by E.) from Woodbridge, containing 163 inhabitants. The living is a discharged rectory, in the archdeaconry of Suffolk, and diocese of Norwich, rated in the king's books at £4. 17. 11., and in the patronage of N. Randall, Esq. The church is dedicated to All Saints. There is a place of worship for Baptists.

WALDRON, a parish in the hundred of SHIPLAKE, rape of PEVENSEY, county of SUSSEX, 5¾ miles (E. S.E.) from Uckfield, containing 965 inhabitants. The living is a rectory, in the archdeaconry of Lewes, and diocese of Chichester, rated in the king's books at £13. 4. 7., and in the patronage of the Rector and Fellows of Exeter College, Oxford. The church, dedicated to All Saints, is partly in the early, and partly in the later, style of English architecture : it has lately received an addition of fifty free sittings, the Incorporated Society for the enlargement of churches and chapels having granted £30 towards defraying the expense. There is a place of worship for Wesleyan Methodists.

WALES, a parish partly within the liberty of ST. PETER of YORK, East riding, but chiefly in the southern division of the wapentake of STRAFFORTH and TICKHILL, West riding of the county of YORK, 8 miles (S. S. E.) from Rotherham, containing 277 inhabitants. The living is a perpetual curacy, annexed to the Prebend of Laughton en le Morthen, endowed with £400 private benefaction, and £400 royal bounty, and in the peculiar jurisdiction and patronage of the Chancellor of the Cathedral Church of York. The church is dedicated to St. John. Five poor children are taught to read for an annuity of £5, the gift of a Mr. Turie.

WALESBY, a parish in the southern division of the wapentake of WALSHCROFT, parts of LINDSEY, county of LINCOLN, 3¼ miles (N. E.) from Market-Rasen, containing 239 inhabitants. The living is a rectory, in the archdeaconry and diocese of Lincoln, rated in the king's books at £23. 18. 1½., and in the patronage of Henry Dalton, Esq. The church is dedicated to All Saints.

WALESBY, a parish in the Hatfield division of the wapentake of BASSETLAW, county of NOTTINGHAM, 3 miles (N. E.) from Ollerton, containing 308 inhabitants. The living is a discharged vicarage, in the archdeaconry of Nottingham, and diocese of York, rated in the king's books at £6. 1. 3., endowed with £200 royal bounty, and in the patronage of the Hon. and Rev. John Lumley Saville. The church, dedicated to St. Edmund, is in the Norman style of architecture, with a low tower surmounted by a pyramidical roof. The Rev. Richard Jackson, in 1760, bequeathed a rent-charge of £2 for teaching poor children ; nine are educated for £5. 5. a year, being the rental of land received in lieu of the annuity. Walesby is in the honour of Tutbury, duchy of Lancaster, and within the jurisdiction of a court of pleas held at Tutbury every third Tuesday, for the recovery of debts under 40s.

WALFORD, a parish in the hundred of GREYTREE, county of HEREFORD, 2¼ miles (S. S. W.) from Ross, containing 1060 inhabitants. The living is a discharged vicarage, with the perpetual curacy of Ruardean annexed, in the archdeaconry and diocese of Hereford, rated in the king's books at £13. 2. 1., and in the patronage of the Precentor in the Cathedral Church of Hereford. The church is dedicated to St. Leonard.

WALFORD, a joint township with Letton and Newton, in the parish of LEINTWARDINE, hundred of WIGMORE, county of HEREFORD, 13 miles (N. W. by N.) from Leominster, containing, with Letton and Newton, 208 inhabitants.

WALGHERTON, a township in the parish of WYBUNBURY, hundred of NANTWICH, county palatine of CHESTER, 3¾ miles (S. E. by E.) from Nantwich, containing 246 inhabitants.

WALGRAVE, a parish in the hundred of ORLINGBURY, county of NORTHAMPTON, 7¼ miles (N. W. by W.) from Wellingborough, containing 529 inhabitants. The living is a rectory, with that of Hannington annexed, in the archdeaconry of Northampton, and diocese of Peterborough, rated in the king's books at £22. 4. 7., and in the patronage of the Bishop of Lincoln. The church is dedicated to St. Peter. There is a place of worship for Baptists. Montague Lane, in 1670, bequeathed £200, directing the interest to be applied for teaching poor children.

WALHAM-GREEN, a chapelry in the parish of FULHAM, Kensington division of the hundred of OSSULSTONE, county of MIDDLESEX, 3 miles (S. W. by W.) from London. The population is returned with the parish. The chapel, dedicated to St. John, was erected in 1829, at an expense of £9683. 17. 9., raised by subscription, and a grant from the parliamentary commissioners : it contains one thousand three hundred and seventy sittings, of which five hundred and forty-four are free.

WALKER, a township in the parish of LONG BENTON, eastern division of CASTLE ward, county of NORTHUMBERLAND, 3¼ miles (E.) from Newcastle upon Tyne. The population is returned with the parish. It is bounded on the south by the river Tyne, along the banks of which are extensive manufactories and coal-staiths.

WALKERINGHAM, a parish in the North-clay division of the wapentake of BASSETLAW, county of NOTTINGHAM, 4 miles (N. W. by W.) from Gainsborough, containing 518 inhabitants. The living is a discharged vicarage, in the peculiar jurisdiction of the manorial court of Gringley on the Hill, rated in the king's books at £7. 11. 4., and in the patronage of the Master and Fellows of Trinity College, Cambridge. The church is dedicated to St. Mary Magdalene. There is a place of worship for Wesleyan Methodists. The Chesterfield canal passes through the parish, and the river Trent forms the eastern boundary, where there is a ferry. Robert Woodhouse, in 1719, bequeathed a rent-charge of £15 for teaching poor children, and another of £1 for providing books.

WALKERITH, a hamlet in the parish of GAINSBOROUGH, wapentake of CORRINGHAM, parts of LINDSEY, county of LINCOLN, 2½ miles (N. W. by N.) from Gainsborough, containing 67 inhabitants.

WALKERN, a parish in the hundred of BROADWATER, county of HERTFORD, 4¾ miles (E. by N.) from Stevenage, containing 631 inhabitants. The living is a rectory, in the archdeaconry of Huntingdon, and diocese of Lincoln, rated in the king's books at £20. 1. 10½., and in the patronage of the Provost and Fellows of King's College, Cambridge. The church, dedicated to St. Mary, contains a curious monument of a Knight Templar. There is a place of worship for Independents. A fair for cattle is held on November 5th.

WALKHAMPTON, a parish in the hundred of ROBOROUGH, county of DEVON, 4½ miles (S.E. by E.) from Tavistock, containing 670 inhabitants. The living is a vicarage, in the archdeaconry of Totness, and diocese of Exeter, rated in the king's books at £9. 14. 7., and in the patronage of Sir M. M. Lopes, Bart. The church is situated on the verge of Dartmoor Forest. The Plymouth railway passes through the parish. Lady Modyford, in 1719, gave a school-house, with the rents and profits of certain premises, now producing about £161 a year, for the education of poor children; about fifty are instructed.

WALKINGHAM-HILL, an extra-parochial liberty, in the upper division of the wapentake of CLARO, West riding of the county of YORK, 4 miles (N.) from Knaresborough, containing, with Occaney, 24 inhabitants. It is within the peculiar jurisdiction of the court of the honour of Knaresborough.

WALKINGTON, a parish partly in the Hunsley-Beacon division of the wapentake of HARTHILL, but chiefly in the wapentake of HOWDENSHIRE, East riding of the county of YORK, 2¾ miles (S. W. by W.) from Beverley, containing, with the township of Provosts-Fee, 533 inhabitants. The living is a rectory, in the

jurisdiction of the peculiar court of Howdenshire, rated in the king's books at £24. 13. 4., and in the patronage of W. Thompson, Esq. The church is dedicated to All Hallows. There is a place of worship for Wesleyan Methodists.

WALKINSTEAD, county of SURREY.—See GODSTONE.

WALKMILL, a township in that part of the parish of WARKWORTH which is in the eastern division of COQUETDALE ward, county of NORTHUMBERLAND, containing 13 inhabitants.

WALL, a chapelry in the parish of ST. JOHN LEE, southern division of TINDALE ward, county of NORTHUMBERLAND, 3¾ miles (N. by W.) from Hexham, containing 465 inhabitants. The living is a perpetual curacy, in the peculiar jurisdiction of the Archbishop of York, endowed with £800 royal bounty, and £600 parliamentary grant, and in the patronage of T. R. Beaumont, Esq. The chapel, dedicated to St. Oswald, was erected by the monks of Hexham, upon the spot where King Oswald, who was afterwards canonized, raised the standard of the cross, and defeated the Britons under Cadwalla. A silver coin of the former was found when the chapel underwent repair, and a mutilated Roman altar lies in the cemetery; adjoining which is a field, where human skulls and fragments of military weapons have been often turned up by the plough.

WALL, a hamlet in that part of the parish of ST. MICHAEL, LICHFIELD, which is in the southern division of the hundred of OFFLOW, county of STAFFORD, 2½ miles (S.S.W.) from Lichfield, containing 84 inhabitants.

WALL-TOWN, a township in the parish of HALTWHISTLE, western division of TINDALE ward, county of NORTHUMBERLAND, 3 miles (N.W. by W.) from Haltwhistle, containing 109 inhabitants. The Roman wall passed through the village; and in this township were the stations, Vindolana, now called Little Chesters, and Æsica, called Great Chesters; the ramparts of which, particularly the latter, where there are also considerable traces of a town, are in a better state of preservation than those of any other on the whole line of the wall. Roman baths, altars, tombstones, inscriptions, curious pieces of sculpture, and numerous other relics of antiquity, have been found in both; and in a neighbouring hill, called Chapel-Steads, many urns have been discovered. Near the military road connecting the two stations are tumuli, termed the "Four Lawes;" and, on an adjoining hill, a rude monument of three large stones, vulgarly called the "Mare and Foals." Part of the ruins of a castellated mansion, formerly the residence of the Ridleys, has been removed for building a modern seat, and the remainder has been converted into a farm-house.

WALLASEA (ISLE OF), partly in the parishes of CANEWDON, EASTWOOD, PAGLESHAM, GREAT STAMBRIDGE, and LITTLE WAKERING, hundred of ROCHFORD, county of ESSEX, 6 miles (E.N.E.) from Rochford. It is now a peninsula, formed by the rivers Crouch and Broomhill, and joined to the main land by a causeway, kept up at the expense of the several parishes to which it belongs.

WALLAZEY, a parish in the lower division of the hundred of WIRRALL, county palatine of CHESTER, comprising the townships of Liscard, Poulton with Seacomb, and Wallazey, and containing 1169 inhabitants, of which number, 444 are in the township of Wallazey, 11¾ miles (N. by E.) from Great Neston. The living is a discharged rectory, in the archdeaconry and diocese of Chester, rated in the king's books at £11. 0. 2½., and in the patronage of the Bishop of Chester. The church, dedicated to St. Hilary, was rebuilt about seventy years ago, excepting the tower, which bears the date 1560: it stands in the centre of the parish, on a hill composed of red sandstone, used for building. There was another church, prior to the dissolution, appropriated to Birkenhead abbey, but there are no traces of it: the way leading to its site is called Kirk-way. Wallazey forms the north-west corner of the county: it is a peninsula of a triangular form, bounded on the west by the Irish sea, on the north-east by the Mersey, and on the south-east by a branch of the Mersey, called Wallazey Pool: there are sand-hills bordering on the sea, which form a natural barrier against its encroachments. Many handsome houses and marine villas have been erected on the banks of the Mersey, this place being much frequented for sea-bathing. The principal house in the village is an ancient mansion by the sea side, denominated Mockbeggar Hall, or, more properly, Leasowe Castle, formerly a seat of the Egertons, which has been converted by its proprietor, Col. Edward Cust, into a commodious hotel for the accommodation of visitors. A handsome pillar near it, with an inscription, has been erected to the memory of the colonel's mother-in-law, Mrs. Bardé, who was thrown out of her carriage and killed on the spot. On the Black rock, at the north-west point of the parish, a very strong fort, mounting fifteen guns of the largest calibre, has been lately built; and, further in the sea, a small lighthouse, on the plan of the Eddystone light-house, is in progress of erection. The masses of sandstone next the Black rock, called the "Red Noses," well merit the attention of the naturalist, being worn, by the action of the sea, into a variety of caverns of the most romantic forms. Between the village and the sea-shore is an enclosure (formerly a common), called the Leasowes, where races were held, which were of very early origin: here the unfortunate Duke of Monmouth ran his horse, in the reign of Charles II., won the plate, and presented it to the daughter of the mayor of Chester: the races were discontinued about the year 1760, and the ground is now under cultivation. The grammar school was founded, in 1666, by Major Henry Moels, and completed by his brother, who, with Mr. Henry Young, endowed it with a house and garden at Poulton cum Seacomb, and about thirty-seven acres of land, now let for £35 a year, with the interest of £100, and some other benefactions, constitutes the salary of the master. The old school-house, which was inconveniently situated near the church, was pulled down and rebuilt on another site, in 1799. It affords a free English education to all boys of the parish. Steam-boats cross the ferry every hour from Seacomb to Liverpool, which is directly opposite to it. At Liscard, on the banks of the river, is a magazine, where all ships entering the port of Liverpool deposit their gunpowder, prior to admission into the docks.

WALLBOTTLE, a township in that part of the parish of NEWBURN which is in the western division of CASTLE ward, county of NORTHUMBERLAND, 4¾ miles

(W. by N.) from Newcastle upon Tyne, containing 676 inhabitants, many of whom are employed in an extensive colliery at this place.

WALLDITCH, a parish in the hundred of GODDER-THORNE, Bridport division of the county of DORSET, 1¾ mile (E. by S.) from Bridport, containing 141 inhabitants. The living is a perpetual curacy, in the archdeaconry of Dorset, and diocese of Bristol, in the patronage of Lord Rolle and another. The church, dedicated to St. Mary, was formerly a free chapel, or chantry.

WALLERSCOAT, a township in the parish of WEAVERHAM, second division of the hundred of ED-DISBURY, county palatine of CHESTER, 1½ mile (W.) from Northwich, containing 10 inhabitants.

WALLERTHWAITE, a joint township with Markington, in that part of the parish of RIPON which is within the liberty of RIPON, West riding of the county of YORK, 4 miles (N. N. E.) from Ripley. The population is returned with Markington. This township is within the ecclesiastical jurisdiction of the peculiar court of Ripon, belonging to the Archbishop of York.

WALLINGFORD, a borough and market town, having exclusive jurisdiction, though locally in the hundred of Moreton, county of BERKS, 15 miles (N. N. W.) from Reading, and 46 (W. by N.) from London, containing, with the extra-parochial liberty of the Castle, but exclusively of the liberty of Clapcot, which is in the parish of

Seal.

Allhallows, 2093 inhabitants, according to the census of 1821, since which period the population has increased to about 2600. The name is derived from the ancient British word Guallen, or the Roman Vallum, each signifying "an old fort," and from a ford over the Thames: subsequently to the Roman invasion, it was converted into a strong fortification by that people, and is supposed to have been the principal station of the Attrebatii. On the arrival of the Saxons, it became one of their principal forts, and continued to be a place of considerable repute, until it was burnt by the Danes, in 1006: from the effects of this calamity it speedily recovered, and, in the reign of Edward the Confessor, had risen to the dignity of a royal prescriptive borough. At the Conquest, William, having arrived with his army, received here the homage of Stigand, Archbishop of Canterbury, and many other prelates and barons. During the civil war between Stephen and the Empress Matilda, the castle was occupied and held for the latter: it was subsequently the place of meeting between John and the barons. The honour, having become vested in the crown, was given by Richard I. to his brother John; and Henry III., on being elected King of the Romans, entertained all the prelates and barons in the castle. Having been subsequently annexed, by act of parliament, to the duchy of Corn-wall, on the reversion of these estates to the crown, the castle and manor were granted to Cardinal Wolsey, who conferred them on his then newly-erected college of Christ Church, Oxford; and, in Camden's time, part of the castle was used, as an occasional retreat in time of sickness, by the students of that college: a portion of these buildings, called the "Priests' Chambers," has been converted into a malthouse. At the commencement of the parliamentary war, it was repaired and garrisoned for the king, and was not surrendered till nearly the close of the war; and, about four years afterwards, in 1653, it was completely demolished, insomuch that, at present, part of a wall towards the river is all that remains of this ancient and celebrated structure.

The town is situated on the road between Reading and Oxford, and has a remarkably neat and clean appearance: it consists principally of two streets, well paved and lighted with oil, according to the provisions of an act obtained in 1795: the inhabitants are abundantly supplied with water. Across the river Thames, which passes on the eastern side of the town, is a fine stone bridge of several arches, about three hundred yards in length, constructed in 1809, in lieu of a dilapidated structure which was supposed to have been built five centuries ago: there is a fund of £42 per annum for its repair, being a rent-charge on houses, under the management of two bridge-masters chosen annually from the burgesses. Some business is done in malting, but it is not so extensive as formerly. A line of communication has been opened with Birmingham, Bath, and Bristol, by means of a canal navigation, running into the Thames, by which river coal is brought hither, and corn and flour are conveyed to London and other places. The market is on Friday; and a statute and pleasure fair is held on the 29th of September. By the charter of incorporation, obtained in the reign of James I., and confirmed and enlarged by Charles I., the government is vested in a mayor, high steward, recorder, six aldermen, and eighteen burgesses, or, as they are generally termed, assistants; with a chamberlain, two bailiffs, and two bridge-men, who are annually elected from the burgesses by the mayor; and a town clerk, who is also chosen, by the corporation, from among the burgesses. The mayor, who is also coroner, aldermen, and recorder, are justices of the peace, exercising exclusive jurisdiction. A court of quarter session is held, at which the mayor, or recorder, presides: it was formerly empowered to inflict capital punishment, but its authority is now limited to transportation. In former times, criminals convicted capitally in this borough, for the first time, had their lives spared on certain conditions; and, in the 45th of Henry III., a return made by the jurors declared, that no person belonging to the borough ought to be executed for one offence. The corporation are empowered, by charter, to hold a court for the recovery of small debts; but this right is seldom exercised, though debts to any amount may be recovered by a process from the town clerk. Petty sessions for the division are held every Friday. The freedom of the borough, although vested in the corporation, is not enforced; every individual may engage in business indiscriminately. This borough sends two members to parliament: the elective franchise is in the corporation, and the inhabitants at large paying scot and lot: the number of voters is about three hundred, and the mayor is the returning officer.

Wallingford comprises the parishes of All Hallows, St. Leonard, St. Mary the More, and St. Peter, all in

VOL. IV.

the archdeaconry and diocese of Salisbury. The living of All Hallows' is a sinecure rectory, in the patronage of the Master and Fellows of Pembroke College, Oxford: the church was demolished in 1648. The living of St. Leonard's is a discharged rectory, with the perpetual curacy of Sotwell annexed, rated in the king's books at £7. 12. 6., and in the patronage of the Crown: the church is a very ancient structure, but destitute of claim to architectural description, with the exception of some few Norman remains. The living of St. Mary's the More is a discharged rectory, rated in the king's books at £4, endowed with £600 private benefaction, and £800 royal bounty, and in the patronage of the Crown: the church is a very handsome edifice, situated in the space near the market-house, with a square embattled tower, ornamented with pinnacles, and on which is the figure of an armed knight on horseback, supposed to represent King Stephen; the tower, which bears the date of 1658, is said to have been built with materials from the castle. The living of St. Peter's is a discharged rectory, rated in the king's books at £6. 1. 3., endowed with £600 private benefaction, £400 royal bounty, and £600 parliamentary grant, and in the patronage of W. S. Blackstone, Esq. The church is a very handsome structure, bearing date 1769, with a square tower, surmounted by an elegant spire of Portland stone, supported on pillars and arches, and erected, in 1777, by voluntary subscriptions, to which the learned Sir William Blackstone, who was an inhabitant of the town, and whose remains are deposited in the church, was a liberal contributor. There are places of worship for Baptists, the Society of Friends, Independents, and Wesleyan Methodists. The free school was founded by Walter Bigg, alderman of London, in 1659, by whom it was endowed with £10 per annum, for six boys, who are elected by the aldermen. In 1672, the fraternity of St. John the Baptist, London, now the Merchant Taylors' Company, gave £32. 10. for the erection of a free school, and £2. 10. for the schoolmaster. A school was established, in 1819, for twenty boys and thirty girls, all of whom are educated and clothed: it is supported by voluntary contributions. An infant school, for an unlimited number of children, is held in a handsome brick building, erected by subscription, at a small distance from the town. An almshouse for six poor widows was founded and endowed with £34 per annum, in 1681, by William Angier and Mary his sister; the endowment has been augmented by subsequent benefactions. On Wittenham hill, in this neighbourhood, are some remains of a Roman camp, where numerous coins have been found. Richard de Wallingford, abbot of St. Albans, a celebrated mathematician and mechanic; and John de Wallingford, a monk of that abbey, are supposed to have been natives of this town: the former invented, and presented to the abbey church, an ingenious clock, that shewed not only the course of the sun, moon, and principal stars, but also the ebbing and flowing of the sea. Joan, the fair maid of Kent, and widow of the Black Prince, died here in 1385. Wallingford confers the title of viscount on the Earl of Banbury.

WALLINGTON, a parish in the hundred of ODSEY, county of HERTFORD, 3 miles (E.) from Baldock, containing 210 inhabitants. The living is a rectory, in the archdeaconry of Huntingdon, and diocese of Lincoln, rated in the king's books at £16. 15. 2½., and in the patronage of the Master of Emanuel College, Cambridge. The church, dedicated to St. Mary, is an ancient structure, with an embattled tower, surmounted by a short spire : attached to the north side of the chancel are several mutilated altar-tombs, and other sepulchral remains. John Brown, in 1736, bequeathed property, producing about £5 a year, for teaching poor children.

WALLINGTON, a parish in the hundred of CLACK-CLOSE, county of NORFOLK, 3½ miles (N. by E.) from Downham-Market, containing, with the hamlet of Thorpland, 72 inhabitants. The living is a rectory, with Holme and South Runcton annexed, in the archdeaconry of Norfolk, and diocese of Norwich, and in the patronage of — Bell, Esq. The church, now in ruins, was dedicated to St. Margaret.

WALLINGTON, a hamlet in the parish of BEDDINGTON, second division of the hundred of WALLINGTON, county of SURREY, 2¾ miles (W. by S.) from Croydon, containing 847 inhabitants. Here was formerly a chapel, now in ruins.

WALLINGTON-DEMESNE, a township in that part of the parish of HARTBURN which is in the north-eastern division of TINDALE ward, county of NORTHUMBERLAND, 12½ miles (W. by S.) from Morpeth, containing 205 inhabitants. In pulling down the remains of Fenwick tower, in 1775, several hundred gold nobles, of the coinage of Edward III., were found in an open stone chest ; it is supposed that they were concealed on the invasion of David, King of Scotland, in 1360, who made prisoners the two sons of Sir John Fenwick, then owner of the castle.

WALLINGWELLS, an extra-parochial liberty, in the Hatfield division of the wapentake of BASSETLAW, county of NOTTINGHAM, 3¾ miles (N. by W.) from Worksop, containing 7 inhabitants. A Benedictine nunnery, in honour of the Virgin Mary, was founded here, in the reign of Stephen, by Ralph de Cheroulcourt, which at the dissolution had a revenue of £88. 11. 6.: it is now the residence of Sir Thomas Woollaston White, Bart. In excavating near the house, in 1829, several stone coffins were found, and amongst them that of Dame Margery Dourant, second abbess of the convent, who died in the reign of Richard I.: on opening it, the body appeared nearly perfect, but, on exposure, soon suffered decomposition ; her shoes were entire, as was also a silver chalice : these relics were again deposited, with the ashes, in the same receptacle, and re-interred.

WALLOP (NETHER), a parish in the hundred of THORNGATE, Andover division of the county of SOUTHAMPTON, 4 miles (W. by N.) from Stockbridge, containing 839 inhabitants. The living is a discharged vicarage, in the archdeaconry and diocese of Winchester, rated in the king's books at £13. 13. 4., and in the patronage of the Dean and Chapter of York. The church is dedicated to St. Andrew. There is a place of worship for Wesleyan Methodists. Twenty-four children are instructed for £17 a year, the bequest of Francis Douce, Esq., in 1759. On a point, or head, of an elevated ridge, called Danebury Hill, or Bill, are considerable remains of a circular fortification, with very lofty ramparts, enclosing an extensive area : a short distance to the westward is an outwork, for the defence of that side; but on the east and north sides, where the ground is more steep,

it is protected by a single ditch only : the entrance is by a winding course, strengthened by great embankments. There are several barrows near this camp, one of which, about a mile distant, is called Canute's barrow.

WALLOP (OVER), a parish in the hundred of THORNGATE, Andover division of the county of SOUTHAMPTON, 5 miles (W. N. W.) from Stockbridge, containing 499 inhabitants. The living is a rectory, in the archdeaconry and diocese of Winchester, rated in the king's books at £27. 5. 2½., and in the patronage of the Earl of Portsmouth. The church is dedicated to St. Peter. Six poor children are instructed for £2 a year, the gift of Mr. Smith, in 1786.

WALLSEND, a parish in the eastern division of CASTLE ward, county of NORTHUMBERLAND, 3½ miles (E. N. E.) from Newcastle upon Tyne, comprising the townships of Howden-Pans, Wallsend, and Wellington, and containing 5103 inhabitants. The living is a perpetual curacy, in the archdeaconry of Northumberland, and diocese of Durham, and in the patronage of the Dean and Chapter of Durham. The church, dedicated to St. Peter, is a neat stone building with a spire, situated at some distance from the village : it was erected at the expense of nearly £5000, of which, about £3300 was raised by tontine ; the first stone was laid in 1807, and it was consecrated in August 1809. The old church, which was dedicated to the Holy Cross, has been pulled down. There are three places of worship for Methodists, and one for Anti-Burghers. The name of this parish is obviously derived from its situation at the extremity of the wall of Severus, on the east : it contained the Roman station *Legedunum*, so called from its situation, and from having been a magazine for corn, whence other stations in the interior were supplied. It was garrisoned by the first cohort of the *Lergi*, who were stationed here for the defence of their shipping, of which the Romans kept, in the rivers on the borders of their settlements, ships called *lusoriæ*, which were always on the alert, either to protect them from the invasion of the inhabitants of the neighbouring coasts, or to assist them in extending their empire, by the invasion of the territories of their neighbours ; and many altars, coins, and urns, with other curious relics, have been discovered upon the spot. Beyond this point the wall does not appear to have been continued ; the Tyne itself, near its influx into the ocean, forming, by its great breadth and depth, a sufficient barrier against the incursions of those enemies, from whose frequent depredations it was originally erected, to protect the inhabitants of this part of the island. The ruins of a quay still further evince that it was anciently a considerable trading colony of the Romans, who, more than one thousand years since, discharged their freights where now are numerous staiths, projecting from the northern bank of the Tyne, whence vessels employed in the coal trade are continually taking in immense quantities of the excellent coal termed "Wallsend," for the London and other markets. Here are several yards for shipbuilding, extensive limekilns, and manufactories for copperas and earthenware. The village is large and well-built, situated near the Shields road, and contains many good houses, with a spacious green in the centre, crossed by a raised causeway. At its eastern extremity is a school-room, with a house and garden for the master, given, in 1748, by Mrs. Stewart and Mrs. Muncaster, for the education of children : the Sunday schools are attended by about six hundred boys and girls. Wallsend is the birthplace of the two brothers, John and William Martin, the first distinguished as historical painter to the king, the other as an ingenious inventor of several useful machines. In October 1821, fifty-two individuals were killed by an explosion in one of the neighbouring collieries.

WALMER, a parish, and a member of the cinque-port liberty of SANDWICH, locally in the hundred of Cornilo, lathe of ST. AUGUSTINE, county of KENT, 2 miles (S.) from Deal, containing 1568 inhabitants. The living is a perpetual curacy, in the archdeaconry and diocese of Canterbury, endowed with £200 private bene-faction, and £200 royal bounty, and in the patronage of the Archbishop of Canterbury. The church, dedicated to St. Mary, has lately received an addition of three hundred and eighty sittings, of which two hundred and eighty are free, the Incorporated Society for the enlargement of churches and chapels having granted £200 towards defraying the expense. Walmer-street, on the high road from London to Dovor, is neatly built, being interspersed with genteel houses, marine villas, &c., and, partly on account of its convenient situation as regards Dovor and Deal, is much frequented during the season for sea-bathing. It is noted for the salubrity of its air, and for the fine prospects, in its vicinity, over the Downs and the straits of Dovor to the French coast ; but chiefly for the celebrated fortress, Walmer Castle, erected by Henry VIII., at the same period with those of Deal and Sandown, for the defence of the coast, and now appropriated to the Lord Warden of the cinque-ports (an office usually held by the first Lord of the Treasury), for whose residence the principal apartments were fitted up a few years ago, and the fosse, at the same time, was converted into a garden. Here are also barracks, but they are partially disused.

WALMERSLEY, a township in that part of the parish of BURY which is in the hundred of SALFORD, county palatine of LANCASTER, 2¼ miles (N. by E.) from Bury, containing 3290 inhabitants, who are chiefly employed in the extensive spinning mills on the river Irwell, which runs through it. There is a place of worship for Independents.

WALMSGATE, a parish in the hundred of HILL, parts of LINDSEY, county of LINCOLN, 8 miles (N. N. W.) from Spilsby, containing 56 inhabitants. The living is a perpetual curacy, annexed to the vicarage of Burwell, in the archdeaconry and diocese of Lincoln.

WALMSLEY, a chapelry in the parish of BOLTON, hundred of SALFORD, county palatine of LANCASTER, 4 miles (N.) from Great Bolton. The population is returned with the parish. The living is a perpetual curacy, in the archdeaconry and diocese of Chester, endowed with £200 private benefaction, and £800 royal bounty, and in the patronage of the Vicar of Bolton in the Moor. There is a place of worship for Unitarians. Ten poor children are instructed in a school-house erected by subscription, upon land given by Miles Lonsdale, in 1716 : the school is partly supported with the interest of £50, the bequest of James Lancashire, in 1737.

WALNEY (ISLE of), a chapelry in the parish of DALTON in FURNESS, hundred of LONSDALE, north of the sands, county palatine of LANCASTER, 5 miles (S. W.)

from Dalton. The population is returned with the parish. The living is a perpetual curacy, in the archdeaconry of Richmond, and diocese of Chester, endowed with £600 royal bounty, and in the patronage of the Vicar of Dalton. Walney, which is insular at high water, is ten miles in length, and about one in breadth, having a lighthouse on its southern extremity, a short distance north from which is a rocky islet, termed the Pile of Fouldrey, i. e., the island of fowls, where are the venerable ruins of a strong castle, built by an abbot of Furness. There are several other small isles in the group, the principal of which is Old Barrow, lying between this and the main land, opposite the small village and port of Barrow. On Walney are some remarkable intermitting springs of fresh water. It is stated to have been once covered with wood, of which it is now extremely barren. West, in his " Antiquities of Furness," describes it as lying on a bed of moss, which is found by digging through a layer of sand and clay, and in which trees have been discovered. To prevent the encroachments of the sea, the abbots of Furness kept up a dyke, which, since the dissolution, has been neglected, and the sea has made considerable inroads.

WALPOLE, a parish in the hundred of BLYTHING, county of SUFFOLK, 2 miles (S. W.) from Halesworth, containing 605 inhabitants. The living is a perpetual curacy, in the archdeaconry of Suffolk, and diocese of Norwich, endowed with £800 royal bounty, and £1000 parliamentary grant. The Rev. B. Philpot was patron in 1817. The church is dedicated to St. Mary. There is a place of worship for Independents. Thomas Neale, in 1704, bequeathed an annuity of £2. 10., for teaching poor children.

WALPOLE (ST. ANDREW), a parish in the Marsh-land division of the hundred of FREEBRIDGE, county of NORFOLK, 8¾ miles (W. by S.) from Lynn-Regis, containing 360 inhabitants. The living is a discharged vicarage, in the archdeaconry and diocese of Norwich, rated in the king's books at £26. 13. 4., and in the patronage of T. Hankinson, Esq. The church is a regular well-built structure, entirely covered with lead. Walpole derives its name from the great wall raised by the Romans to defend it from the encroachments of the sea, and from an extensive pool of water near it. In a garden at the foot of this embankment, many Roman bricks, and the remains of an aqueduct, formed of earthen pipes, twenty-six in number, have been found. The æstuary, called Cross Keys Wash, in the neighbourhood, may be passed on foot, at the reflux of the tides, to Long Sutton, in Lincolnshire.

WALPOLE (ST. PETER), a parish in the Marsh-land division of the hundred of FREEBRIDGE, county of NORFOLK, 9 miles (W. by S.) from Lynn-Regis, containing 1102 inhabitants. The living is a rectory, in the archdeaconry and diocese of Norwich, rated in the king's books at £21, and in the patronage of the Crown. The church, which was built in the reign of Henry VI., is esteemed one of the most beautiful parochial structures in England ; it has thirteen clerestory windows on each side, exhibiting fine specimens of stained glass. There is a place of worship for Wesleyan Methodists.

WALRIDGE, a township in the parish of STAMFORDHAM, north-eastern division of TINDALE ward, county of NORTHUMBERLAND, 5½ miles (N. by W) from Durham, containing 3 inhabitants.

3 B 2

Seal and Arms.

WALSALL, a parish in the southern division of the hundred of OFFLOW, county of STAFFORD, comprising the market town of Walsall, and the township of Walsall-Foreign, which latter includes the chapelry of Bloxwich, and containing, according to the census of 1821 (since which period the number has considerably increased), 11,914 inhabitants, of which number, 5504 are in the town of Walsall, 18 miles (S. E. by S.) from Stafford, and 118 (N. W.) from London. This place is supposed to have derived its name (in various ancient records written *Waleshall* and *Walshale*) from its situation in or near an extensive forest, resorted to by the Druids for the celebration of their religious rites, and in which the Saxons subsequently erected a temple to their god Woden; from which also the town of Wednesbury, in the vicinity, is supposed to have derived its name. In the early part of the tenth century, it was fortified by Ethelfleda, daughter of Alfred, and Countess of Mercia, probably about the same time that she built a castle at Stafford, and surrounded that town with walls. At the time of the Conquest, it was retained by William, and continued to be a royal demesne for nearly twenty years, till it was given by the Conqueror to Robert, son of Asculfus, who accompanied him to Britain. Walsall is not connected with any events of historical interest: Queen Elizabeth, in one of her tours through the country, visited it, and affixed the royal seal and signature, at *Walshale*, on the 13th of July, in the 28th year of her reign, to a deed preserved in the archives of the corporation, containing a grant of certain lands to the town; and, in 1643, Henrietta Maria, queen of Charles I., remained here for a short time previously to joining the king at Edgehill. The town is pleasantly situated on the summit and acclivities of a rock of limestone, and is watered by a small brook called by Erdeswick "Walsal water," which falls into the river Tame, a little below the town: it consists of several regular and spacious streets, in some of which are handsome houses of modern erection, many of them being of a superior description. The environs are interesting, and contain some pleasant villas, and much beautiful and varied scenery. The town is well paved, and lighted with gas, under the superintendence of commissioners, appointed by act of parliament passed in 1824, and amply supplied with water. A subscription library was established in 1800, the plan of which has been recently enlarged, and a splendid edifice, containing reading and news rooms, ornamented by a Doric colonnade thirty feet high, has been erected. Assemblies are held at the principal hotels, at different times, and always during the races, which take place annually, commencing on the Tuesday before Michaelmas-day. The principal hotel, a very spacious and handsome building, has been recently enlarged and beautified at a considerable expense; the handsome portico is formed of pillars formerly belonging to Fisherwick, the noble mansion of Lord Donegall. The principal articles of manufacture are bridle-bits, stirrups, spurs, saddle-trees, and every kind of saddlers' ironmongery; buckles, snuffers, spoons, and various other kinds of hardware; coach harness and furniture, plated ware, locks, chain curbs, dog chains, and other articles, many of which are brought into the town and sold by factors: there are several brass and iron foundries, and in the vicinity are extensive quarries of limestone, which afford employment to a great number of individuals: a considerable trade is also carried on in malt. The situation of the town, in the north-eastern part of an extensive mining and manufacturing district, abundantly supplied with coal, is peculiarly favourable to its manufactures; and a branch of the Old Birmingham canal, which comes up to the west end of the town, and the Wyrley and Essington canal, which passes within a mile north of it, afford every facility of inland navigation. From the wharf, at Park-street, fly-boats ply to Birmingham, on Tuesdays and Fridays. The market is on Tuesday; and the fairs are, February 24th; Whitsun-Tuesday, a pleasure fair; and the Tuesday before Michaelmas-day, chiefly for horses, cattle, and cheese. The inhabitants enjoy several privileges and immunities by prescription: Henry I. granted them exemption from toll throughout England, and from serving upon juries out of the limits of the "borough and foreign," into which Walsall is divided; and the guilds of St. John the Baptist, and of our Lady, appear to have been ancient establishments, exercising various rights and privileges. The last charter of incorporation was granted in the 13th of Charles II., by which the government was vested in a mayor, recorder, and twenty-four capital burgesses (including the mayor), assisted by a town clerk, two serjeants at mace, and other officers. The mayor is annually elected by the capital burgesses, by whom also the recorder, town clerk, and other officers, are appointed. The mayor, the late mayor, the recorder, and two senior burgesses, are justices of the peace, and hold quarterly courts of session for all offences not capital; and a court of record, under the charter of Charles II., as often as may be requisite, for the recovery of debts not exceeding £20. The hundred court is held here, for the recovery of debts under 40s., before a steward appointed by the high sheriff of the county; and the lord of the manor holds an annual court leet, at which constables and other officers are appointed. The town hall, where the several courts are held, and the public business of the corporation is transacted, is a handsome, though rather ancient, building, well adapted to its purpose: the common gaol for the town is a small building, calculated to receive only ten prisoners.

The living is a vicarage, in the archdeaconry of Stafford, and diocese of Lichfield and Coventry, rated in the king's books at £10. 19. 7., and in the patronage of the Earl of Bradford. The church, dedicated to St. Matthew, an ancient and spacious cruciform structure, with several chapels in the aisles, was, with the exception of the tower and chancel, which latter has undergone several alterations, taken down and rebuilt, in the later style of English architecture, from a design by Mr. Goodwin, in 1821, at an expense of £20,000, the Incorporated Society for the enlargement of churches and chapels having granted £2000 for the erection of one thousand one hundred and seventy-three sittings, of which seven hundred and fifty-seven are free: it occupies a commanding situation on the summit of the rock on which the town is built, and the tower, which is in fine proportion, and surmounted by a lofty spire, forms a conspicuous object in the distant view of the town. St. Paul's chapel, a handsome edifice in the Grecian style of architecture, was erected by the governors of the free grammar school, who, having sold some mines under part of the land belonging to that establishment, in 1797, obtained an act of parliament for applying part of the purchase money to the erection of the chapel, which was completed in 1826: the living is a perpetual curacy, in the patronage of the governors, who appoint the head-master of the school to the office of minister. There are places of worship for Independents, Wesleyan Methodists, and Unitarians, and two Roman Catholic chapels, of which one, lately erected from a design by Mr. Ireland, is a handsome edifice in the Grecian style of architecture.

The free grammar school, in Park-street, was founded in 1557, by Queen Mary, who endowed it with lands belonging to the guilds and chantries. which existed here previously to the dissolution, and placed it under the control of certain governors, whom she incorporated: the income is about £780 per annum: the salary of the head-master, including his stipend as minister of the chapel, is £220 per annum; and there are three other masters, whose salaries respectively are £100, £80, and £60: the head, second, and third masters have houses rent-free, and the privilege of taking boarders, and the school is open to all boys of the parish. Bishop Hough received the rudiments of his education in this school: the premises, recently built, are handsome and commodious. An English school is supported from the same funds, in the old school buildings in the churchyard, in which one hundred and twenty boys are instructed gratuitously, with the exception of finding their own books and stationery; and two schoolmistresses are also supported, for the instruction of children of both sexes. The Blue-coat charity school, which was endowed with £19. 4. per annum, for the instruction of twenty-five children of each sex, has been incorporated with a National school, which is principally supported by subscription. There are also Sunday schools in connexion with the established church and the several dissenting congregations, of which one, belonging to the latter, has an endowment in land producing £12 per annum. Some almshouses, founded by Mr. John Harper, in the reign of James I., and endowed with land producing £40 per annum, were rebuilt, in 1790, by the Rev. Mr. Rutter, then vicar, for the reception of six aged widows, among whom £10 per quarter is divided, in equal shares. Almshouses were, in 1825, erected and endowed for eleven aged widows, five from the borough and five from the foreign, of Walsall, and one from the parish of Rushall; to which purpose a dole of one penny, paid by the corporation to every person in the parishes of Walsall and Rushall, on the eve of the Epiphany, was appropriated. In the reign of Henry VI., Mr. Thomas Mollesley gave to the corporation a manor and estates in the county of Warwick, out of the rental of which the dole was paid, and which now constitute part of their extensive possessions. There are also numerous charitable bequests for apprenticing children, and for distribution among the poor. An annual feast, held by the mayor on St. Clement's day, called "Clement's Ac-compt," when the tenants of the corporation pay their rents, appears to have originated in a decree issued by John Arundel, Bishop of Lichfield and Coventry, in 1496, in which, among other things, he directs the wardens to make "a true account before the mayor yearly, on St. Clement's day:" at this festival a custom has prevailed, from time immemorial, of throwing apples and nuts from the town hall into the street, to be scrambled for by the populace.

WALSALL-FOREIGN, a township in the parish of WALSALL, southern division of the hundred of OFF-LOW, county of STAFFORD, containing 6410 inhabitants.

WALSDEN, a township in that part of the parish of ROCHDALE which is in the hundred of SALFORD, county palatine of LANCASTER. The population is returned with the chapelry of Todmorden.

WALSHAM (NORTH), a market town and parish in the hundred of TUNSTEAD, county of NORFOLK, 15 miles (N.N.E.) from Norwich, and 124 (N.E. by N.) from London, containing 2303 inhabitants. In the year 1600, nearly the whole of this town was destroyed by a fire, which, although it continued but three hours, consumed property of the value of £20,000. It is situated on the high road to Norwich, and consists of three streets diverging from a central area, in which stands the church: the inhabitants are well supplied with water. A neat theatre has been lately erected, and is opened for performances once in two years. A navigable canal passes through the parish, a short distance north-east of the town, in its course from Antingham to Yarmouth; and a silk-manufactory has been recently established. The market is on Thursday; and a fair is held on the day before Holy Thursday, for cattle: statutes for hiring servants are held twice a year. The market cross, erected by Bishop Thirlby, in the reign of Edward III., was repaired, after the great fire in 1600, by Bishop Redman. Two courts baron are held annually, one by the Bishop of Norwich, and the other by Lord Suffield. The magistrates for the hundred meet here every week.

The living is a vicarage, with the rectory of Antingham St. Mary annexed, in the archdeaconry of Norfolk, and diocese of Norwich, rated in the king's books at £8, and in the patronage of the Bishop of Norwich. The church, which is dedicated to St. Mary, is a spacious structure; but the tower, having fallen in the year 1724, is in ruins: in the chancel is an elegant mural monument to the memory of Sir William Paston, Knt., a native of this town, and founder of the grammar school; it was erected during his life, and is surmounted by a recumbent statue in armour. There are places of worship for the Society of Friends, Independents, and Primitive and Wesleyan Methodists. The free grammar school was founded by the above-mentioned Sir William Paston, for the education of forty boys, being children of the inhabitants resident in either of the hundreds of North Erpingham, Happing, Tunstead, and Flegg, who endowed it with the rents of certain estates at Horsey and Walcot, to the amount of about £300 per annum, together with a small endowment of £4. 15. by a person unknown: the master's salary is £70 per annum, with a residence; that of the usher £30, and that of the lecturer £10. Admiral Lord Nelson received part of his education at this school. A Sunday school, on the National system, is supported by voluntary subscription. About a mile south of the town is a stone cross, erected to commemorate a victory obtained, in 1382, by Spencer, Bishop of Norwich, over some rebels headed by a dyer, named Leytester.

WALSHAM (SOUTH), a village in the hundred of WALSHAM, county of NORFOLK, 2¾ miles (N.W. by W.) from Acle, comprising the parishes of St. Lawrence and St. Mary, in the archdeaconry and diocese of Norwich, and containing 524 inhabitants. The living of St. Lawrence's is a rectory, rated in the king's books at £13.6.8., and in the patronage of the President and Fellows of Queen's College, Cambridge: that of St. Mary's is a discharged vicarage, rated in the king's books at £5, and in the patronage of the Bishop of Norwich, by lapse. The church of St. Mary only remains.

WALSHAM le WILLOWS, a parish in the hundred of BLACKBOURN, county of SUFFOLK, 4½ miles (E. by N.) from Ixworth, containing 1081 inhabitants. The living is a perpetual curacy, in the archdeaconry of Suffolk, and diocese of Norwich, endowed with £16 per annum private benefaction, £400 royal bounty, and £1400 parliamentary grant. John Sparke, Esq. was patron in 1813. The church is dedicated to St. Mary. There are places of worship for Baptists and Wesleyan Methodists. A small sum, bequeathed by William Withers, in 1632, is applied for teaching poor children.

WALSHFORD, a joint township with Great Ribston, in the parish of HUNSINGORE, upper division of the wapentake of CLARO, West riding of the county of YORK, 3¼ miles (N. by E.) from Wetherby. The population is returned with Great Ribston. It is in the peculiar jurisdiction of the manorial court of Hunsingore.

WALSINGHAM (GREAT), a parish in the northern division of the hundred of GREENHOE, county of NORFOLK, 1 mile (N. by E.) from Little Walsingham, comprising the united parishes of All Saints and St. Peter, and containing 413 inhabitants. The living is a donative, in the patronage of H. Lee Warner, Esq. The church is remarkable for the fine proportions of its architecture, which is in the English style. This place, also called Old Walsingham, was formerly of considerable importance, having contained three churches.

WALSINGHAM (LITTLE), a parish (formerly a market town) in the northern division of the hundred of GREENHOE, county of NORFOLK, 28 miles (N.W.) from Norwich, and 114 (N.N.E.) from London, containing 1067 inhabitants. This place, also denominated New Walsingham, was of great celebrity, for many centuries, as the site of a shrine of the Virgin, or our Lady of Walsingham, constructed of wood, after the plan of the Sancta Casa at Nazareth, and founded, in 1061, by the widow of Ricoldie Faverches, whose son confirmed her endowment, and added a monastery for Augustine canons, with a conventual church: this institution became immensely rich, and at the dissolution its revenue was valued at £446. 14. 4., exclusively of the valuable offerings of the numerous devotees of all nations who had visited the shrine, which are said to have equalled those presented at the shrine of our Lady of Loretto, and that of St. Thomas à Becket at Canterbury. Among the illustrious visitants were several of the kings and queens of England, especially Henry VIII., who, in the second year of his reign, walked hither barefoot from Barsham, to present a valuable necklace to the image of the Virgin. During the prevalence of superstition the credulous were taught to believe that the galaxy, or milky way, in the heavens was the peculiar residence of the Virgin, whence it obtained the name of "Walsingham way." The venerable remains of this once noble and stupendous pile are situated, in the midst of a grove of stately trees, in the pleasure grounds of H. L. Warner, Esq., and contiguous to a fine stream of water, over which that gentleman has built a handsome bridge: they chiefly consist of the great western portal, a lofty and magnificent arch, sixty feet high, which formed the east end of the conventual church; the spacious refectory, seventy-eight feet by twenty-seven, with walls twenty-six feet and a half in height; a portion of the cloisters, and a stone bath with two wells, called St. Mary's, or the "Wishing Wells;" near which is a Saxon arch with zigzag mouldings, removed hither from the mansion as an ornamental object. The devotees who had permission to drink of these wells were taught to believe that, under certain restrictions, they should obtain whatever they might desire. The cross, resting upon a platform on which the pilgrims knelt to receive the water, is still visible. The other relics are, the abbey, a stone pulpit belonging to the refectory, and the ruins of a fine window. Here was also a house of Grey friars, founded, in 1346, by Elizabeth de Burgo, Countess of Clare. The town is situated in a vale, surrounded by bold heights presenting diversified scenery, near a small stream which, within a few miles, falls into the sea: the inhabitants are supplied with water from wells. A fair is held annually a fortnight after Whit-Monday. Quarter sessions are held here by adjournment from Norwich. The bridewell, or house of correction, formerly an hospital for lepers, founded in 1486, has been considerably enlarged. This place was formerly noted for the growth of saffron, which has been discontinued for some years.

The living is a donative, in the patronage of H. Lee Warner, Esq. The church, which is dedicated to St. Mary, is a spacious structure, and contains a very ancient and beautiful font, of octagonal form, resting on a plinth of four ornamented steps, and representing, in compartments, the seven Sacraments of the church of Rome and the Crucifixion: there is also an ancient monument, erected to the memory of a Roman Catholic bishop; and a very fine one to that of Sir Henry Sidney. There is a place of worship for Wesleyan Methodists. A free grammar school was founded by Richard Bond, Esq., in 1639, and endowed with an estate in Great Snoring, in this county, producing £110 per annum, vested in feoffees, for the maintenance of a master and an usher, to teach thirty boys. There are eight almshouses, occupied by paupers having large families. The remains of a Danish encampment are visible towards the sea. This place confers the title of baron on the family of De Grey.

WALSOKEN, a parish in the Marshland division of the hundred of FREEBRIDGE, county of NORFOLK, containing 1240 inhabitants. The living is a rectory, in the archdeaconry and diocese of Norwich, rated in the king's books at £30. 13. 4., and in the patronage of Mrs. Allington. The church, dedicated to All Saints, is a handsome structure with a lofty spire. The village is pleasantly situated adjoining the town of Wisbeach, and extending a mile from it; and the pleasant walks in its vicinity are much frequented by the inhabitants of that town.

WALTERSTONE, a parish in the hundred of EWYASLACY, county of HEREFORD, 15 miles (S. W. by W.) from Hereford, containing 176 inhabitants. The living is a perpetual curacy, in the archdeaconry of Brecon, and diocese of St. David's, endowed with £200 private benefaction, and £800 royal bounty, and in the patronage of the Earl of Oxford. The church is dedicated to St. Mary.

WALTHAM, a parish in the hundred of BRIDGE and PETHAM, lathe of ST. AUGUSTINE, county of KENT, 7 miles (S. S. W.) from Canterbury, containing, with the inmates of the poorhouse of twelve united parishes, 582 inhabitants. The living is a vicarage, annexed to that of Petham, in the archdeaconry and diocese of Canterbury, rated in the king's books at £7. 15. 5. The church, dedicated to St. Bartholomew, is in the early style of English architecture. The parish is bounded on the east by Stane Street.

WALTHAM, a parish in the wapentake of BRADLEY-HAVERSTOE, parts of LINDSEY, county of LINCOLN, 3¾ miles (S. by W.) from Great Grimsby, containing 526 inhabitants. The living is a rectory, in the archdeaconry and diocese of Lincoln, rated in the king's books at £15. 10. 10., and in the patronage of the Chapter of the Collegiate Church of Southwell. The church is dedicated to All Saints. There is a place of worship for Wesleyan Methodists.

WALTHAM (BISHOP'S), a market town and parish in that part of the hundred of BISHOP'S WALTHAM which is in the Portsdown division of the county of SOUTHAMPTON, 10 miles (E. N. E.) from Southampton, and 65 (S. W. by W.) from London, containing 2126 inhabitants. The market is on Friday: fairs are held on the second Friday in May, for horses and toys; July 30th, for cheese and pedlary; and the first Friday after Old Michaelmas-day, for horses, stockings, and toys. A bailiff is appointed at the court of the manor held by the Bishop of Winchester. The living is a rectory, in the peculiar jurisdiction of the Incumbent, rated in the king's books at £26. 12. 8½., and in the patronage of the Bishop of Winchester. The church is dedicated to St. Peter. The river Hamble has its source about half a mile from the village, and passes through the piece of water termed Waltham Pond, which formerly deserved the appellation, given it by historians, of "a large and beautiful lake," but is now contracted by the encroachments of alluvial soil and rushes. On its banks are the remains of the once magnificent palace of the Bishops of Winchester, built, in 1135, by Bishop Henry de Blois, brother of King Stephen, and greatly embellished by Wykeham: it continued to be the principal episcopal residence till the parliamentary war, when it was destroyed by the army under Waller: the extensive park in which it stood was afterwards converted into farms by Bishop Morley, who also founded a free school here, and endowed it with an annuity of £10, which sum has been augmented, by subsequent benefactions, to £38, for which thirty-six boys are instructed.

WALTHAM (BRIGHT), a parish in the hundred of FAIRCROSS, county of BERKS, 5 miles (W. S. W.) from East Ilsley, containing 450 inhabitants. The living is a rectory, in the archdeaconry of Berks, and diocese of Salisbury, rated in the king's books at £11. 15., and in the patronage of Mrs. Plumptre. The church is dedicated to All Saints. The parish is entitled to send two children to the school founded at Chaddleworth by William Saunders.

WALTHAM (COLD), a parish in the hundred of BURY, rape of ARUNDEL, county of SUSSEX, 5½ miles (S. E.) from Petworth, containing 357 inhabitants. The living is a perpetual curacy, in the peculiar jurisdiction and patronage of the Bishop of Chichester, endowed with £1200 royal bounty. The parish is bounded on the north by the Rother, and on the east by the Arun.

WALTHAM (GREAT), a parish in the hundred of CHELMSFORD, county of ESSEX, 4½ miles (N. by W.) from Chelmsford, containing, with the chapelry of Black-Chapel, 1883 inhabitants. The living is a vicarage, in the archdeaconry of Essex, and diocese of London, rated in the king's books at £18. 13. 4., and in the patronage of the President and Fellows of Trinity College, Oxford. The church is dedicated to St. Mary and St. Lawrence. The river Chelmer runs through the parish. Courts leet and baron are held here on the Thursday in Whitsun-week.

WALTHAM (ST. LAWRENCE), a parish in the hundred of WARGRAVE, county of BERKS, 5¾ miles (S. W.) from Maidenhead, containing 638 inhabitants. The living is a vicarage, in the archdeaconry of Berks, and diocese of Salisbury, rated in the king's books at £7. 6. 8., and in the patronage of Lord Braybrooke. The church contains a fine monument in memory of Sir Henry Nevill, one of the gentlemen of the privy chamber to Edward VI., who died in 1593. A fair is held on August 11th: a court baron takes place annually at Wargrave. Michael Wondesford, in 1712, bequeathed land, now let for £6 a year, which, with a smaller bequest from Richard How, in 1652, is applied to the instruction of poor children. A National school is supported by Lord Braybrooke, the lord of the manor, who has an ancient residence at Billingbear, in the parish. In a field between the church and the Bath road was a Roman station, where coins, urns, and tiles, have frequently been dug up.

WALTHAM (LITTLE), a parish in the hundred of CHELMSFORD, county of ESSEX, 4¼ miles (N. by E.) from Chelmsford, containing 620 inhabitants. The living is a rectory, in the archdeaconry of Essex, and diocese of London, rated in the king's books at £11. 10., and in the patronage of T. L. Hodges, Esq. The church is dedicated to St. Martin. There is a place of worship for Independents. A school is supported by annual subscriptions, amounting to about £20. The village is situated on the river Chelmer, and on the high road from Chelmsford to Bury and Norwich.

WALTHAM (NORTH), a parish in the hundred of OVERTON, Kingsclere division of the county of SOUTHAMPTON, 6 miles (S. W. by W.) from Basingstoke, containing 373 inhabitants. The living is a rectory, in the peculiar jurisdiction of the Incumbent, rated in the king's books at £15. 13. 4., and in the patronage of the Bishop of Winchester. The church is dedicated to St. Michael. This parish is within the jurisdiction of the Cheyney Court held at Winchester every Thursday, for the recovery of debts to any amount.

WALTHAM (UP), a parish in the hundred of Box and STOCKBRIDGE, rape of CHICHESTER, county of

SUSSEX, 6½ miles (S. S. W.) from Petworth, containing 99 inhabitants. The living is a discharged rectory, in the archdeaconry and diocese of Chichester, rated in the king's books at £6. 2. 11., and in the patronage of the Earl of Egremont. The church is in the early style of English architecture, with a circular east end.

WALTHAM (WHITE), a parish in the hundred of BEYNHURST, county of BERKS, 4 miles (S. W.) from Maidenhead, containing 795 inhabitants. The living is a vicarage, with the rectory of Shottesbrook united, in the archdeaconry of Berks, and diocese of Salisbury, rated in the king's books at £10. 13. 4., and in the patronage of Arthur Vansittart, Esq. The church is dedicated to St. Mary. Smewin's house, now occupied by a farmer, is surrounded by a moat, and is said to have been a hunting seat of Prince Arthur's, eldest son of Henry VII.: it was also the retreat of the learned Dodwell, first Camden Professor of Ancient History at Oxford, and a celebrated writer on ecclesiastical antiquity. The vicarage-house was partly paved with Roman bricks, and many Roman tiles, coins, and other relics, have been found near the church. Thomas Hearne, the antiquary, was born here in 1678.

WALTHAM on the WOLDS, a parish (formerly a market town) in the hundred of FRAMLAND, county of LEICESTER, 5¼ miles (N. E.) from Melton-Mowbray, containing 622 inhabitants. The living is a rectory, in the archdeaconry of Leicester, and diocese of Lincoln, rated in the king's books at £19. 5., and in the patronage of the Duke of Rutland. The church, dedicated to St. Mary Magdalene, is principally in the decorated style, with portions of earlier date ; it has three enriched stalls, and the font presents a curious admixture of the Norman and early English styles. Joseph and George Noble, in 1776, and Thomas Baker, left trifling sums to be applied in support of a school.

WALTHAM-ABBEY, or HOLY-CROSS, a parish in the hundred of WALTHAM, county of ESSEX, comprising the market town of Waltham-Abbey, and the hamlets of Holyfield, Sewardstone, and Upshire, and containing 3982 inhabitants, of which number, 2097 are in the town of Waltham-Abbey, 23½ miles (W. by S.) from Chelmsford, and 12½ (N. by E.) from London. The name of this place is compounded of the Saxon words Weald and Ham, signifying a residence in, or near, a wood; the adjunct is a term of distinction derived from an ancient abbey which was founded here. The town derived its origin, so long since as the time of Canute the Great, from the facility and inducement for hunting afforded by the neighbourhood, which led Ralph de Toni, standard-bearer to that monarch, to build a few houses. A church was soon afterwards erected, principally for the preservation of the holy cross, to which many legends of miraculous efficacy were attached; and, upon a lapse of the property to the crown, Harold, to whom it had been given by Edward the Confessor, founded, in 1062, a monastery for Secular canons ; for which, in 1177, Henry II. substituted monks of the order of St. Augustine, and dedicated it to the Holy Cross. At the dissolution, the revenue was valued at £1079. 12. 1.: within the choir, or eastern chapel, the body of Harold, who was slain in the battle of Hastings, with those of his brothers, Gurth and Leofwin, was entombed. In a place called Romeland, adjoining the abbey, was a house

at which Henry VIII. occasionally resided ; and to a conversation held here, on the important subject of the king's divorce, Dr. Cranmer was eventually indebted for the royal favour, and his ultimate elevation to the see of Canterbury. The town, which is spacious and irregularly built, consisting chiefly of one long street, is situated on the banks of the river Lea, which here divides into many streams, and separates the two counties of Essex and Herts about half a mile to the west, and also the parishes of Cheshunt and Waltham-Abbey: the inhabitants are well supplied with water. The gunpowder mills belonging to government are situated here, and at present afford employment to nearly two hundred persons, but in time of war from four to five hundred were engaged. About one hundred persons are occupied in printing silk handkerchiefs, and some business is done in the manufacture of pins, though it is by no means so extensive as formerly: here are also a brewery, flour-mill, and two malt-kilns. In the hamlet of Sewardstone is an extensive factory for throwing and spinning silk, in which between two and three hundred persons are employed : at the west end of the town is the new cut from the river Lea. The market is on Tuesday: fairs are held May 14th and September 25th, for horses and cattle ; and on the 26th is a statute fair for hiring servants. Courts leet and baron are held on Whit-Monday.

The living is a perpetual curacy, in the jurisdiction of the Commissary of London, concurrently with the Consistorial Court of the Bishop of London, and in the patronage of certain Trustees. The church, which is dedicated to the Holy Cross and St. Lawrence, and comprises only the nave of the old abbey church, is a spacious structure in the Norman style of architecture, with a tower of later date ; on the south side is the Lady chapel, now used as a vestry and school room. In the interior are three tiers of semicircular arches, enriched with zigzag ornaments, supported on circular massive piers, some of which are also decorated with waving lines ; the windows are of various kinds: beneath the Lady chapel is a fine crypt, now arranged in vaults. Among the various monuments and sepulchral tablets the principal is one to the memory of Sir Edward Denny, who died in 1599 ; under an arch of veined marble are recumbent effigies of him and his lady, and beneath those of their children, in a kneeling posture, surmounted by an appropriate inscription: a slab near the communion-table retains the impression of an abbot with his crosier, the brass having been taken away. There are places of worship for Baptists and Wesleyan Methodists. A free school, in which fifteen boys and eight girls receive instruction, is supported by voluntary contributions. The Leverton school, founded, about 1824, by Mrs. Rebecca Leverton, widow, for the education of fifteen boys and ten girls, who are also clothed at her expense, was extended for four additional boys by Mr. John Edmondson, who, in 1708, bequeathed a piece of land, now let for £18 per annum, for their benefit: this school has an interest in the reversion of £6000 three per cents. consolidated annuities, left by Thomas Leverton, Esq., for charitable purposes, subject to the life of the abovementioned Mrs. Rebecca Leverton, his wife. Green's almshouses, for four poor widows, originally built, and endowed with an orchard and barn, now let for £20 per annum, by — Green, Esq., in 1626, were rebuilt and enlarged, in 1818, with four additional rooms, by means of a bequest from Robert Mason, in 1807. Eight poor widows reside in them: those occupying the additional rooms receive a weekly allowance of two shillings and sixpence each, arising from the interest of £1350, given, in 1826, by Mowbray Woolard; from this bequest also, one shilling weekly is allowed to five poor men and five women in the workhouse. The only remains of the venerable abbey, exclusively of the 'church, are a fine gate with a postern, the bridge leading to it, and some dilapidated walls: in the gardens formerly belonging to the institution, and now let as nursery ground, is an ancient tulip tree, the trunk of which is nine feet six inches in circumference, considered a great curiosity when in flower.

WALTHAM-CROSS, a ward in the parish of CHESHUNT ST. MARY, hundred and county of HERTFORD, 9 miles (S. by E.) from Hertford. The population is returned with the parish. Here is a chapel, the living of which is a donative, in the patronage of the Trustees of the Earl of Norwich. There is a place of worship for Independents. This place received the adjunct to its name from a noble cross erected, on the eastern side of the high road, by Edward I. to his beloved consort Eleanor, whose corpse rested here on its way from Lincolnshire to London: it is hexangular, and highly enriched with tabernacle-work and foliage, having pendant shields bearing the devices of England, Castile, Leon, and Ponthieu, and crowned statues of the queen, the left hand holding a cordon, and the right a sceptre, or globe. This beautiful monument having suffered much from mutilation, was, in 1757, at the instance of the Society of Antiquaries, enclosed by a brick wall, at the expense of Lord Monson, then lord of the manor. Courts leet and baron are held twice a year. The river Lea separates this ward from the parish of Waltham Holy-Cross, and the new river runs through the centre of it. Almshouses for four poor widows, founded and endowed by Beaumont Spital, were taken down in 1830, and are now in progress of re-erection, in the decorated style of English architecture.

WALTHAMSTOW, a parish in the hundred of BECONTREE, county of ESSEX, 6 miles (N.E. by N.) from London, containing 4304 inhabitants. According to the Norman survey, wherein it is written Welannestun, the manor was in the possession of Judith, niece to the Conqueror; and having subsequently belonged to the Earls of Warwick, on the attainder and execution of Earl Thomas, in 1396, it lapsed to the crown. The name appears to be of Saxon origin, consisting of weald, a wood, and ham, a dwelling; the adjunct stowe, a place, being intended to distinguish this from other Walthams within the county; and the entire name being accurately descriptive of the village, which consists of numerous dwelling-houses and mansions, detached and encompassed with trees and woodland, and pleasantly situated on the borders of Epping Forest, through which a new road has been recently cut to Woodford, in order to form a nearer communication with the great road from London to Newmarket. The parish is separated from the county of Middlesex by the navigable river Lea, over which is a bridge, and on its banks are extensive copper-mills and an oil-mill, which furnish employment to about sixty

persons. Courts leet and baron, for the manors within it, are held as occasion requires. The government of the parish was entrusted to a select vestry of seventeen persons, besides the minister and churchwardens, according to a grant of Bishop Montaigne, in 1624, which does not appear to have been otherwise acted upon. The living is a vicarage, in the jurisdiction of the Commissary of London, concurrently with the Consistorial Court of the Bishop of London, rated in the king's books at £13. 6. 8., and in the patronage of the Rev. W. Wilson, B.D.; it has been endowed with about £125 private benefaction. The church, dedicated to St. Mary, is a neat structure, originally built of flint and stone, with a tower at the west end, situated on an eminence; the tower was partly rebuilt by Sir George Monox, who also built the chapel at the east end of the north aisle, in 1535: it was enlarged, repaired, and beautified, in 1817, at an expense of about £2000: in the chancel is a circular window, divided into compartments of stained glass, representing a "Gloria"; it was originally intended for Southampton castle, but was presented to this parish by Miss Russell. Among the various sepulchral memorials which adorn the interior are those of Sir George Monox, Lord Mayor of London in 1514, and his lady; a splendid monument of white marble, with figures as large as life, to Sigismond Trafford, his wife, and infant daughter; and another in memory of Lady Lucy Stanley, erected by her husband, Sir Edward Stanley. In the churchyard is a white marble tomb, by Chantry, in memory of Jesse Russell, Esq., father of the above-named benefactress. At Chapel End, in this parish, a chapel of ease was erected, at an expense of £1800, raised by subscription: it will accommodate about four hundred persons. There are places of worship for Independents and Unitarians.

A free school, for clothing and educating children, and an almshouse for thirteen poor people, at the north side of the churchyard, were founded and endowed with a rent-charge of £42. 17. 4.: the latter was further endowed with a proportion of the income arising from certain land bequeathed for the benefit of the parish by Henry Maynard, in 1686. In 1815, Mr. Richard Banks bequeathed a reversionary legacy, now producing £30. 4. 9.; and in 1825, a bequest of £500 four per cent. annuities was made, in aid of the almshouse fund, by William Bedford, Esq. A National school, in which one hundred and twenty boys and ninety-four girls receive instruction, is supported by voluntary contributions, and bequests of charitable individuals, amounting to £17. 10. per annum: it was established in 1819, and the building was enlarged by subscription in 1825. An infant school, in which are one hundred and seventy children, was established in 1823, and is supported in a similar manner: the building adjoins the churchyard, and comprises a large school-room, with separate houses for the master and mistress. In a school belonging to the Independents thirty girls receive instruction, of whom twenty are clothed. Almshouses for six poor widows were built and endowed by Mrs. Mary Squires, in 1797: the annual income is £78. The sum of £10 per annum was given by Mrs. Mary Newell, in 1810, as an annual apprentice fee; she also gave £200 to the Sunday school. George Gascoigne, a poet of considerable repute, and author of several dramatic pieces, was a native of this village; he died in 1578. The Rev. William Piers, D. D., Bishop of Bath and Wells, lies interred in the chancel of the church; he died at the advanced age of ninety-four, and was at the time the oldest bishop in Christendom, both with respect to years, and date of consecration. Edward Rowe Mores, an eminent scholar and antiquary, and one of the principal agents in forming the Equitable Society for Assurance on Lives, was buried here in 1778. Thomas Cartwright, afterwards Bishop of Chester, and Edmund Chishall, a learned antiquary and divine, author of Travels in Turkey, and Antiquities of Asia before the Christian Era, were respectively vicars of the parish.

WALTON, a parish in the hundred of NEWPORT, county of BUCKINGHAM, 2 miles (N. by E.) from Fenny-Stratford, containing 102 inhabitants. The living is a rectory, in the archdeaconry of Buckingham, and diocese of Lincoln, rated in the king's books at £8. 9. 7., and in the alternate patronage of the Crown and W. Ellis, Esq., as lord of the manor. The church is dedicated to St. Michael.

WALTON, a parish in ESKDALE ward, county of CUMBERLAND, comprising the townships of High and Low Walton, and containing 480 inhabitants, of which number, 177 are in High Walton, 10½ miles (N.E. by E.), and 303 in Low Walton, 10 miles (N. E. by E.), from Carlisle. The living is a perpetual curacy, in the archdeaconry and diocese of Carlisle, endowed with £200 private benefaction, and £600 royal bounty, and in the patronage of Mrs. Dacre. The ancient Roman wall crossed the parish, which contained the station *Petriana*, the site of which is now called Castle Steads, and out of its ruins several houses have been built. From the blackness of the stones, it is thought that the ancient buildings had suffered greatly from fire: numerous inscriptions and other relics of antiquity have been discovered. A charity school, with a small endowment, was founded by J. Boustead, Esq.; and a Sunday school has been established, and is supported, by Mrs. Johnson.

WALTON, a chapelry in the parish of CHESTERFIELD, hundred of SCARSDALE, county of DERBY, 3 miles (S. W. by W.) from Chesterfield, containing 783 inhabitants.

WALTON, or DEERHURST-WALTON, a hamlet in that part of the parish of DEERHURST which is in the lower division of the hundred of WESTMINSTER, county of GLOUCESTER, 3¼ miles (S.) from Tewkesbury, containing 173 inhabitants.

WALTON, a township in the parish of BISHOP'S FROOME, hundred of RADLOW, county of HEREFORD, 4½ miles (S.) from Bromyard, containing 80 inhabitants.

WALTON, a hamlet in that part of the parish of KNAPTOFT which is in the hundred of GUTHLAXTON, county of LEICESTER, 4 miles (N. E. by E.) from Lutterworth, containing 231 inhabitants.

WALTON, a hamlet in the parish of PASTON, liberty of PETERBOROUGH, county of NORTHAMPTON, 2¾ miles (N. N. W.) from Peterborough, containing 151 inhabitants.

WALTON, a parish in the hundred of WHITLEY, county of SOMERSET, 3½ miles (S. W. by W.) from Glastonbury, containing 635 inhabitants. The living is a perpetual curacy, annexed to the rectory of Street,

in the archdeaconry of Wells, and diocese of Bath and Wells. The church, dedicated to the Holy Trinity, has a tower rising from the centre. There is a place of worship for Wesleyan Methodists.

WALTON, a township in the parish of BASWICH, eastern division of the hundred of CUTTLESTONE, county of STAFFORD, 2¾ miles (S. E. by E.) from Stafford. The population is returned with the parish.

WALTON, a township in the parish of ECCLESHALL, northern division of the hundred of PIREHILL, county of STAFFORD, containing 109 inhabitants. It is in the peculiar jurisdiction of the prebendal court of Eccleshall.

WALTON, a parish in the hundred of COLNEIS, county of SUFFOLK, 10 miles (S. E. by E.) from Ipswich, containing 783 inhabitants. The living is a discharged vicarage, with that of Felixtow annexed, in the archdeaconry of Suffolk, and diocese of Norwich, rated in the king's books at £4. 6. 8., and in the patronage of Mr. Eagle and others. The church is dedicated to St. Mary. There is a place of worship for Baptists. The parish has the river Deben on the east, Harwich harbour on the west, and the North sea on the south, where there is a Martello tower for the defence of the coast. A cell of Benedictine monks, subordinate to the monastery of Rochester was founded here in the reign of William Rufus, which continued till 1528, when it was given to Cardinal Wolsey, towards the endowment of his intended colleges.

WALTON, a parish in the ainsty of the city, and East riding of the county, of YORK, 2½ miles (E. by S.) from Wetherby, containing 247 inhabitants. The living is a perpetual curacy, in the archdeaconry and diocese of York, endowed with £400 private benefaction, and £600 royal bounty, and in the patronage of the Impropriators. The church is dedicated to St. Peter. There is a place of worship for Wesleyan Methodists. The old Roman Watling-street crosses the river Wharf at a place called St. Helens, and passes through the parish to that part of the wall now called Redgate.

WALTON, a township in the parish of GREAT SANDALL, lower division of the wapentake of AGBRIGG, West riding of the county of YORK, 3 miles (S. E. by S.) from Wakefield, containing 385 inhabitants.

WALTON le DALE, a chapelry in the parish and lower division of the hundred of BLACKBURN, county palatine of LANCASTER, 2 miles (S. E.) from Preston, containing, according to the last census, 5740 inhabitants, since which period the number has increased to about 7000. The living is a perpetual curacy, in the archdeaconry and diocese of Chester, endowed with £1400 private benefaction, £800 royal bounty, and £1300 parliamentary grant, and in the patronage of the Vicar of Blackburn. The chapel, dedicated to St. Leonard, is principally in the later style of English architecture. It is situated on an eminence which commands fine views of the vale of Ribble on one side, and of the vale of Darwent on the other. Both these vallies are extremely picturesque, the banks of their respective rivers being steep and richly clothed with wood. The back ground of the Ribble is formed by the high and extensive ranges of Longridge and Pendle; and that of the Darwent by Billinge hill, and an abrupt elevation crowned with the ruins of Houghton Tower, the ancient baronial residence of the family of that name. Here are three large cotton-manufactories and several printing-establishments, affording employment to the greater portion of the inhabitants. There is a National school in the village, capable of containing one hundred and fifty children of each sex, established and wholly supported by voluntary contributions : the building is also used as a Sunday school. Another school-house was built by subscription among the inhabitants in 1672; it is endowed with about £16 per annum, for teaching all children who apply. In 1701, the Duke of Norfolk, the Earl of Derwentwater, and other leaders of the jacobites, incorporated themselves by the style of the "Mayor and Corporation of the ancient borough of Walton," and held their meetings in a small public-house here, concealing their real motives under the guise of ludicrous transactions; they kept a register, a mace, a sword of state, and other mock insignia of office : the society, notwithstanding the diminution of the number of its members by the unsuccessful rebellion of 1715, existed till about thirty years ago, when it was entirely dissolved. Walton is distinguished as the scene of a great battle, fought August 17th, 1648, between Cromwell and the Duke of Hamilton ; also for a gallant achievement performed, in 1715, by General, or Parson, Wood and his congregation, in defending the passage of the Ribble against the Scottish rebels.

WALTON (EAST), a parish in the Lynn division of the hundred of FREEBRIDGE, county of NORFOLK, 7 miles (N. W.) from Swaffham, containing 174 inhabitants. The living is a discharged vicarage, in the archdeaconry and diocese of Norwich, rated in the king's books at £6. 3. 4. Andrew Hamond, Esq. was patron in 1818. The church is dedicated to St. Mary.

WALTON in GORDANO, a parish in the hundred of PORTBURY, county of SOMERSET, 11½ miles (W.) from Bristol, containing 161 inhabitants. The living is a discharged rectory, in the archdeaconry of Bath, and diocese of Bath and Wells, rated in the king's books at £9. 15. 5., and in the patronage of P. J. Miles, Esq. The church, dedicated to St. Paul, is a plain modern building : there are some remains of a more ancient structure at the foot of the hill occupied by Walton castle, an octangular pile, embattled and crowned at each angle with a turret : the principal entrance is on the east, and the keep, which is octangular, is situated in the centre of the area.

WALTON on the HILL, a parish in the hundred of WEST DERBY, county palatine of LANCASTER, comprising the chapelries of Everton, Formby, Kirkby, and West Derby, and the townships of Bootle with Linacre, Fazakerley, Kirkdale, Simonswood, and Walton on the Hill, and containing 14,245 inhabitants, of which number, 1171 are in the township of Walton on the Hill, 2¾ miles (N. by E.) from Liverpool. The living is a rectory, in the archdeaconry and diocese of Chester, rated in the king's books at £69. 16. 10¼., and in the patronage of J. S. Leigh, Esq. : the vicarage is separately rated at £6. 13. 4., and in the patronage of the Rector. The church, dedicated to St. Mary, is partly in the decorated style of English architecture. Up to 1698 it was the mother church of Liverpool, and the present church of St. Nicholas there was a chapel of ease under the Vicar of Walton. The church of St. James, in Toxteth Park, is dependent on Walton. In consequence of its proximity to Liverpool, this place has greatly advanced in population, and has become the residence of numerous merchants, retired tradesmen, &c. The house of correction for the county is at Kirkdale, in this parish.

WALTON on the HILL, a parish in the first division of the hundred of COPTHORNE, county of SURREY, 4¼ miles (S. by E.) from Epsom, containing 314 inhabitants. The living is a discharged rectory, in the archdeaconry of Surrey, and diocese of Winchester, rated in the king's books at £12. 6. 5½., and in the patronage of Mrs. Anne Paston Gee. The church is dedicated to St. Peter : the body has been recently rebuilt at the expense of the inhabitants, and an elegant tower has been erected by the patroness; on this occasion the church received an addition of sixty free sittings, the Incorporated Society for the enlargement of churches and chapels having granted £40 towards defraying the expense : it contains a curious ancient font, and the windows exhibit some fragments of ancient stained glass. Walton Place, the old manor-house, now occupied as a farm-house, bears evident marks of having been once strongly fortified. There are some springs in the parish, the water of which is of a mineral quality.

WALTON (INFERIOR), a township in the parish of RUNCORN, hundred of BUCKLOW, county palatin of CHESTER, 2 miles (S.) from Warrington, containing 353 inhabitants. The Mersey and Irwell canal passe in the vicinity. A school is supported by subscriptions amounting to about £7 per annum.

WALTON le SOKEN, a parish in the hundred of TENDRING, county of ESSEX, 13¼ miles (S.E. by E.) from Manningtree, containing 293 inhabitants. The living is a discharged vicarage, consolidated with those of Kirby le Soken and Thorpe le Soken, in the jurisdiction of the peculiar court of the Sokens, and subject to the visitation of the Bishop of London, the wills and records being deposited at the residence of the lord of the manor, at Harwich ; it is rated in the king's books at £9. The church, dedicated to All Saints, was erected and consecrated by Bishop Porteus, about twenty-five years ago, the ancient structure having, a few years previously, been entirely swept away, as well as the churchyard and every house but one of the old village. The parish, which is bounded on three sides by the sea, forms a noted promontory, called the Naze, from the Saxon term, signifying a nose of land. Embedded in the clay, which composes the basis of the cliffs, are found, among various alluvial remains, some curious fossils, the tusks of elephants, with the horns, bones, and teeth of other huge animals, which have been usually discovered after the ebbing of very strong tides. The shore abounds with pyrites, chiefly of wood, of which immense quantities have been here manufactured into green copperas, or sulphate of iron ; but the works having gone to decay, the pyrites are at present merely collected and sent to other places, to undergo the like process. Nodules of argillaceous clay, which continually fall from the cliffs and harden into stone, are gathered up and conveyed to London and Harwich, for making Roman cement. The beach is a delightful promenade, and affords superior facilities for bathing, the ebb tides leaving a firm smooth sand several miles in extent; which advantages have, of late years, occasioned a number of invalids, principally from the eastern parts of the county, to resort hither for the benefit of cold and warm sea-bathing, for whose accommodation convenient machines and baths are in constant readiness. and many commodious lodging - houses have been erected. Adjoining the old hall is a square tower, built by the corporation of the Trinity House, as a mark to guide ships passing, or entering, the port of Harwich; and on other parts of the coast are two Martello towers, also a signal station. The district comprising these three parishes received the distinguishing appellation "le Soken" from some peculiar privileges formerly granted to certain refugees from the Netherlands, who established themselves here and introduced various manufactures, particularly that of cloth.

WALTON (SUPERIOR), a township in the parish of RUNCORN, hundred of BUCKLOW, county palatine of CHESTER; 2¾ miles (S.S.W.) from Warrington, containing 219 inhabitants. The Duke of Bridgewater's canal passes in the vicinity.

WALTON upon THAMES, a parish in the first division of the hundred of ELMBRIDGE, county of SURREY, 2 miles (N.E. by E.) from Weybridge, and 18 (S.W. by W.) from London, containing, with Common-Side, Hersham, Burnwood, and Town divisions, 1891 inhabitants. The living is a discharged vicarage, in the archdeaconry of Surrey, and diocese of Winchester, rated in the king's books at £12. 13. 4., and in the patronage of the Crown. The church, dedicated to St. Mary, is a handsome structure of considerable antiquity, containing many fine monuments, of which the most conspicuous is one by Roubilliac, to the memory of Richard Boyle, Viscount Shannon, who distinguished himself at the memorable battle of the Boyne. It contains the remains of several members of the Rodney family, and of many other eminent persons. There is a place of worship for Independents. Walton probably derived its name from the formidable Roman works yet visible within its precincts, the principal of which, on St. George's hill, is called the Camp of Cæsar, who here gave battle to Cassivelaunus, at the head of the Britons : that chieftain having first taken the precaution of driving stakes into the bed of the Thames, successfully opposed the vigorous attempts of the Romans to force the passage of the river, at a place still called Coway Stakes. Strata of iron-ore appear in different parts of the parish. The village is small, but derives some importance from the many noble mansions in its immediate neighbourhood, and the elegant villas by which it is surrounded. A curious wooden bridge, of three arches, over the Thames was built, about 1750, by Samuel Dicker, Esq.; and, more recently, another of brick and stone, of fifteen arches, across the low meadows, was added to it; but the former, falling to decay, was replaced by the present structure, built uniform with that which remained, and both now appear as one bridge of considerable length and beauty. A fair for cattle, granted by Henry.VIII., is held on Wednesday and Thursday in Easter week. A National school, established by the late Earl of Carhampton, is supported by voluntary contributions : there are also some endowed almshouses, and a remarkable bequest by one Smith, originally a beggar, who, in the course of his wanderings, having amassed a considerable sum, left a portion of it to the poor

of every parish in the county of Surrey, with the exception of those wherein he had experienced punishment as a vagabond. Apps Court, in this parish, was once a residence of Cardinal Wolsey; but the ancient building has given place to a more modern and elegant mansion, the proprietor of which is subject to an old custom of distributing annually a quarter of wheat made into bread, and a barrel of small beer, amongst such travellers as may happen to present themselves on the 13th of November ; he enjoys the privilege of nominating four poor widows of Walton to a charity derived from the parish of Effingham. Ashley House, one of the many edifices built by Wolsey, was occasionally the residence of Oliver Cromwell. A farm-house is also mentioned as having been the seat of Bradshaw, who presided at the trial of Charles I., and which was afterwards occupied by Judge Jeffreys : some of the old carving is still preserved in several of the apartments. Paine's hill, at the foot of which the river Mole is crossed by a neat brick bridge, is partly occupied by the mansion and tasteful plantations of the Dowager Countess of Carhampton. Oatlands, once the property of the late Duke of York, is partly in this parish, the boundary line which separates Walton and Weybridge passing through the house. Block-making, for supplying the navy, was extensively carried on here, till the erection of the celebrated machinery in Portsmouth dock-yard entirely superseded the necessity for its continuance.

WALTON on TRENT, a parish in the hundred of REPTON and GRESLEY, county of DERBY, 4¼ miles (S.W.) from Burton upon Trent, containing 416 inhabitants. The living is a rectory, in the archdeaconry of Derby, and diocese of Lichfield and Coventry, rated in the king's books at £17. 2. 8½., and in the patronage of Marquis Townshend. The church, dedicated to St. John the Baptist, has been lately repaired at a considerable expense, defrayed by subscription : it contains several ancient monumental tombs. A schoolroom has been erected by voluntary contributions, in which all the poor children of the parish are instructed on the National system : it is partly supported by subscription, and partly with £20 a year arising from land bequeathed, in 1760, in support of a school, by two ladies named Levett and Bailey, who also gave a dwelling-house for the master. Edward II. forded the Trent at this place, in pursuit of Thomas, Earl of Lancaster, and the disaffected barons.

WALTON (WEST), a parish in the Marshland division of the hundred of FREEBRIDGE, county of NORFOLK, 2¾ miles (N. by E.) from Wisbeach, containing 735 inhabitants. The living is a rectory, in the archdeaconry and diocese of Norwich, rated in the king's books at £16. 13. 4. H. H. Townshend, Esq. was patron in 1811. The rectory of West Walton Elien is rated at £16, and in the patronage of the Crown. The church is dedicated to St. Mary.

WALTON on the WOLDS, a parish in the eastern division of the hundred of GOSCOTE, county of LEICESTER, 4 miles (E.) from Loughborough, containing 289 inhabitants. The living is a rectory, in the archdeaconry of Leicester, and diocese of Lincoln, rated in the king's books at £15, and in the patronage of the Rev. Augustus Edward Hobart. The church is dedicated to St. Mary. The river Soar runs through the parish.

WALTON (WOOD), a parish in the hundred of NORMAN - CROSS, county of HUNTINGDON, 7 miles (N. by W.) from Huntingdon, containing 211 inhabitants. The living is a rectory, in the archdeaconry of Huntingdon, and diocese of Lincoln, rated in the king's books at £11, and in the patronage of Sir R. H. Bickerton, Bart. The church is dedicated to St. Andrew.

WALTON-CARDIFF, a parish in the lower division of the hundred of TEWKESBURY, county of GLOUCESTER, 1¼ mile (E. S. E.) from Tewkesbury, containing 51 inhabitants. The living is a perpetual curacy, in the archdeaconry and diocese of Gloucester, endowed with £400 royal bounty, and in the patronage of the Warden and Fellows of All Souls' College, Oxford. The church is dedicated to St. James.

WALTON-DEIVILE, a parish in the Warwick division of the hundred of KNIGHTLOW, county of WARWICK, 3¾ miles (W. N.W.) from Kington. The population is returned with the parish of Wellesbourn-Hastings. The living is a rectory, annexed to the vicarage of Wellesbourn-Hastings, in the archdeaconry and diocese of Worcester, rated in the king's books at £4.13.4. The church, dedicated to St. James, was rebuilt by Sir C. Mordaunt, about eighty years ago.

WALWICK, an extra-parochial liberty, locally in the parish of Warden, north-western division of TINDALE ward, county of NORTHUMBERLAND, 5¼ miles (N. W. by N.) from Hexham. The population is returned with Warden. This place, situated on the western bank of the North Tyne, and on the line of Severus' Wall, was the *Cilurnum* of the Romans, and the station of the *Ala Secunda Asturum*; its extent, which may still be traced, was, from east to west, five hundred and seventy feet, and from north to south four hundred. Among the numerous relics discovered are a spacious vault, a mutilated statue of Europa neatly sculptured in freestone, and a curious tablet commemorative of the rebuilding of some edifice by the second wing of the *Astures*. Walwick Grange, formerly the seat of the Errington family, built out of an old tower, has been converted into a farm-house; and in Homer's-lane are fragments of an ancient cross.

WALWORTH, a township in the parish of HEIGHINGTON, south-eastern division of DARLINGTON ward, county palatine of DURHAM, 4½ miles (N. W.) from Darlington, containing 162 inhabitants.

WALWORTH, a chapelry in the parish of ST. MARY, NEWINGTON, eastern division of the hundred of BRIXTON, county of SURREY, 2 miles (S.) from London. The population is returned with the parish. The living is a perpetual curacy, in the peculiar jurisdiction of the Archbishop of Canterbury, and in the patronage of the Rector of Newington. The church, dedicated to St. Peter, is described in the article on NEWINGTON, which see.

WAMBROOK, a parish in the hundred of BEAMINSTER-FORUM and REDHONE, Bridport division of the county of DORSET, 1¾ mile (S. W.) from Chard, containing 201 inhabitants. The living is a rectory, in the peculiar jurisdiction of the Prebendary of Chardstock in the Cathedral Church of Salisbury, rated in the king's books at £8.7.1., and in the patronage of Mrs. Edwards. The church, dedicated to St. Mary, was anciently a chapel to the vicarage of Chardstock.

WAMPOOL, a township in the parish of AIKTON, ward and county of CUMBERLAND, 4¾ miles (N. by W.) from Wigton, containing 97 inhabitants.

WANBOROUGH, an extra-parochial liberty, in the first division of the hundred of WOKING, county of SURREY, 4¼ miles (W.) from Guildford, containing 107 inhabitants.

WANBOROUGH, a parish in the hundred of KINGSBRIDGE, county of WILTS, 3½ miles (E. by S.) from Swindon, containing 903 inhabitants. The living is a vicarage, in the archdeaconry of Surrey, and diocese of Salisbury, rated in the king's books at £21.10.7½., and in the patronage of the Dean and Chapter of Winchester. The church is dedicated to St. Andrew. There is a place of worship for Wesleyan Methodists.

WANDSWORTH, a parish in the western division of the hundred of BRIXTON, county of SURREY, 6 miles (S. W.) from London, containing 6702 inhabitants. The name of this place is derived from its situation on the river Wandle, which falls into the Thames in this parish. It consists chiefly of one street, occupying the declivities of two hills, on each of which are several mansions of a superior description: the inhabitants are supplied with water from springs. The manufactures comprise scarlet-dyeing, established for more than a century; hat - making, introduced by some French emigrants who settled here in the time of Louis XIV.; the making of bolting cloths, the printing of kerseymeres, the whitening and pressing of stuffs, and calico-printing: there are also three corn-mills, and mills for the preparation of iron, white lead, and linseed oil, now on the decline; vinegar works, distilleries, and a large brewery; the whole furnishing employment to several hundred persons. A rail-road extends from the basin, near the junction of the Wandle with the Thames, through Mitcham and Croydon, to Merstham in Surrey, and furnishes means of conveyance for the manufactures and other commodities. A fair is held on Whit-Monday, for cattle, horses, and pigs; and there is a pleasure fair on the two following days. The town is within the jurisdiction of the new police. Petty sessions for the western division of the hundred of Brixton are held every Saturday; and a court of requests, for the recovery of debts under £5, comprises within its jurisdiction the parishes of Barnes, Battersea, Lower Tooting, Mortlake, Merton, Putney, Wandsworth, and Wimbledon.

The living is a vicarage, in the archdeaconry of Surrey, and diocese of Winchester, rated in the king's books at £15. 5. 5., and in the patronage of Mrs. Anne Butcher. The church, dedicated to All Saints, is a plain brick structure, rebuilt in 1780, with the exception of a square tower at the west end; it contains several monuments. A new church, dedicated to St. Anne, and containing one thousand seven hundred and fifty-eight sittings, of which one thousand three hundred and thirty-two are free, has been recently erected, at an expense of £14,600, which was defrayed by His Majesty's commissioners for building new churches. There are places of worship for Baptists, the Society of Friends, Independents, and Wesleyan Methodists: the Society of Friends have two schools, at one of which the eminent citizen, Sir John Barnard, was educated. The free, or Green-coat, school was founded and endowed, in 1710, under the will of William Wicks;

of late years it has been incorporated with the National schools, in which one hundred and twenty-five boys and one hundred girls are educated, twenty-five of the boys and thirty of the girls being also clothed : the produce of the old endowment is appropriated exclusively to the use of thirty-five boys on the original foundation. The school of industry, founded in 1805, in which forty girls are instructed in knitting, spinning, &c., besides apportioning rewards for good behaviour at service, is supported by voluntary contributions. A school for the education of children of every religious denomination, instituted in 1821, affords instruction to one hundred and seventy boys and sixty girls. Fifteen watermen of the parish receive £4 per annum each, the produce of bequests by Nicholas Tonnett, Sir Alan Broderick, and Sir Francis Millington. Here are some small funds for apprenticing. poor children, and relieving the poor, for whose benefit a parochial library was instituted, in 1826. Amongst the miscellaneous charities, those of the famous Alderman Smith, commonly called Dog Smith, who was born and buried here, deserve particular notice, extending not only to Wandsworth, but to most of the principal towns in the county. The first Presbyterian congregation established in the kingdom was at this place, in the year 1572. In Garratt-lane, between Wandsworth and Tooting, a mock election used to be held after every parliamentary election, to which Foote's dramatic production of the Mayor of Garratt has given celebrity.

WANGFORD, a parish in the hundred of BLYTHING, county of SUFFOLK, 3½ miles (N. W. by N.) from Southwold, containing, with the hamlet of Henham, 746 inhabitants. The living is a perpetual curacy, in the archdeaconry of Suffolk, and diocese of Norwich, endowed with £400 royal bounty, and £1400 parliamentary grant, and in the patronage of the Earl of Stradbroke. The church is dedicated to St. Peter. A Cluniac priory, a cell to Thetford, was founded here before 1160, by Doudo Asini, and at the suppression had a revenue of £30. 9. 5.

WANGFORD, a parish in the hundred of LACKFORD, county of SUFFOLK, 3 miles (S. W. by W.) from Brandon Ferry, containing 63 inhabitants. The living is a discharged vicarage, annexed to the rectory of Brandon Ferry, in the archdeaconry of Suffolk, and diocese of Norwich, rated in the king's books at £9. 11. 8½. The church is dedicated to St. Denis. Robert Wright and Joanna his widow, about 1644, bequeathed the respective rent-charges of £30 and £10 towards the establishment of a school for poor children of this parish and those of Brandon, Downham, and Weeting : the former gave also a school-room and house for the master, and the latter certain land to provide for repairs.

WANLIP, a parish in the western division of the hundred of GOSCOTE, county of LEICESTER, 3¼ miles (S. E. by S.) from Mountsorrel, containing 128 inhabitants. The living is a rectory, in the archdeaconry of Leicester, and diocese of Lincoln, rated in the king's books at £14. 4. 4½., and in the patronage of Sir Charles Thomas Palmer, Bart. The church is dedicated to St. Nicholas. The river Soar, or the Leicester and Melton-Mowbray navigation, runs through the parish, and is crossed by a bridge. Near the old Fosse road, which also passes in the vicinity, a Roman tesselated pavement, coins, broken urns, and other relics, have

been found. Wanlip is in the honour of Tutbury, duchy of Lancaster, and within the jurisdiction of a court of pleas held at Tutbury every third Tuesday, for the recovery of debts under 40s.

WANSFORD, a parish in the liberty of PETERBOROUGH, county of NORTHAMPTON, 36 miles (N. E.) from Northampton, containing 179 inhabitants. The living is a perpetual curacy, annexed to the rectory of Thornhaugh, in the archdeaconry of Northampton, and diocese of Peterborough. The church, dedicated to St. Mary, exhibits specimens of various styles of architecture.

WANSFORD, a township in the parish of NAFFERTON, wapentake of DICKERING, East riding of the county of YORK, 3¼ miles (E. S. E.) from Great Driffield, containing 344 inhabitants, many of whom are employed in the manufactures of cotton goods and carpets; the latter establishment, which is situated on the navigable river Hull, is the only one of the kind in this part of the kingdom. There is a place of worship for Wesleyan Methodists.

WANSTEAD, a parish in the hundred of BECONTREE, county of ESSEX, 7 miles (N. E.) from London, containing 1354 inhabitants. This is a genteel village, situated on the borders of Waltham Forest, near the main road from London to Cambridge, and is principally worthy of note as the site of that once princely mansion, Wanstead House, built, in 1715, by Sir Richard, son of Sir Josiah Child, created Viscount Castlemain in 1718, and Earl of Tylney in 1731, and considerably extended and embellished by his descendants. This splendid mansion was surrounded by a very extensive and beautiful park, laid out with great taste, and interspersed with gardens, pleasure grounds, and grottos : it was the temporary residence of the Prince of Condé, but having come, by marriage, into the possession of the Hon. W. T. L. P. Wellesley, it was sold and demolished in 1822, since which time the park has been let out in portions for the grazing of cattle; of the buildings, nothing remains but the stables and out-offices. The living is a rectory, in the archdeaconry of Essex, and diocese of London, rated in the king's books at £6.13.9., and in the patronage of the Hon. Mr. Wellesley. The church, which is dedicated to St. Mary, was rebuilt about the year 1790; it is a handsome edifice of brick and Portland stone, with a fine Doric portico, and, at the west end, a cupola supported on eight Ionic pillars : the interior is of light and elegant appearance, the aisles being separated from the nave by columns of the Corinthian order : in the chancel is a window of beautifully stained glass, by Eginton, representing Christ bearing the Cross, in imitation of the altar-piece in the chapel of Magdalene College, Oxford; also a superb monument to the memory of Sir Josiah Child, Bart., who died in 1699, embellished with a marble effigy of the deceased. A free school, in which sixty children of both sexes are educated, forty of whom are also clothed, is partly supported by the proceeds of £200 three per cents., the bequest of George Bowles, Esq., in 1805. About the year 1735, a tesselated pavement of considerable dimensions, brass and silver coins, fragments of urns, and other relics of antiquity, were dug up on the south side of Wanstead park.

WANSTROW, a parish in the hundred of FROME, county of SOMERSET, 5 miles (N. N. E.) from Bruton, containing, with the hamlet of Weston, 397 inhabitants. The living is a rectory, in the archdeaconry of Wells, and diocese of Bath and Wells, rated in the king's books at £13. 9. 9½., and in the patronage of the Rev. George M. Bethune. The church is dedicated to St. Mary. A new road has been formed in this parish, which has added considerably to its local advantages.

WANTAGE, a parish in the hundred of WANTAGE, county of BERKS, comprising the market town of Wantage, and the hamlets of Charlton, Grove, and West Lockinge, and containing 3256 inhabitants, of which number, 2560 are in the town of Wantage, 24 miles (W. N. W.) from Reading, and 60 (W.) from London. This town, celebrated as the birthplace of Alfred the Great, and as a royal residence in the time of the West Saxons, was made a borough after the Conquest, through the influence of Fulk Fitz-Warine, who had obtained a grant of the manor from Bigod, Earl Marshal of England. It is situated at the edge of the Vale of White Horse, on a branch of the river Ocke : the streets are very irregularly built, and contain but few good houses : an act of parliament has been obtained for paving and lighting it : the inhabitants are supplied with water from wells, and from a brook which runs into the river. The principal branches of trade and manufacture are those of sacking, twine, malt, and flour ; coal is brought hither, and corn, flour, and malt sent to different parts, by means of a branch of the Wilts and Berks canal, which comes up to the town, affording a communication with Bath, Bristol, and London. The market, in which the corn is pitched, is on Saturday, chiefly for corn, also for pigs and cattle: fairs are on the first Saturdays in March and May, for cattle and cheese ; July 18th, for cherries ; and the 18th of October, a statute fair : a cheese fair is also held on the first Saturday in every month. The petty sessions for the division are held here every Saturday : a manorial court is held annually.

The living is a vicarage, in the peculiar jurisdiction and patronage of the Dean and Canons of Windsor, rated in the king's books at £35. 2. 8½. The church, which is dedicated to St. Peter and St. Paul, is a spacious and handsome cruciform structure, with a square embattled tower rising from the intersection ; it is said to have been built by some of the Fitzwarrens, to different members of which family there are several monuments. There are places of worship for Baptists, Independents, and Wesleyan Methodists. A free grammar school for the sons of inhabitants is situated in the churchyard, and is supported from the proceeds of Town Lands, given in the reigns of Henry VI. and Henry VII., and in 1598, vested in twelve trustees : the income is about £200 per annum : an English school is connected with it, in which twenty-four boys are educated. An infant school was established in 1825, and supported by voluntary contributions, but it has been discontinued from want of funds : there are Sunday schools connected with the established church and the dissenters. Seven almshouses were founded and endowed by Richard Styles, in 1680, with land in Hampshire, producing about £70 per annum : twelve poor persons are maintained, and receive a small weekly allowance. King Alfred, whose memory is here retained by a well, called "Alfred's Well," was born in 849, and died in 901. Dr. Joseph Butler, Bishop of Durham, and the well-known author of "The Analogy," was born here in 1692 ; as

was also the Rev. Isaac Kimber, a learned theological writer : the former died in 1752, and the latter in 1755.

WANTISDEN, a parish in the hundred of PLOMESGATE, county of SUFFOLK, 4¾ miles (N. W. by W.) from Orford, containing 128 inhabitants. The living is a perpetual curacy, in the archdeaconry of Suffolk, and diocese of Norwich, endowed with £1200 royal bounty, and £200 parliamentary grant, and in the patronage of N. Barnardiston, Esq. The church is dedicated to St. John the Baptist.

WAPLEY, a parish in the lower division of the hundred of GRUMBALD'S ASH, county of GLOUCESTER, 2½ miles (S. S. W.) from Chipping-Sodbury, containing, with the tything of Codrington, 307 inhabitants. The living is a discharged vicarage, in the archdeaconry and diocese of Gloucester, rated in the king's books at £7. 18., and in the patronage of the Dean and Chapter of Bristol. The church is dedicated to St. Peter.

WAPLINGTON, a township in the parish of ALLERTHORPE, Wilton-Beacon division of the wapentake of HARTHILL, East riding of the county of YORK, 2¾ miles (S. W.) from Pocklington, containing 19 inhabitants.

WAPPENBURY, a parish in the Southam division of the hundred of KNIGHTLOW, county of WARWICK, 6¼ miles (N. N. W.) from Southam, containing, with the hamlet of Eathrope, 284 inhabitants. The living is a vicarage, in the archdeaconry of Coventry, and diocese of Lichfield and Coventry, rated in the king's books at £8, endowed with £400 private benefaction, and £1000 royal bounty, and in the patronage of Lord Clifford. The church is dedicated to St. Esperit.

WAPPENHAM, a parish in the hundred of KING'S SUTTON, county of NORTHAMPTON, 5 miles (W. S. W.) from Towcester, containing, with the hamlet of Falcutt, and the whole of that of Astwell, which is partly in the parish of Syresham, 566 inhabitants. The living is a rectory, in the archdeaconry of Northampton, and diocese of Peterborough, rated in the king's books at £21. 9. 9½., and in the patronage of the Bishop of Lincoln. The church is dedicated to St. Mary. There is a place of worship for Wesleyan Methodists. At Astwell is an ancient mansion-house, formerly the seat of the Earls Ferrars.

WAPPING, a parish adjoining the eastern portion of the city of London, in the Tower division of the hundred of OSSULSTONE, county of MIDDLESEX, containing 3078 inhabitants. This place, originally overflowed by the Thames, was first recovered from inundation, and denominated Wapping Wash, in the reign of Elizabeth, under whose auspices it was enclosed and defended by walls. In the early part of the reign of Charles II., it comprised only one long street, which extended from the Tower along the northern bank of the Thames. In the reign of William and Mary it was made a parish, by act of parliament. About the end of the last century, upwards of sixty houses and other buildings were destroyed by fire, and several lives were lost, from the explosion of some barrels of gunpowder : the damage sustained on this occasion was estimated at more than £200,000. On the abdication of James II., the notorious judge Jeffreys, who had fled in order to escape the probable effects of popular rage, assumed the disguise of a sailor, and concealed himself for a short time in an obscure part of Wapping, but was at last discovered and committed to the Tower, where he died in a few days. The parish, part of which is in the precincts of Wellclose, in the liberty of the Tower, consists of several streets, which are well paved and lighted with gas, the main street having been recently widened in several places; and the inhabitants are well supplied with water. It is within the jurisdiction of the court of requests for the Tower Hamlets, for the recovery of debts not amounting to 40s. The business transacted is chiefly of a maritime and commercial character, to the growth of which the construction of the London docks has materially contributed : they occupy more than twenty acres of ground, extend nearly as far as Ratcliffe-Highway, are enclosed by a wall, and contain numerous and extensive warehouses and cellars ; the larger dock, called St. George's, is capable of receiving five hundred ships, and the smaller, denominated Shadwell dock, will hold about fifty : they are entered from the Thames by means of three basons, and from corresponding stairs, called Hermitage, Old Wapping, and Old Shadwell stairs. The largest tobacco warehouse is seven hundred and sixty-two feet by one hundred and sixty, and the smallest two hundred and fifty feet by two hundred. The first stone of the entrance bason, and those of the respective warehouses, were laid June 26th, 1802 ; and the docks were opened, in the presence of the Chancellor of the Exchequer, and some of the principal officers of state, with appropriate ceremonies, at the commencement of the year 1805. The whole of this immense establishment is under the control of the officers of the customs, and the capital of the Dock Company is estimated at £1,200,000. The living is a rectory not in charge, in the archdeaconry of Middlesex, and diocese of London, and in the patronage of the Principal and Fellows of Brasenose College, Oxford. The church, which is dedicated to St. John the Baptist, contains a very fine monument, by Roubilliac. There is a place of worship for Roman Catholics. The free school was established by subscription, in 1704 ; in 1822, its funds were augmented by a bequest of £5000 from Samuel Troutbeck, of Madras, Esq., and it is further supported by voluntary contributions ; seventy boys and fifty girls are educated. A Roman Catholic school, in this parish, affords instruction to about four hundred children of both sexes. Thomas Dilworth, author of the spelling-book, and system of arithmetic, was master of the parochial free school.

WARBLETON, a parish in the hundred of HAWKESBOROUGH, rape of HASTINGS, county of SUSSEX, 6½ miles (N. by E.) from Hailsham, containing 1167 inhabitants. The living is a rectory, in the archdeaconry of Lewes, and diocese of Chichester, rated in the king's books at £13. 6. 8., and in the patronage of the Trustees of Smith's charities. The church is dedicated to St. Mary.

WARBLINGTON, a parish in the hundred of Bos-MERE, Portsdown division of the county of SOUTHAMPTON, ¾ of a mile (S. E. by E.) from Havant, containing, with the tything of Emsworth, 1850 inhabitants. The living is a rectory, in the archdeaconry and diocese of Winchester, rated in the king's books at £19. 9. 4½., and in the patronage of the Rev. W. Norris. The church is partly in the Norman and partly in the early English style of architecture, with an oratory at the termination of each aisle : several stone coffins are deposited in both aisles. The parish is bounded on the south by Langstone harbour. The ruins called Warblington castle are the remains of a quadrangular mansion of the Montacutes, of which there are only the gateway and tower, the whole being surrounded by a deep fosse.

WARBOROUGH, a parish in the hundred of EWELME, county of OXFORD, 2¾ miles (N.) from Wallingford, containing 684 inhabitants. The living is a perpetual curacy, in the jurisdiction of the peculiar court of Dorchester, and in the patronage of the President and Fellows of Corpus Christi College, Oxford. The church is dedicated to St. Lawrence.

WARBOYS, a parish in the hundred of HURSTINGSTONE, county of HUNTINGDON, 4½ miles (S. S. E.) from Ramsey, containing 1353 inhabitants. The living is a rectory, in the archdeaconry of Huntingdon, and diocese of Lincoln, rated in the king's books at £27. 10., and in the patronage of William Strode, Esq. The church, dedicated to St. Mary Magdalene, has lately received an addition of two hundred and fifty-four sittings, of which one hundred and fifty-eight are free, the Incorporated Society for the enlargement of churches and chapels having granted £200 towards defraying the expense. There is a place of worship for Baptists.

WARBRICK, a joint township with Layton, in the parish of BISPHAM, hundred of AMOUNDERNESS, county palatine of LANCASTER, 2¼ miles (W. S. W.) from Poulton. The population is returned with Layton.

WARBSTOW, a parish in the hundred of LESNEWTH, county of CORNWALL, 8½ miles (N. E.) from Camelford, containing 439 inhabitants. The living is a perpetual curacy, annexed to the vicarage of Treneglos, in the archdeaconry of Cornwall, and diocese of Exeter. The church has a curious Norman font. Here is a remarkable ancient fortification, called Warbstow-Barrow.

WARBURTON, a parish in the hundred of BUCKLOW, county palatine of CHESTER, 6½ miles (E. by N.) from Warrington, containing 509 inhabitants. The living is a perpetual curacy, annexed to the second mediety of the rectory of Lymme, in the archdeaconry and diocese of Chester, and in the patronage of R. E. E. Warburton, Esq. The church is dedicated to St. Werburgh. The rivers Mersey and Botling run through the parish. Here was anciently a monastery of Premonstratensian canons, dedicated to St. Werburgh.

WARCOP, a parish in EAST ward, county of WESTMORLAND, comprising the hamlets of Bleatarn, Burton, Sandford, and Warcop, and containing 713 inhabitants, of which number, 369 are in the hamlet of Warcop, 3 miles (W. by N.) from Brough. The living is a discharged vicarage, in the archdeaconry and diocese of Carlisle, rated in the king's books at £9. 5. 1½., and in the patronage of the Rev. W. M. S. Preston. The church is dedicated to St. Columba. There is a place of worship for Wesleyan Methodists. The river Eden runs through the parish, in the mountainous part of which there is said to be lead, but no mines have been opened. In the village is an ancient cross, which was recently brought from the common, at the expense of the lord of the manor, who holds his court annually in June, or July. Castle hill, near its south-east end, is supposed to be the site of an ancient castle ; and Kirksteads, near it, that of a chapel.

WARDEN, a parish within the liberty of the Isle of SHEPPY, lathe of SCRAY, county of KENT, 6¾ miles (E.) from Queenborough, containing 21 inhabitants. The living is a discharged rectory, in the archdeaconry and diocese of Canterbury, rated in the king's books at £4. 17. 8½., and in the patronage of Mrs. Simpson. The church is dedicated to St. James.

WARDEN, a parish in the north-western division of TINDALE ward, county of NORTHUMBERLAND, comprising the chapelry of Haydon, or Elrington, the townships of Brokenhaugh, Dean-Raw, Lipwood, and Warden, and containing, with the extra-parochial liberty of Walwick, 2072 inhabitants, of which number, 498 are in the township of Warden, 2½ miles (N. W. by N.) from Hexham. The living is a vicarage, in the archdeaconry of Northumberland, and diocese of Durham, rated in the king's books at £8. 16. 3., and in the patronage of Col. and Mrs. Beaumont. The church, dedicated to St. Michael, is a cruciform structure, in the early style of English architecture. The parish lies between the wall of Severus and the North and South Tyne rivers, and near their junction is a petrifying spring. On an eminence, called Castle Hill, are vestiges of a circular British fortification, which was defended by a rampart of rough stone; it was subsequently occupied by the Romans, by whom additional earthworks were raised, and surrounded by a fosse; within the area the foundations of buildings, and several hand-mills, have been discovered. Not far from the vicarage-house are traces of another fort, termed Castle Hill.

WARDEN (CHIPPING), a parish (formerly a market town) in the hundred of CHIPPING-WARDEN, county of NORTHAMPTON, 7¾ miles (N. N. E.) from Banbury, containing 488 inhabitants. The living is a rectory, in the archdeaconry of Northampton, and diocese of Peterborough, rated in the king's books at £26. 10., and in the patronage of the Earl of Guilford. The church is dedicated to St. Peter and St. Paul. In the neighbourhood are some Saxon, or Danish, intrenchments, called Arberry Banks.

WARDEN (OLD), a parish in the hundred of WIXAMTREE, county of BEDFORD, 3¾ miles (W. by S.) from Biggleswade, containing 670 inhabitants. The living is a discharged vicarage, united with that of Southill, in the archdeaconry of Bedford, and diocese of Lincoln, endowed with £200 private benefaction, and £200 royal bounty. The church is dedicated to St. Leonard: in the cemetery is the mausoleum of Lord Ongley. A market and fair, granted in 1218, were formerly held, but both have been long disused. An abbey for Cistercian monks from Rivaulx was founded here, in 1135, by Walter L'Espec: it was dedicated to the Blessed Virgin Mary, and at the dissolution had a revenue of £442. 11. 11.

WARDEN-LAW, a township in the parish of HOUGHTON le SPRING, northern division of EASINGTON ward, county palatine of DURHAM, 8½ miles (N. E.) from Durham, containing 14 inhabitants. It comprises a lofty eminence, crossed by a railway, having a steam-engine on its summit, for drawing up and letting down coal-wagons employed in conveying coal from the Heaton pits.

WARDINGTON, a chapelry in that part of the parish of CROPREDY which is in the hundred of BANBURY, county of OXFORD, 5 miles (N. E. by N.) from Banbury, containing, with the hamlets of Coton and Willscott, 825 inhabitants. The chapel is dedicated to St. Mary

Magdalene. This chapelry is in the jurisdiction of the peculiar court of Banbury in the Cathedral Church of Lincoln.

WARDLE, a township in that part of the parish of BUNBURY which is in the first division of the hundred of EDDISBURY, county palatine of CHESTER, 4¼ miles (N. W.) from Nantwich, containing 129 inhabitants. The Chester canal passes through the parish.

WARDLE, a joint township with Wuerdale, in that part of the parish of ROCHDALE which is in the hundred of SALFORD, county palatine of LANCASTER, 3 miles (N. N. E.) from Rochdale. The population is returned with Wuerdale. There is a place of worship for Wesleyan Methodists.

WARDLEWORTH, a township in that part of the parish of ROCHDALE which is in the hundred of SALFORD, county palatine of LANCASTER, 1½ mile (N. by E.) from Rochdale, containing 6451 inhabitants. The principal part of the town of Rochdale is within this township.

WARDLEY, a parish in the soke of OAKHAM, county of RUTLAND, 2¾ miles (W. by N.) from Uppingham, containing 52 inhabitants. The living is a discharged rectory, with the vicarage of Belton annexed, in the archdeaconry of Northampton, and diocese of Peterborough, rated in the king's books at £10. 16., and in the patronage of the Crown. The church is dedicated to St. Mary. The parish is bounded on the south by the river Eye, which separates it from Leicestershire.

WARDLOW, a township partly in the parish of HOPE, but chiefly in that of BAKEWELL, hundred of HIGH PEAK, county of DERBY, 2 miles (E. by S.) from Tideswell, containing 168 inhabitants. It is in the honour of Tutbury, duchy of Lancaster, and within the jurisdiction of a court of pleas held at Chapel en le Frith every third Tuesday, for the recovery of debts under £5. In making a turnpike-road through the village, in 1759, a circular heap of stones was opened, and found to contain the remains of about seventeen human bodies, interred in rude cells, or coffins of stone, apparently brought from a quarry about a quarter of a mile off: by some they are supposed to have been the bodies of persons slain during the war between the houses of York and Lancaster, but others think that the tomb was a family burial-place.

WARE, a market town and parish in the hundred of BRAUGHIN, county of HERTFORD, 2¼ miles (E. N. E.) from Hertford, and 21 (N.) from London, containing 3844 inhabitants. This place, anciently called Guare, derived both its origin and name from a weare, or dam, constructed on the river Lea, and strongly fortified by the Danes in 894, in order to defend their vessels; but Alfred is said to have drained the bed of the river, thereby stranding them, and destroying the fort. After this, his son Edward built a town here, which continued of no importance till the reign of John, when Sayer de Quincy forced the thoroughfare of the bridge over the river Lea, by breaking the chain placed there until toll was paid to the king's bailiff at Hertford. This led to the diversion of the northern road through this town, instead of Hertford, which essentially conduced to its prosperity. In the reign of Henry III., a tournament was held here by Gilbert Marshall, Earl of Pembroke, in which he was slain; and, in the same reign, a Benedictine priory was founded by Margaret, Countess of Leicester, as a cell to the monastery of Ebralf, at Uttica in Normandy, which was eventually bestowed by Henry V. on the Carthusian monastery of Sheen in Surrey : here was also a house of Franciscan friars. The town is situated in a valley, on the east side of the navigable river Lea, and consists of several streets, the principal extending about a mile along the high road from London to Cambridge : it is lighted, well supplied with both river and spring water, and is in a state of general improvement. A public library was established in 1795. The place was formerly subject to floods, but, from diverting into the river the water that flowed through Baldock-street to near the centre of the town, the inconvenience has been removed. The trade is chiefly in malt, which is made to a very great extent, and most of the London breweries are supplied from this town : there are seventy malting establishments in the town, and others are in progress of erection. The river Lea is navigable hence to Hertford and London, furnishing ample facilities for the conveyance of malt and corn to the metropolis, and for bringing back coal and manure. The market is on Tuesday; and fairs are held on the last Tuesday in April, and on the Tuesday before September 21st, for cattle. A market-house, erected by subscription, supported on sixteen arches, and containing an elegant assembly-room, was completed in 1827 : the site was given by the lord of the manor. The town is under the superintendence of four constables and three head-boroughs : the county magistrates hold a petty session every alternate Tuesday, and a court baron is held annually.

The living is a vicarage, with that of Thundridge annexed, in the archdeaconry of Middlesex, and diocese of London, rated in the king's books at £20. 10., and in the patronage of the Master and Fellows of Trinity College, Cambridge. The church, situated in the centre of the town, is dedicated to St. Mary ; it is an ancient cruciform edifice, with two sepulchral chapels and a west tower, surmounted by a low spire; in the interior is an antique font, in the later style of English architecture. In the churchyard is an ancient tombstone, bearing the following inscription;—"To the memory of William Mead, M.D., who departed this life on the 28th day of October, 1652, aged one hundred and forty-eight years, nine months, three weeks, and four days." There are two places of worship each for Independents and Wesleyan Methodists, and one for the Society of Friends. Humphrey Spencer gave a schoolhouse, and funds for keeping it in repair, and for the salary of the master, to which additions have since been made. A National school, in which one hundred boys are educated, is supported by voluntary contributions ; a British school, in which eighty are instructed, is supported by the Independents; and a free school, for one hundred girls, is chiefly maintained by two ladies, aided by private subscriptions. Here is an old school-house belonging to the Governors of Christ's Hospital, also a range of buildings, for the accommodation of the nurses and children. There are seventeen almshouses for widows and other poor persons, some of which have small endowments : bequests to the amount of about £300 per annum have been left for the poor, for whose further relief a Lying-in-Society and a Friendly Institution have been established. Near the town are two springs of excellent water, of which one, called "the Chadwell Spring," is also denominated the "New River Head," and the other the "Amwell Spring;" these, under the superintendence of the New River Company, supply the metropolis. In the grounds of Amwell House is a beautiful grotto. The great bed of Ware, sufficiently capacious to accommodate six couple, is of uncertain and conjectural origin : at the head is carved the date 1453. Four stone coffins were found in a field, called Bury Field, at the south-west corner of the town, in 1802, supposed to have been the burial-place of the priory.

WAREHAM, a borough and market town, having separate jurisdiction, though locally in the hundred of Winfrith, Blandford (South) division of the county of DORSET, 17 miles (E. by S.) from Dorchester, and 119 (S. W. by W.) from London, containing, with the out portion of the parish of Lady St. Mary, and the liberty of Stowborough, 1931 inhabitants.

Seal and Arms.

This town has been of great note in history ; it existed in the time of the Britons, and was called *Durngneis* ; by the Saxons it was named *Vepham* and *Thornsæta*, and in ancient records it is designated *Warham* and *Varama*, a compound of *Var-Ham*, "a habitation on a fishing shore." It has been supposed to occupy the site of the *Morionium*, or *Moriconium*, of Ravennas, but this is doubtful. That it was known to the Romans is demonstrated by the existence of a Roman way proceeding to Dorchester, and by the discovery of coins in the vicinity. In the Saxon times it was of some importance, and the burial-place of Brithric, the West Saxon king, about the year 800. The Danes soon afterwards massacred the inhabitants, and reduced the town to ruins ; but it had so recovered in the time of Athelstan, that he established two mints in it. In 978, the body of Edward the Martyr, after his assassination at Corfe-Castle, was temporarily interred here, and was removed by St. Dunstan, with much ceremony, to Shaftesbury. After the lapse of twenty years more, the town was again ravaged by the Danes, who, making the Isle of Wight their general place of rendezvous, proceeded thence to the mouth of the river Frome, and kept Wareham in a state of continual alarm. In 1138, the castle and town were seized for the Empress Maud, by Robert de Lincoln, but retaken and burnt by Stephen. On the intended expedition of John against France, in 1205, that monarch landed here, and three years afterwards garrisoned the town, which, in 1213, became the scene of the cruel execution of Peter of Pomfret, a religious enthusiast, and his son, because the former had foretold the deposition of that monarch. During the parliamentary war, Wareham was alternately possessed by the king and the parliament, but was finally given up to the former, on the surrender of Corfe Castle. In 1762, two-thirds of it were destroyed by fire ; but, by a liberal subscription throughout the country, and an act procured for its restoration, it was, within two years, completely rebuilt.

The town is pleasantly situated on an eminence between the mouths of the Frome and the Piddle, which commands a prospect of Poole harbour, and in form resembles a parallelogram, occupying an area of about one hundred acres, enclosed, except on the south, by a high wall, or rampart, of earth ; the intervening space between the wall and the town is laid out in large garden grounds, divided into regular squares by lanes, which still exhibit traces of some ancient buildings. The four principal streets, as well as the minor streets and lanes, diverge at right angles, and the former are open and spacious, corresponding with the cardinal points of the compass. The south and north entrances are formed by bridges over the Frome and the Piddle ; the former is a handsome modern stone structure of five arches, erected in 1775, in lieu of an old bridge, which had stood from the time of William Rufus ; the latter has three arches : from both bridges are raised stone causeways, that from the south leading to Stowborough, and being eight hundred paces in length ; the other to North Port, on the London road. Wareham was formerly a noted port, and, in the time of Edward III., furnished three ships and fifty-nine men for the siege of Calais ; but the retreat of the sea from its harbour has long destroyed its importance, and withdrawn its commercial traffic ; although, at very high tides, the water flows up nearly five miles to Holm bridge : the quay is on the south side of the town. The river Frome was anciently a celebrated salmon fishery, of which the profits formed part of the dowry granted by Henry VII. to his queen ; and so abundant and cheap was this fish, that the curious stipulation inserted in the indentures of apprentices, that they should not be compelled to eat of it more than thrice a week, prevailed here, as in various other places : the fishery has long since declined, very few being now caught. The manufacture of shirt buttons and straw-plat, and the knitting of stockings, employ a great number of females ; pipe-clay is obtained in large quantities from pits in the neighbourhood, and exported, in the proportion of considerably more than ten thousand tons annually, from Poole, for the Staffordshire potteries, also to London, Liverpool, Hull, and Glasgow, for the manufacture of tobacco pipes : coal, manufactured goods, and grocery, are imported. The gardens within the town produce a sufficient quantity of vegetables for the supply of its own market, and also for those of Poole and Portsmouth. The market is on Saturday ; and fairs are held on Midsummer-day, April 17th, and September 11th, for cattle, cheese, and hogs : the toll of the market and fairs belongs to the mayor : of late years six cattle markets have been held during the spring, and are well attended. This is a borough by prescription, and the inhabitants have had their privileges confirmed by several charters : the last, under which the town is now governed, was granted by Queen Anne, in 1703. The municipal body consists of a mayor, and six capital and twelve assistant burgesses, with a recorder, town clerk, and inferior officers. The mayor, who is a justice of the peace and coroner for the town and the isles of Purbeck and Brownsea, and capital burgesses, hold quarter sessions of the peace, having exclusive jurisdiction : a court of record is held on the first Monday in every month, for the recovery of debts under £40. A court baron is held annually by the lord of the manor. The gift of the freedom of the borough is vested in the corporation. This town has returned members to parliament from the time of Edward I. : the elective franchise is in the mayor, magistrates, and inhabitants paying scot and lot, and in the freeholders of lands and tenements who have been, *bonâ fide*, in the occupancy or receipt of the rents and profits thereof for the space of one whole year next before the election ; except the same came to such freeholders by descent, devise, marriage settlement, or appointment to some benefice in the church : the number of voters paying scot and lot are about one hundred and sixty-five, but the whole number of electors is above seven hundred : the mayor is the returning officer.

Wareham comprises the parishes of the Holy Trinity, St. Martin Within and Without, and Lady St. Mary Within and Without, in the archdeaconry of Dorset, and diocese of Bristol. The living of Holy Trinity parish is a rectory, to which those of St. Martin's and St. Mary's were united in 1678, rated in the king's books at £7. 5. 5., and in the patronage of John Calcraft, Esq. ; the church is disused. The living of St. Martin's is rated in the king's books at £8. 2. 6. : this church also is disused. The living of St. Mary's is a rectory not in charge : the church is a spacious and ancient structure, containing early and decorated portions : it is believed to have been conventual, and attached to a priory founded here before 876, when the monastery was destroyed by the Danes, and to have been rebuilt about the period of the Conquest : over a small north door is a rude piece of sculpture, representing the Crucifixion, surmounted by a Saxon arch. In a small south chapel, of which the ceiling is richly groined, are the monuments of two warriors recumbent, and in complete mail : in this chapel the remains of Mr. Hutchins, rector of this place, and author of the " History and Antiquities of the County of Dorset," are deposited ; here also are several mural monuments to the members of the Calcraft family. There were formerly two other parochial churches, St. Peter's and St. Michael's. There are places of worship for Independents, Wesleyan Methodists, and Unitarians : that for the Independents was erected in 1670, and its first minister was one of the confessors of Bartholomew-day : they have recently erected a British free school, reading-room, and library, in which lectures are given during the winter, which is supported by voluntary contributions.

The free school, situated in the parish of Lady St. Mary, was founded by George Pitt, of Stratfieldsaye, Esq., with a salary of £25 per annum for a schoolmaster ; the endowment was further augmented by a bequest from Henry Harbin, in 1703, who left £200 for the purchase of land, to instruct the children of the poor. An almshouse, opposite St. Peter's church, was founded by John Streche, of Exeter, Esq., for six aged men and five women; it was rebuilt, in 1741, by Henry Drax and John Pitt, Esqrs., and valued in the chantry roll at £11. 13. 10. The antiquities of Wareham comprise the walls built by the Danes in the time of Alfred : the west wall is one thousand eight hundred feet in length, the north one thousand nine hundred and sixty, the east one thousand six hundred, and the south one thousand seven hundred, varying as to height in different places : near Bloody bank, the place of execution, in 1684, of Mr. Baxter, Holman, and others, for their attachment to the Duke

3 D 2

of Monmouth, it is thirty feet perpendicular. Of the castle, situated in the south-west angle of the town, and originally supposed to have been built by the Romans, and rebuilt by the Conqueror, only the mound, or keep, called Castle hill, remains. The relics of the priory have been converted into a dwelling - house. At Stowborough, on opening a barrow, called King Barrow, in 1767, a large hollow trunk of an oak was discovered, in which were human bones, wrapped up in a large covering composed of several deer skins, and a small vessel of oak, in the shape of an urn, conjectured by Mr. Hutchins to have been the drinking cup of the deceased, who, in the opinion of Mr. Gough, was some Saxon, or Danish, chieftain. Dr. John Chapman, tutor to the great Lord Camden; and Horace Walpole, Earl of Orford, were natives of this town.

WAREHORNE, a parish in the hundred of HAM, lathe of SHEPWAY, county of KENT, 7¼ miles (S. by W.) from Ashford, containing 493 inhabitants. The living is a rectory, in the archdeaconry and diocese of Canterbury, rated in the king's books at £19, and in the patronage of the Crown. The church is dedicated to St. Matthew. The Grand Military canal from Hythe to Rye passes through the parish, and the rivers Medway, Rother, and Stour, have their sources here. Fairs are held on May 14th, for toys; and October 2nd and 3rd, for cattle; the former on Ham-Street green, the latter on Warehorne green.

WARESLEY, a parish in the hundred of TOSELAND, county of HUNTINGDON, 4¼ miles (N. N. E.) from Potton, containing 231 inhabitants. The living is a discharged vicarage, in the archdeaconry of Huntingdon, and diocese of Lincoln, rated in the king's books at £8. 16. 5½., and in the patronage of the Master and Fellows of Pembroke Hall, Cambridge. The church is dedicated to St. Andrew.

WARFIELD, a parish in the hundred of WARGRAVE, county of BERKS, 6 miles (E. N. E.) from Wokingham, containing 1155 inhabitants. The living is a vicarage, in the archdeaconry of Berks, and diocese of Salisbury, rated in the king's books at £13. 6. 8., and in the patronage of Maxwell Windle, Esq. The church, dedicated to St. Michael, contains some handsome monuments; and in a chapel (the burial-place of the Stavertons) attached to the north side of the chancel, is an ancient brass with an effigy of one of that family. This parish once formed part of Windsor Forest. At New Bracknell, fairs are held on April 25th, August 22nd, and October 1st. The sum of £200, bequeathed by the Hon. Gen. Wm. Hervey, has been expended in the erection of premises for a National school, on land given by the late Lord Braybrooke, the lord of the manor; the school is supported by voluntary contributions.

WARFORD (GREAT), a township in the parish of ALDERLEY, hundred of MACCLESFIELD, county palatine of CHESTER, 5 miles (E. by S.) from Nether Knutsford, containing 336 inhabitants. There is a place of worship for Baptists.

WARFORD (LITTLE), a joint township with Martall, in that part of the parish of ROSTHERN which is in the hundred of BUCKLOW, county palatine of CHESTER, 4½ miles (E. S. E.) from Nether Knutsford. The population is returned with Martall.

WARGRAVE, a parish in the hundred of WARGRAVE, county of BERKS, 6½ miles (N. E. by E.) from

Reading, containing 1409 inhabitants. The living is a vicarage, in the archdeaconry of Berks, and diocese of Salisbury, rated in the king's books at £13. 13. 6½., and in the patronage of Lord Braybrooke, as lord of the manor, and impropriator of the great tithes; to whose ancestor, Sir Henry Nevill, the Billingbear estates, and the hundred of Wargrave, formerly attached to the see of Winchester, were granted by Edward VI. The church, dedicated to St. Mary, has a tower in a later style of English architecture; it has lately received an addition of two hundred and ninety-seven sittings, of which one hundred and fifty are free, the Incorporated Society for the enlargement of churches and chapels having granted £200 towards defraying the expense. The parish is bounded on the north by the river Thames. Richard Aldworth, in 1692, bequeathed an annuity of £5 for teaching four poor children; and Robert Pigot, Esq., in 1796, left by will £6700, three per cent. stock, directing the interest to be applied towards instructing and clothing twenty boys and twenty girls. A market, granted in 1218, to Peter de Rupibus, Bishop of Winchester, which was held here on Monday, has been long disused.

WARHAM, a village in the northern division of the hundred of GREENHOE, county of NORFOLK, 2 miles (S. E. by E.) from Wells, containing 400 inhabitants: it comprises the parishes of All Saints, a discharged rectory, rated in the king's books at £16, and in the patronage of the Crown; St. Mary, and St. Mary Magdalene, united rectories, rated jointly at £11. 6. 8., and in the patronage of Thomas W. Coke, Esq.; all in the archdeaconry and diocese of Norwich. There are small remains of an old baronial mansion, surrounded by a moat, and of some ancient fortifications.

WARK, a parish in the north-western division of TINDALE ward, county of NORTHUMBERLAND, comprising the townships of High Shitlington, Low Shitlington, Wark, and Warksburn, and containing 866 inhabitants, of which number, 367 are in the township of Wark, 4½ miles (S. S. E.) from Bellingham. The living is a rectory not in charge, in the archdeaconry of Northumberland, and diocese of Durham, and in the patronage of the Governors of Greenwich Hospital, who have erected a handsome church, the first stone of which was laid in October 1815, and it was opened for divine service on August 10th, 1818; they also built the parsonage - house. There is a place of worship for Presbyterians. This parish is one of the six into which the late extensive parish of Simonbourn was divided, in 1814, under the authority of an act of parliament obtained in 1811: it is bounded on the east by the North Tyne, across which there is a ferry. Courts leet and baron for the manor are held, annually in October, by the Governors of Greenwich Hospital, who, with the Trustees of Heron's charity, have erected a school-room, in which the poor children of the parish are instructed on the National system. The village is ancient, and has been considerably improved by the recent erection of a handsome row of houses, with stone taken from some extensive ruins. About half a mile northward are the remains of an old church, a tumulus, and a cairn, in which urns and other relics have been found. Within the parish are vestiges of several ancient fortifications, said to have been thrown up by

Edward III.; and on the bank of the river is Moat Hill, formerly occupied by a tower, and more recently used as an observatory to watch the movements of an enemy.

WARKLEY, a parish in the hundred of SOUTH MOLTON, county of DEVON, 5½ miles (W. S. W.) from South Molton, containing 268 inhabitants. The living is a rectory, in the archdeaconry of Barnstaple, and diocese of Exeter, rated in the king's books at £14. 4. 7., and in the patronage of the Bishop of Exeter, by lapse. The church is dedicated to St. John. A school is supported by small annual subscriptions.

WARKSBURN, a township in the parish of WARK, north-western division of TINDALE ward, county of NORTHUMBERLAND, 5¼ miles (S.) from Bellingham, containing 290 inhabitants. Near the farm-house of Roses Bower is a medicinal spring, called Holy Well, the water of which is said to be efficacious in the cure of agues and certain obstructions.

WARKTON, a parish in the hundred of HUXLOE, county of NORTHAMPTON, 2¼ miles (E. N. E.) from Kettering, containing 247 inhabitants. The living is a rectory, in the archdeaconry of Northampton, and diocese of Peterborough, rated in the king's books at £18. 16. 3., and in the patronage of the Duke of Buccleuch. The church, dedicated to St. Edmund, is chiefly remarkable for containing sumptuous monuments of the Montague family, two of which are by Roubilliac.

WARKWORTH, a parish in the hundred of KING'S SUTTON, county of NORTHAMPTON, 2 miles (E.) from Banbury, containing, with the hamlets of Grimsbury and Nethercote, 426 inhabitants. The living is a perpetual curacy, annexed to the vicarage of Marston St. Lawrence, in the archdeaconry of Northampton, and diocese of Peterborough. The church is dedicated to St. Mary.

WARKWORTH, a parish comprising the townships of Birling, Brotherick, High Buston, Low Buston, Sturton-Grange, and Walkmill, in the eastern division of COQUETDALE ward, and the townships of Amble, Acklington, Acklington - Park, Bullock's - Hall, East Chivington, and West Chivington, Glosterhill, Hauxley, Hadston, Morrick, Togston, and Warkworth, in the eastern division of MORPETH ward, county of NORTHUMBERLAND, and containing 2265 inhabitants, of which number, 594 are in the township of Warkworth, 7 miles (S. E.) from Alnwick. The living is a vicarage, in the archdeaconry of Northumberland, and diocese of Durham, rated in the king's books at £18. 5. 7½., and in the patronage of the Bishop of Carlisle. The church, dedicated to St. Lawrence, is a handsome structure, said to have been originally founded by Ceolwulph, King of Northumbria, in 736, and rebuilt at a later period; it has a spire nearly one hundred feet high: in its southwestern extremity is a monument to the memory of Sir Hugh de Morwick, a Knight Templar, who gave the common to the inhabitants. There are places of worship for Scottish Seceders and Wesleyan Methodists. The parish abounds with excellent coal, freestone, limestone, and whinstone. The village is situated a short distance westward from the sea, and is almost surrounded by the river Coquet, which is here crossed by an ancient bridge of two arches, having at the south end a tower gateway, formerly defended by an iron gate, through which the road passes: some valuable gems and pebbles are frequently found in its bed. This place consists of one main street leading from the castle to the bridge, and a short opening to the church, of good modern-built houses, and contains two very commodious inns. At the ancient cross, a market, granted by King John, was formerly held for provisions, but it has been long disused. Fairs for cattle are proclaimed on the first Thursday in May, and on the Thursdays before August 18th and November 23rd, one being held also on the last-mentioned day. Warkworth was anciently a borough, having been probably so constituted by King Ceolwulph, in the time of the Saxons. The Duke of Northumberland holds a court leet on the first Wednesday in October, at which a boroughreeve, two moorgrieves, three constables, and other officers, are annually chosen. A building, now sometimes called the "Town Hall," was erected, in 1736, by Mr. G. Lawson, for a school-house, and is used as such; but a more commodious one was erected by subscription in 1824, the children in which are educated on the Madras system: there are also a girls' National school, and an infants' school for both sexes. Nearly adjoining the churchyard are some remains of a small Benedictine priory, founded by Nicholas de Farnham, Bishop of Durham, who died in 1257. The venerable and magnificent ruins of Warkworth castle occupy a fine elevation, rising from the margin of the river, south of the village, the moat by which it is surrounded enclosing more than five acres: the area is of an oblong form, on the north side of which stands the keep, on a lofty mound, encompassed by a wall thirty-five feet high, both in good preservation; but of the grand entrance to this once stately fortress only a few apartments remain. It is not recorded by whom the castle was erected; the arms of the Percy family, however, appear to have been inserted in different parts of the building, at a much later period than that of its foundation. About a mile westward is an ancient hermitage, with a neat small chapel, curiously adorned, in the early style of English architecture, containing an altar and various other devotional emblems, with the representation of a recumbent female on a table monument placed in a niche near the altar, and that of a hermit standing over it, in a mournful attitude. This interesting retreat is celebrated in the beautiful poem entitled "The Hermit of Warkworth," published by Dr. Percy, Bishop of Dromore, in 1771. Warkworth gives the inferior title of baron to the Duke of Northumberland.

WARLABY, a township in the parish of AINDERBY-STEEPLE, eastern division of the wapentake of GILLING, north riding of the county of YORK, 2¾ miles (S. S. W.) from North Allerton, containing 97 inhabitants.

WARLEGGON, a parish in the hundred of WEST, county of CORNWALL, 5¾ miles (E. N. E.) from Bodmin, containing 296 inhabitants. The living is a discharged rectory, in the archdeaconry of Cornwall, and diocese of Exeter, rated in the king's books at £5. 17. 6., and in the patronage of G. W. F. Gregor, Esq. The church is dedicated to St. Bartholomew. A branch of the river Fowey runs through the parish.

WARLEY, a township in the parish of HALIFAX, wapentake of MORLEY, West riding of the county of YORK, 2½ miles (W.) from Halifax, containing 4982 inhabitants, of whom many are employed in the manufacture of cotton, worsted, and stuffs. The chapelry of

Sowerby-Bridge is in this township. There is a place of worship for Independents. In the neighbourhood is one of those remarkable rocking-stones, supposed to be of Druidical origin.

WARLEY (GREAT), a parish in the hundred of CHAFFORD, county of ESSEX, 3¾ miles (S.) from Brentwood, containing 521 inhabitants. The living is a rectory, in the archdeaconry of Essex, and diocese of London, rated in the king's books at £14, and in the patronage of the Master and Fellows of St. John's College, Cambridge. The church is dedicated to St. Mary.

WARLEY (LITTLE), a parish in the hundred of CHAFFORD, county of ESSEX, 3½ miles (S. by E.) from Brentwood, containing 179 inhabitants. The living is a rectory, in the archdeaconry of Essex, and diocese of London, rated in the king's books at £11. 3. 9., and in the patronage of Earl Brownlow and Miss Tyrell. The church is dedicated to St. Peter. In the reign of George III. a considerable army was encamped in the neighbourhood; and, about twenty years ago, barracks were erected here for two thousand cavalry.

WARLEY-WIGORN, a hamlet in that part of the parish of HALES-OWEN which is in the lower division of the hundred of HALFSHIRE, county of WORCESTER, 3 miles (N. E. by E.) from Hales-Owen, containing 878 inhabitants. John Moore, in 1797, bequeathed £100, now producing £9 a year, for which fourteen poor children are educated.

WARLINGHAM, a parish in the second division of the hundred of TANDRIDGE, county of SURREY, 4¾ miles (S. S. E.) from Croydon, containing 421 inhabitants. The living is a vicarage, with the perpetual curacy of Chelsham annexed, in the archdeaconry of Surrey, and diocese of Winchester, rated in the king's books at £11. 12. 11., and in the patronage of A. W. Wigzell, Esq. The church, dedicated to All Saints, is principally in the early style of English architecture.

WARMFIELD, a parish in the lower division of the wapentake of AGBRIGG, West riding of the county of YORK, comprising the townships of Sharlston, and Warmfield with Heath, and containing 1071 inhabitants, of which number, 741 are in the township of Warmfield with Heath, 3½ miles (E.) from Wakefield. The living is a vicarage, in the archdeaconry and diocese of York, rated in the king's books at £5. 4. 2., and in the patronage of the Master and Fellows of Clare Hall, Cambridge. The church is dedicated to St. Peter. Dame Mary Bowles, in 1660, conveyed to trustees a building, to be used as a school-house, and a rent-charge of £20, for educating and apprenticing ten poor children. John Smyth, Esq., in 1729, left three houses and an annuity of £4, for educating six children.

WARMINGHAM, a parish in the hundred of NORTHWICH, county palatine of CHESTER, comprising the townships of Elton, Moston, Tetton, and Warmingham, and containing 1078 inhabitants, of which number, 386 are in the township of Warmingham, 3¾ miles (W.) from Sandbach. The living is a rectory, in the archdeaconry and diocese of Chester, rated in the king's books at £12. 4. 7., and in the patronage of Lord Crewe. The church is dedicated to St. Leonard. Courts leet and baron are held here. A free school, founded by Thomas Minshull, has an endowment in land, of the annual value of £15.

WARMINGHURST, a parish in the hundred of EAST EASWRITH, rape of BRAMBER, county of SUSSEX, 6 miles (N. W.) from Steyning, containing 116 inhabitants. The living is a perpetual curacy, in the archdeaconry and diocese of Chichester, and in the patronage of the Duke of Norfolk.

WARMINGTON, a parish, comprising the hamlet of Warmington in the hundred of WILLYBROOK, but chiefly in that of POLEBROOK, county of NORTHAMPTON, 3¼ miles (N. E.) from Oundle, containing 519 inhabitants. The living is a discharged vicarage, in the archdeaconry of Northampton, and diocese of Peterborough, rated in the king's books at £13. 6. 8., and in the patronage of the Earl of Westmorland. The church, dedicated to St. Mary, is a beautiful structure, principally in the early English style, with an enriched tower and spire. There is a place of worship for Wesleyan Methodists. The water of Caldwell Spring, in the neighbourhood, possesses some mineral properties. Two small bequests, by Mr. Blowfield and Mr. Elmes, are applied in support of a school.

WARMINGTON, a parish in the Burton-Dassett division of the hundred of KINGTON, county of WARWICK, 5 miles (N. W. by N.) from Banbury, containing, with the township of Arlescote, 437 inhabitants. The living is a rectory, in the archdeaconry of Coventry, and diocese of Lichfield and Coventry, rated in the king's books at £16. 3. 11½., and in the patronage of Mrs. Farrer. The church is dedicated to St. Nicholas. There is a place of worship for Wesleyan Methodists. A Benedictine priory, subordinate to the abbey of St. Peter and St. Paul de Pratellis, or Preaux, in Normandy, was founded here in the time of Henry I., which, after the suppression of Alien houses, was granted by Henry VI. to the Carthusian priory at Witham in Somersetshire. Nadbury camp, in this vicinity, where some fix the ancient *Tripontium*, is of a square form, rounded at the angles, and comprises about twelve acres.

WARMINSTER, a market town and parish in the hundred of WARMINSTER, county of WILTS, 21 miles (W. N. W.) from Salisbury, and 97 (W. S. W.) from London, containing 5612 inhabitants. Antiquaries are at variance respecting the etymology of its name: according to Camden, this was the *Verlucio* of the Romans, and he considers the first syllable to be a corruption of that of its ancient appellation: others deduce it from the *wears* near which the town stood, and from a minster, or monastery, stated to have been once situated in its vicinity; which conjecture receives confirmation from the supposed site being still called "The Nunnery," and a walk upon the neighbouring hill, "Nuns' Path." At the Conquest it was denominated *Guermistre*, and, according to the Norman survey, was then possessed of many privileges: at a later period it became celebrated for its corn market, which, in the time of Henry VIII., appears to have been of considerable note. The town is situated on the river Willey, near the south-western extremity of Salisbury Plain, and consists principally of one street, nearly a mile long, well paved by the commissioners of the roads, and of clean appearance; it is considered one of the most healthy towns in England, and has been remarked for the longevity of its inhabitants. The malt trade was formerly carried on here to a greater extent than in any other town in the West of England, and it is still a respectable branch of trade; the manufacture of broad cloths and kerseymeres was also much more extensive than it is at present: the silk business has been recently introduced, and affords employment to many females and children. The market, which is on Saturday, is very considerable for the sale of corn: the whole is previously warehoused in the town, and a sack from every load is pitched in the market-place: the average quantity sold each market day is from two to three thousand quarters, and the annual value, in 1828, exceeded £160,000. The want of a canal navigation is, however, beginning to affect this trade; and Devizes, which possesses this advantage, promises, within a few years, to rival it successfully. Fairs are held on April 22nd, August 10th, and October 26th; the last is pre-eminently called "The Great Fair," for sheep, cattle, and cheese. A high constable, deputy constables, and tythingmen, are chosen annually at the manorial court of the Marquis of Bath. The county sessions of the peace for the summer quarter are holden here annually in July. A court of requests, for the recovery of debts not exceeding £5, is held every fortnight, on Tuesday, at Warminster and Westbury alternately, the jurisdiction of which extends over the hundreds of Warminster, Westbury, and Heytesbury: petty sessions are held monthly by the neighbouring magistrates. The town hall has been lately pulled down, and the Marquis of Bath has erected, at his own expense, a noble building in the centre of the market-place, in the same elegant style of architecture as his lordship's own mansion at Longleat, comprising every accommodation for holding the sessions, and a handsome suite of apartments for assemblies, public meetings, &c.

The living is a vicarage, in the archdeaconry and diocese of Salisbury, rated in the king's books at £18. 0. 2½., and in the patronage of the Bishop of Salisbury. The parochial church, dedicated to St. Denis, is situated on the Bath road, near the north-western extremity of the town, and is a spacious and handsome structure, of various styles of architecture, with a tower rising from the centre, originally built about the time of Edward III., but the body and aisles were rebuilt, on the old foundation, in 1724. A proprietary chapel, founded in the reign of Edward I., and dedicated to St. Lawrence, stands near the market-place: it was endowed by two maiden sisters, named Hewett, and is vested in feoffees; the original tower remains, but the body of the chapel was rebuilt in 1725, and has lately been repaired and beautified. A new church, called Christ Church, has also been recently built by voluntary subscriptions, aided by a grant from the parliamentary commissioners; it occupies an elevated site, and forms an interesting object in the view of the town: many other improvements have also been made. There are places of worship for Baptists, Independents, Wesleyan Methodists, and Unitarians. A free grammar school was built and endowed by the first Viscount Weymouth: the appointment of the master belongs to the Marquis of Bath; he receives a salary of £30 per annum, for which twenty boys are instructed. A National school for boys and girls, and a Lancasterian school for girls, are supported by voluntary contributions. A variety of Roman coins, both of silver and brass, has been found here. In the vicinity are many British tumuli, and several remains of Roman encampments,

particularly Battlesbury, a strong earthwork with double sides, where spear-heads and other weapons have been occasionally ploughed up. Near this intrenchment, on the edge of the river Willey, a beautiful tesselated pavement, and the foundations of a Roman villa, with its hypocaust, sudatory, &c., were discovered, in 1786: among other portraits was a figure of Diana, with a hare; the former was too much injured to be removed; the latter is carefully preserved at Longleat House. On the west side of the town is Clay hill, a steep and conical eminence surmounted by a tumulus: it is nearly nine hundred feet above low water mark at Bristol, and was formerly used as a beacon. The environs are rich in fossil remains, many of which have been deposited in the British Museum. In the year 1816, a toad and a newt, both living, were found imbedded in a thick stratum of rock, which had not the smallest crack, or orifice; an account of this discovery was published in the thirty-eighth volume of the Medical and Physical Journal, for 1817. Dr. Huntingford, Bishop of Hereford; and Dr. Samuel Squire, Bishop of St. David's, an able and learned writer, were natives of this town.

WARMSWORTH, a parish in the southern division of the wapentake of STRAFFORTH and TICKHILL, West riding of the county of YORK, 3¼ miles (S. W.) from Doncaster, containing 335 inhabitants. The living is a discharged rectory, in the archdeaconry and diocese of York, rated in the king's books at £6. 10. 10., and in the patronage of W. Wrightson, Esq. The church is dedicated to St. Peter; half a mile from it is a steeple, containing a bell. In the neighbourhood are some limekilns. George Fox, founder of the Society of Friends, held his first meetings at this place.

WARMWELL, a parish in the hundred of WINFRITH, Blandford (South) division of the county of DORSET, 5½ miles (S. E.) from Dorchester, containing 82 inhabitants. The living is a rectory, united in 1749 to that of Poxwell, in the archdeaconry of Dorset, and diocese of Bristol, rated in the king's books at £15.

WARNBOROUGH (NORTH), a tything in the parish and hundred of ODIHAM, Basingstoke division of the county of SOUTHAMPTON, 1 mile (N. W.) from Odiham. The population is returned with the parish.

WARNBOROUGH (SOUTH), a parish in the hundred of BERMONDSPIT, Basingstoke division of the county of SOUTHAMPTON, 2¾ miles (S. W. by S.) from Odiham, containing 356 inhabitants. The living is a rectory, in the archdeaconry and diocese of Winchester, rated in the king's books at £14. 12. 3½., and in the patronage of the President and Fellows of St. John's College, Oxford. The church is dedicated to St. Andrew. The Rev. John Duman, D.D., in 1785, gave £200, directing the interest to be applied in support of a Sunday school.

WARNDON, a parish in the lower division of the hundred of OSWALDSLOW, county of WORCESTER, 2½ miles (E. N. E.) from Worcester, containing 177 inhabitants. The living is a rectory, in the archdeaconry and diocese of Worcester, rated in the king's books at £10. 0. 2½., and in the patronage of B. Johnson, Esq., as trustee for R. Berkley, Esq., a Roman Catholic. The church is dedicated to St. Nicholas. The Birmingham and Worcester canal passes through the parish.

WARNFORD, or WARRINGTON, a township in the parish and northern division of BAMBROUGH ward, county of NORTHUMBERLAND, 3½ miles (S. E. by S.) from Belford, containing 27 inhabitants. This was formerly a considerable village, but there are now only a few houses. A Presbyterian chapel, built in 1750, was rebuilt by subscription in 1824, and has a handsome house attached, for the residence of the minister.

WARNFORD, a parish in the hundred of MEON-STOKE, Portsdown division of the county of SOUTHAMPTON, 6¼ miles (N. E.) from Bishop's Waltham, containing 364 inhabitants. The living is a rectory, in the peculiar jurisdiction of the Bishop of Winchester, rated in the king's books at £21. 9. 4½. The church is in the early style of English architecture, with a Norman tower; it was founded by Wilfrid, and rebuilt by Adam de Portu in the reign of the Conqueror. There is a place of worship for Independents. Near the church is a very ancient and curious ruin of a house, called King John's, a corruption of St. John's, which family formerly possessed it. The dimensions of the building were eighty feet by fifty-four, and the walls, composed of flints set in grout work, were four feet thick, with semicircular arched windows and doors: it was divided into two apartments, under a vaulted roof, which, though fallen in, appears to have been once supported by four slender, well-proportioned columns, the bases and capitals of which are still entire, and by four half-columns worked into the east and west walls.

WARNHAM, a parish in the hundred of SINGLE-CROSS, rape of BRAMBER, county of SUSSEX, 3 miles (N. N. W.) from Horsham, containing 914 inhabitants. The living is a vicarage, in the archdeaconry and diocese of Chichester, rated in the king's books at £10. 1. 0½., and in the patronage of the Dean and Chapter of Canterbury. The church is dedicated to St. Margaret.

WARNINGCAMP, a tything in the parish of LEOMINSTER, hundred of POLING, rape of ARUNDEL, county of SUSSEX, 1¾ mile (E.) from Arundel, containing 113 inhabitants.

WARPSGROVE, a parish in the hundred of EWELME, county of OXFORD, containing 27 inhabitants. The living is a rectory, in the archdeaconry and diocese of Oxford, rated in the king's books at £2. 11. 10½., and in the patronage of the Crown. The church is dedicated to St. James.

WARRENTON, a township in the parish, and northern division of the ward, of BAMBROUGH, county of NORTHUMBERLAND, 3 miles (S.) from Belford, containing 128 inhabitants.

WARRINGTON, a parish in the hundred of WEST-DERBY, county palatine of LANCASTER, comprising the market town of Warrington, the chapelry of Burtonwood, and the townships of Poulton with Fearnhead, Rixton, and Woolston with Martinscroft, and containing 16,698 inhabitants, of which number, 13,570 are in the town of Warrington, 52 miles (S. by E.) from Lancaster, and 188 (N. W. by N.) from London. This place, which is unquestionably of very great antiquity, is by some writers supposed to have been originally a British town, and, on the invasion of the Romans under Agricola, in the year 79, to have been converted into a Roman station. This opinion rests chiefly on the circumstance of three Roman roads leading respectively from the stations of *Condate, Coccium,* and *Mancunium,*

to a ford here over the river Mersey; the vestiges of a castrum and fosse, which are still discernible; and in the discovery of some Roman relics, consisting of coins found on both sides of the river near the ancient ford, and other antiquities, which have been subsequently dug up. On its occupation by the Saxons, it obtained the name of *Weringtun,* from the Saxon *Wæring,* a fortification, and *tun,* a town, from which its present appellation is derived. It was at that time of sufficient importance to give name to a wapentake, which afterwards merged into the hundred of West Derby, and formed part of the demesne of Edward the Confessor; it had been previously the head of a deanery, of which the jurisdiction still remains. In Domesday-book it is noticed under the name of *Wallintun;* and in the reign of Edward I., it was in the possession of William le Boteler, who obtained for it the grant of a market, and other privileges. From the earliest period, the river Mersey at this place was passed only by the ancient ford, till the close of the fifteenth century, when Thomas, first Earl of Derby, in compliment to Henry VII., on his visit to Latham and Knowsley, in 1496, erected the first bridge of stone, soon after which, the passage of the river by the ford ceased. In the reign of Henry VIII., Leland, speaking of Warrington, says, "it is a pavid towne of a prety bignes, the paroche chirch is at the tayle of the towne; it is a better market than Manchestre." Nothing of importance is recorded of it from this period till the commencement of the parliamentary war, when the inhabitants openly declared in favour of the royal cause, and the town was garrisoned for the king. In 1643, a detachment of the parliamentary forces, stationed at Manchester, laid siege to it, on which occasion the royalists under Col. Norris, the governor, took refuge in the church, and, fortifying that edifice against the assailants, obstinately resisted their attack for five days; but the enemy having erected a battery, which they brought to bear upon it, the royalists were compelled to surrender. Their number was one thousand six hundred, of whom three hundred were taken prisoners, and ten pieces of ordnance, with a large quantity of arms and ammunition, fell into the hands of the enemy. The royalists seem, however, to have soon regained possession of the town, for in less than three months it was again attacked by the parliamentarians, who carried it by storm, when the former lost six hundred men and eight pieces of cannon. In 1648, a numerous body of Scottish troops, under the command of the Duke of Hamilton, on their retreat after the battle of Ribbledale, rallied at Warrington; and, after an obstinate but unsuccessful encounter with the parliamentary forces under General Lambert, in which one thousand men were slain, the remainder, consisting of two thousand, surrendered themselves prisoners of war. The same general, in 1651, encountered the Scottish army, under the command of the young king, near this town, and repulsed them with considerable loss.

Towards the close of the Interregnum, Sir George Booth, Knight of the shire, who had been a strenuous supporter of the parliament, being dissatisfied with the conduct of public affairs, and anxious for the re-establishment of a free parliament under a legitimate head, raised a considerable force, in 1658; but, after a severe engagement with the forces under General

Lambert, at Winnington bridge, near Delamere Forest, he was defeated, and part of his army retreating to Warrington, the men were arrested in their flight by the parliamentary garrison stationed in that town: the services of Sir George, on this occasion, procured for him, after the Restoration, the title of Baron Delamere of Dunham Massey. Since the erection of the bridge over the Mersey, Warrington, as a military station, was regarded as commanding the entrance into the county of Lancaster; and, in 1745, on the approach of the army under Prince Charles Edward, the young pretender, who was advancing from Manchester, the central arches were demolished by the Liverpool Blues, who, having thus intercepted their progress, captured part of the rebel army, whom they sent prisoners to Chester castle: the bridge was repaired in 1747, but afterwards becoming much dilapidated, it was taken down, and a wooden bridge on stone piers was erected, in 1812, at the joint expense of the counties of Chester and Lancaster.

The town, which is pleasantly situated on the river Mersey, consists of four principal streets diverging from the centre, and intersected by several smaller; they are in general narrow and inconvenient, but are undergoing considerable improvement, under the superintendence of commissioners appointed by an act of parliament obtained in 1813: the houses are, for the greater part, of indifferent appearance, but interspersed with numerous respectable modern edifices, which form a striking contrast. It is well paved, under the provisions of the act; lighted with gas by a company incorporated in 1822, whose works, on a very extensive scale in Mersey-street, were erected at an expense of £15,000, advanced on shares of £20 each; and amply supplied with water by public works. The public subscription library was established in 1760, and is well supported. A Floral and Horticultural Society are now united, the former of which originated in 1817, and in 1824 was extended, to embrace the objects of the latter; a mechanics' institution was established in 1825; a neat and well arranged theatre is opened occasionally; and a handsome suite of assembly-rooms has been recently erected, which are well fitted up for the purpose. About seventy stage coaches pass daily through the town, serving to give it every appearance of bustle and animation.

Warrington has been long celebrated as a place of trade: until the early part of the eighteenth century the principal branches of manufacture were coarse linen and checks, to which succeeded that of sail-cloth, which was carried on so extensively, that one-half of the sail-cloth for the use of the British navy is computed to have been made here: the raw material, imported from Russia into Liverpool, was conveyed up the Mersey. On the decline of this branch of business after the peace, the spinning of cotton was introduced, together with the manufacture of muslin, calico, velveteen, and other cotton goods, which, with sail-cloth on a less extensive scale, constitute a very great portion of the trade of the town, and for the sale of which two cloth halls have been erected. There are several considerable pin-manufactories, which is the principal staple trade; and the making of files, for which the artificers have obtained a high degree of reputation, and other articles of hardware, employs a great number of men. The manufacture of glass and glass bottles is also extensively carried

on, there being several large establishments, of which the Bank Quay Glass Company is the chief. The manufacture of flint-glass has been subject to considerable fluctuation: at one period the export trade in this article to America was exceedingly great, but it is now almost annihilated; the Americans, in order to encourage their own manufactures, having imposed a tariff on English glass, which operates in many instances as a prohibition. A considerable trade is also carried on in malt, and there are several tanneries, soap-manufactories, and breweries: the ale of this place is in high repute. In the production of these different articles of manufacture, about twenty steam-engines, equal in extent of power to nearly four hundred horses, are employed in the town and its vicinity. The soil in the neighbourhood is extremely fertile, and productive of early vegetables for the supply of the neighbouring markets: formerly large quantities of potatoes were exported to the counties bordering on the Mediterranean, but since the increase of the population in the neighbouring districts, that species of traffic has been discontinued. The Mersey and Irwell navigation affords a direct communication with Manchester, and the other districts with which that town is connected, by various canals. The Sankey canal, commencing at the river Mersey, about one mile westward of the town, and approaching very near its northern extremity, was the first formed in the county, the act for its construction having been obtained in 1755: it extends about twelve miles to the collieries near St. Helen's, is crossed by eighteen swivel bridges, and by it about one hundred thousand tons of coal, at one shilling per ton, are conveyed to Liverpool, and for the glass-works at Warrington. In the year 1830, a railway, with two collateral branches, was constructed from this town to join the new one between Manchester and Liverpool, at Newton in Mackerfield, and subsequently an act was obtained to extend it across the latter, until it reached the branch from the borough of Wigan; goods are conveyed by it at rates varying from three halfpence to sixpence per ton per mile.

On the river Mersey was formerly a valuable fishery, which, in 1763, was let for £400 per annum: it abounded with salmon and smelts of very superior quality, but has now greatly declined, not only in the quantity, but also in the size and flavour, of the fish. At spring tides the water in this river rises to a height varying from ten to twelve feet at Warrington bridge, at which times vessels of from seventy to one hundred tons' burden can sail up to the quay a little above the town, where warehouses and other accommodations have been erected. The town, from its situation as regards Liverpool and Manchester, enjoys considerable traffic, having a constant communication, both by land and water, with those places. The market days are Wednesday and Saturday; the former, which is the principal, is abundantly supplied with corn, and the latter with provisions of every kind; there is also a large cattle market every alternate Wednesday. The fairs are July 18th and November 30th, each continuing ten days, for the sale of woollen cloth and other goods, and for horses, cattle, sheep, and pigs. The market hall, a neat and convenient building in the market-place, used on market days for the sale of corn, is, during the fairs, let to different tenants, for the sale of flannels and other goods; over it is a good suite of rooms, in which the assemblies were formerly held. Adjoining the market-house is the principal cloth hall, occupying three sides of a quadrangle; the ground floor is divided into shops for the sale of linen-drapery, fustians, hardware, and toys, during the fairs, and the upper part is used for the sale of cloths. There is also a cloth hall on a smaller scale in Buttermarket-street. The town is within the jurisdiction of the county magistrates, who hold a petty session for the division on the first and third Wednesdays in every month; and constables and other officers are appointed, annually in October, at the court leet of the lord of the manor. The town hall, a neat building, in which the petty sessions are held, was erected in 1820, at an expense of £2800, raised by subscription among the inhabitants.

The living is a rectory, in the archdeaconry and diocese of Chester, rated in the king's books at £40, endowed with £400 private benefaction, £600 royal bounty, and £1200 parliamentary grant, and in the patronage of Lord Lilford. The ancient church, dedicated to St. Elfin, which was of Saxon origin, existed at the time of the Conquest; of this there are few remains, the site being occupied by the present church, dedicated to St. Helen, a spacious and ancient cruciform structure, of various styles of architecture, with a central tower, which, with the piers and arches supporting it, and the chancel, are parts of the original building, being a fine specimen of the decorated style of English architecture: the windows of the chancel, particularly the east window, are enriched with elegant tracery of beautiful design; the north transept is in the later style of English architecture, of an inferior character, and the nave and south transept are modern additions. Two of the ancient sepulchral chapels are remaining, in one of which is the magnificent tomb of Sir Thomas Boteler and his lady, with their effigies, the former in armour, and both surrounded by various sculptured figures; in the other, which formerly belonged to the family of Massey, are several monuments to the Patten family, one of which is embellished with an elegant specimen of Italian sculpture to the memory of Thomas Wilson Patten, Esq., who died at Naples in 1819. This church has recently received an addition of two hundred and eighty-eight sittings, of which one hundred and ninety-eight are free, the Incorporated Society for enlarging and building churches and chapels having granted £100 towards defraying the expense. Trinity chapel, in Sankey-street, is a neat and commodious edifice; the living is a perpetual curacy, in the patronage of Thomas Legh, Esq. The first stone of a new church, to be erected by grant from the parliamentary commissioners, and to be dedicated to St. Paul, was laid in Bewsey-street, on the 11th of August, 1829; the living will be a perpetual curacy, in the patronage of the Rector. There are places of worship for Baptists, the Society of Friends, those in the late Countess of Huntingdon's Connexion, Independents, Independent and Wesleyan Methodists, Unitarians, and Roman Catholics.

The free grammar school was founded and amply endowed, in 1526, by a member of the Boteler family; by a decree of the court of Chancery, in 1820, the trustees were ordered to pay the master a salary of £300 per annum, with the gratuitous use of the school-

house, garden, and land adjoining, and to increase it when the number of scholars should exceed thirty; the same order directs the usher's salary to be from £60 to £100 per annum, and the writing-master's from £40 to £60: the school, which is under the patronage of Lord Lilford, who appoints the master, is open to all boys of the parish who have attained the age of seven: the late Rt. Hon. George Tierney was educated here. The Blue-coat school, in Winwick-street, was established in 1677, and is supported partly by subscription, and partly by an income arising from benefactions and legacies vested in the purchase of land, producing more than £200 per annum: this establishment has also the reversion of an estate at Sankey, worth £6000, granted by John Watkins, Esq., in 1797, and the reversionary interest of an estate in the county of Bedford, given, in 1685, by Arthur Borron, Esq.: one hundred and fifty boys and forty girls are instructed in it, of which number, fourteen boys and ten girls are also clothed. A charity school, established in 1814, in the same street, and in which one hundred and fifty girls are taught to read and sew; and an infant school, opened in 1826, are supported by subscription; and nearly three thousand children are instructed in the various Sunday schools in connexion with the established church and the dissenting congregations. A society for the relief of widows and orphans of clergymen of the archdeaconry of Chester was established in the early part of the last century, under the patronage of the bishop of the diocese, and is liberally supported. The dispensary was established in 1810, and an appropriate building erected for its use in 1818, at an expense of £1030: from this institution, to which a branch of the Royal Humane Society has been annexed, not less than one thousand persons annually derive medical relief. A ladies' society, for affording relief to lying-in women, was established in 1819: there are also various other institutions and provident societies for promoting the religious instruction and the comfort of the poor, and divers funds for charitable uses. Orford Hall, about a mile from the town, was the residence of John Blackburne, Esq., a celebrated botanist; he was the second person that succeeded in raising the pine apple in England; he was also successful in the cultivation of the cotton tree, which he brought to a considerable degree of perfection, and died in 1796, at the advanced age of ninety-six. Litherland, the inventor of the patent lever watch, was a native of this town. Warrington formerly gave the title of earl to the family of Booth, which, after becoming extinct, was revived, in 1796, in the family of Grey, who are now Earls of Stamford and Warrington.

WARSILL, a township in that part of the parish of RIPON which is within the liberty of RIPON, West riding of the county of YORK, containing 86 inhabitants. There is a place of worship for Independents.

WARSLOW, a chapelry in the parish of ALLSTONEFIELD, northern division of the hundred of TOTMONSLOW, county of STAFFORD, 7¼ miles (E. N. E.) from Leek, containing 595 inhabitants. The living is a perpetual curacy, annexed to the vicarage of Allstonefield, in the archdeaconry of Stafford, and diocese of Lichfield and Coventry, endowed with £1200 royal bounty, and £1400 parliamentary grant. The chapel, dedicated to St. John the Baptist, is a neat modern structure. The school, erected by subscription in 1788, is endowed with about £17 per annum, for which twenty children are instructed.

WARSOP, a parish in the Hatfield division of the wapentake of BASSETLAW, county of NOTTINGHAM, 5¼ miles (N. N. E.) from Mansfield, containing, with the township of Sokeholme, 1141 inhabitants. The living is a rectory, in the archdeaconry of Nottingham, and diocese of York, rated in the king's books at £22. 15. 2½., and in the patronage of H. G. Knight, Esq. The church is dedicated to St. Peter and St. Paul. A part of this parish is within the peculiar jurisdiction of the manorial court of Mansfield. The river Meden runs through it, and the village, a considerable place, has been formed into divisions, called Church-Warsop and Market-Warsop. Fairs for cattle and horses are held on May 21st and November 17th. Thomas Whiteman, in 1811, bequeathed £400, now producing £15. 15. per annum, for which twenty-five children are instructed. Dr. Samuel Halifax, Bishop of St. Asaph, died also rector of this parish, in 1790.

WARTER, a parish in the Bainton-Beacon division of the wapentake of HARTHILL, East riding of the county of YORK, 4½ miles (E. by N.) from Pocklington, containing 428 inhabitants. The living is a discharged vicarage, in the archdeaconry of the East riding, and diocese of York, rated in the king's books at £4, endowed with £400 royal bounty, and £400 parliamentary grant, and in the patronage of Lord Muncaster. The church is dedicated to St. James. There is a place of worship for Wesleyan Methodists. A priory of Black canons, in honour of St. James, was founded here, in 1132, by Geoffry Fitz-Pain, which, at the period of the dissolution of the monasteries, possessed a revenue of £221. 3. 10.

WARTHERMASK, a joint township with Swinton, in the parish of MASHAM, partly within the liberty of ST. PETER of YORK, East riding, and partly in the eastern division of the wapentake of HANG, North riding, of the county of YORK, 7¾ miles (S. W. by S.) from Bedale. The population of this township is returned with Swinton.

WARTHILL, a parish partly in the wapentake of BULMER, North riding, and comprising the township of Warthill within the liberty of ST. PETER of YORK, East riding, of the county of YORK, containing 153 inhabitants, of which number, 115 are in the township of Warthill, 5½ miles (N. E. by E.) from York. The living is a discharged vicarage, in the peculiar jurisdiction and patronage of the Prebendary of Warthill in the Cathedral Church of York, rated in the king's books at £3. 1. 8., and endowed with £800 royal bounty. The church is dedicated to St. Mary.

WARTLING, a parish in the hundred of FOXEARLE, rape of HASTINGS, county of SUSSEX, 4½ miles (E. by S.) from Hailsham, containing 990 inhabitants. The living is a vicarage, in the archdeaconry of Lewes, and diocese of Chichester, rated in the king's books at £16. 0. 2¼. The Rev. J. Cazalet was patron in 1811. The church is dedicated to St. Mary Magdalene.

WARTNABY, a chapelry in that part of the parish of ROTHLEY which is in the eastern division of the hundred of GOSCOTE, county of LEICESTER, 4½ miles (N. W.) from Melton-Mowbray, containing 90 inhabitants. It is in the jurisdiction of the peculiar court of the lord of the manor of Rothley. The chapel is dedicated to St. Michael.

WARTON, a chapelry in the parish of KIRKHAM, hundred of AMOUNDERNESS, county palatine of LANCASTER, 3 miles (S. S. W.) from Kirkham, containing 468 inhabitants. The living is a perpetual curacy, in the archdeaconry of Richmond, and diocese of Chester, endowed with £400 private benefaction, £800 royal bounty, and £300 parliamentary grant, and in the patronage of the Vicar of Kirkham. The chapel, which is dedicated to St. Paul, was consecrated in 1725. About forty children are educated in a school built by subscription, and supported by various endowments, producing an annual income of nearly £100.

WARTON, a parish in the hundred of LONSDALE, south of the sands, county palatine of LANCASTER, comprising the chapelry of Silverdale, and the townships of Borwick, Carnforth, Hutton, Warton with Lindeth, Yealand-Conyers, and Yealand-Redmayne, and containing 2050 inhabitants, of which number, 558 are in the township of Warton with Lindreth, 7 miles (N. by E.) from Lancaster. The living is a vicarage, in the archdeaconry of Richmond, and diocese of Chester, rated in the king's books at £74. 10. 2½., endowed with £30 per annum private benefaction, and £1400 parliamentary grant, and in the patronage of the Dean and Chapter of Worcester. The church is dedicated to Holy Trinity. The Lancaster canal passes through the parish. A free grammar school and an hospital were founded and endowed, in 1594, by Matthew Hutton, Archbishop of York, and further endowed with bequests from Robert Lucas and others, but they are at present shut up. The remains of a Roman encampment may still be traced; and under Warton Cragg there is a copper mine, but it is not now worked.

WARTON, a township in the parish of ROTHBURY, western division of COQUETDALE ward, county of NORTHUMBERLAND, 3¼ miles (W. by N.) from Rothbury, containing 46 inhabitants.

WARWICK, a parish comprising the townships of Aglionby and Warwick, in CUMBERLAND ward, and the township of Little Corby, in ESKDALE ward, county of CUMBERLAND, and containing 518 inhabitants, of which number, 257 are in the township of Warwick, 4¾ miles (E. by N.) from Carlisle. The living is a perpetual curacy, annexed to that of Wetheral, in the archdeaconry and diocese of Carlisle. The church, dedicated to St. Leonard, is built of stone, in the Norman style of architecture, with a semicircular east end, and appears to have been formerly much larger. The village is pleasantly situated on the western bank of the river Eden, which is crossed by a bridge of four arches, near the base of an eminence, on which are the remains of trenches, probably thrown up to guard the pass during the border feuds. Besides its ecclesiastical union with Wetheral, the two parishes join in the maintenance of the poor, the workhouse being at Wetheral. A building for a Sunday school was erected by the late Thomas Parker, Esq. The parish is bounded on the north by the river Eden, and on the west by the Irthing; and, from the large earthworks still remaining, is supposed to be the site of the ancient *Virosidum*, where the sixth cohort of the Nervii was stationed.

3 E 2

WARWICK, a borough and market town, having separate jurisdiction, locally in the Warwick division of the hundred of Kington, county of WARWICK, of which it is the chief town, 90 miles (N. W.) from London, containing 8235 inhabitants. This place is said by Rous, the historian of the county, to have been a British town of consider-

Corporate Seal.

able importance prior to the Roman invasion, and this statement is confirmed by Camden, Dugdale, and other writers. The same author relates, that, after its devastation by the frequent incursions of the Picts, it was rebuilt by Caractacus, on whose defeat by Claudius, in the year 50, the Romans, in order to secure their conquests in Britain, erected several fortresses on the banks of the Severn and Avon, of which latter, Warwick castle was one; but this is very doubtful, the nearest Roman station having, probably, been that at Chesterton. Upon the establishment of the Saxons in the island, this town, included in the kingdom of Mercia, fell under the dominion of Warremund, who rebuilt it, and, after his own name, called it *Warre-wyke*: it appears, however, from a coin of Hardicanute, that its Anglo-Saxon name was *Werhica*, but from either of these sources its present name may be derived. Warwick was subsequently destroyed by the Danes, and, according to the most authentic records, Ethelfleda, daughter of Alfred, and Countess of Mercia, restored it, about the year 913, and built a fort, which evidently forms the most ancient part of the present castle. At the time of the Conquest, this fortress was considerably enlarged, and the town was surrounded with walls and a ditch, of which there are still some vestiges, and a memorial is preserved in the appellation of a certain part of the town, called "Wall-dyke." In the reign of Edward I., the fortifications were repaired by Guy, Earl of Warwick, who, in 1312, with the Earl of Lancaster, having taken Piers Gaveston, the favourite of Edward II., brought him from Wallingford castle, where he was secured for the night under the barons' guard, to Blacklow hill, about a mile from the town, where he was tried and beheaded. In 1566, Robert, Earl of Leicester, who had succeeded to the earldom of Warwick, celebrated, in the Beauchamp chapel in St. Mary's church, the ceremony of the order of St. Michael, which, by permission of Elizabeth, had been conferred upon him by Charles XI. of France: William Parr, brother of Catherine, the last consort of Henry VIII., assisted at this ceremony, and, dying soon after, was buried in the chancel of the church. Queen Elizabeth visited Warwick, in 1572, on her route to Kenilworth castle, where she was sumptuously entertained by the Earl of Leicester, for seventeen days, and amused with diversions, spectacles, and other pageants of costly magnificence, at an expense of not less than £1000 per day. In 1617, James I. visited the town, and was splendidly entertained in the great hall of the Earl of Leicester's hospital; in commemoration of which, a tablet, with an appropriate inscription, was put up on one of the walls of that building. During the great civil war, in the reign of Charles I., Robert Greville,

Lord Brooke, embraced the cause of the parliament, and defended the castle against the king. Having occasion to repair to London, in order to procure a supply of arms and ammunition, he deputed Sir Edward Peto governor during his absence. The supply being obtained, he was met on his return by the Earl of Northampton, with a considerable force, near Edge Hill; but an accommodation taking place, Lord Brooke deposited his artillery and ammunition in Banbury castle, and returned to London. After his departure, the earl, having attacked Banbury castle, and taken the military stores, advanced to Warwick, and laid siege to the castle, which was defended by the governor for fourteen days, till Lord Brooke, on his return from London, after a successful skirmish with the earl near Southam, came to his assistance, and compelled the royalists to abandon the siege. William III., in 1695, visited the town, of which, in the course of the preceding year, more than one half was destroyed, by a dreadful conflagration, occasioned by a spark, from a lighted piece of wood, in the hand of a boy, communicating with the thatched roof of a dwelling-house; a great quantity of goods, probably in a state of ignition, having been removed for safety into the collegiate church of St. Mary, set fire to that venerable pile, which, with the exception of the chancel, the Beauchamp chapel, and the chapter-house, was destroyed. In a few years after, the town was rebuilt, in consequence of a National contribution, amounting to £110,000, of which £1000 was bestowed by Queen Anne.

The town is pleasantly situated on a rock of freestone, rising gently from the north side of the river Avon, which winds round its base; the approaches on every side are beautiful, and the surrounding scenery is richly diversified. The entrance from the Banbury road is strikingly picturesque; a handsome stone bridge, of one arch nearly one hundred feet in the span, leads into the town, which rises gradually from the bank of the river, and presents in succession the venerable castle on the left, the spire of St. Nicholas' church in the lower ground, and the lofty tower of St. Mary's in the distance. The entrance from the Birmingham road, after passing through the suburb called Saltisford, commands a view of the priory, the county hall, and the fine tower of St. Mary's church. The entrance from the Stratford road is through a long ancient arched gateway, with a lofty tower on the west; and that from the Emscot road, through an archway, which supports the chapel of St. Peter. The streets are spacious and regularly formed, consisting chiefly of two principal ones running east and west, crossed by another inclining to the centre of the town: the houses are in general modern and well built, interspersed with elegant mansions, and others affording occasional specimens of the style which prevailed before the fire: the town is well paved, lighted with gas, and amply supplied with water, by pipes leading from springs about half a mile distant. The castle, which is situated on the southern side of the town, is one of the most splendid and entire specimens of feudal grandeur in the kingdom, and is not less remarkable for its stately magnificence than for the elegance of its architecture and the beauty of its situation: it encloses within the walls an area of nearly three acres, the plot surrounded by the moat being more than five acres and a half. A winding road cut through the solid rock, the sides of which are covered with ivy and skirted with shrubs, leads from the outer lodge to a massive gateway flanked with two towers connected by an embrasure above, and formerly defended by a portcullis, which leads into the inner court, in the north angle of which is a lofty octangular tower, with a projecting and embattled parapet resting upon corbels; in the south angle is Guy's tower, of nearly similar form, but more ancient, and having an exploratory turret rising from within the battlements; on the north-east side are two low embattled towers, in one of which bears were anciently kept, for the purpose of baiting. The range of state apartments on the east, as viewed from this side of the castle, is strikingly magnificent; the windows are in fine proportion, and every part is in the highest preservation. At the western extremity, and commanding, from its elevated situation, an extensive view of the surrounding country, is the keep, erected by Ethelfleda, as a place of security against any sudden irruption of the Danes, and also as an exploratory tower, from which their movements might be observed; the ascent is by a winding path, now richly planted with forest trees, among which are some beautiful cedars of Lebanon, and laid out in walks and shrubberies. The façade of the castle, rising from the river Avon, is a long line of flat masonry, relieved only by the number and variety of its windows: the broken arches of an ancient bridge, which formerly led into the town, are still preserved, and add greatly to the picturesque beauty of the scene. The state-rooms, the armoury, and the other various apartments, are preserved in a style of appropriate grandeur: the lawns and gardens which surround it are tastefully laid out, and in the green-house, built expressly for its reception, is the beautiful Grecian Vase of Lysippus, which was dug from the ruins of Adrian's palace, at Tivoli near Rome, and brought to England, by Sir William Hamilton, under the direction and at the expense of his nephew, the late Earl of Warwick. This celebrated specimen of ancient sculpture is of white marble, and is placed upon a pedestal of the same material: its form is nearly that of a hemisphere with reverted rim: two intertwining vines, of which the stems form the handles, wreathe their tendrils, with fruit and foliage, round the upper part of the exterior, and the central part is ornamented with antique heads, and enveloped with a panther's skin with the head and paws, the thyrsus of Bacchus, the lituus of the augurs, and other embellishments: it is of large dimensions, being capable of containing one hundred and sixty-three gallons. The public library and news-room is supported by subscription. Assemblies are held in the town-hall, and for larger meetings, and during the races, in the county-hall: the theatre is opened during the race week, and occasionally at other times, by the Cheltenham company. The races are held twice in the year: the spring races generally take place about the middle of March, and continue only for one day; they are principally patronized by the inhabitants of Leamington, the ladies of which place give a plate of £50; there are also, the Leamington cup, worth £50, with £10 for the second horse; a cup of the same value by Bolton King, Esq.; and other stakes: the autumnal races take place in the first week of September, and continue for three days; at this meeting the king's plate of £105, the town plate of £50, the members' plate of £50, the Warwick cup of £100, and the Guy, Leamington, and other stakes, are run for. The course is a fine level, with a little rising ground in one part, and is now undergoing such improvement as will make it one of the best in the kingdom: the grand stand, which is handsome and commodious, affords every accommodation to the numerous visitors.

Very little trade is carried on beyond what is necessary for the supply of the inhabitants: the cotton manufacture, which was formerly introduced, has entirely declined; and a worsted manufactory, subsequently established, is decreasing. There are several large malting-houses, and lime, timber, and coal wharfs on the banks of the Warwick and Napton canal, which comes up to the northern part of the town, and, communicating with the Oxford and Birmingham canal, affords every facility of inland navigation. From the wharfs at Saltisford fly boats start daily, conveying goods to all the intermediate counties, on their way to London; others proceed to Birmingham and Wolverhampton, Manchester and Liverpool, and, on Tuesday and Friday, to Oxford and Banbury. The market, which is abundantly supplied with corn and provisions of every kind, is on Saturday: the fairs are January 21st, February 11th and 23rd, April 1st, May 13th, June 3rd, July 5th, August 12th, September 4th, October 12th (which is a pleasure and a statute fair, and during which an ox is generally roasted in the market-place), November 8th, and December 16th. The market-place is an extensive area surrounded by respectable houses, in the centre of which is the market-house, a neat substantial building of stone, supported on arches affording a sheltered area for the use of the market; the upper story, which is surmounted by a cupola and dome, is appropriated to different uses, chiefly as a depôt for stores belonging to the county militia.

Warwick was made a "mayor town" by Queen Mary, in 1554: by charter of Charles II., in 1694, confirmed and extended by William III., the government is vested in a mayor, recorder, deputy recorder, twelve aldermen, and twelve assistant burgesses, aided by a town clerk, a serjeant at mace, a yeoman serjeant, and subordinate officers. The mayor is elected from among the aldermen, by the burgesses at large, annually on the 29th of September, and sworn into office on the 1st of November; the recorder, who holds his office for life, is chosen by the corporation; the deputy recorder, who is also town clerk, is appointed by the recorder; the aldermen are chosen by the mayor and the rest of the body, who must fill up all vacancies within eight days; the assistant burgesses are elected by the aldermen, and sworn in by the mayor: three years' residence is requisite to qualify for the office of assistant burgess. The mayor, the late mayor, the recorder, deputy recorder, and three senior aldermen, are justices of the peace. They hold quarterly courts of session, for all offences not capital; and a court of record every Wednesday, except in the Christmas, Easter, and Whitsun weeks, for the recovery of debts not exceeding £40, at which the town clerk generally presides. The borough first exercised the elective franchise in the 23rd of Edward I., since which time it has regularly returned two members to parliament: the right of election is vested in the burgesses and inhabitants generally paying scot and lot; the mayor is the returning officer: the Earl of Warwick possesses influence sufficient for the return of one member. The court-house, in which the borough sessions and courts of record are held, is a handsome stone building in High-street, ornamented with fluted Corinthian pilasters, and having over the entrance a sculptured figure of justice, surmounted by the arms of the borough; on the left hand of the vestibule is the court-room, which, though rather dark, is in other respects very well arranged; on the right hand is the mayor's parlour, a handsome room, with a portrait of Henry VIII. over the mantel-piece, and the royal arms at the other end. In the upper story is an elegant assembly-room, sixty feet long and twenty-seven feet wide: the walls are decorated with fluted Corinthian pilasters supporting an entablature and cornice, with an orchestra at one end: from the ceiling, which is lofty, three large and brilliant chandeliers of cut glass are suspended; adjoining it is a card-room, in which is a good portrait of Charles II. The assizes and general quarter sessions of the peace for the county are held at Warwick, as the county town. The county-hall, in Northgate-street, is an elegant building of freestone, in the Grecian style of architecture; the façade is embellished with pilasters of the Corinthian order, and with a central portico of Corinthian columns supporting a triangular pediment; the hall, which is finely proportioned and handsomely decorated, is one hundred and ten feet long, and forty-five feet wide, with a lofty coved ceiling; in the centre of the side fronting the entrance is a vestibule, forming an approach for barristers and attorneys to their respective courts: the criminal court is situated on the right, and the nisi prius court on the left, hand; both are octagonal in form, and are lighted by a lantern dome supported on finely-proportioned Corinthian columns at the angles. On the left of the county-hall is the judges' mansion, a neat stone building with a handsome portico, and having communication with the hall; and on the right hand is the county gaol, a large stone building of the Doric order, with massive columns in front, having a central entrance to the office of the clerk of the peace. The entrance to the prison is through a spacious gateway, over which is the platform for the execution of criminals: the interior is divided into ten wards for the classification of prisoners, with day-rooms, work-rooms, and airing-yards, in one of which is a tread-mill with three compartments: the cells are ranged round the governor's house in the centre, commanding a distinct view of each of the wards, and the greatest order, and, as far as circumstances will allow of it, the greatest comfort and cleanliness, prevail throughout the establishment; a warm bath is appropriated to the use of the prisoners on their entrance, and every precaution is used to prevent contagion: the chapel, capable of containing four hundred persons, is divided by screens, with a view to preserve the same classification. Opposite to the side entrance of the gaol is the county bridewell, enclosed within a high stone wall: having been enlarged at different times, the arrangement is rather inconvenient, the entrance from some of the wards to the chapel and other parts of the prison requiring an ascent of many steps; the same regard to classification, order, and cleanliness, prevails here as in the

county gaol; a flour-mill, worked by hand, and employing twenty-four men, who relieve each other at intervals, grinds a sufficient quantity to supply the county gaol and bridewell, and bread sufficient for the supply of both establishments is made here, and baked in an oven large enough to hold four hundred loaves at once: the boys and the women are employed in heading pins for the manufacturers at Birmingham, and the men in drawing and preparing the wire for that purpose, and in other occupations: the tread-wheel is applied to working a triple pump, which, from an excellent spring, raises seven gallons of water in a minute, and supplies the whole prison.

The town comprises the parishes of St. Mary and St. Nicholas, both in the archdeaconry and diocese of Worcester. The living of St. Mary's is a vicarage, rated in the king's books at £20, and in the patronage of the Crown: the church, formerly collegiate, of which the tower and the greater part were destroyed in the conflagration, and rebuilt in 1704, though comprising an incongruous mixture of styles, blending the Roman and later English architecture, is, notwithstanding, a very stately and magnificent structure; the tower, which rises in successive stages, variously embellished, to the height of one hundred and thirty feet, is supported on four pointed arches, affording a spacious passage underneath, and crowned with lofty pinnacles at the angles, with others in the centre, of less elevation, forming a prominent and beautiful feature in the distant view of the town. The exterior, in many parts, is strikingly handsome, but the eastern part, in particular, is elaborately embellished with panelled and richly-canopied buttresses; and the east front, simple in its arrangement, but elegant in its details, is a beautiful specimen of the original style of architecture. The chancel, which is in its original state, is an elegant and highly enriched specimen of the later style of English architecture, and contains several ancient monuments. The nave, separated from the aisles by lofty clustered columns, is spacious, and well lighted by a range of clerestory windows, and the windows in the aisles and transepts are of large dimensions, but totally destitute of beauty in the details. In the south transept is the entrance to the chapel of St. Mary, erected by Richard Beauchamp, Earl of Warwick, and thence called the Beauchamp chapel: it is an elegant and highly enriched edifice, in the later style of English architecture, and both in its external and internal embellishment, is inferior only to the chapel of Henry VII. at Westminster: the roof is elaborately groined and enriched with fan tracery; the altar is adorned with a well-executed representation of the Salutation, in basso relievo, by Collins; behind it is an apartment within the buttresses, said to have been the library of John Rous, the historian; and on the north side is a chantry, from which an ascent of four stone steps, deeply worn, leads into an apartment formerly used as a confessional. In the centre of the chapel is the splendid monument of the founder, in gilt brass, in which his effigy, recumbent on an altar-tomb decorated with shields of armorial bearings and numerous figures, and surmounted by a canopy, is finely executed; on the north side is a large monument, in the Elizabethan style, to the memory of Robert Dudley, Earl of Leicester. On the north side of the church is the ancient chapter-house, which has been converted into a mausoleum, with a chapel above it, appropriated to the use of the National school. The living of St. Nicholas' is a vicarage, rated in the king's books at £13. 6. 8., and in the patronage of the Corporation: the church was rebuilt in 1780, the tower and spire having been rebuilt about forty years previously: it is a neat edifice in the later style of English architecture; the roof is groined, and supported on clustered columns; the interior is lighted with three handsome windows on each side, and the altar is placed in a recess at the east end. There are places of worship for Baptists, the Society of Friends, Independents, Wesleyan Methodists, and Unitarians.

The free grammar school, situated on the Butts (a place formerly set apart for the young men of the town to exercise themselves in the use of the bow, prior to the invention of gunpowder), was founded by Henry VIII., and endowed with a portion of the lands of the dissolved monasteries; it is under the patronage of the king, who appoints the master, with a salary of £130 per annum, and is open to all boys of the town upon paying £1. 11. 6. entrance, and 5s. half-yearly. There are two exhibitions, of £70 per annum each, to any of the colleges at Oxford, founded by Mr. Fulk Weale, of Warwick, and the school is also entitled to two exhibitions to Trinity College, Cambridge, in failure of candidates from Combrook school, founded by Lady Verney. The premises occupy a quadrangle, with a cloister on two sides, built by Richard Beauchamp, Earl of Warwick, for the dean and canons of the church of St. Mary, in which he founded a collegiate establishment. The charity school now held in the ancient chapel of St. Peter, was endowed by Lady Greville, Lord Brooke, and Mr. T. Oaken, for the instruction of thirty-nine boys and thirty-six girls in reading, writing, and arithmetic; forty of this number are completely clothed, and the remainder receive each a coat and a pair of shoes annually: the master's salary is £70 per annum, out of which he pays a mistress for teaching the girls to sew. The National school, in which two hundred children of both sexes are instructed, is supported by subscription. The school of industry, in Castle-street, was established by the Countess of Warwick, and is supported, under her patronage, by the subscription of ladies in the town and neighbourhood: in this establishment, to which the house formerly occupied by Mr. Oaken, a great benefactor to the town, is appropriated, forty girls are completely clothed, and provided, at a moderate charge, with dinner in the school-room daily, from Michaelmas to Lady-day; they are instructed in reading, writing, and arithmetic, and taught to sew, knit stockings, and spin flax and Jersey: the school is conducted on the National system, and the earnings of the scholars contribute to its support.

The hospital, founded by Robert, Earl of Leicester, occupies the buildings formerly used by the ancient guilds of the Holy Trinity and St. George, which, after being united in the reign of Henry VI., became, at the dissolution, the property of the earl, who converted them into an hospital, which he endowed for a master and twelve aged brethren, especially such as had been maimed or wounded in the service of their country: the increase in the rental having produced

£130 per annum to each of the brethren, and the master's salary, by the deed of endowment, being limited to £50 per annum, an act of parliament was obtained for augmenting it to £400 per annum, and for reducing the yearly stipend of the brethren to £80, till, by the application of the difference, the great hall should be converted into dwellings for ten additional brethren, after which time the revenue is to be equally divided among the brethren. The almsmen wear a blue gown bearing the crest of the founder, a bear and ragged staff, on the left sleeve, without which they are not permitted to appear in public: the appointment of the master, who must be a clergyman, is vested in the heirs of the founder; and the presentation to the vicarage of Hampton in Arden is in the gift of the Master and Brethren. The premises, near the west end of High-street, occupy a quadrangle, on one side of which is the great hall, on another are the master's apartments, the two remaining sides being occupied by the brethren, who have separate dwellings, and a common kitchen. The chapel of St. James, over the west gate of the town, is annexed to, and forms part of, the hospital; and the master reads morning and evening prayers to the brethren, except on those days when there is service in the church: it is neatly fitted up, and the altar is embellished with a painting of the Ascension, by Millar, a pupil of Sir Joshua Reynolds: behind the quadrangle is a spacious and well-planted garden, bounded on one side by part of the ancient walls of the town. Warwick is one of the towns included in Sir Thomas White's charity, by which young tradesmen are assisted with a free loan of £100 for nine years, to enable them to commence business. There are not less than forty almshouses in various parts of the town, chiefly for aged women, who receive small sums of money quarterly, with gowns and coal annually, and other advantages. The corporation have large funds at their disposal for charitable uses and for distribution among the poor.

About a mile from Warwick, on the road to Kenilworth, is Guy's Cliff, the solitary retreat, for some years prior to his death, of the celebrated Guy, Earl of Warwick, of whom so many legendary tales are recorded: the cave in which he is said to have lived in retirement and devotion, and in which he was buried, is hewn in the rock near the bank of the Avon: he is stated to have assumed the disguise of a hermit, and to have daily visited the castle, in which his countess resided, ignorant of his destiny, to whom he made himself known only a few days before his death. Near the cave is a range of cells, having the appearance of a nunnery, and some cloisters hewn in the rock, and rudely arched, called Phillis' Cloisters, after the countess, who survived him only a few days, and was buried near him. Under a Roman arch, built by the late proprietor to sustain an ancient pointed one, which was falling to decay, are preserved two stone basins, called Guy's Well, covered with moss, into which a fine spring of clear water is constantly flowing. On this cliff Richard de Beauchamp, Earl of Warwick, built a chapel, dedicated to St. Margaret, in which he erected a colossal statue of Guy in armour, and in the attitude of drawing his sword; the right arm is wanting, and the left bears a shield: the chapel, now dismantled, is in the later style of English architecture, with a very beautiful porch, the roof of which, like that of the chapel, is richly groined. The mansion built on this cliff by the late Mr. Greatheed is a handsome modern structure, with a stately avenue of noble fir-trees in front; the Avon winds beautifully round the base of the cliff, and through the grounds, in which is a water-mill for grinding corn, erected prior to the Conquest. Nearly opposite to Guy's Cliff, on the other side of the road, is Blacklow hill, a rocky eminence planted with forest trees: in the hollow part of the rock, which appears to have been quarried, Piers Gavestone was beheaded, in commemoration of which event, a monument of an upright shaft, supporting a cross, and resting upon a pedestal, with a suitable inscription, has been erected on the summit.

Numerous monastic establishments anciently existed in the town: the priory was founded by Henry de Newbury, Earl of Warwick, and completed by his son Roger, in the reign of Henry I., for canons Regular of the order of the Holy Sepulchre, and its revenue at the dissolution was £49. 13. 6.: the remains have been converted into a private mansion, but retain very considerable portions of the ancient architecture, and are situated at the entrance into the town from Birmingham. The hospital of St. John the Baptist was founded, in the reign of Henry II., by William, Earl of Warwick, for the reception of strangers and pilgrims, and, at the dissolution, had a revenue valued at £19. 17. 3.: the building, which is a fine specimen of the architecture of the time, is now occupied as a private boarding-school, and is situated near the extremity of the town, on the road to Leamington. Within the precincts of the castle was the collegiate church of All Saints, of which John Rous relates, that St. Dubricius made it an episcopal seat, about the latter end of the sixth century, the Secular priests, or canons, of which establishment were, in 1125, united to the college of St. Mary's. In the north-west part of the town was an abbey, which was destroyed by Canute in 1016, who also reduced to ashes a nunnery, occupying the site of St. Nicholas' churchyard. In the north suburb was the chapel of St. Michael, to which was annexed an hospital, founded about the close of the reign of Henry I., or the beginning of that of Stephen, by Roger, Earl of Warwick, for a master and leprous brethren, the revenue of which, at the dissolution, was £10. 19. 10; the remains are appropriated as an almshouse for aged women. Of the hospital of St. Thomas, stated by Rous to have been founded by William, Earl of Warwick, not even the site is known. The convent of Dominican friars, which was situated in the western suburbs, was founded, in the reign of Henry III., by the Botelers, Lords Studley, and the Mounforts; the revenue, at the time of the dissolution, was £4. 18. 6. Attached to the chapel of St. James, over the west gate of the town, now forming part of the Leicester hospital, was a college for four Secular priests, founded in the reign of Richard II., which continued till the dissolution. There were also numerous churches in the town, of which only St. Mary's and St. Nicholas' are remaining; these being found sufficient for the accommodation of the inhabitants, the others, which were greatly dilapidated, were suffered to fall into decay. Edward Plantagenet, son of George, Duke of Clarence, and the last male heir of that family, was born in War-

wick castle; he was kept a close prisoner in the reigns of Edward IV., Richard III., and Henry VII., and, attempting to effect his escape from the Tower, during the reign of the last-named monarch, was beheaded, in 1499. Warwick gives the title of earl to the family of Greville.

WARWICKSHIRE, an inland county, bounded on the east by Leicestershire and Northamptonshire, on the south by Oxfordshire and Gloucestershire, on the west by Worcestershire, and on the north-west and north by Staffordshire: it extends from 51° 37' 30" to 52° 42' (N. Lat.), and from 1° 7' 30" to 1° 56' 40" (W. Lon.).; and includes an area of nine hundred and two square miles, or five hundred and seventy-seven thousand two hundred and eighty statute acres. The population, in 1821, including that of the city and county of the city of Coventry, was 274,392. At the period of the invasion of Britain by Julius Cæsar, this county was included partly in the territory of the Cornavii, and partly in that of the Wigantes, or Wiccii; the former occupying the northern part of it, and the latter the southern. It was first subjected to Roman sway by Ostorius Scapula, the second Roman governor of Britain, who entered it with his forces about the year 50, and constructed a line of intrenched camps along the banks of the Avon: it was afterwards included in the province called Flavia Cæsariensis. On the complete establishment of the Saxon Octarchy, Warwickshire formed part of the powerful kingdom of Mercia, the sovereigns of which selected Warwick, Tamworth, and Kingsbury, as occasional places of residence. Near Seckington, at the northern extremity of the county, in 757, a sanguinary battle was fought, between Cuthred, King of the West Saxons, and Ethelwald, King of Mercia, in which the latter was treacherously slain by one of his own commanders. This county, in common with most other parts of England, suffered severely, at different periods, from the ravages of the Danes. In 1147, the Earl of Chester, who took an active part in favour of the Empress Matilda, during her contest with Stephen, having received a severe check at Lincoln, hastened towards his castle at Coventry, which, however, had been already seized by the king's forces: he immediately commenced besieging it, but was attacked by Stephen, and, after an obstinate conflict, was compelled to retreat. In 1263, the forces of the revolted barons, already in possession of the castle of Kenilworth, seized and dismantled that of Warwick: in 1266, however, a powerful body of the royal forces, headed by the king, captured the former fortress, after an arduous siege of six months. During the wars of the Roses, though the inhabitants were divided in their attachment to the contending parties, Warwickshire escaped being the scene of any important warfare. The Earl of Richmond's increasing forces marched through it, to meet the army of Richard III. at Bosworth Field, whence, after the battle, the victor, become king, by the title of Henry VII., repaired to Coventry. In the civil war of the seventeenth century, the inhabitants were almost unanimous in favour of the parliament; and the castle of Warwick, a fortress eminent for its strength, was successfully held by the same party, though several times attacked by the royalists. In June and July, 1642, Lord Brooke arrayed the militia of the county, in pursuance of a commission received from the parlia-

WARWICKSHIRE

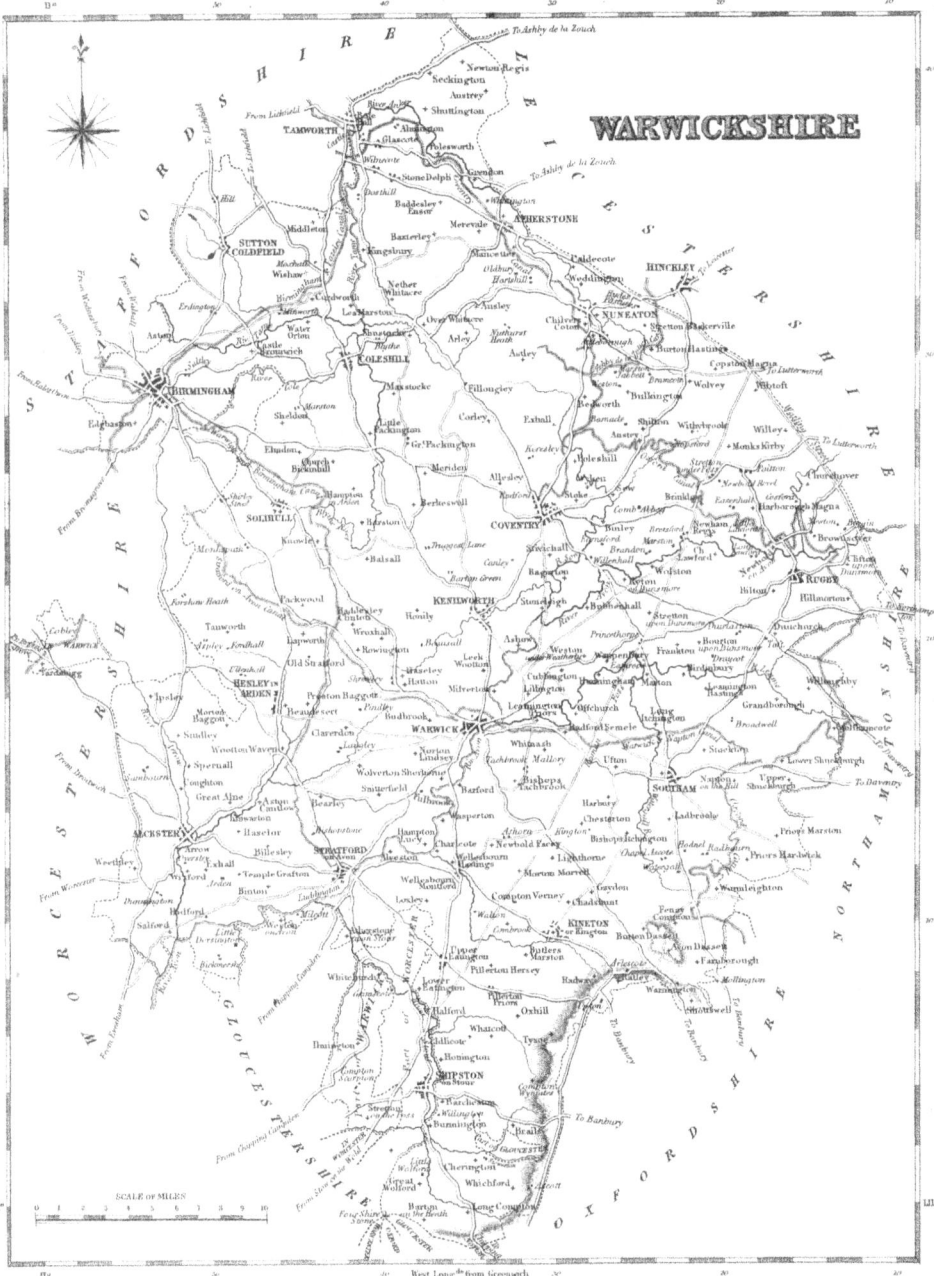

SCALE OF MILES

West Long. from Greenwich

ment. On the 28th of August, Caldecote Hall was attacked by Prince Rupert and Prince Maurice, but without effect. On the 23rd of October, the sanguinary, but indecisive, battle of Edge-hill was fought, near Kington, on the south-eastern border of the county, in which the men of Warwickshire distinguished themselves in the right wing of the parliamentarian army. In January 1643, Lord Brooke was appointed General and Commander in Chief, under the Earl of Essex, of the associated counties of Warwick and Stafford; and in the same year, Prince Rupert, with a detachment of two thousand men, having been commissioned to open a communication between Oxford and York, came to Birmingham, where his entrance was opposed by the inhabitants, aided by a company of infantry, and a troop of cavalry: after a smart skirmish the prince succeeded in driving out the small body of military, and punished the inhabitants by a heavy fine. In this year also a party of royalists, posted at Stratford upon Avon, were driven from that town by a superior parliamentary force under Lord Brooke:. it was, however, soon after retaken by the royalists, and afforded a temporary residence to the queen. In 1643, Warwick castle was again unsuccessfully attacked by the royalists. After the Restoration, in 1662, the walls of Coventry were totally demolished by order of the king, as a punishment for the strenuous adherence of its inhabitants to the cause of the parliament, and their refusal to admit his father within its gates.

Warwickshire is included partly in the diocese of Lichfield and Coventry, and partly in that of Worcester, in the province of Canterbury; the former including the archdeaconry of Coventry, in which are the deaneries of Arden, Coventry, Marton, and Stonely; and the latter the deaneries of Kington and Warwick, in the archdeaconry of Worcester: the total number of parishes is two hundred and one (exclusively of parts of four or five more, which extend into other counties), of which seventy-one are rectories, ninety-one vicarages, and the remainder perpetual curacies. For purposes of civil government it is divided into four hundreds; viz., that of Barlichway, having the divisions of Alcester, Henley, Snitterfield, and Stratford; that of Hemlingford, having those of Atherstone, Birmingham, Solihull, and Tamworth; that of Kington, having those of Brails, Burton-Dassett, Kington, and Warwick; and that of Knightlow, having those of Kenilworth, Kirby, Rugby, and Southam. The county of the city of Coventry comprises an extent of eighteen thousand eight hundred and sixty-one acres, forming nine parishes. Warwickshire contains the city of Coventry (locally), the borough and market town of Warwick, the large manufacturing and market town of Birmingham, and the market towns of Alcester, Atherstone, Coleshill, Henley in Arden, Kenilworth, Kington, or Kineton, Nuneaton, Rugby, Southam, Stratford upon Avon, and Sutton-Coldfield. Two knights are returned to parliament for the shire, two citizens for the city of Coventry, and two burgesses for the borough of Warwick: the county members are elected at Warwick. It is in the Midland circuit: the assizes and quarter sessions for the county are held at Warwick; and those for the city and county of the city of Coventry, at Coventry. There are sixty-one acting magistrates. The rates

raised in the county, for the year ending March 25th, 1827, amounted to £169,537. 4., and the expenditure to £178,425. 5., of which £144,581. 12. was applied to the relief of the poor.

A considerable tract of Warwickshire is separated, on its south-western border, from the rest of the county, by a detached portion of Worcestershire; and a smaller isolated district, lying at a short distance beyond the western confines of the county, is surrounded by Worcestershire. Although the boundaries of the hundreds are extremely irregular, their situations may be generally described as follows: Kington on the south; Knightlow on the east; Hemlingford on the north; and Barlichway on the west: the county of the city of Coventry is bounded on every side by Knightlow hundred, except on the north, where it is bordered for a short distance by a small portion of that of Hemlingford. The general surface consists of gentle hill and dale, and, though seldom presenting romantic scenery, has, for the most part, a rich and pleasing appearance, which is greatly heightened by its numerous small tracts of woodland. The highest points of land are the hills at Corley, and the woods near Packington, in the hundred of Hemlingford. There is an elevated range of limestone hills, in the hundred of Kington, at Walton and Long Compton, including both Edge-hill and the Brails-hill, which, as well as the other heights above named, command rich and extensive prospects. The banks of the Avon, though in some places flat and uninteresting, are in many, particularly near Warwick, highly beautiful and picturesque. The climate is generally esteemed mild and healthy, and is subject to no peculiar excess of wet or cold. The most prevailing winds are from the south-west, and are usually accompanied by rain; but vegetation, in the early spring season, often suffers severely from continued easterly breezes. Corley, from its elevated situation, is colder than any other part of the county, excepting the ridge above Long Compton and the Brails-hill, which, though much lower, are less sheltered and have a stronger and colder soil.

The soils are generally fertile, but very various, comprising almost every kind, except such as contain chalk, or flints. All the southern and south-eastern part of the county, separated from the rest by an imaginary line drawn from the border of Northamptonshire, near Willoughby, south-westward by Grandborough, Long Itchington, Southam, Harbury, Ashorn, and Wellesbourn - Hastings, to the vicinity of Atherstone upon Stour, has, very nearly throughout, a strong clay loam, resting on limestone. A soil of a similar nature occupies the north-eastern extremity of the county, bordering on the course of the small river Anker, and may be separated from the rest by a line passing from the confines of Leicestershire, near Nuneaton, by Oldbury and Kingsbury, to the point where the river Tame begins to form the north-western boundary of Warwickshire, a little above Tamworth. The soil of an extensive tract of Barlichway hundred, reaching from the vicinity of Warwick to the western border of the county, near Tamworth, and in the neighbourhood of Salford, and including the towns of Henley in Arden and Alcester, is a strong clay loam, which rests on marl and limestone. A little westward from Warwick there commences a considerable tract of strong clay, resting on limestone, which extends south-westward to the confines of the county, Stratford upon Avon being situated on the south-eastern side of it: the large detached portion of the county, lying westward of its southern extremity, has a soil of similar quality. A light sandy soil, in several places mixed with sharp gravel, and well adapted for the turnip husbandry, occupies the tract lying between the town of Rugby and the village of Grandborough, bounded on the east by the confines of the county, and on the west by the road from Southam to Coventry. A soil of a similar kind, poor, but also well adapted for the same purpose, extends from the vicinity of the village of Meriden, northward, to the boundary of the county, chiefly bordering on the vallies of the Blythe and the Tame. Between this and the northern tract of clay and limestone land is a considerable extent of various poor and moory soils, which also occupy another large district on the western side of these light lands, in the vicinity of Sutton-Coldfield. The remaining extensive portions of the county consist chiefly of a red sandy loam, and a red clay loam, resting on free-stone, or limestone, and sometimes on a sharp gravel: some of the sand is well adapted for the turnip husbandry. Coventry is also surrounded by a rich deep sandy loam, resting on marl and freestone, which, in different directions, soon becomes intermingled with some of the other soils above mentioned. On the south side of the river Avon, in the vicinity of Castle Bromwich, a good red clayey loam is found, extending eastward to Coleshill, and westward towards Birmingham: near the latter town, and in the vicinities of Aston and Hackley brook, a light, dry, red, sandy soil prevails. A considerable district around Solihull, and various parishes to the north and east of that town, are composed of a strong marl clay soil, on a wet clay substratum. In the vale of the Avon the soil is remarkable for its fertility, and is excellently adapted for the culture of turnips.

The courses of crops are very various: those commonly cultivated are, wheat, barley, oats, peas, beans, turnips, potatoes, and tares, or vetches. On the rich loams wheat is sown only once in four or six years, and on the light sandy soils hardly ever. Much of the barley is made into malt, of which there is a great consumption in the county itself. Rye is seldom sown, except upon the light, poor, sandy soils, and then chiefly for spring food for sheep. The finer kinds of peas are grown to a considerable extent by the market-gardeners and farmers in the vicinity of the towns, and are gathered green: the grey peas are grown only by the farmers, who apply them chiefly to the fattening of hogs. The cultivation of turnips is general on all the lighter and drier soils: they are chiefly eaten upon the land by sheep. Cabbages, carrots, and parsnips, are cultivated only in the gardens; but potatoes are a common agricultural crop, more particularly in the vicinities of the larger towns. Both winter and spring tares are grown: they are chiefly consumed by sheep folded upon them, and are also given green to horses. Flax is cultivated in different places, but not to a great extent. The principal artificial grasses are red and white clover, and ray-grass: most of the young clover is eaten off by sheep. It is computed that the permanent meadow and pasture lands amount to no less than two hundred

and thirty-five thousand acres, and the quantity of land under artificial grasses to sixty thousand, making a total of two hundred and ninety-five thousand acres. Out of this, it is supposed that from eighty to eighty-five thousand acres are meadows, and their produce mown every year for hay: from ten to fifteen thousand acres of the artificial grasses are cut and given green to horses and other cattle, or made into hay: the large remaining portion, of from one hundred and ninety-five, to two hundred and five, thousand acres, is pastured with sheep and cattle; this being a noted grazing county. The most extensive tracts of permanent pasture are towards the eastern and north-eastern confines of the county, bordering on Leicestershire. Towards Oxfordshire, at Radway, Warmington, Avon-Dassett, Shottswell, &c., and along the great road thence towards Warwick, as far as Gaydon, is a large extent of very rich pastures. On each bank of the Avon, during the whole of its course through this county, there is also much rich meadow and grazing land, and numerous other parts abound in fine old pastures. Though meadows exist in almost every part of the county, the most valuable are situated on the banks of its numerous streams: the produce of these is generally from one and a half to two and a half tons of hay per acre; that of the less fertile from one to two tons. About three thousand acres of grass land in the county of the city of Coventry are subject to a common right of pasturage from the 13th of August to the 13th of February, enjoyed by the freemen of Coventry, and not transferable.

The principal manures are, lime, which is burned from the limestone in various parts of the county, and is also imported, in considerable quantities, by the canals, from Staffordshire and Leicestershire; marl, which abounds in the western districts, but in place of which lime has, of late years, been much employed; soap-ashes, horn-scrapings, malt-dust, and soot. Many different breeds of cattle are common in the county, although the Scotch and Herefordshire oxen, and the long-horned heifers and cows, are always preferred for grazing. The cows and oxen bred are chiefly of the long-horned Lancashire sort: the other breeds that have been introduced are principally the Devonshire, the Herefordshire, the Yorkshire, the Tees-water, the Scotch, and the Welch: of these, the Yorkshire and long-horned and the Durham breeds are most esteemed for the dairy. The sheep bred are chiefly of the Old Warwickshire and the New Leicester breeds: the former are a large polled kind, which, when fat, frequently weigh from forty to forty-eight pounds per quarter; the average weight of their wool was nine pounds, but they have been much intermingled with the New Leicester sheep, which are here bred in great perfection. A few Wiltshire, South Down, Small Welch, and Spanish, or Merino, sheep are also kept. Those bred and kept upon the commons are a mixed sort, some having black, and others grey, faces and legs: the best of them, when fattened at three years old, weigh from eighteen to twenty-three pounds per quarter, and carry from four to six pounds of wool each: the inferior sort weigh only from five to ten pounds per quarter, and yield a fleece of from one to three pounds weight of coarse wool: the New Leicester sheep are preferred by the graziers. The extent of ground devoted to horticulture, for which the soil is generally very well adapted, is about five thousand acres : there are few orchards of any considerable extent. The middle, western, and northern parts are those most abounding in timber, of which a large proportion is oak of remarkably fine growth, those parts having been formerly occupied by the extensive forest of Arden : elm is also very common, and grows to the largest size near the banks of the Avon. The coppice woods consist of oak, ash, hazel, alder, birch, and beech ; and their produce is chiefly made into hurdles for folding sheep, hoops, fagots, rails, and broom shafts. There are numerous thriving plantations of different kinds of forest trees in various parts of the county. The hedgerows of the old enclosures contain many timber trees ; those of the northern parts of the county consist chiefly of hazels and brambles on high banks; all of them have a flourishing appearance. The extent of unenclosed land is inconsiderable, consisting chiefly of small commons in different parts of the county : Sutton-Coldfield and Sutton-Park are the only extensive ones.

The chief mineral productions are coal, limestone, freestone, and a blue flag-stone. The coal of the best quality is found at Bedworth, between Coventry and Nuneaton, where the seam varies in thickness from three to four feet, and is worked to a considerable extent. Large quantities of coal are also raised at Griff-hollow, Chilvers-Coton, Nuneaton common, Hunts hall, and Oldbury, lying to the north of the first-mentioned place : that obtained at Oldbury is of an inferior kind, fit only for burning lime : the same bed of coal extends still further northward, by Merevale, to Polesworth and Wilnecote. Limestone is found to a great extent, and is largely quarried at Bearley, Grafton Court, Stretton, Princethorpe, Ufton, Harbury, Wilnecote, Bidford, Newbold on Avon, and numerous other places, where it is also burned into lime; it also abounds along the borders of Oxfordshire and Leicestershire: it is generally of a close texture and a dark blue colour, and produces strong lime. Abundance of freestone exists in the neighbourhood of Warwick, Leamington, Kenilworth, Coventry, and many other places, chiefly where the soil is light and sandy : it is sometimes quarried for building, and is more particularly employed in the erection of all public edifices. The blue flag-stone is found in many places, and large quarries of it are wrought in the neighbourhoods of Bidford and Wilnecote: it is used for paving and flooring. Iron-stone is found at Oldbury and Merevale, near the former of which places it was formerly worked. The western part of the county abounds with marl of different colours and qualities, much of which is strong and excellent. A peculiar kind of blue clay, having some of the properties of soap, exists in great quantities in the eastern part of the county.

The hardware manufactures of Birmingham and its vicinity are the principal in the county. The next in importance is that of silks, ribands, &c., which is calculated to employ not less than sixteen thousand persons in the city of Coventry and the surrounding villages : watch-making is also very extensively carried on in that city. At Berkeswell and Balsall, and the vicinity of Tamworth, are considerable flax-mills ; much linen yarn being spun at those places. At Kenilworth horn-combs of all descriptions are manufactured. At Alcester about six hundred people are employed in making fish hooks and needles; and at Atherstone are several manufactories for hats and ribands ; the latter article is also manufactured at Nuneaton. The commerce of the county, which is greatly facilitated by its numerous canals, consists chiefly in the exportation of the abundant produce of its manufactures, and the importation of the materials necessary for carrying them on, as well as of the usual foreign supplies for its inhabitants, together with some corn. Notwithstanding the great consumption of butchers' meat at Birmingham, Coventry, &c., great numbers of cattle and sheep are annually driven from Warwickshire to London.

The principal rivers are the Avon and the Tame : the former, called the Upper Avon, to distinguish it from the river Avon, which forms the harbour of Bristol, rising on the confines of Leicestershire and Northamptonshire, soon enters this county at Bensford bridge, and thence pursues a westerly course, a little northward of Rugby, to the vicinity of the village of Ryton on Dunsmoor, where it commences a very devious south-westerly course, by Warwick and Stratford on Avon : a little below the latter town it forms, for some miles, the southern boundary of the county, a projecting portion of which it then crosses, and having again formed the boundary line for a short distance, finally quits Warwickshire, a little below Abbots-Salford. It receives the small river Dove, from Leicestershire, a little below Brownsover ; the Sow, from the eastern parts of this county near Stoneleigh ; the Leam, from the borders of Northamptonshire, which is joined by the Watergall, flowing northward by the vicinity of Southam, a little above Warwick ; the Stour, from the southern extremity of the county, about a mile and a half below Stratford; and the Alne, from the western parts of it, which is joined by the small stream of the Arrow, about half a mile below Priors Salford. The current of the Avon, like that of the other streams, is gentle : the river was made navigable for vessels of forty tons' burden up to Stratford, in the year 1637. The Tame enters from Staffordshire, a little above Aston, near Birmingham, having formed the boundary of the county for a short distance, and, taking an easterly direction, is joined, a little below that village, by the small river Rea, which has its source in Worcestershire, and flows north-eastward by Birmingham. Having passed Castle-Bromwich and Water-Overton, it is joined by the Blythe, which, descending from the western border of the county by Solihull, is augmented by the stream of the Cole, a little below the town of Coleshill : at this junction the Tame suddenly turns northward by Lea-Marston and Kingsbury, and having again formed the north-western boundary of the county for some miles, wholly quits it for Staffordshire, at Tamworth, in its further progress to the Trent : the small river Anker, from the eastern border of the county, flowing by Nuneaton and Atherstone, falls into the Tame at Tamworth.

This county possesses an extensive artificial navigation: Birmingham is the grand centre from which most of these important lines of communication radiate, enabling that town to send the produce of its manufactures, by a direct and easy water-carriage, to the four great ports of the kingdom. The Birmingham old canal, entering the county near Birmingham, from the Worcestershire and Staffordshire canal near Wolverhampton, terminates in the Birmingham and Fazely canal, at

Farmer's Bridge, near the former place, where it also communicates with the Worcester and Birmingham canal: by this channel coal and iron are conveyed to Birmingham and other places, from the numerous mines on its banks, and the manufactured goods of that town are forwarded to Liverpool, Manchester, &c. The Birmingham and Worcester canal, the chief objects in the formation of which were, the conveyance of coal, and opening a more direct communication between Birmingham and the river Severn, takes its course from Worcester, through a detached portion of this county, to the Birmingham canal at Farmer's Bridge. The Dudley Extension canal branches from this, a little before it enters the county near Birmingham; and the Stratford on Avon canal, commencing in it at King's Norton in Worcestershire, soon enters Warwickshire, through the western part of which it proceeds, a little eastward of Henley in Arden, to its termination in the navigable channel of the Avon at Stratford: this canal has a short branch to the village of Tanworth, and a longer one to the Grafton limeworks; it also communicates by a short cut with the Warwick and Birmingham canal, near Lapworth-street. The Birmingham and Fazely canal, commencing in the Coventry canal at Whittington brook, proceeds near the course of the Tame, which it crosses a little below Aston, to its junction with the Birmingham, and the Worcester and Birmingham, canal at Farmer's Bridge, a little beyond Birmingham: the great objects of this canal are, the conveyance of the produce of the Birmingham manufactures towards London and Hull, and the supply of Birmingham with grain and other commodities. The Coventry canal, which forms an important line in the communication between London, Birmingham, Manchester, Liverpool, &c., and by means of which great quantities of coal are conveyed from the pits in its vicinity, chiefly to the city of Coventry, enters a little above Tamworth, and pursues its course up the valley of the Anker, by Atherstone and Nuneaton, and thence to Coventry: a branch, of about a mile in length, extends from it to the Griff collieries; and another, having several minor branches, runs to those near Lees-wood, Pool, and Bedworth. The Ashby de la Zouch canal commences from the Coventry canal at Marston bridge, near Nuneaton, and taking an irregular north-easterly course, soon quits the county near Hinckley. The Oxford canal, the course of which is extremely irregular, commencing in the Coventry canal at Longford, about four miles from Coventry, winds south-eastward by Brinklow and Brownsover, crossing the Avon near the latter place, to the eastern border of the county, near which, occasionally crossing small portions of Northamptonshire, it passes by Wolfhamcote, Lower Shuckburgh, Napton on the Hill, and Merstondale, in this county, which it finally quits for Oxfordshire, a little southward of Wormleighton: the Grand Junction canal commences in this last-mentioned at Braunston, on the eastern border of Warwickshire, but in the county of Northampton. The Warwick and Birmingham canal, commencing in the Digbeth cut of the Birmingham and Fazely canal at Digbeth near Birmingham, proceeds south-eastward near Solihull to Warwick, whence the navigation is continued by the Warwick and Napton canal, which commences from the former in the parish of Budbrook, and proceeding eastward near Leamington-Priors, ter-

minates in the Oxford canal near Napton on the Hill: these two canals, with the few miles of the Oxford canal lying between Napton and Braunston, where the Grand Junction canal commences, form an important part of the most direct line of water communication between Birmingham and London, and the first supplies the town of Warwick with coal. The principal roads are, one entering the county near Long Compton, and passing through Shipston, Stratford on Avon, Henley in Arden, and Birmingham, soon after which it quits the county; and another, entering near Willoughby, and proceeding through Coventry to Birmingham: from this road a branch diverges at Packington Magna, and, passing through Coleshill, quits the county for Lichfield a little beyond Middleton.

Warwickshire contained the Roman station of *Manduessedum*, situated on the Watling-street, at Mancetter; and that of *Alauna*, at Alcester; while another was probably fixed at Chesterton: it was traversed by the following great Roman roads; viz., the Watling-street, which, running from south-east to north-west, forms, first, the boundary between this county and the north-western extremity of Northamptonshire, and then the entire boundary between Warwickshire and Leicestershire, until it reaches the vicinity of Atherstone, whence it crosses the northern extremity of the former county, and quits it on passing the Tame, a little above Tamworth, being visible throughout the whole of its course; the Fosse-way, which, crossing the Watling-street into this county at High Cross, passes south-westward, near Monks' Kirby and Stretton, through Brinklow, Bretsford, and Stretton upon Dunsmoor, and a short distance to the west of Chesterton, Lighthorne, and Combrook, to the neighbourhood of Stretton on the Foss, in the south-western detached portion of it, where it enters Gloucestershire, also discernible in many places; the Ryknield-street, which enters from the south, near Bitford, and proceeds, in a northerly direction, across the western parts of Warwickshire, and the eastern extremity of Worcestershire, finally quitting the former for Staffordshire, to the west of Sutton-Coldfield, and being traceable in the vicinity of Bidford, to the north of Alcester (where it is called the Headen-way), and on the north-eastern border of the county; and a minor road, termed the Ridge-way, which skirts the county for some distance on the east: several vicinal ways diverged from each extremity of the great roads. The principal of the Roman camps still visible, which are not very numerous, are situated along the course of the Fosse-way, and on the banks of the river Avon: in the vicinity of these, and of the roads, many tumuli and coins are found, and various other vestiges of Roman occupation have been discovered in almost every part of the county. On Welcombe hills, to the west of the village of Alveston, are extensive earthworks, called the Dingles, supposed to be of Saxon origin.

The number of religious houses, including hospitals and colleges, was about fifty-seven. There yet exist remains of the abbey of Merevale, which comprise some interesting specimens of Saxon architecture; of the priories of Coventry, Kenilworth, and Maxstoke; and of the nunneries of Nuneaton, Pindley, and Polesworth. The churches most remarkable for their antiquity, or otherwise, are those of Astley; St. Martin at Birmingham; Balsall; Beaudesert; Coleshill; St.

John, St. Michael, and the Holy Trinity, at Coventry; Kenilworth; Nuneaton; Shustock; Stoneleigh; Stratford; St. Mary and St. Peter, at Warwick; and Wolston. Different places in the county have curious chapels. There are remains of the castles of Astley, Brandon, Kenilworth, Maxstoke, Tamworth, and Warwick, the latter of which are particularly extensive, and form the chief part of the present magnificent residence of the Earl of Warwick. The most remarkable ancient mansions are, Clopton House, situated about a mile to the north of Stratford, and Compton Wyniates House, on the south-eastern border of the county. The more modern seats of the nobility and gentry are rather numerous : some of the most distinguished, besides Warwick castle before mentioned, are Ragley Hall near Alcester, the residence of the Marquis of Hertford ; Combe Abbey, that of the Earl of Craven; Packington Hall, that of the Earl of Aylesford ; and Stoneleigh Abbey, that of J. Chandos Leigh, Esq. In the vicinity of Birmingham are numerous country houses of opulent merchants and tradesmen of that town, surrounded by ornamented grounds. There are various chalybeate springs, particularly at Birmingham, Ilmington, and Newnham-Regis. But the mineral waters of Leamington, about two miles to the east of Warwick, are by far the most celebrated, and their reputation has of late years converted this formerly obscure village into a place of considerable fashionable resort.

WARWICK-BRIDGE, a township in that part of the parish of WETHERAL which is in ESKDALE ward, county of CUMBERLAND, 5¼ miles (E.) from Carlisle, containing 648 inhabitants. There is a Roman Catholic chapel at this place. The river Eden is here crossed by a fine stone bridge of four arches to the opposite village of Warwick. Extensive cotton-mills and bleaching grounds, established by Messrs. Dixon and Sons, employ more than five hundred persons : these gentlemen support a Sunday school. A strong party of royalists, stationed to defend the passage of the bridge, in June 1648, was put to the rout by General Lambert.

WASDALE, or NETHERWASDALE, a joint chapelry with Eskdale, in the parish of ST. BEES, ALLERDALE ward above Darwent, county of CUMBERLAND, 7 miles (N. N. E.) from Ravenglass. The population is returned with Eskdale. The living is a perpetual curacy, in the archdeaconry of Richmond, and diocese of Chester, endowed with £200 private benefaction, £1400 royal bounty, and £200 parliamentary grant, and in the patronage of the Inhabitants. A fair for sheep is held on the first Monday in September. The beautiful lake Wast-water, in this parish, is three miles long, half a mile broad, and forty-five fathoms deep, or about fifteen fathoms below the level of the sea, which disproportion as to its extent and depth accounts, perhaps, for its never having been known to freeze.

WASDALE-HEAD, a chapelry in the parish of ST. BEES, ALLERDALE ward above Darwent, county of CUMBERLAND, 11 miles (S. W. by S.) from Keswick. The population is returned with Eskdale. The living is a perpetual curacy, in the archdeaconry of Richmond, and diocese of Chester, endowed with £1000 royal bounty, and in the patronage of the Perpetual Curate of St. Bees. The chapel is very small, and, having no

burial-ground attached, the inhabitants inter their dead at Netherwasdale. The chapelry lies at the head of Wast-water lake, in a narrow valley almost surrounded by lofty hills.

WASHAWAY, a hamlet in the parish of EGLOSHAYLE, hundred of TRIGG, county of CORNWALL, 3 miles (N. W.) from Bodmin. The population is returned with the parish. The petty sessions for the division are held here, on the last Monday in every month.

WASHBOURN (GREAT), a parish in the upper division of the hundred of TEWKESBURY, county of GLOUCESTER, 5½ miles (N. N. W.) from Winchcombe, containing 80 inhabitants. The living is a perpetual curacy, in the archdeaconry and diocese of Gloucester, endowed with £800 royal bounty. Henry Fowke, Esq. was patron in 1810. The church is dedicated to St. Mary.

WASHBOURN (LITTLE), a chapelry in the parish of OVERBURY, middle division of the hundred of OSWALDSLOW, county of WORCESTER, 6½ miles (E. by N.) from Tewkesbury, containing 55 inhabitants.

WASHBROOK, a parish in the hundred of SAMFORD, county of SUFFOLK, 4 miles (W. by S.) from Ipswich, containing 377 inhabitants. The living is a discharged vicarage, annexed to the rectory of Copdock, in the archdeaconry of Suffolk, and diocese of Norwich, rated in the king's books at £8. 6. 8. The church, dedicated to St. Mary, contains several ancient stalls, which have been recently renovated; and over the communion-table a window of stained glass has been placed, at the expense of Lord Walsingham.

WASHFIELD, a parish in the western division of the hundred of BUDLEIGH, county of DEVON, 1¾ mile (N. N. W.) from Tiverton, containing 457 inhabitants. The living is a rectory, in the archdeaconry and diocese of Exeter, rated in the king's books at £19. 7. 6., and in the patronage of J. Worth, Esq. The church is dedicated to St. Mary.

WASHFORD-PINE, a parish in the hundred of WITHERIDGE, county of DEVON, 8½ miles (N. by W.) from Crediton, containing 139 inhabitants. The living is a discharged rectory, in the archdeaconry of Barnstaple, and diocese of Exeter, rated in the king's books at £6. 0. 2½., endowed with £200 private benefaction, and £200 royal bounty, and in the patronage of William Comyns, Esq. The church is dedicated to St. Peter. There was formerly a chapel at Whenham, in this parish.

WASHINGBOROUGH, a parish in the second division of the wapentake of LANGOE, parts of KESTEVEN, county of LINCOLN, 2 miles (N. E.) from Lincoln, containing, with the chapelry of Heighington, 874 inhabitants. The living is a rectory, in the archdeaconry and diocese of Lincoln, rated in the king's books at £26. 13. 4., and in the patronage of Sir W. A. Ingilby, Bart. The church, dedicated to St. John the Evangelist, is a large and handsome structure with a lofty tower. The parish is bounded on the north by the navigable river Witham. At Washingborough is a school for young children, with an endowment of about £20 per annum, arising from the bequests of Timothy Pike and others, in 1728. The free grammar school at Heighington was founded in 1619, by Thomas Garrett, who endowed it with lands and houses of the present annual value of £140; he was, in other respects, a great benefactor to the poor. In 1701, Sir Thomas Clack, left land, now producing £70 per annum, for apprenticing poor children.

WASHINGLEY, a parish in the hundred of Norman-Cross, county of Huntingdon, 1½ mile (W.) from Stilton, containing 91 inhabitants. The living is a rectory, united to that of Lutton, in the archdeaconry of Northampton, and diocese of Peterborough. There being no church the inhabitants attend at Lutton.

WASHINGTON, a parish in the eastern division of Chester ward, county palatine of Durham, comprising the townships of Barmston, Great and Little Usworth, and Washington, and containing 2687 inhabitants, of which number, 1243 are in the township of Washington, 5½ miles (S.E.) from Gateshead. The living is a rectory, in the archdeaconry and diocese of Durham, rated in the king's books at £18, and in the patronage of the Bishop of Durham. The church has lately received an addition of one hundred free sittings, the Incorporated Society for the enlargement of churches and chapels having granted £40 towards defraying the expense. There is a place of worship for Wesleyan Methodists. The parish abounds with coal, and there are considerable cast-iron and rope works. A charity school was founded, in 1814, by the late Mrs. Peareth; and another subsequently, by the Rev. J. Davison, late rector.

WASHINGTON, a parish in the hundred of Steyning, rape of Bramber, county of Sussex, 4½ miles (W.N.W.) from Steyning, containing 704 inhabitants. The living is a discharged vicarage, in the archdeaconry and diocese of Chichester, rated in the king's books at £9. 10., and in the patronage of the President and Fellows of Magdalene College, Oxford. The church is in the early style of English architecture.

WASING, a parish in the hundred of Faircross, county of Berks, 7½ miles (E.S.E.) from Newbury, containing 68 inhabitants. The living is a discharged rectory, in the archdeaconry of Berks, and diocese of Salisbury, rated in the king's books at £3. 13. 4., and in the patronage of W. Mount, Esq. The church is dedicated to St. Nicholas.

WASPERTON, a parish in the Warwick division of the hundred of Kington, county of Warwick, 4 miles (S.S.W.) from Warwick, containing 271 inhabitants. The living is a discharged vicarage, in the archdeaconry and diocese of Worcester, rated in the king's books at £5, endowed with £200 private benefaction, and £200 royal bounty, and in the patronage of the Rector of Hampton-Lucy. The church is dedicated to St. John the Baptist. This parish is entitled to participate in the benefit of the grammar school founded at Hampton-Lucy by the Rev. Richard Hill.

WASTE-LANDS, an extra-parochial liberty, locally in the parish of Swineshead, wapentake of Kirton, parts of Holland, county of Lincoln, 6½ miles (W. by S.) from Boston, containing 43 inhabitants.

WATCHETT, a sea-port and market town, in the parish of St. Decuman, hundred of Williton and Freemanners, county of Somerset, 5 miles (E.) from Dunster, and 154 (W. by S.) from London. The population is returned with the parish. This place, anciently called *Weced-poort*, suffered severely from the Danes in 886: it is agreeably situated in a pleasant valley, on a creek of the Bristol channel, and consists chiefly of four paved streets.

It was once a place of extensive trade, and noted for its herring fishery: vessels are now employed in the coasting trade, and in the importation of coal from Newport and Swansea. There is a small manufacture of woollen cloth and paper. A pier, originally erected by the Wyndham family, was repaired by Sir William Wyndham previously to 1740. The cliffs in the vicinity abound with alabaster and limestone. The market is on Saturday; and a fair is held on the 17th of November. Manorial courts are held annually. There are places of worship for Baptists and Wesleyan Methodists. Two packets ply between this place and Bristol every fortnight.

WATCHFIELD, a township (formerly a chapelry) in the parish and hundred of Shrivenham, county of Berks, 4½ miles (S.W. by S.) from Great Farringdon, containing 306 inhabitants. The chapel was pulled down about 1770.

WATERBEACH, a parish in the hundred of Northstow, county of Cambridge, 5¾ miles (N.E. by N.) from Cambridge, containing 814 inhabitants. The living is a discharged vicarage, in the archdeaconry and diocese of Ely, rated in the king's books at £5. 15. 7½., and in the patronage of the Bishop of Ely. The church is dedicated to St. John. A charity school was founded in the year 1687, and endowed with lands, by Grace Clarke and Dorothy Staines: the master's salary is upwards of £40 per annum, with a good house and garden, and the number of scholars is limited to eighteen. An almshouse for six poor widows was founded, in 1628, by a bequest from Mr. John Yaxley, alderman of Cambridge, and endowed with £12 per annum; to which a rent-charge of £15 was added by Mrs. Jane Brigham, in 1705. About the year 1160, a cell to the monastery of Ely was established in a small island, called Elmeneye, but was shortly after removed to Denney, both in this parish: in the following century it was occupied by the Knights Templars, who then possessed the manor of Waterbeach. In 1293, an abbey for minoresses of the order of St. Clare was founded by Dionysia de Mountchensi, which, in 1338 (the order of the Templars being then abolished), was transferred to their house at Denney: at the dissolution there were twenty-five nuns, and the annual value of the lands was estimated at £172: the abbey house and the demesnes have been many years rented as a farm, and the refectory has been converted into a barn.

WATERDEN, a parish in the hundred of Brothercross, county of Norfolk, 4 miles (W. by S.) from Little Walsingham, containing 16 inhabitants. The living is a discharged rectory, annexed to that of Warham St. Margaret, in the archdeaconry of Norfolk, and diocese of Norwich, rated in the king's books at £5. 6. 8. The church is dedicated to All Saints.

WATER-EATON, a township in the parish of Bletchley, hundred of Newport, county of Buckingham, ¾ of a mile (S.) from Fenny-Stratford, containing 276 inhabitants.

WATER-EATON, a township in the parish of Kidlington, hundred of Wootton, county of Oxford, 3¾ miles (N.) from Oxford, containing 113 inhabitants.

WATER-EATON, a township in the parish of Penkridge, eastern division of the hundred of Cuttlestone, county of Stafford, 2¼ miles (S.W. by S.) from Penkridge, with which the population is returned.

WATER-EATON, a township in the parish of EISEY, hundred of HIGHWORTH, CRICKLADE, and STAPLE, county of WILTS, 2¼ miles (E. S. E.) from Cricklade, containing 58 inhabitants.

WATERFALL, a parish in the southern division of the hundred of TOTMONSLOW, county of STAFFORD, 7 miles (E. S. E.) from Leek, containing, with part of the chapelry of Calton, 534 inhabitants. The living is a perpetual curacy, in the archdeaconry of Stafford, and diocese of Lichfield and Coventry, endowed with £200 private benefaction, and £600 royal bounty, and in the patronage of Mrs. Jane Wilmott. The church is. dedicated to St. James. There is a place of worship for Wesleyan Methodists. The river Hamps almost surrounds the parish; it enters the ground at the Waterhouses, and pursues a subterraneous course of about three miles to Ilam, where it emerges and joins the river Manifold. Limestone (a considerable quantity of which is burned), grit-stone, and lead-ore, are found in the neighbourhood; and at the adjoining hamlet of Winkshill are two paper-mills, a flax-mill, and an iron forge and foundry. Eight poor children are instructed, in a school-house built by subscription, for £6. 10. a year, arising from four acres and a half of land.

WATERGALL, an extra-parochial liberty, in the Southam division of the hundred of KNIGHTLOW, county of WARWICK, 4 miles (S.) from Southam, containing 13 inhabitants.

WATERHEAD, a township in the parish of LANERCOST-ABBEY, ESKDALE ward, county of CUMBERLAND, 24 miles (N. E.) from Carlisle, containing 175 inhabitants.

WATERINGBURY, a parish (formerly a market town) in the hundred of TWYFORD, lathe of AYLESFORD, county of KENT, 5 miles (W. by S.) from Maidstone, containing 915 inhabitants. The living is a discharged vicarage, in the archdeaconry and diocese of Rochester, rated in the king's books at £5, endowed with £200 private benefaction, and £200 royal bounty, and in the patronage of the Dean and Chapter of Rochester. The church, dedicated to St. John the Baptist, formerly exhibited a profusion of stained glass, with portraits of Edward III. and his consort Philippa. On a monument in the cemetery, to the memory of Sir Oliver Style, Bart., it is recorded that, in the height of an entertainment given to a party of his friends at Smyrna, every individual, himself excepted, perished by an earthquake. In the neighbourhood of the village are several gentlemen's seats.

WATER-MILLOCK, a chapelry in the parish of GREYSTOCK, LEATH ward, county of CUMBERLAND, 7 miles (S. W.) from Penrith, containing 410 inhabitants. The living is a perpetual curacy, in the archdeaconry and diocese of Carlisle, endowed with £800 royal bounty, and in the patronage of the Rector of Greystock. This place is sometimes called Newchurch, from the present chapel, which was built, in 1558, on a more convenient site than the former. A school is endowed with £500 five per cents., the amount of sundry subscriptions. This chapelry is situated on the north side of Ullswater lake, in a district abounding with diversified scenery, the natural beauties of which have been heightened and improved by the erection of several handsome private residences, with pleasure grounds tastefully laid out. In a deep glen in Gow-Barrow

Park, rushing impetuously through the thick foliage of full-grown trees, is Airey Force, a beautiful cataract, which, dashing violently from rock to rock, emits a considerable spray. The discharge of a gun here produces, from the reverberation of the hills, an effect somewhat like thunder, and one or two French horns that of an harmonious concert of musical instruments.

WATER-OAKLEY, a division in the parish and hundred of BRAY, county of BERKS, containing 475 inhabitants.

WATER-OVERTON, a chapelry in the parish of ASTON, Birmingham division of the hundred of HEMLINGFORD, county of WARWICK, 2½ miles (N. W.) from Coleshill. The population is returned with the parish. The living is a perpetual curacy, in the archdeaconry of Coventry, and diocese of Lichfield and Coventry, endowed with £200 private benefaction, and £200 royal bounty, and in the patronage of Earl Digby. The church, dedicated to St. Peter and St. Paul, has lately received an addition of three hundred and sixty-six sittings, of which three hundred and twenty are free, the Incorporated Society for the enlargement of churches and chapels having granted £380 towards defraying the expense. The navigable river Medway bounds the parish on the south, where it is crossed by a bridge.

WATERPERRY, a parish in the hundred of BULLINGTON, county of OXFORD, 5¾ miles (W.) from Thame, containing 242 inhabitants. The living is a discharged vicarage, in the archdeaconry and diocese of Oxford, rated in the king's books at £8. 1. 5½., endowed with £200 private benefaction, and £500 parliamentary grant, and in the patronage of Joseph Henley, Esq. The church is dedicated to St. Mary.

WATERSTOCK, a parish in the hundred of THAME, county of OXFORD, 5¼ miles (W.) from Thame, containing 132 inhabitants. The living is a rectory, in the archdeaconry and diocese of Oxford, rated in the king's books at £10. 16. 0½., and in the patronage of W. H. Ashurst, Esq. The church is dedicated to St. Leonard.

WATFORD, a parish in the hundred of CASHIO, or liberty of St. ALBANS, county of HERTFORD, comprising the market town of Watford, and the hamlets of Cashio, Levesden, and Oxhey, and containing 4713 inhabitants, of which number, 2960 are in the town of Watford, 20 miles (W. S. W.) from Hertford, and 15 (N. W.) from London. This town, situated on the river Colne, derives its name from the Watlingstreet, which passes in the vicinity, and from a ford over the river, to which latter its origin also is attributed : it consists of one principal street, about a mile in length, is well built, paved, and supplied with water by a forcing pump, erected by subscription. By means of the Grand Junction canal, which passes a mile to the westward, a communication is maintained with the metropolis and the northern part of the kingdom. The manufacture of straw-plat, and three silk-throwsting mills, employ a considerable number of persons ; there are likewise eight malt-kilns, and two extensive breweries. The market, granted by Henry I., is held on Tuesday: the market-house is an indifferent building supported on wooden pillars, with granaries over it, and its situation is very confined. Fairs are on the Tuesday after Whit-Tuesday, and on August 29th and 30th, for cattle and pedlary ; the latter, originally granted by Edward IV., in 1469, had fallen into disuse, but was revived in 1827; there is also a statute fair for hiring servants in September. A meeting of magistrates is held every Tuesday, and there is a weekly court of requests, for the recovery of debts under 40s., the jurisdiction of which is co-extensive with the liberty of St. Albans; this court is constituted of commissioners, whose qualification to act is the possession of £800 real or personal property.

The living is a vicarage, in the archdeaconry of St. Albans, and diocese of London, rated in the king's books at £21. 12. 1., and in the patronage of the Earl of Essex. The church, dedicated to St. Mary, and situated in the centre of the street, on the south side of the town, has two chapels annexed, and a tower at the west end. There are places of worship for Baptists, those in the Connexion of the late Countess of Huntingdon, and Wesleyan Methodists. The free school, founded by Elizabeth Fuller, in 1704, is a handsome structure, at the south-west corner of the churchyard, with a residence for the master and mistress; it was endowed with a rent-charge of £52, imposed on lands in the parishes of Watford and Sarratt, in this county, and at Creek in Northamptonshire, to which an augmentation of £1000 was made by C. Deane, Esq., other benefactors having contributed about £2000 more: fifty boys and thirty girls are taught gratuitously. A parochial free school was founded and endowed by Francis Coombes, in 1641, in which twelve boys are instructed. There are also two small bequests for Sunday schools. A National school is chiefly supported by the Earl of Essex. Almshouses for four poor widows were founded by Sir Christopher Morrison and Sir B. Hicks; and some for eight poor widows were founded and endowed by Francis, Earl of Bedford, and his Countess, in 1580. Dame Morrison bequeathed £50 per annum, and Sarah Eure gave the sum of £200, for apprenticing poor children; and numerous other sums have been left for charitable uses.

WATFORD, a parish in the hundred of GUILSBOROUGH, county of NORTHAMPTON, 4¼ miles (N.N.E.) from Daventry, containing 331 inhabitants. The living is a vicarage, in the archdeaconry of Northampton, and diocese of Peterborough, rated in the king's books at £11. 7. 8½., and in the patronage of the Crown. The church is dedicated to St. Peter and St. Paul. The Union canal passes through the parish, which is bounded on the west by the ancient Watling-street. Sarah Clarke, in 1702, gave £400, now producing £42 a year, for which about thirty children are instructed. Here are some springs strongly impregnated with iron.

WATH, a parish comprising the chapelry of Norton-Conyers, in the wapentake of ALLERTONSHIRE, and the chapelries of Melmerby and Middleton-Quernhow, and the township of Wath, in the wapentake of HALLIKELD, North riding of the county of YORK, and containing 633 inhabitants, of which number, 186 are in the township of Wath, 4¼ miles (N. by E.) from Ripon. The living is a rectory, in the archdeaconry of Richmond, and diocese of Chester, rated in the king's books at £17. 17. 1., and in the patronage of the Marquis of Ailesbury. The church is dedicated to St. Mary. The Rev. Peter Samwaise, in 1690, founded a free school, and endowed it with lands and houses producing about £75 a year, for which forty boys are educated.

WATH, a township in that part of the parish of HOVINGHAM which is in the wapentake of RYEDALE, North riding of the county of YORK, 8 miles (W. by N.) from New Malton, containing 22 inhabitants.

WATH upon DEARN, a parish in the northern division of the wapentake of STRAFFORTH and TICKHILL, West riding of the county of YORK, comprising the chapelries of Nether Hoyland, Swinton, and Wentworth, and the townships of Brompton-Bierlow and Wath upon Dearn, and containing 5812 inhabitants, of which number, 1001 are in the township of Wath upon Dearn, 5¾ miles (N.) from Rotherham. The living is a discharged vicarage, in the archdeaconry and diocese of York, rated in the king's books at £15. 10. 2½., and in the patronage of the Dean and Canons of Christ Church, Oxford. The church is dedicated to All Saints. There is a place of worship for Wesleyan Methodists. The Rev. Thomas Wombwell, in 1663, gave £30 towards the erection of a school-house, which is endowed with £4. 13. 4. per annum, the amount of two rent-charges, bequeathed by Anthony Sawdrie, in 1648, and John Skyers, in 1668, for which seven children are instructed. There are extensive potteries, furnaces, and collieries in the parish. The Roman Iknield-street passed through it.

WATLINGTON, a parish in the hundred of CLACKCLOSE, county of NORFOLK, 5½ miles (N.) from Downham-Market, containing 488 inhabitants. The living is a rectory, in the archdeaconry of Norfolk, and diocese of Norwich, rated in the king's books at £14.16.8., and in the patronage of C. B. Plastow, Esq. The church, dedicated to St. Peter and St. Paul, which has been highly decorated, contains some fine old fragments of stained glass, a curious ancient font, and a number of monuments and inscriptions.

WATLINGTON, a market town and parish in the hundred of PIRTON, county of OXFORD, 15 miles (E. S. E.) from Oxford, and 43 (W. by N.) from London, containing, with the liberty of Greenfield, and the hamlet of Warmscomb, 1479 inhabitants. The name is conjectured to have been derived from the Saxon Watelar, hurdles, or wattles, alluding to the way in which the Britons are described to have built their towns, "as groves fenced in with hewn trees." The town is situated between the two high roads leading from London to Oxford, about half a mile from the line of the Iknield-street; it is irregularly built, and consists of some narrow streets, the houses, with a few exceptions, being but of mean appearance; water is supplied from an adjacent brook, which rises in one of the Chiltern hills, above the town, and on which are four corn-mills. A few females are employed in lace-making; a school, in which from thirty to forty girls attend, having been established to teach them the art. The market, granted in the reign of Richard I., is on Saturday: a substantial market-house was built, in 1666, by Thomas Stonor, Esq., and over it is a room where the public business of the town is transacted. Fairs are held on April 5th and the Saturday before October 10th; and on the Saturday before and after Michaelmas is a statute fair. Two courts leet are held annually, and the petty sessions for the hundred take place once a fortnight. The living is a discharged vicarage, in the archdeaconry and diocese of Oxford, rated in the king's books at £12, endowed with £200 private benefaction, and £200 royal bounty, and in the patronage of John H. Tilson, Esq. The church, standing on the north-western side of the town, is dedicated to St. Leonard; in the chancel is a burial-place of the Horne family, also some interesting monuments. There are places of worship for Baptists, Independents, and Wesleyan Methodists. The free grammar school, once a noted classical school, but now confined to English instruction, was founded in 1664, and endowed with a rent-charge of £10, by Thomas Stonor, Esq., which sum has been augmented by subsequent benefactions: the master, who must be a graduate of one of the Universities, receives a salary of £20 per annum; it is held in a room over the market-place: nineteen boys are instructed. On Bretwell hill there are some remains of trenches, indicating the site of an ancient encampment. Of Watlington castle, which stood southeast of the church, there are only some traces of the moat by which it was surrounded, now filled with water.

WATTISFIELD, a parish in the hundred of BLACK-BOURN, county of SUFFOLK, 2 miles (W. S. W.) from Botesdale, containing 596 inhabitants. The living is a discharged rectory, in the archdeaconry of Sudbury, and diocese of Norwich, rated in the king's books at £8. 11. 8. The Rev. R. Morgan was patron in 1808. The church is dedicated to St. Margaret. There is a place of worship for Independents.

WATTISHAM, a parish in the hundred of COSFORD, county of SUFFOLK, 2 miles (N. E.) from Bildeston, containing 193 inhabitants. The living is a perpetual curacy, in the archdeaconry of Sudbury, and diocese of Norwich, and in the patronage of the Provost and Fellows of King's College, Cambridge. The church is dedicated to St. Nicholas. There is a place of worship for Baptists.

WATTLEFIELD, a division in the parish of WYMONDHAM, hundred of FOREHOE, county of NORFOLK, 2¾ miles (S. by W.) from Wymondham, containing 487 inhabitants.

WATTON, a parish in the hundred of BROADWATER, county of HERTFORD, 4¾ miles (N. N. W.) from Hertford, containing 812 inhabitants. The living is a rectory, in the archdeaconry of Huntingdon, and diocese of Lincoln, rated in the king's books at £19. 8. 6½., and in the patronage of Abel Smith, Esq. The church, dedicated to St. Mary and St. Andrew, has a square western tower, embattled, and a chapel attached to the north side of the chancel. The river Beane runs through the parish, which was also intersected by one of the Roman vicinal ways, on the supposed line of which there is still a large stone, apparently of high antiquity and several coins have been found in the vicinity Maurice and William Thompson, in 1662, founded, and endowed with lands and houses, a free school, to which Abraham Crossland, in 1703, bequeathed a small sum for the purchase of books.

WATTON, a market town and parish in the hundred of WAYLAND, county of NORFOLK, 24 miles (W. by S.) from Norwich, and 94 (N. N. E.) from London, containing 894 inhabitants. This town, which suffered severely, in 1673, from an extensive fire that destroyed property to the amount of £10,000, is situated in the centre of the hundred, on the verge of that part of the county called Filand, or "the open country:" the streets are lighted with oil, and the inhabitants are supplied with water from springs: the

neighbourhood is noted for supplying the metropolis with large quantities of butter, called Cambridge butter. The market is on Wednesday; and the ancient fairs are on July 10th, October 11th, and November 3rd; two others, of modern establishment, being held on the first Wednesday in July and the first Wednesday after Old Michaelmas-day. A manorial court is held annually, and petty sessions for the hundred every month. The living is a discharged vicarage, in the archdeaconry and diocese of Norwich, rated in the king's books at £7. 0. 4., and in the patronage of John Raby Hicks, Esq. The church, dedicated to St. Mary, appears to have been originally built in the time of Henry I., and to have been re-dedicated in that of Henry VI.; the tower is circular at the base, and octangular above; the north porch is surmounted by a much admired crucifix, now partly dilapidated; there are a few brasses. In the centre of the town is a small building, with a clock and one bell, the latter rung on Sundays preparatory to divine service: the lower part is used as a lock-up house. There is a place of worship for Independents, a short distance from the town. A National school, in which about one hundred children are educated, was erected, in 1819, by William Lane Robinson, Esq., and is supported by voluntary contributions. Almshouses for four poor widows were founded and endowed with a small rent-charge by Mr. Goff. In Wayland wood, near this town, supposed to be the scene of the tale of the Babes in the Wood, and which gives name to the hundred, the sheriffs' torn, or court, was anciently held.

WATTON, a parish in the Bainton-Beacon division of the wapentake of HARTHILL, East riding of the county of YORK, 5½ miles (S.) from Great Driffield, containing 307 inhabitants. The living is a perpetual curacy, in the archdeaconry of the East riding, and diocese of York, endowed with £400 royal bounty, and £200 parliamentary grant, and in the patronage of R. Bethell, Esq. The church is dedicated to St. Mary. A nunnery of the Sempringham order, in honour of the Blessed Virgin Mary, was founded here, in 1150, upon the site of a more ancient priory, which existed so early as the year 686: at the dissolution, its revenue was valued at £453. 7. 8., when its site and remains, which are still considerable, were granted to John, Earl of Warwick.

WAULDBY, a township in the parish of ROWLEY, Hunsley-Beacon division of the wapentake of HART-HILL, East riding of the county of YORK, 4¼ miles (E. by S.) from South Cave, containing 44 inhabitants.

WAVENDON, a parish in the hundred of NEW-PORT, county of BUCKINGHAM, 3½ miles (N. E.) from Fenny-Stratford, containing 721 inhabitants. The living is a rectory, in the archdeaconry of Buckingham, and diocese of Lincoln, rated in the king's books at £26. 6. 10¼., and in the patronage of H. Hugh Hoare, Esq. The church is dedicated to St. Mary. There is a place of worship for Wesleyan Methodists. The sum of £1000 was given by Mr. George Wells, who died in 1714, and his niece, Mrs. Miller, with which a charity school was built, and endowed with lands producing upwards of £40 per annum, for teaching, clothing, and apprenticing ten boys.

WAVERLEY, an extra-parochial liberty, in the hundred of FARNHAM, county of SURREY, 2 miles (S. E.

by E.) from Farnham, containing 58 inhabitants. An abbey of Cistercian monks, in honour of the Blessed Virgin Mary, was founded here, in 1128, by William Giffard, Bishop of Winchester, which, at the dissolution, had a revenue of £196. 13. 11. : it is said to have been the first of that order established in England. The remains are still considerable, and, though insufficient to give an idea of its original magnificence, have an interesting effect, much enhanced by the luxuriant ivy with which they are overgrown.

WAVERTON, a parish in the lower division of the hundred of BROXTON, county palatine of CHESTER, comprising the townships of Hatton, Huxley, and Waverton, and containing 707 inhabitants, of which number, 303 are in the township of Waverton, 4½ miles (E. S. E.) from Chester. The living is a rectory, annexed to the bishoprick of Chester, in the archdeaconry and diocese of Chester, rated in the king's books at £23. 6. 8. The church is dedicated to St. Peter. The Chester canal passes through the parish.

WAVERTON (HIGH and LOW), a township in the parish of WIGTON, ward and county of CUMBERLAND, 2½ miles (W. S. W.) from Wigton, containing 477 inhabitants. The river Waver intersects the township, dividing it into what is termed High and Low Waverton.

WAVERTREE, a chapelry in the parish of CHILDWALL, hundred of WEST DERBY, county palatine of LANCASTER, 2½ miles (E. by S.) from Liverpool, containing 1620 inhabitants. The living is a perpetual curacy, in the archdeaconry and diocese of Chester, endowed with £200 parliamentary grant, and in the patronage of certain Trustees. There is a well in the neighbourhood, at which contributions were formerly received by some monks; it bears a curious Latin inscription, and the date 1414.

WAXHAM, a parish in the hundred of HAPPING, county of NORFOLK, 12 miles (E. S. E.) from North Walsham, containing 63 inhabitants. The living is a discharged rectory, with that of Palling annexed, in the archdeaconry of Norfolk, and diocese of Norwich, rated in the king's books at £6. 13. 4., and in the patronage of Sir G. B. Brograve, Bart. The church is dedicated to St. John and St. Margaret.

WAXHOLME, a township in that part of the parish of OWTHORNE which is in the middle division of the wapentake of HOLDERNESS, East riding of the county of YORK, 15¼ miles (E.) from Kingston upon Hull, containing 72 inhabitants.

WAYFORD, a parish in the hundred of CREWKERNE, county of SOMERSET, 2½ miles (S. W.) from Crewkerne, containing, with the tythings of Ashcomb and Oathill, 224 inhabitants. The living is a discharged rectory, in the archdeaconry of Taunton, and diocese of Bath and Wells, rated in the king's books at £5. 1. 5½. John Pinney, Esq. was patron in 1819. Elizabeth Bragge, in 1719, gave a rent-charge of £2. 10. for teaching eight children.

WEALD, a chapelry in the parish of SEVEN-OAKS, hundred of CODSHEATH, lathe of SUTTON at HONE, county of KENT, 2½ miles (S.) from Seven-Oaks, containing 612 inhabitants. The living is a perpetual curacy, annexed to the rectory of Ickham, in the exempt deanery of Shoreham, which is in the peculiar jurisdiction of the Archbishop of Canterbury, endowed with

£200 private benefaction, and £2100 parliamentary grant.

WEALD, a joint hamlet with Greenhill, in the parish of HARROW on the HILL, hundred of GORE, county of MIDDLESEX, 2½ miles (N.) from Harrow on the Hill. The population is returned with the parish.

WEALD (NORTH), a parish partly in the hundred of HARLOW, but chiefly in that of ONGAR, county of ESSEX, 3¼ miles (N. E. by E.) from Epping, containing, with the hamlets of Hastingwood and Thornwood, 827 inhabitants. The living is a vicarage, in the archdeaconry of Essex, and diocese of London, rated in the king's books at £13. 6. 8., and in the patronage of the Bishop of London. The church is dedicated to St. Andrew.

WEALD (SOUTH), a parish in the hundred of CHAFFORD, county of ESSEX, 1½ mile (W.) from Brentwood, containing, with the chapelry of Brentwood and the hamlet of Brookstreet, 2558 inhabitants. The living is a vicarage, in the archdeaconry of Essex, and diocese of London, rated in the king's books at £26. 13. 4., and in the patronage of the Bishop of London. The church is dedicated to St. Peter. Courts leet and baron are occasionally held. The whole parish is entitled to send boys to the free grammar school at Brentwood, founded in 1556, by Sir Anthony Browne. In front of the ancient hall is a mild chalybeate spring, much resorted to in summer, the water possessing properties somewhat similar to those of sea water.

WEARDALE (ST. JOHN), or ST. JOHN'S CHAPEL, a market town and chapelry in the parish of STANHOPE, north-western division of DARLINGTON ward, county palatine of DURHAM, 6¼ miles (W. N. W.) from Stanhope. The population is returned with the parish. The living is a perpetual curacy, in the archdeaconry and diocese of Durham, endowed with £400 private benefaction, and £1800 parliamentary grant, and in the patronage of the Rector of Stanhope. The chapel, which is a handsome structure, was rebuilt at the expense of the late Sir William Blackett, Bart., aided by a bequest of £50 from Dr. Hartwell. Dr. Shute Barrington, the late Bishop of Durham, also erected another chapel, which is presented to by the rector; and, about the same time, a National school. There are places of worship for Independents and Primitive and Wesleyan Methodists. Weardale is a small thriving town, situated in the Vale of Wear, through which runs the river of that name : its chief support is derived from the neighbouring lead mines. A customary market, on Saturday, has been established for more than a century : the market cross was erected at the expense of the late Sir Ralph Milbank, Bart., some time member for the county.

WEARDLEY, a township in that part of the parish of HAREWOOD which is in the upper division of the wapentake of SKYRACK, West riding of the county of YORK, 6½ miles (E.) from Otley, containing 191 inhabitants.

WEARE, a parish in the hundred of BEMPSTONE, county of SOMERSET, 2½ miles (S. W.) from Axbridge, containing 800 inhabitants. The living is a vicarage, in the archdeaconry of Wells, and diocese of Bath and Wells, rated in the king's books at £12. 1. 5½., and in the patronage of the Dean and Chapter of Bristol. The church is dedicated to St. Gregory. The river Ax is crossed by an ancient bridge, and runs through that part of the parish termed Nether Weare; which place, among many other privileges granted by different monarchs, enjoyed that of sending members to parliament in the 34th and 35th of Edward I., and had a weekly market on Wednesday, with an annual fair.

WEAR-GIFFORD, a parish in the hundred of SHEBBEAR, county of DEVON, 2¾ miles (N. N. W.) from Great Torrington, containing 469 inhabitants. The living is a rectory, in the archdeaconry of Barnstaple, and diocese of Exeter, rated in the king's books at £13. 5., and in the patronage of Earl Fortescue. The church is dedicated to the Holy Trinity. Sixteen poor children are taught to read for £15 a year, the bequest of John Lovering, in 1671.

WEARMOUTH (BISHOP), a parish adjoining the town of Sunderland, in the northern division of EASINGTON ward, county palatine of DURHAM, comprising the townships of Bishop-Wearmouth, Bishop-Wearmouth-Pans, Burdon, Ford, Ryhope, Silksworth, and Tunstall, and containing 11,542 inhabitants, of which number, 9477 are in the township of Bishop-Wearmouth. The living is a rectory, in the archdeaconry and diocese of Durham, rated in the king's books at £89. 18. 1½., and in the patronage of the Bishop of Durham. The church, dedicated to St. Michael, was rebuilt in 1807, on the site of the ancient edifice, which existed from the time of Athelstan. There is a place of worship for Methodists of the New Connexion. This parish derived its distinguishing appellation from having been appropriated by King Athelstan, about the year 930, to the church of St. Cuthbert at Durham. It is situated on the south-western side of Sunderland, having, prior to 1719, comprised that town within its limits: the two places are now connected, and may be said to form one large town and port, a regular and continued street, nearly a mile long, with others of uniform character branching from it, having been constructed on the vacant plot of ground that formerly intervened. The rector is lord of the manor, for which he occasionally holds courts. On the side of an eminence, called Building Hill, is a quarry of stone, which, on the division of lands in 1649, was reserved for the free use of the copyholders within the manor; and the inhabitants, from time immemorial, have enjoyed the privilege of bleaching their linen, &c., on a small piece of ground, called Burnfields, a little westward. For a more detailed account, See SUNDERLAND.

WEARMOUTH (MONK), a parish in the eastern division of CHESTER ward, county palatine of DURHAM, comprising the townships of Fulwell, Hylton, Monk-Wearmouth, Monk-Wearmouth-Shore, and Southwick, and containing 7644 inhabitants, of which number, 1278 are in the township of Monk-Wearmouth, ½ a mile (N.) from Sunderland. The name of this place designates its situation on the northern bank of the Wear, near its mouth; while its prefix is one of distinction, derived from a monastery founded about 674, by Biscopius, a Saxon nobleman attached to the court of Oswy, King of Northumberland, and dedicated to St. Peter. In the reign of Ethelred, this establishment was completely destroyed by the Danes: accounts differ with respect to the period of its re-erection, but, in 1083, the majority of the monks were removed to Durham, and this institution became a cell subordinate to the monastery of St. Cuthbert, in that city: at the dissolution, the revenue was valued only at £26. 9. 9. The town consists chiefly of two long streets, stretching east and west, situated on the declivity of an eminence, at the base of which is the river Wear; and of some irregular buildings on the shore, once comprising merely a few fishermen's huts, but now containing the major part of the population; it is on the left bank of the river, opposite to Sunderland, with which it is joined by the suspension bridge. The inhabitants are engaged in the various branches of trade connected with the shipping interests of Sunderland, with which this place and Bishop-Wearmouth are closely united. The living is a perpetual curacy, in the archdeaconry and diocese of Durham, endowed with £1000 private benefaction, £400 royal bounty, and £1200 parliamentary grant, and in the patronage of Sir H. Williamson, Bart. The church, which is dedicated to St. Peter, is of considerable antiquity, believed to have been built about 634; in the tower, which is supported on four circular arches, are some Saxon windows: during some repairs a stone coffin was found. There are places of worship for Baptists, Presbyterians, and Wesleyan Methodists. A free school for boys is supported by an annual subscription of £25 from Lady Williamson, and by voluntary contributions: the number of children is about one hundred. For an account of other charities, see SUNDERLAND. A skeleton of gigantic stature, and some relics of stags' horns have been found in this parish. Some remains of the monastery are still visible near the church. Venerable Bede passed the early part of his monastic life in it, whence he removed to Jarrow: some consider Wearmouth, and others Iscombe, to have been his native place; he was born in 672, and died in 735.

WEARMOUTH-PANS (BISHOP), a township in the parish of BISHOP-WEARMOUTH, northern division of DARLINGTON ward, county palatine of DURHAM, containing 483 inhabitants. It was so called from some salt-pans which formerly existed here, but have long been disused, and of which there is not a single vestige.

WEARMOUTH-SHORE (MONK), a township on the northern bank of the river Wear, adjoining the town of Sunderland, in the parish of MONK-WEARMOUTH, eastern division of CHESTER ward, county palatine of DURHAM, containing 4924 inhabitants. This place is comparatively of modern origin, having risen in consequence of the extensive yards for ship-building which, during the late continental war, were here constructed, and from the increased commerce of the port of Sunderland.

WEASENHAM (ALL SAINTS), a parish in the hundred of LAUNDITCH, county of NORFOLK, 7¼ miles (S. W.) from Fakenham, containing 284 inhabitants. The living is a discharged vicarage, with that of Weasenham St. Peter's annexed, in the archdeaconry and diocese of Norwich, rated in the king's books at £15. 10., endowed with £400 royal bounty, and in the patronage of the Crown.

WEASENHAM (ST. PETER'S), a parish in the hundred of LAUNDITCH, county of NORFOLK, 7¼ miles (S. W.) from Fakenham, containing 293 inhabitants. The living is a discharged vicarage, annexed to that of Weasenham All Saints, in the archdeaconry and diocese of Norwich, endowed with £200 royal bounty,

WEATHERSFIELD, a parish in the hundred of HINCKFORD, county of ESSEX, 6¾ miles (N.N.W.) from Braintree, containing 1558 inhabitants. The living is a vicarage, in the archdeaconry of Middlesex, and diocese of London, rated in the king's books at £12, and in the patronage of the Master and Fellows of Trinity Hall, Cambridge. The church is dedicated to St. Mary Magdalene. There is a place of worship for Independents. Thomas Fitch, in 1702, bequeathed land producing £30 per annum, for teaching and partly clothing twenty boys: and Dorothy Motte gave land, producing about £20 a year, for teaching, partly clothing, and finding books, for twenty girls.

WEAVERHAM, a parish in the second division of the hundred of EDDISBURY, county palatine of CHESTER, comprising the townships of Acton, Crowton, Cuddington, Onston, Wallerscoat, Weaverham *cum* Milton, and the lordship of Weaverham, and containing 2360 inhabitants, of which number, 749 are in the township of Weaverham *cum* Milton, 3¼ miles (W. by N.) from Northwich. The living is a vicarage, in the archdeaconry and diocese of Chester, rated in the king's books at £12. 11. 10½., and in the patronage of the Bishop of Chester. The church is dedicated to St. Mary. The interest of £100, left by Mary Barker, is applied for apprenticing poor children, as is also a rent-charge of £2, bequeathed by Mr. Mobberley. Here is a charity for six poor decayed housekeepers and their wives, or for deserving widowed or maiden women, selected by the vicar.

WEAVERTHORP, a parish partly within the liberty of ST. PETER of YORK, but chiefly in the wapentake of BUCKROSE, East riding of the county of YORK, comprising the townships of Luttons-Ambo and Weaverthorp, and containing 645 inhabitants, of which number, 334 are in the township of Weaverthorp, 10½ miles (N. N. W.) from Great Driffield. The living is a vicarage, in the peculiar jurisdiction and patronage of the Dean and Chapter of York, rated in the king's books at £9. 6. 0½. The church is dedicated to All Saints. There is a place of worship for Wesleyan Methodists.

WEDDINGTON, a parish in the Atherstone division of the hundred of HEMLINGFORD, county of WARWICK, 1¼ mile (N.) from Nuneaton, containing 91 inhabitants. The living is a rectory, in the archdeaconry of Coventry, and diocese of Lichfield and Coventry, rated in the king's books at £8. 10. 7½., and in the patronage of C. B. Adderley, Esq. The church is dedicated to St. James. The Coventry canal passes through the parish.

WEDGWOOD, a township in the parish of WOLSTANTON, northern division of the hundred of PIREHILL, county of STAFFORD, containing 68 inhabitants.

WEDHAMPTON, a tything in the parish of URCHFONT, hundred of SWANBOROUGH, county of WILTS, 3¾ miles (N. E.) from East Lavington, containing 194 inhabitants.

WEDMORE, a parish in the hundred of BEMPSTONE, county of SOMERSET, 4¾ miles (S. by E.) from Axbridge, containing, with the hamlet of Panborough, which is in the hundred of Glaston-Twelve-Hides, 3079 inhabitants. The living is a discharged vicarage, in the peculiar jurisdiction and patronage of the Dean of Wells, rated in the king's books at £20. 8. 6½. The

church, dedicated to St. Mary, is a handsome cruciform edifice, in the early style of English architecture, with a stately tower at the intersection, crowned with balustrades: on each side of the chancel there is a chapel, and annexed to the south aisle is another of smaller dimensions. Over the porch is a library, the gift of the Rev.—Andrews, a former vicar. There are places of worship for Baptists and Wesleyan Methodists. Wedmore was originally written *Wet-moor*, which appellation it retained till a late period. It was the residence of the West Saxon monarchs, and, with their hunting seat at Cheddar, and the *brugge* of Axe, was given by Alfred to one of his sons; the king having previously converted to Christianity the Danish prisoners taken at the battle of Eddington, whom he caused to be baptized at Aller, and afterwards kept the festival of Christmas here. Few places have undergone such rapid and extensive improvement as Wedmore; since, within memory, the immediate neighbourhood was usually under water nine months in the year. At present the situation of the village is extremely pleasant, being considerably elevated above the subjacent level, which, from the extensive drainage effected during the last half-century, has been rendered valuable land. This ancient borough, by which distinction a part of it is still known, is under the superintendence of a portreeve, chosen annually at the manorial court, with water-bailiffs, constables, and other officers. The custom of appointing water-bailiffs, and the discovery of a large vessel, in draining the adjacent moor, have induced an opinion that the sea, at some remote period, came up to the town. A National school, recently established, is supported by voluntary contributions.

WEDNESBURY, a market town and parish in the southern division of the hundred of OFFLOW, county of STAFFORD, 19 miles (S. S. E.) from Stafford, and 117 (N. W.) from London, containing 6471 inhabitants. This place, denominated by the Saxons *Weadesbury*, and now commonly called *Wedgebury*, was fortified, in 916, against the Danes, by Ethelfleda, daughter of Alfred the Great: at the Conquest it was held in royal demesne. The trade consists principally in the manufacture of articles of iron, both cast and wrought, such as locks, screws, nails, horse-shoes, hinges, gun-locks, coach ironmongery, agricultural implements, apparatus for gaslights, &c., many of which are prepared for exportation. In the vicinity of the town are numerous collieries, yielding a superior species of coal, which, from its great heat, is admirably adapted for the forges; and a species of iron is here made, termed Blondi, well suited for the preparation of axes and other sharp instruments. On a small rivulet near the town is an extensive manufactory for edge tools, also some cornmills. A branch of the Birmingham canal passes in the vicinity. The market is on Friday; and fairs are held May 6th and August 3rd, for cattle.

The town is governed by a constable chosen at the manorial court held annually in October. A court of requests for the townships of Bilston and Willenhall, and the parishes of Wednesbury and Darlaston, in the county of Stafford, excepting the manor of Bradley, is held here occasionally, for the recovery of debts not exceeding £5. The living is a discharged vicarage, in the archdeaconry of Stafford, and diocese of Lichfield and Coventry, rated in the king's books at £4. 3. 4., and in the patronage of the Crown. The church, occupying an elevated site, commanding a beautiful prospect, is dedicated to St. Bartholomew: it is a fine structure, principally in the later style of English architecture, with an octagonal east end, and contains some ancient wooden seats, and monuments to several families of eminence. It has undergone complete repair, having received an addition of four hundred and fifty sittings, of which three hundred are free, and towards defraying the expense the Incorporated Society for the building and enlargement of churches and chapels contributed £500: it is supposed to stand on the site of the ancient castle. There are places of worship for Independents and Primitive and Wesleyan Methodists. An almshouse, erected and endowed by Thomas Parkes, in 1602, has received some subsequent benefactions: the same benefactor has also bequeathed a house and land, called Clay Pit Leasow, and his son a small sum, for the education of poor children. The Lancasterian school, in High-street, is amply supported by voluntary subscriptions. William, the first Lord Paget, Secretary of State to Henry VIII., was a native of this town.

WEDNESFIELD, a chapelry in that part of the parish of WOLVERHAMPTON which is in the southern division of the hundred of OFFLOW, county of STAFFORD, 2 miles (N. E. by E.) from Wolverhampton, containing 1468 inhabitants. The living is a perpetual curacy, in the jurisdiction of the royal peculiar court of Wolverhampton, endowed with £400 private benefaction, £400 royal bounty, and £200 parliamentary grant, and in the patronage of J. Gough, Esq. The church, dedicated to St. Giles, was built in 1750. There is a place of worship for Wesleyan Methodists. The Essington and Wyrley canal passes through the parish; and the manufacture of locks, traps, &c., constitutes the principal trade of the place. Edward the Elder, in 911, here defeated the Danes, when two of their kings, two earls, and nine other chiefs, were slain. There were formerly two barrows on the supposed site of the battle, one of which has been levelled.

WEEDON, a hamlet in the parish of HARDWICKE, hundred of COTTESLOE, county of BUCKINGHAM, 2¼ miles (N.) from Aylesbury, containing 420 inhabitants. A school is supported by annual subscriptions.

WEEDON-BECK, a parish in the hundred of FAWSLEY, county of NORTHAMPTON, 4 miles (S. E. by E.) from Daventry, containing 1178 inhabitants. The living is a discharged vicarage, in the archdeaconry of Northampton, and diocese of Peterborough, rated in the king's books at £11, endowed with £800 private benefaction, £200 royal bounty, and £900 parliamentary grant, and in the patronage of T. R. Thornton, Esq. The church, dedicated to St. Peter and St. Paul, exhibits portions in the various styles of English architecture, and has lately received an addition of four hundred and fifty-seven sittings, of which two hundred and fifty-seven are free, the Incorporated Society for the enlargement of churches and chapels having granted £500 towards defraying the expense. There are places of worship for Independents and Wesleyan Methodists. A branch of the Grand Junction canal communicates with the Royal Military depôt here, which magnificent establishment, not surpassed by any other of the kind in Europe, is capable of receiving, besides numerous

pieces of artillery, no less than two hundred thousand stand of small arms, of which number, two-thirds are constantly deposited in it. The storehouses stand on an eminence overlooking the village of Lower Weedon, and have an hospital attached for forty patients, also workshops, or laboratories, for the artizans. Courts leet and baron are annually held. Wulphere, one of the kings of Mercia, had a palace here; and his daughter Werburga, who was afterwards canonized, converted it into a nunnery, which was burned by the Danes. The Roman Watling-street passed through the parish. Nathaniel Billing, in 1712, bequeathed certain houses to be sold, and the money to be applied for the establishment of a school, to which the Rev. John Rogers, in 1736, added £76; the annual income is about £100, for which twenty boys are educated and clothed.

WEEDON-LOYS, a parish in the hundred of GREENS-NORTON, county of NORTHAMPTON, 6¼ miles (W. by S.) from Towcester, containing, with the hamlet of Weston, 477 inhabitants. The living is a vicarage, in the archdeaconry of Northampton, and diocese of Peterborough, rated in the king's books at £6. 17. 6., and in the patronage of the Provost and Fellows of King's College, Cambridge. The church is dedicated to St. Peter and St. Mary. In the neighbourhood is a mineral spring, called St. Loy's, or St. Lewis', Well.

WEEFORD, a parish in the southern division of the hundred of OFFLOW, county of STAFFORD, 4 miles (S. S. E.) from Lichfield, containing, with the hamlet of Swinfen, and the liberty of Packington, 440 inhabitants. The living is a perpetual curacy, in the peculiar jurisdiction of the Prebendary of Alrewas and Weeford in the Cathedral Church of Lichfield, endowed with £10 per annum private benefaction, and £200 royal bounty, and in the patronage of the Chancellor of the Cathedral Church of Lichfield. The church is dedicated to St. Mary. Weeford is supposed to have taken its name from a ford on the line of the Roman Watling-street, called Wayford. Within the parish is the low, termed Offlow, which gives name to the hundred: it is erroneously stated to have been the burial-place of Offa, who was interred at Bedford. A school was founded and is supported by the family of Lawley.

WEEK, a parish in the hundred of BUDDLESGATE, Fawley division of the county of SOUTHAMPTON, 1 mile (N. W. by W.) from Winchester, containing 136 inhabitants. The living is a rectory, in the archdeaconry and diocese of Winchester, rated in the king's books at £12. 19. 2., and in the patronage of the Bishop of Winchester. The church is dedicated to St. Mary. Part of the parish is bounded by the old castle walls of the city of Winchester. Week is within the jurisdiction of the Cheyney Court held at Winchester every Thursday, for the recovery of debts to any amount.

WEEK (ST. MARY), a parish in the hundred of STRATTON, county of CORNWALL, 6 miles (S.) from Stratton, containing 782 inhabitants. The living is a rectory, in the archdeaconry of Cornwall, and diocese of Exeter, rated in the king's books at £17, and in the patronage of the Master and Fellows of Sidney Sussex College, Cambridge. In all ancient records this is termed the borough of Week St. Mary, and the occupiers of certain fields are still called burgage-holders. The custom of electing a mayor is still observed, but the office is little more than nominal. Fairs for bullocks and sheep are held on September 8th and 12th. Adjoining the churchyard is the site of an ancient fortress, called Castle Hill.

WEEKE - CHAMPFLOWER, a chapelry in the parish and hundred of BRUTON, county of SOMERSET, 1½ mile (W.) from Bruton, containing 82 inhabitants. The living is a perpetual curacy, in the archdeaconry of Wells, and diocese of Bath and Wells, endowed with £1000 royal bounty, and in the patronage of Sir R. C. Hoare, Bart. The chapel is dedicated to St. Mary.

WEEKLEY, a parish in the hundred of CORBY, county of NORTHAMPTON, 2¼ miles (N. E. by N.) from Kettering, containing 255 inhabitants. The living is a discharged vicarage, in the archdeaconry of Northampton, and diocese of Peterborough, rated in the king's books at £9. 0. 5., and in the patronage of the Duke of Buccleuch. The church, dedicated to St. Mary, contains a monument to the memory of Lord Chief Justice Montague. Near the south side of it is an hospital for seven poor men.

WEEL, a township in that part of the parish of ST. JOHN, BEVERLEY, which is within the liberties of the borough of BEVERLEY, East riding of the county of YORK, 2¼ miles (E.) from Beverley, containing 101 inhabitants.

WEELEY, a parish in the hundred of TENDRING, county of ESSEX, 9½ miles (S. S. E.) from Manningtree, containing 668 inhabitants. The living is a discharged rectory, in the archdeaconry of Colchester, and diocese of London, rated in the king's books at £12, and in the patronage of the Bishop of London. The church, dedicated to St. Andrew, has an embattled tower built of remarkably large bricks. There is a place of worship for Wesleyan Methodists. Extensive barracks were formerly kept up here.

WEETHLEY, a parish in the Alcester division of the hundred of BARLICHWAY, county of WARWICK, 3¼ miles (S. W. by W.) from Alcester, containing 54 inhabitants. The living is a perpetual curacy, annexed to the rectory of Kinwarton, in the archdeaconry and diocese of Worcester. The church is dedicated to St. James.

WEETING, a parish in the hundred of GRIMSHOE, county of NORFOLK, 1½ mile (N.) from Brandon-Ferry, containing, with the hamlet of Brumhill, 399 inhabitants. The living comprises the united rectories of All Saints and St. Mary, in the archdeaconry of Norfolk, and diocese of Norwich, rated jointly in the king's books at £18. 9. 9½., and in the patronage of the Master and Fellows of Gonville and Caius College, Cambridge. The church of St. Mary has gone to decay.

WEETON, a township in the parish of KIRKHAM, hundred of AMOUNDERNESS, county palatine of LANCASTER, 3¼ miles (N. W. by W.) from Kirkham, containing 473 inhabitants. A fair for cattle and pedlary is held on Trinity-Monday and the following day.

WEETON, a township in that part of the parish of HAREWOOD which is in the upper division of the wapentake of CLARO, West riding of the county of YORK, 6 miles (E. N. E.) from Otley, containing 310 inhabitants. The township is in the Forest division, and within the peculiar jurisdiction of the court of the honour of Knaresborough. There is a place of worship for Wesleyan Methodists.

WEETSTED, a township in the parish of LONG BENTON, eastern division of CASTLE ward, county of NORTHUMBERLAND. The population is returned with the parish.

WEEVER, a township in that part of the parish of MIDDLEWICH which is in the first division of the hundred of EDDISBURY, county palatine of CHESTER, 4¼ miles (W. S. W.) from Middlewich, containing 177 inhabitants.

WEIGHTON (MARKET), a parish partly within the liberty of ST. PETER of YORK, but chiefly in the Holme-Beacon division of the wapentake of HARTHILL, East riding of the county of YORK, comprising the market town of Market-Weighton, the chapelry of Shipton, and the hamlet of Arras, and containing 2093 inhabitants, of which number, 1724 are in the town of Market-Weighton with Arras, 19 miles (E. S. E.) from York, and 190 (N. by W.) from Loudon. This town, which is situated at the western foot of the Wolds, near a branch of the river Foulness, on the high road from York to Beverley, is progressively improving, its trade having been considerably increased by the construction of a canal to the Humber. The market is on Wednesday; and fairs are held on May 14th and September 25th, for horses, cattle, and sheep. The living is a discharged vicarage, in the peculiar jurisdiction and patronage of the Prebendary of Weighton in the Cathedral Church of York, rated in the king's books at £4. 13. 9. The church, dedicated to All Saints, is an ancient edifice. There are places of worship for Independents and Wesleyan Methodists. Two small rent-charges have been assigned for the instruction of ten children. Near the town are many tumuli, which have been found to contain some human bones, and remains of ancient armour, supposed to be Danish.

WELBECK, an extra-parochial liberty, in the Hatfield division of the wapentake of BASSETLAW, county of NOTTINGHAM, 3½ miles (S. W. by S.) from Worksop, containing 64 inhabitants. An abbey for Premonstratensian canons, in honour of St. James, was founded here in 1153, by Thomas le Flemangh, which at the dissolution had a revenue of £298. 4. 8.

WELBORNE, a parish in the hundred of FOREHOE, county of NORFOLK, 6½ miles (N. N. W.) from Wymondham, containing 166 inhabitants. The living is a discharged rectory, annexed to that of Yaxham, in the archdeaconry of Norfolk, and diocese of Norwich, rated in the king's books at £5. 18. 4. The church is dedicated to All Saints.

WELBOURN, a parish in the higher division of the wapentake of BOOTHBY-GRAFFO, parts of KESTEVEN, county of LINCOLN, 9½ miles (N. W.) from Sleaford, containing 489 inhabitants. The living is a rectory, in the archdeaconry and diocese of Lincoln, rated in the king's books at £19. 16. 0½., and in the patronage of the Earl of Buckinghamshire. The church, dedicated to St. Chad, exhibits fine specimens of the early, decorated, and later styles of English architecture: the tower, which is of very early date, is surmounted by a crocketed spire, in the shape of a sugar-loaf, supported by flying buttresses springing from the angles of the tower.

WELBURN, a township in the parish and wapentake of BULMER, North riding of the county of YORK, 5¾ miles (S. W. by W.) from New Malton, containing 352 inhabitants.

WELBURN, a township in that part of the parish of KIRKDALE which is in the wapentake of RYEDALE,

North riding of the county of YORK, 4¾ miles (E. by S.) from Helmsley, containing 112 inhabitants.

WELBURY, a parish in the wapentake of BIRDFORTH, North riding of the county of YORK, 6¾ miles (N. N. E.) from North Allerton, containing 257 inhabitants. The living is a rectory, in the archdeaconry of Cleveland, and diocese of York, rated in the king's books at £7. 2. 11., and in the patronage of the King, as Duke of Lancaster. The church, dedicated to St. Leonard, has been lately rebuilt.

WELBY, a township in the parish of MELTON-MOWBRAY, hundred of FRAMLAND, county of LEICESTER, 2¼ miles (N. W. by W.) from Melton-Mowbray, containing 65 inhabitants.

WELBY, a parish in the wapentake of WINNIBRIGGS and THREO, parts of KESTEVEN, county of LINCOLN, 4½ miles (E. by N.) from Grantham, containing 377 inhabitants. The living is a rectory, in the archdeaconry and diocese of Lincoln, rated in the king's books at £10. 6. 3., and in the patronage of the Prebendary of South Grantham in the Cathedral Church of Salisbury. The church is dedicated to St. Bartholomew.

WELCHES-DAM, an extra-parochial liberty, in the southern division of the hundred of WITCHFORD, Isle of ELY, county of CAMBRIDGE, containing 156 inhabitants.

WELDON (GREAT), a parish (formerly a market town) in the hundred of CORBY, county of NORTHAMPTON, 4¼ miles (E. S. E.) from Rockingham, containing, with the hamlet of Little Weldon, 819 inhabitants. The living is a rectory, in the archdeaconry of Northampton, and diocese of Peterborough, rated in the king's books at £13. 6. 8. D. F. Hatton, Esq. was patron in 1819. The church is dedicated to St. Mary. There is a place of worship for Independents. The market was on Wednesday; and there were four fairs, three of which are still held, viz., on the first Thursdays in February, May, and November, but the fourth is disused. The market-house, erected at the expense of Lord Viscount Hatton, over which were the sessions-chambers, supported by pillars of the Tuscan order, was pulled down about ten years ago. The houses are built of rag-stone from extensive quarries in the neighbourhood. In an enclosure called Chapelfield, the pavements of a Roman villa, forming a double square, measuring one hundred feet by fifty, with the foundations of a stone wall, and a great number of coins of the Lower Empire, besides some of Constantine, Constans, Magnentius, and Constantine, jun., were discovered in 1738: higher up the hill are the remains of an ancient town.

WELDON (LITTLE), a hamlet in the parish of GREAT WELDON, hundred of CORBY, county of NORTHAMPTON, 4 miles (E. S. E.) from Rockingham, containing 480 inhabitants.

WELFORD, a parish partly in the hundred of KINTBURY-EAGLE, but chiefly in that of FAIRCROSS, county of BERKS, 5¼ miles (N. W.) from Speenhamland, containing 1058 inhabitants. The living is a rectory, in the peculiar jurisdiction of the Dean of Salisbury, rated in the king's books at £35. 15. 5., and in the patronage of the Rev. H. Sawbridge. At the period of the Norman survey here were two churches; that remaining, dedicated to St. Gregory, has a rude

Norman round tower supporting an early English stage, crowned with a decorated spire, the body of the structure exhibiting the later style.

WELFORD, a parish partly in the Stratford division of the hundred of BARLICHWAY, county of WARWICK, but chiefly in the upper division of the hundred of DEERHURST, county of GLOUCESTER, 4¼ miles (W. S. W.) from Stratford on Avon, containing, with the hamlet of Bickmersh with Little Dorsington, 702 inhabitants. The living is a rectory, in the archdeaconry and diocese of Gloucester, rated in the king's books at £29. 15. 10., and in the patronage of the Duke of Dorset. The church, dedicated to the Holy Trinity, is principally in the Norman style, with a lofty tower crowned with pinnacles. There is a place of worship for Wesleyan Methodists.

WELFORD, a parish in the hundred of GUILSBOROUGH, county of NORTHAMPTON, 8¾ miles (S. W. by W.) from Market-Harborough, containing 1005 inhabitants. The living is a discharged vicarage, with that of Sibbertoft united, in the archdeaconry of Northampton, and diocese of Peterborough, rated in the king's books at £8, endowed with £200 private benefaction, and £200 royal bounty, and in the patronage of the Bishop of Oxford. The church is dedicated to St. Mary. There are places of worship for Independents and Wesleyan Methodists. The Grand Union canal passes through the parish. The free school and premises here were purchased out of funds arising from the church and poor's lands; the income is £21. 10. a year.

WELHAM, a parish in the hundred of GARTREE, county of LEICESTER, 4¼ miles (N. E. by N.) from Market-Harborough, containing 74 inhabitants. The living is a vicarage, in the archdeaconry of Leicester, and diocese of Lincoln, rated in the king's books at £6. 3. 4., and in the patronage of the Crown. The church is dedicated to St. Andrew.

WELHAM, a township in the parish of NORTON, wapentake of BUCKROSE, East riding of the county of YORK, 1¾ mile (S.) from New Malton, containing 64 inhabitants.

WELL, a parish in the Wold division of the hundred of CALCEWORTH, parts of LINDSEY, county of LINCOLN, 2¼ miles (S. S. W.) from Alford, containing, with the chapelry of Derthorpe and the township of Mawthorpe, 135 inhabitants. The living is a discharged rectory, with the vicarage of Claxby united, in the archdeaconry and diocese of Lincoln, and in the patronage of B. Dashwood, Esq. The church, dedicated to St. Margaret, has been rebuilt in the form of an elegant Grecian temple. Near this place, in 1725, two urns, containing six hundred Roman coins, were found; in the neighbourhood are three Celtic barrows, contiguous to each other.

WELL, a parish in the eastern division of the wapentake of HANG, North riding of the county of YORK, comprising the townships of Snape and Well, and containing 1059 inhabitants, of which number, 370 are in the township of Well, 4½ miles (S.) from Bedale. The living is a discharged vicarage, in the archdeaconry of Richmond and diocese of Chester, rated in the king's books at £8. 13. 7., endowed with £400 private benefaction, £200 royal bounty, and £1100 parliamentary grant, and in the patronage of

Charles Chaplin, Esq. The church, dedicated to St. James, contains several monuments of the lords of Snape. This place derived its name from a celebrated well, dedicated to St. Michael, which, at all times of the year, is supplied with water by a spring issuing from a rock. An hospital, in honour of St. Michael the Archangel, for a master, two priests, and twenty-four poor brethren and sisters, was founded here, in 1342, by Sir Ralph de Neville, Lord of Middleham, which at the dissolution had a revenue of £42. 12. 3. Thomas, Earl of Exeter, in 1605, established a charity, called Neville's workhouse, for the maintenance of a master and mistress and twelve poor girls, the latter of whom are also educated. A school for boys, and another for girls, were founded here, and two others at Snape, in 1788, and are supported from these funds, which amount to about £100 per annum.

WELL-HAUGH, a township in the parish of FALSTONE, north-western division of TINDALE ward, county of NORTHUMBERLAND, 12¼ miles (W. N. W.) from Bellingham, containing 267 inhabitants.

WELLAND, a parish in the lower division of the hundred of OSWALDSLOW, county of WORCESTER, 3 miles (W. by S.) from Upton upon Severn, containing 453 inhabitants. The living is a discharged vicarage, in the peculiar jurisdiction of the Bishop of Worcester, rated in the king's books at £8. 2. 11., and in the patronage of the Crown. The church is dedicated to St. James.

WELLCOMBE, a parish in the hundred of HARTLAND, county of DEVON, 5¾ miles (S. W. by S.) from Hartland, containing 247 inhabitants. The living is a perpetual curacy, in the archdeaconry of Barnstaple, and diocese of Exeter, endowed with £1600 royal bounty, and in the patronage of the Perpetual Curate of Hartland. The church is dedicated to St. Nectan.

WELLESBOURN-HASTINGS, a parish in the Warwick division of the hundred of KINGTON, county of WARWICK, 4¾ miles (N. W.) from Kington, containing, with Walton-Deivile, 600 inhabitants. The living is a discharged vicarage, with the rectory of Walton-Deivile annexed, in the archdeaconry and diocese of Worcester, rated in the king's books at £7. 11. 8., and in the patronage of the Crown. The church, dedicated to St. Peter, is partly in the Norman, and partly in the early English, style of architecture, with a tower of later character: it contains a monument to the memory of Sir Thomas le Strange, lord-lieutenant of Ireland in the reign of Henry VI. About fifty boys and sixty girls receive gratuitous instruction in schools founded, in 1723, by the Rev. Richard Boyse, who endowed them with land and houses now producing nearly £60 per annum, which sum has been subsequently augmented by subscriptions to about £82, for the maintenance of a master and a mistress.

WELLESBOURN-MONTFORD, a parish in the Warwick division of the hundred of KINGTON, county of WARWICK, 5 miles (N. W. by W.) from Kington, containing 525 inhabitants.

WELLINGBOROUGH, a market town and parish in the hundred of HAMFORDSHOE, county of NORTHAMPTON, 10 miles (N. E. by E.) from Northampton, and 67 (N. N. W.) from London, containing 4454 inhabitants. The name is derived from the wells, or springs, that abound here, of which that denominated Red Well

was formerly in such repute for its medicinal properties, that, in 1626, Charles I. and his queen resided in tents during a whole season, for the purpose of drinking its salubrious water at the source. In 1738, the town was nearly destroyed by fire, and rebuilt on the slope of a hill nearly a mile northward from the navigable river Nen : it consists of several streets lighted and pitched, the principal of them meeting in the market-place : the houses, built of red sand-stone, which abounds in the vicinity, are of modern style and handsome appearance. The chief articles of manufacture are boots and shoes, and bobbin-lace : the former was very extensive during the war, and is still considerable; and the latter, though on the decline, employs many females and children : a silk-mill has been recently established. The market was granted by King John, at the request of the monks of Croyland abbey, the proprietors of the manor, which was subsequently held by Queen Elizabeth, after the dissolution· it is on Wednesday, and is a very considerable corn market. Fairs are on the Wednesdays in Easter and Whitsun-weeks, and October 29th; the last is a large one for live stock. Manorial courts are held annually in October; and petty sessions for the division, every week by the county magistrates, who assemble at the town hall, which has been recently erected by the feoffees, and is used for vestries and other public meetings.

The living is a vicarage, in the archdeaconry of Northampton, and diocese of Peterborough, rated in the king's books at £24. 1. 8., and in the patronage of Quintus Vivian, Esq. The church, dedicated to All Saints, is a spacious and handsome structure, combining specimens of the different styles of English architecture, with an elegant tower and spire; on the south side is a Norman door, and in the interior are some ancient screen-work and stalls; the east window is richly ornamented with sculpture and tracery : the exterior is protected by an iron palisade. There are three places of worship for Independents, and one each for Baptists, the Society of Friends, and Wesleyan Methodists. A free grammar school, adjoining the church-yard, was founded in the 2nd of Edward VI., and endowed with the revenue of a guild of the Blessed Virgin, formerly attached to the church; the funds have received considerable augmentation from subsequent benefactors, and are under the management of sixteen feoffees: the head and under masters are elected by the inhabitants assessed to the land tax, and receive certain shares of the annual income. In 1711, a copyhold house was bequeathed by John Freeman, Esq., to be used as a charity school, in which twenty-five boys are taught to read, and twenty-five girls to read, sew, and make lace: the salaries to the master and the mistress are derived from invested legacies given by Samuel Knight, Mary Roan, and John Robinson, together with four-eighths of the rental of fifty-five acres of land, producing about £137. 10. per annum, the remainder of which is appropriated to the head and under master of the free grammar school, and to two aged inhabitants not receiving parochial relief. There is a gift of land for the use of the poor, made, in the reign of Elizabeth, by a person unknown. The chalybeate spring, which flowed about half a mile north-west of the town, is now covered over, and, with other streams, supplies the reservoir of a corn-mill.

WELLINGHAM, a parish in the hundred of LAUNDITCH, county of NORFOLK, 6¼ miles (S. W. by S.) from Fakenham, containing 140 inhabitants. The living is a discharged rectory, annexed to the rectories of Tittleshall and Godwick, in the archdeaconry and diocese of Norwich, rated in the king's books at £5. 8. 6½. The church is dedicated to St. Andrew.

WELLINGLEY, a joint township with Stancill and Wilsick, in the parish of TICKHILL, southern division of the wapentake of STRAFFORTH and TICKHILL, West riding of the county of YORK, 2 miles (N. by W.) from Tickhill. The population is returned with Stancill.

WELLINGORE, a parish in the higher division of the wapentake of BOOTHBY-GRAFFO, parts of KESTEVEN, county of LINCOLN, 9 miles (N. W.) from Sleaford, containing 727 inhabitants. The living is a discharged vicarage, in the peculiar jurisdiction and patronage of the Dean and Chapter of Lincoln, rated in the king's books at £11. 10. The church is dedicated to All Saints. There is a place of worship for Wesleyan Methodists.

WELLINGTON, a parish in the hundred of GIRMSWORTH, county of HEREFORD, 5½ miles (N.) from Hereford, containing 672 inhabitants. The living is a discharged vicarage, in the archdeaconry and diocese of Hereford, rated in the king's books at £6. 13. 4., endowed with £200 private benefaction, and £200 royal bounty, and in the patronage of the Prebendary of Wellington in the Cathedral Church of Hereford. The church is dedicated to St. Margaret.

WELLINGTON, or WILLINGTON, a township in the parish of WALLSEND, eastern division of CASTLE ward, county of NORTHUMBERLAND, 3 miles (W. by S.) from North Shields. The population is returned with the parish. It is situated on the river Tyne, where are a fine quarry, several coal-staiths, a patent ropery, and a corn-mill, worked by steam. There are extensive collieries within the township.

WELLINGTON, a market town and parish in the Wellington division of the hundred of BRADFORD (South), county of SALOP, 11 miles (E.) from Shrewsbury, and 151 (N. W.) from London, containing 8390 inhabitants. During the great civil war, this was the first place of rendezvous of Charles I., who, on the 19th of September, 1642, mustered his forces near the town, and having commanded his military orders to be read, delivered, in person, the remarkable address mentioned by Clarendon. The town occupies a low situation, near the ancient Roman Watling-street, about two miles southward from the Wrekin, which rises from the plain to a height of about eleven hundred feet above the bed of the Severn, embraces an horizon of from three hundred and fifty to four hundred miles in circumference, and is surmounted by an ancient fortification; a part of the parish is bounded by the river Tern. The streets are mostly narrow, but they have recently been much improved, and are now Macadamized, and lighted with gas, and many of the houses are of modern and respectable appearance. The mineral productions of the parish, consisting of coal, iron-stone, and limestone, form the basis of its trade, which chiefly consists in the different branches of iron manufacture, especially that of nails: several companies of iron-masters possess establishments in the neighbourhood, amongst which are, the Hadley, Ketley, Lawley, and Lilleshall companies. There are also a glass manufactory, corn-mills, and

malt-kilns, and some business is transacted in timber. The various articles of manufacture and commerce are conveyed by the Shrewsbury and Shropshire canals, which communicate with the navigable river Severn, and the midland counties. The market, granted to Hugh Burnel, in the 11th of Edward I., is on Thursday, and is on a very extensive scale: fairs, chiefly for live stock, and butter and cheese, are held on March 29th, June 22nd, September 29th, and November 17th. The town is under a mayor and constables, and two clerks are appointed to regulate the market: a manorial court is held every November, at which these officers are appointed: petty sessions for the hundred take place weekly, and a court of record, for the recovery of debts under £20, is held on certain specified days.

The living is a vicarage, with the rectory of Eyton on the Wild Moors annexed, in the archdeaconry of Salop, and diocese of Lichfield and Coventry, rated in the king's books at £9. 5., and in the patronage of T. Eyton, Esq. The church, dedicated to All Saints, is a light and elegant modern edifice of freestone: a part of it is supported by iron pillars, and the same material is employed in the window-frames, one of which is fifteen feet high, thereby giving the whole a light appearance. There are places of worship for Baptists, Independents, and Wesleyan Methodists. A free school has been founded for poor children of both sexes, and there is an almshouse for poor women. A National school is held in a building in the churchyard. There are two valuable springs at Admaston, about a mile and a half from the town, called the Upper and the Lower, the former chalybeate, and the latter sulphureous. A very comfortable inn and baths have been erected here, at considerable expense, the waters having been found highly efficacious, particularly in rheumatic complaints, and it has become a favourite watering-place, being frequented by persons from various parts of the kingdom. Several curious petrifactions of plants and shells are found occasionally in some of the iron mines in the vicinity. Dr. Withering, author of a "Botanical Arrangement of British Plants," and some medical treatises, was born here, in 1741.

WELLINGTON, a market town and parish, forming, with the parish of West Buckland, one of the two unconnected portions which comprise the western division of the hundred of KINGSBURY, county of SOMERSET, 24 miles (W. S. W.) from Somerton, and 149 (W. S. W.) from London, containing 4170 inhabitants. This town is situated on the main road from Bath to Exeter, and is in progress of great improvement, many of the streets having been paved, and a few of the old houses removed. The manufacture of druggets and serges was formerly carried on to a considerable degree, and still prevails on a less extended scale. The Grand Western canal being in an unfinished state, the town at present derives no benefit from it; but it is expected that this undertaking will shortly be renewed, and great advantages are anticipated on its completion. During the manorial possession of the Bishops of Wells, a charter was obtained for a market and two fairs; the former is held on Thursdays, principally for corn; the latter on the Thursdays before Easter and Whitsuntide. The present market-house being in a very dilapidated condition, and not affording suitable accommodation for the market people, is thought to have caused a partial decline in the market of late years; to obviate which, an application has been made to His Grace the Duke of Wellington, lord of the manor, for the erection of a new edifice, which it is considered will shortly be accomplished. The government of the town is in a bailiff and subordinate officers, chosen at the annual court leet held for the manor. The living is a vicarage, with the perpetual curacy of West Buckland annexed, locally in the archdeaconry of Taunton, and diocese of Bath and Wells, rated in the king's books at £15. 10. 2½., and in the patronage of the Rev. W. P. Thomas. The church, which is dedicated to St. John the Baptist, is a handsome edifice, with an embattled tower crowned with pinnacles at the west end, and two sepulchral chapels; in one of these is a splendid monument to the memory of Sir John Popham, Knt., Lord Chief Justice of England in the reigns of Elizabeth and James I., ornamented with a profusion of effigies and carved work. The Rev. Mr. Thomas has erected an elegant chapel, at his own expense, near the west end of the town: it is dedicated to the Holy Trinity, and was lately consecrated for the service of the church of England. There are places of worship for Baptists, the Society of Friends, Independents, and Wesleyan Methodists. Almshouses for six poor men and six poor women were founded in 1604, and endowed with land by Sir John Popham, the master and matron to instruct poor children. Wellington confers the titles of viscount, earl, marquis, and duke, on that distinguished military commander, Arthur Wellesley, Prince of Waterloo; the first created Sept. 4th, 1809; the second, February 28th, 1812; the third, Aug. 18th, of the same year; and the fourth, May 3rd, 1814. At a short distance from the town a magnificent pillar has been erected, by public subscription, in commemoration of the signal victory obtained by his Grace on the plain of Waterloo, in 1815.

WELLOW, a parish in the South-clay division of the wapentake of BASSETLAW, county of NOTTINGHAM, 1½ mile (S. E. by E.) from Ollerton, containing 444 inhabitants. The living is a perpetual curacy, in the archdeaconry of Nottingham, and diocese of York, endowed with £800 royal bounty, and £200 parliamentary grant, and in the patronage of the Hon. and Rev. J. L. Saville. The church is dedicated to St. Swithin. Here is a small school, endowed by an unknown benefactor.

WELLOW, a parish in the hundred of WELLOW, county of SOMERSET, 4¼ miles (S.) from Bath, containing 817 inhabitants. The living is a discharged vicarage, in the archdeaconry of Wells, and diocese of Bath and Wells, rated in the king's books at £20. 6. 10½., and in the patronage of Edward Gardiner, Esq. The church, dedicated to St. Julian, was built by Sir Walter Hungerford, about 1732. There is a place of worship for Wesleyan Methodists. A railway from the Welton collieries, communicating with the Avon and Kennet, and the Radford coal canals, passes through the parish. Ten poor children are educated for £10 a year, the bequest of Rachael Coles, in 1756; and two for a rent-charge of £2, the gift of Daniel Sumner, in 1699. Among numerous other Roman relics discovered in the neighbourhood, a tesselated pavement was found in 1644, another in 1670, and a third in 1685, with altars, pillars, and fragments of pateræ, and other vessels. At the extremity of the parish is an immense barrow, called

Woodeborough, and another smaller one has been found to contain several stone coffins.

WELLOW (EAST), a parish in the hundred of THORNGATE, Andover division of the county of SOUTHAMPTON, 3¾ miles (W.) from Romsey, containing, with the tything of Embley, 288 inhabitants. The living is a vicarage, in the archdeaconry and diocese of Winchester, rated in the king's books at £5, and in the patronage of W. E. Nightingale, Esq. The church is dedicated to St. Margaret. There is a place of worship for Wesleyan Methodists.

WELLOW (WEST), a tything in the parish of EAST WELLOW, hundred of AMESBURY, county of WILTS, 4¾ miles (W. by N.) from Romsey, containing 395 inhabitants.

WELLS, a sea-port town and parish, in the northern division of the hundred of GREENHOE, county of NORFOLK, 33 miles (N. W. by N.) from Norwich, and 120 (N. N. E.) from London, containing 2950 inhabitants. This place, called in Domesday-book Guella, is situated on a creek about a mile from the German Ocean, and consists principally of two streets, partially paved, and well supplied with water. There is a theatre, a plain brick building, neatly fitted up within; and a subscription library has been established: races were formerly held here, but they have been discontinued. The magistrates of the hundred hold their sittings once a fortnight; and courts leet and baron are held annually by the lord of the manor, at which the steward presides. The trade consists in the exportation of grain and malt, and the importation of coal, deals, tiles, bark, linseed and rapeseed cakes, tar, and wine: oysters of an excellent quality are also found, and the fishery furnishes employment to many persons. The harbour, from the accumulation of sand, is rather difficult of access, but considerable improvements have been made in it by the Harbour Commissioners. The custom-house is a brick building, situated on the quay, and the establishment consists of a collector, comptroller, land and tide waiter, &c. A fair is held annually on Shrove-Tuesday. The living is a rectory, in the archdeaconry and diocese of Norwich, rated in the king's books at £26. 13. 4., and in the patronage of the Rev. J. R. Hopper. The church, dedicated to St. Peter, is a handsome spacious edifice of flint, with a lofty embattled tower. The Society of Friends, Independents, and Wesleyan Methodists have each a place of worship. There are free schools for thirty boys and thirty girls, founded and endowed by Christ. Ringer, Esq., of Field Dalling, about a century and a half since.

WELLS, a city, having separate jurisdiction, locally in the hundred of Wells-Forum, county of SOMERSET, 19 miles (S.W.) from Bath, 19 (S.) from Bristol, and 120 (W. by S.) from London, containing, with that part of the parish of St. Cuthbert which is without the limits of the city, 5888 inhabitants. This place derives its name from

Seal and Arms.

the numerous springs with which it abounds, more particularly from St. Andrew's well, the water of which, rising near the episcopal palace, flows through the south-western part of the city: it owes its origin to Ina, King of the West Saxons, who, in 704, founded a collegiate church, which he dedicated to St. Andrew the Apostle. This establishment was subsequently endowed by Cynewulf, one of his successors, with considerable estates in the vicinity, in 766, and continued to flourish till 905; when, in pursuance of an edict of Edward the Elder, for the revival of religion, which, from the frequent incursions of the Danes, had almost fallen into disuse, several new bishops were consecrated by Pligmund, Archbishop of Canterbury, of whom Aldhelm, formerly abbot of Glastonbury, was appointed to preside over Wells, which was then erected into a see, having jurisdiction over the entire county of Somerset. After a succession of twelve bishops, Giso, chaplain to Edward the Confessor, was appointed to the see, to which that monarch gave the extensive possessions of Harold, Earl of Wessex, whom, with his father, Godwin, Earl of Kent, he had banished from the kingdom. Harold, during his exile, made an incursion into this part of Somersetshire, raised contributions on his former tenantry, despoiled the church of its ornaments and treasure, expelled the canons, and converted their possessions to his own use. Giso, on his return from Rome, where he had been consecrated, obtained some compensation for these injuries from the queen, who was Harold's sister; but that prince, on his restoration to favour, procured the banishment of Giso, and, upon his subsequent accession to the throne, resumed all the estates granted by Edward to the church, and greatly impoverished the see. Bishop Giso remained in exile till the Conquest, when he was reinstated; and William, in the second year of his reign, restored to the bishoprick all Harold's estates, with the exception of some small portions which had been granted to the monastery of Glastonbury, adding, in lieu of them, two other manors. Giso exerted himself in augmenting the revenue of his see; he increased the number of canons, over whom he appointed a provost, built a cloister, hall, and dormitory, and enlarged and embellished the choir of the cathedral: these buildings, however, were demolished by his successor, John de Villula, who erected a palace on their site. This prelate removed the seat of the diocese to Bath, and assumed the title of Bishop of Bath, in which he was followed by his two next successors. Great disputes arising between the inhabitants of both cities, each claiming to be regarded as the head of the diocese, the matter was at length referred to the arbitration of the bishop, who decided that the prelates should take the title of Bishops of Bath and Wells, that their election should be made by an equal number of delegates from both places, and that the ceremony of installation should take place in both churches. Reginald Fitz-Jocelyne, who was bishop in the reign of Richard I., granted the town a charter of incorporation, and made it a free borough; and during the captivity of that monarch in Austria, Savaricus, who succeeded Fitz-Jocelyne in the see, and was nearly allied to the emperor, obtained, through his influence, a promise from Richard, as a condition of his restoration, that the abbacy of Glastonbury, then vacant, should be annexed to the see of Bath and Wells: this prelate afterwards removed the seat of his diocese to Glastonbury, and assumed the title of Bishop of Glaston-

bury. After his death, in 1205, the monks under his successor, Joscelyne de Welles, petitioned the court of Rome that they might be restored to their ancient government by an abbot, which indulgence they obtained, on condition of their relinquishing to the bishop a considerable portion of their revenue, and Joscelyne assumed the style of Bishop of Bath and Wells, which the prelates of the see have ever since retained. After the death of Joscelyne, disputes arose in the election of his successors, the monks of Bath frequently exercising that right without the concurrence of the canons of Wells; but an appeal having been made to the pope, the union of the churches appears to have subsequently remained without interruption. At the time of the Reformation, the monastery of Bath was suppressed; and, though the name of the see was retained, the ecclesiastical authority, and the right of electing the bishops, were vested in the Dean and Chapter of Wells, then constituted the sole chapter of the diocese. The revenue of the monastery of Wells, at the period of its dissolution, was valued at £1939. 12. 8.

The city, which appears to have grown up around the ancient ecclesiastical establishment, and to have flourished in proportion to its prosperity, is pleasantly situated on the south side of the Mendip hills, in a fertile plain lying at their base, and is sheltered from the north winds by that mountainous range of richly-wooded eminences, and open on the south side to an extensive tract of fine meadow land. The houses are well built, and of respectable appearance; several of them are ancient, having been erected for ecclesiastical residences, and many are of modern and elegant structure. The grandeur of its cathedral, the beauty of its church, and the character of the conventual buildings, give it an air of peculiar interest. It is divided into four verderies by four principal streets, from which they take their name, and is well paved, and amply supplied with water from a public conduit of great beauty, built by Bishop Beckington, and filled by pipes leading from an aqueduct near the source of St. Andrew's well. The environs, which abound with diversified and picturesque scenery, contain many handsome seats, and afford a variety of pleasing walks and rides. Races are held annually a short distance east of the city, beyond the limits of its liberties. The principal branch of manufacture is the knitting of stockings; and at Wookey, about two miles distant, are several paper-mills, where, from the excellent quality of the water, paper of the best kind is made. The market days are Wednesday and Saturday, for provisions, and on every fourth Saturday a large market is held for corn, cattle, and cheese. The fairs are, January 6th, May 14th, July 6th, October 25th, and November 30th, for cattle, horses, and pedlary. The market-place, on the east side of the city, is a fine spacious area, on the north side of which is a handsome range of twelve houses of stone, built by Bishop Beckington, for twelve priests, now inhabited by townsmen: at the eastern extremity is an ancient gateway, communicating with the Cathedral Close, and, fronting the street, another leading to the episcopal palace, both erected by the same bishop, who intended to rebuild the whole area. Near the site of the ancient cross, which was taken down in 1780, formerly stood the city conduit, an elegant hexagonal structure in the

3 H 2

later style of English architecture, erected by the same bishop, in 1450, richly embellished with canopied niches and delicate ornaments, and crowned with a conical dome; but this being considered an obstruction, it was taken down about thirty years since, and soon afterwards removed to Stowerhead, the seat of Sir R. C. Hoare, Bart., and a very handsome one was erected on the site of the old cross: in the south-east angle is the town hall and market-house, a plain but commodious building. The charter granted by Reginald Fitz-Jocelyne was confirmed by King John, who entrusted the government to a master and commonalty of the borough of Wells. Queen Elizabeth gave the inhabitants a new charter, in the thirty-first of her reign, under which the government is vested in a mayor, recorder, seven masters, and sixteen common council-men, assisted by a town clerk, and other officers: the mayor, recorder, and the senior master, are justices of the peace within the borough. The freedom is inherited by the eldest son of a freeman, obtained by marriage with the eldest daughter, or by servitude of seven years to a freeman. The corporation hold half-yearly courts of session for all offences not capital, arising within the city, but no prisoners have been tried for several years; and a court of record, formerly held for the recovery of debts to any amount, has been discontinued. The assizes for the county are held here every alternate year, and the Epiphany and Easter quarter sessions annually. The inhabitants first exercised the elective franchise in the 23rd of Edward I., since which time they have regularly returned two members to parliament: the right of election is vested in the mayor, masters, and burgesses generally: the mayor is the returning officer.

The present ecclesiastical establishment, as re-founded by Henry VIII., on the dissolution of the monastery, consists of a bishop, dean, precentor, chancellor, three archdeacons, treasurer, subdean, forty-nine prebendaries, four priest-vicars, eight lay-vicars, organist, six choristers, and other officers. The cathedral church, dedicated to St. Andrew, is a

Arms of the Bishoprick.

magnificent cruciform structure, principally in the early style of English architecture, with partial insertions of the decorated and later styles: the foundation was laid by Wiffeline, second bishop of the diocese, and the edifice was completed and improved by Bishop Joscelyne, in 1239. The west front is a striking and superb combination of stately grandeur and splendid embellishment; the whole of it, together with the buttresses, by which it is divided into compartments, is replete with elaborate sculpture, from the base to the summit, in successive tiers of richly-canopied shrines, containing the statues of kings, popes, bishops, cardinals, and abbots; the mullions of the west window and the lower stages of the western towers are similarly enriched; the canopies of the niches in which these figures are enshrined are supported by slender-shafted pillars of polished marble, and the intermediate spaces between the several series are filled with architectural ornaments of elegant de-

sign and appropriate character. In the upper range of the central compartment are the statues of the twelve Apostles, in a series of lofty niches separated by slender shafts, and in the range immediately beneath them are figures of the hierarchs, below which is a sculptured representation of the Resurrection, in alto relievo. The entrance, which is through a deeply-recessed arch, is flanked by the western towers, of which the lower stages are comprised in the general design of the front, and the upper, which are wreathed with pierced parapets, are relieved by fine windows, and with lofty canopies rising from the buttresses, and terminating in crocketed finials. The central tower, which is one hundred and sixty feet from the base, is crowned with a pierced parapet of elegant design, and decorated with lofty angular pinnacles surmounted with vanes, and with smaller pinnacles in the intervals: though of large dimensions, it has an airy appearance, from the proportionate size and elegance of the windows. The interior displays some specimens of the early English style, which are of unfrequent occurrence, and equally remarkable for simplicity and elegance. Of this character are the nave and transepts: the former, one hundred and ninety feet in length, is separated from the aisles by a beautiful range of clustered columns and finely-pointed arches, above which are a triforium of lancet-shaped arches, and a fine range of clerestory windows, in which elegant tracery in the later English style has been inserted; the roof is finely groined, and the great west window is embellished with ancient stained glass of great brilliancy. The choir, which is in the decorated style, and of very elegant character, is one hundred and eight feet long from the organ-screen to the altar, beyond which is the Lady chapel, fifty-five feet in length, both forming parts of one general arrangement, which, for beauty of design, and richness of architectural embellishment, is perhaps unequalled; the piers and arches are of graceful proportion, the roof is elaborately groined, and the windows are of beautiful symmetry, and enriched with tracery of peculiar delicacy. There are numerous chapels in various parts of the cathedral, some of which are enclosed with screens of beautiful design, and in one is an ancient clock, removed from Glastonbury, with an astronomical dial, and a train of figures of knights in armour, which, by the machinery, are moved round in circular procession: in the south transept is an ancient font of the same date as that part of the building. Many of the details of this splendid structure are of singular character, and of exquisite beauty, and, whether taken as a whole, or examined in its several parts, it ranks high among the ecclesiastical edifices of the kingdom. There are many interesting and ancient monuments of the bishops who were interred within its walls, among which are, the tomb of Bishop Beckington, in a chapel in the presbytery, with his effigy in alabaster; the gravestone of Bishop Joscelyne, in the middle of the choir, marking the spot where an elegant marble monument, bearing his effigy in brass, formerly stood; that of King Ina, who was interred in the centre of the nave, and many others. The cloisters form three sides of a quadrangle south of the cathedral: the western range, in which are the school and the treasury, was built by Bishop Beckington, who also began the south side, which was finished by Thomas Henry, treasurer of Wells, and archdeacon

of Cornwall; and the eastern range, containing a chapel and a library, was erected by Bishop Bubwith. The chapter-house is an elegant octagonal structure, of which each side measures fifty feet : the roof, which is finely groined, is supported on an elegant clustered column of Purbeck marble in the centre, and the interior is lighted by windows of handsome design : beneath it is a crypt of good character, with a roof displaying a fine specimen of plain groining, from which a staircase of singular construction leads into the chapter-room, and to several other parts of the adjacent buildings. To the south of the cathedral is the episcopal palace, an ancient castellated mansion, surrounded with walls, enclosing nearly seven acres of ground, and defended by a deep moat, which is supplied from the water of St. Andrew's well : on the north side is a venerable gateway tower leading over a bridge into the outer court, on the east side of which is the palace, containing several spacious and magnificent rooms, and a chapel : opposite the entrance are the remains of the great hall, one hundred and twenty feet long, and seventy feet wide, now in ruins, having been demolished in the reign of Edward VI., for the sake of the materials. The vicar's close was originally built by Walter de Hull, canon of Wells, and archdeacon of Bath, and improved by Bishop Ralph de Salopia, in 1348, who erected a new college for the residence of the vicars and choristers, which he endowed with lands of his own, in addition to what were given by Walter de Hull: it was subsequently enlarged, and its endowment augmented, by Bishop Beckington, who erected the gateways, of which that on the east, adjoining the cathedral buildings, has a long gallery communicating with the church and the vicar's close, with a large flight of steps at each end : at the south end is a hall with a buttery, and other conveniences, under which is an arched gateway : at the north end are the chapel and library, and on the east and west sides are handsome ranges of dwelling-houses. This college, the revenue of which, in the 26th of Henry VIII., was £72. 10. 9½., escaped the general dissolution, and was afterwards refounded by Queen Elizabeth, who appointed the number of vicars to be not less than fourteen, nor more than twenty. The deanery is a spacious and handsome structure, erected by Dean Gunthorp, in allusion to whose name the walls are ornamented with several guns, carved in stone : in this mansion the founder entertained Henry VII., on his return from the West of England. Near the deanery is the west gate, a plain ancient edifice, forming the principal entrance into the city from Bath.

The city comprises only the in-parish of St. Cuthbert, which surrounds the cathedral precincts : the several hamlets, which are without the limits of the city, extending for seven miles in circuit, form the outparish of St. Cuthbert. The living is a vicarage, rated in the king's books at £33. 13. 6., and in the patronage of the Dean and Chapter, who have ecclesiastical jurisdiction over the liberty of St. Andrew, the in-parish being subject to the bishop, and the out-parish to the dean. The church of St. Cuthbert is a spacious and handsome structure, in the later style of English architecture, with a lofty square embattled tower, strengthened with angular buttresses, and crowned with pinnacles, forming one of the most beautiful specimens of a tower in that style of architecture.

Though of large dimensions, it assumes a degree of lightness from the judicious distribution of its ornaments, and the relief afforded by niches of elegant design ; the belfry windows are lofty, and, from the beauty of their composition, give to the tower above the roof the character of a magnificent lantern, and the west door, and the large window over it, are also richly embellished. The interior consists of a nave, aisles, and choir, and contains several sepulchral chapels, among which are traces of an earlier style of architecture than the church : the walls are adorned with several ancient monuments and mural tablets. There are places of worship for Baptists, Independents, and Wesleyan Methodists. The United charity school, founded in 1654, by Mrs. Mary Barkham, Mr. Adrian Hickes, and Mr. Philip Hodges, which last erected a school-house, is endowed with property producing above £500 per annum, which is appropriated to the instruction of thirty-four boys and twenty girls in reading, writing, and arithmetic, of which number twenty of each sex are completely clothed ; the boys, on leaving the school, are apprenticed, with a premium of £10, and an additional sum of £10 on the completion of the fourth year ; at the expiration of their term, upon producing a certificate of good conduct, each receives a present of £5 : the girls are also taught needlework, and placed out in service. On the north side of the churchyard is an hospital, founded and endowed by Bishop Bubwith, who died in 1424, for twelve aged men, twelve aged women, and a chaplain, to which six more aged men were added, in 1607, by Bishop Still, who augmented the endowment for that purpose ; including the previous augmentation, by Bishops Beckington and Bourne, the present income is about £400 per annum: the inmates receive, in summer, a weekly allowance of four shillings and sixpence, and in winter five shillings each, with a supply of coal, clothes, and other necessaries : the buildings are neat, and comprise separate apartments for each, with a common room, and a small chapel at the east end. The almshouses in Priests' Row were founded, in 1614, by Mr. Henry Llewellyn, who endowed them for six aged women, who have each two rooms, an allowance of five shillings and sixpence per week, £1 every two years for clothes, and five shillings yearly for coal : the income arising from the endowment is about £170 per annum, from which fund also, the same weekly allowance is paid to four aged widows not in the almshouses, and an annual payment of twelve shillings and sixpence made to all, on St. Thomas' day. An almshouse for decayed burgesses was founded, in 1638, by Mr. Walter Brick, who placed it under the inspection of the bishop. Almshouses were founded, in 1711, by Mr. Archibald Harper, who endowed them with property, now producing about £70 per annum, for five decayed wool-combers of the city : the buildings comprise five apartments for the men, with a committee-room for the meeting of the trustees, which, at other times, is appropriated as a common room for the inmates, who receive each five shillings per week during the summer, and six shillings during the winter : there are numerous other charitable bequests and funds, at the disposal of the corporation, for distribution among the poor. In the verdery of Southover are the remains of the priory of St. John, founded in 1206, by Hugh, Archdeacon of Wells, afterwards

Bishop of Lincoln, and subsequently augmented by Bishop Joscelyne; the revenue at the dissolution was £41. 3. 6.: the buildings have been converted into a wool-comber's shop. The neighbourhood, especially on the side of the Mendip hills, abounds with geological interest. Among the eminent prelates of the see were Cardinal Wolsey and Archbishop Laud; the celebrated historian, Polydore Virgil, was archdeacon in the sixteenth century; and the learned and pious Dr. George Bull, Bishop of St. David's, was born in this city, in the year 1634; he died in 1709.

WELNETHAM (GREAT), a parish in the hundred of THEDWESTRY, county of SUFFOLK, 3½ miles (S. E. by S.) from Bury-St. Edmunds, containing 399 inhabitants. The living is a rectory, in the archdeaconry of Sudbury, and diocese of Norwich, rated in the king's books at £9. 15. 7½., and in the patronage of Sir H. E. Bunbury, Bart. Here was a priory of Crouched, or Crossed, friars, subordinate to the principal house of that order, near the Tower of London.

WELNETHAM (LITTLE), a parish in the hundred of THEDWESTRY, county of SUFFOLK, 3½ miles (S. E.) from Bury-St. Edmunds, containing 176 inhabitants. The living is a discharged rectory, in the archdeaconry of Sudbury, and diocese of Norwich, rated in the king's books at £4. 13. 4., and in the patronage of Sir Charles Davers, Bart. The church is dedicated to St. Mary.

WELNEY, a chapelry in the parish of UPWELL, partly in the hundred of WISBEACH, Isle of ELY, county of CAMBRIDGE, and partly in the hundred of CLACKCLOSE, county of NORFOLK, 8 miles (E. S. E.) from March, containing 706 inhabitants. Roman coins have been found here in urns, &c. turned up by the plough.

WELTON, a parish in the wapentake of LAWRESS, parts of LINDSEY, county of LINCOLN, 6 miles (N. N. E.) from Lincoln, containing 484 inhabitants. The living is a discharged vicarage, in the peculiar jurisdiction of the Dean and Chapter of Lincoln, rated in the king's books at £7. 6. 8., endowed with £200 private benefaction, and £200 royal bounty, and in the patronage of the five Prebendaries of Welton in the Cathedral Church of Lincoln. The church is dedicated to St. Mary. There is a place of worship for Wesleyan Methodists.

WELTON, a parish in the hundred of FAWSLEY, county of NORTHAMPTON, 2½ miles (N. N. E.) from Daventry, containing 567 inhabitants. The living is a discharged vicarage, in the archdeaconry of Northampton, and diocese of Peterborough, rated in the king's books at £7, endowed with £200 private benefaction, and £200 royal bounty, and in the patronage of the Crown. The church is dedicated to St. Andrew. The Grand Junction and Union canals meet at the south-eastern extremity of the parish, and the latter is previously crossed by Watling-street, which skirts the eastern boundary. The poor children are taught for £8 a year, paid from the receipts of the charity lands; and a Sunday school is supported with £7. 10. per annum from the same fund.

WELTON, a township in the parish of OVINGHAM, eastern division of TINDALE ward, county of NORTHUMBERLAND, 9¼ miles (E. N. E.) from Hexham, containing 67 inhabitants. This was the seat of King

Oswy, and the place where the kings Peada and Segbert received the rites of baptism from Finan, Bishop of Lindisfarne: the Roman wall passed in the vicinity.

WELTON, a parish in the wapentake of HOWDENSHIRE, East riding of the county of YORK, comprising the chapelry of Melton and the township of Welton, and containing 683 inhabitants, of which number 576 are in the township of Welton, 3½ miles (S. E.) from South Cave. The living is a vicarage, in the jurisdiction of the peculiar court of Howdenshire, rated in the king's books at £25, and in the patronage of the Crown. The church, dedicated to St. Helen, is supposed to have been built by William Rufus. There is a place of worship for Wesleyan Methodists. A National school has been established here.

WELTON in the MARSH, a parish in the Wold division of the wapentake of CANDLESHOE, parts of LINDSEY, county of LINCOLN, 6 miles (E. N. E.) from Spilsby, containing, with Boothby, 355 inhabitants. The living is a discharged rectory, in the archdeaconry and diocese of Lincoln, rated in the king's books at £14. 8. 9., and in the patronage of — Massingbard, Esq. The church is dedicated to St. Martin.

WELTON le WOLD, a parish in the Wold division of the hundred of LOUTH-ESKE, parts of LINDSEY, county of LINCOLN, 3¾ miles (W.) from Louth, containing 144 inhabitants. The living is a rectory, in the archdeaconry and diocese of Lincoln, rated in the king's books at £11. 12. 1., and in the patronage of the Crown. The church is dedicated to St. Martin.

WELWICK, a parish in the southern division of the wapentake of HOLDERNESS, East riding of the county of YORK, 2 miles (S. E. by E.) from Patrington, containing 410 inhabitants. The living is a discharged vicarage, in the archdeaconry of the East riding, and diocese of York, rated in the king's books at £6. 13. 4., endowed with £400 royal bounty, and in the patronage of the Crown. The church, dedicated to St. Mary, is principally in the decorated style of English architecture, and contains the remains of a once splendid monument, said to have been removed from Burstall abbey, and bearing marks of high antiquity. There are places of worship for the Society of Friends and Wesleyan Methodists.

WELWYN, a parish in the hundred of BROADWATER, county of HERTFORD, 8 miles (W. N. W.) from Hertford, containing 1287 inhabitants. The living is a rectory, in the archdeaconry of Huntingdon, and diocese of Lincoln, rated in the king's books at £21, and in the patronage of the Warden and Fellows of All Souls' College, Oxford. The church is dedicated to St. Mary. Over the altar is a piece of embroidery, with a suitable inscription, by Lady Betty Young, wife of Dr. Edward Young, author of the "Night Thoughts," who was many years rector of this parish: he died on Good Friday, 1765, and was buried by the side of his lady, under the communion-table. There are places of worship for Huntingtonians and Wesleyan Methodists. The village is situated on the small river Mimram, and on the great north road from London to York; it consists of one principal street, with a smaller leading to Stevenage, and contains several genteel residences, besides which there are many others in the immediate vicinity. In Mill-lane is a fine chalybeate spring, formerly in considerable repute: here is also an assembly-room. Dr. Young built and endowed a school for sixteen poor boys, who are clothed and instructed in reading, writing, and accounts, and in the duties of the Christian religion, according to the principles of the established church. About fifty other boys are educated in a National school supported by subscription.

WEM, a parish partly in the hundred of PIMHILL, but chiefly in the Whitchurch division of the hundred of BRADFORD (North), county of SALOP, comprising the market town of Wem, the chapelries of Edstaston and Newtown, and the townships of Aston, Cotton, Horton, Lacon, Lowe with Ditches, Northwood, Soulton, Tilley, and ·Wolverley, and containing 3608 inhabitants, of which number, 1555 are in the township of Wem, 11 miles (N. by E.) from Shrewsbury, and 172 (N.W.) from London. It has been conjectured by Horsley that this place occupies the site of the ancient *Rutunium*, but there is no authentic account of it prior to the Conquest, at which period William Pandulph, who held twenty-eight manors of Earl Roger de Montgomery, made it the head of a barony, and fixed his residence here; and, on the forfeiture of the estates of Robert de Belesme, son of Earl Roger, for rebellion in the reign of Henry I., Pandulph held it immediately of the crown, and thence became a baron of the realm. After continuing for several generations in this family, and passing through the hands of other proprietors, the barony was, in 1665, purchased by Daniel Wycherley, father of the poet, and by him sold to the unprincipled Judge Jeffreys, who was created Baron of Wem in 1685, being the first who enjoyed that dignity by patent, but at the death of his son the title became extinct. Wem was the first town in the county which declared for the parliament, in 1643, in which year, a party of the king's troops, under Lord Capel, attempted to capture it by storm, but were repulsed by the small garrison, aided, it is said, by the active exertions of the women : in the following year it was reconnoitred by Prince Rupert, who deemed it unworthy of any effort to capture. Under the government of Major-General Mytton, the garrison plundered the possessions of the neighbouring royalists, and the booty brought by them into the town caused it to flourish at that time more than at any antecedent or subsequent period. In 1677, it suffered from a dreadful fire, which consumed the church, market-house, and whole ranges of building, destroying property of the value of upwards of £23,000.

The town, situated in a level district, on the northern bank of the river Roden, consists principally of one spacious street, called High-street, from which several smaller streets and lanes diverge, and is well supplied with good water. There are no manufactures, but tanning and malting is carried on to a very considerable extent. The Ellesmere and Chester canal skirts the north-western boundary of the parish. The market was granted by King John, in 1205, to be held on Sunday, at that time a usual circumstance; since the 24th of Edward III., it has been held on Thursday. The market-house, on the south side of High-street, is a small neat edifice of brick, with stone quoins, commenced in 1702, but not completed until 1728; in the room over it the courts leet are held. The fairs are on March 4th and May 6th, for linen cloth; May 20th and June 29th, for cattle; and September 30th and November 22nd, chiefly for swine. Wem appears to have

been incorporated, though at what period the charter was granted is not known; but, from a copy of court roll, dated 9th of Edward VI., it must have been prior to that period : it never sent members to parliament. The principal officers are two bailiffs, appointed annually at the court leet held after Michaelmas, one by the lord's steward, and the other by the borough jury. Their authority is now very limited, their duties consisting chiefly in the returning of the jury to attend the steward at courts leet, in preventing fraud by the use of false weights and measures, and in being present at public proclamations; but they do not possess magisterial powers. The burgesses are the holders of burgage-tenements, which are about eighty in number. The living is a rectory, in the archdeaconry of Salop, and diocese of Lichfield and Coventry, rated in the king's books at £26. 4. 4½., and in the patronage of Lord Darlington. The church, dedicated to St. Peter and St. Paul, is a spacious edifice with a lofty tower : it appears to have been built at an early period, but the subsequent alterations and repairs it has undergone have left little of the original style. An elevated spot at the north-west corner of the churchyard, now converted into gardens, is supposed to have been the site of the ancient castle. Baptists and Presbyterians have each a place of worship. The free grammar school, in Noble-street, was founded and endowed for three masters, in 1650, by Thomas Adams, Esq., who was born here in 1586, and became a wealthy trader and active magistrate of the city of London, having been created a baronet in 1660. Its management is vested in feoffees, who appoint the masters; and, to increase the original endowment, the statutes of the founder direct that the school shall not be open to the children of those parents who, having the ability, do not contribute towards its support: several subsequent bequests have been added : the present school premises were erected in 1670. This school enjoys the benefit of two exhibitions, founded by Mr. Careswell, for an account of which see BRIDGE-NORTH. Mr. John Ireland, author of "Hogarth Illustrated," was born in this parish.

WEMBDON, a parish in the northern division of the hundred of PETHERTON, county of SOMERSET, 1½ mile (N. W.) from Bridg-water, containing 293 inhabitants. The living is a discharged vicarage, in the archdeaconry of Taunton, and diocese of Bath and Wells, rated in the king's books at £9. 16. 10., and in the patronage of C. K. Tynte, Esq. The church is dedicated to St. George. The river Parret is navigable on the east.

WEMBURY, a parish in the hundred of PLYMPTON, county of DEVON, 5¼ miles (S. by W.) from Earl's Plympton, containing 564 inhabitants. The living is a perpetual curacy, in the archdeaconry of Totness, and diocese of Exeter, endowed with £200 royal bounty, and £1400 parliamentary grant, and in the patronage of the Dean and Canons of Windsor. The chapel is dedicated to St. Werburgh. The parish is bounded on the west and south by the English channel, and on the east by the river Yealm. Here is an almshouse for ten poor people, founded and endowed, in 1625, by Sir Warwick Hele.

WEMBWORTHY, a parish in the hundred of NORTH TAWTON with WINKLEY, county of DEVON, 3½ miles (S. S. W.) from Chulmleigh, containing 349 inhabitants. The living is a rectory, in the archdeaconry of Barnstaple, and diocese of Exeter, rated in the king's books at £11. 13. 4., and in the patronage of the Rev. R. T. Johnson. The church is dedicated to St. Michael.

WENDLEBURY, a parish in the hundred of PLOUGHLEY, county of OXFORD, 2½ miles (S.W.) from Bicester, containing 200 inhabitants. The living is a rectory, in the archdeaconry and diocese of Oxford, rated in the king's books at £11. 9. 4½., and in the patronage of the Dean and Canons of Christ Church, Oxford. The church is dedicated to St. Giles.

WENDLING, a parish in the hundred of LAUN-DITCH, county of NORFOLK, 4¼ miles (W.) from East Dereham, containing 351 inhabitants. The living is a perpetual curacy, in the archdeaconry and diocese of Norwich, endowed with £600 royal bounty, and in the patronage of T. W. Coke, Esq. The church is dedicated to St. Peter and St. Paul. An abbey of Premonstratensian canons, in honour of the Blessed Virgin Mary, was founded here before 1267, by William de Wendling, which at the dissolution had a revenue of £55. 18. 4.: part of the church was lately standing, but it has been removed for the purpose of mending the roads.

WENDON-LOFTS, a parish in the hundred of UTTLESFORD, county of ESSEX, 5¼ miles (W.byN.) from Saffron-Walden, containing 67 inhabitants. The living is a discharged rectory, annexed to the vicarage of Elmdon, in the jurisdiction of the Commissary of Essex and Herts, concurrently with the Consistorial Court of the Bishop of London, rated in the king's books at £9. 10. 10. The church is dedicated to S. Dunstan.

WENDONS-AMBO, a parish in the hundred of UTTLESFORD, county of ESSEX, 2½ miles (S. W. by W.) from Saffron-Walden, containing 336 inhabitants. The living is a discharged vicarage, with the rectory of Little Wendon united, in the jurisdiction of the Commissary of Essex and Herts, concurrently with the Consistorial Court of the Bishop of London, rated jointly in the king's books at £17, and in the patronage of the Marquis of Bristol. The church is dedicated to St. Mary.

WENDOVER, an unincorporated borough, market town, and parish, in the hundred of AYLESBURY, county of BUCKINGHAM, 23 miles (S. E. by S.) from Buckingham, and 35 (N. W. by W.) from London, containing 1602 inhabitants. The manor was given by Henry II. to Faramus de Boulogne, and it was subsequently in the possession of the Fiennes; Sir John Molins; Alice Perrers, a favourite of Edward III.; Thomas Holland, Earl of Kent; Edward, Duke of York, in 1388 (between which period and 1564, it was held either by the queen or some branch of the royal family); and Sir Francis Knollys and Catherine his wife: in 1660 it was purchased by the Hampden family, and continued in their possession until the decease of the late lord. The town, situated at the foot of the Chiltern hills, near the entrance to the Vale of Aylesbury, is indifferently built, containing but few good houses; the inhabitants are well supplied with water from wells. Many of the females are engaged in lace-making. A branch of the Grand Junction canal extends to the town, and affords a medium of conveyance for coal from Staffordshire; it passes through a reservoir in the neighbourhood,

extending over seventy acres. A market was granted in 1403, and confirmed in 1464, with two fairs: the former is on Monday; and the latter are held May 13th and October 2nd, chiefly for cattle. Wendover, which is a borough by prescription, returned members to parliament from the 28th of Edward I. to the 2nd of Edward II.; at which period the right ceased, and, after a discontinuance of more than four hundred years, was restored through the exertions of Mr. Hakeville, a barrister; who, on examining the parliamentary writs in the Tower, in the 21st of James I., discovered that Amersham, Wendover, and Great Marlow, had all sent representatives. Petitions were accordingly presented from these places; and, notwithstanding the opposition of the monarch, who declared that "he was troubled with too many burgesses already," the commons decreed the renewal of the privilege. The right of election is vested in housekeepers not receiving alms: the number of voters is about one hundred and thirty; and the constables, chosen at the court leet of the manor, are the returning officers: the influence of Lord Carrington is predominant. Hampden, the celebrated patriot, represented this borough in five successive parliaments. Petty sessions are held once a fortnight, and courts leet and baron occasionally. The living is a discharged vicarage, in the archdeaconry of Buckingham, and diocese of Lincoln, rated in the king's books at £12. 16. 1., and in the patronage of the Crown. The church, which is dedicated to St. Mary, stands about a quarter of a mile from the town: some remains of a chapel, dedicated to St. John, are still visible. There are places of worship for Baptists and Independents. A school for the instruction of twenty poor children was endowed, in 1723, by William Hill, with £20 per annum. A National school, established in 1816, is supported by voluntary contributions, and held over the market-house in High-street. Roger de Wendover, historiographer to Henry II.; and Richard, Bishop of Rochester, in the reign of Henry III.; were natives of this place.

WENDRON, a parish in the hundred of KERRIER, county of CORNWALL, 2½ miles (N. E. by N.) from Helston, containing, with the borough of Helston, which is in this parish, 6864 inhabitants. The living is a vicarage, with the perpetual curacy of Helston annexed, in the archdeaconry of Cornwall, and diocese of Exeter, rated in the king's books at £26. 19. 4½., and in the patronage of the Provost and Fellows of Queen's College, Oxford. The church is dedicated to St. Wendron. There is a small endowed school for teaching children to read, also two Sunday schools.

WENDY, a parish in the hundred of ARMINGFORD, county of CAMBRIDGE, 6¼ miles (N. N. W.) from Royston, containing 134 inhabitants. The living is a discharged vicarage, with the perpetual curacy of Shingay annexed, in the archdeaconry and diocese of Ely, rated in the king's books at £5. 10. 10., and in the patronage of Lord Sondes.

WENHAM (GREAT), a parish in the hundred of SAMFORD, county of SUFFOLK, 4½ miles (S.E.) from Hadleigh, containing 205 inhabitants. The living is a discharged rectory, in the archdeaconry of Suffolk, and diocese of Norwich, rated in the king's books at £8. 13. 4. The Rev. George H. Deane was patron in 1819. The church is dedicated to St. John.

WENHAM (LITTLE), a parish in the hundred of SAMFORD, county of SUFFOLK, 5 miles (S. E. by E.) from Hadleigh, containing 90 inhabitants. The living is a discharged rectory, annexed to that of Capel St. Mary, in the archdeaconry of Suffolk, and diocese of Norwich, rated in the king's books at £5. 8. 11½. Here are the remains of an old castle, which, from bearing the date 1569, appears to have been either built or repaired in that year; it has been converted into a granary.

WENHASTON, a parish in the hundred of BLYTH-ING, county of SUFFOLK, 2¼ miles (E. S. E.) from Halesworth, containing, with the hamlet of Mells, 887 inhabitants. The living is a discharged vicarage, in the archdeaconry of Suffolk, and diocese of Norwich, rated in the king's books at £6. 0. 10., and in the patronage of the Crown. The church is dedicated to St. Peter.

WENLOCK (LITTLE), a parish within the liberties of the borough of WENLOCK, county of SALOP, 3¼ miles (S.) from Wellington, containing 965 inhabitants. The living is a rectory, in the archdeaconry of Salop, and diocese of Hereford, rated in the king's books at £11.13.4., and in the patronage of Lord Forester. The church, dedicated to St. Lawrence, has lately received an addition of five hundred free sittings, the Incorporated Society for the enlargement of churches and chapels having granted £200 towards defraying the expense. There are coal and iron mines, with extensive quarries of limestone, in the parish.

WENLOCK (MUCH), a borough, market town, and parish, having separate jurisdiction, and the head of a liberty, in the county of SALOP, 12 miles (S. E.) from Shrewsbury, and 148 (N. W.) from London, containing 2200 inhabitants. This town is of considerable antiquity; its British name was *Llan Meilien*, or "St. Milburgh's Church;" and in the Monasticon it is denominated *Winnica*, or "the windy place." Its early importance was derived from the establishment of a convent, about 680, by Milburga, daughter of King Merwald, and niece of Wolphere, King of Mercia, who presided as abbess, and at her death was interred here. Having been destroyed by the Danes, it was restored by Leofric, Earl of Mercia, in the time of Edward the Confessor, after which it fell into decay. It was rebuilt, or repaired, by Roger de Montgomery, soon after the Conquest, who largely endowed it, converted it into a priory for Cluniac monks, and dedicated it to St. Milburga: at the dissolution, the revenue was valued at £434. 1. 2. The ruins, which are situated on the south side of the town, are extensive, and present every variety of the most finished specimens of the latest Norman, and the early and decorated styles of English, architecture. Of the church, the south transept is in the most perfect state: the end and side walls, including the triforium and clerestory windows, are standing, and exhibit the purest specimens of elegant design and elaborate execution; one wall of the north transept also is remaining, in which

Corporate Seal.

is a continuation of the same details: the bases of the four massive piers which supported the tower, and of those which separated the aisles from the nave and choir, are still uncovered by turf, and mark out the ground-plan of a cathedral, which, for its magnificence and elegant decoration, scarcely had its equal in the kingdom. Three beautiful Norman arches, highly ornamented, form an entrance to the chapter-house, the walls of which are embellished with successive series of intersecting arches, with clustered columns of exquisite design. Two of the cloisters also remain in a very perfect state; the one of the lighter decorated style, with a lofty ceiling, richly groined, and ornamented with slender shafts terminating in corbels on the walls; the other of the more massive, but finished Norman style, with low clustered pillars ranged upon circular plinths.

The town is situated in a pleasant vale, and consists principally of one long street, from which another diverges at right angles; the houses are in general of brick, and well built, several of them being modern and handsome, with many cottages of stone, with thatched roofs; the streets are Macadamized, but not lighted; and the inhabitants are supplied with water by pumps attached to the houses. In the time of Richard II. this place was noted for lime quarries and copper mines; the former are still extensive; the latter are not now worked. The market, originally granted to the prior and brethren, is on Monday: fairs are held on the second Monday in March, and May 12th, for horned cattle, horses, and sheep, and for hiring servants; July 5th, for sheep; and October 17th and December 4th, for horned cattle, horses, sheep, and swine. Much-Wenlock enjoys many peculiar privileges, with a jurisdiction extending over seventeen parishes, and the extra-parochial district of Posenall, which constitute the liberty. By virtue of a charter of incorporation granted by Edward IV., in the seventh year of his reign, "to the liege men and residents of the town of Wenlock," and confirmed and extended by subsequent sovereigns, the corporation consists of a bailiff, recorder, and bailiff's peers: the bailiff, recorder, and two of the peers are justices of the peace, and, with the exception of the recorder, who holds office for life, are elected annually by a jury of burgesses on Michaelmas-day: there are also a coroner, treasurer, town clerk, serjeant at mace, and subordinate officers. They are empowered to hold a court of common pleas, every Tuesday fortnight; a court of assize for trying criminals, with the power of life and death, now in part discontinued; a court of record, for the recovery of debts to any amount, at which the bailiff and the recorder preside; as well as a court of requests, under the 22nd of George III., for the recovery of debts under 40s., the jurisdiction of which extends over the parishes of Broseley, Benthall, Madeley-Barrow, Linley, Willey, Little Wenlock, and the extra-parochial place called Posenall: manorial courts are held at Easter and Michaelmas; at the latter constables are appointed. The guildhall is an ancient building of timber frame-work, resting on piazzas, more remarkable for its antiquity than the beauty of its architecture. The elective franchise was granted, in 1478, by Edward IV., when it returned one member; at present it sends two. The right of election is vested in the burgesses: the number of voters is from five to six hundred, and the bailiff is the returning officer: the influence of Lord Forester and Sir W. W. Wynn is predominant. This borough was the first that possessed the right of parliamentary representation by virtue of a charter from the crown. The freedom is obtained by birth after the father has been sworn, and is also conferred upon residents, by election from a common hall.

Wenlock is the head of a deanery: the living is a discharged vicarage, with the perpetual curacies of Burton and Benthall annexed, in the archdeaconry of Salop, and diocese of Hereford, rated in the king's books at £12. 9. 7., and in the patronage of Sir W. W. Wynn, Bart. The church, which is dedicated to the Holy Trinity, is a venerable structure, with a square tower surmounted by a spire: it partakes, in a very remote degree, of the style of the abbey, being partly of the Norman, and partly of the decorated English, style: the interior consists of a chancel, nave, and aisles, separated by clustered piers and obtusely pointed arches. A small theological library, left by one of the vicars for the use of the clergy, has, within the last forty years, been extended by subscription into a circulating library for the use of the inhabitants. There is a place of worship for Wesleyan Methodists. The free school, endowed with the interest of £200, in 1778, by the Rev. Francis Southern, and with other small benefactions, is further supported by voluntary contributions: twelve boys are educated on the foundation. There are almshouses for four poor widows.

WENN (ST.), a parish in the hundred of PYDER, county of CORNWALL, 4 miles (N.E. by E.) from St. Columb-Major, containing 589 inhabitants. The living is a vicarage, in the archdeaconry of Cornwall, and diocese of Exeter, rated in the king's books at £16. 6. 8. P. Rashleigh, Esq. was patron in 1810. At Tregonetha, in this parish, are fairs for cattle on April 25th and August 1st.

WENNINGTON, a parish in the hundred of CHAFFORD, county of ESSEX, 2 miles (N. by W.) from Purfleet, containing 128 inhabitants. The living is a rectory, in the archdeaconry of Essex, and diocese of London, rated in the king's books at £8, and in the patronage of the Bishop of London. The church is dedicated to St. Peter. There are extensive marshes in this parish, stretching southward and westward to the Thames.

WENNINGTON, a township in the parish of MELLING, hundred of LONSDALE, south of the sands, county palatine of LANCASTER, 6½ miles (S. by E.) from Kirkby-Lonsdale, containing 160 inhabitants.

WENSLEY, a parish in the western division of the wapentake of HANG, North riding of the county of YORK, comprising the chapelry of Bolton Castle, and the townships of Leybourn, Preston under Scar, Redmire, and Wensley, and containing 2182 inhabitants, of which number, 317 are in the township of Wensley, 3 miles (N.W. by W.) from Middleham. The living is a rectory, in the archdeaconry of Richmond, and diocese of Chester, rated in the king's books at £49, 9. 9½., and in the patronage of Lord Bolton. The church is dedicated to the Holy Trinity. The river Ure runs through the parish, and is crossed by an ancient bridge of three or four arches, which was erected about the commencement of the fourteenth century, and has been lately widened and repaired, at the expense of the riding.

Above Wensley are the ruins of Bolton castle, built in the reign of Richard II., by Richard, Lord Scroop, Lord High Chancellor of England. According to Leland it consisted of four principal towers, and was eighteen years in building, the expense having amounted to one thousand marks yearly, or £12,000 sterling in the whole. The timber was brought from Inglewood Forest, in Cumberland, the conveyance of which was the chief cause of the great expense incurred in the building.

WENTNOR, a parish in the hundred of PURSLOW, county of SALOP, 5½ miles (N.E. by E.) from Bishop's Castle, containing 583 inhabitants. The living is a rectory, in the archdeaconry of Salop, and diocese of Hereford, rated in the king's books at £7. 2. 11., and in the patronage of the Dean and Canons of Christ Church, Oxford. The church is dedicated to St. Michael.

WENTWORTH, or WINGFORD, a parish in the southern division of the hundred of WITCHFORD, Isle of ELY, county of CAMBRIDGE, 4½ miles (W.S.W.) from Ely, containing 139 inhabitants. The living is a rectory, in the peculiar jurisdiction of the Bishop of Ely, rated in the king's books at £10, and in the patronage of the Dean and Chapter of Ely.

WENTWORTH, a chapelry in the parish of WATH upon DEARN, northern division of the wapentake of STRAFFORTH and TICKHILL, West riding of the county of YORK, 5½ miles (N.W. by N.) from Rotherham, containing 1269 inhabitants. The living is a perpetual curacy, in the archdeaconry and diocese of York, endowed with £400 private benefaction, and £400 royal bounty, and in the patronage of Earl Fitzwilliam. The chapel, dedicated to the Holy Trinity, is principally in the later style of English architecture. A school was erected here, in 1716, by Thomas Wentworth, who endowed it with land and an annuity of £8, towards teaching and clothing fifty poor children: the master occupies the school-house and land rent-free, and receives, besides the above named annuity, one of £12 from Earl Fitzwilliam, and another of £2 left by Ann Pickles, in 1669.

WEOBLEY, an unincorporated borough, market town, and parish, in the hundred of STRETFORD, county of HEREFORD, 12 miles (N.W.) from Hereford, and 145 (W.N.W.) from London, containing 739 inhabitants. This ancient town consists of one principal street on the main road from Hereford to Knighton. The market is on Thursday; and fairs are held on Holy Thursday and three weeks after. A manorial court is held annually in October, the jurisdiction of which extends to the recovery of debts under 40s. The petty sessions for the hundred take place here. The elective franchise was granted in the reign of Edward I., and renewed, or confirmed, by Charles I.: the right of election is vested in "the inhabitants of the ancient vote houses of twenty shillings per annum, resident during forty days previous to the election, and paying scot and lot, also in such owners of ancient vote houses, paying scot and lot, as shall be resident in such houses at the time of election:" the number of voters is about ninety-three; the constables are the returning officers, and the influence of the Marquis of Bath is predominant. The living is a discharged vicarage, in the archdeaconry and diocese of Hereford, rated in the king's books at £9. 1., endowed with £200 private benefaction, and £200 royal bounty, and in the patronage of the Bishop of Hereford. The church is dedicated to St. Peter and St. Paul. The free grammar school was founded in 1655, by William Crother, citizen of London, for the education of children born in the parishes of Weobley, Wormesley, and in the village of Wooton, in the parish of King's Pion, and endowed with £20 per annum for the master, chargeable on Wormesly Grange and another estate in the township of Wooton, in the parish of King's Pion, county of Hereford; he likewise bequeathed £100 to build a school-house. A National school for boys and girls is supported principally by voluntary contributions. On the south side of the town are the remains of an ancient castle, which was taken by Stephen in the war between him and the Empress Matilda, for whom it had been kept by William Talbot.

WEONARD'S (ST.), a parish in the lower division of the hundred of Wormelow, county of Hereford, 7¼ miles (W. by N.) from Ross, containing 642 inhabitants. The living is a perpetual curacy, annexed to the vicarage of Lugwardine, in the archdeaconry and diocese of Hereford. There is a place of worship for Wesleyan Methodists.

WEREHAM, a parish in the hundred of Clackclose, county of Norfolk, 1¾ mile (N. W.) from Stoke-Ferry, containing 546 inhabitants. The living is a perpetual curacy, with that of Wretton annexed, in the archdeaconry of Norfolk, and diocese of Norwich, endowed with £16 per annum private benefaction, and £400 royal bounty, and in the patronage of Edward R. Pratt, Esq. The church is dedicated to St. Margaret. A Benedictine priory, in honour of St. Winwaloe, or St. Guenolo, was founded here, about the beginning of the reign of John, by the Earl of Clare, as a cell to the abbey of Mounstroll in France; it was given, in 1321, to the abbey of West Dereham, and at the dissolution had a revenue of £7. 2. 8.

WERNITH, a township in the parish of Stockport, hundred of Macclesfield, county palatine of Chester, 4¼ miles (E. N. E.) from Stockport, containing 1804 inhabitants, most of whom are employed in the manufacture of hats and cotton goods, with calico-printing. Gee-Cross, so named from a cross erected there by the family of Gee, is the most considerable village in the township: it consists of a spacious street half a mile in length, on the high road from Stockport to Mottram in Longdendale, and is intersected by the Peak Forest canal. There is a place of worship for Unitarians, with an extensive cemetery and a Sunday school attached. A court baron is annually held; and there are fairs for cattle, on April 28th and November 20th. Coal and freestone are plentiful in this township. From a hill, called Wernith Lee, which is enclosed and cultivated to its summit, are most extensive and varied prospects, including views of Manchester, Stockport, Ashton under Line, Oldham, Mottram in Longdendale, &c., bounded by the Cheshire and Derbyshire mountains.

WERRINGTON, a parish in the hundred of Black Torrington, county of Devon, 2½ miles (N. by W.) from Launceston, containing 635 inhabitants. The living is a perpetual curacy, in the archdeaconry of Cornwall, and diocese of Exeter, and in the patronage of the Earl of Buckinghamshire. The church is dedicated to St. Martin and St. Giles.

WERRINGTON, a chapelry in the parish of Paston, liberty of Peterborough, county of Northampton, 3½ miles (N. N. W.) from Peterborough, containing 472 inhabitants.

WERVIN, a township in that part of the parish of St. Oswald, city of Chester, which is in the lower division of the hundred of Broxton, county palatine of Chester, 4¼ miles (N. by E.) from Chester, containing 67 inhabitants. The Ellesmere, or Wirrall, canal bounds the parish on the west.

WESHAM, a joint township with Medlar, in the parish of Kirkham, hundred of Amounderness, county palatine of Lancaster, 1¼ mile (N. by W.) from Kirkham. The population is returned with Medlar.

WESSINGTON, a township in that part of the parish of Crich which is in the hundred of Scarsdale, county of Derby, 3½ miles (N. W. by W.) from Alfreton, containing 488 inhabitants.

WESSINGTON, a joint hamlet with Combe, in the parish of Chipping-Campden, upper division of the hundred of Kiftsgate, county of Gloucester, ½ a mile (S.) from Chipping-Campden, containing, with Combe, 128 inhabitants.

WEST-ACRE, a parish in the Lynn division of the hundred of Freebridge, county of Norfolk, 5¼ miles (N. W. by N.) from Swaffham, containing, with the hamlet of Custhorpe, 362 inhabitants. The living is a perpetual curacy, in the archdeaconry and diocese of Norwich, and in the patronage of P. Hamond, Esq. The church is dedicated to All Saints. A priory of Black canons, in honour of St. Mary and All Saints, was founded here, in the time of William Rufus, by Ralph de Toney, which at the dissolution had a revenue of £308. 19. 11.: the remains of this once celebrated house exhibit specimens of the early and later styles of English architecture.

WESTANSWICK, a township in the parish of Stoke upon Tern, Drayton division of the hundred of Bradforth (North), county of Salop, containing 188 inhabitants.

WESTBEER, a parish in the hundred of Bleangate, lathe of St. Augustine, county of Kent, 3½ miles (N. E. by E.) from Canterbury, containing 194 inhabitants. The living is a rectory, in the archdeaconry and diocese of Canterbury, rated in the king's books at £7, and in the patronage of the Crown. The church is dedicated to All Saints.

WESTBOROUGH, a parish in the wapentake of Loveden, parts of Kesteven, county of Lincoln, 7 miles (N. W. by N.) from Grantham, containing 227 inhabitants. The living is a rectory in medieties, in the archdeaconry and diocese of Lincoln, endowed with £400 royal bounty; the first mediety, with Shefford annexed, is rated in the king's books at £20, and the second, with the vicarage of Dry Doddington annexed, at £6. 13. 4. The Rev. Robert Hall was patron of both in 1809. The church is dedicated to All Saints.

WESTBOURNE, county of Sussex.—See BOURNE (WEST).

WEST-BROMWICH, county of Stafford.—See BROMWICH (WEST).

WESTBROOK, a tything in that part of the parish of Boxford which is in the hundred of Kintbury-Eagle, county of Berks, 3¼ miles (N. W. by N.) from Speenhamland. The population is returned with the parish.

WESTBURY, a parish in the hundred and county of BUCKINGHAM, 4¾ miles (W. N. W.) from Buckingham, containing 345 inhabitants. The living is a vicarage, in the archdeaconry of Buckingham, and diocese of Lincoln, rated in the king's books at £9. 17. 1. Benjamin Price, Esq. was patron in 1817. The church is dedicated to St. Augustine.

WESTBURY, a parish in the hundred of FORD, county of SALOP, comprising the chapelry of Minsterley, and the township of Westbury, and containing 2153 inhabitants, of which number, 1395 are in the township of Westbury (including Westley and Yockleton townships), 8¾ miles (W. by S.) from Shrewsbury. The living is a rectory in two portions, in the archdeaconry of Salop, and diocese of Hereford; Westbury in Dextera Parte, rated in the king's books at £13. 9. 4½., and Westbury in Sinestra Parte, rated at £11. 12. 8½., both in the patronage of Smythe Owen, Esq. The church is dedicated to St. Mary. An extensive colliery is worked in the neighbourhood. Petty sessions for the division are held here during the winter months. The Rev.— Earl, in 1716, gave land producing about £30 per annum, for teaching and apprenticing twenty-four boys and girls.

WESTBURY, a parish in the hundred of WELLS-FORUM, county of SOMERSET, 4 miles (N. W. by W.) from Wells, containing 622 inhabitants. The living is a discharged vicarage, with the perpetual curacy of Priddy annexed, in the peculiar jurisdiction of the Dean of Wells, rated in the king's books at £11. 4. 9½., endowed with £200 private benefaction, and £200 royal bounty, and in the patronage of the Bishop of Bath and Wells. The church is dedicated to St. Lawrence. The parish is bounded on the south-west by the river Ax, which separates it from Wedmore.

WESTBURY, a joint hamlet with Peak, in that part of the parish of EAST MEON which is in the hundred of MEON-STOKE, Portsdown division of the county of SOUTHAMPTON, 6¼ miles (W.) from Petersfield, containing, with Peak, 50 inhabitants.

Seal and Arms.

WESTBURY, a parish forming the hundred of WESTBURY, county of WILTS, and comprising the borough of Westbury, the chapelries of Bratton and Dilton, and the townships of Hawkeridge, Haywood, and Leigh, and containing 6846 inhabitants, of which number, 2117 are in the town of Westbury, 24 miles (N. W. by W.) from Salisbury, and 98 (W. by S.) from London. This place is of very great antiquity, and is generally supposed to have been a British settlement, and to occupy the site of the Roman station Verlucio. The name is of Saxon origin, being intended to designate the importance, or relative position, of the town: here, according to tradition, was a palace belonging to the West Saxon kings. The town is situated under Salisbury Plain, and consists of three principal streets, irregularly built, branching off towards Frome, Bradford, and East Lavington : the inhabitants are supplied with water from springs, and a small stream which falls into the Avon. The clothing trade formerly flourished here, one house alone employing a thousand persons : the principal manufactures are broad cloth and kerseymere, there being in and near the town eight manufactories, and several others within the parish: a considerable quantity of malt is made. The market, now merely nominal, is on Tuesday, for pigs only; and fairs are held on the first Friday in Lent and Whit-Monday, for pedlary, and on Easter-Monday and September 24th, for cattle, horses, and cheese. The charter of incorporation was granted by Henry IV.: the municipal body consists of a mayor, recorder, twelve aldermen, and burgesses, with subordinate officers, none of them possessing magisterial authority. Courts leet are held by the mayor in November, and by the steward of the lord of the manor in May. There is also a court of requests, for the recovery of debts under £5, the jurisdiction of which is co-extensive with the hundreds of Westbury, Warminster, and Heytesbury; it is-held here and at Warminster alternately, every fortnight, on Tuesday. Two high constables are appointed at the manorial court. This borough has constantly returned two members to parliament from the 27th of Henry VI.: the right of election is in the occupiers of burgage tenements, in fee or for lives, or ninety-nine years determinable on lives, or by copy of court roll, paying a burgage rent of fourpence, or twopence, yearly, being resident within the borough, and not receiving alms : the number of voters is sixty-one; the mayor is the returning officer, and the influence of Sir Manasseh Masseh Lopes is predominant, at whose sole expense a handsome town hall, in the centre of the town, was erected in 1815.

The living is a discharged vicarage, in the peculiar jurisdiction and patronage of the Precentor of the Cathedral Church of Salisbury, rated in the king's books at £44. 16. 0½., endowed with £200 private benefaction, and £200 royal bounty. The church, which is dedicated to All Saints, is a spacious and handsome structure, with a central tower, supposed to have been built about nine hundred years ago; in the interior are several handsome monuments: it has recently received an addition of three hundred and thirty free sittings, for which the Incorporated Society for the enlargement of churches contributed £300. There are two places of worship for Independents, three for Baptists, and one for Wesleyan Methodists in the town, besides some others in the parish. A National school, in which about forty boys are instructed, was endowed with £1000 by the late John Matravers, an opulent clothier of this place, and a member of the Society of Friends, who also bequeathed £1000 for clothing twenty poor women at Christmas; and there are some other trifling bequests for the same purpose. Roman coins have been found here in great abundance. William de Westbury, one of the puisne judges of the Court of Common Pleas, and James Ley, Earl of Marlborough, are interred within the church. Bryan Edwards, historian of the British colonies in the West Indies; and Dr. Philip Withers, a writer of some eminence about the close of the last century, were natives of this town.

WESTBURY upon SEVERN, a parish in the hundred of WESTBURY, county of GLOUCESTER, 2½ miles (N. E. by E.) from Newnham, containing, with the township of Rodley, which is locally in the duchy of Lancaster, 1889 inhabitants. The living is a vicarage, in the archdeaconry of Hereford, and diocese of Gloucester, rated in the king's books at £20. 2. 8½., and in the patronage of the Custos of the College of Vicars-Choral in the Cathedral Church of Hereford. The church is dedicated to St. Peter and St. Paul. There is a place of worship for Wesleyan Methodists. The river Severn bounds the parish on the east and south. A National school is partly supported by subscriptions, and partly with an annuity of £4. 10., arising from two small bequests by John Young, in 1650, and Joseph Houlstead, in 1722.

WESTBURY upon TRYM, a parish in the lower division of the hundred of HENBURY, county of GLOUCESTER, 3 miles (N. N. W.) from Bristol, containing, with the chapelry of Shirehampton, and the tything of Bishop's Stoke, 3721 inhabitants. The living is a perpetual curacy, in the peculiar jurisdiction of the Bishop of Bristol, endowed with £200 private benefaction, and £200 royal bounty, and in the alternate patronage of the Rev. J. Baker and S. Edwards, Esq. The church is dedicated to the Holy Trinity. There is a place of worship for Wesleyan Methodists. A monastery existed here early in the ninth century, which was refounded near the close of the eleventh; it was dedicated to the Blessed Virgin, and made a cell to the priory of Worcester, but was dissolved in the reign of Henry I. About 1288, it became a college for a dean and canons, in honour of the Holy Trinity: in 1443 it was rebuilt, and its possessions augmented by Dr. Carpenter, Bishop of Worcester, who styled himself Bishop of Worcester and Westbury, and was buried on the south side of the altar. Its revenue at the dissolution was estimated at £232. 14., and the house, which remained till the reign of Charles I., was burned by Prince Rupert, to prevent its falling into the power of the parliament, but some traces of it are still visible in a mansion erected on its site.

WESTBY, a joint township with Plumptons, in the parish of KIRKHAM, hundred of AMOUNDERNESS, county palatine of LANCASTER, 2½ miles (W.) from Kirkham, containing, with Plumptons, 771 inhabitants.

WESTCOTE, a parish in the upper division of the hundred of SLAUGHTER, county of GLOUCESTER, 4 miles (S. E. by S.) from Stow on the Wold, containing 185 inhabitants. The living is a rectory, in the archdeaconry and diocese of Gloucester, rated in the king's books at £9. 7. 3½., and in the patronage of the Rev. T. P. Pantin. The church is dedicated to St. Mary.

WESTCOTE, a township in the parish of TYSOE, Kington division of the hundred of KINGTON, county of WARWICK, 5 miles (S.E. by E.) from Kington. The population is returned with the parish.

WESTCOTT, a hamlet in the parish of WADDESDON, hundred of ASHENDON, county of BUCKINGHAM, 7 miles (W.N.W.) from Aylesbury, containing 261 inhabitants.

WESTEND, a township in the parish of BURGH upon the SANDS, ward and county of CUMBERLAND, containing 195 inhabitants.

WESTEND, a tything in the parish of WORPLESDON, first division of the hundred of WOKING, county of SURREY. The population is returned with the parish.

WESTENHANGER, or OSTENHANGER, anciently a parish, now a manor, in the parish of STANDFORD, hundred of STOUTING, lathe of SHEPWAY, county of

KENT, 3 miles (N.W.) from Hythe. The population is returned with Standford. The living is a rectory, in the archdeaconry and diocese of Canterbury, rated in the king's books at £7. 12. 6., and in the patronage of the Crown. The church, which was dedicated to St. Thomas à Becket, has been long demolished.

WESTERDALE, a parish in the eastern division of the liberty of LANGBAURGH, North riding of the county of YORK, 7½ miles (S.S.E.) from Guilsbrough, containing 281 inhabitants. The living is a perpetual curacy, in the peculiar jurisdiction of the manorial court of Westerdale, and in the patronage of the Rector of Stokesley. Fifteen children are instructed for £15 per annum, arising from a rent-charge of £3, given by Jane Duck, in 1734, and certain land left by Mary Fish, in 1741.

WESTERFIELD, a parish partly within the borough of IPSWICH, and partly in the hundred of BOSMERE and CLAYDON, county of SUFFOLK, 2½ miles (N.N.E.) from Ipswich, containing 289 inhabitants. The living is a discharged rectory, in the archdeaconry of Suffolk, and diocese of Norwich, rated in the king's books at £11. 10. 7½., and in the patronage of the Bishop of Ely. The church is dedicated to St. Mary Magdalene. Bridget Collett, in 1662, bequeathed land producing about £5 per annum, in support of a school.

WESTERHAM, a market town and parish in the hundred of WESTERHAM, lathe of SUTTON at HONE, county of KENT, 22 miles (W.) from Maidstone, and 21 (S. S. E.) from London, containing 1742 inhabitants. The name of this town implies its situation on the western border of the county. Two remarkable phenomena, called land slips, occurred here in the years 1596 and 1756; in the former, nine acres of ground continued in motion for eleven days, and in the latter, two acres and a half, some parts sinking into pits, and others rising into hills. The town stands on the declivity of an eminence, and is of neat and clean appearance; about the centre is a large obelisk, used as a market-house. The river Darent rises in the neighbourhood, and after watering the ancient park of Squeries, takes a north-eastern direction through the parish. The market, which was granted, in the 25th of Edward III., to the abbot of Westminster, who possessed the manor, is on Wednesday; and a cattle fair is held on the 3rd of May. This place is within the jurisdiction of a court of requests held for the hundred, for the recovery of debts under £5. The living is a vicarage, with the perpetual curacy of Edenbridge annexed, in the archdeaconry and diocese of Rochester, rated in the king's books at £19. 19. 4½., and in the patronage of the Rev. Richard Board. The church, dedicated to St. Mary, is a large, ancient, and venerable structure. There are places of worship for the Society of Friends and Wesleyan Methodists. A National school, for children of both sexes, has been recently built, and is supported by voluntary contributions. Bishop Hoadley and the celebrated General Wolfe were both natives of this town; in the church is a fine cenotaph to the memory of the latter; and in the grounds of Quebec House there is a pillar, with an inscription, erected for the like purpose.

WESTERLEIGH, a parish in the hundred of PUCKLE-CHURCH, county of GLOUCESTER, 3 miles (S. W. by W.) from Chipping-Sodbury, containing 1817 inhabitants. The living is a perpetual curacy, annexed to the vicarage of Puckle-Church, in the archdeaconry and diocese of Gloucester. The church, dedicated to St. James, is a handsome structure in the later English style, with a lofty tower and stone pulpit. Sir John Smyth, in 1715, gave an annuity of £20 in support of two schools, in which ten boys and ten girls are educated. Edward Fowler, a divine and theological writer of the seventeenth century, was born here.

WESTERTON, a township in that part of the parish of St. Andrew, Auckland, which is in the south-eastern division of Darlington ward, county palatine of Durham, 2½ miles (E. by N.) from Bishop-Auckland, containing 77 inhabitants.

WESTFIELD, a parish in the hundred of Mitford, county of Norfolk, 2½ miles (S.) from East Dereham, containing 165 inhabitants. The living is a discharged rectory, united to that of Whinbergh, in the archdeaconry of Norfolk, and diocese of Norwich, rated in the king's books at £4. 4. 2. The church is dedicated to St. Andrew.

WESTFIELD, a parish in the hundred of Baldslow, rape of Hastings, county of Sussex, 4¼ miles (E. by S.) from Battle, containing 897 inhabitants. The living is a vicarage, in the archdeaconry of Lewes, and diocese of Chichester, rated in the king's books at £11. 6. 8., and in the patronage of the Bishop of Chichester. The church, dedicated to St. John the Baptist, is in the early style of English architecture. The parish is bounded on the north by Brede channel.

WESTGATE, a township in that part of the parish of St. John, Newcastle, which is in the western division of Castle ward, county of Northumberland, containing 1360 inhabitants. It forms the north-western suburb of the town of Newcastle, and several streets, containing many handsome residences, have lately been erected.

WESTHALL, a parish in the hundred of Blything, county of Suffolk, 4 miles (N. E.) from Halesworth, containing 440 inhabitants. The living is a discharged vicarage, in the archdeaconry of Suffolk, and diocese of Norwich, rated in the king's books at £10. 2. 3½., and in the patronage of the Dean and Chapter of Norwich. The church is dedicated to St. Andrew. Two small rent-charges, amounting together to £2. 18., given by Anne Clarke, in 1717, and the Rev. William Gregory Clarke, in 1726, are applied for teaching poor children.

WESTHAM, a parish in the lowey and rape of Pevensey, county of Sussex, 5¾ miles (S. E.) from Hailsham, containing 583 inhabitants. The living is a vicarage, in the archdeaconry of Lewes, and diocese of Chichester, rated in the king's books at £21. 10. 10., and in the patronage of Lord George Cavendish. The church, dedicated to St. Mary, is partly in the later style of English architecture, and partly of earlier date. There is an almshouse, containing four tenements, called the hospital of St. John, endowed with thirty acres of land, granted, as it is supposed, by one of the religious societies of Layney and Priest Hawes, the remains of which have been converted into farm-buildings.

WESTHAMPNETT, county of Sussex. — See HAMPNETT (WEST).

WESTHORPE, a parish in the hundred of Hartismere, county of Suffolk, 7¾ miles (N.) from Stow-Market, containing 234 inhabitants. The living

is a discharged rectory, in the archdeaconry of Sudbury, and diocese of Norwich, rated in the king's books at £4. 18. 1½., and in the patronage of the Rev. R. Hewitt, D.D. The church is dedicated to St. Margaret.

WESTLETON, a parish in the hundred of Blything, county of Suffolk, 2¾ miles (E.) from Yoxford, containing 788 inhabitants. The living is a discharged vicarage, with the rectories of Fordley and Middleton annexed, in the archdeaconry of Suffolk, and diocese of Norwich, rated in the king's books at £8. D. Davyd and H. Jermyn, Esqrs. were patrons in 1820. The church is dedicated to St. Peter.

WESTLEY, a township in the parish of Westbury, hundred of Ford, county of Salop, 10 miles (W. S. W.) from Shrewsbury. The population is returned with the township of Westbury.

WESTLEY, a parish in the hundred of Thingoe, county of Suffolk, 2 miles (W.) from Bury-St. Edmunds, containing 124 inhabitants. The living is a rectory, annexed to that of Fornham All Saints, in the archdeaconry of Sudbury, and diocese of Norwich, rated in the king's books at £9. 15. 5. The church, dedicated to St. Thomas à Becket, is a small edifice of mean appearance, covered with lead; the tower fell down in 1744.

WESTLEY-WATERLESS, a parish in the hundred of Radfield, county of Cambridge, 5 miles (S. S. W.) from Newmarket, containing 158 inhabitants. The living is a rectory, in the archdeaconry and diocese of Ely, rated in the king's books at £10. 5., and in the patronage of the Heirs of Mrs. Dresser. The church, dedicated to St. Mary, has a circular tower.

WESTMANCOATE, a hamlet in that part of the parish of Bredon which is in the middle division of the hundred of Oswaldslow, county of Worcester, 4¾ miles (N. E.) from Tewkesbury. The population is returned with the parish. There is a place of worship for Baptists.

WESTMESTON, a parish in the hundred of Street, rape of Lewes, county of Sussex, 5¾ miles (N. W. by W.) from Lewes, containing, with the chapelry of East Chiltington, 494 inhabitants. The living is a rectory, in the archdeaconry of Lewes, and diocese of Chichester, rated in the king's books at £22. 4. 2., and in the patronage of G. Courthope, Jun., Esq. The church, dedicated to St. Martin, is principally in the early style of English architecture, having a plain Norman arch between the nave and the chancel, decorated with the remains of a painting of the signs of the Zodiac: it contains several ancient monumental slabs, and a rudely-constructed circular stone font. At the east end is an ancient chapel, the burial-place of the Marten family. Anthony Shirley, who acquired some celebrity as a traveller and writer, in the time of James I., was born here. A charter for an annual fair on Martinmas-day was granted by Edward II. The dividends arising from £244. 8. 11. three per cents., the amount of sundry subscriptions, are applied for the education of poor children.

WESTMILL, a parish in the hundred of Braughin, county of Hertford, 1½ mile (S. by E.) from Buntingford, containing 415 inhabitants. The living is a rectory, in the archdeaconry of Huntingdon, and diocese of Lincoln, rated in the king's books at £20, and in the patronage of the Earl of Hardwicke. The church is dedicated to St. Mary.

WESTMINSTER, county of MIDDLESEX. — See LONDON.

WESTMORLAND, an inland county, bounded on the north and west by Cumberland, on the south-west and south by Lancashire, on the south-east and east by Yorkshire, and on the north-east by the county of Durham. It extends from 54° 11' 30" to 54° 42' 30" (N. Lat.), and from 2° 20' to 3° 12' (W. Lon.); and includes an area of seven hundred and sixty-three square miles, or four hundred and eighty-eight thousand three hundred and twenty statute acres. The population, in 1821, was 51,359. The ancient British inhabitants of the territory included within the limits of this county were of two tribes of the *Brigantes*, called the *Voluntii* and the *Sistuntii*; the former occupying the eastern parts of it, the latter the western. Under the Roman dominion it was included in the division called *Maxima Cæsariensis*; and, at the period of the Saxon Heptarchy, it formed part of the extensive and powerful kingdom of Northumbria: from its Saxon conquerors it received the name of *West-moringa-land*, or land of the western moors, since contracted into Westmorland. In later ages this county has been very little distinguished in history, except that it several times suffered severely from the hostile incursions of the Scotch. In 1173, King William of Scotland took Appleby castle by surprise, and destroyed the town; for permitting which, Henry II. imposed severe fines on several of the principal families in the county: during this inroad the Scottish monarch also sacked Brough castle. In 1388, Appleby was again reduced to ashes by these northern invaders. At the commencement of the civil war of the seventeenth century, Appleby castle was garrisoned by Anne, Countess of Pembroke, for the king, for whom it held out until the 16th of October, 1648, when it surrendered to the parliamentarian forces under Lieut.-Gen. Ashton, who captured in it a great number of officers, and one thousand two hundred horse, with all their baggage, being the force which he had compelled to abandon the siege of Cockermouth. In 1663, after the restoration of Charles II., some friends of the Commonwealth, who were very numerous in that part of the county, met on Kaber-Rigg, near the village of Kaber, designing to commence an insurrection, but were dispersed by the militia; some of them were taken prisoners, and afterwards tried and executed at Appleby. In 1745, a sharp action took place at Clifton moor between the retreating forces of the Scotch rebels and those of the Duke of Cumberland: some of the rebels who entered Kendal were also attacked by the inhabitants, but with very little effect.

Westmorland is partly in the diocese of Chester, and partly in that of Carlisle, in the province of York: the former includes the barony of Kendal, which is divided between the two deaneries of Kendal and Kirkby-Lonsdale, both of which extend into the adjoining parts of Lancashire; the barony of Westmorland, forming the remaining portion of the county, is in the diocese of Carlisle, and constitutes the deanery of Westmorland. The total number of parishes is thirty-two, of which fourteen are rectories, seventeen vicarages, and one a perpetual curacy. Its great civil divisions

are the two baronies of Kendal and Westmorland; the former containing the wards of Kendal and Lonsdale; the latter, which has in later ages been occasionally styled the "barony of Appleby," and is often called the "Bottom of Westmorland," comprising the East and West wards. The county contains the borough and market town of Appleby, the small market town and sea-port of Milnthorpe, and the market towns of Ambleside, Brough, Burton in Kendal, Kendal, Kirkby-Lonsdale, Kirkby-Stephen, and Orton: two knights are returned to parliament for the shire, and two representatives for the borough of Appleby: the county members are elected at Appleby. Westmorland is included in the northern circuit: the assizes and the Easter and Michaelmas quarter sessions are held at Appleby, and the Epiphany and Midsummer sessions at Kendal. There are thirty-two acting magistrates. The rates raised in the county, for the year ending March 25th, 1827, amounted to £31,029. 15., and the expenditure to £31,514. 12., of which £27,114. 3. was applied to the relief of the poor.

In the later periods of the Saxon dominion, when the ancient kingdom of Northumbria was divided into six shires, one of these was called Appleby-scyre: this, however, does not seem to have included the barony of Kendal, which, according to various records, appears, for some ages after the Norman Conquest, to have continued to form part of the hundred of Lonsdale, county palatine of Lancaster. In Domesday-book many places in the barony of Kendal are noticed, while Westmorland, properly so called, is, with Cumberland, Durham, Northumberland, and part of Lancashire, wholly omitted, those counties having been excluded from the survey. Lands in this county were, for centuries after the Norman Conquest, held by services similar to those of the border counties of Cumberland and Northumberland. The barony of Westmorland was granted by the Conqueror to Ranulph de Meschines, from whom, in a few generations, the possessions attached to it descended, through the families of Trevers, Engain, and Morville, to that of the Veteripònts, from whom it passed to the Cliffords, and from the latter, in the seventeenth century, to the Tuftons, Earls of Thanet, in which family it still remains; the present Earl of Thanet being hereditary sheriff of the county, as owner of that barony.

The county is in general so mountainous, that the soil of a great portion of it must necessarily for ever remain undisturbed by the plough. The mountains are separated by pleasant and fertile vallies, requiring only a greater number of trees and hedge-rows to complete the beauty of their appearance. The most extensive vales are, that of the Eden, reaching from about ten miles south-east of Kirkby-Stephen, north-westward by Appleby, towards Penrith; and that of Kendal, more particularly southward and westward of that town. Loose masses of rock, of various sizes and descriptions, are scattered over all the lower hills and the champaign parts of the county; and on the southern side of Shap, along the road towards Kendal, different streams, and especially Wasdale-beck, force their passage amidst stupendous blocks of rounded granite. Cross-fell, at the north-eastern extremity of the county, which is the highest of the chain of mountains extending along the eastern borders of Westmorland and Cumberland, rises to the height of two thousand nine hundred and one feet above the level of the sea. The other greatest elevations, included wholly or partly within its limits, are Helvellyn, three thousand and fifty-five feet high; Bow-fell, two thousand nine hundred and eleven feet high; Rydal-head, about the same height as the last-mentioned; and the High Street, which is about two thousand seven hundred and thirty feet high, and derives its name from an ancient road that runs along its summit, and on which the people of the neighbourhood have annual horse-races and other sports, on July 10th. All these mountains command magnificent and extensive prospects, and from Rydal-head are seen the lakes Windermere, Elter-water, Grassmere, and Rydal-water.

Many beautiful lakes adorn the numerous romantic and sequestered dales, and, together with those of Cumberland, have afforded an abundant theme for description, and have been the subjects of some of the finest efforts of landscape painting. The principal of those in Westmorland are, Ullswater, Windermere, Grassmere, Haws-water, Elter-water, Broad-water, and Rydal-water. *Ullswater* is on the north-western side of the county: the higher part of it is wholly within the limits of this county, while its lower part is divided between it and Cumberland: it is about nine miles long, its breadth varying from a quarter of a mile to two miles: the lower end is called Ousemere: its depth varies from six to thirty-five fathoms. The shores of this lake are extremely irregular, and, from its making different bold sweeps, only parts of it are seen at once: the lower extremity is bordered by pleasant enclosures, interspersed with woods and cottages, scattered on the sides of gently rising hills; but, advancing upwards towards Patterdale, the enclosures are of smaller extent, and the hills more lofty and rugged, until their aspect becomes wholly wild and mountainous: in its highest expanse are a few small rocky islands. Place-fell, on the east, projects its barren and rugged base into the lake; and on the west rise several rocky hills, one of which, called Stybarrow Crag, is clothed with oaks and birches: these and the other surrounding hills are furrowed with glens and the channels of torrents, causing remarkable echoes. When the sky is uniformly overcast, and the air perfectly calm, this lake, in common with some others, has its surface overspread by a smooth oily appearance, provincially called a *keld*, which term is also applied to the places that are longest in freezing: it contains abundance of fine trout, perch, skellies, and eels, some char, and a species of trout, called grey trout, almost peculiar to it, which frequently attains the weight of thirty pounds. *Windermere* is ten miles and a half long, and lies on the western border of the county, which it separates, for the greater part of its length, from Lancashire, in which county its lower extremity is wholly included: its breadth is from one to two miles, and its area is computed at two thousand five hundred and seventy-four acres, including thirteen islands, occupying a space of about forty acres, the largest of which is now called Curwen's Island, and contains twenty-seven acres. The Westmorland margin of this lake is bordered by enclosures rising gently from the water's edge, adorned with numerous woody and rocky knolls of various elevations and sizes; the Lancashire shore is higher and

more abrupt, and is clothed with wood, though not to the summit; and a simple magnificence is the chief characteristic of the whole surrounding scenery. Its fisheries, which are rented of the crown, are chiefly for common and grey trout, pike, perch, skellies, and eels, and more particularly for char, its most remarkable produce, of which there are two sorts, called, from the difference of their colour, silver and golden char, the former of which is considered the most delicious, and is potted for the London market: great numbers of water fowl resort to this lake, and to a few of the smaller ones. *Grassmere* is a particularly beautiful small lake, situated at the lower end of a valley bearing its name: in the centre of it is one small island, and its head is adorned by the church and village of Grassmere. *Haws-water* is situated in a narrow vale, called Mardale, and is about three miles long, and from a quarter to half a mile broad: near the centre it is nearly divided into two by a low enclosed promontory; and the mountains which environ its head are steep, bold, and craggy, but are skirted at their feet by enclosures. On its northern side is Naddle Forest, a steep mountainous ridge, in the form of a bow, and in the centre of which rises Wallow Crag, a mass of upright rocks: the other portions of its scenery are equally picturesque. The char and trout of this lake are in great esteem; besides these, it produces perch, skellies, and eels. *Elter-water*, at the bottom of Great Langdale, which is rather larger than Grassmere, is inferior to none of the smaller lakes in the variety and beauty of its scenery. *Broad-water*, about a mile above the head of Ullswater, is environed by high and rugged mountains, and is viewed to great advantage from a spot called Hartsop-high-field. *Rydal-water*, on the course of the Rothay, is shallow, and has several picturesque woody islands: it is about a mile in length. The principal of the smaller lakes, most commonly called *tarns*, are Ais-water, about a mile south-west of Hartsop, and under a mile northward of which is Angle-tarn; Grisedale-tarn, at the head of Grisedale; Red-tarn; under the eastern side of Helvellyn, and westward of which lies Kepel-cove-tarn; Red-tarn and Small-water, at the head of Riggindale, the highest branch of Mardale; Skeggles-water, in the mountains between Long-Sleddale and Kentmere; Kentmere, in the valley of the Kent; Sunbiggin-tarn, in the parish of Orton; and Whinfell-tarn, in the parish of Kendal. Some of the finest views are obtained from the high land near Askham, the terrace of Brougham Hall, Farleton Knot, Haverbrack Castle hill, Helsington chapel, Kirkby-Lonsdale church-yard, Mell-fell, Orton Scar, Storr's Point, Whinfell, Whitbarrow Scar, Wildboar-fell, and Wreynose hill. The mountainous character of this county, and its proximity to the Western sea, from which the wind is supposed to blow during eight months of the year, render its climate remarkably moist, and its streams uncommonly numerous. The air on the summits of the hills is pure and healthy, and the winters are generally severe. Along the chain of mountains extending from Cross-fell, in a southern direction, to Stainmore near Brough, a distance of about twenty miles, occurs a singular phenomenon, called the Helm Wind, which blows at various times of the year, but most commonly from October to April. A light-coloured cloud covers the summit of the mountain, and extends nearly half-way

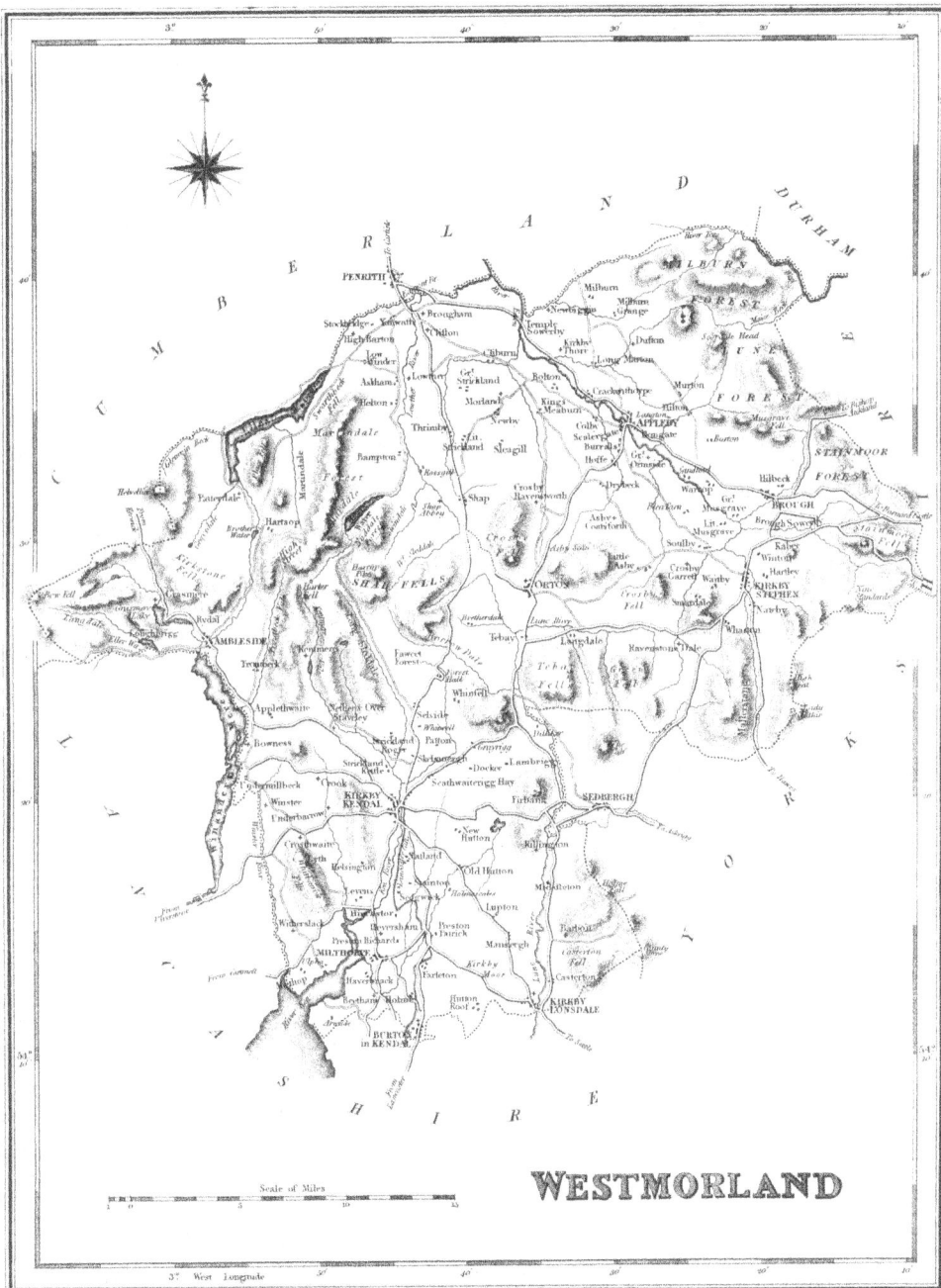

WESTMORLAND

down; above which the blue sky generally appears, and, above that, another cloud somewhat darker than the former: the latter is called, by the country people, the Burr, or Bar, from a popular notion that it represses the fury of the storm. During the time the Helm is forming, a noise is heard something like the distant roaring of the sea, and when it assumes the appearance of one continued and unbroken cloud, with a tremulous motion, the phenomenon is said to be completely formed. The wind then rushes down the mountain with incredible fury, extending its influence in a westerly direction for about three miles, beyond which the air is often quite calm, and occasionally a wind is even found blowing in an opposite direction. Over the top, or eastern side, of the mountain, the cloud extends no farther downwards than on the western side; and after it has passed through, the air there also is often quite calm. The Helm, therefore, is purely a local wind: it is more or less violent at different times of the year, and is most severely felt about the villages of Dufton, Murton, and Hilton, where it occasionally does considerable damage, tearing up trees by the roots, and unroofing houses, and, when it unfortunately occurs in harvest time, destroying the crops within its influence.

The most prevailing soil is a dry gravelly mould. Sand and hazel-mould appear in various places, but chiefly towards the eastern and north-eastern confines. Clay is found on a few farms near the Eden, and bordering on the eastern mountains, and a heavy moist soil in others in the northern parts of the county. Peat-moss occurs in small patches in many of the vallies, and abounds on the tops of several of the higher mountains, which, however, are in general covered with a dry soil upon a hard blue rock, provincially termed rag. The soil resting on a limestone bottom is every where esteemed the best. Notwithstanding the numerous enclosures and improvements that have taken place since the commencement of the present century, the cultivated lands hardly amount to one-half of the whole extent of the county. Upon these the oldest system of husbandry is, when the pastures have become very full of moss, to have, first, a crop of oats, then one of barley manured, and, lastly, oats again, after which they become grass land as before: the farmer does not usually sow seeds with his last crop of oats, the land of itself producing a tolerable herbage, which is greatly encouraged by the humidity of the climate; but, in a few years, it again becomes of little value, on account of the increase of moss amongst it, when it is again brought under a similar course of tillage. This system, however, is nearly exploded, and the turnip and clover husbandry now chiefly prevails, particularly in the Bottom of Westmorland, and in the parishes of Heversham, Burton, and Kirkby-Lonsdale, where considerable quantities of wheat are grown. Many potatoes are also grown and consumed in the county, particularly in the vicinity of Kendal. Hence it is obvious, that the greater part, amounting to about three-fourths, of the enclosed lands, are always under grass, particularly in high situations; and as the farmers, during the summer months, can keep almost any quantity of cattle on the commons, at a very little expense, their chief object is to get as much hay as possible from their enclosed lands against the approach of winter. Many dairy cows, fattening cattle, and young stock, are also

pastured in them, particularly in the rough upland grounds. The artificial irrigation of meadows lying on the borders of streams is practised in many parts, but generally on a small scale. Lime is extensively employed as manure in all parts of the county, limestone being found in inexhaustible quantities in most parts of it: rock-marl obtained from Bolton common is also used, as well as peat ashes. Paring and burning is much practised on the moor lands and the rough pastures.

The cattle formerly bred in the county were chiefly of the long-horned breed, and many farmers, particularly about Kendal and the neighbourhood, are still partial to them; but, of late, the Durham, or short-horned, breed has almost superseded the former, being generally considered much superior. There are few counties where, in proportion to their size, more milch cows are kept than in this, and where the produce of the dairy is an object of greater importance: this is chiefly butter, of which great quantities are annually sent to the London market, in firkins containing fifty-six pounds net. Part of the young cattle not adapted for the dairy are fattened in the county, and the rest sold to the Yorkshire and Lancashire graziers, with whom they are in great request. Not less than ten thousand Scotch cattle are annually brought to Brough Hill fair, whence great numbers are driven towards the rich pastures of the more southern parts of England, though many are retained and fattened within the limits of Westmorland. The breeds of sheep kept on the mountains and commons are either native or have been intermingled with Scotch sheep: they are horned, and have dark or grey faces, thick pelts, and coarse, hairy wool. Silverdale, a small tract in the southern part of the county, in the neighbourhood of Milnthorpe, gives name to a peculiar breed found in the surrounding districts: they are said to be native, and are in every respect superior to the common sort. In Westmorland it is not unusual for the proprietor of the land to be the owner of the sheep upon it, in which case the farmer is little more than a shepherd; and any difference in the value of the flock between the time of his entering upon the farm and that of his quitting it, must be accounted for by either party in money. The hogs, though not large, are considered of a good kind: farmers, butchers, and others, who kill swine, often dispose of the hams to persons who make a trade of curing them, in which state they are highly prized. They are packed in hogsheads, with straw, or the husks of oats, and sent to London, Lancaster, and Liverpool, in such quantities as to form one of the principal articles of export. Considerable quantities of geese, ducks, and common fowls are reared; the two last are generally disposed of in the market towns of the county, or at Lancaster; but great numbers of the geese are annually sold to drovers from Yorkshire. As only so small a portion of the county is under tillage, the horses are not numerous: they are of a small and hardy kind, but are neither strong nor handsome.

In some parts, considerable tracts are covered with coppices, consisting chiefly of oak, ash, alder, birch, and hazel: these underwoods, particularly in the barony of Kendal, are usually cut every sixteenth year, hardly any trees being left for timber, and their produce converted partly into hoops, which are made in the county, and sent coastwise to Liverpool; and partly into charcoal, which is in demand for the neighbouring iron-works. Timber is chiefly found in the plantations, which are numerous, and, at Whinfield Forest and around Lowther Hall, extensive: the larch is generally the most flourishing tree, though indeed most of the woods spring with a degree of vigour hardly to be expected from the bleak and exposed situations which many of them occupy. The extensive wastes are partly subject to common rights, constituting a great part of the value of many farms, to which they are attached, and partly in severalties and stinted pastures. A few of them consist of extensive commons in low situations, possessing a good soil; but by far the greater number is composed of large mountainous tracts, called by the inhabitants *fells* and moors, which produce little besides a very coarse grass, heath, and fern, provincially called *ling* and *brackens:* the soil of these is generally a poor hazel-mould and peat moss. The higher wastes are principally applied to the pasturage of large flocks of sheep, which, during the winter, are all brought down to the enclosures. By the end of April, they are sent back to the wastes. Numerous herds of black cattle are likewise seen on the lower commons: a few are of the breed of the county; the rest are Scotch. The eastern part of Westmorland is supplied with coal from Stainmore, part of which lies in Yorkshire; and the southern from Lancashire, by means of the Lancaster canal: in some districts the most common fuel is peat.

The mineral productions are various, and some of them valuable: they consist chiefly of lead, coal, marble, slate (the finest in England), limestone, freestone, and gypsum; every part of the county presents an interesting field of study to the geologist. The principal lead mines are those at Dunfell, which are considered to be nearly exhausted; at Dufton, where they are unusually rich; at Eagle Crags, in Grisdale, a branch of the vale of Patterdale; and at Greenside near Patterdale. A small quantity of this metal is also annually procured in the hills above Staveley, and large loose masses of ore have been found in different other situations: a very rich and productive vein at Hartley ceased to be worked about the commencement of the last century. Copper has been wrought to a limited extent at Limbrig, Asby, and Rayne, and is found in small quantities in many other parts. Coal is neither abundant, nor of good quality: it is wrought only in the south-eastern extremity of the county, chiefly on Stainmore heath, and in the neighbourhood of Shap: in the vale of Mallerstang a kind of small coal, chiefly used for burning limestone, is procured. Bordering upon the river Kent, about three miles below Kendal, a bed of beautiful white marble, veined with red and other tints, was discovered in 1793, and quarries were immediately opened. Near Ambleside, and between that town and Penrith, is found a marble of a dusky green colour, veined with white; a black sort is also found near Kirkby-Lonsdale, and another species at Kendal Fell. The western mountains produce vast quantities of slate, all the various kinds of which are used in the surrounding districts for covering the roofs of buildings, while the best of them are conveyed by sea to Liverpool, London, Lynn, Hull, &c., and by land into Cumberland, Northumberland, Durham, and Lancashire. The most general colour is blue, of many different shades, some-

times having a greenish cast; one kind is purple; and another, used to make writing slates, is nearly black: the best kinds are obtained at the greatest depth. The prevailing strata in the southern and eastern parts of the county are limestone and freestone, together with a soft laminous schistus, horizontally stratified. The western and north-western mountains, besides the slate before mentioned, consist of masses of the trap genera, chiefly basalt, commonly called whinstone. Around the head of Windermere, and for some distance eastward of it, lies a stratum of dark grey limestone, which is occasionally burned into lime, or polished for tombstones and chimney-pieces. Wasdale Crag is a mass of coarse flesh-coloured granite; higher up the dale, a greenish-coloured granite, of a finer and harder texture, is found: a very coarse species of granite also appears in many other parts of the county. A vein of red porphyry crosses the road between Kendal and Shap; and at Acorn-bank, near Kirkby, there is one of gypsum, which is used for laying floors. In many parts are also detached round pieces of blue rag-stone, of granite, and of a very hard composite stone, called by the masons *callierde*. In Knipe Scar are found talky fibrous bodies, opaque and of an ash-colour, which burn for a considerable time without any sensible diminution. Fossil remains exist only in the strata of the southern and eastern parts of the county: coral-loid bodies are very common, some of them being beautifully variegated.

The manufactures are but of minor importance, and consist chiefly of coarse woollen cloths, called Kendal *cottons* (supposed to be corrupted from *coatings*), linseys, knit-stockings, waistcoat-pieces, flannels, and leather. Nor is the commerce extensive: the principal exports are, the coarse cloths manufactured at Kendal, stockings, slates, tanned hides, gunpowder, hoops, charcoal, hams, bacon, wool, sheep, and cattle: the imports are, grain, and Scotch cattle and sheep. Much fish from the rivers and lakes is annually sent to Lancaster and Liverpool, and some even to London.

The principal rivers are the Eden, Eamont, Lowther, Lune, and Kent. The Eden, issuing from one of the hills at the top of Mallerstang, near the south-eastern border of the county, flows north-westward, by the towns of Kirkby-Stephen and Appleby, to the parish of Brougham, at the northernmost extremity of which, after having formed the boundary of the county for a short distance, it enters Cumberland, having received numerous smaller streams from the mountains which environ its course: this river abounds with fine salmon, trout, and a few other kinds of fish. The Eamont issues, in a rapid and remarkably transparent stream, from the lake of Ullswater, at its lower extremity, and pursues a bending east-north-easterly course, by Penrith, to the Eden, at the point where it quits the county. The Lowther has its source in the moors above Wetsleddale, and passes northward, by Shap, in a narrow and rocky channel, to the Eamont, a little below Penrith, being joined in its course by the water from the Haws-water lake, and by numerous other mountain streams. The Lune rises at the foot of a hill, called the Green Bell, in the parish of Ravenstonedale, and thence runs southward, between craggy banks and in a rugged channel, until it enters Lancashire, a mile below Kirkby-Lonsdale: for the distance of about seven miles, directly eastward of Kendal, it forms the boundary between this county and that of York : this river is much resorted to by salmon during the spawning season, and gives name to the vale through which it has its course. The Kent rises on the south side of the hill called the High Street, and thence flows through Kentmere-tarn, and by the town of Kendal, into the spacious bay of Morecambe, approaching which it spreads into a broad, shallow, and sandy æstuary: amongst the other streams by which it is joined are, the Sprit, from Long Sleddale; the Mint, from Fawcet Forest; the Underbarrow; the Blyth, or Betha, which descends from above Betham, and forms the port of Milnthorpe; and the Winster, which rises on Cleabarrow heath, and at Blackbeck becomes the boundary between this county and the northern portion of Lancashire, which it thenceforward continues to be, falling into the æstuary of the Kent opposite to Arnside Fell. The beds of the Kent, Betha, and Winster, are too rocky, and their waters too rapid, to admit of their being navigated beyond the respective points to which the tide flows up them. The principal of the mountain streams that pour their waters into Windermere, at its head, are the Brathay and the Rothay, which meet about three quarters of a mile below Ambleside : the Troutbeck falls into that lake from Westmorland, near Calgarth : very large trout yearly make their passage up the river Rothay, and great quantities of case, a species of char, up the Brathay. Westmorland derives considerable benefit from the Lancaster canal, which, commencing at Kendal, proceeds for some distance parallel with the course of the Kent, and afterwards across that of the Betha, to the vicinity of Burton, where it enters Lancashire, in the southern part of which county it communicates with the Leeds and Liverpool canal, &c. The roads are in excellent order, durable materials being readily obtained, and the carriage upon them not being heavy. The road from London to Carlisle, through Lancashire, enters the county at Burton, and thence proceeds by Milnthorpe, or by Barras Green, to Kendal, Shap, and across the Eamont to Penrith in Cumberland. A road from London to Kendal, through Bedford, Nottingham, and Skipton in Craven, passes through Kirkby-Lonsdale. That from London to Glasgow and Edinburgh, by Carlisle, enters from Yorkshire to the south-east of Brough, and passes through that town and Appleby to Penrith.

A singular collection of huge stones, called Penhurrock, now nearly destroyed, and a Druidical circle of stones near Oddendale, both in the parish of Crosby-Ravensworth, are supposed to have been British; as also are the rude circle of stones at the head of the stream called the Ellerbeck; that on the waste of Moorduvock, called the Druids' Cross; that of Mayborough, on a gentle eminence on the western side of Eamont bridge; and that about a mile north-eastward of Shap, called the Druids' Temple. Various other relics of this people have been discovered, including several cairns and encampments. Westmorland was traversed by a variety of Roman roads of minor importance, and contained the stations of *Verteræ*, which has been fixed at Brough; *Brovacum*, at Brougham castle; *Galacum*, at the head of Windermere; and another at Natland, the name of which is uncertain. A branch of the great Roman road, called the Watling-street, passed through it from Stainmore to Brougham castle, and several parts

of it between Brough and Kirkby Thore are still tolerably perfect : it is six or seven yards wide, and, on the level plain, is formed of three layers of stones, a yard in thickness, but in other places it is made of gravel or flints, where those materials are the most easily procured. From this the Maiden-way branched off at Kirkby-Thore, and passed over the lower extremity of Cross-fell, by Whitley castle, into Northumberland : this road may still be clearly traced, being uniformly about seven yards broad, and formed of large loose stones. Other vestiges of Roman occupancy are also very numerous, including altars, urns, coins, bricks, tesselated pavements, foundations of buildings, &c., which have been found on the sites of the stations, and in a few other places. There are also, a Roman camp, about one hundred yards southward of Borrowbridge, in Borrowdale, now called Castlehows; others, called Castlesteads and Coney-beds, near the station at Natland; and several between Crackenthorpe and Cross-fell; besides Maiden Castle, upon Stainmore, a very strong square fort, about five miles from Brough; and several other remarkable intrenchments. Near Shap is a stupendous monument of antiquity, called Carl-lofts, supposed to be Danish, consisting of two long lines of huge obelisks of unhewn granite, with different other masses of the same material, arranged in various forms. The religious houses in this county were only the Premonstratensian abbey of Shap, and a monastery of White friars at Appleby, together with an hospital for lepers near Kirkby in Kendal : there are some remains of the abbey of Shap. The churches most worthy of notice are those of Appleby, Asby, Askham, Burton, Brough, Crosby-Ravensworth, Kendal, Kirkby-Thore, Kirkby-Lonsdale, and Kirkby-Stephen. The county also contains several remarkable ancient chapels, and ruins of others. Remains of more modern fortifications are numerous and extensive, comprising the ruins of the castles of Appleby, Beetham, Brough, Brougham, Bewley, Howgill, Kendal, and Pendragon; Arnside tower, Helsback tower, and several other ancient castellated buildings. Of ancient mansions, the most remarkable specimens are, Sizergh Hall, the seat of Thomas Strickland, Esq.; and Levens Hall, that of the Hon. Col. Howard; together with the ruins of Old Calgarth Hall and Preston Hall. Of the more modern seats of the nobility and gentry, those most worthy of notice are, Lowther Castle, the residence of the Earl of Lonsdale, lord lieutenant of the county; Appleby Castle, that of the Earl of Thanet, hereditary high sheriff. The small freeholds are very numerous. The enclosed fields are generally very small, and are fenced partly by hedges, and partly by stone walls. The inhabitants, owing to their secluded situation, have, until recently, been distinguished for their adherence to several antiquated customs : *haver-bread*, from the oat, sometimes called *haver*, made into unleavened cakes, is still in common use : shoes with wooden soles, called clogs, are worn by the common people of both sexes, especially in the winter season. There are mineral springs of various qualities in several places; the principal being that near the village of Clifton, at which a great number of people annually assemble, on the first day of May, to drink its waters; that called Gondsdike, a little to the south of Rounthwaite, which continually casts up small metallic spangles; Shap wells, much resorted to in the summer season by persons afflicted with scorbutic complaints, and by lead-miners from Alston and Arkingartdale; the numerous petrifying springs on the borders of the river Kent; and a petrifying well in the cave called Pate-hole. The most remarkable cascades on the numerous mountain streams are, Leven's Park waterfall, on the Kent; another on the Betha, below Betham— the *Caladupæ* of Camden; and Gill-forth spout, in Long Sleddale, which has an unbroken fall of one hundred feet. Pate-hole, before mentioned, is a very curious and extensive cavern in a limestone rock near Great Asby, from which, in rainy seasons, powerful streams of water issue. Westmorland gives the title of earl to the family of Fane. Baron Vipont of Westmorland is one of the titles borne by the noble family of Clifford.

WESTOE, a chapelry in the parish of JARROW, eastern division of CHESTER ward, county palatine of DURHAM, containing 7618 inhabitants. The living is a perpetual curacy, in the archdeaconry and diocese of Durham, endowed with £200 private benefaction, and £1700 parliamentary grant, and in the patronage of the Perpetual Curate of South Shields. Westoe is a populous suburb to South Shields, the market-place and many of the principal streets of which are comprised in this township.

WESTON, a township in the parish of RUNCORN, hundred of BUCKLOW, county palatine of CHESTER, 3¼ miles (N. N. W.) from Frodsham, containing 294 inhabitants. The Weston canal passes in the vicinity, parallel with the river Mersey.

WESTON, a township in the parish of WYBUNBURY, hundred of NANTWICH, county palatine of CHESTER, 6 miles (E.) from Nantwich, containing 463 inhabitants.

WESTON, a tything in the parish of STALBRIDGE, hundred of BROWNSHALL, Sturminster division of the county of DORSET, containing 224 inhabitants.

WESTON, a parish in the hundred of BROADWATER, county of HERTFORD, 4½ miles (N. E. by N.) from Stevenage, containing 927 inhabitants. The living is a discharged vicarage, in the archdeaconry of Huntingdon, and diocese of Lincoln, rated in the king's books at £10. 6. 8., and in the patronage of William Hale, Esq. The church, dedicated to the Holy Trinity, is partly Norman, and partly of later date. There is a place of worship for Wesleyan Methodists.

WESTON, a parish in the wapentake of ELLOE, parts of HOLLAND, county of LINCOLN, 3¼ miles (N. E. by E.) from Spalding, containing 498 inhabitants. The living is a vicarage not in charge, in the archdeaconry and diocese of Lincoln, and in the patronage of the Crown. The church is dedicated to St. Mary.

WESTON, a parish in the hundred of EYNSFORD, county of NORFOLK, 5¼ miles (S.) from Reepham, containing 392 inhabitants. The living is a discharged rectory, in the archdeaconry of Norfolk, and diocese of Norwich, rated in the king's books at £8. 18. 1½., and in the patronage of the Warden and Fellows of New College, Oxford. The church is dedicated to All Saints.

WESTON, a hamlet in the parish of LOYS WEEDON, hundred of GREEN's NORTON, county of NORTHAMPTON, 7 miles (W. by S.) from Towcester. The population is returned with the parish. There is a place of worship for Baptists. A chalybeate spring in the

neighbourhood was formerly much esteemed, but has fallen into disrepute.

WESTON, a parish in the northern division of the wapentake of THURGARTON, county of NOTTINGHAM, 3 miles (S. E.) from Tuxford, containing 300 inhabitants. The living is a rectory, in the archdeaconry of Nottingham, and diocese of York, rated in the king's books at £19. 2. 11., and in the patronage of Earl Manvers. The church, dedicated to All Saints, exhibits specimens of various styles of architecture. Richard Hawksworth, in 1736, bequeathed £50 for erecting a school-house, and £100 towards its endowment, for the education of ten poor children. Weston is in the honour of Tutbury, duchy of Lancaster, and within the jurisdiction of a court of pleas held at Tutbury every third Tuesday, for the recovery of debts under 40s.

WESTON, a joint township with Nash and Tilsop, in the parish of BURFORD, hundred of OVERS, county of SALOP, 6 miles (E. S. E.) from Ludlow. The population is returned with Nash.

WESTON, a parish in the hundred of BATH-FORUM, county of SOMERSET, 1¾ mile (N. W. by W.) from Bath, containing 1919 inhabitants. The living is a vicarage, in the archdeaconry of Bath, and diocese of Bath and Wells, rated in the king's books at £10. 1. 8., and in the patronage of the Crown. The church, dedicated to All Saints, has lately received an addition of four hundred and fifty-three sittings, of which two hundred and twenty-seven are free, the Incorporated Society for the enlargement of churches and chapels having granted £300 towards defraying the expense. There is a place of worship for Wesleyan Methodists. The parish is bounded on the south by the river Avon, a stream tributary to which has its source in Lansdown Hill, flows through the village, and is crossed by a stone bridge of one arch on the high road from Bath to Bristol.

WESTON, a hamlet in the parish of WANSTROW, hundred of FROME, county of SOMERSET, 5¼ miles (S. W.) from Frome, containing 85 inhabitants.

WESTON, a tything in the parish of BURITON, hundred of FINCH-DEAN, Alton (South) division of the county of SOUTHAMPTON, 1¼ mile (S. S. W.) from Petersfield. The population is returned with the parish. John Goodyer, in 1664, bequeathed premises now let for £79 a year, which is applied to the education of children and the relief of the poor.

WESTON, a parish in the hundred of WANGFORD, county of SUFFOLK, 2¾ miles (S.) from Beccles, containing 179 inhabitants. The living is a discharged rectory, in the archdeaconry of Suffolk, and diocese of Norwich, rated in the king's books at £13. 6. 8., and in the patronage of the Crown. The church is dedicated to St. Peter.

WESTON, a joint hamlet with Ember, in that part of the parish of THAMES-DITTON which is in the second division of the hundred of ELMBRIDGE, county of SURREY. The population is returned with Ember.

WESTON, a hamlet in the parish of BULKINGTON, Kirby division of the hundred of KNIGHTLOW, county of WARWICK, 3½ miles (S. S. E.) from Nuneaton, containing 151 inhabitants.

WESTON, a parish in the upper division of the wapentake of CLARO, West riding of the county of YORK, comprising the townships of Askwith and Weston, and containing 475 inhabitants, of which number, 108 are in the township of Weston, 2 miles (N. W. by W.) from Otley. The living is a discharged vicarage, in the archdeaconry and diocese of York, rated in the king's books at £6. 11. 5½., endowed with £400 royal bounty, and in the patronage of the Governors of the grammar school at Sedbergh. The church is dedicated to All Saints.

WESTON (ALCONBURY), a parish in the hundred of LEIGHTONSTONE, county of HUNTINGDON, 6 miles (N. W.) from Huntingdon, containing 382 inhabitants. The living is a perpetual curacy, annexed to the vicarage of Alconbury, in the archdeaconry of Huntingdon, and diocese of Lincoln.

WESTON upon AVON, a parish partly in the Alcester division of the hundred of BARLICHWAY, county of WARWICK, but chiefly in the upper division of the hundred of KIFTSGATE, county of GLOUCESTER, 4½ miles (S. W. by W.) from Stratford on Avon, containing, with the hamlet of Milcott, 107 inhabitants. The living is a discharged vicarage, in the archdeaconry and diocese of Gloucester, rated in the king's books at £7. 14. 7., endowed with £200 parliamentary grant, and in the patronage of the Duke of Dorset. The church is dedicated to All Saints.

WESTON (COLD), a parish in the hundred of MUNSLOW, county of SALOP, 6¾ miles (N. E. by N.) from Ludlow, containing 24 inhabitants. The living is a discharged rectory, in the archdeaconry of Salop, and diocese of Hereford, rated in the king's books at £2. 8. 4., endowed with £200 private benefaction, and £400 royal bounty. Samuel Davies, Esq. was patron in 1816. The church is dedicated to St. Mary.

WESTON (CONEY), a parish in the hundred of BLACKBOURN, county of SUFFOLK, 6¼ miles (N. N. E.) from Ixworth, containing 261 inhabitants. The living is a discharged rectory, annexed to that of Barningham, in the archdeaconry of Suffolk, and diocese of Norwich, rated in the king's books at £13. 0. 5. The church is dedicated to St. Mary.

WESTON sub EDGE, a parish in the upper division of the hundred of KIFTSGATE, county of GLOUCESTER, 1¾ mile (W. N. W.) from Chipping-Campden, containing 347 inhabitants. The living is a rectory, in the archdeaconry and diocese of Gloucester, rated in the king's books at £31. H. H. Pelly, Esq. was patron in 1817. The church is dedicated to St. Lawrence.

WESTON (EDITH), county of RUTLAND. — See EDITH-WESTON.

WESTON in GORDANO, a parish in the hundred of PORTBURY, county of SOMERSET, 10 miles (W. by N.) from Bristol, containing 111 inhabitants. The living is a discharged rectory, in the archdeaconry of Bath, and diocese of Bath and Wells, rated in the king's books at £6. 3. P. John Mills, Esq. was patron in 1817. The church is dedicated to St. Paul.

WESTON on the GREEN, a parish in the hundred of PLOUGHLEY, county of OXFORD, 4½ miles (S. W. by W.) from Bicester, containing 462 inhabitants. The living is a discharged vicarage, in the archdeaconry and diocese of Oxford, and in the patronage of the Earl of Abingdon. The church is dedicated to St. Mary.

WESTON (KING), county of SOMERSET.——See KINGWESTON.

WESTON (KING'S), a tything in that part of the parish of HENBURY which is in the lower division of the hundred of BERKELEY, county of GLOUCESTER, 4½ miles (N. W.) from Bristol, containing 154 inhabitants. Here was formerly a chapel, which has been demolished.

WESTON (LAWRENCE), a tything in that part of the parish of HENBURY which is in the lower division of the hundred of BERKELEY, county of GLOUCESTER, 5¼ miles (N. W. by N.) from Bristol, containing 335 inhabitants.

WESTON under LIZARD, a parish in the western division of the hundred of CUTTLESTONE, county of STAFFORD, 5¾ miles (N. E. by E.) from Shiffnall, containing 296 inhabitants. The living is a discharged rectory, in the archdeaconry of Stafford, and diocese of Lichfield and Coventry, rated in the king's books at £6. 7. 8½., endowed with £200 private benefaction, and £200 royal bounty, and in the patronage of the Earl of Bradford. The church is dedicated to St. Andrew.

WESTON super MARE, a parish in the hundred of WINTERSTOKE, county of SOMERSET, 9¾ miles (N. W. by W.) from Axbridge, containing, with the hamlets of Ashcombe and Milton, 738 inhabitants. The living is a discharged rectory, in the archdeaconry of Wells, and diocese of Bath and Wells, rated in the king's books at £14. 17. 11., and in the patronage of the Bishop of Bath and Wells. The church, dedicated to St. John, is a neat edifice, lately erected. There are two places of worship for Dissenters. The place is situated on the margin of Uphill bay, near the Bristol channel, and possesses the usual appendages of a neat watering-place, having considerably increased in size within the last twenty years: there are commodious inns and lodging-houses, and good baths. A convenient market-house has recently been erected, at the expense of Richard Parsley, Esq. A few persons are engaged in the sprat and herring fishery. A small school, for the instruction of poor children, is supported by voluntary contributions. At Worteberry, above the village, is a rampart of stones, twenty feet high, with ditches attached; and a well in the parish possesses the unusual properties of being empty at high water, and full when the tide is at its ebb.

WESTON (MARKET), a parish in the hundred of BLACKBOURN, county of SUFFOLK, 7 miles (S.) from East Harling, containing 332 inhabitants. The living is a discharged rectory, in the archdeaconry of Sudbury and diocese of Norwich, rated in the king's books at £8. 19. 7., and in the patronage of Walter Hill, Esq. The church is dedicated to St. Mary.

WESTON (OLD), a parish in the hundred of LEIGHTONSTONE, county of HUNTINGDON, 7¼ miles (N.) from Kimbolton, containing 379 inhabitants. The living is a perpetual curacy, united to the rectory of Brington, in the archdeaconry of Huntingdon, and diocese of Lincoln. The church is dedicated to St. Swithin.

WESTON under PENYARD, a parish in the hundred of GREYTREE, county of HEREFORD, 2¼ miles (E. S. E.) from Ross, containing 674 inhabitants. The living is a rectory, in the archdeaconry and diocese of Hereford, rated in the king's books at £18, and in the patronage of the Bishop of Hereford. The church is dedicated to St. Lawrence.

WESTON under RED-CASTLE, a chapelry in the parish of HODNET, Drayton division of the hundred of BRADFORD (North), county of SALOP, 4 miles (E.) from Wem, containing, with Wixhill, 322 inhabitants.

WESTON (SOUTH), a parish in the hundred of PIRTON, county of OXFORD, 2¾ miles (S. by E.) from Tetsworth, containing 108 inhabitants. The living is a rectory, in the archdeaconry and diocese of Oxford, rated in the king's books at £9. 2. 6., and in the patronage of the Provost and Fellows of Queen's College, Oxford. The church is dedicated to St. Lawrence. There is a place of worship for Wesleyan Methodists.

WESTON upon TRENT, a parish in the hundred of MORLESTON and LITCHURCH, county of DERBY, 7 miles (S. E. by S.) from Derby, containing 397 inhabitants. The living is a rectory, in the archdeaconry of Derby, and diocese of Lichfield and Coventry, rated in the king's books at £11. 16. 3., and in the patronage of Sir Robert Wilmot, Bart. The church is dedicated to St. Mary. The Trent and Mersey canal passes through the parish, which is in the honour of Tutbury, duchy of Lancaster, and within the jurisdiction of a court of pleas held at Tutbury every third Tuesday, for the recovery of debts under 40s.

WESTON upon TRENT, a parish in the southern division of the hundred of PIREHILL, county of STAFFORD, 4½ miles (N. E.) from Stafford, containing, with the liberty of Yarlett, 475 inhabitants. The living is a perpetual curacy, in the archdeaconry of Stafford, and diocese of Lichfield and Coventry, endowed with £200 royal bounty, and £200 parliamentary grant, and in the patronage of — Inge, Esq. The church is an ancient structure, with a large tower and spire. The Grand Trunk canal passes through the parish. Extensive salt-works have been established at the village: the brine is raised in the parish of Ingestre, by means of machinery worked by the waters of the Trent, and is conveyed across that river and under the canal, through pipes, to certain reservoirs, whence it runs into iron pans, is heated, and becomes chrystallized for use. The daily consumption of brine is estimated at one thousand four hundred hogsheads, from which about fourteen thousand tons of salt are annually extracted, including most of the basket, or kiln-dried, salt sold in London.

WESTON under WEATHERLY, a parish in the Southam division of the hundred of KNIGHTLOW, county of WARWICK, 6 miles (N. E. by E.) from Warwick, containing 232 inhabitants. The living is a discharged vicarage, in the archdeaconry of Coventry, and diocese of Lichfield and Coventry, rated in the king's books at £5. 9. 2., endowed with £400 royal bounty, and in the patronage of Lord Clifford. The church is dedicated to St. Michael.

WESTON by WELLAND, a parish in the hundred of CORBY, county of NORTHAMPTON, 4¼ miles (N. E.) from Market-Harborough, containing 220 inhabitants. The living is a vicarage, with that of Sutton-Bassett united, in the archdeaconry of Northampton, and diocese of Peterborough, rated in the king's books at £11. 17. 1., and in the patronage of Lord Sondes. The church is dedicated to St. Mary.

WESTON-BAMFYLD, a parish in the hundred of CATSASH, county of SOMERSET, 5¾ miles (S. S. W.) from Castle-Cary, containing 119 inhabitants. The living is

a rectory, in the archdeaconry of Wells, and diocese of Bath and Wells, rated in the king's books at £8. 15. 10., endowed with £200 private benefaction, and £300 parliamentary grant, and in the patronage of the Rev. J. Goldesbrough. The church is dedicated to Holy Cross.

WESTON-BEGGARD, a parish in the hundred of RADLOW, county of HEREFORD, 5 miles (E.) from Hereford, containing 270 inhabitants. The living is a discharged vicarage, in the archdeaconry and diocese of Hereford, rated in the king's books at £5. 15. 3., endowed with £200 royal bounty, and in the patronage of the Dean and Chapter of Hereford. The church, dedicated to All Saints, has lately received an addition of seventy-six sittings, of which seventy-one are free, the Incorporated Society for the enlargement of churches and chapels having granted £45 towards defraying the expense. There is a place of worship for Wesleyan Methodists.

WESTON-BIRT, a parish in the hundred of LONGTREE, county of GLOUCESTER, 3¾ miles (S. W. by S.) from Tetbury, containing, with Lasborough, 198 inhabitants. The living is a discharged rectory, in the archdeaconry and diocese of Gloucester, rated in the king's books at £6. 2., endowed with £200 private benefaction, and £200 royal bounty. P. Holford, Esq. was patron in 1803. The church is dedicated to St. Catherine.

WESTON-COLLEY, a tything in the parish and hundred of MITCHELDEVER, Basingstoke division of the county of SOUTHAMPTON, 8 miles (N. by E.) from Winchester. The population is returned with the parish. This tything is within the jurisdiction of the Cheyney Court held at Winchester every Thursday, for the recovery of debts to any amount.

WESTON-COLVILLE, a parish in the hundred of RADFIELD, county of CAMBRIDGE, 6 miles (N. E. by N.) from Linton, containing 419 inhabitants. The living is a rectory, in the archdeaconry and diocese of Ely, rated in the king's books at £21. 13. 6½., and in the patronage of John Hall, Esq. The church is dedicated to St. Mary.

WESTON - CORBETT, an extra-parochial liberty, in the hundred of BERMONDSPIT, Basingstoke division of the county of SOUTHAMPTON, 4 miles (S. E.) from Basingstoke, containing 20 inhabitants.

WESTON-COYNEY, a joint township with Hulme, in the parish of CAVERSWALL, northern division of the hundred of TOTMONSLOW, county of STAFFORD, 5 miles (W.) from Cheadle, containing 527 inhabitants.

WESTON-FAVELL, a parish in the hundred of SPELHOE, county of NORTHAMPTON, 2½ miles (E.N.E.) from Northampton, containing 389 inhabitants. The living is a rectory, in the archdeaconry of Northampton, and diocese of Peterborough, rated in the king's books at £16. 16. 3., and in the patronage of the Rev. R. H. Knight. The church is dedicated to St. Peter. Henry and Elizabeth Ekins gave a house and land in support of a school for fifteen children, also a rent-charge of £1 for repairs; and Thomas Green, in 1739, gave certain other land in furtherance of this charity. The Rev. James Hervey, author of "Meditations among the Tombs," for many years held the rectory of this parish, and was buried in the church.

WESTON-JONES, a township in the parish of NORBURY, western division of the hundred of CUTTLE-STONE, county of STAFFORD, 3¼ miles (N. N. E.) from Newport, containing 89 inhabitants.

WESTON-PATRICK, a parish in the hundred of ODIHAM, Basingstoke division of the county of SOUTH-AMPTON, 4¼ miles (S. W. by W.) from Odiham, containing 189 inhabitants. The living is a perpetual curacy, in the archdeaconry and diocese of Winchester, endowed with £800 royal bounty, and in the patronage of the Hon. W. T. L. P. Wellesley. The church is dedicated to St. Lawrence.

WESTON-PEVEREL, or PENNY-CROSS, a chapelry in that part of the parish of St. ANDREW, PLY-MOUTH, which is in the hundred of ROBOROUGH, county of DEVON, 2¾ miles (N. by W.) from Plymouth, containing 238 inhabitants. The chapel is dedicated to St. Pancras.

WESTON-RHYN, a joint township with Bron-y-gath, in the parish of St. MARTIN, hundred of OSWES-TRY, county of SALOP. The population is returned with Bron-y-gath.

WESTON-TURVILLE, a parish in the hundred of AYLESBURY, county of BUCKINGHAM, 2¼ miles (N. by W.) from Wendover, containing 611 inhabitants. The living is a rectory, in the archdeaconry of Buckingham, and diocese of Lincoln, rated in the king's books at £22. 0. 10., and in the patronage of the Warden and Fellows of All Souls' College, Oxford. The church is dedicated to St. Mary. A school is supported by small annual donations.

WESTON-UNDERWOOD, a parish in the hundred of NEWPORT, county of BUCKINGHAM, 1¼ mile (W. S. W.) from Olney, containing 420 inhabitants. The living is a perpetual curacy, in the archdeaconry of Buckingham, and diocese of Lincoln, endowed with a rent-charge of £8 and £200 private benefaction, and £400 royal bounty, and in the patronage of Robert Throckmorton, Esq. The church is dedicated to St. Lawrence. The parish is bounded on the south by the river Ouse, and contains the ancient seat, now uninhabited, of the Throckmorton family, who have also a neat Roman Catholic chapel here, with a handsome residence for the priest. In this pleasant village Cowper resided for several years during the latter part of his life; and the neighbourhood is supposed to have furnished many of his descriptions of rural scenery.

WESTON-UNDERWOOD, a township in the parish of STANTON by DALE, hundred of MORLESTON and LITCHURCH, county of DERBY, 5¾ miles (N. W. by N.) from Derby, containing 228 inhabitants. Weston is in the honour of Tutbury, duchy of Lancaster, and within the jurisdiction of a court of pleas held at Tutbury every third Tuesday, for the recovery of debts under 40s.

WESTON-ZOYLAND, a parish in the hundred of WHITLEY, county of SOMERSET, 4 miles (E. S. E.) from Bridg-water, containing, with a portion of Borough-bridge, which is in the hundred of ANDERSFIELD, 807 inhabitants. The living is a vicarage, in the archdeaconry of Wells, and diocese of Bath and Wells, rated in the king's books at £14. 6. 8., endowed with £200 private benefaction, and £200 royal bounty, and in the patronage of the Bishop of Bath and Wells. The church, dedicated to St. Mary, is a cruciform structure, with a stately western tower, highly enriched, and crowned with pinnacles. The parish is bounded on the south by the navigable river Parret.

WESTONING, a parish in the hundred of MANS-HEAD, county of BEDFORD, 4 miles (S. by W.) from Ampthill, containing 634 inhabitants. The living is a discharged vicarage, in the archdeaconry of Bedford, and diocese of Lincoln, rated in the king's books at £9. 17., and in the patronage of John Everett, Esq. The church is dedicated to St. Mary Magdalene. There is a place of worship for Baptists.

WESTOVER, a tything in the parish and hundred of WHERWELL, Andover division of the county of SOUTHAMPTON, 2½ miles (S. by W.) from Andover. The population is returned with the parish.

WESTOW, a parish in the wapentake of BUCK-ROSE, East riding of the county of YORK, comprising the townships of Eddlethorp, Firby, Menethorpe, and Westow, and containing 660 inhabitants, of which number, 423 are in the township of Westow, 5½ miles (S. S. W.) from New Malton. The living is a discharged vicarage, in the archdeaconry of the East riding, and diocese of York, rated in the king's books at £4. 18. 4., and in the patronage of the Archbishop of York. The church is dedicated to St. Mary. There is a place of worship for Wesleyan Methodists. Three poor children are educated for an annuity of £2. 10., the gift of Elizabeth Sugar.

WEST-PARK, a joint tything with Cole, in the parish and hundred of MALMESBURY, county of WILTS, The population is returned with Cole.

WESTPORT (ST. MARY), a parish in the hundred of MALMESBURY, county of WILTS, adjacent to the north-west side of Malmesbury, containing 1023 inhabitants. The living is a vicarage, with the perpetual curacy of Charlton annexed, in the archdeaconry of Wilts, and diocese of Salisbury, rated in the king's books at £16. 17. 8½., and in the patronage of the Crown. The church is dedicated to St. Mary.

WESTRILL, an extra-parochial liberty, in the hundred of GUTHLAXTON, county of LEICESTER, containing, with Stormore, 6 inhabitants.

WEST-VILLE, a township in the western division of the soke of BOLINGBROKE, parts of LINDSEY, county of LINCOLN, containing 102 inhabitants. This township, with six others, is not dependent on any parish, and was created such by act of parliament, in 1812, on the occasion of a very extensive drainage of Wildmore, and the East and West Fens : the inhabitants attend the chapel at Carrigton, which was consecrated in 1818.

WESTWARD, a parish in ALLERDALE ward below Darwent, county of CUMBERLAND, 2¼ miles (S. E. by S.) from Wigton, comprising the townships of Brocklebank with Stoneraise, Rosley, and Woodside, and containing 1287 inhabitants. The living is a perpetual curacy, in the archdeaconry and diocese of Carlisle, endowed with £1600 parliamentary grant, and in the patronage of the Dean and Chapter of Carlisle. The church stands on an eminence in the township of Stoneraise. The parish is bounded on the east by the Wampool river, and on the south by branches of the Waver. Limestone, red freestone, and slate, all of excellent quality, are quarried here, and there are seams of cannel and other coal within the parish. Seven poor children are instructed for the interest of £60, left by

John Jefferson, in 1744, and of £20, bequeathed by another benefactor, in 1778. About one mile south from Wigton, and one and a half north from the church, on the Roman road from the city of Carlisle to Ellenborough, is Old Carlisle, the supposed site of the *Olenacum* of the Notitia, where the *Ala Herculea* and *Ala Augusta* were quartered. Antiquaries, however, differ as to the name of this important station, the environs of which covered many acres, still overspread with ruins and foundations of innumerable buildings, with fragments of altars, equestrian statues, images, inscriptions, and various other remains. The walls enclosed an oblong area, one hundred and seventy yards long by one hundred and twenty broad, with obtuse angles, and an entrance on each side, and were surrounded by a double ditch. Near a place called the Heights, in another part of the parish, vestiges of several square, as well as circular, intrenchments may be traced, though many of them have been levelled, and enclosed with the waste lands. Ile-Kirk Hall, which is now a farm-house, was once in the possession of the famous Richard Barwise, a man of prodigious strength and stature.

WESTWATER, a tything in the parish and hundred of AXMINSTER, county of DEVON, 2 miles (N. W.) from Axminster, containing 357 inhabitants.

WESTWELL, a parish in the hundred of CALEHILL, lathe of SCRAY, county of KENT, 2½ miles (E. S. E.) from Charing, containing 867 inhabitants. The living is a vicarage, in the peculiar jurisdiction and patronage of the Archbishop of Canterbury, rated in the king's books at £13. The church is dedicated to St. Mary.

WESTWELL, a parish in the hundred of BAMPTON, county of OXFORD, 2 miles (W. S. W.) from Burford, containing 160 inhabitants. The living is a rectory, in the archdeaconry and diocese of Oxford, rated in the king's books at £5. 3. 9., and in the patronage of the Dean and Canons of Christ Church, Oxford. The church is dedicated to St. Mary.

WESTWICK, a hamlet in that part of the parish of OAKINGTON which is in the hundred of CHESTERTON, county of CAMBRIDGE, 5¼ miles (N. N. W.) from Cambridge, containing 47 inhabitants.

WESTWICK, a township in that part of the parish of GAINFORD which is in the south-western division of DARLINGTON ward, county palatine of DURHAM, 2 miles (S. E.) from Barnard-Castle, containing 97 inhabitants.

WESTWICK, a parish in the hundred of TUNSTEAD, county of NORFOLK, 2¾ miles (S.) from North Walsham, containing 182 inhabitants. The living is a discharged rectory, in the archdeaconry of Norfolk, and diocese of Norwich, rated in the king's books at £9. 13. 9., endowed with £200 royal bounty, and in the patronage of J. Petre, Esq. The church is dedicated to St. Botolph. At a short distance from Westwick House is an obelisk, ninety feet high, with a neat room at the top, commanding beautiful and extensive views of the sea-coast on one hand, and of a richly diversified country on the other.

WESTWICK, a township in that part of the parish of RIPON which is within the liberty of RIPON, West riding of the county of YORK, 3¾ miles (W. by S.) from Boroughbridge, containing 27 inhabitants.

WESTWOOD, a township in that part of the parish of THORNBURY which is in the hundred of WOLPHY, county of HEREFORD, 4½ miles (N. W. byN.) from Bromyard. The population is returned with the parish.

WESTWOOD, a parish forming a detached portion of the hundred of ELSTUB and EVERLEY, being locally in that of Bradford, county of WILTS, 2 miles (S. W.) from Bradford, containing, with the hamlet of Iford, 462 inhabitants. The living is a perpetual curacy, annexed to the vicarage of Bradford, in the archdeaconry of Wilts, and diocese of Salisbury.

WESTWOOD, an extra-parochial liberty, in the upper division of the hundred of HALFSHIRE, county of WORCESTER, 2¼ miles (W. N. W.) from Droitwich. A priory, dedicated to the Blessed Virgin, for six nuns of the order of Fontevrault, was founded here in the reign of Henry II., and at the dissolution had a revenue of £75. 18. 11.

WETHERAL, a parish, comprising the townships of Cumwhinton with Coathill, Scotby, and Wetheral, in CUMBERLAND ward, and the townships of Great Corby and Warwick-Bridge, in ESKDALE ward, county of CUMBERLAND, and containing 2192 inhabitants, of which number, 451 are in the township of Wetheral, 5 miles (E. by S.) from Carlisle. The living is a perpetual curacy, with that of Warwick annexed, in the archdeaconry and diocese of Carlisle, endowed with £1200 parliamentary grant, and in the patronage of the Dean and Chapter of Carlisle. The church, dedicated to the Holy Trinity, was built in the reign of Henry VIII.; and a handsome chapel was attached to it, as a burial-place, by Henry Howard, Esq., in 1791. The river Eden runs through the parish, in which there are quarries of red freestone and alabaster. Thomas Graham, in 1760, left £60, directing the interest to be applied for teaching poor children. A priory of Benedictine monks, dedicated to the Holy Trinity, St. Mary, and St. Constantine, was founded here by Ranulph de Meschines, as a cell to the abbey of St. Mary at York; at the dissolution its revenue was estimated at £128. 5. 3. Of the conventual buildings, the gatehouse still remains, and near the site are three ancient cells, excavated in the rock, at the height of forty feet above the river Eden, which flows at its base.

WETHERBY, a market town and chapelry in the parish of SPOFFORTH, upper division of the wapentake of CLARO, West riding of the county of YORK, 12½ miles (W. by S.) from York, and 194 (N. N. W.) from London, containing 1217 inhabitants. The Saxon name of this town, whence the present is obviously deduced, was *Wederbi*, intended to designate its situation on a bend of the river Wharf. During the great civil war it was garrisoned for the parliament, and successfully repulsed two attacks made upon it by Sir Thomas Glemham. About 3½ miles below it is St. Helen's ford, where the Roman military way crossed the Wharf. The town consists chiefly of one long street, behind which is the market-place. Over the river is a handsome stone bridge, and a little above this a wear, formed for the benefit of some mills for grinding corn, extracting oil from rape-seed, and pulverising logwood for the use of clothiers and dyers. Many old houses have been recently removed and new ones erected, under the direction of the lord of the manor. The market is on Thursday; and fairs are held on Holy

Thursday, August 5th, October 10th, and the first Thursday after November 22d; there are also fortnight fairs for the sale of cattle. The quarter sessions for the West riding are held here at Christmas, in rotation with Knaresborough, Skipton, and Wakefield, and courts leet and baron on Lady-day and Michaelmasday. The living is a perpetual curacy, in the archdeaconry and diocese of York, endowed with £200 private benefaction, £400 royal bounty, and £800 parliamentary grant, and in the patronage of the Rector of Spofforth. The church is dedicated to St. James. There are places of worship for Independents and Wesleyan Methodists.

WETHERDEN, a parish in the hundred of STOW, county of SUFFOLK, 4¼ miles (N. W.) from Stow-Market, containing 468 inhabitants. The living is a discharged rectory, in the archdeaconry of Sudbury, and diocese of Norwich, rated in the king's books at £6.13.4., and in the patronage of the Crown. The church is dedicated to St. Mary.

WETHERINGSETT, a parish in the hundred of HARTISMERE, county of SUFFOLK, 2¼ miles (E. N. E.) from Mendlesham, containing, with the hamlet of Brockford, 937 inhabitants. The living is a rectory, in the archdeaconry of Sudbury, and diocese of Norwich, rated in the king's books at £33.9.2., and in the patronage of — Stewart, Esq. The church is dedicated to All Saints.

WETTENHALL, a chapelry in the parish of OVER, first division of the hundred of EDDISBURY, county palatine of CHESTER, 5½ miles (E. by S.) from Tarporley, containing 297 inhabitants. The living is a perpetual curacy, in the archdeaconry and diocese of Chester, endowed with £200 private benefaction, and £800 royal bounty, and in the patronage of the Vicar of Over.

WETTON, a parish in the southern division of the hundred of TOTMONSLOW, county of STAFFORD, 7½ miles (N. W. by N.) from Ashbourn, containing 609 inhabitants. The living is a perpetual curacy, in the archdeaconry of Stafford, and diocese of Lichfield and Coventry, endowed with £800 royal bounty, and £1200 parliamentary grant, and in the patronage of W. Burgoyne, Esq. The church, dedicated to St. Margaret, is ancient and much decayed: over the doorway is a piece of rude sculpture. The river Manifold runs through the parish, as far as Wetton-mill, then suddenly disappears through the fissures of its limestone bed, and, continuing a subterranean course for about five miles, emerges within a few yards of the place where the river Hamps re-appears in like manner from its channel underground. At Ecton hill are extensive lead and copper mines, affording employment to a number of men, women, and children. Within this parish is a remarkable cavern of large dimensions, termed Thor's House, in which the Druids, it is believed, sacrificed to their god Thor. Twelve poor children are instructed for an annuity of £5, the bequest of William Risbridger, in 1754. Wetton is in the honour of Tutbury, duchy of Lancaster, and within the jurisdiction of a court of pleas held at Tutbury every third Tuesday, for the recovery of debts under 40s.

WETWANG, a parish partly within the liberty of ST. PETER of YORK, and partly in the wapentake of BUCKROSE, East riding of the county of YORK, comprising the chapelry of Fimber, and the township of

Wetwang, and containing 526 inhabitants, of which number, 422 are in the township of Wetwang, 5¾ miles (W. by N.) from Great Driffield. The living is a discharged vicarage, in the peculiar jurisdiction and patronage of the Prebendary of Wetwang in the Cathedral Church of York, rated in the king's books at £9.7.8½. The church is dedicated to St. Michael. There is a place of worship for Wesleyan Methodists.

WEXHAM, a parish in the hundred of STOKE, county of BUCKINGHAM, 1½ mile (N. E.) from Slough, containing 154 inhabitants. The living is a rectory, in the archdeaconry of Buckingham, and diocese of Lincoln, rated in the king's books at £5.15., and in the patronage of the Crown. The church is dedicated to St. Mary. Rag-stone abounds in the neighbourhood. The learned Fleetwood, before his elevation to episcopal dignity, was rector of this parish from 1705 to 1708, during which period he published his *Chronicon Pretiosum.*

WEYBOURNE, a parish in the hundred of HOLT, county of NORFOLK, 3¾ miles (N. E.) from Holt, containing 230 inhabitants. The living is a perpetual curacy, in the archdeaconry and diocese of Norwich, and in the patronage of the Earl of Orford. The church is dedicated to All Saints.

WEYBREAD, a parish in the hundred of HOXNE, county of SUFFOLK, 1¾ mile (S. S. W.) from Harleston, containing 680 inhabitants. The living is a discharged vicarage, in the archdeaconry of Suffolk, and diocese of Norwich, rated in the king's books at £4.15., and endowed with £200 royal bounty, and £400 parliamentary grant. The Rev. John Edge was patron in 1814. The church is dedicated to St. Andrew.

WEYBRIDGE, a parish in the first division of the hundred of ELMBRIDGE, county of SURREY, 20 miles (S. W. by W.) from London, containing 897 inhabitants. The living is a rectory, in the archdeaconry of Surrey, and diocese of Winchester, rated in the king's books at £7.0.5., and in the patronage of the Crown. The church, dedicated to St. Nicholas, is a small neat edifice, and contains several ancient and modern monuments: Her Royal Highness the late Duchess of York was interred here. There is a place of worship for Baptists. The parish is bounded on the north by the Thames, where it receives the river Wey, which was formerly crossed by a bridge, and thus gave name to the place. The Wey and Arun canal commences a little to the westward of the village, and the neighbourhood is adorned with many elegant seats; the principal of these is Oatlands, which was the country residence of His Royal Highness the late Duke of York, occupying the brow of an eminence, near a fine sweep of the Thames. Charles Hopton, in 1739, bequeathed £100 for the erection of a school, which is endowed with about £5 per annum, the produce of sundry bequests, for teaching twelve children. Among the various relics of antiquity found here, several curious wedges, or celts, were discovered, in 1725, at Oatlands, about twenty feet below the surface of the earth; which circumstance seems to sanction the opinion that Julius Cæsar attacked the Britons at the place now called Coway Stakes, a short distance from his camp at Walton.

WEYHILL, a parish in the hundred of ANDOVER, Andover division of the county of SOUTHAMPTON, 3¼ miles (W. by N.) from Andover, containing, with Clanville,

Nutbin, and Penton-Grafton, 408 inhabitants. The living is a rectory, in the archdeaconry and diocese of Winchester, rated in the king's books at £26, and in the patronage of the Provost and Fellows of Queen's College, Oxford. The church is dedicated to St. Michael. The village is situated on the edge of Salisbury Plain, and, though only an insignificant place, is celebrated for the great fair held in the neighbourhood, commencing on October 10th, for horses and sheep, of the latter of which it is estimated that more than one hundred and forty thousand are sold on the first day; it continues the five following days, and is visited by persons from all parts of the kingdom; cheese, hops, and leather, are also sold in considerable quantities.

Arms.

WEYMOUTH and MELCOMBE - REGIS, a sea-port, borough, and market town, having separate jurisdiction, in the Dorchester division of the county of DORSET, 8 miles (S. by W.) from Dorchester, and 130 (S. W. by W.) from London, containing 6622 inhabitants. This borough comprises the towns of Weymouth and Melcombe-Regis, forming opposite boundaries of the harbour, in the conveniences of which they had their origin; and to terminate their mutual rivalry for the exclusive possession of which, they were united into one borough, in the reign of Elizabeth. Weymouth, which derives its name from its situation at the mouth of the river Wey, is the more ancient, and was probably known to the Romans; as, in the immediate neighbourhood, there are evident traces of a vicinal way, leading from one of the principal landing stations connected with their camp at Maiden Castle to the *via Iceniana*, where the town of Melcombe-Regis now stands. The earliest authentic notice of it occurs in a grant by Athelstan, in 938, wherein he gives to the abbey of Milton "all that water within the shore of Waymouth, and half the stream of that Waymouth out at sea, a saltern, &c." It is also noticed in the Norman survey, with several other places, under the common name of Wai, or Waia; among which it is clearly identified by the mention of the salterns exclusively belonging to it.

The ports of Weymouth and Melcombe, with their dependencies, were, by the charters of Henry I. and II., granted to the monks of St. Swithin, in Winchester; from whom, by exchange, Weymouth passed into the possession of Gilbert de Clare, Earl of Gloucester, who, in the reigns of Henry III. and Edward I., held it with view

Admiralty Seal.

of frankpledge and other immunities. His successor, Lionel, Duke of Clarence, obtained many privileges for the town, which he made a borough, and which, through his heir, Edward IV., subsequently reverted to the crown, and formed part of the dowry of several queens

of England. In the reign of Edward II. it received the staple of wine, and collectors were appointed, in the 4th and 6th years of that reign, to receive the duties. Weymouth, in the 10th of Edward III., had become a place of some importance, and, with Melcombe and Lyme, contributed several ships towards the equipment of that monarch's expedition to Gascony. In the year 1347, it furnished twenty ships and two hundred and sixty-four mariners towards the fleet destined for the siege of Calais: in this subsidy, Melcombe, though not mentioned, was probably included. In 1471, Margaret of Anjou, with her son, Prince Edward, landed at this port from France, to assist in restoring her husband, Henry VI., to the throne of England; and, in the 20th of Henry VII., Philip, King of Castille, on his voyage from Zealand to Spain, with a fleet of eighty ships, on board of which was his queen, being driven by a storm on the English coast, put into it for safety, intending to re-embark, after having refreshed himself from his toils, before his arrival could be known to the English monarch; but Sir Thomas Trenchard and Sir John Carew, who, fearing some hostile attack, had marched with their forces to the town, detained him till he might have an interview with the king, and for that purpose conducted him to Woolverton, the seat of Sir Thomas Trenchard. This port, in 1588, contributed six ships to oppose the armada of Spain, and one of the enemy's vessels, having been taken in the English channel, was brought into Weymouth harbour. Melcombe-Regis, on the north side of the harbour, derived its name from being situated in a valley, in which was an ancient mill; and its adjunct from its having formed part of the demesnes of the crown. It is not mentioned in Domesday-book, being included in the parish of Radipole, which at that time belonged to Cerne abbey; but it passed from the monks into the possession of the crown at an earlier period than Weymouth, and, in the reign of Edward I., became the dowry of Queen Eleanor, on which account it obtained many valuable and extensive privileges. In the reign of Edward III., it was made one of the staple towns for wool, and flourished considerably; but, in the following reign, having been burnt by the French, it became so greatly impoverished, that the inhabitants petitioned the king to be excused from the payment of their customs. Edward IV., in order to afford relief, granted them a new charter, conferring the same privileges as were enjoyed by the citizens of London.

In the reign of Elizabeth, the lords of the council, wearied by the continual disputes of these two towns, which were both boroughs, and endowed with extensive privileges, by the advice of Cecil, Lord Treasurer, united them into one borough by an act of parliament, which was afterwards confirmed by James I., under the designation of "The United Borough and Town of Weymouth and Melcombe-Regis," from which time their history becomes identified. Weymouth afterwards gradually fell into decay, and suffered greatly during the parliamentary war, having been alternately garrisoned for both parties. In 1644, it was evacuated by the royalists, on which occasion several ships, and a great quantity of arms, fell into the hands of the parliament, who obtained possession of it. The royalists soon afterwards attempted to recover it, but the garrison sustained the attack for eighteen days, and finally obliged them to raise the siege. An additional fort was built, in 1645, on the Weymouth side of the harbour, to defend it from the incursions of the Portlanders; and, four years after, the corporation petitioned for an indemnification for the destruction of their bridge and chapel (the latter, from its commanding situation, having been converted into a fort), and for assistance in the maintenance of the garrison, which application appears to have been disregarded; but, in 1666, a brief was granted to repair the damage; and, in 1673, another was bestowed for the collection of £3000, to repair the injury which the town had received from an accidental fire, whereby a considerable portion of it was destroyed. The rise of the town of Poole, which was rapidly growing into importance, the decay of the haven, and the loss of its trade, with various other causes, contributed powerfully to the decline of the town, which, from an opulent and commercial port, had almost sunk into a mere fishing town, when Ralph Allen, Esq., of Bath, in 1763, first brought it into notice as a bathing-place; and the subsequent visits of George III. and the royal family, with whom it was a favourite place of resort, laid the foundation of its present prosperity.

The town is beautifully situated on the western shore of a fine open bay in the English channel, and separated into two parts by the river Wey, which, expanding to a considerable breadth, in its progress to the bay, forms a small, but secure and commodious, harbour, on the south side of which is Weymouth, at the foot of a high hill near the mouth of the river; and, on the north side, Melcombe-Regis, on a peninsula, connected with the main land by a narrow isthmus, which separates the waters of the bay from those formed by the æstuary of the river, called the Backwater. A long and handsome stone bridge of two arches, with a swivel in the centre, to admit small vessels into the upper part of the harbour, has been erected, by act of parliament in the 1st of George IV., and connects the two parts of the town. In building it, the workmen, on clearing the foundation of some ancient premises, discovered an urn, covered with a thin piece of sheet-iron, containing a great number of crowns, half-crowns, shillings, and sixpences, of the reigns of Elizabeth, James I., and Charles I.; and, in taking down an old house, nearly opposite the bridge, a richly-gilt crucifix in brass, about four inches in length, was found, which, with the exception of a part of the gilding, was in a very perfect state. Since their town has become a place of fashionable resort for sea-bathing, various handsome ranges of building, and a theatre, assembly-rooms, and other places of public entertainment have been erected. Among the former, Belvidere, the Crescent, Gloucester-Row, Royal-Terrace, Chesterfield-Place, York-Buildings, Charlotte-Row, Augusta-Place, and Clarence, Pulteney, and Devonshire Buildings, are conspicuous; to which may be added, Brunswick-Buildings, a handsome range of houses at the entrance of the town. From the windows of these buildings, which front the sea, a most extensive and delightful view is obtained, comprehending, on the left, a noble range of hills and cliffs extending, for many miles, in a direction from west to east, and of the sea in front, with the numerous vessels, yachts, and pleasure-boats, which are continually entering and leaving the harbour. The town, especially on the Melcombe side of the harbour, is regularly built, and consists partly of two principal streets, parallel with each other, intersected by others at right angles; it is well paved and lighted, under the provisions of an act passed in the year 1776, and is supplied, by a public company incorporated by another act, with pure water, conveyed by pipes from the Boiling Rock, at some distance, in the parish of Sutton. The houses, excepting such as have been erected for the accommodation of visitors, are in general built of stone and roofed with tiles, and are low and of indifferent appearance.

About half a mile to the south-west are the remains of Weymouth, or Sandsfoot, castle, erected by Henry VIII., in the year 1539, and described, by Leland, as "a right goodly and warlyke castle, having one open barbicane." It is quadrangular in form: the north front has been nearly destroyed, the masonry with which it was faced having been removed; the apartments on this side are all vaulted, and appear to have been the governor's residence; at the extremity is a tower, on the front of which were the arms of England, having a wyvern and unicorn for supporters. The south front is circular, and was defended by a platform of cannon, the wall of which now overhangs the precipice on which it was raised: on this side is a low building, broader than the castle, and flanking its east and west sides, in which are embrasures for great guns, and loop-holes for small arms: the walls, in some parts, are seven yards in thickness, but in a very dilapidated state, and rapidly falling to decay. On the west of the town are the barracks, a neat and commodious range of building. The Esplanade, a beautiful terrace, thirty feet broad, rising from the sands, and secured by a strong wall extending in a circular direction, parallel with the bay, for nearly a mile, and commanding an extensive and beautiful view of the sea and the mountainous range of cliffs by which the bay is enclosed, is one of the finest marine promenades in the kingdom. Among the buildings that adorn it is the Royal Lodge, where George III. and the royal family resided while visiting this place, comprising several houses of handsome, though not of uniform, appearance: opposite is a noble flight of steps, of Portland stone, leading to the sands, to which also is a gently sloping descent from one extremity of the Esplanade to the other: in the centre is the principal public library, elegantly furnished. The assembly and card rooms, a handsome range of building, comprising also an hotel, with commodious stabling and other appendages, and occupying an area six hundred feet in length, and two hundred and fifty in breadth, were erected at an expense of £6000, advanced on shares of £100 each: they are in every respect well adapted to the meetings which are held there during the season, under the superintendence of a master of the ceremonies. The theatre, of which the box entrance is in Augusta Place, is a neat and well-arranged edifice, handsomely fitted up; it will accommodate three hundred persons in the boxes, and is open four nights in the week during the season. Races were established in 1821, which are generally well attended; they take place in August, and among the prizes contended for are the king's plate of one hundred guineas, the mayor's of fifty guineas, the members' of fifty guineas, the Gordon of £50, and the ladies' and tradesmen's plates : the course, adjoining the town, is conveniently adapted to the purpose.

3 L 2

During the time of the races, a splendid regatta is celebrated in the bay, which has a fine circular sweep of nearly two miles, and, being sheltered from the north and north-east winds by a continuous range of hills, the water is generally calm and transparent. The sands are smooth, firm, and level; and so gradual is the descent towards the sea, that, at the distance of three hundred feet, the water is not more than two feet deep. Numerous bathing machines are in constant attendance, and on the South Parade is an establishment of hot salt-water baths, furnished with dressing-rooms and every requisite accommodation. At the south entrance of the harbour are the Higher and Lower jetties, the latter of which is a little to the east of the former. The sea has for some years been retiring from the eastern side of the harbour, and part of the ground over which it formerly flowed is now covered with buildings, other parts being enclosed with iron railings, which form a prominent feature on the Esplanade. On the Weymouth side are the Look-out and the Nothe, affording extensive and interesting prospects: on the latter is a battery, formerly mounted with six pieces of ordnance, which, on the dismantling of the fort, were removed into Portland castle: within the walls a signal post has been established, which communicates with several other stations, and apartments have been built for the accommodation of a lieutenant and a party of men. The bay almost at all times affords ample facilities for aquatic excursions, its tranquil surface being never disturbed, except by violent storms from the south or south-west; yachts and pleasure-boats are always in readiness, the fares of which are under strict regulations. The air is so mild and pure, that the town is not only frequented during the summer, but has been selected, by many opulent families, as a permanent residence; and the advantages which it possesses in the excellence of its bay, the beauty of its scenery, and the healthfulness of its climate, have contributed to raise it from the low state into which it had fallen, from the depression of its commerce, to one of the most flourishing towns in the kingdom.

The port formerly carried on an extensive trade with France, Spain, Norway, and Newfoundland, in the fishery of which last place it employed eighty vessels; but the war with France, after the Revolution, put an end to its commerce with that country; the trade with Newfoundland was, in a great measure, transferred to Poole; and the accumulation of sand in the harbour, operating with other causes, considerably diminished its importance as a port. A few vessels are still employed in the Mediterranean trade and in the Newfoundland fishery; in addition to which, it carries on a tolerable coasting trade. The principal imports are coal, timber, wine, brandy, geneva, tobacco, and rice, for which it was made a bonding port by an order of council, in 1817: the chief exports are Portland-stone, pipe-clay, Roman cement, bricks, tiles, slates, corn, and flour. The number of vessels belonging to the port, in 1829, was eighty-seven, of the aggregate burden of seven thousand one hundred and seventy-five tons; and, in the course of the year 1828, four hundred and twenty vessels cleared outwards, and four hundred and four entered inwards. Ship-building is carried on to some extent; and many persons are employed in the manufacture of ropes, twine, and cordage, and in the

making of sails. The quay, on which is the custom-house, a neat and commodious building, is well adapted to the loading and unloading of goods, but, from the accumulation of sand in the harbour, it is not accessible to ships of large burden. Three steam-packets sail regularly, on Wednesdays and Saturdays, for Guernsey, Jersey, and the neighbouring islands; and a cutter once a week, which is neatly fitted up for the accommodation of passengers, and the conveyance of merchandize. The market days are Tuesday and Friday: the town is abundantly supplied with fish of every description, with the small mutton from the isle of Portland, and with provisions of all kinds.

Corporate Seal.

Weymouth and Melcombe - Regis, which had been distinct boroughs, and had returned members to parliament, the latter since the 8th, and the former since the 12th, of Edward II., were united into one borough by charter of Elizabeth, confirmed by James I., and upon its loss, in 1803, by neglect in filling up vacancies in the corporate body, renewed by George III. Under this charter, the government is vested in a mayor, recorder, two bailiffs, an indefinite number of aldermen (generally not less than eight), and twenty-four principal burgesses, assisted by a town clerk, two serjeants at mace, and subordinate officers. The mayor, who is also coroner and clerk of the market, and the bailiffs, are elected annually (the former by the inhabitants, and the latter by the corporation), on St. Matthew's day; and the recorder and town clerk are appointed by the mayor and aldermen. The mayor, recorder, and two bailiffs, are justices of the peace, and are empowered to hold a court of session quarterly, for offences not capital, which court is held only at Michaelmas, and merely *pro formâ*, no prisoners having been tried for many years; a court leet is held at the same period. The corporation also hold a court of record every Tuesday, under their charter, for the recovery of debts to any amount. The town hall, in which the courts are held, and the business of the corporation is transacted, is situated in the market-place, and under it is a small prison. The borough, since its union, has continued to return four members to parliament: the right of election is vested in the corporation and freeholders generally not receiving alms, of whom the number is about six hundred, every elector being entitled to vote for four candidates: the mayor is the returning officer.

The living of Weymouth is a perpetual curacy, annexed to the rectory of Wyke-Regis, in the archdeaconry of Dorset, and diocese of Bristol: the church, which was dedicated to St. Nicholas, is in ruins. Melcombe, previously to the reign of James I., was a chapel of ease to Radipole, from which it was separated in 1605, when a new church was built on the site of the former chapel, and made parochial in 1606: the living is a rectory, to which the living of Radipole, now a perpetual curacy, is annexed, in the archdeaconry of Dorset, and diocese of Bristol, rated in the king's books at

£11. 5. 5., and in the patronage of W. Wyndham, Esq. The church, dedicated to St. Mary, having become greatly dilapidated, an act of parliament was obtained, in the 55th of George III., for rebuilding it, which was completed in 1817; it is a spacious neat edifice, containing two thousand sittings, including eight hundred additional ones erected by grant of £800 from the Incorporated Society for the enlargement of churches and chapels, of which one half are free; it is appropriated to the use of the inhabitants of Weymouth and Melcombe-Regis: the interior is neatly fitted up, and the altarpiece is embellished with a painting of the Last Supper, by Sir James Thornhill. There are places of worship for Baptists, the Society of Friends, Independents, and Wesleyan Methodists. The two National schools, in which six hundred, and the Lancasterian, in which about two hundred, children of both sexes are instructed, are supported by subscription; and there are several small bequests for the education of children, especially one amounting to £21. 10. per annum, by Mr. Harbin, in 1703; another of £70, for teaching eight boys, and a third of £28, for teaching two boys navigation, left by Mr. Taylor, in 1753. Sir James Thornhill built an almshouse, in St. Mary's-street, for decayed seamen, but, having no endowment, it fell to decay; a small portion only is remaining, the greater part having been taken down. At Nottington, about two miles and a half distant, on the Dorchester road, is a mineral spring, the water of which is considered efficacious in scrofula. In the centre of the town was a priory of Black canons, dedicated to St. Winifred, founded by some member of the family of Rogers of Bryanston: the buildings occupied a quadrangular area of nearly one acre, but they have been entirely removed, and several small houses erected on the site: in digging up the foundations, a great quantity of human bones was found. The burning cliff at Weymouth has long attracted the notice of naturalists, and is at present (1831) raging with greater fury than it has hitherto been known to display. Certain masses of blue lias, which, when sawn asunder, exhibit beautiful specimens of spar, cornua ammonis, &c., have recently been discovered in the rear of Melcombe. Sir James Thornhill, the celebrated painter, was a native of Melcombe-Regis, and represented that borough in parliament in the reign of George I. Melcombe conferred the title of baron on Bubb Doddington, with whom it became extinct; Weymouth gives that of baron to the family of Thynne.

WHADDON, a parish in the hundred of Cottesloe, county of Buckingham, 4¼ miles (S. by E.) from Stony-Stratford, containing, with the hamlet of Nash, 900 inhabitants. The living is a vicarage, in the archdeaconry of Buckingham, and diocese of Lincoln, rated in the king's books at £10, endowed with £600 private benefaction, £600 royal bounty, and £200 parliamentary grant, and in the patronage of the Warden and Fellows of New College, Oxford. The church is dedicated to St. Mary. A charity school was founded here by a Mr. Coare, who endowed it with £10 per annum for teaching twenty children: he also erected an almshouse, but died before fulfilling his intention of endowing it. A small priory of Benedictine monks, in honour of St. Leonard, was founded at Snelleshall, prior to the time of Henry III., by Ralph Martel, which, at the dissolution, had a revenue of £24. The prior

obtained, in 1227, a grant of a weekly market on Thursday, long since disused. Whaddon Hall was once the seat of Arthur, Lord Grey, who was honoured by a visit from Queen Elizabeth, in 1568, then on her Buckinghamshire progress. Spenser, the poet, his lordship's secretary, was frequently here: it was afterwards purchased and occupied by Browne Willis, the antiquary. Dr. Richard Cox, Bishop of Ely, an eminent champion of the Reformation, and one of the principal composers of the Liturgy, was born in this parish, in 1499.

WHADDON, a parish in the hundred of Armingford, county of Cambridge, 4¼ miles (N.) from Royston, containing 318 inhabitants. The living is a discharged vicarage, in the archdeaconry and diocese of Ely, rated in the king's books at £7. 2. 3½., endowed with £200 private benefaction, and £200 royal bounty, and in the patronage of the Dean and Canons of Windsor. The church is dedicated to St. Mary. The river Cam runs through the parish.

WHADDON, a parish in the middle division of the hundred of Dudstone and King's Barton, county of Gloucester, 3¼ miles (S. by W.) from Gloucester, containing 139 inhabitants. The living is a perpetual curacy, in the archdeaconry and diocese of Gloucester, endowed with £400 royal bounty, and £400 parliamentary grant, and in the patronage of William Capel, Esq. The church is dedicated to St. Margaret.

WHADDON, a parish in the hundred of Melksham, county of Wilts, 2¼ miles (N. E. by N.) from Trowbridge, containing 63 inhabitants. The living is a discharged rectory, in the archdeaconry and diocese of Salisbury, rated in the king's books at £8. 4. 4½., endowed with £200 private benefaction, and £200 royal bounty, and in the joint patronage of the Lords of the Manor. The river Avon, and the Kennet and Avon canal, pass through the parish.

WHALEY, a joint township with Yeardsley, in the parish of Taxall, hundred of Macclesfield, county palatine of Chester, 9¼ miles (S. E.) from Stockport, containing, with Yeardsley, 421 inhabitants. There is a place of worship for Wesleyan Methodists. The Peak Forest canal passes through the parish.

WHALLEY, a parish comprising the borough and market town of Clitheroe, the market towns of Burnley and Colne, the chapelries of Old Accrington, Altham, Bacup, Cliviger, Downham, Goldshaw-Booth, Great Marsden, New-Church with Deadwin-Clough, Padiham, and Pendleton, and the townships of New Accrington, Barley with Whitley-Booths, Barrowford, Higher Booths, Lower Booths, Brierscliffe with Extwistle, Chatburn, Dunnockshaw, Foulridge, Habergham-Eaves, Hapton, Heyhouses, Higham-Booth, Reedly-Hallows with Filly-Close and New Laund-Booth, Huncoat, Ightenhill Park, Little Marsden, Mearley, Little Mitton, Read, Rough-Lee-Booth, Simonstone, Trawden-Forest, Twiston, Whalley, Wheatley-Carr, Wiswell, Worsthorn, Worston, and Yate with Pick-up-Bank, in the higher division of the hundred of Blackburn, and the market town of Haslingden, the chapelry of Church-Town, and the townships of Bowland with Leagram, Clayton le Moors, and Oswaldtwistle, in the lower division of the hundred of Blackburn, county palatine of Lancaster; the township of Willington, in the second division of the hundred of Eddisbury, county palatine of Chester; and the chapelry of Whitewell, in the western division of the wapentake of STAINCLIFFE and EWCROSS, West riding of the county of YORK; and containing 84,198 inhabitants, of which number, 1058 are in the township of Whalley, 4 miles (S. by W.) from Clitheroe. The living is a vicarage, in the archdeaconry and diocese of Chester, rated in the king's books at £6. 3. 9., endowed with £200 private benefaction, £300 royal bounty, and £600 parliamentary grant, and in the patronage of the Archbishop of Canterbury. The church, dedicated to All Saints, is a large structure, principally in the early English style, of which the chancel is a very fine specimen: the interior contains eighteen ancient stalls, and some considerable remains of good screen-work, brought from the old abbey. There is a place of worship for Wesleyan Methodists. This parish is about thirty miles in length by fifteen in breadth, though but little more than half its ancient extent, which included also the present parishes of Blackburn, Chipping, Mitton, Ribchester, Rochdale, and Slaidburn, which have been separated from it at different times. The rivers Calder and Ribble form a junction at the western extremity of the parish. The village is chiefly celebrated for the venerable ruins of its abbey, which exhibit portions in the early, decorated, and later, styles of English architecture: they are still considerable, and possess much interest. This house was founded, in 1296, by Henry Lacy, Earl of Lincoln, in honour of the Blessed Virgin Mary, for monks of the Cistercian order, whose revenue, at the dissolution, was estimated at £551. 4. 6. Here are manufactures of cotton, rope, and nails. The free grammar school, founded by Queen Elizabeth, was rebuilt by subscription, in 1725, with a dwelling-house for the master, who receives an annuity of £12. 8. 2. from the crown rents, and another of £4. 14. arising from the bequests of John Chewe and Sir Edmund Assheton: it is open for the classical instruction of all boys of the township, but there are only twelve at present upon the foundation: this school, in conjunction with those of Burnley and Middleton, has an interest in thirteen scholarships, founded in Brasenose College, Oxford, by Dr. Nowell, in 1572. A National school was erected by subscription in 1819.

WHALTON, a parish in the western division of CASTLE ward, county of NORTHUMBERLAND, comprising the townships of Newnham, Ocle, or Ogle, Riplington, and Whalton, and containing 534 inhabitants, of which number, 285 are in the township of Whalton, 6 miles (S.W. by W.) from Morpeth. The living is a rectory, in the archdeaconry of Northumberland, and diocese of Durham, rated in the king's books at £13. 8. 1½., and in the patronage of — Bates, Esq. The church is an ancient structure; it was repaired in 1783, when parapets and pinnacles were added to the tower. The rivers Blythe and Howburn run through the parish. The village is a neat well-built place, containing many commodious houses. A little to the eastward are the remains of considerable earthworks, supposed to enclose the site of the castle of the ancient barons of Whalton. About a mile and a half south of the village are some slight remains of Ogle castle, surrounded by a double fosse, part of which is in fine preservation. Margaret Moor, in 1720, left a small sum for teaching and clothing children.

WHAPLODE, a parish in the wapentake of ELLOE, parts of HOLLAND, county of LINCOLN, 2¾ miles (W.) from Holbeach, containing, with the chapelry of Whaplode-Drove, 1744 inhabitants. The living is a perpetual curacy, in the archdeaconry and diocese of Lincoln, rated in the king's books at £16. 14. 9½., and in the patronage of the Crown. The church, dedicated to St. Mary, has lately received an addition of two hundred sittings, of which one hundred and thirty are free, the Incorporated Society for the enlargement of churches and chapels having granted £200 towards defraying the expense. Elisha Wilson, and Frances his wife, in 1708, bequeathed land and houses, directing the rents to be applied in support of a school.

WHAPLODE-DROVE, a chapelry in the parish of WHAPLODE, wapentake of ELLOE, parts of KESTEVEN, county of LINCOLN, 5¾ miles (E.N.E.) from Crowland, containing 540 inhabitants. The living is a perpetual curacy, in the archdeaconry and diocese of Lincoln, and in the patronage of certain Trustees. The chapel is dedicated to St. John the Baptist.

WHARLES, a joint township with Treales and Roseacre, in the parish of KIRKHAM, hundred of AMOUNDERNESS, county palatine of LANCASTER, 2½ miles (N.E. by N.) from Kirkham. The population is returned with Treales.

WHARRAM le STREET, a parish comprising the township of Wharram le Street, in the wapentake of BUCKROSE, East riding of the county of YORK, 6¾ miles (S.E. by E.) from New Malton, containing 127 inhabitants. The living is a discharged vicarage, in the peculiar jurisdiction of the court of the Dean and Chapter of York, rated in the king's books at £6, endowed with £400 royal bounty, and in the patronage of Lord Middleton. The church is dedicated to St. Mary.

WHARRAM-PERCY, a parish in the wapentake of BUCKROSE, East riding of the county of YORK, comprising the townships of Raisthorpe with Birdsall, Thixendale, Towthorpe, and Wharram-Percy, and containing 336 inhabitants, of which number, 44 are in the township of Wharram-Percy, 7¼ miles (S.E.) from New Malton. The living is a discharged vicarage, in the archdeaconry of the East riding, and diocese of York, rated in the king's books at £11. 13. 4., endowed with £200 royal bounty, and in the patronage of Miss Isted and Miss Englefield.

WHARTON, a township in the parish of DAVENHAM, hundred of NORTHWICH, county palatine of CHESTER, 2½ miles (W.N.W.) from Middlewich, containing 853 inhabitants.

WHARTON, a township in the parish of BLYTON, wapentake of CORRINGHAM, parts of LINDSEY, county of LINCOLN, 3¾ miles (N.E.) from Gainsborough. The population is returned with the parish.

WHARTON, a township in the parish of KIRKBY-STEPHEN, EAST ward, county of WESTMORLAND, 2¼ miles (S. by W.) from Kirkby-Stephen, containing 81 inhabitants. The hall, once a large quadrangular building, with a tower at each angle, was the princely residence of Philip, the celebrated Duke of Wharton, and his ancestors, but is now occupied as a farm-house. The ancient village was demolished many years ago for the enlargement of the park, when the inhabitants settled at Wharton Dikes, on the other side of the Eden.

WHASHTON, a township in the parish of KIRKBY-RAVENSWORTH, western division of the wapentake of

GILLING, North riding of the county of YORK, 4 miles (N. by W.) from Richmond, containing 140 inhabitants.

WHATBOROUGH, a liberty partly in the parish of TILTON, but chiefly in that of LODDINGTON, eastern division of the hundred of GOSCOTE, county of LEICESTER, 12 miles (E. by N.) from Leicester, containing 18 inhabitants.

WHATCOMBE, a tything in the parish of FAWLEY, hundred of KINTBURY-EAGLE, county of BERKS, 6 miles (S.) from Wantage. The population is returned with the parish.

WHATCOTT, a parish in the Brails division of the hundred of KINGTON, county of WARWICK, 4¼ miles (N. E.) from Shipston upon Stour, containing 199 inhabitants. The living is a rectory, in the archdeaconry and diocese of Worcester, rated in the king's books at £12. 17. 3½., and in the patronage of the Marquis of Northampton. The church is dedicated to St. Peter.

WHATCROFT, a township in the parish of DAVENHAM, hundred of NORTHWICH, county palatine of CHESTER, 3 miles (N. W. by N.) from Middlewich, containing 71 inhabitants. The Grand Trunk canal passes through the parish.

WHATFIELD, a parish in the hundred of Cosford, county of SUFFOLK, 3¼ miles (S. E.) from Bildestone, containing 326 inhabitants. The living is a rectory, in the archdeaconry of Sudbury, and diocese of Norwich, rated in the king's books at £15. 0. 5., and in the patronage of the Master and Fellows of Jesus' College, Cambridge. The church is dedicated to St. Margaret.

WHATLEY, a parish in the hundred of FROME, county of SOMERSET, 2¾ miles (W. by S.) from Frome, containing 354 inhabitants. The living is a rectory, in the archdeaconry of Wells, and diocese of Bath and Wells, rated in the king's books at £12. 17. 1., and in the patronage of T. S. Horner, Esq. The church, dedicated to St. George, has a spire steeple; it is situated on an eminence separated from the parish of Mells by a deep ravine, the sides of which are clothed with thick woods, and at the bottom runs a small rivulet. The parish abounds with freestone, under which is limestone rock to a considerable depth : in the former are embedded fossil shells, which are also found in great abundance over the entire surface. On a bold height, at the western extremity of the parish, are vestiges of a Roman encampment.

WHATLINGTON, a parish in the hundred of BATTLE, rape of HASTINGS, county of SUSSEX, 2 miles (N. by E.) from Battle, containing 285 inhabitants. The living is a discharged rectory, in the archdeaconry of Lewes, and diocese of Chichester, rated in the king's books at £7. 4. 6., and in the patronage of the Duke of Dorset. Edward Theobald, in 1738, bequeathed £20, directing the interest to be applied in support of a school.

WHATTON, a parish in the northern division of the wapentake of BINGHAM, county of NOTTINGHAM, 2¾ miles (E.) from Bingham, containing, with the chapelry of Aslacton, 663 inhabitants. The living is a discharged vicarage, in the archdeaconry of Nottingham, and diocese of York, rated in the king's books at £5. 6. 8., endowed with £200 royal bounty, and in the patronage of G. S. Foljambe, Esq. The church, dedicated to St. John of Beverley, contains the effigy of a Knight Templar in armour, and a monumental tablet in memory of Thomas Cranmer, father of the celebrated Archbishop Cranmer, who was born at Aslacton, in this parish, in 1489. There is a place of worship for Wesleyan Methodists. Whatton is in the honour of Tutbury, duchy of Lancaster, and within the jurisdiction of a court of pleas held at Tutbury every third Tuesday, for the recovery of debts under 40s.

WHATTON (LONG), a parish in the western division of the hundred of GOSCOTE, county of LEICESTER, 4¼ miles (N. W. by W.) from Loughborough, containing 820 inhabitants. The living is a rectory, in the archdeaconry of Leicester, and diocese of Lincoln, rated in the king's books at £13. 6. 8., and in the patronage of the Crown. The church is dedicated to All Saints.

WHEATACRE (ALL SAINTS), a parish in the hundred of CLAVERING, county of NORFOLK, 4¾ miles (N. E. by E.) from Beccles, containing 159 inhabitants. The living is a discharged rectory, with the perpetual curacy of Barnby and the vicarage of Mutford annexed, in the archdeaconry of Norfolk, and diocese of Norwich, rated in the king's books at £6. 6. 5½., and in the patronage of the Master and Fellows of Caius College, Cambridge.

WHEATACRE-BURGH, or BURGH (ST. PETER), a parish in the hundred of CLAVERING, county of NORFOLK, 6¾ miles (E. N. E.) from Beccles, containing 259 inhabitants. The living is a discharged rectory, in the archdeaconry of Norfolk, and diocese of Norwich, rated in the king's books at £7. 6. 8., and in the patronage of the Rev. Samuel Boycatt.

WHEATENHURST, a parish in the lower division of the hundred of WHITSTONE, county of GLOUCESTER, 8 miles (N. W. by W.) from Stroud, containing 370 inhabitants. The living is a perpetual curacy, in the archdeaconry and diocese of Gloucester, rated in the king's books at £7. 12. 3½. Thomas Moore, Esq. and others were patrons in 1813. The church is dedicated to St. Andrew. The Gloucester and Berkeley, and the Thames and Severn, canals pass through the parish; and the river Severn is navigable on its northern boundary, near which there are extensive ironworks.

WHEATFIELD, a parish in the hundred of PIRTON, county of OXFORD, 2¼ miles (S.) from Tetsworth, containing 79 inhabitants. The living is a rectory, in the archdeaconry and diocese of Oxford, rated in the king's books at £9. 10. 10., and in the patronage of the Hon. John Spencer. The manor-house was destroyed by fire in 1814, and is now in ruins.

WHEATHAMPSTEAD, a parish in the hundred of DACORUM, county of HERTFORD, 4¼ miles (W. S. W.) from Welwyn, containing 1584 inhabitants. The living is a rectory, with the perpetual curacy of Harpenden annexed, in the archdeaconry of Huntingdon, and diocese of Lincoln, rated in the king's books at £42. 1. 10½., and in the patronage of the Bishop of Lincoln. The church, dedicated to St. Helen, is an ancient cruciform structure: the font is a curious specimen of the early decorated style. There is a place of worship for Independents. The river Lea runs through the parish. A National school, erected in 1814, is supported by voluntary contributions ; about fifty children of each sex are admitted. Sundry small bequests are annually applied for apprenticing two poor boys. The rebellious barons here assembled their forces against Edward II., in 1311, on which occasion two nuncios, sent by the pope, endeavoured to restore peace between the contending parties, when the papal authority was rejected by the former. John Bostock, abbot of St. Albans, a learned divine and poet in the time of Henry VI., was born here, and was commonly called John of Wheathampstead. The St. Albans races are held on ground, called Nomans land, which extends into this parish.

WHEATHILL, a parish in the hundred of Stottesden, county of Salop, 9½ miles (N. E. by E.) from Ludlow, containing 141 inhabitants. The living is a rectory, in the archdeaconry of Salop, and diocese of Hereford, rated in the king's books at £7. 5. 7½., and in the patronage of T. Holland, Esq. The church is dedicated to the Holy Trinity. A weekly market and an annual fair were granted to this place by Edward I., both which have been long disused.

WHEATHILL, a parish in the hundred of Whitley, county of Somerset, 4 miles (W. by S.) from Castle-Cary, containing 47 inhabitants. The living is a discharged rectory, in the archdeaconry of Wells, and diocese of Bath and Wells, rated in the king's books at £4. 5. 2¼., and in the patronage of Mrs. Phillips. The church is dedicated to St. John the Baptist.

WHEATLEY, a joint township with Thornley, in the parish of Chipping, lower division of the hundred of Blackburn, county palatine of Lancaster, 8½ miles (W. by S.) from Clitheroe. The population is returned with Thornley.

WHEATLEY, a chapelry in the parish of Cuddesden, hundred of Bullington, county of Oxford, 5½ miles (E. by S.) from Oxford, containing 899 inhabitants. The living is a perpetual curacy, in the archdeaconry and diocese of Oxford, endowed with £400 private benefaction, £600 royal bounty, and £300 parliamentary grant, and in the patronage of the Bishop of Oxford. The chapel is dedicated to St. Mary.

WHEATLEY, a joint township with Long Sandal, in that part of the parish of Doncaster which is within the soke of Doncaster, West riding of the county of York, 2 miles (N. E. by N.) from Doncaster. The population is returned with Long Sandal. A school for teaching poor children, and almshouses for twelve aged persons, were erected and are liberally supported by the family of Cooke.

WHEATLEY (NORTH), a parish in the North-clay division of the wapentake of Bassetlaw, county of Nottingham, 5½ miles (N. E.) from East Retford, containing 441 inhabitants. The living is a discharged vicarage, in the archdeaconry of Nottingham, and diocese of York, rated in the king's books at £3. 18. 11¼., and in the patronage of Lord Middleton. The church is dedicated to St. Peter. There is a place of worship for Wesleyan Methodists. The Roman road from Doncaster to Lincoln passes through the parish. Four children are educated for a trifling annuity, the bequest of Thomas James. A National school, in connexion with the parent institution, has been established here.

WHEATLEY (SOUTH), a parish in the North-clay division of the wapentake of Bassetlaw, county of Nottingham, 5½ miles (N. E. by E.) from East Retford, containing 47 inhabitants. The living is a discharged rectory, in the peculiar jurisdiction and patronage of the

Chapter of the Collegiate Church of Southwell, rated in the king's books at £6. 14. 2. The church is dedicated to St. Helen.

WHEATLEY-CARR, a township in that part of the parish of Whalley which is in the higher division of the hundred of Blackburn, county palatine of Lancaster, 3¾ miles (W. S. W.) from Colne, containing 69 inhabitants.

WHEATON-ASTON, a chapelry in the parish of Lapley, western division of the hundred of Cuttlestone, county of Stafford, 5¼ miles (W. by S.) from Penkridge, containing 718 inhabitants.

WHEDDICAR, a township in the parish of St. Bees, Allerdale ward above Darwent, county of Cumberland, 2¾ miles (E. by S.) from Whitehaven, containing 52 inhabitants.

WHEELOCK, a township in that part of the parish of Sandbach which is in the hundred of Northwich, county palatine of Chester, 1½ mile (S. S. W.) from Sandbach, containing 458 inhabitants. There is a place of worship for Wesleyan Methodists. The Grand Trunk canal passes through the parish, and on its banks are commodious wharfs and warehouses. Cotton is manufactured here, and there is a brewery; but the chief trade of the place is in salt, of which large quantities are extracted from the brine found, at the depth of sixty yards, on both sides of the river Wheelock.

WHEELTON, a township in the parish and hundred of Leyland, county palatine of Lancaster, 4 miles (N. E. by N.) from Chorley, containing 1186 inhabitants.

WHELDRAKE, a parish partly within the liberty of St. Peter of York, but chiefly in the wapentake of Ouze and Derwent, East riding of the county of York, 7½ miles (S. E.) from York, containing, with the township of Langwith, 677 inhabitants. The living is a rectory, in the archdeaconry of Cleveland, and diocese of York, rated in the king's books at £25. 17. 3½., and in the patronage of the Archbishop of York. The church, dedicated to St. Helen, was rebuilt in 1789. There are places of worship for Wesleyan Methodists and Methodists of the New Connexion. A manorial court is occasionally held here, for the recovery of small debts, at which a bailiff is appointed. Nineteen children are educated for about £12 a year, arising from the bequests of Silvester Walker, in 1775, and others.

WHELPINGTON (KIRK), a parish in the northeastern division of Tindale ward, county of Northumberland, comprising the townships of Great Bavington, Capheaton, Catcherside, Coldwell, Crogdean, Fawns, Little Harle, West Harle, Kirk-Whelpington, and West-Whelpington, and containing 793 inhabitants, of which number, 277 are in the township of Kirk-Whelpington, 11 miles (E. by N.) from Bellingham. The living is a vicarage, in the archdeaconry of Northumberland, and diocese of Durham, rated in the king's books at £7. 3. 4., and in the patronage of the Bishop of Durham. The church, dedicated to St. Bartholomew, is ancient, and constitutes the remains of a much larger structure. The river Wansbeck has its source in this parish, which is a hilly and extensive district, for the most part composed of sheep and dairy farms. Limestone and sandstone are plentiful, and the moors afford an almost inexhaustible supply of peat for fuel. There is a spring, the water of which is impregnated with sulphur, and has been found efficacious in chronic disorders. In various parts of the parish are traces of circular and rectilinear earthworks, probably thrown up in the border wars, for the protection of cattle from the moss-troopers. Whelpington tower, now the vicarage-house, was anciently fortified.

WHELPINGTON (WEST), a township in the parish of KIRK-WHELPINGTON, north-eastern division of TINDALE ward, county of NORTHUMBERLAND, 15½ miles (W.) from Morpeth, containing 69 inhabitants. Horns castle, situated on a commanding eminence in this township, has been converted into a farm-house.

WHENBY, a parish in the wapentake of BULMER, North riding of the county of YORK, 9¼ miles (E.) from Easingwould, containing 129 inhabitants. The living is a discharged vicarage, in the archdeaconry of Cleveland, and diocese of York, rated in the king's books at £4. 8. 4., and in the patronage of W. Garforth, Esq. The church is dedicated to St. Martin.

WHEPSTEAD, a parish in the hundred of THINGOE, county of SUFFOLK, 4¼ miles (S. S. W.) from Bury-St. Edmunds, containing 664 inhabitants. The living is a rectory, in the archdeaconry of Sudbury, and diocese of Norwich, rated in the king's books at £14. 4. 2., and in the patronage of the Rev. T. Image. Thomas Sparke, in 1721, bequeathed land, now producing an annual income of about £16, for which twelve poor children are educated.

WHERSTEAD, a parish in the hundred of SAMFORD, county of SUFFOLK, 2¾ miles (S. by W.) from Ipswich, containing 242 inhabitants. The living is a discharged vicarage, in the archdeaconry of Suffolk, and diocese of Norwich, rated in the king's books at £5.6.8., and in the patronage of the Crown. The church is dedicated to St. Mary. The parish is bounded on the north-east by the river Orwell.

WHERWELL, a parish in the hundred of WHERWELL, Andover division of the county of SOUTHAMPTON, 3¾ miles (S. S. E.) from Andover, containing, with the tything of Westover, 622 inhabitants. The living is a vicarage, with the perpetual curacies of Bullington and Tufton annexed, in the archdeaconry and diocese of Winchester, rated in the king's books at £14, and in the patronage of Colonel Iremonger, as rector of the sinecure rectory, which was a prebend in the nunnery of Wherwell, and is rated in the king's books at £44. 11. 0½. The church is dedicated to the Holy Cross. The rivers Test and Ande run through the parish; the latter falls into the Redbridge and Andover canal. A fair for cattle is held on September 24th. A Benedictine nunnery was founded and amply endowed here, about 986, by Elfrida, Queen Dowager, in expiation of the murders of her first consort, Athelwold, and her step-son, Edward the Martyr; she spent the latter part of her life in it, and was buried within its walls. It was dedicated to the Holy Cross and St. Peter, and at the dissolution had a revenue of £403. 12. 10. There is a very extensive wood in this parish, in a recess of which is a stone cross, with the following inscription on its base : "About the year of our Lord DCCCCLXIII Upon this spot beyond the time of memory, Called Dead Man's Plack, Tradition reports that Edgar (Sirnamed the Peaceable) King of England, in the ardour of Youth, Love and Indignation, Slew with his own hand his treacherous, and ungrateful Favourite, Earl Athelwold,

owner of this Forest of Harewood, in resentment of the Earl's having basely betrayed his Royal confidence, and perfidiously married his Intended Bride The beautious Elfrida, Daughter of Ordgar, Earl of Devonshire, after Wife to King Edgar and by him Mother of King Etheldred the 2nd, which Queen Elfrida, after Edgar's Death, murdered his eldest Son, King Edward the Martyr, and founded the Nunnery of Whor-well."

WHESSOE, a township in that part of the parish of HAUGHTON le SKERNE which is in the south-eastern division of DARLINGTON ward, county palatine of DURHAM, 2½ miles (N. by W.) from Darlington, containing 99 inhabitants. The Stockton and Darlington railway passes through the parish.

WHETMORE, a joint township with Buraston, in the parish of BURFORD, hundred of OVERS, county of SALOP, 2½ miles (N. N. E.) from Tenbury. The population is returned with Buraston.

WHETSTONE, a hamlet in the parish of TIDESWELL, hundred of HIGH PEAK, county of DERBY, 1¼ mile (W.) from Tideswell, containing 66 inhabitants.

WHETSTONE, a parish in the hundred of GUTHLAXTON, county of LEICESTER, 5¼ miles (S. S. W.) from Leicester, containing 883 inhabitants. The living is a perpetual curacy, annexed to the vicarage of Enderby, in the archdeaconry of Leicester, and diocese of Lincoln. The church is dedicated to St. Peter. The river Soar bounds the parish on the north-west.

WHETSTONE, a hamlet partly in the parish of EAST BARNET, hundred of CASHIO, or liberty of ST. ALBANS, county of HERTFORD, and partly in that of FRYERN-BARNET, Finsbury division of the hundred of OSSULSTONE, county of MIDDLESEX, 8 miles (N. N. W.) from London. The population is returned with the respective parishes.

WHICHAM, a parish in ALLERDALE ward above Darwent, county of CUMBERLAND, 10 miles (S. S. E.) from Ravenglass, containing 301 inhabitants. The living is a discharged rectory, in the archdeaconry of Richmond, and diocese of Chester, rated in the king's books at £8. 15., and in the patronage of the Earl of Lonsdale. The church is dedicated to St. Mary. An annuity of £16, supposed to have been granted by Queen Elizabeth from the Crown revenues of the county, and payable out of the Exchequer, is applied towards the support of a grammar school for the parishes of Whicham and Millom. The school-house was erected at Churchgate, pursuant to a decree of Chancery, in 1688, when trustees were appointed, with power to fix the amount of quarterages to be paid by the scholars, in augmentation of the master's income: from fifty to sixty are educated upon this foundation.

WHICHFORD, a parish in the Brails division of the hundred of KINGTON, county of WARWICK, 6 miles (S. E.) from Shipston upon Stour, containing, with the hamlets of Ascott and Stowerton, 583 inhabitants. The living is a rectory, in the archdeaconry and diocese of Worcester, rated in the king's books at £19. 8. 6½., and in the patronage of Earl Beauchamp. The church is dedicated to St. Michael.

WHICKHAM, a parish in the western division of CHESTER ward, county palatine of DURHAM, comprising the townships of Fellside, Lowside, Swalwell, and Whickham, and containing 3713 inhabitants, of which number, 788 are in the township of Whickham, 3½ miles (W.S.W.)

from Gateshead. The living is a rectory, in the archdeaconry and diocese of Durham, rated in the king's books at £20. 8. 11½., and in the patronage of the Bishop of Durham. The church, dedicated to St. Mary, and the village, which is a genteel place, are pleasantly situated on an eminence. There are extensive coal mines in the parish; also a bed of calcined earth, produced by the English having set fire to their camp, when pressed by the Scottish army under Leslie, which communicated with a seam of coal that burnt with great fury for some years. A charity school was erected, about 1711, by Robert Thomlinson, D.D., then rector of the parish; it is supported by various bequests subsequently made by him and others, and from the rental of certain galleries and pews constructed in the church at the founder's expense: the building was enlarged in 1825, by Archdeacon Bouyer. Ten pounds per annum, and a house and school-room, are also allowed by the Earl of Strathmore to a schoolmaster at Fellside. See SWALWELL.

WHIDHILL, a township in the parish of ST. SAMPSON, borough of CRICKLADE, hundred of HIGHWORTH, CRICKLADE, and STAPLE, county of WILTS, 2¾ miles (S. E.) from Cricklade, containing 21 inhabitants.

WHILE, a joint parish with Puddlestone, in the hundred of WOLPHY, county of HEREFORD, 5½ miles (E. by N.) from Leominster. The population is returned with Puddlestone. The living is a rectory, united to the vicarage of Puddlestone, in the archdeaconry and diocese of Hereford.

WHILLYMOOR, a township in the parish of ARLECDON, ALLERDALE ward above Darwent, county of CUMBERLAND, 5½ miles (E.N.E.) from Whitehaven. The population is returned with the parish.

WHILTON, a parish in the hundred of NOBOTTLE-GROVE, county of NORTHAMPTON, 5 miles (E. N.E.) from Daventry, containing 370 inhabitants. The living is a rectory, in the archdeaconry of Northampton, and diocese of Peterborough, rated in the king's books at £12. 16. 3. Mrs. Rose was patroness in 1814. The church is dedicated to St. Andrew. The old Watling-street, and the Grand Junction canal, pass through the parish. Jonathan Emery, in 1768, bequeathed £500, and Judith Worsfold £1000 three per cent. consols., producing together about £57 per annum, which is applied for teaching from seventy to eighty children.

WHIMPLE, a parish in the hundred of CLISTON, county of DEVON, 4½ miles (W.N.W.) from Ottery St. Mary, containing, with a portion of the tything of Rawleigh, which is in this parish, 557 inhabitants. The living is a rectory, in the archdeaconry and diocese of Exeter, rated in the king's books at £30, and in the patronage of the Duke of Bedford. The church is dedicated to St. Mary. A fair for sheep is held on the Monday before Michaelmas-day.

WHINBERGH, a parish in the hundred of MITFORD, county of NORFOLK, 3½ miles (S.S.E.) from East Dereham, containing 196 inhabitants. The living is a discharged rectory, united to that of Westfield, in the archdeaconry of Norfolk, and diocese of Norwich, rated in the king's books at £6. 18. 6½. The church is dedicated to St. Mary.

WHINFELL, a township in the parish of BRIGHAM, ALLERDALE ward above Darwent, county of CUMBERLAND, 3¾ miles (S.) from Cockermouth, containing 107 inhabitants.

WHINFELL, a township in that part of the parish of KENDAL which is in KENDAL ward, county of WESTMORLAND, 6½ miles (N. E. by N.) from Kendal, containing 204 inhabitants. The school-room was rebuilt by the late Mr. Shepherd, but there is no endowment.

WHIPPINGHAM, a parish in the liberty of EAST MEDINA, Isle of Wight division of the county of SOUTHAMPTON, 3½ miles (N. by E.) from Newport, containing 2068 inhabitants. The living is a rectory, in the archdeaconry and diocese of Winchester, rated in the king's books at £19. 1. 5½., and in the patronage of the Crown. The church, dedicated to St. Mildred, is a large structure, principally in the later English style, with a tower and spire. The parish lies on the east side of the navigable river Medina, and is bounded on the north-east by the Motherbank: it contains the populous hamlet of East Cowes, which is separated from West Cowes by the river. On the brow of a neighbouring hill is East Cowes castle, erected by Mr. Nash, for his own residence and commanding some fine sea views; it has one square, and two circular, embattled towers. Old Castle point, on this coast, is the site of a fort constructed in the reign of Henry VIII. At Barton, in this parish, was an oratory of Augustine monks, founded in 1282, by John de Insula, the remains of which have been converted into a farm-house.

WHIPSNADE, a parish in the hundred of MANSHEAD, county of BEDFORD, 3 miles (S.W.) from Dunstable, containing 199 inhabitants. The living is a discharged rectory, in the archdeaconry of Bedford, and diocese of Lincoln, rated in the king's books at £7. 13. 4., and in the patronage of the Crown. The church is dedicated to St. Mary Magdalene.

WHISBY, a chapelry in the parish of DODDINGTON, lower division of the wapentake of BOOTHBY-GRAFFO, parts of KESTEVEN, county of LINCOLN, 6 miles (S.W. by W.) from Lincoln, containing 68 inhabitants.

WHISSENDINE, a parish in the hundred of ALSTOE, county of RUTLAND, 4½ miles (N.W. by N.) from Oakham, containing 701 inhabitants. The living is a discharged vicarage, in the archdeaconry of Northampton, and diocese of Peterborough, rated in the king's books at £7. 1., and in the patronage of the Earl of Harborough. The church is dedicated to St. Andrew.

WHISSONSETT, a parish in the hundred of LAUNDITCH, county of NORFOLK, 4¾ miles (S.) from Fakenham, containing 522 inhabitants. The living is a discharged rectory, in the archdeaconry and diocese of Norwich, rated in the king's books at £10. 3. 4., and in the patronage of F. R. Reynolds, Esq. The church is dedicated to St. Mary: in the chancel are gravestones, of grey marble, with effigies of some members of the ancient family of Bozoun.

WHISTLEY-HURST, a liberty in that part of the parish of HURST which is in the hundred of CHARLTON, county of BERKS, 5¼ miles (E. by N.) from Reading, containing 847 inhabitants. A school is supported by annual donations of about £12.

WHISTON, a township in the parish of PRESCOT, hundred of WEST DERBY, county palatine of LANCASTER, 1¼ mile (S.) from Prescot, containing 1306 inha-

'bitants, most of whom are employed in the extensive collieries here.

WHISTON, a parish in the hundred of WYMERS-LEY, county of NORTHAMPTON, 6¾ miles (E. by S.) from Northampton, containing 47 inhabitants. The living is a rectory, to which a portion of the rectory of Denton is annexed, in the archdeaconry of Northampton, and diocese of Peterborough, rated in the king's books at £14. 11. 0½., and in the patronage of Lord Boston. The church, dedicated to St. Mary, was built, about 1534, by Anthony Catesby, Esq.: it is remarkable for the beauty of its proportions, and is in the later English style of architecture, with a lofty and elegant tower crowned with rich pinnacles; the font is octagonal, with panelled sides handsomely executed. The river Nene runs through the parish, in which are the remains of a moated building, said to have been the residence of King John. Limestone abounds here.

WHISTON, a township in that part of the parish of PENKRIDGE which is in the eastern division of the hundred of CUTTLESTONE, county of STAFFORD, 2 miles (W.) from Penkridge. The population is returned with the township of Penkridge.

WHISTON, a township in that part of the parish of KINGSLEY which is in the northern division of the hundred of TOTMONSLOW, county of STAFFORD, 3¾ miles (N. E.) from Cheadle, containing 403 inhabitants.

WHISTON, a parish in the southern division of the wapentake of STRAFFORTH and TICKHILL, West riding of the county of YORK, 2½ miles (S. E.) from Rother-ham, containing 859 inhabitants. The living is a rectory, in the archdeaconry and diocese of York, rated in the king's books at £10, and in the patronage of Lord Howard of Effingham. The church is dedicated to St. James. There is a place of worship for Wesleyan Methodists. Francis Mansel, in 1728, bequeathed a rent-charge of £6 for teaching twelve children; Mr. Shaw, in 1719, left £5 a year for the education of ten; and Joseph Hammond, in 1794, among other charitable bequests, gave a proportionate sum for the instruction of twelve.

WHISTONS, a tything in the parish of CLAINES, lower division of the hundred of OSWALDSLOW, county of WORCESTER, adjacent to the north side of the city of Worcester, containing 1344 inhabitants. A priory of White nuns, in honour of St. Mary Magdalene, was founded here, before 1255, by a bishop of Worcester, which at the dissolution had a revenue of £56. 3. 7. An hospital, dedicated to St. Oswald, said to have been founded by Bishop Oswald, for a master and poor brethren, existed here before 1268, and at the dissolution was valued at £15. 18. per ann., when it was granted to the Dean and Chapter of Worcester: it was demolished in the reign of Elizabeth, but after the Restoration was rebuilt by Bishop Fell, who recovered most of its ancient possessions, and it now affords an asylum for twelve poor men. A new gaol has been erected here.

WHITACRE (NETHER), a parish in the Ather-stone division of the hundred of HEMLINGFORD, county of WARWICK, 3¼ miles (N. E.) from Coleshill, containing 408 inhabitants. The living is a perpetual curacy, in the archdeaconry of Coventry, and diocese of Lichfield and Coventry, endowed with £400 private bene-

faction, and £400 royal bounty, and in the patronage of Earl Howe. The church is dedicated to St. Giles. There is a place of worship for Wesleyan Methodists. The river Tame runs through the parish. Charles Jennins, Esq., in 1775, bequeathed one-third of the interest of £1000 in support of a school.

WHITACRE (OVER), a parish in the Atherstone division of the hundred of HEMLINGFORD, county of WARWICK, 3½ miles (E. N. E.) from Coleshill, containing 292 inhabitants. The living is a perpetual curacy, in the archdeaconry of Coventry, and diocese of Lichfield and Coventry, endowed with £400 private benefaction, and £400 royal bounty, and in the patronage of Earl Howe. The church is dedicated to St. Leonard. Six poor children are educated for the interest of £40, bequeathed by the Rev. Thomas Morrall, in 1740.

WHITBECK, a parish in ALLERDALE ward above Darwent, county of CUMBERLAND, 8¾ miles (S. S. E.) from Ravenglass, containing 221 inhabitants. The living is a perpetual curacy, in the archdeaconry of Richmond, and diocese of Chester, endowed with £200 private benefaction, and £600 royal bounty, and in the patronage of W. Parke, Esq. The church is dedicated to St. Mary. The parish is situated between the mountain of Black-Comb and the sea. In the former is a cavity, similar to the crater of a volcano, several hundred yards in diameter and depth; the inside is lined with vitrified and crystallized matter, having at the bottom a fine spring of water. On the west side of the mountain is a cascade, and on the shore a mineral spring, formerly in repute for the cure of gravel and scurvy. Trunks of oak and fir, of an immense size, have been found in the peat mosses, considerably below the surface. Here are the remains of three Druidical temples; one, termed Standing-stones, consists of eight massive stones disposed in a circle; Kirkstones, of thirty, in two circles, like Stonehenge; and the third of twelve stones: there is also a large cairn, encompassed at the base by a circle of huge stones. An hospital, built by the parishioners in 1632, is endowed with a rent-charge of £24 per annum, purchased with the sum of £400 bequeathed by Henry Parke, a native of this place.

WHITBOURNE, a parish in the hundred of BROX-ASH, county of HEREFORD, 6 miles (E. by N.) from Bromyard, containing 821 inhabitants. The living is a rectory, in the archdeaconry and diocese of Hereford, rated in the king's books at £14. 14. 9½., and in the patronage of the Bishop of Hereford. The church is dedicated to St. John the Baptist. The Bishops of Hereford had a palace here, the remains of which are occupied as a farm-house.

WHITBURN, a parish in the eastern division of CHESTER ward, county palatine of DURHAM, 3½ miles (N.) from Sunderland, containing, with the township of Cleadon, 856 inhabitants. The living is a rectory, in the archdeaconry and diocese of Durham, rated in the king's books at £39. 19. 4½., and in the patronage of the Bishop of Durham. There is a place of worship for Wesleyan Methodists. The parish is bounded on the east by the North sea, and on the shore several copper coins of Constantine, Licinius, Maxentius, and Maximian, have been found. Limestone is quarried to a great extent, and conveyed up the river Tyne into Yorkshire: coal also is obtained here, though it lies at a great depth. There are several chalybeate springs in the neighbourhood, the water of which is in great request among the inhabitants.

WHITBY, a township partly in the parish of East-ham, and partly in that of Stoke, higher division of the hundred of Wirrall, county palatine of Chester, 6¼ miles (N.) from Chester, containing 250 inhabitants. The Ellesmere, or Wirrall, canal passes through the parish.

WHITBY, a parish in the liberty of Whitby-Strand, North riding of the county of York, comprising the sea-port and market town of Whitby, and the townships of Aislaby, Eskdale-Side, Hawsker *cum* Stainsacre, Newholm *cum* Dunsley, Ruswarp, and Ugglesbarnby, and containing 12,331 inhabitants, of which number, 8697 are in the town of Whitby, 48 miles (N. N. E.) from York, and 241 (N. by W.) from London. This place was originally called by the Saxons *Streones-halh*, which Bede translates *Sinus-fari*, the bay of the lighthouse, or tower, probably from a tower built there by the Romans. At the time of the Conquest, either from the colour of the houses, or from its conspicuous situation, it was called *Whitteby*, or the White Town, of which its present name is a contraction; and a certain portion of the town, or an appendage belonging to it, was then called *Prestby*, or Priests' Town. Its origin may be ascribed to the monastery founded by Oswy, King of Northumberland, in fulfilment of a vow which he made in 655, prior to his encountering Penda, King of Mercia, who had invaded his dominions, and whom he defeated and killed. In fulfilment of the same vow, his daughter Ælfleda became a nun in this monastery, which was placed under the superintendence of Hilda, grand niece of Edwin, King of Northumberland, who, in 658, came from Hartlepool to commence this establishment, of which she was made the first abbess. A National synod, at which Oswy presided, was held here in 664, for the regulation of some minor observances in ecclesiastical affairs, about which considerable differences at that time prevailed. Under Lady Hilda, and her successor Ælfleda, the monastery became celebrated as a seat of learning, where several bishops and many eminent men received their education; and several cells, or smaller convents, were erected as appendages to the abbey, of which the principal was that of Hackness, founded, in 679, by Hilda, who died in the following year, and whose virtues subsequently obtained for her the honour of canonization. The Danes, in 867, completely destroyed the monastery, laid waste the town, and massacred the inhabitants with the most horrible barbarity : the abbot previously escaped, and is said to have carried with him the relics of St. Hilda to Glastonbury; but so complete was the devastation of these merciless invaders, that the town remained in ruins till its ancient name was lost. Towards the close of the Saxon period, Whitby began to revive, and at the time of the Conquest had become so considerable, that the manor, including its dependencies, was valued in the Norman survey at £112, being the richest in the north-east part of the county of York. The Conqueror granted the site of the town and monastery to his nephew, Hugh, Earl of Chester, who assigned it to William de Percy, by whose assistance the monastery was rebuilt by Reinfrid, a Benedictine monk from the abbey of Evesham, soon

after 1074. William de Percy afterwards endowed it with two hundred and forty acres of land, and its revenues were subsequently augmented by the Earl of Chester, who also granted it a charter conferring many privileges. After having been plundered and greatly injured by a band of pirates, it was again restored and dedicated to St. Peter and St. Hilda, by William de Percy, who appointed his brother Serlo prior. The monastery, notwithstanding the repeated attacks of pirates, to which it was continually exposed, increased in wealth and importance; it was constituted an abbey by Henry I., its privileges were greatly extended by royal charters and pontifical decrees, and it continued to flourish till the dissolution, at which period its revenue was £437. 2. 9. Tradition relates that Robin Hood and Little John paid a visit to Richard de Waterville, who was then abbot, and, to give a proof of their dexterity in archery, shot each of them an arrow from the tower of the abbey to the distance of more than a mile; and that pillars were erected by the abbot on the spots where the arrows fell, to commemorate the event. The enclosures are still called Robin Hood and Little John's fields; and about six miles from the town is Robin Hood's bay, where that celebrated outlaw is said to have kept a small fleet, to assist his escape when pursued by an enemy.

The town is situated on the shore of the German ocean, at the mouth of the river Esk, by which it is divided into two nearly equal parts, and consists of several streets, of which the greater number are narrow, and some steep; the houses are partly of stone and partly of brick, and several of the modern buildings, of both kinds, are spacious and elegant : it is paved under the provisions of an act of parliament obtained in 1789, and is lighted with gas from the works of a company established in 1825. The approaches have been greatly improved; the environs, in which are many gentlemen's seats and pleasant villas, abound with pleasing and picturesque scenery, and the view of the town derives considerable beauty from the ruins of the abbey on the east bank of the river. A handsome stone building of three stories was erected by subscription on the north pier, in 1826, of which the lower story is occupied by baths with spacious ante-rooms, dressing-rooms, and every requisite accommodation; the middle, or principal, story is occupied by the public subscription library, established in 1776; and the upper story by the museum of the Literary and Philosophical Society, instituted in 1823. The museum contains an extensive collection of petrifactions and fossil organic remains, which abound in the rocks of the vicinity, especially in the alum rock. The fossils form a rich variety of plants, shells, and fishes, including some animals of the larger size, among which are the ichthyosaurus, or lizard fish, and the plesiosaurus. The finest specimen in the collection, and perhaps the noblest fossil in the world, is the great crocodile found in the alum rock near Whitby, in 1824; it is nearly entire, and, when alive, must have measured eighteen feet in length. There are also several varieties of the ammonitæ, or snake stones, which are found here in great abundance, and are fabled to have been snakes deprived of their heads, and petrified by St. Hilda : three white snakes on a blue shield were the ancient arms of the abbots of Whitby. A botanic garden was established on the east side of Green-lane, in 1812, but not meeting with a sufficient degree of support, it has fallen into decay. A handsome news-room was erected by subscription, in Haggersgate, in 1814, and a tradesmen's news-room was also established on the opposite side of the river. A commodious theatre was built by subscription, in 1784, but it was destroyed by fire in 1823, and has not been since rebuilt. Assemblies are held in a handsome room forming part of the Angel Inn.

The origin of the commercial prosperity and consequent importance of Whitby may be attributed to the discovery of the alum mines in the latter part of the reign of Elizabeth. Early in the seventeenth century these mines were worked, and very soon became the source of an extensive trade, of which the necessary supply of coal requisite for conducting the works formed an additional branch; ship-building was introduced about thirty years after, and great improvements were made in the harbour by removing rocks and other obstructions. In 1632 the Burgess pier was constructed, principally through the exertions of Sir Hugh Cholmeley, under whose sanction a subscription of £500 was raised for promoting the work, and the town began to assume a considerable degree of maritime importance. An act of parliament was obtained in 1702, imposing certain dues for the improvement of the piers and harbour, which, being in force only for a limited time, was, on its expiration, renewed from time to time, with certain modifications, till 1827, when it was made perpetual. The duties collected under the authority of this act consist of a halfpenny per chaldron (Newcastle measure) on all coal shipped at that port and at Sunderland, with their dependencies, and of some trifling payments on coal, grain, salt, and other commodities delivered in the harbour. By these means the piers and the harbour have been very greatly improved; the former, with the exception of those at Ramsgate, are perhaps the finest in England. The West pier is six hundred and twenty yards in length, and terminates with a circular head, which has been principally rebuilt during the last season, and on which it is contemplated to erect a lighthouse, seventy feet high. The east pier, which is two hundred and fifteen yards long, is also terminated with a substantial circular head, and there are two inner piers to break the force of the waves in stormy weather; the Burgess pier, one hundred and five, and the Fish pier, sixty-five, yards in length. The drawbridge, which crosses the river Esk, was completed in 1767, at an expense of £3000, and will allow vessels of six hundred tons' burden to pass into the inner harbour, which is capable of receiving a large fleet, and affords secure shelter in stormy weather; adjoining the inner harbour are spacious dock-yards, and commodious dry docks for the building and repairing of ships. Ship-building was carried on here to a very considerable extent in the time of the late war, during which the extensive demand for transports was a source of great emolument to the ship-builders and owners: but the return of peace, an alteration in the navigation laws, and other causes, have occasioned the decline of this trade, and of all the branches connected with it. During that period seven large dock-yards were in active operation, and ship-building was the principal trade of the town; at present only four of them are partially employed, and the prosperity

of the town and the amount of its population have consequently decreased. During the last three years, twenty-six ships have been built and registered here, exclusively of several which have been registered at other ports; the larger vessels belonging to the port are employed in the foreign trade, and the smaller coastwise, especially in the coal trade. The Greenland and Davis' Straits fisheries, which formerly were of great benefit to the town, and, in 1819, employed twelve large ships, at present employ only one; and the manufacture of alum, which once constituted a principal branch of the trade, has also very much declined; several of the works have been discontinued, and those which are still carried on are not in full operation. The works at Kettleness were totally destroyed, in December, 1829, by the falling of the rock under which they were situated, but are now being rebuilt. The export trade in alum to France, Holland, and other parts of the continent, was formerly very considerable, but it has long been extinct, and the principal part of the alum now manufactured is sent coastwise to London, Hull, and other towns. The sailcloth manufactured at Whitby is in great repute, but the quantity, though still considerable, is, from the decline of the port, much diminished.

The fishery on the coast, which formed originally the principal employment of the inhabitants, was very much injured by the late war, which afforded more advantageous opportunities for the employment of capital and labour. The fish generally taken are cod, ling, halibut, and haddocks; salmon and salmon-trout have been very scarce for several years, though at one time they were plentiful in the Esk, and were a considerable article of trade; salmon-trout has been lately taken on the coast by a particular method of fishing, and sometimes in considerable quantities. Oats, butter, and bacon, were formerly sent to London in great cargoes, but this trade also has been much reduced within the last twenty years. The foreign exports are inconsiderable: the principal imports are timber from British America, and timber, wooden wares, hemp, and flax, from the Baltic. The principal article sent coastwise is freestone, of which great quantities are procured, for the erection of different public works in various parts of the kingdom, from the quarries at Aislaby, about three miles from the town: the chief articles brought coastwise are groceries, salt, and coal. The number of vessels belonging to the port is two hundred and fifty-nine, being an aggregate burden of forty-one thousand nine hundred and fifty-three tons: four hundred and twenty-nine vessels entered inwards, and two hundred and ten cleared outwards, during the year ending January 5th, 1831. The depth of water in the harbour in common neap tides is about ten feet, and in spring tides from fifteen to sixteen feet, and sometimes more. The great swell occasioned by tempestuous weather renders the harbour difficult of access, and many disastrous accidents had occurred before it attained its present state of security. In November, 1710, the shipping was greatly damaged by a violent storm, in which it suffered injury to the amount of £40,000; and in the night of the 24th of December, 1787, a newly erected quay, on which was a range of houses, eighty feet above the level of the sea, from the insecurity of the foundation, suddenly fell, involving the greater number of them in one common ruin, leaving one hundred and ninety-six families, who had been forewarned of their danger in time to escape, destitute of a home. The custom-house is a commodious building in Sandgate; a small office for the governor of the pilots has been erected on the pier; and there are four marine associations for mutual insurance. Whitby is a station for the preventive coast guard; and regular trading vessels to and from London, Hull, and Newcastle, sail from two wharfs in Church-street. The market, granted by Henry VI., is held on Saturday; and there are fairs on the 25th of August and on Martinmas-day; the former was granted, in 1168, by Henry II., to the abbot, but they are both inconsiderable. The town is under the superintendence of the magistrates of the North riding, who meet every Tuesday, Thursday, and Saturday. A court for the recovery of small debts, every third Monday, and a court leet, annually at Michaelmas, are held in the town hall, a substantial building of the Tuscan order, situated in the market-place, and erected, in 1788, by Nathaniel Cholmeley, Esq. During what was called the equal representation of the people, in the time of the Commonwealth, Whitby was summoned to send members to parliament, but it does not appear to have ever exercised that privilege under a monarchy.

The living is a perpetual curacy, in the archdeaconry of Cleveland, and diocese of York, endowed with £50 per annum and £200 private benefaction, and £1500 parliamentary grant, and in the patronage of the Archbishop of York. The church, dedicated to St. Mary, is supposed to have been built by William de Percy; but it has undergone so much alteration that little of the original structure remains. It is situated on the summit, and near the verge, of a high cliff, and is approached by one hundred and ninety-one stone steps; six hundred new sittings, of which three hundred are free, have been recently added, partly by a grant of £300 from the Incorporated Society for enlarging churches and chapels. In the western division of the town is a neat chapel of ease, erected in 1778. There are two places of worship for Wesleyan Methodists, and one each for the Society of Friends, Independents, Presbyterians, Primitive Methodists, Unitarians, and Roman Catholics. The Lancasterian schools are in a large handsome building in Cliff-lane, which will contain five hundred children; it is divided into separate schools for boys and girls. The dispensary was established in 1786. The Seamen's hospital, erected in 1676, affords a comfortable asylum to forty-two seamen's widows and their children: there are numerous small benefactions and donations applied annually to the relief of the poor, and several societies for administering to their wants, principally formed by the ladies. The remains of Whitby abbey, which stand a small distance from the church, on a cliff two hundred feet above the level of the sea, present one of the most interesting ruins in the country, and consist of the choir, or eastern part of the church; the north transept, which is nearly entire; and considerable portions of the north wall of the nave, and of the western wall, or front, of the building: the beauty of these ruins has been much impaired by the fall of the central tower, one hundred and four feet high, on the 25th of June, 1830, occasioned by one of the four massive clustered columns by which it was supported having given way. About half a mile west of the pier is a chalybeate spring,

celebrated formerly, when baths existed near the spot, but the latter have been demolished, and the former has fallen into disuse. The neighbourhood abounds with petrifactions, which have been frequently investigated by learned naturalists and other scientific enquirers, and are particularly described in Young's "Geological Survey of the Yorkshire Coast." Some lands near Whitby are still held by the tenure formerly called Horngarth, thought to be that now called the Penny Hedge: this service, which is supposed to have been originally intended for the repairs of the quays and piers of the harbour, at that time constructed of wood with stones thrown in between, is still continued by a family of the name of Herbert; it consists in the erection of a small hedge of stake and yether in the harbour, on the eve of Ascension-day.

WHITCHBURY, or WHITSBURY, a parish in the hundred of CAWDEN and CADWORTH, county of WILTS, 3½ miles (N. by W.) from Fordingbridge, containing 156 inhabitants. The living is a discharged vicarage, in the archdeaconry and diocese of Winchester, rated in the king's books at £5. 13. 4., and in the patronage of J. C. Purvis, Esq. The church is dedicated to St. Leonard.

WHITCHESTER, a township in that part of the parish of HEDDON on the WALL which is in the eastern division of TINDALE ward, county of NORTHUMBERLAND, 9½ miles (W. N. W.) from Newcastle upon Tyne, containing 57 inhabitants. Here was the site of a Roman station, defended on almost every side by deep ravines.

WHITCHURCH, a parish in the hundred of COTTESLOE, county of BUCKINGHAM, 4¾ miles (N. by W.) from Aylesbury, containing 845 inhabitants. The living is a discharged vicarage, in the archdeaconry of Buckingham, and diocese of Lincoln, rated in the king's books at £8. 17., and in the patronage of the Crown. The church is dedicated to St. John the Evangelist. There is a place of worship for Wesleyan Methodists. A market on Monday, and a fair on the festival of St. John the Evangelist, granted in 1245, were formerly held here.

WHITCHURCH, a parish in the hundred of ROBOROUGH, county of DEVON, 1¼ mile (S.E.) from Tavistock, containing 692 inhabitants. The living is a vicarage, in the archdeaconry of Totness, and diocese of Exeter, rated in the king's books at £16. 5. 5., and in the patronage of the Rev. Peter Sleeman. The church is dedicated to St. Andrew. A chantry chapel was founded, in 1300, by the abbot of Tavistock. Francis Pengelly, Esq., in 1719, left £6 per annum for teaching six poor children. The Tavistock races are held annually on Whitchurch down.

WHITCHURCH, a parish in the lower division of the hundred of WORMELOW, county of HEREFORD, 6½ miles (S. W. by S.) from Ross, containing 730 inhabitants. The living is a rectory, with that of Ganerew annexed, in the archdeaconry and diocese of Hereford, rated in the king's books at £6. 0. 2½., and in the patronage of Joseph Pyrke, Esq. The church is dedicated to St. Dubritius. There are places of worship for Independents and Wesleyan Methodists. The navigable river Wye runs through the parish. A court leet is occasionally held. Here was formerly an extensive iron forge, but it has been for some years discontinued.

WHITCHURCH, a parish in the hundred of LANG-TREE, county of OXFORD, 6½ miles (N. W.) from Reading, containing 647 inhabitants. The living is a rectory, in the archdeaconry and diocese of Oxford, rated in the king's books at £16. 2. 8½., and in the patronage of the Crown. The church is dedicated to St. Mary.

WHITCHURCH, a parish comprising the market town of Whitchurch, the townships of Alkington, Great Ash, Little Ash, Black Park, Broughall, Chimnell, Dodington, Edgeby, Hinton, and Hollyhurst, and the chapelry of Tilstock, in the Whitchurch division of the hundred of BRADFORD (North), county of SALOP, and the township of Wirswall, in the hundred of NANT-WICH, county palatine of CHESTER, 20 miles (N. by E.) from Shrewsbury, and 160 (N. W. by N.) from London, and containing 5489 inhabitants. This place was anciently called *Album Monasterium* and *Blancminster*, which have the same signification as its present name, and appear to imply the existence of a monastery, of which there is no account; but an hospital was standing here in the reign of Henry III., and was endowed by the lord of the manor with the whole town of Wylnecot, for the relief of the poor at its gate. In 1211, King John assembled his forces here, prior to attacking the Welch, on which occasion he penetrated to the foot of Snowdon. At the commencement of the civil war between Charles I. and his parliament, the inhabitants appear to have taken an active part in favour of the unfortunate monarch, and to have raised a regiment in support of his cause. Of the foundation and history of the ancient castle, a portion of the ruined walls of which was standing in 1760, nothing is known. The town is situated on elevated ground, in a rich and picturesque country, and contains some neat streets and respectable houses: in its neighbourhood are three fine lakes, called Osmere, Blackmere, and Brown Mosswater, and several brooks, one of which, called Red Brook, is the boundary between England and Wales; another separates this county from that of Chester. The trade is principally in malt and hops: shoes are manufactured for the Manchester market: near the town is an establishment for making oak-acid, also several limekilns and brick-ovens. A branch of the Ellesmere canal extends to the town, by means of which boats ply to London and many intervening towns on Saturday, and to Manchester and Shrewsbury, from the canal wharf. The market is on Friday; and there are fairs on the second Friday in April, Whit-Monday, Friday after August 2nd, and October 28th. A high steward, who superintends the affairs of the town, is appointed by the lord of the manor, and presides at courts baron and leet held in October, at the town hall, which is the depository for the rolls and archives of the lordship. The living is a rectory, with that of Marbury annexed, in the archdeaconry of Salop, and diocese of Lichfield and Coventry, rated in the king's books at £44. 11. 8., and in the patronage of the Trustees of the late Earl of Bridgewater. The church, dedicated to St. Alkmund, and erected in 1722, on the site of an ancient edifice, is a noble structure of the Tuscan order, built with freestone, with a square embattled western tower: it contains several handsome monuments of the Shrewsbury family, and amongst them an effigy in alabaster of the renowned John Talbot, Earl of Shrewsbury, who was killed in France in 1453, and who, for his remarkable prowess, was called the English Achilles. Baptists, Independents, Wesleyan Methodists, and Unitarians, have each a place of worship. The free grammar school, situated at Bargates, was founded and endowed by John Talbot, rector of the parish; the master is appointed by the trustees, and the usher by the master, both appointments being subject to the approbation of the rector; the Earl of Shrewsbury is hereditary visitor. A charity school for children of both sexes, and an almshouse for six decayed housekeepers, were endowed by Mrs. Jane Higginson. A National school, in which five hundred boys are instructed, was established in 1827, at Highgate. At the northern extremity of the town is an extensive house of industry: there are some vestiges of a foss in its vicinity. Whitchurch was the birthplace of Dr. Bernard, chaplain and biographer of Archbishop Usher, and of Abraham Wheelock, a celebrated linguist, who died in 1654.

WHITCHURCH, otherwise FELTON, a parish in the hundred of KEYNSHAM, county of SOMERSET, 3 miles (N.) from Pensford, containing 403 inhabitants. The living is a perpetual curacy, in the archdeaconry of Bath, and diocese of Bath and Wells, endowed with £200 private benefaction, and £400 royal bounty, and in the patronage of Sir J. H. Smith, Bart. The church is dedicated to St. Gregory. The name Filton, or Felton, is derived from a very ancient town, situated to the north-west of the present village, in a forest, or chase, once called Filwood: a church having been erected on the site of an ancient chapel, dedicated to St. Whyte, the inhabitants of Filton gradually removed into its vicinity, upon which the new village and the parish assumed their designation.

WHITCHURCH, a borough, decayed market town, and parish, in the hundred of EVINGAR, Kings-clere division of the county of SOUTHAMPTON, 12 miles (N. by E.) from Winchester, and 57 (W. S. W.) from London, containing, with the tythings of Charlcott, Cold Hurley, and Freefolk, with Freefolk Prior, 1434

Corporate Seal.

inhabitants. The town, which is small and irregularly built, is situated on the river Teste, on very low ground, under a range of chalk hills: a few of the inhabitants are employed in silk-weaving, and two silk-mills also furnish work to about seventy persons, but both these branches of manufacture are on the decline: there are some corn-mills on the river. The market was on Friday, but it is now disused: a pleasure fair is held on the third Thursday in June, and there is one on the 19th and 20th of October, for cattle, pigs, &c. Whitchurch is a borough by prescription, and is governed by a corporation consisting of a titular mayor and bailiff, who do not now exercise any authority within the borough: they are chosen, with a constable, at the court leet of the lord of the manor, held annually in October at the town hall, a neat building, erected about fifty years since, and another court is held at the manor farm, in May, under the Dean and Chapter of Winchester, as lords of the manor. Whitchurch first sent members to parliament in the 27th of Queen Elizabeth : the right of election is vested in the freeholders (in their own right, or that of their wives), of lands and tenements, not divided since the act of the 7th and 8th of William III. The number of voters is about eighty-four : the mayor is the returning officer, and the prevailing influence is possessed by Viscount Sydney, and Samuel Scott, Esq., M.P. This place is within the jurisdiction of the Cheyney Court held at Winchester every Thursday, for the recovery of debts to any amount. The living is a vicarage, in the archdeaconry and diocese of Winchester, rated in the king's books at £13. 12. 8½., endowed with £800 private benefaction, £400 royal bounty, and £400 parliamentary grant, and in the patronage of the Bishop of Winchester. The church, which is a low and plain structure, is dedicated to All Saints, and contains a library, chiefly of theological works, bequeathed by the Rev. William Wood, to which access is obtained by permission of the vicar. There are places of worship for Baptists, Independents, and Wesleyan Methodists. A quantity of clothing and bedding, of the value of about £80, is annually distributed amongst the poor of this parish, from the produce of a bequest by Richard Woollaston, Esq., in 1688.

WHITCHURCH, a parish in a detached portion of the Kington division of the hundred of KINGTON, county of WARWICK, 5½ miles (S. S. E.) from Stratford upon Avon, containing, with the hamlets of Broughton, Crimscott, and Wimpstone, 262 inhabitants. The living is a rectory, in the archdeaconry and diocese of Worcester, rated in the king's books at £20. 17. 3½., and in the patronage of James West, Esq. The church is dedicated to St. Mary.

WHITCHURCH-CANONICORUM, a parish in the hundred of WHITCHURCH-CANONICORUM, Bridport division of the county of DORSET, 5 miles (W. N. W.) from Bridport, containing, with Abbotswooten, Barn, Vale, and Wild quarters, 1317 inhabitants. The living is a vicarage, with the perpetual curacy of Stanton annexed, in the archdeaconry of Dorset, and diocese of Bristol, rated in the king's books at £32. 6. 3., and in the patronage of the Bishop of Bath and Wells. The church was originally dedicated to St. Whyte, or Candida, and subsequently to the Holy Cross. This is one of the most ancient and extensive parishes in the county, and gave name to the hundred : it had anciently a market and a fair, granted by Henry III.

WHITCLIFF, a joint township with Thorpe, in that part of the parish of RIPON which is within the liberty of RIPON, West riding of the county of YORK, 1½ mile (S.) from Ripon, containing, with Thorpe, 157 inhabitants.

WHITCOMBE, a parish in the hundred of CULLIFORD-TREE, Dorchester division of the county of DORSET, 2¼ miles (S. E.) from Dorchester, containing 54 inhabitants. The living is a perpetual curacy, in the archdeaconry of Dorset, and diocese of Bristol, and in the patronage of the Impropriators.

WHITCOMBE (MAGNA), a parish in the upper division of the hundred of DUDSTONE and KING'S BARTON, county of GLOUCESTER, 3½ miles (N. E. by N.) from Painswick, containing 155 inhabitants. The living is a discharged rectory, in the archdeaconry and diocese of Gloucester, rated in the king's books at £4. 6. 8., and in the patronage of Sir W. Hicks, Bart. The church is dedicated to St. Mary. Near the foot of Cooper's Hill,

on a delightful spot in this parish, the remains of a Roman villa, with a sacrarium, baths, &c., were discovered in 1818, the walls of which, to the height of nearly six feet, are remaining, some of them being covered with stucco painted in panels of different colours, elegantly ornamented with ivy leaves. Several of the apartments were paved with red sand-stone, others with beautiful mosaic work, and in many of them have been found fragments of columns, and cornices of white marble, numerous coins of the Lower Empire, from Constantine to Valentinian and Valens, various domestic utensils, and other relics in copper and iron, an axe, a British hatchet, and the skulls of bullocks and goats, with fragments of stags' horns, &c.

WHITECHAPEL, a chapelry in the parish of KIRKHAM, hundred of AMOUNDERNESS, county palatine of LANCASTER, 5½ miles (S. E. by E.) from Garstang. The population is returned with the parish. The living is a perpetual curacy, in the archdeaconry of Richmond, and diocese of Chester, endowed with £400 private benefaction, and £600 royal bounty, and in the patronage of the Vicar of Kirkham.

WHITEFIELD, a joint hamlet with Apperley, in that part of the parish of DEERHURST which is in the lower division of the hundred of WESTMINSTER, county of GLOUCESTER, 4¼ miles (S. S. W.) from Tewkesbury, containing 401 inhabitants.

WHITEGATE, otherwise NEWCHURCH, a parish in the first division of the hundred of EDDISBURY, county palatine of CHESTER, 3¼ miles (S. W.) from Northwich, comprising the townships of Darnhall and Marton, and containing 789 inhabitants. The living is a vicarage, in the archdeaconry and diocese of Chester, endowed with £400 private benefaction, £1000 royal bounty, and £200 parliamentary grant, and in the patronage of Lord Delamere. The church, dedicated to St. Mary, has lately received an addition of four hundred and fifty-three sittings, of which two hundred and twenty-seven are free, the Incorporated Society for the enlargement of churches and chapels having granted £300 towards defraying the expense. Whitegate, which once formed part of the parish of Over, was separated from it, and made a distinct parish, in 1541 : it is bounded and partly intersected by the river Weaver. During the confinement at Hereford of Prince Edward, afterwards Edward I., while a prisoner in the hands of the barons, the monks of the neighbouring monastery of Dore visited and consoled him : he afterwards removed them, about the year 1273, to Dernhall, in this parish ; a few years subsequently the king having resolved to build them a new abbey on a neighbouring spot, gave it the name of Vale-Royal, and laid the first stone of the new monastery, in August 1277, wherein the monks took up their abode in 1330, at which period £32,000 had been issued from the royal treasury, for defraying the expense : the solemnity of the removal was observed with much magnificence, being attended by a great concourse of prelates, nobility, and gentry : at the dissolution the revenue was estimated at £518. There are still some small remains of this house in the doorways of the modern mansion that now occupies its site, which, in the great civil war, was plundered and partly destroyed.

WHITEHAVEN, a sea-port and market town, in the parish of ST. BEES, ALLERDALE ward above Darwent, county of CUMBERLAND, 40 miles (S. W.) from Carlisle, and 320 (N. W.) from London, containing 12,438 inhabitants, exclusively of about 800 seamen belonging to registered vessels, or, including these and the suburb of Preston Quarter, nearly 18,000 inhabitants. The derivation of the name is very uncertain : in the record of a trial between the abbot and monks of St. Mary's at York and the crown, relative to a claim to the wreck of the sea in the manor of St. Bees, the place is called *Whitothaven :* by some it is supposed to owe its name to the light-coloured rocks which surmount the bay, though others derive it from the circumstance of a fisherman, named White, having been the first who frequented the bay, and built a cottage here ; but the last account is generally discredited. In the reign of Henry I. the manor formed part of the possessions of the monastery of St. Mary near the Walls at York, to which the priory of St. Bees belonged ; and, so late as that of Elizabeth, the town consisted of only a few small huts inhabited by fishermen. In 1599, the manor of St. Bees was purchased from Sir Thomas Chaloner, Knt., by Gerard Lowther and Thomas Wybergh, Esqrs.; and the whole having come into the possession of Sir John Lowther, Bart., in 1644, Whitehaven, under his auspices, advanced rapidly in prosperity. He obtained from Charles II. a grant of land, estimated at one hundred and fifty acres, between high and low water mark, to the extent of two miles northward ; he materially improved the harbour, extended the collieries, and erected a mansion near the town, which, aided and improved by the patronage of his family, created Earls of Lonsdale, continued to increase until it has become one of the most populous and flourishing places in Cumberland.

The town is situated on a creek of the Irish sea, and consists of several spacious and well-built streets, intersecting each other at right angles, which are paved with pebbles : it is lighted with gas; supplied with water partly from wells, and partly by means of carts, in which it is brought into the town; and is watched under the superintendence of police. The ground, on three approaches to it, rises abruptly and precipitously, and the entrance from the north is under a fine arch of red sand-stone, with a rich entablature bearing the arms of the Lowther family. On the south-east is the castle of the Earl of Lonsdale, a quadrangular building, with square projections at the angles, and a circular bastion in the centre, having fine meadow land to the south, and commanding an extensive prospect of the harbour. The theatre, erected in 1769, in Roper-street, is a handsome and commodious structure. Races are occasionally held in the neighbourhood. The subscription library, established in 1797, occupies a neat building, erected by the Earl of Lonsdale, in Catherine-street, and contains about three thousand volumes : the subscription news-room, also fitted up by his lordship, is well supplied with newspapers. The mechanics' institute and library, in Lowther-street, was established in 1825. Cold, warm, and shower salt water baths have been fitted up in a building erected near the old platform. The harbour has always been an object of importance with those interested in the trade of the town, and many important improvements have been effected in it. Several stone piers extend, some in a diverging and some in a parallel direction, into the harbour ;

and another bends in an angular manner towards the north-west, on which is a battery. A watchhouse and a lighthouse have been built on the pier called the Old Quay, which was constructed in the time of Charles II., or previously, affording protection to the shipping in the harbour, which is capable of sheltering several hundred sail of vessels. At high water, in spring tides, there were about twenty feet, and in neap tides about twelve feet, of water ; but at low water the harbour was dry : to remedy this, a new west pier, twenty yards in thickness, is being constructed to the north-west ; it was commenced in 1824, on a plan by Mr. John Rennie, and sufficient has been done to admit of nine feet at low water within it. The estimated expense was £80,000, but this sum has been found insufficient, and the trustees are empowered to borrow £180,000, to complete the undertaking, which has already extended nearly three hundred yards. The harbour was defended by four batteries, mounting together nearly one hundred guns; but, since the termination of the late war, many of the guns have been removed. At the entrance of the harbour are two lighthouses, that already mentioned, and another on the New Quay, which has a revolving light ; and a life-boat, stationed here since 1803, has frequently been instrumental in saving life.

Whitehaven is a place of very considerable trade, of which coal forms the chief article : in addition to this, it exports lime, freestone, alabaster, and grain : the imports consist chiefly of American, Baltic, and West Indian produce, linen and flax from Ireland, fruit from the Levant, and wine from Spain and Portugal. The principal manufactures are linen, linen yarn, sailcloth, checks, ginghams, cordage, earthenware, copperas, colours, anchors, and nails ; soap and candles are also made for the West India market and for home consumption. The coal mines, which are of a magnitude only inferior to those of Newcastle and Sunderland, furnish the principal employment of the inhabitants ; some have been sunk to a depth of upwards of one hundred and fifty fathoms, and extend to a considerable distance under the sea. They are worked by means of shafts formed at great expense, and to some are entrances, called Bear Mouths, which, opening at the bottom of a hill, lead through passages, by a steep descent, to the bottom of the pit, by which horses are taken into the mines : the coal, after being raised, is carried to the harbour in wagons on railways, the progress of which is aided by the declivity of the ground, and shipped by means of an inclined plane and wooden spouts, called *hurries,* placed sloping over the quays. These mines have suffered occasionally from firedamp, but the safety lamp has removed much of this danger, and the water is emptied by pumps worked with powerful steam-engines. The coal lies in seams varying in thickness from two to eleven feet, in proportion to the depth. A quantity of a very rich iron-ore is sent from the mines here to the iron-works in South Wales. The herring fishery was formerly carried on to a great extent, but now very few of the inhabitants are employed in it. There are several ship-builders' yards, the ships being distinguished for their durability, and for drawing little water. A patent slip was erected, in 1821, by the Earl of Lonsdale, which will admit vessels of seven hundred tons' burden, and, with great convenience, four vessels of one hundred and fifty tons' burden each, and by which a few men can draw a large vessel into the yard to be repaired. A communication with Liverpool, Dublin, Carlisle, the Isle of Man, Dumfries, Annan, and Garliestown, is maintained by steam-boats, which sail regularly for those places. The jurisdiction of the port extends from Maryport, northward, to midstream in the river Duddon, southward, and to the intermediate coast and ports of Workington, Harrington, Ravenglass, and Millom, and as far into the sea as ten fathoms of water. The number of ships belonging to it, in 1828, was one hundred and ninety-seven, the aggregate tonnage of which amounted to thirty thousand nine hundred and sixty. The custom-house, erected in 1811, is a commodious structure; the establishment consists of a collector and comptroller, with the usual subordinate officers. There are three weekly markets, on Tuesday, Thursday, and Saturday, that on Thursday being the principal, and they are all well supplied with provisions : the fair, held on the 12th of August, has nearly fallen into disuse. The market-place is a handsome area, containing a neat market-house, designed by Smirke, in 1813, for the sale of poultry, eggs, and dairy produce; and there is another, erected in 1809, at the expense of the Earl of Lonsdale, for fish, of which there is a good supply: there are also shambles, called the Low and George's markets, for butchers. The regulation of the affairs of the town and harbour was, by acts of parliament passed in the 7th and 11th of Queen Anne, confirmed by subsequent acts, vested in twenty-one trustees, of whom, seven are appointed by the lord of the manor (himself being one), and the remaining fourteen are elected triennially by ballot; such of the inhabitants as pay harbour dues, or possess one-sixteenth share of a vessel belonging to the port, and the masters of vessels, being the electors. The constables of the town are nominated by the trustees, and appointed by the justices of the peace, who meet at the public office, in Lowther-street, on Thursday and Saturday, for the despatch of business. A court leet is held annually, and a court baron monthly; the latter is for the recovery of debts under 40s.

Whitehaven contains three chapels, the livings of which are perpetual curacies, in the archdeaconry of Richmond, and diocese of Chester, and in the patronage of the Earl of Lonsdale. St. James' stands on an eminence at the eastern extremity of the town, and was rebuilt in 1753; it is a neat structure with a square tower, surmounted with pinnacles. St. Nicholas' was erected in 1693, and is a plain building of good proportion and workmanship, with a square tower; the interior is decorated with paintings of the Last Supper, and of Moses and Aaron, by Matthias Reed, an artist of some merit, who came from Holland in the fleet with the Prince of Orange, and settled in this town : the ecclesiastical courts are held in it. That of the Holy Trinity stands near the southern extremity of the town, at the head of Roper-street ; it is a plain building with a lofty tower. There are two places of worship for Presbyterians, and one each for Particular Baptists, the Society of Friends, Independents, Primitive and Wesleyan Methodists, and Roman Catholics. The Marine school, near St. James' church, or chapel, in which sixty boys are instructed in reading, writing, and arithmetic, was endowed by Matthew Piper, Esq., with the interest of £2000; the site was given, and the building erected,

by the Earl of Lonsdale. The National school, a large and commodious stone building, was erected in 1824, at an expense of upwards of £700, raised by donations ; about five hundred children of both sexes receive instruction in it. A Sunday school, erected at Gins in Preston Quarter, in 1817, for five hundred children of both sexes and all denominations, is used during the week as an infant school. The interest of £1000 was bequeathed by Matthew Piper, Esq., for the purchase of soup, to be distributed, during winter, among the poor ; for whose benefit there are also some minor bequests and donations, besides several charitable institutions for providing them with clothing, &c. A dispensary was established in 1783, and a house of recovery in 1819 : about the commencement of the year 1830, a spacious mansion in Howgill-street was purchased, and fitted up for the purpose of an infirmary, which establishment includes the dispensary and house of recovery. A savings bank was instituted in 1818, and, from the accumulation of interest beyond what was paid to the depositors, a new and elegant edifice is about to be erected in Lowther-street, which will be highly ornamental to the town, and displace several old dilapidated houses, a portion of the first built structures, in that part of it. Dean Swift when a child, resided with his attendant in a house in Roper-street, during the disturbance in Ireland about the time of the Revolution ; and Dr. Brownrigs, who by his publications first attracted the notice of strangers to the beauties of Keswick and the surrounding scenery, for many years practised as a physician in this town.

WHITEPARISH, a parish in the hundred of FRUSTFIELD, county of WILTS, 8 miles (S. E. by E.) from Salisbury, containing, with the extra-parochial liberty of Earldoms, 1169 inhabitants. The living is a discharged vicarage, in the archdeaconry and diocese of Salisbury, rated in the king's books at £13. 7. 2., and in the patronage of Robert Bristow, Esq. The church is dedicated to All Saints. Henry Eyre, in 1639, bequeathed £200, directing the interest to be applied for teaching twenty boys ; Elizabeth Hitchcock, in 1721, left a like sum for the instruction of ten girls ; and Ann Hitchcock, in 1746, gave £236 for teaching ten more.

WHITESIDELAW, a township in the parish of CHOLLERTON, north-eastern division of TINDALE ward, county of NORTHUMBERLAND, 7½ miles (N. N. E.) from Hexham. The population is returned with the township of Chollerton.

WHITEWELL, a chapelry in that part of the parish of WHALLEY which is in the western division of the wapentake of STAINCLIFFE and EWCROSS, West riding of the county of YORK, 7 miles (N. W. by W.) from Clitheroe. The population is returned with the parish. The living is a perpetual curacy, in the archdeaconry and diocese of Chester, endowed with £400 private benefaction, £400 royal bounty, and £200 parliamentary grant, and in the patronage of the Vicar of Whalley. The chapel has lately received an addition of seventy free sittings, the Incorporated Society for the enlargement of churches and chapels having granted £25 towards defraying the expense.

WHITFIELD, a township in the parish of GLOSSOP, hundred of HIGH PEAK, county of DERBY, 8¼ miles (N. by W.) from Chapel en le Frith, containing 984 inhabitants. There is a place of worship for Wesleyan Methodists. A school-house was erected, about 1786, by Joseph Hague, Esq., who endowed it with land and houses of the present annual value of £40 ; he also left the interest of £1000 to be expended in clothes for twelve poor men and as many women of this and other townships in the parish.

WHITFIELD, a parish in the hundred of BEWS-BOROUGH, lathe of ST. AUGUSTINE, county of KENT, 3¼ miles (N. N. W.) from Dovor, containing 207 inhabitants. ·The living is a perpetual curacy, in the peculiar jurisdiction and patronage of the Archbishop of Canterbury, rated in the king's books at £5. 18. 8., and endowed with £200 private benefaction, and £200 royal bounty. The church is dedicated to St. Mary.

WHITFIELD, a parish in the hundred of KING'S SUTTON, county of NORTHAMPTON, 2 miles (N. E. by N.) from Brackley, containing 297 inhabitants. The living is a rectory, in the archdeaconry of Northampton, and diocese of Peterborough, rated in the king's books at £8. 15., and in the patronage of the Provost and Fellows of Worcester College, Oxford. The church is dedicated to St. John the Evangelist. About twenty poor children are instructed for £6 a year, arising from land purchased with sundry donations.

WHITFIELD, a parish in the western division of TINDALE ward, county of NORTHUMBERLAND, 11½ miles (W. S. W.) from Hexham, containing 289 inhabitants. The living is a discharged rectory, in the archdeaconry of Northumberland, and diocese of Durham, rated in the king's books at £8, and in the patronage of William Ord, Esq. The church was rebuilt about 1784. The East and West Allen rivers join their streams at Cupola, in this parish, at which place lead-ore, obtained from a mine at Limestone-Cross, was formerly smelted. A new line of road from Alston to Haydon bridge, has been recently formed through the parish. At Redmires there is a chalybeate spring. Mr. Ord allows a house and garden, with £20 a year, to the master of a school, for teaching poor children.

WHITGIFT, a parish in the lower division of the wapentake of OSGOLDCROSS, West riding of the county of YORK, comprising the chapelry of Swinefleet, and the townships of Ousefleet, Reedness, and Whitgift, containing 2202 inhabitants, of which number, 310 are in the township of Whitgift, 6½ miles (S. E.) from Howden. The living is a perpetual curacy, with that of Swinefleet annexed, in the archdeaconry and diocese of York, and in the patronage of N.Yarburgh, Esq. The church is dedicated to St. Mary Magdalene. The river Ouse runs through the parish, in which are two endowed schools.

WHITGREAVE, a township in that part of the parish of ST. MARY, LICHFIELD, which is in the southern division of the hundred of PIREHILL, county of STAFFORD, 3½ miles (N.N.W.) from Stafford, containing 204 inhabitants.

WHITKIRK, a parish in the lower division of the wapentake of SKYRACK, West riding of the county of YORK, 4 miles (E.) from Leeds, comprising the townships of Austhorpe, Seacroft, Temple - Newsom, and Thorp-Stapleton, and containing 2227 inhabitants. The living is a discharged vicarage, in the archdeaconry and diocese of York, rated in the king's books at £13. 5. 7½., endowed with £600 private benefaction, and £900 royal bounty, and in the patronage of the

Master and Fellows of Trinity College, Cambridge. The church is dedicated to St. Mary. In a school, built by subscription, six children are instructed for an annuity of £10, bequeathed by Richard Brooke, in 1702.

WHITLEY, a tything in the parish of CUMNER, hundred of HORMER, county of BERKS, 5 miles (W. by S.) from Oxford, containing 37 inhabitants.

WHITLEY, a hamlet in that part of the parish of ST. GILES, READING, which is in the hundred of READING, county of BERKS, 2 miles (S.) from Reading, containing 276 inhabitants.

WHITLEY, a chapelry in the parish of TYNEMOUTH, eastern division of CASTLE ward, county of NORTHUMBERLAND, 2½ miles (N. by E.) from North Shields, containing 554 inhabitants. The living is a perpetual curacy, in the archdeaconry of Northumberland, and diocese of Durham, endowed with £600 private benefaction, £200 royal bounty, and £600 parliamentary grant. The village, pleasantly situated near the sea, contains many well-built houses. Iron-stone abounds in the neighbourhood; and there are extensive mines of coal, and quarries of limestone, the productions of which are conveyed by means of a rail-road to Shields for exportation. The North Shields Water-works Company have a reservoir here.

WHITLEY, a township in the parish of KELLING-TON, lower division of the wapentake of OSGOLDCROSS, West riding of the county of YORK, 5½ miles (W. by S.) from Snaith, containing 284 inhabitants.

WHITLEY (LOWER), a chapelry in that part of the parish of GREAT BUDWORTH which is in the hundred of BUCKLOW, county palatine of CHESTER, 4¾ miles (N. W. by N.) from Northwich, containing 236 inhabitants. The living is a perpetual curacy, annexed to the vicarage of Great Budworth, in the archdeaconry and diocese of Chester, endowed with £800 parliamentary grant. There is a place of worship for Wesleyan Methodists.

WHITLEY (LOWER), a township in the parish of THORNHILL, lower division of the wapentake of AG-BRIGG, West riding of the county of YORK, 5¼ miles (S.W.) from Wakefield, containing 903 inhabitants. There are two scribbling-mills and a tan-yard in the neighbourhood.

WHITLEY (OVER), a township in that part of the parish of GREAT BUDWORTH which is in the hundred of BUCKLOW, county palatine of CHESTER, 5½ miles (N. N.W.) from Northwich, containing 244 inhabitants.

WHITLEY (UPPER), a township in the parish of KIRK-HEATON, upper division of the wapentake of AGBRIGG, West riding of the county of YORK, 6 miles (E. by N.) from Huddersfield, containing 764 inhabitants.

WHITLEY-BOOTHS, a joint township with Barley, in that part of the parish of WHALLEY which is in the higher division of the hundred of BLACKBURN, county palatine of LANCASTER, 4 miles (W. by N.) from Colne. The population is returned with Barley.

WHITLINGHAM, a parish in the hundred of HENSTEAD, county of NORFOLK, 2½ miles (E.S.E.) from Norwich, containing 33 inhabitants. The living is a perpetual curacy, in the archdeaconry of Norfolk, and diocese of Norwich, and in the patronage of ——

Hare, Esq. The church, which is demolished, was dedicated to St. Andrew.

WHITMORE, a parish in the northern division of the hundred of PIREHILL, county of STAFFORD, 4 miles (S.W.) from Newcastle under Lyne, containing 302 inhabitants. The living is a rectory not in charge, in the archdeaconry of Stafford, and diocese of Lichfield and Coventry, endowed with £400 royal bounty, and in the patronage of E. Mainwaring, Esq. Whitmore is in the honour of Tutbury, duchy of Lancaster, and within the jurisdiction of a court of pleas held at Tutbury every third Tuesday, for the recovery of debts under 40s.

WHITNASH, a parish in the Kenilworth division of the hundred of KNIGHTLOW, county of WARWICK, 3 miles (E.S.E.) from Warwick, containing 287 inhabitants. The living is a rectory, in the archdeaconry of Coventry, and diocese of Lichfield and Coventry, rated in the king's books at £5. 9. 9½., and in the patronage of Chandos Leigh, Esq. The church is dedicated to St. Margaret. Nicholas Chamberlaine, in 1715, bequeathed a rent-charge of £2 in support of a school.

WHITNEY, a parish in the hundred of HUNTINGTON, county of HEREFORD, 5 miles (N.E.) from Hay, containing 268 inhabitants. The living is a discharged rectory, in the archdeaconry and diocese of Hereford, rated in the king's books at £5. 8., and in the patronage of Tomkin Dew, Esq. The church is dedicated to St. Peter and St. Paul.

WHITRIDGE, a township in that part of the parish of HARTBURN which is in the western division of MORPETH ward, county of NORTHUMBERLAND, 9½ miles (W. by N.) from Morpeth, containing 10 inhabitants.

WHITRIGG, a joint township with Torpenhow, in the parish of TORPENHOW, ALLERDALE ward below Darwent, county of CUMBERLAND, 1 mile (S.) from Torpenhow. The population is returned with Torpenhow. On a hill, called Caer Mot, are the remains of a square double intrenchment, intersected by the old road from Keswick to Old Carlisle; near it is a smaller encampment, defended by a rampart and fosse : there are also the remains of a beacon.

WHITSTABLE, a parish in the hundred of WHITSTABLE, lathe of ST. AUGUSTINE, county of KENT, 5¼ miles (N. N.W.) from Canterbury, containing, with the hamlet of Harwich, 1611 inhabitants. The living is a perpetual curacy, in the archdeaconry and diocese of Canterbury, endowed with £400 private benefaction, and £400 royal bounty, and in the patronage of the Archbishop of Canterbury. The church is dedicated to All Saints. There are places of worship for Independents and Wesleyan Methodists. This parish lies near the entrance to the East Swale, opposite the Isle of Sheppy. On the shore by Tankertoṇ are several copper-houses, where considerable quantities of copperas, or green vitriol, are manufactured. Whitstable bay is frequented by a number of colliers, from which Canterbury and the surrounding places are supplied with coal, by means of the Canterbury and Whitstable railway. It is also the station of hoys, which sail to and from London alternately,every week, with goods and passengers. Many boats are employed in the fisheries, Whitstable being a royalty of fishery, or oyster dredging, appendant to the manor, and for the due re-

gulation of the trade a court is held annually in February. There are fairs on Thursday before Whitsuntide, near the water side ; on Midsummer-day, at Church-street ; and on St. James' day, on Greensted-green, in Whitstable-street, which is a thriving and populous village, containing shops well stored with every necessary article of consumption for those engaged in the extensive traffic here carried on. Great quantities of Roman pottery have been found in dredging for oysters round a rock, now called the Pudding-pan, which is supposed by some to have been the island *Caunos* of Ptolemy, though now covered by the sea.

WHIT-STAUNTON, a parish forming a distinct portion of the southern division of the hundred of PETHERTON, being locally in that of Kingsbury, county of SOMERSET, 3½ miles (W.N.W.) from Chard, containing 327 inhabitants. The living is a rectory, in the archdeaconry of Taunton, and ·diocese of Bath and Wells, rated in the king's books at £14. 2. 11., and in the patronage of Isaac Elton, Esq. The church is dedicated to St. Andrew.

WHITSTONE, a parish in the hundred of STRATTON, county of CORNWALL, 5¾ miles (S.S. E.) from Stratton, containing 466 inhabitants. The living is a discharged rectory, in the archdeaconry of Cornwall, and diocese of Exeter, rated in the king's books at £14. 11. 0½., and in the patronage of Thomas Brown, Esq. The Bude and Launceston canal passes through the parish.

WHITSTONE, a parish in the hundred of WONFORD, county of DEVON, 3¾ miles (W.N.W.) from Exeter, containing 585 inhabitants. The living is a rectory, in the archdeaconry and diocese of Exeter, rated in the king's books at £19. 3. 4., and in the patronage of Thomas Brown, Esq. The church is dedicated to St. Catherine. John Splatt, in 1753, bequeathed £20 per annum for teaching the poor children of the parish. He also founded almshouses for five poor people, with an annual allowance of 5s. each.

WHITTERING, a parish in the liberty of PETERBOROUGH, county of NORTHAMPTON, 2½ miles (N.N.W.) from Wansford, containing 183 inhabitants. The living is a discharged rectory, in the archdeaconry of Northampton, and diocese of Peterborough, rated in the king's books at £8. 0. 10., and in the patronage of the Marquis of Exeter. The church is dedicated to All Saints.

WHITTINGHAM, a township in the parish of KIRKHAM, hundred of AMOUNDERNESS, county palatine of LANCASTER, 5¾ miles (N.N.E.) from Preston, containing 661 inhabitants.

WHITTINGHAM, a parish in the northern division of COQUETDALE ward, county of NORTHUMBERLAND, comprising the townships of Callaley with Yetlington, Glanton, Lorbottle, Great Ryle, Little Ryle, Shawdon, and Whittingham, and containing 1749 inhabitants, of which number, 588 are in the township of Whittingham, 8½ miles (W. by S.) from Alnwick. The living is a vicarage, in the archdeaconry of Northumberland, and diocese of Durham, rated in the king's books at £12. 11. 3., and in the patronage of the Dean and Chapter of Carlisle. The church, dedicated to St. Bartholomew, has lately received an addition of one hundred and seventy-two sittings, of which one hundred are free, the Incorporated Society for the enlargement of churches and chapels having granted £50 towards defraying the expense. The river Aln runs through the parish, in which there is a vaulted tower, that has often afforded refuge and defence to the inhabitants during the border warfare.

WHITTINGTON, a parish in the hundred of SCARSDALE, county of DERBY, 2¼ miles (N.) from Chesterfield, containing 680 inhabitants. The living is a rectory, in the archdeaconry of Derby, and diocese of Lichfield and Coventry, rated in the king's books at £7. 10. 10., and in the patronage of the Dean of Lincoln. The church is dedicated to St. Bartholomew: the chancel was built in 1827. The manufacture of earthenware is here carried on. A free school was founded in 1674, by Peter Webster, who, in 1678, gave £200 to purchase lands for its endowment, and directed that twenty children should be taught; and Joshua Webster, in 1681, gave land in Whittington to be applied for teaching ten children: the annual income arising from these bequests is now about £32. 10., for which twenty boys and ten girls receive free instruction, and a small gratuity for shoes and books. A chalybeate spring here was formerly much resorted to, and, for the convenience of visitors, a cold bath was erected in 1769. A public-house on Whittington moor is distinguished by the name of the Revolution House, from the adjournment to it of a select meeting of friends to liberty and the Protestant religion, held on the moor early in 1688, at which the Earl (afterwards Duke) of Devonshire, the Earl of Derby (afterwards Duke of Leeds), Lord Delamere, and Mr. John Darey, eldest son of the Earl of Holderness, attended. When the centenary anniversary of that glorious event was commemorated in Derbyshire, in 1788, the committee dined on the preceding day at this house; and on the anniversary, a sermon was preached in the parish church by Dr. Pegge, the celebrated antiquary, then rector, before the descendants of these illustrious revolutionists, and a large assemblage of the most distinguished families of the county, who afterwards went in procession to take refreshment at the Revolution House, and then proceeded to Chesterfield to dinner. A subscription was then opened for erecting a column on Whittington moor, in memory of the Revolution, but the design was abandoned, in consequence, as it is supposed, of the revolution which so speedily followed in France. The Chesterfield races are held on this moor.

WHITTINGTON, a parish in the hundred of BRADLEY, county of GLOUCESTER, 4½ miles (E. S. E.) from Cheltenham, containing 215 inhabitants. The living is a rectory, in the archdeaconry and diocese of Gloucester, rated in the king's books at £13. 6. 8., and in the patronage of Walter Lawrence Lawrence, Esq. The small river Coln runs through the parish.

WHITTINGTON, a parish in the hundred of LONSDALE, south of the sands, county palatine of LANCASTER, 2 miles (S. S. W.) from Kirkby-Lonsdale, containing 461 inhabitants. The living is a rectory, in the archdeaconry of Richmond, and diocese of Chester, rated in the king's books at £13. 9. 9½., and in the patronage of the Rev. William Carus Wilson. William Margison, in 1762, left £1000 for building and endowing a school, in which six children are now educated.

WHITTINGTON, a parish in the hundred of Oswestry, county of SALOP, 3 miles (E. N. E.) from Os-

westry, containing 1749 inhabitants. The living is a rectory, in the archdeaconry and diocese of St. Asaph, rated in the king's books at £25. 4. 2., and in the patronage of the Trustees of the late Rev. J. R. Lloyd. The church, dedicated to St. John the Baptist, is supposed to have been built, in the reign of Henry II., by Fulk Fitz-warine, lord of the manor, who procured a market and fair to be held here, both which have been long disused: it was rebuilt in 1806. The river Perry runs through the parish; also the Ellesmere canal, which here divides into four branches, called the Chester, Llangollen, Montgomeryshire, and Weston canals. Robert Jones, in 1679, bequeathed two cottages and five acres of land, directing the rents to be applied in support of a school; and, in 1706, Griffith Hughes left seventeen acres of land, one-half to be given to the school here, and the other to that of Ruabon: upwards of one hundred boys are instructed on the National system. There is also a school for fifty girls, founded by Elizabeth Probert, and conducted on the same plan. Lloyd, in his "Archaeologia," imagines this place to have been celebrated, under the name Drêv Wen, or the White Town, by Llowarch Hen, a noble British bard, who flourished about the close of the sixth century; and describes it as the place where Condolanus, a British chieftain, was slain, in an attempt to expel some Irish invaders. According to the bards, it was subsequently the property and chief residence of Tudor Trevor. After the Conquest it was given to Roger, Earl of Shrewsbury, and, on the defection of his son, Earl Robert, and the confiscation of that nobleman's immense estates, in the reign of Henry I., the castle and barony were granted to the Peverells, from whom, by the marriage of Mellet, second daughter of William Peverell, to Guarine de Mets, who received her hand as the reward of his distinguished prowess in a tournament held at the castle in the Peak, in Derbyshire, they passed to the illustrious race of Fitz-warine, whose feats of chivalry and valorous exploits have furnished a subject for romance, and, in modern times, have been beautifully illustrated in a poem by J. F. M. Dovaston, Esq., of West Felton, in the vicinity. The Fitz-warines were lords of the place for nearly four hundred years, and every heir, for nine descents, preserved the Christian name of Fulk. The castle then became a border fortress, and the neighbourhood the frequent scene of battle between the lord's retainers and the Welch: in these conflicts the building, probably, sustained considerable injury, since license was granted by Henry III. to the renowned Fulk Fitz-warine, for repairing and fortifying it. The remains consist of one large tower, with traces of four others, and the exterior gateway, which is inhabited by a farmer. On the green, annually at Midsummer, a gay assemblage of the young people of the vicinity, called the Whittington Club, similar to those at Ellesmere and Oswestry, takes place. A court leet and baron is annually held in a modern portion of the castle, rebuilt, a few years ago, by William Lloyd, Esq., the present lord of the manor. Coal is thought to lie beneath the surface of some parts of the parish, but no mines have yet been opened.

WHITTINGTON, a parish in the northern division of the hundred of OFFLOW, county of STAFFORD, 2½ miles (E. by S.) from Lichfield, containing, with the hamlet of Tamhorn, 723 inhabitants. The living is a perpetual curacy, in the peculiar jurisdiction of the prebendal court of Whittington and Baswich, and in the patronage of T. Levett, Esq. The church is dedicated to St. Giles. The Coventry canal passes near the village. Sarah Neal, in 1741, gave a house and land towards the education of poor children; and, in 1800, the Rev. Richard Levett bequeathed £200 for the like purpose: the income is about £8, and the number taught from twenty to thirty.

WHITTINGTON, a hamlet in the parish of GRENDON, Tamworth division of the hundred of HEMLINGFORD, county of WARWICK, 2 miles (N.W.) from Atherstone. The population is returned with the parish. Whittington is in the honour of Tutbury, duchy of Lancaster, and within the jurisdiction of a court of pleas held at Tutbury every third Tuesday, for the recovery of debts under 40s.

WHITTINGTON, a chapelry in that part of the parish of ST. PETER, WORCESTER, which is in the lower division of the hundred of OSWALDSLOW, county of WORCESTER, 2½ miles (S. E. by E.) from Worcester, containing 207 inhabitants. The chapel, dedicated to St. Philip and St. James, is an ancient structure of wood, with some curious tracery in the windows.

WHITTINGTON (GREAT), a township in the parish of CORBRIDGE, eastern division of TINDALE ward, county of NORTHUMBERLAND, 7 miles (N. E.) from Hexham, containing 224 inhabitants. James Kirsopp, Esq., left £5 a year for the education of ten poor children, in a school built by subscription in 1825.

WHITTINGTON (LITTLE), a township in the parish of CORBRIDGE, eastern division of TINDALE ward, county of NORTHUMBERLAND, 6½ miles (N. E.) from Hexham, containing 19 inhabitants.

WHITTLE, a hamlet in the parish of GLOSSOP, hundred of HIGH PEAK, county of DERBY, 6¼ miles (N.W.) from Chapel en le Frith, containing 1696 inhabitants.

WHITTLE, a township in the parish of SHILBOTTLE, eastern division of COQUETDALE ward, county of NORTHUMBERLAND, 5 miles (S.) from Alnwick, containing 64 inhabitants.

WHITTLE, a township in the parish of OVINGHAM, eastern division of TINDALE ward, county of NORTHUMBERLAND, 11 miles (W.) from Newcastle upon Tyne, containing 32 inhabitants.

WHITTLE (WELCH), a township in the parish of STANDISH, hundred of LEYLAND, county palatine of LANCASTER, 3 miles (S. W.) from Chorley, containing 151 inhabitants.

WHITTLE le WOODS, a township in the parish and hundred of LEYLAND, county palatine of LANCASTER, 2 miles (N.) from Chorley, containing 2083 inhabitants. Here are several valuable millstone quarries; and a lead mine was formerly worked with great success. A school, erected by subscription in 1769, was endowed by Samuel Crooke, in 1770, with £220, now producing about £16 per annum, for which from fifteen to twenty children are educated.

WHITTLEBURY, a parish in the hundred of GREENS-NORTON, county of NORTHAMPTON, 3¾ miles (S. by W.) from Towcester, containing 642 inhabitants. The living is a perpetual curacy, annexed, with that of Silverstone, to the rectory of Greens-Norton, in the archdeaconry of Northampton, and diocese of Peterborough. The church is dedicated to St. Mary. There

is a place of worship for Wesleyan Methodists. A National school has been established, and is partly supported out of the rents of the Slapton charity estate, and partly by subscriptions. About eighty children are instructed on week days, and one hundred and fifty on Sundays.

WHITTLESEY, a village (formerly a market town) containing the parishes of St. Andrew and St. Mary, in the northern division of the hundred of WITCHFORD, Isle of ELY, county of CAMBRIDGE, 6 miles (E. by S.) from Peterborough, containing 5276 inhabitants. The living of St. Andrew's is a discharged vicarage, in the peculiar jurisdiction of the Bishop of Ely, rated in the king's books at £4. 13. 4., and in the patronage of the Crown. The church is a handsome structure, with a stately tower crowned with turrets. The living of St. Mary's is a discharged vicarage, also in the peculiar jurisdiction of the Bishop of Ely, rated in the king's books at £19. 13. 9., and in the patronage of E. C. and H. Waldegrave, Esqrs. The church is a handsome edifice, with a lofty tower of peculiar elegance, surmounted by a slender enriched spire of good proportions. Within the limits of the two parishes are places of worship for Baptists, Independents, and Calvinistic and Wesleyan Methodists. Whittlesey, written *Witesie* in Domesday-book, is supposed to have been a Roman station, from the traces of a military way, and the numerous relics of antiquity discovered in the neighbourhood. The village, which is bounded on the north and south by branches of the river Nene, is still a large and respectable place, though its market, formerly held on Friday, has been for some years disused: the market-house still remains, and there is a fair for horses on June 13th. At the Falcon, the principal inn, courts leet and baron are held twice a year, also a court of requests, for the recovery of debts under 40s., on the third Friday in every month. A public library and news-room have been lately established by subscription. There are two endowed schools, one of them founded, in 1735, by Adam Kelfull, and the other, in 1815, by John Sudbury. William de Whittlesey, Archbishop of Canterbury, was born here in 1367. Adjoining this place, but in the county of Huntingdon, is an expanse of water, termed WhittleseyMere; it bears also the appellation of the White sea, and abounds with a variety of fish, a considerable quantity of which is sent to the metropolis.

WHITTLESFORD, a parish in the hundred of WHITTLESFORD, county of CAMBRIDGE, 6¼ miles (W. by N.) from Linton, containing 486 inhabitants. The living is a discharged vicarage, in the archdeaconry and diocese of Ely, rated in the king's books at £10, and in the patronage of the Master and Fellows of Jesus' College, Cambridge. The church is dedicated to St. Mary and St. Andrew. A market and a fair were formerly held here, but both have been long disused. William Westley, in 1723, bequeathed lands, now let for £50 a year, for teaching poor children. At Whittlesford bridge are the remains of an ancient hospital, said to have been founded before the time of Edward I., by William Colvill, and dedicated to St. John the Baptist.

WHITTON, a township in the parish of GRINDON, north-eastern division of STOCKTON ward, county palatine of DURHAM, 5½ miles (N. W. by W.) from Stockton upon Tees, containing 59 inhabitants.

WHITTON, a joint township with Trippleton, in the parish of LEINTWARDINE, hundred of WIGMORE, county of HEREFORD, containing, with Trippleton, 79 inhabitants.

WHITTON, a parish in the northern division of the wapentake of MANLEY, parts of LINDSEY, county of LINCOLN, 11 miles (W. N. W.) from Barton upon Humber, containing 212 inhabitants. The living is a discharged rectory, with the vicarage of Aukborough united, in the archdeaconry of Stow, and diocese of Lincoln, rated in the king's books at £6. 10., endowed with £200 royal bounty, and in the alternate patronage of the Bishop of Lincoln and T. Goulton, Esq. The church is dedicated to St. John the Baptist.

WHITTON, a township in the parish of ROTHBURY, western division of COQUETDALE ward, county of NORTHUMBERLAND, ½ a mile (S.) from Rothbury, containing 110 inhabitants. Whitton Tower, formerly a very strong fortress, is still a commodious edifice, occupied by the rector of the parish: near it is a circular observatory, built by the late Dr. Sharp.

WHITTON, a township in the parish of BURFORD, hundred of OVERS, county of SALOP, 3¾ miles (N.W. by N.) from Tenbury, containing 68 inhabitants.

WHITTON, a parish within the borough of IPSWICH, county of SUFFOLK, 2½ miles (N. N. W.) from Ipswich, containing 255 inhabitants. The living is a rectory, in the archdeaconry of Suffolk, and diocese of Norwich, rated in the king's books at £6. 11. 5½., and in the patronage of the Bishop of Ely. The church is dedicated to St. Mary. The Stow-Market and Ipswich navigation passes through the parish.

WHITTONSTALL, a chapelry in the parish of BYWELL ST. PETER, eastern division of TINDALE ward, county of NORTHUMBERLAND, 10 miles (S. E. by E.) from Hexham, containing 146 inhabitants. The living is a perpetual curacy, in the archdeaconry of Northumberland, and diocese of Durham, endowed with £600 private benefaction, and £800 royal bounty, and in the patronage of the Dean and Chapter of Durham. The chapel is dedicated to St. Philip and St. James. The Roman Watling-street passes through the parish. The Governors of Greenwich Hospital allow £15 a year to a schoolmaster for teaching poor children.

WHITWELL, a parish in the hundred of SCARSDALE, county of DERBY, 10¾ miles (E. N. E.) from Chesterfield, containing 873 inhabitants. The living is a rectory, in the archdeaconry of Derby, and diocese of Lichfield and Coventry, rated in the king's books at £20. 3. 4., and in the patronage of the Duke of Portland. The church, dedicated to St. Lawrence, has a Norman tower. A school for boys is principally supported by the Duke of Portland, and another for girls by the Duchess, on the National system. Whitwell, together with some of the neighbouring villages, has been on the decline since the opening of the Chesterfield canal; frame-work knitting is still carried on to a small extent. A statute fair for hiring servants, formerly held on November 1st, is now in disuse. The ancient hall has been converted into a farm-house. At Steetley, said to have been at one period a distinct parish, is a desecrated church, exhibiting a curious and good specimen of the later and more enriched style of Norman architecture; it is an interesting ruin, and is preserved with great care.

WHITWELL, a parish in the hundred of EYNSFORD, county of NORFOLK, 1¼ mile (S. W.) from Reepham, containing 414 inhabitants. The living is a discharged vicarage, annexed to the rectory of Lyng, in the archdeaconry of Norfolk, and diocese of Norwich.

WHITWELL, a parish in the hundred of ALSTOE, county of RUTLAND, 4½ miles (E.) from Oakham, containing 112 inhabitants. The living is a rectory, in the archdeaconry of Northampton, and diocese of Peterborough, rated in the king's books at £5, and in the patronage of Sir G. Noel Noel, Bart. The church is dedicated to St. Michael. A small mound in the neighbourhood, bearing the name of Robin Hood's Cave, is supposed to have been a retreat of that celebrated outlaw.

WHITWELL, a parish in the liberty of EAST MEDINA, Isle of Wight division of the county of SOUTHAMPTON, 8 miles (S. by E.) from Newport, containing 488 inhabitants. The living is a perpetual curacy, annexed to the vicarage of Godshill, in the archdeaconry and diocese of Winchester. The church is dedicated to St. Radegund.

WHITWELL, a township in that part of the parish of KENDAL which is in KENDAL ward, county of WESTMORLAND, 4½ miles (N. by E.) from Kendal. The population is returned with the chapelry of Selside. This was an extensive common previously to 1825, when it was enclosed by act of parliament.

WHITWELL, a chapelry in that part of the parish of CATTERICK which is in the eastern division of the wapentake of GILLING, North riding of the county of YORK, 3 miles (E.) from Catterick, containing 99 inhabitants.

WHITWELL on the HILL, a township in the parish of CRAMBE, wapentake of BULMER, North riding of the county of YORK, 5¾ miles (S. W.) from New Malton, containing 182 inhabitants.

WHITWELL-HOUSE, an extra-parochial liberty, in the southern division of EASINGTON ward, county palatine of DURHAM, 2¾ miles (E. S. E.) from Durham, containing 38 inhabitants.

WHITWICK, a parish in the western division of the hundred of GOSCOTE, county of LEICESTER, 5½ miles (E. by S.) from Ashby de la Zouch, containing, with the chapelry of Thringstone with Swannington, 2858 inhabitants. The living is a discharged vicarage, with the perpetual curacy of Thringstone with Swannington annexed, in the archdeaconry of Leicester, and diocese of Lincoln, rated in the king's books at £9.14.7., endowed with £200 private benefaction, and £200 royal bounty, and in the patronage of the King, as Duke of Lancaster. The church is dedicated to St. John the Baptist. There is a place of worship for Wesleyan Methodists.

WHITWOOD, a township in that part of the parish of FEATHERSTONE which is in the lower division of the wapentake of AGBRIGG, West riding of the county of YORK, 4¾ miles (N. W. by W.) from Pontefract, containing 292 inhabitants. There is an extensive manufacture of earthenware at Mere pottery in this township.

WHITWORTH, a parochial chapelry in the southeastern division of DARLINGTON ward, county palatine of DURHAM, comprising the townships of Tudhoe and Whitworth, and containing 409 inhabitants, of which number, 111 are in the township of Whitworth, 5¼ miles (N. E. by N.) from Bishop-Auckland. The living is a perpetual curacy, in the peculiar jurisdiction and patronage of the Dean and Chapter of Durham. The chapel was originally a chapel of ease to the vicarage of Merrington. In the churchyard, among other ancient sepulchral memorials, are a monument of a knight in armour, and the effigies of two ladies.

WHITWORTH, a chapelry in that part of the parish of ROCHDALE which is in the hundred of SALFORD, county palatine of LANCASTER, 2¾ miles (N. by W.) from Rochdale. The population is returned with the parish. The living is a perpetual curacy, in the archdeaconry and diocese of Chester, endowed with £200 private benefaction, £600 royal bounty, and £200 parliamentary grant. — Starky, Esq. and others were patrons in 1804. The chapel is dedicated to St. Bartholomew. Twelve poor children are taught to read for £14. 10. a year, arising from the rents of certain cottages bequeathed by James Starky, in 1724.

WHIXHALL, a chapelry in the parish of PREES, Whitchurch division of the hundred of BRADFORD (North), county of SALOP, 3¾ miles (N. by E.) from Wem, containing 811 inhabitants. The living is a perpetual curacy, in the peculiar jurisdiction of the Prebendary of Prees in the Cathedral Church of Lichfield, endowed with £1000 private benefaction, £800 royal bounty, and £1400 parliamentary grant, and in the patronage of the Bishop of Lichfield and Coventry. The chapel, dedicated to St. Mary, has lately received an addition of one hundred and fifty free sittings, the Incorporated Society for the enlargement of churches and chapels having granted £150 towards defraying the expense. William Higgins, in 1737, bequeathed a rent-charge of £2 for teaching poor children.

WHIXLEY, a parish comprising the township of Thornville, in the lower division, and the townships of Green-Hammerton and Whixley, in the upper division, of the wapentake of CLARO, West riding of the county of YORK, and containing 809 inhabitants, of which number, 467 are in the township of Whixley, 6½ miles (S. S. E.) from Aldborough. The living is a perpetual curacy, in the archdeaconry of Richmond, and diocese of Chester, rated in the king's books at £7. 17. 1., endowed with £600 royal bounty, and £1200 parliamentary grant, and in the patronage of the Trustees of the Tancred charities. There is a place of worship for Wesleyan Methodists.

WHIXOE, a parish in the hundred of RISBRIDGE, county of SUFFOLK, 4 miles (W. S. W.) from Clare, containing 147 inhabitants. The living is a discharged rectory, in the archdeaconry of Sudbury, and diocese of Norwich, rated in the king's books at £5. 13. 1½. J. T. H. Elwes, Esq. was patron in 1808.

WHORLTON, a chapelry in that part of the parish of GAINFORD which is in the south-western division of DARLINGTON ward, county palatine of DURHAM, 4 miles (E. S. E.) from Barnard-Castle, containing 300 inhabitants. The living is a perpetual curacy, in the archdeaconry and diocese of Durham, endowed with £600 private benefaction, and £800 royal bounty, and in the patronage of the Vicar of Gainford. The chapel stands near the edge of a steep cliff above the river Tees. Limestone abounds in the chapelry, in which also there are some petrifying springs.

WHORLTON, a township comprising East and West Whorlton, in that part of the parish of NEWBURN which is in the western division of CASTLE ward, county of NORTHUMBERLAND, 4¾ miles (N. W. by W.) from Newcastle upon Tyne, containing 57 inhabitants.

WHORLTON, a parish in the western division of the liberty of LANGBAURGH, North riding of the county of YORK, comprising the townships of Faceby, Potto, and Whorlton, and containing 968 inhabitants, of which number, 583 are in the township of Whorlton, 5½ miles (S. W. by S.) from Stokesley. The living is a perpetual curacy, in the archdeaconry of Cleveland, and diocese of York, endowed with £600 royal bounty, and £1000 parliamentary grant, and in the patronage of G. Cary, Esq. The church, dedicated to the Holy Cross, is remarkable for a beautiful ivy tree, which ornaments the interior. A school is supported by two small bequests of Isabel and William Harker, the latter of whom also gave a cottage for a school-house. At Scarth, in this parish, in the time of Henry I., a cell of Augustine canons, subordinate to the monastery of Gisburn, was founded by Stephen Meinil. The lofty gateway tower of a castle, supposed to have been built in the reign of Richard II., still remains, and bears the arms of D'Arcy, Meynell, and Gray, its ancient possessors.

WIBSEY, a chapelry in the parish of BRADFORD, wapentake of MORLEY, West riding of the county of YORK, 2¼ miles (S. W. by S.) from Bradford, with which the population is returned. The living is a perpetual curacy, in the archdeaconry and diocese of York, endowed with £600 private benefaction, £400 royal bounty, and £300 parliamentary grant, and in the patronage of the Vicar of Bradford. The chapel, dedicated to the Holy Trinity, has lately received an addition of five hundred sittings, of which three hundred are free, the Incorporated Society for the enlargement of churches and chapels having granted £250 towards defraying the expense. The manufacture of worsted is extensively carried on here.

WIBTOFT, a chapelry in that part of the parish of CLAYBROOKE which is in the Kirby division of the hundred of KNIGHTLOW, county of WARWICK, 5½ miles (W. N. W.) from Lutterworth, containing 112 inhabitants. The old Watling-street and Fosse-way meet at a Roman fort on the Leicestershire boundary, north of this place.

WICHAUGH, a township in the parish of MALPAS, higher division of the hundred of BROXTON, county palatine of CHESTER, 5½ miles (N. W.) from Whitchurch, containing 36 inhabitants.

WICHENFORD, a parish in the lower division of the hundred of OSWALDSLOW, county of WORCESTER, 6¼ miles (N. W. by N.) from Worcester, containing 334 inhabitants. The living is a vicarage, in the archdeaconry and diocese of Worcester, rated in the king's books at £9. 10., and in the patronage of the Rev. William Digby, Prebendary of the Cathedral Church of Worcester. The church is dedicated to St. Lawrence.

WICHNOR, a chapelry in the parish of TATENHILL, northern division of the hundred of OFFLOW, county of STAFFORD, 6½ miles (N. E.) from Lichfield, containing 162 inhabitants. The living is a perpetual curacy, in the archdeaconry of Stafford, and diocese of Lichfield and Coventry, endowed with £400 royal bounty, and in the patronage of T. Levett, Esq. The chapel is dedicated to St. Leonard. The Grand Trunk canal passes through the parish, and communicates with the neighbouring Iron-works. Wichnor is in the honour of Tutbury, duchy of Lancaster, and within the jurisdiction of a court of pleas held at Tutbury every third Tuesday, for the recovery of debts under 40s.

WICK, a hamlet in the chapelry of Abson, hundred of PUCKLE-CHURCH, county of GLOUCESTER, 6 miles (E. by S.) from Bristol. The population is returned with Abson. Five boys are educated for £10. 10. a year, being one-fifth of the income arising from a bequest of £500 by Henry Berrow, in 1718.

WICK (ST. LAWRENCE), a parish in the hundred of WINTERSTOKE, county of SOMERSET, 8½ miles (N. N. W.) from Axbridge, containing 267 inhabitants. The living is a perpetual curacy, annexed to the vicarage of Congresbury, in the archdeaconry of Wells, and diocese of Bath and Wells. The church was formerly a chapel of ease to Congresbury.

WICK near PERSHORE, a chapelry in the parish of ST. ANDREW, PERSHORE, upper division of the hundred of PERSHORE, county of WORCESTER, 1½ mile (E. S. E.) from Pershore, containing 303 inhabitants. The living is a perpetual curacy, in the archdeaconry and diocese of Worcester, endowed with £600 royal bounty, and in the patronage of the Vicar of St. Andrew, Pershore. The chapel is dedicated to St. Lawrence. An Augustine priory was founded here, early in the reign of Stephen by Peter de Corbezon, who, a few years afterwards, removed it to Studley in Warwickshire.

WICK-EPISCOPI, a township in the parish of ST. JOHN BEDWARDINE, lower division of the hundred of OSWALDSLOW, county of WORCESTER, containing 1263 inhabitants.

WICKEN, a parish in the hundred of STAPLOE, county of CAMBRIDGE, 7 miles (S. S. E.) from Ely, containing 752 inhabitants. The living is a perpetual curacy, in the archdeaconry of Sudbury, and diocese of Norwich, endowed with £200 private benefaction, and £400 royal bounty, and in the patronage of Mrs. Rayner. The church is dedicated to St. Lawrence. The Buckingham canal passes through the parish. At Spinney there was a priory founded by Sir Hugh de Malebisse, in the reign of Henry III., for three Augustine canons.

WICKEN, a parish in the hundred of CLELEY, county of NORTHAMPTON, 3½ miles (W. S. W.) from Stony-Stratford, containing, with Wyke-Hamon, 471 inhabitants. The living is a rectory, with Wyke-Hamon, in the archdeaconry of Northampton, and diocese of Peterborough, rated in the king's books at £15. 1. 10½., and in the patronage of — Prowse, Esq. The church is dedicated to St. John the Evangelist : that of Wyke-Hamon has been long demolished.

WICKEN-BONANT, a parish in the hundred of UTTLESFORD, county of ESSEX, 4¾ miles (S. W. by S.) from Saffron-Walden, containing 122 inhabitants. The living is a rectory, in the peculiar jurisdiction of the Commissary of Essex and Herts, concurrently with the Consistorial Court of the Bishop of London, rated in the king's books at £11. A. George, Esq. was patron in 1814. The church is dedicated to St. Margaret.

WICKENBY, a parish in the western division of the wapentake of WRAGGOE, parts of LINDSEY, county

VOL. IV.

of LINCOLN, 5½ miles (N. W.) from Wragby, containing 125 inhabitants. The living is a rectory, in the archdeaconry and diocese of Lincoln, rated in the king's books at £6. 17. 6., and in the patronage of George Neville, Esq. The church is dedicated to St. Peter and St. Lawrence.

WICKERSLEY, a parish in the southern division of the wapentake of STRAFFORTH and TICKHILL, West riding of the county of YORK, 3½ miles (E. by S.) from Rotherham, containing 432 inhabitants. The living is a rectory, in the archdeaconry and diocese of York, rated in the king's books at £8. 0. 2½. H. Kater, Esq. was patron in 1804. The church is dedicated to St. Alban. Here are quarries of excellent grindstone, from which the Sheffield manufacturers are supplied in large quantities.

WICKFORD, a parish in the hundred of BARSTABLE, county of ESSEX, 6 miles (E. by S.) from Billericay, containing 381 inhabitants. The living is a rectory, in the archdeaconry of Essex, and diocese of London, rated in the king's books at £14, and in the patronage of R. B. de Beauvoir, Esq. There is a place of worship for Independents.

WICKHAM, a chapelry in that part of the parish of WELFORD which is in the hundred of KINTBURY-EAGLE, county of BERKS, 5½ miles (N. W. by N.) from Speenhamland. The population is returned with the parish. The chapel is dedicated to St. Swithin.

WICKHAM, a chapelry in the parish of SPALDING, wapentake of ELLOE, parts of HOLLAND, county of LINCOLN, 3¼ miles (N. E. by N.) from Spalding. The population is returned with the parish. The chapel is dedicated to St. Nicholas.

WICKHAM, a parish in the hundred of TITCHFIELD, Portsdown division of the county of SOUTHAMPTON, 4 miles (S. by E.) from Bishop's Waltham, containing 1134 inhabitants. The living is a rectory, in the archdeaconry and diocese of Winchester, rated in the king's books at £8. 2. 8½. P. Rashleigh, Esq. was patron in 1806. The church is dedicated to St. Nicholas. The village, which is situated on the high road from London to Gosport, is remarkable as the birthplace, in 1324, of the distinguished and munificent prelate, William of Wykeham ; and as the residence of Dr. Joseph Warton, the poet, who died here in 1800. Courts leet and baron are held annually ; and there is a fair for cattle on May 20th. John Swann, in 1778, bequeathed £100 three per cent. consols., directing the dividends to be applied for teaching poor children.

WICKHAM (BISHOP'S), a parish in the hundred of THURSTABLE, county of ESSEX, 2½ miles (S. by E.) from Witham, containing 467 inhabitants. The living is a rectory, in the peculiar jurisdiction of the Commissary of Essex and Herts, concurrently with the Consistorial Court of the Bishop of London, rated in the king's books at £12. 3. 4., and in the patronage of the Bishop of London.

WICKHAM (CHILDS), a parish in the lower division of the hundred of KIFTSGATE, county of GLOUCESTER, 5¼ miles (W. by S.) from Chipping-Campden, containing 428 inhabitants. The living is a discharged vicarage, in the archdeaconry and diocese of Gloucester, rated in the king's books at £7. 16. 10., endowed with £200 royal bounty, and in the patronage of S. Young Esq. The church is dedicated to St. Mary.

3 O

WICKHAM (EAST), a parish in the hundred of LESSNESS, lathe of SUTTON at HONE, county of KENT, $3\frac{1}{2}$ miles (W. N. W.) from Crayford, containing 317 inhabitants. The living is a perpetual curacy, annexed to the vicarage of Plumstead, in the archdeaconry and diocese of Rochester. The church is dedicated to St. Michael. Part of the lands and tithes in East Wickham were given, by the famous Admiral, Sir John Hawkins, in the reign of Elizabeth, to the hospital for distressed mariners, founded by him at Chatham, to which they still belong. William Forster, in 1727, gave lands in trust, among other purposes, to erect and endow a school; the income is £68 a year, for which thirty-three boys and nineteen girls are educated.

WICKHAM (ST. PAUL), a parish in the hundred of HINCKFORD, county of ESSEX, $3\frac{1}{4}$ miles (E. by N.) from Castle-Hedingham, containing 328 inhabitants. The living is a rectory, in the peculiar jurisdiction and patronage of the Dean and Chapter of St. Paul's, London, rated in the king's books at £9. The church is dedicated to All Saints.

WICKHAM (WEST), a parish in the hundred of CHILFORD, county of CAMBRIDGE, $4\frac{3}{4}$ miles (N. E. by E.) from Linton, containing 517 inhabitants. The living is a perpetual curacy, in the archdeaconry and diocese of Ely, and in the patronage of Lord Montford. The church is dedicated to St. Mary.

WICKHAM (WEST), a parish in the hundred of RUXLEY, lathe of SUTTON at HONE, county of KENT, $2\frac{3}{4}$ miles (S. S. W.) from Bromley, containing 555 inhabitants. The living is a rectory, in the archdeaconry and diocese of Rochester, rated in the king's books at £11. 10. 10., and in the patronage of the Dowager Lady Farnaby. The church is dedicated to St. John the Baptist: the windows of the chancel are beautifully ornamented with stained glass. There is a place of worship for Wesleyan Methodists. This was formerly a market town; a fair for cattle is held on Easter-Monday. A National school, for forty children of each sex, is supported by subscription. The manor-house is a curious square structure, with angular towers, of the time of Henry VII. The learned Gilbert West, the friend of Gray the poet, long resided in the village, where he was visited by Lyttleton and Pitt, and where, according to Dr. Johnson, he received that conviction which produced the dissertation on the conversion of St. Paul; he was buried here.

WICKHAM-MARKET, a parish (formerly a market town) in the hundred of WILFORD, county of SUFFOLK, $12\frac{1}{2}$ miles (N. E.) from Ipswich, containing 1015 inhabitants. The living is a discharged vicarage, in the archdeaconry of Suffolk, and diocese of Norwich, rated in the king's books at £6. 16. 8., endowed with £200 private benefaction, and £200 royal bounty, and in the patronage of the Crown. The church, dedicated to All Saints, is situated on an eminence commanding a most extensive prospect, including no less than fifty churches; the spire is a conspicuous landmark. There is a place of worship for Independents. The village occupies an elevated and pleasant site, rising from the river Deben, and, as its name implies, was formerly a market town; it had also a shire-hall, where the general quarter sessions were usually held, but the building was, a few years since, taken down by the lord

of the manor; the archdeacon still holds his spiritual courts here. Ann Barker, in 1730, bequeathed one-third of the produce of £300, which, with the rents arising from certain lands given by an unknown individual, is applied for teaching poor children; the annual income is about £46.

WICKHAM-SKEITH, a parish in the hundred of HARTISMERE, county of SUFFOLK, $2\frac{3}{4}$ miles (N.) from Mendlesham, containing 523 inhabitants. The living is a discharged rectory, in the archdeaconry of Sudbury, and diocese of Norwich, rated in the king's books at £5. 8. $1\frac{1}{2}$., and in the patronage of J. Wodehouse, Esq. The church is dedicated to St. Andrew.

WICKHAMBREUX, a parish in the hundred of DOWNHAMFORD, lathe of St. AUGUSTINE, county of KENT, 5 miles (E. by N.) from Canterbury, containing 469 inhabitants. The living is a rectory, in the archdeaconry and diocese of Canterbury, rated in the king's books at £29. 12. 6., and in the patronage of G. W. H. D'Aeth, Esq. The church is dedicated to St. Andrew. The Rev. John Smith, B.D., in 1656, gave a house and school-room in trust to the minister and parish officers, for the education of children.

WICKHAMBROOK, a parish in the hundred of RISBRIDGE, county of SUFFOLK, $6\frac{1}{4}$ miles (N. by W.) from Clare, containing 1295 inhabitants. The living is a vicarage, in the archdeaconry of Sudbury, and diocese of Norwich, rated in the king's books at £8. 6. $10\frac{1}{2}$., and in the patronage of the Crown. The church is dedicated to All Saints. There is a place of worship for Independents.

WICKHAMFORD, a parish in the upper division of the hundred of BLACKENHURST, county of WORCESTER, $2\frac{1}{4}$ miles (E. S. E.) from Evesham, containing 130 inhabitants. The living is a discharged perpetual curacy, in the peculiar jurisdiction of the Chancellor of the Cathedral Church of Worcester: rated in the king's books at £2. 4. $4\frac{1}{2}$., endowed with £200 royal bounty, and in the patronage of the Dean and Canons of Christ Church, Oxford. The church is dedicated to St. John the Baptist. Limestone in abundance is obtained in the neighbourhood.

WICKHAMPTON, a parish in the hundred of WALSHAM, county of NORFOLK, $4\frac{1}{2}$ miles (S. S. E.) from Acle, containing 112 inhabitants. The living is a discharged rectory, in the archdeaconry and diocese of Norwich, rated in the king's books at £4. The Rev. John Love was patron in 1803. The church is dedicated to St. Andrew: the arms of the ancient family of Gerbrigges are exhibited in various parts of the building, though much defaced by time. There is a place of worship for Wesleyan Methodists.

WICKLEWOOD, a parish in the hundred of FOREHOE, county of NORFOLK, 13 miles (W. N. W.) from Wymondham, containing 672 inhabitants. The living comprises the rectory of St. Andrew, consolidated with the discharged vicarage of All Saints, in the archdeaconry of Norfolk, and diocese of Norwich, rated in the king's books at £6. 3. $11\frac{1}{2}$., and in the patronage of Mrs. Kett and R. Heber, Esq. The church of St. Andrew has been long demolished; it stood in the same churchyard with that of All Saints, which is a spacious structure, with a large handsome tower, in the later style of English architecture. A market and two fairs granted in 1440 by Henry VI., were formerly held here.

WICKMERE, a parish in the southern division of the hundred of ERPINGHAM, county of NORFOLK, 5 miles (N. N. W.) from Aylsham, containing 285 inhabitants. The living is a discharged rectory, with that of Wolterton annexed, in the archdeaconry and diocese of Norwich, rated in the king's books at £9, and in the patronage of the Earl of Orford.

WICKTON, a joint township with Risbury, in the parish of STOKE-PRIOR, hundred of WOLPHY, county of HEREFORD, 4½ miles (S. E.) from Leominster, containing, with Risbury, 140 inhabitants.

WICKWAR, a market town and parish in the upper division of the hundred of GRUMBALD'S ASH, county of GLOUCESTER, 24 miles (S. S. W.) from Gloucester, and 111 (W.) from London, containing 919 inhabitants. The town is conveniently situated on two small streams, over one of which is a handsome stone bridge. It formerly participated largely in the clothing trade carried on extensively in the surrounding district, of which it was the central mart, but has greatly decayed. Of late, great improvements have taken place, among which is the formation of a new road to Wotton under Edge, whereby the distance has been shortened three miles, and, from other local advantages, it is expected to recover its former importance. Coal abounds in the adjacent waste lands. The market is on Monday; and there are fairs on the 5th of April and the 2nd of July, for horses and horned cattle. The town, under a very ancient charter, is governed by a mayor, and an indefinite number of aldermen, consisting of all who have held the office of mayor. A manorial court is held annually in October.

The living is a rectory, in the archdeaconry and diocese of Gloucester, rated in the king's books at £18, and in the patronage of the Rev. Thomas Cook. The church, dedicated to the Holy Trinity, is a spacious edifice, with a lofty and handsome tower at the west end. There are places of worship for Independents and Wesleyan Methodists. The free school was founded by Alexander Hosea, a native of this town, who, by a bequest in his will, dated in 1683, endowed it with property producing about £100 per annum : a Latin master, with a salary of £28 per annum, and a writing master, with one of £10 are appointed by the trustees, who consist of the corporation, and some other gentlemen of the town and neighbourhood : the masters have also houses provided for them. The number of boys on the foundation in the classical school rarely exceeds three or four, but in the writing school the average number is about twenty-five. There are several small endowments for the benefit of the poor.

WIDCOMB, a joint parish with Lyncomb, in the hundred of BATH-FORUM, county of SOMERSET, 1½ mile (S. E. by E.) from Bath, containing 5880 inhabitants. The living is a perpetual curacy, annexed to the rectory of St. Peter and St. Paul, Bath, in the archdeaconry of Bath, and diocese of Bath and Wells. The church, dedicated to St. Thomas à Becket, has lately received an addition of six hundred and eighty sittings, of which three hundred and seventy are free, the Incorporated Society for the enlargement of churches and chapels having granted £500 towards defraying the expense. At Holloway, in this parish, John Cantlow, prior of Bath, towards the close of the fifteenth century, built a small chapel, in honour of St. Mary Magdalene;

and adjoining it an hospital for lunatics, which latter was rebuilt in 1761. A fair is held annually on May 14th.

WIDCOMBE, a tything in the parish of CHEWTON-MENDIP, hundred of CHEWTON, county of SOMERSET, 5 miles (S. W. by S.) from Pensford, containing 168 inhabitants.

WIDDINGTON, a parish in the hundred of UTTLESFORD, county of ESSEX, 5 miles (W. by N.) from Thaxted, containing 367 inhabitants. The living is a rectory, in the jurisdiction of the Commissary of Essex and Herts, concurrently with the Consistorial Court of the Bishop of London, rated in the king's books at £25, and in the patronage of Lady Vincent. The church is dedicated to St. Mary.

WIDDINGTON, a township in that part of the parish of LITTLE OUSEBURN which is in the upper division of the wapentake of CLARO, West riding of the county of YORK, 8¼ miles (S. E. by E.) from Aldborough, containing 31 inhabitants.

WIDDRINGTON, a parochial chapelry in the eastern division of MORPETH ward, county of NORTHUMBERLAND, 8 miles (N. E. by N.) from Morpeth, containing 388 inhabitants. The living is a perpetual curacy, in the archdeaconry of Northumberland, and diocese of Durham, endowed with £200 private benefaction, and £800 royal bounty, and in the patronage of the Hon. Mr. and Mrs. Vernon. The church is ancient, and appears to have been once much larger. A Scotch church was erected here in 1765. Widdrington was separated from the parish of Woodhorn, and invested with distinct parochial rights, in 1768. A small colliery is worked near the village. There is a school-room, with a house and garden occupied by the master, whose salary of £25 a year is paid by the lady of the manor, for teaching the poor children of the parish. The ancient castle, which stood in a noble park of six hundred acres, was burned down more than fifty years ago, and the present edifice, which occupies the site of the former, is much out of repair, and now uninhabited. This was long the seat of the family of Widdrington, of whom many have at various periods distinguished themselves against the Scots. Sir William, in 1642, was expelled from the House of Commons for raising forces in defence of Charles I., who, in the following year, elevated him to the dignity of Baron Widdrington of Blankney. After the battle of Marston Moor he left the kingdom, when his estates were confiscated by the parliament; but returning in the service of Charles II., he was slain at the battle of Wigan. His son and successor, William, Lord Widdrington, was attainted in 1715, and his property, to the amount of £100,000, was sold for public use.

WIDECOMBE in the MOOR, a parish forming, with the parish of Buckland in the Moor, a detached portion of the hundred of HAYTOR, being locally in that of Lifton, county of DEVON, 5¾ miles (N. W. by N.) from Ashburton, containing 934 inhabitants. The living is a vicarage, in the archdeaconry of Totness, and diocese of Exeter, rated in the king's books at £25. 13. 9., and in the patronage of the Dean and Chapter of Exeter. The church, dedicated to St. Pancras, was greatly injured by lightning during the performance of divine service, on October 21st, 1638, when portions of the stone and wood work fell in,

The parish is intersected by three rivulets tributary to the river Dart, which bounds it on one side. It comprises several long vallies, enclosed by rugged hills, bordering upon Dartmoor, and exhibits, in many places, marks of stream-works: tin has long been found in the neighbourhood. There are four small schools in different parts of the parish, supported by subscription and the trifling endowments of William Culling and Miss Smith.

WIDFORD, a parish in the hundred of CHELMS-FORD, county of ESSEX, 1½ mile (S. W.) from Chelmsford, containing 118 inhabitants. The living is a discharged rectory, in the archdeaconry of Essex, and diocese of London, rated in the king's books at £8. W. Harding, Esq. was patron in 1814. The church, dedicated to St. Mary, is partly in the early, and partly in the decorated, style of English architecture; it is situated on the west side of the high road from London to Chelmsford.

WIDFORD, a parish in the lower division of the hundred of SLAUGHTER, county of GLOUCESTER, 1½ mile (E. S. E.) from Burford, containing 51 inhabitants. The living is a discharged rectory, in the archdeaconry and diocese of Gloucester, rated in the king's books at £3. 14. 2., and endowed with £400 royal bounty. T. H. H. Gwynne, Esq. was patron in 1812. The church is dedicated to St. Oswald.

WIDFORD, a parish in the hundred of BRAUGHIN, county of HERTFORD, 3¾ miles (E. by N.) from Ware, containing 461 inhabitants. The living is a rectory, in the archdeaconry of Middlesex, and diocese of London, rated in the king's books at £12. 13. 4., and in the patronage of S. Partridge, Esq. The church, dedicated to St. John the Baptist, has a square embattled tower, with a tall slender spire, and occupies a considerable eminence. The river Ash runs through the parish. A rent-charge of £5, from an unknown benefactor, is applied for teaching three boys.

WIDLEY, a parish in the hundred of PORTSDOWN, Portsdown division of the county of SOUTHAMPTON, 5½ miles (E. by N.) from Fareham, containing 544 inhabitants. The living is a rectory, with the vicarage of Wimeringe annexed, in the archdeaconry and diocese of Winchester, rated in the king's books at £14. 11. 10½., and in the alternate patronage of the Warden and Fellows of Winchester College and T. Thistlethwaite, Esq. The church, dedicated to St. Mary Magdalene, has lately received an addition of one hundred and sixty-nine sittings, of which ninety-nine are free, the Incorporated Society for the enlargement of churches and chapels having granted £100 towards defraying the expense. The Rev. John Taylor, in 1771, gave an annuity of £2 in support of a school.

WIDMER-POOL, a parish in the southern division of the wapentake of RUSHCLIFFE, county of NOTTINGHAM, 9 miles (S. S. E.) from Nottingham, containing 229 inhabitants. The living is a rectory, in the archdeaconry of Nottingham, and diocese of York, rated in the king's books at £14. 16. 0½. F. Robinson, Esq. was patron in 1812. The church is dedicated to St. Peter. The parish is bounded on the west by the old Fosse-road.

WIDNESS, a joint township with Appleton, in the parish of PRESCOT, hundred of WEST DERBY, county

palatine of LANCASTER, 6¼ miles (W. by S.) from Warrington, containing 1439 inhabitants.

WIDWORTHY, a parish in the hundred of COLYTON, county of DEVON, 3½ miles (E. by S.) from Honiton, containing 274 inhabitants. The living is a rectory, in the archdeaconry and diocese of Exeter, rated in the king's books at £11. 16. 0½., and in the patronage of J. T. B. Marwood, Esq. The church, dedicated to St. Cuthbert, contains the effigy of a knight in armour, and a fine monument, by Bacon, to the memory of James Marwood, Esq., a liberal benefactor to the parish. Near it is an old earthwork, and in the north-east part of the parish are vestiges of an ancient intrenchment. Benedictus Marwood, Esq., in 1742, gave £100, and the Rev. Joseph Somaster, in 1770, left £50, to be applied for the education of poor children. At Wilmington, in this parish, a fair is held on the morrow of the festival of St. Matthew.

WIELD, a parish in the hundred of FAWLEY, Fawley division of the county of SOUTHAMPTON, 6 miles (W.) from Alton, containing 222 inhabitants. The living is a perpetual curacy, in the archdeaconry and diocese of Winchester, endowed with £400 royal bounty, and in the patronage of the Earl of Portsmouth. The church is dedicated to St. James. Wield is within the jurisdiction of the Cheyney Court held at Winchester every Thursday, for the recovery of debts to any amount.

WIGAN, a parish comprising the borough and market town of Wigan (which has separate jurisdiction), the chapelries of Billinge (Chapel - End), Hindley, and Upholland, and the townships of Abram, Billinge (Higher-End), Dalton, Haigh, Ince, Orrell, Pemberton, and Winstanley, in the hundred of WEST DERBY, and the township of Aspull, in the hundred of SALFORD, county palatine of LANCASTER, and containing 38,318 inhabitants, of which number, 17,716 are in the town of Wigan, 18 miles (W. N. W.) from Manchester, and 199 (N. W. by N.) from London. This place is stated by Camden to have been originally called *Wibiggin*: the vicinity is said to have been the scene of some sanguinary battles between the Britons, under their renowned King Arthur, and the Saxons; and the discovery, rather more than eighty years since, of a large quantity of human bones, and the bones and shoes of horses, over an extensive tract of ground near the town, tends to confirm this opinion. During the great civil war, several battles were fought here by the contending parties, it being the principal station of the king's troops commanded by the Earl of Derby, who was defeated and driven from the town by the parliamentary forces under Sir John Smeaton, early in 1643, and shortly afterwards, in the same year, he was again defeated by Col. Ashton, who, in consequence of the devotion of the inhabitants to the royal cause, ordered the fortifications of the town to be demolished. From this time Wigan remained tranquil (with the exception of Oliver Cromwell pursuing through it, in 1648, the

Corporate Seal.

Scotch army under the Duke of Hamilton, whom he had driven from Preston) until 1651, when the Earl of Derby, having been summoned from the Isle of Man by King Charles II., was again defeated here by a very superior force under Col. Lilburne. To record the courage and loyalty of Sir Thomas Tildesley, who was slain in this action, a monumental pillar was erected, in 1679, by Alexander Rigby, Esq., then high sheriff of the county, on the spot where he fell, at the northern end of the town; in 1745, Prince Charles Edward marched through Wigan on his route from Preston to Manchester.

The town is situated on the eastern bank, and near the source, of the river Douglas, and is described by Leland as "a paved town, as big as Warrington, but better builded;" a patent for paving it and building a bridge over the Douglas was granted so early as the 7th of Edward III. The old and greater part of the town consists of irregular streets and mean houses, but great improvements have recently been made, and two new streets formed, which contain some well-built houses. It is lighted with gas by a company established in 1823, and supplied with good water by works erected by a company formed under the authority of an act in 1761. The manufacture of calicoes, fustians, and other cotton goods, linens, and checks, and the spinning of cotton yarn, are extensively carried on; and there are brass and iron foundries, pewter-works, several manufactures for spades and edge-tools, and some corn-mills, on the river. The steam-engines employed are equal in power to that of six hundred horses; and an increase of more than two thousand inhabitants, since 1821, may convey some idea of the improvement of the trade and manufactures. The Douglas, under the authority of an act obtained in 1720, was made navigable to its junction with the Ribble. The Leeds and Liverpool canal passes the town, and, by its branches and various communications with Manchester and Kendal on one side, and the German ocean on the other, affords every facility for the conveyance of the manufactures and of the coal abounding in this neighbourhood, among which is cannel coal, to all parts of the kingdom: fly boats ply daily upon it to Manchester and Liverpool. The market is held on Monday and Friday, that on the latter day being the principal; and there are fairs on Holy Thursday, June 27th, and October 28th, on which days the commercial hall, a commodious brick building in the market-place, erected in 1816, is open for the use of the clothiers. The first charter of incorporation was granted by Henry III., and the privileges which it bestowed have been confirmed and augmented by succeeding monarchs; but that under which the corporation now acts was granted by Charles II., and vests the government of the borough in a mayor, justice, two bailiffs, and subordinate officers, all elected annually. The mayor is a justice of the peace during, and for one year after, his mayoralty. The corporation are authorized by their charter to try for all civil actions, and hold a court of sessions quarterly for felonies not capital, committed within the borough. Petty sessions for the Warrington division of the hundred are held here. The town hall was rebuilt, in 1720, by the Earl of Barrymore and Sir Roger Bradshaigh, then members for the borough. The gaol is used only for temporary confinement, pri-

soners being committed to the county gaol. The borough first sent members to parliament in the 23rd of Edward I., and again in the thirty-fifth of the same reign, after which period this privilege was not exercised until the 1st of Edward VI.: the right of election is vested in the free burgesses, and the number of voters at the last election was about one hundred and thirty: the mayor and the two bailiffs are the returning officers. The corporation have the power of admitting non-resident and honorary freemen to vote without limitation, which gives them a preponderating influence in returning members.

The living is a rectory, in the archdeaconry and diocese of Chester, rated in the king's books at £80. 13. 4., and in the patronage of the Earl of Bradford. The church, dedicated to All Saints, is an ancient and handsome edifice. St. George's was erected, as a chapel of ease, in 1781: the living is a perpetual curacy, endowed with £600 royal bounty, and £2200 parliamentary grant, and in the gift of the owners of pews and the rector, alternately; the latter has also the patronage of the perpetual curacies of Billinge, Hindley, and Upholland, in this parish. There are two places of worship each for Baptists, Independents, and Roman Catholics, and one each for Presbyterians and Wesleyan Methodists. The free grammar school, at Millgate, appears to have been founded in the early part of the reign of James I., but by whom is uncertain; the earliest recorded benefaction to it is one of £6. 13. 4. per annum, in 1619, by Mr. James Leigh. A considerable increase in the income having arisen from various subsequent donations and benefactions, an act of parliament was passed, in 1812, incorporating fifteen members of the corporation governors of the institution, who appoint a master, with a salary of £130 per annum and the privilege of receiving boarders, and an usher; the number of scholars is limited to eighty. A Blue-coat school, wherein forty boys were clothed and instructed, was established in 1773, but a building for a National school having been erected in 1825, partly by a grant of £350 from the National School Society in London, and partly by subscription, the former has been united to it, and about three hundred boys are taught. A school of industry was instituted in 1823; and about two thousand five hundred children receive instruction in the various Sunday schools connected with the dissenting places of worship. The dispensary was established in 1798, and the building in 1801: it is supported principally by annual subscriptions, and has extended its benefits to a great number of sufferers. There are also many minor bequests and benefactions for the poor, amounting in the aggregate to a considerable sum annually. A clothing society, for furnishing them with warm clothing and bedding during the winter months, was formed in 1817; a savings bank was established in 1821; a Bible society in 1825; and a mechanics' institute and library in 1825. A spring was discovered near Scholes bridge, some years since, the water of which possessed nearly the same medicinal properties as those at Harrogate, and a handsome building was erected for the convenience of persons who wished to drink, or use it for a bath; but it has ceased to be resorted to, the water having lost much of its medicinal virtue, owing, it is supposed, to its being mixed with the produce of the neighbouring coal-pits.

WIGBOROUGH (GREAT), a parish in the hundred of WINSTREE, county of ESSEX, 6½ miles (S. S. W.) from Colchester, containing 410 inhabitants. The living is a rectory, in the archdeaconry of Colchester, and diocese of London, rated in the king's books at £18. 17. 6., and in the patronage of Henry Bewes, Esq. The church, dedicated to St. Stephen, is situated on a considerable eminence, and is visible at a great distance. The parish is bounded on the south by a creek of the Blackwater river, called Verley; it was formerly of much greater importance, as is evident from several green lanes still retaining the name of streets. A quantity of ancient coins, enclosed in an earthen jar, was discovered in the marshes, about forty years ago. There were formerly salt-works in the neighbourhood, whence the place has been called Salcot-Wigborough.

WIGBOROUGH (LITTLE), a parish in the hundred of WINSTREE, county of ESSEX, 7¼ miles (S. by W.) from Colchester, containing 95 inhabitants. The living is a discharged rectory, in the archdeaconry of Colchester, and diocese of Exeter, rated in the king's books at £10, and in the patronage of the Governors of the Charter-house, London. The church is dedicated to St. Nicholas. A creek of the Blackwater, termed Mersea channel, bounds the parish on the east, and another, called Verley channel, on the south.

WIGGENHALL (ST. GERMANS), a parish in the Marshland division of the hundred of FREEBRIDGE, county of NORFOLK, 4¼ miles (S. S. W.) from Lynn-Regis, containing 584 inhabitants. The living is a discharged vicarage, in the archdeaconry and diocese of Norwich, rated in the king's books at £6, endowed with £200 royal bounty, and in the patronage of the Dean and Chapter of Norwich. The church is situated on the east bank of the Ouse.

WIGGENHALL (ST. MARY), a parish in the Marshland division of the hundred of FREEBRIDGE, county of NORFOLK, 5¾ miles (S. W. by S.) from Lynn-Regis, containing 239 inhabitants. The living is a discharged vicarage, in the archdeaconry and diocese of Norwich, rated in the king's books at £12. 10., and in the patronage of the Crown. The church is a stately structure; at the east end is an oaken screen, separating what was once a chapel from the rest of the interior. The windows over the arches of the nave exhibit some remains of ancient stained glass, representing the twelve Apostles, and various portions of sacred history. It contains a fine altar-tomb, bearing the arms of Kervile and Plowden, with the effigies of a knight in armour, his lady, and two children. The parish is bounded on the west by the river Ouse.

WIGGENHALL (ST. MARY MAGDALENE), a parish in the Marshland division of the hundred of FREE-BRIDGE, county of NORFOLK, 6 miles (S. S. W.) from Lynn-Regis, containing 551 inhabitants. The living is a discharged vicarage, in the archdeaconry and diocese of Norwich, rated in the king's books at £5..15. 10. Mrs. Garforth was patroness in 1811. The church is a regular structure, with a square stone tower at the west end, and chapels at the terminations of the north and south aisles: various parts of the building are ornamented with the arms of Kervile, Scales, Berney, and several other ancient families. On the west bank of the Ouse was a hermitage, dedicated to St. John the Evangelist, which in 1181 was appropriated,

by the prior and convent of Reynham, to nuns of the order of St. Augustine, subject to Castle-Acre, whose revenue at the dissolution was valued at £31. 16. 7.

WIGGENHALL (ST. PETER), a parish in the Marshland division of the hundred of FREEBRIDGE, county of NORFOLK, 5 miles (S. by W.) from Lynn-Regis, containing 122 inhabitants. The living is a discharged vicarage, in the archdeaconry and diocese of Norwich, rated in the king's books at £6, and in the patronage of the Crown. The church stands on the east bank of the Ouse: on the font are two cross keys, an emblem of the patron saint.

WIGGESLEY, a hamlet in the parish of THORNEY, northern division of the wapentake of NEWARK, county of NOTTINGHAM, 8½ miles (E. by S.) from Tuxford, containing 78 inhabitants.

WIGGINTHORPE, a joint township with Terrington, in the parish of TERRINGTON, partly within the liberty of ST. PETER of YORK, East riding, and partly in the wapentake of BULMER, North riding, of the county of YORK, 9 miles (W.) from New Malton. The population is returned with Terrington.

WIGGINTON, a parish in the hundred of DACORUM, county of HERTFORD, 1½ mile (S.E.) from Tring, containing 477 inhabitants. The living is a perpetual curacy, united with that of Tring, in the archdeaconry of Huntingdon, and diocese of Lincoln, endowed with £400 private benefaction, and £1200 royal bounty. The church is dedicated to St. Bartholomew.

WIGGINTON, a parish in the hundred of BLOXHAM, county of OXFORD, 5¼ miles (W.N.W.) from Deddington, containing 291 inhabitants. The living is a rectory, in the archdeaconry and diocese of Oxford, rated in the king's books at £17. 2. 8½., and in the patronage of the Principal and Fellows of Jesus College, Oxford. The church is dedicated to St. Giles.

WIGGINTON, a chapelry in that part of the parish of TAMWORTH which is in the southern division of the hundred of OFFLOW, county of STAFFORD, 1¾ mile (N.) from Tamworth, containing 747 inhabitants. The living is a perpetual curacy, in the archdeaconry of Stafford, and diocese of Lichfield and Coventry, endowed with £800 royal bounty, and £1400 parliamentary grant, and in the patronage of the Vicar of Tamworth. The chapel is dedicated to St. Leonard. Thomas Barnes, in 1717, gave property, of the value of about £5 per annum, in support of a school.

WIGGINTON, a parish in the wapentake of BULMER, North riding of the county of YORK, 5 miles (N.) from York, containing 309 inhabitants. The living is a rectory, in the jurisdiction of the peculiar court of Alne and Tollerton, rated in the king's books at £14. 13. 4., and in the patronage of the Crown.

WIGGLESWORTH, a township in the parish of LONG PRESTON, western division of the wapentake of STAINCLIFFE and EWCROSS, West riding of the county of YORK, 6½ miles (S. S. W.) from Settle, containing 479 inhabitants.

WIGGONBY, a township in the parish of AIKTON, ward and county of CUMBERLAND, 4¾ miles (N.E.) from Wigton, containing 169 inhabitants. Near Down hall, within the township, is an encampment sixty yards square, now planted with fir, and surrounded by a deep ditch. Margaret Hodgson, in 1792, left land, now let for about £175 a year, in support of a school.

WIGGONHOLT, a parish in the hundred of WEST EASWRITH, rape of ARUNDEL, county of SUSSEX, 7¼ miles (N.N.E.) from Arundel, containing 47 inhabitants. The living is a rectory, consolidated with that of Greatham, in the archdeaconry and diocese of Chichester, rated in the king's books at £7. 4. 4½. The church is small, and remarkable only for its curious Norman font. The parish is bounded on the west by the river Arun. A great number of Roman urns was found here about seven years since; they were of red pottery, beautifully figured, but, from the unprotected situation in which they were deposited, few of them are in a perfect state. Several Roman coins of the Emperors Nero, Vespasian, Claudius, Adrian, and Marcus Antoninus, were also discovered.

WIGHILL, a parish in the ainsty of the city, and East riding of the county, of YORK, 2½ miles (N. by W.) from Tadcaster, containing 250 inhabitants. The living is a discharged vicarage, in the archdeaconry and diocese of York, rated in the king's books at £5. 3. 6½., endowed with £200 private benefaction, and £200 royal bounty, and in the patronage of — Wilson, Esq. The church, dedicated to All Saints, is situated on an eminence rising from the margin of the river Wharfe.

WIGHT (ISLE OF). — See article on the county of SOUTHAMPTON.

WIGHTON, a parish in the northern division of the hundred of GREENHOE, county of NORFOLK, 2¼ miles (N. by E.) from Little Walsingham, containing 507 inhabitants. The living is a discharged vicarage, in the archdeaconry and diocese of Norwich, rated in the king's books at £11. 11. 8., endowed with £400 royal bounty, and in the patronage of the Dean and Chapter of Norwich. The church is dedicated to All Saints.

WIGLAND, a township in the parish of MALPAS, higher division of the hundred of BROXTON, county palatine of CHESTER, 1¾ mile (S. S. E.) from Malpas, containing 204 inhabitants. At Dirtwich, in this township, are brine springs, from which salt is made. In 1643, the works were destroyed by a detachment of the parliamentary army, but they were soon restored.

WIGMORE, a parish in the hundred of WIGMORE, county of HEREFORD, 10 miles (N.W. by N.) from Leominster, containing, with the township of Limebrook, 429 inhabitants. The living is a discharged vicarage, in the archdeaconry and diocese of Hereford, rated in the king's books at £8, endowed with £400 royal bounty, and in the patronage of the Bishop of Hereford. The church is dedicated to St. James. Limestone abounds here, and it is supposed that coal may be obtained in the neighbourhood. A court leet is occasionally held; and there are fairs for cattle, sheep, &c., on May 6th and August 5th. On a commanding elevation, a little to the westward of the village, are the ivy-mantled ruins of Wigmore castle, the outer works of which are the most perfect: the massive fragments of the keep occupy the summit of a lofty artificial mound, and present an appearance highly grand and picturesque: the founder of this once stately edifice is now unknown, but it is recorded that Edward the Elder caused it to be repaired. It was taken from Edric, Earl of Shrewsbury, by Ranulph de Mortimer, who came over with the Conqueror, and made it his principal seat. The same nobleman, in 1100, established in the parish church a small college of three prebendaries, which continued till 1179, when his son Hugh founded, in honour of St. James, a noble abbey for monks of the order of St. Augustine, about one mile distant from the castle, and endowed it so amply that, at the dissolution, its revenue was estimated at £302. 12. 3. An Alien priory, a cell to that of Aveney in Normandy, is said to have existed, at an early period, at Limebrook in this parish; but it is more certain that a priory of nuns of the order of St. Augustine was founded there by the Mortimers, some time in the reign of Richard I., which at the suppression was valued at £23. 17. 8. In the neighbourhood are traces of a Danish camp.

WIGSTHORPE, a hamlet in the parish of LILFORD, hundred of HUXLOE, county of NORTHAMPTON, 4 miles (S. by E.) from Oundle. The population is returned with the parish. Here was anciently a chapel.

WIGSTON (MAGNA), a parish in the hundred of GUTHLAXTON, county of LEICESTER, 3½ miles (S.S.E.) from Leicester, containing 2089 inhabitants. The living is a discharged vicarage, in the archdeaconry of Leicester, and diocese of Lincoln, rated in the king's books at £9. 8. 9., endowed with £400 private benefaction, and £400 royal bounty, and in the alternate patronage of the Master and Wardens of the Haberdashers' Company, and the Governors of Christ's Hospital, London. The church is dedicated to All Saints. There is a place of worship for Independents. This place was formerly called Wigston Two Steeples, from its having two churches; one of these, now in a very dilapidated state, is used as a school-room, where poor children are taught to read and write at the expense of the parishioners. The Leicester canal runs through the parish. The village is pleasantly situated on the high road between Welford and Leicester, and is chiefly inhabited by persons employed in the manufacture of stockings. Here are a lunatic asylum, and an hospital, or almshouse, for six poor widows and as many widowers; the latter was endowed by a Miss Clarke. At a place called the Gaol Close, during the civil war in the reign of Charles I., a temporary prison was erected, to which the prisoners were removed from the county gaol at Leicester: the royal army lay near this place some days.

WIGSTON (PARVA), a chapelry in the parish of CLAYBROOKE, hundred of GUTHLAXTON, county of LEICESTER, 6½ miles (N.W. by W.) from Lutterworth, containing 79 inhabitants. The chapel is dedicated to St. Mary.

WIGTOFT, a parish in the wapentake of KIRTON, parts of HOLLAND, county of LINCOLN, 3 miles (S.E. by S.) from Swineshead, containing 637 inhabitants. The living is a discharged vicarage, with that of Quadring united, in the archdeaconry and diocese of Lincoln, rated in the king's books at £11. 5., and in the patronage of the Bishop of Lincoln. The church is dedicated to St. Peter and St. Paul. A free school here is endowed with certain land, and bears the name of Cowley's and Blisbury's charity.

WIGTON, a parish in the ward and county of CUMBERLAND, comprising the market town of Wigton, and the townships of Oulton, High and Low Waverton, and Woodside-Quarter, and containing, according to the last census, 5456 inhabitants (since increased to near 7000), of which number, 4056 are in the town of Wigton, 11 miles (S. W. by W.) from Carlisle, and 305 (N. N. W.) from London. Of the early history of this place little is recorded : the barony was given by William de Meschines to Waldeof, Lord of Allerdale, and by him to Odoard, who lived about the period of the Norman Conquest, and who assumed the name of De Wigton. The town was burnt by the Scots when they plundered the abbey of Holme-Cultram, in 1322 ; and during the civil war, in 1648, the van of the Duke of Hamilton's army was quartered here. It consists principally of one spacious street, with a narrower extending transversely at one end of it, containing some handsome, well-built houses ; it is pitched with pebbles, and supplied with water from wells, the property of individuals, and a public well and pump, erected near the centre of the town. There are a public subscription and a circulating library : races formerly took place annually in the month of August, but they have been discontinued. The principal articles of manufacture are checks, muslins, and ginghams, which are made to a considerable extent ; and a large establishment for calico printing and dyeing also affords employment to many of the inhabitants. Coal is obtained within three miles, and copper-ore is found within five miles, of the town. The market days are Tuesday and Friday, the former only for corn, of which a great quantity is pitched in the market-place. Fairs are held on the 20th of February, a very large horse fair ; the 5th of April, for horned cattle ; and on the 21st of December, called Wallet fair, for cattle, butchers' meat, apples, and honey ; there are also statute fairs at Whitsuntide and Martinmas. The county magistrates hold here a petty session every month ; and constables are appointed at the court leet and baron of the lord of the manor, which is held annually in September.

The living is a discharged vicarage, in the archdeaconry and diocese of Carlisle, rated in the king's books at £ 17. 19. 0½., endowed with £200 private benefaction, £200 royal bounty, and £400 parliamentary grant, and in the patronage of the Bishop of Carlisle. The church, dedicated to St. Mary, is said to have been originally erected by Odoard, with materials brought from the neighbouring Roman station, called Old Carlisle, and it subsequently belonged to the abbey of Holme-Cultram ; it was taken down in 1788, and the present edifice, a light and handsome building, erected on its site : attached to it is a library for the use of the clergy, presented by Dr. Bray. There are places of worship for the Society of Friends, Independents, Wesleyan Methodists, and Roman Catholics. The free grammar school, at Market hill, near the entrance of the town, was founded, in 1730, by certain of the inhabitants, who agreed to subscribe towards its erection £1 for every penny for which their houses were assessed to the purvey, on condition of having the privilege of sending their children ; this privilege is retained by their successors in the several houses which have thus contributed : the children of such as are not free pay a quarterage of one guinea to the master. In 1787, the sum of £1000 three per cent. stock was bequeathed by John Allison to this school, for the education of four boys belonging to the parish of Wigton, and not living in free tenements ; and, in 1798, £355 was bequeathed

to it by Thomas Tomlinson, Esq., who also left £100 for the establishment of a public library : the present income is about £71 per annum. The master and usher are elected by those inhabitants whose tenements are entitled to the freedom of the school, and the former has a good dwelling-house : there are at present on the foundation fifteen boys under the head-master, who are studying the classics, and twenty under the usher, who are instructed in writing, arithmetic, and mathematics. The Rev. John Brown, D. D., author of the tragedy of *Barbarossa*, received his early education in this school. At Brookfield, near the town, is a school for sixty boys, founded by the Society of Friends, in 1825. The Sunday school, erected in 1820, is a neat and spacious building of freestone, capable of receiving five hundred children ; the general number attending it is about four hundred and fifty : there are also Sunday schools supported by the dissenting congregations. An hospital for six widows of beneficed clergymen, or curates of two years' standing, of the county of Cumberland, or that part of Westmorland which is in the diocese of Carlisle, or of Rothbury in the county of Northumberland, and above forty-six years of age, was founded, in 1725, by the Rev. John Tomlinson, who endowed it with a rent-charge of £45. 12., to which other benefactions have subsequently been added ; it is under the special superintendence of the Bishop of Carlisle, as visitor, and the chancellor of the diocese, the rectors of Aikton and Caldbeck, and the vicars of Wigton and Bromfield, as governors : the inmates have each three apartments, and an allowance of £9 per annum ; the eldest, who officiates as governess, has an extra allowance of ten shillings per annum. About a mile south of Wigton, on an eminence, are the remains of a Roman station, called Old Carlisle, where a great variety of antiquities has been dug up, consisting of coins, altars, statues, and inscriptions, which prove that the *Ala Augusta* was stationed here, in the reign of the Emperor Gordian. Ewan Clarke, the well-known Cumberland poet ; Joseph Rooke, a self-taught genius, who has become a distinguished mathematician, and philosopher, excelling in his knowledge of music, mechanics, optics, and botany ; R. Smirke, R.A., the celebrated historical painter ; and Mr. George Barnes, professor of mathematics, were natives of this town.

WIGTON, a township in that part of the parish of HAREWOOD which is in the upper division of the wapentake of SKYRACK, West riding of the county of YORK, 5½ miles (N. by E.) from Leeds, containing 164 inhabitants.

WIKE, a township in the parish of BIRSTALL, wapentake of MORLEY, West riding of the county of YORK, 3½ miles (S. by W.) from Bradford, containing 1509 inhabitants. There is a place of worship for Independents.

WIKE, a township in that part of the parish of HAREWOOD which is in the upper division of the wapentake of SKYRACK, West riding of the county of YORK, 6¼ miles (N. N. E.) from Leeds, containing 139 inhabitants.

WILBARSTON, a parish in the hundred of CORBY, county of NORTHAMPTON, 4½ miles (S. W. by W.) from Rockingham, containing 697 inhabitants. The living is a vicarage, in the archdeaconry of Northampton, and diocese of Peterborough, rated in the king's books at £7. 17. 1., and in the patronage of Lord Sondes. The church is dedicated to All Saints. There is a place of worship for Independents.

WILBERFOSS, a parish in the Wilton-Beacon division of the wapentake of HARTHILL, East riding of the county of YORK, comprising the townships of Newton upon Derwent and Wilberfoss, and containing 590 inhabitants, of which number, 385 are in the township of Wilberfoss, 5½ miles (W. N. W.) from Pocklington. The living is a perpetual curacy, in the archdeaconry of the East riding, and diocese of York, endowed with £400 royal bounty, and £1400 parliamentary grant, and in the patronage of W. Wilberforce, Esq. The church is dedicated to St. John the Baptist. A Benedictine nunnery, in honour of the Blessed Virgin Mary, was founded here, before 1153, by Alan de Catton, which at the dissolution had a revenue of £28. 8. 8.

WILBRAHAM (GREAT), a parish in the hundred of STAINE, county of CAMBRIDGE, 7¼ miles (E. by S.) from Cambridge, containing 495 inhabitants. The living is a discharged vicarage, in the archdeaconry and diocese of Ely, rated in the king's books at £11. 18. 4., endowed with £200 private benefaction, and £200 royal bounty, and in the patronage of Mrs. Hicks. The church, dedicated to St. Nicholas, is a cruciform structure, with a tower at the west end; it had originally a tower rising from the centre. The manor-house, an ancient building formerly belonging to the Knights Templars, is still called the Temple.

WILBRAHAM (LITTLE), a parish in the hundred of STAINE, county of CAMBRIDGE, 7¼ miles (E.) from Cambridge, containing 274 inhabitants. The living is a rectory, in the archdeaconry and diocese of Ely, rated in the king's books at £19. 16. 8., and in the patronage of the President and Fellows of Corpus Christi College, Cambridge.. The church is dedicated to St. John the Evangelist.

WILBURTON, a parish in the southern division of the hundred of WITCHFORD, Isle of Ely, county of CAMBRIDGE, 6½ miles (S. W.) from Ely, containing 465 inhabitants. The living is a perpetual curacy, in the archdeaconry and diocese of Ely, endowed with £200 private benefaction, and £500 royal bounty, and in the patronage of the Archdeacon of Ely. The church is a handsome structure, dedicated to St. Peter. There is a place of worship for Baptists. The parsonage-house was anciently the seat of the Archdeacons of Ely, at which Henry VII. and his son, Prince Henry, were entertained for several days, when that sovereign came to visit the shrine of St. Ethelreda at Ely.

WILBY, a parish in the hundred of SHROPHAM, county of NORFOLK, 3½ miles (N. E. by E.) from East Harling, containing 103 inhabitants. The living is a discharged rectory, with that of Hargham annexed, in the archdeaconry of Norfolk, and diocese of Norwich, rated in the king's books at £7. 4. 7½., and in the patronage of Sir Thomas Beevor, Bart. The church is dedicated to All Saints.

WILBY, a parish in the hundred of HAMFORD-SHOE, county of NORTHAMPTON, 2¼ miles (S.W. by W.) from Wellingborough, containing 347 inhabitants. The living is a rectory, in the archdeaconry of Northampton, and diocese of Peterborough, rated in the king's books at £13. 19. 4½., and in the patronage of

Mat. Easton, Esq. The church, dedicated to St. Mary, is partly in the early, and partly in the decorated, style of English architecture, with a beautiful spire steeple of later date.

WILBY, a parish in the hundred of HOXNE, county of SUFFOLK, 6 miles (E. S. E.) from Eye, containing 576 inhabitants. The living is a rectory, in the archdeaconry of Suffolk, and diocese of Norwich, rated in the king's books at £26. 6. 10½., and in the patronage of the Rev. Neville White. The church is dedicated to St. Mary.

WILCOT, a parish in the hundred of SWANBOROUGH, county of WILTS, 1¾ mile (W. N. W.) from Pewsey, containing, with the chapelry of Draycot-Foliatt, and the tythings of Pare and Stowel, 695 inhabitants. The living is a discharged vicarage, in the archdeaconry of Wilts, and diocese of Salisbury, rated in the king's books at £6. 17., endowed with £200 private benefaction, and £200 royal bounty, and in the patronage of Lieut.-Col. George Wroughton Wroughton. The church is dedicated to the Holy Cross. The Kennet and Avon canal passes through the parish. The manor-house is said to have been anciently a monastery, of which there are no further particulars.

WILCOTE, a parish in the hundred of WOOTTON, county of OXFORD, 4 miles (N. by E.) from Witney, containing 11 inhabitants. The living is a discharged rectory, in the archdeaconry and diocese of Oxford, rated in the king's books at £2. 13. 4., and endowed with £600 royal bounty. The Rev. R. Pickering was patron in 1820. The church is dedicated to St. Peter.

WILDBOAR-CLOUGH, a township in the parish of PRESTBURY, hundred of MACCLESFIELD, county palatine of CHESTER, 6½ miles (S. E. by E.) from Macclesfield, containing 414 inhabitants. There is a place of worship for Wesleyan Methodists.

WILDEN, a parish in the hundred of BARFORD, county of BEDFORD, 5¼ miles (N. E. by N.) from Bedford, containing 447 inhabitants. The living is a rectory, in the archdeaconry of Bedford, and diocese of Lincoln, rated in the king's books at £18. 7. 1., and in the patronage of the Duke of Bedford. The church is dedicated to St. Nicholas. John and Thomas Rolle, in 1624, bequeathed land, now producing an annual income of £30, for teaching poor children.

WILDON-GRANGE, a township in the parish of COXWOLD, wapentake of BIRDFORTH, North riding of the county of YORK, 6½ miles (N. by W.) from Easingwould, containing 29 inhabitants.

WILDSWORTH, a hamlet in the parish of LAUGHTON, wapentake of CORRINGHAM, parts of LINDSEY, county of LINCOLN, 7½ miles (N.) from Gainsborough, containing 103 inhabitants.

WILERICK, or WILLCRICK, a parish in the lower division of the hundred of CALDICOTT, county of MONMOUTH, 4½ miles (E. S. E.) from Caerleon, containing 47 inhabitants. The living is a discharged rectory, in the archdeaconry and diocese of Llandaff, rated in the king's books at £2. 10. 2½., endowed with £600 royal bounty, and in the patronage of Sir T. R. Salusbury, Bart.

WILFORD, a parish in the northern division of the wapentake of RUSHCLIFFE, county of NOTTINGHAM, 1¾ mile (S. by W.) from Nottingham, containing 569 inhabitants. The living is a rectory, in the archdeaconry of Nottingham, and diocese of York, rated in the king's books at £18. 17. 6., and in the patronage of Sir R. Clifton, Bart. The church is dedicated to St. Wilfrid. The river Trent is here crossed by a ford and a ferry.

WILKESLEY, a joint township with Dodcot, partly in the parish of WRENBURY, but chiefly in that of AUDLEM, hundred of NANTWICH, county palatine of CHESTER, 3¾ miles (S. W. by W.) from Audlem. The population is returned with Dodcot.

WILKSBY, a parish in the soke of HORNCASTLE, parts of LINDSEY, county of LINCOLN, 5¾ miles (S. S. E.) from Horncastle, containing 58 inhabitants. The living is a discharged rectory, in the archdeaconry and diocese of Lincoln, rated in the king's books at £4. 4. 2., and in the patronage of Henry Dymoke, Esq. The church is dedicated to All Saints.

WILLAND, a parish in the hundred of HALBERTON, county of DEVON, 2¼ miles (N. N. E.) from Cullompton, containing 289 inhabitants. The living is a discharged rectory, in the archdeaconry and diocese of Exeter, rated in the king's books at £7. 10. 5., and in the patronage of the Salter family. The church is dedicated to St. Mary. There is a place of worship for Wesleyan Methodists. The river Culme runs through the parish.

WILLASTON, a township in the parish of WYBUNBURY, hundred of NANTWICH, county palatine of CHESTER, 1½ mile (E. by N.) from Nantwich, containing 209 inhabitants.

WILLASTON, a township in the parish of NESTON, higher division of the hundred of WIRRALL, county palatine of CHESTER, 2¾ miles (E.) from Great Neston, containing 261 inhabitants.

WILLEN, a parish in the hundred of NEWPORT, county of BUCKINGHAM, 1½ mile (S.) from Newport-Pagnell, containing 83 inhabitants. The living is a vicarage, in the archdeaconry of Buckingham, and diocese of Lincoln, rated in the king's books at £7. 10., and in the patronage of the Trustees of the late Dr. Busby, who nominate a Westminster student of Christ Church College, Oxford. The church, dedicated to St. Mary Magdalene, was erected in 1680, at the expense of Dr. Busby, head-master of Westminster school, who endowed it with the great tithes, and gave a library for the use of the vicar : he also appointed twenty-two lectures on the catechism to be preached annually.

WILLENHALL, a chapelry in that part of the parish of WOLVERHAMPTON which is in the southern division of the hundred of OFFLOW, county of STAFFORD, 3¼ miles (E.) from Wolverhampton, containing 3965 inhabitants. The living is a perpetual curacy, in the jurisdiction of the court of the royal peculiar of Wolverhampton, and in the patronage of the inhabitants who possess lands of inheritance. The chapel, dedicated to St. Giles, was built about 1748. There are places of worship for Baptists and Wesleyan Methodists. The Wyrley and Essington canal passes through the parish, in which are extensive collieries and mines of iron-stone. This place, at the period of the Norman survey, was called *Winehala*, the Saxon term for victory, probably from the great battle fought near it in 911. The village began to thrive so early as the reign of Elizabeth, when the iron manufacture was first established here : at present it is noted for its flourishing trade in locks, which it possesses

to a greater extent than any other place of its size in Europe. As an instance of the great ingenuity of the workmen, if is recorded that, in 1776, one Lees, aged sixty-three, produced a padlock and key, wrought by himself, of less weight than a silver twopenny coin. Many other articles of hardware are made, particularly curry-combs, gridirons, screws, &c. Courts leet and baron are annually held ; and there is a court of requests on three Mondays in every alternate month, for the recovery of debts under £5. In the neighbourhood are the remains of an old hall, formerly the seat of the maternal ancestors of the Marquis of Stafford.

WILLENHALL, a hamlet in that part of the parish of the HOLY TRINITY, city of COVENTRY, which is in the Kirby division of the hundred of KNIGHTLOW, county of WARWICK, 2¾ miles (S. E.) from Coventry, containing 100 inhabitants.

WILLERBY, a parish in the wapentake of DICKERING, East riding of the county of YORK, comprising the townships of Binnington, Staxton, and Willerby, and containing 297 inhabitants, of which number, 34 are in the township of Willerby, 7½ miles (S. S. W.) from Scarborough. The living is a discharged vicarage, in the archdeaconry of the East riding, and diocese of York, rated in the king's books at £9. 0. 7½., and in the patronage of the Crown. The church is dedicated to St. Peter.

WILLERBY, a township partly in the parish of COTTINGHAM, Hunsley-Beacon division of the wapentake of HARTHILL, and partly in that of KIRK-ELLA, county of the town of KINGSTON upon HULL, East riding of the county of YORK, 5½ miles (W. N. W.) from Kingston upon Hull : the latter part contains 200 inhabitants, and the former is returned with the parish of Cottingham.

WILLERSEY, a parish in the upper division of the hundred of KIFTSGATE, county of GLOUCESTER, 3 miles (W.) from Chipping-Campden, containing 301 inhabitants. The living is a rectory, in the archdeaconry and diocese of Gloucester, rated in the king's books at £13. 2. 6., and in the patronage of P. Hampton, Esq. The church, dedicated to St. Peter, is a cruciform structure of various dates, with a tower at the intersection, crowned with pinnacles.

WILLERSLEY, a parish in the hundred of HUNTINGTON, county of HEREFORD, 7¼ miles (E. N. E.) from Hay, containing 11 inhabitants. The living is a discharged rectory, in the archdeaconry and diocese of Hereford, rated in the king's books at £3. 6. 8., endowed with £600 royal bounty, and in the patronage of the Representatives of the late John Freeman, Esq. The church is dedicated to St. Mary Magdalene. The parish is bounded on the south by the river Wye.

WILLESBOROUGH, a parish in the hundred of CHART and LONGBRIDGE, lathe of SCRAY, county of KENT, 2 miles (S. E. by E.) from Ashford, containing 483 inhabitants. The living is a vicarage, in the archdeaconry and diocese of Canterbury, rated in the king's books at £8. 16. 8., and in the patronage of the Dean and Chapter of Canterbury. The church, dedicated to St. Mary, is principally in the decorated style of English architecture.

WILLESDEN, or WILSDON, a parish in the Kensington division of the hundred of OSSULSTONE, county of MIDDLESEX, 5 miles (W. N. W.) from London, containing 1413 inhabitants. The living is a vicarage, in the peculiar jurisdiction and patronage of the Dean and Chapter of St. Paul's, London, rated in the king's books at £14. The church, dedicated to St. Mary, is principally in the later style of English architecture.

WILLESLEY, a parish forming, with the parishes of Measham and Stretton en le Fields, a detached portion of the hundred of REPTON and GRESLEY, county of DERBY, being locally in the western division of the hundred of Goscote, county of Leicester, 2½ miles (S. W. by S.) from Ashby de la Zouch, containing 62 inhabitants. The living is a perpetual curacy, in the archdeaconry of Derby, and diocese of Lichfield and Coventry, endowed with £20 per annum private benefaction, and £400 royal bounty, and in the patronage of Sir Charles Abney Hastings, Bart. The church is dedicated to St. Thomas. The Ashby de la Zouch canal skirts the south-western boundary of the parish, whence a rail-road passes to that town. Willesley is in the honour of Tutbury, duchy of Lancaster, and within the jurisdiction of a court of pleas held at Tutbury every third Tuesday, for the recovery of debts under 40s.

WILLEY, a township in that part of the parish of PRESTEIGNE which is in the hundred of WIGMORE, county of HEREFORD, 2¾ miles (N.) from Presteigne, containing 115 inhabitants.

WILLEY, a parish within the liberties of the borough of WENLOCK, county of SALOP, 4¾ miles (N.W. by N.) from Bridgenorth, containing 155 inhabitants. The living is a discharged rectory, in the archdeaconry of Salop, and diocese of Hereford, rated in the king's books at £5. 6. 3., and in the patronage of Lord Forester. The church is dedicated to St. John the Baptist.

WILLEY, a parish in the Kirby division of the hundred of KNIGHTLOW, county of WARWICK, 3½ miles (W.) from Lutterworth, containing 101 inhabitants. The living is a rectory, in the archdeaconry of Coventry, and diocese of Lichfield and Coventry, rated in the king's books at £8. 6. 0½., and in the patronage of the Crown. The church is dedicated to St. Leonard.

WILLIAMSCOTT, or WILLSCOTT, a hamlet in that part of the parish of CROPREDY which is in the hundred of BANBURY, county of OXFORD, 3¾ miles (N. N. E.) from Banbury. The population is returned with the chapelry of Wardington. Walter Calcott, in 1575, gave a rent-charge of £13, and John Ditchfield, in 1708, an annuity of £2, to be applied for teaching poor children.

WILLIAN, a parish in the hundred of BROADWATER, county of HERTFORD, 2¾ miles (E. by N.) from Hitchin, containing 269 inhabitants. The living is a vicarage, in the archdeaconry of Huntingdon, and diocese of Lincoln, rated in the king's books at £5. Francis Pym, Esq. was patron in 1816. The church, dedicated to All Saints, has been recently beautified, at the expense of £250.

WILLINGALE-DOE, a parish in the hundred of DUNMOW, county of ESSEX, 4½ miles (N. E.) from Chipping-Ongar, containing 434 inhabitants. The living is a rectory, with that of Shellow-Bowels consolidated, in the peculiar jurisdiction of the Commissary of Essex and Herts, concurrently with the Consistorial Court of the Bishop of London, rated in the king's books at £16, and in the patronage of T. G. Bramston, Esq. The

church, dedicated to St. Christopher, stands in the same churchyard with that of Willingale-Spain : the parishes are much intermixed, though quite distinct as to ecclesiastical and civil concerns. Robert Cole, in 1733, gave an annuity of £4 for teaching six poor children : there is also a small sum, the bequest of the Rev. Mr. Walker, for purchasing books.

WILLINGALE-SPAIN, a parish in the hundred of DUNMOW, county of ESSEX, 4¼ miles (N. E.) from Chipping-Ongar, containing 203 inhabitants. The living is a rectory, in the archdeaconry of Middlesex, and diocese of London, rated in the king's books at £7. 13. 4., and in the patronage of the Crown, on the nomination of the Bishop of London. The church is dedicated to All Saints.—See WILLINGALE-DOE.

WILLINGDON, a parish in the hundred of WILLINGDON, rape of PEVENSEY, county of SUSSEX, 2¼ miles (N. by W.) from East Bourne, containing 520 inhabitants. The living is a discharged vicarage, annexed to that of Arlington, in the archdeaconry of Lewes, and diocese of Chichester, rated in the king's books at £12, and in the patronage of the Dean and Chapter of Chichester. The church is principally in the early style of English architecture.

WILLINGHAM, a parish in the hundred of PAPWORTH, county of CAMBRIDGE, 6¼ miles (E. by S.) from St. Ives, containing 1170 inhabitants. The living is a rectory, in the peculiar jurisdiction and patronage of the Bishop of Ely, rated in the king's books at £18. 8. 1½. The church is dedicated to St. Mary and All Saints ; on the north side of the chancel is a chapel, in the decorated style of English architecture, with a stone roof of singular construction. There is a place of worship for Baptists. A charity school was founded by subscription, in 1593, and an estate purchased for its endowment, which now produces £20 per annum ; it is also further endowed with a rent-charge of £10, bequeathed, in 1700, by Dr. Saywell, Master of Jesus' College, Cambridge ; the number of children is limited to thirty. An almshouse for four widows was founded, in 1616, by William Smith, Provost of King's College, Cambridge, and endowed with £12 per annum. Much of the cheese which takes its name from the neighbouring village of Cottenham is made in this parish, where about one thousand two hundred milch cows are usually kept.

WILLINGHAM, a chapelry in the parish of CARLTON, hundred of RADFIELD, county of CAMBRIDGE, 5¼ miles (S. by E.) from Newmarket : the population is returned with the parish. It is within the peculiar jurisdiction of the Bishop of Ely. The chapel is dedicated to St. Matthew.

WILLINGHAM, a parish in the wapentake of WELL, parts of LINDSEY, county of LINCOLN, 6 miles (S. E.) from Gainsborough, containing 292 inhabitants. The living is a rectory, in the archdeaconry and diocese of Lincoln, rated in the king's books at £18. 6. 8., and in the patronage of the Heirs of the late Rev. R. Wells. The church is dedicated to St. Helen. There is a place of worship for Wesleyan Methodists.

WILLINGHAM, a parish in the hundred of WANGFORD, county of SUFFOLK, 4 miles (S.) from Beccles, containing 170 inhabitants. The living is a rectory, annexed to that of North Cove, in the archdeaconry of Suffolk, and diocese of Norwich, rated in the king's books at £6. 13. 4.

WILLINGHAM (CHERRY), a parish in the wapentake of LAWRESS, parts of LINDSEY, county of LINCOLN, 4 miles (E. by N.) from Lincoln, containing 89 inhabitants. The living is a discharged vicarage, in the archdeaconry of Stow, and diocese of Lincoln, rated in the king's books at £6. 13. 4., endowed with £600 royal bounty, and in the patronage of Messrs Ellis. The church is dedicated to St. Peter. The parish is bounded on the south by the river Witham.

WILLINGHAM (NORTH), a parish in the southern division of the wapentake of WALSHCROFT, parts of LINDSEY, county of LINCOLN, 4 miles (E. by S.) from Market-Rasen, containing 211 inhabitants. The living is a discharged vicarage, in the archdeaconry and diocese of Lincoln, rated in the king's books at £5. 4. 4½., endowed with £600 royal bounty, and in the patronage of Ayscoghe Boucherett, Esq.

WILLINGHAM (SOUTH), a parish in the eastern division of the wapentake of WRAGGOE, parts of LINDSEY, county of LINCOLN, 5¼ miles (E. N. E.) from Wragby, containing 202 inhabitants. The living is a discharged rectory, in the archdeaconry and diocese of Lincoln, rated in the king's books at £13. 10. 10., and in the patronage of G. R. Heneage, Esq. The church is dedicated to St. Martin.

WILLINGTON, a parish in the hundred of WIXAMTREE, county of BEDFORD, 4 miles (E.) from Bedford, containing 286 inhabitants. The living is a discharged vicarage, in the archdeaconry of Bedford, and diocese of Lincoln, rated in the king's books at £7. 17., and in the patronage of the Duke of Bedford. The church, dedicated to St. Lawrence, is principally in the later style of English architecture, and contains some old monuments to the Gostwicke family. The navigable river Ouse bounds the parish on the north.

WILLINGTON, a township in that part of the parish of WHALLEY which is in the second division of the hundred of EDDISBURY, county palatine of CHESTER, 3 miles (N. N. W.) from Tarporley, containing 101 inhabitants. This township is deemed to be part of the parish of Whalley, it having formerly belonged to the abbey there, though for the performance of ecclesiastical rites the inhabitants resort to the church of St. Oswald, Chester, and pay a portion of the great tithes to the rectors of Wem and Tarvin. There is a place of worship for Unitarians.

WILLINGTON, a parish in the hundred of MORLESTON and LITCHURCH, county of DERBY, 5 miles (N. E.) from Burton upon Trent, containing 411 inhabitants. The living is a discharged vicarage, in the archdeaconry of Derby, and diocese of Lichfield and Coventry, rated in the king's books at £4. 17. 3., endowed with £800 royal bounty, and in the patronage of the Corporation of Etwall and Repton. The church is dedicated to St. Michael. The river Trent and the Grand Trunk canal pass through the parish. The poor are entitled to send their children for gratuitous instruction to Findern school, in the parish of Mickleover.

WILLINGTON, a township in the parish of BRANCEPETH, north-western division of DARLINGTON ward, county palatine of DURHAM, 4 miles (N.) from Bishop-Auckland, containing 221 inhabitants. It is situated on the north side of the river Wear, and is intersected by the great Roman road. There is a place of worship for Wesleyan Methodists.

WILLISHAM, a parish in the hundred of BOSMERE and CLAYDON, county of SUFFOLK, 4 miles (S. S. W.) from Needham, containing 173 inhabitants. The living is a perpetual curacy, in the archdeaconry of Suffolk, and diocese of Norwich, endowed with £1000 royal bounty. A. Upcher, Esq. was patron in 1809. The church is dedicated to St. Mary.

WILLITOFT, a joint township with Gribthorpe, in the parish of BUBWITH, Holme-Beacon division of the wapentake of HARTHILL, East riding of the county of YORK, 5¼ miles (N.) from Howden. The population is returned with Gribthorpe.

WILLITON, a chapelry in the parish of ST. DECUMAN, hundred of WILLITON and FREEMANNERS, county of SOMERSET, 6¼ miles (E. S. E.) from Dunster. The population is returned with the parish. The living is a perpetual curacy, in the peculiar jurisdiction and patronage of the Vicar of St. Decuman's, endowed with £600 royal bounty, and £1400 parliamentary grant. The chapel is dedicated to St. Peter. There are places of worship for Baptists and Wesleyan Methodists.

WILLOUGHBY, a parish in the Wold division of the hundred of CALCEWORTH, parts of LINDSEY, county of LINCOLN, 3½ miles (S. S. E.) from Alford, containing, with the hamlet of Sloothby, 514 inhabitants. The living is a rectory, in the archdeaconry and diocese of Lincoln, rated in the king's books at £39. 10. 2½., and in the patronage of Lord Gwydir. The church is dedicated to St. Helen. There is a place of worship for Wesleyan Methodists. Anthony Barnes, in 1728, bequeathed certain land, now producing more than £25 per annum, for teaching and apprenticing poor children.

WILLOUGHBY, a parish in the Rugby division of the hundred of KNIGHTLOW, county of WARWICK, 3 miles (S. by E.) from Dunchurch, containing 421 inhabitants. This place, in the neighbourhood of which many Roman antiquities have been discovered, is in Domesday-book called *Wilbere* and *Wilebei*, from which its present name is derived. It was a royal demesne in the reign of Henry I., who gave it to Wigan, one of his servants, by one of whose descendants it was granted, in the reign of Henry III., to the hospital of St. John, founded by that monarch without the east gate at Oxford, in the 17th year of his reign. On the dissolution of which, in the reign of Henry VI., William de Wainfleet, Bishop of Winchester, having obtained a grant of the site for the foundation of Magdalene College, procured from the master and brethren the manor of Willoughby, which at present forms part of the endowment of that institution. The parliamentarian army, in their retreat from the battle of Edge Hill, passed through the village, and fastened a rope round the ancient cross, with the intention of pulling it down, from which they were dissuaded by the vicar. Willoughby was formerly a place of much more importance than it is at present, having enjoyed a market and fairs, to which, from the name of a small hamlet in the parish, called "Pie Court," probably a court of pie-powder was attached: part of the foundation of a public gaol was discovered by some labourers, in digging for gravel near the church. The village is situated on the high road from London to Holyhead, from which it extends, in a westerly direction, for nearly three quarters of a mile: the houses, which are chiefly of stone with thatched roofs, occasionally interspersed with a few of more modern construction, have a very rural appearance, and the whole village has a pleasing air of tranquillity and retirement. The lands in the neighbourhood are fertile, and in a high state of cultivation, and the environs abound with pleasing scenery and with various objects of interest. Within the last few years Willoughby has been growing into notice from the discovery of some powerful sulphureous and saline springs, the properties of which have been found similar to those at Harrogate. Two small bathing establishments have been erected, one called Willoughby Lodge Spa, situated in a field at the western extremity of the village, and the New Sulphureous and Saline baths, on the high road opposite to the inn called the Four Crosses. Some neat cottages have been erected as lodging-houses; hot, cold, and shower baths have been constructed, and there is a pump-room for drinking the water, which is efficacious in all cases of scrofula, and in scorbutic and cutaneous diseases; separate baths are provided for the poor. The situation on the high road affords opportunities of direct and expeditious communication with the metropolis and the principal towns in the kingdom.

The living is a discharged vicarage, in the archdeaconry of Coventry, and diocese of Lichfield and Coventry, rated in the king's books at £9. 4. 4., endowed with £200 private benefaction, and £200 royal bounty, and in the patronage of the President and Fellows of Magdalene College, Oxford. The church, dedicated to St. Nicholas, is a spacious and neat structure, in the later style of English architecture, with a low square embattled tower, strengthened with angular buttresses; the exterior, which is plain, is relieved by a north and south porch of good design, and above the western entrance is a large window enriched with tracery. The interior, which is of appropriate character, consists of a nave, aisles, and chancel, the last of which was rebuilt in 1779, and is separated from the nave by an obtusely pointed arch; the nave is separated from the aisles by three clustered columns and arches of a similar character, and from the tower by a lofty arch of good proportion, plainly moulded; the font, which is placed in the south aisle, is a large cylindrical vase of stone, supported on a square pedestal, and is slightly ornamented: the church contains several ancient monuments and brasses, among which is an altar-tomb of the family of Clerke. There is a place of worship for Primitive Methodists. A school was founded in 1816, and a school-house, with accommodation for a master and mistress, was erected, at an expense of £430, paid by the trustees of property, amounting to nearly £500 per annum, bequeathed by various benefactors for pious and charitable uses; children of both sexes are gratuitously instructed in reading, writing, and arithmetic, and the girls also in needlework, by a master and mistress appointed by the trustees, with a salary of £40 per annum: the remainder of the income, after deducting the expense of repairing the church and the roads, is appropriated to apprenticing children, as gratuities to females entering upon service, weekly payments to the poor, donations of coal, and other charitable distributions.

WILLOUGHBY (SCOTT), a parish in the wapentake of AVELAND, parts of KESTEVEN, county of LINCOLN, 4 miles (N.W. by N.) from Falkingham, containing 12 inhabitants. The living is a discharged rectory, in the archdeaconry and diocese of Lincoln, rated in the king's books at £7. 1. 3., and in the patronage of Lord Gwydir. The church is dedicated to St. Andrew.

WILLOUGHBY (SILK), a parish in the wapentake of ASWARDHURN, parts of KESTEVEN, county of LINCOLN, 2¼ miles (S. S. W.) from Sleaford, containing 197 inhabitants. The living is a rectory, in the archdeaconry and diocese of Lincoln, rated in the king's books at £14. 8. 1½., and in the patronage of Lord Huntingtower. The church, dedicated to St. Denis, is a handsome structure, with a well-proportioned tower and spire: the body is principally in the decorated style of English architecture, and the chancel of later date; the latter contains three stalls, some fine screenwork of wood, and fragments of ancient stained glass in the east window: the font is circular, with Norman shafts.

WILLOUGHBY in the WOLDS, a parish in the southern division of the wapentake of RUSHCLIFFE, county of NOTTINGHAM, 7½ miles (N. E. by E.) from Loughborough, containing 450 inhabitants. The living is a discharged vicarage, in the archdeaconry of Nottingham, and diocese of York, rated in the king's books at £6. 18. 6½., endowed with £200 private benefaction, and £200 royal bounty, and in the patronage of the Rev. George Davys. The church is dedicated to St. Mary and All Saints. There is a place of worship for Wesleyan Methodists. The old Fosse road bounds the parish on the west, near which is a tumulus, called Cross Hill, where an annual revel is held. According to Horsley, this was the Roman station *Vernometum*, but Gale and Stukeley place *Margidunum* here. In a field called Herrings, or Black field, are traces of an old town, where many coins, pavements, and other relics of antiquity have been found. In the centre of the village stands a cross, the shaft consisting of one entire stone, fifteen feet high, resting on four steps. Near this place, in the great civil war, a battle was fought, which is commonly termed the battle of Willoughby Field.

WILLOUGHBY-WATERLESS, a parish in the hundred of GUTHLAXTON, county of LEICESTER, 5¾ miles (N. N. E.) from Lutterworth, containing 322 inhabitants. The living is a rectory, with the vicarage of Peatling Magna united, in the archdeaconry of Leicester, and diocese of Lincoln, rated in the king's books at £11. 11. 3., and in the patronage of the Rev. John Miles. The church is dedicated to St. Mary.

WILLOUGHTON, a parish in the western division of the wapentake of ASLACOE, parts of LINDSEY, county of LINCOLN, 8½ miles (E. by N.) from Gainsborough, containing 409 inhabitants. The living is a discharged vicarage, in medieties, in the archdeaconry of Stow, and diocese of Lincoln, rated in the king's books at £7. 4. 2., endowed with £400 royal bounty, and in the alternate patronage of the Provost and Fellows of King's College, Cambridge, and Lord Scarborough. The church is dedicated to St. Andrew. There is a place of worship for Wesleyan Methodists. An Alien priory, a cell to the abbey of St. Nicholas at Angiers, is said to have existed here. Roger de Buslei and Simon de Canci, in the time of Stephen, gave a moiety of the church, and the greatest part of the town, to the

Knights Templars, who had a preceptory here; from that order it came to the hospitallers, and at the dissolution its revenue was estimated at £219. 19. 8.

WILLSBOROUGH, an extra-parochial liberty, in the hundred of SPARKENHOE, county of LEICESTER, 2½ miles (W. by S.) from Market-Bosworth. The population is returned with Temple-Hall.

WILLS-PASTURES, an extra-parochial liberty, in the Southam division of the hundred of KNIGHTLOW, county of WARWICK, containing 12 inhabitants.

WILLSWORTHY, a hamlet in that part of the parish of ST. PETER TAVY which is in the hundred of LIFTON, county of DEVON, 6 miles (N. E. by N.) from Tavistock, containing 86 inhabitants.

WILMINGTON, a parish in the hundred of AXTON, DARTFORD, and WILMINGTON, lathe of SUTTON at HONE, county of KENT, 1 mile (S.) from Dartford, containing 653 inhabitants. The living is a vicarage, in the archdeaconry and diocese of Rochester, rated in the king's books at £6. 17. 6., and in the patronage of the Dean and Chapter of Rochester. The church, dedicated to St. Michael, occupies the summit of a hill near the high road, and has a handsome spire steeple. The great Earl of Warwick, in the reign of Edward IV., resided at the manor-house in the village, which is remarkable for the beauty of its situation.

WILMINGTON, a parish in the hundred of LONGBRIDGE, rape of PEVENSEY, county of SUSSEX, 4½ miles (S. W.) from Hailsham, containing 321 inhabitants. The living is a discharged vicarage, in the archdeaconry of Lewes, and diocese of Chichester, rated in the king's books at £8, endowed with £200 private benefaction, and £200 royal bounty, and in the patronage of Lord George Cavendish. The church, dedicated to St. Mary, is principally in the Norman style of architecture. A Benedictine priory, a cell to the abbey of Grestein in Normandy, was founded here in the time of William Rufus, which, at its suppression, was valued at two hundred and forty marks per annum, and sold by license of Henry IV. to the Dean and Chapter of Chichester, to whom it was confirmed by Henry V., towards founding a chantry for two priests in the cathedral church. Wilmington gives the inferior title of baron to the Marquis of Northampton.

WILMSLOW, a parish in the hundred of MACCLESFIELD, county palatine of CHESTER, 7 miles (N.W. by N.) from Macclesfield, comprising the townships of Bollen-Fee, Chorley, Fulshaw, and Pownal-Fee, and containing 3927 inhabitants. The living is a rectory, in the archdeaconry and diocese of Chester, rated in the king's books at £32. 15., and in the patronage of Thomas Joseph Trafford, Esq. The church, dedicated to St. Bartholomew, is a handsome structure, combining the decorated and later English styles, and containing several old monuments of the Dunham, Trafford, and Newton families: in an adjoining chapel, of modern construction, are several tombs of the family of Leigh, by one of whom it was founded. The small river Bollin, upon which are extensive cotton and silk mills, runs through the parish. There are places of worship for Independents and Wesleyan Methodists. Courts leet and baron are held, the former by the Earl of Stamford and Warrington, and the latter at Pownal-Fee by Mr. Trafford. A school, founded by the Rev. Henry Hough, with a small endowment, affords instruction to ten children. A workhouse was established, about 1780, upon Lindon common, and land, now producing upwards of £200 per annum, was assigned for its support. About a quarter of a mile eastward from the church are some remains of an ancient chapel, supposed to have belonged to the old manor-house.

WILNE (GREAT), a parish in the hundred of MORLESTON and LITCHURCH, county of DERBY, 7¾ miles (S. E.) from Derby, containing, with the township of Shardlow, and the inmates of a large poor-house belonging to several townships, 993 inhabitants. The living is a perpetual curacy, in the peculiar jurisdiction of the prebendal court of Sawley, endowed with £1600 parliamentary grant, and in the patronage of the Perpetual Curate of Sawley. The church is dedicated to St. Chad.

WILNE (LITTLE), a chapelry in the parish of SAWLEY, hundred of MORLESTON and LITCHURCH, county of DERBY, 7¾ miles (E. S. E.) from Derby. The population is returned with the liberty of Draycott.

WILNECOTE, a chapelry in that part of the parish of TAMWORTH which is in the Tamworth division of the hundred of HEMLINGFORD, county of WARWICK, 2¾ miles (S. E. by S.) from Tamworth, containing, with the hamlet of Dosthill, 653 inhabitants. The living is a perpetual curacy, with that of Tamworth, in the archdeaconry of Coventry, and diocese of Lichfield and Coventry, endowed with £1000 royal bounty, and £1200 parliamentary grant. The chapel, dedicated to the Holy Trinity, has lately received an addition of four hundred and eighty-two sittings, of which four hundred and fifty are free, the Incorporated Society for the enlargement of churches and chapels having granted £300 towards defraying the expense. Collieries and brick and lime kilns have been established in this chapelry of late years.

WILPSHIRE, a township in the parish and lower division of the hundred of BLACKBURN, county palatine of LANCASTER, 3¼ miles (N. by E.) from Blackburn, containing 287 inhabitants.

WILSDEN, a township in the parish of BRADFORD, wapentake of MORLEY, West riding of the county of YORK, 4 miles (S. E. by S.) from Keighley, containing 1711 inhabitants. The first stone of a new chapel was laid here in 1823, which was finished in 1825, at an expense of £7710. 13. 6., defrayed by the parliamentary commissioners: it was made a district church in 1828, the right of presentation being vested in the Vicar of Bradford. There are places of worship for Independents and Wesleyan Methodists. The spinning of worsted and cotton is extensively carried on, and there are also manufactories for cotton and linen goods.

WILSFORD, a parish in the wapentake of WINNIBRIGGS and THREO, parts of KESTEVEN, county of LINCOLN, 4½ miles (W. S. W.) from Sleaford, containing 341 inhabitants. The living is a rectory, in the archdeaconry and diocese of Lincoln, rated in the king's books at £10, and in the patronage of Viscount Melbourne. The church, dedicated to St. Mary, has a tower and spire, and exhibits an admixture of the early and decorated styles of English architecture: the font, which is octagonal, with concave sides, is of later date. A Benedictine priory, a cell to the abbey of Bec in Normandy, was founded here in the reign of Stephen; at the suppression of Alien houses it was settled upon the abbey of Bourn, in this county, and at the dissolution was granted to Charles, Duke of Suffolk.

WILSFORD, a parish in the hundred of UNDER-DITCH, county of WILTS, 1¾ mile (S. W. by W.) from Amesbury, containing 120 inhabitants. The living is a vicarage, consolidated with that of Woodford, in the peculiar jurisdiction of the Prebendary of Wilsford and Woodford in the Cathedral Church of Salisbury. The church is dedicated to St. Michael. The parish is bounded on the east by the river Avon. The manor-house of Lake, in this parish, is a remarkably fine specimen of the Elizabethan style of architecture.

WILSFORD-DAUNTSEY, a parish in the hundred of SWANBOROUGH, county of WILTS, 4½ miles (W.S.W.) from Pewsey, containing, with the tything of Manning-ford-Bohune, 487 inhabitants. The living is a vicarage, in the archdeaconry and diocese of Salisbury, rated in the king's books at £8. 17. 11., and in the patronage of the Master of the hospital of St. Nicholas, Salisbury. The church is dedicated to St. Nicholas.

WILSHAMPSTEAD, a parish in the hundred of REDBORNESTOKE, county of BEDFORD, 4 miles (S. by E.) from Bedford, containing 749 inhabitants. The living is a vicarage, in the archdeaconry of Bedford, and diocese of Lincoln, rated in the king's books at £9. 9. 7., and in the patronage of Lord Carteret. The church is dedicated to All Saints. There is a place of worship for Wesleyan Methodists. A small charity school here is endowed with about five acres and a half of land.

WILSICK, a joint township with Stancill and Wel-lingley, in the parish of TICKHILL, southern division of the wapentake of STRAFFORTH and TICKHILL, West riding of the county of YORK, 6 miles (S. by W.) from Doncaster. The population is returned with Stancill.

WILSTHORPE, a chapelry in the parish of GREAT-FORD, wapentake of NESS, parts of KESTEVEN, county of LINCOLN, 5 miles (N. W.) from Market-Deeping, con-taining 102 inhabitants.

WILSTROP, a township in that part of the parish of KIRK-HAMMERTON which is in the ainsty of the city, and East riding of the county, of YORK, 7½ miles (W. by N.) from York, containing 95 inhabitants. It is in the duchy of Lancaster, and within the jurisdic-tion of a court of pleas held at Tutbury every third Tuesday, for the recovery of debts under 40s.

WILTON, a parish in the hundred of GRIMSHOE, county of NORFOLK, 4¼ miles (W.) from Brandon-Ferry. The population is returned with the parish of Hockwold. The living is a discharged vicarage, united to the rectory of Hockwold, in the archdeaconry of Norfolk, and dio-cese of Norwich, rated in the king's books at £6. 7. 6. The church, dedicated to St. James, is built of flint and boulder stones, with a massive embattled tower, sur-mounted by an octangular spire of freestone : on the north side of the building is a curious arch, probably constructed for the burial-place of the founder. There is a place of worship for Wesleyan Methodists.

WILTON, a tything in the parish of MIDSUMMER-NORTON, hundred of CHEWTON, county of SOMERSET, 8½ miles (S. W.) from Bath, containing 885 inhabitants.

WILTON, a parish in the hundred of TAUNTON and TAUNTON-DEAN, county of SOMERSET, containing 579 inhabitants. The living is a perpetual curacy, in the archdeaconry of Taunton, and diocese of Bath and Wells, endowed with £400 private benefaction, £600 royal bounty, and £700 parliamentary grant, and in the pa-tronage of George Stone, Esq. The church, dedicated to St. George, was formerly a chapel to the vicarage of St. Mary Magdalene, in Taunton, to which town Wilton forms an extensive suburb. Here was former-ly an hospital, built by one of the Bishops of Win-chester.

WILTON, a borough (formerly a market town) and parish, having sepa-rate jurisdiction, locally in the hundred of Branch and Dole, county of WILTS, 3 miles (W. by N.) from Sa-lisbury, and 85 (W. S. W.) from London, containing, with the tythings of Bul-bridge and Ditchampton, 2058 inhabitants. This town, which derives its name from the river Wily, on which it is situated, is of great antiquity, and is supposed by Baxter to have been the Caer-Guilon, or capital of the British Prince Caroilius, and subsequently a seat of the West Saxon kings. It was a place of great importance for several centuries preceding the Norman Conquest, possessing an eminent religious establishment, and giving name to the county in which it is situated : it had also a mint. Wilton is stated by Camden and other writers to have been originally called Ellan-dune, and the scene of a sanguinary battle, fought between Egbert, King of the West Saxons, and Beor-wulf, the Mercian king, in which the latter was defeated ; but later writers have controverted this opinion, and the battle is now supposed to have been fought at a place called Ellendune, situated in another part of the county. An engagement took place here in 871, between King Alfred and the Danes, in which the former was successful, obliging the latter to sue for peace. The celebrated monastery was commenced, so early as the year 800, by Wulstan, Earl of Wiltshire, who, having defeated Ethelmund, the Mercian king, founded a chantry, or oratory, and repaired the old church of St. Mary at Wilton, which had been destroyed by the Danes, and placed in it a college of Secular priests, to pray for his own soul and that of the martyr Alqui-mund, who, returning from banishment, was slain by command of the usurper Eardulf. About thirty years after Earl Wulstan's death, his widow Alburga, sister to King Egbert, induced that monarch to convert the oratory into a priory of thirteen sisters, of which she was the first prioress, and hence Egbert has been commonly reputed its founder. Immediately on grant-ing peace to the Danes, King Alfred, at the solicita-tion of his queen, Ealswitha, built a nunnery on the site of the palace, and transferred to it the thirteen sisters of the priory, adding to them an abbess and twelve nuns ; his successors were great benefactors to this establishment, particularly Edgar, who enlarged its buildings and augmented its revenue ; his natural daughter Editha, having been abbess, and, after her death, being canonized, became its patron saint. Editha, daughter of Earl Godwin, and queen of Edward the Confessor, who was educated in this nunnery, rebuilt it in a magnificent manner with stone, it having been originally constructed of wood; and Matilda, queen of

Arms.

Henry I., was also educated in it, under her aunt, the abbess Christina. Early in the tenth century Wilton became the seat of the diocese of Wiltshire, and continued so during the lives of eleven successive bishops, the last of whom, Hermannus, having been also appointed to the see of Sherborne, united the two bishoprics, and removed to Old Sarum, where he founded a cathedral, which continued the seat of the see until its transfer, in 1217, to Salisbury. After the Conquest the town continued to flourish, until the year 1143, when King Stephen took possession of it, intending to convert the nunnery into a place of defence; but being surprised by Robert, Earl of Gloucester, with the troops of the Empress Matilda, who set fire to the town on all sides, the king was obliged to flee, leaving behind him his troops and baggage. Wilton recovered from this disaster; but in the succeeding reign it began to decline, in consequence of the foundation of New Sarum, or Salisbury, and the change in the direction of the great western road, which quickly followed. Its monastic institution, however, continued of importance until the dissolution, when it was granted to Sir William Herbert, afterwards Earl of Pembroke, its revenue being at that time estimated at upwards of £600: a house of Black friars, and two hospitals, dedicated to St. Mary Magdalene and St. John, also existed here at the period of the dissolution. The only historical circumstances connected with this place, in later times, are, its having been visited by Queen Elizabeth, in September 1579, and the residence of the court for a short time, in October 1603.

The town, consisting principally of one street, is situated in a broad and fertile valley, near the confluence of the rivers Nadder and Wily, and is partially paved, and well supplied with water. The manufacture of carpets, for which Wilton has been so much celebrated, was introduced by a former Earl of Pembroke, who brought over workmen from France for that purpose, being the first place in England where this manufacture commenced : though not carried on to the same extent as formerly, it has latterly been incrrasing, and there are at present two manufactories, containing about eighty looms, and employing about three hundred and fifty persons : fancy cloth waistcoatings also formed, at one time, a considerable branch of manufacture, but this is nearly extinct. The market days were on Wednesday and Saturday, but, since the decline of the manufactures, no regular market has been held. The fairs are on the 4th of May and 12th of September, the former for cattle and sheep, and the latter one of the largest sheep fairs in the West of England, the number sold often exceeding one hundred thousand. Wilton is a borough by prescription, its ancient rights and franchises having been confirmed by charters of various monarchs, from the time of Henry I. to that of Henry VI.: it is governed by a mayor, recorder, high steward, five aldermen, and an unlimited number of burgesses, appointed occasionally by the corporation, with a town clerk, two serjeants at mace, and four constables. The mayor is chosen by the corporation at large, on the first Thursday after Michaelmasday, from three persons previously nominated by such members of the corporation as have served the office of mayor, and is sworn into office, with the other officers who are then chosen, on the 13th of October, at

the court leet of the lord of the manor, held at the town hall, an ancient plain brick building, which was repaired and improved, about six years since, by the corporation. The mayor and recorder are justices of the peace, with exclusive jurisdiction. The borough first sent members to parliament in the 23rd of Edward I., and has since done so without interruption : the right of voting is vested in the members of the corporation, resident or non-resident, in number at present between forty and fifty : the mayor is the returning officer. The parliamentary influence is possessed by the Earl of Pembroke. The election of members of parliament for the county takes place here, but the nomination is at Devizes : the hustings are erected near the Hare Warren, a short distance southward of the town.

The living is a rectory, with that of Ditchampton and the vicarage of Bulbridge united, in the archdeaconry and diocese of Salisbury, rated in the king's books at £12. 16. 3., and in the patronage of the Earl of Pembroke. The church, dedicated to St. Mary, is an ancient edifice. The Independents and Methodists have each a place of worship. The free school, situated in North-street, was founded in 1706, by a bequest of £600 from Walter Dyer; and, in 1716, Richard Uphill bequeathed £1000 Bank stock, producing £2090, for its benefit, and for apprenticing poor children. Part of the money left by Mr. Dyer was invested in the purchase of the school-house and premises, in 1719, to which additions have been made, at different times, by the trustees; and the residue, with the legacy of Mr. Uphill, was laid out in an estate at East Knoyle, the rental of which is appropriated to the school, which is also entitled to the interest of £1000, part of a sum of £4200 three per cent. consols., bequeathed, in 1775, by Mr. Robert Sumpton, for various purposes. The master has a salary of £40 per annum, and a dwelling-house, and twenty boys of the parish are clothed and educated, and an apprentice fee of £8. 10. given with each. Of the remainder of Mr. Sumpton's bequest, the interest of £1000 is given annually, as a marriage portion, to four young women, and £2000 is appropriated to the benefit of five poor men, and as many women, natives of Wilton, or residents for seven years previously, who receive £6 per annum each, to which an addition of £2 per annum has been recently made from a bequest by James Swayne, Esq.: there are also several minor charitable bequests for annual distribution. In 1816, Thomas Mease gave to the lord high steward and corporation of Wilton, on the death of his wife, £4000 Navy five per cents., directing that the dividends should be allowed to accumulate for twenty years after her decease; the accumulations to be applied in improving the parish church, and the annual interest of the principal to various charitable purposes. The hospital of St. John, supposed to have been founded by Hubert, who was Bishop of Salisbury in 1189, and Archbishop of Canterbury in 1193, supports a master, or prior, who is a clergyman, nominated by the Dean of Salisbury, and two poor men and two women, chosen by the master, who receive an annual pension of £4. 10. 6., and a suit of clothes: the tenements are going to decay, and the pensioners are lodged in an adjoining cottage; the chapel has been recently fitted up for the performance of divine service. On the site of the celebrated nunnery, Sir William Herbert, to whom it was granted, commenced the erection of that princely pile, now the residence of his descendants, the Earls of Pembroke: it was designed by Holbein and Inigo Jones, and contains a collection of paintings, statues, and various antiquities, not excelled by any in the kingdom: in this house Sir Philip Sidney composed his Arcadia; his sister Mary, the celebrated Countess of Pembroke, being the wife of the earl.

WILTON, a chapelry in the parish of KIRK-LEATHAM, eastern division of the liberty of LANGBAURGH, North riding of the county of YORK, 3½ miles (N. N. W.) from Guilsbrough, containing 405 inhabitants. The living is a perpetual curacy, in the archdeaconry of Cleveland, and diocese of York, endowed with £200 private benefaction, and £400 royal bounty, and in the patronage of the Earl of Lonsdale. The chapel is dedicated to St. Cuthbert. At the west end of the village is Wilton castle, recently erected upon the site of the ancient baronial castle of the Bulmers, which family possessed it for many generations, till Sir John Bulmer, Knt., was attainted of high treason, when his estates were confiscated.

WILTON, a chapelry in the parish of ELLERBURN, PICKERING lythe, North riding of the county of YORK, 3¾ miles (E. by S.) from Pickering, containing 203 inhabitants.

WILTON (BISHOP), a parish partly within the liberty of ST. PETER of YORK, and partly in the Wilton-Beacon division of the wapentake of HARTHILL, East riding of the county of YORK, comprising the townships of Bishop-Wilton with Belthorpe, Bolton, and Youlthorpe with Gowthorpe, and containing 793 inhabitants, of which number, 570 are in the township of Bishop-Wilton with Belthorpe, 4½ miles (N.) from Pocklington. The living is a discharged vicarage, in the peculiar jurisdiction of the court of the Dean of York, rated in the king's books at £7. 3. 6¼., endowed with £400 private benefaction, £800 royal bounty, and £300 parliamentary grant, and in the patronage of Sir Tatton Sykes, Bart. The church is dedicated to St. Edith. There is a place of worship for Wesleyan Methodists. Here was formerly a palace, built in the reign of Edward IV., by Bishop Neville, and encompassed with a moat, which still remains. A trifling sum, bequeathed in 1765, by Elizabeth Barnett, is applied for teaching poor children.

WILTSHIRE, an inland county, bounded on the north and north-west by Gloucestershire, on the west by Somersetshire, on the south-west and south by Dorsetshire, on the south-east and east by Hampshire, and on the north-east by Berkshire. It extends from 50° 55′ to 51° 42′ (N. Lat.), and from 1° 30′ to 2° 22′ (W. Lon.), and comprises an area of eight hundred and eighty-two thousand five hundred and sixty statute acres, or about one thousand three hundred and seventy-nine square miles. The population, in 1821, was 222,157. A large portion of this county was occupied, in the time of Cæsar, by the Belgæ: the Hedui inhabited the north-western parts of it, and the Carvilii another district; the Cangi are also supposed, either at this period or soon after, to have possessed some territory within its northern limits. On the second invasion of the Romans, during the reign of the Emperor Claudius, in the year 44, the Belgæ were found to have subdued nearly the whole, which they occupied as far

north as the rude barrier of the Wansdyke, beyond which the Cangi are, by some writers, supposed to have preserved their dominion. Under the Roman government, Wiltshire was comprised in the division called Britannia Prima. After the withdrawal of the Roman forces, Cerdic, the founder of the kingdom of the West Saxons, who had been engaged in an arduous warfare, for upwards of twenty years, with the Romanized Britons near the place of his landing, on the coast of Hampshire, at last penetrated into this territory, in the year 520, but was defeated in a great battle by the British hero Arthur, and the Saxons did not return hither for upwards of thirty years. In 554, Cynric, son of Cerdic, and his successor in the sovereignty of Wessex, advanced with his army towards Sorbiodunum, or Old Sarum, and defeated a British army opposed to his progress near that place, of which he immediately after took possession. Four years afterwards another decisive battle was fought, at "Beranbyrig," or Barbury Castle, near Marlborough, in which the Britons were again routed, and Wiltshire shortly became incorporated in the kingdom of Wessex. Ceola, or Ceolric, nephew to Ceawlin, Cynric's successor, rebelled against his uncle; and being aided by a party of the Saxons and by some British tribes, defeated him in a pitched battle at Wednesbury, on the Wansdyke: Ceawlin fled, and Ceolric usurped the crown. In the wars maintained against each other by the different kingdoms of the Octarchy, Wessex took an active part, and several times suffered severely in contests with Mercia, which bounded it on the north. In a great battle, however, fought at Great Bedwin in this county, between Wulfhere, King of Mercia, and Eswin, leader of the West Saxon forces, the slaughter was dreadful on both sides, and Wulfhere returned to his own dominions, but Eswin was unable to follow him. In the reign of Ina, an indecisive, but sanguinary, battle was fought at Wednesbury, in this county (the precise situation of which place has not been ascertained), between that monarch and Ceolred, King of Mercia. At Wilton, in 823, Egbert, the active and warlike king of Wessex, who afterwards subdued the rest of England, signally defeated the Mercian army under Beornwulf, which had invaded his dominions. Wiltshire suffered very severely from the ravages of the Danes, who, during the reign of the last-mentioned West Saxon prince, having defeated the Saxon forces at Basingstoke, and at Merantune, supposed to have been Marden, to the south-east of Devizes, in this county, wasted the greater part of it with fire and sword. The illustrious Alfred, in 871, attacked the Danes at Wilton, but was defeated, after an obstinate and doubtful conflict. An invading Danish force, which had surprised Exeter, in 877, advanced to Chippenham, then a royal residence, where they established their winter quarters, and received such numerous reinforcements, that the Saxons ceased to resist, and Alfred himself fled to the Isle of Athelney, in Somersetshire. In 878, having at length mustered a considerable army, near the forest of Selwood, on the western confines of the county, Alfred suddenly and unexpectedly attacked the Danish forces encamped at Ethandune, supposed to be Eddington in this county, under their chief Guthrum, and gained that decisive victory by which he liberated his country. In 1003, Sweyn, King of

Denmark, invading England in revenge for the massacre of the Danes, landed on the coast of Devonshire, and, advancing into the interior, laid waste this county, and destroyed the towns of Wilton and Sarum. In 1006, another army of Danes, having ravaged Hampshire and Berkshire, entered Wiltshire : on the borders of the river Kennet, it was opposed by the men of the county, who, however, were totally defeated. Wiltshire was again visited by a Danish army, in 1011, under Sweyn and his son Canute, who imposed very heavy contributions upon its inhabitants, but were soon after compelled to retire to their ships, by Edmund, surnamed Ironside, who shortly after succeeded to the throne of England, by the death of his father Ethelred, who then lay ill at Corsham, in this county. The Danes then sailed eastward to the mouth of the Thames, which river they entered, and advanced inland to Cricklade, on the northern border of Wiltshire ; and though defeated, by Edmund, at Pen in Somersetshire, yet having received powerful reinforcements, they were enabled to besiege Sarum, and to advance to *Scearstan*, or Sherston, on the north-western confines of the county, where they were again opposed by Edmund, who, after an obstinate battle, which lasted two days, compelled Canute to retire towards the eastern shores of England. After the Norman Conquest, William I., on the completion of the general survey, held a great council at Sarum, in 1086, at which all the principal landholders did homage : at this city also William's successors held various other important councils.

Wiltshire was the scene of much warfare during the sanguinary disputes between King Stephen and the Empress Matilda. In 1139, Stephen forcibly seized the castles of Salisbury, Devizes, and Malmesbury, held by Roger, Bishop of Salisbury, and his partisans : in 1151, Devizes castle was taken by Robert Fitzherbert, who, having shown himself faithless to both parties, was at last seized and hanged by one of Matilda's commanders. The empress herself, on her escape from Winchester in the same year, fled to Ludgershall castle, in this county : in 1142, Old Sarum was taken possession of by her forces. In the course of this war also, Stephen, having marched to Wilton with the design of there raising a fortress to check the garrisons of Wareham and Salisbury, was attacked by Matilda's forces, under the command of the Earl of Gloucester, and his army routed with great slaughter, while he himself narrowly escaped being taken prisoner : the town was then plundered and burned by the victors. In 1150, Trowbridge castle was besieged and taken by Stephen ; and in 1152, Henry of Anjou, shortly after his landing in England, besieged and captured Malmesbury, together with its castle. Malmesbury was one of the places seized upon by Prince John, during the foreign imprisonment of his elder brother, Richard I., and was reduced soon after Richard's return to England. In 1450, at the period of Cade's rebellion, the Bishop of Salisbury's tenants rose in insurrection, and barbarously murdered that prelate. In 1471, Edward IV. passed through Malmesbury, on his road to meet the forces of Margaret, in the decisive battle of Tewkesbury, in which many Wiltshire men fell in the ranks of the Lancastrians. In the great civil war of the seventeenth century, numerous engagements occurred in this county. In May 1643, Wardour castle was besieged and taken by a body of one

thousand three hundred parliamentarians, under the command of Sir Edward Hungerford : in September of the same year, the Earl of Essex, with the parliamentarian army, marching towards London from the siege of Gloucester, was unexpectedly attacked at Albourne, by Charles I., aided by Prince Rupert, when the former was defeated and driven as far as Hungerford, with great loss. In this year also, Sir William Waller, after possessing himself of Chichester, marched with a strong force to Malmesbury, which had been garrisoned for the king, but which immediately surrendered to him ; it was, however, shortly after retaken by the royalists. In 1644, Woodhouse, which had been garrisoned by a party of parliamentarians under Major Wansey, was closely besieged by Lord Inchiquin, with his Irish forces : a small body of parliamentarians advanced to Warminster, with an intent to raise the siege, but was compelled to retreat towards Salisbury with great loss. From the celebrated battle of Lansdown, near Bath, the royalist forces retired to Chippenham, and thence to Devizes, where they were closely besieged by the parliamentarians under Sir William Waller, who, however, were soon obliged to withdraw from before the town, to oppose a body of fifteen hundred horse, under Lord Wilmot, sent by the king from Oxford to its relief. In the action which ensued on Roundaway hill, the parliamentarians were totally defeated, with the loss of two thousand men, and all their cannon, ammunition, baggage, and stores. In 1645, Cromwell took Devizes ; and Malmesbury was stormed and taken by a parliamentary brigade under Col. Massie. The general rising of the royalists, which was planned to take place on the 11th of March, 1655, broke out only at Salisbury. Several gentlemen of the west marched into that city, with a body of two hundred horse, seized the sheriff and judges, who were then present at the assize, and proclaimed Charles II.; but having wandered about for some time without receiving any accession of force, the insurrection was suppressed by a single troop of horse, the leaders taken and executed, and their followers sold for the plantations. In 1688, on the landing of the Prince of Orange, James II. established the head-quarters of his army at Salisbury; but as his affairs became more desperate, he privately withdrew to London.

This county is in the diocese of Salisbury (excepting only the parish of Kingswood, which is in that of Gloucester, and the parish of Whitchbury, in that of Winchester), and province of Canterbury : it forms the two archdeaconries of Sarum and Wilts, the former comprising the deaneries of Amesbury, Chalk, Potterne, Salisbury, Wilton, and Wily ; the latter, those of Avebury, Cricklade, Malmesbury, and Marlborough. The total number of parishes is two hundred and ninety-five, of which one hundred and forty-three are rectories, one hundred and four vicarages, and forty-eight perpetual curacies. For purposes of civil government it is divided into the following hundreds, *viz.*, Alderbury ; Amesbury ; Bradford ; Branch and Dole ; Calne ; Cawden and Cadworth; Chalk ; Chippenham ; Damerham (North and South); Downton ; Dunworth ; Elstub and Everley ; Frustfield ; Heytesbury ; Highworth, Cricklade, and Staple; Kingsbridge ; Kinwardstone ; Malmesbury ; Melksham ; Mere ; Potterne and Cannings ; Ramsbury ; Selkley ; Swanborough ; Underditch ; War-

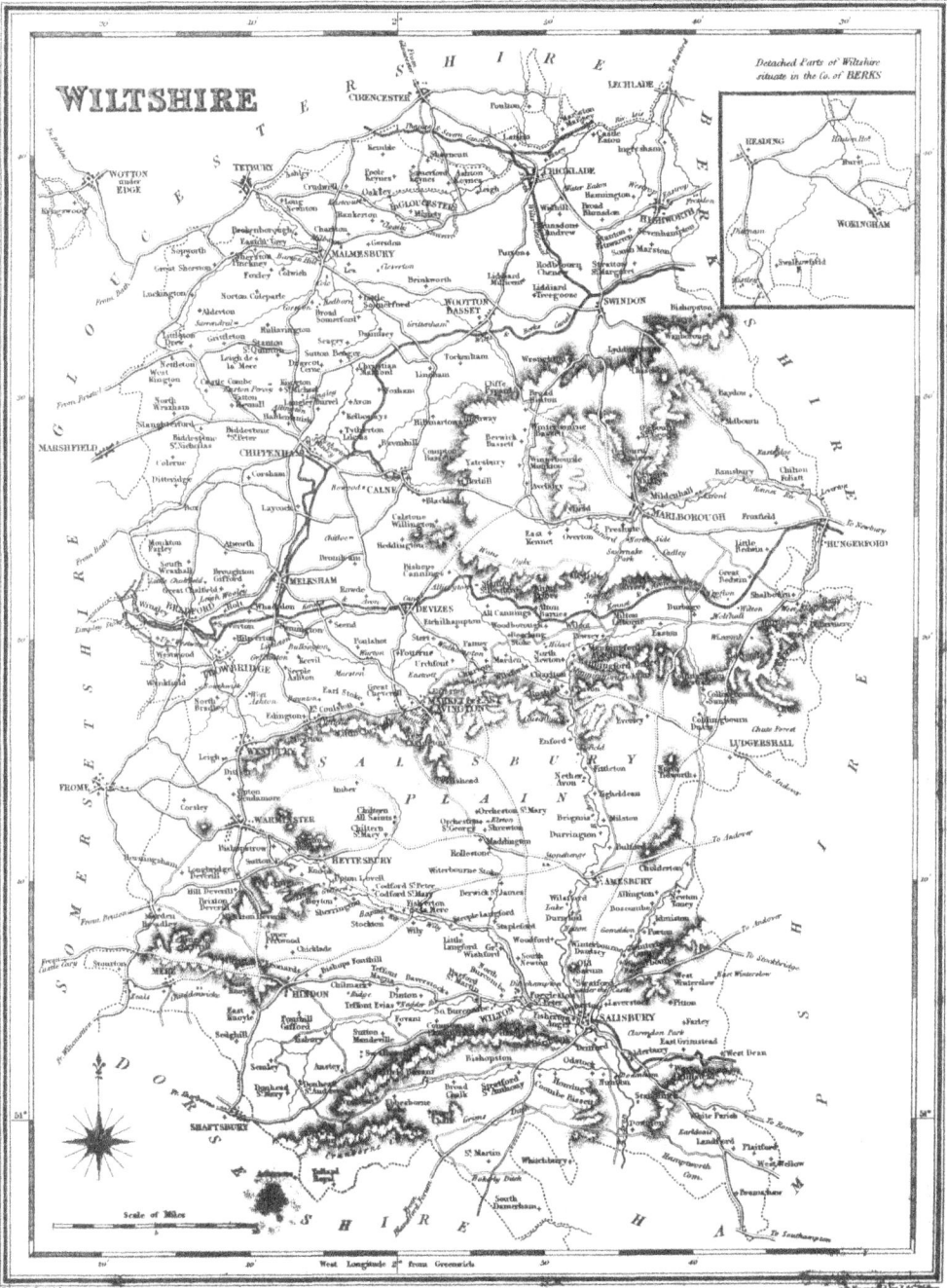

WILTSHIRE

Detached Parts of Wiltshire situate in the Co. of BERKS

Scale of Miles

Drawn by R. Creighton.

minster; Westbury; and Whorwelsdown. It contains the city of Salisbury, or New Sarum; the borough and market towns of Calne, Chippenham, Cricklade, Devizes, Hindon, Malmesbury, Marlborough, Westbury, and Wootton-Bassett; the boroughs of Great Bedwin, Downton, Heytesbury, Ludgershall, Old Sarum, and Wilton; and the market towns of Amesbury, Great Bradford, Market-Lavington, Melksham, Mere, Swindon, Trowbridge, and Warminster. Two knights are returned to parliament for the shire, two citizens for the city of Salisbury, and two burgesses for each of the boroughs: the county members are nominated at Devizes, and elected at Wilton. This county is included in the Western circuit: the assizes are held at Salisbury, and the quarter sessions at Devizes in the winter, at Salisbury in the spring, at Warminster in the summer, and at Marlborough in the autumn: the county gaol is at Fisherton-Anger, the county house of correction at Devizes, and the bridewells at Devizes and Marlborough: there are upwards of one hundred acting magistrates. The parochial rates raised in the county, for the year ending March 25th, 1827, amounted to £192,914. 17., and the expenditure to £190,043. 2., of which £165,443. 2. was applied to the relief of the poor.

Wiltshire derives its name from Wilton, which for a long period anterior to the Norman Conquest, and for a considerable time subsequent to that event, was its principal town, and still continues the county town. This county, which, in the early period of Christianity among the West Saxons, was included in the diocese of Winchester, was afterwards, in the reign of Ina, annexed to that of Sherborne, and so remained for a long succession of years. Soon after the year 905, however, a bishoprick was erected co-extensive with the county, the seat of which was placed successively at Ramsbury and at Wilton. Hermannus, who held it at the Conquest, and who had obtained the bishoprick of Sherborne to be united with it, soon after fixed the seat of his diocese at Old Sarum; whence, in the early part of the thirteenth century, it was removed to its present situation at New Sarum, or Salisbury.

The form of the county is nearly an ellipse, the transverse diameter of which bears north and south: a little beyond its north-western border is a small detached portion, containing the village of Kingswood, and surrounded by Gloucestershire: another detached portion is situated at and near Oakingham, in Berkshire, at the distance of almost thirty miles beyond its eastern confines. A detached portion of the county of Gloucester, containing the principal part of the parish of Minety, is locally in Wiltshire. It is common to consider it as divided into North Wiltshire and South Wiltshire, by a line passing through it from east to west, at or near Devizes; but the natural division is into South-east Wiltshire and North-west Wiltshire, by an irregular line passing from the confines of Berkshire, near Bishopston, south-westward to those of Somersetshire, near Maiden-Bradley. South-east Wiltshire, containing nearly five hundred thousand acres, thus comprehends, and is almost entirely occupied by, the whole of the Wiltshire Downs, with their intersecting vallies, forming the western division of the ranges of chalk hills which occupy so great a portion of Hampshire, and a smaller extent of Berkshire. At a distance, this portion

of the county presents the appearance of one large elevated plain; but on a nearer approach its surface is found to be broken by numerous and frequently extensive vallies, and to possess an almost constant series of gentle eminences, but no where a mountainous elevation: the declivities on one side of some of the ridges are very abrupt, while on the other they sink gently, in irregular gradation, sometimes into a perfect flat. The two grand divisions of the chalk hills are into Marlborough Downs, being those to the north of the Kennet and Avon canal, and Salisbury Downs, or Plain, occupying nearly all the county southward of that line: these great districts are separated by the vale of Pewsey, and the only difference in their general appearance is, that the eminences of the former are more abrupt and elevated than those of the latter. The most extensive level prevails around Stonehenge, where the scenery is peculiarly tame. On Marlborough Downs are scattered many of the singular masses of stone, called "grey wethers," and, when broken, "Sarsden-stones," or, by contraction, "Sarsons." The principal vallies, which display scenes of rich meadow and arable lands, adorned with seats, villages, and occasionally woods, are traversed by streams of excellent water: those descending from Salisbury Plain take a direction towards Wilton and Salisbury. The north-western division of the county presents a remarkably different appearance, being a rich tract of vale land, extending from the base of the Downs to the northern and western confines of the county, and generally so flat that few deviations from the ordinary level are perceptible: approaching the Cotswold hills of Gloucestershire, however, the surface becomes gradually more elevated. This low plain is so well wooded, that, when viewed from any of the surrounding hills, it appears like one vast plantation. The most remarkable eminences in the county, and some of those which command the finest prospects, are, Beacon hill, near Amesbury, which rises to the height of six hundred and ninety feet above the level of the sea; Bidcombe hill, near Maiden-Bradley; Codford hill; the high grounds near Standlinch House; Old Sarum hill, three hundred and thirty-nine feet high; and Westbury Down, seven hundred and seventy-five feet high.

With regard to the climate, it may be observed, that the cold sharp air of the Downs is almost proverbial; but it is also healthy. Although that of the north-western district is somewhat milder, vegetation is there very late, owing chiefly to the cold retentive quality of the soil. The corn harvest is generally as early in the Down district, and in a tract bordering on Gloucestershire, as in any other part of the kingdom; but on the low cold lands it is frequently a month later. The soil of the downs, though varying considerably in quality, is uniformly calcareous: the hills consist of chalk, with its usual accompaniment of flint; and the soil on their sides, where hardly any flints are found, consists of a chalky loam, or rather decomposed chalk, called "white land." The flatter parts have a flinty loam; and in the centre of the principal vallies is a bed of broken flints, covered with black vegetable earth, washed from the hills above: in some of the more extensive vallies are beds of black peat. These hills are bordered at their base by narrow tracts of very fertile soil, called by geologists green sand, from its contain-

3 Q 2

ing little round masses of a green substance, frequently prevailing to such an extent as to give a green hue to the aggregate of which they form a part. One of these lines, entering the county at Mere, on the borders of Dorsetshire and Somersetshire, proceeds by Maiden-Bradley, Warminster, Westbury, and Lavington, to the vicinity of Devizes, where it joins the broader one occupying the Vale of Pewsey, and is afterwards again found to the north-west of the Marlborough Downs. Another enters from Shaftesbury in Dorsetshire, and proceeds eastward, by Donhead, Anstey, Swallowcliffe, Fovant, &c., to the high ground at Burcomb-field, near Wilton; this tract is also joined, near Fovant, by a ridge of sand hills, which extends towards it from West Knoyle, by Stop-Beacon and Ridge. The substratum of the north-westernmost part of the county, separated from the rest of it by a line passing from the border of Somersetshire, near Bradford, through the neighbourhood of Malmesbury, to the confines of Gloucestershire, near Cirencester, consists of a loose irregular mass of the broken strata of a light-coloured, calcareous, and sandy stone, provincially called *corn-grate*, the soil resting upon which is chiefly a reddish calcareous loam, mixed with flat stones, and is called *stonebrash*. The quality of this soil varies much, according to its depth above the stone rock, and the absence or presence of an occasional intervening stratum of blue clay, which has the appearance of marl, but is devoid of its good qualities: its presence is denoted by a spontaneous growth of oak, and that of the drier substratum by a natural and luxuriant growth of elm. About Chippenham, and thence southward by Melksham and Trowbridge, is a much more fertile district, having a greater depth of soil without any of the clay. From Melksham, by Chippenham, to Cricklade, runs a stratum of gravel, in general covered to a good depth with a rich loam : the greatest extent of it is, however, from Tytherton, through Christian-Malford and Dauntsey, to Somerford: this is considered to be the richest soil in the county. In the north-western district are also two tracts of sand of a sharp, loose, gravelly nature, one of which runs from Rodborne, by Seagry, Draycot, and Sutton-Benger, to Langley-Burrel, near Chippenham ; the other from Charlcot, through Bremhill, to Bromham : of the latter there are also detached parts at Rowde and Seend, and the stratum of sand appearing in different places to the north of it is supposed to be the same. The remaining parts of North-west Wiltshire, particularly those extending from Highworth, by Wootton-Bassett, to Clack, have a cold retentive soil on a hard, close, rough kind of limestone. Braden Forest, between Cricklade and Malmesbury, has a soil peculiar to itself, being a cold iron clay, proverbially sterile. Strong clays and clayey loams, of a tolerably rich quality, are found to a small extent in various places on the skirts of the south-eastern district. South-eastern Wiltshire is chiefly appropriated to tillage and to sheep-walks ; the north-western district comprises a very rich and extensive tract of grazing and dairy land, on the borders of the Thames and the Lower Avon, while the rest of it is chiefly arable.

The courses of crops are very various : in the South-eastern district the red wheat is most commonly sown. Barley is a favourite crop in the chalk district, but hardly in any other part of the county : oats are no where sown to a great extent : a few peas and beans are grown in the north-western parts of the county: rye is often sown as spring food for sheep, but is seldom suffered to stand for a corn crop. Turnips are extensively cultivated on the chalky and stonebrash soils : rape, or coleseed, is grown to a great extent on the Downs; as also are vetches in this and in the North-western district. Potatoes are much cultivated, particularly on the rich sands adjoining the chalk. The principal artificial grasses are, ray-grass, broad clover, marl-grass, or Dutch clover, and trefoil ; and the chief object of their cultivation is the maintenance of the sheep for a certain period in the spring. The grass lands of the North-eastern district are of the richest quality, and are partly occupied by dairies, and partly employed in the fattening of cattle. The cheese, which is the only produce of the numerous dairies, excepting the poor kind of butter made from the whey, was, for many years, sold in the London market as Gloucestershire cheese; but it is now well known and much esteemed there under the name of " North Wiltshire." It is customary to graze and mow, the meadow land alternately. Many of the numerous cattle fattened in these rich pastures are taken to Bath, while some are sold at Salisbury, for the supply of the adjoining southern counties, but the greatest number are driven to London. In South Wiltshire are some dairy lands on cold clay soils, from Sedghill and Semley to Wardour Castle, adjoining Dorsetshire; and from Dilton's Marsh, by Westbury and Steeple-Ashton, towards Lavington and Potterne, being on the southern boundary of the North-west district : these assist in supplying the cities of Bath and Salisbury, and other places, with butter: there are also various small tracts of pasture near the towns. Bordering on the streams of the downs are continued narrow tracts of meadow land, under an excellent system of irrigation, which became general about the commencement of the last century : the quantity is estimated at about twenty thousand acres. In the low northern districts there are very few water-meadows; on some small tracts in the vicinity of Hungerford, however, many lambs are bred and fattened for the London market.

With the grass lands of Wiltshire may be classed its spacious downs, which are unenclosed and subject to common rights ; and though a portion of them is always under tillage, yet by far the most extensive tracts are covered with a fine native sward, affording food to no less than five hundred thousand sheep and lambs during the summer and autumn. To find winter food for the sheep is one of the principal objects of the farmers, who, nevertheless, are obliged to send great numbers to be wintered in the contiguous enclosed districts of this and the adjoining counties. Besides the common sheep downs, the unsown common fields adjoining are open to the flocks until they are ploughed and sown with wheat; as also are other similar corn lands, after the harvest. Several parts of the downs, usually the most level and valuable, are pastured with common herds of cattle, which are brought upon them early in May, and remain until the end of harvest, when they are taken to the stubble-fields, and the down then becomes common to the sheep. These lands derive almost their only manure from having the sheep folded upon them, which practice also bestows upon the arable lands in every other part of the county the chief part of that which they receive : the other manures most frequently employed, besides the ordinary ones, are chalk, lime burned from chalk, soot, coal-ashes, peat-ashes, woollen rags, and soap-ashes. The dairy cows of the northern parts of the county are nearly all of the long-horned breed, and are chiefly obtained from the more northern counties of England ; some Devonshire cattle have also been introduced : great numbers of calves are annually sent for the supply of the Bath and London markets with veal. The principal breeds of sheep are the native Wiltshire and the South-Down ; the former, however, on the downs, has been much intermixed with a larger breed, and is now, in its pure state, only occasionally seen in the northern districts. It is computed that not less than one hundred and fifty thousand lambs are annually reared on the downs ; great numbers of sheep are also bred in the North-western district, and some of them fattened there. The native hog is large, white, and long-eared ; but the prevailing kind is a mixed breed between this and a black species : the county is famous for its excellent bacon, which is prepared in very large quantities in the dairy districts. Much land on the rich sands adjoining the chalk, in the vicinities of Devizes, Lavington, Warminster, Westbury, &c., is devoted to horticulture, and supplies the neighbouring towns in this county, and Frome and Bath in Somersetshire, with great quantities of vegetables ; near Wootton-Bassett some small tracts are similarly occupied, and supply the markets of that town, Cricklade, Cirencester, &c. Orchards are common in most parts of the county, and a little cider is, in some places, made for home consumption.

Wiltshire was anciently well-wooded, but its present woodlands are of comparatively small extent. Different parts near its border are occupied by valuable woods, generally in a thriving condition, though much injured by cattle, to which they are common. The only forest still remaining in a well-wooded state is Savernake forest, the property of the Earl of Ailesbury, which is about sixteen miles in circumference, and is situated to the south-east of Marlborough ; it contains many majestic oaks, and exhibits some fine and interesting scenery ; it is also well stocked with deer. Cranborne Chase occupied a long narrow tract on the extreme southern verge of the county, and contained six lodges, with walks appropriated to each, the whole under the care of a ranger deputed by Lord Rivers, as lord of the chase ; but it has lately been disfranchised, his lordship receiving an annual payment from the owners of the woods in it, and the lands adjoining. Vernditch Chase, belonging to the Earl of Pembroke, adjoins the latter on the east, and is now nearly all under cultivation. Grovely Forest, now generally called Grovely woods, also belongs to Lord Pembroke ; it occupies a long narrow tract of the high ground between the vallies of the Nadder and the Wily. The ancient forest of Penchett, or Ponsett, near Salisbury, is now better known as Clarendon park and woods, the property of Sir F. H. Bathurst. Small patches of woodland frequently occur in the vallies, and are more particularly abundant in the North-western district. The cold soils on the western side of the county are peculiarly favourable to the growth of oak, the sands of the southern parts

of it to that of ash, and the gravelly vallies and deep loams of various parts to that of elm ; so that, although many districts are entirely bare of timber, sufficient for the consumption of the county is produced within it. The wastes are comparatively trifling, and consist chiefly of small marshy commons, most of them in the North-western part of the county, where there are also a few small heaths. Fuel is dear and scarce, being partly coal and partly wood : the former is obtained, by means of the canals, chiefly from the Mendip collieries in Somersetshire.

The mineral productions are of little importance. The chalk, forming the substratum of nearly all the extensive South-eastern district, is, in some places, extremely hard, though more frequently of a soft marly texture ; the finest kind is found at Sidbury hill, which furnishes a supply to several of the western counties. Sandstone is obtained in the low grounds both of North and South Wiltshire : the " corn-grate " is frequently found in masses so thin as to be employed in the roofing of houses ; it is also used for building and paving : a more regular stratified sandstone is found under the sandy surface at Swindon, and is in much request for paving, for cisterns, and for tombstones. The inferior kind of limestone, found in the country between Highworth and Clack, is used only for the making and repairing of roads. On the western side of the county, bordering on Somersetshire, are numerous and extensive quarries of a fine kind of freestone : those at Box, near Bath, are among the most celebrated in the vicinity of that city, and produce a great variety of fossil shells and other marine exuviæ. Near Wootton-Bassett, in the blue clay, and near Grittleton, in the freestone strata, other singular fossil remains are found. The freestone quarries at Chilmark, Tisbury, and that neighbourhood, are extensive, and the stone of a very superior quality.

The manufactures are of considerable extent and importance, particularly that of woollen goods. At Salisbury great quantities of flannel were made till within the last twenty years, and also fancy woollens ; but the manufacture has gradually declined, and a very small quantity of flannel and linsey is now made : this city has also a manufacture of cutlery and steel goods of great excellence. Wilton has a manufacture of carpets and of kerseymere and linsey. Bradford, Trowbridge, Westbury, and all the adjacent towns and villages, from Chippenham to Heytesbury inclusive, carry on extensive woollen manufactures, chiefly of superfine broad cloth, kerseymere, and fancy cloths. At Mere and in its vicinity is a manufacture of linen, chiefly dowlas and bed-ticking ; and at Aldbourn is one of cotton goods, chiefly fustians and thicksets. The parishes of Stourton and Maiden-Bradley, and others in their vicinity, participate to a small extent in the neighbouring linen-manufacture of Dorsetshire, and the silk-manufacture of Bruton in Somersetshire. Ale of a superior quality is brewed in some parts of the county, and a considerable quantity of it is sold in London, under the names of "Wiltshire" and "Kennet" ale. The commerce consists chiefly in the exportation of the agricultural and manufacturing produce : of the former there is a considerable surplus, principally wheat, barley, fat cattle, calves, sheep, hogs, and cheese, part of which is taken to the London markets, and the rest to Bath, Bristol, and the eastern parts of Somerset-shire. Great numbers of store sheep bred here are annually sold off to be fattened elsewhere, chiefly in the more eastern counties. Wiltshire, besides supplying its own woollen manufactures with the raw material, also sends a considerable quantity to other counties. The principal imports are the ordinary articles of merchandise, coal, and cows for the supply of the dairy districts.

The rivers and streams are very numerous, and all of them rise either within the county, or near its borders: the principal are the Isis, or Thames, the Lower Avon, the Kennet, and the Salisbury, or Wiltshire and Hampshire Avon, not one of which is navigable within its limits. The Isis, rising among the Cotswold hills in Gloucestershire, enters the county on its northern confines, near Ewen, and winds, first south-eastward, and then eastward, to Cricklade, which town it reaches after having formed the northern boundary of the county for a short distance; below Cricklade it winds east by north, and soon again becomes the boundary, which it continues to be until it finally quits Wilt-shire at its north-eastern extremity: it is joined from the northern part of the county by the streams of the Swill-brook, the Key, the Ray, and the Churn. The Lower Avon, rising on the confines of Wiltshire and Gloucestershire, proceeds eastward to Malmesbury, and thence southward, by Great Somerford and Dauntsey, to Chippenham: from the latter place it takes a winding course, by Melksham and Bradford, to the border of Somersetshire, a little to the west of the latter town, where it makes a bold sweep to the north, and enters that county a little below Winsley. The Kennet is formed by the streams which issue from Marlborough Downs; it is considered to have its principal source close to the village of Uffcott, whence it flows, first south-westward, and then southward, to West Kennet, thence taking an easterly course by the town of Marlborough and the villages of Ramsbury and Chilton, and across the eastern confines of the county to Hungerford in Berkshire; this river is noted for its trout, and for a peculiar species of eels. The Wiltshire and Hampshire Avon is formed by the junction of several small streams in the Vale of Pewsey, whence it flows southward by Amesbury, Old Sarum, Salisbury, and Downton, and enters Hampshire about a mile below the last-mentioned town: its principal tributaries are, the Wily, which rises at the foot of the Clay hills, and flows east-south-easterly, by Warminster, Heytesbury, and Wilton, below which it unites with the Nadder, and runs to Salisbury, where it discharges its waters into the Avon by two channels. The Nadder, which rises at the southern extremity of the county, near Shaftesbury in Dorsetshire, and flows eastward, by Wardour Castle and the village of Hatch, to the Wily, near Wilton; and the Bourne, which rises near the village of Easton, about five miles to the south-west of Great Bedwin, and then takes a southerly course through a small portion of Hampshire, but re-entering this county near Cholderton, it proceeds south-south-eastward, by Newton-Toney and the three Winterbournes, to the Avon, a little to the south-east of the city of Salisbury: the bed of this river is remarkable for being entirely dry during the whole of the summer.

Wiltshire is traversed by four lines of artificial inland navigation. The Kennet and Avon canal, which crosses the centre of it from west to east, and connects the navigation of the Lower Avon with that of the Kennet and the Thames, enters from Bath, near Winsley, where it crosses the Avon, and passes to Bradford, where it again crosses that river, and then proceeds by Trowbridge and Poulshot to Devizes, a little to the north-west of which latter town it makes a considerable ascent, by means of lockage; it then passes through the parishes of Bishops-Cannings, All-Cannings, Stanton St. Bernard, Alton-Barnes, Wilcot, and Wootton-Rivers; and near Burbage is carried through a tunnel to the valley in which Great Bedwin is situated, and down which it proceeds to the banks of the Kennet, near Hungerford, with which river it quits the county. The first act of parliament for its formation was obtained in 1794, and several other acts, for the alteration of the course originally designed for it, and for the raising of additional funds, were afterwards passed: the whole line, however, was not completed and opened until the end of the year 1809. The Wilts and Berks canal, branching from the Kennet and Avon at Semington, about two miles to the west of Devizes, passes northward, by Melksham, to the vicinities of Chippenham and Calne, to each of which towns it has a short branch: it thence proceeds north-eastward to Wootton-Bassett, from that town eastward to Swindon, and then, again north-eastward, to within three miles of Highworth, where it enters Berkshire, in its further course to the navigable channel of the Thames, a short distance below Abingdon: the first act for its formation was obtained in 1795, but the work experienced many delays. The Salisbury and Southampton canal was designed to have commenced at Salisbury, and to have proceeded, first south-eastward and then eastward, into Hampshire; but after a considerable portion of the work had been completed, it was at last abandoned, on encountering an extensive quicksand. The Thames and Severn canal crosses only the northern extremity of the county, passing the northern bank of the Isis, and near the town of Cricklade.

Few counties in the kingdom have such numerous and excellent turnpike-roads as Wiltshire. The great western road from London to Exeter and the Land's End enters it in two branches, one from Andover, and the other from Stockbridge, and passes through Salisbury to Blandford in Dorsetshire: the road from London to Exeter, by Shaftesbury, branches from this near Salisbury. The road from London to Bath, by Chippenham, enters from Hungerford in Berkshire, and passes through Marlborough, Calne, and Chippenham, to Bath; that to Bath, by Devizes, branches from the last-mentioned at Beckhampton, through Devizes and Melksham, to Bath-Ford in Somersetshire: that to Bath, by Sandy Lane, branches off at a short distance from Beckhampton, by Laycock, Corsham, and Box, to Bath-Easton in Somersetshire; the road from London to Bath, by Andover, enters from that town in Hampshire, and passes through Ludgershall to Devizes, where it joins the road to Bath passing through that town. The road from London to Bristol branches from the first-mentioned Bath road at Chippenham, and passes by Wraxhall into Gloucestershire; that to Wells, at Beckhampton, through Devizes and Trowbridge. The road from London to Barnstaple, entering from Andover in Hampshire, passes through Amesbury, Wily, and Chicklade, to Bruton in Somersetshire: the road from London to Frome branches from this a little beyond Amesbury, through Heytesbury and Warminster, to that town in Somersetshire; and a branch from this again, at Warminster, passes through Maiden-Bradley to Bruton. The road from London to Bruton, by Salisbury, branches from the great western road at that city, through Wilton and Hindon. This county contained the Roman stations of *Sorbiodunum*, at Old Sarum; *Verlucio*, in the vicinity of Heddington; and *Cunetio*, a little to the east of Marlborough: this people had also several other permanent settlements in Wiltshire, particularly at Easton-Grey, Wanborough, near Heytesbury, and Littlecot. The principal of the Roman roads which traversed it was a continuation of the *Julia Strata*, which, entering from Bath, proceeded north-eastward, by Medley and Spye Park, to the station of *Verlucio*, and thence by Colston and across the river Kennet to that of *Cunetio*, beyond which it stretched across the eastern confines of the county. The Fosse-way branched from the *Julia Strata* at Bath-Ford, and passed by Banner Down, Easton-Grey, and across the turnpike-road between Tetbury and Malmesbury, to Cirencester in Gloucestershire: another great road entered from Cirencester, and passed south-eastward by Cricklade to Wanborough, at which latter place it separated into two branches, one proceeding by Baydon towards Speen in Berkshire, and the other, by Ogbourne, Mildenhall, Manton, and Chute Park, towards Winchester. *Sorbiodunum* was connected with other stations by three roads, one of which passed by Bemerton, Stratford St. Anthony, and Woodyates - Inn, towards Dorchester; another, by Ford, Winterslow, Buckhold Farm, and Bossington, towards Winchester; and the third, by Porton and Idmiston, towards Silchester, in the north of Hampshire. The Ridge-way, extending north-eastward from Avebury into the adjoining county of Berks, is also mentioned by Whitaker as a Roman road.

Wiltshire is distinguished for remarkably numerous traces (chiefly in its south-eastern districts) of the nations which successively occupied it during the earlier periods of our history. Of these, the stupendous monument of Stonehenge, two miles westward of Amesbury, and that of Avebury, about five miles to the west of Marlborough, are entitled to primary notice. The vast earthwork of the Wansdyke is conjectured by some to have been the northern boundary of the Belgæ, and supposed to have intersected the whole county, from the north of Somersetshire to the north of Hampshire: though in the greater part of its course it can be distinctly traced only in detached spots, yet throughout the range of hills to the south and west of Marlborough, it is still tolerably entire, and in one place is conspicuous, in a bold and connected line, for the distance of ten or twelve miles. The sepulchral mounds, called barrows, or tumuli, are abundant, more particularly around Stonehenge and Avebury: the most remarkable is Silbury hill, near Avebury. There is a cromlech at Clatford Bottom, near the village of Clatford, and another at Littleton-Drew. The Roman roads may yet be distinctly traced in several places; and the Ridge-way is clearly visible on the high chalk ridge extending north-eastward from Avebury into Berkshire.

The encampments, which are so numerous, vary in the period of their formation, in their size, shape, and mode of construction, and in the peculiarities of their situations. Some of these are undoubtedly the work of British tribes and of the Belgæ; others of successive invaders, the Romans, the Saxons, and the Danes. The largest and most noted are, the vast fortifications of Old Sarum, enclosing an area of nearly thirty acres, the foundations of the walls of which are still visible; Chidbury Camp, to the north-west of Tidworth, comprising an area of seventeen acres; and Vespasian's Camp, as it is commonly called, to the westward of Amesbury, enclosing an area of thirty-nine acres. There are many others nearly equal in extent, and scarcely less interesting to the antiquary: the principal are situated at Whitesheet hill, to the north-west of Mere; Clay hill, near Warminster; Warminster down; Whiten hill, near Longbridge-Deverill; Cottley hill, to the north-west of Heytesbury; Knighton down; Pewsey heath; Oldbury hill, near Calne; Roundway hill, near Devizes; Martinsall hill, near Marlborough; Chidbury hill; Blunsden hill, near Highworth; Beacon hill, near Amesbury; Southley wood, to the south of Warminster; Barberry Castle, near Marlborough; Liddington Castle; Hays, on the western border of the county, near the Lower Avon; Bratton, two miles from Eddington; Battlesbury, near Warminster; Scratchbury, near Cottley; Yarnborough, at an angle formed by the old trackway from Salisbury to Bath and the present turnpike-road from Amesbury to Mere; Badbury, near Wily; Groveley Castle, Rolston; Casterley, near Shrewton; the vicinity of Berwick St. John; Haydon hill, near Chute; Ogbury, near Great Durnford; Newton-Toney; Alderbury; Whitchbury; Clearbury, near Downton; Broad-Chalk; Chiselbury, near Fovant; Old Camp, on Boreham Down, near Warminster; Dinton, and Little Path hill. These intrenchments were evidently formed for purposes of military defence, but there is a variety of other earthworks spread over Salisbury Plain and Marlborough Downs, the uses of which are unknown; some of them are considered the sites of British villages, others as denoting places consecrated to religion. Many less vestiges of antiquity, such as tesselated pavements, coins, urns, &c., of the Romans, and fragments of sculpture, daggers, shields, gold and silver ornaments, and a great variety of other articles of British, Saxon, Danish, or Norman manufacture, have been discovered at different periods. The number of religious houses, including colleges and hospitals, was about fifty-seven. There are remains of the abbeys of Kingswood, Laycock, and Malmesbury; of the priory of Bradenstoke; and of the nunnery of Kington St. Michael. The most remarkable specimens of ecclesiastical architecture are the magnificent cathedral of Salisbury, and the churches of Amesbury, Anstey, Avebury, Bishops-Cannings, Boyton, Calne, Chippenham, St. John at Devizes, Great Bedwin, Kington St Michael, Malmesbury, Mere, Oaksey, and Steeple-Ashton. There are ancient and curious fonts in several of the churches, more particularly those of Great Durnford and Preshute. There yet exist extensive remains of the ancient castles of Castle-Combe, Devizes, Farley, Ludgershall, Malmesbury, Marlborough, and Wardour.

Amongst the principal of the numerous seats of the nobility and gentry, the most splendid are Bowood, the residence of the Marquis of Lansdowne, lord lieutenant of the county; Charlton House, that of the Earl of Suffolk; Stowerhead, that of Sir Richard Colt Hoare, Bart.; Longleat, that of the Marquis of Bath; Tottenham Park, that of the Earl of Ailesbury; Wardour Castle, that of Lord Arundel; Wilton House, that of the Earl of Pembroke; Longford Castle, that of the Earl of Radnor; and Corsham House, that of Paul Methuen, Esq. There is a chalybeate spring at Chippenham, also a chalybeate and a saline aperient spring near Melksham, and mineral springs of different other qualities at Heywood, Holt, and Middle Hill Spa, near Box. Wiltshire gives the inferior title of earl to the Marquis of Winchester.

WILY, a parish in the hundred of BRANCH and DOLE, county of WILTS, 7 miles (E. N. E.) from Hindon, containing, with the tything of Deptford, 466 inhabitants. The living is a rectory, in the archdeaconry and diocese of Salisbury, rated in the king's books at £21. 14. 2., and in the patronage of the Earl of Pembroke. The church is dedicated to St. Mary. About one mile from the village is a large British encampment, called Badbury-Rings, or Wily Camp, which occupies a point of down projecting from the principal ridge, and encloses an area of more than seventeen acres.

WIMBISH, a parish in the hundred of UTTLESFORD, county of ESSEX, 4¼ miles (E. S. E.) from Saffron-Walden, containing, with Thunderley, 809 inhabitants. The living is a vicarage, with that of Thunderley united in 1425, in the archdeaconry of Middlesex, and diocese of London, rated in the king's books at £8, and in the patronage of the Rector : the rectory, a sinecure, is rated at £12, and in the patronage of the Rev. John Dolignon. The church is dedicated to All Saints. Sarah Barnard, in 1774, bequeathed an annuity of £4 in support of a school.

WIMBLEDON, a parish in the western division of the hundred of BRIXTON, county of SURREY, 9 miles (S. W.) from London, containing 2195 inhabitants. The name of this place, anciently written *Wymbandune*, *Wymbaldon*, and *Wymbeldon*, is supposed to have been derived from one of its early proprietors. The principal feature in the parish is Wimbledon Park, which comprises about twelve thousand acres, and contains a sheet of water covering a space of thirty acres. The common is surrounded by seats of the nobility and gentry, and exhibits, at the south-west angle, a circular encampment with a single ditch, including a surface of seven acres; the trench is very deep and perfect. It is supposed to mark the site of a battle, fought in 568, between Ceawlin, King of the West Saxons, and Ethelbert, King of Kent. At the north-east angle of the common is the village, consisting of one street, containing many respectable houses; and in detached situations are numerous handsome seats and pleasant villas. In the immediate vicinity of Wimbledon is a well, the water of which has never been known to freeze. The mills of the English Copper Company are in this parish : there are also calico-printing works, a manufactory for Japan ware, and a corn-mill. A pleasure fair is held on the first Monday after Easter, and the two following days.

The living is a rectory, in the peculiar jurisdiction of the Archbishop of Canterbury, rated in the king's books at £35. 2. 11., and in the patronage of the Dean and Chapter of Worcester. The church, dedicated to St. Mary, and situated near the entrance of the village, was erected in 1787, on the site of a former, which had fallen to decay. It is a neat edifice, in the Grecian style of architecture : in the east window are some remains of painted glass, representing the arms of the families of Leeds, Salisbury, Dorset, &c.; and in the churchyard, which is watched by a society formed for that purpose upwards of eight years ago, are several handsome mausoleums. There are places of worship for Independents and Wesleyan Methodists. A National school, in which one hundred and twenty boys and fifty girls are instructed, is supported by voluntary contributions : the school-house, with a garden and field annexed, were given by John, Earl Spencer, in 1773. In 1650, Dorothy Cecil, daughter of Edward, Lord Viscount Wimbledon, gave a rent-charge of £22. 2. 6., for teaching poor children, and keeping her father's tomb in repair.

WIMBLINGTON, a hamlet in the parish of DODDINGTON, northern division of the hundred of WITCHFORD, Isle of ELY, county of CAMBRIDGE, 4 miles (S.) from March, containing 859 inhabitants. There is a place of worship for Wesleyan Methodists. A school was directed to be founded, in 1714, by Mr. Thomas Eaton, for teaching forty children reading, writing, and accounts : it was endowed with lands of considerable value, but, in consequence of a suit in Chancery, it has not been yet established.

WIMBOLDSLEY, a township in that part of the parish of MIDDLEWICH which is in the hundred of NORTHWICH, county palatine of CHESTER, 2½ miles (S. W.) from Middlewich, containing 121 inhabitants. Lea Hall, which is in this township, was for a considerable period the residence of the celebrated physician, Dr. Fothergill.

WIMBORNE (ALL SAINTS, or ALLHALLOWS), a parish in the hundred of WIMBORNE ST. GILES, Shaston (East) division of the county of DORSET, ½ a mile (N.) from Wimborne St. Giles, with which the population is returned. The living is a rectory, united in 1732 with that of Wimborne St. Giles, in the archdeaconry of Dorset, and diocese of Bristol, rated in the king's books at £9. 4. 4½. The church, which formerly appears to have been the mother church of Wimborne St. Giles, was pulled down in 1733.

WIMBORNE (ST. GILES), a parish in the hundred of WIMBORNE ST. GILES, Shaston (East) division of the county of DORSET, 2½ miles (S. W. by W.) from Cranborne, containing, with Wimborne All Saints, 384 inhabitants. The living is a rectory, with that of Wimborne All Saints united, in the archdeaconry of Dorset, and diocese of Bristol, rated in the king's books at £12. 13. 4., and in the patronage of the Earl of Shaftesbury. The church was rebuilt in 1732, on the union of the two livings : it stands near the seat of the Earl of Shaftesbury, and is the burial-place of the family; its tower is crowned with balustrades, and at each angle is an urn surmounted by a steel vane. Here are almshouses for eleven poor people, founded, in 1624, by Sir Anthony Ashley, Bart., and endowed with a large farm at Gussage All Saints.

Corporate Seal.

WIMBORNE - MINSTER, a parish in the hundred of BADBURY, Shaston (East) division of the county of DORSET, comprising the market town of Wimborne-Minster, and the tythings of Abbottstreet, Barnesley,Cowgrove,Leigh, Petersham,Stone,Thornhill, and Wimborne - Borough, and containing 3563 inhabitants, of which number, 1387 are in the town of Wimborne-Minster, 26 miles (E.N.E.) from Dorchester, and 101 (S.W. by W.) from London. This is a place of very remote antiquity; in the time of the Romans it was of considerable importance as a station to their camp at Badbury, and by them was denominated *Vindogladia*, or *Ventageladia*, terms descriptive of its situation near to, or between, two rivers. The Saxon appellation of *Vinburnan*, whence the present name is obviously deduced, is of similar import; the epithet of Minster, from its ancient monastery, having been added as a term of distinction. Some have supposed this to have been the scene of a battle between Kearl, Earl of Devon, and the Danes, in 851, in which the latter were defeated; but Bishop Gibson states this to have occurred at Wenbury, in Devonshire, with which he endeavours to identify *Wicganbeorche*, the place where, in the Saxon Chronicle, it is stated to have taken place. About the commencement of the tenth century, Edward the Elder, in the beginning of his reign, being opposed by Ethelwald, son of his uncle Ethelbert, who aspired to the crown, encamped at Badbury, with a considerable army, and advanced upon Wimborne, where Ethelwald had fortified himself with a small force, which he captured, after an ineffectual resistance from the latter. But the principal cause of its celebrity was a nunnery, founded previously to 705, and dedicated to the Virgin Mary, by St. Cuthberga, daughter of Cenred, and sister of Ina, both kings of the West Saxons, which, about the year 900, being destroyed by the Danes, was subsequently converted into a house for Secular canons, the revenue of which, at the dissolution, was valued at £131. 14. The foundress became an inmate of the nunnery, where she died, and was buried in the church, of which, having been canonized, she was made the tutelar saint. The town is situated in a fertile vale, near the confluence of the rivers Stour and Allen, on the main road from London to Poole : the streets are irregular, and the houses in general of mean appearance. At its eastern extremity the Allen divides into two branches, over which are two bridges. Leland thus describes it :—"the town is yet meatly good, and reasonably well inhabited. It hath bene a very large thing, and was in price in the tyme of the West Saxon kinges. Ther be in and about it diverse chappelles, that in tymes paste were, as I have lernid, paroche chirchis of the very town of Wimburne." And in another place he says ;—"the soile about Wimburn-Minstre self is very good for corne, grasse, and woodde." The town hall, which formerly stood near the square, has long since fallen into decay: it occupied the site of St. Peter's chapel sometimes styled the king's free chapel, which,

the building having been neglected soon after the Reformation, was, with the cemetery, containing about one acre of ground, vested in the corporation, and their successors in fee, for the erection of a town-hall, the residue of the profits to be applied towards the maintenance of the choristers in the church. The market is on Friday; and fairs are held on the Friday before Good Friday and on the 14th of September, each for two days, for horses and cattle. Constables are appointed at the manorial court held annually at Michaelmas.

On the establishment of the Secular canons, when the nunnery was destroyed by the Danes, the church became collegiate, and a royal free chapel, having been declared by letters of Edward II., in the eleventh year of his reign, to be exempt from all ordinary jurisdiction, imposition, &c. In Leland's time the society consisted of a dean, four prebendaries, five cantarists, three vicars, and four secondaries. The dean and prebendaries maintained four priests and four clerks to serve the cure; viz., in the collegiate church, and in St. Peter's, Kingston, and Holt chapels. On the dissolution of the college, its possessions lapsed to the crown; and Elizabeth, in the fifth year of her reign, on re-establishing the school, appointed twelve of the inhabitants governors, whom she incorporated, with a common seal, and granted in trust to them the tithes of the parish, and all other endowments of the college and school, for their future support, with all ecclesiastical rights and spiritual jurisdiction previously belonging to the college and prebends. In the reign of Charles I., the governors having surrendered these possessions, the king re-granted them in full, on the condition of their providing the necessary officers for the service of the church and the school, with all ecclesiastical jurisdiction within the parish, and power to appoint the official and registrar of the peculiar court. Three incumbents are elected by the governors, who serve the church in rotation weekly; they also appoint three clerks, an organist, three singing men, and six singing boys : a visitation court is held annually. The chapels of Kingston and St. Peter have fallen into ruins ; that at Holt remains. The church, commonly called the Minster, is dedicated to St. Cuthberga, and is a large cruciform structure, with a quadrangular tower rising from the intersection, and another at the west end, the former in the Norman style, the latter in the later English; the east window is in the early English style of architecture. A tempest destroyed the spire about 1600, and it has not since been replaced. The chancel and choir are approached from the nave by a flight of steps, and are supported by pillars : the choir consists of sixteen stalls, covered with canopies of carved oak. St. Cuthberga is supposed to have been entombed in the wall of the chancel : here also was King Ethelred's tomb, of which the brass plate fixed in the floor is all that remains. On the south side of the choir is an altar-tomb, with the effigies of the Duke and Duchess of Somerset, the parents of Margaret, Countess of Richmond, mother of Henry VII.; on the opposite side is a similar tomb, but without figures, to the memory of Gertrude, Marchioness of Exeter, mother of the unfortunate Edward Courtenay, last Earl of Devonshire ; and in the south aisle is a monument, with an armed recumbent figure, to Sir Edmund Uvedale, Knt., dated 1606. Under the area

3 R

of the chancel is a small crypt, called the Dungeon, having pointed arches, with bold circular groins to support the roof; it was formerly used as a chantry, of which the church contained a great number. On the outside of the Bell tower is the figure of a soldier, with a hammer in each hand, with which it strikes the quarters of the hour. There are places of worship for Baptists, Independents, and Wesleyan Methodists.

The free grammar school, originally founded by Margaret, Countess of Richmond, in 1497, was re-founded by Queen Elizabeth, in 1563, for the gratuitous instruction of all applicants, without limitation, and designated Queen Elizabeth's free grammar school in Wimborne-Minster : the management is vested in the twelve governors. St. Margaret's hospital, for poor persons, situated at the west end of the town, is of ancient and obscure foundation; the revenues are under the direction of the lord of the manor of Kingston-Lacy, and his steward, who conjointly nominate the almspeople : in a chapel attached to it divine service is occasionally performed. A second hospital, called Courtenay's, situated at the east end of the town, was built pursuant to the will of Gertrude, Marchioness of Exeter, bearing date 1557 ; the governor and poor persons are incorporated and have a common seal : there are six almspeople on the foundation. At Pamphill, in this parish, are a school and almshouse, founded pursuant to the will of Roger Gillingham, dated July 2nd, 1695 : the schoolmaster and almspeople are nominated and appointed by the governors of the free grammar school in this town; the former receives £20, and each of the latter £5, per annum. This is supposed to be the birthplace of Matthew Prior, Esq., the statesman and poet, who was educated at the free grammar school. The Duke of Monmouth, after his escape from the battle of Sedgmoor, is stated to have been arrested in a small enclosure, called Shagsheath, near this place; but this is doubted by some, who are of opinion that his capture took place near Ringwood. Badbury camp, in the vicinity, is a circular intrenchment, surrounded by three ramparts, enclosing an area of eighteen acres : Roman coins, urns, and a sword, were dug up in 1665.

WIMBOTSHAM, a parish in the hundred of CLACK-CLOSE, county of NORFOLK, 1¼ mile (N. by E.) from Downham-Market, containing 413 inhabitants. The living is a discharged rectory, with the vicarage of Stow-Bardolph annexed, in the archdeaconry of Norfolk, and diocese of Norwich, rated in the king's books at £5. 6. 8., and in the patronage of Mrs. Moor. The church is dedicated to St. Mary.

WIMESWOULD, a parish in the eastern division of the hundred of GOSCOTE, county of LEICESTER, 5¼ miles (N. E. by E.) from Loughborough, containing 1061 inhabitants. The living is a discharged vicarage, in the archdeaconry of Leicester, and diocese of Lincoln, rated in the king's books at £9, endowed with £200 private benefaction, and £200 royal bounty, and in the patronage of the Master and Fellows of Trinity College, Cambridge. The church is dedicated to St. Mary. There is a place of worship for Wesleyan Methodists. Joseph Thompson, in 1733, bequeathed land, directing the rents to be applied in support of a school for ten boys.

WIMPOLE, a parish in the hundred of WETHERLEY, county of CAMBRIDGE, 6 miles (S. E. by S.) from Caxton, containing 493 inhabitants. The living is a rectory, in the archdeaconry and diocese of Ely, rated in the king's books at £18, and in the patronage of the Earl of Hardwicke. The church, dedicated to St. Andrew, contains various monuments to the Hardwicke family, among which is that to the memory of Lord Chancellor Hardwicke, who died in 1764, and was here interred. There is a charity school for thirty children.

WINCANTON, a market town and parish in the hundred of NORTON-FERRIS, county of SOMERSET, 34 miles (E.) from Taunton, and 108 (W. by S.) from London, containing 2143 inhabitants. This place is of very great antiquity; it was anciently called Wyndcaleton, and derived its name from its situation on the windings of the river Cale, by which it is bounded on the west. At a very early period it was the scene of many sanguinary conflicts between the Britons and Saxons, and subsequently of numerous encounters between the latter and the Danes, who made frequent irruptions into this part of the country. During the parliamentary war, some of the earliest engagements between the contending parties took place in the immediate vicinity of this town, in which, according to Burnet's "History of his own Times," was shed the first blood in the Revolution of 1688; though some state this to have occurred at Cirencester. In 1747, it suffered material injury from an accidental fire, which destroyed a considerable portion of the town, to which calamity may be attributed the regular and uniform appearance it afterwards assumed. The town is pleasantly situated on the western declivity of a hill rising gently from the river Cale, and consists principally of four regular streets, containing some well built houses. The environs, which are pleasant, abound with interesting scenery, and on the south is an uninterrupted view of the fine Vale of Blackmore, extending for many miles: the land is extremely fertile; and within a short distance of the town are several gentlemen's seats. The manufacture of linen and bed-ticking was formerly carried on to a considerable extent; but within the last few years it has greatly declined, and at present affords employment only to a small number of persons : a branch of the silk manufacture has lately been introduced. The market is on Wednesday, and is well supplied with corn, cattle, cheese, and butter: the fairs are on Easter-Tuesday and September 29th. The town, which is within the jurisdiction of the county magistrates, is divided into two parts, called the borough and the tything ; two constables for the former, and a tythingman for the latter, are annually appointed at the manorial court, and a court leet for the hundred is also held annually. The living is a perpetual curacy, in the archdeaconry of Wells, and diocese of Bath and Wells, endowed with £400 private benefaction, £200 royal bounty, and £1100 parliamentary grant, and in the joint patronage of U. and G. Messiter, Esqrs., as owners of the impropriate rectory. The church, dedicated to St. Peter and St. Paul, is a spacious and neat edifice, with a square embattled tower ; the interior consists of a nave, aisles, and chancel, and, as well as the exterior, has within the last few years undergone a thorough repair. There is a place of worship for Independents. Various charitable bequests have been made for distribution among the poor. At Stavordale, the north-eastern extremity of the parish, a small priory of Augustine canons, dedicated to St. James, is said to have been built by Sir William Zouch, which, in the 24th of Henry VIII., was annexed to the priory of Taunton : the remains, especially the roof and some portions of the chapel, are in good preservation. The Earl of Illchester, among his other inferior titles, enjoys that of Lord Illchester and Stavordale. At Horwood, about a mile south-east of the town, are two mineral springs, resembling in their properties those at Cheltenham. An urn, containing several Roman coins, was discovered in this parish, many years since.

WINCEBY, a parish in the hundred of HILL, parts of LINDSEY, county of LINCOLN, 4 miles (E. by S.) from Horncastle, containing 78 inhabitants. The living is a discharged rectory, in the archdeaconry and diocese of Lincoln, rated in the king's books at £6. 0. 2½., endowed with £200 royal bounty, and in the patronage of the Crown. The church is dedicated to St. Margaret. A battle was fought here during the parliamentary war, in which the king's troops were defeated.

WINCH (EAST), a parish in the Lynn division of the hundred of FREEBRIDGE, county of NORFOLK, 5½ miles (S. E. by E.) from Lynn-Regis, containing 376 inhabitants. The living is a discharged vicarage, in the archdeaconry and diocese of Norwich, rated in the king's books at £8, and in the patronage of Edmund Kent, Esq. The church is dedicated to All Saints. In the east window of the chancel are the arms of Vere and Howard; and on the north side is the ancient chapel of St. Mary, the family burial-place of the latter.

WINCH (WEST), a parish in the Lynn division of the hundred of FREEBRIDGE, county of NORFOLK, 3 miles (S. by S.) from Lynn-Regis, containing 315 inhabitants. The living is a rectory, in the archdeaconry and diocese of Norwich, rated in the king's books at £9. 13. 4., and in the patronage of the Crown. The church is dedicated to St. Mary.

WINCHAM, a township in that part of the parish of GREAT BUDWORTH which is in the hundred of BUCKLOW, county palatine of CHESTER, 2 miles (N. E. by E.) from Northwich, containing 491 inhabitants. The Grand Trunk canal passes through the parish.

WINCHCOMB, a market town and parish in the lower division of the hundred of KIFTSGATE, county of GLOUCESTER, 15½ miles (N. E. by E.) from Gloucester, and 95 (W. N. W.) from London, comprising the chapelries of Greet and Gretton, and the hamlets of Coates, Cockbury, Corndean, Langley with the Abbey demesnes, Naunton with Frampton, Postlip, and Sudeley-Tenements, and containing 2240 inhabitants. This place, which is of equal antiquity and importance, was anciently called *Winchelscomb*, of which its modern name is obviously a contraction. During the Saxon Octarchy, if not the metropolis of the kingdom of Mercia, it was at least the residence of some of the Mercian kings, of whom Offa founded a nunnery here, in 787. Cenulph, who succeeded to the throne of that kingdom, after the death of Egferth, Offa's son, who survived his father only a few months, had a palace here, and in 798, laid the foundation of the stately abbey, for three hundred monks of the Benedictine order; which he endowed with an ample revenue, and dedicated, with unusual splendour, to the Blessed Virgin Mary. After the conclusion of the ceremony, which was conducted by Wulfred,

Archbishop of Canterbury, assisted by twelve other prelates, in the presence of the king himself, Cuthred, King of Kent, Sired, King of the East Saxons, ten dukes, and the flower of the Mercian nobles, Cenulph, leading to the high altar his captive, Ethelbert Pren, the usurper of the kingdom of Kent, whom he had made prisoner, generously restored him to his liberty without fine or ransom. Cenulph, in the year 819, was buried in the abbey which he had founded, where also the remains of his son and successor, Cenelm, were deposited. The young king, after a reign of one year, having been cruelly murdered, at the instigation of his unnatural sister Quendreda, in the hope thereby of securing to herself the throne, was first obscurely buried, and afterwards, on the discovery of the foul deed, removed with much funeral pomp, and interred near his father in the abbey church. He was at length canonized, and the numerous pilgrimages made to his shrine much augmented the revenue of the monastery, which was subsequently re-dedicated to the Virgin Mary and St. Cenelm. It was afterwards in the possession of Secular priests, and had almost fallen into decay, when Oswald, Bishop of Worcester, in 985, reformed its discipline, recovered the lands of which it had been deprived, and restored it to the Benedictine monks, who held it till the dissolution. This was a mitred abbey, and its possessions were numerous ; for, at the period of the Norman survey, no fewer than nineteen manors were annexed to it, independently of Winchcomb itself; but the monks having opposed the Conqueror, were by him deprived of many of their lands. At the dissolution, the revenue was £759. 11. 9. The building is reported to have been exceedingly magnificent, and so prosperous, at one period, was its state, that it is said to have been " equal to a little university." Very few traces of it, however, remain, but the memorial is preserved in the name of part of a hamlet, which is still called the Abbey demesnes. Of the civil history of the place few particulars are recorded : the town appears to have been walled, and to the south of the church there was an ancient fortress, or castle, which, according to Leland, having fallen into decay, and the ruins being overspread with ivy, gave the name of Ivy castle to a spot which is now occupied only by a few cottages and gardens.

Winchcomb is situated in a beautiful vale, at the northern base of the Cotswold hills, by which it is sheltered nearly on every side, and is watered by the little river Isbourne, which flows close to it on the south-east: it consists principally of three streets, extending in a long line from east to west, with North-street, and a few smaller ones, branching from them. The houses are in general low and of indifferent appearance, and, from its being but little of a thoroughfare, the place preserves an air of seclusion and tranquillity, and has that venerable character which denotes an old Anglo-Saxon town : it is abundantly supplied with excellent water from wells and springs. The cultivation of tobacco, which is said to have been first planted here after its introduction into the kingdom, in 1583, was, for a considerable time, a source of much profit to the inhabitants ; but in the 12th of Charles I., that trade being restrained, the plantations were neglected. The principal branches of manufacture at present carried on are those of paper and silk, for the former of which there are in the neighbourhood two large mills, and one for the latter ; there

3 R 2

is also a tan-yard on a moderate scale. Other minor branches are cotton stockings and pins; and agricultural operations, with the spinning of linen and woollen, afford nearly constant employment to the parochial poor. The market is on Saturday : the fairs are on the last Saturday in March, May 6th, and July 28th, for horses, cattle, and sheep ; and two fairs are held at Michaelmas for the hiring of servants. Previously to the time of Canute, Winchcomb, with a small surrounding district, was a county of itself; but, in the reign of that monarch, according to an ancient manuscript in the cathedral church of Worcester, Edric, who governed under him as viceroy, "joined the sheriffdom of Winchelscomb, which was entire within itself, to the county of Gloucester." In the reign of Edward the Confessor the town was made a borough, and the government was vested in two bailiffs and twelve burgesses, of whom the former have till lately been annually elected by the lord of the manor, but exercise no jurisdiction, the charter having for many years ceased to be acted upon.

The living is a discharged vicarage, with the chapelry of Gretton annexed, in the archdeaconry and diocese of Gloucester, rated in the king's books at £3. 4., endowed with £400 private benefaction, £400 royal bounty, and £400 parliamentary grant, and in the patronage of C. H. Tracy, Esq. The church, dedicated to St. Peter, partly erected by Abbot William, in the reign of Henry VI., and completed at the expense of the parishioners, munificently assisted by Ralph Boteler, Lord of Sudeley, is a spacious and handsome structure, in the later style of English architecture, with a lofty square embattled tower, crowned with pinnacles ; the walls are embattled, and strengthened with buttresses, also terminating with pinnacles ; the south porch is a beautiful specimen of the style of which the roof is elaborately groined and highly enriched. The interior, consisting of a nave, aisles, and chancel, is of appropriate character ; the nave is separated from the aisles by octagonal pillars and compressed arches, and from the chancel by an ancient carved oak screen. There are places of worship for Baptists and Wesleyan Methodists. A free grammar school was founded, in 1522, by Henry VIII., who endowed it with £9. 4. 6. per annum, which was afterwards confirmed by Queen Elizabeth. The school, after being long continued in a house belonging to the corporation, now inhabited by some of the parochial poor, was united to a grammar school, subsequently founded by Lady Frances Chandos, for which she erected a school-house in St. Nicholas'-street, endowing it with certain lands and tenements, for the education of fourteen boys : the income, arising from nearly twenty acres of land, is about £40 per annum, which is received by the master of the king's grammar school, who pays a sub-master to teach the boys reading, writing, and arithmetic ; the number of scholars on both these foundations is about thirty-four. A school for teaching children to read was founded by George Townsend, Esq., who endowed it with £5 per annum, as a salary for the master, (since increased to £20 by the trustees,) and also left funds for apprenticing the children, with whom a premium of £15 is given. There are unendowed almshouses for six poor families, founded by Lady Dorothy Chandos, and various charitable bequests for the distribution of bread,

clothing, and money to the poor. There are two mineral springs in the parish, one a strong saline, the other chalybeate, and nearly similar to those of Cheltenham. In addition to the abbey of St. Mary, previously noticed, were a church, dedicated to St. Nicholas, in the east part of the town, of which there are no remains, and an ancient hospital, of which no particulars are recorded. About half a mile from the town are the beautiful remains of the magnificent castle of Sudeley, formerly belonging to the Botelers lords of Sudeley, which is noticed in the article on SUDELEY-MANOR. Tidenham of Winchcomb, Bishop of Worcester, and physician to Richard II., is supposed to have been a native of this town ; and Dr. Christopher Mercet, an eminent naturalist and philosopher, was born here, in 1614.

WINCHELSEA, a borough and parish (formerly a market town), having separate jurisdiction, locally in the hundred of Guestling, rape of HASTINGS, county of SUSSEX, 74 miles (E. by N.) from Chichester, and 66¾ (S. E.) from London, containing 817 inhabitants. The ancient town of this name, situated near the Camber Point, was a place of considerable importance in the time of the Romans, and was subsequently destroyed by an inundation of the sea, about the close of the thirteenth century. The present town, which is situated at the distance of a mile and a half from the sea, was built upon an eminence well adapted to prevent a similar accident, in the reign of Edward I., who gave land for that purpose, and contributed largely towards its erection. The site, originally called Higham, was, by the munificence of that monarch, surrounded with walls, and defended by three strong gates, which formed the principal entrances, and are still in good preservation. In the reign of Henry III., Winchelsea and Rye were annexed to the cinque-ports, but more as appendages than equal ports, being members of the port of Hastings ; in the different charters granted to these towns, they are invariably styled "ancient towns." The new town was invested with the same privileges as the old, and enjoying all the benefits of the cinque-ports, it rapidly acquired a considerable degree of commercial importance. In the reign of Edward III. it sustained material injury from the French, who, having landed on this part of the coast, burnt a considerable portion of it, and it was subsequently plundered by the Spaniards, in the reign of Richard II. But it experienced the greatest injury from the subsequent retiring of the sea, by which its harbour was destroyed, and its commercial importance annihilated. The town occupies a space nearly two miles in circumference, divided into squares by streets intersecting each other at right angles, probably after the plan of the ancient town. Neither any trade, nor any particular branch of manufacture, is carried on at present : the market has fallen into disuse, but a fair is still held on the 14th of May, for cattle. The Royal Military canal commences at Cliff-End, and passes by this town, parallel with the shore, till it enters the sea at Shornecliff, near Hythe.

Arms.

Corporate Seal of Winchelsea.

Obverse. Reverse.

Arms.

WINCHESTER, a city, having separate jurisdiction, locally in the hundred of Buddlesgate, Fawley division of the county of SOUTHAMPTON, of which it is the capital, 63 miles (S. W. by W.) from London, containing 7739 inhabitants, according to the census of 1821. This place, which the ancient Britons called *Caer Gwent*, from the whiteness of its chalky soil, was the *Venta Belgarum* of Ptolemy and Antoninus: on its subsequent occupation by the Saxons, it obtained the appellation of *Wintan-Ceaster*, from which its present name is derived. It was probably first inhabited by the Celtic Britons, who emigrated from the coasts of Armorica in Gaul, and established themselves in this part of the island; where, finding well-watered vallies, fertile plains, and shady forests, adapted to their support, and suited to the exercise of their religious rites, they fixed their chief residence, and continued in undisturbed possession till within a century prior to the Christian era, when they were expelled by a tribe of the Belgæ, who, after having established themselves on the southern coasts, concentrated their forces, and, advancing into the country, made this one of their principal settlements. Among the several towns which were called *Ventæ*, this became the most important, and was, prior to the Roman invasion, the capital of the Belgian territory in Britain: it retained its pre-eminence till it fell under the power of the Romans, who, having achieved the conquest of this part of the island, under Vespasian, made it one of their principal stations. In the year 50, Ostorius Scapula fortified all the cities of the Belgæ between Anton, or the Southampton river, and the Severn, and placed garrisons in them, to defend them from the frequent assaults of the Britons, who were ever on the alert to surprise the enemy, and to recover the towns of which they had been deprived. The fortifications of this station may be still discerned in various places; and on Catherine hill, within a mile of the present town, are vestiges of a Roman camp, quadrangular in form, and defended by strong intrenchments: this, which was probably the *castra æstiva* of the station, communicated with the Roman road between Porchester and Winchester on one side, and with the river on the other, also with the several roads leading to the neighbouring stations of *Vindonum*, or Silchester, and *Sorbiodunum*, or Old Sarum. Two Roman temples are said to have been erected in this place, one consecrated to Apollo, and the other to Concord, near the site of the present cathedral; and, among other evidences of Roman occupation, sepulchres have been recently discovered without the walls of the city to the north and east, nine of which, on being opened in 1789, were found to contain human bones, urns of black pottery elegantly formed, a coin of Augustus Cæsar, fibulæ, and other Roman relics. Carausius and Alectus, who assumed the imperial purple in Britain, are said to have fixed their residence in this place, where their coins have been discovered in greater profusion than in any other part of the kingdom. Soon after the establishment of Chris-

According to the ancient charter, the government is vested in a mayor and twelve jurats, who are justices of the peace within the ancient town and its liberties. The borough received the elective franchise in the 42nd of Edward III., since which time it has regularly returned two members to parliament : the right of election is vested in the freemen, eleven in number : the mayor is the returning officer, and the influence of the Marquis of Cleveland is predominant. It also, jointly with Hastings, sends canopy bearers on the occasion of a coronation, these two places being entitled to every third turn, in common with the other cinque-ports. The living is a discharged rectory, in the archdeaconry of Lewes, and diocese of Chichester, rated in the king's books at £6. 13. 4., and in the patronage of Sir W. Ashburnham. The church, dedicated to St. Thomas, is the only remaining portion of a very fine and ample structure, the whole of which, except the chancel, is gone to decay : it presents an elegant specimen of the early and decorated styles of English architecture. On the north side are some stalls and a piscina of beautiful design, and there are several splendid monuments, of which, one in particular, is hardly excelled by any in the kingdom : among them are three remarkable ones, supposed to be monuments of Knights Templars, cross-legged and in armour. There is a place of worship for Wesleyan Methodists. In addition to the church of St. Thomas, here were anciently two other parochial churches, dedicated respectively to St. Leonard and St. Giles. The remains of antiquity still visible are, the ruins of Camber castle, erected by Henry VIII., a circular fortress with a round tower, which was the keep; the ancient gates of the town; and the interesting ruins of a monastery of Grey friars, founded by Edward II. Robert, Archbishop of Canterbury, who died in 1313, was a native of this town. Winchelsea gives the title of earl to the family of Finch.

WINCHENDON (NETHER), a parish in the hundred of ASHENDON, county of BUCKINGHAM, 7 miles (W. by S.) from Aylesbury, containing 284 inhabitants. The living is a perpetual curacy, in the archdeaconry of Buckingham, and diocese of Lincoln, endowed with £400 private benefaction, and £1000 royal bounty, and in the patronage of Sir W. B. Cave, Bart. The church is dedicated to St. Nicholas.

WINCHENDON (UPPER), a parish in the hundred of ASHENDON, county of BUCKINGHAM, 6 miles (W. by N.) from Aylesbury, containing 216 inhabitants. The living is a donative, rated in the king's books at £7. 17., endowed with £200 parliamentary grant, and in the patronage of the Duke of Marlborough. The church is dedicated to St. Mary Magdalene.

tianity in the island, a monastery was founded here, of which Constans, son of Constantine, was one of the brethren; but being allured by his father from his devotional retirement, to take the command of the forces in Spain, he was, by the revolt of his general, made prisoner, and afterwards put to death.

After the departure of the Romans from Britain, Vortigern, who had previously exercised authority over the western part of it, was elected king, in order to defend it from the incursions of the Picts and Scots, who were making continual depredations : this prince made Winchester the metropolis of the kingdom, and it was subsequently the residence of his successors. On the invasion of the island by the Saxons, under Cerdic, and the defeat of the united Britons in the New Forest, it became the capital of the Saxon kingdom of Wessex, and the residence of the conqueror, who was crowned king of the West Saxons. Cerdic, after having, in conjunction with his son Cenric, spent several years in extending his dominions and in giving security to his conquests, died, and was buried here in 534 : during his government, the monastery was converted into a Pagan temple, and appropriated to the service of the Saxon deities. In 635, St. Birinus, whom Pope Honorius had sent into Britain, to propagate the Christian faith in those parts of the island which were still in Pagan darkness, met with a favourable reception from Cynegils, who, in conjunction with his son Cwichelm, was then king of the West Saxons. Cynegils, by the persuasion of Oswald, King of Northumbria, who afterwards espoused his daughter, Kineburga, was baptized at York; and, in the following year, his son and many of his subjects were converted to Christianity, which from that time began to flourish in this part of the island. Subsequently, he commenced collecting materials for building a cathedral in Winchester, intending to make it the seat of a bishoprick, which St. Birinus had, in the mean time, established at Dorchester, where his son Cwichelm held his court; but the design was frustrated by his death, which happened about six years after that of Cwichelm, who died the year after his conversion. Cenwahl, his second son, succeeding to the throne after the death of his father and elder brother, the people again relapsed into Paganism, under a prince who refused to acknowledge the new religion; but on his conversion to Christianity and baptism by St. Birinus, Cenwahl completed the cathedral in 648, dedicating it to St. Birinus, St. Peter, and St. Paul, and founded, and amply endowed, a monastery near it. About ten years after the death of St. Birinus, who was buried at Dorchester, Cenwahl divided the see into two portions, assigning the northern part of his kingdom to Dorchester, and the southern part to Winchester, to the cathedral of which last the remains of St. Birinus were removed, by Hedda, the fifth bishop. Egbert, who succeeded to the throne of Wessex in 800, after many severe struggles for empire, obtained the sovereignty of all the other kingdoms of the Octarchy, of which he was crowned sole monarch, in the cathedral church of Winchester, in 827, in the presence of a wittenagemote, or great assembly of the people. On this occasion he published an edict, abolishing all distinctions, and commanding all his subjects, in every part of his dominions, to be called English. This union of the kingdoms greatly promoted the importance of Winchester, which, from

being the capital only of Wessex, became the metropolis of the kingdom. Ethelwolf, who succeeded Egbert, dated his charter from this city in 855, for the general establishment of tithes, which was signed by himself, by Bhurred, King of Mercia, and Edmund, King of the East Angles (his tributary vassals), and by the chief nobility and prelates, in the cathedral church.

About this time the city seems to have been in a flourishing condition, and a commercial guild was established in it, under royal protection, at least a century earlier than in any other part of the kingdom. During the reigns of Ethelwolf and Ethelbald, St. Swithin, a native either of the city or of the suburbs, presided over the see: by his advice the latter monarch enclosed the cathedral and the cloisters with a wall and fortifications, to defend them from the predatory attacks of the Danes, who, at this period, were beginning to make frequent incursions upon this part of the coast, and who, in the succeeding reign, having landed in considerable numbers at Southampton, advanced to Winchester, where they committed the most barbarous outrages. They were, however, attacked, on their retreat to their ships, and routed with great slaughter, and the immense quantity of plunder which they had taken in the city was recovered. On this occasion, the cathedral and monastic buildings, which had been previously fortified, escaped without injury. About the year 872, after repeated battles fought with varied success, in which Ethelbert was assisted by his younger brother, Alfred, a band of those rapacious pirates assaulted the city, in which they made dreadful havoc; the cathedral was greatly damaged, and the ecclesiastics were inhumanly massacred. After the victory subsequently obtained over them by Alfred, Winchester was restored to its former importance, and again became the seat of government; and Alfred, who had fixed his chief residence here, ordered a general survey of the country to be made and deposited in the archives of the city, which was thence called the Codex Wintoniensis. This monarch founded a monastery on the north side of the cathedral, for his chaplain, St. Grimbald, intending it also as a place of interment for himself and family; but dying before it was completed, he was buried in the cathedral, from which his remains were subsequently removed, and deposited in the new minster. In the reign of Athelstan, six mints were established in the city, for coining as many different kinds of money : during this reign, the legendary battle between Guido, Earl of Warwick, and a Dane of gigantic stature, named Colbrand, is said to have taken place in a meadow near the city, on a spot of ground still called Danemark. In commemoration of this combat, which many historians regard as fabulous, there are numerous traditionary records; and, in the north wall of the city, the turret, called Athelstan's chair, from which that monarch is said to have viewed the battle, and a representation of it in stone, are stated to have existed formerly; and the battle-axe of Colbrand was kept in the cathedral till after the reign of James I.

In the reign of Edgar, a law was made to prevent frauds arising from the diversity of measures in different parts of the kingdom, and for the establishment of a legal standard measure to be used in every part of his dominions : the standard vessels made by order of that monarch were deposited in this city, from which circumstance originated the appellation "Winchester measure:" the original bushel is still preserved in the guildhall. In this reign, St. Ethelwold, a native of Winchester, who presided over the see, partly rebuilt the cathedral, which, on its completion in the following reign, he re-consecrated, in the presence of King Ethelred, Dunstan, Archbishop of Canterbury, and the principal nobility and prelates of the kingdom; and included in the dedication the name of St. Swithin, whose remains, buried at his own request in the churchyard, were removed and re-interred in the cathedral under a magnificent shrine, which had been prepared for that purpose by King Edgar. During the prelacy of St. Ethelwold, the Secular canons who officiated in the cathedral, being married men, had been, under the directions of Dunstan, Archbishop of Canterbury, replaced by Benedictine monks from the abbey of Abingdon; but on the accession of Edward the Martyr to the throne, Elfrida endeavoured to reverse that measure, which had been adopted generally throughout the kingdom, and by her influence caused the suppression of three Benedictine abbeys, which St. Ethelwold had founded, transferring their possessions to the married clergy. In consequence of these proceedings, a synod was held in the refectory of the old monastery in this city, in which the general dissolution of all monasteries was debated; but the measure was negatived by the intervention of one of those supposed miracles which were not uncommon upon such occasions. Ethelred, in 1002, having resolved upon the extermination of the Danes, by a general massacre throughout the kingdom, dispatched secret letters to every part of his dominions for that purpose, which was carried into effect with the greatest inhumanity: such as were not actually put to death were mutilated and rendered incapable of any military service; and, in commemoration of that barbarous policy, the "Hoctide sports," so called from cutting the hamstrings of the victims, were instituted by that king, and continued, till within the last few ages, to be celebrated on the Monday in the third week after Easter. The retaliating vengeance of the Danes under Sweyn, King of Denmark, did not reach Winchester till some time after it had been inflicted on other parts of the kingdom; and on their approach in 1013, the inhabitants sued for peace, and gave hostages for the performance of any conditions.

After the partition of the kingdom between Edmund Ironside and Canute, the latter having obtained the entire sovereignty, divided it into four parts, three of which he entrusted to the government of subordinate rulers; but, reserving the fourth and most important for his own administration, he fixed his seat of government at Winchester, and greatly enriched the cathedral church, to which, after the memorable reproof of his courtiers at Southampton, for their flattery, he presented his regal crown, depositing it over the high altar, and making a vow never to wear it more. This monarch here held a general assembly of the nobility, in which he enacted laws for the government of the kingdom, and for the preservation of the royal forests and chases. On the death of Hardicanute, in 1041, Edward the Confessor was crowned with great pomp and splendour in the cathedral, to which he granted an additional charter, and ordered a donation of half a mark to the master of the choir, and a cask of wine and one hundred cakes of white bread to the convent, as often as a

king of England should wear his crown in that city. During this reign, Queen Emma, his mother, by her own desire, to vindicate her innocence of the crime of incontinence, with which she had been aspersed, underwent the trial of the fiery ordeal in the cathedral church; and being conducted by two bishops, in the presence of the king and a crowded assembly of nobles and of the people, she is stated to have walked barefoot over nine heated plough-shares, without receiving the smallest injury. In gratitude for her deliverance, she enriched the possessions of the church with nine additional manors; the same number was also added by Bishop Alwyn, her kinsman and her asserted paramour, and the manors of Portland, Weymouth, and Wyke, were given on this occasion by the king: the first great seal of England was, in the course of this reign, made and kept in the city.

At the time of the Conquest, William fixed his principal residence at Winchester, which he made the seat of government, and built a strong castle at the south-west extremity of the city, in order to keep his new subjects in awe. Here he enacted most of his laws, and framed political measures for the security of his government, among which were the institution of the Curfew, and the general survey and estimate of the property of his subjects, called the Roll of Winchester, or Domesday-book, a probable imitation, or enlargement, of the *Codex Wintoniensis* of Alfred. Though he occasionally resided in London, which was growing into importance, and more especially during the latter part of his reign, yet he invariably celebrated the festival of Easter in this city. Soon after his establishment on the throne, Waltheof, who had been married to his niece Judith, and was created Earl of Huntingdon, being charged with entering into a conspiracy against him, was beheaded on St. Giles' hill, near Winchester. In 1079, Walkelyn, a relation of the Conqueror's, and bishop of the see, began to rebuild the cathedral and the adjoining monastery; for which purpose, he obtained from the king a grant of timber from the woods in the vicinity. The building was completed in 1093, and dedicated, with great pomp, in the presence of all the bishops and abbots in the kingdom. On the death of Walkelyn, in 1098, William Rufus, who was crowned here, seized upon the bishoprick, and held it till the year 1100, when, being killed while hunting in the New Forest, his body was brought into the city on the following day, in a cart belonging to a charcoal maker, and interred in the centre of the choir of the cathedral: the lineal descendants of this man, whose name was Purkis, still pursue that occupation in the same place, which is within a few hundred yards of the spot where the monarch fell. On the death of Rufus, his elder brother Robert being then on a crusade, Henry, his younger brother, hastened to Winchester; and having made himself master of the royal treasure; he, in the presence of the reluctant nobles, drew his sword, and secured his pretensions to the crown by seizing and placing it upon his head. In this year he espoused Matilda, daughter of Malcolm III., King of Scotland, who had assumed the veil in the monastery of St. Mary, in this city, but had not taken the vows: by this marriage the royal Saxon and Norman lines were united; on the birth of a son, in the following year, he conferred many additional privileges on the inhabitants.

In the same year also a dreadful fire broke out, which destroyed the royal palace, the mints, the guildhall, a considerable portion of the city, and many of the public records. Henry, by the advice of Roger, Bishop of Sarum, ordered a general meeting of the masters of the several mints to assemble at Winchester, on Christmas-day in 1125, to investigate the state of the coin, which had been generally debased throughout the kingdom : after due examination they were, with the exception of three of the Winchester mint-masters, found guilty of gross fraud, and punished by the loss of their right hands. An entirely new coinage was ordered to be made, and the management of it was exclusively confided to those of the mint-masters of this city who had been declared innocent. About the same time, Henry, to prevent frauds in the measurement of cloth, ordered a standard yard, of the length of his own arm, to be made and deposited here with the standard measures of Edgar.

At this time Winchester appears to have attained its highest degree of prosperity : it was the seat of government, and the residence of the monarch ; the royal mint, the treasury, and the public records were kept here ; it had also a magnificent royal palace, a noble castle erected by the Conqueror, likewise another not less considerable, which was subsequently built as an episcopal palace for the bishops, with various stately public buildings, and numerous mansions for the residence of the nobility and gentry connected with the court : it had three royal monasteries, exclusively of inferior religious houses; a splendid cathedral, in which many of the monarchs of England had been crowned, and were interred ; a vast number of parish churches, of which Stowe relates that not less than forty were destroyed in the war between Stephen and Matilda : its population was great, and its suburbs, in every direction, extended a mile further than they do at present; it was the general thoroughfare from the eastern to the western parts of the kingdom; it had a considerable manufactory for woollen caps, and enjoyed an extensive commerce with the continent, from which it imported wine, in exchange for its manufactures ; and was a place of great resort for its numerous fairs, which were frequented by persons from various parts of the kingdom. On the death of Henry I., Winchester suffered greatly in the war which followed in the reign of Stephen, who, having seized the episcopal palaces throughout the kingdom into his own hands, a synod was held here, to protest against the injustice of that measure, and to concert means of obtaining redress: at this meeting it was resolved that the assembled prelates should prepare an address, and send a deputation to the king, who then resided at the palace of Winchester, which was accordingly done, but the king, without paying the least attention to it, left the city and departed for London.

At this conjuncture the Empress Matilda landed on the coast of Sussex, to dispute Stephen's title to the throne, and the royal castle of Winchester was secured by a party in her interest ; but, through the influence of Henry de Blois, brother of the king, who was then bishop of the see, the city was preserved in its allegiance to Stephen. On the subsequent captivity of the king, who was made prisoner in the war, and the acknowledgment of Matilda's claim to the crown by the greater part of the kingdom, the bishop abandoned the cause of his brother; and, having gone out with a solemn procession of his clergy, to meet the empress at Magdalene hill, he conducted her and her partizans into the city with great ceremony. Her haughtiness, however, having excited disgust in the minds of the citizens, and the public opinion beginning to change in favour of the captive king, the bishop relaxed in his attention and deference to the empress, who, on that account, summoned him to wait upon her at the castle, where she then resided. Having returned an ambiguous answer to her summons, the bishop immediately began to put his castle of Wolvesey into a state of defence, and had scarcely completed its fortifications, when it was closely invested by the forces of Matilda, under the command of Robert, Earl of Gloucester, her natural brother, and her uncle, David, King of Scotland. A considerable body of Stephen's party having taken up arms, marched to the relief of the bishop : the armies on both sides were numerous and well appointed, and the city suffered dreadful havoc from their hostilities, which were carried on in the very centre of it, for several weeks, with the utmost acrimony. The party of the empress had possession of the royal castle and the northern part of the city ; the king's party held the castle of Wolvesey, cathedral, and the southern parts, and, discharging fireballs from Wolvesey castle, destroyed the abbey of St. Mary, the houses of the opposite party, and almost all the north part of the city, and ultimately succeeded in confining his opponents within the limits of the royal castle. The supply of water having been cut off, and provisions beginning to fail, the garrison began to entertain thoughts of surrendering ; but, having previously spread a report of Matilda's sickness and death, they obtained a truce for her interment, and placing her in a coffin, she was carried out through the army and escaped in safety to Gloucester. In the mean time, the Earl of Gloucester, with the King of Scots, taking advantage of the truce, made a sally from the castle; but being pursued, the earl was taken prisoner at Stockbridge, and subsequently exchanged for the captive monarch. Stephen, immediately on his liberation, repaired to Winchester, and began to strengthen the fortifications of the castle by the addition of new works ; but, while engaged in that undertaking, an army, which had been newly raised in the adjoining counties, marched against him, and he was compelled to abandon his design, and save himself by flight. During this war, the bishop held a synod here, by an act of which it was decreed, that ploughs should have the same privileges of sanctuary as churches; and a sentence of excommunication was issued against all who should molest any person employed in agriculture. On the conclusion of this war, during which nearly one-half of the city was destroyed, the treaty between Stephen and Henry, the son of Matilda, the terms of which had been agreed upon at Wallingford castle, was ratified at Winchester, by general consent.

Henry II., on his accession to the throne, was crowned here with his queen Margaret, and held a parliament in 1172; and here also, in 1184, his daughter, the Duchess of Saxony, gave birth to a son, named William, from whom the illustrious house of Hanover is supposed to have sprung. This monarch conferred many privileges upon the city, among which was that of being governed by a mayor and a subordinate bailiff : during his reign a calamitous fire, which began in the mint, destroyed the greater part of the town. On the death of Henry, his son, Richard I., surnamed Cœur de Leon, after having secured the royal treasure in this city, was crowned in London ; but, on his ransom from the captivity into which he had fallen, in returning from the Crusades, he had the ceremony of his coronation performed with great pomp in the cathedral of Winchester. In 1207, King John held a parliament here, in which he imposed a tax of one-thirteenth part on all moveable property; and in the same year his queen gave birth to a son, who, from the place of his nativity, was surnamed Henry of Winchester. In the year following, in consideration of two hundred marks paid down, and an annual payment of one hundred, that monarch granted the inhabitants a charter of incorporation, confirming all previous privileges ; and, on his subsequent submission to the pope, he received absolution in the chapter-house of the monastery from sentence of excommunication, which had been pronounced against him by the legate of Pope Innocent III. Henry III., during his minority, kept his court here, under the guardianship of the Earl of Pembroke, and, after the death of that nobleman, under that of Peter de Rupibus, Bishop of Winchester. The residence of the king contributed materially to restore Winchester to the importance it had enjoyed previously to the war between Stephen and Matilda ; but this advantage was greatly diminished by the numerous bands of lawless plunderers in the city and its vicinity, with which many of the inhabitants, and even members of the king's household, were connected. The depredations committed by these associations for the purpose of rapine were at length suppressed by the firmness and resolution of the king, but not till after thirty of the offenders had been brought to trial and publicly executed. During the war between this monarch and the barons, the city experienced considerable devastation, and suffered severely from the violence of both parties, who alternately had possession of it. After the battle of Evesham, the king held several parliaments here, in which all who had borne arms against him were attainted ; but, with the exception of the Montfort family, none of these attainders were carried into execution, and the highest penalty inflicted did not exceed five years' rent of the forfeited estates. The celebrated trial of John Plantagenet, Earl of Surrey, took place here, for the murder of Alan de la Zouch, Chief Justice of Ireland, whom that nobleman killed on the bench in Westminster Hall, on being summoned before him to give evidence of the tenure by which he held his estates. On his own oath, and on that of twenty-four compurgators, that he did not strike the judge from preconceived malice, the earl was acquitted, and fined one thousand two hundred marks. Edward I. also held several parliaments at Winchester, in one of which the celebrated ordinances, afterwards called the Statutes of Winchester, were passed ; but the royal residence for the greater part was transferred to London, which now having risen into higher importance, had become the metropolis of the kingdom ; and Winchester, which hitherto

VOL. IV.

had held the first rank among the cities of the empire, began to decline. Towards the end of his reign, this monarch, offended at the escape of a foreign hostage, who had been confined in the castle under the custody of the mayor, deprived the city of all its privileges, which were subsequently restored. Soon after the death of Edward II., a parliament was held here by Queen Isabel and Mortimer, in which Edmund of Woodstock, Earl of Kent, was arraigned, on a charge of high treason, and condemned to death. For this purpose he was led to a scaffold erected opposite to the castle gate ; but so strong was the feeling of disgust which that iniquitous sentence excited, that no person could be found to carry it into execution, till, towards evening, a prisoner under sentence of death was prevailed upon, by the offer of pardon, to behead the earl.

Edward III. having made Winchester a staple for the sale of wool, the merchants erected large warehouses for conducting that lucrative trade, and the city began to recover its commercial importance ; but its progress was interrupted by the destruction of Portsmouth and Southampton by the French, in 1337, who were, however, repulsed from this city, and the following year by the plague, which ten years afterwards raged violently in the neighbourhood, and ultimately by the removal of the staple to Calais, in 1363. During this reign, Bishop Edynton, who was treasurer and chancellor to the king, commenced rebuilding the nave of the cathedral, which was completed by his successor, William of Wykeham, who, for his skill in architecture, was employed by Edward III. to superintend the erection of part of Windsor castle. Richard II. and his queen visited Winchester in 1388 ; and, in 1392, that monarch removed to it his parliament from London, which was then suffering a suspension of its privileges under the king's displeasure. The marriage of Henry IV. with the Dowager Duchess of Bretagne was solemnized in the cathedral, by Bishop Wykeham, in 1401 ; and on the death of that prelate, Henry, afterwards Cardinal Beaufort, son of John of Gaunt, was by that monarch appointed to the see. Here Henry V. gave audience to the French ambassadors, and in consequence of their insolence on that occasion, the invasion of France soon followed. Henry VI. was a great benefactor to the city, which he frequently visited ; and, in 1449, he held a parliament here, which continued to sit for several weeks. In the course of this reign, however, its trade and population so greatly declined, that, in petitioning the king for the renewal of a grant conferred by his predecessor in 1440, the inhabitants represent that nine hundred and ninety-seven houses were deserted, and seventeen parish churches closed. Bishop Waynfleet having succeeded to the see, that monarch honoured the ceremony of his installation with his presence, and in the following reign, the queen of Henry VII. resided in the castle, where she gave birth to a son, whom, to conciliate the Welch, the king named Arthur, in honour of the British hero of that name. In 1522, Henry VIII., in company with his royal guest, Charles V., came hither, where he spent several days : on this occasion the celebrated round table, at which the renowned King Arthur and his knights used to dine, and which was preserved in the castle, was fresh painted, and an inscription placed beneath it, in commemoration of the royal visit.

3 S

The dissolution of the monasteries, which took place during this reign, and the demolition of many of the religious establishments, completed the downfall of this once splendid and opulent city, and reduced it to a mere shadow of its former grandeur. On the accession of Mary, some transient gleams of returning prosperity revived, for a time, a hope of restoration: the marriage of that queen with Philip of Spain was solemnized in the cathedral, and several of the estates which had been alienated during the former reigns were restored to the see; but the real importance of Winchester had subsided, and, in a charter obtained for it from Elizabeth, through the solicitation of Sir Francis Walsingham, it is described as "having fallen into great ruin, decay, and poverty." On the death of Elizabeth, Sir Benjamin Tichborne, high sheriff of Hampshire, instantly on learning that event, and without waiting for any instructions from the lords of the privy council, who had been for many hours in close deliberation, proclaimed the accession of James I., in the city of Winchester. For this spirited conduct he was afterwards rewarded with the hereditary grant of the royal castle, and a pension of £100 per annum, during his own life and that of his eldest son, on whom the king also conferred the honour of knighthood. In the first year of this reign, the trial of Sir Walter Raleigh, Lords Cobham and Grey de Wilton, and others, on a charge of conspiracy, took place here, and Sir Walter Raleigh, though reprieved, was removed to the Tower of London, where he passed thirteen years in confinement. At the commencement of the parliamentary war, Sir William Waller took possession of the castle for the parliament; but towards the close of the year 1643, it was re-taken and garrisoned for the king, by Sir William, afterwards Lord Ogle, and the city was appointed the general rendezvous of the army then forming in the west for the re-establishment of the king's authority. Fortifications were at that time constructed round it, and more especially on the east and west sides, where vestiges of the intrenchments are still discernible; but the vigilance and activity of Sir William Waller disconcerted the enterprize, and on the subsequent defeat of Lord Hopton's party on Cheriton Down, Waller obtained possession of the city without difficulty. The castle, notwithstanding, held out for the king; and on the retreat of the parliamentarians to join the forces of the Earl of Essex, who was then laying siege to Oxford, the city also fell into the hands of the royalists. After the battle of Naseby, Cromwell was sent with an army to reduce Winchester, which, after being repeatedly summoned, refused to surrender, and the siege was immediately commenced. The garrison made a resolute defence, but after a week's resistance capitulated on honourable terms; the castle was immediately dismantled, and the works blown up; the fortifications were demolished, together with the Bishop's castle of Wolvesey, and several churches and public buildings. The wanton violence of the parliamentary troops was manifested in defacing the cathedral, destroying its monuments, violating the tombs, and the indiscriminate insult offered to the relics of the illustrious dead, whose bones were scattered about the church; the statues of James and Charles, at the entrance of the choir, were thrown down, and the communion plate and other valuables belonging to the church were carried away. After the restoration of Charles II.,

that monarch chose Winchester for his residence during the intervals of his absence from London, and purchased the remains of the ancient castle; on the site, and with the materials, of which he began to erect an extensive and magnificent palace. The example of the king was followed by many of his nobility, who also began to build splendid mansions, and Winchester once more exhibited signs of retrieving its distinction; but the death of the king, before the completion of these works, put an end to those flattering prospects. The palace, upon which considerable sums had been expended, was left unfinished; and after having been at various times used as a place of confinement for prisoners of war, and for various other purposes, was ultimately converted into barracks for the military. On the defeat of the duke of Monmouth, in the reign of James II., Alice Lisle, widow of John Lisle, Esq., member for the city during the parliamentary war, and one of the judges who passed sentence of condemnation upon Charles I., was brought to trial in this city before the notorious Judge Jeffreys, on a charge of harbouring and concealing parties who were concerned in that rebellion: of this charge, though in opposition to the assertions of the jury that they were not satisfied with the evidence, she was pronounced guilty, and condemned to be burnt, which sentence being changed into decapitation, it was accordingly carried into execution in 1685. Queen Anne, after her accession to the throne, paid a visit to the city, accompanied by Prince George of Denmark, on whom the royal palace of Charles II. had been settled at the time of his marriage, in the event of his surviving the queen, his consort.

The city is pleasantly situated on the eastern acclivity of an eminence rising gradually from the river Itchen, which is navigable to Southampton, and consists of one spacious regular street passing through the centre, and intersected at right angles by several smaller streets, which extend in a parallel direction for about half a mile through the breadth of the city, which is nearly the same as its length: extensive hills, or downs, encircle it on the east and west. The principal parts of the city are within the limits of the ancient walls, which were of flint, strongly cemented with mortar, and defended by turrets at short intervals. The chief entrances from the suburbs were through four ancient gates, of which only the West gate is remaining, which, though it has undergone considerable alteration, still retains much of its ancient character: the other gates were removed by the commissioners appointed in 1770, by act of parliament, for the general improvement of the town. Over the river is a handsome stone bridge, and several smaller branches of the Itchen intersect the town in various places, of which two pass under the High-street. At a small distance beyond the West gate an obelisk has been erected, on the spot where the people of the neighbouring country used to deposit their provisions, for the supply of the city during the time of the plague, the inhabitants leaving the stipulated sum for payment, to prevent any communication of the contagion. In the centre of the High-street is the city cross, forty-three feet high, an elegant pyramidal structure in the later style of English architecture, consisting of three successive stages, richly ornamented with open arches, canopied niches, and crocketed pinnacles, erected by the fraternity of the Holy Cross, instituted by Henry VI. In one of the niches of the second stage is a figure, supposed by some to be that of St. John the Evangelist, but, more probably, by others to be that of St. Lawrence, to whom the church near the spot is dedicated: this beautiful relic owes its preservation to the spirited conduct of the inhabitants, who by force resisted an attempt, on the part of the commissioners of the pavements, to take it down, and drove away the workmen employed for that purpose. The houses are in general substantial and well built, and many of them possess an appearance of great antiquity: the city is indifferently paved, and but partially lighted with oil; but it is amply supplied with water of excellent quality. A public subscription library has been established in High-street, within the last few years, which is supported by one hundred proprietary members, whose shares are five guineas, and annual subscription one guinea and a half, and by annual subscribers of two guineas each. The theatre, in Gaol-street, a neat building handsomely fitted up, is occasionally opened by the Southampton company of comedians, but is very indifferently supported. A triennial musical festival was formerly celebrated in September, for three days, during which oratorios and selections of sacred music were performed in the cathedral; but Dr. Rennell, the present dean, having objected to the use of this sacred edifice for such a purpose, it has for many years been discontinued. Miscellaneous concerts and balls are held in St. John's rooms, in which also the general winter assemblies and subscription concerts usually take place. Hot, cold, vapour, and shower baths have been erected in High-street, for the use of the inhabitants. Races are held annually in July, when the king's plate of one hundred guineas and other stakes are run for, on Worthy down, about four miles from the city, on the road to Oxford. On the site of the ancient castle is the unfinished palace of Charles II., now called the King's House, which, had it been completed according to the original design, would have been one of the most spacious and magnificent palaces in Europe: the front is three hundred and twenty-eight feet in length, and the principal story contained a splendid suite of state apartments: this building has been converted into an extensive and handsome range of barracks for the district, capable of containing two thousand men, with spacious grounds for exercise.

The trade of Winchester is very unimportant; it was formerly considerable for the manufacture of woollen caps, but at present there is only an extensive manufactory for sacking, and a very little business is done in wool-combing: the spinning of silk was introduced here a few years since, but the undertaking totally failed. A canal to Woodmill, about two miles above the Itchen Ferry, near Southampton, supplies the town with coal and the heavier articles of merchandise. The market days are Wednesday and Saturday, the latter for corn: the market-house, erected in 1772, is a handsome and commodious building, in every respect adapted to its use. The fairs are on the first Monday in Lent, August 2nd, September 12th, and October 24th, for horses and pedlary; the first and last are held in the city, and the two others on the hills immediately adjoining; the September fair, which is held on St. Giles' hill, is a very large cheese fair.

Corporate Seal.

Winchester received its first regular charter of incorporation from Henry II., in 1184, twenty-two years before London was incorporated; and among other privileges conferred by that monarch, was the superintendence of the kitchen and laundry of the kings, at the ceremony of their coronation. By this charter, which, after having been confirmed and extended by succeeding sovereigns, was remodelled by Queen Elizabeth, the government is vested in a mayor, recorder, two bailiffs, six aldermen, and twenty-four common councilmen, assisted by a town clerk, two coroners, four serjeants at mace, and subordinate officers. The mayor is chosen, annually in September, from three persons nominated by the aldermen and those who have previously served the office, of which number one is struck off the list by the mayor for the time being, and from the other two his successor is appointed by the corporation at large, who also elect the bailiffs. Four constables, four serjeants at mace, and two coroners, are chosen by the common council, on the first Saturday in December. The mayor, recorder, and the six aldermen, are justices of the peace within the city and liberties, and hold quarterly courts of session for all offences not capital; also a court of record, on Wednesdays and Fridays, for the recovery of debts to any extent. The Cheyney court, so called from its having been anciently held under an oak (chêne being the French word for oak), which makes its origin revert to the time of the Druids, is an ancient court of the Bishops of Winchester, for the determining of actions, and the recovery of debts to any amount: its jurisdiction extends over all places which ever belonged to the see of Winchester, or the convent of St. Swithin, including one hundred parishes, tythings, and hamlets, in the county of Southampton, some of which are thirty miles distant from the city: this court is held in the Cathedral Close weekly; the jury is selected from the liberty, or soke, of Winchester, and the judge is appointed by the bishop. The town hall, a handsome structure in the Grecian style of architecture, and of the Doric order, was rebuilt in 1713, on the site of a more ancient hall, which was erected on the foundation of a former, burnt down in 1112: in it are preserved the public records of the city, the original Winchester bushel, made by order of King Edgar, the standard yard of Henry, and the standard measures of succeeding sovereigns, with various other remains of antiquity: its front is decorated with a well-executed statue in bronze of Queen Anne, which was presented to the corporation by George Brydges, Esq., who represented the city in seven successive parliaments. The common gaol and bridewell is in High-street, an inconvenient building, not adapted to classification, and capable of receiving only twenty prisoners.

The city first exercised the elective franchise in the 23rd of Edward I., since which time it has regularly returned two members to parliament: the right of election is vested in the members of the corporation, who, by the privilege of electing freemen, may add to

3 S 2

their number, which having been augmented by the appointment of additional residents, now amounts to above one hundred, of whom the majority are nonresident: the mayor is the returning officer. The prevailing interest is that of the Duchess of Buckingham and Lady Mildmay. The assizes and general quarter sessions for the county, and the election of knights of the shire, are held at Winchester, as the county town. The several courts are held in the chapel of the old castle, which has been converted into a county hall, and appropriately fitted up for that purpose: it is one hundred and ten feet in length. At the east end is suspended the celebrated round table, attributed to the renowned King Arthur, but which, with greater probability, is said to have been introduced by King Stephen, with a view to prevent disputes for precedence: it is made of oaken planks, and is eighteen feet in diameter, and a figure of King Arthur, and the names of his knights, as collected from the romances of the times, are painted on it, in the costume and characters of the time of Henry VIII.; in several parts it is perforated by bullets, probably by Cromwell's soldiers, while in possession of the city. An extensive common gaol for the county was erected in Gaol-street, in 1788, upon the principle recommended by the philanthropist Howard: it comprises two yards for debtors, two dayrooms on the side for poor debtors, and one day-room on the master's side, five yards and five day-rooms for male felons, and two yards and two day-rooms for females: the prisoners not condemned to hard labour are employed in useful occupations, and receive a portion of their earnings on their discharge: there are four separate infirmaries, a chapel, and other requisite offices. The county bridewell, in Hyde-street, was erected in 1786, and is a spacious structure, containing fourteen wards, six work-rooms, fourteen day-rooms, and eighteen airing-yards, in some of which are tread-wheels and capstans: the prisoners here are also employed in useful labour, and receive one-fourth of their earnings on being discharged: the building, which is well adapted to the classification of the prisoners, comprises an infirmary, and a chapel, in which divine service is performed twice on the Sunday, and morning prayer daily.

Winchester is the seat of a diocese, the jurisdiction of which extends over the counties of Southampton and Surrey: its origin may be traced to the early part of the seventh century, when Cynegils, the first Christian king of the West Saxons, having been converted by St. Birinus, resolved to make his capital the seat of a bishoprick, and began to collect materials for building a cathedral, which was afterwards accomplished by his son Cenwahl, in 646. The establishment having been dispersed by the Danes, in 867, Secular priests were substituted the year following, who remained till 963, when Ethelwold, by command of King Edgar, expelled them, and supplied their place with monks of the Benedictine order from Abendon: these kept possession of it without molestation, and it continued to flourish, en-

Arms of the Bishoprick.

riched with royal donations and ample endowments, till the dissolution, at which time its revenue amounted to £1507. 17. 2. It was afterwards refounded by Henry VIII., for a bishop, dean, chancellor, twelve prebendaries, two archdeacons, six minor canons, ten lay clerks, eight choristers, and other officers. The cathedral, situated in an open space near the centre of the city, towards the south-east, originally dedicated to St. Peter, St. Paul, and St. Swithin, was, upon the establishment of the present society by Henry VIII., dedicated to the Holy and Undivided Trinity. It is a spacious, massive, and splendid cruciform structure, chiefly in the Norman style of architecture, with a low tower rising from the centre, richly ornamented in its upper stages. The original building, as erected by Bishop Walkelyn, in 1079, was one of the most splendid and magnificent specimens of the Norman style in the kingdom: it was subsequently enlarged by Bishop Edington, and a considerable part was rebuilt by the celebrated William of Wykeham, who, adopting the later style of English architecture, which prevailed in his time, endeavoured to make the original style conform to that model. By this means the character of the architecture has been materially changed, though, from its extent and the loftiness of its proportions, it retains, notwithstanding the discrepancy of some parts, an air of stately grandeur, and displays many features of great beauty. The principal parts of the original structure are the transepts, in which the chief alteration is the insertion of windows in the later style; and the tower, which preserves its original character. The west front is an elegant composition, in the later style of English architecture, comprising three highly enriched porches of beautiful design. Some part of the eastern portion is in the finest character of the early English style, with occasional insertions of later date, particularly the clerestory windows of the choir; and in other parts of the building are various specimens of the early English at different periods, all remarkable for the excellence of their details. In some few instances are found small portions of the decorated, merging into the later English, of which, in various parts of the building, there are progressive series, from its commencement to the period of its utmost perfection. The interior, from the amplitude of its dimensions, and the loftiness of its elevation, is strikingly impressive: the nave, which is three hundred and fifty-one feet in length, is separated from the aisles by a long range of massive circular columns, twelve feet in diameter, and of proportionate height, which, in order to make them assimilate with the pointed arches that have been introduced within the circular Norman arches, have been cased with clustered pillars, and embellished with appropriate ornaments. In some of the intervals between the columns, which are two diameters in width, are various chantry and sepulchral chapels: the roof is elaborately groined, and richly ornamented with delicate tracery, embellished with the armorial bearings and devices of John of Gaunt, Cardinal Beaufort, and Bishops Waynfleet and Wykeham, which are continued along the facia, under the arches of the triforium. The transepts, which together are one hundred and eighty-six feet in length, are in the original Norman style of architecture: the central part is divided from the aisles by massive circular columns and arches, rising in successive series and with varied ornaments to the roof. In the transepts are various chapels and altars of exquisite design; the west aisle of the south transept has been partitioned off for a chapter-house, and at the extremity of the north transept is a beautiful Catherine-wheel window. At the eastern extremity of the nave, a flight of steps leads into the choir, through a beautiful screen erected from a modern design within the last few years: in niches on each side of the entrance are old bronze statues of James I. and Charles I.

The choir, which includes the lower stage of the central tower, is one hundred and thirty-six feet in length, and in the early English style, with some insertions: the original roof of the tower is concealed by an embellished ceiling, in the centre of which is an emblematical representation of the Trinity, with an inscription. The vaulting is supported by ribs springing from four busts of James I. and Charles I., in alternate succession, dressed in the costume of their times, above each of which is a motto, and, among various other ornaments, are the initials and devices of Charles I. and his queen, Henrietta Maria, with their profiles in medallions. The roof of the choir, from the tower to the east end, is richly groined, and embellished with a profusion of armorial bearings, devices, and other ornaments exquisitely carved, and richly painted and gilt; among them are the armorial bearings of the houses of Tudor and Lancaster, and those of the sees of Exeter, Bath and Wells, Durham, and Winchester, over which Bishop Fox, who superintended this work, successively presided. From the altar to the east window, the embellishments are emblematical of Scripture history; and among them are the instruments of the Crucifixion, and the faces of Pilate and his wife, and of the high priest and others; the whole of which embellishments have been judiciously renewed during the recent repairs of the edifice. The choir, which is in the early style of English architecture, is lighted by a handsome range of clerestory windows in the later style; the bishop's throne, prebendal stalls, and pulpit, are excellent specimens of tabernacle-work of appropriate character; the altar, in front of which is a beautiful tesselated pavement, is embellished with a painting, West, of Christ raising Lazarus from the dead. Behind the altar, and separating it from the Lady chapel, is a finely-carved stone screen of beautiful design, elaborately enriched with canopied niches and other appropriate ornaments; the statues, which formerly filled the niches now vacant, were destroyed by Cromwell's soldiers. On each side of the altar are partitions of stone, separating the presbytery from the aisles, which are divided into compartments, and richly ornamented with arches, and with shields of armorial bearings and other devices: above the several compartments are placed six mortuary chests, richly carved and gilt, and surmounted by crowns, containing the bones of several of the Saxon kings and prelates, which were collected and deposited in them by Bishop Fox. The east window is of excellent proportion and design, and is embellished with remains of ancient stained glass of rich hue: the subjects are chiefly the Apostles and Prophets, and some of the bishops of the see, with appropriate symbols and legends: many of the figures were mutilated by the soldiery, when they defaced the cathedral, at which time also the painted glass generally was destroyed;

the fragments that remain bear ample testimony to their original merit. In the south aisle of the choir is the sumptuous chapel, or chantry, of Bishop Fox, which, for its richness and minutely elaborate ornaments, is perhaps unequalled, either in the multiplicity of its parts, or in the fidelity of its details: in a niche under one of the arches is a recumbent figure of the founder, wrapped in a winding sheet, with the feet resting on a scull; the roof is finely groined, and embellished with the royal arms of the house of Tudor, richly emblazoned, and with the armorial bearings of the bishop, and the pelican, his favourite device. In the north aisle of the choir is the sepulchral chapel of Bishop Gardiner, an unsightly mixture of the later English and Grecian styles of architecture, and in a greatly dilapidated state. Behind the altar is a chapel, in which was kept the magnificent shrine of St. Swithin, the costly gift of King Edgar, said to have been of silver, richly gilt, and profusely ornamented with jewels. The Lady chapel, fifty-four feet in length, and on each side of which is a smaller chapel, terminates the eastern extremity of the cathedral: it was built by Bishop de Lucy, and enlarged and beautified by Priors Hunton and Silkstede, whose initials and devices are worked into the groinings of the roof; the portrait of the latter, with his insignia of office, are still visible over the piscina, and on the walls are traces of paintings in fresco, representing subjects of scriptural, profane, and legendary history, now in a very imperfect state. The marriage of Queen Mary with Philip of Spain was solemnized in this chapel.

The magnificent chantry of Cardinal Beaufort, of Purbeck marble, is a highly-finished structure in the later style of English architecture, and abounds with architectural beauty of the highest order, and with embellishments of the richest character; the roof, which is delicately groined, and enriched with fan tracery of elegant design, is supported on slender clustered columns of graceful proportion. It contains the tomb of the founder, on which is his effigy in a recumbent posture, in his robes as cardinal; around the cornice was an inscription in brass, which has been torn away by violence; and at the upper end of the chantry, enclosing the altar, are some beautiful canopied niches, crowned with crocketed pinnacles, from which the statues were taken by the parliamentarian soldiers. Bishop Waynfleet's chantry is in the same style, and of equal beauty with that of Cardinal Beaufort's, and, from the attention paid to it by the trustees of his foundation at Magdalene College, is kept in good repair: it contains the tomb of the bishop, on which is his effigy in his pontificals, in the attitude of prayer. There are various other chapels in this spacious and extensive pile, among which are, that of Bishop Langton, containing some fine carvings in oak, his tomb stripped of all its ornaments; and that of Bishop Orleton, of whom no memorial is preserved in the chapel; the roof is vaulted, and profusely ornamented with the figures of angels: on the north side is the tomb of Bishop Mews, a distinguished adherent to the cause of Charles I., who, after having served as officer in the royal army, entered into holy orders, and was promoted to the see of Winchester: in this chapel is also a monument to the memory of Richard Weston, Earl of Portland, and lord high treasurer in the reign of Charles I. Underneath the high altar, and formerly accessible by a stone staircase leading from that part of the cathedral called the " Holy Hole", as being the depository of the remains of saints, are vestiges of the ancient Norman crypt, built by Ethelwold; the walls, pillars, and groining are in their original state, and remarkable for the boldness and simplicity of their style : a new crypt, in the later style, has been built underneath the eastern end of the Lady chapel. Among the monuments, in addition to those in the sepulchral chapels, is the tomb of William Rufus, in the centre of the choir, of grey marble, raised about two feet above the surface of the pavement; his bones had been removed into one of the mortuary chests prior to the parliamentary war, during which the tomb was re-opened, and among the remaining ashes were found a large gold ring, a small silver chalice, and some pieces of cloth embroidered with gold : there are also the tombs of Hardicanute; Earl Beorn, son of Ertrith, sister of Canute; Richard, second son of William the Conqueror; Bishops Peter de Rupibus, Henry de Blois, Hoadly, Willis, and other distinguished prelates; Sir John Clobery, who assisted General Monk in planning the restoration of Charles II.; Sir Isaac Townsend, knight of the garter; the Earl of Banbury; Dr. Joseph Warton; Izaak Walton, and numerous other illustrious and distinguished persons. The ancient font, of black marble, supported on pillars of the same material, is of square form, and has the faces rudely sculptured with designs emblematical of the diffusion of the Holy Spirit, and with subjects from the legendary history of St. Nicholas ; it is supposed to be of the time of Bishop Walkelyn. The whole length of this magnificent cathedral is five hundred and forty-five feet, from east to west, and the breadth along the transepts one hundred and eighty-six; the mean breadth of the nave is eighty-seven, and that of the choir forty; the height of the tower is one hundred and forty feet, and its sides are fifty feet broad. The great cloisters, which enclosed a quadrangular area one hundred and eighty feet in length, and one hundred and seventy-four in breadth, were destroyed in the reign of Queen Elizabeth. On the east side of the quadrangle is a dark passage, ninety feet in length, which led to the infirmary and other offices belonging to the ancient monastery ; and to the south of it is a doorway, that formerly led to the chapter-house, the site of which, ninety feet square, is now occupied by the Dean's garden, in the walls of which are some of the pillars and arches still remaining. The refectory, forty-one feet in length, twenty-three broad, and forty feet high, is now divided into two stories ; under it two kitchens, the roofs of which are vaulted in the Norman style, and supported on a single central column, are still remaining. The Prior's hall and some other apartments now form the deanery, and other remains of the conventual buildings may be traced in the gardens of the prebendal houses, which occupy what is termed the Cathedral Close, an extra-parochial district.

Winchester comprises the parishes of St. Bartholomew, which is partly in the Soke liberty ; St. Lawrence, the mother church; St. Mary Kalendar; St. Maurice; St. Peter Colebrook ; and St. Thomas, within the city : and the parishes of St. Faith, St. John, St. Michael, St. Peter Cheesehill, St. Martin Winnal, and St. Swithin, within the liberty of the Soke, all in the

archdeaconry and diocese of Winchester. The living of St. Bartholomew's is a discharged vicarage, rated in the king's books at £10, endowed with £600 private benefaction, and £600 royal bounty, and in the patronage of the Crown : the church, in Hyde-street, which is well adapted to the accommodation of all the parishioners, is not entitled to particular architectural notice. The living of St. Lawrence's is a discharged rectory, rated in the king's books at £6. 5., endowed with £500 private benefaction, and £600 royal bounty, and in the patronage of the Crown : the church, situated in the square, is an ancient structure with a lofty square tower, and consists only of one large aisle, into which, on taking possession of his see, the bishop makes a solemn entry. The living of St. Mary Kalendar's is a rectory, united to that of St. Maurice, rated in the king's books at £7 : the church has been destroyed. The living of St. Maurice's is a rectory, to which those of St. Mary Kalendar, St. Peter Colebrook, St. George and St. Mary Wood, are united, rated in the king's books at £6. 7. 6., endowed with £200 parliamentary grant, and in the patronage of the Bishop : the church, in High-street, which was formerly the chapel of an ancient priory, is a venerable edifice with a low massive tower, and consists of a nave and two aisles, one of which is very spacious. The living of St. Peter's Colebrook is a rectory, united to that of St. Maurice, rated in the king's books at £3. 4. 2., and endowed with £200 royal bounty: the church has been destroyed, as also have those of St. George and St. Mary Wood, but the livings are still rated in the king's books, the former at £3. 5. 8., and the latter at £2. The living of St. Thomas' is a discharged rectory, with that of St. Clement, rated in the king's books at £13. 17. 8½., endowed with £300 private benefaction, £200 royal bounty, and £200 parliamentary grant, and in the patronage of the Bishop : the church is an ancient structure in the Norman style of architecture, with a low tower ; the interior consists of a nave and one aisle, separated by massive circular columns : the church of St. Clement's has been demolished. The living of St. Faith's is a sinecure rectory, annexed to the mastership of St. Cross. The hospital of St. Cross is extra-parochial, in the chapel of which the parishioners attend divine service, the church of St. Faith having been demolished for more than two centuries. The living of St. John's is a discharged rectory, with that of St. Peter's Southgate united, endowed with £300 private benefaction, £400 royal bounty, and £800 parliamentary grant, and in the patronage of the Crown : the church is an ancient structure in the Norman style of architecture, with a massive tower and turret : the interior consists of a nave and two aisles, separated by massive circular columns : the church of St. Peter's Southgate has been destroyed. The living of St. Michael's is a discharged rectory, rated in the king's books at £5. 17. 11., endowed with £1000 private benefaction, and £800 royal bounty, and in the patronage of the Bishop : the church, which, with the exception of the ancient tower, has been rebuilt, is a handsome edifice in the later style of English architecture, and consists of a spacious nave and chancel. The living of St. Peter's Cheesehill is a discharged rectory, rated in the king's books at £14. 9. 9½., endowed with £600 private benefaction, £400 royal bounty, and

£600 parliamentary grant, and in the patronage of the Crown: the church is a neat plain structure with a tower. The living of *St. Swithin's* is a discharged rectory, rated in the king's books at £6. 6. 10½., endowed with £200 private benefaction, £800 royal bounty, and £200 parliamentary grant, and in the patronage of the Crown: the church is over a postern called King's Gate, which is ascended by a staircase of stone, and formerly used as the church for the servants employed in the great priory of St. Swithin. The living of *St. Martin's Winnal* is a rectory, rated in the king's books at £5, and in the peculiar jurisdiction and patronage of the Rector: the church was rebuilt in 1786, and consists of one aisle and a small tower. There are places of worship for Baptists, Independents, Wesleyan Methodists, and Roman Catholics : that belonging to the last, which is dedicated to St. Peter, is an elegant edifice in the later style of English architecture, erected in 1792, in St. Peter-street, from a design by Mr. Carter: the exterior is richly ornamented with canopies supported on corbels of antique heads of sovereigns and bishops, which crown the lofty windows of elegant tracery, and a frieze embellished with devices illustrative of the history of Winchester, surmounted by a parapet pierced in quatrefoils, and enriched with crocketed pinnacles rising from panelled buttresses, and terminating with crosses richly gilt : the interior is splendidly decorated ; the windows of ground glass are painted in quatrefoil, and embellished with paintings of the principal saints and kings connected with the city, and on the north side, in which there are no windows, are corresponding panels painted in chiaro oscuro, with subjects from Scripture history: the altar-piece is ornamented with a good painting of the Transfiguration, by Mr. Cave, sen., from the original by Raphael. At the entrance of the walk leading to the chapel is an ancient Norman portal, which was removed from the church of St. Mary Magdalene's hospital. Nearly opposite is the convent, a large and handsome brick edifice, called the Bishop's House, consisting of Benedictine nuns removed from Brussels.

Winchester college holds a pre-eminent rank among the public literary institutions of the kingdom, and from a very early period has been distinguished as a seat of preparatory instruction. A grammar school had been established prior to the commencement of the twelfth century, on the site of which, in 1387, Bishop Wykeham, who received his early education in it, erected the present magnificent college, which he amply endowed for a warden, ten Secular priests, who are perpetual fellows, three priests' chaplains, three clerks, sixteen choristers, a first and second master, and seventy scholars, intending it as a preparatory seminary for his foundation of New College, Oxford, which he had completed the year before. For the government of the college, the bishop drew up a code of statutes, which, from their judicious adaptation to the purposes of the institution, were adopted by Henry VI., for the regulation of the establishments founded by that monarch at Eton and Cambridge. Under the influence of those salutary regulations, the college continued to flourish till the time of the dissolution, when its revenue amounted to £639. 8. 7.; but its reputation was held in such estimation, that it obtained a special exemption from the operation of that general measure. The buildings, which were completed in 1393, occupy two spacious

quadrangles, the entrance into the outermost of which is through a noble turreted gateway, under a finely-pointed arch, surmounted by a canopy resting on the bust of a king on the one side, and of a bishop on the other, probably representing the founder and his royal patron. In the groining underneath the tower are the arms of the founder, and on the face of it, over the entrance, is a canopied niche, in which is a crowned statue of the Virgin, holding in its right hand a sceptre, and on the left arm a figure of the infant Jesus. On the opposite side of this quadrangle is a gateway leading into the second court, above which is a tower ornamented in front with three beautiful niches, enriched with canopies and crocketed pinnacles ; in the central niche is a statue of the Virgin, with a book in the left hand, the right raised towards a figure of the angel Gabriel, which occupies the niche on that side, and in the niche on the left hand is the statue of the founder, in his episcopal robes, crowned with a mitre. The buildings surrounding the inner quadrangle are principally in the later style of English architecture, of which they exhibit an elegant specimen : the grand hall and the chapel occupy the south side ; the former is sixty-three feet in length, thirty-three wide, and of proportionate height, and lighted by a handsome range of well-proportioned windows enriched with elegant tracery ; the roof, which is of timber, is finely arched, and the beams, which are handsomely ornamented, are supported by ribs springing from corbels decorated with coloured busts of kings and bishops : this noble room is ascended by a flight of steps at the south-west angle of the quadrangle, and at the western extremity, under an enriched canopy, is a figure of St. Michael piercing the dragon. In the centre of this side is the stately tower of the chapel, surmounted with turrets, and crowned with pinnacles, the work of a later period than the building by Wykeham, and said to have been erected by the Warden Thurbern. The entrance into the chapel is by a vestibule, the ceiling of which is elaborately enriched, and in which are placed the ancient stalls, removed from the chapel, in 1681, by Dr. Nicholas, and some ancient brasses. The interior is beautifully arranged ; the roof is finely groined ; the windows, which are enriched with elegant tracery, ornamented with paintings of kings, saints, prelates, and nuns ; and in the great east window is a representation of the Genealogy of Christ, the Crucifixion, and the Resurrection ; the altar is embellished with a painting of the Salutation, by De Moine, presented to the College by the late head-master, Dr. Burton. Between the stairs leading to the hall and the entrance to the chapel is a passage conducting to the school and play-ground. The school-room, a plain brick building erected in 1687, at an expense of £2600, is ninety feet in length, and thirty-six feet in breadth ; over the entrance is a statue of Bishop Wykeham, finely executed in bronze, and presented to the College by Mr. C. G. Cibber, which has been injudiciously painted and gilt, and at the other extremity of the school-room are the statutes for the government of the students, written in Latin. To the south of the chapel are the cloisters, enclosing a quadrangular area one hundred and thirty-two feet square, and apparently of the date of the fifteenth century : they contain many ancient brasses, and in the centre of the enclosed area is a chantry chapel, erected by Mr. John Fromond, a liberal benefactor to the foundations of Bishop Wykeham. This building, the ceiling of which is strongly vaulted, is now appropriated as the college library, and contains a select and valuable collection of works, and a small museum of natural curiosities. The other sides of the quadrangle are composed of the houses and apartments of the warden, fellows, the head and second masters, and other members of the establishment; and contiguous to the college is a spacious quadrangular building, for the residence of gentlemen commoners not on the foundation, of whom the number is very considerable: the college, chapel, and school, were completely repaired in 1795. An annual visitation is held, in July, by the warden and two of the fellows of New College, Oxford, at which there is an examination of the candidates for the vacant fellowships in that college, which, by the will of the founder, are to be supplied from this establishment, and of which there are, on an average, three in the year. At that time also is held, by the same persons, with the addition of the warden, subwarden, and headmaster, an election of boys for admission on the foundation of Winchester college: the qualification for candidates by the statutes is, that they must be "*pauperes et indigentes scholares;*" boys are not eligible till above eight years of age. There are several scholarships and exhibitions for such as fail in obtaining fellowships in New College; and there is also a superannuated fund belonging to the establishment, founded by Dr. Cobden, Archdeacon of London, in 1784. The bishop of the diocese is visitor of the college; and one of the fellows is annually elected to the office of subwarden, and another to that of bursar. In this noble institution, which maintains undiminished the distinguished reputation it has enjoyed from its foundation, many eminent prelates and literary characters have received their early education: among these were, Sir Thomas Brown, Sir Thomas Wooton, Sir Thomas Ryves; the poets Otway, Philips, Young, Somerville, Pit, Collins, Warton, and Hayley; and others distinguished for their genius and literary acquirements.

Christ's hospital was founded, in 1586, by Peter Symonds, Esq., who endowed it with lands producing more than £420 per annum, for the support of six unmarried men above fifty years of age, who reside in the hospital, and are supplied with clothing and food; and for the clothing, maintenance, and education of four poor boys, from seven till fourteen years of age. There are two exhibitions, of £10 per annum each, tenable for four years, to Oxford and Cambridge, and with such as do not obtain them an apprentice fee of £30 is given, on their leaving the hospital: the corporation, as trustees, appoint the schoolmaster, and elect the inmates and scholars. A charity school for clothing, instructing, and apprenticing fifty boys, and a similar establishment for thirty girls, are supported by subscription: there is a National school in Colebrook-street, for the education of children of both sexes; and there are Sunday schools in connexion with the established church and the several dissenting congregations.

The hospital of St. Cross, about a mile south of the city, and beautifully situated on the bank of the river Itchen, was founded in 1132, by Bishop Henry de Blois, brother of King Stephen, who endowed it for the residence and maintenance of a master, steward, four chaplains, thirteen clerks, seven choristers, and thirteen poor brethren, and for the daily entertainment of one hundred of the most indigent men of the city, who dined together in a common hall, called the "hundred mennes hall." Bishop Wykeham, on his appointment to the see of Winchester, in 1366, finding that the revenue of the hospital was misapplied, succeeded, after a tedious litigation, in re-establishing the institution according to the intention of the founder, and placed it on so secure a basis, that Henry de Beaufort, wishing to found some permanent charity, preferred an augmentation of the original endowment to the foundation of a new institution, and added two priests, increased the number of poor men to thirty-five, appointed three sisters to attend upon them when ill, and greatly enlarged the buildings. At the suppression of monasteries its revenue was valued at £184. 4. 2. : it was exempted from dissolution, but suffered materially during the war in the reign of Charles I. : the present establishment consists of a master, a chaplain, a steward, and thirteen brethren. The buildings occupied two quadrangular areas, but the south side of the inner quadrangle has been taken down. The entrance gateway, erected by Cardinal Beaufort, is a good specimen of the later style of English architecture, surmounted by a lofty tower, the front of which is ornamented with three handsome niches, one of them containing the figure of the Cardinal in a kneeling posture, and on the cornice above the arch are busts of John of Gaunt, Henry IV. and V., and of his predecessor, Bishop Wykeham, with other devices; and in the spandrils, on each side of the arch, are the arms of the founder. In the inner court is the church, or chapel, of St. Cross, in which the parishioners of St. Faith's attend divine service: it is an ancient and interesting cruciform structure, comprising a series of styles, passing, by gradual and almost imperceptible transitions, from the Norman to the early and decorated styles of English architecture. The low tower rising from the centre is in the Norman style: the nave is separated from the aisles by a range of pillars, of which some are of the massive circular character, and others clustered in the style of the early English, with pointed arches, which, towards the west end, merge into the decorated style: most of the arches of the chancel are pointed, and the windows generally towards the east end are Norman, with circular arches and zigzag ornaments: the groining of the roof towards the east is replete with ornaments of the Norman style; and that of the western part, which appears to have been the work of Cardinal Beaufort, is embellished with shields of the armorial bearings of the Cardinal, Bishop Wykeham, and of the College: the whole building, from the variety of its styles, and the facility with which they glide into each other, forms an interesting display of the progressive advances of ancient architecture. The west front is an elegant composition in the early English style, with appropriate embellishments; and the west window, of five lights, is richly ornamented with painted glass, representing the figures of various saints, and emblazoned with armorial devices; over the stalls in the choir are sculptured figures of the most conspicuous subjects of scripture history. Among the funeral monuments are, an ancient brass in memory of John de

Campden, the friend of Wykeham, and a modern mural tablet to Wolfran Cornwall, Esq., Speaker of the House of Commons. The living is a perpetual curacy, united to the rectory of St. Faith's, endowed with £200 private benefaction, and £200 royal bounty, and in the patronage of the Bishop of Winchester. The remaining buildings of the hospital comprise the apartments of the brethren, each of whom has three chambers for his own use, with a separate garden; the refectory; and the master's apartments, which are spacious and commodious. On the east side of the quadrangle, extending from the north transept of the church, is the ancient ambulatory, an open portico one hundred and thirty-five feet long, above which are the infirmary and the nuns' chambers, so called from their having been appropriated to the use of the three sisters placed on the foundation, by Cardinal Beaufort, to attend the brethren when unwell.

The county hospital, or infirmary, in Parchment-street, the first institution of the kind established in the kingdom, was founded in 1736, and is supported by subscription: it has afforded ample relief to numerous patients in the city and county, and is under excellent regulations, being conducted with a liberality which extends relief to every object of distress. The buildings, ascended by a fine flight of steps, comprise a centre and two wings, one having been recently added at the northern end, and are in every respect well adapted to the purposes of the institution. St. John's hospital, now called St. John's House, in High-street, is a very ancient establishment, said to have been founded in the year 933, by St. Brinstan, Bishop of Winchester, and to have become the property of the Knights Templars, upon the suppression of which order it was refounded, by permission of Edward II., for sick and lame soldiers, pilgrims, and necessitous wayfaring men, who had their lodging and other necessaries for one night, or longer, in proportion to their wants. It was placed under the superintendence of the corporation, who, at a very early period, appear to have used it as a public hall for the transaction of their business: after the dissolution, the site and remains having been given to that body, they have converted the great hall into a public room, in which meetings of the corporation, and public assemblies and concerts, are held. The hall, which is sixty-two feet long, thirty-eight broad, and twenty-eight high, is elegantly fitted up, chiefly by a donation of £800 from the late Colonel Bridges: it is embellished with a portrait of that gentleman, and a full-length portrait of Charles II., in his robes of state, painted by Sir Peter Lely, and presented to the corporation by that monarch: in an adjoining room, called the council-chamber, are the city tables, recording a brief chronological account of its principal historical events. The ancient chapel of this hospital is now used as a school-room, in which twenty-four boys are instructed by a master, who is paid £22 annually by the trustees of Mr. William Over, who, in 1701, bequeathed an estate for that purpose. In an inner court of the northern part of the hospital are the almshouses, founded in 1558, by Ralph Lamb, Esq., who endowed them for the support of six poor widows of the city, each of whom receives a weekly allowance, a supply of coal, and a gown every alternate year, with some other sums, which are periodically divided among them: the funds of this hospital have been greatly augmented by the recent successful issue of a suit in Chancery directed to their investigation. Near the cathedral are almshouses, founded in 1672, by Bishop Morley, for the residence and support of ten clergymen's widows. There are various funds for charitable uses at the disposal of the corporation, among which is Sir Thomas White's charity, for loans without interest to young tradesmen; also divers sums for distribution among the poor, and numerous other charitable bequests.

Among the ancient monastic institutions, in addition to those already described, was Hyde abbey, originally the new minster founded by Alfred the Great, adjoining the site of the present cathedral, which, by way of distinction, was thence called the Old Minster. The foundation, after the death of Alfred, was completed by his son, Edward the Confessor, and placed under the superintendence of St. Grimbald, who established a fraternity of canons regular, who were afterwards expelled by Bishop Ethelwold, and replaced by monks of the order of St. Benedict. Alwyn, the eighth abbot in succession from St. Grimbald, was uncle of Harold, and, with twelve of his monks, assisted that monarch at the battle of Hastings, in which he was slain with his brethren. In resentment of this, William the Conqueror treated the New Minster with the utmost rigour, seized upon its revenue, and would not allow a new abbot to be appointed. About three years after, he, however, permitted an abbot to be chosen, and restored some of the abbey lands, giving others in exchange for the remainder. The nuisances which had arisen, from the stagnation of a stream of water brought, in its immediate vicinity, to supply the fosse which had been dug round the castle erected by the Conqueror, and from its contiguity to the Old Minster, induced the fraternity to build a new abbey at a greater distance, and the present edifice was erected on a spot near the north wall of the city, called Hyde meadow, from which it took its name. Into this the remains of Alfred, his queen Alswitha, his sons Ethelred and Edward the Elder, Elfleda, Ethelhida, and King Edwy, were removed and re-interred. In the contest between Stephen and Matilda, the abbey was burnt to the ground by the fire balls thrown from Wolvesey castle, but was rebuilt, with greater magnificence, in the reign of Henry II., and the abbot was invested with the privilege of a seat in parliament. It continued to flourish till the dissolution, at which time its revenue was £865. 1. 6.: it was soon after demolished, and very small portions of the monastic buildings are at present remaining, among which are, the tower of St. Bartholomew's church, some of the offices, and part of a large barn, with one gateway containing a regal head in the groining of the arch. On the site of the abbey a new bridewell has been erected, in digging the foundations of which many stone coffins, chalices, patins, rings, busts, capitals of the ancient columns, and other fragments of sculpture, were found. Of these, the most interesting is a stone inscribed "Alfred Rex, 881," in Saxon characters, which is now in the possession of H. Howard, Esq., of Corby Castle in the county of Cumberland. The abbey of St. Mary was founded by Alswitha, wife of Alfred, and, after the king's death, was the place of her retirement. Edburga, daughter of Edward the Elder, became abbess of this convent, which, in the reign of Edgar, was amply endowed by Bishop Ethelwold, who prescribed for the observance of the nuns the more severe rules of the order of St. Benedict. Many Saxon ladies of royal and noble lineage were sisters in this establishment, in which Matilda, wife of Henry I., received her education. The original buildings were destroyed in the war during the reign of Stephen, and restored in the following reign by Henry II., who was a liberal benefactor. At the time of the dissolution, its revenue was £179. 7. 2.; it remained for a few years after that period, when its abbess and eight of the nuns received a small pension, and the rest of the inmates were dispossessed: the only visible remains are in a large modern mansion, which has been partly built with the materials of the abbey. In the meadow of St. Stephen, near the Bishop's palace of Wolvesey, was a college, founded in 1300, by Bishop Pontoys, which he dedicated to St. Elizabeth, a daughter of the King of Hungary, and endowed for a provost, six chaplains, priests, six clerks, and six choristers: its revenue at the dissolution was £112. 17. 4. A monastery, dedicated to St. James, was founded in the abbey churchyard by John, or Roger, Inkpenne, who, in 1318, endowed it for a warden and several priests. In the church of St. Maurice was the fraternity of St. Peter, and in that of St. Mary Kalendar, a college, the revenue of which was granted to the corporation, in the reign of Philip and Mary. The hospital of St. Mary Magdalene was founded in the reign of Edward I., and endowed for nine poor brothers and sisters; the patronage was in the Bishop of Winchester, but the founder is unknown; it continued till the dissolution, at which time its revenue was £42. 16. There were also convents of Augustine, Carmelite, Dominican, and Franciscan friars, the sites of which were, after the dissolution, granted to the college. Among the illustrious and eminent natives of this city were, Henry III.; Eleanor, youngest daughter of Edward I., who died in her infancy; and Prince Arthur, eldest son of Henry VIII., who died at Ludlow, and was buried in the cathedral church of Worcester. Winchester gives the title of marquis to the distinguished family of Paulet.

WINCHFIELD, a parish in the hundred of ODIHAM, Basingstoke division of the county of SOUTHAMPTON, 2½ miles (N. E.) from Odiham, containing 226 inhabitants. The living is a rectory, in the archdeaconry and diocese of Winchester, rated in the king's books at £8. 16. 10½., and in the patronage of the Rev. H. E. St. John. The church is dedicated to St. Mary. The Basingstoke canal runs through the parish.

WINCHMORE-HILL, a chapelry in the parish and hundred of EDMONTON, county of MIDDLESEX, 8 miles (N.) from London. The population is returned with the parish. The chapel, dedicated to St. Paul, and consecrated in 1828, was erected at an expense of about £5000, of which sum, £3843. 6. 3. was granted by the parliamentary commissioners, the remainder having been raised by subscription: it contains six hundred and fifty sittings, of which two hundred and eighty-six are free. There are places of worship for the Society of Friends, Independents, and Wesleyan Methodists. Dr. Fothergill, an eminent physician, and a member of the Society of Friends, was buried here.

WINCLE, a chapelry in the parish of PRESTBURY, hundred of MACCLESFIELD, county palatine of CHESTER, 5½ miles (S. E. by S.) from Macclesfield, contain-

ing 466 inhabitants. The living is a perpetual curacy, in the archdeaconry and diocese of Chester, endowed with £400 private benefaction, £600 royal bounty, and £1300 parliamentary grant, and in the patronage of the Vicar of Prestbury. The chapel was erected about 1642.

WINDER, a township in the parish of LAMPLUGH, ALLERDALE ward above Darwent, county of CUMBERLAND, 5¼ miles (E. by S.) from Whitehaven. The population is returned with the parish.

WINDER (LOW), a township in the parish of BARTON, WEST ward, county of WESTMORLAND, 5¼ miles (S. by W.) from Penrith, containing 19 inhabitants.

WINDERMERE, a parish in KENDAL ward, county of WESTMORLAND, 9 miles (W. N. W.) from Kendal, comprising the chapelry of Troutbeck, and the townships of Applethwaite and Undermilbeck, and containing, with the chapelry of Winster, which is in the parish of Kendal, but exclusively of a portion of the township of Ambleside, which is in this parish, 1441 inhabitants. The living is a rectory, in the archdeaconry of Richmond, and diocese of Chester, rated in the king's books at £24. 6. 8., and in the patronage of the Rev. Sir R. Fleming, Bart. The church, dedicated to St. Martin, stands in the village of Bowness. The east window, which is of stained glass, formerly belonged to Furness abbey, at the dissolution of which it was purchased by the parishioners and placed here. This parish derives its name from the beautiful lake, anciently called Wynandermere, which is twelve miles in length, by about one in breadth, and is in depth forty fathoms. It is studded with many picturesque islands, the principal of which, Bello, the property of Mr. Curwen, is richly wooded, and adorned with an elegant circular mansion. In the centre of another, bearing the name of the lake, stood Holme House, which was besieged for the parliament by Col. Briggs, who, on the siege of Carlisle being raised, was obliged to abandon it. On a smaller one, called Lady Holme, formerly stood a chapel, dedicated to the Virgin Mary. Great quantities of char, taken in this lake during the winter months, are potted and sent to different parts of the kingdom. On its margin are several good inns for the accommodation of visitors, at two of which, Low Wood and Ferry Inns, regattas are held annually about the beginning of September; these are attended by families of distinction, and terminate with balls, exhibitions of fireworks, &c. For a further account of this lake, see the article on the county of WESTMORLAND.

WINDFORD, a parish in the hundred of HARTCLIFFE with BEDMINSTER, county of SOMERSET, 6½ miles (S. W. by S.) from Bristol, containing 849 inhabitants. The living is a rectory, in the archdeaconry of Bath, and diocese of Bath and Wells, rated in the king's books at £21. 12. 11., and in the patronage of the Provost and Fellows of Worcester College, Oxford. The church is dedicated to St. Mary and St. Peter. Four poor children are instructed for £3 a year, the bequest of Alexander Goodwin, in 1780.

WINDLE, a township in the parish of PRESCOT, hundred of WEST DERBY, county palatine of LANCASTER, 1 mile (N.) from St. Helens, containing 4820 inhabitants.

WINDLESHAM, a parish in the first division of the hundred of WOKING, county of SURREY, 1 mile (E. by N.) from Bagshot, containing 1590 inhabitants. The living is a rectory, in the archdeaconry of Surrey, and diocese of Winchester, rated in the king's books at £10. 9. 7., and in the patronage of the Crown. The church is dedicated to St. John the Baptist. Hool Mill, in this parish, erected by an abbot of Chertsey, in the reign of Edward III., is subject to a permanent rent-charge of £8, in support of the poor.

WINDLESTON, a township in that part of the parish of ST. ANDREW, AUCKLAND, which is in the south-eastern division of DARLINGTON ward, county palatine of DURHAM, 4 miles (E. S. E.) from Bishop-Auckland, containing 173 inhabitants.

WINDLEY, a township in the parish of DUFFIELD, hundred of APPLETREE, county of DERBY, 6¾ miles (N. N. W.) from Derby, containing 199 inhabitants. It is in the honour of Tutbury, duchy of Lancaster, and within the jurisdiction of a court of pleas held at Tutbury every third Tuesday, for the recovery of debts under 40s.

WINDRIDGE, a ward in the parish of ST. STEPHEN, hundred of CASHIO, or liberty of ST. ALBANS, county of HERTFORD, 1¾ mile (W. S. W.) from St. Albans. The population is returned with the parish.

WINDRUSH, a parish in the lower division of the hundred of SLAUGHTER, county of GLOUCESTER, 5¼ miles (E.) from North Leach, containing 317 inhabitants. The living is a discharged vicarage, united to that of Sherborne, in the archdeaconry and diocese of Gloucester, rated in the king's books at £5, and in the patronage of Lord Sherborne. The church is dedicated to St. Peter.

Seal and Arms of the Borough.

WINDSOR (NEW), a borough, market town, and parish, having separate jurisdiction, locally in the hundred of Ripplesmere, county of BERKS, 20 miles (E. by N.) from Reading, and 22½ (W. by S.) from London, containing, with the castle and the lower ward, 4648 inhabitants. This place owes its origin to a more ancient town, about two miles distant, called by the Saxons, from the winding course of the river Thames, *Windleshora*, of which its present name, Windsor, is an abbreviation. The first authentic notice of that town, which had been the residence of the Saxon kings, occurs in an ancient charter of Edward the Confessor, granting it, with all its appendages, to the monks of Westminster, in whose possession it remained till the Conquest. William, soon after his establishment on the throne, struck with the beauty of its situation on the bank of the Thames, and the peculiar adaptation of the surrounding country to the pleasures of the chase, procured it from the monastery of Westminster, in exchange for some lands in the county of Essex, and made it his occasional residence while pursuing the diversion of hunting. On a hill in the neighbourhood, that monarch erected a fortress, where he held his court in 1070; and, two years afterwards, assembled there a synod of the no-

bility and prelates, in which the question of precedency between the sees of Canterbury and York was discussed, and decided in favour of the former. Around this fortress he laid out extensive parks, enlarged the boundaries of the neighbouring forest, and enacted severe laws for the preservation of the game. The palace of Old Windsor continued to be the royal residence of William and his successors till 1110, when Henry I., having partly rebuilt and considerably enlarged the fortress which his father had erected, by the addition of a suite of apartments, converted it into a palace, in which he occasionally resided and kept his court. From this time the importance of the ancient town began to decline, and, subsequently a new town arose in the immediate vicinity of the castle, which was distinguished by the appellation of New Windsor. In the treaty of peace between Stephen and Matilda, the castle is referred to by the name of " Mota de Windsor ;" and after the death of Stephen, Henry II. held a council here, in 1170. When Richard I. embarked on his expedition to the Holy Land, the castle became the residence of the Bishop of Durham, to whom, in conjunction with the Bishop of Ely, Richard had entrusted the administration of the government in his absence. During the contest between King John and the barons, that monarch resided in the castle, which was at that time considered the next strongest fortress after the Tower of London : it was ineffectually besieged by these lords, to whom, in the succeeding reign, it was ceded by treaty ; but, in the following year, it was surprised and taken by the king, who made Windsor the principal rendezvous of his forces. Henry III. erected a barbican, and strengthened the fortifications and outworks of the castle, which, during the baronial wars in that monarch's reign, was alternately taken and retaken by the contending parties, till Prince Edward finally obtained possession and held it for his father. On the succession of that prince to the throne, the castle was frequently the place of his residence, and four of his children were born at Windsor, which was likewise the favourite retreat of his queen Eleanor. Edward III., who was also born here, rebuilt the royal palace on a more extensive and magnificent scale, enlarged the castle with additional towers, erected the keep, and, near it, a tower of high elevation, named Winchester tower, after William of Wykeham, Bishop of Winchester, whom that monarch had made superintendent of his buildings. The same sovereign erected the collegiate chapel of St. George, in which he established a dean and twelve canons ; and the magnificent hall of St. George, as a banqueting house for the knights of the royal order of the garter, of which he was the founder ; and surrounded the whole with a strong wall and rampart, faced with stone, and encompassed with a moat. While this monarch occupied the throne, two sovereigns were prisoners in the castle at the same time, viz., John, King of France, and David, King of Scotland, the latter of whom he captured, after the reduction of that country. Edward IV. enlarged, and partly rebuilt, the collegiate chapel, the choir of which was vaulted by Henry VII., who also erected the lofty pile of building adjoining the state apartments in the upper ward. Henry VIII. added materially to the buildings by the erection of the prebendal houses and the gateway leading into the lower ward. Edward VI. and Queen Mary both made Windsor their residence; and, among other improvements, constructed a fountain in the centre of the upper quadrangle, from which the whole of the castle was supplied with water. Queen Elizabeth, after her accession to the throne, resided occasionally in the palace, to which she added some building adjoining the Norman gateway, and that part adjoining the buildings of Henry VII., which is called Queen Elizabeth's gallery, and raised the noble terrace on the north side of the castle, commanding a beautiful view of Eton College, and an extensive prospect over the vale of the Thames.

During the parliamentary war, the castle, which had received several additions in the reign of Charles I., was seized and garrisoned by the parliament, who, notwithstanding an attack of Prince Rupert, in 1642, to regain possession of it for the king, retained it in their hands till the conclusion of the war. After the Restoration, Charles II. repaired the injuries it had suffered, and greatly embellished the interior; and James II. and William III. ornamented the state apartments with a splendid collection of paintings. In almost every succeeding reign, this interesting structure continued to receive additional embellishment; and, in the reign of George III., the alterations and additions were conducted on a larger scale, and with a stricter regard to the restoration and preservation of the original character of the building, than in that of any of his predecessors since the time of Edward III. In the reign of George IV., the varied attractions of Windsor induced that monarch to make it his principal residence; and, under the influence of a correct and refined taste, which duly appreciated the merits and the beauty of the ancient style of English architecture, a design was formed for the enlargement and decoration of the castle, of which a considerable part was accomplished under his immediate superintendence. For carrying this design into effect, divers sums amounting to £771,000 have been granted by parliament for the buildings alone, and, among the various plans which had been submitted for that purpose, the design of Mr. Jeffrey Wyatt was, on the approbation of his Majesty, adopted by government. Under this plan, several parts of the old building, which had been injudiciously engrafted on the main edifice (and which, not only from their want of harmony with the general character, diminished the unity of its design, but, from their projection into the main avenue, destroyed the perspective and obstructed the approach), have been entirely removed; portions of freehold land within the park, belonging to private individuals, have been purchased, and made to conform, in their appearance, with the varied beauty of the grounds; the height of the buildings generally throughout the castle has been increased by an additional story; several new towers have been erected; windows of lofty dimensions and of elegant and appropriate design generally inserted; some splendid gateway entrances from the principal approaches formed in a style of commensurate grandeur; and other improvements are still in progress, which, when completed, will render this interesting structure, with its appendant gardens, parks, and pleasure grounds, preeminently adapted to the purposes of a royal residence.

The castle occupies more than twelve acres of ground, and comprises the upper, lower, and middle wards. The principal approach is from the Little, or Home, park,

through a lofty gateway, flanked on the one side by the York, and on the other by the Lancaster, tower, both stately and massive structures, one hundred feet high, crowned with projecting battlements supported on corbels. This gateway, which ranges in a line with the noble avenue of stately elms in the Great park, called the Long Walk, was erected by George IV., whose name it bears; the first stone was laid by that sovereign on the 12th of August, 1828, when His Majesty was pleased to change the name of the architect from Wyatt, to Wyatville, upon whom he subsequently conferred the honour of knighthood. It is a noble and stately structure, and forms an entrance of correspondent grandeur into the upper ward, a spacious quadrangle, to which also are entrances through St. George's gate at the south-west, leading from the town, and the ancient Norman gateway at the west, from the middle and lower wards. On the north side of this quadrangle are the state apartments, which are open to the inspection of the public; on the east His Majesty's private apartments; on the south side are apartments for His Majesty's visitors; and on the west, the round tower, or keep, to the front of which has been removed, from the centre of the quadrangle, an equestrian statue in bronze of Charles II., in the Roman costume, on a marble pedestal ornamented with sculpture. The entrance to the state apartments is by a tower of very imposing character, projecting into the quadrangle, and in a line with King George the Fourth's gateway, and the long avenue in the Great park. This entrance leads into the grand hall and staircase, constructed in the reign of George III., under the superintendence of the late Mr. James Wyatt. The approach to the state apartments is by a superb vestibule, forty-five feet long and twenty-eight feet broad, divided into three parts by ranges of finely-clustered columns and gracefully-pointed arches, in the most finished character of the later style of English architecture: the roof is elaborately groined, and decorated with fan-tracery of elegant design: in the walls are four larger and three smaller niches for the reception of statues, richly canopied, and highly embellished with architectural ornaments of beautiful character. The grand staircase, divided in the centre by a broad landing, is defended with a balustrade of bronze, with massive pedestals and capitals of polished brass, and lighted by an octagonal lantern, one hundred feet high from the pavement: the roof is delicately ornamented with fan-tracery depending from the centre, and ending with the royal arms encircled by the garter. At the termination of the grand staircase is the king's drawing-room; over the folding doors are the royal arms in artificial stone, and on each side are shields of arms of several of the British monarchs, supported by angels: the internal decorations of this splendid apartment are of the most superb character; the ceiling is beautifully painted in compartments, representing the Restoration of Charles II., the Labours of Hercules, and other subjects, and bordered with flowers and fruit, and ornaments richly gilt; the mirrors, chandeliers, and furniture, are in a corresponding style of elegance: a choice selection of paintings, by the first masters, is finely displayed, and the embellishments are disposed with the most refined taste, and the various arrangements are on a scale of the most splendid magnificence. The audience-chamber, of which the ceiling is painted with an allegorical representation of the re-establishment of the Church of England, is beautifully decorated with hangings of blue silk richly embroidered : the chair and canopy of state are superbly rich : the collection of paintings, chiefly historical, represent the victories of Edward III., painted by West; the first installation of the knights of the order of the garter, in which more than one hundred figures are finely grouped. The king's presence-chamber, and the whole suite of these magnificent state apartments, are in a style of correspondent grandeur, and equally remarkable for the stateliness of their proportions, and the elegance and splendour of their embellishment.

The new ball-room, a splendid apartment, ninety-six feet in length, thirty-two feet wide, and thirty-one feet high, is finished in the most elaborate style of Louis XIV.: the walls and ceiling are panelled in compartments, highly ornamented and richly gilt; in the larger panels of the former are some superb specimens of rich tapestry, most exquisitely worked, representing the history of Jason and the Golden fleece; the colours are singularly vivid, and at the same time so softened by the skilful combination of light and shade, as to have all the force and delicacy of the finest painting; and in the intermediate panels are six mirrors, of large dimensions and great brilliancy. A pair of elegant folding doors, panelled and ornamented to correspond with the walls, open into St. George's Hall, a spacious and lofty apartment, appropriated as a banquet-room for the knights of the order of the garter: it is nearly two hundred feet in length, and of proportionate width and elevation; the lofty arched ceiling is supported on beams, springing from corbels decorated with shields, on which are richly emblazoned the arms of the original knights, and divided into thirteen compartments, subdivided into panels of bold design, containing nearly seven hundred shields, emblazoned with the arms of the knights of the order up to the present time: at the east end, under a rich canopy, is the throne of His Majesty, who is the sovereign of the order, at the back of which are His Majesty's arms, and on each side are those of twelve preceding sovereigns, richly carved and emblazoned, and also those of Edward III. and the Black Prince: the mantel-piece is a massive and elegant piece of workmanship of Dove marble, richly sculptured in flowers and foliage, with the initials of George IV. In the plan for the general improvement of the castle, after the designs and under the superintendence of Sir Jeffrey Wyatville, R.A., which is now in progress, it is the intention of that eminent architect to remove the grand staircase, which at present occupies the south end of the vestibule, and to leave, by that means, an uninterrupted and magnificent hall, one hundred and forty feet in length, and forty feet wide, commanding, on the north, an extensive prospect over Eton, and, on the south, the long avenue, terminating with the pedestal, on which is to be placed a statue of George III. The new grand staircase will have an open communication with the grand hall below, and lead into an elegant vestibule above, communicating with the royal state apartments, St. George's Hall, the new guard chamber, which is nearly completed, and the Waterloo chamber, which is in a less advanced state. In the guard chamber will be deposited, on pedestals erected for the purpose, under richly canopied niches, suits of ancient armour, the coats of mail of John King of France, and David King of Scotland, with other military trophies, and on pedestals, busts of the Duke of Wellington and the Duke of Marlborough, and on a pedestal formed of the frustum of the mast of the Victory, the bust of Lord Nelson. In the Waterloo chamber, a magnificent apartment, one hundred feet in length, forty-six feet wide, and forty-five feet high, and lighted by a lantern, will be arranged the portraits of the various Sovereigns, Popes, Cardinals, Ministers of State, Ambassadors, Generals, and others connected with the prosecution of the war on the continent, and in the negociation of the late peace, painted for His late Majesty George IV. by Sir Thomas Lawrence, at an expense of more than £36,000, paid from the privy purse. The entrance to His Majesty's private apartments is in the south-east angle of the quadrangle, through a handsome hall, from which is an ascent by a double staircase of great architectural beauty, lighted by a double lantern of elegant design, into a corridor five hundred feet in length, communicating with His Majesty's apartments on the east, and with the visitors' apartments on the south. The ceiling of this splendid gallery is panelled in compartments, with delicate tracery richly gilt, and the walls are decorated with paintings by the most eminent masters of the old and modern schools; the furniture is of the most sumptuous and elegant character, and the whole, enriched with every architectural ornament which the later style has combined, has an air of costly grandeur and stately magnificence. The private apartments consist of a dining-room, fifty feet in length and thirty-seven wide; a drawing-room, sixty-six feet in length and thirty feet wide; a smaller drawing-room, forty feet long, and twenty-five feet wide; library, fifty feet long and forty feet wide; with bed-rooms, dressing-rooms, boudoir, and various other apartments. These rooms are of the most splendid and sumptuous elegance; they are decorated with every ornament that ingenuity can devise, or wealth purchase, and lighted with superb oriel windows of elegant design, enriched with tracery, which not only give an air of impressive beauty to their internal grandeur, but add greatly to the external embellishment of the castle: the rooms for His Majesty's servants occupy the lower and higher stories of the palace. In front of the king's private apartments is a parterre, four hundred feet in length and of equal breadth, surrounded by a broad terrace rampart wall with bastions; in the area are numerous statues finely sculptured, and under the terrace on the north side is an orangery two hundred and fifty feet in length, the front of which forms a long series of finely pointed arches with tracery.

The middle ward comprises the round tower, or keep, which was formerly the residence of the constable, whose office was both of a military and a civil nature. In his military character he was entrusted with the command of the castle, and with the custody of every thing contained in it, and assisted by a lieutenant-governor, or deputy, who possessed equal authority during his absence: in his civil capacity, he was judge of a court of record having jurisdiction over the precincts of the forest, which extends seventy-seven miles and a half in circumference; but that office is now vested in a steward, assisted by a janitor, who is keeper of the prison, though no process has issued from it within the last forty years. The round tower, which is of very spacious dimensions, has been raised thirty-two feet higher than its original elevation, and is crowned with a projecting machicolated battlement, supported on massive corbels and arches; and surmounted on the eastern part of the circumference by a newly erected turret twenty feet high, on the summit of which the royal standard is displayed during His Majesty's presence at the castle. The lower part of the tower is surrounded by a rampart, in which are embrasures for seventeen pieces of cannon: the ascent to it is by a flight of one hundred stone steps; the roof of the staircase is supported by corbels, consisting of busts of kings, knights, angels, and other figures, of which many are in good preservation. At the summit of the staircase is a large piece of cannon, pointed at the entrance through an aperture in the wall; and from the rampart a strong arched gateway, grooved for a portcullis, leads into the main tower, formerly appropriated to the reception of state prisoners of high rank.

The lower ward, or quadrangle, into which is an entrance leading from the town through Henry the Eighth's gateway, flanked with two lofty massive towers, comprises the collegiate chapel of St. George, beyond which, on the north side, are the houses of the dean, canons, minor canons, and other officers of the college, and various towers, among which are those of the Bishop of Winchester, who is prelate, and the Bishop of Salisbury, who is chancellor, of the order of the garter; a tower, formerly belonging to Garter King at Arms, of which a small portion only remains, and a store tower. Apartments have been also fitted up in this ward for the commanding officer and officer on guard, who, though subordinate to the constable, or governor of the castle, has the command of a company of the royal foot guards, who are always on duty here. On the south side are the houses assigned to the thirteen poor knights on the royal foundation, each of whom has a pension of about £40 per annum, and wears a scarlet gown and a purple mantle, with the cross of St. George embroidered on the left shoulder; and a building appropriated to their governor: there are also houses for five additional knights, on the foundations of Sir Peter le Maire and Sir Francis Crane. By the will of Mr. Samuel Travers, in 1728, provision was made for seven disabled, or superannuated, lieutenants of the Royal Navy, to each of whom a pension of £60 per annum was assigned; they are chosen by the trustees, and their residence is at Travers College, Datchet-lane. In an apartment in the deanery, called the garter room, the arms of the sovereign and knights companions of the order are emblazoned; and an ancient screen is decorated with the arms of Edward III., and of the several sovereigns and knights companions of the order from its original foundation: this apartment is at present used as a robing-room on days of installation.

The collegiate chapel of St. George (of which the establishment consists of a dean, twelve canons, seven minor canons, thirteen clerks, ten choristers, a steward, treasurer, and other officers) was, as before observed, originally built by Edward III., on the site of a smaller chapel erected by Henry I., and dedicated to Edward the Confessor. It was considerably enlarged by Edward IV., materially enriched by Henry VII., and repaired, restored,

and greatly embellished by George III., who expended £20,000 in its improvement. It is a beautiful cruciform structure, in the purest character of the later style of English architecture, of which it displays one of the finest specimens in the kingdom: the transepts project in an octagonal form from the main building, and at the extremities of the aisles are lateral octangular projections, forming sepulchral chapels. Pierced parapets of elegant design are principally the external embellishments, and buttresses crowned with square embattled turrets. The interior is finely arranged; the walls are panelled throughout in one general design, of which the windows, enriched with tracery and divided by battlemented transoms, form an integral part. The nave is separated from the aisles by seven pointed arches and piers of peculiar beauty, adapted to the contrast of light and shade with singular effect; its roof and that of the choir are elaborately groined, richly embellished with fan tracery of beautiful design, and splendidly decorated with shields of armorial bearings and heraldic devices, highly emblazoned: it is lighted by an elegant range of clerestory windows, which are continued round the transepts; and the great west window, which occupies the whole of the western extremity above the entrance, of an elaborate and beautiful arrangement of panels, enriched with tracery, and embellished with ancient stained glass of unrivalled brilliancy. The choir, in which the installation of the knights takes place, and of which the general arrangement is, with the exception of the roof being more enriched with fan tracery, similar to that of the nave, is separated from it by a skreen of artificial stone, from the manufactory of Coade, of appropriate character and beautiful design, ornamented with several devices illustrative of the order of the garter. On each side are the stalls of the sovereign and knights companions of the most noble order of the garter, enriched with historical and emblematical carvings, and with the names and heraldic honours of the knights richly emblazoned: the curtains and cushions are of blue velvet with gold fringe, and on the canopies of the several stalls are deposited the sword, helmet, mantle, and crest of the knights, above which are their banners of silk, emblazoned with their several armorial bearings and heraldic honours. The stall of the sovereign, whose banner is of velvet mantled with silk, and considerably larger than that of the knights companions, is on the right hand of the entrance. The other stalls, originally twenty-five in number, and increased to thirty-one, occupy the north and south sides of the western part of the choir. The altar is embellished with a painting of the Last Supper, by West, which is considered to be one of the best productions of that artist; and the wainscot surrounding the presbytery is richly ornamented with the arms of Edward III., Edward the Black Prince, and those of the knights who originally composed the order, finely carved. In the east window is a beautiful painting, on glass, of the Resurrection, in three compartments, finely executed by Jarvis and Forrest, from a design by West, at an expense of £4000; and in the windows on the north and south sides of the altar are the arms of the sovereign, and of the several knights companions who subscribed to defray that expense. The east window of the south aisle is embellished with a painting, on glass, of the Angels appearing to the Shepherds, and in the west window is one of the Nativity; the west window of the north aisle is ornamented with a painting of the Adoration of the Magi; and at the eastern extremity is a chapter-room, forming an approach to the royal closet on the north side of the altar.

The various monumental chapels are separated from the aisles by skreens of elegant and appropriate character, and in the south transept is a modern font of good design. At the east end of the north aisle are deposited the remains of Edward IV.; over the tomb is a black marble slab, on which is the inscription " Edward IV. and his Queen, Elizabeth Widville;" an elegant monument of iron, beautifully wrought, and representing a pair of gates between two antique towers, of elaborate design, which formerly covered the tomb, has been removed to the choir on the north side of the altar. In 1789, a small aperture was discovered in the side of this vault by some workmen, and, upon its enlargement by order of the canons, the skeleton of that monarch was found in a leaden coffin, enclosed in one of wood. In the opposite aisle, near the choir, were deposited the remains of Henry VI., which were removed from Chertsey in Surrey, by order of Henry VIII. Near the ascent to the altar is the royal vault, in which were interred the remains of Henry VIII., and his queen, Jane Seymour; and of Charles I., whose coffin being opened by order of George IV., when Prince Regent, the remains were found in a very perfect state, the countenance being as fresh as when they were interred. In a small chapel at the east end of the south aisle are the monuments of Edward, Earl of Lincoln, and Richard Beauchamp, Bishop of Salisbury, first chancellor of the order of the garter. In the same aisle is a small chantry, erected in 1522, by John Oxenbridge, a canon, and a benefactor to the chapel; adjoining which is King's, or Aldworth, chapel, probably erected by Dr. Oliver King, Bishop of Bath and Wells, whose remains are interred in it. Opposite to this chapel are some panels of oak, on which are carved the arms and devices of Prince Edward (son of Henry VI.), Edward IV., and Henry VII., whose portraits, in full length, are painted on the panels. Near the centre of the aisle is the chapel of Sir Reginald Bray, in which he is interred; and at the west end is the Beaufort chapel, containing the monuments of Henry Somerset, Duke of Beaufort, of white marble, elegantly decorated with sculpture; and of Charles Somerset, Earl of Worcester, and his lady Elizabeth: on this tomb are the effigies of the earl, dressed in the habit of the order, and of his lady, in her robes of state. In the centre of the north aisle is Rutland chapel, in which is an alabaster monument to the memory of Sir George Manners, Lord Roos, and Lady Anne, his wife, niece to Edward IV.: on the tomb are the figures of Sir George in armour, and his lady in her robes of state, and round it are the effigies of their children. In this chapel, in which Sir Thomas Syllinger and his wife, Anne, Duchess of Exeter, and sister of Edward IV., were also interred, is a beautiful marble tablet to the memory of Major Packe, killed at the battle of Waterloo, in which he is represented as being raised from the field by a brother officer, finely sculptured in alto relievo. In the same aisle, near the choir, is the chapel of St. Stephen, decorated internally with paintings illustrative of the life and death of that martyr: this chapel was erected by

Elizabeth, widow of Lord William Hastings, whose remains were deposited in it, after his decapitation by Richard III.: in the south aisle of the choir is the chapel of St. John the Baptist, similarly decorated with paintings illustrative of his history. At the south-west corner of the church is Urswick's chapel, founded by Dr. Christopher Urswick, Dean of Windsor, who contributed greatly, with Sir Reginald Bray, to the completion of the church: it contains the cenotaph of the Princess Charlotte, finely executed in white marble, by Mr. Matthew Wyatt. In the lower compartment is the corpse of the Princess lying on the bier covered with drapery, under which the outline of the form is admirably traced, having the right arm hanging over the side of the bier, and at the corners are female figures kneeling, with their heads resting on it, and veiled with drapery. In the upper compartment, the Princess appears with a countenance animated with hope, and, having drawn aside the curtains of her sepulchre, is rising from the tomb attended by angels, of whom one is bearing her infant in its arms. There are several other chapels; and, in various parts of this imposing and elegant structure, numerous interesting and highly admirable specimens of magnificent decoration and costly embellishment.

At the east end of the collegiate chapel is a chapel erected by Henry VII., as a place of interment for himself and his successors; but that monarch afterwards changing his purpose, it remained in a neglected state till the reign of Henry VIII., when Cardinal Wolsey, by permission of the king, began to erect a splendid tomb, the design of which exceeded in magnificence that of Henry VII., in Westminster abbey. The Cardinal died before it was completed, and was buried in Leicester abbey; and the unfinished sepulchre was destroyed in the parliamentary war. James II. converted this building into a chapel, and employed the artist Verrio to ornament the walls and ceiling with paintings; but the populace, excited by the public performance of the Roman Catholic rites, furiously assailed the building, destroying the windows and interior decorations; and in this ruined state it remained till George III. ordered it to be repaired, and subsequently constructed within it a royal mausoleum for himself and his successors. In clearing away the ground for this purpose, the workmen discovered two coffins in a stone recess, in one of which were the remains of Mary, daughter of Edward IV., and Elizabeth Widville, and in the other, those of their third son, George, Duke of Bedford; the remains of both were re-interred in the same tomb with those of their parents. The mausoleum, an excavation seventy feet in length, twenty in width, and fourteen in depth, occupies the whole extent of the building: the roof is supported on massive octagonal columns and four pointed arches, in each of which are four shelves of stone, capable of containing two coffins; at the east end are five niches for one coffin each, and in the centre is a range of twelve low altar-tombs, intended for the coffins of the sovereigns. The roof is strongly groined with ribs springing from the capitals of the columns: the entrance, through a pair of brazen gates, is by a subterraneous passage under the altar of St. George's chapel, into which is the descent by a platform lowered by machinery. The first coffin placed in the royal mausoleum was that of the Princess Amelia, daughter of George III.; after which, in succession, have been deposited the remains of the Duchess of Brunswick ; the Princess Charlotte, daughter of George IV., and her infant son; Queen Charlotte ; the Duke of Kent, fourth son of George III ; George III ; Princess Elizabeth of Clarence, infant daughter of their present Majesties ; the Duke of York, second son of George III ; and his late Majesty, George IV : the two younger sons of George III., Prince Alfred and Prince Octavius, whose remains were removed from Westminster abbey, were also re-interred in the royal sepulchre. The chapel above the mausoleum is intended as a chapter-house for the order of the garter : it is lighted by a fine range of elegant windows with tracery, which surround the building, and form a beautiful group at the east end, which is hexagonal ; the west end is ornamented with a large window of elegant design, in the compartments of which full-length paintings of the sovereigns and knights companions of the order will be placed.

The palace is surrounded on all sides, except the west, by a spacious and noble terrace, above two thousand five hundred feet in extent, faced with a strong rampart of hewn stone, and having, at convenient intervals, easy slopes leading down to the park. The smaller park, which is also called the Home park, immediately surrounding the north north-east and south sides of the castle, is about four miles in circumference, and was enclosed, by William III., with a brick wall. Immediately under the terrace, on the east side of the castle, is a beautiful lawn, laid out in shrubberies and walks, called the Slopes, and extending, on the east side of the park, from the north terrace to the Adelaide Lodge : the grounds are beautifully diversified with forest trees and sylvan scenery. On the opposite side of the road is Frogmore Lodge, which was purchased by her late Majesty, and is still the favourite retreat of the Princess Augusta : the gardens and pleasure grounds are tastefully laid out, abounding with beautiful scenery, and containing many interesting objects, among which are a hermitage, designed by the Princess Elizabeth, a highly picturesque ruin, by Mr. James Wyatt, situated on the margin of a beautiful piece of water : in the interior is an elegant apartment, in which are, the effigy of an infant reposing on a cushion, and a monumental tablet to the memory of the Princess Charlotte, in which the countenance of the Princess, and the representation of her infant, are exquisitely sculptured. Many festive meetings were held here during the life of Queen Charlotte, the last of which was in honour of the fiftieth anniversary of the accession of George III. The Long Walk, extending from the upper quadrangle of the castle into the Great park, is continued in a direct line for three miles, forming a noble avenue of double rows of elms, seventy-seven yards wide, and, at the opposite extremity, ascending a hill of considerable elevation, on which the first stone of a monument, in honour of his royal father, was laid by his late Majesty, George IV., in 1829. The monument will consist of a colossal statue in bronze, twenty-five feet high, by Westmacott, placed on a pedestal forty feet high, forming a conspicuous object from the castle. Near this spot is Cumberland Lodge, the residence of the late Duke of Cumberland. This park, eighteen miles in circumference, abounds with forest scenery of great beauty, and is agreeably diversified with hill and valley, and with wood and water. Virginia water, issuing from a valley commencing near

the back of Cumberland Lodge, after winding for several miles through the varied scenery of the Great park, expands towards the south-east into a beautiful lake, more than a mile in length and of considerable breadth, bounded by a verdant lawn surrounded with extensive plantations of various kinds of trees, and terminated by a fine cascade, a view of which is obtained from a bridge on the high road over the rivulet formed by the waste water of the lake, and running into the Thames near Chertsey. On the margin of the lake an elegant temple and a fishing gallery, of very light and beautiful design, have been erected. There is also a noble and magnificent ruin, consisting of numerous ancient columns of marble brought from the ruins of Corinth, and classically arranged and re-constructed by Sir Jeffrey Wyatville. The grounds are planted with shrubs and flowers, and laid out in pleasant walks. The surface of the lake is enlivened with pleasure boats and with several beautiful models of ships, among which is an elegant model of the Euryalus frigate, presented by Captain Inglis. George IV. took possession of the castle, after its partial restoration and improvement, on the 9th of December, 1828, and the first public act of that monarch was to confer the honour of knighthood on the architect by whom the additional buildings were erected and the improvements accomplished, and to add to his family arms a quartering of George the Fourth's gateway, with the motto "Windsor," both of His Majesty's suggestion. From the magnificence, extent, and grandeur of its buildings ; the beauty and richness of the surrounding scenery, diversified with hills and vales, and enlivened with the frequent windings of the Thames, and the peaceful waters of its inland lake ; the luxuriant woodlands within its enclosures ; and the extensive and majestic forest in the vicinity, Windsor must unquestionably be regarded as one of the most spacious and magnificent palaces in Europe.

The town is pleasantly situated on the acclivities of the hill on which the castle is built, and consists of six principal streets, intersected by several smaller : it is well paved and lighted with gas, and amply supplied with water: the houses are in general of brick, and of respectable appearance, and several in the more modern part of the town are handsome and well built. The approach from Datchet is strikingly beautiful, and at the other extremity is an elegant iron-bridge of three arches, resting on piers of granite, the first stone of which was laid, in 1822, by the late Duke of York, connecting the town with Eton, on the opposite side of the Thames. The environs abound with varied scenery of every description, and the neighbourhood is enlivened with the windings of the river. Considerable improvements have lately been made, among which are, the removal of the ancient edifices of lath and plaster, and the erection of some handsome ranges of building fronted with stone, in which the materials of the lodges that were taken down for the improvement of the castle have been used: among the more recent erections are York Place, Brunswick Terrace, and Augusta Place. On the west side of High-street is a meadow, comprising more than two acres, called the Bachelors' Acre, which, by the award of the commissioners of the forest enclosure, was appropriated to the commonalty of the borough for their amusements. It is bounded on the east and south sides by a high bank; on the summit is a broad terrace, at the end of which is an obelisk, with inscriptions on the pedestal, commemorative of the fiftieth anniversary of the accession of George III., and of the visit of her Majesty and the Princesses, upon that occasion, to partake of the old English fare provided for the assembled populace. The barracks, for one thousand infantry, form a handsome and commodious range of building: they were erected in 1795, and enlarged to their present extent in 1803. The cavalry barracks, about half a mile from the town, on the road to Winkfield, are handsomely built, and occupy an open, healthy, and pleasant situation. The theatre in Thames-street, a small commodious building erected in 1815, at an expense of £6000, advanced on transferable shares, is open during the Ascot races and the vacations at Eton. The public library, in Castle-street, is well supported, and there is also a subscription circulating library. Windsor, though possessing all the advantages of a navigable river, has neither any particular branch of manufacture nor any trade, except what is necessary for the supply of the inhabitants: it has been long celebrated for the quality of its ale, of which considerable quantities are sent to London and other towns. It is indebted equally for its origin and its continued prosperity to the erection of the castle, and to its selection as a royal residence. The market days are Wednesday and Saturday, the latter chiefly for corn, which is pitched in the market-place: the fairs are, Easter-Tuesday, July 5th, and October 24th. A commodious market-place has been recently constructed for the sale of butchers' meat and other provisions: the area underneath the guildhall is appropriated to the use of the corn market.

The inhabitants were first incorporated in the fifth of Edward I., from which time it was the county town till 1314, when Edward II. transferred that distinction to Reading. The charter was extended and confirmed in various successive reigns till that of Charles II., by whom the government was vested in a mayor, high steward, two bailiffs, and twenty-eight burgesses, assisted by a town clerk, serjeants at mace, and subordinate officers: thirteen of the burgesses are styled benchers of the guildhall, of which number ten are appointed aldermen, and from these the mayor is annually chosen. The mayor and one of the aldermen chosen for that purpose are justices of the peace within the borough, and the former is also coroner and clerk of the market. Quarterly courts of session are held for all offences not capital; The guildhall is a spacious and handsome building in High-street, erected in 1686; it is supported on columns and arches of Portland stone, and ornamented at the north end with a statue of Queen Anne, and at the south, with one of Prince George of Denmark: the chamber, in which the public business of the corporation is transacted, is decorated with portraits of all the sovereigns from James I. to Queen Anne, George III. and his queen, and George IV., and with those of Prince Rupert, Archbishop Laud, and some others. The com-

Seal used by the Corporation for general purposes.

mon gaol and house of correction for the borough, which was rebuilt at the expense of George III. in George-street, and contains seven wards, with an airing-yard, being capable of receiving eighteen prisoners. The borough first exercised the elective franchise in the 30th of Edward I., and sent members to parliament till the 14th of Edward III., from which time it discontinued till the 25th of Henry IV., but since that period it has regularly returned two members: the right of election is vested in the inhabitants generally paying scot and lot, and resident at least six months previously to the election, of whom the number is about six hundred; the mayor is the returning officer.

The living is a discharged vicarage, in the archdeaconry of Berks, and diocese of Salisbury, rated in the king's books at £15. 3. 4., endowed with £200 private benefaction, and £200 royal bounty, and in the patronage of the Crown. The church, dedicated to St. John the Baptist, is a handsome structure in the later style of English architecture, with a lofty square embattled tower crowned with pinnacles, erected, in 1822, upon the site of a former church, which, having become greatly dilapidated, was taken down in 1820: the interior is elegantly arranged; the nave is separated from the aisles by a range of six lofty clustered columns and pointed arches, which support the roof: the altar is embellished with an excellent painting of the Last Supper, found in one of the chantries in St. George's chapel, where it is supposed to have been secreted during the parliamentary war, and, after having been restored to its place over the altar of that chapel, presented to this church by George III., in 1788: the skreen is of oak, richly carved, to correspond with two massive chairs presented by the Princess Augusta; and the rail, which surrounds the chancel, is elaborately carved with beautiful devices of pelicans feeding their young, and with fruit and foliage, supposed to be the work of the celebrated Gibbons, and formerly belonging to the chapel of St. George. Under small arches, at the east end of the church, are the royal closets, fitted up with crimson drapery; and the corporation seat is beautifully ornamented with tabernacle-work, and surmounted by an enriched canopy. Six hundred sittings were provided in this church by the Incorporated Society for promoting the building and enlargement of churches and chapels, who contributed £750 towards its erection, the whole cost of which amounted to £14,040. 17. 3.: towards defraying this expense George III. contributed £1050, £4000 was raised by subscription, and the remainder by a rate on the inhabitants. There are several ancient monuments, among which may be noticed the sarcophagus of Chief Justice Reeve, with busts of himself and his lady, by Schemacker; that of Edward Jobson and Eleanor his wife, with their effigies, and those of their ten children, in the costume of the sixteenth century; and others, which have been carefully preserved on taking down the old church, and replaced in the new edifice. In the churchyard, finely shaded by avenues of yew trees, are many handsome tombs. There are places of worship for Independents and Wesleyan Methodists.

On the north side of the church is the charity school, established, in 1705, by subscription, for clothing and instructing children: the annual income, arising from several benefactions vested in the funds, and an annual

payment of £24. 15. from his Majesty's Exchequer, amounts to £167. 4., which sum is increased by annual subscription and collections after charity sermons. Thirty-six boys and twenty-four girls are completely clothed, and instructed in reading, writing, and arithmetic, and the girls in sewing and knitting : they are nominated by the dean and two senior canons, the mayor and two senior aldermen, and the vicar, of Windsor, who are the trustees. The school-house, with apartments for the master and mistress, was erected by means of a legacy of £500, bequeathed by Theodore Randue, Esq. The ladies' charity school was established, in 1784, by subscription, under the patronage of the late queen : the annual income, arising from endowments by several benefactors, is £56. 7. ; twenty girls are clothed, and instructed in reading and needle-work, and in the principles of the established church, and fitted for domestic service. The National school, in which two hundred boys and two hundred girls are instructed, is supported by subscription ; and there are funds, bequeathed by Mrs. Barker, for teaching children of this parish and the parishes of Egham, in Surrey, and Yateley, in the county of Southampton ; by Mr. Marrat, for teaching children of the parishes of Windsor and Clewer ; by Mr. Panton, for the endowment of the Sunday school, in which two hundred children are instructed. Archbishop Laud bequeathed £50 per annum to the parish, to be employed for two following years in apprenticing poor boys ; and, every third year, in giving marriage portions to poor maidens of the town : this charity has been augmented, with a bequest of £1000, by Theodore Randue, Esq., with which, increased by £250 added by his executors, an estate has been purchased, yielding a rental of £50, of which, £10 each are given, for two successive years, to five such apprentices on Archbishop Laud's foundation as have faithfully served their terms ; and, every third year, to poor maidens who have lived for three years in the same family, with a good character.

An hospital for eight poor men and women was founded, in 1503, and endowed, in 1570, by Mr. Thomas Brotherton, and, subsequently, by Mr. Richard Gallis, with funds producing £35 per annum : the number of inmates has been augmented to twelve, who receive each ten shillings per quarter. Near the Pitfields, four almshouses were founded, in 1676, by Mr. Richard Reeve, who endowed them with funds, from which the inmates receive £2. 10 per annum; and there is an unendowed almshouse, in Park-street, in which twelve poor men are supported by the parish. The royal general dispensary, in Church-street, was established in 1818, and is supported by subscription. The hospital for invalid soldiers was erected by George III., in 1784, on land which had been presented to his Majesty by the corporation ; it is a neat and commodious building, well adapted to the purpose, and capable of receiving forty patients. A charity for the relief of lying-in women was established, in 1801, by a society of ladies, and is supported by subscription. Mrs. Phebe Thomas bequeathed funded property, from the proceeds of which twelve poor widows receive £10 per annum each ; and the number will probably be augmented on the death of some annuitants named in the will of that lady. There are also numerous other bequests for charitable purposes, and for distribution

among the poor : the parochial rates have been materially diminished by three several bequests, and also by three successive grants from the crown as compensation for the loss of rates on houses purchased by the crown, and taken down for the improvements of the castle and approaches. Near the Long Walk, in the park, some labourers discovered a mineral spring, which was fast growing into repute; but the crowds of persons who frequented it proving a great annoyance, it was closed up, and a building of wood erected over the well. Among the illustrious natives of Windsor were, John, eldest son of Edward I., who died in his infancy, and was interred at Westminster, in 1273 ; Eleanor, eldest daughter of the same monarch, who was born in 1266, and married, by proxy, to Alphonso, King of Arragon, who died before the consummation of the marriage (she was afterwards married to Henry, Earl of Burg, in France, from whom the house of Anjou and the kings of Sicily are descended, and died in 1298); Margaret, third daughter of Edward I., born in 1275, and married to John, second Duke of Brabant, from whose son John, the third duke, the Dukes of Burgundy were descended ; Mary, the sixth daughter of the same monarch, born in 1279, who, when ten years of age, entered a nunnery at Amesbury, in the county of Wilts ; Edward III., son of Edward II., in 1312, the first of the English sovereigns who issued gold coin, the pieces having been called rose-nobles; William, the sixth son of Edward, who died in his infancy ; and Henry VI., son of Henry V., who died by violence, in 1471. Windsor gives the title of earl to the family of Stuart, Marquisses of Bute.

WINDSOR (OLD), a parish in the hundred of RIPPLESMERE, county of BERKS, 2 miles (S. E. by S.) from New Windsor, containing 1050 inhabitants. The living is a discharged vicarage, in the archdeaconry of Berks, and diocese of Salisbury, rated in the king's books at £8. 6. 8., endowed with £200 private benefaction, and £200 royal bounty, and in the patronage of the Crown. The church is dedicated to St. Peter : in the churchyard are several tombs of noble individuals, and other distinguished characters. A parochial school, and four cottages with gardens attached, for poor persons, were erected in 1797, and endowed with land : here is also a female school of industry. The Roman road from Silchester passes through a part of the parish. Previously to the Conquest this is said to have been the seat of several Saxon kings.

WINESTEAD, a parish in the southern division of the wapentake of HOLDERNESS, East riding of the county of YORK, 2 miles (N. W. by N.) from Patrington, containing 129 inhabitants. The living is a rectory, in the archdeaconry of the East riding, and diocese of York, rated in the king's books at £12, and in the patronage of T. B. Hildyard, Esq. The church, dedicated to St. German, is an ancient building surrounded by stately trees : in front of the pulpit is a monument, with a recumbent statue in armour, to the memory of Sir Robert Hildyard. The celebrated Andrew Marvel, M. P. for Hull in the time of Charles I., was born here, March 31st, 1621, during the incumbency of his father.

WINFARTHING, a parish in the hundred of DISS, county of NORFOLK, 4¼ miles (N. by W.) from Diss, containing 683 inhabitants. The living is a discharged rectory, in the archdeaconry of Norfolk, and diocese of

Norwich, rated in the king's books at £12, and in the patronage of the Earl of Albemarle. The church is dedicated to St. Mary.

WINFIELD, a township in the parish and hundred of WROTHAM, lathe of AYLESFORD, county of KENT, 5 miles (S.) from Wrotham. The population is returned with the parish.

WINFORD-EAGLE, a parish in the hundred of TOLLERFORD, Dorchester division of the county of DORSET, 8½ miles (W. N. W.) from Dorchester, containing 152 inhabitants. The living is a perpetual curacy, annexed to the vicarage of Toller-Fratrum, in the archdeaconry of Dorset, and diocese of Bristol. The church is dedicated to St. Lawrence. On Fernham down are several barrows, in one of which seventeen urns, containing bones and ashes, have been discovered. Dr. Thomas Sydenham, an eminent physician, was born here, in 1624; he died in 1689.

WINFORTON, a parish in the hundred of HUNTINGTON, county of HEREFORD, 6 miles (N. E. by E.) from Hay, containing 169 inhabitants. The living is a rectory, in the archdeaconry and diocese of Hereford, rated in the king's books at £9. 6. 8., and in the patronage of the Heirs of the late John Freeman, Esq. The church is dedicated to St. Mary. A rail-road from Hay to Kington passes through the parish. A court leet is occasionally held here. A charity school has been endowed by the late Mr. Freeman.

WINFRITH-NEWBURGH, a parish in the hundred of WINFRITH, Blandford (South) division of the county of DORSET, 9 miles (W. by S.) from Wareham, containing 764 inhabitants. The living is a rectory, with the perpetual curacy of West Lullworth annexed, in the archdeaconry of Dorset, and diocese of Bristol, rated in the king's books at £23. 14. 4½., and in the patronage of the Bishop of Salisbury. The church, dedicated to St. Christopher, has a fine Norman doorway and an embattled tower; the nave is covered with lead. This is a very extensive and ancient parish, giving name to the hundred, and formerly belonged to the family of Newburgh, who had a seat here, of which there are no traces. Near the hamlet of Bromehill, a rivulet, tributary to the Frome, is crossed by three bridges, erected in 1769, at the joint expense of Edward Weld and James Frampton, Esqrs. A small school is supported by annual subscriptions.

WING, a parish in the hundred of COTTESLOE, county of BUCKINGHAM, 3 miles (S. W. by W.) from Leighton-Buzzard, containing 1086 inhabitants. The living is a vicarage, in the archdeaconry of Buckingham, and diocese of Lincoln, rated in the king's books at £18. 16. 3., and in the patronage of the Earl of Chesterfield. The church, dedicated to All Saints, is a remarkably fine structure. There is a place of worship for Wesleyan Methodists. An almshouse for eight poor persons was founded, in 1596, by Lady Pelham, with an endowment of £30 per annum, to which Sir William Stanhope, in 1772, bequeathed an annuity of £6. 10. A Benedictine priory, a cell to the monastery of St. Nicholas at Angiers in France, was founded at Ascot, in this parish, by the Empress Maud, which, after the suppression, came into the possession of Cardinal Wolsey.

WING, a parish in the hundred of MARTINSLEY, county of RUTLAND, 3 miles (N. E.) from Uppingham, containing 273 inhabitants. The living is a rectory,

in the archdeaconry of Northampton, and diocese of Peterborough, rated in the king's books at £7. 5. 5., and in the patronage of the Crown, or the Marquis of Exeter. The church is dedicated to St. Peter and St. Paul.

WINGATE, a township in the parish of KELLOE, southern division of EASINGTON ward, county palatine of DURHAM, 6½ miles (E. S. E.) from Durham, containing 131 inhabitants.

WINGATES, a township in the parish of LONG HORSLEY, western division of MORPETH ward, county of NORTHUMBERLAND, 6 miles (S. E. by S.) from Rothbury, containing, with Chirm, Garrotlee, Wholm, and Wingates-Moore, 177 inhabitants. Peter Silcock, in 1818, bequeathed £50, directing the interest to be applied for teaching five children in a school built by subscription.

WINGERWORTH, a parish in the hundred of SCARSDALE, county of DERBY, 2¾ miles (S. by W.) from Chesterfield, containing 459 inhabitants. The living is a perpetual curacy, in the archdeaconry of Derby, and diocese of Lichfield and Coventry, endowed with £200 private benefaction, and £400 royal bounty, and in the patronage of the Dean and Chapter of Lincoln. The Iknield-street passes through the parish, in which large quantities of coal, iron-stone, and freestone, are obtained. A school for twenty children is supported by annual subscriptions, amounting to about £20. On Stonedge cliff are several basins, and two seats, excavated in the rock. The brass head of a caputla was found a few years ago on the Roman road. Wingerworth Hall was taken possession of and garrisoned for the parliament, in 1643; the present large and elegant mansion was erected in 1728.

WINGFIELD, a parish in the hundred of HOXNE, county of SUFFOLK, 5¾ miles (E. by N.) from Eye, containing 578 inhabitants. The living is a perpetual curacy, in the archdeaconry of Suffolk, and diocese of Norwich, endowed with £1000 parliamentary grant, and in the patronage of the Bishop of Norwich. The church, dedicated to St. Andrew, was made collegiate in 1362: it is built of flints and stones of various colours, exhibiting a fine and rather uncommon appearance. In the chancel, of which the architecture is highly enriched, are some superb monuments and ancient brasses of the Wingfields and De la Poles: among those of the latter family is one to the memory of Michael, first Earl of Suffolk, who, in the reign of Richard II., built the castle, of which the south front still remains, and the west side has been converted into a farm-house: these ruins, which are surrounded by a moat, are situated about a quarter of a mile north-west of the church, on a thickly-wooded plain. Of the college, founded on the south side of the church by Sir John Wingfield, in 1362, for a provost and nine priests, all that remains is the west side of the quadrangle, now used as a farm-house; it was valued, at the dissolution, at £50 per annum.

WINGFIELD (NORTH), a parish in the hundred of SCARSDALE, county of DERBY, 4½ miles (S. S. E.) from Chesterfield, comprising the townships of Claylane, Stretton, Tupton, and Woodthorpe, and containing 1657 inhabitants. The living is a rectory, in the archdeaconry of Derby, and diocese of Lichfield and Coventry, rated in the king's books at £21. 6. 3., and in the patronage of G. Barrow, Esq. The church, dedicated to St. Lawrence, is a large handsome structure, situated at a distance from the village. There is a place of worship for Wesleyan Methodists. A school is supported by a trifling endowment; and at Deerleap, near Stretton, is another, erected in 1790, by A. L. Maynard, who endowed it with £15. 15. per annum, for teaching twenty-five children. Wingfield is in the honour of Tutbury, duchy of Lancaster, and within the jurisdiction of a court of pleas held at Tutbury every third Tuesday, for the recovery of debts under 40s. The Roman Iknield-street may be traced in this parish.

WINGFIELD (SOUTH), a parish in the hundred of SCARSDALE, county of DERBY, 2¼ miles (W.) from Alfreton, containing 1051 inhabitants. The living is a discharged vicarage, in the archdeaconry of Derby, and diocese of Lichfield and Coventry, rated in the king's books at £6. 13. 4., and in the patronage of the Duke of Devonshire. The church is dedicated to All Saints. There is a place of worship for Wesleyan Methodists. The ancient Iknield-street passes through the parish, in which coal is obtained. The village is large, and possesses a considerable and increasing trade in the weaving of stockings, for which there are about two hundred frames in operation. Samuel Newton, in 1683, gave £200 for charitable uses, with which sum certain lands were purchased, now producing £33 per annum, £20 of which is applied for teaching twenty children. The estate called Strelley's charity, at Okerthorpe in this parish, is now let for £55 a year, of which income £20 was directed by the donor to be applied for apprenticing two poor boys, and £10 for exhibitions for two poor scholars at the University. The manor-house, now an extensive and interesting ruin, was a splendid and spacious edifice, erected by Ralph, Lord Cromwell, Lord Treasurer in the reign of Henry VI.: it was afterwards, for several generations, one of the principal seats of the Earls of Shrewsbury; and Mary, Queen of Scots, while in the custody of George, the sixth earl, passed some months here, in 1569; she was here also in November and December, 1584. At the commencement of the parliamentary war, Wingfield manor-house was garrisoned for the parliament; but being taken by the Earl of Newcastie, towards the close of the year 1643, it was then made a royal garrison: in 1644 it sustained a siege, but surrendered to the parliament in August: in 1646, it was dismantled by order of parliament. In 1774, a considerable part of the mansion was pulled down, to build a modern house near it with the materials.

WINGHAM, a parish (formerly a market town) in the hundred of WINGHAM, lathe of ST. AUGUSTINE, county of KENT, 34 miles (E.) from Maidstone, containing 1085 inhabitants. The living is a perpetual curacy, in the peculiar jurisdiction of the Archbishop of Canterbury, and in the patronage of Sir B. W. Bridges, Bart., and others. The church is dedicated to St. Mary. There is a place of worship for Independents. This place is situated on the high road from Canterbury to Deal, in a neighbourhood abounding with genteel residences. The market has been disused, but considerable fairs for cattle are held on May 12th and November 12th. The petty sessions for the division are also held here. A college for a provost and six canons in the church was founded in 1286, by John Peckham, Archbishop of Canterbury, which at the dissolution had a revenue of £84, and was granted by Edward VI. to Sir Henry Palmer: on or near its site a stone coffin and some other relics of

antiquity have been found. Sir James Oxendon, Bart., in 1686, founded a free school, and endowed it with £16 per annum, which is paid for the instruction of twenty boys in reading, writing, and accounts. William de Wengham, Bishop of London, and Chancellor in the reign of Henry III., was a native of this parish.

WINGRAVE, a parish in the hundred of COTTESLOE, county of BUCKINGHAM, 5½ miles (N. E.) from Aylesbury, containing, with the hamlet of Rowsham, 675 inhabitants. The living is a discharged vicarage, in the archdeaconry of Buckingham, and diocese of Lincoln, rated in the king's books at £9. 9. 7., and in the patronage of the Trustees of the late Earl of Bridgewater. The church is dedicated to St. Peter and St. Paul. There is a place of worship for Independents. A small school is partly supported by a trifling annual subscription. At Rowsham there was formerly a chapel.

WINKBOURN, a parish in the northern division of the wapentake of THURGARTON, county of NOTTINGHAM, 3 miles (N.) from Southwell, containing 159 inhabitants. The living is a donative, in the patronage of P. Pegge Burnell, Esq. The church, a large ancient edifice, formerly belonged, with the liberty, to the Knights Hospitallers of Newland, in the county of York; at the dissolution they were granted by Edward VI. to the family of Burnell.

WINKFIELD, a parish in the hundred of RIPPLESMERE, county of BERKS, 5½ miles (S. W. by W.) from New Windsor, containing, with Ascot, 1676 inhabitants. The living is a discharged vicarage, in the archdeaconry of Berks, and diocese of Salisbury, rated in the king's books at £8. 5. 10., endowed with £200 private benefaction, and £200 royal bounty, and in the patronage of the Dean and Chapter of Salisbury. The church is dedicated to St. Mary. The Earl of Ranelagh, in 1710, built a chapel on Winkfield Plain, in which service is daily performed, and attached to it a free school for twenty-one boys, and another for twenty-one girls, endowing them with property in Ireland, and directed that the schoolmaster should be in holy orders. In 1715, Thomas Maule, Esq. bequeathed £500; in 1783, Thomas Hatch, who had been educated here, £500; and in 1809, John Tow left £500 four per cent. stock, in augmentation of the income, which altogether amounts to upwards of £250. The children are clothed and educated according to the founder's intention, and afterwards apprenticed, with a premium of £5 each.

WINKFIELD, a parish in the hundred of BRADFORD, county of WILTS, 2 miles (W. S. W.) from Trowbridge, containing, with Rowley, 354 inhabitants. The living is a rectory, in the archdeaconry and diocese of Salisbury, rated in the king's books at £5. 16. 5½. The Rev. E. Spencer was patron in 1817. The church is dedicated to St. Andrew.

WINKLEY, a parish in the hundred of NORTH TAWTON and WINKLEY, county of DEVON, 5¼ miles (S. W.) from Chulmleigh, containing 1436 inhabitants. The living is a vicarage, in the archdeaconry of Barnstaple, and diocese of Exeter, rated in the king's books at £21. 8. 9., and in the patronage of the Dean and Chapter of Salisbury. The church is dedicated to All Saints. There is a place of worship for Wesleyan Methodists. A fair for cattle is held on the first Monday in August; and there is an annual fair at Hollacombe, in this parish, on Michaelmas-day. Here is an endowed almshouse, called Gidley's, for poor widows.

WINKSLEY, a chapelry in that part of the parish of RIPON which is in the lower division of the wapentake of CLARO, West riding of the county of YORK, 4¾ miles (W.) from Ripon, containing 176 inhabitants. The living is a perpetual curacy, in the jurisdiction of the peculiar court of Ripon, belonging to the Archbishop of York, endowed with £400 private benefaction, and £600 royal bounty, and in the patronage of the Dean and Chapter of Ripon. The chapel, dedicated to St. Oswald, has lately received an addition of two hundred and twenty sittings, of which one hundred and ninety-five are free, the Incorporated Society for the enlargement of churches and chapels having granted £150 towards defraying the expense.

WINKTON, a tything in the parish and hundred of CHRISTCHURCH, New Forest (West) division of the county of SOUTHAMPTON, 2½ miles (N. W. by N.) from Christchurch, with which the population is returned.

WINLATON, a parochial district in the western division of CHESTER ward, county palatine of DURHAM, 6¼ miles (W. by S.) from Gateshead, containing 3295 inhabitants. The church was finished in 1828, at an expense of £2500, of which sum £2000. 11. 5. was defrayed by the parliamentary commissioners : it is in the later English style of architecture, and contains eight hundred sittings, of which six hundred and thirty-seven are free. The village occupies an elevated site between the rivers Tyne and Darwent, and owes its rise to the extensive iron works, removed hither from Sunderland by Sir Ambrose Crawley, about 1690, for carrying on which the neighbourhood affords peculiar advantages, in the abundance of coal, the facility of water carriage, &c. Edge-tools, files, and nail-rods, are the principal articles manufactured; and those of a heavier kind, such as anchors, anvils, pumps, and cylinders for steam-engines, chain cables, spades, shovels, saws, and cast-iron utensils of every description, are made at Swalwell. A code of laws for the workmen was also established, which, in a great measure, has superseded the general law, and under which a court of arbitrators sits every ten weeks, by whom justice is promptly administered, at a very trifling expense. The principal manufacturers (Crawley, Millington, and Co.) have large warehouses in Thames-street, London, and at Greenwich, and constantly employ two vessels, of about three hundred tons' burden each, in transporting their goods thither and to Newcastle for sale. A chapel was built here, in 1705, on the site of a more ancient one, which is said to have been demolished in 1569; but having been suffered to go to ruin, a spacious school-room was erected, in 1816, on the spot, in which divine service was occasionally performed by the rector of Ryton, to which parish Winlaton formerly belonged, till the new church was built, when it was made parochial. At the village of Blaydon, in this township, there is a place of worship for Methodists; and there are works for refining lead on the banks of the Tyne.

WINMARLEIGH, a township in the parish of GARSTANG, hundred of AMOUNDERNESS, county palatine of LANCASTER, 2 miles (N. W.) from Garstang, containing 248 inhabitants.

WINNALL, a parish in the hundred of FAWLEY, Fawley division of the county of SOUTHAMPTON, ¾ of a mile (N. N. E.) from Winchester, containing 128 inhabitants. The living is a rectory, in the peculiar jurisdiction of the Rector, rated in the king's books at £5, and in the patronage of the Bishop of Winchester.

WINNERSH, a liberty in that part of the parish of HURST which is in the hundred of SONNING, county of BERKS, containing 491 inhabitants. A school is partly supported here by a trifling annual subscription.

WINNINGTON, a township in that part of the parish of GREAT BUDWORTH which is in the second division of the hundred of EDDISBURY, county palatine of CHESTER, 1 mile (N. W.) from Northwich, containing 230 inhabitants. It is situated on the banks of the Weever, over which there is a stone bridge.

WINNINGTON, a township in that part of the parish of MUCKLESTON which is in the northern division of the hundred of PIREHILL, county of STAFFORD, 4½ miles (N. E.) from Drayton in Hales, containing 226 inhabitants.

WINNOW (ST.), a parish in the hundred of WEST, county of CORNWALL, 2½ miles (S. E.) from Lostwithiel, containing 906 inhabitants. The living is a vicarage, in the peculiar jurisdiction and patronage of the Dean and Chapter of Exeter, rated in the king's books at £5. The navigable river Fowey runs on the west and south of this parish, and is crossed by a bridge, on the high road from Bodmin to Plymouth, at Resprin, where are the ruins of a chapel of ease. On Beacon hill a square battery was constructed by the royalists, a short time before the capitulation of the army of the parliament, in 1644.

WINSCALES, a township in the parish of WORKINGTON, ALLERDALE ward above Darwent, county of CUMBERLAND, 2½ miles (S. E.) from Workington, containing 157 inhabitants.

WINSCOMBE, a parish in the hundred of WINTERSTOKE, county of SOMERSET, 2 miles (N. by W.) from Axbridge, containing 1428 inhabitants. The living is a discharged vicarage, in the archdeaconry of Wells, and diocese of Bath and Wells, rated in the king's books at £16. 2. 11., and in the patronage of the Dean and Chapter of Wells. The church, dedicated to St. James, is a handsome structure, with a stately western tower crowned with pinnacles. Symons Cardinbrook, in 1761, gave the residue of his estate to be applied for teaching poor children : the school-room was erected by subscription, aided by about £60 from this bequest; the permanent annual income is £15.

WINSFORD, a parish in the hundred of WILLITON and FREEMANNERS, county of SOMERSET, 5 miles (N. by W.) from Dulverton, containing 518 inhabitants. The living is a vicarage, in the archdeaconry of Taunton, and diocese of Bath and Wells, rated in the king's books at £14. 13. 9., and in the patronage of the Master and Fellows of Emanuel College, Cambridge. The church is dedicated to St. Mary Magdalene. There is a place of worship for Wesleyan Methodists. The river Ax runs through the parish.

WINSHAM, a parish forming one of the four detached portions which constitute the eastern division of the hundred of KINGSBURY, county of SOMERSET, 4 miles (E. by S.) from Chard, containing 878 inhabitants. The living is a vicarage, in the peculiar jurisdiction of the Consistorial Court of the Dean and Chapter of Wells, rated in the king's books at

£14. 13. 4., and in the patronage of the Dean of Wells. The church is an ancient structure, with a tower rising from the centre. Sir Matthew Holworthy, in 1680, gave certain premises, producing about £6 per annum, which is applied towards the instruction of twenty-four boys and twenty-four girls, in a school erected by subscription in 1818. A considerable manufacture of narrow woollen cloth is carried on in the village.

WINSHILL, a township in that part of the parish of BURTON upon TRENT which is in the hundred of REPTON and GRESLEY, county of DERBY, 1½ mile (E. N. E.) from Burton upon Trent, containing 357 inhabitants.

WINSKILL, a township in the parish of ADDINGHAM, LEATH ward, county of CUMBERLAND, 6¾ miles (N. E. by E.) from Penrith. The population is returned with the township of Hunsonby.

WINSLADE, a parish in the hundred of BASINGSTOKE, Basingstoke division of the county of SOUTHAMPTON, 3 miles (S. by E.) from Basingstoke, containing, with the tything of Kempshot, 158 inhabitants. The living is a discharged rectory, in the archdeaconry and diocese of Winchester, rated in the king's books at £6. 12. 1., and in the patronage of Lord Bolton. The church is dedicated to St. Mary.

WINSLEY, a joint hamlet with Snitterton, in that part of the parish of DARLEY which is in the hundred of WIRKSWORTH, county of DERBY, 3½ miles (W. N. W.) from Matlock, containing, with Snitterton, 665 inhabitants.

WINSLEY, a joint chapelry with Limpley-Stoke, in the parish of GREAT BRADFORD, hundred of BRADFORD, county of WILTS, 1½ mile (W.) from Bradford, containing, with Limpley-Stoke, 2979 inhabitants. The chapel is dedicated to St. Nicholas. There is a place of worship for Wesleyan Methodists.

WINSLEY, a joint chapelry with Hartwith, in the parish of KIRKBY-MALZEARD, lower division of the wapentake of CLARO, West riding of the county of YORK, 3 miles (W. N. W.) from Ripley. The population is returned with Hartwith.

WINSLOW, a market town and parish in the hundred of COTTESLOE, county of BUCKINGHAM, 6½ miles (S. E.) from Buckingham, and 50 (N. W.) from London, containing 1222 inhabitants. This town is of considerable antiquity, having been given by King Offa to the abbey of St. Albans, so early as 794: it is situated on the brow of a hill, and consists of three principal streets, regularly built and of neat appearance ; the houses are chiefly of brick ; water is amply supplied from wells. The land in the vicinity is extremely fertile, and in a high state of cultivation : lace-making is carried on to a small extent. The market, granted by charter of Henry III., is on Thursday; a small quantity of corn is pitched in the market-house. Fairs are held on February 18th, March 20th, Holy Thursday, August 21st, September 22nd, November 26th, for cattle ; the Thursday before Old Michaelmas day, and the first and second Thursday following, are statute fairs. The living is a discharged vicarage, in the archdeaconry of St. Albans, and diocese of London, rated in the king's books at £11. 5. 10., endowed with £200 private benefaction, and £200 royal bounty, and in the patronage of the Crown. The church, which is dedicated to St. Lawrence, is a spacious and venerable structure, in the later style of English architecture, with a square embattled tower at the west end. There are places of worship for Baptists, Independents, and Wesleyan Methodists. Joseph Rogers, in 1724, bequeathed £600 in trust, directing it to be vested in land, and the rental, now amounting to about £22 per annum, to be applied to the instruction of twelve poor children ; and a further sum of £27. 10. was formerly granted by a person unknown, for the charity school at Hanging Stiles. The white poppy was so successfully cultivated here, in 1821, as to produce sixty pounds of opium, worth, at least, £75, from four acres, and one hundred and forty-three pounds, in the next year, from eleven acres ; for which, on both occasions, the prize of thirty guineas was awarded by the Society for the Encouragement of Arts, Manufactures, and Commerce.

WINSLOW, a township in the parish of BROMYARD, hundred of BROXASH, county of HEREFORD, 2½ miles (S. W. by W.) from Bromyard, containing 401 inhabitants.

WINSON, a chapelry in that part of the parish of BIBURY which is in the hundred of BRADLEY, county of GLOUCESTER, 5 miles (S. S. W.) from North Leach, containing 185 inhabitants. The chapel is dedicated to St. Michael. Winson is within the jurisdiction of the peculiar court of Bibury.

WINSTANLEY, a township in that part of the parish of WIGAN which is in the hundred of WEST DERBY, county palatine of LANCASTER, 3¼ miles (S. W. by W.) from Wigan, containing 800 inhabitants.

WINSTER, a market town and chapelry in that part of the parish of YOULGRAVE which is in the hundred of HIGH PEAK, county of DERBY, 19 miles (N.N.W.) from Derby, and 145 (N. N. W.) from London, containing 928 inhabitants. This small town is situated midway between the river Derwent and the Cromford and High Peak railway, about three miles from each, with the latter of which a branch communication is contemplated ; it is badly supplied with water, which in dry seasons is only to be procured at the distance of a mile. The inhabitants are chiefly employed in mining, which was formerly much more extensively carried on ; the cotton trade at one period was established, but has ceased for some years. The market, on Saturday, is very indifferently attended; and the four fairs formerly held annually have declined. Winster is within the jurisdiction of a court of pleas held at Tutbury every third Tuesday, for the recovery of debts under 40s. The living is a perpetual curacy, in the archdeaconry of Derby, and diocese of Lichfield and Coventry, endowed with £400 private benefaction, £200 royal bounty, and £300 parliamentary grant, and in the patronage of the Freeholders. In 1702, Mrs. Anne Phermey and Mrs. H. Fenshaw bestowed one-fourth of the tithes of corn and hay in the township on the minister. The chapel, dedicated to St. John the Baptist, is partly in the Norman style of architecture, and partly of a later date, with a tower nearly covered with ivy. Primitive and Wesleyan Methodists have each a place of worship. Thomas Eyre, Esq., in 1717, bequeathed £20 per annum for the instruction of twenty children ; and an annuity of £5 was left, in 1718, by Robert Moore, for teaching five more. In the neighbourhood are several barrows, in one of which, opened in 1768, two glass vessels were found, containing some clear, but green-coloured, water, a silver bracelet, some glass beads, and other trinkets.

WINSTER, a chapelry in that part of the parish of KENDAL which is in KENDAL ward, county of WESTMORLAND, 7 miles (W.) from Kendal. The population is returned with the township of Undermilbeck, which is in the parish of Windermere. The living is a perpetual curacy, in the archdeaconry of Richmond, and diocese of Chester, endowed with £400 private benefaction, £800 royal bounty, and £300 parliamentary grant, and in the patronage of the Landowners. This chapelry once formed part of the chapelry of Crook, and the inhabitants still contribute towards the reparation of that chapel.

WINSTON, a parish in the south-western division of DARLINGTON ward, county palatine of DURHAM, 6½ miles (E.) from Barnard-Castle, containing 287 inhabitants. The living is a rectory, in the archdeaconry and diocese of Durham, rated in the king's books at £9. 18. 1½., and in the patronage of the Bishop of Durham. The church is dedicated to St. Andrew. The village is situated on an elevation rising from the northern bank of the river Tees, which is crossed by a handsome stone bridge of one arch, one hundred and eleven feet span, built in 1764. A school was founded here by the Earl of Bridgewater, who endowed it with £70 per annum.

WINSTON, a parish in the hundred of THREDLING, county of SUFFOLK, 1¼ mile (S. S. E.) from Debenham, containing 366 inhabitants. The living is a vicarage, in the archdeaconry of Suffolk, and diocese of Norwich, rated in the king's books at £9. 3. 9., and in the patronage of the Dean and Chapter of Ely. The church is dedicated to St. Andrew.

WINSTONE, a parish in the hundred of BISLEY, county of GLOUCESTER, 6¼ miles (N. W. by N.) from Cirencester, containing 192 inhabitants. The living is a discharged rectory, in the archdeaconry and diocese of Gloucester, rated in the king's books at £7. 10., endowed with £200 royal bounty, and in the patronage of Sir E. B. Sandys, Bart. The church is dedicated to St. Bartholomew. There is a place of worship for Baptists. The ancient Ermin-street passes through the parish.

WINTERBOURNE, a chapelry in the parish of CHIEVELEY, hundred of FAIRCROSS, county of BERKS, 3½ miles (N. N. W.) from Speenhamland, containing 321 inhabitants. The chapel is dedicated to St. James. A school here is partly supported by subscriptions, amounting to about £10 per annum.

WINTERBOURNE, a parish in the upper division of the hundred of LANGLEY and SWINEHEAD, county of GLOUCESTER, 6½ miles (N. E. by N.) from Bristol, containing, with the hamlet of Hambrook, 2627 inhabitants. The living is a rectory, in the peculiar jurisdiction of the Consistorial Court of the Bishop of Bristol, rated in the king's books at £27. 7. 6., and in the patronage of the President and Fellows of St. John's College, Oxford. The church is dedicated to St. Mary. There is a place of worship for Wesleyan Methodists. John Silcocks, in 1741, left an annuity of £2. 10. for teaching children to read. A National school, established here and supported by voluntary contributions, affords instruction to about one hundred and eighty children

WINTERBOURNE (EARLS), a parish in the hundred of ALDERBURY, county of WILTS, 3½ miles (N. E. by N.) from Salisbury, containing 210 inhabitants. The living is a perpetual curacy, in the peculiar jurisdiction and patronage of the Prebendary of Chute and Chisenbury in the Cathedral Church of Salisbury, endowed with £800 royal bounty, and £200 parliamentary grant. The church is dedicated to St. Michael. There is a place of worship for Wesleyan Methodists. Near the village is an ancient earthwork, called Chlorus' Camp, or Figbury Ring, from its circular form, including an area of about fifteen acres.

WINTERBOURNE (ST. MARTIN), a parish in the hundred of GEORGE, Dorchester division of the county of DORSET, 3 miles (W. S. W.) from Dorchester, containing 342 inhabitants. The living is a discharged vicarage, in the archdeaconry of Dorset, and diocese of Bristol, rated in the king's books at £9. 15., and in the patronage of the Bishop of Salisbury. The church has a neat embattled tower crowned with pinnacles. A market, granted by Henry III., was formerly held here; and a fair is still kept on St. Martin's day. In this parish is Maiden Castle, one of the strongest and most extensive Roman camps in the west of England, which, according to Ptolemy, was the *castra æstiva* of the garrison of *Dunium*, afterwards called *Durnovaria*, the capital of the Durotriges: it consists of a treble ditch and rampart, enclosing an irregular oval area of forty-four acres, but the entire work covers an extent of one hundred and fifteen acres and a half. There are two very intricate entrances, that at the east end being defended by five, and that at the west end by six, ditches and ramparts. Near the former passes the vicinal road leading from Dorchester to Weymouth, and to the latter extends a branch from the *Via Iceniana*, which passes about a mile north of the camp. The summit commands an extensive prospect of barrows stretching for many miles along the tops of the hills to the southward.

WINTERBOURNE-ABBAS, a parish in the hundred of EGGERTON, Bridport division of the county of DORSET, 4¼ miles (W.) from Dorchester, containing 170 inhabitants. The living is a rectory, with that of Winterbourne-Steepleton united, in the archdeaconry of Dorset, and diocese of Bristol, rated in the king's books at £13. 17. 6., and in the patronage of the Rector and Fellows of Lincoln College, Oxford. The church is dedicated to St. Mary. The stream called the South Winterbourne runs through the parish: it rises about a mile west of this place, in the vicinity of an ancient British temple, consisting of nine rude stones of unequal height, placed in a circular form, the diameter of which is twenty-eight feet. Half a mile to the westward are the remains of a cromlech, and there are several other erect stones in the vicinity. This neighbourhood is supposed to have been the scene of some remarkable action, from the great number of tumuli scattered about in different directions.

WINTERBOURNE-BASSETT, a parish in the hundred of SELKLEY, county of WILTS, 7¾ miles (N. W.) from Marlborough, containing 291 inhabitants. The living is a rectory, in the archdeaconry and diocese of Salisbury, rated in the king's books at £18. 9. 7., and in the patronage of the President and Fellows of Magdalene College, Oxford. The church is dedicated to St.

Catherine. Among various other Druidical remains are, a double circle of rude stones, a barrow surrounded with large stones, and the supposed site of houses once occupied by archdruids.

WINTERBOURNE-CAME, a parish partly in the hundred of CULLIFORD-TREE, Dorchester division, and partly within the liberty of FRAMPTON, Bridport division, of the county of DORSET, 2¾ miles (S. E. by S.) from Dorchester, containing, with the tything of Cripton, 54 inhabitants. The living is a rectory, to which that of Winterbourne-Farringdon was united, in 1751, in the archdeaconry of Dorset, and diocese of Bristol, rated jointly in the king's books at £15. 5., and in the patronage of Lady C. Damer. The church is dedicated to St. Peter. Here was anciently a small Benedictine nunnery, supposed to have been a cell to the abbey of Caen in Normandy.

WINTERBOURNE-CLENSTONE, a parish in the hundred of COOMBS-DITCH, Blandford (North) division of the county of DORSET, 4¼ miles (S. W.) from Blandford-Forum, containing 73 inhabitants. The living is a rectory, in the archdeaconry of Dorset, and diocese of Bristol, rated in the king's books at £6. 18. 1½., and in the patronage of E. M. Pleydell, Esq. The church is dedicated to St. Nicholas. Anciently there were three churches, the livings of which were rectories, and the parish was much more populous, as is evident from the foundations of houses still visible within its limits. A little south of the church, on the side of a hill, commences Coombs-ditch, which gives name to the hundred, and where the courts were formerly held : it is thought by Dr. Stukeley to have been a long rampart and ditch of the first colony of the Belgæ.

WINTERBOURNE-DANTSEY, a parish in the hundred of ALDERBURY, county of WILTS, 3¾ miles (N. E. by N.) from Salisbury, containing 150 inhabitants. The living is a perpetual curacy, in the peculiar jurisdiction and patronage of the Prebendary of Chute and Chisenbury in the Cathedral Church of Salisbury. The church is dedicated to St. Edward.

WINTERBOURNE-FARRINGDON, or ST. GERMAN'S, formerly a parish, now claiming to be extraparochial, in the hundred of CULLIFORD-TREE, Dorchester division of the county of DORSET, 2½ miles (S.) from Dorchester. The population is returned with Herringstone. The living was a discharged rectory, in the archdeaconry of Dorset, and diocese of Bristol, rated in the king's books at £7. 3. 6½.; in 1751 it was united to the rectory of Winterbourne-Came.

WINTERBOURNE-GUNNER, a parish in the hundred of ALDERBURY, county of WILTS, 4 miles (N. E. by N.) from Salisbury, containing 132 inhabitants. The living is a rectory, in the archdeaconry and diocese of Salisbury, rated in the king's books at £12. 16. 10½., and in the patronage of the Rev. C. J. and Mrs. Coleman. The church is dedicated to St. Mary.

WINTERBOURNE-HOUGHTON, county of DORSET. — See HOUGHTON (WINTERBOURNE).

WINTERBOURNE-KINGSTON, a parish in the hundred of BEER-REGIS, Blandford (South) division of the county of DORSET, 6½ miles (S. S. W.) from Blandford-Forum, containing 464 inhabitants. The living is a perpetual curacy, annexed to the vicarage of Beer-Regis, in the jurisdiction of the peculiar court of

the Dean of Salisbury. The church is dedicated to St. Nicholas.

WINTERBOURNE-MONKTON, a parish in the hundred of CULLIFORD-TREE, Dorchester division of the county of DORSET, 2 miles (S. W. by S.) from Dorchester, containing 77 inhabitants. The living is a rectory, in the archdeaconry of Dorset, and diocese of Bristol, rated in the king's books at £8, and in the patronage of the Earl of Ilchester. An Alien priory, subordinate to the priory of Wast, or de Vasto, of the order of Clugny, is said to have existed here before the 15th of John.

WINTERBOURNE-MONKTON, a parish in the hundred of SELKLEY, county of WILTS, 7 miles (W. N. W.) from Marlborough, containing 201 inhabitants. The living is a discharged vicarage, united, in 1747, to that of Avebury, in the archdeaconry and diocese of Salisbury, rated in the king's books at £5. The church is dedicated to St. Mary Magdalene.

WINTERBOURNE-STEEPLETON, a parish in the hundred of UGGSCOMBE, Dorchester division of the county of DORSET, 4 miles (W. by S.) from Dorchester, containing 161 inhabitants. The living is a rectory, united with that of Winterbourne-Abbas, in the archdeaconry of Dorset, and diocese of Bristol, rated in the king's books at £10. 4. 7. The church, dedicated to St. Michael in 1401, is situated in the middle of the parish ; it is covered with lead, and has a tower surmounted by a stone spire, which, and that at Iwerne-Minster, are the only spires in the county.

WINTERBOURNE-STOKE, a parish in the hundred of BRANCH and DOLE, county of WILTS, 5 miles (W. by S.) from Amesbury, containing 281 inhabitants. The living is a discharged vicarage, in the archdeaconry and diocese of Salisbury, rated in the king's books at £11. 2. 8., and in the patronage of Alexander Baring, Esq. The church is dedicated to St. Peter.

WINTERBOURNE-STRICKLAND, a parish in the hundred of PIMPERNE, Blandford (North) division of the county of DORSET, 3¾ miles (W. S. W.) from Blandford-Forum, containing 364 inhabitants. The living is a rectory, in the archdeaconry of Dorset, and diocese of Bristol, rated in the king's books at £16. 6. 3., and in the patronage of Lady C. Damer. The church is nearly in the centre of the parish ; it has an embattled tower crowned with pinnacles, and was repaired about 1716. Quarrelston House, an ancient quadrangular building, formerly the seat of the Binghams, has been, for the greater part, pulled down at different times within the last half century.

WINTERBOURNE-WHITCHURCH, a parish in the hundred of COOMBS-DITCH, Blandford (North) division of the county of DORSET, 5½ miles (S. W.) from Blandford-Forum, containing 493 inhabitants. The living is a discharged vicarage, in the archdeaconry of Dorset, and diocese of Bristol, rated in the king's books at £7. 16. 10½., endowed with £200 private benefaction, and £200 royal bounty, and in the patronage of the Bishop of Salisbury. The church, dedicated to St. Mary, is a long narrow edifice, with a south transept, and a low embattled tower rising from the intersection ; it contains a curious ancient font. The Rev. Samuel Wesley, father of John and Charles Wesley, founders of the sect of Methodists, and author of several poems on religious subjects, was born here, during the incumbency of his father, who was ultimately ejected for non-conformity ; he died in 1735.

WINTERBOURNE-ZELSTONE, a parish in the hundred of RUSHMORE, Blandford (North) division of the county of DORSET, 6¼ miles (S. by E.) from Blandford-Forum, containing 245 inhabitants. The living is a rectory, in the archdeaconry of Dorset, and diocese of Bristol, rated in the king's books at £13. 11. 3., and in the patronage of J. J. Farquharson, Esq. The church, dedicated to St. Mary, has a lofty embattled tower.

WINTERBURN, a joint township with Flasby, in the parish of GARGRAVE, eastern division of the wapentake of STAINCLIFFE and EWCROSS, West riding of the county of YORK, 7 miles (N. W. by N.) from Skipton. The population is returned with Flasby. There is a place of worship for Independents.

WINTERINGHAM, a parish in the northern division of the wapentake of MANLEY, parts of LINDSEY, county of LINCOLN, 7½ miles (W.) from Barton upon Humber, containing 746 inhabitants. The living is a rectory, in the archdeaconry of Stow, and diocese of Lincoln, rated in the king's books at £28, and in the patronage of the Hon. and Rev. J. Lumley Saville. The church is dedicated to All Saints. There is a place of worship for Wesleyan Methodists. According to Dr. Stukeley, the ancient name of this place was *Abontrus*.

WINTERSET, a township in that part of the parish of WRAGBY which is in the wapentake of STAINCROSS, West riding of the county of YORK, 5¾ miles (S. E. by E.) from Wakefield, containing 135 inhabitants.

WINTERSLOW, a parish comprising East and West Winterslow, in the hundred of ALDERBURY, county of WILTS : East Winterslow is 7¼ miles (N. E. by E.), and West Winterslow 6½ miles (E. N. E.), from Salisbury, containing 748 inhabitants. The living is a rectory, in the archdeaconry and diocese of Salisbury, rated in the king's books at £18. 13. 4., and in the patronage of Lord Holland. The church is dedicated to All Saints. There is a place of worship for Wesleyan Methodists. Near Winterslow hut are three barrows, in one of which was discovered, a few years ago, an arched vault, constructed of rude flints, wedged together remarkably secure, enclosing two large sepulchral urns inverted, which were found to contain ashes enveloped in linen of a very fine texture, burnt bones, beads of red amber, a metal pin, a two-edged lance-head of brass, with hair of a beautiful brown colour, and other relics, supposed to have been those of some illustrious British female. The Roman road from Salisbury to Winchester passed through this parish.

WINTERTON, a parish in the northern division of the wapentake of MANLEY, parts of LINDSEY, county of LINCOLN, 8¼ miles (W. S. W.) from Barton upon Humber, containing 1015 inhabitants. The living is a discharged vicarage, in the archdeaconry of Stow, and diocese of Lincoln, rated in the king's books at £8, endowed with £200 parliamentary grant, and in the patronage of the Crown. The church is dedicated to All Saints. There is a place of worship for Wesleyan Methodists. A meeting of farmers, for the sale of corn, &c., takes place here every Wednesday, but there is no now established market. A fair for cattle is held on July 6th, and it is intended to apply for another to be held in the autumn. Ten poor children are instructed for a

VOL. IV.

rent-charge of £3. 3. a year, the bequest of Richard Beck, in 1728. Three curious tesselated pavements were discovered here, in 1747 : the Fosse road terminates at this place.

WINTERTON, a parish in the western division of the hundred of FLEGG, county of NORFOLK, 5½ miles (N. by W.) from Caistor, containing 545 inhabitants. The living is a rectory, with the perpetual curacy of East Somerton annexed, in the archdeaconry and diocese of Norwich, rated in the king's books at £20. 13. 4., and in the patronage of E. Cooper, Esq. The church is dedicated to All Saints; the steeple serves as a noted landmark. Winterton had formerly a market and a fair, which have been long disused : the fishery affords employment to a considerable number of the inhabitants. On a promontory, called Winterton Ness, are two lighthouses, one supplied with coal, the other with oil. Several large bones were found on the cliff, in 1665, one of which, supposed to be that of a man's leg, was three feet two inches in length, and weighed fifty-seven pounds.

WINTHORPE, a parish in the Marsh division of the wapentake of CANDLESHOE, parts of LINDSEY, county of LINCOLN, 11 miles (E. by N.) from Spilsby, containing 233 inhabitants. The living is a discharged vicarage, united, in 1729, to that of Burgh in the Marsh, in the archdeaconry and diocese of Lincoln, rated in the king's books at £8, and endowed with £200 royal bounty, and £800 parliamentary grant. The church is dedicated to St. Mary.

WINTHORPE, a parish in the northern division of the wapentake of NEWARK, county of NOTTINGHAM, 1¾ mile (N. N. E.) from Newark, containing 235 inhabitants. The living is a rectory, in the archdeaconry of Nottingham, and diocese of York, rated in the king's books at £7. 11. 0½., and in the patronage of the Rev. W. Rastall. The church is dedicated to All Saints. The village is situated on the banks of the Trent : the Fosse road passes through the parish.

WINTNEY (HARTLEY), county of SOUTHAMPTON.—See HARTLEY-WINTNEY.

WINTON, a township in the parish of KIRKBY-STEPHEN, EAST ward, county of WESTMORLAND, 1¼ mile (N. N. E.) from Kirkby-Stephen, containing 284 inhabitants. A free school, erected by subscription in 1659, is endowed with about £15 a year, £11 of which arises from land bequeathed, in 1681, by Robert Waller, and the rest from £112 left by Richard Munkhouse, in 1722 : it is open to all children of the township, who pay a small quarterage. John Langhorne, D.D., joint translator of Plutarch, author of "Fables of Flora," and other works; his brother, William Langhorne, M.A., his assistant in the above translation ; and Richard Burn, L.L.D., the eminent law-writer and historian, were natives of this place, and received the rudiments of their education at the school.

WINTON, a township in the parish of KIRBY-SIGSTON, wapentake of ALLERTONSHIRE, North riding of the county of YORK, 3¾ miles (N. E. by E.) from North Allerton, containing 138 inhabitants.

WINTRINGHAM, a parish in the wapentake of BUCKROSE, East riding of the county of YORK, comprising the chapelry of Knapton and the township of Wintringham, and containing 532 inhabitants, of which number, 326 are in the township of Wintringham, 6½ miles (E. by N.) from New Malton. The living is a

3 X

donative, in the patronage of Sir W. Strickland, Bart. The church is dedicated to St. Peter.

WINWICK, a parish partly in the hundred of LEIGHTONSTONE, county of HUNTINGDON, and partly in that of POLEBROOK, county of NORTHAMPTON, 6¼ miles (S. E.) from Oundle, containing 301 inhabitants. The living is a discharged vicarage, in the archdeaconry of Huntingdon, and diocese of Lincoln, rated in the king's books at £7. 16. 10., and in the patronage of Lord Montagu. The church is dedicated to All Saints.

WINWICK, a parish in the hundred of WEST DERBY, county palatine of LANCASTER, comprising the borough town of Newton in Mackerfield, the chapelries of Ashton in Mackerfield, Lowton, and Newchurch, and the townships of Culcheth, Golborne, Haydock, Houghton with Middleton and Arbury, Kenyon, Southworth with Croft, and Winwick, and containing 16,229 inhabitants, of which number, 602 are in the township of Winwick, 3 miles (N.) from Warrington. The living is a rectory, in the archdeaconry and diocese of Chester, rated in the king's books at £102. 9. 9½., and in the patronage of the Earl of Derby. The church, dedicated to St. Oswald, is an ancient edifice with a lofty spire, said to be coeval with the establishment of the Christian religion in this country. There is a place of worship for Wesleyan Methodists. Southworth Hall, in this parish, once belonged to the Roman Catholic college of Stonyhurst, and part of it is still used as a chapel by professors of that religion. Considerable manufactures of cotton, fustian, locks, hinges, and various other articles, are carried on within the parish. A free grammar school was founded, in 1618, by Gualter Legh, Esq., who endowed it with an annuity of £10, which by subsequent benefactions was augmented to £34 : the school-room was built by Sir Peter Legh. One of the prescribed rules for the government of this charity is, that if the school be vacant for one whole year, the salary for that time shall devolve to the heirs of Francis, Thomas, and Peter Legh. Between this village and the town of Newton is an elevated piece of ground, called Redbank, from its having been, in 1648, the scene of an obstinately contested battle between Oliver Cromwell and the Scots, when the latter were defeated with terrible slaughter. In observance of a custom for some time established, the rector pays annually the rental of their cottages for six poor industrious tenants, placing over the door of each a board, on which is inscribed the date when its occupant enjoyed the benefaction.

WINWICK, a parish in the hundred of GUILSBOROUGH, county of NORTHAMPTON, 8¾ miles (N. N. E.) from Daventry, containing 137 inhabitants. The living is a rectory, in the archdeaconry of Northampton, and diocese of Peterborough, rated in the king's books at £15. 6. 8., and in the patronage of the Bishop of Lincoln. The church is dedicated to the Holy Trinity. The Grand Union canal passes through the parish. Here are the remains of an old mansion, which have been converted into a farm-house ; the gateway leading to it is a curious antique structure.

WIRKSWORTH, a parish comprising the market town of Wirksworth, the townships of Cromford, Hopton, and Ible, and the hamlets of Callow and Middleton, in the hundred of WIRKSWORTH ; the townships of Alderwasley, Ashleyhay, Biggin, and Idridgehay with Allton, in the hundred of APPLETREE ; and the hamlet of Iron-Brock-Grange, in the hundred of HIGH PEAK, county of DERBY ; and containing 7315 inhabitants, of which number, 3787 are in the town of Wirksworth, 13 miles (N. N. W.) from Derby, and 139 (N. W. by N.) from London. This place, formerly written Wircesworth, Werchestworde, and Wyrkysworth, is of very great antiquity, and is supposed to derive its name from the valuable lead-works in the neighbourhood, which, by an inscription on a pig of lead, found in 1777, appear to have been worked so early as the time of the Emperor Adrian, at the commencement of the second century ; and the Saxons subsequently carried on mining operations here on an extensive scale. In 714, Eadburga, abbess of Repton, to which abbey Wirksworth then belonged, sent hence to St. Guthlac, patron saint of Croyland abbey, a leaden coffin ; and in 835, Kenwara, another abbess of Repton, granted her estate at Wercesvorde to Humbert, on condition that he gave annually lead worth £15 to Archbishop Ceolnoth, for the use of Christ Church at Canterbury. In Domesday-book Wirksworth is described as the property of the Crown, having a church, a priest, and three lead mines ; and it remained so until King John, in the fifth year of his reign, granted it to William de Ferrers, in whose family it continued until the attainder of his descendant, Robert, in the reign of Henry III., by which monarch it was, in 1265, given to his son Edmund, Earl of Lancaster, and the manor has since that period constituted a part of the possessions of the duchy of Lancaster.

The town is situated in a valley nearly surrounded with hills, at the southern extremity of the mining district ; it is not regularly lighted or paved, and is supplied with water, brought by pipes, from the hills on its eastern side. The chief employment of the inhabitants arises from the lead mines, but some of them are also engaged in the cotton manufacture ; and there are, in the town and its immediate neighbourhood, three establishments in which common ginghams are made, and others for the production of hosiery, hats, tape, silk, and for wool-combing. The Cromford canal, and the Cromford and High Peak railway, commence in this parish ; the former about a mile and a half north of the town, near where it crosses the river Derwent, by means of an aqueduct, the span of whose arch over the river is eighty feet; and the latter about half a mile north. The mines and miners of this neighbourhood are governed by ancient customs, confirmed by a commission of enquiry in 1287 ; and all disputes and offences are determined at the Barmote courts, held twice a year before the steward, in the moothall, a handsome stone building, erected in 1814, by the Hon. Chas. Bathurst, late Chancellor of the duchy. In this hall is deposited the ancient brass dish, the standard from which those used for measuring the ore are made, which must be brought to be corrected by it, at least twice a year, by all the miners. The code of laws and regulations by which these courts are governed is very similar to that in force in the mining districts of the duchy of Cornwall : one remarkable custom is, that each person has the privilege of digging and searching for lead-ore in any part of the king's field, which, with a few exceptions, comprehends the whole wapentake ; and should he discover a vein of lead, he has a right to work it, and erect buildings necessary for that purpose, without making any compensation to the owner of the land. A market on Wednesday, and an annual fair for three days, were granted by Edward I., in 1305, to Thomas, Earl of Lancaster: Tuesday is now the market day, for provisions generally; and there are fairs on Shrove-Tuesday, Easter-Tuesday, May 12th, July 8th, September 8th, and the third Tuesday in November, for cattle, the last being also a statute fair. The town is governed by a constable and headborough, and a petty session is held by the county magistrates, on Tuesday in each week. Two courts baron, at Easter and Michaelmas, and a court leet at Easter, are held annually for the king's manor, by the lessee of the crown; and a court is also held for the rectorial manor, under the Dean of Lincoln, as impropriator: there is also another manor within the parish, for which no courts are held, called the Holland, or Richmond, manor, granted in 1553, by Henry VIII., to Ralph Gell, Esq., which now belongs to his descendant, Philip Gell, Esq., of Hopton.

The living is a vicarage, in the archdeaconry of Derby, and diocese of Lichfield and Coventry, rated in the king's books at £42. 7. 8½., and in the patronage of the Dean of Lincoln. The vicar is entitled, by custom, to every fortieth dish (of fourteen pints) of lead-ore raised in the parish, but the quantity, of late years, has been very small. The church, dedicated to St. Mary, is a handsome structure in the later English style, with a square tower, supported in the centre by four large pillars, and contains some ancient monuments. There are places of worship for Baptists, Independents, and Wesleyan Methodists. The free grammar school, adjoining the churchyard, was founded and endowed by Anthony Gell, Esq., of Hopton, in 1576, and has been recently rebuilt in the English style of architecture, at an expense of about £2000 : the present income is upwards of £250 per annum; the boys on the foundation are taught the classics free, but pay a small sum quarterly for instruction in English grammar, writing, and arithmetic. This school, in common with those of Ashbourn and Chesterfield, is entitled, next after the founder's relatives, to two fellowships and two scholarships at St. John's College, Cambridge, founded by the Rev. James Beresford, vicar of this parish, who died in 1520. Almshouses for six poor men, near the school, were also founded and endowed by Anthony Gell, Esq.; the inmates receive a small monthly allowance. Elizabeth Bagshaw, in 1797, bequeathed £2000 three per cent. consols. to trustees, for the benefit of the poor, the dividends of which, amounting to £56 per annum, are distributed in sums of £1 each : there are many other small donations and bequests, producing together a considerable sum, which is annually given to the poor of the town and parish; and a library for their use has been recently established, and is supported by subscription. In 1736, a quantity of Roman coins was discovered; and spars, fluors, &c., are found in great variety in the neighbourhood. Here were also some mineral springs, but they have been destroyed by draining the mines.

WIRSWALL, a township in that part of the parish of WHITCHURCH which is in the hundred of NANT-

WICH, county palatine of CHESTER, 5½ miles (E. S. E.) from Malpas, containing 113 inhabitants. The Chester canal passes along its western boundary.

WISBECH, or WISBEACH, (ST. PETER), a sea-port and market town in the hundred of WISBECH, Isle of ELY, county of CAMBRIDGE, 44 miles (N.) from Cambridge, and 94 (N. by E.) from London, containing, with Wisbech St. Mary, 7877 inhabitants. This place, which is of great antiquity, is noticed by the name of *Wisbece*, in

Corporate Seal.

a charter of Wulfhere, son of Peada, King of Mercia, by which that prince gave some lands in the vicinity to the abbey of Medehamstead, now Peterborough. The first part of the name is derived from the river Ouse, which was formerly called the Wise, and the latter syllable, of which the orthography has been adapted to that opinion, has been supposed to express its situation near the sea shore : according to other antiquaries, it is derived from the Saxon *bec*, signifying, either a river or a tongue of land at the confluence of two rivers, which, corresponding to its situation at the mouth of the Ouse, or Wise, near its confluence with the Nene, seems to justify the orthography *Wisbech*, generally adopted by the inhabitants, and sanctioned by a charter of Edward VI., in which the name is written *Wisbeche*. From the time of Wulfhere, nothing of importance occurs in the history of the place, till that of William the Conqueror, who, in the last year of his reign, erected a strong castle to keep the refractory barons in submission, and to check the ravages of the outlaws, who made frequent incursions from the neighbouring fens into the upland parts of the county. The castle, which was placed under the command of a governor, who was styled constable, and had a powerful garrison of soldiers, was, with the greater part of the town, destroyed by an inundation of the sea, in 1236, but they were soon afterwards restored, and the former having subsequently become greatly dilapidated, Bishop Morton erected another of brick, on its site, which became an episcopal palace of the Bishops of Ely, and their occasional residence. In the reign of Elizabeth the castle was appropriated as a place of security for the confinement of state prisoners; and during the protectorate of Cromwell, it was purchased by his secretary, Thurloe, who occasionally made it his residence. After the restoration, the castle again reverted to the Bishops of Ely, by whom it was sold : and the site and remains have subsequently disappeared in the recent improvement of the town. Richard I., in 1190, granted the inhabitants an exemption from toll in all fairs and markets throughout the kingdom, which grant, with other privileges, was confirmed by King John, who, in 1216, visited Wisbech, and took up his residence in the castle. On his departure, that monarch attempting to cross the Wash at an improper time, lost all his carriages, treasure, and regalia, by an inundation of the sea. The town is situated on both sides of the river Nene, over which is a handsome stone bridge of one elliptical arch, seventy-two feet in span, and consists of

3 X 2

several streets regularly formed; the houses are in general well-built, and on the site of the ancient castle, which was taken down in 1816, a handsome circus, of fifty well-built houses, has been erected, adding greatly to the general appearance of the town, whichhas been progressively improving, and is at present the most flourishing place in the Isle of Ely. The town is well paved, at the expense of the inhabitants, lighted and watched by the corporation, and amply supplied with water. A Literary Society was established in 1781, who have a library containing more than three thousand volumes: there is also a parochial library, containing many valuable works of eminent divines. Over the corn exchange are billiard and reading rooms; and there are a neat theatre, which is occasionally opened, and an assembly-room, which is appropriately fitted up. A neat and commodious edifice has been recently erected, in which are hot and cold salt water baths, furnished with dressing-rooms, and every requisite accommodation. The trade of the port has been considerably improved, and is still increasing. About a century since considerable quantities of oil, for the preparation of which not less than seven mills were employed in the town, and great quantities of butter, were shipped from this port; of the latter, eight thousand firkins were sent annually to London. From the great improvements that have been made in the system of draining, by which a considerable portion of unproductive land in the neighbourhood has been brought into cultivation, the trade in corn has been greatly increased, and the annual average quantity of that article alone, shipped from the port to Cambridge, Lynn, and other places, is not less than one hundred and twenty thousand quarters: the other exports are rape seed and long wool, of which great quantities are sent to Yorkshire; and timber, for the use of the navy, which is brought hither from the county of Northampton: the principal imports are, wine, deals, and coal. In the year ending January 1826, forty-five foreign vessels, and one thousand one hundred and sixty-four British, cleared out from this port, the latter chiefly coastwise: the aggregate burden was seventy thousand three hundred and twenty tons; and the duties paid at the custom-house amounted to £29,531. 15. 9. The navigation of the Nene has been greatly improved by a straight cut, or river, from Peterborough, by which vessels of one hundred tons' burden can approach the quay, which is commodiously constructed; and a custom-house, forming part of the town hall, was erected on the site of the old Firkin Cross. A packet sails from Peterborough every Tuesday and Friday to Wisbeach, and returns every Wednesday and Sunday. In 1794, a canal was constructed, extending from the river, at Wisbech, to the Old Nene at Outwell, and thence to the Ouse, at Salter's Lode sluice, opening a communication with Norfolk, Suffolk, and the eastern counties. There is no branch of manufacture carried on in the town, but the vicinity abounds with rich pasturage; and great numbers of oxen and sheep, which attain a large size, are sent to the London market. The market is on Saturday: the fairs are on the Saturday before Palm-Sunday, and the Saturday before Lady-day, for hemp and flax; a large fair for horses, which is numerously attended by the London dealers, and which was formerly held on the Wednesday before Whit-Sunday, is now on the

second Wednesday in April; and a very large cattle fair is held on the 12th of August, at which three thousand head of cattle have been sold.

The guild of the Holy Trinity, established in 1379, having been found, at the time of the dissolution, to have supported a grammar school, and maintained certain jetties and piers "against the rage of the sea," was restored by Edward VI., who gave the inhabitants a charter of incorporation, under the provisions of which ten capital burgesses are annually elected by the inhabitants, being freeholders, or occupying houses of the value of forty shillings per annum, for the management of the guild estates, producing from £2000 to £3000 per annum, and of whom one is appointed town bailiff. This charter was renewed by James I., and confirmed by Charles II. The corporation possess no magisterial authority; but the town being situated within the Isle of Ely, which is a royal franchise, assizes are held here in summer, and in Lent at Ely, alternately; quarter sessions are also held at these places alternately; petty sessions are held twice in the week; and a court of requests for the recovery of debts under 40s. is held at the shire-hall, on the second Friday in every month. The town-hall is a part of the custom-house. The shire-hall, where assizes and sessions are held, is annexed to the gaol, which was rebuilt in 1807, and contains seventeen wards for prisoners of both sexes, two for debtors, with a yard, chapel, and tread-mill, at which eleven men can work, and which was erected at an expense of £600.

Wisbech comprises the parishes of St. Mary and St. Peter, in the archdeaconry and diocese of Ely. The living of St. Peter's is a vicarage, with the perpetual curacy of St. Mary and the chapelry of Guyhirn annexed, rated in the king's books at £26. 13. 4., and in the patronage of the Bishop of Ely: the church is a spacious and handsome structure, with a fine tower distinct from the former, principally in the later style of English architecture; the north aisle of the chancel is in the decorated style, with a fine window of the same character at the west end of the south aisle; the naves are divided by light and slender pillars and pointed arches, and separated from their respective aisles by low massive pillars and semicircular Norman arches: the nave bears the date 1586, but the building appears to have been erected much earlier, the noble stone tower having been erected in the year 1500. The living of St. Mary's is a perpetual curacy, annexed to the vicarage of St. Peter: the church is in the later English style, with a plain tower, and is situated about two miles north-west of the town. A chapel of ease, octangular in form, and designed to accommodate one thousand persons, including three hundred free sittings for the poor, is in process of erection near the old market place: it was commenced by subscription, and endowed by Dr. Jobson, the incumbent, with an estate valued at £200 per annum. There are places of worship for Baptists, Independents, Johnsonians, Society of Friends, Presbyterians, Wesleyan Methodists, and Unitarians. The free grammar school is of very ancient foundation, supposed to have been established by the guild of the Holy Trinity, so early as 1379: it is now under the superintendence of the capital burgesses, having been erected on the site of the old town hall in Ship-lane, and is subject to the visitation of the Bishop of Ely. The master, who is chosen by the burgesses, and receives a salary and perquisites to the amount of £160 per annum, holds his situation for life, unless displaced by the visitor; classical instruction is afforded gratuitously to all boys of the town who apply; from twenty to thirty are on the foundation. Attached to this institution, from a bequest by Thomas Parke, in 1628, are four by-fellowships, of £10 per annum each, at Peter House, Cambridge; four scholarships, of £10 per annum each, and two others, at the college of St. Mary Magdalene, the latter now amounting to £70 per annum each. A National school, erected in 1811, at the Church-terrace, in which two hundred and fifty boys are instructed, is supported by various contributions and voluntary contributions. A girls' school, in which are one hundred and twenty scholars, is endowed with lands let for about £55, and is situated in Lower Hill-street. A benefaction for lending sums of money to poor tradesmen, free of interest, was founded by a Mr. John Crane, an apothecary of Cambridge, in 1652, which was further increased by a gift of £300 from a Mr. W. Holmes. In 1813, six almshouses were erected near the church by the burgesses; there are also eleven others erected from various bequests. Here was anciently an hospital of St. John the Baptist, but no traces of it are discernible. Archbishop Herring received his education in the free grammar school of this town.

WISBOROUGH-GREEN, a parish partly in the hundreds of ROTHERBRIDGE and WEST-EASWRITH, but chiefly in the hundred of BURY, rape of ARUNDEL, county of SUSSEX, 6¼ miles (N. E. by E.) from Petworth, containing, with the chapelry of Loxwood End, 1679 inhabitants. The living is a discharged vicarage, in the archdeaconry and diocese of Ely, rated in the king's books at £9. 18. 0½., and in the patronage of the Prebendary of Wisborough in the Cathedral Church of Chichester. The church, dedicated to St. Peter, is principally in the early style of English architecture. There is a place of worship for Independents. The Arun and Wey canal passes through the parish.

WISETON, or WYESTON, a township in the parish of CLAYWORTH, North-clay division of the wapentake of BASSETLAW, county of NOTTINGHAM, 5 miles (E. S. E.) from Bawtry, containing 126 inhabitants. The Chesterfield canal passes in the vicinity.

WISHAW, a parish in the Birmingham division of the hundred of HEMLINGFORD, county of WARWICK, 3¾ miles (E. S. E.) from Sutton-Coldfield, containing, with the hamlet of Moxhall, 219 inhabitants. The living is a rectory, in the archdeaconry of Coventry, and diocese of Lichfield and Coventry, rated in the king's books at £5. 5., and endowed with £400 royal bounty. Mrs. Folliott was patroness in 1816. The church is dedicated to St. Chad. The Birmingham and Fazely canal passes through the parish. Lady Hackett, in 1710, gave £100, directing the interest to be applied for teaching six children: there is also a rent-charge of ten shillings, bequeathed, in 1744, by Thomas Bayliss, for the education of one poor boy.

WISHFORD (GREAT), a parish in the hundred of BRANCH and DOLE, county of WILTS, 2½ miles (N. N. W.) from Wilton, containing 372 inhabitants. The living is a rectory, in the archdeaconry and diocese of Salisbury, rated in the king's books at £17. 10. 7¾., and in

the patronage of the Earl of Pembroke. The church is dedicated to St. Giles. Sir Richard Howe, in 1722, gave a rent-charge of £32 in support of a school for poor boys and girls.

WISHFORD (LITTLE), a tything in the parish of SOUTH NEWTON, hundred of BRANCH and DOLE, county of WILTS, 3 miles (N. N. W.) from Wilton. The population is returned with the parish.

WISLEY, a parish in the second division of the hundred of WOKING, county of SURREY, 2½ miles (N. by E.) from Ripley, containing 141 inhabitants. The living is a discharged rectory, with the vicarage of Pyrford annexed, in the archdeaconry of Surrey, and diocese of Winchester, rated in the king's books at £40. 19., and in the patronage of Earl Onslow.

WISPINGTON, a parish in the southern division of the wapentake of GARTREE, parts of LINDSEY, county of LINCOLN, 4¼ miles (W. N. W.) from Horncastle, containing 70 inhabitants. The living is a discharged vicarage, in the archdeaconry and diocese of Lincoln, endowed with £200 private benefaction, and £200 royal bounty, and in the patronage of Edmund Turnor, Esq. The church is dedicated to St. Margaret.

WISSETT, a parish in the hundred of BLYTHING, county of SUFFOLK, 2 miles (N. W.) from Halesworth, containing 435 inhabitants. The living is a perpetual curacy, in the archdeaconry of Suffolk, and diocese of Norwich, endowed with £24 per annum private benefaction, and £400 royal bounty, and in the patronage of Sir E. C. Hartopp, Bart. The church, dedicated to St. Andrew, has two Norman doors and a round tower.

WISTANSTOW, a parish partly in the hundred of PURSLOW, but chiefly in that of MUNSLOW, county of SALOP, 9¾ miles (N. W. by N.) from Ludlow, containing 883 inhabitants. The living is a rectory, in the archdeaconry of Salop, and diocese of Hereford, rated in the king's books at £18, and in the patronage of the Earl of Craven. The church is dedicated to the Holy Trinity.

WISTASTON, a parish in the hundred of NANTWICH, county palatine of CHESTER, 2½ miles (N. E. by E.) from Nantwich, containing 332 inhabitants. The living is a discharged rectory, in the archdeaconry and diocese of Chester, rated in the king's books at £4. 0. 3., and in the patronage of Peter Walthall, Esq. The church, dedicated to St. Mary, has lately received an addition of one hundred and fifty-eight sittings, of which one hundred and twenty-one are free, the Incorporated Society for the enlargement of churches and chapels having granted £100 towards defraying the expense.

WISTESTON, a chapelry in the parish of MARDEN, hundred of BROXASH, county of HEREFORD, 7 miles (N. by E.) from Hereford. The population is returned with the parish. The living is a perpetual curacy, in the peculiar jurisdiction of the Dean of Hereford, endowed with £200 private benefaction, £800 royal bounty, and £200 parliamentary grant. W. C. Hayton, Esq. was patron in 1810.

WISTON, otherwise WISSINGTON, a parish in the hundred of BABERGH, county of SUFFOLK, 1½ mile (W. by S.) from Nayland, containing 246 inhabitants. The living is a vicarage, in the archdeaconry of Sudbury, and diocese of Norwich, rated in the king's books at £4. 19. 4½., and in the patronage of the Crown. The church, dedicated to St. Mary, has a rich and very curious Norman door. The river Stour bounds the parish on the south, where it is crossed by a bridge.

WISTON, a parish in the hundred of STEYNING, rape of BRAMBER, county of SUSSEX, 1½ mile (N. N. W.) from Steyning, containing 293 inhabitants. The living is a rectory, in the archdeaconry and diocese of Chichester, rated in the king's books at £12. 13. 4., and in the patronage of C. Goring, Esq. The church, dedicated to St. Mary, is principally in the decorated style of English architecture.

WISTOW, a parish in the hundred of HURSTINGSTONE, county of HUNTINGDON, 3¾ miles (S. S. W.) from Ramsey, containing 352 inhabitants. The living is a rectory, in the archdeaconry of Huntingdon, and diocese of Lincoln, rated in the king's books at £10. 17. 8½., and in the patronage of J. Torkington, Esq. The church is dedicated to St. John the Baptist.

WISTOW, a parish in the hundred of GARTREE, county of LEICESTER, 7¼ miles (S. E. by S.) from Leicester, containing, with the chapelry of Newton-Harcourt, 307 inhabitants. The living is a discharged vicarage, in the archdeaconry of Leicester, and diocese of Lincoln, rated in the king's books at £8. 18. 4., endowed with £400 private benefaction, and £400 royal bounty, and in the patronage of Sir H. Halford, Bart. The church is dedicated to St. Winston. The Union canal passes through the parish.

WISTOW, a parish partly within the liberty of ST. PETER of YORK, East riding, but chiefly in the lower division of the wapentake of BARKSTONE-ASH, West riding, of the county of YORK, 3 miles (N. W. by N.) from Selby, containing 633 inhabitants. The living is a discharged vicarage, in the peculiar jurisdiction of the Prebendary of Wistow in the Cathedral Church of York, rated in the king's books at £8, and in the patronage of the Dean of Ripon. The church is dedicated to All Saints. The river Ouse passes near this place. There is an endowed school in the parish for ten poor boys.

WISWELL, a township in that part of the parish of WHALLEY which is in the higher division of the hundred of BLACKBURN, county palatine of LANCASTER, 3 miles (S. by E.) from Clitheroe, containing 683 inhabitants. The extension of the manufacture in spinning cotton thread, and the weaving and printing of calico, have caused a considerable increase in the population of this township within the last few years.

WITCHAM, a parish in the southern division of the hundred of WITCHFORD, Isle of ELY, county of CAMBRIDGE, 5½ miles (W.) from Ely, containing 473 inhabitants. The living is a vicarage, in the archdeaconry and diocese of Ely, rated in the king's books at £8. 11. 0½., and in the patronage of the Dean and Chapter of Ely. The church is dedicated to St. Martin. There is a place of worship for Wesleyan Methodists.

WITCHAMPTON, a parish in that part of the hundred of CRANBORNE which is in the Shaston (East) division of the county of DORSET, 4½ miles (N. by W.) from Wimborne-Minster, containing 442 inhabitants. The living is a rectory, in the archdeaconry of Dorset, and diocese of Bristol, rated in the king's books at £12. 12. 3½., and in the patronage of Mrs. Mary King. The church, dedicated to All Saints, is a large handsome edifice. There is a place of worship for Wesleyan Methodists. The rapid river Allen runs through the parish, and on its bank is an extensive paper-mill. Here

are the remains of an old monastery, once subordinate to the abbots of Crawford, and now converted into a barn.

WITCHFORD, a parish in the southern division of the hundred of WITCHFORD, Isle of ELY, county of CAMBRIDGE, 3 miles (W. S. W.) from Ely, containing 401 inhabitants. The living is a vicarage, in the peculiar jurisdiction and patronage of the Bishop of Ely, rated in the king's books at £9. 18. 9. The church is dedicated to St. Nicholas.

WITCHINGHAM (GREAT), a parish in the hundred of EYNSFORD, county of NORFOLK, 2 miles (S.) from Reepham, containing 514 inhabitants. The living is a discharged vicarage, with the rectory of Little Witchingham annexed, in the archdeaconry and diocese of Norwich, rated in the king's books at £4. 17. 11., endowed with £200 royal bounty, and in the patronage of the Warden and Fellows of New College, Oxford. The church is dedicated to St. Mary.

WITCHINGHAM (LITTLE), a parish in the hundred of EYNSFORD, county of NORFOLK, 2¼ miles (S. E. by S.) from Reepham, containing 52 inhabitants. The living is a rectory, annexed to the vicarage of Great Witchingham, in the archdeaconry and diocese of Norwich, rated in the king's books at £5. The church is dedicated to St. Faith.

WITCHLING, a parish in the hundred of EYHORNE, lathe of AYLESFORD, county of KENT, 2½ miles (N. N. E.) from Lenham, containing 137 inhabitants. The living is a discharged rectory, in the archdeaconry and diocese of Canterbury, rated in the king's books at £4. 1. 8., endowed with £200 private benefaction, and £200 royal bounty, and in the patronage of Thos. W. Wrighte, Esq. The church is dedicated to St. Margaret.

WITHAM, a market town and parish in the hundred of WITHAM, county of ESSEX, 8 miles (N. E. by E.) from Chelmsford, and 37 (N. E. by E.) from London, containing 2578 inhabitants. The original erection of this town, or at least that part of it which is situated on Cheping Hill, is attributed to Edward the Elder, about the commencement of his reign, and was subsequently in the possession of the Knights Templars, who had a preceptory at Cressing, about three miles distant. Some consider this to have been the Roman station *Canonium* of Antoninus, which opinion receives confirmation from the quantity of Roman bricks worked up in the body and tower of the church, and from Roman coins of different Emperors, which have been discovered in levelling the fortifications. There are some remains of a circular camp, defended by a double vallum, yet visible in the vicinity of the town. A mansion here, formerly the property of the Earl of Abercorn, has been repeatedly honoured by the presence of royalty; George II. rested at it in his progress to and from his Hanoverian dominions, and Queen Charlotte, consort of George III., was received here on her first arrival in England. The town, which is pleasantly situated near the confluence of a small stream, called the Braine, with the river Blackwater, on the main road from London to Colchester, is of respectable appearance, and consists principally of one long street; it is partly lighted and paved, and amply supplied with water from wells. There are no branches of manufacture; the principal trade is what arises from its situation on a great public thoroughfare, and the requisite supply of the inhabitants. The market, granted by Richard I., and kept originally at Cheping Hill, from which it was removed by Richard II., is on Tuesday; and fairs are held on the Monday before Whit-Sunday, June 4th, and September 14th. The county magistrates hold here petty sessions for the division, every Tuesday; and manorial courts are held, as occasion requires, at which constables and other officers are appointed. The living is a vicarage, in the archdeaconry of Colchester, and diocese of London, rated in the king's books at £22. 0. 7½., and in the patronage of the Bishop of London. The church, which is situated at Cheping Hill, about half a mile north of the town, is dedicated to St. Nicholas: it is a neat edifice in the later style of English architecture, and contains many ancient monuments, and a large tomb, erected in the reign of Elizabeth, to the memory of Judge Southcote and his lady, by whose effigies it is surmounted. There are places of worship for Baptists, the Society of Friends, Independents, and Roman Catholics. A National school, for eighty-two boys and fifty-five girls, is supported partly by the rent of a house, conditionally bequeathed, in 1630, by Dame Catherine Barnardiston, and partly by voluntary contributions. Two almshouses on Cheping Hill, for four poor widows, were endowed by Thomas Green, Esq., in 1491, with a farm in Springfield, let for upwards of £50 a year; the inmates have an allowance of money and fuel: this bequest having been lost for eighty years, it was recovered in Chancery, chiefly through the care and exertions of Dr. Warley, vicar of the parish. An almshouse for two poor widows was founded, in the reign of Charles I., by means of a bequest from George Armond, Esq. At Cheping Hill are two tenements, with a weekly allowance, for two poor widows, arising from a bequest of £35 per annum by Mr. Green; six others by Matthew Harvey, Esq., for six poor persons chosen by the pastor and deacons of the Independent chapel; and five, by an unknown donor, for ten poor widows, endowed in 1687 with a farm at Goldhanger, and another at Fairstead; the income is about £67 per annum. Dr. Warley, amongst other benefactions, in 1719, bequeathed £100 in aid of an orthodox school for poor children, to be elected by the minister and churchwardens for the time being. There is a mineral spring in the neighbourhood, which was formerly in great repute.

WITHAM on the HILL, a parish in the wapentake of BELTISLOE, parts of KESTEVEN, county of LINCOLN, 4¼ miles (S. W.) from Bourne, containing, with the hamlets of Manthorpe and Toft with Lound, 563 inhabitants. The living is a vicarage, in the archdeaconry and diocese of Lincoln, rated in the king's books at £6. 1. 0½., endowed with £600 private benefaction, £200 royal bounty, and £1000 parliamentary grant, and in the patronage of G. W. Johnson, Esq. The church is dedicated to St. Andrew. There is a place of worship for Wesleyan Methodists. James Thompson, in 1719, bequeathed a rent-charge of £4 and the produce of certain land, for teaching seventeen poor children.

WITHAM (NORTH), a parish in the wapentake of BELTISLOE, parts of KESTEVEN, county of LINCOLN, 1½ mile (S. by W.) from Colsterworth, containing, with the hamlet of Lebthorpe, 209 inhabitants. The living

is a rectory, in the archdeaconry and diocese of Lincoln, rated in the king's books at £6. 19. 2., and in the patronage of Lord Downe. The church is dedicated to St. Mary. The river Witham runs through the parish.

WITHAM (SOUTH), a parish in the wapentake of BELTISLOE, parts of KESTEVEN, county of LINCOLN, 3¾ miles (S. by W.) from Colsterworth, containing 345 inhabitants. The living is a discharged rectory, in the archdeaconry and diocese of Lincoln, rated in the king's books at £3. 12. 11., and in the patronage of Lord Huntingtower. The church is dedicated to St. John the Baptist. The river Witham has its source in this parish. Three poor children are instructed for an annuity of £1. 10., the gift of the Rev. Mr. Troughton. A preceptory of Knights Templars existed here so early as 1164, which afterwards devolved upon the Hospitallers.

WITHAM-FRIARY, a parish (formerly an extra-episcopal liberty), comprising Charter-house on Mendip, in the hundred of FROME, county of SOMERSET, 5½ miles (S. S. W.) from Frome, containing, exclusively of Charterhouse on Mendip, which is in the hundred of Winterstoke, 589 inhabitants. The living is a perpetual curacy, in the archdeaconry of Wells, and diocese of Bath and Wells, and in the patronage of the Duke of Somerset. The church, dedicated to St. Mary, which belonged to the ancient friary, has lately received an addition of one hundred and thirty sittings, of which one hundred are free, the Incorporated Society for the enlargement of churches and chapels having granted £100 towards defraying the expense. Here was anciently a nunnery; and subsequently, in 1181, a monastery, said to be the first establishment of Carthusians in England, was founded by Henry II., in honour of the Blessed Virgin, St. John the Baptist, and All Saints, which at the dissolution had a revenue of £227. 1. 8.: the ruins were taken down in 1764, and a farm-house now stands upon its site. Notwithstanding that this parish was known to be of peculiar and exempt jurisdiction, there are no records shewing that any privileges were exercised prior to the year 1785, when an official was appointed: the manor having come into the possession of the Duke of Somerset, his Grace, in 1826, signified his intention of relinquishing his peculiar rights, provided the Governors of Queen Anne's bounty would contribute to the augmentation of the living; and having charged his estate in the parish with a permanent stipend for the minister, the usual license to the incumbent was issued by the Bishop of Bath and Wells, in 1827, and no peculiar rights whatever are now exercised.

WITHCALL, a parish in the Wold division of the hundred of LOUTH-ESKE, parts of LINDSEY, county of LINCOLN, 3¾ miles (S. W. by W.) from Louth, containing 89 inhabitants. The living is a discharged rectory, in the archdeaconry and diocese of Lincoln, rated in the king's books at £11. 16. 10., and in the patronage of the Crown. The church is dedicated to St. Martin.

WITHCOTE, a parish forming, with the parishes of Cold-Overton and Somerby, a detached portion of the hundred of FRAMLAND, being locally in that of Goscote, county of LEICESTER, 9½ miles (S. S. E.) from Melton-Mowbray, containing 51 inhabitants. The living is a discharged rectory, in the archdeaconry of Leicester, and diocese of Lincoln, rated in the king's books at £6. 9. 4½., endowed with £200 private benefaction, and £400 royal bounty, and in the patronage of the Rev. Henry Palmer.

WITHERIDGE, a parish in the hundred of WITHERIDGE, county of DEVON, 8¼ miles (E.) from Chulmleigh, containing 1121 inhabitants. The living is a vicarage, in the archdeaconry of Barnstaple, and diocese of Exeter, rated in the king's books at £23. 10. 5., and in the patronage of the Rev. W. P. Thomas. The church, dedicated to St. John the Baptist, has a stone pulpit highly enriched. This is a decayed borough and market town. A fair for cattle is held on June 24th; and there are still great markets on the Wednesday after September 21st, and the first Wednesday in November. Richard Melhuish, Esq., in 1799, gave £500 stock, the dividends arising from which are applied for the instruction of forty poor children. William Chapple, the antiquary, was born here; he died in 1755.

WITHERLEY, a parish in the hundred of SPARKENHOE, county of LEICESTER, 1½ mile (E. by S.) from Atherstone, containing, with the hamlet of Atterton, 471 inhabitants. The living is a rectory, in the archdeaconry of Leicester, and diocese of Lincoln, rated in the king's books at £16 .2. 3½., and in the patronage of the Rev. Mr. Roberts. The church, dedicated to St. Peter, has one of the finest spire steeples in the county; it is one hundred and fifty-six feet high. The old Watling-street, which here separates Leicestershire from Warwickshire, crosses the river Anker at Witherley bridge. In this parish is Mancetter, the site of the great Roman station *Manduessuedum*.

WITHERN, a parish in the Wold division of the hundred of CALCEWORTH, parts of LINDSEY, county of LINCOLN, 4½ miles (N. N. W.) from Alford, containing 343 inhabitants. The living is a rectory, in the archdeaconry and diocese of Lincoln, rated in the king's books at £18. 10. 2½. Robert Vyner, Esq. was patron in 1806. The church is dedicated to St. Margaret. There is a place of worship for Wesleyan Methodists. George Stovins, in 1726, bequeathed £100, the interest of which, with that of £50, previously given by the Rev. William Jones, is applied for teaching and partly clothing poor children.

WITHERNSEA, a chapelry in the parish of HOLLYM, southern division of the wapentake of HOLDERNESS, East riding of the county of YORK, 19 miles (E. by S.) from Kingston upon Hull, containing 108 inhabitants. The chapel, dedicated to St. Nicholas, is apparently the remains of a magnificent building, probably the church of a priory which existed here in the reign of John, a cell to the abbey of Albemarle in France.

WITHERNWICK, a parish partly within the liberty of ST. PETER of YORK, but chiefly in the northern division of the wapentake of HOLDERNESS, East riding of the county of YORK, 12 miles (E.) from Beverley, containing 370 inhabitants. The living is a discharged rectory, in the peculiar jurisdiction and patronage of the Prebendary of Holme in the Cathedral Church of York, rated in the king's books at £6. 7. 1. The church, dedicated to St. Alban, is an ancient structure. There is a place of worship for Wesleyan Methodists. Matthias North gave land producing a trifling income for teaching and apprenticing children of this parish.

WITHERSDALE, a parish in the hundred of HOXNE, county of SUFFOLK, 3 miles (S. E. by E.) from Harleston, containing 168 inhabitants. The living is a discharged rectory, annexed to the vicarage of Fressingfield, in the archdeaconry of Suffolk, and diocese of Norwich, rated in the king's books at £6. 16. 8., and endowed with £200 private benefaction, and £200 royal bounty. The church is dedicated to St. Mary Magdalene.

WITHERSFIELD, a parish in the hundred of RISBRIDGE, county of SUFFOLK, 2¼ miles (N. W. by N.) from Haverhill, containing 484 inhabitants. The living is a rectory, in the archdeaconry of Sudbury, and diocese of Norwich, rated in the king's books at £9. 17. 1., and in the patronage of G. T. W. H. Duffield, Esq. The church is dedicated to St. Mary.

WITHERSLACK, a chapelry in the parish of BEETHAM, KENDAL ward, county of WESTMORLAND, 7½ miles (W. N. W.) from Milnthorpe, containing 477 inhabitants. The living is a perpetual curacy, in the archdeaconry of Richmond, and diocese of Chester, endowed with £400 private benefaction, and £400 royal bounty, and in the patronage of the Vicar of Beetham. The chapel, dedicated to St. Paul, was built and endowed, in 1664, by Dr. John Barwick, a native of the place, and Dean of St. Paul's, London, who bequeathed the impropriate rectory of Lazonby, to which his brother, Peter Barwick, Esq., M.D., added an estate near Kirk-Oswald, to provide an annuity of £26 to the curate for teaching forty children, one of £4 for repairing the chapel, and another of £10 for placing out apprentices and as a marriage portion to poor maidens within the chapelry. These allowances have been considerably augmented by the increased value of the lands, which now let for about £400 a year, and the treasurers were enabled, in 1824, to erect a girls' school on the same foundation, and have given several marriage portions, of £30 and £40 each, to deserving females. The fishery in the river Belo, which passes through the chapelry, belongs to the Earl of Derby, who holds his manorial court at the Derby Arms, on the second Tuesday after Trinity: the ancient hall has been converted into a farm-house. About a mile from the chapel a chalybeate spring was discovered, and named Holy Well, in 1656, but it has since disappeared.

WITHERSTONE, a parish in the hundred of EGGERTON, Bridport division of the county of DORSET, 5 miles (E. N. E.) from Bridport. The population is returned with the parish of Poorstock. The living is a rectory, in the archdeaconry of Dorset, and diocese of Bristol, rated in the king's books at £2. 13. 4., and in the patronage of the Earl of Dorchester. This ancient parish is now almost depopulated and reduced to one farm-house, the occupier of which pays church and poor rates to Poorstock, the parish church having been suffered to go to decay soon after the Reformation.

WITHIEL, a parish in the hundred of PYDER, county of CORNWALL, 5 miles (W. by S.) from Bodmin, containing 339 inhabitants. The living is a rectory, in the archdeaconry of Cornwall, and diocese of Exeter, rated in the king's books at £10, and in the patronage of Sir R. R. Vyvyan, Bart. The church is dedicated to St. Uvell. Brynn, in this parish, is the birthplace of Sir Beville Grenville, a distinguished royalist commander in the great civil war.

WITHIELL-FLOREY, a parish in the hundred of TAUNTON and TAUNTON-DEAN, county of SOMERSET, 5¾ miles (N. E.) from Dulverton, containing 86 inhabitants. The living is a perpetual curacy, in the archdeaconry of Taunton, and diocese of Bath and Wells, endowed with £1000 royal bounty, and £400 parliamentary grant, and in the patronage of Sir T. B. Lethbridge, Bart. The church is dedicated to St. Mary Magdalene.

WITHINGTON, a parish in the hundred of BRADLEY, county of GLOUCESTER, 6 miles (W.) from North Leach, containing 759 inhabitants. The living is a rectory, in the peculiar jurisdiction of the Incumbent, rated in the king's books at £30, and in the patronage of the Bishop of Worcester. The church, dedicated to St. Michael, is a cruciform structure, principally in the Norman style, and partly of later date: among the monuments, is a handsome one to the memory of Sir John How, his wife, and nine children, in a small cross aisle on the south side of the church, the burial-place of that family. The river Colne runs through the parish, in which a Roman pavement was discovered in 1811, a part of which was deposited in the British Museum. There are two schools, one for boys and one for girls, and one in the hamlet of Foxcote, supported by the interest of money left to the parish. The Rev. W. Osborn, D.D., who held the living of this parish, left £100 for apprenticing poor children and John Rich, Esq., gave £100 also for the same purpose: there are other benefactions for the use of the poor.

WITHINGTON, a parish in the hundred of BROXASH, county of HEREFORD, 4½ miles (E. N. E.) from Hereford, containing, with the chapelry of Preston-Wynne, 806 inhabitants. The living is a discharged vicarage, with the perpetual curacy of Preston-Wynne annexed, in the peculiar jurisdiction and patronage of the Dean of Hereford, rated in the king's books at £5.1., and endowed with £200 private benefaction, and £200 royal bounty. The church is dedicated to St. Peter. There is a place of worship for Baptists.

WITHINGTON, a township in the parish of MANCHESTER, hundred of SALFORD, county palatine of LANCASTER, 4 miles (S.) from Manchester, containing 892 inhabitants.

WITHINGTON, a parish in the Wellington division of the hundred of BRADFORD (South), county of SALOP, 6¼ miles (E.) from Shrewsbury, containing 179 inhabitants. The living is a perpetual curacy, in the archdeaconry of Salop, and diocese of Lichfield and Coventry, and in the patronage of the Rector of Upton Magna. The church is dedicated to St. John the Baptist. The Shrewsbury canal passes through the parish.

WITHINGTON (LOWER), a township in the parish of PRESTBURY, hundred of MACCLESFIELD, county palatine of CHESTER, 7 miles (N. N. W.) from Congleton, containing 615 inhabitants. There is a place of worship for Wesleyan Methodists. Tunsted, a hill in this township, is supposed, from its Saxon etymology, viz., the place of a town, to have been the site of an ancient ville of some consequence. A school is supported here, by Mr. Parker, for the instruction of poor children.

WITHINGTON (OLD), a township in the parish of PRESTBURY, hundred of MACCLESFIELD, county palatine of CHESTER, 7½ miles (N. N. W.) from Congleton, containing 164 inhabitants.

WITHNELL, a township in the parish and hundred of LEYLAND, county palatine of LANCASTER, 5 miles (N. E. by N.) from Chorley, containing 1146 inhabitants.

WITHYBROOK, a parish in the Kirby division of the hundred of KNIGHTLOW, county of WARWICK, 8 miles (N. E. by E.) from Coventry, containing, with the hamlet of Hopsford, 309 inhabitants. The living is a discharged vicarage, in the archdeaconry of Coventry, and diocese of Lichfield and Coventry, rated in the king's books at £8. 6. 8., endowed with £400 private benefaction, and £800 royal bounty, and in the patronage of the Master and Fellows of Trinity College, Cambridge. The church is dedicated to All Saints. The Oxford canal passes through the parish.

WITHYCOMBE, a parish in the hundred of CARHAMPTON, county of SOMERSET, 2½ miles (S. E.) from Dunster, containing 319 inhabitants. The living is a rectory, in the archdeaconry of Totness, and diocese of Exeter, rated in the king's books at £10. 11. 5½., and in the patronage of T. Hutton, Esq. The church is dedicated to St. Nicholas. In this parish is a Druidical circle, formed of rude stones, not far from which are two cairns.

WITHYCOMBE-RAWLEIGH, a parish in the eastern division of the hundred of BUDLEIGH, county of DEVON, 2½ miles (N. E.) from Exmouth, containing, with a portion of the town of Exmouth, which extends into this parish, 1054 inhabitants. The living is a perpetual curacy, annexed to the vicarage of East Budleigh, in the archdeaconry and diocese of Exeter. The ancient church was taken down about 1745, and a new one erected half a mile from Exmouth. The navigable river Exe bounds the parish on the west. Here is an almshouse with a trifling endowment. The manor was formerly held by the tenure of finding the king two good arrows stuck in an oaten cake, whenever he should hunt in Dartmoor.

WITHYHAM, a parish in the hundred of HARTFIELD, rape of PEVENSEY, county of SUSSEX, 7¼ miles (E. S. E.) from East Grinstead, containing 1393 inhabitants. The living is a rectory, in the archdeaconry of Lewes, and diocese of Chichester, rated in the king's books at £25. 5. 5., and in the patronage of the Duke of Dorset. The church, dedicated to St. Michael, is principally in the later style of English architecture; it was rebuilt in 1624, by Richard, Earl of Dorset, who was interred here.

WITHYPOOLE, a parish in the hundred of WILLITON and FREEMANNERS, county of SOMERSET, 7 miles (N. W.) from Dulverton, containing 204 inhabitants. The living is a perpetual curacy, annexed to the vicarage of Hawkridge, in the archdeaconry of Taunton, and diocese of Bath and Wells. The church is dedicated to St. Andrew.

WITLEY, a parish in the second division of the hundred of GODALMING, county of SURREY, 3¼ miles (S. W. by S.) from Godalming, containing 1264 inhabitants. The living is a discharged vicarage, with the perpetual curacy of Thursley annexed, in the archdeaconry of Surrey, and diocese of Winchester, rated in the king's books at £17. 15. 10. The Rev. J. F. Chandler was patron in 1815. The church, dedicated to All Saints, is principally in the early style of English architecture. Many ancient coins of gold and silver have been discovered here.

WITLEY (GREAT), a parish in the lower division of the hundred of DODDINGTREE, county of WORCESTER, 5 miles (S. W. by S.) from Stourport, containing, with the hamlet of Redmarley, 354 inhabitants. The living is a rectory, in the archdeaconry and diocese of Worcester, rated in the king's books at £7. 6. 3., and in the patronage of Lord Foley. The church, dedicated to St. Michael, is an elegant structure, erected about 1760, by the first Lord Foley and his widow, to whom it contains a superb monument: the windows, painted by Price, in 1719, and the ceiling by Verrio, were brought from the chapel at Canons, when that princely mansion of the late Duke of Chandos was pulled down, and the materials sold.

WITLEY (LITTLE), a chapelry in the parish of Holt, lower division of the hundred of OSWALDSLOW, county of WORCESTER, 6¾ miles (S. S. W.) from Stourport, containing 302 inhabitants. The chapel is dedicated to St. Michael.

WITNESHAM, a parish in the hundred of CARLFORD, county of SUFFOLK, 4½ miles (N. by E.) from Ipswich, containing 515 inhabitants. The living is a rectory, in the archdeaconry of Suffolk, and diocese of Norwich, rated in the king's books at £18. 13. 4., and in the patronage of the Master and Fellows of St. Peter's College, Cambridge. The church is dedicated to St. Mary. A singular discovery took place some time since in this parish; on removing some earth, the skeleton of a man in armour, seated on horseback, supposed to have been buried during some of the civil wars, was exposed to the view.

WITNEY, a parish in the hundred of BAMPTON, county of OXFORD, comprising the market town of Witney, the chapelry of Hailey, and the hamlets of Crawley and Curbridge, and containing 4784 inhabitants, of which number, 2827 are in the town of Witney, 11 miles (W. by N.) from Oxford, and 65 (W. N. W.) from London. This place, anciently called *Whitteney*, was a town of some importance prior to the Conquest, and was one of the manors given to the monastery of St. Swithin at Winchester, in the reign of Edward the Confessor, by Bishop Ailwyn, in gratitude for the deliverance of Queen Emma, mother of that monarch, from the reputed fiery ordeal which she underwent in the cathedral church of that city, in vindication of her innocence of a charge of incontinence. In the 5th of Edward II. it was made a borough, and returned two members to parliament, from which it was released, on petition of the inhabitants, in the 33rd of Edward III. The town is pleasantly situated on the river Windrush, over which a neat and substantial stone bridge of three arches was erected in 1822, and on the high road from London to Cheltenham and Gloucester: it consists principally of two streets, containing neat well-built houses, and has a clean and respectable appearance: the environs are pleasant, and the ground in the vicinity is agreeably varied with hill and dale. Witney has long been celebrated for its staple manufacture of blankets, which have been invariably regarded as superior, both in texture and colour, to all others: the latter quality is, perhaps, attributable to the peculiar properties of the water of the Windrush. The blanket-weavers of the town, and within twenty miles of it, were incorporated in the reign of Queen Anne, under the designation of "the

Master, Assistants, Wardens, and Commonalty of the Blanket-Weavers of Witney, in Oxfordshire." At that time the manufacturers had one hundred and fifty looms in full operation, affording employment to more than three thousand persons, and consuming weekly about one thousand packs of wool. The charter continued in force for some years, and under its provisions the company enacted laws for the regulation of the trade; but, in process of time, it was found to interfere with improvements in the manufacture, and having become incompatible with the interests of the trade, as at present conducted, it has nearly fallen into disuse. The number of persons now employed is about two thousand, and the annual consumption of wool about six thousand packs. Rough coatings, tilting for barges and wagons, and felting for paper-makers, are made also to a considerable extent: the glove trade affords employment to a small number of persons; and wool-stapling, as connected with the manufactures of the town, is carried on extensively: there is also a considerable trade in malt. The market is on Thursday; and the fairs are on the Tuesday in Easter week, Holy Thursday, July 10th, the Thursday after the 8th of Sept., the Thursday before the 10th of October, and December 4th. The town is within the jurisdiction of the county magistrates; and two bailiffs, assisted by two constables and other officers, are appointed by the jury at the court leet for it, held annually: a court baron is held twice in the year by the Duke of Marlborough, as lessee under the Bishop of Winchester. A handsome blanket hall was erected in 1721: the town hall is a neat stone building, with a piazza for the use of the market; and the market cross, in High-street, was erected in 1683, and repaired in 1811.

The living comprises a rectory and a vicarage, united, in the 9th of Charles I., into one benefice, by the designation of the rectory of Witney, with a reservation of the dues and fees of each, as if separate; it is in the archdeaconry and diocese of Oxford, the former rated in the king's books at £47. 9. 4½., and the latter at £9. 12. 6., and in the patronage of the Bishop of Winchester. The church, dedicated to St. Mary, is a spacious and elegant cruciform structure, in the early and decorated styles of English architecture, with a central tower, having octagonal turrets at the angles, and surmounted by a lofty spire, panelled in compartments, and richly ornamented: the nave is separated from the aisles by handsome piers and finely pointed arches, and is lighted by a range of clerestory windows of the later style: the transepts are large, and the northern, which is in the decorated style, is lighted by an elegant window of seven lights: the chancel, which is small, is in the early English style of architecture, and is lighted with windows of delicate tracery: there are several monumental effigies in the transepts, and many ancient tombs in various parts of the church, and in the chancel is a piscina of elegant design. There are places of worship for the Society of Friends, Independents, and Wesleyan Methodists. The free grammar school, in Church Green, was founded, under an act of parliament, in 1663, by Henry Box, Esq., a native of this town, and citizen of London, who endowed it with a rent-charge of £63 on an estate at Longworth, in Berkshire. It is under the direction of the Grocers' Company, who are trustees, and the control of the Provost and four senior Fellows of Oriel College, Oxford, as visitors; and is conducted by a principal and a sub-master: the number of scholars is limited to thirty, who must be natives of Witney. The buildings comprise a spacious school-room, with a library, dwelling-house for the master, and a large play-ground in front. A free school was founded, in 1723, by Mr. John Holloway, who endowed it with lands producing about £135 per annum, for instructing, clothing, and apprenticing the sons of journeymen weavers of Witney and Hailey: there are at present ten scholars from the former, and five from the latter place, who are clothed every year, and with each of whom an apprentice fee of £15 is given, on leaving the school. The same benefactor erected almshouses for six widows of blanket-weavers, and endowed them with lands producing an income of about £85 per annum; the inmates have each two apartments, a garden, and a weekly allowance of four shillings. Mr. William Blake, of the parish of Coggs, in 1693, endowed a school here with £6 per annum, which is paid to a mistress for teaching thirty girls; and a National school, in which eighty boys and seventy girls are instructed, is supported by subscription. Some ancient almshouses, on Church Green, were taken down, and six substantial houses erected, in 1795, by the feoffees of the charity estates: these houses are at present let to tenants, and the rents are distributed among the poor. Six neat almshouses for aged and unmarried women were erected, in 1828, by Mr. Townsend of London. There are also several charitable bequests for distribution among the poor of the parish. The Roman Akeman-street passes near the town.

WITSTON, a parish in the lower division of the hundred of CALDICOTT, county of MONMOUTH, 6½ miles (S. E. by E.) from Newport, containing 91 inhabitants. The living is a discharged vicarage, in the archdeaconry and diocese of Llandaff, rated in the king's books at £6. 7. 8½., and in the alternate patronage of the Bishop of Llandaff and the Provost of Eton College. The church, according to tradition, belonged to Portown, a town once situated in the neighbourhood, but swallowed up by the sea at some remote period.

WITTENHAM (LITTLE), a parish in the hundred of OCK, county of BERKS, 4¼ miles (N. W. by N.) from Wallingford, containing 107 inhabitants. The living is a rectory, in the archdeaconry of Berks, and diocese of Salisbury, rated in the king's books at £17. 10., and in the patronage of the Rev. F. J. Hilliard. The church is dedicated to St. Peter. The parish is bounded on the north by the Isis, which there receives the smaller river Thame from the opposite side. Sinodun hill, in the neighbourhood, is surrounded by an ancient intrenchment, supposed to be of British origin, and to have been afterwards occupied by the Romans.

WITTENHAM (LONG), a parish in the hundred of OCK, county of BERKS, 5 miles (N.W.) from Wallingford, containing 496 inhabitants. The living is a discharged vicarage in the archdeaconry of Berks, and diocese of Salisbury, rated in the king's books at £12. 12. 6. and in the patronage of the Rector and Fellows of Exeter College, Oxford. The church is dedicated to All Saints. There is a place of worship for Wesleyan Methodists. The parish is bounded on the north by the Thames. A National school is supported by voluntary contributions.

WITTERING (EAST), a parish in the hundred of MANHOOD, rape of CHICHESTER, county of SUSSEX, 6¾ miles (S. W. by S.) from Chichester, containing 216 inhabitants. The living is a discharged rectory, in the archdeaconry and diocese of Chichester, rated in the king's books at £6. 16. 8., and in the patronage of the Bishop of Chichester.

WITTERING (WEST), a parish in the hundred of MANHOOD, rape of CHICHESTER, county of SUSSEX, 7¼ miles (S. W.) from Chichester, containing 504 inhabitants. The living is a discharged vicarage, in the archdeaconry and diocese of Chichester, rated in the king's books at £10. 3. 4., endowed with £200 royal bounty, and in the patronage of the Prebendary of Wittering in the Cathedral Church of Chichester. The church exhibits portions in the various styles of English architecture. The parish is bounded on the south-west by the English channel, and on the north-west by the mouth of Chichester harbour. Wittering is included in the privilege of sending four poor boys to the school founded, in 1702, at Chichester, by Oliver Whitby, who also left an annuity of £3 towards supporting a school for six boys at this place.

WITTERSHAM, a parish in the hundred of OXNEY, lathe of SHEPWAY, county of KENT, 5¼ miles (S. by E.) from Tenterden, containing 911 inhabitants. The living is a rectory, in the peculiar jurisdiction and patronage of the Archbishop of Canterbury, rated in the king's books at £15. 8. 6½. The church, dedicated to St. John the Baptist, has portions in various styles of architecture. There is a place of worship for Wesleyan Methodists.

WITTON, a parochial chapelry, included in that part of the parish of GREAT BUDWORTH which is in the hundred of NORTHWICH, county palatine of CHESTER, ¼ of a mile (E.) from Northwich, containing, with the township of Twambrook, and a portion of that of Rudheath, 2405 inhabitants. The living is a perpetual curacy, in the archdeaconry and diocese of Chester, endowed with £400 private benefaction, £400 royal bounty, and £1400 parliamentary grant, and in the patronage of Edward Greenall, Esq. The chapel, dedicated to St. Helen, is a noble and spacious structure, in the later English style of architecture, with an embattled tower. The free grammar school, adjoining the churchyard, was founded in 1588, by Sir John Deane, who endowed it with a salt-work at Northwich, and certain houses and lands in other parts of the county, which property belonged to the college of St. John the Baptist, and its dissolved guild of St. Anne, in the city of Chester; to the priory of Norton, Cheshire; and to that of Basingwerk, in the county of Flint; and now produces an annual income of upwards of £400. In 1624, Thomas Farmer, A.M., who had been forty years master of the school, bequeathed a sum of money for the maintenance of certain scholars, as exhibitioners, in the University of Oxford, until taking the degree of A. M.; and, in 1715, Peter Cotton left a fund in augmentation of the master's salary; but these two bequests are not now available. None, except the kinsfolk of the founder, have claims to admission on the foundation, unless their parents reside within the chapelry; nor does the institution afford to any of the scholars instruction not immediately connected with the prosecution of their studies in Greek, Latin, and the doctrines of Christianity. Its statutes, in some respects, are similar to those of Harrow, but in the most essential points they are the same as those of St. Paul's school, London. The master is elected by the twelve feoffees appointed under the will of the founder, assisted by certain of the inhabitants, and approved by the bishop and the master of the King's school, Chester. The school-house, which was rebuilt about a century ago, is a substantial structure of brick and stone, with a porter's lodge attached, having also a commodious suite of apartments, occupied by the master, with a spacious class room over the school. The King is visitor.

WITTON, or WYTTON, a parish in the hundred of HURSTINGSTONE, county of HUNTINGDON, 2½ miles (W. by N.) from St. Ives, containing 261 inhabitants. The living is a perpetual curacy, annexed to the rectory of Houghton, in the archdeaconry of Huntingdon, and diocese of Lincoln. The church is dedicated to All Saints. The river Ouse passes through the parish.

WITTON, a township in the parish and lower division of the hundred of BLACKBURN, county palatine of LANCASTER, 1¾ mile (W. by N.) from Blackburn, containing 1067 inhabitants. The river Darwent bounds the township on the south. At Wensley Fold an extensive spinning establishment affords employment to upwards of three hundred persons.

WITTON, a parish in the hundred of BLOFIELD, county of NORFOLK, 5½ miles (E.) from Norwich, containing 112 inhabitants. The living is a discharged rectory, consolidated with those of Brundall and Little Plumstead, in the archdeaconry and diocese of Norwich, rated in the king's books at £6. 13. 4. The church is dedicated to St. Margaret.

WITTON, a parish in the hundred of TUNSTEAD, county of NORFOLK, 3½ miles (E. by N.) from North Walsham, containing 236 inhabitants. The living is a discharged vicarage, in the archdeaconry of Norfolk, and diocese of Norwich, rated in the king's books at £4. 13. 1½., endowed with £400 royal bounty, and in the patronage of the Bishop of Ely. The church is dedicated to St. Margaret.

WITTON (EAST), a parish in the western division of the wapentake of HANG, North riding of the county of YORK, 2½ miles (S. E. by S.) from Middleham, containing 747 inhabitants. The living is a vicarage, in the archdeaconry of Richmond, and diocese of Chester, rated in the king's books at £5. 3. 6½., endowed with £600 private benefaction, £200 royal bounty, and £1100 parliamentary grant, and in the patronage of the Marquis of Ailesbury. The church, dedicated to St. Ella, is an elegant structure in the later English style; the first stone was laid in 1809, and the building was completed in 1812, at the expense of the Earl of Ailesbury, in commemoration of the 50th anniversary of the reign of George III. A school was erected, in 1817, by the Marquis of Ailesbury, by whom it is chiefly supported; the master's salary is £60 per annum. In the neighbourhood are quarries of excellent freestone, well adapted for grindstones. About a mile east of the village are the ruins of Jervaulx abbey, founded about the middle of the twelfth century, by Akarius, in honour of the Virgin Mary, which at the dissolution had a revenue of £455. 10. 5. These interesting

remains having been recently cleared from briars and rubbish, considerable portions of the abbey church, with its cross aisles, choir, and chapter-house, also several tombs and stone coffins, are now plainly visible: the tesselated pavement of the great aisle was also discovered, apparently in a perfect state, but, by exposure to the air, it soon crumbled to dust.

WITTON (LONG), a township in that part of the parish of HARTBURN which is in the western division of MORPETH ward, county of NORTHUMBERLAND, 8 miles (W. by N.) from Morpeth, containing 149 inhabitants.

WITTON (NETHER), a parish in the western division of MORPETH ward, county of NORTHUMBERLAND, comprising the townships of Coat-Yards, or Coal-yards, Ewesley, Healy with Comb-Hill, Nether Witton, Nunnikirk, Ritton-Coltpark, and Ritton-Whitehouse, and containing 460 inhabitants, of which number, 277 are in the township of Nether Witton, 7¾ miles (W. N. W.) from Morpeth. The living is a perpetual curacy, annexed to the vicarage of Hartburn, in the archdeaconry of Northumberland, and diocese of Durham. The church is dedicated to St. Giles.

WITTON (UPPER), a chapelry in the parish of ASTON, Birmingham division of the hundred of HEMLINGFORD, county of WARWICK, 3½ miles (N. by E.) from Birmingham. The population is returned with the parish.

WITTON le WEAR, a parish in the north-western division of DARLINGTON ward, county palatine of DURHAM, 4¼ miles (W. N. W.) from Bishop-Auckland, containing 531 inhabitants. The living is a perpetual curacy, in the archdeaconry and diocese of Durham, endowed with £400 private benefaction, and £400 royal bounty, and in the patronage of W. Chaytor, Esq. The church, dedicated to St. Philip and St. James, is an ancient structure. The village is situated on the southern acclivity of an eminence rising from the north bank of the river Wear, which is here crossed by a bridge. There is a commodious grammar school, founded by John Cuthbert, Esq., and formerly endowed with the interest of £200; but the building has been long occupied as a private boarding school, and the endowment transferred to a smaller establishment. On the south side of the river stood Witton castle, built about 1410, formerly the baronial mansion of the Lords de Eure, many of whom signalized themselves in the border warfare: it was a large oblong edifice, with towers and turrets, and, while recently undergoing repair, was accidentally destroyed by fire. In the great civil war it was held by Sir William D'Arcy for the king, and was besieged and taken by the parliamentarians, under Sir Arthur Haslerigg. Coal abounds in the neighbourhood.

WITTON (WEST), a parish in the western division of the wapentake of HANG, North riding of the county of YORK, 4½ miles (W.) from Middleham, containing 519 inhabitants. The living is a perpetual curacy, in the archdeaconry of Richmond, and diocese of Chester, endowed with £200 private benefaction, £800 royal bounty, and £400 parliamentary grant; and in the patronage of Lord Bolton. The church is a small building, supposed to have been erected in the reign of Henry I.: from the churchyard is a delightful view over Wensley-dale. Charles Robinson, in 1790, bequeathed £250, now producing an annual income of about £12, for teaching and clothing poor children of West Witton and Newbiggen. On an eminence, called Penhill, are vestiges of an ancient castle, formerly belonging to Ralph Fitz-Randal.

WITTON-GILBERT, a parish in the western division of CHESTER ward, county palatine of DURHAM, 3½ miles (N. W.) from Durham, containing, with the outside portion of the parish, 364 inhabitants. The living is a perpetual curacy, with the rectory of Kimbleworth annexed, in the archdeaconry and diocese of Durham, and in the patronage of the Dean and Chapter of Durham. The church, dedicated to St. Michael, is a small building, without a tower. An hospital for five lepers was founded near it, at an early period, by Gilbert de la Ley, the only remaining fragment of which is a pointed window in a farm-house now standing on its site. Jane Finney, in 1728, gave certain land, now let for £12 a year, for teaching eight poor children.

WITTON - SHIELS, a township in the parish of LONG HORSLEY, western division of MORPETH ward, county of NORTHUMBERLAND, 7 miles (N. W. by W.) from Morpeth, containing 21 inhabitants. A strong tower, erected in 1608, by Sir Nicholas Thornton, has been converted into a Roman Catholic chapel.

WIVELISCOMBE, a market town and parish, forming, with the parishes of Ash-Priors, Bishop's Lydiard, and Fitzhead, one of the two unconnected portions which constitute the western division of the hundred of KINGSBURY, county of SOMERSET, 28 miles (W.) from Somerton, and 155 (W. by S.) from London, containing 2791 inhabitants. This place is of considerable antiquity, but its origin and etymology cannot be traced with certainty. Conjecture has deduced the latter from the Saxon *Willi*, or *Vili*, signifying many, and *Combe*, a deep ravine, or dell, of which there are several in the immediate environs. The town occupies a gentle eminence, in an extensive valley enclosed by lofty hills, which suddenly break into deep ravines ; the houses are in general neat and well built, and, by the recent removal of several of the more ancient, the streets have been widened, and the general appearance of the town greatly improved. The inhabitants are supplied with water conveyed by pipes from a spring on Mawndown, a hill about a mile distant. A considerable woollen manufacture is carried on, but not to so great an extent as formerly: the articles consist chiefly of slave clothing for the West India markets, swan-skins for the Newfoundland fishery, and blankets for the home trade: the number of persons regularly employed varies from eight hundred to a thousand. The diversion of the mail-road through this town has materially contributed to promote its various interests. The markets are on Tuesday and Saturday ; the former is the principal, and a great deal of business is transacted in corn, &c. A great market for prime oxen, of the North Devon breed, considered to be the largest in the West of England, is held on the last Tuesday in February. Fairs are, May 12th for oxen and other cattle, and September 25th for sheep. The town is under the superintendence of a bailiff and portreeve, with ale-tasters and other officers, all of whom are chosen at a court leet held annually. It is said to have been formerly a parliamentary borough, and that it was relieved from the elective franchise on petition.

The living is a vicarage, in the peculiar jurisdiction and patronage of the Prebendary of Wiveliscombe in the Cathedral Church of Wells, rated in the king's books at £27. 0. 10. The church, dedicated to St. Andrew, has been recently erected, at an expense of £6000, raised on the security of the parish rates, to be paid off in twenty years, aided by a general subscription, and a grant of £500 from the Incorporated Society for the building and enlargement of churches and chapels : it is a very handsome edifice, in the ancient style of English architecture, and contains five hundred and fifty-eight sittings, of which four hundred and fifty-seven are free. There is a place of worship for Independents. An infirmary was established, in 1804, through the exertions of the medical men of the town and neighbourhood. In this parish are two ancient encampments ; the one on an eminence at a place called Castle, of a circular form and very perfect; the other at Courtneys, square and evidently of Roman origin. Here also are some remains of an old episcopal palace, particularly an archway leading into the workhouse, and the kitchen, which is nearly entire. In digging for the foundation of the new church, it was discovered that the tower of the former had been erected upon the foundations of a more ancient building ; a variety of Roman and Saxon coins was also found, together with some Nuremberg counters, used by the monks in their calculations on the Abacus.

WIVELSFIELD, a parish in the hundred of STREET, rape of LEWES, county of SUSSEX, 4 miles (S. E.) from Cuckfield, containing 537 inhabitants. The living is a perpetual curacy, in the archdeaconry of Lewes, and diocese of Chichester, endowed with £800 royal bounty, and £1200 parliamentary grant, and in the patronage of the Impropriators. The church, dedicated to St. John the Baptist, is principally in the early style of English architecture. There are places of worship for Baptists and Wesleyan Methodists. Six poor children are instructed for £5 per annum, arising from the sum of £100 bequeathed by Francis More, in 1723.

WIVENHOE, a parish in the Colchester division of the hundred of LEXDEN, county of ESSEX, 4½ miles (S. E. by E.) from Colchester, containing 1287 inhabitants. The living is a discharged rectory, in the archdeaconry of Colchester, and diocese of London, rated in the king's books at £10, endowed with £200 private benefaction, and £200 royal bounty, and in the patronage of the Executors of the Rev. N. Corsellis. The church is dedicated to St. Mary. There is a place of worship for Independents. The parish is bounded on the west and south by the river Colne. Wivenhoe is considered the port to Colchester, and has a regular custom-house establishment, with a commodious quay, whence the noted Colchester oysters are shipped for the London and other markets. Two pounds a year, the gift of Mr. Potter, is applied for teaching poor boys.

WIVETON, a parish in the hundred of HOLT, county of NORFOLK, ¼ of a mile (W. by S.) from Clay, containing 209 inhabitants. The living is a discharged rectory, in the archdeaconry and diocese of Norwich, rated in the king's books at £15, and in the patronage of G. Wyndham, Esq. The church is dedicated to St. Mary.

WIX, or WEEKS, a parish in the hundred of TENDRING, county of ESSEX, 4½ miles (E. S. E.) from Manningtree, containing 818 inhabitants. The living is a perpetual curacy, in the archdeaconry of Colchester, and diocese of London, endowed with £600 private benefaction, and £600 royal bounty, and in the patronage of Miss Hickeringhill. The church is dedicated to St. Mary. Five pounds a year, bequeathed by a Mr. Clarke, is applied in support of a small school. A Benedictine nunnery, in honour of the Virgin Mary was founded here in the time of Henry I., by Walter, Mascherell and others, which, at its suppression, was valued at £92. 12. 3., and was granted to Cardinal Wolsey towards erecting and endowing his intended colleges.

WIXFORD, a parish in the Stratford division of the hundred of BARLICHWAY, county of WARWICK, 2 miles (S.) from Alcester, containing 110 inhabitants. The living is a perpetual curacy, annexed to the rectory of Exhall, in the archdeaconry and diocese of Worcester. The church is dedicated to St. Milburgh.

WOBURN, a market town and parish in the hundred of MANSHEAD, county of BEDFORD, 15 miles (S. W. by S.) from Bedford, and 42 (N. W. by N.) from London, containing 1656 inhabitants. This town, which, having suffered from fire in 1595, and again in 1724, has been almost entirely rebuilt, occupies a gentle eminence on the main road from London to Leeds, and consists of several broad and handsome streets, which intersect each other at right angles, and are well paved with pebbles; the inhabitants are amply supplied with water from wells: the approaches to it, both from the north and the south, are kept in excellent repair. In the immediate vicinity is Woburn Abbey, with its noble and extensive park, the seat of His Grace the Duke of Bedford, which occupies the site of a Cistercian abbey, founded, in 1145, by Hugh de Bolbeck, the revenue of which, at the dissolution, was valued at £430. 13. 11.: the site, with great part of the lands, was granted, in 1574, by Edward VI., to John, Lord Russell. In the middle of the last century the abbey was almost entirely rebuilt, by Flitcroft, since which time considerable enlargements have been made, under the superintendence of Mr. Holland, architect of Drury-lane theatre. This magnificent pile occupies the four sides of a quadrangle, and comprises various suites of apartments: the principal state-rooms are in the west front, which is of the Ionic order of architecture; and the gallery contains a highly valuable collection of portraits. The park is well stocked with deer, and abundantly supplied with game, and, being open to the inhabitants, affords many interesting walks. Queen Elizabeth made a journey to this place, in 1572; and when Charles I. visited Woburn, in 1645, notwithstanding that the Earl of Bedford was then in the service of the parliament, the monarch slept at the abbey. Assemblies, respectably attended, are occasionally held in the town during the winter months. The principal branches of manufacture are those of straw-plat and thread-lace, which are considerable. The market is on Friday; and fairs are held on January 1st, March 23rd, July 13th, and October 6th: the spring fair is noted for an abundant supply of horses. The market-house, in the centre of the town, is a handsome square brick building, with a stuccoed front; it is three stories high, and is surmounted by

a cupola and vane: the lower part is principally appropriated to the use of the butchers, and the upper end is for corn, butter, and cheese: this edifice was erected, after the great fire in 1724, at the expense of the Bedford family, and has been much improved by the present Duke. Manorial courts are held occasionally, at which constables are appointed. The county magistrates hold here a petty session for the hundred, on the first Friday in every month.

The living is a perpetual curacy, in the peculiar jurisdiction of the Incumbent, and in the patronage of the Duke of Bedford. The church, which is dedicated to St. Mary, was erected by Robert Hobbs, the last abbot of Woburn: it presents a singular appearance, being nearly covered with ivy. About six yards from the north aisle, and detached from the main building, is a quadrangular embattled tower, scarcely fifty feet high, strengthened with buttresses at the angles, terminating in pinnacles, and surmounted by a cupola. In the interior is a curious monument of the Stanton family, consisting of twelve figures in the attitude of prayer, besides several other ancient sepulchral memorials: the fine altar-piece, representing the Nativity, was the gift of the present Duke of Bedford. There are places of worship for Independents and Wesleyan Methodists. The free school, in Bedford-street, established in 1582, by Francis, the fifth Earl of Bedford, has been united to another, founded by one of his successors: to this institution, which is conducted on the Lancasterian system, for an unlimited number of children of both sexes, of whom there are at present about one hundred and fifty, the present Duke contributes £50 per annum, and it is further supported by voluntary contributions. Twelve almshouses were founded, in 1672, and endowed by John, Duke of Bedford, for the residence and maintenance of twenty-four poor widows. Several stone coffins have been discovered at the abbey; and, in 1744, on taking down part of the ancient buildings, a corpse was found, with the flesh so firm as to bear cutting with a knife, though it had, probably, been buried more than two hundred years. About a mile from the town is a piece of water, possessing the power of petrifaction.

WOKEFIELD, a tything in the parish of STRATFIELD-MORTIMER, hundred of THEALE, county of BERKS, containing 105 inhabitants.

WOKING, a parish (formerly a market town) in the first division of the hundred of WOKING, county of SURREY, 2½ miles (W. by N.) from Ripley, containing 1810 inhabitants. The living is a vicarage, in the archdeaconry of Surrey, and diocese of Winchester, rated in the king's books at £11. 0. 5., and in the patronage of Earl Onslow. The church, dedicated to St. Peter, is partly in the early, and partly in the decorated style of English architecture: it contains some brasses and a few monuments, and the windows exhibit fragments of ancient stained glass. The Basingstoke canal passes through the parish, and the town is situated on the river Wey; but its market, formerly held on Tuesday, is now disused. There is a fair on Whit-Tuesday; and courts leet and baron are occasionally held. This was one of the royal demesnes of Edward the Confessor; and was afforested in 1154, by Henry II., whose successor gave it to Alan, Lord Basset; but, in the reign of Edward II., it belonged to the Despencers, and on their attainder was given, by Edward III., to Edmund of

Woodstock, from which time it had various distinguished owners till the time of Edward IV., who, it is recorded, kept his Christmas in 1480, at the royal palace of Woking. Henry VII. afterwards repaired and enlarged it, for the residence of his mother, Margaret, Countess of Richmond, who died there. Henry VIII. used it as a summer retreat, where he sometimes entertained Wolsey, and on one of these occasions, in September 1551, that prelate was first informed, by a letter from the pope, of his elevation to the dignity of Cardinal. James I. granted Woking to Sir Edward Zouch; but, in the reign of Charles I., it again belonged to the Crown, and was bestowed upon Barbara, Duchess of Cleveland; it subsequently passed, by purchase, through various hands to Richard, Lord Onslow, an ancestor of Earl Onslow, its present proprietor. There are now no remains of the palace, except its foundations and a portion of the walls of the guard-room; the Zouches having removed the greater part of the building, to erect another mansion in the neighbourhood. Sutton House, a fine specimen of the style of building which prevailed in the sixteenth century, was erected, in 1529, by Sir Richard Weston: it was of a quadrangular form, enclosing a square area eighty feet in dimensions, with a noble gateway, having lofty hexagonal turrets at the angles. A great part of this magnificent structure was burned down, during a visit of Queen Elizabeth, and the remainder, consisting of the south-west side and north-east front, continued in a ruinous state till 1721, when it was repaired and embellished by the late John Weston, Esq.

Corporate Seal.

WOKINGHAM, a market town and parish, having separate jurisdiction, situated partly in, and forming a detached portion of, the hundred of AMESBURY, county of WILTS, but chiefly in the hundred of SONNING, county of BERKS, 7 miles (E. S. E.) from Reading, and 32 (W. S. W.) from London, comprising the Berkshire and Town divisions, and containing 2810 inhabitants. This town, situated within the prescribed limits of Windsor Forest, is of triangular form, and consists of several streets irregularly built, meeting in a central area; water is supplied from wells in abundance: the atmosphere is considered particularly salubrious, and the inhabitants are remarkable for longevity. The manufacture of silk, gauze, and shoes, and the malting and flour trades, are the only branches of business. The market, which is on Tuesday, is one of the most noted in the kingdom for its abundant supply of poultry: the fairs are, April 23rd, June 11th (both of little importance, and not regularly held), October 11th, and November 2nd, chiefly for cattle. The government of the town is vested in an alderman, seven capital burgesses, a high steward, recorder, and town clerk: the charter has been possessed from time immemorial. The alderman is elected from among the capital burgesses, annually on the Wednesday in Easter week, and becomes the chief magistrate for the year ensuing: the alderman, high steward, and recorder, are justices of the peace, with exclusive jurisdiction. The corporation holds half-yearly courts of session for minor offences, and is authorized by charter to hold a court of requests, for the recovery of small debts; but this power has not been exercised for some years. The gift of freedom is vested in the corporation, and may be acquired by birth, apprenticeship, and purchase. This being the only town in the forest, the forest courts were formerly held here; but they have been discontinued: manorial courts are held as occasion requires. Petty sessions take place, on the first and third Tuesdays in the month, for the Wokingham, or Forest, division of the county. The town hall, which is over the market-house, is an ancient building in the centre of the town; it was repaired about twelve years ago, at an expense of £1100, defrayed by subscription: balls are occasionally held here in the winter season.

The living is a perpetual curacy, in the peculiar jurisdiction and patronage of the Dean of Salisbury, endowed with £400 royal bounty. The church, which is dedicated to All Saints, is an ancient structure. There are places of worship for Baptists and Wesleyan Methodists. The free school, in Down-street, for children of both sexes, is supported by the proceeds of various bequests left for the instruction of children, particularly a rent-charge on certain lands in this parish, by Dr. Charles Palmer, in 1711, amounting to the sum of about £20 per annum, and by voluntary contribution: thirty-four boys and twelve girls receive instruction, and, with the master, are appointed by the corporation: there are likewise other scholars of both sexes in the establishment. The Sunday school in Rose-street, conducted on the National system, in which two hundred children of both sexes are taught, is supported partly by some small bequests, and partly by subscription, and is held in a substantial brick building, erected in 1825, at an expense of £700. Eight almshouses near the church, founded and endowed by Mr. John Westend, an inhabitant of this town, in 1451, are occupied by sixteen poor men and women, who receive a small allowance of fuel. At Luckley Green, in this parish, about a mile from the town, is an hospital, founded in 1665, by Henry Lucas, Esq., for sixteen poor pensioners and a master, under the superintendence of the Drapers' Company in London: the pensioners are chosen alternately from sixteen of the neighbouring parishes in the counties of Berks and Surrey, and receive £14 per annum in weekly payments. Attached to the hospital, which is a handsome brick building, erected at an expense of £2320, is a chapel, with a residence for the minister, who is the perpetual curate of the parish. Archbishop Laud bequeathed £60 per annum, for apprenticing boys two years successively, the third for poor maidens. Dr. Thomas Goodwin, who, after various promotions, was eventually raised to the see of Bath and Wells, was a native of this town, and received the elements of his education in the free school: in the chancel of the church is a monument to his memory, the inscription written by his son, who was Bishop of Hereford.

WOLD, county of NORTHAMPTON.—See OLD.

WOLD-NEWTON, East riding of the county of YORK.— See NEWTON (WOLD).

WOLDINGHAM, a parish in the second division of the hundred of TANDRIDGE, county of SURREY, 3 miles (N. E. by N.) from Godstone, containing 47 inhabitants. The living is a donative, in the patronage of William Bryant, Esq.

WOLFERLOW, a parish in the hundred of BROX-ASH, county of HEREFORD, 5½ miles (N. by E.) from Bromyard, containing 117 inhabitants. The living is a discharged vicarage, in the archdeaconry and diocese of Hereford, rated in the king's books at £4. 4. 9., and in the patronage of Sir T. E. Winnington, Bart. The church is dedicated to St. Andrew.

WOLFHAMCOTE, a parish in the Southam division of the hundred of KNIGHTLOW, county of WAR-WICK, 3¾ miles (N. W. by W.) from Daventry, containing 413 inhabitants. The living is a discharged vicarage, in the archdeaconry of Coventry, and diocese of Lichfield and Coventry, rated in the king's books at £12. 18. 2., endowed with £200 private benefaction, and £400 royal bounty, and in the patronage of — Tibbits, Esq. The church is dedicated to St. Peter. The Oxford canal passes through the parish. In sinking a well here some years ago, a vault, containing several urns and coins, was discovered.

WOLFORD (GREAT), a parish in the Brails division of the hundred of KINGTON, county of WAR-WICK, 4 miles (S. by W.) from Shipston upon Stour, containing, with the hamlet of Little Wolford, 529 inhabitants. The living is a discharged vicarage, in the archdeaconry and diocese of Worcester, rated in the king's books at £8, endowed with £400 private benefaction, £200 royal bounty, and £300 parliamentary grant, and in the patronage of the Warden and Fellows of Merton College, Oxford. The church is dedicated to St. Michael.

WOLFORD (LITTLE), a hamlet in the parish of GREAT WOLFORD, Brails division of the hundred of KINGTON, county of WARWICK, 3 miles (S.) from Shipston upon Stour, containing 257 inhabitants.

WOLLASTON, a parish in the hundred of HIGHAM-FERRERS, county of NORTHAMPTON, 3 miles (S. S. E.) from Wellingborough, containing 991 inhabitants. The living is a discharged vicarage, with that of Irchester annexed, in the archdeaconry of Northampton, and diocese of Peterborough, rated in the king's books at £13. 6. 8., endowed with £200 private benefaction, and £200 royal bounty, and in the patronage of Francis Dickens, Esq. The church, dedicated to St. Mary, is a handsome cruciform structure, with a stately tower rising from the intersection, and surmounted by a spire. There are places of worship for Independents and Wesleyan Methodists. The river Nen runs through the parish.

WOLLASTON, a chapelry in that part of the parish of ALBERBURY which is in the hundred of FORD, county of SALOP, 10½ miles (W.) from Shrewsbury, containing 441 inhabitants. The living is a perpetual curacy, in the archdeaconry of Salop, and diocese of Hereford, endowed with £800 royal bounty, and £1400 parliamentary grant, and in the patronage of the Vicar of Alberbury. The chapel is dedicated to St. Michael.

WOLLASTONE, a parish, forming, with Tidenham, a detached portion of the hundred of WESTBURY, county of GLOUCESTER, 5¼ miles (N. E.) from Chepstow, containing 884 inhabitants. The living is a discharged rectory, in the archdeaconry of Hereford, and diocese of Gloucester, rated in the king's books at £13. 11. 5., and in the patronage of the Duke of Beaufort. The

church, dedicated to St. Andrew, is a small cruciform edifice, partly in the Norman style of architecture. The parish is bounded on the south by the river Severn. A National school was established about seven years ago, and is supported by subscription, aided by the sum of £2 per annum, bequeathed by Richard Clayton, in 1605.

WOLLATON, a parish in the southern division of the wapentake of BROXTOW, county of NOTTINGHAM, 3 miles (W.) from Nottingham, containing 571 inhabitants. The living is a discharged rectory, with the perpetual curacy of Cossal annexed, in the archdeaconry of Nottingham, and diocese of York, rated in the king's books at £14. 2. 6., endowed with £200 private benefaction, and £200 royal bounty, and in the patronage of Lord Middleton. The church, dedicated to St. Leonard, exhibits a mixture of the several styles of English architecture. The Nottingham canal passes through the middle of the parish, in various parts of which coal mines have been wrought from time immemorial. Wollaton Hall, the seat of Lord Middleton, is a large and lofty edifice, in the Elizabethan style, built by Sir Francis Willoughby, entirely of freestone, which was brought from Ancaster, in the county of Lincoln, in exchange for coal obtained upon the estate.

WOLLEY, a parish in the hundred of BATH-FO-RUM, county of SOMERSET, 3 miles (N.) from Bath, containing 101 inhabitants. The living is a rectory, annexed to that of Bathwick, in the archdeaconry of Bath, and diocese of Bath and Wells. The church is dedicated to All Saints.

WOLSINGHAM, a market town and parish in the north-western division of DARLINGTON ward, county palatine of DURHAM, 16 miles (W. S. W.) from Durham, and 259 (N. N. W.) from London, containing 2197 inhabitants. The town, which is irregularly built, is situated on the north bank of the Wear. In 1824, a new town hall was erected and covered with a roof, but it yet remains unfinished, for want of funds to complete the work. There are manufactures of linen, woollen cloth, edge-tools, and implements of agriculture, in which, and in the neighbouring coal, lead, and limestone works, a great proportion of the population is employed. The market and fairs are held by grant from the Bishop of Durham; the former is on Tuesday, and the latter are on May 12th and October 2nd, for cattle and all sorts of merchandise. The county magistrates hold a petty session for the division here, every Wednesday, and a court leet and baron, under the Bishop of Durham, as lord of the manor, is held twice a year, at which debts under 40s. are recoverable : its jurisdiction extends to Stanhope, Bishopley, North and South Bedburn, Lynsack, and Softley. The living is a rectory, in the archdeaconry and diocese of Durham, rated in the king's books at £31. 13. 4., and in the patronage of the Bishop of Durham. The church, situated on rising ground to the north-west of the town, and dedicated to St. Mary and St. Stephen, is a neat plain building with a low tower, and has a font of Weardale marble, beautifully variegated with petrifactions of shells, &c. There are places of worship for Baptists and Primitive and Wesleyan Methodists. The grammar school, founded in 1613, with a residence for the master, was rebuilt, in 1786, upon a piece of waste land granted by the Bishop of Durham and the landholders of the parish, by whom it was endowed with sixteen acres of land. On the enclosure of the moor, seven acres and a quarter more were added, for the maintenance of the master: eighteen boys are appointed by the trustees, who are nine in number. Several bequests in money, particularly by Jonathan and George Wooller, have since been made, amounting to about £200, for the interest of which eight additional boys are taught on this foundation. Forty girls are also instructed in another school, supported by the Misses Wilson, of this place; and there are Sunday schools attended by about one hundred and sixty children. Contiguous to a field, called Chapel-Walls, are the remains of an extensive building, surrounded by a moat, supposed to be those of the manor house of the Bishop of Durham, attached to Wolsingham park. There are two chalybeate springs in the neighbourhood, and a sulphureous spring about two miles east of Wolsingham, on an estate called Bradley.

WOLSTAN, a parish partly in the Kirby, but chiefly in the Rugby, division of the hundred of KNIGHTLOW, county of WARWICK, 5½ miles (E. S. E.) from Coventry, containing, with the hamlets of Brandon with Bretsford, and Marston, 941 inhabitants. The living is a vicarage, in the archdeaconry of Coventry, and diocese of Lichfield and Coventry, rated in the king's books at £15. 10., and in the patronage of Lady Scott. The church, dedicated to St. Margaret, is a large cruciform structure. There is a place of worship for Baptists. An Alien priory, a cell to the abbey of St. Peter *super Divam* in Normandy, was founded here soon after the Conquest, and, at its suppression, granted by Richard II. to the Carthusian priory at Coventry. On the southern bank of the Avon are vestiges of a Roman encampment.

WOLSTANTON, a parish in the northern division of the hundred of PIREHILL, county of STAFFORD, comprising the chapelry of Thursfield, the townships of Chatterley, Chell, Chesterton, Knutton, Oldcott, Rainscliff, Stadmerslow, Wedgwood, and Wolstanton, the hamlet of Brerehurst, and the liberty of Tunstall Court, and containing 8572 inhabitants, of which number, 958 are in the township of Wolstanton, 1½ mile (N. by E.) from Newcastle under Line. The living is a rectory, in the archdeaconry of Stafford, and diocese of Lichfield and Coventry, rated in the king's books at £32. 3. 9., and in the patronage of Walter Sneyd, Esq. The church is dedicated to St. Nicholas. There is also a chapel, called New chapel, the living of which is a perpetual curacy, endowed with £200 private benefaction, and £400 royal bounty, and in the same patronage. The Grand Trunk and Sir N. Gresley's canals pass through the parish, and the former is here conducted under a tunnel one mile and a half in length. Six poor children are educated for £2 a year, bequeathed by John Turner, in 1696. Wolstanton is in the honour of Tutbury, duchy of Lancaster, and within the jurisdiction of a court of pleas held at Tutbury every third Tuesday, for the recovery of debts under 40s.

WOLSTONE, a chapelry in the parish of UFFINGTON, hundred of SHRIVENHAM, county of BERKS, 5¼ miles (S. by E.) from Great Farringdon, containing 247 inhabitants. The chapel is dedicated to All Saints.

WOLTERTON, a parish in the southern division of the hundred of ERPINGHAM, county of NORFOLK, 4¼ miles (N. N. W.) from Aylsham, containing 37 inhabit-

ants. The living is a discharged rectory, annexed to that of Wickmere, in the archdeaconry and diocese of Norwich, rated in the king's books at £8. The church, dedicated to St. Margaret, is supposed to have been rebuilt by John de Wulterton, whose effigy, with that of his wife, still remain in one of the windows, and in others were representations of the twelve Apostles.

WOLVERHAMPTON, a parish comprising the market towns of Bilston and Wolverhampton, in the northern division of the hundred of SEISDON; the chapelries of Pelsall, Wednesfield, and Willenhall, in the southern division of the hundred of OFFLOW; and the townships of Featherstone, Hatherton, Hilton, and Kinvaston, in the eastern division of the hundred of CUTTLESTONE, county of STAFFORD; and containing, according to the last census, 36,838 inhabitants, of which number 18,380 were in the town of Wolverhampton (the population of which has since greatly increased), 16 miles (S.) from Stafford, and 123 (N. W.) from London. This place, which is of considerable antiquity, was called "Hanton," or "Hamton," prior to the year 996, when Wulfruna, sister of King Edgar, and widow of Aldhelm, Duke of Northampton, founded a college here, in which she placed a dean and several prebendaries, or Secular canons, endowing it with so many privileges, that the town, in honour of Wulfrana, was called *Wulfranis Hamton*, of which its present appellation is a corruption. The college, under the same government, continued till the year 1200, when Petrus Blesensis, who was then dean, after fruitless attempts to reform the dissolute lives of the brethren, surrendered the establishment to Hubert, Archbishop of Canterbury; and it was subsequently annexed by Edward IV. to the deanery of Windsor. In 1258, the town obtained from Henry III. the grant of a market and a fair, from which time no circumstance of historical importance occurs till 1590, when a considerable part of it was destroyed by a fire, which continued burning for five days. In the parliamentary war Charles I., accompanied by his sons, Charles, Prince of Wales, and James, Duke of York, visited Wolverhampton, where he was received with every demonstration of loyalty by the inhabitants, who, in aid of the royal cause, raised a liberal subscription, towards which Mr. Gough, ancestor of the learned antiquary of that name, contributed £1200. Prince Rupert, in 1645, fixed his head-quarters in the town, while the king was encamped at Bushbury; and, immediately after the battle of Naseby, Charles marched into it, and quitted the day following.

The town is situated on an eminence, in a district abounding with mines of coal, iron, and limestone, and consists of several streets diverging from the market-place (in the centre of which is a cast-iron pillar, forty-five feet high, supporting a gas lantern) to the several roads from which they take their names. Among the recent improvements effected, under the provisions of an act obtained about 1814, is a new entrance on the east from Bilston, which, by means of a street crossing the town, nearly in a direct line, communicates on the west with Salop-street, leading towards Shrewsbury. The houses are in general substantial and neatly built of brick, many of them being modern and handsome; but in the smaller streets are several dwellings of more ancient appearance: the town is irregularly paved, well lighted with gas, and supplied with water by sinking wells to a great depth in the rock on which it is built. A public subscription library was established in 1794, which contains more than five thousand volumes, and for which a neat and commodious building was erected in 1816, when a news-room was added: over the library is a suite of rooms in which assemblies and concerts, under the superintendence of the Harmonic Society, take place. A neat theatre, well arranged for the purpose, is opened occasionally: prior to its erection, the celebrated Mrs. Siddons, and her brother, J. P. Kemble, performed in the town hall, since taken down, where they first developed those talents which procured for them so distinguished a reputation. Races are held annually in August, and are well attended: the course is an extensive area near the town, on which an elegant stand has lately been erected. The manufacture of the finer steel ornaments, which was formerly carried on extensively, and brought to the highest perfection, in this town, has given place to the heavier articles of steel and iron, of which the principal are, smiths' and carpenters' tools of every description, files, nails, screws, gun-locks, hinges, steel-mills, and machinery; locks, for the making of which the town has long been celebrated; furnishing ironmongery and cabinet brasses, with every branch of the iron manufacture; and brass, tin, Pont-y-pool, and japanned wares, in great variety: there is also a large chemical laboratory. The Birmingham canal, which forms a junction with the Staffordshire and Worcestershire canal, passes close to the town, on the west and north, where it is joined by the Essington and Wyrley canal, which terminates here, and affords facility of conveyance to every part of the kingdom: fly-boats proceed daily for London, Liverpool, and Chester, from the wharfs at Walsall-street and Horsleyfield, and twice a week for Derby, Nottingham, and Hull. The market is on Wednesday; and the fair, which continues for three days, the first being for cattle, commences on the 10th of July. The town is within the jurisdiction of the county magistrates, who hold petty sessions for the north and south divisions. A court of requests, for the recovery of debts not exceeding £5, is held in the public office, Prince's-street, every fourth Friday, under an act passed in the 48th of George III.; the jurisdiction of which extends over Wolverhampton and Wednesfield, and the parishes of Brewood, Pattingham, Busbury, and Penn. The lord of the manor holds a court leet, at which two constables (one of them chosen by the dean) and other officers are annually appointed.

The living is a perpetual curacy, in the jurisdiction of the royal peculiar court of Wolverhampton, and in the patronage of the Dean of Windsor, as incumbent of the ancient deanery of Wolverhampton. The church, dedicated to St. Mary and St. Peter, formerly collegiate, and one of the king's free chapels, to which many immunities were granted, is a spacious cruciform structure, partly in the early decorated, but principally in the later, style of English architecture, with a handsome square embattled tower rising from the centre, the upper part of which is a very fine specimen of the later style. The interior, with the exception of the chancel, which is modern, is generally of more ancient character; the piers and arches of the nave and transepts, if not of the early English, are of that style merging into the decorated; and the pul-

pit, of one entire stone, is richly embellished with sculpture. An octagonal font, of great antiquity, is supported on a shaft, the faces of which are embellished with the figures of St. Anthony, St. Paul, and St. Peter, in bas-relief, and is richly ornamented with bosses, flowers, and foliage. In the chancel are, a fine statue of brass, erected in honour of Admiral Sir Richard Leveson, who commanded, under Sir Francis Drake, against the Spanish Armada, and a monument to the memory of Col. John Lane, the protector of Charles I. after the battle of Worcester: in what was anciently the Lady chapel is an alabaster monument to John Lane and his wife, the former represented in armour. In the churchyard, which has been recently enclosed with a handsome iron palisade, is a column twenty feet high, divided into compartments, highly enriched with sculpture of various designs, supposed to be either of Saxon or Danish origin. Near its south-west corner is a large vault, thirty feet square, the roof of which is finely groined, and supported on one central pillar; the walls are three yards in thickness, and on both sides of the doorway are slight vestiges of sculpture; the interior is in good preservation. It appears to have been the basement story of some edifice, probably connected with the monastery of Wulfrana, the exact site of which has not been ascertained. The living of St. John's is a perpetual curacy, endowed with £200 private benefaction, and £300 parliamentary grant, and in the patronage of the Earl of Stamford. The church is an elegant modern structure, in the Grecian style of architecture, with a handsome tower surmounted by a lofty and finely-proportioned spire; the prevailing character is a mixture of the Ionic and Corinthian orders. A pleasing and appropriate effect is produced from the arrangement of the interior; the altar is ornamented with a good painting of the Descent from the Cross, by Barney, a native of the town. A new church, to be dedicated to St. George, is now being erected, towards defraying the expense of which the inhabitants have subscribed £3500, the remainder to be granted by the parliamentary commissioners: the dean having given up the right of first presentation, application is to be made for an act of parliament to dispose of it. There are places of worship for Baptists, the Society of Friends, Independents, Wesleyan Methodists, Methodists of the New Connexion, Unitarians, and Roman Catholics.

The free grammar school was founded, under letters patent of Henry VIII., in 1513, by Sir Stephen Jenyns, Knt., a native of this town, and lord mayor of London in 1508, who endowed it with estates in the parish of Rushoe, in the county of Worcester, an income, aided by other benefactions, of about £1170 per annum: the management, originally in the Master and Wardens of the Merchant Taylors' Company in London, is now, by a decree of the court of Chancery, vested in forty trustees, including the Bishop of Lichfield and Coventry, and the two county members, for the time being. The head-master has a salary of £500, and the usher £200, per annum, with residences; and there are also writing, French and German, and drawing masters, who have, respectively, salaries of £84, £80, and £70, per annum. The school is open to all boys of the town; the present number on the foundation is one hundred and fifty. The building was erected, in 1713, by the Merchant Taylors' Company, who, on some disagreement with the inhabitants, subsequently petitioned the Lord Chancellor to be released from the governorship. Sir William Congreve; John Abernethy, Esq. ; and John Pearson, Esq., Advocate General of India, were educated at this school. The Blue-coat charity school, for thirty-six boys and thirty girls, of whom six of each are also clothed and maintained, is an ancient establishment of unknown origin : it has an endowment arising from a farm at Siesdon, tenements in the town, and funded property, purchased with accumulated benefactions, producing more than £240 per annum, and is further liberally supported by subscription : residences for the master and mistress are attached. Sunday schools, in connexion with the established church and the various dissenting congregations, have been established. A dispensary was instituted in 1821, and a handsome and commodious building was erected, by subscription, in 1826 : it is under the direction of a committee, of which the Earl of Dudley is president; and its income, arising from bequests and annual subscriptions, is about £400 per annum. There are numerous charitable bequests for distribution among the poor ; but one of the most praiseworthy institutions is the establishment of the "Union Mill," erected, in 1813, at an expense of £14,000, raised in shares, for the purpose of grinding corn for the poor on easy terms, and supplying them with cheap flour and bread. There is a medicinal spring near the town, at Cull Well, on the road to Wednesfield.

WOLVERLEY, a township in that part of the parish of WEM which is in the Whitchurch division of the hundred of BRADFORD (North), county of SALOP, containing 67 inhabitants.

WOLVERLEY, a parish partly in the upper division of the hundred of HALFSHIRE, but chiefly in, and forming a detached portion of, the lower division of the hundred of OSWALDSLOW, county of WORCESTER, 2 miles (N. by W.) from Kidderminster, containing 1529 inhabitants. The living is a vicarage, in the peculiar jurisdiction and patronage of the Dean and Chapter of Worcester, rated in the king's books at £13. 6. 8. The church, dedicated to St. John the Baptist, was erected in 1772 ; it is a neat brick structure, occupying an elevated site. At Cookley there is a place of worship for Wesleyan Methodists; there are also manufactures of iron and tin ware. The Staffordshire and Worcestershire canal, and the river Stour, pass through the parish. William Sebright, Esq., in 1618, erected a free school, in support of which, and for various other public purposes, he bequeathed two houses in Mark-lane, London, with twenty acres of land at Bethnall Green, now producing a considerable income, from which he directed that the master should receive £20 a year, and the overplus be applied to the increase of that stipend, and the repair of the church and bridges, &c : in 1816 the Madras system of education was introduced, on which about ninety boys and seventy girls are taught by a master and a mistress, who have each a salary and a rent-free residence. John Baskerville, an eminent printer, was born here, in 1706 ; he died in 1775.

WOLVERTON, a parish in the Lynn division of the hundred of FREEBRIDGE, county of NORFOLK, 2¾ miles (N. by W.) from Castle-Rising, containing 159 inhabitants. The living is a rectory, in the archdeaconry and diocese of Norwich, rated in the king's books at £12, and in the patronage of H. H. Henley, Esq. The church is dedicated to St. Peter.

WOLVERTON, a parish in the Snitterfield division of the hundred of BARLICHWAY, county of WARWICK, 5 miles (W. S. W.) from Warwick, containing 152 inhabitants. The living is a rectory, in the archdeaconry and diocese of Worcester, rated in the king's books at £7. 10. 7½., and in the patronage of the Rev. James Roberts. The church is dedicated to St. Mary.

WOLVES-NEWTON, a parish in the upper division of the hundred of RAGLAND, county of MONMOUTH, 5¼ miles (E. by S.) from Usk, containing 222 inhabitants. The living is a rectory, in the archdeaconry and diocese of Llandaff, rated in the king's books at £8. 2. 8½., and in the patronage of the Crown. The church is dedicated to St. Thomas à Becket.

WOLVEY, a parish in the Kirby division of the hundred of KNIGHTLOW, county of WARWICK, 5¼ miles (S. E. by E.) from Nuneaton, containing 851 inhabitants. The living is a discharged vicarage, in the peculiar jurisdiction of the Bishop of Lichfield and Coventry, rated in the king's books at £6. 6. 5½., and in the alternate patronage of the Representatives of the late Mr. Foster and the Prebendary of Wolvey in the Cathedral Church of Lichfield. The church, dedicated to St. John the Baptist, contains a monument, five hundred years old, of the Clinton family, formerly resident here. The river Anker rises in the parish.

WOLVISTON, a chapelry in the parish of BILLINGHAM, north-eastern division of STOCKTON ward, county palatine of DURHAM, 4½ miles (N. by E.) from Stockton upon Tees, containing 541 inhabitants. The living is a perpetual curacy, in the archdeaconry and diocese of Durham, endowed with £800 private benefaction, £400 royal bounty, and £600 parliamentary grant, and in the patronage of the Dean and Chapter of Durham. The chapel, dedicated to St Peter, is situated on an eminence; it is a modern brick edifice, and has lately received an addition of one hundred and forty sittings, of which one hundred are free, the Incorporated Society for the enlargement of churches and chapels having granted £75 towards defraying the expense.

WOMBLETON, a township in the parish of KIRKDALE, partly within the liberty of ST. PETER of YORK, East riding, and partly in the wapentake of RYEDALE, North riding, of the county of YORK, 4 miles (E. by S.) from Helmsley, containing 265 inhabitants. There is a place of worship for Wesleyan Methodists.

WOMBOURNE, a parish in the southern division of the hundred of SEISDON, county of STAFFORD, 4 miles (S. W. by S.) from Wolverhampton, containing, with the liberty of Orton, 1478 inhabitants. The living is a discharged vicarage, in the archdeaconry of Stafford, and diocese of Lichfield and Coventry, rated in the king's books at £12. 12. 8½., and in the patronage of certain Trustees. The church is dedicated to St. Benedict. The Staffordshire and Worcestershire canal passes through the parish.

WOMBRIDGE, a parish in the Wellington division of the hundred of BRADFORD (South), county of SALOP, 2¾ miles (E.) from Wellington, containing 1860 inhabitants. The living is a perpetual curacy, in the peculiar jurisdiction and patronage of William Charlton, Esq., as lord of the manor, endowed with £800 royal bounty, and £1200 parliamentary grant. The church, dedicated to St. Mary and St. Leonard, has lately received an addition of three hundred sittings, of which two hundred and ninety-five are free, the Incorporated Society for the enlargement of churches and chapels having granted £270 towards defraying the expense. The Shrewsbury, Shropshire, and Marquis of Stafford's, canals form a junction in this parish, which is intersected by the old Watling - street and the great Holyhead road, also by several railways communicating with the extensive coal and iron mines at Ketley and in the neighbourhood, which have been worked for centuries; but the most considerable iron-works were established here in 1818. At Oaken-Gates a small customary market is held. There are slight remains near the church of a priory of Black canons, founded in the reign of Henry I., by William Fitz-Alan, which at the dissolution had a revenue of £72. 15. 8.

WOMBWELL, a chapelry in that part of the parish of DARFIELD which is in the northern division of the wapentake of STRAFFORTH and TICKHILL, West riding of the county of YORK, 4½ miles (S. E. by E.) from Barnesley, containing 811 inhabitants.

WOMENSWOULD, a parish in the hundred of WINGHAM, lathe of ST. AUGUSTINE, county of KENT, 5 miles (S. by W.) from Wingham, containing 233 inhabitants. The living is a perpetual curacy, annexed to that of Nonington, in the archdeaconry and diocese of Canterbury,. The chapel is dedicated to St. Margaret.

WOMERSLEY, a parish in the lower division of the wapentake of OSGOLDCROSS, West riding of the county of YORK, comprising the townships of Cridling-Stubbs, Little Smeaton, Walden-Stubbs, and Womersley, and containing 746 inhabitants, of which number, 316 are in the township of Womersley, 5 miles (E. S. E.) from Pontefract. The living is a discharged vicarage, in the archdeaconry and diocese of York, rated in the king's books at £6. 11. 5½., endowed with £200 private benefaction, and £200 royal bounty, and in the patronage of Lord Hawke. The church, dedicated to St. Martin, is a handsome structure with a lofty spire, situated on an eminence in the centre of the parish. The river Went runs through the parish, and is crossed by a bridge; on its southern bank are quarries of a fine freestone, whence a rail-road passes over the stream, runs through the township of Little Smeaton, and meets the new line of navigation made by the Aire and Calder Company: there are also extensive quarries of limestone. A neat building has been recently erected, comprising a dwelling-house for a schoolmaster, and two school-rooms for boys and girls, who are taught on the National system: the site was given by Lord Hawke, and the expense of the building was defrayed by liberal grants from the parent institution in London, and the York Diocesan Society, aided by voluntary contributions. At Walden-Stubbs is an ancient hall, once the seat of a family of the name of Shuttleworth, now occupied as a farm-house.

WONASTOW, a parish in the lower division of the hundred of SKENFRETH, county of MONMOUTH, 2 miles (W. S. W.) from Monmouth, containing 149 inhabitants. The living is a discharged vicarage, in the archdeaconry and diocese of Llandaff, rated in the king's books at £4. 15. 5. T. Swineston, Esq. was patron in 1812. The church is dedicated to St. Wonnow.

WONERSH, a parish in the first division of the hundred of BLACKHEATH, county of SURREY, 3½ miles (S. S. E.) from Guildford, containing 918 inhabitants. The living is a discharged vicarage, in the archdeaconry of Surrey, and diocese of Winchester, rated in the king's books at £15. 1. 3., and in the patronage of Lord Grantley. The church is dedicated to St. John the Baptist. The Wey and Arun canal passes through the parish, which abounds with iron-stone. Six poor boys are instructed for a rent-charge of £4, the bequest of Henry Chennell, in 1672; and four are taught for a like sum left by Richard Gwynne, in 1698.

WONSTON, a parish in the hundred of BUDDLESGATE, Fawley division of the county of SOUTHAMPTON, 5¾ miles (S.) from Whitchurch, containing 668 inhabitants. The living is a rectory, in the peculiar jurisdiction of the Incumbent, rated in the king's books at £46. 15. 7½., and in the patronage of the Bishop of Winchester. The church is dedicated to the Holy Trinity. Eleven poor children are educated for £5 a year, the bequest of John Wickham, in 1779. Wonston is within the jurisdiction of the Cheyney Court held at Winchester every Thursday, for the recovery of debts to any amount.

WOOBURN, a parish (formerly a market town) in the hundred of DESBOROUGH, county of BUCKINGHAM, 3 miles (W. S. W.) from Beaconsfield, containing 1831 inhabitants. The living is a discharged vicarage, in the archdeaconry of Buckingham, and diocese of Lincoln, rated in the king's books at £12, and in the patronage of James Dupré, Esq. The church, dedicated to St. Paul, is a stately edifice, in the later style of English architecture, with a very handsome tower and a curiously carved font; it contains some monuments of the Bertie and Wharton families, of whom Philip, Lord Wharton, in 1694, gave a rent-charge of £22. 10., to be paid to the vicar for preaching an evening lecture every Sunday. There are places of worship for Independents and Wesleyan Methodists. A rivulet, rising at West Wycombe, flows through this parish, turning in its course several paper, mill-board, and flour, mills. Several of the female inhabitants are employed in the manufacture of bone-lace. The market, which was held on Friday, and a fair on the festival of the translation of St. Edward, were granted by Henry VI., but they have been long disused, and fairs are now held, for horses, cattle, and sheep, on May 4th and November 12th. A school on the Lancasterian system, and one for infants, are supported by subscription. Wooburn House occupies the site of a noble palace, formerly the residence of the Bishops of Lincoln.

WOOD, a member of the cinque-port liberty of DOVOR, locally in the hundred of Ringslow, or the Isle of Thanet, lathe of ST. AUGUSTINE, county of KENT, 3 miles (S. W. by W.) from Margate, containing 212 inhabitants. Here are the ruins of a chapel of ease to the vicarage of Monkton: it was dedicated to St. Mary Magdalene.

WOOD-DALLING, a parish in the hundred of EYNSFORD, county of NORFOLK, 3 miles (N. by W.) from Reepham, containing 527 inhabitants. The living is a discharged vicarage, annexed to the rectory of Swannington, in the archdeaconry of Norfolk, and diocese of Norwich, rated in the king's books at £8. 8. 4. The church is dedicated to St. Andrew.

WOOD-EATON, a parish in the hundred of BUL-LINGTON, county of OXFORD, 4 miles (N. N. E.) from Oxford, containing 69 inhabitants. The living is a rectory, in the archdeaconry and diocese of Oxford, rated in the king's books at £10. 0. 10., and in the patronage of J. Weyland, Esq. The church is dedicated to the Holy Rood. John Collins, a distinguished mathematician, was born here, in 1624 ; he died in 1683.

WOOD-NORTON, a parish in the hundred of EYNSFORD, county of NORFOLK, 7 miles (N. W.) from Reepham, containing 313 inhabitants. The living comprises the united rectories of All Saints and St. Peter, with the rectory of Swanton-Novers annexed, in the archdeaconry of Norfolk, and diocese of Norwich, rated in the king's books at £7. 12. 3½., and in the patronage of the Dean and Canons of Christ Church, Oxford. The church, dedicated to All Saints, has no steeple, the bells being hung on a frame in the churchyard. The church of St. Peter has been long demolished.

WOOD-RISING, a parish in the hundred of MITFORD, county of NORFOLK, 2½ miles (W. N. W.) from Hingham, containing 119 inhabitants. The living is a discharged rectory, in the archdeaconry of Norfolk, and diocese of Norwich, rated in the king's books at £4. 18. 4. John Weyland, Esq. was patron in 1804. The church is dedicated to St. Nicholas.

WOOD-THORPE, a hamlet in the parish of LOUGH-BOROUGH, western division of the hundred of GOSCOTE, county of LEICESTER, 1½ mile (S.) from Loughborough, containing 77 inhabitants.

WOODBANK, otherwise ROUGH-SHOTWICK, a township in the parish of SHOTWICK, higher division of the hundred of WIRRALL, county palatine of CHESTER, 5½ miles (N. W.) from Chester, containing 39 inhabitants.

WOODBASTWICK, a parish in the hundred of WALSHAM, county of NORFOLK, 5¼ miles (N. W.) from Acle, containing 236 inhabitants. The living is a discharged vicarage, with the rectory of Panxworth annexed, in the archdeaconry and diocese of Norwich, rated in the king's books at £6, and in the patronage of John Cator, Esq. The church is dedicated to St. Fabian and St. Sebastian : the steeple was built about 1518.

WOODBOROUGH, a parish in the southern division of the wapentake of THURGARTON, county of NOTTINGHAM, 7½ miles (N. E. by E.) from Nottingham, containing 717 inhabitants. The living is a perpetual curacy, in the peculiar jurisdiction of the Collegiate Church of Southwell, rated in the king's books at £4, endowed with £200 private benefaction, £400 royal bounty, and £600 parliamentary grant, and in the patronage of the first and second Prebendaries of Oxton in the same collegiate church. The church, dedicated to St. Swithin, has a fine Norman doorway, and the east window exhibits some remains of ancient stained glass. The Doverbeck, a considerable stream turning several mills, runs through the parish. The stocking frame was invented here by William Lew, in 1528 : about one hundred and fifty of them are usually at work in the village. The free school was built and endowed, in 1739, by Mr. Wood, and enlarged by the Rev. Richard Oldanes, the master, in 1763 : the income, about £90 a year, arises from certain land at Blidworth, and other premises at Stapleford, and the school is open to all children of the parish.

WOODBOROUGH, a parish in the hundred of SWANBOROUGH, county of WILTS, 3½ miles (W.) from Pewsey, containing 335 inhabitants. The living is a rectory, in the archdeaconry of Wilts, and diocese of Salisbury, rated in the king's books at £10, and in the patronage of G. W. Heneage, Esq. The church is dedicated to St. Mary Magdalene. There is a place of worship for Wesleyan Methodists. The Kennet and Avon canal passes through the parish.

WOODBRIDGE, a market town and parish in the hundred of LOES, county of SUFFOLK, 7¼ miles (E. N. E.) from Ipswich, and 76¼ (N. E. by E.) from London, containing 4060 inhabitants. This town is of considerable antiquity, for, so early as the time of Edward the Confessor, the prior and convent of Ely had possessions here : the name is thought to be a corruption of Woden-bryge, from the Saxon god Woden. Towards the termination of the twelfth century a priory was founded here, by Ernaldus Rufus and others, and dedicated to the Virgin Mary, the revenue of which, at the dissolution, was valued at £50. 3. 5.: a house built by one of the Seckfords, now in the possession of the Carthew family, still retains the name of the Abbey. In 1666, upwards of three hundred and twenty-seven inhabitants died of the plague, and were buried, according to tradition, at Bearman's Hill in the vicinity. The town is pleasantly situated on the north side of the river Deben, in the direct road from London to Yarmouth, and occupies the slope of a hill surrounded by beautiful walks : it consists of two principal streets, a spacious square called Market Hill, and several narrow streets and lanes, and is paved, lighted, and amply supplied with water : the atmosphere is highly salubrious, and the general appearance of the town is neat and respectable ; from the summit of the hill is a commanding view of the river Deben to its influx into the sea. A small theatre was built in 1813 ; and a concert is held annually. During the war, barracks were erected on the high ground about half a mile north-west of the town, with accommodation for seven hundred and fifty cavalry and four thousand one hundred and sixty-five infantry ; those for the latter were pulled down on the restoration of peace. The trade principally consists in the exportation of corn, flour, and malt ; and in the importation of coal, timber, foreign wine, spirits, porter, grocery, drapery, and ironmongery. The shipping is greatly on the increase, consisting at present of thirty-eight vessels, of an aggregate burden of two thousand six hundred and fifty-nine tons : vessels sail weekly from this port to London, and many others are employed in trading with Newcastle, Hull, and the Continent ; one or two sail direct to Liverpool, from which place they bring back salt ; and there is a small trade to the Baltic for timber. A manufacture of salt, of peculiarly fine quality, was formerly carried on here ; and there was a brisk business in ship-building, but both have declined. The river Deben, near its mouth, forms the haven of Woodbridge, from which it is navigable for vessels of one hundred and twenty tons' burden to the town ; and on its bank are two excellent quays, the common quay, where the general exports and imports are shipped and landed, and the limekiln quay, where there are two docks, in which small ships of war and other vessels were formerly built : at the custom-house, in Quay-lane, the usual officers of collector, comptroller, tide-surveyor, and coast-waiter, are stationed. The market is on Wednesday, for corn, cattle, and provisions; and fairs are held on April 5th and October 23rd. The government of the town is vested, according to the provisions of an act of parliament, called Gilbert's Act, in a visitor and two guardians, chosen by the parishioners not rated under £5 per annum, whose duty it is to determine and superintend the collection and application of the parochial rates; in other respects the churchwardens exercise local authority. The quarter sessions for the liberty of St. Ethelred, and the hundreds of Colneis, Carlford, Loes, Plomesgate, Welford, and Thredling, are held here; and petty sessions take place every Wednesday. The sessions hall, under which is the corn market, in the centre of the market hill, erected in 1587, by Thomas Seckford, Esq., has recently undergone some extensive repairs; it is a handsome and lofty edifice of brick. On an adjacent eminence is the bridewell, rebuilt in 1804.

The living is a perpetual curacy, to which the impropriate rectory has been annexed, in the archdeaconry of Suffolk, and diocese of Norwich, endowed with £200 private benefaction, and £200 royal bounty, and in the patronage of the Rev. T. Carthew. The church, which is dedicated to St. Mary, was built by John, Lord Segrave, in the reign of Edward III., and the tower and north portico in that of Henry VI.: on the north side of the chancel is an elegant private chapel, built in the reign of Elizabeth, by Thomas Seckford, Esq., in which is a tomb without an inscription, over the family vault, probably erected to his memory: the north portico is adorned with sculpture, in relief, representing the conflict of St. Michael and the Dragon. The tower is stately and magnificent, and, like the church, is constructed of dark flint intermixed with freestone, and, towards the upper part, formed into elegant devices; the summit is crowned with battlements, having finials at the angles, which are surmounted by vanes, and decorated in the intervals with badges of the four Evangelists; it is one hundred and eight feet high. There are places of worship for Baptists, the Society of Friends, Independents, and Wesleyan Methodists. The free grammar school, in Well-street, was founded in the year 1662, by Mrs. Dorothy Seckford and others (this lady having also bequeathed the tithes of the parish to the minister), and is endowed with property producing about £37 per annum. The master is elected by the heirs of the founder and the perpetual curate, or, in default of such, by the lord of the priory manor, the perpetual curate, the two churchwardens, and the three principal owners, and three principal occupiers, of land in the parish: his salary is £25 per annum, with land worth about £12 per annum and a rent-free residence, for instructing free scholars, of whom there are about ten, and he has £3 per annum for day scholars, with permission to take boarders. A National school, in Bridewell-street, in which are three hundred and fifty boys and girls, is supported by voluntary contributions, and by grants from the National School Society. A school on the Lancasterian system, in Miller's-lane, affords instruction to about one hundred children of both sexes; and there is a Sunday school, twenty-four of the girls in which are also clothed. Almshouses were erected, in the time of Elizabeth, by Thomas Seckford, Esq., for

the residence of thirteen poor unmarried men, with another house for three poor women, to attend them as nurses, and endowed with an estate in the parish of St. John's, Clerkenwell, London, which, in 1767, produced an income of £568 per annum; but more than £20,000 having been expended on it, such is the improving state of the property, that the rental is expected eventually to produce between £5000 and £6000 per annum. The inmates must be chosen from among the poor inhabitants of Woodbridge, if proper objects can be found, by the minister and churchwardens: the principal of these poor men receives £27 per annum, and each of the other twelve £20, with various extra allowances; the men wear a silver badge, with the arms of the founder. The sum of £10 is given annually to the poor of Clerkenwell, and a like annuity is paid to the minister of this parish, for instructing the almspeople and visiting them when sick; and £5 per annum is given to each of the churchwardens, as paymasters of the establishment: this institution is placed under the government of the Master of the Rolls and the Chief Justice of the Common Pleas, by patent of Queen Elizabeth. There are, besides, different benefactions, amounting to about £150 per annum, for the benefit of the poor. Various relics of antiquity, especially fragments of warlike instruments, have been occasionally found in the vicinity. Christopher Saxton, the publisher of the first county maps, was a native of this place, and servant to Thomas Seckford, Esq., a great benefactor to the town, who resided in a mansion house at Great Bealings, about a mile and a half distant: they were published under his patronage, in 1579, and dedicated to Queen Elizabeth.

WOODBURY, a parish (formerly a market town) in the eastern division of the hundred of BUDLEIGH, county of DEVON, 3 miles (E. by S.) from Topsham, containing 1494 inhabitants. The living is a perpetual curacy, in the peculiar jurisdiction of the Custos and College of Vicars Choral in the Cathedral Church of Exeter, endowed with £800 parliamentary grant, and in the patronage of the Dean and Chapter of Exeter. The church is dedicated to St. Swithin. The navigable river Exe bounds the parish on the west. A charity school is supported by the several endowments of Thomas Weare, in 1691; William Holwell, M.D., in 1707; and Esaias Broadmead, in 1728; amounting in the whole to £50 per annum.

WOODCHESTER, a parish in the hundred of LONGTREE, county of GLOUCESTER, 2½ miles (S. W.) from Stroud, containing 929 inhabitants. The living is a rectory, in the archdeaconry and diocese of Gloucester, rated in the king's books at £10, endowed with £600 royal bounty, and in the patronage of Lord Ducie. The church, dedicated to St. Mary, contains a fine monument to the memory of Sir Robert Huntley. There is a place of worship for Baptists. The village occupies an elevated site, forming part of a range of hills bounding a beautiful and fruitful valley, and has an extensive manufacture of woollen cloth, in which there are eight mills constantly engaged in the neighbourhood. Woodchester, as its name implies, was a Roman station, apparently of considerable importance. Among the numerous interesting relics that have been discovered is a noble tesselated pavement, superior to any thing of the kind yet found in the kingdom, the design of which seemed to be a circular area, in diameter twenty-five feet, enclosed within a frame, or square, of forty-eight feet and ten inches, divided into twenty-four compartments, and enriched with a variety of architectural ornaments, figures of beasts, &c. Ruins of buildings, fragments of statues, glass and pottery, pieces of stags' horns, &c., and many other relics, with numerous coins of the Lower Empire, one of Adrian, and another of Lucilla, have been also found on the spot, and have led to the conclusion that the Roman proprætor, or perhaps the Emperor Adrian himself, made this his residence. In 1795, Samuel Lysons, Esq., F.A.S., having traced the form and extent of the pavement, and procured an engraving to be made of the ground plan of the building to which it belonged, exhibited the plate to the Society of Antiquaries in London; and, in 1797, he published an elaborate account of this and the other relics discovered here. Robert Bridges, in 1722, bequeathed £500, now producing an annual income of £50, for teaching, clothing, and apprenticing poor boys; but St. Loe's school, founded by Nathaniel Cambridge, at Minchinhampton, being open to boys of Woodchester, this charity is only appropriated to clothing and apprenticing them, with premiums of £15 each.

WOODCHURCH, a parish in the lower division of the hundred of WIRRALL, county palatine of CHESTER, comprising the townships of Arrow, Barnston, Irby, Landican, Noctorum, Oxton, Pensby, Prenton, Thingwell, and Woodchurch, and containing 835 inhabitants, of which number, 74 are in the township of Woodchurch, 6¾ miles (N. by W.) from Great Neston. The living is a rectory, in the archdeaconry and diocese of Chester, rated in the king's books at £25. 9. 2., and in the patronage of Mrs. King. The church, dedicated to the Holy Cross, is principally in the Norman style, with a curious ancient font. William Gleave, Esq., alderman of London, in 1665, founded a free school here, and endowed it with lands now producing £80 per annum.

WOODCHURCH, a parish in the hundred of BLACKBOURNE, lathe of SCRAY, county of KENT, 4 miles (E. by N.) from Tenterden, containing 1095 inhabitants. The living is a rectory, in the peculiar jurisdiction and patronage of the Archbishop of Canterbury, rated in the king's books at £26. 13. 4. The church, dedicated to All Saints, is partly in the early, and partly in the later, style of English architecture, with a tower surmounted by a spire; it contains numerous ancient monuments. There is a place of worship for Wesleyan Methodists. A charity school is supported by subscription among the inhabitants.

WOODCOT, a township in the parish of WRENBURY, hundred of NANTWICH, county palatine of CHESTER, 3¾ miles (S. W. by W.) from Nantwich, containing 29 inhabitants.

WOODCOTE, a liberty in the parish of SOUTH STOKE, hundred of DORCHESTER, county of OXFORD, 5½ miles (S. S. E.) from Wallingford. The population is returned with the parish. The chapel is dedicated to St. Leonard.

WOODCOTE, a chapelry in that part of the parish of SHERIFF-HALES which is in the Newport division of the hundred of BRADFORD (South), county of SALOP, 3 miles (S. E. by S.) from Newport, containing 188 inhabitants.

WOODCOTS, a tything in the parish of HANDLEY, in that part of the hundred of SIXPENNY-HANDLEY which is in the Shaston (East) division of the county of DORSET. The population is returned with the parish.

WOODCUTT, a parish in the hundred of PASTROW, Kingsclere division of the county of SOUTHAMPTON, 5 miles (N. N. W.) from Whitchurch, containing 92 inhabitants. The living is a donative. Woodcutt is within the jurisdiction of the Cheyney Court held at Winchester every Thursday, for the recovery of debts to any amount.

WOODEN, a township in that part of the parish of LESBURY which is in the eastern division of COQUETDALE ward, county of NORTHUMBERLAND, 4½ miles (S. E. by E.) from Alnwick. The population is returned with the parish.

WOODEND, a hamlet in the parish of BLAKESLEY, hundred of GREENS-NORTON, county of NORTHAMPTON, 5¼ miles (W. by N.) from Towcester, containing 289 inhabitants.

WOODFORD, a township in the parish of PRESTBURY, hundred of MACCLESFIELD, county palatine of CHESTER, 6 miles (S. by W.) from Stockport, containing 383 inhabitants. Courts leet and baron are held twice a year.

WOODFORD, a parish in the hundred of CHIPPING-WARDEN, county of NORTHAMPTON, 7½ miles (S. S. W.) from Daventry, containing 766 inhabitants. The living is a discharged vicarage, in the archdeaconry of Northampton, and diocese of Peterborough, rated in the king's books at £6. 10., endowed with £200 private benefaction, and £200 royal bounty, and in the patronage of the Crown. The church, dedicated to All Saints, has lately received an addition of eighty sittings, of which forty-seven are free, the Incorporated Society for the enlargement of churches and chapels having granted £30 towards defraying the expense. There is a place of worship for Baptists. At Hinton, in this parish, is a mineral spring.

WOODFORD, a parish in the hundred of HUXLOE, county of NORTHAMPTON, 2½ miles (S. W. by W.) from Thrapstone, containing 572 inhabitants. The living is a rectory in united medieties, in the archdeaconry of Northampton, and diocese of Peterborough, rated jointly in the king's books at £22. 9. 7., and in the patronage of Henry Batley, Esq. The church is dedicated to St. Mary. In the neighbourhood are three tumuli, near which have been found Roman tiles, fragments of a tesselated pavement, an urn, and two small coins of the Lower Empire, inscribed *Constantinopolis.*

WOODFORD, a parish in the hundred of UNDERDITCH, county of WILTS, 4¼ miles (N. N. W.) from Salisbury, containing 363 inhabitants. The living is a vicarage, with that of Wilsford united, rated in the king's books at £13. 10., and in the peculiar jurisdiction and patronage of the Prebendary of Wilsford and Woodford in the Cathedral Church of Salisbury. The church is dedicated to All Saints. The parish is bounded on the east by the river Avon, and here was formerly a palace of the Bishops of Salisbury, but no traces of it are now visible. Charles II., after the battle of Worcester, was concealed in this neighbourhood.

WOODFORD (ST. MARY), a parish in the hundred of BECONTREE, county of ESSEX, 8 miles (N. E. by N.) from London, containing 2699 inhabitants.

Woodford, so called from the ford in the wood, or forest, where is now Woodford-bridge, is a beautiful village, situated on the confines of Epping Forest, on the main road from London to Newmarket, which passes through it: the houses are in general detached, and irregularly arranged on the undulating declivities of a rising ground, beautifully interspersed with trees, and disclosing at intervals mansions of a superior character, which are principally occupied by wealthy merchants of the metropolis. In different parts of the parish some fine and extensive views into the counties of Essex and Kent present themselves. A nearer communication with the metropolis has been recently opened, by the construction of a new road from the highest part of the village, near the Castle Inn, which passes through the forest into the Lea Bridge road. The custom of Borough English, by which the younger son inherits, prevails in this manor.

The living is a rectory, in the peculiar jurisdiction of the Commissary of London, concurrently with the Consistorial Court of the Bishop of London, rated in the king's books at £11. 12. 1., and in the patronage of the Hon. W. T. L. P. Wellesley. The church, which is dedicated to St. Mary, was erected on the site of the former, in 1817, at an expense of nearly £9000, defrayed partly by subscription, and partly by rate: it is situated in the lowest part of the village, on the west side of the London road, and is an elegant edifice in the ancient style of English architecture, with a square embattled tower; the aisles are separated from the nave by six pointed arches carried up to the roof, which is of open wood work, supported on eight pillars, and surmounted in the centre by an octangular lantern tower; the east window is of stained glass, and divided into three compartments, containing figures of our Saviour, the four Evangelists, St. Peter, and St. Paul; there are some good monuments. In the churchyard is a splendid Corinthian column of marble, about forty feet in height, erected to the memory of the family of Godfrey, which flourished many years in Kent; also a tomb with a column entirely covered with ivy, of picturesque appearance, and a remarkably fine old yew tree. There are places of worship for Independents and Wesleyan Methodists. A National school, in which about one hundred and thirty children of both sexes are educated, of whom fifty are clothed, is supported by voluntary contributions. This parish is entitled to send two boys for gratuitous instruction to each of the schools founded at Chigwell, in 1629, by Dr. Samuel Harsnett, Archbishop of York; it has also the perpetual right of presenting two boys to Christ's Hospital, London, granted by Thomas Foulkes, in 1686. In 1828, a parochial library was established in the village. At Woodford Wells is a mineral spring, formerly in high estimation, but now little resorted to.

WOODFORD-GRANGE, an extra-parochial liberty, in the southern division of the hundred of SEISDON, county of STAFFORD, containing 14 inhabitants.

WOODGARSTON, a tything in that part of the parish of MONK's SHERBORNE which is in the hundred of CHUTELY, Kingsclere division of the county of SOUTHAMPTON, 4½ miles (N. W. by W.) from Basingstoke. The population is returned with the parish.

WOODGREEN, an extra-parochial liberty, in the northern division of the hundred of NEW FOREST,

New Forest (East) division of the county of SOUTHAMPTON, 3 miles (N. E. by E.) from Fordingbridge, containing 357 inhabitants.

WOODHALL, a parish in the southern division of the wapentake of GARTREE, parts of LINDSEY, county of LINCOLN, 2¾ miles (W. S. W.) from Horncastle, containing 191 inhabitants. The living is a discharged vicarage, in the peculiar jurisdiction of the manorial court of Kirkstead, rated in the king's books at £13, endowed with £300 private benefaction, and £400 royal bounty, and in the patronage of the Bishop of Lincoln. The church is dedicated to St. Margaret.

WOODHALL, a joint township with Brackenholme, in the parish of HEMINGBROUGH, wapentake of OUZE and DERWENT, East riding of the county of YORK, 5¼ miles (N. W. by W.) from Howden. The population is returned with Brackenholme.

WOODHALL, a township in the parish of HARTHILL, southern division of the wapentake of STRAFFORTH and TICKHILL, West riding of the county of YORK, 9½ miles (S. S. E.) from Rotherham. The population is returned with the parish.

WOODHAM, a hamlet in the parish of WADDESDON, hundred of ASHENDON, county of BUCKINGHAM, 8½ miles (W. N. W.) from Aylesbury, containing 28 inhabitants.

WOODHAM, a township in the parish of AYCLIFFE, south-eastern division of DARLINGTON ward, county palatine of DURHAM, 7 miles (E. S. E.) from Bishop-Auckland, containing 183 inhabitants.

WOODHAM-FERRIS, a parish in the hundred of CHELMSFORD, county of ESSEX, 4½ miles (S. S. E.) from Danbury, containing 865 inhabitants. The living is a rectory, in the archdeaconry of Essex, and diocese of London, rated in the king's books at £28. 13. 4., and in the patronage of Sir B. W. Bridges, Bart. The church, dedicated to St. Mary, contains an elegant monument to the memory of Cecilia, wife of Edwin Sandys, Archbishop of York. The parish is bounded on the south by Crouch river, over which there is a ferry. At Bikinacre, in this parish, there was anciently a hermitage, which was superseded by a priory of Black canons, founded and endowed by Maurice Fitz-Jeffrey, in consideration of certain sums of money due from him to Henry II.; it was dedicated to St. John the Baptist, and, being almost deserted in the time of Henry VII., was then annexed to St. Mary's Spittal, London.

WOODHAM-MORTIMER, a parish in the hundred of DENGIE, county of ESSEX, 2½ miles (S. W. by W.) from Maldon, containing 340 inhabitants. The living is a rectory, in the archdeaconry of Essex, and diocese of London, rated in the king's books at £6. 13. 4. A. Bullen, Esq. was patron in 1814. The church is dedicated to St. Margaret. In the marshes near Crouch river are several barrows.

WOODHAM-WALTER, a parish in the hundred of DENGIE, county of ESSEX, 2½ miles (E. N. E.) from Danbury, containing 454 inhabitants. The living is a rectory, in the archdeaconry of Essex, and diocese of London, rated in the king's books at £12. 13. 1½. The Rev. L. Way was patron in 1819. The church is dedicated to St. Michael. The Chelmer and Blackwater navigation bounds the parish on the north.

WOODHAY (EAST), a parish in the hundred of EVINGAR, Kingsclere division of the county of SOUTH-

AMPTON, 10½ miles (N. N. W.) from Whitchurch, containing 1206 inhabitants. The living is a rectory, in the peculiar jurisdiction of the Incumbent, rated in the king's books at £21. 6. 0½., and in the patronage of the Bishop of Winchester. The church, dedicated to St. Martin, was rebuilt at the expense of the parishioners, in 1823, and contains monuments to Bishops Kenn and Louth, who held the living. Ten children are taught to read for £8 a year, the interest of a bequest from the Rev. Joshua Wakefield, in 1753. A National school for about one hundred children is supported by voluntary contributions. Here was formerly a palace belonging to the Bishops of Winchester. Woodhay is within the jurisdiction of the Cheyney Court held at Winchester every Thursday, for the recovery of debts to any amount.

WOODHAY (WEST), a parish (formerly a market town) in the hundred of KINTBURY-EAGLE, county of BERKS, 6 miles (S.W. by W.) from Newbury, containing 144 inhabitants. The living is a rectory, in the archdeaconry of Wilts, and diocese of Salisbury, rated in the king's books at £4. 4. 3., and in the patronage of R. Sloper, Esq. The church is dedicated to St. Lawrence. The market, which was on Tuesday, was granted to one of the Barons St. Amand, in 1318, but it has been disused from time immemorial.

WOODHEAD, a chapelry in the parish of MOTTRAM in LONGDEN-DALE, hundred of MACCLESFIELD, county palatine of CHESTER, 13¼ miles (E. N. E.) from Stockport. The population is returned with the parish. The living is a perpetual curacy, in the archdeaconry and diocese of Chester, endowed with £200 private benefaction, and £800 royal bounty, and in the patronage of the Bishop of Chester. The chapel is a neat structure. There is a place of worship for Calvinistic Methodists.

WOODHORN, a parish in the eastern division of MORPETH ward, county of NORTHUMBERLAND, comprising the chapelry of Newbiggin, and the townships of Cresswell, Ellington, Hirst, Linmouth, North Seaton, and Woodhorn, and the demesne of Woodhorn, and containing 1378 inhabitants, of which number, 155 are in the township of Woodhorn, 8 miles (E. N. E.) from Morpeth. The living is a vicarage, in the archdeaconry of Northumberland, and diocese of Durham, rated in the king's books at £21. 15. 7½., and in the patronage of the Bishop of Durham. The church, dedicated to St. Mary, is an ancient edifice, with the exception of the chancel, which has been added by the Master and Wardens of the Mercers' Company of London. Mr. Foster, in 1800, left £1200 for founding a free school here, but the bequest has not yet been so applied. The Rev. Thomas Triplett, in 1640, bequeathed a rent-charge of £5 for clothing and apprenticing poor children.

WOODHOUSE, a chapelry in the parish of BARROW upon SOAR, western division of the hundred of GOSCOTE, county of LEICESTER, 3½ miles (W.) from Mountsorrel, containing 1067 inhabitants. The living is a perpetual curacy, in the archdeaconry of Leicester, and diocese of Lincoln, endowed with £600 royal bounty, and £1200 parliamentary grant, and in the patronage of the Vicar of Barrow. The chapel is dedicated to St. Mary. There is a place of worship for Wesleyan Methodists. Thomas Rawlins, in 1691, left a

rent-charge of £89. 17. for teaching twenty-two children and supplying them with books, also for apprenticing one, the residue to be applied to the use of the poor.

WOODHOUSE, a township in the parish of SHILBOTTLE, eastern division of COQUETDALE ward, county of NORTHUMBERLAND, 5¼ miles (S. E. by S.) from Alnwick, containing 25 inhabitants.

WOODHOUSE, a joint township with Burntwood and Edgehill, in that part of the parish of ST. MICHAEL, LICHFIELD, which is in the southern division of the hundred of OFFLOW, county of STAFFORD, 2¾ miles (W. by S.) from Lichfield. The population is returned with Burntwood.

WOODHOUSE-HALL, an extra-parochial liberty, in the Hatfield division of the wapentake of BASSETLAW, county of NOTTINGHAM, 6½ miles (S. W. by S.) from Worksop, containing 5 inhabitants.

WOODHOUSES, a township in the parish of MAYFIELD, southern division of the hundred of TOTMONSLOW, county of STAFFORD, 4 miles (N. W. by W.) from Ashbourn, containing 26 inhabitants. It is in the honour of Tutbury, duchy of Lancaster, and within the jurisdiction of a court of pleas held at Tutbury every third Tuesday, for the recovery of debts under 40s.

WOODHURST, a parish in the hundred of HURSTINGSTONE, county of HUNTINGDON, 4 miles (N.) from St. Ives, containing 335 inhabitants. The living is a perpetual curacy with that of Old Hurst, annexed to the vicarage of St. Ives, in the archdeaconry of Huntingdon, and diocese of Lincoln. The church is dedicated to All Saints.

WOODLAND, a chapelry in the parish of IPPLEPEN, hundred of HAYTOR, county of DEVON, 2 miles (E. by S.) from Ashburton, containing 233 inhabitants. The living is a perpetual curacy with Ipplepen, in the archdeaconry of Totness, and diocese of Exeter, endowed with £600 royal bounty, and £200 parliamentary grant. William Culling, in 1722, gave an annuity of £2 for the education of children.

WOODLAND, a township in the parish of STAINDROP, south-western division of DARLINGTON ward, county palatine of DURHAM, 7¼ miles (N. by E.) from Barnard-Castle, containing 155 inhabitants. There is a place of worship for Wesleyan Methodists. Coal is obtained in the neighbourhood.

WOODLAND, a chapelry in the parish of KIRKBYIRELETH, hundred of LONSDALE, north of the sands, county palatine of LANCASTER, 8¼ miles (N. N. W.) from Ulverstone, containing, with the township of Heathwaite, 267 inhabitants. The living is a perpetual curacy, in the archdeaconry of Richmond, and diocese of Chester, endowed with £200 private benefaction, and £600 royal bounty, and in the patronage of the Vicar of Kirkby-Ireleth.

WOODLAND-EYAM, a township in the parish of EYAM, hundred of HIGH PEAK, county of DERBY, containing 197 inhabitants.

WOODLAND-HOPE, a hamlet in the parish of HOPE, hundred of HIGH PEAK, county of DERBY, containing 225 inhabitants.

WOODLANDS, a tything in the parish of HORTON, hundred of KNOWLTON, Shaston (East) division of the county of DORSET, 4½ miles (S. S. W.) from Cranborne, containing 395 inhabitants. There is a place of worship for Wesleyan Methodists. A fair, which was transferred hither from Knowlton, is held on July 5th. The unfortunate Duke of Monmouth, after his flight from the battle of Sedgmore in Somersetshire, is stated to have been found here by his enemies, in a ditch under an ash tree, which is inscribed with the various names of those who have since visited the spot.

WOODLANDS, a joint tything with Chaddenwicke, in the parish and hundred of MERE, county of WILTS, containing 663 inhabitants.

WOODLEIGH, a parish in the hundred of STANBOROUGH, county of DEVON, 3 miles (N.) from Kingsbridge, containing 298 inhabitants. The living is a rectory, in the archdeaconry of Totness, and diocese of Exeter, rated in the king's books at £22. 8. 4., and in the patronage of the Rev. R. Edmonds. The church, dedicated to St. Mary, contains an altar-tomb, representing the Resurrection of our Saviour.

WOODLESFORD, a township in the parish of ROTHWELL, lower division of the wapentake of AGBRIGG, West riding of the county of YORK, 6 miles (N. N. E.) from Wakefield, containing 590 inhabitants. Here are manufactures of paper and earthenware.

WOODLEY, a joint township with Sandford, in that part of the parish of SONNING which is in the hundred of SONNING, county of BERKS, 3½ miles (E. by N.) from Reading. The population is returned with Sandford. A school for the education of poor children is supported by small annual subscriptions.

WOODMANCOTE, a tything in the parish of NORTH CERNEY, hundred of RAPSGATE, county of GLOUCESTER, 5 miles (N. by W.) from Cirencester. The population is returned with the parish.

WOODMANCOTE, a parish in the hundred of TIPNOAK, rape of BRAMBER, county of SUSSEX, 5 miles (N. E. by E.) from Steyning, containing 294 inhabitants. The living is a rectory, in the archdeaconry of Lewes, and diocese of Chichester, rated in the king's books at £13. 1. 10½., and in the patronage of the Crown. The church is principally in the early style of English architecture.

WOODMANCOTT, a hamlet in the parish of BISHOP'S CLEEVE, hundred of CLEEVE, or BISHOP'S CLEEVE, county of GLOUCESTER, 3½ miles (W. by S.) from Winchcomb, containing 255 inhabitants.

WOODMANCOTT, a parish in the hundred of MAINSBOROUGH, Fawley division of the county of SOUTHAMPTON, 8 miles (S. W.) from Basingstoke, containing 75 inhabitants. The living is a perpetual curacy, annexed to the rectory of Brown Candover, in the archdeaconry and diocese of Winchester. The church is dedicated to St. James: the parishioners inter at Brown Candover.

WOODMANSEY, a joint township with Beverley Park, in that part of the parish of ST. JOHN, BEVERLEY, which is within the liberties of the borough of BEVERLEY, East riding of the county of YORK, 2¼ miles (S. E. by E.) from Beverley, containing, with Beverley Park, 276 inhabitants.

WOODMANSTERNE, a parish in the first division of the hundred of WALLINGTON, county of SURREY, 4½ miles (S. E. by E.) from Ewell, containing 171 inhabitants. The living is a rectory, in the archdeaconry of Surrey, and diocese of Winchester, rated in the king's books at £11. 7. 6., and in the patronage of the Crown.

The church, dedicated to St. Peter, is a small neat edifice. In the grounds of The Oaks, formerly an inn, but converted into a hunting seat by the late General Burgoyne, and now the property of the Earl of Derby, is an old beech tree, remarkable for its boughs having grown fast to one another. Shortes House, in this parish, is a very ancient building with curiously carved wainscoting.

WOODNESBOROUGH, a parish in the hundred of EASTRY, lathe of ST. AUGUSTINE, county of KENT, 1¾ mile (W. S. W.) from Sandwich, containing 689 inhabitants. The living is a vicarage, in the archdeaconry and diocese of Canterbury, rated in the king's books at £10. 0. 7½., and in the patronage of the Dean and Chapter of Rochester. The church, dedicated to St. Mary, is principally in the decorated style of English architecture. On Woodnesborough hill is a lofty artificial mount, supposed by some to have been either the place where the Saxon idol Woden was worshipped, or the burial-place of Vortimer; whilst others state it to be the Woodnesbeorth of the Saxon Chronicle, and the scene of the battle between Celred and Ina, kings of Mercia and the West Saxons, in 715. A fine gold coin, bearing on one side the figure of an armed warrior, and on the other that of Victory, was found here in 1514.

WOODSFIELD, a hamlet in the parish of POWICK, lower division of the hundred of PERSHORE, county of WORCESTER, 5½ miles (S. S. W.) from Worcester, containing 56 inhabitants. Here are the remains of a chapel, formerly dependent upon the church of Great Malvern.

WOODSFORD, a parish in the hundred of WINFRITH, Blandford (South) division of the county of DORSET, 5½ miles (E.) from Dorchester, containing 159 inhabitants. The living is a rectory, in the archdeaconry of Dorset, and diocese of Bristol, rated in the king's books at £4. 9. 9½. Mrs. Sturt was patroness in 1802. The church is a small ancient structure with a low tower. The parish is bounded on the north by the river Frome, upon which are the remains of an ancient castle, built by Guido de Brient, of a quadrangular form, one side of which has been converted into a farm-house, a very lofty building : the principal entrance was on the west, where there is still an ancient staircase, and in the south-east corner is another, both pierced with narrow apertures for arrows, or small arms. The offices on the basement story are all vaulted with stone ; above is an apartment called the Queen's room, and vestiges of a chapel, and around the whole are traces of a moat.

WOODSIDE, a township in the parish of WESTWARD, ALLERDALE ward below Darwent, county of CUMBERLAND, 2 miles (N. W. by N.) from Temple-Sowerby, containing 364 inhabitants. The rivers Eden and Eamont unite their streams here.

WOODSIDE, a township in the parish of SHIFFNALL, Shiffnall division of the hundred of BRIMSTREE, county of SALOP, 3 miles (S. S. E.) from Shiffnall, containing 509 inhabitants.

WOODSIDE-QUARTER, a township in the parish of WIGTON, ward and county of CUMBERLAND, 3 miles (E. by N.) from Wigton, containing 587 inhabitants.

WOODSIDE-WARD, a township in the parish of ELSDON, southern division of COQUETDALE ward, county of NORTHUMBERLAND, 1½ mile (N.) from Elsdon, containing 164 inhabitants.

WOODSTOCK (NEW), a borough, market town, and parish, having separate jurisdiction, though locally within the liberty of the city of Oxford, county of OXFORD, 8 miles (N.N.W.) from Oxford, and 62 (W.N. W.) from London, containing 1455 inhabitants. This place is of Saxon origin, and was called by that people *Vudestoc*, signifying a

Seal and Arms.

woody place. It appears to have been chosen, at an early period, as an abode of royalty, and the manor-house, as it was called, is supposed to have been built upon the site of a Roman villa. Alfred the Great resided here whilst translating Boëtius; Ethelred held a council, or parliament, here, and made several of the statutes enumerated by Lambard, in his collection of Anglo-Saxon laws: it subsequently became a favourite residence of Henry I., who in a great measure rebuilt the place, surrounded the park with a wall, and stocked it with wild animals. In the reign of Henry II., Woodstock is celebrated as the residence of the fair Rosamond, whose romantic adventures are so interwoven with the history of that monarch : Henry here received Rice, Prince of Wales, when he, in 1163, came to do homage. Edmund of Woodstock, the second son of Edward I., was born here in 1330; as were also Edward the Black Prince, and Thomas of Woodstock, sons of Edward III. It was for some time the place of confinement of Queen Elizabeth, during the reign of her sister Mary : on her accession to the throne, it was occasionally selected as her residence, the town was distinguished by her favours. The manor and honour continued in the crown until the reign of Queen Anne, when it was granted to the celebrated Duke of Marlborough, for whom a splendid mansion was erected, at the expense of the nation, called Blenheim, after the scene of one of his victories, as a recompense for his great military and diplomatic services. The town is very pleasantly situated on an eminence, at the eastern bank of the Glyme, an expansion of which forms the lake in Blenheim park, and afterwards joining the Evenlod in the vicinity, both fall into the Isis : the streets are clean and spacious; and the houses, which are mostly built of stone, are generally large and handsome. The manufacture of gloves is the principal branch of trade, and, although fluctuating, is carried on to a considerable extent, furnishing employment to about one hundred men and fifteen hundred women and girls in the town and neighbourhood, upwards of five hundred dozen pair being made weekly. The manufacture of various articles of fine steel has very much decayed since the rise of Birmingham and Sheffield : those made here formerly brought very high prices, from the beauty of the workmanship and the brightness of the polish, and are remarkable from having been generally made of old nails of horse-shoes, formed into bars. Queen Elizabeth, among other privileges, granted a wool staple, of which there are now no remains, and a market to be held on Friday, but the principal market day is Tuesday. There are fairs on Tuesday after February 2nd, April 5th, Tuesday at Whitsuntide, August 2nd, October 2nd (a great mart for cheese), Tuesday after November 1st, and December 17th.

Woodstock, which had long been a borough by prescription, was incorporated in 1453, by Henry VI., whose charter was confirmed and enlarged by succeeding monarchs, the last of whom, Charles II., granted that under which the corporation now acts; a restrictive charter was forced on it by James II., but soon after set aside by proclamation. The members of the corporation are in number twenty-five, viz., five aldermen, from among whom a mayor is annually chosen, a high steward, a recorder, assisted by seventeen common council-men, and a town clerk; two of the common council-men act as chamberlains ¦in rotation. The freedom is acquired by birth, servitude, or gift of the corporation, who, as lords of the manor, hold a court leet annually; and a court for the recovery of debts under £15 within the borough is held every month, but only *pro formâ* for many years past. The town hall is a handsome stone building, erected about the year 1766, by the Duke of Marlborough, after a design by Sir William Chambers. This borough has always been privileged to send two members to parliament, though the right has only been exercised without interruption since the 13th of Elizabeth : the electors are the mayor, aldermen, and freemen; the number of voters is about one hundred and fifty, of whom nearly one half are non-resident : the mayor is the returning officer.

Woodstock, though for all civil purposes a parish, and by far the most populous, is only a chapelry to the rectory of Bladon : a parsonage-house was erected here by Bishop Fell, in which the rector may optionally reside. The chapel, dedicated to St. Mary, was principally rebuilt, in 1785, on the site of a chantry founded by King John : in the original part of the building, which forms the south side of the chapel, is a round-headed doorway of early Norman architecture, composed of red stone, ornamented with chevron work; it consists of withinside of three massy columns supporting pointed arches, their capitals having various grotesque sculptures of the human countenance : the more modern part of the structure has been erected in a style no way corresponding with this ancient part, but it has a tower of good proportions. Particular Baptists and Wesleyan Methodists have each a place of worship. The free grammar school was founded and endowed, in 1585, by Richard Cornwall, a native of the town; the master is appointed by the corporation, who pay him £30 per annum; and he receives fifteen shillings a quarter from each child of a freeman, for instruction in reading, writing, and accounts, the classics being taught free. Eight boys and eight girls, double the original number, are instructed and clothed, under the benefaction of the Rev. Sir Robert Cocks, Bart., formerly rector of Bladon with Woodstock, now producing upwards of £60 per annum; the remainder of the endowment, which fluctuates with the rent of land, being given as apprentice fees with the boys when leaving the school. Almshouses for six poor widows, standing near the southern entrance of the town, were built in 1793, by the late Duchess of Marlborough. There are various bequests for the benefit of the poor, which are distributed amongst them in money, clothing, &c.

In the Rolls of the reign of Henry III., mention is made of an almshouse, built near the king's manor, which Tanner thinks may be the same with the hospital of St. Mary the Virgin and St. Mary Magdalene, for which a protection was granted to beg, by patent of the 1st of Edward III. Roman coins, especially of Constantine, are occasionally dug up within the limits of the borough; and the Akeman-street-way, an ancient Roman road, passes through the northern part of Blenheim park. Chaucer, the father of English poets, resided, and is said by some to have been born, here. Woodstock gives the title of viscount to the Duke of Portland.

WOODSTONE, a parish in the hundred of Norman-Cross, county of Huntingdon, ¾ of a mile (S. W. by W.) from Peterborough, containing 149 inhabitants. The living is a rectory, in the archdeaconry of Huntingdon, and diocese of Lincoln, rated in the king's books at £7. 11. 3., and in the patronage of John Bevis, Esq. The church is dedicated to St. Augustine. John and Mary Walsham, in 1728, gave certain land for the establishment of a school and other charitable purposes.

WOODTHORPE, a township in the parish of North Wingfield, hundred of Scarsdale, county of Derby, 6 miles (E. N. E.) from Chesterfield, containing 211 inhabitants.

WOODTON, a parish in the hundred of Loddon, county of Norfolk, 5 miles (N. W.) from Bungay, containing 505 inhabitants. The living is a rectory, in the archdeaconry of Norfolk, and diocese of Norwich, rated in the king's books at £6. 13. 4., and in the patronage of —Suckling, Esq. The church is dedicated to All Saints.

WOODWALTON, county of Huntingdon. — See WALTON (WOOD).

WOODYATES (WEST), an extra-parochial liberty, in the hundred of Wimborne St. Giles, Shaston (East) division of the county of Dorset, 5½ miles (N. N.W.) from Cranborne, containing 9 inhabitants. On the neighbouring downs are numerous barrows, and a vast rampart and fosse, termed Grimesditch, crossed by the Roman road from Dorchester to Old Sarum.

WOOKEY, a parish in the hundred of Wells-Forum, county of Somerset, 1¾ mile (W.) from Wells, containing 1040 inhabitants. The living is a discharged vicarage, in the peculiar jurisdiction and patronage of the Subdean of Wells, rated in the king's books at £12.15. 10., and endowed with £400 private benefaction, and £400 royal bounty. The church is dedicated to St. Matthew. In the side of the Mendip hills, about a mile and a half from the village, is a curious cavern, termed Wookey Hole, the approach to which is surrounded by scenery extremely wild and picturesque: the entrance is very narrow, but within are several spacious apartments, one of them resembling the interior of a church, the roof and sides of which are encrusted with concretions of most fantastical form, while on the floor are other large petrifactions, formed by the water dropping from above. Beyond it is a smaller cavity, and this leads to a third, the diameter of which is about one hundred and twenty feet its roof cylindrical, and its bottom composed of a fine sand, on one side of which runs a very cold and pure stream of water, the primary source of the river Ax.

WOOL, a parish in the liberty of Bindon, Blandford (South) division of the county of Dorset, 6 miles (W. by S.) from Wareham, containing 453 inhabitants. The living is a perpetual curacy, annexed to the vicarage of Coombe-Keynes, in the archdeaconry of Dorset, and diocese of Bristol. The church, dedicated to the Holy Rood, stands on the south side of the river Frome. Near it are the remains of Bindon abbey, founded, in 1172, by Robert de Newburgh and Matilda his wife, in honour of the Virgin Mary, for monks of the Cistercian order, whose revenue at the dissolution was £229. 2. 1. A fair for cattle is held on May 3rd.

WOOLASCOTT, a township in that part of the parish of St. Mary, Shrewsbury, which is in the hundred of Pimhill, county of Salop, containing 29 inhabitants.

WOOLAVINGTON, a parish in the hundred of Whitley, county of Somerset, 4 miles (N. E.) from Bridg-water, containing 381 inhabitants. The living is a vicarage, with that of Puriton annexed, in the archdeaconry of Wells, and diocese of Bath and Wells, rated in the king's books at £11. 7. 11., and in the patronage of the Dean and Canons of Windsor. The church, dedicated to St. Mary, has a small sepulchral chapel attached. A fair for cattle and sheep is held on October 18th.

WOOLAVINGTON (EAST and WEST), a parish in the hundred of Rotherbridge, rape of Arundel, county of Sussex, 4½ miles (S. W. by S.) from Petworth, containing 272 inhabitants. The living is a rectory, in the archdeaconry and diocese of Chichester, rated in the king's books at £9. J. Sargent, Esq. was patron in 1813.

WOOLBEDING, a parish in the hundred of Easebourne, rape of Chichester, county of Sussex, 1¼ mile (N. W.) from Midhurst, containing 261 inhabitants. The living is a rectory, in the archdeaconry and diocese of Chichester, rated in the king's books at £7. 0.10., and in the patronage of Lord Robert Spencer. The river Rother runs through the parish.

WOOLBOROUGH, or WOLBOROUGH, a parish in the hundred of Haytor, county of Devon, 1 mile (S.) from Newton-Abbots, containing, with the town of Newton-Abbots, 1859 inhabitants. The living is a donative, in the patronage of Viscount Courtenay. The church, dedicated to St. James, has some fine screenwork across the nave and aisles. Ninety children are educated for about £90 a year, arising from certain property, bequeathed in 1788, by Hannah Maria Bearne, for charitable uses. There are almshouses for four clergymen's widows, founded by Lady Lucy Reynell.

WOOLDALE, a township in the parish of Kirk-Burton, upper division of the wapentake of Agbrigg, West riding of the county of York, 6¼ miles (S.) from Huddersfield, containing 3445 inhabitants. Here are fulling and scribbling mills, and an extensive manufacture of woollen cloth. A school was built by means of a legacy, aided by subscriptions, about fifty years ago, on part of the waste given by the Duke of Leeds, and a house for the master was erected, also by subscription, in 1821 : about forty children are instructed, who pay small quarterages.

WOOLER, a market town and parish in the eastern division of Glendale ward, county of Northumberland, 46 miles (N. N. W.) from Newcastle upon Tyne, and 318 (N. N. W.) from London, containing

1830 inhabitants. This place occupies the eastern declivity of the Cheviot hills, and near it is the village of Humbledon, celebrated for the memorable victory gained by Percy, Earl of Northumberland, in the reign of Henry IV., over a Scottish army of ten thousand men, under the command of Earl Douglas: the engagement took place on a plain within a mile north-west of the town, where a stone pillar has been erected, commemorative of the event. A great part of the town was destroyed by fire in 1722, since which period it has not made any considerable advances towards improvement. It consists of several streets diverging from the market-place, which is in the centre, and is indifferently paved, and supplied with water from a fountain erected at the public expense: a good trout stream flows through the lower part of it, and falls into the river Till: the houses are mostly old, and the general appearance of the place is unfavourable. The situation, though mountainous, is extremely salubrious, the town having formerly been much resorted to by invalids, who have ceased to frequent it, probably, from a want of accommodation. A public subscription library is well supported; and a mechanics' institute was established in 1827. The market is on Thursday; and fairs are held on the 4th of May and the 27th of October, for horses, cattle, and sheep; and on the Tuesday in Whitsun-week a general fair is held on a hill at a short distance from the town, which, from that circumstance, is called Whitsun Bank fair. The lord of the manor holds a court leet and baron annually, within three weeks after Easter, at which constables and other officers for the ensuing year are appointed.

The living is a vicarage, in the archdeaconry of Northumberland, and diocese of Durham, rated in the king's books at £5. 8. 1½., and in the patronage of the Bishop of Durham. The church, rebuilt in 1765, on the site of the ancient structure, which was destroyed by fire, is dedicated to St. Mary; it is a neat and appropriate edifice, and occupies an eminence commanding an extensive and richly-varied prospect. There are places of worship for Baptists, Burghers, and Presbyterians, also a Scotch Relief Church and a Roman Catholic chapel. The free grammar school, founded and endowed by the Earl of Tankerville, for six boys of the town, has received an additional endowment, for three more, from the Bishop of Durham, in compensation for a lapsed gift of £100, bequeathed for that purpose by Mrs. Chisholme. There are also Sunday schools in connexion with the established church and the several dissenting congregations. A dispensary has been established here, but it is not well supported, and is consequently on the decline. On a circular mount, near the town, are the remains of an ancient tower, apparently of Norman origin. There are many intrenchments in the vicinity, of which the most remarkable is "Humbledon Hugh," about a mile north-west of the town; it is circular in form, with a large cairn on the summit; the sides of the hill are formed into terraces, about twenty feet broad, of which there are three successive tiers, which, being filled with soldiers, presented a formidable resistance to any assailing force: in the plain beneath is the pillar commemorating the victory of Earl Percy.

WOOLFARDISWORTHY, a parish in the hundred of HARTLAND, county of DEVON, 9½ miles (S. W.

by W.) from Bideford, containing 755 inhabitants. The living is a perpetual curacy, in the archdeaconry of Barnstaple, and diocese of Exeter, endowed with £400 royal bounty, and £1400 parliamentary grant, and in the patronage of the Rev. W. Loggin. The church has an enriched Norman doorway and font.

WOOLFARDISWORTHY, a parish in the hundred of WITHERIDGE, county of DEVON, 6 miles (N. by W.) from Crediton, containing 213 inhabitants. The living is a rectory, in the archdeaconry of Barnstaple, and diocese of Exeter, rated in the king's books at £9. 19. 4½., and in the patronage of the Rev. Thomas Brent. The church is dedicated to the Holy Trinity. Berry Castle, an ancient Roman encampment, is in this parish.

WOOLFERTON, a township in that part of the parish of RICHARD'S CASTLE which is in the hundred of MUNSLOW, county of SALOP, 3 miles (S. E.) from Ludlow. The population is returned with the parish. Stourport canal passes through the township.

WOOLHAMPTON, a parish in the hundred of THEALE, county of BERKS, 7¼ miles (E.) from Newbury, containing 387 inhabitants. The living is a rectory, in the archdeaconry of Berks, and diocese of Salisbury, rated in the king's books at £7. 17. 6., and in the patronage of the Rev. Lancelot Greenthwaite Halton. The church is dedicated to St. Peter. Here is a Roman Catholic chapel. The navigable river Kennet runs through the parish.

WOOLHOPE, a parish in the hundred of GREYTREE, county of HEREFORD, 7¾ miles (W. by S.) from Ledbury, containing, with the townships of Buckenhill and Putley, 825 inhabitants. The living is a discharged vicarage, annexed to that of Fownhope, in the peculiar jurisdiction of the Consistorial Court of the Dean of Hereford, rated in the king's books at £7. 12. 8½., endowed with £200 private benefaction, and £200 royal bounty. The church is dedicated to St. George. A charity school here is supported by voluntary contributions.

WOOLLAND, a parish in the hundred of WHITEWAY, Cerne subdivision of the county of DORSET, 8 miles (W. by N.) from Blandford-Forum, containing 135 inhabitants. The living is a perpetual curacy, annexed to the vicarage of Hilton, in the peculiar jurisdiction of the Consistorial Court of Milton-Abbas. The church was rebuilt in 1745, a little to the westward of the ancient site.

WOOLLEY, a tything in the parish of CHADDLEWORTH, hundred of KINTBURY-EAGLE, county of BERKS, 6 miles (W.) from East Ilsley. The population is returned with the parish.

WOOLLEY, a parish in the hundred of LEIGHTONSTONE, county of HUNTINGDON, 5 miles (N. E. by N.) from Kimbolton, containing 64 inhabitants. The living is a rectory, in the archdeaconry of Huntingdon, and diocese of Lincoln, rated in the king's books at £9. 9. 2. Henry Sweeting, Esq. was patron in 1817. The church, dedicated to St. Mary, has a western tower crowned with a handsome cupola.

WOOLLEY, a chapelry in the parish of ROYSTON, wapentake of STAINCROSS, West riding of the county of YORK, 5¼ miles (N. by W.) from Barnesley, containing, with the township of Emley, 482 inhabitants. The living is a perpetual curacy, in the archdeaconry and diocese of York, endowed with £15 per annum and £200 private benefaction, and £400 royal bounty, and in the patronage of W. Wentworth, Esq. Sixteen poor children are instructed for £11. 11. a year, arising from the rent of certain land bequeathed by Nicholas Burley, with a trifling annuity from the parish fund.

WOOLLOS (ST.), a parish in the upper division of the hundred of WENTLLOOG, county of MONMOUTH, adjacent to the western side of the town of Newport, containing, with that town, 951 inhabitants. The living is a discharged vicarage, in the archdeaconry and diocese of Llandaff, rated in the king's books at £7. 3. 11½., and in the patronage of the Bishop of Gloucester. The church has lately received an addition of one hundred and seventy free sittings, the Incorporated Society for the enlargement of churches and chapels having granted £170 towards defraying the expense. There is a place of worship for Independents.

WOOLPIT, a parish in the hundred of THEDWESTRY, county of SUFFOLK, 5¾ miles (N. W. by W.) from Stow-Market, containing 801 inhabitants. The living is a rectory, in the archdeaconry of Sudbury, and diocese of Norwich, rated in the king's books at £6. 18. 9., and in the patronage of the Rev. T. Cobbold. The church, dedicated to St. Mary, is partly in the decorated, and partly in the later, style of English architecture. Woolpit is on the high road from Ipswich to Bury St. Edmunds, and was formerly a market town. One of the largest cattle fairs in England is held here, on September 16th and several following days. Sunday schools for both sexes are attended by about one hundred children.

WOOLSINGTON, a township in that part of the parish of NEWBURN which is in the western division of CASTLE ward, county of NORTHUMBERLAND, 5¼ miles (N. W. by N.) from Newcastle upon Tyne, containing 36 inhabitants.

WOOLSTANWOOD, a township in the parish and hundred of NANTWICH, county palatine of CHESTER, 3¼ miles (N. N. E.) from Nantwich, containing 65 inhabitants.

WOOLSTASTON, a parish in the hundred of CONDOVER, county of SALOP, 3½ miles (N.) from Church-Stretton, containing 93 inhabitants. The living is a rectory, in the archdeaconry of Salop, and diocese of Hereford, and in the patronage of W. W. Whitmore, Esq.

WOOLSTHORPE, a parish in the wapentake of WINNIBRIGGS and THREO, parts of KESTEVEN, county of LINCOLN, 6¼ miles (W. by S.) from Grantham, containing 566 inhabitants. The living is a rectory, in the archdeaconry and diocese of Lincoln, rated in the king's books at £12. 2. 8½., and in the patronage of the Duke of Rutland. The church is dedicated to St. James.

WOOLSTON, a hamlet in the parish of NORTH CADBURY, hundred of CATSASH, county of SOMERSET, 2¾ miles (S.) from Castle-Cary. The population is returned with the hamlet of Yarlington.

WOOLSTONE, a parish forming a detached portion of the lower division of the hundred of DEERHURST, county of GLOUCESTER, 5 miles (W. N. W.) from Winchcombe, containing 89 inhabitants. The living is a rectory, in the archdeaconry and diocese of Gloucester, rated in the king's books at £13. 6. 0½.,

and in the patronage of the Earl of Coventry. The church is dedicated to St. Martin.

WOOLSTONE, a joint township with Martinscroft, in the parish of WARRINGTON, hundred of WEST DERBY, county palatine of LANCASTER, 2½ miles (E. by N.) from Warrington, containing, with Martinscroft, 596 inhabitants.

WOOLSTONE, a tything in the parish of HOUND, hundred of MANSBRIDGE, Fawley division of the county of SOUTHAMPTON, 1½ mile (S. E. by E.) from Southampton. The population is returned with the parish.

WOOLSTONE (GREAT), a parish in the hundred of NEWPORT, county of BUCKINGHAM, 3½ miles (N.) from Fenny-Stratford, containing 108 inhabitants. The living is a discharged rectory, in the archdeaconry of Buckingham, and diocese of Lincoln, rated in the king's books at £8. 16. 1., endowed with £200 private benefaction, and £200 royal bounty. J. C. Nield, Esq. was patron in 1816. The church is dedicated to the Holy Trinity.

WOOLSTONE (LITTLE), a parish in the hundred of NEWPORT, county of BUCKINGHAM, 3¾ miles (N.) from Fenny-Stratford, containing 114 inhabitants. The living is a discharged rectory, in the archdeaconry of Buckingham, and diocese of Lincoln, rated in the king's books at £8. 6. 1., and in the patronage of the Crown. The church, which was dedicated to the Holy Trinity, has fallen to ruins.

WOOLSTROP, a hamlet in that part of the parish of QUEDGLEY which is in the middle division of the hundred of DUDSTONE and KING'S BARTON, county of GLOUCESTER, 5 miles (S. W. by W.) from Gloucester, containing 36 inhabitants.

WOOLTON (LITTLE), a township in the parish of CHILDWALL, hundred of WEST DERBY, county palatine of LANCASTER, 4½ miles (S. W. by S.) from Prescot, containing 673 inhabitants. A trifling sum, bequeathed by the Rev. Thomas Compton, is applied for teaching poor children.

WOOLTON (MUCH), a chapelry in the parish of CHILDWALL, hundred of WEST DERBY, county palatine of LANCASTER, 5¼ miles (S. W. by S.) from Prescot, containing 970 inhabitants. The chapel has lately received an addition of five hundred and thirty-eight sittings, of which two hundred and sixty-nine are free, the Incorporated Society for the enlargement of churches and chapels having granted £200 towards defraying the expense.

WOOLVERCOTT, a parish in the hundred of WOOTTON, county of OXFORD, 2¾ miles (N. N. W.) from Oxford, containing 493 inhabitants. The living is a perpetual curacy, in the archdeaconry and diocese of Oxford, and in the patronage of the Warden and Fellows of Merton College, Oxford. The church, dedicated to St. Peter, is situated on the banks of the Isis. A National school is supported by voluntary contributions and annual subscriptions, aided by an annuity of £3 from the poor's estate : the income is £52, which is paid to the master and mistress, who are also allowed a dwelling-house rent-free, and teach about sixty-five boys and fifty-five girls. A Benedictine abbey, in honour of the Virgin Mary and St. John the Baptist, was founded here, in 1138, by a pious lady, called Editha, which at the dissolution had a revenue of £319. 18. 8. Henry II. was a great benefactor to it; and within its walls fair Rosamond was interred.

WOOLVERSTONE, a parish in the hundred of SAMFORD, county of SUFFOLK, 4½ miles (S. by E.) from Ipswich, containing 269 inhabitants. The living is a discharged rectory, lately consolidated with the rectory of Erwarton, in the archdeaconry of Suffolk, and diocese of Norwich, rated in the king's books at £5. 8. 9., and in the patronage of Charles Berners, Esq. The church is dedicated to St. Michael. The navigable river Orwell bounds the parish on the north-east.

WOOLVER, a parish in the hundred of NEW-PORT, county of BUCKINGHAM, 1 mile (E. N. E.) from Stony-Stratford, containing 335 inhabitants. The living is a discharged vicarage, in the archdeaconry of Buckingham, and diocese of Lincoln, rated in the king's books at £10. 3. 9., endowed with £400 private benefaction, and £400 royal bounty, and in the patronage of W. Drake, Esq. and others. The church is dedicated to the Holy Trinity.

WOOLVERTON, a parish in the hundred of FROME, county of SOMERSET, 4½ miles (N. by E.) from Frome, containing 184 inhabitants. The living is a discharged rectory, consolidated with that of Road, in the archdeaconry of Wells, and diocese of Bath and Wells, rated in the king's books at £7. 1. 3., and in the patronage of Dr. Starkie. The church is dedicated to St. Lawrence. The river Frome separates the two parishes, that of Road being on the east, and Woolverton on the west. A considerable trade in wool was formerly carried on here.

WOOLVERTON, a parish in the hundred of KINGS-CLERE, Kingsclere division of the county of SOUTH-AMPTON, 7½ miles (N. W.) from Basingstoke, containing 213 inhabitants. The living is a rectory, in the archdeaconry and diocese of Winchester, rated in the king's books at £13. 2. 8½. R. and J. Clarke, Esqrs. were patrons in 1804. The church is dedicated to St. Catherine.

WOOLWICH, a market town and parish in the hundred of BLACKHEATH, lathe of SUTTON at HONE, county of KENT, 8 miles (E. by S.) from London, containing, according to the last census, 17,008 inhabitants, which number has, since that period, considerably decreased. This place, originally a small fishing town, unnoticed by any of the earlier Kentish historians, owes its present importance, among other causes, to its situation on the river Thames, which, in this part, is nearly three quarters of a mile broad, and of sufficient depth, at the lowest state of the tide, for ships of the largest burden. In the reign of Henry VII., a ship of war of one thousand tons' burden was built here, which that monarch named the "Harry Grace de Dieu;" but it does not appear that any regular establishment for ship-building had been formed previously to the reign of Henry VIII., who constructed a royal dock-yard here, which was enlarged by Queen Elizabeth, and has continued progressively to increase in every succeeding reign. The "Sovereign of the Seas," the largest ship that had ever been built in England, was launched from this dock-yard in the reign of Charles I.: this ship, which was of one thousand six hundred and thirty-seven tons' burden, and carried one hundred and seventy-six guns, was richly ornamented with carving and gilding; from which cir-

cumstance, combined with the destructive efficacy of its heavy ordnance in the war with the Dutch, it obtained from that people the appellation of the "Golden Devil." In the reign of George I., the cannon for the Board of Ordnance was cast in a foundry situated in Moorfields, which having been destroyed by an explosion, occasioned by dampness in the moulds at the time of pouring in the liquid metal, the establishment was removed to Woolwich, and placed under the superintendence of Mr. Andrew Schalch, a native of Schaffhausen in Switzerland, who, travelling for improvement, visited the foundry in Moorfields at the time when preparations were in progress for casting several pieces of ordnance on the day following, in the presence of many of the nobility, general officers, and a large concourse of people. Mr. Schalch, who had obtained permission to inspect the process, minutely examined the preparations, and instantly perceiving the improper state of the moulds, warned the surveyor-general of the ordnance, and the superintendent of the foundries, of the lurking danger; and they, sensible of the justness and importance of his apprehensions, retired with their friends and all whom they could persuade to accompany them, in time to escape the effect of the explosion, by which several lives were lost, and many of the workmen dreadfully burnt and mangled. The Board of Ordnance subsequently finding this gentleman duly qualified, authorised him to choose a commodious situation within twelve miles of the metropolis, for the erection of a new foundry; and, after having visited several places, he selected the Warren at Woolwich for that purpose. The first specimens of ordnance cast under his superintendence being highly approved of, he was appointed master founder, which office he held for nearly sixty years, with so much skill and attention, that, during this long period, not a single accident occurred. This circumstance may be considered the origin of the present arsenal, the subsequent extension and establishment of which, with the augmentation of the artillery, whose head-quarters were fixed here, the institution of the Royal Military academy, and various other foundations, have raised the town to a degree of importance, which, as a grand naval and military depôt, is without a parallel in any empire of the world.

The town is situated on elevated ground rising gradually from the south bank of the river Thames, on the opposite side of which, in the county of Essex, is a detached part of the parish: it consists of one main street, extending nearly a mile parallel with the river, from which numerous other streets branch off in various directions, and is partly included in the parish of Plumstead. The houses in that part of it which may be considered the principal street are of ancient appearance, occasionally interspersed with substantial and well-built dwellings; but the other streets consist of modern houses, principally erected for the accommodation of the artificers and labourers employed in the dock-yard, arsenal, and other public works. The upper part of the town, towards the common and the Charlton road, is elevated and pleasant, and contains several ranges of well-built and handsome modern houses: the environs abound with rich woodland scenery, agreeably diversified with the windings of the Thames, sometimes seen in pleasing combination, and at others in striking contrast. The town is partially paved, under the superintendence of commissioners annually chosen under the provisions of an act of parliament passed in the 47th of George III.; lighted with gas by a company established by act of parliament; and amply supplied with water from the works of the Kent Water Company.

The public buildings are all on a scale of vast extent, and most of them in a style of magnificence corresponding with the importance of the purposes to which they are applied. The dock-yard commences near the village of New Charlton on the west, and extends nearly a mile along the bank of the river, to the east; the breadth varies from one to two furlongs: the principal entrance is through a stone portal, of which the piers are ornamented with anchors sculptured in stone. On the left hand, within the walls, is a house for a commissioner, and on the right are the houses belonging to the principal officers of the yard. Beyond these is the smithery, a spacious and lofty building, in which are, a steam-engine of twenty-horse power, which works two large lift-hammers, weighing nearly four tons each, and one of fourteen-horse power, working three tilt-hammers, of less weight; the general fall of these hammers is about nine inches, and the number of strokes from thirty to fifty per minute: there is another steam-engine, of fourteen-horse power, for blowing the fires throughout the smithery, and there are several blast furnaces for converting scrap iron into pigs, and a machine for rolling iron. Kneels, keelsons, breast-pieces, and all other iron work connected with ship-building, are manufactured here, and also anchors of the largest size, great numbers of which, kept in readiness for supplying the Royal Navy, are disposed in extensive ranges in the area in front of the building. There are two dry docks, one of which is double, for the repairing of vessels, and several slips, in which ships of war of the largest dimensions are built, under lofty sheds lighted from the roof; and a capacious basin, four hundred feet long, and two hundred and ninety feet in mean breadth, has been recently excavated, capable of receiving ships of the largest class, the entrance into which from the river is by caisson of large dimensions; the embankment is by strong sloping walls of brick, coped with massive blocks of stone. The line of wharfage is very extensive and of proportionate breadth: there are a mast-pond, a boat-pond, and several mast-houses and boat-houses, also extensive ranges of timber-sheds, storehouses of every kind upon the largest scale, a mould loft, and every requisite arrangement for the purposes of the establishment. Several fine first and second rate ships have recently been built here, among which are, the Lord Nelson, of one hundred and twenty guns; the Invincible, of seventy-four; the Venerable, of seventy-four; the Redoubtable, the Hawk, the Talavera, Black Prince, and others, together with numerous third-rates and frigates; and several fine ships are now on the stocks, among which are, the Trafalgar, of one hundred and twenty guns; the Boscawen, of eighty; the Thunderer, of eighty-four; the Chichester, of fifty-two; the Ambuscade, of thirty-six; the Halcyon and Hyæna sloops; and the Dee, a steam-vessel of seven hundred and one tons' burden. The establishment, under the direction of the Navy Board, consists of a master attendant, a store-keeper, a master shipwright and assistants, a master smith, master painter, with their assistants, a

surgeon and an assistant surgeon, and other officers. In the eastern part of the town is the rope-yard, an extensive range of building, three stories high, and more than one thousand two hundred feet in length, in which ropes of various sizes, cordage for rigging the ships, and cables of the largest size, are made: in the upper story the hemp is spun into yarn, which, in the next story below, is made into lines, cordage, and smaller ropes; and in the lowest story the larger ropes and cables are twisted by the help of powerful machinery, a part of which, by a very ingenious contrivance, is applied to stretching the largest cables, which they strain till they break, in order to ascertain their strength, and the exact weight which they are capable of sustaining; some of the cables made here are one hundred and two fathoms long, and twenty-four inches in circumference: this establishment, which is enclosed with high walls, and is under the superintendence of a resident clerk, is about to be transferred to Chatham, or Portsmouth.

To the east of the rope-yard is the royal arsenal, under the control of the Master-General and the Honourable Board of Ordnance: this magnificent establishment comprises within the boundary walls more than one hundred acres, and, including the canal, more than one hundred and forty-two, the greater part of which is within the adjoining parish of Plumstead. The principal entrance is through a spacious and lofty central gateway for carriages, with smaller entrances on each side; the inner piers are ornamented with small piles of shot, and the outer piers, which are loftier, are surmounted by mortars. Nearly opposite the entrance is a range of handsome houses, appropriated to the commandant of the garrison, the field-officers of the royal artillery, and the principal officers attached to some of the departments; the chief of which are, the inspector of artillery's department, the royal carriage department, the royal engineer's department, the storekeepers' department, superintendant of shipping, the royal laboratory. In addition to these are immense ranges of storehouses, forming a grand national depôt of warlike stores, of every description, for the naval and military departments of the service. On the right hand of the entrance is a range of buildings used, till within the last few years, as an academy for part of the gentlemen cadet company, in connexion with the Royal Military academy, and now occupied partly as store-rooms and partly as dwelling-houses. On the left hand is a handsome guard-house, with a portico of four columns of Portland stone, beyond which is the royal brass-foundry, erected by Vanbrugh, a spacious and lofty building of red brick, ornamented with stone and roofed with slate, which is perforated for ventilation. Over the entrance are the royal arms, handsomely carved in stone, above which is a neat cupola: it contains three large furnaces for casting brass ordnance only, the largest of which will melt eighteen tons of metal at one time: to avoid all danger of explosion, the moulds are heated to a considerable degree before the metal runs into them. To the east of the foundry are appropriate workshops for boring and engraving the cannon: the machine for boring is well adapted to the purpose; the gun is fixed to a shaft turned round by a horizontal wheel, moved by horse power, which, working into another attached to the end of the piece, gives it a vertical motion; the cutter, or borer, is placed in a frame, and adjusted by iron clamps and screws, and is moved gradually forward, as the cavity deepens, by machinery adapted to that purpose: the time requisite for boring a ninepounder is usually three days, and longer in proportion for pieces of a larger calibre. The several duties are performed under the direction of the inspector of artillery, in whose department is also carried on the examination and proving of ordnance, the fitting and adjusting of them with the necessary instruments for taking the degree of elevation, and other arrangements connected with the service. All ordnance used in the Hon. East India Company's, and in the merchants' service are sent here to undergo examination and proof, previously to their being used. To the east of the buildings appropriated to the boring and engraving of cannon are the workshops of the royal carriage department, for the construction and manufacture of gun carriages for naval and land service, and of all carts, ammunition wagons, and other carriages used in the ordnance department; in these workshops are steamengines applied to the working of circular and other saws for converting timber, machinery of ingenious construction for planing wood, and for turning wood and metal. In a line with this range of buildings is the royal engineer department, under the direction of which are the erection and repair of all buildings belonging to the Board of Ordnance within a limited distance of Woolwich. To the north-west of the foundry is the royal laboratory, in which are made up blank and ball cartridges for small arms, cartridges for cannon of all descriptions, grape and case shot, and all combustible articles, and a variety of other important duties relating to the naval and military service is performed. In addition to the workshops for these purposes are the buildings by Vanbrugh, in which are now deposited some ingenious models of fire-ships, completely prepared for explosion, models of various fireworks exhibited on public occasions, and other curiosities: and in the other are various machines for ascertaining the strength of gunpowder, with samples of the different ingredients for making it, in their several stages of purification and refinement; specimens of the various kinds used by different nations, and of the several degrees of fineness, from the coarsest used for the heaviest ordnance to the finest for small arms; numerous models of muskets, and arms of different construction; and a variety of interesting and curious objects.

A line of wharfage, with a commodious quay, accessible to ships of large burden, extends for many hundred yards along the bank of the Thames, on which is a spacious and magnificent range of storehouses, occupying three sides of a quadrangle, the area of which is filled with vast quantities of shot and shell of every size, ranged in regular quadrangular and pyramidal piles, and duly numbered. The buildings are of light brick, with quoins, cornices, pilasters, and pediments of stone, and handsomely embellished with appropriate ornaments: the central range, comprising three stories, is connected with the wings, which are two stories high, by handsome arched portals of stone forming the entrances into the quadrangle, and surmounted with balustraded corridors, communicating with the principal stories of each range. In the basement story of the principal range are deposited general

stores for the naval service; in the second are the harness and other equipments for the royal horse artillery; and in the upper story, stores of various descriptions. The east wing is appropriated to the reception of stores for garrison and field services, with a large assortment of nails and other necessaries: the west contains the stores and various implements used by the sappers and miners, and those for making intrenchments and constructing fortifications, among which are sand-bags, axes, shovels, spades, barrows, grates for heating shot, and numerous other articles, and an extensive collection of samples of different materials, and patterns of various implements, with which the several articles furnished to the Board of Ordnance are compared, before they are received into the depôt. On the ground-floors of these store-rooms are iron tram-roads, upon which carriages constructed for the purpose, once put in motion, will run, when heavily loaded, from one extremity to the other, for the conveyance of stores to the wharf. To the east and west of the principal buildings are smaller quadrangular ranges of storehouses, of one and two stories in height: in both of these, the ranges parallel with the river are of one story, and are appropriated as repositories for carriages; in the lower story of the eastern range are stores of oil and cement; and in the upper, a general repository of stores of various kinds: the lower story of the western range is for the reception of carriages, and the upper is the depôt of clothing for the royal artillery and for the sappers and miners, and in the centre of each of these smaller quadrangles are painters' shops. There are also various ranges of building for warehouses in different parts of the enclosure. To the south of the principal quadrangle are immense quantities of iron ordnance of various calibres, placed on iron skidding, and ranged in double files, extending many hundred yards in length, and, with small intervals between the rows, spreading over several acres of ground: large quantities of iron carriages for guns, and beds for mortars, are ranged at the extremity and around the space occupied by the ordnance; and numerous mortars of the largest calibre are disposed in various parts of the ground.

The arsenal is bounded on the south-east by a canal, thirty-five feet broad, on the banks of which are wooden buildings for the manufacture of the Congreve rockets, under the superintendence of the officers of the royal laboratory; and towards the south-eastern extremity of the boundary wall is pleasantly situated, on the road to Plumstead, the house appropriated to the residence of the storekeeper and paymaster. A little to the west is a saw-mill, worked by a steam-engine of twenty-horse power, for sawing trees and rough timber into planks of any required thickness, to which the saws, fixed in frames and worked perpendicularly with great efficacy, can be adjusted at pleasure; there are also circular and other saws, with machinery of a very ingenious description, for turning and other purposes, all under the direction of the officers belonging to the royal carriage department. At a short distance from the royal arsenal, on the road to Woolwich common, are the barracks for the sappers and miners, a neat substantial range of building, with accommodation for two hundred and fifty to two hundred and seventy men. Adjoining these is the grand depôt of field train artillery, consisting of a central building appropriated as offices for the director-general of the field train, and other officers of the department, and five spacious sheds, averaging each three hundred feet in length, in which are deposited, in double files, an immense number of guns, mounted on field carriages, in readiness for embarkation at a minute's notice, and supplied with a due proportion of stores and ammunition for immediate service. To the south of the depôt is the ordnance hospital, a handsome building, containing apartments for a resident surgeon and apothecary, and other officers, and for the servants of the establishment, with wards for the reception of seven hundred patients, a medical library, and other requisite offices : it is under the superintendence of the director-general and medical staff of the garrison, from which all the ordnance medical establishments abroad are supplied.

The barracks for the royal foot and horse artillery form a spacious and splendid pile of building, of which the principal front, facing the common, is three hundred and forty yards in length. The main entrance is through a central portal of three arches, divided by lofty columns of the Doric order, supporting pedestals surmounted with military trophies, and above the central arch are the royal arms, finely sculptured in stone. The building, which is of light brick, ornamented with Portland stone, consists of six principal ranges, connected by four lower buildings, in front of which are colonnades of the Doric order, surmounted by balustrades : above the second range, on the east side of the entrance, is a handsome cupola, in which is a clock; and above the corresponding building on the west side is a similar cupola, with a wind-dial. The chapel, which is neatly fitted up, contains one thousand sittings, and is regularly open for divine service : the library and reading-room are well supplied with works of general literature and periodical publications. The mess-room is a splendid apartment, sixty feet in length, fifty feet wide, and of proportionate height ; at one end is a circular recess, in which is a music gallery, and at the other, a handsome range of windows looking upon the common : from the ceiling, which is ornamented with groining above the cornice, three elegant cut-glass chandeliers are suspended, and the whole arrangement is in the style of an elegant assembly-room. Attached to it is a suite of apartments, comprising a drawing-room of appropriate character, with retiring and ante-rooms : in this elegant suite of rooms the officers of the garrison give frequent balls to the gentry of the vicinity, and, in 1830, had the honour of entertaining King William IV. and Queen Adelaide, who accompanied His Majesty on his visit to review the royal artillery. From the principal entrance, an avenue, two hundred and twenty yards in length, and terminating with a handsome arched portal, divides the buildings into two spacious quadrangles, round which are the stabling and barracks for the horse artillery ; and at the extremity of the east quadrangle is a spacious riding-school of elegant design : the whole establishment is arranged for the accommodation of from three thousand to four thousand men.

The Parade, in front of the barracks, is about sixty yards in breadth, adjoining the common, which, in this part, is a fine level lawn, appropriated for the exercise of the foot artillery. In the centre of the Parade are ranged several beautiful pieces of artillery, mounted on carriages of bronze, richly chased and ornamented. Among these is a very large piece of ordnance taken at the siege of Bhurtpoor, in the East Indies, and presented by the captors to the King of England : it is mounted on a splendid carriage of bronze : the breech, which is of unusually large proportion, rests upon the shoulders of a lion couchant, beautifully executed : one side of the carriage is ornamented with a view of the citadel of Bhurtpoor in a medallion, and the other bears an inscription commemorative of its capture: the wheels are solid, with a face of Apollo, or the sun, forming the nave, and the beams of the sun the radii. The more distant part of the common is appropriated to the exercise of the horse artillery.

Adjoining the barrack field to the west is the repository, for the exercise and general instruction of all persons belonging to the artillery, occupying an extensive piece of ground, tastefully laid out in parterres and walks leading to the several buildings; nearly opposite to the entrance are the modelling rooms for the use of the officers and men, in which are models, and drawings of projected improvements in the construction of gun-carriages and implements of war, and in which various mechanical experiments are performed for that purpose. In a shed adjoining them are preserved the funeral car of Napoleon, brought from St. Helena ; a travelling oven used by the French army in their campaigns under Buonaparte, and some other curiosities ; and in various parts of the ground are numerous pieces of brass ordnance, of different kinds, taken from the enemy, among which are, two captured at the battle of Malplaquet, with three barrels each, and several others of very singular construction. The ground, which is in many places unequal and precipitous, rising abruptly from several pieces of water, by which it is intersected, is made available for the practice of the artillery corps in the construction of bridges of pontoons, for transporting artillery across rivers, in the managing of gun-boats, and in the more difficult and arduous exercises of their duty; heavy pieces of artillery are manœuvered under every possible disadvantage of situation, lowered down steep declivities, and raised up precipitous heights, by a variety of contrivances : in various parts of the ground are intrenchments of earth and batteries of turf, which are thrown up by the students for their improvement in the art of fortification. On the north of the entrance is the rotunda, or model-room, a spacious circular apartment, one hundred and fifteen feet in diameter, originally erected in the gardens of Carlton palace by George IV., when Prince Regent, for the entertainment of the allied sovereigns, on their visit to this country after the peace, and presented by that monarch to the garrison. The roof, in the form of the awning of a tent, is supported on a lofty central Doric column, on the pedestal of which are various kinds of ancient armour, coats of mail, helmets, and other military trophies; with specimens of the small arms of various nations. The room is lighted by a range of windows in the several compartments into which it is divided, and in which a vast number of beautiful and well-finished models of machinery are arranged, with apparatus for military and naval warfare : among these are guns and weapons of various descriptions, boats, pontoons, carriages, and implements, a variety of missiles, and Congreve and other rockets, with machines for discharging them singly or in vollies; a block of wood, fifteen inches square, pierced through and shattered by a Congreve rocket, which is wedged within the fissure, is preserved as a specimen of the destructive efficacy of this invention. Around the inner circle is arranged a most interesting variety of larger models, finished with the most scrupulous and minute exactness: among these are a bomb ship, with the whole apparatus for throwing the shells; a ship for the transport of horses, with the apparatus for slinging them, and the several arrangements for their management on board; models of all the royal dock-yards; the lines and fortifications of Portsmouth; the breakwater at Plymouth; the island of St. Kits; Cumberland fort; the citadel of Massina; the floating battery at South Carolina; the town of Quebec; the rock of Gibraltar, with the fortifications and batteries formed by excavated passages in the solid rock, and fine specimens of the strata highly polished; Fort William, in Bengal; Rio Janeiro; with a beautiful model of St. James' Park, and the several buildings erected in it on the occasion of the celebration of peace; a pair of kettle drums, of which the larger weighs more than four hundred weight and three quarters, taken from the cathedral of Strasbourgh; a lever target upon a new construction, and an infinite number of interesting and ingenious specimens of the adaptation of science to the invention, or improvement, of machinery connected with the art of war. On the south-west part of the common is the veterinary hospital for the horse artillery, under the control of the commandant and the superintendence of a veterinary surgeon and assistants; this building, which is well adapted to its use, is situated in the parish of Charlton. Between the repository and the veterinary hospital are fifty cottages, neatly built of brick, containing two apartments each, for the accommodation of one hundred married soldiers.

At the south-eastern extremity of the common, opposite to the artillery barracks, is the Royal Military academy, established in 1741, originally for the instruction of officers and men belonging to the military department of the ordnance, but now appropriated exclusively to gentlemen cadets, the number of whom varies from one hundred to one hundred and forty, and is at present one hundred and thirty. The establishment is under the superintendence of a governor, who is always master-general of the ordnance for the time being; a lieutenant-governor and an inspector, who are officers of high rank in the artillery and engineer departments; a professor of mathematics, and four mathematical masters; a professor of fortification, and one master; a drawing-master of military plans, surveying, and perspective; a drawing-master for landscape; a French-master; and a lecturer on chemistry. Examinations of the students are held monthly, when lists of the state of progress are laid before the master-general: from these lists, the number of cadets is selected to supply vacant commissions, and on their nomination, according to merit, they become candidates at the half-yearly examinations. The scale of progress is referred to for promotion to the different classes, and every gradation is exclusively the result of merit. To prevent disappointment in the ultimate nomination to commissions, a minimum of progress within the first year is fixed, the

attainment, or non-attainment, of which decides the prospect of the student, who if unsuccessful is not, by an unnecessary loss of time, precluded from other pursuits. The buildings form a spacious pile in the early English, and partly in the Elizabethan, style of architecture, and comprise a central range with angular octagonal towers crowned with domes, containing on the basement story the entrance-hall and school-rooms, and, in a central situation between them, an apartment originally intended for the inspector, but used only as a receptacle for stores, and as a place from which hot air is distributed for warming the building: above these is the grand hall, in which the public examinations are held. The centre is connected by corridors, with two wings in the Elizabethan style, with turrets at the angles, and containing the apartments for the residence of the cadets: behind the central range is the refectory, a spacious hall with a lofty timber-framed roof, lighted by windows of appropriate character, adjoining which are the kitchen and domestic offices. On the east side of the common are the houses of the professors, and some handsome ranges of building, including the quarters of the field officers of the garrison, and several private residences. The barracks for the Woolwich division of marines are situated at a short distance to the north of the artillery barracks; they are a plain irregular building, having accommodation for about four hundred men, and attached is an hospital for seamen and marines. There is no trade except what is requisite for the supply of the inhabitants, nor any particular branch of manufacture carried on here. The intercourse with the metropolis is great, and is facilitated by passage-boats on the river, by carriages direct, and by vans, which run every half hour from the Ship Tavern to Greenwich, whence there are coaches to London every half hour. There was also an ancient ferry to the Devil's House, originally Du Val's house, on the opposite side of the river, but the present ferry is nearly a mile further up the river. Hulks are moored off Woolwich, for the reception of convicts whose sentence of transportation is commuted for hard labour at home, and who are employed in the dock-yard, arsenal, and public works. The market is on Friday; and under the provisions of the local act before mentioned, markets are also held on Wednesday and Saturday: a market-house was erected a few years since, but it has never been used for that purpose, and the entrances are now closed up, the building having been appropriated to the reception of stores. The town is within the jurisdiction of the county magistrates, who hold their sittings every Monday and Friday at the King's Arms hotel; and a petty session for the division is held at the Green Man, at Blackheath, on the first Thursday in every month. The court of requests for the hundred of Blackheath, and other places in the county of Kent, is held under commissioners annually appointed by the act of the 47th of George III., at the Crown and Anchor tavern, every alternate Friday, for the recovery of debts not exceeding £5.

The living is a rectory, in the archdeaconry and diocese of Rochester, rated in the king's books at £7. 12. 6., and in the patronage of the Bishop of Rochester. The church, dedicated to St. Mary Magdalene, was rebuilt by act of parliament passed in the 5th of George II., at an expense of £6500, towards defraying which £3000 was appropriated from the grant of Queen Anne, for building fifty new churches, and the remainder raised by contribution of the inhabitants : it is situated on an eminence overlooking the dock-yard and the river, and is a neat building of brick with a square tower, ornamented with copings and cornices of stone ; the interior, in which several standards taken from the enemy are deposited, is lofty and well arranged ; the galleries are supported on Ionic columns of good proportion; there are few monuments of any celebrity ; in the churchyard are numerous monuments to officers of the royal artillery, among which is one to the memory of Lieutenant-General Williamson, whose wife was lineally descended from Robert, second King of Scotland. The ordnance chapel, on the road to Plumstead, a plain commodious building, and the chapel in the barracks, are the only additional episcopal churches, to both of which chaplains are appointed by the Honourable the Board of Ordnance. There are places of worship for Baptists, Independents, Wesleyan and Welch Methodists, and for a society calling themselves Arminian Bible Christians, also a Scottish church, and a Roman Catholic chapel. Mrs. Mary Wiseman, in 1758, bequeathed £1000 South Sea annuities for educating and clothing six orphan sons of shipwrights of His Majesty's dock-yard, and for apprenticing them to the same business in the yard : this property, by accumulated savings, now produces £86. 5. per annum, for which ten boys are clothed, educated, and apprenticed, according to the intention of the testator, when practicable, in the dock-yard, or, when not so, to shipwrights out of the yard, or to other trades when such cannot be found. Mrs. Mary Withers, in 1750, bequeathed £600 Old South Sea annuities, of which £100 was to be laid out in building a school-room, with an apartment for a mistress, who was to receive the dividends on the remainder, for instructing thirty girls maintained in the workhouse, in reading, knitting, and needlework ; and the further sum of £600, in the same funds, to augment the salary of the schoolmistress, on condition of her teaching as many children nominated by the rector, as would make up the number to thirty, when so many might not be at any time in the workhouse: the building adjoins the parish workhouse, and the salary arising from the endowment is £33 per annum. The National school, in Powis-street, in which two hundred boys, and a similar establishment in the churchyard, in which one hundred and thirty girls, are instructed, are supported by subscription. There is also a British and foreign school, in which one hundred and sixty-four boys, and one hundred girls, are taught; and an infant school, in which there are one hundred and twenty children of both sexes, supported by the same means. Attached to Enon chapel is an endowed school, in which one hundred and thirty boys and sixty girls are taught free of expense. An almshouse for five aged widows was founded, about the year 1560, by Sir Martin Bowes, who endowed it with a portion of the produce of lands and tenements vested for charitable uses in the Company of Goldsmiths, London, by whom the almshouses were rebuilt in 1771 : the buildings consist of five houses of four apartments each, and are inhabited by five widows, parishioners of Woolwich, above fifty years of age, to each of whom the company pay

£10. 10. per annum, exclusively of a donation of £1 at the annual visitation : they receive, in addition, a chaldron of coal, and a supply of candles. There are also several other bequests for charitable purposes, and for distribution among the poor.

WOOPERTON, a township in the parish of Eg-lingham, northern division of Coquetdale ward, county of Northumberland, 6¼ miles (S. E. by S.) from Wooler, containing 68 inhabitants.

WOORE, a chapelry in that part of the parish of Muckleston which is in the Drayton division of the hundred of Bradford (North), county of Salop, 6¾ miles (N. N. E.) from Drayton in Hales, containing 365 inhabitants. The chapel has lately received an addition of eighty free sittings, the Incorporated Society for the enlargement of churches and chapels having granted £10 towards defraying the expense. About thirty children are taught in a Sunday school, from an annuity of £10, the bequest of William Elkins, in 1593; to which has been added one of £5, bequeathed by Randolph Woolley, in 1615.

WOOTHORPE, a hamlet in the parish of St. Martin, Stamford-Baron, liberty of Peterborough, county of Northampton, 6 miles (N. W. by N.) from Wansford, containing 36 inhabitants. A small Benedictine nunnery, dedicated to St. Mary, existed here so early as the time of Henry I., and was united, in the reign of Edward III., to the convent of our Lady St. Mary and St. Michael, at Stamford-Baron.

WOOTON, a hamlet in that part of the parish of St. Mary de Lode, Gloucester, which is in the upper division of the hundred of Dudstone and King's Barton, county of Gloucester, ¾ of a mile (E. by S.) from Gloucester, containing 397 inhabitants.

WOOTON, a parish in the liberty of East Medina, Isle of Wight division of the county of Southampton, 4 miles (N. E.) from Newport, containing 56 inhabitants. The living is a rectory, in the archdeaconry and diocese of Winchester, rated in the king's books at £7. 16. 0½. The Rev. R. W. White was patron in 1808. The church is dedicated to St. Edmund. There is a place of worship for Wesleyan Methodists. The parish is bounded on the north by the Motherbank, and on the east by an inlet of the sea, across which there is a narrow causeway, called Wooton bridge, upwards of nine hundred feet in length, and on the high road to Newport. On an eminence south of the bridge is Fern Hill, the seat of Charles Chute, Esq., a curious edifice with a lofty handsome tower, having somewhat the appearance of a church : it was erected by the late Lord Bolton, and commands a noble prospect of Spithead and the adjacent parts of Hampshire. At Wooton farm is an ancient oak of remarkably large dimensions, being forty-seven feet in girth.

WOOTTON, a parish in the hundred of Redborne-stoke, county of Bedford, 4½ miles (S. W.) from Bedford, containing 944 inhabitants. The living is a vicarage, in the archdeaconry of Bedford, and diocese of Lincoln, rated in the king's books at £13. 6. 8., and in the patronage of the Representatives of the late Sir P. Monoux, Bart. The church, dedicated to St. Mary, contains numerous monuments to the Monoux family. There is a place of worship for Wesleyan Methodists.

WOOTTON, a parish in the hundred of Hormer, county of Berks, 3½ miles (N. W. by N.) from Abingdon, containing 310 inhabitants. The living is a perpetual curacy, in the archdeaconry of Berks, and diocese of Salisbury, endowed with £200 private benefaction, and £200 royal bounty, and in the patronage of the Earl of Abingdon. The church is dedicated to St. Peter. Wootton, formerly a chapelry in the parish of Cumner, was made a separate parish early in the last century.

WOOTTON, a parish in the hundred of KINGHAM-FORD, lathe of ST. AUGUSTINE, county of KENT, 9½ miles (S. E. by S.) from Canterbury, containing 131 inhabitants. The living is a rectory, in the archdeaconry and diocese of Canterbury, rated in the king's books at £8. 10. 2½., and in the patronage of Sir J. H. Brydges, Bart. The church, dedicated to St. Martin, is in the early style of English architecture.

WOOTTON, a parish in the northern division of the wapentake of YARBOROUGH, parts of LINDSEY, county of LINCOLN, 5¾ miles (S. E.) from Barton upon Humber, containing 397 inhabitants. The living is a discharged vicarage, in the archdeaconry and diocese of Lincoln, rated in the king's books at £4. 18. 4., endowed with £200 royal bounty. William Holt, Esq. was patron in 1814. The church is dedicated to St. Andrew. There is a place of worship for Wesleyan Methodists. Several trifling bequests are applied for teaching poor children.

WOOTTON, a parish in the hundred of WYMERS-LEY, county of NORTHAMPTON, 2½ miles (S. by E.) from Northampton, containing 581 inhabitants. The living is a rectory, in the archdeaconry of Northampton, and diocese of Peterborough, rated in the king's books at £21. 15., and in the patronage of the Rector and Fellows of Exeter College, Oxford. The church is dedicated to St. George the Martyr.

WOOTTON, a parish in the hundred of WOOTTON, county of OXFORD, 2¼ miles (N. by W.) from Woodstock, containing 1084 inhabitants. The living is a rectory, in the archdeaconry and diocese of Oxford, rated in the king's books at £15. 2. 8½., and in the patronage of the Warden and Fellows of New College, Oxford. The church, dedicated to St. Mary, is partly in the Norman style, but principally of later date. A court leet is annually held, at which constables and other officers are appointed. At Old Woodstock, and in other parts of the parish, the manufacture of gloves is carried on. Charles Parrott, in 1785, bequeathed £2300 India annuities, now producing about £70 per annum, for the maintenance, education, and apprenticing of twelve boys. Numerous vestiges of Roman occupation have been discovered at various times; on Chaldon hill are the remains of an exploratory camp, near which passes the old Roman road, Akeman-street.

WOOTTON, a township in the parish of ECCLES-HALL, northern division of the hundred of PIREHILL, county of STAFFORD, containing 146 inhabitants.

WOOTTON, a township in the parish of ELLA-STONE, southern division of the hundred of TOTMONS-LOW, county of STAFFORD, 4½ miles (W. by S.) from Ashbourn, containing 245 inhabitants.

WOOTTON (ST. LAWRENCE), a parish in the hundred of CHUTELY, Kingsclere division of the county of SOUTHAMPTON, 4¼ miles (W. by N.) from Basingstoke, containing 664 inhabitants. The living is a vicarage, in the archdeaconry and diocese of Winchester, rated in the king's books at £10. 2. 3½., and in the patronage of the Dean and Chapter of Winchester. The

church has a Norman doorway and several windows in the early English style.

WOOTTON (NORTH), a parish in the hundred of SHERBORNE, Sherborne division of the county of DORSET, 2 miles (S. E. by S.) from Sherborne, containing 64 inhabitants. The living is a perpetual curacy, in the peculiar jurisdiction of the Dean of Salisbury, endowed with £200 private benefaction, and £400 royal bounty, and in the patronage of Earl Digby. The church was anciently a chapel of ease to the vicarage of Sherborne.

WOOTTON (NORTH), a parish in the Lynn division of the hundred of FREEBRIDGE, county of NORFOLK, 2 miles (W. by S.) from Castle-Rising, containing 187 inhabitants. The living is a discharged vicarage, in the peculiar jurisdiction of the Rector of Castle-Rising, rated in the king's books at £10, and in the patronage of Col. Howard. The church is dedicated to All Saints.

WOOTTON (NORTH), a parish in the hundred of GLASTON-TWELVE-HIDES, county of SOMERSET, 4 miles (W. S. W.) from Shepton-Mallet, containing 278 inhabitants. The living is a perpetual curacy, annexed to the vicarage of Pilton, in the peculiar jurisdiction of the Precentor of the Cathedral Church of Wells. The church is a neat plain building. The interest of £104, bequeathed by John Humphreys, is applied in support of a Sunday school.

WOOTTON (SOUTH), a parish in the Lynn division of the hundred of FREEBRIDGE, county of NORFOLK, 2¼ miles (S. W. by W.) from Castle-Rising, containing 151 inhabitants. The living is a discharged rectory, in the peculiar jurisdiction of the Rector of Castle-Rising, rated in the king's books at £8. 6. 8., and in the patronage of the Crown. The church is dedicated to St. Mary.

WOOTTON under WOOD, a parish in the hundred of ASHENDON, county of BUCKINGHAM, 7 miles (N. by W.) from Thame, containing 344 inhabitants. The living is a perpetual curacy, in the peculiar jurisdiction of the Archbishop of Canterbury, endowed with £400 private benefaction, and £400 royal bounty, and in the patronage of the Duke of Buckingham. The church, dedicated to All Saints, was repaired a few years since, when a stone spire was added to the tower; and in the Grenville chapel, or south aisle, which was built in 1343, a columbarium has been more recently constructed by the Duke of Buckingham, for the interment of his family.

WOOTTON-BASSETT, a borough, market town, and parish, in the hundred of KINGSBRIDGE, county of WILTS, 36 miles (N. by W.) from Salisbury, and 87 (W.) from London, containing 1701 inhabitants. This place, which appears to have been originally of greater importance than it is at present, was, at the time of the Norman Conquest, called Wode-

Seal and Arms.

ton, from wode, a wood, and tun, a town: about a century after that period it became the property of the noble family of Bassett, from whom it derived the adjunct to its name. It is pleasantly situated on elevated ground, commanding extensive and pleasingly diversified prospects of the surrounding country, which is extremely fertile and in a high state of cultivation, and consists principally of one street, nearly half a mile in length, neither paved nor lighted, but the inhabitants are amply supplied with water; the houses are in general indifferently built, and of mean appearance. The manufacture of broad cloth, which was formerly carried on here, has entirely ceased, and there is now neither any branch of manufacture, nor trade, beyond what is requisite for the supply of the inhabitants. The Wilts and Berks canal passes within half a mile to the south of the town. The market is on Tuesday; and the fairs, formerly six in number, have been reduced to two, which are held on the Mondays next after the feasts of Pentecost and St. Bartholomew. The town received its first charter of incorporation in the reign of Henry VI., under which, renewed by Charles II., in the thirty-first year of his reign, the government is vested in a mayor, two aldermen, and twelve capital burgesses, assisted by a town clerk and subordinate officers. The mayor is annually chosen by the corporation, who also elect the town clerk; and the inferior officers are appointed by the mayor, who, with the free tenants in the borough, anciently enjoyed the privilege of free common in Fasterne great park, which contained nearly two thousand acres. The borough first exercised the elective franchise in the 25th of Henry VI., since which time it has regularly returned two members to parliament : the right of election is vested in the inhabitant householders paying scot and lot, the number of whom exceeds two hundred : the mayor is the returning officer.

The living is a vicarage, in the archdeaconry of Wilts, and diocese of Salisbury, rated in the king's books at £12, and in the patronage of the Earl of Clarendon. The church, dedicated to All Saints, is an ancient structure. In cleaning the southern wall, some years since, a curious painting was discovered, the subject of which was the murder of Thomas à Becket, executed in a rude style. There is a place of worship for Independents. The free school was founded, in 1688, by Richard Jones, and endowed with lands vested in trustees, now producing about £25 per annum; eighteen poor children are taught to read and write : there are also a charity school for girls, and a Sunday school. At a short distance below the town is a mineral spring, possessing the same properties as that of Cheltenham waters, and much used by those residing in the neighbourhood, though not generally known. An ancient hospital, dedicated to St. John, which formerly existed here, was, during the reign of Henry IV., granted and united to the priory of Bradenstoke, in this county : the old manor-house has been converted into a farm-house.

WOOTTON-COURTNEY, a parish in the hundred of CARHAMPTON, county of SOMERSET, 3 miles (W.) from Dunster, containing 411 inhabitants. The living is a rectory, in the archdeaconry of Taunton, and diocese of Bath and Wells, rated in the king's books at £16. 8. 9., and in the patronage of the Provost and Fellows of Eton College. The church, dedicated to All Saints, is a handsome structure. Limestone abounds in the parish, and there are kilns for burning it. A fair for cattle, sheep, &c., is held on September 9th.

WOOTTON-FITZPAIN, a parish in the hundred of WHITCHURCH - CANONICORUM, Bridport division of the county of DORSET, 4 miles (N. E. by N.) from Lyme-Regis, containing 446 inhabitants. The living is a rectory, in the archdeaconry of Dorset, and diocese of Bristol, rated in the king's books at £8. 15. The Rev. Thomas Fox and another were patrons in 1817.

WOOTTON-GLANVILLE, a parish in the hundred of BUCKLAND-NEWTON, Cerne subdivision of the county of DORSET, 7½ miles (S. S. E.) from Sherborne, containing, with the tything of Wootton-Newland, 309 inhabitants. The living is a rectory, in the archdeaconry of Dorset, and diocese of Bristol, rated in the king's books at £12, and in the patronage of the Devisees in trust of Humphrey Evans. The church, dedicated to St. Mary, is principally in the decorated style, with a low embattled tower of later date ; in the windows are some fragments of ancient stained glass : it was repaired and new pewed in 1741, and contains an altar-tomb with a recumbent figure, also several monuments and inscriptions.

WOOTTON-NEWLAND, a tything in the parish of WOOTTON-GLANVILLE, hundred of BUCKLAND-NEWTON, Cerne subdivision of the county of DORSET. The population is returned with the parish.

WOOTTON-RIVERS, a parish in the hundred of KINWARDSTONE, county of WILTS, 3 miles (N. E.) from Pewsey, containing 400 inhabitants. The living is a rectory, in the archdeaconry of Wilts, and diocese of Salisbury, rated in the king's books at £7. 10. 5., and in the alternate patronage of the Master and Fellows of St. John's College, Cambridge, and the Principal and Fellows of Brasenose College, Oxford : but it must be given to one who has been a scholar, at either, from Somersetshire. The church is dedicated to St. Andrew.

WOOTTON-WAVEN, a parish in the Henley division of the hundred of BARLICHWAY, county of WARWICK, 1½ mile (S.) from Henley in Arden, containing, with the chapelries of Henley in Arden and Ullenhall, and the hamlet of Aspley with Fordhall, 2248 inhabitants. The living is a discharged vicarage, in the archdeaconry and diocese of Worcester, rated in the king's books at £11. 9. 7., endowed with £200 private benefaction, and £200 royal bounty, and in the patronage of the Provost and Fellows of King's College, Cambridge. The church, dedicated to St. Peter, is a noble edifice, principally in the later style of English architecture, with a fine tower rising from the centre ; the south door is of early English architecture, and a small part of the building is in the decorated style. At the east end of the north aisle there is a large desk, in which is a number of old books, containing expositions, by various authors, on the four Gospels ; each volume is secured by a chain of sufficient length to reach outside the desk : they were originally intended for the use of those who, with the permission of the priest, retired thither for study. There is a Roman Catholic chapel at Gromos, the seat of the Dowager Lady Smythe. The Stratford and Avon canal passes through the parish. A Benedictine priory, a cell to the abbey of Conches in Normandy, was founded here by one of the Stafford family, the revenue of which, at the suppression, was granted by Henry VI. to King's College, Cambridge.

Arms.

WORCESTER, a city and county of itself, having exclusive jurisdiction, locally in the county of Worcester, of which it is the capital, 111 miles (N. W. by W.) from London, containing, according to the last census, 17,023 inhabitants, which number has since increased to about 20,000. This place, which is unquestionably of great antiquity, is, under the name of *Caer Guorangon*, enumerated by Nennius in his catalogue of cities belonging to the Britons, by whom, from the advantages of its situation near a fordable part of the river Severn, and on the confines of a thick forest, it was selected, as a place of strength and security. On the expulsion of that people by the Romans, it was, with other British towns, retained by the conquerors; and if not one of their principal stations, as some (judging from the Roman roads in the vicinity appearing to concentrate here) have supposed, it was very probably one of those fortresses which the prætor Ostorius erected on the banks of the Severn, to secure his conquests on that side of the river. It again, on the departure of the Romans from Britain, came into the possession of its ancient inhabitants, from whom it was taken, in 628, by Penda, King of Mercia, whose son Wulfhere, on his accession to the throne of that kingdom, appointed Osric his viceroy over the province of *Huiccia*, including the counties of Worcester and Gloucester, with part of Warwickshire, and forming a portion of the kingdom of Mercia. Osric, either repairing the Roman fortress, or erecting another in this city, which by the Saxons was called *Wigornaceastre*, made it his residence, and fortified it as a frontier against the Britons, who had retreated into the territories on the other side of the Severn. Sexulf, Bishop of Mercia, founded here the first Christian church within his diocese, which he dedicated to St. Peter; and in the reign of Ethelred, that monarch having resolved to divide the kingdom of Mercia into five separate dioceses, Osric prevailed upon him to establish one of them at *Wigornaceastre*, the metropolis of his province; and, in 679, Bosel was consecrated first bishop, by the style of *Episcopus Huicciorum*, and invested with full authority to preside over the ecclesiastical affairs of the province of Huiccia, or Wiccia. From the death of Osric nothing is recorded, either of the province or of the city, till the time of Offa, in one of whose charters Uhtred, a Wiccian prince, is styled *Regulus et Dux propriæ gentis Huicciorum* (ruler and duke of his own people the Huiccii), and his brother Aldred is described as *Subregulus Wigorniæ civitatis*, lieutenant of the city of Worcester, by license of King Offa. After the union of the kingdoms of the Octarchy, Alfred the Great appointed Duke Ethelred, a Mercian prince, to whom he gave his daughter Elfleda in marriage, to the government of Mercia; and in 894, Ethelred and Elfleda rebuilt the city, which had been destroyed by the Danes. Soon after this, Wærfred, Bishop of Worcester, desirous of defending the city and the cathedral from the future attacks of these rapacious invaders, obtained from Ethelred a grant of one moiety of the royal dues, with which he repaired the ancient seat

of the Huiccian viceroys, and erected several fortresses around the cathedral, of which the only one now remaining is Edgar's tower. In 1041, a tax imposed by Hardicanute excited an insurrection of the citizens, who having seized the collectors, after endeavouring to shelter themselves in Edgar's tower, and put them to death, the king, to punish this outrage, sent an army to Worcester, and the inhabitants abandoning the city, retired to the river island Bevere, in which they fortified themselves, determined to hold out to the last extremity. The forces of Hardicanute having plundered and set fire to the city, attacked the inhabitants in their place of refuge, but were so vigorously repulsed, that, after repeated fruitless attempts to dislodge them, the general was compelled to grant honourable terms of capitulation, and the inhabitants returned to their city, and repaired it.

Soon after the Conquest, a royal castle was erected here, of which Urso d'Abitot, who accompanied the Conqueror into England, was appointed constable, and made sheriff of the county. He extended the buildings of the castle, and, to the great annoyance of the monks, infringed upon the site of the cathedral, the outer ward of which occupied what is now the College Green. In 1074, Roger, Earl of Hereford, Ralph de Guader, Earl of East Anglia, and other powerful barons, entered into a conspiracy against William, and invited aid from Denmark; but their design having been discovered, they were obliged to enter the field before the expected succour arrived; and Bishop Wulstan, Urso d'Abitot, and Agelwy, abbot of Evesham, assisted by Walter de Lacey, assembled a body of troops to guard the passes of the Severn, intercepted their progress, and terminated the rebellion. The inhabitants, in 1088, having embraced the cause of William Rufus, the reigning monarch, Bernard de Neumarché, Lord of Brecknock, Osborn Fitz-Richard, Roger de Lacey, Ralph de Mortimer, and other partizans of his elder brother Robert, assembled a large force, and assaulted the city. On this occasion Bishop Wulstan armed his tenants, and retiring into the castle, with the citizens and their wives and children, animated the garrison to a resolute defence. The assailants set fire to the suburbs; but more intent upon plunder than prudent in securing their ground, they spread themselves over the open country, for the sake of pillage; and the garrison taking advantage of the opportunity, sallied from the castle, and advancing upon them suddenly, while in the act of ravaging the bishop's lands at Wick, captured or killed five hundred men, and put the rest to flight. In 1113, the greater part of the city was destroyed by fire, which nearly consumed the cathedral and the castle: this calamity is supposed to have been inflicted by the Welch, who at that time had resolved on the entire devastation of the English marches.

In the reign of Stephen, William de Beauchamp, constable of the castle, having embraced the cause of Matilda, drew upon him the resentment of that monarch, who deposed him from his government, and appointed in his place Waleran, Count of Meulant, whom he created Earl of Worcester. Matilda, in 1139, having gained several advantages in various parts of the kingdom, and greatly increased the number of her partizans, marched from Gloucester with a considerable force, and arriving before Worcester, laid siege to it; but before her arrival, the inhabitants had deposited every thing valuable in the cathedral, and made the necessary preparations for defending their city: the assailants attacked it on the south side, but being repulsed, they renewed the attack on the north side, and gaining an entrance, set fire to it in several places. Having succeeded in obtaining possession of the castle, William de Beauchamp was reinstated in his government by Matilda, and his appointment was subsequently confirmed by her son, Henry II. In 1149, Stephen, to punish the inhabitants for the assistance which they had given to his opponent, took the city and burnt it; but the castle having been strengthened with additional fortifications, resisted all his attempts, and Eustace, his son, having subsequently invested it without success, again set fire to the city in revenge. Worcester, which was so frequently the victim of intestine war and of accidental calamity, was fortified by Hugh de Mortimer against Henry II.; but on the approach of that monarch to invest it, Mortimer having made his submission, received pardon, and the city escaped being damaged. In 1189, it was almost totally destroyed by an accidental conflagration; and in 1202 it again suffered a similar calamity, when the cathedral and adjacent buildings were consumed, but the walls not being demolished, the injury was speedily repaired.

In the contest between King John and the barons, the latter having obtained the aid of Louis, Dauphin of France, the inhabitants adhered to their cause, and opening the gates of the city, received Mareschall, son of the Earl of Pembroke, as governor of the castle for the Dauphin, in 1216; but Ranulph, Earl of Chester, with a body of the royal forces, took that fortress by surprise, and afterwards obtained possession of the city. The inhabitants were made prisoners, and compelled by torture to discover their treasures; the soldiers of the garrison, who had taken sanctuary in the cathedral, were forcibly dragged out; the church and convent were plundered; and a fine of three hundred marks was imposed upon the inhabitants, for the payment of which they were obliged to melt down the precious metals with which the shrine of St. Wulstan was enriched. In the course of the same year, that king was buried in the cathedral of this city. During this reign, Walter de Beauchamp, who had been appointed governor of the castle, having taken part with the barons, was deposed, and his lands confiscated. In 1217, the outer ward of the castle, which was contiguous to the cathedral, was granted to the monks, for the enlargement of their close, by the Earl of Pembroke, guardian to the young king; since which time the Earls of Worcester have ceased to reside in it; the inner ward, comprising the citadel and keep, was alone kept up as a fortress for the protection of the city. In 1218, Bishop Sylvester obtained from Henry III. the grant of an annual fair for four days, in honour of St. Wulstan, to commence on the festival of St. Barnabas. During the reign of this monarch, a great tournament was celebrated here, in the year 1225, in which all who took part were subsequently excommunicated by Bishop Blois. A great part of the city, in 1233, was destroyed by an accidental fire, which greatly damaged the buildings of the cathedral. In 1263, Robert Ferrers, Earl of Derby, Peter de Montfort, son of Simon de Montfort,

Robert, Earl of Leicester, and others of the confederate barons, laid siege to the city, which they took after several assaults; they spared the church, but plundered the houses of the inhabitants, and put several Jews to death. After the battle of Lewes, in which Henry III. was made prisoner, that monarch was brought by the Earl of Leicester to Worcester, whence, together with his son Prince Edward, he was removed to Hereford castle: the latter, having made his escape, repaired hither, where he assembled an army with which he defeated the earl and the confederate barons in the celebrated battle of Evesham. In 1299, the street leading to the suburb of St. John's was destroyed by an accidental fire, which also burnt down the wooden bridge over the Severn, which was afterwards replaced with one of stone. The city, in 1401, was plundered and partly burnt by the forces of Owen Glyndwr, in his repeated attacks upon the English frontiers in the reign of Henry IV., against whom he maintained a desultory warfare for a considerable time; but that monarch advancing against him, drove him back into Wales, and retiring after his victory to Worcester, took up his residence in that city, whence, after disbanding his army, he withdrew privately to London. In the reign of Edward IV., Queen Margaret, after the defeat of her party at the battle of Tewkesbury, and the subsequent murder of her son, was taken from a convent near that town, into which she had retired the day after the battle, by Lord Stanley, and brought before the king, who was then at Worcester. The Duke of Buckingham, in 1484, having raised an army of Welchmen to oppose the claim of Richard III. to the throne, a sudden inundation of the Severn impeded their progress, and disconcerted the enterprise; and after the battle of Bosworth Field, in which that monarch was slain, Worcester was seized for Henry VII.: several of the partizans of Richard were made prisoners here, and beheaded at the high cross, and a fine of five hundred marks was paid to the king for the redemption of the city. In 1486, Sir Humphrey Stafford and his brother, Lord Lovell, having escaped from their sanctuary at Colchester, levied a force of three or four thousand men, and laid siege to this city; but on the approach of an army sent against them by the king, under the command of the Duke of Bedford, they raised the siege and dispersed. During the prelacy of Archbishop Whitgift, Sir John Russel and Sir Henry Berkeley came to the sessions here, with a large band of armed followers, to decide by force a quarrel which had arisen between them; but by the vigilance and activity of the bishop, who placed strong guards at the city gates, they were arrested and brought to his palace, when he prevailed upon them to deliver up their arms to his servants, and appeased their animosity. During the destructive pestilence that raged here in 1637, the inhabitants again abandoned the city, and shut themselves up in the island of Bevere.

In the parliamentary war, Worcester was the first city that openly declared in favour of the king, and the inhabitants opened their gates to admit Sir John Byron, at the head of three hundred cavaliers, whom they assisted to fortify the city against the parliament. These, being afterwards joined by Lord Coventry with some troops of horse, and expecting further aid from the king, began to act on the defensive;

but before the promised succours arrived, Col. Fynes, at the head of one thousand dragoons, and accompanied by the train bands from Oxford, and a detachment of the troops under Lord Say, arrived before the city, and summoned it to surrender to the parliament. The inhabitants indignantly refusing, he immediately commenced the assault; and a shot having been fired into the city, through a hole made in the gate, by one of the parliamentarians, the cavaliers sallied out on the assailants, and having killed several of Col. Fynes' troops, returned without being pursued. Prince Rupert, with his brother Prince Maurice, arriving soon after with a considerable body of troops, joined Sir John Byron, and the royalists drew out their forces into Pitchcroft meadow, adjoining the town, to give the enemy battle. A spirited encounter took place, and was kept up for some time, but Prince Rupert perceiving a considerable reinforcement, under the Earl of Essex, advancing to the assistance of the parliamentarians, withdrew his forces into the city, where the engagement was continued till night, to the great disadvantage of the Prince, who, with a party of his troops, retreated to Hereford in disorder. On the same evening the Earl of Essex arrived, but, for fear of surprise, did not enter the city till the following morning, when the parliamentary troops were quartered in the cathedral, which they stripped of its ornaments, destroyed the altar, and committed every kind of depredation : having explored the vaults, they found a large store of provisions and supplies which had been sent from Oxford for the king's use, and a considerable quantity of plate. The mayor and aldermen were taken into custody for having surrendered the city to the cavaliers, and sent under a strong guard to London ; and two thousand two hundred pounds' weight of plate was sent off under the same escort. A gallows was erected in the market-place, for the execution of such of the citizens as should be found guilty of having betrayed Col. Fynes' soldiers to Prince Rupert; and a commission was appointed by authority of the parliament, under which Sir Robert Harlow and Serjeant Wilde were sent down, to secure the city and try the delinquents; and these officers, as a preliminary step, imposed a fine of £5000 on the inhabitants. After having repaired the fortifications, and obtained from the citizens a loan of £3000 for the parliament, the Earl of Essex divided his army, consisting of twenty-four thousand men, into three brigades; two of them he detached in different directions, to intercept the king's forces on their march towards London ; and leaving a garrison in the city, he advanced at the head of the third brigade to Shrewsbury, in pursuit of that part of the royal army which was headed by the king in person.

The citizens, after the departure of the earl and his army, still maintained their loyalty, and the corporation passed several resolutions in favour of the royal cause : they elected for mayor and sheriff two ardent royalists, provided additional ordnance and ammunition, strengthened the fortifications, and raised levies of money, which they transmitted for the king's use. These measures again drew upon them the vengeance of the parliament, and in March 1646, Sir William Brereton and Colonels Morgan and Birch appeared before the city, with a force of two thousand five hundred foot

and horse, and demanded its surrender; this being peremptorily refused, they drew off their forces at night towards Droitwich, and advanced to assist in the siege of Lichfield. The citizens sent messengers for instructions to the king, who had escaped from Oxford, and was then at Newark; and in the meantime Gen. Fairfax, who was then at Headington, near Oxford, sent a letter to the governor of Worcester, requiring him to deliver up the city to the parliament, and on his refusal despatched Col. Whalley, with five thousand men, to reduce it. The garrison, which consisted of one thousand five hundred men, made a resolute defence, but after having sent various messengers to the king for instructions, and receiving no reply, their ammunition and provisions beginning to fail, and being in hourly expectation of the arrival of Fairfax, with an army of ten thousand foot and five thousand horse, they capitulated on honourable terms, on the 23rd of July. After a respite of five years, Worcester again became the seat of war ; the citizens, still firm in their loyalty to the king, notwithstanding the opposition of the garrison, opened their gates to Charles II., who arrived at the head of a Scottish army of twelve thousand men, attended by the Dukes of Hamilton and Buckingham, and other officers of distinction, on the 22nd of August, 1651; and, after some slight opposition from the garrison, entered in triumph, preceded by the mayor and corporation, by whom, on the following day, he was solemnly proclaimed. On the 28th, Cromwell, at the head of seventeen thousand men, arrived at Red Hill, within one mile of the city, where he fixed his headquarters ; and being soon after joined by the forces under Generals Fleetwood, Lambert, and Harrison, his army amounted to thirty thousand men. General Lambert having surprised a detachment of the king's forces ordered to guard the pass of the Severn, approached to besiege the city ; and the king having concentrated his forces, advanced with the main body of his army, to give battle to Cromwell; a general engagement now took place, and the parliamentarians were beginning to give way, when a reinforcement arriving from the other side of the Severn, the royal forces were overwhelmed, and compelled to retire into the city in disorder. A part of the Scottish troops laying down their arms, and the enemy advancing on all sides, every hope of victory was dispelled ; Cromwell carried the royal fort by storm, putting all the garrison to the sword, and gained possession of the city : the king, attended only by Lord Wilmot, narrowly escaped by the back entrance of the house in which he was quartered, at the moment Col. Cobbet was entering at the front, to make him prisoner; and mounting a horse which had been prepared for him, rode to Boscobel, where he was hospitably entertained and concealed till he found means of escaping into France. The battle was sustained for some time with desperate valour; the citizens made their last stand at the town hall, but without success, and the city was eventually given up to plunder. Cromwell describes his success upon this occasion as a " crowning mercy;" and, in token of his joy for the victory, he ordered a sixty-gun ship, which was soon after launched at Woolwich, to be named the " Worcester."

The city is pleasantly situated at the base and on the acclivity of elevated ground, rising gently from the east bank of the river Severn, over which is a handsome stone bridge of five elliptical arches, connecting it with the suburb of St. John's, built in 1780, at an expense of £29,843, towards defraying which Henry Crabb Boulton and John Walsh, Esqrs., members for the city, contributed £3000. It consists of several spacious and regular streets, of which the Foregate is a stately and lengthened avenue of handsome well-built houses, terminating with a fine view of St. Nicholas' church. The approaches exhibit rich and beautiful scenery, which, in many parts, is pleasingly diversified and strikingly picturesque. Bromsgrove Lickey to the north-east, the Malvern hills to the south-west, the Shropshire hills and the Welch mountains in the distance, are forcibly contrasted with the windings of the Severn, the luxuriant vales, orchards, hop-grounds, and fertile meadows, for which the surrounding country is distinguished. The streets are well paved, lighted with gas, and amply supplied with river water by means of a steam-engine, erected on the eastern bank of the Severn, at a place called Little Pitchcroft, in 1810. An act of parliament was obtained, in 1823, for more effectually paving, lighting, and watching the city, under the authority of which several improvements have recently taken place. A public subscription library was established in Angel-street, in 1790, containing upwards of five thousand volumes: it is now about to be removed to a more eligible situation on the eastern side of the Foregate, near Sansom fields, where a suitable building has been erected by subscription; on the basement story is a large and elegant reading and news-room, over which is an apartment for the library, appropriately fitted up. Two medical societies have been formed, the first in 1796, and the other, to which an extensive and well-assorted library is attached, in 1815; and a society for the encouragement and improvement of native artists has been formed, whose first exhibition of paintings took place in the town hall, in September 1818. The theatre, a neat and appropriate building, erected in 1780, by a tontine subscription, in shares of £50 each, and handsomely fitted up, is opened occasionally; and assemblies and concerts are held in the large room at the town hall. The musical festivals of the choirs of Worcester, Hereford, and Gloucester, take place here in the cathedral, every third year, and are attended by numerous and fashionable audiences: the surplus amount of receipts is appropriated to the benefit of the widows and orphans of the poorer clergy of the associated dioceses. A society for the promotion of this object was formed, in 1778, under the patronage of Bishop North, whose successors are perpetual presidents; for this purpose the diocese is divided into four districts, to each of which two stewards are appointed. Races take place in August and November; at the former time they continue for three days, and are numerously attended: the course is on Pitchcroft meadow, where a grand stand has been erected, near the margin of the Severn, by which the course is bounded on one side.

The manufacture of broad cloth prevailed here to a very great extent in the reign of Henry VIII., at which time there were three hundred and eighty looms, employing eight thousand persons: on its decline the carpet manufacture was introduced, which, after flourishing for a short time, was transferred to Kidderminster. The present manufactures are those of porcelain and gloves, for the former of which this city has obtained a degree of reputation unequalled at home, and not surpassed abroad: the Worcester china is equally valued for its fineness and transparency, the elegance of its patterns, and the beauty of its embellishments. This branch of manufacture was established, in 1751, by Dr. Wall and some other proprietors, and its progress has been rapid and successful: there are at present three manufactories, which contain splendid shew-rooms, visited by persons travelling through Worcester with infinite gratification; from these the principal shops in the metropolis and other great towns are supplied with the most costly of their wares. The glove manufacture is conducted upon a very extensive scale, affording employment to not less than eight thousand persons in the city, exclusively of many thousands in the neighbouring villages: the gloves made are in high estimation, not only in the several parts of England, but in the foreign markets, to which they are exported in great numbers. The manufacture of lace has been recently established here, and is making rapid progress. A distillery upon a large scale, a rectifying establishment, and a British wine manufactory, are conducted; and extensive iron-foundries have been erected on the banks of the canal and the Severn: a considerable trade is carried on in hops, of which there are extensive plantations in the vicinity. The Worcester and Birmingham canal affords great facility of communication between the latter town and the Severn, and for the conveyance of goods from Manchester and the north of England, through Worcester; and the Severn, which is navigable for barges of considerable tonnage, and on the banks of which are commodious quays and spacious warehouses, contributes greatly to promote the trade and commercial prosperity of the city. The market days are Wednesday, Friday, and Saturday: the fairs are on the Saturday before Palm-Sunday, Saturday in Easter week, August 15th, and September 19th, which is a great fair for hops; a cattle fair is also held on the first Monday in December; and there are markets free of toll on the second Monday in February, and on the first Mondays in May, June, July, and November. The market-place, nearly opposite the town hall in High-street, is a spacious and commodious area, erected in 1804, at an expense of £5050: the entrance is through a handsome arched portal of stone, ornamented with pillars of the Tuscan order, supporting a panelled entablature, on each side of which are smaller entrances; the interior is commodiously arranged for the sale of butchers' meat, fish, poultry, and various other articles, and behind it is the vegetable market. The corn market is held at a place so called, being a spacious area at the eastern end of Silver-street. The hop market is held in a spacious area opposite Berkeley chapel, at the south end of the Foregate: the buildings surrounding this area, formerly used as the city workhouse, have been converted into warehouses and offices, of which the rents are applied by the guardians thereof in aid of the poor rates of the several parishes which contributed to their erection: the sales of hops are very considerable, averaging annually about twenty-five thousand pockets.

Corporate Seal.

Worcester was first constituted a city by Wulfhere, the sixth king of Mercia, and additional privileges were granted by Offa and Edgar; the inhabitants were incorporated by Henry I., whose charter was confirmed by Henry II., Richard I., and King John, and afterwards renewed by Henry III., who vested the government in two bailiffs, two aldermen, two chamberlains, twenty-four common council-men, and forty-eight assistants. The charter of incorporation was subsequently confirmed by Edward I., Edw. II., Edw. III., Rich. II., Hen. VII., Hen. VIII., and Edw. VI., and remodelled by James I., in 1621, who erected the city into a county of itself, under the designation of the "City and County of the City of Worcester." Under this charter the government is vested in a mayor, recorder, sheriff, six aldermen, twenty-four common council-men, and forty-eight capital citizens, with a town clerk, two chamberlains, two coroners, and subordinate officers. The mayor, who is chosen annually on the Monday next after the festival of St. Bartholomew, and the aldermen, are elected from the common council-men generally; and the common council-men, as vacancies occur, are chosen from the forty-eight capital citizens. The mayor, recorder, and aldermen are justices of the peace within the city and county of the city. The freedom is inherited by the eldest sons of freemen, and acquired by servitude or purchase. The corporation hold quarterly courts of session for all offences within the city and county of the city, not capital; and a court of record, every Monday, for the recovery of debts to any amount. The town hall is a handsome building of brick, with quoins, cornices, and ornaments of stone, consisting of a centre and two slightly projecting wings, surmounted by a close panelled parapet, decorated with urns and statues; in the centre is a statue of Justice, on each side of which are those of Peace and Plenty: the entrance is ornamented with two engaged columns of the composite order, on one side of which is a niche containing a statue of Charles I., and on the other a statue of Charles II.; the pediment over the entrance is ornamented with the city arms. In a niche occupying the central window of the principal story is a fine statue of Queen Anne; above is a circular pediment, in the tympanum of which are the arms of England, supported by angels. The lower room, which is one hundred and ten feet in length, and twenty-five feet broad, is divided into two parts by the Crown bar on the north, and the Nisi Prius court on the south, and is decorated with several suits of ancient armour. On the upper story is the grand council-chamber, of the same dimensions as the lower room, with circular terminations, and divided into three compartments by two screens of columns crossing the room near the ends; it is lighted by numerous lustres, and is appropriately decorated for civic entertainments and for assemblies, which occasionally take place in it; opposite the principal entrance is a full-length portrait of George III., presented by that monarch when he visited the city in 1788, and it is embellished with various architectural ornaments. This edifice being too small and inconvenient, it is intended to apply to parliament during the present session (1831) for permission to erect a new town hall on a more enlarged plan. The new city gaol and bridewell was built in 1824, at an expense of £12,578. 12. 11.; it comprises eight distinct wards, eight day-rooms, eight airing-yards, with separate rooms for male and female debtors, and a chapel, in which divine service is regularly performed; in one of the yards is a tread-wheel, which is exclusively used for the pumping of water to supply the prison. The county gaol and house of correction was erected in 1809, at an expense of £19,000: it is situated on the north-west side of the town, and comprises twelve wards, with day-rooms, work-rooms, airing-yards, and other requisites: the several departments are connected, by small bridges, with the keeper's house in the centre, in which is also the chapel: there is a tread-mill with three wheels for grinding corn for the use of the prison; and the prisoners are employed in different trades, the produce of which is applied to the support of the prison. The city first exercised the elective franchise in the 23rd of Edward I., since which time it has regularly returned two members to parliament: the right of election is vested in the freemen not receiving parochial relief, of whom, including those non-resident, the number is about three thousand: the sheriff is the returning officer. The assizes and general quarter sessions and the election of knights of the shire, are held in Worcester, as the county town.

Arms of the Bishoprick.

Worcester was first erected into a see in the reign of Ethelred, and, in 679, Bosel was consecrated first bishop. The establishment, which was amply endowed by successive Saxon monarchs, consisted of Secular canons till the eighth century, when a convent, dedicated to St. Mary, was founded near the cathedral church of St. Peter, of which Ethelburga was abbess; on her death it was converted into a monastery for monks of the Benedictine order. The disputes which subsequently arose between the Secular clergy and the monks terminated, in 969, by the surrender of the church of St. Peter to the latter, and the church of St. Mary became the cathedral of the diocese. After the Conquest the establishment continued to increase, and flourished till the dissolution, at which time its revenue was valued at £1386. 12. 10. It was refounded by Henry VIII., for a bishop, dean, archdeacon, ten prebendaries, ten minor canons, ten lay clerks, ten choristers, two schoolmasters, forty king's scholars, and other members. The jurisdiction of the see, with the exception of fifteen parishes and eight chapelries, extends over the whole of the county of Worcester, nearly one-third of the county of Warwick, the parishes of Brome and Clent in the county of Stafford, and the parish of Hales-Owen in the county of Salop. The ancient cathedral church of St. Peter, after its surrender to the monastery of St. Mary, was rebuilt by St. Oswald in 983, but being destroyed by Hardicanute in 1041, Bishop Wulstan, in

1084, founded the present cathedral, which was subsequently enlarged and improved by several of his successors. It is a spacious and venerable pile, in the form of a double cross, with a noble and lofty square tower rising from the centre to the height of two hundred feet: the prevailing style of architecture is the early English, intermixed with portions in the Norman, the decorated, and the later English styles. The tower is a fine composition, enriched with series of canopied niches, in which are statues of kings and bishops, and embellished with sculpture of elegant design. The exterior possesses a simplicity of elegance arising from the loftiness of its elevation and the justness of its proportions; the interior is remarkable for the airiness and lightness of its appearance, and, in many parts, for the correctness of its details and the appropriate character of its embellishments. Part of the nave contains specimens of the Norman style, and, in some places, portions in the decorated: it is separated from the aisles by lofty ranges of finely-clustered columns and pointed arches, and lighted by a fine range of clerestory windows, the tracery of which is in the later style: the roof is finely groined, and ornamented with bosses of flowers, antique heads, and other devices. The choir, to which is an ascent of several steps, is in the early English style; the groining of the roof and the details are in general of very elegant character and in high preservation; the altar-screen is of carved stone, and the pulpit, also of stone and of octagonal form, is richly sculptured with symbols of the Evangelists and devices illustrative of scripture history: the east window, as well as the great west window of the nave, are modern compositions in the later English style; and the bishop's throne and prebendal stalls are richly embellished with tabernacle-work. The Lady chapel, also in the same style, consisting of a nave and aisles, is among the earlier parts of the cathedral, being equally remarkable for the symmetry of its parts and the goodness of its preservation. In the south-eastern transept is the monumental chapel of Prince Arthur, son of Henry VII., in the later style of English architecture, of which it is an elegant specimen, containing his tomb highly enriched with sculpture, emblematical of the union of the houses of York and Lancaster, and other embellishments; adjoining it is the dean's chapel, and to the north the bishop's chapel, with others in various parts of the building. In the centre of the choir is the tomb of King John; the slab bearing the effigy of that monarch is of a date soon after his decease, but the tomb, which is in the later style, was probably erected at the same time as Prince Arthur's chapel. From a supposition, at that time generally prevailing, that this was only a cenotaph of the monarch, whose remains were interred in the Lady chapel, the Dean and Chapter, in 1797, resolved upon its removal to that spot; but on opening it a stone coffin was found, in which were the remains of the king, in good preservation, but on exposure to the air they mouldered to dust. There are several interesting monuments, among which those of Bishops Hough, Maddox, and Johnson, and of Mrs. Rae, are elegant specimens of sculpture. To the south of the cathedral are the cloisters, in the later style of English architecture, enclosing a spacious quadrangular area, on the south side of which is the ancient refectory of the monastery, in the decorated style of architecture, with some elegant windows, and a doorway highly enriched, now appropriated to the use of the king's school. On the eastern side is the chapter-house, in which is the library, an ancient building in the form of a decagon, the roof of which, finely groined, is supported on a central column: the windows are of modern insertion, and the walls are ornamented with a series of Norman intersecting arches. The episcopal palace is a modern embattled edifice of brick, decorated with stone, containing several spacious apartments; the drawing-room is ornamented with portraits of George III. and Queen Charlotte, between which is a marble tablet, recording their presentation to the bishop by their Majesties, who, when on a visit to Worcester, took up their abode in the palace.

The city comprises the parishes of St. Alban, All Saints, St. Andrew, St. Clement (partly in the lower division of the hundred of Oswaldslow), St. Helen, St. Martin (partly in the lower division of the hundred of Oswaldslow), St. Nicholas, St. Peter (partly in the lower division of the hundred of Oswaldslow), and St. Swithin, all in the archdeaconry and diocese of Worcester. The living of St. Alban's is a discharged rectory, rated in the king's books at £5, endowed with £200 private benefaction, £800 royal bounty, and £500 parliamentary grant, and in the patronage of the Bishop: the church claims no particular architectural notice. The living of All Saints' is a discharged rectory, rated in the king's books at £13. 12. 4½., endowed with £200 private benefaction, and £600 royal bounty, and in the patronage of Crown: the church is not remarkable for any architectural features of importance. The living of St. Andrew's is a discharged vicarage, rated in the king's books at £10. 5. 10., endowed with £400 royal bounty, and £800 parliamentary grant, and in the patronage of the Dean and Chapter. The church has recently undergone extensive reparation; the tower, in 1814, was cased with freestone; it is ninety feet in height, and is surmounted by an octagonal spire, one hundred and fifty-five feet six inches high, regularly and symmetrically diminishing from twenty feet at the base, to only six inches and five-eighths at the top, the height of the tower and spire being two hundred and forty-five feet six inches; the whole is terminated by a Corinthian capital, and surmounted by a gilt weather-cock, and forms one of the most striking ornaments of the city: the spire was erected by Nathaniel Wilkinson, a stone mason of the city. The living of St. Clement's is a discharged rectory, rated in the king's books at £5. 5., endowed with £800 royal bounty, and £600 parliamentary grant, and in the patronage of the Dean and Chapter. The church, a small old structure of stone, stood on the eastern bank of the Severn, although the principal part of the parish was on the western side of that river; but being much decayed, and liable to be flooded by the overflowing of the river, a new church, on an enlarged scale, was built, which was opened in 1823. It is in the style of a Saxon church, and is situated on the upper road to Henwick, &c., and is computed to accommodate eight hundred and two persons, and in consequence of a grant of £1000 from the Incorporated Society for promoting the building and enlargement of churches and chapels, four hundred and seven seats are free. The whole cost of its erection was near £6000. The living of St. Helen's is a discharged rectory, rated in the king's books at £11, endowed with £400 private benefaction;

£400 royal bounty, and £600 parliamentary grant, and in the patronage of the Bishop. The living of St. Martin's is a rectory, rated in the king's books at £15. 3. 4., and in the patronage of the Dean and Chapter. The living of St. Nicholas' is a discharged rectory, rated in the king's books at £16. 10. 7½., and in the patronage of the Bishop: the church is a uniform modern structure, with a handsome steeple, and, from its situation in the more open part of the town, forms a conspicuous and interesting object in the perspective of the Foregate and Broad-street. The living of St. Peter's is a vicarage, rated in the king's books at £12. 4. 2., and in the patronage of the Dean and Chapter. The living of St. Swithin's is a discharged rectory, rated in the king's books at £15. 15., endowed with £200 private benefaction, and £400 royal bounty, and in the patronage of the Dean and Chapter. There are places of worship for Baptists, the Society of Friends, those of the late Countess of Huntingdon's connexion, Independents, Wesleyan Methodists, and Roman Catholics.

The royal grammar school connected with the cathedral was founded, at the time of that establishment by Henry VIII., for forty boys, of which number ten are appointed by the dean, and three by each of the prebendaries: the scholars are admitted only for four years, and are required to undergo an examination in the rudiments of Latin, in which, if found deficient, they pay to the head-master £10 for the first year's instruction; they receive annually £2. 6. 8., out of which they have to find a surplice, and to pay £1. 10. per annum to the writing master: there are two exhibitions to Balliol College, Oxford, founded by Dr. Bell, Bishop of Worcester, which are restricted to this diocese. The free grammar school was founded by Queen Elizabeth, in 1561, for twelve boys, to the three senior of whom she assigned thirteen shillings and fourpence per annum for purchasing books: this school stands the third in claim to six scholarships founded by Sir Thomas Cookes, Bart., founder of Worcester College, Oxford, which lead to the six fellowships in that college by the same founder, as vacancies occur. The Rev. John Meek, in 1665, bequeathed to Magdalene Hall, Oxford, estates then producing £100 per annum for ten scholars from this school. Mr. Joseph Worfield, in 1642, assigned to the corporation certain lands and tenements in the parishes of Powick, Leigh, Wicke, and Bransford, in the county of Worcester, in trust for the maintenance and education of fourteen poor boys of the city, or of those parishes, to be elected from any schools whatever by two able and learned men of the degree of master of arts, appointed by the corporation, and to be sent to either of the Universities for seven years: the income is about £240 per annum, which is appropriated to the payment of £30 each per annum to seven students in the University, who have been selected under the will of the testator. The free school and Trinity almshouses, under the management of the six masters appointed by Queen Elizabeth, on establishing the free grammar school, were founded, in 1558, by Mr. Thomas Wilde, who endowed them with land called Little Pitchcroft, and a part of the meadow of Great Pitchcroft, producing, with subsequent donations, an annual income of nearly £300; the school was intended as preparatory for the free grammar school, and the almshouses for the residence and support of aged inhabitants of

the city: the buildings, situated partly in the parish of St. Nicholas, and partly in that of St. Swithin, consist of a school-room, with a dwelling-house for the master, and twenty-nine apartments for the almspeople, who receive each six shillings per month, and half a ton of coal annually; there are at present six boys, who are maintained, clothed, and instructed. Schools for the education of sixteen boys and eight girls were founded, in 1713, by Bishop Lloyd, who endowed them with a small estate in the parish of Aston, in this county, producing at present about £80 per annum: in 1782, a house was purchased by subscription, and fitted up as a school-house, with dwellings for the master and mistress. A British and foreign school is supported by subscription; and there are various Sunday schools.

St. Oswald's hospital was founded prior to 1268, and originally endowed for a master, chaplain, and four brethren; at the time of the dissolution it was given to the Dean and Chapter, but had been dispossessed of a considerable portion of the lands with which it was endowed. In 1660, Dr. John Fell, Bishop of Oxford, having been appointed to the mastership, successfully exerted himself for the recovery of its alienated property: a new charter of foundation was obtained in the 15th of Charles II., and almshouses for ten men and a chapel were erected. Thomas Haynes, Esq., in 1681, built rooms for six additional brethren, and added £50 per annum to its endowment: its present revenue is about £350, which is appropriated to the support of sixteen aged men and twelve women, who have a weekly allowance of money, gratuitous medical attendance, and other advantages. The almshouses founded by Mr. Inglethorpe, in 1619, for six aged men and a woman to attend upon them, have an endowment of £53 per annum, and have been rebuilt and enlarged for nine inmates, who receive each two shillings per week. Mr. John Nash, alderman of the city, founded ten almshouses, which he endowed with lands and tenements in Powick and in the parish of St. Martin, for eight aged men, and two aged and unmarried women to wait upon them: the endowment produces at present an income of more than £360 per annum, which is appropriated to seventeen almspeople, who receive each a weekly allowance of five shillings, and an annual supply of clothing and coal. Mr. Michael Wyatt, in 1725, left property in trust to the mayor and corporation, for the erection and endowment of almshouses for six freemen of the city: the premises are neatly built of brick, and comprise six tenements for aged men, who receive each two shillings per week, a supply of coal, and other relief: the annual produce of the endowment is about £40. Berkeley's hospital was founded, in 1692, by Robert Berkeley, Esq., of Spetchley, in the county of Worcester, who endowed it with £6000 from the rents of his lands, in annual sums of £400, for twelve aged men and one aged woman of the city, who receive each £10 per annum in quarterly payments; and for the payment of £20 per annum to a chaplain for performing service in the chapel. Geary's almshouses, for four aged women, who receive each two shillings and sixpence per week, with a yearly supply of coal, are endowed with about £30 per annum. Shewringe's hospital was founded, in 1702, by Mr. Thomas Shewringe, alderman of the city, who endowed it with messuages, lands, and tenements, in and near

Worcester, producing at present an income of nearly £150 per annum, for six aged women of the parishes of St. Swithin, All Saints, St. Andrew, St. Helen, and St. Clement, and one of the tything of Whistons, with preference to the kindred of the founder : the premises are neatly built of brick, and the inmates receive each a weekly allowance of eight shillings; under the window in each apartment is a stone inscribed with the name of the parish from which, in case of vacancy, the tenant is to be chosen. Mr. William Jarvies, in 1772, bequeathed property, now producing more than £120 per annum, for the support of three aged freemen and one widow, and for apprenticing boys, of the parish of St. Andrew; the pensioners receive each five shillings per week, and have a tenement free of rent; and, in 1567, Mr. John Walsgrove bequeathed eight almshouses to the poor of this parish, which were subsequently endowed with premises, for keeping them in repair, by his son, and with £4 per annum by his grandson; the houses have been rebuilt at a considerable expense, and contain two apartments for each tenant. Some almshouses, founded by Mr. Steynor, as residences for the poor of the parish, have been taken down, and the rents of some other houses, with which they were endowed, are now divided among eight poor people. Several benefactions by the family of Lilley were given to the charity school of the parish of St. Nicholas, and for other uses; the produce, about £12 per annum, is distributed annually in clothes, coal, and bread to the poor of this parish, there being no parochial school. There are numerous other charitable bequests and donations, under the control of the corporation and other trustees, for apprenticing poor children, lending money without interest to young tradesmen setting up in business, for various charitable uses, and for distribution among the poor; in addition to which, Worcester is one of the cities partaking of Sir Thomas White's charity.

The city and county infirmary was established in 1770, and is under the regulation of a president and committee, being liberally supported by the nobility and gentry of the surrounding neighbourhood; the building, which occupies an airy and appropriate situation, adjoining the Pitchcroft meadow, was completed at an expense of £6085. 9. 9., raised by subscription : it has two handsome fronts : the internal arrangements are well adapted, and a considerable quantity of garden and pleasure ground is attached to it. An institution for the relief of lying-in women has been established, and is supported by subscription, under the patronage and management of a committee of ladies. The house of industry, an extensive brick building, occupying an elevated situation to the east of the town, was erected by act of parliament, obtained in 1792, for the accommodation of eight incorporated parishes of the city, the parish of St. Peter not being included; and is under the control of the mayor, for the time being, and a board of twelve directors : the buildings were erected at an expense of £7318, and the purchase of the land belonging to it was £2273. It consists chiefly of a central elevation and two wings, the first one hundred and sixteen feet in length, forty-four in breadth, and forty in height : on the roof of the southern wing, is a capacious reservoir, filled with water by a pump in the brewhouse, whence it is distributed by pipes to the baths, and every other part of this extensive and well-arranged establishment. Behind the house are workshops for the men, and an hospital : further backward is a burial-ground, for those who die in the house; and in front is an extensive plot of ground, with a small building used for reading the burial service, in which the general poor of the united parishes are interred. A female penitentiary has been recently established, and is supported by subscription; and a new dispensary is about to be erected.

Among the ancient monastic establishments were, an hospital, founded in the south-east part of the city, in honour of St. Wulstan, bishop of the see, in 1088, the revenue of which at the dissolution was £79. 12. 6.; the remains of this establishment, which was subsequently denominated the Commandery, and still retains that name, are considerable : a convent of Grey friars, without St. Martin's gate, founded, about the year 1268, by the family of the Beauchamps, Earls of Warwick, the remains of which were for several years used as the city gaol : a convent of Dominican friars, in the west part of the city, the site of which is now covered with buildings : a convent of White nuns of the Benedictine order, which existed at the time of the Conquest, and at the dissolution had a revenue of £53. 13. 7.; the site still bears the name of the White Ladies; a small portion of its ruined chapel is visible; and a farm, about a mile from the city, called the Nunnery, is probably a part of its ancient demesne. The guild of the Holy Trinity was instituted by Henry IV., and, on its dissolution, was converted into an hospital by Queen Elizabeth. Among the distinguished prelates of the see were, the venerable Dr. Latimer, and Drs. Prideaux, Stillingfleet, and Hurd. Florence and William of Worcester were brethren in the monastery; Nicholas Facio de Duillier, a native of Switzerland, and author of several mathematical and philosophical works, resided here for thirty-three years, and was buried in St. Nicholas' church, in 1753; Dr. Thomas, son of Bishop Thomas, and author of a Survey of the Cathedral Church of Worcester; and Drs. Mackenzie, Johnstone, and Wall, eminent medical practitioners, were also residents; the last introduced the manufacture of porcelain, and contributed, by an analysis of its medicinal springs, to bring Malvern into repute as a watering-place. Among the eminent natives was Edward Kelly, noted for his knowledge of chemistry and astrology, born in 1555; John, Lord Somers, a celebrated lawyer; and Mr. Thomas White, a distinguished sculptor and architect. Worcester gives the inferior title of marquis to the Duke of Beaufort.

WORCESTERSHIRE, an inland county, bounded on the west by Herefordshire, on the south and south-east by Gloucestershire, on the east and north-east by Warwickshire, on the north by Staffordshire and a detached portion of Shropshire, and on the north-west by Shropshire. It extends from 52° 0′ to 52° 30′ (N. Lat.), and from 2° 14′ to 3° 0′ (W. Lon.), and, including the detached portions, comprises an area of upwards of seven hundred and eighty square miles, or about five hundred thousand statute acres. The population, in 1821, was 184,424. At the period of the Roman invasion of Britain, the district now included within the confines of Worcestershire is supposed to have been partly occupied by the ancient British tribe of the Cornavii, and partly by that of the

WORCESTERSHIRE

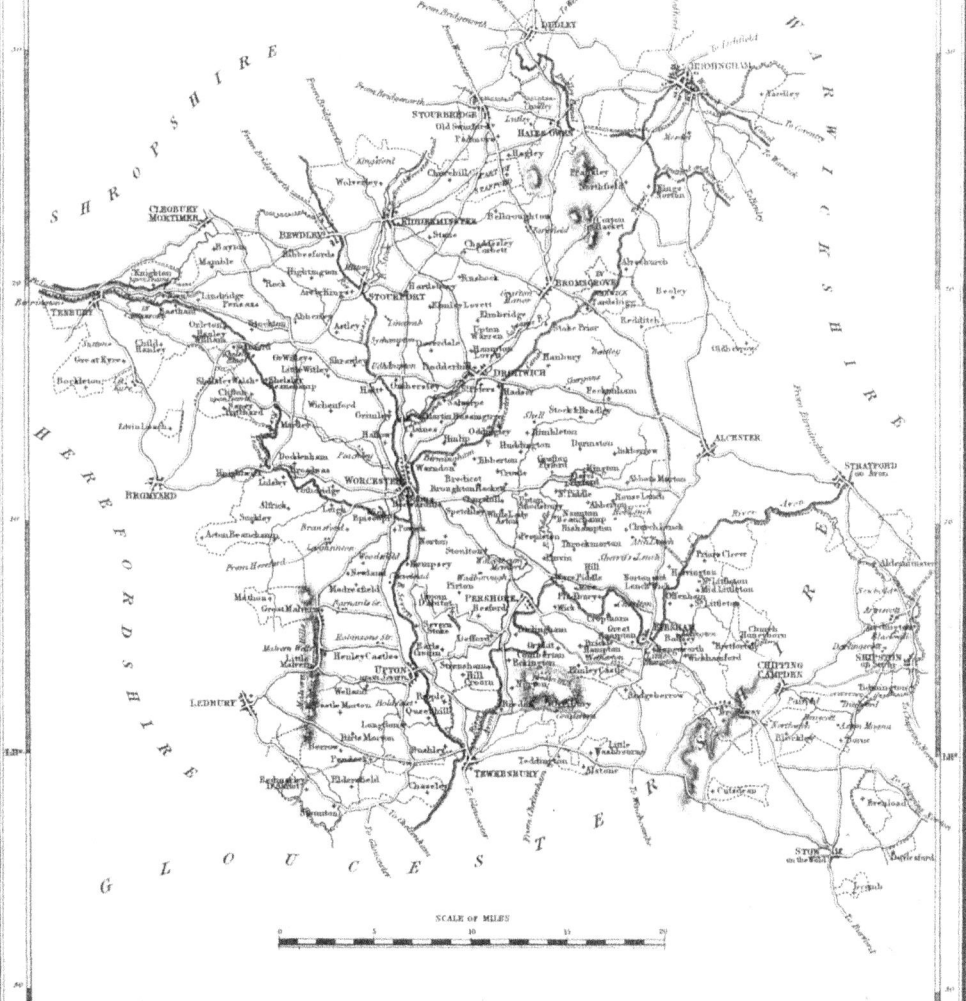

SCALE OF MILES

West 2° Longitude

DRAWN AND ENGRAVED FOR LEWIS TOPOGRAPHICAL DICTIONARY.

Dobuni. Under the Roman dominion it was included in the division called *Flavia Cæsariensis*, but being then for the most part low and woody, it received but little attention from these conquerors. On the complete establishment of the Saxon Octarchy, it was included in the kingdom of Mercia; and in the predatory invasions of the Danes it suffered, at a later period, in common with most other parts of the kingdom. In 1016, the Danish forces under Canute were defeated with great slaughter by Edmund Ironside, near Blockley. During the various internal dissensions which have disturbed the tranquillity of England, no event of importance has transpired within the limits of this county of which the city of Worcester has not been the scene; and as these are minutely narrated in the description of that place, it is unnecessary to recapitulate them here.

This county is in the diocese of Worcester (excepting fifteen parishes and eight chapelries, which are in that of Hereford), and in the province of Canterbury: it forms an archdeaconry, including the deaneries of Blockley, Droitwich, Evesham, Kidderminster, Pershore, Powick, Kington, Warwick, Wich, and Worcester: the total number of parishes is one hundred and seventy-one, of which ninety-two are rectories, fifty-five vicarages, and twenty-four perpetual curacies. For purposes of civil government it is divided into the five hundreds of Blackenhurst, Doddingtree, Halfshire, Oswaldslow, and Pershore, each of which is divided into Upper and Lower, excepting Oswaldslow, which has also a middle division. It contains the city of Worcester; the borough and market towns of Bewdley, Droitwich, and Evesham; and the market towns of Bromsgrove, Dudley, Kidderminster, Pershore, Shipston upon Stour, Stourbridge, Stourport, Tenbury, and Upton upon Severn. Two knights are returned to parliament for the shire, two citizens for the city of Worcester, two burgesses for each of the boroughs of Droitwich and Evesham, and one for that of Bewdley; the county members are elected at Worcester. It is included in the Oxford circuit: the assizes and quarter sessions are held at Worcester, where stands the county gaol and house of correction. There are ninety acting magistrates. The rates raised in the county for the year ending March 25th, 1827, amounted to £93,685. 16., and the expenditure to £92,708. 19., of which £76,954. 6. was applied to the relief of the poor.

The form of the county nearly approaches a parallelogram, two-thirds of the area of which lie to the east of the Severn; but its boundaries are extremely irregular, and its detached portions numerous. Its general appearance, when viewed from the heights bordering it in different parts, is that of a rich plain, the more gentle elevations being hardly discernible. The Vale of the Severn extending through it, from north to south, a distance of about thirty miles, varies in breadth from a quarter of a mile to a mile, and contains about ten thousand acres. The Vale of Evesham is an indefinite tract in the south-eastern part of the county, including the Valley of the Avon, the adjoining uplands to the north of that river, and the whole of the vale land in the southern part of the county and the adjoining parts of Gloucestershire. These vales, together with those of the Avon and the Teme, are but little elevated above the level of the tide in the Severn; and from their level the uplands rise gradually in gen-

tle slopes, swelling to the height of from fifty to two hundred feet. On these elevations there are few instances of extended plains, the country being broken by gentle vales and smoothly swelling hills, the latter of which, towards the north and north-east, and in one or two other directions, much increase in height. To the north-east of Bromsgrove is a ridge of hills, called the Lickey, which extends to Hagley, and has various branches eastward: some of its highest peaks rise to the height of nearly nine hundred feet. The Abberley hills, in the north-western part of the county, extend over the parish of Abberley, and are seen to a great distance, rising to about the same height as the last-mentioned: Witley hill is a little to the southward of these. Bredon hill is another remarkable elevation, to the south of Pershore, and on the south-eastern side of the Avon, rising to the height of nearly nine hundred feet. But by far the loftiest tract is the Malvern hills, a chain extending from north to south, upon a base about six miles in length and from one to two in breadth: a line passing along the summit of this ridge separates Worcestershire from Herefordshire: the most elevated point attains the height of one thousand three hundred and thirteen feet above the Severn. The views obtained from most of these eminences are remarkable for their beauty and extent, particularly those from the Malvern hills; and their rocky summits give a picturesque diversity to much of the scenery. The districts lying between Droitwich and Bromsgrove, and those extending from the latter town northward, possess, however, little of the richness and beauty of the general landscape; but peculiarly pleasing and extensive views are obtained from the Broadway hills, near the village of Broadway; Stagbury hill, near Bewdley; the Witchbury hills, near Hagley; Woodbury hill, near the banks of the Teme; the rising ground to the east of Worcester; and various other points. The climate, more particularly in the middle, southern, and western parts of the county, is mild, salubrious, and favourable to every process of vegetation. The most elevated tracts, more particularly those lying to the north-east of Bromsgrove, are much colder, and have frequently a bleak aspect. The seasons here are much more early than in any of the surrounding counties, more particularly the northern ones, the common meadow flowers making their appearance a fortnight sooner than in Staffordshire.

The soils are remarkable for their general fertility, and add a peculiarly rich verdure to a district presenting great beauty of outline, and enjoying an eminently fine climate. Those of the vallies traversed by the principal rivers consist of a deep rich sediment, which has been deposited by floods during a long series of ages: this sediment is in some places a pure clay, adapted to the making of bricks, but generally consists of a rich mould. The vallies of the Severn, the Avon, the Stour, the Salwarpe, and nearly all the smaller streams, consist of rich natural meadows and pastures; while that of the Teme abounds also with hop-plantations and orchards. In the valley of the Stour some small tracts of peat bog are found: the extent of this kind of soil, bordering on the rivers, is estimated at about fifty thousand acres. Rich clay and loamy soils occupy nearly half the county in its middle, southern, and western districts, and, besides the ordinary crops of other counties, produce great quantities of hops and fruit. The substrata of the Vale of Evesham are various, being sometimes a yellowish gravel, and at others a clay, which is unfit for making bricks, as containing calcareous particles. About Kidderminster and Stourbridge light sandy soils prevail to a very great extent; some of them are poor and barren, as at Mitton and Wolverley; others rich and fertile: the sands of Wolverley are in many places of considerable depth, or terminate in a sandy rock of various depths. To the north-east of Bromsgrove, including the hilly cultivated tracts, a mixed gravel abounding in springs, and a gravelly loam, are found: in this north-eastern part of the county some of the hilly grounds have also a moist clay loam on a broken rocky substratum, and a lighter loam on clay, with a similar substratum: the lands on Bromsgrove Lickey have often a deep substratum of sand; but, on the higher parts of it, they frequently rest immediately upon an irregular granitic rock, or upon a soft pudding-stone. The waste lands in the eastern part of the county, which are but of small extent, have generally a deep black peaty soil. The Abberley hills and Witley hills have a strong wet clay, resting on limestone.

The soil and climate being well adapted to the production of every kind of grain in abundance, the agriculture of the county is less subject to any characteristic system than that of almost any other: the drill husbandry is practised chiefly on the hills and lighter soils. The amount of arable land is estimated at three hundred and sixty thousand acres: the crops most generally cultivated are, wheat, barley, oats, beans, peas, vetches, turnips, and hops. Four varieties of wheat are commonly sown, and annually occupy about forty-three thousand five hundred acres. Nearly one thousand acres in the sandy parts of the county are annually sown with rye, much of the produce of which is sold to be sown as early spring food for sheep. Barley is sown after turnips on all lands where the latter crop is grown, in conjunction with clover and grass seeds, and is calculated to occupy about thirty-three thousand acres annually. Oats are grown on a much smaller scale, being seldom cultivated on the richer soils: beans are grown to a considerable extent on the strong soils, but peas only to a limited degree; vetches are in common cultivation in almost every part of the county, and are chiefly employed as green food for horses. Turnips are extensively and successfully grown on the more friable soils; the Swedish turnip is also cultivated, but only to a small extent: cabbages are sometimes an agricultural crop. The sands of Wolverley are famous for their produce of carrots and carrot seed; an average crop of the former is fifteen tons per acre: for the most part they are sold to persons who carry them to the markets of Birmingham, Stourbridge, or the populous parts of Staffordshire; much of the seed is frequently sold to the London dealers. Potatoes are grown in great plenty, particularly in the neighbourhood of Bromsgrove, and large quantities are sent to Birmingham and the southern parts of Staffordshire. Worcestershire has long been famous for the culture of hops, which annually occupy about six thousand acres, in all cases upon a deep rich loam, or a peaty soil, plentifully manured: many hopgrounds on the banks of the Teme receive occasional irrigation from the overflow of that river, whose waters are of a peculiarly fertilizing quality. Three sorts of hops are here cultivated, distinguished as red, green, and white: the picking is performed, in September, by great numbers of women and children from the neighbouring populous counties and from Wales, some of whom come a distance of from thirty to forty miles: the produce, though varying extremely, is estimated to average about five hundred weight per acre. Flax and hemp are sometimes grown, though not very commonly, nor to a great extent. The principal artificial grasses are, red and white clover, trefoil, and ray-grass; and the seeds of the common grasses are also occasionally sown on the vale lands: much clover is annually seeded: chicory and burnet, though common native plants, are not cultivated.

The extensive vales, particularly that of the Severn, consist of meadows and pastures of a particularly rich quality, maintaining their verdure nearly all the year, and occupying an extent of about fifty thousand acres: almost any proportion of this land may be mown at pleasure, and a great quantity of hay is sent to the mining districts of Shropshire and Staffordshire. There are, besides, nearly fifty thousand acres of permanent upland pasture, including parks and pleasure grounds. Few instances of artificial irrigation occur, but the natural meadows derive nearly all their fertility from the periodical overflow of the rivers which traverse them. A part of the pastures is grazed by cows belonging to the dairies, the produce of which is chiefly butter, for home consumption and the supply of Birmingham, and cheese made of skimmed milk: in some dairies, however, cheese only, of a good quality, is made. Great numbers of sheep and cattle are fattened in the rich meadows, chiefly in the southern and western parts of the county; many cattle are also fattened in stalls during the winter, a very great proportion of them being driven to the London market. Lime is extensively used as a manure on the gravelly and sandy soils of the north-eastern part of the county, where marl is also occasionally employed; horn shavings, leather shreds, ashes, soot, and offal salt from the works at Droitwich, are in some places used for the same purpose to a small extent.

The cattle are of various sorts, few being bred in the county: those most esteemed are the Hereford and long-horned breeds, the latter being chiefly bought at the fairs of Staffordshire and Shropshire: besides these, almost all the other surrounding counties furnish Worcestershire with various kinds of cattle, to be fattened in its rich vales; for which purpose also great numbers of Welch, Yorkshire, and even Scotch, cattle are imported. The only peculiar kind of sheep is the common, or waste-land, breed, occupying all the wastes, except those in the southern parts of the county: they are without horns, and are supposed to have sprung from the same stock as the South Down sheep, and the Cannock-heath sheep of Staffordshire. In the enclosures are found the Cotswold (which also occupy the southern wastes), the Ryeland, the Leicester, the South Down, and various other breeds and mixtures; besides which, many of the Somersetshire, Wiltshire, and Dorsetshire breeds are annually bought in, chiefly for the purpose of being fattened: folding is not commonly practised. The hogs are chiefly of a large white slouch-eared kind: much bacon is consumed in the county; the surplus assists in the supply of the adjoining manufacturing districts of Warwickshire, Staffordshire, &c. Few horses are bred: the sort most commonly used is of a strong black breed. The extent of land applied to the raising of vegetables for human food is estimated at about five thousand acres, for, besides the gardens commonly attached to country houses, there are very considerable horticultural tracts near the principal towns, more particularly on the north-eastern side of Worcester, and on the northern side of the town of Evesham, in the vicinity of which latter place there are about three hundred acres of garden ground, which, besides producing all the other ordinary vegetables, supply the cities of Bath and Bristol, and the town of Birmingham, with considerable quantities of early peas and asparagus: great quantities of cucumbers and onions are exported from the same district, chiefly to the last-mentioned town; much onion seed is also produced there. This county has for many centuries been famous for its orchards, which flourish in a degree unknown to most other parts of the kingdom; they are situated chiefly around the towns, villages, and farm-houses, chiefly of the middle, southern, and western parts of the county, where the various kinds of fruit-trees are also frequently dispersed in the hedge-rows, and form an important source of profit, though their produce is very uncertain. The average quantity of cider and perry made is remarkably great, for, besides supplying the consumption of the county, which is very considerable, a large surplus, together with great quantities of raw fruit, is exported to other parts of the kingdom.

Worcestershire is adorned with a plentiful store of timber: in many parts are oak coppices of different degrees of growth, and in some are small tracts of the finest oak and ash timber, particularly in the neighbourhood of the different seats: the most important produce of the underwoods is, poles for the hop-yards, and charcoal for the iron-works. The Forest of Wyre, on the north-western border of the county, near Bewdley, partly in this county and partly in that of Salop, is a great nursery for oak-poles and underwood, which are cut at stated periods, leaving trees for timber at proper distances: the oak-poles, after being stripped of their bark, are sold, under the name of "black poles," for making rails, hurdles, laths, &c. Some parts possess beech timber of excellent quality, and many of the precipitous heights bordering on the Severn, and the hills in some other places, are ornamented with large plantations of fir. The hedge-rows, too, throughout a large portion of the most fertile districts, are well stocked with some of the most valuable elm timber in the kingdom, more particularly in the parishes of Hartlebury, Elmley-Lovett, Ombersley, &c.; great quantities of which are regularly cut down and sent to Birmingham, or exported by the Severn and the canals. On the borders of the rivers are many poplar and willow plantations, more particularly along the course of the Teme. The waste lands do not, at most, exceed twenty thousand acres, and consist of high hilly tracts, or of small commons and wastes, dispersed in various quarters: at present they are in a state of nature, overrun with furze, heath, and fern, and affording only a scanty summer maintenance for a few sheep of an inferior kind, and for a still smaller number of cows and horses. Of the hilly wastes, the principal are the upper parts of the Malvern hills,

which are very rocky; of Bredon hill, near Pershore; and of the Abberley and Witley hills, together with some of the unenclosed parts of Bromsgrove Lickey. Wyre Forest, to the left of Bewdley, besides its woodlands, comprises also a considerable portion of open land. The fuel consumed is chiefly coal, a small portion of which is obtained from the mines in the county; but by far the greater quantity, which is also of excellent quality, is imported, by the canals and the Severn, from the rich mines of Staffordshire and Shropshire.

The mineral productions are of minor importance. Coal is obtained in the north-western part of the county, particularly at Mamble, which place communicates, by means of an iron railway, with the Leominster canal; and again at Pensax, where the small refuse is partly converted into coke, highly esteemed for the drying of hops, and is partly used for burning the limestone obtained at Witley hill; but the seam is only from two feet to two feet six inches thick, and lies at the depth of about twenty yards, from which the water is raised in buckets. Common rock salt and a species of gypsum are found at Droitwich. Limestone of the lias formation forms the substratum of nearly the whole south-eastern portion of the county, and is worked at South Littleton and other places: the kind called by geologists "mountain limestone" is found in the hills of the north-western part, and is burned in several places, particularly at Witley and Huddington. The town of Dudley is situated at the southern extremity of a range of limestone hills, which extends northward into Staffordshire; and this, upon which stands the castle and part of the town, is completely undermined by stupendous quarries. Freestone for building is obtained in several places. The Malvern hills are formed chiefly of a kind of decomposed granite, with which, on their northern side, gneiss is connected, and on their eastern, sienite. The precipitous swells of Bromsgrove Lickey are composed chiefly of quartz, a siliceous stone, much resembling the granite of the Malvern hills: in the Broadway hills a reddish stone is quarried. In the Vale of Evesham, in the parishes of Badsey, the three Littletons, and Prior's Cleeve, are quarries of a calcareous flag-stone, about three inches thick, and of a very durable quality, some of it bearing a fine polish: considerable quantities are raised for gravestones, kitchen floors, barn floors, &c., and much of it is exported by means of the Avon navigation. Brick clay, gravel, sand, and marl, exist in numerous places. The most remarkable fossil production is that found in the limestone at Dudley, thence called the "Dudley locust."

The manufactures are various, extensive, and important. Those of gloves and porcelain are carried on at Worcester. Stourbridge has an extensive manufacture of glass, which has long flourished both there and at Dudley: and at both places the iron manufacture is carried on to a very considerable extent. Nails, needles, and fish hooks, are made at Bromsgrove, also at Redditch, on the border of Warwickshire. Kidderminster is famous for its carpets; and the manufacture of bombazines is still carried on, but not so extensively as formerly. On the river Stour and its tributary streams are several very considerable iron-works, in which the pig-iron from the foundries of Shropshire, Staffordshire, and other mining districts, is rendered malleable, and worked into bars, rods, sheet-iron, &c. The manufacture of salt, at Droitwich, is known to have been practised so early as the year 816, when this county formed part of the Saxon kingdom of Mercia : it is here made from inexhaustible brine springs, which lie at the depth of about eighty feet, and, when bored into, immediately rise and fill the pit dug to receive their waters. The commerce of the county is greatly facilitated by its extensive canal and river navigation. Worcester is the great mart for the hops, fruit, cider, and perry produced in this county and that of Hereford. The quantity of hops brought to market varies, according to the plentifulness of the crop, but is supposed to average about thirty-six thousand hundred-weight. An idea of the quantity of fruit exported may be formed from the fact, that the cargoes sent northward consisting chiefly of apples and pears, have, in some years, amounted to upwards of two thousand tons; besides which, considerable quantities are carried out of the county from the markets of Bewdley, Kidderminster, Bromsgrove, &c. The cider annually exported amounts to about ten thousand hogsheads, of one hundred and ten gallons each; the perry to about a tenth part of that quantity. Of the wheat, barley, and beans, grown in the county, the surplus is very great, and finds ready carriage to Birmingham and the populous parts of Staffordshire and Shropshire, or down the Severn, to be conveyed coastwise. Fat cattle, sheep, and hogs, are supplied for the London market, and the manufacturing districts of Warwickshire and Staffordshire : about two thousand packs of wool, of two hundred and forty pounds each, are annually exported; as also are clover and grass seeds, hay, and timber.

The principal rivers are the Severn, the Upper Avon, the Teme, and the Stour. The Severn enters on the northern border of the county, a little above Bewdley, and flows southward by that town, Stourport, Worcester, and Upton, to the vicinity of Tewkesbury, where it quits it for Gloucestershire, but forms the eastern border of a projecting portion of Worcestershire for a short distance below that town, in the vicinity of Chaseley. The channel of this noble river, in this part of its course, is generally from eighty to one hundred yards wide, though sometimes considerably more; its depth averages from five to six yards, and it has a fall of about a foot in a mile; shortly before it quits the county it meets the tide, and becomes deep and tranquil. It is navigable for vessels of eighty tons' burden as high as Worcester bridge, and for those of sixty in the higher part of its course through the county; but the navigation, though of great benefit and importance, is frequently impeded in the summer by sands and shoals. Salmon, chad, lamprey, and lampern, are the most remarkable fish in this part of its course, but are not so abundant as formerly. By the statute of the 30th of Charles II., c. ix., the conservancy of the Severn, within the limits of the county, is granted to the magistrates of Worcestershire. The Upper Avon enters the county from Warwickshire, a little above the village of Prior's Cleeve, whence it pursues an extremely devious course through the Vale of Evesham, by the towns of Evesham and Pershore, to that of Tewkesbury in Gloucestershire, where it enters the Severn, after forming, for several miles, the boundary between this county and a projecting por-

tion of Gloucestershire. So early as the year 1637, this river was made navigable, with the aid of locks, in the whole of its course through Worcestershire, a distance of about twenty miles. The Teme, from the borders of Shropshire and Herefordshire, first touches this county at its north-western extremity, and, flowing eastward, enters it a little below Tenbury, then takes a bending south-easterly course until it becomes the western boundary between Martley and Lulsley; hence it flows east-south-eastward, and falls into the Severn about a mile and a half below Worcester : the channel of this river has too great a declivity, and its waters are too shallow, to admit of its being navigated higher than a small distance above Powick bridge : the scenery on its banks is particularly beautiful. The Stour, rising in a detached portion of Staffordshire, nearly surrounded by the northern part of this county, flows northward by Hales-Owen, which is a detached part of Shropshire, and thence eastward to Stourbridge, in this county, which, however, it immediately quits for the southern part of Staffordshire, but re-enters it a little above Wolverley, whence it takes its course southward by Kidderminster to the Severn at Stourport : this stream is navigable for a short distance to some of the iron-works on its banks. Besides these, the stream called the Salwarpe descends from the Lickey, by Bromsgrove and Droitwich, to the Severn, about three miles above Worcester : the Ledden borders the county for a few miles at its south-western extremity; and the Rhea, rising between Frankley and Chadwick, flows north-eastward to Birmingham : the smaller streams are particularly numerous.

The Trent and Severn canal, or, as it is more commonly called, the Staffordshire and Worcestershire, enters the county from Staffordshire, near Wolverley, and thence proceeds down the valley of the Stour, and by the town of Kidderminster, to the navigable channel of the Severn, at Stourport, into which it opens through a spacious basin : the length of that part of its course included in Worcestershire is about nine miles, in which it has nine locks, and a fall of ninety feet : this canal, one of the works of the celebrated Brindley, is that branch of the Grand Trunk canal which unites the navigation of the Severn with the water communication between the rivers Trent and Mersey : the act for its formation was obtained in 1766, and it was completed about the year 1770. The Droitwich canal, from that town to the Severn, down the valley of the Salwarpe, was constructed soon after the above, and by the same engineer : it is five miles and a half long, with five locks and a fall of about sixty feet : the cost of its formation was £25,000. The noble canal from Birmingham to the Severn, immediately below Worcester, called the Birmingham and Worcester canal, for vessels of sixty tons' burden, commences with a short tunnel in the vicinity of the first-mentioned town, where it communicates with the Birmingham, Birmingham and Fazely, and Birmingham and Warwick canals, and proceeds nearly southward, across two valleys, over which it is conveyed by extensive embankments to a little beyond King's Norton, where it passes through another tunnel, upwards of a mile in length, and then, after completing its summit level of sixteen miles and three quarters from the wharfs at Birmingham, descends south-eastward from the towns of Bromsgrove and Droitwich, by a lockage of four hundred and fifty feet fall to the Severn: it has also other tunnels, of smaller extent than the last; the act of parliament for its formation was obtained in 1791: its total length is twenty-nine miles. The Dudley Extension canal branches from it near Selly Oak, and thence proceeds westward, through a long tunnel to Hales-Owen, a short distance beyond which it is carried through another tunnel, and, on emerging, pursues a winding northerly course to Dudley, and there passes through a tunnel under the limestone hills, nearly two miles in length, into the county of Stafford, where it forms a junction with the Birmingham canal from that town to Wolverhampton: its total length is thirteen miles. The Stratford upon Avon canal branches from the Birmingham and Worcester canal near King's Norton, and thence proceeds eastward, through a small tunnel, into Warwickshire. The Kington, Leominster, and Stourport canal was projected towards the close of the last century, the first act of parliament for the execution of the design having been obtained in 1791; but the expense was found far to exceed the sum at first computed, and only the part of its course between Leominster and Stourport has been completed: this enters the county on the northern bank of the Teme, a little below Tenbury.

The turnpike roads are generally in good repair, being relieved from the wear of heavy carriage by the navigable rivers and canals. The road from London to Welchpool, enters from Gloucestershire, and passes through Pershore, Worcester, and Tenbury, to Ludlow in Shropshire: the road from London to Aberystwith branches from this, near Worcester, on the opposite side of the Severn, directly westward to Bromyard in Herefordshire. Another road from London to Worcester enters from Chipping-Campden, and passes through Evesham. The road from London to Shrewsbury and Holywell, by Bridgenorth, enters from Alcester in Warwickshire, and passes through Bromsgrove and Kidderminster, to Bridgenorth in Shropshire. The road from London to Kidderminster, by Birmingham, enters from Hales-Owen, and passes through Stourbridge to Kidderminster. The road from London to Birmingham passes through Shipston upon Stour, and through the north-western extremity of the county, which is also crossed by the road from London to Birmingham, through Warwick. The Roman roads were, the *Iknield-street*, which passed northward, from Alcester in Warwickshire, through its north-western extremity, into Staffordshire; another, which passed from Worcester into Shropshire; a third, from Worcester, southward by Upton, to Tewkesbury, where it joined the *Iknield-street*; and the *Ridge-way*, which bounds the county for several miles, on the east. Numerous vestiges of them are still visible; as also of a fosse-way which passes through the detached parish of Blockley, and an ancient road which crossed Hagley common, now called the King's Head Land. Stukeley supposes Upton, on the banks of the Severn, to have been the *Ypocessa* of the Romans; and Worcester, from the termination of its name and other circumstances, appears to have been either a Roman station, or a fort.

The remains of antiquity include few very remarkable objects. Near the Fourshire Stone, at a point where the counties of Worcester, Gloucester, Warwick and Oxford meet, there is a small earthwork, supposed by Gough to be of British construction; and there are traces of other ancient encampments in the vicinities of Bredon, Kempsey, and Malvern; as also on Witchbury hill, Woodbury hill, and Conderton hill, in the parish of Overbury. Various coins of the Lower Empire have been found in the vicinity of Hagley, particularly near the large camp on Witchbury hill; and on Clent heath, about half a mile from Witchbury, are five barrows, assigned by popular tradition to the Romans, which, on being opened, were found to contain burnt wood, ashes, and bones. The number of religious houses, including colleges and hospitals, was about twenty-eight. There yet exist remains of the abbeys of Bordesley, Evesham, and Pershore; of the Commandery of St. Wulstan at Worcester; of the priories of Dodford and Great Malvern; and of the nunnery of Cokehill, in the parish of Inkberrow. The most remarkable specimens of ecclesiastical architecture are, the cathedral of Worcester, and the churches of Church-Lench, Droitwich, Eastham, All Saints at Evesham, Great Malvern, Holt, Naunton-Beauchamp, Pedmore, Rock, Stockton, and St. Alban, St. Andrew, and St. Clement at Worcester. The fonts most worthy of notice are those of Chaddesley-Corbett and Eastham: at several places are ancient chapels in different states of preservation. There are remains of the ancient castles of Dudley; Ham, near Clifton upon Teme; Hartlebury; and Holt. Worcestershire contains a considerable number of elegant mansions: among the principal are, Croome Park, the seat of the Earl of Coventry, the lord-lieutenant of the county; Hartlebury Castle, that of the Bishop of Worcester; Hewell Park, that of the Earl of Plymouth; Madresfield, that of Earl Beauchamp; Northwick Park, that of Lord Northwick; Ombersley Court, that of the Marchioness of Downshire; Witley Court, that of Lord Foley; Hagley Park, that of Lord Lyttelton; Hanbury Hall, that of John Phillips, Esq.; and Stanford Court, that of Sir Thomas Winnington, Bart. The mineral springs are very numerous: the most noted are the chalybeate waters of Bredon, Bromsgrove (which are also petrifying), Hallow Park near Worcester, Kidderminster, and Worcester; and those of other qualities at Abberton, near Naunton-Beauchamp, and at Churchill. But the Malvern wells, which possess various properties, are by far the most celebrated, and, in conjunction with the fine climate and scenery of the surrounding country, have rendered the town of Great Malvern a place of fashionable resort. The produce of the salt springs of Droitwich has been noticed above.

WORDWELL, a parish in the hundred of BLACK-BOURN, county of SUFFOLK, 6 miles (N. by W.) from Bury St. Edmunds, containing 48 inhabitants. The living is a discharged rectory, in the archdeaconry of Sudbury, and diocese of Norwich, rated in the king's books at £7. 7. 3½., and in the patronage of R. B. de Beauvoir, Esq. The church is dedicated to All Saints.

WORFIELD, a parish in the Hales-Owen division of the hundred of BRIMSTREE, county of SALOP, 3¾ miles (N. E. by E.) from Bridgenorth, containing 1582 inhabitants. The living is a discharged vicarage, in the archdeaconry of Stafford, and diocese of Lichfield and Coventry, rated in the king's books at £16. 15., endowed with £200 private benefaction, and £200 royal bounty, and in the patronage of W. Y. Davenport, Esq. The church is dedicated to St. Peter. William Lloyd and Thomas Parker, in 1613, conveyed certain estates, now producing an annual income of about £46, in trust for the maintenance of a school, in which thirteen children are educated.

WORGRET, a tything in that part of the parish of EAST STOKE which is in the hundred of HUNDREDS-BARROW, Blandford (South) division of the county of DORSET, 1 mile (W.) from Wareham. The population is returned with the parish.

WORKINGTON, a parish in ALLERDALE ward above Darwent, county of CUMBERLAND, comprising the market town and sea-port of Workington, the chapelry of Great Clifton, and the townships of Little Clifton, Stainburn, and Winscales, and containing, exclusively of seamen, 7188 inhabitants, of which number, 6439 are in the town of Workington, 34 miles (S. W. by W.) from Carlisle, and 310 (N. W. by N.) from London. The only historical circumstance of interest connected with Workington is its having been the place where, in 1568, Mary, Queen of Scots, landed, when she sought an asylum in England, after her escape from the field of Langside : she was hospitably entertained at Workington Hall (the apartment she occupied being still called the Queen's chamber), until Queen Elizabeth gave directions for her removal to Carlisle castle. The town is situated on the southern bank of the Derwent, near its influx into the sea; and, in addition to the older part, which is narrow and irregular, contains some more recent streets, in which are many handsome and well-built houses : it is not lighted, and is badly paved with pebbles, but well supplied with water from the Derwent. There is a small theatre in Christian-street, and an assembly and news room in the Square. The Hall, the ancient seat of the Curwens, occupies an eminence on the south side of the river, commanding beautiful views of the surrounding country, the sea, and Scotland. Upon the Cloffocks, an extra-parochial meadow, or island, situated north-east of the town, on the banks of the Derwent, races are annually held in August. A handsome stone bridge, of three arches, crosses the river, at the entrance into the town from Maryport, which was erected, in 1763, at the expense of the county. The trade principally arises from the exportation of coal to Ireland, in which more than one hundred vessels are employed. There were belonging to the port, in 1828, one hundred and twenty-six, with a burden amounting, in the aggregate, to nearly twenty thousand tons. The harbour has been secured by the erection of a breakwater within these few years, and is now one of the safest on the coast : the entrance is lighted with gas. Great improvement has been also effected by enlarging the quays, owing to the indefatigable exertions of the late Mr. Curwen. The collieries give employment to about five hundred persons; the mines are drained by an engine of more than one hundred and fifty horse power. There are three ship-builders' yards, in which vessels of from three hundred to four hundred tons' burden are constructed, besides two patent slips : the manufacture of cordage and other articles connected with the shipping is carried on, though not so extensively as formerly ; there is also a manufactory for imitation Leghorn hats,

giving employment to upwards of four hundred men, women, and children, during the summer months, in the preparation of the straw, which is grown in the neighbourhood : the manufacturer has received a patent for the invention. The salmon fishery, for which Camden mentions this place to have been famous, although not so productive as in his time, is still pursued in the Derwent and along the coast. The markets are on Wednesday and Saturday, that on the former day being the principal : it is a large corn market, and has recently been removed to Washington-street : there is another market-place, for butter, poultry, &c., which is connected with convenient shambles for butchers' meat. The fairs, on the 18th of May and October, have nearly fallen into disuse. Manor courts are held occasionally, and the county magistrates hold petty sessions, every Wednesday, at the Public office in Udale-street.

The living is a rectory, in the archdeaconry of Richmond, and diocese of Chester, rated in the king's books at £23. 5., and in the patronage of Henry Curwen, Esq. The church, dedicated to St. Michael, and rebuilt in 1770, is a handsome structure, in the later style of English architecture, with a square tower, situated at the west end of the town. A chapel of ease, dedicated to St. John, has recently been erected, under the auspices of His Majesty's commissioners for building churches, the first stone of which was laid on the 15th of April, 1822 : it is a handsome building of the Tuscan order, with a portico and cupola, and contains one thousand four hundred and ninety sittings, of which nine hundred and ninety are free; the expense was upwards of £10,000. There are places of worship for Independents, Primitive and Wesleyan Methodists, Presbyterians, and Roman Catholics. A free grammar school was founded, in 1664, by Sir P. Curwen, and endowed, in 1672, by Thomas Curwen ; but, in consequence of a discovery that the endowment was void, from the circumstance of Mr. T. Curwen having only a life interest in the property so assigned, the school has ceased to exist. A school in the Square was founded, in 1808, by the late Mr. Curwen, when the free grammar school was broken up : it is a very commodious building, and affords instruction to about two hundred boys and sixty girls, who pay a small weekly sum each. There is also a school of industry, established in 1816, for thirty girls. A dispensary has been recently formed, and there are several benevolent institutions for clothing the poor, supported by voluntary contributions. On an eminence near the sea, at a short distance hence, are the remains of an ancient dilapidated building, called the Old Chapel; which, as it commanded an extensive view of Solway Frith and the Scottish coast, was probably used as a watch-tower, to guard against the incursions of the Scots.

WORKSOP, a market town and parish in the Hatfield division of the wapentake of BASSETLAW, county of NOTTINGHAM, 26 miles (N.) from Nottingham, and 146 (N. N. W.) from London, containing 4567 inhabitants. This place, which in Domesday book is written Wirchesope, and in other records of that period Wyrksoppe and Wirkensop, appears to have belonged, prior to the Conquest, to Elsi, a Saxon nobleman; after that event it was granted by the Conqueror to Roger de Busli, and subsequently became the property of William de Lovetot, who, in the reign of Henry I., founded here a priory for canons Regular of the order of St. Augustine, the prior of which was, in the reign of Henry III., summoned to parliament. It passed, after a considerable period, by the marriage of the heiress of the Lovetots, to the family of Furnival; then to that of Nevill; and from that family to the Talbots, afterwards Earls of Shrewsbury, to whom, on the dissolution of monastic establishments, the revenue of the priory, then valued at £239, was granted by Henry VIII. From this family the manor descended by marriage to the Earls of Arundel, now Dukes of Norfolk, who still hold it as tenants in chief of the Crown, by the service of a knight's fee, and of procuring a glove for the king's right hand at his coronation, and supporting that hand while holding the sceptre. In December 1460, an engagement took place at Worksop, between the forces of the Duke of York and those of the Duke of Somerset, when the latter were defeated. Gilbert, first Earl of Shrewsbury, who so much distinguished himself in the French wars under Henry V., built the vast and magnificent mansion-house, afterwards the ducal residence. It was the place of confinement of Mary, Queen of Scots, in the sixteenth year of her captivity, she being at that time in the custody of the earl; and her son, James I., on the 20th of April, 1603, rested here, on his way to London to assume the English crown. In 1761, it was accidentally destroyed by fire, but was soon afterwards splendidly rebuilt by His Grace the Duke of Norfolk.

The town is situated in a pleasant valley, near the northern extremity of the forest of Sherwood, in the midst of a well-wooded and picturesque country; and its vicinity is ornamented by the magnificent seats of several noblemen, amongst which are Worksop Manor, the noble mansion of the Duke of Norfolk, alluded to above, standing in a park eight miles in circumference; Welbeck Abbey, the seat of the Duke of Portland; Clumber, the mansion of the Duke of Newcastle; and Thoresby, the seat of Earl Manvers. It is neat in its general appearance, and consists, in the higher and principal part, of one long street, with a second running into it at right angles, which are well built and paved; it is lighted by subscription, and well supplied with water. Camden describes Worksop as famous for the production of liquorice, which has long since ceased to be cultivated. Malt, which is made in considerable quantities, barley being much grown in the surrounding country, is the principal article of trade; and the Chesterfield canal, passing on the northern side of the town, affords every facility for its conveyance to Manchester, and the other markets to which it is chiefly sent: on this canal are wharfs communicating with the town, and to the east it crosses the river Ryton by an aqueduct. The market is on Wednesday; and there are fairs on March 31st and June 21st, for cattle and sheep; on October 14th, for horses and cattle; and a statute fair about three weeks after. Constables are chosen at the annual court leet of the lord of the manor. It is in contemplation to take down the old moot hall (which has been many years in a dilapidated state), and some of the adjoining buildings, and to erect on their site a handsome structure, comprising a town hall, assembly-room, prison, market-house, &c.

The living is a vicarage, in the archdeaconry of Nottingham, and diocese of York, rated in the king's books at £12. 4. 2., and in the patronage of the Duke of Norfolk. The church, dedicated to St. Mary and St. Cuthbert, standing on the eastern side of the town, comprises the western portion of the priory church, and its cathedral-like towers form an interesting object in the view of the town: it is one of the principal remaining specimens of Norman architecture, in which style it was originally entirely constructed, but in the exterior much of the English style has been mixed with it: in form and size it resembles a cathedral. The western entrance is under a beautiful receding Norman arch, with diagonal ornaments, and the towers which surmount it have Anglo-Norman, or circular and pointed, arched windows, in different gradations. The body of the church is one hundred and thirty-five feet in length; the roof of the nave is supported by eight pillars, alternately cylindrical and octangular, joined by circular arches ornamented with quatrefoils; at the east end is the great central tower, supported by arches springing from several massive pillars: the pulpit is curiously ornamented in the Norman style; and the church contains some ancient monuments, principally of the Furnivals and Lovetots. There are places of worship for Independents and Wesleyan Methodists; and near the Manor-house is a chapel for Roman Catholics, who are numerous in the neighbourhood. In the National school, which is supported chiefly by voluntary subscription, upwards of two hundred children of both sexes are educated and partially clothed. There are some small endowments for the benefit of the poor.

The principal gateway to the priory still exists, forming the entrance towards the church: it is twenty yards in front, with a pediment, in which is a niche covered with much tabernacle-work, and in it a figure in a sitting posture. Its style of architecture is the later English, with a pointed roof and flat arch: it is ornamented above with a window of twelve lights, and canopied niches of great beauty, while figures in ecclesiastical costume enrich the interior: the room over the gateway is used as the National school for boys. On the right of the entrance are the remains of the beautiful chapel of St. Mary, forming an interesting ruin, the ornamental parts of which are most richly executed, and the windows considered some of the most perfect models of the lancet shape in the kingdom. On the northern side, and contiguous to the church, are some fragments of the walls of the priory, and in the meadows below are extensive traces of the foundation. The priory well is still in high estimation, for the purity and softness of the water. On a hill, at the western side of the town, the site of the ancient castle of the Lovetots may still be traced; and in the park of the manor are some tumuli, which, from fragments discovered in them, appear to be ancient British. Within the parish are the Shire Oaks, so named from an oak, whose branches are said to overshadow a portion of the three counties of Nottingham, Derby, and York. At Osberton, a hamlet in this parish, human bones, stone coffins, an antique font, some stained glass, &c., have been found at various times, the supposed remains of a church: they are preserved at Osberton Hall. The ruins of the ancient manor-house of Gateford, with its gables, moats, &c., are still visible;

and near them, in 1826, several Roman coins of Nero and Domition were found.

WORLABY, an extra-parochial liberty, in the hundred of HILL, parts of LINDSEY, county of LINCOLN, 7 miles (S.) from Louth, containing 32 inhabitants.

WORLABY, a parish in the northern division of the wapentake of YARBOROUGH, parts of LINDSEY, county of LINCOLN, 5½ miles (N. by E.) from Glandford-Bridge, containing 262 inhabitants. The living is a discharged vicarage, in the archdeaconry and diocese of Lincoln, rated in the king's books at £6. 8. 4. E. Arrowsmith, Esq. and others were patrons in 1806. The church is dedicated to St. Clement.

WORLDHAM (EAST), a parish in the hundred of ALTON, Alton (North) division of the county of SOUTHAMPTON, 2½ miles (E. by S.) from Alton, containing 156 inhabitants. The living is a discharged vicarage, with the donative of West Tisted united, in the archdeaconry and diocese of Winchester, rated in the king's books at £5. 18. 1½., and in the patronage of the President and Fellows of Magdalene College, Oxford.

WORLDHAM (WEST), a parish in the hundred of ALTON, Alton (North) division of the county of SOUTHAMPTON, 2½ miles (S. E. by E.) from Alton, containing 100 inhabitants. The living is a perpetual curacy, in the archdeaconry and diocese of Winchester, endowed with £200 private benefaction, and £1000 royal bounty, and in the patronage of the Warden and Fellows of Winchester College. The church is dedicated to St. Nicholas.

WORLE, a parish in the hundred of WINTERSTOKE, county of SOMERSET, 8 miles (N. W.) from Axbridge, containing 673 inhabitants. The living is a discharged vicarage, in the archdeaconry of Wells, and diocese of Bath and Wells, rated in the king's books at £12. 15., and in the patronage of the Crown. The church, dedicated to St. Martin, is a neat structure, with a tower surmounted by a small spire. There is a place of worship for Wesleyan Methodists. This parish produces very fine limestone and *lapis calaminaris*: here are vestiges of a Roman camp. The inhabitants feed great numbers of poultry, and dispose of them to the visitors at Weston super Mare, which has become a thriving watering-place.

WORLESTON, a township in the parish of ACTON, hundred of NANTWICH, county palatine of CHESTER, 1¾ mile (N.) from Nantwich, containing 369 inhabitants.

WORLINGHAM, a parish in the hundred of WANGFORD, county of SUFFOLK, 1¼ mile (S. E. by S.) from Beccles, containing 221 inhabitants. The living is a rectory, with that of Worlingham Parva annexed, in the archdeaconry of Suffolk, and diocese of Norwich, rated in the king's books at £12, and in the patronage of the Crown. The church is dedicated to All Saints: that of Worlingham Parva, which was dedicated to St. Peter, has been demolished. The navigable river Waveney runs on the northern side of the parish.

WORLINGTON, a parish in the hundred of LACKFORD, county of SUFFOLK, 1¼ mile (W. S. W.) from Mildenhall, containing 360 inhabitants. The living is a rectory, in the archdeaconry of Sudbury, and diocese of Norwich, rated in the king's books at £19. 6. 8., and in the patronage of the Hon. Thomas Windsor. The church is dedicated to All Saints. The parish is bounded on the north by the navigable river Lark, over which there is a ferry.

WORLINGTON (EAST), a parish in the hundred of WITHERIDGE, county of DEVON, 6 miles (E.) from Chulmleigh, containing 253 inhabitants. The living is a rectory, in the archdeaconry of Barnstaple, and diocese of Exeter, rated in the king's books at £7. 15. 10., and in the patronage of the Hon. N. Fellowes. The church is dedicated to St. Mary. In the neighbourhood are the remains of an ancient cross. Roman coins have been found here.

WORLINGTON (WEST), a parish in the hundred of WITHERIDGE, county of DEVON, 5½ miles (E.) from Chulmleigh, containing 172 inhabitants. The living is a rectory, in the archdeaconry of Barnstaple, and diocese of Exeter, rated in the king's books at £8. 15. 10., and in the patronage of L. W. Buck, Esq. The church is dedicated to St. Mary. Within the parish are the ruins of a castellated mansion, the ancient seat of the Affetons.

WORLINGWORTH, a parish in the hundred of HOXNE, county of SUFFOLK, 5 miles (N.W.) from Framlingham, containing 685 inhabitants. The living is a rectory, with the perpetual curacy of Southolt annexed, in the archdeaconry of Suffolk, and diocese of Norwich, rated in the king's books at £19. 12. 3½., and in the patronage of Lord Henniker. The church, dedicated to St. Mary, is principally in the later style of English architecture, and has an enriched font with a lofty and elegant cover. John Baldry, in 1689, bequeathed a house and land; and William Godbold, in 1698, left other land, the rental of which is applied for teaching poor children.

WORMBRIDGE, a parish in the hundred of WEBTREE, county of HEREFORD, 9 miles (S. W.) from Hereford, containing 95 inhabitants. The living is a perpetual curacy, in the peculiar jurisdiction and patronage of Edward Bolton Clive, Esq. The chapel is dedicated to St. Thomas the Apostle.

WORMEGAY, a parish in the hundred of CLACKCLOSE, county of NORFOLK, 7½ miles (N. N. E.) from Downham-Market, containing 362 inhabitants. The living is a perpetual curacy, in the archdeaconry of Norfolk, and diocese of Norwich, endowed with £400 royal bounty, and in the patronage of the Bishop of Norwich. The church is dedicated to the Holy Cross. A priory of Black canons, in honour of the Virgin Mary, the Holy Cross, and St. John the Evangelist, was founded here in the reign of Richard I., or John, and, in 1468, was united to the priory of Pentney, to which it became a cell.

WORMHILL, a chapelry in the parish of TIDESWELL, hundred of HIGH PEAK, county of DERBY, 2¼ miles (W. S. W.) from Tideswell, containing 347 inhabitants. The living is a perpetual curacy, in the peculiar jurisdiction of the Dean and Chapter of Lichfield, endowed with £30 per annum private benefaction, and £400 royal bounty, and in the patronage of certain Trustees. The chapel is dedicated to St. Margaret. A small school, erected by the inhabitants, is supported by several trifling bequests. Wormhill is in the honour of Tutbury, duchy of Lancaster, and within the jurisdiction of a court of pleas held at Tutbury every third Tuesday, for the recovery of debts under 40s. The river Wye runs in the vicinity through the most picturesque scenery, particularly that of Chee dale, in this chapelry: the rocks on both sides of the stream present a bold face of limestone and lava, in alternate strata, which, when viewed from the narrow dell, appear, by the uniformity of their recesses and projections, to have been once united, and torn asunder by some remarkable convulsion of the earth.

WORMINGFORD, a parish in the Colchester division of the hundred of LEXDEN, county of ESSEX, 3¾ miles (W. S. W.) from Nayland, containing 453 inhabitants. The living is a vicarage, in the archdeaconry of Colchester, and diocese of London, rated in the king's books at £7. 13. 4., and in the patronage of John J. Tufnel, Esq. The church is dedicated to St. Andrew. The navigable river Stour bounds the parish on the north.

WORMINGHALL, a parish in the hundred of ASHENDON, county of BUCKINGHAM, 4¾ miles (W. N. W.) from Thame, containing 314 inhabitants. The living is a discharged vicarage, in the archdeaconry of Buckingham, and diocese of Lincoln, rated in the king's books at £6. 18. 10., endowed with £200 royal bounty, and in the patronage of Edward Horne, Esq. The church is dedicated to St. Peter. A market, formerly held here on Thursday, was granted to John de Rivers, in 1304, with a fair on the festival of St. Peter and St. Paul. An almshouse was founded, in 1675, by John King, Esq., for four poor women and six poor single men, who each receive a monthly allowance of eight shillings and fourpence.

WORMINGTON, a parish in the lower division of the hundred of KIFTSGATE, county of GLOUCESTER, 9 miles (N. by E.) from Winchcombe, containing 83 inhabitants. The living is a discharged rectory, in the archdeaconry and diocese of Gloucester, rated in the king's books at £7. 15. 5., and in the patronage of Josiah Gist, Esq. The church is dedicated to the Holy Trinity.

WORMLEIGHTON, a parish in the Burton-Dassett division of the hundred of KINGTON, county of WARWICK, 5¾ miles (S. S. E.) from Southam, containing 171 inhabitants. The living is a discharged vicarage, in the archdeaconry of Coventry, and diocese of Lichfield and Coventry, rated in the king's books at £6. 13. 4., endowed with £200 private benefaction, and £200 royal bounty, and in the patronage of Earl Spencer. The church is dedicated to St. Peter. The Oxford canal passes through the parish.

WORMLEY, a parish in the hundred and county of HERTFORD, 2½ miles (N. by E.) from Cheshunt, containing 492 inhabitants. The living is a rectory, in the jurisdiction of the Archdeacon of Middlesex, concurrently with the Consistorial Court of the Bishop of London, rated in the king's books at £10. 12. 3½., and in the patronage of Sir A. Hume, Bart. The church, dedicated to St. Lawrence, has a Norman doorway, and at the west end, a square wooden tower; it contains several tablets, altar-tombs, and other sepulchral memorials. The New River runs through the parish, and the river Lea bounds it on the east.

WORMSHILL, a parish in the hundred of EYHORNE, lathe of AYLESFORD, county of KENT, 5 miles (S. S. W.) from Sittingbourne, containing 165 inhabitants. The living is a rectory, in the archdeaconry and diocese of Canterbury, rated in the king's books at

£10, and in the patronage of the Governors of Christ's Hospital, London. The church, dedicated to St. Giles, has a tower steeple, and some fine remains of stained glass in the great east window.

WORMSLEY, a parish in the hundred of GRIMSWORTH, county of HEREFORD, 3½ miles (S. E. by S.) from Weobley, containing 131 inhabitants. The living is a perpetual curacy, in the archdeaconry and diocese of Hereford, endowed with £800 royal bounty, and in the patronage of T. A. Knight, Esq. The church is dedicated to St. Mary.

WORPLESDON, a parish in the first division of the hundred of WOKING, county of SURREY, 3½ miles (N. N. W.) from Guildford, containing, with the tythings of Burgham, Perry-Hill, West-End, and Wyke, 1276 inhabitants. The living is a rectory, in the archdeaconry of Surrey, and diocese of Winchester, rated in the king's books at £24. 13. 9., and in the patronage of the Provost and Fellows of Eton College. The church is dedicated to St. Mary. The Rev. Dr. Moore, in 1706, bequeathed £200, directing the interest to be applied in teaching poor children.

WORSALL (HIGH), a chapelry in the parish of NORTH ALLERTON, wapentake of ALLERTONSHIRE, North riding of the county of YORK, 4 miles (S. S. W.) from Yarm, containing 154 inhabitants. The living is a perpetual curacy, in the jurisdiction of the peculiar court of the Dean and Chapter of Durham for Allerton and Allertonshire, endowed with £200 private benefaction, £800 royal bounty, and £200 parliamentary grant, and in the patronage of the Vicar of North Allerton.

WORSALL (LOW), a township in the parish of KIRK-LEAVINGTON, western division of the liberty of LANGBAURGH, North riding of the county of YORK, 3 miles (S. W.) from Yarm, containing 217 inhabitants.

WORSBROUGH, a chapelry in that part of the parish of DARFIELD which is in the wapentake of STAINCROSS, West riding of the county of YORK, 2½ miles (S. by E.) from Barnesley, containing 1392 inhabitants. The living is a perpetual curacy, in the archdeaconry and diocese of York, endowed with £200 private benefaction, £400 royal bounty, and £1000 parliamentary grant, and in the patronage of the Rector of Darfield. The chapel, dedicated to St. Mary, is an elegant building, principally in the later style of English architecture, with a low tower surmounted by a spire. A free school here is endowed with an annual pension of £4. 15. from the Crown, an annuity of £13. 6. 8. bequeathed by John Rayney, in 1631, and a house and land let for £13 per annum: the classics were formerly taught, but for the last fifty years only an English education has been given to about thirty boys. A Sunday school was established, in 1818, by Anna Shaw, who bequeathed £20 towards its support.

WORSLEY, a chapelry in the parish of ECCLES, hundred of SALFORD, county palatine of LANCASTER, 6 miles (W. by N.) from Manchester, containing 7191 inhabitants. The living is a perpetual curacy, in the archdeaconry and diocese of Chester, endowed with £600 royal bounty, and £1400 parliamentary grant, and in the patronage of the Trustees of the late Earl of Bridgewater. The chapel has a Sunday school attached, which is attended by three hundred children. There is a place of worship for Wesleyan Methodists.

In the 10th of George II., an act was obtained for making navigable the river called Worsley brook, but the design was not carried into effect; and, in the 32nd of the same reign, the celebrated Duke of Bridgewater obtained an act, and, subsequently, other acts, enabling him to construct a series of canals from his extensive collieries here to different places, affording the means of conveying coal, &c., through a populous manufacturing district : the underground canals and tunnels at Worsley are said to be eighteen miles in length, and their construction to have cost £168,960. Twelve poor children are instructed for a rent-charge of £5, bequeathed by Thomas Collier, in 1706. Worsley Archers' Society, formed in August 1826, consists of twenty-four members, who hold their meetings every Wednesday at the Grapes' Inn, from the first Wednesday in April to the first in October.

WORSTEAD, a parish (formerly a market town) in the hundred of TUNSTEAD, county of NORFOLK, 2¾ miles (S. S. E.) from North Walsham, and 121 (N. E. by N.) from London, containing 706 inhabitants. This place was formerly celebrated for the invention and manufacture of woollen twists and stuffs, thence called worsted goods; but this branch of trade, soon after its introduction by the Flemings, in the reign of Henry I., was, on the petition of the inhabitants of Norwich, removed to that city in the reign of Richard II., where it was finally established in the reign of Henry IV. The town at present has neither any manufacture nor trade : a navigable canal, which joins the sea at Yarmouth, passes through it. The market is entirely disused; but a fair for cattle is held on the 12th of May, and another at Scotto, an adjoining parish, on Easter-Tuesday. A manorial court is held annually, at which constables and other officers are appointed. The living is a discharged vicarage, in the archdeaconry of Norfolk, and diocese of Norwich, rated in the king's books at £10, and in the patronage of the Dean and Chapter. The church, dedicated to St. Mary, is a spacious and elegant structure, partly in the decorated, and partly in the later, style of English architecture, with a lofty square embattled tower, strengthened with enriched buttresses, and crowned with pinnacles; forming, both in its combinations and details, a beautiful specimen of the decorated style : the chancel and the nave are principally in the later style, and are ornamented with screen-work of wood richly carved: the font is peculiarly rich, the sides being highly ornamented, and the pedestal on which it is supported is relieved with buttresses and canopied niches, and the risers of the steps are panelled in compartments; the cover is of tabernacle-work elegantly designed. There is a place of worship for Baptists, connected with which is a Sunday school, conducted on the National plan, and supported by subscription.

WORSTHORN, a township in that part of the parish of WHALLEY which is in the higher division of the hundred of BLACKBURN, county palatine of LANCASTER, 2¼ miles (E.) from Burnley, containing 631 inhabitants.

WORSTON, a township in that part of the parish of WHALLEY which is in the higher division of the hundred of BLACKBURN, county palatine of LANCASTER, 2¼ miles (E. N. E.) from Clitheroe, containing 178 inhabitants.

WORSTON, a township in that part of the parish of ST. MARY and ST. CHAD, STAFFORD, which is in the southern division of the hundred of PIREHILL, county of STAFFORD, containing 23 inhabitants.

WORTH, a township in the parish of PRESTBURY, hundred of MACCLESFIELD, county palatine of CHESTER, 6 miles (S. S. E.) from Stockport, containing 406 inhabitants, who are chiefly employed in the neighbouring collieries.

WORTH, or WORD, a parish in the hundred of EASTRY, lathe of ST. AUGUSTINE, county of KENT, 1½ mile (S.) from Sandwich, containing 438 inhabitants. The living is a perpetual curacy, annexed to the vicarage of Eastry, in the archdeaconry and diocese of Canterbury. The church is dedicated to St. Peter and St. Paul.

WORTH, a parish in the hundred of BUTTINGHILL, rape of LEWES, county of SUSSEX, 7½ miles (N.) from Cuckfield, containing 1725 inhabitants. The living is a rectory, in the archdeaconry of Lewes, and diocese of Chichester, rated in the king's books at £13. 3. 4. Mrs. Bethune was patroness in 1803. The church has lately received an addition of one hundred and twenty free sittings, the Incorporated Society for the enlargement of churches and chapels having granted £50 towards defraying the expense. There is a place of worship for Dissenters. Sixteen children are instructed for a rent-charge of £8, the gift of Timothy Shelley, in 1767.

WORTH-MATRAVERS, a parish in the hundred of ROWBARROW, Blandford (South) division of the county of DORSET, 3½ miles (S. S. E.) from Corfe-Castle, containing 325 inhabitants. The living is a discharged vicarage, in the archdeaconry of Dorset, and diocese of Bristol, rated in the king's books at £8. 8. 4., and in the patronage of the Rev. T. O. Bartlett. The church, dedicated to St. Nicholas, is a very ancient structure. This parish has the English channel on the south, where is the noted cliff called St. Alban's head, one hundred and forty-seven yards in perpendicular height, with a signal-house on its summit; also the remains of a very ancient chapel, dedicated to St. Aldhelms, built and vaulted with stone, and supported by a single massive pillar, with four arches, meeting in a point at the crown : it is entered through a semicircular doorway in the north side, but has no window, only a hole on the south side. Near Quarr, which anciently belonged to the Cullifords, marble was once quarried.

WORTHAM, a parish in the hundred of HARTISMERE, county of SUFFOLK, 5½ miles (N. W.) from Eye, containing 935 inhabitants. The living is a rectory, formerly in medieties, now consolidated, in the archdeaconry of Sudbury, and diocese of Norwich, and in the patronage of the Rev. R. Cobbold; one, termed Everard, is rated in the king's books at £13. 2. 8½., and the other, named Jervis, at £13. 1. 0½. The church is dedicated to St. Mary.

WORTHEN, a parish partly in the hundred of CAWRSE, county of MONTGOMERY, WALES, but chiefly in the hundred of CHIRBURY, county of SALOP, containing 2116 inhabitants, of which number, 1684 are in that part of the parish which is in the county of Salop, and which is divided into the quarters of Bing-Weston, Bromblow, Upper Heath, and Worthen, 9 miles (N. E.) from

Montgomery. The living is a rectory, with the chapelry of Wolston annexed, in the archdeaconry of Salop, and diocese of Hereford, rated in the king's books at £28. 14. 7., and in the patronage of the Warden and Fellows of New College, Oxford. The church is dedicated to All Saints. This place had formerly a market on Wednesday, and two annual fairs, granted by Henry III. In this and the neighbouring parishes is a very singular ridge of stones, termed Stiperstones, extending several miles towards Shrewsbury, and said to be the ancient boundary between England and Wales; there are still the remains of two old castles upon the same line. In the neighbourhood are considerable lead mines, some of which were worked by the Romans, in the time of Adrian.

WORTHEN, a quarter in that part of the parish of WORTHEN which is in the hundred of CHIRBURY, county of SALOP, containing, with Brockton, Aston-Rogers, Aston-Piggott, Nether and Upper Heath, and Habberley, 708 inhabitants.

WORTHING, a parish in the hundred of LAUNDITCH, county of NORFOLK, 4 miles (N. by E.) from East Dereham, containing 113 inhabitants. The living is a rectory, annexed to that of Swanton-Morley, in the archdeaconry and diocese of Norwich. The church is dedicated to St. Margaret; the steeple, which was round, is much dilapidated.

WORTHING, a sea-port, market-town, and chapelry, in the parish of BROADWATER, hundred of BRIGHT-FORD, rape of BRAMBER, county of SUSSEX, 20 miles (E. by S.) from Chichester, and 56 (S. by W.) from London. The population is returned with the parish. This fashionable and attractive watering-place is comparatively of recent growth, having risen, within a few years from a small fishing village to its present size and importance. Its situation forms a strong recommendation to visitors, more especially to invalids, as the South Down hills, which approach to within a mile of the town, completely shelter it from the north and east winds, and protect it from that degree of cold to which the other bathing places on this coast are in the winter subject. There is every facility for bathing, aided by the beautiful and level beach of sand, extending several miles on each side of the town, and sufficiently firm for exercise on horseback and on foot; there are also warm baths fitted up with every convenience. The town is well lighted with oil, paved, and abundantly supplied with water: it contains some good streets, with many excellent houses: the inns and boarding and lodging houses are generally of the best description. The theatre, a small but neat building, is opened in the season; the libraries and reading-rooms are well supplied, and furnish the sources of amusement usually to be found in them at watering-places, and every description of attraction and accommodation has been provided for the many respectable families who resort hither. The principal market is on Saturday, and there is a corn market on alternate Wednesdays, and one for vegetables daily. A fishery, for mackarel in the spring and herrings in the autumn, has been established here, and great quantities of the former are sent to the London market. The chapel is a handsome building with a portico; it was erected in 1812, at an expense of £12,000, raised by the inhabitants, aided by £150 given by the Incorporated Society for enlarging churches and chapels; it

VOL. IV.

will contain one thousand two hundred persons, having one hundred and fifty-four free sittings. There are places of worship for Independents and Wesleyan Methodists. National schools are supported by subscription, in which about one hundred boys and one hundred girls are instructed; and there is an infant school. A savings bank was established in 1817; and several institutions have been formed for the benefit of the poor, which are supported by voluntary contributions.

WORTHINGTON, a township in the parish of STANDISH, hundred of LEYLAND, county palatine of LANCASTER, 3½ miles (N. by W.) from Wigan, containing 143 inhabitants.

WORTHINGTON, a chapelry in the parish of BREE-DON, western division of the hundred of GOSCOTE, county of LEICESTER, 4¼ miles (N. E.) from Ashby de la Zouch, containing, with the liberty of Newbold, 1257 inhabitants. The living is a perpetual curacy, in the archdeaconry of Leicester, and diocese of Lincoln, endowed with £400 royal bounty, and £1200 parliamentary grant, and in the patronage of Lord Scarsdale. The chapel is dedicated to St. Matthew. Worthington is in the honour of Tutbury, duchy of Lancaster, and within the jurisdiction of a court of pleas held at Tutbury every third Tuesday, for the recovery of debts under 40s.

WORTHY (ABBOT'S), a tything in that part of the parish of KING's WORTHY which is in the hundred of MITCHELDEVER, Basingstoke division of the county of SOUTHAMPTON, 2 miles (N. N. E.) from Winchester. The population is returned with the parish.

WORTHY (HEADBOURN), a parish in the hundred of BARTON-STACEY, Andover division of the county of SOUTHAMPTON, 2 miles (N. by E.) from Winchester, containing 176 inhabitants. The living is a rectory, in the archdeaconry and diocese of Winchester, rated in the king's books at £15. 12. 1., and in the patronage of the Trustees of Dr. Radcliffe, for a member of University College, Oxford. The church is dedicated to St. Martin.

WORTHY (KING'S), a parish partly in the hundred of MITCHELDEVER, Basingstoke division, but chiefly in the hundred of BARTON-STACEY, Andover division, of the county of SOUTHAMPTON, 2¼ miles (N. N. E.) from Winchester, containing, with the tything of Abbot's Worthy, 344 inhabitants. The living is a rectory, in the archdeaconry and diocese of Winchester, rated in the king's books at £22. 12. 6., and in the patronage of Sir Thomas Baring, Bart. The church is dedicated to St. Mary.

WORTHY (MARTYR), a parish partly in the hundred of BOUNTISBOROUGH, but chiefly in that of FAWLEY, Fawley division of the county of SOUTHAMPTON, 3 miles (N. E. by N.) from Winchester, containing, with the hamlet of Chilland, 237 inhabitants. The living is a rectory, in the archdeaconry and diocese of Winchester, rated in the king's books at £15. 10. 2½., and in the patronage of the Bishop of Winchester. The church is dedicated to St. Swithin. This parish is within the jurisdiction of the Cheyney Court held at Winchester every Thursday, for the recovery of debts to any amount. Ten boys are instructed for a rent-charge of £6. 13. 4., the bequest of Agnes Parnell, in 1589.

WORTING, a parish in the hundred of CHUTELY, Kingsclere division of the county of SOUTHAMPTON,

4 E

2¼ miles (W.) from Basingstoke, containing 136 inhabitants. The living is a rectory, in the archdeaconry and diocese of Winchester, rated in the king's books at £8. 17. 8½., and in the patronage of Harris Bigg Wither, Esq. The church is dedicated to St. Thomas à Becket.

WORTLEY, a tything in the parish of WOTTON under EDGE, upper division of the hundred of BERKELEY, county of GLOUCESTER. The population is returned with the parish.

WORTLEY, a chapelry in the parish of ST. PETER'S, town and liberty of LEEDS, West riding of the county of YORK, 2¼ miles (W. S. W.) from Leeds, containing 3179 inhabitants. The living is a perpetual curacy, in the archdeaconry and diocese of York, endowed with £400 private benefaction, and £2000 parliamentary grant, and in the patronage of five Trustees. The chapel is a neat modern structure. There are places of worship for Independents and Wesleyan Methodists. The manufacture of woollen cloth is extensively carried on here. In the neighbourhood coarse earthenware and tobacco pipes are made from clay obtained upon the spot. Langdale Sunderland, in 1677, conveyed certain houses and land, now producing about £40 a year, in support of a free school for all the poor children of the chapelry.

WORTLEY, a chapelry in the parish of TANKERSLEY, wapentake of STAINCROSS, West riding of the county of YORK, 5½ miles (S. S. W.) from Barnesley, containing 904 inhabitants. The living is a perpetual curacy, in the archdeaconry and diocese of York, endowed with £300 private benefaction, £400 royal bounty, and £1700 parliamentary grant, and in the patronage of the Rector of Tankersley. This place, which is delightfully situated on the river Don, and embosomed in fine woods, is celebrated in the ancient poem of "The Dragon of Wantley."

WORTON, a hamlet in the parish of CASSINGTON, hundred of WOOTTON, county of OXFORD, containing 52 inhabitants.

WORTON, a tything in the parish of POTTERNE, hundred of POTTERNE and CANNINGS, county of WILTS, 3½ miles (S. W.) from Devizes, containing 298 inhabitants. There is a place of worship for Wesleyan Methodists.

WORTON (NETHER), a parish in the hundred of WOOTTON, county of OXFORD, 3¾ miles (W. S. W.) from Deddington, containing 96 inhabitants. The living is a perpetual curacy, in the archdeaconry and diocese of Oxford, endowed with £800 royal bounty, and in the patronage of W. Wilson, Esq. The church is dedicated to St. James.

WORTON (OVER), a parish in the hundred of WOOTTON, county of OXFORD, 4 miles (S. W. by W.) from Deddington, containing 56 inhabitants. The living is a rectory, in the archdeaconry and diocese of Oxford, rated in the king's books at £6. 2. 8½., and in the patronage of T. Cartwright, Esq. The church is dedicated to the Holy Trinity.

WORTWELL, a hamlet in the parish of REDDENHALL, hundred of EARSHAM, county of NORFOLK, 2¾ miles (N. E. by E.) from Harleston, containing 486 inhabitants.

WOTHERSOME, a township in the parish of BARDSEY, lower division of the wapentake of SKYRACK,

West riding of the county of YORK, 3½ miles (S.) from Wetherby, containing 16 inhabitants.

WOTTON under EDGE, a market town and parish in the upper division of the hundred of BERKELEY, county of GLOUCESTER, 19 miles (S. S. W.) from Gloucester, and 108 (W. by N.) from London, comprising the tythings of Huntingford, Sinwell with Bradley, Symonds-Hall with Combe, and Wortley, and containing 5004 inhabitants. The name of this place, formerly Wotton under Ridge, is descriptive of its situation beneath a range of well-wooded hills. The old town, which stood on a spot now called "The Brands," was destroyed by fire in the reign of John; and on its restoration, a market and fair, with various municipal privileges, were granted by Henry III. to Maurice, Lord Berkeley, in 1254, which laid the foundation of its subsequent importance. The present town is situated on a gentle eminence, and consists principally of two parallel streets; the houses are in general well built and of neat appearance. It has long been celebrated for the manufacture of fine broad cloth; the trade is in a flourishing state, and affords employment to the inhabitants of the town and vicinity; on a small stream, which flows to the west of the town, are nine water-mills connected with the manufacture. The market is on Friday; and there is a fair annually on September 25th, for cattle and cheese. A mayor is chosen annually in October at the manorial court leet, but he has no magisterial authority; at the termination of his mayoralty he becomes an alderman. Petty sessions for the division are held here.

The living is a vicarage, in the archdeaconry and diocese of Gloucester, rated in the king's books at £13. 10., endowed with £200 private benefaction, and £200 royal bounty, and in the patronage of the Dean and Canons of Christ Church, Oxford. The church, which is dedicated to St. Mary, is a spacious and handsome structure, having a tower with battlements and pinnacles, and containing some curious sepulchral memorials. There are places of worship for Baptists, Independents and Wesleyan Methodists. The free grammar school was founded and endowed by Lady Catherine Berkeley, under letters patent from Richard II., in 1385; and having become forfeited in the reign of Edward I., it was restored, on petition, by James I., under the title of "the Free Grammar School of Lord Berkeley," to consist of one master, and five or more poor scholars, who should be a body corporate, the election of the master being vested in his lordship and his heirs, or, in default of issue, in the lord of the manor : the total annual income is £376. 12. 6. There are ten boys on the foundation, who are allowed £6 per annum for books and other purposes. The Blue-coat school is endowed with £60 per annum from the funds of the general hospital trust, and with the produce of sundry bequests ; the annual income is £136. 13. : thirty boys on the foundation are clothed, educated, and apprenticed, and about ten others receive gratuitous instruction : the school-house was erected about 1714, partly from the funds of Hugh Perry's estate, and partly by subscription. An hospital for twelve persons of both sexes, founded in 1630, by Hugh Perry, Esq., alderman of London ; another for six aged persons of both sexes, founded by Thos. Dawes, in 1712 ; and the general hospital, are situated in Church-lane, and form three sides of a square, with an open court in the middle, and a chapel at the north end. Hugh Perry, Esq. also procured a supply of water for the town at his own expense. Sir Jonathan Dawes, sheriff of London, gave £1000 for the relief of the poor, and for apprenticing poor children. On Westridge, in this parish, are the remains of a square camp, with double intrenchments, partly covered with wood, which is called Becketsbury.

WOTTON-ABBAS, a liberty in the parish and hundred of WHITCHURCH-CANONICORUM, Bridport division of the county of DORSET, 4¾ miles (N. E. by N.) from Lyme-Regis. The population is returned with the parish. The liberty is of great extent, stretching from the river Char to the Ax, which bounds the counties of Devon and Dorset. Courts leet and baron are held here; and an annual fair, granted in the 7th of Queen Anne, on the Wednesday before the festival of St. John the Baptist, is kept on a lofty hill, called Lambert's Castle, the summit of which, in the form of the letter D, is fortified with triple trenches and ramparts, enclosing twelve acres, and having several entrances.

WOTTON-LOW-HILL and UP-HILL, a parish in the first division of the hundred of WOTTON, county of SURREY, 3 miles (W. S. W.) from Dorking, containing 589 inhabitants. The living is a rectory, in the archdeaconry of Surrey, and diocese of Winchester, rated in the king's books at £12. 18. 9., and in the patronage of John Evelyn, Esq. The church is dedicated to St. John the Evangelist.

WOUGHTON on the GREEN, a parish in the hundred of NEWPORT, county of BUCKINGHAM, 2½ miles (N. by W.) from Fenny-Stratford, containing 299 inhabitants. The living is a rectory, in the archdeaconry of Buckingham, and diocese of Lincoln, rated in the king's books at £16. 9. 7., and in the patronage of the Rev. Francis Rose. The church is dedicated to St. Mary. A branch of the river Ouse bounds the parish on the east, and the Grand Junction canal passes through it.

WOULDHAM, a parish in the hundred of LARKFIELD, lathe of AYLESFORD, county of KENT, 2½ miles (S. W.) from Rochester, containing 176 inhabitants. The living is a discharged rectory, in the archdeaconry and diocese of Rochester, rated in the king's books at £14. 6. 5½., endowed with £400 private benefaction, and £400 royal bounty, and in the patronage of the Bishop of Rochester. The church is dedicated to All Saints. The village is situated on the western bank of the Medway.

WRABNESS, a parish in the hundred of TENDRING, county of ESSEX, 4¾ miles (E.) from Manningtree, containing 253 inhabitants. The living is a discharged rectory, in the archdeaconry of Colchester, and diocese of Essex, rated in the king's books at £8, and in the patronage of the Crown. The church is dedicated to All Saints. There is a place of worship for Wesleyan Methodists. The navigable river Stour bounds the parish on the north.

WRAGBY, a market town and parish in the western division of the wapentake of WRAGGOE, parts of LINDSEY, county of LINCOLN, 10½ miles (E. N. E.) from Lincoln, and 139½ (N. by W.) from London, containing 633 inhabitants. This place, noticed by Leland as a village giving name to a small beck, or stream, which flowed by it, in its course from Panton to Bardney abbey, is of some antiquity, but is not distinguished by any

event of historical importance. From an inconsiderable village it was raised to a market town by George, Duke of Buckingham, who, in 1671, obtained for it the grant of a market and three annual fairs, two of which are still held. The town is pleasantly situated on the high road from Lincoln to Horncastle, at the point where it meets the road to Louth, and consists of neatly-built houses. The environs comprise an extensive tract of fertile land, in the cultivation of which the inhabitants are principally employed. There is very little trade, except what arises from its situation on a public road, and is requisite for the supply of the inhabitants. The market is on Thursday; and fairs are annually held on Holy Thursday, and the 29th of September, for sheep and cattle. The town is under the jurisdiction of the county magistrates, and within that of a court of requests for the wapentake of Wraggoe, established by an act passed in the 19th of George III., for the recovery of debts under 40s. The living is a vicarage, united, in 1735, to the rectory of East Torrington, in the archdeaconry and diocese of Lincoln, rated in the king's books at £8. 4. 2., and in the patronage of Edmund Turnor, Esq. The church, dedicated to All Saints, is an ancient structure, principally in the later style of English architecture, and contains several sepulchral memorials. There is a place of worship for Wesleyan Methodists. William Hansard, in 1632, bequeathed a rent-charge of £30 for teaching poor children of the parish. Sir Edmund Turnor, Knt., founded an almshouse, with a chapel, for six clergymen's widows, and for six aged widowers, or widows, of Wragby, which, in 1707, he endowed with a rent-charge of £100, for keeping the buildings in repair, for the support of the inmates, and for the payment of a stipend to the vicar for officiating in the chapel. There are also some charitable bequests for distribution among the poor.

WRAGBY, a parish comprising the townships of West Hardwick, Hasle, Hill-top, and Hurstwick with Nostal, in the upper division of the wapentake of Os-GOLDCROSS, and the townships of Ryhill and Winterset, in the wapentake of STAINCROSS, West riding of the county of YORK, 5 miles (S. W.) from Pontefract, and containing 660 inhabitants. The living is a donative, in the patronage of C. Winn, Esq. The church, dedicated to St. Michael, is principally in the later style of English architecture. An annuity of £6. 5., paid out of the revenue of the duchy of Lancaster, is applied in support of a free school for the poor children of the parish.

WRAMPLINGHAM, a parish in the hundred of FOREHOE, county of NORFOLK, 3 miles (N. by E.) from Wymondham, containing 215 inhabitants. The living is a discharged rectory, in the archdeaconry of Norfolk, and diocese of Norwich, rated in the king's books at £5. 4. 9½. R. Marsham, Esq. was patron in 1811. The church, dedicated to St. Peter and St. Paul, has a round tower.

WRANGLE, a parish in the wapentake of SKIRBECK, parts of HOLLAND, county of LINCOLN, 8¼ miles (N. N. E.) from Boston, containing 995 inhabitants. The living is a vicarage, in the archdeaconry and diocese of Lincoln, rated in the king's books at £9. 18. 6½., and in the patronage of the Rev. T. B. Wright. The church is dedicated to St. Peter and St. Paul. The Rev. Thomas Allenson bequeathed land now producing a considerable income, one moiety of which is applied for teaching poor children, and the other for the maintenance of five poor people.

WRANTAGE, a tything in the parish and hundred of NORTH CURRY, county of SOMERSET, 5½ miles (E. by S.) from Taunton. The population is returned with the parish.

WRATTING (GREAT), a parish in the hundred of RISBRIDGE, county of SUFFOLK, 2¾ miles (N. E. by N.) from Haverhill, containing 263 inhabitants. The living is a rectory, in the archdeaconry of Sudbury, and diocese of Norwich, rated in the king's books at £8, and in the patronage of the Rev. B. Syer, D.D. The church is dedicated to St. Mary.

WRATTING (LITTLE), a parish in the hundred of RISBRIDGE, county of SUFFOLK, 5¼ miles (W. by N.) from Clare, containing 183 inhabitants. The living is a rectory, in the archdeaconry of Sudbury, and diocese of Norwich, rated in the king's books at £4. 19. 9½., and in the patronage of the Rev. B. Syer, D.D.

WRATTING (WEST), a parish in the hundred of RADFIELD, county of CAMBRIDGE, 5¼ miles (N.E. by N.) from Linton, containing 696 inhabitants. The living is a vicarage, in the archdeaconry and diocese of Ely, rated in the king's books at £7. 17. 3½., and in the patronage of the Dean and Chapter of Ely. The church, dedicated to St. Andrew, and the vicarage-house, were repaired and improved, at an expense of £767, defrayed by Sir John Jacob, who died in 1740.

WRATTON, or WRAYTON, a joint township with Melling, in the parish of MELLING, hundred of LONSDALE, south of the sands, county palatine of LANCASTER, 5 miles (S.) from Kirkby-Lonsdale. The population is returned with Melling.

WRAWBY, a parish in the southern division of the wapentake of YARBOROUGH, parts of LINDSEY, county of LINCOLN, 2 miles (N. E. by E.) from Glandford-Bridge, containing, with the chapelry of Glandford-Bridge, and the hamlet of Kettleby, 2130 inhabitants. The living is a discharged vicarage, in the archdeaconry and diocese of Lincoln, rated in the king's books at £9. 14. 7., and in the patronage of the Master and Fellows of Clare Hall, Cambridge. The church is dedicated to St. Mary.

WRAXALL, a parish in the hundred of EGGERTON, Bridport division of the county of DORSET, 8 miles (E. by S.) from Beaminster, containing 62 inhabitants. The living is a rectory, united, in 1758, to that of Rampisham, in the archdeaconry of Dorset, and diocese of Bristol, rated in the king's books at £5. The church is dedicated to the Conception of the Virgin Mary.

WRAXALL, a parish in the hundred of PORTBURY, county of SOMERSET, 6½ miles (W. by S.) from Bristol, containing 769 inhabitants. The living is a rectory, with the perpetual curacies of Flax-Bourton and Nailsea, in the archdeaconry of Bath, and diocese of Bath and Wells, rated in the king's books at £49. 11. 8., and in the patronage of the Rev. James Vaughan. The church, dedicated to All Saints, has lately received an addition of one hundred and sixty sittings, of which one hundred are free, the Incorporated Society for the enlargement of churches and chapels having granted £200 towards defraying the expense. A school adjoining the churchyard was erected by Richard Vaughan, who endowed it with £300, the interest of which, together with about

£6 a year bequeathed by Elizabeth Martindale, is applied for teaching poor children. A fair is held at Allhallow-tide, which continues six days. On Leigh down, about a mile from Fayland's Inn, in this parish, is an irregular intrenchment, and near it another of a circular form, called the Old Fort. On the same down, upon opening a tumulus in 1815, several hundred Roman coins of the Lower Empire were discovered, with fragments of ancient urns ; and many other indications of the residence of the Romans have been observed in the neighbourhood.

WRAXALL (NORTH), a parish in the hundred of CHIPPENHAM, county of WILTS, 7 miles (W. by N.) from Chippenham, containing 345 inhabitants. The living is a rectory, in the archdeaconry of Wilts, and diocese of Salisbury, rated in the king's books at £15. 9. 2. Mrs. Heneage was patroness in 1814. The church is dedicated to St. James.

WRAXALL (SOUTH), a chapelry in the parish of GREAT BRADFORD, hundred of BRADFORD, county of WILTS, 5 miles (W. by N.) from Melksham, containing 435 inhabitants. The chapel is dedicated to St. James.

WRAY, a township in the parish of MELLING, hundred of LONSDALE, south of the sands, county palatine of LANCASTER, 10 miles (N.E. by E.) from Lancaster, containing 808 inhabitants, several of whom are employed in making nails. Richard Pooley, in 1685, bequeathed £20 for the erection of a school, and £200 to purchase land for its support; the annual income is about £35, which sum, with about £4 per annum, arising from a bequest by Mary Thompson, in 1803, is applied to the free instruction of from fifty to sixty children.

WREA, a township in the parish of KIRKHAM, hundred of AMOUNDERNESS, county palatine of LANCASTER, 1¾ miles (W. by S.) from Kirkham. The population is returned with the chapelry of Ribby.

WREAY, a chapelry in that part of the parish of ST. MARY, CARLISLE, which is in CUMBERLAND ward, county of CUMBERLAND, 5¾ miles (S. E. by S.) from Carlisle, containing 130 inhabitants. The living is a perpetual curacy, in the archdeaconry and diocese of Carlisle, endowed with £400 private benefaction, and £400 royal bounty, and in the patronage of the Dean and Chapter of Carlisle. The chapel, dedicated to St. Mary, was consecrated in 1739. A school, erected by subscription in 1760, was endowed by John Brown, in 1763, with £200, which was laid out in land now producing £15 a year, for the education of poor children.

WRECKLESHAM, a joint tything with Bourn, in the parish and hundred of FARNHAM, county of SURREY, 1¾ mile (S. W. by S.) from Farnham, containing 758 inhabitants.

WREIGH-HILL, a township in the parish of ROTHBURY, western division of COQUETDALE ward, county of NORTHUMBERLAND, 5¼ miles (W.) from Rothbury, containing 29 inhabitants. It is bounded on the south by the river Coquet, and was anciently called Wreck Hill, probably from having been destroyed, in 1412, by a band of Scottish freebooters, who killed most of the inhabitants. In 1665, almost the entire population was swept off by the plague, since which event great quantities of human bones have been discovered on the spot where the victims were interred. There are strata of limestone and freestone in this township. George

Coughran, the celebrated youthful mathematician, was born here.

WRELTON, a township in the parish of MIDDLE-TON, PICKERING lythe, North riding of the county of YORK, 2¾ miles (W. N. W.) from Pickering, containing 193 inhabitants.

WRENBURY, a parish in the hundred of NANT-WICH, county palatine of CHESTER, comprising the townships of Bromhall, Chorley, Woodcot, and Wren-bury with Frith, and containing 934 inhabitants, of which number, 526 are in the township of Wrenbury with Frith, 4¾ miles (S. W. by W.) from Nantwich. The living is a perpetual curacy, in the archdeaconry and diocese of Chester, endowed with £600 private benefac-tion, £200 royal bounty, and £2200 parliamentary grant, and in the patronage of the Vicar of Acton. The church, dedicated to St. Margaret, has a fine carved oak ceiling and an elegant tower. A branch of the Chester canal passes through the parish, and a court leet is oc-casionally held here. A school is supported by annual subscriptions amounting to about £12.

WRENINGHAM (GREAT and LITTLE), a parish in the hundred of HUMBLEYARD, county of NORFOLK, 4¼ miles (E. S. E.) from Wymondham, containing 427 inhabitants. The living is a rectory, annexed to that of Ashwellthorpe, in the archdeaconry of Norfolk, and diocese of Norwich, rated in the king's books at £10. The church is dedicated to All Saints: that of Little Wreningham, which was dedicated to St. Mary, has been long demolished.

WRENTHAM, a parish in the hundred of BLYTH-ING, county of SUFFOLK, 4½ miles (N. by W.) from Southwold, containing 995 inhabitants. The living is a rectory, in the archdeaconry of Suffolk, and diocese of Norwich, rated in the king's books at £21. 6. 8., and in the patronage of Miss Buckle. The church is dedi-cated to St. Nicholas. There is a place of worship for Independents. William Wotton, a learned divine, was born here, in 1666; he died in 1726.

WRENTHORP, a joint township with Stanley, in the parish of WAKEFIELD, lower division of the wapen-take of AGBRIGG, West riding of the county of YORK, 1½ mile (N. N. E.) from Wakefield: the population is returned with Stanley. The manufacture of woollen cloth, &c., is carried on here.

WRESSEL, a parish in the Holme-Beacon division of the wapentake of HARTHILL, East riding of the county of YORK, comprising the townships of News-ham with Brind, and Wressel with Loftsome, and con-taining 360 inhabitants, of which number, 183 are in the township of Wressel with Loftsome, 3½ miles (N. W.) from Howden. The living is a discharged vicarage, in the archdeaconry of the East riding, and diocese of York, rated in the king's books at £5. 13. 9., and in the patronage of the Earl of Egremont. The church, dedicated to St. John of Beverley, is a very ancient build-ing. Here are some remains of Wressel castle, built by Thomas Percy, Earl of Worcester, who was made prisoner at the battle of Shrewsbury, and afterwards beheaded: this once princely mansion continued to be a seat of the Northumberland family till the civil war in the reign of Charles I., when it was demolished by order of the parliament.

WRESTLINGWORTH, a parish in the hundred of BIGGLESWADE, county of BEDFORD, 6 miles (E. N. E.)

from Biggleswade, containing 400 inhabitants. The living is a rectory, in the archdeaconry of Bedford, and diocese of Lincoln, rated in the king's books at £7. 6. 8., and in the patronage of the Crown. The church is dedicated to St. Peter.

WRETHAM (EAST), a parish in the hundred of SHROPHAM, county of NORFOLK, 5¾ miles (N. E. by N.) from Thetford, containing, with the parish of West Wretham, 342 inhabitants. The living is a rectory, with that of West Wretham annexed, in the archdea-conry of Norfolk, and diocese of Norwich, rated in the king's books at £11. 12. 3½., and in the patronage of Wyrley Birch, Esq. The church is dedicated to St. Ethelbert.

WRETHAM (WEST), a parish in the hundred of SHROPHAM, county of NORFOLK, 5½ miles (N. N. E.) from Thetford. The population is returned with the parish of East Wretham. The living is a rectory, an-nexed to that of East Wretham, in the archdeaconry of Norfolk, and diocese of Norwich, rated in the king's books at £12. 11. 3. The church is dedicated to St. Lawrence.

WRETTON, a parish in the hundred of CLACK-CLOSE, county of NORFOLK, 1 mile (W.) from Stoke-Ferry, containing 419 inhabitants. The living is a perpetual curacy, annexed to that of Wereham, in the archdeaconry of Norfolk, and diocese of Norwich, en-dowed with £16 per annum private benefaction, and £400 royal bounty. The church is dedicated to All Saints. There is a place of worship for Wesleyan Methodists.

WRIBBENHALL, a hamlet in the parish of KID-DERMINSTER, lower division of the hundred of HALF-SHIRE, county of WORCESTER, situated on the left bank of the Severn, immediately opposite Bewdley, and connected with that town by a noble bridge over the river. The population is returned with the parish. Here is a chapel for the service of the church of England, but not consecrated: it was erect-ed in the year 1701, at the expense of the inhabit-ants of the hamlet, on a plot of waste land belong-ing to Lord Foley, and was subsequently claimed by his lordship, as lord of the manor: this gave rise to litigation, and, after various decisions, it was given in his favour. Since that period his lordship has continued to appoint the minister, who held his situ-ation solely by virtue of such presentation, until its existence was legalized by a clause in an act of par-liament which passed in the early part of the reign of George IV., relating to dissenting places of worship, which excepts from its provisions all chapels wherein the service of the church of England had previously been performed: it is exempt from all ecclesiastical jurisdiction. The inhabitants support, by voluntary subscription, and by a collection after a sermon preached for the purpose, two schools in Bewdley, for children whose parents reside in the hamlet; in these about twelve boys and twenty-five girls are in-structed.

WRIGHTINGTON, a township in the parish of ECCLESTON, hundred of LEYLAND, county palatine of LANCASTER, 4 miles (N. W.) from Wigan, containing 1461 inhabitants.

WRINEHILL, a joint township with Checkley, in the parish of WYBUNBURY, hundred of NANTWICH, county palatine of CHESTER, 7 miles (E. S. E.) from Nantwich. The population is returned with Checkley.

WRINGTON, a parish (formerly a market town) in a detached portion of the hundred of BRENT with WRINGTON, county of SOMERSET, 7 miles (N. N. E.) from Axbridge, containing, with the tything of Broadfield, 1349 inhabitants. This place, which is situated near the Mendip hills, is not distinguished either for trade or for any branch of manufacture; the inhabitants are principally employed in agricultural pursuits, especially in the cultivation of teasel, of which great quantities are produced in the neighbourhood, for the supply of the clothiers in the adjoining districts, who use it in dressing the cloth. The town consists principally of two streets, intersecting each other obliquely, with other houses irregularly built, and in detached situations. The market, originally granted in the reign of Edward II., was held on Tuesday; and a fair was held annually on the 9th of September; but both have fallen into disuse. The county magistrates hold petty sessions here.

The living is a rectory, in the archdeaconry of Bath, and diocese of Bath and Wells, rated in the king's books at £39. 9. 4½., and in the patronage of the Marquis of Cleveland. The church, dedicated to All Saints, and situated at the south-west extremity of the town, is a spacious and handsome structure, in the later style of English architecture, with a square embattled tower, surmounted by angular turrets crowned with pinnacles. There are places of worship for Independents and Wesleyan Methodists. Mr. George Legg, in 1704, bequeathed nine acres of land, now producing £20 per annum, for the instruction of twelve children of both sexes in reading the bible. The school of industry, in which from thirty to forty children were instructed, and which was partly supported by a dividend on £50 stock, the bequest of Mrs. Webb, has been united to the National schools which have been established; and Sunday schools, in connexion with the established church and the dissenting congregations, are supported by subscription. Mrs. Hannah More resided for twenty-five years in a cottage, built by herself and sisters, at Barley Wood, in this parish; and John Locke, the eminent philosopher, was born in an old thatched house on the north side of the churchyard, in 1632; after his decease, in 1704, an urn with an appropriate inscription was presented by Mrs. Montague to Mrs. Hannah More, and erected in the pleasure grounds at Barley Wood. Dr. John Rogers, an eminent divine, held the rectory of this parish, where he passed a considerable portion of his time.

WRITHLINGTON, a parish in the hundred of KILMERSDON, county of SOMERSET, 7 miles (N. W. by N.) from Frome, containing 216 inhabitants. The living is a discharged rectory, in the archdeaconry of Wells, and diocese of Bath and Wells, rated in the king's books at £5. 7. 8½., and in the patronage of the Prebendary of Writhlington in the Cathedral Church of Salisbury. The church is dedicated to St. Mary Magdalene. In this parish are extensive coal mines and quarries of freestone: white lias and fullers' earth are also obtained here.

WRITTLE, a parish (formerly a market town) in the hundred of CHELMSFORD, county of ESSEX, 2½ miles (W. by S.) from Chelmsford, containing 2100 inhabitants. The living is a perpetual curacy, in the jurisdiction of the peculiar court of Writtle with Roxwell annexed, and in the patronage of the Warden and Fellows of New College, Oxford. The church, dedicated to All Saints, is ancient and spacious. There is a place of worship for Independents. Writtle has been long divested of the greater part of its trade by the rising importance of the neighbouring town of Chelmsford, but malting and brewing are still carried on, and there is an oil-mill in the vicinity. Morant and other writers have placed here the *Cæsaromagus* of Antoninus; and the remains of a royal palace, built by King John in 1211, which occupied an acre of ground surrounded by a deep moat, are still visible. Courts leet and baron are held here, and the inhabitants have the privilege of appointing their own coroner. Almshouses for six poor people were endowed by Thomas Hawkins, in 1607; and John Blencowe, in 1774, founded a free school for the education of the poor children of Writtle and Roxwell. A National school also has been recently established within the parish. About four miles northeast of the church, in the middle of a wood, called Highwood Quarter, a hermitage was founded, in the reign of Stephen, which, in that of Henry II., was attached to St. John's abbey, Colchester.

WROCKWARDINE, a parish in the Wellington division of the hundred of BRADFORD (South), county of SALOP, 2 miles (W. by N.) from Wellington, containing 2240 inhabitants. The living is a discharged vicarage, in the archdeaconry of Salop, and diocese of Lichfield and Coventry, rated in the king's books at £7. 8. 6., and in the patronage of the Crown. The church, dedicated to St. Peter, is a venerable edifice of red stone, substantially built, and in good repair. The Shrewsbury canal passes through the parish, which is bounded on the north by the river Tern. In the neighbourhood are extensive mines of coal and ironstone, also a mineral spring of considerable celebrity, called Admaston Spa.

WROOT, a parish in the western division of the wapentake of MANLEY, parts of LINDSEY, county of LINCOLN, 8 miles (N. E. by N.) from Bawtry, containing 285 inhabitants. The living is a rectory, in the archdeaconry of Stow, and diocese of Lincoln, rated in the king's books at £3. 7. 8½., and in the patronage of the Crown. The church is dedicated to St. Pancras. There is a place of worship for Wesleyan Methodists.

WROTHAM, a parish (formerly a market town) in the hundred of WROTHAM, lathe of AYLESFORD, county of KENT, 11 miles (W. N. W.) from Maidstone, and 24 (S. E. by E.) from London, containing, with the townships of Hale, Nepicar, Plaxtol, Winfield, and Roughway, 2357 inhabitants. This is a place of very remote antiquity: that it was a town of the ancient Britons is probable from various discoveries of British coins, and fragments of brass armour and military weapons; other circumstances lead to the conclusion that it was afterwards a Roman station, and the ancient military way from Oldborough to Stane-street passed through it. The town is situated near the foot of the chalk hills, and consists principally of two streets crossing each other on the high road from London to Maidstone; in the centre is the market-place, where is a public well. Some paper is manufactured at Basted. The market has been discontinued for many years: there is a fair on the 4th of May. The living comprises a sinecure rectory and a vicarage, in the exempt deanery of Shoreham, and in the peculiar jurisdiction and patronage of the Archbishop of Canterbury: the former, with the perpetual curacy of Stanstead annexed, is rated in the king's books at £50. 8. 1¼.; and the latter, with the rectory of Woodland annexed, at £22. 5. 10. The church, dedicated to St. George, is an ancient and spacious structure, with a mixture of the various styles, from the Norman to the later English; it contains sixteen stalls. A palace for the Archbishops of Canterbury formerly stood here, of which the terrace and a few offices alone remain. Wrotham hill, immediately above the town, affords one of the finest prospects in England.

WROTTESLEY, a hamlet in that part of the parish of TETTENHALL which is in the southern division of the hundred of SEISDON, county of STAFFORD, containing 258 inhabitants. This place is within the jurisdiction of the court of the royal peculiar of Tettenhall. Here are vestiges of an ancient city, from three to four miles in circuit, with streets running in different directions. Within its limits huge square stones have been dug up, with hinges, a dagger, and other relics, supposed to be Roman.

WROUGHTON, a parish in a detached portion of the hundred of ELSTUB and EVERLEY, county of WILTS, 3 miles (S. W. by S.) from Swindon, containing 1381 inhabitants. The living is a vicarage, in the archdeaconry of Wilts, and diocese of Salisbury, rated in the king's books at £12, and in the patronage of the Rector: the rectory (an impropriation) is rated at £31. 4. 4½., and is in the patronage of the Bishop of Winchester. The church is dedicated to St. John the Baptist and St. Helen. There is a place of worship for Wesleyan Methodists. Thomas Benit, in 1743, gave land, now producing more than £20 a year, for the endowment of a school.

WROXETER, a parish in the Wellington division of the hundred of BRADFORD (South), county of SALOP, 5¾ miles (S. E. by E.) from Shrewsbury, containing 659 inhabitants. The living is a discharged vicarage, in the archdeaconry of Salop, and diocese of Lichfield and Coventry, rated in the king's books at £11. 8., and in the patronage of the Marquis of Cleveland. The church is dedicated to St. Andrew. The old Watling-street passes through the parish, in which coal is obtained. It is bounded on the west by the navigable river Severn, and at low water the foundations of an ancient bridge are discernible. Here are the remains of an old Roman wall, twenty feet high, and two hundred feet in length, built partly of hewn stone and of British bricks, the remains of the celebrated city of *Uriconium*, so called by Antoninus, but by Ptolemy *Viroconium*, the circumference of which was about three miles. Within the area, among various other relics, such as graves, human bones, and other sepulchral memorials, numerous Roman coins have been found, which the tenants are bound by their leases to render to the lord of the manor, and are termed "Dynders," a corruption probably of *Denarius*; but they are so corroded, that their effigies and inscriptions are either very obscure, or entirely obliterated.

WROXHALL, a parish in the Snitterfield division of the hundred of BARLICHWAY, county of WARWICK, 6 miles (N. W. by N.) from Warwick, containing 177 inhabitants. The living is a donative, in the patronage of Christopher Roberts Wren, Esq. The church, dedicated to St. Leonard, forms the north side of the quadrangular edifice called Wroxhall Abbey, founded by Hugh de Hatton, about the close of the reign of Henry I., for Benedictine nuns, whose revenue at the dissolution was valued at £78. 10. 1.: it is occupied by C. R. Wren, Esq., fourth in descent from Sir Christopher Wren, who purchased the estate from the family of Burgoyne, about the year 1713.

WROXHAM, a parish in the hundred of TAVERHAM, county of NORFOLK, 2½ miles (S. E.) from Coltishall, containing 351 inhabitants. The living is a discharged vicarage, united to that of Salhouse, in the archdeaconry and diocese of Norwich, rated in the king's books at £7. 17. 1. The church is dedicated to St. Mary.

WROXTON, a parish in the hundred of BLOXHAM, county of OXFORD, 3 miles (W. N. W.) from Banbury, containing, with the chapelry of Balscott, 792 inhabitants. The living is a vicarage, in the archdeaconry and diocese of Oxford, and in the patronage of the Marquis of Bute. The church is dedicated to All Saints. There is a place of worship for Wesleyan Methodists. A priory of Augustine canons, in honour of the Blessed Virgin Mary, was founded early in the reign of Henry III., by Michael Belet, which at the dissolution was granted to Sir Thomas Pope, who afterwards bestowed it on Trinity College, Oxford.

WUERDALE, a joint township with Wardle, in that part of the parish of ROCHDALE which is in the hundred of SALFORD, county palatine of LANCASTER, 2 miles (N. E.) from Rochdale, containing, with Wardle, 5629 inhabitants. The parliamentary commissioners have proposed a grant towards the erection of a chapel in this township.

WYASTON, a township in the parish of EDLASTON, hundred of APPLETREE, county of DERBY, 3¼ miles (S. by E.) from Ashbourn. The population is returned with the parish.

WYBERTON, a parish in the hundred of KIRTON, parts of HOLLAND, county of LINCOLN, 2¼ miles (S.) from Boston, containing 487 inhabitants. The living is a rectory, in the archdeaconry and diocese of Lincoln, rated in the king's books at £33. 6. 8., and in the patronage of the Rev. Martin Sheath. The church is dedicated to St. Leodegar.

WYBUNBURY, a parish in the hundred of NANTWICH, county palatine of CHESTER, comprising the townships of Bartherton, Basford, Blakenhall, Bridgemere, Checkley with Wrinehill, Chorlton, Doddington, Hatherton, Hough, Hunsterson, Lea, Rope, Shavington with Gresty, Sound, Stapeley, Walgherton, Weston, Willaston, and Wybunbury, and containing 4146 inhabitants, of which number, 429 are in the township of Wybunbury, 3½ miles (E. S. E.) from Nantwich. The living is a vicarage, in the archdeaconry and diocese of Chester, rated in the king's books at £13. 12. 1., and in the patronage of the Bishop of Lichfield and Coventry. The church, dedicated to St. Chad, was rebuilt in 1595; it is a spacious structure, with carved wooden ceilings and a lofty pinnacled tower, which leans a little to the north-east. There is a place of worship for Wesleyan Methodists. A school, founded by the late Sir Thomas Delves, Bart., is conducted on the

National system, and attended by one hundred and thirty-four boys, of whom twenty receive annually a blue coat and cap each : the same individual endowed a school for ten girls, each of whom have a blue gown and bonnet annually ; also four others in different parts of the parish, which afford instruction to sixty-six girls. There is, besides, a boys' school, called the Wybunbury Charity, built by subscription about two hundred years ago, and endowed by several persons for the instruction of twenty boys. An hospital, dedicated to the Holy Cross and St. George, for a master and brethren, existed here before 1464.

WYCLIFFE, a parish in the western division of the wapentake of GILLING, North riding of the county of YORK, 2½ miles (E. N. E.) from Greta-Bridge, containing, with the township of Thorpe, 152 inhabitants. The living is a rectory, in the archdeaconry of Richmond, and diocese of Chester, rated in the king's books at £14. 12. 1., and in the patronage of T. E. Headlam, Esq. The church was rebuilt in the reign of Edward III. This is said to be the birthplace of Wickliffe, the Reformer; though some affirm that he was born at Spreswell, near Richmond, which is only a few miles hence.

WYCOMB, a hamlet in that part of the parish of ROTHWELL which is in the eastern division of the hundred of GOSCOTE, county of LEICESTER, 4½ miles (N.N.E.) from Melton-Mowbray. The population is returned with the chapelry of Chadwell.

Seal and Arms.

WYCOMBE (HIGH, or CHIPPING), a borough, market town, and parish, in the hundred of DESBOROUGH, county of BUCKINGHAM, 31 miles (S. S. E.) from Buckingham, and 29 (W. by N.) from London, containing 5599 inhabitants, of which number, 2864 are in the borough. This place, which is evidently of great antiquity, is by some supposed to have been occupied by the Romans. In the vicinity a tesselated pavement, nine feet square, was discovered in 1774; and among the numerous Roman coins that have been found were some of Antoninus Pius, Marcus Aurelius, and other Roman emperors. Of its occupation by the Saxons, the prefix to its name, "Cheaping," signifying a market, is an evident proof; and in the immediate neighbourhood of the town are the remains of a strong double intrenchment, called Desborough Castle, which was probably thrown up by that people to check the progress of the Danes. The only historical event connected with the place is a successful attack on the parliamentary troops quartered here, by Prince Rupert, after the battle of Reading. The town is pleasantly situated on a fine rivulet, called the Wycombe stream, which, after winding through the adjoining meadows, flows into the Thames below Marlow : it consists of one principal street, on the high road from London to Oxford, from which some smaller streets branch off in various directions. The houses are in general well built ; many of them are spacious and handsome, and the town has a prepossessing appearance of cheerfulness and great respectability. On each side are some

hills, richly wooded ; the environs abound with pleasingly varied scenery, and the surrounding district is luxuriantly fertile, and in the highest state of cultivation. The manufacture of paper is carried on to a very considerable extent, for which there are not less than twelve mills on the banks of Wycombe stream, besides six flour-mills. That of lace affords employment to several of the inhabitants, and chairs are made in great numbers : there is a considerable trade in malt, and the town derives a great degree of traffic from its situation, being on the road to Bath, Bristol, &c. The market, which is extensively supplied with corn, is on Friday; and a fair is annually held on the Monday next before Michaelmas-day, which is also a statute fair.

Wycombe, though governed by a mayor in the reign of Edward III., received its first regular charter of incorporation from Henry VI., which was confirmed and extended in the reigns of Elizabeth, James I., and Charles II., and vests the government in a mayor, recorder, two bailiffs, twelve aldermen, and an indefinite number of burgesses, assisted by a town clerk and other officers. The corporation hold occasional sessions for all offences not capital ; and under their charter they have power to hold a court of record, for the recovery of debts under £40, but no process has issued from it within the last fifty years. The town hall, erected in 1757, at the expense of the Earl of Shelburne, is a commodious and neat structure of brick, supported on stone pillars, and is well adapted to the business of the sessions, to the holding of public meetings, and to the uses of the corporation. The borough prison is a small, but well-arranged, building, capable of accommodating twelve prisoners ; it is divided into four wards for their classification. The borough first exercised the elective franchise in the 28th of Edward I., since which time it has continued to return two members to parliament : the right of election is vested in the mayor, bailiffs, and burgesses not receiving alms : the mayor is the returning officer.

The living is a discharged vicarage, in the archdeaconry of Buckingham, and diocese of Lincoln, rated in the king's books at £23. 17. 1., endowed with £1000 parliamentary grant, and in the patronage of the Marquis of Lansdowne. The church, dedicated to All Saints, is an ancient and venerable structure, in the early style of English architecture, with a square embattled tower, which has been subsequently ornamented and crowned with pinnacles. The interior consists of a nave, aisles, and chancel, the last of which is separated from the nave by an ancient oak screen: it contains several ancient and interesting monuments, among which are, one to the memory of Henry Petty, Earl of Shelburne, who died in 1751; one to the lady of the late earl, and several to the families of Archdale, Llewellyn, and Bradshaw. There are two places of worship for Independents, and one each for Baptists and the Society of Friends. An ancient hospital for lepers, dedicated to St. Margaret and St. Giles, and another, dedicated to St. John the Baptist, for a master, brethren, and sisters, were founded here in the reign of Henry III.; the latter was granted by Elizabeth to the mayor and corporation, and the endowment, augmented by Mr. Bowden, who in 1790 gave £1000 to be vested in the funds, producing at present about £180 per annum, is appropriated to the maintenance of a grammar school, and an almshouse for eight aged widows. The master of the school receives a salary of £60 per annum, and has a house, garden, and an orchard of two acres ; and the residue of the income is divided among the widows. A Lancasterian school for girls is supported by subscription; and there are several charitable bequests for distribution among the poor. Previously to the completion of the Royal Military College at Sandhurst, a department of that institution was established at Wycombe, which was, in 1802, removed to Great Marlow. Dr. Gamble, who wrote the Life of General Monk, and is supposed to have assisted him in effecting the restoration of Charles II., was vicar of this parish. The learned William Alley, Bishop of Exeter, and one of the translators of the Bible, in the reign of Queen Elizabeth ; and Charles Butler, author of a Treatise on Rhetoric, and other works, were natives of this town. Wycombe gives the titles of earl and baron to the Marquis of Lansdowne.

WYCOMBE (WEST), a parish in the hundred of DESBOROUGH, county of BUCKINGHAM, 2½ miles (N. W. by W.) from High Wycombe, containing 1545 inhabitants. The living is a discharged vicarage, in the archdeaconry of Buckingham, and diocese of Lincoln, rated in the king's books at £11. 9. 7., endowed with £800 private benefaction, and £200 royal bounty, and in the patronage of Sir J. Dashwood King, Bart. The church, dedicated to St. Lawrence, which is surrounded by an ancient intrenchment, was erected, in 1763, at the expense of Lord le Despenser ; it is an elegant structure in the Grecian style, with a profusion of Mosaic ornaments, and containing some handsome monuments ; in the adjoining mausoleum is one of considerable beauty to the memory of Sarah, Baroness le Despenser, with many memorials of the Dashwood family and others ; and in one of its recesses was deposited, in 1775, an urn enclosing the heart of Paul Whitehead, the poet, which he had bequeathed to Lord le Despenser. The church occupies an eminence finely clothed with woods, emerging from which the tower and the mausoleum form objects strikingly picturesque. There are places of worship for Independents and Wesleyan Methodists. The inhabitants are chiefly employed in the manufacture of lace and chairs. Catherine Pye, in 1713, bequeathed £7 per annum for teaching poor children. In the neighbourhood is an ancient camp, doubly intrenched, called Desborough Castle, which gives name to the hundred; vestiges of buildings, together with window-frames of stone, similar to those of a church, have been discovered on its site. Under the hill on which the church stands is a cave, but when and by whom dug is uncertain.

WYDDIALL, a parish in the hundred of EDWINS-TREE, county of HERTFORD, 1½ mile (N. E.) from Buntingford, containing 225 inhabitants. The living is a rectory, in the archdeaconry of Middlesex, and diocese of London, rated in the king's books at £16, and in the patronage of John Heaton, Esq. The church, dedicated to St. Giles, has an embattled tower at the west end, and contains several monuments : on the north side of the chancel is a chapel, in which are some remains of fine stained glass, representing the Crucifixion.

WYE, a parish (formerly a market town) in the hundred of WYE, lathe of SCRAY, county of KENT, 4 miles

(N. E.) from Ashford, and 56 (E. S. E.) from London, containing 1508 inhabitants. The town is pleasantly situated near the right bank of the river Stour, over which is a stone bridge of five arches, and consists of two parallel and two cross streets neatly built : on the river a little above the bridge is a corn-mill. The market has been long discontinued, but there are fairs on the 29th of May and the 11th of October. The living is a perpetual curacy, in the archdeaconry and diocese of Canterbury, endowed with £600 parliamentary grant, and in the patronage of the Earl of Winchilsea. The church, which is dedicated to St. Martin and St. Gregory, and anciently belonged to Battle abbey, was rebuilt and made collegiate by John Kemp, a native of this town, first Bishop of Rochester, and afterwards Cardinal, who, in 1431, founded a college for a master and Secular canons, the revenue of which at the dissolution was valued at £93. 2. It was a beautiful cruciform structure, with a central tower surmounted by a spire, and had all the usual parts of a large collegiate church ; in 1572, the spire was injured by lightning, and having been restored, fell in 1685, and destroyed a portion of the east end of the church, which was partly rebuilt in 1701, but on a much smaller scale. There is a place of worship for Wesleyan Methodists. The free grammar school was founded by grant from Charles I. of the rectories of Boughton-Aluph, Beuset, and Newington, and other premises, to Robert Maxwell and his heirs, for affording classical instruction to the poor children of parishioners; for which £16 a year is paid to a master, but there are no children on the foundation. An exhibition, originally of £10 per annum, to Lincoln College, Oxford, was attached to this school by Sir George Wheeler, in 1723, which was augmented to £20, in 1759, by his son, the Rev. Granville Wheeler : in default of candidates from this establishment, it is open to any other grammar school in the kingdom. A free school for children of both sexes was founded and endowed, in 1708, by Lady Joanna Thornhill; the present annual income is £193. 10. 6., for which fifty boys and sixty-one girls are now instructed, the school being open to all children of the poor, who are nominated by the trustees, consisting of the ministers of Wye and the four adjoining parishes, and the heirs of three other persons : the salary of the master is £40, and that of the mistress is £25, per annum. In 1723, Sir George Wheeler devised the ancient collegiate buildings and lands for the respective residences and schools of the master of the grammar school and the master and mistress under Lady Thornhill's charity : these establishments, therefore, now occupy the college green, the former the south, and the latter the north, side. An almshouse for the residence of six poor persons was founded by Sir Thomas Kempe.

WYERSDALE (NETHER), a township in the parish of GARSTANG, hundred of AMOUNDERNESS, county palatine of LANCASTER, 4 miles (N. N. E.) from Garstang, containing 800 inhabitants. Margaret Blackburn, in 1718, bequeathed £40, directing the interest to be applied in teaching poor children; and at Scorton, in this township, thirty other children are educated, at small charges, in a school erected by subscription.

WYERSDALE (OVER), a chapelry in that part of the parish of LANCASTER which is in the hundred of

LONSDALE, south of the sands, county palatine of LANCASTER, 6 miles (N. N. E.) from Garstang, containing 774 inhabitants. The living is a perpetual curacy, in the archdeaconry of Richmond, and diocese of Chester, endowed with £600 private benefaction, and £600 royal bounty, and in the patronage of the Vicar of Lancaster. The river Wyre rises in the neighbourhood. William Cawthorne, in 1683, gave a school-house, with a messuage and land, for the use of a schoolmaster, also a rent-charge of £15, for which thirty boys are instructed. Some monks from the abbey of Furness settled here, but, in 1188, they removed to Ireland, and founded Wythney abbey.

WYFORDBY or WYVERBY, a parish in the hundred of FRAMLAND, county of LEICESTER, 3 miles (E.) from Melton-Mowbray, containing, with the chapelry of Brentingby, 126 inhabitants. The living is a rectory, in the archdeaconry of Leicester, and diocese of Lincoln, rated in the king's books at £6, and in the patronage of Sir E. C. Hartopp, Bart. The church is dedicated to St. Mary. The river Eye and the Oakham canal run through the parish.

WYHAM, a parish in the wapentake of LUDBOROUGH, parts of LINDSEY, county of LINCOLN, 7¼ miles (N. W. by N.) from Louth, containing, with the hamlet of Cadeby, 107 inhabitants. The living is a discharged rectory, in the archdeaconry and diocese of Lincoln, rated in the king's books at £8, endowed with £600 royal bounty, and in the patronage of Viscount and Viscountess Goderich. The church is dedicated to All Saints.

WYKE, a tything in the parish and hundred of AXMINSTER, county of DEVON, containing 351 inhabitants.

WYKE-HAMON, formerly a parish, now a hamlet in that of WICKEN, hundred of CLELEY, county of NORTHAMPTON. The population is returned with Wicken, with which the rectory has long since been consolidated. The church, which has been long demolished, was dedicated to St. James.

WYKE-REGIS, a parish in the liberty of WYKE-REGIS and ETWALL, Dorchester division of the county of DORSET, 1¼ mile (W. S. W.) from Weymouth, containing 914 inhabitants. The living is a rectory, with the perpetual curacy of Weymouth annexed, in the archdeaconry of Dorset, and diocese of Bristol, rated in the king's books at £19. 7. 1., and in the patronage of the Bishop of Winchester. The church, dedicated to All Saints, is a large and ancient pile, with a lofty embattled tower. It is the mother church of Weymouth, and the usual burial-place of its inhabitants. At Smallmouth, in this parish, is a ferry to the Isle of Portland.

WYKEHAM, a parish in PICKERING lythe, North riding of the county of YORK, 6¼ miles (S. W. by W.) from Scarborough, containing 582 inhabitants. The living is a perpetual curacy, in the archdeaconry of Cleveland, and diocese of York, and in the patronage of the Hon. M. Langley. The church, dedicated to All Saints, was repaired and beautified at the expense of the late Richard Langley, Esq. A priory of Cistercian nuns, in honour of the Blessed Virgin Mary, was founded here, about 1153, by Pain Fitz-Osbert, which at the dissolution had a revenue of £25. 17. 6. There are still some remains of the abbey church.

WYKEHAM (EAST), a parish in the Wold division of the hundred of LOUTH ESKE, parts of LINDSEY, county of LINCOLN, 7 miles (W. by N.) from Louth, containing 29 inhabitants. The living is a discharged vicarage, in the archdeaconry and diocese of Lincoln, and in the patronage of —Ferrand, Esq. The church is in ruins.

WYKEHAM (WEST), a parish in the eastern division of the wapentake of WRAGGOE, parts of LINDSEY, county of LINCOLN, 7½ miles (W. by N.) from Louth. The living is a vicarage, in the archdeaconry and diocese of Lincoln, rated in the king's books at £3. 6. 8., and in the patronage of the Crown. The church is in ruins.

WYKEN, a parish in the county of the city of CoVENTRY, 3 miles (N. E. by E.) from Coventry, containing 79 inhabitants. The living is a perpetual curacy, in the archdeaconry of Coventry, and diocese of Lichfield and Coventry, endowed with £400 private benefaction, and £400 royal bounty, and in the patronage of Earl Craven.

WYKIN, a hamlet in the parish of HINCKLEY, hundred of SPARKENHOE, county of LEICESTER, 1½ mile (W. N. W.) from Hinckley, containing 98 inhabitants. Here was formerly a chapel, which has been demolished.

WYLAM, a township in the parish of OVINGHAM, eastern division of TINDALE ward, county of NORTHUMBERLAND, 9 miles (W.) from Newcastle upon Tyne, containing 728 inhabitants, who are mostly employed in the neighbouring collieries, the produce of which is brought hither from the south side of the Tyne, under the river, and conveyed by a rail-road to Leamington. Here are an extensive brewery and a manufactory for patent shot.

WYLDECOURT, a tything in that part of the parish of HAWKCHURCH which is in the hundred of CERNE, TOTCOMBE, and MODBURY, Cerne subdivision of the county of DORSET, containing 298 inhabitants.

WYMERING, a parish in the hundred of PORTSDOWN, Portsdown division of the county of SOUTHAMPTON, 4¼ miles (W.) from Havant, containing 625 inhabitants. The living is a vicarage, annexed to the rectory of Widley, in the archdeaconry and diocese of Winchester. The church is dedicated to St. Peter and St. Paul. The northern end of Portsea island, where Hilsea barracks stand, and across which are strong lines of defence, forms a part of this parish, and is connected with the main portion of it by Pos bridge, which crosses the narrow channel between Portsmouth and Langston harbours, and terminates in a tête-dupont. Great and Little Horsea islands, at the upper end of the former harbour, are also in this parish. An annuity of £2, the bequest of John Taylor, is applied in teaching poor children of the parishes of Wymering and Widley.

WYMINGTON, a parish in the hundred of WILLEY, county of BEDFORD, 6¼ miles (N.) from Harrold, containing 262 inhabitants. The living is a rectory, in the archdeaconry of Bedford, and diocese of Lincoln, rated in the king's books at £10, and in the patronage of — Lee, Esq. The church, dedicated to St. Lawrence, is a handsome structure in the later style of English architecture, said to have been built some time in the fourteenth century, by John Curteys, then lord of the manor, and mayor of the staple at Calais.

WYMONDHAM, a parish in the hundred of FRAMLAND, county of LEICESTER, 6½ miles (E.) from Melton-

Mowbray, containing 624 inhabitants. The living is a rectory, in the archdeaconry of Leicester, and diocese of Lincoln, rated in the king's books at £12, and in the patronage of the Crown. The church is dedicated to St. Peter. This is a place of great antiquity, being still surrounded by the remains of its ancient walls: the Oakham canal runs through the parish. Sir John Sedley, in 1637, liberally endowed, with land at Melton-Mowbray, a free school for all the poor boys of the parish.

WYMONDHAM, or WINDHAM, a parish in the hundred of FOREHOE, county of NORFOLK, 9 miles (W. S. W.) from Norwich, and 100 (N. E. by N.) from London, comprising the market town of Wymondham, which forms the in-soken, and the divisions of Downham, Market-Street, Silfield, Suton, Towngreen, and Wattlefield, which form the out-soken, and containing, according to the last census, 4708 inhabitants, since which the number is supposed to have increased to nearly 7000. This town derives its name from the Saxon words *Win Munde Ham*, which signify "a pleasant village on a mount," and is indebted for its importance to the foundation of a priory of Black monks, at first a cell to the abbey of St. Albans, by William d'Albini, or Daubeny, in the reign of Henry I. This monarch endowed the monastery with lands and with the privilege of appropriating all wrecks between Eccles, Happisburgh, and Tunstead, and with an annual rent, in kind, of two thousand eels from the village of Helgay. About 1448, it was elevated to the rank of an abbey, and at the dissolution its revenue was valued at £72. 5. 4. The two Ketts, who disturbed this county in the reign of Edward VI., were accustomed to assemble their followers under an oak, of which part yet remains, in the vicinity of the town; after their defeat by the Earl of Warwick, the elder was hanged in chains on the castle of Norwich, and the younger upon the lofty steeple of the church of Wymondham, of which town they were both natives. In 1615, three hundred houses were destroyed by fire; and in 1631, the plague raged with great fury among the inhabitants. The town, which is situated on the main road from Norwich to London, is of considerable extent, and is well supplied with water from springs; it has much improved of late years. Different branches of weaving are carried on in private houses, from ten to twelve hundred persons being employed by Messrs. Tipple and Son, the only firm in the town; the chief articles are bombazines and crapes. The market, granted by charter of King John in 1203, is held on Friday: the fairs are on February 14th and May 17th, principally for cattle, horses, and pedlary; statute fairs for hiring servants are held occasionally: in the market place is an ancient cross. A court leet is held annually for the appointment of constables, and manorial courts are held as occasion requires: the inhabitants enjoy the privilege of exemption from serving on juries at assizes and sessions.

' The living is a discharged vicarage, in the archdeaconry of Norfolk, and diocese of Norwich, rated in the king's books at £10. 14. 4½., and in the patronage of the Bishop of Ely. The church, which comprises the eastern part of the abbey church, and is dedicated to the Virgin Mary, is a fine structure in various styles of architecture, with the remains of the central tower, and another at the west end. Amid the ruins of the ancient conventual edifice are some Norman arches with low massive columns, and fragments of old walls: the more modern parts of the building are the north aisle, porch, and towers. In the interior is a large font, adorned with carved work, and elevated on steps; in the chancel is the tomb of the founder, who died in 1156, and several sepulchral memorials to the d'Albini family and other noble persons. There are places of worship for Baptists, the Society of Friends, Independents, and Wesleyan Methodists. A free grammar school was founded in the reign of Elizabeth, and endowed with part of the property of the guilds belonging to the collegiate church: a scholarship in Corpus Christi College, Cambridge, was attached to it, in 1574, by Archbishop Parker; another, in 1580, by John Parker, Esq.; and, in 1659, a share in an exhibition for scholarships to the same college, given by Edward Coleman, Esq.: the scholars must be natives, and have continued at the school for two years without intermission, and be fifteen years of age: the master's salary is about £60 per annum. There is also a bequest of a house and land, by a person unknown, producing about £100 per annum, for this school, part being distributed among the poor. The school is kept in an ancient chapel, dedicated to St. Mary and Thomas à Becket, at the bridge. The Rev. John Hendry, in 1722, bequeathed £400 to be vested in the purchase of land and the rental to be given to the vicar, on condition that two sermons be preached in the church every Sunday throughout the year; also a rent-charge of £13. 10. for preaching a sermon every Friday in Lent: the same benefactor bequeathed a small estate for the use of the charity school, chargeable with the payment of fifty shillings annually to indigent old maids of Wymondham, and ten shillings to the poor of Crownthorpe. A charity school in Churchgate-street, for educating, &c. an unlimited number of children, is supported by voluntary subscriptions.

WYMONDLEY (GREAT), a parish in the hundred of BROADWATER, county of HERTFORD, 2 miles (E. by S.) from Hitchin, containing 329 inhabitants. The living is a vicarage, with that of Ippolitts united, in the archdeaconry of Huntingdon, and diocese of Lincoln, and in the patronage of the Master and Fellows of Trinity College, Cambridge. The church is ancient, having a Norman arch between the nave and the chancel, with an embattled tower. The manor is held by the service of cup-bearer to the kings of England, at their coronation.

WYMONDLEY (LITTLE), a parish in the hundred of BROADWATER, county of HERTFORD, 2¼ miles (S. E. by E.) from Hitchin, containing 227 inhabitants. The living is a perpetual curacy, in the archdeaconry of Huntingdon, and diocese of Lincoln, and in the patronage of S. H. U. Heathcote, Esq. The church, dedicated to St. Mary, is covered with lead, and contains, among other sepulchral memorials, some very ancient gravestones. A priory of Black canons, in honour of St. Lawrence, was founded here, in the time of Henry III., by Richard Argentein, which at the dissolution had a revenue of £37. 10. 6. There are no remains of the building; its site is marked by some avenues of stately box trees, and there is an ancient well, to the water of which tradition ascribes considerable efficacy. In the village is a college for educating Protestant dissenting ministers, founded in 1729, by W. Coward, Esq., with a chapel attached. This establishment originated at Northampton, and the celebrated Dr. Doddridge was its first theological professor. It possesses a valuable library of nearly ten thousand volumes, and an extensive and complete philosophical apparatus. There are two professorships, one including the theological, philosophical, and mathematical departments; the other every branch of classical literature.

WYRARDISBURY, or WRAYSBURY, a parish in the hundred of STOKE, county of BUCKINGHAM, 3 miles (S. W. by S.) from Colnbrook, containing 520 inhabitants. The living is a vicarage, with the perpetual curacy of Langley-Marish annexed, in the archdeaconry of Buckingham, and diocese of Lincoln, rated in the king's books at £14. 10. 5., and in the patronage of the Dean and Canons of Windsor. The church is dedicated to St. Andrew. A Benedictine nunnery, in honour of St. Mary Magdalene, was founded at Ankerwyke, in this parish, in the time of Henry II., by Sir Gilbert de Montfichet, which at the dissolution was valued at £45. 14. 4.

WYRE-PIDDLE, a chapelry in the parish of FLADBURY, middle division of the hundred of OSWALDSLOW, county of WORCESTER, 1¾ mile (N. E. by E.) from Pershore, containing 178 inhabitants.

WYRLEY (GREAT), a township in the parish of CANNOCK, eastern division of the hundred of CUTTLESTONE, county of STAFFORD, 6½ miles (N. N. W.) from Walsall, containing 531 inhabitants.

WYRLEY (LITTLE), a township in the parish of NORTON under CANNOCK, southern division of the hundred of OFFLOW, county of STAFFORD, 7¼ miles (W. S. W.) from Lichfield: the population is returned with the parish. Several of the inhabitants are employed in the Brownhill coal mine, the shaft of which is ninety yards in depth, and the strata three yards thick.

WYSALL, a parish in the southern division of the wapentake of RUSHCLIFFE, county of NOTTINGHAM, 8½ miles (S. by E.) from Nottingham, containing 287 inhabitants. The living is a discharged vicarage, in the archdeaconry of Nottingham, and diocese of York, rated in the king's books at £4. 11. 0½., and in the patronage of the Earl of Gosford. The church is dedicated to the Holy Trinity.

WYTHALL, a chapelry in the parish of KING'S NORTON, upper division of the hundred of HALFSHIRE, county of WORCESTER, 8 miles (N. E. by E.) from Bromsgrove. The population is returned with the parish. The living is a perpetual curacy, in the archdeaconry and diocese of Worcester, endowed with £800 royal bounty, and in the patronage of the Vicar of Bromsgrove. The chapel is dedicated to St. Mary.

WYTHAM, a parish in the hundred of HORMER, county of BERKS, 3 miles (N. W.) from Oxford, containing 241 inhabitants. The living is a rectory, in the archdeaconry of Berks, and diocese of Salisbury, rated in the king's books at £7. 5. 2½., and in the patronage of the Earl of Abingdon. The church is dedicated to All Saints. Here was anciently a nunnery, which was originally founded at Abingdon by the sister of King Ceadwalla, and afterwards removed hither; but, during the war between Offa and Cynewulf, it was demolished by the nuns, who had suffer'd great annoy-

ance from a castle having been erected in the neighbourhood.

WYTHBURN, a joint chapelry with St. John's Castlerigg, in that part of the parish of CROSTHWAITE which is in ALLERDALE ward below Darwent, county of CUMBERLAND, 8¼ miles (S. E. by S.) from Keswick. The population is returned with St. John's Castlerigg, under which also the account of the living is given. The boundaries of the counties of Cumberland and Westmorland are here marked by "Dunmaile-Raise Stones," which are said to commemorate the defeat of the last king of Cumberland, by Edmund, the Saxon monarch, of whom Malcolm, King of Scotland, held Cumberland in fee. Thirlemere lake is within this chapelry.

WYTHOP, a chapelry in the parish of LORTON, ALLERDALE ward above Darwent, county of CUMBERLAND, 5 miles (E. by S.) from Cockermouth, containing 100 inhabitants. The living is a perpetual curacy, in the archdeaconry of Richmond, and diocese of Chester, endowed with £800 royal bounty, and £400 parliamentary grant, and in the patronage of certain Trustees. The chapel is situated on an eminence above the western bank of Bassenthwaite lake. The ancient hall has been converted into a farm-house. The Rev. John Hudson, a learned divine and critic, was born here, in 1662; he died in 1719.

WYTON, a township in that part of the parish of SWINE which is in the middle division of the wapentake of HOLDERNESS, East riding of the county of YORK, 5½ miles (N. E. by E.) from Kingston upon Hull, containing 95 inhabitants.

WYVERSTONE, a parish in the hundred of HARTISMERE, county of SUFFOLK, 6¼ miles (N.) from Stow-Market, containing 260 inhabitants. The living is a discharged rectory, in the archdeaconry of Sudbury, and diocese of Norwich, rated in the king's books at £8. 14. 9½., and in the joint patronage of Mrs. Moseley and John Moseley, Esq. The church is dedicated to St. George.

WYVILL, a parish in the wapentake of WINNIBRIGGS and THREO, parts of KESTEVEN, county of LINCOLN, 6 miles (N. W.) from Colsterworth. The population is returned with the parish of Hungerton. The living is a discharged rectory, united to that of Hungerton, in the archdeaconry and diocese of Lincoln. The church is in ruins: the inhabitants attend that at Harlaxton.

Y.

YADDLETHORPE, a hamlet in that part of the parish of BOTTESFORD which is in the eastern division of the wapentake of MANLEY, parts of LINDSEY, county of LINCOLN, 8 miles (W.) from Glandford-Bridge, containing 87 inhabitants. John Willson, in 1738, bequeathed land, producing upwards of £30 per annum, in support of a free school for teaching all the poor children of the parish of Bottesford.

YAFFORTH, a chapelry in the parish of DANBY-WISK, eastern division of the wapentake of GILLING, North riding of the county of YORK, 1½ mile (W. by N.) from North-Allerton, containing 149 inhabitants.

YALDING, a parish (formerly a market town) in the hundred of TWYFORD, lathe of AYLESFORD, county of KENT, 5 miles (S. W.) from Maidstone, containing 2414 inhabitants. The living is a vicarage, in the archdeaconry and diocese of Rochester, rated in the king's books at £20. 18. 9., and in the patronage of the Rev. Richard Ward. The church, dedicated to St. Peter and St. Paul, is principally in the decorated style of English architecture. The parish is intersected by different branches of the Medway, and upon two of the larger streams stands the village, approached by a long narrow stone bridge, besides which, there are two others in the parish, called Brant and Twyford bridges. The river is navigable to this place for barges, by which a considerable traffic in timber and other naval stores is carried on with Chatham, Sheerness, London, and other ports; the vessels returning with a variety of necessary articles, particularly coal, from which a considerable quantity of coke is made, and distributed through the neighbourhood for drying hops. The market has been long disused; but fairs for cattle and hops are held on Whit-Monday and October 15th. William Cleave, Esq., in 1665, founded a free school, and endowed it with a farm now let for £50 a year, which, with the previous bequests of Julian Kenward and Thomas and John Twiffer, amounting to the additional sum of £17 per annum, is applied to teaching from thirty to forty children. A charity school, founded in 1711, for girls and young children, has been endowed by Mrs. Alchorn and Mrs. Warde, sisters, with a school-house, besides certain lands and other premises, the rents of which are paid half-yearly to a schoolmistress for teaching from twenty to twenty-four children, under the superintendence of the vicar.

YANWATH, a joint township with Eamont-Bridge, in the parish of BARTON, WEST ward, county of WESTMORLAND, 2 miles (S. by W.) from Penrith, containing, with Eamont-Bridge, 244 inhabitants. The ancient hall, a quadrangular castellated building, is now occupied as a farm-house, and about a mile from it are vestiges of a circular camp, called Castle Steads.

YANWORTH, a chapelry in the parish of HAZLETON, hundred of BRADLEY, county of GLOUCESTER, 3½ miles (W. by S.) from North Leach, containing 119 inhabitants. The chapel, dedicated to St. Michael, is a chapel of ease to Hazleton, where the inhabitants of Yanworth anciently buried their dead; but since the latter part of the last century this has been their usual place of sepulture.

YAPHAM, a chapelry in the parish of POCKLINGTON, Wilton - Beacon division of the wapentake of HARTHILL, East riding of the county of YORK, 2½ miles (N.N.W.) from Pocklington, containing 114 inhabitants. The living is a perpetual curacy, with the vicarage of Pocklington, in the peculiar jurisdiction of the Dean of York. Twelve children are educated for an annuity of £12, paid out of the produce of the chapel lands. There is no burial-ground at Yapham; the inhabitants inter their dead at Pocklington.

YAPTON, a parish in the hundred of AVISFORD, rape of ARUNDEL, county of SUSSEX, 5 miles (S. W.) from Arundel, containing 579 inhabitants. The living is a discharged vicarage, united to that of Walberton, in the archdeaconry and diocese of Chichester, rated in the king's books at £7. 10. 11½. The church is principally in the early style of English architecture. The Arundel and Portsmouth canal passes through the parish. Stephen Roe, in 1766, bequeathed £1200 three per cent. South Sea annuities, producing about £36 a year, of which sum £20 is applied for teaching twenty children, and the residue to other charitable purposes.

YARBOROUGH, or YARBURGH, a parish in the Marsh division of the hundred of LOUTH-ESKE parts of LINDSEY, county of LINCOLN, 4¾ miles (N. E. by N.) from Louth, containing 207 inhabitants. The living is a discharged rectory, in the archdeaconry and diocese of Lincoln, rated in the king's books at £9. 13. 6., and in the patronage of N. E. Yarburgh, Esq. The church is dedicated to St. John the Baptist. There is a place of worship for Wesleyan Methodists. Yarborough gives the title of baron to the family of Pelham.

YARBOROUGH, a hamlet in the parish of CROXTON, eastern division of the wapentake of YARBOROUGH, parts of LINDSEY, county of LINCOLN, 8 miles (N. E.) from Glandford-Bridge. The population is returned with the parish. Here are the remains of a very extensive camp, upon the site of which vast numbers of Roman coins have been discovered.

YARCOMBE, a parish in the hundred of AXMINSTER, county of DEVON, 5½ miles (W.) from Chard, containing 793 inhabitants. The living is a discharged vicarage, in the archdeaconry and diocese of Exeter, rated in the king's books at £28, endowed with £200 private benefaction, and £200 royal bounty, and in the patronage of the Crown. The church is dedicated to St. John the Baptist. There is a place of worship for Baptists. A small school is partly supported by annual subscriptions of about £5.

YARDLEY, a parish in the hundred of ODSEY, county of HERTFORD, 4½ miles (W. S. W.) from Buntingford, containing 617 inhabitants. The living is a discharged vicarage, in the archdeaconry of Huntingdon, and diocese of Lincoln, rated in the king's books at £12, endowed with £200 private benefaction, and £200 royal bounty, and in the patronage of the Dean and Chapter of St. Paul's, London. The church, dedicated to St. Lawrence, has an embattled tower surmounted by a spire covered with lead. Chauncey, the historian of Hertfordshire, is interred here.

YARDLEY, a parish in the upper division of the hundred of HALFSHIRE, county of WORCESTER, 4½ miles (E.) from Birmingham, containing 2313 inhabitants. The living is a discharged vicarage, in the archdeaconry and diocese of Worcester, rated in the king's books at £9. 19. 4½., and in the patronage of Edmund Wigley, Esq. The church, dedicated to St. Edburgh, exhibits various specimens of the English style of architecture, with a fine tower and spire of the later date; it has lately received an addition of one hundred and twenty sittings, of which one hundred are free, the Incorporated Society for the enlargement of churches and chapels having granted £100 towards defraying the expense. Here are various bequests, producing a considerable income, for the education and relief of the poor. Great quantities of tiles are made in the neighbourhood, and conveyed to Birmingham, whence they are sent by the canals to various parts of the kingdom.

YARDLEY-GOBION, a hamlet in the parish of POTTERS-PURY, hundred of CLELEY, county of NORTH-

AMPTON, 3½ miles (N. N. W.) from Stony-Stratford, containing 565 inhabitants. There is a place of worship for Independents.

YARDLEY-HASTINGS, a parish in the hundred of WYMERSLEY, county of NORTHAMPTON, 8½ miles (E. S. E.) from Northampton, containing 917 inhabitants. The living is a rectory, to which a portion of the rectory of Denton is annexed, in the archdeaconry of Northampton, and diocese of Peterborough, rated in the king's books at £13. 16. 0½., and in the patronage of the Marquis of Northampton. The church is dedicated to St. Andrew. There is a place of worship for Independents. North of the church are the ruins of an ancient mansion, once the seat of the family of Hastings, Earls of Pembroke. A fair is held on Whit-Monday. The Rev.— Lye, author of the Saxon Dictionary, died rector of this parish, in 1767. A school, in which about two hundred children are educated, is supported by subscription.

YARKHILL, a parish in the hundred of RADLOW, county of HEREFORD, 7¼ miles (E. by N.) from Hereford, containing 435 inhabitants. The living is a discharged vicarage, in the archdeaconry and diocese of Hereford, rated in the king's books at £3. 19. 3., and in the patronage of the Dean and Chapter of Hereford. The church is dedicated to St. John the Baptist.

YARLESIDE, a township in the parish of DALTON in FURNESS, hundred of LONSDALE, north of the sands, county palatine of LANCASTER, 2 miles (S.) from Dalton, containing 509 inhabitants.

YARLETT, a liberty in the parish of WESTON upon TRENT, southern division of the hundred of PIREHILL, county of STAFFORD, containing 33 inhabitants.

YARLINGTON, a parish in the hundred of BRUTON, county of SOMERSET, 3½ miles (W.) from Wincanton, containing 301 inhabitants. The living is a rectory, in the archdeaconry of Wells, and diocese of Bath and Wells, rated in the king's books at £16. 1. 3., and in the patronage of Mrs. Anne Reynolds Rogers. The church, dedicated to St. Mary, has an embattled tower on the south side. On the south-west declivity of Godshill, in this parish, is a double-intrenched camp, from which there is an extensive prospect.

YARLINGTON, a hamlet in the parish of NORTH CADBURY, hundred of CATSASH, county of SOMERSET, containing, with Woolston and Clapton, 140 inhabitants.

YARM, a market town and parish in the western division of the liberty of LANGBAURGH, North riding of the county of YORK, 44 miles (N. N. W.) from York, and 238 (N. by W.) from London, containing 1504 inhabitants. This town, situated on a low peninsula formed by the river Tees, appears to have been formerly of more importance than it is at present, and its decline may be attributed partly to its vicinity to the rising town of Stockton, distant only four miles, and partly to its having been exposed, from its low situation, to floods. On the 17th of February, 1753, from a sudden thaw on the western hills, the water rushed down upon the town,- seven feet in depth, destroying and carrying off live stock and household goods to a considerable extent; but the most destructive of these inundations occurred in November, 1771, when the Tees rose so as to occasion, in some parts of the town, a depth of twenty feet, which, in addition to the destruction of a great quantity of valuable property, occasioned also the loss of some lives: it has been since occasionally subject to similar, though much less violent, calamities. The principal street, which extends north and south, is spacious, and contains some good houses. A bridge of five arches across the Tees, built in 1400, by Walter Skirlaw, Bishop of Durham, has been much improved. A beautiful iron bridge of one arch, of one hundred and eighty feet span, was constructed in 1805; but, owing to some defect in the foundation, it fell down on the 12th of January, 1806, a short time before it was to have been opened to the public, and has not been replaced. The trade principally consists in the exportation of agricultural produce, and the town also participates with Stockton in the salmon fishery of the Tees, the tide flowing a short distance above it: the corn trade, which at one period was carried on to a considerable extent, has much declined. In addition to the advantages derived from the navigation of the river Tees, a branch from the Stockton and Darlington railway facilitates the transit of goods. The market is on Thursday; and there are fairs on the Thursday before April 5th, on Ascension-day, August 2nd, and October 19th and 20th, for horses, cattle, and cheese, of which last article great quantities are sold on the latter day. A court for the recovery of small debts is held here, twice in the year, by the lord of the manor.

The living is a perpetual curacy, in the archdeaconry of Cleveland, and diocese of York, and in the patronage of the Archbishop of York. The church, dedicated to St. Mary Magdalene, situated at the west side of the town, is a plain neat structure, rebuilt in 1730: it has a handsome painted window, containing a full-length figure of Moses delivering the law on Mount Sinai. The Society of Friends, Independents, Primitive and Wesleyan Methodists, and Roman Catholics, have each a place of worship. The free grammar school was founded, in the reign of Queen Elizabeth, by Thomas Conyers, the endowment was increased in 1799, by a bequest from William Chaloner, of £400 three per cent. stock; which, together with the preceding, produces at present an income of £21. 4. as a salary to the master, who has also rent free a small house of two apartments adjoining the school-room. The founder and six other of the inhabitants were, by charter of Elizabeth, incorporated as governors with a common seal, and power to possess lands, to nominate the master, and make statutes for the regulation of the school: but this body is extinct; and the management is in twelve of the principal inhabitants. The usual number of free scholars is fourteen, but none of them are instructed in the classics. The same Mr. Chaloner also bequeathed £100 four per cent. stock to the minister of Yarm for four annual Sunday evening lectures in the parish church. A National school for one hundred and sixty children of both sexes was erected, in 1816, by subscription, and is supported by voluntary contributions: some small bequests are annually distributed among the poor. An hospital, dedicated to St. Nicholas, founded in 1185, and valued at its dissolution at £5 per annum, and a house of Black friars, founded in the thirteenth century, both by the family of De Brus, existed here; but no trace of either is discernible.

Corporate Seal.

YARMOUTH, a borough, market town, and parish, in the liberty of WEST MEDINA, Isle of Wight division of the county of SOUTHAMPTON, 10 miles (W.) from Newport, and 94 (S. W.) from London, by Portsmouth, and 105 by Southampton, containing 564 inhabitants. This place, which derived its name from its situation on the river Yar, was formerly of much greater extent and importance than it is at present; but it had suffered severely from attacks of the French, by whom it was, in the reign of Richard II., pillaged and entirely burned, and on two subsequent occasions it was nearly destroyed by them. The Town field, laid out regularly in right angles, though now destitute of buildings, clearly appears to have been originally the site of a part of the town. Yarmouth is situated on a bank sloping to the sea, on the eastern point of land at the mouth of the Yar, and consists of several neat streets, for the most part running east and west: the houses, which are of freestone, are in general well-built and of neat appearance, and public baths have been recently established. At its western extremity are a castle and small fort, erected by Henry VIII.: the latter, which occupies the site of a church, or ancient religious house, and consists of a platform with eight guns, and houses for the garrison, has recently been granted by the Board of Ordnance to the corporation, who contemplate demolishing it, for the purpose of improving the quay and the landing-places. A large house near the former, which has been converted into an inn, was erected by Sir Robert Holmes, for the reception of Charles II., a portrait of whom, during his stay here, was painted by Sir P. Lely, and is in the possession of the Holmes family. The trade is now very limited: a considerable quantity of fine white sand, used in the manufacture of flint glass and the finer sorts of British china, is obtained here. The principal imports are, coal from Sunderland, and timber from the New Forest: a constant intercourse by boats is kept up with the opposite town of Lymington, and, before the general use of steamboats, this was considered the safest and most expeditious passage to the island. The market is on Friday; and a fair is held on the 25th of July. The markethouse is a neat building, with a hall over it, in which the several courts are held, and the business of the corporation is transacted. The original charter of incorporation was granted by Baldwyn de Kedvers, Earl of Devon, and confirmed by Edward I.; but that under which the corporation now acts was granted in the 7th of James I., which ordains the appointment of a mayor and twelve capital burgesses, with power to choose a steward, a town clerk, and a serjeant at mace, and to create an unlimited number of freemen, but this last privilege is not now exercised. The borough courts are held by the mayor and steward, and the corporation is entitled to all the fines, forfeitures, and profits of the courts, with many other privileges. The borough first sent members to parliament in the 23rd of Edward I., but made no other return until the 27th of Elizabeth,

since which period it has exercised the privilege without interruption: the right of election is vested in the mayor and burgesses; the mayor is the returning officer, and the patronage is possessed by the Trustees of the late Sir L. Worsley Holmes.

The living is a discharged rectory, in the archdeaconry and diocese of Winchester, endowed with £200 private benefaction, and £200 royal bounty, and in the patronage of the Crown. The church, dedicated to St. James, and situated in the centre of the town, is a neat structure, consisting of a nave and chancel, on the south side of which is a sepulchral chapel, containing a handsome statue of the full size, in Parian marble, of Sir Robert Holmes, formerly Governor of the Isle of Wight. There are places of worship for Baptists and Wesleyan Methodists. A National and a Lancasterian school are supported by voluntary subscriptions. The sum of £30, bequeathed by Thomas, Lord Holmes, is distributed annually, in the chapel adjoining the church, to the poor not receiving parochial relief, towards apprenticing a boy out of the parish, and to the minister. Many Saxon customs, not generally observed, are still retained at Yarmouth, such as decorating the coffins of the dead with flowers and evergreens, the mourners carrying bunches of rosemary, &c.

YARMOUTH (GREAT), a sea-port, borough, market town, and parish, having separate jurisdiction, locally in the eastern division of the hundred of Flegg, county of NORFOLK, 23 miles (E. by S.) from Norwich, and 123 (N. E.) from London, containing, according to the last census, 18,040 inhabitants. This place, which, from its extensive and prosperous trade and many other advantages and privileges, may be considered the most flourishing port on this part of the coast, derives its name from its situation at the mouth of the river Yare, which here falls into the ocean. It occupies ground originally covered by the sea, which, on its receding, left a bank of sand, whereon a few fishermen settled, the first of whom, denominated Fuller, imparted name to the higher portion, still called Fuller's hill. As the bank increased in extent and density, the population augmented; but the channel of the northern branch of the Yare, on which the first settlers fixed their habitations, becoming choked up with sand, they, in 1040, removed to the southern branch. The earliest authentic record of Yarmouth is in Domesday-book, in which it is described as "the king's demesne, and having seventy burgesses." Its fishery attracting, at an early period, many residents, a charter was granted, at the request of the inhabitants, by Henry III., allowing them to enclose the burgh, on the land side, with a wall and moat; the former was two thousand two hundred and forty yards in length, and had sixteen towers and ten gates. A castle, having four watch towers, and upon which a fire beacon was placed in 1588, was also built about this time in the centre of the town: in the last-named year a mound, called South Mount, was thrown up and crowned

Arms.

with heavy ordnance, and the place was then considered impregnable. The castle having been demolished in 1621, and the changes introduced into the system of warfare rendering further defences necessary, strong parapets were constructed in front of the town, and cannon planted on them, facing the sea: the circuit of the fortifications thus completed was nearly two miles and a half. The only military operation in which the inhabitants have been ever actually engaged was their gallantly repulsing Kett, when, in his rebellion, he attempted, at the head of twenty thousand men, to take the town by assault. But though Yarmouth has been only slightly visited by the scourge of warfare, it has suffered severely from the plague, to which, in 1348, upwards of seven thousand persons fell victims; in 1579, upwards of two thousand; and more than two thousand five hundred in 1664.

The town occupies an extent of one hundred and fifty-three acres, on the western bank of a peninsula formed by the river Yare and the sea, and is connected with South Town, or Little Yarmouth, which is on the opposite bank, by a drawbridge. It is divided into eight wards, and is of a quadrangular form, about a mile long, and half a mile broad: it consists of four good streets parallel with each other, a handsome new street leading to the quay, on which is a noble range of buildings, and a great number of narrow rows intersecting the principal streets at right angles: it is lighted with gas, and well supplied with fresh water, and the streets are kept remarkably clean. The theatre, a neat and commodious edifice, erected in 1778, near the market-place, is open during the summer months; and races take place, annually in August, on the Denes, a fine down south of the town. The bathing-houses on the beach, near the jetty, possess every accommodation for visitors; and adjoining is a public room, built in 1788, where balls and concerts occasionally take place. There are very pleasant walks on the quay and beach; and the extensive sea view, enlivened by the number of vessels in the roads, is a source of considerable gratification to the frequenters of this sea-port, which is resorted to as a watering-place. The barracks on the South Denes, near the beach, form a magnificent quadrangular range of buildings, designed by Mr. Pilkington, and erected at a cost of £120,000; the building was used as a naval hospital during the war. The armoury in South Town will contain, exclusively of other military and naval stores, ten thousand stand of arms. Between the barracks and the entrance to the harbour, a grand fluted column, one hundred and thirty feet high, and surmounted by a statue of Britannia, has been erected to the memory of Admiral Lord Nelson, and, as a land-mark, well supplies to seamen the loss of Gorleston steeple, which was blown down in 1813. On the quay is the custom-house, with the usual officers of collector, comptroller, surveyor, landing waiters, &c., attached, and a coast waiter at Lowestoft; and within a short distance is a public library, with a good collection of books: there are also subscription reading-rooms adjoining the library. A handsome suspension chain bridge, of eighty-six feet span, has been constructed by Robert Cory, Esq., at the northern part of the quay over the river Bure; and a new road, in communication with this bridge, recently completed under

an act of parliament, will materially shorten the distance between this town and Norwich.

Yarmouth is not a manufacturing town, though a considerable establishment for winding and throwing silk has been recently formed in connexion with a larger concern at Norwich, and for which buildings have been erected on the site formerly occupied by the barracks, at the north of the town. The premises are very extensive; the machinery is worked by a very powerful steam-engine, and the shaft, or chimney, which rises to a height of one hundred and twenty-five feet, is a conspicuous object at a considerable distance both at sea and land. There are extensive yards for ship-building, with corresponding rope-walks, and several large breweries. A considerable business is carried on coastwise in malt, corn, flour, coal, timber, and other articles. A direct trade prevails with the Baltic, the Mediterranean, Portugal, and other parts of the continent; and a regular communication by steam-vessels is kept up internally with Norwich, and coastwise with London and the North of England. But the principal source of trade by which this town is supported is the herring fishery, which is usually productive to a remarkable extent. The fish, when cured, or dried, for both of which processes there are very extensive establishments, are not only sent to all parts of the kingdom, but exported in considerable quantities to other parts of the world, particularly the West Indies, where they are much used as food for the negroes. Many vessels from other parts of the coast fish here, and some, at a defined distance, from other countries, especially France and the Netherlands. The situation of Yarmouth, in a commercial point of view, affords unusual advantages. The Yare is here navigable for vessels of two hundred and fifty tons' burden; and to Norwich, a distance of thirty-two miles, for smaller vessels, without the intervention of locks. The Waveney, which falls into the Yare, is navigable by Beccles to Bungay, a distance of twenty miles; and the Bure, which also joins the Yare, by Horstead to Aylsham, thirty miles, and another branch to North Walsham, twenty-five miles hence, thus opening an extensive and valuable channel of inland communication. Many attempts have been unsuccessfully made to form a safe harbour, at the enormous expense of above £240,000; but the present one, which is the seventh that has been constructed, was projected and executed, at an expense of about £4200 only, by Joas Johnson, a native of Holland, and affords secure anchorage in all weathers: it was defended by two batteries, one on the beach to the north, and the other on Gorleston hill. At the entrance of the Yare are two piers; that on the south is one thousand two hundred and thirty feet long, and forms an agreeable promenade; and that on the north is four hundred feet in length, erected on wooden piles, and secured by iron railing. The quay, which in length and beauty of construction ranks the first in England, is a very great ornament to the town, and its centre is formed into a beautiful walk, planted on each side with trees. A duty of fifteen-pence per chaldron, producing about £8000 per annum, is levied on all coal brought to the port, and applied, under the direction of twelve commissioners, to keeping the jetties and piers in repair, and deepening and clearing the river: the commissioners are chosen, three each, by the corporations of Yarmouth and Norwich, and by the magistrates of Norfolk and Suffolk.

The number of vessels belonging to this port is upwards of five hundred, exclusively of small craft. The navigation of the coast is very dangerous; but the Roads, in which are two floating lighthouses, are frequently resorted to by the North Sea fleet, and merchant vessels are constantly repairing to them for shelter. The market is on Wednesday and Saturday; and fairs are held on the Friday and Saturday in Easter week, and on the Monday and Tuesday at Shrovetide.

Corporate Seal.

Obverse.   Reverse.

Prior to the reign of King John, the town was governed by a provost appointed by the Crown; but a charter of incorporation granted by that monarch, in the ninth year of his reign, empowered the burgesses to choose their own magistrates, called bailiffs, of whom four were elected, who were authorised to hold a court of hustings, now called the Burgh court. These privileges were extended by charters granted by succeeding sovereigns, of which that of Edward II., granted ironage to the burgesses, and that they should not be put on any assizes, juries, or inquisitions, out of the borough. Richard II. united Kirtley-road to Yarmouth; Henry VII. granted power to elect justices of the peace; Elizabeth granted a charter to hold an admiralty court weekly, with power to try all maritime causes, except piracy; James I. confirmed the foregoing, adding the power to try pirates, and defined the admiralty jurisdiction to be from Winterton Ness, in Norfolk, to Easton Ness, in Suffolk, and seven leagues eastward from all sea-banks and shores; ship-owners are also exempted from paying harbour dues at Dover, Ramsgate, Rye, and other harbours on the coast. The charter granted by Queen Anne, in 1702, under the authority of which the corporation now acts, altered the title of bailiff to that of mayor. The members of the corporation are, a mayor, high steward, recorder, sub-steward, eighteen aldermen (including the mayor), and thirty-six common council-men, assisted by a town clerk, registrar of the admiralty court, four proctors, who are also attornies of the Burgh court, a water-bailiff, marshal and gaoler, six serjeants at mace, and pier master. The mayor is chosen, on the 29th of August annually, by the common council-men; and should there not be a sufficient number present, the deficiency is supplied by freemen; he is sworn in on the 29th of September. The aldermen are elected for life, by the members of the body, from the common council; and vacancies in the latter body are filled up from the freemen, the common council nominating two of them, and the aldermen one. The other officers are elected by the corporation in council. The mayor, high steward, recorder, and deputy mayor, and such aldermen as have passed the chair, are justices of the peace. All offences may be

determined at the sessions of oyer and terminer, which are held twice a year by the magistrates, who have the power of life and death, Yarmouth not being included in the circuit.

Admiralty Seal.

In the admiralty court, held every Monday, or Tuesday, at which the mayor presides as judge and admiral, all maritime causes are heard and determined, in the same manner as in the high court of admiralty, an appeal from the court lying only to the delegates: the last admiralty sessions were held in 1823, when two men were convicted of piracy. A borough court, for determining all manner of trespasses and civil contracts arising in the town of which the mayor is judge, is also held every Monday, or Tuesday; and a court of requests, for the recovery of debts under 40s., every Monday: there are thirty-six commissioners, of whom the mayor and aldermen form a part, and vacancies are filled up by the remaining commissioners: the jurisdiction extends throughout the borough and liberties. A court leet and a court of pie powder are also held. The jurisdiction of the corporation, by the charter of the 20th of Charles II., extends to South Town, or Little Yarmouth, in the county of Suffolk, and, as conservators of the Yare, Waveney, and Bure, for ten miles upon each of those rivers. The inhabitants are not liable to serve on juries for the county, nor to the payment of county rates, as the corporation supports the gaol, and maintains the prisoners; and writs, unless accompanied with a non omittas, can only be executed under the warrant of the mayor, and by one of his officers. The freedom is obtained by birth, servitude of seven years to a freeman, and gift of the corporation; all sons of freemen become free on attaining twenty years of age, but cannot vote until they are twenty-one. The town hall, near the centre of the quay, is an elegant building of the Tuscan order, with a handsome portico in front; it is also the mansion-house, and under the control of the mayor for the time being. The council-chamber, in which public meetings and assemblies are held, is a splendid room, ornamented with a fine portrait of George I. in his robes; the card-room is spacious, and contains paintings by Butcher, of the quay, the Roads, and the market-place, and a portrait of Sir Robert Walpole, who was high steward. The borough first sent members to parliament in the reign of Edward I.: the elective franchise is vested in the freemen, in number about two thousand: the mayor is the returning officer.

The living is a perpetual curacy, in the archdeaconry and diocese of Norwich, and in the patronage of the Dean and Chapter of Norwich. In Domesday-book mention is made of a church dedicated to St. Benedict, probably founded by the barons of the cinque-ports. The present church, situated in the north-east part of the town, was founded by Herbert de Lozinga, Bishop of Norwich, about 1101, and appropriated to the prior and monks of the Holy Trinity at Norwich, who had a cell here: he erected only the cross, which constitutes the present nave and transepts; the aisles were added in 1250, and in the following year it was dedicated to St.

Nicholas. It is a handsome cruciform structure, in the early, decorated, and later, styles of English architecture, with a central tower and spire, four turrets at the west end surmounted with pinnacles, and with an elegant south porch. Seventeen oratories, each with an image, altar, lights, &c., and supported by a guild, were founded in it: on the tower was formerly a wooden spire, which appeared crooked from whatever side viewed, but it was replaced by the present one in 1804. The chapel of ease, dedicated to St. George, a handsome edifice, built in 1716, is supported by a duty of one shilling per chaldron on all coal consumed in the parish : two ministers are appointed to serve it by the mayor and corporation. The commissioners for building churches, aided by a subscription raised among some of the inhabitants, have commenced the erection of a new church, or chapel, near the White Iron Gates, on the north side of the road leading to the jetty. There are places of worship for Particular Baptists, the Society of Friends, Independents, Primitive and Wesleyan Methodists, Unitarians, and Roman Catholics. The free grammar school, in the market-place, commonly called the children's hospital school, was founded by the corporation, in 1651, and was part of St. Mary's hospital: it is now a free school for reading, writing, and arithmetic only; thirty boys and twenty girls are clothed, maintained, instructed, and apprenticed, and seventy boys and thirty girls are instructed only. There is also a Lancasterian school on the Chapel Denes, supported by subscription ; and a school in the market-place, under the superintendence of the minister of the parish and twenty-four directors, supported by subscription and the produce of money at interest. In the Sunday school ninety boys and fifty girls are instructed. The fishermen's hospital, of a quadrangular form, contains twenty apartments for the accommodation of that number of fishermen and their wives, who receive each a weekly stipend, and some coal annually ; the wife is obliged to leave on the death of the husband : it is supported by an annual grant from the Crown. Besides the cell belonging to the Holy Trinity at Norwich, and the hospital of St. Mary, here were two lazar-houses, and houses of Black, Grey, and White friars, many fragments of which remain, as well as of the ancient wall of the town. Yarmouth gives the inferior title of earl to the Marquis of Hertford.

YARNFIELD, a hamlet in that part of the parish of MAIDEN-BRADLEY which is in the hundred of NORTON-FERRIS, county of SOMERSET, 5½ miles (E. N. E.) from Bruton, containing 94 inhabitants.

YARNSCOMBE, a parish in the hundred of HARTLAND, county of DEVON, 6 miles (N. E. by E.) from Great Torrington, containing 463 inhabitants. The living is a discharged vicarage, in the archdeaconry of Barnstaple, and diocese of Exeter, rated in the king's books at £7. 1½. 11½, and in the patronage of the Crown. The church is dedicated to St. Andrew.

YARNTON, or YARINGTON, a parish in the hundred of WOOTTON, county of OXFORD, 4¼ miles (N. W. by N.) from Oxford, containing 273 inhabitants. The living is a discharged vicarage, in the archdeaconry and diocese of Oxford, rated in the king's books at £8. 5. 5., and in the patronage of Sir George Dashwood, Bart., for three turns, and of the Warden and Fellows of All Souls' College, Oxford, for one. The church is dedicated to St. Bartholomew. From forty to fifty children are educated in a school built by William Fletcher, in 1818, and supported by voluntary subscription.

YARPOLE, a parish in the hundred of WOLPHY, county of HEREFORD, 5 miles (N. N. W.) from Leominster, containing, with the township of Bircher, 622 inhabitants. The living is a perpetual curacy, annexed to the rectory of Croft, in the archdeaconry and diocese of Hereford, endowed with £200 private benefaction, and £200 royal bounty. The church is dedicated to St. Leonard. Courts leet and baron are occasionally held here. A school, established about 1817, and now attended by one hundred and ten children, is supported by subscription, aided by a small endowment.

YARWELL, a parish in the hundred of WILLYBROOK, county of NORTHAMPTON, 1¼ mile (S. by W.) from Wansford, containing 312 inhabitants. The living is a perpetual curacy, annexed to the vicarage of Nassington, in the peculiar jurisdiction of the Prebendary of Nassington in the Cathedral Church of Lincoln. The church is dedicated to St. Mary Magdalene.

YATE, a parish in the upper division of the hundred of HENBURY, county of GLOUCESTER, 1 mile (W.) from Chipping-Sodbury, containing 827 inhabitants. The living is a rectory, in the archdeaconry and diocese of Gloucester, rated in the king's books at £30. 18. 11½., and in the patronage of Mrs. Goodenough. The church is dedicated to St. Mary.

YATE, a joint township with Pick-up-Bank, in that part of the parish of WHALLEY which is in the higher division of the hundred of BLACKBURN, county palatine of LANCASTER, 4 miles (S. E.) from Blackburn, containing, with Pick-up-Bank, 1359 inhabitants.

YATEHOUSE, a joint township with Byley, in that part of the parish of MIDDLEWICH which is in the hundred of NORTHWICH, county palatine of CHESTER, 1¾ mile (N. by E.) from Middlewich. The population is returned with Byley.

YATELY, a parish in the hundred of CRONDALL, Basingstoke division of the county of SOUTHAMPTON, 3¼ miles (N. E. by E.) from Hartford-Bridge, containing, with the tythings of Cove, Hawley, and Minley, 1801 inhabitants. The living is a perpetual curacy, in the archdeaconry and diocese of Winchester, endowed with £800 private benefaction, £600 royal bounty, and £1000 parliamentary grant, and in the patronage of the Marquis of Winchester. The church is dedicated to St. Peter. Yately is within the jurisdiction of the Cheyney Court held at Winchester every Thursday, for the recovery of debts to any amount. Six boys and six girls are instructed for about £8 a year, being one-third of the income arising from land bequeathed for charitable purposes by Mary Barker, in 1706.

YATESBURY, a parish in the hundred of CALNE, county of WILTS, 4½ miles (E. by N.) from Calne, containing 234 inhabitants. The living is a rectory, in the archdeaconry of Wilts, and diocese of Salisbury, rated in the king's books at £17. 3. 4., and in the patronage of Colonel James Kyrle Money. The church is dedicated to All Saints.

YATTENDON, a parish in the hundred of FAIRCROSS, county of BERKS, 6½ miles (S. E.) from East Ilsley, containing 230 inhabitants. The living is a rectory, in the archdeaconry of Berks, and diocese of Salisbury, rated in the king's books at £14. 6. 8., and in the patronage of the Rev. T. A. Howard. The church is dedicated to St. Peter and St. Paul. Here was formerly a weekly market, on Tuesday, granted in 1258, with a fair on the festival of St. Nicholas, to Peter de Etyndon, and confirmed, in 1319, to John de la Beche, with another fair on the festival of St. Peter and St. Paul; these have long been disused, but an annual fair is held on October 13th. Thomas Carte, the historian, wrote the greater part of his History of England at this place; he died in 1754, and was buried in the church, without any monument to his memory. A castle, said to have been inhabited by King Alfred, once occupied the site of the present manor-house.

YATTON, a chapelry in the parish of MUCH MARCLE, hundred of GREYTREE, county of HEREFORD, 5½ miles (N. E. by N.) from Ross, containing 183 inhabitants.

YATTON, a parish in the hundred of WINTERSTOKE, county of SOMERSET, comprising East and West Yatton, and containing 1516 inhabitants, of which number, 598 are in East, and 918 in West, Yatton, 8 miles (N.) from Axbridge. The living is a vicarage, with the perpetual curacy of Kenn annexed, in the peculiar jurisdiction and patronage of the Prebendary of Yatton in the Cathedral Church of Wells, rated in the king's books at £30. The church, dedicated to St. Mary, is a stately cruciform structure, with a tower in the centre, formerly surmounted by a spire. Eight poor children are instructed for £10. 10. a year, arising from a donation of £120 and certain land, by John Lane. On Cadbury hill, in the vicinity, are vestiges of an ancient fortification. In 1782, thirteen human bodies, some of them fresh and of unusual size, and a stone coffin, were discovered in a limestone quarry, about two feet and a half below the surface of the earth.

YATTON-KEYNALL, a parish in the hundred of CHIPPENHAM, county of WILTS, 4¼ miles (N. W. by W.) from Chippenham, containing 430 inhabitants. The living is a rectory, in the archdeaconry of Wilts, and diocese of Salisbury, rated in the king's books at £8. 7. 1., and in the patronage of the Rev. Thomas Hooper. The church is dedicated to St. Margaret.

YAVERLAND, a parish in the liberty of EAST MEDINA, Isle of Wight division of the county of SOUTHAMPTON, 8 miles (E. S. E.) from Newport, containing 92 inhabitants. The living is a rectory, in the archdeaconry and diocese of Winchester, rated in the king's books at £6. 6. 10½., and in the patronage of J. A. Wright, Esq. The church has a Norman door, but is principally in the later English style.

YAXHAM, a parish in the hundred of MITFORD, county of NORFOLK, 2½ miles (S. E. by S.) from East Dereham, containing 505 inhabitants. The living is a rectory, with that of Weborne annexed, in the archdeaconry of Norfolk, and diocese of Norwich, rated in the king's books at £10. 0. 10., and in the patronage of Mrs. Bodham. The church is dedicated to St. Peter.

YAXLEY, a parish (formerly a market town) in the hundred of NORMAN-CROSS, county of HUNTINGDON, 14 miles (N. N. W.) from Huntingdon, and 73 (N. by W.) from London, containing 1070 inhabitants. The village is irregularly, but neatly, built, extending for a considerable distance along the high road from Stilton to Farcet, and is amply supplied with water. At a short distance to the east is Whittlesea mere, one of the most extensive sheets of water in the king-

dom; it is six miles in length, and three miles broad, and abounds with fish. The barracks at Norman-Cross, in this parish, were used, during the late war, as a place of confinement for French prisoners, but are now partly dismantled. The neighbourhood is extremely productive of sedges and reeds, the preparation of which affords employment to a considerable portion of the inhabitants : a fair is held annually on Holy Thursday, for cattle. The living is a discharged vicarage, in the archdeaconry of Huntingdon, and diocese of Lincoln, rated in the king's books at £11, and in the patronage of the Crown. The church, dedicated to St. Peter, and situated on an eminence at the western extremity of the town, is a handsome structure, principally in the later style of English architecture, with some portions of earlier date; the tower is surmounted by a finely proportioned crocketed spire, supported by flying buttresses. There is a place of worship for Independents. Mrs. Jane Proby, in 1712, bequeathed £600 for building a school-room, and for paying a master to instruct twenty boys of the parish; and, in 1711, Mr. Francis Proby bequeathed £200 towards building a workhouse, and for teaching poor girls to work. There are also some other charitable bequests for distribution among the poor.

YAXLEY, a parish in the hundred of HARTISMERE, county of SUFFOLK, 1½ mile (W.) from Eye, containing 425 inhabitants. The living is a rectory, in the archdeaconry of Sudbury, and diocese of Norwich, rated in the king's books at £6. 6. 5½., and in the patronage of the Rev. J. T. Mott. The church is dedicated to St. Mary.

YAZOR, a parish in the hundred of GRIMSWORTH, county of HEREFORD, 4½ miles (S.) from Weobley, containing 181 inhabitants. The living is a discharged vicarage, annexed to the rectory of Bishopstone, in the archdeaconry and diocese of Hereford, rated in the king's books at £5. 12. 6., endowed with £200 royal bounty, and in the patronage of Sir Uvedale Price, Bart. The church is dedicated to St. John the Baptist.

YEADEN, a township in the parish of GUISLEY, upper division of the wapentake of SKYRACK, West riding of the county of YORK, 7 miles (N. N. E.) from Bradford, containing 2455 inhabitants, many of whom are employed in the manufacture of woollen cloth and worsted goods, and in a scribbling-mill and extensive bleaching grounds in the neighbourhood. There is a place of worship for Wesleyan Methodists.

YEALAND-CONYERS, a township in the parish of WARTON, hundred of LONSDALE, south of the sands, county palatine of LANCASTER, 2¼ miles (W. S. W.) from Burton in Kendal, containing 264 inhabitants, who are chiefly employed in the spinning of flax and the manufacture of linen.

YEALAND-REDMAYNE, a township in the parish of WARTON, hundred of LONSDALE, south of the sands, county palatine of LANCASTER, 3 miles (S. W.) from Burton in Kendal, containing 227 inhabitants.

YEALMPTON, a parish in the hundred of PLYMPTON, county of DEVON, 2¾ miles (S. E. by S.) from Earl's Plympton, containing 1235 inhabitants. The living is a vicarage, with the perpetual curacy of Revelstoke annexed, in the archdeaconry of Totness, and diocese of Exeter, rated in the king's books at £35. 19. 4½., and in the patronage of the Prebendary of Kingsteinton in the Cathedral Church of Salisbury. The church, dedicated to St. Bartholomew, is partly in the early, and partly in the later, style of English architecture, with two stone stalls enriched with trefoil arches. Near it are the ruins of a building, once, probably, the residence of the prebendary : according to tradition, it was a palace of the Saxon kings, having been occupied by Ethelwold, whose lieutenant, Lipsius, was buried here. The navigable river Yealm, which gives name to the town, here flows through much pleasing scenery, and is crossed by a bridge at the village. Yealmpton was anciently denominated a borough; it is now much decayed, though still a very genteel place, the neighbourhood being adorned by some elegant seats. A great cattle market is held on the fourth Wednesday in every month. National and Sunday schools are supported by voluntary subscription. At Kitley, the fine mansion of the family of Bastard, is a collection of the most valuable productions of Sir Joshua Reynolds.

YEARDSLEY, a joint township with Whaley, in the parish of TAXALL, hundred of MACCLESFIELD, county palatine of CHESTER, 9¾ miles (S. E. by E.) from Stockport. The population is returned with Whaley. There is a place of worship for Wesleyan Methodists, with a Sunday school attached. The river Goyt, and the Peak Forest canal, run through the parish, and from the latter a railway passes to the Connesford canal. Here are extensive collieries, and one of the seams of coal is crossed by a rich vein of lead. In the village of Yeardsley, which is a place of considerable antiquity, the manufacture of tape is carried on to a limited extent.

YEARSLEY, a township in the parish of COXWOLD, wapentake of BIRDFORTH, North riding of the county of YORK, 5½ miles (N. E. by E.) from Easingwould, containing 170 inhabitants.

YEAVELEY, a chapelry in the parish of SHIRLEY, hundred of APPLETREE, county of DERBY, 4½ miles (S.) from Ashbourn, containing 250 inhabitants. There is a place of worship for Independents. Here was a preceptory of the Knights Hospitallers, dedicated to St. Mary and St. John the Baptist, to which Sir William Meynell was a great benefactor in 1268, and which, at the dissolution, had a revenue of £107. 3. 8. The chapel, now called Stydd chapel, has fallen to ruins; but there are considerable remains of it.

YEAVERING, a township in the parish of KIRK-NEWTON, western division of GLENDALE ward, county of NORTHUMBERLAND, 4½ miles (W. N. W.) from Wooler, containing 64 inhabitants. In this township is Yeavering Bell, a lofty conical mountain rising to the height of more than two thousand feet from the vale. Its summit, which is level, and one thousand yards in circuit, is encompassed by the remains of an ancient wall, eight yards in breadth, built on the very edge of the hill, with an entrance on the south; within this is another wall, defended by a ditch, and in the centre of the area is a large cairn hollowed like a bowl. There are several smaller circles on other parts of the hill, with vestiges of a grove of oaks, strongly indicating that these works were constructed by the Druids. In the neighbourhood are, an immense cairn, and a cluster of rocks, respectively called Tom Tallan's grave and crag. Yeavering was the residence of some of the Saxon

kings of Northumbria, particularly Edwin, after his conversion : here Paulinus was employed in baptizing other converts in the river Glen, close by. Near the village is a rude column of stone, commemorating the victory gained, in 1415, by the Earl of Westmorland, with a small English force of four hundred and forty men, over Sir Robert Umfranville, at the head of a Scottish army, consisting of four thousand.

YEDDINGHAM, a parish in the wapentake of BUCKROSE, East riding of the county of YORK, 8¼ miles (N. E.) from New Malton, containing 127 inhabitants. The living is a vicarage, in the archdeaconry of the East riding, and diocese of York, rated in the king's books at £5. 4. 2., and in the patronage of Earl Fitzwilliam. The church is dedicated to St. John the Baptist. The village is situated on the navigable river Derwent. A Benedictine nunnery, in honour of the Blessed Virgin Mary, was founded here before 1163, by Roger de Clere, which at the dissolution had a revenue of £26. 6. 8.

YELDERSLEY, a hamlet in that part of the parish of ASHBOURN which is in the hundred of APPLETREE, county of DERBY, 3½ miles (E. S. E.) from Ashbourn, containing 202 inhabitants.

YELDHAM (GREAT), a parish in the hundred of HINCKFORD, county of ESSEX, 3 miles (N. W. by N.) from Castle-Hedingham, containing 552 inhabitants. The living is a rectory, in the archdeaconry of Middlesex, and diocese of London, rated in the king's books at £20, and in the patronage of Sir W. B. Rush, Knt. The church is dedicated to St. Andrew.

YELDHAM (LITTLE), a parish in the hundred of HINCKFORD, county of ESSEX, 4¼ miles (N.) from Castle-Hedingham, containing 287 inhabitants. The living is a rectory, in the peculiar jurisdiction of the Commissary of Essex and Herts, concurrently with the Consistorial Court of the Bishop of London, rated in the king's books at £8, and in the patronage of the Crown.

YELFORD, a parish in the hundred of BAMPTON, county of OXFORD, 3¼ miles (S.) from Witney, containing 16 inhabitants. The living is a discharged rectory, in the archdeaconry and diocese of Oxford, rated in the king's books at £4. 3. 6½., and endowed with £200 royal bounty. W. J. Lenthall, Esq. was patron in 1815. The church is dedicated to St. Nicholas.

YELLING, a parish in the hundred of TOSELAND, county of HUNTINGDON, 6 miles (E. N. E.) from St. Neots, containing 297 inhabitants. The living is a rectory, in the archdeaconry of Huntingdon, and diocese of Lincoln, rated in the king's books at £14. 10. 5., and in the patronage of the Crown. The church is dedicated to the Holy Cross.

YELVERTOFT, a parish in the hundred of GUILS-BOROUGH, county of NORTHAMPTON, 9¾ miles (N. by E.) from Daventry, containing 654 inhabitants. The living is a rectory, in the archdeaconry of Northampton, and diocese of Peterborough, rated in the king's books at £25. 0. 10., and in the patronage of the Earl of Craven. The church is dedicated to All Saints. There is a place of worship for Independents. The Union canal passes through the parish. Twenty poor children are instructed for £35 a year, arising from land bequeathed by Mrs. Ashby, in 1719. A school here was established by subscription.

YELVERTON, a parish in the hundred of HEN-STEAD, county of NORFOLK, 5¾ miles (S. E. by S.) from Norwich, containing 79 inhabitants. The living is a discharged rectory, in the archdeaconry of Norfolk, and diocese of Norwich, rated in the king's books at £10, and in the patronage of the Crown. The church, dedicated to St. Mary, has a Norman font with later enrichments.

YEOVIL, a market town and parish, in the hundred of STONE, county of SOMERSET, 9½ miles (S. S. E.) from Somerton, and 122 (W. S. W.) from London, containing 4655 inhabitants. This town, which, from the discovery of tesselated pavements and other relics of antiquity, is supposed to have been known to the Romans,

Corporate Seal.

derives its name from the river Yeo, or Ivel, the *Velox* of Ravennas, which, having its source in seven springs near Sherborne, separates the counties of Somerset and Dorset, and passes this place at a short distance to the east, beneath a stone bridge of three arches, near which it receives a small stream, turning three mills, which bounds the town on the south. It consists of numerous streets, many of them spacious ; the houses in general are good, several being constructed with stone. The town is well supplied with water from springs, which rise at a short distance, and is sheltered on the north by a range of lofty hills, which, as well as the adjacent country, are in a high state of cultivation ; the metropolis is chiefly supplied with what is called Dorset butter from the numerous dairy farms in this neighbourhood. On the south-east are three remarkable hills, from the summit of one of which, Newton hill, the English and Bristol channels can be discerned. The inhabitants were formerly engaged in the woollen manufacture to a great extent, but this has been superseded by that of leather gloves, which are made here to the extent of four thousand dozen per week, affording employment to many hundred persons in the neighbouring villages. The market is on Friday, and every alternate Friday is the great market : corn, cattle, pigs, bacon, butter, cheese, hemp, and flax, are sold in considerable quantities ; in the purchase and sale of the two latter articles upwards of £1000 is frequently returned in one day. Fairs are held on June 28th and November 17th, for horses, cattle, and pedlary, and continue for two days each. The market-house is supported on stone pillars. The government of the town, which is a corporation by prescription, is vested in a portreeve and eleven burgesses ; a mace bearer and two constables are chosen for the town, and two constables for the parish, which has a distinct jurisdiction : the portreeve exercises magisterial authority while in office. A court of record is held every three weeks, and a court leet for the borough annually, by the lord of the manor.

The living is a vicarage, with the perpetual curacy of Preston annexed, in the archdeaconry of Wells, and diocese of Bath and Wells, rated in the king's books at £18, and in the patronage of John Phelips, Esq. The church, which is dedicated to St. John the Baptist, is a fine old cruciform structure, near the centre of the town, in the ancient style of English architecture, with a tower at the west end surmounted by a balustrade : it has lately received an addition of two hundred free sittings, towards defraying the expense of which the Incorporated Society for building and enlarging churches and chapels contributed £62. At its western end stands an ancient building, now used as a school-room, of much older date than the church itself, which was probably a chapel. There are places of worship for Baptists, Independents, Wesleyan Methodists, and Unitarians. A free school, originally founded in 1707, by subscription, has been endowed with sundry bequests, especially those of Francis Cheesman, in 1711 ; of John Nowes, in 1718, who bequeathed the manor of Lea, and estates in Romsey Extra, producing about £150 per annum, partly extended to Romsey and Fisherton-Anger, for instructing, clothing, and apprenticing poor children, and afterwards for setting some of them up in business ; and of Elen Boucher, in 1725 : about thirty boys are educated on the various foundations, and some of them are also clothed and apprenticed. An almshouse for a master, two wardens, and twelve poor persons, of either sex, was founded, in 1476, by John Woburne, minor canon of St. Paul's Cathedral, and endowed to a considerable extent with landed property ; a chapel is annexed to the institution. The Portreeve's almshouses, in Back-street, for four poor women, each of whom receives a small allowance, is of unknown origin. In 1449, a fire consumed one hundred and seventeen houses in this town, fifty of which belonged to different chantries.

YEOVILTON, a parish in the hundred of SOMERTON, county of SOMERSET, 1½ mile (E.) from Ilchester, containing, with the hamlet of Bridghampton, 255 inhabitants. The living is a rectory, in the archdeaconry of Wells, and diocese of Bath and Wells, rated in the king s books at £26. 9. 2., and in the patronage of the Bishop of Bath and Wells. The church is dedicated to St. Bartholomew. The river Yeo bounds the parish on the south.

YETLINGTON, a joint township with Callaley, in the parish of WHITTINGHAM, northern division of COQUETDALE ward, county of NORTHUMBERLAND, 12 miles (W. S. W.) from Alnwick. The population is returned with Callaley.

YETMINSTER, a parish (formerly a market town) in the hundred of YETMINSTER, Sherborne division of the county of DORSET, 5¼ miles (S. W.) from Sherborne, containing, with the chapelries of Chetnole and Leigh, 1125 inhabitants. The living is a discharged vicarage, in the peculiar jurisdiction and patronage of the Prebendary of Yetminster in the Cathedral Church of Salisbury, rated in the king's books at £20. 14. 7., and endowed with £200 private benefaction, and £200 royal bounty. The church, dedicated to St. Andrew, is a large ancient structure with a lofty tower, crowned with battlements and pinnacles. This extensive parish lies on the western border of the county, and gives name to the hundred. The village, which is situated near the river Ivel, consists of a long well-built street, having still the appearance of a town. In the year 1300, the Bishop of Sarum obtained a grant from Edward I. for a market and fair, which was confirmed by Richard II., but the market has been long disused, and fairs are now held on April 23rd and October 1st. The Hon. Robert Boyle, in 1699, bequeathed an estate, now producing more than £70 per annum, for teaching twenty poor boys.

YIELDING, or YELDEN, a parish in the hundred of STODDEN, county of BEDFORD, 3¾ miles (E.) from Higham-Ferrers, containing 279 inhabitants. The living is a rectory, in the archdeaconry of Bedford, and diocese of Lincoln, rated in the king's books at £13.13.4., and in the patronage of the Rev. E. S. Bunting. The church is dedicated to St. Mary.

YOCKLETON, a township in the parish of WESTBURY, hundred of FORD, county of SALOP, 6 miles (W. by S.) from Shrewsbury. The population is returned with the township of Westbury.

YOKEFLEET, East riding of the county of YORK. —See YORKFLEET.

Arms.

YORK, a city and county of itself, having exclusive jurisdiction, locally in the East riding of the county of YORK, of which it is the capital, 198 miles (N. N. W.) from London, containing 20,787 inhabitants. The origin of this ancient city, in Nennius' catalogue called *Caer Ebrauc*, is involved in obscurity, and the etymology of its name is also uncertain. According to Llwyd, the learned Welch antiquary, it is identified with the city called by the Britons *Caer Effioc*, and, among the towns of the Brigantes mentioned by Ptolemy, with the *Eboracum* of the Romans. The latter name is probably a modification of the former, on its becoming the station of the sixth legion, sent into Britain by Adrian. The early importance of the city must unquestionably be attributed to the Romans, who fixed a colony here, and made this the metropolis of their empire in Britain. The Emperor Adrian fixed his principal station in this city, in 124, while engaged in restraining the incursions of the northern hordes. In the reign of Commodus, the Caledonians having made a successful irruption into Britain, attacked and routed the Roman army, and laid waste the open country as far as the city of York; but Marcellus Ulpius, who had been sent over from Rome, aided by the ninth legion, at that time stationed in the city, quickly routed them with great slaughter, and drove them back within their own territory. The Emperor Severus, in the fourteenth year of his reign, finding that the city of York was besieged by the northern Britons, came over into Britain, with his sons Caracalla and Geta and a numerous army, and attended by his whole court; the besiegers, on his approach, retired towards the north, and intrenched themselves behind the rampart which his predecessor Adrian had constructed, to defend the inhabitants from their assaults. The emperor, leaving his son Geta in the city to administer justice during his absence, advanced with Caracalla to give them battle, and, though from age and infirmity obliged to be carried in a litter, routed them with great slaughter; and leaving Caracalla to complete his victory, and to super-

intend the erection of a strong wall of stone, nearly eighty miles in length, which he ordered to be built near the rampart of earth raised by Adrian, as a more effectual barrier against their future incursions, returned to York, where he spent the remainder of his days. The Caledonians again taking up arms, Severus sent out his legions with positive instructions to give no quarter, but to put men, women, and children indiscriminately to the sword. During this period the city was in its highest degree of splendour; the residence of the court, and the resort of numerous tributary kings and foreign ambassadors, conferred upon it a distinction almost unsurpassed among the cities of the world, and obtained for it the appellation of "*Altera Roma*," to which city, in these respects more than in any fancied resemblance of design, it might not unaptly have been compared. Severus died in his palace here, in 212, and his funeral obsequies were performed with great solemnity on the west side of the city, near Ackham; in the immediate vicinity of the spot are three natural sandhills, called Severus' hills, upon which the ceremony is supposed to have been performed: his remains were deposited in a costly urn, and sent to Rome, where they were placed in the sepulchre of his ancestors. Constantius Chlorus, another of the Roman emperors who resided for some time in Britain, died also in this city, in 307. His son, Constantine the Great, who at the time of his father's death was at York, was proclaimed emperor by the army. Of the grandeur of the city during its occupation by the Romans, numerous vestiges have been discovered, and various remains of Roman architecture have been found. Of these, the principal are, a polygonal tower, with the south wall of the Mint yard; a votive altar to the tutelar genius of the place; an altar, dedicated to the household and other gods by Ælius Marcianus; a cemetery without Micklegate Bar, in which many urns, containing ashes and burnt bones, have been recently dug up; also a small coffin of red clay and a leaden coffin, of large dimensions, enclosed with oak; besides numerous coins and various other relics.

After the departure of the Romans from Britain, the city suffered greatly from the depredations of the Scots and Picts, by whom it was frequently assailed; and after the arrival of the Saxons it experienced considerable devastation in the wars which arose between the Britons and their new allies, in the many contests for empire during the establishment of the several kingdoms of the Octarchy, and in the mutual wars of their several monarchs for the extension of their territories. By the Saxons the city was called *Euro wic, Euore wic*, and *Eofor wic*, all descriptive of its situation on the river Ouse, which, according to Leland, was at that time called the *Eure*; and from these Saxon appellations its present name is most probably contracted. Edwin, King of Northumbria, made this place the metropolis of his kingdom, and upon his conversion to Christianity, soon after his marriage with Ethelburga, daughter of Ethelbert, King of Kent, in 624, erected it into an archiepiscopal see, of which he made Paulinus, Ethelburga's confessor, primate. This monarch founded a church, which he dedicated to St. Peter, and his example in embracing the Christian faith was followed by vast numbers of his subjects, who, under the influence of Paulinus' ministry, were converted to Christianity. On the death of Edwin, who was killed in battle in 633, while resisting an attack of the Britons under Cadwallo, assisted by Penda, King of Mercia, the city suffered severely from the ravages of the confederated armies, who devastated it with fire and sword, and massacred the inhabitants. Ethelburga fled into Kent, accompanied by Paulinus; and the newly-erected church, which was scarcely finished, lay neglected for some time, till it was restored by Oswald, Edwin's successor, who, collecting a small army, after a fierce and sanguinary conflict, slew Cadwallo and the chief of his officers, and regained possession of his kingdom.

After the union of the several kingdoms of the Octarchy, York again became a place of importance, and in the ninth century was the seat of commerce and of literature, as far as they then prevailed in the kingdom. During the Danish incursions it was reduced to ashes, and having been rebuilt, it finally became one of the principal settlements of those rapacious invaders, who kept possession of it till Athelstan attacked and expelled them from the city, and demolished the castle which they had erected for their defence. In the peaceful times which followed, the city gradually recovered, and continued to flourish till the Conquest, at which time, according to the Norman survey, it contained six shires, exclusively of the archbishop's; one of these lay waste in consequence of the demolition of the castles, in the other five were one thousand four hundred and twenty-eight houses, and in the archbishop's two hundred houses. William the Conqueror placed strong garrisons in the two castles which remained, both to overawe the inhabitants, and to protect the city from the attempts of the Saxon nobility, who, refusing to submit to his government, had gone over into Denmark, to incite Sweyn, king of that country, to invade Britain for the recovery of a throne which had descended to him from his ancestors. In 1069, Sweyn sent his two sons, Harold and Canute, with two hundred and forty ships and a numerous army, who, having arrived in the Humber, disembarked their forces and advanced to York, laying waste the country through which they marched: on their arrival before the city they were joined by Edgar Atheling, who, with a large number of the English exiles, had arrived from Scotland for the same purpose. The garrison, to prevent them from fortifying themselves in the suburbs, set fire to the houses; but the wind being high, the flames communicated to the city, and during the consternation of the inhabitants, the enemy entered and made themselves masters of it. The successful Danes then proceeded northward, and after subduing the greater part of Northumberland, finding their further progress arrested by the severity of the winter, returned to York, where they took up their winter quarters. William was unable, from the severity of the weather, to bring an army against them till the spring, when he advanced with his forces and encamped near the confluence of the rivers Humber and Trent, and, after a severe and obstinate battle, obtained a triumphant victory; Harold and Canute escaped, with a few of their principal officers, to their ships, and Edgar Atheling, with great difficulty, effected his retreat into Scotland. William, attributing the first success of the Danes to the treachery of the citizens, took signal vengeance on them, burnt the city, and laid

waste the neighbouring country, which, from the Humber to the Tyne, remained for several years in a state of desolation. From this signal calamity York gradually recovered in the two succeeding reigns. Archbishop Thomas repaired the cathedral, for temporary use, by covering the remaining walls with a roof, and afterwards, finding that they had been essentially injured by the fire, he pulled them down and rebuilt the church. Though continually exposed to the assaults of the Scots, it continued progressively to advance in importance; and, in 1088, a splendid monastery, for monks of the Benedictine order, was erected and dedicated to St. Mary, of which William Rufus laid the first stone. In the reign of Stephen the city was almost entirely consumed by an accidental fire, which is stated to have destroyed the cathedral, the monastery, with some other religious houses, and thirty-nine parish churches.

In 1138, David, King of Scotland, whom Matilda had engaged in her interest, by a promise of ceding to him the county of Northumberland, laid siege to York; but Archbishop Thurstan, though at that time confined to his bed by illness, assembled the nobility and gentry, who, under the conduct of Ralph, Bishop of Durham, his deputy, advanced against him, and put him to flight with considerable loss. In the reign of Henry II., one of the first meetings distinguished in history by the name of Parliament was held here in 1169, at which William, King of Scotland, accompanied by all his barons, abbots, and prelates, attended, and did homage to Henry in the cathedral, acknowledging him and his successors his superior lords. In the reign of Richard I., a general massacre of the resident Jews took place, under circumstances of peculiar atrocity: the fury of the populace had first been excited against them for mingling with the crowd at the king's coronation in London, and in spite of a proclamation in their favour by the king, the same spirit of persecution manifested itself in many of the large towns, especially in York, where many of the victims, having taken refuge in the castle, after defending it for some time against their assailants, perished by their own hands, after putting their wives and children to death. In 1221, Alexander, King of Scotland, who the year before had met Henry III. at York, had another interview with that monarch here, when he espoused the Lady Joan, sister of the king, and at the same time Hubert de Berg married the Lady Margaret, sister of Alexander; these marriages were both solemnized in the city, in presence of the king. In 1237, Cardinal Otto, the pope's legate, negociated a peace between the kings of England and Scotland, who met here for that purpose; and, in 1252, Alexander III., King of Scotland, came to York, attended by a large retinue of his nobility, and celebrated his marriage with Margaret, daughter of Henry III. Upon this occasion considerable festivities took place; the Scottish king, with his retinue, was lodged in a separate part of the city appropriated to their use, and he and twenty of his principal attendants received the honour of knighthood. In the reign of Edward I., a parliament was held here which was attended by most of the barons and principal nobility; the great charter, with the charter of forests, was renewed with great solemnity, and the Bishop of Carlisle pronounced a curse upon all who should attempt to violate it. The Scottish lords, who were summoned to attend this parliament, not making their appearance, the English lords decreed that an army should be sent, under the command of the Earl of Surrey, to relieve Roxburgh, which the Scots were at that time besieging. After the battle of Bannockburn, in 1315, Edward II. came to York, and held a council, in which it was decreed to send a force for the defence of Berwick, then threatened with siege by Robert Bruce; and, in 1322, the Earl of Hereford, who, with the Earl of Lancaster, had rebelled against the king, having been killed at Boroughbridge, by Adam de Hercla, who had been sent against him, his body was conveyed hither, where also many of his partizans were hanged, drawn, and quartered. After the suppression of this rebellion, which had been excited to free the kingdom from the influence of the De Spencers, the king held a parliament in this city, in which the decree, made in the preceding year at London, for alienating their estates, was reversed, and the elder Spencer created Earl of Winchester. At this parliament the several ordinances made at different times were examined, and such of them as were confirmed were, by the king's order, directed to be called statutes ; the clergy of the province of York granted the king a subsidy of fourpence in each mark, and Edward, the king's son, was created Prince of Wales and Duke of Aquitaine. After the breaking up of the parliament, Aymer de Valence was arrested, on his return, by order of the king, and brought back into the city, on a charge of having secretly abetted the barons in their rebellion against the king, and of having contributed to excite the late disturbances ; but, upon the intercession of several noblemen, he was released, on payment of a fine, and taking an oath of fidelity and allegiance to the king. This monarch, having collected an army to oppose Robert Bruce, who was then desolating the English border, was surprised by the enemy, and with difficulty escaped into the city.

In the beginning of the reign of Edward III., the Scots having sent three armies to lay waste the English border, and take possession of the adjoining counties, the king collected an army, with which he marched to York, where he was soon after joined by Lord John Beaumont, of Hainault, with a considerable body of forces. The Scots, being informed of these preparations, sent ambassadors to York, to negociate a treaty of peace ; upon the failure of which, Edward advanced against them with his army, and enclosing them in Stanhope Park, had nearly made them prisoners. By the treachery of Roger Mortimer, who opened a road for their escape, they, however, withdrew their forces, and Sir William Douglas assaulting Edward's camp by night, nearly succeeded in killing the king, but, on the failure of his attempt, the Scots, after doing what mischief they could, retreated within their own territories. Beaumont, after receiving an ample reward for his services, returned to his own dominions, and a marriage was soon after negociated between his niece and the king, which was solemnized at York, in 1327. After the battle of Hallidown Hill, in 1333, Edward retired to York, where he held a parliament, in which Edward Balliol, whose cause he had embraced in opposition to David Bruce, was summoned to attend him ; but Balliol, having sent messengers to excuse his attendance, afterwards met the king at Newcastle. In 1335, Edward

took up his residence in the monastery of the Holy Trinity in this city, and held a council, in which the Bishop of Durham, then Chancellor, resigned the great seal into his hands, and he immediately delivered it to the Archbishop of Canterbury, who took the usual oaths of office in the presence of the council, and on the same day proceeded to the church of the monastery of the Blessed Mary, where he affixed it to several deeds. Richard II., while on his expedition against the Scots, in 1385, passed some time in this city, which he also visited in 1389, in order to adjust some differences that had arisen between the ecclesiastical and civil authorities. On this occasion the monarch took his own sword from his side, and presented it to William de Selby, the mayor, to be borne in all public processions before him and his successors, whom he dignified with the title of Lord Mayor, which honour has been ever since retained, and is possessed by no other city, except those of London and Dublin. This monarch, in the nineteenth year of his reign, erected the city into a county of itself, and appointed two sheriffs, in lieu of the three bailiffs that previously formed a part of the corporation, and presented the first mace to the city, and a cap of maintenance to the sword-bearer: during this reign, Edmund Langley, fifth son of Edward III., was created the first Duke of York. In the reign of Henry IV., the Earl of Northumberland and Lord Bardolph, who, after the defeat of an insurrection against that monarch, headed by the Earl of Nottingham and the Archbishop of York, had retired into Scotland, raised some forces in that country, and made an irruption into the northern part of the kingdom ; but Sir Thomas Rokesby, sheriff of Yorkshire, having levied some forces, defeated them in a battle in which both those noblemen were slain ; and the king, marching into York, found several of the earl's adherents in the city, of whom some were ransomed and others punished ; the earl's head was severed from his body, and, being sent to London, was fixed upon the bridge.

During the war between the houses of York and Lancaster, this city was occasionally connected with the contending parties, and though not actually the seat of war, several of the battles took place in the neighbourhood. In the reign of Henry VI., Edward, Duke of York, who had raised an army in support of his claim to the crown, was killed in the battle of Wakefield, and his body being afterwards found among the slain, the head was struck off by order of Queen Margaret, and fixed upon the gate of York, with a paper crown upon it, in derision of his pretended title. In 1461, after the assumption of the crown by Edward IV., Queen Margaret, having levied an army of sixty thousand men, made another effort to regain the crown, and advancing towards York, was met by Edward and the Earl of Warwick, with forty thousand men ; the armies met at Towton, and a sanguinary battle ensued, in which thirty-six thousand seven hundred and seventy-six men are said to have been slain. During the engagement, Henry and Margaret remained in the city of York, but, on hearing of the total defeat of their army, fled with great precipitation into Scotland. After the restoration of Henry VI., Edward IV. landed at Ravenspur in Yorkshire, in 1471, and advanced to York without opposition. On his arrival he hesitated to enter the gates, for fear of treachery; but being informed by the mayor and citizens, that, provided he sought only to recover his dukedom of York, and not to lay his hand upon the crown, he might enter with safety, he took up his abode there, after swearing to a priest, who met him on his entrance, to treat the citizens with courtesy, and to be faithful and obedient to the king. Having remained at York for some time, he left a garrison in the city and marched towards London; and meeting with the army of the Earl of Warwick, near Barnet, a sanguinary battle took place, in which the earl, his brother, and several of his principal officers, were slain, and Edward, after this victory, was peaceably established on the throne. Richard III. arrived at York in 1483, and was crowned with great solemnity and pomp in the cathedral church, by Archbishop Rotherane. In 1503, Margaret, eldest daughter of Henry VII., visited the city, in which she remained for some days.

In the reign of Henry VIII. the art of printing was first established in York, by Hugo Goes, the son of an ingenious printer at Antwerp. At the time of the dissolution of monasteries, during this reign, there were in the city of York, besides the cathedral, forty-one parish churches, seventeen chapels, sixteen hospitals, and nine religious houses, including the monastery of St. Mary: with the suppression of the monasteries, ten parish churches were demolished, and their revenues and materials appropriated to secular uses. In consequence of these proceedings, the insurrection called the Pilgrimage of Grace originated in Yorkshire, and in a short time forty thousand men, headed by Robert Aske, and attended by priests with sacred banners, took possession of this city and of Hull. The Duke of Norfolk being sent against them, they were ultimately dispersed, their principal leaders were taken and executed, and Aske was brought to York, where he was hanged upon Clifford's tower. After the suppression of this insurrection, Henry made a tour through the county, on the border of which he was met by two hundred of the principal gentry, with four thousand of the yeomanry on horseback, who made their submission to the king, by Sir Matthew Bowes, their speaker, and presented him with £900: on his advance towards the city from Barnsdale, the abbot of York, attended by three hundred priests, went out to meet him, and presented him with £600; and on his entering it, the lord mayor, with the mayors of Newcastle and Hull, who had repaired to York to meet him, received him with great pomp and ceremony, and in token of their submission presented him with £100 each. Henry remained at York for twelve days, and established there a president and council, under the great seal of oyer and terminer, and, after making several other arrangements, departed for Hull, where he threw up some additional fortifications. During the reign of Elizabeth, an insurrection to restore the Roman Catholic religion was headed by Thomas Percy, Earl of Northumberland, and Charles Neville, Earl of Westmorland, on the failure of which, Simon Digby of Askew, and John Fulthorpe of Iselbeck, Esqrs., who had been made prisoners, were taken from York Castle to Knavesmire, where they were executed. The Earl of Westmorland escaped out of the country, but the Earl of Northumberland, being taken prisoner, and attainted by parliament, was beheaded at York, and his head placed

on the Micklegate bar. James I. resided for some time at the manor palace in this city; and, in 1633, Charles I. visited York, where, in 1639, he held a council at the palace, and made the city the chief rendezvous of the troops destined to march against the Scottish rebels. During his visit, the king, who was then thirty-nine years of age, ordered the Bishops of Ely and Winchester to wash the feet of thirty-nine beggars, first in warm water, and afterwards with wine, which ceremony was performed in the south aisle of the cathedral. The king afterwards gave to each of them a purse containing thirty-nine silver pence, several articles of wearing apparel, and a quantity of wine and provisions. Before leaving the city, he dined with the lord mayor and corporation, and expressed his satisfaction at the hospitality with which he had been entertained, by conferring the honour of knighthood on the lord mayor and the recorder. While Charles remained here, the Scots demanded an audience to express their grievances, and ultimately succeeded in obtaining a treaty of peace, after which the king disbanded his army, and returned to London.

Previously to the commencement of the parliamentary war, the king, to avoid the importunity of the parliament, who petitioned for the exclusive control of the militia, and for other privileges subversive of the royal authority, removed to this city, and was received by the inhabitants with every demonstration of loyalty and affection. He sent a message to both houses of parliament, and afterwards advanced to Hull, to secure the magazine which had been left in that town, upon the disbanding of the army raised to oppose the Scots; but, on being denied admission by Sir John Hotham, the parliamentary governor, he returned to York. The parliament soon after appointed a commission to reside in the city, to strengthen their party, and to watch the movements of the king; and on their passing an ordinance for embodying the militia, the king ordered his friends to meet him in this city, whither he directed the several courts to be in future adjourned. The Lord-Keeper Littleton, being ordered by the parliament not to issue the writs, apparently obeyed; but on the first opportunity made his escape to York, and bringing with him the great seal, joined the royal party, for which he was afterwards proclaimed by the parliament a traitor and a felon. On the 27th of May, 1642, the king issued a proclamation, dated from his court at York, appointing a public meeting of the nobility and gentry of the neighbourhood to be held at Heworth moor, on the 3rd of June. This meeting was attended by more than seventy thousand persons, who, on his Majesty's approach, accompanied by his son, Prince Charles, and one hundred and fifty knights in complete armour, and attended with a guard of eight hundred infantry, greeted him with the loudest acclamations of loyalty and respect. The king, in a short address, explained the particulars of the situation in which he was placed, and thanking them for their assurances of loyalty and attachment, returned to the city, where, after keeping his court for more than five months, during which time every attempt at negociation had failed, he advanced to Nottingham, and there erected his standard. In 1644, the parliamentary army, under Sir Thomas Fairfax, the Earl of Leven, and the Earl of Manchester, besieged the city, which was defended by the Marquis of Newcastle, and in a state of great distress; but hearing that Prince Rupert was approaching with an army to its relief, they raised the siege, and encamped on Marston moor, about six miles from York, where they awaited the arrival of the royalists. The armies, which were nearly equal in number, each consisting of about twenty-five thousand men, met on the 2nd of July, when, after a long and sanguinary engagement, the royalists were defeated: the parliamentarians, after this signal victory, returned to the siege of York, which, having held out nearly four months, surrendered upon honourable terms. On the 1st of January, 1645, the great convoy, under the conduct of General Skippon, arrived at York with the sum of £200,000, which, according to treaty, was paid to the Scots for surrendering to the parliament the person of the unfortunate monarch, who, relying upon their fidelity, had entrusted himself to their protection. After the Restoration, Charles II. was proclaimed here with triumphant rejoicings.

York was connected with several of the proceedings which led to the Revolution of 1688: James II. had attempted to introduce the Roman Catholic religion into the city, and for this purpose had converted one of the large rooms in the manor palace into a chapel, in which the service was performed according to the Romish ritual. This attempt, together with some arbitrary proceedings on the part of the court, gave great offence to the citizens; and in a general meeting appointed to vote a loyal address to the king, on the rumoured landing of the Prince of Orange, they resolved to add to their address a petition for a free parliament and redress of grievances. On the 19th of November, the Duke of Newcastle, lord-lieutenant of the county, arrived in the city to preside at a county meeting for the same purpose; but finding that several of the deputy-lieutenants had joined with the citizens in their petition, retired the next day in disgust. The meeting took place in the guildhall, where a petition was framed in addition to the address; but during the proceedings, a rumour being raised of an insurrection of the papists, the party rushed from the hall, and, headed by some gentlemen on horseback, advanced towards the troops of militia, at that time on parade, crying out "A free parliament, the Protestant religion, and No Popery." The militia immediately joined them, and having secured the governor and the few regular troops then in the city, they placed guards at the several entrances leading into the town. On the following day they summoned a public meeting, passed resolutions, and issued a declaration explanatory of their proceedings. On the 24th they attacked, plundered, and destroyed the houses belonging to the principal Roman Catholics in the city, together with their chapels; and, on the 14th of December, a congratulatory address was voted, by the lord mayor and corporation, to the Prince of Orange, who, with his consort, were proclaimed on the 17th of February, by the title of King William and Queen Mary, amidst general acclamation. During the rebellion in 1745, the inhabitants raised four companies of infantry, called the York Blues, for the protection of the city against the attempts of the insurgents. In 1789, their Royal Highnesses the Prince of Wales and the Duke of York visited the races, on the conclusion of which they entered Earl Fitzwilliam's carriage, and

were drawn into the city by the populace, who took the horses from the carriage, amidst the loud congratulation of the assembled inhabitants. On the 2nd of February, 1829, the inhabitants were greatly alarmed by the appearance of smoke issuing from the roof of the cathedral, and, on inspection, had the mortification to find that the choir of that beautiful structure was in flames. Every possible assistance was immediately obtained, but the beautiful tabernacle-work, the roof, and every thing combustible in that part of the church, were destroyed, and several of the piers and the finer masonry materially injured. This lamentable destruction, which was regarded as a national calamity, was the work of a lunatic, who had secreted himself for that purpose in the cathedral, after the performance of the evening service, and, under the influence of a fanatical delusion, set fire to this magnificent pile. Within a very short time after, a sum of £50,000 was subscribed, principally within the county, which, with the addition of well-seasoned timber of the value of £5000, contributed by government from the royal dock yards, will, it is calculated, be sufficient for the restoration of the building.

The city is pleasantly situated on the bank of the river Ouse, near its confluence with the Foss, and is nearly three miles in circumference: it is almost surrounded with walls erected at an early period, and restored in the reign of Edward I., and defended by four ancient gates, forming the principal entrances. Of these, Micklegate Bar, to the south-west, affords an entrance from Tadcaster; Bootham Bar, to the north-west, from the Edinburgh road; Monk Bar, to the north-east, from Malton and Scarborough; and Walmgate Bar, on the south-east, affording an entrance from Beverley and Hull. Terminating that part of the wall which extends from Walmgate Bar, on the north-west, to the edge of the marsh formed by the waters of the Foss and other smaller streams, is the Red Tower, built of brick: the inner face of this part of the wall presents a series of arches, and the same are seen in other parts. Besides these principal gates, there were five posterns, or smaller entrances, which took their names from the streets and parts of the city to which they led, and were severally called North-street, Skeldergate, Castlegate, Fishergate, and Layerthorpe posterns; but Skeldergate and Castlegate posterns have been removed. There are six bridges, of which the principal, over the river Ouse, was begun in 1810, and completed in 1820, at an expense of £80,000: it is a handsome and substantial structure of three arches of freestone, forming a communication between the parts of the city which are on opposite sides of the river. A handsome stone bridge has been erected over the Foss, of which the first stone was laid in 1811; and over the same river are four other bridges, affording communication with the suburbs. The city is divided into four wards, which take their names from the principal gates, and, under the superintendence of forty commissioners, who are triennially chosen under the provisions of an act of parliament obtained in 1825, is rapidly undergoing considerable improvement. The city is well paved, lighted with gas by a company whose extensive works were erected in 1824, and amply supplied with water by the York Company's water-works. Of the ancient castle, erected by William the Conqueror, there remains only the mount, thrown up with prodigious labour, on which is an ancient circular building, called Clifford's tower, appearing to have been the keep, which was reduced to its present ruinous condition by an accidental fire in 1685. The ancient fortress, after it was dismantled by Cromwell, remained in a dilapidated state for several years; its site is now occupied by the county prison.

The subscription library was established, in 1794, by a small number of proprietary subscribers, which at present amounts to about five hundred, who are admitted by ballot, and pay an annual subscription of £1. 6.; the library contains a well-assorted collection in every department of literature, at present exceeding ten thousand volumes. A handsome building was erected for the purpose in 1811, of which the ground-floor is occupied by a subscription news-room, well furnished with periodical publications, and supported by a company of two hundred subscribers, each of whom has the privilege of introducing a visitor, if not resident within the city. There are also two other subscription news-rooms, one called the York Club-room, and the other the Commercial News-room, both of which are well supported. The Philosophical Society was instituted in 1822, and at present consists of more than three hundred members, who are elected by ballot; the institution, among other subjects, embraces the geology, natural history, and antiquities of the county. Its meetings were held, and the museum deposited, in a house at the extremity of Ousebridge; but a handsome and commodious building has been recently erected for the use of the society, on part of the site of the venerable abbey of St. Mary, by voluntary subscription of the members of the society, assisted by the noblemen and gentlemen of the county: it is in the Grecian style of architecture, and of the Ionic order, and is surrounded by about three acres of land laid out as a botanic garden, and ornamented with shrubberies, pleasure grounds, and plantations. The meetings of the society, which are in general well attended, are held on the first Tuesdays in January, February, March, April, July, October, November, and December. The theatre was erected in 1769, and, in 1822, was considerably enlarged, greatly improved, and elegantly fitted up: it is brilliantly lighted with gas, and is opened by the York company of comedians, in the first week in March, and continues open till the first week in May; the company also perform during the assizes and the race week. Concerts and assemblies are held periodically, during the winter season, in a splendid suite of rooms in Blake-street, erected after a design by Lord Burlington, in 1730, upon a scale of sumptuous magnificence, unparalleled in any town in the kingdom: the entrance is by an elegant vestibule, thirty-two feet long and twenty-one feet high, into the principal room, which is one hundred and twelve feet in length, forty feet wide, and forty feet in height, ornamented in the lower part with a range of Corinthian columns and an enriched cornice, from which rises a series of the Composite order, surmounted by an appropriate cornice, and decorated with wreaths of fruit and foliage: this room is lighted by thirteen brilliant chandeliers suspended from the ceiling, each of which consists of eighteen branches. On the right hand of the large room is a smaller, in which the subscription assemblies are held, of which there are generally six

or seven, and the subscription concerts, of which there are generally four, during the season, exclusively of benefit concerts, and the assize and race balls, which are held in the larger room: the smaller room, which is elegantly fitted up, is sixty-six feet in length, and twenty-two feet wide, and the ceiling is richly ornamented: there are also other apartments and ante-rooms, forming, altogether, a splendid suite. The new concert rooms, adjoining the old assembly-rooms, were erected, in 1824, at an expense of nearly £7000, and form an elegant building, the first stone of which was laid by the Right Hon. William Dunslay, lord mayor: the principal room is ninety-two feet long, sixty feet wide, and forty-five feet high, and will afford accommodation for one thousand eight hundred persons.

The York musical festival was instituted in 1823, and has been liberally patronised, not only by the nobility and gentry resident in the county, but also by families of the highest distinction in every part of the kingdom. The nave of the spacious cathedral is fitted up on these occasions for the performance of sacred music: the orchestra combines the united talents of the metropolis with the professional skill of every other part of the kingdom, and the performances rank among the most profitable and attractive of these periodical festivals. Miscellaneous concerts are held also in the large concert rooms during the period of the festival; and the proceeds, after deducting the expenses, are appropriated to the York County Hospital, and the general Infirmaries of Hull, Leeds, and Sheffield. The races are held in May and August, and are in general numerously attended; at the latter meeting, the king's gold cup, for which a plate of one hundred guineas has since been substituted, was first run for in 1713, and there are various other matches and sweepstakes: the course, on Knavesmire, about a mile from the town, on the road to Tadcaster, is well adapted to the purpose, and is furnished with a grand stand and other accommodations, for the numerous spectators who assemble on these occasions. The cold baths, near the New Walk, are provided with dressing-rooms and every requisite accommodation for ladies and gentlemen; and at Lendal tower, adjoining the water-works, is an establishment of hot, cold, tepid, and vapour baths, replete with every accommodation. The cavalry barracks, about a mile to the south-west of the city, were erected in 1796, at an expense of £30,000, including the purchase of twelve acres of ground, which are attached to them, for parade, and for performing the different evolutions: the buildings are handsome and commodious, and include arrangements for three field officers, five captains, nine subalterns, and two hundred and forty non-commissioned officers and privates, with stabling for the requisite number of horses.

The city is not much distinguished either for its commerce or manufactures; the trade principally arises from the supply of the inhabitants and the numerous opulent families in the neighbourhood. Several linen factories have been recently established, but are not carried on to any great extent; the manufacture of glass was introduced in 1797; and some works for white and red lead are conducted upon a moderate scale. Carpets, worsted lace for liveries, gloves, and combs, are made in moderate quantities; and there are some chemical laboratories and iron-foundries. The river Ouse is navigable as far as the bridge, for vessels of eighty tons' burden; and ships of one hundred and fifty tons' burden trade with London. Great quantities of coal are brought hither in barges of thirty and forty tons' burden; and from the junction of the Foss with the Ouse is a navigable communication to the parish of Sheriff-Hutton, in the North riding. The market days are Tuesday, Thursday, and Saturday; the last, which is the principal, is for corn. Fairs for cattle and horses, at which very large quantities of live stock are disposed of, are held every fortnight, and on Whit-Monday, St. Peter's day, Lammas-day, and some other festivals during the year, in a spacious market-place, recently formed and most commodiously fitted up, without the city walls, near Walmgate Bar, in the construction of which, and in the erection of a handsome inn contiguous to it, the corporation have expended upwards of £10,000: a fair for leather is held every month; a fair for wool is held on Peaseholm Green every Thursday, from Lady-day to Michaelmas, which is well attended; a fair for flax on the Saturdays before Michaelmas, Martinmas, Christmas, Lady-day, St. Peter's day, Lammas-day, and Whit-Monday; and a large horse fair, without Micklegate Bar, in the week next before Christmas.

Corporate Seal

Obverse.   Reverse.

The earliest charter of liberties granted to the city, which is now in existence, is dated in the reign of Richard I., but this is rather a confirmation of privileges previously granted by his predecessors. In the reign of Edward I. the city was governed by a mayor, aldermen, and bailiffs; and from the year 1273 the list of mayors, in uninterrupted succession, is nearly complete, though the entire series is supposed to revert to the time of Stephen, or even to an earlier date. Richard II., after confirming the charters of his predecessors, and granting additional privileges, erected the city, with the adjoining district, into a county of itself, dignified the mayor with the title of lord, and, in lieu of the three bailiffs, appointed two sheriffs. The charter now in use was granted by Charles II.: by it the government is vested in a lord mayor, twelve aldermen, two sheriffs, the ex-sheriffs (called the twenty-four, though they generally exceed that number), and seventy-two common council-men, assisted by a recorder, two city counsel, and a town clerk, together with chamberlains, sword bearer, mace bearer, four serjeants at mace, and other officers. The lord mayor is elected annually, from the aldermen, by the corporate body, on the 15th of January, and enters upon his office on the 3rd of February. The sheriffs are elected from the citizens at large, on the 21st of September, and enter upon office on the 29th; the aldermen and common council-men, as vacancies occur, are also elected by the cor-

poration from the citizens generally, together with the six chamberlains, who are chosen annually. The recorder and two city counsel, who must be barristers, and the town clerk, who must be an attorney at law, are chosen by the whole corporation, and the recorder and town clerk must have their appointment confirmed by the king. The lord mayor, aldermen, sheriffs, and such as have served the office of sheriff, constitute what is called the Upper House of the corporation, and possess certain exclusive privileges. The lord mayor, recorder, the two city counsel, and the twelve aldermen, are justices of the peace within the city and county of the city, which latter extends over the whole of the city (except that part which is within the liberty of St. Peter, including the Close of the Cathedral) and the wapentake of the ainsty. The freedom is inherited by all the sons of freemen, on their coming of age, and acquired by apprenticeship for seven years to a resident freeman, and by purchase, or grant, of the corporation, which last privilege is confined to the Upper House exclusively. The corporation hold courts of assize for the city and county of the city, which are opened by the judges of the northern circuit, under a separate commission, on the same day as the assizes for the county: at these courts, which are held in the guildhall, the lord mayor takes the chair in presence of the judge, who sits on his right hand. Courts of quarter session are held before the lord mayor, recorder, and aldermen, for all offences not capital; the lord mayor, and usually one of the aldermen, hold a petty session three times in the week; and a court of record is held weekly by prescription, for the recovery of debts to any amount, in which the sheriffs preside. The mansion-house, erected in 1726, for the residence of the chief magistrate, is a stately and handsome edifice, containing a splendid suite of apartments; the banquet hall, which is forty-nine feet and a half in length, and nearly twenty-eight feet wide, is lighted by a double range of windows, and ornamented with a large collection of well-painted portraits, among which are those of William III.; George II.; George IV., when Prince of Wales, presented by His Royal Highness to the corporation in 1811; Lord Dundas, painted, in 1822, by Jackson; Lord Bingley; Sir William Mordaunt Milner, Bart.; Sir John Lister Kaye, Bart.; and other eminent persons. The guildhall is a handsome structure in the later style of English architecture, erected in 1446: the hall, which is ninety-six feet long and forty-three feet wide, is appropriated to the use of the courts, and for the transaction of corporate affairs and the election of members and officers of the corporation. The council-chamber, adjoining the guildhall, was erected in 1819, when the buildings anciently used for that purpose, and situated on the old bridge over the Ouse, were taken down: the upper room is assigned to the meetings of the lord mayor, recorder, aldermen, and those who constitute the Upper House; and the lower apartment is appropriated to the common council-men. The common gaol for the city and county of the city was erected in 1807, at the joint expense of the city and the ainsty, towards which the former contributed three-fifths, and the latter two-fifths: it is a substantial stone building. It consists of three stories, surrounded by a cupola and vane; the lower story is appropriated to felons, and the second and third stories to debtors.

Behind the gaol is the governor's house, in which is a chapel : there are seven wards, seven day-rooms, and seven airing-yards, for felons, and one for male and one for female debtors. The house of correction for the city and county of the city was erected, in 1814, at the expense of the city and ainsty, and contains six wards, six work-rooms, six day-rooms, and six airing-yards.

The city first exercised the elective franchise in the 49th of Henry III., since which time it has regularly returned two members to parliament : the right of election is vested in the corporation and freemen generally, of whom the number is from three to four thousand : the sheriffs are the returning officers. The general assizes for the county, and the election of the knights of the shire, take place at York, as the county town. The site of the ancient castle, which, on its being dismantled after the parliamentary war, was converted into a prison, is at present occupied by the county hall and common gaol for the county, erected in 1701, and forming three sides of a quadrangle, near the confluence of the Ouse and the Foss. The county hall, which occupies the western range, is a handsome structure, in the Grecian style of architecture, erected in 1777, with a noble portico of six lofty columns of the Ionic order, above which are the king's arms, a figure of Justice, and other emblematical ornaments : the hall is one hundred and fifty feet long, and forty-five feet wide ; at one end is the crown bar, and at the other the court of nisi prius, each lighted by an elegant dome, supported on twelve pillars of the Corinthian order. On the east side of the quadrangle are the apartments of the clerk of assize, the office of the court of record, the indictment office, hospital rooms, and cells for female prisoners : this range, which is one hundred and fifty feet in length, is fronted with a handsome colonnade of the Ionic order. The county gaol occupies the south side of the quadrangle, and contains seven wards, twelve day-rooms, and seven airing-yards, well adapted to the classification of prisoners, who are employed in knitting caps, making shoes, and weaving laces, and receive the whole amount of their earnings.

The city was constituted an archiepiscopal see by Edwin, King of Northumberland, who, after his conversion to Christianity, in 627, erected a church here, which he dedicated to St. Peter, and made Paulinus, the confessor of his queen, Ethelburga, first archbishop. After the death of Edwin, who was killed

Arms of the Archbishoprick.

in battle, Paulinus was compelled to abandon the province to the fury of the Britons, who, under Cadwallo, assisted by the King of Mercia, took possession of the city, and, accompanied by Ethelburga, found an asylum in the kingdom of Kent. During his absence the newly-founded establishment fell into decay, but was restored by Oswald, the successor of Edwin, who, after a successful battle with the Britons, expelled them from the city, and recovered possession of his capital. Paulinus, dying in Kent, was succeeded in the government of the see and province by Cedda, who

held it till the return of Wilfrid from France, whither he had been sent for consecration, and where he remained for three years. The establishment, under Wilfrid and his successors, remained upon its original foundation till after the Conquest, when Thomas, chaplain to William the Conqueror, being made archbishop, constituted the several dignitaries and prebendaries, and established the first regular chapter. After frequent disputes for precedency with the Archbishop of Canterbury, which were carried on for many years with the greatest animosity, it was ultimately decided in favour of Canterbury, the archbishop of that see being styled Primate of all England, as a superior designation to that of the Archbishop of York, who is styled Primate of England. The Archbishop of York, who is also lord high almoner to the king, takes precedence of all dukes who are not of the blood royal, and of all the chief officers of state, with the exception of the lord high chancellor; he places the crown on the head of the queen at coronations; and, in the county of Northumberland, has the power and privileges of a prince palatine : he was formerly styled metropolitan of Scotland. The province of York comprises the sees of York, Carlisle, Chester, Durham, and Sodor and Man, and has jurisdiction over the counties of York, Chester, Cumberland, Durham, Lancaster, Northumberland, Westmorland, and Nottingham. The ecclesiastical establishment consists of an archbishop, dean, chancellor, precentor, subdean, succentor, four archdeacons, four canons residentiary, twenty-four prebendaries, chancellor of the diocese, a subchanter and four vicars choral, seven lay clerks, six choristers, organist, and other officers. The canons residentiary are appointed by the dean, who must choose them out of the prebendaries : the dean and the four residentiaries constitute the chapter. The treasurership, erected in the year 1090, was dissolved and made a lay fee by King Edward VI., as were also the prebends of Wilton and Newthorpe, annexed thereto.

The cathedral, originally founded by Edwin, after having been frequently demolished and restored, was destroyed by an accidental fire in 1137. It remained in a desolate state for some time, till Archbishop Roger, in 1171, rebuilt the choir, and in the reign of Henry III., Walter de Grey built the south transept. In the beginning of the reign of Edward I., John le Romaine, treasurer of the church, built the north transept and a central tower; and, in 1291, his son of the same name, who was made archbishop, laid the foundation of the nave, which was, forty years afterwards, completed by Archbishop William de Melton, who also built the west front and the two western towers. Archbishop Thoresby, in 1361, rebuilt the choir in a style better adapted to the character of the nave, to which it was before greatly inferior; and, in 1370, the central tower was taken down, and in the course of eight years completely rebuilt in a more appropriate manner ; and the whole edifice at present displays a regular series of the richest and purest specimens of the various styles of English architecture, with some remains of the Norman, of which the only portion now entire is the crypt, under the eastern part of the church. The distant view of this extensive and magnificent pile, towering above the churches and other buildings of the city, and equally unrivalled in the magnitude of its dimensions and the richness of its embellishment, is strikingly impressive. The cathedral is a cruciform structure, with the addition of two lateral projections between the central tower and the east end, which are called the little transepts, and is five hundred and twenty-four feet and a half in length from east to west, and two hundred and twenty-two along the principal transepts. The west front, which is divided into three compartments by richly panelled buttresses of four stages, terminating with boldly crocketed finials, is almost covered with a profusion of the most richly varied sculpture, comprising several canopied niches, in which are statues. The central compartment contains the principal entrance, a beautiful pointed and richly moulded arch, supported on a series of slender clustered columns, and surmounted by a straight angular canopy with crocketed pinnacles, and ornamented with canopied niches, in which are statues of the Archbishops Melton, Percy, and Vavasour. The principal arch is divided, by a slender clustered pillar in the centre, into two smaller cinquefoiled arches, forming a double doorway, and having the spandril decorated with a circular window of elegant tracery. On each side of the principal entrance are two series of trefoiled arches, with delicately feathered canopies, terminating in crocketed finials; and above it is the beautiful west window of eight lights, enriched with elegant tracery, and surmounted by an acutely angular canopy and parapet pierced in beautiful design, behind which is seen the gable of the roof of the nave, with an angular pediment, perforated with great delicacy, and having on the apex a richly crocketed pinnacle. The entrances to the aisles are through plainer arches, above which are elegant windows of three lights, with tracery surmounted by canopies similar to that over the west window. The western towers, which are uniform and of graceful elevation, are strengthened with double buttresses at the angles, highly enriched with canopies and pinnacles at the offsets, and which, after diminishing in four successive stages, die away under the cornice, which is carried round the upper part of the towers. Above the windows previously noticed are others of five lights with tracery, and crowned by the embattled parapet, which is carried round the nave; the upper portion of the towers is ornamented with large belfry windows of three lights with tracery, surmounted by a delicately feathered ogee canopy, terminating in a lofty crocketed finial; the summits are wreathed with pierced embattled parapets, and crowned with eight boldly crocketed pinnacles.

The north and south sides of the cathedral are strengthened with buttresses terminating with pinnacles; and a delicately pierced parapet is continued round the walls of the nave. The transepts, which are in the early style of English architecture, are nearly similar in design, though differing in the minuter details: the entrance to the south transept is through an elegant porch, ascended by a double flight of steps, above which are three lofty lancet-shaped windows, divided only by panelled and enriched buttresses; and a large circular window, surrounded with rich and varied mouldings, occupies the centre of a triangular pediment, at each end of which is an octagonal turret, and on the apex a crocketed finial. The front of the north transept is ornamented with five

lofty narrow windows, which occupy the principal part, above which are five others, of unequal height, ranged in the triangular pediment. The central tower, which rises to the height of two hundred and thirteen feet, is a massive square structure, relieved on each of its faces by two large windows of three lights, separated and bounded at each side by enriched buttresses, terminating in crocketed finials; the crown of the arch of the windows is surmounted by an enriched canopy, and the summit of the tower is wreathed with a delicately pierced and embattled parapet. The east front, which is one of the finest compositions extant, is divided into three compartments by four octangular buttresses, terminating in crocketed pinnacles, and profusely ornamented with canopied niches, in which are, a figure of an archbishop seated, holding in his left hand the model of a church, and having the right hand raised; a statue of Vavasour, in tolerable preservation; and one, much mutilated, said to be that of Lord Percy. The magnificent window, of nine lights, filled with rich and intricate tracery, occupies the whole of the central compartment, and is surmounted by an enriched ogee canopy, above which is some highly elaborate and beautiful tabernacle-work, and in the centre, a square turret, with a crocketed finial.

On entering the cathedral from the west end, the vastness of its dimensions, the justness of its proportions, and the simplicity and beauty of the arrangement, produce an intense impression of grandeur and magnificence. The nave, extending two hundred and sixty-one feet from the entrance to the organ screen, and ninety-nine feet in height, is separated from the aisles by long ranges of finely clustered columns, of which the central shafts rise to the roof, which is plainly groined, and the others support a series of gracefully pointed arches, in the decorated style, chastely and appropriately enriched. The triforium consists of openings of five lofty narrow trefoiled arches, with acute angular canopies, richly ornamented. The clerestory is a noble range of windows, divided by slender mullions into five lights, having in the crown of the arch a circular light, with geometrical tracery of beautiful design: the aisles are lighted by an elegant range of windows of three lights, with quatrefoiled circles and tracery; and the walls below them are decorated with panels and tracery, and with canopied niches with crocketed pinnacles. At the eastern extremity of the nave is the lantern tower, supported on four lofty clustered columns and finely pointed arches, the windows of which diffuse a pleasing light over the transepts and eastern portion of the nave, which, when viewed from this point, derives increased effect from the great west window, which is filled with flowing tracery of the most delicate and beautiful character. The transepts, in the early style of English architecture, are dissimilar only in the minuter details and the arrangement of the ends. The central part is separated from the aisles by clustered columns and sharply pointed arches; the triforium consists of four arches, separated by small pillars resembling the Norman, and included in a larger circular arch, having, in the spandril, a cinquefoiled, and on each side of it a quatrefoiled, circle; the clerestory consists of ranges of five sharp pointed arches, of which the three central only admit light; the roof, which is of wood, is groined like that of the nave: the aisles of the transepts are lighted with double lancet-shaped windows, beneath which is a series of blank trefoiled arches. The choir is separated from the nave by a splendid stone screen supporting the organ, and is divided into fifteen compartments, containing a series of richly canopied niches, in which are placed, on elegant pedestals, the statues of the kings of England, from William the Conqueror to Henry VI.: the statue of the last monarch was removed from its niche in the reign of James I., whose statue was substituted in its place; but a statue of Henry VI., from the chisel of Michael Taylor, sculptor, of York, now occupies the niche, from which that of James I. has been removed. Nearly in the centre of the screen is the doorway leading into the choir, an obtuse arch, supported on slender clustered columns, with an ogee canopy, terminating with a crocketed finial. Above the niches in which are the statues of the kings are series of narrow shrines, richly canopied, and containing smaller statues, and above them a series of angels, beautifully sculptured; the whole is surmounted with bands of delicate tracery, and enriched with the most elaborate sculpture.

The choir, of which the roof is loftier and more intricately groined than that of the nave, is one hundred and fifty-seven feet and a half in length, and is a beautiful specimen of the later style of English architecture. The piers and arches are similar to those of the nave, and the intervals between the arches are embellished with shields of armorial bearings; the openings in the triforium consist of a series of five cinquefoiled arches with canopies and crocketed finials, divided in the centre by horizontal transoms; and the clerestory is a beautiful range of windows of five lights, with cinquefoiled heads, having the crown of the arch enriched with elegant tracery. The walls of the aisles of the choir are panelled and enriched with tracery corresponding with the character of the windows, which, as well as the groining of the roof, is similar to those of the nave. The magnificent east window, of nine lights, occupies nearly the whole of the east end of the choir, and is embellished with nearly two hundred subjects from sacred history, painted in glass; the upper section of the window is occupied with intricate tracery, elaborately wrought into a series of canopies, running up to the crown of the arch, and containing projecting busts, and the outer border is enriched with small tabernacles, containing half-length figures; the window is divided, nearly in the centre, by an embattled transom, in which a light gallery is wrought, affording an unobstructed view of the whole cathedral. Behind the altar, to which is an ascent of fifteen steps, and separating it from the Lady chapel, is an elaborately enriched and beautiful stone screen, divided into compartments by slender panelled buttresses terminating with crocketed pinnacles: each compartment contains, in the lower division, a triple shrine of niches richly canopied, and in the upper, a beautiful open arch, separated by slender mullions into three divisions, enriched with elegant tracery, and surmounted by a square head, of which the spandrils are pierced in quatrefoiled circles; above these is a delicate open embattled parapet, pierced alternately into triple cinquefoiled arches and circles of double quatrefoil, with shields of armorial bearings. The intervals of this exquisitely wrought and highly enriched screen have

been filled with plate-glass, affording a view of the eastern portion of the choir and of the magnificent east window. On each side of the choir, and on each side of the entrance under the organ, are the prebendal stalls, of oak richly carved, and surmounted with canopies of tabernacle-work: at the east end are the bishop's throne and pulpit, opposite to each other, both elaborately ornamented; and in the centre is the desk for the vicars choral, enclosed with tabernacle-work, on the north side of which is an eagle of brass on a pedestal. The pavement of the choir and nave has been beautifully relaid in mosaic work, and adds materially to the effect. The Lady chapel is perfectly similar to the choir, of which it is only a continuation, and contains some beautiful monuments. Beneath the altar is an ancient crypt of Norman architecture, with low massive circular columns with varied capitals, supporting a plainly groined roof; it was built of the materials of Archbishop Thomas' church, by Archbishop Thoresby. On the south side of the choir are three chapels, or rather vestries, in which are several ancient chests; in the inner vestry, or council-chamber, is a large press, containing many of the ancient records of the church, and a large horn of ivory, presented by Ulphus, Prince of West Deira, with all his lands and revenues, to the cathedral, which, after having been lost and stripped of its gold ornaments, was restored to the church by Henry, Lord Fairfax.

The monument of Archbishop Walter de Grey consists of two tiers of trefoiled arches, supported on slender columns, sustaining a canopy of niches with angular pediments and finials, under which, on an altar-tomb, is the recumbent effigy of the prelate in his pontifical robes. The tomb of Archbishop Godfrey is in the shape of a coffin, under a canopy of trefoiled arches, having the sides decorated with plain shields in quatrefoiled circles. Beneath an arch at the east end is the monument of Archbishop Henry Bowett, a beautiful composition in the later style: an obtusely pointed arch supports a highly enriched canopy of elaborate and delicate tabernacle-work; above the arch are three lofty shrines, in each of which is a statue on a pedestal, and beneath the canopy is a slab of marble, enclosed with a parapet pierced in quatrefoil. The monument of Archbishop Thomas Savage has a recumbent figure of the prelate on an altar-tomb, under a square-headed straight-lined arch, in the spandrils of which are shields of arms supported by unicorns, and angels lifting up their censers, and the cornice is ornamented with five projecting angels, bearing shields of the same arms. There are also several large stone coffins, some recumbent figures of knights, and numerous tombs of archbishops, of which that of Archbishop Roger is the most ancient. In the north aisle of the choir is a recumbent statue in alabaster, commonly, but erroneously, said to be that of Prince William de Hatfield, second son of Edward III., under a rich and beautiful canopy; and in the north transept is the tomb of John Haxby, treasurer of the church, on which, according to ancient usage, payments of money for the church estates are still occasionally made. There are numerous other monuments and tombs in various parts of the church; among which are those of Sir William Ingram, Knt., commissary of the prerogative court; Charles Howard, Earl of Carlisle; Frances Cecil, Countess of Cumberland; a statue of William Wentworth, Earl of Strafford, son of the Minister of Charles I.; and a monument to William Burgh, L.L.D., on which is an emblematical figure of Faith, finely sculptured by Westmacott. From the north transept a passage leads to the chapter-house, an elegant and highly enriched octagonal structure, in the decorated style of English architecture, with a lofty and elaborately groined roof of wood, without a central pier, profusely ornamented with sculpture in various devices: seven sides of the octagon are occupied by large windows of elegant tracery, embellished with shields of armorial bearings painted on glass; below the windows are forty-four stalls of rich tabernacle-work of Petworth marble: the finely clustered pillars between the windows are perforated for a narrow gallery, which is carried round the whole building above the cornice of the stalls; the eighth side is solid, and enriched with tracery corresponding with the windows, and the arch forming the doorway is divided into two trefoiled arches by a clustered column, in the centre of which is a statue of the Virgin with the Infant in her arms, enshrined in a canopied niche; above the entrance is a series of niches, in which were formerly statues in silver of Our Saviour and the twelve Apostles. The vestibule is of beautiful design; the windows are large and enriched with tracery of exquisite delicacy, and the walls beneath them are ornamented with tracery of corresponding character. The recent removal of ancient buildings to the north of the cathedral has disclosed a series of very beautiful Norman arches, which formed part of the archiepiscopal palace, and which, though greatly mutilated, are peculiarly fine in their details.

PARISHES IN THE CITY OF YORK.

PARISHES.	LIVINGS.	Value in the King's Books.	ENDOWMENTS.			PATRONS.	Population, 1821.
			Private Benefaction.	Royal Bounty.	Parliamentary Grant.		
		£. s. d.	£.	£.	£.		
All Saints, North-street	Discharged Rectory	4 7 11	200	400	800	The Crown	910
All Saints, Pavement } united {	Discharged Rectory }	5 16 10½		200	800	{ The Crown	554
St. Peter the Little }	Discharged Vicarage }						660
St. Crux	Discharged Rectory	6 16 6			1400	The Crown	827
St. Cuthbert }	Discharged Rectory	5 10 10				The Crown	209
St. Helen on the Walls } united {	Discharged Rectory						398
All Saints in Peaseholm }	Discharged Rectory						223
St. Denis in Walmgate, with } united {	Discharged Rectory }	4 0 10			600	{ The Crown and another alternately	1093
St. George and Naburn }	Discharged Vicarage }						
St. Giles } united {	Perpetual Curacy			400	1400		881
St. Olave }							
St. Helen Stonegate	Discharged Vicarage	4 5 5		400	1200	The Crown	678
St. John Delpike }	Discharged Rectory					Archbishop of York	367
St. Maurice without Monkbar } united {	Discharged Rectory	12 4 9½	1200	700	2500		527
St. Trinity in Goodramgate }	Discharged Vicarage						798
St. John at Ousebridge-end	Perpetual Curacy						938
St. Lawrence, with St. Nicholas	Discharged Vicarage	5 10 0		600	800	Dean and Chapter	799
St. Margaret Walmgate } united {	Discharged Rectory }	4 9 9½	200	900	800	{ The Crown	808
St. Peter le Willows }	Discharged Vicarage }						418
St. Martin in Coney-street	Discharged Vicarage	4 0 0	200	200		Dean and Chapter	610
St. Martin Micklegate } united {	Discharged Rectory }	5 16 3	200	200		Giles Earle, Esq. and others	562
St. Gregory }	Discharged Vicarage }						
St. Mary Bishopshill Senior	Discharged Rectory	5 0 10				{ The Crown, and the Dean and Chapter }	881
St. Mary Bishopshill Junior	Discharged Vicarage	10 0 0				Dean and Chapter	1477
St. Mary Castlegate	Discharged Rectory	2 8 6½	200	400	1000	The Crown	989
St. Michael le Belfrey } united {	Perpetual Curacy		} 400	700	800	{ Dean and Chapter	1543
St. Wilfrid }	Discharged Rectory	2 0 10					359
St. Michael Spurrier-gate, or Ouse-bridge	Discharged Rectory	8 12 1	200	400	1000	The Crown	593
St. Sampson	Perpetual Curacy		200	800	600	The Vicars Choral	1041
St. Saviour } united {	Discharged Rectory	5 6 8				{ The Crown	987
St. Andrew }							185
St. Trinity in King's-ct., or Christ-church,	Discharged Vicarage	8 0 0	200	400	1200	Master of Well Hospital	737
St. Trinity in Micklegate	Perpetual Curacy			600	800	The Crown	845

All the above parishes are in the archdeaconry of York, except those of St. Andrew, St. John Delpike, St. John at Ousebridge-end, St. Lawrence, St. Martin (Coney-street), St. Mary Bishopshill Junior, St. Maurice, St. Michael le Belfry, and St. Sampson, which are in the peculiar jurisdiction of the Dean and Chapter of York.

The churches are in general of the later style of English architecture, but several of them contain portions in the Norman and early English styles. The church of *All Saints on the Pavement* is a very ancient structure, said to have been built on the site, and with the ruins, of the Roman *Eboracum*; it has an octagonal lantern tower with large windows of elegant tracery, in which was formerly a lamp to guide travellers across the forest of Galtres : the chancel was taken down, in 1782, for the enlargement of the market-place, but since the removal of the market the site has been added to the cemetery. The church of *All Saints in North-street* has some ancient stained glass in the windows, and, in the south wall, the mutilated remains of a Roman sepulchral monument. The church of *St. Crux* has a neat square tower of brick, surmounted by a dome, and declining considerably from a perpendicular line; in the chancel is a monument to the memory of Sir Robert Walton, twice lord mayor of the city, with the effigies of himself, his wife, and three children. The church of *St. Cuthbert* is a neat edifice in the later style, with some ancient portions: the windows were formerly embellished with stained glass, of which some portions are remaining. Near the site many Roman antiquities have been found, consisting of urns, pateræ, and part of the foundation of an apparently Roman building. The church of *St. Denis in Walmgate*, originally a spacious structure, has been much reduced by taking down the western part, which, from the insecurity of the foundation, was giving way; and the spire, which was perforated by a ball during the parliamentary war, has been replaced with a square tower of indifferent character : little remains of the original architecture, except the entrance door, which belonged to an ancient porch that has been removed. In the interior are, a mural tablet with a female figure in the attitude of prayer, erected to Mrs. Dorothy Hughes; and an elegant marble monument to Robert Welbourne Hotham, Esq., sheriff of York in 1801 : in the north aisle is a sepulchral chapel of the Earls of Northumberland, in which Earl Henry, who fell at the battle of Towton Field, was interred. The church of *St. Helen*, supposed to have been originally a temple of Diana, was rebuilt in the reign of Mary, and the ground of the churchyard, which had risen to an enormous height, was levelled and marked out as the site of St. Helen's square : the present structure, which has an elegant octagonal tower, has been much modernised, and most of the painted glass has been removed. Near the entrance is a Norman font lined with lead, and ornamented with antique sculpture : there are several monuments, and two mural tablets to the memory of Barbara and Elizabeth Davyes, two maiden sisters, who died in 1765 and 1767, each ninety-eight years of age. The steeple of the church of *St. John* was blown down in 1551, and has not been rebuilt : the interior contains a monument to Sir Richard York, Knt., lord mayor of the city in 1469 : the churchyard has been much curtailed by the improvement near Ouse bridge. The church of *St. Lawrence* was nearly destroyed, during the siege of York, by the parliamentarian forces, and lay in ruins till 1669, when it was repaired; it consists only of a nave, with a square embattled tower. Over the altar is a large handsome window, with some remains of ancient stained glass; and there are some neat marble tablets to de-

ceased members of the family of Yarburgh. The porch has been removed, but at the entrance is a fine Norman arch, with three mouldings ornamented with flowers; in the north wall of the church is a large grit-stone, supposed to have been a Roman altar; and in the churchyard wall are two antique statues. The church of *St. Margaret in Walmgate* is an ancient building of brick, with a steeple of the same material : the only interesting feature is a Norman porch, removed from the dissolved hospital of St. Nicholas : at the entrance is a semicircular arch, resting on single columns, and having four mouldings ornamented alternately with the signs of the zodiac, emblematical representations of the seasons, and grotesque figures. The church of *St. Martin in Micklegate* is a neat ancient structure with a more modern steeple, built in 1677; the windows contain some portions of beautiful stained glass, and in the exterior of the walls of the church, and in the walls of the churchyard, are some remains of mutilated Roman sculpture. The church of *St. Martin the Bishop*, in Coney-street, is an elegant structure in the later style of English architecture, with a square embattled tower : the interior is spacious and appropriately arranged. Among the monuments are, one to Sir William Sheffield and his lady, with busts and the family arms; and a plain marble tablet to Elizabeth, wife of Robert Porteus, and mother of Beilby Porteus, Bishop of London. The church of *St. Mary Bishopshill Sen.* has portions in the early and decorated styles of English architecture, of which the details are very good; and that of *St. Mary Bishopshill Jun.* has a Norman tower; some of the piers and arches are in the early English style, with portions of a later date. The church of *St. Mary in Castlegate* has a very handsome and lofty spire, and contains several ancient monumental inscriptions. In digging a grave in this church, a copper plate was found, which had been fastened on the inside of the lid of the coffin of a priest who was executed for the plot of 1680. The church of *St. Maurice* is a very ancient structure : the interior has been recently repaired and modernised. The church of *St. Michael le Belfry* is a spacious and elegant edifice in the later style of English architecture, erected on the site of a more ancient church, which was taken down in 1535 : the nave is separated from the aisles by slender clustered columns and finely pointed arches; and the interior is handsomely arranged, with the exception of the altar, which is of the Corinthian order, and consequently inappropriate to the general character of the building. *St. Michael's in Spurrier-gate* is a very ancient structure; the west end is built of gritstone, in large masses. The church of *St. Olave*, adjoining the ruins of St. Mary's abbey, and a very ancient edifice, was destroyed, during the siege of York, by the parliamentarian forces, who used the roof as a platform for their cannon; it was rebuilt in 1722, with stone taken from the ruins of the abbey. The interior is modern and neatly arranged, the east window contains some excellent stained glass, and there are some neat mural tablets. The church of *St. Sampson* is an ancient edifice, in the later style of English architecture, with a square embattled tower, on the west side of which is a sculptured figure of its tutelar saint, and on which may be perceived its perforation by a cannon ball during the siege of the city. There were formerly three chantry chapels in this church; most of the painted glass has been removed from the windows, and the monumental inscriptions have been greatly defaced. The church of *St. Saviour* is an ancient structure, with a handsome tower surmounted by a wooden cross: the interior is very neatly arranged; the windows contain considerable portions of ancient stained glass, and there are several ancient monuments. The church of *St. Trinity in Micklegate* is an ancient structure, principally in the Norman style of architecture, with portions of a later date; the tower preserves its original Norman character, but the church has been greatly mutilated; it formerly belonged to the priory of the Holy Trinity, of which some ruined arches may be traced, and a gateway is still remaining in good preservation. The church of *St. Trinity in Goodramgate* is an ancient edifice, in which were formerly three chantry chapels; over the altar is a fine window, containing some beautiful specimens of stained glass; there are also some very ancient monumental inscriptions. The church of *St. Trinity in King's-court*, usually called *Christchurch*, is an ancient edifice, to which there is a descent of several steps. The Roman palace was situated near this church, on the side of which is a ditch, still called King's ditch, which is supposed to have bounded the demesne. There are places of worship for Baptists, the Society of Friends, Independents, Primitive and Wesleyan Methodists, Sandemanians, and Unitarians, and two Roman Catholic chapels.

The free grammar school in the Cathedral Close was erected in 1546, and endowed with £12 per annum by Robert Holgate, Archbishop of York; it is under the inspection of the archbishop for the time being, who appoints the master. Another free grammar school, in the "Horseayer," was founded by charter of Philip and Mary, and endowed by the Dean and Chapter with the lands of the hospital of St. Mary, originally founded, in 1330, by Robert de Pykering, Dean of York, the site and revenue of which, on its suppression, were granted to that body: the endowment was subsequently augmented, in the reign of Elizabeth, with £4 per annum, charged on the manor of Harteshohm, in the county of Lincoln, by Robert Dallison, chanter in the cathedral church of that city: the master is appointed by the Dean and Chapter of York, and has a residence rent-free; the number of scholars, which is regulated by the Dean and Chapter, seldom exceeds twenty-three: the school was formerly held in part of the old church of St. Andrew, but has lately been removed into the cathedral; and the old school-room is now occupied by an infant school, supported by subscription. Three schools were erected in Walmgate, Friar Wells, and Bishopshill, respectively, by Mr. John Dodsworth, ironmonger of the city, who endowed them with £10 per annum each, for the gratuitous instruction of children of the parishes near which they are situated; in each of these schools twenty children are taught to read and write. The Blue-coat school for boys, held in an ancient building on Peaseholm Green, called St. Anthony's Hall; and the Grey-coat school for girls, for which an appropriate building was erected near Monkgate bar, were established by the lord mayor and corporation, in 1705; they are liberally supported by subscription, and with the interest of donations

vested in the funds, among which was a legacy of £4000 by Thomas Wilkinson, Esq., of Highthorne, alderman of York, in 1820, which, though void in law, was given to the charity by the testator's relative and executor, William Hotham, Esq., also alderman of the city: sixty boys and forty-four girls are clothed, maintained, and instructed in reading, writing, and arithmetic, in this establishment; the boys are also taught to weave, and are apprenticed on leaving the school; and the girls are qualified to become useful servants, and placed out in respectable families. A charity school was founded, in 1773, by Mr. William Haughton, dancing-master of York, who bequeathed £1300 for its erection and endowment, and £290 more, after the demise of certain annuitants, for the instruction of twenty poor children of the parish of St. Crux, near the church of which a commodious schoolhouse has been erected: the master receives an annual salary of £200, arising from the endowment. The same benefactor left £500, directing the interest to be appropriated to the payment of the rents of poor widows of that parish; and £1000 to be lent without interest to forty poor tradesmen, but this sum has been reduced to £232. 6. by litigation, to establish the will of the testator. At Monkgate is the institution called "Manchester College," removed hither from that town in 1803, for the maintenance and education of young men for the ministry among the Independents, supported by donations and subscriptions. A spinning school was established, in 1782, by Mrs. Cappe and Mrs. Gray, to instruct children in spinning worsted; but the plan was soon changed, and sixty girls are now taught to read, sew, and knit, and are principally clothed from funds raised by subscription. Two schools (in one of which, in a spacious apartment under the banqueting room of the manor, four hundred and eighty-five boys, and another in Merchant Taylors' Hall, two hundred and fifty girls, are educated in the principles of the established church) were formed, under the patronage of the Archbishop, by the Central Diocesan Society, in 1812: the master of the boys' school has a salary of £105 per annum, and the mistress of the girls' school a salary of £40 per annum. A Lancasterian school was originally established, in 1813, and removed, in 1816, to St. Saviour's gate, in which one hundred and twenty girls are instructed in reading, writing, and accounts, on payment of one penny per week; the remainder of the sum necessary for its support is raised by subscription. At the Roman Catholic school in Castlegate sixty boys are gratuitously instructed in reading, writing, and arithmetic, and in the principles of the Roman Catholic religion. There are also Sunday schools in connexion with the established church and the several dissenting congregations; in the former are more than seven hundred children, among whom ninety bibles are annually distributed by the trustees of Lord Wharton's charity.

An hospital was founded by Alderman Agar, who endowed it with lands forming part of the estate of Lord Middleton, for six aged widows, who receive each £1. 8. 4. half-yearly. The hospital of St. Catherine, formerly a house for the reception of poor pilgrims, has been converted into an almshouse for the residence of four aged widows, who, from the augmentation of the original endowment by subsequent benefactions, receive each £18 per annum. An hospital was founded, in

1717, by Dr. Colton and Mary his wife, who endowed it with lands at Cawood and Thorpe-Willoughby, in this county, for eight aged women, who have an annual allowance of £5 each. An hospital was founded at Bootham, in 1640, by Sir Arthur Ingram, alderman of York, who endowed it with £5 per annum each for ten aged women, and twenty nobles to a chaplain, to read prayers : the buildings consist of ten neat cottages, containing two rooms each, with a chapel in the centre ; the inmates, who have also a gown every alternate year, are nominated by the Dowager Marchioness of Hertford, a lineal descendant of the founder. Mason's hospital was founded, in 1732, by Mrs. Mason, who endowed it for six aged widows, each receiving £3. 10. per annum. Dame Anne Middleton bequeathed £2000 for the erection and endowment of an hospital for twenty widows of poor freemen of York, who receive each an allowance from the corporation, of £5. 16. per annum : this hospital was entirely rebuilt by the corporation, in 1829, at an expense of nearly £2000. Near Marygate is the Old Maids' hospital, founded, in 1725, by Miss Mary Wandesford, who endowed it with an estate at Brompton upon Swale, near Richmond, a mortgage of £1200, and £1200 South Sea stock, for ten maiden gentlewomen, members of the church of England, and a reader, or preacher: the inmates receive an annual payment of £16. 17. 4., and the reader a stipend of £15 per annum, for reading morning prayer every Wednesday and Friday in the chapel of the hospital. St. Thomas' hospital, without Micklegate Bar, was originally founded for the fraternity of Corpus Christi : after its dissolution it was repaired, in 1787, and endowed with £1000 by William Luntley, glover ; the endowment was augmented by Lady Conyngham, in 1791, with £25 per annum; from the produce of these sums twelve aged widows receive each £6 per annum. Trinity hospital was founded, in 1373, by John de Rawcliffe, for a priest, five brethren, and five sisters : the Merchants' Company, upon its dissolution, in the reign of Edward VI., having obtained possession of the building, re-endowed it for ten aged persons of both sexes, who receive each £5 per annum. The hospital founded by Sir Thomas Walter, in 1612, and endowed by him with £3 per annum for a reader, and £2 per annum each to ten aged persons, payable out of the lordship of Cundall, has, from some unknown cause, been reduced ; there are at present only seven inmates, who receive £2 per annum each. An almshouse in St. Denis-lane, originally founded by the Company of Cordwainers, after having fallen into a state of dilapidation and decay, was rebuilt by Mr. Hornby, at his own cost, and affords a comfortable residence for four decayed members of that fraternity, but has no endowment. An hospital was founded, early in the last century, by Percival Winterskelf, Gent., who endowed it for six aged persons, who receive each £8 per annum. Lady Hewley's hospital, founded in 1708, is a neat brick building, comprising ten houses, for ten aged women, who receive each £15 per annum from that lady's endowment ; the same person also bequeathed large sums of money for other charitable uses. An hospital, near Foss bridge, was founded by Mrs. Dorothy Wilson, who, in 1717, endowed it with lands at Skipwith and Nun-Monkton, for ten aged women, who receive each £15 per annum from the same

funds : a salary of £20 per annum is paid to a schoolmaster for teaching twenty boys, who have each a new suit of clothes annually ; £2 per annum is given to a schoolmistress, for teaching six children to read, and the same sum to three blind people : the hospital is a neat brick building, rebuilt a second time in 1812.

The county hospital originated in 1740, by the benevolence of Lady Hastings, who bequeathed £500 for the relief of the diseased poor of the county ; other donations and subscriptions being subsequently obtained, the present edifice, in Monkgate, was soon afterwards erected : it is conducted on the most liberal principles, persons meeting with accidents being admitted without recommendation, and is under the direction of a committee, who appoint a treasurer and a steward ; it is gratuitously attended by two physicians, two surgeons, an apothecary, and a chaplain, and is supported by annual subscription. The city dispensary, for which a commodious building was erected in 1828, administers extensive relief, and is liberally supported by subscription. The lunatic asylum, without Bootham Bar, was established in 1774, and has undergone considerable alteration, and received great additions : in 1817, a large building was erected behind the former, intended solely for the reception of female patients ; it is a handsome and commodious edifice, and the whole is surrounded with gardens and pleasure grounds ; it is supported partly by subscription, and by the moderate weekly payment of patients for their board, who are admitted on producing a proper certificate. About a mile from York, in the village of Heslington, is a similar institution, established by the Society of Friends, in 1796, called The Retreat: the building, which was erected at an expense of £12,000, forms a handsome quadrangular range, with an entrance lodge, and is well adapted to the reception of patients, who pay a moderate sum in proportion to their circumstances. There are numerous institutions for relieving the distress and alleviating the sufferings of the poor; among which are the Charitable Society, for the relief of distressed objects resident in the city; the Benevolent Society, for the casual relief of strangers ; the Lying-in Society, the Clothing Society, a society for the encouragement of female servants, and various others. Among the most munificent benefactors to the poor were, the Countess Dowager of Conyngham, who bequeathed £20,000 for charitable purposes ; Mr. John Allen, who, with several other sums, bequeathed £140 per annum for the erection and endowment of an hospital for twelve aged men, who receive each £12 per annum ; and numerous others.

Near the city are the beautiful ruins of the venerable abbey of St. Mary, founded, in 1088, by William Rufus, who laid the first stone of the building, and amply endowed it for monks of the Benedictine order ; it flourished till the dissolution, at which time its revenue was £2085. 1. 5. Among other ancient remains are the crypt of the hospital of St. Leonard, originally founded in the reign of William the Conqueror, and dedicated to St. Peter, previously to erecting a church in 1724 by King Stephen, dedicated to St. Leonard, by which name it was afterwards distinguished ; at the dissolution its revenue was estimated at £500. 11. 1. : the crypt has been for many years used as wine vaults. Considerable portions of the ancient city walls are remaining, though in a greatly dilapidated condition. Among the eminent natives were, Constantine the Great, the first Roman emperor that embraced Christianity ; Flaccus Albanus, the pupil of Bede ; Waltheof, Earl of Northumberland, son of the gallant Siward ; Thomas Morton, successively Bishop of Chester, Lichfield and Coventry, and Durham : and among those of more recent date may be noticed Gent, an eminent printer and historian ; Swinburn, a distinguished lawyer and civilian ; Flaxman, the celebrated sculptor ; and several other eminent characters. York gave the title of duke to Prince Federick, second son of King George III., who died on the 5th of January, 1827.

YORKSHIRE, a maritime county, and by far the largest in England, bounded on the south by the Humber and the counties of Lincoln, Nottingham, and Derby ; on the south-west, for a short distance, by that of Chester ; on the west by Lancashire ; on the north-west by Westmorland ; on the north by Durham ; and on the north-east and east by the North Sea. It extends from 53° 19' to 54° 40' (N. Lat.), and from 10' (E. Lon.) to 2° 40' (W. Lon.), and includes an area of three million eight hundred and fifteen thousand and forty statute acres, or nearly five thousand nine hundred and sixty-one square miles. The population, in 1821, was 1,173,500.

The ancient British inhabitants of this territory were the Brigantes, the most numerous and powerful of all the tribes that shared in the possession of Britain before its Conquest by the Romans. The latter succeeded in subjugating them, about the year 71, after defeating them in several sanguinary battles, and ravaging the whole of their country. The Romans then fixed their principal station in the north at *Eboracum*, now York, which held the rank of a *municipium*, or free city, and from which central point their cohorts, dispersed in every direction, retained the surrounding country in obedience, though the territory at present included within the limits of this county suffered repeatedly during this period from the incursions of the northern barbarians. The Caledonians having overrun a great part of the country to the north of the Humber, the Emperor Adrian arrived in Britain, in the year 120, to oppose them in person, and fixed his residence at *Eboracum :* on his approach the invaders retired, and the emperor, having made provisions for the future security of the province, soon returned to Rome. But no sooner had he departed than the Caledonians renewed their predatory inroads, which became more frequent and extensive, until, in the reign of Antoninus Pius, the Brigantes having at the same time attempted to throw off the Roman yoke, that emperor sent Lollius Urbicus with strong reinforcements to suppress these commotions : this commander having first reduced the revolted Brigantes, drove the Caledonians northward into the highlands of Scotland, and thus restored tranquillity. This people, however, having renewed their irruptions, in the year 207, the Emperor Severus came over with a numerous army, and immediately advanced to York, whence, having rejected all overtures for peace, he marched northward and expelled them, leaving to his son Caracalla the command of the army, and the care of repairing Adrian's rampart. Severus, labouring under indisposition, retired, in the year 211, to York, where he expired, and

his obsequies and apotheosis were solemnized with great magnificence. Constantius Chlorus, Emperor of the West, resided for a long time at York, where he also died, in 307 : he was succeeded by his son Constantius, who was saluted emperor by the Roman soldiery in that city, and who soon after collected a powerful army, composed chiefly of native Britons, and departed for the continent. The barbarians of the north again renewed their incursions, about the year 364, but were at length repelled by the Roman General Theodosius, in 368. In the later period of the Roman empire in Britain, the territory at present contained in Yorkshire was included in the division called *Maxima Cæsariensis*. After the accession of Honorius, one of the sons of Theodosius, to the empire of the West, in 393, the invasions of the Picts and Scots became incessant, and their progress was every where marked with desolation ; and when the Romans, about the year 410, abandoned Britain, in order to defend their continental dominions, the Romanized Britons fell into a state of anarchy, amidst which it is only known of Yorkshire, that it formed the greater part of a British kingdom, named Deifyr, or Deira, the conquest of which by the Saxon chieftains was not achieved until after a lapse of one hundred and eleven years from the first arrival of Hengist in Kent. Bernicia, situated to the north of the Roman wall, having been subjugated by Ida, about the year 547, Ella, another Saxon leader, about the year 560, penetrated southward from that territory, and effected the conquest of Deira : these two kingdoms, afterwards united into one sovereignty by Ethelfrith of Bernicia, derived, from their situation to the north of the Humber, the name of Northumberland, or Northumbria. It was in the year 628, during the reign of Edwin, the next Northumbrian monarch, who had married a Christian Princess, named Ethelburga, sister of Ethelbald, King of Kent, that Christianity was first introduced into this part of Britain. In 633, Penda, King of Mercia, having entered into a league with Cadwallo, King of North Wales, against Edwin of Northumbria, the united forces of these confederate princes invaded the dominions of the latter, who opposed them at Hatfield, in the West riding, about seven miles to the east of Doncaster, where a desperate battle ensued, in which the Northumbrian monarch, together with one of his sons and the greater part of his army, perished : the victors then ravaged Northumbria with merciless cruelty, and this powerful kingdom became once more divided into two separate sovereignties ; Osric, nephew of Edwin, succeeding to the precarious throne of Deira, and restoring paganism in his dominions, while Eanfrid, son of Ethelfrith, ascended that of Bernicia. Osric, having besieged Cadwallo in York, was killed and his army totally routed, in attempting to repulse the Welch prince, who had made a vigorous sortie ; and, during the space of a year, Cadwallo remained master of York, desolating the whole country of Deira : he also put to death Eanfrid, King of Bernicia, but, in 634, was defeated and slain, with the flower of his army, by Oswald, brother of Eanfrid, who thereupon succeeding without opposition to the throne of Northumbria, fixed his residence at York, restored Christianity, and completed the building of the church, which Edwin had left unfinished.

Penda, King of Mercia, preparing to invade Northumbria, Oswald hastily entered his dominions; but was defeated and slain in Shropshire, in 642, and Penda ravaged his territory: the Bernicians placed Oswy, the brother of Oswald, on the throne of their kingdom; and in the following year Oswin, the grandson of Edwin, was elected and crowned king of Deira. Oswy soon asserted his claim to the throne of York; and Oswin, being of a religious and unsuspecting, rather than of a martial, disposition, was betrayed into the hands of Oswy, who inhumanly put him to death. The people of Deira immediately elected Adelwald, nephew of Oswin, for their king; and this monarch, having been induced to enter into a league with the kings of Mercia and East Anglia, against the sovereign of Bernicia, the confederated forces encountered those of Oswy, on the northern bank of the Aire, near Leeds, in 655. But Adelwald, seeing that the victory of either party would be equally dangerous to him, took no part in the action which ensued; and though the Mercian king Penda attacked the Bernicians with great impetuosity, not doubting of success, yet his soldiers, as soon as they perceived Adelwald withdrawing his forces, suspecting treachery, began to give way; and though the kings of Mercia and East Anglia made great efforts to rally their troops, both of them were slain, and their army was routed with terrible slaughter. On the peaceful death of Adelwald, Oswy succeeded to the entire dominion of Northumbria, but his affection for his natural son Alfred induced him to make him king of Deira; and on the death of Oswy, in 670, his son Egfrid succeeded him in the kingdom of Bernicia; the Deirians, however, revolted against Alfred, and put themselves under the dominion of Egfrid, on whose death, after an active reign of fifteen years, Alfred was recalled to assume the sway over Northumbria, the dominion of which was never again divided. A few of the succeeding reigns, though short, were marked by no act of peculiar violence; but the instances of ferocity, treason, and rebellion, which disfigure the annals of this northern kingdom, from the close of the reign of Eadbert to the commencement of the ninth century, present one of the most disgusting pictures to be found in the history of any age or country: within the short space of fifty years eight kings were successively hurled from this blood-stained throne by expulsion or assassination. A region of civil discord was ill prepared to resist the victorious arms of King Egbert, who, from the conquest of Mercia, advanced to that of Northumbria: the reigning prince, Eanred, submitted without an appeal to arms, and accepted the same terms that had been granted to East Anglia and Mercia, according to which Northumbria was to remain a distinct, but tributary, kingdom.

About the middle of the ninth century, Ragnar Lodbrog, a celebrated Danish pirate, was wrecked, with two vessels of a size unusually large at that period, on the coast of Northumbria, in which country fresh disputes for the throne had arisen; and having succeeded in landing, he moved forward to plunder and ravage, regardless of his fate; but was soon opposed by Ella, one of the rival kings, with the whole of his forces, and a fierce, though unequal, conflict ensued, in which, after seeing most of his followers fall around him, Ragnar was at last overpowered and made

prisoner, and soon after cruelly put to death. A more powerful force than had ever before sailed from Denmark soon after approached the English coasts, under command of Inguar and Ubba, two sons of Ragnar, and, in 867, after having wintered on the coast of East Anglia, entered the Humber and ravaged Holderness, slaughtering such of the inhabitants as were unable to save themselves by flight. Advancing with insatiable avidity and ruthless vengeance, they destroyed with fire and sword all the country near the northern shores of the Humber, and near York defeated Osbert, the rival of Ella in the sovereignty of Northumbria, who was slain in the action, together with great numbers of his men. The Danes then entered York, to which city Ella was advancing in aid of his rival, and near which he was met by the North-men, who slew him, and routed his army with great slaughter. Northumbria now, from an Anglo-Saxon, became a Danish kingdom, of which this county formed by far the largest and most important part. Inguar established his throne at York, which city was colonized by his followers, and extended his sway over the whole country from the Humber to the Tyne. The Danes, no longer fighting only for plunder, but for dominion, in 868, moved southward into Mercia, and returned the following year with a rich booty. In the spring of 870, several large bodies of their army again marched into the more southern provinces; and the storm which had been gathering at York, and in its vicinity, extended its direful effects over the whole of them. In the year 878, the Northumbrian Danes acknowledged the paramount sovereignty of the Saxon king, Alfred, but were, notwithstanding, governed by their own chieftains, one of whom bore the title of king, and had his principal residence at York. In 910, hostilities having arisen between the Danes and the Saxons, Edward the Elder ravaged a great part of Northumbria, and totally routed the Danes, slaying two of their kings, Halfden and Eowils, together with many of their great officers, and several thousand of their soldiers. Athelstan, who ascended the Anglo-Saxon throne in 924, with a large army expelled the Danish chieftains, and made himself master of all Northumbria. Anlaf, one of the expelled princes, having entered into alliance with different chieftains of Ireland and Wales, and with Constantine, King of Scotland, soon after entered the Humber with a fleet of six hundred and fifteen ships, filled with warriors: these troops being disembarked, the Saxons abandoned the stations that were weakly fortified; but the stronger fortresses, being well garrisoned, resisted the attacks of the invaders, and gave time for Athelstan to prepare for the contest. Both parties having concentrated their forces, a sanguinary and decisive conflict took place, in which the confederates were totally defeated; and the king of Scotland, and six Welch and Irish kings, with twelve of their earls and general officers, and a vast number of their followers, were slain. The issue left the Anglo-Saxon monarch master of all Northumbria, which (its population being chiefly Danish) he held in subjection by numerous garrisons, and totally destroyed the castle of York. Some time afterwards, Eric, King of Norway, being expelled by his subjects, was kindly received by Athelstan, who placed him on the throne of Northumbria, as a vassal of the Anglo-Saxon crown: Eric fixed his habitation at York, which thus again became a royal residence. On the death of Athelstan, Anlaf, having obtained assistance from Olaus, King of Norway, once more entered this principality, and, appearing before the gates of York, was admitted by the citizens, whose example was followed in most of the other towns, the English garrisons being either expelled or slaughtered by the inhabitants, who were for the most part Danish : Anlaf then extended his conquests into Mercia, and, by a treaty with Edmund, the successor of Athelstan on the Anglo-Saxon throne, was confirmed in his title to the kingdom of Northumbria.

From this period to the final subjugation of the Northumbrian kingdom by Edred, in 951, its imperfect history is very confused : after that event it was governed by a succession of earls, or viceroys, who, like the ancient kings, had their residence at York. In 993, Sweyn, King of Denmark, entered the Humber with a large fleet and army, and ravaged Holderness, which district also suffered from similar Danish descents in 1013 and 1060. Tostig, brother of Harold, afterwards King of England, who was appointed Earl of Northumberland, in 1055, having been expelled by the people for his tyrannical conduct, was prompted to disturb his brother in the possession of the crown of England, to which he acceded in January 1066. Being assisted by his father-in-law, Baldwin, Earl of Flanders, with about fifty vessels, he infested the English coast, in the beginning of that year, and, entering the Humber, made a descent on the Yorkshire side, and committed the most horrible ravages, but soon crossed over to the southern shores of that æstuary, where he was defeated and compelled to flee to his ships by Edwin, Earl of Chester, and Earl Morcar, who had succeeded Tostig in the government of Northumbria. Later in the same year he re-entered the Humber, accompanied by Harold Harfager, King of Norway, with a fleet of five hundred ships : they advanced up the Ouse, landed their army at Riccall, about ten miles below York, and at Fulford, near that city, defeated the inferior forces of the Earls Edwin and Morcar : they then laid siege to York, which city speedily surrendered. On the approach of Harold, King of England, with the powerful army which he had collected to oppose the expected attack from William of Normandy, the Norwegian army withdrew from York, and encamped at Stamford-Bridge, about seven miles eastward of that city, where, on September 23rd, it received from the English that signal and sanguinary defeat in which the King of Norway and Earl Tostig perished, and after which twenty of their ships were sufficient to carry back to Norway their few remaining forces. On the evening after the battle the victorious Harold returned to York, through which city he had passed in his advance to oppose the North-men, and where he shortly afterwards received intelligence of the landing of the Duke of Normandy, whom he immediately marched southward to oppose.

The strenuous resistance which the Conqueror experienced from the inhabitants of the northern parts of England is well known: after he had partially subdued them, and received the submissions of Edwin, Earl of Chester, and Morcar, Earl of Northumberland, these lords, apprehensive of being involved in the same ruin with the rest of the Anglo-Saxon nobility, raised an army in the north, which was increased by a considera-

ble reinforcement of Welch troops, and the city of York, where William had established a sort of advanced post, declared in their favour. On the Conqueror's sudden approach, the Earls and the people of York, aware of their incapacity for effectual resistance, threw themselves upon his mercy: William received their submission, but compelled the inhabitants to pay a heavy fine, at the same time erecting a strong castle in their city, to keep them in awe. The Northumbrians bore the galling yoke of the Norman with the greatest impatience, and at length called Sweyn, King of Denmark, to their assistance. In 1069, the Danish fleet, under Osbern, brother of the king of Denmark, appeared in the Humber : the whole of Northumbria declared against the Conqueror, and the Danish general, having landed his troops, was joined by great numbers of the English, among whom was Edgar Atheling (whom the insurgents recognised as king), Gospatric, and other fugitive noblemen. Osbern marched without opposition to York, where he put to the sword the Norman garrison, which had fired the suburbs. Earl Waltheof, with a strong garrison of English, was left in that city while the Danish general retired to a strong position at the confluence of two rivers in its vicinity. Entering Yorkshire, William began to inflict vengeance for this invasion and revolt by the most destructive ravages : he laid close siege to York, which, after a vigorous defence, he took and razed to the ground; and then so completely desolated the surrounding country, that such of the inhabitants as escaped slaughter perished by famine; the dead bodies lay putrifying in the houses, streets, and highways, none being left alive to cover them with earth, and during the space of nine years the country lay totally uncultivated, presenting one vast wilderness, the retreat of wild beasts and robbers, and the terror of travellers : in this state, indeed, the entire district between York and Durham continued for at least sixty years after. In the reign of Stephen, in the year 1138, David, King of Scotland, entered England with a powerful army, and ravaged this county, as far as York : Thurstan, the archbishop, who acted as Stephen's lieutenant in the north, summoned the neighbouring barons, each of whom mustered his forces, and the whole having placed themselves under the command of Ralph, Bishop of the Orkney Islands, Walter L'Espec, and William de Albemarle, advanced to North Allerton, where they fought and won the famous battle of the Standard, under the banners of St. Peter of York and St. John of Beverley.

During the inauspicious reign of Edward II., Piers Gaveston, that monarch's favourite, was besieged and taken prisoner in Scarborough Castle by the Earls of Pembroke and Warren. In 1318, Douglas, the Scottish leader, ravaging the north of England, burned the towns of North Allerton, Boroughbridge, Scarborough, and Skipton, pillaged Ripon and several other places in the county, and returned northward, carrying with him a vast quantity of plunder and a great number of prisoners. In the following year, the Scots, under the Earl of Murray, again desolated the northern parts of the county, as far as the gates of York, where they set fire to the suburbs: the Archbishop of York, indignant at this insult, hastily mustered about ten thousand men, and, accompanied by the Bishop of Ely, pursued the Scots, and overtook them at Myton, a village on the Swale, distant about twelve miles from York : in the battle which there ensued the English were totally routed, after a feeble resistance, and the fugitives made a precipitate retreat to the city: from the great number of clergymen that were killed in it, this conflict was for many years after called the "White Battle." In 1321, Thomas, Earl of Lancaster, who headed the barons against his nephew, Edward II., was defeated and taken prisoner at Boroughbridge, and, together with several other noblemen of his party, beheaded a few days after at Pontefract. While Edward III., in 1347, was engaged in his memorable continental wars, David Bruce, the Scottish monarch, invaded England, and destroyed the whole country with fire and sword as far south as York: Queen Philippa, whom Edward had appointed regent of the kingdom, and who then kept her court at York, having collected troops in the city and its neighbourhood, marched with them in person against the enemy, who was brought to action and totally defeated in the battle of Nevill's Cross, near Durham. In 1399, Henry of Bolingbroke, Duke of Hereford, afterwards Henry IV., landed at Ravenspur (a port formerly situated near the mouth of the Humber, in Holderness, but long since swallowed up by encroachments either of that arm of the sea, or of the ocean itself), and was immediately joined by the Earls of Northumberland and Westmorland, and other northern barons: being refused admittance into Hull, he proceeded on his march, with increasing forces, by way of Doncaster. Richard II., after his deposition, was confined successively in the castles of Leeds, Knaresborough, and Pontefract. In 1405, Henry IV. being then established on the throne, Richard Scroop, Archbishop of York, whose brother that monarch had beheaded; Henry Percy, Earl of Northumberland; Thomas Mowbray, Earl Marshal; the lords Fauconbridge, Bardolph, Hastings, and several others, having entered into a conspiracy for his deposition, levied a considerable number of troops, which they led to York, the place appointed for the general rendezvous: Henry immediately sent Ralph Nevill, Earl of Westmorland, with a formidable body of troops, to oppose the insurgents; and he, by his artful policy, having succeeded in drawing the archbishop and the earl marshal to a conference, took them prisoners, thus throwing the confederates into such consternation, that the Earl of Northumberland, who was then in York, finding it impossible to keep his army together, retired northward to Berwick: the archbishop, the earl marshal, and several others, were executed near York. In 1408, the Earl of Northumberland again appearing in arms, was defeated and slain at Bramham Moor, by Sir Thomas Rokesby, sheriff of Yorkshire.

This county was the scene of various important events during the wars of the Roses. In 1460, Richard, Duke of York, was defeated and slain by the superior forces of Queen Margaret, in the battle of Wakefield. Shortly after, his son, having assumed the title of Edward IV., commenced his march northward to oppose the Lancastrians, whose forces now amounted to about sixty thousand. Edward, having arrived at Pontefract, sent two of his officers to secure the passage of the Aire, at Ferrybridge, which they easily effected, and posted their detachment on the north side of the river. Henry VI. and his queen, having given the command of their army to the Duke

of Somerset, awaited at York the issue of the approaching conflict; and that nobleman commenced his operations by sending Lord Clifford to dislodge the Yorkists from their post on the northern bank of the Aire, in which he was so successful, that they were driven across the river with great slaughter. Edward then sent William Nevill, Lord Fauconbridge, to pass the Aire at Castleford, between three and four miles above Ferrybridge, which he did unobserved by the enemy, and, marching along the northern side of the river, suddenly attacked a body of horse under Lord Clifford, which was completely routed, and Clifford himself slain. Edward then crossed the Aire with his whole army, consisting of forty-eight thousand six hundred and sixty men, and, advancing towards Tadcaster, encountered the enemy on a ridge of high ground between the villages of Towton and Saxton, where, on Palm-Sunday, March 29th, 1461, was fought the decisive battle of Towton, the most sanguinary of all that occurred in the course of those exterminating wars: the fugitive Lancastrians took their way towards Tadcaster bridge, but despairing to reach it, on account of the close pursuit of their enemies, they turned aside, in order to pass the small river Cock, which movement was performed in such confusion and hurry, that the river was immediately full of those precipitated into it and drowned, whose bodies served as a bridge for their companions: the total number slain is stated at thirty-six thousand seven hundred and seventy-six, among whom were found the Earls of Northumberland and Westmorland, the Lords Dacre and Wells, Sir John Nevill, and Sir Andrew Trollope; the Earl of Devonshire was taken prisoner, and afterwards suffered death on the scaffold; Henry and Margaret fled into Scotland; and the victorious Edward took possession of York. The same prince, after his flight to Flanders, landed, in 1471, at Ravenspur, with a force of two thousand men, and thence, without opposition, marched immediately to York, pretending to claim only his patrimonial inheritance as Duke of York: having left a strong garrison in that city, he proceeded on his march towards London, and meeting the Earl of Warwick at Barnet, won the battle which placed him on the throne. In 1489, during the reign of Henry VII., the people of Yorkshire and Durham refused to pay a land-tax imposed to defray the expenses of the army; and, supposing the Earl of Northumberland to be one of the chief advisers of that measure, they assailed his house at Topcliffe, near Thirsk, and slew him with many of his servants. The populace then openly raised the standard of rebellion, and chose for their leaders Sir John Egremont and a man of mean extraction, called John à Chambre; but their chief force was shortly afterwards defeated by the Earl of Surrey, who took John à Chambre and several others prisoners: the rest of the insurgents fled to York, but, fearing to stand a siege, they dispersed in different directions, and Sir John Egremont escaped to Flanders; John à Chambre was executed at York, with a number of his chief adherents, and the tax was levied with the utmost rigour.

In 1536, the 27th of Henry VIII., the suppression of monasteries, and the other religious changes, excited great commotions in the northern counties, and in Yorkshire caused a formidable insurrection, headed by Robert

Aske, a gentleman of considerable fortune, courage, and capacity, with whom were associated the Lord D'Arcy, Sir Robert Constable, Sir Thomas Percy, brother to the Earl of Northumberland, and different other persons of influence. Professing to take up arms for the cause of religion, they called their march "The Pilgrimage of Grace," and painted on their banners a crucifix, with the five wounds, and a chalice : a number of priests marched at their head, carrying crosses in their hands, and every one wore on his sleeve an emblem of the five wounds of Christ, with the name of Jesus wrought in the middle. Aske, though unsuccessful in an attack upon Scarborough castle, made himself master of that of Pontefract, and afterwards of York and Hull; and either persuaded or compelled most of the nobility and gentry of the county to join his standard. The insurgents then advanced southward, as far as Doncaster, where the Duke of Norfolk was posted with a force of only five thousand men; but the river Don being swollen by heavy rains, they were unable to effect their passage over it, and a negociation being in consequence commenced, a general pardon was granted, and they immediately dispersed. Some of their leaders, however, endeavouring to excite new commotions, were afterwards taken and executed; and Aske, their commander-in-chief, was hanged in chains on one of the towers of York. In 1537, a less considerable rebellion broke out in the neighbourhood of Scarborough, Malton, &c., and the insurgents made a hasty march towards Hull, with the intention of taking that town by surprise; but Sir John Constable and Sir Ralph Ellerker being informed of their intention, hastily collected a few forces, and threw themselves into it, where they stood a siege of several days, and at last compelled the assailants to retire, at the same time sallying out upon their rear, and killing and taking prisoners a considerable number of them. Sir Robert Constable, and others of the insurgent leaders, however, at last made themselves masters of Hull by a stratagem, and held it for the space of a month, when, their partizans in the country being all either killed, taken prisoners, or dispersed by the king's forces, they were attacked by the inhabitants of the town during the night, and quite overpowered, many of them being taken prisoners, and amongst the rest their chief leader, Sir Robert Constable: these were afterwards hanged and quartered. In 1548, a third insurrection, for a like religious purpose, commenced at the village of Seamer, near Scarborough, and in its vicinity, one of the principal leaders of which was Thomas Dale, the parish clerk of Seamer. The beacon at Staxton having been lighted, collected a tumultuous crowd of about three thousand persons, who committed some barbarous excesses; but the lord president of the North, the seat of whose jurisdiction was at York, having sent from that city a detachment to oppose them, bearing a general pardon to those who should immediately return to their duty, most of the insurgents dispersed, though Dale and eight other ringleaders, refusing the proffered mercy, were soon after taken and executed at York. In 1553, at the time of Wyat's rebellion in the south of England, Thomas Stafford, second son of Lord Stafford, seized Scarborough castle by a stratagem, but retained possession of it only for three days, when it was retaken by the Earl of West-

morland, with a strong force; and Stafford and Captain Saunders, together with three other leaders of this insurrectionary movement, being made prisoners, paid the forfeit of their lives. Early in the year 1642, the breach between Charles I. and his parliament widening daily, the former, with his son, Prince Charles, the prince elector, and several noblemen, departed from London, and, on the 18th of March, arrived at York, whither most of the nobility and gentry of the North of England, and many from the southern provinces, resorted to offer their services to him. On the 23rd of April, the king, attended by two or three hundred of his servants, and many gentlemen of the county, left York, and about noon reached Hull, which, by order of the parliament, had been garrisoned by troops under the command of Sir John Hotham, who steadily refused to admit the king, and the latter returned in disappointment to York. Having mustered about three thousand foot and nearly eight hundred horse, and having procured arms, &c., from Holland, Charles determined to commence the war by an attempt on Hull, and, with that view, left York for Beverley, where he summoned the trained bands of the neighbouring districts. By cutting the banks of the Humber, thus covering with a considerable depth of water the meadows and pastures to the distance of two miles on every side of Hull, Sir John Hotham for some time prevented all access to the town, the garrison of which, about the middle of July, received powerful reinforcement by sea, and, at the end of the same month, in a vigorous sally, defeated the beleaguering forces, and compelled them to raise the siege. The king, after a stay of five months at York, departed from that city to erect his standard at Nottingham; but, before his departure, as danger was apprehended from the garrison of Hull, the citizens entreated His Majesty to constitute the Earl of Cumberland military commander of the county, and to appoint Sir Thomas Glemham governor of the city, which was readily granted. Sir Thomas Fairfax and Captain Hotham, son of the governor of Hull, advanced so far from that town towards York as to fortify Tadcaster and Wetherby, and twice repulsed Sir Thomas Glemham in two vigorous assaults which he made upon the last-mentioned place. The success of the parliamentarians induced the royalist gentry of Yorkshire to solicit succours from the Earl of Newcastle, who had raised a considerable force in the north, and who immediately marched to their assistance, entering York on the 30th of November, with six thousand men and ten pieces of artillery. The Earl of Cumberland then resigned his commission to the Earl of Newcastle, who, with four thousand of his men, drove the enemy from Tadcaster, while his lieutenant-general, the Earl of Newport, with two thousand men, took Wetherby. In 1643, on January 16th, Colonel Slingsby, with a force of about six hundred royalists, defeated Sir Hugh Cholmley and his troops at Guisborough. On the 23rd of the same month, Sir Thomas Fairfax, with a strong force, took the town of Leeds by assault; and the same commander, having led reinforcements into Bradford, was there besieged by the Earl of Newcastle, who made unsuccessful attempts to storm the town in several places : Sir Thomas having, however, exhausted his ammunition, offered to capitulate, but his terms being refused, he made his escape by cutting his way through their lines with fifty horse. On the 22d of February, Queen Henrietta Maria landed at Bridlington quay, with a considerable quantity of artillery and small arms, and was thence escorted to York by the lord general, the Earl of Newcastle: after remaining there for three months, she proceeded to meet the king, under the escort of the same nobleman, who, for this service, was created a marquis. This commander having driven Sir Thomas Fairfax out of Beverley with great slaughter, appeared with his whole force before Hull, on the 2d of September, and immediately commenced an arduous siege, which, as well as the defence, was conducted with all the military skill of that age, and with the most determined resolution: it continued nearly six weeks, and many were slain on both sides: the parliamentarians, however, being masters of the sea, and having a squadron on the Humber, the town received ample supplies by water, which rendered its reduction by famine impossible; and the Marquis of Newcastle, after sustaining a grand sortie, made on the 11th of October, was obliged to raise the siege.

In 1644, almost every part of Yorkshire was a scene of war and devastation. Early in this year, Sir Thomas Fairfax, having gained a considerable victory over the royal forces near Selby, was joined by the Scottish general, the Earl of Leven, and on April 19th their united forces commenced the siege of York, in which they were shortly assisted by the Earl of Manchester, with his troops and twelve field-pieces. These three generals, having collectively a force of forty thousand men, pressed the siege with great vigour, and the suburbs were fired by the besieged: numerous sanguinary conflicts took place, until, on the 30th of June, the parliamentarian generals receiving intelligence that Prince Rupert, with an army of twenty thousand men, was advancing, and would quarter that night at Boroughbridge and Knaresborough, they raised the siege and marched to Marston Moor, where they arrayed their army for battle, expecting that the Prince would take that road to York, which city, however, he reached by another route. Prince Rupert, contrary to the advice of the Marquis of Newcastle, but alleging that he had positive orders from the king to bring the enemy to action, marched his whole army out of York, on the 2d of July, and encountered the enemy near the position which they had taken up a few days before: there was fought the celebrated battle of Marston Moor, in which the parliamentarians were completely victorious, after a sanguinary conflict, and which cast the balance between the king and the parliament, entirely overthrowing the power of the former in the north. The loss on each side in this encounter is variously stated, but the peasants employed in burying the dead reported that they interred four thousand one hundred and fifty bodies, and of these it was generally believed that three thousand were royalists: the parliamentarians took prisoners above one hundred officers and one thousand five hundred soldiers, and gained possession of the Prince's train of artillery and military stores: the royalist army having fled into York, soon left that city for Lancashire; and the Marquis of Newcastle, with many other distinguished persons of the same party, embarked at Scarborough for the continent. The siege of York was immediately resumed, and that city surrendered on July 11th, after having, since its commencement, sustained twenty-two assaults, and after between four and five thousand parliamentarians had perished before its walls. Soon after these events, Tickhill castle was taken by Colonel Lilburn; Sheffield castle, on August 10th, by Major General Crawford; and Knaresborough town and castle, and Helmsley castle, towards the close of the year, by Lord Fairfax, who also, in December, made himself master of the town of Pontefract, and besieged the castle, which was, however, relieved in January following by Sir Marmaduke Langdale. Meantime, on the 18th of February, 1644, the parliamentarian officer, Sir John Meldrum, took the town of Scarborough by assault, and commenced a vigorous siege of the castle, which was obstinately defended by Sir Hugh Cholmley, who had declared on behalf of the king. On May 17th, 1645, the parliamentarians made a general assault on the castle, but were repulsed with great loss, their commanding officer receiving a mortal wound, when he was succeeded by Sir Matthew Boynton, who at length compelled this fortress to surrender, on July 22d. March 21st, 1645, the parliamentarians regained possession of the town of Pontefract, and besieged the castle, which surrendered on June 20th. In October, Great Sandall castle surrendered, after a siege of three weeks, to a parliamentarian force under Colonel Overton; Bolton castle surrendered to the parliamentarian troops on November 5th; as also did Skipton castle, on December 20th. On June 6th, 1648, a small party of royalists, headed by Colonel Morrice, seized Pontefract castle for the king, by surprise; and in the month of October commenced the third siege of this celebrated fortress, which was at first conducted by Cromwell in person, and afterwards by General Lambert, to whom it surrendered on March 25th, 1649. Colonel Boynton, governor of Scarborough castle, having declared for the king, that fortress was again besieged by the parliamentarians, about the middle of September 1648, and, the garrison becoming mutinous, surrendered on the 19th of December following.

The year 1663 was marked in this county by an insurrection in the West riding, the leaders of which were conventicle preachers and old parliamentarian soldiers: great numbers of misguided people assembled in arms at Farnley Wood, near Otley, where they were attacked by a body of regular troops, with some of the county militia, and several of them seized: twenty-one of their leaders were tried and executed at York under a special commission. At the period of the rebellion in 1745, Herring, Archbishop of York, projected an association of the nobility, gentry, and other inhabitants of the county, which was entered into at the castle of York, on the 24th of September; the sum of £31,420 was subscribed, which, together with the sums raised in a similar manner from the city and ainsty of York, was expended in raising, clothing, and paying four companies of foot, for the defence of the established government, and of the county in particular. In 1757, several riots occurred in different parts of the county, in consequence of the new regulations then introduced with regard to the levying of the militia. In 1812, serious disturbances broke out in the manufacturing districts of the West riding, chiefly owing to distress occasioned by the depressed state of trade at that time; and in 1819 the same part of the county shared in the ferment which then agitated the manufacturing districts of the kingdom generally, and especially those of Lancashire.

This county is in the diocese of York, excepting only a western portion of the North riding, which is in that of Chester: the whole is in the province of York, and forms the three archdeaconries of York (or of the West riding), the East riding, and Cleveland, in the diocese of York, and part of that of Richmond, in the diocese of Chester: the archdeaconry of York is subdivided into the deaneries of the city and ainsty of York, Craven, Doncaster, and Pontefract; that of the East riding into those of Buckrose, Dickering, Harthill and Hull, and Holderness; and that of Cleveland into those of Bulmer, Cleveland, Ryedale, and Ripon; while that of Richmond comprises, in this county, those of Boroughbridge, Catterick, Richmond, and part of Lonsdale: the total number of parishes is six hundred and four, of which one hundred and eighty-nine are rectories, two hundred and ninety-two vicarages, and one hundred and twenty-three perpetual curacies.

The grand civil and military division of Yorkshire is into three ridings, — West, North, and East, (the term riding being corrupted from trithing, a third part), independent of which is the ainsty, or county of the city of York: the West riding is subdivided into the nine wapentakes of Agbrigg (Upper and Lower), Barkston-Ash (Upper and Lower), Claro (Upper and Lower), Morley, Osgoldcross (Upper and Lower), Skyrack (Upper and Lower), Staincliffe and Ewcross (East and West), Staincross, and Strafforth and Tickhill (North and South), with the liberty of Ripon and soke of Doncaster; the North riding into the eight wapentakes of Allertonshire, Birdforth, Bulmer, Gilling (East and West), Hallikeld, Hang (East and West), Langbaurgh (East and West), and Ryedale, Pickering Lythe, and the liberty of Whitby-Strand; and the East riding into the six wapentakes of Buckrose, Dickering, Harthill (Bainton-Beacon, Holme-Beacon, Hunsley-Beacon, and Wilton-Beacon, divisions), Holderness (Middle, North, and South), Howdenshire, and Ouze-and Derwent, besides which it comprehends within its limits the liberty of St. Peter of York, the ainsty of the city of York, the borough and liberties of Beverley, and the county of the town of Kingston upon Hull, which comprises a few parishes in the neighbourhood of that place. Yorkshire contains the city of York; the borough, market, and sea-port towns of Hull and Scarborough; the borough and market towns of Beverley, Boroughbridge, Doncaster, Hedon, Knaresborough, Malton, North Allerton, Pontefract, Richmond, Ripon, and Thirsk; the borough of Aldborough; the great manufacturing and market towns of Halifax, Leeds, and Sheffield; the market and sea-port towns of Bridlington and Whitby; and the market towns of Askrigg, Barnesley, Bawtry, Bedale, Bingley, Bradford, Dewsbury, Guisborough, Hawes, Helmsley, Howden, Huddersfield, Keighley, Kirkby-Moorside, Leyburn, Masham, Otley, Patrington, Penistone, Pickering, Pocklington, Reeth, Rotherham, Sedbergh, Selby, Settle, Sherburn, Skipton, South Cave, Stokesley, Tadcaster, Thorne, Market-Weighton, Wetherby, and Yarm. The Cornish borough of Grampound

having been recently disfranchised, on the ground of corruption, the right of electing two additional members was granted to this large and populous county, which accordingly sends four representatives to parliament; two citizens are also returned for the city of York, and two burgesses for each of the boroughs: the county members are elected at York. This shire is included in the Northern circuit: the assizes are held at York, where is the county gaol. The quarter sessions for the West riding are held as follows: the Easter sessions at Pontefract; the Midsummer quarter sessions at Skipton, whence they are adjourned to Bradford, and thence to Rotherham; the Michaelmas quarter sessions begin at Knaresborough, whence they are adjourned to Leeds, and thence to Sheffield; the Christmas quarter sessions commence at Wetherby, and are adjourned to Wakefield, and thence to Doncaster: on the termination of each session there is an adjournment to Wakefield, for the purpose of inspecting the prison, which generally takes place within a month or six weeks after that time. In pursuance of an act passed in the year 1704, the office for the registration of deeds, conveyances, and wills, relating to property within the West riding, was established at Wakefield, where also are kept the records of the sessions. The quarter sessions for the North and East ridings are held respectively at North Allerton and Beverley, in each of which towns are also offices for the registration of all deeds relating to landed property within those ridings. There are two hundred and fifty-one acting magistrates. The rates raised in the county for the year ending March 25th, 1827, amounted to £611,411. 8., and the expenditure to £605,372. 9., of which, £470,677. 18. was applied to the relief of the poor.

One of the most remarkable peculiarities in the civil and military jurisdiction of Yorkshire is, that each of its ridings has a distinct lord-lieutenant. The ainsty of York was formerly a wapentake of the West riding; but, in the 27th of Henry VI., it was annexed to the city, and placed under its immediate jurisdiction: in returning to parliament the knights of the shire, the freeholders in the ainsty vote in common with those in other parts of the county. The liberty of St. Peter comprehends all those parts of the city and county of York that belong to the cathedral church of St. Peter at York: the jurisdiction is separate and exclusive, and it has its own magistrates, steward, bailiff, coroners, and constables: amongst its privileges, the inhabitants are exempt from the payment of all manner of tolls throughout England, Wales, and Ireland, on the production of a certificate from the under-steward. Quarter sessions are held for this liberty at the sessions-house in the Minster yard at York; and a court is held in the hall every three weeks, where pleas in actions of debt, trespass, replevin, &c., to any amount whatever, arising within the liberty, are heard. There is also a court leet and view of frankpledge for the whole liberty, held twice a year, viz., on the Wednesday in Easter week, and on the first Wednesday after New Michaelmas-day. Sessions for the Archbishop of York's liberty of Cawood, Wistow, and Otley, are held at Otley, in January and April, and at Cawood, in April and October.

The West riding, which, whether considered with regard to its extent and population, or to its trade and manufactures, is by far the most important, is bounded on the north by the North riding; on the east, by the ainsty, and the river Ouse, to its junction with the Trent; and on the south and west, by the arbitrary limits of the county: its greatest length, from east to west, is ninety-five miles; its extreme breadth, from north to south, forty-eight miles; and its circumference about three hundred and twenty miles, including an area of two thousand four hundred and fifty square miles, or one million five hundred and sixty-eight thousand statute acres: its population, in 1821, was 799,357. The surface of this portion of Yorkshire is much diversified, but may be divided into three large districts, gradually varying from a level and marshy, to a rocky and mountainous, region. The flat and marshy district, forming part of the extensive Vale of York, lies along the borders of the Ouse, and in most places extends westward as far as within three or four miles of an imaginary line drawn from Doncaster to Sherburn: the general level is broken only by low sandy hills, which occur in the vicinities of Snaith, Thorne, and Doncaster, and the altitude of which is seldom more than fifty feet above the level of the sea; so that the great rivers Ouse, Aire, and Don, which traverse this extensive tract, have often changed their channels. The middle parts of the riding, as far westward as Sheffield, Bradford, and Otley, contain a variety of beautiful scenery, formed chiefly by noble hills of gentle ascent; but further westward the county becomes rugged and mountainous, scarcely any thing being seen beyond Sheffield, in that direction, but high black moors, which, running north-westward, join the lofty hills of Blackstone Edge, on the borders of Lancashire. The north-western part of the riding, forming the western part of the district of Craven, presents a confused heap of rocks and mountains, among which Pennygant, Wharnside, and Ingleborough, are particularly conspicuous, the two latter being amongst the highest mountains in England: the height of Wharnside above the level of the sea is two thousand three hundred and eighty-four feet; that of Ingleborough, two thousand three hundred and sixty-one feet; and that of Pennygant, two thousand two hundred and seventy feet. Amidst the mountainous tracts of this riding there are also many romantic vallies, presenting the most beautiful and picturesque scenery: the most extensive of these are, Netherdale, or Nidderdale, watered by the small river Nid, Wharfdale, and the vale of the Aire. Many vallies of less extent vie with these in picturesque beauty, and the greater part of them being enclosed, well-wooded, and thickly scattered with almost continuous villages, present a most delightful appearance when viewed from the neighbouring eminences. In the mountainous districts of Craven are also several small lakes, the principal of which is Malham-water, near the village of Malham, of an almost circular form, about a mile in diameter, and remarkably situated on a high moor. Some of the finest scenery in England, in which beauty and sublimity are pleasingly combined, may be viewed in travelling from Knaresborough, or Ripon, to Pateley-Bridge; from Tadcaster to Otley and Skipton; from Leeds, by Bradford and Keighley, to Skipton; from Bradford to Halifax; and from Halifax, by Dewsbury, to Wakefield.

The North riding, the next most extensive division, is bounded on the north by the river Tees; on the north-east and east by the ocean; on the south-east by the rivers Hertford and Derwent, which separate it from the East riding; on the south by the river Ouse and the West riding; and on the west, by the county of Westmorland: its greatest length is eighty-three miles, from east to west; its extreme breadth forty-seven miles, from north to south; and it comprises an area of one million three hundred and eleven thousand one hundred and eighty-seven acres, or about two thousand and forty-eight square miles: its population, in 1821, was 183,694. The face of the country along the coast, from Scarborough nearly to the mouth of the Tees, is hilly and bold, the cliffs overhanging the beach being generally from sixty or seventy to one hundred and fifty feet high; while Stoupe Brow, vulgarly called "Stow Brow," about seven miles to the south of Whitby, rises to the stupendous height of eight hundred and ninety-three feet. From the ordinary elevation of the cliff the ground rises, in most places very rapidly, to the height of three or four hundred feet; and the maritime tract thus formed, comprising about sixty-four thousand nine hundred and twenty acres, is tolerably productive. A little further inland, successive hills, rising one above another, form the elevated tract of the Eastern Moorlands: this wild and mountainous district, which occupies a space of about thirty miles in length from east to west, and fifteen in breadth from north to south, is intersected by numerous beautiful and fertile dales, some of which are rather extensive, containing from five to ten thousand acres, and Eskdale and Bilsdale, considerably more: the level land at the bottom of these vales is seldom more than two hundred, or three hundred, yards broad, but the soil is generally cultivated from half a mile to a mile and a half up the hills, though the surface is in many places very irregular. Rising to the height of upwards of one thousand feet, the general aspect of this extensive district is bleak and dreary, and the whole is destitute of wood, excepting only a few dwarfish trees, in the vallies among the few scattered habitations. On the roads leading from Whitby to Guisborough, Stokesley, and Pickering, at the distance of a few miles, commence dreary and extensive wastes, bounded only by the horizon. Some of the hills, however, near the edges of this rugged and mountainous region command picturesque and magnificent prospects, particularly the Blue Bank, near Whitby; the hills on the southern border of the moors; the Hamilton hills, which form their western extremity; and the heights near Upleatham, Whorlton, and Arncliffe. But the most remarkable object in the topography of these wilds is the singular peaked mountain called Rosebury-Topping, situated near the village of Newton, about a mile to the eastward of the road from Guisborough to Stokesley which rises to the height of one thousand and twenty-two feet, and is a noted land-mark; the view from its summit is celebrated for its great extent and variety. The total extent of the Eastern Moorland district is two hundred and ninety-eight thousand six hundred and twenty-five acres. The Vale of Cleveland, situated to the north-west of these mountains, is the fruitful tract bordering on the river Tees, in the lower part of its course; in this county it comprises an area of seventy thousand four hundred and forty-four acres, the whole under cultivation, and is lightly marked with gentle eminences. The extensive Vale of York is considered by Mr. Tuke, author of the "General View of the Agriculture of the North riding of York-shire, drawn up for the consideration of the Board of Agriculture," to reach from the border of the Tees to the southern confines of the county, the north-ern part of it only being included in this riding: this part, bounded on each side by the Eastern and the Western Moorlands, has a gentle slope, from the border of the river Tees, southward as far as York, where it sinks into a perfect flat; between the Tees and York, however, its ordinarily level surface is broken by several bold swells; and on the east it is separated from Ryedale by a range of hills, called by Mr. Mar-shall, in his Rural Economy of Yorkshire, the "How-ardian Hills." This part of the vale, together with these hills, comprises an extent of four hundred and fifty-six thousand three hundred and eighty-six acres, of which about fifteen thousand are uncultivated. Ryedale (so called from its being traversed by the river Rye) and the East and West Marishes form one ex-tensive level, situated between the Eastern Moorlands and the river Derwent, and contain one hundred and three thousand eight hundred and seventy-two acres, of which about three thousand are waste : the surface of its lower parts is flat, but towards the north it rises with a gentle ascent for three or four miles towards the foot of the moors ; its lower levels are also broken by several isolated swells of considerable extent and elevation : the Marishes are separated from Ryedale by the Pickering-beck. The Western Moorlands, occu-pying the rest of the North riding, to the west of the Vale of York, and of far greater elevation than the Eastern Moorlands, resemble in general character the mountainous parts of Craven, and are, like them, in-tersected by numerous fertile dales ; of these, Wensley-dale is the most extensive, the bottom of it consisting of rich grazing pastures, through which the river Ure pursues a very winding course, forming, in many places, beautiful cascades. The next in size is Swaledale, which, however, is much inferior to the former in picturesque beauty. The total extent of the Western Moorlands is three hundred and sixteen thousand nine hundred and forty acres : together with the mountainous dis-tricts of the West riding, they form an important part of the long range of mountains reaching northward from Staffordshire into Scotland, and contain several small lakes, the principal of which is Simmer lake, near Askrigg.

The East riding is bounded on the north and north-west by the little river Hertford, and the Derwent as far down as Stamford-Bridge, about a mile above which place an irregular boundary line commences, which joins the Ouse about a mile below York : from this point it is bounded, on the west and south-west, by the Ouse ; on the south by the Humber; and on the east by the North Sea : its greatest length is fifty-two miles, from south-east to north-west ; its extreme breadth forty-two miles, from south-west to north-east ; and it includes an area of eight hundred and nineteen thousand one hundred and ninety-three statute acres, or nearly one thousand two hundred and eighty «square miles : its population, in 1821, including the city and county of the city of York, and the liberty of St. Peter, amounted to 190,449. This division of Yorkshire is far less conspicuously marked with the bolder features of nature than the other parts of the county. It may be distinguished into three districts, viz., the Wolds and the two level tracts, one of which lies to the east, the other to the west and north of that elevated region. The Wolds are a magnificent assemblage of lofty chalk hills, extending from the banks of the Humber in the vicinity of Hessle, in a northerly direction, to the neighbourhood of New Mal-ton on the Derwent, whence they range eastward, within a few miles of the course of that river, to the coast, where they form the lofty promontory of Flam-borough Head, and, in the vicinities of the villages of Flamborough, Bempton, and Specton, rise in cliffs to the height of one hundred, and in some places of one hundred and fifty, feet. The ascent of these hills is steep, except upon their eastern side, where they rise in gentle and successive swells : their height in few places exceeds six hundred feet ; but many parts of them afford magnificent and delightful prospects. Their northern edge overlooks the Vale of the Derwent, be-yond which the black eastern moors immediately rise ; the western hills command the Vale of York ; and the eastern the rich district of Holderness ; but the south-ern extremity of the Wolds is by far the most distin-guished for the beauty and diversity of its prospects, commanding the districts surveyed from the eastern and western heights, together with the vast æstuary of the Humber, and the northern shores of Lincolnshire. The surface of the Wolds is for the most part divided in-to a number of extensive swells, by deep, narrow, and winding vallies, and occupies an extent of about four hundred thousand acres. Their eastern side, at Brid-lington, sinks into a perfect flat, which continues for eight or nine miles southward. At the distance of about seven miles southward of Bridlington, however, the wapentake of Holderness begins, the eastern part of which, towards the sea-coast, is a finely varied coun-try, in which is situated Hornsea mere, the largest lake in the county, being about a mile and three quarters long, and three quarters of a mile across in the broad-est part ; but the western edge is a fenny tract of about four miles in breadth, and extending nearly twenty miles in length, southward, to the banks of the Humber: these fenny lands are provincially called "Cars." The southern part of Holderness also falls into marshes, bordering on the Humber ; and the county terminates south-eastward in the long low promontory of Spurn-head, the *Ocellum Promontorium* of Ptolemy. The Humber is known to have made, in former ages, con-siderable encroachment on the shores of Holderness ; but in later times it has gradually receded from very extensive tracts. About the commencement of the reign of Charles I., an island, since called Sunk Island, began to appear in the Humber, nearly opposite Patring-ton ; at first, a few acres only were left dry at low water ; but, as it increased in extent every year, it was at last embanked, and converted into pasture ground : successive embankments were made, large tracts being at each time secured, until at the present period it comprises about four thousand seven hundred acres of fertile land, and towards the west end is separated from the Holderness marshes only by a ditch a few feet broad : it is held on lease from the crown. The Holderness marshes have also been increased by the re-tiring of the waters of the Humber ; and a large tract of land, called "Cherry-cob Sands," which was left dry and embanked in the same manner as Sunk Island, is more particularly worthy of notice. The third natural division of the East riding, which extends from the western foot of the Wolds to the boundary of the West riding, is commonly called "The Levels," and, though generally fertile, and interspersed with villages and hamlets, is every where flat and uninteresting. One of the most important agricultural improvements in the county is the drainage of the cars and marshes of this division of it, together with those in the North riding, bordering on the course of the Derwent.

The "Holderness Drainage" lies chiefly adjoining to and on the eastern side of the river Hull, extends from north to south about eleven miles, and contains eleven thousand two hundred and eleven acres: in 1762, an act of parliament was obtained for draining this level, much of which before that period was of small value, being usually covered with water for above half the year: the execution of this drainage was vested in trustees, appointed by the owners of land within the limits of its operation. The "Beverley and Barmston Drainage," executed under the provisions of an act passed about the year 1792, lies parallel to the last, but on the opposite side of the river Hull, and extends from the sea-shore at Barmston, a few miles south of Bridlington, along the course of that river nearly to Kingston upon Hull, a distance of about twenty-four miles: its northern part contains more than two thousand acres, and has an outfall into the sea at Barmston; while the southern division, extending southward from Foston, contains upwards of ten thousand acres, and has its outlet into the river Hull, at a place called Wincolmlee. The "Keyingham Drainage," lying between Sunk Island and the main land, was originally completed under an act passed in the year 1722; a new act was obtained in 1802, under which the course of the drainage in some parts was altered, and an additional quantity of land included, making a total of five thousand five hundred acres: the execution of this was vested in three commissioners, and on a vacancy occurring by death or resignation, another commissioner is elected by the proprietors. The "Hertford and Derwent Drainage" contains upwards of ten thousand five hundred acres, of which four thousand five hundred are in the East, and the remainder in the North, riding: the act for this was obtained in the year 1800, and its execution was vested in three directors and three commissioners: the directors have a power to levy an annual assessment, not exceeding an average of three shillings per acre, for the purpose of maintaining and repairing the existing works and drains, and also of further making such new works as may, from time to time, become necessary. Spalding Moor and Walling Fen, lying to the westward of the southern part of the Wolds, were drained, allotted, and enclosed, about fifty years since, under the provisions of the same act of parliament.

The ainsty of York is situated to the west, and on the south-western side, of the Ouse, which borders it from the mouth of the Nid to that of the Wharfe, separating it first from the North, and afterwards from the East, riding: from the West riding it is separated for some distance by the Nid, and afterwards by a line including Wilstrop, Cattle-bridge, Bickerton,

and Thorp-Arch, and terminating at the junction of the Wharfe with the Ouse: its circumference is thirty-two miles, and, in 1821, the population was 8740. The surface and scenery of this tract have the same general character as the rest of the Vale of York, of which it forms a part: the western portion of it is diversified by various gentle swells; while the eastern, adjoining the Ouse, is an entire flat, abounding with excellent meadows and pastures. The whole district of the ainsty was anciently a forest, but it was disforested by the charters of Richard I. and John.

The climate of Yorkshire is as various as its surface. The Levels of the East and West ridings, owing to their being sheltered from the east winds by the Wolds, enjoy a mild atmosphere, but are subject to continual damps and fogs. In the middle district of the West riding the air is sharper, clearer, and more salubrious: at Sheffield the average annual fall of rain is thirty-three inches. On the western mountains of this riding, as well as among the western Moorlands of the North riding, the climate is cold, tempestuous, and rainy: notwithstanding which, the frequent high winds that purify the atmosphere render it salubrious for strong constitutions, and the inhabitants of those districts have a robust and healthy appearance: the quantity of rain which annually falls in the vicinity of Ingleborough is not less than forty-eight inches: on account of their superior elevation and greater distance from the sea, the climate of the Western Moorlands is much colder than that of the Eastern, and the snow remains upon them much later in the spring. In the Vale of York the climate is mild and temperate, except near the Moors, where the influence of the winds from those mountainous regions is often severely felt. On the Howardian hills the air is colder, and the corn later in ripening. Ryedale and the Marishes enjoy a mild air, but are in many parts rendered unhealthy by the want of better drainage. The great altitude of the Eastern Moorlands renders their climate extremely cold, and presents an insuperable obstacle to their improvement: little corn, therefore, except oats and big, a kind of barley, are sown in the higher parts of the dales that penetrate them. About the end of August the clouds begin to descend, and in the form of dense fogs hang upon these Moorland hills, at an elevation of about seven or eight hundred feet; and as they become rarefied by the warmth of the sun, they either ascend above their summits, or remain upon them at an elevation increased in proportion to their rarefaction · as the autumn advances they hang lower on the hills in the morning, and occasionally leave the summits clear, though only for a short time: the whole tract is afterwards, during several months, enveloped in fogs, chilled with rain, or bound up in frost and snow, from an elevation of about six hundred feet upwards, with little interruption. The climate of Cleveland and of the coast is stormy and cold, but the quality of the soil renders the harvest in those districts nearly as early as in the warmer parts of the county. In the East riding, the Wolds and the country lying eastward of them are much exposed to cold raw winds from the German Ocean: the vicinity of the coast is also exposed to fogs from the sea and the Humber. In the county generally the easterly winds prevail in the spring, with great severity, and during a great part of the summer.

as the westerly winds do in the western counties : the conflict between these two currents generally takes place on the western mountains, which also arrest the vapours in their progress from the Western ocean; and to these causes must be attributed the great quantity of rain which falls in those districts. The climate of the eastern part of the county is, however, nearly as much characterized by peculiar dryness, as that of any of the eastern counties of England.

The soils comprise all the varieties common in the kingdom, from the deep strong clay and rich loam to the worst kind of peat earth. In the West riding the prevailing quality is loam, the value of which depends, in a great measure, upon the nature of the substratum. Much of the low ground in this division of the county, bordering on the Ouse, has a clayey soil of a very tenacious quality, the cultivation of which is subject to many difficulties, although it is capable of producing the most abundant crops : this and a rich loamy soil are the predominating kinds, but are intermixed with some sandy and moorish tracts. The middle of the riding is occupied chiefly by loam resting on limestone; and the same kind of soil, with a similar basis, although intermixed in many places with tracts of moor, of different qualities, prevails even to its western limits. In the North riding the soils of the coast district are, a brownish clay, a clayey loam, a lightish soil upon alum shale; a loam upon freestone, or, as it is here called, "gritstone;" and, in some vallies to the west of Whitby, a deep rich loam. The soil of Cleveland is generally a fertile clay, with occasionally some clayey loam, and a fine red sandy soil, the latter of which is found chiefly between Marsh and Worsall, and about Crathorne, near the moors. In the Vale of York, the soil, though varying greatly, is for the most part fertile, and comprises rich gravelly loams; rich strong loams; rich hazel loams; strong and fertile, gravelly, and cold clays; sandy loams of various qualities, sometimes intermixed with cobble-stones and coarse gravel; loamy soils upon limestone; cold and springy soils; and some small tracts of swampy and peaty land : there is also a cold thin clay upon what is called "moorband," a stratum from six inches to a foot in thickness, of a ferruginous and ochreous appearance, which, wherever found, is attended with great sterility. On the southern side of the Howardian hills good clayey and loamy soils prevail, as also at the western extremity : in other places the soil is frequently thin and poor, resting immediately upon a gritstone, or limestone, substratum. The soils of Ryedale are for the most part of extraordinary fertility, comprising a hazel loam upon a clay substratum, and a deep warp, or silt, washed down from the higher country by the floods of many former ages, and deposited upon a gravel or clay; but some cold clayey and yellow loamy soils, mixed with sandy pebbles, of less fertility than the above, are occasionally met with; the detached swells have a rich strong clay, one only excepted, in the vicinity of Normanby, which is sandy : the northern margin of this vale has for the most part a deep loamy soil, resting on an imperfect reddish sandstone; but approaching the moors, the soil gradually becomes stiffer and less fertile, though in some places it is a yellow sand. The soil of the Marishes is chiefly clay, with some sandy loam, gravel, and peat, the whole very

low and wet. Most of the narrow vallies of the Eastern Moorlands contain more or less of a black moory soil, resting upon clay; of a sandy soil, in some places intermixed with large gritstones, upon a shaly rock; and of a light loam lying on gritstone; on their eastern side is also found a stiffish loam upon limestone, and a deep sandy loam upon whin-stone; and in the lowest situation a light loam upon gravel, or freestone. In the Western Moorlands, the soil of the bottom of Wensleydale is generally a rich loamy gravel; that on the sides of the hills, by which it is enclosed, a good loam, in some places rather stiff, and sometimes resting on gritstone, but generally on limestone : there are also some small tracts of clay and peat. Swaledale and the smaller dales are very similar to this in their soils, and several of those which discharge their waters into the Tees are peculiarly fertile.

In the East riding, the whole country to the eastward of the Wolds is occupied by clays and loams, of occasionally varying quality; excepting only a narrow tract of gravelly land, which extends for two or three miles both to the north and south of Rise, near Hornsea, and is excellent turnip land. The Holderness marshes, bordering on the Humber, below Hull, have a strong clayey loam, the fertility of which is almost unequalled. The Wolds are composed almost entirely of chalk; their soils are, therefore, warm and calcareous : the most prevailing kind is a friable and rather light loam, having a mixture of chalky gravel, in some parts very shallow; a deeper sandy loam, resting immediately upon the chalk, is also found in some places. The soil of the "Levels" is, in some parts, clayey; in others, sandy. An extensive sandy, and in some places moory, tract stretches across the middle of them from South Cave, north-westward, to York; but near the banks of the Derwent and the Ouse the predominant soils are a clayey loam and a very strong clay; the latter chiefly prevails from Gilberdike to Howden, and thence extends quite to the Ouse. The tract of ground called "Marshland," situated below the junction of the Aire with the Ouse, is supposed to have been, at some former period, wholly covered with water, and the soil is for the most part of that sort which, in many places, is known by the name of water-fat. The Vale of the Derwent, extending from the vicinity of the coast westward towards York, is remarkable for the great variety of its soils, which, however, are generally fertile; they include a very light fine sand, loams of various qualities, a strong clay of divers colours, lying in some places upon a coarse hard limestone abounding in shells, and a black peat, which extends along the course of the Hertford to its junction with the Derwent, and thence to Yeddingham bridge.

The soils of the ainsty bear a character of general fertility : they are chiefly loams of rather various kinds, some on a calcareous, and others on a gravelly, substratum. The low grounds adjoining the rivers have a soil formed chiefly of the alluvial matter washed from the surrounding higher grounds : those on the banks of the Ouse are most remarkable for their fertility. All that portion of the West riding included between the river Ouse and an imaginary line drawn from Ripley southward by Leeds, Wakefield, and Barnesley, to Rotherham, is principally employed in the production of corn; while the land in the vicinity of the manufacturing towns is under no peculiar system of husbandry: the amount of arable land in the western parts of the West riding is extremely small. In the North riding, in the Vale of York, one-third of the land is in tillage; on the western end of the Howardian hills, and thence to Thirsk, only one-fourth; on the rest of the Howardian hills, nearly one-half; in Ryedale, the Marishes, and the northern part of the coast, about one-third; the southern part of the coast, one-fourth; in Cleveland, one-half; in the dales of the eastern moors, one-fifth; in those of the western moors, hardly any. In the East riding the proportion of land under tillage, on the Wolds, is two-thirds; in Holderness, rather more than one-third, and towards the south-eastern extremity of the county considerably more; and in Howdenshire, and to the west of the Wolds, somewhat less than one-third.

Every kind of agricultural crop is cultivated in this county; and the systems of tillage, on account of the great diversity of soils and situations, are extremely various. Wheat is grown to a great extent on all the lower and more fertile lands; and no other district in the north of England, in proportion to its size, is considered to produce so much of it, or of so good a quality, as Cleveland, whence large quantities are shipped to the southern coasts of England, and much is conveyed to Thirsk and Leybourn, where it is bought up for the manufacturing districts. Rye is sometimes sown on the lighter soils, more particularly of the North riding, where wheat is not unfrequently mixed with it: of this mixture, provincially called "meslin," the common household bread of that portion of the county is chiefly made. The quantity of land annually sown with barley is no where remarkably great, except on the Wolds, the soil of which is peculiarly adapted to its culture: in the North riding, in Ryedale and the dales of the Eastern Moorlands, are occasionally seen plots of the species provincially called big, which is six-rowed barley; and of bear, four-rowed. Besides being occasionally grown in other places, oats are very much cultivated in all the arable parts of the North riding, more particularly in Ryedale, which district is as remarkable for the quantity and excellent quality of its oats, as Cleveland is for those of its wheat: two crops are here always taken in succession, and frequently three: in the western parts of the West riding, too, this corn is the prevailing crop: oaten bread is in common use in the manufacturing districts of the West riding. Peas are not extensively cultivated; they are most common in the North and East ridings. Beans are grown on the stronger soils, more particularly in the East riding: beans and peas mixed, provincially called "blendings," are also sometimes sown on the lighter soils of the North riding. The turnip husbandry prevails in most parts of the county, and the Swedish turnip is occasionally grown to a small extent. Several varieties of cabbages are cultivated in the East riding, as food for cattle and sheep. Potatoes are commonly grown in all parts of the county; and in some districts to a great extent, more particularly on the rich lands near the Ouse and in Holderness, from which great quantities are annually exported to the London market. Rape for seed is extensively cultivated in the North riding, more particularly in Ryedale, upon land pared and

burned: rape is also grown in the level eastern parts of the West riding: in gathering this crop, it is a general custom to thrash it in the field as soon as dry. Winter tares are sown in many places, particularly about Sheffield and Rotherham: in the North riding lentils are sometimes sown with beans, from which, when gathered, their seed is separated with a sieve; and in the East riding they are sometimes grown upon the poorer and shallower soils of the Wolds. Considerable quantities of flax are grown in the West riding, in the neighbourhood of Selby; in the East riding, about Howden and on the eastern bank of the Derwent; and in the North riding, a small quantity in Ryedale, and a few other situations. Woad, for dying, is cultivated in the neighbourhood of Selby, among red clover. In the vicinity of York mustard is a valuable article of cultivation, and fields of it are occasionally seen in different places in the northern and eastern parts of the county: that which is grown near York is prepared for use in mills at that city, and is afterwards sold as Durham mustard. The wapentake of Barkstone-Ash, in the eastern part of the West riding, is distinguished for its extensive growth of teasel, which is also occasionally cultivated to a small extent in different other places having a strong soil: it is purchased by the cloth-dressers, for the purpose of raising the nap on cloth, before it undergoes the operation of shearing. Sainfoin is grown in different situations. On the richer soils the principal artificial grasses are, however, red clover, when the next crop is to be wheat; and white clover and hay-seeds, when the land is to remain in pasture; sometimes only the hay-seeds are sown, or trefoil, or ray-grass added: the produce is partly mown and partly grazed.

In the North riding, the cultivation of grasses is little attended to, except in the country lying between Boroughbridge and Catterick: they are here chiefly sown where the land is intended to remain permanently under grass, and consist generally of white clover, trefoil, rib-grass, and hay-seeds, with which some mix red clover, while others sow ray-grass, instead of the hay-seeds. The grass lands are very extensive, for, besides the tracts included with the arable districts in the large proportion above stated, the productive parts of the western side of the county are kept almost exclusively in grass, and from Ripley to its western extremity the whole country is employed in grazing; while corn, and that almost entirely oats, is raised only in very small quantities on the inferior moorish soils. The old pasture lands, forming by far the greater portion of the grass lands, have remained in that state from time immemorial, and in the West riding are frequently mown, producing hay held in great esteem. Some of them are, nevertheless, of a very mean quality, and, especially in the North riding, are often covered with thistles, ant-hills, and occasionally furze: in the dales of the Western Moorlands, however, remarkably great attention is paid to the meadows. The extent of natural meadow, namely, such as derives the whole, or the greater part, of its fertility from the overflow of rivers, is not very great: many of the old fields of this kind in the Vale of York and Ryedale have been constantly mown for ages, and are still highly productive. The East riding contains the smallest quantity of grass land, its sheep, pastures on the Wolds, for which it was formerly so distinguished, having been mostly brought under various courses of tillage; but it contains, on the banks of the Derwent, above Malton, and again at Cottingwith, low tracts of marshy meadows, occasionally overflowed by that river, which produce abundant crops of coarse flaggy hay, of which that obtained from the last-mentioned district is of a peculiarly nutritive quality. The whole of the West riding is an eminent grazing district, where cattle and sheep of all kinds are fattened to great perfection, chiefly to supply the manufacturing parts of Yorkshire and Lancashire: for this purpose, great numbers of lean cattle and sheep are annually brought from Scotland and the northern counties contiguous to Yorkshire. It has also numerous small dairies, for the supply of its own manufacturing towns and those of Lancashire with butter; and some large ones in the vicinity of the large towns, to which the milk is chiefly sold. In the North riding, the pastures are for the most part appropriated to the dairy; though grazing is also practised in some parts of it, more particularly in the Vale of York: the butter produced in this riding is chiefly packed in firkins, and sold to factors, who ship it for the London and other markets. In the East riding, grazing and fattening, as also stall-feeding, are practised to a very considerable extent.

The manures are, lime, which is used in almost every part of the county; rape-dust; bones, great quantities of which are imported from abroad; horn-shavings, and several other articles of refuse from the manufacturing towns; kelp-ashes and peat-ashes, in the North riding; sea-*wreck*, or sea-weed, which is frequently thrown upon the coast by the tide; sea-sand; whale blubber, and the refuse of the oil; and, in the East riding, chalk: in this division, also, straw is frequently spread upon the land and burned, which operation adds great fertility to the soil: in Cleveland, lime is fetched from Sunderland, in Durham; and in the East riding it is obtained, by water-carriage, from Knottingley, Brotherton, and Doncaster, all in the West riding. Extensive tracts, bordering on the Ouse and the Humber, in the East riding, and the eastern parts of the West riding, are rendered of extraordinary fertility by the practice of warping; this is the admitting of the tide, which rises higher than their level, to overflow them, and afterwards allowing it to retire from them at its ebb, when it deposits a thin bed of mud and salts, provincially called *warp*: this operation is performed chiefly by means of a clough, or inlet in the bank of the river, walled strongly on each side, and a floodgate fixed in the middle, which, as the tide falls, permits the gentle egress of the waters which had been admitted upon the land previously banked and prepared, through a smaller opening on a higher level. The West riding is the only division containing any considerable extent of irrigated meadows, which are most common in the manufacturing districts. A dry limestone ridge, about four miles broad, extending from east to west, northward of Ryedale, and in the vicinity of Kirkby-Moorside, was ingeniously supplied with water, in the latter part of the last century, by means of artificial rills, brought down from the much loftier tract of the Eastern Moorlands. Artificial ponds, of a peculiar construction, for catching and preserving the rain water, are very common on the Wolds of the East riding, and

in different parts of the North riding that require such accommodations. With regard to implements of husbandry, the common Rotherham plough, sometimes called the Dutch plough, is in general use, except upon the Wolds, where the clumsy, heavy, old-fashioned foot-plough, having a short straight wooden mould-board, is chiefly employed.

The cattle for which the West riding is most noted are the hardy, long-horned, or Craven breed: these are both bred and fattened in the western parts of it: some also are brought from the adjoining county of Lancaster. The cattle and sheep brought into this division of the county, for the purpose of being fattened, include almost all the different varieties reared in Britain, though the greater number are Scotch. Short-horned cattle are the prevailing kind in the eastern parts of this riding, in the East riding, and in the North riding, excepting only its westernmost districts. The short-horned cattle of the northern part of the Vale of York, and of Cleveland, where considerable numbers are bred, are generally known by the name of the Teeswater breed; and in the south of England by that of the Holderness cattle, from the district of that name in the East riding, where this breed was either originally established, or first so improved as to bring it into notice, and where, in common with the tracts before mentioned, the best of the sort are still to be met with: these are also occasionally called Durham, or Dutch, cattle, and the cows are in great demand in some of the southern counties of England, more particularly near London, as their produce of milk is remarkably great: very few oxen in these principal breeding districts are used for draught. Many excellent cattle of this same kind are also bred in Ryedale and the Marishes, and on the Howardian hills; as also in the Eastern Moorlands, and along the coast of the North riding, in which districts, however, they are not quite so large as those bred near the Tees. In the neighbourhood of Pocklington, in the East riding, many calves are fattened for the supply of York, Hull, Beverley, &c., with veal. In the Western Moorlands are found some small long-horned cattle, and a mixed breed, between the long-horned and the short-horned species, which also occupies a considerable portion of the West riding, including Nidderdale and the adjacent country, and is held in great esteem: in the lower parts of the dales of the Western Moorlands many of the short-horned breed are also kept. The working of oxen is most common in the eastern part of the North riding: the cattle of these districts being, from their natural strength and hardihood, well adapted to the purpose, are trained to labour at two or two years and a half old, and are worked until five or six years old.

The kinds of sheep are very numerous and much intermixed. Those bred upon the moors of the mountainous parts of the West riding, which are supposed to be native, have horns, are light in the forequarters, and are altogether well made for exploring the mountain wastes which they inhabit; they are generally called the Penistone breed, from the name of the market town at which they are chiefly sold: when fat, they weigh from ten to fifteen pounds per quarter: their meat is of excellent quality. The Dishley breed is common in the southern and eastern parts of this riding. The sheep of the old stock of the northern part of the Vale of York, and of Cleveland, generally called Teeswater sheep, are very large, with long, dry, and harsh wool; but within the last forty years these sheep have been greatly intermixed with the Dishley, Northumberland, and some other breeds, and the varieties thus produced occupy all the low lands and rich cultivated tracts of the North riding. The next in point of number in this division of the county is the hardy unmixed breed which occupies the summits of both the Moorlands : these sheep have black, or speckled, faces and legs, and fleeces of coarse short wool : the greater number of the sheep on the Moorlands are, however, temporary flocks, of a kind called " Short Scots," to distinguish them from a larger breed of Scotch sheep, called " Long Scots." A peculiar, but far less numerous, race occupies a middle region in the western part of the county, the grassy summits of the calcareous hills, and the higher enclosed lands of the Western Moorlands, being a pure, unmixed, and hardy race, much resembling the Old Wiltshire breed : their fleeces are generally thick, dry, and harsh, but some of them produce a very fine wool, used in the hosiery manufacture, for which the dales of these Moorlands are so celebrated. The native sheep of the East riding are the Holderness and the Wolds breeds, which have of late years, been much intermixed with the Leicester ; the former of these resembles the Lincolnshire sheep : the Wolds breed is small, hardy, compact, and active, with a short thick fleece of fine clothing wool. The South Down breed has been introduced upon the Wolds, and is gradually extending itself. The hogs are of various kinds ; the old sort in the North and East ridings has long ears; long legs, a high narrow back, and low shoulders, being very slow feeders; but the Chinese and Berkshire breeds have been introduced throughout the county. In the western part of the West riding many hogs are fattened upon oatmeal, and their flesh sold for the manufacturing districts of Lancashire, excepting only the hams, which are usually sent to the London market : from the East riding many are sold into Lincolnshire, and are thence, in many instances, forwarded to the metropolis.

In the West riding few horses are bred, except in the eastern parts of it : the size of those employed in its mountainous districts is small, but they are hardy, and capable of sustaining great fatigue ; in the other parts of this division they are larger, and those used in the wagons are strong and well made : but the North and East ridings have long been famous for the breeding and rearing of horses, chiefly adapted for the coach and the saddle, for which purposes they are not excelled by any in the kingdom : the strongest of them are chiefly employed as coach-horses ; the lighter for the field, the road, and the army. In the dales of the Eastern Moorlands, and along the coast of the North riding, many horses of a hardy useful kind are reared, but they are generally too small for coach-horses. The horses sold for the London market, if for the carriage, are chiefly bay geldings ; others, which, from some peculiarity, will not sell for a good price at home, are much sought after by foreigners, or others, who eagerly purchase them for exportation abroad. The principal fairs, for horses of every description, are at Beverley, VoL. IV.

Howden, Malton, and York, and are resorted to by numerous dealers from London and all parts of the kingdom. At an annual fair held at Hull, in October, great numbers of colts are also purchased by the Lincolnshire farmers and graziers, who keep them until they are four years old, when they are sold to the London dealers at Horncastle fair. Rabbit-warrens were formerly a very prominent feature of the Wolds, but these are now nearly all destroyed by the progress of cultivation : the East riding, however, still contains several thousand acres of warrens, the produce of which is carried to Leeds, Halifax, and other populous places : a few warrens occur on the detached moors, as also on the skirts of the higher moors in the North riding, but only three are of any considerable extent, and these are situated in the vicinity of Pickering. In the dales of the Moorlands, more particularly of those in the north-eastern part of the county, many considerable stocks of bees are kept; they are extremely fond of the flower of the ling, or common heath, and the honey thus collected is of a high colour, and of a strong and peculiar flavour, and is consequently sold in London at a high price. The season for the bees to collect honey being a month or six weeks earlier in the cultivated parts of the country than on the moors, many owners of bees, who reside within a few miles of the moors, take the honey which they have collected at home, as soon as the flowers have ceased blowing, and then remove their bees to the moors to collect a fresh store for their own support during the winter.

The gardens and orchards present no very remarkable feature; considerable quantities of apples are sent from the North riding to Leeds, and many thence into Lancashire : Sherburn and its vicinity are celebrated for the growing of the winesour plum : in the northern division of the county are also several nursery gardens, in which considerable quantities of forest-trees and shrubs are raised. A great deal of oak and ash timber is produced in the West riding, and great attention is paid to the management of the woods by their proprietors : the timber meets with a ready sale to the ship-building and manufacturing towns : much is also used in the mines and collieries; the small wood is made into laths, baskets, puncheons for coalpits, hedge-stakes and bindings, riddles, charcoal, &c.; that of middle growth into agricultural implements of every description; while the largest timber is worked up by the house, and ship carpenters, coopers, &c. The extent of the woodlands in the North riding is estimated at about twenty-five thousand acres, dispersed in all quarters, the Moorlands and Cleveland having the smallest proportion : exclusively of the above, this division also produces a considerable quantity of timber in its hedge-rows, more particularly in the Vale of York, on the Howardian hills, and in Ryedale. The spontaneous produce of the best woodlands is oak, ash, and broad-leaved, or wych, elm; of those in mountainous situations, chiefly birch and alder ; and of the hedge-rows, various kinds of trees, for the most part of artificial plantation. In this riding it is the custom to sell the falls of wood to professed wood-buyers, who cut up the trees on the spot, according to the purposes for which the different parts of them are best calculated: the ports of Scarborough and Whitby consume most of the ship timber, excepting only such as grows towards its western extremity : the oak timber grown in the greater part of this riding, though not large, is extremely hard and durable: the only peculiar application of the ash timber, which grows abundantly and in great perfection, is in the manufacture of butter-firkins, in which it is chiefly consumed. Plantations have been made on the sides and summits of several of the Moorland and other barren hills, chiefly of Scotch fir, larch, and spruce, a few oaks, &c. The East riding is little remarkable for its timber; the natural woods are confined chiefly to the levels lying between the rivers Ouse and Derwent and the Wolds, where there are also abundance of timber-trees in the hedge-rows of old enclosures: the only woods to the east of the Wolds are those of Rise and Burton-Constable. The fine elevations of the Wolds have been ornamented in different parts by extensive plantations of Scotch and spruce firs, larch, beech, ash, &c., to the amount of several thousand acres; and various other plantations have been made in the low country to the west of them.

The wastes in this county are very extensive, and about the end of the last century were calculated to amount in the whole to eight hundred and forty-nine thousand two hundred and seventy-two acres: of these the high moors of the western parts of the West riding were supposed to comprise three hundred and forty thousand two hundred and seventy-two acres, and the detached moors and wastes of that division sixty-five thousand; the Western Moorlands of the North riding two hundred and twenty-six thousand nine hundred and forty; the Eastern Moorlands of the same division one hundred. and ninety-six thousand six hundred and twenty-five; its detached moors and wastes, eighteen thousand four hundred and thirty-five; and the detached wastes of the East riding two thousand. The amount of waste lands has, however, since that period, been considerably lessened by numerous enclosure acts, obtained both for the detached wastes and for parts of the Moorlands. The surface of some of the higher hills of the Eastern Moorlands is entirely covered with large freestones; while upon others of them are extensive beds of peat bog, in many places very deep, frequently not passable, and never without danger: these are invariably overgrown with ling, in some places mixed with bent and rushes. Near the old enclosures are some considerable tracts of loamy and sandy soils, producing furze, fern (here called "brackens"), thistles, and coarse grass, with but little ling; but wherever ling is the chief produce, the soil is invariably black moor, or peat. The subsoils of these extensive wastes are various: in some places a yellowish, in others a reddish, clay occurs; a loose freestone rubble, resting either upon a freestone rock or upon clay, is also very common; and in different other places is found a rotten earth of a peaty quality (which produces very luxuriant ling, bent, and rushes), a hard cemented reddish sand, or a grey sand; the basis of the whole is freestone. The Hamilton hills, forming the western end of these wastes, are, however, very different, having generally a fine loamy soil on a limestone rock, which produces great quantities of coarse grass and bent, in some places intermixed with ling, more particularly towards the south-western parts of them. The mountains of the western side of the county differ materially in their produce from the Eastern Moorlands: some, instead of black ling, are covered with a fine sweet grass; others with extensive tracts of bent; and though the higher parts produce ling, it is generally mixed with a large proportion of grass, bent, or rushes: the soil on the lower parts is a fine loam, in many places rather stiff, resting upon a hard blue limestone: the bent generally covers a strong soil lying upon a gritstone or freestone rock; the black ling, a reddish peat upon a red subsoil, or, in many places, a loose grit rubble, beneath which is a gritstone rock. Some of the lower tracts of the eastern moors, the lower parts of the western moors in general, and in some instances the higher parts of the latter, are stinted pastures during the summer, and those who have that limited right in summer have a right in winter of turning upon them whatever quantity of stock they choose: these pastures are chiefly stocked with young cattle, horses, and such sheep as are intended to be sold off the same year. The remainder of the moors is common without stint, and is stocked for the most part with sheep, though a small, hardy, and very strong kind of horses are also bred and reared upon the Western Moorlands, and chiefly sold to the manufacturing parts of the West riding and of Lancashire. The Moorland sheep are remarkable for their wretched appearance and great activity: they are wholly supported on these mountain wastes, and their mutton is of a particularly fine quality. The detached wastes are generally pastured by all kinds of stock, and in any proportion which the occupier pleases. The wastes of the East riding consist chiefly of low, sandy, barren, and moory tracts, lying between the Wolds and the rivers Ouse and Derwent, and the chief natural produce of which is short heath. The common fuel throughout the county is coal, with which the North riding, as far south as Thirsk, is for the most part supplied by the collieries in the county of Durham, from which they are brought in one-horse carts to the coast of the East riding from Newcastle and Sunderland, and the rest of the same division from the West riding: in the Moorlands of the North riding much peat is used.

To the geologist Yorkshire affords interesting fields of study: all its strata, with slight variations, dip eastward, those which appear at its western extremities being of the oldest formation. The mineral productions are various and important, and have given rise, and afford support, to some of its principal manufactures: they consist chiefly of coal, iron, lead, stone of various qualities, and alum. The best coal is obtained in the West riding, which comprises one of the most valuable and extensive coal fields in the kingdom. This coal district is bounded on the east by a narrow range of magnesian limestone, extending from Tickhill northward by Doncaster, Ferrybridge, Wetherby, Knaresborough, and Ripon, and consists of a great number of alternations of sand-stone, clay, shale, coal, and iron-stone, which form the substrata of the most populous parts of the riding. Its surface is characterised by successive parallel ranges of high ground, extending in length from north to south: the ascent to these hills on their western sides is abrupt, while on the east they decline more gradually, each one to the foot of the next range, under which its strata dip. Next to the magnesian limestone and its subjacent sand, proceeding westward, appear, first, the blue shale and thin coal of the Vale of Went, and then the grit freestone of Ackworth and

Kirby, beneath which is found the swift-burning coal of Wragby, Shafton, Crofton, and other places in the great clay district of the Dearn below Barnesley, and of the Calder below Wakefield. These various measures rest upon the grit freestone of Rotherham, Barnesley, Newmiller Dam, and East Ardsley, through which pits are sunk near Barnesley to several thick seams of hard furnace coal, one of them as much as ten feet thick. The next great sand-stone stratum forms high grounds, and frequently projects beyond the general range into detached hills: it occurs near Sheffield, Wentworth Park, and Bretton Park, and forms the high ground of Horbury and Dewsbury, and of Middleton, near Leeds: beneath it are found valuable beds of iron-stone, which are worked at Rotherham, Haigh-bridge, Low Moor, and several other places, where an abundance of muscle shells is found in contact with them: contiguous to this iron-stone are several strata of excellent coal. Next in the series lies the sand-stone of Wortley-Chapel, Silkstone, Elmley, and Whitley-hall, with the valuable bituminous coals of Silkstone and Flockton, the best seams of the whole formation: this rock, entering the West riding from Derbyshire, and passing by Sheffield, Penistone, Huddersfield, Elland Edge, and the Clayton heights, afterwards takes its course parallel with the river Aire, by Idle and Chapel-Allerton, towards the magnesian limestone: in this part of the coal district, near Sheffield, Bradford, and Leeds, is dug the *galliard* stone, so much in request for making and mending the roads.

The coal mines are most numerous in the tract between Leeds and Wakefield, and in the neighbourhoods of Bradford, Barnesley, and Sheffield. Characterised by its irregular texture, its numerous quartz pebbles, and its frequently craggy surface, the millstone-grit, with soft alternations both above and below it, occupies the wide and barren moors to the west of Sheffield, Penistone, Huddersfield, Bradford, Otley, Harrogate, Ripley, and Masham: in the numerous alternations of this stone, thin seams of coal frequently occur, and in certain situations are worked with advantage. Of the millstone-grit, an excellent and almost imperishable building stone, great quantities are annually sent down the rivers Don and Aire. The summits of Wharnside, Ingleborough, Pennygant, and other lofty mountains on the western boundary of the county, are crowned with coal measures, but their base consists wholly of limestone. The principal lead mines in the West riding are at Grassington, about ten miles west of Pateley-Bridge, and are found in a limestone tract which occupies also a great part of Craven; but here the ores are far less abundant than in the vales of the Nid and the Wharfe. Hongill Fells, on the western boundary of the county, consist of the kind of slate called by geologists *grey wacke*. In the North riding seams of an inferior kind of coal, which is heavy, sulphureous, and burns entirely away to white ashes, are wrought in different parts of both the Eastern and Western Moorlands, at Gilling Moor on the Howardian hills, and in the Vale of York, between Easingwould and Thirsk. Cleveland and the coast of this riding abound in all their hills with inexhaustible beds of aluminous strata; and extensive works for the manufacture of alum have been established in the vicinity of Whitby, where the art is stated to have been first introduced from Italy, in the year 1595. Alum is also found, but not worked, in the Eastern Moorlands, and in the vicinity of Bradford. In the Western Moorlands are many lead mines, some of which have been, and others still are, very valuable: these are situated in Swaledale, Arkendale, and the neighbouring vallies: their annual produce is estimated at six thousand tons, of which one-half is yielded by the mines of Swaledale.

Veins of copper have been discovered at Richmond and at Middleton-Tyas, at which latter place that metal was worked about the middle of the last century: copper pyrites is also found in considerable quantities in all the alum mines, and copperas was formerly extracted from it. Great quantities of iron-stone are found in Bilsdale, Bransdale, and Rosedale, in the Eastern Moorlands, where iron seems to have been extensively manufactured in ancient times; but Ayton is the only place where forges have been erected at a modern period, and these are now abandoned. The iron-ore found in the northern parts of the Eastern Moorlands is sometimes in detached pieces, but more frequently in regular strata, of from six to fourteen inches thick, dipping towards the south: in the neighbourhood of Whitby, some of these beds are wrought, and their produce carried to the works in the north, where this ore is of great use in fluxing the more obdurate ores there obtained. Freestone, or gritstone, of an excellent quality for building, is found in many parts of this riding, particularly on Gatherly Moor, near Richmond, at Renton, near Boroughbridge, in the neighbourhood of Whitby, in all parts of the Eastern Moorlands, of which it forms the chief basis, and in many parts of the Western. Nor is limestone less abundant: the Western Moorlands in a great measure consist of it; the Hamilton and Howardian hills, almost entirely; and a narrow ridge, producing lime of a peculiarly excellent quality for agricultural purposes, extends for at least thirty miles along the southern edge of the Eastern Moorlands: various isolated masses are also found in different situations. In Coverdale, one of the smaller vallies of the Western Moorlands, and at Pen-hill, between this and Wensleydale, a kind of flag-stone, used for covering roofs is dug, and in Swaledale a kind of purple slate, resembling that of Westmorland, but thicker and coarser, the use of which extends little beyond the spot where it is produced. Marble of various kinds, some much resembling that worked in Derbyshire, and some, in closeness of texture and distinctness of colours, superior to it, is found in many parts of the calcareous hills of the Western Moorlands, but is only used for burning into lime, or mending the roads: some of the limestone on the northern margin of Ryedale also greatly resembles the marble of Derbyshire, and is susceptible of nearly an equal polish. In the vicinity of the small river Greta, and in other places in the north-western extremity of the county, large blocks of a light red granite are found scattered over the surface, and in some places a light grey kind of the same stone. Gypsum, or alabaster, is found in the Vale of York, in the North riding, and in some parts of the levels of the East and West ridings: near Thornton-bridge, on the Swale, where it is worked for the use of the plasterers of the neighbourhood, it lies in strata several feet thick, and in some places not more than

four feet from the surface. The principal mineral productions of the East riding are, the chalk of the
Wolds, which is occasionally used in building, and frequently for burning into lime ; and the coarse hard
limestone of the vale of the Derwent, which is of little
value either for building or burning : the springs in
the chalk are remarkably powerful, and many of them,
breaking out through the gravel at the eastern foot of
the Wolds, combine to form the river Hull. In the
gravel beds resting on the chalk, to the east of where
this substance appears next the surface, very perfect
remains of large animals are found: vertebræ, eighteen
feet in length, and from eight to ten inches in diameter,
have here been exhumed, as are frequently teeth, measuring from eight to ten inches in circumference. The
strata of the West riding contain few fossil remains,
except at Bradford, where, in a stratum of sand-
stone, are found beautiful impressions of· euphorbium,
bamboo cane, and other tropical productions : at a
little distance from Knaresborough a bed of strontian
earth exists, which is very rare in this kingdom. Various remarkable petrifactions of animals have been
discovered in the alum rocks in the vicinity of Whitby,
as also *cornua ammonis*, or snake stones: some of the
strata in the same neighbourhood also contain petrified
cockle, oyster, and scallop shells; jet and petrified wood ;
and *trochitæ*, or "thunderbolts," as they are vulgarly
called, which are singular conical stones of from half
an inch to an inch and a half in diameter at the base,
and from two to five or six inches long. Great quantities of remarkable crystals of *gypsum selenites* and
prismaticum are discovered in a bed of clay at Knapton,
in the East riding.

The manufactures, the most valuable and extensive
of which are confined to the West riding, are of the
highest degree of importance to the kingdom, as well as
to the multitudes to whom they afford subsistence, and,
in numerous instances, wealth. The two distinguishing manufactures are those of woollen goods and cutlery; the seat of the former is the district including
the towns of Leeds, Halifax, Huddersfield, Bradford,
and Wakefield; and that of the latter, Sheffield and
its vicinity. The principal inducement for the establishment of these great works in the situations which
they now occupy, was the plentiful supply of water
and fuel for giving motion to machinery, and for the
various other purposes of their several departments.
The river Aire is the eastern boundary of the clothing
district, which extends over the country thence to
the mountain ridge separating this county from that
of Lancaster. The great bulk of the woollen manufactures consisted formerly of the coarser kinds of
cloth ; but at present "Yorkshire cloth" no longer
conveys the exclusive idea of inferiority, as the manufacturers now produce also great quantities of black
and blue superfine cloths of distinguished merit. Until of late years, when numerous extensive factories
have been erected (in which the whole process of
making cloth, from the first breaking of the wool to
the finishing of the piece ready for the consumer
is completed), the first stages of the manufacture
were carried on in villages and hamlets, where the
wool underwent the respective operations of spinning,
weaving, and fulling : this, however, is now only partially the case : the cloth from these scattered esta-

blishments is sent in its unfinished state to the cloth
halls in the respective towns, where it is sold to
the merchants, who have it dressed under their own
direction. Besides broad and narrow cloths of various qualities, serges, and kerseymeres, the woollen
manufactures of the West riding include also great
quantities of ladies' cloths, such as pelisse-cloths and
shawls ; stuff goods of various kinds ; camblets, shalloons, tammies, duroys, everlastings, calimancoes, mo-
reens, shags, serges, baize, &c. ; blankets, and carpets,
much resembling those made in Scotland. Several
very large factories have been established for spinning flax for canvas, linen, sacking, thread, &c.: an
extensive branch of the Manchester cotton trade is
also carried on. There is a considerable trade in
the spinning of worsted yarn, and in the manufacture of wool cards and combs. The Leeds pottery
enjoys a very considerable reputation both in the British dominions and in foreign countries : the whole-
sale tobacco trade is also carried on to a great extent
in that town, where there are mills for preparing the
raw material.

Sheffield has, from a very remote period, been
famous for its manufacture of cutlery, which, however,
was of very small extent until the early part of the
seventeenth century, when it began gradually to increase ; and by an act of parliament, passed in 1624, the
cutlers of the liberty of Hallamshire, comprising the
town of Sheffield and the adjacent country, were erected
into a corporate body, which at present consists of between three and four thousand members. Even until
the middle of the last century the trade of Sheffield
was still limited and precarious, but at that period
various new branches of manufacture were introduced,
more particularly that of plated goods. Its present
manufactures, branches of which are also carried on in
the numerous villages and hamlets in the surrounding
country, to the distance of about seven miles from
the town, include all kinds of cutlery and plated goods,
edge-tools, combs, cases, buttons, fenders, files, anvils,
joiners' tools, lancets, ink-stands, nails, snuffers, saws,
scythes, hay and straw knives, sickles, shears, awls,
bellows, and an endless variety of other articles of
hardware. There are also several foundries for iron,
brass, and Britannia metal, and extensive works for
the refining of steel : the iron-works at Rotherham are
particularly celebrated, and produce all kinds of articles in cast iron, and much wrought iron, in bars,
sheets, and rods, together with tinned plates and steel.
At Sheffield is also a minor manufacture of hair seating,
besides a more considerable one of carpets. In the dales
of the Eastern Moorlands and in Cleveland some coarse
linens are manufactured by the small farmers ; and at
Crathorne in Cleveland, and various places near the Hamilton hills, are considerable bleaching establishments.
The dales of the Western Moorlands have long been
famous for their manufacture of knit worsted and yarn
stockings, but this has been, in a great measure,
superseded by the spinning of worsted for the manufactures of the West riding. Cotton-mills have been
erected in Wensleydale, at Easingwould, and at Masham,
at which latter place is also a worsted-mill, and in its
vicinity shalloons and shags are manufactured to a
small extent. York and the East riding have various
isolated manufactures, the whole of which are men-

tioned under the heads of the places where they are respectively carried on. In the vicinities of York and Hull a kind of coarse earthenware is made, as well as bricks and tiles; and on Walling Fen, near Howden, great quantities of white bricks are made from a blue clay found there, which are exported in various directions, being in great demand for superior buildings, on account of their beauty of colour, accuracy of form, and durability. Almost every town in the North riding, and many in the other parts of the county have tanners, and tawers, who manufacture the hides and skins produced in their respective neighbourhoods. To this enumeration of manufactures may also be added the building and rigging of ships, which is carried on to a considerable extent at Hull and Whitby, and in a minor degree at Scarborough and Thorne: at the three first-mentioned places are considerable manufactures of sail-cloth and cordage. The chief port of the county is Hull, which may be considered the fourth in England; besides this it possesses, of a smaller class, those of York, Selby, Goole, Thorne, Bridlington, Scarborough, and Whitby. The commerce is of a very extensive and diversified character: the foreign and coasting trade is wholly centred in the above-mentioned ports, more particularly in that of Hull, through which is poured an immense quantity of manufactured goods, coal, stone, &c., from the West riding, and of cotton-twist and manufactured cottons from Lancashire, the latter of which articles are chiefly forwarded to Hamburgh. Hull and Whitby share largely in the Greenland fishery; and their imports of timber, deals, hemp, flax, &c., from the Baltic, are very considerable. The internal commerce of the West riding is very extensive, and is greatly facilitated by an excellent system of artificial navigation. A considerable quantity of corn is exported from Hull, Bridlington, and Scarborough to London and the collieries of the north; and from the various principal markets of the East and North ridings great quantities of grain are sent by water-carriage into the western division of the county, from which the first-mentioned division receives in return coal, lime, flag-stones, bricks and tiles, and sundry other articles. A large quantity of hams and bacon is annually sent from the eastern parts of Yorkshire to the metropolis and other populous districts of the kingdom.

The principal rivers are, the Northern Ouse (so called to distinguish it from the Ouse of Buckinghamshire), the Swale, the Ure, the Wharfe, the Derwent, the Aire, the Calder, the Don, the Hull, the Tees, and the Esk, all of which, except the two latter, pour their waters through the great æstuary of the Humber. The Swale, rising at Hollow Mill Cross, in the Western Moorlands, and watering the romantic valley of Swaledale, flows eastward, by Richmond and Catterick, into the Vale of York, where it gradually assumes a south-south-easterly direction, and is joined by the small stream of the Wiske, which descends from the western edge of Cleveland by the vicinity of North Allerton: proceeding onward it falls into the Ure, a river of about equal magnitude with itself, which, rising at Lady's Pillar, within five miles of the source of the Swale, and winding through Wensleydale, flows, first eastward to Middleham, and then southward by Masham to a little below the town, where it

becomes the boundary between the West and North ridings, and so continues until it reaches the vicinity of Ripon, where, receiving the waters of the Skell, it makes a circuit of a few miles in the first-mentioned division, and then again separates the two ridings until a little below its junction with the Swale, where it takes the name of Ouse, from an inconsiderable stream, which there falls into it. The Ouse, thus formed (and receiving from the west the waters of the river Nid, which descends from Nidderdale by Pateley-Bridge, Ripley, and Knaresborough), flows south-eastward to York, in the vicinity of which city it separates the ainsty of York from the North and East ridings, and thence southward, with greater windings: about eight miles below York, at the influx of the Wharfe, it becomes the boundary between the East and West ridings, which it continues to form throughout the rest of its course, and re-assumes a winding south-easterly direction, by Selby, Howden, and Goole, at which latter place, having successively received the waters of the Derwent, Aire, Calder, and Don, it becomes as wide as the Thames at London; and after making a circuit to the south, near Swinefleet, takes a north-easterly direction to the place where it unites with the Trent to form the Humber, the *Abus* of Ptolemy, which is at first about a mile broad, but rolling its vast collection of waters eastward, its breadth, on reaching Hull, is gradually increased to between two and three miles. Below this port, opposite to Hedon and Paul, the Humber takes a south-easterly direction, and opening into a grand æstuary of between six and seven miles in breadth, joins the ocean between Spurn Head and the coast of Lincolnshire. The Humber is navigable up to Hull for ships of the largest burden; the Ouse, up to the newly-formed port of Goole, for vessels drawing not more than sixteen feet of water, and to York, for those of one hundred and forty tons' burden: above that city it is navigable for barges of thirty tons' burden, as also is the Ure past Boroughbridge to Ripon, and the Swale, only for a very few miles: the spring tides would turn the current of the Ouse to a little above York, were it not that they are obstructed by locks about four miles below that city. The Wharfe rises at the foot of the Craven hills, at Green Field, five miles south of Pennigant, and, flowing south-eastward, waters the beautiful district of Wharfedale, passes the towns of Otley, Wetherby, and Tadcaster, and falls into the Ouse a little below the village of Nun-Appleton: this river is navigable as high as Tadcaster. The Derwent, rising in the Eastern Moorlands, within about four miles of the sea, and eight or nine of Scarborough, at first takes a southerly direction, nearly parallel with the coast, through the romantic village of Hackness, and in a remarkably picturesque valley, until it reaches the northern extremity of the Wolds, where it is joined from the east by the small stream called the Hertford, and then pursues a westerly, and afterwards a south-westerly, course, receiving from the north the waters of the river Rye, formed by numerous streams from the Eastern Moorlands: from this junction the Derwent continues the same course by New Malton and Stamford-Bridge, in the vicinity of which latter place it gradually assumes a southerly direction, and joins the Ouse near the village of Barmby, about three miles and a half above Howden: this river forms the boundary between the North and East ridings, from its junction with the Hertford until within about a mile of Stamford-Bridge, where it enters the latter division: it is navigable for vessels of twenty-five tons' burden to New Malton, above which town the navigation has been continued to Yeddingham bridge, a further distance of about nine miles. It is worthy of observation, that the Rye, together with its tributaries, the Rical, Hodge-beck, Dove, Seven, and Pickering-beck, in their course southward, have subterraneous passages under the narrow range of limestone hills which skirts the southern side of the Eastern Moorlands, and emerge at its foot, on the northern side of Ryedale, having run under ground from half a mile to a mile and a half. The Aire, one of the largest rivers of the county, rises at Malham, in the mountains of Craven, and thence glides with a smooth, slow, and serpentine course through the winding valley of Airedale, which extends nearly in a south-easterly direction to Leeds, being about thirty-five miles in length, though little more than a mile in breadth: at Leeds it becomes navigable, and a few miles lower, near Castleford, is joined by the Calder, which rises in the mountains on the border of Lancashire, and takes a very tortuous course eastward, leaving Halifax at the distance of rather less than two miles on the north, and passing by Dewsbury to Wakefield, whence its course is nearly north-eastward to Castleford: thus augmented, the Aire proceeds eastward by Ferrybridge, until, after passing within a very short distance of Snaith, it turns north-eastward to its confluence with the Ouse, a little below Armin: the Calder is navigable to Salter-Hebble, near Halifax. The Don, rising in the moors above Penistone, towards the south-western border of the county, flows south-eastward to Sheffield, where it is joined by the small river Sheaf, and then takes a north-easterly course to Rotherham: having been joined by the powerful stream of the Rother, it hence passes through a narrow and picturesque vale, by Conisbrough, to Doncaster, where it enters the levels, through which it proceeds, by Thorne, to the Ouse at Goole; the lower part of its channel, from the vicinity of Snaith, being artificial, and usually called the Dutch River: in 1751, this river was made navigable to Tinsley, three miles below Sheffield, and, under the provisions of an act of parliament passed in 1815, this navigation has been continued by a cut, called the Tinsley canal, to Sheffield. The Hull, rising at the eastern foot of the Wolds, in the vicinity of Great Driffield, flows from that town southward, within half a mile of Beverley, to Hull, where it falls into the Humber, and where its mouth forms a secure but narrow haven: this river is navigable to Frodingham bridge, several miles above Beverley (with which town it communicates by means of a short cut), whence the navigation is continued by a canal to Great Driffield. Another canal extends eastward from the river Hull to Leven, a distance of about three miles. The Tees rises in the mountains on the confines of Durham and Westmorland, a little beyond the north-western extremity of this county, of which it immediately becomes the northern boundary, and which, throughout the rest of its course, it separates from that of Durham: at first it flows south-eastward by Barnard Castle, but, a little below Darlington, it changes its direction to the north-east, and winds

placidly by Yarm, the only town situated on its southern bank, to a short distance above which it is navigable for vessels of sixty tons' burden, and where the spring-tides rise about seven feet: below Stockton it spreads into the fine æstuary of Redcar, three miles broad. The Eske, descending from the northern districts of the Eastern Moorlands, flows eastward through a narrow, but beautiful, dale, to which it gives name, and falls into the North Sea at Whitby, after forming the inner harbour of that port. The smaller rivers are very numerous, more particularly in the mountainous regions, where, in some situations, they form beautiful cascades.

The canals are nearly all within the limits of the West riding. Under this head, however, may be classed the small navigable river Foss, the channel of which is believed to have been originally formed by the Romans, to effect the drainage of an extensive level tract lying between the Ouse and the Howardian hills, near the western extremity of which it rises, and thence takes first a south-easterly, and then a southerly, course to the Ouse, at York: at the end of the last century the navigation was made perfect from York up to Sheriff-Hutton, a distance of about fourteen miles, under the provisions of an act of parliament passed in the year 1793. Market-Weighton and Hedon, which are both situated in the East riding, and are considerable markets for corn, have each the advantage of a navigable canal to the Humber. The canals of the West riding, in alphabetical order, are as follows: the Barnesley canal, which commences in the navigable channel of the river Calder, a little below Wakefield, and, taking a southerly direction, unites with the Dearn and Dove canal, near Barnesley: its length is only fifteen miles, but it is of great importance, as forming part of the line of navigation from Sheffield to Barnesley, Wakefield, Leeds, Huddersfield, Manchester, and Liverpool. The Bradford canal, which is only three miles in length, commences in the Leeds and Liverpool canal at Windhill, in the parish of Idle, and terminates at Bradford, where extensive railways connect it with the collieries and iron-works of Low Moor and Bowling. The Dearn and Dove canal commences in a side cut from the river Don, between Swinton and Mexborough, and, passing north-westward, terminates in the Barnesley canal at Eyming's Wood, after a course of nine miles: together with the Barnesley canal it forms a line connecting the navigable channel of the Don with that of the Calder. From the newly-formed commercial docks at Goole a canal passes westward to the river Aire, at Ferrybridge, and thus completes the water communication between that rising port and the manufacturing districts of the West riding, together with the counties of Lancaster, Chester, and Stafford. The Huddersfield canal, nineteen miles and a half long, commences in Sir John Ramsden's canal, on the southern side of that town, and, proceeding westward, passes near Saddleworth, through the range of mountains on the borders of Yorkshire and Lancashire, by one of the largest tunnels in the kingdom, being nearly three miles and a half in length, and terminates in the latter county in the Manchester, Ashton, and Oldham canal. The Leeds and Liverpool canal enters this county from Colne in Lancashire, whence it proceeds by Skipton, Keighley, and Bingley, and across the river Aire, near Shipley, to

Leeds, where it terminates in the Aire navigation: this extensive and important canal connects, by a direct water communication, the ports of Liverpool and Hull with the large manufacturing town of Leeds. The Ramsden canal, four miles in length, commences in the Calder and Hebble navigation at Cooper's bridge, and terminates in the Huddersfield canal at the King's Mills, near Huddersfield; thus completing, in conjunction with the Huddersfield canal, the important line of water communication between Manchester and the great manufacturing towns of Yorkshire. The Rochdale canal, entering from Rochdale in Lancashire, terminates in the Calder and Hebble navigation at Sowerby bridge, two miles from Halifax. The Stainforth and Keadley canal, partly in this county, and partly in the Isle of Axholme, in Lincolnshire, branches from the navigation of the Don at Fishlake, near Stainforth, and, passing by Thorne, terminates in the Trent, at Keadley, after a course of fifteen miles. On the 29th of May, 1830, an act of parliament received the royal assent, for the construction of a railway from the town of Leeds to the Ouse at Selby, a total length of nineteen miles and seven furlongs: it commences at the east side of Marsh-lane, in Leeds, and immediately enters a tunnel, which will be eight hundred yards long, to be cut through a hill, the summit of which is seventy-two feet above the line of the railway: the expense of the undertaking has been estimated at £200,000.

In the West riding many of the roads are very good, though a few are indifferent, particularly near some of the manufacturing towns, where the carriage upon them is heavy, and the materials for their repair of an inferior quality, being chiefly burnt freestone and brick: in the western manufacturing districts footpaths are raised on the sides of most of the public roads, some of which are paved, and the rest formed of fine gravel and sand. Many of the turnpike-roads in the North riding are very good; the rest, for the most part, are in an improving condition; and the bridges are very numerous, good, and handsome; but a large proportion of the roads of this division of the county, and nearly all those of the East riding, are parochial. The roads in Cleveland are distinguished for their excellence; but those along the coast, and in both the Moorlands of the North riding, are narrow, steep, and rugged, particularly in the dales of the Eastern Moorlands: in the larger dales of the Western Moorlands they are, however, generally in tolerably good condition. The roads of the East riding are much better in the lower districts than on the Wolds: in Holderness, they are formed chiefly of gravel, much of which is brought from the sea-shore; while in the levels to the west of the Wolds, burnt bricks of irregular form, and, in the vicinity of Howden, gravel, brought by water from Spurn-point, are frequently used. The road from London to Edinburgh, by Coldstream, or Berwick (the great north road), enters the county from Nottinghamshire at Bawtry, and passes through Doncaster, Ferrybridge, Wetherby, Boroughbridge, and North Allerton, to Darlington, in Durham: the road from London to Edinburgh, by Carlisle, branches from this at Boroughbridge, and proceeds through Leeming, Catterick, and Greta-Bridge, to Brough, in Westmorland; while that from London to Edinburgh, by York, branches from the first-mentioned at Ferrybridge, through Sherburn, Tadcaster, York,

Easingwould, and Thirsk, to North Allerton, where it rejoins it. A branch from the great north road at Bawtry passes through Hatfield, Thorpe, and Howden, to Market-Weighton; and from this again, at Thorne, there is a branch through Snaith and Selby, to Cawood. The road from London to Whitby branches off at York, and passes through New Malton and Pickering; that from London to Scarborough, by York, from this again at New Malton; and that from London to Hartlepool, from the great north road at North Allerton, through Yarm. The road from London to Hexham and Bellingham branches from the Carlisle road at Greta-Bridge, through Barnard-Castle, in Durham; and that to Askrigg, from the great north road at Boroughbridge, through Masham. The road from London to Hull and Scarborough, by Lincoln, enters the county by the ferry across the Humber from Barton, in Lincolnshire, to Hull, from which town it proceeds, by Beverley and Driffield, to Scarborough. The road from London to Leeds and Ripon enters from Chesterfield in Derbyshire, and passes through Sheffield, Barnesley, Wakefield, Leeds, Harrogate, and Ripley, to Ripon, whence it is continued across the great north road to Thirsk. The road from London to Skipton branches from the road to Manchester and Preston, at Manchester, and entering from Clitheroe in Lancashire, passes through Gisburn to Skipton. The road from London to Kendal, through Bedford, Nottingham, and Skipton, entering from the eastern border of Derbyshire, passes through Rotherham, Barnesley, Huddersfield, Halifax, Skipton, and Settle, to Kirkby-Lonsdale, in Westmorland. The road from London to Skipton, by Leeds, passes from the last-mentioned town through Otley.

Besides the great station of *Eboracum*, or York, the chief seat of the Roman power in Britain, this county contained also, in the West riding, the stations of *Isurium*, at Aldborough; *Legiolum*, a little below the junction of the rivers Aire and Calder; *Danum*, at Doncaster; *Olicana*, at Ilkley; *Cambodunum*, at Slack, near Halifax; and *Calcaria*, at Tadcaster: in the North riding, those of *Cataractonium*, at Catterick; and *Derventio*, at Stamford-Bridge, or at Aldby, a mile further northward: and in the East riding, of *Delgovitia*, at Londesborough; and *Prætorium*, at Patrington. The most durable of the works of this people were the roads which they constructed, in order to facilitate the communication between their military stations, several of which traversed Yorkshire in different directions, and remains of some of them may yet be traced in various parts of it: the common centre from which they diverged was *Eboracum*, or York. The line of the great road, since called the Watling-street, which ran the whole length of England, from the coast of Kent to the wall of Severus, enters from Nottinghamshire in the vicinity of Bawtry, and passes through Doncaster, Barnsdale, Pontefract Park, Castleford, Tadcaster, York, Aldborough, and Catterick, into the county of Durham at Pierse-Bridge. Another military road entered from Manchester, and passed through the vicinity of Halifax, and by Wakefield, to the Watling-street. Another similar road, from Chesterfield, on the north-western confines of Derbyshire, passed by Sheffield, Barnesley, Hemsworth, and Ackworth, to the Watling-street, at or near Pontefract: a vicinal way also appears to have passed through Pontefract, in a southerly direction, to the villages of Darrington, Wentbridge, Smeaton, Campsall, and Hatfield. From York a Roman road ran to Malton, and appears to have there divided into two branches, one, now commonly called Wade's Causeway, leading to Dunsley bay, in the neighbourhood of Whitby; the other to Scarborough and Filey: another road passed from York, by Stamford-Bridge, Fridaythorpe, and Sledmere, and across the Wolds, to Bridlington bay, called by Ptolemy *Gabrantovicorum Sinus Portuosus*, or *Salutaris*. Further to the south was a Roman road from York, by Stamford-Bridge and Londesborough, to Patrington: from Londesborough, a branch of this, formerly called Humber-Street, passed in a straight line southward to the village of Brough on the Humber. The most remarkable antiquities exist in the remains of ancient castles and religious edifices; but there are also several specimens of military and other works, of a more remote period. The three gigantic obelisks of single stones, vulgarly called the Devil's Arrows, situated near Boroughbridge, are by some thought to be Druidical, and by others of Roman origin. Traces of Roman encampments are found in several places, and the remains of their roads are more particularly conspicuous on the Eastern Moorlands, where the ancient road from Malton to Dunsley bay, now called Wade's Causeway, is in excellent preservation, being twelve feet broad, in some places raised more than three feet above the surface, and paved with flint pebbles; and on the Wolds, where the Roman road from York to Bridlington bay may be traced for many miles. The only remains of Roman structures now to be seen in York, the site of the ancient *Eboracum*, are the multangular tower and the south wall of the Mint yard. A vast variety of Roman antiquities has at different times been found in York and its vicinity, in digging the cellars, drains, and foundations of houses, such as altars, sepulchral and other urns, sarcophagi, coins, signets (both cameos and intaglios), fibulæ, &c. Roman urns, coins, &c., have been discovered in several other situations near the stations and roads of that people. Many ancient tumuli are discernible in various parts of the county, particularly on the Wolds. Besides the Roman encampments, others of the Saxons and the Danes may be traced in several places in the North and West ridings. The remarkable assemblage of rocks, called Bramham Crags, about nine miles north-west of Ripon, are supposed, from the peculiar marks of rude sculpture which some of them exhibit, to have been a celebrated Druidical temple.

The number of religious houses was about one hundred and six, including seven Alien priories: the ruins of several of them are extremely beautiful and picturesque. The principal ruins of abbeys are those of St. Mary's at York; of Fountains, Kirkstall, Roche, and Selby, in the West riding; and of Byland, Rievaulx, and Whitby, in the North riding; and of priories, those of Bolton and Knaresborough, in the West riding; of Guisborough, Mountgrace, and Wikeham, in the North riding; and of Bridlington, Kirkham and Watton, in the East riding. The most remarkable specimens of ancient ecclesiastical architecture are, the magnificent cathedral church of St. Peter at York; and, in the West riding, the churches of Addle, Guisley, Halifax, Horton, St. Peter at Leeds, Linton, Rotherham, St. Peter at Sheffield, Sherburn, Thornton in Lonsdale, and

All Saints and St. Margaret at York, together with the remains of that of St. Gregory; in the North riding, those of Bowes, Danby-Wisk, Downholme, Grinton, Kirby-Wisk, Kirkdale, Old Malton, Startforth, and Thornton-Steward; and in the East riding, those of Flamborough, Great Driffield, Hemingborough, Howden, North Newbald, and the chapel of Skirlaw in the parish of Swine. There are, besides, several other ancient and curious chapels in the North and West ridings; and the churches of every division of the county possess, in many instances, fonts of ancient date and curious workmanship, among which may be more particularly noticed those of Doncaster, Ingleton, Linton, and Thorpe-Salvin, in the West riding; of Easby and Catterick, in the North riding; and of Everingham, in the East riding. The most distinguished remains of ancient fortresses, besides Clifford's Tower at York, are those of the castles of Cawood, Conisbrough, Harewood, Knaresborough, Pontefract, Great Sandall, Skipton, and Tickhill, in the West riding; of Helmsley, Malton, Mulgrave, Pickering, Richmond, Scarborough, Sheriff-Hutton, and Skelton, in the North riding; and of Wressle, in the East riding. The most remarkable ancient mansions are, Temple-Newsome, near Leeds, the seat of the Marquis of Hertford; and Gilling Castle, near Helmsley, that of the ancient family of Fairfax; besides which, several in different parts of the county are now occupied as farm-houses. Yorkshire contains a great number of elegant seats of more modern erection, belonging to the nobility and gentry who possess estates within its limits: some of those more particularly worthy of mention in the West riding are, Wentworth House, the property and residence of Earl Fitzwilliam; Wentworth Castle, or Stambrough Hall, formerly the seat of the Earls of Strafford, now that of Wentworth Vernon, Esq.; Methley Park, that of the Earl of Mexborough; Thundercliffe Grange, near Rotherham, that of the Earl of Effingham; Sandbeck Park, near Tickhill, that of the Earl of Scarborough; Newby Hall, near Ripon, that of Lord Grantham; Harewood House, near Leeds, that of the Earl of Harewood, lord-lieutenant of the West riding; Scarthingwell Hall, near Tadcaster, that of Lord Hawke; and Allerton-Mauleverer, that of Lord Stourton: in the North riding, Hornby Castle, near Bedale, that of the Duke of Leeds, lord-lieutenant of this division of the county; Stanwick, near Richmond, that of the Duke of Northumberland; Castle-Howard, near Malton, that of the Earl of Carlisle, lord-lieutenant of the East riding; and Mulgrave Castle, near Whitby, that of Lord Mulgrave: in the East riding, Londesborough, near Market-Weighton, that of the Duke of Devonshire: and in the ainsty, Bishopthorpe, near York, the archiepiscopal palace.

The chalybeate and sulphureous springs of Harrogate, discovered in 1571, are of great celebrity, and have rendered that once obscure hamlet one of the principal watering-places in the North of England. Askerne, about eight miles north of Doncaster, has of late years become much noted for its medicinal waters, which much resemble those of Harrogate, both in smell and taste, but differ from them in their operation. The chalybeate and saline springs of Scarborough, discovered early in the seventeenth century, have long been celebrated and greatly resorted to

In May, 1822, a mineral spring was discovered a mile to the south-east of Guisborough; it is greatly resorted to by persons labouring under different complaints: the waters are diuretic. There are, besides, mineral springs of various qualities at Aldfield, Boston, Gilthwaite, Horley Green, Ilkley, and Knaresborough, in the West riding; a chalybeate spring at Bridlington Quay, on the coast of the East riding; and a noted mineral spring at Thorp-Arch, in the ainsty. At Knaresborough is the celebrated dropping and petrifying well; and at the bottom of Giggleswick Scar, near the village of Giggleswick, is a spring which ebbs and flows at irregular periods. On the Wolds, and near Cottingham on their eastern side, are periodical springs, which sometimes emit very powerful streams of water for a few months successively, and then become dry for years. Some of the most remarkable waterfalls are, Thornton Force, formed by a small stream which is driven down a precipice of about thirty yards in height, and is situated near the village of Ingleton, in the West riding, and in the vicinity of Thornton Scar, a tremendous cliff of about three hundred feet in height; the cataract of Malham Cove, which is three hundred feet high; Aysgarth Force; Hardrow Fall; High Force, or Fall, on the Tees; Mallin Spout; Egton; and Mossdale Fall; all in the North riding. Among the natural curiosities of this county must also be enumerated its caves, the principal of which, situated among the Craven mountains, are, Yordas Cave, in a mountain called Greg-roof, and Weathercote Cave, both of them in the vicinity of Ingleton, and in the latter of which is a stupendous cataract of twenty yards' fall; Hurtlepot and Ginglepot, near the head of the subterranean river Wease, or Greta; and Donk Cave, near the foot of Ingleborough. At the foot of the mountain called Pennigant, in the same neighbourhood, are two frightful orifices, called Hulpit and Huntpit Holes, through each of which runs a subterranean brook, passing under ground for about a mile, and then emerging, one at Dowgill Scar, and the other at Bransil-head.

YORKFLEET, a township in the parish of Howden, wapentake of Howdenshire, East riding of the county of York, 6¼ miles (S.E. by E.) from Howden, containing 199 inhabitants. The village is situated on the river Ouse.

YOULGRAVE, a parish comprising the chapelry of Middleton with Smerrill, and the township of Elton, in the hundred of Wirksworth, and the chapelries of Birchover, Stanton, and Winster, the township of Youlgrave, and the hamlet of Gratton, in that of High Peak, county of Derby, and containing 3593 inhabitants, of which number 955 are in the township of Youlgrave, 3 miles (S. by W.) from Bakewell. The living is a discharged vicarage, in the archdeaconry of Derby, and diocese of Lichfield and Coventry, rated in the king's books at £9. 4. 7., endowed with £200 private benefaction, and £200 royal bounty, and in the patronage of the Duke of Devonshire. The church, dedicated to All Saints, is partly Norman and partly of later date. There is a place of worship for Wesleyan Methodists. A school was erected by subscription, about 1765, in which eight children are taught; in 1824, a residence for the master was added, at the expense of the Duke of Rutland. Youlgrave is in the honour of Tutbury,

VOL. IV.

duchy of Lancaster, and within the jurisdiction of a court of pleas held at Tutbury every third Tuesday, for the recovery of debts under 40s.

YOULTHORPE, a joint township with Gowthorpe, in the parish of Bishop-Wilton, partly within the liberty of St. Peter of York, and partly in the Wilton-Beacon division of the wapentake of Harthill, East riding of the county of York, 5¼ miles (N. W. by N.) from Pocklington, containing 111 inhabitants.

YOULTON, a township in the parish of Alne, wapentake of Bulmer, North riding of the county of York, 6½ miles (S.S.W.) from Easingwould, containing 56 inhabitants.

YOXFORD, a parish in the hundred of Blything, county of Suffolk, 23½ miles (N.E.) from Ipswich, containing 1073 inhabitants. The living is a perpetual curacy, in the archdeaconry of Suffolk, and diocese of Norwich, rated in the king's books at £5. 14. 2., and in the patronage of the Earl of Stradbrooke. The church is dedicated to St. Peter. The village is situated in a remarkably pleasant and genteel neighbourhood, on the high road from Ipswich to Yarmouth, and consists principally of one well-built street of modern houses, with two or three commodious inns.

YOXHALL, a parish in the northern division of the hundred of Offlow, county of Stafford, 7½ miles (N.N.E.) from Lichfield, containing, with the township of Hoarcross, 1756 inhabitants. The living is a rectory, in the archdeaconry of Stafford, and diocese of Lichfield and Coventry, rated in the king's books at £17. 6. 8., and in the patronage of the Hon. Mrs. Leigh. The church, dedicated to St. Peter, exhibits various styles of architecture, from the Norman to the later English. A free school, founded in 1695, by Thomas Taylor, is endowed with various bequests producing about £20 per annum. Yoxhall is in the honour of Tutbury, duchy of Lancaster, and within the jurisdiction of a court of pleas held at Tutbury every third Tuesday, for the recovery of debts under 40s. In levelling a piece of ground, about forty vessels of a soft brown earthenware, containing ashes and human bones, were taken up some years ago.

Z.

ZEAL (SOUTH), a chapelry in the parish of South Tawton, hundred of Wonford, county of Devon, 4½ miles (E.S.E.) from Oakhampton. The population is returned with the parish. The chapel, dedicated to St. Mary, is now used as a school-house. This is a decayed borough and market town: the market has been long disused, but there is a fair for cattle on the Tuesday following the martyrdom of Thomas a Becket.

ZEAL-MONACHORUM, a parish in the hundred of North Tawton with Winkley, county of Devon, 1¼ mile (N.) from Bow, containing 681 inhabitants. The living is a rectory, in the archdeaconry of Barnstaple, and diocese of Exeter, rated in the king's books at £17. 8. 9., and in the patronage of the Earl of Morley. The church is dedicated to St. Peter. The river Yeo flows through the parish. Sixteen poor children are educated for an annuity of £5, the bequest of Weekes Hole, Esq., in 1768.

ZEALS, a tything in the parish and hundred of MERE, county of WILTS, 2 miles (W. by S.) from Mere, containing 539 inhabitants.

ZENNOR, a parish in the hundred of PENWITH, county of CORNWALL, 4¼ miles (W. S. W.) from St. Ives, containing 715 inhabitants. The living is a discharged vicarage, in the archdeaconry of Cornwall, and diocese of Exeter, rated in the king's books at £5. 5. 0½., and in the patronage of the Bishop of Exeter. The church is dedicated to St. Sennar. There are here some remains of two ancient chapels; and there is also a place of worship for Wesleyan Methodists. The parish is bounded on the North by St. George's channel. There are some tin mines here, but the substratum of the greater part of the parish is moorstone.

THE END OF VOLUME IV.

www.ingramcontent.com/pod-product-compliance
Lightning Source LLC
Chambersburg PA
CBHW072037020426
42334CB00017B/1300